Bill James presents . . .

STATS™ 1997
Batter vs. Pitcher
Match-Ups!

STATS, Inc. • Bill James

STATS

PUBLISHING

Published by STATS Publishing
A division of Sports Team Analysis & Tracking Systems, Inc.
Dr. Richard Cramer, Chairman • John Dewan, President

Cover by Ron Freer and the Big Blue Image

Photo of Kevin Brown by Ken Babbitt
Photo of Ken Caminiti by David Seelig

© Copyright 1997 by STATS, Inc. and Bill James

STATS is a trademark of Sports Team Analysis and Tracking
Systems, Inc.

First Edition: January, 1997

Printed in the United States of America

ISBN 1-884064-33-7

Acknowledgments

STATS *1997 Batter Versus Pitcher Match-Ups!* may not be the biggest book we do, but it's easy to see that we pack a lot of information into a small package. All of this bang for your buck is available because of the efforts of a dedicated, exacting group of individuals who form the STATS team.

John Dewan may be our President and CEO, but he's a fan first and foremost. We work to bring you closer to the game, and no one works harder towards that end than John. He is assisted by Heather Schwarze, who does a remarkable job of matching his pace.

At the heart of our business, and certainly at the heart of this book, are those wonderful numbers. Keeping track of who hit what where and against whom—and then being able to access that data with the touch of a button—is our calling card, and our Systems Department provides that access. Headed by Sue Dewan, Mike Canter and Art Ashley, this group takes an *ordinary* statistic and makes it extraordinary with just a few keystrokes. We are continually amazed by the magic Dave Carlson, Marty Couvillon, Mike Hammer, Stefan Kretschmann, Steve Moyer, Brent Osland, Dave Pinto, Pat Quinn, Jeff Schinski and Kevin Thomas work every day while weaving their lines of code.

Of course, someone has to collect the data, and that's where our tireless Operations Department comes in to play. Manning the fort here in Skokie all hours of the day and night, this finicky bunch isn't satisfied until every ball and strike of every game is accounted for. Doug Abel oversees the keen eyes and ears of Jeff Chernow, Jason Kinsey, Jim Osborne, Matt Senter, Allan Spear, Peter Woelflein and a vast network of reporters who man the press boxes in every major league park.

Don Zminda heads the STATS Publications Department, with the help of Ethan Cooperson, Kevin Fullam, Jim Henzler, Chuck Miller, Mat Olkin and myself. Books are a big part of our business, and we strive to keep you ahead of the game with our 11 annual publications.

Our Marketing Department does yeoman's work making sure the world knows about STATS. Jim Capuano is Director of National Sales, and he is assisted by Kristen Beauregard and Lori Smith. Ron Freer is our advertising guru, and Jim Musso and Oscar Palacios make our fantasy games the best in the business.

The Departments responsible for Publications Sales, Finances and Administration, headed by Bob Meyerhoff, juggle the other myriad responsibilities here at STATS. The group includes Marc Elman, Drew Faust, Mark Hong, Betty Moy, and Mike Wenz. Stephanie Seburn manages the Administrative group, with the assistance of Grant Blair, Ken Gilbert, Virginia Hamill, Tiffany Heingarten, Antoinette Kelly and Leena Sheth.

And certainly not least, there's Bill James. Here's thanks to an explorer who never tires of discovery.

—Tony Nistler

This book is dedicated to my parents, Clifford and Marilyn, for encouraging me to want to grow up to be a baseball player, and to Todd Nahigian and my wife Karlene, for encouraging me while I still try.
—Mike Wenz

Table of Contents

Introduction

by Tony Nistler

My colleague, Mat Olkin, came to work one morning this past October and immediately began thumbing through his copy of STATS *1996 Batter Versus Pitcher Match-Ups!*. In a few seconds, a smile flashed across his face. It was the kind of "I knew it!" smile which comes from personal vindication. You see, the Braves had just dropped Game 4 of the NLCS to the Cardinals the night before, and in the process had made a very peculiar decision in the top of the ninth. Down 4-3 with Jermaine Dye on second and no outs, the Braves sent Luis Polonia to the plate—pinch hitting for Jeff Blauser—to face Cards closer Dennis Eckersley. With Terry Pendleton on deck, everyone knew Polonia would bunt Dye to third...everyone, that is, except for Atlanta skipper Bobby Cox. Instead, Cox had Polonia swinging away, eschewing the "obvious" decision to sacrifice. Though the call proved fruitless when Polonia popped out to second baseman Luis Alicea and St. Louis held on for the win, Mat stood firmly behind Cox. Why? In his career, Polonia had managed three hits in seven at-bats against Eckersley, while Pendleton was just 2-for-14. Why not give Polonia a chance against a guy he'd enjoyed some success against, even if that guy was Dennis Eckersley? Atlanta may have lost the game, but thanks to Mat's memory and his copy of *Batter Versus Pitcher Match-Ups!*, Cox' move made sense.

Making sense of the game is something we strive for in each of our publications, and the STATS *1997 Batter Versus Pitcher Match-Ups!* goes a long way towards that end. Every big league contest involves quick decisions based on who hits who well, who pitches who well and who hits well where. This book gives *you* the ability to make those decisions right along with major league managers. They go into every game armed with these numbers. . . shouldn't you?

You may even get that smile of vindication when you make the right call as to which moves were right, and which ones should never have been made.

What's In This Book

What we are presenting in this book are two of the most fundamental elements of baseball—the batter/pitcher match-up and the ballpark. The upcoming pages are broken into four sections. The first part is the Batter/Pitcher match-ups. To be included in this section, both the batter and pitcher must have been active in 1996 and there must be a minimum of five career plate appearances between the two. Only position players versus pitchers are included in the match-ups. Our data goes back to 1984, so everything since then is career match-up data. For batters, "*" indicates a left-handed hitter and "#" is for a switch-hitter.

The second and third sections list how players and pitchers perform in each ballpark. Again, everyone who played in 1996 is eligible for this list, but a minimum of 35 plate appearances (or 12 innings pitched for pitchers) at a given park is needed to be included. Not all the current parks have been around since 1984, so the numbers at Oriole Park at Camden Yards are since it opened in 1992, the numbers at SkyDome are since its debut on June 5, 1989, etc. The stats for Colorado are from Coors Field, which opened in 1995. One more thing: the stats for the Oakland Coliseum and Jack Murphy Stadium do *not* include the home games those teams played in Las Vegas and Monterrey (MX) in 1996.

The final section is the Leader Boards. We went through the data and pulled out the most one-sided match-ups in almost 100 categories. Here, you'll see why the Rangers should think about signing Tim Salmon and Harold Baines and why Brian Anderson should never be left on the mound to face Edgar Martinez. We think the numbers are quite enlightening, and we're sure you will as well.

Batter vs. Pitcher

This is the main section of the book, and it's very straightforward. Pitchers are listed alphabetically, from Jim Abbott to Anthony Young, with match-up data for all major league position players who have had at least five career plate appearances against that pitcher. In almost every case, the data is complete for the players' careers. There's one exception: since our play-by-play database only goes back to 1984, we don't have match-up data for batter-pitcher confrontations prior to then. That's no big deal, when you think about it; after all, when Brett Butler comes up to face Fernando Valenzuela, is it all that useful to know how he hit Valenzuela back in 1983?

Have fun browsing through this section, and keep the book handy when you're at the park or watching a game on television. That way, you can do what big league managers and writers do: see how the players in a club's batting order have fared against the man on the mound. You'll discover some of those "mysterious lineup decisions" aren't so mysterious after all.

Batter	Avg	AB	H	HR	BI	BB	SO	OBP	Slg
Alexander, M	.000	7	0	0	1	0	1	.000	.000
Alomar, R#	.258	31	8	3	7	2	5	.351	.581
Alomar Jr, S	.222	18	4	0	5	1	1	.263	.278
Amaral, Rich	.333	27	9	1	2	3	3	.400	.481
Anderson, Brd*	.368	38	14	0	4	7	3	.467	.500
Baerga, C#	.171	41	7	0	5	2	4	.209	.195
Baines, H*	.190	21	4	0	3	1	6	.261	.286
Bautista, D	.111	9	1	1	2	1	1	.200	.444
Becker, Rich*	.143	7	1	0	0	1	2	.250	.286
Bell, Derek	.167	6	1	1	1	0	2	.167	.667
Belle, Albert	.281	32	9	2	4	5	5	.368	.531
Berroa, G	.143	21	3	0	1	2	4	.217	.143
Berry, Sean	.000	3	0	0	0	2	1	.400	.000
Bichette, D	.286	14	4	0	4	2	4	.375	.500
Blowers, Mike	.387	31	12	2	8	1	5	.406	.677
Boggs, Wade*	.286	56	16	0	3	8	4	.375	.357
Bonilla, B*	.400	5	2	0	0	0	1	.400	.400
Borders, Pat	.241	54	13	3	9	4	9	.293	.407
Bordick, Mike	.120	25	3	0	1	7	5	.313	.120
Brosius, S	.455	22	10	1	7	4	2	.538	.682
Buford, Damon	.143	7	1	0	0	1	0	.250	.143
Buhner, Jay	.310	42	13	3	11	6	10	.388	.595
Burks, Ellis	.231	39	9	2	6	2	7	.268	.436
Canseco, Jose	.385	26	10	3	7	1	4	.407	.769
Carreon, Mark	.200	5	1	0	1	0	0	.200	.200
Carter, Joe	.264	53	14	5	13	0	10	.255	.604
Cedeno, D#	.250	4	1	0	0	0	2	.250	.250
Cirillo, Jeff	.200	5	1	0	2	5	0	.600	.200
Clark, Will*	.188	16	3	0	1	0	3	.176	.250
Coleman, V#	.200	10	2	0	0	2	0	.333	.200
Coomer, Ron	.200	5	1	0	0	1	0	.333	.200
Cora, Joey#	.000	16	0	0	0	1	1	.059	.000
Cordova, M	.308	13	4	0	2	0	2	.357	.462
Curtis, Chad	.250	20	5	0	1	4	2	.375	.400
Cuyler, Milt*	.182	11	2	0	1	0	1	.182	.182
Damon, Johnny*	.333	6	2	1	4	0	1	.333	.833
Davis, Chili*	.278	36	10	1	6	4	8	.341	.389
Davis, Russ	.500	6	3	0	0	1	2	.571	.667
Deer, Rob	.214	28	6	1	2	4	7	.313	.357
Devereaux, M	.441	34	15	1	2	9	5	.568	.618
DiSarcina, Al	.200	15	3	0	1	1	2	.250	.267
Durham, Ray#	.200	5	1	0	0	1	1	.333	.200
Easley, D	.105	19	2	0	0	3	1	.227	.158
Edmonds, Jim*	.444	9	4	0	2	1	2	.500	.444
Eisenreich, J	.333	12	4	0	1	0	2	.333	.333
Elster, Kevin	.364	11	4	0	2	0	1	.333	.636
Espinoza, A	.393	28	11	0	1	2	2	.433	.464
Fermin, Felix	.268	41	11	0	4	3	1	.311	.341
Fielder, C	.308	39	12	4	11	1	10	.325	.462
Franco, Julio	.250	36	9	1	4	2	3	.289	.361
Fryman, T	.162	37	6	1	5	3	7	.225	.243
Gaetti, Gary	.143	28	4	1	2	1	2	.172	.250
Gagne, Greg	.333	39	13	0	5	1	3	.350	.462
Gallego, Mike	.409	22	9	1	6	1	3	.435	.591
Gates, Brent#	.100	10	1	0	0	1	3	.250	.100
Giambi, Jason*	.000	5	0	0	0	0	1	.000	.000
Gil, Benji	.500	8	4	0	0	0	2	.500	.500
Gomez, Leo	.304	23	7	0	1	2	3	.385	.348
Gonzales, R	.200	15	3	0	1	4	2	.368	.267
Gonzalez, A	.250	12	3	0	1	2	1	.357	.333
Gonzalez, J	.366	41	15	2	6	3	6	.409	.561
Goodwin, Tom*	.200	10	2	0	0	2	2	.333	.200
Grebeck, M	.217	23	5	0	0	3	3	.308	.261
Greenwell, M*	.357	28	10	1	5	6	4	.457	.536
Greer, Rusty*	.385	13	5	2	4	0	2	.357	.923
Griffey Jr, K*	.317	41	13	3	8	3	2	.356	.610
Guillen, O*	.250	36	9	0	2	1	3	.270	.250
Hall, Mel*	.222	9	2	0	1	0	2	.300	.333
Hamilton, D*	.313	32	10	0	3	2	1	.353	.313
Hammonds, J	.375	8	3	0	2	4	0	.583	.500
Henderson, R	.186	43	8	1	1	9	8	.327	.279
Hiatt, Phil	.385	13	5	1	4	0	1	.385	.692
Hill, G	.227	22	5	0	1	2	6	.292	.364
Hoiles, Chris	.548	31	17	3	9	4	1	.583	.903
Howard, Dave*	.176	17	3	0	0	2	0	.263	.176
Hudler, Rex	.375	8	3	1	2	1	0	.400	.875
Huff, Michael	.125	24	3	0	1	2	4	.192	.125
Hulse, David*	.143	7	1	0	0	0	1	.250	.286
Incaviglia, P	.313	16	5	1	1	2	1	.389	.563
Jaha, John	.250	4	1	0	0	2	1	.500	.500
Javier, Stan#	.222	9	2	0	3	2	1	.364	.333
Jefferies, G#	.167	6	1	1	2	0	0	.167	.667
Jeter, Derek	.400	5	2	0	1	0	1	.400	.800
Johnson, L*	.333	30	10	0	1	1	4	.355	.400
Joyner, Wally*	.375	16	6	0	2	2	1	.444	.438
Karkovice, R	.381	21	8	2	6	6	2	.500	.667
Kelly, Pat	.083	12	1	0	1	0	1	.077	.083
Kelly, R	.360	25	9	0	1	0	3	.360	.440
Knoblauch, C	.400	45	18	0	4	7	5	.481	.578
Kreuter, Chad#	.100	10	1	0	0	1	1	.182	.100
Leius, Scott	.222	36	8	1	1	4	5	.300	.361

Batter	Avg	AB	H	HR	BI	BB	SO	OBP	Slg
Lewis, Darren	.000	5	0	0	0	0	1	.000	.000
Lewis, Mark	.250	12	3	0	2	0	1	.250	.250
Leyritz, Jim	.278	18	5	1	4	2	2	.350	.444
Liriano, N#	.167	6	1	0	0	1	0	.286	.167
Listach, Pat#	.250	20	5	1	3	5	3	.400	.450
Lofton, Kenny*	.429	28	12	0	1	4	2	.500	.500
Macfarlane, M	.350	40	14	1	5	5	6	.447	.575
Martinez, E	.422	45	19	0	6	4	5	.469	.533
Martinez, S*	.375	8	3	0	1	0	0	.375	.625
Martinez, T*	.222	18	4	0	1	0	0	.263	.222
Marzano, John	.000	5	0	0	0	1	3	.167	.000
Matheny, Mike	.400	5	2	0	0	0	1	.400	.400
McCarty, Dave	.250	12	3	1	0	2	2	.250	.250
McGriff, Fred*	.250	20	5	0	0	1	6	.286	.250
McGwire, Mark	.375	40	15	6	11	12	7	.519	.850
McLemore, M#	.188	32	6	0	5	5	2	.297	.219
McRae, Brian#	.226	31	7	0	3	0	4	.226	.258
Meares, Pat	.250	16	4	0	0	3	0	.368	.250
Mieske, Matt	.188	16	3	1	2	1	1	.235	.438
Mitchell, Kei	.167	6	1	0	0	0	0	.167	.167
Mitchell, K	.429	7	3	0	3	1	0	.500	.571
Molitor, Paul	.211	38	8	0	1	9	7	.362	.237
Mouton, Lyle	.333	6	2	0	2	0	1	.333	.333
Munoz, Pedro	.385	39	15	3	8	1	7	.400	.692
Murray, Eddie*	.200	15	3	0	2	1	1	.250	.333
Naehring, Tim	.125	8	1	0	0	1	2	.222	.125
Newfield, M	.000	11	0	0	2	0	0	.000	.000
Nilsson, Dave*	.000	3	0	0	1	2	2	.400	.000
Nixon, Otis#	.444	9	4	0	1	2	0	.545	.444
Norman, Les	.500	6	3	0	1	0	0	.500	.500
O'Brien, C	.111	9	1	0	0	1	2	.200	.111
O'Neill, Paul*	.235	17	4	1	6	0	2	.235	.529
Offerman, J#	.333	12	4	0	0	1	0	.385	.417
Olerud, John*	.219	32	7	1	5	2	3	.286	.344
Palmeiro, R*	.327	52	17	4	10	4	3	.386	.635
Palmer, Dean	.333	27	9	2	5	6	5	.455	.593
Paquette, C	.333	15	5	0	2	3	2	.421	.333
Parent, Mark	.000	4	0	0	0	1	0	.200	.000
Pena, Tony	.250	32	8	1	3	1	1	.273	.438
Perez, E	.000	4	0	0	0	1	1	.200	.000
Perez, Robert	.500	6	3	0	0	0	0	.500	.667
Phillips, T#	.262	42	11	0	1	10	5	.404	.286
Pirkl, Greg	.167	6	1	0	0	0	2	.167	.167
Plantier, P*	.500	8	4	0	0	2	1	.600	.500
Polonia, Luis*	.364	11	4	0	0	1	0	.417	.364
Pulliam, H	.667	6	4	0	1	1	1	.714	.833
Raines, Tim#	.261	23	6	0	2	3	3	.346	.261
Ramirez, M	.467	15	7	2	3	1	1	.471	1.067
Randa, Joe	.200	5	1	0	3	2	0	.429	.200
Reboulet, J	.333	24	8	0	1	2	2	.385	.333
Reed, Jody	.343	35	12	0	4	3	6	.439	.429
Ripken, Billy	.158	19	3	0	1	1	3	.200	.158
Ripken, Cal	.277	47	13	1	4	4	0	.327	.362
Rodriguez, Al	.200	15	3	0	0	1	4	.250	.333
Rodriguez, I	.300	30	9	0	6	0	3	.290	.400
Salmon, Tim	.313	16	5	1	2	3	1	.400	.500
Samuel, Juan	.353	17	6	1	3	1	5	.389	.588
Schofield, D	.600	5	3	0	1	0	0	.600	.600
Sinclair, Ru	.400	5	2	1	1	0	1	.400	1.000
Segui, David#	.357	14	5	0	2	0	0	.333	.429
Seitzer, K	.225	40	9	0	2	5	5	.311	.250
Sheffield, G	.333	9	3	0	0	0	1	.333	.444
Shumpert, T	.167	12	2	0	0	0	3	.167	.250
Sierra, Ruben#	.250	56	14	2	12	4	9	.295	.357
Smith, Mark	.000	5	0	0	0	0	1	.000	.000
Snopek, Chris	.333	6	2	1	3	0	0	.333	1.000
Snow, J.T.#	.267	15	4	1	1	1	3	.313	.467
Sojo, Luis	.385	13	5	0	1	0	0	.385	.462
Sorrento, P*	.444	9	4	0	3	3	3	.444	.556
Sosa, Sammy	.368	19	7	0	1	3	2	.455	.526
Spehr, Tim	.167	6	1	1	4	0	0	.167	.667
Spiers, Bill*	.133	15	2	0	0	1	2	.188	.200
Sprague, D	.385	26	10	2	5	2	4	.433	.615
Stairs, Matt	.417	12	5	0	1	2	6	.500	.583
Stanley, Mike	.313	48	15	0	3	1	8	.353	.375
Steinbach, T	.263	19	5	1	3	2	0	.333	.421
Stillwell, K#	.263	19	5	1	3	2	0	.333	.421
Strange, Doug#	.333	6	2	0	1	0	1	.333	.500
Stynes, Chris	.500	6	3	0	0	0	0	.500	.500
Surhoff, B.J.*	.440	25	11	0	2	1	0	.462	.640
Sveum, Dale#	.143	7	1	0	0	0	1	.143	.143
Tartabull, D	.333	33	7	1	4	8	5	.366	.333
Tettleton, M#	.216	37	8	0	1	5	10	.310	.270
Thomas, Frank	.394	33	13	3	11	5	5	.545	.545
Thome, Jim*	.286	7	2	1	2	1	2	.375	.857
Trammell, A	.361	36	13	3	7	2	4	.395	.639
Tucker, M*	.400	5	2	2	0	0	0	.400	1.600
Turner, Chris	.167	6	1	0	0	0	1	.167	.333
Valentin, Jhn	.286	7	2	0	1	0	1	.286	.286
Valentin, Jse#	.000	6	0	0	0	0	1	.000	.000
Valle, Dave	.343	35	12	1	4	3	7	.395	.486
Vaughn, Greg	.167	30	5	0	2	5	6	.286	.200

4

Jim Abbott, Angels — LHP

Batter	Avg	AB	H	HR	BI	BB	SO	OBP	Slg
Vaughn, Mo*	.200	5	1	0	1	2	1	.429	.200
Velarde, R	.238	21	5	0	0	1	4	.304	.238
Ventura, R*	.182	22	4	0	1	0	6	.182	.273
Vitiello, Joe	.438	16	7	2	6	1	1	.471	.938
Vizquel, Omar#	.259	27	7	0	2	4	2	.355	.296
Voigt, Jack	.167	12	2	0	1	2	0	.286	.167
Walbeck, Matt#	.167	12	2	0	1	2	1	.286	.167
Ward, Turner#	.600	5	3	0	0	0	0	.600	.600
Webster, L	.400	5	2	0	0	0	0	.400	.400
Weiss, Walt#	.000	4	0	0	0	1	0	.200	.000
White, Devon#	.262	42	11	1	6	0	12	.279	.381
Whiten, Mark#	.000	8	0	0	0	1	3	.111	.000
Williams, Ber#	.476	21	10	0	1	1	0	.500	.524
Williams, Ger	.333	12	4	0	2	1	1	.357	.500
Wilson, Dan	.350	20	7	3	9	0	1	.350	.900
Worthington	.083	12	1	0	0	0	2	.083	.083

Kyle Abbott, Angels — LHP

Batter	Avg	AB	H	HR	BI	BB	SO	OBP	Slg
Alou, Moises	.111	9	1	0	0	0	1	.111	.111
Anthony, Eric*	.800	5	4	1	3	1	0	.833	1.400
Bagwell, Jeff	.000	4	0	0	0	1	0	.200	.000
Biggio, Craig	.250	4	1	0	1	1	0	.400	.500
Blauser, Jeff	.333	6	2	0	0	1	1	.333	.333
Bonilla, B#	.300	10	3	0	1	0	0	.300	.300
Cianfrocco, A	.167	6	1	0	1	0	0	.167	.500
Clark, Will*	.583	12	7	0	2	1	0	.615	.583
Clayton, R	.000	4	0	0	0	2	1	.333	.000
Coleman, V#	.000	5	0	0	0	1	0	.000	.000
Dascenzo, D#	.143	7	1	0	0	1	0	.250	.143
DeShields, D*	.429	7	3	0	0	0	0	.500	.429
Finley, Steve*	.143	7	1	0	0	0	1	.143	.143
Gilkey, B	.333	3	1	1	2	2	0	.600	1.333
Girardi, Joe	.600	5	3	0	0	2	0	.714	.600
Grace, Mark*	.364	11	4	0	1	0	0	.364	.364
Grebeck, C	1.000	2	2	1	4	3	0	1.000	3.000
Grissom, M	.375	8	3	1	3	2	1	.455	.875
Gwynn, Tony*	.500	8	4	0	0	0	0	.500	.500
Huff, Michael	.250	4	1	0	0	0	0	.400	.250
Hundley, Todd#	.300	10	3	0	0	0	3	.300	.300
Incaviglia, P	.750	4	3	1	2	1	0	.800	1.750
Justice, Dave*	.000	3	0	0	0	2	2	.400	.000
Karkovice, R	.667	3	2	0	0	2	0	.800	.667
Lewis, Darren	.125	8	1	0	0	0	1	.125	.125
Magadan, Dave*	.571	7	4	0	1	2	0	.667	.714
Manwaring, K	.500	10	5	0	0	0	2	.500	.700
McGee, Willie#	.111	9	1	0	0	0	4	.111	.111
McGriff, Fred*	.083	12	1	0	1	0	5	.083	.083
Murray, Eddie#	.143	7	1	0	2	0	0	.143	.286
O'Brien, C	.000	5	0	0	0	0	0	.000	.000
O'Neill, Paul*	.200	5	1	0	0	0	1	.200	.200
Raines, Tim#	.286	7	2	0	0	0	1	.286	.286
Sanchez, Rey	.600	5	3	0	2	0	0	.600	1.000
Sandberg, R	.000	8	0	0	0	1	2	.111	.000
Santiago, B	.000	6	0	0	0	0	0	.000	.000
Schofield, D	.250	8	2	0	0	0	0	.250	.250
Sheffield, G	.333	6	2	1	3	1	1	.429	1.167
Smith, Ozzie#	.600	5	3	0	0	0	0	.600	.800
Sosa, Sammy	.000	7	0	0	0	1	2	.125	.000
Thomas, Frank	.400	5	2	0	0	1	1	.500	.400
Thompson, Rob	.000	5	0	0	0	1	1	.167	.000
Ventura, R*	.333	6	2	0	0	0	1	.333	.333
Vizcaino, J#	.333	6	2	0	0	0	2	.333	.500
Walker, Larry*	.714	7	5	0	2	0	0	.714	.857
Wallach, Tim	.000	6	0	0	1	1	2	.143	.000
Williams, Ma	.182	11	2	0	0	3	0	.167	.727

Mark Acre, Athletics — RHP

Batter	Avg	AB	H	HR	BI	BB	SO	OBP	Slg
Alomar, R#	.200	5	1	0	0	1	3	.200	.200
Alomar Jr, S	.000	5	0	0	0	0	0	.000	.000
Belle, Albert	.500	4	2	1	2	1	1	.600	1.250
Buhner, Jay	.500	4	2	0	1	0	0	.500	.833
Canseco, Jose	.200	5	1	1	1	0	0	.200	.800
Clark, Will*	.000	3	0	0	0	0	0	.400	.000
Cora, Joey#	.400	5	2	0	0	0	2	.500	.400
Cordova, M	.250	4	1	1	1	1	0	.400	1.000
Devereaux, M	.250	4	1	0	0	0	1	.250	.750
Gonzalez, J	.400	5	2	0	1	0	0	.400	1.000
Griffey Jr, K*	.500	4	2	0	1	0	1	.600	.750
Hoiles, Chris	.167	6	1	0	0	0	1	.286	.333
Martinez, E	.400	5	2	0	0	0	1	.400	.400
Molitor, Paul	.200	5	1	0	0	1	2	.333	.200
Naehring, Tim	.500	4	2	0	0	1	0	.600	.750
O'Leary, Troy*	.333	6	2	1	3	0	0	.333	.833
Palmer, Dean	.400	5	2	0	2	0	0	.400	.400
Raines, Tim#	.143	7	1	0	0	1	0	.143	.143
Ripken, Cal	.167	6	1	0	3	2	0	.375	.500
Salmon, Tim	.500	4	2	1	2	1	0	.600	1.250
Snow, J.T.*	.167	6	1	1	3	1	3	.286	.667
Surhoff, B.J.*	.200	5	1	0	0	0	3	.200	.200

Mark Acre, Athletics — RHP

Batter	Avg	AB	H	HR	BI	BB	SO	OBP	Slg
Valentin, Jhn	.250	4	1	0	0	0	0	.250	.250
Vaughn, Greg	.000	3	0	0	0	1	1	.400	.000
Vaughn, Mo*	.500	2	1	0	0	3	1	.800	.500

Terry Adams, Cubs — RHP

Batter	Avg	AB	H	HR	BI	BB	SO	OBP	Slg
Bagwell, Jeff	.000	4	0	0	0	3	1	.429	.000
Bates, Jason#	.250	4	1	0	2	1	0	.400	.250
Bichette, D	.333	6	2	0	0	0	2	.333	.333
Biggio, Craig	.400	5	2	0	1	0	0	.333	.600
Blowers, Mike	.500	4	2	0	0	1	1	.600	.750
Burks, Ellis	.286	7	2	0	0	0	3	.286	.286
Castilla, V	.400	5	2	0	0	0	0	.400	.400
Cianfrocco, A	.400	5	2	0	2	0	0	.400	.400
Colbrunn, G	.200	5	1	0	0	1	1	.333	.400
DeShields, D*	.000	3	0	0	0	2	0	.400	.000
Galarraga, A	.200	5	1	0	0	0	1	.200	.200
Gant, Ron	.400	5	2	1	1	0	2	.400	1.000
Gilkey, B	.000	5	0	0	0	1	0	.167	.000
Grissom, M	.500	4	2	0	0	1	0	.600	.500
Grudzielanek	.500	4	2	0	0	1	0	.600	.500
Gutierrez, R	.000	4	0	0	0	1	1	.200	.000
Jones, C#	.125	8	1	0	0	0	2	.125	.125
Klesko, Ryan*	.000	4	0	0	0	2	0	.333	.000
Lankford, Ray*	.500	4	2	1	3	0	0	.400	1.250
Larkin, Barry	.000	4	0	0	0	1	0	.200	.000
McGriff, Fred*	.375	8	3	0	0	0	0	.375	.500
Mouton, James	.333	3	1	0	0	2	2	.600	.333
Pendleton, T#	.400	5	2	0	1	0	0	.400	.400
Santiago, B	.000	3	0	0	0	1	0	.400	.000
Wilkins, Rick*	.333	6	2	0	0	1	1	.429	.333

Willie Adams, Athletics — RHP

Batter	Avg	AB	H	HR	BI	BB	SO	OBP	Slg
Belle, Albert	.000	6	0	0	0	0	0	.000	.000
Bragg, Darren*	.000	7	0	0	0	0	2	.000	.000
Frye, Jeff	.429	7	3	0	0	0	0	.429	.429
Jefferson, R*	.286	7	2	0	0	0	4	.286	.286
Lofton, Kenny*	.000	6	0	0	0	0	2	.000	.000
Murray, Eddie#	.200	5	1	1	2	1	2	.333	.800
O'Leary, Troy*	.143	7	1	0	0	1	2	.250	.143
Pena, Tony	.000	5	0	0	0	1	0	.167	.000
Ramirez, M	1.000	5	5	0	0	1	0	1.000	1.600
Thome, Jim*	.500	4	2	1	1	2	1	.667	1.250
Tinsley, Lee#	.167	6	1	0	0	0	2	.167	.167
Valentin, Jhn	.333	6	2	0	1	0	1	.333	.500
Vaughn, Mo*	.200	5	1	0	2	0	2	.429	.200
Vizquel, Omar#	.000	6	0	0	0	0	1	.000	.000

Rick Aguilera, Twins — RHP

Batter	Avg	AB	H	HR	BI	BB	SO	OBP	Slg
Aldrete, Mike*	.095	21	2	0	0	2	5	.174	.095
Alomar, R#	.400	10	4	0	1	0	1	.364	.500
Alomar Jr, S	.250	12	3	1	4	0	3	.250	.583
Anderson, Brd*	.083	12	1	0	0	1	4	.154	.083
Anderson, G*	.200	5	1	0	0	2	0	.200	.200
Baerga, C#	.200	15	3	0	0	2	1	.333	.200
Baines, H*	.167	12	2	0	0	0	5	.167	.167
Belle, Albert	.231	13	3	2	4	0	1	.231	.692
Berroa, G	.143	7	1	0	0	1	3	.250	.143
Bichette, D	.250	8	2	1	5	0	1	.250	.875
Biggio, Craig	.333	3	1	0	1	2	0	.600	.667
Boggs, Wade*	.389	18	7	0	1	0	3	.389	.444
Bonds, Barry*	.188	16	3	0	0	1	1	.235	.250
Bonilla, B#	.167	12	2	0	2	2	3	.333	.167
Borders, Pat	.857	7	6	0	2	0	1	.857	1.429
Bordick, Mike	.167	6	1	0	0	1	0	.286	.167
Bragg, Darren*	.429	7	3	2	3	0	2	.429	1.286
Brosius, S	.556	9	5	0	0	3	0	.556	.556
Buhner, Jay	.000	6	0	0	0	2	2	.250	.000
Burks, Ellis	.222	9	2	0	0	0	0	.222	.222
Burnitz, J*	.400	5	2	0	3	0	0	.400	.600
Canseco, Jose	.188	16	3	0	1	0	6	.188	.188
Carreon, Mark	.167	6	1	0	0	1	1	.286	.167
Carter, Joe	.111	9	1	0	1	3	0	.308	.222
Clark, Tony#	.143	7	1	0	0	0	4	.143	.286
Clark, Will*	.261	23	6	2	4	3	5	.346	.565
Cole, Alex*	.286	7	2	0	1	1	0	.375	.286
Coleman, V#	.400	20	8	0	5	0	1	.400	.450
Cora, Joey#	.364	11	4	0	0	0	0	.364	.455
Curtis, Chad	.235	17	4	1	1	0	2	.235	.471
Daulton, D*	.286	7	2	2	3	0	0	.286	1.143
Davis, Chili#	.208	24	5	1	3	3	7	.296	.333
Davis, Eric	.143	14	2	1	3	2	7	.250	.429
Dawson, Andre	.241	29	7	2	6	3	5	.333	.517
Deer, Rob	.333	6	2	1	2	1	3	.429	.833
Delgado, C*	.333	6	2	2	4	3	1	.500	1.333
Devereaux, M	.231	13	3	1	3	2	1	.333	.615
DiSarcina, G	.000	10	0	0	0	1	4	.091	.000
Dunston, S	.308	13	4	0	0	1	4	.357	.462
Durham, Ray#	.333	6	2	0	0	0	0	.429	.500

Rick Aguilera, Twins — RHP

Batter	Avg	AB	H	HR	BI	BB	SO	OBP	Slg
Easley, D	.400	5	2	1	3	0	0	.400	1.000
Edmonds, Jim*	.429	7	3	2	2	1	1	.500	1.286
Eisenreich, J*	.583	12	7	0	0	0	1	.583	.833
Elster, Kevin	.333	6	2	1	3	0	2	.333	1.000
Espinoza, A	.200	10	2	0	0	0	4	.200	.200
Fermin, Felix	.333	9	3	0	1	1	0	.400	.333
Fielder, C	.333	12	4	1	2	1	1	.385	.583
Franco, Julio	.125	8	1	0	1	1	0	.222	.125
Frye, Jeff	.250	4	1	0	1	0	1	.200	.250
Fryman, T	.118	17	2	0	1	0	5	.118	.176
Gaetti, Gary	.333	9	3	0	1	0	1	.333	.444
Galarraga, A	.200	15	3	2	5	2	5	.333	.600
Gallego, Mike	.000	9	0	0	0	1	0	.000	.000
Gomez, Chris	.000	6	0	0	1	0	0	.000	.000
Gonzales, R	.167	6	1	0	0	0	3	.167	.167
Gonzalez, A	.000	5	0	0	0	2	3	.286	.000
Gonzalez, J	.235	17	4	1	3	1	7	.278	.471
Green, Shawn*	.429	7	3	0	0	0	2	.429	.429
Greenwell, M*	.800	5	4	0	2	1	0	.714	1.000
Greer, Rusty*	.333	9	3	1	3	1	2	.400	.667
Griffey Jr, K*	.182	11	2	0	1	0	4	.182	.273
Guillen, O*	.200	15	3	0	1	0	2	.200	.333
Gwynn, Tony*	.111	9	1	0	0	2	0	.273	.111
Hall, Mel*	.333	9	3	0	0	1	1	.400	.444
Hamilton, D*	.200	15	3	0	1	2	0	.294	.267
Henderson, R	.200	15	3	2	4	0	0	.200	.600
Higginson, B*	.167	6	1	0	0	1	3	.286	.167
Hoiles, Chris	.286	7	2	0	0	0	2	.375	.286
Hudler, Rex	.143	7	1	0	0	0	1	.143	.143
Huson, Jeff*	.333	9	3	0	0	0	3	.333	.333
James, Dion*	.286	7	2	0	0	0	1	.286	.429
Javier, Stan#	.200	5	1	0	1	0	2	.333	.200
Jefferson, R*	.333	9	3	0	0	0	2	.333	.444
Johnson, L*	.333	21	7	0	6	1	2	.348	.571
Joyner, Wally*	.500	4	2	0	1	0	1	.400	.500
Karkovice, A	.267	15	4	0	1	0	5	.353	.333
Kelly, R	.250	16	4	1	2	1	2	.294	.500
Kirby, Wayne*	.200	5	1	0	1	0	0	.200	.400
Larkin, Barry	.000	6	0	0	0	0	1	.000	.000
Lewis, Mark	.300	10	3	0	1	0	2	.417	.400
Leyritz, Jim	.600	5	3	1	1	0	1	.600	1.200
Livingstone*	.200	5	1	0	0	0	0	.200	.200
Lofton, Kenny	.400	15	6	0	3	0	1	.400	.400
Macfarlane, M	.125	8	1	0	0	1	4	.222	.125
Martinez, Da*	.200	10	2	0	0	0	3	.200	.200
Martinez, E	.250	12	3	2	5	1	1	.308	.833
Martinez, T*	.167	6	1	0	0	1	1	.286	.167
Mayne, Brent*	.143	7	1	0	0	2	3	.333	.143
McGee, Willie*	.400	15	6	0	2	0	0	.400	.533
McGwire, Mark	.400	15	6	3	4	0	3	.500	1.067
McLemore, M#	.231	13	3	0	0	1	5	.286	.231
McRae, Brian*	.143	7	1	0	1	0	0	.125	.143
Mitchell, K	.273	11	3	0	0	0	2	.273	.273
Molitor, Paul	.429	14	6	1	5	1	2	.467	.714
Murray, Eddie#	.300	10	3	1	2	1	1	.364	.600
Naehring, Tim	.300	10	3	0	0	0	1	.300	.400
Newson, W*	.429	7	3	0	1	4	2	.636	.429
Nixon, Otis#	.300	20	6	0	2	0	1	.300	.350
O'Brien, C	.333	6	2	0	0	0	1	.333	.333
O'Leary, Troy*	.167	6	1	0	0	0	2	.167	.167
O'Neill, Paul*	.250	12	3	0	2	1	2	.308	.500
Olerud, John*	.300	10	3	0	0	0	0	.300	.400
Orsulak, Joe*	.179	28	5	0	2	0	5	.172	.214
Palmeiro, R*	.143	21	3	1	1	2	9	.250	.286
Palmer, Dean	.333	12	4	2	2	2	3	.429	1.000
Paquette, C	.167	6	1	0	0	0	2	.167	.167
Pena, Terry	.280	25	7	0	0	0	7	.280	.360
Pendleton, T#	.214	14	3	0	0	1	2	.267	.357
Perez, Tomas#	.500	6	3	0	2	0	0	.500	.667
Phillips, T#	.200	20	4	0	1	4	3	.333	.200
Polonia, Luis*	.333	15	5	0	1	0	2	.333	.533
Pozo, A	.000	7	0	0	1	0	0	.000	.000
Raines, Tim#	.167	36	6	0	7	3	3	.250	.167
Ramirez, M	.125	8	1	0	0	0	2	.125	.250
Reed, Jody	.000	6	0	0	0	0	0	.000	.000
Ripken, Cal	.364	11	4	0	1	2	2	.462	.545
Rodriguez, I	.462	13	6	2	4	0	0	.462	1.000
Salmon, Tim	.375	8	3	0	1	1	2	.444	.750
Samuel, Juan	.273	22	6	0	1	2	4	.360	.364
Sandberg, R	.278	18	5	0	3	1	5	.316	.278
Santiago, B	.200	5	1	0	0	0	2	.200	.200
Schu, Rick	.286	7	2	0	0	0	1	.286	.286
Segui, David#	.375	8	3	1	2	0	1	.375	.750
Seitzer, K	.333	9	3	0	0	0	2	.333	.333
Sierra, Ruben#	.294	17	5	2	6	5	3	.455	.765
Smith, Dwight*	.400	5	2	1	2	0	2	.400	1.000
Smith, Ozzie*	.429	14	6	0	4	1	0	.500	.429
Snow, J.T.#	.250	8	2	0	0	0	3	.250	.250
Sojo, Luis	.000	5	1	0	0	0	0	.000	.200
Sorrento, P*	.200	10	2	0	3	2	4	.333	.200
Sosa, Sammy	.000	6	0	0	0	0	4	.000	.000

Rick Aguilera, Twins — RHP

Batter	Avg	AB	H	HR	BI	BB	SO	OBP	Slg
Spiers, Bill*	.333	6	2	0	1	0	3	.333	.667
Sprague, Ed	.222	9	2	1	2	1	2	.300	.556
Stanley, Mike	.600	10	6	2	5	0	0	.600	1.200
Steinbach, T	.400	10	4	0	2	2	3	.462	.600
Stevens, Lee*	.000	5	0	0	0	0	1	.000	.000
Stillwell, K#	.308	13	4	0	0	0	3	.308	.308
Strange, Doug#	.364	11	4	0	1	0	2	.364	.364
Surhoff, B.J.*	.250	12	3	1	5	1	1	.308	.500
Tartabull, D	.316	19	6	0	0	0	6	.316	.368
Tettleton, M#	.267	15	4	0	1	2	4	.353	.400
Thomas, Frank	.250	8	2	1	2	2	1	.400	.750
Thome, Jim*	.333	9	3	2	3	0	3	.333	1.222
Thompson, Mil*	.176	17	3	0	0	0	4	.176	.176
Thompson, Rob	.333	12	4	0	0	2	2	.429	.417
Trammell, A	.091	11	1	0	0	0	1	.091	.091
Valentin, Jhn	.333	12	4	1	2	0	2	.333	.583
Valle, Dave	.250	4	1	0	0	1	0	.400	.250
Vaughn, Greg	.308	13	4	1	4	1	4	.357	.615
Vaughn, Mo*	.250	16	4	1	2	0	7	.250	.438
Velarde, R	.143	7	1	0	0	1	1	.250	.143
Ventura, R*	.188	16	3	0	3	4	4	.350	.250
Vizquel, Omar*	.364	11	4	0	0	2	1	.462	.364
Wallach, Tim	.423	26	11	0	10	4	5	.484	.577
White, Devon#	.111	9	1	0	0	1	4	.200	.222
Williams, Ber#	.111	9	1	0	0	0	3	.111	.111

Jose Alberro, Rangers — RHP

Batter	Avg	AB	H	HR	BI	BB	SO	OBP	Slg
Martinez, T*	.200	5	1	0	3	0	0	.200	.400

Scott Aldred, Twins — LHP

Batter	Avg	AB	H	HR	BI	BB	SO	OBP	Slg
Alomar, R#	.000	4	0	0	0	1	0	.200	.000
Alomar Jr, S	.167	6	1	0	0	0	0	.167	.167
Amaral, Rich	.167	6	1	0	0	1	1	.375	.333
Anderson, Brd*	.429	7	3	0	0	0	2	.429	.429
Anderson, G*	.500	10	5	0	0	0	2	.500	.700
Arias, George	.000	4	0	0	0	0	1	.000	.000
Baerga, C#	.000	8	0	0	2	0	1	.100	.000
Baines, H*	.286	7	2	0	0	0	0	.286	.429
Batista, Tony	.000	6	0	0	0	0	1	.000	.000
Belle, Albert	.400	10	4	3	4	0	2	.400	1.300
Berroa, G	.286	7	2	0	1	0	1	.286	.286
Bichette, D	.111	9	1	0	1	0	1	.111	.222
Boggs, Wade*	.000	5	0	0	0	2	0	.286	.000
Bonilla, B#	.333	6	2	0	2	0	0	.333	.500
Bordick, Mike	.333	9	3	0	4	0	0	.333	.444
Brosius, S	.333	6	2	0	0	1	1	.429	.500
Buhner, Jay	.222	9	2	1	2	4	1	.462	.667
Canseco, Jose	.200	5	1	0	2	1	0	.200	.200
Carreon, Mark	.250	4	1	0	1	1	0	.400	.250
Carter, Joe	.000	4	0	0	0	0	0	.000	.000
Clark, Will*	.375	8	3	0	1	0	1	.375	.375
Cole, Alex*	.714	7	5	0	0	1	0	.750	1.143
Coomer, Ron	.667	3	2	0	3	1	0	.600	.667
Cordero, Wil	.500	4	2	0	1	0	0	.600	.750
Cordova, M	.000	5	0	0	0	0	3	.000	.000
Curtis, Chad	.333	6	2	0	0	1	1	.333	.333
Damon, Johnny*	.250	4	1	0	1	1	0	.400	.500
Davis, Chili#	.286	7	2	0	0	0	2	.286	.429
Devereaux, M	.214	14	3	0	1	0	3	.200	.214
DiSarcina, G	.111	9	1	0	1	0	2	.273	.111
Durham, Ray#	.000	5	0	0	1	0	1	.000	.000
Elster, Kevin	.333	6	2	0	1	1	2	.429	.333
Franco, Julio	.333	6	2	1	3	2	1	.500	1.000
Frye, Jeff	.400	5	2	0	1	0	2	.400	.400
Gaetti, Gary	.333	6	2	0	0	0	1	.333	.333
Girardi, Joe	.400	5	2	0	0	1	0	.500	.600
Gomez, Leo	.167	6	1	1	4	2	1	.375	.667
Goodwin, Tom*	.667	3	2	0	3	1	0	.750	1.000
Greer, Rusty*	.800	5	4	2	6	0	0	.800	2.200
Griffey Jr, K*	.250	12	3	2	5	1	0	.308	.917
Hall, Mel*	.375	8	3	0	1	0	1	.444	.375
Hamilton, D*	.333	6	2	0	2	0	1	.333	.333
Hoiles, Chris	.167	6	1	1	1	1	1	.286	.667
Howard, Dave#	.400	5	2	0	0	1	0	.500	.400
Hudler, Rex	.286	7	2	0	0	1	1	.375	.571
Hunter, Brian	.500	4	2	0	1	0	0	.600	.500
Jefferies, G#	.333	6	2	0	0	0	0	.333	.333
Jeter, Derek	.600	5	3	0	2	0	1	.600	.800
Karkovice, R	.000	4	0	0	0	1	1	.200	.000
Kelly, R	.500	12	6	1	4	0	0	.500	.833
Knoblauch, C	.444	9	4	0	1	0	2	.444	.444
Lewis, Darren	.143	7	1	0	0	0	0	.143	.143
Leyritz, Jim	.000	3	0	0	0	4	2	.571	.000
Lofton, Kenny*	.500	6	3	0	0	0	1	.500	.667
Macfarlane, M	.273	11	3	1	1	0	0	.273	.636
Martin, N	.714	7	5	0	1	0	1	.714	.857
Martinez, E	.444	9	4	2	2	2	0	.545	1.222
Martinez, T*	.429	7	3	0	1	2	0	.556	.429
McGwire, Mark	.333	3	1	0	0	5	1	.778	.333

Scott Aldred, Twins — LHP

Batter	Avg	AB	H	HR	BI	BB	SO	OBP	Slg
McLemore, M#	.000	5	0	0	0	0	0	.000	.000
McRae, Brian#	.600	5	3	0	0	0	2	.600	.600
Molitor, Paul	.385	13	5	2	4	4	1	.500	.923
Murray, Eddie*	.111	9	1	0	1	2	1	.273	.222
Nilsson, Dave*	.167	6	1	0	0	0	3	.167	.167
O'Neill, Paul*	.167	6	1	0	2	1	0	.286	.167
Offerman, J#	.400	5	2	0	1	2	2	.571	.600
Palmeiro, R*	.400	10	4	1	5	0	0	.400	.800
Palmer, Dean	.333	9	3	0	2	2	4	.455	.333
Paquette, C	.400	5	2	0	0	1	2	.500	.400
Phillips, T#	.300	10	3	0	0	0	0	.300	.400
Ramirez, M	.200	5	1	0	0	0	2	.200	.200
Randa, Joe	.167	6	1	0	1	0	1	.167	.167
Ripken, Billy	.333	6	2	0	0	0	0	.333	.500
Ripken, Cal	.571	14	8	2	5	1	1	.600	1.143
Rodriguez, Al	.500	6	3	1	3	1	3	.571	1.000
Rodriguez, I	.167	6	1	0	0	0	1	.167	.333
Salmon, Tim	.222	9	2	1	2	2	1	.364	.556
Seitzer, K	.500	6	3	1	1	0	0	.500	1.000
Sierra, Ruben#	.143	7	1	0	0	2	0	.333	.143
Slaught, Don	.333	9	3	1	3	2	0	.455	.667
Snow, J.T.#	.000	9	0	0	0	1	4	.100	.000
Sojo, Luis	.167	6	1	0	0	0	0	.167	.333
Sprague, Ed	.286	7	2	0	2	0	1	.286	.286
Stanley, Mike	.455	11	5	3	5	0	2	.500	1.273
Steinbach, T	.111	9	1	0	1	0	2	.111	.111
Surhoff, B.J.*	.500	8	4	1	2	2	0	.600	.875
Tartabull, D	.273	11	3	2	4	6	2	.529	.909
Tettleton, M#	.333	3	1	0	2	2	1	.500	.333
Thomas, Frank	.400	5	2	0	0	1	1	.500	.400
Thome, Jim*	.250	4	1	1	1	1	2	.400	1.000
Valentin, Jhn	.500	6	3	0	0	0	2	.500	.500
Vaughn, Greg	.200	10	2	1	2	1	2	.273	.500
Vaughn, Mo*	.167	6	1	0	0	1	2	.286	.167
Velarde, R	.188	16	3	0	1	2	5	.263	.188
Ventura, R*	.286	7	2	1	3	2	1	.444	.857
Vitiello, Joe	.000	5	0	0	0	3	0	.375	.000
Vizquel, Omar#	.600	5	3	0	0	0	0	.600	1.000
Wallach, Tim	.286	7	2	1	2	0	2	.286	.714
Williams, Ber#	.308	13	4	1	3	1	3	.357	.692
Williams, Ger	.250	4	1	1	1	1	0	.400	1.000
Wilson, Dan	.143	7	1	1	1	0	0	.143	.571
Young, Ernie	.200	5	1	0	0	1	0	.200	.200
Young, Kevin	.333	6	2	1	3	0	1	.333	.833

Tavo Alvarez, Expos — RHP

Batter	Avg	AB	H	HR	BI	BB	SO	OBP	Slg
Bonds, Barry*	.250	4	1	0	1	2	1	.500	.250
Butler, Brett*	.200	5	1	0	0	1	0	.333	.200
Carreon, Mark	.500	6	3	0	0	0	0	.500	.500
Clayton, R	.400	5	2	0	1	0	0	.400	.400
DeShields, D*	.250	4	1	0	0	1	1	.400	.250
Fonville, C#	.600	5	3	0	1	0	0	.600	.600
Howard, T*	.500	4	2	0	1	0	0	.500	.500
Jones, C#	.500	5	1	0	0	1	0	.200	.200
Karros, Eric	.167	6	1	0	1	0	3	.167	.167
Lopez, Javy	.400	5	2	0	1	0	1	.400	.600
Manwaring, K	.250	4	1	1	1	1	1	.500	.250
Mondesi, Raul	.200	5	1	0	1	1	1	.333	.400
Offerman, J#	.500	4	2	0	0	1	0	.667	.750
Piazza, Mike	.500	6	3	0	1	0	0	.500	.500
Williams, Ma	.167	6	1	1	1	0	1	.167	.667

Wilson Alvarez, White Sox — LHP

Batter	Avg	AB	H	HR	BI	BB	SO	OBP	Slg
Alomar, R#	.448	29	13	2	9	4	4	.515	.690
Alomar Jr, S	.000	9	0	0	0	0	1	.000	.000
Amaral, Rich	.176	34	6	0	1	8	7	.341	.235
Anderson, Brd*	.310	29	9	0	3	5	1	.412	.448
Anderson, G*	.417	12	5	1	1	0	3	.429	.667
Baerga, C#	.286	42	12	1	6	2	2	.318	.452
Bartee, K	.429	7	3	0	0	0	2	.429	.429
Battle, Allen	.333	6	2	0	0	1	1	.333	.333
Becker, Rich*	.333	6	2	0	1	0	2	.333	.333
Belle, Albert	.268	41	11	2	7	6	9	.362	.463
Beltre, E	.200	5	1	0	0	0	1	.200	.200
Berroa, G	.238	21	5	0	1	0	8	.238	.286
Blowers, Mike	.238	21	5	3	5	5	9	.385	.714
Boggs, Wade*	.333	21	7	0	1	3	5	.400	.381
Bonilla, B#	.143	7	1	0	1	1	1	.250	.286
Boone, Bret	.200	5	1	0	0	1	2	.333	.200
Borders, Pat	.350	20	7	0	2	2	1	.409	.450
Bordick, Mike	.333	24	8	1	2	9	2	.529	.458
Brosius, S	.083	24	2	0	0	4	3	.214	.083
Buford, Damon	.333	6	2	0	0	1	0	.333	.500
Buhner, Jay	.241	29	7	1	5	6	7	.371	.379
Canseco, Jose	.429	14	6	3	9	2	1	.500	1.071
Carr, Chuck	.000	7	0	0	0	0	2	.000	.000
Carter, Joe	.238	21	5	1	3	1	4	.273	.381
Cirillo, Jeff	.421	19	8	0	3	3	3	.500	.789
Clark, Will*	.200	15	3	0	3	2	1	.294	.267

Wilson Alvarez, White Sox — LHP

Batter	Avg	AB	H	HR	BI	BB	SO	OBP	Slg
Coleman, V#	.000	10	0	0	0	0	3	.000	.000
Coomer, Ron	.333	12	4	1	4	1	4	.385	.833
Cordova, M	.273	11	3	0	1	1	2	.333	.455
Curtis, Chad	.414	29	12	0	2	8	2	.541	.586
Cuyler, Milt#	.154	13	2	0	0	0	5	.154	.154
Damon, Johnny*	.444	9	4	0	3	1	1	.500	.667
Davis, Chili#	.171	41	7	1	3	5	11	.261	.268
Davis, Eric	.111	9	1	0	0	0	2	.111	.111
Davis, Russ	.000	8	0	0	0	1	5	.111	.000
Dawson, Andre	.400	5	2	0	0	1	1	.500	.400
Devereaux, M	.107	28	3	0	0	0	7	.107	.107
DiSarcina, G	.346	26	9	0	4	1	2	.370	.423
Easley, D	.368	19	7	2	4	2	5	.429	.737
Edmonds, Jim*	.200	10	2	0	1	3	5	.385	.300
Elster, Kevin	.600	5	3	1	5	1	1	.667	1.400
Erstad, Darin*	.333	6	2	0	0	1	0	.429	.333
Espinoza, A	.211	19	4	0	2	2	3	.318	.263
Fermin, Felix	.368	19	7	0	3	3	0	.455	.421
Fielder, C	.345	29	10	5	8	3	9	.406	.931
Flaherty, J	.429	7	3	0	0	0	0	.429	.571
Franco, Julio	.250	8	2	0	1	0	2	.250	.500
Frye, Jeff	.333	12	4	0	2	1	1	.385	.417
Fryman, T	.188	32	6	1	9	3	5	.257	.281
Gaetti, Gary	.115	26	3	0	0	1	6	.148	.115
Gagne, Greg	.200	20	4	0	0	4	6	.333	.250
Gallego, Mike	.364	22	8	0	2	2	6	.417	.455
Gates, Brent#	.158	19	3	0	0	3	3	.273	.158
Giambi, Jason*	.000	7	0	0	0	0	5	.000	.000
Gil, Benji	.000	5	0	0	1	0	2	.000	.000
Gomez, Chris	.143	14	2	0	3	1	3	.200	.214
Gomez, Leo	.267	15	4	0	3	3	5	.389	.333
Gonzales, R	.333	9	3	1	3	1	2	.400	.667
Gonzalez, A	.000	9	0	0	0	0	3	.000	.000
Gonzalez, J	.174	23	4	1	2	1	4	.208	.304
Goodwin, Tom*	.429	14	6	0	2	2	0	.500	.429
Greenwell, M*	.333	9	3	0	1	2	1	.455	.444
Greer, Rusty*	.389	18	7	0	3	1	1	.421	.500
Griffey Jr, K*	.111	27	3	1	3	1	4	.172	.222
Hall, Mel*	.000	6	0	0	0	0	0	.000	.000
Hamilton, D*	.167	18	3	0	1	4	5	.318	.222
Hammonds, J	.125	8	1	0	0	1	2	.222	.250
Haselman, B	.333	6	2	0	2	2	0	.500	.333
Henderson, R	.167	12	2	0	0	6	3	.444	.167
Hill, G	.000	5	0	0	0	2	2	.286	.000
Hoiles, Chris	.200	20	4	1	3	6	2	.370	.350
Howard, Dave#	.176	17	3	0	1	1	4	.222	.235
Hudler, Rex	.588	17	10	1	3	0	3	.588	.882
Jaha, John	.467	15	7	1	8	3	4	.556	.800
Javier, Stan#	.409	22	9	0	0	4	1	.500	.409
Jordan, Ricky	.167	6	1	0	0	0	1	.167	.167
Joyner, Wally*	.308	13	4	0	2	0	2	.308	.308
Kelly, Pat	.111	18	2	0	0	2	6	.200	.111
Kelly, R	.333	15	5	1	2	1	3	.412	.533
Kirby, Wayne*	.250	4	1	0	1	3	1	.625	.250
Knoblauch, C	.417	24	10	0	3	2	1	.464	.542
Knorr, Randy	.111	9	1	0	0	0	2	.111	.111
Kreuter, Chad#	.000	7	0	0	0	1	0	.000	.000
Leius, Scott	.091	11	1	0	0	2	1	.231	.091
Lewis, Mark	.158	19	3	0	1	1	2	.200	.158
Leyritz, Jim	.154	26	4	2	4	4	4	.267	.423
Listach, Pat#	.133	15	2	0	0	1	1	.133	.133
Lockhart, K*	.143	7	1	0	0	0	1	.143	.286
Lofton, Kenny*	.265	49	13	0	3	6	9	.345	.306
Loretta, Mark	.000	6	0	0	0	0	0	.000	.000
Lovullo, S	.250	8	2	0	0	1	0	.250	.375
Macfarlane, M	.100	10	1	0	2	3	3	.286	.100
Martinez, E	.304	23	7	1	4	9	3	.500	.565
Martinez, T*	.158	19	3	0	3	4	3	.292	.263
Matheny, Mike	.125	8	1	0	0	1	2	.222	.250
McGwire, Mark	.250	8	2	1	3	3	2	.455	.625
McLemore, M#	.370	27	10	0	1	0	2	.370	.407
McRae, Brian#	.333	12	4	0	1	1	0	.385	.417
Meares, Pat	.071	14	1	0	1	0	4	.071	.071
Mieske, Matt	.350	20	7	2	7	1	5	.381	.800
Molitor, Paul	.360	25	9	1	3	5	3	.467	.600
Munoz, Pedro	.176	17	3	0	1	3	8	.300	.176
Murray, Eddie#	.115	26	3	0	0	2	1	.179	.115
Naehring, Tim	.308	13	4	0	1	2	1	.400	.308
Newfield, M	.300	10	3	0	2	0	1	.300	.500
Nieves, M#	.143	7	1	1	1	1	3	.250	.571
Nilsson, Dave*	.400	10	4	0	0	3	3	.571	.400
Nixon, Otis#	.278	18	5	0	0	2	1	.350	.278
O'Neill, Paul*	.556	9	5	0	0	2	0	.636	.556
Offerman, J#	.250	8	2	0	0	0	1	.250	.250
Olerud, John*	.385	13	5	1	4	5	0	.526	.615
Orsulak, Joe*	.500	6	3	0	1	0	0	.429	.833
Ortiz, Luis	.333	3	1	0	2	1	0	.400	1.000
Palmeiro, R*	.450	20	9	2	6	2	1	.500	.850
Palmer, Dean	.278	18	5	0	0	3	6	.381	.278
Paquette, C	.143	14	2	1	3	3	5	.294	.357
Pena, Tony	.407	27	11	0	0	0	2	.407	.444

7

Wilson Alvarez, White Sox — LHP

Batter	Avg	AB	H	HR	BI	BB	SO	OBP	Slg
Perez, Robert	.167	6	1	0	0	0	1	.167	.167
Perry, H	.000	8	0	0	0	0	1	.000	.000
Phillips, T#	.467	15	7	0	1	8	3	.652	.533
Plantier, P*	.000	6	0	0	0	1	2	.143	.000
Polonia, Luis*	.000	10	0	0	0	0	3	.000	.000
Ramirez, M	.308	26	8	1	5	5	4	.419	.462
Randa, Joe	.333	12	4	1	2	0	2	.333	.667
Reboulet, J	.462	13	6	0	1	3	1	.563	.615
Reed, Jody	.100	10	1	0	0	1	1	.182	.200
Ripken, Billy	.429	7	3	0	2	1	0	.500	.571
Ripken, Cal	.189	37	7	1	6	4	6	.268	.324
Rodriguez, Al	.111	9	1	1	1	5	3	.429	.444
Rodriguez, I	.318	22	7	2	6	3	3	.400	.591
Salmon, Tim	.207	29	6	1	2	6	9	.343	.345
Samuel, Juan	.350	20	7	1	1	3	1	.381	.500
Schofield, D	.000	6	0	0	1	0	1	.000	.000
Segui, David*	.231	13	3	0	0	2	0	.333	.231
Seitzer, K	.444	27	12	1	8	5	2	.531	.667
Sheets, Andy	.500	4	2	0	1	2	0	.667	.500
Shumpert, T	.167	6	1	0	0	0	1	.167	.167
Sierra, Ruben#	.235	34	8	2	3	5	5	.333	.559
Slaught, Don	.200	5	1	1	2	1	1	.333	.800
Snow, J.T.#	.087	23	2	0	0	1	6	.125	.087
Sojo, Luis	.091	22	2	0	3	1	0	.130	.136
Sorrento, P*	.000	9	0	0	0	1	4	.100	.000
Sprague, Ed	.111	18	2	0	2	5	7	.304	.167
Stankiewicz	.250	4	1	0	0	0	0	.400	.250
Stanley, Mike	.250	24	6	4	6	6	8	.387	.750
Steinbach, T	.333	27	9	3	5	8	5	.486	.741
Stevens, Lee*	.250	5	1	0	1	0	1	.200	.200
Stinnett, K	.000	5	0	0	0	0	3	.000	.000
Surhoff, B.J.*	.375	16	6	0	2	1	4	.444	.500
Tartabull, D	.375	16	6	3	8	5	3	.524	.938
Tettleton, M#	.125	16	2	1	1	13	6	.517	.375
Thome, Jim*	.316	19	6	0	2	4	4	.435	.526
Trammell, A	.280	25	7	3	7	1	0	.308	.680
Turner, Chris	.286	7	2	0	0	1	1	.375	.286
Valentin, Jhn	.333	12	4	0	1	3	1	.467	.583
Valentin, Jse#	.111	9	1	0	1	4	5	.385	.111
Valle, Dave	.294	17	5	0	2	1	4	.333	.353
Vaughn, Greg	.176	17	3	0	1	1	2	.222	.235
Vaughn, Mo*	.167	18	3	0	2	5	5	.348	.167
Velarde, R	.231	26	6	2	4	7	8	.394	.577
Vina, F*	.286	7	2	0	0	0	0	.286	.286
Vitiello, Joe	.143	7	1	0	0	0	1	.143	.143
Vizquel, Omar#	.229	35	8	0	5	5	3	.325	.314
Voigt, Jack	.000	4	0	0	0	1	3	.200	.000
Walbeck, Matt#	.364	11	4	0	1	1	2	.417	.455
Wallach, Tim	.250	12	3	1	1	1	1	.308	.583
Ward, Turner#	.000	5	0	0	0	1	0	.000	.000
White, Devon#	.333	15	5	0	2	1	2	.375	.400
Whiten, Mark#	.000	7	0	0	0	1	2	.125	.000
Williams, Ber#	.227	22	5	1	2	6	5	.379	.409
Williams, E	.000	8	0	0	0	0	5	.000	.000
Williams, Ger	.063	16	1	0	0	1	3	.118	.063
Wilson, Dan	.167	18	3	0	1	3	1	.211	.167
Young, Ernie	.125	8	1	0	0	0	3	.222	.125
Young, Kevin	.286	7	2	0	0	2	1	.286	.571

Brian Anderson, Indians — LHP

Batter	Avg	AB	H	HR	BI	BB	SO	OBP	Slg
Greenwell, M*	.250	8	2	0	0	1	0	.333	.250
Greer, Rusty*	.300	10	3	0	1	0	0	.300	.400
Griffey Jr, K*	.308	13	4	2	5	1	1	.357	.846
Guillen, O*	.000	6	0	0	0	0	1	.000	.000
Hamelin, Bob*	.200	5	1	0	1	0	1	.200	.200
Hamilton, D*	.222	9	2	1	1	0	2	.300	.556
Hammonds, J	.400	5	2	0	0	1	0	.333	.600
Henderson, R	.429	7	3	0	1	1	0	.500	.571
Hoiles, Chris	.400	10	4	2	2	1	2	.455	1.000
Hunter, Brian	.500	4	2	0	1	0	0	.400	.750
Javier, Stan#	.667	6	4	2	4	0	0	.667	1.833
Johnson, L*	.143	7	1	0	1	0	2	.143	.429
Joyner, Wally*	.286	7	2	0	0	3	3	.286	.429
Karkovice, R	.286	7	2	1	1	0	2	.286	.714
Kelly, Pat	.333	9	3	0	1	0	1	.333	.444
Knoblauch, C	.500	8	4	1	3	0	0	.500	.875
Leyritz, Jim	.000	6	0	0	0	1	1	.143	.000
Listach, Pat#	.429	7	3	0	1	0	1	.500	.571
Macfarlane, M	.333	6	2	0	0	0	0	.333	.833
Martin, N	.333	9	3	0	0	0	0	.333	.444
Martinez, E	.765	17	13	3	4	2	0	.789	1.471
Martinez, T*	.375	8	3	3	5	0	2	.375	1.500
McLemore, M#	.111	9	1	0	0	0	2	.111	.111
Mieske, Matt	.200	5	1	1	2	0	0	.167	.800
Molitor, Paul	.300	10	3	0	1	0	1	.300	.500
Mouton, Lyle	.200	5	1	0	0	0	2	.200	.400
Munoz, Pedro	.286	7	2	0	3	0	1	.286	.286
Naehring, Tim	.571	7	4	0	2	1	1	.556	.714
Nixon, Otis#	.286	7	2	0	1	0	1	.286	.571
O'Neill, Paul*	.583	12	7	4	9	0	3	.583	1.667
Olerud, John*	.500	8	4	0	1	0	0	.556	.625
Palmeiro, R*	.364	11	4	0	1	3	0	.500	.364
Palmer, Dean	.222	9	2	0	0	1	1	.222	.222
Phillips, T#	.167	6	1	0	1	1	2	.286	.333
Raines, Tim#	.000	4	0	0	0	0	0	.000	.000
Ripken, Cal	.308	13	4	1	4	1	1	.357	.615
Rodriguez, Al	.333	6	2	0	0	0	0	.333	.333
Rodriguez, I	.455	11	5	0	0	2	1	.538	.636
Sabo, Chris	.000	3	0	0	0	2	1	.400	.000
Salmon, Tim	.000	3	0	0	0	2	2	.400	.000
Samuel, Juan	.143	7	1	0	1	0	2	.125	.143
Seitzer, K	.000	5	0	0	1	0	0	.000	.000
Sierra, Ruben#	.429	7	3	0	4	0	0	.429	.429
Sojo, Luis	.231	13	3	1	1	0	0	.231	.462
Sprague, Ed	.000	5	0	0	1	2	0	.250	.000
Stanley, Mike	.455	11	5	2	3	1	0	.455	1.091
Steinbach, T	.400	5	2	0	0	0	0	.400	.400
Surhoff, B.J.*	.800	5	4	0	0	0	0	.800	.800
Tartabull, D	.154	13	2	0	0	2	2	.154	.154
Tettleton, M#	.200	10	2	0	2	3	1	.385	.300
Thomas, Frank	.625	8	5	2	4	1	0	.600	1.500
Trammell, A	.143	7	1	0	0	0	0	.143	.143
Valentin, Jhn	.333	6	2	1	2	1	1	.429	1.000
Vaughn, Mo*	.286	7	2	0	2	0	2	.375	.429
Velarde, R	.357	14	5	0	1	2	3	.438	.571
Ventura, R*	.300	10	3	1	4	0	1	.300	.600
Ward, Turner#	.250	4	1	0	0	1	0	.400	.250
White, Devon#	.222	9	2	0	1	0	0	.222	.222
Williams, Ber#	.333	9	3	0	0	4	0	.538	.333
Williams, Ger	.375	8	3	0	2	0	1	.375	.625
Wilson, Dan	.111	9	1	0	0	0	2	.111	.273

Brian Anderson, Indians — LHP

Batter	Avg	AB	H	HR	BI	BB	SO	OBP	Slg
Alomar, R#	.091	11	1	0	0	0	0	.167	.091
Amaral, Rich	.105	19	2	0	0	1	1	.150	.105
Anderson, Brd*	.400	15	6	1	1	0	1	.400	.733
Anderson, G*	.600	5	3	1	4	0	0	.600	1.400
Beltre, E	.333	3	1	0	0	0	1	.333	.667
Berroa, G	.400	5	2	1	1	1	1	.500	1.000
Blowers, Mike	.300	10	3	0	1	2	2	.417	.300
Boggs, Wade*	.375	8	3	0	0	0	1	.375	.375
Bonilla, B#	.429	7	3	2	2	0	1	.429	1.286
Borders, Pat	.500	8	4	0	1	1	0	.556	.500
Buford, Damon	.600	5	3	0	2	0	1	.600	.600
Buhner, Jay	.158	19	3	1	3	0	1	.158	.368
Canseco, Jose	.167	6	1	1	1	0	1	.167	.667
Carter, Joe	.375	8	3	1	2	1	1	.444	.875
Clark, Will*	.273	11	3	0	2	1	0	.308	.364
Coleman, V#	.143	7	1	0	0	1	0	.143	.286
Curtis, Chad	.167	6	1	0	1	1	2	.286	.333
Davis, Russ	.200	5	1	0	0	0	1	.200	.200
Devereaux, M	.250	4	1	0	1	0	1	.200	.250
Diaz, Alex#	.000	5	0	0	0	0	0	.000	.000
Durham, Ray#	.667	6	4	0	1	0	0	.667	1.333
Elster, Kevin	.000	4	0	0	1	0	1	.000	.000
Fermin, Felix	.222	9	2	0	0	0	0	.222	.333
Fielder, C	.167	6	1	0	1	0	1	.167	.333
Flaherty, J	.111	9	1	0	1	0	2	.111	.111
Fryman, T	.375	8	3	2	3	1	0	.455	1.250
Gaetti, Gary	.111	9	1	0	0	0	1	.111	.111
Gagne, Greg	.125	8	1	0	0	2	1	.125	.250
Gomez, Chris	.200	10	2	1	1	0	0	.200	.500
Gonzalez, A	.000	6	0	0	0	1	1	.143	.000

Luis Andujar, Blue Jays — RHP

Batter	Avg	AB	H	HR	BI	BB	SO	OBP	Slg
Becker, Rich*	.571	7	4	0	1	0	1	.571	1.000
Coomer, Ron	.333	6	2	0	0	0	0	.333	.333
Cordova, M	.250	8	2	1	3	1	1	.333	.750
Elster, Kevin	.250	8	2	1	1	1	3	.333	.625
Gonzalez, J	.333	9	3	0	0	0	0	.333	.333
Greer, Rusty*	.167	6	1	1	1	0	1	.167	.667
Hamilton, D*	.222	9	2	0	1	1	1	.300	.222
Hocking, D#	.200	5	1	0	0	0	0	.200	.200
Knoblauch, C	.429	7	3	0	1	2	0	.556	.857
Lawton, Matt*	.500	8	4	0	2	1	0	.556	.625
McLemore, M#	.200	5	1	0	0	1	1	.333	.200
Palmer, Dean	.500	8	4	0	0	1	0	.556	.750
Rodriguez, I	.286	7	2	1	1	0	0	.286	.857
Stevens, Lee*	.143	7	1	1	1	0	0	.222	.143
Tettleton, M#	.000	6	0	0	0	1	1	.143	.000

Kevin Appier, Royals — RHP

Batter	Avg	AB	H	HR	BI	BB	SO	OBP	Slg
Aldrete, Mike*	.333	24	8	0	0	4	6	.429	.417
Alomar, R#	.163	43	7	1	2	6	12	.260	.279
Alomar Jr, S	.231	26	6	0	1	2	2	.286	.231
Amaral, Rich	.400	5	2	0	1	0	0	.400	.400
Anderson, Brd*	.182	33	6	0	1	6	7	.325	.273
Anderson, G*	.500	10	5	0	1	0	2	.500	1.000
Ausmus, Brad	.000	6	0	0	0	0	2	.000	.000
Baerga, C#	.302	43	13	0	7	3	5	.340	.395
Baines, H*	.372	43	16	2	8	7	9	.451	.605

Batter	Avg	AB	H	HR	BI	BB	SO	OBP	Slg
Barberie, B#	.000	5	0	0	0	0	3	.000	.000
Batista, Tony	.222	9	2	0	1	0	4	.222	.222
Becker, Rich*	.000	9	0	0	0	1	4	.100	.000
Belle, Albert	.205	44	9	2	7	3	14	.250	.409
Beltre, E	.000	2	0	0	0	2	1	.500	.000
Berroa, G	.267	15	4	0	0	1	3	.353	.400
Bichette, D	.143	7	1	0	0	0	2	.143	.143
Blowers, Mike	.111	9	1	0	0	0	3	.111	.222
Boggs, Wade*	.222	45	10	1	3	12	3	.379	.289
Bonilla, B#	.375	8	3	0	0	0	1	.375	.500
Borders, Pat	.125	8	1	0	0	1	2	.222	.125
Bordick, Mike	.212	33	7	0	2	2	7	.257	.273
Bragg, Darren*	.333	6	2	0	2	0	4	.333	.333
Brosius, S	.190	21	4	0	2	1	4	.227	.286
Buhner, Jay	.160	25	4	1	2	2	9	.222	.320
Burks, Ellis	.208	24	5	0	2	1	8	.231	.333
Cangelosi, J#	.375	8	3	0	0	0	2	.375	.375
Canseco, Jose	.167	24	4	1	3	2	10	.259	.333
Carter, Joe	.245	49	12	0	8	1	8	.255	.327
Cedeno, D#	.143	7	1	0	0	0	2	.143	.143
Cirillo, Jeff	.250	16	4	0	3	1	2	.294	.438
Clark, Tony#	.167	6	1	1	1	1	4	.286	.667
Clark, Will*	.235	17	4	0	3	6	6	.435	.294
Cole, Alex*	.231	26	6	0	0	2	5	.286	.346
Cora, Joey#	.237	38	9	0	5	4	5	.310	.342
Cordero, Wil	.167	6	1	0	0	0	1	.167	.333
Cordova, M	.083	12	1	0	1	1	5	.154	.083
Curtis, Chad	.120	25	3	0	1	1	6	.148	.120
Cuyler, Milt#	.143	7	1	0	0	2	1	.333	.286
Davis, Chili*	.220	41	9	3	8	4	15	.289	.488
Dawson, Andre	.200	15	3	0	2	1	3	.250	.200
Deer, Rob	.087	23	2	0	0	2	9	.160	.130
Delgado, C*	.083	12	1	0	0	1	5	.154	.083
Devereaux, M	.214	28	6	1	3	1	2	.241	.464
Diaz, Alex#	.200	20	4	0	0	1	2	.238	.200
DiSarcina, Gary	.314	35	11	1	5	3	3	.359	.429
Durham, Ray#	.500	6	3	0	1	0	0	.571	.500
Easley, D	.176	17	3	0	3	0	3	.176	.176
Edmonds, Jim*	.259	27	7	0	2	2	8	.333	.333
Espinoza, A	.250	12	3	0	1	0	1	.250	.333
Fabregas, Jorge*	.300	10	3	0	0	1	1	.364	.300
Fermin, Felix	.348	23	8	0	3	0	1	.348	.391
Fielder, C	.150	40	6	2	4	2	16	.209	.300
Flaherty, J	.200	5	1	0	0	0	2	.200	.200
Fox, Andy*	.400	5	2	0	0	0	1	.400	.400
Franco, Julio	.273	33	9	1	3	3	7	.333	.424
Frye, Jeff	.250	12	3	0	2	0	3	.400	.375
Fryman, T	.333	42	14	3	10	4	12	.383	.619
Gaetti, Gary	.077	13	1	0	0	0	6	.077	.077
Gagne, Greg	.333	9	3	0	0	0	3	.333	.444
Gallego, Mike	.192	26	5	1	1	1	6	.222	.308
Gates, Brent#	.263	19	5	0	2	0	4	.250	.316
Giambi, Jason*	.125	8	1	0	0	0	2	.125	.125
Gil, Benji	.143	7	1	0	2	0	3	.143	.143
Girardi, Joe	.333	6	2	0	0	0	2	.333	.333
Gomez, Chris	.000	9	0	0	0	0	2	.100	.000
Gomez, Leo	.391	23	9	2	4	2	5	.440	.696
Gonzales, R	.444	9	4	0	0	1	2	.500	.444
Gonzalez, A	.167	6	1	0	0	3	4	.444	.167
Gonzalez, J	.235	34	8	1	3	1	12	.278	.353
Grebeck, C	.200	10	2	0	2	0	1	.200	.300
Green, Shawn*	.133	15	2	0	2	2	3	.235	.200
Greenwell, M*	.333	42	14	1	6	4	8	.391	.548
Greer, Rusty*	.133	15	6	0	2	1	4	.438	.600
Griffey Jr, K*	.217	46	10	2	6	5	5	.294	.348
Guillen, O*	.242	33	8	0	6	1	4	.250	.303
Hall, Mel*	.364	11	4	1	6	0	0	.364	.727
Hamilton, D*	.538	26	14	0	2	7	2	.618	.654
Hammonds, J	.500	6	3	0	0	0	0	.571	.667
Haselman, B	.333	9	3	0	2	2	2	.455	.333
Henderson, R	.299	31	9	0	2	5	2	.405	.323
Herrera, Jose*	.200	10	2	0	1	0	1	.200	.200
Higginson, B*	.625	8	5	2	3	1	2	.600	1.375
Hill, G	.222	9	2	0	0	0	0	.222	.333
Hoiles, Chris	.154	13	2	0	1	2	6	.267	.231
Howell, Jack*	.500	14	7	1	3	1	4	.533	.786
Hudler, Rex	.000	5	0	0	0	1	4	.167	.000
Hulse, David*	.318	22	7	0	2	1	5	.348	.455
Huson, Jeff*	.143	21	3	0	3	5	3	.250	.190
Incaviglia, P	.143	14	2	0	1	0	8	.200	.143
Jaha, John	.133	15	2	0	0	2	7	.235	.200
James, Dion*	.308	13	4	0	2	4	1	.471	.385
Javier, Stan#	.500	6	3	1	1	1	1	.571	1.000
Jeter, Derek	.375	8	3	0	1	0	0	.375	.375
Johnson, L*	.206	34	7	0	0	1	1	.229	.294
Joyner, Wally*	.444	9	4	0	1	0	0	.444	.444
Karkovice, R	.294	17	5	0	0	4	3	.429	.412
Kelly, Pat	.100	10	1	0	0	0	2	.100	.100
Kelly, R	.167	6	1	0	0	0	2	.167	.167
Kent, Jeff	.167	6	1	0	0	2	2	.167	.167
Kirby, Wayne*	.462	13	6	0	3	1	2	.500	.538

Batter	Avg	AB	H	HR	BI	BB	SO	OBP	Slg
Knoblauch, C	.355	31	11	0	3	4	6	.429	.452
Knorr, Randy	.000	8	0	0	0	0	4	.000	.000
Kreuter, Chad#	.313	16	5	0	2	3	6	.400	.313
Leius, Scott	.235	17	4	0	2	1	3	.278	.235
Lewis, Darren	.250	8	2	0	0	0	2	.250	.250
Lewis, Mark	.280	25	7	0	0	0	4	.280	.320
Leyritz, Jim	.250	8	2	0	1	2	4	.400	.250
Listach, Pat#	.316	16	5	0	3	4	3	.476	.438
Livingstone*	.235	17	4	0	0	0	3	.235	.294
Lofton, Kenny*	.325	40	13	0	1	2	0	.357	.375
Lovullo, T#	.125	8	1	0	0	0	1	.125	.250
Manto, Jeff	.333	6	2	0	1	0	1	.333	.333
Martinez, Da*	.091	11	1	0	0	0	4	.091	.091
Martinez, E	.186	43	8	0	1	8	11	.314	.209
Martinez, T*	.182	33	6	1	4	6	9	.308	.333
Marzano, John	.250	8	2	0	2	0	1	.250	.250
McCarty, Dave	.100	10	1	0	0	0	5	.100	.200
McGwire, Mark	.161	31	5	1		4	8	.278	.290
McLemore, M#	.240	25	6	0	1	2	3	.296	.240
Meares, Pat	.214	14	3	0	1	1	5	.267	.214
Mieske, Matt	.222	9	2	0	1	0	3	.222	.333
Mitchell, K	.222	9	2	0	0	0	0	.222	.333
Molitor, Paul	.209	43	9	1	3	3	3	.261	.279
Munoz, Pedro	.091	11	1	0	0	0	4	.091	.091
Murray, Eddie*	.353	17	6	2	5	2	3	.421	.882
Myers, Greg*	.290	31	9	0	3	2	4	.324	.290
Naehring, Tim	.143	21	3	0	2	1	5	.182	.143
Newson, W*	.500	4	2	0	1	4	1	.750	.750
Nieves, M#	.333	9	3	1	3	2	4	.455	.667
Nilsson, Dave*	.143	21	3	0	2	0	4	.136	.238
Nixon, Otis#	.389	18	7	0	0	3	2	.476	.444
O'Brien, C	.000	6	0	0	0	0	1	.000	.000
O'Leary, Troy*	.100	10	1	0	0	2	3	.250	.200
O'Neill, Paul*	.346	26	9	3	9	2	5	.367	.769
Olerud, John*	.267	45	12	0	2	6	5	.353	.289
Oliver, Joe	.222	9	2	0	0	0	2	.222	.333
Orsulak, Joe*	.167	18	3	0	0	1	1	.211	.167
Palmeiro, R*	.205	44	9	1	2	6	11	.300	.341
Palmer, Dean	.182	22	4	1	3	1	7	.217	.318
Paquette, C	.222	9	2	0	1	0	1	.222	.222
Peltier, Dan*	.250	4	1	0	0	1	1	.400	.250
Pena, Tony	.214	28	6	0	1		6	.241	.286
Perez, Tomas#	.000	6	0	0	0	0	1	.000	.000
Phillips, T#	.191	47	9	2	4	8	22	.309	.340
Plantier, P*	.333	15	5	0	0	4	3	.474	.533
Polonia, Luis*	.386	44	17	0	4	5	2	.413	.545
Pride, Curtis*	.429	7	3	1	1	1	2	.500	1.143
Raines, Tim#	.353	34	12	1	5	6	5	.450	.588
Ramirez, M	.071	14	1	0	1	1	8	.188	.143
Reboulet, J	.000	8	0	0	0	0	3	.000	.000
Reed, Jody	.281	32	9	0	2	3	2	.343	.344
Ripken, Billy	.200	10	2	0	3	1	2	.273	.300
Ripken, Cal	.326	43	14	0	7	3	11	.370	.395
Rodriguez, Al	.200	10	2	0	0	0	2	.200	.200
Rodriguez, I	.333	33	11	1	5	1	6	.353	.515
Salmon, Tim	.167	30	5	0	0	3	7	.242	.300
Schofield, D	.105	19	2	0	0	2	8	.190	.158
Segui, David#	.333	6	2	0	1	1	0	.429	.500
Seitzer, K	.160	25	4	0	3	1	5	.192	.160
Sheffield, G	.167	6	1	0	0	0	0	.167	.167
Sierra, Ruben*	.229	48	11	2	7	5	10	.296	.396
Snow, J.T.#	.190	21	4	1	3	7	5	.393	.381
Sojo, Luis	.200	15	3	0	1	0	2	.200	.333
Sorrento, P	.343	35	12	1	3	1	7	.361	.543
Sosa, Sammy	.111	9	1	0	1	0	2	.111	.111
Spiers, Bill*	.500	14	7	0	4	2	1	.563	.571
Sprague, Ed	.120	25	3	0	2	2	10	.172	.120
Stahoviak, S*	.143	7	1	0	0	0	1	.143	.286
Stairs, Matt*	.400	5	2	0	0	2	2	.571	.600
Stanley, Mike	.188	16	3	0	0	0	5	.188	.188
Steinbach, T	.206	34	7	0	4	2	13	.237	.235
Stevens, Lee*	.500	4	2	0	0	0	1	.500	.625
Strange, Doug*	.222	18	4	0	1	1	3	.263	.333
Strawberry, D*	.167	6	1	0	0	0	3	.167	.167
Surhoff, B.J.*	.200	25	5	0	1	4	6	.310	.320
Tartabull, D	.000	18	0	0	0	1	11	.053	.000
Tettleton, M#	.111	36	4	0	1	7	13	.256	.111
Thomas, Frank	.333	36	12	0	4	8	8	.435	.472
Thome, Jim*	.333	18	6	1	2	6	9	.500	.556
Tinsley, Lee#	.333	3	1	0	0	0	1	.500	.333
Trammell, A	.250	12	3	0	2	0	3	.231	.250
Valentin, Jhn	.150	20	3	0	1	2	5	.227	.200
Valentin, Jse#	.200	15	3	0	0	3	4	.333	.333
Valle, Dave	.320	25	8	1	4	0	2	.370	.480
Vaughn, Greg	.333	27	9	1	4	2	13	.400	.556
Vaughn, Mo*	.265	34	9	1	8	3	15	.419	.529
Velarde, R	.308	13	4	1	3	1	2	.438	.615
Ventura, R*	.350	40	14	1	8	7	5	.420	.475
Vina, F*	.125	8	1	1	1	1	1	.222	.500
Vizquel, Omar#	.235	34	8	0	1	6	4	.350	.235
Walbeck, Matt#	.286	7	2	0	0	1	0	.375	.286

Kevin Appier, Royals — RHP

Kevin Appier, Royals — RHP

Batter	Avg	AB	H	HR	BI	BB	SO	OBP	Slg
Ward, Turner#	.263	19	5	0	3	3	3	.364	.316
Weiss, Walt*	.273	11	3	0	1	2	2	.385	.455
White, Devon#	.268	41	11	0	1	2	7	.318	.366
Whiten, Mark#	.176	17	3	2	3	2	2	.263	.529
Williams, Ber#	.111	27	3	1	2	4	8	.226	.222
Williams, Geo#	.250	8	2	0	1	0	3	.250	.250
Wilson, Dan	.429	7	3	1	2	0	1	.429	.857

Andy Ashby, Padres — RHP

Batter	Avg	AB	H	HR	BI	BB	SO	OBP	Slg
Abbott, Kurt	.333	6	2	2	5	0	1	.333	1.333
Alicea, Luis#	.250	8	2	0	0	0	1	.250	.250
Alou, Moises	.200	15	3	2	4	1	1	.235	.600
Andrews, S	.333	6	2	0	0	0	2	.333	.333
Anthony, Eric*	.000	6	0	0	1	1	2	.143	.000
Arias, Alex	.250	4	1	0	1	1	1	.500	.250
Ashley, Billy	.400	5	2	0	0	1	1	.500	.800
Bagwell, Jeff	.231	26	6	2	4	3	6	.310	.615
Barberie, B#	.429	7	3	0	1	1	1	.500	.429
Bates, Jason#	.111	9	1	1	1	0	0	.111	.444
Batiste, Kim	.167	6	1	0	0	0	1	.167	.167
Bell, Derek	.143	14	2	0	1	0	4	.133	.143
Bell, Jay	.077	26	2	0	0	4	7	.250	.077
Benard, M*	.400	10	4	0	0	1	1	.455	.500
Benjamin, M	.167	6	1	0	0	0	2	.167	.167
Berry, Sean	.400	15	6	0	1	0	4	.400	.467
Bichette, D	.350	20	7	2	3	0	5	.350	.750
Biggio, Craig	.370	27	10	1	6	7	6	.500	.704
Blauser, Jeff*	.375	16	6	1	5	0	3	.353	.688
Bonds, Barry*	.417	24	10	5	6	5	3	.500	1.125
Bonilla, B#	.250	16	4	1	4	3	2	.368	.500
Boone, Bret	.400	5	2	0	1	0	1	.400	.400
Branson, Jeff*	.125	8	1	1	2	0	0	.125	.500
Brogna, Rico*	.188	16	3	1	1	2	1	.278	.438
Brumfield, J	.333	6	2	0	1	1	1	.429	.333
Burks, Ellis	.214	14	3	0	0	0	5	.214	.214
Butler, Brett*	.304	23	7	0	2	1	2	.333	.304
Caminiti, Ken#	.333	15	5	0	2	2	1	.412	.467
Carr, Chuck	.250	12	3	0	0	3	1	.400	.250
Carreon, Mark	.125	8	1	0	1	1	1	.222	.125
Castilla, V	.533	15	8	3	9	0	1	.533	1.133
Cedeno, A	.133	15	2	1	2	0	4	.133	.333
Clark, Dave*	.200	5	1	0	1	1	1	.333	.400
Clark, Will*	.500	6	3	2	2	0	0	.500	1.500
Clayton, R	.182	22	4	0	3	0	3	.182	.182
Colbrunn, G	.250	8	2	0	0	0	1	.250	.250
Coleman, V#	.167	6	1	0	0	1	0	.286	.167
Conine, Jeff	.412	17	7	0	2	0	2	.412	.412
Cordero, Wil	.273	11	3	0	1	0	2	.308	.273
Cummings, M*	.000	5	0	0	0	1	1	.167	.000
Daulton, D*	.357	14	5	1	5	4	1	.500	.786
Dawson, Andre	.333	9	3	0	3	1	1	.400	.444
DeShields, D*	.233	30	7	0	2	3	1	.303	.267
Dunston, S	.333	12	4	1	3	0	4	.308	.583
Dykstra, L*	.533	15	8	0	2	2	1	.588	.733
Eisenreich, J*	.667	12	8	0	6	0	1	.667	.917
Eusebio, Tony	.333	6	2	0	1	0	2	.333	.500
Everett, Carl#	.400	10	4	0	2	2	3	.500	.400
Finley, Steve*	.091	11	1	0	0	3	3	.286	.091
Fletcher, D*	.429	14	6	1	3	4	0	.579	.714
Floyd, Cliff*	.300	10	3	1	3	0	2	.300	.800
Frazier, Lou*	.200	5	1	0	0	2	1	.429	.200
Gaetti, Gary	.000	4	0	0	0	0	1	.000	.000
Gagne, Greg	.167	6	1	0	0	0	0	.167	.167
Galarraga, A	.450	20	9	3	9	1	4	.522	1.000
Gant, Ron	.182	11	2	0	0	0	3	.182	.182
Garcia, C	.118	17	2	0	2	1	2	.150	.235
Gilkey, Otis	.263	19	5	0	1	2	3	.333	.421
Girardi, Joe	.385	13	5	0	0	1	3	.429	.538
Goff, Jerry*	.200	5	1	0	1	1	1	.333	.400
Gonzalez, L*	.241	29	7	0	5	1	3	.267	.276
Grace, Mark*	.320	25	8	1	7	4	3	.414	.600
Grissom, M	.375	16	6	0	2	0	0	.375	.500
Grudzielanek	.167	12	2	0	0	1	2	.286	.250
Gutierrez, R	.333	9	3	0	1	0	0	.333	.444
Hansen, Dave*	.333	9	3	0	0	0	0	.333	.444
Hayes, C	.200	15	3	0	0	0	0	.200	.200
Hernandez, Ca	.333	6	2	0	0	0	1	.333	.500
Hernandez, Jo	.556	9	5	0	1	1	2	.600	.556
Hill, G	.750	8	6	1	2	1	1	.778	1.625
Hollandsworth*	.182	11	2	0	0	0	0	.182	.182
Hollins, Dave#	.167	12	2	0	2	2	4	.250	.250
Hundley, Todd#	.500	14	7	0	1	3	1	.588	.571
Hunter, Brian	.143	7	1	0	0	0	2	.143	.286
Hunter, Bri L	.400	10	4	0	2	0	1	.400	.400
Huskey, Butch	.375	8	3	0	0	0	1	.375	.375
Incaviglia, J	.222	9	2	0	2	1	3	.300	.333
Jefferies, G#	.353	17	6	0	2	1	2	.389	.412
Johnson, Char	.222	9	2	0	0	0	2	.222	.222
Johnson, L*	.286	7	2	0	1	0	0	.286	.286
Johnson, Mark*	.333	6	2	1	1	1	1	.429	.833

Andy Ashby, Padres — RHP (continued)

Batter	Avg	AB	H	HR	BI	BB	SO	OBP	Slg
Jones, C#	.111	9	1	0	0	0	1	.111	.111
Jordan, Brian	.471	17	8	0	0	0	1	.471	.706
Justice, Dave*	.231	13	3	1	5	3	2	.375	.462
Karros, Eric	.143	28	4	2	2	2	6	.226	.357
Kelly, R	.400	10	4	0	1	0	2	.400	.500
Kent, Jeff	.261	23	6	2	5	1	8	.292	.609
King, Jeff	.111	9	1	0	0	1	0	.200	.111
Kingery, Mike*	.467	15	7	0	1	1	0	.500	.667
Kirby, Wayne*	.429	7	3	0	0	1	0	.500	.714
Klesko, Ryan*	.556	9	5	0	2	2	1	.636	.556
Lankford, Ray*	.227	22	5	0	0	2	2	.292	.273
Lansing, Mike	.421	19	8	1	7	1	0	.450	.632
Larkin, Barry	.375	16	6	1	3	3	3	.474	.625
Lemke, Mark#	.222	9	2	0	0	1	0	.300	.222
Lewis, Darren	.083	12	1	0	0	2	1	.267	.083
Liriano, N#	.200	5	1	0	1	0	0	.200	.200
Mabry, John*	.200	10	2	0	1	0	2	.273	.200
Magadan, Dave*	.545	11	6	1	2	0	0	.615	.818
Manwaring, K	.429	14	6	0	2	2	0	.500	.500
Martin, Al*	.389	18	7	1	4	0	4	.389	.778
Martinez, Da*	.250	12	3	1	1	0	1	.308	.500
May, Derrick*	.267	15	4	1	1	1	3	.313	.467
Mayne, Brent*	.250	4	1	0	0	1	1	.400	.250
McGee, Willie#	.667	9	6	0	1	0	0	.667	.667
McGriff, Fred*	.333	12	4	0	3	0	3	.467	.333
McRae, Brian#	.462	13	6	0	2	0	2	.462	.615
Merced, O*	.320	25	8	0	0	2	5	.370	.320
Miller, Orl	.143	7	1	0	1	1	2	.250	.286
Mitchell, K	.750	4	3	0	2	2	0	.833	1.250
Mondesi, Raul	.200	20	4	1	2	0	4	.200	.400
Morandini, M*	.348	23	8	1	3	3	4	.423	.609
Morris, Hal*	.417	12	5	1	2	2	3	.500	.750
Mouton, James	.286	7	2	0	0	0	0	.286	.286
Murray, Eddie#	.429	7	3	0	0	1	1	.500	.571
Nixon, Otis#	.500	4	2	0	0	1	0	.600	.750
O'Brien, C	.333	6	2	1	3	4	2	.600	.833
O'Neill, Paul*	.400	5	2	1	4	1	1	.500	1.000
Offerman, J#	.231	13	3	0	2	1	1	.267	.231
Oliver, Joe	.429	7	3	0	4	2	0	.500	.429
Ordonez, Rey	.667	6	4	0	1	0	1	.667	.833
Orsulak, Joe*	.231	13	3	0	2	0	0	.231	.231
Pagnozzi, Tom	.368	19	7	0	4	0	1	.368	.526
Parent, Mark	.167	6	1	0	0	0	2	.167	.333
Pena, G#	.375	8	3	1	2	1	3	.444	.750
Pendleton, T#	.222	18	4	2	6	0	1	.222	.556
Phillips, J*	.000	5	0	0	0	1	2	.167	.000
Piazza, Mike	.250	28	7	0	1	3	3	.323	.286
Plantier, P*	.333	6	2	0	0	0	2	.333	.500
Reed, Jeff*	.100	10	1	0	1	2	2	.250	.200
Reed, Jody	.500	4	2	0	0	0	0	.500	.750
Roberts, Bip#	.250	8	2	0	3	2	3	.364	.250
Rodriguez, H*	.294	17	5	0	2	0	3	.294	.412
Sabo, Chris	.250	8	2	0	3	0	2	.222	.375
Sanchez, Rey	.154	13	2	1	3	0	2	.154	.385
Sandberg, R	.188	16	3	0	0	0	2	.188	.313
Sanders, R	.286	7	2	1	3	2	1	.444	.857
Santangelo, F	.125	8	1	0	0	0	0	.125	.125
Santiago, B	.300	10	3	0	1	0	0	.300	.300
Scarsone, S	.100	10	1	1	1	0	4	.200	.500
Segui, David#	.182	11	2	0	0	0	2	.182	.273
Servais, S	.200	10	2	1	2	1	1	.273	.500
Sheaffer, D	.400	5	2	0	0	1	1	.500	.400
Sheffield, G	.200	10	2	1	2	1	0	.357	.500
Slaught, Don	.143	7	1	0	1	2	2	.333	.286
Smith, Dwight*	.250	12	3	1	4	0	3	.231	.500
Smith, Ozzie#	.214	14	3	0	0	0	0	.214	.214
Sosa, Sammy	.467	15	7	2	4	1	1	.471	.933
Stinnett, K	.250	4	1	0	0	1	1	.400	.250
Stocker, K#	.182	11	2	0	1	4	1	.438	.273
Sweeney, Mark*	.167	6	1	0	0	0	2	.167	.167
Tarasco, Tony*	.200	5	1	0	0	0	4	.200	.200
Taubensee, E*	.222	9	2	0	1	1	2	.300	.222
Thompson, Mil*	.400	15	6	0	1	3	2	.500	.400
Thompson, Rob	.000	3	0	0	0	3	1	.500	.000
Thompson, Ry	.143	14	2	0	0	0	5	.143	.143
VanderWal, J*	.250	4	1	0	0	1	1	.500	.250
Veras, Q#	.200	10	2	0	0	1	3	.273	.300
Vizcaino, J#	.273	22	6	0	2	4	4	.360	.364
Walker, Larry*	.316	19	6	0	1	1	3	.364	.421
Wallach, Tim	.231	26	6	1	2	3	6	.333	.385
Weiss, Walt*	.217	23	5	1	1	3	4	.333	.348
White, R	.300	10	3	0	1	0	4	.364	.500
Whiten, Mark#	.143	14	2	0	2	0	3	.250	.143
Williams, Ma	.200	20	4	1	2	1	1	.238	.350
Young, Eric	.300	10	3	1	2	1	1	.364	.600
Young, Kevin	.222	12	3	0	1	1	3	.308	.250
Zeile, Todd	.333	15	5	1	4	5	1	.524	.600

Paul Assenmacher, Indians — LHP

Batter	Avg	AB	H	HR	BI	BB	SO	OBP	Slg
Aldrete, Mike*	.250	8	2	0	1	0	0	.250	.375
Alomar, R#	.267	15	4	1	1	4	2	.421	.600
Anderson, Brd*	.125	8	1	0	1	1	2	.300	.250
Anderson, G*	.000	5	0	0	0	1	0	.000	.000
Baines, H*	.143	7	1	0	0	0	0	.143	.143
Barberie, B#	.143	7	1	0	1	1	1	.333	.143
Bell, Jay	.455	11	5	1	2	1	2	.500	1.000
Belliard, R	.167	6	1	0	2	1	3	.286	.167
Biggio, Craig	.273	11	3	0	1	1	1	.333	.273
Blauser, Jeff	.200	5	1	1	3	3	2	.500	.800
Boggs, Wade*	.429	7	3	0	0	1	0	.500	.429
Bonds, Barry*	.135	37	5	1	4	4	12	.220	.297
Bonilla, B#	.281	32	9	3	7	3	6	.333	.625
Butler, Brett*	.692	13	9	0	4	1	2	.714	.769
Caminiti, Ken#	.385	13	5	0	2	0	3	.385	.385
Candaele, C#	.600	5	3	0	1	1	0	.667	.800
Carreon, Mark	.000	8	0	0	0	0	4	.000	.000
Clark, Will*	.267	30	8	0	6	2	7	.324	.333
Coleman, V#	.208	24	5	0	2	1	5	.240	.250
Damon, Johnny*	.250	4	1	0	2	0	0	.250	.250
Daulton, D*	.300	20	6	2	4	3	6	.417	.600
Davis, Chili#	.200	10	2	0	0	0	3	.200	.300
Davis, Eric	.625	8	5	2	4	2	2	.727	1.375
Dawson, Andre	.333	6	2	1	1	1	1	.429	.833
DeShields, D*	.286	14	4	0	3	3	3	.412	.357
Devereaux, M	.286	7	2	0	0	1	1	.375	.286
Duncan, M	.400	10	4	0	0	1	1	.455	.500
Dykstra, L*	.571	14	8	1	4	0	3	.533	.929
Easley, D	.000	5	0	0	0	1	1	.167	.000
Edmonds, Jim*	.167	6	1	0	1	0	3	.167	.333
Elster, Kevin	.000	8	0	0	1	2	4	.200	.000
Finley, Steve*	.375	8	3	1	2	0	1	.375	.750
Galarraga, A	.167	12	2	1	3	0	5	.167	.417
Gant, Ron	.333	9	3	1	2	0	2	.333	.667
Grace, Mark*	.000	6	0	0	0	0	2	.000	.000
Greenwell, M*	.125	8	1	0	1	0	2	.111	.125
Greer, Rusty*	.400	5	2	0	2	1	1	.500	.600
Grissom, M	.200	10	2	0	0	1	2	.273	.200
Guillen, O*	.000	6	0	0	0	0	2	.000	.000
Gwynn, Tony*	.258	31	8	1	3	1	3	.281	.387
Hamelin, Bob*	.000	5	0	0	0	1	3	.167	.000
Harris, Lenny*	.833	6	5	0	0	0	0	.833	.833
Hayes, C	.200	5	1	0	0	0	0	.200	.200
Hollins, Dave#	.286	14	4	0	4	0	1	.333	.357
Hudler, Rex	.167	6	1	0	0	0	4	.167	.333
Hundley, Todd#	.000	3	0	0	0	1	3	.250	.000
Javier, Stan#	.250	4	1	0	1	1	0	.400	.250
Jefferies, G#	.176	17	3	0	3	2	3	.300	.176
Jordan, Ricky	.273	11	3	1	3	0	2	.250	.545
Joyner, Wally*	.000	6	0	0	0	0	1	.000	.000
Justice, Dave*	.400	10	4	1	1	0	3	.400	.700
King, Jeff	.091	11	1	0	1	0	2	.091	.091
Lankford, Ray*	.500	12	6	0	3	4	2	.625	.667
Larkin, Barry	.400	10	4	1	2	3	2	.538	.800
Lemke, Mark#	.429	7	3	0	1	1	1	.500	.429
Lewis, Darren	.000	4	0	0	0	1	0	.200	.000
Magadan, Dave*	.350	20	7	0	5	2	5	.409	.400
Manwaring, K	.200	5	1	0	0	0	2	.200	.200
Martinez, Da*	.100	20	2	0	1	1	9	.182	.100
Martinez, T*	.167	6	1	0	1	0	1	.167	.333
McGee, Willie*	.500	16	8	0	3	1	3	.529	.563
McGriff, Fred*	.091	11	1	1	3	4	5	.333	.364
McLemore, M*	.167	6	1	0	1	0	1	.167	.167
Merced, O*	.375	8	3	0	3	1	1	.444	.625
Mitchell, K	.100	10	1	0	0	3	3	.308	.100
Morandini, M*	.286	7	2	0	0	0	2	.286	.429
Morris, Hal*	.333	6	2	0	1	0	3	.333	.333
Murray, Eddie*	.182	11	2	1	2	2	2	.286	.455
Nilsson, Dave*	.000	7	0	0	2	0	2	.000	.000
Nixon, Otis#	.143	7	1	0	0	0	4	.143	.143
O'Brien, C	.500	4	2	0	0	0	0	.500	.500
O'Neill, Paul*	.143	21	3	0	2	1	9	.182	.143
Olerud, John*	.222	9	2	0	1	1	2	.300	.222
Oliver, Joe	.300	10	3	0	0	0	1	.300	.400
Pagnozzi, Tom	.333	6	2	0	1	1	1	.429	.333
Palmeiro, R*	.222	18	4	0	1	0	3	.222	.222
Pena, Tony	.111	9	1	0	0	1	2	.200	.111
Pendleton, T#	.318	22	7	0	3	1	2	.348	.409
Phillips, T#	.333	6	2	0	1	1	0	.429	.333
Raines, Tim#	.444	9	4	0	4	1	1	.455	.444
Randa, Joe	.400	5	2	0	1	0	2	.400	.800
Reed, Jeff*	.167	6	1	0	0	1	2	.286	.333
Roberts, Bip#	.375	16	6	0	0	3	3	.375	.438
Sabo, Chris	.417	12	5	1	2	3	2	.533	.667
Samuel, Juan	.150	20	3	1	2	1	5	.190	.300
Santiago, B	.500	10	5	0	2	2	2	.583	.600
Sierra, Ruben#	.600	5	3	0	1	0	1	.600	1.000
Slaught, Don	.400	5	2	0	0	0	2	.400	.400
Smith, Ozzie*	.208	24	5	0	2	2	3	.269	.208
Stillwell, K#	.143	7	1	0	0	0	1	.143	.143
Strawberry, D*	.107	28	3	0	0	4	9	.219	.143

Paul Assenmacher, Indians — LHP

Batter	Avg	AB	H	HR	BI	BB	SO	OBP	Slg
Surhoff, B.J.*	.500	10	5	1	3	0	1	.500	.800
Tettleton, M#	.000	7	0	0	0	1	7	.125	.000
Thompson, Mil*	.053	19	1	0	1	1	2	.100	.105
Thompson, Rob	.545	11	6	0	3	0	1	.583	.727
Vaughn, Mo*	.500	8	4	0	2	2	2	.636	.500
Ventura, R*	.286	7	2	0	1	0	4	.286	.286
Walker, Larry*	.111	18	2	0	2	2	5	.200	.111
Wallach, Tim	.111	9	1	0	0	4	4	.385	.111
Williams, Ma	.400	10	4	1	1	0	3	.400	.700
Zeile, Todd	.250	8	2	0	0	4	3	.500	.250

Pedro Astacio, Dodgers — RHP

Batter	Avg	AB	H	HR	BI	BB	SO	OBP	Slg
Abbott, Kurt	.417	12	5	0	0	1	0	.462	.750
Alfonzo, E	.100	10	1	0	0	0	0	.100	.100
Alicea, Luis#	.333	9	3	0	1	2	0	.417	.333
Alou, Moises	.412	17	7	0	2	2	1	.474	.412
Andrews, S	.400	10	4	1	2	0	3	.400	.800
Anthony, Eric*	.182	11	2	0	0	1	0	.250	.182
Arias, Alex	.167	6	1	0	0	0	0	.167	.167
Ausmus, Brad	.000	5	0	0	0	0	1	.000	.000
Bagwell, Jeff	.333	18	6	1	3	2	1	.400	.611
Barberie, B#	.200	10	2	0	3	2	0	.333	.200
Batiste, Kim	.000	5	0	0	0	0	2	.000	.000
Beamon, Trey*	.143	7	1	0	0	1	0	.143	.143
Bell, Derek	.000	4	0	0	2	1	1	.143	.000
Bell, Jay	.111	9	1	0	2	0	4	.111	.222
Benard, M*	.500	6	3	0	0	0	0	.500	.833
Benjamin, M	.143	7	1	0	0	2	1	.333	.143
Berry, Sean	.143	7	1	0	0	2	2	.333	.143
Bichette, D	.200	30	6	0	3	3	4	.265	.233
Biggio, Craig	.409	22	9	2	4	3	5	.462	.682
Blauser, Jeff	.300	20	6	0	1	3	7	.391	.350
Bonds, Barry*	.750	8	6	1	3	3	0	.750	1.500
Bonilla, B#	.385	13	5	1	2	4	3	.529	.769
Boone, Bret	.067	15	1	0	0	0	1	.067	.067
Branson, Jeff*	.421	19	8	1	1	0	2	.421	.684
Brogna, Rico*	.222	9	2	1	2	2	0	.364	.333
Brumfield, J	.333	6	2	0	0	1	1	.429	.333
Burks, Ellis	.077	13	1	0	3	2	7	.200	.077
Burnitz, D*	.400	5	2	1	2	3	2	.625	1.000
Butler, Brett*	.000	7	0	0	0	1	0	.000	.000
Caminiti, Ken#	.192	26	5	1	5	2	9	.241	.308
Carr, Chuck	.214	14	3	0	1	0	0	.214	.214
Castilla, V	.250	20	5	1	2	1	6	.286	.450
Cedeno, A	.115	26	3	0	0	0	10	.115	.154
Clark, Dave*	.455	11	5	0	1	0	1	.455	.545
Clark, Will*	.200	5	1	0	2	0	0	.167	.400
Clayton, R	.176	17	3	0	0	2	3	.263	.176
Colbrunn, G	.429	7	3	0	1	2	0	.636	.571
Cole, Alex*	.429	7	3	0	0	1	1	.500	.429
Coleman, V#	.333	12	4	0	0	1	1	.385	.500
Conine, Jeff	.348	23	8	0	3	0	5	.348	.435
Cordero, Wil	.286	14	4	0	2	1	1	.333	.429
Daulton, D*	.231	13	3	1	3	2	2	.313	.462
Davis, Eric	.200	5	1	0	1	1	1	.286	.200
Dawson, Andre	.571	7	4	0	1	0	0	.571	.714
Decker, Steve	.000	3	0	0	0	1	0	.250	.000
DeShields, D*	.200	10	2	1	2	0	0	.200	.500
Duncan, M	.222	9	2	1	3	0	1	.222	.556
Dykstra, L*	.154	13	2	1	2	4	2	.353	.385
Eisenreich, J*	.476	21	10	2	7	2	0	.522	1.000
Eusebio, Tony	.333	6	2	0	0	0	2	.333	.333
Finley, Steve*	.219	32	7	0	0	3	5	.286	.281
Fletcher, D*	.095	21	2	0	1	0	1	.130	.143
Floyd, Cliff*	.214	14	3	0	1	0	1	.214	.214
Galarraga, A	.333	27	9	5	9	1	6	.379	.889
Gant, Ron	.000	7	0	0	0	3	2	.300	.000
Garcia, C	.400	5	6	1	3	1	1	.471	.600
Gilkey, B	.389	18	7	0	2	2	4	.450	.611
Girardi, Joe	.235	17	4	1	2	2	4	.316	.412
Gomez, Chris	.444	9	4	0	0	1	3	.500	.556
Gomez, Leo	.250	4	1	0	0	1	2	.500	.250
Gonzalez, L*	.226	31	7	0	3	2	5	.273	.258
Grace, Mark*	.429	21	9	0	1	1	1	.455	.571
Greene, W*	.182	11	2	0	0	0	0	.182	.182
Grissom, M	.160	25	4	0	1	3	1	.276	.240
Grudzielanek	.462	13	6	0	0	0	0	.462	.462
Gwynn, Tony*	.250	12	3	1	2	1	1	.308	.500
Haney, Todd	.400	5	2	0	1	0	2	.400	.600
Harris, Lenny*	.333	6	2	0	0	0	0	.333	.333
Hayes, C	.333	27	9	0	5	1	1	.357	.444
Henderson, R	.000	8	0	0	0	0	2	.000	.000
Hernandez, Jo	.333	6	2	0	1	0	1	.333	.333
Hill, G	.182	11	2	0	1	0	2	.182	.273
Hollins, Dave#	.176	17	3	0	2	2	2	.263	.235
Howard, T*	.333	6	2	0	0	1	0	.429	.500
Hundley, Todd#	.316	19	6	3	5	0	3	.316	.842
Incaviglia, R	.273	11	3	0	0	0	5	.385	.273
Jefferies, G#	.111	18	2	1	2	1	0	.158	.278
Johnson, Bri	.250	12	3	0	2	0	0	.250	.250

Pedro Astacio, Dodgers — RHP

Batter	Avg	AB	H	HR	BI	BB	SO	OBP	Slg
Johnson, Char	.000	7	0	0	0	1	0	.125	.000
Johnson, Mark*	.143	7	1	0	0	2	2	.333	.143
Jones, C#	.222	9	2	0	1	1	3	.300	.222
Jordan, Brian	.176	17	3	1	2	0	4	.222	.353
Joyner, Wally*	.400	5	2	0	0	1	1	.500	.600
Justice, Dave*	.211	19	4	1	1	0	4	.211	.474
Kelly, R	.167	6	1	0	0	1	0	.286	.167
Kendall, J	.571	7	4	0	1	1	0	.667	.857
Kent, Jeff	.235	17	4	0	1	2	5	.350	.235
King, Jeff	.412	17	7	0	1	2	1	.450	.412
Kingery, Mike*	.125	8	1	0	2	0	0	.111	.250
Klesko, Ryan*	.417	12	5	3	5	1	2	.462	1.250
Lankford, Ray*	.381	21	8	1	6	3	7	.458	.571
Lansing, Mike	.333	24	8	0	4	2	4	.407	.458
Larkin, Barry	.370	27	10	0	3	2	0	.414	.370
Lemke, Mark#	.167	18	3	0	2	3	0	.286	.167
Lewis, Darren	.214	14	3	0	0	1	0	.267	.214
Liebenthal, M	.636	11	7	1	1	0	1	.636	.909
Liriano, N#	.500	22	11	1	4	0	2	.500	.864
Lopez, Javy	.333	9	3	1	2	1	4	.417	.667
Mabry, John*	.286	7	2	0	0	0	0	.286	.571
Manwaring, K	.308	13	4	0	1	0	3	.357	.385
Martin, Al*	.217	23	5	1	3	1	7	.250	.391
Martinez, Da*	.273	11	3	0	1	1	1	.333	.273
May, Derrick*	.286	7	2	0	3	0	0	.286	.286
McCracken, Q#	.000	4	0	0	1	2	1	.333	.000
McGee, Willie#	.000	7	0	0	0	0	0	.000	.000
McGriff, Fred*	.143	14	2	1	1	2	3	.250	.357
McRae, Brian#	.273	11	3	0	0	1	2	.333	.273
Merced, O*	.000	10	0	0	0	1	3	.091	.000
Mitchell, K	.250	8	2	1	1	3	2	.455	.625
Morandini, M*	.280	25	7	0	2	7	6	.438	.440
Morris, Hal*	.391	23	9	0	1	1	2	.417	.652
Mouton, James	.111	9	1	0	0	0	1	.111	.111
Murray, Eddie*	.273	11	3	0	1	0	1	.250	.545
Murray, Glenn	.250	4	1	0	0	2	1	.500	.250
Natal, Bob	.000	5	0	0	0	0	1	.000	.000
Newfield, M	.167	6	1	0	0	0	2	.167	.167
Nieves, M#	.286	7	2	1	2	0	2	.286	.857
Nixon, Otis#	.364	11	4	0	0	0	1	.364	.364
O'Brien, C	.000	2	0	0	0	3	0	.600	.000
O'Neill, Paul*	.273	11	3	0	0	0	1	.273	.273
Oliver, Joe	.300	10	3	0	2	0	1	.273	.300
Orsulak, Joe*	.227	22	5	1	4	0	1	.227	.364
Otero, Ricky#	.200	5	1	0	0	0	0	.200	.200
Owens, Eric	.286	7	2	0	1	0	0	.286	.429
Owens, J	.167	6	1	0	0	1	1	.167	.333
Pagnozzi, Tom	.125	8	1	0	0	0	1	.125	.125
Pendleton, T#	.321	28	9	2	5	0	7	.321	.679
Plantier, P*	.000	3	0	0	0	1	2	.400	.000
Reed, Jeff*	.200	5	1	0	1	0	0	.200	.200
Reed, Jody	.300	10	3	0	0	2	1	.417	.300
Renteria, E	.500	8	4	0	2	0	0	.500	.625
Roberts, Bip#	.353	17	6	0	0	4	2	.476	.412
Rodriguez, H*	.125	8	1	0	0	0	1	.125	.250
Sanchez, Rey	.222	9	2	0	1	1	1	.273	.222
Sandberg, R	.200	15	3	1	3	3	2	.316	.467
Sanders, R	.267	15	4	1	2	2	1	.333	.467
Santangelo, F#	.364	11	4	0	4	1	2	.417	.636
Santiago, B	.176	17	3	1	2	0	4	.176	.412
Segui, David#	.250	12	3	0	1	1	0	.308	.250
Servais, S	.222	9	2	0	0	1	3	.364	.333
Sheaffer, D	.333	6	2	0	1	0	1	.333	.333
Sheffield, G	.333	12	4	1	2	3	2	.467	.667
Smith, Dwight*	.500	10	5	1	3	1	0	.545	1.100
Smith, Ozzie#	.286	14	4	0	1	3	0	.444	.286
Sosa, Sammy	.222	18	4	0	2	2	4	.333	.278
Stocker, K#	.294	17	5	0	1	2	4	.368	.294
Taubensee, E*	.087	23	2	0	0	0	5	.087	.087
Tavarez, Je#	.000	5	0	0	0	1	0	.000	.000
Thompson, Mil*	.444	9	4	1	3	0	1	.444	.778
Thompson, Rob	.333	15	5	0	1	0	2	.333	.400
Thompson, Ry	.400	5	2	0	1	0	2	.500	.600
VanderWal, J*	.333	12	4	0	0	1	3	.385	.333
Veras, Q#	.200	10	2	0	0	1	3	.200	.200
Vizcaino, J#	.227	22	5	0	1	3	2	.320	.273
Walker, Larry*	.455	22	10	1	4	1	3	.458	.727
Weiss, Walt#	.333	24	8	0	2	1	2	.360	.333
White, Devon#	.143	7	1	1	2	0	0	.143	.571
White, R	.222	9	2	0	0	0	2	.222	.333
Whiten, Mark#	.333	12	4	0	1	0	2	.333	.417
Wilkins, Rick*	.417	12	5	1	3	3	3	.533	.667
Williams, E	.500	6	3	0	0	0	2	.500	.667
Williams, Ma	.214	14	3	1	3	0	3	.200	.429
Young, Eric	.353	34	12	1	5	3	3	.405	.500
Young, Kevin	.333	6	2	0	0	1	1	.500	.833
Zeile, Todd	.320	25	8	0	1	2	5	.370	.400

Steve Avery, Braves — LHP

Batter	Avg	AB	H	HR	BI	BB	SO	OBP	Slg
Abbott, Kurt	.333	18	6	0	2	1	7	.350	.444
Alfonzo, E	.286	7	2	0	1	0	3	.250	.429
Alicea, Luis#	.313	16	5	0	5	1	2	.353	.500
Alomar, R#	.500	2	1	0	1	2	0	.750	.500
Alou, Moises	.207	29	6	1	3	1	3	.226	.379
Andrews, S	.000	4	0	0	0	1	2	.200	.000
Anthony, Eric*	.231	13	3	0	2	0	3	.231	.231
Arias, Alex	.500	6	3	0	2	0	0	.429	.500
Ashley, Billy	.400	10	4	1	4	1	2	.455	.900
Bagwell, Jeff	.324	34	11	3	6	6	3	.405	.618
Barberie, B#	.000	7	0	0	0	0	2	.000	.000
Batiste, Kim	.222	9	2	0	0	0	1	.222	.222
Bell, David	.125	8	1	0	1	0	1	.125	.125
Bell, Derek	.429	14	6	0	1	3	2	.556	.429
Bell, Jay	.354	48	17	1	4	4	5	.404	.500
Benjamin, M	.143	14	2	0	0	2	1	.250	.286
Berry, Sean	.313	16	5	0	0	0	2	.313	.438
Bichette, D	.375	24	9	2	4	0	4	.400	.750
Biggio, Craig	.333	45	15	0	3	6	4	.404	.356
Blowers, Mike	.250	4	1	0	2	1	2	.333	.250
Bogar, Tim	.429	7	3	0	1	1	1	.444	.429
Bonds, Barry*	.243	37	9	1	4	5	2	.364	.351
Bonilla, B#	.235	34	8	2	5	5	3	.325	.412
Boone, Bret	.182	11	2	0	0	1	3	.250	.273
Brogna, Rico*	.000	9	0	0	0	0	3	.000	.000
Burks, Ellis	.375	11	2	1	2	0	2	.182	.455
Butler, Brett*	.341	41	14	0	3	3	6	.386	.366
Caminiti, Ken#	.229	48	11	1	5	2	7	.260	.354
Candaele, C#	.214	14	3	0	0	2	0	.313	.286
Cangelosi, J#	.167	6	1	0	0	2	0	.375	.167
Carr, Chuck	.222	18	4	0	0	3	2	.333	.278
Carreon, Mark	.391	23	9	0	1	1	0	.417	.522
Carter, Joe	.167	6	1	0	1	0	2	.167	.167
Castilla, V	.389	18	7	0	5	0	1	.389	.556
Cedeno, A	.217	23	5	0	3	0	5	.217	.391
Cedeno, Roger#	.250	4	1	0	0	0	1	.250	.250
Cianfrocco, A	.286	7	2	1	1	0	1	.286	.714
Clark, Phil	.125	8	1	0	1	2	0	.333	.125
Clark, Will*	.370	27	10	1	5	1	3	.393	.667
Clayton, R	.406	32	13	2	5	1	8	.412	.750
Colbrunn, G	.269	26	7	0	4	2	8	.321	.346
Coleman, V#	.222	9	2	0	1	3	2	.417	.222
Conine, Jeff	.391	23	9	1	7	3	7	.429	.696
Cordero, Wil	.278	18	5	2	5	2	5	.350	.667
Cummings, M*	.375	8	3	0	2	0	2	.375	.500
Dascenzo, D#	.273	11	3	0	0	1	1	.333	.364
Daulton, D*	.217	23	5	2	5	4	3	.333	.522
Davis, Eric	.294	17	5	0	4	5	3	.455	.471
Dawson, Andre	.263	19	5	2	8	0	3	.250	.684
Decker, Steve	.000	5	0	0	0	0	2	.000	.000
DeShields, D*	.250	36	9	0	4	4	11	.325	.306
Duncan, M	.250	36	9	1	4	0	9	.250	.389
Dunston, S	.308	26	8	1	4	1	6	.333	.462
Dykstra, L*	.381	21	8	1	6	5	2	.481	.714
Elster, Kevin	.400	15	6	0	6	0	1	.400	.667
Eusebio, Tony	.250	8	2	0	0	0	3	.250	.250
Everett, Carl#	.125	8	1	0	2	1	2	.300	.250
Finley, Steve*	.250	40	10	0	0	4	3	.318	.300
Gaetti, Gary	.250	8	2	0	2	0	1	.250	.250
Galarraga, A	.161	31	5	0	3	4	10	.257	.226
Gant, Ron	.357	14	5	2	2	1	5	.438	.786
Garcia, C	.231	26	6	1	1	2	5	.286	.423
Gilkey, S	.226	31	7	1	6	4	5	.314	.355
Girardi, Joe	.353	17	6	2	4	3	2	.450	.824
Gonzalez, L*	.067	15	1	0	0	2	1	.176	.133
Grace, Mark*	.390	41	16	0	5	1	5	.405	.439
Greene, W*	.000	6	0	0	0	0	5	.000	.000
Grissom, M	.258	31	8	0	1	2	5	.303	.258
Grudzielanek	.222	9	2	0	0	1	1	.300	.333
Gutierrez, R	.333	12	4	1	1	0	1	.333	.583
Gwynn, Tony*	.357	28	10	0	6	2	1	.400	.536
Hayes, C	.324	34	11	3	4	1	6	.343	.676
Hernandez, Ca	.500	6	3	0	1	0	1	.500	.833
Hernandez, Jo	.333	6	2	1	1	0	3	.333	.833
Hollins, Dave#	.250	16	4	1	2	2	2	.333	.563
Howard, T*	.200	5	1	0	0	0	0	.200	.400
Hudler, Rex	.250	8	2	0	0	0	1	.250	.375
Hundley, Todd#	.348	23	8	1	4	2	8	.400	.565
Hunter, Brian	.154	13	2	0	1	0	1	.154	.154
Hunter, Bri L	.333	6	2	0	1	0	0	.333	.667
Huskey, Butch	.167	12	2	0	0	1	3	.231	.333
Incaviglia, P	.286	28	8	3	5	1	5	.333	.607
Javier, Stan#	.188	16	3	0	1	1	1	.235	.188
Jefferies, G#	.250	28	7	0	3	3	1	.323	.321
Johnson, Bri	.286	7	2	0	0	0	0	.286	.286
Johnson, Char	.200	10	2	0	2	3	3	.385	.200
Johnson, L*	.167	6	1	0	0	0	0	.167	.167
Jones, Chris	.174	23	4	1	2	3	6	.269	.348
Jordan, Brian	.429	21	9	1	4	1	2	.455	.857
Jordan, Ricky	.316	19	6	1	6	0	4	.316	.474
Karros, Eric	.265	34	9	0	3	2	2	.306	.324
Kelly, R	.333	6	2	0	1	0	1	.333	.500

Batter	Avg	AB	H	HR	BI	BB	SO	OBP	Slg
Kent, Jeff	.194	31	6	0	2	1	3	.242	.355
King, Jeff	.324	37	12	2	11	4	4	.381	.622
Lankford, Ray*	.194	31	6	0	3	2	13	.242	.258
Lansing, Mike	.150	20	3	1	3	0	2	.143	.300
Larkin, Barry	.392	51	20	1	4	4	1	.436	.529
Lewis, Darren	.207	29	6	0	3	1	3	.226	.310
Lewis, Mark	.500	6	3	1	2	0	0	.500	1.167
Liriano, N#	.286	7	2	0	1	2	1	.444	.286
Magadan, Dave*	.310	29	9	0	2	3	3	.375	.379
Manwaring, K	.379	29	11	0	2	2	5	.419	.414
Martin, Al*	.273	11	3	0	1	1	4	.308	.364
McGee, Willie*	.176	34	6	0	0	2	8	.222	.176
McGriff, Fred*	.190	21	4	1	5	0	4	.182	.333
McRae, Brian#	.294	17	5	1	3	0	4	.294	.529
Merced, O*	.500	8	4	0	1	2	0	.600	.625
Mitchell, K	.500	12	6	1	6	0	3	.500	.833
Mondesi, Raul	.455	11	5	0	0	1	2	.500	.727
Morandini, M*	.308	13	4	0	1	0	5	.308	.308
Morris, Hal*	.222	18	4	1	0	5	2	.222	.222
Mouton, James	.182	11	2	0	1	0	3	.182	.182
Murray, Eddie#	.219	32	7	1	2	1	2	.242	.313
Nixon, Otis#	.333	6	2	0	1	0	0	.333	.333
O'Brien, C	.273	11	3	0	0	1	2	.333	.273
O'Neill, Paul*	.200	5	1	0	0	1	2	.333	.400
Ochoa, Alex	.143	7	1	0	0	0	1	.143	.143
Offerman, J#	.048	21	1	0	0	1	2	.091	.048
Oliver, Joe	.250	36	9	1	7	5	4	.357	.389
Ordonez, Rey	.167	6	1	0	0	1	1	.286	.167
Owens, J	.200	5	1	0	0	0	1	.200	.200
Pagnozzi, Tom	.367	30	11	1	5	1	2	.387	.533
Pena, G#	.429	14	6	0	1	1	1	.467	.714
Pendleton, T#	.231	13	3	0	0	0	0	.231	.308
Piazza, Mike	.333	15	5	1	5	3	2	.444	.533
Plantier, P*	.250	4	1	0	2	3	0	.571	.500
Prince, Tom	.000	5	0	0	0	0	0	.000	.000
Reed, Jody	.333	9	3	0	0	3	0	.500	.333
Roberts, Bip#	.316	38	12	2	3	2	3	.350	.500
Rodriguez, H*	.000	5	0	0	0	0	2	.000	.000
Sabo, Chris	.441	34	15	1	7	3	6	.487	.618
Samuel, Juan	.129	31	4	0	2	0	6	.129	.161
Sanchez, Rey	.370	27	10	0	2	1	1	.393	.407
Sandberg, R	.300	20	6	1	3	4	3	.417	.550
Sanders, R	.219	32	7	2	4	3	3	.286	.500
Santangelo, F#	.333	9	3	0	0	1	1	.400	.333
Santiago, B	.333	21	7	1	4	0	5	.333	.619
Schofield, D	.100	10	1	0	1	2	1	.250	.100
Segui, David*	.318	22	7	0	2	1	4	.348	.409
Servais, S	.158	19	3	1	1	3	2	.273	.316
Sheaffer, D	.000	8	0	0	0	0	0	.000	.000
Sheffield, G	.333	36	12	3	6	3	3	.385	.611
Shipley, C	.077	13	1	0	0	1	3	.143	.077
Simms, Mike	.300	10	3	1	1	2	1	.417	.700
Slaught, Don	.227	22	5	0	3	4	2	.357	.273
Smith, Ozzie*	.160	25	4	0	1	3	1	.250	.200
Sosa, Sammy	.417	24	10	3	5	0	6	.417	.833
Stinnett, K	.300	10	3	0	1	0	0	.300	.400
Stocker, K#	.333	12	4	0	0	2	2	.429	.417
Strawberry, D*	.118	17	2	0	0	1	3	.167	.118
Thompson, Rob	.276	29	8	1	5	6	3	.389	.483
Thompson, Ry	.125	16	2	0	0	1	3	.176	.125
Timmons, O	.308	13	4	0	1	0	0	.308	.385
Veras, Q#	.308	13	4	0	1	0	3	.400	.385
Vizcaino, J#	.269	26	7	1	1	3	3	.321	.269
Walker, Larry*	.344	32	11	2	7	3	10	.417	.531
Wallach, Tim	.360	25	9	1	5	5	4	.452	.520
Walton, J	.100	10	1	1	1	3	1	.357	.400
Webster, L	.000	4	0	0	0	2	0	.333	.000
Wehner, John	.250	8	2	0	1	1	1	.333	.375
Weiss, Walt#	.250	16	4	0	1	2	4	.333	.250
White, Devon#	.600	5	3	0	3	1	1	.667	.600
White, R	.333	15	5	1	3	0	2	.333	.600
Whiten, Mark#	.400	5	2	0	0	2	0	.571	.400
Wilkins, Rick*	.000	7	0	0	0	1	3	.125	.000
Williams, E	.429	7	3	1	3	0	0	.500	.857
Williams, Ma	.194	31	6	1	3	1	2	.212	.323
Young, Eric	.161	31	5	0	3	0	0	.161	.226
Young, Kevin	.250	16	4	0	1	3	1	.294	.375
Zeile, Todd	.244	41	10	2	5	4	5	.311	.463

Batter	Avg	AB	H	HR	BI	BB	SO	OBP	Slg
Cedeno, D#	.600	5	3	0	0	0	1	.600	1.000
Clark, Will*	.143	7	1	0	3	2	1	.300	.286
Clayton, C	.429	7	3	0	2	0	2	.500	.429
Coleman, V#	.167	6	1	0	1	1	1	.286	.333
Cordova, M	.333	6	2	0	1	0	1	.333	.500
Curtis, Chad	.300	10	3	2	2	0	2	.300	.900
Daulton, D*	.600	5	3	1	2	1	1	.667	1.200
Davis, Chili#	.286	7	2	0	0	0	3	.286	.286
Delgado, C*	.333	6	2	1	3	2	2	.500	.833
Devereaux, M	.000	4	0	0	0	1	0	.200	.000
DiSarcina, G	.333	6	2	0	1	0	2	.333	.333
Duncan, M	.111	9	1	0	0	0	2	.111	.111
Durham, Ray#	.333	6	2	0	2	0	2	.333	.500
Dykstra, L*	.250	4	1	0	1	3	2	.571	.500
Edmonds, Jim*	.200	5	1	0	0	0	0	.200	.200
Eisenreich, J*	.250	4	1	0	0	1	1	.500	.250
Fabregas, Jor*	.400	5	2	0	1	0	1	.400	.400
Fielder, C	.000	8	0	0	0	0	4	.111	.000
Frye, Jeff	.667	3	2	0	0	1	0	.800	.667
Fryman, T	.000	8	0	0	0	0	3	.000	.000
Gaetti, Gary	.000	6	0	0	0	2	0	.200	.000
Gant, Ron	.400	5	2	1	4	0	0	.400	1.000
Gonzalez, A	.600	5	3	1	3	0	1	.667	1.000
Gonzalez, J	.091	11	1	0	0	0	2	.091	.091
Greenwell, M*	.333	9	3	1	5	0	0	.333	.667
Greer, Rusty*	.143	7	1	1	1	0	5	.143	.571
Grissom, M	.400	5	2	0	0	1	0	.500	.400
Guillen, O*	.200	5	1	0	0	1	0	.333	.200
Hale, Chip*	.250	4	1	0	0	1	1	.400	.250
Hamilton, D*	.000	5	0	0	0	1	0	.167	.000
Haselman, B	.250	4	1	0	0	1	2	.400	.250
Hayes, C	.400	5	2	0	1	0	1	.400	.600
Higginson, B*	.200	5	1	0	0	0	2	.200	.200
Hoiles, Chris	.250	4	1	0	1	1	2	.400	.500
Hollins, Dave#	.400	5	2	1	3	2	1	.571	1.000
Hundley, Todd#	.000	5	0	0	0	0	3	.000	.000
Incaviglia, P	1.000	5	5	2	5	2	0	1.000	2.200
Kent, Jeff	.333	6	2	0	0	0	0	.333	.333
Knoblauch, C	.500	6	3	0	2	0	1	.500	.500
Lewis, Darren	.333	9	3	0	2	0	0	.333	.333
Listach, Pat#	.000	5	0	0	0	0	2	.000	.000
Manwaring, K	.200	5	1	0	0	0	0	.200	.200
McGee, Willie#	.000	7	0	0	0	0	0	.000	.000
McGriff, Fred*	.571	7	4	1	3	3	2	.700	1.286
McLemore, M#	.200	5	1	0	0	0	1	.200	.600
Molitor, Paul	.000	5	0	0	0	2	1	.286	.000
Murray, Eddie#	.375	8	3	0	0	1	2	.444	.625
Myers, Greg*	.200	5	1	1	1	0	2	.200	.800
Newson, W*	.400	5	2	0	2	1	1	.500	.400
Nixon, Otis#	.364	11	4	0	1	2	3	.462	.364
O'Leary, Troy*	.200	5	1	1	2	1	2	.333	.800
O'Neill, Paul*	.375	8	3	0	6	2	2	.455	.625
Offerman, J#	.167	6	1	0	1	1	1	.286	.333
Olerud, John*	.400	5	2	0	2	1	0	.500	.400
Palmer, Dean	.286	7	2	0	1	1	4	.375	.429
Phillips, T#	.000	5	0	0	0	2	2	.375	.000
Polonia, Luis*	.000	4	0	0	0	0	1	.000	.000
Raines, Tim#	.125	8	1	0	1	1	3	.222	.125
Ripken, Cal	.286	7	2	0	0	0	1	.286	.286
Rodriguez, I	.182	11	2	0	0	1	1	.250	.273
Salmon, Tim	.444	9	4	1	3	1	2	.500	.778
Sandberg, R	.333	3	1	0	0	2	2	.600	.667
Sheffield, G	.286	7	2	1	1	2	1	.444	.714
Snow, J.T.#	.571	7	4	1	2	0	1	.571	1.143
Sprague, Ed	.222	9	2	2	5	1	3	.300	.889
Stahoviak, S*	.200	5	1	0	1	0	2	.200	.200
Stanley, Mike	.250	4	1	0	2	1	2	.400	.500
Steinbach, T	.250	4	1	0	0	1	1	.400	.750
Stillwell, K#	.286	7	2	0	0	0	2	.286	.286
Tettleton, M#	.111	9	1	1	3	1	4	.250	.444
Thomas, Frank	.200	5	1	0	0	1	0	.200	.200
Thompson, Rob	.500	6	3	0	3	0	1	.571	.500
Thompson, Ry	.143	7	1	0	0	0	3	.143	.286
Valentin, Jhn	.500	6	3	0	0	0	2	.500	.667
Vaughn, Mo*	.000	9	0	0	0	0	5	.000	.000
Velarde, R	.400	5	2	0	1	0	0	.429	.400
Ventura, R*	.000	3	0	0	0	2	2	.400	.000
Vina, F*	.400	5	2	0	2	0	1	.400	.400
Walbeck, Matt#	.400	5	2	0	2	0	1	.400	.400
Williams, Ber#	.250	8	2	0	2	2	0	.400	.500
Williams, Ma	.286	7	2	1	3	0	2	.286	.714

Batter	Avg	AB	H	HR	BI	BB	SO	OBP	Slg
Anderson, Brd*	.400	5	2	1	1	1	1	.500	1.000
Anderson, G*	.750	4	3	0	1	0	0	.800	1.000
Arias, Alex	.000	5	0	0	0	0	0	.000	.000
Becker, Rich*	.333	6	2	0	3	1	2	.429	.500
Berroa, G	.400	5	2	0	3	0	3	.400	.600
Boggs, Wade*	.333	9	3	0	2	3	1	.500	.444
Bonilla, B#	.375	8	3	1	2	3	2	.545	.750
Butler, Brett*	.250	4	1	0	0	1	0	.500	.250
Canseco, Jose	.000	4	0	0	1	2	1	.200	.000
Carter, Joe	.125	8	1	0	1	0	2	.125	.125

Batter	Avg	AB	H	HR	BI	BB	SO	OBP	Slg
Bichette, D	.000	5	0	0	0	0	0	.000	.000
Grissom, M	.200	5	1	0	0	0	0	.200	.200
Zeile, Todd	.200	5	1	0	0	0	2	.200	.200

Batter	Avg	AB	H	HR	BI	BB	SO	OBP	Slg
Alou, Moises	.167	6	1	0	1	0	1	.167	.167

13

Roger Bailey, Rockies — RHP

Batter	Avg	AB	H	HR	BI	BB	SO	OBP	Slg
Andrews, S	.167	6	1	1	3	0	0	.167	.667
Bell, Jay	.250	8	2	0	0	1	1	.333	.375
Benard, M*	.200	5	1	0	1	3	1	.500	.600
Blowers, Mike	.250	4	1	1	3	1	0	.400	1.000
Bonds, Barry*	.000	4	0	0	0	4	0	.500	.000
Boone, Bret	.200	5	1	0	0	0	1	.200	.200
Branson, Jeff*	.500	4	2	0	0	4	2	.750	.750
Brumfield, J	.200	5	1	0	0	0	0	.200	.200
DeShields, D*	.400	5	2	0	1	2	0	.571	.400
Dunston, S	.333	9	3	0	0	0	0	.333	.667
Finley, Steve*	.600	5	3	0	1	0	0	.600	1.000
Fonville, C#	.250	4	1	0	2	2	0	.500	.750
Gaetti, Gary	.200	5	1	0	0	2	0	.429	.200
Gagne, Greg	.750	4	3	0	1	1	0	.800	1.000
Gant, Ron	.625	8	5	0	1	1	0	.667	.750
Garcia, C	.250	4	1	0	1	0	1	.250	.250
Gilkey, B	.375	8	3	0	0	0	1	.375	.375
Gonzalez, L*	.333	6	2	0	0	0	0	.333	.500
Grace, Mark*	.600	5	3	0	3	1	1	.571	.600
Grissom, M	.400	10	4	0	2	0	1	.400	.600
Grudzielanek	.600	5	3	0	2	0	0	.600	.600
Harris, Lenny*	.000	5	0	0	1	0	1	.000	.000
Hollandsworth*	.500	4	2	0	0	1	1	.600	.500
Howard, T*	.500	4	2	0	1	1	0	.600	1.250
Jones, C#	.286	7	2	0	0	3	2	.500	.429
Jordan, Brian	.375	8	3	1	1	0	0	.375	.875
Karros, Eric	.500	8	4	2	3	0	0	.500	1.375
King, Jeff	.286	7	2	0	0	1	1	.286	.429
Klesko, Ryan*	.444	9	4	1	6	0	0	.400	1.111
Lankford, Ray*	.333	12	4	2	4	1	2	.385	.917
Lansing, Mike	.600	5	3	0	2	0	2	.600	1.000
Larkin, Barry	.200	5	1	0	1	2	0	.429	.200
Lemke, Mark#	.000	6	0	0	0	0	0	.000	.000
Lewis, Darren	.000	4	0	0	0	0	1	.000	.000
Lopez, Javy	.222	9	2	0	1	0	2	.222	.333
Mabry, John*	.286	7	2	0	2	0	0	.286	.286
Manwaring, K	.200	5	1	0	0	1	0	.333	.200
Martin, Al*	.500	6	3	0	1	3	0	.667	.667
McCarty, Dave	.400	5	2	0	1	0	2	.400	.600
McGee, Willie#	.000	7	0	0	0	0	2	.000	.000
McGriff, Fred*	.500	6	3	1	2	0	0	.667	1.000
McRae, Brian#	.500	8	4	0	0	1	0	.556	.875
Merced, O*	.333	9	3	0	5	0	0	.333	.444
Mondesi, Raul	.222	9	2	0	0	1	2	.300	.333
Mordecai, M	.000	5	0	0	0	0	2	.000	.000
Morris, Hal*	.167	6	1	0	1	3	0	.444	.333
Pagnozzi, Tom	.000	4	0	0	1	0	0	.200	.000
Parent, Mark	.167	6	1	0	0	1	1	.286	.333
Pendleton, T#	.333	6	2	0	2	0	1	.333	.500
Piazza, Mike	.333	9	3	0	1	0	2	.333	.333
Rodriguez, H*	.000	6	0	0	0	0	3	.000	.000
Sanchez, Rey	.500	6	3	0	2	0	0	.429	.500
Sanders, R	.500	6	3	1	1	2	0	.625	1.167
Servais, S	.333	6	2	0	3	0	1	.333	.500
Smith, Dwight*	.500	4	2	0	1	1	1	.600	1.000
Smith, Ozzie#	.000	7	0	0	0	3	0	.300	.000
Sosa, Sammy	.125	8	1	1	3	0	1	.125	.500
Taubensee, E*	.000	4	0	0	1	1	1	.200	.000
Thompson, Rob	.000	5	1	0	1	0	0	.333	.200
Webster, L	.000	4	0	0	0	1	1	.200	.000
White, R	.500	4	2	0	0	1	0	.600	.500
Williams, Ma	.600	5	3	1	5	0	0	.600	1.200
Young, Kevin	.500	5	2	0	0	0	0	.400	.400
Zeile, Todd	.167	6	1	0	0	1	0	.286	.333

James Baldwin, White Sox — RHP

Batter	Avg	AB	H	HR	BI	BB	SO	OBP	Slg
Giambi, Jason*	.333	6	2	0	0	0	0	.333	.333
Goodwin, Tom*	.429	7	3	0	1	0	1	.429	.429
Greenwell, M*	.429	7	3	0	0	0	2	.429	.429
Greer, Rusty*	.400	5	2	0	0	1	1	.500	.400
Hamilton, D*	.333	6	2	0	0	0	3	.333	.333
Hammonds, J	.286	7	2	1	1	0	1	.286	.714
Higginson, B*	.286	7	2	0	0	1	0	.375	.286
Hoiles, Chris	.400	5	2	1	1	0	1	.400	1.200
Jaha, John	.500	6	3	0	1	0	0	.500	.667
Jefferson, R*	.500	4	2	0	1	1	1	.600	.750
Jeter, Derek	.429	7	3	1	1	0	1	.429	1.000
Lewis, Mark	.333	9	3	0	1	1	1	.400	.333
Lockhart, K*	.222	9	2	1	2	0	1	.222	.667
Lofton, Kenny*	.143	7	1	0	1	0	2	.143	.286
Macfarlane, M	.429	7	3	0	2	0	0	.500	.571
Martinez, E	.000	5	0	0	0	2	2	.000	.000
Martinez, T*	.500	6	3	1	1	0	1	.500	1.000
McLemore, M#	.167	6	1	0	1	0	0	.167	.167
Murray, Eddie#	.333	9	3	1	1	0	0	.333	.667
Naehring, Tim	.200	5	1	0	1	0	1	.200	.200
Nieves, M#	.100	10	1	0	0	0	6	.100	.100
Nilsson, Dave*	.600	5	3	1	2	0	0	.600	1.200
Nixon, Otis#	.000	7	0	0	0	1	0	.000	.000
O'Leary, Troy*	.200	5	1	0	0	1	1	.333	.200
O'Neill, Paul*	.167	6	1	0	0	1	0	.286	.167
Offerman, J#	.222	9	2	0	0	1	0	.300	.222
Palmeiro, R*	.111	9	1	0	1	1	0	.100	.222
Palmer, Dean	.375	8	3	0	0	0	2	.375	.375
Paquette, C	.111	9	1	1	1	0	5	.111	.444
Pena, Tony	.000	9	0	0	0	0	1	.000	.000
Pride, Curtis*	.400	5	2	1	3	4	1	.667	1.200
Ramirez, M	.125	8	1	0	1	1	0	.222	.125
Randa, Joe	.111	9	1	0	0	0	1	.200	.111
Ripken, Cal	.000	7	0	0	0	0	0	.000	.000
Roberts, Bip#	.167	6	1	0	1	0	1	.167	.167
Rodriguez, I	.286	7	2	0	3	1	0	.375	.429
Salmon, Tim	.500	8	4	1	2	1	0	.600	.875
Seitzer, K	.333	6	2	0	0	0	0	.333	.333
Sierra, Ruben*	.333	9	3	0	0	0	2	.333	.333
Snow, J.T.#	.286	7	2	0	2	1	1	.444	.286
Sprague, Ed	.250	4	1	0	0	1	2	.400	.500
Stairs, Matt*	.167	6	1	0	0	0	0	.167	.167
Steinbach, T	.000	6	0	0	0	0	3	.000	.000
Surhoff, B.J.*	.000	6	0	0	0	2	2	.250	.000
Tettleton, M#	.500	6	3	2	3	2	1	.625	1.667
Thome, Jim*	.200	5	1	0	0	1	1	.333	.200
Trammell, A	.250	4	1	0	1	0	0	.400	.250
Tucker, M*	.429	7	3	0	2	0	1	.429	.571
Valentin, Jhn	.571	7	4	0	0	0	0	.571	.714
Valentin, Jse#	.000	5	0	0	0	1	2	.167	.000
Vaughn, Mo*	.167	6	1	1	3	1	1	.286	.667
Vina, F	.000	5	0	0	1	1	0	.400	.500
Vizquel, Omar#	.600	5	3	0	0	1	0	.667	.600
Williams, Ber#	.000	7	0	0	0	1	1	.333	.400

Shawn Barton, Giants — LHP

Batter	Avg	AB	H	HR	BI	BB	SO	OBP	Slg
Daulton, D*	.200	5	1	0	1	0	0	.200	.200
Eisenreich, J*	.000	4	0	0	0	1	0	.000	.000

Jose Bautista, Giants — RHP

Batter	Avg	AB	H	HR	BI	BB	SO	OBP	Slg
Alicea, Luis#	.250	8	2	1	1	0	0	.250	.625
Alou, Moises	.083	12	1	1	3	0	2	.083	.333
Bagwell, Jeff	.364	11	4	2	7	1	2	.385	.909
Baines, H*	.000	6	0	0	0	0	1	.000	.000
Barberie, B#	.375	8	3	0	1	0	2	.375	.375
Bell, Derek	.143	7	1	0	1	0	1	.125	.143
Bell, Jay	.462	13	6	0	1	0	2	.462	.538
Belliard, R	.500	6	3	0	0	0	0	.500	.500
Berry, Sean	.400	5	2	0	2	1	2	.429	.600
Bichette, D	.467	15	7	0	2	0	2	.500	.667
Biggio, Craig	.500	12	6	0	3	0	2	.538	.750
Blauser, Jeff	.222	9	2	0	1	1	2	.364	.333
Boggs, Wade*	.118	17	2	0	1	3	2	.250	.118
Bonds, Barry*	.000	4	0	0	0	1	1	.200	.000
Bonilla, B#	.167	6	1	1	2	0	2	.167	.667
Boone, Bret	.125	8	1	1	1	0	1	.125	.500
Brumfield, J	.500	4	2	0	1	0	1	.400	.750
Burks, Ellis	.286	14	4	0	2	3	3	.421	.429
Butler, Brett*	.500	5	1	0	0	2	0	.429	.200
Caminiti, Ken#	.200	10	2	0	1	5	2	.467	.300
Carr, Chuck	.167	12	2	0	0	0	1	.167	.167
Carter, Joe	.167	6	1	1	3	1	2	.286	.667
Castilla, V	.250	8	2	0	1	0	3	.333	.500
Cedeno, A	.286	7	2	0	1	4	3	.500	.429
Clark, Dave*	.500	6	3	1	2	1	1	.571	1.000
Clayton, R	.400	10	4	1	1	0	2	.400	.700
Colbrunn, G	.286	7	2	1	3	0	0	.286	.714
Cole, Alex*	.400	5	2	0	0	0	0	.400	.800
Conine, Jeff	.111	9	1	0	1	1	1	.182	.111

James Baldwin, White Sox — RHP

Batter	Avg	AB	H	HR	BI	BB	SO	OBP	Slg
Alomar, R#	.400	10	4	0	1	0	2	.400	.400
Anderson, Brd*	.800	5	4	2	1	0	1	.833	2.200
Anderson, G*	.000	6	0	0	0	0	4	.000	.000
Ausmus, Brad	.500	4	2	0	0	1	1	.600	.750
Baerga, C	.333	6	2	0	1	0	1	.333	.333
Belle, Albert	.000	3	0	0	0	3	1	.500	.000
Boggs, Wade*	.333	6	2	0	1	0	1	.429	.333
Bonilla, B#	.250	8	2	0	1	4	3	.333	.250
Bordick, Mike	.200	5	1	1	2	0	0	.200	.800
Bragg, Darren*	.714	7	5	0	0	2	0	.778	.714
Brosius, S	.000	6	0	0	0	1	0	.000	.000
Buhner, Jay	.250	4	1	0	1	0	0	.400	.250
Clark, Tony*	.400	5	2	1	1	1	2	.500	1.000
Clark, Will*	.000	6	0	0	0	0	1	.000	.000
Curtis, Chad	.333	6	2	2	2	1	0	.429	1.333
Damon, Johnny*	.222	9	2	0	0	0	2	.222	.444
Davis, Chili#	.375	8	3	0	1	1	2	.444	.375
Delgado, C*	.200	5	1	0	0	0	2	.200	.200
DiSarcina, G	.000	4	0	0	1	0	0	.000	.000
Edmonds, Jim*	.200	5	1	1	0	0	0	.200	.800
Elster, Kevin	.600	5	3	1	4	0	0	.600	1.400
Fielder, C	.333	9	3	2	5	1	0	.400	1.000
Frye, Jeff	.625	8	5	0	2	0	0	.625	.875
Fryman, T	.083	12	1	0	0	0	3	.083	.083

Batter	Avg	AB	H	HR	BI	BB	SO	OBP	Slg
Cordero, Wil	.308	13	4	2	3	0	1	.308	.846
Davis, Chili#	.143	14	2	0	0	0	2	.143	.143
Davis, Eric	.143	7	1	0	0	1	3	.250	.143
Deer, Rob	.077	13	1	0	1	0	5	.077	.077
DeShields, D*	.143	7	1	0	0	1	2	.250	.143
Duncan, M	.500	8	4	0	2	0	3	.500	.500
Dunston, S	.400	5	2	1	1	0	0	.400	1.400
Dykstra, L*	.500	6	3	1	3	2	0	.625	1.167
Eisenreich, J*	.500	8	4	0	0	2	0	.600	.875
Fermin, Felix	.000	5	0	0	0	0	0	.000	.000
Finley, Steve*	.500	10	5	0	3	2	0	.583	.600
Fletcher, D*	.143	7	1	0	1	0	1	.143	.143
Franco, Julio	.714	7	5	0	3	1	0	.750	1.286
Gaetti, Gary	.125	8	1	0	1	0	1	.125	.125
Gagne, Greg	.600	5	3	1	2	0	0	.600	1.200
Galarraga, A	.308	13	4	1	4	1	2	.357	.615
Gant, Ron	.286	7	2	0	0	0	1	.286	.429
Garcia, C	.100	10	1	0	0	1	0	.182	.100
Gilkey, B	.263	19	5	0	2	0	1	.250	.316
Girardi, Joe	.500	8	4	0	2	0	2	.500	.625
Gonzalez, L*	.444	9	4	0	0	1	0	.444	.444
Grace, Mark*	.222	9	2	1	2	0	0	.222	.667
Greenwell, M*	.500	18	9	4	7	2	0	.550	1.333
Grissom, M	.200	10	2	0	0	0	3	.200	.200
Grudzielanek	.286	7	2	0	0	0	0	.286	.286
Guillen, O*	.500	6	3	0	0	1	0	.571	.500
Gwynn, Chris*	.167	6	1	0	0	0	2	.167	.167
Hansen, Dave*	.250	4	1	0	0	1	0	.400	.250
Harris, Lenny*	.200	5	1	0	1	1	1	.333	.600
Hayes, C	.182	11	2	0	0	1	1	.250	.182
Henderson, R	.556	9	5	0	0	3	0	.667	.778
Howard, T*	.750	4	3	0	0	1	1	.800	.750
Howell, Jack*	.333	12	4	1	3	0	0	.333	.583
Hundley, Todd#	.333	6	2	1	3	1	0	.429	1.000
Incaviglia, P	.222	9	2	1	2	0	2	.222	.556
Javier, Stan*	.000	5	0	0	0	0	0	.000	.000
Jefferies, G#	.286	7	2	0	2	2	0	.444	.286
Jones, Chris	.000	4	0	0	1	0	0	.000	.000
Jordan, Brian	.077	13	1	0	0	0	0	.143	.154
Joyner, Wally*	.231	13	3	0	2	1	0	.286	.308
Justice, Dave*	.429	7	3	1	1	0	0	.429	.857
Karros, Eric	.250	16	4	2	4	0	2	.250	.688
Kelly, R	.100	10	1	0	0	1	0	.100	.100
Kent, Jeff	.571	7	4	1	2	0	1	.571	1.143
King, Jeff	.083	12	1	0	0	0	0	.083	.167
Kingery, Mike*	.286	7	2	0	0	0	0	.286	.286
Lankford, Ray*	.200	15	3	2	4	3	3	.333	.667
Lansing, Mike	.143	7	1	0	0	0	0	.143	.143
Larkin, Barry	.750	8	6	1	3	2	1	.800	1.125
Lewis, Darren	.222	9	2	0	0	0	0	.222	.222
Livingstone*	.200	5	1	0	0	0	0	.200	.200
Magadan, Dave*	.500	4	2	0	2	1	0	.600	.500
Manwaring, K	.000	6	0	0	0	0	0	.000	.000
Martin, Al*	.444	9	4	2	3	0	1	.444	1.111
McGee, Willie*	.286	7	2	1	1	0	0	.286	.714
McGriff, Fred*	.308	13	4	1	3	2	5	.400	.692
McGwire, Mark	.111	9	1	1	2	0	0	.111	.444
McRae, Brian#	.286	7	2	0	0	1	1	.375	.429
Merced, O*	.125	8	1	0	1	1	1	.200	.125
Miller, Orl	.286	7	2	1	2	0	1	.286	.857
Mitchell, K	.400	5	2	0	0	1	1	.500	.600
Molitor, Paul	.250	12	3	0	1	0	2	.250	.417
Mondesi, Raul	.364	11	4	0	0	0	0	.364	.364
Morandini, M*	.333	9	3	0	0	1	0	.400	.333
Morris, Hal*	.000	3	0	0	0	2	0	.400	.000
Mouton, James	.000	4	0	0	0	0	0	.000	.000
Offerman, J#	.385	13	5	0	0	0	2	.385	.385
Orsulak, Joe*	.167	6	1	0	1	0	0	.167	.167
Pagnozzi, Tom	.100	10	1	0	2	0	0	.100	.100
Palmeiro, R*	.400	5	2	0	2	0	0	.400	.400
Pena, G#	.400	5	2	0	1	0	0	.400	.600
Pendleton, T#	.333	6	2	0	0	0	0	.333	.333
Piazza, Mike	.500	16	8	2	5	0	1	.471	.938
Polonia, Luis*	.222	9	2	0	1	0	0	.222	.222
Reed, Jody	.286	14	4	0	2	3	0	.412	.286
Rodriguez, H*	.200	10	2	0	0	0	3	.200	.300
Sabo, Chris	.250	8	2	0	0	1	1	.333	.250
Sanchez, Rey	.111	9	1	0	1	0	0	.111	.222
Sanders, R	.400	5	2	0	2	0	0	.400	.400
Santiago, B	.308	13	4	0	1	0	2	.308	.385
Schofield, D	.500	12	6	0	0	1	4	.538	.500
Segui, David#	.600	10	6	2	6	2	0	.667	1.400
Seitzer, K	.417	12	5	0	1	2	0	.500	.417
Servais, S	.200	5	1	0	1	0	0	.200	.400
Sheaffer, D	.000	7	0	0	1	0	0	.000	.000
Sheffield, G	.333	6	2	0	1	1	2	.375	.333
Sierra, Ruben#	.400	10	4	0	2	0	1	.455	.600
Slaught, Don	.091	11	1	0	1	0	3	.091	.091
Smith, Ozzie#	.250	8	2	1	2	0	0	.250	.625
Sosa, Sammy	.222	9	2	1	2	1	2	.300	.556
Steinbach, T	.200	5	1	0	0	1	0	.333	.200
Stillwell, K#	.333	12	4	0	1	1	1	.385	.583
Stocker, K#	.167	6	1	0	0	2	0	.375	.167
Surhoff, B.J.*	.333	9	3	0	0	0	1	.333	.444
Sveum, Dale#	.143	7	1	0	0	0	4	.143	.143
Tarasco, Tony*	.571	7	4	0	2	0	0	.571	.857
Tartabull, D	.200	15	3	1	3	0	3	.200	.533
Thompson, Mil*	.667	6	4	0	0	0	1	.667	.667
Thompson, Rob	.400	5	2	0	0	0	0	.400	.400
Trammell, A	.333	6	2	0	0	1	0	.429	.333
Veras, Q#	.800	5	4	0	0	0	0	.800	1.200
Vizcaino, A*	.286	7	2	0	0	0	1	.286	.286
Walker, Larry*	.200	5	1	0	0	2	0	.429	.200
Weiss, Walt#	.111	9	1	0	0	4	1	.385	.222
White, Devon#	.273	11	3	2	3	1	1	.333	.818
White, R	.250	8	2	0	1	0	1	.333	.250
Whiten, Mark#	.714	7	5	0	0	1	0	.750	.714
Williams, Ma	.000	9	0	0	0	0	3	.000	.000
Young, Eric	.200	5	1	0	0	0	0	.200	.200
Young, Kevin	.200	5	1	0	0	1	1	.333	.600
Zeile, Todd	.353	17	6	2	6	0	3	.353	.706

Batter	Avg	AB	H	HR	BI	BB	SO	OBP	Slg
Amaro, Ruben#	.333	6	2	0	2	0	2	.333	.500
Anthony, Eric*	.167	6	1	0	0	0	2	.167	.167
Bagwell, Jeff	.333	9	3	1	2	2	1	.455	.889
Bell, Derek	.143	7	1	0	3	0	0	.125	.143
Bell, Jay	.231	13	3	1	3	1	5	.286	.462
Belliard, R	.000	6	0	0	0	0	1	.000	.000
Berry, Sean	.250	8	2	0	0	0	2	.250	.250
Bichette, D	.333	6	2	0	0	0	0	.333	.333
Biggio, Craig	.273	11	3	0	2	1	2	.333	.273
Blauser, Jeff	.400	10	4	0	0	2	4	.500	.600
Bonilla, B#	.167	6	1	0	0	2	3	.375	.167
Branson, Jeff*	.400	5	2	1	2	0	2	.400	1.000
Brumfield, J	.333	6	2	1	1	0	2	.429	.833
Butler, Brett*	.167	6	1	0	0	0	0	.167	.167
Caminiti, Ken#	.250	12	3	0	0	1	1	.308	.250
Candaele, C#	.000	4	0	0	0	1	1	.200	.000
Carr, Chuck	.500	4	2	0	0	1	1	.600	.500
Castilla, V	.000	7	0	0	0	1	0	.000	.000
Cedeno, A	.364	11	4	2	5	0	4	.364	.909
Cianfrocco, A	.000	4	0	0	0	0	3	.000	.000
Clark, Dave*	.286	7	2	1	2	0	2	.286	.714
Clark, Phil	.400	5	2	0	0	0	0	.500	.400
Colbrunn, G	.600	5	3	1	2	1	1	.667	1.400
Conine, Jeff	.250	8	2	0	2	0	2	.250	.375
Daulton, D*	.125	8	1	0	1	1	6	.300	.125
Davis, Eric	.250	8	2	0	1	0	3	.333	.333
DeShields, D*	.231	13	3	0	1	1	6	.286	.308
Duncan, M	.333	6	2	0	0	1	1	.333	.333
Dykstra, L*	.143	7	1	0	1	0	1	.143	.286
Eisenreich, J*	.000	6	0	0	1	1	1	.143	.000
Eusebio, Tony	.500	4	2	1	3	1	2	.600	1.250
Finley, Steve*	.500	12	6	3	4	0	0	.500	1.417
Fletcher, D*	.182	11	2	0	0	0	3	.182	.182
Frazier, Lou*	.200	5	1	0	0	0	0	.200	.200
Galarraga, A	.200	10	2	0	0	1	5	.273	.200
Gant, Ron	.154	13	2	0	0	0	3	.154	.154
Garcia, C	.200	5	1	0	0	1	0	.333	.200
Gilkey, B	.222	9	2	0	0	1	1	.300	.222
Girardi, Joe	.333	6	2	0	0	0	1	.429	.333
Gonzalez, L*	.313	16	5	0	0	1	4	.353	.438
Grace, Mark*	.222	18	4	1	2	1	3	.263	.444
Greene, W*	.167	6	1	0	0	0	3	.167	.333
Grissom, M	.143	14	2	0	1	1	6	.200	.143
Hansen, Dave*	.250	8	2	0	1	0	0	.250	.250
Hayes, C	.375	8	3	0	3	0	3	.375	.500
Hollins, Dave#	.200	5	1	0	0	1	1	.429	.200
Howard, T*	.333	6	2	0	2	0	0	.286	.833
Hundley, Todd#	.083	12	1	0	2	0	3	.077	.083
Hunter, Brian	.200	5	1	1	1	0	2	.333	.800
Incaviglia, P	.125	8	1	0	0	0	0	.125	.250
Johnson, Mark*	.000	5	0	0	0	0	3	.000	.000
Jordan, Brian	.000	4	0	0	1	1	1	.200	.000
Jordan, Ricky	.000	7	0	0	0	0	2	.000	.000
Justice, Dave*	.375	8	3	1	2	2	4	.500	.750
Karros, Eric	.182	11	2	1	2	0	3	.182	.455
Kent, Jeff	.167	6	1	0	0	0	2	.167	.167
King, Jeff	.200	10	2	0	0	0	1	.200	.200
Kingery, Mike*	.000	4	0	0	1	1	0	.167	.000
Lankford, Ray*	.125	8	1	1	2	0	4	.125	.500
Lansing, Mike	.750	8	6	0	2	0	0	.778	.875
Larkin, Barry	.500	6	3	0	2	1	2	.571	.500
Lemke, Mark#	.167	6	1	0	0	0	2	.167	.167
Liriano, N#	.000	5	0	0	1	1	1	.143	.000
Livingstone*	.000	5	0	0	0	0	0	.000	.000
Mabry, John*	.500	6	3	0	1	0	0	.429	.500
Magadan, Dave*	.750	4	3	0	2	3	0	.857	.750
Martin, Al*	.111	9	1	0	0	0	4	.111	.111
Martinez, Da*	.333	9	3	0	1	1	1	.400	.333

15

Rod Beck, Giants — RHP

Batter	Avg	AB	H	HR	BI	BB	SO	OBP	Slg
May, Derrick*	.273	11	3	1	1	2	2	.385	.545
McGriff, Fred*	.273	11	3	1	3	0	2	.273	.545
McRae, Brian*	.167	6	1	0	0	0	0	.167	.167
Merced, O*	.182	11	2	0	0	0	4	.182	.273
Miller, Orl	.000	4	0	0	0	1	1	.200	.000
Mondesi, Raul	.400	5	2	0	0	0	1	.400	.600
Morandini, M*	.143	14	2	0	0	1	2	.200	.143
Morris, Hal*	.625	8	5	1	1	1	0	.667	1.250
Nixon, Otis*	.250	4	1	0	0	1	1	.400	.250
O'Neill, Paul*	.000	6	0	0	0	0	2	.000	.000
Offerman, J#	.125	8	1	0	2	1	2	.222	.375
Pagnozzi, Tom	.400	5	2	0	1	1	0	.500	.400
Pendleton, T#	.111	18	2	0	0	1	6	.158	.167
Piazza, Mike	.143	14	2	1	2	0	3	.143	.357
Plantier, P*	.400	5	2	1	4	0	2	.400	1.000
Reed, Jody	.400	5	2	0	0	1	1	.500	.400
Roberts, Bip#	.000	8	0	0	0	0	3	.000	.000
Rodriguez, H*	.077	13	1	0	0	0	3	.077	.077
Sabo, Chris	.167	6	1	0	0	0	1	.167	.167
Sanchez, Rey	.250	8	2	0	0	0	1	.250	.375
Sandberg, R	.111	9	1	0	1	0	3	.100	.111
Sanders, R	.100	10	1	0	0	1	3	.182	.200
Santiago, B	.417	12	5	0	2	0	1	.417	.500
Segui, David#	.400	5	2	0	0	0	0	.400	.400
Servais, S	.000	4	0	0	0	0	1	.000	.000
Sheffield, G	.375	8	3	2	4	1	1	.444	1.125
Shipley, C	.500	8	4	1	4	0	1	.500	1.000
Slaught, Don	.400	5	2	0	0	0	0	.400	.400
Smith, Dwight*	.250	4	1	0	0	1	1	.400	.250
Sosa, Sammy	.231	13	3	0	0	0	1	.231	.231
Stocker, K#	.333	9	3	1	4	1	2	.364	.889
Thompson, Mil*	.222	9	2	0	0	0	2	.222	.333
VanderWal, J*	.200	10	2	0	0	0	3	.200	.200
Vizcaino, J#	.250	8	2	0	1	0	1	.250	.250
Walker, Larry*	.400	5	2	1	1	1	3	.500	1.000
Wallach, Tim	.273	11	3	0	1	0	4	.273	.273
Weiss, Walt#	.250	8	2	0	0	0	3	.250	.250
Wilkins, Rick*	.000	5	0	0	0	2	2	.286	.000
Young, Eric	.286	7	2	0	0	1	0	.286	.286
Young, Kevin	.429	7	3	1	2	0	2	.429	.857
Zeile, Todd	.308	13	4	1	2	1	2	.357	.538

Matt Beech, Phillies — LHP

Batter	Avg	AB	H	HR	BI	BB	SO	OBP	Slg
Belliard, R	.200	5	1	0	0	0	1	.200	.400
Caminiti, Ken#	.500	6	3	0	2	0	1	.429	.500
Dye, Jermaine	.333	6	2	0	0	0	0	.333	.667
Gomez, Chris	.200	5	1	0	0	0	2	.200	.200
Grissom, M	.167	6	1	1	1	1	0	.286	.667
Gwynn, Tony*	.571	7	4	0	0	0	0	.571	.714
Henderson, R	.286	7	2	1	1	0	1	.286	.857
Jones, C#	.500	6	3	0	0	0	2	.500	.500
Klesko, Ryan*	.000	5	0	0	0	0	3	.167	.000
McGriff, Fred*	.000	6	0	0	0	0	1	.000	.000
Reed, Jody	.250	4	1	0	1	0	1	.200	.250

Tim Belcher, Royals — RHP

Batter	Avg	AB	H	HR	BI	BB	SO	OBP	Slg
Aldrete, Mike*	.167	18	3	0	1	3	5	.286	.222
Alicea, Luis#	.455	11	5	1	3	0	1	.455	.818
Alomar, R#	.282	39	11	1	4	5	2	.356	.385
Alomar Jr, S	.389	18	7	2	4	1	1	.450	.833
Anderson, Brd*	.300	20	6	1	1	2	1	.364	.600
Anderson, G*	.294	17	5	1	1	3	1	.400	.529
Anthony, Eric*	.182	11	2	1	3	0	2	.167	.455
Arias, George	.333	6	2	1	2	0	1	.333	.833
Ausmus, Brad	.200	5	1	0	0	0	1	.200	.200
Baerga, C#	.154	26	4	0	3	1	1	.185	.269
Bagwell, Jeff	.136	22	3	0	1	3	8	.240	.182
Baines, H*	.200	20	4	0	2	3	1	.304	.200
Batiste, Kim	.000	5	0	0	0	0	1	.000	.000
Becker, Rich*	.600	10	6	1	7	2	0	.667	1.200
Bell, Derek	.143	7	1	0	0	0	2	.250	.143
Bell, Jay	.242	33	8	0	0	5	9	.342	.333
Belle, Albert	.222	27	6	1	2	2	5	.276	.370
Belliard, R	.105	19	2	0	0	1	3	.150	.158
Beltre, E	.286	7	2	0	0	0	1	.286	.286
Berroa, G	.211	19	4	0	1	1	3	.250	.263
Biggio, Craig	.229	48	11	0	2	4	10	.288	.333
Blauser, Jeff	.111	36	4	2	5	2	10	.158	.361
Blowers, Mike	.167	6	1	0	0	0	2	.167	.333
Boggs, Wade*	.524	21	11	0	3	4	2	.600	.667
Bonds, Barry*	.154	39	6	1	3	6	11	.261	.282
Bonilla, B#	.149	47	7	0	2	1	12	.163	.234
Bordick, Mike	.105	19	2	0	0	1	3	.227	.105
Bragg, Darren*	.167	6	1	0	1	1	0	.286	.333
Brosius, S	.333	15	5	0	1	1	2	.389	.467
Buhner, Jay	.538	13	7	2	6	1	0	.571	1.077
Burnitz, J*	.250	4	1	0	0	0	2	.400	.250
Butler, Brett*	.267	30	8	0	2	4	6	.353	.267
Caminiti, Ken#	.156	45	7	1	3	1	9	.174	.289

Tim Belcher, Royals — RHP

Batter	Avg	AB	H	HR	BI	BB	SO	OBP	Slg
Candaele, C#	.222	9	2	0	0	0	1	.222	.333
Canseco, Jose	.385	13	5	2	2	4	2	.556	.923
Carr, Chuck	.500	4	2	0	0	0	0	.500	.500
Carreon, Mark	.143	7	1	0	0	0	1	.143	.143
Carter, Joe	.321	28	9	2	9	0	3	.321	.607
Cedeno, A	.231	13	3	0	1	0	2	.231	.231
Cedeno, D#	.000	6	0	0	1	0	3	.333	.000
Cianfrocco, A	.167	6	1	0	1	0	1	.167	.167
Cirillo, Jeff	.500	8	4	0	2	1	0	.600	.625
Clark, Dave*	.438	16	7	2	8	0	1	.438	1.000
Clark, Will*	.270	63	17	2	8	4	12	.309	.429
Clayton, R	.625	8	5	0	1	0	0	.667	1.000
Cole, Alex*	.400	10	4	0	1	1	1	.455	.500
Coleman, V#	.368	38	14	0	2	3	7	.415	.447
Conine, Jeff	.333	6	2	0	1	0	2	.333	.333
Cora, Joey#	.333	9	3	0	0	0	0	.333	.333
Cordero, Wil	.500	6	3	0	3	0	1	.500	.500
Cordova, M	.167	6	1	1	1	4	0	.500	.667
Curtis, Chad	.400	10	4	1	2	1	1	.455	.800
Dascenzo, D#	.333	6	2	0	0	3	0	.556	.500
Daulton, D*	.214	28	6	1	6	5	6	.333	.321
Davis, Chili#	.333	21	7	2	5	3	4	.417	.714
Davis, Eric	.294	34	10	2	4	2	10	.333	.471
Dawson, Andre	.313	48	15	3	10	2	5	.353	.583
Decker, Steve	.000	9	0	0	0	0	3	.000	.000
Delgado, C*	.071	14	1	0	0	1	5	.133	.071
DeShields, D*	.556	9	5	0	2	3	1	.667	.556
Devereaux, M	.091	11	1	0	1	0	3	.091	.182
DiSarcina, A	.385	13	5	0	0	1	0	.429	.385
Duncan, M	.320	25	8	0	4	0	4	.346	.400
Dunston, S	.174	23	4	0	1	0	6	.174	.174
Durham, Ray#	.125	16	2	0	1	0	1	.125	.125
Dykstra, L*	.296	27	8	0	0	7	3	.441	.407
Easley, D	.200	10	2	0	0	0	2	.200	.300
Edmonds, Jim*	.407	27	11	2	4	1	4	.429	.704
Elster, Kevin	.143	7	1	1	1	2	1	.400	.571
Espinoza, A	.200	5	1	0	1	0	2	.200	.200
Fabregas, Jor*	.471	17	8	0	1	3	0	.550	.471
Fermin, Felix	.400	5	2	0	1	0	0	.400	.600
Fielder, C	.429	7	3	0	2	2	0	.556	.571
Finley, Steve*	.368	19	7	0	0	2	5	.429	.526
Franco, Julio	.308	13	4	0	4	1	1	.357	.385
Frye, Jeff	.300	10	3	0	0	1	1	.364	.600
Fryman, T	.545	11	6	0	5	2	1	.615	.909
Gaetti, Gary	.500	16	8	1	3	1	1	.529	.813
Gagne, Greg	.333	18	6	1	4	3	2	.429	.611
Galarraga, A	.235	34	8	1	1	0	14	.235	.353
Gallego, Mike	.200	5	1	0	1	1	0	.333	.200
Gant, Ron	.237	38	9	2	6	5	6	.326	.553
Garcia, C	.125	8	1	0	0	1	3	.222	.250
Gates, Brent#	.500	16	8	0	2	0	0	.500	.625
Giambi, Jason*	.222	9	2	0	1	1	1	.300	.222
Gilkey, B	.143	7	1	0	1	0	1	.143	.286
Girardi, Joe	.188	16	3	0	0	0	2	.188	.188
Gomez, Chris	.167	6	1	0	0	2	2	.375	.333
Gonzalez, A	.133	15	2	0	1	1	3	.188	.267
Gonzalez, J	.292	24	7	1	6	2	1	.346	.500
Gonzalez, L*	.300	20	6	1	3	2	2	.364	.550
Goodwin, Tom*	.333	6	2	0	0	1	0	.429	.333
Grace, Mark*	.271	48	13	0	3	7	1	.357	.313
Green, Shawn*	.176	17	3	0	0	0	5	.176	.235
Greenwell, M*	.400	25	10	1	2	3	2	.448	.640
Greer, Rusty*	.333	18	6	0	1	3	0	.429	.389
Griffey Jr, K*	.154	13	2	0	0	1	1	.214	.154
Grissom, M	.182	11	2	0	2	2	2	.286	.182
Guillen, O*	.300	20	6	0	3	0	1	.300	.400
Gutierrez, R	.750	4	3	0	1	2	1	.833	1.750
Gwynn, Tony*	.333	45	15	0	3	8	2	.434	.444
Hamelin, Bob*	.444	9	4	1	2	2	1	.545	.778
Hamilton, D*	.167	7	1	0	0	0	0	.143	.143
Hammonds, J	.250	4	1	0	0	1	0	.400	.250
Hansen, Dave*	.429	7	3	0	0	2	1	.556	.571
Harris, Lenny*	.316	19	6	0	0	2	0	.350	.316
Haselman, B	.000	6	0	0	0	0	1	.000	.000
Hayes, C	.286	7	2	0	3	0	0	.286	.286
Henderson, R	.364	11	4	0	3	1	0	.417	.636
Herrera, Jose*	.400	10	4	0	0	3	0	.400	.400
Higginson, B*	.200	5	1	0	0	1	1	.429	.400
Hoiles, Chris	.500	4	2	0	1	5	0	.778	.500
Hollins, Dave#	.353	17	6	0	3	10	3	.593	.412
Howell, Jack*	.222	9	2	1	2	0	2	.222	.778
Hudler, Rex	.429	7	3	0	1	0	0	.500	.429
Hulse, David*	.167	12	2	0	1	0	1	.167	.167
Hundley, Todd#	.125	8	1	0	0	0	1	.125	.250
Huson, Jeff*	.000	4	0	0	0	0	0	.200	.000
Incaviglia, P	.167	6	1	0	0	0	1	.167	.167
Jaha, John	.250	12	3	3	6	1	2	.308	1.000
James, Dion*	.238	21	5	0	0	4	0	.360	.333
Javier, Stan#	.214	14	3	0	2	2	0	.294	.214
Jefferies, G#	.471	17	8	0	5	0	0	.471	.647
Jefferson, R*	.200	20	4	0	1	0	1	.200	.400

16

Tim Belcher, Royals — RHP

Batter	Avg	AB	H	HR	BI	BB	SO	OBP	Slg
Jeter, Derek	.444	9	4	0	2	4		.545	.444
Johnson, L*	.357	14	5	0	1	1	0	.400	.429
Jordan, Ricky	.217	23	5	0	2	0	5	.240	.261
Joyner, Wally*	.389	18	7	0	3	5	0	.500	.556
Justice, Dave*	.222	27	6	1	5	6	4	.364	.481
Karkovice, S	.111	9	1	1	2	2	1	.273	.444
Karros, Eric	.357	14	5	2	6	1	2	.400	.929
King, Jeff	.083	12	1	0	1	1	2	.154	.083
Kirby, Wayne*	.118	17	2	0	1	0	3	.118	.118
Knoblauch, C	.417	24	10	0	1	2	1	.462	.708
Lankford, Ray*	.294	17	5	0	3	4	3	.455	.471
Larkin, Barry	.367	30	11	1	7	4	2	.417	.600
Leius, Scott	.444	9	4	0	3	3	1	.583	.778
Lemke, Mark*	.182	33	6	0	2	2	7	.229	.273
Lewis, Darren	.353	17	6	0	2	1	1	.389	.412
Lewis, Mark	.000	6	0	0	0	0	3	.000	.000
Leyritz, Jim	.167	6	1	0	1	0	1	.167	.333
Lockhart, K*	.167	6	1	0	1	0	2	.286	.500
Lofton, Kenny*	.333	24	8	1	2	2	2	.385	.583
Macfarlane, M	.250	16	4	1	3	1	4	.400	.500
Magadan, Dave*	.450	20	9	0	3	2	4	.500	.550
Manwaring, K	.091	11	1	0	0	0	3	.091	.091
Martin, Al*	.200	10	2	0	1	0	3	.200	.200
Martinez, Da*	.244	41	10	0	1	7	4	.354	.268
Martinez, E	.444	9	4	0	2	0	1	.545	1.000
Martinez, S*	.111	9	1	0	0	0	1	.111	.111
Martinez, T*	.250	8	2	1	4	2	1	.400	.625
Matheny, Mike	.000	6	0	0	0	0	2	.000	.000
May, Derrick*	.214	14	3	0	1	0	0	.214	.214
Mayne, Brent*	.167	12	2	0	2	0	1	.167	.167
McGee, Willie#	.333	27	9	0	1	1	2	.357	.333
McGriff, Fred*	.286	21	6	0	3	4	4	.375	.333
McGwire, Mark	.154	13	2	1	2	0	5	.154	.385
McLemore, M#	.250	16	4	0	0	1	0	.294	.250
McRae, Brian#	.231	13	3	0	3	1	4	.286	.231
Meares, Pat	.176	17	3	0	1	0	1	.176	.235
Merced, O*	.300	20	6	0	2	4	5	.417	.400
Mitchell, K	.172	29	5	0	1	5	5	.294	.241
Molitor, Paul	.158	19	3	0	2	1	4	.190	.316
Morandini, M*	.150	20	3	0	1	1	8	.190	.150
Morris, Hal*	.250	12	3	0	0	1	2	.308	.500
Munoz, Pedro	.143	7	1	0	0	1	5	.250	.143
Murray, Eddie#	.217	23	5	1	5	1	2	.250	.348
Myers, Greg*	.385	13	5	0	3	1	0	.429	.615
Naehring, Tim	.318	22	7	0	1	1	0	.348	.364
Nieves, M#	.200	10	2	1	4	0	5	.200	.500
Nilsson, Dave*	.182	11	2	0	2	3	3	.357	.455
Nixon, Otis#	.273	44	12	0	1	7	9	.373	.318
Nunnally, Jon*	.167	6	1	1	1	1	1	.167	.667
O'Brien, C	.000	6	0	0	0	0	3	.000	.000
O'Leary, Troy*	.333	15	5	0	2	1	1	.375	.600
O'Neill, Paul*	.267	60	16	5	10	7	12	.353	.550
Offerman, J#	.308	13	4	0	3	3	4	.438	.462
Olerud, John*	.412	17	7	2	2	5	0	.545	.765
Oliver, Joe	.143	14	2	1	3	0	2	.143	.357
Pagnozzi, Tom	.333	12	4	0	3	1	0	.385	.417
Palmeiro, R*	.286	28	8	2	7	5	3	.382	.571
Palmer, Dean	.050	20	1	0	0	0	5	.050	.050
Paquette, C	.250	8	2	1	3	0	3	.222	.625
Parent, Mark	.200	5	1	1	1	1	1	.333	.800
Pena, Tony	.250	8	2	0	1	1	0	.300	.375
Pendleton, T	.261	46	12	1	5	1	6	.265	.391
Phillips, T#	.333	15	5	1	4	7	2	.545	.533
Piazza, Mike	.167	6	1	1	2	0	0	.167	.667
Plantier, P*	.143	7	1	1	2	1	1	.250	.571
Polonia, Luis*	.188	16	3	0	0	1	1	.235	.188
Pride, Curtis*	.300	10	3	0	0	0	1	.300	.300
Raines, Tim#	.350	40	14	0	1	4	5	.409	.400
Ramirez, M	.292	24	7	3	9	1	2	.320	.750
Reboulet, J	.250	8	2	0	0	1	3	.333	.375
Reed, Jeff*	.304	23	7	0	2	1	5	.333	.348
Reed, Jody	.364	11	4	0	2	0	2	.364	.545
Ripken, Cal	.353	17	6	0	2	1	3	.389	.588
Roberts, Bip#	.067	15	1	0	0	2	2	.176	.067
Rodriguez, I	.348	23	8	0	4	2	1	.385	.565
Sabo, Chris	.229	35	8	0	2	4	6	.308	.257
Salmon, Tim	.333	24	8	1	7	3	5	.333	.458
Samuel, Juan	.286	14	4	0	1	0	3	.286	.286
Sanchez, Rey	.250	12	3	0	0	0	0	.250	.250
Sandberg, R	.173	52	9	2	8	4	7	.228	.327
Santiago, B	.209	43	9	4	7	0	8	.209	.512
Schofield, D	.125	8	1	0	0	0	2	.125	.125
Seitzer, K*	.353	17	6	0	3	1	0	.389	.471
Servais, S	.400	5	2	1	1	1	0	.500	1.000
Sheffield, G	.133	15	2	0	2	0	2	.167	.133
Shipley, C	.182	11	2	0	2	0	1	.182	.182
Sierra, Ruben#	.222	27	6	3	6	3	3	.290	.630
Singleton, D*	.333	6	2	0	0	0	1	.333	.333
Slaught, Don	.143	7	1	0	0	2	2	.400	.286
Smith, Dwight*	.300	20	6	0	0	3	3	.391	.400
Smith, Mark	.000	6	0	0	0	0	2	.000	.000

Tim Belcher, Royals — RHP

Tim Belcher, Royals — RHP

Batter	Avg	AB	H	HR	BI	BB	SO	OBP	Slg
Smith, Ozzie*	.500	28	14	0	1	3	1	.548	.536
Snow, J.T.#	.273	22	6	0	1	2	0	.360	.273
Sorrento, P*	.211	19	4	1	3	0	3	.211	.368
Sosa, Sammy	.000	13	0	0	0	0	1	.000	.000
Sprague, Ed	.050	20	1	1	1	0	6	.095	.200
Stahoviak, S*	.300	10	3	0	2	1	0	.364	.500
Stanley, Mike	.235	17	4	0	0	5	3	.409	.294
Steinbach, T	.429	14	6	0	1	1	2	.467	.500
Stillwell, K#	.231	13	3	0	0	1	0	.231	.385
Strange, Doug#	.333	12	4	0	0	1	0	.385	.417
Strawberry, D*	.222	9	2	0	1	0	1	.222	.222
Surhoff, B.J.*	.375	8	3	0	0	2	0	.500	.375
Tartabull, D	.067	15	1	1	1	4	7	.263	.267
Taubensee, E*	.200	5	1	0	0	1	0	.333	.400
Tettleton, M#	.111	9	1	1	3	1	3	.273	.444
Thomas, Frank	.313	16	5	2	3	6	1	.500	.688
Thome, Jim*	.333	21	7	0	0	9	4	.533	.333
Thompson, Mil*	.241	29	7	0	4	2	7	.290	.276
Thompson, Rob	.194	36	7	0	4	3	9	.256	.278
Thompson, Ry	.250	4	1	0	1	0	0	.200	.250
Valentin, Jhn	.143	21	3	1	2	3	3	.269	.286
Valentin, Jse#	.500	12	6	0	1	2	3	.571	.750
Valle, Dave	.000	6	0	0	0	0	0	.000	.000
VanderWal, J*	.400	5	2	0	1	0	0	.400	.800
Vaughn, George	.313	16	5	2	3	1	2	.353	.750
Vaughn, Mo*	.207	29	6	2	5	1	5	.226	.448
Velarde, R	.304	23	7	1	4	1	3	.333	.478
Ventura, R*	.545	22	12	1	9	2	0	.583	.773
Vina, F*	.143	7	1	0	0	0	1	.143	.143
Vizcaino, J#	.563	16	9	0	4	1	2	.611	.750
Vizquel, Omar#	.318	22	7	0	3	3	4	.370	.364
Walbeck, Matt#	.000	8	0	0	2	0	0	.000	.000
Walker, Larry*	.429	14	6	1	4	1	2	.500	.857
Walker, Tim	.355	31	11	2	5	4	4	.444	.581
Walton, J	.167	6	1	0	1	1	2	.286	.333
Ward, Turner#	.111	9	1	0	0	3	1	.333	.111
Weiss, Walt*	.250	4	1	0	0	1	1	.400	.250
White, Devon#	.250	12	3	0	1	0	2	.250	.250
Wilkins, Rick*	.250	18	5	0	0	4	2	.409	.278
Williams, Ber#	.261	23	6	0	2	2	1	.320	.261
Williams, Ma	.268	41	11	2	6	1	7	.286	.512
Young, Kevin	.250	8	2	0	0	0	2	.250	.250
Zaun, Greg#	.250	8	2	0	0	1	1	.333	.500
Zeile, Todd	.200	15	3	0	3	0	2	.188	.333

Stan Belinda, Red Sox — RHP

Batter	Avg	AB	H	HR	BI	BB	SO	OBP	Slg
Aldrete, Mike*	.222	9	2	0	1	2	1	.364	.444
Alomar, R#	.375	8	3	0	0	2	2	.500	.375
Alou, Moises	.125	8	1	0	0	0	2	.125	.250
Amaro, Ruben*	.000	4	0	0	0	1		.000	.000
Bagwell, Jeff	.000	8	0	0	0	0	1	.000	.000
Belle, Albert	.000	7	0	0	0	1	0	.000	.000
Berroa, G	.000	4	0	0	0	1	2	.200	.000
Biggio, Craig	.250	8	2	0	1	2	4	.364	.250
Blauser, Jeff	.333	6	2	0	1	1	0	.429	.333
Bonilla, B#	.750	4	3	1	2	1	0	.800	1.500
Bordick, Mike	.143	7	1	0	0	0	2	.143	.143
Buhner, Jay	.125	8	1	0	0	0	3	.125	.125
Butler, Brett*	.500	4	2	0	1	0	0	.600	.500
Caminiti, Ken#	.143	7	1	0	0	1	3	.222	.143
Candaele, C#	.400	5	2	0	2	1	0	.429	.600
Carreon, Mark	.250	4	1	0	0	1	2	.400	.250
Carter, Joe	.250	16	4	2	4	1	6	.294	.625
Coleman, V#	.333	3	1	0	0	2	0	.600	.333
Cordova, M	.000	6	0	0	0	0	2	.000	.000
Curtis, Chad	.333	6	2	0	1	0	2	.333	.333
Dascenzo, D#	.000	7	0	0	0	1	2	.125	.000
Daulton, D*	.000	7	0	0	0	1	1	.000	.000
Davis, Chili#	.333	6	2	0	1	3	1	.556	.333
Davis, Eric	.250	8	2	0	1	2	1	.500	.333
Dawson, Andre	.385	13	5	4	10	0	1	.467	1.308
DeShields, D*	.143	7	1	0	0	0	3	.143	.429
Diaz, Alex#	.250	4	1	0	0	0	0	.200	.200
DiSarcina, G	.250	4	1	0	0	1	2	.250	.250
Duncan, M	.200	10	2	0	0	0	2	.200	.300
Dunston, S	.250	8	2	0	0	0	1	.250	.500
Elster, Kevin	.000	5	0	0	0	0	3	.000	.000
Fielder, C	.167	6	1	0	1	1	1	.286	.167
Finley, Steve*	.400	5	2	0	0	0	0	.400	.600
Franco, Julio	.000	4	0	0	4	1	0	.600	1.000
Fryman, T	.250	4	1	0	1	2	1	.500	.250
Galarraga, A	.167	18	3	0	1	7	0	.167	.167
Gant, Ron	.250	12	3	0	2	1	3	.308	.333
Gates, Brent#	.250	8	2	0	0	0	1	.250	.250
Gilkey, B	.500	2	1	0	2	4	0	.833	.500
Gomez, Chris	.000	6	0	0	0	0	3	.000	.000
Gonzalez, A	.667	6	4	1	3	0	1	.714	1.500
Gonzalez, J	.000	5	0	0	0	0	3	.000	.000
Grace, Mark*	.300	10	3	0	1	5	0	.533	.400
Greer, Rusty*	.000	5	0	0	0	0	3	.000	.000

17

Stan Belinda, Red Sox — RHP

Batter	Avg	AB	H	HR	BI	BB	SO	OBP	Slg
Grissom, M	.273	11	3	1	4	1	3	.333	.545
Hale, Chip*	.500	6	3	0	3	0	0	.500	.500
Hammonds, J	.167	6	1	0	1	0	0	.286	.333
Harris, Lenny*	.667	3	2	0	0	2	0	.800	.667
Hayes, C	.083	12	1	0	1	0	0	.083	.083
Hoiles, Chris	.000	9	0	0	0	0	3	.000	.000
Hollins, Dave#	.250	8	2	1	3	0	0	.250	.625
Hudler, Rex	.000	7	0	0	0	0	3	.000	.000
Huff, Michael	.250	4	1	0	2	1	1	.400	.250
Hundley, Todd#	.000	6	0	0	2	0	0	.000	.000
Incaviglia, P	.250	4	1	0	2	0	2	.250	.250
Javier, Stan#	.250	8	2	1	3	3	1	.455	.625
Jefferies, G#	.800	5	4	0	3	1	0	.833	.800
Justice, Dave*	.167	6	1	1	3	0	2	.167	.667
Knoblauch, C	.111	9	1	0	2	0	0	.200	.111
Lankford, Ray*	.000	5	0	0	0	0	2	.000	.000
Larkin, Barry	.444	9	4	0	3	1	0	.455	.667
Lemke, Mark#	.167	6	1	1	1	0	0	.167	.667
Magadan, Dave*	.500	6	3	0	1	0	0	.500	.500
Martinez, Da*	.143	7	1	0	0	1	1	.143	.143
Martinez, E	.500	4	2	0	1	2	0	.714	.750
May, Derrick*	.200	5	1	0	0	0	0	.200	.200
McGee, Willie#	.429	7	3	0	1	0	3	.429	.429
McGriff, Fred*	.600	5	3	2	2	2	1	.714	1.800
McLemore, M#	.000	5	0	0	0	1	0	.167	.000
Mieske, Matt	.333	6	2	0	2	1	0	.429	.500
Mitchell, K	.429	7	3	1	4	0	1	.429	.857
Molitor, Paul	.429	14	6	0	1	1	0	.467	.500
Morandini, M*	.000	7	0	0	0	1	0	.000	.000
Morris, Hal*	.500	8	4	1	1	2	0	.600	1.125
Murray, Eddie*	.125	8	1	0	0	1	1	.125	.125
Myers, Greg*	.400	5	2	1	2	1	1	.500	1.000
Nixon, Otis#	.333	9	3	0	2	3	1	.500	.333
O'Brien, C	.200	5	1	0	0	1	2	.333	.400
O'Neill, Paul*	.167	6	1	0	1	0	2	.167	.333
Offerman, J#	.000	6	0	0	0	1	0	.143	.000
Olerud, John*	.125	8	1	0	0	2	1	.300	.250
Oliver, Joe	.250	8	2	0	1	2	1	.364	.375
Paquette, C	.200	5	1	0	0	0	0	.200	.200
Pendleton, T#	.167	12	2	1	3	0	3	.167	.417
Raines, Tim#	.333	3	1	0	0	2	0	.600	.333
Ramirez, M	.200	5	1	0	1	1	2	.333	.200
Reboulet, J	.286	7	2	0	0	0	0	.286	.286
Ripken, Cal	.286	7	2	1	2	0	0	.250	.857
Roberts, Bip#	.286	7	2	0	2	0	3	.286	.429
Rodriguez, I	.000	5	0	0	0	0	0	.000	.000
Sabo, Chris	.125	8	1	0	1	1	1	.222	.125
Salmon, Tim	.375	8	3	1	4	0	1	.375	.875
Samuel, Juan	.429	7	3	0	4	4	0	.636	.714
Sandberg, R	.385	13	5	1	3	1	2	.429	.615
Santiago, B	.286	7	2	0	1	1	2	.375	.286
Schofield, D	.400	5	2	1	1	1	0	.500	1.000
Seitzer, K	.143	7	1	0	0	0	2	.143	.143
Sierra, Ruben#	.200	5	1	0	1	0	1	.167	.200
Smith, Ozzie#	.143	7	1	0	1	2	1	.333	.143
Sosa, Sammy	.167	6	1	1	2	0	2	.167	.667
Sprague, Ed	.000	4	0	0	1	3	1	.556	.000
Steinbach, T	.000	6	0	0	0	0	0	.000	.000
Tettleton, M#	.167	6	1	0	0	1	2	.286	.167
Thomas, Frank	.500	6	3	0	2	1	1	.500	.667
Thome, Jim*	.250	4	1	0	0	3	1	.571	.500
Thompson, Mil*	.444	9	4	0	1	0	1	.444	.444
Thompson, Rob	.000	6	0	0	0	0	2	.000	.000
Vaughn, Greg	.200	5	1	0	0	1	1	.333	.200
Walbeck, Matt#	.167	6	1	0	0	0	0	.167	.167
Walker, Larry*	.125	8	1	0	0	1	2	.222	.125
Wallach, Tim	.211	19	4	0	2	2	3	.286	.263
Walton, J	.000	3	0	0	0	2	1	.400	.000
White, Devon#	.667	6	4	1	4	0	1	.667	1.667
Williams, Ma	.167	6	1	0	0	1	1	.286	.500
Zeile, Todd	.167	12	2	1	4	4	2	.375	.500

Alan Benes, Cardinals — RHP

Batter	Avg	AB	H	HR	BI	BB	SO	OBP	Slg
Alou, Moises	.000	5	0	0	1	1	0	.143	.000
Aurilia, Rich	.800	5	4	0	1	0	0	.800	.800
Bagwell, Jeff	.333	6	2	1	1	1	0	.429	.833
Bell, Derek	.000	7	0	0	0	0	2	.000	.000
Bell, Jay	.250	12	3	1	3	0	4	.250	.500
Benard, M*	.429	7	3	0	1	0	0	.500	.571
Berry, Sean	.167	6	1	0	0	0	0	.286	.167
Bichette, D	.222	9	2	1	1	2	2	.364	.667
Biggio, Craig	.167	6	1	0	0	0	0	.286	.167
Bonds, Barry*	.500	8	4	1	3	1	0	.556	1.000
Boone, Bret	.400	5	2	0	1	1	0	.500	.600
Brogna, Rico*	.286	7	2	0	2	0	0	.444	.429
Burks, Ellis	.250	12	3	1	3	1	4	.308	.583
Caminiti, Ken#	.286	7	2	0	1	0	1	.250	.286
Castilla, V	.500	8	4	0	1	2	0	.600	.625
Clark, Dave*	.500	4	2	0	1	0	0	.600	.500
Davis, Eric	.000	5	0	0	0	1	2	.167	.000

Alan Benes, Cardinals — RHP

Batter	Avg	AB	H	HR	BI	BB	SO	OBP	Slg
DeShields, D*	.182	11	2	0	0	0	2	.182	.182
Eisenreich, J*	.000	5	0	0	0	1	1	.167	.000
Encarnacion	.200	5	1	0	0	0	3	.200	.200
Finley, Steve*	.250	8	2	0	1	1	0	.333	.250
Fletcher, D*	.400	5	2	0	0	1	1	.500	.600
Gagne, Greg	.375	8	3	0	0	1	2	.444	.500
Galarraga, A	.300	10	3	2	4	0	4	.300	.900
Garcia, C	.250	8	2	1	1	0	2	.250	.625
Gilkey, B	.100	10	1	0	2	0	2	.091	.100
Gomez, Leo	.286	7	2	0	2	0	3	.286	.429
Gonzalez, L*	.429	7	3	0	4	1	1	.444	.429
Grace, Mark*	.857	7	6	0	0	2	1	.889	1.143
Grissom, M	.500	5	2	1	1	1	0	.500	1.000
Grudzielanek	.286	7	2	0	0	0	0	.286	.286
Gwynn, Tony*	.500	6	3	0	2	3	0	.667	.500
Hayes, C	.250	4	1	0	2	1	1	.400	.500
Henderson, R	.400	5	2	0	0	4	1	.667	.400
Hernandez, Jo	.600	5	3	1	2	0	0	.500	1.400
Hill, G	.000	4	0	0	0	1	0	.200	.000
Hollandsworth*	.400	10	4	2	2	1	1	.455	1.000
Hundley, Todd#	.500	5	1	1	2	2	2	.429	.800
Hunter, Bri L	.167	6	1	0	2	0	0	.167	.167
Huskey, Butch	.222	9	2	0	1	2	2	.300	.222
Johnson, L*	.455	11	5	2	4	2	1	.538	1.273
Johnson, Mark*	.167	6	1	0	0	1	0	.167	.167
Jones, C#	.167	6	1	0	0	0	0	.167	.167
Karros, Eric	.111	9	1	0	1	3	1	.333	.111
Kendall, J	.286	7	2	0	0	0	1	.286	.286
Kent, Jeff	.125	8	1	0	0	0	2	.125	.125
King, Jeff	.100	10	1	0	2	3	5	.250	.100
Kingery, Mike*	.286	7	2	0	0	0	5	.286	.286
Kirby, Wayne*	.200	5	1	0	0	0	0	.200	.200
Klesko, Ryan*	.400	5	2	1	1	1	1	.500	1.200
Lansing, Mike	.200	5	1	0	0	2	1	.429	.200
Larkin, Barry	.500	4	2	1	2	1	0	.600	1.250
Lemke, Mark#	.167	6	1	0	0	0	0	.167	.167
Lopez, Javy	.667	6	4	2	3	0	1	.667	1.833
Lopez, Luis#	.167	6	1	0	1	0	2	.167	.167
Manwaring, K	.000	4	0	0	0	1	1	.200	.000
Martin, Al*	.500	12	6	1	1	3	1	.625	.917
May, Derrick*	.250	4	1	0	1	1	1	.400	.250
McGriff, Fred*	.000	6	0	0	0	0	0	.000	.000
McRae, Brian#	.333	6	2	0	1	1	1	.429	.333
Merced, O*	.545	11	6	0	5	4	0	.667	.545
Miller, Orl	.167	6	1	0	0	0	1	.167	.333
Mondesi, Raul	.300	10	3	1	2	2	2	.417	.800
Morandini, M*	.333	6	2	0	1	0	0	.286	.333
Morris, Hal*	.400	5	2	0	3	1	1	.500	.800
Mueller, Bill#	.333	3	1	0	0	2	0	.600	.667
Ordonez, Rey	.300	10	3	0	1	0	0	.300	.300
Piazza, Mike	.286	7	2	0	0	1	0	.375	.286
Reed, Jeff*	.600	5	3	0	0	0	1	.600	.600
Reed, Jody	.333	6	2	0	2	0	1	.333	.500
Rodriguez, H*	.000	7	0	0	0	4	0	.000	.000
Sandberg, R	.000	4	0	0	0	1	1	.200	.000
Santiago, B	.250	4	1	0	2	1	2	.400	.500
Servais, S	.000	5	0	0	0	1	0	.286	.000
Sosa, Sammy	.222	9	2	1	3	0	6	.222	.556
Stocker, K#	.000	2	0	0	2	1	0	.600	.000
Vizcaino, J#	1.000	9	9	0	1	0	0	1.000	1.556
Walker, Larry*	.143	7	1	0	0	3	0	.143	.143
Wallach, Tim	.143	7	1	0	1	0	0	.250	.143
Weiss, Walt#	.286	7	2	0	2	1	1	.444	.286
Whiten, Mark#	.250	8	2	0	2	1	1	.333	.250
Wilkins, Rick*	.333	6	2	0	0	0	2	.333	.333
Young, Eric	.167	12	2	1	2	1	0	.231	.583
Zeile, Todd	.200	5	1	0	1	1	2	.429	.200

Andy Benes, Cardinals — RHP

Batter	Avg	AB	H	HR	BI	BB	SO	OBP	Slg
Abbott, Kurt	.333	6	2	0	0	0	3	.333	.333
Alfonzo, E	.250	4	1	0	0	1	0	.400	.250
Alicea, Luis*	.364	11	4	0	0	2	2	.462	.364
Alou, Moises	.348	23	8	1	5	0	5	.348	.652
Amaro, Ruben*	.000	6	0	0	0	0	2	.143	.000
Anderson, G*	.333	6	2	1	1	0	0	.333	.833
Anthony, Eric*	.250	20	5	1	5	4	6	.360	.400
Arias, Alex	.100	10	1	0	0	0	4	.100	.100
Ashley, Billy	.000	5	0	0	0	0	4	.000	.000
Aurilia, Rich	.111	9	1	0	0	0	0	.111	.111
Bagwell, Jeff	.306	49	15	3	7	9	12	.426	.612
Barberie, M#	.067	15	1	0	1	3	3	.222	.067
Bell, Derek	.375	16	6	1	3	3	5	.500	.688
Bell, Jay	.224	49	11	0	0	2	10	.255	.286
Belliard, R	.115	26	3	0	1	0	4	.148	.115
Benard, M	.111	9	1	0	0	2	2	.273	.111
Benjamin, M	.150	20	3	1	3	4	6	.261	.300
Berry, Sean	.267	15	4	1	2	0	3	.267	.533
Bichette, D	.321	28	9	1	5	0	8	.310	.464
Biggio, Craig	.262	65	17	1	4	7	12	.338	.400
Blauser, Jeff	.064	47	3	0	1	4	9	.135	.064

Andy Benes, Cardinals — RHP

Batter	Avg	AB	H	HR	BI	BB	SO	OBP	Slg
Bonds, Barry*	.278	36	10	3	16	11	4	.442	.583
Bonilla, B#	.282	39	11	1	4	3	8	.333	.436
Boone, Bret	.600	15	9	1	7	1	4	.625	1.067
Branson, Jeff*	.308	13	4	0	1	1	1	.333	.385
Brogna, Rico*	.278	18	5	0	0	1	7	.316	.333
Brumfield, J	.000	5	0	0	0	1	1	.000	.000
Burks, Ellis	.231	13	3	0	2	0	1	.231	.308
Butler, Brett*	.378	45	17	0	4	11	6	.500	.489
Caminiti, Ken#	.180	50	9	3	8	3	9	.236	.420
Candaele, C#	.222	18	4	0	2	0	4	.222	.333
Canseco, Jose	.400	5	2	0	0	0	0	.400	.800
Carr, Chuck	.167	6	1	0	0	1	1	.286	.167
Carreon, Mark	.273	11	3	1	3	0	1	.273	.727
Castilla, V	.222	18	4	0	2	1	2	.263	.333
Cedeno, A	.222	27	6	3	4	1	9	.250	.630
Clark, Dave*	.316	19	6	0	2	2	2	.381	.421
Clark, Will*	.233	43	10	1	5	2	8	.261	.326
Clayton, R	.261	23	6	0	2	0	9	.261	.304
Colbrunn, G	.417	12	5	1	1	1	3	.462	.667
Cole, Alex*	.200	10	2	0	1	2	2	.385	.200
Coleman, V#	.316	19	6	0	2	0	4	.316	.316
Conine, Jeff	.200	20	4	0	0	0	9	.200	.250
Cordero, Wil	.500	12	6	3	6	1	0	.538	1.333
Dascenzo, D#	.286	7	2	0	0	0	0	.286	.286
Daulton, D*	.212	33	7	1	5	5	6	.308	.364
Davis, Chili#	.400	5	2	0	0	1	0	.500	.400
Davis, Eric	.308	26	8	0	4	3	8	.379	.385
Dawson, Andre	.318	22	7	1	4	1	1	.348	.455
Decker, Steve	.167	12	2	1	1	3	6	.333	.500
DeShields, D*	.238	42	10	0	3	4	8	.304	.286
DiSarcina, A	.200	5	1	0	0	0	1	.200	.200
Duncan, M	.292	24	7	0	2	0	7	.280	.417
Dunston, S	.304	23	7	0	1	1	5	.320	.391
Durham, Ray#	.400	5	2	0	1	0	1	.400	.400
Dye, Jermaine	.400	5	2	0	0	1	0	.500	.400
Dykstra, L*	.189	37	7	1	2	4	1	.268	.297
Edmonds, Jim*	.400	5	2	0	0	1	2	.571	.400
Eisenreich, J*	.208	24	5	0	1	0	4	.208	.250
Elster, Kevin	.167	6	1	1	3	0	0	.167	.667
Eusebio, Tony	.357	14	5	0	2	2	2	.412	.429
Finley, Steve*	.233	43	10	1	1	2	7	.267	.349
Fletcher, D*	.300	30	9	2	7	3	2	.364	.567
Floyd, Cliff*	.364	11	4	0	3	1	3	.417	.727
Gagne, Greg	.200	5	1	1	3	1	0	.333	.800
Galarraga, A	.227	44	10	1	6	2	15	.277	.341
Gant, Ron	.313	32	10	1	6	7	6	.425	.438
Garcia, C	.241	29	7	0	0	1	3	.290	.241
Gilkey, B	.167	18	3	1	1	3	1	.318	.333
Girardi, Joe	.278	18	5	0	3	2	1	.350	.278
Goff, Jerry*	.200	5	1	0	0	0	2	.200	.200
Gomez, Leo	.000	5	0	0	0	1	0	.167	.000
Gonzalez, L*	.220	50	11	1	6	5	8	.291	.360
Grace, Mark*	.280	50	14	0	4	6	3	.351	.360
Grebeck, C	.200	5	1	0	0	0	1	.200	.200
Greene, W*	.167	6	1	0	0	1	0	.286	.333
Greenwell, M*	.333	3	1	0	2	1	0	.400	.667
Grissom, M	.245	53	13	1	4	5	9	.310	.396
Guillen, O*	.200	5	1	0	0	0	0	.200	.200
Gwynn, Chris*	.286	7	2	0	0	1	0	.375	.286
Hansen, Dave*	.444	9	4	0	1	1	1	.500	.444
Harris, Lenny*	.262	42	11	2	4	2	4	.295	.429
Hayes, C	.195	41	8	0	4	6	9	.298	.244
Hernandez, Ca	.167	6	1	1	1	0	2	.167	.667
Hernandez, Jo	.000	8	0	0	0	0	3	.000	.000
Hill, G	.417	12	5	1	3	0	2	.417	.750
Hollins, Dave#	.160	25	4	0	2	4	4	.241	.160
Howard, T*	.143	7	1	0	0	0	0	.143	.143
Hundley, Todd#	.229	35	8	2	5	0	7	.229	.457
Hunter, Brian	.357	14	5	2	2	0	4	.357	.929
Hunter, Bri'L	.357	14	5	1	1	1	2	.400	.571
Huskey, Butch	.200	5	1	0	0	1	2	.333	.200
Incaviglia, P	.429	7	3	0	0	1	4	.500	.429
Javier, Stan#	.143	21	3	0	1	0	0	.182	.143
Jefferies, G#	.250	36	9	1	5	1	3	.270	.333
Johnson, Char	.000	5	0	0	0	0	1	.000	.000
Johnson, L*	.357	14	5	1	1	0	1	.357	.643
Johnson, Mark*	.400	10	4	1	3	1	3	.417	.800
Jones, C#	.308	13	4	0	1	4	0	.471	.308
Jordan, Brian	.143	7	1	0	2	0	1	.143	.143
Jordan, Ricky	.240	25	6	4	11	0	5	.240	.760
Joyner, Wally*	.000	5	0	0	0	2	1	.286	.000
Justice, Dave*	.260	50	13	5	11	7	9	.362	.620
Karros, Eric	.217	23	5	0	2	3	6	.308	.304
Kelly, R	.313	16	5	1	2	0	2	.313	.500
Kent, Jeff	.231	26	6	1	2	0	10	.231	.346
King, Jeff	.379	29	11	3	7	7	0	.500	.724
Kingery, Mike*	.208	24	5	0	2	2	4	.269	.250
Klesko, Ryan*	.286	21	6	2	2	2	4	.348	.619
Lampkin, Tom*	.333	6	2	0	1	1	0	.429	.500
Lankford, Ray*	.217	23	5	1	6	2	8	.280	.478
Lansing, Mike	.333	15	5	0	1	0	5	.333	.467

Andy Benes, Cardinals — RHP

Batter	Avg	AB	H	HR	BI	BB	SO	OBP	Slg
Larkin, Barry	.292	48	14	1	5	2	6	.320	.417
Lemke, Mark#	.300	30	9	1	2	5	0	.400	.467
Lewis, Darren	.316	19	6	0	2	2	2	.381	.421
Lieberthal, M	.286	7	2	1	2	1	1	.400	.714
Liriano, N#	.100	10	1	0	0	3	4	.308	.300
Lopez, Javy	.294	17	5	2	5	0	3	.294	.706
Magadan, Dave*	.320	25	8	1	3	5	5	.433	.440
Manwaring, K	.182	11	2	0	1	1	0	.231	.182
Martin, Al*	.355	31	11	1	3	2	3	.394	.581
Martinez, Da*	.298	47	14	0	6	2	4	.320	.383
May, Derrick*	.240	25	6	0	2	1	3	.269	.280
McGee, Willie#	.314	35	11	0	3	1	9	.333	.429
McGriff, Fred*	.318	22	7	1	3	2	4	.360	.636
McRae, Brian#	.286	14	4	1	1	1	1	.375	.500
Merced, O*	.333	39	13	2	10	12	5	.481	.513
Miller, Orl	.214	14	3	0	0	0	5	.214	.286
Mitchell, K	.367	30	11	5	10	2	8	.406	1.067
Mondesi, Raul	.100	10	1	0	0	1	3	.182	.100
Morandini, M*	.405	37	15	0	0	4	5	.463	.541
Morris, Hal*	.256	39	10	0	1	2	3	.293	.333
Mouton, James	.444	9	4	0	1	1	3	.500	.556
Mueller, Bill#	.571	7	4	0	0	0	0	.571	.714
Murray, Eddie#	.324	34	11	0	3	4	2	.395	.382
Nixon, Otis#	.385	26	10	0	2	5	1	.484	.423
O'Neill, Paul*	.344	32	11	1	6	3	12	.400	.531
Offerman, J#	.222	18	4	0	1	2	5	.300	.222
Oliver, Joe	.167	12	2	0	1	1	4	.231	.167
Ordonez, Rey	.000	4	0	0	0	1	0	.200	.000
Orsulak, Joe*	.150	20	3	0	0	2	4	.261	.150
Osik, Keith	.286	7	2	0	1	1	0	.375	.429
Otero, Ricky#	.000	7	0	0	0	1	2	.125	.000
Pagnozzi, Tom	.059	17	1	1	2	0	2	.059	.235
Pena, G#	.333	6	2	1	1	1	1	.429	.333
Pendleton, G	.286	49	14	1	7	5	8	.364	.388
Perez, Eddie	.333	6	2	0	0	0	0	.333	.500
Phillips, J*	.333	12	4	1	4	1	4	.385	.750
Phillips, T#	.000	6	0	0	0	1	1	.143	.000
Piazza, Mike	.333	13	4	1	5	0	5	.308	.538
Plantier, P*	.200	5	1	0	0	1	0	.200	.400
Prince, Tom	.125	8	1	1	3	0	4	.125	.500
Raines, Tim#	.500	16	8	2	4	1	3	.529	1.063
Reed, Jeff*	.500	34	17	2	10	8	5	.568	.735
Reed, Jody	.167	6	1	0	0	1	1	.167	.167
Renteria, E	.125	8	1	0	0	0	3	.125	.125
Roberts, Bip#	.300	20	6	0	3	1	2	.364	.400
Rodriguez, H*	.231	13	3	0	1	2	4	.333	.308
Sabo, Chris	.143	21	3	0	3	4	5	.280	.190
Salmon, Tim	.286	7	2	0	0	0	1	.286	.286
Samuel, Juan	.333	24	5	1	1	2	9	.269	.333
Sanchez, Rey	.385	13	5	0	0	1	5	.385	.462
Sandberg, R	.191	47	9	1	6	4	5	.255	.362
Sanders, D	.250	20	5	1	2	2	7	.318	.450
Santiago, B	.400	15	6	2	4	2	6	.471	.933
Scarsone, S	.250	8	2	0	0	1	4	.333	.375
Schofield, D	.000	6	0	0	1	0	0	.000	.000
Segui, David#	.143	7	1	0	0	0	2	.143	.286
Servais, S	.333	18	6	2	4	2	5	.400	.667
Sheaffer, D	.375	8	3	1	1	1	2	.444	.750
Sheffield, G	.214	14	3	0	1	1	5	.313	.286
Simms, Mike	.000	5	0	0	0	0	1	.000	.000
Smith, Dwight*	.278	18	5	1	2	1	3	.316	.556
Smith, Ozzie#	.346	26	9	0	3	2	2	.393	.423
Snow, J.T.#	.000	6	0	0	0	0	2	.000	.000
Sosa, Sammy	.208	24	5	0	2	2	9	.269	.333
Spiers, Bill*	.250	4	1	0	1	2	2	.500	.250
Stocker, K#	.000	19	0	0	0	6	0	.000	.000
Strawberry, D*	.238	21	5	1	2	2	7	.304	.476
Taubensee, E*	.118	17	2	0	0	2	5	.211	.118
Thomas, Frank	.000	4	0	0	0	2	1	.333	.000
Thompson, Mil*	.273	22	6	0	1	4	4	.385	.409
Thompson, Rob	.314	35	11	2	4	2	9	.351	.486
Thompson, Ry	.167	12	2	0	1	0	5	.167	.167
Tomberlin, A*	.250	4	1	0	1	1	1	.400	.750
Valentin, Jhn	.250	4	1	1	3	0	0	.200	1.000
VanderWal, J*	.286	14	4	0	2	1	3	.333	.429
Vaughn, Mo*	.250	4	1	0	1	0	0	.400	.250
Ventura, R*	.000	3	0	0	0	3	1	.500	.000
Vizcaino, J	.303	33	10	0	2	1	6	.343	.333
Walker, Larry*	.265	34	9	3	10	5	9	.359	.647
Wallach, Tim	.121	33	4	1	2	6	8	.268	.212
Weiss, Walt*	.111	27	3	0	1	3	4	.200	.111
White, Devon#	.500	10	5	0	0	0	2	.500	.600
Whiten, Mark#	.231	13	3	1	2	1	3	.286	.615
Wilkins, Rick*	.500	10	5	0	0	1	6	.333	.150
Williams, Ma	.370	46	17	5	10	2	9	.408	.761
Young, Eric	.435	23	10	0	1	2	4	.480	.652
Young, Kevin	.250	8	2	0	3	0	1	.250	.500
Zeile, Todd	.275	40	11	0	3	4	7	.341	.275

Armando Benitez, Orioles — RHP

Batter	Avg	AB	H	HR	BI	BB	SO	OBP	Slg
Belle, Albert	.000	5	0	0	0	0	2	.000	.000
Berroa, G	.000	5	0	0	0	1	2	.143	.000
Carter, Joe	.000	7	0	0	0	0	2	.000	.000
Gates, Brent#	.000	5	0	0	0	2	5	.286	.000
Leius, Scott	.000	4	0	0	0	1	2	.200	.000
Martinez, E	.200	5	1	1	4	1	3	.333	.800
McGwire, Mark	.000	3	0	0	0	2	3	.400	.000
Molitor, Paul	.000	4	0	0	0	2	1	.333	.000
Paquette, C	.167	6	1	0	1	0	1	.167	.167
Ramirez, M	.000	5	2	1	4	0	1	.400	1.000

Jason Bere, White Sox — RHP

Batter	Avg	AB	H	HR	BI	BB	SO	OBP	Slg
Alomar, R#	.571	7	4	0	0	3	1	.700	.571
Amaral, Rich	.667	3	2	0	0	3	0	.833	.667
Anderson, Brd*	.375	8	3	1	1	8	2	.688	.750
Baerga, C	.467	15	7	0	1	2	1	.556	.600
Baines, H*	.154	13	2	0	1	3	2	.313	.231
Becker, Rich*	.250	4	1	0	0	3	0	.571	.250
Belle, Albert	.292	24	7	3	3	0	3	.320	.667
Berroa, G	.417	12	5	1	4	1	1	.462	.667
Boggs, Wade*	.167	6	1	0	0	2	2	.375	.167
Bordick, Mike	.200	10	2	0	0	0	3	.200	.200
Brosius, S	.200	10	2	0	0	1	2	.333	.300
Buhner, Jay	.286	7	2	1	1	1	2	.444	.714
Canseco, Jose	.100	10	1	0	2	2	3	.250	.100
Carter, Joe	.000	8	0	0	0	1	4	.111	.000
Clark, Will*	.500	6	3	0	1	4	0	.700	.833
Cole, Alex*	.250	4	1	0	2	1	0	.400	.250
Coleman, V#	.625	8	5	0	2	1	0	.667	.750
Cordova, M	.125	8	1	1	2	0	4	.125	.500
Curtis, Chad	.280	25	7	1	4	1	7	.308	.480
Davis, Chili#	.333	18	6	1	6	6	6	.480	.611
Davis, Eric	.111	9	1	0	0	0	2	.111	.222
Dawson, Andre	.200	5	1	0	0	0	1	.200	.200
Devereaux, M	.273	11	3	1	2	0	4	.273	.545
DiSarcina, G	.389	18	7	1	4	1	2	.421	.667
Easley, D	.083	12	1	0	1	2	5	.200	.083
Edmonds, Jim*	.313	16	5	2	4	2	9	.389	.750
Espinoza, A	.444	9	4	0	1	0	2	.444	.556
Fabregas, Jor*	.500	6	3	1	3	1	1	.571	1.000
Fermin, Felix	.273	11	3	0	1	2	1	.385	.273
Fielder, C	.200	20	4	1	5	1	11	.273	.350
Franco, Julio	.400	5	2	0	0	1	0	.500	.400
Fryman, T	.261	23	6	0	1	2	6	.320	.304
Gaetti, Gary	.471	17	8	1	6	0	5	.471	.706
Gagne, Greg	.211	19	4	0	2	2	8	.286	.263
Gallego, Mike	.143	7	1	0	1	0	1	.143	.143
Gates, Brent#	.231	13	3	0	0	2	3	.333	.385
Gomez, Chris	.200	5	1	0	0	1	3	.333	.200
Gomez, Leo	.167	6	1	0	2	2	2	.375	.167
Gonzalez, J	.385	13	5	2	5	2	4	.438	.846
Goodwin, C*	.400	5	2	0	1	0	0	.400	.400
Goodwin, Tom*	.400	5	2	0	0	1	0	.500	.400
Green, Shawn*	.000	3	0	0	0	2	0	.400	.000
Greenwell, M*	.154	13	2	0	3	1	2	.214	.231
Greer, Rusty*	.375	8	3	0	1	1	1	.444	.375
Grifley Jr, K*	.143	7	1	1	3	2	1	.333	.571
Hamelin, Bob*	.250	12	3	0	1	2	4	.357	.333
Hamilton, D*	.455	11	5	0	0	4	2	.600	.545
Hammonds, J	.167	6	1	0	2	0	1	.167	.167
Henderson, R	.417	12	5	0	4	5	2	.588	.583
Hiatt, Phil	.167	6	1	0	1	0	3	.167	.500
Higginson, B*	.200	5	1	0	1	1	0	.333	.200
Hoiles, Chris	.200	10	2	0	1	3	2	.385	.300
Hulse, David*	.250	8	2	0	1	1	3	.333	.250
Jaha, John	.200	10	2	0	1	0	8	.182	.500
Javier, Stan#	.294	17	5	0	1	2	2	.368	.353
Jefferson, R*	.286	7	2	0	1	1	2	.375	.286
Joyner, Wally*	.278	18	5	1	2	3	3	.381	.500
Kirby, Wayne*	.154	13	2	0	0	2	0	.267	.231
Knoblauch, C	.222	9	2	0	1	8	3	.588	.222
Kreuter, Chad#	.400	5	2	0	0	0	0	.400	.800
Levis, Jesse*	.500	6	3	0	2	0	1	.500	.667
Listach, Pat#	.000	5	0	0	0	2	2	.286	.000
Livingstone*	.167	6	1	0	0	1	0	.286	.167
Lofton, Kenny*	.292	24	7	1	3	5	3	.414	.417
Lovullo, T#	.200	5	1	0	0	1	1	.333	.400
Macfarlane, M	.429	14	6	3	6	5	4	.579	1.071
Martinez, E	.143	7	1	0	1	1	0	.222	.286
Martinez, T*	.000	5	0	0	0	0	2	.000	.000
Matheny, Mike	.200	5	1	0	0	1	0	.200	.200
Mayne, Brent*	.200	5	1	0	0	1	2	.333	.200
McGwire, Mark	.400	5	2	1	3	1	1	.429	1.000
McLemore, M#	.143	14	2	0	2	1	3	.200	.214
McRae, Brian#	.111	18	2	0	0	3	4	.238	.111
Meares, Pat	.308	13	4	1	1	0	1	.308	.538
Mieske, Matt	.500	6	3	1	1	0	2	.500	1.167
Molitor, Paul	.400	10	4	0	2	0	0	.400	.500
Munoz, Pedro	.167	6	1	0	0	0	4	.167	.167
Murray, Eddie#	.273	11	3	0	3	3	2	.400	.364

Jason Bere, White Sox — RHP

Batter	Avg	AB	H	HR	BI	BB	SO	OBP	Slg
Myers, Greg*	.200	5	1	0	0	0	1	.200	.200
Naehring, Tim	.182	11	2	0	0	2	4	.308	.273
Nilsson, Dave*	.133	15	2	0	1	3	1	.278	.200
Nixon, Otis#	.000	1	0	0	0	5	0	.833	.000
O'Neill, Paul*	.333	6	2	0	0	1	1	.429	.333
Olerud, John*	.167	6	1	0	0	3	1	.444	.167
Palmeiro, R*	.176	17	3	0	0	4	3	.333	.176
Palmer, Dean	.273	11	3	1	1	1	0	.385	.636
Pena, Tony	.250	4	1	0	0	1	1	.400	.250
Perez, E	.200	5	1	0	0	0	4	.333	.200
Phillips, T#	.333	15	5	0	1	9	6	.583	.333
Polonia, Luis*	.231	13	3	0	0	1	4	.286	.231
Ramirez, M	.100	10	1	1	4	1	5	.182	.400
Reed, Jody	.250	8	2	0	0	2	0	.400	.375
Ripken, Cal	.313	16	5	1	5	0	1	.313	.563
Rodriguez, I	.154	13	2	1	4	0	3	.143	.385
Salmon, Tim	.294	17	5	2	3	5	5	.455	.765
Seitzer, K	.400	10	4	0	1	3	1	.538	.500
Sierra, Ruben#	.176	17	3	1	2	1	5	.222	.412
Snow, J.T.#	.235	17	4	2	5	1	6	.278	.588
Sorrento, P*	.333	15	5	2	3	5	6	.500	.733
Spiers, Bill*	.167	6	1	0	0	1	0	.286	.167
Sprague, Ed	.429	7	3	1	3	1	1	.556	.857
Stahoviak, S*	.333	6	2	0	4	0	3	.286	.500
Steinbach, T	.250	16	4	0	2	1	1	.294	.313
Strange, Doug#	.000	4	0	0	0	3	0	.429	.000
Surhoff, B.J.*	.083	12	1	0	0	1	5	.154	.083
Tartabull, D	.000	5	0	0	0	2	1	.286	.000
Tettleton, M#	.000	14	0	0	0	6	9	.300	.000
Thome, Jim*	.286	14	4	2	5	3	2	.389	.714
Tinsley, Lee*	.400	5	2	1	2	0	1	.400	1.000
Trammell, A	.375	8	3	1	1	0	1	.375	.875
Tucker, M*	.286	7	2	0	3	0	3	.286	.429
Turner, Chris	.200	5	1	0	0	0	3	.200	.200
Valentin, Jhn	.444	9	4	1	3	2	2	.545	.889
Valentin, Jse#	.167	6	1	0	1	2	1	.375	.333
Vaughn, Greg	.385	13	5	1	6	0	2	.385	.769
Vaughn, Mo*	.231	13	3	0	0	1	6	.286	.231
Velarde, R	.400	5	2	0	1	1	2	.500	.400
Vizquel, Omar#	.333	12	4	0	1	1	2	.385	.333
Voigt, Jack	.000	4	0	0	0	1	0	.200	.000
Walbeck, Matt#	.400	10	4	0	2	1	4	.455	.500
Ward, Turner#	.333	9	3	1	2	1	4	.400	.667
White, Devon#	.000	5	0	0	0	2	2	.286	.000
Williams, Ber#	.286	7	2	0	1	0	2	.286	.286
Wilson, Dan	.200	5	1	0	1	1	3	.286	.400

Sean Bergman, Padres — RHP

Batter	Avg	AB	H	HR	BI	BB	SO	OBP	Slg
Alfonzo, E	.400	5	2	0	2	1	0	.500	.400
Alicea, Luis#	.200	5	1	0	1	0	0	.286	.200
Alomar, R#	.444	9	4	1	1	2	1	.545	.778
Anderson, Brd*	.625	8	5	1	6	1	0	.667	1.375
Baerga, C#	.250	12	3	1	5	0	0	.250	.500
Bagwell, Jeff	.167	6	1	0	0	0	3	.167	.167
Baines, H*	.500	6	3	0	0	2	0	.625	.833
Becker, Rich*	.167	6	1	0	0	1	1	.286	.167
Bell, Derek	.333	6	2	0	1	1	1	.429	.667
Belle, Albert	.250	8	2	0	3	1	2	.333	.500
Biggio, Craig	.000	6	0	0	0	0	0	.000	.000
Blauser, Jeff	.500	4	2	0	0	1	0	.600	.750
Boggs, Wade*	.500	4	2	0	1	2	0	.667	.500
Boone, Bret	.286	7	2	0	0	0	0	.286	.286
Branson, Jeff*	.250	4	1	1	1	2	1	.500	1.000
Brogna, Rico*	.167	6	1	0	0	0	2	.167	.167
Buhner, Jay	.400	5	2	0	1	0	1	.400	.600
Carter, Joe	.333	9	3	0	0	0	2	.333	.444
Cirillo, Jeff	.375	8	3	0	0	2	1	.500	.500
Conine, Jeff	.250	4	1	0	1	0	0	.250	.250
Cora, Joey#	.000	4	0	0	1	0	0	.200	.000
Cordova, M	.500	6	3	0	0	0	0	.500	.500
Davis, Eric	.667	3	2	1	3	1	0	.800	1.667
Devereaux, M	.286	7	2	0	0	0	0	.286	.286
Durham, Ray#	.200	5	1	0	0	1	0	.200	.200
Fermin, Felix	.200	5	1	0	0	0	0	.200	.200
Gaetti, Gary	.714	7	5	1	3	3	2	.800	1.429
Gagne, Greg	.429	7	3	0	1	0	0	.429	.571
Gilkey, B	.429	7	3	2	3	1	1	.500	1.286
Green, Shawn*	.625	8	5	0	1	0	0	.625	.875
Greenwell, M*	.375	8	3	0	1	0	0	.375	.375
Greer, Rusty*	.167	6	1	1	3	0	1	.167	.667
Grissom, M	.833	6	5	0	0	0	1	.833	.833
Guillen, O*	.286	7	2	0	0	0	0	.286	.286
Hamilton, D*	.500	6	3	0	1	1	1	.571	.500
Howard, T*	.750	4	3	0	2	1	1	.800	.750
Hulse, David*	.000	5	0	0	0	1	2	.167	.000
Hundley, Todd#	.167	6	1	0	0	0	1	.167	.167
Hunter, Bri L	.167	6	1	0	0	0	0	.167	.167
Incaviglia, P	.400	5	2	1	1	0	0	.500	1.000
Jaha, John	.444	9	4	1	1	0	2	.444	.778
Javier, Stan#	.000	5	0	0	0	0	1	.000	.000

20

Sean Bergman, Padres — RHP

Batter	Avg	AB	H	HR	BI	BB	SO	OBP	Slg
Johnson, L*	.526	19	10	0	0	0	0	.526	.684
Jones, C#	.200	5	1	0	3	1	0	.333	.400
Joyner, Wally*	.143	7	1	0	1	1	2	.250	.143
King, Jeff	.400	5	2	0	1	0	0	.400	.600
Kirby, Wayne	.667	6	4	1	4	0	0	.667	1.500
Klesko, Ryan*	.800	5	4	2	3	0	0	.800	2.200
Knoblauch, C	.462	13	6	0	0	1	2	.500	.462
Lemke, Mark#	.500	4	2	0	0	0	1	.500	.500
Lofton, Kenny*	.444	9	4	2	3	2	0	.583	1.333
Martinez, Da*	.167	6	1	0	1	0	1	.143	.167
May, Derrick*	.222	9	2	1	1	0	3	.222	.556
Mayne, Brent*	.000	4	0	0	0	0	0	.000	.000
McCarty, Dave	.000	6	0	0	0	0	1	.000	.000
McGriff, Fred*	.333	6	2	0	2	0	1	.333	.333
McLemore, M*	.500	4	2	0	0	2	1	.667	.500
McRae, Brian#	.333	6	2	0	0	1	2	.429	.333
Meares, Pat	.500	10	5	0	2	0	1	.500	.700
Miller, Orl	.200	5	1	0	0	0	1	.200	.200
Molitor, Paul	.200	10	2	1	1	2	1	.333	.300
Morandini, M*	.286	7	2	0	1	1	1	.375	.571
Morris, Hal*	.000	7	0	0	0	0	3	.000	.000
Murray, Eddie#	.500	6	3	1	3	2	0	.625	1.000
Naehring, Tim	.000	4	0	0	1	1	1	.000	.000
Nilsson, Dave*	.500	4	2	0	2	4	0	.750	.500
Nixon, Otis#	.333	6	2	0	0	1	1	.429	.333
O'Leary, Troy*	.000	6	0	0	0	0	2	.000	.000
O'Neill, Paul*	.333	6	2	0	1	0	1	.333	.333
Olerud, John*	.125	8	1	0	0	3	3	.364	.250
Oliver, Joe	.000	5	0	0	0	0	2	.000	.000
Ordonez, Rey	.125	8	1	0	0	0	1	.125	.125
Palmeiro, R*	.500	8	4	3	5	0	1	.500	1.625
Pena, Tony	.000	5	0	0	0	0	1	.000	.000
Pendleton, T#	.600	5	3	0	0	0	1	.600	.600
Raines, Tim#	.000	8	0	0	1	1	1	.111	.000
Ramirez, M	.143	7	1	0	0	0	2	.250	.143
Ripken, Cal	.444	9	4	2	4	0	1	.444	1.111
Rodriguez, I	.429	7	3	1	2	0	0	.429	.857
Seitzer, K	.333	12	4	0	1	0	3	.333	.333
Sheffield, G	.000	5	0	0	0	0	1	.000	.000
Sierra, Ruben#	.200	5	1	0	1	1	1	.333	.200
Sorrento, P*	.286	7	2	0	1	1	1	.375	.286
Sprague, Ed	.300	10	3	0	1	1	1	.300	.300
Stahoviak, S*	.200	5	1	0	1	1	1	.333	.400
Stocker, K#	.000	4	0	0	1	0	2	.000	.000
Surhoff, B.J.*	.333	6	2	0	3	1	2	.429	.333
Taubensee, E*	.400	5	2	0	1	0	0	.400	.400
Tettleton, M#	.400	5	2	1	2	1	1	.500	1.000
Thomas, Frank	.333	6	2	0	0	3	0	.556	.333
Thome, Jim*	.600	5	3	1	4	3	1	.750	1.400
Tinsley, Lee#	.333	9	3	0	0	1	2	.400	.333
Valentin, Jhn	.286	7	2	0	2	2	2	.444	.286
Valentin, Jse#	.143	7	1	0	0	0	2	.143	.143
Vaughn, Greg	.500	6	3	0	2	3	0	.667	.833
Vaughn, Mo*	.167	6	1	0	0	2	2	.444	.167
Velarde, R	.200	5	1	0	0	0	1	.200	.200
Ventura, R*	.286	7	2	2	4	1	1	.375	1.143
Vina, F*	.143	7	1	0	0	0	1	.250	.143
Vizquel, Omar#	.429	7	3	0	1	2	0	.556	.571
Ward, Turner#	.143	7	1	0	1	0	1	.125	.286
White, Devon#	.182	11	2	0	1	1	4	.250	.273
Whiten, Mark#	.250	4	1	0	2	1	0	.400	.250
Williams, Bern#	.167	6	1	0	0	0	2	.167	.167
Zeile, Todd	.400	5	2	0	2	1	0	.500	.400

Mike Bertotti, White Sox — LHP

Batter	Avg	AB	H	HR	BI	BB	SO	OBP	Slg
Fielder, C	.000	5	0	0	0	0	4	.000	.000
Girardi, Joe	.000	4	0	0	0	1	0	.200	.000
Jeter, Derek	.400	5	2	0	0	1	2	.500	.600
Martinez, T*	.500	4	2	0	0	3	1	.714	.750
O'Neill, Paul*	.400	5	2	1	3	1	0	.500	1.000
Williams, Ber#	.200	5	1	1	1	0	3	.200	.800

Andres Berumen, Padres — RHP

Batter	Avg	AB	H	HR	BI	BB	SO	OBP	Slg
McRae, Brian#	.250	4	1	0	0	0	1	.400	.250

Brian Bevil, Royals — RHP

Batter	Avg	AB	H	HR	BI	BB	SO	OBP	Slg
Seitzer, K	.333	6	2	0	0	0	2	.333	.500

Mike Bielecki, Braves — RHP

Batter	Avg	AB	H	HR	BI	BB	SO	OBP	Slg
Aldrete, Mike*	.143	7	1	0	0	1	3	.250	.143
Alicea, Luis#	.417	12	5	1	4	1	1	.462	.833
Alomar, R#	.500	16	8	1	4	2	1	.556	.688
Alou, Moises	.200	5	1	0	0	0	0	.200	.200
Anthony, Eric*	.400	10	4	1	1	1	3	.455	.700
Bagwell, Jeff	.267	15	4	0	1	3	5	.421	.267
Batiste, Kim	.250	4	1	0	0	1	0	.400	.250
Bell, Jay	.571	21	12	0	6	3	4	.625	.952
Belliard, R	.417	12	5	0	2	1	2	.462	.500
Bichette, D	.400	5	2	1	2	0	1	.400	1.000
Biggio, Craig	.429	28	12	0	1	4	3	.500	.536
Blauser, Jeff	.273	11	3	0	1	0	0	.273	.273
Bonds, Barry*	.088	34	3	1	3	6	8	.225	.206
Bonilla, B#	.353	34	12	4	10	6	5	.452	.794
Bordick, Mike	.125	8	1	0	0	2	1	.300	.125
Bullett, S*	.600	5	3	0	1	1	1	.667	.600
Butler, Brett*	.450	20	9	0	3	3	1	.522	.600
Caminiti, Ken#	.304	23	7	0	0	3	3	.385	.391
Candaele, C#	.429	7	3	0	2	1	0	.444	.429
Carter, Joe	.375	8	3	0	4	1	0	.400	.500
Clark, Will*	.280	25	7	1	5	0	6	.259	.440
Clayton, C	.000	5	0	0	0	2	2	.286	.000
Coleman, V#	.375	32	12	0	0	2	4	.412	.500
Curtis, Chad	.000	3	0	0	0	2	1	.400	.000
Daulton, D*	.207	29	6	2	4	5	8	.314	.483
Davis, Chili#	.000	4	0	0	0	1	1	.200	.000
Davis, Eric	.250	24	6	1	4	4	7	.357	.375
Dawson, Andre	.313	16	5	0	2	2	4	.389	.438
DeShields, D*	.250	12	3	0	1	2	3	.357	.333
Duncan, M	.267	15	4	0	1	1	2	.313	.333
Dunston, S	.400	10	4	0	3	2	2	.500	.500
Durham, Ray#	.167	6	1	0	0	0	2	.167	.167
Dykstra, L*	.333	48	16	2	7	7	2	.418	.604
Elster, Kevin	.286	14	4	0	2	0	2	.267	.500
Fielder, C	.833	6	5	2	3	2	0	.889	1.833
Finley, Steve*	.529	17	9	1	2	1	1	.579	1.000
Fletcher, D*	.000	5	0	0	0	0	2	.000	.000
Fryman, T	.429	7	3	1	2	2	0	.556	1.000
Gaetti, Gary	.167	6	1	1	3	0	0	.167	.667
Galarraga, A	.161	31	5	1	3	2	10	.206	.323
Gant, Ron	.300	10	3	0	2	2	2	.417	.300
Gilkey, B	.400	5	2	0	1	2	0	.571	.800
Goff, Jerry*	.333	3	1	0	0	3	0	.667	.333
Gonzalez, L*	.353	17	6	0	2	2	1	.421	.471
Goodwin, C*	.500	6	3	0	1	0	0	.500	.500
Grace, Mark*	.200	10	2	0	2	1	0	.273	.200
Greenwell, M*	.083	12	1	0	0	1	3	.154	.083
Greer, Rusty*	.000	4	0	0	0	1	0	.200	.000
Grissom, M	.091	11	1	0	0	3	0	.286	.091
Guillen, O*	.000	5	0	0	0	0	0	.000	.000
Gwynn, Tony*	.382	34	13	0	6	3	3	.475	.529
Hansen, Dave*	.000	7	0	0	0	2	0	.000	.000
Harris, Lenny*	.263	19	5	0	0	1	0	.300	.263
Hayes, C	.290	31	9	1	3	1	3	.313	.452
Henderson, R	.300	10	3	0	4	2	1	.417	.400
Hernandez, Jo	.167	6	1	0	0	0	3	.167	.167
Hoiles, Chris	.500	4	2	0	2	0	0	.400	.500
Hollins, Dave#	.500	8	4	0	3	0	0	.500	.625
Howard, T*	.300	10	3	0	1	0	0	.300	.500
Howell, Jack*	.400	5	2	1	2	0	0	.400	1.000
Hudler, Rex	.200	5	1	0	1	1	2	.333	.400
Hundley, Todd#	.286	7	2	1	1	0	0	.375	.714
Huson, Jeff*	.286	7	2	0	0	0	0	.286	.286
Incaviglia, P	.000	5	0	0	0	2	0	.000	.000
James, Dion*	.250	8	2	0	0	2	1	.400	.375
Javier, Stan#	.000	8	0	0	0	0	2	.000	.000
Jefferies, G#	.280	25	7	0	4	0	0	.280	.360
Jefferson, R*	.000	5	0	0	1	1	1	.333	.000
Johnson, L*	.273	11	3	0	0	0	1	.273	.364
Jones, Chris	.250	4	1	0	0	1	2	.400	.250
Jordan, Ricky	.421	19	8	0	2	0	0	.421	.474
Joyner, Wally*	.250	4	1	0	0	2	1	.500	.500
Justice, Dave*	.750	4	3	0	0	1	1	.800	1.000
Karros, Eric	.000	7	0	0	0	0	3	.000	.000
King, Jeff	.091	11	1	0	0	1	3	.167	.091
Kingery, Mike*	.286	7	2	0	0	1	0	.375	.429
Knoblauch, C	.222	9	2	0	0	0	0	.222	.333
Lankford, Ray*	.385	13	5	0	1	2	0	.467	.462
Larkin, Barry	.308	26	8	1	3	4	8	.400	.538
Mabry, John*	.250	4	1	0	1	1	1	.400	.250
Macfarlane, M	.000	6	0	0	0	1	1	.143	.000
Magadan, Dave*	.241	29	7	1	4	4	3	.324	.379
Manwaring, K	.200	5	1	0	0	1	0	.333	.400
Martinez, Da*	.250	36	9	3	3	2	4	.289	.528
Mayne, Brent*	.167	6	1	0	0	0	1	.167	.333
McCarty, Dave	.200	5	1	0	0	0	1	.200	.200
McGee, Willie*	.278	36	10	0	4	1	2	.297	.361
McGriff, Fred*	.625	8	5	0	1	1	0	.667	.875
McGwire, Mark	.333	9	3	0	0	1	2	.400	.444
McRae, Brian#	.556	9	5	1	1	0	1	.556	.889
Meares, Pat	.125	8	1	0	0	0	1	.125	.125
Merced, O*	.400	5	2	0	0	2	0	.571	.400
Mitchell, K	.313	16	5	2	6	2	2	.389	1.000
Morandini, M*	.357	14	5	0	2	2	2	.471	.500
Morris, Hal*	.263	19	5	0	2	2	3	.333	.316
Munoz, Pedro	.167	6	1	0	1	0	1	.167	.167
Murray, Eddie#	.412	17	7	0	3	1	2	.444	.588
Naehring, Tim	.800	5	4	0	2	3	0	.875	.800
Newson, W*	.250	4	1	0	0	2	1	.500	.250

Mike Bielecki, Braves — RHP

Batter	Avg	AB	H	HR	BI	BB	SO	OBP	Slg
Nilsson, Dave*	.250	4	1	0	1	0	0	.200	.250
Nixon, Otis#	.500	16	8	0	3	1	4	.529	.688
O'Brien, C	.333	6	2	0	0	1	1	.429	.500
O'Leary, Troy*	.429	7	3	0	1	0	0	.429	.429
O'Neill, Paul*	.241	29	7	1	2	1	4	.267	.414
Offerman, J#	.000	8	0	0	0	1	0	.000	.000
Oliver, Joe	.400	10	4	1	3	0	1	.400	.800
Pagnozzi, Tom	.176	17	3	0	2	0	4	.176	.176
Palmeiro, R*	.333	6	2	1	2	1	0	.429	.833
Parent, Mark	.000	6	0	0	0	0	1	.000	.000
Pena, Tony	.231	13	3	0	2	0	0	.231	.231
Pendleton, T#	.235	34	8	1	8	0	5	.235	.382
Phillips, T#	.167	6	1	0	0	0	1	.167	.167
Raines, Tim#	.359	39	14	1	3	3	5	.405	.538
Reed, Jeff	.118	17	2	0	1	3	4	.238	.118
Roberts, Bip#	.333	18	6	0	3	0	0	.429	.444
Sabo, Chris	.258	31	8	1	5	1	5	.281	.387
Samuel, Juan	.500	20	10	2	8	2	2	.500	.900
Sanchez, Rey	.400	5	2	0	0	1	1	.500	.800
Sandberg, R	.217	23	5	2	3	4	2	.333	.565
Santiago, B	.360	25	9	1	6	2	3	.407	.640
Seitzer, K	.200	5	1	0	0	0	1	.200	.200
Sheffield, G	.571	7	4	0	1	0	1	.571	1.000
Sierra, Ruben#	.100	10	1	0	3	0	0	.100	.200
Smith, Ozzie#	.211	38	8	0	1	5	2	.302	.211
Steinbach, T	.429	7	3	0	0	0	0	.429	.571
Stillwell, K	.200	5	1	0	2	1	1	.333	.600
Strawberry, D*	.200	25	5	2	6	7	5	.364	.440
Surhoff, B.J.*	.750	4	3	1	3	1	0	.800	1.500
Taubensee, E*	.200	5	1	0	1	0	1	.167	.200
Tettleton, M#	.429	7	3	2	3	1	3	.556	1.286
Thomas, Frank	.400	5	2	1	1	2	1	.571	1.000
Thompson, Mil*	.280	25	7	0	1	5	2	.387	.360
Thompson, Rob	.238	21	5	2	5	2	3	.304	.619
Valentin, Jhn	.167	6	1	0	1	0	0	.167	.167
Vaughn, Greg	.000	4	0	0	2	1	3	.333	.000
Vaughn, Mo*	.500	10	5	1	3	1	3	.545	.900
Ventura, R*	.400	5	2	0	0	1	0	.500	.400
Walker, Larry*	.100	10	1	0	0	1	3	.182	.100
Wallach, Tim	.250	36	9	0	1	5	5	.341	.306
Williams, Ma	.316	19	6	0	4	2	5	.381	.368
Zeile, Todd	.353	17	6	1	1	6	4	.522	.765

Willie Blair, Padres — RHP

Batter	Avg	AB	H	HR	BI	BB	SO	OBP	Slg
Abbott, Kurt	.125	8	1	0	0	0	2	.125	.375
Alou, Moises	.333	9	3	1	2	0	1	.333	.667
Ausmus, Brad	.500	4	2	0	0	1	0	.600	.500
Bagwell, Jeff	.100	10	1	0	0	0	3	.100	.200
Barberie, B#	.167	6	1	0	0	1	0	.286	.167
Batiste, Kim	.000	6	0	0	0	1	0	.000	.000
Bell, Derek	.313	16	5	1	2	0	5	.294	.500
Bell, Jay	.385	13	5	0	0	1	3	.429	.462
Belliard, R	.200	5	1	0	0	0	2	.200	.200
Benjamin, M	.111	9	1	0	0	0	1	.111	.111
Berry, Sean	.250	16	4	1	5	1	2	.333	.500
Bichette, D	.273	11	3	1	3	2	1	.385	.545
Biggio, Craig	.111	9	1	0	0	1	1	.333	.111
Blauser, Jeff	.188	16	3	0	2	1	1	.235	.250
Boggs, Wade*	.600	5	3	0	2	1	0	.667	.600
Bonds, Barry*	.333	9	3	1	7	5	2	.571	.778
Bonilla, Rob	.400	10	4	0	0	1	2	.455	.600
Boone, Bret	.417	12	5	0	4	0	0	.417	.500
Branson, Jeff*	.417	12	5	0	1	2	2	.500	.417
Brogna, Rico*	.375	8	3	1	1	0	2	.375	.750
Brumfield, J	.125	8	1	0	0	0	0	.125	.250
Buford, Damon	.200	5	1	0	0	1	0	.333	.200
Burks, Ellis	.333	6	2	0	3	2	1	.500	.500
Butler, Brett*	.160	25	4	0	2	1	1	.192	.240
Carr, Chuck	.111	9	1	0	0	1	1	.200	.222
Carreon, Mark	.286	7	2	0	0	0	0	.286	.286
Castilla, V	.500	10	5	2	5	0	2	.500	1.100
Clark, Phil	.800	5	4	0	0	0	0	.800	.800
Clark, Will*	.200	5	1	0	3	1	1	.429	.800
Clayton, R	.214	14	3	0	0	0	2	.214	.357
Colbrunn, G	.000	5	0	0	0	1	0	.000	.000
Conine, Jeff	.500	8	4	0	2	2	2	.600	.500
Cordero, Wil	.400	10	4	0	0	2	0	.400	.500
Daulton, D*	.400	10	4	0	4	4	2	.533	.500
Davis, Chili*	.167	6	1	0	0	1	0	.286	.167
Davis, Eric	.167	6	1	0	1	1	4	.375	.167
DeShields, D*	.400	10	4	0	2	0	0	.500	.500
Duncan, M	.000	4	0	0	1	1	1	.200	.000
Dunston, S	.000	4	0	0	0	0	0	.000	.000
Dykstra, L*	.267	15	4	1	2	1	3	.294	.533
Eisenreich, J*	.286	14	4	0	1	0	0	.286	.286
Everett, Carl#	.167	6	1	1	4	1	1	.286	.667
Fletcher, D*	.222	9	2	0	0	1	0	.300	.222
Fonville, C#	.250	8	2	0	0	0	1	.250	.250
Gaetti, Gary	.400	5	2	0	4	0	0	.400	.800
Gagne, Greg	.167	6	1	1	2	0	1	.167	.667
Galarraga, A	.364	11	4	2	5	0	1	.417	1.000
Gant, Ron	.308	13	4	1	3	1	4	.357	.538
Garcia, C	.200	10	2	0	0	0	2	.200	.200
Gilkey, B	.167	12	2	0	1	0	2	.231	.250
Girardi, Joe	.500	4	2	0	2	1	1	.600	.500
Gonzalez, L*	.333	6	2	0	1	2	0	.444	.667
Grace, Mark*	.385	13	5	0	0	5	1	.556	.462
Greene, W*	.000	4	0	0	0	1	3	.200	.000
Greenwell, M*	.600	5	3	0	1	0	0	.600	1.000
Grissom, M	.444	9	4	1	4	0	1	.444	.778
Guillen, O*	.600	5	3	0	0	0	0	.600	1.000
Gutierrez, R	.333	12	4	0	2	0	3	.333	.333
Gwynn, Tony*	.231	13	3	0	1	1	1	.286	.231
Hall, Mel*	.200	5	1	1	1	0	0	.200	.800
Hansen, Dave*	.200	5	1	0	0	0	1	.333	.200
Harris, Lenny*	.143	7	1	0	0	0	2	.143	.143
Hernandez, Ca	.200	5	1	0	1	0	1	.167	.200
Hernandez, Jo	.417	12	5	0	1	1	4	.462	.583
Hill, G	.000	4	0	0	0	2	1	.333	.000
Hollins, Dave#	.364	11	4	0	2	3	3	.500	.455
Howard, T*	.182	11	2	0	2	0	3	.182	.364
Hundley, Todd#	.333	6	2	0	3	0	0	.333	.667
Hunter, Bri L	.400	5	2	0	2	0	1	.400	.400
Huskey, Butch	.400	5	2	0	1	1	1	.500	.400
Incaviglia, P	.375	8	3	1	1	1	1	.444	.750
Jefferies, G#	.222	9	2	0	0	1	0	.300	.222
Johnson, L*	.571	7	4	0	0	0	1	.571	.714
Jones, C#	.667	3	2	0	2	2	0	.800	.667
Jordan, Brian	.400	10	4	1	3	0	2	.400	.700
Justice, Dave*	.077	13	1	0	0	1	1	.143	.077
Karros, Eric	.308	26	8	2	6	0	4	.308	.615
Kelly, R	.455	11	5	0	1	2	2	.538	.636
Kent, Jeff	.300	10	3	0	1	2	0	.364	.300
King, Jeff	.200	10	2	0	2	0	1	.182	.200
Kingery, Mike*	.200	5	1	0	1	0	2	.200	.200
Lankford, Ray*	.286	7	2	2	4	1	3	.375	1.143
Lansing, Mike	.500	14	7	0	1	0	3	.500	.714
Larkin, Barry	.188	16	3	0	3	0	2	.176	.250
Lemke, Mark#	.273	11	3	0	2	0	0	.273	.273
Lewis, Darren	.267	15	4	0	3	2	3	.389	.400
Lopez, Javy	.500	6	3	0	2	0	1	.500	.500
Mabry, John*	.200	5	1	0	1	0	0	.200	.400
Magadan, Dave*	.250	8	2	0	1	2	1	.400	.375
Manwaring, K	.000	9	0	0	0	1	1	.100	.000
Martin, Al*	.600	10	6	2	4	0	0	.600	1.400
Martinez, Da*	.167	6	1	0	2	1	1	.286	.333
Martinez, E	.333	6	2	0	0	1	1	.429	.667
May, Derrick*	.333	15	5	0	2	1	4	.353	.333
McGee, Willie*	.667	6	4	0	2	0	0	.571	1.167
McGriff, Fred*	.263	19	5	1	3	3	1	.364	.579
McRae, Brian*	.400	10	4	0	1	1	2	.455	.700
Merced, O*	.300	10	3	0	2	2	1	.417	.500
Mitchell, K	.667	3	2	0	3	2	0	.800	1.333
Molitor, Paul	.333	3	1	0	0	2	0	.600	.333
Mondesi, Raul	.385	13	5	0	0	0	2	.385	.385
Morandini, M*	.533	15	8	0	0	1	1	.533	.733
Morris, Hal*	.364	22	8	0	2	2	1	.417	.364
Mouton, James	.167	6	1	0	0	1	1	.286	.167
Murray, Eddie#	.167	6	1	0	1	1	0	.286	.167
Nixon, Otis#	.167	6	1	0	0	0	1	.167	.167
O'Brien, C	.333	3	1	0	0	2	1	.600	.667
Offerman, J#	.533	15	8	0	1	2	0	.588	.800
Oliver, Joe	.375	8	3	2	5	0	1	.375	1.125
Orsulak, Joe*	.286	7	2	0	0	1	1	.375	.286
Pagnozzi, Tom	.500	4	2	0	1	2	0	.667	.500
Palmeiro, R*	.200	5	1	0	0	0	0	.200	.400
Pena, G#	.600	5	3	0	0	1	1	.667	.600
Pendleton, T#	.188	16	3	1	1	0	5	.235	.438
Piazza, Mike	.381	21	8	1	3	2	4	.458	.619
Plantier, P*	.400	15	6	0	3	1	4	.526	.467
Raines, Tim#	.600	5	3	0	0	0	0	.600	.600
Reed, Jeff*	.000	4	0	0	0	2	1	.333	.000
Reed, Jody	.571	14	8	2	5	0	2	.571	1.071
Roberts, Bip#	.500	4	2	0	1	1	0	.600	.500
Rodriguez, H*	.154	13	2	0	0	1	3	.214	.154
Sabo, Chris	.143	7	1	0	1	0	0	.250	.286
Sanchez, Rey	.273	11	3	0	1	0	2	.273	.273
Sandberg, R	.143	14	2	0	2	1	1	.200	.214
Sanders, R	.231	13	3	1	4	3	3	.421	.615
Santangelo, F#	.000	4	0	0	0	0	1	.200	.000
Santiago, B	.400	15	6	1	4	0	3	.400	.733
Segui, David#	.231	13	3	0	1	3	1	.375	.308
Servais, S	.250	8	2	1	1	0	1	.333	.625
Sheffield, G	.304	23	7	4	8	4	1	.407	.870
Shipley, C	.571	7	4	0	1	0	0	.571	.571
Sierra, Ruben#	.400	5	2	0	0	0	1	.400	.400
Smith, Ozzie#	.111	9	1	0	0	0	2	.273	.111
Sosa, Sammy	.476	21	10	2	10	3	6	.542	.905
Stillwell, K#	.250	8	2	0	0	2	1	.400	.250
Stinnett, S	.200	5	1	0	0	1	2	.429	.200
Stocker, K#	.125	8	1	0	1	2	1	.300	.125

Willie Blair, Padres — RHP

Batter	Avg	AB	H	HR	BI	BB	SO	OBP	Slg
Strawberry, D*	.000	4	0	0	0	1	2	.200	.000
Tarasco, Tony*	.000	5	0	0	0	0	3	.000	.000
Taubensee, E*	.500	4	2	1	2	2	1	.667	1.250
Thomas, Frank	.667	6	4	0	0	0	0	.667	.667
Thompson, Mil*	.143	7	1	0	2	2	0	.333	.286
Thompson, Rob	.444	9	4	1	2	0	1	.444	.778
Thompson, Ry	.143	7	1	0	0	1	2	.250	.143
Ventura, R*	.167	6	1	1	3	0	1	.167	.667
Vizcaino, J#	.200	20	4	0	2	0	3	.200	.200
Walker, Larry*	.143	7	1	0	1	1	1	.250	.286
Wallach, Tim	.217	23	5	0	4	2	3	.280	.348
Weiss, Walt*	.143	14	2	0	1	1	2	.200	.143
White, Devon#	.333	3	1	0	2	3	1	.667	.333
White, R	.200	10	2	0	1	0	7	.200	.200
Whiten, Mark#	.500	8	4	1	2	1	2	.556	1.000
Wilkins, Rick*	.357	14	5	2	4	3	4	.471	.786
Williams, Ma	.154	13	2	1	3	3	1	.313	.538
Young, Eric	.333	9	3	0	0	1	0	.400	.444
Young, Kevin	.400	5	2	0	3	0	0	.400	.800
Zeile, Todd	.438	16	7	1	1	2	4	.500	.625

Ron Blazier, Phillies — RHP

Batter	Avg	AB	H	HR	BI	BB	SO	OBP	Slg
Conine, Jeff	.600	5	3	0	2	0	0	.600	1.000
Sheffield, G	.400	5	2	0	0	0	0	.400	.400

Doug Bochtler, Padres — RHP

Batter	Avg	AB	H	HR	BI	BB	SO	OBP	Slg
Bates, Jason#	.000	5	0	0	0	0	1	.000	.000
Bonds, Barry*	.250	4	1	1	1	1	0	.400	1.000
Boone, Bret	.250	4	1	1	2	0	1	.250	1.000
Castilla, V	.400	5	2	0	1	0	0	.400	.800
Clayton, R	.429	7	3	0	1	0	2	.429	.571
Gant, Ron	.250	4	1	0	1	1	2	.400	.250
Jones, C#	.000	5	0	0	0	0	2	.000	.000
Karros, Eric	.000	4	0	0	0	1	3	.200	.000
Klesko, Ryan*	.250	4	1	0	0	2	1	.500	.750
McGriff, Fred*	.250	4	1	0	0	1	0	.400	.500
McRae, Brian#	.000	5	0	0	0	0	3	.000	.000
Mondesi, Raul	.333	6	2	1	3	0	1	.333	.833
Morris, Hal*	.000	4	0	0	0	1	0	.200	.000
Scarsone, S	.000	5	0	0	0	0	4	.000	.000

Brian Boehringer, Yankees — RHP

Batter	Avg	AB	H	HR	BI	BB	SO	OBP	Slg
Baerga, C#	.600	5	3	1	1	0	0	.600	1.200
Franco, Julio	.500	4	2	0	0	2	0	.667	.750
Fryman, T	.000	5	0	0	0	1	2	.167	.000
Johnson, L*	.600	5	3	0	1	1	0	.667	1.000
Lofton, Kenny*	.333	6	2	0	0	0	1	.333	.667
Murray, Eddie*	.200	5	1	0	2	1	2	.286	.200
Raines, Tim*	.600	5	3	0	1	1	0	.667	.800
Ramirez, M	.200	5	1	1	2	0	2	.200	.800
Thomas, Frank	.500	2	1	0	3	0	0	.800	.500
Thome, Jim*	.600	5	3	0	2	1	1	.667	.800
Velarde, R	.250	4	1	1	1	0	0	.500	.500
Vizquel, Omar#	.000	3	0	0	1	1	0	.200	.000

Joe Boever, Pirates — RHP

Batter	Avg	AB	H	HR	BI	BB	SO	OBP	Slg
Aldrete, Mike*	.500	6	3	0	1	2	1	.625	.500
Alicea, Luis#	.222	9	2	0	1	1	2	.300	.333
Alomar, R#	.333	18	6	0	2	2	2	.400	.333
Alomar Jr, S	.250	8	2	0	0	0	0	.250	.250
Amaral, Rich	.333	6	2	0	1	0	0	.333	.500
Anderson, Brd*	.125	8	1	0	0	2	3	.300	.125
Anderson, G*	.200	5	1	1	1	0	0	.200	.800
Baerga, C#	.400	10	4	1	6	1	0	.455	.700
Baines, H*	.600	5	3	0	1	1	0	.571	.600
Bell, Jay	.111	9	1	0	1	2	0	.200	.111
Belle, Albert	.364	11	4	2	5	1	1	.417	1.000
Belliard, R	.571	7	4	0	2	0	1	.571	.571
Biggio, Craig	.333	3	1	0	0	3	1	.667	.333
Blauser, Jeff	.667	6	4	1	6	3	0	.778	1.500
Blowers, Mike	.429	7	3	0	0	1	1	.500	.571
Boggs, Wade*	.200	5	1	0	1	1	1	.333	.400
Bonds, Barry*	.000	10	0	0	1	2	3	.167	.000
Bonilla, B#	.167	12	2	0	1	0	2	.167	.167
Borders, Pat	.500	4	2	0	3	1	0	.600	.750
Buhner, Jay	.143	7	1	0	0	1	2	.250	.286
Butler, Brett*	.273	11	3	0	2	2	0	.385	.455
Caminiti, Ken#	.308	13	4	0	2	1	1	.357	.308
Candaele, C#	.000	4	0	0	1	1	1	.167	.000
Canseco, Jose	.143	7	1	0	1	1	5	.250	.143
Carter, Joe	.556	9	5	1	2	1	1	.600	.889
Cedeno, A	.800	5	4	0	2	0	1	.800	1.200
Clark, Will*	.143	21	3	1	5	2	5	.217	.286
Clayton, R	.000	5	0	0	0	1	2	.167	.000
Cole, Alex*	.500	6	3	0	0	1	1	.571	.500
Coleman, V#	.158	19	3	0	2	2	5	.238	.211
Cora, Joey#	.222	9	2	0	0	0	1	.222	.222

Joe Boever, Pirates — RHP

Batter	Avg	AB	H	HR	BI	BB	SO	OBP	Slg
Cordova, M	.000	4	0	0	0	1	1	.200	.000
Curtis, Chad	.250	8	2	1	2	1	1	.300	.625
Dascenzo, D#	.400	5	2	0	0	0	1	.400	.400
Daulton, D*	.111	9	1	0	2	2	2	.273	.222
Davis, Chili#	.182	11	2	0	2	1	4	.250	.182
Davis, Eric	.308	13	4	1	3	1	3	.333	.615
Dawson, Andre	.333	21	7	2	4	1	1	.364	.762
Decker, Steve	.333	3	1	0	1	1	0	.400	.333
Deer, Rob	.000	6	0	0	0	4	0	.000	.000
DeShields, D*	.400	5	2	0	1	3	3	.625	.400
Devereaux, M	.429	7	3	0	1	1	2	.500	.571
DiSarcina, G	.167	12	2	0	0	0	1	.231	.333
Duncan, M	.133	15	2	1	1	0	2	.133	.333
Dunston, S	.267	15	4	1	2	0	2	.267	.533
Dykstra, L*	.200	5	1	0	0	2	0	.429	.200
Easley, D	.333	6	2	0	1	2	0	.500	.500
Edmonds, Jim*	.167	6	1	1	2	1	2	.250	.667
Elster, Kevin	.000	5	0	0	0	3	0	.000	.000
Espinoza, A	.250	4	1	0	0	1	0	.400	.250
Fabregas, Jor*	.167	6	1	0	1	1	0	.286	.167
Fermin, Felix	.333	6	2	0	0	0	0	.333	.333
Finley, Steve*	.571	7	4	1	3	1	0	.625	1.000
Franco, Julio	.143	7	1	0	1	0	0	.143	.143
Gaetti, Gary	.429	7	3	1	2	0	1	.429	1.000
Gagne, Greg	.071	14	1	1	3	2	2	.188	.286
Galarraga, A	.429	21	9	2	7	1	5	.455	.762
Gallego, Mike	.600	5	3	0	0	1	2	.667	.600
Gant, Ron	.400	5	2	0	0	1	0	.400	.400
Gilkey, B	.250	8	2	0	0	1	2	.333	.375
Girardi, Joe	.500	6	3	0	1	1	0	.571	.500
Gomez, Leo	.143	7	1	0	1	0	0	.143	.286
Gonzales, R	.167	6	1	0	0	1	0	.286	.333
Gonzalez, J	.571	7	4	2	2	1	0	.625	1.429
Grace, Mark*	.556	9	5	0	4	4	1	.692	.667
Grebeck, C	.500	4	2	0	0	1	1	.600	.500
Griffey Jr, K*	.200	5	1	1	2	1	1	.333	.800
Grissom, M	.333	6	2	0	0	2	0	.500	.333
Guillen, O*	.083	12	1	0	1	0	1	.077	.083
Gwynn, Chris*	.125	8	1	0	0	1	1	.125	.125
Gwynn, Tony*	.471	17	8	0	1	1	0	.500	.529
Hale, Chip*	.167	6	1	0	0	0	2	.167	.167
Hamelin, Bob*	.250	4	1	0	0	1	1	.400	.250
Hamilton, D*	.600	5	3	0	1	0	0	.600	.600
Harris, Lenny*	.556	9	5	1	1	2	0	.636	.778
Hayes, C	.400	5	2	0	0	1	0	.400	.400
Henderson, R	.250	4	1	0	1	0	0	.200	.250
Hoiles, Chris	.167	6	1	0	1	1	2	.375	.167
Hollins, Dave#	.000	6	0	0	0	2	0	.000	.000
Hudler, Rex	.556	9	5	2	2	0	1	.556	1.222
Hulse, David*	.000	3	0	0	1	0	1	.000	.000
Hunter, Brian	.000	5	0	0	0	0	4	.167	.000
Huson, Jeff*	.000	5	0	0	0	0	2	.000	.000
Jaha, John	.500	4	2	0	0	1	1	.600	.750
Javier, Stan#	.000	7	0	0	1	1	0	.125	.000
Jefferies, G#	.000	4	0	0	0	2	0	.000	.000
Jefferson, R*	.000	4	0	0	0	0	3	.200	.000
Johnson, L*	.111	9	1	0	0	1	0	.200	.111
Joyner, Wally*	.455	11	5	0	1	1	2	.500	.636
Justice, Dave*	.400	5	2	1	1	2	2	.571	1.000
Karkovice, R	.000	7	0	0	0	0	2	.000	.000
Kelly, Pat	.333	6	2	0	1	1	2	.375	.333
King, Jeff	.250	4	1	0	1	2	0	.500	.250
Knoblauch, C	.714	7	5	0	0	2	0	.778	1.000
Lankford, Ray*	.429	7	3	0	2	1	1	.500	.714
Larkin, Barry	.444	18	8	1	4	1	2	.450	.611
Lemke, Mark#	.167	6	1	0	0	2	2	.375	.333
Lewis, Darren	.400	5	2	0	1	1	1	.500	.600
Lofton, Kenny*	.500	10	5	0	1	2	1	.583	.700
Macfarlane, M	.143	7	1	1	2	4	1	.500	.571
Magadan, Dave*	.308	13	4	0	4	3	2	.438	.308
Manwaring, K	.125	8	1	0	0	1	1	.222	.125
Martinez, Da*	.250	12	3	2	6	2	2	.357	.833
Martinez, E	.600	5	3	0	3	1	0	.714	.800
Martinez, T*	.250	4	1	0	0	2	2	.500	.250
McCarty, Dave	.375	8	3	0	2	0	1	.375	.375
McGee, Willie#	.176	17	3	0	0	2	2	.263	.176
McGriff, Fred*	.500	6	3	0	0	1	0	.571	.667
McLemore, M#	.100	10	1	0	1	0	1	.100	.100
McRae, Brian#	.143	7	1	0	1	0	0	.250	.143
Meares, Pat	.286	7	2	0	2	0	1	.286	.714
Mitchell, K	.000	9	0	0	0	1	2	.100	.000
Molitor, Paul	.200	5	1	0	1	1	1	.333	.200
Morris, Hal*	.167	6	1	0	0	1	0	.286	.167
Munoz, Pedro	.333	6	2	0	0	0	2	.333	.500
Murray, Eddie#	.333	18	3	1	7	4	0	.611	.846
Myers, Greg*	.364	11	4	0	2	0	2	.364	.455
Naehring, Tim	.286	7	2	0	1	2	0	.444	.286
Nixon, Otis#	.300	20	6	0	2	4	0	.364	.300
O'Brien, C	.200	5	1	0	2	0	1	.200	.400
O'Leary, Troy*	.800	5	4	1	1	1	0	.833	1.800
O'Neill, Paul*	.450	20	9	1	6	9	3	.621	.900

Joe Boever, Pirates — RHP

Batter	Avg	AB	H	HR	BI	BB	SO	OBP	Slg
Offerman, J#	.500	4	2	0	0	1	1	.600	1.000
Olerud, John*	.200	5	1	0	0	0	1	.200	.200
Oliver, Joe	.154	13	2	0	0	1	3	.214	.154
Pagnozzi, Tom	.333	6	2	0	1	0	2	.333	.500
Palmeiro, R*	.200	5	1	1	1	0	1	.200	.800
Pena, Tony	.250	4	1	0	0	1	0	.250	.250
Pendleton, T#	.154	13	2	0	1	1	2	.214	.154
Phillips, T#	.167	6	1	0	2	2	0	.375	.167
Polonia, Luis*	.000	5	0	0	0	1	1	.167	.000
Raines, Tim#	.294	17	5	0	1	4	1	.429	.471
Ramirez, M	.286	7	2	1	3	1	3	.375	.857
Reed, Jody	.400	5	2	0	1	0	0	.400	.400
Ripken, Cal	.200	10	2	0	0	0	0	.200	.200
Roberts, Bip#	.300	10	3	0	0	0	2	.300	.300
Rodriguez, I	.000	5	0	0	1	0	1	.000	.000
Sabo, Chris	.364	11	4	1	2	1	2	.429	.636
Salmon, Tim	.444	18	8	2	6	1	4	.474	.833
Samuel, Juan	.143	7	1	0	0	2	1	.333	.143
Sandberg, R	.188	16	3	1	4	0	2	.188	.438
Sanders, R	.167	6	1	0	0	0	3	.167	.167
Santiago, B	.200	15	3	1	3	0	5	.200	.467
Schofield, D	.000	4	0	0	0	2	1	.333	.000
Seitzer, K	.600	5	3	0	0	1	0	.600	.800
Sierra, Ruben#	.000	3	0	0	1	1	2	.200	.000
Slaught, Don	.250	8	2	0	1	0	1	.250	.250
Smith, Dwight*	.750	8	6	0	3	1	0	.778	1.000
Smith, Ozzie#	.333	9	3	0	0	0	0	.333	.778
Snow, J.T.#	.000	5	0	0	1	2	1	.250	.000
Sojo, Luis	.600	5	3	0	2	0	0	.600	1.000
Sorrento, P*	.429	7	3	1	2	3	1	.600	.857
Spiers, Bill*	.400	5	2	0	1	2	0	.571	.800
Sprague, Ed	.250	8	2	0	0	0	0	.250	.250
Stanley, Mike	.400	10	4	0	1	1	1	.455	.500
Stillwell, K#	.000	6	0	0	0	1	1	.000	.000
Strange, Doug#	.000	6	0	0	0	0	1	.000	.000
Strawberry, D*	.200	10	2	1	2	1	2	.273	.500
Surhoff, B.J.*	.200	5	1	0	0	0	0	.200	.200
Tartabull, D	.125	8	1	0	1	0	3	.111	.125
Tettleton, M#	.333	6	2	0	3	2	1	.500	.333
Thomas, Frank	.556	9	5	2	7	5	1	.714	1.333
Thome, Jim*	.400	5	2	0	0	0	1	.400	.400
Thompson, Mil*	.375	8	3	1	1	1	2	.444	.750
Thompson, Rob	.056	18	1	0	2	5	4	.292	.056
Tinsley, Lee#	.500	4	2	0	1	1	0	.833	1.000
Valentin, Jhn	.500	6	3	0	1	1	0	.625	.667
Valentin, Jse#	.143	7	1	1	1	0	3	.143	.571
Vaughn, Greg	.200	10	2	0	5	2	2	.333	.200
Vaughn, Mo*	.222	9	2	1	4	0	2	.222	.556
Velarde, R	.400	5	2	0	1	0	0	.400	.600
Ventura, R*	.500	8	4	1	4	2	1	.545	1.000
Vizquel, Omar#	.500	8	4	0	1	0	2	.500	.500
Walker, Larry*	.000	8	0	0	1	0	3	.000	.000
Wallach, Tim	.368	19	7	0	2	2	2	.429	.526
Walton, J	.500	6	3	1	1	0	2	.500	1.167
Ward, Turner#	.200	5	1	0	0	0	1	.200	.200
White, Devon#	.333	6	2	0	0	0	3	.333	.333
Williams, Ber#	.333	15	5	0	3	0	2	.333	.467
Williams, Ma	.222	18	4	1	1	0	3	.222	.389
Zeile, Todd	.000	7	0	0	1	2	1	.222	.000

Brian Bohanon, Blue Jays — LHP

Batter	Avg	AB	H	HR	BI	BB	SO	OBP	Slg
Alomar, R#	.000	6	0	0	0	0	2	.000	.000
Alomar Jr, S	.100	10	1	0	1	0	1	.091	.100
Amaral, Rich	.231	13	3	0	1	0	4	.214	.308
Anderson, Brd*	.333	9	3	0	0	4	2	.538	.556
Baerga, C#	.435	23	10	0	5	0	1	.435	.522
Baines, H*	.375	8	3	1	3	1	0	.444	.750
Belle, Albert	.600	15	9	1	6	3	0	.667	1.000
Blowers, Mike	.000	5	0	0	0	2	3	.286	.000
Boggs, Wade*	.200	15	3	0	1	1	3	.250	.267
Bordick, Mike	.429	7	3	0	0	0	0	.429	.571
Buhner, Jay	.143	14	2	0	2	5	2	.381	.143
Canseco, Jose	.333	3	1	0	1	4	0	.750	.667
Carter, Joe	.400	10	4	0	2	1	0	.400	.500
Cole, Alex*	.000	5	0	0	0	0	2	.000	.000
Coleman, V#	.667	3	2	0	1	2	0	.800	.667
Cora, Joey#	.000	5	0	0	0	0	0	.000	.000
Cordova, M	.167	6	1	1	2	2	3	.375	.667
Curtis, Chad	.556	9	5	0	1	1	0	.636	.778
Davis, Chili*	.429	7	3	1	4	2	1	.556	1.000
Davis, Russ	.333	6	2	1	3	2	1	.500	1.000
Deer, Rob	.500	4	2	1	2	0	0	.400	1.250
Devereaux, M	.083	12	1	0	2	0	1	.083	.083
Diaz, Alex#	.000	5	0	0	1	1	1	.167	.000
DiSarcina, G	.400	10	4	0	3	2	0	.500	.500
Durham, Ray#	.125	8	1	0	0	0	1	.125	.125
Easley, D	.429	7	3	0	0	1	1	.500	.571
Edmonds, Jim*	.600	5	3	0	1	1	1	.667	.800
Espinoza, A	.167	6	1	0	1	0	0	.167	.167
Fermin, Felix	.444	9	4	0	1	0	1	.444	.444

Brian Bohanon, Blue Jays — LHP

Batter	Avg	AB	H	HR	BI	BB	SO	OBP	Slg
Fielder, C	.250	8	2	0	0	2	2	.400	.375
Fryman, T	.500	6	3	0	1	1	0	.571	.667
Gaetti, Gary	.154	13	2	0	0	1	3	.214	.231
Gagne, Greg	.636	11	7	0	2	0	1	.583	.818
Gallego, Mike	.333	6	2	0	0	1	0	.429	.333
Gates, Brent#	.167	6	1	1	2	0	1	.286	.667
Gonzalez, A	.400	5	2	0	1	1	0	.500	.400
Goodwin, Tom*	.200	5	1	0	0	0	1	.200	.200
Grebeck, C	.143	7	1	0	0	0	1	.143	.143
Greenwell, M*	.000	4	0	0	0	1	0	.200	.000
Griffey Jr, K*	.545	11	6	0	2	3	1	.667	.545
Guillen, O*	.455	11	5	0	2	0	1	.455	.636
Hall, Mel*	.429	7	3	0	2	1	1	.500	.429
Henderson, R	.000	6	0	0	0	0	3	.000	.000
Hiatt, Phil	.125	8	1	0	0	0	3	.125	.125
Hill, G	.200	5	1	0	1	0	0	.200	.200
Hoiles, Chris	.167	6	1	0	0	1	0	.286	.333
Howard, Dave#	.167	6	1	0	0	0	1	.167	.167
Howard, T*	.000	3	0	0	0	2	1	.400	.000
Javier, Stan#	.200	5	1	1	3	0	0	.200	.800
Johnson, L*	.294	17	5	1	1	0	3	.294	.471
Joyner, Wally*	.500	14	7	0	7	0	1	.467	.571
Karkovice, A	.200	5	1	1	1	0	0	.200	.800
Kelly, Pat	.222	9	2	0	1	0	2	.222	.333
Kelly, R	.429	7	3	0	2	1	0	.500	.571
Knoblauch, C	.375	16	6	0	3	4	1	.500	.625
Knorr, Randy	.429	7	3	1	3	0	2	.429	.857
Leius, Scott	.500	12	6	0	4	2	0	.571	.667
Lewis, Mark	.500	6	3	0	0	0	1	.500	.500
Leyritz, Jim	.400	5	2	1	3	2	1	.571	1.200
Lofton, Kenny*	.385	13	5	0	3	0	4	.385	.462
Macfarlane, M	.250	4	1	0	0	2	0	.500	.250
Manto, Jeff	.400	5	2	0	0	0	1	.400	.400
Martin, N	.000	5	0	0	0	1	0	.167	.000
Martinez, E	.294	17	5	1	4	0	0	.294	.529
Martinez, T*	.417	12	5	2	5	0	3	.385	1.083
Mayne, Brent*	.400	5	2	0	1	0	0	.400	.400
McCarty, Dave	.000	5	0	0	0	0	1	.000	.000
McGwire, Mark	.600	5	3	2	4	0	1	.600	1.800
McLemore, M#	.429	7	3	0	0	1	1	.500	.429
McRae, Brian#	.538	13	7	0	2	0	0	.538	.846
Meares, Pat	.091	11	1	0	0	0	0	.091	.091
Molitor, Paul	.250	12	3	0	2	2	0	.357	.417
Munoz, Pedro	.357	14	5	2	4	2	4	.438	.929
Murray, Eddie#	.375	8	3	0	0	1	1	.444	.375
Myers, Greg*	.250	4	1	0	1	1	1	.400	.250
O'Neill, Paul*	.333	12	4	0	1	0	3	.385	.333
Olerud, John*	.364	11	4	1	7	3	2	.500	.636
Palmeiro, R*	.429	7	3	0	0	0	0	.429	.571
Pena, Tony	.000	7	0	0	1	0	1	.000	.000
Phillips, T#	.250	8	2	0	0	6	2	.571	.250
Polonia, Luis*	.000	6	0	0	1	0	0	.000	.000
Raines, Tim#	.200	5	1	0	0	1	1	.333	.200
Ramirez, M	.250	4	1	1	1	1	1	.400	1.000
Reboulet, J	.429	7	3	0	0	0	0	.429	.571
Ripken, Cal	.300	10	3	1	2	1	0	.333	.600
Salmon, Tim	.400	5	2	0	1	0	1	.400	.600
Segui, David#	.429	7	3	0	1	1	2	.500	.429
Shumpert, T	.200	5	1	0	0	0	1	.200	.200
Sierra, Ruben#	.429	7	3	0	0	2	1	.556	.571
Snow, J.T.#	.333	6	2	0	3	1	1	.429	.500
Sojo, Luis	.429	7	3	0	0	0	0	.429	.571
Sorrento, P*	.273	11	3	2	6	0	0	.333	.909
Sprague, Ed	.250	8	2	0	0	1	1	.333	.250
Stanley, Mike	.500	8	4	0	3	4	1	.667	.500
Steinbach, T	.500	4	2	0	1	0	1	.667	.500
Stevens, Lee*	.400	5	2	0	1	0	0	.400	.400
Surhoff, B.J.*	.286	7	2	0	0	0	1	.250	.286
Tartabull, D	.286	14	4	0	2	0	5	.267	.500
Tettleton, M#	.143	7	1	1	3	4	4	.417	.571
Thomas, Frank	.375	8	3	0	0	1	0	.545	.375
Thome, Jim*	.231	13	3	0	4	2	5	.333	.231
Trammell, A	.333	6	2	1	4	0	0	.333	1.000
Vaughn, Greg	.143	7	1	0	0	0	2	.143	.143
Vaughn, Mo*	.143	7	1	0	1	1	3	.333	.286
Velarde, R	.529	17	9	0	1	0	3	.529	.588
Ventura, R*	.308	13	4	1	2	2	1	.400	.538
Vizquel, Omar#	.353	17	6	0	3	2	1	.400	.412
Walbeck, Matt#	.250	4	1	0	1	0	0	.400	.250
White, Devon#	.364	11	4	1	2	0	2	.364	.636
Whiten, Mark#	.250	8	2	0	1	0	0	.222	.375
Williams, Ber#	.300	20	6	2	6	1	2	.318	.650
Williams, Ger	.800	5	4	0	3	0	1	.800	1.400

Ricky Bones, Yankees — RHP

Batter	Avg	AB	H	HR	BI	BB	SO	OBP	Slg
Aldrete, Mike*	.200	10	2	1	2	0	0	.200	.500
Alexander, M	.000	7	0	0	0	0	0	.000	.000
Alicea, Luis#	.375	8	3	0	2	1	0	.400	.500
Alomar, R#	.259	27	7	0	2	1	1	.286	.407
Alomar Jr, S	.333	18	6	0	6	0	0	.333	.444

Ricky Bones, Yankees — RHP

Batter	Avg	AB	H	HR	BI	BB	SO	OBP	Slg
Anderson, Brd*	.314	35	11	4	9	5	2	.415	.743
Anderson, G*	.375	8	3	0	1	0	0	.333	.500
Baerga, C#	.231	26	6	0	3	1	1	.286	.308
Baines, H*	.188	32	6	3	5	1	0	.212	.500
Bautista, D	.167	6	1	0	0	0	0	.167	.333
Becker, Rich*	.333	15	5	1	2	1	1	.375	.533
Bell, Jay	.200	5	1	0	0	0	2	.200	.200
Belle, Albert	.269	26	7	3	9	6	2	.424	.692
Berroa, G	.077	13	1	1	2	2	5	.200	.308
Boggs, Wade*	.313	32	10	0	1	0	1	.313	.344
Bonds, Barry*	.667	3	2	0	2	1	0	.600	.667
Bonilla, B#	.200	10	2	0	0	3	1	.385	.200
Borders, Pat	.200	15	3	2	3	0	2	.188	.600
Bordick, Mike	.318	22	7	1	2	3	1	.385	.545
Bragg, Darren*	.143	7	1	0	1	3	0	.364	.286
Brosius, S	.222	9	2	0	0	1	0	.300	.222
Buhner, Jay	.292	24	7	3	6	2	6	.333	.792
Burks, Ellis	.200	10	2	0	1	0	2	.200	.300
Butler, Brett*	.333	6	2	0	0	2	1	.333	.500
Canseco, Jose	.250	12	3	0	1	2	2	.357	.500
Carter, Joe	.280	25	7	1	2	2	2	.357	.440
Clark, Tony*	.200	5	1	1	1	1	1	.333	.800
Clark, Will*	.267	15	4	0	1	1	1	.313	.333
Cole, Alex*	.571	7	4	0	2	1	0	.625	1.000
Coleman, V#	.182	11	2	0	0	0	0	.182	.273
Cora, Joey#	.217	23	5	0	1	2	0	.280	.304
Cordova, M	.250	12	3	2	2	1	3	.308	.750
Curtis, Chad	.231	26	6	2	2	4	0	.333	.500
Cuyler, Milt*	.364	11	4	0	1	1	1	.385	.455
Damon, Johnny*	.417	12	5	0	2	2	1	.500	.667
Davis, Chili#	.391	23	9	2	2	4	1	.481	.652
Dawson, Andre	.308	13	4	0	0	1	0	.308	.385
Deer, Rob	.111	9	1	1	0	0	1	.111	.444
Delgado, C*	.667	3	2	1	2	2	0	.800	1.667
Devereaux, M	.364	22	8	0	1	3	1	.440	.364
Diaz, Alex#	.200	5	1	0	0	0	0	.333	.200
DiSarcina, G	.182	22	4	0	1	0	3	.182	.273
Duncan, M	.385	13	5	0	0	0	2	.385	.538
Durham, Ray#	.667	6	4	0	0	1	0	.714	1.000
Easley, D	.167	6	1	0	0	0	0	.286	.167
Edmonds, Jim*	.286	14	4	2	6	0	0	.286	.714
Eisenreich, J*	.444	9	4	0	0	0	1	.444	.778
Espinoza, A	.429	7	3	0	1	0	1	.429	.429
Fabregas, Jor*	.250	8	2	0	0	1	1	.333	.250
Fasano, Sal	.375	8	3	0	2	0	1	.375	.500
Fermin, Felix	.000	8	0	0	0	0	2	.000	.000
Fielder, C	.214	28	6	0	3	3	7	.290	.286
Flaherty, J	.400	5	2	2	2	1	1	.500	1.600
Franco, Julio	.250	20	5	2	3	3	0	.348	.550
Frye, Jeff	.333	9	3	0	2	1	0	.400	.444
Fryman, T	.318	22	7	0	2	5	2	.444	.318
Gaetti, Gary	.095	21	2	0	0	1	2	.174	.095
Gagne, Greg	.344	32	11	1	6	0	0	.364	.656
Gallego, Mike	.200	10	2	0	2	1	3	.273	.200
Gates, Brent#	.333	15	5	0	0	2	0	.412	.533
Giambi, Jason*	.375	8	3	0	2	2	0	.545	.500
Girardi, Joe	.375	8	3	0	2	0	0	.375	.500
Gomez, Chris	.143	14	2	0	0	1	3	.200	.143
Gomez, Leo	.278	18	5	1	3	4	2	.409	.556
Gonzales, R	.167	6	1	0	0	0	0	.167	.167
Gonzalez, A	.125	8	1	0	1	0	2	.125	.250
Gonzalez, J	.100	20	2	1	3	2	1	.217	.250
Goodwin, C*	.333	6	2	0	0	1	2	.429	.333
Goodwin, Tom*	.476	21	10	0	2	1	2	.500	.476
Grebeck, D	.375	8	3	0	2	0	1	.444	.500
Green, Shawn*	.444	9	4	1	2	1	0	.500	.778
Greenwell, M*	.276	29	8	0	1	2	1	.313	.310
Greer, Rusty*	.667	6	4	0	0	3	1	.778	.833
Griffey Jr, K*	.273	11	3	1	2	2	0	.385	.545
Guillen, O*	.304	23	7	1	3	0	1	.304	.435
Gwynn, Chris*	.000	6	0	0	0	0	1	.000	.000
Hale, Chip*	.250	4	1	0	0	1	0	.400	.250
Hall, Mel*	.125	8	1	0	0	0	0	.125	.250
Hamelin, Bob*	.471	17	8	2	3	3	3	.550	.882
Hammonds, J	.000	6	0	0	1	1	1	.143	.000
Harris, Lenny*	.500	4	2	0	0	1	0	.600	.500
Haselman, B	.714	7	5	2	5	1	0	.750	1.714
Hayes, C	.333	6	2	0	0	1	3	.429	.333
Henderson, R	.333	15	5	1	2	2	3	.412	.533
Higginson, B*	.455	11	5	1	2	1	0	.417	.909
Hill, G	.375	8	3	0	0	0	0	.375	.625
Hoiles, Chris	.389	18	7	2	5	7	2	.560	.722
Howard, Dave#	.154	13	2	0	0	1	1	.214	.385
Howard, T*	.000	7	0	0	0	0	0	.000	.000
Hudler, Rex	.400	5	2	0	0	0	2	.400	.600
Hulse, David*	.200	10	2	0	0	1	0	.273	.200
Huson, Jeff*	.333	9	3	1	1	1	0	.400	.667
James, Dion*	.111	9	1	0	0	0	0	.200	.111
Javier, Stan#	.500	6	3	0	0	1	0	.500	.500
Jefferies, G#	.125	8	1	0	0	2	0	.300	.125
Jefferson, R*	.263	19	5	0	1	1	2	.300	.368
Jeter, Derek	.125	8	1	0	1	1	2	.222	.125
Johnson, L*	.346	26	9	0	0	1	0	.370	.346
Joyner, Wally	.226	31	7	0	2	3	4	.294	.355
Karkovice, R	.214	14	3	0	2	3	3	.353	.286
Kelly, Pat	.300	10	3	1	2	1	2	.364	.700
Kirby, Wayne*	.385	13	5	1	3	0	0	.385	.615
Knoblauch, C	.250	28	7	0	2	5	5	.364	.393
Knorr, Randy	.286	7	2	2	3	2	2	.444	1.143
Larkin, Barry	.250	8	2	0	1	0	1	.250	.375
Leius, Scott	.250	4	1	0	0	1	1	.400	.250
Lewis, Darren	.250	4	1	0	0	2	0	.500	.250
Lewis, Mark	.286	14	4	1	2	0	2	.286	.500
Leyritz, Jim	.000	5	0	0	0	0	1	.167	.000
Livingstone*	.333	9	3	0	1	0	0	.333	.444
Lockhart, K*	.462	13	6	0	0	0	0	.500	.462
Lofton, Kenny*	.188	32	6	0	2	2	3	.235	.281
Lovullo, T#	.455	11	5	0	0	0	0	.455	.727
Macfarlane, M	.321	28	9	0	2	2	5	.387	.429
Martinez, Da*	.750	4	3	0	1	0	0	.800	1.000
Martinez, E	.389	18	7	3	7	1	3	.400	1.111
Martinez, T*	.190	21	4	1	1	0	0	.227	.333
Mayne, Brent*	.200	10	2	1	4	0	0	.182	.500
McGwire, Mark	.083	12	1	1	2	5	3	.333	.333
McLemore, M#	.233	30	7	2	3	1	1	.258	.500
McRae, Brian#	.050	20	1	0	1	2	2	.130	.050
Meares, Pat	.167	18	3	0	1	0	3	.211	.389
Merced, O*	.400	5	2	0	0	1	1	.500	.400
Molitor, Paul	.407	27	11	1	5	2	1	.452	.667
Morris, Hal*	.400	5	2	0	2	0	0	.400	.600
Munoz, Pedro	.500	26	13	3	6	2	0	.536	1.077
Murray, Eddie#	.545	11	6	1	2	4	0	.667	.909
Myers, Greg*	.250	8	2	0	1	0	0	.250	.250
Naehring, Tim	.389	18	7	2	5	2	3	.450	.722
Newson, W*	.273	11	3	0	0	1	3	.333	.273
Nixon, Otis#	.429	14	6	0	0	1	0	.467	.429
Nunnally, Jon*	.333	9	3	1	1	1	1	.400	.778
O'Leary, Troy*	.278	18	5	0	3	0	1	.278	.333
O'Neill, Paul*	.267	30	8	0	3	2	4	.303	.300
Offerman, J#	.333	6	2	0	0	1	0	.429	.333
Olerud, John*	.455	22	10	2	7	5	1	.571	.818
Orsulak, Joe*	.571	7	4	0	1	0	0	.571	.714
Palmeiro, R*	.207	29	6	1	4	3	0	.303	.310
Palmer, Dean	.118	17	2	0	0	0	9	.118	.118
Paquette, C	.000	10	0	0	1	0	2	.000	.000
Pena, Tony	.273	11	3	1	1	2	2	.385	.545
Perez, E	.077	13	1	0	0	1	2	.143	.077
Phillips, T#	.346	26	9	0	3	3	2	.400	.462
Plantier, P*	.167	6	1	0	0	0	1	.167	.333
Polonia, Luis*	.350	20	7	0	1	3	1	.417	.400
Pozo, A	.200	5	1	0	0	0	0	.200	.400
Raines, Tim#	.353	34	12	1	3	4	1	.421	.500
Ramirez, M	.417	12	5	1	3	0	1	.417	.750
Randa, Joe	.222	9	2	0	2	0	2	.222	.333
Reboulet, J	.429	14	6	1	3	2	0	.500	.714
Reed, Jeff*	.000	5	0	0	0	0	1	.000	.000
Reed, Jody	.000	4	0	0	0	0	0	.000	.000
Ripken, Cal	.282	39	11	1	4	2	4	.317	.487
Rodriguez, Al	.167	6	1	0	1	1	1	.286	.333
Rodriguez, I	.100	20	2	0	1	0	3	.143	.200
Sabo, Chris	.250	8	2	1	4	1	1	.364	.750
Salmon, Tim	.333	24	8	1	3	2	8	.385	.542
Schofield, D	.111	9	1	0	0	0	1	.111	.111
Segui, David#	.667	6	4	0	0	2	0	.750	.667
Sierra, Ruben#	.125	32	4	1	0	0	4	.121	.125
Snow, J.T.#	.167	12	2	1	1	0	0	.231	.417
Sojo, Luis	.400	15	6	2	3	0	0	.400	.800
Sorrento, P*	.257	35	9	0	4	1	4	.278	.343
Sprague, Ed	.105	19	2	0	2	2	2	.190	.105
Stahoviak, S*	.600	10	6	2	3	0	0	.600	1.500
Stankiewicz	.000	6	0	0	0	0	0	.000	.000
Stanley, Mike	.227	22	5	0	1	4	3	.370	.273
Steinbach, T	.385	13	5	1	3	1	2	.467	.462
Stevens, Lee*	.200	5	1	1	2	0	1	.200	.800
Strange, Doug#	.222	18	4	0	1	2	2	.300	.278
Strawberry, D*	.143	7	1	1	4	1	1	.250	.571
Tartabull, D	.316	19	6	1	6	3	3	.409	.579
Tettleton, M#	.200	20	4	1	5	5	1	.360	.450
Thomas, Frank	.419	31	13	3	17	5	2	.486	.839
Thome, Jim*	.385	13	5	1	1	6	1	.579	.615
Tinsley, Lee#	.273	11	3	1	2	2	0	.385	.545
Trammell, A	.250	8	2	0	3	2	1	.364	.375
Tucker, M*	.333	12	4	0	1	0	0	.385	.417
Turner, Chris	.375	8	3	0	1	0	1	.375	.500
Valentin, Jhn	.280	25	7	1	6	6	3	.394	.560
Valle, Dave	.167	6	1	1	1	1	1	.286	.667
Vaughn, Mo*	.289	38	11	3	10	5	5	.378	.605
Velarde, R	.250	12	3	0	1	0	1	.250	.250
Ventura, R*	.345	29	10	1	4	5	1	.441	.552
Vitiello, Joe	.200	5	1	0	1	1	0	.286	.200
Vizquel, Omar*	.286	14	4	1	3	0	2	.267	.500

Ricky Bones, Yankees — RHP

Batter	Avg	AB	H	HR	BI	BB	SO	OBP	Slg
Walbeck, Matt#	.000	5	0	0	0	0	0	.000	.000
Webster, L	.167	6	1	0	0	0	0	.167	.333
White, Devon#	.355	31	11	2	2	2	4	.394	.677
Whiten, Mark#	.250	12	3	0	2	0	1	.250	.333
Williams, Ber#	.148	27	4	0	2	4	3	.258	.222
Williams, Geo#	.000	5	0	0	0	1	2	.167	.000
Wilson, Dan	.300	10	3	0	0	3	3	.462	.400
Young, Ernie	.333	9	3	0	0	1	2	.400	.333

Pedro Borbon, Braves — LHP

Batter	Avg	AB	H	HR	BI	BB	SO	OBP	Slg
Alfonzo, E	.500	4	2	0	2	1	1	.600	1.000
Morandini, M*	.167	6	1	0	0	1	2	.286	.167
Pendleton, T	.200	5	1	0	0	0	0	.200	.400
Stocker, K#	.600	5	3	0	1	0	0	.600	.600

Toby Borland, Phillies — RHP

Batter	Avg	AB	H	HR	BI	BB	SO	OBP	Slg
Abbott, Kurt	.143	7	1	0	0	1	4	.333	.429
Alou, Moises	.333	6	2	0	1	0	2	.333	.500
Andrews, S	.000	6	0	0	0	0	2	.000	.000
Ausmus, Brad	.000	4	0	0	0	1	1	.200	.000
Bagwell, Jeff	.375	8	3	0	2	0	1	.375	.500
Bell, Derek	.400	5	2	0	0	2	1	.625	.400
Bell, Jay	.143	7	1	0	0	1	1	.250	.143
Berry, Sean	.143	7	1	0	1	0	2	.143	.286
Bichette, D	.000	5	0	0	0	1	0	.286	.000
Biggio, Craig	.500	6	3	0	1	3	1	.667	.667
Blauser, Jeff	.143	7	1	0	0	0	2	.143	.143
Bogar, Tim	.400	5	2	0	0	0	1	.400	.400
Bonds, Barry*	.000	3	0	0	0	4	1	.571	.000
Boone, Bret	.250	4	1	0	0	1	1	.400	.250
Burks, Ellis	.167	6	1	0	0	1	3	.286	.167
Butler, Brett*	.000	2	0	0	1	2	0	.500	.000
Caminiti, Ken#	.333	6	2	0	1	0	1	.333	.333
Castilla, V	.000	5	0	0	0	1	3	.286	.000
Clayton, R	.250	8	2	0	3	0	3	.250	.250
Colbrunn, G	.333	6	2	2	5	0	2	.333	1.333
Conine, Jeff	.167	6	1	1	1	1	2	.286	.667
DeShields, D*	.429	7	3	0	0	2	1	.556	.429
Finley, Steve*	.500	6	3	0	0	1	0	.571	.667
Galarraga, A	.200	5	1	1	1	0	1	.200	.800
Gant, Ron	.600	5	3	0	0	0	1	.600	.600
Gilkey, B	.000	7	0	0	1	1	2	.125	.000
Grissom, M	.500	8	4	0	1	2	0	.600	.625
Gwynn, Chris*	.000	4	0	0	0	1	0	.200	.000
Gwynn, Tony*	.400	5	2	0	3	1	2	.571	.400
Hansen, Dave*	.250	4	1	0	1	1	1	.400	.250
Hayes, C	.000	5	0	0	0	0	3	.000	.000
Henderson, R	.000	3	0	0	0	3	0	.500	.000
Hill, G	.286	7	2	0	3	0	2	.286	.286
Huskey, Butch	.250	4	1	0	1	1	1	.333	.250
Johnson, Char	.250	4	1	0	1	1	0	.400	.250
Johnson, Mark*	.167	6	1	0	0	0	2	.167	.167
Jones, C	.500	8	4	0	0	1	0	.556	.625
Justice, Dave*	.667	3	2	0	1	2	0	.800	.667
Karros, Eric	.000	7	0	0	0	0	0	.000	.000
Kelly, R	.200	5	1	0	0	1	2	.333	.200
Kendall, J	.333	6	2	0	1	0	0	.333	.333
Kent, Jeff	.600	5	3	0	0	0	1	.600	.600
King, Jeff	.286	7	2	0	3	0	2	.286	.429
Klesko, Ryan*	.250	4	1	0	0	2	0	.500	.250
Lansing, Mike	.167	6	1	0	0	1	0	.286	.333
Lemke, Mark#	.375	8	3	0	1	0	0	.375	.500
Livingstone*	.429	7	3	0	2	0	2	.429	.429
Lopez, Javy	.200	5	1	0	0	0	3	.200	.200
Mabry, John*	.333	6	2	0	0	0	0	.333	.333
Martin, Al*	.286	7	2	0	0	0	1	.286	.429
McGriff, Fred*	.500	6	3	2	2	3	2	.667	1.667
Merced, O*	.400	5	2	0	0	0	0	.400	.400
Miller, Orl	.167	6	1	0	2	0	2	.286	.333
Mondesi, Raul	.500	8	4	0	1	1	2	.556	.500
Mouton, James	.333	6	2	1	4	0	2	.500	1.000
Orsulak, Joe*	.333	6	2	0	1	0	0	.333	.333
Pendleton, T#	.600	5	3	0	0	2	2	.714	.600
Piazza, Mike	.167	6	1	0	0	0	2	.167	.167
Reed, Jody	.250	4	1	0	1	0	0	.500	.500
Rodriguez, H*	.200	5	1	0	2	0	1	.200	.200
Sanders, R	.200	5	1	0	0	3	1	.800	1.000
Segui, David#	.000	5	0	0	0	1	0	.167	.000
Sheffield, G	.286	7	2	0	2	1	3	.400	.429
Veras, Q#	.000	7	0	0	0	0	1	.000	.000
Vizcaino, J#	.200	5	1	0	1	0	0	.200	.200
Weiss, Walt#	.333	6	2	0	2	0	1	.333	.333
White, R	.667	6	4	0	1	0	0	.667	1.000
Wilkins, Rick*	.167	6	1	0	0	0	3	.167	.167
Williams, E	.250	4	1	0	0	1	0	.400	.500
Williams, Ma	.000	6	0	0	0	0	2	.000	.000

Chris Bosio, Mariners — RHP

Batter	Avg	AB	H	HR	BI	BB	SO	OBP	Slg
Aldrete, Mike*	.167	6	1	0	0	0	0	.167	.167
Alicea, Luis#	.571	7	4	0	1	0	1	.571	.714
Alomar, R#	.297	37	11	0	3	3	1	.341	.486
Alomar Jr, S	.235	17	4	0	1	0	2	.222	.235
Anderson, Brd*	.250	32	8	1	3	7	2	.385	.438
Baerga, C#	.353	34	12	2	7	1	4	.395	.559
Baines, H*	.288	59	17	3	9	9	6	.386	.475
Barberie, B#	.500	4	2	0	0	1	1	.600	.750
Becker, Rich*	.200	15	3	0	0	1	2	.250	.200
Belle, Albert	.303	33	10	2	7	6	3	.410	.606
Berroa, G	.286	14	4	0	0	1	0	.286	.286
Bichette, D	.000	7	0	0	0	0	2	.000	.000
Boggs, Wade*	.188	48	9	0	4	2	3	.216	.229
Borders, Pat	.235	17	4	0	1	0	3	.222	.353
Bordick, Mike	.227	22	5	0	5	1	2	.261	.273
Brosius, S	.500	14	7	1	4	1	1	.533	.857
Buhner, Jay	.000	7	0	0	0	0	3	.000	.000
Burks, Ellis	.238	21	5	0	0	2	5	.304	.238
Butler, Brett*	.250	4	1	0	0	1	0	.400	.250
Canseco, Jose	.286	42	12	3	8	7	14	.392	.595
Carter, Joe	.293	58	17	2	6	3	7	.339	.448
Cirillo, Jeff	.375	8	3	0	0	0	0	.375	.375
Clark, Dave*	.000	12	0	0	0	0	5	.000	.000
Clark, Will*	.182	11	2	1	3	1	0	.231	.455
Cole, Alex*	.500	14	7	0	3	1	1	.500	.714
Cora, Joey#	.385	13	5	0	0	1	5	.429	.615
Cora, V#	.231	13	3	0	3	1	2	.267	.385
Cordova, M	.222	9	2	0	0	0	1	.222	.222
Curtis, Chad	.167	18	3	0	2	2	5	.238	.167
Cuyler, Milt#	.333	9	3	0	1	1	1	.400	.556
Damon, Johnny*	.250	4	1	0	0	0	0	.250	.250
Davis, Chili#	.237	38	9	2	5	1	2	.250	.421
Dawson, Andre	.267	15	4	1	3	0	3	.250	.533
Deer, Rob	.250	16	4	1	2	1	5	.294	.438
Devereaux, M	.217	23	5	2	5	1	4	.250	.522
DiSarcina, G	.231	13	3	0	1	0	2	.231	.231
Durham, Ray#	.667	3	2	0	1	1	0	.833	.667
Easley, D	.167	6	1	0	0	0	1	.167	.167
Eisenreich, J*	.160	25	4	0	1	1	5	.192	.200
Espinoza, A	.300	20	6	0	1	0	6	.300	.450
Fermin, Felix	.240	25	6	0	0	2	0	.296	.280
Fielder, C	.317	41	13	2	7	3	13	.364	.561
Finley, Steve*	.200	5	1	0	1	0	2	.200	.200
Franco, Julio	.268	41	11	1	6	3	3	.311	.366
Frye, Jeff	.167	6	1	0	0	2	1	.375	.333
Fryman, T	.242	33	8	2	9	0	11	.229	.485
Gaetti, Gary	.314	35	11	2	7	0	5	.297	.571
Gagne, Greg	.367	49	18	1	4	4	8	.415	.490
Gallego, Mike	.302	43	13	1	4	1	7	.318	.442
Gates, Brent#	.333	18	6	0	4	0	1	.316	.500
Giambi, Jason*	.000	4	0	0	0	2	0	.333	.000
Gil, Benji	.400	5	2	1	1	1	1	.500	1.000
Gomez, Chris	.600	10	6	3	5	1	1	.636	1.500
Gomez, Leo	.333	15	5	1	2	0	2	.333	.600
Gonzales, R	.278	18	5	0	2	0	4	.278	.389
Gonzalez, A	.000	5	0	0	0	0	3	.000	.000
Gonzalez, J	.167	30	5	0	0	2	9	.219	.200
Goodwin, Tom*	.429	7	3	0	1	1	0	.444	.429
Grebeck, C	.200	10	2	0	0	1	3	.333	.200
Green, Shawn*	.200	5	1	0	0	0	1	.200	.200
Greenwell, M*	.370	54	20	1	7	4	0	.424	.537
Greer, Rusty*	.357	14	5	0	1	0	3	.357	.571
Griffey Jr, K*	.304	23	7	1	3	2	3	.360	.565
Guillen, O*	.341	41	14	0	2	2	2	.372	.537
Hall, Mel*	.185	27	5	1	4	1	3	.214	.370
Hamelin, Bob*	.200	10	2	1	2	4	2	.429	.500
Hamilton, D*	.217	23	5	0	1	3	0	.308	.304
Hammonds, J	.444	9	4	0	0	0	1	.444	.444
Hayes, C	.500	8	4	1	4	0	2	.500	1.125
Henderson, R	.306	36	11	0	3	6	5	.395	.389
Higginson, B*	.273	11	3	0	2	0	1	.273	.455
Hoiles, Chris	.200	15	3	2	2	1	2	.250	.667
Howard, Dave#	.333	9	3	0	2	2	1	.417	.333
Howard, T*	.182	11	2	0	0	0	2	.182	.182
Howell, Jack*	.389	18	7	1	4	2	3	.450	.667
Hulse, David*	.250	8	2	0	2	1	1	.400	.375
Huson, Jeff*	.292	24	7	1	7	4	1	.379	.500
Incaviglia, P	.200	30	6	3	6	1	12	.242	.533
Jaha, John	.100	10	1	1	1	1	5	.308	.400
James, Dion*	.522	23	12	0	3	2	2	.560	.652
Javier, Stan#	.206	34	7	0	0	1	5	.229	.206
Jefferies, G#	.143	7	1	0	0	0	1	.143	.143
Jefferson, R*	.438	16	7	0	2	3	0	.438	.438
Johnson, L*	.292	24	7	0	0	4	1	.393	.417
Joyner, Wally*	.275	51	14	1	8	1	3	.296	.392
Karkovice, R	.182	22	4	1	6	3	10	.269	.318
Kelly, Pat	.083	12	1	0	1	2	4	.250	.083
Kelly, R	.077	13	1	0	0	0	4	.077	.077
Kirby, Wayne*	.200	15	3	0	0	0	1	.200	.200
Knoblauch, C	.179	39	7	0	2	5	2	.273	.256
Kreuter, Chad#	.400	5	2	0	1	0	1	.400	.400

Chris Bosio, Mariners — RHP

Batter	Avg	AB	H	HR	BI	BB	SO	OBP	Slg
Leius, Scott	.375	16	6	1	2	1	3	.412	.688
Lewis, Mark	.214	14	3	0	1	0	2	.214	.214
Leyritz, Jim	.400	5	2	0	1	1	2	.500	.500
Liriano, N#	.150	20	3	0	0	1	1	.190	.150
Listach, Pat#	.125	8	1	0	0	0	1	.125	.125
Livingstone*	.455	11	5	0	2	0	2	.455	.455
Lofton, Kenny*	.222	27	6	0	2	1	2	.250	.370
Lovullo, T#	.286	7	2	0	0	2	2	.444	.286
Macfarlane, M	.238	21	5	1	4	2	5	.304	.429
Manto, Jeff	.200	5	1	0	0	0	1	.200	.200
Martinez, E	.313	16	5	0	0	2	3	.389	.375
Martinez, S*	.500	4	2	0	0	1	0	.600	.500
Martinez, T*	.600	10	6	1	7	0	0	.600	1.200
Marzano, John	.364	11	4	0	1	0	2	.364	.455
Matheny, Mike	.111	9	1	0	0	0	4	.111	.111
Mayne, Brent*	.278	18	5	0	2	0	2	.278	.333
McGriff, Fred*	.143	21	3	0	0	5	4	.308	.190
McGwire, Mark	.250	48	12	3	7	3	14	.294	.479
McLemore, Mark	.300	30	9	1	5	2	6	.344	.433
McRae, Brian#	.211	19	4	0	0	3	3	.318	.263
Meares, Pat	.333	18	6	1	5	0	4	.333	.500
Molitor, Paul	.438	16	7	0	0	2	2	.526	.625
Munoz, Pedro	.200	10	2	0	1	0	4	.200	.200
Murray, Eddie#	.231	26	6	0	2	1	3	.259	.269
Myers, Greg*	.353	17	6	1	3	1	1	.389	.647
Naehring, Tim	.214	14	3	0	2	2	3	.313	.214
Newson, W*	.545	11	6	0	2	3	0	.643	.727
Nieves, M#	.200	5	1	0	0	0	3	.200	.200
Nilsson, Dave*	.300	10	3	0	3	1	0	.385	.400
Nixon, Otis#	.278	18	5	0	0	3	3	.278	.389
O'Leary, Troy*	.111	9	1	0	1	2	0	.273	.222
O'Neill, Paul*	.750	8	6	0	0	2	0	.800	1.250
Offerman, J#	.200	5	1	0	0	0	1	.200	.200
Olerud, John*	.297	37	11	1	8	3	3	.350	.459
Orsulak, Joe*	.200	20	4	0	2	0	2	.190	.250
Palmeiro, R*	.339	62	21	2	4	3	8	.369	.500
Palmer, Dean	.148	27	4	0	0	1	9	.179	.185
Paquette, C	.000	10	0	0	0	1	4	.091	.000
Parent, Mark	.000	3	0	0	0	0	2	.000	.000
Pena, Tony	.148	27	4	0	1	0	5	.179	.148
Phillips, T#	.209	43	9	0	3	6	8	.300	.209
Plantier, P*	.200	5	1	1	1	1	2	.333	.800
Polonia, Luis*	.200	60	12	0	1	3	7	.234	.300
Raines, Tim#	.125	24	3	0	0	4	1	.250	.125
Ramirez, M	.143	14	2	0	0	2	6	.294	.143
Reed, Jody	.156	32	5	0	2	6	6	.308	.156
Ripken, Billy	.346	26	9	0	1	0	5	.346	.385
Ripken, Cal	.236	55	13	1	4	7	7	.323	.291
Rodriguez, I	.385	26	10	0	2	0	3	.385	.423
Salmon, Tim	.200	10	2	1	2	1	4	.273	.500
Schofield, D	.118	17	2	0	1	2	2	.211	.176
Schu, Rick	.167	6	1	0	0	0	2	.167	.500
Seitzer, K	.200	25	5	0	1	2	1	.259	.200
Shumpert, T	.286	7	2	0	2	1	0	.375	.286
Sierra, Ruben*	.294	68	20	2	13	3	7	.311	.441
Slaught, Don	.417	12	5	1	2	0	2	.417	.750
Snow, J.T.#	.600	5	3	1	4	1	0	.667	1.200
Sojo, Luis	.182	11	2	0	0	0	3	.182	.182
Sorrento, P*	.160	25	4	1	3	2	3	.222	.280
Spiers, Bill*	.400	5	2	0	0	1	0	.333	.600
Sprague, Ed	.000	15	0	0	0	0	3	.000	.000
Stahoviak, S*	.667	6	4	0	0	0	1	.667	.667
Stanley, Mike	.222	18	4	0	1	4	3	.364	.278
Steinbach, T	.317	41	13	1	7	4	9	.370	.463
Stevens, Lee*	.143	7	1	0	0	0	1	.143	.143
Stillwell, K#	.308	13	4	0	1	1	2	.400	.385
Strange, Doug#	.125	8	1	0	0	1	1	.222	.125
Strawberry, D*	.400	5	2	0	0	0	2	.500	.400
Surhoff, B.J.*	.313	16	5	0	0	2	1	.389	.375
Tartabull, D	.343	35	12	3	8	4	9	.390	.657
Tettleton, M#	.133	30	4	2	2	11	8	.366	.333
Thomas, Frank	.130	23	3	0	0	7	5	.333	.174
Thome, Jim*	.278	18	5	0	2	1	3	.316	.333
Tinsley, Lee#	.000	4	0	0	1	0	0	.000	.000
Trammell, A	.308	39	12	1	4	1	0	.317	.436
Tucker, M*	.250	4	1	0	1	1	0	.400	.250
Valentin, Jhn	.172	29	5	2	2	1	7	.200	.379
Valentin, Jse#	.333	9	3	2	2	0	1	.333	1.111
Valle, Dave	.286	7	2	0	0	0	1	.286	.286
Vaughn, Greg	.417	12	5	1	3		2	.533	.750
Vaughn, Mo*	.310	29	9	1	6	3	7	.375	.448
Velarde, R	.286	7	2	0	1	1	0	.375	.286
Ventura, R*	.345	29	10	0	0	5	4	.441	.345
Vina, F*	.286	7	2	0	0	0	0	.375	.857
Vizquel, Omar	.333	27	9	0	2	1	2	.345	.333
Walbeck, Matt#	.200	15	3	0	0	0	3	.200	.200
Ward, Turner#	.063	16	1	1	1	1	2	.118	.250
Weiss, Walt#	.241	29	7	0	0	0	7	.267	.241
White, Devon#	.231	52	12	1	3	3	9	.273	.327
Whiten, Mark#	.333	9	3	1	3	1	4	.364	.667
Williams, Ber#	.154	13	2	1	1	2	1	.267	.385
Williams, E	.200	5	1	0	0	0	3	.200	.200
Worthington	.250	12	3	0	2	2	3	.357	.250

Shawn Boskie, Angels — RHP

Batter	Avg	AB	H	HR	BI	BB	SO	OBP	Slg
Abbott, Kurt	.000	5	0	0	0	0	1	.000	.000
Aldrete, Mike*	.000	6	0	0	0	0	0	.000	.000
Alicea, Luis#	.143	7	1	0	1	5	0	.462	.143
Alomar, R#	.333	21	7	1	2	2	3	.391	.619
Alomar Jr, S	.167	12	2	0	0	0	0	.167	.167
Alou, Moises	.429	7	3	1	3	0	1	.429	1.000
Amaral, Rich	.429	7	3	0	0	0	0	.429	.429
Anderson, Brd*	.231	13	3	1	3	1	5	.333	.462
Anthony, Eric*	.222	9	2	1	1	1	1	.300	.556
Ausmus, Brad	.500	6	3	1	0	0	2	.500	1.000
Baerga, C#	.286	7	2	0	1	0	0	.286	.286
Bagwell, Jeff	.300	10	3	0	4	0	1	.273	.300
Baines, H*	.333	9	3	0	0	2	1	.455	.444
Barberie, B#	.300	10	3	0	0	0	3	.300	.300
Becker, Rich*	.300	10	3	1	1	2	4	.417	.700
Bell, Derek	.400	5	2	1	2	0	2	.400	1.000
Bell, Jay	.261	23	6	0	2	1	3	.292	.304
Belle, Albert	.250	12	3	1	3	1	2	.308	.667
Belliard, R	.364	11	4	0	1	0	2	.417	.455
Berroa, G	.375	8	3	1	2	2	1	.500	.750
Berry, Sean	.667	6	4	0	0	1	1	.714	.833
Biggio, Craig	.308	13	4	0	0	2	3	.400	.385
Blauser, Jeff	.667	6	4	0	0	1	0	.714	.667
Boggs, Wade*	.333	6	2	0	1	1	1	.429	.333
Bonds, Barry*	.400	15	6	2	7	5	2	.550	1.133
Bonilla, B#	.429	28	12	3	7	4	2	.529	.857
Bordick, Mike	.182	11	2	0	1	2	1	.308	.273
Bragg, Darren*	.250	12	3	0	1	3	3	.308	.333
Brosius, S	.300	10	3	1	1	1	3	.364	.700
Buhner, Jay	.368	19	7	0	3	1	3	.400	.526
Burnitz, J*	.000	5	0	0	0	2	0	.286	.000
Butler, Brett*	.320	25	8	0	1	3	2	.393	.400
Caminiti, Ken#	.133	15	2	0	0	1	1	.188	.133
Canseco, Jose	.286	7	2	0	1	1	3	.375	.286
Carr, Chuck	.286	7	2	0	0	0	0	.375	.286
Carter, Joe	.214	14	3	1	1	0	1	.267	.500
Cedeno, A	.250	12	3	1	2	0	3	.250	.583
Cianfrocco, A	.000	5	0	0	0	1	0	.000	.000
Cirillo, Jeff	.500	6	3	1	1	0	0	.500	1.000
Clark, Dave*	.500	4	2	1	3	1	0	.600	1.250
Clark, Tony#	.000	6	0	0	0	0	4	.000	.000
Clark, Will*	.083	12	1	0	0	5	2	.353	.167
Clayton, R	.000	5	0	0	0	0	3	.167	.000
Cole, Alex*	.300	10	3	0	2	0	2	.300	.300
Coleman, V#	.167	12	2	0	0	4	5	.375	.333
Conine, Jeff	.000	4	0	0	0	1	2	.200	.000
Cora, Joey#	.300	20	6	1	2	1	1	.364	.450
Cordero, Wil	.667	6	4	0	1	0	0	.714	.833
Cordova, M	.429	14	6	1	2	0	0	.429	.714
Curtis, Chad	.000	5	0	0	0	1	0	.000	.000
Damon, Johnny*	.333	6	2	0	0	0	0	.333	.333
Davis, Eric	.000	5	0	0	0	1	0	.167	.000
Decker, Steve	.750	4	3	0	0	0	0	.800	1.000
Delgado, C*	.000	3	0	0	0	2	1	.400	.000
DeShields, D*	.364	11	4	1	2	1	2	.417	.727
Devereaux, M	.000	5	0	0	0	1	1	.167	.000
Dunston, S	.167	6	1	0	1	0	0	.167	.167
Durham, Ray#	.273	11	3	2	4	0	2	.273	.818
Dykstra, L*	.000	5	0	0	0	4	1	.444	.000
Elster, Kevin	.125	8	1	0	0	2	3	.300	.250
Fasano, Sal	.500	4	2	0	1	0	0	.600	.500
Finley, Steve*	.364	11	4	1	1	1	1	.417	.636
Fletcher, D*	.333	9	3	0	1	0	1	.300	.444
Franco, Julio	.444	9	4	1	2	1	0	.545	.778
Frye, Jeff	.333	6	2	0	0	1	2	.429	.500
Fryman, T	.500	6	3	0	2	0	0	.500	.667
Gaetti, Gary	.000	6	0	0	0	0	3	.000	.000
Gagne, Greg	.000	4	0	0	1	0	0	.000	.000
Galarraga, A	.133	15	2	0	0	0	2	.188	.133
Gant, Ron	.385	13	5	1	3	0	1	.357	.692
Garcia, C	.091	11	1	1	2	0	1	.091	.364
Gates, Brent#	.125	8	1	0	0	1	1	.222	.125
Giambi, Jason*	.286	7	2	0	0	1	1	.375	.571
Gilkey, B	.500	12	6	3	2		1	.600	1.083
Gonzalez, A	.000	8	0	0	1	0	5	.000	.000
Gonzalez, J	.429	7	3	2	5	0	1	.429	1.286
Gonzalez, L*	.300	10	3	0	4	1	2	.364	.700
Goodwin, Tom*	.000	9	0	0	1	0	2	.000	.000
Grace, Mark*	.000	4	0	0	0	2	0	.333	.000
Green, Shawn*	.125	8	1	1	2	1	0	.222	.500
Greenwell, M*	.500	10	5	0	4	1	0	.545	.600
Griffey Jr, K*	.417	12	5	1	5	2	1	.500	.750
Grissom, M	.182	11	2	0	0	1	0	.182	.273
Guillen, O*	.125	8	1	0	0	0	1	.125	.125
Gwynn, Tony*	.167	12	2	0	1	2	0	.286	.250

Shawn Boskie, Angels — RHP

Batter	Avg	AB	H	HR	BI	BB	SO	OBP	Slg
Hamelin, Bob*	.429	7	3	0	1	0	0	.500	.714
Hamilton, D*	.333	6	2	1	1	0	0	.333	.833
Hammonds, J	.375	8	3	0	3	0	0	.375	.500
Hansen, Dave*	.667	6	4	1	2	1	0	.714	1.500
Harris, Lenny*	.333	18	6	0	3	0	0	.333	.500
Haselman, B	.000	6	0	0	0	0	2	.000	.000
Hayes, C	.231	13	3	0	0	0	1	.231	.231
Henderson, R	.333	6	2	0	1	0	0	.333	.333
Herrera, Jose*	.500	8	4	0	0	0	2	.500	.625
Higginson, B*	.333	6	2	0	1	1	0	.429	.500
Hoiles, Chris	.091	11	1	0	0	0	4	.091	.091
Hollins, Dave*	.313	16	5	2	3	2	1	.389	.688
Howard, Dave#	.400	5	2	0	0	0	1	.400	.400
Hundley, Todd#	.375	8	3	0	1	0	1	.375	.625
Jaha, John	.500	4	2	1	2	1	0	.600	1.250
James, Dion*	.167	6	1	0	0	0	0	.167	.333
Javier, Stan#	.333	3	1	0	2	2	1	.455	.333
Jefferies, G#	.333	9	3	1	6	0	1	.333	.667
Jefferson, R*	.400	10	4	0	1	1	2	.417	.500
Jordan, Brian	.286	7	2	0	0	1	0	.375	.286
Jordan, Ricky	.125	8	1	1	2	0	1	.125	.500
Joyner, Wally*	.429	7	3	1	3	0	0	.429	1.000
Justice, Dave*	.200	15	3	0	1	2	3	.278	.267
Karkovice, R	.333	9	3	0	0	0	1	.333	.333
Karros, Eric	.250	4	1	0	1	1	0	.400	.250
Kent, Jeff	.200	5	1	0	0	0	0	.333	.200
King, Jeff	.300	10	3	0	4	0	1	.273	.500
Kingery, Mike*	.176	4	0	0	0	1	1	.200	.000
Knoblauch, C	.385	13	5	0	0	0	0	.500	.385
Lankford, Ray*	.176	17	3	0	0	5	2	.364	.294
Larkin, Barry	.333	12	4	0	0	1	0	.385	.417
Lawton, Matt*	.250	4	1	0	1	0	0	.200	.250
Leius, Scott	.500	6	3	0	2	0	0	.500	.833
Lemke, Mark#	.300	10	3	0	0	2	0	.417	.400
Lewis, Darren	.500	12	6	1	3	0	1	.500	.750
Lockhart, K*	.200	5	1	1	3	0	1	.200	.800
Lofton, Kenny*	.385	13	5	1	1	0	0	.385	.615
Magadan, Dave*	.500	6	3	0	0	1	1	.571	.667
Manwaring, K	.167	6	1	0	1	0	0	.167	.167
Martin, Al*	.286	7	2	0	0	1	1	.375	.286
Martinez, Da*	.156	32	5	0	0	5	4	.270	.156
Martinez, E	.263	19	5	1	3	3	1	.364	.526
Martinez, T*	.143	7	1	0	1	0	0	.250	.286
May, Derrick*	.000	6	0	0	0	0	1	.000	.000
Mayne, Brent*	.667	6	4	0	1	0	0	.667	.833
McGee, Willie#	.200	5	1	0	0	0	0	.200	.200
McGriff, Fred*	.286	7	2	0	0	2	2	.444	.286
McGwire, Mark	.417	12	5	2	7	1	2	.462	1.083
McLemore, M#	.125	8	1	0	0	2	1	.300	.250
Meares, Pat	.273	11	3	1	4	0	1	.273	.636
Merced, O*	.538	13	7	2	4	1	2	.571	1.231
Mitchell, K	.200	15	3	0	1	0	2	.200	.200
Molitor, Paul	.200	15	3	0	1	0	0	.200	.200
Morandini, M*	.333	9	3	0	0	1	2	.400	.444
Morris, Hal*	.222	9	2	0	2	0	0	.182	.333
Mouton, Lyle	.200	5	1	0	0	0	0	.200	.200
Munoz, Pedro	.333	6	2	1	1	0	1	.429	.833
Murray, Eddie#	.308	26	8	2	6	3	6	.379	.615
Myers, Greg*	.429	7	3	0	1	0	1	.429	.429
Naehring, Tim	.556	9	5	0	2	0	1	.556	.889
Newson, W*	.200	5	1	0	0	2	3	.429	.200
Nieves, M#	.333	6	2	1	1	0	3	.333	1.000
Nixon, Otis*	.267	15	4	0	1	0	2	.267	.333
Nunnally, Jon*	.167	6	1	0	0	1	1	.286	.500
O'Brien, C	.500	5	2	1	1	0	0	.571	1.000
O'Leary, Troy*	.357	14	5	0	2	0	2	.333	.500
O'Neill, Paul*	.467	15	7	2	3	1	3	.556	.933
Offerman, J#	.500	8	4	0	1	2	0	.600	.500
Olerud, John*	.000	8	0	0	0	2	1	.200	.000
Oliver, Joe	.000	10	0	0	0	1	0	.000	.000
Orsulak, Joe*	.400	5	2	0	0	1	1	.500	.400
Pagnozzi, Tom	.333	15	5	0	1	0	1	.333	.400
Palmeiro, R*	.267	15	4	1	2	2	1	.389	.467
Palmer, Dean	.286	7	2	1	2	0	2	.286	.714
Pena, G#	.111	9	1	0	3	0	2	.111	.222
Pendleton, T#	.471	17	8	1	1	1	1	.500	.882
Phillips, T#	.286	7	2	1	3	1	1	.375	.714
Plantier, P*	.000	5	0	0	0	0	3	.000	.000
Polonia, Luis*	.250	12	3	0	0	1	3	.308	.333
Raines, Tim#	.167	12	2	1	1	0	0	.167	.250
Ramirez, M	.444	9	4	1	1	0	3	.444	.889
Ripken, Billy	.600	5	3	0	0	1	0	.600	1.200
Ripken, Cal	.313	16	5	1	1	0	0	.353	.500
Roberts, Bip#	.250	12	3	0	1	3	0	.375	.250
Rodriguez, Al	.538	13	7	2	6	0	3	.538	1.154
Rodriguez, I	.125	8	1	0	0	0	1	.125	.250
Rodriguez, T	.000	5	0	0	0	0	0	.000	.000
Sabo, Chris	.273	11	3	0	1	1	1	.333	.364
Samuel, Juan	.357	14	5	1	3	1	2	.438	.571
Sandberg, R	.286	7	2	1	1	0	1	.286	.714
Sanders, R	.000	7	0	0	0	1	0	.222	.000

Shawn Boskie, Angels — RHP

Batter	Avg	AB	H	HR	BI	BB	SO	OBP	Slg
Santiago, B	.167	6	1	0	0	0	1	.167	.167
Seitzer, K	.333	6	2	0	2	2	2	.500	.333
Sheffield, G	.167	6	1	1	1	1	1	.286	.667
Shipley, C	.400	5	2	0	1	0	1	.400	.600
Slaught, Don	.800	5	4	1	3	0	0	.800	1.800
Smith, Ozzie#	.167	12	2	0	0	2	2	.286	.167
Sojo, Luis	.000	7	0	0	0	0	1	.000	.000
Sorrento, P*	.250	8	2	2	3	4	2	.500	1.000
Sosa, Sammy	.000	6	0	0	0	0	3	.000	.000
Sprague, Ed	.250	8	2	0	1	0	2	.300	.375
Stahoviak, S*	.167	12	2	0	0	2	3	.286	.333
Stairs, Matt*	.333	6	2	1	2	0	1	.333	.833
Stanley, Mike	.286	7	2	0	0	3	0	.500	.286
Steinbach, T	.250	12	3	0	2	0	0	.250	.250
Strange, Doug#	.375	8	3	0	0	1	0	.444	.500
Strawberry, D*	.125	8	1	0	2	1	0	.222	.125
Tartabull, D	.400	10	4	1	3	0	2	.400	.900
Tettleton, M#	.167	6	1	0	0	1	3	.286	.167
Thomas, Frank	.455	11	5	1	3	1	0	.500	.818
Thome, Jim*	.250	12	3	2	4	1	3	.308	.833
Thompson, Mil*	.333	9	3	1	2	1	2	.400	.667
Thompson, Rob	.267	15	4	1	3	1	1	.313	.533
Thompson, Ry	.250	8	2	0	2	0	1	.300	.375
Valentin, Jhn	.438	16	7	0	3	1	1	.500	.750
Valentin, Jse#	.600	5	3	1	1	0	1	.600	1.400
Vaughn, Greg	.500	4	2	0	0	1	0	.600	.500
Vaughn, Mo*	.467	15	7	2	8	3	2	.526	1.067
Ventura, R*	.182	11	2	2	4	0	2	.167	.727
Vina, F*	.444	9	4	0	0	0	1	.444	.444
Vizcaino, J#	.222	9	2	0	1	0	1	.222	.222
Vizquel, Omar#	.222	9	2	0	2	1	0	.364	.222
Walker, Larry*	.400	10	4	0	1	4	2	.600	.500
Wallach, Tim	.278	18	5	0	0	2	1	.350	.444
White, Devon#	.333	6	2	0	0	1	1	.429	.667
Whiten, Mark#	.125	8	1	0	0	1	3	.222	.125
Wilkins, Rick*	.200	5	1	0	0	0	1	.200	.400
Williams, Ber#	.400	5	2	0	0	1	2	.500	.600
Williams, Ma	.391	23	9	3	8	0	1	.391	.913
Wilson, Dan	.500	12	6	0	1	0	1	.500	.500
Young, Ernie	.000	3	0	0	0	2	0	.400	.000
Zeile, Todd	.250	16	4	2	3	0	1	.368	.688

Ricky Bottalico, Phillies — RHP

Batter	Avg	AB	H	HR	BI	BB	SO	OBP	Slg
Abbott, Kurt	.000	5	0	0	0	0	2	.000	.000
Alou, Moises	.000	5	0	0	0	0	1	.000	.000
Bagwell, Jeff	.000	4	0	0	0	1	2	.200	.000
Biggio, Craig	.250	8	2	0	1	0	4	.250	.250
Bonds, Barry*	.000	5	0	0	0	0	2	.000	.000
Carreon, Mark	.000	6	0	0	0	0	3	.000	.000
Castilla, V	.429	7	3	1	2	0	1	.429	.857
Colbrunn, G	.125	8	1	0	0	1	2	.222	.125
Conine, Jeff	.250	8	2	1	3	1	0	.333	.625
Grudzielanek	.200	5	1	0	1	1	1	.333	.200
Hill, G	.000	6	0	0	0	0	1	.000	.000
Hunter, Bri L	.333	6	2	0	0	0	2	.333	.833
Johnson, Char	.286	7	2	0	0	0	3	.286	.286
Johnson, Mark*	.500	2	1	1	2	2	0	.800	2.000
Jones, C#	.000	6	0	0	0	1	2	.000	.000
Jordan, Brian	.600	5	3	0	1	0	0	.600	.800
Karros, Eric	.333	6	2	1	2	0	2	.333	.833
King, Jeff	.250	4	1	0	1	0	0	.400	.250
Kingery, Mike*	.250	4	1	0	2	1	0	.400	.250
Lansing, Mike	.250	4	1	0	0	1	0	.400	.250
Lemke, Mark#	.750	4	3	0	1	1	0	.800	.750
Martin, Al*	.167	6	1	1	2	0	1	.167	.667
Mondesi, Raul	.000	6	0	0	1	0	3	.143	.000
Mouton, James	.000	5	0	0	1	1	2	.167	.000
Orsulak, Joe*	.000	7	0	0	0	1	1	.125	.000
Pendleton, T#	.286	7	2	0	0	0	3	.286	.286
Segui, David#	.250	8	2	0	0	0	3	.250	.375
Sheffield, G	.167	6	1	1	4	0	0	.167	.667
VanderWal, J*	.667	3	2	0	1	1	1	.600	.667
Veras, Q#	.500	4	2	0	0	2	0	.667	.500
Vizcaino, J#	.250	4	1	0	0	1	1	.400	.250
Wallach, Tim	.000	5	0	0	0	0	1	.000	.000
Weiss, Walt#	.000	4	0	0	0	2	0	.333	.000
White, R	.250	4	1	0	0	1	1	.400	.250
Williams, Ma	.000	5	0	0	0	1	3	.286	.000

Kent Bottenfield, Cubs — RHP

Batter	Avg	AB	H	HR	BI	BB	SO	OBP	Slg
Anthony, Eric*	.200	4	0	0	0	1	1	.200	.200
Arias, Alex	.286	7	2	0	0	0	1	.286	.286
Bell, Jay	.200	10	2	0	1	0	0	.200	.200
Berry, Sean	.667	3	2	1	2	1	1	.800	1.667
Bichette, D	.167	6	1	0	2	0	0	.143	.167
Biggio, Craig	.444	9	4	1	1	0	2	.444	.889
Bonds, Barry*	.500	8	4	1	1	3	0	.667	.875
Bonilla, B#	.429	7	3	0	1	3	0	.600	.571
Boone, Bret	.500	6	3	0	0	0	0	.500	.500

Kent Bottenfield, Cubs — RHP

Batter	Avg	AB	H	HR	BI	BB	SO	OBP	Slg
Branson, Jeff*	.222	9	2	0	0	0	1	.222	.333
Brumfield, J	.286	7	2	0	1	0	1	.286	.429
Burnitz, J*	.167	6	1	1	1	0	0	.167	.667
Butler, Brett*	.111	9	1	0	2	3	1	.333	.111
Caminiti, Ken#	.400	5	2	0	2	0	0	.400	.800
Carr, Chuck	.286	7	2	0	0	1	0	.375	.429
Castilla, V	.667	3	2	0	0	1	0	.800	.667
Cedeno, A	.286	7	2	0	0	0	2	.286	.429
Cianfrocco, A	.333	3	1	0	1	1	1	.500	.333
Clark, Dave*	.500	4	2	0	1	1	0	.600	.500
Clark, Will*	.200	5	1	0	0	3	0	.500	.200
Clayton, R	.375	8	3	0	3	4	1	.583	.500
Cole, Alex*	.250	4	1	0	0	3	0	.571	.250
Conine, Jeff	.000	6	0	0	0	1	2	.250	.000
Daulton, D*	.429	7	3	0	0	1	2	.429	.571
Davis, Eric	.083	12	1	0	2	1	1	.154	.167
Duncan, M	.250	4	1	0	0	2	2	.500	.500
Dykstra, L*	.400	5	2	0	0	1	0	.500	.600
Finley, Steve*	.429	7	3	0	1	0	0	.429	.429
Galarraga, A	.364	11	4	1	3	0	0	.364	.636
Gant, Ron	.500	4	2	0	1	2	1	.667	.500
Garcia, C	.125	8	1	0	1	0	0	.222	.125
Gilkey, B	.778	9	7	2	3	0	0	.800	1.667
Girardi, Joe	.000	5	0	0	0	0	1	.000	.000
Gonzalez, L*	.333	6	2	0	0	1	0	.429	.500
Grace, Mark*	.000	7	0	0	0	1	0	.125	.000
Grissom, M	.333	6	2	1	3	0	0	.333	.833
Gutierrez, R	.250	4	1	0	0	1	1	.400	.750
Harris, Lenny*	.375	8	3	0	0	0	0	.375	.375
Hayes, C	.571	7	4	1	2	1	0	.625	1.000
Hollins, Dave#	.000	3	0	0	0	2	2	.400	.000
Hundley, Todd#	.400	5	2	0	1	1	0	.500	.400
Incaviglia, P	.000	6	0	0	0	0	3	.000	.000
Jefferies, G#	.222	9	2	0	0	0	0	.222	.222
Karros, Eric	.385	13	5	1	1	1	0	.429	.615
Kent, Jeff	.333	9	3	1	2	1	1	.455	.667
King, Jeff	.250	8	2	0	1	0	0	.250	.250
Lankford, Ray*	.571	7	4	1	3	3	0	.700	1.000
Lansing, Mike	.167	6	1	0	0	1	1	.286	.167
Larkin, Barry	.000	5	0	0	1	1	1	.167	.000
Lemke, Mark*	.429	7	3	0	0	0	0	.429	.714
Lewis, Darren	.125	8	1	0	0	0	0	.125	.125
Manwaring, K	.200	10	2	0	0	0	2	.273	.200
Martin, Al*	.571	7	4	1	3	1	0	.625	1.429
May, Derrick*	.286	7	2	1	1	0	0	.286	.857
McGee, Willie*	.200	10	2	0	0	0	1	.200	.300
Merced, O*	.200	10	2	0	0	4	2	.429	.300
Mitchell, K	.400	5	2	0	0	0	0	.400	.400
Mondesi, Raul	.200	5	1	0	0	0	2	.200	.200
Morandini, M*	.333	9	3	0	1	0	0	.333	.333
Morris, Hal*	.375	8	3	0	2	1	1	.500	.500
Murray, Eddie#	.375	8	3	0	0	0	1	.375	.375
Offerman, J#	.250	8	2	0	0	1	1	.333	.250
Oliver, Joe	.500	8	4	0	7	0	1	.500	.875
Orsulak, Joe*	.100	10	1	0	0	1	1	.182	.100
Pagnozzi, Tom	.000	8	0	0	0	0	0	.000	.000
Pendleton, T*	.200	5	1	0	0	0	0	.200	.200
Piazza, Mike	.222	9	2	1	7	1	0	.300	.556
Reed, Jody	.375	8	3	0	1	0	0	.375	.375
Rodriguez, H*	.400	5	2	0	0	1	0	.500	.600
Sandberg, R	.286	7	2	0	0	1	1	.375	.429
Sanders, R	.222	9	2	0	2	1	1	.300	.222
Santiago, B	.333	6	2	1	3	1	1	.375	.833
Scarsone, S	.000	4	0	0	0	0	1	.000	.000
Sheffield, G	.556	9	5	1	3	1	0	.600	1.000
Smith, Dwight*	.333	6	2	1	2	1	0	.429	.833
Smith, Ozzie#	.455	11	5	0	0	1	0	.500	.545
Strawberry, D*	.000	4	0	0	0	0	0	.000	.000
Thompson, Mil*	.600	5	3	1	4	0	1	.600	1.200
Thompson, Rob	.200	5	1	0	0	0	2	.200	.200
Thompson, Ry	.286	7	2	1	4	2	2	.444	.714
Walker, Larry*	.750	4	3	2	3	1	0	.800	2.250
Wallach, Tim	.444	9	4	0	1	1	1	.500	.444
Weiss, Walt*	.600	5	3	0	0	2	0	.714	.600
White, R	.000	7	0	0	0	1	1	.125	.000
Whiten, Mark#	.200	5	1	0	0	1	0	.333	.200
Wilkins, Rick*	.333	6	2	1	1	0	1	.333	1.000
Williams, Ma	.222	9	2	1	3	1	1	.300	.667
Young, Eric	.333	9	3	1	1	0	0	.400	.778
Young, Kevin	.333	3	1	0	0	1	0	.500	.333
Zeile, Todd	.167	6	1	0	1	2	0	.375	.167

Steve Bourgeois, Giants — RHP

Batter	Avg	AB	H	HR	BI	BB	SO	OBP	Slg
Bichette, D	.250	4	1	0	0	1	0	.400	.250
Burks, Ellis	.250	4	1	0	0	0	1	.250	.250
Castilla, V	.200	5	1	0	0	0	1	.200	.200
Galarraga, A	.600	5	3	0	2	0	1	.600	1.000
McCracken, Q#	.250	4	1	0	1	2	1	.500	.500
Weiss, Walt#	.600	5	3	0	0	0	0	.600	.800
Young, Eric	.714	7	5	0	0	0	0	.714	.714

Marshall Boze, Brewers — RHP

Batter	Avg	AB	H	HR	BI	BB	SO	OBP	Slg
Gonzalez, A	.600	5	3	0	2	1	0	.667	.600
Nixon, Otis#	.600	5	3	0	0	0	0	.600	.600

Mark Brandenburg, Red Sox — RHP

Batter	Avg	AB	H	HR	BI	BB	SO	OBP	Slg
Amaral, Rich	.333	6	2	0	0	0	2	.333	.333
Anderson, G*	.250	4	1	0	2	1	1	.400	.250
Baines, H*	.000	4	0	0	0	1	2	.200	.000
Bordick, Mike	.200	5	1	0	0	0	0	.200	.200
Buhner, Jay	.200	10	2	0	0	1	3	.333	.300
Cora, Joey#	.600	5	3	0	3	2	0	.714	1.200
Fielder, C	.250	4	1	0	1	1	0	.400	.250
Hollins, Dave#	.250	4	1	0	1	0	3	.400	.250
Jaha, John	.143	7	1	1	2	1	4	.250	.571
Martinez, E	.000	5	0	0	3	0	0	.375	.000
Phillips, T#	.167	6	1	0	0	3	0	.167	.167
Ripken, Cal	.400	5	2	0	1	0	0	.400	.400
Rodriguez, Al	.400	5	2	0	1	0	2	.400	.400
Sojo, Luis	.444	9	4	0	2	0	2	.444	.444
Sorrento, P*	.000	7	0	0	0	2	3	.222	.000
Steinbach, T	.750	4	3	1	2	1	1	.800	1.750
Strange, Doug*	.200	5	1	0	0	0	2	.200	.200
Ventura, R*	.250	4	1	0	0	1	1	.400	.250
Wilson, Dan	.286	7	2	0	1	0	2	.286	.286

Jeff Brantley, Reds — RHP

Batter	Avg	AB	H	HR	BI	BB	SO	OBP	Slg
Alomar, R#	.200	10	2	0	1	2	0	.333	.200
Alou, Moises	.333	9	3	2	2	2	0	.455	1.000
Anthony, Eric*	.143	7	1	0	0	2	2	.333	.143
Ausmus, Brad	.000	5	0	0	0	0	4	.000	.000
Bagwell, Jeff	.389	18	7	2	9	6	1	.520	.722
Barberie, B#	.167	6	1	0	1	0	3	.167	.333
Bell, Derek	.273	11	3	1	4	0	4	.273	.636
Bell, Jay	.227	22	5	0	2	1	1	.261	.227
Belliard, R	.143	14	2	0	0	0	2	.143	.143
Berry, Sean	.000	12	0	0	0	0	6	.000	.000
Bichette, D	.250	4	1	0	0	1	1	.400	.250
Biggio, Craig	.174	23	4	0	2	2	2	.259	.261
Blauser, Jeff	.318	22	7	2	6	3	4	.464	.636
Bonds, Barry*	.111	18	2	1	3	4	5	.273	.278
Bonilla, B#	.188	16	3	0	0	2	3	.278	.250
Butler, Brett*	.350	20	7	0	3	3	2	.417	.400
Caminiti, Ken#	.250	20	5	0	4	5	6	.407	.400
Candaele, C#	.000	8	0	0	1	2	1	.200	.000
Cangelosi, J#	.111	9	1	0	0	1	3	.200	.222
Carr, Chuck	.250	4	1	0	1	1	0	.400	.250
Carreon, Mark	.500	8	4	1	1	1	1	.556	1.000
Carter, Joe	.000	5	0	0	0	0	1	.000	.000
Castilla, V	.250	8	2	0	1	0	2	.250	.250
Cedeno, A	.143	14	2	1	3	1	2	.200	.357
Cianfrocco, A	.167	6	1	0	0	0	4	.167	.167
Clark, Dave*	.000	5	0	0	0	0	3	.000	.000
Clayton, R	.000	5	0	0	0	0	3	.000	.000
Colbrunn, G	.111	9	1	0	1	0	3	.111	.111
Coleman, V#	.000	7	0	0	1	2	1	.125	.000
Conine, Jeff	.250	8	2	1	6	2	3	.364	.625
Cora, Joey*	.250	4	1	0	1	1	2	.400	.250
Cordero, Wil	.286	7	2	0	0	0	1	.286	.286
Daulton, D*	.067	15	1	0	1	1	0	.125	.067
Davis, Eric	.364	11	4	0	3	5	0	.563	.364
Dawson, Andre	.357	14	5	1	1	0	0	.357	.571
DeShields, D*	.286	14	4	1	1	1	3	.333	.286
Duncan, M	.211	19	4	1	1	1	5	.250	.421
Dunston, S	.375	16	6	0	3	2	1	.444	.438
Dykstra, L*	.278	18	5	0	1	2	1	.350	.333
Eisenreich, J*	.286	7	2	0	1	1	3	.333	.286
Elster, Kevin	.000	4	0	0	0	1	0	.200	.000
Eusebio, Tony	.200	5	1	0	0	0	0	.200	.200
Everett, Carl#	.000	3	0	0	0	2	1	.400	.000
Finley, Steve*	.214	14	3	1	1	1	0	.267	.500
Fletcher, D*	.000	6	0	0	0	1	0	.143	.000
Frazier, Lou#*	.400	5	2	0	0	2	0	.400	.400
Galarraga, A	.267	15	4	2	4	2	6	.353	.667
Gant, Ron	.292	24	7	3	6	2	5	.346	.708
Garcia, C	.167	12	2	0	1	1	4	.231	.167
Gilkey, B	.200	10	2	0	0	0	2	.200	.200
Girardi, Joe	.500	8	4	1	3	0	0	.500	.875
Gonzalez, L*	.222	18	4	1	5	0	6	.211	.389
Grace, Mark*	.217	23	5	1	3	2	1	.280	.478
Grissom, M	.214	14	3	0	3	2	5	.313	.214
Gwynn, Chris*	.143	7	1	0	0	1	3	.250	.143
Gwynn, Tony*	.593	27	16	0	1	5	1	.656	.630
Hansen, Dave*	.200	5	1	0	0	1	2	.429	.200
Harris, Lenny*	.308	13	4	0	1	4	1	.471	.385
Hayes, C	.133	15	2	1	2	0	3	.133	.333
Hill, G	.250	8	2	0	0	1	1	.250	.250
Hollins, Dave#	.182	11	2	1	3	3	3	.375	.455
Hundley, Todd#	.333	9	3	2	5	3	2	.500	1.000
Hunter, Brian	.000	5	0	0	0	0	2	.000	.000
Hunter, Bri L	.167	6	1	0	0	0	3	.167	.167

Jeff Brantley, Reds — RHP

Batter	Avg	AB	H	HR	BI	BB	SO	OBP	Slg
Incaviglia, P	.000	6	0	0	1	0	4	.143	.000
James, Dion*	.200	5	1	0	1	3	1	.500	.200
Javier, Stan#	.100	10	1	0	2	0	5	.100	.200
Jefferies, G#	.400	10	4	0	1	2	0	.500	.500
Jones, C#	.200	5	1	0	0	0	1	.200	.200
Jordan, Brian	.250	8	2	0	2	0	4	.250	.250
Jordan, Ricky	.286	14	4	0	4	0	3	.286	.429
Joyner, Wally*	.000	4	0	0	0	1	1	.200	.000
Justice, Dave*	.158	19	3	0	0	3	2	.273	.211
Karros, Eric	.235	17	4	1	2	1	4	.278	.471
Kent, Jeff	.444	9	4	0	2	1	3	.500	.556
King, Jeff	.278	18	5	1	3	3	2	.381	.556
Klesko, Ryan*	.250	4	1	0	0	1	2	.400	.250
Lankford, Ray*	.143	7	1	0	0	2	3	.333	.286
Lansing, Mike	.143	7	1	0	0	0	0	.143	.143
Larkin, Barry	.133	15	2	0	0	0	1	.133	.133
Lemke, Mark#	.235	17	4	0	1	2	3	.316	.235
Lieberthal, M	.250	4	1	0	0	1	2	.400	.250
Liriano, N#	.200	5	1	0	0	0	1	.200	.200
Lopez, Javy	.167	6	1	0	1	0	4	.143	.167
Mabry, John*	.400	5	2	1	1	0	0	.400	1.000
Magadan, Dave*	.333	9	3	0	0	2	1	.455	.333
Martin, Al*	.250	8	2	1	1	1	1	.333	.750
Martinez, Da*	.100	10	1	0	1	2	0	.250	.100
May, Derrick*	.364	11	4	0	0	0	0	.364	.455
McGee, Willie#	.500	8	4	0	0	0	1	.500	.500
McGriff, Fred*	.222	18	4	2	2	3	6	.333	.611
McRae, Brian#	.200	5	1	0	0	1	1	.333	.200
Merced, O*	.556	9	5	0	2	7	1	.750	.667
Miller, Orl	.250	8	2	1	1	0	2	.250	.625
Mondesi, Raul	.286	7	2	0	0	0	0	.286	.571
Morandini, M*	.125	8	1	0	0	1	3	.222	.250
Morris, Hal*	.500	6	3	0	0	3	0	.667	.500
Murray, Eddie#	.333	18	6	1	4	0	2	.333	.500
Nieves, M#	.250	4	1	0	1	1	3	.333	.500
Nixon, Otis*	.167	12	2	0	1	2	4	.286	.167
O'Brien, C	.250	4	1	0	1	1	1	.500	.250
O'Neill, Paul*	.364	11	4	2	6	6	1	.588	.909
Offerman, J#	.214	14	3	0	0	3	1	.353	.214
Oliver, Joe	.143	7	1	0	0	1	2	.250	.143
Orsulak, Joe*	.167	6	1	0	0	1	1	.286	.167
Pagnozzi, Tom	.333	9	3	0	0	0	3	.333	.333
Pena, G#	.000	4	0	0	0	1	1	.200	.000
Pendleton, T#	.286	28	8	0	3	0	7	.286	.393
Piazza, Mike	.417	12	5	1	4	0	1	.417	.667
Plantier, P*	.200	5	1	0	3	1	1	.500	.200
Prince, Tom	.000	5	0	0	1	1	1	.167	.000
Raines, Tim#	.143	7	1	0	1	0	1	.125	.143
Reed, Jeff*	.000	6	0	0	0	2	2	.250	.000
Reed, Jody	.250	8	2	1	2	0	0	.250	.875
Roberts, Bip#	.400	15	6	0	0	0	0	.400	.467
Rodriguez, H*	.091	11	1	0	0	0	5	.091	.091
Sabo, Chris	.286	14	4	1	1	2	5	.375	.571
Samuel, Juan	.273	11	3	0	0	0	6	.273	.364
Sanchez, Rey	.000	5	0	0	0	0	0	.000	.000
Sandberg, R	.417	12	5	1	3	3	3	.563	.750
Sanders, R	.200	5	1	0	0	1	1	.333	.200
Santiago, B	.300	20	6	0	1	1	4	.364	.300
Servais, S	.000	5	0	0	0	0	4	.000	.000
Sheffield, G	.625	8	5	1	4	0	1	.667	1.125
Smith, Dwight*	.083	12	1	0	1	2	2	.214	.083
Smith, Ozzie#	.250	12	3	0	1	1	1	.286	.333
Sosa, Sammy	.214	14	3	1	2	0	7	.214	.429
Stillwell, K#	.200	5	1	0	1	0	0	.200	.200
Strawberry, D*	.231	13	3	1	2	1	3	.286	.538
Tarasco, Tony*	.600	5	3	0	1	0	0	.600	.800
Taubensee, E*	.400	5	2	0	0	0	0	.400	.400
Thompson, Mil*	.273	11	3	0	1	2	1	.385	.455
VanderWal, J*	.286	7	2	1	2	2	1	.444	.714
Vizcaino, J#	.333	12	4	1	1	2	4	.429	.583
Walker, Larry*	.313	16	5	1	3	5	3	.421	.563
Wallach, Tim	.208	24	5	2	3	0	3	.240	.458
Walton, J	.286	7	2	0	0	0	1	.286	.429
Weiss, Walt#	.250	4	1	0	0	1	0	.400	.250
Whiten, Mark#	.600	5	3	1	1	0	0	.600	1.200
Wilkins, Rick*	.364	11	4	0	0	1	4	.417	.455
Williams, Ma	.333	6	2	1	3	0	1	.333	1.000
Young, Eric	.167	6	1	0	0	1	0	.286	.167
Young, Kevin	.000	6	0	0	1	1	2	.222	.000
Zeile, Todd	.136	22	3	0	0	0	5	.136	.182

Billy Brewer, Yankees — LHP

Batter	Avg	AB	H	HR	BI	BB	SO	OBP	Slg
Anderson, Brd*	.200	5	1	0	1	0	2	.200	.200
Baerga, C#	.286	7	2	0	2	0	2	.286	.286
Becker, Rich*	.200	5	1	0	0	0	1	.200	.200
Belle, Albert	.167	6	1	0	0	1	0	.286	.167
Griffey Jr, K*	.429	7	3	3	6	0	1	.429	1.714
Guillen, O*	.167	6	1	0	0	1	1	.286	.167
Hamilton, D*	.143	7	1	0	0	2	2	.333	.143
Johnson, L*	.200	5	1	0	0	0	0	.200	.200

Billy Brewer, Yankees — LHP

Batter	Avg	AB	H	HR	BI	BB	SO	OBP	Slg
Kirby, Wayne*	.200	5	1	0	0	0	0	.200	.200
Lofton, Kenny*	.200	5	1	0	0	3	2	.500	.200
Martinez, T*	.200	5	1	1	2	0	0	.200	.800
Murray, Eddie#	.200	5	1	0	0	0	0	.200	.200
O'Neill, Paul*	.500	6	3	0	1	1	3	.571	.833
Olerud, John*	.250	8	2	0	1	2	3	.455	.250
Phillips, T#	.000	2	0	0	1	3	2	.600	.000
Raines, Tim#	.400	5	2	0	1	1	0	.500	.400
Reboulet, J	.000	3	0	0	0	2	0	.400	.000
Snow, J.T.#	.250	4	1	0	0	1	0	.400	.250
Sorrento, P*	.286	7	2	0	1	1	1	.375	.286
Spiers, Bill*	.000	6	0	0	0	1	2	.143	.000
Sprague, Ed	.200	5	1	0	1	0	0	.200	.200
Surhoff, B.J.*	.400	5	2	0	1	2	0	.571	.400
Tettleton, M#	.000	3	0	0	0	3	1	.500	.000
Vaughn, Mo*	.500	6	3	3	3	1	1	.571	2.000
Ventura, R*	.000	7	0	0	2	1	1	.125	.000
Vizquel, Omar#	.333	6	2	0	1	0	0	.333	.667
Williams, Ber#	.500	4	2	1	2	1	0	.600	1.250

John Briscoe, Athletics — RHP

Batter	Avg	AB	H	HR	BI	BB	SO	OBP	Slg
Anderson, Brd*	.500	6	3	0	0	3	2	.667	.500
Baerga, C#	.000	4	0	0	0	0	1	.000	.000
Baines, H*	1.000	3	3	1	5	2	0	1.000	2.000
Boggs, Wade*	.286	7	2	0	1	0	2	.286	.429
Canseco, Jose	.167	6	1	0	0	0	2	.167	.333
Carter, Joe	.000	4	0	0	1	0	1	.000	.000
Clark, Will*	.600	5	3	1	2	0	0	.600	1.200
Curtis, Chad	.200	5	1	0	2	1	2	.333	.200
Devereaux, M	.375	8	3	2	3	0	5	.375	1.250
Durham, Ray#	.400	5	2	0	0	0	0	.400	.400
Fielder, C	.200	5	1	0	0	1	1	.429	.200
Flaherty, J	.250	4	1	0	2	1	1	.400	.250
Franco, Julio	.000	5	0	0	0	0	2	.000	.000
Fryman, T	.222	9	2	1	1	1	3	.300	.556
Gomez, Chris	.000	4	0	0	0	1	0	.200	.000
Gonzalez, J	.125	8	1	0	0	0	1	.125	.250
Guillen, O*	.250	4	1	0	2	2	0	.500	.250
Hale, Chip*	.200	5	1	0	0	1	0	.200	.400
Hoiles, Chris	.200	5	1	0	1	1	1	.333	.400
Johnson, L*	.167	6	1	0	1	0	1	.167	.167
Karkovice, R	.600	5	3	0	1	0	0	.600	.800
Knoblauch, C	.600	5	3	0	1	0	0	.667	.600
Lewis, Mark	.000	6	0	0	0	0	1	.000	.000
Meares, Pat	.200	5	1	0	0	0	1	.200	.200
O'Neill, Paul*	.250	4	1	0	0	1	1	.400	.250
Palmeiro, R*	.400	5	2	0	3	2	0	.571	.600
Palmer, Dean	.167	6	1	1	2	1	2	.286	.667
Phillips, T#	.250	4	1	0	2	5	1	.600	.250
Polonia, Luis*	.333	3	1	0	0	2	0	.600	.333
Raines, Tim#	.500	4	2	0	2	2	0	.667	.500
Ripken, Cal	.000	4	0	0	1	2	1	.333	.000
Rodriguez, I	.400	5	2	1	1	1	0	.500	1.000
Sprague, Ed	.000	3	0	0	0	2	1	.400	.000
Strange, Doug#	.250	4	1	0	0	1	0	.400	.250
Tartabull, D	.250	4	1	0	1	1	1	.400	.250
Thomas, Frank	.667	3	2	1	2	2	0	.800	1.667
Velarde, R	.000	3	0	0	0	2	1	.400	.000

Doug Brocail, Astros — RHP

Batter	Avg	AB	H	HR	BI	BB	SO	OBP	Slg
Abbott, Kurt	.400	5	2	0	0	0	2	.400	.400
Alou, Moises	.167	12	2	0	0	0	3	.167	.167
Anthony, Eric*	.000	6	0	0	0	0	2	.000	.000
Ausmus, Brad	.250	4	1	0	1	2	0	.500	.250
Bagwell, Jeff	.571	7	4	0	0	0	2	.571	.714
Bell, Jay	.333	9	3	0	1	1	2	.455	.667
Berry, Sean	.125	8	1	0	2	0	2	.125	.375
Bichette, D	.125	8	1	0	0	0	1	.125	.125
Biggio, Craig	.000	6	0	0	0	1	1	.143	.000
Blauser, Jeff	.308	13	4	0	0	2	2	.400	.385
Bonds, Barry*	.300	10	3	2	3	0	1	.300	.900
Brumfield, J	.286	7	2	0	1	0	1	.286	.286
Butler, Brett*	.250	12	3	0	1	1	0	.286	.250
Caminiti, Ken#	.308	13	4	0	0	2	2	.308	.385
Castilla, V	.143	7	1	0	2	0	1	.143	.429
Cedeno, A	.200	10	2	0	0	0	5	.250	.200
Clark, Dave*	.286	7	2	0	0	0	1	.286	.286
Clark, Will*	.375	8	3	1	6	2	1	.455	.875
Clayton, R	.385	13	5	0	0	1	3	.429	.385
Colbrunn, G	.500	8	4	1	3	0	0	.556	1.000
Cole, Alex*	.750	4	3	0	0	1	0	.800	.750
Conine, Jeff	.300	10	3	0	2	0	1	.300	.500
Cordero, Wil	.143	7	1	0	0	0	1	.250	.143
Davis, Eric	.125	8	1	0	0	0	4	.125	.250
DeShields, D*	.143	7	1	0	1	1	1	.250	.143
Dykstra, L*	.000	4	0	0	0	1	0	.200	.000
Eisenreich, J*	.222	9	2	0	1	0	3	.222	.222
Finley, Steve*	.231	13	3	0	1	0	1	.286	.308
Fletcher, D*	.333	6	2	0	1	2	0	.556	.500

Doug Brocail, Astros — RHP

Batter	Avg	AB	H	HR	BI	BB	SO	OBP	Slg
Galarraga, A	.286	7	2	0	0	0	1	.286	.429
Gant, Ron	.222	9	2	0	0	1	0	.300	.222
Garcia, C	.375	8	3	0	0	1	0	.444	.375
Gilkey, B	.286	7	2	0	3	0	2	.222	.429
Gonzalez, L*	.444	9	4	0	1	0	2	.444	.556
Grace, Mark*	.625	8	5	0	1	0	0	.556	.750
Grissom, M	.182	11	2	0	1	0	1	.182	.182
Grudzielanek	.143	7	1	1	1	0	0	.143	.571
Gwynn, Tony*	.000	5	0	0	0	1	0	.167	.000
Hayes, C	.200	10	2	0	0	2	0	.333	.400
Henderson, R	.667	3	2	0	0	2	0	.800	.667
Hill, G	.333	6	2	0	0	0	1	.333	.500
Hundley, Todd*	.200	5	1	0	0	1	0	.333	.200
Jefferies, G#	.667	6	4	0	0	1	0	.714	.833
Johnson, Bri	.500	6	3	0	2	0	1	.500	.667
Justice, Dave*	.308	13	4	2	3	0	1	.357	.846
Karros, Eric	.111	9	1	0	0	0	3	.111	.111
Kent, Jeff	.167	6	1	0	2	0	1	.143	.167
King, Jeff	.200	5	1	0	2	2	0	.429	.200
Kingery, Mike*	.400	5	2	0	1	1	1	.500	.400
Lankford, Ray*	.000	4	0	0	0	2	2	.333	.000
Lansing, Mike	.278	18	5	0	1	0	0	.278	.389
Larkin, Barry	.000	5	0	0	0	0	2	.000	.000
Lemke, Mark#	.200	5	1	0	0	1	0	.333	.200
Lewis, Darren	.455	11	5	0	0	0	1	.455	.455
Liriano, N#	.222	9	2	0	1	0	1	.222	.222
Lopez, Javy	.250	4	1	0	0	0	0	.400	.500
Manwaring, K	.143	7	1	0	1	2	0	.333	.143
Martin, Al*	.000	8	0	0	0	0	2	.000	.000
McGee, Willie#	.583	12	7	0	1	0	1	.583	.667
McGriff, Fred*	.000	7	0	0	0	1	1	.125	.000
McRae, Brian*	.000	4	0	0	0	1	1	.200	.000
Merced, O*	.125	8	1	0	1	2	1	.300	.125
Mondesi, Raul	.200	5	1	0	0	0	2	.200	.400
Morandini, M*	.333	6	2	0	3	0	1	.333	.333
Morris, Hal*	.500	6	3	0	0	0	0	.500	.500
Nixon, Otis*	.375	8	3	0	0	1	0	.444	.375
Offerman, Jer*	.500	6	3	0	1	1	0	.571	.833
Oliver, Joe	.000	4	0	0	0	1	0	.000	.000
Orsulak, Joe*	.000	5	0	0	1	1	0	.143	.000
Pagnozzi, Tom	.167	6	1	0	1	0	0	.167	.333
Pendleton, T#	.235	17	4	1	3	1	3	.278	.471
Piazza, Mike	.364	11	4	2	5	2	3	.462	1.091
Reed, Jody	.400	10	4	0	2	4	1	.571	.500
Roberts, Bip#	.200	5	1	0	0	0	0	.200	.200
Rodriguez, H*	.400	10	4	2	4	0	2	.364	1.100
Sabo, Chris	.200	5	1	0	0	0	0	.200	.200
Sanchez, Rey	.333	6	2	0	2	0	0	.333	.500
Sandberg, R	.400	5	2	0	1	0	0	.400	.400
Sanders, R	.200	5	1	0	0	0	0	.200	.200
Segui, David#	.333	9	3	0	0	0	0	.333	.556
Servais, Scott	.600	5	3	1	3	0	0	.600	1.200
Sheaffer, D	.333	9	3	1	3	0	0	.333	.667
Sheffield, G	.200	5	1	1	3	0	1	.200	.800
Smith, Ozzie*	.556	9	5	0	1	1	0	.600	.778
Sosa, Sammy	.400	5	2	1	2	1	0	.429	1.000
Stocker, K#	.500	10	5	0	1	0	1	.545	.700
Tarasco, Tony*	.500	4	2	1	1	1	0	.600	1.250
Tavarez, Je#	.286	7	2	0	0	0	0	.286	.571
Thompson, Rob	.100	10	1	0	0	1	1	.182	.100
Veras, Q#	.571	7	4	0	1	2	1	.667	.714
Vizcaino, Jr	.167	6	1	0	0	1	0	.375	.333
Walker, Larry*	.143	7	1	0	2	1	0	.250	.429
Wallach, Tim	.200	5	1	1	1	1	2	.333	.800
Webster, L	.571	7	4	0	1	0	1	.571	.571
Weiss, Walt*	.286	7	2	0	0	1	1	.375	.286
Whiten, Mark#	.250	4	1	0	0	2	0	.500	.250
Wilkins, Rick*	.333	6	2	0	2	1	2	.429	.333
Williams, M	.300	10	3	1	4	1	0	.364	.700
Young, Eric	.571	7	4	0	1	0	0	.571	.714

Scott Brow, Braves — RHP

Batter	Avg	AB	H	HR	BI	BB	SO	OBP	Slg
Anderson, Brd*	.250	8	2	1	1	0	2	.250	.625
Baines, H*	.400	5	2	0	1	0	0	.400	.400
Fielder, C	.250	4	1	0	1	0	0	.400	.250
Fryman, T	.167	6	1	0	0	0	1	.167	.167
Hoiles, Chris	.200	5	1	1	3	1	1	.286	.800
Knoblauch, C	.000	2	0	0	0	3	1	.600	.000
McLemore, M#	.167	6	1	0	0	2	0	.375	.167
Ripken, Cal	.429	7	3	0	1	1	0	.556	.429

Kevin Brown, Marlins — RHP

Batter	Avg	AB	H	HR	BI	BB	SO	OBP	Slg
Aldrete, Mike*	.200	20	4	0	0	0	4	.200	.200
Alicea, Luis*	.000	5	0	0	0	0	3	.167	.000
Alomar, R#	.393	28	11	0	4	6	3	.500	.536
Alomar Jr, S	.267	30	8	0	3	0	6	.290	.300
Alou, Moises	.333	6	2	0	0	0	1	.333	.667
Anderson, Brd*	.474	19	9	0	1	0	3	.474	.632
Anderson, G*	.286	7	2	0	1	0	1	.286	.286

Kevin Brown, Marlins — RHP

Batter	Avg	AB	H	HR	BI	BB	SO	OBP	Slg
Anthony, Eric*	.250	16	4	0	1	0	6	.250	.313
Baerga, C#	.263	57	15	2	7	5	8	.323	.421
Bagwell, Jeff	.200	5	1	0	0	1	2	.333	.200
Baines, H*	.323	31	10	2	4	4	2	.400	.516
Bates, Jason#	.200	5	1	0	1	0	1	.200	.200
Bell, Derek	.200	5	1	0	1	1	1	.333	.200
Bell, Jay	.333	9	3	0	0	0	1	.333	.333
Belle, Albert	.333	51	17	1	8	4	13	.386	.490
Benard, M*	.375	8	3	0	0	0	0	.375	.375
Berroa, G	.000	5	0	0	0	2	2	.286	.000
Berry, Sean	.167	6	1	0	0	0	2	.167	.500
Bichette, D	.158	19	3	1	2	1	4	.200	.421
Biggio, Craig	.333	3	1	0	1	2	0	.500	.333
Blowers, Mike	.333	15	5	0	4	1	5	.375	.333
Boggs, Wade*	.325	40	13	1	5	6	4	.396	.450
Bonds, Barry*	.100	10	1	0	0	2	1	.250	.100
Boone, Bret	.200	5	1	0	0	1	1	.333	.400
Borders, Pat	.143	21	3	0	3	0	4	.143	.190
Bordick, Mike	.154	26	4	0	2	1	5	.207	.192
Bragg, Darren*	.167	6	1	0	0	1	1	.286	.167
Branson, Jeff*	.000	4	0	0	0	1	0	.200	.000
Brosius, S	.409	22	9	0	1	0	0	.409	.455
Buhner, Jay	.265	34	9	1	7	6	7	.366	.412
Burks, Ellis	.314	35	11	0	4	2	8	.351	.429
Butler, Brett*	.286	7	2	0	0	0	1	.286	.286
Caminiti, Ken#	.400	5	2	0	2	0	2	.333	.600
Canseco, Jose	.419	31	13	0	5	2	6	.471	.516
Carreon, Mark	.357	14	5	0	2	0	1	.357	.357
Carter, Joe	.303	33	10	3	10	2	3	.378	.636
Castilla, V	.167	6	1	0	0	0	2	.167	.167
Clark, Will*	.333	6	2	0	0	0	0	.333	.333
Cole, Alex*	.292	24	7	0	1	1	7	.320	.375
Coleman, V#	.375	16	6	0	0	0	3	.375	.563
Cora, Joey#	.276	29	8	0	3	7	2	.462	.345
Curtis, Chad	.250	28	7	0	2	3	5	.323	.321
Cuyler, Milt#	.133	15	2	0	1	3	4	.278	.133
Davis, Chili#	.170	47	8	0	1	7	8	.278	.170
Davis, Eric	.000	11	0	0	0	1	5	.083	.000
Dawson, Andre	.385	13	5	0	1	0	0	.429	.538
Deer, Rob	.200	20	4	1	3	3	7	.333	.450
Delgado, C*	.400	5	2	0	0	1	1	.500	.400
DeShields, D*	.091	11	1	0	0	0	2	.091	.091
Devereaux, M	.276	29	8	1	6	0	5	.267	.517
Diaz, Alex#	.125	8	1	0	1	1	2	.222	.125
DiSarcina, S	.095	21	2	0	2	1	3	.136	.143
Dunston, S	.375	8	3	0	0	0	0	.375	.375
Easley, D	.111	9	1	0	0	0	3	.111	.111
Edmonds, Jim*	.273	11	3	0	2	3	0	.429	.364
Eisenreich, J*	.333	24	8	0	3	2	3	.385	.458
Espinoza, A	.174	23	4	0	0	2	3	.240	.174
Fermin, Felix	.204	49	10	0	5	1	6	.235	.204
Fielder, C	.261	46	12	4	10	3	14	.320	.543
Finley, Steve*	.154	13	2	0	2	0	2	.154	.154
Flaherty, J	.182	11	2	1	1	0	1	.182	.455
Fletcher, D*	.200	5	1	0	1	1	0	.333	.200
Floyd, Cliff*	.667	6	4	0	0	0	1	.667	.833
Franco, Julio	.250	4	1	0	0	1	2	.500	.250
Frye, Jeff	.400	4	0	0	0	1	0	.200	.200
Fryman, T	.368	38	14	1	5	3	9	.442	.500
Gaetti, Gary	.161	31	5	0	4	1	6	.206	.161
Gagne, Greg	.130	46	6	0	1	2	6	.184	.152
Gallego, Mike	.240	25	6	0	2	1	2	.296	.240
Garcia, C	.400	10	4	0	1	1	1	.455	.700
Gates, Brent#	.278	18	5	0	0	0	1	.278	.333
Gil, Benji	.500	4	2	0	0	0	0	.500	.750
Gilkey, B	.600	5	3	1	2	2	0	.778	1.400
Gomez, Chris	.000	10	0	0	0	0	1	.167	.000
Gomez, Leo	.182	11	2	0	1	0	1	.182	.273
Gonzales, R	.444	9	4	0	0	2	0	.545	.444
Gonzalez, L*	.200	10	2	0	0	0	2	.200	.300
Grace, Mark*	.250	8	2	0	0	1	0	.333	.375
Grebeck, C	.143	7	1	0	0	2	2	.333	.143
Greenwell, M*	.295	44	13	0	5	4	4	.354	.341
Greer, Rusty*	.200	5	1	1	1	1	0	.333	.800
Griffey Jr, K*	.238	42	10	1	3	1	3	.256	.333
Grissom, M	.300	10	3	0	0	1	0	.364	.300
Guillen, O*	.135	37	5	0	0	0	3	.135	.162
Gwynn, Chris*	.250	8	2	0	0	0	0	.250	.375
Hall, Mel*	.250	24	6	1	3	1	3	.280	.417
Hamelin, Bob*	.200	10	2	1	4	0	2	.200	.600
Hamilton, D*	.314	35	11	0	4	0	5	.314	.429
Harris, Lenny*	.250	8	2	0	1	0	0	.250	.250
Hayes, C	.077	13	1	0	0	0	3	.077	.077
Henderson, R	.391	46	18	1	5	4	6	.431	.522
Higginson, B*	.222	9	2	0	0	1	0	.300	.222
Hill, G	.211	19	4	0	1	0	2	.211	.211
Hoiles, Chris	.167	6	1	1	2	0	2	.167	.667
Hollandsworth	.222	9	2	0	2	1	1	.222	.222
Howard, Dave*	.200	5	1	0	0	0	1	.200	.200
Howard, T*	.353	17	6	0	1	0	2	.353	.529
Howell, Jack*	.200	10	2	1	2	1	1	.273	.500

Batter	Avg	AB	H	HR	BI	BB	SO	OBP	Slg
Hudler, Rex	.250	4	1	1	2	1	0	.400	1.000
Huff, Michael	.300	10	3	0	0	2	0	.417	.600
Hundley, Todd#	.111	9	1	1	1	0	4	.111	.444
Incaviglia, P	.000	4	0	0	1	0	1	.000	.000
Jaha, John	.320	25	8	1	7	1	6	.357	.520
James, Dion*	.269	26	7	0	3	6	1	.406	.269
Javier, Stan#	.150	20	3	0	0	2	4	.261	.150
Jefferies, G#	.167	18	3	0	1	1	1	.211	.278
Jefferson, R*	.389	18	7	0	3	1	0	.421	.444
Johnson, L*	.333	54	18	0	7	3	2	.368	.426
Jones, C#	.200	10	2	0	2	1	4	.273	.200
Joyner, Wally*	.288	52	15	0	7	4	6	.328	.365
Karkovice, R	.261	23	6	1	3	1	5	.346	.435
Karros, Eric	.444	9	4	1	4	1	0	.500	.778
Kelly, Pat	.077	13	1	0	0	0	2	.143	.077
Kelly, R	.190	21	4	0	0	2	3	.261	.190
Kendall, J	.500	8	4	0	1	0	0	.556	.625
King, Jeff	.091	11	1	0	0	0	4	.091	.091
Kingery, Mike*	.250	8	2	0	0	0	1	.250	.250
Kirby, Wayne*	.333	24	8	0	4	1	1	.360	.417
Klesko, Ryan*	.125	8	1	1	2	0	0	.125	.500
Knoblauch, C	.276	29	8	0	1	6	2	.400	.345
Knorr, Randy	.000	5	0	0	0	0	1	.000	.000
Kreuter, Chad#	.167	18	3	0	2	1	6	.211	.222
Lampkin, Tom*	.100	10	1	0	0	0	4	.100	.100
Lansing, Mike	.333	6	2	0	0	0	1	.333	.333
Larkin, Barry	.200	10	2	0	1	1	2	.273	.200
Leius, Scott	.375	8	3	1	4	0	2	.375	.750
Lemke, Mark#	.375	8	3	0	1	0	0	.375	.500
Liriano, N#	.182	11	2	0	0	0	1	.182	.182
Listach, Pat#	.318	22	7	0	1	1	5	.348	.409
Livingstone*	.227	22	5	0	1	2	5	.292	.227
Lofton, Kenny*	.333	39	13	1	4	4	3	.395	.564
Lopez, Javy	.125	8	1	1	2	0	0	.125	.500
Lovullo, T#	.333	9	3	1	1	2	3	.455	.667
Macfarlane, M	.235	17	4	0	3	0	6	.235	.294
Magadan, Dave*	.167	6	1	0	0	0	0	.167	.167
Martin, Al	.182	11	2	0	0	0	1	.182	.182
Martinez, E	.370	46	17	1	3	2	10	.408	.565
Martinez, T*	.118	34	4	0	0	1	6	.143	.118
Marzano, John	.200	5	1	0	1	0	0	.333	.200
Matheny, Mike	.167	6	1	0	0	1	1	.375	.167
Mayne, Brent*	.375	16	6	0	2	1	3	.444	.500
McGriff, Fred*	.296	27	8	1	2	3	8	.367	.444
McGwire, Mark	.156	32	5	1	2	4	8	.243	.250
McLemore, M#	.167	12	2	0	0	4	1	.375	.167
McRae, Brian#	.263	38	10	0	2	1	7	.300	.395
Meares, Pat	.400	5	2	0	0	0	1	.400	.400
Merced, O*	.100	10	1	0	0	0	0	.100	.100
Mitchell, K	.467	15	7	0	2	0	1	.467	.533
Molitor, Paul	.364	33	12	0	2	2	3	.400	.455
Mondesi, Raul	.111	9	1	0	0	0	1	.111	.111
Morandini, M*	.100	10	1	0	0	0	2	.100	.100
Morris, Hal*	.273	11	3	0	1	0	1	.250	.273
Munoz, Pedro	.238	21	5	0	3	2	5	.304	.286
Murray, Eddie#	.350	20	7	0	3	1	2	.381	.500
Myers, Greg*	.200	35	7	0	1	1	5	.222	.257
Naehring, Tim	.200	10	2	0	0	1	2	.273	.200
Newfield, M	.111	9	1	0	0	0	1	.200	.111
Newson, W*	.500	6	3	0	0	2	0	.625	.500
Nilsson, Dave*	.524	21	11	0	4	0	0	.524	.619
Nixon, Otis*	.182	11	2	0	1	0	2	.182	.182
O'Leary, Troy*	.833	6	5	1	4	1	0	.857	1.333
O'Neill, Paul*	.263	19	5	0	2	0	0	.263	.368
Olerud, John*	.457	35	16	1	8	3	5	.500	.657
Ordonez, Rey	.333	6	2	0	1	1	1	.429	.333
Orsulak, Joe*	.400	20	8	1	7	4	1	.500	.700
Otero, Ricky*	.125	8	1	0	0	0	3	.125	.125
Paquette, C	.000	8	0	0	0	0	1	.000	.000
Pena, Tony	.276	29	8	0	2	3	5	.344	.276
Phillips, J*	.000	4	0	0	0	1	1	.200	.000
Phillips, T#	.378	45	17	1	6	7	8	.472	.467
Piazza, Mike	.400	10	4	0	1	1	2	.455	.500
Plantier, P*	.250	4	1	0	0	1	1	.400	.250
Polonia, Luis*	.263	57	15	0	3	4	3	.311	.298
Raines, Tim#	.216	37	8	0	1	2	5	.275	.378
Ramirez, M	.333	9	3	0	1	0	3	.333	.444
Reboulet, J	.375	8	3	0	0	0	1	.375	.375
Reed, Jeff*	.000	3	0	0	0	1	1	.250	.000
Reed, Jody	.219	32	7	0	3	6	3	.342	.313
Ripken, Billy	.300	10	3	0	0	0	4	.300	.400
Ripken, Cal	.250	32	8	0	4	3	2	.351	.313
Rodriguez, H*	.167	6	1	0	0	0	1	.167	.167
Rodriguez, I	.167	6	1	0	0	0	0	.167	.333
Salmon, Tim	.467	15	7	0	2	1	3	.500	.600
Sanchez, Rey	.167	6	1	0	0	0	1	.167	.167
Sandberg, R	.250	8	2	0	0	0	2	.250	.375
Santangelo, F#	.500	6	3	0	0	2	1	.500	.500
Santiago, B	.000	6	0	0	0	0	0	.000	.000
Scarsone, S	.286	7	2	0	0	0	2	.286	.429
Schofield, D	.348	23	8	0	1	0	1	.375	.348

Batter	Avg	AB	H	HR	BI	BB	SO	OBP	Slg
Segui, David#	.083	12	1	0	1	1	0	.154	.167
Seitzer, K	.389	36	14	0	5	6	5	.488	.500
Servais, S	.000	5	0	0	0	0	0	.167	.000
Sheffield, G	.286	7	2	0	0	1	1	.375	.286
Shumpert, T	.176	17	3	0	0	0	5	.222	.176
Sierra, Ruben#	.308	26	8	0	3	0	4	.308	.346
Slaught, Don	.429	7	3	0	2	1	0	.444	.429
Snow, J.T.#	.462	13	6	0	2	1	3	.467	.462
Sojo, Luis	.333	18	6	0	1	1	2	.368	.389
Sorrento, P*	.154	39	6	3	5	4	7	.233	.385
Sosa, Sammy	.250	12	3	2	3	0	4	.250	.750
Spiers, Bill*	.211	19	4	1	2	3	5	.318	.368
Sprague, Ed	.364	11	4	0	2	0	1	.462	.545
Stankiewicz	.200	5	1	0	0	1	0	.429	.200
Stanley, Mike	.250	12	3	2	1	1	7	.308	.750
Steinbach, T	.194	31	6	0	5	0	5	.182	.194
Stevens, Lee*	.333	12	4	0	1	1	3	.385	.417
Stillwell, K#	.300	20	6	0	0	1	4	.333	.350
Stocker, K#	.000	8	0	0	0	0	2	.111	.000
Strange, Doug#	.308	13	4	0	1	0	2	.357	.308
Surhoff, B.J.*	.154	39	6	0	3	0	3	.175	.256
Sveum, Dale#	.143	7	1	0	0	0	0	.143	.143
Tartabull, D	.267	15	4	1	3	3	3	.368	.600
Taubensee, E*	.429	7	3	1	1	0	2	.429	.857
Tettleton, M#	.281	32	9	1	7	10	7	.465	.531
Thomas, Frank	.306	36	11	1	6	8	6	.422	.389
Thome, Jim*	.250	28	7	2	3	2	7	.300	.571
Tinsley, Lee#	.111	9	1	0	1	0	2	.111	.111
Tomberlin, A*	.143	7	1	0	0	1	0	.250	.143
Trammell, A	.313	32	10	0	3	0	2	.313	.375
Valentin, Jhn	.182	22	4	1	1	3	3	.280	.364
Valentin, Jse#	.200	5	1	0	0	1	3	.333	.200
Valle, Dave	.417	12	5	0	1	3	3	.588	.417
VanderWal, J*	.333	6	2	0	0	0	1	.333	.333
Vaughn, Greg	.171	41	7	1	3	4	16	.244	.244
Vaughn, Mo*	.333	30	10	3	5	4	4	.412	.633
Velarde, R	.083	12	1	0	0	1	3	.214	.083
Ventura, R*	.349	43	15	2	9	2	2	.370	.581
Vina, F*	.200	10	2	0	0	0	0	.200	.200
Vizquel, Omar#	.097	31	3	0	4	10	4	.310	.097
Walbeck, Matt#	.200	5	1	1	1	0	3	.200	.800
Ward, Turner#	.286	14	4	1	3	1	4	.333	.643
Weiss, Walt#	.273	11	3	0	0	2	2	.467	.273
White, Devon#	.158	38	6	1	3	2	9	.200	.263
Whiten, Mark#	.304	23	7	2	6	5	5	.429	.609
Williams, Ber#	.235	17	4	0	0	2	3	.316	.294
Williams, E	.000	5	0	0	0	0	1	.000	.000
Williams, Ma	.273	11	3	0	1	0	3	.273	.273
Wilson, Dan	.333	12	4	0	1	0	4	.333	.500
Worthington	.333	12	4	0	0	1	3	.385	.417
Zeile, Todd	.200	10	2	0	1	0	3	.200	.200

Batter	Avg	AB	H	HR	BI	BB	SO	OBP	Slg
Abbott, Kurt	.000	4	0	0	0	2	1	.333	.000
Alfonzo, E	.400	5	2	0	0	1	0	.500	.600
Alicea, Luis#	.429	7	3	0	2	0	1	.429	.571
Alou, Moises	.294	17	5	0	4	3	0	.294	.412
Andrews, S	.167	6	1	0	1	0	2	.167	.167
Anthony, Eric*	.250	8	2	0	1	2	2	.400	.250
Arias, Alex	.000	7	0	0	0	0	1	.000	.000
Ashley, Billy	.400	5	2	0	0	0	2	.400	.400
Ausmus, Brad	.000	9	0	0	0	0	4	.000	.000
Bagwell, Jeff	.429	14	6	1	5	5	3	.550	.786
Barberie, B#	.000	5	0	0	0	1	0	.167	.000
Batiste, Kim	.400	5	2	0	2	0	2	.400	.600
Bell, Derek	.167	6	1	0	0	1	1	.286	.167
Bell, Jay	.273	11	3	0	3	2	2	.385	.455
Belliard, R	.125	8	1	0	1	0	1	.111	.125
Benard, M*	.200	5	1	0	0	0	0	.200	.200
Benjamin, M	.400	5	2	0	0	2	0	.400	.400
Bichette, D	.294	17	5	1	3	1	2	.333	.471
Biggio, Craig	.294	17	5	0	0	1	2	.400	.294
Blauser, Jeff	.500	6	3	0	2	1	1	.500	.667
Bonds, Barry*	.364	11	4	1	3	3	3	.533	.727
Boone, Bret	.300	10	3	0	0	0	0	.385	.300
Branson, Jeff*	.364	11	4	1	1	3	1	.500	.727
Brogna, Rico*	.000	6	0	0	0	0	0	.000	.000
Brumfield, J	.167	6	1	0	0	1	1	.167	.167
Burks, Ellis	.400	5	2	1	2	1	0	.500	1.200
Butler, Brett*	.462	13	6	1	2	0	0	.462	.846
Caminiti, Ken#	.231	13	3	0	2	0	2	.231	.231
Cangelosi, J#	.167	6	1	0	1	1	0	.286	.167
Carr, Chuck	.250	4	1	0	0	1	1	.400	.500
Castilla, V	.500	6	3	1	5	2	0	.600	1.000
Cedeno, A	.667	6	4	2	4	0	0	.667	1.667
Cianfrocco, A	.250	8	2	0	0	0	2	.250	.250
Clark, Dave*	.000	5	0	0	0	2	2	.286	.000
Clark, Will*	.000	6	0	0	0	0	2	.000	.000
Clayton, R	.458	24	11	0	3	1	1	.480	.542
Colbrunn, G	.154	13	2	0	1	0	1	.214	.308

Batter	Avg	AB	H	HR	BI	BB	SO	OBP	Slg
Coleman, V#	.000	6	0	0	0	0	2	.000	.000
Conine, Jeff	.231	13	3	1	4	1	4	.286	.615
Cordero, Wil	.200	5	1	0	0	2	1	.429	.200
Daulton, D*	.500	6	3	0	1	4	0	.700	1.000
Davis, Eric	.250	4	1	0	0	2	1	.500	.250
DeShields, D*	.100	10	1	0	0	4	2	.357	.100
Duncan, M	.222	9	2	0	1	0	1	.222	.333
Dykstra, L*	.250	4	1	0	0	3	0	.571	.500
Eisenreich, J*	.000	8	0	0	0	2	1	.200	.000
Finley, Steve*	.333	12	4	0	1	3	2	.467	.417
Fletcher, D*	.333	12	4	0	2	2	0	.400	.667
Fonville, C#	.429	7	3	0	1	0	0	.429	.714
Gaetti, Gary	.500	2	1	0	0	2	1	.800	1.000
Galarraga, A	.368	19	7	2	4	0	4	.368	.684
Gallego, Mike	.000	5	0	0	0	2	2	.000	.000
Gant, Ron	.182	11	2	0	0	0	4	.250	.182
Garcia, C	.167	12	2	0	1	0	5	.167	.167
Gilkey, B	.259	27	7	0	1	4	4	.375	.296
Girardi, Joe	.000	4	0	0	0	1	1	.200	.000
Gonzalez, L*	.500	8	4	0	2	1	0	.556	.750
Greene, W*	.000	6	0	0	0	0	4	.000	.000
Grissom, M	.250	12	3	0	0	2	1	.357	.250
Grudzielanek	.333	6	2	1	2	1	0	.429	.833
Gutierrez, R	.000	4	0	0	0	1	1	.200	.000
Gwynn, Chris*	.200	5	1	0	0	0	0	.200	.200
Gwynn, Tony*	.182	11	2	0	1	1	0	.250	.182
Hansen, Dave*	.250	4	1	0	0	1	0	.400	.250
Harris, Lenny*	.286	7	2	0	0	0	1	.286	.286
Hayes, C	.200	10	2	0	0	3	2	.385	.200
Hill, G	.250	4	1	0	1	0	0	.400	.500
Hollins, Dave#	.000	5	0	0	0	1	1	.167	.000
Howard, T*	.182	11	2	0	0	0	3	.182	.273
Hubbard, Tr	.200	5	1	0	0	0	1	.200	.200
Hundley, Todd*	.286	7	2	0	1	1	0	.375	.286
Hunter, Bri L	.333	6	2	0	1	0	1	.333	.333
Incaviglia, P	.000	6	0	0	0	1	0	.143	.000
Jefferies, G#	.190	21	4	0	2	0	2	.190	.286
Johnson, L*	.286	7	2	0	2	0	0	.286	.571
Jones, C#	.400	10	4	2	3	2	1	.500	1.000
Jordan, Brian	.353	17	6	2	4	0	1	.353	.706
Justice, Dave*	.143	7	1	0	0	3	2	.400	.143
Karros, Eric	.250	20	5	1	3	0	3	.238	.450
Kelly, R	.000	6	0	0	0	1	1	.143	.000
Kent, Jeff	.500	8	4	0	0	1	0	.500	.625
King, Jeff	.429	7	3	0	1	0	0	.429	.429
Kingery, Mike*	.333	6	2	0	0	0	1	.333	.667
Klesko, Ryan*	.556	9	5	3	7	1	2	.600	1.778
Lankford, Ray*	.259	27	7	2	7	3	3	.333	.556
Lansing, Mike	.333	9	3	0	1	1	2	.400	.333
Larkin, Barry	.235	17	4	0	1	4	1	.364	.235
Lemke, Mark#	.167	12	2	0	2	2	0	.286	.333
Lewis, Darren	.286	7	2	0	3	1	1	.375	.714
Liriano, N#	.250	8	2	0	1	4	3	.500	.250
Livingstone*	.333	6	2	0	1	0	1	.333	.333
Lopez, Javy	.583	12	7	1	1	0	2	.583	.917
Mabry, John*	.364	11	4	0	1	3	0	.500	.364
Magadan, Dave*	.500	10	5	0	4	1	0	.545	.700
Manwaring, K	.182	11	2	1	3	1	0	.231	.455
Martin, Al*	.200	10	2	1	1	1	1	.273	.700
Martinez, Da*	.286	7	2	0	0	0	0	.286	.286
May, Derrick*	.500	6	3	0	2	1	0	.571	.500
McCracken, Q#	.429	7	3	0	2	0	0	.429	.571
McGee, Willie#	.286	7	2	0	1	0	1	.286	.286
McGriff, Fred*	.250	16	4	1	3	0	6	.235	.438
Merced, O*	.200	10	2	1	2	1	0	.273	.500
Mondesi, Raul	.286	14	4	1	3	4	4	.412	.357
Morandini, M*	.167	12	2	0	0	1	1	.286	.167
Morris, Hal	.357	14	5	0	1	3	3	.471	.500
Newfield, M	.250	4	1	0	1	1	1	.400	.250
Offerman, J#	.333	12	4	0	1	0	0	.385	.333
Ordonez, Rey	.000	4	0	0	0	1	0	.000	.000
Orsulak, Joe*	.000	6	0	0	0	0	0	.000	.000
Otero, Ricky#	.200	5	1	0	1	0	1	.200	.200
Pagnozzi, Tom	.421	19	8	0	4	0	4	.421	.474
Pena, G#	.385	13	5	1	5	2	1	.471	.846
Pendleton, T#	.143	7	1	0	1	3	0	.455	.143
Piazza, Mike	.385	13	5	1	4	1	3	.429	.615
Plantier, P*	.000	5	0	0	0	1	0	.167	.000
Prince, Tom	.333	6	2	0	2	0	0	.333	.500
Reed, Jeff*	.250	8	2	0	1	0	0	.250	.375
Reed, Jody	.222	9	2	0	0	1	0	.300	.222
Rodriguez, H*	.111	9	1	1	1	2	3	.333	.444
Sanders, R	.400	10	4	0	2	1	3	.538	.500
Santangelo, F#	.667	6	4	1	5	0	1	.667	1.500
Santiago, B	.200	10	2	0	0	1	0	.273	.400
Scarsone, S	.500	4	2	1	1	1	0	.600	1.250
Segui, David*	.000	6	0	0	1	1	0	.125	.000
Servais, J	.167	6	1	0	0	0	2	.167	.167
Sheaffer, D	.000	5	0	0	0	1	1	.167	.000
Sheffield, G	.250	12	3	1	2	3	1	.400	.500
Shipley, C	.000	6	0	0	0	1	1	.143	.000

Batter	Avg	AB	H	HR	BI	BB	SO	OBP	Slg
Slaught, Don	.167	6	1	0	1	0	1	.167	.167
Smith, Dwight*	.500	4	2	0	0	2	0	.667	.750
Smith, Ozzie#	.125	8	1	0	1	3	0	.333	.125
Stocker, K#	.500	6	3	0	0	1	2	.571	.500
Sweeney, Mark*	.167	6	1	0	0	0	1	.167	.167
Tarasco, Tony*	.333	6	2	0	1	1	0	.429	.333
Taubensee, E*	.444	9	4	0	1	1	2	.500	.556
Thompson, Rob	.000	5	0	0	0	1	0	.000	.000
VanderWal, J*	.143	7	1	0	0	1	1	.250	.143
Vizcaino, J#	.222	9	2	0	1	0	0	.222	.444
Walker, Larry*	.286	7	2	0	0	2	0	.444	.286
Wallach, Tim	.286	14	4	2	3	1	3	.333	.714
Weiss, Walt#	.125	16	2	0	1	3	4	.263	.188
White, Devon#	.250	4	1	0	1	1	0	.333	.250
White, R	.375	8	3	0	1	0	0	.444	.375
Whiten, Mark#	.125	8	1	0	0	1	3	.222	.125
Wilkins, Rick*	.500	4	2	0	1	2	0	.667	.750
Williams, Ma	.133	15	2	0	1	2	8	.222	.133
Young, Eric	.211	19	4	2	4	0	2	.211	.579
Zeile, Todd	.235	17	4	0	1	4	3	.381	.412

Batter	Avg	AB	H	HR	BI	BB	SO	OBP	Slg
Alicea, Luis*	.000	3	0	0	0	2	1	.400	.000
Alou, Moises	.294	17	5	2	4	2	4	.368	.647
Andrews, S	.600	5	3	1	4	2	2	.714	1.600
Anthony, Eric*	.333	6	2	0	0	2	0	.500	.833
Ausmus, Brad	.143	7	1	0	0	0	3	.143	.143
Bagwell, Jeff	.071	14	1	0	1	5	2	.316	.143
Barberie, B#	.250	8	2	0	1	0	2	.250	.250
Bates, Jason#	.250	4	1	1	1	1	0	.400	1.000
Batiste, Kim	.000	4	0	0	0	0	1	.200	.000
Bell, David	.200	5	1	0	1	0	2	.200	.400
Bell, Derek	.200	10	2	1	2	3	3	.357	.500
Bell, Jay	.364	11	4	0	1	2	2	.500	.364
Benard, M*	.200	5	1	0	0	1	1	.333	.400
Berry, Sean	.000	7	0	0	1	0	2	.000	.000
Bichette, D	.313	16	5	2	4	2	6	.421	.750
Biggio, Craig	.250	20	5	1	2	5	2	.400	.450
Blauser, Jeff	.400	5	2	0	3	4	2	.667	1.000
Blowers, Mike	.200	5	1	0	0	0	1	.200	.200
Bonds, Barry*	.333	9	3	1	2	1	1	.400	.889
Bonilla, B#	.667	6	4	2	6	2	0	.750	1.833
Boone, Bret	.167	6	1	0	0	1	2	.286	.167
Branson, Jeff*	.000	5	0	0	0	0	2	.000	.000
Brogna, Rico*	.286	7	2	0	1	1	1	.375	.286
Burks, Ellis	.444	9	4	0	1	1	5	.500	.556
Butler, Brett*	.200	10	2	0	1	0	1	.200	.300
Caminiti, Ken#	.188	16	3	0	2	1	6	.211	.313
Candaele, C#	.250	8	2	0	1	0	1	.250	.250
Carr, Chuck	.600	5	3	0	1	0	0	.600	.600
Castilla, V	.333	15	5	0	3	1	0	.375	.533
Cedeno, A	.333	6	2	0	0	1	0	.429	.333
Cianfrocco, A	.429	7	3	0	2	0	3	.429	.571
Clark, Dave*	.267	15	4	0	2	0	5	.267	.267
Clayton, R	.200	5	1	0	0	0	1	.200	.200
Colbrunn, G	.200	10	2	0	0	2	3	.333	.300
Conine, Jeff	.083	12	1	0	0	2	4	.214	.083
Cordero, Wil	.167	12	2	0	1	1	4	.231	.250
Daulton, D*	.000	5	0	0	0	2	2	.286	.000
Dawson, Andre	.667	6	4	1	6	0	0	.571	1.333
DeShields, D*	.227	22	5	0	1	1	1	.261	.227
Dorsett, B	.250	4	1	0	0	1	0	.400	.250
Duncan, M	.750	4	3	1	2	1	1	.800	1.500
Dunston, S	.000	6	0	0	0	0	3	.000	.000
Dykstra, L*	.250	8	2	0	0	1	1	.333	.250
Eisenreich, J*	.400	5	2	0	0	0	0	.400	.600
Encarnacion	.167	6	1	0	0	0	0	.167	.333
Eusebio, Tony	.667	3	2	0	1	3	0	.833	1.000
Everett, Carl#	.286	7	2	0	2	1	1	.375	.286
Finley, Steve*	.190	21	4	0	0	1	1	.227	.238
Flaherty, J	.333	6	2	0	1	0	0	.333	.333
Fletcher, D*	.474	19	9	0	7	0	2	.474	.579
Gagne, Greg	.500	4	2	0	1	0	1	.600	.500
Galarraga, A	.313	16	5	0	2	1	7	.389	.375
Gant, Ron	.375	8	3	0	3	1	1	.444	.375
Garcia, C	.412	17	7	0	1	2	5	.474	.412
Gilkey, B	.600	15	9	1	4	0	1	.563	1.067
Girardi, Joe	.357	14	5	0	1	2	3	.438	.500
Gomez, Chris	.167	6	1	1	1	0	2	.167	.667
Gomez, Leo	.250	8	2	1	1	5	1	.333	.750
Gonzalez, J	.600	6	3	1	5	0	1	.500	1.167
Gonzalez, L*	.211	19	4	0	3	2	4	.286	.316
Grace, Mark*	.304	23	7	0	1	3	4	.385	.391
Grebeck, C	.714	7	5	0	3	2	0	.700	1.286
Grissom, M	.333	21	7	1	2	0	6	.333	.476
Grudzielanek	.083	12	1	0	0	0	0	.083	.083
Gutierrez, R	.375	8	3	0	1	1	0	.444	.375
Gwynn, Tony*	.471	17	8	0	1	2	1	.526	.529
Hayes, C	.333	15	5	2	6	1	4	.375	.733
Hernandez, Jo	.100	10	1	0	2	0	5	.100	.300

Dave Burba, Reds — RHP

Batter	Avg	AB	H	HR	BI	BB	SO	OBP	Slg
Hill, G	.400	5	2	0	2	1	1	.500	.600
Hollandsworth*	.222	9	2	0	0	1	3	.300	.333
Hollins, Dave#	.250	4	1	0	0	3	1	.571	.250
Hundley, Todd#	.143	7	1	0	2	6	4	.538	.286
Hunter, Brian	.200	5	1	0	2	1	1	.333	.400
Hunter, Bri L	.500	6	3	0	0	1	0	.571	.500
Incaviglia, P	.294	17	5	2	8	0	7	.294	.706
Jefferies, G#	.222	9	2	0	2	1	1	.300	.222
Johnson, Bri	.600	5	3	0	2	1	0	.667	.800
Johnson, Char	.500	4	2	0	2	1	1	.500	.750
Johnson, L*	.500	12	6	0	0	1	1	.538	.667
Jones, C#	.222	9	2	1	1	1	2	.300	.556
Jordan, Brian	.200	10	2	0	0	0	3	.200	.300
Joyner, Wally*	.250	8	2	1	2	1	0	.333	.625
Justice, Dave*	.429	7	3	1	3	2	2	.556	.857
Karros, Eric	.211	19	4	2	3	2	4	.286	.526
Kelly, R	.571	7	4	0	2	1	3	.625	.714
Kent, Jeff	.333	18	6	1	4	0	2	.333	.500
King, Jeff	.333	15	5	0	1	5	0	.476	.467
Kingery, Mike*	.333	9	3	0	1	0	0	.333	.333
Klesko, Ryan*	.400	5	2	1	1	0	1	.400	1.000
Lankford, Ray*	.545	11	6	0	2	0	0	.615	.636
Lansing, Mike	.353	17	6	0	0	2	3	.421	.412
Larkin, Barry	.000	3	0	0	0	4	2	.571	.000
Lemke, Mark#	.400	10	4	1	2	1	1	.417	.800
Liriano, N#	.300	10	3	0	2	1	2	.364	.400
Livingstone*	.400	5	2	0	0	0	0	.400	.600
Lopez, Javy	.500	4	2	1	2	0	1	.400	1.250
Lopez, Luis#	.000	4	0	0	0	1	1	.200	.000
Mabry, John*	.500	6	3	0	1	0	1	.500	.500
Magadan, Dave*	.214	14	3	0	1	2	2	.313	.214
Martin, Al*	.333	18	6	0	1	3	2	.429	.556
May, Derrick*	.267	15	4	1	1	1	1	.353	.600
McGriff, Fred*	.077	13	1	1	2	4	3	.294	.308
McRae, Brian#	.143	14	2	1	1	3	3	.333	.429
Merced, O*	.267	15	4	1	5	1	0	.313	.533
Miller, Orl	.200	5	1	0	2	1	1	.333	.200
Mitchell, K	.500	4	2	0	1	2	1	.667	1.000
Mondesi, Raul	.214	14	3	0	0	4	8	.389	.214
Morandini, M*	.111	9	1	0	1	2	0	.250	.333
Murray, Eddie*	.200	5	1	0	2	0	1	.200	.200
O'Brien, C	.333	6	2	0	2	0	1	.333	.333
Offerman, J#	.200	5	1	0	2	0	3	.444	.200
Ordonez, Rey	.167	6	1	0	0	0	1	.167	.333
Orsulak, Joe*	.143	7	1	0	0	0	1	.143	.143
Otero, Ricky*	.333	6	2	0	0	0	0	.333	.500
Pagnozzi, Tom	.111	9	1	0	0	3	0	.111	.111
Palmeiro, R*	.333	3	1	0	0	2	0	.600	.333
Pendleton, T#	.267	15	4	1	3	2	4	.353	.533
Piazza, Mike	.375	16	6	2	5	2	0	.421	.813
Raines, Tim#	.250	4	1	0	0	1	1	.400	.250
Reed, Jody	.125	16	2	0	1	0	2	.125	.125
Renteria, E	.286	7	2	0	0	1	0	.375	.286
Roberts, Bip#	.000	7	0	0	0	1	1	.125	.000
Rodriguez, H*	.462	13	6	0	3	4	3	.588	.615
Sabo, Chris	.000	4	0	0	0	1	1	.200	.000
Sanchez, Rey	.154	13	2	0	0	2	4	.267	.154
Sandberg, R	.364	22	8	0	1	1	5	.391	.455
Sanders, R*	.400	10	4	1	4	0	5	.400	.900
Santangelo, F#	.000	3	0	0	0	1	1	.400	.000
Santiago, B	.056	18	1	0	0	4	5	.227	.056
Segui, David*	.000	8	0	0	0	0	0	.000	.000
Servais, Jim	.273	11	3	0	1	0	3	.250	.364
Sheaffer, D	.250	8	2	0	0	2	2	.250	.375
Sheffield, G	.400	10	4	1	4	3	1	.500	.800
Shipley, C	.167	6	1	0	2	0	3	.167	.333
Sierra, Ruben#	.333	3	1	0	0	2	0	.600	.333
Slaught, Don	.250	4	1	0	1	1	1	.400	.250
Smith, Dwight*	.167	6	1	0	0	0	1	.286	.167
Smith, Ozzie#	.333	9	3	0	1	1	1	.400	.444
Sosa, Sammy	.077	26	2	0	1	10	5	.111	.077
Spiers, Bill*	.429	7	3	0	1	0	0	.429	.429
Stocker, K#	.000	7	0	0	0	5	0	.000	.000
Sweeney, Mark*	.667	3	2	0	2	3	1	.833	.667
Tarasco, Tony*	.500	4	2	0	1	1	0	.600	.500
Taubensee, E*	.143	7	1	0	0	2	2	.143	.143
Thomas, Frank	.200	5	1	1	1	0	0	.200	.800
Thompson, Mil*	.200	10	2	1	2	0	3	.333	.600
Thompson, Ry	.125	8	1	0	1	0	3	.200	.125
VanderWal, J*	.400	10	4	0	4	1	0	.455	.400
Vaughn, Greg	.000	7	0	0	0	2	0	.222	.000
Ventura, R*	.400	5	2	1	1	0	0	.400	1.200
Vizcaino, J#	.143	21	3	0	1	0	3	.143	.286
Walker, Larry*	.467	15	7	1	2	2	1	.556	.733
Wallach, Tim	.000	10	0	0	0	1	3	.091	.000
Webster, L	.250	4	1	0	0	0	1	.400	.250
Weiss, Walt#	.250	12	3	0	1	1	2	.286	.333
White, Devon#	.250	8	2	0	0	1	1	.333	.625
White, R	.500	5	1	0	0	1	1	.333	.200
Whiten, Mark#	.000	5	0	0	0	4	1	.444	.000
Wilkins, Rick*	.100	10	1	0	1	2	4	.250	.200

Dave Burba, Reds — RHP

Batter	Avg	AB	H	HR	BI	BB	SO	OBP	Slg
Young, Eric	.545	11	6	0	1	2	1	.615	.727
Young, Kevin	.333	3	1	0	0	0	2	.333	.333
Zeile, Todd	.077	13	1	0	1	4	3	.278	.154

John Burkett, Rangers — RHP

Batter	Avg	AB	H	HR	BI	BB	SO	OBP	Slg
Aldrete, Mike*	.167	12	2	0	2	1	1	.231	.167
Alicea, Luis#	.100	10	1	0	0	1	1	.250	.100
Alomar, R#	.000	5	0	0	0	1	0	.167	.000
Alomar Jr, S	.200	5	1	0	0	0	1	.200	.400
Alou, Moises	.421	19	8	1	4	3	1	.500	.737
Amaro, Ruben*	.000	6	0	0	0	0	1	.000	.000
Anderson, G*	.333	6	2	1	2	0	1	.333	.833
Anthony, Eric*	.241	29	7	1	3	1	4	.267	.345
Aurilia, Rich	.200	5	1	1	1	0	0	.200	.800
Ausmus, Brad	.250	16	4	1	2	0	1	.250	.563
Bagwell, Jeff	.400	40	16	1	5	6	8	.490	.575
Barberie, B#	.375	8	3	0	2	0	1	.500	.375
Bell, Derek	.250	12	3	0	1	0	1	.250	.333
Bell, Jay	.171	35	6	0	3	0	7	.194	.171
Belle, Albert	.500	4	2	0	1	1	1	.600	.500
Belliard, R	.188	16	3	0	0	2	3	.350	.188
Benard, M*	.222	9	2	0	0	1	0	.300	.222
Berry, Sean	.385	13	5	1	3	1	2	.429	.615
Bichette, D	.185	27	5	1	3	1	3	.214	.296
Biggio, Craig	.286	63	18	1	4	4	6	.328	.397
Blauser, Jeff	.350	40	14	1	4	5	1	.435	.475
Bonds, Barry*	.278	36	10	4	10	9	4	.422	.722
Bonilla, B#	.361	36	13	1	8	5	3	.429	.583
Boone, Bret	.083	12	1	0	1	0	2	.214	.083
Branson, Jeff*	.200	15	3	0	0	0	5	.200	.200
Brogna, Rico*	.294	17	5	1	4	2	5	.350	.529
Brumfield, J	.100	10	1	0	0	0	1	.100	.100
Bullett, S*	.500	4	2	0	0	1	0	.600	.500
Burks, Ellis	.308	13	4	0	1	3	2	.438	.308
Burnitz, J*	.400	10	4	0	2	1	3	.500	.700
Butler, Brett*	.286	35	10	1	2	2	7	.324	.400
Caminiti, Ken#	.362	47	17	1	2	3	3	.400	.447
Candaele, C#	.318	22	7	1	4	0	2	.348	.545
Carr, Chuck	.429	7	3	0	0	0	0	.429	.429
Carreon, Mark	.556	18	10	1	7	0	2	.579	.833
Carter, Joe	.200	10	2	0	0	0	3	.273	.300
Castilla, V	.250	24	6	0	0	0	2	.250	.333
Clark, Dave*	.231	13	3	0	3	1	0	.286	.308
Clayton, R	.125	8	1	0	0	0	0	.125	.125
Cole, Alex*	.250	16	4	0	4	0	1	.250	.375
Coleman, V#	.583	12	7	0	0	2	0	.643	.583
Conine, Jeff	.250	8	2	0	0	1	2	.333	.250
Cordero, Wil	.467	15	7	3	6	1	1	.500	1.200
Damon, Johnny*	.167	6	1	0	0	1	1	.286	.167
Daulton, D*	.391	23	9	0	5	7	3	.500	.522
Davis, Chili#	.167	6	1	0	0	0	1	.167	.167
Davis, Eric	.208	24	5	1	3	2	5	.296	.333
Dawson, Andre	.357	14	5	0	1	0	2	.357	.357
Delgado, C*	.167	6	1	0	0	1	3	.286	.167
DeShields, D*	.325	40	13	0	1	2	6	.357	.425
DiSarcina, G	.333	6	2	0	0	0	0	.333	.500
Dorsett, B	.000	4	0	0	0	1	1	.200	.000
Duncan, M	.179	28	5	0	0	0	6	.179	.214
Dunston, S	.344	32	11	2	3	0	2	.344	.563
Dykstra, L*	.276	29	8	0	2	4	5	.353	.379
Eisenreich, J*	.250	28	7	0	2	1	5	.276	.250
Elster, Kevin	.250	4	1	0	1	1	2	.333	.250
Fabregas, Jor*	.000	6	0	0	0	0	1	.000	.000
Finley, Steve*	.273	55	15	1	5	2	7	.298	.473
Fletcher, D*	.174	23	4	0	1	1	3	.200	.217
Floyd, Cliff*	.143	7	1	0	0	0	1	.143	.286
Frazier, Lou#	.143	7	1	0	0	2	2	.143	.143
Gagne, Greg	.333	6	2	0	0	0	0	.333	.500
Galarraga, A	.206	34	7	0	4	0	6	.206	.235
Gant, Ron	.308	52	16	2	12	3	11	.345	.481
Garcia, C	.385	13	5	1	4	2	0	.467	.692
Gilkey, B	.207	29	6	0	1	0	8	.233	.276
Girardi, Joe	.286	21	6	0	5	1	3	.304	.333
Gonzalez, A	.167	6	1	0	1	0	1	.167	.167
Gonzalez, L*	.315	54	17	0	7	0	5	.309	.407
Grace, Mark*	.237	38	9	0	2	4	2	.310	.263
Green, Shawn*	.286	7	2	0	0	0	2	.286	.286
Greene, W*	.167	6	1	0	0	1	2	.286	.167
Grissom, M	.300	40	12	0	3	4	3	.364	.400
Gutierrez, R	.091	11	1	0	2	1	1	.167	.091
Gwynn, Tony*	.290	31	9	0	5	3	2	.343	.355
Hansen, Dave*	.400	15	6	1	6	0	3	.375	.667
Harris, Lenny*	.241	29	7	0	2	2	4	.290	.310
Hayes, C	.216	37	8	1	1	1	8	.237	.351
Henderson, R	.167	6	1	0	0	2	1	.375	.167
Hill, G	.389	18	7	1	5	0	4	.389	.556
Hollandsworth*	.500	6	3	0	2	0	0	.500	.667
Hollins, Dave#	.308	26	8	1	6	3	4	.367	.462
Howard, T*	.214	14	3	0	0	0	3	.214	.214

34

Batter	Avg	AB	H	HR	BI	BB	SO	OBP	Slg
Howell, Jack*	.125	8	1	0	0	0	2	.125	.125
Hudler, Rex	.429	7	3	1	1	0	0	.429	.857
Hundley, Todd#	.250	24	6	2	4	1	5	.269	.583
Hunter, Brian	.083	12	1	0	0	0	0	.083	.167
Huskey, Butch	.167	6	1	1	1	0	0	.167	.667
Hyers, Tim*	.429	7	3	0	0	0	0	.429	.429
Incaviglia, P	.167	6	1	0	1	0	0	.167	.167
Javier, Stan#	.600	10	6	0	0	1	1	.636	.600
Jefferies, G#	.324	34	11	0	2	1	2	.343	.324
Johnson, L*	.000	6	0	0	0	1	0	.143	.000
Jones, C#	.400	15	6	0	6	2	4	.444	.600
Jones, Chris	.250	4	1	0	0	2	0	.500	.250
Jordan, Brian	.304	23	7	0	1	1	3	.333	.391
Jordan, Ricky	.417	12	5	1	1	1	3	.462	.667
Justice, Dave*	.244	41	10	1	3	8	5	.320	.467
Karros, Eric	.179	28	5	0	2	1	8	.233	.250
Kelly, R	.286	14	4	1	3	1	2	.333	.500
Kendall, J	.167	6	1	0	0	0	1	.167	.167
Kent, Jeff	.407	27	11	2	5	1	4	.429	.704
King, Jeff	.267	30	8	2	6	0	4	.267	.600
Kingery, Mike*	.000	14	0	0	0	0	2	.000	.000
Klesko, Ryan*	.200	25	5	2	4	1	7	.231	.520
Lampkin, Tom*	.000	4	0	0	0	1	1	.200	.000
Lankford, Ray*	.319	47	15	4	8	5	8	.385	.596
Lansing, Mike	.412	17	7	0	1	1	0	.421	.471
Larkin, Barry	.306	36	11	2	4	4	5	.390	.556
Lemke, Mark#	.238	42	10	0	2	2	3	.273	.286
Lewis, Darren	.000	5	0	0	0	1	1	.286	.000
Liriano, N#	.429	14	6	0	1	2	0	.500	.571
Livingstone*	.625	8	5	1	1	0	0	.625	1.000
Lockhart, K*	.167	6	1	0	1	0	0	.143	.333
Lofton, Kenny*	.273	11	3	0	1	2	2	.385	.273
Lopez, Javy	.278	18	5	1	2	1	1	.350	.444
Mabry, John*	.273	11	3	0	1	0	0	.250	.273
Magadan, Dave*	.240	25	6	0	5	2	3	.296	.360
Manwaring, N	.333	6	2	0	1	1	1	.429	.500
Martin, Al*	.350	20	7	0	2	0	4	.350	.550
Martinez, Da*	.391	23	9	0	2	0	1	.391	.522
Martinez, S*	.400	5	2	0	0	1	1	.500	.400
May, Derrick*	.211	19	4	1	2	0	3	.211	.421
McGriff, Fred*	.267	45	12	1	6	6	11	.353	.378
McRae, Brian#	.125	8	1	0	0	1	2	.222	.125
Merced, O*	.176	34	6	0	2	2	5	.243	.176
Miller, Orl	.500	6	3	0	1	0	2	.500	.833
Mitchell, K	.308	13	4	0	1	1	2	.357	.462
Mondesi, Raul	.300	10	3	2	3	2	0	.417	.900
Morandini, M*	.256	39	10	0	2	3	5	.310	.308
Morris, Hal*	.342	38	13	2	5	5	1	.419	.526
Mouton, James	.000	7	0	0	0	0	0	.000	.000
Murray, Eddie#	.385	26	10	2	6	2	3	.414	.654
Newfield, M	.300	10	3	0	1	0	1	.300	.300
Nieves, M*	.200	5	1	0	1	2	2	.429	.200
Nixon, Otis*	.188	16	3	0	0	3	2	.316	.250
O'Brien, C	.182	11	2	1	1	1	0	.308	.455
O'Neill, Paul*	.290	31	9	1	6	4	3	.313	.419
Offerman, J#	.355	31	11	0	3	2	10	.394	.452
Olerud, John*	.000	6	0	0	0	2	0	.000	.000
Oliver, Joe	.083	12	1	0	0	0	3	.083	.083
Ordonez, Rey	.000	4	0	0	0	1	0	.200	.000
Orsulak, Joe*	.091	11	1	0	0	1	0	.091	.091
Otero, Ricky#	.400	5	2	0	0	1	0	.500	.600
Pagnozzi, Tom	.261	23	6	0	4	1	1	.292	.391
Paquette, C	.571	7	4	0	1	0	0	.571	.571
Parent, Mark	.200	5	1	0	0	0	0	.200	.200
Pena, G#	.143	14	2	0	0	1	4	.200	.143
Pendleton, T#	.268	41	11	1	1	2	6	.302	.366
Piazza, Mike	.250	24	6	1	6	2	4	.308	.417
Plantier, P*	.333	6	2	1	2	0	1	.333	.833
Raines, Tim#	.143	7	1	0	0	2	0	.333	.143
Ramirez, M	.400	5	2	0	1	0	1	.400	.600
Reed, Jeff*	.278	18	5	1	4	1	1	.316	.500
Reed, Jody	.200	15	3	0	1	3	3	.333	.267
Roberts, Bip#	.353	34	12	0	3	3	3	.405	.441
Rodriguez, H*	.250	20	5	0	0	2	0	.250	.300
Sabo, Chris	.333	33	11	1	5	4	6	.405	.545
Salmon, Tim	.429	7	3	0	2	1	1	.500	.429
Samuel, Juan	.167	18	3	0	2	2	4	.238	.167
Sanchez, Rey	.313	16	5	0	2	1	2	.353	.375
Sandberg, R	.381	21	8	1	1	1	2	.409	.524
Sanders, R	.087	23	2	0	4	2	2	.148	.130
Santiago, B	.484	31	15	1	2	1	2	.515	.613
Scarsone, S	.250	12	3	0	2	0	5	.250	.333
Schall, Gene	.167	6	1	0	1	1	2	.286	.167
Schofield, D	.400	5	2	0	1	1	1	.500	.600
Segui, David#	.222	9	2	0	0	1	1	.300	.333
Servais, S	.154	13	2	1	2	0	3	.214	.385
Sheaffer, S	.333	6	2	0	0	0	0	.333	.333
Sheffield, G	.417	12	5	3	6	1	0	.462	1.250
Slaught, Don	.333	9	3	0	1	0	0	.400	.444
Smith, Dwight*	.143	21	3	0	1	0	4	.143	.143
Smith, Ozzie#	.278	36	10	0	3	3	0	.333	.389

Batter	Avg	AB	H	HR	BI	BB	SO	OBP	Slg
Snow, J.T.#	.000	6	0	0	0	0	1	.000	.000
Sosa, Sammy	.214	28	6	1	5	0	9	.214	.429
Sprague, Ed	.286	7	2	0	0	0	0	.286	.429
Stillwell, K#	.500	6	3	0	0	0	1	.500	.667
Stocker, K#	.188	16	3	0	1	2	3	.278	.313
Strange, Doug*	.000	4	0	0	0	1	2	.200	.000
Strawberry, D*	.625	8	5	1	5	2	1	.700	1.250
Sweeney, Mark*	.600	5	3	1	2	1	0	.667	1.600
Sweeney, Mike	.167	6	1	0	0	0	0	.167	.167
Tarasco, Tony*	.250	8	2	1	5	0	1	.250	.875
Tatum, Jimmy	.200	5	1	0	0	0	1	.200	.200
Taubensee, E*	.273	33	9	0	6	0	7	.273	.364
Thome, Jim*	.500	4	2	0	3	1	1	.500	.750
Thompson, Mil*	.308	39	12	2	6	1	4	.341	.487
Thompson, Rob	.250	12	3	0	0	0	5	.250	.333
Thompson, Ry	.455	11	5	0	3	1	2	.500	.727
Thompsons, O	.000	5	0	0	0	0	0	.600	1.500
Tucker, M*	.000	5	0	0	0	2	0	.286	.000
VanderWal, J*	.571	7	4	0	3	0	1	.571	1.000
Velarde, R	.125	8	1	0	0	0	3	.125	.250
Vizcaino, J#	.372	43	16	0	2	2	4	.400	.535
Vizquel, Omar*	.600	5	3	0	1	0	0	.600	1.000
Walker, Larry*	.425	40	17	4	12	2	6	.465	.850
Wallach, Tim	.348	23	8	2	4	5	4	.448	.609
Webster, L	.600	5	3	1	1	1	0	.667	1.400
Weiss, Walt#	.393	28	11	0	4	4	1	.485	.393
Whiten, Mark#	.192	26	5	0	2	2	14	.250	.231
Wilkins, Rick*	.263	19	5	0	1	1	6	.300	.316
Williams, Ma	.286	14	4	1	2	2	2	.375	.500
Wilson, Dan	.286	7	2	0	0	0	0	.286	.286
Young, Eric	.520	25	13	0	3	1	0	.556	.720
Young, Kevin	.222	9	2	1	3	0	2	.222	.556
Zeile, Todd	.244	45	11	2	6	5	11	.320	.444

Terry Burrows, Brewers   LHP

Batter	Avg	AB	H	HR	BI	BB	SO	OBP	Slg
Baerga, C#	.400	5	2	1	1	0	0	.400	1.200
Belle, Albert	.500	4	2	0	0	1	1	.600	.500
Goodwin, Tom*	.750	4	3	0	0	1	1	.800	.750
O'Neill, Paul*	.333	6	2	0	1	0	0	.333	.333
Ramirez, M	.333	3	1	0	1	2	0	.600	.333
Thome, Jim*	.400	5	2	1	4	0	1	.400	1.000
Vizquel, Omar*	.143	7	1	0	1	0	2	.143	.143
Williams, Ber*	.600	5	3	1	2	0	0	.600	1.200

Paul Byrd, Mets   RHP

Batter	Avg	AB	H	HR	BI	BB	SO	OBP	Slg
Biggio, Craig	.000	5	0	0	0	0	0	.000	.000

Mike Campbell, Cubs   RHP

Batter	Avg	AB	H	HR	BI	BB	SO	OBP	Slg
Baines, H*	.167	12	2	0	0	4	2	.375	.167
Boggs, Wade*	.500	8	4	0	0	0	1	.500	.750
Borders, Pat	.200	5	1	1	1	0	1	.200	.800
Burks, Ellis	.125	8	1	0	0	0	3	.125	.250
Caminiti, Ken*	.200	5	1	1	2	0	0	.200	.800
Carter, Joe	.286	7	2	0	0	0	1	.286	.286
Clark, Dave*	.000	5	0	0	0	1	2	.167	.000
Davis, Chili#	.333	6	2	0	1	0	1	.333	.500
Deer, Rob	.667	6	4	1	2	3	1	.778	1.500
Eisenreich, J*	.167	6	1	0	1	1	0	.143	.167
Franco, Julio	.333	6	2	0	1	0	0	.286	.333
Greenwell, M*	.800	5	4	2	5	0	0	.800	2.000
Guillen, O*	.118	17	2	0	0	1	0	.118	.118
Hamilton, D*	.400	5	2	0	1	0	0	.400	.600
Henderson, R*	.154	13	2	0	1	1	0	.214	.154
Howell, Jack*	.000	4	0	0	0	0	0	.200	.000
Johnson, L*	.250	8	2	0	0	0	0	.250	.375
Joyner, Wally*	.286	7	2	0	1	0	1	.286	.286
Liriano, N#	.286	7	2	0	0	0	3	.500	.400
McGriff, Fred*	.571	7	4	3	5	1	1	.625	1.857
McLemore, Mark*	.400	5	2	0	0	2	0	.571	.600
Molitor, Paul	.600	10	6	0	0	2	1	.667	.700
Seitzer, K	.571	7	4	1	1	0	0	.571	1.143
Sheffield, G	.000	4	0	0	0	1	0	.000	.000
Sierra, Ruben#	.375	8	3	0	0	1	3	.375	.375
Surhoff, B.J.*	.111	9	1	0	1	1	3	.200	.111
Tartabull, D	.333	6	2	0	0	1	3	.429	.333
Velarde, R	.200	5	1	0	0	1	1	.333	.400
Weiss, Walt*	.000	3	0	0	0	2	2	.400	.000
White, Devon#	.143	7	1	0	2	0	1	.143	.143

Tom Candiotti, Dodgers   RHP

Batter	Avg	AB	H	HR	BI	BB	SO	OBP	Slg
Abbott, Kurt	.111	9	1	0	0	0	3	.200	.222
Alfonzo, E	.286	14	4	0	0	1	0	.286	.286
Alicea, Luis*	.167	18	3	0	0	4	4	.318	.167
Alomar, R#	.000	7	0	0	0	0	0	.000	.000
Alou, Moises	.111	18	2	1	2	3	3	.227	.278
Amaro, Ruben#	.400	5	2	0	0	0	1	.400	.400
Anderson, Brd*	.250	8	2	0	1	0	1	.250	.250

Tom Candiotti, Dodgers — RHP

Batter	Avg	AB	H	HR	BI	BB	SO	OBP	Slg
Anthony, Eric*	.375	16	6	1	1	0	4	.375	.563
Arias, Alex	.000	5	0	0	0	2	1	.400	.000
Ausmus, Brad	.222	9	2	0	1	0	0	.222	.333
Baerga, C#	.286	7	2	0	0	0	0	.286	.286
Bagwell, Jeff	.250	24	6	1	3	6	5	.400	.417
Baines, H*	.256	39	10	1	6	5	5	.341	.333
Barberie, B#	.364	11	4	1	1	0	1	.364	.727
Batiste, Kim	.333	9	3	0	0	0	0	.333	.333
Battle, Allen	.500	4	2	0	0	0	1	.600	.750
Bell, David	.000	4	0	0	0	0	2	.000	.000
Bell, Derek	.286	21	6	0	6	1	6	.318	.429
Bell, Jay	.360	25	9	0	1	4	3	.448	.600
Belliard, R	.143	7	1	0	0	0	0	.143	.143
Benard, M*	.444	9	4	0	1	0	0	.444	.444
Benjamin, M	.100	10	1	0	0	0	4	.100	.100
Berry, Sean	.357	14	5	0	1	0	2	.357	.429
Bichette, D	.292	24	7	0	2	4	4	.346	.333
Biggio, Craig	.276	29	8	0	2	2	4	.333	.483
Blauser, Jeff	.130	23	3	0	1	1	7	.200	.174
Bogar, Tim	.333	12	4	0	2	0	2	.385	.333
Boggs, Wade*	.375	40	15	1	3	5	3	.444	.500
Bonds, Barry*	.318	44	14	0	6	11	9	.446	.364
Bonilla, B#	.167	30	5	0	4	4	4	.257	.267
Boone, Bret	.222	9	2	1	2	2	1	.364	.556
Branson, Jeff*	.444	9	4	1	2	0	2	.444	1.000
Brogna, Rico*	.381	21	8	2	8	0	0	.381	.857
Buhner, Jay	.231	13	3	1	3	0	3	.333	.538
Burks, Ellis	.200	40	8	2	6	2	8	.238	.400
Burnitz, J*	.167	12	2	0	2	0	2	.167	.333
Butler, Brett*	.167	6	1	0	0	2	1	.375	.167
Caminiti, Ken#	.364	33	12	0	5	2	4	.400	.424
Cangelosi, J#	.250	8	2	0	0	1	3	.333	.250
Canseco, Jose	.371	35	13	2	10	8	4	.467	.629
Carr, Chuck	.211	19	4	0	2	2	3	.286	.263
Carreon, Mark	.571	7	4	0	5	0	0	.625	1.000
Carter, Joe	.429	7	3	1	2	0	1	.429	1.000
Castilla, V	.091	11	1	0	0	1	5	.167	.091
Cedeno, A	.182	22	4	0	2	1	2	.217	.227
Clark, Dave*	.286	14	4	0	3	2	1	.375	.429
Clark, Will*	.200	15	3	0	0	5	6	.400	.333
Clayton, R	.326	46	15	2	8	1	7	.340	.543
Colbrunn, G	.385	13	5	1	5	1	2	.429	.692
Cole, Alex*	.286	14	4	0	1	0	0	.333	.286
Coleman, V#	.000	10	0	0	0	0	1	.000	.000
Conine, Jeff	.400	25	10	2	4	0	1	.400	.720
Cora, Joey*	.571	7	4	0	2	0	0	.571	1.000
Cordero, Wil	.273	11	3	1	1	0	4	.273	.455
Cuyler, Milt#	.200	10	2	0	0	1	5	.273	.400
Daulton, D*	.111	18	2	0	3	5	2	.304	.167
Davis, Chili#	.348	23	8	1	5	7	4	.500	.522
Deer, Rob	.273	44	12	6	11	3	13	.310	.705
DeShields, D*	.000	8	0	0	0	3	2	.273	.000
Devereaux, B	.400	15	6	0	0	2	3	.471	.467
Dorsett, B	.167	6	1	0	1	1	0	.286	.167
Duncan, M	.263	19	5	0	0	0	7	.263	.316
Dunston, S	.294	17	5	2	7	1	0	.333	.647
Dykstra, L*	.286	14	4	0	0	1	1	.333	.286
Eisenreich, J*	.386	44	17	2	9	4	3	.438	.591
Espinoza, A	.118	17	2	0	0	0	5	.118	.118
Everett, Carl#	.125	8	1	0	0	1	1	.222	.250
Fielder, C	.400	20	8	1	5	1	7	.429	.650
Finley, Steve*	.341	44	15	4	10	3	7	.383	.614
Fletcher, D*	.250	16	4	0	0	1	0	.294	.375
Floyd, Cliff*	.167	12	2	0	1	0	1	.231	.333
Franco, Julio	.286	14	4	0	1	1	3	.333	.286
Fryman, T	.214	14	3	1	1	0	4	.214	.429
Gaetti, Gary	.408	49	20	3	15	4	10	.455	.653
Gagne, Greg	.400	35	14	1	3	0	5	.417	.714
Galarraga, A	.118	17	2	0	0	0	4	.111	.118
Gallego, Mike	.250	28	7	0	4	0	2	.250	.250
Gant, Ron	.174	23	4	0	3	2	9	.231	.174
Garcia, C	.308	13	4	0	1	0	2	.308	.385
Gilkey, B	.147	34	5	0	4	2	6	.189	.206
Girardi, Joe	.286	7	2	0	0	0	2	.286	.286
Goff, Jerry*	.200	5	1	0	0	0	2	.200	.200
Gomez, Chris	.600	5	3	0	0	1	0	.667	.600
Gomez, Leo	.444	9	4	1	1	0	1	.444	.778
Gonzalez, J	.167	6	1	1	1	0	4	.167	.667
Gonzalez, L*	.194	31	6	1	2	1	3	.219	.290
Grace, Mark*	.333	21	7	0	3	3	2	.417	.429
Greenwell, M*	.429	35	15	3	10	4	0	.487	.771
Griffey Jr, K*	.222	18	4	0	4	4	2	.348	.222
Grissom, M	.290	31	9	0	3	1	9	.303	.387
Grudzielanek	.222	9	2	0	0	0	0	.222	.222
Guillen, O*	.295	44	13	0	5	2	2	.319	.318
Gutierrez, R	.385	13	5	0	2	0	2	.385	.462
Gwynn, Tony*	.417	36	15	0	3	4	3	.452	.500
Hall, Mel*	.235	17	4	0	2	1	2	.278	.353
Hamilton, D*	.300	10	3	0	0	1	2	.300	.400
Harris, Lenny*	.222	9	2	0	0	1	1	.222	.222
Hayes, C	.267	15	4	1	5	2	1	.368	.533

Tom Candiotti, Dodgers — RHP

Batter	Avg	AB	H	HR	BI	BB	SO	OBP	Slg
Henderson, R	.278	36	10	1	1	5	6	.381	.389
Hernandez, Jo	.125	8	1	0	1	0	2	.125	.250
Hill, G	.429	21	9	4	8	3	3	.500	1.048
Hoiles, Chris	.000	8	0	0	0	1	1	.111	.000
Hollins, Dave#	.455	11	5	0	1	4	1	.563	.545
Howard, Dave#	.200	5	1	0	1	0	0	.200	.400
Howard, T*	.188	16	3	0	1	0	3	.188	.250
Howell, Jack*	.333	9	3	0	2	0	1	.333	.444
Hundley, Todd#	.188	32	6	2	2	2	3	.235	.375
Huskey, Butch	.364	11	4	0	2	0	0	.364	.364
Huson, Jeff*	.000	9	0	0	0	1	1	.100	.000
Incaviglia, P	.149	47	7	1	4	2	15	.184	.255
Javier, Stan#	.267	15	4	0	0	1	4	.313	.267
Jefferies, G#	.194	31	6	1	2	3	2	.265	.323
Johnson, Bri	.200	5	1	0	1	1	1	.286	.200
Johnson, Char	.143	7	1	0	1	1	1	.222	.143
Johnson, L*	.292	24	7	0	2	2	3	.346	.292
Johnson, Mark*	.200	5	1	0	0	0	0	.200	.200
Jones, C#	.100	10	1	0	0	1	0	.182	.100
Jones, Chris	.429	7	3	0	1	0	0	.429	.571
Jordan, Brian	.348	23	8	1	3	1	3	.400	.478
Jordan, Ricky	.000	6	0	0	0	1	2	.143	.000
Joyner, Wally*	.382	34	13	1	7	7	1	.476	.647
Justice, Dave*	.250	16	4	1	3	5	3	.409	.500
Karkovice, R	.200	5	1	0	0	0	1	.200	.200
Kelly, Pat	.500	4	2	0	3	1	0	.600	.750
Kelly, R	.226	31	7	2	2	0	1	.226	.452
Kendall, J	.600	5	3	0	0	0	1	.600	.600
Kent, Jeff	.281	32	9	1	1	1	8	.378	.406
King, Jeff	.400	20	8	0	7	3	2	.458	.650
Kingery, Mike*	.235	17	4	0	0	1	1	.235	.235
Klesko, Ryan*	.333	9	3	1	2	2	2	.455	.667
Knoblauch, C	.167	6	1	0	0	0	1	.167	.167
Lankford, Ray*	.250	40	10	1	2	5	9	.326	.375
Lansing, Mike	.273	22	6	0	4	2	2	.333	.455
Larkin, Barry	.360	25	9	1	8	1	2	.385	.600
Lemke, Mark#	.235	17	4	0	0	5	2	.409	.235
Lewis, Darren	.229	35	8	0	1	0	4	.250	.286
Leyritz, Jim	.000	6	0	0	0	0	2	.143	.000
Lieberthal, M	.286	7	2	0	0	0	0	.286	.429
Liriano, N#	.333	12	4	0	1	1	3	.385	.583
Livingstone, S	.333	18	6	0	3	0	3	.316	.556
Lopez, Javy	.375	8	3	1	2	0	1	.375	.875
Lopez, Luis#	.333	6	2	0	0	0	0	.333	.333
Mabry, John*	.368	19	7	0	2	2	4	.429	.474
Macfarlane, M	.250	8	2	0	1	3	3	.333	.375
Magadan, Dave*	.273	11	3	1	1	2	2	.385	.727
Manwaring, K	.292	24	7	0	4	1	3	.320	.333
Martin, A*	.333	18	6	3	7	0	4	.333	.833
Martinez, Da*	.200	15	3	0	3	2	3	.294	.200
Martinez, E	.083	12	1	0	0	1	5	.154	.083
May, Derrick*	.125	8	1	0	2	0	1	.300	.375
Mayne, Brent*	.000	7	0	0	0	1	1	.125	.000
McGee, Willie#	.222	18	4	0	1	1	3	.263	.222
McGriff, Fred*	.340	47	16	2	3	14	12	.492	.511
McGwire, Mark	.315	35	11	3	5	4	3	.385	.657
McLemore, M#	.000	3	0	0	0	1	0	.250	.000
McRae, Brian*	.174	23	4	0	2	4	5	.296	.217
Merced, O*	.267	15	4	0	2	3	2	.389	.267
Miller, Orl	.750	4	3	0	3	1	1	.800	.750
Mitchell, K	.200	5	1	0	1	0	2	.200	.200
Molitor, Paul	.300	50	15	0	4	2	7	.327	.320
Morandini, M	.270	37	10	0	2	4	4	.308	.270
Morris, Hal*	.125	16	2	0	1	4	6	.300	.250
Mouton, James	.429	7	3	0	1	1	4	.500	.714
Murray, Eddie#	.140	43	6	1	3	6	8	.245	.209
Myers, Greg*	.286	14	4	1	3	2	0	.375	.571
Naehring, Tim	.000	4	0	0	0	2	2	.333	.000
Nixon, Otis#	.222	9	2	0	2	1	1	.300	.333
O'Brien, C	.167	12	2	0	1	0	2	.231	.167
O'Neill, Paul*	.000	6	0	0	0	0	2	.000	.000
Olerud, John*	.167	12	2	0	0	1	3	.231	.167
Oliver, Joe	.250	8	2	0	1	0	0	.222	.250
Ordonez, Rey	.300	10	3	0	0	2	1	.417	.400
Orsulak, Joe*	.439	41	18	0	1	5	6	.500	.488
Pagnozzi, Tom	.357	28	10	1	7	0	3	.345	.571
Palmeiro, R*	.438	16	7	1	2	1	2	.471	.750
Pena, G#	.200	5	1	0	0	0	2	.200	.200
Pena, Tony	.154	13	2	0	1	2	1	.267	.231
Pendleton, T#	.296	27	8	0	1	1	4	.321	.333
Petagine, Rob*	.500	6	3	0	1	1	1	.500	.500
Phillips, J*	.143	7	1	0	0	0	4	.143	.143
Phillips, T#	.257	35	9	0	4	1	10	.270	.314
Plantier, P*	.190	21	4	0	3	0	7	.182	.333
Polonia, Luis*	.217	23	5	0	2	2	4	.280	.217
Raines, Tim*	.143	7	1	0	0	0	1	.250	.143
Reed, Jeff*	.200	10	2	0	0	0	0	.200	.200
Reed, Jody	.167	24	4	0	0	0	5	.167	.208
Ripken, Billy	.150	20	3	0	0	0	2	.150	.150
Ripken, Cal	.163	43	7	1	4	11	7	.327	.233
Roberts, Bip#	.235	17	4	0	1	2	5	.316	.235

Tom Candiotti, Dodgers — RHP

Batter	Avg	AB	H	HR	BI	BB	SO	OBP	Slg
Rodriguez, H*	.143	7	1	0	0	0	1	.143	.143
Sabo, Chris	.222	9	2	0	0	0	0	.222	.222
Sanchez, Rey	.286	14	4	0	0	0	4	.286	.286
Sandberg, R	.364	11	4	0	1	1	1	.417	.636
Sanders, R	.353	17	6	1	2	0	3	.389	.647
Santangelo, F#	.143	7	1	0	1	0	1	.143	.143
Santiago, B	.063	16	1	0	1	4	4	.238	.063
Scarsone, S	.222	9	2	0	0	0	2	.222	.222
Schofield, D	.200	30	6	0	3	0	2	.194	.300
Schu, Rick	.273	11	3	0	0	0	2	.273	.364
Segui, David#	.125	16	2	0	1	2	0	.222	.188
Seitzer, K	.235	34	8	0	2	5	5	.333	.265
Servais, S	.348	23	8	0	4	0	3	.348	.478
Sheaffer, D	.111	9	1	0	1	1	0	.200	.111
Sheffield, G	.265	34	9	2	4	2	6	.306	.529
Shipley, C	.125	8	1	0	1	0	4	.125	.125
Shumpert, T	.333	6	2	0	0	1	1	.429	.333
Sierra, Ruben#	.276	29	8	2	6	0	5	.267	.621
Silvestri, D	.400	5	2	0	1	0	3	.400	.400
Slaught, Don	.118	17	2	0	1	0	3	.118	.235
Smith, Ozzie*	.167	30	5	0	2	3	1	.242	.167
Sojo, Luis	.125	8	1	0	0	0	1	.125	.125
Sosa, Sammy	.286	35	10	3	6	1	8	.306	.629
Spiers, Bill*	.100	20	2	0	3	1	5	.136	.100
Steinbach, T	.176	17	3	0	2	2	4	.250	.176
Stillwell, K#	.241	29	7	1	1	1	3	.267	.345
Stinnett, K	.222	9	2	0	1	0	4	.222	.333
Stocker, K#	.167	12	2	0	2	4	2	.375	.167
Strange, Doug#	.400	5	2	0	0	0	0	.400	.400
Surhoff, B.J.*	.242	33	8	0	1	1	4	.265	.333
Sveum, Dale#	.292	24	7	1	3	1	2	.320	.500
Sweeney, Mark*	.143	7	1	0	1	1	0	.250	.143
Tartabull, D	.286	28	8	0	3	6	7	.412	.393
Taubensee, E*	.200	10	2	0	0	2	1	.333	.300
Tettleton, M#	.267	15	4	0	2	4	3	.450	.333
Thomas, Frank	.222	9	2	0	1	1	3	.300	.222
Thompson, Mil*	.222	9	2	1	2	1	5	.300	.556
Thompson, Rob	.269	26	7	1	3	5	8	.387	.423
Thompson, Ry	.154	13	2	0	1	2	4	.294	.231
Trammell, A	.359	39	14	1	5	4	4	.419	.513
Valle, Dave	.353	17	6	1	6	1	6	.389	.588
VanderWal, J*	.000	8	0	0	0	1	5	.111	.000
Vaughn, Greg	.333	9	3	1	1	0	3	.333	.667
Ventura, R*	.300	20	6	1	6	0	0	.300	.450
Veras, Q#	.250	8	2	0	0	2	2	.400	.500
Vizcaino, J#	.400	25	10	0	3	2	4	.444	.400
Vizquel, Omar#	.353	17	6	1	1	1	1	.389	.647
Walker, Larry*	.444	18	8	4	7	3	0	.500	1.111
Webster, L	.286	7	2	0	1	1	1	.375	.286
Wehner, John	.200	5	1	0	0	1	1	.200	.200
Weiss, Walt#	.296	27	8	0	4	3	2	.367	.333
White, Devon#	.143	28	4	1	3	2	4	.200	.250
Whiten, Mark#	.250	20	5	0	1	1	8	.286	.400
Wilkins, Rick*	.250	16	4	1	2	0	1	.250	.438
Williams, E	.375	8	3	0	2	0	0	.375	.625
Williams, Ma	.226	31	7	1	3	7	6	.385	.452
Young, Eric	.300	10	3	0	2	2	2	.300	.400
Young, Kevin	.200	5	1	0	0	0	2	.200	.400
Zeile, Todd	.276	29	8	1	2	2	4	.323	.448

Rafael Carmona, Mariners — RHP

Batter	Avg	AB	H	HR	BI	BB	SO	OBP	Slg
Baines, H*	.250	4	1	0	1	2	2	.500	.500
Becker, Rich*	.667	6	4	0	0	1	1	.714	.667
Boggs, Wade*	.800	5	4	0	2	0	0	.667	1.000
Cirillo, Jeff	.000	3	0	0	0	1	0	.250	.000
Cordova, M	.000	6	0	0	0	1	1	.250	.000
Curtis, Chad	.000	4	0	0	0	1	2	.200	.000
DiSarcina, G	.333	6	2	0	0	0	0	.333	.500
Edmonds, Jim*	.500	4	2	0	2	0	0	.400	.500
Elster, Kevin	.200	5	1	0	1	0	1	.200	.200
Fielder, C	.400	5	2	0	0	1	0	.500	.400
Fryman, T	.125	8	1	1	4	0	2	.125	.500
Gaetti, Gary	.667	3	2	1	2	2	1	.800	2.000
Gonzalez, J	.250	4	1	1	1	2	0	.500	1.000
Goodwin, Tom*	.143	7	1	0	0	0	1	.143	.143
Greenwell, M*	.200	5	1	0	1	1	0	.333	.200
Greer, Rusty*	.800	5	4	0	0	0	1	.800	1.000
Howard, Dave#	.000	5	0	0	0	1	0	.167	.000
Jefferson, R*	.500	6	3	0	3	1	1	.500	.667
Jeter, Derek	.125	8	1	0	2	0	0	.125	.125
Macfarlane, M	.000	3	0	0	0	2	1	.400	.000
Meares, Pat	.429	7	3	0	1	1	0	.500	.571
Molitor, Paul	.500	4	2	0	2	2	0	.667	.750
Naehring, Tim	.667	6	4	0	3	2	0	.750	1.000
O'Leary, Troy*	.333	6	2	1	4	0	0	.333	1.000
Offerman, J#	.250	4	1	0	0	1	0	.400	.250
Palmer, Dean	.000	5	0	0	0	3	0	.200	.000
Polonia, Luis*	.333	3	1	0	0	2	1	.600	1.000
Reboulet, J	.000	4	0	0	0	1	0	.000	.000
Ripken, Cal	.000	4	0	0	0	1	0	.200	.000

Rafael Carmona, Mariners — RHP

Batter	Avg	AB	H	HR	BI	BB	SO	OBP	Slg
Salmon, Tim	.143	7	1	0	1	1	2	.250	.143
Seitzer, K	.500	2	1	0	0	3	0	.800	.500
Snow, J.T.#	.333	3	1	0	0	3	0	.667	.667
Stahoviak, S*	.667	3	2	1	3	2	0	.800	1.667
Stanley, Mike	.500	6	3	0	0	0	0	.500	.833
Tucker, M*	.250	4	1	0	0	1	1	.400	.500
Valentin, Jhn	.286	7	2	0	0	2	0	.444	.429
Valentin, Jse#	.000	5	0	0	0	0	2	.000	.000
Vaughn, Greg	.000	3	0	0	0	2	1	.400	.000
Vaughn, Mo*	.167	6	1	0	0	3	2	.500	.167
Velarde, R	.286	7	2	1	2	0	1	.286	.714
Williams, Ber#	.200	5	1	0	0	1	0	.333	.200

Cris Carpenter, Brewers — RHP

Batter	Avg	AB	H	HR	BI	BB	SO	OBP	Slg
Anthony, Eric*	.000	5	0	0	0	1	2	.167	.000
Bagwell, Jeff	.400	5	2	1	3	1	0	.571	1.200
Bell, Jay	.000	10	0	0	0	0	4	.000	.000
Belliard, R	.222	9	2	0	0	0	2	.222	.222
Berroa, G	.500	6	3	0	1	0	1	.500	.500
Biggio, Craig	.308	13	4	0	3	0	0	.308	.538
Blauser, Jeff	.000	5	0	0	0	0	3	.000	.000
Bonds, Barry*	.000	9	0	0	0	3	3	.250	.000
Bonilla, B#	.385	13	5	0	0	3	1	.500	.615
Bordick, Mike	.167	6	1	0	2	0	0	.167	.167
Caminiti, Ken#	.333	6	2	0	0	3	1	.556	.500
Candaele, C#	.200	5	1	0	1	1	0	.333	.200
Carter, Joe	.250	4	1	0	1	1	2	.400	.250
Cedeno, A	.250	4	1	0	0	0	1	.250	.250
Clark, Will*	.250	4	1	0	0	0	1	.400	.250
Colbrunn, D	.250	4	1	0	0	1	2	.400	.250
Coleman, V#	.500	4	2	0	0	1	0	.600	.500
Curtis, Chad	.000	5	0	0	0	1	0	.167	.000
Dascenzo, D#	.111	9	1	0	1	0	1	.111	.222
Daulton, D*	.214	14	3	0	2	1	3	.267	.286
Davis, Chili#	.429	7	3	1	6	0	1	.375	.857
Davis, Eric	.077	13	1	0	0	0	2	.077	.077
Dawson, Andre	.214	14	3	0	1	1	0	.250	.214
Duncan, M	.167	6	1	0	2	0	1	.167	.167
Dunston, S	.500	12	6	0	4	0	2	.538	.750
Dykstra, L*	.385	13	5	0	3	4	0	.529	.538
Edmonds, Jim*	.400	5	2	0	0	1	0	.400	.800
Fielder, C	.167	6	1	0	0	0	0	.167	.167
Finley, Steve*	.333	6	2	0	0	0	0	.333	.333
Galarraga, A	.182	11	2	1	2	2	2	.357	.636
Gant, Ron	.308	13	4	1	4	0	1	.286	.692
Girardi, Joe	.250	8	2	0	1	0	1	.250	.250
Gonzalez, L*	.500	4	2	1	2	1	1	.600	1.250
Grace, Mark*	.538	13	7	0	1	1	1	.571	.615
Grissom, M	.400	5	2	1	1	0	0	.400	1.000
Gwynn, Tony*	.200	5	1	0	1	1	0	.333	.400
Harris, Lenny*	.500	6	3	0	0	0	1	.571	.667
Hayes, C	.286	7	2	0	1	0	1	.286	.429
Hollins, Dave#	.167	6	1	0	0	0	0	.167	.167
Javier, Stan#	.444	9	4	0	1	2	0	.545	.444
Jefferies, G#	.167	6	1	0	0	0	1	.167	.167
Jordan, Ricky	.100	10	1	0	0	0	0	.100	.100
Justice, Dave*	.143	7	1	0	0	1	0	.250	.286
King, Jeff	.100	10	1	0	0	0	2	.100	.100
Larkin, Barry	.214	14	3	0	1	0	3	.214	.357
Lewis, Darren	.200	5	1	0	0	0	0	.200	.200
Magadan, Dave*	.200	5	1	0	2	1	0	.333	.200
Martinez, Da*	.182	11	2	0	0	1	1	.250	.182
McGee, Willie#	.200	5	1	0	0	0	2	.200	.200
Merced, O*	.600	5	3	0	4	2	1	.714	1.200
Molitor, Paul	.400	5	2	0	0	0	2	.400	.400
Morris, Hal*	.429	7	3	1	2	0	0	.429	.857
Munoz, Pedro	.200	5	1	0	0	0	2	.200	.200
Murray, Eddie#	.273	11	3	1	3	1	0	.333	.545
Nixon, Otis#	.400	10	4	0	1	2	0	.500	.500
O'Neill, Paul*	.308	13	4	1	3	2	1	.400	.615
Palmeiro, R*	.667	6	4	0	1	0	1	.714	.833
Pendleton, T#	.200	10	2	0	2	1	1	.250	.300
Raines, Tim#	.429	7	3	0	1	4	0	.636	.714
Reed, Jeff*	.400	5	2	0	2	0	0	.400	.800
Sabo, Chris	.333	6	2	0	1	1	1	.375	.500
Salmon, Tim	.250	4	1	0	0	1	1	.400	.250
Samuel, Juan	.500	6	3	0	0	1	0	.571	.667
Sandberg, R	.400	20	8	0	0	2	2	.455	.450
Schofield, D	.000	5	0	0	0	0	0	.000	.000
Slaught, Don	.333	3	1	0	1	0	1	.500	.333
Smith, Dwight*	.455	11	5	0	1	1	2	.500	.727
Tettleton, M#	.500	4	2	0	0	1	2	.600	.500
Thompson, Mil*	.250	4	1	0	0	0	1	.400	.250
Walker, Larry*	.286	7	2	1	1	0	3	.286	.857
Wallach, Tim	.267	15	4	0	2	1	3	.294	.333
Walton, J	.167	6	1	0	0	0	0	.167	.167
White, Devon#	.000	5	0	0	0	1	0	.000	.000
Williams, Ma	.200	5	1	1	2	0	0	.333	.800

Giovanni Carrara, Reds — RHP

Batter	Avg	AB	H	HR	BI	BB	SO	OBP	Slg
Baerga, C#	.500	6	3	0	4	0	0	.500	.667
Belle, Albert	.500	4	2	1	2	1	1	.600	1.500
Bichette, D	.667	3	2	1	1	2	0	.800	1.667
Burks, Ellis	.333	6	2	0	0	0	0	.333	.333
Castilla, V	.200	5	1	1	3	0	1	.200	.800
Galarraga, A	.500	4	2	0	1	0	0	.500	.500
Lofton, Kenny*	.714	7	5	0	5	0	1	.714	.714
Murray, Eddie#	.600	5	3	1	4	1	1	.667	1.200
Ramirez, M	.250	4	1	0	1	2	1	.500	.250
Sorrento, P*	.250	4	1	1	1	2	1	.500	1.000
Thome, Jim*	.500	6	3	0	0	1	0	.571	.667
Vizquel, Omar*	.500	6	3	0	0	1	0	.571	.667
Young, Eric	.000	5	0	0	0	0	0	.000	.000

Larry Casian, Cubs — LHP

Batter	Avg	AB	H	HR	BI	BB	SO	OBP	Slg
Baerga, C#	.600	5	3	0	1	0	0	.667	1.000
Boggs, Wade*	.400	5	2	0	2	0	0	.333	.400
Bordick, Mike	.250	4	1	0	1	1	0	.400	.250
Buhner, Jay	.333	9	3	1	3	2	0	.455	.889
Carter, Joe	.000	4	0	0	0	2	0	.333	.000
Cora, Joey#	.600	5	3	0	2	0	1	.600	1.200
Curtis, Chad	.500	4	2	0	1	1	0	.600	.500
Gaetti, Gary	.500	6	3	1	2	0	0	.500	1.167
Gallego, Mike	.333	6	2	0	0	0	0	.333	.333
Gates, Brent*	.000	3	0	0	0	0	0	.000	.000
Greenwell, M*	.400	5	2	0	0	0	0	.400	.600
Griffey Jr, K*	.250	8	2	1	2	0	2	.250	.625
Guillen, O*	.333	6	2	0	0	0	0	.333	.333
Hamilton, D*	.200	5	1	0	0	0	0	.200	.200
Jefferson, R*	.600	5	3	0	1	0	0	.600	.600
Johnson, L*	.222	9	2	0	1	0	1	.222	.333
Jones, C#	.167	6	1	0	1	0	0	.167	.167
Joyner, Wally*	.375	8	3	1	1	1	1	.500	.750
Kelly, Pat	.750	4	3	0	3	0	0	.750	1.250
Klesko, Ryan*	.600	5	3	0	1	0	0	.600	.600
Lofton, Kenny*	.667	6	4	1	3	0	0	.571	1.167
Macfarlane, M	.167	6	1	0	0	2	2	.375	.167
Martin, Al*	.000	7	0	0	0	0	0	.000	.000
Martinez, E	.333	3	1	0	0	2	0	.600	.333
Martinez, T*	.500	6	3	0	2	0	2	.429	.500
McGriff, Fred*	.400	5	2	1	4	0	1	.400	1.000
McRae, Brian*	.600	10	6	0	0	1	0	.600	.800
Merced, O*	.333	6	2	0	2	1	1	.375	.500
Myers, Greg*	.000	5	0	0	0	1	0	.000	.000
O'Neill, Paul*	.000	5	0	0	2	1	1	.143	.000
Olerud, John*	.714	7	5	0	7	0	0	.714	1.000
Palmeiro, R*	.143	7	1	0	2	0	1	.125	.286
Raines, Tim#	.250	4	1	0	0	2	0	.500	.250
Schofield, D	.750	4	3	0	3	0	0	.857	1.000
Sorrento, P*	.285	7	2	1	1	0	3	.286	.714
Surhoff, B.J.*	.400	5	2	0	0	1	1	.400	.600
Tartabull, D	.500	4	2	0	1	0	0	.500	.500
Thome, Jim*	.400	5	2	0	1	0	2	.400	.600
Ventura, R*	.000	6	0	0	0	0	2	.000	.000
Vizquel, Omar*	.375	8	3	0	1	1	1	.444	.375
Walker, Larry*	.600	5	3	0	1	0	0	.600	.800
Weiss, Walt#	.167	6	1	0	0	0	0	.167	.167
White, Devon#	.200	5	1	1	1	0	0	.200	.800
Williams, Ber#	.429	7	3	0	3	0	1	.429	.714

Hector Carrasco, Reds — RHP

Batter	Avg	AB	H	HR	BI	BB	SO	OBP	Slg
Abbott, Kurt	.000	7	0	0	0	0	2	.000	.000
Andrews, S	.333	6	2	0	0	0	1	.333	.333
Arias, Alex	.167	6	1	0	0	0	2	.167	.167
Ausmus, Brad	.000	4	0	0	0	1	1	.200	.000
Bagwell, Jeff	.154	13	2	0	2	2	4	.267	.308
Bates, Jason#	.500	4	2	0	0	2	0	.667	1.000
Bell, Derek	.273	11	3	0	0	1	3	.333	.273
Bell, Jay	.000	6	0	0	0	2	3	.250	.000
Berry, Sean	.000	5	0	0	0	0	0	.000	.000
Bichette, D	.375	8	3	0	1	2	0	.500	.500
Biggio, Craig	.000	8	0	0	3	2	3	.333	.000
Blauser, Jeff	.000	3	0	0	0	2	0	.400	.000
Burks, Ellis	.000	5	0	0	2	0	2	.000	.000
Caminiti, Ken#	.167	6	1	0	0	1	1	.286	.167
Cangelosi, J#	.333	6	2	0	1	1	4	.429	.333
Carr, Chuck	.125	8	1	0	0	0	2	.125	.125
Castilla, V	.500	12	6	2	2	0	1	.500	1.000
Clayton, R	.000	4	0	0	0	1	3	.200	.000
Colbrunn, G	.000	5	0	0	0	1	0	.167	.000
Conine, Jeff	.400	10	4	0	0	1	1	.455	.400
Cordero, Wil	.400	5	2	0	1	0	2	.400	.600
Eisenreich, J*	.400	5	2	0	2	1	1	.500	.400
Eusebio, Tony	.167	6	1	0	0	0	0	.167	.167
Finley, Steve*	.429	7	3	0	1	1	1	.444	.429
Fletcher, D*	.400	5	2	0	0	0	0	.400	.400
Galarraga, A	.125	8	1	0	1	0	3	.111	.125
Garcia, G	.167	6	1	0	0	0	1	.167	.167
Gilkey, B	.333	6	2	0	2	2	0	.500	.333
Girardi, Joe	.200	5	1	0	0	1	0	.200	.400
Gonzalez, L*	.333	6	2	0	1	1	0	.429	.333
Grace, Mark*	.111	9	1	0	0	0	0	.111	.111
Grissom, M	.286	7	2	0	0	1	2	.444	.429
Grudzielanek	.625	8	5	0	4	0	0	.556	.625
Gwynn, Tony*	.500	5	1	0	0	2	0	.429	.200
Hayes, C	.333	6	2	0	1	1	2	.375	.500
Hill, G	.333	6	2	0	1	1	3	.429	.333
Hollandsworth*	.200	5	1	0	0	0	1	.200	.400
Hundley, Todd#	.167	6	1	0	1	1	2	.286	.500
Hunter, Bri L	.000	6	0	0	0	0	0	.000	.000
Jefferies, G#	.400	5	2	0	0	0	1	.400	.600
Jones, C#	.286	7	2	1	1	0	1	.375	.857
Jordan, Brian	.667	3	2	0	1	1	1	.600	1.000
Karros, Eric	.250	8	2	0	1	0	4	.250	.375
Kent, Jeff	.167	6	1	0	2	1	3	.286	.333
King, Jeff	.000	3	0	0	0	2	0	.400	.000
Kingery, Mike*	.000	3	0	0	0	1	0	.250	.000
Lankford, Ray*	.400	5	2	0	1	0	1	.400	.400
Lansing, Mike	.200	5	1	0	0	1	0	.200	.200
Lemke, Mark#	.375	8	3	0	1	1	1	.444	.500
Magadan, Dave*	.143	7	1	0	0	2	2	.444	.143
Martin, Al*	.200	5	1	0	0	0	0	.200	.200
May, Derrick*	.250	4	1	0	1	1	1	.400	.250
McGriff, Fred*	.571	7	4	1	1	1	1	.625	1.000
McRae, Brian*	.167	6	1	0	0	1	2	.286	.167
Merced, O*	.200	5	1	1	1	0	0	.200	.800
Mondesi, Raul	.600	5	3	0	0	1	1	.667	.800
Morandini, M*	.500	4	2	0	0	1	0	.600	.500
Orsulak, Joe*	.400	5	2	0	1	1	1	.500	.600
Piazza, Mike	.333	3	1	0	1	3	1	.667	.333
Sanchez, Rey	.250	4	1	0	0	2	2	.500	.500
Sheffield, G	.286	7	2	0	1	4	3	.545	.286
Sosa, Sammy	.333	9	3	0	1	0	0	.333	.333
Thompson, Mil*	.167	6	1	0	0	0	2	.167	.167
Thompson, Ry	.200	5	1	0	0	0	0	.200	.200
VanderWal, J*	.600	5	3	0	6	0	0	.600	1.400
Veras, Q#	.000	5	0	0	0	0	0	.000	.000
Vizcaino, J#	.167	6	1	0	1	1	1	.250	.167
Walker, Larry*	.200	5	1	1	3	2	0	.429	.800
Wallach, Tim	.167	6	1	0	0	0	2	.167	.667
Weiss, Walt#	.222	9	2	0	1	1	2	.300	.222
Wilkins, Rick*	.000	5	0	0	0	0	0	.167	.000
Young, Eric	.400	5	2	0	2	2	0	.571	.600
Zeile, Todd	.000	4	0	0	0	1	1	.200	.000

Frank Castillo, Cubs — RHP

Batter	Avg	AB	H	HR	BI	BB	SO	OBP	Slg
Abbott, Kurt	.167	6	1	0	0	0	0	.167	.167
Alfonzo, E	.200	5	1	0	1	0	0	.200	.400
Alicea, Luis#	.000	9	0	0	0	1	4	.100	.000
Alou, Moises	.417	24	10	1	1	3	4	.481	.667
Amaro, Ruben*	.125	8	1	0	0	1	1	.222	.125
Anthony, Eric*	.200	15	3	0	1	1	4	.250	.333
Arias, Alex	.167	12	2	0	1	1	0	.231	.250
Ashley, Billy	.333	6	2	1	1	0	1	.333	1.000
Aurilia, Rich	.000	6	1	0	0	0	0	.167	.167
Ausmus, Brad	.250	16	4	1	1	1	1	.294	.500
Bagwell, Jeff	.207	29	6	1	6	4	1	.333	.379
Barberie, B#	.316	19	6	0	1	0	5	.316	.368
Bates, Jason#	.300	10	3	0	0	1	3	.364	.400
Batiste, Kim	.143	14	2	1	2	0	3	.143	.357
Bell, Derek	.294	17	5	0	3	1	4	.333	.412
Bell, Jay	.233	30	7	3	6	4	4	.324	.567
Belliard, R	.444	9	4	0	2	0	1	.444	.444
Benard, M*	.308	13	4	0	0	1	2	.357	.385
Benjamin, M	.400	5	2	0	0	0	2	.400	.400
Berry, Sean	.500	10	5	1	2	1	3	.545	.800
Bichette, D	.423	26	11	3	5	0	0	.423	.808
Biggio, Craig	.290	31	9	1	7	1	3	.371	.419
Blauser, Jeff	.278	18	5	2	2	0	4	.278	.722
Blowers, Mike	.400	5	2	0	0	0	0	.400	.400
Bonds, Barry*	.233	30	7	3	9	9	2	.400	.567
Bonilla, B#	.308	26	8	2	5	2	6	.357	.615
Boone, Bret	.333	6	2	0	1	0	1	.333	.333
Branson, Jeff*	.250	8	2	0	0	1	1	.333	.500
Brogna, Rico*	.000	8	0	0	0	0	2	.000	.000
Brumfield, J	.182	11	2	0	0	0	3	.182	.273
Burks, Ellis	.333	12	4	2	2	1	4	.385	.833
Butler, Brett*	.125	32	4	0	0	2	5	.176	.125
Caminiti, Ken#	.276	29	8	1	5	8	5	.432	.379
Candaele, C#	.667	6	4	0	1	1	0	.700	.889
Cangelosi, J*	.250	4	1	0	1	2	1	.500	.250
Carr, Chuck	.250	16	4	0	0	1	1	.294	.313
Carreon, Mark	.400	10	4	0	2	0	2	.455	.500
Castilla, V	.273	22	6	1	2	1	4	.304	.409
Cedeno, A	.063	16	1	0	0	0	1	.118	.063
Cianfrocco, A	.400	10	4	1	3	0	4	.400	.800
Clark, Will*	.167	6	1	0	0	0	1	.167	.167
Clayton, R	.250	16	4	0	2	0	4	.250	.250
Colbrunn, G	.200	10	2	1	3	0	0	.273	.500
Cole, Alex*	.364	11	4	0	0	1	1	.417	.364

Frank Castillo, Cubs — RHP

Batter	Avg	AB	H	HR	BI	BB	SO	OBP	Slg
Coleman, V#	.462	13	6	0	1	0	1	.462	.462
Conine, Jeff	.375	24	9	2	4	2	2	.423	.708
Cordero, Wil	.529	17	9	1	3	0	1	.556	.941
Daulton, D*	.235	17	4	1	6	2	3	.316	.529
Davis, Eric	.286	14	4	1	3	1	3	.333	.643
Decker, Steve	.200	10	2	0	0	0	3	.200	.200
DeShields, D*	.389	18	7	1	1	1	1	.421	.611
Duncan, M	.231	13	3	0	2	0	2	.231	.462
Dunston, S	.429	7	3	0	0	0	0	.429	.571
Dykstra, L*	.000	10	0	0	0	4	1	.636	1.600
Eisenreich, J*	.333	6	2	0	1	0	1	.333	.333
Everett, Carl#	.000	5	0	0	0	0	2	.000	.000
Finley, Steve*	.211	38	8	0	0	2	1	.250	.289
Fletcher, D*	.353	17	6	1	5	0	0	.333	.529
Floyd, Cliff*	.167	6	1	0	0	0	4	.167	.167
Fonville, C#	.250	8	2	0	0	0	1	.250	.250
Gaetti, Gary	.000	5	0	0	0	0	2	.000	.000
Galarraga, A	.211	19	4	1	2	0	4	.200	.368
Gallego, Mike	.200	5	1	0	0	0	1	.200	.200
Gant, Ron	.421	19	8	0	2	3	5	.522	.421
Garcia, J	.188	16	3	0	1	0	0	.235	.313
Gilkey, B	.292	24	7	0	1	1	3	.320	.458
Girardi, Joe	.125	8	1	0	0	1	0	.222	.125
Gonzalez, L*	.154	13	2	0	1	0	3	.154	.154
Grissom, M	.360	25	9	1	4	1	2	.385	.640
Grudzielanek	.125	8	1	0	1	0	0	.125	.125
Gutierrez, R	.429	7	3	0	1	2	1	.556	.429
Gwynn, Tony*	.345	29	10	0	2	3	0	.406	.414
Hansen, Dave*	.100	10	1	0	0	3	1	.308	.100
Harris, Lenny*	.154	13	2	0	1	0	4	.143	.154
Hayes, C	.375	8	3	0	0	0	1	.375	.500
Henderson, R	.000	5	0	0	0	2	2	.286	.000
Hill, G	.200	10	2	0	2	1	2	.273	.300
Hollandsworth*	.333	3	1	0	0	2	0	.600	.333
Hollins, Dave#	.300	20	6	2	3	2	1	.364	.600
Hubbard, Tr	.000	5	0	0	0	0	1	.000	.000
Hundley, Todd#	.222	27	6	2	8	0	4	.222	.481
Hunter, Brian	.000	6	0	0	0	0	3	.000	.000
Hunter, Bri L	.333	15	5	0	0	1	1	.375	.400
Huskey, Butch	.600	5	3	1	3	0	1	.600	1.200
Incaviglia, P	.333	6	2	0	0	0	0	.333	.500
Javier, Stan#	.200	5	1	0	0	0	2	.200	.200
Jefferies, G#	.333	24	8	1	3	1	1	.360	.625
Johnson, Char	.600	5	3	1	2	0	1	.600	1.200
Johnson, L*	.167	6	1	0	0	0	0	.167	.167
Johnson, Mark*	.308	13	4	1	1	0	5	.308	.769
Jones, C#	.333	9	3	1	6	2	2	.455	.667
Jones, Chris	.600	5	3	0	0	1	2	.667	.600
Jordan, Brian	.200	15	3	0	2	0	5	.188	.333
Justice, Dave*	.154	13	2	2	2	3	3	.313	.615
Karros, Eric	.550	20	11	1	2	2	4	.609	.900
Kelly, R	.250	8	2	0	1	0	1	.333	.250
Kent, Jeff	.308	13	4	2	4	0	1	.308	.769
King, Jeff	.208	24	5	2	4	0	3	.208	.500
Kingery, Mike*	.125	16	2	0	1	1	2	.176	.125
Klesko, Ryan*	.222	9	2	0	0	0	1	.222	.222
Lampkin, Tom*	.500	6	3	0	0	0	1	.500	.667
Lankford, Ray*	.161	31	5	0	0	3	9	.235	.226
Lansing, Mike	.375	16	6	0	2	1	2	.474	.375
Larkin, Barry	.368	19	7	0	3	2	2	.429	.579
Lemke, Mark#	.167	12	2	0	2	2	1	.267	.167
Lewis, Darren	.133	15	2	0	0	1	0	.188	.133
Livingstone*	.000	6	0	0	0	2	2	.250	.000
Lopez, Javy	.286	7	2	0	0	1	1	.375	.286
Lopez, Luis#	.000	5	0	0	0	0	2	.000	.000
Mabry, John*	.125	8	1	0	1	0	1	.125	.125
Magadan, Dave*	.357	14	5	0	2	3	4	.471	.357
Manwaring, K	.286	14	4	1	2	0	2	.267	.500
Martin, Al*	.429	21	9	2	5	1	3	.455	.762
Martinez, Da*	.500	8	4	2	2	1	2	.556	1.250
May, Derrick*	.375	8	3	1	2	1	3	.444	.875
McCracken, Q#	.200	5	1	0	2	1	3	.333	.200
McGee, Willie#	.091	11	1	0	0	1	1	.167	.091
McGriff, Fred*	.250	16	4	1	4	2	4	.333	.625
Merced, O*	.167	36	6	1	3	3	7	.225	.278
Miller, Orl	.500	10	5	0	4	0	1	.500	.700
Mitchell, K	.286	7	2	0	2	0	2	.286	.429
Mondesi, Raul	.222	9	2	2	3	0	0	.222	.889
Morandini, M*	.240	25	6	0	0	0	2	.269	.280
Morris, Hal*	.231	13	3	2	3	3	1	.375	.692
Mouton, James	.500	8	4	0	2	0	2	.500	.750
Murray, Eddie#	.588	17	10	1	8	1	1	.579	.882
Newfield, M	.143	7	1	0	0	0	0	.143	.143
Nixon, Otis#	.333	9	3	0	1	0	0	.333	.556
O'Neill, Paul*	.143	7	1	0	0	1	1	.250	.143
Offerman, J#	.261	23	6	0	2	2	5	.320	.261
Oliver, Joe	.214	14	3	0	2	0	1	.267	.214
Ordonez, Rey	.400	5	2	0	0	0	1	.400	.400
Orsulak, Joe*	.429	14	6	0	1	0	1	.429	.571
Osik, Keith	.500	4	2	0	1	0	2	.600	.500
Pagnozzi, Tom	.300	20	6	1	5	0	2	.300	.600
Pena, G#	.500	8	4	1	6	4	2	.615	1.000
Pendleton, T#	.250	28	7	0	3	1	6	.267	.321
Petagine, Rob*	.000	4	0	0	0	1	3	.200	.000
Piazza, Mike	.190	21	4	0	1	0	5	.190	.190
Plantier, P*	.000	5	0	0	0	0	3	.000	.000
Reed, Jeff*	.167	6	1	0	0	2	0	.375	.167
Reed, Jody	.263	19	5	1	1	0	2	.263	.421
Renteria, E	.286	7	2	0	0	0	0	.286	.286
Roberts, Bip#	.263	19	5	0	0	4	1	.391	.263
Rodriguez, H*	.091	11	1	0	1	0	3	.091	.091
Sabo, Chris	.278	18	5	0	2	1	1	.333	.444
Samuel, Juan	.375	8	3	0	2	1	3	.444	.500
Sanders, R	.300	10	3	2	4	1	0	.417	1.000
Santangelo, F#	.857	7	6	0	2	0	0	.857	.857
Santiago, B	.150	20	3	1	2	0	6	.150	.350
Scarsone, S	.000	7	0	0	0	0	2	.000	.000
Schofield, D	.250	4	1	0	1	2	0	.500	.250
Segui, David#	.333	9	3	0	0	0	2	.333	.333
Servais, S	.000	3	0	0	0	1	0	.250	.000
Sheffield, G	.318	22	7	0	2	2	2	.385	.500
Smith, Ozzie#	.520	25	13	0	1	5	1	.600	.640
Spiers, Bill*	.400	5	2	0	0	0	2	.400	.400
Stillwell, K#	.333	6	2	0	1	2	1	.500	.500
Stocker, K#	.800	5	4	0	1	1	0	.857	1.000
Strawberry, D*	.000	3	0	0	0	2	1	.400	.000
Tarasco, Tony*	.600	5	3	0	0	1	2	.667	1.000
Taubensee, E*	.400	10	4	0	3	1	1	.455	.700
Tavarez, Je#	.000	6	0	0	0	0	1	.143	.000
Thompson, Ja*	.333	3	1	1	2	1	1	.400	1.333
Thompson, Mil*	.077	13	1	0	0	2	3	.250	.077
Thompson, Rob	.188	16	3	0	0	2	4	.350	.250
Thompson, Ry	.286	7	2	1	1	1	2	.375	1.000
VanderWal, J*	.188	16	3	0	0	0	7	.188	.188
Veras, Q#	.429	7	3	0	0	1	2	.500	.429
Vizcaino, J#	.364	11	4	0	0	1	2	.417	.455
Walker, Larry*	.138	29	4	1	3	2	5	.219	.276
Wallach, Tim	.417	12	5	1	2	0	0	.417	.750
Weiss, Walt#	.263	19	5	0	1	1	2	.300	.263
White, Devon#	.167	6	1	0	0	0	0	.167	.167
White, R	.182	11	2	0	0	0	4	.182	.273
Whiten, Mark#	.250	8	2	0	1	0	1	.250	.250
Wilkins, Rick*	.143	7	1	0	0	1	3	.250	.143
Williams, E	.167	12	2	0	0	1	1	.231	.167
Williams, Ma	.429	28	12	4	11	1	5	.448	.964
Young, Eric	.278	18	5	0	0	1	2	.316	.389
Zeile, Todd	.333	24	8	2	2	3	2	.407	.583

Tony Castillo, White Sox — LHP

Batter	Avg	AB	H	HR	BI	BB	SO	OBP	Slg
Alexander, M	.000	4	0	0	0	0	1	.000	.000
Alicea, Luis#	.167	6	1	0	1	0	1	.167	.167
Alomar, R#	.333	6	2	0	1	1	0	.429	.500
Alomar Jr, S	.400	5	2	0	0	0	0	.400	.400
Amaral, Rich	.250	8	2	0	1	0	3	.222	.250
Anderson, Brd*	.267	15	4	0	0	0	3	.267	.400
Baerga, C#	.100	10	1	0	2	0	2	.083	.100
Baines, H*	.000	5	0	0	0	1	1	.167	.000
Becker, Rich*	.167	6	1	0	1	0	1	.286	.167
Belle, Albert	.375	8	3	1	2	1	5	.500	.875
Berroa, G	.400	5	2	1	4	0	0	.500	1.000
Blowers, Mike	.143	7	1	0	0	1	0	.143	.143
Boggs, Wade*	.333	9	3	0	2	0	0	.333	.444
Bonds, Barry*	.500	6	3	0	0	0	2	.429	.500
Bonilla, B#	.444	9	4	1	7	1	0	.500	1.111
Bordick, Mike	.000	4	0	0	1	3	1	.375	.000
Brosius, S	.000	5	0	0	0	1	1	.167	.000
Buhner, Jay	.250	8	2	0	2	2	1	.400	.250
Butler, Brett*	.333	6	2	0	2	1	1	.429	.333
Caminiti, Ken#	.200	5	1	0	1	0	1	.200	.200
Carter, Joe	.500	6	3	0	2	1	1	.571	.667
Clark, Tony*	.400	5	2	0	0	0	1	.400	.400
Clark, Will*	.273	11	3	0	1	1	4	.333	.273
Coleman, V#	.455	11	5	0	2	0	1	.455	.636
Cora, Joey#	.167	6	1	0	0	0	1	.167	.167
Davis, Chili*	.375	8	3	2	3	0	3	.375	1.125
Davis, Eric	.750	4	3	0	2	2	0	.833	1.000
DeShields, D*	.000	4	0	0	0	0	3	.000	.000
Devereaux, M	.600	5	3	1	2	1	0	.667	1.400
DiSarcina, G	.250	8	2	0	0	0	0	.250	.250
Duncan, M	.286	7	2	0	0	0	0	.286	.286
Fielder, C	.000	4	0	0	0	2	2	.333	.000
Franco, Julio	.000	8	0	0	0	1	0	.000	.000
Frye, Jeff	.600	5	3	1	3	0	0	.600	1.200
Fryman, T	.125	8	1	0	0	1	4	.222	.125
Gagne, Greg	.429	7	3	0	0	2	0	.556	.571
Gates, Brent#	.333	12	4	0	2	2	1	.429	.500
Gomez, Chris	.600	5	3	0	4	0	1	.600	.600
Grace, Mark*	.250	8	2	0	0	0	0	.250	.250
Greenwell, M*	.364	11	4	0	3	0	0	.385	.364
Griffey Jr, K*	.200	5	1	1	1	0	0	.200	.800
Guillen, O*	.286	7	2	0	1	0	0	.286	.286

Tony Castillo, White Sox — LHP

Batter	Avg	AB	H	HR	BI	BB	SO	OBP	Slg
Gwynn, Tony*	.500	4	2	0	2	1	0	.500	.500
Hamilton, D*	.375	8	3	0	2	1	0	.444	.375
Henderson, R	.400	5	2	0	2	2	1	.571	.400
Hoiles, Chris	.182	11	2	1	2	3	2	.357	.455
Howard, Dave#	.000	4	0	0	1	1	1	.167	.000
Hudler, Rex	.167	6	1	0	0	0	0	.167	.167
Jaha, John	.400	5	2	1	2	2	0	.571	1.200
Javier, Stan#	.143	7	1	0	0	2	3	.333	.286
Jefferson, R*	.250	8	2	0	1	0	2	.250	.250
Johnson, L*	.167	6	1	0	0	0	1	.167	.167
Joyner, Wally*	.200	10	2	0	0	2	3	.333	.300
Kreuter, Chad*	.250	8	2	0	1	0	2	.250	.250
Lankford, Ray*	.400	5	2	0	1	0	2	.400	.400
Lewis, Mark	.400	5	2	0	1	0	2	.333	.400
Leyritz, Jim	.333	6	2	0	2	2	1	.500	.333
Listach, Pat	.000	6	0	0	0	0	3	.000	.000
Lofton, Kenny*	.300	10	3	0	2	1	0	.364	.400
Macfarlane, M	.077	13	1	0	0	1	1	.143	.077
Martinez, Da*	.333	6	2	0	0	0	2	.333	.500
Martinez, T*	.333	6	2	0	1	2	1	.500	.500
McGee, Willie*	.333	6	2	0	2	0	0	.333	.500
McLemore, M#	.286	7	2	0	0	1	1	.375	.571
McRae, Brian#	.333	9	3	1	2	0	1	.333	.667
Meares, Pat	.400	5	2	0	1	1	1	.500	.600
Mieske, Matt	.200	5	1	0	0	1	1	.200	.200
Mitchell, K	.500	4	2	0	0	2	1	.667	.500
Molitor, Paul	.000	4	0	0	1	1	0	.167	.000
Morris, Hal*	.200	5	1	0	1	0	1	.200	.200
Munoz, Pedro	.250	4	1	0	1	0	1	.200	.250
Murray, Eddie#	.111	9	1	0	0	2	3	.273	.111
Naehring, Tim	.000	4	0	0	1	0	1	.000	.000
Nixon, Otis#	.222	9	2	0	0	3	1	.417	.222
O'Leary, Troy*	.444	9	4	0	2	0	0	.444	.667
O'Neill, Paul*	.235	17	4	0	4	2	6	.316	.294
Offerman, J#	.200	5	1	0	1	0	0	.200	.200
Oliver, Joe	.429	7	3	1	3	1	1	.500	1.000
Palmeiro, R*	.222	9	2	1	2	0	0	.222	.667
Paquette, C	.000	6	0	0	0	0	3	.000	.000
Phillips, T#	.000	5	0	0	0	3	0	.375	.000
Raines, Tim#	.250	4	1	0	0	1	0	.400	.250
Ramirez, M	.000	6	0	0	0	1	2	.143	.000
Reboulet, J	.750	4	3	0	0	0	0	.750	.750
Ripken, Cal	.545	11	6	1	2	0	1	.545	.909
Roberts, B*	.429	7	3	0	0	1	0	.500	.429
Sabo, Chris	.300	10	3	0	1	1	1	.364	.400
Salmon, Tim	.667	6	4	2	2	0	1	.667	1.667
Samuel, Juan	.667	6	4	0	1	1	1	.625	.667
Sandberg, R	.000	5	0	0	0	1	0	.000	.000
Seitzer, K	.231	13	3	0	1	1	1	.286	.385
Sierra, Ruben*	.250	16	4	1	5	1	3	.278	.438
Slaught, Don	.500	4	2	0	0	1	1	.600	.750
Smith, Ozzie*	.200	5	1	0	1	1	0	.333	.400
Snow, J.T.#	.125	8	1	0	0	0	2	.125	.125
Sorrento, P*	.273	11	3	0	3	0	2	.273	.364
Stanley, Mike	.444	9	4	2	3	1	3	.455	1.111
Steinbach, T	.333	9	3	0	0	0	1	.333	.333
Strange, Doug#	.200	5	1	0	0	0	0	.200	.200
Surhoff, B.J.*	.364	11	4	0	3	1	0	.462	.364
Tartabull, D	.571	7	4	0	1	3	0	.700	.857
Tettleton, M#	.000	10	0	0	1	2	2	.154	.000
Thomas, Frank	.400	5	2	0	1	0	0	.400	.600
Thome, Jim*	.250	8	2	0	0	1	2	.333	.375
Thompson, Rob	.143	7	1	0	0	1	4	.250	.286
Tinsley, Lee#	.000	5	0	0	0	0	1	.000	.000
Trammell, A	.500	6	3	0	0	0	0	.500	.500
Valentin, Jhn	.222	9	2	0	0	0	2	.222	.222
Valentin, Jse#	.400	5	2	1	2	0	0	.400	1.000
Vaughn, Greg	.250	4	1	0	2	3	1	.500	.250
Vaughn, Mo*	.400	15	6	1	4	0	2	.412	.733
Velarde, R	.143	7	1	0	0	0	0	.143	.143
Ventura, R*	.250	8	2	1	3	0	1	.250	.625
Vizquel, Omar#	.167	6	1	0	0	0	1	.167	.167
Wallach, Tim	.000	8	0	0	0	0	1	.000	.000
Williams, Ber#	.143	7	1	0	1	1	2	.250	.143
Wilson, Dan	.167	6	1	0	0	0	2	.167	.167

Norm Charlton, Mariners — LHP

Batter	Avg	AB	H	HR	BI	BB	SO	OBP	Slg
Alomar, R#	.263	19	5	0	0	7	1	.462	.316
Alomar Jr, S	.500	4	2	0	0	1	0	.600	.500
Anderson, Brd*	.000	7	0	0	0	2	1	.222	.000
Anderson, G*	.000	3	0	0	0	1	0	.000	.000
Bagwell, Jeff	.500	8	4	1	2	3	1	.636	1.000
Baines, H*	.000	4	0	0	1	0	2	.000	.000
Bell, Jay	.500	14	7	1	2	0	0	.500	.714
Berroa, G	.000	6	0	0	0	2	1	.000	.000
Biggio, Craig	.292	24	7	1	3	1	5	.320	.500
Blauser, Jeff	.286	14	4	0	1	0	4	.267	.357
Boggs, Wade*	.000	7	0	0	0	1	0	.143	.143
Bonds, Barry*	.263	19	5	0	0	3	3	.263	.421
Bonilla, B#	.346	26	9	0	0	2	7	.393	.462
Bordick, Mike	.000	3	0	0	1	3	1	.500	.000
Butler, Brett*	.190	21	4	0	1	3	2	.320	.190
Caminiti, Ken#	.037	27	1	0	3	2	7	.103	.148
Candaele, C#	.222	18	4	0	1	0	5	.222	.278
Carreon, Mark	.429	7	3	0	0	2	1	.556	.429
Carter, Joe	.333	12	4	0	3	0	2	.333	.500
Clark, Will*	.091	22	2	0	0	3	7	.259	.091
Coleman, V#	.231	13	3	0	0	0	1	.231	.308
Cora, Joey#	.400	5	2	0	0	0	0	.400	.400
Dascenzo, D#	.273	11	3	0	1	1	3	.333	.364
Daulton, D*	.333	6	2	0	0	1	3	.600	.667
Davis, Chili#	.000	4	0	0	0	1	3	.000	.000
Dawson, Andre	.263	19	5	1	6	1	4	.286	.421
DeShields, D*	.200	5	1	0	0	1	1	.333	.200
Devereaux, M	.000	4	0	0	0	1	1	.200	.000
DiSarcina, A	.500	6	3	0	0	0	0	.500	.667
Dunston, S	.417	12	5	0	2	0	3	.417	.417
Durham, Ray#	.000	5	0	0	0	1	3	.167	.000
Dykstra, L*	.000	10	0	0	0	1	4	.091	.000
Elster, Kevin	.200	10	2	0	1	1	2	.273	.200
Finley, Steve*	.375	16	6	0	2	0	1	.375	.375
Galarraga, A	.286	7	2	0	1	1	0	.375	.571
Gant, Ron	.125	16	2	0	1	3	6	.300	.125
Gilkey, B	.100	10	1	0	0	2	1	.100	.100
Girardi, Joe	.111	9	1	0	0	2	0	.273	.111
Gonzalez, J	.167	6	1	0	0	0	3	.167	.333
Gonzalez, L*	.000	6	0	0	0	1	5	.250	.000
Grace, Mark*	.238	21	5	1	9	1	1	.261	.429
Grissom, M	.333	9	3	0	0	2	2	.333	.444
Gwynn, Tony*	.333	24	8	0	4	2	2	.385	.417
Hamilton, D*	.000	4	0	0	0	1	0	.200	.000
Harris, Lenny*	.000	6	0	0	0	1	0	.000	.000
Hayes, C	.300	10	3	0	1	1	3	.364	.300
Hoiles, Chris	.143	7	1	1	4	0	4	.143	.571
Hollins, Dave#	.600	10	6	1	2	0	4	.600	.900
Hudler, Rex	.100	10	1	0	0	1	3	.182	.100
Hunter, Brian	.000	7	0	0	0	1	3	.125	.000
Javier, Stan#	.273	11	3	0	1	0	3	.273	.364
Jefferies, G#	.286	7	2	0	0	0	2	.286	.429
Jordan, Ricky	.400	10	4	0	4	2	2	.500	.500
Justice, Dave*	.308	13	4	1	5	2	3	.400	.615
King, Jeff	.000	10	0	0	0	1	1	.000	.000
Lankford, Ray*	.200	5	1	0	1	1	1	.286	.200
Lemke, Mark#	.188	16	3	0	1	1	1	.235	.188
Lewis, Darren	.429	7	3	0	1	0	2	.429	.571
Magadan, Dave*	.182	11	2	0	0	1	0	.250	.273
Manwaring, K	.250	4	1	0	0	1	0	.400	.750
Martin, N	.250	4	1	0	0	0	3	.250	.250
McGee, Willie#	.143	14	2	0	0	0	6	.143	.143
McGriff, Fred*	.000	11	0	0	0	6	4	.353	.000
McLemore, M#	.125	8	1	0	1	1	1	.222	.125
Merced, O*	.000	5	0	0	0	1	1	.000	.000
Mitchell, K	.267	15	4	1	2	0	4	.267	.467
Murray, Eddie#	.313	16	5	0	2	5	3	.476	.313
Naehring, Tim	.333	3	1	0	0	2	1	.600	.333
Nixon, Otis#	.125	8	1	0	0	1	1	.222	.125
O'Neill, Paul*	.000	5	0	0	0	1	1	.167	.000
Offerman, J#	.143	7	1	0	0	0	2	.143	.143
Pagnozzi, Tom	.000	10	0	0	0	1	2	.091	.000
Palmeiro, R*	.091	11	1	0	1	0	2	.091	.091
Paquette, C	.200	5	1	0	0	0	2	.200	.200
Parent, Mark	.143	7	1	0	0	0	3	.143	.143
Pena, Tony	.000	5	0	0	0	1	0	.000	.000
Pendleton, T#	.500	18	9	1	6	1	1	.526	.833
Phillips, T#	.000	5	0	0	0	0	4	.000	.000
Raines, Tim#	.111	9	1	0	0	1	1	.200	.111
Ripken, Cal	.250	8	2	0	3	1	2	.300	.375
Roberts, Bip#	.300	20	6	0	0	1	5	.364	.300
Rodriguez, I	.125	8	1	0	0	0	2	.125	.125
Salmon, Tim	.400	5	2	0	0	0	1	.400	.400
Samuel, Juan	.385	13	5	0	2	1	6	.429	.385
Sandberg, R	.188	16	3	0	0	2	3	.278	.250
Santiago, B	.111	18	2	0	1	2	4	.200	.111
Seitzer, K	.200	5	1	0	0	0	2	.200	.200
Slaught, Don	.308	13	4	1	3	1	4	.357	.615
Smith, Ozzie*	.333	21	7	0	3	2	2	.391	.571
Snow, J.T.#	.286	7	2	0	1	1	3	.375	.429
Stanley, Mike	.200	5	1	0	0	1	0	.200	.200
Strawberry, D*	.250	8	2	0	4	1	1	.400	.375
Surhoff, B.J.*	.000	5	0	0	0	1	5	.167	.000
Thompson, Rob	.083	12	1	0	1	0	4	.083	.083
Valentin, Jhn	.143	7	1	0	1	1	2	.250	.143
Vaughn, Greg	.250	4	1	1	1	2	1	.400	1.000
Vaughn, Mo*	.000	6	0	0	0	1	3	.143	.000
Velarde, R	.167	6	1	0	0	0	3	.167	.333
Ventura, R*	.200	5	1	0	3	1	0	.500	.200
Vizquel, Omar*	.400	5	2	1	0	0	0	.400	1.000
Walker, Larry*	.571	7	4	0	1	0	2	.571	.714
Wallach, Tim	.000	9	0	0	0	0	2	.000	.000
Walton, J	.125	8	1	0	1	0	1	.125	.125
Williams, Ber#	.125	8	1	0	1	1	5	.222	.125

Norm Charlton, Mariners — LHP

Batter	Avg	AB	H	HR	BI	BB	SO	OBP	Slg
Williams, E	.500	4	2	0	0	2	0	.667	.500
Williams, Ma	.333	12	4	1	3	5	3	.529	.583
Zeile, Todd	.364	11	4	0	0	2	1	.462	.364

Bobby Chouinard, Athletics — RHP

Batter	Avg	AB	H	HR	BI	BB	SO	OBP	Slg
Buhner, Jay	.167	6	1	0	0	0	1	.286	.167
Cora, Joey#	.000	6	0	0	0	1	1	.143	.000
Gonzalez, J	.167	6	1	1	3	0	1	.167	.667
Greer, Rusty	.600	5	3	1	2	1	0	.667	1.400
Hamilton, D*	.167	6	1	0	0	0	0	.167	.167
Martinez, E	.400	5	2	1	1	2	0	.571	1.200
Newson, W*	.000	5	0	0	0	0	2	.000	.000
Palmer, Dean	.000	5	0	0	0	1	1	.167	.000
Ripken, Billy	.400	5	2	0	0	0	0	.400	.600
Rodriguez, J	.500	6	3	2	4	1	2	.571	1.667
Rodriguez, I	.833	6	5	1	1	0	0	.833	1.500
Sojo, Luis	.200	5	1	0	0	0	0	.200	.200
Sorrento, P*	.333	6	2	0	0	0	0	.333	.333

Jason Christiansen, Pirates — LHP

Batter	Avg	AB	H	HR	BI	BB	SO	OBP	Slg
Bonds, Barry*	.400	5	2	0	1	2	2	.571	.600
Caminiti, Ken#	.333	3	1	0	0	2	0	.600	.333
DeShields, D*	.000	8	0	0	0	1	4	.111	.000
Finley, Steve*	.250	8	2	1	2	0	1	.250	.750
Grace, Mark*	.200	5	1	0	0	2	1	.333	.200
Gwynn, Tony*	.200	5	1	0	0	2	0	.429	.400
Klesko, Ryan*	.400	4	0	0	0	2	3	.333	.000
Lankford, Ray*	.000	6	0	0	1	0	4	.000	.000
Lansing, Mike	.500	4	2	0	0	1	0	.600	.500
McGriff, Fred*	.000	7	0	0	0	1	4	.125	.000
Morandini, M*	.375	8	3	0	0	0	2	.375	.625
Veras, Q#	.200	5	1	0	0	0	1	.200	.200

Mike Christopher, Tigers — RHP

Batter	Avg	AB	H	HR	BI	BB	SO	OBP	Slg
Alomar, R#	.333	6	2	0	0	0	1	.333	.333
Becker, Rich*	.500	4	2	0	0	1	0	.600	.500
Borders, Pat	.167	6	1	0	0	0	1	.167	.167
Brosius, S	.400	5	2	0	1	0	1	.400	.400
Buhner, Jay	.250	4	1	0	0	1	1	.400	.250
Carter, Joe	.500	5	2	1	1	1	1	.500	1.200
Cora, Joey#	.000	7	0	0	0	0	0	.000	.000
Cordova, M	.000	5	0	0	0	1	1	.167	.000
Davis, Chili*	.200	5	1	0	1	0	2	.200	.200
Diaz, Alex#	.200	5	1	0	0	0	1	.200	.200
DiSarcina, G	.000	6	0	0	0	1	0	.143	.000
Fabregas, Jor*	.600	5	3	1	1	0	0	.600	1.200
Gagne, Greg	.600	5	3	0	1	0	0	.600	.800
Greer, Rusty*	.400	5	2	0	1	1	1	.500	.400
Hollins, Dave#	.667	3	2	0	0	2	1	.800	.667
Knoblauch, C	.167	6	1	0	0	1	0	.286	.333
Lawton, Matt*	.200	5	1	0	0	1	0	.200	.200
Martinez, E	.800	5	4	0	0	0	1	.800	1.200
Molitor, Paul	.000	9	0	0	0	0	1	.000	.000
Munoz, Pedro	.167	6	1	1	1	0	4	.167	.667
Naehring, Tim	.000	4	0	0	1	1	0	.000	.000
Olerud, John*	.250	4	1	1	1	1	0	.400	1.000
Palmer, Dean	.333	6	2	0	1	0	2	.333	.500
Reboulet, J	.250	4	1	0	1	1	0	.400	.500
Rodriguez, I	.286	7	2	0	1	0	0	.286	.286
Sprague, Ed	.200	5	1	1	2	0	2	.200	.800
Tettleton, M#	.500	4	2	0	1	2	1	.667	.500
Vaughn, Mo*	.600	5	3	2	2	0	0	.600	1.800
Velarde, R	.167	6	1	0	0	0	0	.167	.167
Wilson, Dan	.500	4	2	2	2	1	2	.600	2.000

Mark Clark, Mets — RHP

Batter	Avg	AB	H	HR	BI	BB	SO	OBP	Slg
Aldrete, Mike*	.300	10	3	1	2	0	1	.300	.600
Alicea, Luis#	.125	8	1	0	1	4	2	.417	.125
Alomar, R#	.333	15	5	0	1	2	1	.412	.400
Amaral, Rich	.500	6	3	0	1	0	1	.500	.500
Amaro, Ruben*	.571	7	4	1	2	1	2	.556	1.143
Anderson, Brd*	.200	15	3	1	1	2	0	.294	.400
Arias, Alex	.286	7	2	0	1	1	1	.375	.286
Bagwell, Jeff	.375	8	3	0	2	1	0	.444	.375
Baines, H*	.125	8	1	0	0	2	0	.300	.125
Barberie, B#	.400	10	4	0	2	2	0	.500	.400
Becker, Rich*	.231	13	3	1	4	1	2	.286	.462
Bell, Derek	.000	6	0	0	0	0	2	.000	.000
Bell, Jay	.176	17	3	1	1	1	4	.222	.412
Berroa, G	.300	10	3	0	0	0	2	.300	.300
Berry, Sean	.333	6	2	0	0	0	0	.333	.333
Bichette, D	.286	7	2	0	1	1	0	.375	.286
Biggio, Craig	.250	8	2	0	1	0	2	.333	.375
Blauser, Jeff	.333	6	2	0	0	0	2	.333	.333
Blowers, Mike	.100	10	1	0	1	0	4	.100	.100
Boggs, Wade*	.500	6	3	0	0	1	0	.571	.500
Bonds, Barry*	.091	11	1	1	2	4	1	.333	.364
Bonilla, B#	.571	7	4	0	0	1	1	.625	.714
Boone, Bret	.333	6	2	0	0	0	3	.333	.333
Borders, Pat	.263	19	5	0	0	0	2	.263	.263
Bordick, Mike	.300	10	3	1	1	1	0	.364	.600
Branson, Jeff*	.000	5	0	0	0	1	0	.167	.000
Brosius, S	.000	4	0	0	0	1	0	.200	.000
Buford, Damon	.000	2	0	0	1	2	1	.400	.000
Buhner, Jay	.143	7	1	0	2	2	2	.333	.286
Burks, Ellis	.231	13	3	0	0	0	3	.231	.231
Caminiti, Ken#	.600	5	3	1	1	1	0	.667	1.200
Cangelosi, J#	.000	6	0	0	0	1	1	.143	.000
Canseco, Jose	.286	14	4	0	4	2	0	.353	.357
Carreon, Mark	.000	6	0	0	0	0	0	.000	.000
Carter, Joe	.211	19	4	2	4	0	4	.200	.526
Castilla, V	.500	6	3	0	0	0	0	.500	.833
Cedeno, Roger#	.000	6	0	0	0	0	0	.000	.000
Clark, Dave*	.333	6	2	1	3	1	0	.429	.833
Clark, Will*	.333	6	2	0	1	2	1	.444	.333
Clayton, R	.000	5	0	0	0	0	0	.000	.000
Colbrunn, G	.364	11	4	0	0	1	1	.417	.455
Cole, Alex*	.267	15	4	0	2	1	1	.313	.467
Coleman, V#	.154	13	2	0	1	2	3	.250	.154
Conine, Jeff	.400	10	4	0	1	0	2	.400	.600
Cora, Joey#	.182	11	2	0	1	2	0	.308	.182
Cordova, M	.000	5	0	0	0	0	0	.000	.000
Curtis, Chad	.200	15	3	1	3	0	4	.200	.467
Damon, Johnny*	.333	6	2	0	0	0	1	.333	.333
Dascenzo, D#	.167	6	1	0	1	0	1	.167	.167
Daulton, D*	.429	7	3	0	2	2	1	.556	.714
Davis, Chili#	.100	10	1	1	1	1	2	.182	.400
Davis, Eric	.357	14	5	0	2	1	1	.375	.357
Dawson, Andre	.333	6	2	0	2	0	2	.286	.667
DeShields, D*	.071	14	1	0	0	1	3	.133	.071
Devereaux, M	.400	5	2	1	4	0	1	.400	1.400
DiSarcina, G	.125	8	1	0	2	0	0	.125	.250
Duncan, M	.333	6	2	0	0	0	0	.333	.500
Dunston, S	.111	9	1	0	0	0	2	.111	.222
Dykstra, L*	.333	6	2	0	0	1	0	.429	.500
Easley, D	.571	7	4	0	0	1	0	.625	.857
Eisenreich, J*	.500	6	3	0	1	1	1	.571	.500
Fielder, C	.125	8	1	0	0	2	3	.300	.125
Finley, Steve*	.200	5	1	0	0	1	1	.333	.200
Flaherty, J	.222	9	2	0	1	1	2	.300	.333
Franco, Julio	.429	7	3	0	0	0	1	.429	.429
Frye, Jeff	.750	4	3	0	0	1	0	.800	1.250
Fryman, T	.125	8	1	0	0	3	0	.364	.125
Gaetti, Gary	.053	19	1	0	0	0	6	.053	.105
Gagne, Greg	.500	16	8	0	2	0	1	.500	.563
Galarraga, A	.444	9	4	2	3	1	2	.500	1.222
Gant, Ron	.000	7	0	0	1	0	2	.000	.000
Gates, Brent*	.154	13	2	0	0	0	1	.154	.154
Gomez, Chris	.429	14	6	0	0	0	2	.429	.571
Gomez, Leo	.143	14	2	0	2	1	2	.200	.214
Gonzalez, J	.250	12	3	1	1	0	0	.250	.583
Goodwin, Tom*	.429	14	6	1	2	1	1	.500	.643
Grace, Mark*	.500	12	6	0	1	1	0	.538	.667
Green, Shawn*	.429	7	3	0	0	1	1	.500	.714
Greenwell, M*	.222	9	2	0	1	1	0	.300	.333
Greer, Rusty*	.600	5	3	0	4	0	0	.500	.600
Griffey Jr, K*	.500	4	2	0	0	1	0	.600	.750
Grissom, M	.235	17	4	0	1	0	1	.235	.294
Guillen, O*	.273	11	3	0	2	0	2	.273	.364
Gwynn, Tony*	.500	12	6	0	2	0	0	.500	.667
Hamelin, Bob*	.143	7	1	1	5	0	4	.111	.571
Hamilton, D*	.167	6	1	0	0	0	1	.167	.167
Hansen, Dave*	.222	9	2	0	0	1	2	.300	.222
Harris, Lenny*	.182	11	2	0	1	0	2	.182	.182
Haselman, B	.167	6	1	0	1	0	0	.167	.500
Hayes, C	.125	8	1	0	0	1	0	.222	.125
Henderson, R	.235	17	4	1	1	2	5	.316	.412
Higginson, R	.200	5	1	0	1	0	1	.167	.400
Hoiles, Chris	.400	10	4	0	0	3	0	.538	.500
Hollandsworth*	.250	12	3	1	3	0	4	.250	.583
Hollins, Dave#	.286	7	2	0	1	1	0	.333	.286
Howard, T*	.250	8	2	1	2	0	1	.250	.625
Hulse, David*	.643	14	9	0	2	0	1	.643	.786
Hundley, Todd#	.250	4	1	1	2	1	0	.400	1.000
Jaha, John	.111	9	1	0	0	1	1	.273	.111
Javier, Stan#	.333	9	3	0	1	0	0	.333	.300
Jefferies, G#	.167	12	2	0	3	1	0	.214	.167
Johnson, L*	.333	9	3	0	1	0	0	.333	.333
Johnson, Mark*	.167	6	1	0	1	1	0	.167	.333
Jones, Andruw	.000	4	0	0	0	1	1	.200	.000
Jones, C#	.500	8	4	1	2	2	1	.600	1.000
Jordan, Brian	.200	5	1	0	1	0	0	.200	.200
Joyner, Wally*	.313	16	5	0	2	2	4	.389	.313
Karkovice, B	.286	7	2	0	0	0	0	.286	.571
Karros, Eric	.385	13	5	0	2	3	3	.500	.462
Kelly, Pat	.200	5	1	0	0	0	0	.200	.200
Kendall, J	.286	7	2	0	0	0	0	.286	.286
King, Jeff	.250	12	3	1	1	2	1	.357	.500

Mark Clark, Mets — RHP

Batter	Avg	AB	H	HR	BI	BB	SO	OBP	Slg
Kirby, Wayne*	.250	8	2	0	1	0	0	.250	.375
Klesko, Ryan*	.286	7	2	0	1	1	3	.375	.286
Knoblauch, C	.294	17	5	0	1	0	1	.294	.294
Kreuter, Chad*	.000	4	0	0	0	1	1	.200	.000
Lampkin, Tom*	.500	8	4	0	1	0	0	.500	.500
Lansing, Mike	.600	5	3	1	1	0	0	.600	1.200
Larkin, Barry	.429	7	3	0	1	1	0	.500	.714
Leius, Scott	.222	9	2	1	1	2	0	.364	.556
Leyritz, Jim	.286	7	2	0	2	0	1	.286	.429
Liriano, N#	.500	6	3	0	1	0	0	.500	.500
Lockhart, K*	.222	9	2	1	2	0	0	.222	.556
Lopez, Javy	.125	8	1	0	0	0	2	.125	.125
Macfarlane, M	.625	8	5	2	2	0	2	.700	1.500
Magadan, Dave*	.400	5	2	0	0	0	0	.400	.600
Manwaring, K	.000	5	0	0	0	0	1	.000	.000
Martin, Al*	.333	9	3	0	1	0	1	.333	.333
Martinez, Da*	.625	8	5	0	0	0	0	.625	.625
Martinez, E	.250	4	1	1	2	3	0	.571	1.000
Martinez, S*	.400	5	2	1	2	0	0	.400	1.200
Martinez, T*	.625	8	5	0	2	1	0	.667	.875
May, Derrick*	.231	13	3	0	2	0	3	.214	.231
Mayne, Brent*	.500	6	3	0	0	2	0	.625	.667
McGriff, Fred*	.091	11	1	0	1	4	1	.333	.091
McLemore, M#	.500	6	3	1	3	1	0	.571	1.000
McRae, Brian#	.300	10	3	0	1	0	1	.364	.400
Meares, Pat	.200	10	2	0	1	0	2	.200	.200
Merced, O*	.286	14	4	0	3	0	1	.267	.429
Mieske, Matt	.333	6	2	0	1	0	2	.333	.500
Miller, Orl	.143	7	1	1	1	0	2	.143	.571
Molitor, Paul	.353	17	6	1	5	3	2	.450	.647
Mondesi, Raul	.231	13	3	0	2	0	5	.231	.308
Morandini, M*	.300	20	6	0	1	0	3	.300	.400
Morris, Hal*	.286	7	2	0	1	1	0	.375	.714
Munoz, Pedro	.125	8	1	0	0	1	2	.222	.125
Murray, Eddie#	.250	4	1	0	0	1	1	.400	.250
Naehring, Tim	.250	4	1	0	0	1	0	.400	.250
Nilsson, Dave*	.286	7	2	0	0	1	0	.375	.571
Nixon, Otis#	.000	5	0	0	0	0	2	.000	.000
O'Leary, Troy*	.429	14	6	0	0	1	3	.500	.643
O'Neill, Paul*	.455	11	5	3	5	0	0	.417	1.273
Offerman, J#	.000	6	0	0	1	0	2	.000	.000
Olerud, John*	.375	16	6	1	3	2	1	.444	.563
Oliver, Joe	.143	7	1	0	0	0	1	.143	.143
Otero, Ricky#	.364	11	4	0	0	0	0	.364	.364
Palmeiro, R*	.250	16	4	0	3	0	3	.250	.313
Palmer, Dean	.333	9	3	0	2	1	4	.400	.333
Pendleton, D	.267	15	4	0	1	0	2	.267	.333
Phillips, T#	.250	8	2	1	1	0	1	.250	.625
Piazza, Mike	.143	7	1	0	0	3	1	.400	.143
Polonia, Luis*	.111	9	1	0	2	0	3	.111	.111
Raines, Tim	.286	7	2	0	1	0	1	.375	.286
Reboulet, J	.333	6	2	0	0	2	1	.500	.500
Reed, Jeff*	.000	5	0	0	0	1	3	.167	.000
Reed, Jody	.500	6	3	0	0	0	0	.500	.500
Renteria, E	.250	8	2	0	0	0	3	.250	.250
Ripken, Cal	.267	15	4	1	1	0	1	.267	.467
Roberts, Bip#	.250	4	1	0	1	2	1	.500	.500
Rodriguez, H*	.375	8	3	1	4	0	0	.375	.875
Rodriguez, I	.571	7	4	0	1	0	0	.571	.571
Sabo, Chris	.429	7	3	0	0	0	2	.429	.429
Salmon, Tim	.100	10	1	1	1	1	1	.182	.400
Sanchez, Rey	.250	4	1	0	0	1	0	.400	.250
Sandberg, R	.500	12	6	2	3	3	2	.563	1.167
Sanders, R	.333	6	2	0	1	0	3	.333	.500
Santangelo, F#	.000	5	0	0	0	2	0	.000	.000
Santiago, B	.375	8	3	0	0	0	1	.375	.500
Schofield, D	.333	12	4	0	0	1	2	.385	.500
Segui, David#	.500	6	3	0	1	1	0	.571	.667
Seitzer, K	.400	5	2	0	0	1	1	.571	.400
Sheffield, G	.154	13	2	0	1	3	2	.313	.154
Shipley, C	.000	5	0	0	0	0	0	.000	.000
Sierra, Ruben#	.200	15	3	0	0	0	4	.200	.200
Smith, Dwight*	.200	15	3	0	1	0	2	.200	.333
Snow, J.T.#	.286	7	2	1	1	0	0	.286	.714
Sojo, Luis	.250	4	1	0	0	1	1	.400	.250
Sosa, Sammy	.444	9	4	3	3	0	2	.444	1.444
Spiers, Bill*	.250	8	2	0	1	0	0	.250	.250
Sprague, Ed	.235	17	4	2	2	1	2	.278	.647
Steinbach, T	.200	10	2	0	1	0	2	.182	.200
Stocker, K#	.500	8	4	1	1	1	2	.556	.875
Strange, Doug#	.375	8	3	0	0	0	0	.375	.375
Strawberry, D*	.600	5	3	0	0	1	0	.667	.800
Surhoff, B.J.*	.444	9	4	0	0	0	2	.500	.667
Taubensee, E*	.200	5	1	0	0	1	0	.333	.200
Tettleton, M#	.444	9	4	1	3	2	2	.545	.889
Thomas, Frank	.100	10	1	0	0	1	1	.182	.100
Thompson, Rob	.286	7	2	0	0	0	1	.286	.286
Tucker, M*	.429	7	3	0	1	0	0	.429	.714
Valentin, Jhn	.250	12	3	0	0	0	2	.308	.250
Valentin, Jse#	.222	9	2	1	3	0	0	.200	.667
Vaughn, Greg	.176	17	3	1	4	1	2	.222	.471

Mark Clark, Mets — RHP

Batter	Avg	AB	H	HR	BI	BB	SO	OBP	Slg
Vaughn, Mo*	.333	12	4	0	2	0	4	.333	.417
Velarde, R	1.000	4	4	0	2	1	0	1.000	1.250
Ventura, R*	.500	8	4	1	4	1	2	.556	.875
Vitiello, Joe	.400	5	2	0	0	0	0	.400	.400
Vizcaino, J#	.000	8	0	0	0	0	1	.000	.000
Walbeck, Matt#	.000	6	0	0	1	1	3	.143	.000
Walker, Larry*	.357	14	5	1	3	0	2	.357	.714
Wallach, Tim	.200	10	2	0	2	1	4	.250	.200
Ward, Turner#	.300	10	3	0	0	0	0	.300	.300
Wehner, John	.500	4	2	0	0	1	0	.600	.750
Weiss, Walt#	.429	7	3	0	0	1	1	.500	.429
White, Devon#	.333	24	8	3	6	0	3	.333	.792
Wilkins, Rick*	.333	9	3	0	2	0	4	.333	.444
Williams, Ber#	.000	4	0	0	0	1	1	.200	.000
Williams, Ma	.143	7	1	0	0	0	2	.143	.286
Zeile, Todd	.429	7	3	0	2	0	2	.429	.571

Terry Clark, Astros — RHP

Batter	Avg	AB	H	HR	BI	BB	SO	OBP	Slg
Berroa, G	.200	5	1	0	0	0	0	.200	.200
Boggs, Wade*	.667	9	6	0	1	1	0	.700	.667
Bordick, Mike	.600	5	3	1	2	0	0	.600	1.200
Buhner, Jay	.600	5	3	0	3	1	0	.667	.600
Burks, Ellis	.333	6	2	0	2	1	0	.429	.500
Canseco, Jose	.000	6	0	0	1	2	4	.250	.000
Carter, Joe	.125	8	1	0	1	0	0	.125	.125
Franco, Julio	.333	6	2	0	0	2	0	.500	.333
Greenwell, M	.375	8	3	0	2	0	0	.375	.625
Hall, Mel*	.167	6	1	0	0	0	1	.167	.167
Henderson, R	.556	9	5	0	1	0	1	.556	.778
Jaha, John	.000	6	0	0	0	0	0	.000	.000
Javier, Stan*	.500	6	3	0	0	1	0	.625	.500
Listach, Pat#	.500	4	2	0	1	1	2	.600	.750
McGwire, Mark	.375	8	3	0	0	2	1	.500	.500
Molitor, Paul	.143	7	1	0	1	0	0	.143	.143
Reed, Jody	.400	5	2	0	0	2	1	.571	.600
Seitzer, K	.000	5	0	0	1	1	0	.167	.000
Sierra, Ruben#	.429	7	3	0	3	0	1	.375	.571
Stanley, Mike	.200	5	1	0	2	0	0	.167	.200
Velarde, R	.200	4	2	0	2	1	0	.600	1.000

Roger Clemens, Red Sox — RHP

Batter	Avg	AB	H	HR	BI	BB	SO	OBP	Slg
Aldrete, Mike*	.267	15	4	2	3	4	4	.421	.667
Alexander, M	.167	6	1	0	0	0	1	.167	.167
Alomar, R#	.191	47	9	0	5	5	4	.269	.255
Alomar Jr, S	.318	22	7	0	1	1	6	.348	.318
Amaral, Rich	.125	8	1	0	1	0	1	.125	.125
Anderson, Brd*	.323	31	10	1	3	6	9	.475	.581
Anderson, G*	.235	17	4	0	0	0	3	.235	.235
Anthony, Eric*	.167	6	1	0	0	0	2	.167	.167
Ausmus, Brad	.333	6	2	0	0	0	1	.333	.500
Baerga, C#	.169	59	10	1	5	0	10	.169	.237
Baines, H*	.308	78	24	2	7	10	15	.386	.423
Bautista, D	.200	5	1	0	0	0	3	.200	.200
Becker, Rich	.222	9	2	0	0	2	2	.417	.222
Belle, Albert	.200	50	10	1	6	7	18	.298	.340
Berroa, G	.200	20	4	1	1	1	9	.238	.400
Berry, Sean	.200	5	1	0	0	0	2	.200	.200
Bichette, D	.412	17	7	0	1	0	6	.412	.471
Blowers, Mike	.200	5	1	0	1	1	2	.333	.400
Boggs, Wade*	.231	13	3	0	1	8	1	.524	.231
Bonilla, B#	.154	13	2	0	1	2	4	.267	.154
Boone, Bret	.333	6	2	0	1	0	1	.429	.500
Borders, Pat	.290	31	9	1	3	1	5	.313	.387
Bordick, Mike	.143	21	3	0	2	1	3	.269	.238
Bragg, Darren*	.125	8	1	0	2	0	0	.200	.125
Brosius, S	.125	8	1	0	0	1	3	.222	.125
Buhner, Jay	.162	37	6	2	5	5	13	.262	.351
Butler, Brett*	.345	29	10	0	1	0	3	.367	.414
Cangelosi, J#	.300	10	3	0	1	2	0	.417	.300
Canseco, Jose	.176	51	9	3	7	5	20	.250	.353
Carter, Joe	.231	91	21	5	11	6	18	.297	.451
Cedeno, D#	.167	6	1	0	0	1	3	.286	.167
Cirillo, Jeff	.000	12	0	0	0	0	7	.000	.000
Clark, Dave*	.182	11	2	0	0	2	1	.308	.182
Clark, Tony#	.000	7	0	0	0	0	6	.000	.000
Clark, Will*	.571	7	4	1	4	2	1	.667	1.286
Cole, Alex*	.267	30	8	0	2	2	11	.313	.367
Cora, Joey#	.316	19	6	0	5	2	3	.348	.421
Cordova, M	.286	7	2	0	0	0	1	.375	.286
Curtis, Chad	.237	38	9	1	3	2	12	.275	.368
Cuyler, Milt*	.200	5	1	0	0	0	2	.200	.200
Damon, Johnny*	.182	11	2	0	0	0	2	.182	.182
Davis, Chili*	.282	78	22	3	9	7	28	.349	.462
Deer, Rob	.171	41	7	1	3	1	18	.190	.317
Delgado, C*	.600	5	3	0	1	1	3	.667	.800
Devereaux, M	.156	32	5	0	5	1	10	.176	.156
Diaz, Alex*	.500	6	3	0	1	0	2	.500	.667
DiSarcina, G	.167	36	6	0	1	1	6	.211	.194
Durham, Ray#	.333	6	2	0	1	0	1	.333	.333

Roger Clemens, Red Sox — RHP

Batter	Avg	AB	H	HR	BI	BB	SO	OBP	Slg
Easley, D	.154	26	4	0	3	1	7	.185	.192
Edmonds, Jim*	.143	21	3	1	3	6	10	.333	.286
Eisenreich, J*	.182	33	6	0	1	1	4	.200	.242
Elster, Kevin	.000	4	0	0	0	0	1	.000	.000
Espinoza, A	.207	29	6	0	1	1	5	.233	.241
Fabregas, Jor*	.143	21	3	0	0	0	7	.143	.143
Fermin, Felix	.188	48	9	0	3	1	10	.220	.208
Fielder, C	.024	41	1	0	2	3	20	.091	.024
Finley, Steve*	.333	6	2	0	0	1	1	.500	.333
Flaherty, J	.222	9	2	0	0	0	3	.222	.222
Fox, Andy*	.300	10	3	0	1	2	2	.417	.300
Franco, Julio	.212	85	18	0	6	4	11	.247	.306
Frye, Jeff	.750	4	3	0	0	1	0	.800	.750
Fryman, T	.179	39	7	2	4	2	17	.220	.359
Gaetti, Gary	.194	67	13	4	18	6	10	.257	.433
Gagne, Greg	.103	39	4	1	4	4	15	.186	.179
Gallego, Mike	.250	24	6	0	1	4	7	.379	.250
Gates, Brent*	.368	19	7	0	4	2	3	.429	.474
Giambi, Jason*	.250	12	3	0	1	1	4	.308	.250
Gil, Benji	.250	4	1	0	0	1	3	.400	.250
Girardi, Joe	.143	7	1	0	1	0	2	.143	.143
Gomez, Chris	.200	5	1	0	0	0	3	.200	.400
Gomez, Leo	.222	9	2	0	0	1	6	.300	.222
Gonzales, R	.136	22	3	0	0	0	4	.136	.182
Gonzalez, A	.300	10	3	1	1	2	2	.417	.600
Gonzalez, J	.296	27	8	3	9	5	6	.412	.741
Goodwin, C*	.444	9	4	0	1	1	2	.500	.556
Goodwin, Tom*	.286	14	4	0	0	2	2	.375	.286
Grebeck, C	.222	9	2	0	1	0	3	.222	.444
Green, Shawn*	.231	13	3	0	0	1	4	.286	.385
Greer, Rusty*	.100	10	1	0	0	3	2	.308	.100
Griffey Jr, K*	.413	46	19	3	8	9	7	.509	.717
Guillen, O*	.264	53	14	0	1	0	6	.264	.283
Gwynn, Chris*	.000	4	0	0	0	1	1	.200	.000
Hale, Chip*	.500	12	6	0	1	2	1	.600	.500
Hall, Mel*	.188	69	13	0	5	4	12	.233	.232
Hamelin, Bob*	.000	10	0	0	0	1	4	.167	.000
Hamilton, D*	.200	30	6	0	3	1	4	.219	.267
Hammonds, J	.400	5	2	0	1	2	0	.571	.400
Hayes, C	.333	9	3	0	1	0	3	.400	.333
Henderson, R	.182	55	10	0	2	10	14	.308	.218
Herrera, Jose*	.091	11	1	0	1	1	3	.167	.091
Higginson, B*	.133	15	2	1	3	1	6	.176	.400
Hill, G	.313	16	5	1	2	1	7	.353	.500
Hoiles, Chris	.250	36	9	0	5	1	9	.308	.278
Hollins, Dave#	.333	6	2	0	1	1	2	.375	.333
Howard, Dave#	.000	10	0	0	0	0	4	.000	.000
Howard, T*	.333	12	4	0	0	1	2	.385	.333
Howell, Jack*	.173	52	9	0	0	3	17	.218	.269
Hulse, David*	.000	14	0	0	0	1	4	.067	.000
Huson, Jeff*	.176	17	3	0	1	1	6	.211	.235
Incaviglia, P	.136	22	3	2	6	0	15	.136	.455
Jaha, John	.263	19	5	1	3	2	7	.333	.526
James, Dion*	.333	33	11	0	3	2	1	.371	.515
Javier, Stan#	.071	14	1	0	0	3	1	.316	.071
Jefferson, R*	.400	20	8	0	2	1	7	.455	.550
Jeter, Derek	.167	12	2	0	1	1	3	.231	.250
Johnson, L*	.125	40	5	0	0	0	7	.125	.125
Joyner, Wally*	.282	71	20	1	7	6	7	.338	.465
Karkovice, M	.000	6	0	0	0	0	2	.000	.000
Kelly, Pat	.000	9	0	0	0	1	3	.100	.000
Kelly, R	.262	42	11	1	6	1	12	.295	.405
Kent, Jeff	.143	7	1	0	0	0	1	.143	.143
Kingery, Mike*	.214	14	3	0	2	2	5	.313	.286
Kirby, Wayne*	.000	10	0	0	0	2	1	.231	.000
Knoblauch, C	.325	40	13	0	4	5	5	.400	.475
Kreuter, Chad*	.000	5	0	0	0	0	4	.429	.000
Lampkin, Tom*	.400	5	2	0	1	1	1	.500	.400
Leius, Scott	.143	7	1	1	1	1	1	.250	.571
Levis, Jesse*	.182	11	2	0	1	2	2	.286	.182
Lewis, Mark	.154	13	2	0	0	0	6	.154	.154
Leyritz, Jim	.500	10	5	1	4	0	2	.500	.900
Liriano, N#	.375	16	6	0	2	0	3	.412	.438
Listach, Pat#	.083	24	2	0	0	0	7	.083	.125
Livingstone*	.600	5	3	1	1	0	0	.600	1.200
Lockhart, K*	.385	13	5	0	2	2	1	.467	.538
Lofton, Kenny*	.233	30	7	0	2	3	11	.303	.300
Loretta, Mark	.667	6	4	0	0	0	0	.667	.667
Lovullo, T#	.167	12	2	1	1	0	5	.167	.500
Macfarlane, M	.290	31	9	0	4	1	10	.333	.290
Martin, N	.000	6	0	0	0	1	0	.000	.000
Martinez, Da*	.333	6	2	0	0	2	2	.500	.667
Martinez, E	.222	45	10	1	2	9	9	.255	.356
Martinez, S*	.273	11	3	1	3	0	2	.273	.636
Martinez, T*	.152	33	5	2	3	7	7	.263	.182
Mayne, Brent*	.391	23	9	0	2	3	5	.500	.435
McGriff, Fred*	.219	32	7	2	4	5	13	.324	.500
McGwire, Mark	.095	42	4	2	2	5	13	.191	.262
McLemore, M#	.206	34	7	0	2	6	13	.325	.265
McRae, Brian*	.280	25	7	1	2	2	5	.333	.520
Meares, Pat	.200	5	1	0	0	2	1	.429	.200
Mieske, Matt	.000	9	0	0	0	0	4	.000	.000
Mitchell, K	.333	6	2	1	3	0	1	.333	.833
Molitor, Paul	.348	89	31	1	11	7	15	.396	.461
Morman, Russ	.167	6	1	0	0	0	1	.167	.167
Murray, Eddie#	.350	40	14	2	4	6	4	.435	.575
Myers, Greg*	.185	27	5	0	0	0	6	.185	.185
Newfield, M	.200	5	1	0	0	0	1	.333	.200
Newson, W*	.222	9	2	0	1	2	5	.364	.333
Nieves, M#	.200	5	1	0	0	1	2	.333	.200
Nilsson, Dave*	.167	24	4	0	0	2	6	.231	.167
O'Brien, C	.333	6	2	0	0	1	3	.500	.333
O'Neill, Paul*	.211	19	4	0	2	7	2	.423	.316
Offerman, J#	.250	8	2	0	2	2	1	.400	.250
Olerud, John*	.152	46	7	2	11	10	10	.333	.326
Orsulak, Joe*	.292	24	7	0	2	1	2	.320	.292
Palmeiro, R*	.304	56	17	3	8	8	12	.391	.500
Palmer, Dean	.353	17	6	0	0	3	7	.450	.353
Paquette, C	.167	6	1	0	1	0	3	.167	.167
Pena, Tony	.333	6	2	0	0	0	2	.333	.500
Phillips, T#	.347	75	26	0	5	6	16	.395	.467
Plantier, P*	.250	8	2	0	0	1	5	.333	.250
Polonia, Luis*	.256	78	20	0	2	4	15	.293	.333
Raines, Tim#	.200	35	7	0	0	4	8	.282	.257
Ramirez, M	.444	9	4	3	3	1	2	.500	1.444
Randa, Joe	.333	6	2	0	2	0	1	.333	.667
Reboulet, J	.231	13	3	0	1	4	3	.412	.385
Reed, Jeff*	.167	6	1	0	0	0	2	.167	.333
Reed, Jody	.200	10	2	0	0	1	1	.273	.300
Ripken, Billy	.190	21	4	0	0	0	0	.190	.190
Ripken, Cal	.253	79	20	1	8	9	10	.326	.316
Roberts, Bip#	.167	6	1	0	0	1	3	.286	.167
Rodriguez, Al	.333	12	4	0	2	0	2	.286	.333
Rodriguez, I	.238	21	5	2	6	1	4	.304	.667
Salmon, Tim	.139	36	5	1	2	1	13	.184	.222
Samuel, Juan	.000	5	0	0	0	0	2	.000	.000
Schofield, D	.302	43	13	0	3	2	8	.348	.372
Schu, Rick	.286	7	2	0	0	0	1	.286	.286
Segui, David#	.455	11	5	0	3	1	0	.500	.545
Seitzer, K	.329	70	23	0	4	8	12	.405	.386
Sheffield, G	.533	15	8	0	2	1	1	.563	.600
Shumpert, T	.250	12	3	0	1	0	4	.250	.333
Sierra, Ruben#	.224	67	15	0	5	3	13	.257	.343
Slaught, Don	.125	8	1	1	1	0	2	.222	.500
Smith, Mark	.143	7	1	0	0	1	4	.250	.143
Snow, J.T.#	.088	34	3	0	2	2	15	.139	.118
Sojo, Luis	.250	8	2	0	0	0	0	.250	.250
Sorrento, P*	.214	42	9	0	6	3	9	.261	.262
Sosa, Sammy	.077	13	1	1	1	0	6	.077	.308
Spiers, Bill*	.292	24	7	1	1	0	6	.292	.625
Sprague, Ed	.136	22	3	0	1	1	8	.167	.227
Stahoviak, S*	.300	10	3	0	3	1	4	.364	.400
Stankiewicz	.286	7	2	0	0	0	3	.286	.286
Stanley, Mike	.200	5	1	0	2	1	3	.333	.200
Steinbach, T	.194	36	7	1	4	2	7	.237	.278
Stevens, Lee*	.182	11	2	0	0	2	4	.308	.182
Stillwell, K#	.200	35	7	0	2	0	8	.222	.200
Strange, Doug#	.167	18	3	0	0	5	6	.348	.222
Strawberry, D*	.222	9	2	0	1	1	5	.300	.333
Surhoff, B.J.*	.338	65	22	4	12	5	6	.386	.631
Sveum, Dale#	.083	24	2	0	0	2	12	.154	.125
Tartabull, D	.182	55	10	2	8	4	21	.233	.309
Tettleton, M#	.205	39	8	2	5	9	13	.340	.410
Thomas, Frank	.360	25	9	3	7	11	4	.541	.760
Thome, Jim*	.421	19	8	3	8	5	2	.538	1.000
Trammell, A	.364	66	24	2	14	3	7	.391	.561
Tucker, M*	.333	9	3	0	1	1	4	.400	.444
Valentin, Jse#	.250	16	4	1	3	1	4	.294	.563
Valle, Dave	.300	20	6	1	2	1	2	.333	.550
Vaughn, Greg	.069	29	2	0	0	4	16	.182	.069
Velarde, R	.225	40	9	0	3	4	13	.295	.350
Ventura, R*	.308	39	12	1	6	3	4	.349	.462
Vina, F*	.308	13	4	0	0	3	2	.471	.308
Vizquel, Omar*	.209	43	9	0	2	9	2	.244	.209
Voigt, Jack	.000	6	0	0	0	3	0	.000	.000
Walbeck, Matt#	.111	9	1	0	1	2	4	.250	.111
Ward, Turner*	.250	8	2	0	0	1	2	.333	.250
Webster, L	.000	5	0	0	0	0	0	.000	.000
Weiss, Walt*	.375	16	6	0	1	1	5	.412	.500
White, Devon*	.158	76	12	1	1	3	23	.190	.250
Whiten, Mark*	.200	15	3	0	1	1	7	.250	.267
Williams, Ber#	.143	28	4	1	4	6	7	.314	.286
Williams, E	.000	7	0	0	0	3	0	.000	.000
Wilson, Dan	.167	12	2	0	0	0	3	.167	.250
Worthington	.273	11	3	1	2	1	1	.308	.545
Young, Ernie	.167	6	1	0	1	1	0	.286	.167

Brad Clontz, Braves — RHP

Batter	Avg	AB	H	HR	BI	BB	SO	OBP	Slg
Abbott, Kurt	.111	9	1	0	0	1	2	.200	.111
Alou, Moises	.167	6	1	1	2	0	1	.286	.667
Bagwell, Jeff	.250	4	1	0	0	2	0	.500	.250

Brad Cliontz, Braves — RHP

Batter	Avg	AB	H	HR	BI	BB	SO	OBP	Slg
Bell, Derek	.600	5	3	0	4	1	0	.667	.600
Bichette, D	.125	8	1	0	0	0	1	.125	.250
Biggio, Craig	.600	5	3	0	0	0	0	.600	.600
Boone, Bret	.000	5	0	0	0	0	0	.000	.000
Burks, Ellis	.333	6	2	0	3	0	0	.429	.333
Castilla, V	.375	8	3	0	1	0	1	.375	.375
Clayton, R	.600	5	3	0	1	0	0	.500	.800
Colbrunn, G	.000	6	0	0	0	0	0	.000	.000
Conine, Jeff	.250	8	2	0	2	0	0	.222	.250
Gaetti, Gary	.000	4	0	0	0	1	0	.200	.000
Galarraga, A	.625	8	5	1	4	0	0	.667	1.000
Gant, Ron	.375	8	3	1	5	0	1	.375	1.000
Gilkey, B	.429	7	3	1	3	0	1	.429	.857
Grace, Mark*	.250	4	1	0	0	1	0	.400	.500
Harris, Lenny*	.250	4	1	0	1	0	0	.250	.250
Hayes, C	.286	7	2	2	2	0	1	.286	1.143
Hernandez, Jo	.167	6	1	0	0	0	3	.167	.167
Hundley, Todd#	.333	6	2	0	0	0	0	.429	.333
Johnson, Char	.167	6	1	0	0	0	3	.167	.167
Jones, Chris	.250	4	1	0	0	1	0	.400	.250
Jordan, Brian	.125	8	1	0	1	0	1	.125	.125
Karros, Eric	.143	7	1	1	2	0	5	.143	.571
Kent, Jeff	.400	5	2	0	2	0	0	.400	.400
King, Jeff	.000	7	0	0	0	0	2	.000	.000
Lansing, Mike	.167	6	1	0	0	0	0	.167	.167
Larkin, Barry	.400	5	2	0	0	2	0	.571	.400
Mabry, John*	.200	5	1	0	0	0	0	.200	.400
McRae, Brian#	.200	5	1	0	0	2	1	.429	.400
Merced, O*	.200	5	1	0	0	0	0	.200	.200
Mondesi, Raul	.333	6	2	0	0	0	1	.333	.333
Pendleton, T#	.750	4	3	0	2	3	0	.750	.750
Piazza, Mike	.200	5	1	1	3	0	1	.200	.800
Santiago, B	.200	5	1	0	0	0	3	.200	.200
Segui, David#	.600	5	3	0	1	0	0	.600	.800
Sheffield, G	.200	5	1	0	0	0	1	.333	.200
Zeile, Todd	.167	6	1	0	0	1	1	.286	.167

David Cone, Yankees — RHP

Batter	Avg	AB	H	HR	BI	BB	SO	OBP	Slg
Aldrete, Mike*	.261	23	6	0	5	1	6	.292	.304
Alicea, Luis#	.200	20	4	0	0	0	4	.200	.300
Alomar, R#	.170	47	8	1	1	9	5	.304	.277
Alomar Jr, S	.300	10	3	1	1	0	1	.300	.700
Anderson, Brd*	.350	20	7	1	3	4	2	.480	.500
Anderson, G*	.167	12	2	0	2	0	3	.167	.250
Anthony, Eric*	.261	23	6	1	1	2	10	.320	.435
Baerga, C#	.240	25	6	0	0	1	3	.269	.320
Bagwell, Jeff	.214	14	3	1	3	2	4	.313	.429
Baines, H*	.409	22	9	2	5	3	2	.480	.773
Parberie, B#	.333	15	5	0	2	4	4	.500	.400
Becker, Rich*	.000	8	0	0	0	0	4	.000	.000
Bell, Jay	.185	27	5	0	2	6	9	.333	.222
Belle, Albert	.250	24	6	2	3	6	6	.400	.583
Belliard, R	.176	17	3	0	0	2	6	.263	.176
Beltre, E	.000	5	0	0	0	1	2	.167	.000
Berroa, G	.412	17	7	1	1	1	6	.444	.706
Biggio, Craig	.200	25	5	1	2	2	8	.259	.320
Blauser, Jeff	.077	13	1	0	0	2	6	.200	.077
Blowers, Mike	.000	9	0	0	1	0	4	.000	.000
Boggs, Wade*	.250	16	4	1	1	4	0	.400	.250
Bonds, Barry*	.175	40	7	1	4	5	5	.267	.275
Bonilla, B#	.244	41	10	2	6	10	10	.392	.463
Boone, Bret	.200	5	1	0	0	0	1	.200	.200
Borders, Pat	.320	25	8	0	4	0	3	.320	.480
Bordick, Mike	.250	24	6	1	1	1	3	.280	.458
Brosius, S	.083	12	1	0	0	2	3	.267	.083
Buhner, Jay	.308	13	4	2	6	2	4	.400	.769
Burks, Ellis	.125	8	1	1	1	1	3	.333	.250
Butler, Brett*	.300	40	12	1	4	6	6	.404	.525
Caminiti, Ken#	.222	20	4	0	1	2	6	.273	.250
Candaele, C#	.118	17	2	0	0	2	4	.211	.176
Canseco, Jose	.286	14	4	0	1	1	6	.375	.429
Carter, Joe	.152	33	5	2	5	2	14	.200	.333
Cedeno, A	.200	5	1	0	0	0	2	.200	.200
Cirillo, Jeff	.000	6	0	0	0	1	2	.143	.000
Clark, Tony*	.000	5	0	0	2	0	2	.000	.000
Clark, Will*	.250	40	10	0	2	10	8	.400	.300
Coleman, V#	.255	47	12	0	2	3	13	.300	.277
Cora, Joey#	.270	37	10	0	3	3	2	.341	.324
Cordova, M	.143	7	1	0	0	1	1	.250	.143
Curtis, Chad	.208	24	5	0	2	1	3	.240	.208
Cuyler, Milt#	.222	9	2	0	0	2	3	.417	.222
Dascenzo, D#	.182	11	2	0	3	3	2	.357	.273
Daulton, D*	.261	23	6	4	9	10	5	.514	.478
Davis, Chili#	.212	33	7	1	3	8	11	.366	.364
Davis, Eric	.217	23	5	1	3	6	12	.379	.435
Dawson, Andre	.281	57	16	3	13	5	16	.333	.491
Deer, Rob	.182	11	2	0	0	1	8	.250	.182
Delgado, C*	.000	9	0	0	0	0	5	.000	.000
DeShields, D*	.342	38	13	0	0	3	11	.390	.447
Devereaux, M	.091	11	1	0	0	2	5	.231	.091
Diaz, Alex*	.250	8	2	0	0	0	0	.250	.375
DiSarcina, G	.278	18	5	0	2	0	0	.278	.278
Duncan, M	.125	16	2	0	1	0	8	.125	.250
Dunston, S	.267	30	8	0	2	0	11	.267	.267
Dykstra, L*	.381	21	8	1	1	3	1	.458	.667
Easley, D	.444	9	4	0	0	1	2	.500	.444
Edmonds, Jim*	.200	15	3	0	1	1	1	.250	.200
Espinoza, A	.000	7	0	0	0	0	1	.125	.000
Fabregas, Jor*	.100	10	1	0	0	2	1	.250	.100
Fermin, Felix	.176	17	3	0	1	1	3	.286	.176
Fielder, C	.188	32	6	1	4	3	14	.257	.313
Finley, Steve*	.438	16	7	0	0	3	2	.526	.438
Flaherty, J	.375	8	3	0	1	0	1	.375	.500
Fletcher, D*	.143	7	1	0	1	0	0	.143	.143
Franco, Julio	.263	19	5	1	3	1	6	.333	.474
Fryman, T	.300	30	9	0	3	3	7	.364	.467
Gaetti, Gary	.300	10	3	1	2	0	2	.300	.600
Gagne, Greg	.500	12	6	0	2	0	2	.500	.750
Galarraga, A	.244	41	10	3	3	2	16	.279	.293
Gallego, Mike	.167	12	2	0	1	1	6	.231	.167
Gant, Ron	.281	32	9	1	2	1	7	.294	.406
Gates, Brent#	.467	15	7	0	2	3	1	.556	.533
Giambi, Jason*	.200	5	1	1	2	2	0	.429	.800
Gilkey, B	.167	6	1	0	0	1	3	.286	.167
Girardi, Joe	.167	6	1	0	0	0	1	.167	.167
Gomez, Chris	.000	7	0	0	0	0	4	.000	.000
Gonzalez, A	.250	4	1	0	0	1	1	.400	.250
Gonzalez, J	.176	17	3	2	3	1	3	.300	.529
Gonzalez, L*	.111	9	1	0	0	4	2	.467	.111
Goodwin, Tom*	.417	12	5	0	0	1	4	.462	.500
Grace, Mark*	.370	46	17	1	6	3	6	.408	.522
Green, Shawn*	.333	6	2	1	2	0	1	.333	1.000
Greenwell, M*	.250	20	5	1	2	2	3	.318	.450
Greer, Rusty*	.231	13	3	0	0	2	2	.231	.231
Griffey Jr, K*	.200	20	4	1	1	2	5	.273	.350
Grissom, M	.240	25	6	0	2	2	5	.296	.360
Guillen, O*	.375	24	9	0	3	0	2	.360	.375
Gwynn, Chris*	.250	8	2	2	2	0	1	.250	1.000
Gwynn, Tony*	.294	34	10	2	6	1	2	.314	.529
Hale, Chip*	.313	16	5	1	1	2	2	.389	.563
Hamelin, Bob*	.000	5	0	0	1	1	4	.167	.000
Hamilton, D*	.240	25	6	0	1	2	4	.296	.360
Hansen, Dave*	.000	7	0	0	0	0	1	.000	.000
Harris, Lenny*	.278	36	10	1	4	1	2	.297	.417
Haselman, B	.000	7	0	0	0	0	4	.000	.000
Hayes, C	.053	19	1	0	1	0	7	.053	.105
Henderson, R	.250	12	3	0	1	1	2	.357	.500
Herrera, Jose*	.250	4	1	0	0	2	1	.500	.250
Higginson, B*	.500	10	5	0	1	2	2	.583	.600
Hoiles, Chris	.300	10	3	1	2	4	3	.533	.700
Hollins, Dave*	.111	9	1	0	0	0	5	.200	.222
Howard, Dave#	.000	4	0	0	0	1	0	.200	.000
Howard, T*	.429	7	3	0	2	0	1	.429	.714
Huff, Michael	.167	6	1	0	0	0	2	.167	.333
Hulse, David*	.091	22	2	0	1	0	1	.091	.136
Huson, Jeff*	.300	10	3	0	0	0	2	.300	.300
Incaviglia, P	.333	6	2	0	0	1	3	.429	.333
Jaha, John	.188	16	3	1	1	3	2	.316	.375
James, Dion*	.333	21	7	0	1	3	3	.417	.333
Javier, Stan#	.214	28	6	1	4	2	8	.250	.393
Jefferson, R*	.176	17	3	1	2	0	6	.211	.412
Johnson, L*	.192	26	5	0	2	2	0	.250	.308
Jordan, Brian	.333	6	2	0	0	0	2	.333	.833
Jordan, Ricky	.227	22	5	2	4	0	7	.227	.500
Joyner, Wally*	.556	9	5	1	3	3	0	.667	.889
Justice, Dave*	.154	13	2	0	1	4	5	.353	.231
Karkovice, R	.176	17	3	0	0	1	7	.222	.235
Karros, Eric	.000	9	0	0	0	0	6	.000	.000
Kelly, Pat	.300	10	3	0	0	0	1	.300	.400
King, Jeff	.313	16	5	0	0	1	5	.353	.375
Kingery, Mike*	.125	8	1	0	0	0	2	.125	.250
Kirby, Wayne*	.286	14	4	0	0	0	0	.286	.357
Knoblauch, C	.190	21	4	0	0	4	4	.346	.286
Kreuter, Chad#	.167	12	2	1	1	2	4	.286	.583
Lankford, Ray*	.242	33	8	0	7	0	13	.235	.394
Larkin, Barry	.176	34	6	0	2	2	2	.222	.206
Lemke, Mark#	.200	5	1	0	0	2	1	.429	.200
Lewis, Darren	.250	8	2	0	0	2	1	.400	.250
Listach, Pat#	.444	9	4	0	1	1	1	.500	.444
Livingstone*	.000	7	0	0	1	0	0	.000	.000
Lockhart, K*	.000	3	0	0	0	1	0	.500	.000
Lofton, Kenny*	.185	27	5	0	2	3	7	.267	.222
Lovullo, T#	.286	7	2	0	0	2	1	.444	.429
Manwaring, K	.000	7	0	0	0	0	2	.000	.000
Martinez, Da*	.259	54	14	0	4	3	4	.298	.407
Martinez, E	.316	19	6	2	5	4	3	.435	.684
Martinez, S*	.200	5	1	0	0	0	1	.333	.200
Martinez, T*	.182	22	4	1	2	4	2	.308	.409
Matheny, Mike	.143	7	1	0	0	0	2	.143	.143
May, Derrick*	.188	16	3	0	2	1	1	.222	.250
Mayne, Brent*	.000	7	0	0	0	0	2	.000	.000

David Cone, Yankees — RHP

Batter	Avg	AB	H	HR	BI	BB	SO	OBP	Slg
McCarty, Dave	.000	4	0	0	0	1	2	.200	.000
McGee, Willie#	.313	48	15	1	5	4	7	.377	.458
McGriff, Fred*	.100	10	1	0	0	2	4	.250	.200
McGwire, Mark	.000	6	0	0	0	1	3	.250	.000
McLemore, Mark	.294	17	5	0	2	0	4	.278	.294
Meares, Pat	.000	8	0	0	0	1	3	.111	.000
Merced, O*	.125	16	2	0	1	1	5	.176	.125
Mitchell, K	.375	24	9	2	9	0	7	.375	.625
Molitor, Paul	.346	26	9	3	7	3	2	.400	.692
Morandini, M*	.273	11	3	0	0	2	4	.385	.364
Morris, Hal*	.333	18	6	0	1	0	2	.333	.389
Murray, Eddie#	.326	43	14	3	7	6	7	.408	.581
Myers, Greg*	.167	12	2	1	2	0	3	.231	.417
Naehring, Tim	.214	14	3	0	0	0	3	.214	.286
Newson, W*	.300	10	3	1	2	3	2	.462	.700
Nilsson, Dave*	.200	10	2	0	0	3	0	.385	.300
Nixon, Otis#	.235	17	4	0	0	1	2	.278	.294
Nunnally, Jon*	.167	6	1	0	1	1	2	.286	.500
O'Leary, Troy*	.143	7	1	1	3	0	2	.143	.571
O'Neill, Paul*	.333	36	12	2	7	7	10	.442	.667
Offerman, J	.059	17	1	0	0	6	0	.059	.059
Olerud, John*	.286	21	6	3	5	3	7	.360	.714
Pagnozzi, Tom	.217	23	5	0	1	0	7	.217	.261
Palmeiro, R*	.258	31	8	2	5	12	5	.465	.581
Palmer, Dean	.063	16	1	0	0	2	11	.167	.063
Paquette, C	.286	7	2	0	1	0	3	.250	.429
Parent, Mark	.100	10	1	0	0	0	6	.100	.100
Pena, G*	.154	13	2	0	0	1	4	.214	.308
Pena, Tony	.263	38	10	0	3	4	9	.333	.342
Pendleton, T#	.184	38	7	2	4	2	6	.225	.395
Perez, E	.333	9	3	0	3	1	2	.400	.556
Perez, Tomas#	.200	5	1	0	0	1	1	.333	.200
Phillips, T#	.289	38	11	1	3	4	10	.349	.421
Polonia, Luis*	.273	22	6	0	3	1	1	.292	.409
Raines, Tim#	.222	45	10	1	3	14	8	.407	.378
Ramirez, M	.100	10	1	0	1	1	3	.182	.100
Reboulet, J	.000	7	0	0	0	2	4	.222	.000
Reed, Jeff*	.095	21	2	0	2	3	7	.208	.095
Ripken, Cal	.095	21	2	0	2	0	4	.095	.095
Roberts, Bip#	.250	20	5	0	0	0	5	.250	.450
Rodriguez, I	.100	20	2	0	0	0	2	.100	.100
Sabo, Chris	.158	19	3	0	0	2	8	.238	.211
Salmon, Tim	.240	25	6	3	5	4	9	.333	.680
Samuel, Juan	.150	40	6	0	2	3	18	.209	.175
Sanchez, Rey	.333	9	3	0	1	0	1	.333	.333
Sandberg, R	.300	50	15	1	10	5	13	.357	.460
Santiago, B	.219	32	7	2	7	0	9	.212	.406
Schofield, D	.100	10	1	0	0	1	3	.182	.100
Segui, David#	.000	5	0	0	1	0	2	.000	.000
Seitzer, K	.235	17	4	0	2	2	2	.300	.294
Sheffield, G	.250	8	2	1	3	2	1	.455	.625
Shipley, C	.000	4	0	0	0	1	0	.200	.000
Sierra, Ruben#	.053	19	1	0	2	0	3	.053	.105
Smith, Dwight*	.375	16	6	1	3	2	1	.444	.750
Smith, Ozzie*	.152	46	7	0	2	13	6	.333	.174
Snow, J.T.#	.227	22	5	1	3	4	12	.320	.455
Sojo, Luis	.000	11	0	0	1	1	2	.083	.000
Sorrento, P*	.045	22	1	0	0	3	5	.160	.045
Spiers, Bill*	.333	6	2	0	2	1	2	.429	.333
Sprague, Ed	.143	21	3	0	0	3	4	.250	.190
Stahoviak, S*	.000	4	0	0	0	2	4	.333	.000
Stanley, Mike	.000	4	0	0	0	2	1	.333	.000
Steinbach, T	.357	14	5	0	1	0	4	.357	.429
Stillwell, K#	.111	9	1	0	3	0	0	.083	.111
Strange, Doug#	.154	13	2	0	1	1	1	.214	.231
Strawberry, D*	.250	8	2	1	3	1	3	.333	.625
Surhoff, B.J.*	.167	18	3	0	0	3	4	.286	.222
Tartabull, D	.000	15	0	0	0	2	4	.118	.000
Taubensee, E*	.400	5	2	0	1	2	1	.571	.400
Tettleton, M#	.208	24	5	1	3	13	6	.296	.417
Thomas, Frank	.286	28	8	1	5	1	4	.300	.536
Thome, Jim*	.231	13	3	0	0	4	5	.412	.308
Thompson, Mil*	.360	50	18	1	7	9	9	.458	.500
Thompson, Rob	.314	35	11	1	2	5	14	.400	.486
Tinsley, Lee#	.200	5	1	0	1	0	1	.200	.200
Trammell, A	.238	21	5	0	3	6	4	.407	.333
Tucker, M*	.000	5	0	0	0	1	4	.167	.000
Valentin, Jhn	.176	17	3	1	1	1	1	.222	.471
Valentin, Jse#	.250	12	3	1	3	1	5	.308	.667
Valle, Dave	.000	6	0	0	0	1	1	.143	.000
VanderWal, J*	.300	10	3	0	0	0	1	.300	.300
Vaughn, Greg	.111	18	2	0	4	3	6	.238	.417
Vaughn, Mo*	.304	23	7	1	5	4	4	.448	.522
Velarde, R	.500	6	3	0	0	0	3	.500	.500
Ventura, R*	.238	21	5	2	4	8	4	.433	.571
Vina, F*	.538	13	7	0	1	1	1	.571	.615
Vizcaino, J#	.333	12	4	0	1	1	3	.385	.333
Vizquel, Omar*	.261	23	6	0	5	1	3	.292	.348
Voigt, Jack	.167	6	1	0	0	0	3	.167	.167
Walbeck, Matt#	.250	8	2	0	1	1	2	.333	.250
Walker, Larry*	.217	23	5	0	2	5	6	.345	.304

David Cone, Yankees — RHP

Batter	Avg	AB	H	HR	BI	BB	SO	OBP	Slg
Wallach, Tim	.286	56	16	1	6	7	8	.365	.393
Walton, J	.357	14	5	0	1	1	5	.375	.357
Ward, Turner#	.077	13	1	0	2	2	2	.200	.077
White, Devon#	.222	18	4	0	3	2	2	.333	.389
Wilkins, Rick*	.154	13	2	0	1	1	6	.214	.231
Williams, Ber#	.278	18	5	0	1	1	4	.316	.278
Williams, Ma	.375	24	9	2	4	0	6	.375	.667
Wilson, Dan	.417	12	5	0	2	0	4	.417	.500
Young, Ernie	.143	7	1	0	0	0	3	.143	.143
Zeile, Todd	.270	37	10	1	5	6	7	.364	.432

Dennis Cook, Rangers — LHP

Batter	Avg	AB	H	HR	BI	BB	SO	OBP	Slg
Alicea, Luis#	.333	3	1	0	1	1	0	.400	.333
Alomar, R#	.304	23	7	1	2	3	3	.385	.478
Alomar Jr, S	.250	4	1	0	0	1	0	.400	.250
Anderson, Brd*	.143	21	3	0	2	0	6	.143	.143
Anderson, G*	.000	6	0	0	0	0	1	.000	.000
Anthony, Eric*	.250	8	2	0	0	0	1	.250	.375
Baines, H*	.286	7	2	0	1	0	1	.286	.286
Barberie, B#	.250	4	1	0	0	1	0	.400	.500
Bell, Jay	.000	9	0	0	0	1	0	.000	.000
Belle, Albert	.250	4	1	0	0	1	2	.400	.250
Beltre, E	.125	8	1	0	0	0	1	.125	.125
Berroa, G	.000	6	0	0	0	0	2	.000	.000
Bichette, D	.200	5	1	0	0	1	0	.200	.200
Biggio, Craig	.286	7	2	0	0	1	1	.375	.286
Blauser, Jeff	.091	11	1	0	0	0	1	.091	.091
Boggs, Wade*	.300	10	3	0	4	4	1	.412	.400
Bonds, Barry*	.000	8	0	0	0	0	0	.000	.000
Bonilla, B#	.059	17	1	0	0	1	1	.111	.059
Borders, Pat	.143	7	1	0	0	0	1	.143	.143
Buhner, Jay	.000	6	0	0	0	0	2	.143	.000
Burnitz, J*	.250	4	1	0	2	0	2	.400	.500
Butler, Brett*	.333	12	4	0	2	2	1	.467	.500
Caminiti, Ken#	.222	9	2	0	1	2	1	.364	.222
Canseco, Jose	.667	6	4	2	4	1	0	.714	1.667
Carreon, Mark	.000	9	0	0	0	1	1	.100	.000
Carter, Joe	.308	13	4	1	1	5	0	.500	.615
Clark, Will*	.158	19	3	0	2	6	0	.238	.211
Coleman, V#	.240	25	6	1	6	3	3	.321	.440
Cora, Joey#	.500	8	4	0	0	0	0	.500	.500
Curtis, Chad	.222	9	2	0	1	0	2	.200	.333
Cuyler, Milt#	.375	8	3	1	4	0	1	.375	.875
Davis, Chili*	.167	12	2	0	0	0	5	.167	.167
Davis, Eric	.111	9	1	0	0	4	2	.385	.111
Decker, Steve	.400	5	2	0	0	0	0	.400	.400
Deer, Rob	.429	7	3	2	2	2	0	.556	1.286
Delgado, C*	.400	5	2	1	4	1	2	.571	1.000
DeShields, D*	.333	6	2	0	0	2	1	.500	.333
Devereaux, M	.000	12	0	0	0	1	3	.077	.000
DiSarcina, G	.222	9	2	0	0	0	1	.222	.333
Duncan, M	.000	8	0	0	0	0	2	.000	.000
Easley, D	.000	4	0	0	1	1	1	.200	.000
Edmonds, Jim*	.200	5	1	0	1	1	1	.333	.200
Elster, Kevin	.375	8	3	0	1	2	1	.500	.375
Fielder, C	.091	11	1	1	3	3	3	.286	.364
Frye, Jeff	.143	7	1	0	0	1	2	.250	.143
Fryman, T	.308	13	4	1	3	1	1	.357	.692
Gaetti, Gary	.364	11	4	1	4	2	4	.462	.727
Gagne, Greg	.250	8	2	0	0	0	2	.250	.250
Galarraga, A	.000	9	0	0	0	1	2	.100	.000
Gant, Ron	.222	9	2	0	0	2	0	.364	.333
Gomez, Leo	.000	5	0	0	0	0	2	.000	.000
Gonzales, R	.250	8	2	0	0	0	0	.250	.250
Gonzalez, J	.100	10	1	0	0	1	3	.182	.200
Goodwin, Tom*	.167	6	1	0	0	0	1	.286	.167
Greenwell, M*	.000	5	0	0	0	0	0	.167	.000
Griffey Jr, K*	.545	11	6	1	7	1	3	.583	.818
Grissom, M	.286	7	2	0	1	0	2	.286	.286
Guillen, O*	.000	6	0	0	0	0	0	.000	.000
Gwynn, Tony*	.333	6	2	0	1	0	0	.286	.500
Hamelin, Bob*	.250	4	1	0	2	1	1	.333	.250
Harris, Lenny*	.400	5	2	0	0	1	0	.400	.400
Hoiles, Chris	.200	5	1	0	0	1	0	.333	.200
Howard, Dave*	.143	7	1	0	0	0	1	.250	.143
Hudler, Rex	.250	12	3	1	2	0	3	.250	.500
Huff, Michael	.200	10	2	1	2	0	5	.200	.500
Jaha, John	.100	10	1	0	0	1	4	.182	.100
Javier, Stan#	.167	6	1	0	0	0	0	.167	.167
Jefferies, G#	.313	16	5	1	2	0	0	.313	.563
Johnson, L*	.273	11	3	0	0	0	1	.333	.273
Joyner, Wally	.200	10	2	0	1	1	1	.273	.200
Justice, Dave*	.250	4	1	0	0	2	0	.500	.500
Kelly, Pat	.667	6	4	2	4	0	0	.667	1.833
Kelly, R	.800	5	4	0	1	0	2	.833	1.000
King, Jeff	.125	8	1	0	0	1	1	.222	.125
Knoblauch, C	.444	9	4	0	0	1	0	.444	.667
Larkin, Barry	.429	7	3	0	1	0	0	.429	.429
Lemke, Mark#	.273	11	3	0	1	0	0	.273	.364
Leyritz, Jim	.400	5	2	0	1	0	2	.400	.600

Batter	Avg	AB	H	HR	BI	BB	SO	OBP	Slg
Listach, Pat#	.250	8	2	0	0	2	2	.455	.250
Lofton, Kenny*	.500	6	3	0	0	1	1	.571	.500
Macfarlane, M	.444	9	4	0	2	0	3	.444	.778
Magadan, Dave*	.333	6	2	0	3	0	0	.333	.333
Martinez, Da*	.300	10	3	0	3	1	3	.364	.400
Martinez, E	.333	9	3	0	1	0	2	.333	.444
Martinez, T*	.333	9	3	0	2	2	1	.417	.444
McGee, Willie*	.267	15	4	0	1	0	1	.250	.333
McLemore, M#	.500	6	3	0	0	0	1	.500	.667
McRae, Brian#	.200	5	1	0	1	2	0	.429	.200
Mitchell, K	.333	12	4	1	2	2	0	.429	.583
Molitor, Paul	.444	9	4	0	1	0	1	.444	.444
Morris, Hal*	.500	4	2	0	0	2	1	.667	.500
Munoz, Pedro	.143	7	1	1	2	1	3	.250	.571
Murray, Eddie*	.417	12	5	0	0	1	1	.462	.500
Myers, Greg*	.000	4	0	0	0	1	2	.200	.000
Nilsson, Dave*	.000	6	0	0	1	0	3	.000	.000
Nixon, Otis#	.385	13	5	0	4	0	1	.385	.462
O'Leary, Troy*	.200	5	1	0	0	2	2	.429	.200
O'Neill, Paul*	.217	23	5	3	10	3	7	.296	.696
Offerman, J#	.400	5	2	0	1	0	0	.400	.400
Olerud, John*	.273	11	3	1	4	1	1	.385	.636
Oliver, Joe	.333	6	2	0	0	0	0	.333	.333
Pagnozzi, Tom	.333	6	2	0	0	0	0	.333	.500
Palmeiro, R*	.444	27	12	1	5	1	4	.464	.667
Palmer, Dean	.333	9	3	1	2	4	3	.538	.889
Pena, Tony	.222	9	2	0	1	1	2	.273	.222
Pendleton, T	.217	23	5	1	2	2	1	.280	.478
Phillips, T#	.211	19	4	1	2	1	3	.250	.368
Polonia, Luis*	.182	11	2	0	0	1	2	.250	.273
Raines, Tim#	.000	7	0	0	0	1	1	.125	.000
Reed, Jody	.500	6	3	1	1	1	0	.571	1.167
Ripken, Cal	.077	13	1	0	0	1	1	.200	.077
Roberts, Bip#	.333	6	2	0	0	1	2	.429	.667
Rodriguez, I	.273	11	3	1	2	2	1	.385	.636
Sabo, Chris	.556	9	5	1	2	1	1	.600	1.222
Salmon, Tim	.333	6	2	1	1	0	2	.500	1.000
Samuel, Juan	.222	9	2	1	1	1	4	.300	.556
Santiago, B	.000	8	0	0	0	1	0	.000	.000
Seitzer, K	.154	13	2	0	0	1	2	.214	.154
Sierra, Ruben*	.364	11	4	1	3	4	1	.533	.727
Smith, Ozzie#	.222	18	4	0	2	3	1	.333	.278
Snow, J.T.#	.250	12	3	0	4	0	3	.231	.500
Sojo, Luis	.429	7	3	1	2	0	1	.429	1.000
Sorrento, P*	.167	6	1	1	4	0	3	.167	.667
Spiers, Bill*	.200	5	1	0	0	0	0	.200	.400
Stanley, Mike	.375	8	3	0	3	0	1	.375	.500
Strawberry, D*	.333	9	3	1	3	4	0	.538	.667
Surhoff, B.J.*	.100	10	1	0	0	1	1	.182	.200
Tartabull, D	.600	5	3	0	2	1	2	.667	1.000
Tettleton, M	.167	12	2	0	0	1	4	.231	.167
Thomas, Frank	.444	9	4	1	1	3	0	.583	1.000
Thome, Jim*	.111	9	1	0	0	0	4	.111	.111
Thompson, Mil*	.167	12	2	0	2	1	4	.214	.250
Thompson, Rob	.250	4	1	1	2	0	0	.200	1.000
Tinsley, Lee#	.000	6	0	0	0	0	3	.000	.000
Trammell, A	.000	3	0	0	0	2	0	.400	.000
Valentin, Jhn	.333	6	2	0	0	2	0	.500	.500
Valentin, Jose#	.400	5	2	0	2	1	2	.500	.600
Valle, Dave	.000	5	0	0	0	1	2	.167	.000
Vaughn, Greg	.333	6	2	2	2	3	0	.556	1.333
Vaughn, Mo*	.444	9	4	1	3	1	1	.500	.889
Velarde, A	.500	2	1	0	1	2	0	.600	.500
Ventura, R*	.357	14	5	1	5	2	3	.438	.643
Vina, F*	.200	5	1	0	2	0	0	.200	.400
Vizquel, Omar#	.000	9	0	0	0	1	0	.100	.000
Wallach, Tim	.111	9	1	0	0	2	3	.273	.222
White, Devon#	.100	10	1	1	1	0	2	.182	.400
Williams, Ber#	.231	13	3	2	3	1	3	.286	.692
Williams, Ger	.571	7	4	0	1	0	0	.571	1.000
Williams, Ma	.267	15	4	1	1	1	0	.313	.533
Zeile, Todd	.750	8	6	0	2	2	0	.800	.875

Batter	Avg	AB	H	HR	BI	BB	SO	OBP	Slg
Carr, Chuck	.235	17	4	1	2	0	3	.235	.412
Carreon, Mark	.267	15	4	0	3	1	4	.313	.333
Cedeno, A	.333	6	2	0	0	0	2	.333	.333
Cianfrocco, A	.500	8	4	0	2	0	2	.500	.875
Clark, Phil	.571	7	4	2	2	0	0	.571	1.429
Clark, Will*	.286	7	2	1	5	0	2	.250	.714
Clayton, R	.438	16	7	1	1	2	2	.500	.813
Colbrunn, G	.429	7	3	2	5	0	2	.429	1.286
Coleman, V#	.250	4	1	0	0	1	1	.400	.250
Conine, Jeff	.467	15	7	0	2	0	0	.467	.533
Cordero, Wil	.385	13	5	0	1	2	0	.500	.692
Daulton, D*	.222	9	2	0	0	1	4	.300	.333
DeShields, D*	.400	15	6	0	2	1	2	.471	.733
Dorsett, B	.200	5	1	0	0	1	1	.333	.400
Duncan, M	.222	9	2	1	1	0	1	.222	.556
Dykstra, L*	.154	13	2	1	3	3	1	.313	.385
Finley, Steve*	.429	7	3	0	2	1	0	.500	.571
Fletcher, D*	.500	6	3	1	4	0	1	.500	1.333
Gant, Ron	.125	8	1	1	2	1	0	.200	.500
Gilkey, B	.429	7	3	0	3	0	0	.429	.714
Gonzalez, L*	.250	8	2	0	2	1	2	.333	.375
Grace, Mark*	.286	7	2	0	2	0	0	.250	.429
Grissom, M	.222	18	4	0	0	2	5	.300	.333
Gutierrez, R	.154	13	2	0	1	1	3	.214	.231
Gwynn, Tony*	.643	14	9	0	3	1	0	.667	.786
Hollins, Dave#	.667	9	6	0	2	0	0	.667	1.000
Hunter, Brian	.250	4	1	0	2	0	0	.250	.250
Incaviglia, P	.278	18	5	1	4	2	5	.350	.500
Jefferies, G#	.333	9	3	0	0	0	1	.333	.444
Jordan, Brian	.571	7	4	2	3	0	1	.571	1.429
Jordan, Ricky	.143	14	2	1	1	0	1	.143	.357
Justice, Dave*	.429	14	6	0	0	5	0	.467	.500
Karros, Eric	.333	6	2	0	0	1	0	.429	.333
Kelly, Mike	.333	6	2	1	1	0	0	.333	1.000
Kelly, R	.571	7	4	1	0	0	0	.571	.714
Kent, Jeff	.308	13	4	1	1	0	0	.308	.615
Lankford, Ray*	.300	10	3	0	1	2	2	.417	.500
Lansing, Mike	.235	17	4	0	2	0	3	.316	.353
Larkin, Barry	.182	11	2	1	2	1	1	.250	.455
Lemke, Mark#	.300	10	3	1	2	0	4	.417	.600
Lewis, Darren	.286	14	4	0	0	4	2	.444	.357
Lopez, Javy	.000	9	0	0	0	0	6	.000	.000
Magadan, Dave*	.333	6	2	0	2	2	1	.444	.333
Manwaring, K	.091	11	1	0	0	1	3	.231	.091
May, Derrick*	.400	5	2	0	0	1	0	.400	.400
McGee, Willie*	.200	10	2	0	1	1	1	.273	.200
McGriff, Fred*	.364	11	4	2	3	3	1	.500	.909
Mitchell, K	.143	7	1	0	1	1	0	.250	.143
Mondesi, Raul	.500	8	4	1	3	0	0	.500	1.125
Morandini, M*	.333	6	2	0	0	2	0	.500	.500
Morris, Hal*	.600	5	3	0	1	1	0	.667	.800
Murray, Eddie*	.308	13	4	0	0	2	2	.400	.462
Nixon, Otis#	.429	7	3	1	2	1	1	.500	.857
O'Brien, C	.400	10	4	1	1	0	0	.400	.800
Offerman, J#	.125	8	1	0	0	1	0	.300	.125
Oliver, Joe	.500	6	3	0	1	0	0	.500	.500
Pagnozzi, Tom	.250	8	2	1	2	0	1	.250	.625
Pena, G#	.143	7	1	0	0	1	2	.250	.143
Pendleton, T#	.154	13	2	0	1	1	1	.214	.154
Piazza, Mike	.429	7	3	0	1	0	0	.429	.429
Plantier, P*	.000	7	0	0	0	2	2	.222	.000
Reed, Jody	.167	6	1	0	0	1	1	.286	.167
Roberts, Bip#	.125	8	1	1	3	2	0	.300	.500
Sabo, Chris	.000	6	0	0	0	0	0	.000	.000
Sanders, R	.273	11	3	0	1	0	3	.333	.273
Santiago, B	.231	13	3	1	0	1	4	.286	.308
Servais, S	.286	7	2	0	2	1	0	.375	.429
Sheffield, G	.000	3	0	0	1	3	0	.429	.000
Smith, Ozzie#	.273	11	3	0	1	0	1	.333	.364
Snow, Sammy	.143	7	1	1	1	1	2	.250	.143
Spehr, Tim	.000	4	0	0	0	1	1	.200	.000
Stocker, K#	.444	9	4	1	2	0	3	.545	.889
Thompson, Rob	.200	15	3	0	0	1	2	.250	.267
Thompson, Ry	.300	10	3	1	4	0	2	.300	.700
Vizcaino, J#	.167	6	1	0	0	0	2	.167	.167
Walker, Larry*	.143	14	2	0	2	2	4	.250	.143
Wallach, Tim	.182	11	2	1	2	0	2	.182	.545
Webster, L	.333	6	2	0	0	0	0	.333	.500
Weiss, Walt#	.000	6	0	0	1	1	3	.143	.000
White, R	.200	5	1	0	0	1	1	.333	.400
Whiten, Mark#	.125	8	1	0	0	1	5	.111	.125
Williams, Ma	.250	20	5	2	4	1	0	.286	.650
Zeile, Todd	.300	10	3	0	0	0	3	.364	.500

Batter	Avg	AB	H	HR	BI	BB	SO	OBP	Slg
Alou, Moises	.267	15	4	1	5	2	3	.353	.667
Ausmus, Brad	.429	7	3	0	1	1	0	.500	.571
Bagwell, Jeff	.636	11	7	2	5	1	0	.667	1.273
Barberie, B#	.200	10	2	0	1	0	1	.200	.300
Batiste, Kim	.333	12	4	0	0	1	2	.385	.417
Bell, Derek	.167	12	2	0	1	0	2	.167	.250
Berry, Sean	.222	9	2	0	0	1	1	.300	.222
Biggio, Craig	.273	11	3	0	0	1	0	.333	.364
Blauser, Jeff	.235	17	4	0	1	2	1	.316	.353
Bogar, Tim	.200	5	1	0	0	1	0	.333	.200
Bonds, Barry*	.125	16	2	0	0	1	1	.176	.188
Bonilla, B#	.308	13	4	0	0	1	4	.357	.538
Boone, Bret	.200	5	1	0	0	0	1	.200	.200
Brumfield, J	.571	7	4	1	2	0	1	.571	1.286
Butler, Brett*	.333	12	4	0	1	0	0	.333	.333
Caminiti, Ken#	.286	7	2	0	2	0	0	.250	.286

Batter	Avg	AB	H	HR	BI	BB	SO	OBP	Slg
Belle, Albert	.600	5	3	2	5	1	0	.667	1.800
Berroa, G	.400	5	2	0	0	1	1	.500	.400
Bordick, Mike	.200	5	1	0	0	0	1	.200	.200
Brosius, S	.167	6	1	0	0	0	2	.167	.333
Brumfield, J	.250	8	2	0	1	1	2	.333	.250

Rocky Coppinger, Orioles — RHP

Batter	Avg	AB	H	HR	BI	BB	SO	OBP	Slg
Buhner, Jay	.667	3	2	1	2	2	0	.667	1.667
Canseco, Jose	.000	3	0	0	0	3	0	.500	.000
Carreon, Mark	.000	5	0	0	0	2	0	.000	.000
Carter, Joe	.100	10	1	0	0	0	4	.100	.000
Cirillo, Jeff	.333	6	2	1	3	0	0	.333	1.000
Clark, Tony*	.429	7	3	2	4	1	2	.500	1.429
Cora, Joey#	.200	5	1	0	0	0	1	.200	.200
Damon, Johnny*	.000	4	0	0	0	1	1	.200	.000
Delgado, C*	.125	8	1	0	0	1	0	.222	.125
Frye, Jeff	.000	6	0	0	0	1	0	.143	.000
Fryman, T	.000	5	0	0	0	1	0	.167	.000
Giambi, Jason*	.333	3	1	0	1	2	2	.500	.333
Giles, B*	.500	4	2	0	1	2	1	.667	1.000
Gonzalez, A	.222	9	2	0	0	0	3	.222	.333
Goodwin, Tom*	.400	5	2	0	0	0	1	.400	.600
Green, Shawn*	.200	10	2	0	0	0	3	.200	.200
Griffey Jr, K*	.500	6	3	1	0	0	0	.500	.500
Higginson, B*	.750	8	6	2	4	1	0	.778	1.750
Hollins, Dave#	.600	5	3	0	0	0	0	.600	.600
Jaha, John	.167	6	1	0	0	0	3	.167	.167
Jefferson, R*	.400	5	2	1	2	1	0	.500	1.000
Lewis, Mark	.143	7	1	0	0	0	4	.143	.143
Lockhart, K*	.750	4	3	0	1	1	0	.800	1.250
Lofton, Kenny*	.600	5	3	1	1	1	0	.667	1.200
Martinez, E	.500	6	3	1	1	0	0	.500	1.000
Martinez, S*	.400	5	2	1	1	1	1	.500	1.000
Mieske, Matt	.000	4	0	0	0	1	3	.200	.000
Naehring, Tim	.200	5	1	0	0	1	1	.333	.200
Newfield, M	.400	5	2	0	0	0	1	.400	.400
Nilsson, Dave*	.250	4	1	1	1	2	1	.500	1.000
O'Leary, Troy*	.400	5	2	0	1	0	0	.400	.800
Olerud, John*	.429	7	3	1	1	2	0	.556	.857
Paquette, C	.200	5	1	0	0	1	2	.200	.200
Perez, Tomas#	.000	6	0	0	0	1	0	.143	.000
Plantier, P*	.200	5	1	0	0	1	2	.333	.600
Pride, Curtis*	.000	5	0	0	0	1	2	.167	.000
Ramirez, M	.000	6	0	0	0	0	1	.000	.000
Rodriguez, Al	.400	5	2	0	1	1	0	.500	.800
Sorrento, P*	.333	3	1	1	4	2	0	.600	1.333
Sprague, Ed	.000	9	0	0	0	0	4	.100	.000
Steinbach, T	.333	6	2	2	5	0	2	.333	1.333
Thome, Jim*	.667	3	2	0	2	2	0	.667	.667
Valentin, Jse#	.000	6	0	0	0	0	4	.000	.000
Vaughn, Mo*	.000	6	0	0	0	0	3	.000	.000
Vizquel, Omar#	.400	5	2	0	0	1	0	.500	.400
Whiten, Mark#	.667	3	2	0	0	2	1	.800	.667
Young, Ernie	.200	5	1	0	0	1	1	.333	.200

Archie Corbin, Orioles — RHP

Batter	Avg	AB	H	HR	BI	BB	SO	OBP	Slg
Anderson, G*	.250	4	1	0	0	1	0	.400	.250
Davis, Chili*	.500	4	2	0	2	2	1	.667	1.000
DiSarcina, G	.000	5	0	0	0	0	2	.000	.000
Salmon, Tim	.500	4	2	0	1	0	0	.500	.500
Snow, J.T.#	.250	4	1	0	0	2	0	.500	.250
Velarde, R	.400	5	2	0	2	2	2	.571	.400

Francisco Cordova, Pirates — RHP

Batter	Avg	AB	H	HR	BI	BB	SO	OBP	Slg
Aurilia, Rich	.000	5	0	0	0	0	3	.000	.000
Bagwell, Jeff	.286	7	2	2	3	0	3	.286	1.143
Bell, Derek	.000	6	0	0	0	0	4	.000	.000
Biggio, Craig	.500	6	3	1	1	0	1	.500	1.000
Boone, Bret	.167	6	1	0	0	0	1	.167	.167
Brown, Brant*	.167	6	1	0	0	0	1	.167	.167
Caminiti, Ken#	.500	4	2	1	2	1	0	.600	1.250
Davis, Eric	.333	6	2	0	0	0	2	.333	.667
Finley, Steve*	.200	5	1	0	0	0	2	.200	.400
Gutierrez, R	.200	5	1	0	0	0	4	.200	.400
Harris, Lenny*	.200	5	1	0	0	0	0	.200	.600
Houston, T*	.833	6	5	0	1	0	0	.833	1.167
Hunter, Bri L	.200	5	1	0	0	0	2	.200	.200
Jennings, R*	.500	6	3	0	2	0	0	.500	.833
Joyner, Wally*	.250	4	1	0	0	1	1	.400	.500
Reed, Jody	.000	5	0	0	0	1	0	.167	.000

Rheal Cormier, Expos — LHP

Batter	Avg	AB	H	HR	BI	BB	SO	OBP	Slg
Alfonzo, E	.400	5	2	0	0	0	0	.400	.800
Alomar, R#	.400	5	2	0	0	0	1	.400	.400
Alou, Moises	.250	16	4	0	1	0	2	.250	.313
Amaral, Rich	.167	6	1	0	0	0	0	.167	.167
Amaro, Ruben#	.167	12	2	0	0	2	1	.286	.250
Anderson, Brd*	.143	7	1	0	0	2	2	.333	.143
Anthony, Eric*	.417	12	5	1	4	2	2	.500	.750
Arias, Alex	.200	5	1	0	0	1	0	.333	.200
Ashley, Billy	.500	6	3	0	3	0	0	.500	1.000
Ausmus, Brad	.000	3	0	0	2	0	0	.000	.000
Bagwell, Jeff	.333	21	7	1	6	4	3	.440	.524
Barberie, B#	.263	19	5	0	4	3	5	.348	.368
Batiste, Kim	.286	7	2	0	0	0	0	.286	.286

Rheal Cormier, Expos — LHP

Batter	Avg	AB	H	HR	BI	BB	SO	OBP	Slg
Bell, Derek	.111	9	1	1	2	1	1	.200	.444
Bell, Jay	.125	24	3	0	0	1	10	.160	.167
Belle, Albert	.200	5	1	0	1	0	0	.200	.200
Berroa, G	.250	4	1	0	1	1	0	.400	.250
Berry, Sean	.273	11	3	1	1	0	1	.273	.545
Bichette, D	.308	13	4	0	0	0	3	.308	.385
Biggio, Craig	.333	21	7	1	5	3	2	.417	.571
Blauser, Jeff	.100	10	1	0	1	1	3	.167	.200
Blowers, Mike	.222	9	2	0	0	2	4	.417	.333
Bonds, Barry*	.231	13	3	1	2	0	2	.333	.611
Bonilla, B#	.231	13	3	0	1	2	0	.333	.231
Boone, Bret	.200	5	1	0	0	2	0	.429	.200
Bordick, Mike	.143	7	1	0	1	0	0	.143	.143
Brosius, S	.333	6	2	2	3	1	1	.429	1.333
Brumfield, J	.250	4	1	0	0	1	1	.400	.250
Buhner, Jay	.200	5	1	0	0	1	1	.333	.200
Burks, Ellis	.714	7	5	1	5	1	1	.750	1.429
Butler, Brett*	.278	18	5	0	0	2	0	.278	.278
Caminiti, Ken#	.250	20	5	1	2	1	1	.286	.450
Carr, Chuck	.167	6	1	0	0	1	0	.286	.167
Carreon, Mark	.353	17	6	1	3	0	0	.389	.588
Castilla, V	.222	9	2	0	1	0	2	.300	.222
Cedeno, A	.267	15	4	0	2	0	3	.267	.467
Cedeno, Roger#	.333	6	2	0	0	0	2	.333	.333
Cianfrocco, A	.083	12	1	0	1	1	5	.214	.083
Clark, Will*	.231	13	3	0	0	1	4	.286	.231
Clayton, R	.389	18	7	0	0	0	4	.389	.444
Colbrunn, G	.400	10	4	2	2	1	2	.455	1.000
Coleman, V#	.417	12	5	1	2	0	0	.417	.833
Conine, Jeff	.333	15	5	1	3	1	1	.375	.533
Cordero, Wil	.300	10	3	0	2	0	0	.364	.400
Dascenzo, D#	.667	6	4	0	2	0	0	.667	.833
Daulton, D*	.091	11	1	0	0	4	4	.091	.091
Davis, Eric	.250	16	4	0	3	0	5	.250	.250
Dawson, Andre	.250	8	2	1	2	0	2	.250	.625
DeShields, D*	.316	19	6	1	4	3	5	.409	.474
Duncan, M	.313	16	5	0	1	0	4	.313	.375
Dykstra, L*	.333	15	5	0	1	1	3	.375	.533
Elster, Kevin	.300	10	3	0	1	3	3	.364	.300
Fermin, Felix	.500	6	3	0	2	0	0	.500	.833
Finley, Steve*	.214	14	3	0	0	1	3	.267	.286
Gaetti, Gary	.111	9	1	0	0	3	3	.200	.111
Galarraga, A	.143	14	2	0	3	2	2	.222	.214
Gant, Ron	.308	13	4	0	4	1	1	.333	.385
Garcia, C	.231	13	3	0	0	0	1	.231	.308
Gates, Brent#	.333	6	2	0	0	0	1	.333	.333
Girardi, Joe	.429	7	3	0	0	0	0	.429	.571
Gomez, Chris	.400	5	2	0	0	0	1	.400	.400
Gomez, Leo	.400	5	2	0	0	0	1	.400	.600
Gonzalez, L*	.444	9	4	0	0	0	2	.444	.444
Goodwin, C*	.400	5	2	0	1	0	1	.400	.600
Grace, Mark*	.300	20	6	1	2	1	1	.333	.500
Griffey Jr, K*	.667	6	4	1	2	1	1	.714	1.167
Grissom, M	.345	29	10	1	4	1	4	.367	.586
Gutierrez, R	.333	6	2	0	1	0	1	.333	.667
Gwynn, Tony*	.444	18	8	0	3	0	0	.444	.722
Hayes, C	.286	14	4	0	3	0	2	.286	.357
Henderson, R	.143	7	1	0	3	2	1	.250	.571
Hernandez, Ca	.143	7	1	0	0	1	0	.333	.143
Hoiles, Chris	1.000	4	4	1	2	3	0	1.000	2.000
Hollins, Dave#	.238	21	5	1	2	0	5	.238	.381
Hundley, Todd#	.222	9	2	1	2	0	2	.222	.556
Hunter, Bri L	.333	6	2	0	0	0	1	.333	.500
Huskey, Butch	.200	5	1	0	0	0	1	.200	.200
Incaviglia, P	.263	19	5	2	4	1	3	.300	.632
Javier, Stan#	.435	23	10	0	1	0	2	.435	.522
Jefferies, G#	.500	16	8	0	1	0	1	.500	.750
Johnson, Char	.000	5	0	0	0	1	1	.167	.000
Johnson, L*	.300	10	3	0	0	1	0	.300	.300
Jones, Chris	.400	5	2	0	1	0	0	.400	.600
Jordan, Brian	.143	7	1	0	0	0	2	.143	.143
Jordan, Ricky	.571	7	4	0	0	0	2	.571	.857
Joyner, Wally*	.182	11	2	0	0	0	2	.182	.182
Justice, Dave*	.500	8	4	0	1	1	0	.556	.625
Karros, Eric	.286	21	6	0	2	1	4	.318	.333
Kelly, Pat	.600	5	3	0	2	0	0	.600	1.000
Kent, Jeff	.167	12	2	1	2	0	4	.167	.417
King, Jeff	.368	19	7	1	5	2	0	.435	.579
Lankford, Ray*	.000	7	0	0	0	0	3	.000	.000
Lansing, Mike	.250	4	1	0	0	1	0	.400	.250
Larkin, Barry	.500	12	6	1	1	0	0	.538	.833
Lemke, Mark#	.071	14	1	0	0	1	0	.133	.071
Lewis, Darren	.111	18	2	0	0	1	0	.158	.111
Leyritz, Jim	.571	7	4	0	1	0	1	.571	.714
Lofton, Kenny*	.000	3	0	0	0	2	1	.400	.000
Mabry, John*	.167	6	1	0	0	1	0	.167	.167
Magadan, Dave*	.143	7	1	0	1	1	1	.250	.143
Manto, Jeff	.333	6	2	0	0	2	1	.500	.333
Manwaring, K	.267	15	4	0	0	1	3	.353	.267
Martin, Al*	.667	9	6	1	2	0	0	.667	1.000
Martinez, E	.500	6	3	0	1	0	0	.500	.667

Rheal Cormier, Expos — LHP

Batter	Avg	AB	H	HR	BI	BB	SO	OBP	Slg
Martinez, T*	.667	6	4	0	0	1	0	.714	.833
May, Derrick*	.214	14	3	0	0	0	1	.214	.214
McGee, Willie#	.200	10	2	0	0	0	0	.200	.200
McGriff, Fred*	.313	16	5	1	3	0	3	.313	.625
McRae, Brian#	.200	5	1	0	1	1	0	.333	.200
Merced, O*	.357	14	5	0	3	1	0	.400	.500
Milliard, R	.200	5	1	0	0	1	1	.333	.200
Mitchell, K	.167	6	1	0	1	1	1	.250	.167
Mondesi, Raul	.000	5	0	0	0	1	0	.167	.000
Morandini, M*	.154	13	2	0	0	0	1	.214	.154
Morris, Hal*	.125	16	2	0	1	0	4	.125	.125
Mouton, James	.167	6	1	0	0	1	1	.286	.167
Murray, Eddie#	.348	23	8	2	6	2	0	.400	.652
Nixon, Otis#	.364	11	4	0	0	1	0	.417	.364
O'Brien, C	.353	17	6	0	0	1	1	.389	.471
O'Neill, Paul*	.333	6	2	0	2	1	1	.429	.500
Ochoa, Alex	.000	5	0	0	0	0	0	.000	.000
Offerman, J#	.364	11	4	0	0	3	0	.364	.545
Oliver, Joe	.533	15	8	1	3	0	0	.533	.800
Owens, Eric	.167	6	1	0	0	0	0	.167	.167
Owens, J	.286	7	2	0	1	0	2	.286	.286
Pagnozzi, Tom	.333	6	2	0	0	0	1	.333	.500
Palmeiro, R*	.333	9	3	0	0	0	2	.333	.444
Paquette, C	.200	5	1	0	0	0	0	.200	.400
Pendleton, T#	.357	14	5	0	0	1	2	.400	.357
Piazza, Mike	.571	7	4	1	3	1	1	.625	1.000
Plantier, P*	.200	5	1	0	0	1	1	.333	.200
Reed, Jody	.429	7	3	0	1	0	0	.429	.571
Renteria, E	.429	7	3	0	0	1	0	.500	.429
Ripken, Cal	.250	8	2	1	1	1	0	.333	.750
Roberts, Bip#	.100	10	1	0	0	0	1	.100	.100
Sabo, Chris	.333	6	2	0	0	1	2	.429	.333
Samuel, Juan	.364	11	4	1	3	1	1	.462	.818
Sanchez, Rey	.000	10	0	0	0	1	0	.091	.000
Sandberg, R	.333	18	6	0	1	3	2	.429	.444
Sanders, R	.625	8	5	2	3	1	1	.667	1.375
Santiago, B	.417	12	5	3	7	1	2	.462	1.333
Schofield, D	.200	5	1	0	0	0	2	.200	.200
Servais, S	.214	14	3	0	2	1	2	.235	.357
Sheffield, G	.158	19	3	0	0	3	1	.304	.158
Shipley, C	.167	6	1	0	0	0	1	.167	.167
Slaught, Don	.267	15	4	0	2	0	1	.250	.267
Sojo, Luis	.250	8	2	0	1	0	0	.250	.250
Sosa, Sammy	.417	12	5	4	8	1	1	.462	1.500
Stillwell, K	.400	5	2	0	0	0	3	.400	.600
Stocker, K#	.200	5	1	0	0	0	1	.200	.200
Strawberry, D*	.250	12	3	0	1	0	3	.250	.333
Taubensee, E*	.200	5	1	0	0	0	3	.200	.400
Thompson, Rob	.308	13	4	0	0	2	5	.400	.308
Thompson, Ry	.333	6	2	0	0	0	3	.333	.500
Timmons, O	.200	5	1	0	0	0	0	.200	.200
Vizcaino, J#	.200	5	1	0	0	0	2	.286	.357
Walker, Larry*	.250	24	6	0	1	1	3	.308	.333
Wallach, Tim	.316	19	6	1	6	0	6	.333	.526
Webster, L	.500	4	2	1	1	0	0	.600	1.500
Wehner, John	.222	9	2	0	0	0	0	.222	.333
Weiss, Walt#	.091	11	1	0	0	1	2	.167	.091
White, Devon#	.182	11	2	0	0	0	3	.250	.273
Williams, Ber#	.500	6	3	0	3	0	0	.500	.833
Williams, Geo#	.500	4	2	0	0	1	2	.600	.750
Williams, Ma	.353	17	6	3	5	0	1	.333	.882
Young, Eric	.462	13	6	0	0	1	1	.500	.538
Young, Kevin	.143	7	1	0	0	0	2	.143	.286

Jim Corsi, Athletics — RHP

Batter	Avg	AB	H	HR	BI	BB	SO	OBP	Slg
Grace, Mark*	.600	5	3	0	0	0	0	.600	.600
Greenwell, M*	.200	5	1	0	1	0	0	.200	.200
Grissom, M	.400	5	2	0	2	0	0	.400	.400
Guillen, O*	.000	4	0	0	0	0	0	.000	.000
Hayes, C	.167	6	1	0	0	0	1	.167	.167
Howard, Dave#	.167	6	1	0	0	0	2	.167	.167
Jefferies, G#	.200	5	1	0	0	0	0	.200	.200
Joyner, Wally*	.333	3	1	0	1	2	0	.600	.333
Knoblauch, C	.000	8	0	0	0	1	2	.111	.000
Lewis, Darren	.000	3	0	0	0	1	0	.250	.000
Manto, Jeff	.333	3	1	0	0	2	0	.600	.333
Martinez, Da*	.500	4	2	0	1	1	0	.600	.500
Martinez, E	.400	5	2	1	2	3	1	.625	1.000
McGriff, Fred*	.200	5	1	0	0	0	2	.200	.200
Meares, Pat	.000	5	0	0	0	0	0	.000	.000
Merced, O*	.000	3	0	0	0	2	1	.400	.000
Molitor, Paul	.000	4	0	0	0	0	0	.000	.000
Murray, Eddie#	.400	5	2	0	2	1	0	.429	.400
Naehring, Tim	.000	3	0	0	0	3	0	.500	.000
Newson, W*	.000	3	0	0	0	2	2	.400	.000
O'Leary, Troy*	.000	4	0	0	0	0	1	.000	.000
Palmer, Dean	.167	6	1	0	0	0	1	.167	.167
Phillips, T#	.333	6	2	0	0	3	3	.556	.333
Raines, Tim#	.667	3	2	0	2	0	0	.800	.667
Ripken, Cal	.000	4	0	0	0	2	1	.333	.000
Rodriguez, Al	.000	4	0	0	0	0	2	.000	.000
Rodriguez, I	.000	5	0	0	0	0	1	.000	.000
Sabo, Chris	.000	6	0	0	1	0	1	.000	.000
Salmon, Tim	.500	4	2	0	1	0	1	.600	.500
Sandberg, R	.250	4	1	0	1	0	2	.200	.250
Seitzer, K	.800	5	4	0	0	1	0	.833	.800
Sojo, Luis	.000	5	0	0	0	0	1	.000	.000
Stanley, Mike	.429	7	3	0	0	1	0	.429	.714
Stillwell, K#	.200	5	1	0	0	0	0	.200	.200
Strawberry, D*	.333	6	2	2	6	0	1	.333	1.333
Tartabull, D	.000	8	0	0	0	1	0	.000	.000
Tettleton, M#	.167	6	1	0	0	0	1	.167	.167
Thomas, Frank	.600	5	3	0	3	0	0	.750	.600
Valentin, Jhn	.500	6	3	0	2	0	1	.500	.500
Vaughn, Greg	.500	4	2	0	1	1	0	.600	.750
Velarde, R	.200	5	1	0	0	0	2	.200	.200
Ventura, R*	.250	4	1	0	1	3	0	.571	.500
Vizcaino, J#	.200	5	1	0	0	0	0	.200	.200
Whiten, Mark#	.000	4	0	0	1	1	2	.200	.000
Williams, Ber#	.500	4	2	0	0	0	1	.600	.750
Wilson, Dan	.200	5	1	0	0	1	0	.200	.200

Tim Crabtree, Blue Jays — RHP

Batter	Avg	AB	H	HR	BI	BB	SO	OBP	Slg
Anderson, G*	.125	8	1	0	0	0	1	.125	.125
Canseco, Jose	.500	4	2	1	1	1	0	.667	1.500
Cordero, Wil	.400	5	2	0	3	0	0	.400	.600
DiSarcina, G	.333	6	2	0	1	0	0	.333	.333
Giambi, Jason*	.167	6	1	0	0	0	1	.167	.333
Greer, Rusty*	.250	4	1	0	2	1	3	.500	.250
Jaha, John	.000	4	0	0	0	1	1	.200	.000
Naehring, Tim	.143	7	1	0	2	1	2	.250	.143
O'Leary, Troy*	.250	4	1	0	1	1	0	.400	.250
Rodriguez, I	.333	6	2	0	2	0	1	.333	.500
Seitzer, K	.333	3	1	0	0	1	0	.600	.333
Snow, J.T.#	.400	5	2	0	1	0	0	.400	.400
Stanley, Mike	.000	9	0	0	0	1	1	.100	.000
Williams, Ber#	.200	5	1	0	0	0	1	.200	.200

Jim Corsi, Athletics — RHP

Batter	Avg	AB	H	HR	BI	BB	SO	OBP	Slg
Baines, H*	.400	5	2	1	3	1	1	.500	1.000
Belle, Albert	.250	4	1	1	2	1	3	.400	1.000
Boggs, Wade*	.500	4	2	0	0	1	1	.600	.500
Bonilla, B#	.143	7	1	0	1	0	0	.143	.143
Borders, Pat	.000	5	0	0	0	0	0	.000	.000
Buhner, Jay	.375	8	3	0	0	1	2	.444	.375
Canseco, Jose	.500	4	2	0	2	1	0	.600	.500
Carreon, Mark	.250	4	1	0	0	0	0	.250	.500
Carter, Joe	.125	8	1	0	2	1	1	.222	.125
Cora, Joey*	.200	5	1	0	0	0	0	.200	.200
Curtis, Chad	.250	4	1	1	1	1	0	.400	1.000
Daulton, D*	.200	5	1	0	1	0	0	.200	.400
Davis, Chili#	.400	5	2	0	0	1	1	.500	.400
Devereaux, M	.200	5	1	0	1	2	1	.429	.200
DiSarcina, G	.143	7	1	0	0	1	2	.250	.143
Duncan, M	.429	7	3	0	1	0	2	.375	.429
Durham, Ray#	.000	5	0	0	0	1	2	.286	.000
Eisenreich, J*	.000	7	0	0	0	1	2	.125	.000
Elster, Kevin	.429	7	3	0	1	0	2	.429	.571
Fielder, C	.250	4	1	0	0	1	0	.400	.250
Franco, Julio	.000	4	0	0	1	1	1	.167	.000
Fryman, T	.250	4	1	0	0	1	0	.400	.250
Gaetti, Gary	.000	6	0	0	0	2	0	.000	.000
Gagne, Greg	.000	4	0	0	0	1	2	.200	.000
Galarraga, A	.000	3	0	0	1	1	2	.200	.000

Doug Creek, Giants — LHP

Batter	Avg	AB	H	HR	BI	BB	SO	OBP	Slg
Caminiti, Ken#	.750	4	3	1	2	1	1	.800	1.500
DeShields, D*	.000	5	0	0	0	1	1	.167	.000
Finley, Steve*	.286	7	2	1	1	0	1	.286	1.000
Klesko, Ryan*	.600	5	3	0	3	1	0	.667	.600
McGriff, Fred*	.000	6	0	0	0	1	1	.143	.000
Servais, S	.667	3	2	1	2	2	1	.800	2.000

John Cummings, Tigers — LHP

Batter	Avg	AB	H	HR	BI	BB	SO	OBP	Slg
Alomar, R#	.143	7	1	0	0	2	2	.333	.143
Anderson, Brd*	.167	6	1	0	0	0	1	.286	.167
Baerga, C#	.250	4	1	0	1	0	1	.200	.250
Baines, H*	.500	6	3	0	3	0	1	.500	.667
Belle, Albert	.250	4	1	1	1	1	0	.400	1.000
Boggs, Wade*	.571	7	4	0	0	2	0	.667	.714
Canseco, Jose	.167	6	1	0	2	1	0	.286	.167
Carter, Joe	.500	4	2	1	3	1	0	.600	1.250
Clark, Will*	.400	5	2	0	0	1	0	.400	.400
Curtis, Chad	.167	6	1	0	2	3	1	.444	.333
Davis, Chili#	.143	7	1	0	0	0	2	.143	.143
Dawson, Andre	.000	2	0	0	1	1	0	.000	.000
DiSarcina, G	.500	6	3	0	2	0	0	.500	.500
Edmonds, Jim*	.500	4	2	0	0	1	0	.600	.500
Fielder, C	.000	1	0	0	2	2	0	.400	.000
Franco, Julio	.500	4	2	0	1	1	0	.600	.750

John Cummings, Tigers — LHP

Batter	Avg	AB	H	HR	BI	BB	SO	OBP	Slg
Gallego, Mike	1.000	4	4	0	2	0	0	1.000	1.000
Gonzalez, L*	.000	6	0	0	0	0	2	.000	.000
Greenwell, M*	.250	8	2	1	2	1	1	.333	.625
Greer, Rusty*	.000	5	0	0	0	1	0	.167	.000
Guillen, O*	.200	5	1	0	1	0	0	.200	.200
Hamilton, D*	.200	5	1	0	0	0	0	.200	.200
Howard, T*	.400	5	2	0	0	0	0	.400	.400
Johnson, L*	.143	7	1	0	0	0	0	.143	.143
Kelly, Pat	.167	6	1	0	1	0	0	.167	.333
Knorr, Randy	.200	5	1	0	0	1	2	.333	.200
Leyritz, Jim	.455	11	5	2	5	0	1	.455	1.091
Lofton, Kenny*	.167	6	1	0	0	0	0	.167	.167
Martin, N	.333	3	1	0	1	1	1	.500	.333
Molitor, Paul	.400	5	2	0	0	1	1	.500	.400
Murray, Eddie#	.667	6	4	1	2	0	0	.667	1.167
Myers, Greg*	.600	5	3	0	1	1	0	.714	.600
O'Neill, Paul*	.143	7	1	1	4	2	2	.333	.571
Palmeiro, R*	.167	6	1	0	0	0	0	.167	.167
Palmer, Dean	.000	6	0	0	0	0	2	.000	.000
Ripken, Cal	.500	4	2	0	0	1	1	.600	.750
Rodriguez, I	.125	8	1	0	0	0	0	.125	.125
Salmon, Tim	.167	6	1	0	0	1	4	.286	.167
Snow, J.T.#	.000	4	0	0	1	1	0	.167	.000
Sprague, Ed	.444	9	4	1	2	0	0	.444	.778
Stanley, Mike	.300	10	3	0	3	0	3	.300	.300
Surhoff, B.J.*	.750	4	3	0	4	1	0	.800	1.000
Tartabull, D	.000	7	0	0	0	6	2	.462	.000
Thomas, Frank	.600	5	3	1	2	3	0	.750	1.200
Valentin, Jhn	.333	6	2	1	1	1	2	.429	1.000
Vaughn, Mo*	.143	7	1	0	0	1	4	.250	.143
Velarde, R	.100	10	1	0	0	0	0	.100	.200
Ventura, R*	.100	10	6	1	6	0	0	.600	1.000
Ward, Turner#	.125	8	1	0	0	0	2	.125	.125
White, Devon#	.500	6	3	0	0	0	1	.500	.500
Williams, Ber#	.231	13	3	0	1	2	2	.333	.231
Williams, Ger	.400	5	2	0	0	0	0	.400	.400

Jeff D'Amico, Brewers — RHP

Batter	Avg	AB	H	HR	BI	BB	SO	OBP	Slg
Alomar, R#	.750	4	3	1	1	1	0	.800	1.750
Ausmus, Brad	.250	4	1	0	0	1	1	.400	.250
Bartee, K	.200	5	1	0	0	0	2	.200	.200
Becker, Rich*	.333	6	2	0	0	0	1	.333	.333
Belle, Albert	.250	4	1	0	2	1	1	.400	.500
Bonilla, B#	.400	5	2	1	3	0	0	.400	1.000
Carter, Joe	.200	5	1	0	1	0	0	.200	.200
Clark, Tony#	.500	8	4	3	4	0	1	.500	1.625
Cordova, M	.167	6	1	0	1	0	1	.167	.167
Cruz, Fausto	.000	5	0	0	0	0	0	.000	.000
Curtis, Chad	.250	4	1	1	2	0	1	.200	1.000
Delgado, C*	.000	5	0	0	0	1	2	.167	.000
Fryman, T	.111	9	1	0	0	1	0	.200	.222
Higginson, B*	.333	9	3	1	1	2	2	.455	.667
Knoblauch, C	.000	4	0	0	0	2	1	.333	.000
Lofton, Kenny*	.400	5	2	1	2	0	1	.400	1.200
Molitor, Paul	.167	6	1	0	0	0	0	.167	.333
Nieves, M#	.200	10	2	1	1	0	6	.200	.600
Nixon, Otis#	.000	4	0	0	0	2	1	.333	.000
Palmeiro, R*	.250	4	1	0	1	2	0	.400	.250
Perez, Tomas#	.400	5	2	0	0	1	0	.400	.400
Pride, Curtis*	.667	3	2	0	1	2	0	.800	1.333
Sierra, Ruben#	.167	6	1	1	2	0	1	.167	.667
Stahoviak, S*	.333	6	2	0	0	0	3	.333	.333
Thome, Jim*	.333	3	1	0	0	2	1	.600	.333

Omar Daal, Expos — LHP

Batter	Avg	AB	H	HR	BI	BB	SO	OBP	Slg
Bell, Jay	.500	4	2	0	1	0	0	.600	.500
Bonds, Barry*	.429	7	3	1	7	0	0	.429	1.000
Bonilla, B#	.000	4	0	0	1	0	1	.000	.000
Caminiti, Ken#	.333	6	2	1	1	1	1	.429	.833
Conine, Jeff	.500	6	3	1	2	0	1	.500	1.000
Daulton, D*	.400	5	2	1	3	1	0	.429	1.000
Duncan, M	.500	5	1	0	1	0	0	.200	.200
Dykstra, L*	.125	8	1	0	1	0	0	.200	.125
Eisenreich, J*	.333	9	3	0	3	1	0	.400	.444
Finley, Steve*	.111	9	1	0	0	1	1	.200	.222
Fletcher, D*	.167	6	1	0	1	1	1	.286	.333
Gonzalez, L*	.250	4	1	0	2	1	2	.400	.250
Grace, Mark*	.500	8	4	0	1	0	1	.500	.750
Gwynn, Tony*	.308	13	4	0	5	1	1	.357	.462
Henderson, R#	.333	3	1	1	1	2	1	.600	1.333
Hollins, Dave#	.571	7	4	0	0	0	1	.571	.857
Jones, C#	.000	3	0	0	0	3	0	.500	.000
King, Jeff	.500	4	2	1	3	0	0	.714	1.250
Klesko, Ryan*	.200	5	1	0	0	0	0	.200	.200
Lankford, Ray*	.200	5	1	0	1	2	0	.375	.200
Mabry, John*	.571	7	4	0	1	0	1	.571	.571
Martin, Al*	.125	8	1	0	1	0	6	.125	.125
McGriff, Fred*	.400	10	4	0	2	3	0	.538	.500
Merced, O*	.000	9	0	0	1	0	3	.000	.000

Omar Daal, Expos — LHP

Batter	Avg	AB	H	HR	BI	BB	SO	OBP	Slg
Morandini, M*	.133	15	2	0	1	1	3	.188	.133
Morris, Hal*	.222	9	2	0	1	1	2	.300	.333
Mouton, James	.333	6	2	0	1	1	1	.429	.333
Pendleton, T#	.000	4	0	0	1	1	1	.200	.000
Plantier, P*	.000	3	0	0	2	1	1	.250	.000
Reed, Jody	.000	4	0	0	0	0	0	.200	.000
Stocker, K#	.500	6	3	0	0	1	1	.571	.667
Tavarez, Je#	.400	5	2	0	1	0	0	.400	.400
Thompson, Mil*	.143	7	1	0	0	0	2	.143	.143
Vizcaino, J#	.143	7	1	0	2	0	2	.143	.143
Walker, Larry*	.200	10	2	1	2	1	0	.273	.500
Wilkins, Rick*	.400	4	0	0	0	2	1	.333	.000

Danny Darwin, Astros — RHP

Batter	Avg	AB	H	HR	BI	BB	SO	OBP	Slg
Abbott, Kurt	.000	6	0	0	0	0	1	.000	.000
Aldrete, Mike*	.269	26	7	1	3	6	5	.406	.385
Alicea, Luis#	.143	14	2	0	0	3	3	.200	.143
Alomar, R#	.475	40	19	1	5	2	2	.488	.625
Alomar Jr, S	.429	7	3	0	1	1	2	.556	.571
Alou, Moises	.375	8	3	0	4	0	0	.333	.625
Amaral, Rich	.400	5	2	0	0	0	0	.400	.600
Anderson, Brd*	.278	18	5	0	1	3	3	.409	.389
Anderson, G*	.600	5	3	1	1	0	0	.600	1.200
Andrews, S	.000	6	0	0	1	0	0	.000	.000
Ausmus, Brad	.000	5	0	0	0	2	0	.000	.000
Baerga, C#	.261	23	6	1	3	1	1	.292	.435
Bagwell, Jeff	.500	6	3	1	1	0	0	.500	1.000
Baines, H*	.400	40	16	3	9	4	2	.457	.650
Bell, Derek	.250	8	2	0	1	1	3	.333	.500
Bell, Jay	.100	10	1	0	0	0	5	.100	.100
Belle, Albert	.261	23	6	2	6	1	4	.292	.565
Belliard, R	.250	12	3	0	0	2	1	.357	.250
Beltre, E	.250	4	1	0	1	1	0	.400	.250
Bichette, D	.125	16	2	0	0	0	5	.125	.125
Biggio, Craig	.000	5	0	0	0	1	2	.286	.000
Blauser, Jeff	.053	19	1	0	0	3	8	.182	.053
Blowers, Mike	.100	10	1	0	0	0	2	.100	.100
Boggs, Wade*	.300	20	6	0	4	6	1	.462	.350
Bonds, Barry*	.200	20	4	2	3	4	2	.385	.550
Bonilla, B#	.063	16	1	0	1	1	2	.118	.063
Borders, Pat	.222	18	4	1	2	1	3	.263	.389
Bordick, Mike	.313	16	5	0	2	0	1	.313	.313
Brogna, Rico*	.500	6	3	0	0	0	1	.500	.667
Brosius, S	.167	6	1	0	0	0	2	.167	.167
Buhner, Jay	.273	11	3	1	2	1	3	.333	.545
Bullett, S*	.167	6	1	0	0	0	2	.167	.167
Burks, Ellis	.182	11	2	1	2	0	1	.182	.545
Butler, Brett*	.200	25	5	1	3	5	6	.333	.360
Caminiti, Ken#	.000	7	0	0	0	0	1	.000	.000
Candaele, C#	.000	6	0	0	0	2	1	.250	.000
Cangelosi, J#	.143	7	1	0	1	2	3	.333	.143
Canseco, Jose	.314	35	11	2	6	2	7	.368	.543
Carreon, Mark	.167	6	1	0	0	0	0	.167	.167
Carter, Joe	.375	40	15	2	9	1	5	.381	.625
Clark, Will*	.450	40	18	2	7	4	5	.478	.650
Colbrunn, G	.200	10	2	0	0	1	2	.200	.400
Cole, Alex*	.333	3	1	0	1	1	0	.400	.333
Coleman, V#	.289	38	11	0	1	1	7	.308	.421
Conine, Jeff	.000	7	0	0	0	1	2	.125	.000
Cora, Joey#	.350	20	7	0	3	1	2	.381	.600
Curtis, Chad	.125	16	2	0	1	1	5	.176	.125
Cuyler, Milt#	.200	10	2	0	0	0	4	.200	.200
Dascenzo, D	.000	9	0	0	0	0	0	.000	.000
Daulton, D*	.111	9	1	0	1	0	2	.111	.111
Davis, Chili#	.412	17	7	2	3	6	4	.565	.824
Davis, Eric	.172	29	5	0	0	3	11	.250	.241
Dawson, Andre	.500	14	7	2	4	3	3	.556	1.000
Deer, Rob	.125	8	1	0	0	0	4	.125	.125
Delgado, C*	.200	5	1	0	0	0	1	.200	.200
DeShields, D	.167	12	2	0	0	1	1	.231	.250
Devereaux, M	.182	22	4	1	4	1	6	.217	.455
DiSarcina, G	.412	17	7	1	4	0	3	.412	.588
Duncan, M	.000	4	0	0	0	2	0	.200	.000
Dunston, S	.179	28	5	0	2	9	2	.233	.179
Dykstra, L*	.394	33	13	0	2	2	7	.444	.545
Easley, D	.462	13	6	0	1	1	1	.533	.462
Edmonds, Jim*	.200	5	1	0	0	1	1	.333	.400
Eisenreich, J*	.250	8	2	0	0	1	1	.333	.250
Elster, Kevin	.250	12	3	0	0	1	3	.308	.333
Espinoza, A	.000	6	0	0	0	0	2	.000	.000
Fermin, Felix	.400	10	4	0	0	1	0	.455	.500
Fielder, C	.250	24	6	3	5	0	2	.250	.667
Finley, Steve*	.571	7	4	1	1	0	2	.571	1.143
Fletcher, D*	.714	7	5	1	2	0	0	.750	1.286
Franco, Julio	.280	25	7	0	3	2	5	.333	.320
Frye, Jeff	.417	12	5	0	1	0	3	.417	.500
Fryman, T	.192	26	5	1	1	3	8	.276	.308
Gaetti, Gary	.237	38	9	1	4	1	10	.262	.342
Gagne, Greg	.267	15	4	1	3	1	5	.294	.533
Galarraga, A	.400	25	10	1	3	1	2	.407	.680

Batter	Avg	AB	H	HR	BI	BB	SO	OBP	Slg
Gallego, Mike	.167	6	1	1	1	0	0	.167	.667
Gant, Ron	.321	28	9	0	7	1	4	.345	.429
Gates, Brent#	.143	7	1	0	0	0	2	.143	.143
Gil, Benji	.333	6	2	0	3	1	2	.429	.500
Gilkey, B	.286	7	2	0	1	0	0	.286	.429
Gomez, Chris	.000	6	0	0	0	0	1	.000	.000
Gomez, Leo	.235	17	4	0	2	2	1	.300	.294
Gonzales, R	.000	5	0	0	0	0	0	.000	.000
Gonzalez, J	.190	21	4	0	1	1	3	.227	.190
Gonzalez, L*	.400	5	2	1	2	1	0	.500	1.000
Goodwin, Tom*	.400	5	2	0	0	1	1	.500	.600
Grace, Mark*	.389	18	7	0	2	2	3	.476	.500
Grebeck, C	.200	5	1	0	0	0	0	.200	.200
Greenwell, M*	.250	4	1	0	0	1	0	.400	.500
Greer, Rusty*	.727	11	8	0	2	0	0	.727	1.091
Griffey Jr, K*	.412	17	7	2	5	1	1	.444	.882
Grissom, M	.222	9	2	0	0	0	1	.222	.222
Grudzielanek	.400	5	2	0	0	1	0	.500	.600
Guillen, O*	.174	23	4	0	4	0	0	.174	.174
Gutierrez, R	.200	5	1	0	0	0	1	.200	.200
Gwynn, Chris*	.375	16	6	0	0	0	3	.375	.563
Gwynn, Tony*	.344	32	11	0	4	1	1	.364	.469
Hale, Chip*	.429	7	3	0	1	1	0	.500	.571
Hall, Mel*	.500	8	4	1	1	1	1	.556	1.000
Hamelin, Bob*	.400	5	2	0	0	0	0	.500	.400
Hamilton, D*	.333	18	6	1	6	2	1	.381	.556
Hammonds, J	.000	6	0	0	0	0	1	.000	.000
Harris, Lenny*	.444	9	4	0	1	0	0	.444	.444
Hayes, C	.143	7	1	0	0	0	1	.143	.143
Henderson, R	.273	33	9	3	6	4	4	.375	.606
Hernandez, Jo	.000	6	0	0	0	0	1	.000	.000
Hill, G	.125	8	1	0	0	0	3	.125	.250
Hoiles, Chris	.167	18	3	2	4	0	5	.158	.500
Hollandsworth*	.333	6	2	0	0	0	0	.333	.333
Howard, Dave#	.286	7	2	0	1	1	2	.375	.286
Howard, T*	.400	5	2	0	1	0	0	.400	.600
Hulse, David*	.308	13	4	0	3	0	1	.286	.385
Hunter, Bri L	.000	7	0	0	0	0	2	.000	.000
Huson, Jeff*	.000	5	0	0	0	0	2	.000	.000
Incaviglia, P	.111	9	1	0	0	0	3	.111	.111
Jaha, John	.250	20	5	1	4	1	6	.286	.450
James, Dion*	.296	27	8	2	3	4	3	.387	.630
Javier, Stan#	.000	7	0	0	0	1	0	.000	.000
Jefferies, G#	.500	10	5	0	2	0	0	.500	.600
Jefferson, R*	.600	10	6	1	5	0	1	.600	1.200
Johnson, Char	.429	7	3	0	2	1	1	.444	.571
Johnson, L*	.143	28	4	0	3	2	1	.200	.286
Jones, C#	.667	6	4	0	3	0	0	.667	.833
Jordan, Brian	.200	5	1	0	0	2	0	.333	.400
Jordan, Ricky	.375	8	3	0	2	0	1	.375	.375
Joyner, Wally*	.385	26	10	2	9	2	3	.414	.808
Justice, Dave*	.167	12	2	0	1	2	5	.286	.250
Karkovice, R	.100	10	1	1	1	1	6	.182	.400
Karros, Eric	.375	8	3	0	0	0	0	.375	.500
Kent, Jeff	.000	6	0	0	0	3	0	.000	.000
King, Jeff	.333	9	3	3	6	1	2	.364	1.333
Kingery, Mike*	.308	13	4	0	1	1	2	.357	.308
Kirby, Wayne*	.600	5	3	1	1	1	1	.667	1.200
Klesko, Ryan*	.500	4	2	0	0	1	1	.600	.500
Knoblauch, C	.200	10	2	0	1	0	2	.200	.400
Kreuter, Chad#	.462	13	6	2	4	1	3	.500	1.077
Lampkin, Tom*	.000	4	0	0	0	2	0	.333	.000
Lankford, Ray*	.444	9	4	1	1	1	2	.500	.889
Lansing, Mike	.250	8	2	0	0	0	0	.333	.500
Larkin, Barry	.226	31	7	0	3	2	3	.286	.290
Lemke, Mark#	.375	8	3	0	1	0	4	.444	.500
Lewis, Mark	.000	5	0	0	0	3	0	.000	.000
Listach, Pat#	.200	20	4	0	0	0	5	.200	.200
Livingstone*	.176	17	3	0	2	1	4	.211	.176
Lofton, Kenny*	.350	20	7	0	1	3	1	.435	.500
Lopez, Javy	.400	5	2	0	0	0	2	.400	.400
Lopez, Luis#	.333	6	2	0	0	0	1	.333	.333
Lovullo, T#	.143	7	1	0	0	0	0	.143	.286
Mabry, John*	.667	6	4	0	1	0	0	.667	.667
Macfarlane, M	.333	18	6	1	6	1	3	.368	.500
Magadan, Dave*	.389	18	7	0	2	2	2	.450	.389
Martinez, Da*	.280	25	7	0	1	1	0	.280	.320
Martinez, E	.333	9	3	1	3	0	0	.333	.667
Martinez, T*	.111	9	1	0	0	1	0	.200	.111
May, Derrick*	.167	6	1	0	0	0	0	.167	.167
Mayne, Brent*	.364	11	4	0	1	0	1	.364	.364
McGee, Willie*	.263	19	5	0	2	2	2	.318	.263
McGriff, Fred*	.000	5	0	0	0	1	0	.000	.000
McGwire, Mark	.167	6	1	1	1	0	3	.167	.667
McLemore, M#	.450	20	9	0	3	1	1	.476	.500
McRae, Brian#	.045	22	1	1	1	1	3	.087	.182
Mitchell, K	.174	23	4	1	5	4	5	.321	.304
Molitor, Paul	.222	27	6	0	4	0	1	.214	.296
Mondesi, Raul	.143	7	1	0	0	0	0	.143	.143
Murray, Eddie#	.389	36	14	1	4	3	2	.436	.500
Myers, Greg*	.200	10	2	0	1	0	1	.200	.300

Batter	Avg	AB	H	HR	BI	BB	SO	OBP	Slg
Newfield, M	.429	7	3	0	0	0	0	.429	.429
Nilsson, Dave*	.286	14	4	0	2	3	2	.412	.286
Nixon, Otis#	.250	16	4	0	1	1	4	.294	.250
O'Leary, Troy*	.400	5	2	1	1	1	2	.500	1.200
O'Neill, Paul*	.269	26	7	1	2	2	3	.321	.423
Olerud, John*	.444	18	8	1	7	3	1	.524	.778
Oliver, Joe	.500	6	3	1	1	1	1	.571	1.000
Ordonez, Rey	.200	5	1	0	0	0	0	.200	.600
Orsulak, Joe*	.333	9	3	0	2	1	2	.400	.556
Pagnozzi, Tom	.400	5	2	0	0	0	0	.400	.400
Palmeiro, R*	.333	33	11	2	4	3	3	.378	.606
Palmer, Dean	.286	21	6	3	7	1	9	.318	.857
Pena, Tony	.263	19	5	1	3	2	1	.333	.474
Pendleton, T#	.320	25	8	0	2	0	2	.320	.400
Phillips, T#	.268	41	11	1	2	4	10	.333	.390
Piazza, Mike	.143	7	1	1	1	1	2	.250	.571
Polonia, Luis*	.211	19	4	0	0	0	3	.211	.211
Raines, Tim#	.314	35	11	4	8	5	5	.400	.686
Ramirez, M	.250	4	1	1	1	2	3	.500	1.000
Reboulet, J	.143	7	1	0	0	1	3	.250	.286
Reed, Jeff*	.333	15	5	0	2	2	1	.412	.667
Reed, Jody	.111	9	1	0	0	1	0	.200	.111
Renteria, E	.222	9	2	0	1	0	1	.222	.333
Ripken, Cal	.216	51	11	1	4	1	4	.241	.294
Roberts, Bip#	.444	9	4	0	0	1	2	.500	.778
Rodriguez, H*	.375	8	3	2	3	0	1	.444	1.125
Rodriguez, I	.250	24	6	1	3	2	4	.296	.500
Sabo, Chris	.227	22	5	0	0	1	3	.292	.409
Salmon, Tim	.250	12	3	0	2	2	3	.333	.250
Samuel, Juan	.133	15	2	0	1	1	3	.176	.133
Sandberg, R	.346	26	9	3	6	3	5	.400	.731
Santiago, B	.367	30	11	1	3	1	8	.387	.500
Schofield, D	.167	18	3	0	0	2	4	.250	.222
Segui, David#	.429	14	6	0	1	0	1	.400	.714
Seitzer, K	.280	25	7	0	3	3	1	.357	.360
Servais, S	.000	6	0	0	0	0	2	.000	.000
Sheffield, G	.500	4	2	0	2	4	0	.750	.750
Shumpert, T	.200	5	1	0	0	0	2	.200	.200
Sierra, Ruben#	.333	15	5	1	2	0	2	.333	.600
Slaught, Don	.333	9	3	1	1	0	3	.333	.778
Smith, Dwight*	.273	11	3	0	4	0	0	.273	.455
Smith, Ozzie#	.300	30	9	0	2	3	2	.364	.433
Snow, J.T.#	.182	11	2	0	0	0	2	.182	.364
Sojo, Luis	.167	6	1	0	0	0	0	.167	.167
Sorrento, P*	.143	14	2	0	0	3	2	.294	.214
Spiers, Bill*	.286	14	4	0	2	0	5	.286	.286
Sprague, Ed	.143	14	2	0	0	0	5	.143	.214
Stahoviak, S*	.000	6	0	0	0	0	2	.000	.000
Stankiewicz	.000	3	0	0	0	1	0	.400	.000
Stanley, Mike	.000	6	0	0	0	1	4	.143	.000
Steinbach, T	.381	21	8	3	4	1	2	.409	.810
Stevens, Lee*	.143	7	1	0	1	0	3	.143	.286
Stillwell, K#	.200	5	1	1	2	1	1	.333	.800
Stocker, K#	.667	3	2	0	1	2	1	.800	1.000
Strange, Doug#	.125	8	1	0	2	0	3	.100	.125
Strawberry, D*	.235	17	4	1	4	1	9	.263	.647
Surhoff, B.J.*	.143	28	4	0	1	2	2	.200	.214
Tartabull, D	.308	13	4	0	3	0	5	.308	.462
Tettleton, M#	.314	35	11	2	6	5	9	.400	.514
Thomas, Frank	.000	15	0	0	0	4	1	.211	.000
Thome, Jim*	.143	7	1	0	0	2	1	.333	.143
Thompson, Mil*	.150	20	3	0	0	2	6	.227	.250
Thompson, Rob	.125	24	3	0	2	3	6	.250	.125
Trammell, A	.240	25	6	0	0	0	3	.240	.320
Valentin, Jse#	.500	8	4	1	2	1	2	.556	1.250
Valle, Dave	.000	5	0	0	0	1	0	.167	.000
Vaughn, Greg	.259	27	7	3	7	2	9	.300	.593
Velarde, R	.000	5	0	0	0	0	2	.000	.000
Ventura, R*	.316	19	6	3	10	2	1	.381	.789
Vina, F*	.500	4	2	0	0	0	0	.600	1.000
Vizcaino, J#	.400	5	2	0	0	1	0	.500	.800
Vizquel, Omar#	.333	18	6	0	2	0	2	.316	.389
Walker, Larry*	.250	8	2	1	1	0	5	.333	.625
Wallach, Tim	.167	30	5	0	5	1	6	.194	.233
Walton, J	.000	5	0	0	0	1	0	.167	.000
Ward, Turner#	.091	11	1	0	3	1	1	.167	.182
Weiss, Walt#	.286	7	2	0	0	0	3	.375	.286
White, Devon#	.345	29	10	2	4	0	3	.333	.655
Whiten, Mark#	.200	10	2	0	0	1	3	.273	.200
Wilkins, Rick*	.833	6	5	1	2	0	0	.833	1.500
Williams, Ber#	.333	6	2	1	4	0	1	.333	1.000
Williams, Ma	.167	18	3	0	0	0	5	.211	.167
Zeile, Todd	.000	14	0	0	1	0	2	.000	.000

Batter	Avg	AB	H	HR	BI	BB	SO	OBP	Slg
Anderson, G*	.500	6	3	0	0	0	0	.500	.667
Davis, Chili*	.167	6	1	0	0	2	2	.375	.167
DiSarcina, G	.500	4	2	0	3	0	0	.400	.750
Edmonds, Jim*	.000	4	0	0	1	1	1	.200	.000
Greenwell, M*	.600	5	3	1	3	2	0	.714	1.400

Tim Davis, Mariners — LHP

Batter	Avg	AB	H	HR	BI	BB	SO	OBP	Slg
Guillen, O*	.000	9	0	0	1	0		.100	.000
Johnson, L*	.375	8	3	0	2	2	0	.455	.375
Joyner, Wally*	.500	6	3	0	0	0	0	.500	.667
Macfarlane, M	.400	5	2	0	2	2	2	.571	.400
McLemore, M#	.286	7	2	0	0	0	2	.286	.429
Naehring, Tim	.000	4	0	0	0	2	2	.333	.000
Nixon, Otis*	.143	7	1	0	0	0	3	.143	.143
O'Neill, Paul*	.000	5	0	0	0	2	2	.286	.000
Palmeiro, R*	.000	7	0	0	0	0	1	.000	.000
Phillips, T#	.500	2	1	0	0	4	1	.833	.500
Raines, Tim#	.167	6	1	0	0	1	1	.286	.167
Salmon, Tim	.000	4	0	0	0	1	2	.200	.000
Snow, J.T.#	.400	5	2	0	0	1	0	.500	.400
Stanley, Mike	.400	5	2	0	2	0	0	.400	.400
Thomas, Frank	.250	4	1	0	1	2	1	.500	.250
Tinsley, Lee#	.250	4	1	0	0	1	0	.250	.250
Valentin, Jhn	.200	5	1	0	1	3	0	.444	.200
Vaughn, Mo*	.429	7	3	0	4	1	3	.500	.429
Ventura, R*	.667	6	4	1	6	0	1	.667	1.333
Williams, Ber#	.600	5	3	0	1	1	0	.667	.600

Rich DeLucia, Giants — RHP

Batter	Avg	AB	H	HR	BI	BB	SO	OBP	Slg
Kirby, Wayne*	.333	3	1	0	1	1	0	.500	.667
Knoblauch, C	.222	9	2	1	3	2	4	.333	.556
Lansing, Mike	.600	5	3	0	0	0	0	.600	1.000
Larkin, Barry	.200	5	1	0	0	1	1	.333	.200
Lewis, Mark	.111	9	1	0	1	0	2	.111	.111
Leyritz, Jim	.333	6	2	0	0	0	2	.333	.500
Liriano, N#	.600	5	3	0	3	0	0	.600	.800
Livingstone*	.286	7	2	0	0	0	1	.286	.286
Magadan, Dave*	.500	2	1	0	1	3	0	.800	1.000
Manwaring, K	.500	5	0	0	0	0	0	.000	.000
Mayne, Brent*	.429	7	3	0	1	1	1	.500	.571
McGwire, Mark	.118	17	2	0	0	1	3	.167	.176
McRae, Brian#	.250	12	3	0	3	1	0	.308	.583
Merced, O*	.500	2	1	0	1	3	0	.800	1.000
Molitor, Paul	.300	10	3	1	3	0	0	.300	.600
Mondesi, Raul	.286	7	2	1	2	2	2	.444	.714
Morris, Hal*	.750	5	4	3	1	1	0	.800	1.500
Mouton, James	.167	6	1	0	0	1	2	.286	.167
Munoz, Pedro	.800	5	4	1	3	0	0	.800	1.600
Olerud, John*	.500	6	3	0	2	2	0	.556	.833
Orsulak, Joe*	.250	12	3	0	0	1	0	.308	.250
Palmeiro, R*	.333	12	4	1	1	0	1	.333	.583
Palmer, Dean	.000	3	0	0	0	2	1	.400	.000
Phillips, T#	.267	15	4	0	3	0	4	.267	.333
Piazza, Mike	.250	4	1	1	2	1	3	.400	1.000
Polonia, Luis*	.438	16	7	0	0	1	1	.471	.625
Raines, Tim#	.222	9	2	0	0	1	2	.300	.333
Reed, Jody	.533	15	8	0	3	2	1	.588	.800
Ripken, Billy	.000	4	0	0	0	1	0	.200	.000
Ripken, Cal	.375	16	6	2	3	0	1	.375	.875
Sanders, R	.200	5	1	0	0	0	2	.333	.200
Santiago, B	.000	5	0	0	0	2	1	.286	.000
Schofield, D	.400	5	2	0	0	1	0	.500	.400
Segui, David#	.429	7	3	1	2	1	2	.500	1.000
Sheffield, G	.143	7	1	1	2	1	1	.250	.571
Shumpert, T	.125	8	1	0	0	0	3	.125	.125
Sierra, Ruben#	.389	18	7	1	2	0	4	.368	.556
Sojo, Luis	.125	8	1	1	1	0	0	.125	.500
Sosa, Sammy	.000	10	0	0	0	0	4	.000	.000
Spiers, Bill*	.571	7	4	1	2	1	1	.556	1.000
Stanley, Mike	.400	5	2	0	1	0	0	.400	.400
Steinbach, T	.333	12	4	1	1	0	2	.429	.583
Stillwell, K#	.286	7	2	0	0	0	0	.286	.429
Stocker, K#	.200	5	1	0	0	0	0	.200	.200
Surhoff, B.J.*	.333	6	2	0	0	1	1	.429	.333
Tartabull, D	.250	8	2	1	2	1	2	.333	.625
Tettleton, M#	.333	6	2	0	2	3	3	.500	.333
Thomas, Frank	.389	18	7	0	4	2	6	.450	.500
Trammell, A	.000	6	0	0	0	3	1	.333	.000
Vaughn, Greg	.000	7	0	0	0	3	0	.000	.000
Ventura, R*	.176	17	3	1	2	3	2	.300	.412
Ward, Turner#	.000	4	0	0	0	0	2	.000	.000
Weiss, Walt*	.250	8	2	0	0	0	0	.250	.250
White, Devon#	.167	12	2	0	0	1	3	.231	.250
Whiten, Mark#	.286	7	2	1	1	1	1	.375	.714
Williams, E	.000	4	0	0	0	1	0	.200	.000
Worthington	.200	5	1	1	1	0	1	.200	.800
Zeile, Todd	.000	6	0	0	0	1	0	.143	.000

Rich DeLucia, Giants — RHP

Batter	Avg	AB	H	HR	BI	BB	SO	OBP	Slg
Abbott, Kurt	.250	4	1	0	0	1	2	.400	.250
Alfonzo, E	.250	4	1	0	0	1	1	.400	.250
Alomar, R#	.273	11	3	0	3	0	2	.273	.455
Alou, Moises	.400	5	2	1	2	0	1	.400	1.000
Anderson, Brd*	.143	7	1	1	1	0	2	.143	.571
Baerga, C	.462	13	6	0	2	1	1	.467	.462
Bagwell, Jeff	.200	5	1	1	1	2	0	.429	.800
Baines, H*	.333	15	5	0	1	2	2	.389	.400
Bell, Derek	.375	8	3	0	0	1	3	.500	.500
Bell, Jay	.333	6	2	0	0	0	2	.333	.333
Belle, Albert	.200	10	2	1	1	0	1	.200	.500
Bichette, D	.333	9	3	0	2	0	2	.333	.444
Biggio, Craig	.125	8	1	0	0	0	1	.125	.125
Boggs, Wade*	.375	8	3	0	0	2	0	.500	.500
Boone, Bret	.143	7	1	0	2	0	4	.143	.143
Borders, Pat	.333	6	2	0	1	1	0	.429	.333
Bordick, Mike	.000	8	0	0	0	1	1	.111	.000
Branson, Jeff*	.250	4	1	0	1	0	0	.200	.750
Burks, Ellis	.071	14	1	0	1	0	4	.067	.071
Caminiti, Ken*	.286	7	2	0	2	0	0	.286	.571
Canseco, Jose	.313	16	5	3	3	1	4	.353	.938
Carter, Joe	.000	11	0	0	0	5	0	.000	.000
Castilla, V	.200	5	1	0	0	0	1	.200	.200
Clayton, R	.143	7	1	0	1	0	3	.143	.143
Cole, Alex*	.400	5	2	0	0	2	0	.571	.600
Conine, Jeff	.400	5	2	0	0	0	0	.400	1.000
Curtis, Chad	.333	6	2	0	0	0	1	.333	.333
Cuyler, Milt*	.250	12	3	1	2	0	1	.308	.667
Davis, Chili#	.455	11	5	1	2	2	2	.538	.727
Deer, Rob	.556	9	5	2	5	2	3	.636	1.444
Devereaux, M	.125	16	2	0	0	1	3	.176	.188
DiSarcina, G	.500	8	3	0	0	2	0	.500	.667
Eisenreich, J*	.250	8	2	0	2	1	2	.300	.250
Espinoza, A	.600	5	3	0	0	0	0	.600	.800
Fermin, Felix	.500	8	4	0	2	0	0	.444	.500
Fielder, C	.333	12	4	3	11	2	2	.429	1.083
Franco, Julio	.308	13	4	0	1	1	3	.357	.308
Fryman, T	.000	10	0	0	0	2	3	.231	.000
Gaetti, Gary	.400	10	4	1	1	1	0	.455	.700
Gagne, Greg	.250	8	2	0	1	0	2	.250	.250
Galarraga, A	.000	5	0	0	0	1	4	.167	.000
Gallego, Mike	.231	13	3	1	2	0	3	.231	.538
Gant, Ron	.400	5	2	0	0	1	2	.500	.400
Garcia, C	.250	4	1	0	2	1	0	.400	.250
Gomez, Leo	.000	6	0	0	1	0	2	.000	.000
Gonzalez, J	.500	6	3	0	1	2	2	.625	.667
Gonzalez, L*	.500	5	1	0	0	1	2	.333	.200
Grebeck, C	.143	7	1	0	2	1	1	.250	.286
Greenwell, M*	.500	4	2	0	1	3	0	.714	.500
Grissom, M	.400	5	2	0	1	0	1	.400	.400
Guillen, O*	.222	9	2	0	1	0	0	.222	.333
Hamilton, D*	.200	5	1	1	2	1	0	.333	.800
Hayes, C	.429	7	3	0	2	0	2	.429	.571
Henderson, R	.125	8	1	0	0	3	4	.364	.125
Hill, G	.000	6	0	0	0	1	3	.143	.000
Hoiles, Chris	.111	9	1	0	0	0	1	.111	.111
Howell, Jack*	.000	4	0	0	0	1	0	.200	.000
Huff, Michael	.250	4	1	0	0	0	2	.400	.500
Huson, Jeff	.100	10	1	0	0	0	2	.100	.100
Incaviglia, P	.167	6	1	1	1	2	3	.375	.667
Johnson, Char	.000	5	0	0	0	0	0	.000	.000
Johnson, L*	.500	20	10	0	3	1	0	.524	.700
Joyner, Wally*	.667	6	4	1	3	4	1	.800	1.333
Karros, Eric	.500	6	3	1	2	1	2	.571	1.000
Kelly, Pat	.200	5	1	0	2	0	2	.200	.400
Kelly, R	.200	5	1	0	1	2	1	.333	.200
Kent, Jeff	.000	4	0	0	1	0	1	.000	.000
King, Jeff	.000	5	0	0	0	1	2	.167	.000

Elmer Dessens, Pirates — RHP

Batter	Avg	AB	H	HR	BI	BB	SO	OBP	Slg
Gant, Ron	.333	3	1	0	0	1	0	.500	.667
Jordan, Brian	.800	5	4	1	4	0	0	.800	1.600
Lankford, Ray*	.600	5	3	0	0	0	0	.600	.800

Mark Dewey, Giants — RHP

Batter	Avg	AB	H	HR	BI	BB	SO	OBP	Slg
Alfonzo, E	.333	6	2	0	0	0	2	.333	.333
Alicea, Luis#	.500	6	3	0	5	0	1	.500	.667
Alou, Moises	.250	4	1	0	0	2	0	.500	.500
Arias, Alex	.250	4	1	0	1	0	1	.200	.250
Bagwell, Jeff	.500	4	2	0	2	1	1	.500	1.000
Bell, Derek	.400	5	2	0	3	1	0	.571	.400
Bell, Jay	.167	6	1	0	0	1	2	.286	.167
Berry, Sean	.444	9	4	0	4	0	0	.444	.444
Bichette, D	.250	8	2	0	0	1	2	.400	.250
Biggio, Craig	.167	6	1	0	1	0	0	.167	.167
Blauser, Jeff	.500	5	2	0	2	1	1	.500	.600
Bogar, Tim	.000	6	0	0	0	1	3	.143	.000
Boone, Bret	.286	7	2	0	1	0	0	.375	.286
Brumfield, J	.250	5	1	0	0	0	1	.200	.400
Burks, Ellis	.000	6	0	0	0	1	4	.143	.000
Butler, Brett*	.333	3	1	0	2	2	0	.600	.333
Caminiti, Ken*	.000	2	0	0	0	3	0	.600	.000
Castilla, V	.300	10	3	1	3	0	1	.273	.800
Cianfrocco, A	.250	4	1	0	2	0	1	.400	.250
Clayton, R	.400	5	2	0	0	0	1	.400	.400
Colbrunn, G	.000	6	0	0	0	0	3	.000	.000
Conine, Jeff	.167	6	1	0	0	0	2	.167	.167
Cordero, Wil	.167	6	1	1	3	0	0	.167	.667
Davis, Eric	.400	5	2	1	5	1	1	.500	1.000

Mark Dewey, Giants — RHP

Batter	Avg	AB	H	HR	BI	BB	SO	OBP	Slg
Finley, Steve*	.750	4	3	0	0	1	1	.800	1.250
Galarraga, A	.273	11	3	0	1	1	0	.385	.455
Gilkey, B	.200	10	2	0	0	1	1	.333	.200
Grace, Mark*	.333	6	2	1	1	1	0	.429	.833
Grissom, M	.111	9	1	0	0	0	2	.111	.111
Grudzielanek	.400	5	2	1	2	0	1	.500	1.000
Gutierrez, R	.000	5	0	0	0	1	2	.167	.000
Harris, Lenny*	.286	7	2	0	1	0	1	.286	.286
Hayes, C	.400	5	2	0	0	1	2	.500	.400
Hollandsworth*	.500	4	2	0	0	1	0	.600	.500
Jefferies, G#	.500	4	2	0	0	1	0	.600	.500
Jordan, Brian	.333	9	3	0	2	1	1	.400	.556
Karros, Eric	.250	12	3	0	2	1	3	.357	.333
Kent, Jeff	.167	6	1	0	1	2	2	.375	.167
King, Jeff	.000	4	0	0	0	1	0	.200	.000
Kingery, Mike*	.000	5	0	0	0	0	0	.000	.000
Lankford, Ray*	.500	4	2	0	0	1	0	.600	.750
Lansing, Mike	.111	9	1	0	0	1	1	.200	.111
Larkin, Barry	.667	6	4	0	2	1	0	.714	.833
Lemke, Mark*	.500	6	3	0	3	0	0	.500	.500
Lopez, Javy	.000	4	0	0	0	2	1	.333	.000
May, Derrick*	.500	6	3	0	1	1	0	.571	.500
Mondesi, Raul	.500	12	6	0	2	1	2	.538	.500
Morris, Hal*	.571	7	4	1	4	0	1	.571	1.000
O'Neill, Paul*	.000	4	0	0	0	1	1	.200	.000
Orsulak, Joe*	.500	4	2	1	3	1	0	.600	1.250
Pagnozzi, Tom	.111	9	1	0	2	0	2	.111	.222
Pendleton, T#	.286	7	2	1	2	1	1	.333	.714
Piazza, Mike	.143	7	1	0	1	1	1	.250	.143
Reed, Jody	.000	5	0	0	0	0	1	.000	.000
Sanchez, Rey	.286	7	2	0	1	1	1	.375	.286
Sandberg, R	.000	8	0	0	0	0	2	.000	.000
Sanders, R	.400	5	2	0	1	0	0	.400	.600
Santiago, B	.000	6	0	0	0	1	2	.143	.000
Segui, David#	.000	4	0	0	0	1	1	.200	.000
Servais, S	.200	5	1	0	0	0	0	.200	.200
Sheffield, G	.000	5	0	0	0	0	1	.000	.000
Smith, Ozzie#	.000	4	0	0	0	0	0	.000	.000
Sosa, Sammy	.375	8	3	1	4	1	3	.444	.750
Stinnett, K	.000	4	0	0	0	0	3	.200	.000
Taubensee, E*	.500	4	2	1	2	1	0	.600	1.250
Thompson, Ry	.000	4	0	0	0	1	2	.200	.000
Walker, Larry*	.167	6	1	0	0	1	0	.286	.333
Wallach, Tim	.200	5	1	0	1	1	1	.333	.200
Webster, L	.000	4	0	0	0	1	2	.200	.000
Weiss, Walt#	.000	5	0	0	0	2	1	.286	.000
White, R	.375	8	3	0	0	1	0	.444	.500
Whiten, Mark#	.500	4	2	0	3	1	0	.600	1.000
Wilkins, Rick*	.333	6	2	0	0	2	1	.500	.333
Zeile, Todd	.200	10	2	0	1	1	6	.273	.200

Jason Dickson, Angels — RHP

Batter	Avg	AB	H	HR	BI	BB	SO	OBP	Slg
Clark, Will*	.143	7	1	0	0	0	1	.143	.143
Duncan, M	.200	5	1	0	0	0	1	.200	.400
Elster, Kevin	.250	4	1	0	0	1	0	.400	.250
Girardi, Joe	.500	4	2	0	0	1	0	.600	.500
Gonzalez, J	.429	7	3	1	2	0	1	.429	.857
Greer, Rusty*	.429	7	3	0	1	0	2	.375	.571
Hamilton, D*	.000	6	0	0	0	2	1	.250	.000
Jeter, Derek	.500	6	3	1	3	0	0	.600	1.200
Martinez, T*	.250	4	1	0	0	1	0	.400	.250
McLemore, M#	.400	5	2	0	0	1	1	.500	.400
O'Neill, Paul*	.750	4	3	0	1	0	0	.800	1.000
Palmer, Dean	.286	7	2	1	1	0	1	.286	.714
Rodriguez, I	.000	6	0	0	0	2	0	.250	.000
Strawberry, D*	.500	4	2	0	0	1	0	.600	.500
Tettleton, M	.500	6	3	0	0	0	2	.500	.500
Williams, Ber#	.500	4	2	0	1	0	1	.600	.750

Jerry DiPoto, Mets — RHP

Batter	Avg	AB	H	HR	BI	BB	SO	OBP	Slg
Bagwell, Jeff	.500	6	3	0	3	3	1	.571	.500
Bates, Jason#	.000	5	0	0	0	0	0	.000	.000
Bell, Derek	.333	9	3	0	2	0	2	.333	.444
Berry, Sean	.000	6	0	0	0	0	1	.000	.000
Bichette, D	.500	6	3	0	1	0	1	.500	.667
Biggio, Craig	.333	6	2	0	0	1	1	.429	.333
Bonds, Barry*	.200	5	1	0	1	1	0	.429	.667
Boone, Bret	.500	6	3	0	1	0	0	.429	.667
Branson, Jeff*	.000	5	0	0	0	0	2	.000	.000
Buhner, Jay	.500	5	0	0	1	1	0	.000	.000
Cangelosi, J#	.000	3	0	0	0	2	1	.500	.000
Castilla, V	.400	5	2	0	0	0	0	.400	.600
Cedeno, A	.200	5	1	0	0	1	0	.200	.200
Clayton, R	.200	5	1	0	0	0	0	.200	.200
Colbrunn, G	.600	5	3	0	1	1	1	.800	1.000
Conine, Jeff	.600	5	3	1	3	1	1	.571	1.400
DeShields, D*	.500	4	2	1	0	0	0	.500	.500
Finley, Steve*	.400	5	2	0	1	0	0	.400	.400
Gaetti, Gary	.250	4	1	0	2	1	1	.500	.250

Jerry DiPoto, Mets — RHP

Batter	Avg	AB	H	HR	BI	BB	SO	OBP	Slg
Gant, Ron	.333	6	2	1	3	0	1	.333	.833
Grace, Mark*	.333	3	1	0	2	2	0	.600	.333
Grudzielanek	.000	5	0	0	1	0	1	.000	.000
Gwynn, Chris*	.500	4	2	0	2	1	0	.600	.500
Hayes, C	.250	4	1	0	0	0	0	.200	.250
Henderson, R	.400	5	2	0	1	2	0	.571	.400
Hernandez, Jo	.000	4	0	0	0	1	0	.000	.000
Hill, G	.500	6	3	1	2	0	2	.500	1.167
Howard, T*	.500	5	0	0	0	0	0	.000	.000
Johnson, Char	.500	4	2	0	0	1	0	.600	.750
Karros, Eric	.000	6	0	0	0	2	1	.250	.000
Kelly, R	.200	5	1	0	0	1	1	.333	.200
Knoblauch, C	.167	6	1	0	1	1	1	.286	.167
Lankford, Ray*	.600	5	3	0	0	0	0	.600	1.200
Lansing, Mike	.333	3	1	0	0	3	0	.667	.333
Larkin, Barry	.400	5	2	0	1	2	0	.571	.400
Livingstone*	.667	6	4	0	1	1	0	.714	.667
Mabry, John*	.500	4	2	0	1	1	0	.600	.750
McCarty, Dave	.333	6	2	0	0	0	2	.333	.500
McRae, Brian#	.667	6	4	1	4	1	0	.714	1.333
Merced, O*	.000	3	0	0	1	1	0	.200	.000
Mondesi, Raul	.400	5	2	0	1	0	1	.333	.600
Morandini, M*	.400	5	2	0	0	1	1	.500	.600
Pendleton, T#	.375	8	3	0	1	0	1	.375	.500
Piazza, Mike	.500	4	2	0	2	3	0	.714	.750
Polonia, Luis*	.200	5	1	0	0	1	0	.200	.200
Segui, David#	.333	6	2	0	2	1	0	.429	.500
Sosa, Sammy	.667	6	4	1	4	0	0	.667	1.167
Stocker, K#	.500	6	3	0	2	2	0	.625	.500
Weiss, Walt#	.300	3	0	0	0	1	0	.250	.000
White, Devon#	.000	3	0	0	1	3	0	.400	.000
Young, Eric	.333	3	1	0	1	0	1	.600	.333

Glenn Dishman, Tigers — LHP

Batter	Avg	AB	H	HR	BI	BB	SO	OBP	Slg
Abbott, Kurt	.333	6	2	0	0	0	2	.333	.333
Bichette, D	.333	9	3	0	2	0	1	.333	.444
Blauser, Jeff	.200	5	1	0	0	1	1	.333	.200
Burks, Ellis	.167	6	1	1	1	0	1	.167	.667
Carr, Chuck	.333	6	2	0	0	0	1	.333	.333
Castilla, V	.000	7	0	0	0	1	0	.000	.000
Colbrunn, G	.000	5	0	0	0	1	0	.167	.000
Galarraga, A	.333	6	2	0	1	0	0	.286	.500
Gilkey, B	.250	8	2	0	0	0	1	.250	.375
Grissom, M	.286	7	2	1	1	0	0	.375	.857
Hayes, C	.667	6	4	0	4	0	0	.667	.833
Jefferies, G#	.333	6	2	0	1	0	0	.333	.333
Jordan, Brian	.286	7	2	1	3	0	0	.286	.714
Justice, Dave*	.000	5	0	0	0	1	0	.167	.000
Lankford, Ray*	.600	5	3	0	3	2	0	.714	1.200
Lopez, Javy	.333	6	2	0	0	0	0	.333	.667
McGriff, Fred*	.000	6	0	0	0	1	0	.000	.000
Morman, Russ	.400	5	2	1	2	1	1	.500	1.000
Walker, Larry*	.333	6	2	0	1	0	0	.500	.500
Weiss, Walt#	.500	8	4	0	1	0	0	.500	.625
Whiten, Mark#	.200	5	1	0	0	1	2	.333	.200
Young, Eric	.625	8	5	1	2	1	0	.667	1.250

John Doherty, Red Sox — RHP

Batter	Avg	AB	H	HR	BI	BB	SO	OBP	Slg
Aldrete, Mike*	.222	9	2	1	4	0	0	.222	.556
Alomar, R#	.200	10	2	0	0	1	2	.273	.200
Alomar Jr, S	.364	11	4	1	4	0	1	.364	.636
Anderson, Brd*	.160	25	4	0	0	2	3	.222	.160
Baerga, C#	.211	19	4	0	3	1	1	.273	.316
Baines, H*	.200	20	4	1	2	4	2	.273	.250
Belle, Albert	.263	19	5	2	7	3	0	.364	.684
Berroa, G	.167	6	1	0	0	0	0	.167	.167
Blowers, Mike	.125	8	1	0	1	0	1	.125	.125
Boggs, Wade*	.267	15	4	0	1	1	1	.313	.267
Boone, Bret	.167	6	1	0	0	0	0	.167	.167
Borders, Pat	.200	5	1	1	1	0	0	.200	.800
Bordick, Mike	.200	15	3	0	1	1	1	.294	.200
Brosius, S	.333	9	3	0	1	0	0	.300	.333
Buhner, Jay	.313	16	5	0	3	1	1	.333	.438
Canseco, Jose	.294	17	5	0	2	0	1	.294	.412
Carter, Joe	.250	8	2	0	0	0	0	.250	.250
Cirillo, Jeff	.143	7	1	0	0	0	0	.143	.143
Clark, Will*	.500	6	3	0	2	4	0	.636	.500
Cora, Joey#	.294	17	5	1	4	0	0	.333	.588
Cordova, M	.200	5	1	0	0	0	0	.200	.200
Curtis, Chad	.231	13	3	0	1	2	2	.333	.231
Davis, Chili#	.222	18	4	0	2	0	0	.222	.278
Dawson, Andre	.286	7	2	0	0	0	0	.286	.286
Devereaux, M	.222	18	4	0	1	3	2	.333	.222
DiSarcina, G	.250	8	2	0	1	1	0	.333	.375
Durham, Ray#	.400	5	2	0	0	1	0	.400	.600
Edmonds, Jim*	.400	5	2	0	1	0	2	.400	.600
Espinoza, A	.250	4	1	0	0	0	0	.250	.250
Fermin, Felix	.250	12	3	0	2	1	0	.286	.333
Franco, Julio	.364	22	8	1	2	0	1	.364	.591

John Doherty, Red Sox — RHP

Batter	Avg	AB	H	HR	BI	BB	SO	OBP	Slg
Frye, Jeff	.250	8	2	0	1	0	0	.333	.250
Gaetti, Gary	.273	11	3	0	3	0	1	.333	.273
Gagne, Greg	.400	15	6	0	1	0	0	.400	.400
Gates, Brent#	.700	10	7	1	2	0	1	.636	1.200
Gil, Benji	.000	5	0	0	0	0	2	.000	.000
Gomez, Leo	.143	7	1	0	0	0	1	.143	.143
Gonzales, R	.000	5	0	0	0	1	0	.167	.000
Gonzalez, A	.400	5	2	0	1	0	0	.400	.400
Gonzalez, J	.364	22	8	1	7	0	2	.417	.591
Grebeck, C	.250	8	2	0	0	1	0	.333	.250
Greenwell, M*	.444	9	4	0	2	1	0	.500	.667
Greer, Rusty*	.333	9	3	0	0	2	1	.455	.333
Griffey Jr, K*	.368	19	7	3	6	2	2	.429	.895
Guillen, O*	.364	11	4	0	0	1	0	.364	.364
Gwynn, Tony*	.286	7	2	0	0	0	1	.286	.286
Hall, Mel*	.167	6	1	0	0	0	0	.167	.167
Hamilton, D*	.278	18	5	0	0	1	0	.278	.278
Henderson, D	.333	12	4	0	1	2	0	.429	.333
Hoiles, Chris	.267	15	4	0	1	1	3	.353	.267
Hudler, Rex	.000	5	0	0	0	0	0	.000	.000
Hulse, David*	.412	17	7	0	1	0	3	.412	.412
Huson, Jeff	.250	8	2	0	1	0	1	.222	.250
Jaha, John	.222	9	2	0	1	1	0	.273	.444
Jefferson, R	.400	10	4	0	0	0	0	.400	.500
Johnson, L*	.167	12	2	0	1	1	0	.231	.167
Joyner, Wally*	.500	12	6	1	5	1	0	.538	.750
Karkovice, R	.250	8	2	1	2	1	0	.300	.625
Kelly, Pat	.300	10	3	0	1	0	0	.364	.400
Kelly, R	.714	7	5	0	0	0	0	.714	.857
Kirby, Wayne*	.500	6	3	0	3	0	0	.500	.833
Knoblauch, C	.381	21	8	1	4	0	0	.381	.571
Leius, Scott	.000	7	0	0	0	2	0	.000	.000
Listach, Pat#	.118	17	2	0	0	0	4	.118	.118
Lofton, Kenny*	.474	19	9	1	4	1	0	.500	.789
Lovullo, T#	.000	5	0	0	0	0	2	.000	.000
Macfarlane, M	.286	7	2	0	0	0	0	.286	.286
Martinez, E	.333	15	5	1	4	2	1	.412	.667
Martinez, T*	.429	14	6	1	2	2	2	.500	.643
Mayne, Brent*	.000	5	0	0	1	0	0	.000	.000
McGwire, Mark	.500	6	3	1	2	3	1	.667	1.000
McLemore, M#	.409	22	9	0	2	1	4	.435	.455
McRae, Brian#	.667	12	8	1	5	0	1	.615	1.083
Meares, Pat	.200	5	1	0	1	0	0	.200	.400
Molitor, Paul	.450	20	9	0	2	0	0	.450	.500
Murray, Eddie#	.273	11	3	0	1	3	2	.429	.273
Myers, Greg*	.000	5	0	0	0	0	1	.000	.000
Naehring, Tim	.333	6	2	0	1	1	4	.429	.333
Nilsson, Dave*	.250	8	2	0	0	1	2	.333	.500
Nixon, Otis#	.250	4	1	0	0	1	2	.400	.250
O'Leary, Troy*	.286	7	2	0	0	0	1	.286	.286
O'Neill, Paul*	.444	9	4	0	2	0	1	.444	.444
Olerud, John*	.500	10	5	0	0	2	0	.583	.700
Palmeiro, R*	.240	25	6	0	2	1	1	.269	.240
Palmer, Dean	.333	15	5	1	5	1	0	.375	.667
Peltier, Dan*	.167	6	1	0	1	0	0	.167	.167
Pena, Tony	.214	14	3	0	3	0	0	.214	.214
Polonia, Luis*	.300	10	3	0	1	3	1	.462	.300
Raines, Tim#	.333	15	5	0	1	3	2	.444	.333
Ramirez, M	.100	10	1	0	0	2	1	.250	.200
Reboulet, J	.000	5	0	0	1	0	1	.000	.000
Reed, Jody	.125	8	1	0	0	0	0	.125	.125
Ripken, Cal	.360	25	9	0	1	2	1	.407	.400
Rodriguez, I	.500	14	7	1	4	1	0	.588	.786
Salmon, Tim	.125	8	1	0	1	1	3	.222	.250
Segui, David#	.100	10	1	1	1	2	1	.250	.400
Seitzer, K	.308	13	4	0	2	1	0	.438	.385
Sierra, Ruben#	.182	22	4	1	1	2	2	.250	.364
Snow, J.T.#	.333	9	3	0	0	0	0	.333	.444
Sojo, Luis	.286	14	4	0	0	0	0	.286	.429
Sorrento, P*	.636	11	7	0	2	2	0	.692	.727
Spiers, Bill*	.200	5	1	0	0	0	0	.200	.200
Sprague, Ed	.222	9	2	0	1	2	0	.364	.444
Stanley, Mike	.300	10	3	0	3	0	2	.364	.300
Steinbach, T	.182	11	2	0	0	0	0	.182	.273
Strange, Doug#	.000	8	0	0	0	0	1	.000	.000
Surhoff, B.J.*	.333	12	4	0	2	3	1	.438	.417
Tartabull, D	.545	11	6	0	3	3	1	.643	.636
Tettleton, M*	.200	5	1	0	0	0	0	.200	.200
Thomas, Frank	.412	17	7	2	6	3	1	.476	.882
Thome, Jim*	.538	13	7	3	5	2	2	.600	1.308
Valentin, John	.500	12	6	0	6	2	1	.600	.667
Valentin, Jse#	.000	6	0	0	0	2	0	.000	.000
Valle, Dave	.000	3	0	0	0	0	0	.000	.000
Vaughn, Greg	.313	16	5	2	6	3	0	.400	.750
Vaughn, Mo*	.182	11	2	0	0	2	2	.357	.182
Velarde, R	.222	9	2	0	1	0	0	.300	.333
Ventura, R*	.231	13	3	1	3	1	0	.286	.538
Vizquel, Omar#	.412	17	7	0	2	0	1	.474	.412
Walbeck, Matt#	.200	5	1	0	0	0	2	.200	.400
Ward, Turner#	.250	4	1	0	0	1	0	.400	.500
White, Devon#	.333	9	3	0	1	0	1	.333	.667

John Doherty, Red Sox — RHP

Batter	Avg	AB	H	HR	BI	BB	SO	OBP	Slg
Williams, Ber#	.357	14	5	1	3	2	2	.438	.714
Wilson, Dan	.400	10	4	0	5	0	1	.400	.600

Jim Dougherty, Astros — RHP

Batter	Avg	AB	H	HR	BI	BB	SO	OBP	Slg
Bell, Jay	.400	5	2	0	0	0	0	.400	.400
Boone, Bret	.167	6	1	0	0	0	0	.167	.167
Colbrunn, G	.000	5	0	0	0	0	0	.000	.000
Conine, Jeff	.800	5	4	0	4	0	1	.800	1.000
Dunston, S	.400	5	2	0	1	0	0	.333	.600
Johnson, Char	.167	6	1	0	0	0	2	.167	.333
Kent, Jeff	.400	5	2	0	0	0	1	.400	.600
McRae, Brian#	.250	4	1	0	1	0	1	.400	.250
Nieves, M#	.500	4	2	0	2	0	1	.600	.500
Sanchez, Rey	.167	6	1	0	0	0	0	.167	.167
Sosa, Sammy	.333	6	2	1	3	0	0	.333	.833
Timmons, J	.250	4	1	0	0	1	2	.400	.250

Doug Drabek, Astros — RHP

Batter	Avg	AB	H	HR	BI	BB	SO	OBP	Slg
Abbott, Kurt	.200	10	2	0	1	0	3	.250	.400
Aldrete, Mike*	.222	18	4	1	3	3	3	.333	.389
Alfonzo, E	.286	7	2	0	2	0	0	.286	.714
Alicea, Luis#	.227	22	5	1	2	5	7	.370	.409
Alomar, R#	.300	20	6	0	2	2	3	.348	.350
Alou, Moises	.250	24	6	2	7	0	10	.280	.542
Amaro, Ruben#	.077	13	1	0	0	1	4	.143	.154
Andrews, S	.125	8	1	0	0	1	4	.222	.250
Anthony, Eric*	.158	19	3	0	1	4	5	.304	.158
Arias, Alex	.250	8	2	0	2	4	4	.455	.250
Ausmus, Brad	.111	9	1	0	0	0	4	.111	.111
Bagwell, Jeff	.125	8	1	0	1	3	2	.200	.125
Barberie, B#	.222	9	2	0	0	3	1	.417	.222
Batiste, Kim	.091	11	1	1	1	0	3	.091	.364
Bell, Derek	.286	7	2	0	0	1	1	.375	.286
Bell, Jay	.375	24	9	0	3	1	5	.400	.417
Belliard, R	.158	19	3	0	0	0	4	.158	.263
Benard, M*	.250	8	2	0	0	0	0	.250	.250
Berry, Sean	.000	6	0	0	0	3	3	.000	.000
Bichette, D	.333	33	11	0	3	0	5	.324	.455
Biggio, Craig	.355	31	11	0	0	1	7	.375	.387
Blauser, Jeff	.205	39	8	1	4	5	6	.304	.385
Blowers, Mike	.333	6	2	0	1	0	2	.333	.333
Bonds, Barry*	.444	27	12	2	4	7	4	.559	.926
Bonilla, B#	.304	23	7	0	2	2	6	.360	.435
Boone, Bret	.357	14	5	0	0	1	4	.400	.500
Branson, Jeff*	.333	27	9	1	3	2	4	.379	.556
Brogna, Rico*	.600	5	3	0	0	2	1	.714	.600
Bullett, S*	.167	6	1	0	0	0	1	.167	.167
Burks, Ellis	.385	13	5	1	2	0	3	.385	.692
Burnitz, J*	.200	10	2	0	0	2	1	.333	.200
Butler, Brett*	.446	65	29	2	7	4	5	.471	.662
Caminiti, Ken#	.367	30	11	0	3	4	6	.441	.467
Candaele, C#	.182	22	4	0	1	0	0	.182	.227
Carreon, Mark	.200	10	2	2	4	0	1	.200	.800
Carter, Joe	.111	9	1	0	0	0	1	.111	.111
Castilla, V	.222	18	4	3	5	0	5	.222	.722
Cedeno, A	.300	10	3	0	0	0	2	.300	.400
Cianfrocco, A	.500	6	3	0	0	0	2	.500	.500
Clark, Dave*	.300	10	3	0	0	0	2	.300	.400
Clark, Will*	.366	41	15	2	5	6	7	.438	.585
Clayton, R	.133	15	2	1	3	1	2	.188	.333
Colbrunn, G	.000	8	0	0	0	0	1	.000	.000
Cole, Alex*	.259	54	14	1	6	2	10	.286	.352
Conine, Jeff	.333	15	5	0	1	0	3	.375	.400
Cordero, Wil	.125	16	2	0	0	1	0	.125	.125
Cummings, M*	.333	9	3	0	0	0	1	.333	.444
Dascenzo, D	.059	17	1	0	1	4	0	.238	.059
Daulton, D*	.176	51	9	2	9	7	9	.267	.373
Davis, Eric	.290	38	11	3	9	4	11	.349	.632
Dawson, Andre	.186	59	11	1	3	4	11	.238	.271
Deer, Rob	.250	4	1	0	1	2	1	.500	.250
DeShields, D*	.267	60	16	1	5	5	11	.316	.367
Duncan, M	.206	34	7	1	2	0	8	.206	.324
Dunston, Shaw	.284	67	19	3	8	2	13	.300	.433
Dykstra, L*	.130	69	9	0	3	5	9	.200	.145
Eisenreich, J*	.217	23	5	0	2	3	0	.308	.217
Elster, Kevin	.370	27	10	2	7	4	4	.452	.704
Encarnacion	.250	4	1	0	0	1	2	.400	.250
Finley, Steve*	.214	28	6	0	1	3	6	.241	.250
Fletcher, D*	.395	38	15	3	7	1	2	.410	.684
Floyd, Cliff*	.000	11	0	0	0	0	3	.000	.000
Fonville, C#	.143	7	1	0	0	2	0	.333	.143
Gaetti, Gary	.556	9	5	0	0	0	0	.556	.667
Gagne, Greg	.250	12	3	0	1	0	1	.308	.250
Galarraga, A	.352	88	31	5	11	5	21	.394	.614
Gant, Ron	.225	40	9	4	7	6	14	.326	.550
Garcia, C	.429	14	6	0	1	3	2	.556	.571
Gilkey, B	.255	47	12	0	4	2	8	.286	.362
Girardi, Joe	.118	17	2	0	2	1	3	.167	.235

Doug Drabek, Astros — RHP

Batter	Avg	AB	H	HR	BI	BB	SO	OBP	Slg
Goff, Jerry*	.000	5	0	0	0	1	2	.167	.000
Gomez, Leo	.600	5	3	1	4	0	0	.600	1.200
Gonzalez, L*	.429	21	9	1	2	2	3	.458	.667
Grace, Mark*	.388	85	33	3	12	9	5	.447	.576
Grissom, M	.148	54	8	0	0	1	9	.164	.204
Grudzielanek	.308	13	4	0	0	0	2	.308	.462
Gutierrez, R	.167	6	1	0	1	0	0	.167	.167
Gwynn, Chris*	.273	11	3	0	0	0	1	.273	.273
Gwynn, Tony*	.469	49	23	0	2	1	2	.480	.694
Hansen, Dave*	.286	14	4	0	0	3	2	.412	.357
Harris, Lenny*	.152	33	5	0	1	4	0	.200	.182
Hayes, C	.260	50	13	1	4	3	11	.302	.340
Hernandez, Ca	.167	6	1	0	0	0	0	.167	.167
Hill, G	.200	10	2	0	0	2	2	.333	.300
Hollandsworth*	.100	10	1	0	1	1	1	.182	.100
Hollins, Dave#	.222	27	6	0	1	2	3	.276	.222
Howard, T*	.286	14	4	0	0	0	2	.286	.429
Hundley, Todd#	.200	30	6	0	5	2	8	.250	.333
Hunter, Brian	.200	5	1	0	0	0	1	.200	.400
Huskey, Butch	.667	6	4	0	2	0	1	.667	.667
Incaviglia, P	.083	12	1	0	0	0	4	.154	.083
James, Dion*	.417	12	5	0	1	1	0	.462	.417
Javier, Stan#	.250	8	2	0	1	2	1	.400	.375
Jefferies, G#	.304	56	17	0	3	5	5	.361	.357
Johnson, Char	.143	7	1	1	1	2	2	.333	.571
Johnson, L*	.625	8	5	0	3	1	0	.667	1.125
Johnson, Mark*	.167	6	1	0	0	0	1	.167	.333
Jones, C#	.235	17	4	2	2	3	3	.350	.647
Jones, Chris	.000	5	0	0	0	1	2	.167	.000
Jordan, Brian	.208	24	5	0	4	1	10	.231	.375
Jordan, Ricky	.105	19	2	0	1	0	8	.105	.158
Joyner, Wally*	.167	6	1	0	0	1	0	.286	.167
Justice, Dave*	.324	37	12	4	9	8	5	.426	.703
Karros, Eric	.409	22	9	2	7	3	3	.462	.818
Kelly, R	.235	17	4	0	0	4	4	.235	.412
Kent, Jeff	.423	26	11	1	4	6	2	.545	.692
King, Jeff	.364	22	8	0	3	0	1	.364	.455
Kingery, Mike*	.211	19	4	0	2	2	1	.273	.263
Klesko, Ryan*	.286	21	6	1	5	7	2	.348	.619
Lankford, Ray*	.288	59	17	1	8	2	16	.306	.390
Lansing, Mike	.296	27	8	2	8	1	2	.310	.519
Larkin, Barry	.343	67	23	2	3	5	7	.389	.537
Lemke, Mark*	.154	39	6	0	1	2	6	.195	.154
Lewis, Darren	.343	35	12	0	1	2	3	.378	.343
Liriano, N#	.067	15	1	0	0	3	3	.222	.067
Lopez, Javy	.417	17	5	0	1	3	3	.333	.294
Mabry, John*	.333	12	4	1	2	1	2	.385	.583
Magadan, Dave*	.419	43	18	0	5	5	1	.479	.488
Manwaring, K	.333	33	11	0	5	2	4	.378	.394
Martin, Al*	.211	19	4	0	1	1	4	.250	.421
Martinez, Da*	.241	87	21	1	5	3	13	.267	.333
May, Derrick*	.138	29	4	1	4	2	0	.188	.276
McGee, Willie*	.263	57	15	1	8	5	7	.323	.404
McGriff, Fred*	.528	36	19	4	7	7	8	.591	.889
McRae, Brian#	.286	14	4	1	1	3	2	.444	.571
Merced, O*	.313	16	5	0	1	0	1	.313	.313
Mitchell, K	.308	39	12	4	10	3	6	.372	.667
Molitor, Paul	.143	7	1	0	1	0	0	.143	.143
Mondesi, Raul	.154	13	2	0	0	0	2	.154	.231
Morandini, M*	.296	54	16	0	2	1	7	.304	.352
Morris, Hal*	.225	40	9	3	3	3	3	.279	.475
Murray, Eddie#	.447	47	21	3	7	6	6	.509	.681
Nixon, Otis#	.172	29	5	0	0	3	3	.250	.172
O'Brien, C	.222	9	2	0	1	4	0	.500	.222
O'Neill, Paul*	.286	35	10	2	4	2	4	.316	.486
Ochoa, Alex	1.000	8	8	0	4	0	0	.889	1.125
Offerman, J#	.250	12	3	0	2	2	2	.333	.333
Oliver, Joe	.278	18	5	0	1	0	1	.278	.278
Orsulak, Joe*	.217	23	5	1	1	2	2	.280	.391
Owens, J	.333	6	2	0	0	0	0	.333	.500
Pagnozzi, Tom	.278	36	10	0	1	4	4	.366	.306
Palmeiro, R*	.273	22	6	1	1	1	2	.304	.500
Parent, Mark	.385	13	5	1	4	1	2	.400	.615
Pena, G#	.125	16	2	0	4	5	5	.176	.188
Pena, Tony	.353	17	6	0	2	0	1	.353	.471
Pendleton, T#	.217	60	13	1	9	3	9	.250	.300
Petagine, Rob*	.000	5	0	0	0	1	2	.167	.000
Phillips, J*	.000	9	0	0	0	4	0	.000	.000
Piazza, Mike	.474	19	9	1	5	1	3	.500	.684
Plantier, P*	.600	10	6	2	6	2	1	.692	1.500
Quinlan, Tom	.250	4	1	1	2	1	1	.400	1.000
Raines, Tim#	.250	36	9	3	11	4	2	.325	.583
Reed, Jeff*	.200	20	4	0	2	3	2	.304	.250
Reed, Jody	.286	14	4	0	0	2	0	.286	.357
Renteria, E	.429	7	3	0	0	0	2	.429	.714
Ripken, Cal	.000	6	0	0	0	0	0	.000	.000
Roberts, Bip#	.185	27	5	0	1	2	2	.214	.222
Rodriguez, H*	.188	16	3	0	0	0	2	.188	.188
Sabo, Chris	.216	37	8	1	4	1	0	.225	.324
Samuel, Juan	.278	54	15	2	2	3	9	.328	.500
Sanchez, Rey	.241	29	7	0	1	2	2	.290	.241

Doug Drabek, Astros — RHP

Batter	Avg	AB	H	HR	BI	BB	SO	OBP	Slg
Sanderg, R	.227	88	20	1	6	5	10	.266	.273
Sanders, R	.231	26	6	2	3	1	6	.259	.462
Santangelo, F#	.143	7	1	0	0	0	2	.143	.143
Santiago, B	.034	29	1	0	3	2	5	.125	.103
Scarsone, S	.071	14	1	0	2	0	5	.071	.071
Schofield, D	.071	14	5	0	1	1	1	.400	.500
Segui, David#	.400	15	6	0	4	0	1	.400	.467
Servais, S	.333	6	2	0	1	0	1	.286	.333
Sheaffer, D	.286	7	2	0	0	1	0	.375	.286
Sheffield, G	.375	16	6	2	4	3	2	.500	.750
Shipley, C	.250	4	1	0	0	0	2	.250	.250
Slaught, Don	.286	14	4	1	2	2	1	.375	.571
Smith, Dwight*	.227	44	10	0	3	3	9	.271	.273
Smith, Ozzie*	.333	66	22	0	3	2	2	.353	.364
Sosa, Sammy	.265	34	9	2	4	2	7	.306	.441
Stillwell, K#	.400	10	4	0	2	1	1	.455	.800
Stocker, M#	.278	18	5	0	0	2	3	.381	.278
Strawberry, D*	.250	48	12	5	11	5	6	.321	.604
Tartabull, D	.167	6	1	1	2	0	4	.167	.667
Taubensee, E*	.217	23	5	0	0	3	2	.308	.217
Tavarez, Je#	.200	5	1	0	0	0	1	.200	.200
Thompson, Mil*	.169	65	11	1	2	3	13	.206	.231
Thompson, Rob	.278	36	10	4	4	2	9	.350	.389
Thompson, R	.071	14	1	0	0	2	3	.188	.071
Trammell, A	.250	4	1	0	0	2	1	.500	.250
VanderWal, J*	.360	25	9	1	7	4	1	.448	.720
Veras, Q#	.333	9	3	0	2	1	0	.364	.444
Vina, F*	.400	5	2	0	0	1	0	.500	.400
Vizcaino, J#	.263	38	10	0	2	1	5	.282	.289
Walker, Larry*	.300	40	12	1	4	2	6	.349	.400
Wallach, Tim	.148	81	12	1	7	3	21	.188	.235
Walton, J	.273	33	9	0	1	1	8	.314	.333
Weiss, Walt*	.250	12	3	0	1	3	3	.438	.333
White, Devon#	.111	9	1	0	0	0	1	.111	.111
White, R	.385	13	5	0	5	1	2	.429	.692
Whiten, Mark#	.316	19	6	2	10	2	4	.381	.632
Wilkins, Rick*	.200	30	6	1	3	4	5	.278	.367
Williams, E	.000	3	0	0	0	1	1	.000	.000
Williams, Ma	.182	44	8	1	6	2	11	.213	.295
Young, Eric	.375	24	9	0	2	2	1	.423	.417
Young, Kevin	.250	8	2	0	0	1	2	.333	.250
Zeile, Todd	.246	57	14	1	1	2	11	.271	.333

Darren Dreifort, Dodgers — RHP

Batter	Avg	AB	H	HR	BI	BB	SO	OBP	Slg
Alou, Moises	.600	5	3	0	1	0	1	.600	.800
Grissom, M	.200	5	1	0	0	1	3	.333	.200
Walker, Larry*	.000	3	0	0	0	2	0	.400	.000

Mike Dyer, Expos — RHP

Batter	Avg	AB	H	HR	BI	BB	SO	OBP	Slg
Alfonzo, E	.600	5	3	0	1	0	0	.600	.600
Alicea, Luis*	.250	4	1	0	0	1	2	.400	.250
Arias, Alex	.500	8	4	0	0	0	0	.500	.500
Bagwell, Jeff	.300	10	3	0	1	1	2	.364	.300
Bichette, D	.333	6	2	0	2	0	0	.333	.500
Biggio, Craig	.286	7	2	0	1	3	2	.500	.286
Blauser, Jeff	.200	5	1	0	0	0	0	.200	.200
Boone, Bret	.333	9	3	0	3	0	1	.333	.333
Branson, Jeff*	.571	7	4	0	2	0	0	.625	.857
Castilla, V	.333	6	2	2	2	1	4	.429	1.333
Cedeno, A	.000	5	0	0	0	0	0	.000	.000
Clayton, B	.286	7	2	0	1	0	0	.286	.286
Colbrunn, G	.200	5	1	0	0	0	1	.200	.200
DeShields, D*	.500	4	2	0	0	0	0	.500	.500
Eisenreich, J*	.400	5	2	0	2	0	0	.400	.800
Franco, Julio	.667	3	2	0	2	0	0	.800	1.333
Galarraga, A	.250	8	2	1	2	0	4	.250	.750
Gant, Ron	.600	5	3	1	4	0	1	.600	1.400
Griffey Jr, K*	.400	5	2	1	2	1	0	.500	1.200
Harris, Lenny*	.200	5	1	0	2	0	1	.200	.200
Henderson, R	.200	5	1	0	0	0	0	.200	.200
Hernandez, Jo	.571	7	4	2	3	0	1	.625	1.571
Howell, Jack*	.333	3	1	0	0	2	0	.500	.333
Hundley, Todd#	.400	5	2	0	2	0	0	.400	.400
Incaviglia, P	.000	7	0	0	0	0	4	.000	.000
Johnson, Char	.000	4	0	0	0	0	1	.200	.000
Johnson, L*	.250	4	1	0	0	1	1	.400	.250
Joyner, Wally*	.167	6	1	0	0	2	1	.375	.167
Karros, Eric	.500	8	4	0	1	1	3	.556	.625
Kelly, R	.250	8	2	0	1	0	0	.250	.250
Lankford, Ray*	.000	3	0	0	0	3	0	.571	.000
Larkin, Barry	.250	8	2	0	0	1	1	.333	.375
Lewis, Darren	.000	4	0	0	0	1	0	.200	.000
Livingstone, S	.250	4	1	0	2	1	0	.400	.250
Manwaring, K	.250	4	1	0	0	0	2	.250	.250
McRae, Brian#	.375	8	3	1	5	0	1	.333	.750
Mondesi, Raul	.500	6	3	1	2	1	0	.500	1.000
Morris, Hal*	.667	3	2	0	0	3	0	.833	.667
Pendleton, T#	.400	5	2	0	0	1	0	.400	.400
Piazza, Mike	.000	5	0	0	0	1	2	.167	.000

Mike Dyer, Expos — RHP

Batter	Avg	AB	H	HR	BI	BB	SO	OBP	Slg
Reed, Jody	.000	6	0	0	0	0	1	.000	.000
Sanchez, Rey	.500	4	2	0	1	0	1	.500	.500
Sanders, R	.250	8	2	0	0	1	1	.333	.250
Sierra, Ruben#	.600	5	3	0	0	0	0	.600	.600
Sosa, Sammy	.143	7	1	0	1	1	1	.250	.143
Strange, Doug#	.000	4	0	0	1	0	1	.000	.000
Taubensee, E*	.200	5	1	0	0	1	1	.333	.400
Tavarez, Je#	.400	5	2	0	1	1	1	.500	.600
Veras, Q#	.000	4	0	0	0	1	2	.200	.000
Wallach, Tim	.200	5	1	0	0	0	1	.200	.200
Weiss, Walt#	.167	6	1	0	0	0	0	.167	.167
White, Devon#	.286	7	2	1	1	0	2	.286	.857
Wilkins, Rick*	.250	4	1	0	2	2	0	.500	.250
Zeile, Todd	.333	6	2	1	2	0	2	.429	.833

Dennis Eckersley, Cardinals — RHP

Batter	Avg	AB	H	HR	BI	BB	SO	OBP	Slg
Alomar, R#	.100	10	1	0	0	0	2	.100	.100
Alomar Jr, S	.000	7	0	0	1	0	3	.000	.000
Anderson, Brd*	.111	18	2	1	1	0	4	.111	.278
Baerga, C#	.417	12	5	0	0	0	2	.462	.417
Baines, H*	.313	16	5	0	3	3	2	.421	.375
Bell, Jay	.200	5	1	0	0	0	0	.200	.200
Belle, Albert	.077	13	1	0	0	0	5	.077	.231
Belliard, R	.333	9	3	0	1	1	0	.400	.444
Bichette, D	.600	5	3	0	0	1	1	.667	.800
Boggs, Wade*	.300	20	6	0	2	1	5	.304	.400
Bonds, Barry*	.429	7	3	0	0	1	0	.500	.571
Boone, Bret	.200	10	2	0	0	0	4	.200	.200
Borders, Pat	.167	6	1	1	1	0	4	.167	.667
Buhner, Jay	.000	8	0	0	0	0	2	.000	.000
Burks, Ellis	.227	22	5	2	4	0	5	.227	.545
Butler, Brett*	.300	10	3	0	0	1	2	.364	.500
Carter, Joe	.150	20	3	0	2	0	5	.150	.150
Clark, Dave*	.200	5	1	0	0	0	0	.200	.400
Clark, Will*	.500	8	4	0	2	0	0	.500	.750
Coleman, V#	.375	16	6	0	2	2	2	.444	.563
Cora, Joey#	.200	5	1	0	1	2	2	.429	.400
Davis, Chili*	.257	35	9	1	5	1	10	.278	.343
Dawson, Andre	.195	41	8	1	3	0	4	.190	.390
Deer, Rob	.167	12	2	0	2	0	8	.167	.167
Devereaux, M	.000	9	0	0	0	0	5	.000	.000
DiSarcina, G	.000	7	0	0	0	0	2	.000	.000
Duncan, M	.100	10	1	0	0	1	3	.182	.200
Dykstra, L*	.333	15	5	0	0	0	1	.333	.467
Eisenreich, J*	.455	11	5	0	1	1	3	.500	.636
Espinoza, A	.500	8	4	0	1	0	1	.500	.500
Fermin, Felix	.200	5	1	0	0	0	1	.200	.200
Fielder, C	.133	15	2	0	4	1	10	.188	.133
Franco, Julio	.273	22	6	0	1	1	4	.304	.318
Frye, Jeff	.400	5	2	0	1	0	0	.400	.400
Fryman, T	.231	13	3	0	0	0	6	.231	.308
Gaetti, Gary	.160	25	4	1	4	1	6	.222	.440
Gagne, Greg	.231	13	3	1	1	0	3	.231	.462
Galarraga, A	.000	5	0	0	0	0	2	.000	.000
Gomez, Leo	.143	7	1	0	2	0	4	.143	.143
Gonzalez, J	.500	6	3	2	4	0	2	.500	1.500
Greenwell, M*	.333	18	6	1	5	0	0	.368	.556
Griffey Jr, K*	.091	11	1	1	1	0	3	.091	.364
Guillen, O*	.286	14	4	0	1	0	1	.286	.286
Gwynn, Tony*	.333	12	4	0	0	0	1	.333	.500
Hale, Chip*	.200	5	1	0	0	0	2	.200	.200
Hall, Mel*	.200	10	2	1	1	0	2	.200	.500
Hamilton, D*	.375	8	3	0	0	0	0	.375	.375
Harris, Lenny*	.400	5	2	0	0	0	1	.400	.400
Henderson, R	.111	9	1	0	0	0	4	.111	.111
Hoiles, Chris	.000	5	0	0	0	1	2	.167	.000
Howard, T*	.571	7	4	1	1	0	1	.571	1.000
Howell, Jack*	.000	7	0	0	0	0	1	.000	.000
Huson, Jeff*	.000	7	0	0	0	0	1	.000	.000
Incaviglia, P	.143	14	2	0	0	0	5	.143	.214
James, Dion*	.333	9	3	0	2	1	2	.400	.333
Jefferson, R*	.000	5	0	0	0	0	4	.000	.000
Johnson, L*	.167	12	2	0	1	2	0	.286	.167
Joyner, Wally*	.091	11	1	0	2	3	3	.286	.091
Karkovice, A	.143	7	1	0	0	0	4	.143	.143
Kelly, Pat	.000	5	0	0	0	0	2	.000	.000
Kelly, R	.000	6	0	0	0	3	0	.000	.000
Kingery, Mike*	.333	9	3	0	1	0	2	.333	.444
Knoblauch, C	.182	11	2	0	4	0	4	.182	.273
Leyritz, Jim	.250	4	1	0	0	0	2	.250	.250
Liriano, N	.125	8	1	0	0	0	1	.125	.125
Livingstone*	.667	6	4	0	2	0	0	.667	.833
Macfarlane, M	.083	12	1	0	1	0	4	.154	.083
Martinez, E	.333	12	4	0	0	0	4	.333	.417
Martinez, T*	.444	9	4	3	5	0	0	.444	1.444
Mayne, Brent*	.182	11	2	0	2	0	2	.182	.182
McGee, Willie#	.346	26	9	0	3	0	3	.346	.423
McGriff, Fred*	.100	10	1	0	0	1	6	.182	.200
McLemore, M	.267	15	4	0	2	1	0	.353	.267
McRae, Brian#	.545	11	6	1	3	0	1	.545	.909

Dennis Eckersley, Cardinals — RHP

Batter	Avg	AB	H	HR	BI	BB	SO	OBP	Slg
Mitchell, K	.500	8	4	0	2	0	2	.500	.875
Molitor, Paul	.364	11	4	1	4	0	1	.364	.727
Murray, Eddie*	.200	5	1	0	1	0	3	.200	.200
Myers, Greg*	.600	5	3	0	1	0	0	.600	.800
Nilsson, Dave*	.333	6	2	0	0	0	1	.333	.333
Nixon, Otis#	.571	7	4	0	3	1	1	.625	.714
O'Neill, Paul*	.000	5	0	0	0	1	2	.167	.000
Olerud, John*	.400	10	4	0	0	0	4	.400	.400
Orsulak, Joe*	.417	12	5	0	0	1	1	.462	.500
Palmeiro, R*	.375	8	3	0	1	0	1	.375	.375
Palmer, Dean	.400	10	4	1	3	0	4	.400	.800
Pena, Tony	.208	24	5	0	0	2	7	.296	.208
Pendleton, T#	.143	14	2	0	0	0	3	.143	.143
Phillips, T#	.182	11	2	0	0	1	4	.250	.182
Polonia, Luis*	.429	7	3	0	0	0	0	.429	.857
Raines, Tim#	.333	51	17	0	5	3	6	.370	.431
Reed, Jody	.375	8	3	0	0	0	1	.375	.500
Ripken, Cal	.053	19	1	1	1	1	1	.100	.211
Rodriguez, I	.100	10	1	0	0	0	1	.100	.100
Salmon, Tim	.250	8	2	0	0	1	4	.333	.375
Samuel, Juan	.243	37	9	1	5	2	13	.275	.432
Schofield, D	.143	14	2	0	1	0	5	.143	.143
Schu, Rick	.286	7	2	0	1	0	3	.286	.286
Segui, David#	.143	7	1	1	2	0	0	.143	.571
Seitzer, K	.316	19	6	0	1	1	2	.350	.316
Sierra, Ruben#	.267	15	4	0	2	0	3	.267	.333
Smith, Ozzie#	.389	18	7	0	5	3	0	.476	.667
Snow, J.T.#	.200	5	1	1	2	0	1	.200	.800
Sojo, Luis	.600	5	3	0	1	0	1	.600	1.000
Sorrento, P*	.333	6	2	0	2	0	2	.333	.500
Sosa, Sammy	.143	7	1	0	1	0	4	.143	.143
Spiers, Bill*	.600	5	3	0	0	1	2	.667	.800
Stanley, Mike	.111	9	1	0	0	1	3	.200	.111
Stevens, Lee*	.167	6	1	0	0	0	2	.167	.167
Stillwell, K#	.111	9	1	0	1	0	0	.111	.222
Strange, Doug#	.200	5	1	0	0	0	1	.200	.200
Strawberry, D*	.143	14	2	0	2	0	3	.143	.214
Surhoff, B.J.*	.308	13	4	0	2	2	1	.375	.462
Sveum, Dale#	.111	9	1	0	0	0	3	.111	.111
Tartabull, D	.273	22	6	0	3	0	9	.273	.409
Tettleton, M#	.095	21	2	1	2	1	4	.130	.238
Thomas, Frank	.077	13	1	0	0	0	4	.077	.077
Thompson, Rob	.333	9	3	0	0	0	3	.333	.444
Trammell, A	.278	18	5	0	2	1	6	.316	.389
Valentin, Jhn	.000	5	0	0	0	0	2	.000	.000
Valle, Dave	.000	9	0	0	0	1	3	.100	.000
Vaughn, Greg	.182	11	2	1	2	0	4	.182	.455
Vaughn, Mo*	.333	6	2	0	1	0	1	.333	.333
Velarde, R	.000	5	0	0	0	0	2	.000	.000
Ventura, R*	.111	9	1	1	2	3	1	.333	.444
Vizquel, Omar#	.250	8	2	0	0	0	0	.250	.250
Wallach, Tim	.371	35	13	1	6	2	4	.421	.514
White, Devon#	.200	15	3	0	2	0	3	.188	.200
Whiten, Mark#	.125	8	1	0	0	1	4	.222	.250
Williams, Ber#	.417	12	5	0	4	0	3	.462	.500
Worthington	.167	6	1	0	0	0	2	.167	.333

Mark Eichhorn, Angels — RHP

Batter	Avg	AB	H	HR	BI	BB	SO	OBP	Slg
Aldrete, Mike*	.250	4	1	0	3	0	1	.200	.500
Alomar, R#	.182	11	2	0	2	1	1	.250	.273
Alomar Jr, S	.071	14	1	0	2	0	5	.071	.071
Anderson, Brd*	.400	10	4	0	0	1	2	.455	.400
Baerga, C#	.462	13	6	0	2	1	2	.500	.615
Baines, H*	.455	11	5	0	2	1	2	.500	.455
Belle, Albert	.533	15	8	0	4	1	0	.500	.600
Berroa, G	.400	5	2	0	3	0	1	.400	.400
Bichette, D	.667	6	4	0	0	0	0	.667	1.000
Biggio, Craig	.000	5	0	0	0	0	3	.000	.000
Blowers, Mike	.000	5	0	0	0	1	1	.167	.000
Boggs, Wade*	.316	19	6	0	0	2	0	.381	.316
Borders, Pat	.333	12	4	0	2	1	4	.385	.583
Bordick, Mike	.250	12	3	0	1	1	5	.308	.250
Brosius, S	.500	6	3	0	2	1	1	.571	.833
Buhner, Jay	.308	13	4	0	2	1	2	.357	.462
Burks, Ellis	.143	14	2	0	1	0	4	.143	.286
Butler, Brett*	.300	10	3	0	1	0	0	.300	.300
Canseco, Jose	.261	23	6	0	4	7	7	.452	.261
Caminiti, Ken#	.250	4	1	0	0	1	0	.250	.250
Carreon, Mark	.500	4	2	0	1	1	0	.600	.500
Carter, Joe	.217	23	5	0	3	3	6	.308	.261
Cora, Joey#	.571	7	4	0	1	0	0	.571	.571
Curtis, Chad	.400	5	2	0	1	0	0	.400	.400
Cuyler, Milt#	.111	9	1	0	0	0	1	.111	.111
Davis, Chili#	.300	10	3	0	0	0	0	.300	.300
Deer, Rob	.150	20	3	1	1	0	10	.150	.300
Devereaux, M	.375	8	3	0	1	0	0	.375	.375
Duncan, M	.000	5	0	0	0	0	5	.000	.000
Eisenreich, J*	.444	9	4	0	0	2	0	.545	.556
Elster, Kevin	.400	5	2	0	1	0	0	.400	.400
Fermin, Felix	.100	10	1	0	2	2	0	.250	.100

Mark Eichhorn, Angels — RHP

Batter	Avg	AB	H	HR	BI	BB	SO	OBP	Slg
Fielder, C	.095	21	2	0	3	1	6	.130	.095
Franco, Julio	.267	15	4	0	1	0	1	.267	.467
Fryman, J	.316	19	6	0	4	0	4	.316	.579
Gaetti, Gary	.235	17	4	0	3	1	3	.278	.294
Gagne, Greg	.235	17	4	0	2	1	4	.316	.294
Gallego, Mike	.250	12	3	0	1	1	1	.308	.250
Gates, Brent#	.167	6	1	0	2	0	0	.167	.333
Gonzalez, J	.143	7	1	0	2	0	1	.143	.286
Greenwell, M*	.333	12	4	0	1	0	1	.333	.417
Griffey Jr, K*	.375	8	3	0	1	1	1	.444	.375
Guillen, O*	.375	16	6	0	3	0	1	.375	.563
Hall, Mel*	.267	15	4	0	2	1	2	.313	.333
Hamelin, Bob*	.000	2	0	0	1	3	2	.600	.000
Hamilton, D*	.364	11	4	1	10	0	1	.364	.727
Henderson, R	.381	21	8	0	3	4	2	.480	.476
Hill, G	.000	4	0	0	0	1	0	.200	.000
Hoiles, Chris	.000	5	0	0	0	0	0	.000	.000
Howell, Jack*	.571	7	4	0	2	0	2	.571	.571
Huff, Michael	.400	5	2	0	1	0	1	.400	.400
Hulse, David*	.333	6	2	0	0	0	0	.333	.333
Huson, Jeff*	.167	6	1	0	1	0	0	.167	.500
Incaviglia, P	.214	14	3	0	1	1	5	.267	.214
Jaha, John	.200	10	2	0	1	0	2	.273	.300
Javier, Stan#	.444	9	4	0	1	2	0	.545	.556
Jefferson, R*	.200	5	1	0	0	0	3	.200	.200
Johnson, L*	.300	10	3	0	4	0	1	.300	.300
Joyner, Wally*	.600	10	6	0	2	1	1	.636	.700
Karkovice, R	.143	7	1	0	0	1	4	.250	.143
Kelly, Pat	.000	7	0	0	0	0	3	.000	.000
Kelly, R	.286	7	2	0	2	0	0	.286	.429
Kingery, Mike*	.143	7	1	0	1	0	0	.125	.429
Knoblauch, C	.600	5	3	1	5	2	1	.714	1.200
Kreuter, Chad#	.400	5	2	0	0	0	1	.400	.600
Lewis, Mark	.000	2	0	0	1	0	0	.250	.000
Listach, Pat#	.143	7	1	0	1	0	3	.143	.143
Livingstone*	.000	4	0	0	0	1	2	.200	.000
Lofton, Kenny*	.375	8	3	0	1	1	0	.444	.625
Macfarlane, M	.100	10	1	0	2	0	5	.100	.100
Martinez, E	.556	9	5	0	3	0	0	.556	.889
Martinez, T*	.333	3	1	0	0	3	1	.667	.333
McGwire, Mark	.471	17	8	1	5	1	3	.500	.647
McLemore, M#	.200	5	1	0	1	1	0	.333	.200
McRae, Brian#	.000	6	0	0	1	1	2	.143	.000
Mieske, Matt	.000	4	0	0	0	0	3	.200	.000
Molitor, Paul	.286	28	8	1	7	3	3	.344	.500
Murray, Eddie*	.167	12	2	0	0	0	4	.167	.167
Naehring, Tim	.200	5	1	0	0	0	1	.200	.200
Nilsson, Dave*	.400	5	2	0	0	0	1	.400	.400
Olerud, John*	.444	9	4	0	2	0	0	.400	.667
Orsulak, Joe*	.286	7	2	0	0	0	0	.286	.286
Palmeiro, R*	.500	4	2	0	1	2	0	.667	.750
Palmer, Dean	.000	7	0	0	0	0	2	.000	.000
Pena, Tony	.375	8	3	0	4	1	2	.444	.500
Phillips, T#	.231	26	6	0	3	2	5	.300	.308
Polonia, Luis*	.000	6	0	0	0	1	1	.143	.000
Reed, Jeff	.200	5	1	0	0	0	2	.200	.600
Reed, Jody	.083	12	1	0	0	2	3	.214	.083
Ripken, Billy	.333	9	3	0	1	0	2	.333	.444
Ripken, Cal	.200	25	5	2	8	1	6	.233	.440
Roberts, Bip#	.500	4	2	0	1	1	1	.600	.500
Rodriguez, I	.143	7	1	0	0	0	1	.143	.143
Santiago, B	.000	6	0	0	0	0	3	.000	.000
Schofield, D	.091	11	1	0	1	1	0	.154	.091
Seitzer, K	.462	13	6	0	1	0	0	.429	.462
Sierra, Ruben#	.294	17	5	0	2	1	1	.333	.412
Slaught, Don	.100	10	1	0	0	0	3	.182	.100
Sorrento, P*	.571	7	4	0	2	0	1	.571	.571
Sosa, Sammy	.200	5	1	0	0	0	1	.200	.200
Spiers, Bill*	.400	5	2	0	0	1	0	.571	.600
Stanley, Mike	.000	4	0	0	0	0	2	.000	.000
Steinbach, T	.400	15	6	0	2	0	2	.400	.533
Stillwell, K#	.500	4	2	0	0	1	1	.600	.500
Surhoff, B.J.*	.313	16	5	0	2	3	0	.400	.438
Sveum, Dale#	.500	14	7	1	6	0	1	.500	.786
Tartabull, D	.278	18	5	0	1	3	5	.409	.444
Tettleton, M#	.400	15	6	4	7	3	5	.474	1.200
Thomas, Frank	.154	13	2	1	4	0	3	.154	.385
Thome, Jim*	.200	5	1	0	0	1	2	.333	.200
Trammell, A	.350	20	7	1	8	0	5	.350	.550
Valle, Dave	.385	13	5	0	3	1	1	.467	.538
Vaughn, Greg	.188	16	3	0	0	2	3	.278	.188
Velarde, R	.400	10	4	0	3	0	1	.400	.600
Ventura, R*	.250	12	3	0	1	0	2	.250	.250
Vizquel, Omar#	.143	7	1	0	0	0	1	.143	.429
Ward, Turner#	.200	5	1	0	0	0	0	.200	.200
Weiss, Walt*	.571	7	4	0	2	1	1	.667	.571
White, Devon#	.118	17	2	0	2	0	6	.111	.176
Whiten, Mark#	.222	9	2	0	1	1	2	.300	.222
Williams, Ber#	.167	6	1	0	0	0	1	.167	.167
Wilson, Dan	.000	4	0	0	0	1	0	.200	.000
Worthington	.143	7	1	0	0	0	1	.143	.286

Joey Eischen, Tigers — LHP

Batter	Avg	AB	H	HR	BI	BB	SO	OBP	Slg
Anderson, Brd*	.000	4	0	0	1	1	3	.200	.000
Bagwell, Jeff	.000	5	0	0	1	0	1	.000	.000
Biggio, Craig	.500	4	2	0	1	1	1	.600	.500
Eisenreich, J*	.250	4	1	0	1	1	0	.400	.250
Hunter, Bri L	.400	5	2	0	1	0	0	.400	.600
Miller, Orl	.200	5	1	1	1	0	1	.333	.800
Mouton, James	.333	3	1	0	1	2	1	.600	.333
Sosa, Sammy	.333	3	1	0	0	2	1	.600	.667
Vizcaino, J#	.200	5	1	0	1	0	0	.200	.200

Cal Eldred, Brewers — RHP

Batter	Avg	AB	H	HR	BI	BB	SO	OBP	Slg
Aldrete, Mike*	.333	6	2	1	3	1	0	.429	1.000
Alomar, R#	.391	23	9	0	1	2	2	.440	.522
Alomar Jr, S	.250	8	2	1	4	1	1	.333	.750
Amaral, Rich	.100	10	1	0	0	2	2	.250	.200
Anderson, Brd*	.286	28	8	0	1	4	5	.394	.429
Anthony, Eric*	.143	7	1	0	0	1	3	.250	.143
Baerga, C#	.235	17	4	1	2	0	5	.235	.412
Baines, H*	.217	23	5	0	2	2	3	.280	.261
Becker, Rich*	.429	7	3	0	1	2	1	.556	.429
Belle, Albert	.438	16	7	3	7	3	2	.550	1.125
Berroa, G	.000	4	0	0	0	2	1	.333	.000
Blowers, Mike	.083	12	1	0	0	1	5	.154	.083
Boggs, Wade*	.333	15	5	0	1	3	1	.444	.333
Boone, Bret	.300	10	3	0	1	1	3	.364	.300
Borders, Pat	.375	16	6	0	0	0	2	.375	.500
Bordick, Mike	.125	8	1	0	1	1	0	.200	.125
Bragg, Darren*	.400	5	2	0	0	1	1	.500	.400
Brosius, S	.154	13	2	0	0	0	1	.154	.154
Brumfield, J	.000	6	0	0	0	0	0	.000	.000
Buhner, Jay	.423	26	11	1	6	4	7	.500	.654
Burks, Ellis	.167	12	2	1	2	1	6	.231	.417
Canseco, Jose	.000	8	0	0	1	1	2	.100	.000
Carter, Joe	.158	19	3	1	2	1	2	.200	.316
Coleman, V#	.125	8	1	0	1	0	0	.125	.250
Cora, Joey#	.304	23	7	0	3	2	3	.360	.435
Curtis, Chad	.273	22	6	0	6	0	2	.261	.318
Cuyler, Milt*	.125	8	1	0	0	1	3	.222	.375
Davis, Chili#	.067	15	1	1	2	0	8	.067	.267
Dawson, Andre	.667	6	4	0	2	0	0	.667	.667
Deer, Rob	.000	6	0	0	0	0	6	.000	.000
Delgado, C*	.333	9	3	1	3	0	1	.333	.667
Devereaux, M	.222	18	4	1	1	2	4	.300	.444
DiSarcina, G	.214	14	3	0	0	0	2	.214	.286
Durham, Ray#	.250	8	2	0	1	0	1	.250	.375
Easley, D	.000	12	0	0	0	1	0	.000	.000
Espinoza, A	.250	12	3	0	0	1	3	.308	.250
Fermin, Felix	.333	15	5	0	1	0	1	.333	.333
Fielder, C	.300	20	6	3	7	2	4	.391	.524
Franco, Julio	.333	21	7	1	6	2	0	.391	.524
Frye, Jim*	.600	10	6	1	2	0	1	.600	1.000
Fryman, T	.364	22	8	0	2	3	3	.440	.364
Gaetti, Gary	.250	12	3	0	2	0	2	.250	.250
Gagne, Greg	.182	11	2	0	1	1	3	.250	.273
Gallego, Mike	.200	5	1	0	0	0	0	.200	.200
Gates, Brent#	.200	10	2	0	1	1	2	.273	.300
Gomez, Chris	.556	9	5	1	1	3	1	.667	1.111
Gomez, Leo	.091	11	1	1	2	1	3	.154	.364
Gonzales, R	.000	2	0	0	1	3	1	.600	.000
Gonzalez, A	.000	4	0	0	0	0	2	.000	.000
Gonzalez, J	.286	14	4	2	7	1	3	.333	.786
Grebeck, C	.333	9	3	0	0	0	2	.333	.333
Green, Shawn*	.273	11	3	1	1	2	2	.385	.545
Greenwell, M*	.154	13	2	1	1	1	1	.214	.385
Griffey Jr, K*	.292	24	7	1	6	3	2	.400	.500
Guillen, O*	.385	26	10	1	4	0	1	.385	.577
Hale, Chip*	.250	8	2	0	0	1	0	.455	.250
Hall, Mel*	.200	5	1	0	0	1	0	.333	.200
Hamelin, Bob*	.000	8	0	0	0	3	0	.273	.000
Haselman, B	.000	4	0	0	0	1	2	.200	.000
Henderson, R	.214	14	3	0	1	2	1	.313	.357
Higginson, B*	.167	6	1	0	0	1	2	.286	.333
Hill, G	.333	6	2	0	0	0	3	.333	.333
Hoiles, Chris	.313	16	5	1	2	6	5	.500	.500
Hulse, David*	.313	16	5	0	1	1	3	.353	.313
James, Dion*	.200	10	2	0	0	1	2	.273	.200
Javier, Stan#	.333	9	3	0	1	0	0	.364	.333
Jefferson, R*	.250	12	3	0	1	0	3	.250	.250
Johnson, L*	.286	28	8	0	0	2	1	.333	.429
Joyner, Wally*	.143	14	2	1	0	0	5	.143	.357
Karkovice, R	.385	13	5	0	2	3	4	.529	.538
Kelly, Pat	.333	9	3	0	1	2	2	.455	.444
Kelly, R	.429	7	3	0	1	4	0	.636	.714
Kirby, Wayne*	.286	7	2	0	0	0	1	.286	.286
Knoblauch, C	.333	12	4	1	3	1	1	.500	.583
Kreuter, Chad*	.250	12	3	1	2	3	3	.438	.500
Leius, Scott	.143	7	1	0	1	2	1	.333	.143
Lewis, Mark	.111	9	1	0	0	0	1	.111	.111
Leyritz, Jim	.333	6	2	0	2	2	1	.500	.333
Livingstone*	.176	17	3	0	0	0	0	.176	.176

Cal Eldred, Brewers — RHP

Batter	Avg	AB	H	HR	BI	BB	SO	OBP	Slg
Lofton, Kenny*	.353	17	6	2	2	4	2	.476	.765
Macfarlane, M	.182	11	2	1	3	0	1	.182	.455
Magadan, Dave*	.167	6	1	0	1	1	0	.286	.167
Martinez, Da*	.167	6	1	1	1	0	2	.167	.667
Martinez, E	.167	6	1	0	0	1	2	.286	.333
Martinez, T*	.222	18	4	1	1	1	2	.263	.444
Mayne, Brent*	.571	7	4	1	2	3	0	.700	1.000
McGwire, Mark	.250	8	2	1	1	0	1	.250	.750
McLemore, M#	.105	19	2	1	2	3	4	.227	.263
McRae, Brian#	.188	16	3	0	0	4	2	.350	.188
Meares, Pat	.083	12	1	0	0	2	1	.267	.167
Molitor, Paul	.286	21	6	1	2	3	1	.360	.429
Munoz, Pedro	.333	6	2	0	0	1	0	.333	.500
Murray, Eddie#	.000	8	0	0	0	1	0	.111	.000
Myers, Greg*	.167	12	2	0	1	0	1	.167	.167
Naehring, Tim	.000	7	0	0	0	2	2	.222	.000
Newson, W*	.333	9	3	0	0	0	5	.333	.444
Nixon, Otis#	.250	8	2	0	1	2	0	.400	.250
O'Leary, Troy*	.000	6	0	0	0	0	1	.000	.000
O'Neill, Paul*	.267	15	4	1	2	1	1	.313	.533
Olerud, John*	.136	22	3	1	2	0	2	.136	.318
Palmeiro, R*	.300	20	6	2	4	3	1	.375	.650
Palmer, Dean	.063	16	1	0	0	2	6	.167	.063
Pena, Tony	.125	8	1	0	0	0	2	.125	.125
Perez, E	.000	6	0	0	0	1	2	.143	.000
Phillips, T#	.182	22	4	0	2	7	5	.367	.182
Plantier, P*	.400	5	2	0	1	0	1	.400	.400
Polonia, Luis*	.211	19	4	0	0	1	3	.250	.421
Raines, Tim#	.174	23	4	0	0	2	2	.269	.304
Ramirez, M	.200	5	1	0	0	2	1	.429	.200
Reboulet, J	.143	7	1	0	2	1	0	.250	.143
Reed, Jody	.500	6	3	0	1	0	0	.500	.500
Ripken, Billy	.000	7	0	0	1	0	1	.125	.000
Ripken, Cal	.179	28	5	2	6	1	2	.207	.429
Rodriguez, I	.200	5	1	0	0	1	2	.333	.200
Rodriguez, I	.111	9	1	0	0	2	4	.273	.111
Sabo, Chris	.000	7	0	0	0	0	1	.000	.000
Salmon, Tim	.143	14	2	0	0	4	1	.333	.143
Schofield, D	.333	6	2	0	1	0	0	.333	.500
Segui, David#	.231	13	3	0	0	1	2	.286	.308
Shumpert, T	.400	5	2	0	0	1	0	.500	.400
Sierra, Ruben#	.071	14	1	0	1	2	2	.176	.071
Smith, Dwight*	.286	7	2	0	2	0	3	.286	.429
Snow, J.T.#	.250	4	1	0	1	0	1	.400	.250
Sorrento, P*	.167	24	4	0	0	0	4	.200	.208
Sprague, Ed	.100	20	2	0	0	0	4	.100	.100
Stanley, Mike	.250	16	4	2	4	0	0	.250	.625
Steinbach, T	.300	10	3	2	6	0	2	.300	.900
Strange, Doug#	.250	12	3	0	2	1	1	.333	.250
Tartabull, D	.143	14	2	1	2	0	3	.133	.429
Tettleton, M#	.417	24	10	2	7	3	4	.481	.792
Thomas, Frank	.370	27	10	2	5	6	3	.485	.741
Thome, Jim*	.286	7	2	1	2	2	2	.444	.857
Trammell, A	.462	13	6	2	5	1	0	.500	1.000
Valentin, Jhn	.111	9	1	0	1	0	1	.100	.111
Valle, Dave	.200	10	2	1	2	2	1	.333	.500
Vaughn, Mo*	.273	22	6	1	3	1	5	.360	.500
Velarde, R	.000	6	0	0	0	1	2	.143	.000
Ventura, Robin	.308	26	8	1	5	7	5	.457	.500
Vizquel, Omar#	.250	16	4	0	1	1	1	.278	.313
Walbeck, Matt#	.143	7	1	0	0	1	2	.250	.143
Webster, L	.000	5	0	0	0	0	0	.000	.000
White, Devon#	.000	18	0	0	1	2	4	.095	.000
Whiten, Mark#	.333	3	1	0	0	2	0	.600	.333
Williams, Ber#	.250	16	4	0	0	2	1	.333	.250
Wilson, Dan	.444	9	4	0	3	1	0	.500	.667

Alan Embree, Indians — LHP

Batter	Avg	AB	H	HR	BI	BB	SO	OBP	Slg
Alomar, R#	.250	4	1	0	1	2	1	.429	.750
Anderson, Brd*	.000	5	0	0	0	2	2	.400	.000
Martinez, T*	.200	5	1	0	0	0	0	.200	.400
Olerud, John*	.167	6	1	0	0	0	0	.167	.333
Ripken, Cal	.400	5	2	0	1	0	0	.400	.400
Sierra, Ruben*	.500	4	2	1	2	0	0	.400	1.250
Velarde, R	.000	3	0	0	0	2	0	.400	.000
Williams, Ber#	.200	5	1	1	3	2	1	.429	.800
Williams, Ger	.200	5	1	1	1	0	2	.200	.667

John Ericks, Pirates — RHP

Batter	Avg	AB	H	HR	BI	BB	SO	OBP	Slg
Abbott, Kurt	.333	6	2	0	2	0	1	.333	.333
Alfonzo, E	.200	5	1	0	0	1	0	.200	.200
Alou, Moises	.667	6	4	2	3	2	0	.750	1.667
Andrews, S	.000	6	0	0	0	0	2	.000	.000
Bagwell, Jeff	.600	5	3	0	1	0	0	.600	1.000
Bichette, D	.200	5	1	1	3	0	1	.200	.800
Biggio, Craig	.286	7	2	0	2	1	1	.375	.571
Caminiti, Ken#	.167	6	1	0	1	2	1	.333	.167
Cangelosi, J#	.333	3	1	0	0	2	0	.600	.333
Colbrunn, G	.400	5	2	1	1	0	0	.400	1.000
Cordero, Wil	.000	5	0	0	1	0	0	.000	.000
Daulton, D*	.167	6	1	0	1	0	2	.167	.333
Dunston, S	.333	6	2	0	2	1	2	.429	.333
Dykstra, L*	.333	6	2	0	0	2	0	.500	.667
Eisenreich, J*	.556	9	5	0	1	1	1	.600	.556
Finley, Steve*	.167	6	1	0	0	2	2	.375	.167
Gonzalez, L*	.500	4	2	0	3	2	1	.571	1.000
Grace, Mark*	.375	8	3	0	0	0	2	.375	.375
Grudzielanek	.250	4	1	0	0	1	1	.400	.250
Gutierrez, R	.000	3	0	0	0	2	0	.400	.000
Gwynn, Tony*	.714	7	5	0	0	0	0	.714	.857
Hayes, C	.167	6	1	0	0	0	2	.167	.167
Hernandez, Jo	.167	6	1	0	2	0	5	.143	.333
Hunter, Bri L	.222	9	2	0	0	0	4	.222	.333
Jefferies, G#	.143	7	1	0	0	1	0	.250	.143
Karros, Eric	.500	4	2	0	1	1	1	.600	.750
Lankford, Ray*	.333	6	2	0	2	0	2	.333	.333
Lansing, Mike	.125	8	1	0	0	1	0	.222	.125
Mabry, John*	.000	5	0	0	0	1	0	.000	.000
Magadan, Dave*	.200	5	1	0	0	1	0	.333	.200
May, Derrick*	.000	6	0	0	0	1	0	.143	.000
McRae, Brian#	.250	8	2	1	1	1	1	.333	.625
Morandini, M*	.500	8	4	0	0	2	1	.600	.500
Pendleton, T#	.333	6	2	1	1	0	0	.333	.333
Piazza, Mike	.333	6	2	0	1	0	1	.333	.333
Reed, Jody	.200	5	1	0	1	1	0	.333	.200
Santiago, B	.000	3	0	0	1	1	1	.200	.000
Segui, David#	.500	8	4	1	3	0	1	.500	1.000
Sosa, Sammy	.000	4	0	0	0	3	2	.429	.000
Stocker, K#	.100	10	1	0	1	0	3	.100	.100
Veras, Q#	.429	7	3	0	0	1	1	.429	.429
White, R	.333	9	3	0	1	0	0	.333	.333
Young, Eric	.000	3	0	0	0	2	0	.400	.000
Zeile, Todd	.286	7	2	0	0	2	1	.444	.429

Scott Erickson, Orioles — RHP

Batter	Avg	AB	H	HR	BI	BB	SO	OBP	Slg
Aldrete, Mike*	.370	27	10	0	3	2	5	.414	.481
Alexander, M	.000	6	0	0	0	1	1	.143	.000
Alicea, Luis#	.200	5	1	0	0	0	0	.200	.200
Alomar, R#	.259	27	7	0	2	7	0	.412	.259
Alomar Jr, S	.160	25	4	0	1	0	2	.160	.160
Amaral, Rich	.364	11	4	0	2	2	2	.500	.364
Anderson, Brd*	.265	34	9	3	4	5	4	.375	.529
Anderson, G*	.125	16	2	0	0	0	1	.125	.125
Arias, George	.200	5	1	0	0	0	0	.200	.200
Ausmus, Brad	.250	4	1	0	1	0	0	.200	.250
Baerga, C#	.264	53	14	1	9	1	7	.273	.358
Baines, H*	.275	40	11	0	7	10	3	.404	.350
Becker, Rich*	.286	7	2	0	1	0	0	.286	.286
Bell, Derek	.000	4	0	0	0	2	2	.333	.000
Belle, Albert	.375	40	15	2	7	6	3	.468	.675
Beltre, E	.500	4	2	1	3	1	3	.600	1.222
Berroa, G	.444	9	4	2	3	1	3	.500	1.222
Bichette, D	.286	7	2	0	0	0	2	.286	.571
Blowers, Mike	.182	11	2	0	1	1	4	.250	.182
Boggs, Wade*	.349	43	15	0	4	4	2	.404	.465
Borders, Pat	.120	25	3	0	2	2	5	.185	.160
Bordick, Mike	.308	26	8	0	3	2	6	.379	.346
Bragg, Darren*	.125	8	1	0	0	2	2	.300	.125
Brosius, S	.300	10	3	0	0	1	0	.300	.300
Brumfield, J	.100	10	1	0	0	1	3	.182	.100
Buhner, Jay	.250	36	9	3	8	5	9	.341	.611
Burks, Ellis	.300	20	6	0	1	2	3	.391	.350
Burnitz, J*	.400	5	2	0	2	0	0	.400	.600
Canseco, Jose	.324	34	11	3	4	5	6	.410	.618
Carter, Joe	.233	43	10	2	8	2	5	.283	.442
Cirillo, Jeff	.333	12	4	0	3	1	1	.385	.417
Clark, Tony*	.462	13	6	0	3	0	4	.462	.538
Clark, Will*	.286	14	4	0	2	2	0	.353	.357
Cole, Alex*	.571	14	8	0	0	1	0	.600	.571
Coleman, V#	.286	7	2	0	0	1	1	.375	.429
Cora, Joey#	.095	21	2	0	2	2	1	.167	.095
Cordova, M	.333	6	2	1	1	0	0	.333	.833
Curtis, Chad	.185	27	5	0	0	4	4	.290	.185
Cuyler, Milt*	.143	14	2	0	0	3	1	.294	.143
Damon, Johnny*	.375	8	3	0	0	0	0	.375	.500
Davis, Chili#	.231	26	6	0	0	2	3	.286	.269
Dawson, Andre	.077	13	1	0	2	0	4	.077	.154
Deer, Rob	.238	21	5	0	3	1	5	.273	.238
Delgado, C*	.231	13	3	1	2	1	6	.333	.615
Devereaux, M	.135	37	5	1	5	4	6	.220	.270
Diaz, Alex#	.000	8	0	0	0	1	0	.000	.000
DiSarcina, G	.292	24	7	0	3	2	0	.346	.333
Duncan, M	.222	9	2	0	0	2	0	.222	.333
Durham, Ray#	.529	17	9	0	4	0	3	.529	.647
Easley, D	.316	19	6	0	0	2	4	.381	.316
Edmonds, Jim*	.292	24	7	2	6	0	7	.292	.625
Eisenreich, J	.278	18	5	0	4	0	1	.278	.444
Elster, Kevin	.167	6	1	0	2	0	1	.167	.333
Espinoza, A	.222	18	4	0	3	0	3	.263	.389

Scott Erickson, Orioles — RHP

Batter	Avg	AB	H	HR	BI	BB	SO	OBP	Slg
Fabregas, Jor*	.455	11	5	0	1	0	0	.455	.545
Fermin, Felix	.375	16	6	0	0	2	1	.444	.375
Fielder, C	.217	46	10	0	7	1	9	.250	.283
Finley, Steve*	.167	6	1	0	1	0	0	.167	.167
Flaherty, J	.500	6	3	1	3	0	0	.500	1.167
Franco, Julio	.286	35	10	1	2	2	7	.342	.371
Frye, Jeff	.375	8	3	0	1	2	1	.500	.500
Fryman, T	.220	41	9	1	6	4	8	.283	.366
Gaetti, Gary	.278	18	5	1	3	0	6	.300	.444
Gagne, Greg	.111	9	1	0	0	0	1	.111	.111
Gallego, Mike	.286	14	4	0	1	1	2	.333	.429
Gates, Brent#	.188	16	3	0	2	0	2	.188	.250
Gil, Benji	.000	4	0	0	0	1	0	.200	.000
Girardi, Joe	.250	4	1	0	2	1	0	.400	.250
Gomez, Chris	.200	10	2	0	0	0	0	.200	.400
Gomez, Leo	.231	26	6	0	4	2	5	.310	.346
Gonzales, R	.000	5	0	0	0	1	0	.167	.000
Gonzalez, A	.231	13	3	1	2	3	4	.375	.538
Gonzalez, J	.263	38	10	5	8	1	8	.282	.658
Goodwin, Tom*	.300	10	3	0	1	2	1	.417	.300
Grebeck, C	.000	5	0	0	1	1	1	.167	.000
Green, Shawn*	.286	7	2	0	0	1	0	.444	.286
Greenwell, M*	.333	39	13	0	2	1	1	.350	.410
Greer, Rusty*	.200	10	2	0	1	3	0	.385	.200
Griffey Jr, K*	.465	43	20	4	11	6	3	.510	.907
Guillen, O*	.324	34	11	0	3	1	0	.343	.324
Gwynn, Chris*	.500	4	2	0	0	1	0	.600	1.000
Hall, Mel*	.167	12	2	0	0	1	0	.231	.167
Hamelin, Bob*	.273	11	3	1	1	1	2	.333	.545
Hamilton, D*	.448	29	13	0	5	2	0	.484	.586
Hammonds, J	.333	6	2	1	4	0	1	.333	1.000
Haselman, B	.400	5	2	0	0	0	2	.500	.400
Hayes, C	.286	7	2	0	0	0	1	.286	.286
Henderson, R	.391	23	9	1	7	6	3	.517	.652
Hiatt, Phil	.125	8	1	0	0	0	2	.125	.125
Higginson, B*	.429	14	6	0	0	1	0	.429	.571
Hoiles, Chris	.471	17	8	1	1	0	2	.526	.824
Hollins, Dave#	.333	6	2	0	2	0	0	.333	.500
Howard, Dave#	.231	13	3	0	1	1	0	.286	.231
Howell, Jack*	.250	4	1	0	0	1	0	.400	.250
Hudler, Rex	.143	7	1	0	0	0	1	.143	.143
Hulse, David*	.200	15	3	0	1	0	2	.200	.333
Huson, Jeff*	.150	20	3	0	2	4	1	.292	.150
Incaviglia, P	.167	6	1	0	0	0	2	.167	.167
Jaha, John	.263	19	5	0	0	2	3	.364	.316
James, Dion*	.154	13	2	0	0	1	1	.214	.231
Javier, Stan#	.538	13	7	0	3	0	0	.538	.615
Jefferies, G#	.667	6	4	1	2	1	0	.714	1.333
Jefferson, R*	.357	14	5	0	1	1	3	.400	.357
Jeter, Derek	.222	9	2	0	0	1	0	.300	.222
Johnson, L*	.417	36	15	0	6	1	1	.432	.500
Joyner, Wally*	.308	26	8	0	1	0	1	.308	.385
Karkovice, M	.250	20	5	1	3	1	4	.273	.500
Kelly, Pat	.300	20	6	0	2	0	3	.286	.450
Kelly, R	.313	16	5	0	2	1	3	.368	.438
Kirby, Wayne*	.500	18	9	0	4	4	2	.565	.556
Knoblauch, C	.600	5	3	0	1	0	1	.714	.800
Kreuter, Chad#	.167	6	1	0	1	0	1	.167	.333
Levis, Jesse*	.333	9	3	0	0	0	1	.333	.444
Lewis, Darren	.000	5	0	0	0	2	1	.286	.000
Lewis, Mark	.318	22	7	0	2	2	1	.375	.500
Listach, Pat#	.176	17	3	0	0	1	5	.222	.235
Livingstone*	.333	12	4	0	3	1	0	.385	.417
Lockhart, K*	.308	13	4	1	2	1	0	.357	.538
Lofton, Kenny*	.381	42	16	2	7	5	2	.447	.595
Lovullo, T#	.167	6	1	0	0	0	0	.167	.167
Macfarlane, M	.261	23	6	1	4	1	3	.292	.435
Magadan, Dave*	.167	6	1	0	0	1	1	.286	.167
Manto, Jeff	.000	5	0	0	0	0	2	.000	.000
Martinez, Da*	.533	15	8	0	2	1	0	.563	.533
Martinez, E	.414	29	12	0	5	6	5	.541	.586
Martinez, S*	.200	5	1	0	0	0	1	.333	.400
Martinez, T*	.290	31	9	1	8	2	3	.324	.484
Marzano, John	.143	7	1	0	0	0	0	.143	.143
Matheny, Mike	.000	3	0	0	1	0	1	.000	.000
May, Derrick*	.167	6	1	1	3	0	1	.167	.667
Mayne, Brent*	.136	22	3	0	3	1	2	.174	.227
McGwire, Mark	.429	28	12	5	11	3	6	.484	1.071
McLemore, M#	.313	32	10	0	2	6	5	.421	.344
McRae, Brian#	.300	30	9	0	5	2	4	.344	.433
Meares, Pat	.200	5	1	0	0	1	0	.200	.200
Mieske, Matt	.222	9	2	0	0	1	3	.300	.333
Molitor, Paul	.231	39	9	0	3	4	6	.302	.231
Murray, Eddie#	.364	22	8	2	8	1	3	.391	.682
Myers, Greg*	.381	21	8	0	2	0	2	.381	.429
Naehring, Tim	.211	19	4	0	2	0	4	.211	.211
Newson, B*	.143	7	1	0	2	3	2	.400	.143
Nieves, M#	.167	6	1	0	0	0	1	.167	.167
Nilsson, Dave*	.357	14	5	0	7	2	2	.389	.429
Nixon, Otis*	.375	16	6	0	0	3	5	.474	.375
Nunnally, Jon*	.250	4	1	0	0	1	1	.500	.250

Scott Erickson, Orioles — RHP

Batter	Avg	AB	H	HR	BI	BB	SO	OBP	Slg
O'Brien, C	.333	6	2	0	1	0	1	.333	.500
O'Leary, Troy*	.364	11	4	0	3	0	0	.364	.364
O'Neill, Paul*	.435	23	10	0	1	2	1	.480	.478
Olerud, John*	.293	41	12	1	8	5	3	.375	.439
Oliver, Joe	.167	6	1	0	0	0	4	.167	.167
Orsulak, Joe*	.313	16	5	0	4	0	2	.450	.563
Palmeiro, R*	.270	37	10	1	6	2	4	.317	.351
Palmer, Dean	.267	15	4	1	4	4	5	.400	.467
Paquette, C	.368	19	7	0	4	0	2	.368	.474
Pena, Tony	.100	20	2	0	1	3	5	.217	.100
Perez, E	.333	6	2	0	0	0	1	.333	.333
Perez, Tomas#	.167	6	1	0	0	0	1	.167	.167
Phillips, T#	.354	48	17	5	9	15	7	.508	.750
Plantier, P*	.250	12	3	0	0	0	1	.250	.250
Polonia, Luis*	.226	31	7	0	2	1	4	.250	.355
Pride, Curtis*	.286	7	2	1	2	0	0	.286	.714
Raines, Tim#	.300	40	12	0	5	1	7	.317	.325
Ramirez, M	.313	16	5	0	1	1	2	.353	.500
Reed, Jody	.174	23	4	0	0	3	5	.269	.217
Ripken, Billy	.000	7	0	0	0	0	1	.125	.000
Ripken, Cal	.231	39	9	2	6	4	8	.295	.436
Rodriguez, Al	.750	8	6	2	5	1	1	.778	1.750
Rodriguez, I	.304	23	7	0	2	2	1	.385	.348
Salmon, Tim	.185	27	5	3	3	0	5	.290	.222
Schofield, D	.200	10	2	0	1	0	1	.200	.300
Segui, David#	.125	8	1	0	0	0	1	.125	.125
Seitzer, K	.125	32	4	0	1	3	3	.222	.156
Sheffield, G	.333	3	1	0	1	1	0	.600	.333
Shumpert, T	.167	6	1	0	0	1	2	.286	.167
Sierra, Ruben*	.292	48	14	1	3	2	7	.320	.479
Snow, J.T.#	.360	25	9	0	1	2	1	.407	.480
Sorrento, P*	.314	35	11	5	7	7	7	.429	.400
Spiers, Bill*	.444	9	4	0	1	3	0	.583	.444
Sprague, Ed	.367	30	11	0	6	0	6	.406	.467
Stahoviak, S*	.600	5	3	0	1	0	0	.600	1.000
Stanley, Mike	.222	18	4	1	1	0	2	.263	.444
Steinbach, T	.438	16	7	0	0	0	2	.471	.500
Stevens, Lee*	.429	7	3	0	0	2	2	.429	.429
Stillwell, K#	.182	11	2	0	1	0	2	.250	.273
Strange, Doug#	.316	19	6	0	2	0	0	.316	.421
Surhoff, B.J.*	.143	14	2	0	1	0	0	.200	.143
Sveum, Dale#	.500	6	3	0	0	0	1	.571	.667
Tartabull, D	.200	15	3	1	6	2	4	.278	.467
Tettleton, M#	.317	41	13	2	5	8	8	.429	.512
Thomas, Frank	.342	38	13	1	5	9	3	.458	.553
Thome, Jim*	.400	25	10	2	4	9	4	.559	.800
Tinsley, Lee#	.308	13	4	0	2	1	2	.400	.308
Trammell, A	.188	16	3	0	0	1	3	.278	.188
Tucker, M*	.333	6	2	0	0	0	1	.429	.333
Valentin, Jhn	.355	31	11	0	2	0	4	.394	.484
Valentin, Jse#	.240	25	6	0	1	0	2	.240	.320
Valle, Dave	.000	17	0	0	1	4	6	.261	.000
Vaughn, Greg	.394	33	13	4	12	2	7	.429	.879
Vaughn, Mo*	.306	36	11	2	10	5	4	.381	.583
Velarde, R	.250	16	4	1	5	3	2	.368	.500
Ventura, R*	.400	35	14	2	10	9	3	.500	.686
Vina, F*	.167	12	2	1	1	1	0	.231	.417
Vitiello, Joe	.333	6	2	0	1	1	1	.429	.333
Vizquel, Omar#	.378	45	17	0	5	4	0	.429	.467
Ward, Turner#	.278	18	5	0	1	2	3	.350	.278
Weiss, Walt#	.100	10	1	0	1	3	0	.100	.100
White, Devon#	.367	30	11	1	3	3	6	.457	.567
Whiten, Mark#	.200	15	3	0	0	2	5	.294	.200
Williams, Ber#	.320	25	8	0	1	3	4	.393	.480
Wilson, Dan	.385	13	5	0	0	0	2	.385	.385
Worthington	.000	3	0	0	0	2	1	.400	.000

Vaughn Eshelman, Red Sox — LHP

Batter	Avg	AB	H	HR	BI	BB	SO	OBP	Slg
Alomar, R#	.200	5	1	0	0	0	2	.200	.200
Amaral, Rich	.000	9	0	0	2	1	0	.100	.000
Anderson, G*	.500	6	3	0	0	0	0	.500	.667
Baerga, C#	.667	6	4	0	2	0	0	.667	1.167
Bautista, D	.200	5	1	0	0	1	0	.200	.400
Becker, Rich*	.200	5	1	0	2	3	0	.167	.200
Belle, Albert	.000	7	0	0	0	0	2	.000	.000
Boggs, Wade*	.000	3	0	0	0	1	1	.400	.000
Buhner, Jay	.500	8	4	1	5	1	1	.556	1.000
Carter, Joe	.166	6	1	0	1	0	0	.143	.166
Cirillo, Jeff	.400	10	4	2	3	1	0	.455	1.000
Cordova, M	.500	6	3	1	1	1	0	.571	.667
Curtis, Chad	.286	7	2	0	0	0	0	.375	.286
Davis, Chili*	.600	5	3	1	3	3	2	.750	1.200
Davis, Russ	.600	5	4	0	2	1	0	.833	1.000
Durham, Ray#	.600	5	3	0	0	0	0	.600	.800
Edmonds, Jim*	.000	6	0	0	0	2	0	.000	.000
Fielder, C	.500	6	3	0	1	0	1	.571	.500
Fryman, T	.000	7	0	0	0	0	0	.000	.000
Gomez, Chris	.000	4	0	0	3	1	0	.429	.000
Gonzalez, A	.333	3	1	0	0	2	1	.600	.333

Vaughn Eshelman, Red Sox — LHP

Batter	Avg	AB	H	HR	BI	BB	SO	OBP	Slg
Gonzalez, J	.800	5	4	1	4	0	0	.800	1.600
Greer, Rusty*	.200	5	1	0	0	0	1	.333	.200
Griffey Jr, K*	.400	10	4	2	8	0	2	.400	1.100
Hollins, Dave#	.000	3	0	0	0	2	0	.400	.000
Hudler, Rex	.667	6	4	0	0	0	0	.667	.667
Hunter, Brian	.286	7	2	0	3	1	0	.375	.286
Jaha, John	.500	8	4	0	0	2	2	.600	.625
Kelly, Pat	.250	4	1	0	1	2	1	.500	.250
Kelly, R	.571	7	4	1	2	0	1	.571	1.000
Knoblauch, C	.000	5	0	0	0	1	2	.167	.000
Lewis, Darren	.000	4	0	0	1	0	0	.000	.000
Leyritz, Jim	.100	10	1	1	3	1	2	.182	.400
Listach, Pat#	.000	7	0	0	0	0	2	.000	.000
Lofton, Kenny*	.200	5	1	0	3	1	1	.333	.400
Loretta, Mark	.000	4	0	0	0	2	1	.333	.000
Martinez, E	.500	4	2	0	1	3	0	.667	.500
Martinez, T*	.333	3	1	0	0	2	0	.600	.333
Matheny, Mike	.429	7	3	0	1	0	0	.429	.571
Mieske, Matt	.167	6	1	0	0	1	0	.286	.333
Molitor, Paul	.375	8	3	0	4	2	0	.455	.625
Mouton, Lyle	.667	6	4	0	1	0	1	.667	.667
Murray, Eddie#	.000	3	0	0	1	1	1	.200	.000
Nilsson, Dave*	.000	6	0	0	0	2	1	.143	.000
Paquette, C	.500	5	1	0	0	1	2	.333	.200
Perry, H	.400	5	2	0	1	0	0	.400	.800
Phillips, T#	.250	8	2	1	1	3	0	.455	.750
Ramirez, M	.429	7	3	0	1	0	2	.429	.429
Ripken, Cal	.333	3	1	1	3	2	0	.600	1.333
Rodriguez, Al	.500	8	4	0	2	1	3	.556	.500
Salmon, Tim	.600	5	3	1	2	0	1	.600	1.400
Samuel, Juan	.200	5	1	0	2	1	3	.333	.200
Seitzer, K	.143	7	1	0	2	1	2	.250	.143
Snopek, Chris	.000	6	0	0	0	0	0	.000	.000
Snow, J.T.#	.000	8	0	0	0	0	2	.000	.000
Sojo, Luis	.250	4	1	0	0	1	0	.400	.250
Sprague, Ed	.333	6	2	0	1	0	2	.333	.333
Stanley, Mike	.143	7	1	0	0	1	1	.250	.143
Surhoff, B.J.*	.750	4	3	0	0	0	0	.750	1.000
Tartabull, D	.250	8	2	0	1	3	2	.455	.250
Thomas, Frank	.286	7	2	0	0	1	0	.375	.286
Thome, Jim*	.667	6	4	0	0	0	1	.667	.833
Trammell, A	.571	7	4	0	0	0	0	.571	.571
Velarde, R	.100	10	1	0	0	3	0	.308	.100
Ventura, R*	.000	5	0	0	0	1	2	.167	.000
Vizquel, Omar*	.250	8	2	0	0	1	1	.333	.250
Walbeck, Matt#	.600	5	3	1	3	0	0	.600	1.200
Williams, Ber#	.200	10	2	0	0	2	0	.333	.200
Williams, Ger	.250	8	2	0	0	0	2	.250	.625
Wilson, Dan	.333	3	1	0	0	3	0	.667	.333

John Farrell, Tigers — RHP

Batter	Avg	AB	H	HR	BI	BB	SO	OBP	Slg
Alomar, R#	.250	4	1	1	3	1	0	.400	1.000
Anderson, Brd*	.125	8	1	0	0	0	2	.125	.125
Baerga, C#	.200	5	1	1	2	0	1	.200	.800
Baines, H*	.333	9	3	0	1	2	0	.455	.333
Belle, Albert	.000	5	0	0	0	0	2	.000	.000
Boggs, Wade*	.375	24	9	1	2	4	4	.464	.542
Buhner, Jay	.100	10	1	0	0	1	3	.182	.100
Burks, Ellis	.368	19	7	1	5	3	6	.435	.632
Canseco, Jose	.200	20	4	0	2	1	4	.238	.250
Cora, Joey*	.250	4	1	0	0	1	0	.500	.250
Davis, Chili*	.375	16	6	0	3	1	2	.368	.438
Deer, Rob	.077	13	1	0	2	3	7	.250	.077
Devereaux, M	.273	11	3	1	1	0	4	.273	.545
Eisenreich, J*	.200	10	2	0	0	0	2	.200	.300
Espinoza, A	.500	8	4	0	0	1	0	.556	.500
Fielder, C	.364	11	4	2	7	1	4	.417	1.000
Finley, Steve*	.455	11	5	0	2	0	1	.455	.545
Franco, Julio	.286	14	4	0	0	1	0	.333	.286
Fryman, D	.429	7	3	0	0	1	2	.556	.714
Gaetti, Gary	.286	28	8	1	1	2	3	.355	.393
Gagne, Greg	.227	22	5	2	3	0	5	.227	.500
Gallego, Mike	.500	10	5	0	0	2	1	.583	.600
Gomez, Leo	.400	5	2	0	1	0	1	.400	.400
Gonzalez, J	.143	7	1	1	3	0	1	.143	.571
Greenwell, M*	.286	21	6	0	3	1	1	.318	.476
Griffey Jr, K*	.364	22	8	1	1	3	1	.440	.591
Guillen, O*	.333	12	4	0	2	2	0	.429	.583
Gwynn, Chris*	.250	4	1	0	0	1	0	.400	.250
Hall, Mel*	.571	7	4	0	4	1	0	.556	.714
Hamelin, Bob*	.286	7	2	0	2	1	1	.375	.571
Henderson, R	.273	11	3	1	1	1	1	.333	.545
Howard, Dave#	.200	5	1	0	0	0	2	.200	.200
Howell, Jack*	.250	16	4	0	1	1	5	.294	.250
Hulse, David*	.500	6	3	0	0	1	0	.571	.667
Incaviglia, P	.333	12	4	0	2	1	3	.385	.417
Javier, Stan#	.154	13	2	0	0	0	6	.154	.154
Johnson, L*	.444	9	4	0	1	1	0	.500	.556
Joyner, Wally*	.200	25	5	1	2	3	6	.286	.360
Karkovice, R	.667	6	4	3	7	2	1	.750	2.167
Kelly, R	.250	4	1	0	0	2	0	.500	.250
Kreuter, Chad#	.375	8	3	0	1	2	2	.500	.625
Liriano, N#	.188	16	3	0	1	3	1	.316	.250
Lofton, Kenny*	.600	5	3	0	0	1	0	.667	.800
Macfarlane, M	.222	18	4	1	3	0	1	.222	.389
Martinez, E	.400	15	6	1	2	1	0	.438	.667
McGriff, Fred*	.381	21	8	0	1	2	2	.435	.524
McGwire, Mark	.294	17	5	1	3	0	7	.294	.471
McLemore, M#	.700	10	7	0	2	0	0	.700	.800
McRae, Brian*	.143	7	1	0	0	0	1	.143	.143
Molitor, Paul	.261	23	6	0	2	5	3	.393	.391
Murray, Eddie#	.000	8	0	0	0	2	0	.200	.000
Myers, Greg*	.200	5	1	0	0	0	0	.200	.200
Olerud, John*	.571	7	4	3	5	0	0	.571	1.857
Orsulak, Joe*	.353	17	6	0	1	1	0	.389	.412
Palmeiro, R*	.200	15	3	1	4	1	1	.250	.400
Palmer, Dean	.667	6	4	2	2	1	0	.714	1.667
Phillips, T#	.185	27	5	1	5	3	4	.267	.296
Polonia, Luis*	.389	18	7	0	2	2	4	.450	.389
Raines, Tim#	.167	6	1	0	0	0	0	.167	.333
Reed, Jody	.235	17	4	2	4	3	1	.350	.706
Ripken, Billy	.250	12	3	0	2	0	0	.250	.333
Ripken, Cal	.200	25	5	1	2	2	4	.259	.360
Rodriguez, I	.167	6	1	0	0	0	0	.167	.333
Schofield, D	.111	9	1	0	0	0	0	.111	.111
Schu, Rick	.429	7	3	0	0	2	0	.600	.714
Seitzer, K	.250	20	5	0	1	2	1	.318	.250
Sheffield, G	.250	4	1	0	0	1	0	.400	.250
Sierra, Ruben#	.188	16	3	0	0	1	4	.278	.188
Sosa, Sammy	.286	7	2	0	1	0	3	.286	.571
Spiers, Bill*	.143	7	1	0	1	0	3	.125	.286
Stanley, Mike	.200	5	1	0	0	0	0	.200	.200
Steinbach, T	.231	13	3	2	2	0	2	.286	.692
Stillwell, K#	.222	18	4	0	1	2	0	.333	.333
Strange, Doug#	.333	6	2	0	2	1	2	.429	.667
Surhoff, B.J.*	.227	22	5	0	0	1	1	.261	.227
Sveum, Dale#	.333	12	4	1	4	0	2	.333	.667
Tartabull, D	.059	17	1	0	0	6	6	.059	.059
Tettleton, M#	.300	10	3	2	7	2	2	.385	.900
Thomas, Frank	.667	6	4	1	2	1	1	.714	1.167
Trammell, A	.333	15	5	0	0	0	0	.333	.467
Valle, Dave	.250	12	3	0	2	1	3	.308	.333
Ventura, R*	.167	6	1	0	0	2	0	.375	.333
Vizquel, Omar*	.286	14	4	0	0	2	1	.375	.429
Weiss, Walt#	.625	8	5	0	0	1	1	.667	.875
White, Devon#	.391	23	9	0	1	2	3	.440	.522
Worthington	.333	12	4	0	1	1	0	.385	.333

Shawn Estes, Giants — LHP

Batter	Avg	AB	H	HR	BI	BB	SO	OBP	Slg
Alfonzo, E	.200	5	1	0	0	1	0	.333	.200
Andrews, S	.200	5	1	0	0	1	2	.333	.200
Ashley, Billy	.000	4	0	0	0	2	2	.333	.000
Bell, Jay	.500	8	3	0	1	0	2	.500	.667
Cedeno, Roger#	.000	4	0	0	0	3	2	.429	.000
Espinoza, A	.333	6	2	0	3	0	2	.333	.500
Gagne, Greg	.400	5	2	0	0	1	1	.500	.400
Gilkey, B	.571	7	4	0	2	0	1	.571	1.000
Grudzielanek	.500	6	3	0	0	0	2	.500	.500
Hundley, Todd#	.000	6	0	0	0	1	4	.143	.000
Johnson, L*	.200	5	1	0	0	2	0	.429	.200
Karros, Eric	.167	6	1	1	1	0	0	.167	.667
Lansing, Mike	.000	5	0	0	0	1	1	.167	.000
Mondesi, Raul	.167	6	1	0	0	0	4	.167	.167
Ochoa, Alex	.500	4	2	0	0	3	0	.714	1.000
Ordonez, Rey	.000	5	0	0	0	0	1	.000	.000
Santangelo, F#	.250	4	1	0	1	1	1	.500	.250
Segui, David#	.200	5	1	0	1	1	0	.333	.200
Webster, L	.200	5	1	0	0	1	0	.333	.400
Wehner, John	.400	5	2	0	1	0	2	.400	.400
White, R	.167	6	1	0	0	0	0	.167	.333

Mike Farmer, Rockies — LHP

Batter	Avg	AB	H	HR	BI	BB	SO	OBP	Slg
Bell, Jay	.600	5	3	1	2	0	0	.600	1.200
Blauser, Jeff	.333	6	2	0	1	0	1	.333	.333
Garcia, C	.500	6	3	0	1	0	1	.500	.500
Grissom, M	.000	4	0	0	0	2	1	.333	.000
Jones, C#	.000	5	0	0	0	1	1	.167	.000
Kendall, J	.000	5	0	0	0	0	0	.000	.000
King, Jeff	.500	6	3	3	5	0	1	.500	2.000
Klesko, Ryan*	.000	5	0	0	0	1	2	.167	.000
Lopez, Javy	.500	6	3	1	4	0	0	.500	1.000
Martin, Al*	.167	6	1	0	1	1	1	.286	.167
McGriff, Fred*	.500	6	3	1	3	0	0	.500	1.167
Merced, O*	.500	4	2	0	0	1	0	.600	.750

Jeff Fassero, Expos — LHP

Batter	Avg	AB	H	HR	BI	BB	SO	OBP	Slg
Abbott, Kurt	.333	18	6	0	4	1	4	.368	.500
Alfonzo, E	.500	8	4	0	1	0	2	.500	.875

Jeff Fassero, Expos — LHP

Batter	Avg	AB	H	HR	BI	BB	SO	OBP	Slg
Alicea, Luis#	.154	13	2	0	0	0	5	.154	.154
Amaro, Ruben#	.167	6	1	0	0	0	1	.167	.167
Anthony, Eric*	.200	5	1	0	2	0	1	.200	.400
Arias, Alex	.333	6	2	0	0	0	1	.333	.333
Ashley, Billy	.111	9	1	0	1	3	6	.308	.111
Aude, Rich	.000	5	0	0		1	0	.167	.000
Ausmus, Brad	.200	20	4	1	1	1	5	.238	.350
Bagwell, Jeff	.192	26	5	2	5	7	7	.364	.462
Barberie, B#	.500	6	3	0	1	0	0	.500	.500
Batiste, Kim	.143	7	1	0	1	1	1	.250	.286
Bell, Derek	.286	21	6	1	1	2	3	.348	.476
Bell, Jay	.367	30	11	2	7	6	4	.472	.667
Belliard, R	.300	10	3	0	0	1	2	.364	.300
Berry, Sean	.286	7	2	0	1	0	1	.250	.286
Bichette, D	.321	28	9	3	8	2	2	.355	.643
Biggio, Craig	.304	23	7	1	2	7	4	.452	.478
Blauser, Jeff	.267	15	4	0	1	1	6	.353	.333
Bogar, Tim	.000	8	0	0	0	0	2	.000	.000
Bonds, Barry*	.318	22	7	1	4	6	3	.464	.500
Bonilla, B#	.400	15	6	3	6	2	0	.471	1.000
Boone, Bret	.200	10	2	1	4	0	3	.200	.500
Bournigal, R	.200	5	1	0	0	0	0	.200	.200
Branson, Jeff*	.200	5	1	0	0	0	1	.200	.200
Brumfield, J	.400	15	6	0	0	1	2	.438	.467
Burks, Ellis	.389	18	7	2	3	2	4	.450	.778
Busch, Mike	.200	5	1	0	2	0	4	.200	.200
Butler, Brett*	.211	19	4	0	0	2	2	.286	.211
Caminiti, Ken#	.226	31	7	1	3	4	5	.314	.452
Carr, Chuck	.500	18	9	0	2	0	3	.500	.833
Carreon, Mark	.231	13	3	0	1	0	2	.286	.231
Castilla, V	.136	22	3	0	1	1	3	.174	.136
Cedeno, A	.348	23	8	1	3	3	7	.423	.522
Cianfrocco, A	.087	23	2	0	1	0	8	.087	.130
Clark, Phil	.188	16	3	0	0	1	5	.278	.188
Clark, Will*	.429	7	3	1	2	1	1	.500	.857
Clayton, D	.111	18	2	0	0	0	5	.111	.111
Colbrunn, G	.222	18	4	0	1	2	2	.300	.278
Conine, Jeff	.500	26	13	1	4	1	4	.519	.654
Curtis, Chad	.429	7	3	0	0	0	1	.429	.571
Dascenzo, D#	.333	6	2	0	0	1	0	.429	.333
Daulton, D*	.313	16	5	1	5	3	8	.400	.563
Davis, Eric	.333	9	3	1	1	2	2	.455	.889
Dawson, Andre	.444	9	4	0	3	0	1	.400	.556
DeShields, D	.217	23	5	0	1	0	4	.217	.261
Duncan, M	.235	17	4	0	3	5	4	.409	.353
Dunston, S	.111	9	1	0	0	0	2	.111	.111
Dye, Jermaine	.000	8	0	0	0	0	0	.000	.000
Dykstra, L*	.375	16	6	0	3	3	2	.474	.500
Eusebio, Tony	.143	7	1	0	1	2	2	.333	.143
Everett, Carl*	.200	10	2	1	2	2	4	.333	.500
Finley, Steve*	.235	34	8	0	5	2	9	.297	.324
Fonville, C#	.364	11	4	0	1	0	0	.364	.455
Gaetti, Gary	.250	8	2	1	2	0	2	.250	.625
Gagne, Greg	.375	8	3	1	5	0	1	.375	.875
Galarraga, A	.185	27	5	2	4	1	6	.214	.444
Gant, Ron	.208	24	5	1	4	2	3	.269	.333
Garcia, C	.250	24	6	1	3	0	2	.250	.417
Gilkey, B	.208	24	5	0	1	5	9	.345	.375
Girardi, Joe	.350	20	7	0	2	0	5	.350	.350
Gomez, Leo	.333	9	3	2	4	0	5	.300	1.000
Gonzalez, L*	.067	15	1	0	0	1	6	.125	.133
Grace, Mark*	.333	30	10	0	1	2	3	.375	.333
Grissom, M	.375	16	6	1	2	2	0	.444	.563
Gutierrez, R	.273	11	3	0	0	2	3	.385	.273
Gwynn, Tony*	.294	34	10	0	3	1	4	.314	.324
Hayes, C	.292	24	7	0	1	1	6	.320	.417
Henderson, R	.286	7	2	1	2	1	3	.375	.714
Hernandez, Ca	.250	8	2	0	0	0	2	.250	.250
Hernandez, Jo	.250	8	2	0	0	0	5	.250	.250
Hill, G	.467	15	7	1	2	1	1	.500	.667
Hollins, Dave#	.143	14	2	0	1	2	1	.250	.357
Hubbard, Tr	.000	8	0	0	0	0	3	.000	.000
Hundley, Todd#	.111	18	2	0	1	3	10	.238	.111
Hunter, Brian	.000	7	0	0	0	0	6	.000	.000
Hunter, Bri L	.375	16	6	0	3	1	3	.412	.500
Huskey, Butch	.167	12	2	0	0	2	4	.286	.167
Incaviglia, J	.133	15	2	0	1	2	7	.235	.133
Javier, Stan#	.667	6	4	0	0	2	1	.750	.667
Jefferies, G#	.409	22	9	0	1	3	2	.480	.455
Johnson, Bri	.125	8	1	0	0	0	2	.125	.125
Johnson, Char	.143	14	2	0	2	1	5	.200	.214
Johnson, L*	.400	15	6	0	2	0	1	.400	.467
Jones, Andruw	.400	5	2	0	0	1	0	.400	.600
Jones, C#	.214	14	3	0	0	1	3	.267	.357
Jones, Chris	.077	13	1	0	1	0	5	.077	.154
Jordan, Brian	.125	16	2	0	1	1	2	.176	.188
Jordan, Ricky	.500	6	3	0	0	1	2	.571	.667
Justice, Dave*	.294	17	5	0	3	2	7	.350	.412
Karros, Eric	.143	28	4	1	4	5	10	.233	.250
Kelly, Mike	.250	12	3	0	0	1	3	.250	.500
Kelly, R	.286	14	4	0	1	0	3	.286	.357
Kendall, J	.600	5	3	0	1	0	0	.600	1.000
Kent, Jeff	.368	19	7	0	4	1	1	.400	.474
King, Jeff	.222	27	6	0	4	0	4	.214	.222
Lankford, Ray*	.143	21	3	0	2	1	4	.182	.238
Larkin, Barry	.214	14	3	0	0	2	3	.313	.286
Lemke, Mark#	.321	28	9	2	4	2	2	.367	.571
Lewis, Darren	.118	17	2	0	0	5	2	.318	.118
Lewis, Mark	.429	7	3	0	1	1	0	.500	.429
Lopez, Javy	.389	18	7	1	2	0	3	.389	.611
Lopez, Luis#	.000	4	0	0	0	1	0	.200	.000
Magadan, Dave*	.000	6	0	0	0	1	0	.143	.000
Manwaring, K	.083	12	1	1	1	1	3	.154	.333
Martin, Al*	.063	16	1	0	1	0	7	.063	.063
McCarty, Dave	.400	5	2	0	0	1	0	.571	.600
McCracken, Q#	.000	5	0	0	0	0	2	.000	.000
McGee, Willie#	.267	15	4	0	1	0	6	.267	.267
McGriff, Fred*	.172	29	5	0	4	2	10	.219	.172
McRae, Brian#	.100	10	1	0	0	1	1	.182	.100
Merced, O*	.111	18	2	0	0	2	5	.200	.167
Miller, Orl	.250	12	3	0	3	0	4	.250	.417
Mondesi, Raul	.478	23	11	1	6	4	3	.556	.696
Morandini, M*	.294	17	5	0	3	4	1	.429	.471
Munson, Russ	.000	5	0	0	0	0	2	.000	.000
Morris, Hal*	.364	11	4	0	2	3	4	.500	.455
Mouton, James	.375	16	6	0	0	0	3	.375	.500
Murray, Eddie#	.417	12	5	0	2	0	0	.417	.667
Natal, Bob	.000	4	0	0	0	1	0	.200	.000
Nixon, Otis#	.100	10	1	0	0	1	1	.182	.100
O'Brien, C	.250	4	1	0	0	1	1	.400	.250
O'Neill, Paul*	.286	7	2	0	2	0	2	.286	.429
Ochoa, Alex	.200	10	2	0	0	0	4	.200	.300
Offerman, J#	.563	16	9	0	0	2	4	.611	.688
Oliver, Joe	.250	12	3	0	2	0	2	.250	.250
Ordonez, Rey	.333	12	4	0	0	0	2	.333	.417
Otero, Ricky#	.214	14	3	0	0	1	3	.267	.214
Owens, J	.000	4	0	0	0	3	2	.429	.000
Pagnozzi, Tom	.250	12	3	0	1	2	2	.357	.250
Parent, Mark	.100	10	1	0	0	2	4	.250	.100
Pena, G#	.667	6	4	0	0	0	0	.667	.833
Pendleton, T#	.250	24	6	0	2	3	8	.321	.333
Piazza, Mike	.263	19	5	1	3	1	10	.300	.474
Plantier, P*	.000	5	0	0	0	0	1	.000	.000
Prince, Tom	.000	8	0	0	0	2	1	.200	.000
Reed, Jody	.222	18	4	0	3	1	2	.263	.333
Renteria, E	.125	8	1	0	1	0	0	.125	.125
Roberson, K#	.000	6	0	0	0	0	1	.000	.000
Roberts, Bip#	.208	24	5	0	2	1	3	.240	.250
Sabo, Chris	.375	8	3	1	3	2	0	.500	.875
Sanchez, Rey	.071	14	1	0	0	1	3	.133	.071
Sandberg, R	.179	28	5	0	1	2	4	.233	.214
Sanders, R	.500	12	6	1	3	4	2	.625	.750
Santiago, B	.200	15	3	0	3	6	4	.429	.400
Scarsone, S	.222	9	2	0	0	1	3	.300	.222
Segui, David#	.333	3	1	0	1	0	1	.500	1.000
Servais, M	.214	14	3	0	2	1	4	.250	.214
Sheffield, G	.154	13	2	0	1	3	4	.313	.154
Shipley, C	.214	14	3	0	0	0	2	.214	.286
Simms, Mike	.250	8	2	0	0	1	4	.333	.375
Slaught, Don	.333	9	3	0	1	1	1	.400	.333
Smith, Ozzie#	.211	19	4	1	1	1	2	.250	.368
Sosa, Sammy	.300	20	6	0	1	1	4	.333	.400
Stocker, K#	.100	10	1	0	0	1	3	.182	.100
Strawberry, D*	.286	7	2	0	2	0	4	.250	.286
Taubensee, E*	.200	5	1	0	0	1	0	.200	.200
Tavarez, Jo#	.250	8	2	0	1	0	1	.250	.250
Thompson, Rob	.250	12	3	0	1	1	2	.308	.333
Thompson, Ry	.500	6	3	0	0	1	2	.571	.500
Timmons, O	.111	9	1	0	0	1	3	.200	.222
Veras, Q#	.000	6	0	0	0	1	1	.143	.000
Vizcaino, J#	.364	22	8	0	0	1	2	.391	.409
Walker, Larry*	.333	6	2	0	0	0	2	.286	.333
Wallach, Tim	.333	18	6	1	4	1	3	.368	.556
Walton, J	.286	7	2	0	0	1	1	.375	.429
Wehner, John	.300	10	3	0	1	0	2	.300	.300
Weiss, Walt#	.240	25	6	0	2	3	5	.321	.240
White, Devon#	.714	7	5	0	1	0	0	.714	.857
Whiten, Mark#	.273	11	3	1	2	3	3	.429	.545
Wilkins, Rick*	.278	18	5	1	1	1	6	.316	.500
Williams, E	.154	13	2	0	2	0	4	.154	.154
Williams, Ma	.316	19	6	3	6	2	4	.381	.789
Young, Eric	.364	22	8	0	1	1	3	.391	.364
Young, Kevin	.133	15	2	0	0	0	6	.133	.133
Zeile, Todd	.333	15	5	1	2	3	1	.444	.533

Alex Fernandez, White Sox — RHP

Batter	Avg	AB	H	HR	BI	BB	SO	OBP	Slg
Aldrete, Mike*	.250	20	5	0	3	0	6	.238	.400
Alicea, Luis#	.400	5	2	0	0	1	2	.500	.600
Alomar, R#	.244	41	10	3	6	4	5	.311	.512
Alomar Jr, R	.385	13	5	0	0	1	5	.385	.385
Amaral, Rich	.444	9	4	0	0	1	1	.545	.556

Batter	Avg	AB	H	HR	BI	BB	SO	OBP	Slg
Anderson, Brd*	.250	28	7	0	2	1	6	.276	.321
Anderson, G*	.364	11	4	0	1	0	3	.364	.364
Baerga, C	.257	35	9	2	3	1	6	.278	.457
Baines, H*	.192	26	5	3	5	5	3	.323	.538
Becker, Rich*	.250	12	3	0	1	2	4	.357	.333
Belle, Albert	.250	44	11	2	7	1	9	.267	.386
Berroa, G	.389	18	7	2	4	2	2	.450	.778
Bichette, D	.429	7	3	1	2	0	2	.429	1.000
Blowers, Mike	.071	14	1	0	2	4	8	.250	.071
Boggs, Wade*	.317	41	13	2	7	3	5	.364	.512
Bonilla, B#	.300	10	3	0	1	1	2	.333	.300
Borders, Pat	.050	20	1	0	0	0	7	.050	.050
Bordick, Mike	.303	33	10	0	2	1	4	.324	.364
Bragg, Darren*	.071	14	1	1	1	2	7	.188	.286
Brito, Tilson	.000	5	0	0	0	1	0	.000	.000
Brosius, S	.313	16	5	1	5	2	3	.389	.500
Buhner, Jay	.359	39	14	2	7	7	9	.468	.641
Burks, Ellis	.231	13	3	0	0	4	3	.412	.462
Canseco, Jose	.242	33	8	2	8	3	15	.297	.455
Carter, Joe	.171	41	7	0	2	2	8	.222	.171
Cirillo, Jeff	.143	14	2	0	0	3	3	.143	.214
Clark, Will*	.143	14	2	0	2	1	4	.200	.143
Cole, Alex*	.294	17	5	0	4	1	5	.333	.294
Coleman, V#	.571	7	4	0	1	0	0	.571	1.000
Cora, Joey#	.353	17	6	0	2	0	1	.353	.353
Cordova, M	.308	13	4	1	4	3	2	.444	.615
Curtis, Chad	.212	33	7	0	5	2	3	.257	.242
Cuyler, Milt#	.278	18	5	0	1	0	5	.278	.333
Damon, Johnny*	.214	14	3	0	0	0	2	.214	.286
Davis, Chili#	.320	25	8	4	9	4	6	.414	.880
Davis, Eric	.429	7	3	2	3	0	2	.429	1.286
Dawson, Andre	.214	14	3	0	1	0	1	.214	.214
Deer, Rob	.250	12	3	1	1	3	5	.400	.500
Delgado, C*	.308	13	4	1	2	2	2	.400	.538
Devereaux, S	.250	24	6	0	4	2	4	.357	.333
Diaz, Alex#	.200	10	2	0	1	1	2	.273	.200
DiSarcina, M	.292	24	7	0	3	2	3	.346	.333
Duncan, M	.333	6	2	0	0	0	1	.333	.333
Easley, D	.200	5	1	0	0	0	1	.200	.200
Edmonds, Jim*	.300	20	6	1	2	0	5	.333	.450
Eisenreich, J*	.375	8	3	0	0	0	0	.375	.500
Elster, Kevin	.000	5	0	0	0	0	3	.000	.000
Espinoza, A	.182	11	2	0	1	1	0	.250	.273
Fabregas, Jor*	.000	5	0	0	1	0	2	.000	.000
Fasano, Sal	.000	5	0	0	0	1	2	.167	.000
Fermin, Felix	.286	21	6	0	0	0	2	.286	.286
Fielder, C	.191	47	9	4	8	8	14	.309	.447
Flaherty, J	.167	6	1	0	0	0	0	.167	.167
Fox, Andy*	.333	6	2	0	0	0	2	.333	.500
Franco, Julio	.233	30	7	0	3	2	6	.281	.300
Frye, Jeff	.235	17	4	0	0	1	1	.278	.235
Fryman, T	.273	44	12	2	4	3	8	.313	.523
Gaetti, Gary	.200	25	5	0	1	2	1	.259	.280
Gagne, Greg	.222	27	6	0	2	1	4	.241	.222
Gallego, Mike	.389	18	7	1	5	2	3	.429	.667
Gates, Brent#	.357	28	10	0	1	3	5	.419	.500
Giambi, Jason*	.200	10	2	0	0	0	5	.200	.200
Girardi, Joe	.333	9	3	0	0	0	1	.333	.333
Gomez, Chris	.294	17	5	1	3	1	1	.333	.471
Gomez, Leo	.385	13	5	1	4	1	2	.429	.692
Gonzales, R	.364	11	4	0	1	1	1	.417	.545
Gonzalez, A	.000	10	0	0	0	0	4	.000	.000
Gonzalez, J	.324	34	11	3	6	5	9	.425	.618
Goodwin, Tom*	.167	18	3	0	1	0	3	.167	.167
Green, Shawn*	.278	18	5	0	2	1	5	.316	.278
Greenwell, M*	.206	34	7	0	3	3	3	.270	.235
Greer, Rusty*	.211	19	4	1	3	2	5	.286	.421
Griffey Jr, K*	.176	34	6	2	2	7	9	.317	.353
Gwynn, Chris*	.333	9	3	0	0	1	0	.400	.444
Hall, Mel*	.200	15	3	0	1	0	1	.200	.267
Hamelin, Bob*	.143	7	1	0	0	1	3	.250	.143
Hamilton, D*	.265	34	9	0	4	2	6	.306	.324
Hammonds, J	.300	10	3	0	3	2	2	.417	.400
Haselman, B	.133	15	2	2	3	0	2	.133	.533
Hayes, C	.571	7	4	0	1	0	1	.571	.571
Henderson, R	.240	25	6	1	2	11	5	.459	.400
Higginson, B*	.200	5	1	0	0	3	0	.500	.200
Hoiles, Chris	.130	23	3	0	1	3	5	.231	.130
Hollins, Dave#	.333	6	2	0	1	1	1	.429	.333
Howard, Dave#	.267	15	4	0	1	0	3	.267	.467
Howell, Jack*	.200	5	1	1	1	0	1	.200	.800
Hulse, David*	.458	24	11	1	2	1	2	.480	.667
Huson, Jeff*	.000	10	0	0	1	4	1	.267	.000
Incaviglia, P	.429	7	3	0	1	2	1	.556	.429
Jaha, John	.231	26	6	1	5	0	7	.231	.385
Javier, Stan#	.111	9	1	0	0	1	3	.200	.111
Jefferies, G#	.300	10	3	1	4	1	2	.364	.600
Jefferson, R*	.333	6	2	1	1	0	2	.333	.833
Jeter, Derek	.077	13	1	0	2	0	3	.067	.077
Joyner, Wally*	.188	32	6	1	8	2	5	.229	.313
Kelly, Pat	.000	9	0	0	0	0	4	.000	.000

Batter	Avg	AB	H	HR	BI	BB	SO	OBP	Slg
Kelly, R	.353	17	6	0	3	0	3	.353	.471
Kirby, Wayne*	.250	8	2	0	0	0	1	.250	.250
Knoblauch, C	.367	49	18	1	2	5	6	.426	.449
Knorr, Randy	.333	6	2	0	1	0	1	.333	.333
Kreuter, Chad#	.222	9	2	0	0	0	3	.222	.333
Lawton, Matt*	.273	11	3	0	0	1	2	.333	.273
Leius, Scott	.182	11	2	0	0	0	5	.182	.182
Levis, Jesse*	.500	8	4	0	1	0	0	.500	.625
Lewis, Mark	.200	10	2	0	1	0	2	.200	.300
Leyritz, Jim	.200	5	1	1	2	1	0	.333	.800
Listach, Pat#	.222	18	4	0	2	2	7	.300	.222
Livingstone*	.250	12	3	1	5	0	0	.250	.583
Lockhart, K*	.333	18	6	1	1	0	1	.333	.611
Lofton, Kenny*	.361	36	13	2	5	0	8	.351	.583
Macfarlane, J	.321	28	9	1	6	5	2	.457	.536
Martinez, E	.139	36	5	0	0	7	2	.279	.194
Martinez, S*	.167	6	1	0	1	0	1	.167	.167
Martinez, T*	.304	46	14	5	9	6	3	.385	.674
Mayne, Brent*	.429	14	6	1	3	0	2	.429	.714
McCarty, Dave	.200	5	1	0	0	0	1	.200	.200
McGee, Willie#	.182	11	2	0	0	1	2	.250	.182
McGriff, Fred*	.667	6	4	0	1	1	0	.714	.833
McGwire, Mark	.227	22	5	4	6	5	6	.370	.773
McLemore, M#	.346	26	9	0	2	0	4	.346	.385
McRae, Brian#	.343	35	12	0	2	3	3	.395	.514
Meares, Pat	.083	12	1	0	0	0	1	.083	.083
Mieske, Matt	.200	10	2	1	1	0	2	.200	.500
Mitchell, K	.333	6	2	0	0	0	2	.333	.500
Molitor, Paul	.318	44	14	0	2	4	2	.375	.545
Munoz, Pedro	.320	25	8	1	2	2	5	.370	.520
Murray, Eddie#	.138	29	4	1	2	0	6	.133	.241
Myers, Greg*	.300	20	6	1	2	1	1	.333	.500
Naehring, Tim	.333	18	6	1	1	1	6	.368	.556
Newfield, M	.545	11	6	2	4	0	0	.545	1.182
Nilsson, Dave*	.265	34	9	2	5	4	4	.342	.471
Nixon, Otis#	.300	20	6	0	1	4	6	.417	.300
Nunnally, Jon*	.500	4	2	0	0	2	0	.667	.750
O'Brien, C	.000	4	0	0	0	1	2	.200	.000
O'Leary, Troy*	.231	13	3	0	1	0	4	.231	.462
O'Neill, Paul*	.238	21	5	2	2	2	0	.304	.524
Offerman, J#	.000	8	0	0	0	0	1	.000	.000
Olerud, John*	.256	43	11	3	7	4	8	.319	.558
Oliver, Joe	.125	8	1	0	0	0	1	.125	.125
Orsulak, Joe*	.467	15	7	0	2	0	0	.467	.800
Palmeiro, R*	.381	42	16	2	8	6	9	.458	.643
Palmer, Dean	.353	34	12	1	8	1	3	.371	.559
Paquette, C	.143	14	2	0	2	0	4	.143	.143
Peltier, Dan*	.200	5	1	0	1	0	2	.200	.400
Pena, Tony	.242	33	8	0	1	1	5	.265	.273
Perez, Tomas#	.286	7	2	0	0	1	2	.375	.286
Phillips, T#	.167	36	6	0	1	4	13	.244	.194
Plantier, P*	.375	8	3	1	4	1	3	.444	1.000
Polonia, Luis*	.385	39	15	0	3	2	2	.405	.436
Ramirez, M	.375	24	9	2	6	2	4	.423	.667
Reboulet, J	.333	21	7	0	3	0	1	.333	.381
Reed, Jody	.345	29	10	0	1	1	1	.355	.345
Ripken, Billy	.250	8	2	0	0	0	1	.333	.250
Ripken, Cal	.229	35	8	1	3	2	4	.263	.400
Rodriguez, A	.222	9	2	0	0	1	4	.300	.222
Rodriguez, I	.395	38	15	1	3	4	2	.452	.553
Salmon, Tim	.217	23	5	2	4	2	7	.280	.522
Samuel, Juan	.308	13	4	1	1	1	2	.357	.538
Schofield, D	.091	11	1	0	0	1	6	.167	.091
Seitzer, K	.275	40	11	3	8	6	3	.370	.550
Sheffield, G	.400	5	2	1	2	0	0	.400	1.200
Shumpert, T	.167	6	1	1	2	0	1	.167	.667
Sierra, Ruben*	.286	42	12	4	10	3	7	.333	.619
Singleton, C*	.000	6	0	0	0	0	3	.000	.000
Snow, J.T.#	.167	18	3	1	2	2	5	.250	.389
Sojo, Luis	.188	16	3	0	2	2	0	.278	.313
Sorrento, P*	.182	33	6	1	2	1	9	.229	.303
Spiers, Bill*	.238	21	5	1	2	1	2	.273	.381
Sprague, Ed	.188	32	6	0	1	2	6	.257	.188
Stahoviak, S*	.308	13	4	0	0	0	2	.308	.385
Stairs, Matt*	.250	4	1	0	0	1	0	.400	.250
Stankiewicz	.333	9	3	0	0	0	0	.333	.333
Stanley, Mike	.286	6	1	0	2	1	2	.250	.167
Steinbach, T	.250	40	10	2	9	2	9	.286	.425
Stevens, Lee*	.136	22	3	0	2	1	7	.208	.227
Stillwell, K#	.333	6	2	1	1	1	0	.429	.833
Strange, Doug#	.050	20	1	0	0	0	2	.050	.050
Strawberry, D*	.200	5	1	0	0	1	2	.333	.200
Surhoff, B.J.*	.316	38	12	0	1	5	6	.395	.447
Sveum, Dale*	.000	4	0	0	0	1	4	.200	.000
Tartabull, D	.273	22	6	1	4	1	7	.304	.455
Tettleton, M#	.222	36	8	2	3	7	14	.349	.444
Thome, Jim*	.333	27	9	2	4	7	6	.471	.630
Tomberlin, A*	.167	6	1	0	0	0	3	.167	.167
Trammell, A	.400	10	4	0	0	3	0	.538	.400
Tucker, M*	.286	7	2	0	0	1	2	.375	.286
Valentin, Jhn	.286	14	4	1	1	2	2	.375	.643

61

Alex Fernandez, White Sox — RHP

Batter	Avg	AB	H	HR	BI	BB	SO	OBP	Slg
Valentin, Jse#	.357	14	5	1	2	1	5	.400	.714
Valle, Dave	.188	16	3	0	2	3	4	.316	.250
Vaughn, Greg	.167	36	6	1	5	0	12	.189	.361
Vaughn, Mo*	.333	27	9	0	3	4	7	.406	.370
Velarde, R	.320	25	8	0	1	2	6	.357	.400
Vina, F*	.238	21	5	0	2	0	2	.238	.286
Vitiello, Joe	.100	10	1	0	0	0	4	.100	.200
Vizquel, Omar#	.267	45	12	0	1	4	4	.327	.267
Voigt, Jack	.000	4	0	0	0	2	1	.333	.000
Walbeck, Matt#	.091	11	1	0	0	2	0	.231	.091
Ward, Turner*	.154	13	2	0	2	5	2	.389	.308
Webster, L	.000	5	0	0	0	0	1	.000	.000
Weiss, Walt#	.167	12	2	0	1	1	1	.231	.167
White, Devon#	.139	36	5	0	0	4	11	.244	.167
Whiten, Mark*	.100	10	1	0	0	0	5	.100	.100
Williams, Bern	.345	29	10	2	3	2	2	.387	.724
Williams, Ger	.000	7	0	0	1	1	0	.111	.000
Wilson, Dan	.316	19	6	0	5	0	6	.316	.368
Young, Ernie	.000	4	0	0	0	1	2	.000	.000

Osvaldo Fernandez, Giants — RHP

Batter	Avg	AB	H	HR	BI	BB	SO	OBP	Slg
Abbott, Kurt	.222	9	2	0	0	0	2	.222	.333
Alfonzo, E	.000	5	0	0	0	0	2	.000	.000
Alicea, Luis#	.500	6	3	1	3	1	1	.571	1.167
Bagwell, Jeff	.833	6	5	1	4	0	1	.833	1.667
Bell, Derek	.250	4	1	0	1	1	2	.500	.250
Benjamin, M	.200	5	1	0	0	0	2	.200	.400
Bichette, D	.286	7	2	0	0	0	1	.286	.571
Biggio, Craig	.400	5	2	0	2	1	0	.500	.800
Blowers, Mike	.250	4	1	0	1	1	2	.400	.250
Boone, Bret	.400	5	2	0	0	1	1	.500	.800
Burks, Ellis	.143	7	1	0	0	0	2	.143	.143
Caminiti, Ken#	.250	8	2	1	1	0	1	.250	.625
Colbrunn, G	.286	7	2	0	1	0	0	.333	.286
Conine, Jeff	.111	9	1	0	0	0	2	.111	.111
Davis, Eric	.286	7	2	0	0	0	3	.286	.286
DeShields, D*	.000	6	0	0	0	1	3	.143	.000
Espinoza, A	.200	5	1	0	0	0	0	.200	.200
Finley, Steve*	.200	5	1	0	0	3	0	.500	.200
Flaherty, J	.333	6	2	0	1	0	1	.333	.500
Fletcher, D*	.333	6	2	0	0	0	1	.333	.667
Gaetti, Gary	.571	7	4	0	0	0	1	.571	.571
Gagne, Greg	.500	4	2	1	2	0	0	.400	1.250
Galarraga, A	.167	6	1	0	0	0	1	.167	.167
Gant, Ron	.000	6	0	0	0	2	2	.000	.000
Gilkey, B	.500	6	3	0	0	0	1	.500	.667
Gomez, Chris	.286	7	2	0	0	1	0	.375	.286
Gomez, Leo	.200	5	1	0	0	1	0	.200	.200
Gonzalez, L*	.400	5	2	0	3	1	0	.500	.600
Grace, Mark*	.571	7	4	0	2	0	0	.571	1.000
Greene, W*	.400	5	2	1	3	0	1	.400	1.000
Grudzielanek	.182	11	2	0	2	0	1	.182	.273
Henderson, R	.200	5	1	1	3	0	0	.200	.800
Hollandsworth*	.250	4	1	0	1	1	0	.400	.250
Hundley, Todd#	.200	5	1	1	2	1	2	.333	.800
Incaviglia, P	.500	6	3	1	3	0	0	.571	1.000
Johnson, Char	.250	8	2	0	0	1	3	.333	.375
Johnson, L*	.600	5	3	0	2	1	0	.667	.800
Jordan, Kevin	.143	7	1	0	2	0	0	.143	.286
Karros, Eric	.250	4	1	0	1	1	2	.400	.250
Lankford, Ray*	.444	9	4	0	0	2	0	.545	.667
Lansing, Mike	.111	9	1	0	0	1	2	.200	.111
Mabry, John*	.400	10	4	0	3	0	0	.400	.400
McGee, Willie*	.286	7	2	1	2	0	1	.286	.714
Mondesi, Raul	.400	5	2	0	0	0	0	.400	.400
Morandini, M*	.286	7	2	0	0	0	0	.286	.429
Morris, Hal*	.167	6	1	0	0	0	2	.167	.167
Obando, S	.500	4	2	0	0	1	0	.600	.500
Orsulak, Joe*	.500	4	2	0	0	1	0	.500	.500
Pagnozzi, Tom	.625	8	5	0	2	1	1	.667	.750
Pendleton, T#	.125	8	1	0	0	0	0	.222	.125
Piazza, Mike	.571	7	4	1	2	0	1	.571	1.000
Reed, Jeff*	.500	6	3	0	0	0	1	.500	.667
Reed, Jody	.500	6	2	0	0	0	0	.400	.400
Rodriguez, H*	.400	10	4	2	3	0	5	.400	1.100
Sanchez, Rey	.400	5	2	0	0	0	1	.400	.400
Santangelo, F#	.500	6	3	1	3	0	1	.571	1.000
Santiago, B	.250	4	1	0	0	1	1	.400	.250
Segui, David#	.333	6	2	0	0	0	0	.500	.333
Servais, A	.500	4	2	0	1	0	0	.500	.500
Sheffield, G	.500	6	3	2	3	4	1	.700	1.500
Silvestri, D	.333	6	2	0	1	0	1	.333	.333
Smith, Ozzie#	.500	8	2	0	1	2	0	.455	.250
Sosa, Sammy	.000	6	0	0	0	0	2	.000	.000
Sweeney, Mark*	.250	4	1	0	0	2	1	.500	.250
VanderWal, J*	.400	5	2	0	1	1	1	.571	.400
Weiss, Walt	.600	5	3	0	1	1	0	.667	.600
White, Devon#	.000	8	0	0	0	2	0	.000	.000
Young, Eric	.429	7	3	0	1	0	0	.500	.857
Zeile, Todd	.200	5	1	0	0	1	0	.333	.200

Sid Fernandez, Phillies — LHP

Batter	Avg	AB	H	HR	BI	BB	SO	OBP	Slg
Alicea, Luis#	.091	11	1	0	1	1	3	.154	.182
Alomar, R#	.200	25	5	2	3	2	7	.259	.520
Alou, Moises	.188	16	3	1	3	0	4	.188	.375
Amaral, Rich	.286	7	2	0	0	2	1	.444	.429
Amaro, Ruben*	.400	10	4	0	0	3	0	.538	.500
Andrews, S	.333	6	2	0	0	0	3	.333	.333
Anthony, Eric*	.100	10	1	1	1	1	5	.182	.400
Bagwell, Jeff	.200	20	4	1	5	2	2	.261	.450
Bell, David	.250	4	1	0	0	1	3	.400	.250
Bell, Derek	.143	7	1	0	1	0	2	.143	.286
Bell, Jay	.300	10	3	1	4	0	2	.273	.600
Belliard, R	.139	36	5	0	0	4	6	.225	.167
Berroa, G	.200	25	5	0	0	2	8	.259	.200
Berry, Sean	.308	13	4	0	0	3	4	.438	.385
Bichette, D	.000	7	0	0	0	1	0	.125	.000
Biggio, Craig	.167	12	2	0	0	4	5	.375	.167
Blauser, Jeff	.179	28	5	2	2	5	7	.324	.429
Blowers, Mike	.222	18	4	1	2	4	6	.391	.556
Bonds, Barry*	.364	11	4	1	4	1	3	.417	.636
Bonilla, B#	.261	69	18	1	8	10	14	.363	.362
Borders, Pat	.289	45	13	3	5	6	5	.373	.556
Bordick, Mike	.273	11	3	0	1	0	2	.273	.273
Brosius, S	.286	7	2	2	2	2	0	.444	1.143
Buhner, Jay	.375	8	3	1	2	0	2	.375	.750
Burks, Ellis	.250	4	1	0	1	2	1	.500	.500
Butler, Brett*	.375	8	3	1	2	0	0	.375	.875
Caminiti, Ken#	.233	30	7	0	1	5	7	.343	.267
Candaele, C#	.208	24	5	1	4	0	3	.208	.458
Cangelosi, J#	.111	18	2	1	3	1	4	.143	.278
Carr, Chuck	.071	14	1	0	0	1	1	.188	.071
Carreon, Mark	.250	4	1	0	0	1	0	.400	.500
Carter, Joe	.143	7	1	0	0	0	1	.143	.143
Castilla, V	.364	11	4	2	2	2	4	.462	.909
Cedeno, A	.125	8	1	0	1	0	1	.125	.250
Cianfrocco, A	.167	6	1	0	0	1	2	.286	.333
Clark, Phil	.200	5	1	0	0	0	1	.333	.200
Clark, Will*	.303	33	10	2	6	0	6	.294	.545
Clayton, R	.211	19	4	0	3	2	8	.286	.316
Coleman, V#	.186	43	8	2	5	5	16	.286	.419
Conine, Jeff	.200	5	1	0	0	0	0	.200	.400
Cora, Joey#	.100	10	1	0	0	1	2	.182	.100
Cordero, Wil	.286	7	2	1	2	0	0	.286	.857
Curtis, Chad	.286	7	2	1	1	0	0	.286	.714
Dascenzo, D#	.188	16	3	0	1	2	0	.278	.313
Daulton, D*	.100	20	2	0	2	3	4	.217	.150
Davis, Chili#	.273	11	3	1	1	2	5	.385	.545
Davis, Eric	.148	27	4	0	3	4	6	.258	.259
Dawson, Andre	.214	56	12	4	11	1	13	.237	.500
DeShields, D*	.333	21	7	0	5	4	9	.440	.476
DiSarcina, G	.167	6	1	0	0	0	0	.167	.167
Duncan, M	.405	42	17	0	5	3	5	.447	.643
Dunston, S	.229	48	11	1	6	3	10	.275	.458
Dykstra, L*	.296	27	8	0	2	6	4	.424	.407
Easley, D	.000	6	0	0	0	1	1	.143	.000
Fermin, Felix	.400	5	2	0	0	0	0	.400	.400
Finley, Steve*	.188	16	3	0	0	4	3	.350	.250
Fonville, C	.200	5	1	0	0	0	1	.200	.200
Franco, Julio	.167	6	1	0	0	1	1	.286	.333
Gaetti, Gary	.143	7	1	0	0	1	3	.250	.143
Galarraga, A	.214	56	12	4	12	1	21	.224	.464
Gallego, Mike	.500	4	2	0	1	1	1	.600	1.000
Gant, Ron	.091	22	2	0	2	6	7	.276	.091
Garcia, C	.400	5	2	1	0	1	0	.400	1.000
Gilkey, B	.273	11	3	0	0	0	3	.273	.364
Girardi, Joe	.211	19	4	1	2	0	2	.211	.526
Gonzalez, L*	.182	11	2	0	0	0	2	.182	.364
Grace, Mark*	.296	27	8	0	2	6	9	.412	.407
Griffey Jr, K*	.167	6	1	0	1	0	1	.286	.333
Grissom, M	.182	22	4	1	4	4	4	.296	.409
Guillen, O*	.500	6	3	0	0	0	0	.500	.500
Gutierrez, R	.333	9	3	0	0	2	0	.455	.333
Gwynn, Tony*	.309	55	17	1	4	2	2	.345	.400
Haselman, B	.250	4	1	0	0	1	0	.400	.250
Hayes, C	.087	23	2	0	0	2	7	.160	.130
Henderson, R	.167	6	1	0	2	1	3	.286	.167
Hernandez, Ca	.333	9	3	0	0	0	0	.333	.333
Hill, G	.286	7	2	0	0	1	2	.375	.571
Hollins, Dave#	.214	14	3	0	3	6	3	.353	.429
Hudler, Rex	.217	23	5	0	1	1	6	.250	.348
Huff, Michael	.000	4	0	0	0	1	2	.200	.000
Hunter, Brian	.000	4	0	0	0	0	1	.000	.000
Hunter, Bri L	.000	5	0	0	0	1	3	.167	.000
Incaviglia, P	.200	5	1	0	0	0	4	.200	.400
Javier, Stan#	.286	21	6	0	2	0	3	.286	.476
Jones, Chris	.111	9	1	0	0	0	6	.111	.222
Jordan, Brian	.091	11	1	0	0	1	7	.167	.091
Jordan, Ricky	.212	33	7	1	4	1	6	.229	.424
Justice, Dave*	.273	11	3	0	1	1	1	.333	.636
Karkovice, R	.167	6	1	0	0	0	4	.167	.167
Karros, Eric	.300	10	3	1	5	1	2	.364	.600

Sid Fernandez, Phillies — LHP

Batter	Avg	AB	H	HR	BI	BB	SO	OBP	Slg
Kelly, Pat	.500	4	2	0	0	1	2	.600	.750
King, Jeff	.152	33	5	1	1	5	4	.263	.333
Knoblauch, C	.667	9	6	1	1	0	0	.667	1.222
Lankford, Ray*	.167	18	3	0	2	3	6	.273	.278
Lansing, Mike	.400	5	2	0	0	1	1	.500	.400
Larkin, Barry	.286	35	10	0	4	3	1	.350	.514
Lemke, Mark#	.000	6	0	0	0	2	0	.250	.000
Lewis, Darren	.143	7	1	0	0	0	2	.143	.143
Lewis, Mark	.000	6	0	0	0	1	4	.143	.000
Leyritz, Jim	.167	6	1	0	0	2	2	.375	.167
Mabry, John*	.143	7	1	0	0	0	3	.143	.143
Manwaring, K	.125	16	2	0	1	1	9	.176	.188
Martinez, E	.200	5	1	0	0	1	1	.333	.400
McCarty, Dave	.167	6	1	0	0	0	3	.167	.167
McGee, Willie*	.295	61	18	1	7	3	17	.328	.443
McGriff, Fred*	.280	20	4	0	1	1	6	.238	.200
McGwire, Mark	.000	6	0	0	0	1	2	.143	.000
McRae, Brian#	.200	5	1	1	1	1	1	.333	.800
Meares, Pat	.200	5	1	0	0	0	1	.333	.200
Merced, O*	.000	6	0	0	0	0	0	.000	.000
Mitchell, K	.320	25	8	4	5	1	5	.346	.880
Molitor, Paul	.400	5	2	0	0	1	1	.500	.600
Mondesi, Raul	.400	5	2	0	0	0	3	.400	.400
Morandini, M*	.200	10	2	0	0	1	2	.273	.200
Morris, Hal*	.143	7	1	0	0	1	1	.250	.286
Mouton, James	.000	6	0	0	0	0	4	.000	.000
Munoz, Pedro	.375	8	3	1	2	0	2	.375	1.000
Murray, Eddie#	.280	25	7	3	5	3	3	.357	.640
Naehring, Tim	.167	6	1	0	1	0	2	.167	.333
Newfield, M	.000	5	0	0	0	0	3	.000	.000
Nixon, Otis#	.200	25	5	0	0	3	12	.286	.200
O'Neill, Paul*	.000	10	0	0	0	3	5	.231	.000
Offerman, J#	.333	9	3	0	0	3	0	.500	.333
Olerud, John*	.500	4	2	0	0	1	1	.600	.500
Oliver, Joe	.200	15	3	1	3	3	4	.316	.467
Owens, J	.250	4	1	1	1	1	1	.400	1.000
Pagnozzi, Tom	.278	18	5	1	2	4	4	.435	.444
Palmeiro, R*	.375	8	3	0	1	0	2	.375	.625
Pena, G#	.364	11	4	1	1	0	2	.364	.636
Pena, Tony	.209	43	9	1	4	5	5	.292	.302
Pendleton, T#	.270	63	17	0	7	3	5	.299	.349
Piazza, Mike	.500	6	3	2	3	0	3	.500	1.500
Prince, Tom	.300	10	3	0	0	2	2	.417	.500
Raines, Tim#	.289	45	13	4	7	8	5	.400	.600
Reboulet, J	.200	5	1	1	1	0	1	.200	.800
Reed, Jody	.000	5	0	0	0	1	0	.000	.000
Roberts, Bip#	.409	22	9	1	4	2	6	.458	.545
Sabo, Chris	.037	27	1	0	0	2	6	.103	.074
Salmon, Tim	.000	5	0	0	0	1	1	.167	.000
Samuel, Juan	.109	55	6	1	2	5	16	.180	.218
Sanchez, Rey	.333	6	2	0	1	1	0	.429	.667
Sandberg, Ryne	.209	67	14	2	5	9	12	.303	.373
Sanders, R	.000	9	0	0	0	1	5	.100	.000
Santiago, B	.167	36	6	1	3	0	13	.158	.250
Schu, Rick	.211	19	4	0	0	3	5	.318	.316
Segui, David#	.500	6	3	1	1	0	0	.500	1.000
Servais, S	.214	14	3	0	1	1	1	.267	.214
Sheffield, G	.333	12	4	2	5	0	2	.333	.833
Shipley, C	.375	8	3	0	0	0	0	.375	.500
Sierra, Ruben#	.444	9	4	2	4	1	2	.500	1.333
Simms, Mike	.200	5	1	0	0	0	3	.200	.200
Slaught, Don	.286	14	4	0	1	1	1	.333	.286
Smith, Ozzie#	.151	53	8	0	2	5	6	.224	.151
Sosa, Sammy	.200	5	1	0	0	1	1	.333	.400
Sprague, Ed	.250	4	1	1	1	1	0	.400	1.000
Stanley, Mike	.400	5	2	1	4	0	0	.400	1.200
Steinbach, T	.375	8	3	0	1	0	1	.375	.500
Stillwell, K*	.125	8	1	0	0	0	3	.222	.125
Tartabull, D	.571	7	4	0	2	1	1	.625	.857
Thomas, Frank	.400	5	2	2	2	2	1	.571	1.600
Thompson, Mil*	.190	21	4	0	1	0	8	.227	.286
Thompson, Rob	.270	37	10	1	4	2	8	.308	.432
Tinsley, Lee*	.400	5	2	1	2	0	2	.500	1.000
Turner, Chris	.000	5	0	0	0	0	3	.000	.000
Vaughn, Mo*	.333	6	2	1	3	0	2	.333	1.000
Velarde, R	.333	6	2	0	1	0	1	.333	.333
Vizcaino, J#	.143	7	1	0	0	0	1	.143	.143
Walker, Larry*	.375	16	6	2	5	1	7	.474	.750
Wallach, Tim	.176	51	9	0	3	1	5	.200	.216
Walton, J	.111	18	2	0	0	6	3	.385	.111
Wehner, John	.143	7	1	0	0	2	4	.333	.143
Weiss, Walt#	.000	9	0	0	0	1	2	.182	.000
White, R	.200	5	1	1	2	1	2	.333	.800
Whiten, Mark#	.000	6	0	0	0	1	1	.143	.000
Williams, Ber#	.286	7	2	0	1	2	3	.444	.286
Williams, Ger	.400	5	2	0	1	2	0	.571	1.000
Williams, Ma	.161	31	5	1	1	1	11	.188	.290
Young, Eric	.154	13	2	0	1	5	2	.389	.154
Zeile, Todd	.278	18	5	2	5	3	3	.364	.611

Mike Fetters, Brewers — RHP

Batter	Avg	AB	H	HR	BI	BB	SO	OBP	Slg
Alomar, R#	.333	6	2	0	0	1	1	.429	.333
Alomar Jr, S	.167	6	1	0	0	0	3	.167	.167
Anderson, Brd*	.273	11	3	0	2	1	1	.333	.273
Baerga, C#	.222	9	2	0	2	0	0	.200	.333
Baines, H*	.364	11	4	1	2	0	1	.364	.636
Becker, Rich*	.200	5	1	0	0	0	1	.200	.200
Belle, Albert	.111	9	1	0	0	3	6	.333	.222
Blowers, Mike	.333	3	1	0	0	2	0	.600	.333
Boggs, Wade*	.273	11	3	0	0	3	3	.429	.273
Borders, Pat	.167	12	2	0	1	0	3	.167	.250
Buhner, Jay	.250	12	3	1	3	1	5	.308	.500
Burks, Ellis	.200	5	1	0	0	0	1	.200	.200
Canseco, Jose	.429	7	3	1	5	1	2	.444	.857
Carter, Joe	.300	10	3	1	5	0	1	.300	.600
Cora, Joey#	.333	6	2	0	0	0	1	.333	.667
Curtis, Chad	.250	8	2	0	0	3	1	.455	.250
Davis, Chili*	.143	7	1	0	0	3	2	.400	.143
Deer, Rob	.222	9	2	0	1	1	3	.300	.222
Devereaux, M	.000	9	0	0	0	0	1	.000	.000
DiSarcina, G	.333	6	2	0	2	0	2	.333	.500
Espinoza, A	.500	6	3	0	3	1	0	.500	.667
Fermin, Felix	.143	7	1	0	0	0	1	.250	.143
Fielder, C	.214	14	3	1	3	0	1	.214	.429
Franco, Julio	.357	14	5	0	2	3	4	.471	.357
Fryman, T	.417	12	5	0	2	0	1	.417	.417
Gagne, Greg	.500	6	3	0	0	0	2	.500	.500
Gallego, Mike	.111	9	1	0	0	0	2	.111	.111
Gonzalez, J	.375	8	3	0	0	2	3	.500	.500
Grebeck, C	.167	6	1	0	3	0	1	.143	.333
Greenwell, M*	.167	6	1	0	0	0	1	.286	.167
Griffey Jr, K*	.250	8	2	0	1	2	1	.455	.250
Guillen, O*	.333	6	2	0	2	0	1	.286	.333
Hale, Chip*	.125	8	1	0	1	2	0	.300	.125
Henderson, R	.333	9	3	0	0	0	2	.333	.333
Hoiles, Chris	.500	4	2	0	0	2	1	.667	.500
Howard, Dave*	.167	6	1	0	0	1	2	.286	.167
Hulse, David*	.000	4	0	0	1	0	0	.000	.000
Huson, Jeff*	.333	6	2	0	0	1	1	.429	.333
Johnson, L*	.333	6	2	0	0	3	1	.556	.500
Joyner, Wally*	.250	4	1	0	1	1	0	.400	.250
Karkovice, R	.000	6	0	0	0	0	2	.143	.000
Kelly, Pat	.200	5	1	1	2	1	0	.429	.800
Kelly, R	.000	5	0	0	0	0	1	.000	.000
Knoblauch, C	.273	11	3	0	2	1	4	.333	.364
Leius, Scott	.200	5	1	0	0	1	1	.333	.400
Macfarlane, M	.000	5	0	0	0	0	1	.167	.000
Martinez, E	.125	8	1	0	1	3	0	.417	.125
McGriff, Fred*	.200	5	1	1	1	1	2	.333	.800
McGwire, Mark	.308	13	4	0	1	2	3	.400	.385
McLemore, M#	.300	10	3	0	1	1	0	.364	.300
McRae, Brian#	.286	7	2	0	0	0	1	.286	.286
Molitor, Paul	.429	7	3	0	0	3	3	.636	.571
Munoz, Pedro	.000	4	0	0	2	0	1	.000	.000
Myers, Greg*	.000	5	0	0	0	0	1	.000	.000
Newson, W*	.000	3	0	0	0	2	1	.400	.000
Nixon, Otis#	.500	4	2	0	0	1	0	.600	.750
O'Neill, Paul*	.429	7	3	0	1	0	2	.429	.429
Olerud, John*	.231	13	3	0	3	2	1	.333	.308
Palmeiro, R*	.444	9	4	1	4	3	0	.615	1.000
Palmer, Dean	.333	9	3	2	9	0	1	.400	1.111
Phillips, T#	.571	7	4	0	1	1	1	.625	.571
Plantier, P*	.400	5	2	0	1	0	1	.400	.400
Raines, Tim*	.167	6	1	0	0	1	1	.286	.167
Reed, Jody	.200	5	1	0	2	0	0	.429	.200
Ripken, Cal	.167	6	1	0	3	1	1	.444	.333
Rodriguez, I	.333	9	3	0	1	1	2	.417	.333
Salmon, Tim	.167	6	1	0	1	0	2	.143	.167
Sierra, Ruben#	.333	15	5	1	5	1	0	.353	.533
Sorrento, P	.125	8	1	0	1	2	2	.300	.125
Spiers, Bill*	.500	4	2	0	3	1	1	.600	.500
Sprague, Ed	.333	9	3	0	1	2	1	.455	.556
Stanley, Mike	.000	9	0	0	0	0	3	.000	.000
Steinbach, T	.273	11	3	0	1	1	0	.273	.364
Stillwell, K#	.375	8	3	0	1	1	0	.444	.500
Surhoff, B.J.*	.143	7	1	0	0	1	0	.250	.143
Tartabull, D	.455	11	5	1	2	5	5	.538	.636
Tettleton, M#	.357	14	5	0	2	2	2	.438	.571
Thomas, Frank	.300	10	3	0	2	0	0	.417	.300
Trammell, A	.222	9	2	0	0	0	2	.222	.222
Valentin, Jhn	.143	7	1	0	0	1	2	.250	.143
Valle, Dave	.143	7	1	0	2	0	2	.143	.143
Vaughn, Mo*	.250	8	2	0	1	1	1	.333	.250
Velarde, R	.700	10	7	1	2	0	1	.750	1.000
Ventura, R*	.100	10	1	0	0	3	1	.308	.200
Vizquel, Omar#	.000	5	0	0	0	2	2	.286	.000
Walbeck, Matt#	.286	7	2	0	1	0	4	.286	.429
Weiss, Walt*	.429	7	3	0	0	1	1	.429	.429
White, Devon#	.125	8	1	0	1	1	2	.222	.125
Whiten, Mark#	.143	7	1	0	0	0	0	.143	.286
Williams, Ber#	.417	12	5	0	2	1	2	.429	.500

Batter	Avg	AB	H	HR	BI	BB	SO	OBP	Slg
Aldrete, Mike*	.000	6	0	0	0	0	3	.000	.000
Alicea, Luis#	.400	5	2	0	1	0	0	.400	.600
Alomar, R#	.258	31	8	2	6	2	4	.303	.548
Alomar Jr, S	.321	28	9	0	4	1	5	.345	.357
Amaral, Rich	.267	30	8	1	1	3	8	.333	.433
Anderson, Brd*	.343	35	12	1	2	7	8	.477	.457
Baerga, C#	.362	47	17	1	8	2	2	.404	.468
Baines, H*	.297	37	11	1	5	2	6	.333	.378
Bautista, D	.200	10	2	0	0	1	3	.273	.200
Becker, Rich*	.429	14	6	0	3	0	2	.429	.500
Belle, Albert	.295	44	13	3	14	8	6	.396	.545
Beltre, E	.250	4	1	0	0	2	0	.500	.250
Berroa, J	.308	26	8	1	4	1	7	.321	.500
Bichette, D	.222	9	2	0	0	1	4	.300	.222
Blowers, Mike	.320	25	8	1	2	2	7	.370	.480
Boggs, Wade*	.222	36	8	0	2	5	3	.317	.250
Bonilla, B#	.429	7	3	0	0	1	1	.500	.429
Boone, Bret	.200	5	1	0	0	2	2	.429	.200
Borders, Pat	.222	36	8	1	3	1	7	.282	.361
Bordick, Mike	.143	42	6	0	4	3	3	.213	.143
Bragg, Darren*	.000	7	0	0	0	2	2	.222	.000
Brosius, S	.160	25	4	1	2	5	8	.300	.280
Brumfield, J	.400	5	2	1	1	1	0	.571	1.200
Buford, Damon	.375	8	3	2	3	1	3	.444	1.125
Buhner, Jay	.255	51	13	3	7	5	13	.316	.490
Burks, Ellis	.185	27	5	0	1	3	5	.267	.296
Butler, Brett*	.000	3	0	0	0	3	1	.500	.000
Canseco, Jose	.289	38	11	0	2	14	15	.491	.395
Carreon, Mark	.222	9	2	1	1	1	3	.300	.556
Carter, Joe	.255	51	13	2	4	5	9	.321	.412
Cedeno, D#	.286	7	2	0	0	0	3	.286	.286
Cirillo, Jeff	.429	14	6	1	3	2	3	.500	.786
Clark, Will*	.375	16	6	0	5	2	4	.444	.500
Cole, Alex*	.429	7	3	0	0	2	1	.556	.429
Coleman, V#	.154	13	2	0	0	0	4	.154	.154
Coomer, Ron	.286	14	4	0	0	0	2	.286	.286
Cora, Joey#	.313	16	5	0	2	2	2	.389	.375
Cordero, Wil	.375	8	3	0	1	0	2	.375	.500
Cordova, M	.150	20	3	1	4	1	3	.261	.300
Curtis, Chad	.267	15	4	0	1	1	3	.294	.400
Cuyler, Milt*	.150	20	3	0	3	2	4	.217	.150
Dascenzo, D#	.167	6	1	0	0	0	2	.167	.167
Davis, Chili*	.125	16	2	2	4	4	5	.300	.500
Davis, Russ	.250	8	2	0	1	1	2	.333	.500
Dawson, Andre	.091	11	1	0	0	0	3	.091	.091
Deer, Rob	.152	33	5	3	5	18	.263	.424
Devereaux, M	.218	55	12	3	7	2	9	.246	.455
Duncan, M	.000	5	0	0	0	1	2	.167	.000
Durant, Mike	.167	6	1	0	0	0	1	.167	.167
Durham, Ray#	.429	14	6	0	1	2	4	.529	.500
Eisenreich, J*	.111	9	1	0	0	2	0	.273	.111
Elster, Kevin	.125	8	1	0	1	1	1	.222	.250
Espinoza, A	.333	12	4	0	0	1	2	.385	.333
Fermin, Felix	.235	34	8	0	0	4	1	.350	.235
Fielder, C	.340	53	18	4	11	14	13	.493	.660
Finley, Steve*	.385	13	5	0	0	0	2	.385	.385
Flaherty, J	.077	13	1	0	1	1	1	.143	.077
Franco, Julio	.372	43	16	1	5	6	9	.449	.488
Frazier, Lou#	.400	5	2	0	1	2	2	.571	.800
Frye, Jeff	.286	14	4	0	1	3	2	.444	.286
Fryman, T	.283	46	13	2	6	14	14	.358	.457
Gaetti, Gary	.132	38	5	0	3	2	7	.171	.184
Gagne, Greg	.269	52	14	2	9	5	8	.339	.500
Gallego, Mike	.243	37	9	4	8	2	2	.282	.595
Gates, Brent#	.333	18	6	0	1	2	2	.400	.333
Gil, Benji	.222	9	2	0	1	2	5	.364	.222
Girardi, Joe	.300	10	3	0	0	0	3	.300	.300
Gomez, Chris	.059	17	1	0	0	2	5	.158	.059
Gomez, Leo	.304	23	7	2	7	2	7	.333	.652
Gonzales, R	.154	13	2	0	0	2	2	.267	.231
Gonzalez, A	.200	10	2	0	1	2	5	.333	.200
Gonzalez, J	.263	38	10	2	10	5	11	.349	.500
Goodwin, Tom*	.200	5	1	0	0	0	0	.200	.200
Grebeck, C	.192	26	5	0	2	2	4	.250	.231
Greenwell, M*	.314	51	16	1	9	0	3	.321	.392
Greer, Rusty*	.286	14	4	0	2	1	5	.313	.286
Griffey Jr, K*	.244	45	11	1	2	3	9	.292	.400
Guillen, O*	.179	28	5	0	1	2	2	.233	.179
Hall, Mel*	.467	15	7	0	1	0	0	.467	.533
Hamelin, Bob*	.000	5	0	0	1	0	0	.167	.000
Hamilton, D	.385	13	5	0	1	1	0	.429	.385
Hammonds, J	.182	11	2	0	0	0	3	.182	.182
Haselman, B	.217	23	5	0	3	0	4	.217	.304
Hayes, C	.091	11	1	1	2	1	2	.167	.364
Henderson, R	.207	58	12	2	6	11	.281	.362
Hiatt, Phil	.200	5	1	0	0	1	3	.333	.400
Higginson, B*	.200	5	1	0	1	0	2	.200	.400
Hill, G	.174	23	4	1	1	1	7	.208	.348
Hocking, D#	.000	5	0	0	1	0	2	.167	.000
Hoiles, Chris	.345	29	10	4	8	4	7	.412	.793
Hollins, Dave#	.333	12	4	0	0	1	2	.385	.333

Batter	Avg	AB	H	HR	BI	BB	SO	OBP	Slg
Howard, Dave#	.167	12	2	0	0	1	6	.231	.167
Huff, Michael	.250	12	3	0	0	6	4	.500	.333
Hulse, David*	.400	5	2	0	0	0	2	.400	.400
Hunter, Brian	.000	6	0	0	0	0	3	.000	.000
Incaviglia, P	.167	24	4	1	1	2	11	.231	.333
Jaha, John	.250	20	5	0	3	6	5	.423	.250
Javier, Stan#	.320	25	8	0	5	4	6	.414	.480
Jefferies, G#	.143	7	1	1	1	1	0	.250	.571
Jefferson, R*	.000	6	0	0	0	0	2	.000	.000
Jeter, Derek	.133	15	2	0	0	1	4	.235	.133
Johnson, L*	.333	33	11	0	3	1	2	.353	.364
Joyner, Wally*	.476	21	10	0	1	3	1	.542	.524
Karkovice, R	.188	32	6	1	6	2	15	.222	.313
Kelly, Pat	.265	34	9	1	4	2	10	.342	.412
Kelly, R	.357	28	10	1	3	2	4	.419	.536
Kent, Jeff	.125	8	1	0	0	1	2	.222	.125
Kingery, Mike*	.143	7	1	0	0	0	0	.143	.143
Knoblauch, C	.333	66	22	0	9	5	7	.375	.409
Kreuter, Chad*	.316	19	6	2	3	2	4	.381	.737
Leius, Scott	.346	26	9	0	2	6	2	.469	.385
Lewis, Darren	.000	6	0	0	1	1	1	.143	.000
Lewis, Mark	.273	33	9	2	2	4	4	.351	.485
Leyritz, Jim	.238	42	10	1	6	4	21	.319	.381
Liriano, N#	.000	6	0	0	0	0	1	.000	.000
Listach, Pat#	.208	24	5	0	1	3	6	.321	.250
Lofton, Kenny*	.448	29	13	0	2	3	2	.500	.517
Macfarlane, M	.234	47	11	0	5	4	8	.283	.298
Manto, Jeff	.100	10	1	0	0	1	2	.250	.100
Martin, N	.429	14	6	0	0	0	0	.429	.429
Martinez, E	.200	50	10	1	4	8	7	.310	.310
Martinez, T*	.308	26	8	1	2	1	8	.333	.538
Matheny, Mike	.300	10	3	0	3	0	2	.273	.400
McCarty, Dave	.111	9	1	0	0	1	1	.273	.111
McGriff, Fred*	.500	6	3	0	0	0	1	.500	.667
McGwire, Mark	.186	43	8	2	7	16	11	.410	.326
McLemore, M#	.267	15	4	0	0	3	3	.389	.400
McRae, Brian#	.342	38	13	2	8	4	5	.405	.526
Meares, Pat	.304	23	7	1	4	1	7	.320	.435
Mieske, Matt	.308	13	4	1	5	2	2	.400	.538
Mitchell, K	.333	6	2	0	0	1	0	.429	.500
Molitor, Paul	.288	59	17	2	6	8	11	.373	.407
Morman, Russ	.400	10	4	0	0	0	2	.400	.700
Mouton, Lyle	.300	10	3	0	0	6	5	.563	.400
Munoz, Pedro	.194	31	6	0	6	2	4	.235	.194
Murray, Eddie*	.286	14	4	0	1	1	1	.333	.286
Naehring, Tim	.348	23	8	2	7	3	2	.423	.696
Nieves, Mel	.000	6	0	0	0	0	3	.000	.000
Nilsson, Dave*	.300	10	3	0	1	0	3	.300	.300
Nixon, Otis#	.435	23	10	0	2	0	5	.435	.435
O'Brien, C	.235	17	4	0	2	1	2	.316	.294
O'Leary, Troy*	.273	11	3	0	2	1	1	.333	.273
O'Neill, Paul*	.182	22	4	2	4	7	9	.379	.455
Olerud, John*	.125	16	2	0	0	2	4	.222	.188
Ortiz, Luis	.400	10	4	1	1	0	2	.400	.900
Palmeiro, R*	.444	36	16	3	4	4	4	.500	.750
Palmer, Dean	.333	30	10	2	4	1	6	.355	.633
Paquette, C	.182	11	2	1	2	2	6	.308	.455
Pena, Tony	.148	27	4	0	2	2	4	.207	.185
Perez, Robert	.200	10	2	0	1	0	2	.200	.200
Perry, H	.333	6	2	0	0	0	1	.333	.667
Phillips, T#	.283	60	17	1	6	12	10	.405	.417
Pirkl, Greg	.300	10	3	0	1	0	3	.300	.400
Pose, Scott*	.200	5	1	0	0	1	0	.200	.200
Raines, Tim#	.244	41	10	0	3	2	8	.289	.341
Ramirez, M	.273	11	3	1	2	5	2	.500	.636
Reboulet, J	.267	30	8	1	1	2	4	.313	.367
Reed, Jody	.185	27	5	0	1	2	6	.241	.222
Ripken, Billy	.323	31	10	0	3	4	4	.400	.355
Ripken, Cal	.288	66	19	3	11	2	6	.304	.470
Rodriguez, Al	.222	9	2	0	0	2	1	.364	.333
Rodriguez, I	.310	29	9	1	2	3	7	.375	.448
Samuel, Juan	.278	18	5	2	8	1	8	.316	.722
Schofield, D	.125	8	1	0	1	1	2	.222	.125
Schu, Rick	.333	6	2	0	0	1	1	.429	.500
Segui, David#	.263	19	5	0	0	7	5	.462	.368
Seitzer, K	.277	65	18	0	7	14	3	.405	.308
Sheffield, G	.333	12	4	0	2	2	0	.429	.667
Shumpert, T	.063	16	1	0	0	1	2	.118	.063
Sierra, Ruben#	.227	75	17	1	10	5	13	.275	.347
Slaught, Don	.375	8	3	0	0	0	1	.375	.375
Snopek, Chris	.286	7	2	0	0	4	3	.545	.286
Sojo, Luis	.125	16	2	0	0	3	2	.263	.125
Sosa, Sammy	.316	19	6	1	2	1	8	.350	.474
Spiers, Bill*	.235	17	4	0	0	1	1	.278	.235
Sprague, Ed	.167	24	4	1	2	2	4	.276	.333
Stankiewicz	.286	7	2	0	1	0	2	.286	.286
Stanley, Mike	.343	70	24	3	14	12	14	.439	.557
Steinbach, T	.371	62	23	5	18	2	13	.400	.661
Stillwell, K#	.200	27	9	6	0	1	4	5	.303	.345
Strange, Doug#	.286	7	2	0	1	0	3	.286	.286
Surhoff, B.J.*	.143	28	4	0	3	3	4	.226	.179

Chuck Finley, Angels — LHP

Batter	Avg	AB	H	HR	BI	BB	SO	OBP	Slg
Sveum, Dale#	.300	20	6	1	5	1	6	.318	.500
Tartabull, D	.219	73	16	5	13	11	23	.321	.452
Tettleton, M#	.196	51	10	3	5	10	18	.333	.451
Thomas, Frank	.277	47	13	1	6	10	9	.404	.447
Thome, Jim*	.333	12	4	0	0	1	5	.385	.333
Trammell, A	.210	62	13	1	5	6	6	.279	.274
Valentin, Jhn	.243	37	9	2	4	6	9	.349	.459
Valentin, Jse#	.273	11	3	0	0	2	4	.385	.273
Valle, Dave	.121	33	4	1	2	8	4	.293	.242
Vaughn, Greg	.189	37	7	2	5	4	12	.268	.405
Vaughn, Mo*	.267	30	8	0	5	8	11	.450	.367
Velarde, R	.256	39	10	0	1	2	10	.293	.333
Ventura, R*	.245	49	12	3	6	5	10	.316	.490
Vitiello, Joe	.000	6	0	0	0	0	0	.000	.000
Vizcaino, J#	.286	7	2	0	0	1	0	.286	.286
Vizquel, Omar#	.161	31	5	0	1	3	6	.235	.226
Voigt, Jack	.176	17	3	0	0	2	3	.263	.176
Walbeck, Matt#	.500	14	7	0	0	2	2	.563	.500
Ward, Turner#	.000	9	0	0	0	1	4	.100	.000
Webster, L	.500	6	3	0	0	0	1	.500	.500
Weiss, Walt	.316	19	6	0	3	1	0	.333	.368
White, Devon#	.212	33	7	2	3	1	4	.235	.394
Whiten, Mark#	.421	19	8	0	1	2	6	.476	.684
Williams, Ber#	.362	47	17	2	7	6	10	.434	.638
Williams, E	.125	8	1	0	1	2	2	.300	.125
Williams, Ger	.211	19	4	0	0	1	6	.250	.263
Wilson, Dan	.143	14	2	0	0	0	3	.143	.214
Worthington	.222	18	4	0	1	4	4	.364	.278
Young, Ernie	.500	6	3	2	2	0	1	.500	1.500

Huck Flener, Blue Jays — LHP

Batter	Avg	AB	H	HR	BI	BB	SO	OBP	Slg
Anderson, Brd*	.125	8	1	0	0	0	1	.125	.125
Bonilla, B#	.000	6	0	0	0	0	2	.000	.000
Durham, Ray#	.750	4	3	0	0	1	1	.800	1.000
Hamilton, D*	.000	5	0	0	0	1	1	.167	.000
McLemore, M#	.333	3	1	0	0	2	0	.600	.333
Murray, Eddie#	.000	5	0	0	0	0	0	.000	.000
Palmeiro, R*	.167	6	1	1	2	0	1	.167	.667
Phillips, T#	.250	4	1	0	0	1	3	.400	.250
Ripken, Cal	.200	10	2	0	0	0	0	.200	.300
Surhoff, B.J.*	.250	4	1	0	0	1	0	.400	.250
Tartabull, D	1.000	2	2	1	4	4	0	1.000	3.000
Thomas, Frank	.750	4	3	0	2	1	0	.800	1.000
Ventura, R*	.000	5	0	0	0	0	0	.000	.000

Bryce Florie, Brewers — RHP

Batter	Avg	AB	H	HR	BI	BB	SO	OBP	Slg
Bell, Derek	.333	3	1	0	0	2	2	.600	.667
Bell, Jay	.400	5	2	0	0	1	3	.500	.400
Bichette, D	.000	7	0	0	0	0	1	.000	.000
Boone, Bret	.600	5	3	0	3	0	0	.600	.600
Castilla, V	.000	5	0	0	0	0	1	.000	.000
Clayton, R	.000	5	0	0	0	0	4	.000	.000
Conine, Jeff	.333	3	1	0	2	2	0	.600	.333
DeShields, D*	.333	3	1	0	0	2	0	.600	.667
Galarraga, A	.000	4	0	0	0	1	3	.333	.000
Grissom, M	.333	3	1	0	0	2	0	.600	.333
Jones, C#	.400	5	2	1	1	1	1	.500	1.000
Karros, Eric	.250	4	1	0	0	1	2	.500	.250
Klesko, Ryan*	.000	5	0	0	0	0	2	.000	.000
Martin, Al*	.000	4	0	0	0	1	0	.200	.000
McGriff, Fred*	.200	5	1	0	0	0	1	.200	.400
Miller, Orl	.200	5	1	0	0	1	2	.333	.200
Mondesi, Raul	.429	7	3	0	2	0	1	.429	.714
Orsulak, Joe*	.000	4	0	0	0	1	2	.200	.000
Piazza, Mike	.333	6	2	1	1	2	1	.500	.833
Reed, Jeff*	.000	4	0	0	0	1	2	.200	.000
Sosa, Sammy	.200	5	1	0	0	0	2	.200	.200
Vizcaino, J	.600	5	3	0	0	0	1	.600	.600
Wallach, Tim	.167	6	1	0	0	0	3	.167	.167
Weiss, Walt#	.400	5	2	0	0	1	0	.500	.400

Tony Fossas, Cardinals — LHP

Batter	Avg	AB	H	HR	BI	BB	SO	OBP	Slg
Anderson, Brd*	.444	9	4	0	0	0	4	.500	.556
Baerga, C#	.250	4	1	0	0	1	0	.400	.250
Baines, H*	.200	5	1	0	1	2	1	.429	.200
Bichette, D	.333	3	1	0	2	2	0	.600	.333
Boggs, Wade*	.200	15	3	0	1	2	3	.294	.200
Bonds, Barry*	.182	11	2	1	2	1	4	.250	.455
Borders, Pat	.500	6	3	0	2	1	0	.571	.500
Brogna, Rico*	.000	4	0	0	1	0	3	.000	.000
Buhner, Jay	.143	7	1	0	0	1	0	.250	.286
Canseco, Jose	.000	2	0	0	0	3	1	.600	.000
Clark, Dave*	.200	5	1	0	1	1	3	.333	.200
Cora, Joey#	.286	7	2	0	0	0	0	.286	.429
Cuyler, Milt#	.000	5	0	0	0	0	0	.000	.000
Davis, Chili#	.500	8	4	0	3	1	1	.556	.750
Dykstra, L*	.500	4	2	0	0	1	0	.600	.500
Eisenreich, J*	.308	13	4	0	2	0	3	.308	.308

Tony Fossas, Cardinals — LHP

Batter	Avg	AB	H	HR	BI	BB	SO	OBP	Slg
Espinoza, A	.200	5	1	0	0	0	0	.200	.200
Fielder, C	.667	3	2	1	3	4	0	.857	1.667
Finley, Steve*	.300	10	3	1	1	0	1	.300	.600
Gaetti, Gary	.800	5	4	1	4	0	0	.800	1.800
Gonzalez, J	.500	6	3	1	2	0	2	.500	1.167
Grace, Mark*	.333	6	2	0	3	0	1	.333	.500
Greenwell, M*	.300	10	3	0	1	0	3	.300	.300
Griffey Jr, K*	.130	23	3	1	3	1	7	.167	.261
Guillen, O*	.267	15	4	0	2	1	6	.313	.267
Gwynn, Tony	.167	6	1	1	3	0	1	.167	.667
Hall, Mel*	.333	9	3	2	4	0	0	.333	1.000
Hamilton, D*	.333	6	2	0	1	0	1	.333	.333
Henderson, R	.400	5	2	0	0	0	1	.400	.800
Hill, G	.286	7	2	0	2	0	0	.286	.286
Huff, Michael	.500	4	2	0	2	1	1	.600	.500
Incaviglia, P	.000	6	0	0	0	0	1	.000	.000
Javier, Stan#	.000	3	0	0	0	2	0	.400	.000
Johnson, L*	.167	12	2	0	1	0	1	.167	.167
Jones, C#	.429	7	3	0	0	0	3	.429	.571
Joyner, Wally*	.133	15	2	1	6	0	7	.133	.333
Justice, Dave*	.222	9	2	0	0	1	3	.300	.222
King, Jeff	.600	5	3	1	1	0	0	.600	1.200
Klesko, Ryan*	.100	10	1	0	1	1	4	.182	.200
Liriano, N#	.500	6	3	0	1	0	0	.500	.667
Martinez, T*	.286	7	2	0	3	0	2	.286	.571
McGriff, Fred*	.150	20	3	0	1	1	6	.190	.200
Merced, O*	.429	7	3	0	0	0	2	.429	.571
Morandini, M*	.000	6	0	0	0	1	2	.143	.000
Myers, Greg*	.000	4	0	0	0	0	3	.000	.000
Nilsson, Dave*	.000	5	0	0	0	0	3	.000	.000
O'Neill, Paul*	.000	8	0	0	0	1	3	.111	.000
Olerud, John*	.167	6	1	0	3	1	0	.333	.333
Orsulak, Joe*	.125	8	1	0	2	0	0	.125	.125
Palmeiro, R*	.286	14	4	0	1	2	7	.375	.286
Phillips, T#	.214	14	3	0	1	0	3	.214	.286
Polonia, Luis*	.000	9	0	0	0	0	5	.000	.000
Raines, Tim#	.375	8	3	0	1	0	0	.375	.375
Ripken, Cal	.167	6	1	0	1	0	1	.167	.167
Seitzer, K	.125	8	1	0	1	2	0	.300	.125
Sierra, Ruben#	.286	7	2	0	3	0	1	.286	.429
Sorrento, P*	.000	4	0	0	0	0	1	.000	.000
Stanley, Mike	.250	4	1	0	1	1	2	.400	.250
Surhoff, B.J.*	.375	8	3	0	3	0	1	.375	.500
Tartabull, D	.400	5	2	0	0	1	1	.500	.600
Tettleton, M#	.333	12	4	2	5	2	3	.429	.917
Trammell, A	.333	6	2	1	4	5	0	.636	.833
Valle, Dave	.200	5	1	0	2	0	0	.200	.400
Ventura, R*	.500	8	4	1	2	4	2	.667	.875
Vizquel, Omar#	.000	7	0	0	2	1	0	.125	.000
Weiss, Walt#	.833	6	5	0	2	0	0	.833	.833
White, Devon#	.429	7	3	1	1	0	2	.429	1.000
Whiten, Mark#	.000	5	0	0	0	1	2	.167	.000

Kevin Foster, Cubs — RHP

Batter	Avg	AB	H	HR	BI	BB	SO	OBP	Slg
Abbott, Kurt	.000	6	0	0	0	1	4	.143	.000
Alou, Moises	.000	11	0	0	0	1	0	.083	.000
Arias, Alex	.300	10	3	1	2	1	2	.417	.800
Ausmus, Brad	.200	10	2	0	1	2	2	.333	.300
Bagwell, Jeff	.286	7	2	0	1	2	3	.400	.429
Bates, Jason#	.500	4	2	1	1	3	1	.714	1.250
Batiste, Kim	.000	5	0	0	0	0	2	.000	.000
Bell, Derek	.333	9	3	0	0	0	2	.333	.333
Bell, Jay	.500	12	6	1	5	3	2	.625	.750
Benard, M*	.200	5	1	0	0	1	3	.333	.400
Benjamin, M	.333	6	2	0	1	0	3	.333	.333
Bichette, D	.250	12	3	0	1	1	2	.308	.500
Biggio, Craig	.375	8	3	0		3	4	.545	.625
Blowers, Mike	.333	3	1	0	3	1	1	.400	.667
Bonds, Barry*	.176	17	3	1	2	1	4	.222	.353
Boone, Bret	.333	12	4	4	5	1	3	.385	1.333
Bradshaw, T*	.000	7	0	0	0	0	3	.000	.000
Branson, Jeff*	.111	9	1	0	0	1	5	.200	.111
Brogna, Rico*	.333	6	2	1	3	0	1	.333	.833
Brumfield, J	.444	9	4	0	0	1	1	.545	.778
Butler, Brett*	.400	10	4	0	0	3	0	.538	.400
Caminiti, Ken#	.444	18	8	1	2	1	5	.474	.778
Carreon, Mark	.250	12	3	1	1	0	0	.250	.583
Castilla, V	.182	11	2	0	2	0	2	.182	.364
Castillo, J	.400	5	2	0	0	0	2	.400	.400
Cedeno, A	.125	8	1	0	0	0	1	.222	.125
Cianfrocco, A	.167	6	1	0	2	1	1	.286	.167
Clark, Dave*	.333	12	4	1	3	1	1	.385	.583
Clayton, R	.300	10	3	0	2	1	2	.364	.300
Colbrunn, M	.333	12	4	1	5	2	1	.467	.667
Conine, Jeff	.250	16	4	0	5	1	4	.294	.313
Cordero, Wil	.429	7	3	0	0	1	0	.500	.429
Cummings, M*	.091	11	1	0	0	0	2	.091	.091
Daulton, D*	.200	5	1	0	0	0	0	.200	.200
Dawson, Andre	.250	8	2	0	1	1	0	.333	.375
Decker, Steve	.250	8	2	1	2	0	1	.250	.625

Kevin Foster, Cubs — RHP

Batter	Avg	AB	H	HR	BI	BB	SO	OBP	Slg
DeShields, D*	.375	8	3	1	1	1	1	.444	.750
Dykstra, L*	.000	6	0	0	0	0	0	.000	.000
Finley, Steve*	.231	13	3	1	2	0	2	.214	.462
Fletcher, D*	.000	6	0	0	0	0	2	.000	.000
Floyd, Cliff*	.143	7	1	0	0	0	3	.143	.286
Fonville, C#	.167	6	1	0	0	0	0	.167	.167
Galarraga, A	.300	10	3	2	2	1	4	.364	.900
Garcia, C	.200	5	1	0	0	1	2	.333	.200
Gilkey, B	.500	14	7	1	7	1	1	.533	.857
Girardi, Joe	.100	10	1	0	1	0	2	.100	.100
Gonzalez, L*	.333	9	3	1	3	2	3	.455	.667
Grissom, M	.143	14	2	0	0	1	0	.200	.286
Gutierrez, R	.167	6	1	0	0	0	0	.167	.333
Gwynn, Tony*	.385	13	5	1	3	0	0	.357	.692
Hayes, C	.000	4	0	0	0	1	3	.000	.000
Hill, G	.273	11	3	2	2	1	2	.333	.818
Hollandsworth*	.000	4	0	0	0	1	1	.200	.000
Howard, T*	.000	7	0	0	0	1	1	.125	.000
Hundley, Todd*	.143	7	1	0	2	1	2	.250	.286
Hunter, Bri L	.000	5	0	0	0	1	2	.167	.000
Jefferies, G#	.333	6	2	0	0	0	2	.333	.333
Johnson, Char	.250	4	1	0	0	1	0	.400	.250
Johnson, L*	.000	4	0	0	0	1	0	.200	.000
Johnson, Mark*	.250	8	2	0	1	0	0	.250	.375
Jones, C#	.111	9	1	0	1	0	3	.100	.111
Karros, Eric	.000	6	0	0	0	0	2	.000	.000
Kelly, R	.200	5	1	0	0	0	1	.200	.200
Kent, Jeff	.333	3	1	0	2	0	0	.600	.667
King, Jeff	.250	8	2	0	1	4	0	.538	.375
Kingery, Mike*	.286	7	2	0	1	2	1	.444	.286
Klesko, Ryan*	.333	6	2	1	2	2	2	.500	.833
Lankford, Ray*	.250	8	2	1	2	0	2	.250	.750
Lansing, Mike	.091	11	1	0	0	0	1	.167	.182
Larkin, Barry	.333	15	5	1	4	0	6	.333	.667
Lemke, Mark#	.250	8	2	0	1	0	1	.250	.375
Lewis, Darren	.286	7	2	0	0	2	1	.444	.429
Liriano, N#	.636	11	7	0	1	1	1	.667	.818
Livingstone*	.636	11	7	0	1	0	1	.636	.727
Lopez, Javy	.375	8	3	0	1	0	0	.375	.375
Mabry, John*	.500	6	3	0	2	1	1	.625	.667
Manwaring, K	.143	7	1	0	1	0	1	.143	.143
Martin, Al*	.286	14	4	1	4	0	1	.267	.571
McGriff, Fred*	.111	9	1	0	0	0	1	.111	.111
Merced, O*	.231	13	3	0	2	3	4	.375	.231
Mitchell, K	.200	5	1	0	0	1	4	.333	.200
Mondesi, Raul	.222	9	2	1	4	0	1	.222	.556
Morandini, M*	.200	5	1	0	0	1	0	.333	.200
Morris, Hal*	.364	11	4	0	1	0	3	.364	.636
Pagnozzi, Tom	.167	6	1	0	0	1	2	.286	.333
Pendleton, T#	.300	20	6	0	0	1	1	.333	.350
Piazza, Mike	.375	8	3	1	1	1	0	.444	.750
Plantier, P*	.143	7	1	1	2	0	0	.143	.571
Reed, Jeff*	.667	3	2	1	2	2	0	.800	1.667
Reed, Jody	.444	9	4	0	0	3	1	.583	.556
Roberts, Bip#	.400	10	4	0	1	0	1	.400	.500
Sanders, R	.083	12	1	1	1	0	8	.083	.333
Santiago, B	1.000	3	3	3	6	1	0	1.000	4.000
Scarsone, S	.000	7	0	0	0	2	3	.222	.000
Segui, David#	.429	7	3	1	1	0	0	.429	.857
Servais, A	.333	6	2	0	0	0	1	.333	.333
Sheffield, G	.300	10	3	1	4	3	0	.462	.700
Shipley, C	.333	6	2	0	0	0	2	.333	.333
Slaught, Don	.167	6	1	0	0	0	4	.167	.167
Smith, Ozzie*	.250	4	1	0	0	1	0	.400	.250
Stocker, K*	.400	5	2	0	0	2	0	.571	.600
Taubensee, E*	.500	8	4	1	2	0	1	.500	1.000
Tavarez, Je#	.250	8	2	0	0	0	1	.250	.250
Thompson, Rob	.000	4	0	0	0	2	0	.333	.000
Veras, Q#	.286	7	2	0	0	3	0	.500	.429
Vizcaino, O	.750	4	3	0	0	1	1	.800	1.500
Walker, Larry*	.222	9	2	1	1	2	3	.364	.556
Walton, J	.333	6	2	0	0	0	0	.333	.333
Weiss, Walt#	.375	8	3	1	2	1	2	.444	.875
White, R	.250	8	2	2	2	1	0	.333	1.000
Williams, E	.167	6	1	1	2	0	2	.167	.444
Williams, Ma	.333	9	3	1	2	0	1	.333	.778
Womack, Tony*	.400	5	2	0	0	3	1	.625	.400
Young, Eric	.333	3	1	0	0	3	0	.667	.667
Zeile, Todd	.250	4	1	1	2	1	1	.400	1.000

John Franco, Mets — LHP

Batter	Avg	AB	H	HR	BI	BB	SO	OBP	Slg
Aldrete, Mike*	.167	6	1	0	0	0	1	.167	.167
Alicea, Luis#	.250	4	1	0	0	2	0	.500	.250
Alomar, R#	.111	9	1	0	0	1	0	.200	.111
Arias, Alex	.167	6	1	0	0	0	0	.167	.167
Bagwell, Jeff	.500	4	2	0	2	2	1	.667	.750
Bates, Jason#	.000	4	0	0	0	1	0	.200	.000
Bell, Derek	.000	5	0	0	0	0	1	.000	.000
Bell, Jay	.231	13	3	0	1	1	3	.286	.385
Belliard, R	.000	7	0	0	0	0	3	.000	.000

John Franco, Mets — LHP

Batter	Avg	AB	H	HR	BI	BB	SO	OBP	Slg
Biggio, Craig	.364	11	4	0	1	1	0	.462	.455
Blauser, Jeff	.182	11	2	0	1	0	1	.167	.182
Bonds, Barry*	.207	29	6	0	6	2	3	.250	.276
Bonilla, B#	.214	14	3	1	2	2		.313	.429
Boone, Bret	.200	5	1	0	0	0	1	.200	.200
Butler, Brett*	.267	15	4	0	0	1	1	.353	.333
Caminiti, Ken#	.250	8	2	1	2	1	2	.333	.625
Candaele, C#	.111	9	1	0	0	0	0	.111	.111
Cangelosi, J#	.250	4	1	0	0	1	2	.400	.250
Castilla, V	.167	6	1	0	0	0	3	.167	.167
Cedeno, A	.400	5	2	0	0	0	2	.400	.600
Cianfrocco, A	.167	6	1	1	2	0	2	.167	.667
Clark, Dave*	.500	6	3	1	2	0	2	.500	1.000
Clark, Phil	.200	5	1	0	1	0	1	.200	.200
Clark, Will*	.286	21	6	0	2	0	4	.286	.381
Clayton, R	.143	7	1	0	0	1	2	.250	.286
Colbrunn, G	.000	6	0	0	1	0	0	.000	.000
Coleman, V#	.261	23	6	0	1	0	6	.261	.261
Dascenzo, D	.333	6	2	0	1	0	1	.333	.500
Daulton, D*	.077	13	1	0	0	1	6	.143	.154
Davis, Chili#	.000	6	0	0	0	1	3	.143	.000
Davis, Eric	.143	7	1	0	0	0	4	.143	.143
Dawson, Andre	.333	21	7	0	4	0	1	.333	.333
DeShields, D*	.000	13	0	0	0	0	6	.000	.000
Duncan, M	.500	20	10	0	1	2	5	.545	.550
Dunston, S	.316	19	6	0	1	0	5	.316	.421
Dykstra, L*	.176	17	3	0	1	1	4	.222	.176
Finley, Steve*	.571	7	4	0	1	1	0	.625	.571
Galarraga, A	.286	21	6	2	5	0	7	.273	.619
Gant, Ron	.300	10	3	1	3	2	2	.417	.700
Garcia, C	.714	7	5	0	2	0	0	.714	1.286
Gilkey, B	.167	6	1	0	0	0	4	.143	.167
Girardi, Joe	.167	6	1	0	0	0	1	.167	.167
Grace, Mark*	.100	20	2	0	0	4	2	.250	.100
Grissom, M	.111	9	1	0	0	2	2	.273	.111
Grudzielanek	.000	5	0	0	0	0	0	.000	.000
Gutierrez, R	.200	5	1	0	1	0	0	.333	.200
Gwynn, Tony*	.319	47	15	0	9	1	1	.327	.362
Hayes, C	.364	11	4	0	0	0	0	.364	.364
Hill, G	.667	6	4	2	3	0	1	.667	1.667
Hudler, Rex	.111	9	1	1	3	1	1	.200	.444
Hunter, Brian	.400	5	2	1	3	0	2	.333	1.000
Incaviglia, P	.200	5	1	0	0	0	1	.200	.200
Jefferies, G#	.333	12	4	0	1	0	0	.333	.500
Johnson, Bri	.500	6	3	0	1	0	1	.500	.667
Jordan, Brian	.333	6	2	0	2	2	2	.500	.667
Justice, Dave*	.250	4	1	0	0	1	0	.400	.250
Karros, Eric	.250	8	2	0	0	1	2	.333	.250
Kelly, R	.200	5	1	0	1	0	1	.200	.200
King, Jeff	.188	16	3	0	3	2	5	.278	.188
Klesko, Ryan*	.167	6	1	0	0	0	1	.167	.167
Lankford, Ray*	.400	10	4	0	3	0	4	.400	.500
Lansing, Mike	.222	9	2	0	2	0	3	.222	.222
Larkin, Barry	.375	8	3	0	1	2	0	.500	.500
Lemke, Mark#	.333	6	2	0	1	0	1	.333	.333
Lewis, Darren	.375	8	3	0	1	0	0	.375	.375
Liriano, N#	.400	5	2	0	1	1	1	.500	.600
Lopez, Javy	.333	6	2	0	0	1	1	.333	.333
Manwaring, K	.143	7	1	0	0	1	2	.250	.143
Martin, Al*	.000	6	0	0	0	1	1	.143	.000
Martinez, Da*	.714	7	5	0	0	0	0	.750	.714
McGee, Willie*	.310	29	9	1	2	0	8	.310	.483
McGriff, Fred*	.600	5	3	0	1	2	1	.714	.600
Merced, O*	.000	5	0	0	0	3	0	.000	.000
Miller, Orl	.000	4	0	0	0	1	0	.000	.000
Mitchell, K	.357	14	5	2	2	6	3	.550	.786
Mondesi, Raul	.600	5	3	0	1	0	2	.600	.600
Morandini, M*	.000	5	0	0	0	1	0	.000	.000
Nixon, Otis#	.167	6	1	0	1	1	1	.286	.167
Offerman, J*	.143	7	1	1	1	0	1	.143	.571
Oliver, Joe	.286	7	2	0	2	0	0	.286	.571
Pagnozzi, Tom	.000	14	0	0	1	2	6	.125	.000
Parent, Mark	.000	5	0	0	0	0	3	.000	.000
Pena, Tony	.308	13	4	0	1	4	2	.471	.308
Pendleton, T#	.421	19	8	0	2	1	1	.450	.474
Piazza, Mike	.167	6	1	0	0	0	1	.167	.167
Prince, Tom	.000	4	0	0	0	1	1	.200	.000
Raines, Tim#	.316	19	6	0	2	2	0	.316	.368
Roberts, Bip#	.417	12	5	0	1	2	2	.500	.417
Sabo, Chris	.143	7	1	0	0	0	2	.143	.143
Samuel, Juan	.316	19	6	0	1	2	4	.381	.316
Sandberg, R	.273	22	6	0	4	7	3	.448	.364
Santiago, B	.300	20	6	1	2	3	2	.391	.450
Scarsone, S	.000	4	0	0	0	1	2	.200	.000
Schu, Rick	.200	5	1	0	0	1	0	.429	.200
Shipley, C	.333	9	3	0	2	0	0	.333	.444
Slaught, Don	.286	7	2	0	1	0	1	.286	.429
Smith, Dwight*	.400	5	2	0	2	0	0	.400	.600
Smith, Ozzie#	.273	22	6	0	2	1	3	.304	.273
Sosa, Sammy	.125	8	1	0	1	0	3	.125	.125
Stocker, K#	.000	3	0	0	0	0	2	.000	.000

John Franco, Mets — LHP

Batter	Avg	AB	H	HR	BI	BB	SO	OBP	Slg
Strawberry, D*	.143	14	2	2	3	4	4	.368	.571
Thompson, Mil*	.308	13	4	0	2	1	2	.357	.385
Thompson, Rob	.125	16	2	0	1	2	1	.222	.125
Vizcaino, J#	.200	5	1	0	0	0	0	.200	.200
Walker, Larry*	.667	6	4	0	2	2	2	.667	.833
Wallach, Tim	.296	27	8	2	5	3	4	.367	.556
Walton, J	.333	6	2	0	2	1	2	.429	.333
Wehner, John	.000	3	0	0	1	0	0	.250	.000
Weiss, Walt#	.333	6	2	0	1	2	1	.500	.333
Whiten, Mark#	.375	8	3	0	0	0	1	.375	.375
Wilkins, Rick*	.333	6	2	1	2	1	4	.429	1.000
Williams, E	.250	4	1	1	1	0	1	.250	1.000
Williams, Ma	.333	18	6	1	7	2	4	.400	.556
Zeile, Todd	.467	15	7	1	1	2	3	.529	.667

Marvin Freeman, White Sox — RHP

Batter	Avg	AB	H	HR	BI	BB	SO	OBP	Slg
Joyner, Wally*	.333	9	3	0	2	0	2	.333	.444
Justice, Dave*	.333	9	3	1	1	2	1	.455	.667
Karros, Eric	.267	15	4	2	5	1	1	.294	.667
Kelly, R	.500	10	5	1	1	0	3	.500	.800
Kent, Jeff	.125	8	1	0	1	1	3	.222	.125
King, Jeff	.400	10	4	1	6	0	4	.400	.700
Klesko, Ryan*	.500	12	6	2	7	0	1	.500	1.083
Lankford, Ray*	.600	15	9	2	5	3	2	.667	1.067
Lansing, Mike	.154	13	2	0	2	2	3	.313	.154
Larkin, Barry	.048	21	1	0	1	0	1	.048	.048
Lemke, Mark#	.444	9	4	0	2	1	1	.500	.444
Lewis, Darren	.429	7	3	0	0	2	1	.600	.714
Lopez, Javy	.333	9	3	0	4	0	1	.333	.444
Mabry, John*	.500	10	5	0	1	0	1	.500	.800
Magadan, Dave*	.250	12	3	0	1	3	1	.400	.500
Manwaring, K	.250	8	2	0	1	1	0	.333	.375
Martin, Al*	.091	11	1	1	1	0	0	.091	.364
Martinez, Da*	.333	9	3	1	2	0	1	.400	.667
May, Derrick*	.385	13	5	0	0	1	0	.429	.385
McGee, Willie*	.111	9	1	0	1	0	1	.111	.111
McGriff, Fred*	.200	15	3	0	0	2	5	.294	.267
McRae, Brian*	.250	8	2	1	2	1	1	.333	.875
Merced, O*	.067	15	1	0	0	2	5	.176	.067
Miller, Orl	.500	6	3	0	0	0	0	.500	.667
Mitchell, K	.125	8	1	0	1	0	2	.222	.125
Mondesi, Raul	.214	14	3	0	0	0	3	.214	.286
Morandini, M*	.167	6	1	0	0	0	0	.167	.167
Morris, Hal*	.471	17	8	1	4	0	0	.471	.765
Murray, Eddie*	.600	5	3	1	3	1	0	.667	1.200
Newfield, M	.250	8	2	1	3	1	0	.333	.625
O'Neill, Paul*	.400	5	2	1	1	0	0	.400	1.000
Offerman, J#	.273	11	3	0	1	2	1	.385	.273
Oliver, Joe	.444	9	4	1	1	0	3	.444	.778
Orsulak, Joe*	.200	10	2	0	0	1	2	.273	.300
Pagnozzi, Tom	.333	15	5	0	6	3	2	.444	.400
Pendleton, T#	.333	15	5	1	5	0	4	.333	.600
Piazza, Mike	.375	16	6	0	0	1	1	.375	.438
Plantier, P*	.500	4	2	1	1	1	2	.600	1.500
Pride, Curtis*	.000	5	0	0	0	0	0	.000	.000
Reed, Jody	.600	10	6	0	2	5	1	.733	.700
Roberts, Bip#	.313	16	5	0	1	3	0	.421	.313
Rodriguez, H*	.417	12	5	0	2	0	5	.417	.500
Sabo, Chris	.111	9	1	0	0	0	0	.200	.111
Samuel, Juan	.400	5	2	0	2	0	0	.400	.400
Sanchez, Rey	.462	13	6	0	1	0	1	.429	.538
Sandberg, R	.300	20	6	2	4	2	3	.364	.650
Sanders, R	.250	12	3	0	0	2	5	.357	.333
Santiago, R	.200	20	4	0	2	0	2	.200	.200
Segui, David#	.714	14	10	0	4	3	0	.765	1.000
Servais, S	.000	7	0	0	0	1	3	.125	.000
Sheffield, G	.412	17	7	1	5	0	0	.565	.706
Slaught, Don	.600	5	3	0	1	1	0	.667	.600
Smith, Dwight*	.250	12	3	0	1	4	4	.308	.250
Smith, Ozzie#	.417	12	5	0	1	3	0	.533	.583
Sosa, Sammy	.182	11	2	1	2	1	2	.231	.455
Stinnett, K	.500	6	3	0	0	0	2	.500	.500
Strawberry, D*	.286	14	4	1	2	2	2	.412	.643
Sweeney, Mark*	.000	6	0	0	0	2	2	.000	.000
Tarasco, Tony*	.000	5	0	0	0	2	0	.286	.000
Taubensee, E*	.455	11	5	2	4	1	0	.500	1.091
Thompson, Rob	.125	16	2	0	3	1	3	.176	.188
Thompson, Ry	.750	4	3	1	2	1	0	.800	1.500
Veras, Q#	.100	10	1	0	0	2	0	.250	.100
Vizcaino, J#	.429	14	6	0	1	0	1	.429	.429
Walker, Larry*	.571	7	4	0	1	0	1	.571	.714
Wallach, Tim	.545	11	6	1	3	3	2	.643	.818
Wehner, John	.143	7	1	0	0	0	2	.143	.143
White, Devon#	.556	9	5	0	4	0	0	.556	1.000
White, R	.000	6	0	0	0	1	3	.143	.000
Whiten, Mark#	.500	6	3	0	3	0	0	.500	.833
Wilkins, Rick*	.444	9	4	1	3	1	2	.545	.889
Williams, Ma	.250	20	5	1	3	1	7	.286	.400
Zeile, Todd	.095	21	2	0	1	1	8	.136	.095

Marvin Freeman, White Sox — RHP

Batter	Avg	AB	H	HR	BI	BB	SO	OBP	Slg
Abbott, Kurt	.222	9	2	0	1	2	2	.333	.222
Aldrete, Mike*	.000	4	0	0	0	2	2	.333	.000
Alfonzo, E	.000	5	0	0	0	0	2	.000	.000
Alicea, Luis#	.200	10	2	0	2	1	2	.273	.300
Alou, Moises	.143	14	2	0	1	2	1	.250	.143
Andrews, S	.500	8	4	0	4	1	2	.556	1.375
Anthony, Eric*	.200	10	2	0	1	1	2	.273	.300
Arias, Alex	.571	7	4	1	1	0	0	.571	1.000
Ausmus, Brian	.333	6	2	0	1	2	1	.500	.833
Bagwell, Jeff	.357	14	5	2	4	1	2	.375	1.000
Barberie, B#	.125	8	1	0	1	0	1	.125	.125
Bell, David	.000	2	0	0	1	1	2	.400	.000
Bell, Derek	.100	10	1	0	0	0	4	.100	.100
Bell, Jay	.375	16	6	1	2	2	2	.444	.625
Benjamin, M	.125	8	1	0	0	0	2	.125	.125
Berry, Sean	.500	6	3	0	4	1	0	.571	.667
Biggio, Craig	.467	15	7	1	2	1	3	.500	.800
Blauser, Jeff	.250	12	3	0	0	0	1	.250	.250
Bonds, Barry*	.500	16	8	0	1	4	0	.600	.688
Bonilla, B#	.438	16	7	1	6	3	3	.526	.875
Boone, Bret	.333	9	3	0	1	0	0	.333	.333
Branson, Jeff*	.125	8	1	0	0	0	1	.125	.125
Brogna, Rico*	.333	9	3	0	0	1	0	.400	.556
Butler, Brett*	.364	22	8	0	3	5	4	.481	.364
Caminiti, Ken#	.240	25	6	0	2	3	3	.321	.320
Candaele, C#	.000	4	0	0	1	1	0	.200	.000
Carr, Chuck	.000	6	0	0	0	0	0	.000	.000
Cedeno, A	.222	9	2	0	0	2	2	.364	.222
Cianfrocco, A	.000	9	0	0	0	0	1	.000	.000
Clark, Dave*	.250	12	3	0	1	0	1	.250	.250
Clark, Will*	.167	6	1	0	1	2	3	.375	.333
Clayton, O	.300	10	3	0	1	1	1	.364	.300
Colbrunn, G	.111	9	1	1	2	1	2	.273	.444
Coleman, V#	.200	5	1	0	0	0	2	.200	.200
Conine, Jeff	.667	15	10	3	5	2	1	.684	1.400
Cordero, Wil	.077	13	1	0	1	1	4	.143	.077
Dascenzo, D#	.333	9	3	0	2	1	1	.455	.333
Davis, Eric	.250	12	3	0	0	1	4	.308	.250
Dawson, Andre	.182	11	2	1	1	1	2	.250	.455
DeShields, D*	.333	12	4	1	2	3	0	.467	.583
Duncan, M	.333	6	2	0	0	0	1	.333	.333
Dunston, S	.176	17	3	0	0	0	4	.176	.176
Dykstra, L*	.000	5	0	0	0	2	0	.375	.000
Elster, Kevin	.250	4	1	0	0	1	2	.400	.250
Finley, Steve*	.350	20	7	0	3	4	2	.458	.700
Flaherty, J	.333	6	2	0	2	0	0	.333	.333
Fletcher, D*	.286	14	4	0	2	0	0	.286	.286
Floyd, Cliff*	.500	4	2	1	1	1	1	.600	1.250
Gaetti, Jim	.200	5	1	1	1	1	0	.429	.800
Galarraga, A	.400	5	2	0	3	0	1	.400	.800
Gant, Ron	.250	4	1	0	0	2	0	.500	.250
Garcia, C	.400	10	4	0	0	0	2	.400	.400
Gilkey, M	.375	8	3	2	3	1	2	.444	1.125
Gomez, Chris	.500	6	3	0	0	0	0	.500	.667
Gonzalez, L*	.333	9	3	0	1	1	0	.400	.333
Grace, Mark*	.185	27	5	0	2	2	2	.241	.222
Grissom, M	.200	20	4	0	2	1	4	.273	.300
Grudzielanek	.429	7	3	0	1	0	2	.429	.714
Gutierrez, R	.500	4	2	0	1	1	0	.600	.750
Gwynn, Tony*	.467	15	7	0	1	0	0	.467	.600
Harris, Lenny*	.333	9	3	0	1	0	0	.333	.444
Hayes, C	.200	5	1	0	0	0	2	.200	.400
Henderson, R	.000	6	0	0	0	1	1	.000	.000
Hollandsworth*	.400	5	2	0	2	0	0	.400	.400
Howard, T*	.273	11	3	0	0	0	0	.273	.364
Hundley, Todd#	.143	7	1	0	0	1	1	.143	.143
Hunter, Bri L	.167	6	1	0	0	1	2	.286	.333
Incaviglia, P	.429	7	3	0	1	0	3	.429	.429
Javier, Stan#	.400	4	1	0	0	0	0	.400	.500
Jefferies, G#	.214	14	3	1	5	3	0	.353	.429
Johnson, Char	.167	6	1	0	0	2	1	.375	.167
Johnson, Mark*	.400	5	2	0	1	2	1	.500	.400
Jones, C#	.400	10	4	0	3	1	3	.455	.500
Jordan, Brian	.231	13	3	1	1	1	3	.286	.538

Steve Frey, Phillies — LHP

Batter	Avg	AB	H	HR	BI	BB	SO	OBP	Slg
Alomar, R#	.000	5	0	0	0	1	0	.167	.000
Anderson, Brd*	.000	8	0	0	1	0	1	.111	.000
Baerga, C#	.143	7	1	0	1	0	1	.143	.143
Bell, Jay	.250	8	2	0	0	1	0	.250	.250
Biggio, Craig	.250	4	1	0	1	0	0	.400	.250
Blauser, Jeff	.250	4	1	0	1	0	0	.400	.250
Boggs, Wade*	.333	3	1	0	0	2	0	.600	.333
Bonds, Barry*	.500	12	6	1	6	1	1	.538	.833
Bonilla, B#	.400	10	4	0	0	1	0	.455	.400
Butler, Brett*	.429	7	3	1	2	3	3	.636	.857
Clark, Will*	.400	5	2	0	3	1	0	.429	.400
Coleman, V#	.167	6	1	0	0	0	0	.167	.167
Dawson, Andre	.400	5	2	0	0	0	0	.400	.400
Devereaux, M	.400	5	2	0	1	0	0	.400	.400
Duncan, M	.250	4	1	0	0	1	1	.400	.250

67

Steve Frey, Phillies — LHP

Batter	Avg	AB	H	HR	BI	BB	SO	OBP	Slg
Eisenreich, J*	.000	4	0	0	0	2	2	.333	.000
Gilkey, B	.400	5	2	1	2	2	0	.571	1.200
Grace, Mark*	.364	11	4	0	1	2	1	.462	.364
Griffey Jr, K*	.200	5	1	1	1	0	1	.200	.800
Gwynn, Tony*	.556	9	5	0	3	1	0	.600	.778
Harris, Lenny*	.400	5	2	1	1	0	0	.400	1.000
Hayes, C	.333	6	2	0	0	0	0	.333	.333
Hundley, Todd#	.000	5	0	0	0	0	0	.000	.000
Jefferies, G#	.286	7	2	0	1	2	0	.444	.286
Johnson, L*	.800	5	4	0	1	0	0	.800	1.000
Jordan, Ricky	.200	5	1	0	0	0	2	.200	.200
Joyner, Wally*	.143	7	1	0	1	3	1	.400	.143
Justice, Dave*	.000	6	0	0	0	1	0	.143	.000
King, Jeff	.500	10	5	0	4	2	0	.583	.700
Lankford, Ray*	.125	8	1	0	0	3	3	.111	.125
Livingstone*	.200	5	1	0	0	0	2	.200	.200
Lofton, Kenny*	.250	4	1	0	0	0	0	.400	.500
Macfarlane, M	.000	6	0	0	0	0	1	.000	.000
Magadan, Dave*	.200	5	1	0	1	1	2	.333	.400
Martin, Al*	.400	5	2	1	5	1	1	.429	1.000
McGriff, Fred*	.400	10	4	1	1	0	1	.400	.900
McRae, Brian*	.444	9	4	0	0	0	0	.444	.444
Mitchell, K	.667	3	2	0	0	2	0	.800	1.000
Morris, Hal*	.250	4	1	0	2	0	0	.250	.250
Murray, Eddie#	.000	4	0	0	0	2	2	.333	.000
O'Neill, Paul*	.286	7	2	1	3	2	3	.400	.857
Offerman, J#	.000	5	0	0	0	1	0	.167	.000
Pena, G#	.400	5	2	1	1	0	2	.400	1.000
Pendleton, T#	.333	6	2	0	1	0	0	.333	.500
Phillips, T#	.250	4	1	0	0	2	2	.500	.250
Raines, Tim#	.400	5	2	0	1	0	0	.400	.400
Roberts, Bip#	.200	5	1	0	0	0	1	.200	.200
Samuel, Juan	.714	7	5	1	2	0	0	.714	1.143
Santiago, B	.750	4	3	0	1	0	0	.800	.750
Segui, David*	.667	6	4	1	2	0	0	.667	1.333
Slaught, Don	.000	2	0	0	3	0	0	.000	.000
Smith, Ozzie*	.286	7	2	1	2	2	0	.444	.714
Strawberry, D*	.333	9	3	0	1	1	4	.400	.444
Tartabull, D	.000	3	0	0	0	2	1	.400	.000
Tettleton, M#	.667	3	2	0	0	2	0	.800	.667
Thompson, Mil*	.500	6	3	0	0	0	0	.500	.667
Vaughn, M*	.400	5	2	1	3	0	1	.400	1.000
Ventura, R*	.167	6	1	0	1	1	0	.286	.333
White, Devon#	.400	5	2	1	4	1	0	.500	1.000
Wilkins, Rick*	.000	5	0	0	0	0	3	.000	.000

Todd Frohwirth, Angels — RHP

Batter	Avg	AB	H	HR	BI	BB	SO	OBP	Slg
Alomar, R#	.286	7	2	0	1	2	0	.444	.286
Alomar Jr, S	.111	9	1	0	0	0	0	.111	.111
Baerga, C#	.273	11	3	0	2	1	1	.333	.273
Baines, H*	.500	8	4	0	2	1	0	.556	.500
Belle, Albert	.333	12	4	0	1	1	2	.385	.333
Boggs, Wade*	.429	7	3	0	3	2	0	.556	.714
Bonds, Barry*	.286	7	2	0	0	0	0	.286	.286
Bonilla, B#	.250	4	1	0	3	1	0	.400	.250
Borders, Pat	.000	5	0	0	0	0	3	.000	.000
Bordick, Mike	.182	11	2	0	0	0	1	.182	.182
Buhner, Jay	.571	7	4	0	1	0	1	.571	.714
Burks, Ellis	.167	6	1	0	0	1	2	.286	.167
Canseco, Jose	.200	15	3	1	3	2	4	.294	.400
Carter, Joe	.200	10	2	0	2	1	5	.273	.200
Cora, Joey#	.000	4	0	0	0	2	0	.000	.000
Curtis, Chad	.000	2	0	0	0	3	0	.600	.000
Cuyler, Milt#	.333	6	2	0	1	1	1	.429	.333
Davis, Chili#	.167	6	1	0	0	1	1	.286	.167
Deer, Rob	.200	10	2	0	1	1	6	.273	.200
DiSarcina, G	.000	5	0	0	0	0	0	.000	.000
Dunston, S	.333	6	2	0	0	0	0	.333	.333
Espinoza, A	.167	6	1	0	0	0	0	.167	.500
Fielder, C	.462	13	6	0	3	1	1	.500	.462
Franco, Julio	.400	5	2	0	2	1	0	.500	.600
Frye, Jeff	.429	7	3	0	0	0	0	.429	.571
Fryman, T	.308	13	4	0	0	0	3	.308	.385
Gaetti, Gary	.250	8	2	0	1	0	0	.250	.250
Gagne, Greg	.273	11	3	0	0	0	2	.273	.273
Galarraga, A	.000	6	0	0	1	1	0	.143	.000
Gallego, Mike	.111	9	1	0	1	1	1	.200	.111
Gomez, Chris	.400	5	2	0	3	0	1	.400	.600
Gonzales, R	.000	6	0	0	0	1	1	.143	.000
Gonzalez, J	.143	14	2	0	0	3	3	.143	.143
Grace, Mark*	.250	4	1	0	0	1	0	.400	.250
Grebeck, C	.000	4	0	0	0	1	0	.200	.000
Griffey Jr, K*	.250	4	1	0	0	1	1	.400	.250
Guillen, O*	.400	5	2	1	2	1	0	.500	1.000
Hamilton, D*	.200	5	1	0	0	0	1	.200	.200
Henderson, R	.273	11	3	0	0	1	3	.333	.364
Howard, T*	.000	5	0	0	0	0	0	.000	.000
Huff, Michael	.400	4	1	0	0	1	2	.400	.500
Hulse, David*	.286	7	2	0	0	0	0	.286	.286
Jefferies, G#	.167	6	1	0	0	0	0	.167	.167

Todd Frohwirth, Angels — RHP

Batter	Avg	AB	H	HR	BI	BB	SO	OBP	Slg
Johnson, L*	.125	8	1	0	0	0	1	.125	.125
Joyner, Wally	.667	6	4	1	2	0	0	.667	1.167
Karkovice, R	.375	8	3	0	0	0	1	.375	.375
Kelly, Pat	.400	5	2	0	0	1	1	.571	.400
Kelly, R	.800	5	4	0	2	0	0	.800	.800
Knoblauch, C	.235	17	4	0	1	0	1	.235	.294
Leius, Scott	.000	8	0	0	0	1	1	.200	.000
Lewis, Mark	.000	7	0	0	1	1	1	.125	.000
Leyritz, Jim	.400	5	2	0	1	0	1	.400	.400
Lofton, Kenny*	.667	3	2	0	1	2	0	.800	.667
Macfarlane, M	.167	12	2	0	1	0	4	.167	.167
Martinez, E	.667	6	4	1	5	0	0	.667	1.167
Mayne, Brent*	.167	6	1	0	3	0	1	.143	.167
McGwire, Mark	.600	5	3	0	1	2	0	.714	.600
McRae, Brian#	.400	10	4	0	1	1	2	.455	.600
Molitor, Paul	.250	8	2	0	3	1	0	.333	.500
Murray, Eddie#	.500	4	2	1	3	0	0	.400	1.000
Myers, Greg*	.250	4	1	0	0	1	0	.400	.500
Olerud, John*	.000	6	0	0	0	1	1	.250	.000
Palmeiro, R*	.500	8	4	0	0	1	0	.556	.750
Palmer, Dean	.077	13	1	1	1	3	3	.250	.308
Pena, Tony	.250	12	3	0	2	1	5	.308	.250
Phillips, T#	.375	8	3	1	2	4	0	.583	1.000
Raines, Tim#	.500	8	4	0	3	2	1	.600	.875
Reed, Jody	.000	10	0	0	1	2	4	.167	.000
Rodriguez, I	.214	14	3	0	0	1	2	.267	.214
Salmon, Tim	.200	5	1	0	0	1	0	.333	.200
Samuel, Juan	.167	6	1	0	1	0	3	.286	.167
Schofield, D	.000	6	0	0	0	1	2	.143	.000
Seitzer, K	.333	6	2	0	3	2	0	.500	.333
Sierra, Ruben#	.083	12	1	0	1	0	0	.083	.083
Sojo, Luis	.400	5	2	0	0	0	0	.400	.400
Stanley, Mike	.833	6	5	1	3	0	0	.833	1.333
Steinbach, T	.125	8	1	0	2	1	2	.222	.125
Stillwell, K#	.000	3	0	0	0	2	2	.400	.000
Surhoff, B.J.*	.200	5	1	0	1	1	1	.333	.200
Tartabull, D	.267	15	4	1	4	0	1	.267	.533
Tettleton, M#	.267	15	4	0	2	0	3	.267	.267
Thomas, Frank	.375	8	3	1	3	1	0	.444	.875
Trammell, A	.000	7	0	0	0	0	1	.000	.000
Valentin, Jhn	.143	7	1	0	0	1	2	.250	.143
Vaughn, Greg	.111	9	1	0	0	0	2	.111	.111
Vaughn, Mo*	.667	3	2	1	3	1	1	.667	1.667
Ventura, R*	.250	4	1	0	0	1	0	.400	.500
Wallach, Tim	.000	4	0	0	0	1	1	.200	.000
White, Devon#	.000	6	0	0	1	2	3	.250	.000
Williams, Ber#	.333	6	2	0	1	0	1	.333	.333

Rich Garces, Red Sox — RHP

Batter	Avg	AB	H	HR	BI	BB	SO	OBP	Slg
Elster, Kevin	.000	5	0	0	0	0	2	.000	.000
Fielder, C	.200	5	1	0	0	1	1	.333	.200
Fryman, T	.667	3	2	0	4	0	0	.400	1.000
Gonzalez, J	.154	5	1	1	1	0	2	.200	.000
Tettleton, M#	.400	5	2	0	2	0	2	.400	.800

Ramon Garcia, Brewers — RHP

Batter	Avg	AB	H	HR	BI	BB	SO	OBP	Slg
Baerga, C#	.286	7	2	0	1	0	0	.286	.286
Belle, Albert	.111	9	1	0	0	0	1	.111	.111
Burks, Ellis	.167	6	1	0	0	0	1	.167	.167
Davis, Chili#	.143	7	1	1	2	2	2	.333	.571
Franco, Julio	.500	14	7	2	4	1	2	.533	.929
Girardi, Joe	.500	4	2	0	1	0	0	.500	1.000
Gonzalez, J	.143	14	2	0	1	0	3	.143	.214
Greenwell, M*	.571	7	4	1	2	1	0	.625	1.143
Griffey Jr, K*	.250	4	1	1	2	0	0	.200	1.000
Hamilton, D*	.200	5	1	0	0	0	0	.200	.200
Huson, Jeff*	.000	5	0	0	0	1	1	.250	.000
Knoblauch, C	.143	7	1	0	0	1	0	.143	.143
McGwire, Mark	.333	3	1	0	0	2	0	.600	.333
Palmeiro, R*	.273	11	3	0	0	1	0	.333	.364
Palmer, Dean	.000	5	0	0	0	1	0	.167	.000
Reed, Jody	.167	6	1	1	2	0	0	.167	.667
Rodriguez, I	.400	5	2	0	0	0	0	.400	.400
Sierra, Ruben#	.154	13	2	0	1	1	0	.200	.231
Valentin, Jhn	.000	5	0	1	0	1	0	.200	.000
Vaughn, Mo*	.364	11	4	1	0	2	0	.364	.636
Vizquel, Omar#	.500	6	3	0	0	0	0	.500	.500

Mark Gardner, Giants — RHP

Batter	Avg	AB	H	HR	BI	BB	SO	OBP	Slg
Alicea, Luis#	.294	17	5	0	1	2	3	.400	.294
Allensworth	.333	6	2	1	4	1	0	.429	1.000
Alomar, R#	.286	14	4	0	1	1	2	.333	.286
Alou, Moises	.154	13	2	0	1	0	1	.154	.154
Anthony, Eric*	.200	15	3	0	1	1	7	.250	.267
Ausmus, Brad	.250	4	1	0	1	2	1	.400	.250
Baerga, C#	.250	4	1	0	2	1	0	.400	.250
Bagwell, Jeff	.217	23	5	1	3	3	0	.308	.348
Baines, H*	.000	5	0	0	0	0	3	.000	.000

Batter	Avg	AB	H	HR	BI	BB	SO	OBP	Slg
Bates, Jason#	.200	5	1	0	1	0	2	.200	.200
Bell, Derek	.556	9	5	0	3	0	1	.556	.889
Bell, Jay	.154	26	4	1	2	3	5	.241	.269
Belliard, R	.154	13	2	0	0	0	4	.154	.231
Benjamin, M	.400	5	2	0	1	0	2	.400	.800
Berry, Sean	.583	12	7	1	4	0	1	.615	1.000
Bichette, D	.222	18	4	1	5	1	4	.263	.389
Biggio, Craig	.300	30	9	0	1	3	3	.432	.333
Blauser, Jeff	.235	17	4	0	0	3	3	.381	.235
Bonds, Barry*	.444	9	4	2	5	3	1	.583	1.222
Bonilla, B#	.200	10	2	0	6	6	2	.500	.400
Boone, Bret	.250	12	3	0	3	0	1	.231	.417
Bordick, Mike	.500	4	2	0	0	1	1	.600	.750
Branson, Jeff*	.300	10	3	0	0	1	2	.364	.400
Brogna, Rico*	.400	5	2	0	0	0	1	.400	.600
Brumfield, J	.600	5	3	0	0	1	0	.667	.800
Burks, Ellis	.091	11	1	1	1	1	5	.167	.364
Butler, Brett*	.281	32	9	0	1	4	5	.361	.344
Caminiti, Ken#	.292	24	7	2	6	4	4	.393	.625
Candaele, C	.333	12	4	0	2	1	2	.385	.417
Cangelosi, J#	.571	7	4	0	0	1	0	.625	.571
Carreon, Mark	.200	5	1	0	1	0	1	.333	.400
Carter, Joe	.125	8	1	0	2	0	1	.200	.125
Castilla, V	.357	14	5	1	5	2	3	.438	.714
Cedeno, A	.286	14	4	0	0	1	2	.333	.429
Clark, Dave*	.000	8	0	0	0	1	2	.111	.000
Clark, Will*	.182	22	4	1	2	2	5	.240	.364
Clayton, R	.417	12	5	1	1	1	3	.462	.667
Coleman, V#	.231	13	3	0	1	2	1	.375	.231
Cordero, Wil	.300	10	3	0	0	1	3	.364	.500
Dascenzo, D	.333	6	2	0	0	0	1	.333	.333
Daulton, D*	.231	13	3	0	0	2	1	.333	.385
Davis, Eric	.222	9	2	0	0	1	1	.300	.222
Dawson, Andre	.385	26	10	3	11	0	5	.407	.885
Decker, Steve	.400	5	2	0	1	0	0	.400	.600
DeShields, D*	.400	10	4	0	2	1	2	.455	.500
Devereaux, M	.333	6	2	0	2	0	1	.333	.333
Duncan, M	.091	11	1	1	1	1	2	.167	.364
Dunston, S	.273	22	6	1	2	0	4	.273	.455
Dye, Jermaine	.333	6	2	1	1	0	3	.333	1.000
Dykstra, L*	.143	21	3	1	1	7	3	.217	.286
Eisenreich, J*	.273	11	3	0	0	2	1	.385	.364
Elster, Kevin	.143	7	1	1	1	0	2	.250	.571
Eusebio, Tony	.167	6	1	0	1	1	1	.286	.167
Everett, Carl#	.200	5	1	0	0	0	0	.200	.200
Finley, Steve*	.233	30	7	1	3	2	3	.281	.367
Fletcher, D*	.350	20	7	2	3	6	2	.500	.700
Floyd, Cliff	.100	10	1	0	1	1	2	.250	.100
Frazier, Lou*	.429	7	3	0	0	0	1	.429	.429
Galarraga, A	.294	17	5	0	4	3	3	.409	.294
Gant, Ron	.389	18	7	3	8	3	3	.476	.944
Garcia, C	.273	11	3	0	2	0	2	.273	.364
Gates, Brent#	.200	5	1	0	0	1	0	.333	.200
Gilkey, B	.200	10	2	1	2	1	1	.273	.500
Girardi, Joe	.143	14	2	0	0	4	1	.333	.143
Gomez, Leo	.500	2	1	1	1	4	1	.857	2.000
Gonzalez, L*	.286	21	6	0	4	3	3	.375	.381
Grace, Mark*	.318	44	14	2	6	2	3	.348	.523
Greene, W*	.100	10	1	0	1	1	4	.182	.100
Griffey Jr, K*	.800	5	4	0	0	3	0	.875	1.200
Grissom, M	.217	23	5	1	3	1	5	.250	.348
Grudzielanek	.400	10	4	0	2	0	2	.400	.400
Gwynn, Chris*	.000	5	0	0	1	0	4	.000	.000
Gwynn, Tony*	.478	23	11	0	4	1	0	.500	.696
Hamilton, D*	.400	5	2	0	0	1	0	.500	.400
Haney, Todd	.000	5	0	0	0	0	0	.000	.000
Hansen, Dave*	.200	15	3	1	2	0	3	.200	.467
Harris, Lenny*	.370	27	10	1	2	1	1	.393	.519
Hayes, Charlie	.350	20	7	2	7	2	3	.435	.800
Henderson, R	.444	9	4	3	4	3	2	.583	1.444
Hernandez, Jo	.000	4	0	0	0	1	2	.200	.000
Hoiles, Chris	.400	5	2	0	0	1	0	.400	.600
Hollandsworth	.429	7	3	1	3	0	2	.429	1.000
Hollins, Dave#	.250	8	2	0	1	1	1	.400	.375
Howard, T*	.250	12	3	0	2	0	2	.250	.417
Javier, Stan#	.500	6	3	0	0	1	2	.571	.500
Jefferies, G#	.320	25	8	0	2	6	2	.469	.440
Johnson, Mark*	.375	8	3	0	1	1	1	.444	.500
Jones, C#	.308	13	4	1	2	0	2	.308	.538
Jordan, Brian	.143	14	2	0	2	1	7	.188	.143
Jordan, Ricky	.500	10	5	0	4	0	1	.545	.500
Justice, Dave*	.240	25	6	2	6	3	5	.345	.480
Karros, Eric	.261	23	6	0	4	0	9	.261	.348
Kelly, R	.364	11	4	1	3	0	2	.364	.727
Kent, Jeff	.111	9	1	0	1	0	2	.111	.222
King, Jeff	.294	17	5	0	4	1	3	.333	.412
Kingery, Mike*	.400	20	8	0	2	1	3	.429	.650
Kirby, Wayne*	.364	11	4	1	2	0	0	.333	.818
Klesko, Ryan*	.154	13	2	1	6	3	6	.294	.538
Knoblauch, C	.167	6	1	0	0	0	2	.167	.167
Lankford, Ray*	.290	31	9	2	3	4	7	.378	.613

Batter	Avg	AB	H	HR	BI	BB	SO	OBP	Slg
Lansing, Mike	.235	17	4	1	1	2	2	.316	.529
Larkin, Barry	.417	24	10	0	3	3	3	.464	.458
Lemke, Mark#	.269	26	7	0	0	0	2	.269	.269
Lewis, Darren	.250	4	1	0	0	0	1	.400	.250
Lieberthal, M	.333	6	2	0	0	0	1	.333	.500
Livingstone*	.000	5	0	0	0	0	0	.000	.000
Lofton, Kenny*	.250	4	1	0	0	1	2	.400	.250
Lopez, Javy	.083	12	1	0	0	0	2	.083	.083
Mabry, John*	.250	8	2	0	0	1	2	.333	.250
Magadan, Dave*	.176	17	3	0	4	6	0	.417	.176
Magee, W	.333	6	2	0	2	0	3	.333	.333
Manwaring, K	.333	9	3	0	4	1	2	.462	.444
Martin, Al*	.357	14	5	1	2	2	3	.438	.571
Martinez, Da*	.500	8	4	0	1	0	1	.500	.625
Martinez, T*	.500	6	3	1	3	0	1	.500	1.000
May, Derrick*	.143	14	2	0	0	0	1	.143	.143
McCracken, Q#	.333	6	2	0	0	0	1	.333	.333
McGee, Willie*	.211	19	4	0	1	2	4	.286	.263
McGriff, Fred*	.261	23	6	2	3	4	4	.370	.565
McLemore, M#	.600	5	3	0	2	0	0	.600	.800
McRae, Brian#	.800	5	4	1	1	0	0	.800	1.600
Merced, O*	.304	23	7	2	7	4	2	.414	.652
Miller, Orl	.500	2	1	0	1	1	0	.750	1.000
Mitchell, K	.250	20	5	0	1	3	5	.348	.250
Mondesi, Raul	.500	10	5	1	1	1	1	.545	.900
Morandini, M*	.308	26	8	0	0	1	5	.357	.385
Morris, Hal*	.286	28	8	0	5	2	3	.323	.321
Mouton, James	.400	5	2	0	2	0	0	.400	.400
Munoz, Pedro	.000	5	0	0	0	0	2	.000	.000
Murray, Eddie#	.227	22	5	0	2	5	3	.370	.227
Murray, Glenn	.000	4	0	0	0	1	3	.200	.000
Nixon, Otis#	.167	12	2	0	0	1	1	.231	.167
O'Brien, C	.167	6	1	0	0	0	1	.167	.333
O'Neill, Paul*	.316	19	6	1	5	1	3	.350	.579
Offerman, J#	.154	13	2	0	0	3	7	.313	.154
Oliver, Joe	.200	15	3	1	3	1	6	.250	.400
Osik, Keith	.400	5	2	0	0	1	1	.500	.400
Owens, Eric	.500	4	2	0	1	0	1	.600	.750
Pagnozzi, Tom	.370	27	10	1	2	1	4	.393	.481
Pena, G#	.286	7	2	0	0	1	0	.375	.286
Pendleton, T#	.471	17	8	0	2	2	2	.526	.529
Piazza, Mike	.400	10	4	1	4	3	1	.538	.700
Reed, Jody	.182	11	2	1	1	0	2	.182	.455
Ripken, Cal	.200	5	1	0	0	0	0	.200	.600
Roberts, Bip#	.400	15	6	0	4	1	1	.526	.467
Rodriguez, H*	.083	12	1	1	2	1	4	.154	.333
Rolen, Scott	.333	6	2	0	1	0	1	.333	.333
Sabo, Chris	.143	7	1	0	1	3	1	.364	.286
Samuel, Juan	.167	12	2	0	1	1	4	.231	.167
Sanchez, Rey	.200	10	2	1	3	0	1	.250	.500
Sandberg, R	.243	37	9	1	3	2	9	.282	.405
Sanders, R	.500	10	5	0	1	4	4	.643	.600
Santangelo, F#	.375	8	3	2	3	0	0	.375	1.125
Santiago, B	.333	18	6	1	4	1	1	.381	.667
Schofield, D	.200	10	2	0	0	4	3	.429	.300
Segui, David#	.455	11	5	1	2	1	1	.500	.818
Servais, A	.200	10	2	1	2	0	3	.200	.500
Sheffield, G	.143	7	1	0	0	2	1	.333	.143
Sierra, Ruben#	.200	5	1	0	0	0	0	.200	.200
Silvestri, D	.000	3	0	0	1	2	2	.333	.000
Smith, Dwight*	.375	16	6	1	3	2	2	.421	.750
Smith, Ozzie*	.147	34	5	0	2	3	8	.194	.176
Sosa, Sammy	.158	19	3	2	5	1	7	.200	.474
Spiers, Bill*	.200	5	1	0	1	0	0	.167	.200
Steinbach, T	.200	5	1	0	0	0	1	.200	.200
Stillwell, K#	.250	8	2	0	0	0	0	.333	.833
Stocker, K#	.250	12	3	0	1	1	4	.308	.250
Strawberry, D*	.222	18	4	0	1	6	7	.417	.333
Tarasco, Tony*	.500	2	1	0	0	3	1	.800	.500
Taubensee, E*	.357	14	5	0	4	2	3	.412	.429
Thompson, Mil*	.125	24	3	0	1	4	4	.250	.125
Thompson, Rob	.300	20	6	0	0	3	7	.391	.400
Valle, Dave	.000	5	0	0	0	0	2	.000	.000
Vaughn, Greg	.400	5	2	2	6	0	0	.400	1.600
Vizcaino, J#	.182	11	2	0	1	0	3	.182	.273
Vizquel, Omar*	.400	5	2	0	0	0	0	.400	.400
Walker, Larry*	.467	15	7	0	2	0	1	.467	.667
Wallach, Tim	.333	6	2	0	0	0	0	.333	.333
Weiss, Walt#	.417	12	5	0	0	1	2	.500	.500
White, Devon#	.286	7	2	0	0	0	4	.286	.429
White, R	.375	8	3	2	3	2	0	.500	1.125
Whiten, Mark#	.333	9	3	0	2	1	3	.400	.556
Wilkins, Rick*	.222	18	4	0	1	4	6	.263	.278
Williams, Ma	.409	22	9	1	2	1	6	.435	.636
Young, Eric	.286	14	4	1	5	1	1	.353	.500
Zeile, Todd	.394	33	13	1	7	6	6	.475	.576

Batter	Avg	AB	H	HR	BI	BB	SO	OBP	Slg
Alomar, R#	.286	7	2	0	0	0	3	.286	.286
Anderson, Brd*	.250	12	3	0	4	3	2	.375	.250

Paul Gibson, Yankees — LHP

Batter	Avg	AB	H	HR	BI	BB	SO	OBP	Slg
Baerga, C#	.333	6	2	0	0	0	0	.333	.333
Baines, H*	.286	7	2	1	5	2	1	.400	.714
Belle, Albert	.000	5	0	0	0	0	2	.000	.000
Bichette, D	.600	5	3	0	2	2	1	.714	1.200
Blowers, Mike	.571	7	4	1	4	0	1	.571	1.429
Boggs, Wade*	.250	16	4	0	0	0	2	.250	.250
Borders, Pat	.400	10	4	1	3	5	0	.563	.900
Buhner, Jay	.111	9	1	0	0	1	3	.200	.111
Burks, Ellis	.571	14	8	0	4	1	0	.588	.643
Canseco, Jose	.000	5	0	0	0	1	4	.167	.000
Carter, Joe	.571	7	4	1	5	0	0	.571	1.143
Cole, Alex*	.400	5	2	0	0	0	0	.400	.400
Dascenzo, D#	.600	5	3	0	0	1	0	.667	.600
Daulton, D*	.250	5	1	0	1	0	0	.200	.200
Davis, Chili#	.250	12	3	0	2	3	0	.400	.250
Deer, Rob	.385	13	5	2	3	3	4	.500	1.000
Devereaux, M	.200	5	1	0	0	0	0	.200	.200
Eisenreich, J*	.375	8	3	0	2	0	1	.375	.375
Espinoza, A	.400	10	4	0	0	2	2	.500	.400
Fermin, Felix	.200	5	1	0	0	0	0	.200	.200
Finley, Steve*	.333	6	2	1	1	0	0	.333	.833
Franco, Julio	.333	12	4	0	0	2	1	.429	.417
Gaetti, Gary	.500	8	4	1	2	2	2	.600	1.000
Gagne, Greg	.500	8	4	1	3	1	1	.500	1.000
Gallego, Mike	.364	11	4	0	2	0	2	.333	.545
Gonzales, R	.000	4	0	0	0	1	1	.200	.000
Grace, Mark*	.286	7	2	0	0	0	0	.286	.286
Greenwell, M*	.238	21	5	0	5	0	0	.273	.286
Griffey Jr, K*	.556	18	10	2	3	3	0	.619	1.000
Guillen, O*	.313	16	5	0	2	0	0	.313	.438
Hall, Mel*	.200	10	2	1	3	1	3	.273	.500
Hamilton, D*	.200	5	1	0	0	0	0	.200	.200
Henderson, D	.143	7	1	0	0	1	0	.250	.143
Hill, G	.400	5	2	1	1	0	2	.400	1.200
Hollins, Dave#	.250	4	1	0	0	1	0	.400	.250
Howell, Jack*	.000	9	0	0	0	2	1	.182	.000
Huson, Jeff*	.600	5	3	0	2	0	0	.500	.600
Incaviglia, P	.167	6	1	1	3	0	1	.167	.667
Jaha, John	.333	6	2	1	2	0	1	.333	.833
Johnson, L*	.300	10	3	0	2	0	0	.300	.300
Joyner, Wally*	.263	19	5	0	2	1	3	.273	.316
Karkovice, R	.286	7	2	1	3	1	0	.375	.714
Kelly, R	.333	9	3	0	0	1	0	.400	.333
Knoblauch, C	.286	7	2	0	0	1	2	.375	.571
Lankford, Ray*	.200	5	1	0	0	1	2	.333	.200
Leius, Scott	.000	4	0	0	0	2	2	.333	.000
Liriano, N#	.200	10	2	0	0	0	4	.200	.300
Macfarlane, M	.364	11	4	0	2	0	4	.364	.364
Martinez, E	.500	8	4	1	3	2	1	.600	.875
Martinez, T*	.167	6	1	0	1	2	0	.375	.167
May, Derrick*	.167	6	1	0	0	2	1	.375	.167
McGriff, Fred*	.125	16	2	0	1	3	5	.263	.188
McGwire, Mark	.300	10	3	0	0	3	2	.462	.300
McRae, Brian*	.250	8	2	1	1	0	0	.333	.500
Molitor, Paul	.300	20	6	1	1	3	0	.391	.500
Naehring, Tim	.500	6	3	0	2	1	1	.571	.667
Nilsson, Dave*	.429	7	3	0	0	1	1	.429	.714
O'Brien, C	.000	5	0	0	0	0	0	.000	.000
Olerud, John*	.250	8	2	0	2	2	1	.400	.250
Orsulak, Joe*	.444	9	4	0	0	2	0	.545	.444
Palmeiro, R*	.278	18	5	0	3	1	4	.316	.278
Palmer, Dean	.400	5	2	1	2	0	1	.400	1.000
Phillips, T#	.333	6	2	0	0	1	1	.429	.333
Polonia, Luis*	.286	7	2	0	2	0	0	.286	.286
Raines, Tim#	.333	3	1	0	1	2	0	.600	.333
Reed, Jody	.273	11	3	0	1	1	0	.333	.273
Ripken, Billy	.400	10	4	0	1	1	0	.500	.400
Ripken, Cal	.214	14	3	0	1	1	0	.267	.286
Rodriguez, I	.250	4	1	0	0	0	0	.400	.250
Schofield, D	.267	15	4	1	1	1	1	.313	.467
Seitzer, K	.182	11	2	0	2	1	2	.250	.182
Sheffield, G	.400	5	2	0	0	0	2	.400	.400
Sierra, Ruben#	.313	16	5	0	2	3	1	.421	.375
Slaught, Don	.250	4	1	0	0	1	0	.400	.500
Smith, Dwight*	.400	5	2	1	3	0	1	.333	1.200
Spiers, Bill*	.308	13	4	0	1	1	2	.357	.308
Steinbach, T	.308	13	4	0	1	0	0	.308	.385
Stillwell, K#	.100	10	1	0	0	4	3	.357	.100
Surhoff, B.J.*	.250	24	6	1	5	0	1	.250	.458
Sveum, Dale#	.333	15	5	0	2	0	3	.375	.400
Tartabull, D	.273	11	3	1	2	2	4	.429	.545
Tettleton, M#	.375	8	3	1	2	1	2	.444	.875
Thome, Jim*	.000	6	0	0	0	0	0	.000	.000
Valle, Dave	.000	7	0	0	0	0	2	.000	.000
Vaughn, Greg	.143	7	1	1	2	2	2	.333	.571
Vaughn, Mo*	.600	5	3	1	4	0	0	.600	1.200
Velarde, R	.125	8	1	0	0	1	2	.222	.125
Ventura, R*	.625	8	5	0	2	1	1	.667	.625
Vizquel, Omar#	.222	9	2	0	1	1	0	.300	.222
Weiss, Walt#	.250	8	2	0	0	1	1	.333	.250
White, Devon#	.071	14	1	0	1	1	4	.188	.143

Paul Gibson, Yankees — LHP

Batter	Avg	AB	H	HR	BI	BB	SO	OBP	Slg
Wilkins, Rick*	.400	5	2	0	0	0	1	.400	.600
Worthington	.429	7	3	0	2	0	2	.375	.571

Brian Givens, Brewers — LHP

Batter	Avg	AB	H	HR	BI	BB	SO	OBP	Slg
Anderson, Brd*	.000	3	0	0	0	2	1	.400	.000
Anderson, G*	.800	5	4	0	1	0	1	.800	1.000
Becker, Rich*	.400	5	2	0	0	0	2	.400	.400
Berroa, G	.167	6	1	0	1	0	1	.167	.333
Bonilla, B#	.600	5	3	2	4	0	1	.600	1.800
Coomer, Ron	.667	3	2	0	0	1	0	.800	.667
Cordova, M	.600	5	3	0	0	1	0	.600	.800
Curtis, Chad	.143	7	1	0	0	2	1	.333	.143
Devereaux, M	.000	8	0	0	0	1	0	.111	.000
Durham, Ray#	.375	8	3	0	2	2	0	.500	.500
Fielder, C	.286	7	2	0	0	1	2	.375	.286
Fryman, T	.500	8	4	0	1	1	2	.556	.750
Gomez, Chris	.250	8	2	0	4	1	0	.333	.500
Gonzalez, J	.600	5	3	1	3	0	1	.600	1.200
Grebeck, C	.333	3	1	0	0	0	1	.333	.444
Higginson, B*	.000	5	0	0	0	0	1	.000	.000
Hudler, Rex	.000	5	0	0	0	0	1	.000	.000
Johnson, L*	.333	6	2	0	0	2	0	.500	.333
Karkovice, R	.556	9	5	0	3	0	1	.556	.778
Kelly, Pat	.200	5	1	0	0	0	0	.200	.400
Knoblauch, C	.500	6	3	0	3	0	0	.500	.667
Leius, Scott	.000	5	0	0	1	0	1	.000	.000
McGwire, Mark	.667	6	4	2	4	0	1	.667	1.833
Munoz, Pedro	.000	6	0	0	1	0	1	.000	.000
Palmeiro, R*	.000	5	0	0	0	1	0	.000	.000
Raines, Tim#	.286	7	2	0	0	1	0	.375	.429
Reboulet, J	.500	4	2	0	1	2	0	.667	1.000
Ripken, Cal	.667	3	2	1	4	2	0	.800	1.667
Rodriguez, I	.400	5	2	0	3	1	0	.500	.400
Samuel, Juan	.000	5	0	0	0	0	1	.000	.000
Sierra, Ruben#	.429	7	3	0	1	1	1	.444	.429
Stanley, Mike	.000	5	0	0	0	2	1	.333	.000
Steinbach, T	.000	5	0	0	0	0	1	.167	.000
Tettleton, M#	.250	4	1	0	0	1	0	.400	.250
Thomas, Frank	.429	7	3	0	2	2	1	.556	.714
Trammell, A	.250	4	1	0	0	1	0	.400	.250
Velarde, R	.500	6	3	0	3	1	0	.571	.833
Ventura, R*	.600	5	3	1	1	1	1	.667	.600
Vitiello, Joe	.400	5	2	0	0	0	0	.400	.600
Williams, Ber#	.500	4	2	0	1	2	1	.667	.750
Williams, Ger	.200	5	1	0	0	0	2	.200	.400

Tom Glavine, Braves — LHP

Batter	Avg	AB	H	HR	BI	BB	SO	OBP	Slg
Abbott, Kurt	.313	16	5	0	0	0	2	.389	.313
Alfonzo, E	.167	6	1	0	0	0	2	.167	.167
Alicea, Luis#	.421	19	8	0	5	2	3	.455	.526
Alomar, R#	.371	35	13	0	5	4	4	.371	.457
Alou, Moises	.182	33	6	0	2	5	6	.289	.242
Andrews, S	.111	9	1	0	0	0	1	.111	.111
Anthony, Eric*	.000	11	0	0	0	1	5	.083	.000
Arias, Alex	.133	15	2	0	1	1	0	.188	.133
Ashley, Billy	.400	10	4	0	1	4	2	.571	.500
Ausmus, Brad	.000	14	0	0	1	0	0	.000	.000
Bagwell, Jeff	.382	34	13	2	5	5	7	.462	.618
Barberie, B#	.250	12	3	0	1	2	2	.308	.417
Batiste, Kim	.182	11	2	1	0	0	1	.182	.455
Bell, David	.400	5	2	0	0	0	2	.400	.400
Bell, Derek	.313	16	5	0	2	2	2	.389	.313
Bell, Jay	.311	61	19	1	3	4	8	.354	.410
Belliard, R	.250	4	1	0	0	1	0	.400	.250
Benjamin, M	.143	7	1	0	0	0	1	.143	.143
Berry, Sean	.154	13	2	0	1	0	2	.154	.154
Bichette, D	.414	29	12	1	5	1	4	.419	.621
Biggio, Craig	.259	54	14	2	6	4	5	.310	.426
Blowers, Mike	.250	8	2	0	1	1	2	.333	.375
Bogar, Tim	.500	6	3	0	1	1	1	.571	.500
Bonds, Barry*	.333	48	16	2	9	7	9	.429	.583
Bonilla, B#	.188	48	9	4	6	0	5	.235	.364
Boone, Bret	.242	33	8	1	6	0	5	.235	.364
Branson, Jeff*	.083	12	1	0	0	0	4	.083	.083
Brumfield, J	.304	23	7	0	0	1	2	.333	.391
Burks, Ellis	.474	19	9	0	3	3	3	.545	.789
Butler, Brett*	.292	65	19	0	4	7	7	.370	.292
Caminiti, Ken#	.246	61	15	1	6	5	9	.303	.344
Candaele, C#	.269	26	7	0	6	0	4	.296	.500
Cangelosi, J#	.231	13	3	0	0	3	5	.375	.308
Carr, Chuck	.211	19	4	0	2	4	3	.333	.263
Carreon, Mark	.148	27	4	0	1	1	1	.179	.185
Carter, Joe	.111	9	1	1	1	4	0	.385	.444
Castilla, V	.300	30	9	0	4	2	1	.333	.467
Castro, Juan	.286	7	2	0	0	1	0	.375	.286
Cedeno, A	.300	20	6	1	2	4	5	.417	.600
Cedeno, Roger#	.286	7	2	1	3	0	2	.286	.714
Cianfrocco, A	.467	15	7	0	4	0	3	.412	.467
Clark, Phil	.091	11	1	0	0	1	1	.167	.091

Tom Glavine, Braves — LHP

Batter	Avg	AB	H	HR	BI	BB	SO	OBP	Slg
Clark, Will*	.283	53	15	0	3	5	11	.350	.340
Clayton, R	.130	23	3	0	0	2	3	.200	.174
Colbrunn, G	.269	26	7	0	4	1	1	.286	.385
Coleman, V#	.208	24	5	0	0	2	3	.269	.250
Conine, Jeff	.188	32	6	0	5	4	6	.278	.250
Cordero, Wil	.318	22	7	0	3	1	2	.348	.409
Cummings, M*	.333	6	2	0	1	0	3	.333	.333
Dascenzo, D#	.286	7	2	0	1	0	0	.286	.286
Daulton, D*	.313	32	10	0	7	8	2	.450	.469
Davis, Eric	.310	42	13	3	7	7	6	.408	.643
Dawson, Andre	.200	30	6	2	4	2	3	.250	.500
Decker, Steve	.188	16	3	1	3	0	0	.188	.438
DeShields, D*	.200	50	10	0	2	2	14	.226	.200
Dorsett, B	.250	12	3	1	1	1	3	.308	.583
Duncan, D	.145	55	8	0	2	0	10	.161	.200
Dunston, S	.171	35	6	0	3	1	4	.189	.171
Dykstra, L*	.385	39	15	0	4	13	5	.538	.462
Elster, Kevin	.250	16	4	0	3	3	1	.350	.375
Everett, Carl#	.167	6	1	0	0	1	1	.286	.167
Finley, Steve*	.333	42	14	0	2	2	10	.356	.381
Fletcher, D*	.000	4	0	0	1	2	1	.333	.000
Gagne, Greg	.250	8	2	0	0	1	1	.333	.250
Galarraga, A	.262	61	16	2	9	4	14	.303	.426
Gant, Ron	.364	11	4	0	1	5	1	.563	.455
Garcia, C	.133	15	2	0	0	2	3	.235	.133
Gilkey, B	.242	33	8	1	3	6	6	.375	.364
Girardi, Joe	.154	26	4	0	0	2	5	.214	.154
Gomez, Leo	.308	13	4	0	1	0	4	.308	.462
Gonzalez, L*	.333	27	9	1	2	3	6	.419	.519
Goodwin, C*	.200	5	1	0	0	1	1	.200	.200
Grace, Mark*	.297	64	19	0	3	5	5	.348	.391
Grissom, M	.205	44	9	0	0	1	6	.222	.250
Grudzielanek	.053	19	1	0	0	0	2	.053	.053
Guerrero, V	.000	5	0	0	0	0	1	.000	.000
Gutierrez, R	.200	15	3	0	0	0	3	.200	.200
Gwynn, Tony*	.338	80	27	1	6	4	2	.369	.425
Harris, Lenny*	.200	10	2	0	0	0	3	.200	.200
Hayes, C	.364	11	4	0	1	0	0	.364	.455
Hernandez, Ca	.364	11	4	0	0	0	0	.364	.455
Hernandez, Jo	.364	11	4	0	2	1	2	.417	.545
Hill, G	.400	20	8	1	5	1	1	.429	.650
Hollins, Dave#	.364	22	8	0	1	2	2	.462	.409
Howard, T*	.154	13	2	0	0	0	4	.154	.154
Hubbard, Tr	.250	8	2	0	0	0	3	.250	.250
Hudler, Rex	.190	21	4	1	3	1	2	.227	.333
Hundley, Todd#	.429	7	3	0	1	2	1	.556	.429
Hunter, Brian	.111	9	1	0	2	0	2	.111	.111
Incaviglia, P	.250	20	5	2	5	6	5	.423	.650
Javier, Stan#	.000	19	0	0	0	3	3	.136	.000
Jefferies, G	.300	40	12	3	7	0	2	.300	.550
Johnson, Bri	.500	4	2	0	0	1	1	.600	.500
Johnson, Char	.214	14	3	1	2	0	1	.214	.429
Jones, Chris	.231	13	3	0	0	0	5	.231	.308
Jordan, Brian	.286	14	4	0	2	2	4	.375	.429
Jordan, Ricky	.290	31	9	0	6	0	2	.290	.419
Joyner, Wally*	.400	5	2	0	2	1	0	.500	.400
Karros, Eric	.367	30	11	0	9	4	7	.417	.433
Kelly, R	.125	8	1	0	0	2	0	.300	.125
Kent, Jeff	.188	16	3	0	1	0	4	.188	.188
King, Jeff	.205	39	8	1	3	6	2	.311	.282
Lankford, Ray*	.364	33	12	0	4	5	5	.447	.455
Lansing, Mike	.250	32	8	0	1	2	1	.294	.281
Larkin, Barry	.313	80	25	3	11	12	3	.398	.525
Lewis, Darren	.222	27	6	0	0	4	5	.323	.296
Lewis, Mark	.091	11	1	0	1	1	4	.167	.091
Liriano, N#	.200	10	2	0	1	1	2	.273	.300
Mabry, John*	.400	5	2	0	0	0	0	.400	.400
Magadan, Dave*	.455	33	15	0	4	4	2	.514	.485
Manwaring, K	.214	42	9	0	3	2	10	.244	.262
Martin, Al*	.000	11	0	0	0	0	4	.000	.000
Martinez, Da*	.200	5	1	1	1	2	2	.429	.800
McCracken, Q#	.111	9	1	0	0	0	1	.111	.111
McGee, Willie#	.289	45	13	1	5	2	7	.319	.400
McGriff, Fred*	.364	22	8	0	5	4	4	.444	.500
McRae, Brian#	.304	23	7	0	1	1	2	.333	.348
Merced, O*	.222	18	4	0	1	0	3	.222	.222
Mitchell, K	.356	45	16	5	12	10	7	.473	.756
Mondesi, Raul	.143	21	3	0	1	0	10	.143	.143
Morandini, M*	.286	21	6	0	2	3	3	.375	.286
Morris, Hal*	.185	27	5	0	4	4	4	.290	.222
Mouton, James	.333	12	4	0	0	2	3	.429	.417
Murray, Eddie#	.259	54	14	0	4	0	7	.255	.278
Nixon, Otis#	.263	19	5	0	0	2	2	.333	.263
O'Brien, C	.389	18	7	0	2	1	1	.421	.611
O'Neill, Paul*	.050	20	1	0	0	0	7	.050	.050
Obando, S	.250	4	1	0	0	2	0	.500	.250
Ochoa, Alex	.429	7	3	0	0	0	2	.429	.429
Offerman, J#	.318	22	7	1	3	5	3	.444	.545
Oliver, Joe	.260	50	13	0	3	3	11	.302	.340
Owens, Eric	.100	10	1	0	0	0	0	.222	.125
Owens, J	.222	9	2	0	0	0	1	.222	.333
Pagnozzi, Tom	.182	22	4	0	3	0	2	.182	.273
Palmeiro, R*	.000	4	0	0	0	1	0	.200	.000
Parent, Mark	.050	20	1	0	0	0	2	.050	.050
Parker, Rick	.400	10	4	0	0	0	2	.400	.500
Pena, G#	.200	15	3	1	1	2	7	.294	.467
Pena, Tony	.182	11	2	0	0	1	3	.250	.182
Pendleton, T#	.370	27	10	1	6	0	2	.370	.519
Piazza, Mike	.421	19	8	2	3	1	2	.450	.789
Plantier, P*	.000	6	0	0	0	0	3	.000	.000
Prince, Tom	.316	19	6	0	1	3	2	.409	.474
Raines, Tim*	.308	13	4	0	4	3	2	.412	.308
Reed, Jody	.250	20	5	0	4	3	3	.348	.250
Renteria, E	.333	6	2	0	0	0	3	.333	.333
Roberts, Bip#	.313	48	15	0	3	4	6	.389	.396
Rodriguez, H*	.000	6	0	0	0	0	4	.000	.000
Sabo, Chris	.293	58	17	1	5	3	3	.323	.414
Samuel, Juan	.333	48	16	2	6	7	11	.429	.500
Sanchez, Rey	.045	22	1	0	0	0	0	.045	.045
Sandberg, R	.286	49	14	1	5	4	7	.340	.490
Sanders, R	.282	39	11	1	3	5	7	.378	.436
Santangelo, F#	.200	2	0	0	1	1	1	.333	.200
Santiago, B	.271	59	16	1	4	5	6	.328	.339
Scarsone, S	.125	8	1	0	0	0	3	.125	.125
Segui, David#	.400	15	6	1	3	2	3	.500	.667
Servais, M	.138	29	4	0	0	4	5	.242	.207
Sheaffer, D	.214	14	3	0	5	0	2	.200	.286
Sheffield, G	.296	27	8	4	7	9	1	.472	.741
Shipley, C	.385	13	5	0	0	0	2	.385	.385
Silvestri, D	.200	5	1	0	1	0	2	.200	.400
Slaught, Don	.250	32	8	0	1	3	0	.314	.250
Smith, Ozzie*	.320	50	16	0	3	3	3	.358	.480
Sosa, Sammy	.207	29	6	2	4	5	7	.324	.448
Stillwell, K#	.125	8	1	0	1	0	2	.125	.125
Stocker, K#	.222	18	4	0	0	2	3	.300	.278
Strawberry, D*	.250	32	8	3	7	2	9	.294	.594
Tavarez, Je#	.000	5	0	0	0	0	1	.000	.000
Thompson, Rob	.393	56	22	4	7	6	10	.452	.786
Thompson, Ry	.100	10	1	0	1	1	6	.182	.200
Timmons, O	.357	14	5	0	1	1	4	.400	.500
Veras, Q#	.286	14	4	0	1	0	2	.286	.286
Vizcaino, J#	.375	16	6	0	1	5	0	.524	.375
Walker, Larry*	.333	48	16	3	8	6	5	.407	.563
Wallach, Tim	.367	60	22	5	12	5	2	.415	.733
Walton, J	.281	32	9	0	1	3	6	.351	.406
Webster, L	.176	17	3	0	1	1	3	.222	.235
Wehner, John	.143	14	2	0	0	1	0	.200	.143
Weiss, Walt#	.231	26	6	0	2	5	4	.344	.308
White, Devon#	.000	5	0	0	0	1	0	.167	.000
White, R	.333	21	7	0	1	2	5	.391	.429
Whiten, Mark#	.500	18	6	0	2	0	2	.500	.625
Wilkins, Rick*	.333	6	2	0	0	3	3	.556	.500
Williams, Ma	.157	51	8	1	4	3	10	.204	.333
Young, Eric	.243	37	9	0	1	4	3	.317	.297
Young, Kevin	.154	13	2	1	2	2	3	.267	.385
Zeile, Todd	.283	46	13	0	6	5	8	.353	.326

Greg Gohr, Angels — RHP

Batter	Avg	AB	H	HR	BI	BB	SO	OBP	Slg
Alomar, R#	.250	4	1	0	0	0	1	.400	.250
Alomar Jr, S	.429	7	3	0	0	0	1	.429	.429
Baerga, C#	.000	6	0	0	0	0	0	.000	.000
Battle, Allen	.167	6	1	0	0	0	0	.167	.333
Becker, Rich*	.000	6	0	0	0	1	1	.143	.000
Belle, Albert	.600	10	6	2	3	0	2	.600	1.200
Berroa, G	.375	8	3	0	1	1	1	.444	.500
Boggs, Wade*	.333	6	2	0	0	0	1	.333	.333
Bonilla, B#	.600	5	3	0	2	0	0	.600	.800
Bordick, Mike	.000	7	0	0	0	1	1	.125	.000
Brosius, S	.429	7	3	2	3	1	2	.500	1.286
Buhner, Jay	.000	5	0	0	0	2	1	.286	.000
Canseco, Jose	.600	5	3	1	2	0	1	.667	1.200
Carter, Joe	.286	7	2	1	2	0	0	.286	1.000
Clark, Will	.600	5	3	0	0	0	0	.714	.600
Cora, Joey#	.375	8	3	0	0	0	0	.375	.500
Cordova, Julio	.667	6	4	1	1	0	1	.714	1.167
Davis, Chili*	.200	5	1	0	1	1	0	.333	.200
DiSarcina, G	.400	5	2	0	0	0	0	.400	.400
Edmonds, Jim*	.250	4	1	0	1	2	2	.500	.250
Fox, Andy*	.333	6	2	0	0	1	0	.429	.333
Franco, Julio	.400	10	4	1	2	1	2	.455	.800
Frye, Jeff	.286	7	2	0	0	1	1	.375	.286
Gates, Brent#	.857	7	6	0	1	2	0	.889	1.000
Giambi, Jason*	.600	5	3	1	2	1	1	.667	1.400
Girardi, Joe	.429	7	3	0	0	0	0	.429	.571
Gonzalez, J	.143	7	1	0	0	0	0	.143	.143
Greer, Rusty*	.333	6	2	0	0	1	1	.429	.333
Griffey Jr, K*	.400	5	2	2	4	1	0	.500	1.600
Guillen, O*	.333	6	2	0	0	0	0	.333	.333
Hamilton, D*	.333	6	2	0	0	0	1	.333	.500
Hoiles, Chris	.167	6	1	1	3	0	5	.167	.667
Hollins, Dave#	.333	6	2	1	3	1	0	.429	.833

Greg Gohr, Angels — RHP

Batter	Avg	AB	H	HR	BI	BB	SO	OBP	Slg
Jeter, Derek	.571	7	4	0	3	3	1	.700	.714
Johnson, L*	.400	5	2	0	1	0	0	.400	.600
Knoblauch, C	.333	6	2	0	0	1	3	.429	.333
Leyritz, Jim	.400	5	2	0	0	1	1	.571	.400
Lofton, Kenny*	.200	10	2	1	1	0	1	.200	.500
Martinez, T*	.333	9	3	0	0	0	2	.333	.333
Meares, Pat	.500	6	3	0	0	0	2	.500	.500
Molitor, Paul	.364	11	4	0	0	0	0	.364	.364
Munoz, Pedro	.429	7	3	1	2	0	2	.429	.857
Murray, Eddie#	.500	8	4	1	2	0	0	.500	.875
Naehring, Tim	.167	6	1	0	0	0	2	.167	.167
Newson, W*	.500	4	2	0	1	2	2	.667	.500
O'Leary, Troy*	.333	6	2	0	3	0	1	.333	.500
O'Neill, Paul*	.222	9	2	0	1	1	0	.300	.222
Olerud, John*	.200	5	1	0	0	0	0	.200	.200
Palmer, Dean	.000	5	0	0	0	1	3	.167	.000
Raines, Tim#	.417	12	5	1	6	0	1	.385	.667
Ramirez, M	.250	8	2	1	3	0	1	.222	.625
Ripken, Cal	.000	6	0	0	1	1	1	.143	.000
Rodriguez, Al	.500	4	2	1	2	1	0	.600	1.250
Rodriguez, I	.200	5	1	0	1	0	1	.200	.200
Salmon, Tim	.167	6	1	0	0	1	1	.286	.167
Sierra, Ruben*	.000	11	0	0	1	0	3	.000	.000
Snow, J.T.#	.200	5	1	0	1	0	1	.200	.200
Sorrento, P*	.167	6	1	0	0	0	2	.167	.333
Sprague, Ed	.286	7	2	0	0	0	2	.286	.286
Stahoviak, S*	.200	5	1	0	0	1	1	.333	.200
Stanley, Mike	.500	4	2	1	1	1	0	.600	1.250
Steinbach, T	.571	7	4	1	3	1	2	.667	1.143
Surhoff, B.J.*	.250	4	1	0	0	2	0	.500	.250
Thomas, Frank	.167	6	1	0	0	1	1	.286	.167
Thome, Jim*	.571	7	4	2	4	3	3	.700	1.429
Valentin, Jhn	.600	5	3	2	2	0	1	.600	2.000
Vaughn, Mo*	.167	6	1	0	0	0	2	.167	.333
Velarde, R	.250	4	1	0	0	1	1	.400	.250
Ventura, R*	.286	7	2	1	5	0	0	.286	.714
Vizquel, Omar*	.222	9	2	0	0	1	2	.300	.222
Williams, Ber#	.400	5	2	0	0	1	2	.571	.400
Wilson, Dan	.600	5	3	1	2	0	1	.600	1.400

Dwight Gooden, Yankees — RHP

Batter	Avg	AB	H	HR	BI	BB	SO	OBP	Slg
Aldrete, Mike*	.273	22	6	0	2	1	7	.304	.318
Alicea, Luis#	.200	10	2	0	0	1	1	.273	.200
Alomar, R#	.320	25	8	0	2	0	3	.320	.360
Alou, Moises	.667	6	4	2	6	0	3	.571	1.667
Amaro, Ruben#	.417	12	5	0	0	1	1	.462	.583
Anderson, Brd*	.167	6	1	0	0	1	0	.286	.167
Anthony, Eric*	.120	25	3	1	6	1	10	.143	.280
Baerga, C#	.286	7	2	1	2	0	0	.286	.857
Bagwell, Jeff	.214	14	3	0	3	3	4	.368	.357
Baines, H*	.125	8	1	0	1	1	2	.222	.250
Barberie, B#	.133	15	2	0	0	2	1	.235	.133
Batista, Tony	.167	6	1	0	1	0	3	.167	.333
Batiste, Kim	.444	9	4	0	2	1	1	.500	.556
Bell, Derek	.125	8	1	0	3	0	3	.250	.375
Bell, Jay	.333	39	13	1	2	4	7	.395	.436
Belle, Albert	.200	5	1	0	0	2	1	.429	.200
Belliard, R	.250	24	6	0	1	5	5	.379	.250
Berroa, G	.333	6	2	0	0	2	2	.500	.333
Bichette, D	.167	6	1	0	0	0	2	.286	.167
Biggio, Craig	.282	39	11	0	4	3	11	.333	.385
Blauser, Jeff	.214	14	3	0	0	1	2	.267	.214
Bonds, Barry*	.323	62	20	3	8	12	10	.440	.548
Bonilla, B#	.320	50	16	0	7	5	9	.382	.440
Bordick, Mike	.429	7	3	0	1	0	1	.429	.429
Bragg, Darren*	.231	13	3	0	3	1	5	.286	.385
Branson, J*	.200	5	1	0	0	0	2	.200	.200
Brosius, S	.333	6	2	1	1	0	1	.333	.833
Buhner, Jay	.125	8	1	1	3	1	3	.300	.500
Butler, Brett*	.370	27	10	0	2	8	3	.514	.444
Caminiti, Ken#	.136	22	3	0	3	1	5	.160	.136
Candaele, C#	.148	27	4	0	0	1	4	.179	.148
Carr, Chuck	.083	12	1	0	0	0	4	.083	.083
Carter, Joe	.444	9	4	1	4	1	2	.500	.889
Cedeno, A	.286	7	2	0	0	0	0	.286	.286
Cianfrocco, A	.250	8	2	0	1	1	2	.333	.500
Cirillo, Jeff	.200	5	1	0	1	1	1	.333	.200
Clark, Dave*	.467	15	7	2	5	4	0	.579	.867
Clark, Will*	.321	56	18	2	8	8	15	.406	.500
Clayton, R	.200	10	2	0	0	0	2	.200	.200
Colbrunn, G	.333	9	3	1	2	0	2	.333	.667
Cole, Alex*	.214	14	3	0	0	1	1	.267	.214
Coleman, V#	.192	52	10	0	1	6	9	.276	.269
Conine, Jeff	.385	13	5	0	4	1	2	.429	.462
Cora, Joey#	.385	13	5	0	0	0	1	.385	.385
Cordero, Wil	.400	5	2	0	0	0	0	.400	.400
Cordova, M	.600	5	3	0	1	0	1	.600	1.000
Curtis, Chad	.333	6	2	0	0	1	0	.429	.667
Damon, Johnny*	.000	5	0	0	0	1	0	.167	.000
Dascenzo, D#	.167	24	4	0	1	1	1	.231	.250

Dwight Gooden, Yankees — RHP

Batter	Avg	AB	H	HR	BI	BB	SO	OBP	Slg
Daulton, D*	.263	57	15	1	4	6	11	.333	.421
Davis, Chili#	.444	27	12	0	2	4	10	.516	.519
Davis, Eric	.323	31	10	2	4	1	7	.344	.516
Dawson, Andre	.243	74	18	1	9	1	15	.260	.365
DeShields, D*	.269	26	7	0	3	2	3	.321	.346
Duncan, Mariano	.167	36	6	1	3	1	13	.189	.361
Dunston, S	.156	45	7	1	4	1	16	.170	.311
Durham, Ray#	.125	8	1	0	0	2	2	.364	.125
Dykstra, L*	.303	33	10	0	3	2	3	.343	.424
Eisenreich, J*	.143	7	1	0	0	0	3	.143	.143
Elster, Kevin	.400	5	2	1	1	1	2	.500	1.200
Fielder, C	.000	5	0	0	0	1	2	.167	.000
Finley, Steve*	.294	17	5	0	1	3	0	.400	.353
Fletcher, D*	.333	9	3	0	1	1	1	.400	.333
Frye, Jeff	.167	6	1	0	0	0	1	.167	.167
Galarraga, A	.273	44	12	1	3	1	18	.304	.409
Gant, Ron	.333	42	14	1	4	1	6	.349	.548
Garcia, C	.167	6	1	0	0	0	0	.167	.167
Garciaparra	.667	3	2	1	2	1	1	.600	1.667
Giambi, Jason*	.250	8	2	0	1	1	2	.333	.375
Gilkey, B	.238	21	5	0	2	2	1	.304	.286
Girardi, Joe	.067	15	1	0	1	2	2	.222	.067
Gomez, Chris	.167	6	1	0	2	0	1	.167	.167
Gonzalez, J	.286	7	2	0	0	0	0	.375	.286
Gonzalez, L*	.526	19	10	1	3	1	3	.550	.895
Goodwin, Tom*	.300	10	3	0	0	0	1	.300	.400
Grace, Mark*	.411	56	23	1	6	4	4	.450	.518
Greene, W*	.000	5	0	0	0	0	2	.000	.000
Greenwell, M*	.333	6	2	0	0	0	0	.333	.333
Greer, Rusty*	.000	9	0	0	0	0	2	.000	.000
Griffey Jr, K*	.375	8	3	1	3	5	2	.615	.750
Grissom, M	.333	21	7	0	2	3	4	.417	.524
Guillen, O*	.125	8	1	0	1	0	1	.125	.375
Gutierrez, R	.143	7	1	0	0	1	4	.250	.286
Gwynn, Chris*	.143	7	1	0	1	2	2	.300	.143
Gwynn, Tony*	.243	70	17	0	1	7	6	.312	.314
Hall, Mel*	.667	3	2	0	1	2	0	.800	1.333
Hamelin, Bob*	.167	6	1	0	0	0	1	.167	.333
Hamilton, D*	.222	9	2	0	0	1	2	.300	.222
Harris, Lenny	.320	25	8	0	5	0	3	.320	.320
Hayes, C	.207	29	6	0	3	2	7	.250	.241
Hollins, Dave#	.227	22	5	1	3	0	8	.227	.409
Howard, David*	.200	5	1	0	0	0	0	.333	.200
Howard, T*	.182	11	2	0	0	1	3	.250	.182
Jaha, John	.200	5	1	0	0	1	1	.333	.200
James, Dion*	.150	20	3	1	1	3	4	.261	.300
Javier, Stan#	.167	12	2	0	0	0	2	.167	.333
Jefferies, Gr#	.375	8	3	0	0	0	1	.375	.500
Jefferson, R*	.333	6	2	0	1	0	2	.333	.333
Jordan, Brian	.429	7	3	0	2	2	1	.556	.429
Jordan, Ricky	.310	29	9	0	5	0	5	.333	.345
Justice, Dave*	.278	18	5	2	4	2	5	.350	.667
Karkovice, J	.333	6	2	1	2	0	1	.333	1.000
Karros, Eric	.143	14	2	0	1	0	2	.143	.214
Kelly, R	.714	7	5	0	0	1	0	.778	1.000
King, Jeff	.375	16	6	0	7	2	2	.474	.500
Knoblauch, C	.400	5	2	0	0	0	0	.400	.400
Lankford, Ray*	.440	25	11	2	7	5	4	.533	.760
Larkin, Barry	.382	34	13	1	6	2	3	.405	.588
Lawton, Matt*	.200	5	1	0	0	0	1	.200	.200
Lemke, Mark#	.091	11	1	0	2	0	1	.083	.182
Lewis, Darren	.333	21	7	0	1	0	2	.333	.476
Lockhart, K*	.143	7	1	0	0	0	0	.143	.143
Lofton, Kenny*	.500	8	4	0	0	0	1	.500	.500
Macfarlane, M	.000	6	0	0	0	0	0	.000	.000
Magadan, Dave*	.250	4	1	0	1	0	0	.400	.500
Manwaring, K	.286	7	2	0	1	0	1	.286	.286
Martin, Al*	.364	11	4	0	3	3	3	.500	.364
Martinez, Da*	.230	74	17	1	6	7	13	.296	.324
Martinez, E	.250	8	2	1	6	4	1	.462	.625
Marzano, John	.200	5	1	0	0	0	0	.200	.200
May, Derrick*	.346	26	9	0	4	1	3	.370	.423
McGee, Willie#	.329	79	26	0	8	5	11	.365	.405
McGriff, Fred*	.240	25	6	0	1	3	10	.310	.240
McGwire, Mark	.500	4	2	0	0	1	0	.600	.750
McLemore, M*	.125	8	1	0	0	0	2	.125	.250
Merced, O*	.290	31	9	0	2	1	5	.313	.355
Mitchell, K	.269	26	7	2	4	6	8	.394	.538
Molitor, Paul	.250	4	1	0	1	1	1	.400	.250
Morandini, M*	.370	27	10	0	3	3	5	.433	.481
Morris, Hal*	.250	12	3	1	4	1	4	.286	.583
Murray, Eddie#	.111	27	3	0	4	3	7	.194	.111
Myers, Greg*	.000	5	0	0	0	0	0	.000	.000
Nilsson, Dave*	.750	4	3	0	3	2	0	.833	1.250
Nixon, Otis#	.250	12	3	0	0	0	0	.308	.250
O'Leary, Troy*	.000	4	0	0	0	0	0	.200	.000
O'Neill, Paul*	.292	24	7	0	4	3	6	.370	.458
Offerman, J#	.190	21	4	1	2	2	1	.261	.333
Oliver, Joe	.267	15	4	1	2	0	6	.267	.533
Orsulak, Joe*	.313	16	5	0	2	1	1	.421	.438
Pagnozzi, Tom	.464	28	13	0	4	0	1	.483	.536

72

Dwight Gooden, Yankees — RHP

Batter	Avg	AB	H	HR	BI	BB	SO	OBP	Slg
Palmeiro, R*	.194	31	6	3	6	4	5	.286	.484
Palmer, Dean	.286	7	2	0	2	1	2	.333	.286
Pena, G#	.167	12	2	0	0	0	5	.167	.167
Pena, Tony	.143	42	6	0	4	0	14	.143	.190
Pendleton, T#	.257	74	19	3	13	4	13	.300	.405
Phillips, T#	.333	6	2	0	0	5	1	.636	.333
Piazza, Mike	.375	8	3	1	2	2	2	.500	.750
Plantier, P*	.083	12	1	0	1	0	2	.083	.083
Polonia, Luis*	.000	5	0	0	0	1	0	.167	.000
Raines, Tim#	.174	46	8	0	4	11	6	.333	.239
Ramirez, M	.000	6	0	0	0	0	1	.000	.000
Reed, Jeff*	.167	18	3	0	2	1	4	.211	.222
Ripken, Cal	.600	5	3	1	4	1	1	.667	1.400
Roberts, Bip#	.222	36	8	0	1	2	4	.263	.250
Rodriguez, Al	.600	10	6	1	1	3	0	.692	1.100
Rodriguez, H*	.333	6	2	1	1	0	2	.333	.833
Rodriguez, I	.167	6	1	0	0	0	0	.167	.167
Sabo, Chris	.357	28	10	1	5	2	3	.400	.643
Samuel, Juan	.183	71	13	0	4	3	24	.216	.310
Sanchez, Rey	.333	9	3	0	2	0	0	.333	.556
Sandberg, R	.313	112	35	1	13	5	23	.342	.411
Sanders, M	.375	8	3	1	3	2	3	.455	.750
Santiago, B	.191	47	9	1	5	0	7	.191	.319
Schu, Rick	.375	8	3	2	3	1	3	.444	1.125
Seitzer, K	.500	4	2	1	1	2	1	.667	1.250
Servais, S	.333	3	1	0	1	2	0	.500	.333
Sheffield, G	.316	19	6	0	1	1	2	.333	.316
Slaught, Don	.500	12	6	0	3	2	2	.533	.500
Smith, Dwight*	.269	26	7	0	3	3	6	.345	.423
Smith, Ozzie#	.321	84	27	0	2	10	3	.394	.369
Sorrento, P*	.273	11	3	1	2	1	2	.333	.545
Sosa, Sammy	.000	9	0	0	0	1	6	.100	.000
Steinbach, T	.286	7	2	0	1	0	2	.250	.286
Stillwell, K#	.250	8	2	0	1	1	3	.333	.250
Strange, Doug#	.182	11	2	1	1	1	2	.250	.545
Strawberry, D*	.167	6	1	0	0	1	2	.286	.167
Surhoff, B.J.*	.286	7	2	0	0	0	3	.286	.286
Tettleton, M#	.500	4	2	1	4	2	2	.667	1.500
Thomas, Frank	.200	5	1	0	0	4	1	.556	.200
Thome, Jim*	.600	5	3	1	2	1	1	.667	1.400
Thompson, Mil*	.160	50	8	0	0	7	17	.276	.180
Thompson, Rob	.310	42	13	0	1	4	7	.383	.333
Trammell, A	.286	7	2	0	0	0	0	.286	.286
Tucker, M*	.286	7	2	0	0	0	1	.286	.286
Valentin, Jse#	.000	3	0	0	0	2	1	.400	.000
Vaughn, Greg	.000	3	0	0	2	1	0	.333	.000
Vaughn, Mo*	.200	5	1	0	0	1	3	.333	.400
Ventura, R*	.000	8	0	0	1	3		.111	.000
Vina, F*	.500	6	3	0	0	0	0	.571	.500
Vizcaino, J#	.304	23	7	0	0	1	4	.333	.348
Vizquel, Omar#	.429	7	3	0	1	0	1	.429	.571
Walker, Larry*	.222	27	6	0	2	4	9	.323	.296
Wallach, Tim	.268	82	22	2	15	6	27	.337	.378
Walton, J	.188	16	3	0	1	2	4	.278	.188
Wehner, John	.000	5	0	0	0	1	1	.000	.000
Weiss, Walt#	.333	9	3	0	0	1	0	.400	.333
Whiten, Mark#	.250	12	3	1	5	0	3	.333	.368
Williams, Ma	.267	30	8	0	1	2	7	.353	.367
Wilson, Dan	.000	8	0	0	0	2	1	.200	.000
Young, Eric	.143	7	1	0	1	1	0	.250	.143
Young, Ernie	.333	6	2	0	0	1	2	.429	.500
Zaun, Greg#	.000	5	0	0	0	1	2	.167	.000
Zeile, Todd	.345	29	10	0	5	1	3	.355	.483

Tom Gordon, Red Sox — RHP

Batter	Avg	AB	H	HR	BI	BB	SO	OBP	Slg
Aldrete, Mike*	.000	6	0	0	0	0	3	.000	.000
Alicea, Luis*	.500	6	3	0	0	0	0	.500	.667
Alomar, R	.400	20	8	0	3	5	2	.520	.600
Alomar Jr, S*	.286	14	4	0	0	2	1	.375	.429
Amaral, Rich	.000	7	0	0	0	1	1	.125	.000
Anderson, Brd*	.273	33	9	2	7	6	8	.400	.515
Anderson, G*	.316	19	6	0	1	0	1	.316	.316
Anthony, Eric*	.125	8	1	0	0	0	1	.125	.125
Ausmus, Brad	.400	5	2	0	1	1	0	.500	.400
Baerga, C#	.321	28	9	0	4	1	3	.345	.429
Baines, H*	.244	45	11	1	6	8	9	.358	.356
Bautista, D	.000	6	0	0	0	0	1	.000	.000
Becker, Rich*	.455	11	5	0	1	2	4	.500	.545
Belle, Albert	.310	29	9	2	8	3	5	.364	.586
Beltre, G	.273	11	3	0	1	4	4	.333	.273
Berroa, G	.100	10	1	0	0	2	0	.250	.100
Bichette, D	.000	8	0	0	1	3		.111	.000
Blowers, Mike	.429	7	3	0	0	2	2	.556	.571
Boggs, Wade*	.452	31	14	0	3	10	1	.571	.516
Bonilla, B#	.000	6	0	0	1	0	2	.000	.000
Boone, Bret	.000	6	0	0	0	0	0	.000	.000
Borders, Pat	.167	18	3	0	2	0	6	.167	.222
Bordick, Mike	.292	24	7	0	2	5	3	.433	.333
Bragg, Darren*	.000	7	0	0	0	0	1	.000	.000
Brosius, S	.571	7	4	0	0	1	0	.625	.714
Buhner, Jay	.179	28	5	0	0	3	7	.258	.250
Burks, Ellis	.238	21	5	1	3	1	7	.273	.524
Burnitz, J*	.257	35	9	3	10	4	10	.325	.600
Canseco, Jose	.211	38	8	2	14	4	6	.273	.421
Carter, Joe	.000	6	0	0	0	0	0	.000	.000
Cedeno, A	.250	16	4	0	2	2	4	.333	.250
Cedeno, D#	.267	15	4	1	4	0	1	.267	.467
Cirillo, Jeff	.273	11	3	1	2	0	5	.273	.545
Clark, Tony*	.400	20	8	1	5	4	3	.480	.550
Clark, Will*	.353	17	6	0	1	3	2	.450	.412
Cole, Alex*	.308	26	8	0	1	1	4	.333	.346
Cora, Joey*	.417	12	5	1	3	0	3	.385	.667
Cordova, M	.217	23	5	0	2	5	9	.345	.261
Curtis, Chad	.250	8	2	0	0	1	4	.333	.250
Cuyler, Milt*	.286	42	12	2	9	9	11	.404	.476
Davis, Chili#	.000	6	0	0	1	0	0	.125	.000
Dawson, Andre	.217	23	5	3	5	2	8	.269	.609
Deer, Rob	.111	18	2	0	1	4	5	.261	.111
Delgado, C*	.136	22	3	0	2	1	3	.174	.273
Devereaux, M	.000	10	0	0	0	1	2	.091	.000
Diaz, Alex#	.242	33	8	1	5	2	1	.286	.485
DiSarcina, G	.000	6	0	0	0	1	0	.143	.000
Durham, Ray#	.125	8	1	0	0	2	1	.364	.125
Easley, D	.435	23	10	0	1	4	2	.519	.609
Edmonds, Jim*	.500	6	3	1	3	0	1	.500	1.167
Elster, Kevin	.063	16	1	0	2	1	5	.118	.063
Espinoza, A	.333	21	7	0	1	0	3	.318	.333
Fabregas, Jor*	.100	10	1	0	0	2	1	.250	.100
Fermin, Felix	.225	40	9	3	9	3	11	.279	.525
Fielder, C	.333	6	2	0	1	0	0	.333	.500
Flaherty, J	.400	35	14	1	6	7	9	.500	.571
Franco, Julio	.167	6	1	0	0	1	1	.286	.167
Frazier, Lou#	.182	11	2	0	1	0	1	.167	.273
Frye, Jeff	.429	35	15	3	9	4	7	.487	.829
Fryman, T	.105	19	2	0	0	4	6	.261	.105
Gaetti, Gary	.364	11	4	0	2	3	3	.500	.455
Gagne, Greg	.190	21	4	0	3	5	6	.346	.238
Gallego, Mike	.211	19	4	1	1	2	3	.286	.368
Gates, Brent#	.167	6	1	1	3	0	1	.286	.667
Giambi, Jason*	.000	4	0	0	0	1	4	.200	.000
Gil, Benji	.111	9	1	0	1	1	1	.200	.111
Gomez, Chris	.100	10	1	0	1	4	3	.375	.100
Gomez, Leo	.125	8	1	0	0	0	3	.125	.125
Gonzales, R	.214	14	3	0	2	1	6	.267	.357
Gonzalez, A	.341	44	15	2	7	3	6	.396	.705
Gonzalez, J	.000	5	0	0	0	0	3	.000	.000
Goodwin, C*	.273	22	6	0	1	0	1	.273	.318
Green, Shawn*	.182	22	4	0	1	6	4	.357	.318
Greenwell, M*	.333	21	7	0	2	3	4	.417	.333
Greer, Rusty*	.361	36	13	6	13	6	5	.452	.889
Griffey Jr, K*	.452	31	14	0	5	2	1	.485	.548
Guillen, O*	.200	10	2	0	1	0	2	.200	.300
Hale, Chip*	.071	14	1	0	1	0	5	.067	.071
Hall, Mel*	.250	32	8	0	1	3	3	.306	.281
Hamilton, D*	.333	6	2	0	0	0	2	.333	.500
Hammonds, J	.143	35	5	1	3	12	4	.362	.257
Henderson, R#	.333	12	4	0	2	6	3	.556	.417
Higginson, B*	.000	5	0	0	0	0	1	.000	.000
Hill, G	.263	19	5	0	2	1	4	.333	.368
Hoiles, Chris	.250	12	3	1	2	0	5	.308	.500
Hollins, Dave#	.188	16	3	0	0	1	5	.235	.188
Howell, Jack*	.308	13	4	1	3	1	1	.357	.692
Hudler, Rex	.400	5	2	0	2	0	1	.400	.600
Huff, Michael	.294	17	5	0	0	1	6	.333	.294
Hulse, David*	.333	18	6	0	3	1	4	.368	.500
Huson, Jeff*	.333	9	3	1	4	0	3	.300	.667
Incaviglia, P	.278	18	5	1	3	3	4	.381	.500
Jaha, John	.286	14	4	0	0	0	1	.286	.286
James, Dion*	.250	16	4	0	1	3	3	.368	.313
Javier, Stan#	.200	5	1	0	0	0	3	.200	.400
Jefferson, R*	.333	6	2	1	1	0	2	.333	1.000
Jeter, Derek	.290	31	9	0	3	4	3	.371	.387
Johnson, L*	.333	12	4	0	2	2	3	.429	.583
Joyner, Wally*	.273	11	3	0	2	1	5	.333	.636
Karkovice, R	.000	5	0	0	0	1	0	.167	.000
Kelly, Pat	.095	21	2	0	1	0	8	.095	.095
Kelly, R	.000	6	0	0	0	2	2	.250	.000
Kirby, Wayne*	.344	32	11	0	1	11	1	.523	.531
Knoblauch, C	.000	5	0	0	0	1	0	.000	.000
Knorr, Randy	.300	10	3	0	1	3	4	.462	.400
Kreuter, Chad#	.429	7	3	1	2	0	1	.429	.857
Lawton, Matt*	.182	11	2	1	2	2	2	.308	.455
Leius, Scott	.200	5	1	0	0	1	1	.333	.200
Lewis, Darren	.250	8	2	0	0	2	2	.455	.375
Lewis, Mark	.444	9	4	1	1	1	2	.545	.778
Leyritz, Jim	.176	17	3	0	1	2	4	.263	.176
Liriano, N#	.278	18	5	0	2	0	4	.278	.333
Listach, Pat#	.500	6	3	0	0	1	1	.571	.500
Livingstone, S*	.500	26	13	0	3	3	3	.552	.500
Lofton, Kenny*	.500	26	13	0	3	3	3	.552	.500

Tom Gordon, Red Sox — RHP

Batter	Avg	AB	H	HR	BI	BB	SO	OBP	Slg
Lovullo, T#	.286	7	2	0	1	0	2	.286	.286
Macfarlane, M	.100	10	1	1	1	0	5	.100	.400
Manto, Jeff	.400	5	2	1	1	1	0	.500	1.000
Martinez, Da*	.455	11	5	0	1	2	0	.538	.545
Martinez, E	.290	31	9	1	2	11	7	.476	.452
Martinez, S*	.333	6	2	0	1	0	0	.333	.333
Martinez, T*	.400	25	10	2	8	3	2	.464	.680
Matheny, Mike	.000	4	0	0	0	1	1	.200	.000
McGriff, Fred*	.267	15	4	0	0	6	3	.476	.333
McGwire, Mark	.425	40	17	4	9	8	6	.510	.775
McLemore, M#	.333	18	6	1	6	5	3	.478	.500
Meares, Pat	.231	13	3	0	1	2	4	.375	.231
Mieske, Matt	.357	14	5	1	4	1	3	.400	.571
Molitor, Paul	.346	52	18	0	7	5	5	.404	.462
Munoz, Pedro	.231	13	3	0	2	0	6	.231	.231
Murray, Eddie*	.333	24	8	2	9	0	6	.320	.583
Myers, Greg*	.095	21	2	0	1	1	4	.136	.095
Naehring, Tim	.063	16	1	0	0	2	5	.167	.063
Newfield, M	.000	7	0	0	0	0	4	.000	.000
Newson, W*	.500	10	5	0	0	3	3	.615	.500
Nieves, Melvin	.125	8	1	0	0	2	3	.300	.125
Nilsson, Dave*	.381	21	8	1	5	4	2	.480	.762
Nixon, Otis#	.276	29	8	0	2	4	3	.364	.276
O'Brien, C	.333	12	4	0	0	0	4	.333	.417
O'Leary, Troy*	.400	5	2	0	0	1	1	.500	.400
O'Neill, Paul*	.333	15	5	2	4	2	0	.389	.733
Olerud, Joe*	.175	40	7	1	2	7	7	.298	.275
Oliver, Joe	.167	6	1	0	0	0	1	.167	.167
Orsulak, Joe*	.167	12	2	2	4	2	3	.286	.667
Palmeiro, R*	.211	38	8	0	6	13	5	.404	.395
Palmer, Dean	.100	20	2	0	0	2	9	.182	.150
Paquette, C	.182	11	2	1	2	0	5	.182	.455
Pena, Tony	.182	22	4	0	1	2	3	.250	.227
Perez, Tomas#	.000	8	0	0	0	1	3	.111	.000
Phillips, T#	.302	43	13	0	6	13	15	.474	.442
Plantier, P*	.286	7	2	0	2	0	2	.250	.286
Polonia, Luis*	.400	30	12	0	3	2	4	.438	.433
Raines, Tim#	.208	24	5	0	2	4	6	.321	.333
Ramirez, M	.200	15	3	1	3	3	2	.333	.400
Reboulet, J	.313	16	5	0	2	3	2	.421	.375
Reed, Jody	.259	27	7	0	1	6	2	.394	.333
Ripken, Billy	.214	14	3	0	1	2	1	.313	.214
Ripken, Cal	.333	33	11	3	6	5	2	.421	.697
Rodriguez, Al	.333	12	4	1	2	2	2	.429	.583
Rodriguez, I	.357	28	10	0	4	3	6	.406	.464
Salmon, Tim	.219	32	7	0	2	3	11	.286	.250
Schofield, D	.235	17	4	0	1	3	4	.350	.235
Schu, Rick	.333	3	1	0	1	2	0	.600	.667
Segui, David#	.500	4	2	0	1	1	0	.600	.750
Seitzer, K	.290	31	9	0	4	1	5	.303	.323
Sheffield, G	.273	11	3	0	1	0	0	.273	.273
Sierra, Ruben#	.205	44	9	2	10	3	10	.250	.364
Snow, J.T.#	.174	23	4	2	3	4	4	.296	.435
Sojo, Luis	.000	7	0	0	0	0	2	.000	.000
Sorrento, P*	.368	19	7	2	7	10	3	.586	.842
Sosa, James	.222	9	2	0	1	0	5	.222	.333
Spiers, Bill*	.310	29	9	0	2	2	9	.355	.379
Sprague, Ed	.286	28	8	2	4	1	9	.310	.571
Stahoviak, S*	.000	5	0	0	1	1	2	.143	.000
Stairs, Matt*	.286	7	2	1	1	0	2	.286	.857
Stanley, Mike	.500	2	1	0	2	0	0	.667	.750
Steinbach, T	.231	26	6	1	3	4	10	.333	.346
Stevens, Lee*	.500	4	2	0	1	1	1	.500	.750
Stillwell, K#	.400	5	2	0	0	0	1	.400	.400
Strange, Doug#	.333	18	6	0	2	0	1	.333	.444
Surhoff, B.J.*	.205	39	8	0	5	2	6	.244	.205
Sveum, Dale#	.000	4	0	0	0	1	2	.200	.000
Tartabull, D	.176	17	3	0	2	2	8	.238	.235
Tettleton, M#	.265	34	9	2	8	13	9	.395	.324
Thomas, Frank	.231	26	6	1	5	9	6	.417	.385
Thome, Jim*	.381	21	8	2	7	5	6	.500	.762
Tomberlin, A*	.000	5	0	0	0	2	3	.286	.000
Trammell, A	.350	20	7	2	3	3	1	.435	.700
Valentin, Jhn	.273	11	3	0	0	2	1	.385	.364
Valentin, Jse#	.389	18	7	1	6	2	7	.450	.667
Valle, Dave	.071	14	1	0	0	4	6	.278	.071
Vaughn, Greg	.147	34	5	1	5	4	15	.231	.265
Vaughn, Mo*	.238	21	5	0	2	1	7	.261	.238
Velarde, R	.118	17	2	0	2	3	5	.250	.118
Ventura, R*	.167	30	5	0	1	6	6	.306	.167
Vina, F*	.143	7	1	0	0	1	0	.333	.143
Vizquel, Omar#	.281	32	9	0	2	3	3	.343	.344
Walbeck, Matt#	.118	17	2	0	2	0	5	.118	.118
Ward, Turner#	.143	7	1	0	1	0	0	.571	.143
Weiss, Walt*	.143	7	1	0	0	4	2	.455	.143
White, Devon#	.270	37	10	0	2	2	15	.325	.324
Whiten, Mark#	.261	23	6	0	3	2	6	.320	.304
Widger, Chris	.000	5	0	0	0	0	0	.000	.000
Williams, Ber#	.167	18	3	0	1	1	5	.200	.333
Wilson, Dan	.000	10	0	0	0	0	4	.167	.000
Worthington	.200	10	2	0	2	0	1	.182	.200

Mike Grace, Phillies — RHP

Batter	Avg	AB	H	HR	BI	BB	SO	OBP	Slg
Ausmus, Brad	.167	6	1	0	0	0	2	.167	.167
Blowers, Mike	.400	5	2	0	0	0	1	.400	.400
Caminiti, Ken#	.400	5	2	0	2	0	1	.400	.600
Cedeno, Roger#	.143	7	1	0	3	0	1	.143	.143
DeShields, D*	.125	8	1	0	0	0	1	.125	.125
Finley, Steve*	.000	4	0	0	0	2	0	.333	.000
Gwynn, Tony*	.556	9	5	0	1	0	0	.556	.778
Henderson, R	.000	3	0	0	0	3	0	.500	.000
Hollandsworth*	.200	5	1	0	0	2	1	.429	.400
Joyner, Wally*	.250	4	1	1	3	1	0	.400	1.000
Karros, Eric	.000	9	0	0	0	0	4	.000	.000
Livingstone*	.500	6	3	0	1	0	1	.500	.833
Mondesi, Raul	.375	8	3	1	1	0	0	.375	.875
Piazza, Mike	.500	6	3	1	2	1	0	.571	1.167
Reed, Jody	.125	8	1	0	0	1	0	.125	.125

Jeff Granger, Royals — LHP

Batter	Avg	AB	H	HR	BI	BB	SO	OBP	Slg
Hudler, Rex	.667	6	4	1	3	0	1	.667	1.667
Salmon, Tim	.667	3	2	0	2	1	1	.600	1.667

Danny Graves, Indians — RHP

Batter	Avg	AB	H	HR	BI	BB	SO	OBP	Slg
Cordova, M	.500	4	2	0	1	1	0	.600	.500
Meares, Pat	.200	5	1	0	0	0	2	.200	.400

Jason Grimsley, Angels — RHP

Batter	Avg	AB	H	HR	BI	BB	SO	OBP	Slg
Alomar, R#	.286	7	2	1	2	2	1	.444	.714
Anderson, Brd*	.385	13	5	1	1	1	1	.429	.615
Baines, H*	.111	18	2	0	1	2	2	.200	.111
Bautista, D	.167	6	1	0	0	0	1	.167	.167
Becker, Rich*	.444	9	4	0	2	1	0	.500	.667
Bell, Jay	.333	6	2	0	0	0	1	.333	.333
Berroa, G	.000	5	0	0	0	1	2	.167	.000
Boggs, Wade*	.333	9	3	0	0	1	0	.400	.333
Bonds, Barry*	.000	6	0	0	0	2	0	.250	.000
Bonilla, B#	.500	10	5	0	4	1	0	.500	.900
Bournigal, R	.167	6	1	0	0	1	1	.286	.167
Bragg, Darren*	.143	7	1	0	0	0	1	.143	.143
Brosius, S	.667	3	2	0	0	1	1	.833	.667
Buhner, Jay	.222	9	2	0	2	1	2	.300	.333
Butler, Brett*	.444	9	4	0	0	3	1	.615	.444
Canseco, Jose	.250	4	1	1	1	1	1	.400	1.000
Carreon, Mark	.286	7	2	0	0	1	0	.444	.286
Carter, Joe	.333	12	4	1	7	1	1	.385	.583
Cedeno, D#	.333	9	3	0	0	0	1	.333	.333
Clark, Will*	.333	12	4	1	1	4	1	.385	.583
Cole, Alex*	.400	5	2	0	0	1	0	.500	.400
Coleman, V#	.167	6	1	0	0	1	2	.286	.167
Cora, Joey#	.364	11	4	0	1	2	0	.462	.545
Cordova, M	.100	10	1	0	3	2	1	.231	.200
Curtis, Chad	.000	3	0	0	0	3	2	.500	.000
Damon, Johnny*	.200	5	1	0	3	0	0	.200	.200
Dascenzo, D#	.167	6	1	0	0	0	0	.167	.333
Dawson, Andre	.143	7	1	0	1	1	2	.333	.143
DeShields, D*	.000	8	0	0	0	2	3	.200	.000
Devereaux, M	.143	7	1	0	0	0	3	.143	.143
Duncan, M	.333	6	2	0	0	0	1	.333	.500
Dunston, S	.200	5	1	0	0	1	1	.333	.200
Durham, Ray#	.286	7	2	0	1	1	1	.444	.429
Elster, Kevin	.250	4	1	0	1	1	1	.333	.250
Fielder, C	.125	16	2	0	1	1	7	.176	.125
Flaherty, J	.200	5	1	0	0	0	2	.200	.400
Franco, Julio	.333	6	2	0	0	1	1	.429	.333
Frye, Jeff	.400	5	2	0	1	2	0	.571	.600
Fryman, T	.333	15	5	1	3	3	4	.474	.667
Galarraga, A	.400	10	4	0	0	3	2	.538	.700
Giambi, Jason*	.500	6	3	1	4	1	0	.571	1.167
Goff, Jerry*	.250	4	1	0	0	1	2	.400	.250
Gomez, Chris	.200	5	1	0	1	0	1	.167	.200
Gomez, Leo	.000	5	0	0	0	0	3	.000	.000
Gonzalez, A	.500	4	2	0	3	1	0	.600	1.000
Grace, Mark*	.250	8	2	0	2	1	0	.333	.250
Greene, Shawn*	.400	5	2	1	3	0	1	.400	1.000
Greenwell, M*	.333	6	2	0	1	1	0	.429	.333
Greer, Rusty*	.200	5	1	0	0	0	2	.200	.200
Griffey Jr, K*	.667	9	6	2	5	1	0	.700	1.444
Grissom, M	.333	3	1	0	0	3	0	.667	.333
Guillen, O*	.214	14	3	0	1	1	2	.214	.214
Gwynn, Chris*	.400	5	2	0	0	1	1	.500	.400
Gwynn, Tony*	.400	5	2	0	0	0	0	.400	.400
Hale, Chip*	.200	5	1	1	1	0	0	.333	.800
Hamelin, Bob*	.400	5	2	0	2	0	1	.333	.400
Hammonds, J	.667	6	4	1	2	0	1	.800	1.333
Harris, Lenny*	.500	8	4	0	0	1	0	.500	.500
Herrera, Jose*	.429	7	3	0	1	0	2	.429	.429
Higginson, R*	.400	5	2	1	1	0	0	.400	1.200
Hocking, D#	.000	5	0	0	0	0	0	.000	.000
Hoiles, Chris	.444	9	4	0	1	1	1	.455	.444
Hollins, Dave#	.000	5	0	0	1	2	2	.286	.000

Jason Grimsley, Angels — RHP

Batter	Avg	AB	H	HR	BI	BB	SO	OBP	Slg
Howard, Dave#	.600	5	3	0	3	0	1	.500	.800
Hulse, David*	.200	5	1	0	2	0	1	.200	.200
Jaha, John	.000	7	0	0	0	1	1	.125	.000
Jefferies, G#	.143	7	1	1	1	2	2	.333	.571
Karkovice, R	.286	7	2	0	1	1	2	.375	.429
King, Jeff	.200	5	1	1	0	0	0	.200	.800
Knoblauch, C	.300	20	6	0	2	5	1	.440	.300
Lewis, Darren	.333	9	3	0	0	1	1	.400	.333
Lewis, Mark	.750	4	3	0	1	1	1	.800	1.000
Leyritz, Jim	.400	5	2	0	2	0	1	.400	.600
Listach, Pat#	.000	4	0	0	0	1	2	.200	.000
Lockhart, K*	.000	5	0	0	0	0	0	.000	.000
Lofton, Kenny*	.200	5	1	0	0	0	1	.200	.600
Macfarlane, M	.500	2	1	0	1	1	0	.800	.500
Magadan, Dave*	.000	5	0	0	1	3	1	.375	.000
Martin, N	.200	5	1	0	1	0	2	.200	.200
Martinez, Da*	.083	12	1	0	0	1	0	.154	.083
Martinez, E	.375	8	3	0	1	2	0	.500	.375
Martinez, T*	.182	11	2	0	0	0	5	.182	.182
May, Derrick*	.000	6	0	0	0	2	0	.000	.000
McCarty, Dave	.429	7	3	0	0	0	1	.429	.571
McGwire, Mark	1.000	2	2	0	0	4	0	1.000	1.000
McLemore, M#	.231	13	3	0	0	0	3	.231	.308
Meares, Pat	.067	15	1	0	3	0	2	.125	.133
Merced, O*	.200	5	1	0	0	1	2	.333	.200
Mieske, Matt	.125	8	1	0	0	1	2	.222	.125
Mitchell, K	.125	8	1	0	0	2	0	.300	.125
Molitor, Paul	.250	12	3	2	3	3	3	.400	.750
Munoz, Pedro	.714	7	5	1	3	2	0	.778	1.143
Murray, Eddie#	.333	9	3	0	0	0	3	.333	.333
Myers, Greg*	.375	8	3	1	1	2	0	.500	.875
Naehring, Tim	.667	9	6	0	2	1	0	.727	1.000
Newson, W*	.000	7	0	0	0	0	0	.000	.000
Nilsson, Dave*	.000	5	0	0	0	3	0	.375	.000
Nixon, Otis#	.286	14	4	0	0	3	1	.412	.286
O'Brien, C	.200	5	1	0	0	1	1	.333	.200
O'Neill, Paul*	.250	8	2	0	0	2	0	.400	.250
Olerud, John*	.444	9	4	0	2	2	0	.545	.667
Palmeiro, R*	.667	9	6	0	3	1	0	.700	1.000
Palmer, Dean	.000	4	0	0	0	1	2	.200	.000
Phillips, T#	.385	13	5	0	0	6	2	.579	.385
Polonia, Luis*	.400	5	2	0	1	0	0	.400	.600
Raines, Tim#	.267	15	4	0	2	3	1	.389	.400
Reboulet, J	.250	4	1	0	1	4	0	.625	.250
Ripken, Cal	.364	11	4	0	1	2	4	.500	.364
Rivera, Ruben	.200	5	1	0	0	0	0	.200	.600
Roberts, Bip#	.000	3	0	0	3	0	0	.500	.000
Rodriguez, Al	.750	4	3	0	1	1	0	.833	1.000
Rodriguez, I	.400	5	2	0	1	0	0	.500	.600
Sabo, Chris	.250	8	2	0	1	0	0	.250	.375
Samuel, Juan	.182	11	2	0	0	0	4	.182	.273
Sandberg, R	.500	4	2	0	0	1	1	.600	.750
Santiago, B	.000	5	0	0	0	0	2	.000	.000
Smith, Dwight*	.250	4	1	0	0	1	1	.500	.250
Sojo, Luis	.333	9	3	0	3	0	1	.333	.556
Sorrento, P*	.000	5	0	0	0	0	1	.000	.000
Sprague, Ed	.500	4	2	0	1	2	1	.667	.500
Stahoviak, S*	.200	10	2	0	2	0	4	.200	.300
Stanley, Mike	.333	6	2	1	3	0	1	.333	1.000
Strawberry, D*	.000	7	0	0	0	2	0	.222	.000
Surhoff, B.J.*	.200	5	1	0	1	0	1	.200	.200
Tartabull, D	.000	5	0	0	0	0	2	.000	.000
Tettleton, M#	.167	6	1	0	0	4	2	.545	.333
Thomas, Frank	.200	10	2	0	1	9	3	.579	.200
Thompson, Rob	.400	4	0	0	0	1	1	.200	.000
Trammell, A	.375	8	3	0	1	0	2	.375	.750
Tucker, M*	.400	4	2	0	2	1	0	.600	.750
Valentin, Jhn	.455	11	5	0	4	2	0	.571	.636
Valentin, Jse#	.125	8	1	0	0	0	2	.125	.125
Vaughn, Greg	.250	4	1	1	1	1	1	.400	1.000
Vaughn, Mo*	.154	13	2	1	3	0	3	.267	.385
Ventura, R*	.438	16	7	0	2	0	3	.438	.500
Walbeck, Matt#	.400	5	2	0	2	1	0	.500	.600
Walker, Larry*	.273	11	3	0	0	0	2	.273	.364
Wallach, Tim	.273	11	3	0	0	0	2	.273	.273
Williams, Ber#	.444	9	4	0	2	1	2	.500	.444
Williams, Ma	.333	6	2	0	0	1	0	.429	.500
Wilson, Dan	.222	9	2	0	1	1	1	.300	.222

Buddy Groom, Athletics — LHP

Batter	Avg	AB	H	HR	BI	BB	SO	OBP	Slg
Alicea, Luis#	.500	4	2	0	1	1	0	.600	.500
Alomar Jr, S	.000	5	0	0	0	0	2	.000	.000
Amaral, Rich	.600	5	3	0	0	1	0	.667	.600
Anderson, Brd*	.111	9	1	0	0	1	3	.200	.111
Anderson, G*	.500	6	3	0	3	0	0	.500	.500
Baerga, C#	.286	7	2	2	3	2	1	.444	1.143
Baines, H*	.000	7	0	0	0	0	2	.000	.000
Boggs, Wade*	.222	9	2	0	1	1	0	.300	.333
Buhner, Jay	.800	5	4	1	4	0	0	.667	1.400
Canseco, Jose	.167	6	1	1	2	0	3	.167	.667

Buddy Groom, Athletics — LHP

Batter	Avg	AB	H	HR	BI	BB	SO	OBP	Slg
Clark, Will*	.200	5	1	0	0	2	0	.429	.200
Cora, Joey#	.125	8	1	0	0	0	2	.125	.125
DiSarcina, G	.400	5	2	0	0	1	0	.400	.400
Devereaux, M	.182	11	2	0	1	0	2	.182	.273
Durham, Ray#	.167	6	1	0	0	2	1	.375	.333
Edmonds, Jim*	.200	5	1	1	2	0	2	.333	.800
Espinoza, A	.400	5	2	0	1	0	0	.400	.400
Gaetti, Gary	.250	4	1	0	0	1	0	.400	.250
Gonzalez, J	.500	4	2	0	0	1	0	.600	.750
Grebeck, C	.333	6	2	0	0	1	1	.429	.667
Green, Shawn*	.200	5	1	0	0	0	2	.200	.200
Greenwell, M*	.500	8	4	0	2	0	0	.500	.625
Greer, Rusty*	.500	6	3	0	0	0	0	.500	.500
Griffey Jr, K*	.333	9	3	0	0	2	2	.333	.444
Guillen, O*	.125	8	1	0	0	0	1	.125	.125
Hamelin, Bob*	.000	5	0	0	0	0	4	.000	.000
Hamilton, D*	.222	9	2	0	0	0	0	.222	.222
Haselman, B	.250	4	1	0	1	1	1	.400	.250
Hoiles, Chris	.400	5	2	0	1	1	1	.500	.400
Hollins, Dave#	.000	3	0	0	0	2	0	.500	.000
Johnson, L*	.500	8	4	0	1	0	1	.500	.750
Karkovice, R	.429	7	3	1	2	0	2	.429	1.000
Knoblauch, C	.250	4	1	0	0	0	0	.400	.500
Listach, Pat#	.333	3	1	0	2	1	1	.400	.333
Lofton, Kenny*	.000	7	0	0	0	0	3	.000	.000
Macfarlane, M	.286	7	2	0	1	1	1	.375	.429
Martinez, E	.000	4	0	0	0	3	0	.429	.000
Martinez, T*	.400	10	4	1	4	1	1	.455	.700
McCarty, Dave	.250	4	1	0	0	0	0	.400	.250
McLemore, M#	.000	6	0	0	0	1	0	.143	.000
McRae, Brian#	.400	5	2	0	0	0	0	.400	.400
Meares, Pat	.200	5	1	0	1	0	1	.167	.200
Molitor, Paul	.167	6	1	0	1	0	1	.167	.167
Naehring, Tim	.333	6	2	0	0	1	0	.429	.333
Nilsson, Dave*	.375	8	3	0	2	0	1	.333	.375
Nixon, Otis#	.000	5	0	0	0	1	1	.167	.000
O'Leary, Troy*	.200	5	1	0	1	2	3	.429	.200
O'Neill, Paul*	.778	9	7	1	6	0	0	.778	1.333
Olerud, John*	.250	4	1	0	0	1	0	.400	.250
Palmeiro, R*	.273	11	3	0	4	2	2	.357	.364
Palmer, Dean	.125	8	1	0	0	0	3	.125	.125
Pena, Tony	.250	4	1	0	1	1	0	.250	.500
Phillips, T#	.500	6	3	2	4	1	1	.571	1.500
Polonia, Luis*	.667	3	2	0	0	1	0	.750	.667
Raines, Tim#	.400	10	4	1	1	2	0	.500	.800
Ramirez, M	.000	5	0	0	0	1	3	.167	.000
Ripken, Cal	.333	9	3	0	0	0	0	.333	.556
Rodriguez, I	.571	7	4	0	0	1	0	.625	.571
Seitzer, K	.600	5	3	0	2	0	0	.600	.600
Sierra, Ruben#	.857	7	6	0	0	0	0	.857	1.143
Snow, J.T.#	.000	5	0	0	0	0	2	.000	.000
Sojo, Luis	.429	7	3	0	1	1	1	.500	.571
Sorrento, P*	.333	6	2	0	1	1	1	.429	.333
Surhoff, B.J.*	.200	5	1	0	0	1	0	.333	.400
Tartabull, D	.250	4	1	0	0	1	1	.400	.250
Tettleton, M#	.333	3	1	0	2	0	0	.600	.333
Thomas, Frank	.667	6	4	1	3	9	0	.867	1.167
Thome, Jim*	.500	6	3	1	2	1	1	.571	1.000
Tinsley, Lee#	.000	3	0	0	1	2	1	.400	.000
Valentin, Jhn	.647	17	11	1	6	0	0	.647	.882
Vaughn, Greg	.250	4	1	0	0	1	0	.400	.250
Vaughn, Mo*	.214	14	3	1	2	3	5	.389	.429
Ventura, R*	.077	13	1	0	1	0	4	.071	.077
Vizquel, Omar#	.714	7	5	0	1	0	1	.750	.857
Whiten, Mark#	.250	4	1	0	0	1	0	.400	.250
Williams, Ber#	.400	5	2	0	2	2	1	.571	.400

Kevin Gross, Rangers — RHP

Batter	Avg	AB	H	HR	BI	BB	SO	OBP	Slg
Aldrete, Mike*	.389	18	7	1	3	5	1	.542	.611
Alicea, Luis#	.333	12	4	0	1	3	2	.467	.500
Alomar, R#	.273	33	9	1	1	3	7	.333	.364
Alomar Jr, S	.500	6	3	1	1	0	2	.500	1.000
Alou, Moises	.364	11	4	0	1	0	1	.364	.455
Amaral, Rich	.571	7	4	0	1	1	0	.625	.714
Anderson, Brd*	.500	10	5	4	5	1	2	.583	1.800
Anthony, Eric*	.250	12	3	0	0	0	1	.250	.250
Ausmus, Brad	.375	16	6	0	0	0	2	.375	.438
Baerga, C#	.300	10	3	0	2	0	0	.300	.300
Bagwell, Jeff	.400	25	10	2	3	3	4	.467	.720
Baines, H*	.200	5	1	0	0	0	0	.200	.200
Barberie, B#	.250	12	3	0	1	5	4	.471	.250
Bautista, D	.000	5	0	0	0	0	0	.000	.000
Becker, Rich*	.100	10	1	0	0	0	3	.100	.100
Bell, Derek	.391	23	9	1	4	0	4	.391	.522
Bell, Jay	.289	45	13	2	6	2	11	.319	.444
Belle, Albert	.200	10	2	1	3	2	1	.385	.500
Belliard, R	.111	18	2	0	0	2	6	.200	.111
Berroa, G	.455	11	5	0	4	4	0	.563	.545
Berry, Sean	.250	8	2	0	0	1	1	.333	.375
Bichette, D	.167	6	1	0	0	0	0	.167	.333

75

Batter	Avg	AB	H	HR	BI	BB	SO	OBP	Slg
Biggio, Craig	.071	42	3	0	2	2	8	.114	.071
Blauser, Jeff	.360	25	9	0	2	0	5	.360	.440
Blowers, Mike	.300	10	3	2	2	0	1	.300	.900
Bogar, Tim	.333	6	2	0	0	1	1	.429	.500
Boggs, Wade*	.500	2	1	0	1	3	0	.800	.500
Bonds, Barry*	.232	56	13	2	6	16	8	.403	.411
Bonilla, B#	.190	63	12	3	8	11	19	.311	.365
Boone, Bret	.167	6	1	0	1	0	3	.167	.333
Bordick, Mike	.091	11	1	0	0	1	1	.167	.091
Bragg, Darren*	.000	3	0	0	1	1	1	.200	.000
Branson, Jeff*	.125	8	1	0	0	0	1	.125	.125
Brosius, S	.200	10	2	0	0	1	2	.273	.200
Buhner, Jay	.235	17	4	1	2	1	3	.278	.471
Burnitz, J*	.333	12	4	0	1	0	2	.333	.417
Butler, Brett*	.400	25	10	0	1	5	1	.500	.440
Caminiti, Ken#	.351	37	13	1	6	6	8	.442	.568
Candaele, C#	.111	36	4	0	0	5	4	.220	.222
Canseco, Jose	.333	12	4	0	1	2	1	.429	.417
Carr, Chuck	.286	7	2	0	0	0	0	.286	.286
Carter, Joe	.231	13	3	0	0	0	0	.231	.231
Cedeno, A	.263	19	5	1	5	2	7	.333	.526
Cedeno, D#	.667	6	4	1	1	0	1	.667	1.333
Cianfrocco, A	.286	7	2	1	1	0	2	.375	.714
Cirillo, Jeff	.400	10	4	0	0	2	0	.500	.500
Clark, Dave*	.400	20	8	2	6	1	3	.429	.750
Clark, Tony#	.167	6	1	0	0	1	1	.286	.167
Clark, Will*	.328	58	19	1	9	3	15	.355	.517
Clayton, R	.438	16	7	0	1	0	2	.438	.563
Cole, Alex*	.000	6	0	0	0	2	1	.250	.000
Coleman, V#	.270	63	17	0	5	9	15	.361	.381
Conine, Jeff	.667	6	4	0	0	0	1	.667	.667
Cora, Joey#	.188	16	3	0	2	3	1	.300	.188
Cordero, Wil	.308	13	4	1	1	1	1	.357	.538
Cordova, M	.375	8	3	0	0	0	1	.375	.500
Curtis, Chad	.400	20	8	1	3	1	2	.429	.700
Damon, Johnny*	.400	5	2	0	0	0	1	.400	.600
Dascenzo, D	.200	5	1	0	0	1	0	.333	.200
Daulton, D*	.182	22	4	1	3	6	9	.345	.318
Davis, Chili#	.250	20	5	0	1	2	6	.318	.250
Davis, Eric	.385	26	10	3	5	6	8	.500	.885
Dawson, Andre	.228	57	13	2	11	6	7	.302	.368
Decker, Steve	.000	4	0	0	0	1	2	.200	.000
DeShields, D*	.286	21	6	1	5	2	7	.348	.429
Devereaux, M	.286	14	4	0	1	1	1	.333	.286
Diaz, Alex#	.000	5	0	0	0	0	1	.167	.000
Dorsett, B	.400	5	2	0	2	0	1	.400	.400
Duncan, M	.214	42	9	1	4	4	7	.283	.333
Dunston, S	.333	42	14	0	3	2	10	.362	.333
Durham, Ray#	.250	12	3	0	2	3	1	.400	.250
Dykstra, L*	.295	61	18	1	2	11	9	.403	.410
Eisenreich, J*	.400	5	2	0	2	2	0	.571	.600
Elster, Kevin	.154	26	4	0	2	0	4	.154	.231
Fermin, Felix	.000	3	0	0	0	0	1	.250	.000
Fielder, C	.267	15	4	2	5	2	2	.333	.667
Finley, Steve*	.269	26	7	0	1	1	3	.296	.308
Flaherty, J	.143	7	1	0	0	0	0	.143	.143
Fletcher, D*	.294	17	5	0	2	2	3	.350	.412
Floyd, Cliff*	.667	6	4	0	0	0	1	.667	.667
Frazier, Lou#	.375	8	3	0	0	0	1	.375	.375
Frye, Jeff	.200	5	1	0	0	1	0	.200	.200
Fryman, T	.286	21	6	0	1	0	4	.304	.381
Gaetti, Gary	.500	8	4	2	2	0	0	.500	1.375
Gagne, Greg	.000	7	0	0	0	0	0	.000	.000
Galarraga, A	.260	50	13	0	4	0	14	.275	.320
Gant, Ron	.182	33	6	1	2	2	6	.229	.333
Garcia, C	.211	19	4	0	0	0	4	.211	.211
Gates, Brent#	.000	9	0	0	1	0	1	.000	.000
Giambi, Jason*	.167	6	1	0	1	0	0	.167	.167
Gilkey, R	.455	11	5	0	2	1	1	.500	.455
Girardi, Joe	.167	18	3	0	1	3	5	.286	.167
Gomez, Chris	.000	10	0	0	0	1	5	.091	.000
Gonzalez, L*	.208	24	5	0	4	1	3	.240	.375
Goodwin, Tom*	.375	8	3	0	2	0	3	.444	.625
Grace, Mark*	.227	44	10	0	10	8	3	.340	.295
Green, Shawn*	.000	5	0	0	0	1	1	.286	.000
Greene, W*	.500	4	2	1	1	1	1	.600	1.250
Greenwell, M*	.222	9	2	0	0	0	0	.222	.333
Griffey Jr, K*	.417	12	5	1	1	2	1	.500	.750
Grissom, M	.259	27	7	0	1	2	2	.300	.296
Guillen, O*	.333	12	4	0	1	0	0	.333	.583
Gutierrez, R	.214	14	3	0	2	1	2	.267	.286
Gwynn, Tony*	.379	58	22	1	10	9	4	.449	.552
Hamilton, D*	.000	7	0	0	0	0	0	.000	.000
Harris, Lenny*	.300	20	6	0	2	1	1	.333	.350
Haselman, B	.200	5	1	1	4	0	2	.200	.800
Hayes, C	.556	18	10	2	4	2	0	.600	.944
Herrera, Jose*	.400	5	2	0	0	0	0	.400	.400
Higginson, R*	.250	16	4	1	1	1	2	.294	.438
Hollins, Dave#	.091	11	1	0	3	1	3	.167	.091
Howard, T*	.143	7	1	0	0	1	2	.250	.143

Batter	Avg	AB	H	HR	BI	BB	SO	OBP	Slg
Hudler, Rex	.167	6	1	0	0	0	1	.167	.167
Hulse, David*	1.000	3	3	0	1	2	0	1.000	1.333
Hundley, Todd#	.083	12	1	1	1	0	3	.083	.333
Hyers, Tim*	.000	6	0	0	0	0	0	.000	.000
Incaviglia, P	.500	12	6	2	5	0	2	.500	1.000
Jaha, John	.250	12	3	1	3	1	1	.308	.583
James, Dion*	.455	22	10	0	2	2	0	.500	.545
Javier, Stan#	.462	13	6	0	1	4	1	.588	.538
Jefferies, G#	.273	22	6	0	1	4	4	.407	.318
Jefferson, R*	.250	8	2	0	0	0	1	.250	.375
Johnson, L*	.400	10	4	1	4	0	0	.400	.700
Jordan, Ricky	.143	14	2	0	0	1	6	.200	.143
Joyner, Wally*	.500	6	3	0	5	2	0	.556	.833
Justice, Dave*	.400	20	8	2	5	4	5	.462	.700
Karkovice, R	.250	4	1	0	0	1	1	.250	.250
Kelly, R	.250	8	2	0	0	0	1	.250	.250
Kent, Jeff	.385	13	5	0	4	0	1	.385	.615
King, Jeff	.333	24	8	1	5	1	3	.360	.500
Kingery, Mike*	.375	8	3	0	1	0	2	.375	.375
Klesko, Ryan*	.167	6	1	0	0	0	2	.167	.167
Knoblauch, C	.778	9	7	1	1	0	1	.778	1.333
Lankford, Ray*	.467	15	7	1	4	1	3	.500	.867
Lansing, Mike	.286	14	4	0	3	0	1	.286	.286
Larkin, Barry	.269	26	7	0	1	2	6	.321	.346
Lemke, Mark#	.500	14	7	0	0	4	1	.611	.500
Lewis, Darren	.368	19	7	0	3	0	3	.400	.474
Lewis, Mark	.333	6	2	0	1	2	0	.500	.500
Listach, Pat#	.333	6	2	0	0	0	0	.333	.333
Livingstone*	.250	8	2	0	0	0	3	.250	.375
Lockhart, K*	.500	6	3	0	0	0	0	.500	.667
Lofton, Kenny*	.071	14	1	0	1	0	0	.067	.071
Lopez, Luis*	.100	10	1	0	0	1	3	.182	.100
Magadan, Dave*	.333	33	11	0	2	8	4	.463	.364
Manwaring, K	.222	18	4	0	1	0	2	.222	.222
Martin, Al*	.375	16	6	1	1	1	6	.412	.625
Martinez, Da*	.154	52	8	0	1	7	11	.267	.154
Martinez, E	.545	11	6	2	3	8	0	.737	1.273
Martinez, T*	.231	13	3	0	2	1	1	.267	.385
Matheny, Mike	.000	6	0	0	0	0	1	.000	.000
May, Derrick*	.300	20	6	1	4	3	4	.391	.550
Mayne, Brent*	.750	4	3	0	1	1	0	.800	.750
McGee, Willie*	.313	67	21	2	8	4	13	.350	.403
McGriff, Fred*	.258	31	8	1	7	3	11	.306	.419
McGwire, Mark	.625	8	5	4	7	6	1	.800	2.125
Meares, Pat	.000	7	0	0	0	0	1	.000	.000
Merced, O*	.346	26	9	0	3	4	3	.433	.423
Mitchell, K	.128	39	5	0	6	3	12	.222	.205
Molitor, Paul	.167	6	1	0	1	0	0	.167	.167
Morandini, M*	.467	15	7	0	4	4	2	.579	.600
Morris, Hal*	.450	20	9	0	3	2	2	.500	.500
Mouton, Lyle	.500	4	2	0	3	1	2	.600	.750
Murray, Eddie#	.406	32	13	4	7	7	2	.513	.875
Naehring, Tim	.125	8	1	0	0	1	0	.222	.125
Nieves, M#	.250	8	2	0	0	1	2	.333	.250
Nilsson, Dave*	.500	10	5	0	3	1	2	.545	.800
Nixon, Otis*	.250	12	3	0	0	3	3	.400	.250
Nunnally, Jon*	.250	8	2	0	1	0	2	.250	.250
O'Leary, Troy*	.176	17	3	1	3	0	3	.176	.353
O'Neill, Paul*	.270	37	10	5	11	9	4	.413	.757
Offerman, J#	.400	5	2	0	1	0	3	.400	.400
Olerud, John*	.286	7	2	1	1	1	2	.375	.714
Oliver, Joe	.286	28	8	2	6	2	4	.333	.536
Orsulak, Joe*	.314	35	11	1	5	3	2	.368	.429
Pagnozzi, Tom	.286	14	4	0	1	0	3	.286	.286
Palmeiro, R*	.400	25	10	2	6	3	2	.464	.840
Parent, Mark	.364	11	4	0	2	0	2	.333	.455
Pena, Tony	.316	38	12	0	2	3	2	.366	.342
Pendleton, T#	.282	71	20	0	13	6	7	.346	.408
Plantier, P*	.143	21	3	1	1	7	7	.250	.333
Polonia, Luis*	.167	6	1	0	0	1	2	.286	.167
Pride, Curtis*	.500	6	3	1	1	0	0	.500	1.167
Raines, Tim#	.341	44	15	1	3	10	11	.473	.455
Ramirez, M	.500	6	3	0	2	3	3	.667	.667
Reed, Jeff*	.227	22	5	0	2	3	4	.320	.273
Ripken, Cal	.500	10	5	0	1	1	0	.545	.600
Roberts, Bip#	.357	42	15	0	3	5	7	.417	.476
Sabo, Chris	.267	30	8	1	3	3	4	.333	.433
Samuel, Juan	.250	20	5	0	0	2	3	.318	.250
Sanchez, Rey	.500	8	4	0	1	1	1	.556	.500
Sandberg, R	.273	77	21	1	7	3	16	.309	.403
Sanders, R	.050	20	1	0	0	2	6	.136	.050
Santiago, B	.250	36	9	0	4	3	8	.308	.250
Segui, David#	.286	7	2	0	0	0	1	.286	.286
Seitzer, K	.267	15	4	0	0	1	3	.313	.333
Selby, Bill*	.286	7	2	0	0	0	1	.286	.286
Servais, S	.000	11	0	0	0	1	0	.000	.000
Sheffield, G	.391	23	9	0	2	3	2	.462	.478
Shipley, C	.364	11	4	0	2	0	3	.364	.364
Sierra, Ruben#	.125	8	1	0	2	0	1	.125	.125
Slaught, Don	.304	23	7	0	3	0	3	.304	.348
Smith, Dwight*	.192	26	5	0	2	4	6	.323	.231

Kevin Gross, Rangers — RHP

Batter	Avg	AB	H	HR	BI	BB	SO	OBP	Slg
Smith, Ozzie*	.310	58	18	0	10	11	6	.420	.362
Sojo, Luis	.231	13	3	0	0	0	0	.231	.308
Sorrento, P*	.333	6	2	2	5	1	3	.375	1.333
Sosa, Sammy	.409	22	9	2	5	0	2	.409	.682
Sprague, Ed	.143	7	1	0	0	0	2	.143	.143
Stahoviak, S*	.500	4	2	0	0	2	0	.667	.750
Stairs, Matt*	.500	4	2	1	1	2	0	.667	1.750
Stanley, Mike	.273	11	3	1	2	2	4	.385	.727
Steinbach, T	.100	10	1	0	0	1	3	.182	.100
Stillwell, K#	.143	14	2	0	1	2	2	.250	.143
Stocker, K#	.444	9	4	0	0	1	0	.500	.556
Strawberry, D*	.203	59	12	3	10	6	16	.290	.390
Surhoff, B.J.*	.083	12	1	0	0	1	1	.154	.083
Tartabull, D	.222	9	2	0	2	1	2	.300	.333
Taubensee, E*	.222	9	2	1	2	0	0	.222	.667
Thomas, Frank	.200	10	2	0	3	6	3	.500	.300
Thome, Jim*	.182	11	2	0	0	0	4	.182	.273
Thompson, Mil*	.290	31	9	0	4	3	6	.371	.323
Thompson, Rob	.240	50	12	1	3	7	12	.339	.320
Thompson, Ry	.333	6	2	1	2	0	1	.333	.833
Tinsley, Lee#	.375	8	3	0	0	0	3	.375	.375
Tucker, M*	.200	5	1	0	0	0	2	.200	.200
Valentin, Jhn	.143	14	2	0	2	4	1	.333	.214
Valentin, Jse#	.143	7	1	0	1	0	0	.125	.286
VanderWal, J*	.143	14	2	0	1	0	4	.143	.143
Vaughn, Greg	.125	8	1	0	1	1	2	.222	.250
Vaughn, Mo*	.300	10	3	0	1	4	4	.500	.700
Ventura, R*	.455	11	5	0	0	3	3	.571	.636
Vina, F*	.286	7	2	0	1	1	0	.444	.286
Vizcaino, J#	.214	28	6	0	1	4	7	.313	.214
Vizquel, Omar#	.750	12	9	0	3	0	0	.750	.917
Walbeck, Matt#	.000	5	0	0	1	1	0	.167	.000
Walker, Larry*	.263	19	5	0	0	2	4	.333	.368
Wallach, Tim	.250	52	13	2	5	5	11	.316	.442
Walton, J	.385	13	5	0	0	2	3	.500	.385
Weiss, Walt*	.182	11	2	0	1	2	3	.250	.182
Wilkins, Rick*	.400	20	8	2	4	2	3	.455	.850
Williams, Ber#	.571	7	4	0	0	0	0	.571	.571
Williams, E	.375	8	3	1	2	0	2	.375	.750
Williams, Geo#	.000	3	0	0	1	1	2	.200	.000
Williams, Ma	.300	30	9	0	3	2	4	.364	.433
Wilson, Dan	.231	13	3	0	0	0	3	.286	.308
Young, Kevin	.083	12	1	0	1	0	6	.143	.083
Zaun, Greg#	.222	9	2	0	0	0	1	.222	.222
Zeile, Todd	.200	15	3	0	1	1	1	.235	.267

Eddie Guardado, Twins — LHP

Batter	Avg	AB	H	HR	BI	BB	SO	OBP	Slg
Martinez, T*	.111	9	1	0	2	1	1	.182	.333
McLemore, M#	.333	12	4	0	1	2	0	.429	.417
McRae, Brian#	.500	8	4	1	5	0	0	.500	1.125
Mieske, Matt	.400	5	2	1	2	2	0	.571	1.200
Molitor, Paul	.429	7	3	0	1	2	0	.556	.571
Murray, Eddie#	.400	5	2	1	2	0	0	.333	1.000
Nilsson, Dave*	.571	7	4	1	6	0	2	.571	1.286
Nixon, Otis#	.444	9	4	0	0	0	1	.444	.556
O'Neill, Paul*	.200	10	2	0	2	1	4	.250	.300
Palmeiro, R*	.200	10	2	0	1	0	3	.200	.300
Palmer, Dean	.600	5	3	0	0	5	0	.800	.800
Paquette, C	.375	8	3	2	2	1	1	.444	1.250
Pena, Tony	.286	7	2	0	0	0	2	.286	.286
Perez, E	.000	4	0	0	0	1	2	.200	.000
Phillips, T#	.200	5	1	1	2	4	1	.556	.800
Raines, Tim#	.375	8	3	0	0	1	1	.444	.375
Ramirez, M	.400	5	2	0	0	0	3	.400	.600
Ripken, Cal	.200	10	2	0	1	3	3	.385	.300
Rodriguez, I	.000	6	0	0	0	2	1	.250	.000
Salmon, Tim	.250	8	2	0	0	3	3	.455	.375
Samuel, Juan	.500	4	2	0	2	0	0	.667	.500
Schofield, D	.250	4	1	0	0	1	1	.400	.250
Segui, David#	.200	5	1	0	0	1	0	.333	.400
Seitzer, K	.333	9	3	1	2	1	2	.400	.778
Sierra, Ruben#	.167	12	2	0	0	2	1	.286	.250
Snow, J.T.#	.167	6	1	0	1	1	2	.286	.167
Sorrento, P*	.273	11	3	1	5	0	3	.333	.545
Sprague, Ed	.333	6	2	0	4	2	1	.500	.500
Stanley, Mike	.167	6	1	0	0	3	1	.444	.167
Steinbach, T	.333	6	2	2	2	0	0	.333	1.333
Surhoff, B.J.*	.300	10	3	1	2	0	2	.300	.600
Tartabull, D	.286	7	2	1	3	0	2	.286	.714
Tettleton, M#	.375	8	3	0	3	2	1	.500	.625
Thomas, Frank	.500	6	3	2	5	0	0	.429	1.500
Thome, Jim*	.273	11	3	0	0	0	5	.273	.364
Valentin, Jhn	.200	5	1	0	0	1	0	.333	.400
Valentin, Jse#	.250	4	1	0	0	1	0	.400	.250
Vaughn, Greg	.500	8	4	2	3	1	0	.556	1.500
Vaughn, Mo*	.200	10	2	0	2	0	2	.200	.200
Velarde, R	.500	4	2	0	0	1	0	.600	.750
Ventura, R*	.182	11	2	1	3	0	3	.182	.545
Vina, F*	.273	11	3	0	0	0	1	.273	.273
Vizquel, Omar#	.200	10	2	0	0	0	0	.200	.200
Voigt, Jack	.333	6	2	0	3	1	1	.375	.500
White, Devon#	.500	6	3	1	2	0	0	.500	1.333
Williams, Ber#	.385	13	5	2	4	1	2	.429	1.000

Eddie Guardado, Twins — LHP

Batter	Avg	AB	H	HR	BI	BB	SO	OBP	Slg
Alomar, R#	.500	6	3	0	3	1	1	.500	.667
Amaral, Rich	.571	7	4	0	4	1	2	.625	.714
Anderson, Brd*	.167	12	2	0	0	1	2	.231	.250
Baerga, C	.300	10	3	0	2	1	0	.364	.400
Baines, H*	.200	5	1	0	1	0	1	.200	.400
Belle, Albert	.571	7	4	1	2	1	0	.625	1.000
Boggs, Wade*	.300	10	3	0	1	0	0	.300	.400
Bordick, Mike	.375	8	3	0	2	1	1	.444	.375
Carter, Joe	.300	10	3	1	3	0	1	.300	.800
Cedeno, D#	.111	9	1	0	0	0	2	.111	.111
Cirillo, Jeff	.286	7	2	1	1	2	1	.444	.857
Clark, Will*	.182	11	2	0	0	1	2	.250	.182
Cora, Joey#	.400	5	2	0	0	0	0	.400	.400
Curtis, Chad	.333	6	2	0	1	1	2	.429	.333
Davis, Chili#	.444	9	4	2	6	2	4	.500	1.111
Devereaux, M	.444	9	4	0	3	0	2	.444	.667
DiSarcina, G	.500	8	4	0	2	0	0	.500	.750
Durham, Ray#	.000	3	0	0	0	2	1	.400	.000
Edmonds, Jim*	.400	10	4	1	5	0	4	.364	.800
Espinoza, A	.500	4	2	1	1	1	1	.600	1.250
Frye, Jeff	.500	4	2	0	0	2	0	.667	.500
Gaetti, Gary	.222	9	2	0	0	0	3	.222	.333
Gagne, Greg	.500	10	5	0	4	1	1	.545	.900
Gates, Brent#	.100	10	1	0	0	0	0	.100	.100
Giambi, Jason*	.600	5	3	0	1	0	1	.600	.600
Gomez, Chris	.167	6	1	0	1	0	2	.167	.167
Gonzalez, J	.500	6	3	1	2	0	0	.500	1.333
Goodwin, Tom*	.333	6	2	0	2	0	3	.333	.667
Greenwell, M*	.571	7	4	0	3	0	0	.571	.571
Griffey Jr, K*	.000	8	0	0	0	0	5	.111	.000
Guillen, O*	.222	9	2	0	1	0	2	.222	.222
Hamilton, D*	.231	13	3	0	0	0	2	.231	.308
Hammonds, J	.500	6	3	0	2	0	0	.429	1.000
Hoiles, Chris	.200	5	1	0	2	1	1	.286	.400
Jaha, John	.333	6	2	0	0	1	0	.429	.333
Johnson, L*	.333	6	2	0	0	1	1	.429	.333
Joyner, Wally*	.333	9	3	0	1	1	1	.400	.333
Kelly, Pat	.167	6	1	0	0	0	0	.167	.167
Knorr, Randy	.200	5	1	0	0	0	2	.200	.200
Listach, Pat#	.167	6	1	0	0	0	0	.167	.167
Lofton, Kenny*	.214	14	3	0	0	1	3	.267	.214
Macfarlane, M	.300	10	3	0	1	0	1	.300	.400
Martinez, Da*	.250	4	1	0	0	1	2	.400	.250

Mark Gubicza, Royals — RHP

Batter	Avg	AB	H	HR	BI	BB	SO	OBP	Slg
Aldrete, Mike*	.381	21	8	0	3	2	2	.435	.571
Alicea, Luis#	.600	5	3	0	0	0	0	.600	.800
Alomar, R#	.476	21	10	1	7	3	3	.520	.667
Amaral, Rich	.250	4	1	0	0	1	1	.400	.500
Anderson, Brd*	.425	40	17	2	7	3	3	.477	.725
Anderson, G*	.286	7	2	0	0	0	0	.286	.286
Anthony, Eric*	.500	8	4	1	1	0	0	.500	.875
Baerga, C#	.200	15	3	0	2	3	4	.333	.333
Baines, H*	.346	52	18	1	7	4	10	.393	.538
Becker, Rich*	.182	11	2	0	2	0	0	.167	.273
Bell, Jay	.182	11	2	0	0	0	4	.182	.182
Belle, Albert	.429	14	6	2	5	2	2	.500	.857
Beltre, E	.400	5	2	0	0	0	0	.400	.400
Berroa, G	.250	20	5	1	2	0	4	.250	.400
Bichette, D	.300	10	3	0	0	3	0	.300	.500
Blowers, Mike	.250	4	1	0	0	1	3	.400	.500
Boggs, Wade*	.367	79	29	1	5	17	3	.474	.494
Bonilla, B#	.375	8	3	0	2	1	1	.444	.375
Borders, Pat	.333	9	3	0	2	0	2	.300	.333
Bordick, Mike	.257	35	9	0	4	1	3	.278	.257
Bragg, Darren*	.400	5	2	0	0	1	1	.500	.400
Brosius, S	.143	21	3	0	1	3	1	.217	.238
Buhner, Jay	.375	24	9	2	9	3	7	.429	.708
Burks, Ellis	.286	35	10	1	4	4	5	.375	.457
Butler, Brett*	.281	32	9	0	2	1	1	.303	.375
Canseco, Jose	.250	56	14	4	7	4	20	.300	.500
Carreon, Mark	.286	7	2	0	0	0	1	.286	.286
Carter, Joe	.257	74	19	2	8	3	11	.304	.419
Cedeno, D#	.222	9	2	0	0	1	0	.300	.222
Cirillo, Jeff	.133	15	2	0	1	2	2	.222	.133
Clark, Dave*	.375	8	3	1	1	0	3	.375	.875
Clark, Will*	.278	18	5	0	1	1	4	.316	.389
Cole, Alex*	.263	19	5	0	0	0	1	.263	.368
Cora, Joey#	.190	21	4	0	1	0	0	.190	.190
Cordero, Wil	.400	5	2	0	0	1	1	.500	.400
Cordova, M	.000	15	0	0	1	1	1	.063	.000
Curtis, Chad	.600	10	6	0	0	0	0	.636	.700
Cuyler, Milt#	.167	12	2	0	0	2	2	.167	.250
Davis, Chili#	.250	36	9	0	1	2	8	.289	.361
Dawson, Andre	.286	7	2	1	0	0	2	.286	.286
Deer, Rob	.212	33	7	2	7	2	12	.257	.455
Delgado, C*	.167	6	1	0	0	0	0	.167	.167

Mark Gubicza, Royals									RHP
Batter	Avg	AB	H	HR	BI	BB	SO	OBP	Slg
Devereaux, M	.280	25	7	0	2	2	4	.333	.400
Díaz, Alex#	.400	5	2	0	1	0	0	.400	.600
DiSarcina, G	.250	16	4	0	0	0	0	.250	.250
Durham, Ray#	.167	6	1	0	0	0	1	.167	.167
Easley, D	.000	5	0	0	0	1	1	.167	.000
Edmonds, Jim*	.462	13	6	0	1	0	1	.462	.538
Elster, Kevin	.250	4	1	0	1	1	0	.400	.500
Espinoza, A	.368	19	7	0	3	0	3	.368	.474
Fabregas, Jor*	.167	6	1	0	0	0	1	.167	.167
Fermin, Felix	.300	20	6	0	2	0	2	.300	.400
Fielder, C	.290	31	9	2	3	2	9	.333	.484
Finley, Steve*	.167	6	1	0	0	1	1	.286	.167
Franco, Julio	.371	70	26	0	4	4	8	.405	.400
Frazier, Lou#	.167	6	1	0	0	0	1	.167	.167
Fryman, T	.304	23	7	0	0	1	8	.333	.348
Gaetti, Gary	.265	49	13	0	4	4	7	.315	.265
Gagne, Greg	.333	33	11	0	6	3	7	.378	.394
Gallego, Mike	.053	19	1	0	0	3	3	.182	.053
Gates, Brent#	.154	26	4	0	3	1	4	.179	.192
Giambi, Jason*	.615	13	8	2	4	1	0	.643	1.154
Gil, Benji	.333	6	2	0	0	0	1	.333	.500
Gomez, Chris	.143	7	1	0	1	0	2	.143	.286
Gomez, Leo	.182	11	2	1	1	2	2	.308	.455
Gonzales, R	.250	16	4	0	1	5	3	.409	.313
Gonzalez, J	.476	21	10	2	8	0	2	.476	.857
Goodwin, C*	.000	5	0	0	0	0	0	.000	.000
Grebeck, C	.273	11	3	0	1	0	1	.273	.273
Green, Shawn*	.444	9	4	1	1	0	1	.444	.778
Greenwell, M*	.417	36	15	0	8	3	2	.475	.611
Greer, Rusty*	.500	14	7	0	2	0	0	.563	.786
Griffey Jr, K*	.524	21	11	2	3	8	3	.655	.905
Guillen, O*	.279	61	17	0	2	3	6	.313	.295
Hall, Mel*	.434	53	23	2	7	5	3	.483	.585
Hamilton, D*	.242	33	8	0	1	1	1	.265	.242
Hammonds, J	.000	4	0	0	0	1	0	.200	.000
Hayes, C	.167	6	1	0	0	0	3	.167	.167
Henderson, R	.229	70	16	1	2	10	6	.325	.357
Herrera, Jose*	.500	8	4	0	0	0	1	.500	.500
Hill, G	.286	7	2	0	1	0	2	.286	.286
Hoiles, Chris	.385	13	5	0	3	1	4	.467	.538
Howell, Jack*	.208	24	5	1	2	3	7	.296	.375
Hulse, David*	.200	20	4	0	0	0	2	.200	.200
Huson, Jeff*	.429	7	3	0	1	3	1	.600	.571
Incaviglia, P	.286	28	8	2	7	2	8	.333	.643
Jaha, John	.318	22	7	1	4	2	3	.375	.455
James, Dion*	.313	16	5	1	3	2	1	.389	.563
Javier, Stan#	.000	19	0	0	0	0	2	.000	.000
Jefferson, R*	.667	9	6	0	5	0	0	.667	1.000
Johnson, L*	.344	32	11	0	3	5	1	.432	.375
Joyner, Wally*	.435	23	10	1	5	2	3	.480	.565
Karkovice, R	.182	22	4	1	2	4	11	.308	.318
Kelly, Pat	.286	21	6	1	3	0	4	.273	.476
Kelly, Jeff	.417	24	10	0	4	1	2	.440	.500
Kent, Jeff	.200	5	1	0	1	1	1	.333	.200
Kingery, Mike*	.143	14	2	0	0	2	5	.250	.214
Kirby, Wayne	.400	5	2	0	1	0	1	.500	.600
Knoblauch, C	.417	36	15	1	6	1	4	.447	.583
Kreuter, Chad#	.200	10	2	0	3	1	2	.250	.400
Lawton, Matt*	.400	5	2	1	5	1	1	.571	1.000
Leius, Scott	.364	11	4	0	1	4	1	.417	.364
Levis, Jesse*	.200	5	1	0	0	1	0	.333	.200
Leyritz, Jim	.200	10	2	0	0	1	2	.273	.200
Liriano, N#	.167	6	1	0	1	0	0	.167	.167
Listach, Pat#	.176	17	3	0	2	1	2	.222	.294
Livingstone*	.000	6	0	0	0	0	1	.000	.000
Lofton, Kenny*	.300	10	3	0	0	1	0	.300	.300
Macfarlane, M	.400	5	2	0	0	0	0	.400	.400
Manto, Jeff	.000	5	0	0	0	1	0	.167	.000
Martin, N	.000	8	0	0	0	1	0	.000	.000
Martinez, Da*	.429	7	3	0	1	0	0	.429	.429
Martinez, E	.333	33	11	1	3	2	4	.389	.515
Martinez, S*	.375	8	3	0	2	1	1	.444	.500
Martinez, T*	.211	19	4	1	4	3	0	.318	.474
Matheny, Mike	.333	6	2	0	1	1	0	.429	.333
McGriff, Fred*	.500	20	10	4	4	3	3	.583	1.250
McGwire, Mark	.239	46	11	6	9	6	9	.345	.435
McLemore, M#	.115	26	3	0	1	1	2	.148	.115
Meares, Pat	.143	7	1	0	0	1	2	.250	.286
Molitor, Paul	.321	56	18	2	7	6	9	.387	.482
Munoz, Pedro	.300	10	3	1	1	2	2	.364	.600
Murray, Eddie*	.281	32	9	1	7	2	2	.324	.594
Myers, Greg*	.182	11	2	1	3	3	1	.357	.455
Naehring, Tim	.250	8	2	0	1	1	1	.250	.375
Newson, W*	.370	27	10	1	3	2	6	.414	.593
Nilsson, Dave*	.200	25	5	0	2	0	2	.200	.200
Nixon, Otis#	.150	20	3	0	0	4	4	.292	.150
O'Leary, Troy*	.143	14	2	0	0	0	1	.143	.143
O'Neill, Paul*	.500	16	8	0	1	1	5	.529	.563
Olerud, John*	.300	30	9	0	2	4	5	.400	.467
Oliver, Joe	.222	9	2	1	1	0	1	.222	.556
Orsulak, Joe*	.233	30	7	0	3	1	5	.258	.267

Mark Gubicza, Royals									RHP
Batter	Avg	AB	H	HR	BI	BB	SO	OBP	Slg
Palmeiro, R*	.294	34	10	2	5	3	2	.351	.559
Palmer, Dean	.211	19	4	1	4	1	7	.250	.421
Paquette, C	.167	6	1	0	1	0	3	.167	.167
Pena, Tony	.167	6	1	0	1	0	2	.167	.167
Perez, Tomas#	.400	5	2	0	0	1	0	.500	.400
Phillips, T#	.158	57	9	2	5	9	11	.273	.351
Plantier, P*	.000	3	0	0	1	3	3	.500	.000
Polonia, Luis*	.258	62	16	0	7	3	8	.288	.306
Raines, Tim#	.258	31	8	0	7	6	3	.385	.323
Reboulet, J	.167	6	1	0	0	0	1	.167	.167
Reed, Jody	.310	29	9	0	5	2	2	.355	.379
Ripken, Billy	.059	17	1	0	0	4	3	.238	.059
Ripken, Cal	.333	72	24	0	12	6	6	.375	.458
Rodriguez, I	.308	26	8	0	5	0	3	.296	.308
Salmon, Tim	.400	15	6	0	2	2	3	.471	.533
Schofield, D	.000	28	0	0	0	2	6	.067	.000
Schu, Rick	.286	7	2	0	0	3	2	.500	.286
Seitzer, K	.378	37	14	2	9	4	1	.452	.703
Sheffield, G	.333	15	5	0	3	1	1	.375	.467
Sierra, Ruben#	.293	58	17	0	9	5	8	.338	.328
Slaught, Don	.296	27	8	0	1	2	6	.345	.333
Snow, J.T.#	.214	14	3	1	4	0	2	.214	.429
Sojo, Luis	.545	22	12	1	8	1	0	.565	.727
Sorrento, P*	.286	14	4	0	0	1	1	.333	.286
Spiers, Bill*	.429	14	6	0	3	0	2	.429	.571
Sprague, Ed	.444	18	8	1	3	0	4	.421	.722
Stahoviak, S*	.125	8	1	0	0	1	2	.222	.250
Stankiewicz	.375	8	3	0	0	0	2	.375	.500
Stanley, Mike	.333	6	2	0	3	0	0	.333	.333
Steinbach, T	.306	62	19	0	6	3	7	.338	.435
Strange, Doug#	.286	14	4	0	3	0	2	.286	.429
Surhoff, B.J.*	.178	45	8	0	3	5	1	.260	.222
Sveum, Dale#	.333	12	4	0	3	5	4	.529	.583
Tartabull, D	.316	19	6	0	5	3	4	.409	.474
Tettleton, M#	.286	42	12	4	5	7	10	.380	.595
Thomas, Frank	.308	26	8	2	6	8	3	.457	.577
Tinsley, Lee#	.500	6	3	0	2	0	0	.500	.500
Tomberlin, A*	.286	7	2	1	1	1	2	.375	.714
Trammell, A	.196	46	9	1	3	3	8	.255	.283
Valentin, Jhn	.250	12	3	0	5	0	1	.214	.417
Valentin, Jse#	.259	27	7	0	0	2	2	.310	.444
Valle, Dave	.176	17	3	0	0	0	2	.176	.176
Vaughn, Greg	.268	41	11	4	5	4	7	.333	.561
Vaughn, Mo*	.222	18	4	0	3	2	3	.300	.278
Velarde, R	.474	19	9	1	3	0	2	.474	.632
Ventura, R*	.200	30	6	0	4	5	2	.314	.233
Vina, F*	.400	20	8	0	4	0	2	.400	.400
Vizquel, Omar#	.182	11	2	0	0	0	1	.182	.182
Walbeck, Matt#	.100	10	1	0	1	0	0	.182	.100
Ward, Turner#	.130	23	3	0	1	0	2	.130	.174
Weiss, Walt	.125	16	2	0	1	1	4	.263	.125
White, Devon#	.182	33	6	0	1	2	8	.229	.212
Whiten, Mark#	.167	12	2	0	0	1	3	.231	.167
Williams, Ber#	.308	26	8	1	6	2	1	.357	.500
Wilson, Dan	.308	13	4	1	3	0	2	.308	.615
Worthington	.214	14	3	1	2	1	4	.267	.571

Lee Guetterman, Mariners									LHP
Batter	Avg	AB	H	HR	BI	BB	SO	OBP	Slg
Alomar, R#	.000	4	0	0	1	0	4	.000	.000
Anderson, Brd*	.111	9	1	0	1	0	4	.111	.222
Anthony, Eric*	.333	6	2	1	2	0	1	.333	.833
Bagwell, Jeff	.200	5	1	0	1	0	0	.167	.200
Baines, H*	.333	21	7	0	2	3	3	.417	.429
Bell, Derek	.200	5	1	0	1	0	1	.200	.400
Bichette, D	.200	5	1	0	0	0	2	.429	.400
Boggs, Wade*	.261	23	6	1	5	0	1	.261	.435
Bonds, Barry*	.167	6	1	0	0	1	1	.286	.167
Borders, Pat	.357	14	5	0	1	1	1	.400	.429
Buhner, Jay	.500	4	2	1	3	1	0	.600	1.500
Burks, Ellis	.133	15	2	0	0	0	3	.133	.133
Butler, Brett*	.200	10	2	0	0	0	0	.273	.200
Cangelosi, J#	.667	3	2	0	1	4	1	.857	.667
Canseco, Jose	.500	12	6	1	5	0	0	.500	.917
Carter, Joe	.417	12	5	0	1	2	3	.467	.417
Cole, Alex*	.500	4	2	0	0	1	0	.600	.500
Cuyler, Milt#	.500	4	2	0	0	1	0	.714	.500
Daulton, D*	.400	5	2	0	1	1	0	.500	.600
Davis, Chili#	.364	11	4	2	3	0	1	.364	.909
Deer, Rob	.429	7	3	2	3	4	1	.636	1.429
Devereaux, M	.571	7	4	0	1	1	0	.625	.857
Eisenreich, J*	.462	13	6	0	0	2	1	.533	.615
Fermin, Felix	.250	8	2	0	0	0	0	.250	.250
Fielder, C	.600	5	3	1	3	1	2	.667	1.200
Finley, Steve*	.000	5	0	0	0	0	1	.000	.000
Franco, Julio	.250	12	3	0	1	2	1	.357	.250
Gaetti, Gary	.550	20	11	0	6	0	1	.524	.550
Gagne, Greg	.286	14	4	1	3	1	2	.333	.714
Gallego, Mike	.167	6	1	0	0	0	0	.167	.167
Gomez, Leo	.200	5	1	1	1	1	0	.333	.800
Gonzales, R	.300	10	3	0	0	0	1	.300	.300

Lee Guetterman, Mariners — LHP

Batter	Avg	AB	H	HR	BI	BB	SO	OBP	Slg
Gonzalez, J	.200	5	1	0	1	1	1	.333	.200
Gonzalez, L*	.750	4	3	0	0	2	0	.833	.750
Greenwell, M*	.471	17	8	1	4	2	2	.550	.765
Griffey Jr, K*	.273	11	3	1	4	0	3	.273	.727
Guillen, O*	.444	18	8	0	6	0	1	.421	.500
Gwynn, Tony*	.250	4	1	0	0	1	0	.400	.250
Hamilton, D*	.000	5	0	0	0	1	1	.167	.000
Henderson, R	.200	5	1	1	2	1	1	.333	.800
Hoiles, Chris	.167	6	1	0	2	1	0	.286	.500
Hollins, Dave#	.600	5	3	1	6	1	1	.667	1.600
Howard, Dave#	.400	5	2	0	3	0	1	.400	.400
Howell, Jack*	.250	4	1	0	0	1	0	.400	.250
Huson, Jeff*	.200	5	1	0	0	0	0	.200	.200
Incaviglia, P	.467	15	7	0	3	0	3	.467	.667
Johnson, L*	.000	11	0	0	1	1	3	.083	.000
Joyner, Wally*	.200	20	4	0	3	2	1	.273	.300
Karkovice, R	.250	4	1	1	2	0	0	.200	1.000
Kent, Jeff	.250	4	1	1	2	0	0	.500	1.000
Knoblauch, C	.400	5	2	0	0	0	0	.400	.400
Lemke, Mark#	.000	4	0	0	0	1	0	.200	.000
Liriano, N#	.100	10	1	0	2	1	1	.250	.100
Macfarlane, M	.500	4	2	0	1	1	0	.600	.750
Martinez, Da*	.250	4	1	0	0	2	2	.500	.250
Martinez, E	.250	4	1	0	0	2	0	.500	.250
McGriff, Fred*	.313	16	5	0	1	1	4	.353	.313
McGwire, Mark	.200	5	1	0	2	1	0	.250	.400
Molitor, Paul	.455	11	5	0	2	0	0	.455	.545
Murray, Eddie#	.333	6	2	0	3	1	1	.429	.333
Olerud, John*	.222	9	2	1	4	1	1	.417	.667
Orsulak, Joe*	.111	9	1	0	1	0	2	.111	.111
Palmeiro, R*	.313	16	5	0	3	1	2	.353	.438
Phillips, T#	.500	8	4	0	0	2	0	.600	.500
Plantier, P*	.250	4	1	0	0	2	2	.500	.250
Polonia, Luis*	.143	7	1	0	0	0	1	.143	.143
Reed, Jody	.444	9	4	0	1	0	0	.444	.778
Ripken, Billy	.000	3	0	0	0	1	1	.000	.000
Ripken, Cal	.250	16	4	0	0	2	2	.333	.375
Schofield, D	.333	6	2	0	0	1	0	.429	.333
Schu, Rick	.333	9	3	0	2	1	0	.400	.333
Seitzer, K	.235	17	4	0	1	3	2	.350	.353
Sheffield, G	.429	7	3	1	1	0	0	.500	.857
Sierra, Ruben#	.276	29	8	1	3	0	3	.276	.414
Slaught, Don	.167	6	1	0	0	0	1	.167	.167
Spiers, Bill*	.125	8	1	0	0	0	2	.125	.125
Stanley, Mike	.250	8	2	0	0	1	1	.333	.250
Steinbach, T	.375	8	3	0	0	0	1	.375	.375
Stillwell, K	.000	5	0	0	1	0	0	.000	.000
Surhoff, B.J.*	.154	13	2	0	1	0	1	.143	.154
Sveum, Dale#	.273	11	3	0	3	0	1	.273	.455
Tartabull, D	.400	15	6	1	6	4	3	.526	.733
Tettleton, M#	.333	15	5	2	6	0	3	.333	.800
Trammell, A	.385	13	5	0	4	1	1	.429	.462
Vaughn, Greg	.167	6	1	0	0	0	0	.167	.500
Vaughn, Mo*	.400	5	2	0	0	0	0	.400	.400
Ventura, R*	.100	10	1	0	0	1	1	.182	.100
Vizquel, Omar#	.400	5	2	0	0	0	0	.400	.400
Walker, Larry*	.250	4	1	0	0	0	0	.400	.250
Weiss, Walt#	.250	4	1	0	0	0	0	.250	.500
White, Devon#	.250	12	3	0	4	0	2	.231	.417
Worthington	.167	6	1	0	0	0	0	.167	.167

Eric Gunderson, Red Sox — LHP

Batter	Avg	AB	H	HR	BI	BB	SO	OBP	Slg
Anderson, G*	.000	5	0	0	0	0	2	.000	.000
Caminiti, Ken#	.400	5	2	0	0	0	0	.400	.800
Griffey Jr, K*	.400	5	2	1	3	0	1	.286	1.200
Gwynn, Tony*	.250	8	2	0	1	1	1	.333	.250
Justice, David*	.400	4	0	0	0	1	2	.200	.400
Nilsson, Dave*	.200	5	1	0	0	0	1	.200	.200
O'Neill, Paul*	.333	3	1	0	1	2	2	.600	.667
Roberts, Bip#	.429	6	2	0	1	1	0	.429	.333

Mark Guthrie, Dodgers — LHP

Batter	Avg	AB	H	HR	BI	BB	SO	OBP	Slg
Alicea, Luis#	.000	3	0	0	1	1	0	.200	.000
Alomar, R#	.600	5	3	1	2	1	0	.667	1.600
Alomar Jr, S	.143	7	1	0	1	1	1	.250	.143
Anderson, Brd*	.222	9	2	0	1	3	4	.417	.222
Baerga, C#	.267	15	4	0	1	0	2	.250	.333
Baines, H*	.222	9	2	1	1	0	1	.222	.556
Bell, Derek	.429	7	3	1	2	0	1	.429	1.143
Belle, Albert	.200	10	2	0	1	0	5	.200	.300
Boggs, Wade*	.250	16	4	0	2	0	1	.235	.250
Bonds, Barry*	.333	3	1	1	1	2	0	.600	1.333
Borders, Pat	.167	18	3	0	0	0	2	.167	.222
Buhner, Jay	.250	12	3	0	0	3	2	.400	.250
Burks, Ellis	.333	6	2	0	1	3	1	.556	.667
Caminiti, Ken#	.400	5	2	1	2	0	3	.333	1.000
Canseco, Jose	.375	8	3	0	0	4	3	.583	.375
Carter, Joe	.429	7	3	0	2	0	1	.429	.714
Cole, Alex*	.333	6	2	0	0	0	0	.333	.500

Mark Guthrie, Dodgers — LHP

Batter	Avg	AB	H	HR	BI	BB	SO	OBP	Slg
Conine, Jeff	.000	6	0	0	0	0	3	.000	.000
Cuyler, Milt#	.444	9	4	0	1	0	0	.444	.556
Davis, Chili#	.400	10	4	1	3	0	0	.400	.900
Deer, Rob	.214	14	3	1	2	3	6	.353	.429
Devereaux, M	.400	10	4	0	0	1	2	.455	.400
Eisenreich, J*	.316	19	6	0	2	0	3	.316	.526
Espinoza, A	.444	9	4	1	1	0	2	.500	.778
Fermin, Felix	.833	12	10	0	4	0	1	.769	.917
Fielder, C	.267	15	4	0	1	2	3	.353	.333
Finley, Steve*	.375	8	3	0	1	2	1	.500	.375
Franco, Julio	.000	3	0	0	0	2	0	.400	.000
Fryman, T	.188	16	3	1	4	2	6	.263	.500
Gaetti, Gary	.286	7	2	0	0	0	2	.286	.286
Gallego, Mike	.182	11	2	0	0	1	3	.250	.273
Gomez, Chris	.000	6	0	0	1	0	1	.000	.000
Gomez, Leo	.300	10	3	1	1	1	2	.364	.700
Gonzales, R	.000	4	0	0	0	1	3	.200	.000
Gonzalez, L*	.167	6	1	0	0	0	1	.167	.167
Grebeck, C	.000	5	0	0	0	0	0	.000	.000
Greenwell, M*	.100	10	1	0	0	0	1	.100	.100
Griffey Jr, K*	.500	20	10	1	2	2	3	.545	.650
Guillen, O*	.227	22	5	0	0	1	4	.261	.273
Gwynn, Tony*	.600	5	3	0	2	1	0	.667	.600
Hall, Mel*	.500	10	5	0	2	0	1	.455	.600
Hamilton, D*	.125	8	1	0	0	0	2	.125	.125
Hayes, C	.125	8	1	1	1	0	3	.125	.500
Henderson, R	.231	13	3	0	1	0	4	.231	.308
Hernandez, Jo	.000	4	0	0	0	1	1	.200	.000
Hill, G	.467	15	7	1	4	0	3	.467	.800
Hoiles, Chris	.429	7	3	0	0	1	1	.500	.571
Huff, Michael	.800	5	4	1	2	3	0	.875	1.400
Incaviglia, P	.250	8	2	0	0	0	2	.333	.250
Jefferies, G#	.400	5	2	0	1	0	0	.400	.400
Johnson, L*	.240	25	6	0	4	2	2	.296	.240
Joyner, Wally*	.238	21	5	0	2	1	4	.273	.286
Kelly, Pat	.250	8	2	0	0	0	3	.250	.375
Kelly, R	.182	11	2	0	0	2	3	.308	.273
King, Jeff	.000	5	0	0	0	1	0	.000	.000
Kirby, Wayne*	.000	4	0	0	0	1	1	.200	.000
Lankford, Ray*	.400	5	2	0	2	0	1	.400	.400
Leyritz, Jim	.000	5	0	0	0	0	2	.000	.000
Lofton, Kenny*	.417	12	5	0	3	1	0	.462	.667
Macfarlane, M	.211	19	4	0	3	1	4	.238	.211
Martin, Al*	.200	5	1	0	1	0	0	.200	.200
Martinez, E	.125	8	1	0	0	1	1	.222	.250
Martinez, T*	.125	8	1	0	1	0	3	.222	.125
McGee, Willie*	.429	7	3	0	0	0	1	.429	.429
McGriff, Fred*	.438	16	7	0	1	0	5	.438	.438
McGwire, Mark	.556	9	5	0	2	3	0	.667	.556
McIntosh, Tim	.000	5	0	0	0	0	2	.000	.000
McLemore, M#	.200	10	2	0	2	0	1	.200	.200
McRae, Brian#	.313	16	5	0	1	3	3	.421	.313
Molitor, Paul	.133	15	2	0	1	0	4	.133	.133
Morandini, M*	.500	4	2	0	2	0	0	.400	.500
Morman, Russ	.000	4	0	0	0	1	1	.000	.000
Murray, Eddie#	.500	4	2	0	0	1	0	.600	.500
Naehring, Tim	.000	5	0	0	0	0	2	.000	.000
Nilsson, Dave*	.167	6	1	0	1	0	2	.167	.167
O'Neill, Paul*	.500	4	2	0	1	1	0	.600	.750
Olerud, John*	.000	6	0	0	1	1	4	.125	.000
Orsulak, Joe*	.200	10	2	0	1	1	2	.273	.200
Palmeiro, R*	.444	9	4	1	2	0	0	.444	.889
Pena, Tony	.222	9	2	0	1	0	0	.222	.333
Phillips, T#	.167	18	3	1	3	3	4	.261	.389
Polonia, Luis*	.000	5	0	0	0	1	0	.167	.000
Raines, Tim#	.100	10	1	0	1	0	3	.100	.100
Reed, Jody	.500	10	5	0	0	4	3	.643	.600
Ripken, Cal	.364	11	4	0	1	2	0	.462	.545
Segui, David#	.333	6	2	0	0	0	0	.333	.333
Seitzer, K	.188	16	3	2	3	0	2	.188	.563
Servais, S	.667	3	2	0	0	1	0	.750	.667
Sheffield, G	.222	9	2	0	0	1	1	.300	.333
Shumpert, T	.286	7	2	0	0	0	3	.286	.286
Sierra, Ruben#	.625	8	5	0	2	2	2	.700	.625
Sojo, Luis	.400	10	4	0	1	0	2	.400	.600
Sorrento, P*	.143	7	1	0	0	0	3	.143	.143
Sosa, Sammy	.375	24	9	0	3	0	7	.333	.458
Sprague, Ed	.200	5	1	0	0	0	1	.200	.200
Stanley, Mike	.200	5	1	0	1	1	1	.333	.400
Steinbach, T	.545	11	6	3	13	1	1	.583	1.364
Stillwell, K	.286	14	4	0	1	0	1	.286	.500
Surhoff, B.J.*	.333	3	1	0	0	1	0	.500	.333
Sveum, Dale#	.125	8	1	0	0	0	3	.125	.125
Tartabull, D	.429	14	6	2	5	6	4	.600	.857
Tettleton, M#	.000	7	0	0	0	2	3	.222	.000
Thomas, Frank	.231	13	3	2	3	2	5	.333	.692
Thome, Jim*	.400	5	2	0	0	0	2	.400	.400
Trammell, A	.357	14	5	1	3	2	3	.438	.786
Valle, Dave	.462	13	6	1	4	0	2	.462	.692
Vaughn, Greg	.000	13	0	0	0	1	4	.071	.000
Vaughn, Mo*	.125	8	1	0	3	1	2	.200	.125

79

Mark Guthrie, Dodgers — LHP

Batter	Avg	AB	H	HR	BI	BB	SO	OBP	Slg
Velarde, R	.222	9	2	0	0	0	3	.222	.222
Ventura, R*	.200	15	3	0	2	2	1	.294	.200
Vizquel, Omar#	.353	17	6	0	1	0	2	.353	.529
Ward, Turner#	.250	4	1	0	0	1	0	.400	.500
Weiss, Walt#	.400	5	2	0	0	1	1	.500	.400
White, Devon#	.250	12	3	0	1	0	3	.250	.500
Whiten, Mark#	.667	3	2	1	1	2	1	.800	1.667
Williams, Ber#	.200	5	1	0	1	1	0	.333	.200

Juan Guzman, Blue Jays — RHP

Batter	Avg	AB	H	HR	BI	BB	SO	OBP	Slg
Aldrete, Mike*	.400	20	8	1	3	8	2	.571	.550
Alexander, M	.143	7	1	0	0	0	1	.143	.143
Alicea, Luis#	.167	6	1	0	0	1	0	.286	.167
Alomar Jr, S	.286	28	8	0	2	0	4	.286	.393
Amaral, Rich	.200	5	1	0	0	0	2	.200	.200
Anderson, Brd*	.043	23	1	0	0	3	6	.185	.043
Anderson, G*	.600	10	6	2	2	0	0	.600	1.300
Anthony, Eric*	.500	6	3	1	5	0	1	.500	1.000
Baerga, C#	.282	39	11	0	4	3	5	.333	.333
Baines, H*	.241	29	7	1	2	6	4	.371	.379
Becker, Rich*	.182	11	2	0	2	1	1	.250	.182
Belle, Albert	.324	37	12	3	8	3	5	.375	.676
Berroa, G	.353	17	6	1	2	0	3	.353	.588
Blowers, Mike	.125	8	1	0	0	2	4	.300	.125
Boggs, Wade*	.222	27	6	0	6	5	3	.344	.259
Bonilla, B#	.286	7	2	0	0	0	1	.286	.286
Boone, Bret	.500	8	4	1	4	0	0	.500	.875
Bordick, Mike	.394	33	13	0	7	2	10	.429	.455
Bournigal, R	.143	7	1	0	0	0	1	.143	.143
Bragg, Darren*	.500	4	2	0	1	3	0	.714	.500
Brosius, S	.182	22	4	0	1	0	5	.182	.182
Buford, Damon	.400	5	2	1	2	0	3	.400	1.000
Buhner, Jay	.138	29	4	1	6	4	11	.242	.276
Burks, Ellis	.400	15	6	0	1	0	6	.400	.533
Canseco, Jose	.233	30	7	1	8	3	7	.303	.400
Carreon, Mark	.400	5	2	1	1	1	3	.500	1.000
Cirillo, Jeff	.400	10	4	2	5	2	1	.500	1.000
Clark, Tony*	.000	5	0	0	0	0	3	.000	.000
Clark, Will*	.353	17	6	1	5	4	3	.455	.529
Cole, Alex*	.364	22	8	1	2	5	4	.481	.591
Coleman, V#	.400	5	2	0	0	0	1	.400	.600
Cora, Joey#	.250	24	6	0	1	2	0	.308	.333
Cordova, M	.250	8	2	1	1	0	1	.333	.625
Curtis, Chad	.087	23	2	1	1	0	6	.087	.217
Cuyler, Milt*	.357	14	5	0	0	2	2	.438	.429
Damon, Johnny*	.167	6	1	0	0	0	1	.167	.167
Davis, Chili*	.238	21	5	0	1	3	4	.320	.286
Deer, Rob	.125	8	1	0	0	3	4	.364	.125
Devereaux, M	.333	15	5	0	2	5	4	.500	.467
DiSarcina, G	.273	22	6	1	2	0	4	.304	.455
Durham, Ray#	.125	8	1	0	0	0	2	.125	.125
Easley, D	.467	15	7	2	7	3	3	.556	1.000
Edmonds, Jim*	.278	18	5	0	1	2	3	.350	.444
Eisenreich, J*	.167	6	1	0	1	0	2	.167	.167
Elster, Kevin	.143	7	1	0	0	1	1	.250	.143
Espinoza, A	.125	8	1	0	0	0	1	.125	.125
Fabregas, Jor*	.400	10	4	0	7	0	0	.400	.500
Fermin, Felix	.059	17	1	0	0	1	0	.059	.059
Fielder, C	.091	33	3	1	6	8	10	.256	.212
Flaherty, J	.100	10	1	0	0	0	0	.100	.100
Franco, Julio	.238	21	5	1	2	2	5	.304	.429
Frye, Jeff	.375	8	3	0	0	0	1	.375	.500
Fryman, T	.184	38	7	2	6	0	16	.175	.395
Gaetti, Gary	.125	8	1	0	0	0	3	.125	.125
Gagne, Greg	.176	17	3	1	4	1	8	.222	.412
Gallego, Mike	.000	9	0	0	0	5	3	.357	.000
Gates, Brent#	.118	17	2	0	0	4	6	.286	.118
Giambi, Jason*	.357	14	5	1	3	3	1	.471	.714
Gil, Benji	.333	6	2	0	0	0	2	.333	.333
Gomez, Chris	.000	13	0	0	0	2	6	.133	.000
Gomez, Leo	.263	19	5	0	3	4	3	.391	.316
Gonzales, R	.400	5	2	0	1	1	1	.500	.400
Gonzalez, J	.107	28	3	1	5	1	8	.161	.250
Goodwin, Tom*	.125	8	1	0	1	0	0	.125	.125
Grebeck, C	.000	5	0	0	0	1	0	.167	.000
Greenwell, M*	.409	22	9	0	5	2	0	.458	.545
Greer, Rusty*	.583	12	7	0	5	5	1	.706	.750
Griffey Jr, K*	.345	29	10	2	3	7	6	.472	.655
Guillen, O*	.273	22	6	1	5	2	2	.333	.455
Gwynn, Chris*	.222	9	2	0	0	3	0	.417	.222
Hale, Chip*	.111	9	1	0	0	3	0	.333	.111
Hall, Mel*	.167	12	2	0	1	0	0	.167	.250
Hamelin, Bob*	.091	11	1	0	0	1	3	.167	.182
Hamilton, D	.400	25	10	0	2	2	4	.444	.480
Hammonds, J	.333	6	2	0	1	0	0	.333	.500
Haselman, B	.250	8	2	0	0	0	1	.250	.375
Hayes, C	.222	9	2	0	0	0	1	.222	.222
Henderson, R	.167	18	3	0	2	0	4	.167	.222
Hiatt, Phil	.000	6	0	0	0	1	3	.143	.000
Higginson, B*	.200	10	2	0	0	0	2	.200	.300
Hill, G	.167	6	1	0	0	0	3	.167	.167
Hoiles, Chris	.154	13	2	0	2	2	7	.267	.154
Hollins, Dave#	.167	6	1	0	0	0	4	.167	.333
Howard, Dave*	.182	11	2	0	0	1	6	.250	.182
Howell, Jack*	.200	5	1	0	0	0	1	.200	.200
Hulse, David*	.348	23	8	0	2	1	3	.375	.348
Huson, Jeff*	.400	5	2	0	0	2	1	.571	.400
Jaha, John	.294	17	5	2	4	3	4	.400	.706
James, Dion*	.350	20	7	0	4	2	2	.409	.350
Jefferies, G#	.286	7	2	0	0	1	0	.375	.429
Jefferson, R*	.400	20	8	0	0	0	6	.400	.400
Johnson, L*	.483	29	14	0	6	0	1	.483	.621
Joyner, Wally*	.471	17	8	1	3	2	1	.526	.824
Karkovice, R	.231	26	6	0	2	2	8	.286	.346
Kelly, Pat	.143	14	2	1	1	2	8	.294	.357
Kelly, R	.462	13	6	0	1	2	2	.533	.462
Kirby, Wayne*	.333	12	4	1	2	0	4	.333	.583
Knoblauch, C	.295	44	13	1	5	7	8	.407	.432
Kreuter, Chad#	.182	11	2	0	1	0	4	.182	.182
Leius, Scott	.267	15	4	0	1	5	4	.429	.400
Levis, Jesse*	.250	4	1	0	0	1	0	.400	.500
Lewis, Mark	.143	7	1	0	0	0	2	.143	.286
Leyritz, Jim	.200	5	1	0	0	4	3	.600	.200
Listach, Pat#	.000	9	0	0	0	1	1	.100	.000
Livingstone, S	.091	11	1	0	0	0	1	.091	.091
Lockhart, K*	.429	7	3	0	0	0	1	.429	.429
Lofton, Kenny*	.226	31	7	0	1	4	6	.306	.258
Lovullo, T#	.000	6	0	0	0	1	1	.143	.000
Macfarlane, M	.280	25	7	0	2	2	5	.333	.360
Magadan, Dave*	.286	7	2	0	1	0	1	.286	.286
Martinez, Da*	.500	8	4	0	1	0	2	.500	.625
Martinez, E	.227	22	5	1	2	5	7	.370	.409
Martinez, T*	.167	12	2	0	1	7	4	.474	.167
Marzano, John	.000	5	0	0	0	0	3	.000	.000
Mayne, Brent*	.188	16	3	1	4	1	4	.235	.375
McCarty, Dave	.111	9	1	0	0	1	2	.200	.222
McGwire, Mark	.000	11	0	0	0	2	5	.214	.000
McLemore, M#	.269	26	7	0	5	1	2	.296	.385
McRae, Brian*	.138	29	4	0	1	1	7	.167	.172
Meares, Pat	.133	15	2	0	1	0	6	.133	.133
Mieske, Matt	.125	8	1	0	1	1	3	.222	.125
Mitchell, K	.167	6	1	0	0	1	0	.167	.167
Molitor, Paul	.400	15	6	1	1	0	5	.438	.733
Mouton, Lyle	.333	6	2	1	1	0	2	.333	.833
Munoz, Pedro	.273	22	6	2	2	2	6	.360	.545
Murray, Eddie*	.333	12	4	1	4	2	2	.429	.583
Myers, Greg*	.333	6	2	0	3	3	0	.556	.500
Naehring, Tim	.300	10	3	0	2	5	4	.417	.300
Newson, W*	.000	8	0	0	0	3	3	.273	.000
Nieves, M#	.600	5	3	0	0	0	1	.600	1.000
Nilsson, Dave*	.167	12	2	1	3	6	3	.333	.417
Nixon, Otis#	.500	8	4	0	0	1	1	.556	.500
O'Leary, Troy*	.158	19	3	0	0	1	6	.200	.158
O'Neill, Paul*	.267	15	4	1	4	3	2	.389	.600
Offerman, J#	.143	7	1	0	0	0	1	.143	.286
Orsulak, Joe*	.000	9	0	0	0	0	1	.000	.000
Palmeiro, R*	.273	33	9	0	0	6	4	.385	.273
Palmer, Dean	.250	28	7	1	5	5	13	.364	.429
Paquette, C	.100	10	1	0	1	0	3	.100	.200
Parent, Mark	.200	5	1	0	2	0	2	.200	.200
Peltier, Dan*	.750	4	3	0	1	1	0	.800	.750
Pena, Tony	.200	5	1	0	0	1	1	.167	.200
Perez, E	.000	3	0	0	0	2	1	.400	.000
Phillips, T#	.128	39	5	0	0	13	14	.346	.154
Plantier, P*	.333	15	5	0	0	1	4	.375	.333
Polonia, Luis*	.391	23	9	0	1	1	3	.417	.391
Raines, Tim#	.240	25	6	0	3	5	3	.367	.280
Ramirez, M	.111	9	1	0	0	2	1	.273	.111
Reboulet, J	.111	18	2	0	3	3	5	.238	.222
Reed, Jody	.462	13	6	1	3	2	1	.533	.769
Ripken, Cal	.207	29	6	1	5	2	1	.273	.345
Rodriguez, I	.424	33	14	0	3	1	5	.457	.485
Sabo, Chris	.143	7	1	0	0	0	2	.143	.143
Salmon, Tim	.286	21	6	2	8	2	7	.348	.667
Seitzer, K	.158	19	3	0	1	4	4	.304	.158
Sierra, Ruben#	.190	21	4	1	4	0	3	.190	.333
Slaught, Don	.143	7	1	0	0	0	1	.143	.143
Smith, Dwight*	.286	7	2	0	1	0	0	.286	.429
Snow, J.T.#	.455	11	5	0	4	3	0	.571	.455
Sojo, Luis	.200	15	3	1	1	1	2	.250	.467
Sorrento, P*	.300	30	9	2	7	8	6	.447	.533
Spiers, Bill*	.250	8	2	0	0	0	0	.250	.250
Stahoviak, S*	.273	11	3	0	0	1	4	.333	.273
Stankiewicz	.200	5	1	0	1	1	1	.333	.200
Stanley, Mike	.333	12	4	1	4	0	5	.308	.750
Steinbach, T	.278	36	10	2	8	0	10	.278	.500
Stevens, Lee*	.000	6	0	0	0	1	4	.143	.000
Strange, Doug*	.250	12	3	0	0	2	1	.357	.333
Surhoff, B.J.*	.273	22	6	1	4	2	4	.308	.455
Tartabull, D	.160	25	4	2	3	8	12	.364	.400
Tettleton, M#	.200	30	6	1	4	10	5	.400	.367

Juan Guzman, Blue Jays — RHP

Batter	Avg	AB	H	HR	BI	BB	SO	OBP	Slg
Thomas, Frank	.250	28	7	1	3	6	3	.400	.393
Thome, Jim*	.227	22	5	0	0	2	7	.292	.227
Tinsley, Lee#	.143	7	1	0	1	0	1	.143	.429
Trammell, A	.375	16	6	0	0	3	3	.474	.438
Tucker, M*	.200	5	1	0	0	1	1	.333	.200
Valentin, Jhn	.313	16	5	1	4	2	5	.389	.563
Valentin, Jse#	.214	14	3	1	2	1	6	.267	.500
Valle, Dave	.154	13	2	0	1	1	4	.214	.231
Vaughn, Greg	.261	23	6	1	2	4	6	.357	.478
Vaughn, Mo*	.318	22	7	2	4	5	4	.444	.591
Velarde, R	.158	19	3	0	1	1	5	.238	.211
Ventura, R*	.200	30	6	2	4	4	1	.294	.433
Vina, F*	.250	12	3	1	1	1	1	.308	.500
Vizquel, Omar#	.320	30	13	0	2	6	2	.528	.500
Walbeck, Matt#	.353	17	6	0	3	1	2	.389	.353
Whiten, Mark#	.125	8	1	0	2	0	3	.125	.125
Williams, Ber#	.350	20	7	0	1	3	7	.435	.450
Wilson, Dan	.182	11	2	0	1	1	5	.250	.182
Young, Ernie	.182	11	2	0	1	1	3	.231	.273

John Habyan, Expos — RHP

Batter	Avg	AB	H	HR	BI	BB	SO	OBP	Slg
Abbott, Kurt	.600	5	3	1	6	0	0	.600	1.400
Alicea, Luis#	.400	5	2	0	0	0	0	.400	.600
Alomar, R#	.833	6	5	0	4	1	0	.857	1.667
Alomar Jr, S	.000	4	0	0	0	1	1	.200	.000
Alou, Moises	.200	5	1	1	2	0	1	.200	.800
Amaral, Rich	.000	4	0	0	0	1	1	.200	.000
Anderson, Brd*	.400	5	2	0	1	0	0	.400	1.000
Baerga, C#	.286	7	2	0	1	0	0	.286	.286
Bagwell, Jeff	.000	4	0	0	0	1	2	.200	.000
Baines, H*	.167	6	1	0	0	0	1	.167	.167
Bell, Derek	.200	5	1	0	2	0	1	.200	.200
Belle, Albert	.429	7	3	1	2	1	1	.500	.857
Bichette, D	.000	7	0	0	0	0	3	.000	.000
Blowers, Mike	.600	5	3	0	0	0	1	.600	.800
Boggs, Wade*	.357	14	5	0	3	2	1	.412	.429
Boone, Bret	.429	7	3	0	1	1	1	.444	.714
Borders, Pat	.400	5	2	0	3	0	1	.400	.800
Bordick, Mike	.300	10	3	0	0	0	1	.300	.300
Buhner, Jay	.000	9	0	0	0	0	2	.000	.000
Burks, Ellis	.417	12	5	0	1	1	1	.462	.417
Canseco, Jose	.222	18	4	1	6	1	5	.286	.500
Carter, Joe	.333	12	4	2	4	0	4	.333	1.000
Clayton, R	.400	5	2	0	1	1	1	.500	.800
Cora, Joey#	.500	2	1	0	0	2	0	.600	.500
Curtis, Chad	.500	4	2	0	1	2	0	.667	.500
Cuyler, Milt#	.333	6	2	0	0	0	1	.333	.333
Deer, Rob	.133	15	2	0	1	1	5	.188	.133
Devereaux, M	.111	9	1	0	1	1	5	.200	.222
Fermin, Felix	.400	5	2	0	0	0	0	.400	.400
Fielder, C	.273	11	3	1	1	1	2	.385	.545
Franco, Julio	.300	10	3	0	1	2	2	.417	.300
Fryman, T	.182	11	2	0	2	3	4	.357	.273
Gaetti, Gary	.000	8	0	0	0	0	0	.000	.000
Gagne, Greg	.429	7	3	0	0	0	3	.429	.571
Gallego, Mike	.250	4	1	0	0	2	0	.500	.500
Gomez, Leo	.000	8	0	0	0	0	2	.000	.000
Gonzalez, J	.200	5	1	0	0	0	0	.200	.200
Grace, Mark*	.800	5	4	0	2	0	0	.800	1.200
Grebeck, C	.250	8	2	0	0	0	2	.250	.250
Greenwell, M*	.300	10	3	0	1	1	1	.364	.300
Griffey Jr, K*	.200	5	1	0	0	1	1	.333	.200
Grissom, M	.600	5	3	0	1	0	0	.600	1.000
Guillen, O*	.125	8	1	0	2	0	0	.125	.125
Hamilton, D*	.000	5	0	0	0	1	0	.167	.000
Henderson, R	.429	7	3	1	3	2	1	.556	1.143
Hill, G	.286	7	2	0	1	0	0	.286	.571
Hoiles, Chris	.143	7	1	0	2	1	2	.250	.286
Howard, T*	.500	6	3	0	1	0	0	.500	.500
Howell, Jack*	.167	6	1	1	1	0	3	.167	.667
Incaviglia, P	.273	11	3	0	2	0	3	.250	.455
Joyner, Wally*	.364	11	4	1	2	1	2	.462	.818
Kelly, R	.333	6	2	0	1	0	1	.333	.333
Kent, Jeff	.000	6	0	0	0	0	2	.000	.000
King, Jeff	.200	5	1	0	1	1	2	.333	.400
Kingery, Mike*	.222	9	2	0	0	0	2	.222	.333
Knoblauch, C	.000	5	0	0	1	1	1	.167	.000
Kreuter, Chad#	.600	5	3	0	0	1	0	.600	.600
Larkin, Barry	.333	6	2	0	1	0	0	.333	.333
Lewis, Darren	.200	5	1	0	0	1	0	.200	.200
Lewis, Mark	.111	9	1	0	0	1	4	.200	.111
Liriano, N#	.400	5	2	0	1	0	1	.400	.400
Listach, Pat#	.000	5	0	0	0	0	1	.000	.000
Lofton, Kenny*	.600	5	3	0	1	0	0	.600	.800
Marzano, John	.400	5	2	0	1	0	1	.500	.400
McGriff, Fred*	.250	8	2	0	0	0	3	.333	.375
McGwire, Mark	.091	11	1	1	1	2	5	.286	.364
McLemore, M	.125	8	1	0	0	1	2	.222	.125
McRae, Brian*	.143	7	1	0	0	0	3	.143	.143
Molitor, Paul	.083	12	1	0	0	1	4	.154	.083
Orsulak, Joe*	.200	5	1	0	0	1	1	.333	.200
Palmeiro, R*	.200	5	1	0	2	0	0	.200	.200
Palmer, Dean	.300	10	3	0	0	0	4	.364	.300
Phillips, T#	.083	12	1	0	0	1	1	.154	.083
Polonia, Luis*	.500	8	4	0	3	0	0	.500	.875
Raines, Tim#	.222	9	2	0	0	0	2	.222	.333
Reed, Jody	.500	6	3	0	0	1	0	.571	.667
Ripken, Billy	.000	5	0	0	0	0	0	.000	.000
Ripken, Cal	.300	10	3	0	1	0	2	.300	.300
Rodriguez, I	.400	10	4	0	2	0	2	.400	.400
Sanchez, Rey	.667	3	2	0	0	0	2	.800	.667
Schofield, D	.125	8	1	0	0	1	3	.222	.250
Segui, David#	.000	5	0	0	0	2	1	.286	.000
Seitzer, K	.571	7	4	0	1	0	0	.571	.857
Sierra, Ruben#	.143	14	2	0	3	0	3	.125	.143
Sosa, Sammy	.200	5	1	0	1	1	2	.333	.200
Stanley, Mike	.400	5	2	0	0	1	0	.400	.600
Steinbach, T	.154	13	2	0	1	0	3	.214	.154
Surhoff, B.J.*	.125	8	1	1	0	0	2	.125	.250
Sveum, Dale#	.111	9	1	1	1	0	2	.111	.444
Tartabull, D	.333	6	2	1	2	0	2	.333	.833
Tettleton, M#	.333	9	3	1	3	1	3	.400	.667
Thomas, Frank	.500	10	5	0	1	1	2	.583	.500
Trammell, A	.316	19	6	0	1	1	1	.350	.421
Valle, Dave	.300	10	3	0	2	0	0	.300	.300
Vaughn, Greg	.111	9	1	1	1	0	3	.111	.444
Ventura, R*	.167	6	1	1	1	0	0	.167	.667
Vizquel, Omar#	.333	12	4	0	1	0	1	.333	.333
Weiss, Walt#	.600	5	3	0	2	0	0	.600	.800
White, Devon#	.357	14	5	0	1	0	1	.357	.429

Joey Hamilton, Padres — RHP

Batter	Avg	AB	H	HR	BI	BB	SO	OBP	Slg
Abbott, Kurt	.111	9	1	0	0	1	4	.200	.333
Alfonzo, E	.444	9	4	0	0	0	1	.444	.556
Alicea, Luis#	.000	5	0	0	0	1	2	.167	.000
Alou, Moises	.357	14	5	1	1	0	1	.357	.571
Andrews, S	.200	5	1	0	1	1	0	.333	.200
Arias, Alex	.375	8	3	0	1	2	1	.500	.375
Bagwell, Jeff	.100	10	1	0	0	3	3	.308	.100
Barberie, B#	.000	6	0	0	0	1	0	.143	.000
Bell, David	.000	5	0	0	0	0	0	.000	.000
Bell, Derek	.091	11	1	0	0	1	2	.167	.091
Bell, Jay	.400	10	4	0	0	0	0	.400	.400
Belliard, R	.000	7	0	0	0	0	1	.000	.000
Benjamin, M	.125	8	1	0	0	3	2	.364	.125
Berry, Sean	.133	15	2	0	2	3	2	.263	.133
Bichette, D	.462	13	6	1	2	1	3	.500	.769
Biggio, Craig	.250	12	3	0	1	2	1	.438	.333
Blauser, Jeff	.222	9	2	0	1	2	3	.364	.222
Blowers, Mike	.750	4	3	0	1	1	0	.800	.750
Bonds, Barry*	.333	15	5	2	4	1	2	.375	.867
Bonilla, B#	.364	11	4	1	2	1	2	.417	.636
Boone, Bret	.000	11	0	0	0	1	2	.154	.000
Branson, Jeff*	.111	9	1	0	0	1	2	.200	.333
Brogna, Rico*	.250	16	4	1	3	0	4	.235	.500
Brumfield, J	.167	6	1	0	2	1	0	.286	.333
Burks, Ellis	.545	11	6	1	4	1	1	.583	1.091
Butler, Brett*	.263	19	5	0	2	2	3	.318	.263
Cangelosi, J#	.286	7	2	0	0	1	1	.375	.286
Carr, Chuck	.167	6	1	0	0	0	1	.167	.167
Carreon, Mark	.333	12	4	0	4	0	0	.333	.333
Castilla, V	.231	13	3	0	1	0	4	.231	.385
Clark, Dave*	.300	10	3	0	0	0	4	.300	.300
Clayton, R	.273	11	3	0	0	2	0	.385	.273
Colbrunn, G	.250	8	2	0	2	0	1	.333	.375
Conine, Jeff	.400	15	6	1	4	1	3	.438	.600
Cordero, Wil	.294	17	5	1	5	1	4	.368	.471
DeShields, D*	.125	24	3	0	1	2	6	.192	.167
Duncan, M	.571	7	4	0	0	0	1	.571	.571
Dunston, S	.267	15	4	1	4	1	4	.313	.467
Eisenreich, J	.222	9	2	0	1	2	1	.333	.222
Espinoza, A	.167	6	1	0	0	0	1	.167	.167
Eusebio, Tony	.167	6	1	0	0	0	1	.167	.500
Everett, Carl#	.200	10	2	0	0	0	2	.200	.200
Fletcher, D*	.071	14	1	0	0	1	0	.133	.071
Fonville, C#	.083	12	1	0	1	1	3	.154	.083
Frazier, Lou#	.286	7	2	0	0	0	0	.286	.286
Gagne, Greg	.571	7	4	0	2	2	0	.667	.714
Galarraga, A	.353	17	6	0	1	1	3	.389	.412
Garcia, C	.385	13	5	0	3	1	2	.429	.538
Gilkey, B	.158	19	3	0	1	0	6	.150	.158
Girardi, Joe	.375	8	3	1	4	0	2	.444	.750
Gomez, Leo	.167	6	1	0	0	1	2	.286	.167
Gonzalez, L*	.176	17	3	0	4	2	3	.263	.235
Grace, Mark*	.429	21	9	0	3	0	0	.429	.571
Greene, W*	.182	11	2	0	1	0	2	.182	.273
Grissom, M	.400	20	8	1	3	1	0	.455	.600
Grudzielanek	.000	7	0	0	0	0	3	.125	.000
Haney, Todd	.200	5	1	0	0	0	2	.200	.200
Hansen, Dave*	.200	5	1	0	0	0	3	.200	.200

Joey Hamilton, Padres — RHP

Batter	Avg	AB	H	HR	BI	BB	SO	OBP	Slg
Harris, Lenny*	.286	7	2	0	0	0	0	.286	.286
Hayes, C	.375	8	3	0	0	2	1	.500	.375
Hernandez, Jo	.111	9	1	1	2	2	3	.273	.444
Hill, G	.100	10	1	0	1	0	0	.100	.100
Hollandsworth*	.273	11	3	0	1	0	2	.273	.273
Howard, T*	.250	12	3	0	0	1	1	.357	.250
Hundley, Todd#	.154	13	2	1	2	1	3	.267	.462
Jefferies, G#	.333	9	3	1	4	0	1	.300	.778
Johnson, Char	.333	6	2	0	1	0	1	.333	.667
Johnson, L*	.417	12	5	0	1	0	1	.417	.417
Johnson, Mark*	.400	5	2	1	2	1	0	.500	1.200
Jones, C#	.357	14	5	1	2	2	1	.438	.643
Jordan, Brian	.231	13	3	1	2	0	2	.231	.462
Jordan, Kevin	.200	5	1	0	0	1	0	.200	.400
Justice, Dave*	.417	12	5	0	2	0	2	.417	.417
Karros, Eric	.136	22	3	0	0	3	6	.240	.227
Kelly, R	.500	6	3	0	0	0	0	.500	.667
Kent, Jeff	.250	16	4	1	4	1	4	.294	.438
King, Jeff	.231	13	3	1	2	2	2	.333	.462
Kingery, Mike*	.222	9	2	0	2	1	3	.300	.444
Klesko, Ryan*	.462	13	6	2	3	2	2	.533	.923
Lankford, Ray*	.188	16	3	1	1	1	6	.235	.375
Lansing, Mike	.063	16	1	0	0	0	3	.063	.063
Larkin, Barry	.500	14	7	1	2	1	0	.500	.714
Lemke, Mark*	.222	9	2	0	0	1	1	.300	.222
Lewis, Darren	.364	11	4	0	0	1	0	.417	.364
Lieberthal, M	.600	5	3	0	0	0	0	.667	1.000
Liriano, N#	.000	6	0	0	0	1	0	.000	.000
Lopez, Javy	.250	12	3	0	1	0	2	.250	.250
Mabry, John*	.375	8	3	0	1	2	0	.500	.625
Magadan, Dave*	.250	8	2	0	1	1	2	.333	.250
Magee, W	.000	5	0	0	0	4	0	.000	.000
Manwaring, K	.333	9	3	0	1	2	0	.500	.444
Martin, Al*	.300	10	3	0	1	2	1	.385	.300
May, Derrick*	.067	15	1	0	1	0	2	.125	.067
Mayne, Brent*	.250	4	1	0	2	1	1	.500	.250
McGee, Willie#	.000	6	0	0	0	1	1	.143	.000
McGriff, Fred*	.333	15	5	1	6	0	2	.333	.667
McRae, Brian*	.294	17	5	0	1	5	3	.500	.353
Merced, O*	.286	14	4	2	9	1	2	.333	.786
Miller, Orl	.143	7	1	0	0	0	3	.143	.143
Mitchell, K	.333	6	2	0	1	1	1	.429	.333
Mondesi, Raul	.238	21	5	0	1	2	3	.304	.333
Morandini, M*	.200	20	4	0	0	2	2	.273	.350
Morris, Hal*	.313	16	5	0	4	1	1	.389	.375
Offerman, J#	.250	4	1	0	2	0	1	.500	.250
Oliver, Joe	.000	5	0	0	0	0	1	.000	.000
Ordonez, Rey	.375	8	3	0	0	0	0	.375	.375
Orsulak, Joe*	.278	18	5	0	0	2	0	.278	.278
Otero, Ricky*	.750	8	6	0	1	0	1	.778	.875
Pagnozzi, Tom	.167	6	1	0	0	1	1	.286	.333
Parent, Mark	.400	5	2	1	2	0	0	.400	1.000
Pendleton, T#	.167	6	1	0	1	0	3	.286	.167
Petagine, Rob*	.400	5	2	0	2	0	1	.400	.400
Phillips, J*	.200	5	1	0	0	0	1	.200	.200
Piazza, Mike	.400	25	10	2	4	3	3	.464	.680
Reed, Jeff*	.200	5	1	0	0	2	2	.429	.200
Renteria, E	.500	6	3	0	1	1	1	.571	.500
Rodriguez, H*	.235	17	4	1	2	0	3	.235	.471
Rolen, Scott	.167	6	1	0	1	1	1	.167	.167
Sanchez, Rey	.167	12	2	0	0	0	1	.231	.167
Sandberg, R	.100	10	1	1	1	1	3	.182	.400
Sanders, B	.400	10	4	0	0	0	2	.400	.500
Santiago, B	.400	15	6	1	3	1	5	.438	.667
Schall, Gene	.400	5	2	0	1	0	0	.400	.800
Segui, David#	.357	14	5	0	1	0	1	.357	.357
Servais, S	.125	8	1	0	0	2	2	.300	.125
Sheffield, G	.375	8	3	1	2	2	2	.500	.875
Smith, Ozzie*	.182	11	2	0	1	1	1	.250	.273
Sosa, Sammy	.435	23	10	2	7	2	5	.480	.783
Stocker, K#	.438	16	7	0	1	0	4	.412	.563
Tarasco, Tony*	.077	13	1	0	1	1	0	.200	.077
Thompson, Mil*	.125	8	1	0	0	2	2	.300	.125
Thompson, Rob	.250	8	2	0	0	3	3	.333	.250
Thompson, Ry	.222	9	2	0	2	0	2	.417	.222
Veras, Q#	.429	7	3	0	1	0	0	.500	.571
Vizcaino, J#	.211	19	4	0	2	0	3	.286	.211
Walker, Larry*	.222	9	2	1	1	1	0	.300	.556
Wallach, Tim	.214	14	3	1	3	1	3	.313	.500
Webster, L	.222	9	2	0	1	1	2	.300	.222
Weiss, Walt#	.231	13	3	0	0	3	4	.375	.231
White, Devon#	.286	7	2	1	1	0	1	.286	.714
White, R	.364	11	4	0	0	2	0	.364	.455
Whiten, Mark*	.600	5	3	1	4	1	0	.667	1.200
Wilkins, Rick*	.353	17	6	1	1	0	2	.353	.647
Williams, Ma	.125	8	1	0	0	0	3	.222	.125
Young, Eric	.105	19	2	0	0	1	0	.150	.105
Zeile, Todd	.125	16	2	0	0	1	4	.176	.125

Chris Hammond, Marlins — LHP

Batter	Avg	AB	H	HR	BI	BB	SO	OBP	Slg
Alfonzo, E	.333	6	2	0	0	0	0	.333	.333
Alicea, Luis#	.143	7	1	0	1	1	1	.250	.143
Alou, Moises	.133	15	2	0	0	1	4	.188	.133
Amaro, Ruben*	.000	5	0	0	0	0	0	.000	.000
Anthony, Eric*	.231	13	3	0	0	1	4	.286	.385
Ashley, Billy	.111	9	1	1	1	0	2	.111	.444
Aude, Rich	.571	7	4	0	1	0	1	.571	.857
Ausmus, Brad	.300	10	3	0	1	0	3	.273	.500
Bagwell, Jeff	.276	29	8	2	7	10	3	.475	.517
Bates, Jason#	.250	4	1	0	0	1	1	.400	.250
Batiste, Kim	.000	6	0	0	0	2	0	.000	.000
Bell, Derek	.308	13	4	1	4	1	0	.357	.615
Bell, Jay	.213	47	10	0	5	4	2	.275	.255
Belliard, R	.444	9	4	0	0	0	1	.444	.444
Benjamin, M	.167	6	1	1	2	1	2	.286	.667
Berry, Sean	.111	9	1	0	0	0	2	.111	.111
Bichette, D	.176	17	3	0	0	2	2	.263	.235
Biggio, Craig	.290	31	9	0	1	4	2	.371	.323
Blauser, Jeff	.273	11	3	0	0	0	1	.273	.273
Bogar, Tim	.286	7	2	0	0	0	1	.286	.429
Bonds, Barry*	.406	32	13	3	10	3	6	.457	.750
Bonilla, B#	.154	26	4	0	0	4	6	.267	.192
Boone, Bret	.231	13	3	0	1	1	0	.267	.385
Branson, Jeff*	.600	5	3	0	1	0	0	.600	.800
Brogna, Rico*	.000	5	0	0	0	1	3	.167	.000
Brumfield, J	.222	9	2	0	0	1	2	.300	.333
Burks, Ellis	.364	11	4	3	3	0	1	.417	1.182
Butler, Brett*	.208	24	5	0	0	4	4	.321	.208
Caminiti, Ken#	.176	34	6	0	3	2	4	.222	.206
Candaele, C#	.417	12	5	0	1	0	0	.462	.417
Carreon, Mark	.462	13	6	2	5	0	2	.462	1.077
Castilla, V	.222	9	2	0	0	1	1	.222	.333
Cedeno, A	.176	17	3	0	1	0	2	.176	.176
Cianfrocco, A	.250	4	1	0	1	0	1	.400	.500
Clark, Phil	.100	10	1	0	0	0	1	.100	.100
Clark, Will*	.400	15	6	0	2	1	2	.444	.600
Clayton, R	.267	15	4	0	1	1	3	.313	.467
Coleman, V#	.250	8	2	0	3	1	1	.333	.250
Cordero, Wil	.083	12	1	0	2	1	0	.143	.083
Dascenzo, D*	.267	15	4	2	5	1	3	.313	.667
Davis, Eric	.400	5	2	0	1	0	1	.400	.400
Dawson, Andre	.400	5	2	1	3	1	0	.500	1.000
DeShields, D*	.190	21	4	0	0	6	2	.370	.238
Dorsett, B	.500	4	2	0	1	2	0	.667	.750
Duncan, M	.368	19	7	0	3	2	2	.429	.526
Dunston, S	.313	16	5	0	2	1	1	.353	.375
Dykstra, L*	.000	11	0	0	0	4	2	.267	.000
Elster, Kevin	.400	5	2	0	0	1	0	.500	.400
Encarnacion	.333	6	2	1	2	0	0	.333	1.000
Eusebio, Tony	.500	6	3	1	4	0	0	.571	1.167
Everett, Carl#	.167	6	1	0	0	1	0	.286	.167
Faneyte, R	.200	5	1	0	0	1	3	.333	.200
Finley, Steve*	.263	38	10	0	3	2	5	.326	.368
Fletcher, D*	.333	3	1	0	0	2	0	.600	.333
Gagne, Greg	.200	5	1	0	0	0	0	.200	.200
Galarraga, A	.286	21	6	2	6	2	4	.348	.714
Gant, Ron	.154	13	2	1	1	2	2	.267	.385
Garcia, C	.185	27	5	1	2	0	5	.185	.333
Gilkey, M	.560	25	14	0	5	5	1	.633	.640
Girardi, Joe	.286	7	2	0	1	3	0	.500	.286
Gonzalez, L*	.314	35	11	4	9	2	3	.342	.743
Grace, Mark*	.148	27	4	0	2	1	2	.226	.148
Greene, W*	.000	5	0	0	0	1	2	.167	.000
Grissom, M	.391	23	9	0	2	2	1	.440	.565
Grudzielanek	.286	7	2	0	0	0	1	.286	.286
Gutierrez, R	.182	11	2	0	0	0	2	.182	.364
Gwynn, Tony*	.409	22	9	0	6	5	0	.519	.545
Hayes, C	.400	20	8	1	3	2	2	.455	.600
Henderson, R	.250	4	1	0	0	3	1	.571	.250
Hernandez, Ca	.200	5	1	0	0	0	2	.200	.200
Hernandez, Jo	.200	5	1	0	0	0	0	.200	.400
Hill, G	.231	13	3	0	2	0	4	.231	.385
Hollins, Dave#	.167	12	2	1	2	1	1	.286	.417
Hudler, Rex	.286	7	2	0	0	0	3	.286	.429
Hundley, Todd#	.250	8	2	0	2	3	3	.400	.375
Hunter, Brian	.182	11	2	1	3	0	3	.182	.455
Hunter, Bri L	.200	5	1	0	0	2	2	.200	.200
Incaviglia, P	.348	23	8	2	4	0	3	.348	.696
Javier, Stan#	.400	5	2	0	0	0	0	.400	.400
Jefferies, G#	.409	22	9	0	4	3	2	.480	.455
Jones, C#	.250	8	2	0	3	1	1	.250	.375
Jones, Chris	.417	12	5	0	1	0	2	.417	.500
Jordan, Brian	.250	8	2	0	0	1	0	.333	.250
Jordan, Ricky	.091	11	1	0	0	0	2	.091	.182
Justice, Dave*	.231	13	3	1	1	0	1	.214	.231
Karros, Eric	.222	27	6	2	6	4	4	.323	.444
Kelly, R	.188	16	3	1	2	0	3	.188	.438
Kent, Jeff	.067	15	1	0	1	0	3	.067	.133
King, Jeff	.125	24	3	0	2	3	4	.222	.208
Lankford, Ray*	.217	23	5	1	3	6	7	.400	.391
Lansing, Mike	.333	15	5	0	4	1	2	.353	.467

Chris Hammond, Marlins — LHP

Batter	Avg	AB	H	HR	BI	BB	SO	OBP	Slg
Larkin, Barry	.316	19	6	3	6	4	1	.435	.789
Lemke, Mark#	.500	10	5	0	1	1	0	.545	.600
Lewis, Darren	.000	7	0	0	0	0	2	.000	.000
Lewis, Mark	.400	5	2	0	0	0	1	.400	.400
Lieberthal, M	.000	4	0	0	0	1	0	.200	.000
Lopez, Javy	.625	8	5	2	3	0	1	.625	1.375
Magadan, Dave*	.286	7	2	0	1	3	0	.500	.429
Manwaring, K	.111	18	2	0	1	1	3	.158	.167
Martin, Al*	.167	12	2	0	1	0	3	.167	.250
May, Derrick*	.400	5	2	0	1	0	0	.400	.400
McGee, Willie*	.333	12	4	0	1	0	1	.333	.417
McGriff, Fred*	.091	22	2	0	1	3	4	.200	.136
McRae, Brian#	.625	8	5	0	2	0	0	.625	.875
Merced, O*	.231	13	3	0	0	1	3	.286	.231
Mitchell, K	.000	10	5	1	3	1	0	.545	.900
Mondesi, Raul	.158	19	3	1	2	1	5	.200	.368
Morandini, M*	.286	14	4	0	1	2	0	.375	.429
Morris, Hal*	.286	14	4	0	1	2	3	.333	.500
Mouton, James	.364	11	4	0	0	1	3	.417	.455
Murray, Eddie*	.375	16	6	0	4	2	1	.444	1.000
Nixon, Otis#	.000	7	0	0	0	1	1	.125	.000
O'Brien, C	.100	10	1	0	1	1	1	.182	.100
Ochoa, Alex	.500	4	2	1	2	2	0	.667	1.250
Offerman, J#	.292	24	7	0	2	2	6	.346	.292
Oliver, Joe	.167	6	1	1	2	0	2	.167	.667
Pagnozzi, Tom	.533	15	8	0	4	3	1	.611	.600
Parent, Mark	.000	5	0	0	1	1	0	.167	.000
Pena, G#	.286	7	2	0	3	2	1	.400	.286
Pendleton, T#	.100	10	1	0	0	0	0	.100	.100
Piazza, Mike	.154	13	2	0	1	2	1	.250	.154
Plantier, P*	.333	6	2	1	1	0	2	.333	.833
Reed, Jody	.500	12	6	0	2	2	0	.600	.667
Roberts, Bip#	.364	11	4	0	1	2	1	.462	.455
Rodriguez, H*	.000	4	0	0	0	0	1	.200	.000
Sabo, Chris	.600	5	3	1	4	1	0	.667	1.200
Samuel, Juan	.500	8	4	0	0	0	2	.500	.625
Sanchez, Rey	.357	14	5	0	1	0	0	.400	.429
Sandberg, R	.300	10	3	0	2	1	1	.417	.400
Sanders, R	.438	16	7	1	6	2	1	.500	1.063
Santiago, B	.250	12	3	0	1	0	0	.250	.333
Schofield, D	.143	7	1	0	0	0	2	.143	.143
Segui, David#	.500	10	5	0	0	1	2	.545	.600
Servais, S	.429	21	9	1	4	3	7	.500	.667
Sheaffer, D	.300	10	3	1	1	0	1	.300	.600
Sheffield, G	.750	4	3	1	5	3	0	.857	1.750
Shipley, C	.273	11	3	1	2	2	1	.357	.545
Slaught, Don	.276	29	8	0	2	3	2	.344	.345
Smith, Ozzie*	.421	19	8	0	3	0	3	.500	.474
Sosa, Sammy	.280	25	7	1	3	0	5	.280	.440
Stocker, K#	.000	5	0	0	0	1	1	.000	.000
Strawberry, D*	.500	8	4	0	2	1	1	.556	.500
Tarasco, Tony*	.167	6	1	0	0	0	1	.167	.167
Taubensee, E*	.600	5	3	1	2	0	2	.600	1.200
Thompson, Rob	.545	22	12	0	2	3	0	.600	.636
Thompson, Ry	.286	7	2	0	0	0	2	.286	.429
Timmons, O	.667	6	4	0	5	0	1	.667	1.167
Vizcaino, J#	.467	15	7	0	0	1	2	.500	.467
Walker, Larry*	.600	15	9	2	3	1	2	.647	1.000
Wallach, Tim	.136	22	3	0	0	1	4	.174	.136
Walton, J	.300	10	3	1	1	0	2	.300	.600
Wehner, John	.417	12	5	0	1	0	2	.417	.667
Weiss, Walt#	.571	7	4	0	0	2	1	.667	.714
White, R	.273	11	3	0	2	0	2	.273	.273
Whiten, Mark#	.077	13	1	0	2	0	6	.077	.077
Williams, Ma	.412	17	7	2	5	2	1	.474	.765
Young, Eric	.333	9	3	1	1	2	1	.455	.778
Young, Kevin	.286	14	4	2	4	1	2	.375	.714
Zeile, Todd	.429	28	12	0	9	2	4	.452	.571

Mike Hampton, Astros — LHP

Batter	Avg	AB	H	HR	BI	BB	SO	OBP	Slg
Colbrunn, G	.200	5	1	0	0	1	0	.333	.200
Coleman, V#	.143	7	1	0	0	0	1	.143	.143
Conine, Jeff	.286	7	2	0	0	0	1	.286	.286
Daulton, D*	.200	5	1	0	0	0	1	.200	.200
Davis, Eric	.625	8	5	1	3	2	2	.727	1.000
Deer, Rob	.500	2	1	0	1	3	0	.800	1.000
DeShields, D*	.300	10	3	0	0	0	2	.300	.500
Duncan, M	.400	5	2	0	0	0	0	.400	.400
Dunston, S	.176	17	3	0	0	0	4	.176	.294
Dye, Jermaine	.500	8	4	0	0	0	1	.500	.500
Dykstra, L*	.571	7	4	0	0	1	1	.625	.571
Everett, Carl#	.167	6	1	0	0	0	1	.167	.167
Finley, Steve*	.250	12	3	0	1	0	1	.250	.250
Flaherty, J	.600	5	3	0	1	1	0	.667	.600
Galarraga, A	.308	13	4	1	3	1	3	.333	.615
Gant, Ron	.143	7	1	1	2	0	1	.143	.571
Gilkey, B	.154	13	2	0	1	0	4	.143	.154
Girardi, Joe	.111	9	1	0	0	0	6	.111	.111
Gomez, Chris	.000	6	0	0	0	0	3	.000	.000
Grace, Mark*	.278	18	5	1	3	0	1	.278	.500
Grissom, M	.300	20	6	2	4	0	0	.300	.450
Gwynn, Tony*	.300	10	3	0	0	3	0	.462	.300
Hayes, C	.529	17	9	0	3	0	1	.529	.647
Henderson, R	.111	9	1	0	1	1	1	.200	.222
Hernandez, Jo	.300	10	3	0	1	0	2	.300	.500
Hill, G	.111	9	1	0	0	1	4	.200	.111
Incaviglia, P	.333	6	2	0	0	0	3	.333	.500
Jefferies, G#	.368	19	7	1	3	1	0	.400	.632
Johnson, Char	.000	6	0	0	0	1	1	.200	.000
Johnson, L*	1.000	5	5	0	4	0	0	1.000	2.000
Jones, C#	.333	18	6	0	1	1	0	.368	.333
Jordan, Brian	.412	17	7	1	2	1	0	.444	.588
Jordan, Kevin	.286	7	2	0	0	0	0	.286	.286
Justice, Dave*	.167	6	1	1	1	4	1	.500	.667
Karros, Eric	.200	5	1	0	0	1	0	.333	.200
Kendall, J	.333	6	2	0	1	1	0	.429	.333
Kent, Jeff	.200	10	2	0	0	0	3	.200	.200
King, Jeff	.333	9	3	0	2	2	0	.417	.444
Kingery, Mike*	.625	8	5	0	0	2	0	.700	.625
Klesko, Ryan*	.071	14	1	0	0	0	6	.071	.071
Lankford, Ray*	.125	16	2	0	0	1	5	.263	.125
Larkin, Barry	.429	14	6	0	3	1	1	.467	.643
Lemke, Mark#	.067	15	1	0	0	4	2	.263	.067
Lopez, Javy	.429	14	6	0	1	0	5	.429	.500
Manwaring, K	.375	8	3	1	1	1	1	.444	.875
Martin, Al*	.750	4	3	0	0	1	1	.800	1.500
McCarty, Dave	.000	5	0	0	1	1	2	.167	.000
McGriff, Fred*	.353	17	6	2	6	0	4	.389	.765
McRae, Brian#	.333	15	5	0	0	0	2	.333	.467
Merced, O*	.429	7	3	1	5	0	0	.429	1.000
Mondesi, Raul	.000	5	0	0	0	1	2	.167	.000
Morandini, M*	.000	9	0	0	0	1	1	.100	.000
Morris, Hal*	.231	13	3	0	2	2	5	.333	.308
Offerman, J#	.200	5	1	0	1	0	0	.200	.200
Oliver, Joe	.200	10	2	1	3	0	1	.182	.500
Otero, Ricky*	.250	4	1	0	0	2	0	.500	.250
Owens, Eric	.200	10	2	0	0	0	1	.200	.200
Pendleton, T#	.375	8	3	0	0	0	1	.375	.375
Piazza, Mike	.333	6	2	0	0	0	1	.333	.333
Reed, Jody	.375	8	3	0	1	2	0	.500	.375
Sabo, Chris	.250	4	1	0	0	4	0	.625	.250
Sanchez, Rey	.143	7	1	0	0	0	3	.143	.143
Sanders, D	.000	5	0	0	0	0	1	.100	.000
Santiago, B	.400	10	4	0	0	2	2	.500	.400
Scarsone, S	.250	12	3	0	0	2	3	.357	.333
Servais, S	.250	8	2	1	3	1	0	.333	.625
Sheaffer, D	.083	12	1	0	0	0	3	.083	.083
Sheffield, G	.250	8	2	1	2	0	0	.250	.750
Smith, Ozzie*	.000	7	0	0	0	0	2	.000	.000
Sosa, Sammy	.000	12	0	0	0	1	5	.077	.000
Stinnett, K	1.000	3	3	0	3	3	0	1.000	1.000
Stocker, K#	.273	11	3	0	0	1	0	.273	.455
Thompson, Ry	.200	5	1	0	0	0	0	.200	.200
Timmons, O	.364	11	4	1	3	1	2	.417	.727
Veras, Q#	.167	6	1	0	0	0	1	.286	.167
Vizcaino, J#	.333	9	3	0	0	0	0	.333	.333
Walker, Larry*	.154	13	2	0	2	0	3	.154	.308
Webster, L	.167	6	1	0	1	1	2	.286	.167
Wehner, John	.222	9	2	0	2	1	3	.273	.444
Weiss, Walt#	.222	9	2	0	0	3	2	.417	.222
Whiten, Mark#	.143	7	1	0	0	1	3	.250	.143
Williams, Ma	.273	11	3	0	3	1	1	.333	.455
Young, Eric	.538	13	7	0	4	1	0	.600	.615
Zeile, Todd	.333	12	4	0	4	1	1	.385	.500

Mike Hampton, Astros — LHP

Batter	Avg	AB	H	HR	BI	BB	SO	OBP	Slg
Allensworth	.167	6	1	0	0	1	0	.286	.167
Battle, Allen	.250	4	1	0	0	1	1	.400	.250
Bell, Jay	.545	11	6	2	4	2	2	.615	1.273
Belliard, R	.400	5	2	0	0	0	0	.400	.400
Benard, M*	.500	4	2	0	0	2	1	.667	.500
Benjamin, M	.200	5	1	0	1	1	1	.333	.200
Bichette, D	.231	13	3	2	6	1	4	.267	.692
Blauser, Jeff	.500	10	5	0	1	1	2	.545	.500
Bogar, Tim	.286	7	2	0	0	0	0	.286	.429
Bonds, Barry*	.375	16	6	2	3	1	1	.412	.813
Boone, Bret	.364	11	4	0	4	0	2	.333	.545
Brogna, Rico*	.500	8	2	0	0	1	1	.333	.375
Buford, Damon	.333	6	2	2	3	0	0	.333	1.333
Burks, Ellis	.250	12	3	1	1	0	5	.250	.500
Butler, Brett*	.286	7	2	0	2	1	2	.375	.286
Caminiti, Ken#	.500	12	6	0	3	0	1	.500	.750
Carreon, Mark	.182	11	2	0	1	1	2	.250	.273
Castilla, V	.231	13	3	0	2	0	2	.231	.385
Cianfrocco, A	.333	6	2	0	2	0	0	.429	.333
Clayton, R	.222	9	2	0	1	1	0	.300	.333

Ryan Hancock, Angels — RHP

Batter	Avg	AB	H	HR	BI	BB	SO	OBP	Slg
Herrera, Jose*	.667	6	4	0	1	0	0	.667	.667

Batter	Avg	AB	H	HR	BI	BB	SO	OBP	Slg
Alomar, R#	.357	14	5	0	1	3	3	.471	.571
Alomar Jr, S	.250	8	2	0	0	1	1	.333	.375
Amaral, Rich	.400	20	8	0	4	2	2	.455	.600
Anderson, Brd*	.313	16	5	1	2	1	5	.353	.625
Anderson, G*	.167	6	1	0	0	0	1	.167	.167
Baerga, C#	.294	17	5	0	2	0	1	.294	.294
Bagwell, Jeff	.500	4	2	0	2	2	0	.667	.750
Becker, Rich*	.000	7	0	0	0	0	3	.000	.000
Bell, Jay	.600	5	3	0	1	0	0	.667	.800
Belle, Albert	.261	23	6	3	6	2	1	.308	.652
Berroa, G	.375	16	6	0	1	1	1	.412	.438
Biggio, Craig	.500	4	2	1	1	3	0	.714	1.250
Blowers, Mike	.333	12	4	1	6	1	3	.385	.750
Boggs, Wade*	.400	10	4	0	0	2	0	.500	.400
Bonds, Barry*	.750	4	3	1	2	1	1	.800	1.500
Bonilla, B#	.286	14	4	0	2	2	0	.353	.286
Boone, Bret	.250	8	2	0	0	0	2	.250	.375
Borders, Pat	.143	7	1	0	1	0	1	.143	.143
Bordick, Mike	.375	16	6	1	3	1	0	.412	.563
Bragg, Darren*	.000	5	0	0	0	1	0	.000	.000
Brosius, S	.364	11	4	0	0	1	0	.417	.818
Brumfield, J	.400	10	4	0	4	0	1	.400	.400
Buford, Damon	.222	9	2	0	1	1	1	.300	.333
Buhner, Jay	.235	17	4	0	0	3	8	.350	.294
Butler, Brett*	.200	5	1	0	2	0	0	.333	.400
Caminiti, Ken	.400	5	2	0	1	1	0	.500	.600
Carreon, Mark	.375	8	3	0	0	0	1	.375	.500
Carter, Joe	.350	20	7	0	3	2	3	.409	.550
Cedeno, D#	.125	8	1	0	1	0	1	.111	.125
Cirillo, Jeff	.188	16	3	0	0	1	1	.235	.188
Clark, Will*	.357	14	5	0	2	4	0	.500	.429
Coomer, Ron	.000	8	0	0	0	0	1	.000	.000
Cordova, M	.500	4	2	0	1	1	1	.600	.750
Curtis, Chad	.667	6	4	1	2	2	0	.750	1.333
Daulton, D*	.000	6	0	0	0	0	0	.000	.000
Davis, Chili*	.417	12	5	1	3	2	2	.500	.667
Dawson, Andre	.417	12	5	1	3	2	0	.500	.667
Devereaux, M	.400	20	8	1	3	0	2	.400	.700
Duncan, M	.308	13	4	0	3	0	3	.308	.308
Dunston, S	.500	4	2	0	0	0	0	.600	.800
Durham, Ray#	.400	10	4	1	2	0	2	.400	.800
Dykstra, L*	.400	5	2	0	1	1	0	.500	.400
Edmonds, Jim*	.333	6	2	0	0	0	0	.333	.500
Elster, Kevin	.095	21	2	0	0	0	3	.095	.143
Espinoza, J	.250	12	3	0	2	0	0	.250	.417
Fermin, Felix	.500	6	3	0	0	0	0	.500	.833
Fielder, C	.250	4	1	1	2	3	2	.571	1.000
Finley, Steve*	.400	5	2	0	0	1	0	.500	.400
Franco, Julio	.444	9	4	1	2	1	2	.500	.778
Frye, Jeff	.111	9	1	0	0	1	1	.200	.111
Fryman, T	.429	7	3	0	1	0	0	.429	.429
Gates, Brent#	.077	13	1	0	1	1	1	.133	.077
Giambi, Jason*	.000	9	0	0	0	0	1	.000	.000
Girardi, Joe	.300	10	3	0	1	0	2	.300	.400
Gonzales, R	.250	8	2	0	0	1	1	.333	.250
Gonzalez, A	.200	10	2	0	0	0	0	.200	.200
Gonzalez, J	.333	15	5	3	4	2	1	.412	1.000
Grace, Mark*	.400	5	2	0	1	1	1	.500	.600
Grebeck, T	.286	7	2	0	1	0	1	.286	.286
Greenwell, M*	.286	7	2	0	0	0	0	.286	.286
Greer, Rusty*	.364	11	4	0	0	0	1	.417	.364
Griffey Jr, K*	.250	16	4	1	3	4	1	.429	.500
Guillen, O*	.250	8	2	0	1	0	0	.250	.250
Hamilton, D*	.167	18	3	0	0	2	1	.250	.167
Hammonds, J	.300	10	3	0	0	0	4	.300	.400
Hayes, C	.125	8	1	0	1	0	2	.125	.250
Henderson, R	.000	9	0	0	0	2	0	.182	.000
Hocking, D	.333	6	2	0	0	0	0	.333	.500
Hoiles, Chris	.400	10	4	1	2	2	1	.500	.700
Hollins, Dave#	.500	8	4	0	3	3	3	.636	.500
Hudler, Rex	.000	6	0	0	0	0	2	.000	.000
Hulse, David*	.333	6	2	0	0	1	0	.333	.333
Hunter, Brian	.250	8	2	0	0	0	2	.250	.375
Jaha, John	.364	11	4	2	3	1	1	.417	.909
Javier, Stan#	.429	7	3	1	2	0	0	.500	1.143
Jeter, Derek	.571	7	4	0	0	1	0	.625	.571
Johnson, L*	.083	12	1	0	0	1	2	.154	.167
Karkovice, R	.429	14	6	0	1	2	3	.500	.500
Kelly, Pat	.333	9	3	0	1	0	1	.333	.333
Kelly, R	.250	8	2	0	2	0	2	.250	.375
Kent, Jeff	.333	3	1	0	0	2	0	.600	.667
Kirby, Wayne*	.200	5	1	0	0	0	0	.200	.200
Knoblauch, C	.364	22	8	2	4	2	1	.417	.636
Lankford, Ray*	.125	8	1	0	0	2	1	.300	.125
Larkin, Barry	.600	5	3	0	3	2	0	.625	1.200
Leius, Scott	.125	8	1	0	1	1	2	.222	.125
Lewis, Darren	.200	5	1	0	0	0	0	.200	.400
Leyritz, Jim	.462	13	6	2	5	4	4	.588	1.077
Listach, Pat	.385	13	5	0	2	1	0	.429	.615
Lofton, Kenny*	.478	23	11	0	3	3	2	.538	.565
Loretta, Mark	.167	6	1	0	0	0	0	.167	.167
Martin, N	.200	5	1	0	0	0	1	.200	.200
Martinez, E	.000	10	0	0	1	3	1	.214	.000
Martinez, T*	.214	14	3	0	2	2	1	.313	.214
Matheny, Mike	.333	12	4	0	2	0	0	.333	.500
McCarty, Dave	.500	4	2	0	0	2	0	.667	.500
McGwire, Mark	.364	11	4	1	2	6	0	.588	.727
McLemore, M#	.238	21	5	0	0	3	1	.333	.286
Meares, Pat	.333	12	4	0	3	0	1	.333	.417
Mieske, Matt	.267	15	4	1	2	2	0	.353	.533
Molitor, Paul	.286	14	4	0	1	2	1	.375	.500
Morris, Hal*	.200	5	1	0	1	0	2	.200	.200
Mouton, Lyle	.286	7	2	0	1	0	1	.286	.286
Munoz, Pedro	.182	11	2	0	0	1	6	.250	.364
Murray, Eddie#	.278	18	5	0	4	1	5	.316	.333
Naehring, Tim	.000	6	0	0	1	0	1	.143	.000
Nilsson, Dave*	.143	7	1	0	0	0	2	.143	.286
Nixon, Otis#	.273	11	3	0	0	1	0	.273	.455
O'Brien, C	.000	7	0	0	0	3	1	.300	.000
O'Neill, Paul*	.118	17	2	0	3	1	2	.211	.118
Olerud, John*	.308	13	4	0	4	1	0	.308	.308
Oliver, Joe	.077	13	1	1	2	1	2	.143	.308
Palmeiro, R*	.350	20	7	0	3	1	5	.381	.450
Palmer, Dean	.148	27	4	1	2	0	10	.148	.259
Paquette, C	.250	8	2	0	3	0	2	.250	.500
Pena, G#	.400	5	2	0	0	0	2	.400	.400
Pena, Tony	.455	11	5	1	1	0	0	.455	.727
Perez, Robert	.333	9	3	0	0	0	0	.333	.444
Perez, Tomas#	.167	6	1	0	0	0	0	.167	.167
Phillips, T#	.167	6	1	0	0	1	2	.375	.167
Polonia, Luis*	.400	5	2	0	0	0	0	.400	.400
Raines, Tim#	.385	13	5	1	2	0	0	.385	.615
Ramirez, M	.429	21	9	1	5	0	0	.429	.762
Reboulet, J	.300	10	3	0	0	2	3	.417	.300
Ripken, Billy	.400	5	2	0	1	0	0	.400	.400
Ripken, Cal	.400	15	6	3	7	1	1	.412	1.000
Roberts, Bip#	.500	6	3	0	0	1	0	.571	.833
Rodriguez, Al	.333	9	3	0	0	1	1	.400	.444
Rodriguez, I	.296	27	8	1	3	0	3	.296	.481
Sabo, Chris	.286	7	2	1	2	0	2	.286	.714
Salmon, Tim	.333	6	2	1	1	2	0	.429	.833
Samuel, Juan	.364	11	4	1	3	1	1	.417	.636
Sandberg, R	.400	5	2	0	0	1	1	.500	.600
Schofield, D	.500	4	2	0	0	1	0	.600	1.250
Seitzer, K	.440	25	11	0	6	4	3	.517	.640
Sierra, Ruben#	.313	16	5	0	2	1	0	.333	.375
Slaught, Don	.500	6	3	0	1	1	0	.571	.500
Smith, Ozzie*	.444	9	4	0	2	1	1	.500	.444
Snopek, Chris	.500	6	3	2	4	0	1	.500	1.667
Snow, J.T.#	.167	6	1	0	0	0	0	.167	.167
Sojo, Luis	.250	4	1	0	0	0	0	.250	.250
Sprague, Ed	.368	19	7	1	2	1	1	.429	.737
Stanley, Mike	.167	12	2	2	3	2	3	.286	.667
Steinbach, T	.133	15	2	0	0	2	0	.235	.133
Strange, Doug#	.000	5	0	0	0	1	0	.000	.000
Strawberry, D*	.250	4	1	1	2	1	3	.400	1.000
Surhoff, B.J.*	.500	16	8	1	4	0	0	.500	.875
Tartabull, D	.167	12	2	0	0	2	6	.333	.167
Tettleton, M#	.350	20	7	0	3	1	4	.364	.500
Thomas, Frank	.625	8	5	1	2	2	0	.636	1.000
Thome, Jim*	.071	14	1	1	1	1	2	.188	.286
Valentin, Jhn	.333	6	2	0	0	0	0	.333	.500
Valentin, Jse#	.300	10	3	0	1	0	3	.300	.300
Valle, Dave	.167	12	2	0	1	0	2	.167	.167
Vaughn, Greg	.316	19	6	1	3	4	2	.417	.526
Vaughn, Mo*	.250	8	2	0	1	2	1	.455	.250
Velarde, R	.286	14	4	0	1	0	1	.286	.429
Ventura, R*	.250	16	4	1	4	1	1	.278	.438
Vina, F*	.000	4	0	0	0	2	0	.333	.000
Vizquel, Omar*	.240	25	6	1	4	1	0	.250	.360
Voigt, Jack	.200	5	1	0	0	0	0	.200	.200
Walbeck, Matt#	.375	8	3	0	2	0	0	.333	.500
Ward, Turner#	.000	8	0	0	0	0	3	.000	.000
White, Devon#	.222	9	2	0	3	1	6	.385	.333
Williams, Ber#	.438	16	7	0	3	3	1	.500	.625
Williams, Geo#	.000	5	0	0	0	1	1	.167	.000
Williams, Ger	.600	5	3	0	1	1	0	.571	.800
Wilson, Dan	.143	7	1	0	1	0	1	.222	.143
Young, Ernie	.444	9	4	0	0	2	2	.444	.667
Zeile, Todd	.200	5	1	0	0	2	1	.429	.200

Greg Hansell, Twins RHP

Batter	Avg	AB	H	HR	BI	BB	SO	OBP	Slg
Baerga, C#	.600	5	3	0	1	0	0	.667	1.000
Carreon, Mark	.600	5	3	0	1	0	0	.600	1.000
Cedeno, A	.400	5	2	1	3	0	1	.400	1.000
Cordero, Wil	.200	5	1	0	0	0	0	.200	.200
McGwire, Mark	.500	4	2	1	1	1	0	.600	1.250
Nieves, M#	.000	4	0	0	0	2	3	.333	.000
Pena, Tony	.167	6	1	0	3	0	0	.167	.333
Ramirez, M	.000	5	0	0	0	1	0	.000	.000
Young, Ernie	.333	3	1	1	2	2	0	.600	1.333

Batter	Avg	AB	H	HR	BI	BB	SO	OBP	Slg
Abbott, Kurt	.200	5	1	0	1	0	3	.200	.200
Aldrete, Mike*	.143	7	1	0	1	0	1	.143	.143
Alomar, R#	.147	34	5	1	6	3	2	.211	.235
Alomar Jr, S	.407	27	11	0	3	0	2	.393	.444
Anderson, Brd*	.375	32	12	1	8	5	5	.447	.656
Anderson, G*	.500	6	3	0	2	0	1	.500	.833
Ausmus, Brad	.500	6	3	0	0	2	1	.625	.667
Baerga, C#	.195	41	8	1	3	0	5	.214	.317
Bagwell, Jeff	.400	5	2	0	0	1	1	.500	.400
Baines, H*	.273	44	12	0	5	6	11	.353	.341
Becker, Rich*	.188	16	3	0	1	1	6	.235	.188
Bell, Jay	.286	7	2	0	1	2	1	.500	.571
Belle, Albert	.302	43	13	4	12	2	4	.333	.674
Beltre, E	.167	6	1	0	2	1	0	.286	.333
Berroa, G	.222	18	4	1	3	3	3	.333	.389
Bichette, Dante	.211	19	4	0	3	1	1	.238	.263
Biggio, Craig	.167	6	1	0	1	0	0	.167	.167
Blowers, Mike	.125	8	1	0	1	0	4	.125	.250
Boggs, Wade*	.333	54	18	1	3	8	2	.419	.537
Bonds, Barry*	.143	7	1	1	1	1	2	.250	.571
Bonilla, B#	.400	5	2	0	2	1	1	.500	.400
Borders, Pat	.125	8	1	0	0	0	3	.125	.125
Bordick, Mike	.429	28	12	0	3	1	3	.448	.500
Bragg, Darren*	.222	9	2	0	1	0	2	.222	.444
Brosius, S	.348	23	8	3	4	1	4	.375	.783
Buhner, Jay	.429	14	6	0	1	0	4	.429	.500
Burks, Ellis	.481	27	13	3	8	2	4	.517	.852
Burnitz, J*	.200	10	2	0	0	0	2	.200	.200
Caminiti, Ken#	.400	5	2	1	3	0	0	.400	1.000
Canseco, Jose	.043	23	1	0	0	3	11	.154	.043
Carreon, Mark	.000	5	0	0	0	1	0	.167	.000
Carter, Joe	.265	34	9	1	8	1	6	.289	.382
Cirillo, Jeff	.357	14	5	2	0	2	2	.357	.429
Clark, Dave*	.167	6	1	1	1	0	2	.167	.667
Clark, Tony#	.000	5	0	0	0	1	2	.167	.000
Clark, Will*	.455	11	5	0	5	3	2	.571	.636
Clayton, B	.250	8	2	0	1	0	4	.250	.375
Coleman, V#	.200	5	1	0	0	1	2	.333	.200
Conine, Jeff	.400	5	2	0	2	0	0	.400	.800
Cora, Joey#	.292	24	7	0	1	0	2	.292	.458
Cordova, M	.333	9	3	0	1	3	3	.500	.333
Curtis, Chad	.429	21	9	1	5	3	0	.520	.714
Cuyler, Milt#	.071	14	1	0	0	2	5	.188	.071
Damon, Johnny*	.167	6	1	0	1	1	1	.286	.167
Daulton, D*	.750	4	3	2	4	1	1	.800	2.250
Davis, Chili#	.237	38	9	0	3	4	16	.310	.263
Deer, Rob	.100	20	2	1	1	0	10	.100	.300
Devereaux, M	.391	23	9	1	5	5	1	.500	.565
DiSarcina, John	.222	27	6	1	3	1	0	.250	.407
Duncan, M	.500	12	6	1	3	0	3	.500	.833
Durham, Ray*	.000	5	0	0	0	1	4	.167	.000
Dykstra, L*	.500	6	3	0	1	0	0	.500	.500
Easley, D	.500	8	2	0	0	1	1	.333	.375
Edmonds, Jim*	.250	12	3	0	1	2	5	.357	.250
Eisenreich, J*	.333	21	7	0	1	1	1	.364	.381
Elster, Kevin	.000	5	0	0	0	1	3	.167	.000
Espinoza, A	.308	13	4	0	0	0	1	.308	.308
Fabregas, Jor*	.333	6	2	0	0	0	0	.333	.333
Fermin, Felix	.222	18	4	0	0	1	0	.222	.222
Fielder, C	.143	42	6	1	4	8	17	.294	.238
Finley, Steve*	.167	12	2	0	0	0	2	.167	.250
Franco, Julio	.520	25	13	1	2	5	1	.600	.680
Frye, Jeff	.500	12	6	0	2	0	3	.500	.667
Fryman, T	.118	34	4	0	4	2	9	.158	.176
Gaetti, Gary	.172	29	5	0	4	0	11	.167	.310
Gagne, Greg	.438	16	7	0	0	1	2	.471	.438
Galarraga, A	.667	6	4	0	2	0	1	.667	1.000
Gallego, Mike	.222	18	4	1	2	3	5	.333	.389
Garcia, C	.300	10	3	0	2	0	1	.300	.300
Gates, Brent#	.522	23	12	0	0	3	3	.577	.696
Giambi, Jason*	.333	9	3	1	4	0	2	.300	.778
Gil, Benji	.000	5	0	0	0	0	2	.000	.000
Girardi, Joe	.333	9	3	0	0	0	2	.333	.333
Gomez, Leo	.467	15	7	1	3	5	5	.571	.667
Gonzales, R	.389	18	7	0	3	1	0	.421	.389
Gonzalez, J	.474	19	9	2	6	2	5	.500	.842
Gonzalez, L*	.800	5	4	1	3	0	0	.800	2.200
Goodwin, Tom*	.500	8	4	0	1	0	1	.500	.500
Grace, Mark*	.375	8	3	0	0	1	0	.444	.375
Grebeck, C	.167	12	2	0	0	2	2	.286	.167
Greenwell, M*	.176	34	6	0	6	4	3	.256	.206
Greer, Rusty*	.250	16	4	0	3	1	2	.294	.250
Griffey Jr, K*	.222	9	2	2	3	1	1	.300	.889
Guillen, O*	.156	32	5	0	1	0	7	.156	.188
Gwynn, Chris*	.250	8	2	0	0	0	1	.250	.375
Hale, Chip*	.571	7	4	0	0	2	0	.625	.714
Hall, Mel*	.400	20	8	1	6	0	5	.400	.750
Hamelin, Bob*	.000	4	0	0	0	2	2	.333	.000
Hamilton, D*	.324	34	11	0	4	5	9	.410	.412
Hayes, C	.400	10	4	1	2	0	0	.400	.800
Henderson, R	.364	33	12	3	7	7	9	.463	.758

Batter	Avg	AB	H	HR	BI	BB	SO	OBP	Slg
Hernandez, Jo	.167	6	1	0	0	0	3	.167	.167
Higginson, B*	.600	10	6	3	5	1	1	.636	1.700
Hill, G	.308	13	4	1	3	1	6	.357	.615
Hoiles, Chris	.364	22	8	1	3	5	5	.500	.636
Hollins, Dave*	.250	12	3	1	2	1	3	.357	.667
Howard, Dave#	.200	5	1	0	0	0	0	.200	.200
Howell, Jack*	.231	13	3	0	1	1	1	.286	.385
Hudler, Rex	.000	7	0	0	0	0	1	.000	.000
Hulse, David*	.125	16	2	0	2	0	0	.125	.188
Hunter, Brian	.000	5	0	0	0	1	2	.167	.000
Huson, Jeff*	.364	11	4	0	0	1	0	.417	.545
Incaviglia, P	.167	6	1	0	0	0	3	.167	.167
Jaha, John	.368	19	7	0	1	4	3	.478	.526
James, Dion*	.350	20	7	0	3	0	1	.350	.350
Javier, Stan#	.400	25	10	1	5	2	4	.444	.640
Jefferies, G#	.154	13	2	0	1	1	1	.214	.154
Jefferson, R*	.000	11	0	0	0	1	3	.083	.000
Jeter, Derek	.556	9	5	0	0	0	0	.556	.667
Johnson, L*	.273	33	9	0	4	0	6	.273	.303
Joyner, Wally*	.333	27	9	2	9	4	4	.419	.630
Karkovice, R	.167	12	2	0	1	1	4	.231	.250
Kelly, Pat	.071	14	1	0	0	0	5	.071	.071
Kelly, R	.308	26	8	1	4	1	5	.333	.654
Kent, Jeff	.286	7	2	0	1	0	0	.375	.286
King, Jeff	.222	9	2	0	0	0	2	.222	.333
Kingery, Mike*	.200	5	1	0	1	0	2	.200	.200
Klesko, Ryan*	.333	6	2	0	0	0	1	.333	.833
Knoblauch, C	.278	36	10	0	3	6	6	.381	.333
Kreuter, Chad#	.400	5	2	0	1	1	1	.500	.600
Lawton, Matt*	.000	5	0	0	0	1	0	.167	.000
Leius, Scott	.250	4	1	0	0	1	0	.400	.250
Lemke, Mark#	.500	6	3	0	0	0	2	.500	.500
Lewis, Darren	.250	12	3	0	0	1	0	.250	.250
Lewis, Mark	.111	9	1	0	1	1	2	.200	.111
Leyritz, Jim	.167	12	2	0	0	0	3	.167	.167
Liriano, N#	.154	13	2	0	0	0	6	.154	.154
Listach, Pat#	.150	20	3	0	4	1	6	.190	.200
Livingstone*	.105	19	2	0	1	0	4	.100	.105
Lockhart, K*	.167	6	1	0	0	2	2	.375	.167
Lofton, Kenny*	.175	40	7	0	3	4	2	.250	.175
Loretta, Mark	.400	5	2	0	1	0	0	.400	.600
Lovullo, T#	.200	10	2	0	1	1	3	.273	.200
Macfarlane, M	.200	15	3	1	1	4	0	.368	.467
Manwaring, K	.600	5	3	0	0	0	0	.600	.600
Martin, Al*	.250	8	2	0	0	0	2	.250	.250
Martin, N	.500	4	2	0	0	0	0	.400	.400
Martinez, Da*	.267	15	4	0	2	1	3	.313	.467
Martinez, E	.455	11	5	4	5	4	0	.600	1.545
Martinez, T*	.385	13	5	1	2	2	2	.467	.615
Matheny, Mike	.143	7	1	0	1	3	2	.364	.286
May, Derrick*	.286	14	4	0	1	0	1	.286	.357
Mayne, Brent*	.167	6	1	0	1	0	2	.167	.167
McGee, Willie*	.571	7	4	0	2	0	1	.571	.714
McGriff, Fred*	.375	8	3	2	3	5	1	.615	1.125
McGwire, Mark	.318	22	7	1	5	8	5	.516	.500
McLemore, M#	.400	20	8	0	1	5	3	.520	.400
McRae, Brian#	.167	12	2	0	0	2	5	.286	.250
Meares, Pat	.143	14	2	0	1	0	5	.143	.214
Merced, O*	.222	9	2	0	1	0	3	.222	.222
Mieske, Matt	.167	6	1	0	1	0	0	.167	.167
Molitor, Paul	.482	56	27	1	8	5	5	.525	.643
Morandini, M*	.250	4	1	0	0	1	0	.400	.250
Mouton, James	.400	5	2	0	1	0	0	.400	.400
Munoz, Pedro	.313	16	5	1	4	1	1	.353	.500
Murray, Eddie*	.136	22	3	0	3	1	4	.174	.136
Myers, Greg*	.136	22	3	0	7	2	5	.192	.227
Naehring, Tim	.000	6	0	0	0	1	3	.143	.000
Newson, W*	.143	14	2	0	0	5	5	.143	.143
Nieves, Mel*	.167	6	1	0	0	1	2	.286	.333
Nilsson, Dave*	.176	17	3	1	1	0	3	.176	.471
Nixon, Otis#	.286	7	2	0	1	0	0	.286	.286
O'Neill, Paul*	.194	31	6	0	2	1	12	.212	.258
Offerman, J#	.286	7	2	0	0	0	1	.286	.286
Olerud, John*	.290	31	9	1	7	3	6	.343	.419
Oliver, Joe	.286	7	2	0	1	0	0	.286	.286
Orsulak, Joe*	.350	20	7	1	4	0	2	.368	.250
Palmeiro, R*	.212	33	7	1	5	3	5	.278	.303
Palmer, Dean	.136	22	3	1	1	1	7	.174	.318
Paquette, J	.200	20	4	0	1	0	6	.200	.250
Pena, Tony	.294	17	5	0	1	3	1	.400	.353
Phillips, T#	.227	44	10	2	3	7	10	.333	.364
Plantier, P*	.091	11	1	0	0	3	5	.286	.091
Polonia, Luis*	.264	53	14	0	3	6	4	.304	.283
Raines, Tim#	.296	27	8	1	4	3	2	.367	.444
Ramirez, M	.167	18	3	0	2	1	5	.200	.278
Reboulet, J	.600	10	6	0	2	0	3	.600	.700
Reed, Jody	.259	27	7	0	0	2	1	.310	.259
Ripken, Billy	.200	10	2	1	2	1	3	.333	.500
Ripken, Cal	.275	40	11	0	2	0	3	.275	.350
Rodriguez, Al	.429	7	3	1	4	0	1	.500	.857

Erik Hanson, Blue Jays — RHP

Batter	Avg	AB	H	HR	BI	BB	SO	OBP	Slg
Rodriguez, I	.360	25	9	0	2	0	4	.360	.600
Salmon, Tim	.435	23	10	1	4	3	1	.500	.696
Sanchez, Rey	.250	8	2	0	0	0	1	.250	.375
Schofield, D	.133	15	2	0	0	2	4	.235	.133
Segui, David#	.455	11	5	1	2	0	2	.455	.727
Seitzer, K	.436	39	17	0	4	11	5	.560	.590
Servais, S	.200	5	1	1	2	0	0	.200	.800
Sheffield, G	.316	19	6	0	2	0	0	.300	.474
Shumpert, T	.429	7	3	0	1	0	2	.429	.429
Sierra, Ruben#	.158	38	6	1	4	1	10	.175	.316
Slaught, Don	.444	9	4	0	1	1	1	.545	.556
Snow, J.T.#	.250	16	4	0	3	3	5	.368	.313
Sojo, Luis	.211	19	4	0	1	5	2	.375	.316
Sorrento, P*	.182	33	6	1	2	3	7	.250	.333
Sosa, Sammy	.154	13	2	0	0	0	3	.154	.154
Spiers, Bill*	.100	20	2	0	0	0	5	.100	.100
Sprague, Ed	.300	10	3	0	0	2	2	.417	.400
Stahoviak, S*	.500	10	5	0	1	2	2	.583	.500
Stankiewicz	.444	9	4	0	0	0	0	.444	.556
Stanley, Mike	.267	15	4	0	3	0	4	.250	.333
Steinbach, T	.286	42	12	1	3	3	6	.333	.381
Stevens, Lee*	.111	9	1	0	0	1	1	.200	.111
Stillwell, K#	.231	13	3	0	3	1	4	.267	.385
Strange, Doug*	.429	7	3	0	2	0	2	.429	.571
Strawberry, D*	.375	8	3	1	3	1	2	.444	.750
Surhoff, B.J.*	.217	46	10	1	5	1	4	.245	.326
Sveum, Dale#	.400	5	2	0	0	0	0	.400	.400
Tartabull, D	.378	37	14	2	6	4	12	.439	.649
Tettleton, M#	.065	31	2	1	2	3	15	.147	.161
Thomas, Frank	.333	33	11	3	5	8	4	.463	.636
Thome, Jim*	.143	21	3	0	1	6	8	.333	.190
Trammell, A	.313	16	5	1	5	0	1	.294	.688
Valentin, Jhn	.400	5	2	0	0	1	0	.500	.600
Valentin, Jse#	.167	12	2	1	1	3	4	.333	.417
Valle, Dave	.375	8	3	0	1	0	2	.375	.500
Vaughn, Greg	.289	38	11	1	9	1	13	.308	.447
Vaughn, Mo*	.133	15	2	1	2	1	6	.188	.400
Velarde, R	.263	19	5	1	2	1	3	.300	.474
Ventura, R*	.194	36	7	0	3	8	8	.256	.222
Vina, F*	.176	17	3	0	4	1	2	.222	.353
Vizquel, Omar*	.308	26	8	0	3	2	0	.345	.346
Walbeck, Matt#	.286	7	2	0	3	2	3	.444	.429
Wallach, Tim	.333	6	2	1	2	0	2	.333	.833
Ward, Turner#	.167	6	1	0	0	3	3	.167	.167
Webster, L	.000	7	0	0	0	0	1	.000	.000
Weiss, Walt#	.182	22	4	0	2	1	7	.217	.273
White, Devon#	.314	35	11	0	3	2	7	.342	.343
Whiten, Mark#	.267	15	4	0	1	2	5	.353	.333
Wilkins, Rick*	.125	8	1	0	0	1	3	.222	.125
Williams, Ber#	.286	35	10	0	3	1	6	.306	.314
Williams, E	.125	8	1	0	0	0	3	.125	.250
Williams, Ger	.167	6	1	0	0	0	2	.167	.167
Williams, Ma	.125	8	1	1	1	0	2	.125	.500
Wilson, Dan	.375	8	3	0	2	1	1	.500	.375
Worthington	.100	10	1	0	2	0	3	.100	.100
Young, Ernie	.000	6	0	0	1	0	4	.143	.000
Zeile, Todd	.000	6	0	0	0	1	2	.143	.000

Pete Harnisch, Mets — RHP

Batter	Avg	AB	H	HR	BI	BB	SO	OBP	Slg
Abbott, Kurt	.167	6	1	1	2	0	1	.167	.667
Alicea, Luis#	.333	12	4	0	2	4	1	.500	.500
Alomar Jr, S	.250	8	2	1	1	0	1	.250	.625
Alou, Moises	.222	18	4	1	5	1	1	.250	.444
Amaro, Ruben#	.250	8	2	0	0	0	0	.400	.375
Andrews, S	.500	8	4	0	1	0	0	.444	.625
Arias, Alex	.375	8	3	0	0	1	0	.444	.500
Ashley, Billy	.000	6	0	0	0	1	5	.143	.000
Aurilia, Rich	.000	6	0	0	0	0	1	.000	.000
Ausmus, Brad	.000	12	0	0	1	2	0	.000	.000
Baerga, C#	.250	4	1	0	0	1	1	.400	.250
Baines, H*	.417	12	5	0	2	1	2	.429	.500
Barberie, J	.167	6	1	0	0	1	1	.286	.167
Bates, Jason#	.333	9	3	0	0	1	3	.400	.444
Bell, Derek	.267	15	4	1	2	0	3	.267	.533
Bell, Jay	.214	28	6	0	3	5	11	.324	.286
Belliard, R	.278	18	5	0	0	3	2	.381	.333
Benard, M*	.500	6	3	2	3	2	0	.625	1.833
Benjamin, M	.200	5	1	0	0	1	0	.200	.200
Berry, Sean	.200	5	1	1	2	2	0	.429	.800
Bichette, D	.219	32	7	2	5	1	4	.242	.438
Blauser, Jeff	.240	25	6	0	3	7	7	.424	.320
Blowers, Mike	.167	6	1	1	1	0	1	.167	.667
Boggs, Wade*	.385	13	5	0	2	1	1	.467	.692
Bonds, Barry*	.292	24	7	3	9	8	1	.471	.667
Bonilla, Bob	.238	21	5	1	4	3	4	.333	.524
Boone, Bret	.364	11	4	1	3	1	2	.417	.818
Branson, Jeff*	.364	11	4	0	1	1	4	.417	.455
Burks, Ellis	.313	16	5	0	1	3	4	.421	.375
Burnitz, J*	.500	6	3	2	2	2	1	.625	1.500
Butler, Brett*	.200	20	4	0	4	3	3	.333	.300

Pete Harnisch, Mets — RHP

Batter	Avg	AB	H	HR	BI	BB	SO	OBP	Slg
Caminiti, Ken*	.000	6	0	0	0	1	4	.143	.000
Canizaro, Jay	.167	6	1	0	0	0	0	.167	.167
Carr, Chuck	.267	15	4	0	0	0	2	.267	.267
Carreon, Mark	.000	5	0	0	0	0	2	.000	.000
Castilla, V	.364	22	8	1	5	0	2	.364	.591
Castro, Juan	.000	4	0	0	0	1	0	.200	.000
Cedeno, A	.143	7	1	0	0	0	3	.143	.143
Cianfrocco, A	.444	9	4	1	1	0	1	.444	.778
Clark, Dave*	.286	14	4	0	1	2	1	.375	.357
Clark, Will*	.250	20	5	1	3	1	2	.286	.450
Clayton, R	.071	14	1	0	1	1	1	.125	.071
Colbrunn, A	.417	12	5	1	2	1	0	.462	.750
Cole, Alex*	.250	12	3	0	0	1	1	.308	.333
Coleman, V#	.091	11	1	0	0	0	3	.091	.182
Conine, Jeff	.231	13	3	0	1	2	5	.313	.231
Cordero, Wil	.364	11	4	0	3	0	1	.364	.364
Cummings, M*	.333	6	2	0	0	0	1	.333	.333
Daulton, D*	.276	29	8	2	4	1	4	.300	.483
Davis, Chili*	.167	6	1	0	0	1	3	.286	.167
Davis, Eric	.200	5	1	0	0	3	1	.500	.200
Dawson, Andre	.118	17	2	0	3	0	3	.105	.176
Decker, Steve	.000	5	0	0	0	2	3	.286	.000
DeShields, D*	.179	28	5	1	2	2	4	.233	.393
Duncan, M	.211	19	4	0	4	1	5	.250	.421
Dunston, S	.133	15	2	1	1	0	1	.133	.400
Dykstra, L*	.214	14	3	1	2	4	2	.389	.500
Eisenreich, J*	.318	22	7	0	1	3	1	.400	.636
Elster, Kevin	.167	6	1	0	1	0	1	.167	.333
Espinoza, A	.250	8	2	0	0	0	1	.250	.250
Fermin, Felix	.111	9	1	0	0	2	0	.273	.111
Finley, Steve*	.556	9	5	0	1	1	0	.600	1.333
Fletcher, D*	.235	17	4	1	2	2	0	.316	.412
Floyd, Cliff*	.231	13	3	0	1	0	5	.286	.231
Fonville, C#	.143	7	1	0	0	0	2	.143	.143
Franco, Julio	.200	15	3	0	0	2	4	.294	.267
Gaetti, Gary	.316	19	6	3	5	0	3	.316	.842
Gagne, Greg	.200	10	2	0	0	0	2	.200	.300
Galarraga, A	.286	21	6	2	6	0	7	.273	.619
Gallego, Mike	.250	4	1	0	0	2	2	.500	.250
Gant, Ron	.179	56	10	2	5	5	12	.246	.357
Garcia, C	.095	21	2	0	2	0	5	.095	.095
Gilkey, B	.133	15	2	1	1	0	3	.188	.333
Girardi, Joe	.273	11	3	0	0	0	5	.273	.273
Gonzalez, L*	.400	10	4	0	3	1	0	.417	.400
Grace, Mark*	.300	40	12	1	2	7	1	.404	.400
Greenwell, M	.333	6	2	0	0	2	0	.500	.500
Griffey Jr, K*	.375	16	6	1	3	1	1	.412	.563
Grissom, M	.265	34	9	0	1	1	3	.286	.353
Grudzielanek	.333	12	4	0	1	0	4	.333	.500
Guillen, O*	.364	11	4	0	1	0	1	.364	.545
Gutierrez, R	.100	10	1	0	0	1	4	.182	.100
Gwynn, Tony*	.400	30	12	1	5	4	2	.457	.633
Hall, Mel*	.100	10	1	0	0	1	0	.100	.200
Hamilton, D*	.500	6	3	0	2	0	0	.500	.500
Hansen, Dave*	.214	14	3	1	2	0	5	.214	.429
Harris, Lenny*	.417	12	5	0	1	0	0	.417	.500
Hayes, C	.235	17	4	0	2	1	3	.278	.294
Henderson, R	.125	8	1	0	1	2	3	.273	.125
Hernandez, Jo	.222	9	2	1	1	0	2	.222	.556
Hill, G	.167	12	2	1	1	1	5	.231	.417
Hollandsworth	.125	8	1	0	0	1	2	.222	.125
Hollins, Dave#	.300	20	6	2	5	4	4	.462	.650
Howard, T*	.429	14	6	2	2	0	5	.429	.929
Howell, Jack*	.000	6	0	0	0	4	2	.400	.000
Hundley, Todd#	.067	15	1	1	2	1	1	.125	.267
Hunter, Brian	.167	6	1	0	1	0	3	.167	.167
Huson, Jeff*	.250	8	2	0	0	0	0	.333	.250
Incaviglia, R	.000	7	0	0	0	1	4	.125	.000
James, Dion*	.111	9	1	0	0	1	1	.200	.111
Javier, Stan#	.125	8	1	0	4	4	1	.417	.250
Jefferies, G#	.125	24	3	0	0	4	1	.250	.125
Johnson, Char	.250	4	1	0	1	1	0	.333	.250
Johnson, L*	.214	14	3	0	3	2	0	.313	.357
Jones, C#	.417	12	5	1	2	1	0	.462	.667
Jordan, Brian	.273	11	3	0	1	0	2	.273	.273
Jordan, Ricky	.375	8	3	0	0	0	2	.375	.625
Joyner, Wally*	.400	5	2	0	0	2	2	.571	.400
Justice, Dave*	.118	34	4	1	2	5	8	.231	.265
Karros, Eric	.115	26	3	2	4	1	5	.148	.346
Kelly, R	.333	30	10	2	3	1	8	.375	.633
Kent, Jeff	.125	8	1	1	2	0	0	.125	.500
King, Jeff	.192	26	5	2	4	2	7	.241	.423
Kingery, Mike*	.231	13	3	0	1	0	2	.231	.538
Kirby, Wayne*	.167	6	1	0	0	1	0	.286	.167
Klesko, Ryan*	.286	7	2	0	1	3	0	.500	.429
Lampkin, Tom*	.250	8	2	0	1	0	0	.250	.250
Lankford, Ray*	.371	35	13	1	10	3	8	.410	.600
Lansing, Mike	.143	21	3	0	1	0	3	.143	.143
Larkin, Barry	.395	43	17	0	7	4	2	.447	.465
Lemke, Mark#	.292	24	7	0	4	3	4	.370	.333
Lewis, Darren	.158	19	3	0	1	3	2	.273	.158

Pete Harnisch, Mets — RHP

Batter	Avg	AB	H	HR	BI	BB	SO	OBP	Slg
Liriano, N#	.400	10	4	1	1	2	1	.500	.700
Lopez, Javy	.167	6	1	0	0	0	1	.167	.167
Lopez, Luis#	.333	6	2	0	1	0	0	.333	.333
Mabry, John*	.200	10	2	0	0	0	2	.200	.400
Magadan, Dave*	.364	22	8	1	3	6	1	.500	.636
Magee, W	.400	5	2	0	0	1	0	.500	.400
Manwaring, K	.083	12	1	0	1	2	8	.214	.167
Martin, Al*	.143	14	2	0	0	4	3	.333	.286
Martinez, Da*	.200	25	5	1	4	1	2	.231	.360
Martinez, E	.222	9	2	0	0	1	1	.300	.222
May, Derrick*	.370	27	10	0	8	0	1	.370	.481
McCracken, Q#	.286	7	2	0	1	2	1	.500	.571
McGee, Willie#	.429	28	12	1	4	2	0	.467	.679
McGriff, Fred*	.256	43	11	1	6	9	6	.377	.395
McGwire, Mark	.400	5	2	1	1	1	2	.500	1.000
McRae, Brian#	.300	10	3	1	2	3	3	.385	.700
Merced, O*	.240	25	6	2	4	4	4	.345	.560
Mitchell, K	.222	18	4	1	2	2	5	.300	.389
Molitor, Paul	.375	8	3	0	1	2	1	.455	.625
Mondesi, Raul	.286	21	6	2	4	0	5	.286	.667
Morandini, M*	.250	28	7	2	7	1	6	.290	.464
Morris, Hal*	.176	34	6	1	5	5	5	.282	.265
Mueller, Bill*	.571	7	4	0	1	1	1	.625	1.000
Murray, Eddie#	.348	23	8	1	3	2	4	.400	.565
Myers, Greg*	.167	6	1	0	0	0	0	.167	.167
Nixon, Otis*	.296	27	8	0	1	5	3	.406	.296
O'Neill, Paul*	.238	21	5	2	2	2	4	.304	.524
Offerman, J#	.214	14	3	0	0	0	4	.267	.214
Oliver, Joe	.133	15	2	1	2	1	4	.188	.333
Orsulak, Joe*	.231	13	3	0	0	1	2	.286	.231
Otero, Ricky*	.286	7	2	0	0	1	0	.375	.429
Pagnozzi, Tom	.250	12	3	0	1	2	1	.357	.250
Palmeiro, R*	.357	14	5	0	0	3	0	.471	.357
Pena, G#	.000	7	0	0	0	0	2	.000	.000
Pendleton, T#	.320	50	16	1	10	1	7	.321	.440
Phillips, T#	.333	9	3	0	1	2	2	.455	.556
Piazza, Mike	.375	16	6	2	4	2	1	.444	.750
Plantier, P*	.333	9	3	0	2	1	1	.455	.444
Polonia, Luis*	.231	13	3	0	1	1	1	.286	.231
Prince, Tom	.400	5	2	1	3	0	0	.400	1.200
Reed, Jeff*	.111	18	2	0	1	5	5	.304	.167
Reed, Jody	.273	22	6	1	3	3	0	.360	.455
Relaford, D#	.286	7	2	0	1	1	1	.375	.429
Renteria, E	.500	10	5	0	1	0	1	.500	.500
Roberts, Bip#	.200	25	5	0	0	4	7	.333	.280
Rodriguez, I#	.273	11	3	1	3	1	4	.333	.636
Sabo, Chris	.059	17	1	0	0	3	7	.200	.059
Samuel, Juan	.125	8	1	0	1	0	1	.125	.125
Sanchez, Rey	.071	14	1	0	0	2	2	.235	.071
Sandberg, R	.212	33	7	1	3	2	10	.257	.364
Sanders, R	.167	24	4	1	1	2	11	.231	.292
Santangelo, F#	.000	8	0	0	0	1	0	.111	.000
Santiago, B	.172	29	5	0	3	0	9	.172	.276
Schofield, D	.000	3	0	0	0	1	2	.250	.000
Sefcik, Kevin	.000	6	0	0	0	0	2	.143	.000
Segui, David*	.500	4	2	0	0	1	1	.600	.500
Seitzer, K	.182	11	2	0	0	1	1	.250	.182
Servais, K	.125	8	1	0	0	0	1	.222	.125
Sheaffer, D	.200	5	1	0	0	0	2	.200	.400
Sheffield, D	.313	32	10	0	4	5	5	.421	.406
Sierra, Ruben#	.067	15	1	0	1	1	3	.118	.067
Slaught, Don	.368	19	7	2	9	2	1	.478	.789
Smith, Dwight*	.167	12	2	0	0	0	2	.167	.500
Smith, Ozzie#	.276	29	8	0	1	2	3	.300	.276
Sorrento, P*	.400	5	2	1	2	0	2	.400	1.200
Sosa, Sammy	.308	39	12	2	5	4	13	.364	.487
Spiers, Bill*	.091	11	1	0	0	1	3	.167	.091
Stillwell, K#	.250	16	4	0	1	2	0	.333	.250
Stocker, K#	.583	12	7	0	6	0	0	.538	.667
Strange, Doug#	.333	6	2	0	0	1	1	.429	.333
Strawberry, D*	.200	10	2	0	2	1	3	.250	.500
Surhoff, B.J.*	.100	10	3	0	0	1	1	.364	.300
Tarasco, Tony*	.286	7	2	0	0	0	0	.286	.286
Tartabull, S	.000	4	0	0	1	0	1	.400	.000
Taubensee, E*	.500	6	3	1	2	0	1	.429	1.000
Thompson, Mil*	.400	25	10	1	2	1	4	.444	.560
Thompson, Rob	.100	20	2	0	1	4	6	.250	.150
Thompson, Ry	.375	8	3	1	3	0	3	.375	1.000
Trammell, A	.250	4	1	0	2	2	1	.500	.750
Valle, Dave	.200	10	2	0	1	3	0	.385	.200
VanderWal, J*	.375	8	3	0	2	3	1	.545	.500
Velarde, R	.143	7	1	0	1	0	2	.143	.429
Ventura, R*	.250	8	2	0	1	2	1	.400	.375
Vizcaino, J#	.231	13	3	0	0	2	1	.333	.231
Vizquel, Omar#	.143	7	1	0	0	1	0	.250	.143
Walker, Larry*	.320	25	8	2	3	1	6	.370	.640
Wallach, Tim	.160	25	4	0	0	2	7	.222	.200
Weiss, Walt#	.240	25	6	0	1	2	4	.296	.280
White, Devon#	.000	13	0	0	0	0	3	.071	.000
White, R	.000	6	0	0	0	0	0	.000	.000
Whiten, Mark#	.600	5	3	0	1	0	1	.600	.600
Wilkins, Rick*	.100	20	2	1	1	4	5	.250	.250
Williams, Ma	.321	28	9	1	3	0	5	.321	.536
Young, Eric	.278	18	5	0	0	0	3	.278	.389
Young, Kevin	.300	10	3	0	1	1	0	.364	.400
Zeile, Todd	.346	26	9	1	7	3	3	.400	.577
Zuber, Jon*	.250	4	1	0	1	0	0	.200	.500

Pep Harris, Angels — RHP

Batter	Avg	AB	H	HR	BI	BB	SO	OBP	Slg
Alomar, R#	.000	3	0	0	1	2	0	.333	.000
Anderson, Brd*	.500	6	3	1	1	0	1	.500	1.167
Bonilla, B#	.400	5	2	0	1	1	0	.500	.400
Hoiles, Chris	.167	6	1	0	0	0	2	.167	.167
Murray, Eddie*	.200	5	1	0	1	0	0	.167	.400
Palmeiro, R*	.200	5	1	0	0	1	0	.333	.400
Ripken, Cal	.250	4	1	0	0	1	0	.500	.250
Surhoff, B.J.*	.200	5	1	0	0	1	1	.333	.200

Dean Hartgraves, Braves — LHP

Batter	Avg	AB	H	HR	BI	BB	SO	OBP	Slg
Grace, Mark*	.429	7	3	0	0	0	1	.429	.571
Howard, T*	.000	3	0	0	0	2	1	.400	.000
Jefferies, G#	.000	5	0	0	0	0	0	.000	.000
Justice, Dave*	.250	4	1	0	1	1	0	.400	.250
McGriff, Fred*	.200	5	1	0	4	1	0	.286	.600
Morandini, M*	.000	5	0	0	0	0	2	.000	.000

LaTroy Hawkins, Twins — RHP

Batter	Avg	AB	H	HR	BI	BB	SO	OBP	Slg
Alomar, R#	.333	6	2	0	2	0	1	.333	.500
Anderson, Brd*	.333	6	2	0	1	0	1	.375	.833
Damon, Johnny*	.200	5	1	1	2	1	0	.333	.800
Durham, Ray#	.333	6	2	0	0	1	0	.429	.500
Gaetti, Gary	.200	5	1	0	1	1	0	.333	.200
Gagne, Greg	.400	5	2	1	4	1	0	.500	1.000
Goodwin, Tom*	.167	6	1	0	0	0	2	.167	.167
Guillen, O*	.500	6	3	0	2	0	0	.500	.500
Hamelin, Bob	.286	7	2	0	0	1	0	.375	.429
Johnson, L*	.375	8	3	0	0	1	0	.375	.625
Joyner, Wally*	.600	5	3	0	1	0	0	.667	1.200
Lockhart, K*	.833	6	5	0	1	0	0	.833	1.000
Mayne, Brent*	.200	5	1	0	1	0	0	.200	.200
Palmeiro, R*	.286	7	2	0	0	0	1	.286	.286
Raines, Tim#	.000	4	0	0	1	3	0	.375	.000
Ripken, Cal	.333	6	2	0	2	0	1	.333	.333
Snopek, Chris	.200	5	1	0	0	0	1	.200	.200
Thomas, Frank	.333	6	2	1	4	1	2	.375	1.000
Tucker, M*	.400	5	2	1	2	0	1	.400	1.000
Ventura, R*	.250	8	2	0	1	0	0	.250	.375

Jimmy Haynes, Orioles — RHP

Batter	Avg	AB	H	HR	BI	BB	SO	OBP	Slg
Anderson, G*	.600	5	3	0	1	0	0	.667	.800
Becker, Rich*	.250	4	1	0	0	4	0	.625	.750
Buhner, Jay	.400	5	2	0	1	1	1	.500	.400
Clark, Will*	.667	3	2	1	4	3	0	.833	1.667
Cora, Joey#	.286	7	2	0	0	0	0	.286	.286
Curtis, Chad	.286	7	2	1	1	0	2	.286	.714
Davis, Chili#	.000	5	0	0	0	0	1	.000	.000
DiSarcina, G	.667	6	4	1	5	0	0	.667	1.167
Edmonds, Jim*	.250	4	1	0	0	1	0	.400	.250
Elster, Kevin	.000	5	0	0	0	2	2	.286	.000
Fielder, C	.500	4	2	0	0	1	1	.600	.500
Fryman, T	.400	5	2	0	3	1	3	.500	.400
Gonzalez, J	.250	8	2	1	2	0	2	.250	.625
Greer, Rusty*	.200	5	1	0	1	1	2	.333	.600
Griffey Jr, K*	.500	4	2	0	0	3	0	.714	.750
Hamilton, D*	.000	7	0	0	0	2	1	.222	.000
Hollins, Dave#	.250	8	2	1	2	1	0	.333	.625
Howell, Jack*	.000	3	0	0	0	2	1	.400	.000
Hudler, Rex	.500	6	3	1	2	0	0	.500	1.000
Jaha, John	.143	7	1	0	0	3	2	.400	.143
Kelly, R	.714	7	5	0	3	0	0	.625	.714
Knoblauch, C	.286	7	2	0	2	2	0	.444	.714
Lawton, Matt*	.500	4	2	0	1	2	0	.667	.500
Listach, Pat#	.111	9	1	0	1	0	1	.111	.111
Martinez, E	.500	4	2	0	3	2	1	.667	.500
Matheny, Mike	.125	8	1	0	2	0	5	.125	.125
Meares, Pat	.250	8	2	0	0	1	1	.250	.500
Mieske, Matt	.143	7	1	0	0	2	0	.333	.286
Molitor, Paul	.333	6	2	0	2	1	0	.333	.500
Myers, Greg*	.750	4	3	0	2	1	1	.800	1.000
Nilsson, Dave*	.333	6	2	0	3	0	0	.333	.500
O'Brien, C	.250	4	1	0	0	0	0	.400	.250
Palmer, Dean	.000	5	0	0	0	2	2	.286	.000
Perez, Robert	.500	4	2	0	0	0	0	.500	.500
Perez, Tomas*	.250	4	1	0	1	1	1	.400	.250
Rodriguez, Al	.571	7	4	0	2	0	1	.571	.857
Rodriguez, I	.444	9	4	0	1	0	3	.444	.556
Salmon, Tim	.500	4	2	0	2	1	0	.600	.750
Seitzer, K	.143	7	1	0	0	4	1	.455	.143

Jimmy Haynes, Orioles — RHP

Batter	Avg	AB	H	HR	BI	BB	SO	OBP	Slg
Snow, J.T.#	.200	5	1	1	1	1	0	.333	.800
Sorrento, P*	.250	4	1	0	1	1	1	.400	.250
Stahoviak, S*	.556	9	5	0	2	0	4	.556	.778
Valentin, Jse#	.333	6	2	1	1	1	1	.429	.833
Vaughn, Greg	.333	6	2	1	3	0	3	.333	.833
Vina, F*	.333	6	2	0	0	1	0	.429	.333
Wilson, Dan	.200	5	1	0	0	1	2	.429	.200

Rick Helling, Marlins — RHP

Batter	Avg	AB	H	HR	BI	BB	SO	OBP	Slg
Alomar, R#	.400	5	2	0	0	1	0	.500	.600
Alou, Moises	.000	7	0	0	0	0	2	.000	.000
Anderson, Brd*	.125	8	1	0	1	1	2	.222	.125
Baerga, C#	.250	4	1	0	2	0	1	.200	.250
Bagwell, Jeff	.000	4	0	0	0	2	1	.333	.000
Baines, H*	.400	5	2	1	1	1	1	.500	1.000
Bell, Derek	.000	6	0	0	0	0	2	.000	.000
Belle, Albert	.000	5	0	0	0	0	0	.000	.000
Berroa, G	.167	6	1	0	0	0	1	.167	.167
Biggio, Craig	.167	6	1	0	0	0	0	.167	.167
Bordick, Mike	.250	5	2	0	2	0	0	.400	.800
Brosius, S	.250	4	1	0	0	1	0	.400	.500
Cangelosi, J#	.000	6	0	0	0	2	0	.000	.000
Davis, Chili#	.500	4	2	1	2	1	0	.600	1.750
Devereaux, M	.167	6	1	0	1	2	0	.375	.167
Easley, D	.000	5	0	0	0	0	0	.000	.000
Eusebio, Tony	.000	6	0	0	0	0	0	.000	.000
Fielder, C	.250	4	1	1	1	1	2	.400	1.000
Fletcher, D*	.200	5	1	0	1	1	1	.333	.200
Fryman, T	.250	5	1	0	0	0	1	.250	.200
Grudzielanek	.167	6	1	0	0	0	1	.167	.167
Hammonds, J	.333	6	2	1	1	0	1	.333	.833
Hoiles, Chris	.333	6	2	0	0	1	1	.429	.333
Lansing, Mike	.143	7	1	0	0	0	4	.143	.143
Lofton, Kenny*	.750	4	3	0	0	1	0	.800	.750
McLemore, M#	.750	4	3	0	1	1	0	.800	1.000
Miller, Orl	.200	5	1	0	0	0	3	.200	.200
Murray, Eddie*	.750	4	3	2	4	1	0	.800	2.250
Palmeiro, R*	.333	6	2	2	6	0	0	.286	1.333
Phillips, T#	.286	7	2	0	1	2	1	.444	.429
Ripken, Cal	.000	7	0	0	0	0	1	.000	.000
Rodriguez, H*	.600	5	3	1	1	1	0	.667	1.400
Sabo, Chris	.000	5	0	0	0	0	2	.000	.000
Salmon, Tim	.600	5	3	1	2	0	0	.600	1.200
Segui, David#	.200	5	1	0	0	2	1	.429	.200
Sorrento, P*	.250	4	1	0	0	1	0	.400	.250
Spiers, Bill*	.200	5	1	0	0	1	0	.333	.600
Steinbach, T	.400	5	2	0	1	1	0	.500	.400
Thome, Jim*	.000	4	0	0	0	0	0	.200	.000
White, R	.000	5	0	0	0	0	2	.000	.000

Mike Henneman, Rangers — RHP

Batter	Avg	AB	H	HR	BI	BB	SO	OBP	Slg
Alomar, R#	.333	9	3	0	1	3	2	.500	.556
Alomar Jr, S	.286	7	2	0	1	0	0	.286	.286
Anderson, Brd*	.357	14	5	1	5	4	1	.500	.643
Baerga, C#	.091	11	1	0	0	1	1	.167	.182
Baines, H*	.500	10	5	0	2	0	0	.500	.500
Belle, Albert	.125	8	1	0	1	1	3	.200	.250
Blowers, Mike	.250	8	2	0	1	0	2	.250	.250
Boggs, Wade*	.333	18	6	1	2	1	1	.400	.389
Borders, Pat	.167	6	1	0	0	0	1	.167	.167
Bordick, Mike	.000	7	0	0	0	1	0	.000	.000
Buhner, Jay	.235	17	4	0	3	1	5	.278	.235
Burks, Ellis	.250	16	4	0	0	0	1	.250	.250
Butler, Brett*	.250	4	1	0	0	1	2	.400	.250
Canseco, Jose	.250	16	4	1	5	2	5	.333	.500
Carter, Joe	.111	27	3	0	0	1	7	.172	.111
Clark, Will*	.000	8	0	0	0	0	3	.000	.000
Cole, Alex*	.750	4	3	0	1	2	0	.833	.750
Cora, Joey#	.000	4	0	0	0	1	0	.333	.000
Curtis, Chad	.500	4	2	0	0	2	0	.667	.500
Davis, Chili#	.667	6	4	0	3	3	1	.700	.833
Dawson, Andre	.200	5	1	0	0	0	1	.200	.200
Deer, Rob	.444	9	4	0	0	0	2	.444	.444
Devereaux, M	.250	12	3	1	4	1	2	.308	.667
DiSarcina, G	.222	9	2	0	0	0	1	.222	.222
Eisenreich, J*	.000	5	0	0	0	2	0	.286	.000
Espinoza, A	.125	8	1	0	0	0	2	.125	.125
Fermin, Felix	.333	9	3	0	1	1	0	.400	.333
Franco, Julio	.259	27	7	0	6	2	6	.310	.296
Frye, Jeff	.200	5	1	0	1	0	1	.200	.400
Gaetti, Gary	.357	14	5	1	3	1	2	.400	.571
Gagne, Greg	.353	17	6	0	2	0	3	.353	.412
Gallego, Mike	.111	9	1	0	0	0	2	.200	.111
Gomez, Leo	.400	5	2	0	2	0	1	.400	.600
Gonzales, R	.143	7	1	0	0	0	1	.143	.143
Gonzalez, J	.357	14	5	3	10	0	3	.313	1.071
Greenwell, M*	.278	18	5	0	4	3	1	.381	.333
Griffey Jr, K*	.375	8	3	0	1	7	2	.667	.500
Guillen, O*	.278	18	5	0	3	4	1	.375	.333

Mike Henneman, Rangers — RHP

Batter	Avg	AB	H	HR	BI	BB	SO	OBP	Slg
Hale, Chip*	.667	3	2	0	1	1	0	.750	.667
Hall, Mel*	.263	19	5	1	2	0	3	.263	.474
Hamelin, Bob*	.000	5	0	0	0	0	2	.000	.000
Hamilton, D*	.125	8	1	0	0	0	2	.125	.250
Henderson, R	.231	13	3	0	0	2	1	.333	.231
Hoiles, Chris	.400	5	2	0	1	1	2	.500	.400
Howell, Jack*	.250	8	2	0	1	4	1	.500	.375
Huson, Jeff	.250	4	1	0	0	1	0	.400	.250
Incaviglia, P	.077	13	1	0	1	0	3	.071	.077
Jaha, John	.000	4	0	0	0	0	2	.200	.000
James, Dion*	.429	7	3	0	0	0	0	.429	.571
Javier, Stan#	.000	5	0	0	0	1	3	.167	.000
Jefferson, R*	.667	6	4	2	5	0	1	.667	1.833
Johnson, L*	.417	12	5	0	0	1	1	.462	.417
Joyner, Wally*	.400	15	6	0	2	1	0	.438	.467
Karkovice, R	.143	7	1	0	0	0	2	.143	.143
Kelly, Pat	.429	7	3	0	0	1	1	.429	.571
Kelly, R	.000	7	0	0	0	1	3	.125	.000
Knoblauch, C	.400	10	4	0	1	1	1	.455	.500
Lewis, Mark	.000	5	0	0	0	0	4	.000	.000
Leyritz, Jim	.333	6	2	0	0	2	2	.333	.333
Liriano, N#	.200	10	2	0	1	1	0	.273	.200
Lofton, Kenny*	.000	4	0	0	0	1	0	.200	.000
Macfarlane, M	.308	13	4	1	1	1	2	.357	.462
Martinez, E	.125	8	1	0	0	3	4	.364	.125
McGriff, Fred*	.000	17	0	0	1	1	4	.056	.000
McGwire, Mark	.308	13	4	1	1	4	4	.471	.538
McLemore, M#	.000	6	0	0	0	1	1	.143	.000
McRae, Brian*	.214	14	3	0	0	0	4	.214	.286
Molitor, Paul	.348	23	8	3	11	1	4	.346	.826
Myers, Greg*	.167	12	2	0	0	0	3	.167	.167
Newson, W*	.400	5	2	0	0	3	1	.625	.600
Nixon, Otis#	.200	5	1	0	0	0	2	.200	.200
O'Brien, C	.333	3	1	0	0	1	0	.600	.333
Olerud, John*	.308	13	4	0	1	3	1	.438	.308
Orsulak, Joe*	.300	10	3	0	2	1	2	.364	.300
Palmeiro, R*	.250	16	4	0	0	3	4	.368	.375
Palmer, Dean	.143	7	1	0	0	0	2	.143	.143
Pena, Tony	.100	10	1	0	0	0	0	.100	.100
Polonia, Luis*	.538	13	7	0	2	1	0	.571	.615
Raines, Tim#	.300	10	3	0	4	2	1	.417	.400
Reed, Jody	.412	17	7	0	3	2	3	.474	.529
Ripken, Billy	.125	8	1	0	0	0	0	.125	.125
Ripken, Cal	.318	22	7	0	4	2	3	.375	.409
Salmon, Tim	.000	6	0	0	0	1	3	.143	.000
Schofield, D	.357	14	5	0	3	1	2	.438	.429
Segui, David*	.500	4	2	0	1	1	1	.600	.500
Seitzer, K	.200	15	3	0	0	0	1	.250	.200
Sierra, Ruben*	.077	13	1	0	2	2	3	.188	.154
Slaught, Don	.083	12	1	0	1	3		.214	.083
Sojo, Luis	.000	6	0	0	0	0	0	.000	.000
Sorrento, P*	.000	7	0	0	0	0	0	.000	.000
Sosa, Sammy	.300	10	3	0	2	0	4	.300	.400
Spiers, Bill*	.125	8	1	0	0	1	2	.222	.250
Sprague, Ed	.000	6	0	0	0	0	2	.000	.000
Stanley, Mike	.111	9	1	0	1	0	2	.222	.222
Steinbach, T	.214	14	3	0	1	0	5	.200	.286
Stillwell, K#	.222	9	2	0	2	3	4	.385	.333
Strange, Doug*	.167	6	1	0	0	0	0	.167	.167
Surhoff, B.J.*	.313	16	5	0	3	1	1	.353	.563
Sveum, Dale*	.556	9	5	1	3	0	1	.500	.889
Tartabull, D	.167	18	3	1	3	4		.286	.333
Tettleton, M#	.300	10	3	0	0	1	6	.364	.300
Thomas, Frank	.313	16	5	1	2	3	1	.421	.625
Thome, Jim*	.000	5	0	0	0	0	1	.000	.000
Valentin, Jhn	.375	8	3	1	2	0	2	.375	.750
Valle, Dave	.429	7	3	1	5	1	1	.500	.857
Vaughn, Greg	.111	9	1	0	0	0	3	.111	.222
Vaughn, Mo*	.385	13	5	2	4	2	3	.467	.846
Velarde, R	.143	14	2	0	0	1	2	.200	.143
Ventura, R*	.400	10	4	0	3	1	0	.417	.400
Vizquel, Omar*	.167	6	1	0	0	1	0	.286	.167
Weiss, Walt*	.000	5	0	0	0	0	2	.000	.000
White, Devon#	.313	16	5	0	0	2	4	.389	.438
Whiten, Mark#	.333	6	2	1	2	0	0	.333	1.000
Williams, Ber#	.273	11	3	0	1	0	2	.273	.364
Worthington	.250	12	3	1	0	1	0	.250	.500

Doug Henry, Mets — RHP

Batter	Avg	AB	H	HR	BI	BB	SO	OBP	Slg
Alomar, R#	.286	7	2	0	0	1	1	.375	.286
Anderson, Brd*	.286	7	2	0	0	1	0	.375	.286
Baerga, C#	.000	5	0	0	0	0	0	.200	.000
Bagwell, Jeff	.000	5	0	0	0	0	2	.000	.000
Baines, H*	.200	4	0	0	0	1	2	.200	.200
Bates, Jason#	.286	7	2	0	1	1	1	.375	.429
Bell, Derek	.167	6	1	0	0	0	1	.167	.167
Belle, Albert	.167	6	1	1	1	0	2	.167	1.071
Bichette, D	.333	9	3	0	3	0	0	.333	.556
Blauser, Jeff	.200	5	1	0	0	1	0	.200	.400
Boggs, Wade*	.500	8	4	1	2	0	0	.500	.875

Doug Henry, Mets — RHP

Batter	Avg	AB	H	HR	BI	BB	SO	OBP	Slg
Borders, Pat	.300	10	3	1	2	0	4	.300	.600
Burks, Ellis	.182	11	2	0	1	0	3	.182	.182
Carreon, Mark	.250	4	1	0	0	1	1	.400	.500
Carter, Joe	.286	7	2	1	3	1	3	.375	.714
Castilla, V	.200	10	2	0	0	0	2	.200	.200
Davis, Chili#	.333	6	2	0	1	2	2	.500	.500
Deer, Rob	.333	6	2	1	1	0	1	.333	.833
DeShields, D*	.200	5	1	0	0	1	4	.333	.200
Devereaux, M	.000	9	0	0	0	1	2	.100	.000
Eisenreich, J*	.200	5	1	0	0	3	0	.500	.400
Fielder, C	.200	5	1	0	0	1	0	.333	.200
Finley, Steve*	.167	6	1	0	1	0	1	.167	.167
Franco, Julio	.000	6	0	0	1	0	1	.000	.000
Fryman, T	.500	8	4	0	7	0	2	.500	.750
Gaetti, Gary	.000	7	0	0	0	0	1	.000	.000
Gagne, Greg	.222	9	2	0	0	0	1	.222	.222
Galarraga, A	.167	6	1	0	0	1	1	.286	.167
Gallego, Mike	.286	7	2	0	1	0	0	.286	.286
Gant, Ron	.000	4	0	0	1	1	1	.200	.000
Gomez, Leo	.400	5	2	0	1	3	1	.625	.600
Gonzales, R	.500	4	2	0	0	2	0	.667	.750
Gonzalez, L*	.200	5	1	0	0	1	1	.333	.200
Grebeck, C	.500	6	3	1	3	0	1	.500	1.167
Greenwell, M*	.000	5	0	0	0	0	0	.000	.000
Gwynn, Tony*	.333	3	1	0	0	2	1	.600	.333
Hall, Mel*	.167	6	1	0	1	0	0	.167	.167
Hansen, Dave*	.200	5	1	0	0	0	1	.200	.200
Hayes, C	.250	4	1	0	0	1	0	.400	.500
Henderson, R	.400	5	2	0	1	0	2	.400	.800
Hernandez, Jo	.600	5	3	0	2	0	0	.600	1.200
Hill, G	.000	7	0	0	0	0	3	.000	.000
Hoiles, Chris	.286	7	2	0	1	2	2	.444	.429
Howard, T*	.111	9	1	0	1	0	2	.111	.111
Jefferies, G#	.400	5	2	0	1	0	0	.400	.600
Johnson, L*	.200	5	1	0	1	1	0	.333	.200
Johnson, Mark*	.000	3	0	0	0	1	0	.400	.000
Jones, C#	.200	5	1	0	1	0	2	.167	.200
Joyner, Wally*	.000	5	0	0	0	0	2	.000	.000
Karros, Eric	.000	6	0	0	0	1	1	.143	.000
Kelly, Pat	.300	3	0	0	0	2	2	.400	.000
Kelly, R	.143	7	1	0	2	0	1	.143	.143
Kingery, Mike*	.167	6	1	0	0	0	0	.167	.167
Kirby, Wayne*	.250	4	1	0	0	1	0	.400	.250
Knoblauch, C	.000	5	0	0	0	1	1	.000	.000
Lansing, Mike	.400	5	2	1	3	0	0	.400	1.000
Liriano, N#	.250	4	1	1	2	0	1	.200	1.000
Livingstone*	.167	6	1	0	1	2	1	.375	.167
Lofton, Kenny*	.200	5	1	0	0	0	1	.200	.200
Mabry, John*	.000	5	0	0	0	0	0	.000	.000
Martin, Al*	.400	5	2	0	1	0	0	.400	.400
Martinez, E	.333	3	1	0	0	2	0	.600	.333
McLemore, M#	.500	4	2	0	2	1	1	.600	.750
McRae, Brian#	.286	7	2	1	1	0	1	.286	.714
Mondesi, Raul	.400	5	2	1	3	0	0	.500	1.000
Morandini, M*	.000	6	0	0	0	1	0	.000	.000
Olerud, John*	.286	7	2	0	1	2	3	.444	.286
Orsulak, Joe*	.400	5	2	0	0	1	1	.500	.600
Palmeiro, R*	.000	5	0	0	0	3	1	.375	.000
Palmer, Dean	.200	5	1	0	0	1	2	.333	.400
Pendleton, T#	.167	6	1	0	1	0	0	.167	.167
Phillips, T*	.571	7	4	1	3	0	2	.571	1.286
Piazza, Mike	.500	6	3	0	0	1	2	.571	.500
Polonia, Luis*	.000	5	0	0	0	0	0	.333	.000
Reed, Jeff*	.200	5	1	0	0	1	1	.333	.200
Reed, Jody	.400	10	4	0	0	0	2	.400	.400
Ripken, Cal	.000	5	0	0	0	0	0	.167	.000
Rodriguez, I	.250	4	1	0	0	1	1	.400	.250
Salmon, Tim	.250	4	1	0	1	1	0	.333	.500
Sierra, Ruben#	.333	6	2	1	2	0	1	.333	.833
Snow, J.T.#	.750	4	3	1	2	1	0	.800	1.500
Steinbach, T	.000	6	0	0	0	1	0	.143	.000
Tartabull, D	.500	6	3	0	2	1	0	.571	1.000
Tettleton, M#	.429	7	3	2	4	3	1	.600	1.429
Thomas, Frank	.200	5	1	0	1	2	1	.429	.200
Trammell, A	.200	5	1	0	0	0	1	.200	.200
Vaughn, Mo*	.333	3	1	1	2	3	1	.667	1.333
Velarde, R	.000	5	0	0	0	1	2	.167	.000
Ventura, R*	.500	4	2	1	3	1	1	.600	1.500
Vizquel, Omar#	.400	5	2	0	0	0	2	.400	.600
Walker, Larry*	.333	3	1	0	0	2	1	.600	.667
Weiss, Walt*	.600	5	3	0	0	1	0	.667	.600
White, Devon#	.333	6	2	0	0	1	2	.429	.667
White, R	.667	3	2	0	1	1	0	.600	1.000
Williams, Ber#	.200	5	1	0	0	0	2	.200	.200
Young, Eric	.667	6	4	0	3	0	1	.667	.667

Pat Hentgen, Blue Jays — RHP

Batter	Avg	AB	H	HR	BI	BB	SO	OBP	Slg
Aldrete, Mike*	.200	10	2	0	0	0	3	.200	.200
Alexander, M	.286	7	2	0	0	0	0	.286	.286
Alomar, R#	.250	8	2	0	0	0	0	.250	.375
Alomar Jr, S	.000	11	0	0	0	2	1	.154	.000
Anderson, Brd*	.407	27	11	2	4	8	6	.543	.741
Anderson, G*	.357	14	5	0	1	0	2	.357	.429
Arias, George	.200	5	1	0	0	1	2	.333	.200
Ausmus, Brad	.000	4	0	0	0	2	0	.333	.000
Baerga, C#	.318	22	7	0	1	0	0	.348	.455
Baines, H*	.227	22	5	1	1	0	4	.346	.364
Bautista, D	.375	8	3	0	2	0	2	.375	.625
Becker, Rich*	.231	13	3	0	0	3	1	.375	.385
Belle, Albert	.190	21	4	0	1	3	3	.292	.238
Berroa, G	.176	17	3	0	1	1	1	.222	.235
Blowers, Mike	.400	5	2	0	2	1	0	.500	.400
Boggs, Wade*	.441	34	15	2	4	4	4	.487	.706
Bonilla, B#	.375	16	6	1	3	2	1	.444	.625
Bordick, Mike	.222	27	6	0	3	5	2	.344	.296
Bragg, Darren*	.154	13	2	0	1	0	3	.154	.154
Brosius, S	.250	20	5	0	1	0	4	.250	.250
Buhner, Jay	.154	13	2	1	4	6	7	.381	.385
Burks, Ellis	.000	7	0	0	1	0	1	.000	.000
Canseco, Jose	.400	15	6	0	4	3	4	.500	.400
Carreon, Mark	.200	5	1	0	1	0	1	.200	.400
Cedeno, A	.167	6	1	0	0	0	0	.167	.167
Cirillo, Jeff	.300	10	3	0	0	1	2	.364	.400
Clark, Tony#	.273	11	3	1	3	1	3	.308	.455
Clark, Will*	.385	13	5	0	0	0	2	.385	.462
Cole, Alex*	.091	11	1	0	0	1	2	.167	.091
Coleman, V#	.167	12	2	0	0	0	7	.167	.250
Cora, Joey*	.385	26	10	1	2	1	0	.407	.577
Cordero, Wil	.333	6	2	0	0	0	0	.333	.333
Cordova, M	.278	18	5	1	4	0	5	.263	.444
Curtis, Chad	.167	36	6	0	1	4	4	.268	.194
Cuyler, Milt*	.231	13	3	0	2	0	1	.231	.385
Damon, Johnny*	.286	14	4	1	3	1	0	.375	.571
Davis, Chili#	.310	29	9	3	7	5	6	.400	.655
Dawson, Andre	.222	9	2	0	0	0	1	.222	.333
Deer, Rob	.375	8	3	1	1	0	5	.375	.875
Devereaux, M	.357	14	5	0	0	3	3	.471	.500
Diaz, Alex#	.133	15	2	0	0	0	0	.133	.133
DiSarcina, G	.333	21	7	0	4	5	1	.462	.476
Duncan, M	.455	11	5	0	0	0	3	.455	.636
Durham, Ray#	.357	14	5	1	4	1	2	.400	.643
Easley, D	.300	10	3	0	1	0	0	.300	.400
Edmonds, Jim*	.267	15	4	1	1	0	3	.267	.467
Espinoza, A	.167	6	1	1	1	0	1	.167	.667
Fabregas, Jor*	.167	6	1	0	0	0	0	.167	.167
Fermin, Felix	.167	6	1	0	1	0	0	.167	.167
Fielder, C	.350	40	14	7	14	3	7	.395	.925
Flaherty, J	.200	5	1	1	1	1	1	.333	.800
Franco, Julio	.182	11	2	0	1	3	2	.357	.182
Frye, Jeff	.167	12	2	0	0	1	2	.231	.167
Fryman, T	.225	40	9	1	4	2	6	.262	.350
Gaetti, Gary	.333	18	6	0	1	2	1	.400	.500
Gagne, Greg	.158	19	3	1	1	2	0	.238	.316
Gallego, Mike	.067	15	1	0	0	1	2	.125	.067
Gates, Brent*	.222	18	4	0	5	1	3	.263	.278
Giambi, Jason*	.250	16	4	0	1	1	2	.294	.375
Girardi, Joe	.125	8	1	0	0	1	2	.222	.125
Gomez, Chris	.278	18	5	2	2	1	5	.316	.667
Gomez, Leo	.133	15	2	0	0	0	4	.133	.133
Gonzalez, J	.211	19	4	0	1	3	5	.348	.211
Goodwin, C*	.333	9	3	0	0	1	0	.400	.444
Goodwin, Tom*	.353	17	6	0	1	4	8	.389	.353
Grebeck, C	.400	10	4	0	1	0	2	.400	.500
Greenwell, M*	.310	29	9	3	8	2	0	.355	.655
Greer, Rusty*	.333	6	2	2	2	0	0	.333	1.333
Griffey Jr, K*	.071	14	1	0	1	2	1	.176	.071
Guillen, O*	.263	19	5	0	3	0	5	.263	.316
Gwynn, Chris*	.500	6	3	0	1	0	0	.500	.500
Hale, Chip*	.200	10	2	0	1	1	0	.200	.300
Hamelin, Bob*	.273	11	3	0	1	3	4	.429	.273
Hamilton, D*	.286	28	8	0	2	0	5	.286	.393
Hammonds, J	.111	9	1	0	1	0	2	.111	.111
Hayes, C	.333	6	2	0	1	0	1	.333	.333
Henderson, R	.278	18	5	1	2	1	3	.316	.500
Herrera, Jose*	.000	9	0	0	0	0	3	.000	.000
Higginson, B*	.182	22	4	0	2	4	5	.308	.227
Hoiles, Chris	.067	15	1	0	0	4	2	.263	.067
Hollins, Dave#	.000	10	0	0	0	2	1	.167	.000
Howard, Dave*	.214	14	3	0	0	1	4	.267	.214
Howard, T*	.600	5	3	0	1	0	0	.600	.600
Hudler, Rex	.500	10	5	0	3	0	0	.500	.500
Hulse, David*	.389	18	7	0	2	2	2	.450	.500
Huson, Jeff*	.500	4	2	0	1	1	0	.600	1.000
Jaha, John	.393	28	11	2	2	5	7	.485	.643
James, Dion*	.333	20	7	0	3	2	1	.409	.400
Javier, Stan#	.278	18	5	0	1	1	3	.316	.278
Jefferson, R*	.400	15	6	2	2	0	2	.438	.533
Jeter, Derek	.200	10	2	1	2	0	4	.200	.500
Johnson, L*	.300	20	6	1	3	2	0	.417	.650
Joyner, Wally*	.200	15	3	0	1	3	3	.333	.200
Karkovice, R	.143	14	2	0	1	1	4	.200	.143

Pat Hentgen, Blue Jays — RHP

Batter	Avg	AB	H	HR	BI	BB	SO	OBP	Slg
Kelly, Pat	.263	19	5	0	4	1	5	.286	.263
Kelly, R	.250	8	2	0	1	0	1	.250	.375
Knoblauch, C	.179	28	5	0	1	2	6	.233	.214
Kreuter, Chad#	.300	10	3	0	1	1	3	.364	.400
Lewis, Mark	.000	10	0	0	0	0	4	.000	.000
Leyritz, Jim	.353	17	6	0	3	3	4	.450	.412
Listach, Pat#	.261	23	6	0	0	2	7	.320	.304
Livingstone*	.143	7	1	0	0	0	1	.143	.143
Lockhart, K*	.200	15	3	0	0	0	1	.200	.200
Lofton, Kenny*	.208	24	5	0	0	2	2	.269	.292
Lovullo, T#	.091	11	1	0	1	0	0	.091	.091
Macfarlane, M	.320	25	8	3	7	0	6	.333	.720
Martinez, Da*	.417	12	5	0	0	0	1	.417	.583
Martinez, E	.222	9	2	0	4	5	3	.500	.444
Martinez, T*	.111	18	2	1	3	4	5	.273	.278
Matheny, Mike	.286	14	4	0	3	1	2	.333	.357
Mayne, Brent*	.182	11	2	0	0	1	2	.250	.182
McCarty, Dave	.333	9	3	0	1	2	0	.455	.556
McGwire, Mark	.200	10	2	1	3	3	5	.385	.300
McLemore, M#	.500	16	8	0	3	0	1	.500	.500
McRae, Brian#	.238	21	5	0	0	1	5	.273	.286
Meares, Pat	.000	14	0	0	0	0	6	.000	.000
Mieske, Matt	.286	14	4	0	1	0	2	.286	.429
Molitor, Paul	.357	14	5	0	2	2	0	.412	.571
Munoz, Pedro	.133	15	2	0	0	1	3	.188	.200
Murray, Eddie#	.083	12	1	0	0	0	1	.083	.083
Myers, Greg*	.200	25	5	1	3	3	6	.286	.360
Naehring, Tim	.333	12	4	0	3	4	2	.500	.500
Nevin, Phil	.143	7	1	0	0	0	3	.143	.143
Newson, W*	.250	8	2	0	1	0	6	.250	.500
Nieves, M*	.000	9	0	0	0	0	6	.000	.000
Nilsson, Dave*	.217	23	5	1	5	0	6	.217	.348
Nixon, Otis	.333	6	2	0	2	2	0	.500	.333
Nunnally, Jon*	.300	10	3	1	4	1	5	.364	.700
O'Leary, Troy*	.211	19	4	0	1	5	2	.375	.211
O'Neill, Paul*	.300	30	9	0	5	5	2	.432	.433
Offerman, J#	.000	9	0	0	0	1	2	.100	.000
Palmeiro, R*	.156	32	5	0	1	4	4	.250	.156
Palmer, Dean	.263	19	5	2	5	2	3	.333	.579
Paquette, J	.167	6	1	0	0	0	3	.167	.167
Peltier, Dan*	.400	5	2	0	0	0	0	.400	.600
Pena, Tony	.000	12	0	0	0	1	4	.077	.000
Perez, E	.333	9	3	0	0	1	1	.400	.333
Phillips, T#	.360	25	9	4	11	3	3	.429	.920
Plantier, P*	.286	7	2	1	1	1	1	.375	.714
Polonia, Luis*	.364	33	12	0	1	2	4	.400	.424
Pride, Curtis*	.400	5	2	0	0	0	2	.400	.400
Raines, Tim#	.200	25	5	0	1	0	3	.200	.240
Ramirez, M	.250	12	3	2	3	2	2	.357	.750
Reboulet, J	.167	6	1	0	0	1	0	.286	.167
Reed, Jody	.182	11	2	0	1	1	0	.250	.182
Ripken, Billy	.333	6	2	1	1	0	1	.333	1.000
Ripken, Cal	.306	36	11	2	8	1	4	.324	.500
Rivera, Ruben	.000	6	0	0	1	0	1	.000	.000
Roberts, Bip#	.286	7	2	0	1	0	1	.286	.286
Rodriguez, Al*	.000	5	1	0	0	1	1	.333	.400
Rodriguez, I	.143	14	2	1	2	1	1	.200	.357
Rodriguez, T	.500	6	3	1	3	0	1	.500	1.000
Sabo, Chris	.333	6	2	1	1	0	1	.429	1.000
Salmon, Tim	.200	30	6	1	2	3	10	.273	.433
Segui, David#	.333	6	2	0	0	0	2	.333	.333
Seitzer, K	.333	33	11	0	3	3	1	.405	.394
Sierra, Ruben*	.158	19	3	1	6	3	9	.273	.368
Slaught, Don	.429	7	3	1	2	0	1	.429	.857
Snow, J.T.#	.320	25	8	0	6	3	4	.393	.440
Sojo, Luis	.500	8	4	0	1	0	0	.500	.500
Sorrento, P*	.313	16	5	2	2	7	3	.522	.750
Spiers, Bill*	.000	8	0	0	0	1	3	.111	.000
Stahoviak, S*	.150	20	3	0	0	1	5	.190	.200
Stanley, Mike	.167	30	5	1	1	4	8	.265	.333
Steinbach, T	.333	21	7	0	1	3	7	.417	.476
Strange, Doug#	.467	15	7	0	5	1	1	.500	.467
Surhoff, B.J.*	.241	29	7	0	1	2	2	.313	.241
Tartabull, D	.208	24	5	2	5	2	8	.269	.500
Tettleton, M#	.231	13	3	1	4	6	3	.450	.538
Thomas, Frank	.273	22	6	1	2	5	2	.407	.409
Thome, Jim*	.250	16	4	0	1	3	5	.368	.313
Tinsley, Lee#	.200	5	1	0	0	1	1	.333	.200
Trammell, A	.375	8	3	1	1	3	0	.545	.875
Tucker, M*	.400	10	4	1	4	4	3	.571	.800
Turner, Chris	.500	6	3	1	4	0	0	.500	1.000
Valentin, John	.217	23	5	2	4	3	5	.308	.522
Valentin, Jse#	.333	18	6	0	3	5	2	.478	.444
Valle, Dave	.222	9	2	0	0	0	0	.222	.222
Vaughn, Greg	.235	34	8	3	4	3	11	.316	.500
Vaughn, Mo*	.333	39	13	4	9	1	10	.366	.692
Velarde, R	.118	17	2	0	2	6	11	.348	.118
Ventura, R*	.304	23	7	1	9	3	2	.370	.609
Vina, F*	.182	11	2	0	0	1	1	.250	.273
Vizquel, Omar*	.421	19	8	2	3	2	0	.476	.895
Ward, Turner#	.125	8	1	0	0	0	1	.125	.125
Williams, Ber#	.286	35	10	0	1	3	5	.342	.343
Wilson, Dan	.250	8	2	0	0	3	1	.455	.250
Young, Ernie	.133	15	2	0	0	0	3	.133	.200
Zaun, Greg#	.000	4	0	0	0	2	0	.333	.000
Zeile, Todd	.000	6	0	0	0	1	1	.143	.000

Pat Hentgen, Blue Jays RHP

Gil Heredia, Rangers — RHP

Batter	Avg	AB	H	HR	BI	BB	SO	OBP	Slg
Abbott, Kurt	.833	6	5	0	0	0	1	.833	1.000
Alicea, Luis*	.333	9	3	0	0	2	2	.455	.333
Anthony, Eric*	.200	5	1	0	1	1	2	.333	.400
Ashley, Billy	.400	5	2	0	2	0	1	.400	.400
Bagwell, Jeff	.333	12	4	1	1	2	2	.429	.583
Bell, Jay	.125	8	1	0	0	1	2	.222	.250
Belliard, R	.000	4	0	0	0	0	1	.200	.000
Bichette, D	.800	5	4	0	1	0	0	.800	.800
Biggio, Craig	.222	18	4	1	3	2	1	.300	.389
Blauser, Jeff	.333	9	3	1	2	0	2	.333	.667
Bonds, Barry*	.385	13	5	2	3	6	2	.600	.846
Bonilla, B#	.143	7	1	0	0	0	5	.143	.143
Bordick, Mike	.400	5	2	0	2	0	1	.400	.400
Branson, Jeff*	.111	9	1	0	1	0	1	.111	.111
Brosius, S	.600	5	3	0	1	0	1	.600	1.000
Butler, Brett*	.571	7	4	0	0	1	1	.625	.571
Caminiti, Ken#	.357	14	5	1	4	1	1	.400	.643
Cangelosi, J#	.600	5	3	0	0	0	0	.600	.600
Carr, Chuck	.273	11	3	0	1	2	1	.385	.273
Carreon, Mark	.375	8	3	1	3	0	0	.375	.750
Carter, Joe	.000	5	0	0	1	0	1	.000	.000
Cedeno, A	.364	11	4	1	3	2	2	.429	.636
Clark, Dave*	.111	9	1	0	1	0	4	.111	.111
Clayton, R	.231	13	3	0	1	2	2	.333	.308
Colbrunn, G	.500	4	2	0	2	0	0	.600	.500
Conine, Jeff	.100	10	1	0	3	0	3	.100	.200
Cummings, M*	.333	6	2	0	1	0	0	.333	.500
Daulton, D*	.667	9	6	2	9	1	2	.700	1.444
DeShields, D*	.300	10	3	0	1	0	4	.300	.300
Duncan, M	.100	10	1	0	0	1	0	.100	.100
Durham, Ray#	.400	5	2	0	0	0	0	.400	.600
Dykstra, L*	.167	6	1	0	0	1	1	.286	.333
Eisenreich, J*	.500	8	4	0	1	0	1	.500	.625
Eusebio, Tony	.000	6	0	0	0	0	3	.000	.000
Finley, Steve*	.214	14	3	0	0	1	2	.267	.214
Galarraga, A	.167	6	1	0	1	0	2	.167	.167
Gant, Ron	.500	8	4	2	3	4	2	.615	1.250
Gilkey, B	.182	11	2	0	0	0	3	.182	.182
Girardi, Joe	.444	9	4	0	1	0	2	.444	.444
Gonzalez, L*	.385	13	5	0	4	1	3	.429	.538
Grace, Mark*	.400	5	2	0	1	2	0	.571	.400
Gwynn, Tony*	.375	8	3	0	1	0	0	.375	.375
Hayes, C	.444	9	4	0	0	0	1	.444	.444
Hill, G	.500	10	5	0	1	0	0	.545	.600
Hollins, Dave#	.200	5	1	0	1	1	1	.333	.200
Howard, T*	.375	8	3	0	1	0	0	.375	.375
Hundley, Todd#	.200	5	1	0	0	0	0	.167	.200
Jefferies, G#	.143	7	1	0	0	0	0	.143	.143
Jeter, Derek	.250	4	1	0	2	1	1	.400	.250
Justice, Dave*	.222	9	2	0	1	2	3	.300	.222
Karkovice, R	.200	5	1	0	1	0	2	.200	.400
Karros, Eric	.444	9	4	0	1	1	1	.500	.556
Kelly, R	.400	10	4	0	2	0	2	.400	.400
Kent, Jeff	.000	5	0	0	0	1	3	.167	.000
King, Jeff	.455	11	5	0	0	2	1	.538	.455
Lankford, Ray*	.250	12	3	1	1	0	1	.250	.500
Larkin, Barry	.357	14	5	0	1	1	1	.400	.429
Lemke, Mark*	.100	10	1	0	0	0	4	.100	.100
Lewis, Darren	.308	13	4	0	1	0	0	.357	.385
Lofton, Kenny*	.429	7	3	0	0	0	0	.429	.429
Magadan, Dave*	.333	6	2	0	0	1	1	.333	.333
Manwaring, K	.231	13	3	0	2	0	3	.231	.231
Martin, Al*	.167	6	1	0	1	1	3	.286	.500
Martinez, Da*	.364	11	4	0	1	0	2	.364	.364
May, Derrick*	.000	4	0	0	0	1	0	.000	.000
McGriff, Fred*	.300	10	3	1	8	0	2	.300	.700
Merced, O*	.125	8	1	0	0	1	1	.222	.125
Miller, Orl	.400	5	2	0	1	0	1	.400	.400
Mondesi, Raul	.500	10	5	0	0	0	2	.500	.800
Morandini, M*	.333	9	3	0	0	0	1	.333	.556
Morris, Hal*	.278	18	5	0	2	0	0	.278	.333
Mouton, James	.286	7	2	0	1	0	1	.286	.429
Nixon, Otis#	.250	4	1	0	0	0	1	.400	.250
O'Brien, C	.000	4	0	0	1	0	2	.000	.000
O'Neill, Paul*	.182	11	2	0	0	1	1	.250	.273
Offerman, J#	.182	11	2	0	2	0	2	.182	.273
Oliver, Joe	.222	9	2	0	0	0	0	.222	.222
Orsulak, Joe*	.400	5	2	0	1	0	0	.333	.400
Pagnozzi, Tom	.125	8	1	0	0	0	2	.125	.250
Pendleton, T#	.200	15	3	1	1	0	0	.200	.467
Piazza, Mike	.500	8	4	1	3	0	0	.500	.875
Roberts, Bip#	.563	16	9	0	3	0	1	.563	.750
Sabo, Chris	.571	7	4	2	2	0	1	.571	1.571

Gil Heredia, Rangers — RHP

Batter	Avg	AB	H	HR	BI	BB	SO	OBP	Slg
Sanders, R	.250	12	3	0	0	1	4	.308	.250
Santiago, B	.333	6	2	0	2	0	0	.333	.500
Scarsone, S	.143	7	1	1	2	0	2	.143	.571
Servais, S	.400	5	2	0	2	0	1	.400	.400
Sheffield, G	.250	4	1	0	1	4	1	.667	.250
Shipley, C	.200	5	1	0	0	0	0	.200	.200
Slaught, Don	.333	6	2	0	1	0	2	.333	.333
Smith, Ozzie#	.364	11	4	0	0	0	1	.364	.455
Sosa, Sammy	.400	5	2	0	0	0	0	.400	.400
Sprague, Ed	.500	6	3	1	3	0	1	.500	1.000
Stocker, K#	.250	8	2	0	0	2	0	.400	.250
Tartabull, D	.000	5	0	0	0	0	3	.000	.000
Thompson, Rob	.000	6	0	0	1	0	0	.000	.000
Thompson, Ry	.000	5	0	0	0	0	4	.000	.000
Vizcaino, J#	.300	10	3	0	0	0	0	.300	.300
Wallach, Tim	.100	10	1	0	0	0	2	.100	.100
Whiten, Mark#	.182	11	2	0	0	0	3	.182	.182
Wilkins, Rick*	.143	7	1	0	0	0	1	.143	.143
Williams, Ma	.455	11	5	1	4	1	2	.500	.727
Wilson, Dan	.200	5	1	1	1	0	1	.200	.800
Young, Ernie	.000	4	0	0	0	1	0	.200	.000
Zeile, Todd	.200	10	2	0	0	1	1	.273	.300

Dustin Hermanson, Padres — RHP

Batter	Avg	AB	H	HR	BI	BB	SO	OBP	Slg
Jordan, Brian	.200	5	1	0	0	0	0	.200	.400

Roberto Hernandez, White Sox — RHP

Batter	Avg	AB	H	HR	BI	BB	SO	OBP	Slg
Aldrete, Mike*	.000	7	0	0	0	3	0	.000	.000
Alomar, R#	.400	10	4	1	2	2	2	.500	.800
Alomar Jr, S	.167	6	1	0	0	0	2	.167	.167
Anderson, Brd*	.300	10	3	0	1	3	4	.462	.300
Anderson, G*	.000	3	0	0	1	1	0	.400	.000
Baerga, C#	.200	5	1	0	0	1	0	.429	.200
Baines, H*	.500	4	2	0	2	2	0	.667	.500
Belle, Albert	.364	11	4	0	3	0	2	.364	.364
Berroa, G	.222	9	2	1	2	0	1	.222	.556
Boggs, Wade*	.400	5	2	0	1	0	2	.400	.600
Borders, Pat	.000	5	0	0	0	0	0	.000	.000
Bordick, Mike	.333	12	4	0	1	1	0	.385	.333
Bragg, Darren*	.250	4	1	0	1	1	2	.400	.250
Brosius, S	.222	9	2	0	1	0	4	.300	.444
Buhner, Jay	.364	11	4	0	1	1	3	.417	.636
Canseco, Jose	.000	5	0	0	0	1	0	.000	.000
Carter, Joe	.000	11	0	0	0	1	0	.000	.000
Cirillo, Jeff	.500	6	3	0	1	2	0	.625	.500
Coleman, V#	.200	5	1	0	0	0	3	.200	.600
Cora, Joey#	.429	7	3	0	1	0	0	.429	.429
Cordova, M	.200	5	1	0	0	0	0	.200	.200
Curtis, Chad	.300	10	3	0	1	0	2	.300	.300
Cuyler, Milt#	.000	5	0	0	0	1	0	.000	.000
Davis, Chili#	.333	9	3	1	4	1	2	.400	.667
Deer, Rob	.000	6	0	0	0	1	0	.000	.000
Devereaux, M	.429	7	3	0	1	0	0	.429	.429
Diaz, Alex#	.286	7	2	0	1	1	2	.375	.286
DiSarcina, G	.222	9	2	0	1	1	0	.300	.222
Easley, D	.000	4	0	0	0	1	1	.200	.000
Edmonds, Jim*	.000	4	0	0	1	1	0	.200	.000
Fielder, C	.200	10	2	0	1	4	2	.467	.200
Franco, Julio	.125	8	1	0	1	0	1	.125	.125
Frye, Jeff	.200	5	1	0	2	0	1	.200	.200
Fryman, T	.231	13	3	1	3	1	6	.286	.462
Gaetti, Gary	.111	9	1	1	1	0	1	.111	.444
Gagne, Greg	.200	5	1	0	0	1	1	.333	.200
Gates, Brent#	.250	8	2	0	3	1	3	.300	.250
Gonzalez, J	.300	10	3	2	5	1	2	.364	.900
Goodwin, Tom*	.200	5	1	0	0	0	0	.200	.200
Green, Shawn*	.333	6	2	1	2	0	2	.333	.833
Greenwell, M*	.600	5	3	0	1	0	0	.600	.600
Greer, Rusty*	.500	5	0	0	1	5	0	.167	.167
Griffey Jr, K*	.571	7	4	0	2	1	2	.625	.571
Hale, Chip*	.100	10	1	0	1	0	4	.100	.100
Hamilton, D*	.444	9	4	0	3	0	1	.444	.556
Henderson, R	1.000	5	5	0	4	1	0	1.000	1.800
Hoiles, Chris	.100	10	1	0	0	0	4	.100	.100
Howard, Dave#	.000	7	0	0	2	1	5	.125	.000
Hulse, David*	.500	6	3	0	1	0	2	.500	.500
Jaha, John	.100	10	1	0	0	1	3	.182	.100
Javier, Stan#	.200	5	1	0	1	1	2	.333	.200
Jefferson, R*	.333	6	2	0	1	1	2	.429	.333
Joyner, Wally*	.429	7	3	0	1	0	0	.429	.429
Kelly, R	.000	6	0	0	0	0	1	.000	.000
Kirby, Wayne*	.000	5	0	0	1	2	0	.167	.000
Knoblauch, C	.250	8	2	0	2	2	1	.400	.625
Lewis, Mark	.400	5	2	0	1	0	1	.400	.600
Livingstone*	.333	6	2	0	1	0	0	.333	.333
Lofton, Kenny*	.000	10	0	0	0	3	0	.000	.000
Macfarlane, M	.400	5	2	0	0	0	1	.400	.600
Martinez, E	.200	10	2	0	2	2	0	.333	.300
Martinez, T*	.333	9	3	0	0	1	2	.400	.333

Roberto Hernandez, White Sox — RHP

Batter	Avg	AB	H	HR	BI	BB	SO	OBP	Slg
Mayne, Brent*	.111	9	1	0	0	0	1	.111	.111
McGwire, Mark	.500	4	2	1	3	1	0	.600	1.250
McLemore, M#	.143	7	1	0	0	1	5	.250	.286
McRae, Brian#	.000	7	0	0	0	1	2	.125	.000
Molitor, Paul	.375	8	3	0	3	0	0	.375	.375
Munoz, Pedro	.143	7	1	0	0	0	2	.143	.143
Murray, Eddie#	.333	6	2	0	1	0	2	.286	.333
Naehring, Tim	.200	5	1	0	0	0	2	.200	.200
Nilsson, Dave*	.167	6	1	0	0	0	3	.167	.167
Nixon, Otis#	.000	2	0	0	0	3	1	.600	.000
O'Leary, Troy*	.400	5	2	0	1	0	2	.400	.400
Offerman, J#	.286	7	2	0	3	0	3	.286	.571
Olerud, John*	.000	6	0	0	3	0	2	.333	.000
Palmeiro, R*	.143	7	1	0	0	0	0	.143	.143
Palmer, Dean	.143	7	1	1	1	1	4	.250	.571
Phillips, T#	.000	6	0	0	0	1	4	.143	.000
Polonia, Luis*	.000	8	0	0	1	1	5	.111	.111
Ramirez, M	.286	7	2	1	2	1	3	.375	.714
Reed, Jody	.333	3	1	0	0	2	0	.600	.333
Ripken, Cal	.000	6	0	0	0	1	1	.143	.000
Rodriguez, I	.375	8	3	0	1	2	3	.500	.375
Salmon, Tim	.333	9	3	1	2	2	3	.455	.667
Schofield, D	.400	5	2	0	1	0	0	.400	.400
Seitzer, K	.250	8	2	0	0	0	3	.250	.250
Sierra, Ruben#	.417	12	5	2	7	2	1	.500	1.000
Snow, J.T.#	.286	7	2	0	1	0	2	.286	.286
Sorrento, P*	.125	16	2	0	2	0	5	.125	.125
Sprague, Ed	.250	12	3	0	1	0	5	.250	.417
Stanley, Mike	.000	7	0	0	0	0	4	.000	.000
Steinbach, T	.364	11	4	0	1	1	3	.417	.455
Strange, Doug#	.333	9	3	0	0	1	2	.400	.333
Surhoff, B.J.*	.167	6	1	0	0	2	2	.375	.167
Tartabull, D	.000	8	0	0	1	0	0	.000	.000
Tettleton, M#	.308	13	4	0	1	1	5	.357	.308
Thome, Jim*	.400	5	2	0	0	1	1	.500	.400
Trammell, A	.250	8	2	0	0	1	1	.250	.250
Valentin, Jhn	.300	10	3	1	2	0	0	.300	.600
Valentin, Jse#	.000	5	0	0	1	0	4	.167	.000
Vaughn, Greg	.222	9	2	1	3	0	3	.222	.667
Vaughn, Mo*	.000	12	0	0	0	0	8	.000	.000
Velarde, R	.000	3	0	0	0	4	1	.571	.000
Vina, F*	.250	4	1	0	0	2	0	.500	.250
Vizquel, Omar#	.250	4	1	0	0	1	0	.400	.250
Ward, Turner#	.000	6	0	0	0	0	1	.000	.000
White, Devon#	.000	4	0	0	0	2	3	.333	.000
Williams, Ber#	.182	11	2	0	1	0	3	.182	.273
Wilson, Dan	.400	5	2	0	0	0	0	.400	.800

Xavier Hernandez, Astros — RHP

Batter	Avg	AB	H	HR	BI	BB	SO	OBP	Slg
Abbott, Kurt	.286	7	2	0	0	1	2	.375	.286
Alfonzo, E	.800	5	4	0	1	0	0	.800	1.200
Alicea, Luis#	.375	8	3	0	0	0	4	.375	.375
Alomar, R#	.200	5	1	0	0	0	0	.200	.200
Alou, Moises	.429	7	3	0	1	0	1	.429	.429
Andrews, S	.200	5	1	0	0	1	3	.333	.200
Bagwell, Jeff	.000	3	0	0	0	1	2	.400	.000
Barberie, B#	.200	5	1	0	0	4	1	.556	.400
Bell, Derek	.167	6	1	0	0	1	3	.286	.167
Bell, Jay	.143	21	3	0	1	0	8	.143	.143
Belliard, R	.333	6	2	0	1	0	0	.333	.333
Benjamin, M	.167	6	1	0	0	0	2	.167	.333
Bichette, D	.600	10	6	0	5	0	3	.600	.900
Biggio, Craig	.000	4	0	0	0	0	0	.200	.000
Blauser, Jeff	.444	18	8	0	5	1	4	.474	.556
Bogar, Tim	.000	5	0	0	0	0	0	.000	.000
Bonds, Barry*	.714	7	5	3	6	2	0	.778	2.000
Bonilla, B#	.200	5	1	0	0	1	1	.333	.200
Burks, Ellis	.143	7	1	0	3	1	1	.222	.143
Butler, Brett*	.182	11	2	0	0	5	1	.438	.273
Carr, Chuck	.167	6	1	0	0	0	1	.167	.167
Carreon, Mark	.200	5	1	0	1	0	4	.167	.200
Carter, Joe	.200	5	1	0	1	0	0	.200	.400
Castilla, V	.375	8	3	0	1	0	0	.375	.375
Cianfrocco, A	.167	6	1	0	0	0	2	.167	.167
Clark, Dave*	.500	6	3	0	2	0	2	.500	.833
Clark, Will*	.385	13	5	1	3	3	0	.500	.615
Clayton, R	.273	11	3	0	0	0	0	.273	.273
Colbrunn, G	.143	7	1	0	1	1	4	.222	.143
Coleman, V#	.250	4	1	0	0	0	2	.250	.250
Conine, Jeff	.273	11	3	1	2	2	2	.385	.636
Cordero, Wil	.200	5	1	0	0	0	2	.200	.400
Daulton, D*	.333	6	2	0	1	4	0	.600	.333
Davis, Eric	.273	11	3	3	5	2	3	.385	1.091
Dawson, Andre	.167	12	2	1	4	0	1	.167	.417
Decker, Steve	.500	4	2	0	0	1	0	.600	.750
Duncan, M	.200	10	2	0	0	0	4	.200	.200
Dunston, S	.545	11	6	0	1	0	1	.583	.636
Dykstra, L*	.222	9	2	0	1	1	1	.300	.222
Fletcher, D*	.333	6	2	1	1	0	3	.333	1.000
Galarraga, A	.364	11	4	0	2	1	1	.385	.545

Xavier Hernandez, Astros — RHP

Batter	Avg	AB	H	HR	BI	BB	SO	OBP	Slg
Gant, Ron	.111	9	1	1	3	1	5	.200	.444
Garcia, C	.125	8	1	0	0	2	1	.300	.125
Gilkey, B	.214	14	3	0	2	1	7	.267	.286
Girardi, Joe	.000	8	0	0	0	0	2	.000	.000
Gomez, Leo	.400	5	2	0	0	1	0	.500	.600
Gonzalez, L*	.333	6	2	0	2	1	1	.429	.667
Grace, Mark*	.375	16	6	1	4	2	0	.444	.563
Grissom, M	.300	10	3	0	1	1	1	.364	.400
Grudzielanek	.500	8	4	1	2	0	0	.500	1.000
Gwynn, Tony*	.429	14	6	0	2	1	1	.438	.500
Hansen, Dave*	.400	5	2	0	0	0	1	.400	.400
Harris, Lenny*	.308	13	4	0	2	1	2	.357	.385
Hayes, C	.154	13	2	1	5	1	2	.214	.462
Henderson, R	.400	5	2	0	0	3	1	.625	.400
Hernandez, Ca	.000	4	0	0	0	1	2	.200	.000
Hollins, Dave#	.000	6	0	0	0	1	2	.143	.000
Howard, T*	.400	5	2	0	2	2	0	.571	.400
Hundley, Todd#	.222	9	2	1	2	0	2	.222	.667
Javier, Stan#	.429	7	3	0	2	1	2	.444	.571
Jefferies, G#	.143	7	1	0	1	1	1	.250	.143
Jones, Chris	.125	8	1	0	1	1	3	.222	.250
Jordan, Brian	.091	11	1	0	1	0	3	.091	.091
Jordan, Ricky	.200	5	1	0	1	0	1	.200	.200
Justice, Dave*	.200	10	2	0	1	1	3	.273	.200
Karros, Eric	.071	14	1	0	1	1	7	.133	.071
Kent, Jeff	.400	5	2	0	0	1	0	.400	1.000
King, Jeff	.278	18	5	1	6	1	2	.300	.500
Kingery, Mike*	.167	6	1	0	0	0	1	.167	.333
Lankford, Ray*	.182	11	2	0	1	0	0	.182	.364
Lansing, Mike	.375	8	3	1	2	2	2	.500	.875
Larkin, Barry	.350	20	7	0	1	1	2	.409	.350
Lemke, Mark#	.375	16	6	0	2	2	1	.444	.375
Lewis, Darren	.375	8	3	0	0	0	0	.375	.375
Mabry, John*	.200	5	1	0	3	0	1	.200	.400
Magadan, Dave*	.571	7	4	1	3	0	0	.571	1.143
Manwaring, K	.300	10	3	0	1	0	1	.300	.500
Martin, Al*	.273	11	3	0	0	0	6	.273	.364
Martinez, Da*	.500	6	3	0	2	1	0	.571	.500
May, Derrick*	.400	5	2	0	0	0	1	.400	.600
McGee, Willie#	.222	9	2	0	0	2	2	.364	.222
McGriff, Fred*	.222	9	2	1	2	4	3	.462	.667
McGwire, Mark	.429	7	3	1	1	0	0	.429	.857
McRae, Brian#	.500	6	3	0	1	2	2	.625	.500
Merced, O*	.667	9	6	1	2	2	2	.727	1.111
Mitchell, K	.333	6	2	0	2	0	1	.286	.333
Morris, Hal*	.200	15	3	0	1	2	3	.294	.267
Murray, Eddie#	.182	11	2	0	0	3	4	.357	.273
Nixon, Otis*	.100	10	1	0	1	0	1	.091	.100
O'Neill, Paul*	.133	15	2	0	2	4	3	.316	.133
Offerman, J#	.100	10	1	0	2	1	3	.182	.300
Oliver, Joe	.182	11	2	0	0	0	4	.182	.182
Orsulak, Joe*	.429	7	3	1	4	1	3	.500	1.143
Pagnozzi, Tom	.100	10	1	1	1	1	3	.182	.400
Pendleton, T#	.063	16	1	1	2	2	5	.167	.250
Piazza, Mike	.375	8	3	1	2	0	1	.375	.875
Plantier, P*	.400	5	2	1	1	0	1	.400	1.000
Reed, Jeff*	.200	5	1	0	0	5	2	.600	.200
Reed, Jody	.250	12	3	0	0	0	2	.250	.250
Roberts, Bip#	.188	16	3	0	1	2	5	.278	.188
Rodriguez, H*	.250	4	1	1	2	1	2	.400	1.000
Sabo, Chris	.190	21	4	0	1	0	3	.190	.286
Samuel, Juan	.500	4	2	0	3	2	1	.571	.667
Sanchez, Rey	.125	8	1	0	0	0	1	.125	.125
Sandberg, R	.214	14	3	2	3	0	3	.214	.643
Sanders, R	.000	7	0	0	0	1	2	.125	.000
Santiago, B	.200	15	3	1	1	1	5	.250	.467
Scarsone, S	.200	5	1	0	0	0	3	.200	.200
Segui, David#	.400	5	2	0	2	1	1	.500	.400
Servais, S	.167	6	1	0	0	1	1	.286	.167
Sheffield, G	.333	12	4	0	0	0	4	.333	.333
Silvestri, D	.500	4	2	0	1	2	0	.667	.500
Slaught, Don	.000	8	0	0	0	1	1	.111	.000
Smith, Dwight*	.400	5	2	0	1	1	2	.500	.800
Smith, Ozzie#	.385	13	5	0	2	0	1	.385	.385
Sosa, Sammy	.231	13	3	0	1	0	1	.231	.231
Steinbach, T	.400	5	2	0	0	0	1	.400	.400
Stillwell, K#	.000	1	0	0	0	0	1	.000	.000
Strawberry, D*	.444	9	4	2	5	1	0	.500	1.111
Thompson, Mil*	.167	6	1	0	3	0	3	.167	.333
Thompson, Rob	.250	16	4	0	4	1	1	.333	.375
VanderWal, J*	.167	6	1	0	0	0	2	.167	.333
Veras, Q#	.286	7	2	0	1	0	1	.286	.429
Walker, Larry*	.200	10	2	0	1	0	3	.200	.200
Wallach, Tim	.200	10	2	0	1	1	3	.333	.200
Walton, J	.000	8	0	0	0	3	0	.000	.000
Weiss, Walt#	.286	7	2	0	2	0	2	.250	.714
White, Devon#	.250	4	1	0	2	0	0	.250	.250
White, R	.200	5	1	0	0	0	2	.200	.200
Whiten, Mark#	.000	4	0	0	2	0	0	.333	.000
Williams, Ma	.400	15	6	2	8	0	2	.400	.933
Young, Eric	.500	8	4	0	1	3	0	.667	.500
Young, Kevin	.000	5	0	0	0	0	2	.000	.000
Zeile, Todd	.222	9	2	1	1	2	0	.364	.556

Orel Hershiser, Indians — RHP

Batter	Avg	AB	H	HR	BI	BB	SO	OBP	Slg
Aldrete, Mike*	.214	42	9	0	5	5	5	.298	.238
Alicea, Luis#	.222	18	4	0	1	3	3	.333	.333
Alomar, R#	.243	37	9	0	1	5	5	.333	.270
Alou, Moises	.083	12	1	0	1	0	2	.083	.167
Anderson, Brd*	.267	15	4	1	2	1	4	.389	.467
Anderson, G*	.357	14	5	1	4	1	1	.400	.571
Anthony, Eric*	.111	9	1	0	0	1	1	.200	.222
Ausmus, Brad	.250	12	3	0	2	0	1	.250	.417
Bagwell, Jeff	.261	23	6	0	5	1	5	.269	.304
Baines, H*	.467	15	7	0	0	0	2	.467	.667
Barberie, B#	.300	20	6	0	2	1	4	.333	.300
Batiste, Kim	.375	8	3	0	2	0	0	.375	.500
Bell, Derek	.211	19	4	0	1	0	3	.211	.263
Bell, Jay	.278	18	5	0	2	0	0	.278	.389
Belliard, R	.282	39	11	0	2	4	7	.349	.282
Benjamin, M	.000	4	0	0	0	1	1	.200	.000
Bichette, D	.286	14	4	0	2	1	2	.333	.357
Biggio, Craig	.423	52	22	1	3	1	8	.434	.615
Blauser, Jeff	.147	34	5	0	1	5	6	.293	.147
Blowers, Mike	.200	5	1	1	1	0	1	.200	.800
Bogar, Tim	.200	5	1	0	1	0	1	.200	.200
Boggs, Wade*	.300	10	3	0	2	0	1	.300	.400
Bonds, Barry*	.250	60	15	5	11	14	11	.392	.517
Bonilla, B#	.295	61	18	4	12	6	7	.362	.574
Bordick, Mike	.125	8	1	0	0	1	1	.222	.125
Brosius, S	.200	5	1	0	1	0	1	.200	.200
Buhner, Jay	.333	12	4	3	6	1	4	.385	1.083
Burnitz, J*	.111	9	1	0	0	0	2	.200	.111
Butler, Brett*	.250	32	8	0	1	3	1	.314	.281
Caminiti, Ken#	.326	46	15	3	9	1	7	.354	.565
Candaele, C#	.267	15	4	0	0	0	2	.313	.467
Cangelosi, J#	.000	5	0	0	0	2	2	.286	.000
Canseco, Jose	.182	11	2	0	1	1	5	.250	.182
Carr, Chuck	.286	14	4	0	0	1	1	.333	.357
Carter, Joe	.167	18	3	1	2	1	5	.211	.333
Castilla, V	.200	5	1	1	1	0	0	.200	.800
Cedeno, A	.278	18	5	0	4	0	5	.316	.444
Cirillo, Jeff	.500	8	4	0	1	2	0	.600	.500
Clark, Tony#	.500	6	3	1	1	0	1	.500	1.000
Clark, Will*	.319	69	22	1	5	12	18	.427	.406
Clayton, R	.074	27	2	0	0	1	2	.107	.074
Cole, Alex*	.333	9	3	0	0	3	3	.500	.333
Coleman, V#	.310	42	13	0	1	6	8	.396	.405
Conine, Jeff	.417	12	5	1	1	1	3	.462	.667
Cora, Joey*	.318	22	7	0	0	1	2	.375	.409
Cordero, Wil	.375	8	3	0	1	1	0	.444	.625
Cordova, M	.333	6	2	0	0	0	0	.333	.500
Curtis, Chad	.200	15	3	0	1	0	5	.200	.267
Cuyler, Milt#	.333	3	1	0	1	1	1	.600	.333
Damon, Johnny*	.250	12	3	0	2	0	2	.231	.333
Dascenzo, D#	.333	6	2	0	0	1	1	.429	.333
Daulton, D*	.250	32	8	1	4	6	5	.368	.344
Davis, Chili#	.231	39	9	0	2	4	8	.302	.282
Davis, Eric	.300	40	12	0	5	6	10	.388	.325
Dawson, Andre	.282	39	11	2	7	3	8	.349	.462
Deer, Rob	.000	6	0	0	0	3	5	.333	.000
Delgado, C*	.444	9	4	0	2	2	2	.583	.444
DeShields, D*	.200	15	3	0	0	3	1	.333	.267
Devereaux, M	.500	6	3	0	2	0	0	.500	.667
Diaz, Alex#	.250	8	2	0	1	0	1	.250	.250
DiSarcina, G	.250	8	2	0	0	2	1	.400	.250
Duncan, M	.222	18	4	0	5	0	4	.200	.278
Dunston, S	.333	33	11	0	0	4	4	.421	.394
Durham, Ray#	.167	6	1	0	0	0	1	.167	.167
Dykstra, L*	.387	31	12	0	2	5	2	.474	.548
Easley, D	.000	5	0	0	0	2	1	.286	.000
Edmonds, Jim*	.300	10	3	2	2	2	3	.417	.900
Eisenreich, J*	.286	7	2	0	0	0	1	.286	.286
Elster, Kevin	.412	17	7	1	2	0	2	.444	.706
Fabregas, Jor*	.273	11	3	0	0	0	0	.273	.273
Fielder, C	.182	11	2	0	0	2	2	.308	.273
Finley, Steve*	.400	25	10	1	1	5	2	.500	.600
Flaherty, J	.300	10	3	0	1	0	1	.364	.500
Fletcher, D*	.600	10	6	0	1	2	0	.667	.700
Frazier, Lou*	.200	5	1	0	2	0	0	.200	.200
Frye, Jeff	.273	11	3	0	0	1	1	.333	.364
Fryman, T	.263	19	5	0	2	0	4	.286	.263
Gaetti, Gary	.000	5	0	0	0	2	2	.286	.000
Gagne, Greg	.250	4	1	0	0	2	1	.500	.250
Galarraga, A	.214	42	9	2	4	1	12	.227	.429
Gant, Ron	.216	37	8	0	2	4	7	.310	.270
Garcia, C	.273	11	3	1	2	1	1	.308	.545
Gates, Brent#	.667	6	4	0	0	0	0	.667	.667
Giambi, Jason*	.333	9	3	0	1	0	0	.333	.333
Gilkey, B	.154	13	2	0	0	0	3	.154	.231
Girardi, Joe	.286	21	6	0	0	1	1	.318	.381

Batter	Avg	AB	H	HR	BI	BB	SO	OBP	Slg
Gomez, Chris	.091	11	1	0	0	2	3	.231	.091
Gonzalez, A	.133	15	2	1	1	1	5	.188	.333
Gonzalez, L*	.308	26	8	1	3	1	0	.333	.538
Goodwin, C*	.333	6	2	0	1	0	1	.333	.667
Goodwin, Tom*	.214	14	3	0	0	0	1	.214	.286
Grace, Mark*	.179	39	7	0	0	2	1	.220	.205
Green, Shawn*	.214	14	3	1	3	0	3	.267	.429
Greenwell, M*	.545	11	6	2	6	1	1	.583	1.182
Greer, Rusty*	.125	8	1	0	0	0	0	.125	.250
Griffey Jr, K*	.333	6	2	0	0	0	0	.333	.333
Grissom, M	.357	14	5	0	0	1	2	.438	.429
Guillen, O*	.273	11	3	0	0	0	1	.273	.273
Gutierrez, R	.167	6	1	0	0	2	0	.375	.167
Gwynn, Tony*	.303	76	23	0	5	8	2	.365	.408
Hamelin, Bob*	.214	14	3	0	3	3	5	.353	.429
Hamilton, D*	.125	8	1	0	0	0	0	.125	.125
Harris, Lenny*	.375	8	3	1	3	0	0	.375	.750
Hayes, C	.273	11	3	0	0	0	1	.273	.364
Higginson, B*	.333	15	5	1	4	0	1	.333	.667
Hoiles, Chris	.222	9	2	1	2	0	3	.300	.556
Hollins, Dave#	.261	23	6	0	3	1	4	.320	.304
Howard, Dave#	.000	7	0	0	0	2	0	.222	.000
Howard, T*	.286	7	2	0	3	0	1	.286	.429
Howell, Jack*	.300	10	3	0	0	0	2	.300	.300
Hudler, Rex	.235	17	4	1	2	0	5	.278	.412
Hulse, David*	.250	8	2	1	3	1	2	.333	.625
Hundley, Todd#	.286	14	4	0	1	1	1	.313	.286
Hunter, Brian	.167	6	1	0	1	0	0	.167	.167
Huson, Jeff*	.500	4	2	0	1	1	0	.600	.750
Incaviglia, P	.273	11	3	0	0	0	3	.333	.273
Jaha, John	.333	12	4	1	3	1	1	.385	.750
James, Dion*	.188	32	6	0	0	2	5	.235	.188
Jefferies, G*	.417	24	10	0	0	1	2	.440	.500
Jefferson, R*	.455	11	5	0	2	1	0	.500	.545
Johnson, L*	.286	7	2	0	0	0	0	.286	.286
Justice, Dave*	.217	23	5	0	3	6	1	.379	.304
Karkovice, R	.000	7	0	0	1	1	2	.125	.000
Kelly, R	.455	11	5	0	1	1	2	.500	.455
Kent, Jeff	.167	12	2	0	1	0	2	.154	.167
King, Jeff	.364	11	4	0	0	1	0	.417	.455
Kingery, Mike*	.333	12	4	0	0	0	0	.333	.667
Knoblauch, C	.143	7	1	0	0	0	0	.143	.143
Lankford, Ray*	.333	21	7	0	4	2	1	.391	.429
Lansing, Mike	.182	11	2	1	2	0	2	.182	.455
Larkin, Barry	.304	46	14	0	0	5	4	.373	.326
Lemke, Mark#	.189	37	7	0	2	1	4	.211	.189
Lewis, Darren	.069	29	2	0	2	1	5	.100	.069
Lewis, Mark	.200	5	1	0	1	2	1	.429	.400
Leyritz, Jim	.000	5	0	0	0	1	3	.167	.000
Liriano, N#	.143	7	1	0	0	2	0	.333	.143
Livingstone*	.000	7	0	0	1	0	0	.000	.000
Lockhart, K*	.182	11	2	0	0	1	2	.250	.455
Lopez, Javy	.400	5	2	0	1	0	0	.500	.400
Lopez, Luis#	.750	8	6	0	0	1	0	.750	1.000
Macfarlane, M	.000	6	0	0	0	1	2	.143	.000
Magadan, Dave*	.192	26	5	1	4	3	3	.276	.423
Manwaring, K	.158	19	3	0	0	2	2	.158	.211
Martin, Al*	.000	8	0	0	0	1	0	.111	.000
Martin, N	.167	6	1	0	0	0	0	.167	.167
Martinez, Da*	.222	45	10	0	4	4	6	.286	.244
Martinez, E	.375	8	3	1	3	1	1	.444	1.000
Martinez, S*	.333	6	2	0	0	0	1	.333	.333
Martinez, T*	.143	7	1	0	0	2	1	.333	.286
Matheny, Mike	.600	5	3	1	3	1	1	.714	1.200
May, Derrick*	.333	12	4	0	3	3	1	.467	.500
Mayne, Brent*	.429	7	3	0	0	1	2	.500	.429
McGee, Willie*	.240	50	12	0	6	5	5	.321	.340
McGriff, Fred*	.188	32	6	2	4	2	8	.229	.406
McGwire, Mark	.500	6	3	1	3	0	1	.500	1.000
McLemore, M#	.333	6	2	0	2	2	2	.500	.667
Meares, Pat	.167	6	1	0	0	0	4	.167	.333
Merced, O*	.400	15	6	0	2	1	2	.438	.533
Mieske, Matt	.222	9	2	0	1	0	3	.222	.222
Mitchell, K	.294	51	15	1	8	3	16	.333	.392
Molitor, Paul	.300	10	3	0	1	0	3	.300	.300
Morandini, M*	.286	14	4	0	3	3	0	.412	.500
Morris, Hal*	.214	14	3	0	0	2	1	.313	.286
Murray, Eddie=	.250	20	5	0	0	0	4	.250	.250
Myers, Greg*	.286	7	2	0	0	0	1	.286	.429
Myers, Rod*	.667	6	4	0	1	1	1	.714	.833
Naehring, Tim	.167	12	2	0	0	0	3	.167	.250
Nevin, Phil	.600	5	3	0	0	1	0	.667	.800
Newfield, M	.000	6	0	0	1	0	2	.000	.000
Newson, M*	.375	8	3	0	2	0	2	.375	.500
Nieves, M#	.500	6	3	0	0	0	2	.500	.500
Nilsson, Dave*	.273	11	3	0	0	2	0	.385	.455
Nixon, Otis#	.171	41	7	0	4	1	9	.186	.220
Nunnally, Jon*	.000	4	0	0	0	1	0	.200	.000
O'Brien, C	.000	8	0	0	0	0	2	.000	.000
O'Leary, Troy*	.214	14	3	0	2	1	2	.267	.286
O'Neill, Paul*	.231	52	12	1	5	3	4	.273	.346

Batter	Avg	AB	H	HR	BI	BB	SO	OBP	Slg
Offerman, J#	.556	9	5	0	1	2	1	.636	.778
Olerud, John*	.500	14	7	0	2	0	1	.533	.643
Oliver, Joe	.071	14	1	1	2	0	5	.071	.286
Orsulak, Joe*	.273	22	6	0	1	0	2	.273	.500
Pagnozzi, Tom	.250	12	3	0	4	1	0	.308	.417
Palmeiro, R*	.421	19	8	1	6	6	1	.538	.737
Palmer, Dean	.500	6	3	1	5	0	0	.500	1.167
Paquette, C	.000	7	0	0	0	0	2	.000	.000
Parent, Mark	.111	9	1	0	1	0	2	.100	.111
Pena, G#	.250	4	1	0	0	1	1	.400	.500
Pena, Tony	.258	31	8	0	3	4	8	.343	.323
Pendleton, T#	.296	71	21	2	6	3	9	.324	.507
Phillips, T#	.300	10	3	0	1	0	2	.300	.400
Plantier, P*	.211	19	4	1	3	3	4	.318	.368
Polonia, Luis*	.333	6	2	0	0	1	0	.429	.333
Pride, Curtis*	.250	8	2	0	0	0	2	.250	.250
Raines, Tim#	.369	65	24	1	6	6	8	.423	.523
Randa, Joe	.125	8	1	0	2	0	1	.125	.250
Reed, Jeff*	.258	31	8	0	0	4	2	.343	.323
Ripken, Cal	.000	12	0	0	1	3	1	.188	.000
Roberts, Bip#	.278	36	10	0	2	1	2	.297	.361
Rodriguez, Al	.400	5	2	1	1	1	1	.500	1.000
Rodriguez, I	.333	6	2	1	1	0	1	.429	.833
Sabo, Chris	.349	43	15	2	5	3	2	.391	.558
Salmon, Tim	.100	10	1	0	1	1	2	.182	.100
Samuel, Juan	.163	49	8	0	1	3	16	.241	.245
Sandberg, R	.310	58	18	1	9	4	12	.355	.483
Sanders, B	.400	10	4	0	3	0	2	.400	.600
Santiago, B	.184	49	9	0	4	2	6	.226	.184
Scarsone, S	.200	5	1	0	0	0	2	.200	.200
Schofield, D	.500	6	3	0	1	1	0	.625	.833
Schu, Rick	.000	8	0	0	0	0	4	.111	.000
Seitzer, K	.500	12	6	0	1	2	1	.571	.583
Servais, S	.200	5	1	0	0	0	1	.200	.200
Sheffield, G	.320	25	8	1	2	0	3	.357	.480
Shipley, C	.364	11	4	0	1	0	0	.417	.364
Sierra, Ruben#	.273	11	3	1	5	1	0	.333	.727
Simms, Mike	.200	5	1	0	1	1	3	.333	.200
Slaught, Don	.222	9	2	0	2	0	2	.222	.222
Smith, Dwight*	.286	14	4	0	0	0	4	.286	.286
Smith, Ozzie#	.300	50	15	0	9	9	0	.400	.300
Snow, J.T.#	.333	15	5	0	0	0	3	.333	.400
Sojo, Luis	.200	5	1	0	0	0	0	.200	.200
Sorrento, P*	.500	6	3	0	0	1	2	.571	.667
Sosa, Sammy	.533	15	8	3	6	1	2	.563	1.200
Sprague, Ed	.357	14	5	1	3	1	3	.400	.643
Stahoviak, S*	.000	6	0	0	0	0	1	.000	.000
Stanley, Mike	.250	12	3	0	0	0	3	.250	.250
Steinbach, T	.111	9	1	1	2	0	3	.111	.444
Stillwell, K#	.391	23	9	0	2	3	2	.462	.609
Stocker, K#	.000	5	0	0	0	1	0	.167	.000
Strawberry, D*	.282	39	11	1	8	7	7	.391	.462
Surhoff, B.J.*	.571	7	4	0	3	1	0	.625	.857
Sweeney, Mike	.400	5	2	2	2	0	1	.400	1.600
Tarasco, Tony*	.571	7	4	1	2	0	0	.571	1.286
Tartabull, D	.333	6	2	0	0	0	2	.333	.333
Taubensee, E*	.300	10	3	0	0	2	1	.417	.300
Tettleton, M#	.714	7	5	1	1	3	0	.800	1.143
Thomas, Frank	.583	12	7	1	3	1	1	.571	1.000
Thompson, Mil*	.246	57	14	1	4	6	12	.328	.316
Thompson, Rob	.250	68	17	1	5	1	11	.261	.397
Thompson, Ry	.400	5	2	0	0	0	2	.400	.600
Tinsley, Lee#	.200	5	1	0	0	0	2	.200	.200
Tucker, M*	.182	11	2	0	0	1	4	.250	.273
Valentin, Jhn	.250	16	4	0	0	0	1	.294	.375
Valentin, Jse#	.375	16	6	3	5	0	3	.375	1.000
VanderWal, J*	.250	12	3	2	2	2	2	.357	.833
Vaughn, Greg	.100	10	1	0	0	1	2	.182	.100
Vaughn, Mo*	.333	15	5	1	3	3	4	.444	.533
Velarde, R	.111	9	1	0	0	1	3	.200	.111
Ventura, R*	.100	10	1	0	0	0	1	.250	.100
Vina, F*	.389	18	7	0	0	0	0	.389	.444
Vitiello, Joe	.250	8	2	1	1	0	1	.250	.625
Vizcaino, J#	.389	18	7	0	0	2	2	.450	.556
Walker, Larry*	.375	16	6	0	3	3	3	.474	.563
Wallach, Tim	.317	60	19	2	6	4	12	.364	.483
Walton, J	.000	8	0	0	0	0	0	.000	.000
Weiss, Walt*	.267	15	4	0	3	3	2	.389	.400
White, Devon*	.500	8	4	0	0	0	3	.500	.500
Whiten, Mark#	.333	12	4	1	6	1	1	.385	.667
Wilkins, Rick*	.222	18	4	0	2	0	6	.263	.333
Williams, Ber#	.444	9	4	0	0	1	2	.500	.556
Williams, Ma	.226	53	12	4	8	1	20	.236	.509
Wilson, Dan	.167	12	2	0	1	0	1	.167	.333
Young, Eric	.429	7	3	0	2	0	2	.429	.714
Young, Ernie	.333	6	2	1	3	0	0	.333	.833
Young, Kevin	.333	15	5	0	0	1	3	.375	.400
Zaun, Greg#	.500	4	2	0	1	0	0	.400	.500
Zeile, Todd	.263	19	5	0	1	4	3	.375	.316

Ken Hill, Rangers									RHP
Batter	Avg	AB	H	HR	BI	BB	SO	OBP	Slg
Abbott, Kurt	.400	5	2	0	1	2	1	.571	.400
Alicea, Luis#	.118	17	2	0	2	3	2	.250	.176
Alomar, R#	.421	19	8	0	2	0	1	.400	.579
Amaro, Ruben*	.000	10	0	0	0	0	1	.091	.000
Anderson, Brd*	.429	7	3	0	0	3	1	.600	.571
Anderson, G*	.417	12	5	0	2	2	2	.500	.417
Anthony, Eric*	.100	20	2	0	0	3	3	.217	.100
Arias, Alex	.125	8	1	0	1	2	3	.300	.125
Arias, George	.000	7	0	0	0	1	2	.125	.000
Ausmus, Brad	.294	17	5	1	1	0	4	.294	.471
Bagwell, Jeff	.226	31	7	1	3	3	6	.314	.387
Baines, H*	.125	8	1	1	2	1	1	.300	.500
Barberie, B#	.333	3	1	0	2	0	0	.600	.667
Bartee, K	.143	7	1	0	0	1	3	.250	.143
Becker, Rich*	.250	16	4	0	0	1	3	.294	.438
Bell, Derek	.300	10	3	0	1	2	2	.417	.300
Bell, Jay	.226	31	7	2	6	4	9	.306	.516
Belliard, R	.222	9	2	0	1	0	1	.222	.333
Benjamin, M	.625	8	5	0	1	0	2	.625	.750
Berroa, G	.333	6	2	1	3	0	3	.286	.833
Bichette, D	.300	10	3	0	1	0	1	.273	.500
Biggio, Craig	.209	43	9	0	2	5	9	.292	.326
Blauser, Jeff	.214	28	6	1	5	4	6	.343	.357
Bogar, Tim	.333	6	2	0	3	1	0	.429	.500
Boggs, Wade*	.188	16	3	0	0	3	2	.316	.250
Bonds, Barry*	.276	29	8	3	4	11	1	.475	.586
Bonilla, B#	.325	40	13	2	7	8	9	.449	.575
Boone, Bret	.333	3	1	1	2	1	2	.500	1.333
Bordick, Mike	.400	5	2	0	0	1	2	.500	.400
Bournigal, R	.125	8	1	0	0	0	1	.125	.125
Brosius, S	.200	5	1	0	1	0	2	.333	.200
Brumfield, J	.000	4	0	0	0	0	1	.000	.000
Buhner, Jay	.000	11	0	0	0	0	5	.000	.000
Bullett, S*	.000	7	0	0	0	0	0	.000	.000
Burnitz, J*	.250	8	2	0	3	2	1	.400	.250
Butler, Brett*	.242	33	8	0	1	2	3	.286	.242
Caminiti, Ken#	.292	48	14	0	7	3	3	.333	.354
Candaele, C	.200	10	2	0	1	1	2	.273	.400
Canseco, Jose	.400	15	6	2	5	0	4	.400	.867
Carr, Chuck	.143	14	2	0	0	3	1	.294	.143
Carreon, Mark	.333	9	3	1	2	1	2	.455	.778
Cedeno, A	.214	28	6	1	1	2	8	.290	.393
Cedeno, D#	.286	7	2	0	0	0	0	.286	.286
Cianfrocco, A	.600	5	3	1	1	0	1	.600	1.400
Cirillo, Jeff	.286	14	4	0	1	2	0	.375	.429
Clark, Dave*	.250	12	3	0	0	1	2	.308	.250
Clark, Phil	.600	5	3	1	2	1	0	.667	1.200
Clark, Tony*	.143	7	1	0	0	0	2	.143	.286
Clark, Will*	.294	17	5	0	1	1	2	.333	.353
Clayton, R	.231	13	3	0	2	0	1	.231	.308
Coleman, V#	.200	15	3	0	0	1	3	.250	.267
Conine, Jeff	.083	12	1	0	2	1	5	.154	.083
Coomer, Ron	.400	5	2	0	0	0	0	.400	.600
Cora, Joey*	.091	11	1	0	1	0	0	.091	.091
Cordero, Wil	.571	7	4	0	0	0	0	.571	.714
Cordova, M	.133	15	2	0	0	1	7	.188	.133
Curtis, Chad	.000	6	0	0	0	2	0	.000	.000
Damon, Johnny*	.182	11	2	0	1	1	1	.231	.182
Dascenzo, D	.333	12	4	0	0	2	3	.429	.417
Daulton, D*	.231	26	6	1	4	10	5	.421	.346
Davis, Chili*	.250	8	2	0	1	2	2	.400	.375
Davis, Eric	.000	9	0	0	2	3	5	.231	.000
Dawson, Andre	.143	21	3	1	5	1	7	.182	.381
DeShields, D*	.400	10	4	0	3	1	3	.429	.450
DiSarcina, G	.143	14	2	0	0	0	2	.143	.143
Duncan, M	.257	35	9	0	5	1	5	.263	.486
Dunston, S	.200	25	5	0	1	0	6	.200	.240
Dykstra, L*	.467	30	14	2	2	10	0	.600	.733
Edmonds, Jim*	.286	7	2	0	1	0	2	.286	.286
Eisenreich, J*	.429	7	3	0	1	1	0	.500	.571
Elster, Kevin	.235	17	4	1	3	2	2	.316	.412
Erstad, Darin*	.273	11	3	0	1	1	3	.333	.364
Fabregas, Jor*	.444	9	4	0	0	1	0	.444	.444
Fasano, Sal	.000	6	0	0	0	0	2	.000	.000
Fielder, C	.125	8	1	0	0	1	2	.222	.125
Finley, Steve*	.263	38	10	1	3	6	1	.364	.395
Frye, Jeff	.333	6	2	0	0	2	1	.500	.667
Fryman, T	.083	12	1	0	0	1	2	.154	.083
Galarraga, A	.290	31	9	0	6	5	5	.436	.355
Gant, Ron	.281	32	9	3	11	5	3	.395	.625
Garcia, C	.273	11	3	0	2	0	1	.273	.273
Giambi, Jason*	.200	5	1	0	0	1	0	.333	.400
Gilkey, B	.250	24	6	0	0	1	5	.280	.250
Girardi, Joe	.192	26	5	0	5	1	5	.222	.231
Gonzalez, L*	.059	34	2	0	3	1	5	.086	.118
Goodwin, Tom*	.267	15	4	0	0	0	3	.267	.267
Grace, Mark*	.319	47	15	1	5	4	3	.373	.426
Green, Shawn*	.571	7	4	0	1	0	0	.571	.857
Greenwell, M*	.143	7	1	0	1	0	0	.143	.143
Grissom, M	.182	11	2	0	0	1	0	.250	.273
Guillen, O*	.222	9	2	0	1	0	0	.222	.444

Ken Hill, Rangers									RHP
Batter	Avg	AB	H	HR	BI	BB	SO	OBP	Slg
Gutierrez, R	.200	5	1	0	0	0	2	.200	.200
Gwynn, Chris*	.000	6	0	0	1	0	3	.000	.000
Gwynn, Tony*	.283	46	13	1	5	1	3	.298	.413
Hamelin, Bob*	.273	11	3	0	1	1	3	.333	.364
Harris, Lenny*	.278	18	5	0	2	2	2	.350	.333
Hayes, C	.316	19	6	0	6	1	5	.350	.421
Higginson, B*	.231	13	3	0	0	0	1	.231	.231
Hoiles, Chris	.375	8	3	2	2	1	3	.444	1.250
Hollins, Dave#	.219	32	7	2	6	6	8	.342	.438
Howard, Dave#	.111	9	1	0	0	0	2	.111	.111
Howard, T*	.100	10	1	0	0	1	1	.182	.200
Hudler, Rex	.308	13	4	1	2	0	1	.308	.615
Hulse, David*	.222	9	2	0	0	0	1	.222	.222
Hundley, Todd#	.111	18	2	1	1	1	4	.158	.278
Hunter, Brian	.444	18	8	0	5	0	2	.444	.778
Jaha, John	.429	14	6	3	7	3	1	.529	1.286
James, Dion*	.125	8	1	0	0	1	0	.222	.125
Javier, Stan#	.222	9	2	0	1	0	5	.300	.222
Jefferies, G#	.313	32	10	0	4	9	1	.463	.344
Jefferson, R*	.400	5	2	0	1	2	1	.571	.400
Jeter, Derek	.273	11	3	0	1	0	3	.333	.455
Johnson, Mark*	.250	4	1	0	0	2	1	.500	.500
Jones, C#	.333	6	2	1	1	2	0	.500	.833
Jordan, Brian	.222	9	2	0	0	0	0	.222	.222
Jordan, Ricky	.133	15	2	0	0	0	1	.133	.133
Justice, Dave*	.040	25	1	1	1	12	5	.351	.160
Karkovice, R	.167	6	1	0	0	0	3	.167	.167
Karros, Eric	.278	18	5	0	2	0	3	.278	.333
Kelly, R	.320	25	8	1	3	2	2	.370	.560
Kent, Jeff	.583	12	7	2	6	0	1	.583	1.083
King, Jeff	.375	16	6	0	2	1	1	.412	.438
Kingery, Mike*	.667	6	4	0	0	1	0	.714	1.000
Klesko, Ryan*	.214	14	3	1	1	2	0	.313	.571
Knoblauch, C	.450	20	9	1	3	3	5	.500	.650
Lankford, Ray*	.320	25	8	2	5	8	4	.471	.640
Larkin, Barry	.320	25	8	1	3	3	5	.393	.560
Lawton, Matt*	.200	5	1	0	2	1	0	.333	.600
Lemke, Mark#	.219	32	7	0	1	6	6	.342	.250
Lewis, Darren	.105	19	2	0	1	0	0	.105	.105
Lewis, Mark	.000	9	0	0	0	1	5	.100	.000
Leyritz, Jim	.200	5	1	0	1	2	2	.333	.400
Listach, Pat#	.200	5	1	0	0	1	1	.333	.200
Lockhart, K*	.357	14	5	0	1	0	0	.357	.429
Lopez, Javy	.333	9	3	0	0	0	0	.333	.333
Lopez, Luis#	.000	6	0	0	0	3	0	.000	.000
Macfarlane, M	.250	8	2	0	0	2	1	.400	.250
Magadan, Dave*	.250	28	7	1	6	7	1	.378	.393
Manwaring, K	.250	8	2	0	3	1	0	.333	.500
Martin, Al*	.188	16	3	0	0	1	3	.235	.250
Martinez, Da*	.174	46	8	0	2	3	3	.224	.217
Martinez, E	.375	8	3	0	0	3	2	.545	.500
Martinez, S*	.286	7	2	0	1	0	1	.286	.286
Martinez, T*	.286	14	4	0	0	2	2	.375	.357
Matheny, Mike	.250	8	2	1	2	0	3	.250	.625
May, Derrick*	.345	29	10	0	6	1	3	.355	.517
McGee, Willie#	.200	10	2	0	1	1	3	.273	.300
McGriff, Fred*	.273	33	9	3	7	9	3	.442	.606
McRae, Brian#	.143	7	1	0	0	1	0	.250	.143
Meares, Pat	.471	17	8	1	2	1	3	.500	.706
Merced, O*	.333	30	10	0	2	1	4	.355	.400
Mieske, Matt	.500	4	2	0	0	1	0	.600	.500
Mitchell, K	.100	10	4	1	3	1	0	.455	.800
Molitor, Paul	.250	16	4	0	2	3	1	.368	.375
Mondesi, Raul	.333	6	2	0	1	0	0	.333	.667
Morandini, M*	.353	34	12	0	7	3	4	.405	.588
Morris, Hal*	.250	20	5	0	2	0	3	.250	.350
Mouton, Lyle	.571	7	4	1	1	0	0	.571	1.143
Munoz, Pedro	.111	9	1	0	0	0	4	.111	.111
Murray, Eddie#	.324	37	12	0	4	3	9	.375	.378
Myers, Greg*	.167	6	1	0	1	0	0	.167	.167
Naehring, Tim	.286	7	2	1	2	1	0	.375	.714
Nilsson, Dave*	.333	12	4	0	4	2	2	.400	.583
Nixon, Otis#	.550	20	11	0	0	5	2	.640	.650
O'Brien, C	.333	12	4	0	3	0	1	.308	.500
O'Leary, Troy*	.100	10	1	0	2	1	3	.167	.200
O'Neill, Paul*	.250	28	7	0	4	9	3	.436	.286
Offerman, J#	.280	25	7	0	2	1	3	.308	.320
Olerud, John*	.500	6	3	0	3	1	0	.571	.667
Oliver, Joe	.250	16	4	0	2	2	5	.316	.250
Orsulak, Joe*	.250	12	3	0	0	1	0	.308	.250
Pagnozzi, Tom	.250	20	5	0	0	2	4	.318	.300
Palmeiro, R*	.429	7	3	2	5	3	1	.600	1.286
Paquette, C	.417	12	5	0	1	0	4	.417	.500
Parent, Mark	.000	5	0	0	0	0	2	.000	.000
Pena, G#	.500	6	3	0	1	1	2	.625	.500
Pendleton, T#	.077	26	2	1	4	1	7	.111	.231
Phillips, T#	.571	7	4	0	2	1	1	.625	.714
Piazza, Mike	.375	16	6	0	3	0	1	.375	.375
Plantier, P*	.200	10	2	1	3	2	1	.333	.500
Pride, Curtis*	.286	7	2	0	0	1	1	.375	.429
Prince, Tom	.400	5	2	0	0	1	0	.571	.400

94

Ken Hill, Rangers — RHP

Batter	Avg	AB	H	HR	BI	BB	SO	OBP	Slg
Raines, Tim#	.588	17	10	0	5	7	1	.708	.882
Reed, Jeff*	.250	20	5	0	0	3	3	.348	.250
Reed, Jody	.200	10	2	0	0	1	0	.273	.200
Ripken, Cal	.286	7	2	0	2	2	1	.444	.286
Roberts, Bip#	.303	33	10	0	1	3	4	.361	.424
Rodriguez, Al	.000	6	0	0	0	1	1	.250	.000
Rodriguez, H*	.167	6	1	0	2	0	1	.167	.500
Sabo, Chris	.176	17	3	2	2	2	4	.300	.529
Salmon, Tim	.667	12	8	1	2	2	1	.714	.917
Samuel, Juan	.211	19	4	0	0	5	5	.400	.263
Sanchez, Rey	.238	21	5	0	0	5	2	.407	.286
Sandberg, R	.279	43	12	1	4	7	4	.380	.395
Sanders, R	.400	15	6	1	2	2	4	.471	.667
Santiago, B	.250	28	7	0	0	1	2	.300	.286
Schofield, D	.333	6	2	0	0	0	1	.333	.333
Segui, David#	.667	6	4	0	2	0	0	.667	1.167
Seitzer, K	.333	12	4	0	2	1	0	.385	.333
Servais, S	.333	9	3	0	2	0	0	.333	.444
Sheffield, G	.333	18	6	1	2	2	0	.400	.556
Shipley, C	.300	10	3	0	3	0	2	.300	.400
Sierra, Ruben#	.300	20	6	1	2	0	0	.300	.450
Simms, Mike	.200	5	1	0	0	1	1	.333	.200
Slaught, Don	.400	15	6	0	0	1	1	.438	.467
Smith, Dwight*	.200	30	6	2	6	7	4	.351	.467
Smith, Ozzie#	.382	34	13	1	3	2	0	.417	.588
Snow, J.T.#	.214	14	3	0	0	0	2	.214	.214
Sorrento, P*	.333	6	2	0	1	0	2	.429	.500
Sosa, Sammy	.500	12	6	2	2	3	1	.600	1.083
Sprague, Ed	.143	7	1	0	1	0	1	.143	.143
Stahoviak, S*	.083	12	1	0	0	1	3	.154	.083
Stanley, Mike	.000	7	0	0	0	1	2	.125	.000
Steinbach, T	.167	6	1	0	0	0	3	.167	.167
Stillwell, K#	.333	9	3	0	3	1	1	.400	.444
Stocker, K#	.250	8	2	0	0	0	1	.250	.500
Strawberry, D*	.273	33	9	0	3	5	4	.368	.394
Surhoff, B.J.*	.100	10	1	0	1	1	3	.167	.100
Taubensee, E*	.250	20	5	1	1	1	5	.286	.450
Thomas, Frank	.286	7	2	0	1	1	3	.375	.429
Thompson, Mil*	.000	7	0	0	0	0	2	.000	.000
Thompson, Rob	.050	20	1	0	0	1	2	.095	.050
Thompson, Ry	.273	11	3	0	1	1	4	.333	.273
Tinsley, Lee#	.333	9	3	0	1	1	0	.400	.333
Tucker, M*	.429	7	3	0	0	1	1	.500	.571
Valentin, Jim	.200	15	3	0	1	1	2	.250	.333
Valentin, Jse#	.444	9	4	0	1	2	2	.545	.778
VanderWal, J*	.400	5	2	0	1	0	1	.400	.400
Vaughn, Greg	.400	5	2	0	1	1	0	.500	.400
Vaughn, Mo*	.571	14	8	1	3	1	1	.600	1.000
Velarde, R	.375	8	3	0	1	0	3	.375	.375
Ventura, R*	.111	9	1	0	1	2	2	.273	.222
Vina, F*	.353	17	6	0	0	1	1	.389	.353
Vitiello, Joe	.286	7	2	0	0	1	1	.375	.286
Vizcaino, J#	.143	14	2	0	0	0	3	.143	.143
Walbeck, Matt#	.556	9	5	0	2	2	0	.667	.556
Walker, Larry*	.111	9	1	1	2	1	0	.182	.444
Wallach, Tim	.282	39	11	1	7	2	7	.326	.487
Walton, J	.200	20	4	1	2	1	2	.238	.500
Weiss, Walt#	.364	11	4	0	1	1	0	.417	.364
Whiten, Mark#	.313	16	5	1	3	2	2	.389	.625
Wilkins, Rick*	.480	25	12	2	5	2	3	.517	.880
Williams, Ber#	.200	15	3	0	0	3	1	.333	.267
Williams, E	.143	7	1	0	0	0	1	.143	.143
Williams, Ma	.211	19	4	1	2	0	2	.211	.368
Wilson, Dan	.333	3	1	0	1	1	0	.400	.333
Young, Eric	.125	8	1	0	0	0	0	.125	.125
Zeile, Todd	.258	31	8	2	6	3	3	.324	.516

Sterling Hitchcock, Mariners — LHP

Batter	Avg	AB	H	HR	BI	BB	SO	OBP	Slg
Alexander, M	.200	5	1	0	1	0	2	.200	.200
Alicea, Luis#	.333	6	2	0	0	1	1	.429	.333
Alomar, R*	.500	16	8	0	1	0	2	.500	.833
Alomar Jr, S	.231	13	3	0	0	0	5	.231	.308
Amaral, Rich	.000	5	0	0	0	1	1	.167	.000
Anderson, Brd*	.185	27	5	1	3	3	6	.267	.333
Anderson, G*	.214	14	3	1	5	0	3	.214	.429
Baerga, C#	.043	23	1	0	1	2	6	.148	.043
Barberie, B#	.000	4	0	0	0	1	1	.333	.000
Bautista, D	.333	6	2	0	0	0	0	.333	.333
Becker, Rich*	.167	6	1	0	1	0	1	.167	.167
Belle, Albert	.333	27	9	1	2	0	8	.333	.519
Berroa, G	.200	10	2	0	3	2	2	.308	.500
Blowers, Mike	.500	6	3	1	2	3	1	.667	1.000
Boggs, Wade*	.273	11	3	0	0	1	0	.273	.273
Bonilla, B#	.091	11	1	0	0	4	1	.333	.091
Borders, Pat	.333	6	2	0	0	0	0	.333	.500
Bordick, Mike	.429	7	3	0	2	2	1	.556	.571
Brito, Tilson	.400	5	2	0	0	1	0	.500	.600
Brosius, S	.286	28	8	1	2	2	1	.364	.750
Buford, Damon	.167	6	1	0	0	0	2	.167	.167
Buhner, Jay	.167	6	1	1	1	0	3	.167	.667

Sterling Hitchcock, Mariners — LHP

Batter	Avg	AB	H	HR	BI	BB	SO	OBP	Slg
Canseco, Jose	.333	12	4	2	2	0	3	.333	.833
Carter, Joe	.188	16	3	1	2	1	1	.235	.438
Cirillo, Jeff	.316	19	6	0	0	3	1	.409	.316
Clark, Will*	.429	7	3	0	2	2	1	.556	.857
Coomer, Ron	.500	6	3	0	2	0	0	.500	.833
Cora, Joey#	.167	6	1	0	0	0	1	.167	.167
Cordova, M	.375	8	3	0	2	1	1	.444	.625
Curtis, Chad	.417	12	5	0	1	1	3	.429	.417
Davis, Chili#	.167	12	2	1	4	3	1	.313	.500
Delgado, C*	.167	6	1	0	1	1	4	.286	.333
Devereaux, M	.083	12	1	0	1	0	2	.083	.167
DiSarcina, G	.500	10	5	0	0	0	0	.500	.500
Duncan, M	.286	7	2	0	2	0	2	.222	.429
Durham, Ray#	.250	8	2	1	2	2	0	.400	.625
Easley, D	.167	6	1	0	0	0	1	.167	.167
Edmonds, Jim*	.364	11	4	1	3	1	3	.417	.727
Elster, Kevin	.333	6	2	0	0	1	4	.429	.500
Erstad, Darin*	.333	9	3	0	1	0	2	.300	.333
Espinoza, A	.143	7	1	0	0	0	3	.143	.143
Fermin, Felix	.182	11	2	0	0	0	1	.182	.182
Fielder, C	.278	18	5	0	2	2	4	.350	.389
Fielder, C	.333	6	2	0	0	0	2	.333	.333
Flaherty, J	.333	9	3	1	3	1	1	.400	.778
Franco, Julio	.286	7	2	0	0	1	0	.375	.286
Fryman, T	.167	12	2	0	1	2	2	.286	.167
Gaetti, Gary	.250	4	1	0	0	0	0	.400	.500
Gagne, Greg	.429	7	3	1	2	0	0	.429	.857
Gates, Brent#	.400	5	2	0	0	0	0	.400	.600
Gil, Benji	.000	5	0	0	0	1	4	.167	.000
Girardi, Joe	.100	10	1	0	0	0	1	.100	.100
Gonzales, R	.200	5	1	0	0	1	2	.333	.400
Gonzalez, A	.182	11	2	0	1	2	6	.357	.182
Gonzalez, J	.375	16	6	3	7	1	2	.412	1.000
Goodwin, Tom*	.400	5	2	0	0	1	1	.500	.400
Greenwell, M*	.143	14	2	0	0	4	4	.333	.143
Greer, Rusty*	.200	10	2	0	1	1	2	.250	.200
Guillen, O*	.143	7	1	0	0	0	0	.143	.143
Hamilton, D*	.083	12	1	0	2	0	1	.214	.083
Hammonds, J	.167	6	1	0	3	1	2	.222	.333
Henderson, R	.333	6	2	0	0	3	2	.556	.333
Hoiles, Chris	.278	18	5	2	6	5	6	.417	.667
Hollins, Dave#	.750	4	3	1	2	0	1	.800	1.750
Howard, Dave#	.000	8	0	0	0	0	0	.000	.000
Hudler, Rex	.429	7	3	0	1	0	1	.429	.429
Huff, Michael	.231	13	3	0	1	1	2	.286	.462
Hulse, David*	.000	6	0	0	0	1	3	.143	.000
Jaha, John	.500	8	4	0	2	1	1	.556	.625
Javier, Stan#	.333	6	2	0	0	0	1	.333	.333
Jeter, Derek	.273	11	3	1	2	1	2	.333	.545
Joyner, Wally*	.250	8	2	0	1	1	1	.333	.375
Karkovice, R	.333	15	5	1	1	0	4	.333	.533
Kelly, R	.800	5	4	0	3	1	1	.833	1.000
Knoblauch, C	.714	7	5	0	1	2	0	.778	1.000
Knorr, Randy	.000	5	0	0	0	0	0	.000	.000
Lewis, Darren	.000	7	0	0	0	0	0	.000	.000
Lewis, Mark	.429	7	3	0	0	0	2	.429	.429
Leyritz, Jim	.556	9	5	0	1	1	1	.556	.667
Listach, Pat#	.235	17	4	0	0	1	3	.278	.294
Lofton, Kenny*	.345	29	10	0	4	2	4	.387	.517
Loretta, Mark	.600	5	3	0	1	0	0	.600	.600
Macfarlane, M	.267	15	4	0	1	3	2	.389	.333
Manto, Jeff	.333	9	3	1	2	0	4	.333	.889
Martin, N	.556	9	5	0	0	1	1	.556	.667
Martinez, E	.167	6	1	1	3	2	1	.444	.667
Martinez, T*	.333	18	6	1	4	0	3	.316	.611
Matheny, Mike	.000	8	0	0	0	2	1	.200	.000
McGee, Willie#	.143	7	1	0	0	0	0	.143	.286
McGwire, Mark	.111	9	1	1	2	4	1	.385	.444
McLemore, M#	.154	13	2	0	0	3	2	.313	.154
McRae, Brian*	.333	6	2	0	0	0	1	.333	.333
Meares, Pat	.429	7	3	0	1	0	1	.429	.714
Mieske, Matt	.389	18	7	0	4	0	3	.368	.389
Molitor, Paul	.188	16	3	0	2	1	2	.235	.250
Mouton, Lyle	.600	5	3	0	2	2	0	.714	.800
Murray, Eddie#	.400	20	8	1	3	1	1	.429	.600
Naehring, Tim	.286	14	4	0	0	0	1	.286	.286
Newfield, M	.000	5	0	0	0	0	2	.167	.000
Nieves, M#	.250	4	1	0	1	0	1	.333	.250
Nixon, Dave*	.167	6	1	0	1	1	3	.286	.167
Nixon, Otis#	.455	11	5	0	1	2	2	.538	.545
O'Brien, C	.250	4	1	0	1	1	0	.500	.250
O'Neill, Paul*	.250	8	2	0	1	0	2	.400	.250
Olerud, John*	.286	14	4	1	2	2	4	.375	.643
Oliver, Joe	.143	7	1	0	0	0	1	.250	.143
Palmeiro, R*	.440	25	11	2	7	4	2	.517	.880
Palmer, Dean	.125	8	1	0	0	0	2	.125	.125
Paquette, C	.250	8	2	0	0	0	2	.250	.250
Pena, Tony	.300	10	3	1	2	1	0	.417	.600
Perez, Robert	.286	7	2	0	0	0	0	.286	.286
Perry, H	.400	5	2	0	0	1	2	.500	.600
Phillips, T#	.429	14	6	0	2	3	3	.529	.429

95

Sterling Hitchcock, Mariners — LHP

Batter	Avg	AB	H	HR	BI	BB	SO	OBP	Slg
Raines, Tim#	.300	10	3	1	3	0	2	.300	.600
Ramirez, M	.313	16	5	2	4	5	1	.476	.688
Reboulet, J	.200	5	1	0	0	0	0	.333	.200
Ripken, Cal	.250	24	6	2	5	3	1	.333	.542
Rodriguez, I	.278	18	5	1	2	0	1	.278	.444
Salmon, Tim	.444	9	4	0	3	2	1	.500	.556
Samuel, Juan	.111	9	1	1	1	1	1	.200	.444
Seitzer, K	.238	21	5	0	3	3	2	.320	.381
Sierra, Ruben#	.000	7	0	0	1	2	2	.200	.000
Smith, Mark	.250	8	2	1	2	1	2	.333	.750
Snow, J.T.#	.333	9	3	0	0	3	1	.538	.333
Sojo, Luis	.200	5	1	0	0	0	1	.200	.200
Sprague, Ed	.500	14	7	1	5	0	1	.500	.714
Steinbach, T	.400	10	4	2	4	1	3	.417	1.000
Surhoff, B.J.*	.333	9	3	1	2	0	0	.333	.889
Tartabull, D	.000	8	0	0	0	2	4	.200	.000
Tettleton, M#	.313	16	5	3	5	2	4	.389	.875
Thomas, Frank	.571	14	8	2	4	2	1	.625	1.214
Thome, Jim*	.263	19	5	0	1	3	7	.391	.316
Tinsley, Lee#	.111	9	1	0	0	1	4	.200	.111
Trammell, A	.333	9	3	0	0	1	1	.333	.333
Valentin, Jhn	.313	16	5	1	5	0	4	.313	.500
Valentin, Jse#	.077	13	1	0	0	0	6	.077	.077
Vaughn, Greg	.333	15	5	0	3	1	2	.375	.400
Vaughn, Mo*	.167	18	3	1	2	0	5	.211	.389
Velarde, A	.400	5	2	0	0	3	1	.625	.400
Ventura, R*	.250	12	3	0	1	3	1	.400	.333
Vizquel, Omar#	.294	17	5	1	3	1	4	.316	.529
Voigt, Jack	.000	3	0	0	0	3	1	.500	.000
Walbeck, Matt#	.600	5	3	0	1	0	0	.600	.600
Ward, Turner#	.125	8	1	0	1	0	0	.111	.125
Williams, Ber#	.500	4	2	0	0	3	0	.714	.750
Williams, Gee	.250	4	1	0	0	4	1	.625	.500
Wilson, Dan	.167	6	1	0	2	2	2	.375	.333
Young, Ernie	.600	5	3	0	3	0	2	.600	.600

Trevor Hoffman, Padres — RHP

Batter	Avg	AB	H	HR	BI	BB	SO	OBP	Slg
Martin, Al*	.143	7	1	0	0	0	2	.333	.143
McGee, Willie#	.000	4	0	0	0	1	0	.200	.000
McGriff, Fred*	.200	10	2	1	2	2	2	.333	.600
McRae, Brian#	.143	7	1	0	0	1	0	.250	.143
Merced, O*	.200	5	1	0	0	1	3	.333	.200
Miller, Orl	.000	5	0	0	0	0	3	.000	.000
Mitchell, K	.000	3	0	0	0	4	3	.571	.000
Mondesi, Raul	.250	8	2	1	1	1	3	.333	.625
Morandini, M*	.000	6	0	0	0	1	1	.143	.000
Morris, Hal*	.200	5	1	0	0	1	2	.333	.200
Orsulak, Joe*	.286	7	2	0	0	1	2	.375	.286
Pagnozzi, Tom	.143	7	1	0	0	0	0	.143	.143
Pendleton, T#	.000	9	0	0	0	1	1	.100	.000
Piazza, Mike	.200	5	1	1	3	0	2	.200	.800
Reed, Jeff*	.000	6	0	0	0	0	4	.000	.000
Sabo, Chris	.333	3	1	0	0	0	0	.333	.500
Sanchez, Rey	.800	5	4	0	0	1	1	.833	1.000
Sandberg, R	.167	6	1	0	0	1	3	.286	.167
Sanders, R	.300	10	3	0	4	2	2	.417	.600
Santiago, B	.143	7	1	0	0	0	1	.143	.143
Segui, David#	.167	6	1	0	0	0	2	.167	.333
Servais, S	.143	7	1	0	0	0	2	.143	.143
Sheffield, G	.167	6	1	0	0	0	2	.167	.167
Sosa, Sammy	.250	12	3	1	2	0	4	.250	.500
Stocker, K#	.222	9	2	0	0	3	4	.417	.333
Tarasco, Tony*	.000	7	0	0	0	0	1	.000	.000
Taubensee, E*	.444	9	4	0	2	1	1	.500	.667
Thompson, Mil*	.286	7	2	1	1	1	2	.375	.714
Thompson, Rob	.571	7	4	0	0	0	1	.625	.857
Timmons, O	.000	5	0	0	0	0	2	.000	.000
VanderWal, J*	.000	4	0	0	0	1	3	.200	.000
Vizcaino, J#	.250	4	1	0	0	1	1	.400	.500
Walker, Larry*	.143	7	1	0	0	2	2	.333	.286
Wallach, Tim	.143	7	1	0	0	0	2	.143	.143
Weiss, Walt#	.167	6	1	0	0	1	0	.286	.167
Whiten, Mark#	.125	8	1	0	0	2	2	.300	.125
Wilkins, Rick*	.000	8	0	0	0	3	5	.273	.000
Williams, Ma	.111	9	1	0	1	0	0	.111	.111
Young, Eric	.200	5	1	0	1	0	2	.429	.200
Zeile, Todd	.200	5	1	0	1	2	3	.429	.200

Trevor Hoffman, Padres — RHP

Batter	Avg	AB	H	HR	BI	BB	SO	OBP	Slg
Alicea, Luis*	.000	5	0	0	0	0	2	.000	.000
Alou, Moises	.375	8	3	1	2	0	3	.375	.875
Bagwell, Jeff	.273	11	3	0	1	0	3	.273	.455
Bell, Derek	.000	6	0	0	0	1	3	.143	.000
Bell, Jay	.333	9	3	0	3	1	1	.364	.556
Berry, Sean	.143	7	1	0	0	0	4	.143	.143
Bichette, D	.364	11	4	2	5	0	3	.364	1.000
Biggio, Craig	.125	8	1	0	1	1	2	.222	.250
Blauser, Jeff	.000	6	0	0	0	2	2	.000	.000
Bonds, Barry*	.444	9	4	1	3	3	0	.583	.778
Bonilla, B#	.000	2	0	0	0	4	0	.667	.000
Boone, Bret	.143	7	1	1	2	0	3	.143	.571
Branson, Jeff	.273	11	3	0	0	1	2	.333	.273
Carreon, Mark	.000	7	0	0	1	1	1	.111	.000
Castilla, D	.143	7	1	0	3	0	0	.125	.143
Clark, Dave*	.250	4	1	0	2	1	0	.400	.250
Clayton, R	.333	6	2	0	1	0	2	.333	.333
Conine, Jeff	.375	8	3	0	1	0	1	.375	.750
Davis, Eric	.000	4	0	0	0	1	2	.200	.000
DeShields, D*	.143	7	1	0	0	2	2	.143	.143
Duncan, M	.375	8	3	0	0	1	1	.375	.625
Dunston, S	.333	6	2	0	0	0	0	.333	.333
Eisenreich, J*	.100	10	1	0	0	2	0	.100	.100
Finley, Steve*	.000	5	0	0	0	1	1	.000	.000
Fletcher, D*	.286	7	2	0	1	0	2	.286	.286
Gagne, Greg	.167	6	1	0	0	0	2	.167	.167
Galarraga, A	.143	7	1	0	0	0	5	.143	.286
Gant, Ron	.200	5	1	1	1	0	1	.200	.800
Garcia, C	.556	9	5	0	1	1	1	.600	.889
Gilkey, B	.333	6	2	0	0	1	1	.429	.667
Girardi, Joe	.400	5	2	1	1	0	1	.400	1.000
Gonzalez, L*	.333	9	3	0	1	1	0	.400	.778
Grace, Mark*	.600	5	3	0	2	0	0	.600	.600
Grissom, M	.250	8	2	0	2	0	4	.250	.375
Hansen, Dave*	.125	8	1	0	0	1	5	.125	.125
Hayes, C	.333	12	4	1	3	1	1	.385	.750
Hernandez, Jo	.200	5	1	0	0	0	2	.200	.200
Hill, G	.000	7	0	0	0	0	3	.000	.000
Howard, T*	.000	8	0	0	1	0	0	.250	.000
Hundley, Todd#	.000	3	0	0	0	1	2	.250	.000
Incaviglia, P	.250	4	1	0	0	1	2	.400	.250
Jefferies, G#	.400	5	2	0	2	1	0	.429	.400
Justice, Dave*	.444	9	4	1	1	1	2	.500	1.222
Karros, Eric	.429	7	3	0	1	0	0	.375	.571
Kelly, R	.333	6	2	0	0	0	1	.333	.667
Kent, Jeff	.125	8	1	0	0	0	3	.125	.125
King, Jeff	.125	8	1	0	1	0	1	.125	.125
Lansing, Mike	.091	11	1	0	0	0	1	.091	.091
Larkin, Barry	.111	9	1	1	2	0	1	.111	.444
Lemke, Mark#	.200	5	1	0	0	0	2	.200	.400
Lewis, Darren	.250	4	1	0	1	1	2	.400	.250
Liriano, N#	.000	3	0	0	0	2	1	.400	.000
Lopez, Javy	.200	5	1	0	0	0	2	.200	.600

Darren Holmes, Rockies — RHP

Batter	Avg	AB	H	HR	BI	BB	SO	OBP	Slg
Alicea, Luis*	.000	4	0	0	1	1	1	.200	.000
Alomar, R#	.600	5	3	0	2	0	0	.600	.600
Alou, Moises	.250	4	1	0	0	1	0	.400	.250
Anthony, Eric*	.250	4	1	0	1	1	1	.400	.250
Arias, Alex	.200	5	1	0	0	0	2	.167	.200
Ausmus, Brad	.222	9	2	0	1	0	2	.222	.222
Baerga, C#	.167	6	1	0	0	0	0	.167	.333
Bagwell, Jeff	.222	9	2	0	1	2	3	.364	.222
Bell, Derek	.308	13	4	0	1	0	3	.308	.385
Bell, Jay	.286	7	2	0	1	3	2	.500	.571
Biggio, Craig	.300	10	3	0	2	2	4	.417	.300
Blauser, Jeff	.400	5	2	1	2	0	1	.400	1.000
Bonds, Barry*	.200	5	1	0	0	1	0	.200	.200
Bonilla, B#	.000	3	0	0	0	2	0	.400	.000
Branson, Jeff*	.167	6	1	0	0	1	0	.286	.167
Butler, Brett*	.200	5	1	0	1	0	0	.200	.400
Caminiti, Ken#	.250	12	3	0	0	1	0	.250	.333
Candaele, C#	.600	5	3	0	0	0	0	.600	.800
Carter, Joe	.000	4	0	0	0	3	3	.429	.000
Cedeno, A	.083	12	1	0	0	0	5	.083	.083
Cianfrocco, A	.400	5	2	0	0	0	2	.400	.600
Clark, Dave*	.000	4	0	0	0	1	1	.200	.000
Clark, Phil	.000	6	0	0	0	0	3	.000	.000
Clayton, R	.000	7	0	0	0	0	3	.000	.000
Colbrunn, G	.333	9	3	2	0	3	0	.333	.500
Conine, Jeff	.286	7	2	1	4	2	4	.444	.857
Cordero, Wil	.600	5	3	1	3	0	2	.600	1.400
Davis, Chili#	.429	7	3	0	2	0	0	.429	.714
Dawson, Andre	.200	5	1	0	0	0	0	.200	.200
DeShields, D*	.500	2	1	0	0	2	1	.750	.500
Duncan, M	.600	5	3	0	2	0	1	.600	1.200
Eisenreich, J*	.125	8	1	0	2	1	2	.222	.125
Finley, Steve*	.500	6	3	0	1	0	0	.500	.833
Gagne, Greg	.000	5	0	0	0	0	3	.000	.000
Gant, Ron	.667	6	4	0	1	0	1	.667	.667
Garcia, C	.429	7	3	0	0	0	1	.429	.429
Gilkey, B	.333	12	4	2	4	1	5	.385	.917
Gomez, Leo	.429	7	3	0	2	1	1	.500	.429
Gonzalez, L*	.125	8	1	0	2	1	1	.364	.125
Grace, Mark*	.500	6	3	0	2	0	0	.500	.800
Grissom, M	.545	11	6	0	2	0	3	.545	.545
Gutierrez, R	.200	5	1	0	1	0	1	.200	.200
Gwynn, Tony*	.600	5	3	0	0	0	0	.667	.800
Hill, G	.111	9	1	0	1	1	3	.182	.111
Hollins, Dave#	.250	4	1	0	0	1	0	.400	.250
Hundley, Todd#	.400	5	2	0	0	0	1	.400	.400
Hunter, Bri L	.400	5	2	0	0	0	1	.400	.400
Incaviglia, P	.000	5	0	0	0	0	4	.000	.000

Darren Holmes, Rockies — RHP

Batter	Avg	AB	H	HR	BI	BB	SO	OBP	Slg
Jefferies, G#	.182	11	2	0	1	0	0	.182	.182
Johnson, L*	.333	6	2	0	2	1	0	.429	.667
Jordan, Brian	.333	9	3	0	2	0	2	.333	.333
Joyner, Wally*	.400	5	2	0	0	1	0	.500	1.000
Kelly, R	.600	5	3	0	0	0	0	.600	.800
Kent, Jeff	.333	9	3	1	2	1	2	.400	.778
King, Jeff	.100	10	1	0	0	0	4	.100	.100
Klesko, Ryan*	.600	5	3	0	1	0	1	.600	.600
Lankford, Ray*	.444	9	4	1	2	2	0	.545	.778
Lansing, Mike	.556	9	5	1	4	1	1	.600	1.000
Lemke, Mark#	.286	7	2	0	0	0	0	.286	.286
Lewis, Mark	.167	6	1	0	1	0	1	.167	.167
Livingstone*	.000	5	0	0	0	0	0	.000	.000
Lopez, Javy	.143	7	1	0	0	0	1	.143	.143
Mabry, John*	.143	7	1	0	2	0	2	.143	.143
Magadan, Dave*	.000	5	0	0	0	0	0	.000	.000
Manwaring, K	.167	6	1	0	0	1	1	.286	.167
Martin, Al*	.500	10	5	3	4	0	2	.500	1.500
May, Derrick*	.000	5	0	0	1	0	0	.000	.000
Mayne, Brent*	.000	5	0	0	1	0	0	.000	.000
McGriff, Fred*	.750	4	3	1	2	0	0	.800	1.750
McRae, Brian#	.100	10	1	0	1	0	5	.100	.100
Merced, O*	.286	7	2	0	0	1	0	.375	.286
Morris, Hal*	.500	4	2	0	2	1	0	.600	.750
Ordonez, Rey	.200	5	1	0	0	0	0	.200	.200
Orsulak, Joe*	.250	12	3	0	0	0	0	.250	.250
Pagnozzi, Tom	.200	5	1	0	1	1	0	.333	.200
Pena, G#	.000	3	0	0	1	1	2	.333	.000
Pendleton, T#	.000	6	0	0	0	0	1	.000	.000
Piazza, Mike	.000	5	0	0	0	0	2	.000	.000
Plantier, P*	.143	7	1	1	2	1	3	.250	.571
Reed, Jody	.455	11	5	0	2	0	0	.455	.727
Ripken, Billy	.200	5	1	0	0	0	1	.200	.200
Ripken, Cal	.333	6	2	0	1	0	0	.333	.333
Roberts, Bip#	.333	6	2	0	0	1	1	.429	.333
Sanchez, Rey	.333	6	2	0	0	1	0	.429	.500
Sanders, R	.250	4	1	0	0	2	2	.500	.250
Santiago, B	.500	6	3	1	6	1	0	.500	1.167
Servais, S	.000	5	0	0	0	0	1	.000	.000
Sheffield, G	.500	6	3	0	0	3	2	.667	.833
Shipley, C	.400	5	2	0	0	0	1	.400	.400
Sierra, Ruben#	.000	6	0	0	0	1	3	.143	.000
Smith, Dwight*	.000	3	0	0	0	2	1	.400	.000
Smith, Ozzie*	.250	8	2	0	2	0	0	.250	.250
Sosa, Sammy	.417	12	5	2	6	0	3	.417	1.000
Taubensee, E*	.333	6	2	0	3	2	1	.500	.500
Thomas, Frank	.250	4	1	0	0	1	0	.400	.250
Vizcaino, J#	.000	4	0	0	0	1	1	.200	.000
Wallach, Tim	.000	5	0	0	0	1	1	.167	.000
Weiss, Walt*	.250	4	1	0	0	1	1	.400	.250
White, Devon*	.000	4	0	0	0	1	2	.200	.000
Whiten, Mark#	.250	8	2	1	1	3	4	.455	.625
Wilkins, Rick*	.000	6	0	0	0	0	5	.000	.000
Williams, Ma	.333	6	2	0	2	0	3	.286	.333
Zeile, Todd	.273	11	3	0	1	1	1	.333	.455

Mark Holzemer, Angels — LHP

Batter	Avg	AB	H	HR	BI	BB	SO	OBP	Slg
Anderson, Brd*	.000	6	0	0	1	0	2	.125	.000
Baines, H*	.143	7	1	0	0	0	1	.143	.143
Devereaux, M	.200	5	1	0	0	2	1	.429	.200
Hamilton, D*	.500	6	3	0	1	2	0	.625	.500
Hoiles, Chris	.625	8	5	1	5	0	1	.625	1.250
Jaha, John	.125	8	1	0	1	0	1	.125	.125
Listach, Pat#	.286	7	2	0	1	0	0	.286	.286
Nilsson, Dave*	.200	5	1	0	0	1	1	.333	.400
Palmeiro, R*	.600	5	3	1	2	1	0	.667	1.200
Ripken, Cal	.571	7	4	1	3	0	0	.571	1.000
Seitzer, K	.833	6	5	1	4	0	0	.857	1.500
Surhoff, B.J.*	.500	10	5	0	6	2	0	.583	.500
Vaughn, Greg	.286	7	2	0	2	0	0	.375	.571

Rick Honeycutt, Cardinals — LHP

Batter	Avg	AB	H	HR	BI	BB	SO	OBP	Slg
Alomar, R#	.375	8	3	0	0	0	2	.375	.375
Alomar Jr, S	.200	5	1	0	0	0	0	.200	.200
Anderson, Brd*	.118	17	2	0	0	0	6	.167	.118
Baerga, C#	.200	10	2	0	1	0	2	.182	.200
Baines, H*	.296	27	8	1	5	2	6	.345	.630
Belle, Albert	.000	3	0	0	0	2	2	.400	.000
Belliard, F	.500	10	5	0	2	1	0	.500	.700
Boggs, Wade*	.500	14	7	0	3	2	1	.529	.500
Bonds, Barry*	.083	12	1	0	1	1	2	.143	.167
Borders, Pat	.667	6	4	0	2	1	1	.714	.833
Burks, Ellis	.286	7	2	0	0	1	2	.375	.714
Carter, Joe	.200	10	2	0	1	2	3	.333	.300
Clark, Will*	.222	9	2	0	2	0	2	.222	.333
Coleman, V#	.200	15	3	0	0	1	2	.294	.333
Davis, Chili#	.367	30	11	4	8	1	1	.387	.800
Davis, Eric	.200	15	3	1	1	6	1	.429	.400
Dawson, Andre	.233	30	7	0	3	3	7	.303	.300

Rick Honeycutt, Cardinals — LHP

Batter	Avg	AB	H	HR	BI	BB	SO	OBP	Slg
Devereaux, M	.250	4	1	0	0	1	1	.400	.250
Dunston, S	.333	15	5	0	0	0	2	.333	.467
Eisenreich, J*	.364	11	4	0	2	0	1	.364	.364
Fermin, Felix	.400	5	2	0	2	0	0	.400	.400
Fielder, C	.250	4	1	0	1	1	1	.400	.250
Finley, Steve*	.000	6	0	0	0	1	0	.000	.000
Franco, Julio	.385	13	5	0	0	1	2	.429	.385
Fryman, T	.000	8	0	0	0	0	4	.000	.000
Gaetti, Gary	.000	8	0	0	0	2	3	.200	.000
Gagne, Greg	.300	10	3	0	1	1	1	.364	.400
Galarraga, A	.200	5	1	0	0	2	0	.429	.200
Gomez, Leo	.000	5	0	0	0	0	1	.000	.000
Gonzales, R	.750	4	3	1	1	2	1	.833	1.500
Gonzalez, J	.200	5	1	1	2	0	1	.200	.800
Greenwell, M*	.214	14	3	0	1	0	2	.267	.357
Griffey Jr, K*	.235	17	4	0	1	1	1	.278	.235
Guillen, O*	.233	30	7	0	3	0	2	.226	.333
Gwynn, Tony*	.262	42	11	0	0	2	2	.295	.333
Hall, Mel*	.500	6	3	1	3	0	2	.500	1.000
Hamilton, D*	.500	6	3	0	0	1	0	.571	.833
Hill, G	.250	4	1	0	0	1	1	.400	.250
Howell, Jack*	.200	5	1	0	0	0	1	.200	.200
Incaviglia, P	.200	5	1	0	1	0	0	.200	.400
James, Dion*	.000	4	0	0	1	1	0	.200	.000
Jefferies, G#	.143	7	1	0	2	0	0	.125	.143
Johnson, L*	.200	20	4	0	3	2	4	.273	.200
Joyner, Wally*	.217	23	5	0	2	4	1	.357	.217
Karkovice, R	.286	7	2	0	0	0	4	.286	.286
Larkin, Barry	.167	12	2	1	2	0	0	.167	.417
Liriano, N#	.167	6	1	0	1	2	2	.375	.167
Lofton, Kenny*	.375	8	3	0	0	0	0	.375	.500
Lovullo, T#	.250	4	1	0	1	1	1	.400	.500
Macfarlane, M	.400	5	2	0	0	0	0	.500	.400
Martinez, E	.000	4	0	0	0	1	1	.200	.000
Martinez, T*	.400	5	2	1	3	1	1	.500	1.000
McGee, Willie*	.278	18	5	1	3	0	6	.278	.556
McGriff, Fred*	.125	16	2	1	4	1	5	.167	.313
McLemore, M#	.250	8	2	0	0	1	1	.333	.250
McRae, Brian*	.125	8	1	0	2	0	0	.125	.125
Mitchell, K	.538	13	7	2	3	0	0	.538	1.154
Molitor, Paul	.667	3	2	0	1	1	1	.600	.667
Olerud, John*	.200	10	2	0	0	1	5	.273	.300
Orsulak, Joe*	.333	9	3	0	2	0	0	.333	.444
Palmeiro, R*	.143	28	4	0	2	1	2	.200	.179
Parent, Mark	.143	7	1	0	2	0	0	.143	.143
Pena, Tony	.364	11	4	0	3	1	0	.417	.455
Pendleton, T#	.200	15	3	0	0	0	1	.200	.200
Phillips, T#	.625	8	5	1	4	1	0	.667	1.000
Polonia, Luis*	.100	10	1	0	0	0	2	.100	.200
Raines, Tim#	.286	35	10	0	2	3	4	.342	.286
Ripken, Billy	.200	5	1	0	1	1	0	.333	.200
Ripken, Cal	.250	8	2	0	0	4	0	.500	.250
Roberts, Bip#	.000	11	0	0	0	1	2	.083	.000
Rodriguez, H*	.200	5	1	1	1	0	2	.200	.800
Samuel, Juan	.154	13	2	0	1	2	3	.267	.231
Sandberg, R	.333	30	10	1	2	2	3	.375	.500
Santiago, B	.375	8	3	1	2	0	2	.375	.875
Schu, Rick	.333	9	3	1	1	2	0	.455	.667
Segui, David#	.571	7	4	0	1	0	0	.571	.571
Seitzer, K	.333	6	2	0	0	2	2	.500	.333
Sheffield, G	.600	5	3	1	0	0	0	.600	.600
Sierra, Ruben#	.250	24	6	0	1	3	4	.333	.292
Smith, Ozzie*	.412	17	7	0	0	3	2	.500	.588
Sorrento, P	.167	6	1	0	1	1	3	.286	.167
Spiers, Bill*	.200	5	1	0	0	0	3	.200	.200
Stanley, Mike	.091	11	1	0	0	2	3	.231	.182
Stillwell, K#	.214	14	3	0	1	1	2	.267	.286
Strawberry, D*	.000	10	0	0	0	0	3	.000	.000
Surhoff, B.J.*	.000	9	0	0	0	1	0	.100	.000
Tartabull, D	.250	4	1	0	0	3	3	.455	.250
Tettleton, M#	.222	9	2	0	0	1	1	.300	.333
Thome, Jim*	.200	5	1	0	1	0	3	.167	.200
Thompson, Mil*	.222	9	2	0	1	1	1	.300	.222
Thompson, Rob	.400	5	2	0	0	2	0	.571	.600
Trammell, A	.286	7	2	0	0	1	0	.375	.286
Vaughn, Mo*	.222	9	2	1	5	0	2	.222	.556
Velarde, R	.500	4	2	1	3	1	1	.600	1.500
Ventura, R*	.214	14	3	0	1	1	2	.267	.286
Vizquel, Omar*	.000	6	0	0	0	0	0	.000	.000
Wallach, Tim	.273	22	6	2	9	3	4	.333	.545
White, Devon#	.238	21	5	0	4	1	9	.273	.381
Whiten, Mark*	.250	4	1	0	0	0	1	.400	.250

Chris Hook, Giants — RHP

Batter	Avg	AB	H	HR	BI	BB	SO	OBP	Slg
Bell, Jay	.500	6	3	0	2	0	0	.500	.667
Castilla, V	.400	5	2	0	2	0	0	.333	.800
Garcia, C	.400	5	2	0	1	0	0	.400	.400
Segui, David#	.500	4	2	0	0	1	0	.600	.500

John Hope, Pirates — RHP

Batter	Avg	AB	H	HR	BI	BB	SO	OBP	Slg
Bichette, D	.400	5	2	1	2	0	1	.500	1.200
Clark, Phil	.200	5	1	0	0	0	0	.200	.200
Conine, Jeff	.167	6	1	1	2	0	0	.143	.667
DeShields, D*	.600	5	3	0	0	0	0	.600	.600
Galarraga, A	.500	6	3	1	4	0	0	.500	1.000
Hayes, C	.286	7	2	0	0	0	1	.286	.429
Mondesi, Raul	.250	4	1	1	3	1	0	.400	1.000
Orsulak, Joe*	.250	8	2	0	0	1	1	.333	.250
Thompson, Ry	.250	4	1	0	1	0	0	.200	.500
Young, Eric	.000	4	0	0	1	0	1	.200	.000

Steve Howe, Yankees — LHP

Batter	Avg	AB	H	HR	BI	BB	SO	OBP	Slg
Alomar, R#	.571	7	4	1	3	0	1	.571	1.000
Alomar Jr, S	.200	5	1	0	0	0	0	.200	.200
Anderson, Brd*	.167	6	1	0	0	0	1	.286	.167
Baerga, C#	.667	6	4	1	2	0	0	.667	1.333
Baines, H*	.111	9	1	0	2	0	3	.111	.111
Belle, Albert	1.000	4	4	1	1	0	0	1.000	1.750
Blowers, Mike	.200	5	1	0	1	0	1	.200	.200
Boggs, Wade*	.600	6	3	0	0	0	1	.500	.833
Borders, Pat	.000	4	0	0	0	1	0	.200	.000
Bordick, Mike	.500	6	3	0	1	1	0	.571	.667
Buhner, Jay	.250	12	3	0	1	1	2	.357	.250
Clark, Will*	.167	6	1	0	0	0	1	.167	.333
Curtis, Chad	.200	5	1	0	1	0	0	.200	.200
Davis, Chili*	1.000	5	5	1	5	1	0	1.000	1.800
Espinoza, A	.200	5	1	0	0	0	0	.200	.200
Fermin, Felix	.000	5	0	0	0	0	1	.167	.000
Fielder, C	.286	7	2	0	0	0	0	.286	.429
Franco, Julio	.000	5	0	0	0	1	3	.167	.000
Gaetti, Gary	.167	6	1	1	1	0	1	.286	.667
Gonzalez, J	.600	5	3	0	1	1	0	.667	.800
Greenwell, M*	.200	15	3	0	2	0	1	.200	.333
Griffey Jr, K*	.235	17	4	1	5	0	3	.235	.412
Guillen, O*	.333	6	2	0	0	0	2	.333	.500
Hamilton, D*	.167	6	1	0	0	0	2	.167	.167
Henderson, R	.200	5	1	0	0	1	1	.333	.200
Huff, Michael	.222	9	2	0	0	0	2	.222	.333
Hulse, David*	.000	5	0	0	0	0	2	.000	.000
Joyner, Wally*	.385	13	5	0	0	0	3	.385	.385
Karkovice, R	.000	4	0	0	0	1	1	.200	.000
Leius, Scott	.250	4	1	0	0	1	0	.400	.250
Lofton, Kenny*	.500	10	5	0	2	0	0	.500	.700
Martinez, E	.400	5	2	0	0	1	0	.500	.600
Martinez, T*	.083	12	1	1	1	0	2	.154	.333
McLemore, M#	.167	6	1	0	0	1	0	.286	.167
Molitor, Paul	.200	5	1	0	0	2	0	.429	.200
Munoz, Pedro	.167	6	1	1	2	0	1	.167	.667
Myers, Greg*	.400	5	2	0	0	0	1	.400	.400
Nixon, Otis#	.200	5	1	0	0	0	1	.200	.200
Olerud, John*	.214	14	3	0	0	0	5	.214	.214
Palmeiro, R*	.154	13	2	0	0	0	2	.154	.154
Pena, Tony	.000	7	0	0	0	0	2	.000	.000
Phillips, T#	.200	5	1	0	0	1	1	.333	.200
Polonia, Luis*	.167	6	1	0	0	0	0	.167	.167
Ripken, Billy	.000	5	0	0	0	0	0	.000	.000
Ripken, Cal	.400	5	2	0	0	2	0	.571	.600
Segui, David#	.000	5	0	0	0	0	0	.000	.000
Seitzer, K	.000	6	0	0	0	0	1	.000	.000
Sierra, Ruben#	.625	8	5	1	4	0	0	.625	1.125
Snow, J.T.#	.500	6	3	0	2	2	0	.625	.500
Sorrento, P*	.200	5	1	0	0	0	0	.200	.200
Sprague, Ed	.250	4	1	0	1	0	0	.250	.250
Steinbach, T	.222	9	2	1	1	0	3	.222	.556
Surhoff, B.J.*	.400	10	4	0	0	0	2	.400	.400
Tettleton, M#	.286	7	2	0	1	2	2	.444	.286
Thome, Jim*	.400	5	2	0	0	0	1	.400	.400
Trammell, A	.200	5	1	0	2	0	1	.200	.400
Vaughn, Greg	.333	6	2	1	1	1	2	.429	1.000
Vaughn, Mo*	.333	6	2	0	0	1	0	.429	.500
Vizquel, Omar#	.200	5	1	0	0	0	0	.200	.200
White, Devon#	.500	6	3	1	1	0	2	.500	1.000
Whiten, Mark#	.167	6	1	0	0	0	1	.167	.333

John Hudek, Astros — RHP

Batter	Avg	AB	H	HR	BI	BB	SO	OBP	Slg
Abbott, Kurt	.250	4	1	1	3	0	1	.250	1.000
Colbrunn, G	.200	5	1	0	0	0	1	.200	.200
Conine, Jeff	.000	5	0	0	0	0	3	.000	.000
Lankford, Ray*	.200	5	1	0	0	0	4	.200	.200
Sheffield, G	.400	5	2	0	0	0	0	.400	.600

Joe Hudson, Red Sox — RHP

Batter	Avg	AB	H	HR	BI	BB	SO	OBP	Slg
Belle, Albert	.333	6	2	0	1	2	0	.500	.667
Carter, Joe	.000	7	0	0	0	0	3	.000	.000
Cordova, M	.333	6	2	0	1	1	0	.429	.500
Fielder, C	.000	4	0	0	0	1	2	.200	.000
Matheny, Mike	.250	4	1	0	0	1	0	.400	.250
Meares, Pat	.000	4	0	0	0	0	0	.200	.000

Joe Hudson, Red Sox — RHP

Batter	Avg	AB	H	HR	BI	BB	SO	OBP	Slg
Molitor, Paul	.400	5	2	0	1	0	0	.400	.600
Murray, Eddie#	1.000	2	2	0	0	4	0	1.000	1.500
Ramirez, M	.333	6	2	0	3	1	2	.429	.333
Sprague, Ed	.400	5	2	0	0	0	2	.400	.600
Stahoviak, S*	.250	4	1	0	2	2	0	.500	.250
Thome, Jim*	.250	4	1	0	0	1	0	.400	.250
Williams, Ber#	.000	4	0	0	1	1	1	.200	.000

Rich Hunter, Phillies — RHP

Batter	Avg	AB	H	HR	BI	BB	SO	OBP	Slg
Alicea, Luis#	.333	6	2	0	0	0	1	.429	.333
Aurilia, Rich	.600	5	3	0	1	0	0	.600	.600
Benard, M*	.333	3	1	0	0	1	1	.500	.333
Caminiti, Ken#	.667	3	2	0	0	1	1	.750	1.000
Clayton, R	.333	6	2	0	0	1	2	.429	.333
Finley, Steve*	.500	4	2	0	1	0	1	.600	.500
Flaherty, J	.250	4	1	0	2	0	0	.200	.250
Gant, Ron	.000	5	0	0	0	0	0	.167	.000
Gonzalez, L*	.400	5	2	0	0	1	0	.500	.400
Grace, Mark*	.500	5	3	0	1	0	0	.500	.600
Gwynn, Tony*	.000	5	0	0	0	0	0	.000	.000
Henderson, R	.250	4	1	0	0	1	0	.400	.250
Hill, G	.000	3	0	0	1	1	0	.400	.000
Joyner, Wally*	.750	4	3	0	3	1	0	.800	.750
Lankford, Ray*	.167	6	1	0	1	0	1	.167	.167
Mabry, John*	.333	6	2	0	0	0	0	.333	.333
Magadan, Dave*	.167	6	1	0	2	0	0	.167	.333
McRae, Brian#	.167	6	1	0	0	0	1	.167	.333
Mueller, Bill#	.400	5	2	0	0	0	1	.400	.400
Sanchez, Rey	.250	4	1	0	0	1	0	.400	.250
Sandberg, R	.200	5	1	0	1	0	0	.333	.200
Servais, S	.200	5	1	0	0	0	0	.200	.400
Sheaffer, D	.333	6	2	0	0	0	1	.333	.500
Timmons, O	.200	5	1	0	0	1	0	.333	.200
Wilkins, Rick*	.333	3	1	0	1	1	1	.400	.333

Edwin Hurtado, Mariners — RHP

Batter	Avg	AB	H	HR	BI	BB	SO	OBP	Slg
Alomar Jr, S	.200	5	1	0	0	0	0	.333	.200
Amaral, Rich	.333	6	2	0	0	0	1	.333	.333
Becker, Rich*	.167	6	1	0	0	2	1	.375	.333
Belle, Albert	.200	5	1	0	1	1	1	.286	.400
Buhner, Jay	.250	4	1	1	2	2		.500	1.000
Cirillo, Jeff	.333	3	1	0	0	2	0	.600	.333
Cora, Joey#	.143	7	1	0	0	0	0	.143	.143
Cordova, M	.286	7	2	0	1	1	1	.375	.429
Curtis, Chad	.143	7	1	0	0	1	3	.250	.143
Durham, Ray#	.250	4	1	0	0	2	0	.500	.250
Fielder, C	.375	8	3	0	0	0	0	.375	.375
Fryman, T	.400	5	2	0	1	3	0	.625	.400
Gomez, Chris	.125	8	1	0	0	1	1	.222	.125
Gonzalez, A	.000	5	0	0	0	0	1	.000	.000
Guillen, O*	.200	5	1	0	0	0	0	.200	.200
Higginson, B*	.625	8	5	1	3	1	1	.667	1.000
Knoblauch, C	.500	4	2	0	2	0	0	.400	.750
Lewis, Mark	.600	5	3	0	1	0	1	.600	.600
Lofton, Kenny*	.143	7	1	0	1	0	0	.250	.143
Martinez, Da*	.500	4	2	0	1	0	0	.600	.750
Martinez, E	.333	6	2	0	1	0	1	.429	.500
Martinez, T*	.300	10	3	1	1	0	2	.300	.600
Meares, Pat	.286	7	2	0	1	0	1	.286	.429
Murray, Eddie#	.571	7	4	0	1	0	0	.571	.571
Nixon, Otis#	.250	4	1	0	0	2	0	.500	.250
O'Brien, C	.200	5	1	0	1	0	0	.200	.200
Raines, Tim#	.000	4	0	0	0	2	0	.333	.000
Ramirez, M	.000	3	0	0	4	2		.571	.000
Stahoviak, S*	.429	7	3	0	1	1	0	.500	.571
Thomas, Frank	.250	4	1	0	0	0	0	.400	.250
Thome, Jim*	.000	5	0	0	1	1	0	.167	.000
Ventura, R*	.000	4	0	0	1	1	1	.200	.000
Vizquel, Omar#	.167	6	1	0	1	0	2	.286	.167

Mark Hutton, Marlins — RHP

Batter	Avg	AB	H	HR	BI	BB	SO	OBP	Slg
Alou, Moises	.333	6	2	0	1	0	0	.333	.333
Baerga, C#	.000	3	0	0	0	1	0	.400	.000
Gaetti, Gary	.200	5	1	0	0	0	1	.200	.200
Grudzielanek	.143	7	1	0	0	0	0	.143	.286
Lansing, Mike	.333	6	2	0	0	0	0	.333	.500
Polonia, Luis*	.333	3	1	0	0	2	0	.600	.333
Rodriguez, H*	.167	6	1	0	1	0	0	.167	.167
Segui, David#	.000	4	0	0	0	3	0	.429	.000
White, R	.333	6	2	0	0	0	0	.333	.333

Batter	Avg	AB	H	HR	BI	BB	SO	OBP	Slg
Abbott, Kurt	.000	4	0	0	1	0	1	.000	.000
Alou, Moises	.182	11	2	1	3	3	0	.357	.455
Andrews, S	.111	9	1	0	0	1	3	.200	.111
Arias, Alex	.200	5	1	0	0	1	0	.333	.200
Bagwell, Jeff	.500	6	3	0	1	4	0	.700	.500
Bates, Jason#	.000	5	0	0	0	1	0	.167	.000
Bell, Derek	.333	9	3	0	2	0	2	.333	.444
Bell, Jay	.250	12	3	0	1	2	0	.357	.250
Benard, M*	.571	7	4	0	0	1	0	.571	.714
Berry, Sean	.111	9	1	0	0	0	0	.111	.111
Bichette, D	.250	12	3	0	0	3	3	.400	.250
Biggio, Craig	.444	9	4	0	1	1	1	.500	.556
Blauser, Jeff	.000	6	0	0	0	0	0	.000	.000
Bonds, Barry*	.000	6	0	0	0	1	1	.143	.000
Burks, Ellis	.455	11	5	2	5	3	0	.600	1.364
Caminiti, Ken#	.375	8	3	0	0	1	1	.444	.375
Carreon, Mark	.200	5	1	0	1	1	3	.286	.200
Castilla, V	.429	14	6	2	3	0	2	.429	.857
Clayton, R	.286	7	2	0	0	0	1	.286	.286
Colbrunn, G	.385	13	5	0	1	0	3	.385	.538
Conine, Jeff	.250	12	3	1	1	1	1	.308	.500
Dunston, S	.000	4	0	0	1	0	1	.167	.000
Eisenreich, J*	.571	7	4	0	0	0	0	.571	.571
Finley, Steve*	.273	11	3	0	0	2	0	.385	.273
Fletcher, D*	.417	12	5	0	2	1	0	.462	.583
Floyd, Cliff*	.222	9	2	0	1	0	1	.300	.222
Gaetti, Gary	.143	7	1	0	0	0	1	.143	.286
Galarraga, A	.308	13	4	0	1	2	4	.400	.308
Gant, Ron	.300	10	3	2	5	1	3	.333	1.000
Gonzalez, L*	.200	5	1	0	2	0	1	.167	.400
Grace, Mark*	.250	4	1	0	0	2	2	.500	.250
Grissom, M	.273	11	3	1	2	0	1	.273	.727
Grudzielanek	.350	20	7	0	0	0	1	.350	.400
Gutierrez, R	.750	4	3	0	0	0	0	.833	1.000
Gwynn, Tony*	.167	12	2	0	1	1	2	.231	.167
Hayes, C	.250	16	4	0	0	1	3	.294	.250
Henderson, R	.200	5	1	0	0	2	1	.429	.200
Hernandez, Jo	.200	5	1	0	0	0	0	.200	.200
Jefferies, G#	.429	7	3	0	0	0	0	.429	.429
Johnson, Bri	.333	9	3	0	2	1	2	.417	.333
Johnson, Char	.250	8	2	0	1	0	1	.333	.375
Johnson, Mark*	.375	8	3	0	3	0	3	.333	.375
Jones, C#	.222	9	2	0	1	1	1	.273	.222
Joyner, Wally*	.400	5	2	0	0	1	1	.500	.400
Justice, Dave*	.167	6	1	0	1	0	0	.167	.167
Kendall, J	.000	6	0	0	0	1	1	.143	.000
King, Jeff	.143	7	1	1	2	0	1	.143	.571
Kingery, Mike*	.300	10	3	0	1	1	1	.364	.300
Klesko, Ryan*	.333	9	3	1	1	1	0	.400	.778
Knorr, Randy	.167	6	1	0	1	0	1	.167	.167
Lampkin, Tom*	.250	4	1	0	0	1	1	.500	.250
Lankford, Ray*	.429	7	3	0	0	1	1	.500	.714
Lansing, Mike	.333	18	6	1	3	2	4	.400	.500
Larkin, Barry	.286	7	2	0	0	0	0	.286	.286
Lemke, Mark#	.286	7	2	0	0	1	0	.375	.286
Liriano, N#	.364	11	4	0	1	0	0	.364	.455
Livingstone*	.556	9	5	0	3	0	0	.556	.556
Lopez, Javy	.100	10	1	0	1	0	2	.100	.100
Mabry, John*	.286	7	2	0	1	0	2	.286	.286
Martin, Al*	.455	11	5	0	3	2	2	.500	.545
May, Derrick*	.600	5	3	1	3	1	0	.667	1.200
McCracken, Q#	.500	6	3	0	2	0	0	.500	.500
McGriff, Fred*	.167	6	1	0	1	3	1	.444	.167
McRae, Brian#	.333	6	2	0	1	0	0	.333	.500
Merced, O*	.429	14	6	2	4	1	1	.467	.929
Miller, Or	.400	5	2	0	2	1	2	.500	.400
Morandini, M*	.143	7	1	0	0	0	1	.143	.429
Morris, Hal*	.500	6	3	0	0	0	0	.500	.667
Mouton, James	.333	6	2	0	0	1	1	.429	.333
Pendleton, T#	.300	10	3	0	1	1	1	.364	.300
Reed, Jeff*	.600	5	3	0	0	2	1	.714	.600
Reed, Jody	.100	10	1	0	0	0	1	.250	.100
Renteria, E	.000	7	0	0	0	0	2	.000	.000
Roberts, Bip#	.000	7	0	0	0	0	0	.000	.000
Rodriguez, H*	.267	15	4	0	2	0	5	.353	.267
Sanders, R	.200	5	1	0	0	1	1	.333	.200
Santangelo, F#	.111	9	1	0	1	1	0	.250	.111
Segui, David*	.200	10	2	1	4	3	2	.385	.500
Sheaffer, D	.200	5	1	0	1	0	1	.333	.200
Sheffield, J	.333	9	3	0	0	1	2	.455	.333
Sosa, Sammy	.000	5	0	0	1	1	0	.167	.000
Stocker, K#	.167	6	1	0	0	2	0	.286	.167
Tarasco, Tony*	.000	6	0	0	0	3	0	.000	.000
Veras, Q#	.833	6	5	0	0	0	0	.833	.833
Webster, D	.400	5	2	1	1	0	0	.400	1.000
Weiss, Walt*	.200	10	2	0	0	1	0	.200	.200
White, Devon&	.364	11	4	0	2	0	4	.364	.364
White, R	.429	14	6	0	1	0	4	.467	.429
Whiten, Mark#	.143	7	1	0	0	0	0	.143	.143
Williams, Ma	.200	5	1	0	2	1	1	.429	.600
Young, Eric	.500	10	5	0	1	1	0	.545	.500

Batter	Avg	AB	H	HR	BI	BB	SO	OBP	Slg
Abbott, Kurt	.167	6	1	0	0	0	1	.167	.167
Alicea, Luis#	.500	8	4	0	3	0	0	.444	.750
Alomar, R#	.364	22	8	1	1	3	4	.440	.682
Alou, Moises	.273	22	6	0	2	0	2	.261	.318
Amaro, Ruben#	.429	7	3	0	1	0	1	.500	1.000
Anthony, Eric*	.200	5	1	0	0	1	1	.333	.200
Arias, Alex	.000	4	0	0	0	2	1	.333	.000
Ashley, Billy	.333	6	2	0	2	0	0	.429	.333
Ausmus, Brad	.333	9	3	1	3	0	2	.333	.889
Bagwell, Jeff	.467	15	7	0	2	0	4	.467	.867
Baines, H*	.308	26	8	0	3	1	7	.333	.346
Barberie, B#	.231	13	3	0	0	0	1	.231	.231
Bell, Derek	.107	28	3	0	2	0	5	.107	.143
Bell, Jay	.357	28	10	0	4	5	7	.457	.464
Belliard, R	.143	7	1	0	2	0	2	.143	.143
Berry, Sean	.222	9	2	0	1	0	3	.417	.222
Bichette, D	.350	20	7	2	5	0	3	.350	.750
Biggio, Craig	.500	22	11	1	6	7	2	.645	.682
Blauser, Jeff	.389	36	14	2	8	7	5	.488	.750
Bogar, Tim	.333	6	2	0	0	0	0	.333	.667
Boggs, Wade*	.444	18	8	0	3	1	2	.545	.500
Bonds, Barry*	.371	35	13	2	11	5	2	.450	.571
Bonilla, B#	.214	42	9	2	5	3	6	.267	.381
Boone, Bret	.154	13	2	0	3	1	6	.200	.231
Bournigal, R	.200	5	1	0	0	1	0	.333	.200
Branson, Jeff*	.500	14	7	0	1	1	3	.533	.571
Brumfield, J	.125	16	2	0	3	0	3	.125	.250
Burks, Ellis	.417	12	5	0	0	3	3	.533	.833
Burnitz, J*	.200	5	1	0	1	0	1	.200	.400
Butler, Brett*	.238	63	15	0	7	12	12	.355	.286
Caminiti, Ken#	.522	23	12	1	5	1	1	.520	.783
Candaele, C#	.333	6	2	0	0	0	1	.333	.333
Cangelosi, J#	.143	7	1	0	1	1	1	.250	.143
Canseco, Jose	.294	17	5	0	2	2	1	.368	.412
Carr, Chuck	.133	15	2	0	0	0	2	.133	.133
Carreon, Mark	.235	17	4	1	4	3	3	.333	.529
Carter, Joe	.273	22	6	1	2	0	2	.273	.500
Castilla, V	.308	13	4	0	3	0	0	.308	.462
Cedeno, A	.200	10	2	0	0	1	2	.273	.200
Cianfrocco, A	.067	15	1	0	0	1	4	.125	.067
Clark, Phil	.471	17	8	1	4	1	2	.500	.765
Clark, Will*	.349	43	15	1	7	5	8	.420	.442
Clayton, R	.294	17	5	1	5	2	5	.381	.529
Colbrunn, G	.231	13	3	0	0	0	2	.231	.385
Coleman, V#	.276	29	8	0	4	0	6	.276	.379
Conine, Jeff	.214	14	3	0	1	2	3	.313	.429
Cora, Joey#	.500	3	3	0	0	0	0	.500	.500
Cordero, Wil	.467	15	7	0	1	4	0	.571	.733
Dascenzo, D#	.333	15	5	0	1	0	1	.333	.333
Daulton, D*	.222	18	4	1	6	0	0	.222	.444
Davis, Eric	.143	7	1	0	0	0	2	.333	.143
Dawson, Andre	.071	14	1	0	0	0	3	.071	.071
Deer, Rob	.364	11	4	2	7	4	4	.500	.909
DeShields, D*	.353	17	6	0	2	6	2	.522	.412
Dorsett, B	.167	6	1	0	0	0	1	.167	.167
Duncan, M	.067	15	1	0	1	1	3	.125	.067
Dunston, S	.261	23	6	1	3	1	1	.292	.522
Dykstra, L*	.235	17	4	0	1	9	2	.500	.235
Elster, Kevin	.294	17	5	0	2	2	3	.368	.353
Eusebio, Tony	.600	5	3	0	0	1	0	.667	1.000
Fielder, C	.364	11	4	1	3	0	1	.364	.636
Finley, Steve*	.167	6	1	0	0	0	2	.167	.167
Franco, Julio	.222	18	4	0	0	3	1	.333	.333
Gaetti, Gary	.238	21	5	1	3	4	2	.360	.381
Gagne, Greg	.190	21	4	0	0	1	2	.227	.190
Galarraga, A	.359	39	14	2	8	2	4	.395	.590
Gallego, Mike	.625	8	5	0	4	0	0	.625	.750
Gant, Ron	.170	47	8	2	5	8	6	.291	.340
Garcia, C	.211	19	4	0	2	0	4	.200	.316
Gilkey, B	.375	32	12	0	2	2	1	.412	.469
Girardi, Joe	.455	11	5	0	1	1	1	.500	.455
Gonzalez, L*	.438	16	7	2	4	1	5	.471	.875
Grace, Mark*	.240	25	6	0	6	3	4	.310	.280
Grissom, M	.323	31	10	0	1	5	2	.417	.387
Guillen, O*	.526	19	10	0	2	0	2	.526	.526
Gutierrez, R	.200	15	3	0	1	2	5	.294	.333
Gwynn, Tony*	.321	53	17	0	5	2	3	.345	.358
Hayes, C	.111	27	3	0	3	2	4	.194	.111
Henderson, R	.222	9	2	0	0	9	2	.611	.222
Hernandez, Ca	.333	15	5	0	1	0	2	.333	.333
Hernandez, Jo	.200	5	1	0	0	1	0	.200	.200
Hill, G	.333	13	4	0	1	1	3	.357	.308
Hollins, Dave#	.500	10	5	1	4	3	1	.600	1.100
Hudler, Rex	.250	20	5	0	0	2	5	.318	.300
Hundley, Todd#	.000	8	0	0	0	4	0	.000	.000
Hunter, Brian	.333	24	8	2	6	3	3	.407	.708
Hunter, Bri L	.500	6	3	0	0	0	0	.500	.500
Incaviglia, P	.250	12	3	0	2	1	2	.308	.417
Javier, Stan#	.389	18	7	0	2	1	2	.450	.500
Jefferies, G#	.300	30	9	0	3	1	2	.313	.400
Jones, Chris	.167	6	1	0	0	1	0	.286	.167

Danny Jackson, Cardinals — LHP

Batter	Avg	AB	H	HR	BI	BB	SO	OBP	Slg
Jordan, Brian	.364	11	4	0	0	1	1	.417	.364
Jordan, Ricky	.250	16	4	0	1	0	4	.250	.250
Joyner, Wally*	.143	14	2	0	0	0	4	.143	.143
Justice, Dave*	.296	27	8	3	6	3	6	.375	.667
Karkovice, R	.111	9	1	1	4	0	4	.111	.444
Karros, Eric	.435	23	10	0	4	3	3	.481	.478
Kelly, R	.250	20	5	0	0	3	4	.348	.300
Kent, Jeff	.294	17	5	0	3	0	0	.294	.471
King, Jeff	.300	30	9	1	4	1	1	.323	.500
Lankford, Ray*	.278	18	5	0	1	4	6	.409	.278
Lansing, Mike	.214	14	3	0	1	2	2	.313	.214
Larkin, Barry	.133	15	2	0	0	8	1	.435	.133
Lemke, Mark#	.308	26	8	0	4	4	1	.400	.500
Lewis, Darren	.290	31	9	0	2	2	5	.333	.355
Lopez, Javy	.667	6	4	1	2	0	1	.667	1.167
Magadan, Dave*	.077	13	1	0	2	0	2	.077	.077
Manwaring, K	.306	36	11	0	3	5	4	.390	.333
McGee, Willie#	.190	21	4	1	2	2	2	.261	.429
McGriff, Fred*	.292	24	7	1	7	5	7	.433	.458
McGwire, Mark	.625	8	5	0	2	2	0	.667	.625
McRae, Brian#	.429	7	3	0	1	0	2	.429	.429
Merced, O*	.313	16	5	0	0	0	4	.313	.313
Miller, Orl	.429	6	2	0	2	1	0	.429	.333
Mitchell, Kei	.000	5	0	0	0	0	0	.000	.000
Mitchell, K	.242	33	8	3	9	2	5	.286	.606
Molitor, Paul	.267	15	4	0	0	1	2	.313	.400
Mondesi, Raul	.200	15	3	0	1	0	3	.200	.333
Morman, Russ	.444	9	4	1	1	1	0	.500	.778
Morris, Hal*	.364	11	4	0	0	0	2	.417	.455
Mouton, James	.500	10	5	0	1	0	1	.500	.700
Murray, Eddie#	.239	71	17	0	8	3	10	.267	.324
Nixon, Otis#	.349	43	15	0	2	7	4	.431	.395
O'Brien, C	.333	24	8	0	2	1	1	.360	.417
Offerman, J#	.455	22	10	0	2	1	6	.478	.455
Oliver, Joe	.222	9	2	0	1	3	1	.417	.222
Owens, Eric	.000	5	0	0	0	2	0	.286	.000
Pagnozzi, Tom	.231	26	6	0	4	3	2	.310	.269
Palmeiro, R*	.571	7	4	0	0	0	0	.571	.714
Parent, Mark	.231	13	3	0	0	2	1	.333	.231
Parker, Rick	.500	6	3	0	0	0	0	.500	.500
Pena, G#	.500	18	9	1	3	1	0	.550	.778
Pena, Tony	.222	9	2	0	0	0	0	.222	.444
Pendleton, T#	.229	48	11	0	4	2	5	.255	.271
Perez, E	.000	5	0	0	1	1	2	.167	.000
Phillips, T#	.231	13	3	0	1	4	4	.412	.231
Piazza, Mike	.333	9	3	1	4	0	1	.300	.778
Plantier, P*	.222	9	2	0	0	1	5	.300	.222
Prince, Tom	.250	8	2	0	2	1	0	.300	.500
Raines, Tim#	.250	8	2	0	0	2	1	.400	.250
Reed, Jody	.250	8	2	0	0	3	1	.455	.375
Ripken, Billy	.286	7	2	0	0	0	0	.286	.286
Ripken, Cal	.261	23	6	0	4	4	2	.393	.348
Roberson, K#	.429	7	3	1	2	0	0	.429	.857
Roberts, Bip#	.192	26	5	0	1	3	4	.276	.192
Sabo, Chris	.222	9	2	0	0	1	4	.300	.333
Samuel, Juan	.286	42	12	1	4	2	7	.318	.452
Sanchez, Rey	.182	11	2	0	0	3	1	.357	.182
Sandberg, R	.308	26	8	0	4	1	5	.333	.385
Sanders, R	.438	16	7	2	9	1	2	.471	.813
Santiago, B	.294	34	10	1	4	4	7	.359	.471
Scarsone, S	.600	10	6	0	3	2	1	.667	.700
Schofield, D	.359	39	14	0	0	6	2	.444	.359
Segui, David#	.222	9	2	0	2	1	1	.300	.222
Servais, S	.167	6	1	0	1	1	1	.250	.333
Sheaffer, D	.167	6	1	0	0	0	0	.167	.333
Sheffield, G	.267	15	4	0	1	0	1	.267	.267
Shipley, C	.273	22	6	0	0	1	2	.333	.273
Sierra, Ruben#	.273	11	3	1	2	0	1	.250	.545
Slaught, Don	.222	27	6	0	0	1	3	.250	.222
Smith, Ozzie#	.342	38	13	0	2	4	2	.386	.395
Sosa, Sammy	.250	20	5	0	4	1	2	.286	.250
Spehr, Tim	.400	5	2	0	1	0	0	.400	.600
Stocker, K#	.167	6	1	0	0	1	0	.375	.167
Strawberry, D*	.056	18	1	0	1	4	6	.227	.056
Sveum, Dale#	.353	17	6	0	2	2	3	.421	.412
Tarasco, Tony*	.125	8	1	0	0	0	0	.125	.125
Tartabull, D	.250	4	1	1	2	1	1	.400	1.000
Tettleton, M#	.267	15	4	0	1	4	3	.450	.267
Thompson, Rob	.297	37	11	0	4	4	7	.366	.432
Thompson, Ry	.143	14	2	0	0	1	2	.200	.143
Trammell, A	.148	27	4	1	3	1	4	.179	.333
Valle, Dave	.444	9	4	0	1	0	2	.444	.667
Vizcaino, J#	.333	9	3	0	1	2	1	.455	.333
Walker, Larry*	.227	22	5	0	4	0	4	.217	.273
Wallach, Tim	.378	37	14	2	7	3	3	.425	.622
Walton, J	.400	10	4	0	0	0	2	.400	.400
Webster, L	.400	10	4	0	3	0	0	.400	.500
Wehner, John	.250	4	1	0	1	1	0	.400	.250
Weiss, Walter	.200	15	3	0	1	0	1	.188	.200
White, Devon#	.111	9	1	0	0	2	2	.273	.111
White, R	.375	8	3	0	2	2	1	.500	.500

Danny Jackson, Cardinals — LHP (continued)

Batter	Avg	AB	H	HR	BI	BB	SO	OBP	Slg
Whiten, Mark#	.200	10	2	1	1	0	3	.200	.500
Williams, E	.444	9	4	0	0	0	2	.444	.556
Williams, Ma	.135	37	5	1	5	4	6	.220	.216
Young, Eric	.167	18	3	0	1	3	0	.286	.167
Young, Kevin	.200	5	1	0	0	1	0	.333	.200
Zeile, Todd	.050	20	1	0	1	11	1	.387	.050

Mike Jackson, Mariners — RHP

Batter	Avg	AB	H	HR	BI	BB	SO	OBP	Slg
Alicea, Luis*	.200	5	1	0	0	0	1	.200	.400
Alomar, R#	.500	4	2	0	2	1	0	.600	.750
Alomar Jr, S	.000	3	0	0	1	0	3	.250	.000
Alou, Moises	.143	7	1	0	0	0	1	.143	.143
Anderson, Brd*	.167	6	1	0	0	1	1	.375	.333
Anthony, Eric*	.200	5	1	0	0	1	0	.333	.200
Baerga, C	.143	7	1	0	0	1	2	.250	.143
Bagwell, Jeff	.300	10	3	1	4	1	3	.364	.600
Baines, H*	.333	9	3	0	5	3	1	.500	.444
Barberie, B#	.400	5	2	0	1	1	0	.500	.400
Bell, Derek	.167	6	1	0	0	1	2	.286	.167
Bell, Jay	.222	9	2	0	1	1	3	.300	.333
Belle, Albert	.111	9	1	0	1	0	4	.111	.222
Belliard, R	.200	5	1	0	0	1	2	.333	.200
Berroa, G	.167	6	1	0	0	1	3	.286	.167
Berry, Sean	.000	5	0	0	0	0	3	.000	.000
Bichette, D	.100	10	1	0	0	1	4	.182	.100
Biggio, Craig	.286	7	2	0	0	0	2	.375	.286
Blauser, Jeff	.100	10	1	0	0	0	3	.100	.100
Boggs, Wade*	.143	7	1	0	0	4	0	.455	.143
Bonds, Barry*	.200	5	1	0	0	1	0	.333	.200
Bonilla, B#	.250	12	3	0	3	1	2	.308	.417
Borders, Pat	.167	6	1	0	0	0	2	.167	.167
Bordick, Mike	.400	5	2	0	0	0	0	.400	.400
Brosius, S	.500	4	2	1	3	2	2	.667	1.250
Burks, Ellis	.250	16	4	2	4	2	4	.333	.625
Butler, Brett*	.000	4	0	0	0	2	2	.333	.000
Caminiti, Ken#	.143	7	1	0	0	4	2	.455	.143
Candaele, C#	.100	10	1	0	1	1	0	.091	.100
Cangelosi, J#	.200	5	1	0	1	2	1	.429	.200
Canseco, Jose	.000	14	0	0	0	2	4	.125	.000
Carr, Chuck	.200	5	1	0	0	0	3	.200	.200
Carter, Joe	.214	14	3	0	0	1	2	.313	.357
Clark, Will*	.500	6	3	1	1	0	0	.500	1.000
Colbrunn, G	.167	6	1	0	1	0	1	.167	.167
Conine, Jeff	.167	6	1	0	0	0	2	.286	.167
Cora, Joey#	.200	5	1	0	0	1	0	.333	.200
Cordova, M	.000	5	0	0	0	0	0	.000	.000
Daulton, D*	.375	8	3	0	2	0	0	.375	.625
Davis, Chili#	.667	9	6	0	2	6	0	.765	.667
Dawson, Andre	.444	9	4	1	2	2	0	.545	.778
Deer, Rob	.000	12	0	0	0	1	8	.077	.000
DeShields, D*	.333	6	2	0	0	0	2	.333	.333
Devereaux, M	.375	8	3	0	0	1	2	.444	.375
Duncan, M	.167	6	1	0	0	0	3	.167	.500
Dunston, S	.222	9	2	0	0	0	3	.222	.333
Eisenreich, J*	.273	11	3	1	2	1	2	.333	.636
Espinoza, A	.500	10	5	0	1	0	1	.500	.700
Fermin, Felix	.000	5	0	0	0	1	1	.167	.000
Fielder, C	.000	6	0	0	0	1	2	.143	.000
Finley, Steve*	.333	9	3	0	1	1	1	.400	.333
Fletcher, D*	.400	5	2	0	0	1	1	.500	.600
Franco, Julio	.294	17	5	0	3	3	3	.400	.353
Fryman, T	.167	6	1	0	0	1	2	.286	.167
Gaetti, Gary	.231	13	3	0	4	1	1	.333	.308
Galarraga, A	.133	15	2	0	0	6	0	.133	.200
Gallego, Mike	.167	6	1	0	0	1	1	.286	.167
Gant, Ron	.143	7	1	0	0	1	1	.250	.143
Garcia, C	.167	6	1	0	0	0	0	.167	.167
Gilkey, B	.333	9	3	0	1	1	3	.364	.444
Girardi, Joe	.125	8	1	0	0	1	0	.222	.250
Gonzales, R	.250	4	1	1	0	0	0	.250	1.000
Gonzalez, J	.250	8	2	1	2	0	2	.250	.750
Gonzalez, L*	.250	4	1	1	2	1	0	.400	1.000
Grace, Mark*	.200	5	1	1	1	0	0	.200	.800
Greenwell, M*	.182	11	2	0	1	2	1	.308	.273
Grissom, M	.286	7	2	0	0	0	2	.286	.571
Guillen, O*	.143	7	1	0	1	4	0	.455	.286
Gwynn, Tony*	.667	6	4	0	3	0	0	.800	.833
Hall, Mel*	.400	5	2	0	0	2	0	.571	.400
Hamilton, D*	.333	6	2	0	1	0	1	.333	.333
Harris, Lenny*	.333	6	2	0	0	1	0	.333	.333
Henderson, R	.429	7	3	0	1	1	1	.556	.429
Hollins, Dave#	.222	9	2	0	0	3	2	.222	.222
Hoiles, Chris	.200	5	1	0	0	0	3	.200	.200
Howell, Jack*	.333	9	3	2	3	1	3	.400	1.000
Hundley, Todd#	.000	4	0	0	0	1	0	.000	.000
Incaviglia, P	.267	15	4	0	0	0	6	.353	.333
Javier, Stan#	.143	7	1	0	0	0	2	.222	.143
Jordan, Brian	.333	6	2	1	3	0	2	.333	.833
Joyner, Wally*	.286	7	2	0	2	0	1	.250	.286
Justice, Dave*	.400	5	2	0	0	0	2	.400	.400

Batter	Avg	AB	H	HR	BI	BB	SO	OBP	Slg
Karkovice, R	.000	4	0	0	0	1	3	.200	.000
Karros, Eric	.400	10	4	0	3	1	5	.455	.500
Kelly, R	.091	11	1	0	0	1	5	.231	.091
Kent, Jeff	.167	6	1	1	1	0	3	.286	.667
King, Jeff	.000	5	0	0	0	0	3	.000	.000
Knoblauch, C	.600	5	3	0	2	0	0	.600	.600
Kreuter, Chad#	.000	5	0	0	0	0	0	.000	.000
Lankford, Ray*	.167	6	1	1	1	2	1	.375	.667
Lansing, Mike	.000	5	0	0	0	1	1	.286	.000
Larkin, Barry	.125	8	1	1	2	1	2	.222	.500
Lemke, Mark*	.200	10	2	0	0	1	1	.273	.200
Liriano, N#	.333	6	2	0	1	1	0	.429	.333
Macfarlane, M	.000	5	0	0	0	0	2	.167	.000
Magadan, Dave*	.200	5	1	0	2	1	0	.333	.200
Martin, Al*	.200	5	1	0	0	0	2	.200	.400
Martinez, Da*	.500	8	4	0	1	3	2	.583	.500
May, Derrick*	.000	4	0	0	0	1	0	.200	.000
McGriff, Fred*	.286	7	2	0	0	1	2	.375	.571
McGwire, Mark	.176	17	3	0	4	5	9	.348	.176
McLemore, M#	.364	11	4	0	3	1	1	.417	.455
McRae, Brian#	.000	5	0	0	0	1	0	.000	.000
Mitchell, K	.286	7	2	2	4	1	1	.375	1.143
Molitor, Paul	.063	16	1	0	1	1	4	.118	.125
Morris, Hal*	.200	5	1	0	0	2	1	.429	.200
Murray, Eddie#	.214	14	3	1	4	1	3	.267	.429
Naehring, Tim	.250	4	1	1	2	1	0	.400	1.000
Nixon, Otis#	.125	8	1	0	0	0	1	.125	.125
O'Brien, C	.000	5	0	0	0	0	0	.000	.000
O'Neill, Paul*	.500	4	2	0	0	1	0	.600	.750
Offerman, J#	.429	7	3	0	1	0	2	.429	.571
Oliver, Joe	.200	5	1	0	0	0	2	.200	.200
Orsulak, Joe*	.250	12	3	2	7	2	1	.333	.750
Pagnozzi, Tom	.000	6	0	0	0	2	0	.000	.000
Palmeiro, R*	.636	11	7	2	3	2	1	.714	1.273
Palmer, Dean	.200	5	1	0	0	1	1	.333	.200
Pena, Tony	.250	12	3	1	2	0	4	.250	.500
Pendleton, T#	.250	12	3	2	4	0	1	.250	.833
Phillips, T#	.111	9	1	0	0	1	1	.200	.111
Piazza, Mike	.333	6	2	0	0	1	2	.429	.500
Plantier, P*	.000	4	0	0	0	1	2	.200	.000
Polonia, Luis*	.500	6	3	0	0	3	1	.667	.500
Raines, Tim#	.300	10	3	0	1	2	0	.417	.500
Ramirez, M	.000	4	0	0	1	1	2	.200	.000
Reed, Jody	.100	10	1	0	1	5	2	.438	.100
Ripken, Billy	.000	5	0	0	0	0	4	.000	.000
Ripken, Cal	.375	16	6	3	10	1	2	.412	1.000
Sabo, Chris	.143	7	1	0	2	1	3	.250	.286
Sandberg, R	.250	12	3	1	2	1	2	.308	.583
Sanders, R	.000	4	0	0	0	2	2	.333	.000
Santiago, B	.000	6	0	0	0	0	3	.000	.000
Schofield, D	.385	13	5	0	3	1	1	.429	.385
Seitzer, K	.286	7	2	0	1	1	2	.375	.286
Sheffield, G	.235	17	4	0	1	2	2	.316	.235
Sierra, Ruben#	.182	11	2	1	0	3	1	.357	.273
Slaught, Don	.111	9	1	1	2	0	4	.111	.444
Smith, Ozzie#	.300	10	3	0	2	3	1	.462	.600
Sosa, Sammy	.000	7	0	0	0	2	5	.222	.000
Stanley, Mike	.250	8	2	0	0	1	3	.333	.250
Steinbach, T	.167	12	2	0	2	0	5	.231	.167
Stillwell, K#	.333	12	4	0	2	1	1	.385	.417
Surhoff, B.J.*	.111	9	1	0	0	1	1	.200	.222
Sveum, Dale#	.400	5	2	0	0	0	1	.400	.400
Tartabull, D	.143	14	2	1	2	1	7	.250	.357
Tettleton, M#	.250	8	2	1	1	3	3	.333	.625
Thomas, Frank	.333	9	3	1	4	1	2	.400	.778
Thompson, Rob	.000	4	0	0	0	1	1	.200	.000
Trammell, A	.100	10	1	0	1	2	3	.250	.100
Vaughn, Greg	.000	4	0	0	2	1	2	.167	.000
Velarde, R	.125	8	1	0	0	1	2	.222	.125
Ventura, R*	.333	3	1	0	0	2	0	.600	.333
Vizcaino, J#	.429	7	3	0	0	2	1	.556	.571
Walker, Larry*	.400	5	2	1	2	3	0	.625	1.000
Wallach, Tim	.250	16	4	0	1	1	3	.294	.313
Weiss, Walt#	.375	8	3	0	1	2	0	.400	.750
White, Devon#	.200	10	2	1	4	3	1	.385	.700
Whiten, Mark#	.429	7	3	0	1	1	0	.500	.429
Worthington,	.000	7	0	0	0	1	5	.125	.000
Young, Eric	.400	5	2	0	0	1	0	.500	.400
Zeile, Todd	.167	12	2	0	2	0	4	.167	.167

Batter	Avg	AB	H	HR	BI	BB	SO	OBP	Slg
Alomar, R#	.286	7	2	0	0	2	0	.444	.286
Alou, Moises	.400	5	2	0	3	0	0	.400	.800
Amaral, Rich	.500	4	2	0	0	1	0	.600	.750
Anderson, Brd*	.333	6	2	0	2	0	0	.333	.333
Anderson, G*	.000	5	0	0	0	1	4	.167	.000
Andrews, S	.250	4	1	0	1	1	0	.400	.750
Ausmus, Brad	.167	6	1	0	0	0	2	.167	.167
Becker, Rich*	.333	6	2	0	0	0	0	.333	.333
Bell, Derek	.000	5	0	0	1	0	1	.000	.000

Batter	Avg	AB	H	HR	BI	BB	SO	OBP	Slg
Berroa, G	.333	6	2	0	0	0	0	.333	.333
Berry, Sean	.500	4	2	0	0	1	0	.600	.750
Bordick, Mike	.286	7	2	0	1	1	0	.375	.286
Brosius, S	.000	7	0	0	0	0	2	.000	.000
Cirillo, Jeff	.286	7	2	0	1	0	1	.286	.286
Clark, Will*	.000	5	0	0	1	0	0	.000	.000
Coomer, Ron	.333	6	2	0	1	1	2	.429	.333
Cordero, Wil	.429	7	3	0	3	0	0	.429	.571
Cordova, M	.600	5	3	0	1	0	0	.600	1.000
Davis, Chili#	.500	6	3	0	0	0	0	.500	.500
Devereaux, M	.333	6	2	0	0	0	0	.333	.333
Durham, Ray#	.400	5	2	0	3	0	0	.400	.800
Frye, Jeff	.600	5	3	0	0	0	1	.600	.600
Gallego, Mike	.400	5	2	0	1	0	0	.400	.400
Giambi, Jason*	.600	5	3	1	1	0	0	.667	1.400
Girardi, Joe	.333	6	2	0	0	0	2	.333	.333
Gonzalez, J	.400	5	2	1	2	0	1	.400	1.200
Greer, Rusty*	.000	4	0	0	0	1	0	.200	.000
Griffey Jr, K*	.600	5	3	0	0	0	2	.600	.600
Gutierrez, R	.250	4	1	0	1	1	1	.333	.250
Gwynn, Tony*	.800	5	4	0	1	0	0	.833	1.200
Hamilton, D*	.200	5	1	0	0	0	0	.200	.200
Herrera, Jose*	.333	3	1	0	2	2	0	.500	.333
Hudler, Rex	.000	5	0	0	0	1	2	.167	.000
Johnson, L*	.500	6	3	1	2	0	0	.500	1.000
Karkovice, R	.250	4	1	1	4	2	0	.500	1.000
Kelly, R	.429	7	3	0	0	0	0	.429	.571
Knoblauch, C	.143	7	1	0	2	1	1	.143	.429
Lansing, Mike	.667	3	2	1	4	1	0	.600	1.667
Leius, Scott	.333	3	1	0	1	0	0	.400	.333
Lewis, Darren	.167	6	1	0	0	1	1	.286	.167
Listach, Pat#	.400	5	2	0	0	0	0	.400	.400
Martinez, T*	.000	4	0	0	0	1	0	.200	.000
Meares, Pat	.143	7	1	0	0	0	2	.143	.143
Mieske, Matt	.200	5	1	0	2	0	0	.200	.400
Molitor, Paul	.286	7	2	0	0	0	0	.286	.286
Mouton, Lyle	.143	7	1	0	0	0	0	.143	.143
Munoz, Pedro	.429	7	3	1	2	0	0	.429	1.000
Myers, Greg*	.400	5	2	0	0	0	1	.400	.400
Nilsson, Dave*	.200	5	1	0	0	1	0	.200	.200
Nixon, Otis#	.143	7	1	0	0	0	0	.143	.143
O'Neill, Paul*	.286	7	2	0	1	0	2	.286	.429
Paquette, C	.000	5	0	0	0	1	1	.000	.000
Phillips, T#	.500	4	2	0	1	1	0	.600	.750
Roberts, Bip#	.167	6	1	0	0	0	1	.167	.333
Rodriguez, I	.600	5	3	0	1	0	0	.600	.800
Salmon, Tim	.000	6	0	0	1	0	0	.000	.000
Santiago, B	.400	5	2	0	0	0	0	.400	.400
Seitzer, K	.429	7	3	0	1	1	1	.500	.429
Shipley, C	.500	8	4	0	1	0	0	.500	.625
Snopek, Chris	.571	7	4	1	3	0	0	.571	1.143
Snow, J.T.#	.750	4	3	1	2	1	0	.800	1.500
Steinbach, T	.400	5	2	0	1	0	1	.400	.400
Surhoff, B.J.*	.100	10	1	0	0	0	1	.100	.100
Tartabull, D	.750	4	3	1	1	1	0	.800	1.500
Tettleton, M#	.400	5	2	0	0	1	2	.500	.600
Thomas, Frank	.500	6	3	1	2	1	1	.571	1.167
Vaughn, Greg	.167	6	1	0	0	0	3	.167	.167
Velarde, R	.500	4	2	1	2	1	1	.600	1.250
Ventura, R*	.600	5	3	0	1	0	0	.600	.600
White, R	.250	4	1	0	0	2	0	.500	.500
Williams, Ber#	.286	7	2	0	0	0	0	.286	.286
Williams, E	.400	5	2	0	1	1	0	.500	.600
Wilson, Dan	.167	6	1	0	0	0	0	.167	.167

Batter	Avg	AB	H	HR	BI	BB	SO	OBP	Slg
Alomar, R#	.000	4	0	0	0	1	0	.200	.000
Bordick, Mike	.400	5	2	0	1	0	0	.500	.400
Bragg, Darren*	1.000	1	1	0	0	4	0	1.000	2.000
Buhner, Jay	.286	7	2	1	1	0	0	.286	.714
Canseco, Jose	.500	4	2	0	0	0	0	.600	.500
Cora, Joey#	.200	5	1	0	0	0	0	.200	.200
Cordova, M	.333	6	2	0	0	0	1	.333	.333
Fielder, C	.000	8	0	0	0	1	1	.111	.000
Fryman, T	.167	6	1	0	0	1	1	.286	.167
Gonzalez, A	.333	6	2	0	1	1	1	.429	.333
Higginson, B*	.000	4	0	0	0	1	1	.200	.000
Macfarlane, M	.200	5	1	0	0	1	1	.333	.200
Martinez, E	.250	4	1	0	1	2	2	.500	.500
McLemore, M#	.200	5	1	0	0	1	0	.200	.200
Meares, Pat	.000	5	0	0	0	0	2	.000	.000
Molitor, Paul	.167	6	1	0	0	0	0	.167	.167
Naehring, Tim	.167	6	1	0	0	0	1	.167	.167
Ripken, Cal	.400	5	2	0	0	0	0	.400	.400
Stanley, Mike	.333	3	1	0	2	1	0	.600	.333
Steinbach, T	.200	5	1	0	0	0	1	.333	.200
Tartabull, D	.000	5	0	0	0	0	1	.000	.000
Thomas, Frank	.500	4	2	1	2	3	0	.714	1.500
Valentin, Jhn	.444	9	4	1	4	0	0	.444	.778
Valentin, Jse#	.250	4	1	0	0	1	0	.400	.250

Mike James, Angels — RHP

Batter	Avg	AB	H	HR	BI	BB	SO	OBP	Slg
Vaughn, Mo*	.000	6	0	0	0	2	2	.250	.000

Marty Janzen, Blue Jays — RHP

Batter	Avg	AB	H	HR	BI	BB	SO	OBP	Slg
Boggs, Wade*	.250	4	1	0	0	1	0	.400	.500
Cirillo, Jeff	.143	7	1	0	0	0	0	.143	.143
Clark, Tony#	.429	7	3	1	2	1	0	.500	1.000
Curtis, Chad	.600	5	3	2	3	1	1	.667	1.800
Fielder, C	.167	6	1	1	3	0	2	.167	.667
Fryman, T	.625	8	5	1	3	1	2	.667	1.000
Higginson, B*	.429	7	3	1	1	1	0	.500	.857
Jaha, John	.000	3	0	0	0	3	1	.500	.000
Lewis, Mark	.125	8	1	0	0	0	2	.125	.125
Matheny	.000	5	0	0	0	0	2	.000	.000
Pride, Curtis*	.222	9	2	1	2	0	3	.222	.556
Seitzer, K	.500	6	3	1	2	0	0	.500	1.167
Valentin, Jse#	.400	5	2	1	2	1	1	.500	1.000
Vaughn, Greg	.333	6	2	1	1	0	0	.333	1.000
Vina, F*	.333	6	2	0	1	1	0	.429	.333

Kevin Jarvis, Reds — RHP

Batter	Avg	AB	H	HR	BI	BB	SO	OBP	Slg
Abbott, Kurt	.000	6	0	0	0	1	0	.143	.000
Alou, Moises	.300	10	3	0	3	0	1	.273	.300
Andrews, S	.833	6	5	1	4	1	0	.857	1.500
Arias, Alex	.167	6	1	0	1	0	1	.167	.167
Bates, Jason#	.286	7	2	0	0	0	1	.286	.286
Bell, Jay	.200	10	2	0	0	1	3	.273	.200
Benard, M*	.200	5	1	0	0	1	1	.333	.400
Bichette, D	.417	12	5	0	3	1	0	.462	.583
Bonds, Barry*	.667	3	2	0	1	5	0	.875	1.000
Brumfield, J	.250	4	1	0	0	1	0	.400	.250
Burks, Ellis	.200	5	1	0	1	0	0	.200	.400
Butler, Brett*	.400	5	2	0	0	1	0	.500	.400
Caminiti, Ken#	.400	10	4	1	2	0	2	.400	.700
Carr, Chuck	.000	4	0	0	0	1	0	.200	.000
Castilla, V	.250	12	3	2	2	1	2	.308	.750
Castillo, L#	.600	5	3	0	0	2	1	.714	.600
Cianfrocco, A	.400	5	2	0	0	0	2	.400	.600
Clark, Dave*	.400	5	2	0	1	1	0	.400	.600
Colbrunn, G	.400	10	4	0	1	1	0	.455	.600
Conine, Jeff	.167	12	2	0	3	1	2	.231	.167
Cordero, Wil	.400	5	2	0	0	0	0	.400	.600
DeShields, D*	.000	3	0	0	0	2	1	.400	.000
Doster, David	.333	6	2	0	0	0	1	.333	.333
Eisenreich, J*	.000	6	0	0	0	0	1	.000	.000
Encarnacion	.200	5	1	0	1	0	1	.200	.400
Finley, Steve*	.300	10	3	0	0	1	1	.364	.400
Fletcher, D*	.500	6	3	0	1	1	1	.500	.500
Floyd, Cliff*	.400	5	2	0	0	0	1	.400	.800
Galarraga, A	.364	11	4	2	3	0	1	.364	.909
Garcia, C	.286	7	2	1	1	0	0	.286	.714
Gilkey, B	.429	14	6	0	0	1	1	.467	.500
Girardi, Joe	.200	5	1	0	2	0	0	.200	.400
Gomez, Chris	.400	5	2	0	0	0	1	.400	.400
Gomez, Leo	.250	4	1	0	1	1	1	.400	.250
Gonzalez, L*	.167	6	1	0	0	0	0	.167	.167
Grace, Mark*	.222	9	2	0	0	0	0	.222	.222
Grudzielanek	.333	9	3	1	3	0	1	.333	.778
Gwynn, Tony*	.400	10	4	1	1	0	1	.400	.700
Hayes, C	.333	9	3	0	1	0	2	.333	.444
Henderson, R	.375	8	3	0	0	2	1	.500	.375
Hernandez, Jo	.000	5	0	0	0	2	0	.000	.000
Hill, G	.333	6	2	0	1	0	0	.333	.667
Hundley, Todd#	.500	8	4	3	6	0	0	.500	1.625
Huskey, Butch	.167	6	1	0	1	1	2	.286	.167
Jefferies, G#	.091	11	1	0	0	0	0	.091	.091
Johnson, Bri	.250	4	1	0	0	1	0	.400	.250
Johnson, Char	.500	4	2	0	3	0	0	.600	.750
Johnson, L*	.286	7	2	0	0	0	1	.286	.571
Johnson, Mark*	.400	5	2	1	1	0	0	.500	1.000
Jordan, Brian	.500	6	3	1	2	1	0	.571	1.000
Joyner, Wally*	.400	5	2	0	2	1	0	.400	.500
Karros, Eric	.500	6	3	0	2	0	0	.571	.833
Kelly, R	.800	5	4	0	1	0	0	.800	1.000
Kent, Jeff	.500	6	3	0	0	0	1	.500	.500
King, Jeff	.273	11	3	0	1	1	1	.333	.364
Kingery, Mike*	.364	11	4	1	1	1	1	.417	.818
Lankford, Ray*	.500	6	3	1	2	2	0	.625	1.000
Lansing, Mike	.222	9	2	0	0	1	0	.222	.444
Manwaring, K	.200	5	1	0	1	0	1	.200	.200
Martin, Al*	.250	12	3	1	3	0	1	.250	.667
McRae, Brian#	.250	4	1	0	1	1	0	.400	.500
Merced, O*	.111	9	1	0	0	0	0	.111	.111
Mondesi, Raul	.500	6	3	0	3	0	0	.500	.500
Murray, Glenn	.000	7	0	0	0	2	0	.000	.000
Otero, Ricky#	.667	3	2	0	2	1	0	.600	1.333
Pagnozzi, Tom	.167	6	1	0	0	0	0	.167	.333
Pendleton, T#	.167	6	1	1	1	0	1	.167	.667
Reed, Jeff*	.200	5	1	1	0	1	0	.200	.800
Reed, Jody	.000	4	0	0	0	2	0	.333	.000

Kevin Jarvis, Reds — RHP

Batter	Avg	AB	H	HR	BI	BB	SO	OBP	Slg
Renteria, E	.167	6	1	0	1	1	0	.286	.167
Rodriguez, H*	.500	6	3	1	4	0	1	.500	1.000
Sandberg, R	.250	8	2	0	0	0	1	.250	.250
Scarsone, S	.000	6	0	0	0	1	2	.143	.000
Selcik, Kevin	.667	6	4	0	0	0	0	.667	1.167
Sheffield, G	.400	10	4	1	4	1	0	.455	.800
Sosa, Sammy	.286	7	2	2	3	0	2	.286	1.143
Tarasco, Tony*	.200	5	1	0	0	0	0	.200	.200
Veras, Q#	.143	7	1	0	0	0	1	.143	.143
Vizcaino, J#	.143	7	1	0	0	1	1	.250	.429
Walker, Larry*	.500	6	3	0	2	1	0	.500	.833
Wallach, Tim	.429	7	3	0	1	0	3	.429	.571
Weiss, Walt*	.100	10	1	1	1	3	0	.357	.400
Wilkins, Rick*	.500	6	3	1	2	0	0	.500	1.000
Young, Eric	.429	7	3	0	0	1	0	.500	.429
Zeile, Todd	.364	11	4	1	2	2	0	.429	.636

Doug Johns, Athletics — LHP

Batter	Avg	AB	H	HR	BI	BB	SO	OBP	Slg
Alexander, M	.000	6	0	0	0	0	0	.000	.000
Alomar, R#	.600	10	6	0	2	2	1	.667	.800
Anderson, Brd*	.333	15	5	2	3	3	3	.444	1.000
Anderson, G*	.286	14	4	0	2	0	1	.267	.286
Baerga, C#	.286	7	2	0	2	0	0	.286	.429
Baines, H*	.571	7	4	0	0	2	1	.667	.714
Bautista, D	.200	5	1	0	1	0	1	.200	.200
Belle, Albert	.000	3	0	0	1	1	2	.200	.000
Boggs, Wade*	.400	5	2	0	0	1	0	.500	.400
Bonilla, B#	.214	14	3	0	2	2	2	.313	.357
Buford, Damon	.286	7	2	0	0	1	2	.375	.286
Buhner, Jay	.600	5	3	2	5	1	1	.667	2.000
Canseco, Jose	.333	6	2	1	2	0	0	.429	.833
Carter, Joe	.000	4	0	0	0	0	0	.200	.000
Cirillo, Jeff	.200	10	2	0	0	0	4	.200	.300
Curtis, Chad	.333	6	2	0	0	0	0	.333	.333
Damon, Johnny*	.375	8	3	0	0	0	0	.375	.375
Davis, Chili#	.500	14	7	0	3	2	1	.529	.643
Devereaux, M	.222	9	2	0	1	1	1	.300	.333
DiSarcina, G	.250	12	3	0	0	1	1	.250	.250
Durham, Ray#	.167	6	1	0	0	0	3	.167	.333
Edmonds, Jim*	.091	11	1	0	0	0	0	.091	.091
Elster, Kevin	.429	7	3	0	0	0	2	.429	.429
Erstad, Darin*	.333	6	2	0	0	1	0	.429	.333
Fielder, C	.333	9	3	1	2	1	1	.400	.667
Franco, Julio	.500	6	3	0	1	1	0	.571	.667
Fryman, T	.333	6	2	0	2	0	0	.333	.500
Girardi, Joe	.167	6	1	0	1	0	0	.167	.167
Gonzales, R	.000	4	0	0	0	2	1	.333	.000
Gonzalez, J	.800	5	4	1	1	2	0	.857	1.600
Goodwin, Tom*	.167	6	1	0	0	0	0	.167	.167
Greer, Rusty*	.400	10	4	0	2	1	1	.455	.500
Hamilton, D*	.200	5	1	0	0	1	0	.333	.200
Hammonds, J	.400	5	2	0	0	1	1	.500	.400
Haselman, B	.667	3	2	0	0	2	0	.800	.667
Hoiles, Chris	.143	7	1	0	0	0	0	.250	.143
Howard, Dave#	.667	6	4	0	1	0	0	.667	.667
Hudler, Rex	.500	8	4	1	1	1	1	.600	1.000
Jaha, John	.429	7	3	1	4	3	1	.600	.857
Jeter, Derek	.000	4	0	0	0	1	0	.200	.000
Lewis, Darren	.000	4	0	0	1	0	0	.200	.000
Lewis, Mark	.200	5	1	0	1	0	0	.333	.600
Listach, Pat#	.111	9	1	0	0	1	0	.200	.111
Lofton, Kenny*	.500	8	4	1	1	1	1	.556	1.000
Loretta, Mark	.200	5	1	0	1	0	0	.333	.200
Macfarlane, M	.250	8	2	1	2	1	0	.333	.750
Martinez, E	.400	5	2	0	2	3	0	.714	.750
Martinez, T*	.100	10	1	0	0	0	2	.182	.200
Matheny, Mike	.000	8	0	0	0	0	2	.000	.000
McGee, Willie#	.400	5	2	0	1	0	2	.400	.400
McLemore, M#	.250	8	2	1	1	1	0	.333	.625
Mieske, Matt	.250	8	2	0	1	0	2	.250	.375
Mouton, Lyle	.167	6	1	0	0	0	1	.167	.333
Murray, Eddie#	.167	6	1	1	2	2	1	.375	.667
Naehring, Tim	.333	3	1	0	0	3	1	.714	.667
O'Leary, Troy*	.500	4	2	0	1	0	0	.500	.750
O'Neill, Paul*	.143	7	1	0	0	0	1	.143	.286
Palmeiro, R*	.250	16	4	1	5	2	0	.333	.563
Palmer, Dean	.200	5	1	0	0	1	0	.200	.200
Paquette, C	.000	4	0	0	0	0	1	.200	.000
Phillips, T#	.125	8	1	0	1	2	1	.364	.125
Ramirez, M	.250	4	1	1	1	1	1	.400	1.000
Ripken, Billy	.500	4	2	0	1	0	0	.600	.750
Ripken, Cal	.133	15	2	1	2	0	1	.133	.400
Rodriguez, Al	.250	4	1	0	1	0	0	.400	.500
Rodriguez, I	.200	10	2	1	1	3	0	.273	.500
Salmon, Tim	.200	10	2	1	1	3	0	.385	.500
Samuel, Juan	.333	6	2	1	2	0	2	.333	.833
Seitzer, K	.556	9	5	0	2	2	1	.636	.889
Slaught, Don	.250	8	2	1	1	0	0	.333	.375
Snopek, Chris	.333	6	2	1	0	0	0	.333	.833
Snow, J.T.#	.200	15	3	0	1	1	4	.250	.200

Batter	Avg	AB	H	HR	BI	BB	SO	OBP	Slg
Sojo, Luis	.250	4	1	0	0	1	0	.400	.250
Tartabull, D	.571	7	4	0	1	0	1	.571	.571
Tettleton, M#	.286	7	2	0	0	1	3	.375	.429
Valentin, Jhn	.167	6	1	0	1	1	0	.286	.333
Vaughn, Greg	.500	4	2	0	1	2	0	.667	.500
Vaughn, Mo*	.375	8	3	0	1	0	3	.375	.375
Velarde, R	.286	7	2	0	0	0	2	.286	.286
Ventura, R*	.333	6	2	0	1	1	0	.429	.333
Vizquel, Omar#	.167	6	1	0	0	0	0	.167	.333
Wallach, Tim	.400	5	2	0	0	1	0	.500	.600
Williams, Ber#	.333	6	2	0	1	0	0	.333	.333
Williams, E	.333	3	1	0	1	2	1	.600	.333
Wilson, Dan	.429	7	3	0	3	0	0	.429	.429

Batter	Avg	AB	H	HR	BI	BB	SO	OBP	Slg
Alexander, M	.250	4	1	0	0	2	1	.500	.250
Alomar, R#	.216	37	8	0	3	6	12	.341	.216
Alomar Jr, S	.200	15	3	0	1	5	1	.429	.200
Anderson, Brd*	.296	27	8	0	7	3	10	.387	.370
Anderson, G*	.000	6	0	0	1	0	3	.000	.000
Baerga, C#	.324	37	12	0	9	1	7	.350	.432
Barberie, B#	.000	5	0	0	0	1	1	.167	.000
Bautista, D	.500	4	2	0	0	1	1	.600	.750
Becker, Rich*	.000	7	0	0	0	0	6	.000	.000
Bell, Derek	.125	8	1	0	0	2	3	.300	.250
Belle, Albert	.243	37	9	3	9	3	13	.317	.568
Beltre, E	.167	12	2	0	0	1	6	.231	.167
Berroa, G	.308	13	4	0	1	1	1	.357	.308
Bichette, D	.200	10	2	1	1	1	6	.273	.600
Blowers, Mike	.500	8	4	0	4	0	0	.500	.625
Boggs, Wade*	.118	17	2	0	0	1	8	.167	.118
Bonds, Barry*	.500	3	3	0	1	0	2	.500	.667
Bonilla, B#	.308	13	4	1	3	0	3	.308	.615
Borders, Pat	.205	39	8	1	2	3	9	.262	.333
Bordick, Mike	.161	31	5	0	2	4	8	.257	.258
Brosius, S	.071	14	1	0	0	2	6	.316	.071
Burks, Ellis	.400	15	6	2	6	2	5	.471	.867
Cangelosi, J#	.333	6	2	0	1	2	0	.500	.333
Canseco, Jose	.192	26	5	1	4	2	14	.250	.385
Carter, Joe	.280	50	14	3	8	3	14	.327	.500
Cirillo, Jeff	.333	12	4	0	1	0	4	.333	.583
Clark, Will*	.214	14	3	0	0	0	4	.214	.286
Coleman, V#	.250	8	2	0	0	0	2	.250	.250
Cora, Joey#	.182	11	2	0	1	4	2	.400	.182
Cordova, M	.364	11	4	0	2	1	4	.462	.545
Curtis, Chad	.300	30	9	0	2	4	6	.382	.467
Cuyler, Milt*	.333	12	4	0	0	4	3	.500	.333
Dascenzo, D#	.000	5	0	0	0	0	1	.000	.000
Davis, Chili*	.224	49	11	3	9	6	21	.309	.449
Dawson, Andre	.133	15	2	1	1	3	3	.278	.400
Deer, Rob	.095	21	2	0	1	2	12	.174	.095
Devereaux, M	.176	34	6	1	7	11	11	.362	.324
Diaz, Alex#	.333	9	3	0	0	0	5	.333	.333
DiSarcina, G	.229	35	8	0	1	2	3	.270	.343
Durham, Ray#	.556	9	5	0	1	0	2	.556	.667
Easley, D	.120	25	3	0	2	0	6	.120	.120
Edmonds, Jim*	.154	13	2	0	1	0	4	.214	.308
Eisenreich, J*	.300	10	3	1	6	0	3	.333	.600
Espinoza, A	.304	23	7	1	3	3	8	.385	.522
Fermin, Felix	.308	26	8	0	1	6	3	.455	.462
Fielder, C	.192	26	5	1	8	11	12	.432	.308
Finley, Steve*	.333	3	1	0	2	2	0	.600	.667
Flaherty, J	.125	8	1	0	0	1	4	.222	.250
Franco, Julio	.231	26	6	0	3	5	10	.364	.269
Frazier, Lou#	.000	6	0	0	0	1	1	.143	.000
Frye, Jeff	.214	14	3	0	0	1	1	.267	.214
Fryman, T	.276	29	8	4	9	4	11	.354	.690
Gaetti, Gary	.178	45	8	2	4	3	16	.224	.378
Gagne, Greg	.182	33	6	1	1	3	17	.250	.273
Gallego, Mike	.235	17	4	0	1	7	5	.480	.235
Gates, Brent#	.095	21	2	0	0	2	7	.174	.095
Gil, Benji	.000	8	0	0	0	0	8	.000	.000
Gomez, Chris	.250	8	2	0	1	2	3	.400	.375
Gomez, Leo	.200	15	3	1	2	7	7	.478	.467
Gonzales, R	.500	16	8	1	2	5	2	.667	.813
Gonzalez, A	.000	6	0	0	1	1	3	.143	.000
Gonzalez, J	.231	39	9	3	6	4	10	.318	.487
Goodwin, Tom*	.222	9	2	0	0	2	4	.364	.222
Grebeck, C	.000	17	0	0	0	4	5	.227	.000
Greenwell, M*	.278	18	5	1	6	1	4	.350	.556
Greer, Rusty*	.167	6	1	0	1	1	3	.286	.167
Guillen, O*	.182	11	2	0	0	1	4	.250	.182
Hall, Mel*	.188	16	3	0	2	2	0	.278	.188
Hamilton, D*	.111	9	1	0	0	3	1	.111	.111
Hammonds, J	.200	5	1	0	0	0	3	.200	.200
Hayes, C	.000	9	0	0	2	0	2	.091	.000
Henderson, R	.139	36	5	0	0	17	18	.415	.194
Hiatt, Phil	.250	8	2	1	2	0	5	.250	.625
Hill, G	.182	22	4	1	4	3	8	.259	.318
Holles, Chris	.250	24	6	2	4	3	12	.357	.500

Batter	Avg	AB	H	HR	BI	BB	SO	OBP	Slg
Howard, Dave#	.087	23	2	0	1	0	7	.087	.130
Howard, T*	.167	12	2	0	2	2	4	.286	.167
Howell, Jack*	.000	5	0	0	0	1	3	.167	.000
Hudler, Rex	.389	18	7	1	5	0	7	.389	.722
Huff, Michael	.083	12	1	0	0	2	9	.214	.083
Hulse, David*	.083	12	1	0	1	0	4	.083	.250
Incaviglia, P	.294	17	5	0	2	3	6	.455	.353
Jaha, John	.100	20	2	0	0	3	9	.217	.100
James, Dion*	.000	7	0	0	0	0	2	.000	.000
Javier, Stan#	.192	26	5	0	1	2	6	.250	.231
Jefferies, G#	.273	11	3	0	0	1	2	.333	.455
Jefferson, R*	.143	14	2	0	1	1	7	.200	.143
Jeter, Derek	.286	7	2	0	1	0	3	.286	.429
Johnson, L*	.297	27	8	0	0	1	6	.321	.296
Joyner, Wally*	.115	26	3	1	1	3	9	.258	.231
Karkovice, R	.160	25	4	1	1	3	12	.250	.320
Kelly, Pat	.192	26	5	0	0	2	8	.276	.269
Kelly, R	.250	20	5	1	1	2	5	.348	.450
Knoblauch, C	.146	41	6	0	0	2	10	.205	.195
Kreuter, Chad	.154	13	2	1	1	1	5	.214	.462
Lampkin, Tom*	.000	6	0	0	0	0	3	.000	.000
Leius, Scott	.200	25	5	0	5	3	4	.394	.240
Lewis, Mark	.182	11	2	0	1	3	2	.375	.182
Leyritz, Jim	.136	22	3	1	3	8	11	.424	.273
Listach, Pat#	.286	28	8	0	5	1	8	.333	.357
Lofton, Kenny*	.231	26	6	0	5	10	5	.355	.269
Macfarlane, M	.077	26	2	1	2	4	14	.219	.231
Manto, Jeff	.333	9	3	0	0	2	2	.500	.556
Martin, N	.100	10	1	0	0	0	4	.100	.100
Matheny, Mike	.300	10	3	0	2	1	4	.364	.400
Mayne, Brent*	.000	4	0	0	0	1	2	.200	.000
McCarty, Dave	.100	10	1	0	0	0	7	.100	.100
McGriff, Fred*	.000	5	0	0	1	1	2	.143	.000
McGwire, Mark	.190	21	4	1	3	5	8	.346	.333
McLemore, M#	.214	14	3	0	1	5	4	.450	.214
McRae, Brian#	.162	37	6	1	6	4	9	.238	.324
Meares, Pat	.217	23	5	2	3	1	8	.250	.522
Mieske, Matt	.214	14	3	2	4	2	2	.353	.643
Molitor, Paul	.222	36	8	1	6	7	10	.341	.361
Munoz, Pedro	.278	36	10	1	4	0	13	.278	.500
Murray, Eddie*	.000	5	0	0	0	1	0	.000	.000
Myers, Greg*	.600	5	3	0	2	0	2	.600	.800
Naehring, Tim	.211	19	4	0	1	0	7	.211	.211
Nixon, Otis#	.278	18	5	0	0	4	5	.409	.333
Norman, Les	.200	5	1	0	0	1	2	.333	.200
O'Brien, C	.214	14	3	0	1	2	1	.353	.286
Offerman, J#	.000	5	0	0	0	0	4	.000	.000
Palmeiro, R*	.048	21	1	0	0	5	8	.048	.048
Palmer, Dean	.172	29	5	1	4	5	18	.294	.276
Paquette, C	.217	23	5	1	3	2	12	.280	.391
Pena, Tony	.143	14	2	0	0	1	6	.368	.143
Perez, E	.182	11	2	0	1	0	3	.182	.182
Phillips, T#	.256	43	11	1	4	9	9	.385	.372
Polonia, Luis*	.200	10	2	0	0	2	5	.385	.300
Pulliam, H	.500	10	5	0	2	0	3	.500	.800
Raines, Tim#	.227	22	5	0	2	2	6	.292	.273
Ramirez, M	.143	7	1	0	3	0	2	.143	.286
Rebouler, J	.276	29	8	0	3	3	8	.344	.345
Reed, Jody	.385	13	5	0	0	6	4	.579	.692
Ripken, Billy	.269	26	7	0	4	1	2	.296	.308
Ripken, Cal	.239	46	11	1	4	5	6	.314	.370
Rodriguez, I	.242	33	8	1	4	3	7	.306	.394
Sabo, Chris	.250	8	2	0	0	2	1	.400	.250
Salmon, Tim	.161	31	5	1	2	1	16	.188	.258
Samuel, Juan	.200	10	2	1	2	0	2	.333	.500
Sandberg, R	.286	7	2	0	0	0	3	.286	.286
Schofield, D	.182	22	4	0	2	4	6	.308	.182
Schu, Rick	.500	6	3	1	1	2	1	.625	1.167
Segui, David#	.444	9	4	0	2	1	3	.500	.444
Seitzer, K	.143	28	4	0	6	12	6	.381	.214
Sheffield, G	.125	8	1	0	1	4	1	.385	.125
Shumpert, T	.286	7	2	0	1	0	7	.444	.571
Sierra, Ruben#	.269	67	18	2	7	7	13	.338	.388
Silvestri, D	.100	10	1	1	2	1	7	.167	.400
Slaught, Don	.333	6	2	0	1	0	1	.333	.500
Snow, J.T.#	.190	21	4	0	0	3	9	.292	.238
Sojo, Luis	.176	17	3	0	1	1	4	.222	.235
Sosa, Sammy	.238	21	5	1	3	1	9	.273	.381
Spiers, Bill*	.500	4	2	0	1	1	0	.600	.500
Sprague, Ed	.154	26	4	0	0	3	13	.241	.192
Stankiewicz	.333	12	4	0	0	2	1	.429	.417
Stanley, Mike	.200	45	9	3	7	12	11	.362	.400
Steinbach, T	.143	42	6	0	2	4	14	.217	.167
Stillwell, K#	.300	10	3	0	2	1	3	.364	.400
Strange, Doug#	.200	5	1	0	1	0	1	.200	.200
Surhoff, B.J.*	.167	12	2	0	0	3	2	.333	.167
Sveum, Dale#	.000	8	0	0	3	4	3	.273	.000
Tartabull, D	.200	40	8	1	5	19	13	.450	.350
Tettleton, M#	.200	40	10	3	6	8	18	.375	.550
Thomas, Frank	.267	30	8	3	7	10	14	.450	.633
Tinsley, Lee#	.143	7	1	0	0	1	4	.250	.143

Randy Johnson, Mariners — LHP

Batter	Avg	AB	H	HR	BI	BB	SO	OBP	Slg
Trammell, A	.364	22	8	0	3	3	2	.440	.455
Turner, Chris	.333	9	3	0	1	2	4	.455	.333
Valentin, Jhn	.313	16	5	0	0	4	3	.476	.563
Valentin, Jse#	.000	10	0	0	0	2	5	.167	.000
Valle, Dave	.250	4	1	0	0	1	1	.400	.250
Vaughn, Greg	.167	30	5	2	6	4	12	.257	.367
Vaughn, Mo*	.200	10	2	1	2	0	4	.200	.500
Velarde, R	.462	39	18	0	7	4	9	.512	.538
Ventura, R*	.188	32	6	0	2	6	12	.308	.219
Vina, F*	.000	6	0	0	0	0	2	.143	.000
Vitiello, Joe	.143	7	1	0	1	2	3	.333	.143
Vizquel, Omar#	.286	7	2	0	0	1	0	.375	.286
Voigt, Jack	.400	10	4	1	2	0	4	.400	.700
Walbeck, Matt#	.222	9	2	0	0	2	3	.364	.333
Ward, Turner#	.556	9	5	0	2	0	2	.556	.778
Weiss, Walt#	.167	6	1	0	2	2	1	.333	.167
White, Devon#	.235	51	12	2	3	8	16	.339	.431
Whiten, Mark#	.250	16	4	0	1	1	5	.294	.250
Williams, Ber#	.286	28	8	0	6	1	10	.394	.393
Williams, Ger	.263	19	5	2	5	3	6	.391	.632
Worthington	.304	23	7	1	2	4	5	.407	.478

John Johnstone, Astros — RHP

Batter	Avg	AB	H	HR	BI	BB	SO	OBP	Slg
Bichette, D	.000	4	0	0	0	1	1	.200	.000
Gilkey, B	.333	6	2	0	1	0	1	.333	.667
Whiten, Mark#	.333	3	1	0	1	2	0	.600	.333

Bobby Jones, Mets — RHP

Batter	Avg	AB	H	HR	BI	BB	SO	OBP	Slg
Abbott, Kurt	1.000	5	5	0	0	1	0	1.000	1.400
Alicea, Luis#	.167	6	1	0	0	0	2	.167	.167
Alou, Moises	.667	9	6	2	6	1	1	.700	1.444
Anthony, Eric*	.200	10	2	0	2	1	0	.273	.200
Arias, Alex	.286	7	2	0	1	0	0	.286	.286
Aurilia, Rich	.000	6	0	0	0	0	2	.000	.000
Ausmus, Brad	.375	8	3	0	0	1	2	.444	.375
Bagwell, Jeff	.304	23	7	2	4	2	5	.346	.609
Batiste, Kim	.167	6	1	0	1	0	0	.167	.167
Bell, Derek	.263	19	5	0	2	1	3	.286	.368
Bell, Jay	.385	13	5	1	3	3	1	.556	.692
Belliard, R	.250	4	1	0	0	0	0	.250	.500
Berry, Sean	.400	10	4	0	0	2	3	.500	.500
Bichette, D	.389	18	7	2	6	0	2	.400	.833
Biggio, Craig	.208	24	5	0	1	4	4	.321	.250
Blauser, Jeff	.522	23	12	2	3	2	2	.560	.913
Blowers, Mike	.167	6	1	1	2	0	2	.167	.667
Bonds, Barry*	.250	28	7	1	4	1	7	.276	.429
Boone, Bret	.333	24	8	1	4	1	3	.360	.542
Branson, Jeff*	.333	18	6	0	1	1	4	.368	.444
Brumfield, T	.222	9	2	0	1	0	2	.300	.333
Burks, Ellis	.571	7	4	3	5	2	2	.667	2.143
Butler, Brett*	.333	9	3	0	0	1	1	.400	.556
Caminiti, Ken#	.214	14	3	1	2	1	4	.267	.429
Cangelosi, J#	.286	7	2	0	0	2	1	.444	.571
Carreon, Mark	.250	8	2	0	0	0	1	.250	.500
Castilla, V	.417	12	5	2	3	2	5	.467	1.083
Cedeno, A	.111	9	1	0	1	2	3	.333	.111
Cedeno, Roger#	.571	7	4	0	0	1	1	.571	.571
Clark, Dave*	.286	7	2	0	1	1	0	.333	.286
Clayton, R	.367	30	11	0	5	1	3	.387	.567
Colbrunn, G	.444	9	4	0	0	0	0	.444	.556
Cole, Alex*	.600	5	3	0	0	1	0	.667	1.200
Conine, Jeff	.231	13	3	1	3	0	2	.231	.462
Cordero, Wil	.143	7	1	0	0	0	1	.143	.143
Daulton, D*	.154	13	2	0	2	2	3	.313	.231
Decker, Steve	.333	6	2	0	1	0	1	.333	.333
DeShields, D*	.214	14	3	1	2	3	3	.353	.500
Duncan, M	.278	18	5	0	1	0	5	.278	.389
Dykstra, L*	.267	15	4	0	1	0	4	.267	.267
Eisenreich, J*	.294	17	5	0	0	2	0	.368	.412
Eusebio, Tony	.200	10	2	0	2	0	0	.200	.200
Finley, Steve*	.160	25	4	0	1	1	3	.192	.200
Fletcher, D*	.200	15	3	1	1	1	1	.250	.467
Floyd, Cliff*	.300	10	3	0	0	1	0	.364	.300
Fonville, C#	.222	9	2	0	0	1	2	.300	.222
Gaetti, Gary	.375	8	3	0	0	1	1	.444	.375
Galarraga, A	.333	15	5	0	1	0	1	.333	.400
Gant, Ron	.250	20	4	1	6	3	4	.292	.400
Garcia, C	.278	18	5	1	2	0	2	.278	.444
Gilkey, B	.308	13	4	0	0	2	3	.308	.308
Girardi, Joe	.500	8	4	0	1	0	0	.500	.625
Gomez, Leo	.143	7	1	1	3	1	0	.250	.571
Gonzalez, L*	.250	28	7	2	5	1	4	.276	.464
Grace, Mark*	.333	18	6	1	3	1	0	.368	.667
Greene, W*	.250	4	1	1	1	1	0	.400	1.000
Grissom, M	.261	23	6	1	3	1	1	.280	.435
Grudzielanek	.857	7	6	0	1	0	0	.857	1.000
Gutierrez, R	.100	10	1	0	0	1	1	.182	.100
Gwynn, Tony*	.417	24	10	0	3	3	2	.481	.500
Harris, Lenny*	.250	12	3	0	1	1	1	.308	.250
Hayes, C	.400	15	6	2	5	0	3	.375	.800
Henderson, R	.125	8	1	0	0	0	1	.125	.125
Hernandez, Jo	.091	11	1	0	0	0	3	.091	.091
Hill, G	.333	15	5	1	2	0	4	.333	.533
Hollandsworth*	.429	7	3	0	2	0	1	.429	.714
Hollins, Dave#	.167	6	1	0	0	1	3	.286	.167
Howard, T*	.391	23	9	1	3	2	3	.440	.565
Hunter, Bri L	.231	13	3	0	1	0	2	.231	.231
Incaviglia, P	.125	8	1	0	2	0	2	.111	.375
Jefferies, G#	.143	14	2	0	0	3	0	.294	.214
Johnson, Bri	.364	11	4	0	0	0	2	.364	.364
Johnson, Mark*	.500	2	1		2	1	1	.600	1.250
Jones, C#	.235	17	4	1	2	1	2	.278	.412
Jordan, Brian	.200	10	2	0	0	0	2	.200	.200
Joyner, Wally*	.375	8	3	1	2	1	0	.444	.875
Justice, Dave*	.286	14	4	1	4	1	1	.333	.571
Karros, Eric	.154	13	2	0	1	2	2	.267	.231
Kelly, R	.200	10	2	0	0	0	1	.200	.200
King, Jeff	.333	15	5	0	4	0	1	.313	.333
Kingery, Mike*	.083	12	1	0	0	0	1	.083	.167
Klesko, Ryan*	.421	19	8	2	6	3	3	.500	.737
Lankford, Ray*	.300	20	6	0	0	1	1	.333	.450
Lansing, Mike	.250	12	3	0	1	0	2	.308	.333
Larkin, Barry	.222	27	6	0	5	1	2	.276	.333
Lemke, Mark#	.100	20	2	0	0	1	1	.143	.100
Lewis, Darren	.250	20	5	0	2	3	2	.348	.300
Livingstone*	.286	14	4	0	1	0	2	.286	.286
Lopez, Javy	.250	12	3	0	1	0	1	.308	.333
Lopez, Luis#	.143	7	1	0	0	2	0	.333	.286
Mabry, John*	.182	11	2	1	2	0	0	.167	.455
Magadan, Dave*	.308	13	4	0	1	4	1	.471	.462
Manwaring, K	.118	17	2	0	0	0	5	.118	.118
Martin, Al*	.357	14	5	1	1	2	3	.438	.643
Martinez, Da*	.286	7	2	0	1	0	0	.286	.286
May, Derrick*	.333	15	5	0	4	1	1	.375	.533
McGee, Willie*	.375	8	3	1	3	1	1	.444	.750
McGriff, Fred*	.333	30	10	2	3	1	8	.355	.567
McRae, Brian#	.462	13	6	0	0	2	2	.533	.692
Merced, O*	.294	17	5	0	1	2	1	.368	.412
Miller, Orl	.167	12	2	0	0	0	0	.167	.167
Mondesi, Raul	.091	11	1	0	0	3	0	.286	.091
Morandini, M*	.333	15	5	0	4	2	2	.412	.467
Morris, Hal*	.211	19	4	1	2	0	5	.200	.421
Mueller, Bill#	.400	5	2	0	0	1	1	.500	.600
Offerman, J#	.000	5	0	0	0	1	2	.167	.000
Oliver, Joe	.400	5	2	0	0	0	1	.400	.400
Otero, Ricky#	.500	10	5	0	4	0	1	.500	.600
Owens, Eric	.000	6	0	0	0	2	0	.000	.000
Pagnozzi, Tom	.333	6	2	0	0	0	1	.333	.333
Pendleton, T#	.190	21	4	0	2	1	4	.217	.286
Perez, Eddie	.429	7	3	0	2	1	0	.500	.429
Phillips, J*	.167	6	1	0	0	1	1	.286	.333
Piazza, Mike	.462	13	6	1	1	0	1	.462	.692
Plantier, P*	.222	9	2	0	0	4	4	.300	.222
Reed, Jeff*	.111	9	1	0	0	2	1	.273	.222
Reed, Jody	.214	14	3	0	0	2	0	.313	.214
Roberts, Bip#	.286	14	4	0	1	1	3	.333	.357
Rodriguez, H*	.000	11	0	0	0	0	3	.000	.000
Sanchez, Rey	.125	8	1	0	1	0	0	.125	.125
Sandberg, R	.222	18	4	0	0	2	2	.300	.222
Sanders, R	.412	17	7	0	1	2	4	.500	.471
Santangelo, F#	.600	5	3	0	1	1	1	.667	.800
Santiago, B	.333	9	3	0	1	0	0	.333	.333
Scarsone, S	.250	8	2	0	2	0	2	.333	.250
Segui, David#	.000	6	0	0	0	1	0	.143	.000
Servais, S	.067	15	1	0	0	1	1	.176	.067
Sheaffer, D	.167	12	2	1	5	0	0	.231	.417
Silvestri, D	.000	5	0	0	0	1	2	.167	.000
Slaught, Don	.250	4	1	0	1	0	0	.400	.250
Smith, Dwight*	.400	15	6	1	2	1	2	.438	.667
Sosa, Sammy	.318	22	7	2	4	1	3	.348	.636
Stocker, K#	.476	21	10	0	4	3	0	.542	.667
Taubensee, E*	.308	13	4	0	3	0	4	.308	.385
Tavarez, Je#	.200	5	1	0	0	0	0	.200	.200
Thompson, Mil*	.125	8	1	0	0	0	1	.125	.125
Thompson, Rob	.286	7	2	0	0	0	0	.286	.429
Veras, Q#	.000	6	0	0	0	1	0	.143	.000
Walker, Larry*	.200	15	3	0	3	0	1	.200	.400
Wallach, Tim	.857	7	6	0	1	0	0	.857	1.000
Weiss, Walt#	.400	10	4	1	1	0	0	.400	.700
White, R	.333	9	3	0	1	0	1	.300	.444
Whiten, Mark#	.000	8	0	0	0	1	0	.000	.000
Wilkins, Rick*	.222	9	2	1	1	2	0	.364	.556
Williams, E	.125	8	1	0	0	1	0	.222	.125
Williams, Ma	.353	17	6	1	4	2	2	.421	.588
Wilson, Desi*	.167	6	1	0	0	0	0	.167	.167
Young, Eric	.400	10	4	0	0	3	0	.455	.400
Zeile, Todd	.143	14	2	0	0	1	6	.200	.143

Doug Jones, Brewers · RHP

Batter	Avg	AB	H	HR	BI	BB	SO	OBP	Slg
Alicea, Luis*	.333	9	3	0	1	0	4	.333	.556
Alou, Moises	.083	12	1	0	2	0	3	.083	.167
Baines, H*	.273	11	3	1	3	1	1	.333	.818
Barberie, B#	.200	5	1	0	0	0	1	.200	.200
Bell, Derek	.500	6	3	1	3	0	1	.500	1.000
Bell, Jay	.000	9	0	0	0	1	2	.100	.000
Belle, Albert	.400	5	2	0	2	0	1	.400	.600
Bichette, D	.308	13	4	1	3	0	1	.357	.538
Blauser, Jeff	.083	12	1	0	1	0	5	.083	.083
Boggs, Wade*	.125	8	1	0	1	3	1	.364	.125
Bonds, Barry*	.300	10	3	0	0	0	1	.300	.400
Bonilla, B#	.250	8	2	0	0	2	1	.400	.250
Buhner, Jay	.286	7	2	0	1	0	1	.286	.286
Burks, Ellis	.182	11	2	0	0	0	1	.182	.182
Butler, Brett*	.333	12	4	0	0	1	3	.385	.333
Canseco, Jose	.357	14	5	1	6	2	6	.438	.571
Carr, Chuck	.000	7	0	0	0	0	0	.000	.000
Clark, Phil	.400	5	2	0	0	0	2	.400	.600
Clark, Will*	.125	8	1	0	0	3	2	.364	.125
Clayton, R	.000	7	0	0	0	1	2	.125	.000
Cole, Alex*	.200	5	1	0	1	0	0	.200	.200
Cordero, Wil	.125	8	1	0	0	0	4	.125	.250
Cuyler, Milt*	.143	7	1	0	1	0	2	.143	.143
Davis, Chili*	.455	11	5	0	1	0	3	.455	.545
Davis, Eric	.222	9	2	1	2	0	2	.222	.667
Deer, Rob	.188	16	3	0	2	1	10	.316	.250
DeShields, D*	.400	5	2	0	4	1	1	.500	.600
Devereaux, M	.000	8	0	0	0	0	1	.000	.000
Duncan, M	.250	8	2	0	1	0	1	.250	.250
Dykstra, L*	.143	7	1	0	0	1	0	.250	.143
Eisenreich, J*	.250	12	3	0	0	1	1	.308	.250
Fielder, C	.214	14	3	1	1	0	5	.214	.429
Finley, Steve*	.000	5	0	0	0	0	0	.000	.000
Fletcher, D*	.250	8	2	1	2	0	1	.333	.750
Franco, Julio	.417	12	5	0	1	0	1	.417	.500
Fryman, T	.545	11	6	0	3	0	2	.545	.818
Gaetti, Gary	.231	13	3	1	1	2	4	.333	.462
Gagne, Greg	.000	8	0	0	0	0	3	.000	.000
Galarraga, A	.429	7	3	0	3	0	2	.429	.571
Gant, Ron	.286	7	2	0	1	0	1	.286	.429
Girardi, Joe	.333	6	2	0	0	0	2	.333	.333
Gonzalez, J	.375	8	3	0	3	0	0	.375	.500
Grace, Mark*	.333	6	2	0	0	1	0	.429	.333
Greenwell, M*	.444	9	4	0	3	1	1	.500	.667
Griffey Jr, K*	.111	9	1	0	0	0	1	.111	.111
Grissom, M	.125	8	1	0	0	0	2	.125	.125
Guillen, O*	.133	15	2	0	1	0	1	.133	.133
Gwynn, Tony*	.455	11	5	0	1	0	0	.455	.455
Hall, Mel*	.333	6	2	1	4	0	0	.286	.833
Hamilton, D*	.308	12	3	0	2	1	0	.308	.250
Hansen, Dave*	.250	8	2	0	0	0	0	.250	.250
Harris, Lenny*	.571	7	4	1	3	1	0	.625	1.000
Hayes, C	.333	6	2	1	4	1	2	.429	1.000
Henderson, R	.385	13	5	0	0	2	2	.467	.462
Hill, G	.000	6	0	0	0	0	2	.000	.000
Hollins, Dave#	.000	6	0	0	0	0	2	.000	.000
Howell, Jack*	.500	6	3	0	2	0	1	.500	.500
Hundley, Todd#	.111	9	1	0	0	0	2	.111	.222
Incaviglia, R	.174	23	4	0	1	1	8	.208	.174
Javier, Stan#	.375	8	3	0	2	1	1	.444	.625
Johnson, L*	.500	6	3	0	0	0	1	.500	.500
Jordan, Brian	.400	5	2	1	3	0	1	.400	1.000
Jordan, Ricky	.600	5	3	0	0	0	0	.600	.600
Joyner, Wally*	.389	18	7	0	4	0	3	.389	.556
Justice, Dave*	.429	7	3	0	0	0	2	.429	.429
Karros, Eric	.267	15	4	0	1	0	3	.267	.267
Kelly, R	.167	12	2	0	1	0	3	.154	.167
Kent, Jeff	.167	6	1	0	0	1	1	.286	.167
Klesko, Ryan*	.250	8	2	0	0	4	4	.250	.375
Knoblauch, C	.333	3	1	0	0	1	1	.600	.667
Lansing, Mike	.333	6	2	0	0	0	1	.333	.333
Larkin, Barry	.222	9	2	0	0	0	2	.222	.222
Lemke, Mark#	.333	12	4	0	2	1	1	.385	.333
Lewis, Darren	.714	7	5	0	3	0	0	.714	.714
Liriano, N#	.400	10	4	1	2	3	0	.500	.700
Livingstone*	.000	5	0	0	1	0	2	.000	.000
Macfarlane, M	.286	7	2	0	0	0	0	.286	.286
Magadan, Dave*	.200	5	1	0	0	0	0	.200	.200
Manwaring, K	.300	10	3	0	0	0	3	.300	.300
Martinez, Da*	.444	9	4	0	1	1	1	.500	.444
Martinez, E	.500	6	3	1	4	2	1	.667	1.333
May, Derrick*	.250	8	2	0	0	1	1	.333	.250
McGee, Willie*	.500	10	5	0	1	0	2	.500	.500
McGriff, Fred*	.059	17	1	0	1	2	5	.158	.059
McGwire, Mark	.389	18	7	1	5	2	4	.450	.611
McLemore, M#	.500	6	3	0	0	1	1	.500	.500
Merced, O*	.429	7	3	0	3	0	2	.429	.571
Mitchell, K	.600	5	3	1	3	0	2	.600	1.200
Molitor, Paul	.125	24	3	0	2	0	3	.125	.125
Mondesi, Raul	.167	6	1	0	3	0	2	.167	.167
Morandini, M*	.250	4	1	1	3	0	0	.333	1.000

Doug Jones, Brewers · RHP

Batter	Avg	AB	H	HR	BI	BB	SO	OBP	Slg
Morris, Hal*	.300	10	3	1	2	0	1	.300	.800
Murray, Eddie#	.412	17	7	1	8	2	4	.474	.824
Nixon, Otis#	.500	4	2	0	0	1	0	.600	.500
Offerman, J#	.125	8	1	0	0	1	0	.125	.125
Olerud, John*	.400	5	2	0	0	1	0	.500	.600
Oliver, Joe	.333	6	2	0	2	0	0	.333	.333
Orsulak, Joe*	.182	11	2	0	2	0	1	.182	.182
Pagnozzi, Tom	.200	10	2	0	0	0	3	.200	.200
Palmeiro, R*	.125	8	1	1	2	0	1	.125	.500
Pena, Tony	.300	10	3	0	1	0	1	.364	.500
Pendleton, T#	.333	6	2	0	1	0	0	.333	.500
Phillips, T#	.273	11	3	0	0	0	3	.273	.545
Piazza, Mike	.250	12	3	0	2	1	3	.308	.250
Plantier, P*	.333	6	2	0	1	0	0	.286	.333
Polonia, Luis*	.385	13	5	1	3	0	3	.385	.615
Reed, Jeff*	.400	5	2	0	1	0	0	.400	.400
Reed, Jody	.300	10	3	0	2	0	0	.300	.300
Ripken, Billy	.167	6	1	0	0	0	3	.167	.167
Ripken, Cal	.500	20	10	1	6	2	3	.545	.800
Roberts, Bip#	.000	4	0	0	0	2	2	.333	.000
Rodriguez, H*	.667	6	4	0	2	1	0	.714	1.000
Sabo, Chris	.400	5	2	0	0	1	0	.500	.600
Sanders, R	.250	12	3	1	2	0	4	.250	.583
Santiago, B	.250	8	2	0	1	0	4	.250	.250
Schofield, D	.333	12	4	0	0	0	2	.333	.333
Segui, David#	.250	4	1	0	1	1	0	.400	.250
Seitzer, K	.077	13	1	0	1	0	1	.077	.077
Sheffield, G	.250	12	3	0	0	0	1	.250	.250
Sierra, Ruben#	.125	16	2	0	1	0	3	.125	.125
Slaught, Don	.375	8	3	0	0	0	4	.375	.375
Smith, Ozzie#	.333	6	2	0	1	1	0	.429	.333
Sosa, Sammy	.364	11	4	0	0	0	2	.364	.364
Spiers, Bill*	.357	14	5	0	2	1	1	.400	.500
Stanley, Mike	.200	5	1	0	2	0	1	.200	.400
Steinbach, T	.625	8	5	0	4	0	1	.556	.750
Stillwell, K#	.000	9	0	0	0	2	3	.182	.000
Strange, Doug*	.500	6	3	0	0	0	2	.500	.500
Surhoff, B.J.*	.348	23	8	0	2	0	1	.348	.391
Sveum, Dale#	.333	12	4	0	1	2	2	.429	.500
Tartabull, D	.214	14	3	0	0	1	5	.267	.214
Tettleton, M#	.267	15	4	0	1	2	6	.353	.267
Thompson, Rob	.300	10	3	1	2	0	2	.333	.600
Trammell, A	.286	14	4	0	0	2	0	.375	.357
Valle, Dave	.333	6	2	0	1	1	1	.429	.500
Vaughn, Greg	.500	14	7	1	3	0	2	.500	1.000
Ventura, R*	.000	5	0	0	1	1	3	.167	.000
Vizquel, Omar*	.250	4	1	0	0	0	0	.250	.250
Weiss, Walt#	.200	10	2	0	0	2	1	.333	.200
White, Devon#	.273	11	3	0	0	0	4	.273	.364
Wilkins, Rick*	.182	11	2	1	1	0	2	.182	.455
Williams, Ma	.231	13	3	0	0	0	3	.231	.231
Young, Eric	.000	4	0	0	0	1	0	.200	.000
Zeile, Todd	.333	9	3	0	1	1	2	.400	.333

Todd Jones, Astros · RHP

Batter	Avg	AB	H	HR	BI	BB	SO	OBP	Slg
Abbott, Kurt	.333	6	2	0	1	0	1	.429	.500
Alicea, Luis*	.250	4	1	1	2	1	1	.400	1.000
Alou, Moises	.100	10	1	1	2	0	1	.100	.400
Arias, Alex	.286	7	2	0	1	0	2	.286	.571
Ausmus, Brad	.000	8	0	0	0	0	2	.000	.000
Bell, Derek	.000	5	0	0	0	0	1	.000	.000
Bell, Jay	.125	8	1	0	0	0	2	.125	.125
Berry, Sean	.200	5	1	1	1	0	0	.200	.800
Bichette, D	.429	7	3	1	4	1	1	.556	.857
Blauser, Jeff	.250	8	2	1	2	0	3	.250	.625
Bonds, Barry*	.250	4	1	0	0	4	1	.625	.250
Boone, Bret	.222	9	2	0	0	0	1	.222	.222
Branson, Jeff*	.500	6	3	1	2	0	1	.556	1.000
Brogna, Rico*	.200	5	1	0	1	1	1	.333	.600
Brumfield, J	.000	2	0	0	0	3	0	.600	.000
Bullett, S*	.167	6	1	0	1	1	3	.286	.167
Butler, Brett*	.333	6	2	0	1	0	1	.333	.333
Carr, Chuck	.000	4	0	0	0	0	3	.200	.000
Carreon, Mark	.333	9	3	0	3	1	1	.400	.444
Castilla, V	.250	4	1	0	0	2	1	.571	.250
Clark, Dave*	.333	6	2	0	1	0	2	.333	.667
Clayton, R	.000	7	0	0	0	1	3	.111	.000
Colbrunn, G	.000	7	0	0	0	1	0	.222	.000
Conine, Jeff	.333	9	3	0	1	0	1	.400	.444
Cordero, Wil	.400	5	2	0	0	0	0	.400	.400
Cummings, M*	.200	5	1	0	0	0	2	.200	.200
DeShields, D*	.000	6	0	0	0	0	0	.000	.000
Dunston, S	.333	6	2	0	0	0	0	.333	.500
Everett, Carl#	.400	5	2	0	0	0	0	.400	.600
Finley, Steve*	.000	5	0	0	0	0	0	.000	.000
Fletcher, D*	.556	9	5	0	2	1	0	.636	.667
Galarraga, A	.455	11	5	1	7	0	2	.455	.818
Gant, Ron	.600	5	3	2	6	1	0	.667	1.800
Garcia, C	.600	5	3	1	2	1	0	.667	1.200
Gilkey, B	.000	12	0	0	3	1	1	.143	.000

105

Todd Jones, Astros — RHP

Batter	Avg	AB	H	HR	BI	BB	SO	OBP	Slg
Girardi, Joe	.200	5	1	0	0	0	1	.200	.200
Grace, Mark*	.667	6	4	0	0	0	0	.667	1.000
Grissom, M	.286	7	2	0	1	1	3	.375	.286
Gwynn, Tony*	.400	5	2	0	0	1	0	.500	.400
Hayes, C	.167	6	1	0	0	3	1	.444	.167
Hernandez, Jo	.000	4	0	0	0	0	2	.000	.000
Hill, G	.000	8	0	0	1	1	3	.111	.000
Hundley, Todd#	.167	6	1	0	0	2	0	.375	.167
Jefferies, G#	.667	6	4	1	2	0	0	.667	1.167
Johnson, L*	.200	5	1	0	0	0	0	.200	.200
Johnson, Mark*	.250	4	1	0	2	1	1	.400	.500
Jones, C#	.200	5	1	0	2	0	2	.200	.200
Jordan, Brian	.286	7	2	0	1	0	2	.286	.571
Justice, Dave*	.200	5	1	0	0	0	0	.200	.200
Karros, Eric	.286	7	2	0	2	0	3	.286	.286
Kelly, R	.167	6	1	0	0	0	2	.167	.333
Kent, Jeff	.375	8	3	2	3	0	1	.444	1.125
King, Jeff	.250	8	2	0	0	1	0	.333	.375
Kingery, Mike*	.000	5	0	0	0	0	2	.000	.000
Lankford, Ray*	.200	5	1	0	2	2	4	.429	.400
Lansing, Mike	.000	10	0	0	1	1	0	.091	.000
Larkin, Barry	.111	9	1	0	1	4	5	.385	.222
Lemke, Mark#	.200	5	1	0	0	0	1	.200	.200
Lewis, Darren	.333	6	2	0	0	0	1	.333	.333
Liriano, N#	.250	4	1	0	0	1	0	.400	.250
Livingstone*	.333	6	2	0	0	0	1	.333	.667
Lopez, Javy	.333	6	2	0	0	0	2	.333	.333
Mabry, John*	1.000	2	2	0	0	3	0	1.000	1.500
Martin, Al*	.250	4	1	0	1	1	1	.333	.250
McGriff, Fred*	.143	7	1	1	1	2	0	.333	.571
McRae, Brian#	.200	5	1	0	0	2	0	.200	.200
Merced, O*	.125	8	1	0	0	2	3	.300	.125
Mondesi, Raul	.200	5	1	0	0	0	2	.200	.200
Morandini, M*	.250	4	1	0	0	1	0	.400	.250
Morris, Hal*	.375	8	3	1	3	1	1	.400	.750
Orsulak, Joe*	.556	9	5	0	1	0	1	.556	.556
Pagnozzi, Tom	.333	6	2	0	2	0	1	.333	.333
Pena, C	.000	4	0	0	0	0	2	.000	.000
Pendleton, T#	.125	8	1	0	0	2	2	.300	.125
Piazza, Mike	.200	5	1	0	1	0	0	.200	.200
Reed, Jeff*	.400	5	2	0	0	2	0	.571	.400
Reed, Jody	.000	8	0	0	2	1	0	.111	.000
Rodriguez, H*	.250	4	1	0	0	2	0	.500	.500
Sanchez, Rey	.167	6	1	0	0	0	2	.167	.167
Sanders, R	.077	13	1	0	1	1	6	.143	.077
Santiago, B	.333	6	2	0	1	0	0	.333	.333
Segui, David#	.333	9	3	0	0	1	0	.400	.333
Sheffield, G	.333	6	2	0	0	0	0	.333	.333
Slaught, Don	.500	2	1	0	0	3	1	.800	.500
Smith, Ozzie*	.400	5	2	0	0	0	0	.400	.400
Sosa, Sammy	.000	6	0	0	0	2	4	.250	.000
Taubensee, E*	.167	6	1	0	0	1	2	.286	.167
Tavarez, Je#	.400	5	2	1	3	0	0	.400	1.000
Thompson, Ry	.400	5	2	0	0	0	2	.400	.400
VanderWal, J*	.000	6	0	0	0	3	0	.000	.000
Veras, Q	.250	4	1	0	3	1	2	.333	.250
Vizcaino, J#	.167	6	1	0	0	1	0	.286	.167
Walker, Larry*	.200	5	1	0	0	0	2	.200	.400
Wallach, Tim	.250	4	1	0	2	1	2	.400	.500
Weiss, Walt*	.200	5	1	0	0	2	0	.429	.200
Whiten, Mark	.167	6	1	0	0	0	2	.167	.167
Young, Eric	.571	7	4	0	1	1	0	.625	.714
Young, Kevin	.600	5	3	0	0	0	0	.600	.600
Zeile, Todd	.364	11	4	0	2	1	3	.417	.364

Jeff Juden, Expos — RHP

Batter	Avg	AB	H	HR	BI	BB	SO	OBP	Slg
Bagwell, Jeff	.500	6	3	0	2	0	2	.429	.833
Bell, Derek	.000	7	0	0	1	2	4	.222	.000
Bell, Jay	.600	5	3	0	3	0	1	.600	.800
Belliard, R	.000	6	0	0	0	0	1	.000	.000
Biggio, Craig	.429	7	3	0	0	0	1	.429	.571
Bonds, Barry*	.200	5	1	0	3	3	3	.500	.200
Boone, Bret	.286	7	2	0	0	0	1	.444	.286
Brogna, Rico*	.500	6	3	2	2	0	1	.500	1.500
Buford, Damon	.000	2	0	0	0	2	0	.600	.000
Butler, Brett*	.200	5	1	0	1	0	0	.167	.200
Cangelosi, J#	.250	4	1	0	0	1	0	.400	.500
Clayton, R	.000	6	0	0	2	1	3	.125	.000
Colbrunn, G	.000	4	0	0	0	1	0	.200	.000
DeShields, D*	.200	5	1	0	1	3	1	.500	.200
Duncan, M	.333	6	2	1	3	0	2	.333	.833
Eusebio, Tony	.000	6	0	0	0	1	1	.143	.000
Flaherty, J	.400	5	2	1	4	0	1	.400	1.000
Fonville, C#	.125	8	1	0	0	0	2	.125	.125
Gant, Ron	.500	8	4	0	2	1	3	.556	.750
Gomez, Chris	.400	5	2	0	0	1	0	.500	.400
Greene, W*	.333	3	1	0	0	3	1	.667	.333
Gutierrez, R	.333	6	2	0	0	1	0	.429	.333
Gwynn, Tony*	.222	9	2	1	1	0	0	.222	.556
Hansen, Dave*	.200	5	1	0	1	0	0	.200	.200

Jeff Juden, Expos — RHP

Batter	Avg	AB	H	HR	BI	BB	SO	OBP	Slg
Henderson, R	.000	3	0	0	0	3	0	.500	.000
Hunter, Bri L	.143	7	1	0	0	0	1	.125	.286
Justice, Dave*	.167	6	1	1	1	3	1	.444	.667
Karros, Eric	.143	7	1	0	2	1	1	.222	.143
Kelly, R	.222	9	2	0	2	2	2	.364	.222
Kent, Jeff	.000	5	0	0	0	0	2	.000	.000
Larkin, Barry	.364	11	4	0	2	2	1	.462	.636
Lemke, Mark#	.455	11	5	1	3	2	1	.538	.909
Lewis, Darren	.333	9	3	0	0	2	1	.455	.333
Lewis, Mark	.250	4	1	0	0	1	0	.400	.500
Lopez, Javy	.500	4	2	1	2	0	1	.600	1.250
Lopez, Luis#	.167	6	1	0	0	0	4	.167	.167
Magadan, Dave*	.600	5	3	0	0	1	0	.667	.600
Manwaring, K	.200	5	1	0	1	1	2	.333	.400
May, Derrick*	.400	5	2	0	1	1	0	.500	.400
Miller, Orl	.750	4	3	0	0	0	1	.800	1.250
Mitchell, K	.000	6	0	0	0	3	0	.000	.000
Mondesi, Raul	.143	7	1	0	0	1	1	.250	.143
Morris, Hal*	.500	16	8	2	4	1	4	.500	1.000
O'Neill, Paul*	.400	5	2	0	0	0	0	.400	.400
Pendleton, T#	.231	13	3	2	2	0	4	.231	.692
Piazza, Mike	.250	4	1	0	0	3	0	.571	.250
Sabo, Chris	.200	5	1	0	1	1	0	.333	.200
Sanders, R	.231	13	3	0	2	0	4	.214	.231
Simms, Mike	.167	6	1	1	2	0	2	.167	.667
Taubensee, E*	.000	5	0	0	0	1	0	.000	.000
Thompson, Rob	.200	5	1	1	1	0	0	.200	.800
Vizcaino, J	.400	5	2	0	0	0	1	.400	.400
Williams, Ma	.143	7	1	0	0	0	1	.143	.571

Scott Kamieniecki, Yankees — RHP

Batter	Avg	AB	H	HR	BI	BB	SO	OBP	Slg
Alomar, R#	.357	14	5	0	0	1	0	.400	.500
Alomar Jr, S	.167	12	2	0	1	0	0	.167	.250
Amaral, Rich	.250	8	2	0	0	2	1	.400	.250
Anderson, Brd*	.250	20	5	1	1	5	6	.400	.400
Anthony, Eric*	.333	6	2	1	2	0	0	.333	.833
Baerga, C#	.333	21	7	2	6	2	2	.375	.667
Baines, H*	.300	20	6	1	2	6	1	.462	.550
Bautista, D	.200	5	1	0	0	1	3	.333	.200
Becker, Rich*	.400	5	2	0	0	0	1	.400	.400
Belle, Albert	.318	22	7	2	3	1	2	.348	.727
Berroa, G	.500	6	3	2	5	2	1	.625	1.500
Bichette, D	.667	6	4	0	0	0	0	.667	.833
Boggs, Wade*	.250	4	1	0	0	1	0	.400	.250
Bonilla, B#	.429	7	3	0	1	0	1	.429	.857
Bordick, Mike	.318	22	7	0	0	0	3	.318	.364
Brosius, S	.125	8	1	0	1	0	1	.125	.125
Buhner, Jay	.167	24	4	1	3	4	5	.286	.292
Burks, Ellis	.500	8	4	1	2	1	1	.556	.875
Canseco, Jose	.316	19	6	3	4	4	5	.435	.842
Carter, Joe	.059	17	1	0	0	0	1	.059	.118
Cole, Alex*	.444	9	4	0	1	1	1	.455	.556
Coleman, V#	.000	6	0	0	0	1	1	.143	.000
Cora, Joey#	.167	12	2	0	0	4	1	.375	.250
Cordova, M	.167	6	1	0	0	0	0	.167	.167
Curtis, Chad	.250	24	6	0	1	2	3	.308	.333
Cuyler, Milt#	.400	5	2	0	0	0	1	.400	.600
Davis, Chili#	.267	15	4	2	7	4	3	.421	.800
Dawson, Andre	.091	11	1	0	1	0	0	.091	.091
Deer, Rob	.308	13	4	0	3	3	5	.412	.308
Devereaux, M	.231	13	3	1	1	2	1	.333	.462
Diaz, Alex#	.000	6	0	0	0	0	1	.000	.000
DiSarcina, G	.231	13	3	0	0	0	2	.286	.231
Easley, D	.333	6	2	0	0	0	1	.333	.333
Edmonds, Jim*	.333	6	2	0	0	2	1	.500	.333
Eisenreich, J*	.429	7	3	0	1	0	0	.429	.714
Espinoza, A	.000	5	0	0	0	0	1	.000	.000
Fermin, Felix	.222	9	2	0	0	1	0	.300	.222
Fielder, C	.136	22	3	0	2	4	6	.259	.182
Franco, Julio	.143	14	2	0	0	2	1	.250	.143
Fryman, T	.300	20	6	0	1	6	5	.444	.400
Gaetti, Gary	.474	19	9	0	3	1	2	.500	.474
Gagne, Greg	.267	15	4	1	4	1	1	.313	.533
Gates, Brent#	.375	8	3	0	0	0	1	.375	.500
Giambi, Jason*	.200	5	1	0	1	0	1	.200	.200
Gomez, Chris	.500	5	2	0	1	1	0	.571	.500
Gomez, Leo	.286	7	2	0	0	1	3	.375	.286
Gonzales, R	.375	8	3	0	1	1	2	.444	.500
Gonzalez, J	.286	7	2	0	2	1	0	.444	.429
Goodwin, C*	.143	7	1	0	0	0	3	.143	.143
Goodwin, Tom*	.500	8	4	0	0	1	1	.556	.500
Green, Shawn*	.000	7	0	0	0	0	2	.000	.000
Greenwell, M*	.389	18	7	0	1	1	1	.421	.444
Griffey Jr, K*	.231	26	6	1	3	2	3	.286	.423
Guillen, O*	.200	10	2	0	1	0	1	.200	.400
Hamelin, Bob*	.333	6	2	0	0	3	2	.556	.500
Hamilton, D*	.368	19	7	1	3	3	0	.455	.684
Henderson, R	.292	24	7	0	3	6	2	.419	.292
Higginson, B*	.000	6	0	0	0	2	2	.333	.000
Hill, G	.000	5	0	0	0	0	0	.000	.000

Scott Kamieniecki, Yankees — RHP

Batter	Avg	AB	H	HR	BI	BB	SO	OBP	Slg
Hoiles, Chris	.286	7	2	0	1	3	0	.500	.286
Howard, Dave#	.000	6	0	0	1	0	0	.000	.000
Howard, T*	.111	9	1	0	1	1	4	.200	.111
Hulse, David*	.429	7	3	1	1	0	0	.429	.857
Huson, Jeff*	.200	5	1	0	0	1	0	.333	.200
Jaha, John	.143	7	1	0	0	0	1	.143	.143
Javier, Stan#	.333	6	2	0	0	0	0	.333	.333
Jefferies, G#	.333	6	2	0	1	0	0	.333	.333
Jefferson, R*	.385	13	5	1	3	1	3	.429	.692
Johnson, L*	.182	11	2	0	0	1	0	.250	.182
Joyner, Wally*	.167	18	3	0	2	5	1	.333	.167
Karkovice, R	.167	6	1	1	1	1	1	.286	.667
Kirby, Wayne*	.286	7	2	0	0	1	1	.375	.286
Knoblauch, C	.321	28	9	0	0	3	0	.387	.393
Kreuter, Chad#	.250	4	1	0	0	2	0	.500	.250
Leius, Scott	.235	17	4	0	0	1	4	.278	.294
Lewis, Mark	.286	7	2	0	0	0	4	.286	.286
Listach, Pat#	.167	12	2	0	0	1	2	.231	.167
Livingstone*	.429	7	3	0	1	0	1	.429	.571
Lockhart, K*	.000	6	0	0	0	0	0	.000	.000
Lofton, Kenny*	.368	19	7	2	6	1	4	.400	.789
Lovullo, T#	.167	6	1	0	0	0	0	.167	.167
Macfarlane, M	.417	12	5	0	1	0	2	.417	.667
Magadan, Dave*	.200	5	1	0	2	1	0	.286	.200
Martinez, E	.385	13	5	1	5	2	1	.500	.846
Martinez, T*	.273	22	6	1	1	1	2	.304	.455
Mayne, Brent*	.143	7	1	0	0	0	0	.143	.143
McCarty, Dave	.333	6	2	0	0	0	1	.333	.333
McGwire, Mark	.444	18	8	4	8	2	3	.500	1.222
McLemore, M#	.273	11	3	0	1	1	3	.333	.455
McRae, Brian#	.125	8	1	0	1	1	1	.222	.125
Meares, Pat	.200	10	2	0	3	0	3	.200	.400
Mieske, Matt	.000	3	0	0	0	3	1	.500	.000
Molitor, Paul	.367	30	11	0	5	3	1	.412	.500
Munoz, Pedro	.143	14	2	2	4	1	4	.200	.571
Murray, Eddie#	.571	7	4	0	0	0	2	.571	.571
Myers, Greg*	.000	10	0	0	0	1	5	.091	.000
Naehring, Tim	.500	8	4	1	5	5	0	.692	1.000
Newson, W*	.250	4	1	0	1	1	1	.400	.250
Nilsson, Dave*	.333	18	6	0	1	1	2	.368	.389
Nixon, Otis#	.333	6	2	0	0	2	0	.500	.333
Nunnally, Jon*	.429	7	3	0	0	1	3	.500	.429
O'Leary, Troy*	.500	4	2	0	0	1	1	.667	.500
Olerud, John*	.267	15	4	1	2	2	2	.353	.467
Orsulak, Joe*	.167	6	1	0	0	1	0	.286	.167
Palmeiro, R*	.421	19	8	0	5	2	1	.476	.737
Palmer, Dean	.333	9	3	0	0	2	3	.455	.444
Paquette, C	.400	5	2	0	0	0	1	.400	.400
Pena, Tony	.100	10	1	0	1	0	1	.182	.100
Phillips, T*	.412	17	7	0	1	4	2	.500	.471
Plantier, P*	.286	7	2	0	0	3	1	.500	.429
Polonia, Luis*	.467	15	7	0	2	3	1	.556	.533
Raines, Tim#	.143	14	2	0	0	1	1	.200	.143
Ramirez, M	.400	5	2	0	0	1	2	.500	.600
Reboulet, J	.143	7	1	0	1	1	2	.250	.143
Reed, Jody	.200	15	3	0	0	2	1	.294	.333
Ripken, Billy	.250	4	1	1	2	0	0	.250	1.000
Ripken, Cal	.318	22	7	0	5	1	2	.348	.455
Rodriguez, Al	.400	5	2	0	0	1	2	.500	.400
Rodriguez, I	.182	11	2	0	3	0	0	.182	.182
Salmon, Tim	.727	11	8	2	5	1	2	.750	1.455
Schofield, D	.400	5	2	0	1	1	1	.500	.400
Segui, David#	.143	7	1	0	0	1	0	.143	.143
Seitzer, K	.158	19	3	0	0	3	1	.273	.158
Sierra, Ruben#	.231	13	3	0	0	0	2	.231	.231
Snow, J.T.#	.400	10	4	0	2	0	2	.500	.600
Sojo, Luis	.250	8	2	0	3	0	0	.250	.375
Sorrento, P*	.429	14	6	1	2	0	1	.429	.643
Spiers, Bill*	.462	13	6	0	0	0	0	.500	.615
Sprague, Ed	.167	12	2	0	1	0	2	.167	.167
Stahoviak, S*	.250	4	1	0	0	3	2	.571	.500
Steinbach, T	.250	16	4	1	2	0	2	.250	.438
Surhoff, B.J.*	.292	24	7	0	3	1	2	.320	.333
Sveum, Dale#	.125	8	1	0	0	0	2	.125	.125
Tettleton, M#	.429	14	6	2	2	1	5	.500	.929
Thomas, Frank	.467	15	7	2	5	5	1	.600	.933
Thome, Jim*	.286	7	2	1	3	3	0	.500	.714
Tinsley, Lee#	.000	6	0	0	0	0	1	.000	.000
Trammell, A	.133	15	2	0	1	0	3	.133	.200
Valentin, John	.429	21	9	1	2	6	1	.556	.619
Valentin, Jse#	.143	7	1	0	0	1	0	.250	.286
Valle, Dave	.167	12	2	0	0	1	1	.231	.167
Vaughn, Greg	.190	21	4	0	4	5	5	.333	.238
Vaughn, Mo*	.318	22	7	2	4	4	6	.464	.682
Ventura, R*	.167	12	2	1	1	6	2	.444	.417
Vizquel, Omar*	.294	17	5	0	0	2	4	.368	.353
Voigt, Jack	.000	4	0	0	0	2	1	.333	.000
Walbeck, Matt#	.222	9	2	0	1	0	0	.222	.333
Ward, Turner#	.000	4	0	0	0	6	0	.600	.000
White, Devon#	.429	14	6	2	4	0	3	.429	1.000
Wilson, Dan	.000	6	0	0	0	1	4	.143	.000

Matt Karchner, White Sox — RHP

Batter	Avg	AB	H	HR	BI	BB	SO	OBP	Slg
Berroa, G	.400	5	2	0	1	1	0	.500	.400
Brosius, S	.500	4	2	1	2	3	1	.714	1.500
Clark, Will*	.500	4	2	1	1	1	1	.600	1.250
Gonzalez, J	.500	6	3	1	2	0	1	.500	1.000
Greer, Rusty*	.250	8	2	0	1	0	0	.222	.250
Hamilton, D*	.000	5	0	0	0	0	1	.000	.000
Naehring, Tim	.400	5	2	1	1	0	0	.400	1.000
Palmer, Dean	.571	7	4	0	0	0	1	.571	.571
Rodriguez, I	.286	7	2	0	0	0	1	.286	.286
Sojo, Luis	.000	4	0	0	0	1	1	.000	.000
Steinbach, T	.750	4	3	0	5	2	1	.833	1.000
Tettleton, M#	.250	4	1	1	1	1	1	.400	1.000
Wilson, Dan	.250	4	1	1	1	0	2	.400	1.000

Scott Karl, Brewers — LHP

Batter	Avg	AB	H	HR	BI	BB	SO	OBP	Slg
Alexander, M	.400	5	2	0	1	0	0	.400	.400
Alicea, Luis#	.200	5	1	0	0	0	0	.200	.200
Alomar, R#	.071	14	1	1	1	2	2	.188	.286
Alomar Jr, S	.571	14	8	2	6	1	2	.563	1.286
Amaral, Rich	.412	17	7	0	2	0	2	.412	.647
Anderson, Brd*	.333	6	2	0	1	0	1	.333	.500
Anderson, G*	.375	8	3	1	3	1	0	.444	.750
Baerga, C#	.273	11	3	0	2	1	0	.273	.364
Becker, Rich*	.143	7	1	0	0	1	2	.333	.286
Belle, Albert	.286	14	4	0	3	3	2	.389	.500
Berroa, G	.333	12	4	0	0	1	3	.385	.417
Blowers, Mike	.600	5	3	0	2	1	0	.667	.800
Boggs, Wade*	.077	13	1	0	0	1	0	.143	.077
Bonilla, B#	.444	9	4	0	1	1	0	.500	.556
Bordick, Mike	.167	12	2	0	0	1	1	.231	.250
Brosius, S	.000	6	0	0	0	3	2	.333	.000
Brumfield, J	.200	5	1	0	1	0	1	.200	.200
Buhner, Jay	.250	12	3	2	4	4	5	.438	.750
Canseco, Jose	.125	8	1	0	1	1	2	.222	.250
Carter, Joe	.533	15	8	1	4	1	1	.563	.933
Cedeno, D#	.400	10	4	0	0	0	0	.400	.500
Clark, Will*	.333	6	2	1	2	0	1	.333	.833
Coomer, Ron	.467	15	7	3	6	1	1	.500	1.200
Cordova, M	.200	15	3	0	1	1	1	.235	.200
Curtis, Chad	.400	5	2	0	0	0	1	.400	.800
Cuyler, Milt#	.000	5	0	0	0	1	0	.167	.000
Damon, Johnny*	.167	6	1	0	0	0	0	.167	.333
Davis, Chili#	.333	6	2	0	1	0	1	.333	.333
Davis, Russ	.167	6	1	0	0	1	2	.286	.167
Devereaux, M	.125	8	1	0	2	3	2	.364	.125
DiSarcina, G	.143	7	1	0	0	0	0	.143	.143
Duncan, M	.250	8	2	0	1	0	1	.250	.250
Durant, Mike	.333	6	2	0	0	0	0	.333	.333
Durham, Ray#	.600	5	3	0	2	1	0	.571	.800
Erstad, Darin*	.286	7	2	0	1	0	1	.286	.286
Espinoza, A	.333	6	2	1	2	0	0	.333	1.000
Fielder, C	.429	7	3	0	0	0	1	.429	.714
Franco, Julio	.300	10	3	0	2	0	3	.300	.400
Frye, Jeff	.556	9	5	0	0	2	0	.636	.667
Fryman, T	.333	7	3	0	4	0	0	.429	.429
Gates, Brent#	.167	6	1	0	0	0	0	.167	.333
Giambi, Jason*	.000	8	0	0	0	1	1	.111	.000
Girardi, Joe	.333	6	2	0	0	0	0	.333	.667
Gonzalez, A	.273	11	3	0	1	0	2	.273	.455
Gonzalez, J	.333	6	2	0	1	0	1	.333	.333
Greenwell, M*	.000	10	0	0	0	0	0	.000	.000
Griffey Jr, K*	.222	9	2	1	2	1	3	.300	.667
Hammonds, J	.111	9	1	1	3	0	1	.182	.444
Haselman, B	.333	6	2	0	0	1	0	.429	.333
Higginson, B*	.167	6	1	0	1	1	1	.286	.167
Hocking, D#	.000	6	0	0	0	1	0	.000	.000
Hoiles, Chris	.400	10	4	0	2	1	1	.417	.500
Hollins, Dave#	.143	7	1	0	0	0	1	.143	.143
Hosey, Dwayne#	.286	7	2	0	0	0	0	.286	.429
Howard, Dave#	.167	6	1	0	0	1	0	.286	.167
Hudler, Rex	.222	9	2	0	0	0	4	.222	.333
Jeter, Derek	.400	10	4	1	3	0	1	.400	.800
Jordan, Ricky	.143	7	1	0	0	0	0	.143	.143
Kelly, R	.333	9	3	1	2	2	0	.455	.667
Kent, Jeff	.143	7	1	0	0	0	0	.143	.143
Knoblauch, C	.231	13	3	0	1	4	0	.444	.231
Leius, Scott	.500	6	3	0	1	0	0	.500	.833
Leyritz, Jim	.222	9	2	0	1	4	3	.462	.222
Lofton, Kenny*	.190	21	4	0	1	1	1	.227	.190
Macfarlane, M	.200	10	2	0	0	1	1	.200	.200
Martin, N	.250	4	1	0	0	1	0	.400	.250
Martinez, E	.333	12	4	0	0	1	1	.385	.333
Martinez, T*	.000	13	0	0	1	1	2	.067	.000
Mashore, D	.143	7	1	0	0	0	3	.143	.143
McGee, Willie#	.333	6	2	0	0	0	0	.333	.333
McGwire, Mark	.286	7	2	2	3	0	1	.500	.286
Meares, Pat	.286	14	4	0	3	0	1	.267	.500
Molitor, Paul	.125	16	2	0	0	2	1	.222	.125
Munoz, Pedro	.500	8	4	0	0	1	3	.556	.500
Murray, Eddie#	.389	18	7	0	0	0	4	.389	.444

Scott Karl, Brewers — LHP

Batter	Avg	AB	H	HR	BI	BB	SO	OBP	Slg
Naehring, Tim	.000	8	0	0	0	1	1	.111	.000
Nixon, Otis#	.167	12	2	0	0	0	1	.167	.167
O'Brien, C	.429	7	3	1	3	1	0	.500	1.000
O'Neill, Paul*	.182	11	2	2	3	1	0	.308	.727
Offerman, J#	.000	5	0	0	0	1	0	.000	.000
Olerud, John*	.333	6	2	1	2	1	0	.500	.833
Palmeiro, R*	.231	13	3	1	3	2	2	.375	.462
Paquette, C	.000	5	0	0	0	3	0	.000	.000
Perez, Robert	.300	10	3	2	4	1	1	.364	.900
Phillips, T#	.667	3	2	0	0	3	0	.833	1.000
Ramirez, M	.286	14	4	0	1	2	2	.412	.357
Randa, Joe	.400	5	2	0	2	0	1	.400	.400
Ripken, Cal	.214	14	3	0	1	2	1	.313	.313
Rodriguez, Al	.333	9	3	0	2	0	1	.333	.667
Rodriguez, I	.000	5	0	0	0	0	0	.000	.000
Salmon, Tim	.857	7	6	1	4	2	1	.889	1.429
Samuel, Juan	.375	8	3	0	1	0	3	.375	.625
Seitzer, K	.500	4	2	0	0	1	1	.600	.500
Sheets, Andy	.667	6	4	0	1	0	2	.667	1.167
Sierra, Ruben*	.286	14	4	0	2	0	0	.286	.357
Slaught, Don	.333	6	2	0	0	0	0	.333	.333
Sojo, Luis	.313	16	5	1	6	2	1	.389	.563
Sprague, Ed	.231	13	3	1	4	2	1	.333	.538
Steinbach, T	.400	10	4	0	1	2	0	.500	.400
Strawberry, D*	.600	5	3	1	2	1	1	.667	1.400
Surhoff, B.J.*	.111	9	1	0	0	0	0	.200	.111
Tartabull, D	.000	6	0	0	0	0	5	.000	.000
Tettleton, M#	.200	5	1	0	0	1	1	.333	.200
Thomas, Frank	.500	4	2	2	4	3	1	.714	2.000
Thome, Jim*	.375	8	3	0	2	2	3	.500	.500
Valentin, Jhn	.273	11	3	0	1	0	0	.385	.273
Vaughn, Mo*	.300	10	3	0	0	0	0	.417	.300
Velarde, R	.600	10	6	0	1	2	0	.667	.900
Ventura, R*	.333	6	2	0	0	1	1	.429	.500
Vitiello, Joe	.250	4	1	0	0	3	1	.625	.250
Vizcaino, J#	.286	7	2	0	1	0	0	.286	.286
Vizquel, Omar#	.154	13	2	0	1	1	1	.214	.154
Walbeck, Matt*	.333	9	3	0	1	1	2	.400	.444
Williams, Ber#	.071	14	1	0	0	1	4	.133	.071
Williams, Gee	.364	11	4	0	0	2	3	.462	.455
Wilson, Dan	.214	14	3	0	4	2	1	.313	.286
Young, Ernie	.375	8	3	2	3	4	0	.583	1.250

Greg Keagle, Tigers — RHP

Batter	Avg	AB	H	HR	BI	BB	SO	OBP	Slg
Alomar, R#	.500	4	2	0	2	1	0	.600	.500
Anderson, Brd*	.250	4	1	0	2	1	1	.500	.250
Baines, H*	.333	3	1	0	0	2	1	.600	.333
Berroa, G	.333	9	3	0	0	0	3	.333	.333
Bonilla, B#	.500	4	2	0	2	1	0	.500	.500
Bordick, Mike	.143	7	1	0	1	1	0	.222	.143
Bournigal, R	.286	7	2	0	0	0	0	.286	.571
Carter, Joe	.333	3	1	0	0	2	0	.600	.667
Frye, Jeff	.500	4	2	0	5	1	0	.600	.500
Gates, Brent*	.500	4	2	0	1	1	1	.600	.500
Giambi, Jason*	.125	8	1	1	3	1	3	.200	.500
Gonzalez, A	.333	4	1	0	0	0	2	.333	.500
Herrera, Jose*	.250	4	1	0	0	2	0	.571	.500
McGwire, Mark	.000	6	0	0	0	3	0	.000	.000
Palmeiro, R*	.333	3	1	0	1	2	1	.600	.333
Plantier, P*	.143	7	1	1	1	0	0	.143	.571
Ripken, Cal	.333	6	2	0	1	1	1	.429	.667
Sprague, Ed	.200	5	1	0	0	1	0	.200	.200
Steinbach, T	.375	8	3	1	3	1	1	.444	.875
Surhoff, B.J.*	.250	4	1	0	2	2	1	.500	.250
Thomas, Frank	.667	3	2	1	5	1	0	.600	1.667
Young, Ernie	.286	7	2	0	0	2	3	.500	.429

Jimmy Key, Yankees — LHP

Batter	Avg	AB	H	HR	BI	BB	SO	OBP	Slg
Alomar, R#	.294	17	5	0	0	3	2	.400	.294
Alomar Jr, S	.100	10	1	0	1	0	1	.091	.200
Amaral, Rich	.421	19	8	0	4	2	4	.455	.579
Anderson, Brd*	.148	27	4	1	3	3	4	.303	.333
Anderson, G*	.000	6	0	0	0	0	1	.000	.000
Arias, George	.200	5	1	1	1	0	0	.200	.800
Ausmus, Brad	.000	2	0	0	0	3	0	.600	.000
Baerga, C#	.472	36	17	1	2	0	3	.472	.722
Baines, H*	.188	32	6	1	3	1	5	.235	.281
Bartee, K	.200	5	1	0	0	0	2	.200	.200
Bautista, D	.000	4	0	0	0	1	2	.200	.000
Bell, Jay	.222	9	2	0	1	0	1	.222	.222
Belle, Albert	.385	26	10	4	10	4	1	.452	.846
Beltre, E	.167	6	1	0	0	0	1	.167	.167
Berroa, G	.167	6	1	0	1	0	2	.167	.167
Bichette, D	.063	16	1	0	1	0	2	.059	.063
Blowers, Mike	.353	17	6	0	1	3	5	.450	.471
Boggs, Wade*	.292	65	19	0	4	1	8	.303	.385
Bonilla, B#	.143	7	1	0	0	1	2	.250	.143
Borders, Pat	.222	9	2	0	2	1	3	.300	.222
Bordick, Mike	.294	17	5	0	1	0	2	.294	.353
Bragg, Darren*	.200	5	1	0	0	1	4	.333	.200
Brosius, S	.111	9	1	0	0	0	2	.111	.111
Brumfield, J	.182	11	2	1	1	0	1	.182	.455
Buhner, Jay	.371	35	13	1	2	3	4	.421	.514
Burks, Ellis	.111	36	4	0	1	3	7	.179	.139
Butler, Brett*	.267	30	8	1	1	4	3	.353	.433
Cangelosi, J#	.000	4	0	0	0	1	1	.200	.000
Canseco, Jose	.264	53	14	0	8	6	10	.339	.283
Carter, Joe	.264	72	19	3	9	3	10	.289	.444
Cedeno, D#	.400	5	2	0	1	1	2	.500	.600
Cirillo, Jeff	.364	11	4	0	0	1	1	.417	.455
Clark, Tony#	.500	5	3	0	4	0	1	.500	.500
Clark, Will*	.417	12	5	0	5	1	1	.462	.667
Cole, Alex*	.333	9	3	0	0	2	1	.455	.333
Coomer, Ron	.200	5	1	0	0	0	0	.200	.200
Cora, Joey*	.000	6	0	0	0	1	3	.143	.000
Cordova, M	.400	5	2	0	0	1	2	.500	.400
Curtis, Chad	.160	25	4	1	1	3	3	.250	.320
Cuyler, Milt#	.250	16	4	0	0	1	4	.294	.313
Damon, Johnny*	.000	5	0	0	0	0	2	.000	.000
Davis, Chili#	.250	40	10	2	5	5	6	.326	.450
Dawson, Andre	.333	9	3	1	1	0	0	.333	.667
Deer, Rob	.140	50	7	4	4	5	22	.218	.380
Devereaux, M	.366	41	15	2	7	1	2	.372	.659
DiSarcina, G	.207	29	6	0	0	0	0	.207	.241
Easley, D	.333	18	6	1	2	2	2	.400	.556
Edmonds, Jim*	.200	10	2	0	1	0	0	.200	.300
Espinoza, A	.258	31	8	0	4	0	3	.250	.323
Fermin, Felix	.256	43	11	0	0	0	5	.256	.279
Fielder, C	.341	44	15	7	12	2	8	.370	.841
Franco, Julio	.361	61	22	1	8	7	7	.420	.443
Frye, Jeff	.429	21	9	0	1	2	3	.478	.571
Fryman, T	.318	44	14	1	7	1	4	.319	.455
Gaetti, Gary	.225	40	9	0	2	1	7	.262	.250
Gagne, Greg	.207	29	6	0	1	2	6	.258	.241
Gallego, Mike	.400	25	10	0	3	4	1	.467	.440
Garciaparra	.333	6	2	0	2	0	0	.333	.667
Gates, Brent#	.385	26	10	1	5	1	1	.393	.577
Gomez, Leo	.385	26	10	1	5	1	1	.393	.577
Gonzales, P	.222	9	2	0	1	2	2	.333	.222
Gonzalez, A	.385	13	5	1	3	0	1	.385	.615
Gonzalez, J	.294	34	10	1	6	1	3	.314	.412
Goodwin, Tom*	.125	8	1	0	1	0	1	.125	.250
Grebeck, C	.208	24	5	0	3	1	2	.231	.250
Greene, Todd	.333	6	2	0	0	0	0	.333	.500
Greenwell, M*	.313	48	15	0	2	1	7	.327	.354
Greer, Rusty*	.500	8	4	0	0	2	1	.600	.500
Griffey Jr, K*	.317	41	13	3	6	3	6	.364	.561
Guillen, O*	.207	58	12	0	2	2	9	.233	.207
Hall, Mel*	.091	11	1	0	0	1	0	.167	.091
Hamilton, D*	.227	22	5	0	1	1	3	.261	.318
Haselman, B	.364	11	4	0	1	1	0	.417	.545
Hayes, C	.222	9	2	0	1	0	1	.222	.333
Henderson, R	.412	85	35	9	14	13	8	.485	.800
Hiatt, Phil	.286	7	2	0	1	0	1	.250	.286
Hill, G	.333	6	2	0	0	0	1	.333	.333
Hoiles, Chris	.217	23	5	0	1	5	3	.357	.304
Hollins, Dave#	.500	4	2	1	2	1	1	.600	1.250
Howard, Dave#	.222	18	4	1	2	0	1	.222	.389
Howard, T*	.000	8	0	0	0	0	3	.000	.000
Howell, Jack*	.063	16	1	0	1	1	4	.118	.188
Hudler, Rex	.250	16	4	0	1	0	3	.250	.500
Huff, Michael	.227	22	5	0	1	0	1	.227	.318
Hulse, David*	.333	12	4	0	1	0	2	.333	.417
Hunter, Brian	.000	2	0	0	0	3	0	.600	.000
Incaviglia, P	.281	32	9	2	5	2	5	.324	.531
Jaha, John	.136	22	3	1	2	0	5	.136	.273
Javier, Stan#	.556	9	5	1	2	0	2	.556	1.000
Jefferies, G#	.231	13	3	0	0	1	2	.286	.231
Jefferson, R*	.182	11	2	0	0	0	4	.182	.273
Johnson, L*	.200	25	5	0	0	1	5	.231	.200
Joyner, Wally*	.255	51	13	1	4	6	8	.345	.353
Karkovice, A	.222	36	8	2	4	4	7	.300	.500
Kelly, Pat	.231	13	3	0	0	0	2	.231	.385
Kelly, R	.353	34	12	0	5	1	4	.361	.471
Knoblauch, A	.344	32	11	0	0	5	5	.344	.375
Kreuter, Chad#	.200	5	1	0	0	2	3	.429	.200
Leius, Scott	.231	13	3	0	2	0	0	.333	.231
Lennon, P	.200	5	1	0	0	0	0	.200	.200
Lewis, Mark	.188	16	3	0	0	2	2	.188	.188
Leyritz, Jim	.273	11	3	0	0	0	0	.273	.455
Liriano, N#	.200	5	1	0	0	0	2	.000	.000
Listach, Pat#	.379	29	11	0	1	2	4	.419	.552
Lofton, Kenny*	.118	17	2	0	1	0	4	.118	.118
Loretta, Mark	.250	4	1	0	0	1	0	.250	.250
Macfarlane, M	.273	44	12	3	6	1	9	.289	.591
Malave, Jose	.200	5	1	0	0	0	1	.200	.200
Manto, Jeff	.154	13	2	0	1	1	3	.214	.154
Martinez, E	.344	44	14	2	5	4	3	.375	.568
Martinez, T*	.316	19	6	2	5	0	3	.316	.684
Matheny, Mike	.000	5	0	0	0	1	3	.167	.000

Jimmy Key, Yankees — LHP

Batter	Avg	AB	H	HR	BI	BB	SO	OBP	Slg
McCarty, Dave	.100	10	1	0	1	1	3	.182	.100
McGwire, Mark	.214	28	6	2	7	3	5	.281	.429
McLemore, M#	.333	15	5	0	2	1	6	.375	.400
McRae, Brian*	.120	25	3	0	0	1	5	.154	.240
Meares, Pat	.333	15	5	0	1	0	4	.333	.400
Mieske, Matt	.385	13	5	1	1	0	1	.385	.923
Mitchell, Kei	.200	15	3	0	2	1	0	.333	.200
Mitchell, K	.200	5	1	0	0	0	1	.200	.200
Molitor, Paul	.286	77	22	3	9	6	9	.333	.481
Morman, Russ	.143	7	1	0	0	2	3	.333	.143
Munoz, Pedro	.125	16	2	0	1	0	5	.125	.188
Murray, Eddie*	.182	33	6	0	3	1	6	.206	.212
Naehring, Tim	.296	27	8	2	5	0	5	.296	.556
Nieves, M#	.333	6	2	0	1	0	1	.333	.333
Nilsson, Dave*	.000	6	0	0	0	2	2	.250	.000
Nixon, Otis*	.353	17	6	0	1	3	0	.450	.412
O'Brien, J	.154	13	2	1	1	1	2	.214	.385
Offerman, J#	.250	8	2	0	0	1	1	.333	.500
Olerud, John*	.154	13	2	0	1	0	5	.154	.154
Orsulak, Joe*	.300	10	3	0	1	0	1	.300	.500
Palmeiro, R*	.308	39	12	0	4	2	8	.333	.385
Palmer, Dean	.240	25	6	1	2	0	7	.240	.440
Paquette, C	.300	10	3	0	0	1	4	.364	.500
Pemberton, R	.600	5	3	0	2	0	1	.600	.800
Pena, Tony	.444	36	16	2	6	0	1	.444	.667
Perez, Robert	.000	10	0	0	1	0	1	.000	.000
Phillips, T#	.224	58	13	2	6	7	14	.303	.379
Polonia, Luis*	.182	22	4	0	0	0	2	.182	.182
Pulliam, H	.333	6	2	0	1	0	0	.333	.333
Raines, Tim#	.233	30	7	0	0	1	5	.258	.267
Ramirez, M	.222	9	2	0	0	0	2	.222	.222
Randa, Joe	.000	9	0	0	1	1	4	.100	.000
Reboulet, J	.231	13	3	0	2	1	2	.286	.308
Reed, Jody	.310	29	9	0	1	0	1	.310	.414
Ripken, Billy	.357	28	10	0	0	1	0	.379	.464
Ripken, Cal	.356	73	26	1	6	7	5	.413	.438
Roberts, Bip#	.091	11	1	0	0	1	3	.167	.091
Rodriguez, Al	.500	8	4	0	1	1	1	.556	.750
Rodriguez, I	.375	24	9	2	7	2	3	.423	.667
Sabo, Chris	.143	7	1	0	0	0	0	.143	.429
Salmon, Tim	.067	15	1	0	2	2	6	.167	.067
Samuel, Juan	.077	13	1	0	1	0	3	.077	.077
Schofield, D	.200	45	9	1	3	3	7	.265	.356
Schu, Rick	.286	7	2	0	0	1	3	.375	.286
Segui, David#	.118	17	2	0	0	0	5	.118	.176
Seitzer, K	.241	54	13	1	6	4	5	.293	.333
Sheffield, G	.250	16	4	0	3	0	2	.235	.375
Shumpert, T	.333	6	2	0	2	0	0	.333	.500
Sierra, Ruben#	.235	51	12	5	10	6	3	.310	.608
Slaught, Don	.263	19	5	0	1	0	2	.300	.474
Snow, J.T.#	.071	14	1	0	0	1	5	.133	.071
Sojo, Luis	.273	11	3	0	0	1	1	.333	.273
Sosa, Sammy	.313	16	5	1	3	1	6	.353	.500
Spiers, Bill*	.000	9	0	0	0	0	0	.000	.000
Sprague, Ed	.130	23	3	1	2	3	4	.231	.304
Stankiewicz	.200	5	1	0	0	0	1	.333	.200
Stanley, Mike	.314	35	11	0	1	5	8	.400	.343
Steinbach, T	.310	42	13	1	4	1	7	.326	.452
Stevens, Lee*	.000	7	0	0	0	0	1	.000	.000
Stillwell, R	.125	8	1	0	1	0	2	.222	.250
Strange, Doug#	.000	6	0	0	2	0	2	.000	.000
Surhoff, B.J.*	.306	36	11	1	3	5	7	.390	.444
Sveum, Dale*	.167	24	4	1	3	0	4	.167	.292
Sweeney, Mike	.000	5	0	0	0	0	1	.000	.000
Tartabull, D	.303	33	10	0	0	7	8	.425	.424
Tettleton, M#	.269	52	14	5	12	6	15	.359	.596
Thomas, Frank	.250	32	8	1	5	7	4	.375	.406
Tinsley, Lee*	.071	14	1	0	0	0	5	.133	.071
Trammell, A	.246	61	15	1	4	6	4	.313	.393
Turner, Chris	.556	9	5	0	2	0	0	.556	.667
Valentin, Jhn	.286	21	6	0	0	7	3	.464	.381
Valentin, Jse#	.500	4	2	0	1	0	0	.500	1.000
Valle, Dave	.139	36	5	1	1	2	4	.205	.222
Vaughn, Greg	.200	40	8	1	6	3	5	.256	.300
Vaughn, Mo*	.273	33	9	3	8	3	6	.351	.576
Velarde, R	.381	21	8	0	0	1	4	.409	.524
Ventura, R*	.160	25	4	0	1	3	5	.276	.160
Vina, F*	.200	5	1	0	0	0	2	.200	.200
Vitiello, Joe	.500	4	2	1	4	0	2	.400	1.500
Vizquel, Omar#	.240	25	6	1	3	0	1	.240	.400
Voigt, Jack	.222	9	2	0	0	0	3	.222	.222
Walbeck, Matt#	.000	5	0	0	0	0	0	.000	.000
Weiss, Walt	.167	12	2	0	0	0	0	.167	.167
White, Devon#	.250	40	10	0	2	1	6	.286	.350
Whiten, Mark#	.429	7	3	0	0	2	1	.556	.429
Williams, Ber#	.500	4	2	0	0	2	0	.667	.750
Williams, G	.071	14	1	0	0	0	3	.071	.143
Wilson, Dan	.286	7	2	0	0	0	2	.286	.286
Worthington	.154	13	2	0	0	0	2	.154	.231

Brian Keyser, White Sox — RHP

Batter	Avg	AB	H	HR	BI	BB	SO	OBP	Slg
Alexander, M	.000	4	0	0	0	0	0	.200	.000
Alomar, R#	.500	8	4	0	1	0	0	.500	.750
Amaral, Rich	.200	5	1	0	0	0	1	.200	.200
Anderson, G*	.429	7	3	0	2	0	0	.429	.571
Bordick, Mike	.500	5	2	0	1	0	1	.400	.400
Bragg, Darren*	.333	3	1	0	0	2	1	.600	.333
Brosius, S	.250	4	1	0	1	1	1	.400	.500
Carter, Joe	.000	6	0	0	0	0	0	.000	.000
Cora, Joey#	.600	5	3	0	1	1	0	.667	.600
Cordova, M	.167	6	1	0	1	1	0	.286	.167
Curtis, Chad	.333	6	2	0	2	1	1	.429	.500
Davis, Chili#	.333	6	2	0	0	2	0	.500	.333
DiSarcina, G	.200	5	1	0	0	1	0	.200	.200
Edmonds, Jim*	.333	6	2	0	0	1	0	.429	.500
Fabregas, Jor*	.200	5	1	0	1	0	0	.200	.200
Fielder, C	.167	6	1	0	0	1	3	.286	.167
Flaherty, J	.000	6	0	0	0	0	1	.000	.000
Fryman, T	.375	8	3	0	1	0	0	.375	.500
Gates, Brent#	.200	5	1	0	0	0	1	.200	.200
Goodwin, Tom*	.625	8	5	0	1	0	0	.625	.750
Green, Shawn*	.200	5	1	0	0	0	0	.200	.400
Hamilton, D*	.143	7	1	0	1	0	0	.125	.143
Hammonds, J	.600	5	3	0	0	1	0	.667	.800
Hoiles, Chris	.250	4	1	0	0	1	1	.400	.500
Howard, Dave*	.286	7	2	0	1	0	0	.286	.571
Hulse, David*	.286	7	2	0	0	0	0	.286	.286
Knoblauch, C	.250	4	1	0	1	2	0	.500	.750
Lockhart, K*	.600	5	3	0	0	0	0	.600	.600
Martinez, E	.600	5	3	0	3	0	1	.667	1.000
Matheny, Mike	.200	5	1	0	0	1	0	.333	.400
Molitor, Paul	.333	6	2	0	1	1	2	.429	.333
Munoz, Pedro	.400	5	2	0	0	0	1	.400	.400
Nilsson, Dave*	.375	8	3	0	0	0	1	.375	.500
Nixon, Otis*	.400	5	2	0	2	0	0	.400	.600
Nunnally, Jon*	.200	5	1	0	0	3	2	.200	.200
Olerud, John*	.500	4	2	0	0	1	0	.600	.500
Palmeiro, R*	.200	5	1	0	0	1	0	.333	.200
Phillips, T#	.600	5	3	1	1	0	1	.600	1.400
Ripken, Cal	.167	6	1	0	0	0	1	.167	.167
Rodriguez, Al	.250	4	1	0	1	1	1	.400	.250
Salmon, Tim	.250	8	2	1	3	0	2	.250	.625
Seitzer, K	.333	9	3	0	1	0	0	.333	.333
Snow, J.T.#	.250	8	2	1	2	0	1	.250	.625
Stahoviak, S*	1.000	4	4	1	1	1	0	1.000	2.000
Steinbach, T	.400	5	2	1	3	0	2	.400	1.000
Surhoff, B.J.*	.222	9	2	0	1	0	2	.222	.222
Valentin, Jse#	.625	8	5	0	3	0	1	.625	.750
Vaughn, Greg	.143	7	1	1	1	0	0	.143	.571
Vaughn, Mo*	.600	5	3	0	0	0	0	.600	.800
Vina, F*	.143	7	1	0	0	1	0	.250	.143
Walbeck, Matt#	.571	7	4	0	0	0	0	.571	.571
Wilson, Dan	.000	6	0	0	0	0	0	.000	.000

Mark Kiefer, Royals — RHP

Batter	Avg	AB	H	HR	BI	BB	SO	OBP	Slg
Carter, Joe	.200	5	1	0	1	0	0	.200	.400
Gil, Benji	.000	6	0	0	0	0	4	.000	.000
Gonzalez, A	.333	3	1	0	0	2	2	.600	.333
Nixon, Otis#	.400	5	2	0	0	0	0	.400	.400
Pena, Tony	.500	4	2	0	1	1	1	.600	.500
Sprague, Ed	.250	4	1	0	1	1	1	.400	.250

Darryl Kile, Astros — RHP

Batter	Avg	AB	H	HR	BI	BB	SO	OBP	Slg
Abbott, Kurt	.167	12	2	0	1	0	7	.231	.167
Alicea, Luis*	.455	22	10	0	5	4	3	.536	.591
Alou, Moises	.333	24	8	1	6	0	6	.360	.583
Amaro, Ruben*	.400	5	2	0	1	1	1	.500	.400
Andrews, S	.200	5	1	0	2	2	2	.429	.400
Anthony, Eric*	.167	6	1	0	1	0	3	.167	.167
Ashley, Billy	.125	8	1	0	0	2	3	.300	.125
Ausmus, Brad	.286	7	2	0	0	0	3	.286	.286
Barberie, B	.143	14	2	0	0	3	2	.333	.143
Bates, Jason#	.333	6	2	1	2	2	1	.500	.833
Batiste, Kim	.571	7	4	0	2	0	0	.571	.571
Bell, Derek	.273	11	3	0	0	0	4	.273	.273
Bell, Jay	.205	39	8	0	3	3	10	.262	.256
Belliard, R	.444	9	4	0	0	0	2	.444	.444
Benard, M*	.375	8	3	0	0	0	2	.375	.500
Berry, Sean	.429	14	6	0	1	4	3	.556	.500
Bichette, D	.267	15	4	0	0	0	4	.267	.267
Blauser, Jeff	.125	32	4	0	3	4	7	.222	.125
Bonds, Barry*	.407	27	11	2	8	4	3	.484	.741
Bonilla, B#	.375	8	3	1	3	2	3	.500	.750
Boone, Bret	.250	12	3	0	2	2	4	.357	.333
Branson, Jeff*	.222	9	2	0	3	1	4	.273	.222
Brogna, Rico*	.200	5	1	1	1	1	3	.333	.800
Brumfield, J	.222	9	2	0	0	1	3	.364	.333
Bullett, S*	.250	8	2	0	0	1	1	.333	.250
Burks, Ellis	.000	5	0	0	0	2	2	.286	.000
Butler, Brett*	.143	21	3	0	0	9	2	.400	.143

Darryl Kile, Astros — RHP

Batter	Avg	AB	H	HR	BI	BB	SO	OBP	Slg
Caminiti, Ken#	.182	11	2	0	0	6	0	.471	.182
Carr, Chuck	.059	17	1	0	0	0	4	.059	.118
Carreon, Mark	.300	10	3	1	3	1	0	.364	.600
Castilla, V	.154	13	2	0	0	0	5	.154	.154
Castillo, L#	.600	5	3	0	0	2	2	.714	.600
Cedeno, A	.500	8	4	0	1	0	0	.500	.875
Clark, Dave*	.278	18	5	0	2	4	2	.409	.333
Clark, Will*	.217	23	5	0	3	3	6	.308	.304
Clayton, R	.308	26	8	1	4	2	7	.357	.500
Colbrunn, G	.500	6	3	0	2	1	0	.500	.500
Conine, Jeff	.286	14	4	0	3	3	3	.444	.286
Cordero, Wil	.222	9	2	0	1	2	1	.462	.444
Cummings, M*	.000	7	0	0	0	0	2	.000	.000
Daulton, D*	.286	14	4	2	4	4	3	.444	.786
Davis, Eric	.105	19	2	1	1	1	9	.150	.263
Dawson, Andre	.200	10	2	0	1	2	1	.333	.200
Decker, Steve	.200	5	1	0	0	0	0	.200	.200
DeShields, D*	.222	18	4	0	3	7	5	.423	.222
Duncan, M	.267	15	4	0	1	0	2	.313	.267
Dunston, S	.125	16	2	0	0	1	4	.176	.125
Dykstra, L*	.385	13	5	0	3	4	2	.529	.385
Eisenreich, J*	.438	16	7	2	5	0	2	.438	.938
Elster, Kevin	.250	4	1	0	0	1	0	.400	.250
Everett, Carl#	.500	6	3	0	1	0	0	.500	.500
Finley, Steve*	.385	13	5	0	1	4	4	.529	.385
Fletcher, D*	.087	23	2	1	2	2	2	.192	.217
Floyd, Cliff*	.167	6	1	0	2	1	3	.250	.500
Gaetti, Gary	.273	11	3	0	0	0	3	.385	.273
Galarraga, A	.370	27	10	2	7	1	6	.414	.630
Gant, Ron	.222	27	6	2	3	3	12	.300	.519
Garcia, C	.296	27	8	1	2	1	6	.321	.481
Gilkey, B	.172	29	5	2	6	5	6	.286	.379
Girardi, Joe	.364	11	4	0	2	2	0	.462	.455
Gomez, Leo	.667	3	2	0	2	2	0	.800	1.000
Gonzalez, L*	.333	9	3	1	2	1	1	.400	.667
Goodwin, Tom*	.400	5	2	0	0	2	1	.571	.400
Grace, Mark*	.258	31	8	0	4	7	5	.395	.323
Greene, W*	.000	5	2	0	2	1	2	.500	1.200
Grissom, M	.311	45	14	2	4	4	9	.367	.511
Grudzielanek	.200	10	2	0	0	0	2	.273	.200
Gutierrez, R	.286	7	2	0	1	2	3	.500	.286
Gwynn, Tony*	.379	29	11	1	7	6	4	.486	.517
Hansen, Dave*	.067	15	1	0	0	1	0	.125	.133
Harris, Lenny*	.185	27	5	0	2	3	2	.267	.222
Hayes, C	.348	23	8	0	8	1	4	.385	.522
Henderson, Jo	.200	10	2	0	0	1	4	.273	.300
Hernandez, Jo	.231	13	3	0	3	3	5	.412	.231
Hill, G	.500	8	4	1	6	6	2	.733	1.125
Hollins, Dave#	.267	15	4	0	3	1	1	.294	.400
Howard, T*	.333	12	4	0	1	2	3	.429	.500
Hundley, Todd#	.333	21	7	1	2	1	4	.364	.476
Huskey, Butch	.231	13	3	0	3	1	5	.286	.385
Incaviglia, P	.250	8	2	0	1	0	3	.250	.375
Jefferies, G#	.176	34	6	0	4	4	6	.256	.176
Johnson, Bri	.111	9	1	0	1	0	4	.111	.111
Johnson, Char	.167	6	1	0	0	0	2	.167	.167
Johnson, L*	.500	12	6	0	0	0	0	.500	.583
Johnson, Mark*	.000	2	0	0	1	4	2	.571	.000
Jones, C#	.250	12	3	0	0	6	4	.500	.333
Jordan, Brian	.278	18	5	0	2	2	6	.381	.389
Jordan, Ricky	.000	10	0	0	0	2	0	.000	.000
Joyner, Wally*	.250	4	1	0	0	5	1	.667	.500
Justice, Dave*	.143	14	2	1	2	9	3	.478	.357
Karros, Eric	.182	22	4	0	2	0	4	.217	.227
Kelly, R	.400	5	2	0	0	2	0	.625	.600
Kendall, J	.000	7	0	0	0	0	1	.000	.000
Kent, Jeff	.200	20	4	2	3	0	3	.238	.500
King, Jeff	.355	31	11	1	7	2	10	.394	.548
Kingery, Mike*	.421	19	8	0	4	2	2	.476	.684
Klesko, Ryan*	.263	19	5	1	5	4	3	.391	.526
Lankford, Ray*	.286	28	8	2	5	8	8	.459	.607
Lansing, Mike	.063	16	1	0	0	3	4	.211	.063
Larkin, Barry	.182	22	4	0	1	3	3	.308	.227
Lemke, Mark#	.172	29	5	1	4	4	5	.273	.276
Lewis, Darren	.067	15	1	0	0	2	4	.176	.067
Liriano, N#	.455	11	5	0	2	3	2	.571	.636
Livingstone*	.429	7	3	0	0	0	1	.429	.429
Lopez, Javy	.143	14	2	0	1	1	5	.188	.143
Lopez, Luis#	.250	8	2	0	1	0	0	.250	.375
Mabry, John*	.438	16	7	1	3	0	1	.438	.688
Magadan, Dave*	.333	18	6	0	4	3	2	.409	.444
Manwaring, K	.500	8	1	0	4	0	0	.300	.125
Marrero, O*	.250	8	2	0	0	0	4	.250	.375
Martin, Al*	.261	23	6	0	2	2	3	.393	.304
Martinez, Da*	.333	11	3	0	2	0	0	.273	.364
May, Derrick*	.385	13	5	0	1	0	2	.385	.385
McGee, Willie#	.519	27	14	0	5	4	4	.581	.667
McGriff, Fred*	.244	41	10	4	10	0	6	.244	.585
McRae, Brian#	.174	46	8	0	2	5	7	.286	.261
Merced, O*	.313	32	10	0	5	3	5	.405	.406
Mitchell, K	.500	10	5	2	5	3	0	.571	1.200

Darryl Kile, Astros — RHP

Batter	Avg	AB	H	HR	BI	BB	SO	OBP	Slg
Mondesi, Raul	.167	6	1	1	1	0	2	.167	.667
Morandini, M*	.269	26	7	0	1	8	5	.457	.269
Morris, Hal*	.056	18	1	0	0	1	3	.150	.111
Murray, Eddie#	.400	15	6	1	4	4	3	.526	.733
Nieves, M#	.200	5	1	0	0	1	2	.333	.200
Nixon, Otis#	.333	15	5	0	0	0	3	.333	.333
O'Brien, C	.143	7	1	0	0	1	3	.333	.143
O'Neill, Paul*	.000	3	0	0	0	2	0	.400	.000
Ochoa, Alex	.167	6	1	0	0	1	0	.286	.167
Offerman, J#	.273	22	6	0	2	2	5	.333	.409
Oliver, Joe	.200	5	1	0	0	1	3	.333	.200
Ordonez, Rey	.125	8	1	0	0	0	2	.125	.125
Orsulak, Joe*	.333	12	4	0	2	3	1	.467	.667
Otero, Ricky#	.273	11	3	0	0	0	2	.273	.273
Pagnozzi, Tom	.185	27	5	0	2	1	5	.233	.296
Pena, G#	.125	8	1	0	0	1	1	.222	.125
Pendleton, T#	.185	27	5	1	3	3	3	.267	.296
Phillips, J*	.125	8	1	0	0	2	4	.300	.125
Piazza, Mike	.353	17	6	0	2	1	4	.389	.353
Plantier, P*	.200	10	2	1	2	4	3	.467	.500
Reed, Jeff*	.438	16	7	0	2	1	1	.471	.563
Reed, Jody	.385	13	5	0	3	2	1	.471	.462
Renteria, E	.400	5	2	0	0	0	2	.500	.400
Roberts, Bip#	.429	7	3	0	1	4	1	.636	.429
Rodriguez, H*	.318	22	7	0	2	1	7	.348	.364
Sabo, Chris	.333	6	2	1	2	1	0	.500	.833
Samuel, Juan	.222	9	2	0	0	0	1	.222	.222
Sanchez, Rey	.182	11	2	0	0	4	2	.400	.364
Sandberg, R	.313	16	5	1	5	6	3	.538	.625
Sanders, R	.250	16	4	1	4	3	6	.400	.438
Santangelo, F#	.500	6	3	0	0	2	1	.625	.667
Santiago, B	.261	23	6	0	0	3	6	.346	.478
Scarsone, S	.300	10	3	0	1	1	4	.364	.600
Schofield, D	.333	6	2	0	0	0	1	.333	.333
Segui, David#	.125	8	1	0	1	2	2	.273	.125
Servais, S	.556	9	5	0	0	1	0	.600	.667
Sheaffer, D	.222	9	2	0	2	0	0	.300	.444
Sheffield, G	.211	19	4	0	2	2	5	.273	.316
Shipley, C	.250	8	2	0	0	0	3	.400	.250
Slaught, Don	.333	12	4	0	1	2	4	.429	.333
Smith, Dwight*	.200	5	1	0	0	1	2	.333	.200
Smith, Ozzie#	.333	33	11	1	5	3	0	.389	.545
Sosa, Sammy	.158	19	3	0	1	0	7	.158	.158
Stocker, K#	.313	16	5	0	1	1	3	.389	.375
Strawberry, D*	.300	10	3	0	0	2	2	.417	.500
Tarasco, Tony*	.000	5	0	0	0	0	2	.000	.000
Taubensee, E*	.364	11	4	1	1	1	2	.462	.636
Thompson, Mil*	.250	8	2	0	1	3	2	.455	.250
Thompson, Rob	.125	16	2	0	0	3	4	.364	.188
Thompson, Ry	.000	7	0	0	0	1	6	.125	.000
VanderWal, J*	.000	12	0	0	0	2	3	.143	.000
Vizcaino, J#	.238	21	5	0	4	1	3	.261	.238
Walker, Larry*	.333	30	10	1	5	3	8	.382	.533
Wallach, Tim	.316	19	6	0	0	2	1	.409	.368
Walton, J	.125	8	1	0	0	1	1	.125	.125
Weiss, Walt#	.176	17	3	0	2	4	3	.318	.176
White, R	.333	6	2	0	0	0	1	.429	.333
Whiten, Mark#	.526	19	10	1	4	2	1	.571	.842
Wilkins, Rick*	.286	21	6	0	1	1	6	.318	.381
Williams, E	.000	7	0	0	0	0	1	.000	.000
Williams, Ma	.250	28	7	1	8	5	9	.371	.393
Young, Eric	.350	20	7	0	3	3	0	.435	.500
Young, Kevin	.333	6	2	0	1	1	3	.429	.333
Zeile, Todd	.300	30	9	1	3	2	3	.333	.433

Scott Klingenbeck, Twins — RHP

Batter	Avg	AB	H	HR	BI	BB	SO	OBP	Slg
Baerga, C#	.167	6	1	0	0	0	0	.167	.167
Belle, Albert	.750	4	3	2	3	4	0	.875	2.250
Blowers, Mike	.333	3	1	0	0	2	1	.600	.333
Buhner, Jay	.455	11	5	4	8	0	4	.455	1.636
Canseco, Jose	.286	7	2	0	1	0	3	.286	.429
Cirillo, Jeff	.600	5	3	0	1	0	0	.600	.600
Cora, Joey*	.200	5	1	0	0	2	1	.500	.200
Davis, Chili#	.000	4	0	0	0	1	2	.200	.000
Easley, D	.000	5	0	0	0	0	2	.000	.000
Edmonds, Jim*	.200	5	1	1	2	0	2	.200	.800
Fielder, C	.250	4	1	0	0	0	1	.400	.500
Fryman, T	.200	5	1	0	0	0	2	.200	.200
Goodwin, Tom*	.250	4	1	0	0	1	1	.400	.500
Greenwell, M*	.625	8	5	1	3	0	0	.625	1.000
Griffey Jr, K*	.300	10	3	0	4	1	2	.364	.400
Lockhart, K*	.600	5	3	1	1	0	0	.600	1.600
Lofton, Kenny*	.500	6	3	0	0	0	0	.500	.667
Macfarlane, M	.333	3	1	0	0	0	0	.600	.333
Martinez, E	.429	7	3	0	1	1	2	.500	.571
Murray, Eddie#	.400	5	2	0	2	0	2	.400	.600
Naehring, Tim	.125	8	1	0	0	0	1	.125	.250
Nilsson, Dave*	.400	5	2	2	5	0	0	.400	1.600
O'Leary, Troy*	.556	9	5	0	0	0	2	.556	.667
Pena, Tony	.000	5	0	0	0	0	2	.000	.000

Scott Klingenbeck, Twins — RHP

Batter	Avg	AB	H	HR	BI	BB	SO	OBP	Slg
Phillips, T#	.429	7	3	0	0	1	1	.500	.429
Ramirez, M	.500	4	2	0	0	2	0	.667	.500
Rodriguez, Al	.333	6	2	0	0	0	1	.333	.500
Salmon, Tim	.571	7	4	2	3	0	1	.571	1.857
Snow, J.T.#	.200	5	1	0	1	0	0	.200	.400
Sojo, Luis	.500	4	2	0	0	1	0	.600	.500
Sorrento, P*	.000	8	0	0	0	1	1	.111	.000
Stanley, Mike	.500	4	2	1	3	2	0	.667	1.500
Strange, Doug#	.400	5	2	0	0	0	1	.400	.400
Tartabull, D	.250	4	1	0	0	1	1	.400	.250
Thome, Jim*	.429	7	3	0	1	1	2	.500	.571
Tinsley, Lee#	.400	5	2	0	0	1	0	.500	.600
Valentin, Jhn	.200	5	1	1	1	3	0	.500	.800
Vaughn, Mo*	.429	7	3	2	7	2	0	.556	1.571
Vina, F*	.500	4	2	0	0	1	1	.600	.500
Vizquel, Omar*	.400	5	2	0	1	2	0	.571	.400
Wilson, Dan	.556	9	5	2	6	1	1	.600	1.222

Joe Klink, Mariners — LHP

Batter	Avg	AB	H	HR	BI	BB	SO	OBP	Slg
Butler, Brett*	.000	4	0	0	0	4	3	.500	.000
Daulton, D*	.000	5	0	0	0	0	1	.000	.000
Eisenreich, J*	.000	4	0	0	0	3	1	.429	.000
Fermin, Felix	.600	5	3	0	1	0	0	.600	.800
Gonzalez, L*	.400	5	2	0	0	0	0	.400	.400
Griffey Jr, K*	.167	6	1	0	0	0	2	.167	.167
Guillen, O*	.200	5	1	0	0	0	2	.200	.200
Hall, Mel*	.333	6	2	0	1	0	0	.333	.333
Johnson, L*	.333	6	2	0	0	1	0	.429	.333
Offerman, J#	.000	6	0	0	1	1	0	.143	.000
Orsulak, Joe*	.125	8	1	0	1	0	3	.125	.125
Ripken, Cal	.250	4	1	0	0	1	0	.400	.250
Sosa, Sammy	.400	5	2	0	0	1	0	.571	.800
Spiers, Bill*	.000	3	0	0	0	2	1	.400	.000
Thomas, Frank	1.000	3	3	0	0	2	0	1.000	1.000
Trammell, A	.500	6	3	1	1	0	1	.500	1.000
Ventura, R*	.286	7	2	0	0	0	0	.286	.286
Wilkins, Rick*	.400	5	2	0	1	0	1	.400	.400

Rick Krivda, Orioles — LHP

Batter	Avg	AB	H	HR	BI	BB	SO	OBP	Slg
Anderson, G*	.200	5	1	0	0	0	2	.200	.200
Belle, Albert	.000	5	0	0	0	1	1	.167	.000
Berroa, G	.111	9	1	0	0	2	2	.273	.111
Blowers, Mike	.667	3	2	0	1	1	1	.600	1.000
Boggs, Wade*	.333	6	2	0	1	0	0	.333	.500
Bordick, Mike	.333	9	3	1	1	0	0	.333	.667
Brosius, S	.143	7	1	0	0	1	3	.333	.143
Brumfield, J	.333	9	3	1	2	0	2	.333	.778
Buhner, Jay	.000	5	0	0	0	0	2	.000	.000
Canseco, Jose	.167	6	1	1	3	0	3	.167	.667
Carter, Joe	.182	11	2	1	1	1	1	.250	.545
Cedeno, D#	.500	4	2	0	0	1	1	.600	.500
Coleman, V#	.429	7	3	0	0	0	1	.429	.571
Curtis, Chad	.333	3	1	0	0	2	0	.600	.333
Davis, Russ	.250	4	1	0	1	0	1	.250	.500
Devereaux, M	.500	6	3	1	3	0	1	.500	1.167
Durham, Ray#	.364	11	4	1	2	0	3	.364	.727
Espinoza, A	.000	4	0	0	1	0	0	.000	.000
Fermin, Felix	.400	5	2	0	0	0	0	.400	.400
Fielder, C	.000	4	0	0	0	2	1	.333	.000
Gates, Brent#	.222	9	2	0	1	0	0	.222	.333
Gonzalez, A	.222	9	2	0	0	2	4	.364	.222
Greenwell, M*	.167	6	1	0	0	0	0	.167	.167
Henderson, R	.200	5	1	0	0	2	0	.429	.400
Hudler, Rex	.333	6	2	1	1	0	2	.333	.833
Javier, Stan#	.600	5	3	1	2	0	0	.600	1.400
Johnson, L*	.333	6	2	0	0	0	0	.333	.667
Lofton, Kenny*	.600	5	3	0	1	0	1	.600	.800
Martin, N	.750	4	3	0	1	1	0	.800	1.000
Martinez, E	.250	4	1	0	2	2	0	.429	.250
Martinez, T*	.250	8	2	0	0	0	4	.250	.250
McGwire, Mark	.500	6	3	0	1	1	2	.571	.500
Mouton, Lyle	.143	7	1	0	0	0	1	.143	.143
Nixon, Otis#	.286	7	2	0	2	0	2	.286	.286
O'Brien, C	.286	7	2	0	0	0	1	.286	.429
O'Neill, Paul*	.286	7	2	0	1	3	1	.500	.286
Paquette, C	.250	8	2	1	2	0	1	.250	.625
Pena, Tony	.200	5	1	0	0	0	0	.200	.200
Perez, Robert	.167	6	1	0	0	1	2	.286	.333
Perez, Tomas#	.429	7	3	0	2	1	1	.500	.714
Ramirez, M	1.000	5	5	0	0	1	0	1.000	1.200
Salmon, Tim	.167	6	1	0	0	0	2	.167	.167
Samuel, Juan	.400	5	2	1	3	1	1	.500	1.000
Sierra, Ruben#	.300	10	3	1	3	0	0	.300	.700
Slaught, Don	.200	5	1	1	1	0	1	.200	.800
Sojo, Luis	.429	7	3	0	0	0	0	.429	.571
Sprague, Ed	.333	12	4	1	4	0	1	.333	.667
Steinbach, T	.000	6	0	0	0	1	3	.143	.000
Thomas, Frank	.250	8	2	1	1	2	0	.400	.625
Thome, Jim*	.250	4	1	0	1	1	1	.400	.750

Rick Krivda, Orioles — LHP

Batter	Avg	AB	H	HR	BI	BB	SO	OBP	Slg
Vaughn, Mo*	.333	6	2	0	0	0	3	.333	.333
Velarde, R	.143	7	1	0	1	2	2	.333	.143
Ventura, R*	.500	10	5	0	0	1	1	.545	.500
Vizquel, Omar*	.000	5	0	0	0	1	0	.167	.000
Williams, Ber#	.250	8	2	1	1	1	1	.400	.625
Williams, Ger	.000	8	0	0	0	0	2	.000	.000
Young, Ernie	.200	5	1	0	0	0	2	.200	.200

Mark Langston, Angels — LHP

Batter	Avg	AB	H	HR	BI	BB	SO	OBP	Slg
Alomar, R#	.207	29	6	0	4	3	4	.281	.276
Alomar Jr, S	.125	8	1	0	0	1	1	.222	.125
Amaral, Rich	.455	22	10	1	4	2	2	.480	.682
Anderson, Brd*	.147	34	5	0	3	4	12	.237	.235
Baerga, C#	.192	26	5	1	3	0	5	.185	.346
Baines, H*	.139	36	5	1	3	0	12	.139	.222
Barberie, B#	.556	9	5	0	1	0	1	.556	.778
Bautista, D	.167	12	2	0	1	1	1	.231	.167
Becker, Rich*	.286	7	2	0	0	1	5	.375	.429
Bell, Jay	.176	17	3	0	1	2	3	.263	.235
Belle, Albert	.286	21	6	2	5	4	3	.385	.619
Beltre, E	.286	7	2	0	0	1	2	.375	.429
Berroa, G	.214	14	3	0	1	0	5	.214	.214
Berry, Sean	.333	6	2	0	3	1	0	.429	.667
Bichette, D	.300	20	6	1	2	0	5	.333	.650
Blowers, Mike	.370	27	10	1	3	3	8	.433	.630
Boggs, Wade*	.276	76	21	1	4	15	6	.391	.382
Bonds, Barry*	.000	5	0	0	0	1	0	.167	.000
Bonilla, B#	.176	17	3	0	1	5	7	.364	.294
Boone, Bret	.286	7	2	1	1	1	4	.375	.714
Borders, Pat	.179	28	5	0	2	3	7	.250	.179
Bordick, Mike	.222	27	6	0	1	2	3	.276	.222
Bournigal, R	.000	7	0	0	0	0	1	.000	.000
Brosius, S	.238	21	5	1	3	1	1	.273	.476
Brumfield, J	.286	7	2	0	2	0	2	.286	.571
Buhner, Jay	.167	36	6	1	5	6	18	.302	.278
Burks, Ellis	.273	44	12	0	5	3	8	.333	.409
Butler, Brett*	.233	30	7	0	2	5	10	.361	.267
Cangelosi, J#	.267	15	4	0	1	3	4	.389	.267
Canseco, Jose	.160	50	8	3	7	12	17	.323	.340
Carreon, Mark	.500	14	7	0	1	3	1	.588	.643
Carter, Joe	.288	80	23	4	18	8	18	.360	.538
Cedeno, D#	.273	11	3	0	1	0	3	.273	.273
Cirillo, Jeff	.267	15	4	1	2	1	2	.313	.467
Clark, Will*	.280	25	7	1	1	4	4	.379	.480
Coleman, V#	.276	29	8	0	1	4	4	.300	.379
Cora, Joey#	.444	9	4	0	0	0	1	.500	.444
Curtis, Chad	.308	13	4	0	0	2	3	.400	.308
Cuyler, Milt*	.083	12	1	0	0	0	1	.083	.083
Davis, Chili#	.280	25	7	2	5	2	6	.333	.560
Davis, Eric	.250	12	3	1	2	0	5	.250	.500
Davis, Russ	.250	4	1	0	0	1	2	.400	.250
Dawson, Andre	.286	14	4	1	3	2	3	.375	.571
Deer, Rob	.289	38	11	2	3	9	11	.426	.500
Devereaux, M	.224	58	13	0	5	2	7	.246	.328
Dunston, S	.800	5	4	0	2	0	0	.800	1.200
Durham, Ray#	.154	13	2	0	0	0	1	.154	.154
Dykstra, L*	.200	5	1	0	0	2	2	.429	.400
Eisenreich, J*	.600	5	3	0	0	1	1	.667	1.000
Elster, Kevin	.143	14	2	0	1	1	4	.188	.143
Espinoza, A	.154	26	4	0	0	1	2	.185	.154
Fermin, Felix	.333	24	8	0	4	0	0	.333	.333
Fielder, C	.239	46	11	5	12	9	14	.351	.652
Flaherty, J	.111	9	1	0	1	0	2	.111	.333
Franco, Julio	.333	60	20	3	12	8	13	.400	.600
Frye, Jeff	.211	19	4	1	2	0	3	.211	.421
Fryman, T	.235	34	8	1	5	8	6	.381	.412
Gaetti, Gary	.184	49	9	0	2	3	10	.226	.306
Gagne, Greg	.167	42	7	0	4	5	17	.255	.214
Gallego, Mike	.133	30	4	1	2	7	12	.297	.233
Gates, Brent#	.286	14	4	0	1	1	2	.313	.286
Gil, Benji	.333	9	3	0	0	2	3	.455	.333
Gomez, Chris	.167	6	1	0	1	1	0	.250	.167
Gomez, Leo	.053	19	1	1	1	2	7	.143	.211
Gonzales, R	.353	17	6	0	3	2	3	.421	.471
Gonzalez, A	.231	13	3	0	1	1	3	.286	.462
Gonzalez, J	.222	45	10	3	9	4	16	.286	.467
Goodwin, Tom*	.333	15	5	0	2	0	3	.333	.333
Grebeck, C	.094	32	3	0	1	3	5	.171	.094
Greenwell, M*	.293	41	12	1	3	2	5	.326	.439
Greer, Rusty*	.143	7	1	1	2	0	2	.143	.571
Griffey Jr, K*	.270	37	10	1	7	4	7	.341	.432
Guillen, O*	.298	57	17	0	4	1	3	.310	.386
Hall, Mel*	.000	11	0	0	0	0	4	.000	.000
Hamilton, D*	.125	16	2	0	0	3	0	.176	.125
Hammonds, J	.333	15	5	0	1	1	1	.375	.333
Hayes, C	.188	16	3	0	3	2	0	.188	.188
Henderson, R	.275	51	14	3	6	12	8	.413	.490
Hiatt, Phil	.200	10	2	0	1	0	3	.200	.300
Hill, G	.192	26	5	1	3	0	11	.192	.308
Hoiles, Chris	.160	25	4	0	3	3	5	.250	.200

Mark Langston, Angels — LHP

Batter	Avg	AB	H	HR	BI	BB	SO	OBP	Slg
Howard, Dave#	.133	15	2	0	2	0	1	.133	.133
Howard, T*	.286	14	4	0	0	1	4	.333	.286
Howell, Jack*	.158	19	3	1	2	0	12	.158	.368
Huff, Michael	.240	25	6	0	1	2	3	.296	.320
Hulse, David*	.200	5	1	0	0	0	4	.200	.200
Incaviglia, P	.133	15	2	0	1	3	8	.278	.200
Jaha, John	.148	27	4	2	3	6	8	.303	.370
Javier, Stan#	.111	18	2	0	0	0	5	.111	.111
Jefferies, G#	.333	6	2	1	2	1	0	.429	1.000
Jefferson, R*	.111	9	1	0	0	0	2	.111	.111
Johnson, L*	.138	29	4	0	1	3	1	.219	.172
Jordan, Ricky	.300	10	3	1	1	0	1	.300	.600
Joyner, Wally*	.103	39	4	1	2	1	6	.125	.179
Karkovice, R	.116	43	5	1	5	2	18	.174	.233
Kelly, Pat	.400	25	10	1	4	2	4	.444	.520
Kelly, R	.226	31	7	0	1	3	7	.294	.355
King, Jeff	.000	7	0	0	0	1	2	.125	.000
Knoblauch, C	.158	19	3	1	3	6	4	.360	.316
Knorr, Randy	.286	7	2	0	0	1	3	.375	.429
Kreuter, Chad#	.200	15	3	0	1	2	7	.278	.333
Leius, Scott	.059	17	1	1	1	3	3	.200	.235
Lewis, Mark	.188	16	3	1	3	1	2	.235	.438
Leyritz, Jim	.125	32	4	0	0	2	12	.176	.125
Liriano, N#	.286	7	2	0	2	0	0	.286	.571
Listach, Pat#	.250	44	11	1	1	1	9	.267	.364
Lofton, Kenny*	.182	11	2	0	1	3	2	.333	.273
Loretta, Mark	.000	6	0	0	0	2	0	.250	.000
Macfarlane, M	.321	53	17	2	6	3	15	.357	.509
Manto, Jeff	.111	9	1	0	1	0	4	.111	.111
Manwaring, K	.000	4	0	0	0	1	2	.200	.000
Martin, N	.250	20	5	0	1	2	2	.318	.350
Martinez, E	.378	37	14	2	5	6	4	.465	.595
Martinez, T*	.308	13	4	0	0	1	4	.357	.308
Matheny, Mike	.222	9	2	0	2	1	4	.300	.333
McCarty, Dave	.333	6	2	0	0	0	2	.333	.333
McGriff, Fred*	.111	9	1	0	0	0	3	.111	.111
McGwire, Mark	.313	48	15	4	15	5	13	.370	.625
McIntosh, Tim	.000	5	0	0	0	0	0	.000	.000
McLemore, M#	.236	55	13	1	4	4	13	.288	.291
McRae, Brian#	.290	31	9	1	4	1	5	.313	.484
Meares, Pat	.167	12	2	0	0	0	5	.167	.167
Mercedes, H	.600	5	3	0	0	0	2	.600	.600
Mieske, Matt	.368	19	7	0	1	0	3	.400	.526
Mitchell, K	.467	15	7	1	4	0	2	.467	.800
Molitor, Paul	.429	63	27	4	15	11	9	.507	.714
Morman, Russ	.286	7	2	1	1	1	3	.375	.714
Mouton, Lyle	.231	13	3	0	1	1	6	.267	.231
Munoz, Pedro	.105	19	2	1	1	0	4	.105	.316
Murray, Eddie#	.304	46	14	1	9	8	5	.407	.522
Naehring, Tim	.250	16	4	0	0	3	4	.368	.375
Nieves, M#	.167	6	1	0	1	0	3	.167	.167
Nilsson, Dave*	.333	6	2	1	3	2	1	.444	.833
Nixon, Otis#	.167	36	6	0	3	2	7	.211	.222
O'Brien, C	.188	16	3	1	3	2	5	.278	.375
O'Neill, Paul*	.313	16	5	0	4	2	1	.368	.375
Obando, S	.333	6	2	0	1	0	3	.333	.333
Offerman, J#	.375	8	3	1	2	0	0	.375	.875
Olerud, John*	.190	21	4	1	4	7	5	.379	.333
Oliver, Joe	.286	7	2	0	1	2	4	.400	.286
Orsulak, Joe*	.111	9	1	0	0	2	2	.273	.111
Ortiz, Luis	.400	5	2	0	1	0	0	.400	.600
Palmeiro, R*	.268	41	11	4	8	5	4	.348	.634
Palmer, Dean	.259	27	7	4	6	5	8	.375	.741
Paquette, C	.278	18	5	1	1	0	4	.278	.500
Parent, Mark	.167	6	1	1	2	0	2	.167	.667
Pena, Tony	.207	29	6	1	5	1	4	.233	.310
Pendleton, T#	.286	7	2	0	1	0	1	.375	.286
Perez, Robert	.222	9	2	0	1	0	0	.222	.333
Phillips, T#	.274	62	17	0	4	17	11	.438	.355
Pirkl, Greg	.167	6	1	1	3	0	1	.167	.667
Plantier, P*	.250	4	1	0	0	2	2	.500	.250
Pulliam, H	.143	7	1	0	0	0	5	.143	.143
Raines, Tim#	.304	46	14	1	4	4	5	.360	.435
Randa, Joe	.222	9	2	0	0	0	0	.222	.222
Rebolulet, J	.000	6	0	0	0	1	1	.143	.000
Reed, Jody	.152	33	5	0	1	5	3	.243	.212
Ripken, Billy	.263	38	10	0	4	3	4	.302	.368
Ripken, Cal	.344	93	32	2	10	13	14	.425	.452
Rodriguez, I	.242	33	8	0	4	1	9	.265	.273
Sabo, Chris	.333	9	3	1	2	2	2	.455	.778
Samuel, Juan	.222	36	8	1	5	3	10	.282	.389
Sandberg, R	.000	8	0	0	0	3	3	.273	.000
Schofield, D	.143	35	5	1	5	6	8	.268	.229
Segui, David#	.353	17	6	1	3	3	2	.450	.588
Seitzer, K	.329	70	23	2	6	11	13	.420	.457
Sheffield, G	.296	27	8	1	4	1	3	.321	.481
Shumpert, T	.200	15	3	1	1	3	7	.333	.400
Sierra, Ruben#	.245	53	13	3	9	6	6	.306	.434
Silvestri, D	.167	6	1	0	1	1	0	.286	.500
Slaught, Don	.158	19	3	0	3	6	2	.375	.211
Smith, Ozzie#	.167	6	1	0	1	2	0	.375	.333

Mark Langston, Angels — LHP

Batter	Avg	AB	H	HR	BI	BB	SO	OBP	Slg
Sojo, Luis	.308	13	4	0	3	2	1	.400	.385
Sosa, Sammy	.222	18	4	1	1	1	6	.263	.500
Spiers, William	.286	7	2	0	0	0	3	.286	.286
Sprague, Ed	.111	27	3	0	2	4	9	.226	.111
Stankiewicz	.143	7	1	0	0	0	2	.143	.143
Stanley, Mike	.256	43	11	1	5	7	14	.360	.349
Steinbach, T	.280	50	14	1	10	8	7	.367	.460
Stillwell, K#	.278	18	5	0	6	1	3	.316	.500
Strange, Doug#	.000	6	0	0	0	0	1	.000	.000
Surhoff, B.J.*	.188	32	6	1	3	3	3	.257	.281
Sveum, Dale#	.389	18	7	0	4	3	5	.435	.444
Tartabull, D	.298	47	14	3	11	11	13	.431	.596
Tettleton, M#	.175	63	11	1	6	3	22	.212	.254
Thomas, Frank	.435	46	20	5	11	17	7	.578	.804
Thompson, Mil*	.000	6	0	0	0	1	2	.143	.000
Thompson, Rob	.400	5	2	0	0	1	0	.500	.400
Trammell, A	.380	71	27	3	10	5	7	.421	.606
Tucker, M*	.500	6	3	0	0	0	1	.500	.500
Valentin, Jhn	.118	17	2	0	2	2	4	.211	.176
Valentin, Jse#	.267	15	4	0	2	1	6	.313	.400
Valle, Dave	.306	36	11	1	6	1	7	.359	.389
Vaughn, Greg	.220	50	11	3	6	7	10	.316	.420
Vaughn, Mo*	.200	15	3	0	2	0	4	.200	.333
Velarde, R	.333	36	12	1	3	10	6	.468	.500
Ventura, R*	.288	59	17	0	6	6	14	.354	.305
Vitiello, Joe	.250	12	3	2	5	2	5	.357	.750
Vizquel, Omar#	.192	26	5	0	1	1	4	.222	.269
Voigt, Jack	.000	12	0	0	0	0	3	.000	.000
Walbeck, Matt#	.200	10	2	0	0	0	1	.200	.300
Walton, J	.300	10	3	0	1	1	4	.364	.300
Ward, Turner#	.200	5	1	0	0	0	2	.200	.400
Weiss, Walt*	.100	10	1	0	0	1	2	.182	.100
White, Devon#	.193	57	11	1	2	3	9	.233	.316
Whiten, Mark#	.222	9	2	0	0	0	2	.222	.333
Williams, Ber#	.300	30	9	1	3	4	6	.382	.433
Williams, E	.400	10	4	0	1	0	2	.400	.500
Williams, Ger	.200	10	2	0	3	0	4	.182	.400
Williams, Ma	.400	5	2	1	3	0	3	.400	1.200
Wilson, Dan	.300	10	3	1	2	0	2	.300	.700
Worthington	.188	16	3	0	1	5	4	.381	.250
Young, Ernie	.200	5	1	0	0	1	3	.333	.400
Young, Kevin	.200	5	1	0	0	1	3	.333	.400

Phil Leftwich, Angels — RHP

Batter	Avg	AB	H	HR	BI	BB	SO	OBP	Slg
Alomar, R#	.143	7	1	0	1	3	1	.400	.143
Alomar Jr, S	.286	7	2	0	0	0	0	.286	.429
Anderson, Brd*	.500	10	5	1	3	0	0	.615	.900
Baerga, C#	.286	7	2	0	0	0	0	.286	.286
Baines, H*	.333	9	3	1	2	2	2	.455	.778
Belle, Albert	.000	5	0	0	0	2	1	.286	.000
Berroa, G	.333	9	3	1	1	0	1	.333	.667
Blowers, Mike	.200	5	1	0	0	0	2	.200	.200
Boone, Bret	.167	6	1	0	0	0	1	.167	.167
Borders, Pat	.375	8	3	0	0	0	1	.375	.500
Bordick, Mike	.600	10	6	0	2	1	1	.636	.900
Brosius, S	.429	7	3	0	2	0	0	.429	.429
Buhner, Jay	.400	5	2	1	2	1	0	.571	1.200
Carter, Joe	.250	8	2	0	1	0	2	.333	.500
Cora, Joey#	.500	8	4	0	2	0	0	.600	.750
Dawson, Andre	.250	8	2	0	0	0	1	.250	.250
Devereaux, M	.200	10	2	0	0	0	2	.200	.200
Franco, Julio	.429	7	3	1	6	1	1	.444	1.000
Gaetti, Gary	.167	6	1	0	0	0	2	.167	.333
Gagne, Greg	.222	9	2	0	1	1	0	.300	.333
Gates, Brent#	.000	9	0	0	0	1	1	.100	.000
Gonzalez, J	.250	4	1	0	0	1	0	.400	.250
Greenwell, M*	.182	11	2	0	1	2	0	.357	.273
Griffey Jr, K*	.000	4	0	0	1	0	0	.000	.000
Guillen, O*	.000	6	0	0	0	0	0	.000	.000
Gwynn, Chris*	.500	6	3	0	1	0	1	.571	.667
Hamelin, Bob*	.000	5	0	0	0	3	0	.375	.000
Hamilton, D*	.286	7	2	0	1	0	1	.286	.429
Hammonds, A	.750	4	3	1	3	1	1	.800	1.750
Henderson, R	.188	16	3	1	1	0	3	.188	.375
Hoiles, Chris	.400	10	4	0	1	1	1	.455	.500
Jaha, John	.167	6	1	0	0	0	1	.167	.333
Javier, Stan#	.429	7	3	0	0	0	2	.429	.429
Johnson, L*	.111	9	1	0	2	0	0	.111	.333
Joyner, Wally*	.500	6	3	0	1	0	1	.500	.500
Kirby, Wayne*	.333	6	2	0	1	0	0	.333	.333
Listach, Pat#	.000	5	0	0	0	1	0	.000	.000
Lofton, Kenny*	.286	7	2	0	1	0	0	.286	.429
Macfarlane, M	.400	5	2	0	0	0	2	.400	.400
Magadan, Dave*	.167	6	1	0	1	0	0	.286	.167
Martinez, E	.500	6	3	1	0	0	0	.500	1.000
Mayne, Brent*	.167	6	1	0	0	0	1	.286	.167
McLemore, M#	.273	11	3	0	1	0	1	.273	.364
Molitor, Paul	.300	10	3	0	2	0	1	.300	.400
Murray, Eddie#	.286	7	2	0	0	0	1	.286	.286
Naehring, Tim	.333	9	3	0	1	0	2	.400	.333

112

Phil Leftwich, Angels — RHP

Batter	Avg	AB	H	HR	BI	BB	SO	OBP	Slg
Nilsson, Dave*	.333	6	2	0	1	0	0	.333	.333
Nixon, Otis#	.286	7	2	0	1	3	0	.455	.286
Olerud, John*	.286	7	2	0	1	2	0	.444	.286
Palmeiro, R*	.000	7	0	0	1	0	1	.000	.000
Raines, Tim#	.667	9	6	0	1	0	1	.600	.667
Ripken, Cal	.100	10	1	0	1	1	0	.182	.200
Sabo, Chris	.500	4	2	1	3	1	0	.600	1.500
Segui, David#	.167	6	1	0	0	0	0	.167	.167
Sierra, Ruben#	.300	10	3	0	2	0	1	.300	.300
Sorrento, P*	.400	5	2	1	1	2	0	.571	1.200
Sprague, Ed	.125	8	1	0	0	0	2	.125	.125
Steinbach, J	.444	9	4	0	1	0	1	.444	.444
Strange, Doug#	.000	4	0	0	1	1	1	.200	.000
Thomas, Frank	.500	8	4	0	2	2	0	.600	.625
Thome, Jim*	.333	6	2	0	2	1	1	.429	.500
Valentin, Jhn	.300	10	3	0	3	0	0	.300	.400
Valle, Dave	.300	10	3	0	0	2	3	.300	.400
Vaughn, Mo*	.250	12	3	1	3	2	5	.357	.583
Ventura, R*	.286	7	2	1	2	2	1	.444	.714
Vizquel, Omar#	.143	7	1	0	0	0	0	.143	.143
White, Devon#	.667	6	4	0	0	0	1	.667	.667

Dave Leiper, Expos — LHP

Batter	Avg	AB	H	HR	BI	BB	SO	OBP	Slg
Anderson, Brd*	.000	5	0	0	0	0	0	.167	.000
Baines, H*	.286	7	2	0	0	2	1	.444	.286
Blauser, Jeff	.000	4	0	0	0	1	1	.200	.000
Boggs, Wade*	.000	10	0	0	0	2	1	.167	.000
Bonds, Barry*	.500	6	3	0	0	1	0	.571	.500
Bonilla, B#	.500	6	3	0	2	1	1	.571	.500
Butler, Brett*	.125	8	1	0	1	1	0	.222	.125
Caminiti, Ken#	.143	7	1	0	0	0	1	.143	.286
Cangelosi, J#	.250	4	1	0	0	0	1	.400	.250
Clark, Will*	.125	8	1	0	2	0	2	.222	.125
Davis, Eric	.200	5	1	0	1	0	2	.200	.600
Fielder, C	.333	3	1	0	0	2	1	.600	.333
Finley, Steve*	.200	5	1	1	4	0	0	.200	.800
Gagne, Greg	.500	4	2	0	0	1	1	.600	1.500
Galarraga, A	.600	5	3	0	1	0	0	.667	.600
Gant, Ron	.500	6	3	0	0	2	2	.625	.500
Greer, Rusty*	.250	4	1	0	0	1	0	.400	.500
Guillen, O*	.600	5	3	0	1	1	0	.667	.600
Gwynn, Tony*	.333	3	1	0	0	2	0	.600	.333
Hall, Mel*	.000	4	0	0	0	1	1	.200	.000
James, Dion*	.333	3	1	0	0	3	1	.667	.333
Joyner, Wally	.200	5	1	1	3	2	0	.429	.800
Justice, Dave*	.400	5	2	1	1	0	0	.400	1.000
Kingery, Mike*	.000	6	0	0	0	0	1	.000	.000
Klesko, Ryan*	.333	6	2	1	1	0	2	.333	1.000
Larkin, Barry	.000	6	0	0	0	1	1	.143	.000
McGee, Willie#	.000	4	0	0	0	1	2	.200	.000
McGriff, Fred*	.600	5	3	0	0	0	1	.600	.800
O'Neill, Paul*	.545	11	6	1	4	2	1	.615	.818
Palmeiro, R*	.000	5	0	0	0	0	0	.000	.000
Polonia, Luis*	.333	6	2	1	1	0	0	.333	1.000
Raines, Tim#	.250	4	1	0	0	1	0	.400	.250
Reed, Jeff*	.250	4	1	0	0	1	0	.400	.250
Ripken, Cal	.000	4	0	0	0	1	1	.200	.000
Sabo, Chris	.333	9	3	0	1	0	1	.333	.444
Sandberg, R	.750	4	3	0	0	1	0	.800	1.000
Smith, Ozzie*	.750	4	3	0	0	0	0	.750	1.000
Strawberry, D*	.000	4	0	0	1	0	1	.200	.000
Thompson, Rob	.000	4	0	0	1	0	0	.000	.000
Trammell, A	.250	4	1	0	2	0	1	.200	.250

Al Leiter, Marlins — LHP

Batter	Avg	AB	H	HR	BI	BB	SO	OBP	Slg
Alicea, Luis#	.250	8	2	0	0	1	1	.455	.250
Alomar Jr, S	.500	6	3	0	0	1	1	.500	.500
Alou, Moises	.250	4	1	0	1	0	2	.200	.500
Amaral, Rich	.200	10	2	0	0	2	3	.333	.200
Anderson, Brd*	.000	9	0	0	1	2	0	.167	.000
Andrews, S	.250	4	1	0	1	1	3	.400	.500
Baerga, C#	.174	23	4	0	2	1	4	.208	.174
Bagwell, Jeff	.200	5	1	0	0	4	2	.556	.200
Barberie, B#	.167	6	1	0	0	0	2	.167	.167
Becker, Rich*	.000	4	0	0	0	1	2	.000	.000
Bell, Derek	.333	9	3	1	3	0	2	.333	.778
Bell, Jay	.333	6	2	0	0	4	1	.600	.333
Belle, Albert	.286	14	4	1	4	6	2	.500	.571
Berroa, G	.250	12	3	0	2	0	2	.250	.417
Berry, Sean	.000	5	0	0	0	1	1	.167	.000
Bichette, D	.250	12	3	0	1	2	4	.357	.333
Biggio, Craig	.286	7	2	0	3	3	0	.500	.429
Blauser, Jeff	.000	5	0	0	0	5	4	.500	.000
Blowers, Mike	.235	17	4	1	4	1	3	.278	.529
Boggs, Wade*	.000	7	0	0	0	5	1	.417	.000
Boone, Bret	.100	10	1	0	0	0	1	.100	.100
Bordick, Mike	.214	14	3	0	2	0	4	.200	.214
Brosius, S	.250	12	3	0	3	1	6	.308	.417
Brumfield, J	.000	7	0	0	0	1	1	.125	.000
Buhner, Jay	.333	12	4	0	0	1	3	.385	.417
Burks, Ellis	.250	16	4	1	6	3	3	.400	.500
Butler, Brett*	.750	4	3	0	2	1	0	.667	1.250
Cameron, Mike	.167	6	1	0	0	1	2	.286	.333
Caminiti, Ken#	.222	9	2	1	2	0	2	.300	.556
Canseco, Jose	.125	8	1	0	1	4	3	.417	.125
Carter, Joe	.125	8	1	0	0	0	3	.125	.125
Castilla, V	.000	7	0	0	0	1	2	.222	.000
Clark, Will*	.200	15	3	1	2	1	1	.250	.467
Clayton, R	.667	6	4	0	1	1	0	.714	.667
Cole, Alex*	.167	6	1	0	0	2	2	.375	.167
Coleman, V#	.200	10	2	0	0	3	2	.200	.200
Cora, Joey*	.250	4	1	0	0	1	1	.400	.250
Curtis, Chad	.188	16	3	0	0	4	3	.350	.188
Cuyler, Milt*	.500	6	3	0	1	1	0	.571	.667
Davis, Chili#	.111	18	2	1	3	3	7	.238	.278
Davis, Eric	.000	3	0	0	0	3	2	.500	.000
Davis, Russ	.000	7	0	0	0	0	4	.000	.000
Deer, Rob	.125	8	1	1	1	2	4	.300	.500
DeShields, D*	.375	8	3	0	0	1	4	.444	1.000
Devereaux, M	.231	13	3	0	3	1	5	.286	.231
DiSarcina, G	.273	11	3	0	1	1	2	.333	.364
Durham, Ray#	.000	9	0	0	0	1	2	.100	.000
Dye, Jermaine	.300	10	3	0	0	0	1	.300	.300
Easley, D	.250	12	3	1	3	0	2	.250	.500
Edmonds, Jim*	.400	5	2	0	2	0	1	.400	.600
Espinoza, A	.000	6	0	0	1	0	1	.000	.000
Fermin, Felix	.438	16	7	0	3	2	0	.500	.438
Fielder, C	.083	12	1	0	2	2	8	.214	.083
Finley, Steve*	.111	9	1	0	1	1	2	.273	.222
Flaherty, J	.000	5	0	0	0	3	0	.444	.167
Franco, Julio	1.000	3	3	0	0	3	0	1.000	1.333
Frye, Jeff	.286	7	2	0	2	1	2	.375	.286
Fryman, T	.300	10	3	0	0	1	3	.364	.300
Gaetti, Gary	.222	18	4	2	2	3	7	.364	.611
Gagne, Greg	.000	20	0	0	0	2	8	.091	.000
Galarraga, A	.667	6	4	1	3	3	1	.778	1.333
Gallego, Mike	.375	8	3	0	2	3	0	.545	.375
Gant, Ron	.000	4	0	0	1	3	1	.429	.000
Garcia, C	.286	7	2	0	0	0	2	.286	.429
Gates, Brent#	.222	9	2	0	1	0	3	.200	.333
Gil, Benji	.167	6	1	0	0	3	3	.444	.333
Gilkey, B	.200	5	1	0	0	1	3	.333	.200
Gomez, Chris	.200	10	2	0	0	3	2	.385	.200
Gomez, Leo	.056	18	1	0	0	3	6	.190	.056
Gonzales, R	.273	11	3	0	1	1	1	.333	.455
Gonzalez, J	.400	10	4	1	3	0	1	.417	.800
Grace, Mark*	.000	8	0	0	0	2	1	.200	.000
Grebeck, C	.375	8	3	0	0	1	1	.444	.625
Greenwell, M*	.267	15	4	0	1	4	1	.313	.333
Griffey Jr, K*	.200	10	2	0	0	1	1	.273	.200
Grissom, M	.200	10	2	0	0	0	1	.200	.200
Guillen, O*	.000	5	0	0	0	1	0	.000	.000
Hamilton, D*	.250	4	1	0	0	1	1	.400	.250
Hammonds, J	.222	9	2	0	0	0	3	.222	.222
Haselman, B	.250	8	2	0	1	1	3	.333	.250
Hayes, C	.000	8	0	0	0	1	3	.111	.000
Henderson, R	.211	19	4	0	1	4	6	.333	.211
Hoiles, Chris	.154	13	2	0	0	3	5	.313	.154
Howard, Dave#	.333	3	1	0	0	0	1	.667	.333
Howard, T*	.286	7	2	0	0	0	0	.286	.286
Hudler, Rex	.375	8	3	0	0	1	1	.444	.375
Hulse, David*	.167	12	2	0	0	1	7	.231	.167
Hundley, Todd#	.375	8	3	0	2	1	5	.444	.625
Huskey, Butch	.250	8	2	1	1	1	4	.333	.750
Incaviglia, P	.400	5	2	2	4	1	3	.500	1.600
Jaha, John	.400	5	2	0	1	3	1	.625	.600
Javier, Stan#	.182	11	2	0	2	1	0	.250	.273
Jefferson, R*	.000	5	0	0	0	0	2	.000	.000
Johnson, L*	.444	18	8	0	2	2	1	.500	.500
Jones, C#	.222	9	2	1	2	0	1	.222	.667
Jones, Chris	.125	8	1	0	0	1	5	.222	.125
Jordan, Brian	.200	5	1	0	1	1	0	.333	.200
Joyner, Wally	.412	17	7	0	0	1	3	.444	.412
Karkovice, R	.167	12	2	0	3	1	4	.231	.333
Karros, Eric	.000	6	0	0	0	2	0	.250	.000
Kelly, Pat	.333	9	3	0	0	0	2	.400	.333
Kendall, J	.250	4	1	0	0	3	1	.571	.250
Kent, Jeff	.333	6	2	0	0	0	3	.333	.333
King, Jeff	.100	10	1	0	0	1	4	.182	.200
Kirby, Wayne*	.250	8	2	0	0	0	2	.250	.250
Knoblauch, C	.182	11	2	1	1	2	4	.308	.455
Knorr, Randy	.250	8	2	0	0	0	2	.250	.500
Lansing, Mike	.400	5	2	0	0	0	1	.400	.600
Larkin, Barry	.400	5	2	1	1	6	1	.727	1.000
Leius, Scott	.222	9	2	0	0	2	1	.364	.222
Lemke, Mark#	.125	8	1	0	1	1	1	.200	.125
Leyritz, Jim	.167	6	1	0	0	2	3	.444	.167
Liriano, N#	.333	9	3	1	2	0	1	.400	.667
Listach, Pat#	.333	9	3	0	0	2	0	.455	.556
Lofton, Kenny*	.313	16	5	0	0	4	5	.450	.625

Al Leiter, Marlins — LHP

Batter	Avg	AB	H	HR	BI	BB	SO	OBP	Slg
Lopez, Javy	.286	7	2	0	0	2	4	.444	.286
Macfarlane, M	.182	11	2	1	2	4	2	.400	.455
Martin, Al*	.143	7	1	0	0	0	1	.143	.286
Martin, N	.000	5	0	0	0	0	1	.000	.000
Martinez, T*	.111	9	1	0	1	0	2	.111	.111
McCracken, Q#	.000	6	0	0	0	2	0	.250	.000
McGee, Willie#	.400	5	2	0	1	0	2	.333	.800
McGriff, Fred*	.333	9	3	0	1	0	2	.333	.333
McLemore, M#	.500	18	9	1	3	3	1	.571	.833
McRae, Brian#	.077	13	1	0	0	3	2	.294	.077
Meares, Pat	.286	7	2	0	0	1	3	.375	.286
Merced, O*	.000	9	0	0	0	1	5	.100	.000
Mieske, Matt	.333	9	3	1	2	0	1	.333	.667
Miller, Orl	.000	7	0	0	1	1	2	.125	.000
Molitor, Paul	.333	3	1	0	0	3	0	.667	.333
Mondesi, Raul	.333	6	2	0	1	1	0	.429	.500
Morris, Hal*	.091	11	1	0	1	0	0	.091	.091
Mouton, James	.375	8	3	0	0	2	0	.500	.500
Mouton, Lyle	.250	8	2	0	1	2	3	.400	.250
Munoz, Pedro	.333	6	2	0	0	6	1	.667	.333
Murray, Eddie#	.267	15	4	0	2	2	3	.353	.333
Naehring, Tim	.273	11	3	1	5	6	1	.529	.636
Nixon, Otis*	.231	13	3	0	1	5	3	.444	.231
O'Leary, Troy*	.333	9	3	0	0	1	2	.333	.333
O'Neill, Paul*	.167	6	1	1	4	2	0	.375	.667
Obando, S	.500	6	3	0	1	1	2	.571	.500
Oliver, Joe	.067	15	1	0	2	1	6	.125	.133
Ordonez, Rey	.143	7	1	0	0	0	0	.143	.143
Owens, J	.000	8	0	0	0	1	5	.111	.000
Pagnozzi, Tom	.500	6	3	0	0	1	1	.500	.833
Palmeiro, R*	.533	15	8	0	4	1	2	.563	.667
Palmer, Dean	.250	8	2	1	2	0	2	.250	.250
Paquette, C	.000	6	0	0	0	1	2	.143	.000
Pena, Tony	.333	9	3	0	3	0	1	.333	.556
Perez, E	.286	7	2	0	1	2	1	.444	.571
Perry, H	.667	3	2	0	1	0	0	.667	.667
Phillips, T#	.143	7	1	0	1	2	1	.300	.143
Piazza, Mike	.250	4	1	1	2	2	2	.500	1.000
Polonia, Luis*	.375	8	3	0	0	0	1	.375	.375
Raines, Tim#	.375	8	3	0	1	4	0	.615	.375
Ramirez, M	.500	14	7	1	3	0	2	.533	.786
Reboulet, J	.167	6	1	0	0	0	1	.167	.167
Reed, Jody	.250	8	2	0	0	4	0	.500	.375
Ripken, Cal	.294	17	5	0	4	0	1	.263	.353
Rodriguez, I	.214	14	3	0	1	3	1	.353	.214
Sabo, Chris	.200	5	1	0	1	4	1	.556	.200
Salmon, Tim	.222	9	2	0	0	7	1	.563	.222
Samuel, Juan	.000	4	0	0	0	1	2	.200	.000
Sanchez, Rey	.000	6	0	0	0	0	3	.000	.000
Sandberg, R	.333	9	3	3	5	1	2	.400	1.333
Sanders, R	.167	6	1	0	0	1	2	.286	.167
Santangelo, F*	.000	1	0	0	1	3	1	.800	.000
Schofield, D	.250	8	2	0	0	1	0	.250	.250
Segui, David#	.222	9	2	0	0	1	2	.300	.333
Seltzer, K	.333	15	5	0	2	3	1	.444	.400
Servais, S	.200	5	1	0	2	1	2	.333	.200
Sierra, Ruben*	.182	11	2	0	0	4	4	.182	.182
Snow, J.T.#	.200	5	1	0	1	2	2	.429	.200
Sosa, Sammy	.000	6	0	0	0	0	1	.000	.000
Stanley, Mike	.500	10	5	0	2	6	2	.688	.700
Steinbach, T	.500	10	5	0	1	2	3	.583	.800
Stillwell, K#	.250	4	1	0	2	1	0	.400	.250
Strange, Doug#	.111	9	1	0	0	0	1	.111	.111
Surhoff, B.J.*	.286	14	4	0	5	2	2	.353	.357
Sveum, Dale#	.000	6	0	0	0	2	2	.000	.000
Tartabull, D	.200	10	2	1	3	4	3	.400	.500
Tettleton, M#	.308	13	4	0	2	4	5	.471	.308
Thomas, Frank	.182	11	2	1	2	4	1	.400	.545
Thome, Jim	.100	10	1	1	3	2	4	.231	.400
Timmons, O	.143	7	1	0	0	2	2	.333	.143
Tinsley, Lee#	.333	15	5	0	1	0	3	.333	.467
Trammell, A	.125	8	1	0	0	3	0	.417	.250
Turner, Chris	.000	5	0	0	0	0	3	.000	.000
Valentin, Jhn	.313	16	5	0	2	2	2	.389	.438
Valentin, Jse#	.200	5	1	0	0	0	2	.200	.200
Valle, Dave	.400	5	2	0	1	1	1	.500	.600
Vaughn, Greg	.200	10	2	0	0	3	1	.385	.200
Vaughn, Mo*	.263	19	5	1	4	1	8	.333	.474
Velarde, R	.111	9	1	0	0	1	4	.273	.111
Ventura, R*	.200	10	2	0	1	2	3	.300	.300
Vizcaino, J#	.571	7	4	0	0	0	2	.571	.571
Vizquel, Omar#	.222	18	4	1	2	4	1	.364	.500
Voigt, Jack	.000	8	2	1	1	2	2	.333	.625
Walbeck, Matt#	.444	9	4	0	2	0	1	.444	.444
Webster, L	.400	5	2	0	0	1	0	.500	.600
Wehner, John	.333	6	2	1	1	3	0	.556	.833
Weiss, Walt#	.000	5	0	0	1	0	1	.167	.000
Whiten, Mark*	.385	13	5	0	1	0	4	.385	.615
Williams, Ber#	.100	10	1	0	0	1	2	.100	.100
Williams, Ger	.500	8	4	0	0	1	0	.556	.625
Wilson, Dan	.000	6	0	0	0	1	1	.000	.000

Al Leiter, Marlins — LHP

Batter	Avg	AB	H	HR	BI	BB	SO	OBP	Slg
Young, Eric	.111	9	1	0	0	1	4	.200	.111

Mark Leiter, Expos — RHP

Batter	Avg	AB	H	HR	BI	BB	SO	OBP	Slg
Abbott, Kurt	.267	15	4	0	1	0	5	.267	.333
Aldrete, Mike*	.400	5	2	0	0	1	1	.500	.600
Aloma, R#	.200	10	2	0	2	5	2	.467	.400
Alou, Moises	.222	9	2	0	0	0	2	.222	.333
Amaral, Rich	.000	5	0	0	0	0	1	.000	.000
Anderson, Brd*	.250	16	4	0	1	1	3	.333	.375
Anthony, Eric*	.375	8	3	2	3	0	2	.375	1.250
Arias, Alex	.167	6	1	0	0	0	0	.167	.167
Ashley, Billy	.400	5	2	0	2	0	1	.400	.400
Aurilia, Rich	.000	3	0	0	0	1	2	.250	.000
Ausmus, Brad	.500	6	3	0	3	0	0	.500	.667
Baerga, C#	.100	10	1	0	0	1	2	.250	.200
Bagwell, Jeff	.412	17	7	1	4	3	6	.524	.647
Baines, H*	.105	19	2	1	6	3	2	.227	.263
Bates, Jason#	.125	8	1	0	0	2	4	.300	.125
Bell, Derek	.471	17	8	1	3	1	3	.500	.824
Bell, Jay	.200	5	1	0	0	2	1	.429	.400
Belle, Albert	.286	7	2	2	2	1	1	.444	1.143
Benard, M*	.143	7	1	0	0	0	1	.143	.143
Berry, Sean	.231	13	3	1	7	0	3	.250	.538
Bichette, D	.471	17	8	0	4	1	4	.500	.706
Biggio, Craig	.158	19	3	0	1	1	3	.273	.158
Blauser, Jeff	.600	5	3	1	3	2	0	.750	1.400
Blowers, Mike	.600	5	3	0	3	2	0	.714	.600
Boggs, Wade*	.462	13	6	0	2	4	1	.588	.692
Boone, Bret	.400	10	4	1	1	2	3	.500	.700
Borders, Pat	.000	7	0	0	0	0	0	.000	.000
Bordick, Mike	.071	14	1	0	1	0	3	.071	.071
Branson, Jeff*	.250	8	2	0	1	0	1	.250	.250
Brogna, Rico*	.333	9	3	0	0	1	5	.400	.333
Brosius, S	.571	7	4	1	4	0	1	.625	1.286
Buhner, Jay	.000	10	0	0	1	2	5	.154	.000
Burks, Ellis	.143	21	3	0	1	0	4	.143	.143
Butler, Brett*	.400	5	2	0	1	0	1	.333	.400
Caminiti, Ken#	.286	14	4	0	2	1	4	.333	.357
Cangelosi, J#	.167	6	1	0	0	1	1	.286	.167
Canseco, Jose	.357	14	5	1	4	0	2	.400	.571
Carter, Joe	.308	13	4	1	3	3	3	.438	.538
Castilla, V	.250	12	3	0	3	0	0	.308	.250
Cedeno, A	.400	5	2	0	2	0	2	.500	.400
Colbrunn, G	.125	16	2	0	0	3	0	.222	.188
Cole, Alex*	.250	4	1	0	0	2	1	.500	.250
Conine, Jeff	.100	20	2	1	2	0	4	.100	.250
Cora, Joey#	.154	13	2	0	1	2	1	.267	.154
Cordero, Wil	.125	8	1	0	1	0	1	.222	.250
Daulton, D*	.000	6	0	0	0	1	1	.143	.000
Davis, Chili#	.000	5	0	0	0	1	1	.286	.000
Davis, Eric	.250	5	1	1	2	1	0	.333	.800
Dawson, Andre	.333	9	3	1	3	0	2	.333	.778
DeShields, D*	.357	17	6	1	3	5	6	.500	.647
Devereaux, M	.158	19	3	0	0	1	8	.200	.158
Dunston, S	.250	8	2	0	1	0	0	.333	.375
Dye, Jermaine	.600	5	3	1	1	0	0	.600	1.400
Eisenreich, J*	.400	15	6	0	0	1	1	.438	.400
Eusebio, Tony	.167	6	1	0	0	0	0	.167	.167
Everett, Carl#	.167	6	1	0	1	4	0	.500	.167
Fermin, Felix	.286	7	2	0	0	0	0	.286	.429
Fielder, C	.250	12	3	1	2	0	4	.250	.500
Finley, Steve*	.333	15	5	2	6	1	2	.375	.800
Flaherty, J	.375	8	3	1	1	0	3	.375	.875
Fletcher, D*	.182	11	2	0	2	0	2	.182	.182
Fonville, C#	.364	11	4	0	1	0	1	.364	.364
Franco, Julio	.263	19	5	1	5	1	3	.333	.421
Fryman, T	.400	10	4	1	3	0	1	.364	.800
Gaetti, Gary	.350	20	7	1	2	0	2	.350	.650
Gagne, Greg	.435	23	10	1	5	1	4	.458	.739
Galarraga, A	.417	12	5	1	5	2	1	.500	1.000
Gallego, Mike	.200	15	3	0	1	0	3	.250	.200
Gant, Ron	.333	6	2	1	1	0	1	.333	.833
Gilkey, B	.353	17	6	2	4	0	5	.353	.824
Girardi, Joe	.714	7	5	1	2	0	0	.714	1.286
Gomez, Chris	.444	9	4	0	5	1	3	.500	.556
Gomez, Leo	.091	11	1	0	0	1	6	.167	.091
Gonzales, R	.400	5	2	0	1	0	1	.400	.400
Gonzalez, J	.143	21	3	0	4	2	4	.208	.143
Gonzalez, L*	.500	4	2	0	0	2	1	.667	.500
Grace, Mark*	.364	11	4	1	1	1	0	.417	.727
Grebeck, C	.200	5	1	0	0	0	0	.200	.200
Greenwell, M*	.500	4	2	0	1	1	1	.600	.750
Griffey Jr, K*	.286	7	2	0	1	4	0	.545	.429
Grissom, M	.375	8	3	1	1	0	0	.375	.750
Grudzielanek	.364	11	4	0	0	2	0	.462	.545
Guillen, O*	.364	11	4	0	2	0	1	.545	.727
Gwynn, Chris*	.385	13	5	0	1	1	0	.357	.615
Gwynn, Tony*	.300	10	3	0	0	1	0	.364	.300
Hamilton, D*	.357	14	5	0	4	2	1	.438	.429
Hammonds, J	.200	5	1	0	2	0	0	.200	.400

Mark Leiter, Expos — RHP

Batter	Avg	AB	H	HR	BI	BB	SO	OBP	Slg
Hansen, Dave*	.286	7	2	0	0	0	2	.286	.286
Harris, Lenny*	.200	5	1	0	0	2	0	.429	.200
Hayes, C	.222	9	2	1	1	0	3	.300	.556
Henderson, R	.308	13	4	0	0	3	4	.500	.308
Hernandez, Ca	.000	4	0	0	0	0	1	.200	.000
Hill, G	.500	8	4	0	0	1	2	.556	.500
Hoiles, Chris	.154	13	2	0	0	1	2	.267	.154
Hollandsworth*	.400	15	6	0	3	3	2	.500	.467
Hollins, Dave#	.333	6	2	0	0	1	2	.429	.333
Howard, T*	.250	8	2	0	0	0	3	.250	.375
Hundley, Todd#	.200	5	1	0	1	0	1	.333	.200
Hunter, Bri L	.222	9	2	1	3	1	2	.300	.556
Huskey, Butch	.400	10	4	0	2	0	0	.400	.400
Huson, Jeff*	.333	6	2	0	0	2	1	.500	.333
Incaviglia, P	.400	5	2	0	0	0	0	.500	.400
Jaha, John	.300	10	3	1	1	1	3	.364	.700
James, Dion*	.000	5	0	0	0	2	2	.286	.000
Jefferies, G#	.143	14	2	0	0	0	0	.143	.143
Johnson, Char	.286	14	4	0	0	2	4	.412	.429
Johnson, L*	.333	21	7	0	1	0	2	.333	.381
Johnson, Mark*	.429	7	3	2	5	0	0	.429	1.429
Jones, Andruw	.200	5	1	0	0	0	0	.200	.200
Jordan, Brian	.300	10	3	0	0	0	1	.300	.300
Joyner, Wally*	.176	17	3	1	3	0	4	.176	.412
Karkovice, R	.125	8	1	0	1	0	3	.125	.125
Karros, Eric	.333	21	7	1	4	2	5	.391	.524
Kelly, Pat	.333	9	3	1	4	0	3	.333	.889
Kelly, R	.300	10	3	1	1	0	1	.364	.600
Kent, Jeff	.100	10	1	0	0	0	3	.100	.200
Kingery, Mike*	.222	9	2	1	1	0	0	.222	.556
Kirby, Wayne*	.500	14	7	0	2	1	0	.533	.714
Klesko, Ryan*	.111	9	1	1	2	1	2	.200	.444
Knoblauch, C	.300	10	3	0	1	3	2	.429	.300
Knorr, Randy	.000	5	0	0	0	0	1	.000	.000
Lampkin, Tom*	.250	4	1	0	1	1	1	.333	.500
Lankford, Ray*	.091	11	1	1	1	2	3	.231	.364
Lansing, Mike	.200	10	2	0	0	0	2	.200	.200
Larkin, Barry	.125	8	1	0	3	0	0	.111	.375
Leius, Scott	.000	5	0	0	0	0	0	.000	.000
Lemke, Mark#	.250	4	1	0	0	0	0	.250	.250
Lewis, Mark	.250	8	2	0	1	0	0	.250	.375
Listach, Pat#	.286	7	2	0	0	1	2	.375	.429
Livingstone*	.222	9	2	1	1	2	2	.364	.556
Lofton, Kenny*	.400	10	4	0	0	0	0	.400	.400
Lopez, Javy	.000	5	0	0	0	0	1	.000	.000
Mabry, John*	.250	12	3	0	0	1	0	.308	.250
Macfarlane, M	.273	11	3	2	5	0	3	.273	.818
Magadan, Dave*	.333	9	3	0	2	0	3	.333	.444
Martin, Al*	.500	6	3	0	0	1	1	.571	.500
Martinez, E	.250	8	2	0	0	3	0	.455	.250
Martinez, T*	.167	6	1	0	1	0	1	.167	.333
May, Derrick*	.200	15	3	0	1	1	0	.250	.200
Mayne, Brent*	.100	10	1	0	0	0	0	.100	.100
McCarty, David	.200	5	1	0	0	0	2	.200	.200
McGriff, Fred*	.250	8	2	1	2	1	4	.333	.625
McGwire, Mark	.100	10	1	0	0	2	3	.250	.200
McLemore, Mark#	.375	8	3	0	1	1	1	.400	.375
McRae, Brian#	.235	34	8	0	3	1	5	.297	.294
Miller, Orl	.200	15	3	0	3	0	5	.333	.333
Mitchell, K	.500	4	2	0	0	1	1	.600	.750
Molitor, Paul	.450	20	9	1	3	2	3	.500	.650
Mondesi, Raul	.190	21	4	0	0	1	7	.261	.238
Morandini, M*	.222	9	2	0	0	1	0	.300	.444
Mordecai, M	.200	5	1	1	1	0	0	.200	.800
Morris, Hal*	.200	5	1	0	0	0	1	.333	.200
Mueller, Bill#	.333	6	2	0	0	1	1	.429	.500
Munoz, Pedro	.091	11	1	0	0	1	4	.167	.182
Naehring, Tim	.250	4	1	0	0	0	0	.250	.250
Newson, W*	.500	4	2	1	1	1	2	.600	1.250
Nilsson, Dave*	.400	5	2	1	1	0	2	.400	1.000
Nixon, Otis#	.000	5	0	0	0	0	1	.000	.000
O'Neill, Paul*	.600	10	6	2	4	2	0	.667	1.200
Obando, S	.167	6	1	0	1	0	5	.167	.167
Offerman, J#	.400	10	4	1	4	0	1	.400	.800
Olerud, John*	.667	9	6	0	4	3	1	.750	1.000
Ordonez, Rey	.400	5	2	0	1	0	0	.400	.400
Orsulak, Joe*	.160	25	4	0	2	1	5	.185	.200
Pagnozzi, Tom	.167	6	1	0	1	0	1	.167	.167
Palmeiro, R*	.632	19	12	3	7	5	1	.708	1.211
Palmer, Dean	.167	12	2	1	1	1	8	.286	.500
Pendleton, T#	.222	18	4	1	3	0	5	.211	.500
Petagine, Rob*	.400	5	2	1	1	1	0	.500	1.000
Phillips, T#	.000	10	0	0	1	0	2	.000	.000
Piazza, Mike	.500	14	7	0	4	1	1	.563	.714
Plantier, P*	.000	5	0	0	0	0	0	.000	.000
Polonia, Luis*	.313	16	5	0	2	1	0	.353	.438
Raines, Tim#	.467	15	7	3	4	4	2	.579	1.067
Reboulet, J	.250	4	1	0	0	3	1	.571	.250
Reed, Jody	.250	20	5	0	0	1	3	.286	.250
Renteria, E	.273	11	3	0	1	0	1	.273	.364
Ripken, Billy	.200	5	1	0	0	1	0	.333	.200
Ripken, Cal	.364	22	8	0	0	1	3	.417	.409
Rodriguez, H*	.500	12	6	2	4	0	2	.500	1.083
Rodriguez, I	.167	12	2	0	1	0	4	.167	.250
Sabo, Chris	.000	5	0	0	0	0	2	.000	.000
Sanchez, Rey	.455	11	5	0	0	1	0	.500	.545
Sanders, R	.222	9	2	1	1	0	2	.222	.667
Santangelo, F#	.167	6	1	0	0	0	0	.167	.167
Santiago, B	.200	5	1	1	1	0	3	.200	.800
Schofield, D	.333	6	2	0	0	0	1	.333	.333
Segui, David*	.294	17	5	0	1	2	3	.368	.471
Seitzer, K	.000	7	0	0	0	0	2	.000	.000
Servais, S	.500	6	3	1	2	0	0	.500	1.333
Sheffield, G	.333	15	5	2	5	8	2	.542	.800
Shumpert, T	.091	11	1	0	0	0	2	.091	.091
Sierra, Ruben#	.118	17	2	1	3	1	3	.158	.353
Silvestri, D	.500	8	4	1	1	1	1	.556	1.000
Smith, Ozzie*	.167	6	1	0	1	1	0	.286	.167
Sojo, Luis	.400	5	2	1	1	1	1	.500	1.000
Sorrento, P*	.375	8	3	1	1	0	2	.375	.750
Sosa, Sammy	.417	12	5	0	2	0	4	.417	.583
Spiers, Bill*	.400	15	6	1	1	6	2	.571	.667
Sprague, Ed	.000	6	0	0	0	1	0	.000	.000
Stanley, Mike	.111	9	1	0	0	0	5	.111	.222
Steinbach, T	.357	14	5	0	1	1	3	.375	.500
Stinnett, K	.143	7	1	0	0	0	0	.143	.143
Stocker, K#	.143	7	1	0	0	0	1	.143	.143
Surhoff, B.J.*	.222	18	4	0	0	0	1	.222	.222
Tarasco, Tony*	.222	9	2	1	1	2	1	.364	.556
Tartabull, D	.071	14	1	0	0	3	7	.235	.143
Taubensee, E*	.286	7	2	1	1	0	1	.286	1.000
Tettleton, M#	.500	2	1	1	1	3	1	.833	2.000
Thomas, Frank	.200	15	3	0	2	2	2	.316	.400
Thompson, Mil*	.000	5	0	0	0	1	0	.167	.000
Thompson, Ry	.167	6	1	0	0	1	1	.286	.167
Valle, Dave	.800	5	4	1	2	0	0	.857	1.800
Vaughn, Greg	.300	20	6	1	7	1	6	.333	.450
Vaughn, Mo*	.400	5	2	0	0	1	1	.571	.400
Velarde, R	.286	7	2	0	0	0	3	.286	.429
Ventura, R*	.188	16	3	1	3	1	1	.235	.375
Veras, Q#	.143	7	1	0	0	3	1	.400	.143
Vizcaino, J#	.100	10	1	1	1	0	1	.100	.400
Vizquel, Omar#	.286	7	2	0	1	0	2	.286	.286
Walker, Larry*	.333	9	3	1	3	0	1	.400	.778
Wallach, Tim	.111	9	1	0	0	1	2	.200	.111
Ward, Turner#	.200	5	1	0	0	0	1	.200	.200
Weiss, Walt*	.308	13	4	0	2	2	2	.400	.462
White, Devon#	.229	35	8	1	1	1	4	.270	.314
White, R	.455	11	5	0	2	0	1	.455	.636
Wilkins, Rick*	.500	10	5	1	2	5	4	.667	.800
Williams, Ber#	.250	16	4	1	2	1	3	.294	.563
Young, Eric	.400	5	2	1	1	1	0	.500	1.000
Zeile, Todd	.143	7	1	1	1	2	3	.333	.571

Curt Leskanic, Rockies — RHP

Batter	Avg	AB	H	HR	BI	BB	SO	OBP	Slg
Abbott, Kurt	.000	4	0	0	0	3	0	.429	.000
Alfonzo, E	.200	5	1	0	2	1	1	.333	.200
Anthony, Eric*	.286	7	2	0	2	0	1	.286	.571
Arias, Alex	.000	6	0	0	0	0	0	.000	.000
Ausmus, Brad	.400	5	2	1	2	1	2	.500	1.000
Bagwell, Jeff	.250	4	1	0	0	1	2	.400	.250
Bell, Derek	.333	6	2	0	1	1	0	.429	.333
Bell, Jay	.250	4	1	1	1	1	0	.400	1.000
Biggio, Craig	.500	4	2	0	0	2	2	.667	.500
Blauser, Jeff	.250	4	1	0	2	2	1	.500	.500
Bonds, Barry*	.375	8	3	2	6	1	0	.444	1.125
Boone, Bret	.167	6	1	0	0	0	0	.167	.167
Branson, Jeff	.250	8	2	1	1	1	2	.333	.625
Bullett, S*	.200	5	1	0	0	0	2	.200	.200
Butler, Brett*	.667	3	2	0	0	3	0	.833	1.000
Caminiti, Ken#	.429	7	3	0	0	1	1	.500	.429
Carr, Chuck	.000	6	0	0	0	0	0	.000	.000
Clark, Will*	.500	4	2	0	0	1	0	.600	.500
Clayton, R	.125	8	1	0	0	0	2	.222	.125
Colbrunn, G	.125	8	1	0	0	0	0	.125	.125
Conine, Jeff	.357	14	5	0	2	2	4	.438	.429
Cordero, Wil	.000	5	1	0	0	2	0	.200	.200
DeShields, D*	.125	8	1	0	0	2	3	.300	.125
Finley, Steve*	.385	13	5	0	1	0	3	.385	.538
Gant, Ron	.500	8	4	0	0	1	1	.500	.500
Garcia, C	.500	6	3	0	1	0	0	.500	.500
Gilkey, B	.273	11	3	0	1	4	2	.273	.364
Gonzalez, L*	.429	7	3	0	1	2	1	.556	.571
Grace, Mark*	.200	10	2	0	0	3	2	.385	.200
Grissom, M	.222	9	2	0	1	0	1	.222	.222
Hayes, C	.333	6	2	0	1	0	2	.333	.500
Henderson, R	.500	4	2	0	0	1	0	.600	.750
Hernandez, Jo	.167	6	1	1	1	0	0	.167	.667
Hill, G	.500	5	2	1	1	0	0	.400	1.000
Hollandsworth*	.250	4	1	1	3	0	0	.200	1.000
Howard, T*	.000	4	0	0	0	1	3	.000	.000

Curt Leskanic, Rockies — RHP

Batter	Avg	AB	H	HR	BI	BB	SO	OBP	Slg
Johnson, Char	.200	5	1	1	2	0	2	.200	.800
Jordan, Brian	.125	8	1	0	1	0	2	.125	.125
Justice, Dave*	.600	5	3	1	1	1	0	.667	.600
Karros, Eric	.364	11	4	1	2	1	2	.417	.636
Kent, Jeff	.500	4	2	1	3	0	2	.400	1.250
King, Jeff	.400	5	2	0	2	0	3	.400	.600
Lankford, Ray*	.571	7	4	1	1	2	0	.667	1.143
Lansing, Mike	.000	5	0	0	0	0	1	.000	.000
Larkin, Barry	.400	5	2	0	1	2	1	.571	.400
Lemke, Mark*	.125	8	1	0	1	0	1	.125	.125
Lewis, Darren	.500	4	2	0	0	0	0	.500	.750
Livingstone*	.250	4	1	1	3	1	1	.400	1.000
Lopez, Javy	.200	5	1	0	1	1	1	.333	.400
Manwaring, K	.333	3	1	0	0	2	1	.600	.667
Martin, Al*	.400	5	2	0	1	0	2	.400	.600
May, Derrick*	.500	8	4	1	5	0	0	.500	.875
McGee, Willie#	.714	7	5	0	2	0	0	.714	1.000
McGriff, Fred*	.444	9	4	1	1	1	2	.500	.778
McRae, Brian#	.000	8	0	0	0	0	0	.000	.000
Miller, Orl	.167	6	1	0	0	0	2	.167	.167
Mondesi, Raul	.385	13	5	0	0	1	3	.429	.615
Morris, Hal*	.000	7	0	0	0	1	2	.125	.000
Offerman, J#	.000	3	0	0	0	1	1	.250	.000
Orsulak, Joe*	.250	8	2	1	1	0	1	.250	.625
Parent, Mark	.000	5	0	0	0	0	3	.000	.000
Pendleton, T#	.000	11	0	0	1	2	4	.154	.000
Piazza, Mike	.333	9	3	0	1	1	1	.400	.444
Reed, Jeff*	.000	4	0	0	0	1	0	.200	.000
Reed, Jody	.000	6	0	0	0	2	2	.250	.000
Roberson, K#	.000	3	0	0	0	2	1	.400	.000
Rodriguez, H*	.333	6	2	0	3	0	1	.333	.667
Sanchez, Rey	.250	12	3	0	0	0	2	.250	.250
Sandberg, R	.200	10	2	0	0	2	2	.333	.200
Sanders, R	.286	7	2	0	0	2	2	.444	.429
Santiago, B	.375	8	3	1	3	0	3	.375	.875
Sheffield, G	.286	7	2	0	1	2	2	.444	.429
Smith, Dwight*	.625	8	5	0	4	0	0	.625	.750
Smith, Ozzie*	.200	5	1	0	2	1	2	.333	.200
Sosa, Sammy	.333	18	6	1	5	2	6	.400	.667
Stocker, K#	.500	4	2	1	2	1	1	.600	1.250
Sweeney, Mark*	.000	4	0	0	0	1	1	.200	.000
Taubensee, E*	.250	4	1	0	0	0	1	.250	.250
Veras, Q#	.333	3	1	0	0	2	1	.600	.333
Vizcaino, J#	.375	8	3	0	1	2	1	.500	.375
Wallach, Tim	.286	7	2	0	0	0	1	.286	.286
Wilkins, Rick*	.000	11	0	0	0	0	7	.000	.000
Williams, Ma	.300	10	3	0	2	0	2	.273	.300
Zeile, Todd	.250	8	2	0	0	1	2	.333	.375

Richie Lewis, Tigers — RHP

Batter	Avg	AB	H	HR	BI	BB	SO	OBP	Slg
Alicea, Luis*	.333	3	1	1	4	3	2	.667	1.333
Bagwell, Jeff	.167	6	1	1	1	0	2	.167	.667
Baines, H*	.167	6	1	0	1	0	0	.167	.167
Bell, Jay	.600	5	3	1	1	1	1	.667	1.400
Belle, Albert	.333	3	1	0	0	2	0	.600	.333
Berry, Sean	.333	6	2	1	2	0	1	.333	.833
Blauser, Jeff	.000	7	0	0	0	0	3	.000	.000
Boggs, Wade*	.600	5	3	0	0	1	0	.667	.600
Boone, Bret	.250	4	1	0	1	1	2	.400	.500
Bordick, Mike	.750	4	3	0	0	1	1	.800	.750
Bournigal, R	.200	5	1	0	2	0	1	.200	.200
Branson, Jeff*	.200	5	1	0	0	0	1	.200	.200
Canseco, Jose	.333	3	1	0	1	1	1	.600	.667
Cedeno, A	.400	5	2	0	2	1	2	.500	.400
Clayton, R	.167	6	1	0	0	0	1	.167	.167
Cordero, Wil	.250	8	2	0	0	0	1	.250	.250
Duncan, M	.000	8	0	0	0	0	3	.000	.000
Dykstra, L*	.400	5	2	0	1	4	0	.667	.400
Eisenreich, J*	.000	3	0	0	0	2	0	.400	.000
Elster, Kevin	.200	5	1	1	1	0	0	.200	.800
Fletcher, D*	.333	9	3	0	6	0	2	.333	.667
Floyd, Cliff*	.200	5	1	1	1	0	3	.200	.400
Galarraga, A	.500	6	3	0	1	2	1	.625	.500
Gilkey, B	.333	6	2	0	1	2	1	.500	.333
Gonzalez, L*	.333	6	2	0	0	0	0	.333	.333
Grissom, M	.714	7	5	1	2	1	0	.750	1.429
Guillen, O*	.333	6	2	0	0	0	0	.333	.333
Hayes, C	.125	8	1	0	0	0	0	.125	.250
Hollins, Dave#	.111	9	1	0	1	0	2	.111	.111
Hundley, Todd#	.250	4	1	0	1	1	2	.333	.250
Incaviglia, P	.250	4	1	0	0	1	2	.400	.750
Jefferies, G#	.250	4	1	0	0	1	1	.400	.250
Justice, Dave*	.600	5	3	1	2	1	1	.667	1.200
Karros, Eric	.000	2	0	0	2	1	0	.200	.000
Kelly, R	.200	10	2	0	4	1	2	.250	.300
Kent, Jeff	.286	7	2	1	4	1	0	.375	.857
King, Jeff	.000	6	0	0	0	0	3	.000	.000
Lankford, Ray*	.400	5	2	0	0	1	1	.500	.600
Lansing, Mike	.286	7	2	0	0	1	2	.375	.429
Larkin, Barry	.200	5	1	0	0	2	0	.429	.200

Jon Lieber, Pirates — RHP

Batter	Avg	AB	H	HR	BI	BB	SO	OBP	Slg
Abbott, Kurt	.125	8	1	0	0	0	3	.125	.125
Alicea, Luis#	.286	7	2	0	1	0	1	.286	.286
Alou, Moises	.357	14	5	0	2	0	5	.375	.429
Aurilia, Rich	.429	7	3	0	0	1	0	.500	.429
Ausmus, Brad	.400	5	2	0	0	1	0	.400	.800
Bagwell, Jeff	.267	15	4	0	7	0	3	.267	.267
Batiste, Kim	.000	6	0	0	0	0	1	.000	.000
Bell, David	.400	5	2	0	1	0	1	.400	.400
Benard, M*	.000	6	0	0	0	1	1	.143	.000
Berry, Sean	.000	4	0	0	0	1	1	.200	.000
Bichette, Dan	.182	11	2	0	0	0	2	.182	.182
Biggio, Craig	.167	12	2	1	4	2	1	.333	.417
Bonds, Barry*	.000	13	0	0	1	2	4	.133	.000
Boone, Bret	.444	9	4	0	1	0	2	.500	.444
Bradshaw, T*	.750	4	3	0	2	1	0	.800	1.000
Branson, Jeff*	.375	8	3	1	1	0	2	.375	1.125
Brumfield, J	.400	5	2	0	1	0	1	.400	.600
Bullett, S*	.429	7	3	1	3	0	1	.429	1.000
Burks, Ellis	.167	6	1	0	0	0	1	.167	.167
Caminiti, Ken#	.533	15	8	1	5	1	2	.563	.933
Carr, Chuck	.500	4	2	0	0	1	0	.600	.500
Castilla, V	.455	11	5	1	2	0	0	.455	.818
Cedeno, A	.333	9	3	0	3	1	2	.400	.444
Clayton, R	.182	11	2	0	0	0	3	.182	.364
Colbrunn, G	.250	8	2	0	0	0	2	.250	.250
Conine, Jeff	.000	4	0	0	0	1	1	.200	.000
Cordero, Wil	.000	5	0	0	0	1	0	.000	.000
Daulton, D*	.333	6	2	0	1	2	0	.333	.333
Davis, Eric	.500	6	3	1	2	1	1	.667	1.400
DeShields, D*	.429	7	3	0	0	1	1	.429	.429
Dykstra, L*	.000	4	0	0	0	2	1	.333	.000
Eisenreich, J*	.571	14	8	0	1	0	1	.571	.643
Finley, Steve*	.412	17	7	0	2	0	0	.412	.588
Fletcher, D*	.167	12	2	1	2	0	1	.167	.500
Floyd, Cliff*	.500	12	6	0	0	1	1	.538	.667
Gaetti, Gary	.200	5	1	0	0	0	1	.200	.400
Galarraga, A	.333	12	4	0	1	0	5	.333	.333
Gant, Ron	.600	5	3	1	2	1	1	.667	1.200
Gonzalez, L*	.385	13	5	1	3	2	1	.467	.769
Grace, Mark*	.286	7	2	0	0	2	0	.444	.429
Greene, W*	.167	6	1	0	0	0	0	.167	.167
Grissom, M	.667	9	6	0	3	2	1	.727	.667
Grudzielanek	.429	7	3	1	1	0	1	.429	.857
Gwynn, Tony*	.364	11	4	1	1	1	1	.417	.727
Harris, Lenny*	.182	11	2	0	1	0	1	.167	.273
Hernandez, Jo	.000	5	0	0	1	2	1	.429	.200
Hill, G	.471	17	8	1	3	0	0	.471	.824
Howard, T*	.231	13	3	1	4	0	2	.231	.615
Hundley, Todd#	.250	8	2	1	1	0	3	.250	.750
Hunter, Bri LL	.800	5	4	1	3	0	0	.800	1.400
Incaviglia, P	.000	4	0	0	0	1	2	.167	.000
Jefferies, G#	.222	9	2	0	0	0	1	.222	.222
Johnson, Char	.375	8	3	0	0	0	0	.375	.375
Jones, Andruw	.143	7	1	0	0	0	0	.143	.143

Jon Lieber, Pirates — RHP

Batter	Avg	AB	H	HR	BI	BB	SO	OBP	Slg
Jones, C#	.250	8	2	1	2	0	2	.250	.625
Jones, Chris	.600	5	3	1	2	0	1	.600	1.200
Jordan, Brian	.125	8	1	0	0	0	2	.125	.125
Karros, Eric	.444	9	4	2	2	0	2	.444	1.111
Kelly, R	.125	8	1	0	1	0	1	.125	.125
Kent, Jeff	.286	7	2	0	1	0	2	.286	.429
Klesko, Ryan*	.571	7	4	0	3	1	1	.625	.857
Lankford, Ray*	.429	7	3	0	0	1	2	.500	.429
Lansing, Mike	.235	17	4	0	1	0	1	.235	.353
Larkin, Barry	.182	11	2	1	1	1	0	.308	.545
Lemke, Mark#	.375	8	3	0	2	1	1	.444	.500
Lewis, Darren	.429	7	3	0	1	0	1	.429	.429
Magadan, Dave*	.000	4	0	0	1	2	2	.286	.000
McGriff, Fred*	.400	10	4	0	0	0	0	.400	.400
McRae, Brian#	.000	6	0	0	0	1	0	.143	.000
Mondesi, Raul	.400	5	2	0	1	0	0	.333	.600
Morandini, M*	.250	12	3	0	0	1	0	.308	.333
Morris, Hal*	.500	10	5	0	3	0	1	.500	.700
Mueller, Bill#	.857	7	6	0	2	0	0	.857	.857
Offerman, J#	.333	6	2	0	2	0	1	.333	.667
Otero, Ricky#	.143	7	1	0	1	0	0	.143	.143
Pagnozzi, Tom	.000	5	0	0	0	0	1	.000	.000
Pendleton, T#	.071	14	1	0	1	0	1	.071	.071
Phillips, J*	.200	5	1	1	1	0	2	.200	.800
Piazza, Mike	.571	7	4	0	2	0	2	.571	.571
Plantier, P*	.200	5	1	0	1	0	1	.167	.200
Reed, Jeff*	.333	12	4	0	2	0	1	.333	.417
Reed, Jody	.500	4	2	0	0	1	1	.600	.500
Roberts, Bip#	.625	8	5	0	2	0	0	.625	.750
Rodriguez, H*	.333	3	1	0	0	2	0	.600	.667
Sanchez, Rey	.200	5	1	0	0	0	1	.333	.200
Sanders, R	.286	14	4	0	1	2	2	.375	.357
Santiago, B	.125	8	1	0	0	0	3	.125	.125
Scarsone, S	.400	5	2	0	0	0	0	.400	.600
Servais, S	.000	7	0	0	1	0	0	.000	.000
Sheffield, G	.286	7	2	1	2	0	0	.250	.714
Shipley, C	.400	5	2	0	2	0	0	.400	.800
Sosa, Sammy	.222	9	2	0	1	0	1	.222	.222
Stocker, K#	.333	9	3	0	1	1	1	.400	.444
Taubensee, E*	.364	11	4	0	2	0	2	.364	.636
Thompson, Mil*	.000	5	0	0	0	0	0	.000	.000
Thompson, Rob	.400	5	2	0	0	0	0	.400	.400
Veras, Q#	.000	6	0	0	0	1	1	.143	.000
Vizcaino, J#	.200	5	1	0	1	0	0	.333	.200
Walker, Larry*	.235	17	4	3	5	0	2	.222	.882
Weiss, Walt#	.500	10	5	0	2	0	1	.500	.500
White, R	.400	5	2	1	2	1	1	.500	1.400
Wilkins, Rick*	.200	10	2	1	3	1	3	.273	.500
Williams, E	.250	4	1	0	2	0	1	.333	.250
Williams, Ma	.250	8	2	0	0	0	3	.250	.250
Wilson, Desi*	.400	5	2	0	0	1	1	.500	.400
Young, Eric	.429	7	3	0	0	0	1	.429	.429
Zeile, Todd	.333	9	3	1	2	0	4	.333	.778

Derek Lilliquist, Reds — LHP

Batter	Avg	AB	H	HR	BI	BB	SO	OBP	Slg
Johnson, L*	.375	8	3	0	0	0	0	.375	.375
Jordan, Ricky	.400	5	2	1	1	0	0	.400	1.000
Joyner, Wally*	.111	9	1	0	1	1	3	.200	.222
Justice, Dave*	1.000	5	5	0	1	0	0	1.000	1.000
King, Jeff	.333	6	2	0	1	1	0	.429	.500
Larkin, Barry	.571	7	4	0	0	0	0	.571	.714
Leyritz, Jim	.333	6	2	0	1	1	1	.429	.500
Lovullo, T#	.000	3	0	0	0	2	1	.400	.000
Magadan, Dave*	.200	10	2	0	0	1	0	.273	.200
Manwaring, K	.750	4	3	0	2	1	1	.800	.750
Martinez, T*	.250	4	1	0	0	1	1	.400	.250
McGee, Willie*	.538	13	7	1	2	1	0	.571	.923
McLemore, M#	.000	5	0	0	0	1	3	.167	.000
Mitchell, K	.214	14	3	0	0	2	0	.353	.214
Munoz, Pedro	.400	5	2	0	1	0	0	.400	.400
Murray, Eddie#	.429	7	3	1	4	0	1	.429	.857
Nixon, Otis#	.250	12	3	0	4	0	2	.250	.333
O'Neill, Paul*	.250	16	4	1	5	0	5	.250	.563
Olerud, John*	.300	10	3	0	1	0	1	.273	.300
Oliver, Joe	.250	8	2	0	0	0	2	.250	.375
Palmeiro, R*	.167	6	1	0	1	1	2	.286	.167
Parent, Mark	.400	5	2	1	3	0	1	.400	1.000
Pena, Tony	.429	7	3	0	2	2	0	.556	.429
Pendleton, T#	.412	17	7	1	4	1	1	.444	.824
Phillips, T#	.500	4	2	0	1	2	0	.667	.750
Polonia, Luis*	.000	8	0	0	1	1	3	.111	.000
Raines, Tim#	.000	6	0	0	1	1	1	.125	.000
Reed, Jody	.000	5	0	0	0	0	1	.000	.000
Ripken, Cal	.200	5	1	0	1	1	0	.333	.400
Roberts, Bip#	.750	8	6	1	1	1	0	.778	1.500
Sabo, Chris	.333	9	3	2	3	1	0	.400	1.000
Samuel, Juan	.444	9	4	0	0	1	0	.500	.556
Sandberg, R	.308	13	4	0	0	0	0	.308	.385
Santiago, B	.167	6	1	0	1	1	0	.286	.167
Sierra, Ruben#	.333	3	1	0	2	0	1	.200	.333
Slaught, Don	.500	4	2	0	0	2	0	.667	.500
Smith, Ozzie#	.286	14	4	0	0	2	1	.375	.357
Snow, J.T.#	.000	6	0	0	0	0	2	.000	.000
Strawberry, D*	.333	9	3	2	4	0	5	.333	1.111
Surhoff, B.J.*	.600	5	3	0	2	0	1	.600	.600
Tartabull, D	.429	7	3	2	2	1	2	.500	1.429
Thompson, Mil*	.273	11	3	0	3	0	3	.273	.273
Thompson, Rob	.350	20	7	2	5	0	2	.381	.750
Vaughn, Mo*	.250	8	2	0	0	0	2	.333	.250
Velarde, R	.286	7	2	1	3	0	0	.286	.714
Ventura, R*	.200	10	2	0	2	0	3	.200	.200
Vizquel, Omar#	.250	4	1	0	0	1	0	.400	.250
Wallach, Tim	.200	10	2	1	2	1	0	.273	.500
Walton, J	.167	6	1	0	0	0	1	.167	.167
Williams, Ber#	.333	6	2	0	0	0	1	.333	.500
Williams, Ma	.364	11	4	0	2	2	2	.429	.364
Zeile, Todd	.000	6	0	0	0	0	0	.000	.000

Derek Lilliquist, Reds — LHP

Batter	Avg	AB	H	HR	BI	BB	SO	OBP	Slg
Alomar, R#	.250	12	3	1	2	2	2	.357	.500
Anderson, Brd*	.200	10	2	0	0	1	0	.273	.200
Bell, Jay	.286	7	2	0	0	0	0	.286	.429
Biggio, Craig	.500	10	5	1	2	1	1	.545	.800
Blauser, Jeff	.000	5	0	0	0	2	0	.286	.000
Boggs, Wade*	.182	11	2	0	3	0	2	.154	.182
Bonds, Barry*	.273	11	3	0	0	3	1	.429	.455
Bonilla, B#	.250	12	3	0	1	1	0	.308	.250
Butler, Brett*	.294	17	5	0	0	0	4	.294	.412
Caminiti, Ken#	.333	15	5	0	2	1	2	.375	.400
Carter, Joe	.200	5	1	0	1	0	1	.167	.400
Clark, Will*	.500	20	10	2	3	2	2	.565	.950
Coleman, V#	.200	15	3	2	2	3	3	.333	.600
Cora, Joey#	.000	3	0	0	0	1	0	.250	.000
Dascenzo, D#	.100	10	1	0	1	0	0	.091	.100
Daulton, D*	.000	5	0	0	0	1	0	.167	.000
Davis, Chili#	.000	5	0	0	1	0	0	.000	.000
Davis, Eric	.333	12	4	1	2	1	3	.385	.583
Dawson, Andre	.300	10	3	2	3	0	1	.300	1.000
Deer, Rob	.500	6	3	1	1	0	1	.500	1.167
DiSarcina, G	.000	9	0	0	0	0	0	.000	.000
Duncan, M	.400	10	4	1	2	1	1	.455	.800
Dunston, S	.333	9	3	0	1	0	0	.333	.556
Easley, D	.500	6	3	0	0	1	0	.571	.667
Elster, Kevin	.400	5	2	1	1	1	1	.500	1.200
Galarraga, A	.364	11	4	0	0	0	5	.364	.455
Gant, Ron	.333	3	1	0	0	2	1	.600	.667
Grace, Mark*	.250	12	3	0	0	0	2	.250	.250
Greenwell, M*	.250	8	2	0	1	0	1	.250	.250
Griffey Jr, K*	.286	7	2	0	1	0	2	.444	.429
Gwynn, Tony*	.333	12	4	0	2	1	0	.385	.500
Hayes, C	.333	9	3	0	0	0	3	.333	.333
Hudler, Rex	.214	14	3	1	1	1	1	.267	.429
Javier, Stan#	.200	5	1	0	0	1	2	.333	.200
Jefferies, G#	.222	9	2	0	0	0	0	.222	.222

Jose Lima, Tigers — RHP

Batter	Avg	AB	H	HR	BI	BB	SO	OBP	Slg
Anderson, G*	.600	5	3	0	2	0	0	.600	.800
Baerga, C#	.400	5	2	0	2	1	1	.500	.800
Belle, Albert	.400	5	2	0	2	2	0	.625	.800
Boggs, Wade*	.333	6	2	0	0	0	0	.333	.500
Buhner, Jay	.250	4	1	0	0	2	0	.400	.250
Canseco, Jose	.200	5	1	0	0	2	0	.429	.200
Carter, Joe	.143	7	1	0	0	0	3	.143	.286
Clark, Will*	.364	11	4	0	3	0	2	.364	.364
Coleman, V#	.500	6	3	0	0	0	0	.500	.500
Cora, Joey#	.400	5	2	0	1	0	0	.400	.400
DiSarcina, G	.167	6	1	0	1	0	0	.167	.167
Durham, Ray#	.600	5	3	0	0	0	0	.600	.800
Edmonds, Jim*	.333	6	2	1	2	1	0	.429	.833
Elster, Kevin	.500	4	2	1	3	0	1	.500	1.250
Gaetti, Gary	.250	4	1	1	3	0	1	.400	1.000
Gagne, Greg	.200	5	1	0	1	0	0	.200	.200
Gonzalez, A	.500	6	3	0	2	0	2	.500	.833
Gonzalez, J	.125	8	1	0	1	1	4	.222	.125
Goodwin, Tom*	.000	4	0	0	0	1	1	.200	.000
Green, Shawn*	.000	4	0	0	0	1	1	.200	.000
Greer, Rusty*	.143	7	1	0	0	1	1	.250	.143
Guillen, O*	.500	4	2	1	4	0	0	.500	1.250
Hamilton, D*	.200	10	2	0	1	0	0	.200	.200
Howard, Dave#	.400	5	2	0	0	0	0	.400	.400
Hudler, Rex	.000	5	0	0	0	1	0	.000	.000
Hulse, David*	.167	6	1	0	0	0	0	.167	.167
Jaha, John	.167	6	1	0	0	0	1	.167	.167
Jefferson, R*	.400	5	2	2	3	0	2	.400	1.600
Joyner, Wally*	.250	4	1	0	1	1	1	.400	.250
Kelly, Pat	.500	4	2	0	0	1	0	.600	.750
Lofton, Kenny*	.500	8	4	0	0	0	1	.500	.625
Macfarlane, M	.250	4	1	0	0	1	3	.400	.250
McLemore, M#	.500	8	4	0	1	2	1	.600	.625
Murray, Eddie#	.333	9	3	0	2	1	2	.400	.333
Naehring, Tim	.500	4	2	1	0	0	0	.600	1.500
Newson, W*	.500	6	3	0	1	0	0	.500	.833

Jose Lima, Tigers — RHP

Batter	Avg	AB	H	HR	BI	BB	SO	OBP	Slg
Nilsson, Dave*	.400	5	2	0	0	0	0	.400	.400
Nixon, Otis#	.200	5	1	0	0	0	1	.333	.200
O'Leary, Troy*	.400	5	2	0	0	0	1	.400	.800
O'Neill, Paul*	.167	6	1	0	0	0	0	.167	.333
Palmer, Dean	.286	7	2	0	0	0	1	.286	.286
Phillips, T#	.500	8	4	0	2	0	0	.444	.750
Ramirez, M	.750	4	3	1	3	3	0	.857	1.500
Rodriguez, I	.182	11	2	0	1	0	0	.182	.182
Salmon, Tim	.167	6	1	0	1	0	2	.167	.167
Seitzer, K	.000	6	0	0	0	0	1	.000	.000
Sierra, Ruben#	.333	6	2	1	2	0	0	.333	1.000
Snow, J.T.#	.400	5	2	0	1	0	2	.400	.400
Sprague, Ed	.143	7	1	0	0	0	2	.250	.143
Stanley, Mike	.400	10	4	1	2	0	1	.400	.700
Surhoff, B.J.*	.000	7	0	0	0	0	2	.000	.000
Tettleton, M#	.000	5	0	0	0	1	2	.143	.000
Thomas, Frank	.429	7	3	1	4	0	0	.375	.857
Thome, Jim*	.333	6	2	1	2	1	1	.429	.833
Tinsley, Lee#	.167	6	1	0	0	0	2	.167	.167
Valentin, Jhn	.333	9	3	0	0	0	0	.333	.444
Vaughn, Mo*	.500	6	3	1	2	1	0	.571	1.167
Velarde, R	.000	5	0	0	0	1	2	.167	.000
Ventura, R*	.286	7	2	1	1	0	2	.286	.714
Vitiello, Joe	.400	5	2	0	0	0	1	.400	.400
Vizquel, Omar#	.167	6	1	0	0	0	0	.167	.167
Williams, Ber#	.375	8	3	1	4	0	1	.375	.875

Doug Linton, Royals — RHP

Batter	Avg	AB	H	HR	BI	BB	SO	OBP	Slg
Aldrete, Mike*	.167	6	1	0	1	0	1	.167	.333
Alomar, R#	.200	5	1	0	1	0	1	.200	.200
Anderson, Brd*	.222	9	2	1	2	1	2	.300	.556
Baines, H*	.500	6	3	0	0	0	1	.500	.667
Becker, Rich*	.200	5	1	0	0	0	1	.200	.200
Berroa, G	.167	6	1	0	2	0	1	.167	.167
Bichette, D	.400	5	2	0	0	0	0	.400	.400
Boggs, Wade*	.000	6	0	0	0	1	0	.143	.000
Bordick, Mike	.000	7	0	0	0	1	1	.222	.000
Bournigal, R	.000	3	0	0	0	0	1	.000	.000
Bragg, Darren*	.400	5	2	0	1	0	1	.400	.600
Brosius, S	.500	8	4	0	2	0	1	.500	.625
Buhner, Jay	.111	9	1	1	3	0	5	.111	.444
Butler, Brett*	.667	3	2	0	1	2	0	.800	.667
Carr, Chuck	.000	4	0	0	0	1	2	.000	.000
Clark, Tony*	.200	5	1	1	1	0	2	.200	.800
Cora, Joey#	.200	5	1	0	0	1	0	.429	.200
Devereaux, M	.222	9	2	0	1	0	2	.222	.333
Durham, Ray*	.167	6	1	1	2	0	3	.167	.667
Fielder, C	.250	12	3	1	2	1	2	.308	.583
Fryman, T	.308	13	4	2	3	0	3	.308	.769
Galarraga, A	.333	6	2	0	0	0	3	.333	.333
Gates, Brent#	.333	6	2	0	3	1	2	.375	.333
Girardi, Joe	.167	6	1	0	0	1	1	.286	.167
Griffey Jr, K*	.250	8	2	0	0	2	1	.400	.250
Guillen, O*	.143	7	1	0	0	0	0	.143	.143
Hamilton, D*	.286	7	2	0	0	0	0	.286	.286
Hayes, C	.200	5	1	0	0	0	0	.200	.400
Henderson, R	.800	5	4	0	1	1	0	.833	1.200
Herrera, Jose*	.250	4	1	0	0	0	2	.250	.250
Higginson, B*	.500	4	2	0	0	1	0	.600	1.000
Hollins, Dave#	.333	6	2	1	2	2	2	.556	.833
Jaha, John	.571	7	4	0	0	2	0	.667	.571
Kingery, Mike*	.400	5	2	0	1	1	0	.500	.400
Knoblauch, C	.333	6	2	0	2	1	0	.429	.500
Kreuter, Chad#	.250	4	1	0	0	0	1	.400	.250
Lawton, Matt*	.800	5	4	0	1	0	0	.800	1.000
Lewis, Darren	.111	9	1	0	1	0	0	.111	.111
Lewis, Mark	.250	8	2	0	0	0	2	.250	.375
Listach, Pat#	.500	8	4	0	2	0	0	.600	.500
Martinez, D*	.333	9	3	0	0	1	2	.400	.444
Martinez, E	.364	11	4	0	2	0	0	.364	.545
Marzano, John	.000	5	0	0	0	0	0	.000	.000
McLemore, M#	.222	9	2	0	3	0	1	.222	.556
Meares, Pat	.200	5	1	0	2	0	3	.200	.400
Molitor, Paul	.100	10	1	0	1	1	2	.182	.100
Nieves, M#	.429	7	3	0	1	0	4	.429	.714
Nilsson, Dave*	.167	6	1	0	0	1	1	.286	.167
Olerud, John*	.400	5	2	0	1	0	0	.400	.600
Paquette, C	.200	5	1	0	1	0	0	.167	.200
Pena, Tony	.000	6	0	0	0	0	2	.000	.000
Phillips, T#	.273	11	3	0	0	2	3	.385	.364
Pride, Curtis*	.125	8	1	0	0	1	3	.222	.125
Ripken, Cal	.200	10	2	0	0	0	0	.200	.300
Rodriguez, Al	.625	8	5	1	3	1	1	.667	1.125
Seitzer, K	.250	8	2	0	1	0	3	.250	.250
Sierra, Ruben#	.200	10	2	1	2	0	3	.200	.600
Sorrento, P*	.333	12	4	1	4	0	2	.333	.750
Stahoviak, S*	.400	5	2	0	0	0	2	.400	.600
Steinbach, T	.375	8	3	0	0	1	1	.444	.375
Surhoff, B.J.*	.333	3	1	0	0	2	1	.600	.333
Tartabull, D	.143	7	1	1	2	0	2	.125	.571

Doug Linton, Royals — RHP

Batter	Avg	AB	H	HR	BI	BB	SO	OBP	Slg
Tettleton, M#	.600	5	3	1	2	1	1	.667	1.200
Thomas, Frank	.167	6	1	0	1	0	3	.167	.167
Trammell, A	.200	5	1	0	0	0	0	.200	.200
Valentin, Jhn	.250	4	1	0	0	1	0	.400	.500
Valentin, Jse#	.500	4	2	0	1	1	2	.600	.750
Vaughn, Greg	.333	9	3	3	7	2	2	.455	1.333
Ventura, R*	.333	9	3	0	0	3	1	.500	.444
Weiss, Walt#	.333	6	2	0	1	0	1	.333	.333
Williams, Ber#	.333	6	2	0	0	0	2	.333	.500

Felipe Lira, Tigers — RHP

Batter	Avg	AB	H	HR	BI	BB	SO	OBP	Slg
Alexander, M	.667	6	4	0	0	0	0	.667	.833
Alomar, R#	.182	11	2	0	2	1	1	.214	.182
Alomar Jr, S	.182	11	2	1	1	0	2	.182	.455
Amaral, Rich	.333	6	2	0	1	0	0	.333	.333
Anderson, Brd*	.333	12	4	0	2	1	1	.529	.333
Anderson, G*	.455	11	5	1	3	0	1	.455	.727
Arias, George	.286	7	2	0	0	0	2	.286	.429
Baerga, C#	.571	7	4	1	3	1	0	.625	1.143
Baines, H*	.200	15	3	0	0	0	2	.200	.267
Battle, Allen	.143	7	1	0	0	0	2	.143	.286
Becker, Rich*	.167	12	2	0	0	2	2	.286	.250
Belle, Albert	.167	12	2	0	1	3	1	.333	.250
Berroa, G	.167	12	2	0	0	0	2	.167	.167
Boggs, Wade*	.500	14	7	0	2	3	1	.588	.571
Bonilla, B#	.364	11	4	1	4	0	1	.364	.818
Bordick, Mike	.364	11	4	0	0	0	1	.364	.400
Bragg, Darren*	.455	11	5	0	0	0	1	.455	.727
Brosius, S	.333	9	3	0	0	0	1	.333	.333
Buhner, Jay	.100	10	1	0	0	2	4	.250	.100
Canseco, Jose	.571	7	4	0	0	3	2	.700	.571
Carter, Joe	.417	12	5	1	2	0	1	.417	.917
Cirillo, Jeff	.000	7	0	0	0	0	1	.000	.000
Clark, Will*	.111	9	1	0	1	3	2	.333	.111
Coleman, V#	.167	6	1	1	2	0	1	.167	.667
Cora, Joey#	.364	11	4	0	0	1	1	.417	.364
Cordova, M	.364	11	4	0	2	2	0	.462	.455
Davis, Chili#	.333	9	3	2	3	0	3	.333	1.000
Delgado, C*	.125	8	1	0	3	1	2	.222	.250
DiSarcina, G	.286	7	2	1	2	0	0	.250	.714
Duncan, M	.333	6	2	0	1	0	1	.286	.333
Durham, Ray*	.429	7	3	0	0	0	0	.500	.429
Edmonds, Jim*	.500	10	5	3	4	2	1	.583	1.400
Elster, Kevin	.000	5	0	0	0	1	1	.000	.000
Fabregas, Jor*	.000	4	0	0	0	1	0	.200	.000
Fielder, C	.333	6	2	1	4	1	1	.429	1.000
Frye, Jeff	.100	10	1	0	0	1	2	.182	.100
Gates, Brent#	.333	9	3	0	0	1	2	.400	.444
Giambi, Jason*	.167	12	2	1	2	0	1	.167	.417
Gil, Benji	.200	5	1	0	0	0	0	.200	.200
Girardi, Joe	.143	7	1	0	1	0	0	.222	.286
Gonzalez, A	.429	7	3	0	4	0	2	.375	.571
Gonzalez, J	.222	9	2	0	1	0	0	.300	.444
Goodwin, C*	.167	6	1	0	0	0	2	.167	.333
Goodwin, Tom*	.222	9	2	0	0	0	2	.222	.222
Green, Shawn*	.300	10	3	0	1	0	1	.300	.300
Greer, Rusty*	.429	14	6	1	2	2	1	.500	.714
Griffey Jr, K*	.300	10	3	1	1	0	3	.300	.600
Guillen, O*	.400	10	4	0	2	0	0	.400	.700
Hamelin, Bob*	.200	5	1	0	0	1	1	.333	.200
Hamilton, D*	.200	10	2	0	0	0	0	.200	.300
Haselman, B	.333	3	1	0	0	2	1	.600	.333
Henderson, R	.400	5	2	0	0	1	1	.500	.600
Hoiles, Chris	.143	7	1	1	1	2	1	.333	.571
Hollins, Dave#	.500	4	2	0	2	1	0	.600	.750
Howard, Dave#	.571	7	4	0	0	0	0	.571	.857
Jaha, John	.429	7	3	0	0	0	0	.429	.571
Jefferson, R*	.444	9	4	0	1	0	1	.444	.667
Jeter, Derek	.500	10	5	0	1	0	1	.500	.500
Joyner, Wally*	.000	5	0	0	0	1	3	.167	.000
Karkovice, R	.300	10	3	2	4	2	4	.417	.900
Kelly, Pat	.000	4	0	0	0	1	1	.200	.000
Knoblauch, C	.273	11	3	0	1	3	1	.467	.273
Lawton, Matt*	.400	5	2	0	2	0	0	.400	.400
Lewis, Darren	.200	5	1	0	1	0	0	.200	.200
Leyritz, Jim	.400	4	0	0	0	1	1	.167	.000
Lockhart, K*	.250	4	1	0	1	0	0	.200	.500
Lofton, Kenny*	.353	17	6	1	3	0	2	.353	.588
Manto, Jeff	.143	7	1	0	0	0	2	.143	.143
Martinez, Da*	.222	9	2	2	5	1	1	.300	.889
Martinez, E	.286	7	2	0	1	1	3	.375	.286
Martinez, S*	.143	7	1	0	0	0	2	.143	.143
Martinez, T*	.357	14	5	2	4	1	1	.400	.786
Mayne, Brent*	.250	4	1	0	1	0	0	.250	.500
McLemore, M#	.200	12	4	1	1	0	2	.231	.167
Meares, Pat	.333	12	4	1	1	0	2	.333	.583
Molitor, Paul	.250	16	4	3	1	0	2	.294	.438
Munoz, Pedro	.333	9	3	0	1	0	1	.571	.500
Murray, Eddie#	.111	9	1	1	2	1	1	.273	.444
Myers, Greg*	.167	6	1	0	1	1	1	.250	.167

Felipe Lira, Tigers — RHP

Batter	Avg	AB	H	HR	BI	BB	SO	OBP	Slg
Naehring, Tim	.286	7	2	1	4	1	0	.375	.714
Newson, W*	.333	6	2	0	1	1	2	.429	.333
Nixon, Otis*	.167	12	2	0	0	2	1	.286	.167
Nunnally, Jon*	.000	7	0	0	0	1	1	.125	.000
O'Leary, Troy*	.300	10	3	0	0	1	1	.417	.300
O'Neill, Paul*	.375	16	6	0	2	3	3	.474	.438
Olerud, John*	.364	11	4	0	1	1	1	.417	.455
Palmeiro, R*	.500	16	8	2	5	0	0	.500	.875
Palmer, Dean	.143	7	1	1	2	0	2	.143	.571
Paquette, C	.286	7	2	2	2	0	0	.286	1.143
Perez, Tomas*	.571	7	4	0	1	1	1	.625	1.143
Phillips, T#	.364	11	4	0	1	1	2	.417	.636
Polonia, Luis*	.400	5	2	0	0	1	1	.500	.400
Raines, Tim#	.000	9	0	0	0	4	2	.308	.000
Ramirez, M	.231	13	3	0	2	1	2	.267	.231
Ripken, Cal	.333	12	4	1	3	3	1	.467	.583
Rodriguez, Al	.333	6	2	0	2	2	0	.556	.500
Rodriguez, I	.167	6	1	1	3	2	0	.444	.667
Salmon, Tim	.222	9	2	1	0	2	2	.222	.333
Seitzer, K	.250	8	2	0	0	0	1	.250	.375
Sierra, Ruben#	.333	9	3	0	1	1	2	.364	.333
Snow, J.T.#	.100	10	1	1	2	2	2	.250	.400
Sorrento, P*	.125	8	1	1	2	2	4	.273	.500
Sprague, Ed	.182	11	2	0	0	0	4	.250	.273
Stahoviak, S*	.091	11	1	0	0	2	2	.231	.182
Stairs, Matt*	.200	5	1	0	0	0	1	.200	.200
Stanley, Mike	.200	5	1	0	0	0	0	.167	.200
Steinbach, T	.200	5	1	0	0	0	2	.200	.400
Stillwell, K#	.250	4	1	0	0	0	0	.400	.250
Strawberry, D*	.444	9	4	0	1	1	1	.500	.889
Surhoff, B.J.*	.222	9	2	1	4	0	1	.222	.556
Tartabull, D	.286	7	2	2	3	1	3	.375	1.143
Tettleton, M#	.091	11	1	0	1	0	5	.083	.091
Thomas, Frank	.200	10	2	0	3	2	2	.308	.200
Thome, Jim*	.455	11	5	1	1	4	2	.625	.818
Tinsley, Lee#	.400	10	4	0	0	0	0	.400	.400
Valentin, Jhn	.333	15	5	1	3	1	2	.375	.533
Valle, Dave	.400	5	2	0	0	0	0	.400	.600
Vaughn, Greg	.400	5	2	0	1	0	1	.400	.600
Vaughn, Mo*	.231	13	3	1	4	1	5	.286	.462
Velarde, R	.471	17	8	0	4	1	3	.500	.647
Ventura, R*	.455	11	5	0	0	2	3	.538	.545
Vina, F*	.000	7	0	0	0	0	0	.000	.000
Vizcaino, J	.000	6	0	0	0	0	0	.000	.000
Vizquel, Omar#	.091	11	1	0	1	2	1	.154	.364
Walbeck, Matt#	.286	7	2	0	0	0	2	.286	.286
Williams, Ber#	.176	17	3	0	2	1	3	.211	.235
Williams, Geo#	.200	5	1	0	0	1	1	.333	.400
Wilson, Dan	.143	7	1	1	1	0	2	.143	.571
Young, Ernie	.500	4	2	0	1	1	1	.500	.750

Graeme Lloyd, Yankees — LHP

Batter	Avg	AB	H	HR	BI	BB	SO	OBP	Slg
Alomar, R#	.143	7	1	0	3	0	1	.125	.143
Alomar Jr, S	.000	4	0	0	0	1	1	.200	.000
Anderson, Brd*	.429	7	3	0	2	1	0	.500	.571
Anderson, G*	.333	6	2	0	2	0	1	.333	.500
Baerga, C#	.333	6	2	1	2	0	0	.333	.833
Baines, H*	.400	5	2	1	2	1	0	.500	1.000
Belle, Albert	.400	5	2	0	0	0	0	.400	.800
Boggs, Wade*	.600	5	3	0	2	2	0	.714	.600
Clark, Will*	.286	7	2	0	0	0	2	.286	.286
Cora, Joey#	.400	5	2	0	1	0	0	.400	.400
Curtis, Chad	.600	5	3	0	0	0	0	.600	.600
Davis, Chili#	.375	8	3	0	2	1	0	.444	.500
Devereaux, M	.400	5	2	0	0	0	0	.400	.400
DiSarcina, G	.333	6	2	1	3	0	0	.333	.833
Edmonds, Jim*	.400	5	2	0	3	0	1	.400	.400
Espinoza, A	.500	6	3	0	0	0	0	.500	.667
Franco, Julio	.400	5	2	1	3	1	0	.500	1.000
Goodwin, Tom*	.143	7	1	0	0	0	1	.143	.143
Greenwell, M*	.200	10	2	0	1	0	0	.200	.200
Griffey Jr, K*	.000	3	0	0	1	2	0	.333	.000
Guillen, O*	.000	9	0	0	0	0	2	.000	.000
Jefferson, R*	.250	4	1	1	1	1	2	.400	1.000
Johnson, L*	.417	12	5	0	1	0	0	.417	.417
Joyner, Wally*	.375	8	3	0	0	1	1	.375	.375
Karkovice, R	.286	7	2	0	1	0	2	.286	.429
Lofton, Kenny*	.154	13	2	0	0	1	1	.154	.231
Macfarlane, M	.400	5	2	1	2	1	2	.500	1.200
McLemore, M#	.000	6	0	0	0	1	0	.143	.000
McRae, Brian#	.333	6	2	0	0	0	1	.429	.333
Meares, Pat	.667	6	4	0	0	0	0	.667	.667
Murray, Eddie#	.429	7	3	0	4	0	0	.429	.571
Nixon, Otis#	.333	6	2	0	0	0	0	.333	.500
O'Neill, Paul*	.182	11	2	0	1	1	1	.250	.182
Olerud, John*	.000	5	0	0	0	0	0	.000	.000
Palmeiro, R*	.188	16	3	0	0	1	3	.235	.188
Palmer, Dean	.000	4	0	0	0	1	3	.333	.000
Phillips, T#	.400	5	2	0	0	0	2	.400	.400
Polonia, Luis*	.250	4	1	0	3	1	0	.400	.250

Graeme Lloyd, Yankees — LHP

Batter	Avg	AB	H	HR	BI	BB	SO	OBP	Slg
Raines, Tim*	.375	8	3	0	1	2	0	.500	.375
Reboulet, J	.200	5	1	0	1	0	0	.200	.200
Ripken, Cal	.125	8	1	0	1	0	1	.111	.125
Salmon, Tim	.286	7	2	1	4	1	3	.375	.714
Sierra, Ruben#	.200	5	1	0	1	0	0	.200	.200
Snow, J.T.#	.167	6	1	0	1	1	3	.286	.167
Sorrento, P*	.000	7	0	0	0	0	1	.000	.000
Sprague, Ed	.200	5	1	0	0	0	1	.200	.200
Stanley, Mike	.250	8	2	0	0	0	2	.333	.375
Strange, Doug*	.000	4	0	0	0	1	1	.200	.000
Tartabull, D	.000	4	0	0	0	3	1	.429	.000
Thome, Jim*	.000	5	0	0	1	1	2	.167	.000
Valentin, Jhn	.143	7	1	1	1	0	2	.143	.571
Vaughn, Mo*	.091	11	1	0	1	2	4	.231	.091
Velarde, R	.333	6	2	0	0	0	1	.429	.333
Ventura, R*	.111	9	1	0	2	0	3	.111	.333
Vitiello, Joe	.600	5	3	0	1	0	0	.600	.800
Vizquel, Omar#	.167	6	1	0	0	0	0	.286	.167
Williams, Ber#	.333	3	1	0	3	2	1	.500	.333

Esteban Loaiza, Pirates — RHP

Batter	Avg	AB	H	HR	BI	BB	SO	OBP	Slg
Abbott, Kurt	.375	8	3	2	2	0	2	.375	1.125
Alfonzo, E	.333	6	2	0	2	0	0	.333	.500
Bagwell, Jeff	.000	8	0	0	0	1	1	.111	.000
Bates, Jason#	.200	5	1	0	1	0	1	.200	.400
Bell, David	.400	5	2	0	1	0	1	.400	.400
Bell, Derek	.455	11	5	2	4	2	2	.538	1.000
Benard, M*	.143	7	1	0	0	0	2	.143	.143
Bichette, D	.400	10	4	0	1	0	1	.364	.400
Biggio, Craig	.308	13	4	0	3	1	0	.357	.385
Blauser, Jeff	.143	7	1	0	0	0	1	.143	.143
Bonds, Barry*	.500	8	4	0	0	2	1	.636	.750
Boone, Bret	.200	10	2	0	1	1	1	.333	.300
Branson, Jeff*	.333	6	2	0	1	1	3	.429	.500
Brogna, Rico*	.429	7	3	0	0	1	1	.429	.571
Butler, Brett*	.000	8	0	0	1	4	0	.333	.000
Caminiti, Ken#	.400	5	2	0	0	2	2	.400	.600
Carreon, Mark	.429	7	3	2	2	0	1	.429	1.286
Castilla, V	.444	9	4	1	1	0	0	.444	1.111
Colbrunn, G	.333	6	2	0	2	0	0	.286	.500
Conine, Jeff	.200	5	1	1	1	0	3	.200	.800
Daulton, D*	.200	5	1	0	0	1	1	.200	.200
Dunston, S	.222	9	2	0	4	1	0	.300	.222
Dykstra, L*	.000	5	0	0	0	1	1	.286	.000
Eisenreich, J*	.200	5	1	0	2	0	1	.200	.200
Eusebio, Tony	.364	11	4	0	0	1	1	.364	.545
Finley, Steve*	.000	4	0	0	0	1	1	.200	.000
Fonville, C#	.000	4	0	0	0	0	1	.200	.000
Galarraga, A	.400	10	4	0	0	1	1	.400	.600
Gilkey, B	.364	11	4	1	2	0	3	.364	.636
Girardi, Joe	.200	5	1	0	1	1	0	.286	.200
Gonzalez, L*	.556	9	5	0	0	0	0	.556	.667
Grace, Mark*	.333	9	3	0	0	1	1	.400	.444
Grissom, M	.286	7	2	0	0	2	0	.444	.286
Gwynn, Tony*	.400	5	2	0	3	0	1	.400	.400
Hayes, C	.600	5	3	0	1	0	0	.600	.800
Hernandez, Jo	.400	5	2	0	1	0	1	.400	.400
Hill, G	.167	6	1	0	0	0	1	.167	.333
Hollins, Dave#	.000	5	0	0	0	0	1	.000	.000
Howard, T*	.250	8	2	0	0	1	0	.333	.375
Hundley, Todd#	.200	5	1	1	1	1	1	.333	.800
Hunter, Bri L	.300	10	3	0	0	0	0	.300	.300
Jefferies, G#	.250	4	1	0	0	1	0	.400	.250
Jones, C#	.500	6	3	0	1	1	1	.571	.500
Jordan, Brian	.417	12	5	0	4	0	0	.462	.417
Justice, Dave*	.000	4	0	0	0	2	2	.333	.000
Karros, Eric	.222	9	2	1	2	0	1	.200	.556
Kelly, R	.400	5	2	0	1	0	0	.400	.600
Kingery, Mike*	.000	7	0	0	1	0	1	.125	.000
Klesko, Ryan*	.286	7	2	2	3	0	2	.286	1.143
Lankford, Ray*	.273	11	3	0	1	3	2	.429	.364
Larkin, Barry	.400	10	4	1	2	3	2	.538	.900
Lemke, Mark#	.333	6	2	0	1	1	1	.429	.333
Lewis, Darren	.364	11	4	0	3	0	1	.364	.545
Mabry, John*	.200	10	2	0	3	1	2	.250	.200
Magadan, Dave*	.000	6	0	0	0	1	1	.000	.000
McGriff, Fred*	.286	7	2	1	2	0	0	.286	.714
McRae, Brian#	.200	5	1	1	1	2	0	.429	.800
Miller, Orl	.625	8	5	3	5	0	1	.625	1.750
Mondesi, Raul	.250	8	2	0	1	0	1	.250	.500
Morandini, M*	.500	4	2	0	0	0	0	.500	.750
Morris, Hal*	.250	8	2	0	1	1	3	.333	.250
O'Brien, C	.200	5	1	0	0	1	0	.333	.200
Offerman, J#	.400	5	2	0	0	0	0	.400	.400
Orsulak, Joe*	.000	4	0	0	1	1	1	.167	.000
Pendleton, T#	.500	8	4	0	4	0	2	.500	.875
Piazza, Mike	.500	8	4	1	2	0	1	.500	.875
Reed, Jeff*	.000	6	0	0	0	1	1	.200	.000
Reed, Jody	.000	3	0	0	0	2	0	.400	.000
Sanders, R	.125	8	1	0	3	0	1	.111	.500

119

Esteban Loaiza, Pirates — RHP

Batter	Avg	AB	H	HR	BI	BB	SO	OBP	Slg
Santiago, B	.500	4	2	0	0	2	0	.667	.500
Sheffield, G	.500	6	3	0	0	0	0	.500	.500
Smith, Ozzie#	.167	6	1	0	0	0	0	.167	.167
Sosa, Sammy	.333	6	2	0	1	0	0	.333	.333
Stocker, K#	.000	5	0	0	0	0	0	.000	.000
Veras, Q#	.250	8	2	0	0	1	1	.333	.250
Vizcaino, J#	.500	6	3	0	2	0	1	.429	.833
Walker, Larry*	.300	10	3	0	0	0	1	.300	.400
Wallach, Tim	.500	6	3	0	0	0	0	.500	.500
Weiss, Walt#	.556	9	5	1	4	1	1	.600	1.222
Young, Eric	.143	7	1	0	0	0	1	.143	.143

Rich Loiselle, Pirates — RHP

Batter	Avg	AB	H	HR	BI	BB	SO	OBP	Slg
Grace, Mark*	.167	6	1	0	0	0	1	.167	.333
Magadan, Dave*	.200	5	1	0	0	1	0	.333	.200
McRae, Brian*	.333	6	2	1	1	0	0	.333	.833
Sanchez, Rey	.200	5	1	0	0	0	1	.200	.200
Servais, S	.400	5	2	0	0	0	1	.400	.400

Albie Lopez, Indians — RHP

Batter	Avg	AB	H	HR	BI	BB	SO	OBP	Slg
Aldrete, Mike*	.200	5	1	0	0	0	1	.200	.200
Alomar, R#	.429	7	3	0	1	2	0	.556	.429
Anderson, Brd*	.222	9	2	0	2	1	1	.300	.222
Baines, H*	.286	7	2	2	2	1	0	.375	1.143
Bordick, Mike	.000	5	0	0	0	1	0	.167	.000
Buhner, Jay	.400	10	4	2	0	0	0	.400	1.000
Carter, Joe	.462	13	6	2	4	0	0	.462	1.000
Cedeno, D#	.375	8	3	0	0	1	3	.444	.375
Clark, Tony#	.000	6	0	0	0	0	3	.000	.000
Cora, Joey*	.167	6	1	0	0	2	1	.375	.333
Curtis, Chad	.333	6	2	0	0	1	1	.429	.333
Davis, Chili#	.200	5	1	0	1	0	2	.200	.400
Delgado, C*	.571	7	4	1	4	0	0	.571	1.143
Devereaux, M	.286	7	2	0	0	0	2	.286	.429
DiSarcina, A	.333	6	2	0	0	0	0	.333	.500
Easley, D	.000	4	0	0	1	0	2	.000	.000
Fielder, C	.111	9	1	1	4	0	4	.100	.444
Fryman, T	.100	10	1	0	0	2	1	.250	.100
Gates, Brent#	.500	4	2	0	0	1	1	.600	.750
Giambi, Jason*	.200	5	1	0	0	0	3	.200	.200
Gomez, Chris	.167	6	1	0	0	0	1	.167	.167
Gonzalez, A	.400	5	2	0	0	1	2	.500	.400
Gonzalez, J	.333	6	2	1	3	0	0	.333	.833
Green, Shawn*	.000	5	0	0	0	1	0	.167	.000
Griffey Jr, K*	.375	8	3	1	2	0	2	.333	.750
Guillen, O*	.000	5	0	0	0	0	2	.000	.000
Hammonds, J	.400	5	2	0	0	0	1	.400	.400
Henderson, R	.167	6	1	0	0	3	1	.444	.167
Higginson, B*	.000	4	0	0	0	1	1	.000	.000
Hoiles, Chris	.200	5	1	0	0	0	1	.200	.200
Martinez, E	.600	6	3	3	4	1	0	.571	2.000
McLemore, M#	.444	9	4	1	1	0	2	.444	.889
Molitor, Paul	.100	10	1	0	0	0	1	.100	.100
Nixon, Otis#	.143	7	1	0	0	2	1	.143	.143
Olerud, John*	.364	11	4	1	2	1	0	.417	.636
Palmeiro, R*	.375	8	3	1	2	1	0	.500	.875
Palmer, Dean	.167	6	1	0	0	2	0	.167	.167
Phillips, T#	.455	11	5	0	0	1	0	.500	.455
Polonia, Luis*	.750	4	3	0	1	1	1	.800	.750
Raines, Tim#	.250	4	1	0	0	0	1	.400	.250
Ripken, Cal	.143	7	1	0	1	1	2	.250	.286
Rodriguez, I	.333	6	2	0	1	0	0	.333	.500
Salmon, Tim	.000	4	0	0	0	2	2	.333	.000
Sierra, Ruben*	.400	5	2	0	1	0	0	.400	.600
Snow, J.T.#	.000	5	0	0	0	0	1	.000	.000
Sorrento, P*	.000	4	0	0	0	1	1	.000	.000
Sprague, Ed	.444	9	4	1	2	1	0	.500	.778
Steinbach, T	.286	7	2	0	2	0	1	.286	.429
Strange, Doug#	.000	5	0	0	0	0	1	.000	.000
Tettleton, M#	.000	8	0	0	0	2	3	.273	.000
Thomas, Frank	.200	5	1	0	0	2	1	.429	.200
White, Devon#	.000	6	0	0	0	0	1	.000	.000
Wilson, Dan	.000	5	0	0	0	0	2	.000	.000

Bob MacDonald, Mets — LHP

Batter	Avg	AB	H	HR	BI	BB	SO	OBP	Slg
Anderson, Brd*	.000	5	0	0	0	4	2	.444	.000
Baerga, C#	.167	6	1	0	1	0	1	.143	.167
Boggs, Wade*	.091	11	1	0	0	1	2	.167	.091
Buhner, Jay	1.000	2	2	1	3	4	0	1.000	2.500
Burks, Ellis	.400	5	2	0	0	0	0	.571	.400
Cora, Joey#	.500	10	5	0	1	0	0	.500	.500
Devereaux, M	.500	8	4	1	2	0	0	.500	.875
Espinoza, A	.200	5	1	0	0	0	0	.200	.200
Franco, Julio	.714	7	5	2	8	0	1	.714	1.714
Greenwell, M	.273	11	3	0	1	0	1	.273	.273
Griffey Jr, K*	.500	6	3	0	0	1	2	.571	.833
Guillen, O*	.000	6	0	0	0	0	0	.000	.000
Hall, Mel*	.000	5	0	0	0	0	0	.000	.000

Bob MacDonald, Mets — LHP

Batter	Avg	AB	H	HR	BI	BB	SO	OBP	Slg
Hamilton, D*	.286	7	2	1	2	0	2	.286	.714
Huff, Michael	.000	5	0	0	0	0	4	.000	.000
Johnson, L*	.167	6	1	0	0	1	1	.286	.167
Joyner, Wally*	.364	11	4	1	5	2	0	.462	.727
Kelly, Pat	.250	4	1	0	0	0	0	.250	.250
Macfarlane, M	.400	5	2	0	2	1	2	.500	.600
Martinez, E	.200	5	1	0	0	0	2	.200	.200
Martinez, T*	.273	11	3	2	4	0	3	.273	.818
McRae, Brian*	.500	8	4	1	4	2	0	.600	1.000
Molitor, Paul	.600	5	3	0	4	1	0	.667	1.000
Myers, Greg*	.600	5	3	0	1	0	2	.600	1.200
O'Neill, Paul*	.400	5	2	0	0	1	1	.400	.600
Olerud, John*	.200	5	1	0	1	0	1	.200	.200
Palmeiro, R*	.500	10	5	0	3	7	1	.706	.500
Raines, Tim#	.333	6	2	0	1	4	0	.600	.333
Reed, Jody	.143	7	1	0	0	0	0	.143	.143
Segui, David#	.000	5	0	0	0	0	1	.000	.000
Seitzer, K	.200	5	1	0	0	2	0	.429	.200
Sierra, Ruben#	.500	10	5	0	1	0	1	.500	.800
Spiers, Bill*	.286	7	2	0	1	1	1	.375	.286
Surhoff, B.J.*	.500	8	4	0	2	0	1	.500	.625
Tartabull, D	.125	8	1	0	2	2	3	.300	.125
Thomas, Frank	.800	5	4	1	4	1	0	.750	1.400
Vaughn, Greg	.200	5	1	0	1	0	1	.167	.400
Vaughn, Mo*	.000	6	0	0	0	1	3	.143	.000
Ventura, R*	.250	8	2	1	4	1	2	.333	.625

Greg Maddux, Braves — RHP

Batter	Avg	AB	H	HR	BI	BB	SO	OBP	Slg
Abbott, Kurt	.000	6	0	0	0	0	2	.000	.000
Aldrete, Mike*	.176	17	3	0	2	4	5	.333	.235
Alfonzo, E	.375	8	3	0	0	0	1	.375	.500
Alicea, Luis#	.297	37	11	0	3	3	3	.350	.351
Alomar, R#	.261	23	6	0	2	1	1	.292	.391
Alou, Moises	.226	31	7	0	3	1	4	.250	.355
Amaro, Ruben*	.182	11	2	0	1	0	4	.308	.182
Andrews, S	.250	8	2	0	0	0	1	.250	.250
Anthony, Eric*	.212	33	7	0	2	0	6	.212	.303
Arias, Alex	.300	10	3	1	2	1	1	.364	.600
Ausmus, Brad	.333	12	4	0	0	2	3	.429	.417
Bagwell, Jeff	.234	47	11	3	9	21	11	.308	.468
Barberie, B#	.375	24	9	0	0	0	7	.400	.500
Batiste, Kim	.333	6	2	0	0	0	0	.333	.333
Bell, David	.000	3	0	0	0	0	2	.000	.000
Bell, Derek	.206	34	7	0	2	0	4	.206	.265
Bell, Jay	.258	66	17	0	2	1	18	.269	.318
Belliard, R	.238	21	5	0	1	0	1	.238	.238
Benard, M*	.143	7	1	0	0	0	0	.143	.286
Berry, Sean	.370	27	10	0	2	0	2	.370	.407
Bichette, D	.200	15	3	0	2	1	3	.294	.200
Biggio, Craig	.232	69	16	0	2	6	5	.312	.261
Blauser, Jeff	.333	9	3	0	0	0	1	.333	.444
Bogar, Tim	.000	6	0	0	0	0	1	.000	.000
Bonds, Barry*	.299	87	26	7	14	15	13	.402	.586
Bonilla, B#	.237	76	18	2	13	4	14	.272	.408
Boone, Bret	.200	20	4	0	1	1	2	.304	.300
Borders, Pat	.000	5	0	0	0	1	1	.167	.000
Branson, Jeff*	.190	21	4	0	1	0	7	.190	.238
Brogna, Rico*	.250	16	4	0	0	1	5	.294	.250
Brumfield, J	.000	5	0	0	0	3	4	.375	.000
Bullett, S*	.167	6	1	0	0	0	3	.167	.167
Burks, Ellis	.167	6	1	0	0	1	2	.286	.167
Burnitz, J*	.200	10	2	0	0	1	3	.273	.200
Butler, Brett*	.239	46	11	0	5	5	4	.314	.261
Caminiti, Ken#	.229	70	16	0	2	3	21	.260	.243
Candaele, C#	.354	24	9	0	3	2	2	.306	.294
Cangelosi, J#	.214	14	3	0	0	2	3	.313	.214
Carr, Chuck	.143	12	2	0	0	2	3	.286	.250
Carreon, Mark	.188	16	3	0	1	0	0	.235	.250
Carter, Joe	.455	11	5	0	1	1	0	.500	.545
Castilla, V	.143	14	2	1	3	0	4	.143	.357
Cedeno, A	.286	21	6	0	4	1	5	.333	.333
Cianfrocco, A	.000	11	0	0	1	0	3	.000	.000
Clark, Dave*	.214	14	3	0	0	1	4	.267	.214
Clark, Will*	.225	40	9	1	3	6	12	.340	.350
Clayton, R	.161	31	5	0	2	4	2	.212	.161
Colbrunn, G	.000	8	0	0	0	1	0	.000	.000
Cole, Alex*	.286	7	2	0	1	1	1	.375	.571
Coleman, V#	.328	61	20	0	6	4	15	.369	.344
Conine, Jeff	.409	22	9	0	5	1	4	.417	.455
Cordero, Wil	.320	25	8	1	3	0	3	.308	.480
Daulton, D*	.234	47	11	3	10	9	11	.357	.468
Davis, Eric	.204	49	10	0	3	14	14	.264	.245
DeShields, D*	.214	42	9	0	2	5	11	.292	.238
Duncan, M	.184	38	7	0	5	1	11	.205	.289
Dunston, S	.308	13	4	1	3	0	1	.308	.615
Dykstra, L*	.277	47	19	0	11	5	14	.298	.338
Eisenreich, J*	.233	30	7	0	3	2	3	.281	.300
Elster, Kevin	.111	18	2	1	3	3	1	.227	.333
Eusebio, Tony	.200	10	2	0	0	2	0	.200	.200
Everett, Carl#	.300	10	3	0	0	0	4	.300	.300

Greg Maddux, Braves — RHP

Batter	Avg	AB	H	HR	BI	BB	SO	OBP	Slg
Finley, Steve*	.220	50	11	1	3	0	10	.220	.300
Fletcher, D*	.143	42	6	0	5	1	10	.174	.190
Floyd, Cliff*	.308	13	4	1	4	1	4	.357	.615
Frazier, Lou#	.250	4	1	0	1	1	2	.400	.250
Gaetti, Gary	.286	7	2	0	0	0	1	.286	.429
Gagne, Greg	.286	7	2	0	0	0	0	.286	.429
Galarraga, A	.239	67	16	1	8	0	20	.271	.299
Gant, Ron	.171	41	7	1	3	2	11	.217	.244
Garcia, C	.143	7	1	0	0	0	1	.143	.143
Gilkey, B	.306	49	15	1	9	2	8	.327	.469
Girardi, Joe	.250	12	3	0	1	0	2	.250	.250
Goff, Jerry*	.000	5	0	0	0	1	2	.167	.000
Gonzalez, L*	.268	56	15	4	10	3	6	.305	.554
Grace, Mark*	.250	20	5	1	3	1	1	.286	.400
Grissom, M	.405	42	17	1	3	0	3	.409	.571
Grudzielanek	.200	10	2	0	2	0	1	.200	.200
Gutierrez, R	.077	13	1	0	0	0	2	.077	.154
Gwynn, Chris*	.000	5	0	0	0	0	2	.000	.000
Gwynn, Tony*	.444	63	28	0	8	9	0	.514	.540
Hansen, Dave*	.154	13	2	0	0	2	2	.267	.154
Hardtke, J#	.500	6	3	0	0	0	1	.500	1.000
Harris, Lenny*	.250	28	7	0	1	1	2	.276	.250
Hayes, C	.196	46	9	1	2	1	6	.213	.261
Henderson, R	.200	10	2	0	0	0	0	.273	.300
Hill, G	.200	5	1	0	0	0	3	.200	.200
Hollins, Dave#	.139	36	5	0	3	3	11	.225	.167
Howard, T*	.286	21	6	0	2	0	4	.304	.333
Howell, Jack*	.250	4	1	0	0	1	0	.400	.250
Hudler, Rex	.273	11	3	0	1	1	2	.333	.364
Hundley, Todd#	.250	56	14	0	2	1	12	.263	.286
Hunter, Bri L	.375	8	3	0	0	0	3	.375	.500
Huskey, Butch	.250	12	3	0	3	0	0	.250	.417
Huson, Jeff*	.200	5	1	0	0	0	0	.200	.400
Hyers, Tim*	.000	5	0	0	0	0	0	.000	.000
Incaviglia, J	.200	5	1	0	0	0	0	.200	.200
James, Dion*	.333	12	4	1	5	2	2	.429	.833
Javier, Stan#	.000	9	0	0	1	0	3	.000	.000
Jefferies, G#	.355	76	27	2	7	6	4	.402	.487
Johnson, Char	.200	5	1	0	0	0	0	.200	.200
Johnson, L*	.273	11	3	0	0	0	1	.273	.273
Johnson, Mark*	.100	10	1	0	1	0	6	.100	.100
Jordan, Brian	.188	32	6	0	1	0	5	.182	.188
Jordan, Ricky	.176	34	6	0	5	1	9	.216	.206
Joyner, Wally*	.167	6	1	0	0	0	2	.167	.167
Justice, Dave*	.235	17	4	0	2	2	4	.316	.294
Karros, Eric	.083	24	2	0	2	1	4	.120	.125
Kelly, R	.462	13	6	0	1	1	3	.500	.462
Kent, Jeff	.226	31	7	0	1	7	7	.250	.290
King, Jeff	.250	40	10	0	5	2	4	.286	.400
Kingery, Mike*	.200	20	4	0	3	0	2	.200	.200
Lampkin, Tom*	.000	8	0	0	0	0	1	.000	.000
Lankford, Ray*	.268	71	19	1	9	3	20	.297	.437
Lansing, Mike	.269	26	7	0	1	1	1	.296	.269
Larkin, Barry	.315	73	23	1	5	2	9	.351	.479
Lewis, Darren	.238	21	5	0	1	4	1	.360	.238
Liriano, N#	.067	15	1	0	0	0	5	.067	.067
Mabry, John*	.353	17	6	0	1	0	4	.353	.471
Magadan, Dave*	.203	69	14	0	4	11	13	.313	.246
Manwaring, V	.217	23	5	0	2	0	2	.280	.261
Martin, Al*	.393	28	11	0	1	1	5	.414	.500
Martinez, Da*	.143	56	8	0	4	7	7	.200	.196
May, Derrick*	.158	19	3	0	1	0	3	.158	.158
McGee, Willie#	.262	61	16	0	3	1	14	.270	.295
McGriff, Fred*	.250	28	5	2	7	5	5	.385	.600
McLemore, M#	.143	7	1	0	0	0	1	.143	.143
McRae, Brian*	.182	11	2	0	1	2	2	.182	.182
Merced, O*	.167	42	7	1	3	2	10	.222	.262
Miller, Orl	.333	12	4	0	0	0	3	.333	.417
Mitchell, K	.200	45	9	2	8	2	9	.234	.422
Mondesi, Raul	.500	12	6	0	1	1	0	.538	.667
Morandini, M*	.292	65	19	0	1	3	13	.324	.431
Morris, Hal*	.375	48	18	0	4	4	8	.423	.458
Mouton, James	.250	4	1	0	0	0	0	.250	.250
Murray, Eddie*	.225	40	9	1	4	6	6	.326	.375
Nieves, M#	.000	5	0	0	0	0	3	.000	.000
Nixon, Otis*	.000	8	0	0	0	1	2	.111	.000
O'Brien, C	.500	4	2	0	1	1	0	.600	.500
O'Neill, Paul*	.189	37	7	0	2	6	7	.318	.243
Offerman, J#	.176	17	3	0	3	0	6	.176	.294
Oliver, Joe	.136	22	3	1	3	1	4	.167	.318
Ordonez, Rey	.167	6	1	0	2	1	3	.250	.167
Orsulak, Joe*	.206	34	7	0	0	0	7	.206	.206
Osik, Keith	.500	8	4	0	0	0	0	.500	.500
Otero, Ricky#	.375	8	3	0	0	0	1	.375	.375
Owens, Eric	.000	5	0	0	1	0	1	.000	.000
Pagnozzi, Tom	.216	37	8	0	3	2	2	.250	.297
Parent, Mark	.182	11	2	0	0	1	0	.250	.182
Pena, G#	.200	20	4	1	2	2	7	.273	.400
Pena, Tony	.200	20	4	1	5	2	4	.357	.462
Pendleton, T#	.300	40	12	0	2	3	6	.349	.400
Phillips, J*	.083	12	1	1	1	0	4	.083	.333

Greg Maddux, Braves — RHP

Batter	Avg	AB	H	HR	BI	BB	SO	OBP	Slg
Piazza, Mike	.263	19	5	1	2	1	3	.300	.474
Plantier, P*	.059	17	1	0	0	0	5	.059	.059
Raines, Tim*	.275	40	11	2	3	7	3	.396	.475
Reed, Jeff*	.340	50	17	1	7	5	3	.400	.420
Reed, Jody	.235	17	4	0	0	1	2	.278	.294
Roberts, Bip#	.471	34	16	0	3	7	4	.561	.588
Rodriguez, H*	.190	21	4	1	2	0	6	.190	.333
Rolen, Scott	.333	6	2	0	0	2	0	.500	.333
Sabo, Chris	.227	44	10	1	5	0	3	.227	.364
Samuel, Juan	.275	40	11	0	5	0	7	.293	.425
Sanchez, Rey	.083	12	1	0	0	0	1	.083	.083
Sandberg, R	.385	13	5	0	0	0	2	.385	.385
Sanders, R	.286	28	8	0	1	3	7	.355	.429
Santangelo, F#	.000	4	0	0	0	1	0	.200	.000
Santiago, B	.283	60	17	6	16	5	10	.348	.650
Scarsone, S	.200	5	1	0	0	1	1	.333	.200
Schofield, D	.250	8	2	0	1	2	1	.400	.375
Segui, David#	.200	15	3	0	0	0	3	.200	.200
Servais, S	.222	9	2	0	0	0	2	.222	.333
Sheaffer, D	.300	10	3	0	0	0	1	.300	.400
Sheffield, G	.269	26	7	0	1	3	7	.367	.423
Shipley, C	.273	22	6	0	1	0	4	.273	.318
Slaught, Don	.091	11	1	0	0	0	3	.091	.091
Smith, Ozzie*	.191	89	17	1	3	3	5	.217	.270
Sosa, Sammy	.400	15	6	0	1	3	5	.500	.467
Spiers, Bill*	.400	5	2	0	0	0	2	.400	.400
Stillwell, K#	.182	11	2	0	0	1	1	.250	.182
Stocker, K	.111	18	2	0	2	0	5	.158	.111
Strawberry, D*	.162	37	6	3	8	6	7	.289	.459
Sweeney, Mark*	.200	5	1	0	0	0	0	.200	.200
Tarasco, Tony*	.000	7	0	0	0	0	3	.000	.000
Taubensee, E*	.184	38	7	0	2	3	11	.244	.263
Thompson, M#	.338	68	23	0	9	2	10	.357	.382
Thompson, Rob	.188	48	9	0	3	3	15	.250	.208
Thompson, Ry	.304	23	7	0	2	1	1	.333	.391
Veras, Q#	.143	7	1	0	0	1	1	.250	.143
Vina, F*	.000	3	0	0	0	0	0	.250	.000
Vizcaino, J#	.158	19	3	0	1	1	6	.190	.158
Walker, Larry*	.222	45	10	0	4	6	12	.314	.267
Wallach, Tim	.260	77	20	1	4	2	4	.288	.351
Wehner, John	.143	7	1	0	0	0	2	.143	.143
Weiss, Walt#	.217	23	5	0	2	3	6	.308	.217
White, R	.111	18	2	0	0	0	2	.111	.222
Whiten, Mark#	.188	16	3	0	3	0	8	.188	.188
Wilkins, Rick*	.091	11	1	0	1	2	3	.214	.182
Williams, E	.250	8	2	0	1	0	2	.250	.375
Williams, Ma	.271	48	13	1	8	1	6	.286	.375
Young, Eric	.182	22	4	0	3	2	1	.240	.182
Young, Kevin	.000	6	0	0	0	0	3	.000	.000
Zeile, Todd	.233	73	17	1	7	5	10	.275	.329

Mike Maddux, Red Sox — RHP

Batter	Avg	AB	H	HR	BI	BB	SO	OBP	Slg
Aldrete, Mike*	.400	5	2	0	1	0	0	.500	.600
Alomar, R#	.750	8	6	0	2	0	0	.778	1.250
Alou, Moises	.286	7	2	0	1	0	2	.250	.286
Anderson, Brd*	.000	4	0	0	0	2	2	.333	.000
Anthony, Eric*	.000	6	0	0	0	0	0	.000	.000
Bagwell, Jeff	.222	9	2	0	1	2	2	.364	.222
Barberie, B#	.000	5	0	0	0	1	0	.000	.000
Batista, Tony	.333	6	2	0	0	1	0	.429	.333
Becker, Rich*	.400	5	2	0	1	0	1	.400	.600
Bell, Derek	.400	5	2	0	1	1	0	.500	.400
Bell, Jay	.118	17	2	0	0	1	1	.118	.235
Belle, Albert	.400	5	2	0	1	0	1	.400	.600
Belliard, R	.167	6	1	0	0	1	0	.286	.167
Berroa, G	.111	9	1	0	0	1	3	.200	.111
Bichette, D	.400	5	2	0	2	0	1	.400	.400
Biggio, Craig	.286	14	4	0	3	0	3	.286	.571
Blauser, Jeff	.333	9	3	0	0	2	2	.333	.333
Boggs, Wade*	.000	5	0	0	0	0	0	.000	.000
Bonds, Barry*	.167	24	4	1	4	3	4	.259	.375
Bonilla, B	.292	24	7	0	3	1	5	.308	.375
Bordick, Mike	.333	9	3	1	5	0	0	.333	.778
Branson, Jeff*	.400	5	2	0	1	0	2	.400	.600
Brosius, S	.500	8	4	1	2	0	0	.500	1.000
Buhner, Jay	.125	8	1	1	1	1	2	.222	.500
Caminiti, Ken*	.200	10	2	0	0	1	2	.200	.200
Candaele, C#	.000	6	0	0	0	0	0	.000	.000
Carter, Joe	.333	9	3	0	2	1	0	.364	.556
Cedeno, A	.167	6	1	0	0	1	1	.167	.167
Clark, Will*	.250	24	6	1	5	2	7	.308	.375
Clayton, R	.125	8	1	0	0	0	0	.125	.125
Coleman, V#	.333	21	7	0	0	2	6	.391	.333
Cora, Joey#	.364	11	4	0	0	0	0	.364	.636
Cordero, Wil	.000	5	0	0	0	0	0	.000	.000
Daulton, D*	.400	5	2	0	1	0	0	.500	.400
Davis, Chili#	.400	5	2	0	0	1	0	.400	.400
Davis, Eric	.143	7	1	0	0	2	3	.333	.143
Dawson, Andre	.250	16	4	0	3	0	4	.250	.313

Mike Maddux, Red Sox — RHP

Batter	Avg	AB	H	HR	BI	BB	SO	OBP	Slg
Delgado, C*	.143	7	1	0	1	1	2	.250	.143
DeShields, D*	.182	11	2	0	0	2	3	.308	.182
Duncan, M	.176	17	3	1	3	1	5	.222	.353
Dunston, S	.333	18	6	1	2	2	6	.400	.667
Dykstra, L*	.385	13	5	1	3	1	2	.429	.846
Elster, Kevin	.167	6	1	1	2	1	1	.375	.667
Fielder, C	.333	6	2	0	1	1	1	.429	.500
Finley, Steve*	.667	9	6	1	2	1	1	.700	1.000
Fletcher, Darr	.429	7	3	1	2	0	0	.429	.857
Galarraga, A	.500	18	9	2	7	1	2	.526	.944
Gant, Ron	.273	22	6	2	3	2	5	.333	.727
Girardi, Joe	.600	10	6	0	1	0	1	.600	.600
Gonzalez, Juan	.000	6	0	0	0	1	1	.143	.000
Gonzalez, L*	.143	7	1	0	1	0	2	.143	.286
Goodwin, C*	.333	6	2	0	1	0	1	.333	.500
Grace, Mark*	.409	22	9	1	6	3	2	.462	.591
Green, Shawn*	.000	5	0	0	0	0	0	.000	.000
Griffey Jr, K*	.222	9	2	0	3	0	3	.222	.556
Grissom, M	.154	13	2	0	0	0	5	.154	.154
Gwynn, Chris*	.400	5	2	0	0	0	2	.400	.400
Gwynn, Tony*	.200	15	3	1	2	3	0	.333	.467
Hansen, Dave*	.000	6	0	0	0	0	1	.000	.000
Harris, Lenny*	.000	7	0	0	0	0	0	.000	.000
Hayes, C	.300	10	3	0	0	2	1	.417	.300
Hoiles, Chris	.200	5	1	0	0	0	1	.200	.200
Hollins, Dave#	.100	10	1	0	0	1	6	.182	.100
Hudler, Rex	.250	4	1	0	0	1	0	.400	.250
Hunter, Brian	.167	6	1	0	0	1	2	.286	.167
James, Dion*	.400	5	2	0	0	3	1	.625	.400
Javier, Stan#	.200	5	1	0	1	0	1	.200	.200
Jefferies, G#	.200	5	1	0	1	0	0	.200	.400
Jordan, Ricky	.000	6	0	0	1	0	1	.000	.000
Justice, Dave*	.000	9	0	0	1	4	2	.286	.000
Karros, Eric	.500	8	4	0	4	1	1	.556	.750
Kelly, R	.000	8	0	0	0	0	0	.000	.000
King, Jeff	.154	13	2	0	0	0	1	.154	.154
Kingery, Mike*	.500	4	2	0	2	1	1	.600	.750
Knoblauch, C	.200	5	1	0	0	0	0	.333	.200
Lansing, Mike	.125	8	1	0	0	0	1	.125	.125
Larkin, Barry	.250	12	3	0	1	0	1	.250	.250
Lemke, Mark#	.308	13	4	0	0	1	4	.357	.308
Lewis, Darren	.500	6	3	0	2	0	0	.500	.833
Magadan, Dave*	.167	6	1	0	1	0	0	.167	.333
Martinez, Da*	.583	12	7	0	0	3	1	.688	.583
Martinez, E	.222	9	2	0	1	0	1	.300	.222
Martinez, T*	.400	5	2	0	0	1	0	.500	.600
May, Derrick*	.200	5	1	0	1	1	0	.333	.400
McGee, Willie*	.250	12	3	0	1	2	2	.357	.333
McGriff, Fred*	.667	3	2	1	1	1	0	.800	1.667
McGwire, Mark	.250	8	2	0	1	1	3	.333	.250
McLemore, M#	.200	5	1	0	0	0	0	.200	.200
Merced, O*	.143	7	1	0	0	1	1	.250	.143
Mitchell, K	.364	11	4	0	2	1	3	.417	.545
Molitor, Paul	.667	3	2	0	1	1	0	.800	1.333
Morandini, M*	.500	4	2	0	1	1	0	.600	.500
Morris, Hal*	.125	8	1	0	1	0	1	.125	.125
Murray, Eddie*	.125	8	1	0	1	2	0	.273	.125
Nixon, Otis#	.227	22	5	0	0	3	5	.320	.227
O'Neill, Paul*	.250	12	3	1	1	1	2	.308	.500
Offerman, J*	.556	9	5	0	0	2	1	.636	.556
Olerud, John*	.714	7	5	0	2	0	0	.750	1.143
Oliver, Joe	.222	9	2	0	1	0	1	.222	.333
Orsulak, Joe*	.286	7	2	0	0	1	1	.375	.429
Pagnozzi, Tom	.200	5	1	0	2	1	0	.286	.200
Palmeiro, R*	.368	19	7	0	1	0	1	.400	.526
Pena, Tony	.429	7	3	0	1	0	1	.429	.571
Pendleton, T#	.179	28	5	0	5	0	4	.179	.214
Perez, Tomas#	.500	4	2	0	0	2	1	.667	1.000
Plantier, P*	.429	7	3	1	1	1	0	.500	.857
Raines, Tim#	.375	8	3	1	3	0	0	.333	.750
Reed, Jeff*	.143	7	1	0	0	0	1	.143	.286
Ripken, Cal	.000	6	0	0	0	1	3	.143	.000
Roberts, Bip#	.455	11	5	0	0	0	0	.455	.545
Rodriguez, Al	.167	6	1	0	0	0	1	.167	.333
Sabo, Chris	.154	13	2	0	0	0	2	.154	.154
Samuel, Juan	.143	7	1	0	0	1	2	.250	.143
Sanchez, Rey	.000	5	0	0	0	0	0	.000	.000
Sandberg, R	.382	34	13	1	7	4	6	.436	.529
Slaught, Don	.111	9	1	0	0	1	4	.200	.111
Smith, Dwight*	.429	7	3	0	4	2	2	.556	.571
Smith, Ozzie*	.267	15	4	0	0	1	0	.313	.267
Sojo, Luis	.375	8	3	0	1	0	0	.375	.375
Sorrento, P*	.000	4	0	0	0	1	0	.200	.000
Sosa, Sammy	.333	9	3	0	1	0	2	.400	.444
Sprague, Ed	.222	9	2	0	0	1	2	.364	.333
Steinbach, T	.143	7	1	0	0	0	0	.143	.143
Strawberry, D*	.154	13	2	0	0	0	4	.267	.308
Tettleton, M#	.333	3	1	1	3	2	1	.600	1.333
Thome, Jim*	.167	6	1	1	3	0	2	.167	.667
Thompson, Mil*	.333	6	2	0	1	2	0	.500	.500
Thompson, Rob	.471	17	8	2	6	0	2	.471	1.000
VanderWal, J*	.250	8	2	0	0	0	1	.250	.250
Vizcaino, J#	.286	7	2	0	2	0	1	.286	.286
Walker, Larry*	.000	8	0	0	1	0	2	.000	.000
Wallach, Tim	.278	18	5	0	3	3	2	.381	.278
Weiss, Walt*	.000	4	0	0	0	0	2	.000	.000
Whiten, Mark#	.429	7	3	1	1	0	3	.429	1.143
Wilkins, Rick*	.222	9	2	1	2	1	2	.300	.556
Williams, Ber#	.200	5	1	0	0	0	1	.200	.200
Williams, Ma	.214	14	3	0	2	1	3	.313	.214
Wilson, Dan	.143	7	1	0	0	1	0	.250	.143
Young, Eric	.400	5	2	0	1	0	0	.400	.400
Zeile, Todd	.333	3	0	0	0	2	1	.500	.000

Calvin Maduro, Phillies — RHP

Batter	Avg	AB	H	HR	BI	BB	SO	OBP	Slg
Everett, Carl#	.600	5	3	0	0	1	1	.667	.800
Hardtke, J#	.000	4	0	0	0	0	2	.000	.000
Hundley, Todd#	.000	5	0	0	0	1	1	.167	.000
Huskey, Butch	.500	6	3	1	4	0	0	.500	1.333
Johnson, L*	.333	6	2	0	0	0	0	.333	.333
Ochoa, Alex	.167	6	1	0	0	0	1	.167	.167
Petagine, Rob*	.200	5	1	0	0	0	3	.200	.200

Mike Magnante, Royals — LHP

Batter	Avg	AB	H	HR	BI	BB	SO	OBP	Slg
Alomar, R#	.429	14	6	0	1	2	1	.500	.571
Alomar Jr, S	.500	8	4	0	2	1	0	.556	.500
Amaral, Rich	.222	9	2	0	2	0	0	.222	.222
Anderson, Brd*	.333	15	5	0	1	1	3	.412	.467
Baerga, C#	.500	10	5	1	4	0	0	.455	.800
Baines, H*	.235	17	4	1	3	0	3	.235	.412
Belle, Albert	.667	6	4	0	3	2	1	.600	.667
Boggs, Wade*	.308	13	4	0	0	3	1	.438	.308
Bonilla, B#	.200	5	1	0	0	0	0	.200	.200
Borders, Pat	.200	5	1	0	0	0	0	.200	.200
Bordick, Mike	.250	8	2	0	2	1	1	.333	.250
Buhner, Jay	.200	10	2	0	0	1	0	.273	.200
Burks, Ellis	.000	5	0	0	0	1	0	.000	.000
Carter, Joe	.273	11	3	0	0	0	3	.273	.273
Clark, Will*	.400	5	2	0	1	1	0	.500	.400
Cole, Alex*	.600	5	3	0	1	0	0	.600	1.000
Davis, Chili#	.222	9	2	0	1	3	0	.300	.222
Devereaux, M	.200	10	2	0	1	1	3	.273	.200
Fielder, C	.000	5	0	0	0	0	3	.000	.000
Fryman, T	.333	6	2	1	1	0	1	.333	1.000
Gagne, Greg	.125	8	1	0	1	0	1	.125	.250
Gallego, Mike	.875	8	7	1	4	0	0	.875	1.750
Gomez, Leo	.600	5	3	1	5	3	1	.667	1.400
Gonzalez, J	.167	6	1	0	0	0	0	.167	.167
Grebeck, C	.375	8	3	0	1	2	1	.500	.750
Greenwell, M*	.571	7	4	1	1	0	0	.571	1.000
Griffey Jr, K*	.308	13	4	1	2	1	2	.357	.615
Guillen, O*	.444	9	4	0	2	1	0	.500	.889
Hall, Mel*	.714	7	5	0	1	0	1	.714	1.000
Hamilton, D*	.300	10	3	0	0	0	0	.300	.300
Hammonds, J	.000	6	0	0	0	0	1	.000	.000
Henderson, R	.000	3	0	0	0	2	1	.400	.000
Hollins, Dave#	.200	5	1	0	0	0	1	.200	.200
Huff, Michael	.125	8	1	0	0	0	0	.125	.125
Jaha, John	.333	6	2	1	4	0	0	.333	.833
Johnson, L*	.111	9	1	0	0	0	0	.111	.222
Karkovice, R	.111	9	1	0	0	1	2	.200	.111
Kelly, Pat	.222	9	2	0	1	0	1	.222	.222
Kelly, R	.667	3	2	0	2	1	0	.600	.667
Kent, Jeff	.333	3	1	0	3	0	0	.333	.333
Knoblauch, C	.278	18	5	1	3	2	1	.350	.611
Leius, Scott	.375	8	3	0	0	3	0	.545	.500
Leyritz, Jim	.250	4	1	0	0	3	0	.571	.250
Listach, Pat#	.167	6	1	1	2	0	0	.286	.667
Livingstone*	.400	5	2	0	0	0	1	.400	.400
Lofton, Kenny*	.250	8	2	0	1	1	0	.333	.250
Martinez, E	.286	7	2	0	1	1	2	.375	.429
Martinez, T*	.250	12	3	0	0	0	2	.250	.250
McCarty, Dave	.200	5	1	0	0	1	0	.200	.200
McGwire, Mark	.250	4	1	0	0	3	1	.571	.250
Meares, Pat	.200	10	2	0	2	0	2	.200	.200
Molitor, Paul	.400	5	2	0	0	1	0	.500	.400
Munoz, Pedro	.273	11	3	0	0	1	0	.333	.273
Myers, Greg*	.286	7	2	0	2	1	3	.375	.286
Naehring, Tim	.333	6	2	0	2	0	0	.333	.667
Nilsson, Dave*	.429	7	3	1	2	0	1	.429	.857
O'Neill, Paul*	.125	8	1	0	0	0	2	.125	.125
Olerud, John*	.182	11	2	0	0	1	1	.250	.182
Orsulak, Joe*	.286	7	2	0	3	0	1	.286	.286
Palmeiro, R*	.294	17	5	0	2	2	0	.368	.353
Palmer, Dean	.500	4	2	0	2	0	2	.500	.500
Phillips, T#	.429	7	3	0	2	1	1	.500	.571
Polonia, Luis*	.000	7	0	0	1	1	1	.125	.000
Raines, Tim#	.214	14	3	0	1	2	1	.313	.286
Ramirez, M	.600	5	3	0	2	2	0	.714	1.000
Reed, Jody	.600	5	3	0	0	0	0	.600	.600

Mike Magnante, Royals — LHP

Batter	Avg	AB	H	HR	BI	BB	SO	OBP	Slg
Ripken, Billy	.200	5	1	1	0	0	0	.200	.800
Ripken, Cal	.455	11	5	0	2	0	0	.455	.636
Rodriguez, I	.833	6	5	1	2	0	0	.833	1.500
Seitzer, K	.000	8	0	0	0	0	1	.000	.000
Sierra, Ruben#	.333	6	2	0	2	0	1	.333	.333
Sojo, Luis	.125	8	1	0	0	0	0	.125	.125
Sorrento, P*	.111	9	1	0	0	1	2	.200	.111
Stanley, Mike	.286	7	2	1	3	1	0	.500	.714
Surhoff, B.J.*	.000	6	0	0	0	1	0	.250	.000
Tartabull, D	.250	8	2	0	3	1	3	.300	.375
Tettleton, M#	.600	5	3	1	2	1	1	.667	1.200
Thomas, Frank	.385	13	5	0	0	1	2	.429	.462
Thome, Jim*	.167	6	1	0	2	2	1	.375	.333
Valentin, Jhn	.000	3	0	0	0	2	0	.400	.000
Valentin, Jse#	.250	4	1	0	0	0	1	.250	.500
Vaughn, Greg	.200	5	1	0	0	2	0	.429	.200
Vaughn, Mo*	.400	5	2	1	5	1	0	.500	1.000
Velarde, R	.286	7	2	1	3	0	2	.286	.714
Ventura, R*	.400	15	6	1	1	2	1	.471	.600
Vizquel, Omar#	.167	6	1	0	0	1	1	.286	.167
White, Devon#	.333	12	4	0	1	0	0	.385	.333
Whiten, Mark#	.333	3	1	0	0	2	0	.600	.333
Williams, Ber#	.182	11	2	0	0	2	3	.308	.273
Wilson, Dan	.333	6	2	0	1	0	0	.286	.333
Zaun, Greg#	.167	6	1	0	0	2	1	.375	.167

Joe Magrane, White Sox — LHP

Batter	Avg	AB	H	HR	BI	BB	SO	OBP	Slg
Aldrete, Mike*	.500	6	3	0	0	0	0	.500	.500
Alomar, R#	.333	18	6	0	1	1	4	.368	.444
Alou, Moises	.200	10	2	0	1	1	0	.273	.200
Amaral, Rich	.563	16	9	0	3	1	1	.588	.625
Anthony, Eric*	.286	7	2	0	0	2	2	.444	.429
Bagwell, Jeff	.429	7	3	0	4	0	0	.429	.571
Bell, Jay	.269	26	7	0	0	4	6	.367	.385
Belliard, R	.125	8	1	0	0	0	1	.125	.125
Berroa, G	.400	10	4	1	3	0	3	.400	.700
Biggio, Craig	.211	19	4	0	3	5	1	.375	.211
Blauser, Jeff	.182	22	4	0	0	2	3	.250	.227
Blowers, Mike	.455	11	5	2	6	0	5	.455	1.000
Boggs, Wade*	.250	4	1	0	0	1	0	.400	.250
Bonds, Barry*	.296	27	8	1	4	7	4	.441	.593
Bonilla, B#	.273	44	12	0	4	5	4	.360	.295
Brosius, S	.400	5	2	0	0	0	0	.400	.600
Buhner, Jay	.273	11	3	1	2	5	2	.500	.727
Butler, Brett*	.320	25	8	0	1	2	2	.370	.360
Caminiti, Ken#	.346	26	9	0	3	4	5	.433	.423
Cangelosi, J#	.294	17	5	0	0	2	1	.368	.471
Canseco, Jose	.273	11	3	1	3	1	3	.333	.636
Carr, Chuck	.300	10	3	0	2	0	0	.300	.400
Carreon, Mark	.167	6	1	0	0	0	2	.167	.167
Carter, Joe	.167	12	2	0	2	2	1	.267	.250
Cedeno, A	.333	6	2	0	1	0	0	.333	.500
Clark, Will*	.333	24	8	1	6	5	6	.452	.500
Colbrunn, G	.000	12	0	0	1	0	4	.000	.000
Coleman, V#	.182	11	2	0	0	0	2	.182	.182
Conine, Jeff	.250	4	1	1	1	2	1	.500	1.000
Cora, Joey#	.250	8	2	0	1	0	1	.250	.250
Cordero, Wil	.400	10	4	0	0	0	0	.400	.400
Dascenzo, D#	.167	12	2	0	1	0	1	.167	.167
Daulton, D*	.222	9	2	0	0	2	2	.364	.444
Davis, Chili#	.286	7	2	0	0	1	1	.375	.286
Davis, Eric	.222	18	4	1	3	3	4	.333	.444
Dawson, Andre	.190	21	4	0	1	2	6	.261	.238
DeShields, D	.500	14	7	1	2	3	1	.611	.786
Duncan, M	.300	20	6	1	1	0	1	.300	.450
Dunston, S	.250	8	2	0	0	0	2	.318	.450
Dykstra, L*	.074	27	2	0	0	2	1	.138	.074
Elster, Kevin	.333	15	5	0	1	1	0	.375	.467
Fermin, Felix	.214	14	3	0	0	0	2	.214	.286
Fielder, C	.111	9	1	0	0	0	3	.111	.222
Franco, Julio	.333	3	1	0	1	1	0	.400	.667
Frye, Jeff	.222	9	2	0	1	5	0	.500	.222
Fryman, T	.429	7	3	1	3	1	1	.444	.857
Gaetti, Gary	.400	5	2	2	4	2	1	.571	1.600
Gagne, Greg	.250	8	2	0	2	1	1	.333	.375
Galarraga, A	.310	42	13	0	5	2	3	.341	.405
Gant, Ron	.368	19	7	3	4	1	0	.400	.895
Garcia, C	.800	5	4	0	0	0	0	.800	1.600
Girardi, Joe	.583	12	7	0	3	0	1	.538	.667
Gomez, Chris	.714	7	5	0	2	1	0	.778	.857
Gonzalez, J	.286	7	2	0	2	1	0	.375	.571
Gonzalez, L*	.600	6	4	0	1	0	0	.714	.833
Grace, Mark*	.182	11	2	0	2	1	2	.250	.455
Griffey Jr, K*	.333	15	5	2	4	2	2	.412	.733
Grissom, M	.250	16	4	0	1	1	2	.294	.250
Gwynn, Tony*	.289	38	11	0	1	4	0	.308	.368
Hamilton, D*	.333	9	3	0	0	0	3	.333	.556
Haney, Todd	.333	6	2	0	1	0	0	.333	.333
Hayes, C	.250	20	5	0	3	1	0	.333	.250
Hollins, Dave#	.667	6	4	2	4	2	0	.750	1.667
Hudler, Rex	.400	15	6	2	6	1	1	.444	1.000
Hunter, Brian	.286	7	2	1	2	0	0	.286	.857
Jaha, John	.250	8	2	0	2	3	2	.455	.250
Javier, Stan#	.286	7	2	0	0	0	0	.286	.286
Jefferies, G#	.417	12	5	0	3	0	0	.533	.667
Jordan, Ricky	.368	38	14	0	8	2	3	.390	.474
Justice, Dave*	.375	8	3	0	2	1	2	.444	.375
Kelly, R	.143	7	1	0	0	0	0	.250	.286
Kent, Jeff	.500	6	3	0	0	1	1	.571	.667
King, Jeff	.308	26	8	0	2	1	0	.321	.500
Lansing, Mike	.333	6	2	0	0	1	1	.429	.333
Larkin, Barry	.474	19	9	0	5	5	1	.560	.632
Lemke, Mark#	.333	9	3	0	1	1	2	.400	.333
Leyritz, Jim	.000	4	0	0	0	1	1	.333	.000
Listach, Pat#	.143	7	1	0	1	1	0	.250	.286
Macfarlane, M	.571	7	4	0	2	0	1	.625	.857
Magadan, Dave*	.133	15	2	0	1	0	4	.133	.267
Malave, Jose	.500	6	3	2	2	0	0	.500	1.500
Manwaring, K	.200	5	1	0	0	0	2	.200	.200
Martinez, Da*	.500	6	3	0	3	1	1	.571	.833
Martinez, E	.500	8	4	2	8	6	0	.667	1.500
Martinez, T*	.600	5	3	0	1	1	0	.667	.600
McGriff, Fred*	.400	5	2	2	3	1	0	.500	1.600
McRae, Brian#	.167	6	1	0	1	2	0	.375	.167
Mieske, Matt	.200	5	1	0	0	1	0	.333	.400
Mitchell, K	.217	23	5	0	3	1	5	.250	.348
Morandini, M*	.286	7	2	0	1	0	0	.286	.286
Munoz, Pedro	.167	6	1	0	1	0	2	.167	.333
Murray, Eddie#	.227	22	5	1	1	1	3	.261	.409
Naehring, Tim	.200	5	1	0	0	1	2	.333	.200
Nixon, Otis#	.121	33	4	0	1	4	3	.216	.121
O'Brien, C	.333	9	3	0	0	0	0	.333	.444
O'Leary, Troy*	.200	5	1	0	0	0	1	.333	.200
O'Neill, Paul*	.200	20	4	0	3	2	3	.273	.250
Oliver, Joe	.133	15	2	0	0	0	2	.133	.133
Palmeiro, R*	.308	13	4	1	5	1	1	.357	.615
Palmer, Dean	.600	5	3	2	4	1	0	.667	1.800
Parent, Mark	.200	10	2	0	0	2	0	.333	.300
Parker, Rick	.000	6	0	0	0	0	1	.000	.000
Pendleton, T#	.286	7	2	1	2	1	0	.333	.714
Phillips, T#	.333	6	2	0	1	5	1	.636	.333
Plantier, P*	.200	5	1	0	0	1	3	.333	.200
Prince, Tom	.000	7	0	0	0	0	1	.000	.000
Raines, Tim#	.257	35	9	1	4	3	2	.316	.429
Reed, Jody	.200	5	1	0	0	1	0	.333	.200
Ripken, Billy	.000	5	0	0	0	1	0	.167	.000
Roberts, Bip#	.143	14	2	0	0	1	2	.200	.143
Rodriguez, Al	.167	6	1	1	3	1	0	.286	.667
Rodriguez, I	.429	7	3	0	0	0	0	.429	.429
Sabo, Chris	.333	21	7	0	0	1	1	.417	.429
Samuel, Juan	.407	27	11	2	3	2	4	.467	.741
Sandberg, R	.222	27	6	3	4	4	3	.313	.370
Sanders, R	.167	6	1	0	0	0	2	.167	.167
Santiago, B	.174	23	4	0	1	1	2	.240	.174
Schu, Rick	.667	3	2	0	0	0	0	.800	.667
Seitzer, K	.222	9	2	0	0	0	0	.222	.222
Shumpert, T	.200	5	1	1	0	0	0	.200	.800
Sierra, Ruben#	.250	4	1	0	3	1	1	.333	.250
Slaught, Don	.455	11	5	1	1	0	1	.455	.727
Sojo, Luis	.000	8	0	0	2	0	0	.200	.000
Stanley, Mike	.125	8	1	0	0	1	0	.222	.125
Strawberry, D*	.435	23	10	0	5	3	5	.500	.522
Surhoff, B.J.*	.200	10	2	0	1	0	2	.200	.200
Tettleton, M#	.429	7	3	0	0	2	2	.556	.714
Thompson, Rob	.389	18	7	0	2	2	2	.476	.444
Trammell, A	.000	7	0	0	0	1	2	.125	.000
Valentin, Jhn	.800	5	4	1	2	2	0	.857	2.600
Vaughn, Greg	.222	9	2	0	3	0	1	.417	.333
Vaughn, Mo*	.333	6	2	0	0	0	3	.333	.500
Velarde, R	.000	5	0	0	0	1	0	.167	.000
Walker, Larry*	.143	7	1	0	0	0	0	.333	.143
Wallach, Tim	.348	46	16	2	9	4	11	.392	.674
Walton, J	.167	6	1	0	0	0	2	.167	.333
Weiss, Walt#	.000	4	0	0	0	1	0	.333	.000
Williams, Ber#	.200	5	1	0	0	0	2	.200	.200
Williams, Ma	.250	8	2	0	2	1	0	.400	.250
Wilson, Dan	.250	12	3	0	0	0	0	.250	.333
Young, Kevin	.200	5	1	0	1	1	0	.333	.200

Pat Mahomes, Red Sox — RHP

Batter	Avg	AB	H	HR	BI	BB	SO	OBP	Slg
Alomar, R#	.182	11	2	0	0	1	1	.357	.182
Amaral, Rich	.333	6	2	0	0	1	0	.333	.500
Anderson, Brd*	.250	12	3	1	1	1	0	.308	.583
Baerga, C#	.231	13	3	0	1	0	0	.231	.308
Baines, H*	.375	16	6	1	5	3	1	.450	.563
Bautista, D	.000	5	0	0	0	0	1	.000	.000
Bell, Derek	.750	4	3	0	1	1	0	.800	1.000
Belle, Albert	.385	13	5	1	5	3	1	.500	.846
Beltre, E	.000	6	0	0	0	0	0	.000	.000
Berroa, G	.364	11	4	1	3	1	2	.417	.727

Pat Mahomes, Red Sox — RHP

Batter	Avg	AB	H	HR	BI	BB	SO	OBP	Slg
Blowers, Mike	.286	7	2	1	4	1	1	.375	.714
Boggs, Wade*	.182	11	2	1	1	2	1	.308	.455
Borders, Pat	.000	8	0	0	0	1	1	.111	.000
Bordick, Mike	.091	11	1	0	2	1	1	.167	.091
Brosius, S	.429	7	3	2	4	0	1	.375	1.286
Buhner, Jay	.300	10	3	1	4	3	4	.429	.600
Burks, Ellis	.500	6	3	0	3	0	1	.500	1.167
Canseco, Jose	.158	19	3	1	2	0	10	.158	.316
Carr, Chuck	.333	6	2	0	0	0	1	.333	.500
Carter, Joe	.278	18	5	0	2	0	1	.278	.500
Cedeno, D#	.200	5	1	0	0	0	1	.200	.200
Cirillo, Jeff	.143	7	1	0	2	0	1	.143	.143
Clark, Wade*	.600	15	9	2	4	2	0	.647	1.067
Coleman, V#	.500	2	1	0	0	3	0	.800	.500
Cora, Joey#	.250	16	4	0	3	3	1	.368	.375
Curtis, Chad	.333	6	2	0	1	1	1	.375	.500
Delgado, C*	.600	5	3	0	0	1	0	.667	.800
Devereaux, M	.143	7	1	0	2	0	1	.143	.429
Durham, Ray#	.200	5	1	0	0	0	1	.200	.400
Fielder, C	.083	12	1	1	2	1	5	.154	.333
Franco, Julio	.167	6	1	0	0	0	2	.167	.167
Frye, Jeff	.400	5	2	0	0	0	1	.400	.400
Fryman, T	.364	11	4	0	6	4	1	.471	.455
Gaetti, Gary	.333	6	2	0	0	2	2	.500	.333
Gagne, Greg	.143	7	1	0	1	1	0	.250	.143
Gallego, Mike	.333	9	3	0	1	0	1	.333	.333
Gates, Brent#	.615	13	8	3	7	1	0	.667	1.385
Giambi, Jason*	.500	4	2	0	0	1	0	.600	.500
Girardi, Joe	.250	4	1	0	0	1	0	.250	.250
Gomez, Chris	.091	11	1	0	0	1	1	.167	.091
Gomez, Leo	.091	11	1	0	0	2	2	.231	.091
Gonzalez, J	.273	22	6	1	3	0	0	.273	.409
Goodwin, Tom*	.600	5	3	0	0	1	0	.667	1.200
Green, Shawn*	.400	5	2	0	1	0	3	.400	.400
Greenwell, M*	.500	4	2	0	2	1	0	.600	.750
Greer, Rusty*	.286	7	2	0	0	3	1	.500	.429
Griffey Jr, K*	.231	13	3	2	7	0	3	.231	.846
Guillen, O*	.200	10	2	0	2	0	0	.200	.200
Hamelin, Bob*	.625	8	5	1	3	0	1	.625	1.000
Hamilton, D*	.250	4	1	0	0	2	0	.500	.500
Hammonds, J	.333	9	3	0	0	0	1	.333	.444
Henderson, R	.333	12	4	2	2	3	3	.467	.833
Higginson, B*	.500	4	2	0	1	2	0	.667	.500
Hoiles, Chris	.000	6	0	0	0	1	1	.143	.000
Hulse, David*	.111	9	1	0	1	1	2	.200	.111
Jaha, John	.286	7	2	2	4	4	2	.545	1.143
Javier, Stan#	.500	6	3	0	0	0	1	.500	.500
Johnson, L*	.529	17	9	0	3	0	0	.529	.706
Joyner, Wally*	.375	8	3	0	3	2	0	.500	.625
Karkovice, R	.250	12	3	1	2	2	3	.357	.667
Kelly, Pat	.200	5	1	0	0	2	2	.400	.400
Kreuter, Chad#	.333	6	2	1	2	0	1	.333	.833
Levis, Jesse*	.250	4	1	0	0	1	0	.400	.500
Lewis, Mark	.333	6	2	0	0	0	0	.333	.500
Leyritz, Jim	.200	5	1	0	0	0	2	.200	.200
Lockhart, K*	.333	6	2	0	1	0	2	.333	.500
Lofton, Kenny*	.143	7	1	0	1	4	1	.455	.143
Macfarlane, M	.000	8	0	0	0	0	0	.000	.000
Martinez, E	.444	9	4	0	3	2	0	.545	.556
Martinez, S*	.000	4	0	0	0	1	2	.200	.000
Martinez, T*	.000	7	0	0	0	0	2	.000	.000
McGwire, Mark	.364	11	4	1	2	3	2	.533	.727
McLemore, M	.429	14	6	1	3	5	3	.579	.786
McRae, Brian#	.000	5	0	0	0	0	1	.000	.000
Mieske, Matt	.222	9	2	1	3	1	0	.300	.556
Molitor, Paul	.571	7	4	0	0	1	0	.625	.857
Murray, Eddie#	.385	13	5	2	6	0	2	.385	1.000
Newson, W*	.429	7	3	2	2	0	1	.429	1.286
Nilsson, Dave*	.222	9	2	1	1	0	1	.222	.556
Nixon, Otis#	.250	4	1	0	0	1	1	.400	.250
O'Leary, Troy*	.500	4	2	1	3	2	0	.667	1.500
O'Neill, Jeff*	.375	8	3	1	2	0	1	.375	.875
Olerud, John*	.200	15	3	1	5	1	1	.222	.467
Palmeiro, R	.313	16	5	1	2	3	2	.421	.625
Palmer, Dean	.250	8	2	1	1	4	2	.500	.625
Paquette, C	.167	6	1	0	0	0	1	.167	.167
Pena, Tony	.000	6	0	0	0	0	3	.000	.000
Phillips, T#	.308	13	4	1	3	0	1	.308	.615
Plantier, P*	.000	6	0	0	0	0	1	.000	.000
Polonia, Luis*	.333	9	3	0	0	2	0	.455	.333
Raines, Tim#	.286	14	4	1	3	3	4	.444	.500
Ramirez, M	.286	7	2	1	3	3	2	.500	.857
Reed, Jody	.500	4	2	0	1	1	0	.600	.500
Ripken, Cal	.267	15	4	1	3	3	1	.389	.667
Rodriguez, I	.000	11	0	0	1	0	0	.000	.000
Seitzer, K	.455	11	5	1	4	1	1	.500	.818
Sierra, Ruben#	.231	13	3	2	3	1	2	.286	.692
Smith, Dwight*	.600	5	3	0	0	1	0	.667	.600
Sojo, Luis	.000	4	0	0	0	2	1	.333	.000
Sorrento, P*	.364	11	4	0	3	0	0	.364	.455
Sprague, Ed	.143	7	1	0	0	0	1	.143	.286
Stanley, Mike	.286	7	2	0	0	0	2	.286	.571
Steinbach, T	.167	12	2	1	3	3	3	.333	.500
Strange, Doug#	.333	9	3	0	0	0	1	.333	.333
Tartabull, D	.250	4	1	0	1	2	0	.500	.250
Tettleton, M#	.500	6	3	2	3	5	2	.727	1.667
Thomas, Frank	.235	17	4	2	6	1	1	.263	.647
Thome, Jim*	.375	8	3	1	1	2	2	.500	.750
Tinsley, Lee#	.000	3	0	0	0	2	0	.400	.000
Valentin, Jhn	.400	5	2	0	1	1	1	.500	.400
Valentin, Jse#	.250	8	2	0	1	1	0	.333	.250
Valle, Dave	.100	10	1	0	0	1	2	.182	.200
Vaughn, Greg	.429	7	3	0	1	3	2	.600	.429
Vaughn, Mo*	.000	4	0	0	0	1	2	.200	.000
Ventura, R*	.333	15	5	0	0	4	0	.474	.400
Vina, F*	.375	8	3	0	0	0	1	.375	.625
Vizquel, Omar#	.444	9	4	0	0	1	0	.500	.556
Voigt, Jack	.200	5	1	0	0	0	2	.200	.200
White, Devon#	.286	14	4	1	2	0	3	.286	.500
Williams, Ber#	.200	5	1	0	1	3	0	.500	.200
Wilson, Dan	.143	7	1	0	0	0	3	.143	.143

Matt Mantei, Marlins — RHP

Batter	Avg	AB	H	HR	BI	BB	SO	OBP	Slg
Cedeno, A	.500	4	2	0	0	0	1	.600	.500
Thompson, Rob	.333	3	1	0	0	2	1	.600	.333

Barry Manuel, Expos — RHP

Batter	Avg	AB	H	HR	BI	BB	SO	OBP	Slg
Gaetti, Gary	.000	5	0	0	0	0	1	.000	.000
Hayes, C	.000	5	0	0	0	0	2	.000	.000
Sanders, R	.400	5	2	1	2	0	0	.400	1.200

Dennis Martinez, Indians — RHP

Batter	Avg	AB	H	HR	BI	BB	SO	OBP	Slg
Aldrete, Mike*	.433	30	13	0	2	1	5	.452	.467
Alicea, Luis#	.200	20	4	0	0	0	3	.200	.250
Alomar, R#	.229	35	8	0	2	0	2	.229	.257
Anderson, Brd*	.118	17	2	0	1	2	1	.211	.118
Anderson, G*	.200	5	1	0	1	0	0	.200	.200
Anthony, Eric*	.286	28	8	1	3	1	9	.300	.393
Bagwell, Jeff	.389	18	7	0	3	1	2	.450	.444
Baines, H*	.323	31	10	2	7	2	3	.353	.581
Barberie, B#	.308	13	4	0	0	1	1	.357	.308
Becker, Rich*	.368	19	7	0	0	0	4	.368	.368
Bell, Derek	.400	10	4	0	0	0	0	.400	.500
Bell, Jay	.164	67	11	0	2	2	10	.188	.224
Belliard, R	.174	23	4	0	4	2	5	.269	.174
Beltre, E	.125	8	1	0	0	0	2	.125	.125
Berroa, G	.545	11	6	1	2	0	3	.545	.909
Bichette, D	.231	13	3	0	1	0	5	.231	.231
Biggio, Craig	.300	40	12	1	5	4	7	.364	.550
Blauser, Jeff	.242	33	8	0	0	2	4	.306	.273
Blowers, Mike	.167	6	1	0	0	0	0	.167	.167
Boggs, Wade*	.361	36	13	1	2	4	3	.425	.556
Bonds, Barry*	.228	92	21	1	7	7	8	.283	.337
Bonilla, B#	.225	80	18	0	7	8	18	.295	.363
Bordick, Mike	.091	11	1	0	1	2	1	.231	.091
Bragg, Darren*	.400	5	2	0	0	1	0	.500	.400
Branson, Jeff*	.200	10	2	1	1	0	2	.200	.500
Brosius, S	.429	7	3	0	0	1	1	.429	.714
Buhner, Jay	.333	12	4	0	1	1	0	.385	.667
Butler, Brett*	.314	51	16	0	1	6	3	.386	.392
Caminiti, Ken#	.200	35	7	0	0	5	8	.300	.200
Candaele, C#	.200	8	2	0	3	0	0	.250	.250
Cangelosi, J#	.353	17	6	0	2	0	2	.353	.471
Canseco, Jose	.200	10	2	1	3	1	3	.273	.500
Carr, Chuck	.083	12	1	0	1	0	1	.083	.083
Carter, Joe	.156	32	5	0	1	4	4	.250	.188
Castilla, V	.400	5	2	0	0	0	0	.500	.400
Cedeno, A	.000	9	0	0	0	3	0	.000	.000
Cedeno, D#	.000	10	2	0	0	1	0	.200	.200
Cianfrocco, A	.000	3	0	0	0	2	2	.500	.000
Cirillo, Jeff	.375	8	3	0	1	1	1	.444	.500
Clark, Dave*	.100	10	1	0	1	4	2	.357	.100
Clark, Will*	.286	63	18	3	9	7	12	.357	.476
Clayton, R	.125	8	1	0	0	1	0	.222	.125
Cole, Alex*	.290	31	9	0	3	6	7	.405	.419
Coleman, V#	.216	74	16	0	3	5	10	.275	.257
Conine, Jeff	.333	6	2	0	0	1	0	.429	.333
Cora, Joey#	.125	16	2	0	0	0	3	.125	.188
Cordero, Wil	.167	6	1	0	0	0	0	.167	.167
Cordova, M	.333	9	3	0	2	0	1	.333	.556
Curtis, Chad	.100	10	1	0	0	1	3	.091	.000
Dascenzo, D#	.389	18	7	0	0	2	1	.450	.389
Daulton, D*	.200	16	3	1	5	4	3	.282	.343
Davis, Chili#	.364	11	4	1	6	3	2	.467	.636
Davis, Eric	.400	45	18	1	4	6	13	.481	.489
Dawson, Andre	.281	57	16	2	8	4	4	.339	.509
Delgado, C*	.556	9	5	0	1	2	0	.583	.667
Devereaux, M	.222	9	2	0	2	1	3	.300	.222
DiSarcina, G	.250	8	2	0	0	0	1	.250	.250

Batter	Avg	AB	H	HR	BI	BB	SO	OBP	Slg
Duncan, M	.310	29	9	1	4	0	5	.310	.448
Dunston, S	.186	43	8	0	3	0	4	.186	.326
Durham, Ray#	.182	11	2	0	0	0	4	.182	.182
Dykstra, L*	.219	64	14	4	8	7	10	.296	.516
Edmonds, Jim*	.250	8	2	0	0	1	1	.333	.375
Eisenreich, J*	.273	11	3	1	2	0	0	.250	.636
Elster, Kevin	.185	27	5	1	3	0	2	.185	.370
Fermin, Felix	.000	6	0	0	0	0	0	.000	.000
Fielder, C	.273	11	3	0	0	0	1	.273	.273
Finley, Steve*	.238	21	5	0	0	0	1	.238	.333
Flaherty, J	.333	9	3	0	0	0	0	.333	.556
Fletcher, D*	.167	6	1	0	0	0	0	.167	.167
Franco, Julio	.267	15	4	0	4	3	4	.368	.333
Fryman, C	.545	11	6	0	0	4	2	.667	.636
Gaetti, Gary	.412	17	7	0	2	1	1	.421	.529
Gagne, Greg	.273	11	3	0	2	0	1	.333	.455
Galarraga, A	.389	18	7	2	7	1	4	.450	.889
Gant, Ron	.263	38	10	2	4	0	8	.282	.500
Gates, Brent#	.200	10	2	0	2	1	0	.231	.200
Giambi, Jason*	.333	9	3	0	0	1	1	.400	.333
Gilkey, B	.200	10	2	1	3	0	2	.200	.500
Girardi, Joe	.241	29	7	0	2	3	6	.313	.345
Gomez, Chris	.333	9	3	0	0	0	0	.333	.333
Gomez, Leo	.556	9	5	0	2	0	1	.556	.778
Gonzalez, A	.000	7	0	0	0	3	1	.300	.000
Gonzalez, J	.200	5	1	0	1	0	0	.200	.200
Gonzalez, L*	.154	13	2	0	1	0	2	.154	.154
Grace, Mark*	.255	55	14	2	6	5	6	.317	.400
Green, Shawn*	.533	15	8	1	2	1	0	.588	.800
Greene, W*	.600	5	3	0	0	0	1	.600	.800
Greenwell, M*	.375	16	6	0	1	2	1	.444	.375
Griffey Jr, K*	.308	13	4	1	2	1	4	.357	.615
Guillen, O*	.042	24	1	0	0	0	1	.042	.042
Gutierrez, R	.250	8	2	1	1	0	2	.250	.625
Gwynn, Tony*	.265	49	13	0	3	1	1	.280	.327
Hale, Chip*	.222	9	2	0	0	0	2	.222	.333
Hall, Mel*	.000	5	0	0	1	0	1	.000	.000
Hamelin, Bob*	.111	9	1	0	0	2	1	.111	.111
Hamilton, D*	.143	7	1	0	0	0	1	.143	.143
Hammonds, J	.111	9	1	0	0	0	0	.111	.111
Hansen, Dave*	.286	7	2	0	0	0	0	.286	.286
Harris, Lenny*	.179	28	5	0	0	0	3	.179	.179
Hayes, C	.194	31	6	0	2	1	7	.212	.290
Henderson, R*	.421	19	8	1	1	3	1	.522	.737
Hoiles, Chris	.000	4	0	0	1	1	4	.167	.000
Hollins, Dave#	.200	20	4	1	2	0	3	.200	.400
Hosey, Dwayne*	.000	4	0	0	0	4	1	.500	.000
Howard, T*	.154	13	2	1	1	2	1	.267	.385
Howell, Jack*	.000	8	0	0	0	2	0	.200	.000
Hudler, Rex	.250	4	1	0	0	1	1	.400	.500
Hulse, David*	.368	19	7	0	3	0	0	.368	.526
Hundley, Todd#	.154	13	2	0	0	1	1	.214	.231
Incaviglia, J	.250	12	3	1	2	2	2	.357	.750
Jaha, John	.400	15	6	1	2	1	3	.438	.667
James, Dion*	.211	19	4	0	0	1	2	.250	.316
Javier, Stan#	.053	19	1	1	1	0	3	.053	.211
Jefferies, G#	.400	30	12	0	3	5	2	.486	.533
Jefferson, R*	.125	8	1	0	0	1	2	.222	.125
Jeter, Derek	.429	7	3	1	3	0	1	.429	.857
Johnson, L*	.100	20	2	0	1	1	1	.143	.100
Jordan, Ricky	.364	11	4	1	3	0	2	.364	.636
Joyner, Wally*	.000	7	0	0	0	0	0	.000	.000
Justice, Dave*	.310	29	9	2	6	6	3	.429	.621
Karkovice, R	.273	11	3	0	0	0	3	.273	.364
Karros, Eric	.267	15	4	2	3	0	1	.267	.667
Kelly, Pat	.000	8	0	0	0	2	0	.200	.000
Kelly, R	.571	7	4	0	0	0	0	.571	.714
Kent, Jeff	.444	9	4	1	3	1	0	.500	1.000
King, Jeff	.136	22	3	0	1	0	2	.136	.182
Knoblauch, C	.250	20	5	0	0	2	3	.400	.450
Knorr, Randy	.286	7	2	0	0	0	1	.286	.286
Lankford, Ray*	.286	14	4	0	0	3	3	.412	.286
Larkin, Barry	.244	41	10	0	3	2	3	.311	.341
Leius, Scott	.286	14	4	0	2	3	2	.412	.429
Lemke, Mark#	.353	17	6	0	0	2	3	.421	.412
Lewis, Darren	.375	8	3	1	3	1	1	.444	.750
Lewis, Mark	.125	8	1	0	0	0	0	.125	.125
Listach, Pat#	.250	12	3	0	1	0	3	.250	.250
Macfarlane, M	.111	9	1	0	2	0	2	.200	.222
Magadan, Dave*	.341	44	14	1	2	5	6	.413	.488
Manwaring, K	.083	12	1	0	1	0	1	.083	.083
Martinez, Da*	.219	32	7	1	3	2	2	.257	.344
Martinez, E	.400	10	4	1	2	1	1	.500	.800
Martinez, S*	.400	5	2	0	2	0	1	.400	.400
Martinez, T*	.125	16	5	1	5	1	1	.438	.600
Matheny, Mike	.167	6	1	0	0	0	0	.167	.500
May, Derrick*	.400	20	8	2	8	2	1	.455	.800
McGee, Willie*	.269	52	14	1	4	0	7	.269	.385
McGriff, Fred*	.348	23	8	2	5	5	3	.464	.696
McGwire, Mark	.200	5	1	0	1	3	3	.333	.200
McLemore, M#	.333	9	3	0	1	4	1	.538	.333

Batter	Avg	AB	H	HR	BI	BB	SO	OBP	Slg
McRae, Brian#	.167	6	1	0	0	0	1	.167	.167
Meares, Pat	.273	11	3	0	1	1	2	.357	.545
Merced, O*	.250	32	8	1	3	5	5	.351	.344
Mieske, Matt	.083	12	1	0	0	0	4	.154	.167
Mitchell, K	.323	31	10	5	8	2	4	.364	.839
Molitor, Paul	.235	17	4	0	0	1	3	.316	.353
Morandini, M*	.045	22	1	0	0	1	3	.087	.045
Morris, Hal*	.250	24	6	0	2	2	2	.308	.250
Munoz, Pedro	.143	7	1	0	0	0	2	.143	.286
Murray, Eddie*	.277	47	13	0	9	2	5	.306	.362
Naehring, Tim	.273	11	3	0	2	0	0	.308	.364
Newson, W*	.333	6	2	0	0	1	0	.429	.333
Nieves, M#	.286	7	2	0	0	0	1	.286	.286
Nilsson, Dave*	.250	12	3	1	3	3	2	.400	.500
Nixon, Otis#	.135	37	5	0	2	1	2	.158	.162
O'Brien, C	.333	12	4	0	2	0	0	.385	.500
O'Leary, Troy*	.462	13	6	2	3	0	1	.462	1.154
O'Neill, Paul*	.373	59	22	4	11	4	7	.413	.712
Offerman, J#	.412	17	7	1	2	0	2	.389	.647
Olerud, John*	.111	18	2	0	0	4	1	.273	.167
Oliver, Joe	.250	20	5	0	4	5	2	.407	.300
Orsulak, Joe*	.286	14	4	0	0	1	0	.333	.429
Pagnozzi, Tom	.231	13	3	0	1	0	0	.286	.385
Palmeiro, R*	.154	26	4	1	1	0	3	.154	.269
Pena, Tony	.194	36	7	0	0	3	3	.256	.194
Pendleton, T#	.222	63	14	0	7	3	10	.258	.302
Perez, Tomas#	.167	6	1	0	0	0	0	.167	.167
Phillips, T#	.118	17	2	0	1	2	6	.211	.118
Piazza, Mike	.167	6	1	0	1	0	1	.167	.167
Plantier, P*	.250	8	2	0	1	1	2	.333	.250
Polonia, Luis*	.286	7	2	0	1	0	0	.286	.571
Pride, Curtis*	.000	4	0	0	0	1	2	.200	.000
Raines, Tim#	.250	16	4	0	0	2	0	.333	.313
Reboulet, J	.143	7	1	0	2	0	0	.143	.286
Reed, Jeff*	.267	15	4	1	2	4	2	.421	.467
Reed, Jody	.400	10	4	1	1	0	0	.455	.700
Ripken, Cal	.250	12	3	0	0	2	1	.400	.333
Roberts, Bip#	.425	40	17	0	3	0	5	.415	.500
Rodriguez, I	.250	8	2	0	0	0	0	.250	.375
Sabo, Chris	.214	42	9	2	4	2	7	.250	.429
Salmon, Tim	.286	7	2	1	2	1	1	.444	.714
Samuel, Juan	.213	47	10	3	4	3	8	.288	.468
Sanchez, Rey	.071	14	1	0	0	1	1	.133	.143
Sandberg, R	.352	71	25	4	11	2	5	.365	.620
Sanders, R	.250	12	3	1	1	1	7	.308	.583
Santiago, B	.256	43	11	0	1	1	5	.273	.349
Schofield, D	.235	17	4	0	1	2	1	.350	.294
Seitzer, K	.182	22	4	0	2	0	4	.182	.227
Sheffield, G	.333	15	5	1	7	2	1	.389	.733
Sierra, Ruben#	.308	13	4	1	4	4	0	.471	.538
Singleton, D*	.000	7	0	0	0	2	0	.000	.000
Slaught, Don	.429	21	9	1	4	1	0	.478	.762
Smith, Dwight*	.227	44	10	1	2	1	11	.244	.295
Smith, Ozzie#	.310	42	13	0	3	7	2	.400	.310
Snow, J.T.#	.600	5	3	1	3	2	0	.600	1.200
Sojo, Luis	.222	9	2	0	0	0	0	.222	.222
Sorrento, P*	.000	4	0	0	0	2	1	.333	.000
Sosa, Sammy	.429	14	6	1	3	1	4	.529	.643
Spiers, Bill*	.286	7	2	0	0	0	1	.286	.286
Sprague, Ed	.273	22	6	0	0	0	2	.273	.318
Stahoviak, S*	.125	8	1	0	1	0	1	.125	.125
Stanley, Mike	.273	11	3	1	1	2	1	.467	.545
Steinbach, T	.333	9	3	1	2	0	0	.333	.667
Stillwell, K#	.118	17	2	0	1	4	3	.286	.118
Stocker, K#	.333	3	1	0	0	1	0	.600	.333
Strawberry, D*	.242	62	15	2	10	8	10	.329	.371
Surhoff, B.J.*	.333	15	5	0	2	0	0	.333	.400
Tartabull, D	.250	8	2	1	2	1	2	.333	.625
Taubensee, E*	.182	11	2	0	0	0	5	.182	.273
Tettleton, M#	.000	7	0	0	0	2	0	.222	.000
Thomas, Frank	.353	17	6	3	7	6	2	.522	.941
Thompson, Mil*	.118	34	4	0	0	2	8	.167	.176
Thompson, Rob	.311	45	14	1	7	1	7	.380	.444
Tinsley, Lee#	.500	6	3	0	0	0	2	.500	.500
Trammell, A	.412	17	7	0	4	0	0	.389	.412
Valentin, Jhn	.348	23	8	1	1	0	2	.348	.609
Valentin, Jse#	.263	19	5	2	6	1	4	.300	.632
Vaughn, Greg	.381	21	8	1	2	1	2	.409	.619
Vaughn, Mo*	.333	18	6	1	3	2	4	.381	.667
Velarde, R	.143	7	1	0	0	1	1	.250	.143
Ventura, R*	.353	17	6	1	2	4	0	.476	.529
Vina, F	.500	6	3	0	0	0	0	.500	.500
Vizcaino, J#	.217	23	5	0	0	1	6	.250	.261
Walbeck, Matt#	.158	19	3	0	1	0	3	.158	.158
Wallach, Tim	.111	9	1	1	1	0	1	.111	.444
Walton, J	.364	11	4	1	1	0	0	.364	.818
Ward, Turner#	.286	7	2	1	1	0	0	.286	.714
Weiss, Walt*	.167	6	1	0	0	0	1	.167	.167
White, Devon#	.071	14	1	0	0	0	3	.133	.071
Whiten, Mark#	.222	9	2	0	0	0	2	.222	.222
Wilkins, Rick*	.100	10	1	0	0	2	3	.250	.200

Dennis Martinez, Indians — RHP

Batter	Avg	AB	H	HR	BI	BB	SO	OBP	Slg
Williams, Ber#	.381	21	8	1	5	3	2	.458	.619
Williams, Ger	.000	5	0	0	0	0	1	.000	.000
Williams, Ma	.167	30	5	0	2	1	6	.242	.233
Wilson, Dan	.250	12	3	0	3	2	3	.357	.333
Young, Eric	.250	4	1	0	0	1	0	.500	.250
Young, Kevin	.400	5	2	0	0	1	0	.500	.500
Zeile, Todd	.200	15	3	0	3	2	2	.294	.400

Pedro Martinez, Expos — RHP

Batter	Avg	AB	H	HR	BI	BB	SO	OBP	Slg
Abbott, Kurt	.111	9	1	0	0	0	6	.111	.111
Alfonzo, E	.000	6	0	0	0	1	1	.143	.000
Alicea, Luis#	.167	6	1	0	0	1	3	.286	.167
Alou, Moises	.333	6	2	0	0	1	1	.429	.333
Anthony, Eric*	.167	6	1	0	0	0	1	.167	.167
Arias, Alex	.000	5	0	0	0	1	1	.167	.000
Aurilia, Rich	.000	3	0	0	0	3	1	.500	.000
Ausmus, Brad	.000	10	0	0	0	2	4	.167	.000
Bagwell, Jeff	.267	15	4	1	4	2	4	.368	.467
Bates, Jason#	.333	6	2	0	1	1	1	.429	.500
Batiste, Kim	.111	9	1	0	0	1	3	.200	.111
Bell, Derek	.227	22	5	0	5	1	9	.261	.227
Bell, Jay	.143	14	2	0	0	5	3	.368	.143
Benard, M*	.100	10	1	0	0	0	3	.100	.100
Benjamin, M	.000	5	0	0	0	0	1	.000	.000
Berry, Sean	.333	6	2	1	3	1	1	.429	.833
Bichette, D	.143	14	2	1	1	0	4	.143	.357
Biggio, Craig	.450	20	9	0	2	6	3	.577	.800
Blauser, Jeff	.067	15	1	1	1	3	8	.333	.133
Bonds, Barry*	.458	24	11	1	3	9	5	.606	.792
Bonilla, B#	.133	15	2	2	1	5		.176	.200
Boone, Bret	.222	9	2	0	0	0	2	.222	.222
Branson, Jeff*	.200	15	3	0	2	1	2	.250	.333
Brogna, Rico*	.100	10	1	0	0	0	3	.100	.100
Brumfield, J	.143	7	1	0	0	0	2	.250	.143
Burks, Ellis	.500	4	2	2	2	1	1	.600	2.000
Burnitz, J*	.167	6	1	0	0	0	4	.167	.167
Butler, Brett*	.364	11	4	1	2	2	1	.462	.909
Caminiti, Ken#	.333	21	7	2	7	0	7	.333	.667
Cangelosi, J#	.214	14	3	0	0	1	2	.267	.214
Carr, Chuck	.364	11	4	0	1	1	2	.417	.455
Carreon, Mark	.273	11	3	0	1	2	2	.385	.364
Castilla, V	.000	8	0	0	0	0	4	.000	.000
Cedeno, A	.100	10	1	0	2	1	4	.182	.100
Cianfrocco, A	.333	6	2	0	0	0	1	.333	.333
Clark, Dave*	.000	7	0	0	0	1	4	.125	.000
Clayton, R	.235	17	4	0	2	2	5	.316	.412
Colbrunn, G	.273	11	3	0	1	4	3	.467	.273
Coleman, V#	.250	8	2	0	1	1	4	.333	.250
Conine, Jeff	.000	11	0	0	0	3	7	.214	.000
Cummings, M*	.000	5	0	0	0	1	1	.167	.000
Daulton, D*	.167	6	1	0	1	4	2	.455	.167
Davis, Eric	.250	8	2	0	1	1	2	.333	.375
DeShields, D*	.500	10	5	0	0	0	4	.500	.600
Dunston, S	.286	14	4	0	0	1	3	.333	.357
Dykstra, L*	.333	12	4	0	0	3	1	.467	.667
Eisenreich, J*	.263	19	5	0	2	1	5	.300	.368
Eusebio, Tony	.364	11	4	1	3	1	1	.417	.727
Everett, Carl*	.250	8	2	0	0	1	3	.333	.375
Finley, Steve*	.269	26	7	0	1	1	3	.321	.423
Fletcher, D*	.429	7	3	0	1	0	1	.429	.429
Gaetti, Gary	.333	6	2	2	3	0	1	.333	1.333
Galarraga, A	.273	11	3	0	0	3	5	.429	.545
Gant, Ron	.083	12	1	0	0	3	2	.267	.167
Garcia, C	.316	19	6	0	3	1	5	.381	.368
Gilkey, B	.133	15	2	0	1	2	6	.278	.200
Girardi, Joe	.429	7	3	0	1	1	1	.429	.333
Gonzalez, L*	.375	16	6	0	1	2	3	.474	.438
Grace, Mark*	.333	12	4	1	4	3	1	.438	.833
Greene, W*	.154	13	2	0	2	1	7	.214	.231
Grissom, M	.571	21	12	1	2	2	2	.609	.952
Gutierrez, R	.333	6	2	0	2	2	3	.500	.333
Gwynn, Tony*	.296	27	8	0	4	1	0	.321	.333
Harris, Lenny*	.333	6	2	0	0	0	0	.333	.333
Hayes, C	.231	13	3	0	2	2	2	.313	.308
Henderson, R	.400	5	2	0	0	1	2	.500	.400
Hernandez, Jo	.375	8	3	1	2	2	2	.500	.750
Hill, G	.105	19	2	0	1	0	8	.100	.105
Hollins, Dave#	.143	7	1	0	0	1	1	.250	.429
Howard, T*	.077	13	1	0	1	0	4	.071	.154
Hundley, Todd#	.200	25	5	1	3	3	5	.310	.360
Hunter, Bri L	.273	11	3	0	0	1	0	.333	.364
Huskey, Butch	.333	9	3	0	1	1	0	.364	.444
Javier, Stan*	.286	7	2	0	0	0	3	.286	.429
Jefferies, G#	.545	22	12	1	3	1	1	.583	.864
Johnson, Bri	.100	10	1	0	0	0	4	.100	.100
Johnson, Char	.333	6	2	1	2	0	1	.333	.833
Johnson, L*	.167	12	2	0	0	0	0	.167	.333
Johnson, Mark*	.222	9	2	0	0	1	2	.364	.222
Jones, C#	.077	13	1	0	1	2	2	.200	.077
Jordan, Brian	.500	8	4	0	0	0	2	.500	.625
Joyner, Wally*	.125	8	1	0	0	0	3	.125	.125
Justice, Dave*	.313	16	5	0	3	4	4	.450	.375
Karros, Eric	.286	7	2	1	1	2	3	.444	.857
Kelly, Mike	.167	6	1	1	2	0	4	.167	.667
Kelly, R	.000	8	0	0	0	0	5	.000	.000
Kendall, J	.182	11	2	0	1	0	0	.182	.182
Kent, Jeff	.200	20	4	1	2	1	4	.238	.350
King, Jeff	.280	25	7	1	2	1	4	.296	.400
Kingery, Mike*	.294	17	5	2	7	2	0	.350	.706
Klesko, Ryan*	.333	18	6	2	4	2	2	.400	.722
Lampkin, Tom*	.167	6	1	0	0	2	0	.375	.167
Lankford, Ray*	.143	14	2	0	0	0	6	.143	.214
Lansing, Mike	.000	5	0	0	0	0	3	.000	.000
Larkin, Barry	.217	23	5	1	3	0	3	.217	.391
Lemke, Mark*	.143	14	2	0	0	0	4	.333	.143
Lewis, Darren	.400	10	4	0	1	1	2	.455	.500
Lieberthal, M	.250	4	1	1	2	1	0	.400	1.000
Liriano, N#	.263	19	5	1	4	2	1	.333	.579
Livingstone*	.231	13	3	1	2	0	3	.231	.462
Lopez, Javy	.125	8	1	0	0	0	2	.125	.125
Lopez, Luis#	.429	7	3	1	2	1	2	.500	.857
Mabry, John*	.111	9	1	1	0	0	4	.111	.444
Magadan, Dave*	.167	12	2	0	0	2	4	.286	.167
Manwaring, K	.000	9	0	0	1	1	5	.250	.000
Martin, Al*	.304	23	7	0	1	2	8	.360	.478
Martinez, Da*	.231	13	3	1	1	0	2	.231	.538
May, Derrick*	.222	18	4	0	1	1	3	.250	.278
McGee, Willie#	.333	12	4	0	1	0	3	.333	.417
McGriff, Fred*	.250	24	6	2	4	2	7	.333	.542
McRae, Brian#	.462	13	6	0	0	1	1	.500	.769
Merced, O*	.241	29	7	0	2	0	7	.241	.276
Miller, Orl	.182	11	2	0	0	0	5	.182	.182
Mitchell, K	.000	6	0	0	0	0	2	.000	.000
Mondesi, Raul	.000	9	0	0	0	0	4	.000	.000
Morandini, M*	.350	20	7	0	2	1	3	.409	.450
Morris, Hal*	.095	21	2	0	0	0	4	.095	.095
Mouton, James	.250	12	3	0	0	0	0	.250	.333
Mueller, Bill#	.143	7	1	0	0	0	0	.143	.286
O'Brien, C	.091	11	1	1	1	1	4	.167	.364
Ochoa, Alex	.429	7	3	0	1	0	2	.429	.429
Oliver, Joe	.000	8	0	0	0	0	3	.000	.000
Ordonez, Rey	.125	8	1	0	0	0	0	.125	.125
Orsulak, Joe*	.250	16	4	0	0	3	3	.368	.375
Otero, Ricky#	.375	8	3	0	0	0	0	.375	.500
Pagnozzi, Tom	.167	6	1	0	1	1	3	.286	.333
Pena, G#	.000	4	0	0	0	0	3	.000	.000
Pendleton, T#	.231	13	3	1	1	2	4	.333	.462
Phillips, J*	.000	9	0	0	0	0	5	.000	.000
Piazza, Mike	.455	11	5	2	4	0	2	.455	1.091
Plantier, P*	.000	9	0	0	0	0	3	.000	.000
Reed, Jeff*	.143	7	1	0	0	2	1	.333	.286
Reed, Jody	.100	10	1	0	0	0	2	.182	.200
Renteria, E	.500	8	4	0	0	0	1	.500	.500
Roberson, K#	.143	7	1	0	0	0	2	.143	.143
Roberts, Bip#	.438	16	7	1	2	3	1	.526	.875
Rodriguez, H*	.400	5	2	0	0	0	0	.400	.400
Sanchez, Rey	.143	14	2	0	3	1	4	.200	.214
Sandberg, R	.214	14	3	0	0	1	8	.267	.357
Sanders, R	.222	18	4	0	2	0	6	.263	.333
Santiago, B	.167	12	2	0	0	0	5	.286	.167
Scarsone, S	.300	10	3	0	1	0	4	.300	.500
Segui, David#	.000	10	0	0	0	1	5	.091	.000
Servais, S	.400	5	2	0	2	0	2	.500	.600
Sheaffer, D	.167	6	1	0	0	0	2	.167	.167
Sheffield, G	.375	16	6	2	7	3	4	.429	.875
Shipley, A	.429	7	3	0	0	0	0	.429	.571
Slaught, Don	.000	9	0	0	0	2	3	.182	.000
Smith, Ozzie#	.417	12	5	0	4	1	1	.462	.417
Sosa, Sammy	.182	22	4	0	2	1	12	.250	.227
Spiers, Bill*	.000	5	0	0	0	1	0	.167	.000
Stocker, K#	.200	10	2	0	1	2	1	.385	.300
Taubensee, E*	.385	13	5	0	2	2	2	.467	.385
Thompson, Mil*	.200	5	1	0	0	1	1	.333	.200
Thompson, Rob	.091	11	1	0	0	1	6	.167	.182
Thompson, Ry	.000	4	0	0	0	2	2	.333	.000
VanderWal, J*	.000	5	0	0	0	0	4	.000	.000
Vina, F*	.200	5	1	0	0	0	1	.200	.400
Vizcaino, J#	.200	30	6	0	2	1	7	.226	.233
Walker, Larry*	.286	7	2	1	1	1	1	.375	.714
Wallach, Tim	.125	8	1	1	2	0	4	.125	.500
Weiss, Walt#	.250	12	3	0	0	2	1	.357	.250
White, Devon#	.400	5	2	0	1	1	2	.500	.400
Whiten, Mark#	.333	9	3	1	2	0	1	.333	.667
Wilkins, Rick*	.467	15	7	0	3	6	6	.591	.533
Williams, E	.143	7	1	0	0	0	1	.143	.143
Williams, Ma	.136	22	3	2	3	0	10	.136	.409
Young, Eric	.333	6	2	1	2	0	0	.500	1.167
Zeile, Todd	.294	17	5	1	3	3	5	.400	.471

Pedro A. Martinez, Reds — LHP

Batter	Avg	AB	H	HR	BI	BB	SO	OBP	Slg
Bichette, D	.600	5	3	1	4	0	0	.600	1.200
Blauser, Jeff	.000	6	0	0	0	0	4	.000	.000
Bonilla, B#	.250	4	1	0	0	2	0	.500	.250
Caminiti, Ken#	.200	5	1	0	2	1	3	.333	.200
Carr, Chuck	.500	4	2	0	2	0	1	.500	.750
Daulton, D*	.500	4	2	0	0	4	0	.750	.750
Duncan, Sean	.333	6	2	0	0	0	1	.333	.333
Dykstra, L*	.286	7	2	0	0	0	0	.286	.429
Eisenreich, J*	.167	6	1	0	1	0	0	.167	.167
Finley, Steve*	.000	5	0	0	0	0	2	.000	.000
Galarraga, A	.400	5	2	1	2	0	1	.400	1.000
Gonzalez, L*	.286	7	2	1	4	1	1	.375	.857
Grace, Mark*	.500	8	4	1	4	1	0	.556	1.000
Hayes, C	.000	6	0	0	0	1	1	.143	.000
Hollins, Dave#	.000	5	0	0	1	1	1	.167	.000
Justice, Dave*	.200	5	1	1	2	0	0	.200	.800
Karros, Eric	.000	3	0	0	0	2	1	.400	.000
Kent, Jeff	.500	6	3	0	0	0	0	.500	.500
Lankford, Ray*	.000	2	0	0	1	2	0	.400	.000
Lemke, Mark#	.333	3	1	0	1	2	1	.600	.667
Martin, Al*	.429	7	3	0	1	0	2	.429	.429
McGriff, Fred*	.250	4	1	0	1	2	0	.500	.250
Merced, O*	.500	4	2	0	1	1	0	.600	.750
Morandini, M*	.500	4	2	0	1	0	1	.600	.500
Morris, Hal*	.000	4	0	0	0	1	3	.200	.000
Sanchez, Rey	.200	5	1	0	0	0	0	.333	.200
Sosa, Sammy	.667	6	4	2	4	2	1	.750	1.667
Stocker, K#	.571	7	4	0	1	0	2	.571	.714
Vizcaino, J#	.500	4	2	0	0	1	1	.600	.500
Weiss, Walt#	.250	4	1	0	0	2	1	.500	.250
Wilkins, Rick*	.000	6	0	0	0	1	2	.250	.000

Ramon Martinez, Dodgers — RHP

Batter	Avg	AB	H	HR	BI	BB	SO	OBP	Slg
Dykstra, L*	.267	45	12	2	4	6	5	.353	.511
Eisenreich, J*	.444	18	8	1	5	2	1	.500	.667
Elster, Kevin	.250	4	1	0	0	1	0	.400	.250
Eusebio, Tony	.300	10	3	0	1	1	0	.364	.300
Everett, Carl#	.000	9	0	0	1	2	4	.182	.000
Finley, Steve*	.359	39	14	1	5	3	4	.405	.538
Flaherty, J	.167	6	1	0	0	0	2	.167	.167
Fletcher, D*	.250	28	7	0	1	5	0	.353	.321
Floyd, Cliff*	.250	8	2	0	0	2	2	.400	.250
Frazier, Lou*	.167	12	2	0	1	3	2	.313	.250
Gaetti, Gary	.167	6	1	0	0	0	0	.167	.167
Galarraga, A	.366	41	15	2	9	3	11	.383	.585
Gant, Ron	.314	51	16	4	7	4	9	.375	.608
Garcia, C	.125	16	2	0	2	0	2	.125	.188
Gilkey, B	.387	31	12	0	3	4	3	.472	.484
Girardi, Joe	.257	35	9	0	4	0	6	.257	.343
Goff, Jerry*	.143	7	1	1	1	1	4	.250	.571
Gomez, Chris	.200	10	2	0	1	0	2	.200	.200
Gonzalez, L*	.160	25	4	1	1	3	7	.250	.360
Grace, Mark*	.385	39	15	2	8	5	5	.455	.615
Grissom, M	.314	35	11	1	6	1	7	.351	.543
Grudzielanek	.211	19	4	0	0	1	1	.286	.211
Gutierrez, R	.250	8	2	1	2	0	2	.333	.625
Gwynn, Tony*	.344	32	11	1	3	6	1	.436	.469
Harris, Lenny*	.000	9	0	0	0	2	2	.182	.000
Hayes, C	.282	39	11	2	4	2	9	.333	.462
Henderson, R	.000	5	0	0	0	4	2	.444	.000
Hill, G	.333	9	3	0	2	1	1	.400	.667
Hollins, Dave#	.158	19	3	1	1	9	3	.429	.316
Howard, T*	.385	26	10	2	2	2	1	.429	.731
Hudler, Rex	.333	6	2	0	0	1	2	.429	.333
Hundley, Todd#	.278	18	5	1	5	4	2	.409	.444
Hunter, Brian	.250	8	2	0	0	0	3	.250	.250
Hunter, Bri L	.100	10	1	0	0	0	1	.100	.100
Huskey, Butch	.000	10	0	0	0	1	2	.091	.000
Javier, Stan#	.125	8	1	0	1	1	0	.222	.125
Jefferies, G#	.310	42	13	0	3	4	4	.370	.452
Johnson, Bri	.800	5	4	0	1	0	0	.667	.800
Johnson, Char	.000	6	0	0	0	0	3	.000	.000
Johnson, L*	.286	7	2	0	0	3	1	.500	.429
Johnson, Mark*	.125	8	1	1	2	1	3	.222	.500
Jordan, Brian	.125	8	1	0	1	1	1	.222	.125
Jordan, Ricky	.412	17	7	1	4	0	1	.444	.706
Joyner, Wally*	.000	6	0	0	0	1	0	.143	.000
Justice, Dave*	.258	31	8	1	7	7	6	.395	.387
Kelly, R	.429	7	3	0	0	0	1	.500	.714
Kent, Jeff	.333	15	5	0	4	2	0	.444	.400
King, Jeff	.318	22	7	1	6	1	3	.333	.455
Kingery, Mike*	.300	20	6	0	1	4	1	.417	.400
Klesko, Ryan*	.200	5	1	0	1	0	2	.200	.200
Lankford, Ray*	.229	35	8	1	5	5	14	.325	.371
Lansing, Mike	.281	32	9	0	2	3	4	.361	.313
Larkin, Barry	.196	46	9	0	2	3	4	.245	.304
Lemke, Mark#	.143	28	4	0	0	7	5	.314	.179
Lewis, Darren	.259	27	7	0	1	2	5	.300	.370
Liriano, M	.231	13	3	0	0	5	0	.444	.308
Mabry, John*	.375	8	3	0	1	1	1	.444	.375
Magadan, Dave*	.324	34	11	0	2	6	2	.415	.324
Manwaring, K	.323	31	10	0	2	2	4	.364	.323
Martin, Al*	.211	19	4	0	0	3	3	.318	.368
Martinez, Da*	.300	30	9	0	3	3	3	.364	.400
May, Derrick*	.375	24	9	2	7	2	4	.407	.625
McGee, Willie#	.243	37	9	0	2	5	10	.333	.243
McGriff, Fred*	.167	18	3	0	2	11	1	.483	.222
McRae, Brian#	.250	12	3	0	0	2	2	.400	.417
Merced, O*	.174	23	4	0	2	3	3	.269	.217
Miller, Orl	.077	13	1	0	1	0	4	.077	.077
Mitchell, K	.212	52	11	1	6	7	11	.295	.288
Morandini, M*	.259	27	7	0	4	4	4	.310	.407
Morris, Hal*	.327	49	16	1	8	5	5	.389	.429
Mouton, James	.214	14	3	0	0	0	3	.214	.214
Murray, Eddie#	.364	11	4	2	3	3	2	.500	.909
Newfield, M	.333	6	2	0	2	0	2	.429	.500
Nixon, Otis#	.158	19	3	0	0	2	5	.238	.211
O'Neill, Paul*	.222	27	6	1	4	2	5	.300	.370
Oliver, Joe	.200	20	4	0	5	2	7	.273	.300
Ordonez, Rey	.000	9	0	0	0	0	2	.000	.000
Orsulak, Joe*	.278	18	5	1	2	3	1	.381	.444
Pagnozzi, Tom	.286	28	8	0	2	2	5	.333	.286
Parent, Mark	.111	9	1	0	0	0	3	.111	.222
Pendleton, T#	.149	47	7	2	3	3	9	.200	.277
Petagine, Rob*	.375	8	3	0	2	0	1	.444	.375
Plantier, P*	.000	3	0	0	1	2	3	.333	.000
Raines, Tim#	.364	11	4	0	2	2	3	.462	.364
Reed, Jeff*	.320	25	8	0	1	1	5	.346	.360
Reed, Jody	.143	14	2	0	1	1	2	.200	.214
Roberts, Bip#	.353	34	12	0	1	6	5	.450	.441
Rodriguez, H*	.091	11	1	0	1	3	4	.286	.091
Sabo, Chris	.321	28	9	3	7	1	7	.345	.714
Samuel, Juan	.200	15	3	0	2	1	0	.200	.267
Sanchez, Rey	.308	13	4	0	1	2	0	.400	.615

Ramon Martinez, Dodgers — RHP

Batter	Avg	AB	H	HR	BI	BB	SO	OBP	Slg
Abbott, Kurt	.000	9	0	0	0	0	4	.000	.000
Alfonzo, E	.333	9	3	0	2	0	1	.333	.444
Alicea, Luis#	.389	18	7	0	0	3	3	.476	.444
Alomar, R#	.450	20	9	0	3	1	1	.476	.500
Alou, Moises	.320	25	8	0	5	2	2	.345	.320
Amaro, Ruben*	.167	6	1	0	0	0	0	.167	.167
Andrews, S	.188	16	3	0	1	1	4	.278	.250
Anthony, Eric*	.143	14	2	1	3	1	2	.200	.357
Ausmus, Brad	.167	6	1	0	0	0	1	.167	.167
Bagwell, Jeff	.222	36	8	3	6	5	8	.310	.472
Barberie, B#	.273	11	3	0	4	3	2	.375	.273
Bell, Derek	.375	24	9	0	1	0	6	.375	.458
Bell, Jay	.091	33	3	0	4	2	10	.139	.091
Belliard, R	.071	14	1	0	0	1	2	.188	.071
Benard, M*	.083	12	1	1	2	1	5	.154	.333
Benjamin, M	.000	8	0	0	0	0	2	.000	.000
Berry, Sean	.133	15	2	0	1	3	3	.316	.200
Bichette, D	.278	36	10	3	9	2	8	.316	.556
Biggio, Craig	.192	52	10	2	4	4	7	.250	.346
Blauser, Jeff	.300	30	9	1	1	4	13	.382	.433
Bonds, Barry*	.349	43	15	3	14	10	4	.472	.581
Bonilla, B#	.333	33	11	6	12	3	9	.389	.939
Boone, Bret	.286	21	6	1	2	2	4	.348	.429
Branson, Jeff*	.167	12	2	0	0	1	2	.231	.167
Brogna, Rico*	.286	7	2	1	2	2	1	.444	.714
Brumfield, J	.214	14	3	0	0	0	2	.214	.214
Burks, Ellis	.429	7	3	0	0	2	3	.556	.429
Burnitz, J*	.200	5	1	1	1	1	1	.333	.800
Butler, Brett*	.208	24	5	0	2	1	4	.231	.208
Caminiti, Ken#	.244	41	10	2	7	12	10	.411	.463
Candaele, C#	.400	10	4	0	2	2	3	.500	.400
Cangelosi, J#	.375	8	3	0	0	1	0	.444	.375
Carr, Chuck	.188	16	3	0	1	1	3	.235	.188
Carreon, Mark	.333	9	3	0	0	3	0	.333	.444
Carter, Joe	.313	16	5	0	2	1	1	.353	.438
Castilla, V	.296	27	8	1	2	3	3	.345	.444
Cedeno, A	.238	21	5	1	3	2	3	.304	.429
Cianfrocco, A	.222	9	2	0	1	0	4	.222	.222
Clark, Dave*	.071	14	1	0	0	0	2	.071	.071
Clark, Will*	.415	41	17	3	8	4	4	.478	.732
Clayton, R	.208	24	5	0	2	2	7	.269	.333
Colbrunn, G	.375	8	3	0	0	0	2	.375	.375
Cole, Alex*	.400	10	4	0	0	3	1	.538	.500
Coleman, V#	.167	24	4	0	1	2	6	.231	.167
Conine, Jeff	.150	20	3	0	1	1	4	.190	.150
Cora, Joey*	.100	10	1	0	0	0	0	.100	.100
Cordero, Wil	.280	25	7	0	1	4	5	.400	.400
Cummings, M*	.000	5	0	0	0	1	2	.167	.000
Dascenzo, D#	.200	5	1	0	1	0	1	.200	.200
Daulton, D*	.257	35	9	1	2	13	9	.469	.400
Davis, Eric	.286	21	6	1	4	2	6	.348	.476
Dawson, Andre	.263	19	5	1	3	0	2	.263	.474
Decker, Steve	.100	10	1	1	3	0	0	.100	.400
DeShields, D*	.387	31	12	1	3	5	2	.472	.548
Dorsett, B	.000	5	0	0	0	3	0	.000	.000
Duncan, M	.368	38	14	1	5	1	5	.385	.553
Dunston, S	.375	24	9	2	6	0	6	.375	.667

Ramon Martinez, Dodgers — RHP

Batter	Avg	AB	H	HR	BI	BB	SO	OBP	Slg
Sandberg, R	.189	37	7	1	1	1	6	.211	.297
Sanders, R	.174	23	4	1	2	4	8	.296	.348
Santangelo, F#	.250	8	2	0	0	2	1	.400	.375
Santiago, B	.229	48	11	2	8	1	10	.245	.438
Scarsone, S	.000	12	0	0	0	0	5	.000	.000
Schofield, D	.167	6	1	0	0	0	2	.286	.167
Segui, David#	.100	20	2	0	2	2	5	.182	.150
Servais, S	.111	9	1	0	0	0	3	.111	.111
Sheaffer, D	.222	9	2	0	1	0	1	.200	.444
Sheffield, G	.333	15	5	0	4	1	2	.375	.400
Slaught, Don	.375	16	6	0	0	2	1	.444	.500
Smith, Dwight*	.300	20	6	0	3	0	2	.300	.400
Smith, Ozzie#	.080	25	2	0	1	6	3	.258	.080
Sosa, Sammy	.280	25	7	3	7	1	2	.308	.640
Stillwell, K#	.000	5	0	0	0	0	0	.000	.000
Stinnett, K	.167	6	1	0	0	1	4	.286	.167
Stocker, K#	.231	13	3	0	2	5	2	.444	.231
Strawberry, D*	.067	15	1	0	1	0	4	.067	.067
Sveum, Dale#	.333	6	2	1	2	0	2	.333	.833
Tarasco, Tony*	.222	9	2	1	1	4	2	.462	.556
Taubensee, E*	.000	10	0	0	0	2	2	.091	.000
Thompson, Mil*	.211	38	8	0	4	4	6	.286	.316
Thompson, Rob	.118	51	6	0	0	2	15	.182	.157
Thompson, Ry	.125	8	1	0	1	1	4	.222	.125
VanderWal, J*	.133	15	2	0	0	2	3	.235	.200
Veras, Q#	.250	8	2	0	0	3	0	.455	.375
Vizcaino, J#	.303	33	10	0	2	1	4	.343	.364
Walker, Larry	.333	27	9	1	6	8	6	.486	.444
Wallach, Tim	.350	20	7	0	2	1	6	.381	.400
Webster, L	.200	5	1	0	1	0	1	.200	.200
Weiss, Walt#	.190	21	4	0	2	5	1	.333	.286
White, R	.286	14	4	0	1	1	2	.313	.357
Whiten, Mark#	.267	15	4	0	0	1	2	.313	.400
Wilkins, Rick*	.212	33	7	1	3	2	6	.278	.333
Williams, Ma	.338	71	24	7	10	3	9	.382	.704
Young, Eric	.364	22	8	0	2	4	0	.517	.455
Young, Kevin	.000	5	0	0	0	1	3	.167	.000
Zeile, Todd	.308	39	12	1	3	2	5	.341	.410

T.J. Mathews, Cardinals — RHP

Batter	Avg	AB	H	HR	BI	BB	SO	OBP	Slg
Andrews, S	.000	5	0	0	0	0	1	.000	.000
Bagwell, Jeff	.000	5	0	0	0	0	1	.000	.000
Bell, Derek	.500	4	2	0	0	1	0	.600	.500
Berry, Sean	.200	5	1	0	1	0	1	.200	.400
Bichette, D	.400	5	2	1	2	0	2	.400	1.200
Biggio, Craig	.000	4	0	0	0	1	0	.200	.000
Boone, Bret	.167	6	1	0	2	0	2	.167	.500
Burks, Ellis	.000	3	0	0	0	0	3	.000	.000
Caminiti, Ken#	.000	2	0	0	0	3	1	.600	.000
Galarraga, A	.400	5	2	0	0	1	0	.400	.400
Grissom, M	.167	6	1	0	0	0	1	.167	.167
Karros, Eric	.222	9	2	1	1	0	3	.222	.667
King, Jeff	.200	5	1	0	0	0	1	.200	.200
Larkin, Barry	.333	6	2	0	0	0	0	.333	.500
Lemke, Mark#	.000	3	0	0	1	2	1	.400	.000
Lewis, Darren	.250	4	1	0	0	0	3	.250	.250
Martin, Al*	.600	5	3	0	0	0	0	.600	.800
Mondesi, Raul	.250	8	2	0	0	0	2	.250	.375
Piazza, Mike	.333	6	2	0	0	1	1	.429	.333
Reed, Jody	.600	5	3	0	0	1	0	.143	.600
Santiago, B	.000	6	0	0	1	1	1	.400	.400
Sosa, Sammy	.400	5	2	0	1	0	1	.400	.400
Young, Eric	.200	5	1	0	2	0	2	.200	.200
Zeile, Todd	.000	5	0	0	0	0	1	.000	.000

Terry Mathews, Orioles — RHP

Batter	Avg	AB	H	HR	BI	BB	SO	OBP	Slg
Anthony, Eric*	.400	5	2	1	1	0	1	.400	1.000
Bagwell, Jeff	.000	4	0	0	0	2	1	.333	.000
Baines, H*	.250	4	1	0	1	1	0	.400	.250
Bates, Jason#	.167	6	1	0	1	0	2	.167	.167
Bell, Jay	.600	5	3	0	2	0	0	.600	1.000
Berry, Sean	.400	5	2	1	3	1	2	.500	1.000
Bichette, D	.167	12	2	1	3	0	4	.167	.417
Biggio, Craig	.400	5	2	0	0	0	0	.400	.400
Boone, Bret	.200	10	2	1	3	0	1	.200	.500
Borders, Pat	.200	5	1	0	1	0	2	.200	.400
Buhner, Jay	.286	7	2	0	0	1	2	.375	.429
Burks, Ellis	.200	5	1	0	1	1	1	.333	.200
Caminiti, Ken#	.250	4	1	0	1	1	0	.400	.250
Cangelosi, J#	1.000	3	3	0	0	2	0	1.000	1.333
Canseco, Jose	.400	10	4	2	5	2	1	.500	1.100
Carreon, Mark	.000	5	0	0	0	0	2	.000	.000
Castilla, V	.600	10	6	1	2	1	1	.636	.900
Cuyler, Milt#	.250	4	1	1	3	1	1	.400	1.000
Deer, Rob	.000	7	0	0	0	0	4	.000	.000
Devereaux, M	.400	5	2	0	0	2	1	.571	.400
Duncan, M	.286	7	2	0	2	0	1	.286	.286
Eisenreich, J*	.000	4	0	0	0	1	2	.200	.000
Fielder, C	.286	7	2	0	3	1	2	.375	.429

Terry Mathews, Orioles — RHP

Batter	Avg	AB	H	HR	BI	BB	SO	OBP	Slg
Fletcher, D*	.400	5	2	0	1	0	0	.400	.600
Gaetti, Gary	.000	6	0	0	0	0	3	.000	.000
Galarraga, A	.200	10	2	0	1	0	8	.273	.300
Gant, Ron	.167	6	1	0	0	0	1	.167	.333
Gilkey, B	.000	7	0	0	0	0	2	.000	.000
Gomez, Leo	.000	7	0	0	0	0	4	.000	.000
Hayes, C	.300	10	3	0	2	1	3	.333	.300
Henderson, R	.333	6	2	0	1	2	1	.500	.500
Hundley, Todd#	.400	5	2	0	1	0	1	.400	.600
Incaviglia, P	.000	5	0	0	0	1	1	.167	.000
Jefferies, G#	.200	5	1	0	1	0	0	.200	.400
Jordan, Brian	.286	7	2	0	2	0	1	.286	.429
Justice, Dave*	.200	5	1	0	0	0	0	.200	.200
Karros, Eric	.500	6	3	1	4	1	0	.571	1.000
Kelly, R	.364	11	4	1	2	1	1	.417	.636
Kent, Jeff	.375	8	3	0	2	1	1	.444	.500
King, Jeff	.167	6	1	1	3	0	0	.167	.667
Kingery, Mike*	.000	5	0	0	0	1	1	.167	.000
Knoblauch, C	.500	4	2	0	2	1	0	.600	.750
Lankford, Ray*	.500	6	3	1	1	1	0	.571	1.333
Lansing, Mike	.429	7	3	0	2	0	0	.429	.571
Larkin, Barry	.200	5	1	0	0	1	1	.333	.400
Lewis, Mark#	.500	6	3	0	0	1	0	.571	.500
Martinez, E	.500	6	3	0	0	0	1	.500	.500
McRae, Brian#	.500	8	4	0	0	1	0	.500	.500
Merced, O*	.000	5	0	0	0	0	3	.000	.000
Mitchell, K	.000	5	0	0	0	0	1	.000	.000
Mondesi, Raul	.000	4	2	0	0	2	0	.667	.750
Morandini, M*	.250	4	1	1	1	1	0	.500	1.000
Morris, Hal*	.167	6	1	1	1	0	0	.167	.667
Mouton, James	.400	5	2	0	1	1	1	.400	.600
O'Brien, C	.500	4	2	0	1	1	1	.600	.750
Orsulak, Joe*	.286	7	2	1	3	0	1	.286	.714
Pagnozzi, Tom	.125	8	1	0	0	0	2	.125	.125
Pena, G#	.000	5	0	0	0	0	0	.000	.000
Phillips, T#	.500	4	2	0	0	1	0	.600	.500
Piazza, Mike	.000	7	0	0	0	2	2	.222	.000
Raines, Tim#	.000	2	0	0	0	3	0	.600	.000
Ripken, Cal	.000	8	0	0	1	0	2	.100	.000
Sanchez, Rey	.000	5	0	0	0	0	0	.000	.000
Sanders, R	.222	9	2	0	0	0	5	.222	.222
Santiago, B	.167	6	1	0	0	0	1	.167	.500
Segui, David#	.250	4	1	0	0	1	1	.400	.500
Sosa, Sammy	.250	8	2	0	1	0	3	.250	.250
Steinbach, T	.200	5	1	0	0	0	1	.200	.400
Stocker, K#	.250	8	2	0	0	2	1	.400	.375
Tarasco, Tony*	.250	4	1	0	0	1	0	.400	.250
Vaughn, Greg	.200	5	1	0	0	0	1	.200	.400
Walker, Larry*	.429	5	2	1	1	1	0	.500	1.000
Weiss, Walt#	.429	7	3	0	0	3	1	.600	.429
Whiten, Mark#	.333	9	3	1	3	1	0	.400	.667
Young, Eric	.500	6	3	0	0	0	0	.500	.667

Brian Maxcy, Cardinals — RHP

Batter	Avg	AB	H	HR	BI	BB	SO	OBP	Slg
Alomar, R#	.200	5	1	0	0	0	0	.200	.200
Cordova, M	.400	5	2	0	1	2	2	.571	.400
Molitor, Paul	.333	6	2	1	3	1	0	.429	.833
Thomas, Frank	.500	2	1	0	0	2	1	.800	.500

Kirk McCaskill, White Sox — RHP

Batter	Avg	AB	H	HR	BI	BB	SO	OBP	Slg
Aldrete, Mike*	.364	11	4	0	0	0	0	.364	.364
Alomar, R#	.407	27	11	0	0	2	1	.448	.481
Alomar Jr, S	.273	11	3	0	2	0	0	.273	.545
Amaral, Rich	.222	9	2	0	1	0	3	.222	.222
Anderson, Brd*	.313	16	5	0	4	3	0	.421	.375
Baerga, C#	.222	18	4	0	2	3	1	.318	.222
Baines, H*	.288	52	15	0	6	10	9	.403	.423
Becker, Rich*	.667	6	4	1	4	0	1	.667	1.167
Bell, Derek	.167	6	1	0	0	0	0	.167	.167
Belle, Albert	.219	32	7	3	4	1	7	.242	.531
Bichette, D	.250	4	1	0	1	0	0	.200	.250
Blowers, Mike	.250	8	2	0	3	0	3	.250	.250
Boggs, Wade*	.333	60	20	2	8	4	4	.375	.500
Bonilla, B#	.400	5	2	0	2	2	1	.571	.600
Borders, Pat	.053	19	1	0	2	0	2	.053	.158
Bordick, Mike	.286	14	4	0	2	4	1	.450	.286
Buhner, Jay	.194	31	6	1	7	2	11	.265	.323
Burks, Ellis	.200	35	7	0	3	2	1	.243	.200
Butler, Brett*	.211	19	4	0	0	2	0	.286	.263
Cangelosi, J#	.091	11	1	0	0	4	3	.333	.091
Canseco, Jose	.326	46	15	5	12	9	10	.429	.717
Carter, Joe	.382	55	21	3	8	3	15	.414	.655
Clark, Dave*	.200	10	2	1	2	1	4	.273	.500
Clark, Will*	.500	6	3	0	1	0	0	.500	.500
Cole, Alex*	.400	5	2	1	3	1	0	.500	1.000
Cora, Joey#	.429	7	3	0	1	0	1	.429	.429
Cordova, M	.429	7	3	0	0	3	1	.636	.429
Curtis, Chad	.235	17	4	0	0	2	2	.316	.294
Cuyler, Milt#	.333	6	2	0	0	0	0	.333	.333

128

Kirk McCaskill, White Sox — RHP

Batter	Avg	AB	H	HR	BI	BB	SO	OBP	Slg
Davis, Chili#	.357	14	5	2	4	4	3	.500	.857
Deer, Rob	.261	23	6	2	5	4	9	.370	.652
Devereaux, M	.321	28	9	2	4	2	2	.367	.643
DiSarcina, G	.250	8	2	0	0	0	0	.250	.250
Eisenreich, J*	.348	23	8	0	4	1	2	.375	.435
Espinoza, A	.091	11	1	0	0	0	2	.091	.091
Fermin, Felix	.192	26	5	0	0	1	2	.222	.269
Fielder, C	.167	30	5	1	3	4	6	.265	.300
Finley, Steve*	.222	9	2	0	0	0	0	.222	.222
Flaherty, J	.375	8	3	0	0	1	0	.444	.500
Franco, Julio	.360	50	18	0	7	5	8	.421	.460
Frye, Jeff	.600	5	3	0	1	0	0	.600	.800
Fryman, T	.233	30	7	2	3	1	5	.258	.467
Gaetti, Gary	.279	43	12	0	2	3	8	.326	.326
Gagne, Greg	.242	33	8	0	4	1	9	.286	.333
Gallego, Mike	.250	28	7	0	1	2	8	.290	.357
Gates, Brent#	.333	6	2	0	2	1	0	.375	.333
Gomez, Chris	.250	8	2	0	1	0	1	.250	.250
Gomez, Leo	.235	17	4	1	3	1	1	.278	.412
Gonzales, R	.222	9	2	0	0	0	4	.222	.222
Gonzalez, J	.167	12	2	0	1	0	4	.167	.167
Goodwin, Tom*	.250	4	1	0	1	0	0	.400	.250
Greenwell, M*	.350	40	14	0	6	4	2	.400	.425
Greer, Rusty*	.333	6	2	0	1	0	2	.286	.500
Griffey Jr, K*	.258	31	8	2	6	2	0	.303	.581
Guillen, O*	.265	34	9	0	4	0	4	.265	.412
Hall, Mel*	.314	35	11	2	7	1	2	.324	.543
Hamilton, D*	.176	17	3	0	1	1	2	.222	.176
Hammonds, J	.400	5	2	1	3	0	0	.400	1.200
Hayes, C	.111	9	1	0	0	0	3	.111	.222
Henderson, R	.394	33	13	2	4	8	3	.500	.636
Hill, G	.500	8	4	0	2	5	1	.692	.500
Hoiles, Chris	.313	16	5	1	4	2	2	.389	.563
Howard, Dave#	.333	12	4	0	1	0	1	.333	.500
Hulse, David*	.400	5	2	0	0	0	0	.400	.400
Huson, Jeff*	.125	16	2	0	1	1	1	.176	.188
Incaviglia, P	.167	24	4	0	0	2	11	.231	.208
Jaha, John	.231	13	3	0	3	0	4	.214	.308
James, Dion*	.273	11	3	1	1	1	0	.333	.636
Javier, Stan#	.462	13	6	1	3	1	3	.500	.692
Jefferies, G#	.286	7	2	0	1	0	1	.250	.286
Johnson, L*	.100	10	1	0	0	1	0	.182	.300
Joyner, Wally*	.667	6	4	0	0	3	0	.778	.667
Karkovice, R	.000	6	0	0	0	2	3	.250	.000
Kelly, Pat	.375	8	3	0	0	0	1	.375	.500
Kelly, R	.318	22	7	1	6	3	6	.400	.455
Kingery, Mike*	.444	18	8	1	4	1	0	.474	.778
Knoblauch, C	.130	23	3	0	2	6	1	.300	.217
Kreuter, Chad#	.286	14	4	0	2	1	2	.313	.429
Leius, Scott	.111	9	1	0	1	1	3	.182	.111
Lewis, Mark	.429	7	3	0	0	1	2	.500	.429
Leyritz, Jim	.286	7	2	1	2	1	0	.375	.714
Liriano, N#	.500	8	4	1	3	1	0	.556	1.125
Listach, Pat#	.333	18	6	0	2	4	0	.455	.333
Livingstone*	.333	6	2	0	1	0	0	.333	.333
Lofton, Kenny*	.588	17	10	0	3	2	1	.650	.588
Lovullo, T#	.200	5	1	0	0	0	1	.200	.400
Macfarlane, M	.261	23	6	0	4	0	1	.240	.348
Martinez, E	.207	29	6	0	1	9	5	.395	.241
Martinez, T*	.143	7	1	0	3	1	0	.250	.286
Mayne, Brent*	.375	8	3	1	2	1	2	.444	.875
McGriff, Fred*	.333	18	6	2	5	6	4	.500	.667
McGwire, Mark	.233	30	7	2	6	7	7	.395	.500
McLemore, M#	.250	12	3	0	2	1	0	.308	.333
McRae, Brian#	.318	22	7	0	3	1	3	.348	.409
Meares, Pat	.200	5	1	0	1	0	0	.167	.200
Mieske, Matt	.571	7	4	0	1	1	0	.625	.714
Mitchell, K	.200	5	1	0	1	1	1	.333	.400
Molitor, Paul	.351	57	20	1	11	4	8	.393	.509
Morman, Russ	.167	6	1	0	1	0	1	.167	.167
Munoz, Pedro	.111	9	1	0	0	0	3	.111	.111
Murray, Eddie*	.375	32	12	1	6	7	2	.487	.531
Myers, Greg*	.273	11	3	1	3	0	0	.273	.727
Naehring, Tim	.600	10	6	0	3	1	0	.636	.700
Newson, W*	.000	5	0	0	1	0	1	.000	.000
Nieves, M#	.400	5	2	0	0	0	2	.400	.600
Nilsson, Dave*	.100	10	1	0	1	0	1	.100	.200
Nixon, Otis#	.000	5	0	0	0	0	0	.000	.000
O'Neill, Paul*	.333	3	1	0	0	3	0	.667	.333
Olerud, John*	.259	27	7	0	3	2	3	.300	.296
Orsulak, Joe*	.242	33	8	1	4	2	2	.286	.333
Palmeiro, R*	.273	33	9	1	7	4	8	.351	.424
Palmer, Dean	.250	16	4	0	2	1	4	.333	.250
Paquette, C	.500	6	3	1	3	0	1	.500	1.167
Pena, Tony	.083	24	2	0	2	1	5	.120	.083
Perez, E	.400	5	2	0	0	0	0	.400	.500
Phillips, T#	.263	38	10	1	2	11	10	.429	.421
Plantier, P*	.250	8	2	0	0	1	1	.333	.250
Polonia, Luis*	.238	21	5	0	1	0	2	.238	.238
Ramirez, M	.500	6	3	0	1	0	0	.571	.833
Reboulet, J	.250	4	1	0	0	1	0	.400	.250
Reed, Jody	.268	41	11	0	2	2	2	.302	.341
Ripken, Billy	.200	20	4	0	4	0	2	.190	.200
Ripken, Cal	.230	61	14	1	10	12	6	.368	.344
Rodriguez, Al	.200	5	1	0	0	0	1	.200	.400
Rodriguez, I	.400	10	4	0	0	0	1	.400	.500
Salmon, Tim	.500	12	6	0	3	0	0	.500	.667
Samuel, Juan	.250	12	3	0	0	0	1	.250	.250
Schofield, D	.250	4	1	0	0	1	1	.400	.250
Segui, David#	.600	5	3	0	0	1	0	.667	.600
Seitzer, K	.333	36	12	0	2	5	2	.429	.444
Sheffield, G	.250	8	2	0	2	0	1	.250	.250
Shumpert, T	.333	6	2	0	2	0	1	.333	.333
Sierra, Ruben#	.240	50	12	1	5	3	10	.296	.360
Singleton, D*	.200	5	1	0	0	1	1	.333	.400
Slaught, Don	.308	13	4	1	2	1	1	.357	.615
Snow, J*	.000	5	0	0	0	1	0	.167	.000
Sojo, Luis	.143	7	1	0	0	1	0	.250	.143
Sorrento, P*	.417	12	5	1	5	3	4	.533	.917
Sosa, Sammy	.000	6	0	0	0	2	2	.250	.000
Spiers, Bill*	.333	18	6	0	3	1	0	.368	.444
Sprague, Ed	.214	14	3	0	0	2	3	.313	.214
Stankiewicz	.000	4	0	0	0	3	2	.429	.000
Stanley, Mike	.000	13	0	0	1	0	7	.071	.000
Steinbach, T	.241	29	7	1	5	6	3	.389	.414
Stillwell, K#	.391	23	9	0	5	2	3	.440	.522
Strange, Doug#	.250	4	1	0	1	1	1	.400	.250
Surhoff, B.J.*	.154	26	4	0	1	2	1	.214	.192
Tartabull, D	.214	28	6	2	5	5	10	.324	.464
Tettleton, M#	.333	36	12	3	8	5	16	.415	.639
Thomas, Frank	.333	3	1	0	0	3	0	.667	.333
Thome, Jim*	.333	6	2	0	0	2	0	.500	.333
Trammell, A	.231	39	9	0	2	1	2	.250	.256
Valentin, Jhn	.333	6	2	0	1	0	2	.333	.500
Valle, Dave	.121	33	4	0	2	4	6	.216	.182
Vaughn, Greg	.370	27	10	0	4	3	5	.433	.444
Vaughn, Mo*	.533	15	8	3	7	3	0	.632	1.200
Velarde, R	.125	16	2	0	1	0	1	.176	.188
Ventura, R*	.091	11	1	0	0	1	2	.167	.091
Vizquel, Omar#	.323	31	10	1	4	2	2	.364	.452
Walbeck, Matt#	.111	9	1	0	0	0	3	.111	.111
Ward, Turner#	.333	6	2	0	0	2	1	.333	.500
Weiss, Walt#	.182	22	4	0	0	3	5	.280	.182
White, Devon#	.333	18	6	1	5	2	3	.400	.500
Whiten, Mark#	.214	14	3	1	2	2	2	.313	.429
Williams, Ber#	.091	11	1	0	1	2	1	.231	.091
Williams, E	.500	6	3	0	0	0	0	.500	.500
Wilson, Dan	.250	8	2	0	0	2	0	.400	.250
Worthington	.214	14	3	0	0	2	2	.313	.286

Jeff McCurry, Tigers — RHP

Batter	Avg	AB	H	HR	BI	BB	SO	OBP	Slg
Biggio, Craig	.000	4	0	0	1	0	0	.333	.000
Boone, Bret	.000	3	0	0	0	2	0	.500	.000
Karros, Eric	.000	7	0	0	0	1	0	.000	.000
Sanders, R	.333	6	2	0	0	0	1	.333	.500

Ben McDonald, Brewers — RHP

Batter	Avg	AB	H	HR	BI	BB	SO	OBP	Slg
Aldrete, Mike*	.250	8	2	0	0	3	2	.455	.375
Alomar, R#	.387	31	12	1	8	4	2	.457	.516
Alomar Jr, S	.286	21	6	0	4	1	2	.318	.429
Amaral, Rich	.364	11	4	0	0	2	1	.462	.455
Anderson, Brd*	.000	5	0	0	0	1	0	.167	.000
Anderson, G*	.333	12	4	0	1	0	2	.333	.417
Arias, George	.143	7	1	0	0	0	1	.143	.143
Baerga, C#	.297	37	11	2	5	2	6	.333	.541
Baines, H*	.409	22	9	2	6	5	3	.500	.727
Bautista, D	.400	5	2	0	1	1	2	.500	.400
Belle, Albert	.342	38	13	4	8	1	4	.359	.684
Berroa, G	.250	12	3	0	1	1	4	.308	.333
Bichette, D	.222	9	2	0	0	0	4	.222	.333
Blowers, Mike	.182	11	2	0	1	1	4	.250	.182
Boggs, Wade*	.222	27	6	0	1	4	2	.313	.259
Bonilla, B#	.000	5	0	0	0	1	0	.000	.000
Boone, Bret	.167	6	1	0	0	1	2	.286	.167
Borders, Pat	.143	21	3	1	1	1	9	.182	.286
Bordick, Mike	.200	20	4	0	3	2	5	.250	.200
Bournigal, R	.000	6	0	0	0	1	0	.000	.000
Bragg, Darren*	.250	8	2	0	0	2	2	.400	.250
Brosius, S	.231	13	3	0	0	1	4	.286	.308
Buhner, Jay	.385	26	10	3	7	5	2	.484	.808
Burks, Ellis	.077	13	1	1	2	0	3	.077	.308
Canseco, Jose	.240	25	6	2	11	2	3	.345	.480
Carreon, Mark	.500	6	3	0	1	0	0	.500	.667
Carter, Joe	.344	32	11	4	11	0	2	.364	.844
Cirillo, Joe	.250	4	1	0	1	2	0	.500	.250
Clark, Tony#	.071	14	1	0	0	3	4	.235	.071
Clark, Will*	.182	11	2	1	1	2	2	.308	.455
Cole, Alex*	.111	18	2	0	0	0	3	.111	.111
Coleman, V#	.250	8	2	0	0	2	1	.400	.500
Cora, Joey#	.192	26	5	0	3	1	2	.222	.269

Ben McDonald, Brewers — RHP

Batter	Avg	AB	H	HR	BI	BB	SO	OBP	Slg
Cruz, Fausto	.200	5	1	0	0	0	3	.200	.200
Curtis, Chad	.314	35	11	0	3	5	5	.400	.371
Cuyler, Milt#	.000	9	0	0	0	0	5	.000	.000
Damon, Johnny*	.125	8	1	0	0	1	1	.222	.125
Davis, Chili#	.167	36	6	1	2	9	6	.333	.306
Dawson, Andre	.273	11	3	1	1	0	2	.273	.545
Deer, Rob	.286	14	4	1	3	0	2	.286	.571
Delgado, C*	.500	8	4	1	3	1	2	.556	1.000
Devereaux, M	.167	6	1	0	0	0	1	.167	.167
Diaz, Alex#	.250	8	2	1	3	0	2	.250	.625
DiSarcina, G	.300	30	9	0	0	0	3	.344	.300
Durham, Ray#	.250	12	3	0	2	2	2	.357	.417
Easley, D	.333	12	4	0	0	2	0	.429	.417
Edmonds, Jim*	.304	23	7	1	2	1	7	.333	.478
Eisenreich, J*	.333	9	3	0	0	1	0	.333	.444
Elster, Kevin	.273	11	3	0	0	1	1	.333	.273
Erstad, Darin*	.125	8	1	0	0	0	0	.125	.125
Espinoza, A	.182	11	2	0	0	0	1	.182	.273
Fabregas, Jor*	.111	9	1	0	0	0	0	.111	.111
Fermin, Felix	.286	14	4	0	0	1	1	.333	.286
Fielder, C	.323	31	10	4	6	7	7	.447	.742
Franco, Julio	.368	19	7	0	4	2	1	.429	.368
Frye, Jeff	.125	8	1	0	0	1	3	.222	.125
Fryman, T	.171	35	6	1	3	7	11	.310	.257
Gaetti, Gary	.231	26	6	1	1	1	5	.259	.346
Gagne, Greg	.077	13	1	0	0	1	3	.143	.154
Gallego, Mike	.056	18	1	0	0	2	5	.150	.056
Gates, Brent#	.154	13	2	0	2	0	4	.200	.154
Giambi, Jason*	.143	7	1	0	0	0	1	.143	.143
Gonzales, Rb	.400	10	4	1	2	0	3	.400	.700
Gonzalez, A	.500	4	2	0	1	1	1	.600	.500
Gonzalez, J	.313	32	10	0	1	1	4	.333	.344
Goodwin, Tom*	.091	11	1	0	0	0	2	.091	.091
Grebeck, C	.200	5	1	0	0	0	1	.200	.400
Green, Shawn*	.222	9	2	0	0	0	2	.222	.333
Greenwell, M*	.292	24	7	0	2	4	4	.393	.375
Greer, Rusty*	.200	5	1	0	0	0	1	.200	.200
Griffey Jr, K*	.286	35	10	3	7	3	12	.333	.600
Guillen, O*	.355	31	11	0	5	1	3	.375	.516
Gwynn, Chris*	.167	6	1	0	0	0	1	.167	.167
Hale, Chip*	.000	5	0	0	0	1	0	.000	.000
Hall, Mel*	.235	17	4	3	6	1	4	.278	.765
Hamelin, Bob*	.308	13	4	0	0	2	5	.400	.385
Hamilton, D*	.238	42	10	0	4	2	3	.273	.342
Hammonds, J	.250	4	1	1	3	0	1	.250	1.000
Haselman, B	.333	6	2	0	1	0	0	.333	.500
Hayes, C	.400	10	4	1	3	0	2	.400	.700
Henderson, R	.345	29	10	2	5	10	3	.513	.621
Hiatt, Phil	.000	4	0	0	0	0	0	.000	.000
Higginson, B*	.333	18	6	1	4	1	5	.350	.611
Hill, G	.111	9	1	0	1	1	2	.200	.111
Howard, Dave#	.000	9	0	0	0	0	2	.000	.000
Howard, T*	.222	9	2	0	1	0	3	.222	.222
Hulse, David*	.400	10	4	0	1	1	3	.455	.400
Huson, Jeff	.100	10	1	0	1	2	1	.182	.400
Jaha, John	.235	17	4	0	0	2	3	.235	.235
James, Dion*	.368	19	7	0	2	0	3	.368	.368
Javier, Stan#	.143	7	1	0	0	0	1	.143	.143
Jefferson, R*	.188	16	3	1	1	1	2	.235	.375
Johnson, L*	.222	27	6	0	2	2	1	.276	.296
Joyner, Wally*	.292	24	7	1	3	6	2	.419	.458
Karkovice, R	.071	14	1	0	1	0	3	.067	.143
Kelly, Pat	.333	18	6	0	0	1	3	.368	.444
Kelly, R	.158	19	3	1	2	0	4	.158	.316
Kirby, Wayne*	.389	18	7	0	1	1	1	.421	.389
Knoblauch, C	.391	23	9	0	2	4	1	.481	.478
Kreuter, Chad#	.250	8	2	1	2	3	3	.455	.625
Leius, Scott	.250	16	4	0	0	1	2	.294	.250
Levis, Jesse*	.333	6	2	0	0	0	2	.333	.333
Lewis, Darren	.375	8	3	0	0	0	1	.375	.375
Lewis, Mark	.300	20	6	0	2	0	1	.300	.400
Leyritz, Jim	.200	10	2	0	1	2	1	.333	.300
Listach, Pat#	.286	14	4	0	0	1	3	.333	.357
Livingstone*	.333	9	3	0	3	0	2	.333	.556
Lockhart, K*	.273	11	3	0	2	0	5	.273	.364
Lofton, Kenny*	.214	42	9	0	5	1	9	.233	.333
Macfarlane, M	.118	17	2	0	0	1	6	.250	.176
Martinez, Da*	.250	12	3	0	0	0	1	.250	.250
Martinez, E	.320	25	8	1	5	0	3	.333	.600
Martinez, S*	.000	5	0	0	0	0	2	.000	.000
Martinez, T*	.375	24	9	3	4	2	4	.423	.875
Mayne, Brent*	.353	17	6	1	3	1	5	.368	.529
McCarty, Dave	.000	8	0	0	1	0	2	.000	.000
McGriff, Fred*	.571	7	4	0	0	0	1	.571	.714
McGwire, Mark	.188	16	3	0	0	3	5	.316	.313
McLemore, M#	.400	10	4	0	0	0	1	.400	.600
McRae, Brian#	.375	24	9	0	2	1	6	.400	.500
Meares, Pat	.231	13	3	0	0	1	3	.286	.385
Mieske, Matt	.333	6	2	0	1	1	1	.429	.500
Mitchell, K	.125	8	1	0	1	0	2	.222	.125
Molitor, Paul	.353	34	12	1	3	3	1	.405	.559

Ben McDonald, Brewers — RHP

Batter	Avg	AB	H	HR	BI	BB	SO	OBP	Slg
Mouton, Lyle	.400	10	4	1	1	2	1	.500	.800
Munoz, Pedro	.222	9	2	1	3	0	2	.222	.556
Murray, Eddie#	.400	15	6	1	4	1	1	.438	.600
Myers, Greg*	.235	17	4	1	3	2	3	.286	.412
Naehring, Tim	.143	7	1	0	0	4	2	.455	.143
Nevin, Phil	.286	7	2	1	1	0	3	.375	.714
Newson, W*	.133	15	2	1	1	2	3	.235	.333
Nieves, M#	.300	10	3	0	0	1	5	.364	.700
Nilsson, Dave*	.429	14	6	1	2	4	1	.556	.714
Nixon, Otis#	.267	15	4	0	2	2	3	.353	.333
O'Leary, Troy*	.200	5	1	0	0	0	0	.200	.200
O'Neill, Paul*	.200	10	2	0	0	3	1	.385	.300
Offerman, J#	.250	4	1	0	0	1	1	.400	.250
Olerud, John*	.333	36	12	5	8	5	5	.415	.833
Palmeiro, R*	.192	26	5	0	0	2	3	.250	.269
Palmer, Dean	.278	18	5	0	2	2	3	.350	.389
Paquette, C	.455	11	5	0	2	0	2	.455	.545
Pena, Tony	.381	21	8	0	3	6	4	.519	.476
Perez, E	.200	10	2	1	1	0	3	.200	.500
Phillips, T#	.220	41	9	0	3	5	3	.304	.293
Plantier, P*	.083	12	1	0	1	2	3	.214	.083
Polonia, Luis*	.303	33	10	1	4	2	5	.361	.515
Pride, Curtis*	.429	7	3	0	0	0	2	.429	.429
Raines, Tim#	.318	22	7	1	2	3	4	.400	.591
Ramirez, M	.200	10	2	1	3	2	1	.333	.500
Randa, Joe	.000	5	0	0	0	0	0	.000	.000
Reed, Jody	.176	17	3	0	2	4	1	.333	.235
Ripken, Cal	.143	7	1	0	0	1	1	.250	.143
Roberts, Bip#	.600	5	3	0	0	1	0	.667	.600
Rodriguez, A	.286	7	2	0	1	0	2	.286	.286
Rodriguez, I	.464	28	13	1	4	1	3	.483	.679
Salmon, Tim	.171	35	6	0	3	1	7	.216	.171
Schofield, D	.182	11	2	0	0	1	1	.250	.182
Seitzer, K	.171	35	6	0	3	2	6	.211	.257
Sierra, Ruben#	.033	30	1	0	0	1	5	.065	.033
Snow, J.T.#	.138	29	4	1	4	4	7	.242	.241
Sojo, Luis	.300	20	6	0	0	1	0	.300	.300
Sorrento, P*	.182	33	6	0	3	1	9	.206	.182
Spiers, Bill*	.450	20	9	0	1	1	1	.476	.550
Sprague, Ed	.235	17	4	3	3	1	5	.278	.765
Stankiewicz	.333	9	3	0	0	1	2	.400	.444
Stanley, Mike	.250	8	2	1	2	1	3	.333	.625
Steinbach, T	.190	21	4	0	0	1	4	.227	.238
Stevens, Lee*	.111	9	1	0	0	0	1	.111	.111
Stillwell, K#	.154	13	2	0	0	1	2	.214	.154
Strange, Doug#	.357	14	5	0	1	0	1	.357	.571
Surhoff, B.J.*	.244	41	10	5	7	2	2	.279	.634
Tarasco, Tony*	.000	4	0	0	0	0	1	.200	.000
Tartabull, D	.136	22	3	1	1	0	9	.136	.273
Tettleton, M#	.167	24	4	1	1	3	9	.259	.375
Thomas, Frank	.212	33	7	2	6	7	2	.372	.424
Thome, Jim*	.412	17	7	1	2	9	5	.615	.647
Trammell, A	.200	15	3	1	1	3	1	.333	.400
Tucker, M*	.444	9	4	0	1	0	1	.444	.778
Valentin, Jhn	.200	15	3	0	0	2	6	.294	.267
Valentin, Jse#	.100	10	1	0	0	2	3	.308	.100
Valle, Dave	.375	16	6	0	2	3	2	.500	.563
Vaughn, Greg	.216	37	8	1	3	5	10	.326	.297
Vaughn, Mo*	.174	23	4	1	5	4	7	.296	.391
Velarde, R	.333	30	10	1	3	4	2	.412	.433
Ventura, R*	.293	41	12	3	10	3	4	.333	.537
Vizcaino, J#	.000	5	0	0	1	0	0	.000	.000
Vizquel, Omar#	.250	32	8	1	5	5	1	.333	.438
Walbeck, Matt#	.143	7	1	0	0	0	2	.143	.143
Ward, Turner#	.154	13	2	0	2	0	3	.143	.154
Weiss, Walt#	.286	7	2	0	0	2	2	.444	.429
White, Devon#	.207	29	6	1	2	2	14	.258	.345
Whiten, Mark#	.182	11	2	0	0	1	5	.250	.273
Williams, Ber#	.143	21	3	0	0	0	4	.143	.143
Wilson, Dan	.100	10	1	0	0	1	4	.182	.200
Young, Ernie	.500	6	3	0	2	0	2	.500	1.000

Jack McDowell, Indians — RHP

Batter	Avg	AB	H	HR	BI	BB	SO	OBP	Slg
Aldrete, Mike*	.160	25	4	0	2	3	5	.250	.200
Alicea, Luis#	.600	5	3	0	1	2	0	.714	.600
Alomar, R#	.552	29	16	3	8	7	6	.639	.897
Alomar Jr, S	.200	15	3	0	0	1	2	.250	.200
Anderson, Brd*	.167	42	7	0	2	4	7	.239	.167
Anderson, G*	.267	15	4	1	2	0	4	.267	.533
Baerga, C#	.378	45	17	1	7	4	8	.440	.467
Baines, H*	.167	60	10	4	6	6	13	.239	.400
Barberie, B#	.143	7	1	0	0	3	0	.143	.143
Bautista, D	.333	6	2	0	1	0	0	.333	.500
Becker, Rich*	.154	13	2	1	2	1	2	.214	.385
Belle, Albert	.233	43	10	0	2	2	12	.267	.302
Berroa, G	.176	17	3	1	2	3	4	.300	.353
Bichette, D	.167	6	1	0	1	0	3	.167	.167
Blowers, Mike	.077	13	1	0	0	0	3	.077	.077
Boggs, Wade*	.300	40	12	0	5	8	2	.408	.400
Bonilla, B#	.500	8	4	0	1	1	0	.556	.500

Batter	Avg	AB	H	HR	BI	BB	SO	OBP	Slg
Boone, Bret	.333	9	3	0	1	0	2	.300	.556
Borders, Pat	.467	15	7	0	2	0	1	.467	.600
Bordick, Mike	.286	42	12	0	4	0	2	.286	.381
Brosius, S	.111	18	2	0	0	3	10	.238	.111
Buhner, Jay	.146	41	6	0	2	3	20	.217	.171
Burks, Ellis	.235	17	4	0	2	2	6	.316	.412
Canseco, Jose	.245	49	12	2	6	5	16	.327	.408
Carreon, Mark	.250	4	1	0	0	1	1	.400	.250
Carter, Joe	.225	40	9	1	4	1	4	.256	.325
Cirillo, Jeff	.111	9	1	0	0	0	1	.111	.111
Clark, Will*	.150	20	3	0	2	2	4	.227	.200
Cole, Alex*	.077	13	1	0	0	1	4	.143	.154
Coleman, V#	.125	8	1	0	0	0	4	.125	.125
Cordero, Wil	.000	7	0	0	0	0	2	.000	.000
Cordova, M	.750	8	6	1	4	2	2	.800	1.250
Curtis, Chad	.200	25	5	0	5	4	4	.300	.200
Cuyler, Milt#	.000	7	0	0	0	1	1	.125	.000
Damon, Johnny*	.357	14	5	0	0	2	0	.357	.500
Davis, Chili#	.220	59	13	0	5	6	12	.288	.254
Dawson, Andre	.231	13	3	1	4	1	1	.286	.538
Deer, Rob	.182	22	4	3	5	2	8	.250	.636
Delgado, C*	.200	5	1	0	0	0	3	.200	.200
Devereaux, M	.195	41	8	0	2	6	11	.298	.317
Diaz, Alex*	.357	14	5	0	0	0	0	.357	.643
DiSarcina, G	.300	30	9	0	3	2	3	.344	.333
Durham, Ray#	.214	14	3	0	0	0	3	.267	.286
Easley, D	.154	13	2	1	2	1	2	.267	.385
Edmonds, Jim*	.227	22	5	0	2	1	5	.261	.318
Eisenreich, J*	.286	14	4	0	1	2	2	.375	.429
Elster, Kevin	.286	7	2	0	0	2	0	.375	.286
Espinoza, A	.333	15	5	1	2	3	1	.444	.533
Fabregas, Jor*	.200	10	2	1	0	0	0	.200	.300
Fermin, Felix	.242	33	8	0	0	1	6	.265	.242
Fielder, C	.317	41	13	1	11	3	14	.364	.488
Flaherty, J	.500	10	5	1	3	1	2	.545	.900
Fox, Andy*	.250	4	1	0	0	0	0	.250	.250
Franco, Julio	.250	28	7	0	3	2	2	.300	.321
Frye, Jeff	.308	13	4	0	1	1	1	.357	.385
Fryman, T	.250	32	8	1	3	6	9	.368	.500
Gaetti, Gary	.226	53	12	1	4	1	12	.241	.358
Gagne, Greg	.304	46	14	3	6	0	8	.304	.565
Gallego, Mike	.313	16	5	1	4	4	2	.450	.563
Gates, Brent#	.138	29	4	0	2	1	3	.167	.138
Giambi, Jason*	.500	10	5	0	2	3	2	.615	.700
Gil, Benji	.500	6	3	0	3	0	1	.500	1.000
Gomez, Chris	.167	12	2	0	1	3	5	.333	.167
Gomez, Leo	.091	11	1	0	0	1	3	.167	.182
Gonzales, R	.267	15	4	0	3	0	3	.267	.400
Gonzalez, A	.375	8	3	0	2	0	4	.333	.375
Gonzalez, J	.409	44	18	3	15	3	3	.447	.705
Goodwin, Tom*	.400	10	4	0	4	0	1	.400	.600
Green, Shawn*	.500	8	4	0	2	1	1	.556	1.000
Greenwell, M*	.261	46	12	1	5	6	3	.340	.413
Greer, Rusty	.294	17	5	1	4	3	4	.400	.647
Griffey Jr, K*	.233	43	10	1	3	2	7	.267	.372
Guillen, O*	.333	15	5	0	1	0	1	.333	.600
Gwynn, Chris*	.143	7	1	0	0	1	0	.143	.143
Hale, Chip*	.182	11	2	0	0	0	3	.182	.273
Hall, Mel*	.222	18	4	0	3	3	1	.292	.222
Hamelin, Bob*	.250	12	3	0	1	1	2	.308	.333
Hamilton, D*	.306	49	15	0	4	3	5	.340	.408
Hammonds, J	.000	6	0	0	0	0	1	.000	.000
Haselman, B	.300	10	3	0	1	1	4	.364	.400
Henderson, R	.422	45	19	1	4	10	8	.518	.600
Herrera, Jose*	.385	13	5	0	0	0	2	.385	.462
Higginson, B*	.500	6	3	1	1	0	0	.500	1.167
Hill, G	.143	7	1	0	0	0	3	.143	.143
Hocking, D#	.571	7	4	0	1	0	1	.571	.571
Hoiles, Chris	.385	39	15	2	5	2	8	.415	.667
Hollins, Dave#	.000	5	0	0	0	1	1	.167	.000
Howard, Dave&	.357	14	5	0	1	3	2	.471	.500
Howell, Jack*	.235	17	4	1	3	2	4	.316	.471
Hudler, Rex	.273	11	3	0	0	0	2	.273	.273
Hulse, David*	.211	19	4	0	1	0	2	.211	.211
Huson, Jeff	.381	21	8	0	2	3	3	.458	.476
Incaviglia, J	.333	12	4	1	2	2	4	.429	.583
Jaha, John	.167	18	3	0	0	1	3	.211	.167
James, Dion*	.375	8	3	0	1	0	0	.375	.375
Javier, Stan#	.344	32	11	0	2	3	5	.400	.375
Jefferies, G#	.091	11	1	0	0	1	0	.167	.091
Jefferson, R*	.263	19	5	0	1	1	4	.286	.421
Jeter, Derek	.429	7	3	0	0	2	1	.556	.429
Johnson, L*	.500	8	4	0	0	0	1	.500	.750
Joyner, Wally*	.222	54	12	1	5	8	9	.323	.389
Karkovice, M	.111	9	1	0	0	0	3	.111	.111
Kelly, Pat	.273	11	3	0	2	1	3	.385	.455
Kelly, R	.000	9	0	0	0	2	5	.182	.000
Kirby, Wayne*	.214	14	3	0	2	0	4	.214	.286
Knoblauch, C	.396	48	19	1	4	4	4	.453	.500
Knorr, Randy	.500	4	2	0	1	1	1	.600	.750
Koslofski, K*	.333	6	2	0	0	0	1	.333	.333

Jack McDowell, Indians   RHP

Batter	Avg	AB	H	HR	BI	BB	SO	OBP	Slg
Kreuter, Chad	.222	9	2	0	2	1	4	.300	.222
Leius, Scott	.250	20	5	0	1	2	2	.318	.250
Levis, Jesse*	.091	11	1	0	0	1	1	.167	.091
Lewis, Mark	.083	12	1	0	1	0	2	.083	.083
Leyritz, Jim	.467	15	7	0	3	1	1	.529	.467
Liriano, N#	.417	12	5	0	1	1	0	.462	.417
Listach, Pat	.350	20	7	0	0	0	1	.350	.400
Livingstone*	.143	7	1	0	0	0	1	.143	.143
Lockhart, K*	.333	9	3	0	1	0	0	.333	.333
Lofton, Kenny	.306	36	11	0	1	3	2	.359	.333
Lovullo, T#	.250	8	2	0	0	3	1	.455	.375
Macfarlane, M	.135	37	5	0	1	3	7	.220	.189
Magadan, Dave*	.000	7	0	0	0	0	3	.000	.000
Manto, Jeff	.000	5	0	0	0	0	2	.000	.000
Martin, N	.500	6	3	0	2	0	1	.500	.833
Martinez, Da*	.333	18	6	2	4	1	3	.368	.667
Martinez, E	.303	33	10	0	4	4	6	.378	.424
Martinez, T*	.368	38	14	4	8	6	4	.455	.816
Mayne, Brent*	.000	15	3	0	0	2	1	.294	.200
McCarty, Dave	.143	7	1	0	0	1	0	.250	.143
McGriff, Fred*	.400	10	4	1	1	1	3	.455	1.000
McGwire, Mark	.194	31	6	4	8	7	9	.366	.581
McLemore, M#	.298	47	14	0	4	4	4	.346	.340
McRae, Brian#	.161	31	5	0	0	4	5	.278	.194
Meares, Pat	.286	14	4	0	3	0	2	.286	.429
Mieske, Matt	.125	8	1	0	0	0	3	.125	.250
Molitor, Paul	.241	54	13	2	6	6	8	.317	.370
Munoz, Pedro	.053	19	1	0	0	0	2	.053	.143
Murray, Eddie*	.250	20	5	1	4	1	4	.286	.500
Myers, Greg*	.222	27	6	1	2	0	4	.222	.370
Myers, Rod*	.545	6	1	0	3	1	2	.286	.167
Naehring, Tim	.545	11	6	0	2	0	1	.500	.636
Newfield, M	.429	7	3	0	1	1	1	.556	.429
Newson, W*	.143	7	1	1	1	1	1	.250	.571
Nilsson, Dave*	.346	26	9	1	2	6	4	.469	.500
Nixon, Otis*	.364	11	4	0	0	1	0	.417	.364
O'Leary, Troy*	.375	16	6	0	2	0	2	.375	.438
O'Neill, Paul*	.286	21	6	2	4	3	2	.375	.571
Offerman, J	.833	6	5	0	2	1	0	.857	1.167
Olerud, John*	.344	32	11	2	5	5	4	.432	.594
Orsulak, Joe*	.458	24	11	2	5	1	1	.480	.792
Palmeiro, R*	.224	49	11	2	7	1	6	.245	.347
Palmer, Dean	.250	32	8	3	5	3	9	.324	.594
Paquette, C	.190	21	4	0	1	0	5	.217	.333
Pena, Tony	.313	32	10	0	1	0	3	.313	.406
Phillips, T#	.188	64	12	1	3	8	14	.278	.266
Plantier, P*	.385	13	5	0	1	1	2	.429	.462
Polonia, Luis*	.400	45	18	0	5	6	6	.471	.489
Raines, Tim#	.125	8	1	1	1	2	1	.300	.500
Ramirez, M	.000	8	0	0	0	0	3	.000	.000
Randa, Joe	.444	9	4	0	2	1	0	.500	.667
Reboulet, J	.214	14	3	0	0	3	3	.353	.214
Reed, Jody	.375	32	12	0	4	5	2	.447	.438
Ripken, Billy	.077	13	1	0	0	0	2	.077	.077
Ripken, Cal	.266	64	17	1	6	2	9	.288	.391
Rodriguez, I	.178	45	8	1	3	3	8	.229	.267
Salmon, Tim	.167	30	5	0	0	3	8	.265	.200
Samuel, Juan	.300	10	3	0	1	1	2	.364	.300
Schofield, D	.167	18	3	0	0	2	2	.250	.167
Segui, David#	.200	10	2	0	0	0	0	.200	.300
Seitzer, K	.354	48	17	2	8	5	5	.411	.583
Sheffield, G	.545	11	6	0	2	0	0	.615	.727
Shumpert, T	.167	6	1	0	0	1	4	.286	.333
Sierra, Ruben#	.217	60	13	2	10	5	12	.273	.367
Slaught, Don	.455	11	5	1	1	1	0	.500	.909
Snow, J.T.#	.192	26	5	0	2	2	4	.250	.192
Sojo, Luis	.316	19	6	0	1	2	1	.381	.316
Sorrento, P*	.250	36	9	4	7	6	10	.357	.639
Spiers, Bill*	.321	28	9	0	2	0	7	.321	.464
Sprague, Ed	.308	13	4	1	3	3	4	.471	.692
Stahoviak, S*	.111	9	1	0	0	1	4	.200	.111
Stanley, Mike	.462	13	6	1	2	3	2	.533	.769
Steinbach, T	.222	27	6	1	3	0	7	.222	.370
Stevens, Lee*	.111	9	1	0	0	0	3	.111	.111
Stillwell, K#	.000	10	0	0	1	2	1	.154	.000
Strange, Doug#	.176	17	3	0	1	1	2	.222	.235
Surhoff, B.J.*	.275	40	11	1	1	4	6	.341	.450
Sveum, Dale#	.000	6	0	0	0	0	1	.000	.000
Tartabull, D	.273	33	9	2	7	0	7	.265	.636
Tettleton, M#	.167	36	6	2	2	8	17	.333	.333
Thomas, Frank	.421	19	8	2	4	3	3	.500	.789
Thome, Jim*	.154	13	2	2	3	2	4	.267	.615
Tinsley, Lee*	.222	9	2	0	1	0	2	.222	.333
Trammell, A	.360	25	9	0	2	2	2	.407	.360
Tucker, M*	.000	3	0	3	1	0	0	.300	.600
Valentin, Jhn	.091	22	2	1	3	2	6	.167	.227
Valentin, Jse#	.263	19	5	1	4	0	4	.263	.632
Valle, Dave	.160	25	4	0	1	1	3	.192	.200
Vaughn, Greg	.170	53	9	1	2	0	22	.170	.283
Vaughn, Mo*	.175	40	7	0	2	4	10	.250	.175
Velarde, R	.294	17	5	1	2	1	1	.333	.471

Jack McDowell, Indians — RHP

Batter	Avg	AB	H	HR	BI	BB	SO	OBP	Slg
Ventura, R*	.158	19	3	0	1	2	5	.238	.211
Vina, F*	.100	10	1	0	0	2	0	.308	.100
Vizquel, Omar#	.268	41	11	0	2	4	7	.348	.317
Walbeck, Matt#	.167	12	2	0	0	1	2	.231	.250
Wallach, Tim	.000	6	0	0	0	0	1	.000	.000
Ward, Turner#	.211	19	4	0	3	1	3	.250	.263
Webster, L	.200	10	2	0	0	0	2	.200	.200
Weiss, Walt*	.048	21	1	0	1	0	4	.048	.048
White, Devon*	.271	48	13	2	12	2	7	.300	.479
Whiten, Mark#	.333	24	8	0	1	3	3	.407	.500
Williams, Ber#	.308	26	8	1	4	1	5	.333	.538
Williams, Geo#	.200	5	1	0	0	1	2	.333	.200
Williams, Ger	.000	5	0	0	0	0	1	.000	.000
Wilson, Dan	.182	11	2	0	0	0	2	.182	.182
Worthington	.000	5	0	0	0	1	2	.167	.000
Young, Ernie	.125	8	1	0	0	0	5	.125	.125

Roger McDowell, Orioles — RHP

Batter	Avg	AB	H	HR	BI	BB	SO	OBP	Slg
Aldrete, Mike*	.267	15	4	0	1	3	1	.421	.333
Alicea, Luis#	.429	7	3	0	3	0	0	.600	.714
Alomar, R#	.273	11	3	0	1	3	0	.400	.273
Amaro, Ruben#	.333	3	1	0	0	2	2	.600	.333
Anthony, Eric*	.167	6	1	0	1	1	1	.286	.167
Bagwell, Jeff	.538	13	7	1	4	1	1	.533	.846
Bell, Derek	.500	4	2	0	2	1	0	.600	.750
Bell, Jay	.154	13	2	0	1	0	0	.214	.154
Belle, Albert	.125	8	1	0	1	0	1	.125	.125
Belliard, R	.077	13	1	0	1	3	4	.250	.077
Benjamin, M	.250	4	1	0	0	1	0	.400	.250
Berroa, G	.500	8	4	1	2	0	1	.556	.875
Bichette, D	.429	7	3	0	3	0	1	.429	.571
Biggio, Craig	.167	18	3	0	1	2	2	.250	.278
Blauser, Jeff	.333	12	4	0	1	2	2	.429	.417
Bonds, Barry*	.214	14	3	0	1	5	0	.421	.286
Bonilla, B#	.471	17	8	0	2	6	2	.583	.588
Bordick, Mike	.250	4	1	0	1	0	2	.500	.250
Buhner, Jay	.444	9	4	2	6	0	1	.444	1.111
Butler, Brett*	.545	11	6	0	0	1	2	.583	.545
Caminiti, Ken#	.118	17	2	0	1	8	2	.400	.176
Candaele, C#	.333	21	7	0	3	0	1	.333	.381
Cangelosi, J#	.286	7	2	0	0	1	1	.375	.286
Carreon, Mark	.167	6	1	0	0	1	1	.286	.167
Carter, Joe	.429	7	3	0	1	0	0	.429	.429
Cedeno, A	.250	12	3	0	0	0	2	.250	.250
Clark, Will*	.238	21	5	1	5	6	2	.429	.476
Clayton, D	.333	6	2	0	0	0	1	.333	.333
Cole, Alex*	.600	5	3	0	1	1	0	.667	1.000
Coleman, V#	.250	28	7	0	2	2	3	.300	.250
Cora, Joey*	.000	6	0	0	0	0	0	.000	.000
Cordero, Wil	.375	8	3	0	2	1	2	.444	.500
Curtis, Chad	.000	4	0	0	0	2	1	.333	.000
Dascenzo, D#	.111	9	1	0	0	2	1	.333	.222
Daulton, D*	.250	8	2	0	0	2	3	.400	.250
Davis, Chili*	.333	9	3	0	3	2	4	.385	.444
Davis, Eric	.222	9	2	0	4	1	1	.300	.222
Dawson, Andre	.200	30	6	0	2	1	7	.226	.200
DeShields, D*	.556	9	5	0	2	0	1	.556	.556
Duncan, M	.385	13	5	0	1	0	2	.385	.538
Dunston, S	.227	22	5	0	2	1	1	.250	.273
Durham, Ray#	.500	6	3	1	1	0	0	.571	1.000
Dykstra, L*	.400	5	2	0	0	1	1	.500	.400
Elster, Kevin	.333	6	2	0	0	1	1	.429	.500
Fielder, C	.143	7	1	0	0	0	1	.143	.143
Finley, Steve*	.455	11	5	0	2	2	0	.500	.818
Fryman, T	.167	6	1	0	0	0	0	.167	.167
Galarraga, A	.174	23	4	0	0	0	4	.174	.174
Gant, Ron	.214	14	3	0	5	2	2	.278	.285
Gates, Brent#	.167	6	1	0	0	0	1	.167	.167
Gilkey, B	.250	8	2	0	2	1	1	.333	.375
Girardi, Joe	.444	9	4	0	1	0	0	.500	.444
Gomez, Chris	.167	6	1	0	0	1	3	.286	.167
Gonzalez, J	.000	4	0	0	0	2	0	.333	.000
Gonzalez, L*	.250	12	3	1	2	1	0	.308	.583
Grace, Mark*	.400	20	8	0	1	5	0	.520	.450
Grissom, M	.250	16	4	0	2	1	2	.294	.250
Guillen, O*	.000	5	0	0	0	0	0	.000	.000
Gutierrez, R	.333	6	2	0	1	0	0	.333	.333
Gwynn, Tony*	.370	27	10	0	2	4	2	.452	.370
Harris, Lenny*	.375	8	3	0	1	2	1	.500	.375
Hollins, Dave#	.200	5	1	1	2	1	0	.200	.800
Hundley, Todd#	.500	4	2	0	3	1	1	.667	.750
Hunter, Brian	.250	8	2	0	0	0	1	.250	.375
James, Dion*	.333	30	10	0	1	0	0	.273	.500
Javier, Stan#	.222	9	2	0	1	0	2	.200	.222
Jefferies, G#	.231	13	3	0	2	1	1	.286	.308
Justice, Dave*	.167	6	1	0	5	0	1	.167	.167
Karkovice, R	.200	5	1	0	0	0	2	.200	.200
Kent, Jeff	.333	6	2	0	1	1	1	.429	.500
King, Jeff	.364	11	4	0	1	0	0	.364	.364
Kingery, Mike*	.000	4	0	0	0	1	0	.200	.000
Knoblauch, C	.600	5	3	0	0	0	2	.600	.600
Lankford, Ray*	.182	11	2	1	2	2	3	.308	.455
Lansing, Mike	.000	5	0	0	1	2	0	.286	.000
Larkin, Barry	.471	17	8	0	1	1	1	.500	.529
Lemke, Mark#	.111	9	1	0	0	0	1	.111	.111
Lewis, Darren	.273	11	3	0	3	0	2	.273	.364
Listach, Pat*	.000	5	0	0	0	0	0	.000	.000
Magadan, Dave*	.500	10	5	1	5	2	3	.538	.900
Manwaring, K	.250	4	1	0	3	0	1	.250	.250
Martinez, Da*	.333	12	4	0	4	2	1	.429	.417
Martinez, E	.000	5	0	0	1	0	2	.000	.000
May, Derrick*	.500	8	4	0	0	0	0	.500	.500
McGee, Willie#	.269	26	7	0	3	7	2	.424	.269
McGriff, Fred*	.222	9	2	0	0	1	1	.300	.333
McGwire, Mark	.429	7	3	0	1	1	0	.500	.429
Merced, O*	.500	6	3	0	1	0	1	.500	.667
Mieske, Matt	.000	3	0	0	1	1	1	.200	.000
Mitchell, K	.200	15	3	0	0	1	3	.294	.200
Molitor, Paul	.250	4	1	0	0	1	0	.400	.500
Morris, Hal*	.375	8	3	0	0	2	1	.500	.500
Munoz, Pedro	.375	8	3	0	1	0	1	.375	.375
Murray, Eddie#	.455	11	5	0	2	2	0	.571	.667
Nixon, Otis#	.385	13	5	0	0	2	3	.500	.385
O'Neill, Paul*	.455	11	5	0	2	4	0	.600	.545
Offerman, J#	.000	5	0	0	0	0	3	.000	.000
Oliver, Joe	.333	9	3	0	1	0	0	.333	.444
Orsulak, Joe*	.300	10	3	0	1	0	1	.300	.500
Pagnozzi, Tom	.333	18	6	0	1	1	1	.368	.444
Palmeiro, R*	.375	8	3	0	0	0	1	.375	.625
Palmer, Dean	.333	6	2	1	2	0	0	.333	.833
Pena, Tony	.240	25	6	0	2	0	3	.231	.240
Pendleton, T	.389	36	14	4	12	6	6	.476	.778
Plantier, P*	.200	5	1	0	1	0	1	.200	.200
Raines, Tim#	.227	22	5	0	1	4	0	.346	.227
Ramirez, M	.143	7	1	0	1	1	1	.250	.143
Reed, Jeff*	.375	8	3	0	3	1	0	.400	.375
Roberts, Bip#	.438	16	7	0	3	0	3	.438	.500
Rodriguez, I	.000	5	0	0	0	0	0	.000	.000
Sabo, Chris	.286	14	4	0	0	0	0	.286	.357
Samuel, Juan	.154	26	4	0	3	4	3	.258	.154
Sandberg, R	.267	45	12	1	8	1	7	.283	.356
Sanders, R	.125	8	1	0	0	1	2	.222	.125
Santiago, B	.348	23	8	0	4	0	4	.333	.435
Schu, Rick	.200	5	1	0	1	1	1	.333	.200
Sheffield, G	.600	5	3	0	2	0	0	.500	.600
Shipley, C	.286	7	2	0	2	0	0	.286	.286
Slaught, Don	.444	9	4	0	4	0	1	.444	.556
Smith, Dwight*	.083	12	1	0	0	0	0	.154	.083
Smith, Ozzie#	.206	34	7	0	5	7	1	.341	.235
Sorrento, P*	.667	6	4	1	3	0	0	.667	1.333
Sosa, Sammy	.571	7	4	0	0	1	1	.571	.571
Sprague, Ed	.500	6	3	0	0	0	0	.600	.800
Steinbach, T	.200	5	1	0	0	0	0	.200	.200
Stillwell, K#	.143	7	1	0	0	0	0	.143	.143
Strange, Doug*	.400	5	2	0	0	0	0	.400	.400
Strawberry, D*	.143	7	1	0	1	2	3	.333	.143
Tartabull, D	.200	5	1	0	2	0	2	.200	.200
Taubensee, E*	.500	4	2	0	2	1	0	.600	.500
Tettleton, M#	.667	3	2	0	2	2	0	.800	.667
Thomas, Frank	.286	7	2	0	1	1	1	.444	.286
Thompson, Mil*	.286	26	13	0	4	1	2	.519	.500
Thompson, Rob	.296	27	8	0	4	0	3	.321	.296
Valentin, Jhn	.000	4	0	0	1	0	1	.000	.000
Ventura, R*	.333	3	1	0	0	2	0	.600	.333
Vina, F*	.000	5	0	0	0	0	1	.167	.000
Vizcaino, J#	.375	8	3	0	3	1	0	.444	.500
Walker, Larry*	.429	7	3	0	0	3	0	.600	.429
Wallach, Tim	.250	32	8	0	4	3	3	.314	.344
Walton, J	.000	8	0	0	1	1	3	.111	.000
Wilkins, Rick*	.000	5	0	0	0	0	2	.000	.000
Williams, Ma	.182	22	4	0	1	2	2	.250	.273
Young, Eric	.500	6	3	0	1	0	0	.500	.667
Zeile, Todd	.194	31	6	0	4	1	6	.389	.548

Chuck McElroy, Angels — LHP

Batter	Avg	AB	H	HR	BI	BB	SO	OBP	Slg
Alicea, Luis#	.333	3	1	0	0	1	0	.500	.333
Anthony, Eric*	.400	5	2	1	2	2	1	.571	1.000
Ausmus, Brad	.200	5	1	0	0	0	1	.200	.200
Bagwell, Jeff	.167	6	1	1	3	2	1	.444	.667
Barberie, B#	.200	5	1	0	0	1	1	.333	.200
Bell, Jay	.583	12	7	1	2	2	1	.643	1.000
Belliard, R	.000	5	0	0	0	1	4	.143	.000
Bichette, D	.000	3	0	0	0	2	0	.400	.000
Biggio, Craig	.286	7	2	0	0	2	1	.444	.429
Blauser, Jeff	.500	6	3	0	1	2	1	.625	.667
Bonds, Barry*	.042	24	1	0	1	4	8	.077	.083
Bonilla, B#	.500	14	7	0	0	2	4	.563	.714
Butler, Brett*	.364	11	4	0	2	6	4	.588	.545
Caminiti, Ken#	.727	11	8	1	3	0	1	.727	1.091
Castilla, V	.000	7	0	0	0	0	1	.000	.000

Batter	Avg	AB	H	HR	BI	BB	SO	OBP	Slg
Clark, Will*	.429	7	3	0	2	0	0	.429	.571
Coleman, V#	.222	9	2	0	0	3	3	.417	.333
Dascenzo, D#	.200	5	1	0	0	1	0	.333	.200
Daulton, D*	.133	15	2	0	0	0	6	.125	.133
DeShields, D*	.231	13	3	0	2	3	6	.353	.231
Duncan, M	.250	8	2	0	0	0	3	.250	.375
Dykstra, L*	.375	8	3	0	2	3	0	.545	.625
Eisenreich, J*	.250	4	1	0	0	1	0	.400	.250
Elster, Kevin	.000	4	0	0	1	0	1	.000	.000
Finley, Steve*	.214	14	3	0	1	1	0	.267	.286
Fletcher, D*	.286	7	2	0	1	1	1	.375	.286
Galarraga, A	.167	12	2	1	4	0	4	.167	.500
Gant, Ron	.200	5	1	0	0	0	2	.200	.200
Garcia, C	.286	7	2	0	2	0	1	.286	.286
Gilkey, B	.571	7	4	0	1	3	0	.700	.714
Girardi, Joe	.500	4	2	0	1	1	1	.600	.750
Gonzalez, L*	.000	9	0	0	0	1	2	.100	.000
Grace, Mark*	.571	7	4	0	3	2	0	.667	.714
Grissom, M	.286	7	2	0	0	0	1	.286	.286
Gwynn, Tony*	.400	15	6	0	3	3	3	.500	.400
Harris, Lenny*	.500	8	4	1	5	0	0	.500	.875
Hayes, C	.250	4	1	0	1	2	1	.500	.250
Hollins, Dave#	.250	8	2	0	0	1	1	.333	.250
Hundley, Todd#	.091	11	1	0	0	1	5	.167	.091
Hunter, Brian	.167	6	1	0	0	0	2	.167	.167
Incaviglia, P	.000	6	0	0	0	0	4	.000	.000
Javier, Stan#	.000	5	0	0	0	0	2	.000	.000
Jefferies, G#	.300	10	3	0	1	1	0	.364	.300
Jones, C#	.750	4	3	0	2	2	1	.833	1.250
Jordan, Ricky	.500	4	2	0	1	1	0	.600	.500
Justice, Dave*	.313	16	5	0	4	0	2	.313	.375
Kelly, R	.000	5	0	0	0	0	3	.000	.000
Kent, Jeff	.500	6	3	0	1	0	0	.500	.667
King, Jeff	.125	8	1	0	1	4	3	.417	.125
Kingery, Mike*	.200	5	1	0	0	0	1	.200	.200
Lankford, Ray*	.294	17	5	0	1	7	9	.500	.353
Larkin, Barry	.250	4	1	0	0	2	2	.500	.750
Lemke, Mark#	.200	5	1	0	0	1	1	.333	.200
Lewis, Darren	.200	5	1	0	0	0	0	.200	.200
Magadan, Dave*	.250	8	2	0	0	0	1	.250	.250
Manwaring, K	.200	5	1	0	0	0	1	.200	.200
Martin, Al*	.222	9	2	0	2	3	2	.417	.222
Martinez, Da*	.143	14	2	0	0	0	8	.143	.143
McGee, Willie*	.571	7	4	0	2	0	2	.571	.571
McGriff, Fred	.333	21	7	2	6	2	5	.391	.762
Merced, O*	.313	16	5	1	5	2	1	.389	.563
Morandini, M*	.143	7	1	0	1	5	0	.500	.143
Morris, Hal*	.000	7	0	0	0	0	5	.000	.000
Murray, Eddie*	.375	8	3	0	3	5	0	.615	.375
Nixon, Otis#	.400	5	2	0	0	2	0	.571	.600
O'Brien, C	.333	6	2	0	1	0	0	.333	.500
O'Neill, Paul*	.400	10	4	1	3	0	3	.364	.700
Offerman, J#	.000	4	0	0	0	1	1	.200	.000
Oliver, Joe	.333	6	2	0	1	0	0	.333	.333
Orsulak, Joe*	.500	4	2	0	4	1	0	.429	.750
Pagnozzi, Tom	.143	7	1	0	1	1	2	.222	.143
Pena, G#	.500	4	2	0	1	3	1	.714	.500
Pendleton, T#	.286	14	4	0	1	1	1	.333	.357
Roberts, Bip#	.250	8	2	0	1	1	2	.333	.375
Sabo, Chris	.000	6	0	0	0	1	2	.143	.000
Samuel, Juan	.200	5	1	0	1	0	3	.200	.200
Santiago, B	.250	8	2	1	2	0	5	.250	.625
Slaught, Don	.667	6	4	0	1	1	0	.714	1.000
Smith, Ozzie*	.154	13	2	0	3	2	3	.267	.308
Stocker, K#	.000	5	0	0	0	1	1	.167	.000
Strawberry, D*	.500	4	2	0	1	3	1	.714	.750
Thompson, Mil*	.231	13	3	0	0	2	3	.333	.308
Walker, Larry*	.333	15	5	0	3	3	4	.474	.400
Wallach, Tim	.286	7	2	1	1	1	2	.375	.714
Wehner, John	.000	4	0	0	0	1	0	.200	.000
Williams, Ma	.125	8	1	1	2	2	4	.300	.500
Young, Kevin	.200	5	1	0	0	1	1	.333	.200
Zeile, Todd	.071	14	1	0	0	2	1	.188	.071

Batter	Avg	AB	H	HR	BI	BB	SO	OBP	Slg
Alicea, Luis*	.333	6	2	1	2	2	1	.500	.833
Alou, Moises	.000	6	0	0	0	1	0	.143	.000
Anthony, Eric*	.222	9	2	0	0	0	2	.222	.222
Arias, Alex	.333	3	1	0	2	2	0	.600	.333
Bagwell, Jeff	.500	6	3	0	0	0	0	.500	.500
Bell, Derek	.364	11	4	0	0	1	2	.417	.364
Bell, Jay	.000	7	0	0	0	1	0	.000	.000
Berry, Sean	.000	6	0	0	0	1	2	.143	.000
Bichette, D	.200	10	2	0	1	1	2	.250	.300
Biggio, Craig	.143	7	1	0	0	1	2	.250	.143
Bonds, Barry*	.182	11	2	0	1	1	2	.250	.182
Boone, Bret	.500	8	4	0	0	0	0	.500	.625
Branson, Jeff*	.400	5	2	0	0	0	1	.400	.600
Brogna, Rico*	.667	6	4	0	2	0	0	.667	.667
Brumfield, J	.667	3	2	0	2	3	0	.714	.667

Batter	Avg	AB	H	HR	BI	BB	SO	OBP	Slg
Bullett, S*	.000	6	0	0	0	0	4	.000	.000
Burks, Ellis	.200	5	1	0	0	1	3	.333	.200
Butler, Brett*	.250	4	1	0	0	1	0	.400	.250
Caminiti, Ken#	.250	8	2	0	1	1	3	.400	.250
Carr, Chuck	.286	7	2	0	0	1	2	.375	.286
Castilla, V	.200	5	1	0	0	1	1	.333	.200
Cedeno, A	.167	6	1	0	1	1	1	.286	.167
Cianfrocco, A	.400	5	2	0	0	0	2	.400	.600
Clark, Dave*	.375	8	3	0	1	1	3	.444	.375
Clayton, R	.308	13	4	0	3	0	2	.308	.462
Colbrunn, G	.182	11	2	0	0	0	4	.182	.182
Conine, Jeff	.267	15	4	0	1	2	1	.353	.267
Cordero, Wil	.111	9	1	0	1	0	2	.111	.111
Daulton, D*	.500	6	3	1	3	1	1	.571	1.000
DeShields, D*	.143	7	1	0	0	1	2	.250	.143
Duncan, M	.444	9	4	0	0	0	1	.444	.444
Dunston, S	.000	6	0	0	0	0	2	.000	.000
Dykstra, L*	.375	8	3	0	4	1	0	.400	.625
Eisenreich, J*	.333	6	2	0	0	0	0	.333	.500
Everett, Carl*	.143	7	1	0	0	1	4	.250	.143
Finley, Steve*	.222	9	2	0	1	1	1	.300	.444
Fletcher, D*	.200	5	1	0	0	0	2	.200	.400
Galarraga, A	.100	10	1	0	0	0	5	.100	.100
Gant, Ron	.333	6	2	0	0	1	1	.429	.333
Garcia, C	.250	4	1	0	0	2	1	.500	.250
Gilkey, B	.200	10	2	0	2	1	1	.273	.300
Girardi, Joe	.143	7	1	0	0	0	1	.143	.143
Gonzalez, L*	.364	11	4	0	3	1	1	.417	.545
Grace, Mark*	.111	9	1	0	0	1	3	.200	.111
Grissom, M	.000	6	0	0	0	0	1	.000	.000
Gutierrez, R	.286	7	2	0	0	0	2	.286	.286
Harris, Lenny*	.333	3	1	1	4	1	0	.500	1.333
Hayes, C	.214	14	3	0	0	1	3	.267	.214
Hollins, Dave#	.500	4	2	0	0	1	0	.600	.750
Hundley, Todd#	.625	8	5	1	4	0	0	.625	1.000
Jefferies, G#	.250	8	2	0	2	1	0	.333	.250
Johnson, Mark*	.000	5	0	0	0	0	3	.000	.000
Jones, Chris	1.000	3	3	0	2	1	0	1.000	1.333
Jordan, Brian	.286	7	2	0	0	1	3	.375	.286
Karros, Eric	.333	9	3	0	0	0	2	.333	.444
Kent, Jeff	.300	10	3	1	1	1	4	.364	.700
King, Jeff	.300	10	3	0	1	1	2	.364	.400
Kingery, Mike*	.333	6	2	0	0	0	1	.333	.333
Lankford, Ray*	.083	12	1	1	1	1	4	.154	.333
Lansing, Mike	.400	10	4	0	1	1	2	.455	.500
Larkin, Barry	.375	8	3	1	4	3	1	.545	.875
Liriano, N#	.167	6	1	0	0	1	3	.286	.167
Mabry, John*	.125	8	1	0	0	0	2	.125	.125
Magadan, Dave*	.000	7	0	0	0	1	2	.125	.000
Manwaring, K	.333	6	2	0	1	0	0	.333	.500
Martin, Al*	.444	9	4	0	0	0	1	.444	.778
McGee, Willie#	.273	11	3	0	2	0	2	.273	.455
McRae, Brian#	.400	5	2	0	0	0	1	.400	.600
Morandini, M*	.273	11	3	0	2	0	3	.273	.273
Morris, Hal*	.167	6	1	0	0	0	2	.167	.333
Mouton, James	.200	5	1	0	2	2	1	.429	.200
Oliver, Joe	.500	8	4	0	1	0	1	.500	.500
Orsulak, Joe*	.143	7	1	0	0	1	1	.143	.143
Otero, Ricky#	.200	5	1	0	1	0	2	.200	.200
Pagnozzi, Tom	.143	7	1	0	0	0	2	.143	.143
Pendleton, T#	.000	8	0	0	0	0	1	.000	.000
Piazza, Mike	.250	4	1	0	1	4	2	.625	.250
Plantier, P*	.143	7	1	0	0	0	3	.143	.286
Reed, Jody	.000	4	0	0	0	1	0	.200	.000
Rodriguez, H*	.286	7	2	0	0	0	4	.286	.286
Sanchez, Rey	.167	6	1	0	0	0	2	.167	.167
Sanders, R	.333	9	3	0	1	1	2	.400	.333
Santiago, B	.111	9	1	0	1	0	4	.111	.111
Segui, David*	.556	9	5	1	3	0	1	.556	1.000
Sheffield, G	.300	10	3	0	2	3	2	.462	.400
Shipley, C	.200	5	1	0	1	1	1	.333	.200
Slaught, Don	.250	4	1	0	0	1	1	.250	.250
Sosa, Sammy	.400	5	2	0	0	2	2	.571	.600
Stocker, K#	.333	9	3	0	0	1	3	.400	.444
Sweeney, Mark*	.143	7	1	0	0	0	1	.143	.143
Taubensee, E*	.167	6	1	0	0	0	2	.167	.333
Thompson, Mil*	.000	7	0	0	0	1	1	.125	.000
Thompson, Rob	.222	9	2	0	1	0	3	.200	.333
VanderWal, J*	.400	5	2	0	0	1	0	.500	.400
Veras, Q#	.400	5	2	0	0	1	0	.500	.400
Vizcaino, J#	.375	8	3	0	3	0	1	.375	.500
Walker, Larry*	.444	9	4	1	1	1	0	.500	.778
Wallach, Tim	.000	6	0	0	0	0	3	.000	.000
Webster, L	.250	4	1	0	0	1	0	.400	.250
Weiss, Walt#	.182	11	2	0	1	0	4	.182	.182
White, B	.400	5	2	1	1	0	0	.400	1.200
Whiten, Mark#	.000	8	0	0	0	0	4	.000	.000
Wilkins, Rick*	.222	9	2	0	0	1	5	.300	.222
Williams, Ma	.111	9	1	1	1	1	1	.200	.444
Young, Eric	.154	13	2	0	0	3	2	.313	.154

Greg McMichael, Braves — RHP

Batter	Avg	AB	H	HR	BI	BB	SO	OBP	Slg
Zeile, Todd	.444	9	4	0	1	0	1	.444	.667

Rusty Meacham, Mariners — RHP

Batter	Avg	AB	H	HR	BI	BB	SO	OBP	Slg
Aldrete, Mike*	.500	4	2	0	1	1	0	.600	.500
Alomar, R#	.500	6	3	0	2	1	0	.571	.667
Alomar Jr, S	.500	6	3	0	0	0	0	.500	.500
Anderson, Brd*	.333	6	2	0	2	1	1	.429	.667
Baerga, C#	.500	6	3	0	0	1	0	.500	.500
Baines, H*	.143	7	1	0	1	0	1	.143	.143
Belle, Albert	.222	9	2	1	1	0	2	.222	.556
Blowers, Mike	.000	7	0	0	0	0	5	.000	.000
Boggs, Wade*	.300	10	3	0	0	1	0	.364	.400
Borders, Pat	.000	5	0	0	0	0	1	.000	.000
Bordick, Mike	.300	10	3	0	0	0	3	.300	.300
Brosius, S	.500	4	2	0	1	1	0	.500	1.000
Buhner, Jay	.143	7	1	1	3	1	2	.222	.571
Burks, Ellis	.333	6	2	0	0	1	2	.429	.333
Canseco, Jose	.429	7	3	0	0	1	1	.500	.571
Carter, Joe	.250	8	2	1	4	1	2	.273	.625
Clark, Will*	.167	6	1	0	0	0	0	.167	.167
Cole, Alex*	.429	7	3	0	1	0	0	.429	.571
Cora, Joey#	.500	6	3	0	0	1	0	.571	.667
Cordova, M	.250	4	1	0	0	1	2	.400	.250
Davis, Chili*	.500	8	4	0	1	3	1	.636	.625
Deer, Rob	.400	5	2	0	0	0	0	.400	.800
Devereaux, M	.375	8	3	0	2	0	2	.375	.375
Diaz, Alex#	.250	4	1	0	1	0	0	.250	.250
DiSarcina, G	.182	11	2	0	1	0	0	.182	.182
Edmonds, Jim*	.400	5	2	1	1	0	1	.400	1.000
Elster, Kevin	.333	6	2	0	3	0	1	.333	.500
Erstad, Darin*	.286	7	2	0	1	0	0	.286	.429
Fabregas, Jor*	.333	6	2	0	2	0	1	.333	.333
Fermin, Felix	.286	7	2	0	0	1	1	.375	.429
Fielder, C	.455	11	5	0	2	0	2	.455	.545
Franco, Julio	.400	5	2	0	0	1	0	.500	.400
Frye, Jeff	.400	5	2	0	1	0	0	.400	.400
Fryman, T	.500	10	5	1	1	1	1	.545	1.000
Gagne, Greg	.400	5	2	0	0	1	1	.500	.600
Gallego, Mike	.500	4	2	0	3	0	0	.400	.750
Gomez, Leo	.556	9	5	0	3	0	1	.556	.778
Gonzalez, J	.235	17	4	1	1	1	5	.278	.471
Greer, Rusty*	.500	8	4	0	1	1	2	.556	.500
Hamilton, D*	.400	10	4	0	1	0	0	.364	.600
Henderson, R	.000	3	0	0	1	1	1	.200	.000
Hoiles, Chris	.000	5	0	0	0	0	2	.167	.000
Huff, Michael	.400	5	2	0	0	0	0	.400	.400
Huson, Jeff*	.286	7	2	1	2	0	0	.286	.714
Jaha, John	.333	6	2	0	0	0	2	.333	.333
Javier, Stan#	.250	4	1	0	2	1	1	.400	.250
Johnson, L*	.000	6	0	0	0	0	0	.000	.000
Karkovice, R	.286	7	2	1	1	0	2	.286	.714
Knoblauch, C	.308	13	4	0	3	2	1	.412	.462
Leius, Scott	.200	10	2	0	1	0	1	.200	.300
Martinez, E	.250	8	2	0	2	0	0	.250	.375
Martinez, T*	.429	7	3	1	4	1	0	.444	1.286
McGwire, Mark	.600	5	3	2	4	0	2	.500	1.800
McLemore, M#	.375	8	3	1	1	3	0	.545	.750
Molitor, Paul	.429	7	3	0	0	1	0	.500	.429
Munoz, Pedro	.143	7	1	0	0	0	1	.143	.143
Newson, W*	.200	5	1	0	0	0	1	.200	.400
Nilsson, Dave*	.400	5	2	1	2	0	0	.500	1.000
Olerud, John*	.167	6	1	0	0	0	0	.167	.167
Palmeiro, R*	.300	10	3	0	0	0	3	.300	.300
Palmer, Dean	.000	13	0	0	0	1	1	.071	.000
Pena, Tony	.143	7	1	0	0	0	0	.143	.143
Phillips, T#	.200	5	1	0	1	1	1	.333	.200
Polonia, Luis*	.286	7	2	0	1	0	2	.286	.286
Raines, Tim#	.375	8	3	0	1	1	1	.444	.750
Reboulet, J	.333	6	2	0	0	0	1	.333	.333
Reed, Jody	.222	9	2	0	0	0	1	.222	.333
Ripken, Cal	.143	7	1	0	1	0	0	.143	.143
Rodriguez, I	.381	21	8	1	1	0	4	.381	.571
Salmon, Tim	.167	6	1	0	0	2	3	.375	.167
Seitzer, K	.125	8	1	0	2	0	1	.111	.125
Sierra, Ruben#	.364	11	4	1	4	0	3	.333	.727
Snow, J.T.#	.857	7	6	0	0	1	1	.875	.857
Sojo, Luis	.200	5	1	0	0	0	1	.200	.200
Sprague, Ed	.143	7	1	0	1	0	2	.125	.143
Stanley, Mike	.167	6	1	0	0	0	2	.167	.167
Steinbach, T	.000	3	0	0	0	2	0	.400	.000
Tartabull, D	.500	6	3	0	3	0	3	.500	.500
Tettleton, M#	.167	12	2	0	0	2	1	.333	.167
Thomas, Frank	.222	9	2	0	1	1	0	.300	.333
Trammell, A	.200	5	1	0	1	0	1	.200	.200
Valentin, John	.200	5	1	0	1	0	1	.200	.200
Valentin, Jse#	.200	5	1	0	1	0	0	.200	.400
Vaughn, Greg	.091	11	1	0	1	1	5	.154	.091
Vaughn, Mo*	.333	6	2	1	1	0	2	.333	.833
Velarde, R	.375	8	3	2	3	0	1	.375	1.125
Ventura, R*	.333	6	2	0	0	0	0	.333	.333

Rusty Meacham, Mariners — RHP

Batter	Avg	AB	H	HR	BI	BB	SO	OBP	Slg
Vina, F*	.250	4	1	0	1	0	0	.200	.250
White, Devon#	.400	5	2	0	1	0	0	.400	.600
Whiten, Mark#	.333	6	2	0	2	0	0	.333	.333
Wilson, Dan	.000	5	0	0	0	0	0	.000	.000

Jim Mecir, Yankees — RHP

Batter	Avg	AB	H	HR	BI	BB	SO	OBP	Slg
Durham, Ray*	.400	5	2	0	0	1	1	.500	.400
Karkovice, R	.167	6	1	0	1	0	4	.167	.167

Ramiro Mendoza, Yankees — RHP

Batter	Avg	AB	H	HR	BI	BB	SO	OBP	Slg
Bragg, Darren*	.125	8	1	0	0	0	0	.125	.125
Carter, Joe	.600	5	3	1	2	0	1	.600	1.400
Cordova, M	.400	5	2	0	1	0	0	.400	.400
Frye, Jeff	.286	7	2	0	2	0	3	.286	.571
Garciaparra	.000	5	0	0	0	0	0	.000	.000
Green, Shawn*	.200	5	1	1	2	0	0	.200	.800
Greenwell, M*	.200	5	1	0	0	0	0	.200	.400
Jefferson, R*	.667	6	4	0	1	0	0	.667	1.000
Molitor, Paul	.500	6	3	0	2	0	0	.500	.667
Olerud, John*	.333	3	1	0	0	0	0	.600	.333
Sprague, Ed	.000	4	0	0	0	0	2	.200	.000
Stahoviak, S*	.800	5	4	0	1	0	1	.800	1.200
Vaughn, Mo*	.286	7	2	0	1	0	2	.286	.429

Paul Menhart, Mariners — RHP

Batter	Avg	AB	H	HR	BI	BB	SO	OBP	Slg
Alomar Jr, S	.200	5	1	0	1	0	1	.200	.200
Anderson, Brd*	.333	6	2	0	0	1	0	.429	.500
Baerga, C#	.167	6	1	0	0	1	0	.167	.167
Baines, H*	.429	7	3	1	1	1	1	.500	.857
Belle, Albert	.286	7	2	0	0	0	1	.286	.286
Boggs, Wade*	.429	7	3	0	1	2	0	.556	.429
Bonilla, B#	.167	6	1	0	0	0	1	.167	.333
Cirillo, Jeff	.111	9	1	0	1	1	1	.182	.111
Curtis, Chad	.167	6	1	1	3	3	1	.444	.667
Damon, Johnny*	.182	11	2	0	0	0	2	.182	.364
Fielder, C	.600	5	3	1	4	1	0	.667	1.400
Fryman, T	.667	6	4	0	1	1	2	.714	.833
Gaetti, Gary	.333	6	2	1	3	1	1	.444	.833
Gagne, Greg	.250	8	2	0	0	0	2	.250	.250
Gomez, Chris	.000	6	0	0	0	0	0	.000	.000
Goodwin, Tom*	.300	10	3	0	1	3	1	.462	.300
Hamelin, Bob*	.143	7	1	1	1	1	0	.250	.571
Higginson, B*	.000	5	0	0	2	2	2	.286	.000
Hoiles, Chris	.000	6	0	0	0	0	2	.000	.000
Howard, Dave#	.333	3	1	0	1	1	1	.500	.333
Huson, Jeff*	.000	6	0	0	0	0	0	.000	.000
Jaha, John	.000	7	0	0	1	1	1	.125	.000
Joyner, Wally*	.111	9	1	0	1	2	0	.273	.111
Listach, Pat#	.167	6	1	0	0	0	1	.167	.167
Lockhart, K*	.286	7	2	0	3	1	1	.333	.429
Lofton, Kenny*	.000	5	0	0	0	0	0	.000	.000
Mayne, Brent*	.375	8	3	0	0	0	2	.375	.500
Mieske, Matt	.375	8	3	2	6	1	1	.444	1.125
Murray, Eddie#	.333	3	1	0	0	2	0	.600	.333
Nixon, Otis#	.250	4	1	0	1	1	0	.400	.250
Nunnally, Jon*	.125	8	1	0	1	1	2	.300	.375
O'Neill, Paul*	.500	4	2	0	3	0	0	.714	.500
Palmeiro, R*	.000	5	0	0	0	1	1	.167	.000
Ripken, Cal	.333	6	2	0	2	0	0	.333	.500
Seitzer, K	.375	8	3	0	2	2	0	.500	.375
Sierra, Ruben#	.667	6	4	1	3	1	0	.714	1.333
Stanley, Mike	.400	5	2	1	2	0	0	.400	1.200
Thome, Jim*	.000	2	0	0	0	4	2	.667	.000
Valentin, Jse#	.333	3	1	0	2	3	0	.667	1.000
Vaughn, Greg	.800	5	4	1	2	2	0	.857	1.400
Velarde, R	.200	5	1	0	0	0	1	.429	.400
Vina, F*	.714	7	5	0	2	0	0	.714	1.429
Vizquel, Omar#	.400	5	2	0	0	0	1	.400	.400

Jose Mercedes, Brewers — RHP

Batter	Avg	AB	H	HR	BI	BB	SO	OBP	Slg
Carter, Joe	.250	4	1	0	2	1	0	.400	1.000

Kent Mercker, Indians — LHP

Batter	Avg	AB	H	HR	BI	BB	SO	OBP	Slg
Abbott, Kurt	.222	9	2	0	0	1	1	.300	.333
Alfonzo, E	.167	6	1	0	0	0	0	.167	.167
Alou, Moises	.294	17	5	0	2	2	0	.368	.294
Anthony, Eric*	.000	7	0	0	0	1	2	.125	.000
Ashley, Billy	.000	9	0	0	0	1	6	.100	.000
Ausmus, Brad	.286	7	2	0	0	1	0	.375	.286
Bagwell, Jeff	.333	9	3	1	5	0	1	.300	.667
Barberie, B#	.333	6	2	0	0	1	2	.500	.333
Bates, Jason#	.000	7	0	0	0	3	0	.000	.000
Battle, Allen	.000	3	0	0	2	0	0	.400	.000
Bell, Derek	.357	14	5	1	5	2	0	.412	.786
Bell, Jay	.176	17	3	0	1	0	4	.222	.176
Benjamin, M	.333	3	1	0	0	4	1	.714	.333
Berry, Sean	.000	8	0	0	1	2	1	.200	.000

Kent Mercker, Indians — LHP

Batter	Avg	AB	H	HR	BI	BB	SO	OBP	Slg
Bichette, D	.400	15	6	1	4	0	3	.400	.733
Biggio, Craig	.188	16	3	0	1	4	1	.350	.250
Bogar, Tim	.444	9	4	2	5	1	1	.500	1.111
Bonds, Barry*	.176	17	3	0	1	0	6	.176	.235
Bonilla, B#	.286	21	6	2	4	2	3	.348	.619
Borders, Pat	.000	5	0	0	0	0	2	.000	.000
Brogna, Rico*	.429	7	3	1	1	0	2	.429	.857
Brumfield, J	.333	9	3	1	2	0	0	.333	.667
Burks, Ellis	.333	6	2	1	1	3	1	.556	.833
Burnitz, J*	.000	5	0	0	0	0	3	.000	.000
Butler, Brett*	.333	9	3	0	1	6	3	.563	.333
Caminiti, Ken#	.235	17	4	1	2	1	3	.278	.529
Carr, Chuck	.200	10	2	0	2	0	3	.200	.300
Carreon, Mark	.200	5	1	0	0	1	0	.333	.200
Carter, Joe	.167	6	1	0	1	0	0	.167	.167
Castilla, V	.100	10	1	0	0	1	0	.182	.200
Cedeno, A	.000	4	0	0	0	1	1	.200	.000
Cianfrocco, A	.000	6	0	0	0	0	2	.000	.000
Clark, Phil	.143	7	1	0	0	0	0	.143	.143
Clark, Will*	.471	17	8	2	7	1	0	.526	.941
Clayton, R	.125	8	1	0	0	0	2	.125	.125
Colbrunn, G	.000	5	0	0	0	0	1	.000	.000
Coleman, V#	.200	5	1	0	0	1	0	.333	.200
Conine, Jeff	.750	8	6	1	1	1	0	.778	1.125
Coomer, Ron	.200	5	2	0	2	2	0	.571	.600
Cordero, Wil	.444	18	8	0	5	1	4	.474	.556
Daulton, D*	.000	7	0	0	0	4	5	.364	.000
Dawson, Andre	.286	7	2	1	1	0	1	.286	.714
DeShields, D*	.125	24	3	0	1	3	6	.222	.125
Duncan, M	.250	12	3	0	1	0	4	.231	.333
Dunston, S	.077	13	1	0	0	0	4	.077	.231
Dykstra, L*	.222	9	2	0	0	2	3	.364	.333
Elster, Kevin	.091	11	1	1	1	0	1	.091	.364
Finley, Steve*	.231	13	3	1	1	1	4	.286	.538
Galarraga, A	.412	17	7	2	6	1	6	.444	.765
Garcia, C	.143	7	1	0	0	1	4	.250	.143
Gilkey, B	.267	15	4	0	1	1	1	.313	.467
Girardi, Joe	.083	12	1	0	0	1	2	.154	.083
Gonzalez, J	.500	6	3	3	7	1	1	.571	2.000
Gonzalez, L*	.200	5	1	0	1	3	3	.333	.200
Grace, Mark*	.400	15	6	0	3	1	1	.412	.467
Greer, Rusty*	.400	5	2	0	1	1	0	.500	.600
Grissom, M	.438	16	7	0	0	0	3	.471	.500
Grudzielanek	.400	5	2	0	0	0	2	.400	.400
Gutierrez, R	.273	11	3	0	1	0	3	.273	.364
Gwynn, Tony*	.227	22	5	1	2	2	1	.292	.409
Hamilton, D*	.571	7	4	0	0	1	1	.625	.571
Hayes, C	.357	14	5	1	5	1	4	.400	.714
Hill, G	.333	12	4	0	1	0	5	.333	.417
Hollins, Dave#	.333	6	2	0	3	5	1	.636	.667
Hudler, Rex	.200	5	1	1	1	1	3	.333	.800
Hundley, Todd#	.091	11	1	0	0	1	3	.167	.091
Hunter, Brian	.125	8	1	0	0	2	0	.300	.125
Hunter, Bri L	.000	6	0	0	0	0	1	.000	.000
Incaviglia, P	.125	8	1	0	0	0	2	.125	.250
Jefferies, G#	.467	15	7	0	0	1	1	.500	.600
Jones, Chris	.429	7	3	0	0	0	1	.429	.429
Jordan, Brian	.286	7	2	1	2	0	2	.286	.714
Jordan, Ricky	.375	8	3	1	2	0	0	.333	.750
Karros, Eric	.375	16	6	0	4	2	1	.444	.625
Kelly, R	.462	13	6	0	5	2	1	.500	.615
Kent, Jeff	.154	13	2	0	1	0	1	.214	.154
King, Jeff	.000	10	0	0	0	0	2	.000	.000
Knoblauch, C	.333	6	2	0	0	0	1	.333	.333
Lankford, Ray*	.273	11	3	0	0	3	3	.429	.455
Lansing, Mike	.182	11	2	1	1	3	2	.357	.455
Larkin, Barry	.167	6	1	1	1	1	0	.286	.667
Lewis, Darren	.300	10	3	0	1	5	1	.533	.300
Magadan, Dave*	.200	10	2	0	0	4	6	.429	.200
Manwaring, K	.333	6	2	0	1	0	2	.333	.333
Martinez, Da*	.273	11	3	0	0	0	3	.273	.273
McGee, Willie#	.300	10	3	0	1	0	2	.333	.300
McGriff, Fred*	.111	9	1	1	1	1	3	.200	.444
McLemore, M#	.000	4	0	0	0	1	0	.000	.000
Meares, Pat	.000	4	0	0	0	1	0	.000	.000
Merced, O*	.125	8	1	0	0	3	1	.364	.250
Mitchell, K	.167	6	1	1	1	1	2	.286	.667
Molitor, Paul	.667	6	4	0	1	0	0	.667	.833
Mondesi, Raul	.091	11	1	1	3	0	2	.143	.364
Morandini, M*	.333	9	3	0	3	1	2	.400	.667
Morris, Hal*	.364	11	4	0	1	1	1	.417	.364
Mouton, James	.125	8	1	0	0	1	0	.222	.375
Murray, Eddie#	.222	9	2	0	0	2	1	.364	.333
O'Neill, Paul*	.000	4	0	0	0	0	1	.000	.000
Offerman, J#	.333	21	7	1	2	3	4	.417	.571
Oliver, Joe	.000	5	0	0	0	2	3	.286	.000
Pagnozzi, Tom	.111	9	1	0	0	0	3	.111	.111
Palmer, Dean	.333	3	1	1	2	2	0	.667	1.333
Parent, Mark	.167	6	1	0	1	2	3	.375	.167
Pena, G#	.000	2	0	0	0	3	1	.600	.000
Pendleton, T#	.444	9	4	1	4	0	1	.444	.889
Phillips, T#	.200	5	1	0	0	0	1	.200	.200
Piazza, Mike	.200	10	2	0	0	0	3	.200	.200
Plantier, P*	.000	6	0	0	0	2	2	.250	.000
Prince, Tom	.000	3	0	0	0	3	2	.500	.000
Randa, Joe	1.000	5	5	0	0	0	0	1.000	1.200
Reed, Jody	.250	4	1	0	0	2	0	.500	.250
Roberts, Bip#	.400	10	4	1	6	1	2	.417	.700
Rodriguez, I	.286	7	2	0	1	0	0	.286	.571
Sabo, Chris	.167	6	1	0	0	0	3	.167	.167
Samuel, Juan	.100	10	1	0	1	2	3	.231	.100
Sanchez, Rey	.333	9	3	0	0	1	0	.400	.556
Sandberg, R	.364	11	4	0	1	2	1	.462	.364
Sanders, R	.143	7	1	0	0	0	3	.143	.143
Santiago, B	.444	9	4	0	0	1	1	.500	.667
Segui, David#	.385	13	5	0	3	3	2	.529	.538
Servais, S	.250	4	1	0	1	0	0	.400	.250
Sheffield, G	.250	12	3	1	3	3	2	.400	.500
Shipley, C	.154	13	2	0	1	2	2	.267	.154
Simms, Mike	.200	10	2	2	2	1	2	.273	.800
Slaught, Don	.182	11	2	0	0	0	5	.182	.182
Smith, Ozzie#	.278	18	5	0	3	3	1	.381	.333
Sosa, Sammy	.125	8	1	0	0	3	5	.364	.125
Stinnett, K	.000	6	0	0	0	1	1	.143	.000
Stocker, K#	.400	5	2	0	1	0	1	.400	.400
Strawberry, D*	.286	7	2	0	0	0	0	.286	.286
Tarasco, Tony*	.200	5	1	0	0	1	1	.333	.200
Tettleton, M#	.000	4	0	0	0	1	1	.200	.000
Thompson, Rob	.600	5	3	0	1	3	1	.750	.600
Thompson, Ry	.000	10	0	0	0	1	2	.091	.000
Veras, Q#	.000	6	0	0	0	0	2	.000	.000
Vitiello, Joe	.333	3	1	0	1	2	1	.600	.333
Vizcaino, J#	.222	9	2	0	1	0	5	.222	.222
Walker, Larry*	.353	17	6	0	3	3	4	.450	.471
Wallach, Tim	.300	20	6	2	4	1	3	.364	.600
Wehner, John	.429	7	3	0	1	1	1	.500	.429
Weiss, Walt#	.333	12	4	0	0	0	0	.333	.333
White, R	.286	14	4	0	1	1	2	.375	.357
Whiten, Mark#	.167	6	1	0	0	1	1	.286	.167
Wilkins, Rick*	.000	6	0	0	0	0	2	.000	.000
Williams, E	.400	5	2	0	0	2	1	.571	.400
Williams, Ma	.500	10	5	1	4	0	2	.500	.800
Young, Eric	.182	11	2	0	1	1	2	.250	.364
Zeile, Todd	.333	9	3	2	6	3	0	.500	1.111

Jose Mesa, Indians — RHP

Batter	Avg	AB	H	HR	BI	BB	SO	OBP	Slg
Aldrete, Mike*	.375	8	3	0	0	0	3	.375	.375
Alomar, R#	.235	17	4	0	0	1	0	.278	.294
Amaral, Rich	.429	7	3	0	1	0	1	.429	.571
Anderson, Brd*	.176	17	3	0	1	2	1	.300	.176
Baines, H*	.150	20	3	1	4	3	4	.261	.300
Becker, Rich*	.143	7	1	0	1	0	4	.143	.286
Berroa, G	.500	6	3	0	1	0	0	.500	.500
Bichette, D	.333	6	2	0	1	0	0	.333	.500
Blowers, Mike	.333	3	1	0	0	1	1	.500	.333
Boggs, Wade*	.355	31	11	0	5	6	3	.459	.452
Bonilla, B#	.000	5	0	0	0	1	0	.167	.000
Borders, Pat	.462	13	6	0	2	0	1	.462	.615
Bordick, Mike	.125	16	2	0	1	1	3	.176	.125
Brosius, S	.333	9	3	0	0	0	3	.333	.333
Buhner, Jay	.105	19	2	0	2	3	5	.227	.158
Burks, Ellis	.222	18	4	0	0	0	0	.222	.278
Canseco, Jose	.259	27	7	0	3	1	4	.286	.407
Carter, Joe	.292	24	7	3	10	0	8	.280	.750
Cirillo, Jeff	.600	5	3	0	0	1	0	.667	.600
Clark, Will*	.400	5	2	0	0	1	0	.500	.400
Cole, Alex*	.333	3	1	0	0	2	0	.600	.333
Cora, Joey#	.500	8	4	0	0	4	1	.714	.625
Curtis, Chad	.467	15	7	1	1	0	2	.467	.667
Cuyler, Milt#	.300	10	3	0	1	0	1	.300	.500
Damon, Johnny*	.250	4	1	0	0	1	1	.400	.250
Davis, Chili#	.400	20	8	0	0	1	2	.429	.550
Davis, Eric	.500	4	2	1	2	1	1	.600	1.250
Dawson, Andre	.385	13	5	1	3	0	2	.385	.769
Deer, Rob	.300	9	3	0	3	2	3	.455	.556
Devereaux, M	.200	10	2	0	0	3	0	.385	.300
Diaz, Alex#	.200	5	1	0	0	0	2	.200	.200
DiSarcina, G	.364	11	4	0	3	0	0	.364	.364
Easley, D	.250	8	2	0	1	1	2	.300	.250
Eisenreich, J*	.571	7	4	0	2	0	0	.571	.714
Fermin, Felix	.400	5	2	0	3	1	1	.429	.400
Fielder, C	.120	25	3	0	0	1	12	.154	.120
Franco, Julio	.333	15	5	1	1	0	2	.333	.533
Frye, Jeff	.333	6	2	0	1	0	2	.333	.500
Fryman, T	.375	24	9	1	2	3	1	.444	.542
Gaetti, Gary	.091	11	1	0	0	0	2	.091	.091
Gagne, Greg	.267	15	4	0	0	1	0	.313	.267
Gates, Brent#	.333	9	3	0	2	1	1	.400	.333
Gomez, Leo	.100	10	1	1	2	2	2	.250	.400
Gonzales, R	.667	6	4	0	0	0	0	.667	.833
Gonzalez, J	.259	27	7	3	8	0	7	.286	.630

135

Batter	Avg	AB	H	HR	BI	BB	SO	OBP	Slg
Greenwell, M*	.118	34	4	0	2	1	3	.143	.118
Greer, Rusty*	.000	2	0	0	0	3	1	.600	.000
Griffey Jr, K*	.478	23	11	1	3	2	1	.520	.652
Guillen, O*	.375	8	3	0	0	0	0	.375	.375
Gwynn, Chris*	.625	8	5	0	1	0	0	.625	.750
Hale, Chip*	.286	7	2	0	1	1	1	.375	.286
Hall, Mel*	.222	9	2	0	0	0	0	.222	.222
Hamelin, Bob*	.000	6	0	0	0	3	0	.000	.000
Hamilton, D*	.333	15	5	0	0	4	1	.474	.333
Hammonds, J	.167	6	1	0	0	1	3	.286	.167
Henderson, R	.409	22	9	0	0	9	2	.581	.545
Hernandez, Jo	.500	4	2	0	1	1	1	.600	.500
Hiatt, Phil	.143	7	1	0	0	0	4	.143	.143
Hoiles, Chris	.000	9	0	0	1	3	5	.231	.000
Howard, Dave*	.000	9	0	0	0	3	4	.250	.000
Howell, Jack*	.000	4	0	0	0	1	1	.200	.000
Hulse, David*	.188	16	3	0	1	0	4	.235	.250
Huson, Jeff*	.000	11	0	0	0	1	0	.000	.000
Incaviglia, P	.400	5	2	0	1	1	1	.500	.600
Jaha, John	.250	16	4	0	0	0	5	.250	.313
James, Dion*	.375	8	3	0	2	0	0	.375	.500
Jefferies, G#	.615	13	8	1	1	0	0	.615	1.000
Jefferson, R*	.250	4	1	0	3	0	0	.167	.250
Johnson, L*	.357	14	5	0	0	1	1	.400	.357
Joyner, Wally*	.391	23	9	1	6	2	2	.423	.652
Kelly, Pat	.000	7	0	0	0	0	3	.000	.000
Kelly, R	.308	13	4	0	1	1	1	.357	.385
Knoblauch, C	.059	17	1	0	1	2	3	.190	.059
Koslofski, K*	.286	7	2	0	0	1	0	.375	.286
Kreuter, Chad#	.500	12	6	1	4	1	1	.571	.917
Leius, Scott	.125	8	1	0	2	1	1	.222	.125
Listach, Pat	.300	10	3	0	4	1	1	.364	.400
Livingstone*	.533	15	8	0	4	2	0	.556	.600
Lovullo, T#	.750	4	3	1	3	3	0	.857	1.500
Macfarlane, M	.111	18	2	1	2	1	5	.200	.278
Martinez, E	.111	18	2	1	2	1	5	.200	.278
Martinez, T*	.364	11	4	0	2	2	0	.429	.364
Marzano, John	.400	5	2	0	1	0	2	.400	.400
Mayne, Brent*	.313	16	5	0	1	0	1	.313	.375
McCarty, Dave	.167	6	1	0	0	0	2	.167	.167
McGriff, Fred*	.250	8	2	0	1	1	1	.333	.250
McGwire, Mark	.000	10	0	0	0	6	7	.375	.000
McLemore, M#	.231	13	3	0	0	3	3	.375	.231
McRae, Brian#	.212	33	7	0	0	1	6	.235	.242
Meares, Pat	.250	8	2	0	1	0	0	.250	.250
Mieske, Matt	.167	6	1	0	0	2	1	.375	.167
Molitor, Paul	.222	27	6	0	4	3	4	.300	.407
Munoz, Pedro	.167	6	1	1	0	0	2	.167	.667
Myers, Greg*	.167	12	2	0	0	1	3	.231	.167
Naehring, Tim	.286	7	2	0	1	1	1	.375	.429
Newson, W*	.500	4	2	0	0	1	2	.600	.750
Nilsson, Dave*	.278	18	5	0	0	0	2	.278	.278
Nixon, Otis#	.750	4	3	0	0	2	1	.833	.750
O'Neill, Paul*	1.000	4	4	0	1	2	0	1.000	1.000
Olerud, John*	.286	21	6	0	0	3	4	.375	.381
Orsulak, Joe*	.333	6	2	0	0	0	0	.333	.333
Palmeiro, R*	.154	26	4	2	5	5	3	.273	.385
Palmer, Dean	.227	22	5	1	3	1	5	.261	.409
Paquette, C	.286	7	2	0	1	0	1	.286	.429
Pena, Tony	.318	22	7	1	3	2	3	.375	.500
Phillips, T#	.333	21	7	0	3	4	3	.423	.381
Plantier, P*	.333	6	2	0	1	0	1	.333	.500
Polonia, Luis*	.368	19	7	0	5	0	0	.400	.421
Raines, Tim#	.077	13	1	0	0	0	0	.077	.077
Reboulet, J	.250	4	1	0	0	1	0	.400	.250
Reed, Jody	.375	24	9	0	4	0	0	.375	.500
Ripken, Billy	.143	7	1	0	1	0	1	.143	.143
Ripken, Cal	.250	24	6	1	6	1	4	.280	.458
Rodriguez, I	.200	25	5	2	6	0	6	.231	.520
Salmon, Tim	.357	14	5	1	1	1	4	.400	.571
Schofield, D	.222	9	2	0	0	1	3	.300	.222
Segui, David*	.500	8	4	0	0	0	0	.500	.500
Seitzer, K	.333	18	6	0	1	2	3	.400	.389
Sheffield, G	.600	5	3	0	0	1	0	.667	1.400
Shumpert, T	.222	9	2	1	1	0	1	.222	.556
Sierra, Ruben#	.258	31	8	1	2	0	5	.250	.355
Snow, J.T.#	.385	13	5	0	2	1	4	.429	.462
Sojo, Luis	.111	9	1	0	0	0	3	.111	.111
Spiers, Bill*	.133	15	2	0	1	1	3	.176	.133
Sprague, Ed	.231	13	3	1	4	0	0	.214	.538
Stanley, Mike	.500	10	5	0	1	0	1	.500	.600
Steinbach, T	.211	19	4	1	2	1	0	.238	.421
Strange, Doug*	.294	17	5	0	1	2	2	.368	.294
Surhoff, B.J.*	.360	25	9	0	4	2	1	.407	.440
Sveum, Dale#	.000	5	0	0	0	1	1	.167	.000
Tartabull, D	.545	11	6	0	2	0	1	.545	.818
Tettleton, M#	.167	18	3	2	5	6	2	.360	.500
Thomas, Frank	.200	15	3	0	1	4	2	.350	.200
Trammell, Ala	.286	14	4	0	4	0	1	.286	.357
Valentin, Jhn	.667	6	4	1	4	2	0	.750	1.167
Valentin, Jse#	.222	9	2	0	1	2	3	.364	.222

Batter	Avg	AB	H	HR	BI	BB	SO	OBP	Slg
Valle, Dave	.200	10	2	0	0	1	0	.273	.200
Vaughn, Greg	.300	20	6	1	3	1	3	.333	.500
Vaughn, Mo*	.333	18	6	1	1	4	2	.455	.500
Velarde, R	.176	17	3	1	3	1	4	.222	.353
Ventura, R*	.467	15	7	0	0	3	0	.556	.533
Vizquel, Omar*	.385	13	5	0	2	3	1	.471	.462
Walbeck, Matt#	.200	5	1	0	0	0	2	.200	.400
Webster, L	.500	4	2	1	2	2	0	.667	1.500
White, Devon#	.429	21	9	0	4	1	6	.455	.524
Williams, Ber#	.111	9	1	0	0	3	4	.333	.111
Williams, Ger	.400	5	2	0	0	0	2	.400	.400

Batter	Avg	AB	H	HR	BI	BB	SO	OBP	Slg
Abbott, Kurt	.143	7	1	0	0	0	5	.143	.143
Alfonzo, E	.600	5	3	0	0	0	0	.600	.600
Alou, Moises	.143	7	1	0	2	0	1	.125	.286
Bagwell, Jeff	.500	6	3	1	3	2	1	.556	1.333
Bell, Derek	.250	8	2	0	4	0	0	.333	.250
Berry, Sean	.000	4	0	0	0	3	2	.429	.000
Bichette, D	.250	4	1	0	0	1	1	.400	.250
Biggio, Craig	.625	8	5	0	2	2	1	.700	.750
Burks, Ellis	.500	6	3	1	5	1	0	.571	1.333
Caminiti, Ken#	.167	6	1	0	1	1	1	.286	.500
Cangelosi, J#	.750	4	3	0	0	2	1	.857	1.000
Castilla, V	.250	4	1	0	1	1	0	.400	.250
Clayton, R	.600	5	3	0	0	0	0	.667	.600
Colbrunn, G	.200	5	1	0	0	0	0	.200	.200
Conine, Jeff	.286	7	2	0	1	3	1	.500	.429
Dunston, S	.200	5	1	0	0	0	3	.200	.400
Eisenreich, J*	.500	8	4	1	2	0	0	.500	1.250
Eusebio, Tony	.400	5	2	0	1	2	2	.500	.400
Finley, Steve*	.143	7	1	0	0	0	1	.143	.286
Fletcher, D*	.200	5	1	0	0	0	0	.200	.400
Galarraga, A	.200	5	1	0	1	2	4	.429	.400
Gant, Ron	.000	3	0	0	0	2	0	.400	.000
Gilkey, B	.200	5	1	0	1	3	0	.500	.200
Gonzalez, L*	.500	8	4	0	1	0	1	.500	.750
Grissom, M	.800	5	4	1	5	0	0	.800	1.600
Gwynn, Tony*	.400	5	2	0	0	1	0	.500	.400
Harris, Lenny*	.250	4	1	0	0	1	0	.400	.250
Hill, G	.250	8	2	1	2	0	1	.250	.625
Howard, T*	.250	4	1	0	0	1	0	.200	.500
Hunter, Bri L	.333	6	2	0	0	0	0	.333	.333
Jefferies, G#	.375	8	3	1	1	1	1	.444	.750
Johnson, L*	.200	5	1	0	0	0	0	.200	.200
Jordan, Brian	.333	6	2	0	0	0	0	.333	.333
Karros, Eric	.833	6	5	0	3	0	0	.833	1.167
Kelly, R	.000	6	0	0	0	0	2	.000	.000
Lansing, Mike	.000	5	0	0	0	0	0	.000	.000
Larkin, Barry	.500	6	3	1	2	0	0	.500	1.000
McRae, Brian#	.600	5	3	2	2	1	0	.600	2.000
Miller, Orl	.250	4	1	0	1	0	2	.500	.250
Mondesi, Raul	.571	7	4	1	2	1	1	.625	1.000
Morandini, M*	.000	5	0	0	0	0	0	.000	.000
Morris, Hal*	.000	5	0	0	0	1	1	.200	.000
Mouton, James	.000	6	0	0	0	1	1	.143	.000
O'Brien, C	.200	5	1	0	1	0	2	.200	.200
Otero, Ricky#	.250	4	1	0	0	2	0	.500	.250
Pendleton, T#	.333	6	2	0	1	0	0	.333	.333
Sanders, R	.167	6	1	0	0	0	4	.167	.167
Santiago, B	.400	5	2	1	3	1	1	.500	1.000
Segui, David#	.400	5	2	0	0	0	1	.400	.600
Servais, S	.167	6	1	0	1	0	0	.167	.167
Shipley, C	.333	6	2	1	4	0	1	.333	.833
Sosa, Sammy	.286	7	2	0	0	1	0	.286	.286
Stocker, K#	.167	6	1	0	2	2	1	.444	.500
Walker, Larry*	1.000	3	3	1	5	1	0	.800	2.333
Webster, L	.143	7	1	0	1	0	3	.143	.143
Weiss, Walt#	.000	3	0	0	0	2	0	.400	.000
Whiten, Mark#	.500	6	3	0	1	0	2	.500	.667
Wilkins, Rick*	.000	5	0	0	0	1	2	.167	.000
Young, Eric	.400	5	2	0	0	1	1	.500	.400
Zeile, Todd	.000	6	0	0	1	3	2	.300	.000

Batter	Avg	AB	H	HR	BI	BB	SO	OBP	Slg
Aldrete, Mike*	.333	3	1	0	1	0	0	.400	.333
Alomar, R#	.167	18	3	0	0	0	2	.167	.167
Alomar Jr, S	.000	13	0	0	0	0	1	.000	.000
Anderson, Brd*	.571	7	4	1	1	1	0	.625	.857
Baerga, C#	.238	21	5	0	1	1	0	.273	.286
Baines, H*	.222	27	6	0	1	5	1	.344	.259
Belle, Albert	.231	13	3	0	1	1	2	.286	.308
Bichette, D	.125	16	2	1	0	0	4	.125	.250
Boggs, Wade*	.333	30	10	1	2	2	0	.364	.533
Borders, Pat	.200	5	1	0	0	0	0	.200	.200
Bordick, Mike	.250	8	2	0	0	1	2	.333	.375
Buhner, Jay	.000	6	0	0	0	1	2	.143	.000
Burks, Ellis	.308	13	4	0	2	2	2	.400	.462
Canseco, Jose	.333	18	6	3	6	2	4	.364	.833

Bob Milacki, Mariners — RHP

Batter	Avg	AB	H	HR	BI	BB	SO	OBP	Slg
Carter, Joe	.316	19	6	2	6	4	6	.435	.737
Clark, Dave*	.200	5	1	0	0	0	0	.200	.200
Cole, Alex*	.308	13	4	0	0	1	2	.357	.385
Cora, Joey#	.000	6	0	0	0	0	0	.000	.000
Curtis, Chad	.333	6	2	0	2	0	1	.333	.333
Cuyler, Milt#	.462	13	6	0	0	0	3	.462	.538
Davis, Chili#	.160	25	4	1	1	3	2	.250	.360
Deer, Rob	.467	15	7	1	4	3	3	.556	.933
Devereaux, M	.400	5	2	0	3	0	0	.400	.400
DiSarcina, G	.556	9	5	1	3	0	1	.556	1.000
Eisenreich, J*	.188	16	3	1	3	2	0	.278	.438
Espinoza, A	.217	23	5	0	0	0	2	.217	.261
Fermin, Felix	.227	22	5	0	1	1	2	.261	.273
Fielder, C	.211	19	4	2	4	4	2	.348	.526
Franco, Julio	.316	19	6	0	4	1	4	.350	.316
Fryman, T	.294	17	5	1	2	4	0	.429	.471
Gaetti, Gary	.417	24	10	0	3	1	2	.423	.500
Gagne, Greg	.154	13	2	0	1	0	2	.143	.231
Gallego, Mike	.190	21	4	0	0	1	1	.227	.286
Gonzales, R	.333	6	2	0	0	0	1	.333	.500
Gonzalez, J	.444	9	4	0	1	1	0	.500	.667
Grebeck, C	.143	7	1	0	0	0	0	.143	.143
Greenwell, M*	.188	16	3	0	0	4	2	.350	.250
Griffey Jr, K*	.583	12	7	0	3	2	0	.643	.667
Guillen, O*	.222	18	4	0	0	1	1	.263	.222
Hall, Mel*	.154	26	4	0	2	1	2	.185	.154
Hamilton, D*	.222	9	2	1	2	2	0	.364	.778
Henderson, R	.190	21	4	0	0	3	1	.320	.238
Hill, G	.500	10	5	0	0	0	1	.500	.500
Howell, Jack*	.333	12	4	1	2	4	2	.500	.583
Huff, Michael	.000	4	0	0	0	1	0	.200	.000
Huson, Jeff*	.200	5	1	0	0	1	0	.333	.200
Incaviglia, P	.462	13	6	3	8	2	3	.533	1.385
James, Dion*	.667	6	4	0	1	0	0	.667	.833
Johnson, L*	.350	20	7	0	0	1	0	.381	.350
Joyner, Wally*	.235	17	4	1	2	0	1	.222	.412
Kelly, R	.407	27	11	0	3	3	6	.467	.481
Knoblauch, C	.333	15	5	0	1	0	0	.333	.400
Leius, Scott	.167	6	1	0	1	1	0	.250	.167
Lewis, Mark	.200	10	2	1	1	1	2	.273	.500
Liriano, N#	.286	7	2	0	2	1	1	.375	.429
Livingstone*	.400	5	2	0	0	0	0	.400	.600
Macfarlane, M	.286	7	2	0	0	0	0	.286	.429
Martinez, E	.300	10	3	0	1	1	1	.417	.400
McGriff, Fred*	.250	8	2	1	3	2	1	.400	.625
McGwire, Mark	.368	19	7	1	4	2	3	.429	.526
McLemore, M*	.200	5	1	0	1	0	1	.200	.200
McRae, Brian#	.000	6	0	0	0	0	3	.000	.000
Molitor, Paul	.367	30	11	1	3	3	3	.412	.533
Munoz, Pedro	.500	8	4	1	3	0	2	.500	1.000
Myers, Greg*	.200	10	2	0	0	0	1	.200	.200
Naehring, Tim	.571	7	4	1	1	0	0	.571	1.000
Newson, W*	.250	4	1	0	0	1	2	.400	.250
O'Neill, Paul*	.000	8	0	0	1	0	1	.111	.000
Olerud, John*	.250	16	4	1	4	1	2	.294	.563
Palmeiro, R*	.476	21	10	2	5	5	0	.577	.857
Pena, Tony	.250	12	3	0	3	1	1	.308	.250
Phillips, T#	.120	25	3	0	1	5	6	.267	.120
Plantier, P*	.111	9	1	0	2	0	4	.111	.222
Polonia, Luis*	.345	29	10	0	1	3	3	.406	.414
Raines, Tim#	.333	15	5	0	0	1	2	.375	.533
Reed, Jody	.211	19	4	0	1	3	0	.318	.263
Ripken, Cal	.400	5	2	1	1	2	0	.571	1.000
Schofield, D	.200	10	2	0	2	0	0	.250	.200
Seitzer, K	.200	25	5	0	1	3	1	.286	.240
Sheffield, G	.000	7	0	0	1	0	1	.000	.000
Shumpert, T	.000	6	0	0	0	1	1	.143	.000
Sierra, Ruben#	.333	18	6	0	0	4	4	.333	.444
Slaught, Don	.429	7	3	0	0	1	1	.500	.714
Sojo, Luis	.333	6	2	0	0	0	0	.333	.333
Sorrento, P*	.167	6	1	1	3	1	1	.286	.667
Sosa, Sammy	.200	5	1	0	0	0	0	.200	.200
Spiers, Bill*	.313	16	5	0	3	0	2	.313	.438
Sprague, G	.600	5	3	1	4	0	1	.600	1.400
Stankiewicz	.333	6	2	0	1	0	0	.333	.833
Stanley, Mike	.125	8	1	0	1	2	0	.300	.125
Steinbach, T	.313	16	5	0	1	2	1	.389	.313
Stillwell, K#	.250	16	4	0	1	0	1	.250	.250
Strange, Doug#	.200	5	1	0	0	1	1	.333	.200
Surhoff, B.J.*	.292	24	7	0	0	1	0	.320	.375
Tartabull, D	.323	31	10	2	13	2	5	.353	.613
Tettleton, M#	.500	14	7	1	5	4	2	.611	.786
Thomas, Frank	.583	12	7	2	6	1	0	.615	1.167
Thome, Jim*	.500	4	2	0	3	1	0	.600	.750
Trammell, A	.094	32	3	0	1	5	5	.216	.125
Valentin, Jhn	.333	6	2	1	1	2	1	.500	.833
Vaughn, Greg	.105	19	2	1	2	0	1	.105	.263
Vaughn, Mo*	.444	9	4	2	4	6	4	.667	1.111
Velarde, R	.333	21	7	1	2	1	5	.364	.571
Ventura, R*	.278	18	5	2	5	2	3	.350	.611
Vizquel, Omar#	.375	8	3	0	0	0	0	.375	.375

Bob Milacki, Mariners — RHP

Batter	Avg	AB	H	HR	BI	BB	SO	OBP	Slg
Weiss, Walt*	.250	12	3	0	0	2	0	.357	.250
White, Devon#	.227	22	5	0	0	5	8	.370	.227
Whiten, Mark#	.429	7	3	0	0	0	2	.429	.714
Williams, Ber#	.071	14	1	0	0	1	0	.133	.071

Kurt Miller, Marlins — RHP

Batter	Avg	AB	H	HR	BI	BB	SO	OBP	Slg
Bichette, D	.250	4	1	0	1	0	0	.400	.250
Dunston, S	.400	5	2	0	0	0	0	.400	.600
Grace, Mark*	.500	6	3	0	3	0	0	.500	.833
Howard, T*	.400	5	2	0	0	0	0	.400	.400
Sanchez, Rey	.400	5	2	0	1	1	0	.500	.400
Segui, David#	.200	5	1	0	0	0	1	.200	.400
Sosa, Sammy	.500	4	2	0	1	1	1	.600	.500
Vizcaino, J#	.000	6	0	0	0	1	0	.000	.000
Young, Eric	.400	5	2	0	0	0	0	.400	.400

Travis Miller, Twins — LHP

Batter	Avg	AB	H	HR	BI	BB	SO	OBP	Slg
Seitzer, K	.400	5	2	0	0	0	0	.400	.400

Trever Miller, Tigers — LHP

Batter	Avg	AB	H	HR	BI	BB	SO	OBP	Slg
Alomar, R#	.000	4	0	0	0	2	0	.333	.000
Alomar, Brd*	.333	6	2	1	1	0	1	.333	.833
Bonilla, B#	.600	5	3	1	1	0	0	.600	1.200
Palmeiro, R*	.500	4	2	1	3	0	0	.400	1.250
Ripken, Cal	.400	5	2	0	0	0	0	.400	.600
Zeile, Todd	.000	5	0	0	0	1	0	.167	.000

Alan Mills, Orioles — RHP

Batter	Avg	AB	H	HR	BI	BB	SO	OBP	Slg
Aldrete, Mike*	.400	5	2	1	4	5	0	.700	1.000
Alomar, R#	.400	5	2	0	0	0	0	.400	.400
Alomar Jr, S	.200	5	1	1	2	0	0	.333	.800
Amaral, Rich	.000	5	0	0	0	1	3	.167	.000
Baerga, C#	.167	12	2	0	0	3	2	.333	.167
Belle, Albert	.231	13	3	1	3	2	3	.333	.538
Berroa, G	.333	6	2	0	3	1	2	.429	.333
Blowers, Mike	.125	8	1	0	0	0	5	.125	.125
Boggs, Wade*	.222	9	2	0	1	1	0	.300	.222
Boone, Bret	.200	5	1	0	2	0	2	.200	.200
Borders, Pat	.429	7	3	0	2	0	0	.429	.429
Bordick, Mike	.167	12	2	1	2	1	3	.231	.417
Brosius, S	.143	7	1	0	1	2	2	.333	.143
Buhner, Jay	.250	8	2	2	4	4	4	.462	1.000
Burks, Ellis	.750	4	3	2	4	2	1	.833	2.500
Canseco, Jose	.286	7	2	2	4	0	3	.286	1.143
Carter, Joe	.286	7	2	0	1	0	1	.375	.571
Cole, Alex*	.200	5	1	0	0	0	1	.333	.200
Cora, Joey#	.250	8	2	0	0	1	1	.333	.250
Curtis, Chad	.231	13	3	0	0	1	4	.286	.308
Cuyler, Milt#	.000	6	0	0	0	0	2	.000	.000
Davis, Chili#	.273	11	3	0	1	3	1	.429	.364
Deer, Rob	.143	7	1	1	3	1	2	.250	.571
DiSarcina, G	.250	8	2	0	1	0	0	.222	.250
Easley, D	.000	4	0	0	0	2	0	.333	.000
Fermin, Felix	.100	10	1	0	1	1	4	.182	.100
Fielder, C	.188	16	3	1	4	5	2	.409	.438
Franco, Julio	.000	9	0	0	0	2	4	.182	.000
Fryman, T	.294	17	5	1	3	1	4	.333	.529
Gaetti, Gary	.333	6	2	0	1	2	0	.500	.500
Gagne, Greg	.200	5	1	0	0	1	2	.333	.600
Gallego, Mike	.400	5	2	0	0	1	1	.500	.400
Gates, Brent#	.000	4	0	0	0	1	2	.200	.000
Gomez, Chris	.000	4	0	0	0	1	2	.200	.000
Gonzales, R	.000	2	0	0	0	4	0	.667	.000
Gonzalez, J	.462	13	6	3	9	0	6	.462	1.308
Grebeck, C	.000	5	0	0	0	1	2	.000	.000
Griffey Jr, K*	.200	10	2	0	1	3	3	.385	.400
Guillen, O*	.333	3	1	1	2	1	0	.500	1.333
Hall, Mel*	.333	6	2	0	0	0	0	.333	.500
Hamilton, D*	.500	6	3	0	1	3	0	.667	.667
Hayes, C	.250	4	1	0	0	0	1	.250	.250
Henderson, R	.143	7	1	0	0	2	0	.333	.143
Higginson, B*	.750	4	3	1	4	1	1	.800	1.750
Jaha, John	.111	9	1	0	0	2	7	.333	.111
Javier, Stan#	.000	5	0	0	0	0	1	.000	.000
Jefferson, R*	.111	9	1	0	0	1	1	.200	.222
Jeter, Derek	.400	5	2	0	0	1	0	.400	.600
Johnson, L*	.500	10	5	0	2	1	0	.545	.500
Joyner, Wally*	.333	6	2	1	2	1	0	.429	1.000
Karkovice, R	.375	8	3	1	1	1	2	.444	.750
Kelly, Pat	.000	5	0	0	0	1	2	.167	.000
Kelly, R	.286	7	2	0	0	0	1	.286	.429
Knoblauch, C	.375	8	3	0	0	1	0	.444	.375
Kreuter, Chad#	.333	6	2	0	0	1	4	.429	.333
Leius, Scott	.333	3	1	0	0	3	0	.667	.333
Lewis, Mark	.000	5	0	0	0	0	0	.000	.000
Leyritz, Jim	.000	4	0	0	0	1	2	.200	.000
Listach, Pat#	.200	10	2	0	0	0	3	.200	.300

Alan Mills, Orioles — RHP

Batter	Avg	AB	H	HR	BI	BB	SO	OBP	Slg
Lofton, Kenny*	.667	6	4	0	1	0	0	.667	.667
Macfarlane, M	.444	9	4	2	3	1	3	.500	1.222
Martinez, E	.333	9	3	0	1	4	1	.538	.444
Martinez, T*	.286	7	2	1	1	1	1	.375	.714
McGwire, Mark	.000	3	0	0	0	2	0	.400	.000
McRae, Brian#	.400	5	2	0	0	0	1	.400	.400
Mieske, Matt	.000	5	0	0	0	0	1	.000	.000
Molitor, Paul	.250	8	2	0	1	0	2	.222	.250
Munoz, Pedro	.200	5	1	0	0	0	3	.200	.400
Newfield, M	.167	6	1	0	2	1	1	.286	.333
Nilsson, Dave*	.000	7	0	0	0	1	0	.000	.000
Newson, W*	.000	2	0	0	0	3	0	.600	.000
Olerud, John*	.667	3	2	1	1	2	0	.800	1.667
Palmeiro, R*	.500	6	3	0	1	2	0	.625	.500
Palmer, Dean	.100	10	1	0	0	1	5	.182	.100
Paquette, C	.200	5	1	1	4	1	1	.333	.800
Pena, Tony	.333	9	3	0	1	0	1	.333	.333
Phillips, T#	.111	9	1	0	0	1	2	.200	.111
Plantier, P*	.750	4	3	1	1	2	0	.833	1.500
Polonia, Luis*	.286	7	2	0	0	0	0	.286	.286
Raines, Tim#	.500	8	4	0	1	1	0	.556	.625
Reed, Jody	.167	6	1	0	1	2	0	.375	.167
Ripken, Billy	.200	5	1	0	2	0	1	.200	.400
Rodriguez, I	.143	7	1	0	3	1	0	.250	.286
Salmon, Tim	.222	9	2	0	1	1	2	.273	.222
Samuel, Juan	.500	6	3	0	2	0	1	.500	.667
Seitzer, K	.143	14	2	0	1	1	1	.200	.214
Sierra, Ruben#	.273	11	3	0	3	3	2	.400	.364
Sojo, Luis	.400	5	2	0	1	1	0	.571	.400
Sorrento, P*	.167	6	1	0	1	1	1	.286	.167
Sprague, Ed	.333	6	2	0	0	0	3	.429	.333
Stankiewicz	.333	3	1	1	2	3	0	.667	1.333
Stanley, Mike	.500	4	2	0	0	1	1	.600	.500
Steinbach, T	.100	10	1	0	0	1	0	.182	.100
Strange, Doug#	.167	6	1	1	2	1	1	.375	.667
Surhoff, B.J.*	.222	9	2	0	0	1	1	.300	.333
Tartabull, D	.100	10	1	0	2	1	6	.167	.100
Tettleton, M#	.200	10	2	1	2	4	5	.429	.700
Thomas, Frank	.133	15	2	0	1	7	4	.391	.133
Thome, Jim*	.167	6	1	0	0	1	1	.375	.167
Trammell, A	.200	10	2	0	1	2	0	.333	.200
Valentin, John	.333	6	2	0	0	0	0	.333	.500
Valentin, Jse#	.250	4	1	0	0	1	0	.400	.500
Valle, Dave	.000	9	0	0	1	0	1	.000	.000
Vaughn, Greg	.214	14	3	1	2	3	3	.353	.429
Vaughn, Mo*	.167	6	1	0	0	1	1	.286	.667
Velarde, R	.000	5	0	0	0	1	2	.167	.000
Ventura, R*	.250	12	3	1	2	2	1	.333	.583
Vizquel, Omar#	.250	8	2	0	0	1	0	.333	.375
White, Devon#	.400	5	2	0	1	0	0	.400	.600
Whiten, Mark#	.375	8	3	0	1	1	1	.444	.375
Williams, Ber#	.300	10	3	1	6	0	0	.300	.300
Wilson, Dan	.000	6	0	0	1	0	1	.000	.000

Michael Mimbs, Phillies — LHP

Batter	Avg	AB	H	HR	BI	BB	SO	OBP	Slg
Abbott, Kurt	.111	9	1	0	1	2	3	.273	.111
Alfonzo, E	.154	13	2	0	1	0	2	.154	.154
Alou, Moises	.500	4	2	0	1	2	0	.667	.500
Andrews, S	.250	8	2	1	3	1	2	.333	.625
Arias, Alex	.200	5	1	0	0	1	1	.333	.200
Ashley, Billy	.000	8	0	0	0	0	6	.000	.000
Ausmus, Brad	.400	5	2	0	0	1	1	.500	.400
Battle, Allen	.000	2	0	0	0	3	0	.600	.000
Blauser, Jeff	.167	12	2	2	7	3	5	.333	.667
Bogar, Tim	.083	12	1	0	0	0	4	.083	.167
Bonilla, B#	.500	6	3	0	1	0	0	.429	.500
Boone, Bret	.100	10	1	0	0	0	1	.100	.100
Brogna, Rico*	.400	5	2	0	0	0	2	.400	.800
Caminiti, Ken#	.375	16	6	1	4	1	0	.412	.625
Carr, Chuck	.000	6	0	0	0	1	0	.143	.000
Cedeno, A	.200	15	3	0	1	0	4	.200	.267
Cianfrocco, A	.400	5	2	0	0	1	1	.500	.400
Colbrunn, G	.111	9	1	0	3	0	1	.111	.111
Conine, Jeff	.273	11	3	0	1	4	0	.467	.364
Davis, Eric	.400	5	2	0	1	1	2	.500	.400
Dawson, Andre	.500	4	2	1	2	0	0	.600	1.500
DeShields, D*	.167	6	1	0	0	2	0	.375	.167
Dunston, S	.500	6	3	0	1	0	0	.600	.800
Everett, Carl#	.600	5	3	0	1	1	0	.714	.800
Finley, Steve*	.421	19	8	0	0	2	1	.476	.526
Fletcher, D*	.333	6	2	0	0	0	0	.333	.500
Gant, Ron	.400	5	2	0	1	0	1	.500	.400
Gilkey, B	.333	3	1	0	2	0	0	.600	.667
Grace, Mark*	.333	9	3	0	1	2	1	.455	.333
Grissom, M	.353	17	6	1	2	0	0	.353	.647
Grudzielanek	.125	8	1	0	0	0	2	.125	.125
Gwynn, Tony*	.083	12	1	0	0	1	1	.200	.083
Henderson, R	.400	5	2	0	0	3	1	.556	.333
Hernandez, Ca	.250	4	1	0	0	1	1	.400	.250
Hundley, Todd#	.500	4	2	0	1	1	1	.600	.500

Michael Mimbs, Phillies — LHP

Batter	Avg	AB	H	HR	BI	BB	SO	OBP	Slg
Huskey, Butch	.200	5	1	1	1	1	0	.333	.800
Johnson, Bri	.500	10	5	1	1	1	0	.583	.900
Johnson, Char	.167	6	1	0	1	1	1	.250	.167
Johnson, L*	.429	7	3	0	2	0	0	.429	.571
Jones, C#	.600	10	6	0	1	6	2	.750	.900
Jones, Chris	.143	7	1	0	1	0	1	.125	.143
Jordan, Brian	.400	5	2	1	2	1	0	.500	1.000
Joyner, Wally*	.250	4	1	0	0	1	0	.400	.250
Justice, Dave*	.200	10	2	0	2	5	2	.467	.200
Karros, Eric	.143	7	1	0	0	1	1	.250	.143
Kelly, R	.000	4	0	0	0	1	0	.333	.000
Kent, Jeff	.300	10	3	1	1	0	1	.300	.700
Klesko, Ryan*	.143	7	1	0	0	0	2	.143	.286
Lankford, Ray*	.375	8	3	0	4	0	0	.375	.375
Lansing, Mike	.333	9	3	0	0	1	0	.400	.333
Larkin, Barry	.500	10	5	2	6	1	0	.545	1.100
Lemke, Mark#	.417	12	5	1	2	1	1	.462	.750
Lopez, Javy	.286	7	2	0	1	0	2	.250	.286
Mabry, John*	.286	7	2	0	0	1	0	.375	.429
McGriff, Fred*	.231	13	3	0	1	2	0	.333	.231
McRae, Brian#	.364	11	4	0	2	0	0	.364	.455
Mondesi, Raul	.125	8	1	0	2	1	1	.222	.250
Nieves, M#	.250	4	1	0	0	1	1	.400	.250
Obando, S	.143	7	1	0	0	1	2	.250	.143
Ochoa, Alex	.167	6	1	0	0	0	0	.167	.167
Offerman, J#	.250	4	1	0	0	3	0	.571	.500
Owens, Eric	.200	5	1	0	1	1	2	.286	.200
Pena, Gr	.250	4	1	0	0	1	2	.400	.250
Pendleton, T#	.000	5	0	0	0	1	0	.000	.000
Reed, Jody	.000	4	0	0	0	1	0	.200	.000
Roberts, Bip#	.167	12	2	0	1	1	2	.231	.167
Sabo, Chris	.000	4	0	0	0	0	1	.000	.000
Sanchez, Rey	.429	7	3	0	0	0	1	.429	.714
Sandberg, R	.500	4	2	1	1	1	1	.600	1.250
Sanders, R	.222	9	2	0	0	1	3	.300	.222
Santangelo, A*	.286	7	2	0	0	0	1	.286	.429
Segui, David#	.000	5	0	0	0	0	1	.000	.000
Sheaffer, D	.600	5	3	0	2	0	0	.600	.600
Sheffield, G	.375	8	3	0	2	3	1	.583	.500
Sosa, Sammy	.250	4	1	1	1	1	1	.400	1.000
Stinnett, K	.429	7	3	1	2	0	2	.429	.857
Thompson, Ry	.500	6	3	0	0	0	0	.500	.500
Timmons, O	.111	9	1	1	1	1	1	.200	.444
Veras, Q#	.417	12	5	0	4	2	.588	.417
Vizcaino, J#	.333	9	3	0	2	1	1	.400	.444
Wallach, Tim	.600	5	3	0	0	1	1	.667	.600
White, Devon#	.200	5	1	0	0	1	0	.333	.400
Williams, E	.222	9	2	1	2	1	2	.300	.667
Zeile, Todd	.200	5	1	0	0	0	0	.200	.200

Nate Minchey, Red Sox — RHP

Batter	Avg	AB	H	HR	BI	BB	SO	OBP	Slg
Alomar, R#	.625	8	5	1	3	1	2	.667	1.375
Baerga, C#	.200	5	1	0	0	0	0	.200	.400
Belle, Albert	.833	6	5	0	1	0	0	.833	.833
Boggs, Wade*	.000	3	0	0	0	2	0	.400	.000
Borders, Pat	.167	6	1	1	1	1	2	.286	.667
Carter, Joe	.222	9	2	0	0	0	2	.222	.222
Fryman, T	.400	5	2	0	2	0	0	.400	.600
Henderson, R	.400	5	2	0	0	0	0	.400	.400
Lofton, Kenny*	.400	5	2	0	1	0	0	.400	.400
Molitor, Paul	.167	6	1	0	3	1	1	.222	.167
O'Neill, Paul*	.200	5	1	1	1	0	1	.200	.800
Olerud, John*	.286	7	2	1	1	1	1	.375	.857
Ramirez, M	.500	6	3	0	2	0	1	.500	.833
Sorrento, P*	.333	3	1	0	1	1	0	.400	.333
Tettleton, M#	.667	3	2	0	0	2	0	.800	.667
Thome, Jim*	.200	5	1	0	2	0	1	.200	.400
White, Devon#	.250	4	1	0	0	2	0	.500	.250

Blas Minor, Mariners — RHP

Batter	Avg	AB	H	HR	BI	BB	SO	OBP	Slg
Alou, Moises	.500	6	3	2	3	0	1	.500	1.500
Ausmus, Brad	.400	5	2	0	0	1	0	.500	.600
Bagwell, Jeff	.833	6	5	0	4	0	0	.833	1.167
Bell, Derek	.167	6	1	0	0	0	2	.167	.167
Bichette, D	.125	8	1	0	0	0	3	.125	.125
Biggio, Craig	.500	4	2	1	3	2	1	.667	1.500
Blauser, Jeff	.200	10	2	0	1	1	1	.273	.200
Bonilla, B#	.500	4	2	1	3	1	1	.600	1.250
Boone, Bret	.286	7	2	0	1	0	1	.286	.429
Brumfield, J	.286	7	2	0	2	1	1	.444	.429
Castilla, V	.000	5	0	0	0	1	0	.000	.000
Cedeno, A	.167	6	1	0	0	0	4	.167	.167
Cianfrocco, A	.600	5	3	0	1	0	0	.600	.600
Clayton, R	.000	6	0	0	0	0	2	.000	.000
Colbrunn, G	.200	5	1	0	1	2	0	.200	.200
Conine, Jeff	.125	8	1	0	0	0	4	.125	.125
Cordero, Wil	.000	5	0	0	0	0	2	.167	.000
Davis, Eric	.000	5	0	0	1	2	.167	.000
DeShields, D*	.500	6	3	0	1	1	1	.571	.833

Bias Minor, Mariners — RHP

Batter	Avg	AB	H	HR	BI	BB	SO	OBP	Slg
Finley, Steve*	.000	4	0	0	1	0	1	.000	.000
Galarraga, A	.429	7	3	0	1	0	1	.429	.429
Gant, Ron	.125	8	1	0	0	0	3	.125	.250
Gilkey, B	.000	5	0	0	0	0	2	.000	.000
Girardi, Joe	.000	6	0	0	0	1	0	.000	.000
Grissom, M	.400	5	2	1	2	0	1	.400	1.000
Hayes, C	.500	8	4	2	2	0	0	.500	1.250
Jefferies, G#	.000	3	0	0	0	2	0	.400	.000
Justice, Dave*	.750	4	3	0	0	1	1	.800	.750
Karros, Eric	.375	8	3	2	4	0	0	.375	1.125
Kelly, R	.333	6	2	1	3	1	1	.429	1.000
Kingery, Mike*	.200	5	1	0	2	0	0	.200	.200
Lankford, Ray*	.333	3	1	0	0	2	0	.600	.333
Lansing, Mike	.500	6	3	0	2	2	1	.625	.833
Larkin, Barry	.143	7	1	0	0	1	0	.250	.143
Lemke, Mark#	.200	5	1	0	2	0	0	.167	.200
Lewis, C	.250	4	1	0	0	1	0	.400	.250
May, Derrick*	.200	5	1	0	0	0	2	.200	.200
McGriff, Fred*	.200	5	1	0	0	0	3	.200	.400
Mitchell, K	.571	7	4	0	2	1	1	.625	.714
Morris, Hal*	.667	6	4	2	4	1	1	.714	1.667
Nieves, M#	.500	4	2	3	2	3	2	.667	2.000
Nixon, Otis#	.167	6	1	0	0	0	0	.167	.167
Offerman, J#	.000	5	0	0	0	0	0	.000	.000
Oliver, Joe	.400	5	2	0	1	0	1	.400	.400
Pendleton, T#	.286	7	2	0	0	2	0	.444	.286
Piazza, Mike	.000	5	0	0	0	1	3	.167	.000
Reed, Jody	.556	9	5	0	1	0	0	.556	.889
Sabo, Chris	.250	4	1	1	1	1	0	.400	1.000
Sandberg, R	.200	5	1	0	0	0	1	.200	.200
Sanders, R	.000	7	0	0	0	0	4	.000	.000
Santiago, B	.000	3	0	0	0	2	2	.400	.000
Sheffield, G	.250	4	1	0	0	1	2	.400	.250
Smith, Ozzie*	.400	5	2	0	0	0	0	.400	.600
Walker, Larry*	.000	4	0	0	0	0	1	.200	.000
Wallach, Tim	.333	6	2	0	1	0	0	.286	.500
Weiss, Walt#	.250	8	2	0	0	3	0	.250	.250
Whiten, Mark#	.833	6	5	1	5	0	0	.833	1.500
Young, Eric	.250	4	1	0	0	1	0	.400	.250
Zeile, Todd	.143	7	1	0	0	0	1	.143	.143

Angel Miranda, Brewers — LHP

Batter	Avg	AB	H	HR	BI	BB	SO	OBP	Slg
Alomar, R#	.133	15	2	0	1	3	3	.278	.133
Alomar Jr, S	.286	7	2	0	0	0	0	.286	.286
Amaral, Rich	.333	9	3	0	1	1	1	.400	.333
Anderson, Brd*	.000	7	0	0	0	2	2	.222	.000
Anderson, G*	.333	6	2	0	1	0	0	.286	.333
Baerga, C#	.333	12	4	0	1	3	3	.500	.500
Becker, Rich*	.200	5	1	0	0	0	1	.200	.400
Belle, Albert	.400	10	4	3	5	4	0	.571	1.400
Blowers, Mike	.200	5	1	0	0	2	1	.429	.200
Boone, Bret	.167	6	1	0	1	1	2	.286	.333
Bordick, Mike	.000	8	0	0	1	0	2	.000	.000
Brosius, S	.250	8	2	1	2	1	1	.333	.750
Buhner, Jay	.182	11	2	0	2	1	2	.250	.273
Burks, Ellis	.167	6	1	1	1	0	0	.167	.667
Carter, Joe	.200	15	3	0	1	1	1	.250	.267
Cedeno, D#	.111	9	1	0	0	0	3	.111	.111
Clark, Will*	.000	5	0	0	0	1	0	.167	.000
Cole, Alex*	.250	4	1	0	0	2	1	.500	.250
Cora, Joey#	.000	8	0	0	0	0	2	.000	.000
Cordova, M	.429	7	3	2	6	3	0	.600	1.286
Cuyler, Milt*	.000	5	0	0	1	0	0	.000	.000
Davis, Chili#	.000	5	0	0	0	5	0	.625	.000
Dawson, Andre	.200	5	1	0	0	0	2	.200	.200
Deer, Rob	.333	3	1	0	1	3	1	.667	.333
Delgado, C*	.200	5	1	0	0	0	2	.200	.200
Devereaux, M	.100	10	1	0	1	2	2	.250	.100
DiSarcina, G	.333	6	2	0	1	0	1	.333	.833
Durham, Ray#	.200	5	1	0	2	0	2	.167	.200
Fielder, C	.125	8	1	0	0	1	1	.222	.125
Franco, Julio	.308	13	4	1	2	3	5	.438	.692
Frye, Jeff	.286	7	2	0	0	1	1	.375	.286
Fryman, T	.000	8	0	0	0	0	2	.000	.000
Gagne, Greg	.333	6	2	0	0	1	1	.429	.500
Gates, Brent#	.000	6	0	0	0	0	0	.000	.000
Gonzalez, A	.333	9	3	1	3	1	2	.364	.889
Grebeck, C	.000	8	0	0	1	2	1	.200	.000
Greenwell, M*	.200	5	1	0	0	2	1	.333	.600
Griffey Jr, K*	.125	8	1	1	2	5	2	.462	.500
Guillen, O*	.400	5	2	0	1	0	0	.400	.400
Hammonds, J	.143	7	1	0	0	1	0	.250	.143
Henderson, R	.000	5	0	0	0	1	1	.167	.000
Hoiles, Chris	.300	10	3	1	2	4	3	.500	.667
Hollins, Dave#	.500	6	3	0	0	0	0	.500	.667
Johnson, L*	.143	7	1	0	1	0	2	.250	.143
Joyner, Wally*	.250	8	2	0	0	0	0	.250	.375
Karkovice, R	.154	13	2	1	2	2	4	.250	.385
Kelly, Pat	.000	4	0	0	1	3	1	.429	.000
Knoblauch, C	.333	9	3	0	0	1	2	.400	.667

Dave Mlicki, Mets — RHP

Batter	Avg	AB	H	HR	BI	BB	SO	OBP	Slg
Abbott, Kurt	.286	7	2	0	1	0	2	.286	.286
Alou, Moises	.250	4	1	0	0	2	1	.500	.250
Arias, Alex	.143	7	1	0	2	0	1	.143	.286
Ausmus, Brad	.000	3	0	0	2	2	0	.286	.000
Bagwell, Jeff	.154	13	2	1	1	0	3	.154	.385
Bell, Derek	.273	11	3	1	3	1	0	.333	.636
Bell, Jay	.200	5	1	0	0	1	1	.333	.200
Berry, Sean	.600	5	3	0	0	0	0	.600	.800
Bichette, D	.750	4	3	0	1	1	0	.800	.750
Biggio, Craig	.067	15	1	0	0	1	2	.125	.067
Blauser, Jeff*	.600	10	6	0	1	1	0	.636	.800
Bonds, Barry*	.556	9	5	2	3	1	0	.600	1.444
Boone, Bret	.125	8	1	0	1	0	1	.125	.125
Branson, Jeff*	.250	8	2	0	0	0	3	.250	.500
Burks, Ellis	.250	8	2	0	0	0	1	.250	.250
Butler, Brett*	.667	6	4	0	1	1	1	.625	.667
Caminiti, Ken#	.429	7	3	0	3	1	0	.600	.714
Cangelosi, J#	.375	8	3	0	1	1	0	.444	.375
Carreon, Mark	.500	6	3	1	1	0	1	.500	1.000
Castilla, V	.250	4	1	0	0	0	0	.400	.250
Clayton, C	.000	6	0	0	0	1	2	.143	.000
Colbrunn, G	.182	11	2	0	0	0	3	.182	.273
Colemore, J	.091	11	1	0	0	3	3	.286	.091
Cora, Joey#	.750	4	3	0	0	0	0	.833	.750
Cordero, Wil	.000	6	0	0	0	0	0	.000	.000
Dawson, Andre	.143	7	1	0	0	0	2	.143	.143
DeShields, D*	.333	9	3	0	0	2	1	.455	.333
Finley, Steve*	.154	13	2	1	3	0		.154	.385
Fletcher, D*	.200	5	1	0	0	0	0	.333	.200
Floyd, Cliff	.200	5	1	0	0	0	1	.200	.400
Fonville, C#	.714	7	5	0	0	0	0	.714	.714
Gant, Ron	.500	6	3	1	5	0	1	.429	1.333

Dave Mlicki, Mets — RHP

Batter	Avg	AB	H	HR	BI	BB	SO	OBP	Slg
Gilkey, B	.250	4	1	0	2	1	0	.333	.500
Gonzalez, L*	.250	8	2	0	0	0	2	.250	.250
Grace, Mark*	.250	8	2	1	2	0	1	.250	.625
Grissom, M	.308	13	4	0	0	0	3	.308	.308
Grudzielanek	.500	6	3	0	1	0	1	.500	.667
Gutierrez, R	.400	5	2	0	1	0	1	.400	.400
Gwynn, Tony*	.444	9	4	0	0	0	0	.444	.556
Hansen, Dave*	.400	5	2	0	0	1	0	.400	.400
Hayes, C	.667	9	6	0	4	2	0	.727	.667
Hernandez, Jo	.143	7	1	0	0	0	1	.143	.143
Hill, G	.286	7	2	0	2	2	3	.444	.429
Howard, T*	.000	7	0	0	0	0	2	.000	.000
Johnson, Char	.286	7	2	0	0	0	3	.286	.429
Johnson, L*	.500	6	3	0	0	1	0	.571	.833
Jones, C#	.417	12	5	1	4	2	1	.500	.833
Jordan, Brian	.667	6	4	2	3	0	0	.667	1.833
Justice, Dave*	.125	8	1	0	1	0	1	.125	.250
Karkovice, R	.167	6	1	0	1	1	3	.286	.167
Karros, Eric	.143	14	2	1	1	1	5	.200	.429
Kelly, R	.154	13	2	0	1	1	3	.214	.154
King, Jeff	.000	5	0	0	0	0	2	.000	.000
Kingery, Mike*	.000	4	0	0	1	1	0	.167	.000
Klesko, Ryan*	.444	9	4	1	2	4	2	.615	.889
Lankford, Ray*	.333	6	2	1	2	4	2	.600	.833
Lansing, Mike	.333	6	2	0	1	0	0	.429	.333
Larkin, Barry	.000	5	0	0	0	1	0	.167	.000
Lemke, Mark*	.500	8	4	0	0	0	0	.500	.500
Lewis, Darren	.250	8	2	0	1	0	1	.250	.250
Livingstone*	.300	10	3	0	2	1	0	.364	.400
Lopez, Javy	.429	7	3	1	0	0	3	.429	.857
Mabry, John*	.000	7	0	0	0	1	1	.125	.000
Magadan, Dave*	.333	6	2	0	0	1	0	.429	.333
Manwaring, K	.000	6	0	0	0	0	2	.000	.000
Martin, Al*	.429	7	3	2	3	0	1	.429	1.286
May, Derrick*	.375	8	3	0	1	2	0	.500	.500
McGriff, Fred*	.385	13	5	1	4	1	1	.429	.615
McRae, Brian*	.400	5	2	0	0	1	1	.571	.400
Merced, O*	.000	4	0	0	0	1	2	.200	.000
Miller, Orl	.300	10	3	0	0	0	2	.300	.300
Mondesi, Raul	.067	15	1	1	1	0	7	.067	.267
Mouton, James	.143	7	1	0	0	1	2	.250	.143
O'Brien, C	.200	5	1	0	0	0	1	.200	.200
Offerman, J#	.333	9	3	0	1	4	0	.571	.556
Pendleton, T#	.308	13	4	0	2	0	2	.308	.385
Phillips, J*	.000	7	0	0	0	0	0	.000	.000
Piazza, Mike	.286	7	2	0	0	3	4	.500	.429
Raines, Tim#	.111	9	1	1	1	0	1	.111	.444
Reed, Jody	.286	7	2	0	2	0	1	.286	.429
Roberts, Bip#	.125	8	1	0	0	0	1	.125	.250
Rodriguez, H*	.333	6	2	0	0	0	4	.333	.333
Sandberg, R	.000	4	0	0	0	1	2	.200	.000
Sanders, R*	.286	7	2	0	1	0	3	.286	.571
Scarsone, S	.250	8	2	1	2	1	4	.333	.625
Segui, David#	.167	6	1	1	1	0	0	.167	.667
Servais, A	.250	8	2	1	1	1	2	.333	.625
Sheaffer, D	.250	4	1	0	1	2	2	.500	.250
Smith, Dwight*	.000	4	0	0	0	0	0	.000	.000
Sosa, Sammy	.000	5	0	0	0	1	4	.286	.000
Sveum, Dale#	.250	4	1	0	0	0	2	.250	.250
Taubensee, E*	.200	5	1	1	1	0	1	.200	.800
Tavarez, Je#	.333	6	2	0	0	0	2	.333	.333
Thomas, Frank	.000	4	0	0	0	2	3	.333	.000
Ventura, R*	.400	5	2	0	1	3	1	.625	.600
Veras, Q#	.200	5	1	0	0	3	0	.200	.200
Wallach, Tim	.333	9	3	0	2	0	1	.333	.444
Weiss, Walt#	.500	6	3	0	0	1	0	.500	.500
White, R	.333	3	1	0	0	3	0	.667	.333
Wilkins, Rick*	.167	6	1	1	1	2	2	.286	.667
Zeile, Todd	.500	4	2	0	0	1	0	.600	.500

Brian Moehler, Tigers — RHP

Batter	Avg	AB	H	HR	BI	BB	SO	OBP	Slg
Burnitz, J*	.000	4	0	0	0	1	0	.200	.000
Cirillo, Jeff	.400	5	2	0	2	1	0	.500	.400
Jaha, John	.333	6	2	1	3	0	1	.333	1.000
Levis, Jesse*	.667	3	2	0	0	0	2	.800	1.000
Nilsson, Dave*	.167	6	1	0	3	0	0	.167	.500
Valentin, Jse#	.000	4	0	0	0	2	0	.333	.000
Vina, F*	.250	4	1	0	0	1	0	.400	.500
Williams, Ger	.250	4	1	0	0	1	0	.400	.500

Mike Mohler, Athletics — LHP

Batter	Avg	AB	H	HR	BI	BB	SO	OBP	Slg
Alomar, R#	.600	5	3	0	2	0	0	.500	.600
Alomar Jr, S	.000	5	0	0	0	0	0	.000	.000
Anderson, Brd*	.000	4	0	0	2	3	0	.333	.000
Anderson, G*	.000	5	0	0	0	0	1	.000	.000
Baerga, C#	.143	7	1	0	0	0	2	.250	.143
Baines, H*	.200	5	1	0	1	2	1	.429	.200
Belle, Albert	.250	4	1	0	0	1	2	.500	.250
Boggs, Wade*	.250	8	2	0	1	1	2	.333	.250

Mike Mohler, Athletics — LHP

Batter	Avg	AB	H	HR	BI	BB	SO	OBP	Slg
Canseco, Jose	.000	1	0	0	0	4	1	.800	.000
Carter, Joe	.167	6	1	0	0	0	1	.167	.333
Cora, Joey#	.143	7	1	0	0	1	1	.250	.143
Cuyler, Milt*	.500	4	2	0	0	1	1	.600	.500
Davis, Chili#	.000	4	0	0	0	3	0	.429	.000
Delgado, C*	.250	4	1	0	0	1	3	.400	.250
Elster, Kevin	.000	5	0	0	0	0	2	.000	.000
Fielder, C	.333	9	3	0	0	1	2	.400	.333
Fryman, T	.250	8	2	2	5	1	0	.333	1.000
Gonzalez, A	.250	4	1	0	0	1	1	.400	.250
Green, Shawn*	.167	6	1	0	1	0	2	.167	.333
Greer, Rusty*	.286	7	2	0	1	1	1	.375	.429
Griffey Jr, K*	.286	7	2	1	1	1	1	.375	.714
Guillen, O*	.200	5	1	0	0	0	0	.200	.200
Hamilton, D*	.000	9	0	0	0	1	2	.100	.000
Hollins, Dave#	.750	4	3	0	2	1	0	.800	.750
Johnson, L*	.250	4	1	0	0	1	0	.400	.250
Kirby, Wayne*	.250	4	1	0	0	1	2	.400	.250
Lofton, Kenny*	.000	9	0	0	0	4	2	.308	.000
Martinez, T*	.500	6	3	2	6	0	1	.500	1.667
McLemore, M#	.000	5	0	0	0	1	1	.167	.000
Nixon, Otis#	.000	5	0	0	0	0	0	.000	.000
O'Neill, Paul*	.375	8	3	0	1	2	0	.455	.500
Olerud, John*	.286	7	2	0	1	2	2	.444	.286
Palmeiro, R*	.400	10	4	1	6	1	2	.455	.800
Phillips, T#	.500	4	2	0	0	5	1	.778	.500
Reboulet, J	.000	3	0	0	0	1	2	.250	.000
Ripken, Cal	.200	5	1	0	0	0	0	.200	.200
Rodriguez, I	.333	6	2	0	1	1	0	.375	.333
Snow, J.T.#	.167	6	1	1	2	2	2	.375	.667
Sorrento, P*	.400	5	2	0	1	0	2	.400	1.000
Sprague, Ed	.500	6	3	1	0	0	0	.500	1.000
Tartabull, D	.400	5	2	0	1	2	1	.571	.600
Tettleton, M#	.167	6	1	1	3	1	2	.286	.667
Thomas, Frank	.000	3	0	0	0	2	1	.400	.000
Valentin, Jhn	.333	3	1	0	1	0	0	.500	1.000
Vaughn, Mo*	.222	9	2	1	3	0	4	.222	.556
Ventura, R*	.125	8	1	0	0	0	6	.125	.375
White, Devon#	.000	3	0	0	0	1	0	.400	.000
Williams, Ber#	.286	7	2	0	0	1	2	.375	.429

Rich Monteleone, Angels — RHP

Batter	Avg	AB	H	HR	BI	BB	SO	OBP	Slg
Alomar, R#	.167	6	1	0	2	2	1	.375	.167
Alomar Jr, S	.286	7	2	0	0	0	1	.286	.286
Alou, Moises	.333	6	2	0	0	0	2	.333	.500
Anderson, Brd*	.100	10	1	0	0	0	3	.100	.100
Baerga, C#	.444	9	4	0	2	0	0	.444	.778
Baines, H*	.000	9	0	0	0	2	3	.182	.000
Belle, Albert	.125	8	1	0	3	0	1	.125	.250
Bichette, D	.200	5	1	0	0	0	1	.200	.200
Boggs, Wade*	.571	7	4	0	1	1	0	.625	.714
Borders, Pat	.111	9	1	0	0	0	1	.111	.111
Bordick, Mike	.222	9	2	0	0	0	2	.222	.222
Brosius, S	.600	5	3	2	3	0	0	.600	1.800
Buhner, Jay	.286	7	2	0	1	2	1	.444	.286
Burks, Ellis	.250	8	2	0	0	0	1	.250	.500
Canseco, Jose	.308	13	4	1	6	1	3	.357	.615
Carter, Joe	.333	12	4	0	1	0	2	.333	.667
Cora, Joey#	.286	7	2	1	4	0	0	.250	1.000
Davis, Chili#	.333	3	1	1	1	2	2	.600	1.333
Deer, Rob	.143	7	1	0	0	3	0	.143	.143
Devereaux, M	.273	11	3	1	2	0	1	.273	.727
DiSarcina, Ga	.333	9	3	0	3	0	1	.333	.333
Eisenreich, J*	.250	4	1	0	2	1	0	.400	.500
Fermin, Felix	.250	4	1	0	1	1	0	.400	.250
Fielder, C	.000	5	0	0	0	2	3	.286	.000
Franco, Julio	.273	11	3	1	2	0	2	.273	.636
Fryman, T	.333	9	3	0	0	0	0	.400	.444
Gaetti, Gary	.000	4	0	0	0	1	0	.200	.000
Gagne, Greg	.143	7	1	0	0	0	0	.125	.143
Gomez, Leo	.167	6	1	0	0	0	2	.167	.167
Gonzalez, J	.133	15	2	0	1	0	3	.133	.200
Greenwell, M*	.429	7	3	0	0	0	1	.429	.429
Griffey Jr, K*	.500	6	3	1	2	1	0	.571	1.500
Grissom, M	.200	5	1	0	0	0	0	.200	.200
Guillen, O*	.667	6	4	0	1	0	0	.667	.833
Hamilton, D*	.200	5	1	0	0	0	0	.200	.200
Henderson, R	.444	9	4	0	2	1	0	.500	.667
Hill, G	.167	6	1	0	0	0	3	.167	.500
Hoiles, Chris	.111	9	1	0	0	1	2	.200	.111
Jaha, John	.167	6	1	0	0	1	1	.286	.167
Johnson, L*	.143	7	1	0	0	0	0	.143	.143
Joyner, Wally*	.600	5	3	0	0	0	0	.600	.600
Karkovice, R	.571	7	4	0	2	1	2	.625	.571
Kent, Jeff	.400	5	2	1	4	0	2	.400	1.400
Knoblauch, C	.286	7	2	0	2	0	0	.286	.286
Lofton, Kenny*	.143	7	1	0	1	0	2	.125	.143
Macfarlane, M	.333	6	2	1	3	0	0	.333	.833
Martinez, E	.250	4	1	0	0	1	0	.400	.250
McGwire, Mark	.333	3	1	0	0	3	0	.667	.333

Rich Monteleone, Angels — RHP

Batter	Avg	AB	H	HR	BI	BB	SO	OBP	Slg
Molitor, Paul	.200	10	2	0	1	0	1	.200	.200
Orsulak, Joe*	.125	8	1	0	2	0	1	.125	.125
Palmeiro, R*	.313	16	5	2	3	0	1	.313	.688
Palmer, Dean	.222	9	2	1	1	1	3	.300	.556
Pena, Tony	.167	6	1	0	0	1	0	.286	.333
Phillips, T#	.200	5	1	0	0	5	2	.600	.400
Polonia, Luis*	.167	6	1	0	0	0	1	.167	.167
Raines, Tim#	.667	3	2	1	1	2	0	.800	1.667
Reed, Jody	.400	5	2	0	0	1	1	.500	.400
Ripken, Billy	.167	6	1	0	1	0	1	.167	.333
Ripken, Cal	.308	13	4	0	0	0	1	.308	.308
Rodriguez, I	.222	9	2	0	0	1	1	.300	.222
Salmon, Tim	.333	3	1	0	1	1	1	.400	.667
Sanders, R	.400	5	2	0	2	0	0	.400	.400
Segui, David#	.600	5	3	0	1	1	0	.667	.600
Seitzer, K	.444	9	4	0	1	0	1	.444	.444
Sierra, Ruben#	.333	9	3	0	1	3	1	.500	.556
Sorrento, P*	.250	8	2	0	0	1	1	.333	.250
Sprague, Ed	.000	5	0	0	0	0	1	.000	.000
Surhoff, B.J.*	.333	6	2	0	0	1	1	.429	.500
Tartabull, D	.429	7	3	1	1	0	1	.429	1.000
Tettleton, M#	.250	8	2	0	0	2	1	.400	.250
Thomas, Frank	.300	10	3	0	2	1	3	.364	.400
Trammell, A	.111	9	1	0	0	0	1	.111	.111
Valentin, Jhn	.400	5	2	0	1	1	0	.500	.400
Vaughn, G	.375	8	3	1	2	1	2	.444	.875
Ventura, R*	.250	8	2	0	2	1	0	.333	.250
Vizquel, Omar#	.500	6	3	0	0	1	1	.571	.667
Weiss, Walt	.286	7	2	0	0	0	0	.286	.286
White, Devon	.125	8	1	0	0	1	3	.222	.125

Jeff Montgomery, Royals — RHP

Batter	Avg	AB	H	HR	BI	BB	SO	OBP	Slg
Aldrete, Mike*	.500	6	3	0	1	0	0	.500	.500
Alomar, R#	.375	8	3	0	3	2	0	.538	.500
Alomar Jr, S	.182	11	2	0	1	0	4	.182	.182
Amaral, Rich	.333	6	2	0	2	0	2	.333	.333
Anderson, Brd*	.267	15	4	1	3	0	2	.267	.533
Anderson, G*	.200	5	1	0	0	0	0	.200	.200
Baerga, C#	.313	16	5	0	3	0	5	.313	.438
Baines, H*	.235	17	4	2	5	1	4	.278	.588
Becker, Rich*	.000	1	0	0	0	2	1	.400	.000
Belle, Albert	.200	10	2	0	1	0	0	.200	.200
Bichette, D	.200	5	1	0	0	0	2	.200	.200
Blowers, Mike	.000	6	0	0	0	0	2	.000	.000
Boggs, Wade*	.313	16	5	0	2	3	0	.421	.313
Borders, Pat	.100	10	1	0	0	0	2	.100	.100
Bordick, Mike	.125	8	1	0	2	1	2	.222	.125
Brosius, S	.143	7	1	0	0	0	5	.143	.143
Buhner, Jay	.222	9	2	0	0	1	2	.300	.222
Burks, Ellis	.364	11	4	0	5	1	2	.385	.545
Canseco, Jose	.400	10	4	1	2	1	2	.455	.800
Carter, Joe	.111	18	2	2	6	0	5	.105	.444
Cirillo, Jeff	.600	5	3	0	1	0	0	.600	.600
Clark, Will*	.286	7	2	0	1	2	1	.444	.286
Cole, Alex*	.250	8	2	0	0	0	1	.250	.250
Cora, Joey*	.167	18	3	0	1	1	1	.211	.167
Curtis, Chad	.100	10	1	0	1	2	4	.250	.100
Cuyler, Milt#	.000	6	0	0	0	1	5	.143	.000
Davis, Chili#	.050	20	1	0	0	5	7	.240	.050
Deer, Rob	.143	14	2	0	1	2	8	.294	.214
Devereaux, M	.235	17	4	0	0	0	7	.235	.235
DiSarcina, G	.333	9	3	0	1	0	1	.333	.333
Edmonds, Jim*	.200	5	1	0	0	0	1	.200	.200
Fermin, Felix	.571	7	4	0	0	0	1	.571	.857
Fielder, C	.333	15	5	1	1	0	4	.333	.733
Franco, Julio	.176	17	3	0	0	2	4	.263	.176
Fryman, T	.250	16	4	2	5	0	4	.250	.625
Gaetti, Gary	.167	12	2	1	1	0	0	.167	.417
Gagne, Greg	.100	10	1	0	0	1	1	.182	.100
Gates, Brent#	.286	7	2	0	0	2	0	.286	.286
Gomez, Leo	.250	8	2	0	0	1	2	.333	.375
Gonzales, R	.200	5	1	0	0	1	1	.333	.200
Gonzalez, J	.235	17	4	1	1	0	8	.278	.412
Green, Shawn*	.750	4	3	1	2	1	1	.800	1.500
Greenwell, M*	.375	16	6	1	2	0	0	.375	.625
Greer, Rusty*	.300	10	3	1	3	0	2	.300	.700
Griffey Jr, K*	.308	13	4	0	3	1	2	.357	.538
Guillen, O*	.227	22	5	0	2	1	0	.261	.227
Hale, Chip*	.286	7	2	0	2	1	1	.375	.429
Hall, Mel*	.111	9	1	0	3	0	1	.111	.222
Hamilton, D*	.118	17	2	0	1	1	1	.167	.118
Henderson, R	.286	14	4	0	1	1	4	.333	.286
Higginson, B	.250	4	1	0	0	1	3	.400	.250
Hoiles, Chris	.143	7	1	1	4	0	3	.143	.571
Howell, Jack*	.143	7	1	0	0	0	1	.143	.143
Huson, Jeff*	.250	4	1	0	0	1	1	.400	.250
Incaviglia, P	.083	12	1	0	1	2	5	.214	.083
Jaha, John	.200	10	2	0	0	0	1	.200	.200
James, Dion*	.333	9	3	0	0	1	1	.400	.333
Javier, Stan#	.200	10	2	0	2	0	4	.200	.200

Jeff Montgomery, Royals — RHP (continued)

Batter	Avg	AB	H	HR	BI	BB	SO	OBP	Slg
Jefferson, R*	.400	5	2	0	1	0	0	.400	.400
Johnson, L*	.211	19	4	1	3	3	4	.304	.526
Karkovice, R	.222	9	2	0	0	0	3	.222	.333
Kelly, R	.182	11	2	0	2	1	5	.250	.273
Knoblauch, C	.250	12	3	0	1	2	0	.357	.417
Kreuter, Chad	.000	6	0	0	0	1	4	.143	.000
Leius, Scott	.600	5	3	0	0	0	0	.600	.800
Levis, Jesse	.800	5	4	0	2	0	0	.800	1.000
Listach, Pat#	.167	6	1	0	0	3	1	.444	.167
Lofton, Kenny*	.000	5	0	0	0	2	1	.286	.000
Martinez, E	.182	11	2	0	0	2	6	.308	.182
Martinez, T*	.385	13	5	0	4	0	4	.385	.462
McGriff, Fred*	.000	6	0	0	0	0	2	.000	.000
McGwire, Mark	.231	13	3	0	3	4	6	.389	.231
McLemore, M#	.111	9	1	0	0	0	3	.111	.111
Meares, Pat	.333	6	2	0	0	0	1	.333	.333
Molitor, Paul	.292	24	7	0	4	2	4	.370	.292
Murray, Eddie#	.000	5	0	0	0	0	0	.000	.000
Myers, Greg*	.333	12	4	0	0	1	0	.385	.583
Newson, W*	.333	9	3	0	1	2	2	.400	.333
Nilsson, Dave*	.250	4	1	0	3	1	1	.333	.500
Nixon, Otis*	.333	6	2	0	0	1	0	.429	.333
O'Brien, C	.400	5	2	0	0	0	2	.400	.600
O'Neill, Paul*	.750	4	3	0	2	1	0	.800	1.250
Olerud, John*	.368	19	7	1	1	3	1	.400	.684
Oliver, Joe	.000	5	0	0	0	0	2	.000	.000
Orsulak, Joe*	.462	13	6	0	2	1	0	.500	.615
Palmeiro, R*	.150	20	3	0	2	1	6	.190	.200
Palmer, Dean	.231	13	3	2	3	0	6	.231	.846
Pena, Tony	.000	5	0	0	0	0	0	.000	.000
Phillips, T#	.200	20	4	1	3	0	5	.190	.350
Polonia, Luis*	.154	13	2	0	0	1	1	.214	.154
Raines, Tim#	.200	10	2	0	2	2	0	.308	.200
Reed, Jody	.100	10	1	0	0	2	5	.308	.200
Ripken, Cal	.444	18	8	0	1	6	1	.583	.667
Rodriguez, I	.333	9	3	0	2	1	2	.400	.333
Salmon, Tim	.167	6	1	0	1	1	1	.375	.167
Schofield, D	.000	6	0	0	0	2	5	.333	.000
Segui, David#	.250	4	1	0	0	1	1	.400	.500
Seitzer, K	.143	7	1	0	2	3	0	.400	.143
Sheffield, G	.143	7	1	0	3	0	2	.143	.143
Sierra, Ruben#	.227	22	5	0	2	4	3	.346	.227
Snow, J.T.#	.200	10	2	0	1	0	0	.273	.200
Sojo, Luis	.200	5	1	0	0	1	0	.333	.200
Sorrento, P*	.429	7	3	1	1	3	2	.600	1.000
Spiers, Bill*	.143	7	1	0	0	2	2	.333	.143
Sprague, Ed	.100	10	2	0	0	0	2	.200	.300
Stanley, Mike	.167	12	2	0	0	1	6	.231	.167
Steinbach, T	.368	19	7	0	5	1	5	.400	.474
Strange, Doug*	.111	9	1	0	0	0	4	.111	.111
Surhoff, B.J.*	.294	17	5	0	5	1	1	.333	.412
Sveum, Dale#	.273	11	3	0	3	2	5	.273	.455
Tartabull, D	.182	11	2	1	2	1	6	.250	.455
Tettleton, M#	.125	16	2	0	0	2	4	.222	.188
Thomas, Frank	.250	12	3	1	3	3	4	.400	.583
Thome, Jim*	.200	5	1	0	0	1	2	.333	.200
Trammell, A	.000	7	0	0	0	0	3	.000	.000
Valentin, Jhn	.000	9	0	0	0	0	4	.000	.000
Valle, Dave	.200	10	2	1	1	0	2	.273	.600
Vaughn, Greg	.200	15	3	0	0	0	2	.200	.200
Vaughn, Mo*	.286	7	2	1	4	1	2	.375	.714
Velarde, R	.000	11	0	0	0	1	7	.083	.000
Ventura, R*	.211	19	4	0	1	1	4	.250	.263
Vizquel, Omar*	.000	4	0	0	0	2	1	.333	.000
Ward, Turner#	.143	7	1	0	1	2	2	.364	.143
White, Devon#	.300	10	3	0	1	1	2	.364	.300
Whiten, Mark#	.200	5	1	0	1	2	1	.429	.400
Williams, Ber#	.250	8	2	0	0	1	4	.333	.500

Marcus Moore, Reds — RHP

Batter	Avg	AB	H	HR	BI	BB	SO	OBP	Slg
Bell, Jay	.400	5	2	0	1	0	0	.400	.800
Clark, Dave*	.333	3	1	0	0	2	2	.600	.333
Dykstra, L*	.000	4	0	0	0	1	2	.200	.000
Garcia, C	.400	5	2	0	3	0	0	.400	.400
Hollins, Dave#	.200	5	1	0	2	0	0	.400	.400
Kent, Jeff	.000	2	0	0	0	3	1	.600	.000
Lemke, Mark#	.200	5	1	0	0	0	0	.200	.400
Manwaring, K	.000	4	0	0	0	1	3	.200	.000
Stocker, R	.400	5	2	0	0	0	1	.400	.800

Ramon Morel, Pirates — RHP

Batter	Avg	AB	H	HR	BI	BB	SO	OBP	Slg
Gilkey, B	.200	5	1	0	0	0	0	.200	.200

Mike Morgan, Reds — RHP

Batter	Avg	AB	H	HR	BI	BB	SO	OBP	Slg
Aldrete, Mike*	.250	4	1	0	1	1	0	.400	.500
Alfonzo, E	.429	7	3	1	2	0	0	.429	1.000
Alomar, R#	.286	7	2	0	0	1	0	.375	.571
Alou, Moises	.250	24	6	0	6	1	1	.259	.292

Mike Morgan, Reds — RHP

Batter	Avg	AB	H	HR	BI	BB	SO	OBP	Slg
Amaro, Ruben#	.125	16	2	0	0	0	4	.176	.125
Andrews, S	.222	9	2	0	0	0	0	.222	.222
Anthony, Eric*	.300	20	6	0	3	1	2	.333	.400
Arias, Alex	.250	4	1	0	2	1	1	.400	.250
Ashley, Billy	.000	4	0	0	0	1	0	.200	.000
Ausmus, Brad	.286	7	2	0	0	0	1	.286	.429
Bagwell, Jeff	.279	43	12	2	9	2	6	.298	.465
Baines, H*	.455	11	5	1	4	0	0	.417	.727
Barberie, B#	.154	13	2	0	0	2	1	.267	.154
Bates, Jason#	.143	7	1	0	0	1	1	.333	.143
Batiste, Kim	.600	5	3	0	1	0	1	.600	.600
Bell, Derek	.125	8	1	0	0	1	3	.222	.125
Bell, Jay	.254	63	16	0	4	5	6	.309	.333
Belliard, A	.455	11	5	0	0	1	2	.500	.545
Benard, M*	.250	4	1	0	0	1	1	.400	.250
Benjamin, M	.000	6	0	0	0	0	1	.000	.000
Berry, Sean	.000	6	0	0	0	0	2	.000	.000
Bichette, D	.346	26	9	1	5	0	3	.346	.500
Biggio, Craig	.250	48	12	0	5	6	10	.333	.333
Blauser, Jeff	.244	41	10	1	4	2	7	.279	.390
Boggs, Wade*	.500	8	4	0	2	2	0	.600	.750
Bonds, Barry*	.340	50	17	2	11	5	7	.379	.540
Bonilla, B#	.333	39	13	3	9	1	10	.350	.667
Boone, Bret	.250	16	4	0	1	2	7	.333	.313
Branson, Jeff*	.333	12	4	0	0	2	3	.429	.500
Brumfield, J	.364	11	4	0	0	1	1	.417	.455
Bullett, S*	.000	5	0	0	0	0	1	.000	.000
Burks, Ellis	.333	12	4	1	3	1	3	.429	.667
Burnitz, J*	.600	5	3	0	2	3	0	.750	1.400
Butler, Brett*	.375	56	21	0	2	4	3	.417	.518
Caminiti, Ken#	.250	52	13	3	6	7	11	.350	.500
Candaele, C#	.182	22	4	1	2	1	2	.217	.318
Canseco, Jose	.250	12	3	0	1	4	3	.438	.333
Carr, Chuck	.429	7	3	0	0	3	1	.600	.571
Carter, Joe	.250	40	10	1	6	0	2	.250	.375
Castilla, V	.222	18	4	0	1	0	0	.211	.333
Cedeno, A	.053	19	1	0	1	0	8	.143	.105
Cianfrocco, A	.100	10	1	0	0	3	1	.308	.100
Clark, Dave*	.261	23	6	1	3	0	6	.261	.391
Clark, Will*	.357	28	10	0	3	7	3	.459	.571
Clayton, R	.417	24	10	0	2	2	5	.481	.500
Colbrunn, G	.154	13	2	0	1	0	4	.154	.154
Cole, Alex*	.100	10	1	0	0	0	2	.100	.100
Coleman, V#	.130	23	3	0	1	1	3	.167	.174
Conine, Jeff	.250	12	3	0	1	1	0	.250	.250
Cordero, Wil	.200	15	3	0	2	0	3	.200	.200
Cummings, M*	.667	6	4	0	0	1	0	.714	.667
Daulton, D*	.235	34	8	0	2	5	6	.333	.294
Davis, Eric	.250	24	6	0	2	3	8	.333	.292
Dawson, Andre	.333	18	6	1	3	1	0	.368	.500
Deer, Rob	.118	17	2	1	1	2	2	.211	.294
DeShields, D*	.200	35	7	1	4	7	8	.326	.286
Duncan, M	.258	31	8	0	1	2	7	.303	.258
Dunston, S	.333	21	7	1	3	2	1	.391	.571
Dykstra, L*	.275	40	11	0	1	8	8	.408	.375
Eisenreich, J*	.455	11	5	0	5	0	0	.417	.455
Elster, Kevin	.125	8	1	0	1	2	2	.300	.125
Espinoza, A	.000	4	0	0	0	0	2	.000	.000
Eusebio, Tony	.400	10	4	0	0	1	2	.455	.500
Everett, Carl#	.200	5	1	0	0	0	0	.200	.400
Finley, Steve*	.340	50	17	2	4	5	4	.400	.560
Fletcher, D*	.304	23	7	0	4	0	0	.333	.435
Floyd, Cliff*	.000	4	0	0	0	1	0	.200	.000
Fonville, C#	.500	6	3	0	2	0	0	.500	.667
Franco, Julio	.345	29	10	0	5	0	0	.345	.414
Frazier, Lou*	.500	6	3	0	0	1	0	.571	.500
Gaetti, Gary	.242	33	8	2	5	2	6	.286	.515
Gagne, Greg	.154	13	2	0	1	0	4	.235	.438
Galarraga, A	.345	29	10	3	7	4	4	.424	.690
Gallego, Mike	.000	5	0	0	0	0	1	.000	.000
Gant, Ron	.205	39	8	2	5	1	3	.244	.359
Garcia, C	.467	15	7	0	0	1	1	.500	.600
Gilkey, B	.400	10	4	0	0	0	1	.400	.700
Girardi, Joe	.200	10	2	0	2	1	0	.333	.300
Gonzalez, L*	.292	48	14	1	4	5	7	.364	.438
Grace, Mark*	.258	31	8	1	7	2	1	.294	.419
Grissom, M	.200	55	11	0	6	4	6	.250	.255
Grudzielanek	.143	7	1	0	0	0	0	.143	.143
Guillen, O*	.273	11	3	0	2	1	0	.333	.273
Gutierrez, R	.200	5	1	0	1	1	0	.200	.200
Gwynn, Tony*	.308	39	12	0	2	4	1	.372	.308
Hall, Mel*	.414	29	12	0	3	2	1	.452	.655
Hansen, Dave*	.462	13	6	0	2	3	1	.563	.538
Harris, Lenny*	.313	32	10	0	2	1	3	.333	.438
Hayes, Charlie	.448	29	13	0	5	0	0	.448	.621
Henderson, R	.500	12	6	3	3	2	2	.571	1.250
Hernandez, Jo	.000	4	0	0	1	0	0	.000	.000
Hill, G	.400	10	4	0	0	1	0	.400	.500
Hollandsworth*	.000	0	0	0	0	0	0	.000	.000
Hollins, Dave#	.310	29	9	2	5	7	7	.444	.621
Howard, T*	.545	11	6	0	1	1	2	.583	.818

Mike Morgan, Reds — RHP

Batter	Avg	AB	H	HR	BI	BB	SO	OBP	Slg
Howell, Jack*	.100	10	1	0	0	1	0	.182	.200
Hundley, Todd#	.407	27	11	3	4	2	3	.448	.852
Hunter, Brian	.429	7	3	1	7	0	1	.429	1.000
Huskey, Butch	.400	5	2	0	0	1	0	.500	.400
Incaviglia, P	.375	24	9	0	1	2	6	.423	.500
James, Dion*	.500	6	3	1	1	0	1	.500	1.000
Jefferies, G#	.321	28	9	0	3	2	2	.367	.357
Johnson, Char	.000	4	0	0	0	1	0	.200	.000
Johnson, L*	.400	10	4	0	0	0	0	.400	.800
Jones, C#	.357	14	5	0	2	2	2	.438	.571
Jones, Chris	.167	6	1	0	1	0	1	.167	.167
Jordan, Brian	.500	6	3	0	1	0	1	.500	.500
Jordan, Ricky	.333	18	6	0	2	0	4	.333	.389
Joyner, Wally*	.357	14	5	1	4	0	1	.357	.714
Justice, Dave*	.323	31	10	3	10	5	5	.395	.645
Karros, Eric	.273	22	6	1	5	0	4	.273	.455
Kelly, R	.167	12	2	0	1	0	1	.167	.167
Kent, Jeff	.400	15	6	4	7	0	2	.400	1.200
King, Jeff	.259	27	7	1	4	4	5	.355	.407
Kingery, Mike*	.154	13	2	0	1	2	2	.267	.231
Klesko, Ryan*	.200	15	3	1	4	4	5	.350	.400
Lankford, Ray*	.235	17	4	1	3	2	4	.316	.412
Lansing, Mike	.500	12	6	0	0	2	2	.600	.667
Larkin, Barry	.213	47	10	0	4	5	2	.283	.255
Lemke, Mark#	.045	22	1	0	0	3	4	.160	.045
Lewis, Darren	.294	17	5	0	1	2	1	.368	.412
Lopez, Javy	.400	5	2	0	1	0	0	.400	.400
Mabry, John*	.200	5	1	1	1	0	0	.200	.800
Magadan, Dave*	.394	33	13	0	4	3	3	.444	.424
Manwaring, K	.103	29	3	0	1	2	5	.156	.103
Martin, Al*	.400	20	8	0	3	3	5	.478	.400
Martinez, Da*	.346	26	9	0	0	2	1	.393	.346
McGee, Willie#	.395	38	15	0	1	2	8	.425	.500
McGriff, Fred*	.422	45	19	0	5	6	5	.481	.556
McGwire, Mark	.200	5	1	0	1	1	1	.333	.200
McLemore, M#	.000	5	0	0	0	1	0	.000	.000
McRae, Brian#	.167	6	1	0	0	0	0	.167	.333
Merced, O*	.357	42	15	0	13	7	7	.440	.405
Miller, Orl	.750	4	3	0	1	0	1	.800	.750
Mitchell, K	.211	19	4	2	5	3	3	.318	.526
Molitor, Paul	.500	16	8	0	1	1	2	.529	.625
Mondesi, Raul	.200	10	2	0	0	1	1	.333	.200
Morandini, M*	.205	39	8	0	1	5	3	.295	.282
Morris, Hal*	.357	28	10	1	7	1	2	.367	.536
Murray, Eddie*	.211	38	8	1	2	6	3	.318	.289
Nixon, Otis#	.267	15	4	0	0	0	3	.267	.267
O'Brien, C	.267	15	4	1	1	0	2	.267	.467
O'Neill, Paul*	.400	30	12	2	5	5	1	.486	.633
Offerman, J#	.273	11	3	0	1	1	2	.333	.455
Oliver, Joe	.273	22	6	2	6	3	3	.360	.591
Orsulak, Joe*	.111	9	1	0	1	2	1	.273	.111
Owens, J	.000	4	0	0	0	0	2	.000	.000
Pagnozzi, Tom	.273	11	3	0	1	0	2	.273	.364
Pena, G#	.000	7	0	0	0	1	3	.125	.000
Pendleton, T#	.257	35	9	0	5	4	6	.333	.314
Phillips, T#	.500	4	2	0	1	1	1	.600	.500
Piazza, Mike	.375	16	6	1	3	0	0	.375	.563
Plantier, P*	.714	7	5	3	6	1	0	.750	2.000
Prince, Tom	.167	6	1	0	0	0	2	.167	.167
Raines, Tim#	.167	12	2	0	0	0	0	.167	.167
Reed, Jeff*	.136	22	3	0	0	0	1	.136	.136
Reed, Jody	.444	9	4	0	0	1	1	.500	.444
Ripken, Cal	.091	22	2	0	0	0	4	.091	.091
Roberts, Bip#	.194	31	6	1	4	4	4	.286	.387
Rodriguez, H*	.063	16	1	0	0	2	3	.167	.125
Sabo, Chris	.216	37	8	0	5	2	4	.256	.216
Samuel, Juan	.600	5	3	0	0	0	0	.600	.600
Sandberg, R	.333	27	9	0	2	2	1	.379	.333
Sanders, R	.208	24	5	0	2	2	8	.269	.250
Santiago, B	.267	30	8	0	2	2	2	.313	.333
Scarsone, S	.300	10	3	0	0	0	1	.300	.300
Schofield, D	.313	16	5	1	2	0	2	.313	.563
Segui, David#	.000	6	0	0	0	3	0	.333	.000
Seitzer, K	.438	16	7	0	0	2	1	.500	.500
Servais, S	.188	16	3	0	1	1	2	.278	.188
Sheaffer, D	.000	4	0	0	0	1	0	.333	.000
Sheffield, G	.333	21	7	2	6	0	1	.333	.714
Sierra, Ruben#	.235	17	4	1	3	1	5	.278	.529
Simms, Mike	.500	5	3	0	0	0	0	.500	.500
Slaught, Don	.533	15	8	2	4	3	0	.632	1.000
Smith, Dwight*	.118	17	2	0	0	1	4	.167	.118
Smith, Ozzie#	.080	25	2	0	0	3	1	.179	.080
Sosa, Sammy	.200	5	1	0	0	1	0	.333	.200
Stairs, Mike	.250	4	1	0	0	1	0	.400	.250
Stillwell, K#	.200	10	2	0	0	0	1	.273	.200
Stocker, D*	.167	6	1	0	0	0	1	.167	.167
Strawberry, D*	.211	19	4	2	2	3	6	.318	.526
Surhoff, B.J.*	.364	11	4	0	4	0	1	.333	.727
Sveum, Dale#	.133	15	2	1	1	1	5	.188	.333
Tarasco, Tony*	.000	4	0	0	0	2	0	.333	.000
Tartabull, D	.727	11	8	1	4	1	0	.750	1.000

RHP

Batter	Avg	AB	H	HR	BI	BB	SO	OBP	Slg
Taubensee, E*	.105	19	2	0	2	0	5	.100	.105
Tettleton, M#	.167	6	1	0	1	0	3	.167	.167
Thompson, Mil*	.120	25	3	1	1	4	1	.241	.240
Thompson, Rob	.220	41	9	0	5	2	3	.250	.268
Thompson, Ry	.375	8	3	2	7	1	1	.500	1.250
Trammell, A	.300	10	3	2	2	0	0	.300	.900
VanderWal, J*	.250	8	2	0	1	1	0	.333	.750
Vizcaino, J#	.167	6	1	1	2	1	0	.250	.667
Walker, Larry*	.382	34	13	2	6	5	1	.462	.676
Wallach, Tim	.256	39	10	1	3	0	3	.256	.359
Walton, J	.250	16	4	0	0	0	0	.250	.313
Wehner, John	.000	4	0	0	0	1	1	.200	.000
Weiss, Walt#	.313	16	5	0	1	3	3	.421	.313
White, Devon#	.400	10	4	0	1	0	0	.364	.500
White, R	.000	6	0	0	0	1	0	.143	.000
Whiten, Mark#	.200	5	1	0	0	1	2	.333	.200
Wilkins, Rick*	.286	7	2	0	2	0	2	.286	.429
Williams, E	.500	6	3	0	1	0	0	.500	.667
Williams, Ma	.318	44	14	4	9	2	11	.348	.591
Young, Eric	.214	14	3	0	2	2	0	.294	.214
Zeile, Todd	.261	23	6	1	8	2	2	.320	.435

LHP

Batter	Avg	AB	H	HR	BI	BB	SO	OBP	Slg
Finley, Steve*	.000	5	0	0	1	0	0	.000	.000
Morris, Hal*	.200	5	1	0	0	1	1	.333	.200

LHP

Batter	Avg	AB	H	HR	BI	BB	SO	OBP	Slg
Alicea, Luis#	.200	5	1	0	0	0	2	.200	.200
Alomar, R#	.192	26	5	0	1	3	4	.276	.269
Alomar Jr, S	.250	12	3	1	2	0	2	.250	.500
Amaral, Rich	.524	21	11	0	2	1	3	.545	.619
Anderson, Brd*	.625	8	5	3	4	0	1	.625	1.750
Anderson, G*	.600	5	3	1	2	0	0	.600	1.200
Baerga, C#	.250	16	4	0	0	3	1	.368	.313
Batista, Tony	.286	7	2	1	2	0	0	.286	.714
Bautista, D	.200	10	2	0	1	0	0	.200	.300
Belle, Albert	.588	17	10	0	5	2	1	.619	.882
Belliard, R	.231	13	3	0	0	1	2	.286	.231
Berroa, G	.214	14	3	0	2	3	1	.333	.357
Biggio, Craig	.200	5	1	0	0	0	2	.200	.200
Blauser, Jeff	.200	5	1	0	1	1	1	.333	.400
Blowers, Mike	.211	19	4	0	1	0	4	.211	.263
Boggs, Wade*	.368	38	14	2	8	2	2	.400	.579
Bonds, Barry*	.280	25	7	5	6	1	4	.308	.880
Bonilla, B#	.270	37	10	1	5	2	5	.300	.405
Borders, Pat	.316	19	6	1	2	1	1	.350	.579
Bordick, Mike	.150	20	3	0	0	0	0	.150	.200
Bragg, Darren*	.333	6	2	0	0	1	1	.429	.333
Brosius, S	.211	19	4	1	1	1	7	.250	.421
Buhner, Jay	.313	16	5	0	0	0	2	.313	.438
Burks, Ellis	.286	7	2	0	1	2	0	.400	.286
Candaele, C#	.462	13	6	0	0	1	0	.500	.769
Cangelosi, J#	.500	6	3	0	3	1	1	.571	.667
Canseco, Jose	.143	7	1	1	2	0	2	.143	.571
Carter, Joe	.143	21	3	1	3	0	5	.136	.286
Cedeno, A	.200	5	1	1	1	0	0	.200	.800
Cirillo, Jeff	.214	14	3	0	0	0	1	.214	.214
Clark, Will*	.148	27	4	0	0	1	5	.179	.185
Coleman, V#	.176	17	3	0	1	2	5	.250	.176
Cora, Joey#	.000	8	0	0	0	1	0	.000	.000
Curtis, Chad	.471	17	8	0	4	2	3	.526	.529
Damon, Johnny*	.250	12	3	0	0	1	0	.308	.250
Davis, Chili#	.323	31	10	2	7	3	7	.382	.581
Davis, Eric	.350	20	7	2	6	3	2	.435	.650
Dawson, Andre	.316	19	6	1	5	0	1	.316	.579
Deer, Rob	.167	6	1	0	0	1	0	.286	.167
DeShields, D*	.667	3	2	0	0	2	0	.800	.667
Devereaux, M	.227	22	5	1	3	0	1	.227	.455
DiSarcina, G	.200	15	3	0	1	1	2	.250	.200
Duncan, M	.333	18	6	0	4	0	3	.316	.389
Dykstra, L*	.500	6	3	1	2	0	0	.500	1.167
Easley, D	.091	11	1	0	0	1	2	.231	.091
Edmonds, Jim*	.286	7	2	0	0	1	2	.375	.286
Elster, Kevin	.214	14	3	0	0	2	2	.313	.214
Espinoza, A	.154	13	2	1	2	0	1	.154	.385
Fabregas, Jor*	.333	6	2	0	2	0	0	.333	.333
Fermin, Felix	.222	18	4	0	2	1	0	.263	.278
Fielder, C	.240	25	6	1	3	2	6	.296	.400
Franco, Julio	.400	10	4	0	3	0	1	.400	.400
Fryman, T	.188	16	3	1	2	2	4	.278	.438
Gaetti, Gary	.222	18	4	0	4	1	4	.263	.278
Gagne, Greg	.318	22	7	0	2	1	5	.348	.455
Galarraga, A	.379	29	11	1	3	2	8	.419	.552
Gallego, Mike	.300	20	6	0	2	0	2	.300	.300
Gant, Ron	.000	6	0	0	1	0	0	.143	.000
Gates, Brent#	.364	11	4	1	1	0	1	.364	.727
Girardi, Joe	.000	6	0	0	0	0	0	.000	.000
Gomez, Chris	.333	9	3	0	0	1	1	.400	.333
Gonzalez, A	.429	7	3	0	1	0	0	.429	.571

LHP

Batter	Avg	AB	H	HR	BI	BB	SO	OBP	Slg
Gonzalez, J	.083	12	1	0	1	5	5	.353	.083
Goodwin, Tom*	.318	22	7	0	2	0	3	.318	.364
Grebeck, C	.273	11	3	0	0	2	0	.385	.273
Greenwell, M*	.400	10	4	0	1	2	0	.462	.500
Greer, Rusty*	.333	3	1	0	1	2	0	.600	.333
Griffey Jr, K*	.364	22	8	1	5	2	5	.417	.636
Grissom, M	.750	4	3	0	1	0	0	.750	1.000
Guillen, O*	.118	17	2	0	1	0	2	.111	.176
Gwynn, Tony*	.389	18	7	1	3	3	1	.455	.556
Hamelin, Bob*	.286	7	2	0	1	0	4	.286	.429
Hamilton, D*	.188	16	3	0	0	0	1	.188	.188
Haselman, B	.143	7	1	0	0	0	0	.143	.286
Henderson, R	.333	15	5	0	1	2	1	.412	.533
Hiatt, Phil	.000	7	0	0	0	3	3	.000	.000
Hill, G	.071	14	1	0	0	2	4	.188	.143
Hoiles, Chris	.286	7	2	0	0	1	1	.375	.286
Howard, Dave#	.286	14	4	1	1	1	1	.333	.500
Hudler, Rex	.375	16	6	3	5	1	1	.412	1.063
Huff, Michael	.143	7	1	0	0	0	1	.143	.286
Hulse, David*	.167	6	1	0	0	1	0	.286	.167
Jaha, John	.444	18	8	3	5	2	1	.500	1.000
Javier, Stan#	.083	12	1	0	2	2	1	.267	.083
Jeter, Derek	.333	9	3	0	0	0	0	.333	.333
Johnson, L*	.133	15	2	0	1	0	2	.133	.133
Jordan, Ricky	.300	10	3	0	0	0	3	.300	.300
Joyner, Wally*	.500	16	8	0	4	0	0	.500	.563
Karkovice, R	.000	6	0	0	1	1	5	.125	.000
Kelly, Pat	.235	17	4	1	3	1	3	.278	.471
Kirby, Wayne*	.167	6	1	0	0	0	0	.167	.167
Knoblauch, C	.231	13	3	1	2	0	2	.231	.538
Larkin, Barry	.364	11	4	1	2	3	1	.500	.727
Leius, Scott	.286	7	2	0	3	1	0	.375	.286
Lesher, Brian	.200	5	1	0	1	0	0	.200	.200
Lewis, Mark	.600	5	3	0	0	0	0	.600	.600
Leyritz, Jim	.118	17	2	0	0	2	6	.211	.118
Listach, Pat#	.200	10	2	0	0	0	1	.200	.300
Lofton, Kenny*	.308	26	8	1	1	0	6	.308	.423
Lovullo, T#	.429	7	3	0	0	1	1	.500	.429
Macfarlane, M	.227	22	5	1	5	1	5	.250	.409
Martin, N	.200	5	1	0	0	0	0	.200	.200
Martinez, E	.444	9	4	0	3	5	0	.643	.556
Martinez, T*	.333	15	5	1	3	3	5	.444	.667
Matheny, Mike	.167	6	1	0	0	0	2	.167	.167
McCarty, Dave	.250	16	4	1	2	0	2	.250	.438
McGee, Willie*	.250	16	4	0	3	0	1	.250	.438
McGriff, Fred*	.250	12	3	1	2	0	2	.250	.583
McGwire, Mark	.250	16	4	1	2	2	5	.333	.563
McLemore, M#	.000	6	0	0	1	2	1	.250	.000
McRae, Brian#	.111	9	1	0	0	1	1	.200	.111
Meares, Pat	.143	7	1	0	0	0	2	.143	.429
Mieske, Matt	.188	16	3	0	1	1	3	.235	.188
Mitchell, K	.200	15	3	1	1	1	3	.250	.467
Molitor, Paul	.400	20	8	1	4	0	2	.381	.550
Morris, Hal*	.400	5	2	0	1	0	1	.400	.600
Munoz, Pedro	.500	6	3	0	1	0	2	.500	.833
Murray, Eddie#	.167	12	2	0	1	1	1	.167	.250
Newfield, M	.333	6	2	1	2	0	1	.333	.833
Nieves, M#	.400	5	2	0	0	0	0	.400	.400
Nilsson, Dave*	.308	13	4	1	4	3	1	.471	.538
Nixon, Otis#	.091	11	1	0	0	0	1	.091	.091
O'Brien, C	.400	5	2	1	1	0	0	.400	1.000
O'Neill, Paul*	.375	24	9	1	3	3	4	.444	.625
Offerman, J#	.286	14	4	0	1	0	2	.286	.429
Olerud, John*	.333	12	4	0	1	2	1	.429	.417
Oliver, Joe	.200	5	1	0	0	1	1	.333	.400
Pagnozzi, Tom	.143	7	1	0	1	1	1	.250	.143
Palmeiro, R*	.231	13	3	1	2	0	1	.286	.538
Palmer, Dean	.222	9	2	0	2	3	3	.364	.222
Paquette, C	.333	21	7	0	2	3	2	.417	.381
Pena, Tony	.323	31	10	1	1	1	1	.344	.484
Pendleton, T	.308	13	4	1	3	0	1	.308	.538
Perez, E	.000	6	0	0	0	0	0	.000	.000
Phillips, T#	.333	24	8	2	4	2	3	.385	.667
Pirkl, Greg	.200	10	2	1	2	0	0	.200	.500
Raines, Tim#	.458	24	11	1	4	3	2	.519	.625
Ramirez, M	.250	12	3	1	2	1	2	.308	.500
Randa, Joe	.333	12	4	0	2	0	1	.333	.500
Reboulet, J	.375	8	3	0	1	0	0	.375	.625
Reed, Jody	.455	11	5	0	2	0	0	.455	.545
Ripken, Billy	.111	9	1	0	1	0	2	.111	.111
Ripken, Cal	.188	16	3	0	0	3	1	.316	.188
Roberts, Bip#	.154	13	2	0	1	1	0	.200	.154
Rodriguez, I	.500	18	9	1	2	0	0	.500	.833
Sabo, Chris	.125	8	1	0	0	0	4	.125	.125
Salmon, Tim	.280	25	7	3	6	0	6	.280	.720
Samuel, Juan	.366	41	15	1	8	4	13	.447	.585
Santiago, B	.250	8	2	1	1	0	1	.250	.625
Schofield, D	.500	4	2	1	1	0	0	.500	1.250
Schu, Rick	.263	19	5	1	3	1	3	.300	.474
Seitzer, K	.333	30	10	1	1	2	1	.375	.467
Sheffield, G	.750	4	3	1	1	3	0	.857	1.500

143

Jamie Moyer, Mariners — LHP

Batter	Avg	AB	H	HR	BI	BB	SO	OBP	Slg
Sierra, Ruben#	.235	17	4	0	1	0	2	.263	.353
Smith, Ozzie#	.235	17	4	0	4	1	0	.278	.412
Snow, J.T.#	.625	16	10	1	2	0	0	.625	.938
Sojo, Luis	.125	8	1	0	0	0	1	.125	.125
Sosa, Sammy	.125	8	1	0	0	1	1	.222	.125
Spiers, Bill*	.200	5	1	0	0	2	1	.429	.200
Sprague, Ed	.357	14	5	0	1	1	0	.400	.429
Stanley, Mike	.333	27	9	1	6	0	3	.333	.593
Steinbach, T	.353	17	6	2	3	1	2	.389	.765
Stillwell, K#	.600	5	2	0	1	1	1	.429	.667
Strawberry, D*	.238	21	5	1	1	6	5	.407	.429
Stynes, Chris	.600	5	3	0	0	0	0	.600	.600
Surhoff, B.J.*	.346	26	9	0	3	2	1	.414	.500
Sweeney, Mike	.333	6	2	1	3	1	1	.429	.833
Tartabull, D	.238	21	5	0	2	4	7	.360	.429
Tettleton, M#	.118	17	2	1	4	2	5	.211	.294
Thomas, Frank	.500	12	6	1	4	3	1	.563	.833
Thome, Jim*	.375	8	3	1	3	1	0	.500	.750
Thompson, Rob	.091	11	1	0	1	1	2	.167	.091
Trammell, A	.176	17	3	0	0	2	2	.263	.176
Turner, Chris	.200	5	1	0	0	1	1	.333	.200
Valentin, Jhn	.250	8	2	0	1	0	1	.250	.250
Valentin, Jse#	.250	16	4	0	1	2	1	.368	.250
Vaughn, Greg	.348	23	8	1	6	3	3	.423	.522
Vaughn, Mo*	.400	5	2	2	3	1	0	.625	1.600
Velarde, R	.192	26	5	1	3	0	6	.192	.308
Ventura, R*	.250	8	2	0	0	2	1	.400	.250
Vina, F*	.000	5	0	0	0	2	0	.286	.000
Vitiello, Joe	.250	8	2	0	2	1	2	.333	.500
Vizquel, Omar#	.429	14	6	1	2	2	1	.500	.714
Wallach, Tim	.250	32	8	1	5	1	3	.294	.406
Ward, Turner#	.000	5	0	0	0	1	1	.167	.000
White, Devon#	.364	11	4	0	3	2	2	.462	.545
Whiten, Mark#	.000	4	0	0	0	1	2	.200	.000
Williams, Ber#	.324	34	18	4	8	2	3	.556	1.059
Williams, Ger	.176	17	3	0	0	1	4	.222	.235
Williams, Ma	.200	5	1	0	0	0	3	.200	.200
Wilson, Dan	.200	10	2	1	1	0	2	.200	.500
Worthington	.500	6	3	0	1	3	2	.667	.500
Young, Ernie	.000	6	0	0	0	0	2	.000	.000
Young, Kevin	.222	9	2	0	0	1	1	.300	.222

Terry Mulholland, Mariners — LHP

Batter	Avg	AB	H	HR	BI	BB	SO	OBP	Slg
Alfonzo, E	.273	11	3	1	3	1	1	.333	.545
Alicea, Luis#	.308	13	4	0	0	2	0	.400	.308
Alomar, R#	.188	16	3	1	1	1	2	.235	.375
Alomar Jr, S	.000	6	0	0	0	0	1	.000	.000
Alou, Moises	.241	29	7	2	4	1	1	.267	.517
Anderson, Brd*	.286	7	2	0	0	0	1	.286	.429
Andrews, S	.333	12	4	0	1	0	0	.333	.333
Anthony, Eric*	.294	34	10	0	5	1	8	.297	.324
Arias, Alex	.667	6	4	0	0	1	0	.714	.833
Ausmus, Brad	.429	7	3	1	2	3	1	.600	.857
Bagwell, Jeff	.314	35	11	0	2	2	3	.351	.400
Bates, Jason#	.250	4	1	0	0	1	0	.400	.250
Batista, Tony	.250	4	1	0	0	1	0	.400	.250
Bell, Derek	.643	14	9	1	8	0	3	.600	.857
Bell, Jay	.173	52	9	0	4	4	8	.232	.192
Belle, Albert	.000	7	0	0	0	2	2	.222	.000
Belliard, R	.294	17	5	0	2	1	2	.333	.471
Benjamin, M	.200	5	1	0	0	0	0	.200	.400
Berroa, G	.467	15	7	1	4	2	1	.529	.733
Bichette, D	.435	23	10	2	6	0	3	.435	.870
Biggio, Craig	.300	40	12	0	2	8	5	.417	.350
Blauser, Jeff	.364	33	12	1	6	6	3	.462	.485
Bogar, Tim	.625	8	5	0	2	0	1	.625	.750
Boggs, Wade*	.400	5	2	0	1	0	0	.333	.400
Bonilla, B#	.387	31	12	4	10	1	1	.441	.871
Boone, Bret	.333	6	2	0	1	0	1	.333	.333
Borders, Pat	.333	6	2	0	0	0	0	.333	.333
Bordick, Mike	.600	5	3	0	3	3	0	.667	.600
Branson, Jeff*	.200	5	1	0	0	1	2	.333	.200
Brosius, S	.125	8	1	0	0	0	2	.125	.250
Brumfield, J	.267	15	4	0	2	0	1	.267	.400
Buford, Damon	.286	7	2	0	0	1	0	.444	.429
Burks, Ellis	.417	12	5	1	5	2	4	.533	.917
Butler, Brett*	.186	43	8	0	1	4	5	.255	.186
Caminiti, Ken#	.350	40	14	2	14	0	3	.341	.600
Candaele, C#	.000	8	0	0	0	1	1	.111	.000
Carr, Chuck	.111	9	1	0	1	0	4	.111	.111
Carreon, Mark	.192	26	5	0	0	0	1	.192	.192
Carter, Joe	.250	12	3	1	4	0	0	.231	.583
Castilla, V	.357	14	5	0	1	2	2	.438	.429
Cedeno, A	.273	22	6	0	1	3	3	.360	.273
Cianfrocco, A	.667	12	8	0	4	0	1	.615	.917
Clark, Phil	.167	6	1	0	1	0	0	.167	.333
Clark, Will*	.132	38	5	1	10	1	9	.171	.263
Clayton, G	.167	6	1	0	0	0	2	.167	.167
Colbrunn, G	.222	9	2	0	1	0	2	.222	.556

Terry Mulholland, Mariners — LHP

Batter	Avg	AB	H	HR	BI	BB	SO	OBP	Slg
Coleman, V#	.293	41	12	0	4	4	8	.370	.512
Conine, Jeff	.200	5	1	0	1	1	0	.333	.400
Cordero, Wil	.300	10	3	0	0	0	2	.300	.300
Curtis, Chad	.429	7	3	0	1	1	2	.500	.429
Dascenzo, D#	.158	19	3	0	0	0	1	.158	.158
Daulton, D*	.750	4	3	0	0	1	0	.800	1.500
Davis, Chili#	.714	7	5	1	5	0	1	.714	1.286
Davis, Eric	.174	46	8	3	5	2	11	.208	.391
Dawson, Andre	.277	47	13	1	6	2	11	.320	.383
Decker, Steve	.556	9	5	1	2	0	0	.556	.889
DeShields, D*	.184	38	7	0	3	2	4	.220	.211
Duncan, M	.357	14	5	0	3	2	3	.438	.500
Dunston, S	.256	43	11	0	5	1	6	.267	.326
Easley, D	.250	8	2	0	2	0	1	.222	.375
Eisenreich, J*	.250	4	1	0	0	1	0	.400	.250
Elster, Kevin	.278	18	5	0	1	0	1	.278	.333
Eusebio, Tony	.000	5	0	0	0	1	1	.167	.000
Everett, Carl#	.375	8	3	0	2	0	1	.444	.750
Fielder, C	.286	7	2	0	0	1	2	.375	.286
Finley, Steve*	.267	30	8	0	1	0	4	.290	.300
Fletcher, D*	.429	7	3	0	0	0	0	.429	.429
Fonville, C	.250	4	1	0	0	1	1	.400	.250
Franco, Julio	.250	4	1	0	0	1	1	.400	.250
Fryman, T	.500	4	2	0	1	1	1	.667	1.000
Gaetti, Gary	.111	9	1	0	2	0	1	.100	.111
Gagne, Greg	.000	6	0	0	0	0	3	.000	.000
Galarraga, A	.226	53	12	0	6	0	8	.236	.321
Gant, Ron	.405	37	15	5	9	1	2	.410	.865
Garcia, C	.714	7	5	0	0	0	0	.714	.714
Gilkey, B	.424	33	14	1	4	2	1	.457	.667
Girardi, Joe	.241	29	7	0	4	3	3	.313	.276
Gomez, Leo	.222	9	2	0	0	1	2	.300	.333
Gonzalez, J	.167	6	1	1	2	0	1	.167	.667
Gonzalez, L*	.000	6	0	0	0	0	0	.000	.000
Goodwin, Tom*	.500	2	1	0	0	1	0	.667	.500
Grace, Mark*	.290	62	18	3	11	7	4	.362	.500
Grissom, M	.260	50	13	2	5	4	8	.309	.440
Grudzielanek	.267	15	4	1	2	0	0	.267	.667
Gutierrez, R	.333	9	3	0	2	1	3	.400	.333
Gwynn, Tony*	.258	62	16	0	6	4	0	.303	.387
Harris, Lenny*	.143	7	1	0	0	1	1	.250	.143
Haselman, B	.200	5	1	0	0	1	0	.333	.200
Hayes, C	.167	18	3	0	2	0	1	.167	.222
Henderson, R	.333	12	4	0	0	1	2	.429	.333
Hernandez, Ca	.100	10	1	0	0	0	0	.100	.100
Hernandez, Jo	.143	7	1	0	0	1	1	.250	.143
Hill, G	.429	7	3	1	0	0	0	.429	.857
Hoiles, Chris	.333	6	2	0	1	1	1	.429	.333
Hudler, Rex	.179	28	5	0	0	0	3	.179	.214
Hundley, Todd#	.300	10	3	1	4	0	2	.300	.700
Hunter, Brian	.385	13	5	1	1	0	0	.429	.692
Huskey, Butch	.455	11	5	1	3	1	2	.500	.727
Incaviglia, P	.200	15	3	0	2	0	3	.235	.267
Javier, Stan#	.316	19	6	0	2	2	2	.381	.368
Jefferies, G#	.320	25	8	0	6	2	1	.367	.400
Jeter, Derek	.400	5	2	0	0	0	0	.400	.400
Johnson, Bri	.167	6	1	0	0	0	1	.167	.167
Johnson, L*	.333	9	3	0	2	0	1	.300	.444
Jones, C#	.364	11	4	1	4	0	1	.364	.636
Jones, Chris	.429	21	9	1	4	1	3	.435	.619
Jordan, Brian	.200	5	1	0	1	0	1	.200	.200
Jordan, Kevin	.667	6	4	1	2	0	0	.667	1.333
Joyner, Wally*	.167	12	2	0	2	0	2	.154	.167
Justice, Dave*	.357	28	10	3	6	3	1	.406	.750
Karros, Eric	.292	24	7	1	1	1	2	.320	.417
Kelly, Mike	.000	7	0	0	0	0	3	.000	.000
Kendall, J	.600	5	3	0	1	0	0	.600	.800
Kent, Jeff	.381	21	8	1	3	2	1	.435	.667
King, Jeff	.233	43	10	2	5	2	2	.267	.442
Lankford, Ray*	.240	25	6	0	2	1	7	.259	.320
Lansing, Mike	.235	17	4	1	1	2	2	.316	.412
Larkin, Barry	.361	36	13	1	5	6	1	.442	.500
Lemke, Mark#	.154	26	4	0	0	0	6	.154	.192
Lewis, Darren	.250	12	3	0	0	0	3	.250	.250
Lewis, Mark	.400	5	2	0	0	0	0	.400	.600
Liriano, N#	.182	11	2	0	0	0	3	.182	.273
Lofton, Kenny*	.273	11	3	0	0	0	0	.273	.273
Lopez, Javy	.556	9	5	1	2	0	1	.556	.778
Macfarlane, M	.300	10	3	1	2	0	2	.300	.700
Magadan, Dave*	.313	16	5	0	1	1	0	.353	.313
Manwaring, K	.313	16	5	1	1	1	2	.389	.563
Martinez, Da*	.286	7	2	0	0	0	1	.286	.286
Martinez, T*	.250	4	1	0	0	2	0	.500	.250
May, Derrick*	.222	9	2	1	3	1	0	.300	.556
McGee, Willie#	.313	32	10	0	3	0	7	.313	.375
McGriff, Fred*	.429	42	18	3	10	5	5	.489	.714
McGwire, Mark	.182	11	2	0	0	1	2	.250	.273
McRae, Brian#	.318	22	7	0	0	1	2	.375	.409
Merced, O*	.143	14	2	0	1	2	2	.250	.143
Mieske, Matt	.500	6	3	1	3	0	1	.500	1.000
Miller, Orl	.400	5	2	0	0	0	0	.400	.600

Terry Mulholland, Mariners — LHP

Batter	Avg	AB	H	HR	BI	BB	SO	OBP	Slg
Mitchell, K	.200	25	5	0	1	3	3	.286	.280
Molitor, Paul	.500	6	3	0	1	1	0	.571	.500
Mondesi, Raul	.200	5	1	0	0	1	1	.333	.200
Morris, Hal*	.250	16	4	0	2	1	1	.278	.250
Murray, Eddie#	.320	25	8	0	1	1	1	.346	.360
Naehring, Tim	.400	5	2	1	1	1	1	.500	1.000
Newfield, M	.400	5	2	0	0	1	0	.500	.400
Nixon, Otis#	.207	29	6	0	1	1	2	.233	.241
O'Brien, C	.167	18	3	0	1	1	2	.211	.167
O'Neill, Paul*	.148	27	4	0	3	1	4	.179	.185
Obando, S	.333	9	3	0	2	2	2	.455	.444
Ochoa, Alex	.500	6	3	0	1	0	0	.500	1.000
Offerman, J#	.379	29	11	0	1	3	4	.438	.517
Olerud, John*	.333	6	2	0	0	0	1	.429	.333
Oliver, Joe	.320	25	8	1	5	2	3	.370	.520
Ordonez, Rey	.200	5	1	0	1	0	0	.200	.200
Owens, J	.167	6	1	0	0	0	3	.167	.167
Pagnozzi, Tom	.423	26	11	1	6	0	3	.407	.615
Palmeiro, R*	.385	13	5	1	4	0	2	.385	.769
Palmer, Dean	.400	5	2	0	0	0	1	.400	.600
Paquette, C	.500	4	2	0	2	1	0	.500	.750
Pena, G#	.071	14	1	0	1	2	5	.176	.143
Pena, Tony	.455	11	5	0	1	0	0	.500	.545
Pendleton, T#	.250	40	10	0	9	1	6	.268	.325
Piazza, Mike	.429	7	3	0	0	1	0	.556	.571
Plantier, P*	.250	8	2	0	3	0	1	.222	.375
Prince, Tom	.143	7	1	0	0	2	2	.333	.143
Raines, Tim#	.471	17	8	0	3	1	2	.500	.529
Ramirez, M	.444	9	4	0	0	0	1	.444	.778
Randa, Joe	.400	5	0	0	0	0	1	.000	.000
Reed, Jody	.318	22	7	0	3	3	1	.400	.455
Ripken, Cal	.333	6	2	0	0	1	0	.429	.333
Roberts, Bip#	.200	30	6	0	3	2	2	.273	.267
Rodriguez, H*	.308	13	4	0	0	0	3	.308	.462
Rodriguez, I	.200	5	1	0	1	0	0	.200	.200
Sabo, Chris	.378	37	14	0	6	2	2	.410	.568
Salmon, Tim	.167	6	1	1	1	1	1	.286	.667
Samuel, Juan	.364	22	8	1	2	1	3	.391	.591
Sanchez, Rey	.176	17	3	0	1	0	1	.176	.176
Sandberg, R	.333	54	18	7	15	5	7	.383	.778
Sanders, R	.583	12	7	1	2	0	1	.583	1.000
Santangelo, F#	.000	5	0	0	0	0	0	.000	.000
Santiago, B	.382	34	13	1	5	0	4	.371	.500
Scarsone, S	.167	6	1	0	0	0	1	.167	.167
Schofield, D	.375	8	3	0	1	0	1	.375	.625
Segui, David#	.300	10	3	0	1	1	1	.364	.400
Seitzer, K	.250	4	1	0	2	3	2	.571	.250
Servais, S	.280	25	7	1	3	1	5	.333	.520
Sheffield, G	.350	20	7	0	1	0	2	.350	.400
Shipley, C	.333	9	3	0	0	0	0	.333	.444
Shumpert, T	.500	4	2	2	4	0	1	.400	2.000
Sierra, Ruben#	.400	10	4	2	6	0	0	.400	1.200
Slaught, Don	.360	25	9	0	4	2	1	.429	.480
Smith, Ozzie#	.235	51	12	0	1	3	4	.278	.275
Sosa, Sammy	.188	32	6	2	6	0	9	.188	.406
Spiers, Bill*	.000	5	0	0	0	0	1	.167	.000
Sprague, Ed	.167	6	1	0	2	0	1	.167	.333
Steinbach, T	.667	6	4	0	1	1	1	.714	.833
Stillwell, K	.294	17	5	0	0	3	0	.400	.294
Stinnett, K	.375	8	3	0	2	0	1	.375	.500
Strawberry, D*	.294	17	5	0	2	1	0	.333	.294
Sweeney, Mike	.000	6	0	0	0	0	2	.000	.000
Taubensee, E*	.167	6	1	0	0	0	1	.167	.167
Tettleton, M#	.000	5	0	0	1	1	1	.167	.000
Thome, Jim*	.333	9	3	0	3	1	1	.400	.444
Thompson, Mil*	.167	12	2	0	2	0	3	.167	.167
Thompson, Rob	.407	27	11	1	1	1	4	.429	.630
Thompson, Ry	.333	15	5	1	2	0	5	.333	.600
Timmons, O	.222	9	2	0	0	0	0	.222	.222
Tinsley, Lee#	.333	6	2	0	0	1	0	.333	.333
Turner, Chris	.200	5	1	0	0	0	1	.200	.200
Valentin, Jhn	.000	5	0	0	1	0	1	.000	.000
Vaughn, Mo*	.500	8	4	4	5	1	2	.556	2.000
Vizcaino, J#	.227	22	5	0	0	1	1	.261	.273
Vizquel, Omar#	.167	6	1	0	2	2	0	.375	.167
Walker, Larry*	.179	28	5	1	5	1	2	.200	.286
Wallach, Tim	.234	47	11	1	4	0	2	.229	.298
Walton, J	.300	10	6	0	4	2	1	.348	.450
Ward, Turner#	.000	6	0	0	0	2	0	.000	.000
Webster, L	.429	7	3	1	1	0	0	.429	1.000
Wehner, John	.182	11	2	0	0	0	0	.182	.182
Weiss, Walt#	.455	11	5	0	2	4	2	.600	.455
White, Devon#	.000	7	0	0	0	1	0	.000	.000
Whiten, Mark#	.313	16	5	1	2	0	1	.313	.500
Wilkins, Rick*	.600	5	3	0	0	0	0	.600	.800
Williams, Ber#	.400	5	2	0	0	0	0	.400	.400
Williams, E	.111	9	1	0	0	0	2	.111	.111
Williams, Ma	.250	36	9	4	8	1	7	.263	.583
Young, Eric	.385	13	5	1	2	2	2	.467	.692
Young, Kevin	.222	9	2	3	1	2	0	.300	.889
Zeile, Todd	.366	41	15	1	8	2	6	.386	.561

Bobby Munoz, Phillies — RHP

Batter	Avg	AB	H	HR	BI	BB	SO	OBP	Slg
Allensworth	.000	5	0	0	0	0	0	.000	.000
Alou, Moises	.714	7	5	0	1	1	0	.750	1.286
Ausmus, Brad	.167	6	1	0	0	0	0	.167	.167
Bell, Derek	.571	7	4	0	1	0	1	.571	.714
Bell, Jay	.556	9	5	0	2	0	1	.556	.667
Berry, Sean	.500	6	3	0	1	0	0	.500	.500
Bichette, D	.200	5	1	0	1	1	0	.333	.400
Blauser, Jeff	.200	5	1	0	0	0	1	.333	.200
Bonilla, B#	.400	5	2	0	2	0	0	.400	.600
Bournigal, R	.500	2	1	0	0	3	0	.800	.500
Burks, Ellis	.400	5	2	0	3	1	0	.500	.600
Butler, Brett*	.000	6	0	0	1	0	0	.000	.000
Clark, Dave*	.250	4	1	0	0	2	1	.500	.250
Cordero, Wil	.286	7	2	0	0	0	1	.286	.429
DeShields, D*	.143	7	1	0	0	0	2	.143	.143
Fielder, C	.000	5	0	0	0	1	0	.000	.000
Fletcher, D*	.000	5	0	0	1	1	2	.143	.000
Floyd, Cliff*	.375	8	3	0	1	0	2	.375	.500
Fryman, T	.400	5	2	0	0	0	2	.400	.600
Galarraga, A	.167	6	1	0	0	0	0	.167	.167
Gilkey, B	.167	6	1	0	1	1	0	.286	.333
Gonzalez, L*	.000	8	0	0	1	0	0	.111	.000
Grace, Mark*	.333	6	2	0	0	0	0	.333	.333
Grissom, M	.300	10	3	0	2	1	0	.385	.300
Gwynn, Tony*	.600	5	3	0	1	0	2	.625	.600
Hayes, C	.250	8	2	0	2	1	1	.333	.375
Henderson, R	.333	3	1	0	0	2	0	.600	.333
Johnson, Mark*	.500	4	2	0	0	1	0	.600	.500
Justice, Dave*	.667	3	2	1	1	2	1	.800	1.667
Karros, Eric	.400	5	2	0	0	0	0	.400	.400
Kendall, J	.500	4	2	0	1	0	0	.600	.500
King, Jeff	.375	8	3	0	1	0	0	.375	.500
Klesko, Ryan*	.167	6	1	0	0	1	1	.286	.167
Lankford, Ray*	.167	6	1	0	1	2	2	.375	.167
Lemke, Mark#	.600	5	3	0	2	1	0	.667	1.000
Livingstone*	.500	8	4	0	0	0	0	.500	.750
Lopez, Javy	.200	5	1	1	2	1	1	.333	.800
Lopez, Luis#	.333	6	2	1	1	0	0	.333	.833
Martin, Al*	.600	5	3	0	0	0	0	.600	.600
McGriff, Fred*	.429	7	3	0	3	0	1	.429	.571
McRae, Brian#	.167	6	1	0	0	0	1	.286	.333
Merced, O*	.167	6	1	1	3	0	0	.167	.667
Mondesi, Raul	.200	5	1	1	1	0	1	.200	.800
Morris, Hal*	.000	4	0	0	1	0	0	.000	.000
Orsulak, Joe*	.000	3	0	0	1	1	0	.000	.000
Piazza, Mike	.400	5	2	0	1	1	1	.500	.600
Roberts, Bip#	.200	5	1	0	0	1	0	.333	.200
Rodriguez, H*	.200	5	1	0	0	1	0	.333	.200
Sandberg, R	.600	5	3	0	3	1	1	.667	1.000
Smith, Ozzie#	.250	4	1	0	0	1	0	.400	.250
Sosa, Sammy	.500	6	3	1	4	3	1	.667	1.000
Wallach, Tim	.400	5	2	1	3	1	0	.500	1.000
Williams, E	.333	6	2	1	5	0	0	.333	.833
Zeile, Todd	.250	4	1	0	2	3	0	.571	.250

Mike Munoz, Rockies — LHP

Batter	Avg	AB	H	HR	BI	BB	SO	OBP	Slg
Bell, Derek	.333	6	2	0	1	1	2	.429	.333
Bell, Jay	.000	3	0	0	0	1	0	.250	.000
Bonds, Barry*	.143	7	1	0	0	0	1	.143	.143
Butler, Brett*	.400	5	2	0	2	3	1	.556	.600
Caminiti, Ken#	.333	15	5	2	3	1	3	.375	.800
Carr, Chuck	.250	4	1	0	2	0	2	.200	.500
Clark, Dave*	.143	7	1	0	0	0	1	.143	.143
Conine, Jeff	.250	4	1	0	1	0	1	.400	.250
Daulton, D*	.250	4	1	0	0	1	0	.400	.250
Davis, Chili#	.167	6	1	0	0	1	1	.286	.167
DeShields, D*	.200	10	2	0	2	2	4	.333	.300
Dykstra, L*	.444	9	4	1	3	2	1	.545	.778
Eisenreich, J*	.250	8	2	0	2	1	1	.333	.375
Eusebio, Tony	.000	5	0	0	0	0	0	.000	.000
Finley, Steve*	.111	9	1	0	0	3	1	.333	.111
Fletcher, D*	.500	8	4	0	0	0	0	.556	.500
Garcia, C	.500	4	2	0	0	1	0	.600	.500
Gonzalez, L*	.429	7	3	0	1	0	0	.429	.714
Grace, Mark*	.154	13	2	0	0	1	2	.154	.231
Gwynn, Tony*	.125	8	1	0	0	0	0	.125	.125
Jefferies, G#	.200	5	1	0	0	1	1	.333	.200
Johnson, L*	.000	7	0	0	0	1	0	.000	.000
Jones, C#	.167	6	1	0	0	1	1	.286	.167
Joyner, Wally*	.143	7	1	0	2	0	0	.333	.143
Justice, Dave*	.286	14	4	0	1	0	6	.286	.286
King, Jeff	.600	5	3	0	1	2	0	.714	.600
Klesko, Ryan*	.000	2	0	0	0	3	1	.667	.000
Lankford, Ray*	.286	7	2	0	0	1	1	.444	.286
Larkin, Barry	.000	0	0	0	0	1	0	.000	.000
Martin, Al*	.333	7	1	1	1	2	3	.333	.571
Martinez, T*	.000	5	0	0	0	0	1	.000	.000
McGriff, Fred*	.214	14	3	1	5	1	3	.267	.500
Merced, O*	.200	10	2	0	1	3	0	.273	.200
Morris, Hal*	.167	6	1	0	0	0	3	.167	.333

Mike Munoz, Rockies — LHP

Batter	Avg	AB	H	HR	BI	BB	SO	OBP	Slg
Pendleton, T#	.333	6	2	0	4	0	2	.333	.500
Plantier, P*	.286	7	2	2	2	1	3	.375	1.143
Reed, Jody	.250	4	1	0	0	1	0	.400	.250
Roberts, Bip#	.250	4	1	0	0	1	0	.400	.250
Segui, David#	.286	7	2	1	4	0	2	.286	.714
Shipley, C	.600	5	3	0	2	2	2	.714	1.000
Smith, Ozzie#	.000	5	0	0	0	1	1	.167	.000
Sosa, Sammy	.600	5	3	2	4	0	0	.600	2.000
Stocker, K#	.400	5	2	0	0	2	1	.571	.600
Vizcaino, J#	.250	4	1	0	0	0	0	.250	.250
Walker, Larry*	.286	7	2	0	0	0	2	.286	.571
Webster, L	.200	5	1	0	1	1	0	.333	.200
Wilkins, Rick*	.000	7	0	0	0	1	5	.125	.000

Mike Mussina, Orioles — RHP

Batter	Avg	AB	H	HR	BI	BB	SO	OBP	Slg
Aldrete, Mike*	.200	25	5	0	0	1	3	.231	.280
Alicea, Luis#	.375	8	3	0	1	1	3	.444	.625
Alomar, R#	.143	28	4	0	1	1	3	.167	.179
Alomar Jr, S	.375	8	3	1	3	0	1	.375	.750
Amaral, Rich	.222	9	2	0	0	0	4	.222	.222
Anderson, G*	.091	11	1	0	0	1	4	.167	.091
Arias, George	.167	6	1	0	0	0	1	.167	.167
Baerga, C#	.360	25	9	0	2	0	0	.360	.520
Baines, H*	.200	20	4	0	1	1	4	.238	.250
Batista, Tony	.429	7	3	0	0	0	0	.429	.429
Bautista, D	.333	9	3	1	2	1	2	.400	.889
Becker, Rich*	.154	13	2	0	0	0	6	.154	.231
Belle, Albert	.346	26	9	3	6	2	4	.393	.846
Berroa, G	.217	23	5	1	4	0	4	.217	.391
Blowers, Mike	.300	10	3	0	0	0	3	.300	.400
Boggs, Wade*	.235	34	8	1	2	2	2	.278	.382
Borders, Pat	.250	12	3	1	3	1	1	.308	.500
Bordick, Mike	.297	37	11	0	2	5	0	.364	.378
Bournigal, R	.400	5	2	0	0	0	0	.400	.400
Bragg, Darren*	.125	8	1	0	0	0	3	.125	.125
Brosius, S	.438	16	7	1	3	1	2	.471	.750
Buhner, Jay	.429	21	9	3	4	1	6	.455	.905
Canseco, Jose	.194	31	6	0	5	0	5	.194	.290
Carter, Joe	.323	31	10	1	3	1	2	.344	.516
Cedeno, D#	.143	7	1	0	0	0	5	.143	.143
Cirillo, Jeff	.125	16	2	0	0	1	4	.176	.250
Clark, Tony#	.000	11	0	0	0	0	8	.000	.000
Clark, Will*	.286	7	2	0	2	3	0	.400	.286
Cole, Alex	.143	7	1	0	0	0	3	.143	.143
Coleman, V#	.211	19	4	0	0	1	4	.250	.368
Conine, Jeff	.000	6	0	0	0	0	2	.000	.000
Cora, Joey*	.233	30	7	1	3	2	5	.281	.333
Cordova, M	.250	8	2	1	3	0	1	.250	.625
Curtis, Chad	.385	39	15	3	5	4	4	.455	.641
Cuyler, Milt#	.273	11	3	0	1	0	4	.273	.273
Damon, Johnny*	.364	11	4	0	1	0	3	.364	.545
Davis, Chili#	.244	45	11	1	4	10	10	.382	.422
Dawson, Andre	.100	10	1	0	0	0	1	.100	.100
Deer, Rob	.500	10	5	0	0	2	2	.583	.600
Delgado, C*	.231	13	3	0	0	2	3	.333	.308
Devereaux, M	.167	6	1	0	0	0	1	.167	.167
Diaz, Alex#	.167	6	1	0	0	1	1	.286	.333
DiSarcina, Ga	.233	30	7	0	3	1	0	.258	.233
Durham, Ray#	.222	9	2	0	2	1	0	.222	.222
Easley, D	.389	18	7	0	3	0	4	.389	.611
Edmonds, Jim*	.200	25	5	1	3	3	11	.276	.440
Eisenreich, J*	.091	11	1	0	0	0	1	.091	.182
Elster, Kevin	.125	8	1	1	1	1	4	.222	.500
Espinoza, A	.091	11	1	0	0	0	1	.091	.182
Fabregas, Jor*	.364	11	4	0	4	0	1	.333	.545
Fermin, Felix	.182	11	2	0	1	0	0	.182	.182
Fielder, C	.167	36	6	1	6	6	11	.286	.278
Flaherty, J	.111	9	1	0	0	0	0	.111	.111
Franco, Julio	.200	15	3	0	1	1	5	.235	.200
Frye, Jeff	.133	15	2	0	0	0	3	.188	.133
Fryman, T	.295	44	13	2	6	2	5	.326	.432
Gaetti, Gary	.111	9	1	0	0	0	1	.200	.111
Gagne, Greg	.235	34	8	1	4	0	5	.235	.382
Gallego, Mike	.286	7	2	1	1	2	0	.444	.857
Gates, Brent#	.300	20	6	0	1	3	3	.391	.350
Giambi, Jason*	.167	6	1	0	0	1	2	.286	.167
Gil, Benji	.000	8	0	0	0	0	4	.000	.000
Gomez, Chris	.214	14	3	0	0	1	2	.267	.286
Gonzales, R	.000	5	0	0	0	0	1	.000	.000
Gonzalez, A	.091	11	1	0	0	0	3	.167	.091
Gonzalez, J	.229	35	8	5	8	1	10	.250	.657
Goodwin, Tom*	.125	16	2	0	0	1	5	.176	.125
Grebeck, C	.400	10	4	0	2	1	3	.455	.500
Green, Shawn*	.100	10	1	0	0	2	1	.250	.200
Greenwell, M*	.355	31	11	1	4	5	4	.444	.516
Greer, Rusty*	.231	13	3	0	1	1	1	.286	.231
Griffey Jr, K*	.125	24	3	0	0	1	7	.160	.208
Guillen, O*	.333	21	7	0	3	0	2	.333	.476
Gwynn, Chris*	.400	10	4	0	1	0	1	.400	.700
Hamelin, Bob*	.000	18	0	0	0	1	2	.053	.000

Mike Mussina, Orioles — RHP

Batter	Avg	AB	H	HR	BI	BB	SO	OBP	Slg
Hamilton, D*	.419	31	13	0	3	1	4	.438	.516
Haselman, B	.182	11	2	1	1	0	2	.250	.455
Henderson, R	.238	21	5	0	0	2	3	.304	.333
Herrera, Jose*	.385	13	5	0	3	1	5	.429	.538
Hiatt, Phil	.600	5	3	0	3	0	1	.600	.600
Higginson, B*	.250	12	3	1	1	3	2	.400	.500
Hollins, Dave#	.125	8	1	0	0	2	3	.300	.125
Howard, Dave#	.190	21	4	0	2	0	3	.190	.238
Huff, Michael	.400	5	2	0	0	0	2	.400	.600
Hulse, David*	.111	9	1	0	0	0	3	.111	.111
Huson, Jeff*	.333	6	2	0	0	0	3	.333	.333
Incaviglia, P	.000	5	0	0	0	1	0	.167	.000
Jaha, John	.368	19	7	3	7	2	7	.429	1.000
James, Dion*	.286	7	2	0	1	0	3	.286	.286
Javier, Stan#	.286	14	4	1	3	1	3	.333	.571
Jefferies, G#	.273	11	3	0	2	1	0	.308	.273
Jefferson, R*	.308	13	4	0	1	0	3	.308	.308
Jeter, Derek	.286	7	2	1	4	1	1	.375	.714
Johnson, L*	.393	28	11	1	4	0	1	.393	.536
Joyner, Wally*	.270	37	10	0	4	0	0	.333	.405
Karkovice, R	.136	22	3	1	4	1	9	.167	.273
Kelly, Pat	.429	14	6	1	5	0	2	.429	.786
Kelly, R	.133	15	2	0	1	0	2	.125	.133
Kirby, Wayne	.000	9	0	0	0	0	0	.000	.000
Knoblauch, C	.256	39	10	2	2	3	6	.326	.462
Koslofski, K*	.000	5	0	0	0	1	2	.167	.000
Lawton, Matt*	.125	8	1	0	0	0	2	.125	.125
Leius, Scott	.364	11	4	0	0	1	1	.417	.455
Lewis, Mark	.222	9	2	0	1	0	2	.222	.222
Leyritz, Jim	.222	9	2	0	3	0	3	.300	.222
Listach, Pat#	.133	15	2	0	0	3	1	.278	.133
Livingstone*	.286	21	6	0	1	0	1	.286	.286
Lockhart, K*	.375	16	6	0	1	0	1	.375	.438
Lofton, Kenny*	.310	29	9	0	0	4	4	.333	.345
Lovullo, T#	.000	5	0	0	0	1	2	.167	.000
Macfarlane, M	.357	28	10	4	5	2	5	.387	.857
Martin, N	.625	8	5	0	1	0	0	.625	1.000
Martinez, Da*	.429	14	6	0	3	1	1	.467	.429
Martinez, E	.400	25	10	3	7	3	1	.464	1.000
Martinez, S*	.333	12	4	0	2	0	2	.333	.500
Martinez, T*	.296	27	8	1	3	0	3	.296	.481
Matheny, Mike	.250	8	2	0	1	0	0	.250	.250
Mayne, Brent*	.286	14	4	0	1	0	0	.286	.500
McGwire, Mark	.150	20	3	1	2	3	6	.261	.300
McLemore, M#	.308	13	4	0	2	2	1	.400	.615
McRae, Brian*	.217	23	5	0	1	2	2	.280	.217
Meares, Pat	.353	17	6	0	0	0	3	.353	.471
Mieske, Matt	.357	14	5	1	1	1	1	.400	.643
Mitchell, K	.167	6	1	0	0	0	0	.167	.333
Molitor, Paul	.273	33	9	1	2	1	2	.294	.455
Munoz, Pedro	.125	16	2	0	0	0	4	.125	.125
Murray, Eddie#	.308	13	4	1	4	3	0	.438	.615
Myers, Greg*	.150	20	3	0	1	1	4	.182	.200
Naehring, Tim	.313	16	5	1	4	2	1	.389	.625
Nevin, Phil	.111	9	1	0	0	0	2	.111	.111
Newfield, M	.250	8	2	1	2	1	0	.333	.625
Nieman, W*	.222	9	2	1	1	3	2	.417	.556
Nieves, M#	.000	5	0	0	0	0	4	.000	.000
Nilsson, Dave*	.059	17	1	0	1	0	5	.059	.059
Nixon, Otis*	.188	16	3	0	1	0	2	.188	.250
Nunnally, Jon*	.250	8	2	0	0	0	2	.250	.500
O'Leary, Troy*	.250	20	5	0	0	3	0	.250	.250
O'Neill, Paul*	.300	20	6	0	0	5	6	.440	.400
Offerman, J#	.333	6	2	0	0	0	1	.333	.333
Olerud, John*	.367	30	11	0	2	2	3	.394	.367
Oliver, Joe	.400	5	2	0	1	0	1	.400	.400
Palmeiro, R*	.091	22	2	0	1	1	3	.125	.136
Palmer, Dean	.133	33	6	2	2	1	10	.206	.394
Paquette, C	.250	12	3	1	2	0	4	.250	.500
Pena, Tony	.353	17	6	0	1	0	3	.353	.529
Perez, E	.000	6	0	0	0	0	3	.000	.000
Phillips, T	.136	44	6	0	1	3	15	.191	.182
Plantier, P*	.150	20	3	0	0	3	1	.150	.200
Polonia, Luis*	.259	27	7	0	1	0	3	.259	.259
Pride, Curtis*	.429	7	3	0	0	1	1	.500	.429
Raines, Tim#	.241	29	7	0	3	5	1	.343	.241
Ramirez, M	.200	10	2	1	3	0	4	.200	.500
Reboulet, J	.000	5	0	0	0	0	1	.000	.000
Reed, Jody	.250	16	4	0	0	0	3	.250	.313
Ripken, Billy	.600	5	3	0	1	1	1	.600	.500
Rodriguez, Al	.143	14	2	0	0	0	3	.143	.143
Rodriguez, I	.273	22	6	0	1	1	5	.304	.409
Salmon, Tim	.317	41	13	5	10	2	11	.364	.756
Samuel, Juan	.600	5	3	0	3	0	1	.600	.800
Seitzer, K	.333	30	10	1	6	0	2	.323	.533
Shumpert, T	.000	5	0	0	0	0	2	.000	.000
Sierra, Ruben#	.240	50	12	1	5	3	8	.283	.380
Snow, J.T.#	.200	30	6	1	3	3	3	.273	.333
Sojo, Luis	.444	9	4	0	1	0	0	.444	.889
Sorrento, P*	.167	24	4	0	0	4	8	.286	.208
Spiers, Bill*	.500	8	4	0	3	0	0	.500	.625

Mike Mussina, Orioles — RHP

Batter	Avg	AB	H	HR	BI	BB	SO	OBP	Slg
Sprague, Ed	.227	22	5	0	3	2	6	.292	.273
Stahoviak, S*	.364	11	4	1	2	0	5	.364	.636
Stairs, Matt*	.125	8	1	0	0	1	2	.222	.125
Stanley, Mike	.353	17	6	1	4	5	4	.500	.647
Steinbach, T	.294	34	10	3	6	1	6	.306	.647
Stevens, Lee*	.125	8	1	0	0	0	2	.125	.250
Stillwell, K	.286	7	2	0	0	0	1	.286	.429
Strange, Doug#	.333	12	4	1	1	0	3	.333	.667
Strawberry, D*	.000	6	0	0	0	1	2	.143	.000
Surhoff, B.J.*	.267	15	4	0	1	2	4	.353	.333
Tartabull, D	.429	14	6	3	4	1	4	.467	1.071
Tettleton, M#	.212	33	7	1	1	6	16	.333	.303
Thomas, Frank	.556	36	20	6	11	7	4	.628	1.194
Thome, Jim*	.316	19	6	3	8	1	3	.350	.789
Tinsley, Lee*	.250	12	3	1	2	2	3	.357	.583
Trammell, A	.267	15	4	0	0	0	3	.267	.467
Tucker, M*	.286	7	2	0	0	1	2	.375	.429
Valentin, Jhn	.333	30	10	0	3	1	1	.355	.400
Valentin, Jse#	.200	20	4	1	3	1	4	.238	.450
Valle, Dave	.250	8	2	0	0	1	3	.333	.375
Vaughn, Greg	.318	22	7	0	2	3	7	.400	.364
Vaughn, Mo*	.341	41	14	1	7	7	11	.449	.463
Velarde, R	.294	17	5	1	1	0	3	.294	.529
Ventura, R*	.128	39	5	1	7	2	7	.171	.231
Vina, F*	.308	13	4	0	0	2	0	.400	.385
Vizquel, Omar#	.412	17	7	0	1	0	3	.412	.529
Walbeck, Matt#	.000	8	0	0	0	1	2	.111	.000
Webster, L	.200	5	1	0	0	1	0	.333	.200
Weiss, Walt#	.250	4	1	0	0	0	0	.250	.250
White, Devon#	.167	24	4	0	1	1	3	.200	.167
Whiten, Mark#	.222	9	2	1	1	1	2	.300	.556
Williams, Ber#	.412	17	7	0	0	4	2	.524	.588
Williams, Ger	.167	6	1	0	0	0	2	.167	.333
Wilson, Dan	.474	19	9	2	4	0	2	.474	.895
Young, Ernie	.273	11	3	0	3	0	1	.273	.455

Mike Myers, Tigers — LHP

Batter	Avg	AB	H	HR	BI	BB	SO	OBP	Slg
Anderson, Brd*	.200	5	1	0	1	0	2	.200	.200
Anderson, G*	.000	6	0	0	0	0	2	.000	.000
Arias, George	.500	4	2	0	0	2	0	.667	.500
Boggs, Wade*	.250	4	1	0	0	1	0	.400	.250
Cirillo, Jeff	.333	3	1	0	0	2	0	.600	.667
Damon, Johnny*	.286	7	2	0	0	0	2	.286	.286
Lawton, Matt*	.400	5	2	0	0	0	2	.400	.600
Levis, Jesse*	.250	4	1	0	0	1	1	.400	.250
Martinez, T*	.375	8	3	0	1	0	2	.375	.625
Nilsson, Dave*	.333	3	1	0	0	2	1	.600	.333
O'Neill, Paul*	.200	5	1	0	0	2	3	.429	.200
Palmeiro, R*	1.000	4	4	0	1	1	0	1.000	1.250
Sierra, Ruben*	.667	3	2	0	3	2	0	.800	.667
Snow, J.T.#	.250	4	1	0	1	0	2	.333	.250
Ventura, R*	.250	4	1	0	1	1	0	.333	.250

Randy Myers, Orioles — LHP

Batter	Avg	AB	H	HR	BI	BB	SO	OBP	Slg
Alicea, Luis#	.400	5	2	0	0	0	0	.400	.600
Alomar, R#	.429	7	3	0	0	0	0	.429	.429
Alou, Moises	.250	8	2	0	1	0	1	.250	.500
Anthony, Eric*	.167	6	1	0	0	1	2	.286	.167
Bagwell, Jeff	.417	12	5	2	5	1	4	.462	1.167
Barberie, B#	.600	5	3	0	0	1	0	.667	.800
Bell, Jay	.286	14	4	1	7	4	4	.444	.714
Belliard, R	.250	4	1	0	0	1	2	.400	.250
Benjamin, M	.200	5	1	0	0	0	2	.200	.200
Berroa, G	.200	5	1	1	1	0	2	.200	.800
Bichette, D	.333	6	2	0	2	1	0	.429	.500
Biggio, Craig	.067	15	1	0	0	3	3	.222	.067
Blauser, Jeff	.250	8	2	0	0	3	1	.455	.250
Bonds, Barry*	.250	36	9	2	11	6	12	.349	.528
Bonilla, B#	.417	24	10	1	7	6	4	.500	.583
Brumfield, J	.111	9	1	0	1	0	5	.111	.111
Butler, Brett*	.318	22	7	0	0	5	8	.444	.409
Caminiti, Ken#	.300	20	6	0	0	1	3	.333	.400
Candaele, C#	.214	14	3	0	0	1	4	.267	.214
Cangelosi, J#	.111	9	1	0	0	1	4	.200	.111
Carr, Chuck	.286	7	2	0	0	0	2	.286	.286
Carreon, Mark	.250	16	4	0	2	1	5	.294	.375
Castilla, V	.600	5	3	0	1	1	0	.667	.800
Cedeno, A	.286	7	2	0	0	0	1	.286	.429
Cianfrocco, A	.000	4	0	0	0	1	2	.200	.000
Clark, Phil	.333	6	2	1	1	0	2	.333	.833
Clark, Will*	.120	25	3	1	2	3	12	.207	.240
Clayton, D	.143	7	1	0	0	1	2	.250	.143
Colbrunn, G	.167	6	1	1	3	0	5	.167	.667
Coleman, V#	.154	13	2	0	1	2	4	.267	.154
Dascenzo, D#	.333	3	1	0	0	2	0	.600	.333
Daulton, D*	.167	18	3	1	2	1	6	.211	.333
Davis, Eric	.000	4	0	0	0	1	1	.200	.000
Dawson, Andre	.389	18	7	1	4	0	1	.389	.667
DeShields, D*	.167	6	1	0	0	3	4	.444	.167
Duncan, M	.700	10	7	1	8	0	0	.700	1.200
Dunston, S	.222	9	2	0	0	0	2	.222	.222
Dykstra, L*	.000	10	0	0	0	4	4	.286	.000
Elster, Kevin	.143	7	1	0	1	1	3	.250	.143
Eusebio, Tony	.400	5	2	0	0	0	1	.400	.400
Finley, Steve*	.000	7	0	0	0	3	4	.300	.000
Frye, Jeff	.500	4	2	0	3	1	0	.600	.750
Galarraga, A	.350	20	7	3	11	5	7	.480	.800
Gant, Ron	.188	16	3	1	1	2	4	.278	.438
Gilkey, B	.235	17	4	0	1	0	4	.235	.294
Girardi, Joe	.364	11	4	0	1	1	2	.417	.364
Gonzalez, L*	.385	13	5	0	5	1	3	.429	.615
Grace, Mark*	.429	14	6	1	6	1	3	.467	.929
Grissom, M	.267	15	4	0	2	2	2	.353	.400
Gutierrez, R	.000	5	0	0	0	1	2	.167	.000
Gwynn, Tony*	.214	14	3	0	1	3	2	.353	.357
Harris, Lenny*	.364	11	4	0	0	2	3	.462	.364
Hayes, Dave#	.273	11	3	0	1	0	1	.273	.273
Hollins, Dave#	.000	7	0	0	0	0	3	.000	.000
Hudler, Rex	.235	17	4	0	0	0	2	.235	.235
Hundley, Todd#	.143	7	1	0	1	0	3	.143	.143
Hunter, Brian	.308	13	4	0	4	3	2	.438	.385
Incaviglia, P	.200	5	1	0	1	2	2	.333	.200
Javier, Stan*	.333	6	2	0	1	1	1	.429	.333
Jefferies, G#	.091	11	1	1	1	2	0	.231	.364
Jones, Chris	.600	5	3	0	3	0	1	.600	.600
Jordan, Brian	.333	9	3	0	0	0	4	.333	.333
Jordan, Ricky	.083	12	1	0	0	2	3	.214	.083
Justice, Dave*	.176	17	3	1	3	2	6	.250	.412
Karros, Eric	.000	6	0	0	0	0	1	.000	.000
Kelly, R	.500	6	3	1	3	0	2	.500	1.000
Kent, Jeff	.000	6	0	0	0	1	2	.143	.000
King, Jeff	.000	8	0	0	1	1	0	.111	.000
Kingery, Mike*	.200	5	1	0	0	0	2	.200	.200
Lankford, Ray*	.118	17	2	0	0	1	2	.167	.118
Larkin, Barry	.333	12	4	0	0	3	3	.467	.333
Lemke, Mark#	.364	11	4	0	2	2	2	.462	.455
Lewis, Darren	.167	12	2	0	2	0	0	.286	.250
Lofton, Kenny*	.400	5	2	0	0	2	1	.571	.400
Lopez, Javy	.000	7	0	0	0	0	0	.000	.000
Magadan, Dave*	.375	8	3	0	3	3	3	.545	.375
Manwaring, K	.214	14	3	0	1	3	3	.353	.286
Martinez, Da*	.000	6	0	0	0	1	5	.143	.000
McGee, Willie#	.259	27	7	0	3	0	6	.259	.296
McGriff, Fred*	.000	5	0	0	0	1	2	.167	.000
Merced, O*	.231	13	3	0	1	1	3	.286	.231
Mitchell, K	.235	17	4	1	3	5	4	.409	.471
Morandini, M*	.000	6	0	0	0	0	4	.000	.000
Morris, Hal*	.250	8	2	0	1	0	3	.250	.375
Murray, Eddie*	.111	18	2	0	1	2	3	.200	.111
Nixon, Otis#	.364	11	4	0	0	2	4	.462	.364
O'Brien, C	.250	8	2	1	2	2	0	.400	.750
O'Neill, Paul*	.375	8	3	0	0	3	0	.545	.500
Offerman, J#	.143	14	2	0	0	1	6	.200	.143
Oliver, Joe	.143	7	1	0	2	0	2	.125	.286
Pagnozzi, Tom	.182	22	4	1	3	3	3	.280	.318
Palmeiro, R*	.000	6	0	0	0	0	1	.000	.000
Parker, Rick	.400	5	2	0	1	0	0	.400	.400
Pena, G#	.000	5	0	0	0	1	3	.167	.000
Pena, Tony	.250	12	3	0	1	1	2	.308	.333
Pendleton, T#	.375	24	9	1	3	0	5	.375	.583
Raines, Tim#	.214	14	3	0	0	3	3	.389	.286
Roberts, Bip#	.235	17	4	0	0	2	4	.316	.353
Sabo, Chris	.286	7	2	1	1	0	1	.286	.714
Samuel, Juan	.348	23	8	0	4	1	4	.375	.522
Sandberg, R	.188	16	3	1	1	2	3	.278	.375
Sanders, R	.273	11	3	0	1	1	3	.333	.364
Santiago, B	.421	19	8	0	3	1	3	.450	.474
Sheaffer, D	.400	5	2	0	1	0	0	.400	.400
Sheffield, G	.500	4	2	0	1	0	1	.600	.500
Shipley, C	.250	8	2	0	1	0	1	.222	.375
Slaught, Don	.364	11	4	0	1	2	4	.462	.364
Smith, Ozzie#	.217	23	5	0	2	3	3	.296	.348
Strawberry, D*	.167	12	2	0	1	3	5	.333	.250
Thompson, Mil*	.500	8	4	0	1	1	3	.600	.750
Thompson, Rob	.300	20	6	0	2	2	7	.391	.350
Tinsley, Lee#	.250	4	1	0	0	1	2	.400	.250
Vaughn, Mo*	.333	6	2	1	4	0	1	.333	.833
Walker, Larry*	.071	14	1	0	2	2	4	.176	.143
Wallach, Tim	.455	11	5	1	4	2	1	.571	.818
Walton, J	.000	4	0	0	1	1	2	.167	.000
Weiss, Walt#	.250	8	2	0	0	2	1	.400	.375
Whiten, Mark#	.429	7	3	1	4	2	0	.556	1.000
Williams, Ma	.200	20	4	1	2	0	6	.200	.400
Young, Eric	.200	5	1	0	0	1	0	.333	.200
Zeile, Todd	.133	15	2	0	0	1	5	.188	.200

Rodney Myers, Cubs — RHP

Batter	Avg	AB	H	HR	BI	BB	SO	OBP	Slg
Castilla, V	.000	4	0	0	1	3	0	.429	.000
Galarraga, A	.400	5	2	0	2	0	1	.400	.400

Rodney Myers, Cubs — RHP

Batter	Avg	AB	H	HR	BI	BB	SO	OBP	Slg
Garcia, C	.167	6	1	0	0	0	1	.167	.333

Charles Nagy, Indians — RHP

Batter	Avg	AB	H	HR	BI	BB	SO	OBP	Slg
Aldrete, Mike*	.333	6	2	0	2	1	0	.429	.333
Alexander, M	.200	5	1	0	0	0	0	.200	.200
Alomar, R#	.246	57	14	0	3	0	3	.241	.281
Amaral, Rich	.250	12	3	0	1	2	2	.357	.250
Anderson, Brd*	.361	36	13	1	3	3	5	.410	.556
Ausmus, Brad	.000	5	0	0	0	0	0	.000	.000
Baines, H*	.375	32	12	3	9	3	4	.417	.719
Bartee, K	.200	5	1	0	0	1	3	.333	.200
Batista, Tony	.286	7	2	0	0	0	2	.286	.286
Bautista, D	.333	6	2	0	0	0	2	.333	.333
Becker, Rich*	.273	11	3	0	2	2	1	.385	.364
Beltre, E	.250	8	2	0	1	0	0	.250	.375
Berroa, G	.333	15	5	0	0	0	2	.333	.400
Blowers, Mike	.250	12	3	0	1	3	2	.400	.250
Boggs, Wade*	.180	50	9	0	3	4	1	.236	.200
Bonilla, B#	.625	8	5	0	4	2	0	.700	1.000
Borders, Pat	.304	23	7	0	2	2	5	.346	.478
Bordick, Mike	.375	32	12	0	2	2	5	.429	.469
Brosius, S	.231	13	3	2	2	1	2	.286	.692
Buhner, Jay	.303	33	10	2	8	3	10	.361	.576
Burks, Ellis	.389	18	7	0	1	3	1	.476	.444
Canseco, Jose	.094	32	3	1	1	2	8	.147	.188
Carter, Joe	.353	51	18	4	11	2	7	.382	.647
Cedeno, A	.333	6	2	0	0	0	1	.333	.500
Cedeno, D#	.333	6	2	0	2	1	1	.375	.333
Cirillo, Jeff	.200	5	1	0	0	2	0	.429	.200
Clark, Tony#	.143	7	1	0	0	0	3	.143	.143
Clark, Will*	.238	21	5	1	3	5	4	.407	.381
Cole, Alex*	.111	9	1	0	0	1	1	.200	.333
Coleman, V#	.154	13	2	0	0	1	2	.214	.231
Coomer, Ron	.333	6	2	0	3	0	0	.333	.500
Cora, Joey#	.161	31	5	0	2	3	3	.235	.194
Cordova, M	.353	17	6	1	2	2	5	.421	.647
Curtis, Chad	.097	31	3	0	0	3	5	.176	.097
Cuyler, Milt#	.208	24	5	0	0	1	5	.240	.292
Damon, Johnny*	.286	7	2	0	0	0	0	.286	.286
Davis, Chili#	.310	29	9	1	4	2	9	.344	.552
Davis, Russ	.143	7	1	0	0	0	2	.143	.143
Deer, Rob	.222	9	2	0	2	0	1	.222	.333
Delgado, C*	.083	12	1	0	2	1	6	.143	.167
Devereaux, M	.296	27	8	1	1	0	2	.296	.481
Diaz, Alex#	.167	6	1	0	0	0	0	.167	.167
DiSarcina, G	.182	22	4	0	1	0	3	.217	.227
Durham, Ray#	.273	11	3	0	0	0	1	.273	.364
Easley, D	.167	6	1	0	0	0	2	.167	.167
Edmonds, Jim*	.000	6	0	0	0	1	3	.143	.000
Eisenreich, J*	.429	7	3	0	1	0	0	.429	.571
Elster, Kevin	.143	7	1	1	1	1	2	.250	.571
Espinoza, A	.000	6	0	0	0	0	0	.000	.000
Fabregas, Jor*	.286	7	2	0	3	0	1	.286	.286
Fielder, C	.286	42	12	1	5	1	8	.302	.357
Flaherty, J	.200	20	4	0	0	0	4	.200	.300
Fox, Andy*	.167	6	1	0	0	0	0	.167	.167
Franco, Julio	.467	15	7	1	4	0	1	.438	.733
Frye, Jeff	.250	12	3	0	1	1	1	.308	.333
Fryman, T	.192	52	10	1	7	2	15	.222	.308
Gaetti, Gary	.267	15	4	2	4	3	3	.389	.733
Gagne, Greg	.391	23	9	0	1	0	3	.391	.522
Gallego, Mike	.267	15	4	0	1	2	2	.353	.333
Gates, Brent#	.071	14	1	0	1	1	4	.133	.071
Giambi, Jason*	.278	18	5	1	3	0	3	.278	.500
Gil, Benji	.000	5	0	0	0	0	2	.000	.000
Gomez, Chris	.214	14	3	0	1	1	4	.267	.286
Gomez, Leo	.154	13	2	0	0	0	3	.154	.154
Gonzales, R	.167	6	1	0	3	0	1	.167	.167
Gonzalez, A	.200	10	2	0	0	0	4	.200	.300
Gonzalez, J	.300	30	9	2	5	1	9	.323	.500
Goodwin, C*	.600	5	3	0	2	0	1	.600	.600
Goodwin, Tom*	.385	13	5	0	1	1	1	.385	.385
Grebeck, C	.500	8	4	0	0	0	2	.500	.500
Green, Shawn*	.143	14	2	0	0	2	3	.250	.286
Greenwell, M*	.222	18	4	0	2	2	2	.300	.333
Greer, Rusty*	.263	19	5	0	3	1	5	.364	.263
Griffey Jr, K*	.371	35	13	2	6	3	11	.421	.714
Guillen, O*	.308	26	8	0	3	1	0	.333	.308
Hall, Mel*	.353	17	6	1	5	0	1	.353	.588
Hamelin, Bob*	.000	9	0	0	0	0	5	.000	.000
Hamilton, D*	.250	24	6	0	1	0	0	.250	.417
Hammonds, J	.417	12	5	0	1	1	5	.462	.500
Hayes, C	.111	9	1	0	0	0	2	.111	.111
Henderson, R	.188	16	3	0	2	2	1	.316	.188
Herrera, Jose*	.500	12	6	2	3	0	1	.500	1.167
Higginson, B*	.125	16	2	0	1	1	6	.176	.188
Hocking, D#	.200	15	3	0	0	0	5	.200	.200
Hoiles, Chris	.313	16	5	0	2	3	8	.421	.375
Hollins, Dave#	.000	6	0	0	0	1	1	.000	.000
Howard, Dave*	.182	11	2	0	0	0	2	.357	.182

Charles Nagy, Indians — RHP

Batter	Avg	AB	H	HR	BI	BB	SO	OBP	Slg
Howell, Jack*	.000	5	0	0	0	0	1	.000	.000
Huff, Michael	.167	6	1	0	0	0	0	.286	.167
Hulse, David*	.235	17	4	0	1	2	1	.316	.235
Huson, Jeff*	.444	9	4	0	1	0	1	.444	.556
Incaviglia, P	.286	7	2	0	0	0	1	.286	.286
Jaha, John	.455	11	5	0	1	1	2	.538	.455
James, Dion*	.250	4	1	0	0	1	0	.400	.250
Jeter, Derek	.000	7	0	0	0	0	1	.000	.000
Johnson, L*	.263	38	10	0	0	2	2	.300	.316
Joyner, Wally*	.167	18	3	0	2	2	4	.238	.167
Karkovice, R	.174	23	4	1	1	2	9	.240	.391
Kelly, Pat	.368	19	7	0	2	1	1	.400	.421
Kelly, R	.143	14	2	0	0	1	1	.200	.286
Knoblauch, C	.242	33	8	0	3	0	5	.257	.333
Kreuter, Chad*	.111	9	1	0	0	0	3	.111	.222
Lawton, Matt*	.000	3	0	0	1	2	1	.400	.000
Leius, Scott	.231	13	3	0	0	1	3	.286	.308
Lewis, Mark	.143	14	2	1	1	1	2	.200	.357
Leyritz, Jim	.200	5	1	0	1	0	1	.200	.200
Listach, Pat#	.250	8	2	0	1	0	2	.250	.375
Livingstone*	.111	9	1	0	1	0	1	.111	.111
Lockhart, K*	.364	11	4	0	2	0	0	.333	.545
Macfarlane, M	.438	16	7	2	4	0	5	.438	.813
Martin, N	.500	4	2	0	0	1	1	.600	.750
Martinez, Da*	.286	7	2	0	0	0	1	.286	.429
Martinez, E	.263	38	10	2	6	6	8	.364	.421
Martinez, S*	.500	4	2	0	0	1	0	.600	.500
Martinez, T*	.167	18	3	0	1	4	1	.318	.167
McGwire, Mark	.167	30	5	2	3	8	12	.342	.400
McLemore, M#	.125	24	3	0	1	2	4	.185	.167
McRae, Brian#	.231	13	3	0	1	0	2	.231	.308
Meares, Pat	.300	10	3	0	1	0	1	.364	.300
Mieske, Matt	.222	9	2	0	1	0	5	.222	.222
Molitor, Paul	.289	38	11	0	3	9	5	.426	.421
Munoz, Pedro	.143	7	1	0	0	0	0	.143	.143
Murray, Eddie#	.167	6	1	0	1	0	1	.167	.333
Myers, Greg*	.273	22	6	0	0	2	6	.333	.409
Naehring, Tim	.143	14	2	0	0	0	1	.143	.143
Newson, W*	.091	11	1	0	0	2	1	.231	.091
Nieves, M#	.300	10	3	1	1	1	3	.364	.600
Nilsson, Dave*	.400	5	2	0	1	1	1	.429	.400
Nixon, Otis#	.421	19	8	0	1	0	0	.421	.474
Nunnally, Jon*	.333	6	2	0	1	3	1	.556	.667
O'Leary, Troy*	.286	7	2	0	0	0	0	.286	.286
O'Neill, Paul*	.304	23	7	2	4	2	2	.346	.652
Offerman, J#	.333	6	2	0	0	0	2	.333	.333
Olerud, John*	.267	45	12	2	8	5	7	.327	.489
Oliver, Joe	.143	7	1	0	2	0	1	.143	.143
Orsulak, Joe*	.350	20	7	0	0	1	2	.381	.400
Palmeiro, R*	.286	28	8	1	4	2	4	.333	.464
Palmer, Dean	.400	30	12	4	13	0	5	.400	.900
Parent, Mark	.200	5	1	0	0	0	1	.200	.200
Pena, Tony	.182	11	2	0	0	1	2	.250	.273
Phillips, T#	.182	22	4	0	1	2	7	.250	.182
Plantier, P*	.313	16	5	0	1	3	3	.389	.438
Polonia, Luis*	.375	32	12	0	4	5	0	.459	.469
Pride, Curtis*	.125	16	2	1	3	0	9	.125	.313
Raines, Tim#	.452	31	14	2	5	3	4	.486	.710
Randa, Joe	.429	7	3	1	0	2	2	.429	.857
Reboulet, J	.333	18	6	0	1	1	2	.368	.444
Reed, Jody	.217	23	5	1	2	2	5	.280	.391
Ripken, Billy	.000	11	0	0	1	1	3	.083	.000
Ripken, Cal	.278	36	10	1	4	2	4	.316	.417
Rodriguez, Al	.333	9	3	0	0	1	2	.400	.333
Rodriguez, I	.300	30	9	1	2	0	3	.323	.433
Sabo, Chris	.500	4	2	0	0	0	1	.600	.500
Salmon, Tim	.182	11	2	1	3	2	4	.308	.455
Schofield, D	.250	20	5	0	0	1	4	.286	.350
Segui, David#	.000	8	0	0	0	3	0	.000	.000
Seitzer, K	.478	23	11	0	3	1	2	.500	.652
Shumpert, T	.000	5	0	0	0	0	1	.000	.000
Sierra, Ruben#	.233	30	7	0	2	5	3	.343	.333
Singleton, D*	.286	7	2	0	1	1	2	.375	.286
Smith, Dwight*	.200	5	1	0	1	0	1	.200	.200
Snopek, Chris	.200	5	1	0	0	1	2	.333	.200
Snow, J.T.#	.625	8	5	1	5	1	1	.667	1.000
Sojo, Luis	.318	22	7	1	1	0	2	.318	.455
Sorrento, P*	.300	10	3	0	0	1	2	.364	.400
Sosa, Sammy	.200	5	1	0	1	0	0	.200	.200
Spiers, Bill*	.222	9	2	0	0	1	1	.222	.333
Sprague, Ed	.242	33	8	0	3	2	12	.286	.303
Stahoviak, S*	.333	15	5	1	3	1	3	.375	.533
Stankiewicz	.200	5	1	0	0	0	0	.200	.200
Stanley, Mike	.476	21	10	3	9	3	2	.542	.952
Steinbach, T	.308	39	12	2	5	1	5	.325	.538
Stevens, Lee*	.200	10	2	0	0	0	2	.200	.200
Stillwell, K#	.125	8	1	0	0	0	3	.125	.125
Strange, Doug*	.250	8	2	1	3	0	2	.250	.750
Strawberry, D	.500	5	0	0	0	0	2	.167	.000
Surhoff, B.J.*	.393	28	11	0	4	2	2	.433	.429
Sveum, Dale#	.143	7	1	0	0	0	4	.143	.143

Charles Nagy, Indians — RHP

Batter	Avg	AB	H	HR	BI	BB	SO	OBP	Slg
Tartabull, D	.367	30	11	1	4	4	8	.429	.500
Tettleton, M	.382	34	13	5	9	8	12	.488	.853
Thomas, Frank	.342	38	13	1	7	7	8	.435	.474
Trammell, A	.375	24	9	1	2	0	4	.375	.542
Tucker, M*	.250	8	2	0	0	0	5	.250	.250
Valentin, Jhn	.071	14	1	0	1	0	2	.071	.071
Valentin, Jose#	.200	10	2	0	1	1	3	.273	.300
Valle, Dave	.368	19	7	1	2	0	3	.368	.632
Vaughn, Greg	.263	19	5	1	4	3	5	.364	.474
Vaughn, Mo*	.214	14	3	1	1	2	4	.313	.429
Velarde, R	.250	16	4	0	3	0	4	.250	.375
Ventura, R*	.310	42	13	0	3	5	8	.375	.333
Vina, F*	.600	5	3	0	0	0	0	.600	.600
Vizquel, Omar#	.250	20	5	0	0	1	4	.286	.300
Walbeck, Matt#	.313	16	5	0	3	1	2	.353	.313
Ward, Turner*	.286	7	2	0	1	0	1	.286	.286
Webster, L	.000	8	0	0	0	1	3	.111	.000
Weiss, Walt#	.462	13	6	0	2	0	1	.462	.615
White, Devon#	.302	43	13	0	2	3	10	.348	.349
Whiten, Mark#	.000	9	0	0	0	1	0	.000	.000
Williams, Ber#	.267	30	8	0	1	3	3	.333	.300
Williams, Ger	.500	6	3	0	2	0	1	.500	1.000
Wilson, Dan	.385	13	5	0	4	0	2	.385	.385
Young, Ernie	.000	11	0	0	0	1	1	.000	.000

Dan Naulty, Twins — RHP

Batter	Avg	AB	H	HR	BI	BB	SO	OBP	Slg
Belle, Albert	.250	4	1	0	0	2	1	.500	.250
Fielder, C	.250	4	1	0	2	1	1	.400	.500
Jeter, Derek	.250	4	1	0	1	1	1	.400	.250

Jaime Navarro, Cubs — RHP

Batter	Avg	AB	H	HR	BI	BB	SO	OBP	Slg
Aldrete, Mike*	.500	4	2	1	3	2	1	.667	1.250
Alfonzo, E	.111	9	1	0	0	0	1	.111	.111
Alicea, Luis#	.000	4	0	0	0	2	0	.333	.000
Alomar, R#	.550	20	11	0	0	0	0	.550	.750
Alomar Jr, S	.273	11	3	0	1	1	1	.333	.364
Alou, Moises	.231	13	3	1	1	0	1	.231	.462
Amaral, Rich	.250	8	2	0	1	1	1	.333	.250
Anderson, Brd*	.241	29	7	1	5	0	5	.233	.379
Andrews, S	.125	8	1	0	0	1	5	.222	.125
Anthony, Eric*	.222	9	2	1	3	1	5	.300	.667
Arias, Alex	.400	10	4	1	1	0	1	.400	.700
Ausmus, Brad	.222	9	2	0	0	0	2	.222	.333
Baerga, C#	.314	35	11	1	4	0	2	.314	.429
Bagwell, Jeff	.364	22	8	2	4	2	4	.400	.636
Baines, Harold	.469	32	15	0	5	5	3	.513	.594
Bell, Derek	.222	18	4	2	5	0	2	.222	.556
Bell, Jay	.250	16	4	0	2	2	6	.368	.313
Belle, Albert	.250	24	6	2	6	0	7	.240	.500
Benjamin, M	.412	17	7	2	4	0	3	.412	.765
Berry, Sean	.333	9	3	0	2	0	0	.400	.556
Bichette, D	.316	19	6	2	7	0	5	.316	.684
Biggio, Craig	.227	22	5	0	0	1	2	.320	.273
Blauser, Jeff	.167	6	1	0	0	0	2	.286	.167
Blowers, Mike	.182	11	2	0	0	3	3	.357	.273
Boggs, Wade*	.323	31	10	0	5	6	1	.421	.355
Bonds, Barry*	.308	13	4	1	2	5	6	.444	.615
Boone, Bret	.357	14	5	1	2	0	1	.357	.571
Borders, Pat	.150	20	3	0	1	0	1	.150	.150
Bordick, Mike	.059	17	1	0	0	1	1	.111	.176
Branson, Jeff*	.333	9	3	0	1	1	0	.400	.889
Brosius, S	.000	4	0	0	1	0	0	.000	.000
Brumfield, J	.100	10	1	0	0	1	1	.182	.100
Buhner, Jay	.381	21	8	0	2	2	7	.435	.476
Burks, Ellis	.259	27	7	0	1	2	3	.333	.370
Butler, Brett*	.071	14	1	0	0	0	3	.071	.071
Caminiti, Ken	.091	11	1	0	0	1	4	.167	.091
Cangelosi, J#	.000	4	0	0	0	1	1	.200	.000
Canseco, Jose	.421	19	8	1	9	4	4	.522	.684
Carreon, Mark	.600	5	3	1	3	1	0	.667	1.200
Carter, Joe	.240	25	6	2	5	0	3	.296	.480
Castilla, V	.333	15	5	0	1	0	1	.333	.467
Cedeno, A	.333	6	2	0	0	0	0	.333	.500
Clark, Dave*	.250	8	2	1	2	0	1	.400	.375
Clark, Will*	.400	5	2	1	2	1	1	.500	1.000
Clayton, R	.235	17	4	0	2	1	1	.278	.235
Colbrunn, G	.364	11	4	1	3	2	1	.467	.636
Cole, Alex*	.389	18	7	0	1	1	1	.389	.556
Coleman, V	.286	7	2	0	3	0	2	.286	.429
Conine, Jeff	.250	16	4	0	0	1	5	.294	.250
Cora, Joey#	.308	13	4	0	1	0	1	.357	.615
Cordero, Wil	.200	10	2	0	1	1	0	.200	.300
Curtis, Chad	.133	15	2	0	0	1	4	.188	.133
Cuyler, Milt#	.368	19	7	0	0	1	3	.400	.368
Davis, Chili#	.308	26	8	2	5	4	3	.400	.577
Davis, Eric	.500	6	3	0	0	0	2	.500	.500
Dawson, Andre	.167	6	1	0	0	0	1	.167	.167
Deer, Rob	.176	17	3	0	0	0	6	.176	.176
DeShields, D*	.273	11	3	0	2	2	0	.385	.364
Devereaux, M	.359	39	14	2	6	3	2	.405	.590
DiSarcina, G	.133	15	2	0	1	0	0	.188	.133
Eisenreich, J*	.357	28	10	1	6	1	2	.379	.536
Espinoza, A	.200	25	5	0	1	1	3	.231	.200
Eusebio, Tony	.167	6	1	0	0	1	1	.286	.167
Faneyte, R	.200	5	1	0	0	1	1	.200	.200
Fermin, Felix	.143	28	4	0	0	2	0	.200	.143
Fielder, C	.343	35	12	3	9	0	4	.333	.629
Finley, Steve*	.263	19	5	1	3	1	3	.300	.421
Flaherty, J	.250	8	2	0	1	0	2	.222	.250
Fletcher, D*	.500	10	5	1	1	2	0	.583	.800
Fonville, C#	.364	11	4	0	0	2	0	.462	.455
Franco, Julio	.458	24	11	0	4	2	3	.500	.542
Frye, Jeff	.333	6	2	0	0	1	1	.429	.500
Fryman, T	.296	27	8	2	7	4	5	.387	.667
Gaetti, Gary	.192	26	5	0	3	0	5	.222	.308
Gagne, Greg	.222	27	6	0	3	6	4	.353	.370
Galarraga, A	.333	15	5	1	1	0	7	.375	.533
Gallego, Mike	.318	22	7	0	1	4	4	.423	.409
Gant, Ron	.625	8	5	1	3	3	0	.727	1.250
Garcia, C	.176	17	3	0	0	1	2	.222	.235
Gates, Brent#	.400	5	2	0	2	0	1	.400	.400
Gilkey, B	.333	12	4	0	1	3	1	.467	.500
Girardi, Joe	.333	6	2	0	1	0	1	.333	.333
Gomez, Chris	.000	5	0	0	0	1	0	.167	.000
Gomez, Leo	.261	23	6	0	1	3	2	.346	.261
Gonzales, R	.500	8	4	0	1	2	0	.636	.625
Gonzalez, J	.231	26	6	1	2	3	5	.323	.346
Goodwin, C*	.000	6	0	0	0	1	2	.143	.000
Grebeck, C	.200	15	3	0	0	1	2	.250	.200
Greenwell, M*	.111	27	3	0	1	3	5	.200	.185
Griffey Jr, K*	.412	34	14	1	7	2	3	.444	.559
Grissom, M	.200	10	2	0	0	0	0	.200	.200
Grudzielanek	.333	6	2	0	1	0	0	.333	.667
Guillen, O*	.381	21	8	0	3	1	0	.391	.381
Gutierrez, R	.462	13	6	0	5	3	2	.563	.538
Gwynn, Chris*	.222	9	2	0	1	0	3	.222	.222
Gwynn, Tony*	.083	12	1	0	0	0	0	.083	.167
Hall, Mel*	.267	15	4	0	4	0	1	.235	.267
Hansen, Dave*	.250	8	2	0	1	1	0	.333	.375
Harris, Lenny*	.429	7	3	0	2	0	0	.429	.857
Hayes, C	.308	13	4	0	1	0	0	.308	.462
Henderson, R	.179	28	5	0	1	6	3	.314	.179
Hill, G	.174	23	4	0	1	0	3	.174	.174
Hoiles, Chris	.227	22	5	1	1	1	5	.261	.409
Hollandsworth*	.429	7	3	0	2	0	2	.429	.571
Howard, T*	.462	13	6	0	1	1	1	.500	.538
Howell, Jack*	.200	5	1	0	0	1	1	.333	.200
Hulse, David*	.300	10	3	0	0	0	3	.300	.500
Hundley, Todd*	.273	11	3	1	1	2	3	.385	.545
Hunter, Bri L	.429	21	9	0	2	3	8	.478	.476
Huson, Jeff*	.375	16	6	0	3	2	1	.444	.625
Incaviglia, P	.133	15	2	0	1	1	6	.188	.267
James, Dion*	.316	19	6	2	3	1	2	.333	.684
Javier, Stan#	.400	5	2	0	2	1	1	.429	.600
Jefferies, G#	.250	24	6	0	1	1	2	.280	.292
Jefferson, R*	.111	9	1	0	1	1	1	.200	.111
Johnson, Char	.077	13	1	0	0	0	1	.077	.077
Johnson, L*	.293	41	12	0	4	0	2	.286	.390
Johnson, Mark*	.167	12	2	1	2	2	4	.286	.417
Jones, C#	.273	11	3	0	3	1	2	.308	.273
Jones, Chris	.000	5	0	0	0	0	0	.000	.000
Jordan, Brian	.333	9	3	0	3	1	0	.400	.444
Joyner, Wally*	.156	32	5	2	5	5	2	.270	.375
Justice, Dave*	.000	6	0	0	0	0	1	.000	.000
Karkovice, R	.000	14	0	0	0	1	7	.125	.000
Karros, Eric	.250	12	3	3	6	1	3	.308	1.000
Kelly, Pat	.222	9	2	0	1	1	2	.333	.333
Kelly, R	.303	33	10	2	6	0	4	.324	.515
Kendall, J	.200	5	1	0	0	1	1	.333	.200
Kent, Jeff	.500	6	3	0	0	1	0	.571	.667
King, Jeff	.529	17	9	2	8	0	0	.529	.941
Kingery, Mike*	.500	8	4	0	1	0	0	.444	.500
Kirby, Wayne*	.235	17	4	1	3	0	2	.222	.471
Klesko, Ryan*	.111	9	1	0	1	1	4	.200	.111
Knoblauch, C	.257	35	9	0	4	3	3	.333	.314
Kreuter, Chad#	.400	5	2	1	1	0	2	.400	1.000
Lankford, Ray*	.125	8	1	0	0	2	4	.300	.250
Lansing, Mike	.400	10	4	0	2	0	2	.400	.700
Larkin, Barry	.231	13	3	0	0	1	2	.286	.308
Leius, Scott	.222	9	2	0	0	0	2	.222	.333
Lemke, Mark#	.417	12	5	0	1	0	0	.462	.417
Lewis, Darren	.250	8	2	0	1	0	2	.250	.375
Lewis, Mark	.150	20	3	0	0	0	1	.150	.200
Leyritz, Jim	.111	9	1	0	0	2	0	.273	.222
Liriano, N#	.500	12	6	0	1	0	0	.500	.500
Livingstone*	.375	8	3	0	1	0	0	.375	.500
Lofton, Kenny*	.182	22	4	0	2	4	2	.308	.227
Lopez, Javy	.000	5	0	0	0	0	1	.000	.000
Lopez, Luis#	.000	5	0	0	0	0	0	.000	.000
Lovullo, T#	.500	12	6	0	2	0	0	.500	.583

Jaime Navarro, Cubs — RHP

Batter	Avg	AB	H	HR	BI	BB	SO	OBP	Slg
Mabry, John*	.250	12	3	0	1	0	0	.250	.250
Macfarlane, M	.500	10	5	0	2	1	0	.538	.600
Magadan, Dave*	.286	7	2	0	1	3	2	.500	.429
Magee, W	.167	6	1	0	2	0	1	.167	.333
Manwaring, K	.333	15	5	0	1	0	1	.333	.333
Martin, Al*	.278	18	5	0	1	1	5	.300	.500
Martinez, E	.276	29	8	0	1	3	4	.364	.310
Martinez, T*	.176	17	3	0	4	1	3	.211	.176
Marzano, John	.286	7	2	0	0	0	3	.286	.429
May, Derrick*	.455	11	5	0	1	0	3	.455	.636
Mayne, Brent*	.471	17	8	0	0	1	2	.500	.529
McGriff, Fred*	.450	20	9	2	2	2	4	.500	.750
McGwire, Mark	.250	16	4	1	2	5	5	.429	.438
McLemore, Mark	.500	14	7	0	3	2	2	.500	.500
McRae, Brian*	.321	28	9	1	6	4	7	.394	.500
Meares, Pat	.143	7	1	0	0	0	1	.143	.143
Merced, O*	.421	19	8	0	5	2	4	.455	.474
Mitchell, K	.167	6	1	0	0	1	0	.286	.167
Molitor, Paul	.600	10	6	1	4	0	0	.600	.900
Mondesi, Raul	.313	16	5	0	1	0	2	.294	.438
Morandini, M*	.000	13	0	0	0	3	2	.188	.000
Morris, Hal*	.200	10	2	1	1	0	4	.273	.500
Mouton, James	.250	8	2	0	1	1	2	.333	.250
Munoz, Pedro	.286	14	4	0	1	0	5	.286	.286
Myers, Greg*	.400	10	4	0	0	0	1	.400	.500
Naehring, Tim	.364	11	4	0	4	1	2	.385	.364
O'Brien, C	.167	6	1	0	0	0	0	.167	.167
O'Neill, Paul*	.333	15	5	0	2	1	2	.375	.467
Ochoa, Alex	.500	4	2	0	0	1	1	.600	.500
Olerud, John*	.435	23	10	0	3	2	1	.480	.652
Ordonez, Rey	.000	8	0	0	0	0	0	.000	.000
Orsulak, Joe*	.259	27	7	1	3	1	2	.286	.407
Otero, Ricky#	.273	11	3	0	0	3	1	.429	.273
Pagnozzi, Tom	.125	8	1	0	0	0	2	.125	.125
Palmeiro, R*	.282	39	11	1	4	0	4	.282	.410
Palmer, Dean	.200	20	4	0	0	6	1	.385	.350
Parent, Mark	.375	8	3	0	2	0	0	.375	.375
Pena, Tony	.235	17	4	0	0	2	3	.316	.353
Pendleton, T#	.200	15	3	0	0	1	5	.250	.333
Perez, E	.400	5	2	0	0	1	2	.500	.600
Phillips, J*	.100	10	1	0	0	0	2	.100	.100
Phillips, T#	.306	36	11	1	5	1	3	.316	.417
Piazza, Mike	.333	15	5	0	2	2	3	.412	.400
Plantier, P*	.400	5	2	0	1	3	0	.625	.800
Polonia, Luis*	.394	33	13	0	4	0	5	.459	.455
Raines, Tim#	.217	23	5	0	1	0	2	.250	.304
Reed, Jeff*	.250	8	2	0	1	2	1	.400	.250
Reed, Jody	.200	25	5	0	2	6	2	.344	.280
Renteria, E	.333	12	4	0	0	0	1	.333	.417
Ripken, Billy	.308	13	4	0	0	3	2	.438	.308
Ripken, Cal	.182	44	8	1	5	3	3	.234	.295
Rodriguez, I	.375	16	6	0	3	0	0	.375	.375
Salmon, Tim	.364	11	4	0	1	1	1	.417	.364
Sanders, D	.250	4	1	0	0	3	1	.571	.250
Santiago, B	.417	12	5	2	4	1	2	.462	1.083
Schofield, D	.500	6	3	0	1	0	0	.500	.500
Sefcik, Kevin	.400	5	2	0	0	0	0	.400	.600
Segui, David#	.167	12	2	0	0	1	1	.231	.167
Seitzer, K	.400	10	4	0	1	4	0	.571	.500
Sheffield, G	.455	11	5	2	5	4	0	.625	1.000
Shumpert, T	.000	5	0	0	0	0	1	.000	.000
Sierra, Ruben#	.214	42	9	1	3	0	4	.214	.333
Slaught, Don	.250	8	2	0	0	0	0	.250	.250
Smith, Dwight*	.000	6	0	0	0	0	2	.000	.000
Smith, Ozzie#	.667	6	4	0	0	0	0	.667	1.000
Snow, J.T.#	.143	7	1	0	0	0	2	.143	.143
Sojo, Luis	.273	11	3	0	0	0	2	.333	.273
Sorrento, P*	.533	15	8	0	1	4	1	.632	.600
Sosa, Sammy	.364	11	4	0	3	1	3	.417	.636
Sprague, Ed	.167	6	1	0	0	2	2	.375	.167
Stanley, Mike	.267	15	4	0	3	2	2	.353	.333
Steinbach, T	.091	11	1	0	2	1	2	.167	.091
Stevens, Lee*	.500	6	3	0	0	2	1	.625	.833
Stillwell, K#	.263	19	5	0	3	1	2	.300	.263
Stocker, K#	.667	9	6	0	1	0	0	.667	1.000
Strange, Doug#	.200	5	1	0	1	0	1	.200	.200
Tarasco, Tony*	.375	8	3	1	2	1	1	.444	.875
Tartabull, D	.480	25	12	3	8	4	8	.567	.880
Taubensee, E*	.400	5	2	0	3	1	0	.429	.600
Tavarez, Je#	.286	7	2	0	0	0	0	.286	.286
Tettleton, M#	.188	32	6	3	5	4	8	.278	.500
Thomas, Frank	.391	23	9	0	5	4	4	.464	.565
Thome, Jim*	.500	8	4	0	2	0	1	.444	.500
Thompson, Ja*	.167	6	1	0	0	0	2	.167	.500
Thompson, Mil*	.111	9	1	0	2	0	1	.111	.111
Thompson, Rob	.091	11	1	0	0	1	4	.167	.091
Trammell, A	.286	14	4	1	1	1	1	.333	.714
Valentin, Jhn	.455	11	5	1	3	2	2	.500	.818
Valle, Dave	.233	30	7	0	4	0	2	.233	.267
Vaughn, Mo*	.310	29	9	4	14	3	4	.364	.793
Velarde, R	.455	11	5	0	2	2	2	.538	.455

Jaime Navarro, Cubs — RHP

Batter	Avg	AB	H	HR	BI	BB	SO	OBP	Slg
Ventura, R*	.172	29	5	0	6	4	1	.273	.207
Veras, Q#	.167	6	1	0	0	1	1	.286	.167
Vizcaino, J#	.500	6	3	0	1	1	1	.571	.500
Vizquel, Omar#	.429	28	12	0	2	1	1	.448	.464
Walbeck, Matt#	.333	6	2	0	0	0	0	.429	.333
Walker, Larry*	.300	10	3	1	4	0	1	.300	.700
Ward, Turner*	.200	5	1	0	0	1	0	.333	.200
Weiss, Walt#	.227	22	5	0	2	4	5	.333	.273
White, Devon#	.219	32	7	0	2	6	4	.359	.313
White, R	.333	6	2	1	1	1	0	.429	.833
Whiten, Mark#	.133	15	2	0	2	0	3	.133	.133
Williams, Ber#	.217	23	5	0	0	4	8	.333	.304
Williams, Ma	.375	8	3	0	1	1	1	.500	.375
Worthington	.214	14	3	0	0	0	0	.214	.286
Young, Eric	.167	12	2	0	0	1	0	.231	.167
Zeile, Todd	.143	7	1	0	0	0	1	.143	.143

Denny Neagle, Braves — LHP

Batter	Avg	AB	H	HR	BI	BB	SO	OBP	Slg
Abbott, Kurt	.300	20	6	0	2	0	4	.300	.500
Alfonzo, E	.200	15	3	0	1	2	1	.278	.200
Alicea, Luis#	.500	4	2	0	0	1	1	.600	.750
Alou, Moises	.370	27	10	0	5	0	1	.370	.481
Amaro, Ruben*	.500	4	2	0	1	0	0	.600	.500
Andrews, S	.455	11	5	1	2	0	2	.455	.909
Anthony, Eric*	.400	5	2	0	2	2	1	.571	.600
Arias, Alex	.429	7	3	0	0	0	0	.429	.571
Aurilia, Rich	.250	4	1	0	0	1	0	.400	.250
Bagwell, Jeff	.263	19	5	0	3	0	5	.263	.368
Barberie, B#	.100	10	1	0	0	2	5	.250	.100
Bell, Derek	.438	16	7	0	2	0	1	.471	.500
Belliard, R	.200	5	1	0	0	0	2	.200	.200
Benjamin, M	.091	11	1	0	0	0	3	.091	.091
Berry, Sean	.100	10	1	0	0	1	2	.250	.100
Bichette, D	.522	23	12	1	5	2	3	.560	.739
Biggio, Craig	.188	16	3	0	1	2	2	.278	.188
Blauser, Jeff	.333	21	7	1	2	4	8	.423	.571
Bogar, Tim	.333	15	5	0	2	0	2	.333	.467
Bonds, Barry*	.357	28	10	3	5	4	2	.438	.714
Bonilla, B#	.438	16	7	2	5	1	2	.471	.875
Boone, Bret	.250	20	5	1	4	1	3	.273	.600
Brogna, Rico*	.400	5	2	0	0	0	2	.400	.600
Brumfield, J	.400	5	2	1	2	0	0	.400	1.200
Burks, Ellis	.438	16	7	1	6	0	2	.438	.688
Butler, Brett*	.533	15	8	0	0	1	2	.563	.800
Caminiti, Ken#	.294	17	5	0	1	1	3	.333	.412
Candaele, C#	.000	5	0	0	0	0	0	.000	.000
Carr, Chuck	.444	9	4	0	1	3	2	.583	.778
Carreon, Mark	.200	15	3	1	2	1	2	.235	.400
Castilla, V	.375	16	6	1	4	0	0	.375	.688
Cedeno, A	.250	8	2	0	0	1	1	.333	.250
Cedeno, Roger*	.600	5	3	0	1	1	0	.667	.800
Clark, Will*	.000	5	0	0	0	0	0	.000	.000
Clayton, R	.217	23	5	1	3	0	7	.208	.348
Colbrunn, G	.412	17	7	1	3	0	2	.412	.647
Coleman, V#	.600	5	3	0	1	1	0	.667	1.600
Conine, Jeff	.417	24	10	2	8	3	1	.433	.667
Cordero, Wil	.400	10	4	0	0	2	1	.500	.400
Dascenzo, D#	.250	8	2	0	0	0	2	.250	.375
Daulton, D*	.100	10	1	0	1	0	4	.100	.200
Davis, Eric	.100	10	1	0	1	0	1	.100	.100
Dawson, Andre	.375	16	6	1	2	1	0	.412	.563
Decker, Steve	.400	5	2	0	2	1	0	.500	.400
DeShields, D*	.190	21	4	0	0	3	2	.320	.190
Dorsett, B	.000	4	0	0	0	2	0	.333	.000
Dunston, S	.350	20	7	0	2	1	1	.381	.550
Dye, Jermaine	.500	6	3	1	2	0	1	.500	1.333
Dykstra, L*	.100	10	1	0	0	2	4	.250	.100
Espinoza, A	.167	6	1	0	0	0	1	.167	.167
Eusebio, Tony	.571	7	4	0	1	0	2	.571	.714
Everett, Carl*	.500	8	4	0	2	1	1	.556	.625
Finley, Steve*	.250	12	3	0	3	1	3	.308	.417
Fonville, C#	.444	9	4	0	0	0	1	.444	.556
Gaetti, Gary	.000	4	0	0	0	2	2	.333	.000
Galarraga, R	.318	22	7	2	6	0	5	.304	.591
Gant, Ron	.111	9	1	0	0	3	3	.333	.111
Gilkey, B	.400	25	10	2	5	3	7	.464	.680
Girardi, Joe	.385	13	5	0	0	1	1	.467	.462
Gomez, Leo	.200	5	1	0	1	2	2	.556	.200
Gonzalez, L*	.364	22	8	1	9	1	4	.391	.636
Grace, Mark*	.343	35	12	0	2	4	7	.410	.429
Grissom, M	.278	36	10	2	2	3	3	.333	.500
Grudzielanek	.333	12	4	0	0	0	3	.333	.417
Gutierrez, R	.333	6	2	0	1	0	0	.333	.667
Gwynn, Tony*	.105	19	2	0	1	2	1	.190	.158
Harris, Lenny*	.000	4	0	0	0	1	0	.000	.000
Hayes, C	.500	6	3	0	1	3	1	.667	.833
Hernandez, Ca	.455	11	5	0	0	0	1	.455	.455
Hernandez, Jo	.063	16	1	0	0	0	5	.063	.063
Hill, G	.333	21	7	4	5	1	5	.364	.905
Hollins, Dave#	.400	5	2	1	1	1	1	.500	1.000

Denny Neagle, Braves — LHP

Batter	Avg	AB	H	HR	BI	BB	SO	OBP	Slg
Howard, T*	.200	5	1	0	1	0	1	.200	.200
Hundley, Todd#	.100	20	2	1	3	2	8	.182	.250
Hunter, Brian	.286	7	2	0	1	2	2	.400	.286
Hunter, Bri L	.333	9	3	0	0	0	0	.333	.444
Huskey, Butch	.200	10	2	0	0	1	1	.273	.200
Incaviglia, P	.400	10	4	0	0	3	3	.538	.500
Javier, Stan#	.167	6	1	1	1	0	1	.167	.667
Jefferies, G#	.333	21	7	1	2	2	0	.391	.476
Johnson, Bri	.000	5	0	0	0	0	0	.000	.000
Johnson, Char	.133	15	2	0	0	2	2	.235	.133
Johnson, L*	.429	7	3	0	0	0	0	.429	.714
Jones, Andruw	.667	6	4	2	2	1	0	.714	2.167
Jones, C#	.150	20	3	0	1	1	3	.190	.200
Jones, Chris	.154	13	2	0	1	0	3	.154	.154
Jordan, Brian	.273	11	3	1	4	1	2	.308	.727
Joyner, Wally*	.429	7	3	0	2	0	0	.429	.714
Justice, Dave*	.353	17	6	1	2	7	1	.542	.529
Karros, Eric	.263	19	5	1	2	2	7	.333	.421
Kelly, Mike	.000	9	0	0	0	0	5	.000	.000
Kelly, R	.308	13	4	1	4	3	3	.438	.692
Kent, Jeff	.250	12	3	0	3	0	0	.231	.417
Klesko, Ryan*	.222	9	2	1	1	3	3	.417	.556
Lankford, Ray*	.269	26	7	1	5	2	9	.321	.500
Lansing, Mike	.269	26	7	0	0	0	2	.269	.346
Larkin, Barry	.160	25	4	1	2	5	1	.290	.360
Lemke, Mark#	.192	26	5	2	3	2	4	.241	.462
Lewis, Darren	.250	16	4	0	0	3	0	.368	.313
Lewis, Mark	.375	8	3	0	1	0	1	.375	.500
Lopez, Javy	.167	18	3	1	1	1	3	.211	.389
Magadan, Dave*	.125	8	1	0	1	1	3	.222	.125
Manwaring, K	.217	23	5	0	2	1	1	.250	.261
Martinez, Da*	.200	5	1	0	0	0	3	.200	.200
Martinez, M	.500	6	3	0	0	0	0	.500	.833
McGee, Willie*	.167	6	1	0	0	1	0	.286	.167
McGriff, Fred*	.290	31	9	2	4	2	12	.333	.516
McRae, Brian#	.300	20	6	2	3	2	4	.364	.650
Miller, Orl	.000	6	0	0	0	0	4	.000	.000
Mitchell, K	.500	6	3	0	1	1	1	.571	.833
Mondesi, Raul	.286	14	4	1	2	0	1	.286	.500
Morandini, M*	.375	16	6	0	1	1	3	.412	.625
Morris, Hal*	.333	18	6	0	1	1	3	.400	.444
Mouton, James	.250	12	3	0	1	5	3	.308	.250
Murray, Eddie*	.333	9	3	0	2	1	0	.364	.556
Nixon, Otis#	.333	6	2	0	0	1	1	.429	.333
Obando, S	.000	7	0	0	0	0	2	.000	.000
Ochoa, Alex	.364	11	4	0	2	0	0	.364	.636
Offerman, J#	.278	18	5	0	0	1	1	.278	.333
Oliver, Joe	.385	13	5	0	1	0	0	.429	.385
Ordonez, Rey	.000	7	0	0	0	0	2	.000	.000
Orsulak, Joe*	.400	5	2	0	0	1	0	.400	.400
Otero, Ricky#	.222	9	2	0	3	0	1	.222	.222
Owens, Eric	.375	8	3	0	0	0	0	.375	.375
Owens, J	.000	5	0	0	0	0	4	.000	.000
Pagnozzi, Tom	.125	16	2	0	0	1	1	.176	.125
Parent, Mark	.000	5	0	0	1	0	2	.000	.000
Pena, D	.000	3	0	0	0	4	2	.571	.000
Pendleton, T#	.313	32	10	1	6	2	4	.353	.438
Perez, Eddie	.333	6	2	0	0	0	0	.333	.333
Piazza, Mike	.250	8	2	0	0	0	1	.250	.250
Plantier, P*	.500	4	2	2	2	1	2	.600	2.000
Reed, Jody	.091	11	1	0	0	2	1	.231	.182
Renteria, E	.375	16	6	0	1	1	1	.444	.625
Roberts, Bip#	.250	12	3	0	1	2	2	.357	.250
Rodriguez, H*	.000	6	0	0	1	0	3	.000	.000
Sabo, Chris	.333	12	4	0	0	0	3	.333	.417
Sanchez, Rey	.105	19	2	0	0	1	2	.150	.105
Sandberg, R	.333	15	5	1	4	0	2	.333	.667
Sanders, R	.429	21	9	3	8	2	7	.478	.952
Santiago, B	.438	16	7	3	4	2	1	.500	1.063
Scarsone, S	.200	15	3	0	1	1	6	.294	.200
Schofield, D	.250	4	1	0	1	1	1	.400	.250
Segui, David#	.125	16	2	0	0	1	5	.176	.188
Servais, S	.211	19	4	0	0	1	4	.286	.263
Sheaffer, D	.500	4	2	0	2	1	1	.600	.500
Sheffield, G	.333	24	8	0	5	0	1	.333	.417
Shipley, C	.200	5	1	0	0	0	1	.200	.200
Smith, Ozzie#	.188	16	3	0	0	1	2	.235	.250
Sosa, Sammy	.207	29	6	2	6	2	7	.258	.448
Stankiewicz	.250	4	1	1	3	1	0	.400	1.000
Stinnett, K	.333	9	3	0	0	0	2	.333	.333
Stocker, K#	.444	9	4	0	4	2	2	.545	.556
Tavarez, Je#	.333	6	2	0	0	1	1	.333	.375
Thompson, Rob	.278	18	5	0	1	3	5	.381	.389
Thompson, Ry	.000	6	0	0	0	0	2	.143	.000
Timmons, O	.333	12	4	0	0	0	2	.333	.333
Vaughn, Greg	.200	5	1	1	1	0	0	.200	.800
Veras, Q#	.200	15	3	1	3	1	3	.294	.400
Vizcaino, J#	.333	9	3	0	0	1	1	.400	.444
Walker, Larry*	.296	27	8	2	8	3	9	.367	.556
Wallach, Tim	.222	18	4	0	2	1	2	.263	.333
Walton, J	.211	19	4	0	0	0	4	.211	.211

Denny Neagle, Braves — LHP (continued)

Batter	Avg	AB	H	HR	BI	BB	SO	OBP	Slg
Webster, L	.385	13	5	1	1	2	2	.467	.615
Weiss, Walt#	.400	15	6	0	1	2	4	.471	.400
White, Devon#	.300	10	3	1	0	1	0	.300	.700
White, R	.250	16	4	0	1	0	2	.250	.250
Whiten, Mark#	.231	13	3	1	3	1	3	.286	.538
Wilkins, Rick*	.000	5	0	0	0	1	3	.167	.000
Williams, E	.333	6	2	0	0	0	0	.333	.333
Williams, Ma	.286	21	6	1	3	1	3	.318	.429
Young, Eric	.235	17	4	1	3	1	0	.278	.471
Zeile, Todd	.348	23	8	0	6	1	1	.360	.522

Jeff Nelson, Yankees — RHP

Batter	Avg	AB	H	HR	BI	BB	SO	OBP	Slg
Alomar, R#	.200	5	1	0	0	1	0	.333	.200
Alomar Jr, S	.429	7	3	0	0	1	0	.500	.429
Anderson, Brd*	.000	3	0	0	0	2	1	.400	.000
Baerga, C#	.500	6	3	0	0	1	0	.571	.500
Baines, H*	.400	5	2	1	1	1	0	.500	1.000
Bautista, D	.200	5	1	0	1	0	4	.200	.200
Becker, Rich*	.200	5	1	0	1	0	2	.200	.200
Belle, Albert	.273	11	3	2	6	2	1	.385	.909
Berroa, G	.000	5	0	0	0	3	3	.333	.000
Bichette, D	.400	5	2	0	2	0	0	.400	.600
Boggs, Wade*	.250	4	1	0	0	1	1	.400	.250
Borders, Pat	.222	9	2	0	0	1	2	.222	.333
Bordick, Mike	.375	8	3	0	2	2	2	.545	.375
Brosius, S	.111	9	1	0	1	1	3	.182	.222
Canseco, Jose	.400	15	6	1	4	1	3	.438	.733
Carter, Joe	.077	13	1	0	0	2	2	.200	.077
Clark, Will*	.667	3	2	0	0	2	0	.800	.667
Coleman, V#	.667	3	2	0	0	1	1	.750	.667
Cordova, M	.500	6	3	0	1	0	3	.571	.833
Curtis, Chad	.400	10	4	0	1	1	2	.500	.400
Davis, Chili#	.167	6	1	1	2	1	2	.286	.667
Devereaux, M	.364	11	4	0	3	0	3	.364	.727
DiSarcina, G	.143	7	1	0	1	0	0	.250	.143
Durham, Ray#	.667	3	2	0	0	1	0	.750	.667
Easley, D	.250	4	1	0	0	0	2	.250	.250
Espinoza, A	.000	6	0	0	0	1	3	.143	.000
Fielder, C	.250	16	4	0	1	0	5	.250	.313
Franco, Julio	.250	8	2	0	1	3	2	.417	.375
Frye, Jeff	.667	6	4	0	0	0	0	.714	.667
Fryman, T	.364	11	4	0	5	1	5	.417	.636
Gaetti, Gary	.250	12	3	0	0	0	2	.250	.250
Gagne, Greg	.125	8	1	0	0	1	4	.300	.125
Gallego, Mike	.000	4	0	0	1	2	1	.333	.000
Gates, Brent#	.667	3	2	0	1	2	0	.800	.667
Gomez, Chris	.143	7	1	0	0	1	3	.250	.143
Gomez, Leo	.200	5	1	0	0	0	2	.200	.200
Gonzales, R	.000	5	0	0	0	2	1	.125	.000
Gonzalez, A	.000	7	0	0	0	0	5	.000	.000
Gonzalez, J	.357	14	5	0	4	1	4	.400	.429
Greenwell, M*	.500	2	1	0	1	2	0	.800	1.000
Greer, Rusty*	.500	4	2	0	0	1	1	.600	.500
Hale, Chip*	.167	6	1	0	1	1	2	.286	.167
Hamilton, D*	.333	6	2	0	1	2	0	.500	.500
Henderson, R	.250	4	1	0	3	2	1	.444	.250
Hoiles, Chris	.273	11	3	0	3	2	2	.385	.273
Howard, Dave#	.200	5	1	0	0	0	3	.200	.400
Jaha, John	.000	5	0	0	0	1	3	.167	.000
James, Dion*	.250	4	1	0	0	1	0	.400	.250
Javier, Stan#	.222	9	2	1	2	0	2	.222	.556
Jefferson, R*	.333	6	2	1	2	0	3	.333	.833
Johnson, L*	.333	6	2	0	0	1	2	.429	.667
Joyner, Wally*	.000	3	0	0	0	2	0	.400	.000
Kelly, Pat	.000	5	0	0	1	1	0	.286	.000
Knoblauch, C	.091	11	1	0	1	6	3	.412	.091
Lewis, Mark	.200	5	1	0	1	0	1	.200	.200
Leyritz, Jim	.143	7	1	0	0	0	1	.143	.143
Lofton, Kenny*	.333	6	2	0	1	0	1	.286	.333
Macfarlane, M	.000	8	0	0	0	0	3	.111	.000
McGwire, Mark	.286	7	2	1	2	2	1	.444	.857
McRae, Brian#	.000	5	0	0	0	2	1	.000	.000
Meares, Pat	.167	6	1	0	0	0	2	.286	.167
Molitor, Paul	.231	13	3	0	3	1	4	.333	.308
Murray, Eddie#	.167	6	1	0	1	1	0	.167	.167
Naehring, Tim	.167	6	1	0	0	0	2	.167	.333
O'Leary, Troy*	.333	3	1	0	0	3	1	.667	.333
Olerud, John*	.333	6	2	0	0	1	1	.429	.333
Palmeiro, R*	.000	4	0	0	0	1	2	.200	.000
Palmer, Dean	.071	14	1	0	1	2	8	.188	.071
Paquette, C	.200	5	1	0	2	1	3	.333	.200
Pena, Tony	.500	6	3	0	0	1	0	.500	.500
Phillips, T#	.800	5	4	0	1	1	1	.857	.800
Polonia, Luis*	.143	7	1	0	0	0	0	.143	.143
Ramirez, M	.167	6	1	1	2	1	3	.286	.667
Ripken, Cal	.300	10	3	0	0	1	0	.364	.300
Rodriguez, Al	.600	5	3	0	0	0	1	.600	.600
Rodriguez, I	.000	12	0	0	0	4	4	.250	.000
Salmon, Tim	.750	4	3	0	0	1	0	.800	.750
Seitzer, K	.400	5	2	0	0	0	0	.500	.400

Jeff Nelson, Yankees — RHP

Batter	Avg	AB	H	HR	BI	BB	SO	OBP	Slg
Shumpert, T	.250	4	1	0	0	1	1	.400	.250
Sierra, Rub*	.250	8	2	0	1	3	1	.455	.500
Sorrento, P*	.000	8	0	0	0	2	3	.200	.000
Sprague, Ed	.167	6	1	0	2	0	3	.286	.333
Stahoviak, S*	.167	6	1	0	0	0	3	.167	.333
Stanley, Mike	.167	12	2	0	2	1	3	.214	.250
Steinbach, T	.222	9	2	0	2	3	2	.417	.222
Surhoff, B.J.*	.500	6	3	0	2	1	0	.571	.500
Tartabull, D	.273	11	3	1	4	2	5	.385	.636
Tettleton, M#	.000	8	0	0	0	1	6	.111	.000
Thomas, Frank	.214	14	3	0	2	4	5	.368	.214
Trammell, A	.250	8	2	0	2	0	3	.250	.250
Valentin, Jhn	.000	9	0	0	1	1	1	.100	.000
Vaughn, Greg	.111	9	1	0	1	3	3	.333	.111
Vaughn, Mo*	.429	7	3	0	1	1	2	.500	.714
Velarde, R	.077	13	1	0	0	0	5	.143	.231
Ventura, R*	.000	6	0	0	0	2	1	.250	.000
Vizquel, Omar*	.333	6	2	0	0	0	0	.333	.500
White, Devon#	.429	7	3	0	4	0	4	.500	.429
Williams, Ber#	.333	6	2	0	2	0	2	.556	.333
Young, Ernie	.000	4	0	0	0	1	3	.200	.000

Robb Nen, Marlins — RHP

Batter	Avg	AB	H	HR	BI	BB	SO	OBP	Slg
Alou, Moises	.200	5	1	0	1	0	3	.200	.200
Bagwell, Jeff	.667	6	4	0	0	2	0	.750	1.000
Bell, Derek	.429	7	3	0	2	0	0	.429	.571
Berry, Sean	.200	5	1	0	0	0	0	.200	.200
Bichette, D	.400	5	2	0	1	0	2	.571	.600
Biggio, Craig	.222	9	2	1	4	0	1	.222	.556
Blauser, Jeff	.000	4	0	0	0	1	2	.200	.000
Bonilla, B#	.400	5	2	1	1	0	1	.400	1.000
Boone, Bret	.000	8	0	0	0	0	2	.000	.000
Branson, Jeff*	.125	8	1	0	0	0	5	.125	.125
Brogna, Rico*	.000	5	0	0	1	3	.167	.000
Brumfield, J	.400	5	2	0	1	1	0	.333	.600
Burks, Ellis	.143	7	1	0	1	0	2	.125	.143
Caminiti, Ken#	.200	5	1	0	0	0	2	.200	.200
Cangelosi, Ja	.125	8	1	0	0	2	1	.300	.125
Carreon, Mark	.200	5	1	0	0	0	2	.200	.200
Castilla, V	.600	5	3	0	0	1	1	.667	.800
Cedeno, A	.400	5	2	0	0	0	1	.400	.600
Clark, Dave*	.200	5	1	0	0	0	1	.200	.200
Clayton, R	.400	5	2	0	2	2	2	.571	.600
Cordero, Wil	.500	6	3	1	2	0	1	.500	1.167
Duncan, M	.400	5	2	0	1	0	2	.400	.800
Dunston, S	.400	5	2	1	1	0	1	.400	1.200
Eisenreich, J*	.400	5	2	0	0	0	1	.400	.400
Eusebio, Tony	.250	4	1	0	0	0	0	.250	.250
Finley, Steve*	.000	5	0	0	0	2	3	.286	.000
Floyd, Cliff*	.000	6	0	0	0	0	2	.000	.000
Galarraga, A	.111	9	1	1	3	0	2	.111	.444
Garcia, C	.000	6	0	0	0	1	3	.143	.000
Gilkey, B	.333	6	2	1	1	1	1	.429	.833
Girardi, Joe	.143	7	1	0	0	1	1	.250	.143
Gonzalez, L*	.143	7	1	0	2	0	1	.143	.286
Grace, Mark*	.000	8	0	0	0	1	2	.111	.000
Grissom, M	.286	7	2	1	2	1	2	.375	.714
Grudzielanek	.200	5	1	0	0	0	1	.200	.200
Gwynn, Tony*	.600	5	3	0	3	0	0	.600	.600
Harris, Lenny*	.000	6	0	0	0	0	1	.000	.000
Hayes, C	.000	10	0	0	0	1	4	.091	.000
Hollandsworth*	.000	5	0	0	0	1	0	.000	.000
Jefferies, G#	.167	6	1	0	0	2	1	.375	.167
Johnson, L*	.571	7	4	0	0	1	1	.571	.714
Johnson, Mark*	.250	4	1	0	1	1	1	.400	.500
Jones, C#	.833	6	5	1	6	0	1	.833	1.500
Jordan, Brian	.333	6	2	0	1	0	1	.333	.667
Justice, Dave*	.200	5	1	0	1	1	1	.286	.200
Karros, Eric	.400	5	2	0	0	3	.400	.400
Kelly, R	.600	5	3	0	0	0	.600	1.000
Kent, Jeff	.182	11	2	0	0	0	7	.182	.273
King, Jeff	.143	7	1	0	2	0	3	.143	.143
Kingery, Mike*	.000	3	0	0	0	2	1	.400	.000
Klesko, Ryan*	.200	5	1	0	0	0	2	.200	.200
Lampkin, Tom*	.167	6	1	0	2	0	1	.167	.333
Lankford, Ray*	.571	7	4	0	1	1	1	.625	.714
Lansing, Mike	.375	8	3	0	1	1	0	.375	.500
Larkin, Barry	.000	5	3	0	1	0	0	.667	.800
Lemke, Mark*	.600	5	3	0	2	2	1	.714	1.000
Liriano, N#	.250	4	1	0	1	1	0	.400	.500
Lopez, Javy	.333	6	2	0	1	0	1	.333	.333
Magadan, Dave*	.333	9	3	0	4	1	1	.400	.333
Manwaring, K	.400	5	2	0	0	0	2	.400	.400
Martin, Al*	.200	5	1	0	1	2	3	.429	.400
May, Derrick*	.167	6	1	0	0	0	2	.167	.333
McGee, Willie*	.000	4	0	0	0	2	0	.333	.000
McGriff, Fred*	.000	5	0	0	0	0	2	.000	.000
McRae, Brian#	.000	4	0	0	1	1	0	.167	.000
Merced, O*	.333	6	2	0	0	0	1	.333	.667
Mondesi, Raul	.250	4	1	0	0	1	2	.400	.250

Robb Nen, Marlins — RHP

Batter	Avg	AB	H	HR	BI	BB	SO	OBP	Slg
Morandini, M*	.222	9	2	0	1	0	1	.222	.333
Morris, Hal*	.200	10	2	0	0	0	4	.200	.300
Mouton, James	.286	7	2	0	1	1	3	.375	.286
Pagnozzi, Tom	.625	8	5	0	2	0	0	.625	.750
Sanchez, Rey	.000	5	0	0	0	0	2	.000	.000
Sandberg, R	.333	6	2	0	1	0	2	.333	.500
Sanders, R	.222	9	2	1	2	0	4	.222	.667
Segui, David#	.333	6	2	0	0	1	1	.429	.333
Sosa, Sammy	.444	9	4	3	5	0	3	.444	1.667
Spiers, Bill*	.000	6	0	0	1	2	0	.250	.000
Stocker, K#	.200	5	1	0	0	2	1	.429	.400
Thompson, Mil*	.200	5	1	0	0	0	1	.200	.200
Thompson, Rob	.333	9	3	2	2	0	5	.333	1.111
VanderWal, J*	.167	6	1	0	0	0	2	.167	.500
Vizcaino, J#	.375	8	3	0	0	0	2	.375	.875
Weiss, Walt#	.000	4	0	0	0	2	2	.333	.000
Whiten, Mark#	.200	5	1	0	0	1	1	.333	.200
Wilkins, Rick*	.200	5	1	0	0	0	1	.200	.400
Williams, Ma	.286	7	2	0	0	0	1	.286	.286
Young, Eric	.200	5	1	0	0	0	0	.200	.400
Zeile, Todd	.167	6	1	1	2	3	2	.444	.667

Dave Nied, Rockies — RHP

Batter	Avg	AB	H	HR	BI	BB	SO	OBP	Slg
Abbott, Kurt	.429	7	3	0	0	0	1	.429	.571
Alou, Moises	.500	6	3	0	1	0	0	.500	.500
Anthony, Eric*	.286	7	2	0	2	0	2	.250	.286
Ausmus, Brad	.500	4	2	0	0	1	1	.500	.600
Bagwell, Jeff	.385	13	5	0	2	1	2	.467	.538
Barberie, B#	.571	7	4	1	3	1	0	.625	1.143
Bell, Derek	.429	7	3	1	1	0	2	.429	.857
Bell, Jay	.000	3	0	0	0	2	0	.400	.000
Biggio, Craig	.389	18	7	0	1	1	2	.421	.444
Blauser, Jeff	.500	8	4	0	0	4	1	.667	.875
Bonds, Barry*	.444	9	4	0	1	2	1	.545	.667
Bonilla, B#	.333	9	3	1	1	1	0	.400	.889
Boone, Bret	.000	7	0	0	0	0	3	.000	.000
Butler, Brett*	.375	8	3	0	0	1	0	.444	.750
Caminiti, Ken#	.100	10	1	0	0	1	1	.182	.100
Carr, Chuck	.143	7	1	0	0	1	2	.333	.143
Cedeno, A	.154	13	2	0	1	0	3	.214	.154
Clark, Will*	.429	7	3	1	1	0	0	.429	1.000
Clayton, R	.500	6	3	0	1	2	0	.625	.667
Coleman, V#	.333	9	3	0	0	2	0	.333	.556
Conine, Jeff	.400	10	4	2	7	1	1	.455	1.000
Cordero, Wil	.000	6	0	0	0	0	0	.000	.000
Finley, Steve*	.143	14	2	0	0	0	1	.143	.143
Gant, Ron	.143	7	1	0	2	1	1	.250	.429
Garcia, C	.000	5	0	0	0	0	0	.000	.000
Gonzalez, L*	.333	15	5	1	4	1	1	.375	.667
Grace, Mark*	.455	11	5	0	1	1	0	.500	.455
Grissom, M	.429	7	3	0	2	0	1	.429	.429
Gutierrez, R	.000	6	0	0	0	1	0	.250	.000
Gwynn, Tony*	.200	5	1	0	0	2	0	.429	.200
Hill, G	.750	4	3	1	5	1	0	.800	1.500
Hundley, Todd#	.200	5	1	0	0	1	1	.333	.400
Jefferies, G#	.167	6	1	0	0	0	1	.167	.167
Jordan, Brian	.167	6	1	0	0	0	1	.167	.167
Justice, Dave*	.375	8	3	1	3	1	0	.444	.750
Karros, Eric	.125	8	1	0	0	2	2	.125	.125
Kelly, R	.429	7	3	0	1	0	2	.429	.429
Kent, Jeff	.100	10	1	0	0	0	3	.100	.100
King, Jeff	.200	5	1	0	0	1	1	.200	.200
Lankford, Ray*	.400	10	4	2	4	0	2	.400	1.100
Lansing, Mike	.200	5	1	0	1	0	0	.200	.200
Larkin, Barry	.571	7	4	1	2	3	0	.700	1.143
Lemke, Mark#	.333	6	2	0	0	1	0	.429	.500
Lewis, Darren	.000	8	0	0	1	2	0	.200	.000
Magadan, Dave*	.429	7	3	0	1	3	0	.600	.571
Martin, Al*	.333	3	1	0	0	2	1	.600	.667
May, Derrick*	.500	8	4	0	2	0	0	.545	.500
McGee, Willie#	.000	5	0	0	0	1	0	.167	.000
McGriff, Fred*	.571	7	4	1	4	1	0	.625	1.143
Merced, O*	.200	5	1	0	0	0	0	.200	.200
Morris, Hal*	.714	7	5	1	6	0	0	.714	1.286
Murray, Eddie#	.429	7	3	0	1	3	0	.600	.571
Nixon, Otis#	.200	5	1	0	1	1	2	.286	.200
O'Brien, C	.000	6	0	0	0	0	2	.000	.000
Offerman, J#	.143	7	1	0	1	1	1	.250	.143
Pagnozzi, Tom	.333	6	2	0	0	0	1	.333	.333
Pena, G#	.333	9	3	0	3	1	2	.400	.444
Pendleton, T#	.667	6	4	0	1	1	0	.714	.667
Piazza, Mike	.375	8	3	1	4	0	1	.375	.750
Plantier, P*	.286	7	2	0	1	3	0	.375	.429
Roberts, Bip#	.429	7	3	0	0	2	0	.556	.429
Sanchez, Rey	.000	5	0	0	1	1	1	.167	.000
Sandberg, R	.500	6	3	1	4	0	1	.500	1.333
Sanders, R	.286	7	2	2	4	0	3	.250	1.143
Santiago, B	.250	8	2	0	0	0	2	.250	.250
Servais, S	.143	7	1	0	1	0	2	.143	.286
Sheffield, G	.600	5	3	0	0	3	0	.750	.600

Dave Nied, Rockies — RHP

Batter	Avg	AB	H	HR	BI	BB	SO	OBP	Slg
Smith, Ozzie#	.500	8	4	0	0	1	1	.556	.750
Sosa, Sammy	.545	11	6	1	4	1	0	.615	1.091
Taubensee, E*	.364	11	4	1	2	1	0	.417	.636
Thompson, Rob	.400	5	2	0	0	1	1	.500	.800
Thompson, Ry	.000	6	0	0	0	0	2	.000	.000
Wallach, Tim	.286	7	2	0	1	0	2	.250	.286
Whiten, Mark#	.125	8	1	0	0	2	2	.300	.125
Wilkins, Rick*	.500	10	5	1	5	2	2	.538	.800
Williams, Ma	.250	8	2	0	2	0	1	.250	.375
Zeile, Todd	.273	11	3	0	1	0	1	.273	.455

C.J. Nitkowski, Tigers — LHP

Batter	Avg	AB	H	HR	BI	BB	SO	OBP	Slg
Anderson, G*	.571	7	4	0	1	0	0	.571	.714
Arias, George	.000	5	0	0	0	0	2	.000	.000
Brumfield, J	.222	9	2	0	0	2	1	.364	.222
Canseco, Jose	.200	5	1	0	0	2	1	.429	.200
Carter, Joe	.500	4	2	1	3	1	1	.600	1.250
Cirillo, Jeff	.000	4	0	0	0	1	1	.200	.000
Clark, Will*	.750	4	3	0	2	0	0	.600	1.250
Davis, Chili#	.250	4	1	1	4	2	1	.429	1.000
DiSarcina, G	.000	6	3	0	0	1	0	.571	.667
Duncan, M	.600	5	3	1	1	0	1	.600	1.200
Edmonds, Jim*	.000	4	0	0	0	2	3	.429	.000
Frye, Jeff	.000	4	2	0	1	2	0	.667	.750
Gonzalez, A	.167	6	1	0	1	1	1	.286	.500
Hudler, Rex	.000	6	3	1	1	1	1	.571	1.167
Knoblauch, C	.400	5	2	1	4	0	0	.400	1.200
Meares, Pat	.000	4	2	0	1	0	0	.600	.750
Naehring, Tim	.250	4	1	0	0	2	1	.500	.250
Nilsson, Dave*	.200	5	1	0	0	0	1	.200	.200
Nixon, Otis	.444	9	4	0	0	3	1	.583	.444
O'Brien, C	.429	7	3	0	1	0	2	.429	.571
Perez, Robert	.600	5	3	0	2	0	0	.600	.600
Perez, Tomas#	.200	5	1	0	2	1	0	.333	.600
Rodriguez, I	.000	3	0	0	1	1	0	.200	.000
Salmon, Tim	.250	4	1	0	1	3	1	.571	.500
Sprague, Ed	.000	5	0	0	0	2	1	.286	.000
Tettleton, M#	.000	3	0	0	0	2	0	.400	.000
Valentin, Jhn	.429	7	3	1	4	0	0	.556	.857
Vaughn, Mo*	.444	9	4	0	2	1	1	.500	.556

Hideo Nomo, Dodgers — RHP

Batter	Avg	AB	H	HR	BI	BB	SO	OBP	Slg
Abbott, Kurt	.091	11	1	1	1	0	6	.091	.364
Alfonzo, E	.167	6	1	0	0	1	2	.286	.167
Alicea, Luis#*	.167	6	1	0	0	1	2	.286	.333
Bagwell, Jeff	.556	9	5	3	4	3	0	.667	1.667
Bates, Jason#	.167	6	1	0	0	0	1	.167	.167
Bell, Derek	.100	10	1	0	2	1	2	.182	.200
Bell, Jay	.083	12	1	0	0	1	7	.154	.083
Benard, M*	.143	7	1	0	0	1	0	.250	.143
Berry, Sean	.125	16	2	0	1	0	2	.125	.188
Bichette, D	.211	19	4	2	5	0	8	.211	.579
Biggio, Craig	.538	13	7	0	0	0	2	.538	.846
Blauser, Jeff	.300	10	3	0	0	0	2	.300	.400
Bonds, Barry*	.167	18	3	1	1	3	6	.286	.389
Bonilla, B#	.600	5	3	1	2	1	0	.667	1.400
Boone, Bret	.444	9	4	0	0	0	0	.444	.556
Branson, Jeff*	.000	6	0	0	0	0	5	.000	.000
Brogna, Rico*	.133	15	2	0	1	1	6	.188	.133
Brumfield, J	.333	6	2	0	2	1	4	.429	.500
Burks, Ellis	.273	11	3	0	2	4	2	.467	.455
Butler, Brett*	.143	7	1	0	0	1	2	.250	.143
Caminiti, Ken#	.400	10	4	0	1	3	4	.538	.500
Cangelosi, J#	.333	6	2	0	0	1	0	.429	.333
Carr, Chuck	.143	7	1	0	1	0	2	.143	.143
Carreon, Mark	.200	5	1	0	1	3	0	.444	.200
Castilla, V	.368	19	7	1	1	0	8	.368	.579
Clayton, R	.190	21	4	0	0	1	8	.227	.238
Colbrunn, G	.200	10	2	0	0	1	6	.273	.200
Conine, Jeff	.111	18	2	0	2	2	9	.190	.111
Cordero, Wil	.500	4	2	0	0	4	0	.750	.500
Dunston, S	.167	12	2	0	0	2	4	.286	.250
Eisenreich, J*	.333	12	4	0	2	3	2	.438	.417
Eusebio, Tony	.000	3	0	0	0	2	0	.400	.000
Everett, Carl#	.167	6	1	1	1	0	5	.167	.667
Finley, Steve*	.333	12	4	2	3	2	2	.429	.833
Fletcher, D*	.286	7	2	1	1	0	1	.286	.714
Gaetti, Gary	.200	5	1	0	0	1	2	.333	.400
Galarraga, A	.133	15	2	0	1	1	7	.188	.133
Gant, Ron	.250	8	2	2	3	1	3	.333	1.000
Garcia, C	.222	9	2	0	0	0	3	.222	.222
Gilkey, B	.167	12	2	0	2	2	2	.286	.250
Girardi, Joe	.000	6	0	0	0	0	3	.000	.000
Gomez, Chris	.750	4	3	0	1	2	0	.833	1.250
Gonzalez, L*	.333	9	3	0	0	0	3	.333	.444
Grace, Mark*	.250	8	2	0	1	0	0	.250	.375
Greene, W*	.200	5	1	1	2	0	4	.200	.800
Grissom, M	.231	13	3	0	1	2	1	.333	.231
Grudzielanek	.250	4	1	0	0	2	0	.500	.250
Gwynn, Tony*	.364	11	4	0	1	2	0	.462	.636
Harris, Lenny*	.000	5	0	0	0	2	1	.400	.000
Hayes, C	.000	7	0	0	1	3	3	.300	.000
Henderson, R	.333	6	2	0	0	1	1	.429	.500
Hill, G	.100	10	1	0	0	3	4	.308	.100
Hundley, Todd#	.250	8	2	0	0	1	4	.333	.250
Hunter, Bri L	.167	12	2	0	1	1	3	.231	.167
Huskey, Butch	.286	7	2	1	1	1	0	.375	.714
Incaviglia, P	.333	6	2	0	0	0	2	.333	.333
Jefferies, G#	.556	9	5	1	4	1	0	.600	1.111
Johnson, Bri	.000	8	0	0	0	0	1	.000	.000
Johnson, Char	.111	9	1	0	0	1	6	.200	.111
Johnson, Mark*	.200	15	3	1	3	0	4	.200	.400
Jones, C#	.000	12	0	0	0	3	5	.000	.000
Jordan, Brian	.143	14	2	1	1	2	6	.250	.357
Jordan, Kevin	.600	5	3	0	1	0	1	.600	.600
Joyner, Wally*	.333	6	2	0	0	0	1	.333	.333
Justice, Dave*	.200	5	1	0	0	2	0	.429	.200
Kendall, J	.286	7	2	0	2	1	0	.375	.429
Kent, Jeff	.071	14	1	0	1	0	6	.067	.071
King, Jeff	.214	14	3	0	1	1	3	.267	.214
Kingery, Mike*	.438	16	7	0	1	1	3	.471	.500
Klesko, Ryan*	.167	12	2	0	1	2	5	.286	.250
Lampkin, Tom*	.500	4	2	1	2	0	0	.714	1.500
Lankford, Ray*	.071	14	1	0	1	0	3	.071	.071
Lansing, Mike	.000	5	0	0	0	1	1	.167	.000
Larkin, Barry	.000	3	0	0	0	3	0	.500	.000
Lemke, Mark*	.167	6	1	0	0	1	2	.333	.167
Lewis, Darren	.364	11	4	0	0	0	0	.364	.364
Liriano, N#	.000	4	0	0	0	0	1	.200	.000
Livingstone*	.000	5	0	0	0	1	3	.167	.000
Lopez, Javy	.222	9	2	0	1	1	3	.300	.333
Mabry, John*	.182	11	2	0	1	1	3	.250	.182
Magee, W	.167	6	1	1	1	1	2	.286	.667
Manwaring, K	.091	11	1	0	3	0	4	.091	.182
Martin, Al*	.313	16	5	0	1	1	8	.389	.313
McCracken, Q#	.100	10	1	0	0	1	1	.182	.100
McGriff, Fred*	.308	13	4	0	0	2	4	.400	.308
McRae, Brian#	.333	12	4	0	1	0	3	.333	.333
Merced, O*	.125	8	1	0	0	0	2	.125	.125
Miller, Orl	.333	3	1	0	1	1	1	.400	.667
Morandini, M*	.211	19	4	0	2	0	8	.211	.316
Morris, Hal*	.200	10	2	0	0	0	2	.200	.300
Nieves, M#	.200	5	1	0	1	0	3	.200	.400
Oliver, Joe	.250	4	1	0	0	0	0	.250	.250
Orsulak, Joe*	.278	18	5	1	4	3	1	.381	.500
Owens, J	.400	5	2	0	0	1	1	.500	.400
Pagnozzi, Tom	.100	10	1	0	2	1	2	.250	.200
Parent, Mark	.250	8	2	0	0	1	2	.333	.250
Pendleton, T#	.176	17	3	0	2	0	3	.167	.176
Reed, Jeff*	.200	5	1	0	0	3	0	.200	.200
Reed, Jody	.182	11	2	0	1	0	3	.167	.182
Renteria, E	.167	6	1	0	0	0	2	.167	.167
Rodriguez, H*	.000	4	0	0	0	2	2	.333	.000
Rolen, Scott	.333	6	2	1	2	0	1	.333	.833
Sanchez, Rey	.600	5	3	0	1	0	0	.667	.600
Santiago, B	.100	10	1	0	0	1	1	.182	.100
Scarsone, S	.000	6	0	0	0	2	3	.250	.000
Segui, David#	.333	6	2	1	1	0	1	.333	.833
Servais, S	.000	6	0	0	0	0	0	.000	.000
Sheffield, G	.583	12	7	2	4	1	1	.615	1.083
Sosa, Sammy	.222	9	2	0	1	1	5	.300	.333
Stinnett, K	.167	6	1	0	0	0	4	.167	.167
Stocker, K#	.333	12	4	0	3	0	3	.333	.500
Sweeney, Mark*	.417	12	5	1	1	1	1	.462	.667
Tarasco, Tony*	.250	8	2	0	0	1	0	.250	.250
Thompson, Rob	.111	9	1	0	0	0	2	.111	.222
Thompson, Ry	.000	8	0	0	0	0	5	.111	.000
VanderWal, J*	.000	5	0	0	0	1	0	.000	.000
Veras, Q#	.222	18	4	1	1	3	3	.364	.389
Vizcaino, J#	.154	13	2	1	4	0	7	.154	.385
Walker, Larry*	.111	9	1	1	1	0	4	.200	.444
Webster, L	.250	4	1	0	0	1	1	.400	.250
Weiss, Walt#	.200	15	3	0	3	2	5	.294	.267
White, Devon#	.000	6	0	0	0	0	2	.000	.000
White, D	.111	9	1	0	0	2	4	.273	.111
Wilkins, Rick*	.000	6	0	0	0	0	2	.000	.000
Williams, Ma	.333	12	4	2	5	1	4	.385	.833
Young, Eric	.286	14	4	1	2	2	0	.375	.500
Zeile, Todd	.167	12	2	0	1	2	5	.286	.250

Chad Ogea, Indians — RHP

Batter	Avg	AB	H	HR	BI	BB	SO	OBP	Slg
Alicea, Luis#*	.200	5	1	0	0	1	0	.333	.200
Alomar, R#	.333	12	4	0	3	1	0	.385	.417
Anderson, Brd*	.316	19	6	1	3	1	2	.333	.737
Anderson, G*	.222	9	2	0	2	0	2	.222	.222
Arias, George	.333	6	2	0	0	0	3	.333	.667
Baines, H*	.154	13	2	1	1	2	1	.267	.385
Barberie, B#	.200	5	1	0	0	1	1	.333	.200
Becker, Rich*	.583	12	7	2	6	2	2	.643	1.250

Chad Ogea, Indians — RHP

Batter	Avg	AB	H	HR	BI	BB	SO	OBP	Slg
Berroa, G	.400	5	2	0	1	0	0	.400	.800
Blowers, Mike	.400	5	2	2	5	0	0	.400	1.600
Boggs, Wade*	.200	5	1	0	1	1	1	.286	.200
Bonilla, B#	.125	8	1	0	2	3	2	.308	.125
Brosius, S	.600	5	3	0	2	0	0	.600	.600
Buhner, Jay	.000	7	0	0	0	1	1	.125	.000
Canseco, Jose	.091	11	1	0	1	1	4	.167	.182
Carter, Joe	.333	12	4	1	3	0	3	.333	.583
Cirillo, Jeff	.167	6	1	0	1	1	1	.286	.333
Cora, Joey*	.182	11	2	0	0	0	0	.182	.182
Cordova, M	.143	14	2	2	4	0	3	.143	.571
Damon, Johnny*	.000	6	0	0	0	1	0	.000	.000
Davis, Chili#	.500	6	3	0	1	0	0	.500	.500
Delgado, C*	.250	4	1	1	2	1	2	.400	1.000
Diaz, Alex#	.167	6	1	0	0	0	2	.167	.167
DiSarcina, G	.167	6	1	0	0	0	0	.167	.333
Durham, Ray#	.333	3	1	0	0	2	1	.600	.333
Easley, D	.000	5	0	0	0	1	2	.167	.000
Edmonds, Jim*	.375	8	3	1	2	1	0	.444	.875
Fabregas, Jor*	.167	6	1	0	0	0	1	.167	.167
Gaetti, Gary	.200	5	1	0	0	0	1	.200	.200
Gonzalez, A	.273	11	3	0	0	0	1	.273	.273
Goodwin, C*	.111	9	1	0	0	0	1	.111	.111
Goodwin, Tom*	.429	7	3	0	0	0	2	.429	.429
Green, Shawn*	.375	8	3	1	3	1	0	.400	1.000
Greenwell, M*	.111	9	1	0	0	0	1	.111	.111
Hamilton, D*	.500	6	3	0	0	0	0	.500	.500
Hammonds, J	.286	7	2	1	2	1	1	.375	.714
Hocking, D#	.200	5	1	0	1	0	0	.200	.200
Hoiles, Chris	.313	16	5	1	4	2	4	.389	.563
Hollins, Dave*	.167	6	1	0	0	0	2	.167	.167
Hosey, Dwayne*	.200	5	1	0	0	0	0	.200	.200
Howard, Dave#	.000	7	0	0	0	0	2	.000	.000
Huson, Jeff*	.000	6	0	0	0	0	1	.000	.000
Jaha, John	.300	10	3	1	3	1	0	.364	.600
Karkovice, R	.333	6	2	0	1	0	2	.333	.667
Knoblauch, C	.300	10	3	0	0	4	1	.533	.300
Lockhart, K*	.182	11	2	0	0	0	1	.182	.182
Macfarlane, M	.455	11	5	0	1	1	1	.571	.636
Martinez, E	.167	6	1	0	0	0	1	.167	.167
Martinez, T*	.250	8	2	1	1	0	1	.250	.625
McLemore, M#	.400	5	2	0	0	1	1	.500	.400
Meares, Pat	.400	10	4	0	1	1	0	.455	.500
Molitor, Paul	.267	15	4	0	2	1	3	.313	.400
Murray, Eddie*	.400	5	2	0	0	0	1	.400	.400
Myers, Greg*	.333	9	3	0	1	0	0	.333	.333
Myers, Rod*	.000	5	0	0	0	0	2	.000	.000
Naehring, Tim	.364	11	4	0	2	0	1	.364	.455
Newfield, M	.333	6	2	0	0	0	1	.333	.333
Nilsson, Dave*	.333	6	2	0	1	2	0	.500	.333
Nixon, Otis*	.222	9	2	0	0	0	3	.222	.333
Nunnally, Jon*	.000	6	0	0	0	0	4	.000	.000
O'Leary, Troy*	.167	6	1	0	0	0	0	.167	.167
O'Neill, Paul*	.000	5	0	0	0	1	1	.167	.000
Offerman, J	.400	5	2	0	1	2	1	.571	.400
Olerud, John*	.500	10	5	0	0	0	0	.500	.600
Palmeiro, R*	.353	17	6	2	3	2	1	.400	.824
Paquette, C	.455	11	5	1	1	0	1	.455	.909
Perez, Tomas#	.200	5	1	0	0	0	1	.200	.200
Phillips, T#	.333	9	3	0	2	0	0	.333	.444
Randa, Joe	.200	5	1	1	1	0	0	.200	.200
Ripken, Cal	.105	19	2	0	0	2	2	.190	.105
Salmon, Tim	.333	9	3	0	0	0	4	.333	.444
Seitzer, K	.167	6	1	0	0	0	1	.167	.333
Sierra, Ruben*	.182	11	2	0	1	2	1	.308	.182
Snow, J.T.#	.300	10	3	1	2	0	2	.300	.700
Sprague, Ed	.000	7	0	0	0	3	2	.364	.000
Stahoviak, S*	.364	11	4	1	4	2	3	.462	.727
Stynes, Chris	.400	5	2	0	0	0	0	.400	.400
Surhoff, B.J.*	.375	8	3	1	1	0	1	.375	.750
Tartabull, D	.167	6	1	0	0	0	1	.167	.167
Thomas, Frank	.333	6	2	0	2	1	1	.429	.333
Tinsley, Lee#	.222	9	2	0	1	1	3	.300	.222
Tucker, M*	.400	5	2	0	0	0	1	.400	.400
Valentin, Jhn	.267	15	4	0	0	1	1	.353	.267
Valentin, Jse#	.111	9	1	0	0	1	0	.200	.333
Vaughn, Mo*	.313	16	5	0	2	2	1	.389	.313
Velarde, R	.571	7	4	0	0	0	0	.571	.714
Ventura, R	.571	7	4	1	4	0	2	.571	1.000
Vina, F*	.250	8	2	0	0	0	0	.250	.375
Walbeck, Matt#	.111	9	1	0	1	0	4	.111	.111
White, Devon#	.400	5	2	0	2	0	1	.286	.400
Williams, Ber#	.250	4	1	0	0	2	1	.500	.250
Wilson, Dan	.125	8	1	0	0	0	0	.125	.125

Omar Olivares, Tigers — RHP

Batter	Avg	AB	H	HR	BI	BB	SO	OBP	Slg
Alomar, R#	.455	11	5	1	2	2	1	.538	.818
Alou, Moises	.455	11	5	1	3	0	1	.500	.727
Amaral, Rich	.000	7	0	0	1	1	2	.125	.000
Amaro, Ruben#	.286	7	2	1	2	1	1	.375	.714

Omar Olivares, Tigers — RHP

Batter	Avg	AB	H	HR	BI	BB	SO	OBP	Slg
Anderson, Brd*	.357	14	5	0	0	0	1	.357	.357
Anthony, Eric*	.167	6	1	0	1	2	1	.375	.333
Bagwell, Jeff	.182	11	2	0	2	0	2	.182	.182
Baines, H*	.333	6	2	0	0	3	2	.556	.500
Barberie, B#	.429	21	9	0	1	2	2	.520	.571
Batiste, Kim	.200	5	1	0	0	0	0	.200	.400
Battle, Allen	.400	5	2	0	0	0	0	.400	.400
Becker, Rich*	.286	7	2	0	0	1	0	.375	.571
Bell, Derek	.667	6	4	0	1	1	0	.750	.667
Bell, Jay	.231	26	6	0	1	4	2	.333	.308
Belliard, R	.300	10	3	0	0	0	1	.300	.300
Berroa, G	.571	7	4	0	0	0	0	.571	.571
Berry, Sean	.222	9	2	0	0	0	0	.222	.222
Bichette, D	.364	11	4	0	4	0	3	.333	.455
Biggio, Craig	.313	16	5	1	4	5	3	.476	.563
Blauser, Jeff	.160	25	4	0	0	3	4	.250	.160
Bonds, Barry*	.308	13	4	0	0	3	1	.438	.385
Bonilla, B#	.310	29	9	0	1	7	4	.459	.379
Bordick, Mike	.167	6	1	0	0	0	0	.167	.167
Branson, Jeff*	.143	7	1	0	0	0	1	.143	.143
Brogna, Rico*	.714	7	5	0	2	0	0	.714	1.143
Brosius, S	.286	7	2	1	2	0	0	.286	.714
Buhner, Jay	.000	5	0	0	0	2	5	.286	.000
Burnitz, J*	.400	5	2	0	0	0	0	.400	.400
Butler, Brett*	.222	9	2	0	0	3	3	.533	.222
Caminiti, Ken#	.182	11	2	0	0	0	1	.182	.182
Candaele, C#	.167	6	1	0	0	1	0	.286	.167
Carr, Chuck	.286	7	2	0	0	1	0	.375	.286
Carter, Joe	.200	5	1	1	2	1	0	.333	.800
Cedeno, A	.200	5	1	0	0	0	1	.200	.400
Cirillo, Jeff	.000	4	0	0	0	1	0	.333	.000
Clark, Dave*	.500	6	3	2	4	4	0	.700	1.500
Clark, Will*	.211	19	4	3	6	5	5	.375	.737
Clayton, R	.250	12	3	0	0	1	3	.308	.333
Cole, Alex*	.444	9	4	0	0	1	3	.500	.444
Coleman, V#	.353	17	6	0	3	1	2	.389	.471
Conine, Jeff	.625	8	5	0	1	1	0	.667	.625
Cora, Joey*	.364	11	4	1	2	2	0	.462	.818
Cordero, Wil	.333	9	3	0	0	3	3	.538	.444
Cordova, M	.429	7	3	1	2	0	2	.429	1.000
Damon, Johnny*	.250	4	1	0	0	1	0	.400	.250
Daulton, D*	.304	23	7	3	8	3	3	.370	.696
Davis, Eric	.286	7	2	0	1	2	1	.444	.286
Dawson, Andre	.429	14	6	2	7	0	1	.467	.857
Delgado, C*	.667	6	4	1	3	0	1	.667	1.167
DeShields, D*	.208	24	5	1	3	4	7	.321	.458
Duncan, M	.267	15	4	0	2	0	5	.267	.400
Dunston, S	.600	5	3	0	0	0	1	.600	.800
Durham, Ray#	.167	6	1	0	0	1	2	.286	.167
Dykstra, L*	.333	18	6	0	0	1	1	.368	.389
Eisenreich, J*	.286	7	2	0	1	2	0	.444	.286
Elster, Kevin	.056	18	1	1	1	1	6	.105	.222
Finley, Steve*	.500	8	4	0	2	0	1	.500	.875
Fletcher, D*	.438	16	7	0	2	0	1	.438	.563
Floyd, Cliff*	.400	5	2	0	1	0	0	.400	.600
Galarraga, A	.296	27	8	1	6	1	3	.321	.481
Gant, Ron	.455	22	10	3	7	4	3	.538	1.091
Garcia, C	.417	12	5	1	2	0	0	.417	.667
Giambi, Jason*	.333	6	2	1	4	1	0	.375	.833
Girardi, Joe	.167	6	1	0	0	0	0	.167	.500
Gonzalez, J	.286	7	2	0	1	1	2	.375	.286
Gonzalez, L*	.100	10	1	0	0	2	0	.250	.100
Grace, Mark*	.360	25	9	1	4	3	2	.429	.560
Green, Shawn*	.500	5	3	0	0	1	0	.667	1.000
Greer, Rusty*	.125	8	1	0	1	0	0	.125	.250
Griffey Jr, K*	.222	9	2	0	1	1	2	.300	.333
Grissom, M	.273	22	6	0	1	2	0	.333	.273
Guillen, O*	.167	6	1	0	0	0	1	.167	.167
Gutierrez, R	.000	4	0	0	0	1	1	.200	.000
Gwynn, Tony*	.059	17	1	1	2	1	0	.111	.235
Hamilton, D*	.500	8	4	0	0	1	0	.556	.875
Hansen, Dave*	.333	6	2	1	3	0	1	.333	1.000
Harris, Lenny*	.462	13	6	0	1	2	1	.533	.615
Hayes, C	.100	20	2	1	3	2	2	.217	.250
Hill, G	.333	3	1	0	0	2	2	.600	.333
Hoiles, Chris	.167	6	1	0	1	1	0	.375	.167
Hollins, Dave#	.273	22	6	0	2	3	5	.360	.318
Howard, T*	.125	8	1	0	0	1	0	.222	.125
Hundley, Todd#	.250	16	4	0	2	4	3	.400	.313
Incaviglia, P	.143	7	1	0	0	0	3	.143	.143
Jaha, John	.222	9	2	0	0	1	1	.300	.222
Javier, Stan#	.143	7	1	0	1	1	3	.250	.286
Jefferies, G#	.000	3	0	0	0	2	0	.500	.000
Jordan, Brian	.400	5	2	0	0	0	0	.400	.400
Jordan, Ricky	.500	18	9	0	1	0	3	.500	.556
Justice, Dave*	.273	22	6	1	3	3	2	.360	.591
Karros, Eric	.429	7	3	1	1	0	0	.429	.857
Kelly, R	.412	17	7	0	3	1	0	.421	.471
Kent, Jeff	.375	8	3	1	4	0	1	.375	.750
King, Jeff	.231	13	3	0	2	3	1	.353	.231
Kingery, Mike*	.375	8	3	0	0	1	0	.444	.625

Omar Olivares, Tigers — RHP

Batter	Avg	AB	H	HR	BI	BB	SO	OBP	Slg
Klesko, Ryan*	.222	9	2	0	2	0	1	.222	.222
Knoblauch, C	.167	6	1	0	1	1	0	.375	.167
Lansing, Mike	.000	6	0	0	0	0	0	.143	.000
Larkin, Barry	.333	15	5	1	6	2	2	.412	.533
Lemke, Mark#	.211	19	4	0	0	3	2	.318	.263
Lewis, Darren	.250	16	4	0	1	1	2	.333	.313
Loretta, Mark	.143	7	1	0	0	0	0	.143	.143
Magadan, Dave*	.188	16	3	0	1	6	2	.391	.250
Manto, Jeff	.333	6	2	0	0	1	0	.429	.667
Manwaring, K	.222	9	2	0	1	1	1	.300	.222
Martin, Al*	.000	6	0	0	0	1	3	.143	.000
Martinez, Da*	.192	26	5	0	1	1	2	.222	.192
Marzano, John	.333	6	2	0	0	0	0	.429	.333
Matheny, Mike	.400	5	2	0	0	1	1	.500	.600
May, Derrick*	.600	10	6	0	3	1	1	.636	.800
McGee, Willie*	.333	12	4	0	0	3	4	.500	.500
McGriff, Fred*	.261	23	6	1	5	1	2	.280	.435
McLemore, Ma	.286	7	2	0	0	0	2	.286	.429
Merced, O*	.273	22	6	1	6	4	3	.370	.455
Molitor, Paul	.375	8	3	0	2	0	1	.375	.375
Morandini, M*	.059	17	1	0	0	1	1	.111	.059
Morris, Hal*	.200	10	2	1	1	3	1	.385	.500
Murray, Eddie*	.300	20	6	1	2	3	1	.391	.500
Nilsson, Dave*	.625	8	5	0	2	2	1	.700	.750
Nixon, Otis*	.214	28	6	0	2	2	8	.267	.321
O'Brien, C	.143	14	2	0	2	3	2	.294	.214
O'Neill, Paul*	.500	8	4	0	2	0	0	.500	.500
Offerman, J#	.462	13	6	0	3	1	1	.500	.615
Olerud, John*	.250	4	1	0	0	1	0	.400	.500
Oliver, Joe	.250	12	3	0	0	0	2	.250	.417
Orsulak, Joe*	.143	7	1	1	1	0	0	.143	.571
Palmeiro, R*	.091	11	1	0	0	1	4	.167	.091
Palmer, Dean	.143	7	1	0	0	0	2	.250	.143
Paquette, C	.800	5	4	1	1	0	0	.800	1.000
Pendleton, T#	.421	19	8	2	2	2	4	.476	.789
Phillips, T#	.000	5	0	0	0	4	1	.444	.000
Plantier, P*	.455	11	5	0	1	1	1	.500	.636
Polonia, Luis*	.000	7	0	0	0	0	0	.000	.000
Ripken, Cal	.273	11	3	0	1	1	2	.333	.364
Roberts, Bip#	.429	14	6	0	1	1	1	.467	.500
Rodriguez, Al	.400	10	4	0	1	0	1	.400	.600
Rodriguez, I	.222	9	2	0	0	0	2	.222	.333
Sabo, Chris	.333	9	3	0	1	1	1	.400	.333
Samuel, Juan	.200	5	1	0	1	0	1	.200	.200
Sandberg, R	.478	23	11	2	3	4	1	.556	.783
Sanders, R	.667	9	6	0	1	1	0	.700	1.222
Santiago, B	.167	12	2	1	2	0	1	.167	.417
Schofield, D	.111	9	1	0	0	0	1	.111	.111
Seitzer, K	.000	8	0	0	0	1	0	.111	.000
Servais, S	.167	6	1	0	0	0	1	.167	.167
Sheaffer, D	.143	7	1	0	0	0	1	.143	.143
Sheffield, G	.455	11	5	1	2	2	2	.538	.909
Slaught, Don	.200	5	1	0	0	1	1	.333	.200
Smith, Dwight*	.421	19	8	1	6	1	3	.476	.842
Sorrento, P*	.125	8	1	0	1	3	0	.364	.250
Sosa, Sammy	.100	10	1	0	0	1	1	.182	.100
Sprague, Ed	.500	4	2	1	1	0	0	.600	1.500
Stahoviak, S*	.500	2	1	0	0	5	0	.857	1.000
Stillwell, K#	.000	5	0	0	1	0	0	.000	.000
Stocker, K#	.200	5	1	0	1	1	2	.333	.400
Strange, Doug#	.167	6	1	0	1	1	0	.286	.167
Strawberry, D*	.429	7	3	0	2	1	2	.500	.429
Surhoff, B.J.*	.143	7	1	0	0	1	2	.250	.429
Tarasco, Tony*	.000	4	0	0	0	1	0	.333	.000
Tartabull, D	.429	7	3	0	2	2	0	.556	.429
Taubensee, E*	.000	9	0	0	0	3	0	.000	.000
Thomas, Frank	.375	8	3	0	3	0	0	.333	.500
Thompson, Mil*	.600	5	3	0	5	0	0	.600	1.000
Thompson, Rob	.167	12	2	0	1	2	3	.333	.250
Thompson, Ry	.286	7	2	0	0	0	2	.375	.286
Valentin, Jse#	.125	8	1	0	0	1	2	.222	.250
VanderWal, J*	.118	17	2	1	2	0	2	.118	.294
Vaughn, Greg	.000	5	0	0	0	2	3	.375	.000
Ventura, R*	.500	8	4	1	5	0	0	.444	1.000
Vina, F*	.333	6	2	0	1	1	0	.375	.667
Vitiello, Joe	.167	6	1	0	1	0	0	.167	.167
Vizcaino, J#	.105	19	2	0	0	1	1	.150	.105
Walker, Larry*	.481	27	13	0	3	4	3	.576	.667
Wallach, Tim	.130	23	3	0	1	3	5	.167	.130
Walton, J	.143	7	1	0	0	0	0	.143	.143
Weiss, Walt*	.273	11	3	0	0	3	2	.429	.455
Wilkins, Rick*	.200	10	2	0	1	1	0	.273	.300
Williams, Ma	.167	18	3	1	2	2	1	.250	.333
Young, Eric	.000	4	0	0	0	1	0	.200	.000
Zeile, Todd	.500	10	5	1	4	0	0	.500	.800

Darren Oliver, Rangers — LHP

Batter	Avg	AB	H	HR	BI	BB	SO	OBP	Slg
Alexander, M	.000	5	0	0	0	0	1	.000	.000
Alomar, R#	.143	7	1	0	1	0	0	.143	.143
Alomar Jr, S	.333	9	3	1	1	1	2	.400	.667

Darren Oliver, Rangers — LHP

Batter	Avg	AB	H	HR	BI	BB	SO	OBP	Slg
Amaral, Rich	.333	12	4	0	4	3	2	.467	.333
Anderson, Brd*	.286	7	2	1	2	3	3	.500	.714
Anderson, G*	.000	6	0	0	0	0	2	.000	.000
Arias, George	.333	6	2	1	1	0	0	.333	.833
Baerga, C#	.182	11	2	0	0	0	3	.182	.182
Bautista, D	.000	5	0	0	0	1	5	.167	.000
Belle, Albert	.231	13	3	3	3	2	1	.333	.923
Berroa, G	.300	10	3	0	4	1	1	.364	.600
Bonilla, B#	.125	8	1	0	0	0	2	.125	.125
Borders, Pat	.000	6	0	0	0	0	2	.000	.000
Bordick, Mike	.333	6	2	0	0	1	1	.429	.500
Bournigal, R	.333	6	2	0	1	0	0	.333	.333
Brosius, S	.571	7	4	1	3	2	3	.667	1.000
Brumfield, J	.000	9	0	0	1	2	1	.182	.000
Buhner, Jay	.222	9	2	0	1	3	3	.462	.333
Canseco, Jose	.400	5	2	1	2	0	1	.333	1.000
Carter, Joe	.231	13	3	0	0	0	4	.231	.385
Cedeno, D#	.286	7	2	0	0	0	1	.286	.286
Cirillo, Jeff	.500	4	2	0	1	2	0	.667	.750
Cordova, M	.000	5	0	0	0	1	1	.167	.000
Curtis, Chad	.500	10	5	0	2	2	0	.538	.700
Davis, Chili#	.455	11	5	1	4	0	4	.455	.727
Devereaux, M	.286	7	2	1	1	3	0	.500	.714
DiSarcina, G	.273	11	3	1	1	0	0	.273	.545
Durham, Ray*	.500	4	2	0	1	1	0	.500	1.000
Edmonds, Jim*	.000	6	0	0	0	4	1	.400	.000
Erstad, Darin*	.143	7	1	0	0	0	2	.143	.143
Espinoza, A	.000	9	0	0	0	1	0	.000	.000
Fielder, C	.143	7	1	0	0	1	2	.250	.143
Franco, Julio	.200	10	2	0	2	3	2	.385	.200
Frye, Jeff	.800	5	4	0	1	1	1	.833	1.000
Fryman, T	.333	9	3	0	1	1	3	.400	.444
Gates, Brent#	.333	3	1	0	1	0	0	.500	.333
Giambi, Jason*	.429	7	3	0	0	0	2	.429	.571
Gomez, Chris	.000	4	0	0	0	2	1	.333	.000
Gonzalez, A	.273	11	3	0	0	1	2	.333	.273
Goodwin, Tom*	.400	5	2	0	1	0	0	.400	.600
Greene, Todd	.167	6	1	1	1	0	2	.167	.667
Griffey Jr, K*	.222	9	2	1	3	1	2	.300	.556
Guillen, O*	.000	6	0	0	0	0	0	.000	.000
Hamilton, D*	.200	5	1	0	0	1	1	.333	.400
Hoiles, Chris	.400	5	2	1	1	2	0	.571	1.000
Hollins, Dave#	.250	4	1	0	2	0	2	.400	.500
Howard, Dave*	1.000	4	4	0	2	1	0	1.000	1.750
Hudler, Rex	.000	5	0	0	1	0	3	.000	.000
Hunter, Brian	.000	5	0	0	1	0	0	.000	.000
Jaha, John	.000	6	0	0	0	2	2	.250	.000
Johnson, L*	.125	8	1	0	0	1	3	.222	.125
Karkovice, M	.286	7	2	0	0	1	3	.375	.429
Knoblauch, C	.714	7	5	0	1	3	2	.800	1.000
Lofton, Kenny*	.231	13	3	0	1	2	4	.333	.462
Malave, Jose	.000	5	0	0	0	0	2	.000	.000
Martin, N	.200	10	2	1	4	0	4	.182	.500
Martinez, Da*	.400	5	2	0	2	1	1	.500	.800
Martinez, E	.250	8	2	1	1	5	1	.538	.625
Martinez, T*	.333	6	2	0	2	1	4	.429	.333
Mashore, D	.333	6	2	0	0	0	2	.333	.333
Matheny, Mike	.200	5	1	0	0	0	0	.333	.200
McGwire, Mark	.400	5	2	1	1	2	2	.571	1.000
Meares, Pat	.200	5	1	0	1	1	1	.286	.400
Mieske, Matt	.429	7	3	1	2	1	1	.500	.857
Mouton, Lyle	.286	7	2	0	0	1	3	.375	.286
Munoz, Pedro	.167	6	1	0	0	0	1	.167	.333
Murray, Eddie#	.167	12	2	0	0	0	1	.167	.167
Naehring, Tim	.200	5	1	0	1	1	0	.200	.200
Nixon, Otis#	.400	10	4	0	3	0	3	.538	.400
Norman, Les	.167	6	1	0	0	0	1	.286	.167
O'Brien, C	.182	11	2	0	0	0	2	.250	.273
O'Neill, Paul*	.333	3	1	0	0	2	1	.600	.333
Offerman, J#	.000	6	0	0	0	0	0	.000	.000
Palmeiro, R*	.250	8	2	0	0	1	1	.333	.375
Paquette, Robert	.375	8	3	1	1	0	1	.375	.750
Perez, Robert	.250	12	3	0	0	0	2	.250	.250
Perez, Tomas#	.000	9	0	0	0	1	1	.100	.000
Phillips, T#	.400	5	2	0	0	3	0	.625	.800
Raines, Tim*	.200	5	1	0	2	2	0	.429	.200
Ramirez, M	.308	13	4	0	0	2	2	.400	.308
Randa, Joe	.250	4	1	0	1	0	0	.200	.500
Ripken, Billy	.333	6	2	0	0	0	1	.333	.333
Ripken, Cal	.143	7	1	0	0	1	1	.250	.143
Rodriguez, Al	.000	4	0	0	0	3	0	.429	.000
Salmon, Tim	.375	8	3	0	0	4	0	.615	.375
Samuel, Juan	.125	16	2	0	0	2	5	.300	.125
Seitzer, K	.333	6	2	0	1	0	0	.333	.333
Sheets, Andy	.000	5	0	0	1	2	2	.250	.000
Snopek, Chris	.600	5	3	0	1	0	0	.600	.800
Snow, J.T.#	.375	8	3	0	2	0	1	.444	.375
Sojo, Luis	.500	12	6	2	6	0	0	.500	1.083
Sorrento, P*	.182	11	2	0	1	0	4	.182	.273
Sprague, Ed	.333	15	5	0	2	0	1	.333	.333

Darren Oliver, Rangers — LHP

Batter	Avg	AB	H	HR	BI	BB	SO	OBP	Slg
Stanley, Mike	.250	4	1	0	2	2	2	.571	.250
Steinbach, T	.500	8	2	2	3	1	0	.333	1.000
Tartabull, D	.200	5	1	0	1	2	1	.429	.200
Thomas, Frank	.125	8	1	0	0	1	0	.222	.125
Thome, Jim*	.000	7	0	0	0	1	2	.125	.000
Trammell, A	.125	8	1	0	0	0	2	.125	.125
Valentin, Jhn	.400	5	2	0	1	1	0	.500	.400
Vaughn, Mo*	.286	7	2	0	0	0	2	.286	.286
Velarde, R	.333	6	2	0	1	1	0	.429	.333
Ventura, R*	.273	11	3	1	4	0	5	.273	.545
Vina, F*	.375	8	3	0	0	1	1	.375	.375
Vizquel, Omar	.222	9	2	0	0	2	0	.417	.222
Walbeck, Matt#	.500	4	2	0	1	1	0	.600	.750
Williams, Ber#	.400	5	2	1	4	0	0	.400	1.000
Williams, Ger	.286	7	2	0	0	0	0	.286	.286
Wilson, Dan	.333	12	4	0	3	0	0	.333	.333
Young, Ern	.000	4	0	0	0	3	2	.429	.000

Gregg Olson, Astros — RHP

Batter	Avg	AB	H	HR	BI	BB	SO	OBP	Slg
Alomar, R#	.250	8	2	0	1	1	1	.333	.375
Alomar Jr, S	.500	8	4	0	3	2	2	.600	.500
Amaral, Rich	.500	6	3	0	0	0	1	.500	.833
Baerga, C#	.083	12	1	1	2	0	5	.083	.333
Baines, H*	.333	9	3	1	3	1	1	.400	.667
Belle, Albert	.000	8	0	0	0	1	1	.111	.000
Berroa, G	.000	5	0	0	0	0	0	.000	.000
Bichette, D	.100	10	1	0	0	0	3	.100	.100
Boggs, Wade*	.300	10	3	0	1	2	0	.417	.300
Borders, Pat	.667	6	4	1	3	1	0	.714	1.167
Bordick, Mike	.250	8	2	0	0	0	1	.250	.250
Buhner, Jay	.167	12	2	0	0	2	5	.286	.250
Burks, Ellis	.231	13	3	0	0	1	3	.286	.231
Canseco, Jose	.182	11	2	0	2	3	4	.357	.273
Carter, Joe	.273	11	3	0	1	0	2	.273	.455
Cole, Alex*	.000	5	0	0	0	0	1	.000	.000
Cora, Joey#	.400	5	2	0	1	1	0	.500	.600
Cordova, M	.143	7	1	0	4	1	0	.250	.286
Davis, Chili#	.250	8	2	0	2	1	2	.333	.375
Deer, Rob	.333	6	2	1	1	1	3	.429	.500
Durham, Ray#	.600	5	3	0	1	1	1	.667	.600
Eisenreich, J*	.333	3	1	0	0	4	0	.714	.667
Fielder, C	.111	9	1	0	0	1	4	.200	.111
Franco, Julio	.000	4	0	0	0	2	3	.333	.000
Fryman, T	.000	8	0	0	1	1	4	.100	.000
Gaetti, Gary	.231	13	3	0	0	0	0	.231	.308
Gagne, Greg	.286	7	2	0	1	1	3	.375	.286
Gallego, Mike	.250	4	1	0	2	1	2	.400	.250
Gonzales, R	.200	5	1	0	0	0	1	.200	.200
Gonzalez, J	.400	5	2	0	0	0	1	.400	.400
Greenwell, M*	.200	10	2	0	0	0	1	.273	.300
Greer, Rusty*	.400	5	2	0	2	0	0	.400	.400
Griffey Jr, K*	.000	5	0	0	0	4	0	.444	.000
Guillen, O*	.357	14	5	0	1	0	1	.357	.357
Hamilton, D*	.000	5	0	0	0	1	2	.167	.000
Henderson, R	.375	8	3	0	0	1	2	.444	.375
Howell, Jack*	.167	6	1	0	1	0	2	.167	.167
Incaviglia, P	.000	8	0	0	0	0	6	.000	.000
Jaha, John	.667	3	2	0	0	2	0	.800	.667
James, Dion*	.143	7	1	0	0	0	1	.143	.143
Johnson, L*	.286	7	2	0	0	0	2	.286	.286
Joyner, Wally*	.167	12	2	0	2	0	3	.154	.167
Karkovice, R	.333	9	3	0	2	1	1	.400	.444
Kelly, Pat	.250	4	1	0	0	1	0	.400	.250
Kelly, R	.222	9	2	1	2	0	3	.222	.556
Knoblauch, C	.273	11	3	0	1	1	2	.333	.273
Liriano, N#	.286	7	2	0	4	0	2	.286	.571
Lofton, Kenny*	.000	5	0	0	0	1	1	.167	.000
Macfarlane, M	.333	6	2	0	1	2	2	.500	.667
Martinez, E	.400	10	4	0	0	2	0	.400	.400
Martinez, T*	.125	8	1	0	1	0	4	.125	.250
Mayne, Brent*	.333	6	2	0	1	0	1	.333	.333
McGwire, Mark	.400	10	4	1	4	3	3	.538	.700
McLemore, M#	.000	5	0	0	0	0	2	.000	.000
McRae, Brian*	.143	7	1	0	1	1	3	.250	.143
Molitor, Paul	.182	11	2	0	1	0	0	.250	.182
Myers, Greg*	.200	5	1	0	0	0	0	.200	.400
Olerud, John*	.625	8	5	0	3	0	1	.625	.625
Palmeiro, R*	.083	12	1	0	2	1	2	.154	.083
Palmer, Dean	.167	6	1	0	0	0	3	.167	.167
Phillips, T#	.333	12	4	0	2	2	0	.429	.417
Plantier, P*	.167	6	1	0	0	1	3	.286	.167
Polonia, Luis*	.444	9	4	0	0	0	0	.444	.444
Raines, Tim#	.111	9	1	0	2	3	0	.111	.222
Reed, Jody	.400	5	2	0	1	2	1	.571	.600
Seitzer, K	.250	12	3	0	0	1	3	.308	.333
Sierra, Ruben*	.000	12	0	0	1	0	3	.077	.000
Sojo, Luis	.250	4	1	0	0	1	0	.400	.250
Sorrento, P*	.250	4	1	1	2	1	2	.333	1.000
Spiers, Bill*	.200	5	1	0	2	0	1	.167	.200
Sprague, Ed	.200	5	1	0	2	2	3	.429	.400

Gregg Olson, Astros — RHP

Batter	Avg	AB	H	HR	BI	BB	SO	OBP	Slg
Stanley, Mike	.333	3	1	0	0	3	1	.667	.333
Steinbach, T	.250	12	3	1	5	2	3	.357	.500
Stillwell, K#	.000	9	0	0	0	1	7	.100	.000
Strange, Doug*	.400	5	2	1	2	0	0	.400	1.000
Surhoff, B.J.*	.100	10	1	0	1	3	0	.286	.200
Tartabull, D	.400	15	6	1	7	3	4	.500	.600
Tettleton, M#	.333	6	2	1	4	1	2	.429	.833
Thomas, Frank	.273	11	3	1	1	2	2	.385	.545
Thome, Jim*	.143	7	1	1	4	1	2	.250	.571
Trammell, A	.375	8	3	0	4	2	3	.500	.500
Valle, Dave	.333	9	3	0	0	0	0	.333	.444
Vaughn, Greg	.000	4	0	0	0	1	0	.200	.000
Vaughn, Mo*	.143	7	1	0	1	1	4	.250	.286
Velarde, R	.200	5	1	0	0	2	2	.429	.400
Ventura, R*	.400	10	4	0	1	1	0	.455	.400
Vizquel, Omar	.167	6	1	0	1	0	1	.167	.167
Weiss, Walt#	.143	7	1	0	1	1	0	.250	.143
White, Devon#	.133	15	2	0	0	2	7	.235	.200
Whiten, Mark#	.250	4	1	0	0	1	1	.400	.500

Mike Oquist, Padres — RHP

Batter	Avg	AB	H	HR	BI	BB	SO	OBP	Slg
Alomar, R#	.667	9	6	0	2	2	1	.727	.667
Bautista, D	.167	6	1	0	0	0	2	.167	.333
Belle, Albert	.600	5	3	2	3	0	0	.600	2.000
Blowers, Mike	.500	4	2	0	2	0	0	.500	.750
Borders, Pat	.125	8	1	0	0	0	1	.125	.375
Canseco, Jose	.500	4	2	0	0	1	0	.600	.500
Carter, Joe	.333	6	2	0	3	1	1	.400	.333
Cordova, M	.000	6	0	0	0	0	3	.000	.000
Fermin, Felix	.800	5	4	0	1	0	0	.833	.800
Fielder, C	.600	5	3	1	3	2	1	.625	1.400
Fryman, T	.625	8	5	0	0	0	1	.625	.875
Gallego, Mike	.000	5	0	0	0	0	2	.000	.000
Gomez, Chris	.500	4	2	0	2	1	0	.600	.750
Green, Shawn*	.000	5	0	0	0	0	0	.000	.000
Greenwell, M*	.200	5	1	0	1	0	0	.200	.200
Griffey Jr, K*	.600	5	3	0	2	0	0	.500	.600
Jefferson, R*	.000	4	0	0	0	1	3	.200	.000
Kelly, Pat	.500	8	4	0	0	2	0	.500	.500
Knoblauch, C	.167	6	1	0	1	3	1	.444	.167
Leius, Scott	.333	6	2	0	2	0	1	.333	.833
Leyritz, Jim	.429	7	3	0	2	2	2	.556	.571
Lofton, Kenny*	.250	4	1	0	1	0	0	.200	.250
Martinez, E	.143	7	1	0	0	0	3	.143	.143
Martinez, T*	.400	5	2	0	2	0	0	.400	.600
Meares, Pat	.500	6	3	1	4	0	0	.500	1.167
Molitor, Paul	.182	11	2	0	0	0	0	.182	.273
Munoz, Pedro	.167	6	1	0	1	0	4	.286	.167
Murray, Eddie#	.500	4	2	1	2	1	0	.600	1.250
Olerud, John*	.000	5	0	0	0	3	2	.375	.000
Phillips, T#	.143	7	1	0	1	2	2	.333	.143
Ramirez, M	.500	4	2	0	3	1	0	.600	.750
Sprague, Ed	.333	9	3	1	4	1	0	.500	.778
Tartabull, D	.143	7	1	0	0	1	1	.250	.143
Tettleton, M#	.333	3	1	0	0	2	0	.667	.667
Thome, Jim*	.000	4	0	0	0	1	0	.200	.000
Valentin, Jhn	.200	5	1	0	0	1	1	.333	.200
Vaughn, Mo*	.333	3	1	1	1	2	0	.600	1.333
Velarde, R	.000	6	0	0	0	0	0	.000	.000
Vizquel, Omar	.333	6	2	0	0	1	0	.429	.333
Walbeck, Matt#	.667	6	4	0	1	0	0	.667	1.167
White, Devon#	.143	7	1	0	0	2	1	.333	.143
Williams, Ber*	.000	7	0	0	1	1	2	.125	.000
Williams, Ger	.333	6	2	1	4	0	1	.333	.833
Wilson, Dan	.000	6	0	0	0	0	3	.000	.000

Jesse Orosco, Orioles — LHP

Batter	Avg	AB	H	HR	BI	BB	SO	OBP	Slg
Alomar, R#	.000	9	0	0	1	0	2	.000	.000
Anderson, Brd*	.200	10	2	0	0	1	4	.273	.300
Baines, H*	.222	9	2	1	3	0	4	.222	.556
Boggs, Wade*	.143	14	2	0	2	3	2	.294	.143
Bonds, Barry*	.176	17	3	1	3	1	6	.222	.353
Bonilla, B#	.182	11	2	0	0	1	1	.308	.182
Borders, Pat	.000	4	0	0	0	1	1	.200	.000
Bordick, Mike	.200	5	1	0	0	1	1	.333	.200
Brosius, S	.000	4	0	0	0	1	2	.200	.000
Buhner, Jay	.250	8	2	0	0	1	4	.333	.375
Burks, Ellis	.375	8	3	1	1	2	2	.500	.875
Candaele, C#	.333	6	2	0	0	0	1	.333	.333
Canseco, Jose	.222	9	2	1	1	2	5	.364	.778
Carter, Joe	.000	3	0	0	0	2	1	.400	.000
Clark, Tony#	.250	4	1	0	0	1	2	.400	.250
Clark, Will*	.250	16	4	0	4	2	3	.333	.375
Coleman, E#	.200	20	4	0	2	2	7	.273	.200
Cora, Joey#	.167	6	1	0	1	1	1	.375	.333
Cuyler, Milt*	.500	4	2	0	2	1	1	.500	1.000
Davis, Chili#	.063	16	1	0	1	5	8	.286	.063
Davis, Eric	.500	4	2	0	3	0	0	.714	.500
Dawson, Andre	.545	11	6	1	3	1	2	.583	.909

Batter	Avg	AB	H	HR	BI	BB	SO	OBP	Slg
Devereaux, M	.182	11	2	1	3	1	1	.231	.455
Duncan, M	.286	7	2	0	0	1	4	.375	.429
Edmonds, Jim*	.400	5	2	1	3	0	1	.400	1.000
Eisenreich, J*	.375	8	3	0	1	0	1	.375	.375
Espinoza, A	.250	8	2	0	0	0	0	.250	.250
Fermin, Felix	.250	4	1	0	0	1	1	.400	.250
Franco, Julio	.200	5	1	0	0	2	2	.429	.200
Fryman, T	.000	3	0	0	0	2	1	.400	.000
Gaetti, Gary	.500	8	4	1	3	2	2	.600	.875
Gagne, Greg	.333	9	3	0	0	0	3	.333	.556
Galarraga, A	.429	7	3	0	1	0	1	.429	.571
Gallego, Mike	.500	5	0	0	0	0	1	.000	.000
Gomez, Leo	.000	4	0	0	1	0	0	.000	.000
Gonzalez, J	.250	8	2	0	2	1	2	.333	.375
Goodwin, Tom*	.000	3	0	0	0	2	1	.400	.000
Greenwell, M*	.158	19	3	1	4	2	1	.238	.368
Greer, Rusty*	.200	5	1	0	0	1	0	.333	.200
Griffey Jr, K*	.438	16	7	0	1	2	4	.526	.438
Guillen, O*	.000	13	0	0	0	0	4	.000	.000
Gwynn, Tony*	.375	16	6	1	4	2	0	.444	.563
Hall, Mel*	.200	5	1	0	1	2	2	.429	.200
Hayes, C	.200	5	1	0	0	0	0	.200	.200
Henderson, R	.250	4	1	0	0	1	2	.400	.250
Hill, G	.000	4	0	0	1	1	3	.167	.000
Hoiles, Chris	.167	6	1	0	1	1	0	.286	.167
Howard, Dave#	.000	6	0	0	0	1	2	.143	.000
Howell, Jack*	.000	5	0	0	0	1	2	.167	.000
Incaviglia, P	.400	5	2	0	0	1	0	.500	.400
James, Dion*	.250	4	1	0	1	1	2	.400	.250
Javier, Stan#	.400	5	2	0	1	0	2	.400	.400
Johnson, L*	.333	12	4	0	0	0	4	.333	.333
Joyner, Wally*	.200	15	3	1	2	3	4	.333	.400
Karkovice, R	.143	7	1	1	1	0	4	.143	.571
Kelly, Pat	.000	5	0	0	0	0	4	.000	.000
Kelly, R	.400	5	2	0	1	0	0	.400	.400
Kreuter, Chad#	.750	4	3	0	0	1	0	.800	1.000
Lockhart, K*	.200	5	1	0	0	0	2	.200	.400
Lofton, Kenny*	.091	11	1	0	0	1	2	.167	.091
Macfarlane, M	.125	8	1	0	0	0	3	.222	.250
Martinez, Da*	.600	5	3	0	0	1	2	.667	.600
Martinez, E	.250	4	1	1	2	5	0	.667	1.000
Martinez, T*	.143	14	2	0	1	1	5	.200	.214
McGee, Willie*	.167	24	4	1	2	2	9	.231	.292
McGriff, Fred*	.200	10	2	1	1	1	4	.273	.500
McLemore, M#	.143	7	1	0	0	0	3	.143	.143
McRae, Brian#	.167	6	1	0	0	0	3	.167	.167
Mitchell, K	.333	6	2	0	0	0	3	.333	.500
Molitor, Paul	.400	5	2	0	0	0	1	.400	.800
Naehring, Tim	.000	4	0	0	0	1	1	.200	.000
Nilsson, Dave*	.286	7	2	0	1	0	3	.286	.429
O'Brien, C	.000	5	0	0	0	1	4	.167	.000
O'Neill, Paul*	.000	9	0	0	0	5	2	.357	.000
Olerud, John*	.300	10	3	0	1	2	2	.385	.300
Orsulak, Joe*	.143	7	1	0	0	3	1	.400	.286
Palmeiro, R*	.200	15	3	0	4	2	3	.294	.267
Palmer, Dean	.250	8	2	2	5	1	3	.333	1.000
Pena, Tony	.250	20	5	0	4	3	3	.348	.300
Pendleton, T#	.063	16	1	0	0	4	4	.250	.063
Phillips, T#	.214	14	3	0	2	3	3	.353	.429
Polonia, Luis*	.333	6	2	0	0	0	0	.333	.333
Raines, Tim#	.167	18	3	1	4	2	7	.286	.333
Reed, Jody	.400	5	2	0	1	1	0	.429	.600
Ripken, B	.200	5	1	0	0	0	2	.200	.200
Ripken, Cal	.133	15	2	0	2	0	4	.188	.133
Rodriguez, I	.000	5	1	0	0	2	2	.429	.200
Samuel, Juan	.188	16	3	0	0	1	6	.235	.250
Sandberg, R	.400	5	2	0	0	1	0	.500	.400
Schu, Rick	.125	8	1	0	0	0	0	.125	.125
Seitzer, K	.333	6	2	0	0	1	1	.429	.500
Sierra, Ruben#	.333	18	6	1	7	0	0	.333	.667
Smith, Ozzie*	.222	18	4	0	2	7	2	.440	.278
Snow, J.T.#	.167	6	1	0	0	1	2	.286	.167
Sorrento, P*	.250	8	2	0	4	0	3	.222	.375
Sosa, Sammy	.250	4	1	0	0	0	2	.250	.500
Spiers, Bill*	.333	6	2	0	0	0	3	.333	.333
Stanley, Mike	.400	10	4	1	2	0	2	.400	.800
Steinbach, T	.000	7	0	0	0	0	2	.000	.000
Stillwell, K#	.167	6	1	0	0	1	2	.286	.167
Surhoff, B.J.*	.200	10	2	0	0	0	2	.200	.300
Tartabull, D	.600	5	3	2	6	3	1	.750	2.000
Tettleton, M#	.300	10	3	0	2	0	3	.273	.400
Thomas, Frank	.400	5	2	0	0	0	0	.400	.400
Thome, Jim*	.000	9	0	0	0	5	6	.357	.000
Thompson, Rob	.750	4	3	1	2	1	1	.667	1.500
Trammell, A	.000	8	0	0	0	2	2	.200	.000
Valentin, Jhn	.286	7	2	0	1	1	1	.375	.429
Valle, Dave	.250	8	2	0	2	1	2	.333	.250
Vaughn, Mo*	.200	15	3	1	3	2	3	.294	.400
Velarde, R	.250	4	1	1	1	0	1	.400	1.000
Ventura, R*	.500	12	6	2	4	3	3	.600	1.250
Vizquel, Omar#	.273	11	3	0	1	1	2	.333	.273

Batter	Avg	AB	H	HR	BI	BB	SO	OBP	Slg
Wallach, Tim	.250	8	2	1	2	1	2	.333	.750
Weiss, Walt#	.000	6	0	0	1	0	0	.000	.000
White, Devon#	.222	9	2	0	0	1	3	.300	.222
Whiten, Mark#	.000	2	0	0	0	2	1	.667	.000
Williams, Ger	.000	5	0	0	0	2	1	.286	.000

Donovan Osborne, Cardinals   LHP

Batter	Avg	AB	H	HR	BI	BB	SO	OBP	Slg
Alou, Moises	.417	12	5	1	2	1	2	.462	.917
Amaro, Ruben#	.333	12	4	0	2	0	2	.333	.667
Andrews, S	.286	7	2	0	2	1	2	.375	.429
Anthony, Eric*	.182	11	2	0	1	1	3	.250	.273
Arias, Alex	.083	12	1	0	0	0	1	.083	.083
Ashley, Billy	.600	5	3	1	1	0	0	.600	1.200
Aude, Rich	.333	6	2	0	1	0	2	.333	.500
Aurilia, Rich	.333	6	2	0	1	0	1	.333	.333
Ausmus, Brad	.125	8	1	1	1	1	1	.222	.500
Bagwell, Jeff	.217	23	5	0	4	6	8	.367	.348
Barberie, B#	.375	8	3	0	0	0	1	.375	.375
Batiste, Kim	.000	5	0	0	0	0	0	.000	.000
Bell, Derek	.143	28	4	0	1	0	6	.143	.143
Bell, Jay	.222	27	6	0	0	3	6	.300	.259
Belliard, R	.167	6	1	0	0	0	3	.167	.167
Berry, Sean	.538	13	7	1	3	1	1	.571	1.077
Bichette, D	.167	6	1	0	0	3	2	.500	.333
Biggio, Craig	.241	29	7	1	3	3	4	.324	.379
Blauser, Jeff	.273	11	3	1	1	2	2	.385	.545
Bogar, Tim	.286	7	2	0	1	0	1	.286	.286
Bonds, Barry*	.250	24	6	1	4	4	2	.357	.500
Bonilla, B#	.125	16	2	1	2	2	0	.222	.313
Boone, Bret	.214	14	3	0	1	1	0	.267	.214
Brogna, Rico*	.200	5	1	0	0	0	1	.200	.200
Brumfield, J	.125	8	1	0	0	1	1	.222	.125
Butler, Brett*	.200	15	3	0	0	1	5	.250	.467
Caminiti, Ken#	.350	20	7	3	5	1	1	.364	.850
Carr, Chuck	.167	6	1	0	0	0	3	.286	.167
Carreon, Mark	.273	11	3	0	2	0	0	.273	.364
Castilla, V	.333	6	2	0	1	0	1	.333	.500
Castillo, L#	.500	6	3	0	0	0	1	.500	.500
Cedeno, A	.400	15	6	1	2	0	0	.438	.733
Cianfrocco, A	.182	11	2	0	0	1	5	.250	.273
Clark, Phil	.571	7	4	1	2	0	0	.571	1.286
Clark, Will*	.231	13	3	0	0	1	4	.286	.231
Clayton, R	.308	13	4	0	2	1	3	.357	.385
Colbrunn, G	.643	14	9	2	4	0	2	.643	1.143
Coleman, V#	.571	7	4	1	1	0	0	.571	1.286
Conine, Jeff	.353	17	6	2	3	2	4	.421	.706
Cordero, Wil	.000	4	0	0	0	0	2	.000	.000
Daulton, D*	.455	11	5	2	7	4	2	.600	1.091
Davis, Eric	.125	16	2	0	0	2	7	.222	.125
Decker, Steve	.222	9	2	0	0	0	0	.222	.222
DeShields, D*	.545	11	6	1	2	0	1	.545	.909
Doster, David	.500	6	3	0	1	0	0	.500	.667
Duncan, M	.435	23	10	2	7	1	1	.458	.739
Dykstra, L*	.400	15	6	1	3	3	2	.500	.667
Eusebio, Tony	.167	6	1	0	0	0	0	.167	.167
Everett, Carl#	.400	5	2	1	1	0	1	.400	1.200
Finley, Steve*	.227	22	5	0	0	1	5	.261	.364
Flaherty, J	.000	5	0	0	0	0	1	.000	.000
Fonville, C#	.286	7	2	0	0	0	1	.286	.286
Galarraga, A	.400	10	4	1	0	0	4	.400	.700
Gant, Ron	.294	17	5	2	6	0	2	.294	.824
Garcia, C	.400	20	8	1	3	0	1	.400	.700
Girardi, Joe	.400	5	2	0	0	0	1	.400	.400
Glanville, D	.167	6	1	0	0	0	1	.167	.333
Gomez, Leo	.125	8	1	0	0	2	3	.300	.125
Gonzalez, L*	.273	11	3	0	1	1	3	.333	.545
Grace, Mark*	.222	18	4	1	4	0	2	.211	.389
Grissom, M	.250	16	4	1	2	0	3	.250	.500
Grudzielanek	.333	9	3	0	1	1	1	.400	.444
Gutierrez, R	.250	12	3	0	1	1	4	.308	.250
Gwynn, Tony*	.333	36	12	0	0	1	0	.351	.361
Hayes, C	.286	14	4	2	5	1	3	.333	.714
Henderson, R	.286	7	2	0	0	5	0	.583	.286
Hernandez, Ca	.000	4	0	0	1	1	0	.200	.000
Hernandez, Jo	.167	6	1	0	0	0	1	.167	.333
Hill, G	.500	10	5	1	5	3	1	.615	.800
Hollandsworth*	.000	4	0	0	0	1	2	.000	.000
Hollins, Dave#	.400	15	6	0	1	1	3	.471	.600
Hundley, Todd*	.250	8	2	0	0	0	2	.250	.375
Hunter, Brian	.545	11	6	2	2	0	1	.545	1.091
Hunter, Bri L	.118	17	2	0	1	1	2	.158	.176
Incaviglia, P	.167	12	2	0	1	0	2	.167	.167
Javier, Stan#	.222	9	2	0	0	3	0	.417	.333
Jefferies, G#	.333	9	3	0	1	0	0	.333	.444
Jones, C	.400	5	2	0	1	0	0	.400	.400
Jones, Chris	.000	5	0	0	1	0	2	.000	.000
Jordan, Ricky	.231	13	3	0	1	0	2	.231	.308
Joyner, Wally*	.000	9	0	0	0	0	2	.000	.000
Justice, Dave*	.333	18	6	1	4	0	2	.316	.556
Karros, Eric	.238	21	5	1	3	1	1	.273	.381

Donovan Osborne, Cardinals — LHP

Batter	Avg	AB	H	HR	BI	BB	SO	OBP	Slg
Kendall, J	.400	5	2	0	1	0	0	.400	.800
Kent, Jeff	.333	6	2	0	0	0	3	.333	.500
King, Jeff	.087	23	2	0	0	1	1	.125	.087
Knorr, Randy	.333	6	2	0	1	0	2	.333	.333
Lansing, Mike	.462	13	6	0	2	0	0	.462	.538
Larkin, Barry	.273	22	6	3	4	3	4	.346	.682
Lemke, Mark#	.188	16	3	0	0	0	0	.188	.188
Lewis, Darren	.067	15	1	0	0	1	2	.125	.200
Lopez, Javy	.400	5	2	0	3	0	1	.400	.400
Magadan, Dave*	.000	9	0	0	0	0	2	.000	.000
Manwaring, K	.273	22	6	0	0	1	3	.304	.455
May, Derrick*	.400	10	4	0	2	0	0	.400	.400
McGee, Willie#	.333	12	4	0	0	1	4	.385	.333
McGriff, Fred*	.136	22	3	0	1	1	4	.174	.136
McRae, Brian#	.308	13	4	0	0	0	1	.308	.308
Merced, O*	.267	15	4	1	3	4	2	.421	.533
Miller, Orl	.333	6	2	0	0	1	1	.429	.500
Mondesi, Raul	.444	9	4	1	3	2	1	.583	.778
Morandini, M*	.091	11	1	0	0	0	0	.091	.091
Morris, Hal*	.462	13	6	0	0	1	1	.500	.538
Mouton, James	.350	20	7	0	3	1	3	.381	.450
Murray, Eddie#	.364	11	4	0	2	1	0	.462	.545
Newfield, M	.000	4	0	0	0	1	2	.200	.000
Nixon, Otis#	.385	13	5	0	1	1	0	.429	.462
O'Brien, C	.200	5	1	0	0	0	0	.200	.200
O'Neill, Paul*	.500	8	4	0	4	0	0	.500	.750
Offerman, J#	.286	14	4	0	2	2	2	.375	.500
Oliver, Joe	.375	8	3	0	1	2	0	.455	.500
Otero, Ricky*	.167	6	1	0	0	0	1	.167	.167
Owens, Eric	.143	7	1	0	0	0	1	.143	.143
Owens, J	.167	6	1	0	2	0	1	.167	.333
Pendleton, T#	.167	18	3	1	2	1	1	.211	.333
Perez, E	.400	5	2	1	1	1	1	.500	1.000
Piazza, Mike	.308	13	4	0	0	2	0	.400	.385
Plantier, P*	.250	4	1	1	4	1	2	.400	1.000
Reed, Jody	.111	18	2	0	1	0	0	.158	.111
Renteria, E	.444	9	4	0	0	0	3	.444	.778
Roberts, Bip#	.143	7	1	0	0	1	1	.250	.143
Rodriguez, H*	.417	12	5	1	3	0	3	.417	.833
Sabo, Chris	.417	12	5	1	1	1	0	.462	.833
Sanchez, Rey	.250	12	3	0	1	1	0	.308	.417
Sandberg, R	.538	13	7	2	6	4	2	.647	1.154
Sanders, R	.353	17	6	0	2	0	4	.353	.471
Santiago, B	.227	22	5	1	3	0	6	.227	.409
Scarsone, S	.125	8	1	0	0	1	0	.222	.125
Schofield, D	.000	6	0	0	0	1	1	.143	.000
Segui, David#	.143	7	1	1	2	0	1	.125	.571
Servais, S	.263	19	5	0	3	1	4	.300	.316
Sheffield, G	.360	25	9	2	8	2	2	.407	.640
Shipley, C	.227	22	5	0	1	1	2	.261	.318
Simms, Mike	.286	7	2	1	1	1	2	.375	.857
Slaught, Don	.200	15	3	0	0	1	1	.333	.200
Sosa, Sammy	.286	14	4	1	3	2	1	.375	.500
Stankiewicz	.250	4	1	0	1	1	1	.400	.250
Stillwell, K#	.125	8	1	0	0	0	1	.125	.125
Stocker, K#	.200	5	1	0	1	3	2	.500	.400
Strawberry, D*	.400	5	2	0	1	1	0	.500	.600
Thompson, Rob	.250	12	3	0	2	1	2	.308	.333
Timmons, O	.167	6	1	0	0	0	0	.167	.167
Vaughn, Greg	.200	5	1	0	1	1	0	.333	.200
Vizcaino, J#	.286	7	2	0	1	3	0	.500	.286
Walker, Larry*	.357	14	5	1	2	0	2	.357	.571
Wallach, Tim	.176	17	3	0	2	0	5	.176	.235
Walton, J	.667	9	6	0	1	0	1	.667	.889
Webster, J	.333	6	2	0	1	0	1	.333	.333
Wehner, John	.250	12	3	0	0	2	0	.357	.250
White, Devon#	.250	12	3	0	0	0	2	.250	.333
White, R	.500	6	3	0	1	0	0	.500	.500
Wilkins, Rick*	.167	6	1	1	1	1	2	.286	.667
Williams, Ma	.286	14	4	2	6	1	1	.375	.786
Young, Eric	.400	10	4	0	2	2	2	.500	.400
Young, Kevin	.091	11	1	0	0	0	7	.091	.091
Zeile, Todd	.500	6	3	1	2	0	0	.500	1.000

Al Osuna, Padres — LHP

Batter	Avg	AB	H	HR	BI	BB	SO	OBP	Slg
Bell, Jay	.286	7	2	0	1	2	1	.444	.429
Bonds, Barry*	.357	14	5	2	2	5	3	.526	.786
Bonilla, B#	.111	9	1	1	2	2	0	.250	.444
Butler, Brett*	.000	7	0	0	0	5	3	.417	.000
Clark, Will*	.429	7	3	1	3	1	0	.500	.857
Daulton, D*	.167	6	1	0	2	2	1	.333	.167
DeShields, D*	.750	4	3	0	1	1	0	.800	.750
Duncan, M	.000	5	0	0	0	0	0	.000	.000
Gant, Ron	.250	4	1	1	1	4	1	.400	1.000
Grace, Mark*	.500	8	4	0	1	2	0	.556	.625
Grissom, M	.000	6	0	0	1	3	0	.143	.000
Gwynn, Tony*	.333	12	4	0	1	0	0	.333	.333
Harris, Lenny*	.429	7	3	0	1	0	1	.500	.429
Javier, Stan#	.000	5	0	0	0	0	2	.000	.000
Jordan, Ricky	.250	4	1	0	0	1	1	.400	.500

Al Osuna, Padres — LHP

Batter	Avg	AB	H	HR	BI	BB	SO	OBP	Slg
Justice, Dave*	.333	12	4	1	3	4	1	.500	.583
Kent, Jeff	.250	4	1	1	1	1	0	.400	1.000
Lankford, Ray*	.375	8	3	0	1	1	2	.444	.500
Larkin, Barry	.286	7	2	0	0	3	0	.500	.286
Magadan, Dave*	.286	7	2	0	0	0	0	.286	.286
Manwaring, K	1.000	4	4	0	3	1	0	1.000	1.000
Martinez, Da*	.375	8	3	0	3	2	0	.500	.375
May, Derrick*	.200	5	1	0	0	1	0	.200	.200
McGriff, Fred*	.273	11	3	0	1	2	4	.385	.455
Merced, O*	.100	10	2	0	2	2	1	.308	.200
Morandini, M*	.000	6	0	0	0	0	2	.000	.000
Morris, Hal*	.154	13	2	0	2	0	2	.143	.154
Murray, Eddie#	.083	12	1	0	3	1	3	.133	.083
O'Neill, Paul*	.100	10	1	0	0	2	5	.250	.200
Oliver, Joe	.200	5	1	0	0	2	1	.429	.200
Pagnozzi, Tom	.667	3	2	1	1	3	0	.833	2.000
Pendleton, T#	.500	8	4	0	2	1	2	.556	.500
Sabo, Chris	.200	5	1	0	0	1	0	.333	.200
Samuel, Juan	.167	6	1	0	2	1	4	.286	.333
Sandberg, R	.000	6	0	0	0	1	0	.143	.000
Sheffield, G	.000	4	0	0	1	0	2	.000	.000
Slaught, Don	.000	2	0	0	0	3	0	.600	.000
Strawberry, D*	.250	8	2	1	5	1	5	.300	.625
Walker, Larry*	.333	6	2	0	0	1	1	.333	.333
Wilkins, Rick*	.400	5	2	0	1	1	1	.500	.600
Zeile, Todd	.000	5	1	0	0	1	1	.333	.200

Antonio Osuna, Dodgers — RHP

Batter	Avg	AB	H	HR	BI	BB	SO	OBP	Slg
Bell, Jay	.333	6	2	0	2	0	2	.333	.333
Bichette, D	.125	8	1	1	2	1	4	.222	.500
Blauser, Jeff	.167	6	1	0	0	0	0	.167	.167
Burks, Ellis	.000	3	0	0	2	1	1	.167	.000
Castilla, V	.143	7	1	1	2	0	2	.143	.571
Clayton, R	.250	4	1	0	0	1	2	.400	.250
Fletcher, D*	.200	5	1	0	0	0	1	.200	.200
Galarraga, A	.400	5	2	0	1	0	0	.571	.400
Gilkey, B	.600	5	3	2	6	0	1	.600	2.200
Gomez, Chris	.500	4	2	0	2	1	1	.600	.750
Gonzalez, L*	.200	5	1	0	0	0	1	.200	.400
Grissom, M	.222	9	2	0	0	0	0	.222	.333
Hill, G	.200	5	1	1	1	1	2	.333	.800
Johnson, Bri	.167	6	1	0	0	0	1	.167	.167
Jones, C#	.000	4	0	0	0	1	1	.200	.000
Jordan, Brian	.200	5	1	0	1	0	4	.200	.200
Manwaring, K	.600	5	3	0	0	1	0	.600	.600
Reed, Jody	.571	7	4	0	1	1	2	.625	.571
Santiago, B	.400	5	2	0	0	1	0	.500	.400
Servais, S	.000	5	0	0	0	0	1	.000	.000
Sosa, Sammy	.200	5	1	0	1	0	1	.200	.200
Stocker, K#	.333	6	2	0	0	1	0	.333	.500
Weiss, Walt#	.200	5	1	0	0	1	0	.333	.200
Williams, Ma	.200	5	1	0	0	0	2	.200	.200
Zeile, Todd	.000	5	0	0	0	0	2	.000	.000

Lance Painter, Rockies — LHP

Batter	Avg	AB	H	HR	BI	BB	SO	OBP	Slg
Alfonzo, E	.400	5	2	0	0	0	0	.400	.400
Alou, Moises	.625	8	5	0	2	0	2	.625	.750
Anthony, Eric*	.000	6	0	0	0	3	0	.600	.000
Bagwell, Jeff	.500	10	5	1	2	1	1	.545	.900
Barberie, B#	.000	5	0	0	0	2	0	.000	.000
Bell, Derek	.571	7	4	0	1	1	1	.625	.571
Bell, Jay	.286	7	2	0	0	1	0	.375	.286
Biggio, Craig	.222	9	2	1	1	3	0	.417	.667
Blauser, Jeff	.429	7	3	0	2	0	1	.375	.571
Bonilla, B#	.375	8	3	0	2	1	1	.444	.625
Brogna, Rico*	.400	5	2	0	0	1	2	.500	.600
Butler, Brett*	.286	7	2	0	0	0	0	.286	.286
Caminiti, Ken#	.538	13	7	0	5	2	1	.600	.692
Carr, Chuck	.000	5	0	0	0	1	1	.167	.000
Cedeno, A	.111	9	1	0	0	0	2	.111	.222
Conine, Jeff	.500	6	3	1	2	0	0	.500	1.333
Daulton, D*	.500	4	2	1	1	2	0	.714	1.250
Dykstra, L*	.167	6	1	0	0	1	0	.286	.167
Finley, Steve*	.250	8	2	0	0	0	0	.250	.250
Fonville, C#	.167	6	1	0	2	0	3	.167	.167
Garcia, C	.429	7	3	0	0	0	0	.429	.429
Gilkey, B	.500	8	4	1	2	0	0	.444	.875
Gonzalez, L*	.100	10	1	0	0	1	0	.100	.100
Grace, Mark*	.286	7	2	0	2	1	0	.375	.286
Grissom, M	.000	9	0	0	0	0	0	.000	.000
Grudzielanek	.500	6	3	0	0	0	1	.500	.667
Gutierrez, R	.600	5	3	0	0	1	0	.667	.800
Gwynn, Tony*	.333	9	3	0	0	0	0	.333	.333
Incaviglia, P	.750	4	3	0	0	1	0	.800	.750
Jefferies, G#	.000	12	0	0	0	1	0	.000	.000
Jones, C#	.125	8	1	1	1	0	2	.125	.500
Jordan, Brian	.000	5	0	0	0	1	1	.000	.000
Justice, Dave*	.571	7	4	0	1	2	0	.667	.857
Karros, Eric	.200	5	1	0	1	0	0	.286	.400

Lance Painter, Rockies — LHP

Batter	Avg	AB	H	HR	BI	BB	SO	OBP	Slg
Kent, Jeff	.286	7	2	0	0	1	0	.375	.429
King, Jeff	.222	9	2	0	1	0	0	.200	.444
Lansing, Mike	.000	9	0	0	0	1	6	.100	.000
Lemke, Mark#	.429	7	3	0	1	0	0	.429	.429
Lopez, Javy	.143	7	1	1	1	0	0	.143	.571
McGriff, Fred*	.313	16	5	1	6	1	4	.353	.563
McRae, Brian#	.286	7	2	0	1	0	0	.286	.286
Merced, O*	.500	6	3	0	2	2	3	.625	1.167
Mondesi, Raul	.462	6	4	0	1	1	0	.714	1.000
Morandini, M*	.000	5	0	0	0	1	3	.167	.000
Morris, Hal*	.400	5	2	0	0	0	0	.400	.600
Mouton, James	.222	9	2	0	0	0	1	.222	.222
O'Brien, C	.167	6	1	1	1	0	1	.167	.667
Offerman, J#	.333	6	2	0	0	0	1	.333	.333
Pagnozzi, Tom	.600	5	3	0	0	2	1	.714	1.000
Pena, J	.000	5	0	0	0	1	1	.167	.000
Piazza, Mike	.625	8	5	3	6	0	0	.625	1.875
Roberts, Bip#	.600	5	3	0	0	0	0	.600	.600
Rodriguez, H*	.250	4	1	0	0	1	2	.400	.250
Sandberg, R	.000	4	0	0	0	1	0	.200	.000
Santiago, B	.333	6	2	0	1	1	1	.429	.333
Segui, David#	.125	8	1	0	0	1	1	.222	.125
Servais, S	.250	8	2	0	0	0	1	.333	.500
Sheffield, G	.333	9	3	1	2	1	2	.400	.889
Shipley, C	.400	5	2	0	0	0	1	.400	.400
Silvestri, D	.000	5	0	0	0	0	2	.000	.000
Smith, Ozzie*	.000	7	0	0	1	0	1	.000	.000
Stinnett, K	.400	5	2	0	1	0	0	.400	.800
Thompson, Ry	.286	7	2	1	2	0	0	.375	.714
Vizcaino, J#	.000	4	0	0	1	0	2	.000	.000
Webster, L	.250	4	1	0	0	1	1	.400	.250
White, R	.250	4	1	0	0	0	0	.250	.250
Whiten, Mark#	.333	9	3	0	0	1	1	.400	.333
Young, Kevin	.400	5	2	1	1	0	0	.400	1.000
Zeile, Todd	.333	3	1	1	0	0	0	.333	1.000

Donn Pall, Marlins — RHP

Batter	Avg	AB	H	HR	BI	BB	SO	OBP	Slg
McGwire, Mark	.385	13	5	1	2	3	2	.500	.692
McRae, Brian#	.167	6	1	0	0	0	1	.167	.167
Molitor, Paul	.364	11	4	0	4	0	1	.364	.364
Munoz, Pedro	.600	5	3	1	3	0	0	.500	1.400
Nilsson, Dave*	.250	4	1	1	4	0	0	.250	1.000
Olerud, John*	.200	5	1	0	0	2	0	.429	.200
Orsulak, Joe*	.375	8	3	0	1	1	1	.444	.375
Palmeiro, R*	.364	11	4	1	2	3	0	.500	.818
Palmer, Dean	.182	11	2	0	2	0	1	.167	.182
Pena, Tony	.250	8	2	0	1	0	0	.250	.250
Phillips, T#	.143	21	3	0	0	2	2	.217	.143
Polonia, Luis*	.333	9	3	0	1	1	0	.400	.333
Reed, Jody	.462	13	6	0	1	2	0	.533	.462
Ripken, Billy	.500	4	2	0	0	0	0	.500	.750
Ripken, Cal	.200	10	2	0	0	0	1	.200	.200
Rodriguez, I	.286	7	2	0	0	0	0	.286	.286
Schofield, D	.333	6	2	0	2	1	1	.429	.333
Segui, David#	.125	8	1	0	0	0	2	.125	.125
Seitzer, K	.214	14	3	0	1	1	0	.267	.286
Sheffield, G	.400	5	2	0	0	1	1	.400	.400
Sierra, Ruben#	.200	15	3	0	1	0	2	.200	.200
Sojo, Luis	.200	5	1	0	0	0	0	.200	.200
Sorrento, P*	.400	5	2	0	1	0	0	.400	.400
Spiers, Bill*	.333	6	2	0	0	0	0	.333	.333
Stanley, Mike	.750	4	3	1	2	1	0	.833	1.500
Steinbach, T	.154	13	2	0	0	1	3	.214	.154
Strange, Doug#	.000	5	0	0	0	0	0	.000	.000
Surhoff, B.*	.714	7	5	0	0	2	1	.778	.714
Sveum, Dale#	.200	5	1	0	2	1	2	.333	.400
Tartabull, D	.250	8	2	1	1	0	2	.250	.625
Tettleton, M#	.364	11	4	1	3	1	3	.417	.545
Trammell, A	.231	13	3	1	1	2	0	.333	.462
Valle, Dave	.200	5	1	0	0	0	2	.333	.200
Vaughn, Greg	.250	4	1	0	2	0	0	.250	.500
Velarde, R	.286	7	2	0	0	0	0	.286	.429
Vizquel, Omar#	.400	10	4	0	0	1	1	.400	.400
Weiss, Walt#	.286	7	2	0	1	1	1	.375	.286
White, Devon#	.250	12	3	0	2	1	4	.308	.333

Donn Pall, Marlins — RHP

Batter	Avg	AB	H	HR	BI	BB	SO	OBP	Slg
Alomar, R#	.833	6	5	0	1	0	0	.875	.833
Amaral, Rich	.000	4	0	0	0	1	0	.200	.000
Anderson, Brd*	.200	5	1	0	1	0	1	.333	.200
Baerga, C	.000	8	0	0	0	1	0	.111	.000
Baines, H*	.091	11	1	0	4	0	1	.091	.364
Belle, Albert	.167	6	1	0	0	1	2	.286	.167
Bichette, D	.500	6	3	1	3	0	0	.500	1.000
Boggs, Wade*	.400	15	6	0	2	5	2	.550	.400
Borders, Pat	.000	4	0	0	0	1	2	.200	.000
Bordick, Mike	.167	6	1	0	1	1	3	.375	.167
Buhner, Jay	.250	8	2	2	0	0	0	.250	.250
Burks, Ellis	.286	7	2	2	4	2	2	.500	1.143
Canseco, Jose	.364	11	4	0	3	2	3	.462	.455
Carter, Joe	.083	12	1	0	0	1	1	.154	.083
Curtis, Chad	.111	9	1	0	0	0	1	.111	.111
Davis, Chili#	.364	11	4	0	0	1	2	.417	.545
Deer, Rob	.385	13	5	3	9	2	4	.500	1.077
Devereaux, M	.111	9	1	0	0	0	1	.111	.333
DiSarcina, G	.667	9	6	0	0	0	0	.667	.778
Eisenreich, J*	.571	7	4	0	1	0	0	.571	.571
Espinoza, A	.250	8	2	0	0	0	3	.250	.250
Fermin, Felix	.231	13	3	1	2	0	0	.231	.538
Fielder, C	.250	12	3	0	1	3	1	.400	.250
Franco, Julio	.364	11	4	1	1	2	1	.462	.727
Fryman, T	.167	12	2	0	2	0	0	.167	.167
Gaetti, Gary	.083	12	1	0	0	0	0	.154	.083
Gagne, Greg	.200	10	2	0	2	0	1	.200	.200
Gallego, Mike	.500	10	5	0	0	0	1	.500	.700
Gomez, Leo	.800	5	4	2	4	0	1	.667	2.200
Gonzalez, J	.143	7	1	0	0	2	1	.333	.143
Greenwell, M*	.400	10	4	1	1	1	1	.455	.800
Griffey Jr, K*	.167	6	1	0	0	1	1	.286	.167
Hall, Mel*	.167	6	1	0	0	0	0	.167	.333
Henderson, R	.462	13	6	1	7	2	0	.533	.769
Hoiles, Chris	.143	7	1	0	0	0	0	.143	.143
Howell, Jack*	.333	6	2	0	1	0	1	.333	.500
Huson, Jeff*	.333	6	2	0	1	1	1	.429	.500
Incaviglia, P	.286	7	2	1	2	0	3	.286	.714
James, Dion*	.000	8	0	0	1	0	2	.000	.000
Javier, Stan#	.333	6	2	0	2	1	2	.429	.500
Joyner, Wally*	.200	5	1	0	0	1	0	.333	.200
Kelly, Pat	.000	7	0	0	2	0	2	.000	.000
Kelly, R	.333	6	2	0	0	1	0	.429	.333
Knoblauch, C	.000	5	0	0	0	2	0	.286	.000
Kreuter, Chad*	.000	5	0	0	0	0	0	.000	.000
Leius, Scott	.600	5	3	1	1	0	0	.600	1.600
Leyritz, Jim	.167	6	1	0	0	0	1	.167	.167
Liriano, N#	.200	5	1	0	0	0	1	.200	.200
Listach, Pat#	.286	7	2	0	1	0	0	.286	.286
Livingstone, S	.333	6	2	0	1	0	1	.286	.500
Macfarlane, M	.400	5	2	1	1	0	0	.400	1.200
Martinez, E	.500	4	2	0	0	2	1	.667	.500
McGriff, Fred*	.167	6	1	1	1	0	2	.167	.667

Jose Paniagua, Expos — RHP

Batter	Avg	AB	H	HR	BI	BB	SO	OBP	Slg
Jones, Andruw	.400	5	2	0	1	0	1	.400	.400
Jones, C#	.000	4	0	0	0	1	1	.200	.000

Chan Ho Park, Dodgers — RHP

Batter	Avg	AB	H	HR	BI	BB	SO	OBP	Slg
Bagwell, Jeff	.250	4	1	0	0	1	1	.400	.500
Bell, Derek	.200	5	1	0	3	0	1	.200	.200
Benard, M*	.333	6	2	1	1	1	2	.429	.833
Bichette, D	.600	5	3	1	1	0	1	.600	1.400
Biggio, Craig	.250	4	1	0	0	0	1	.400	.250
Bonds, Barry*	.333	3	1	0	1	3	0	.667	.333
Castilla, V	.200	5	1	0	1	0	0	.200	.200
Clark, Dave*	.333	3	1	0	0	2	0	.600	.333
Clayton, R	.000	3	0	0	0	2	1	.400	.000
Galarraga, A	.250	4	1	0	0	1	2	.400	.250
Gomez, Leo	.000	5	0	0	0	2	3	.286	.000
Gonzalez, L*	.750	4	3	0	0	3	0	.857	1.000
Grace, Mark*	.250	4	1	0	0	2	0	.500	.250
Grissom, M	.167	6	1	0	0	1	1	.286	.167
Hernandez, Jo	.000	4	0	0	0	1	2	.200	.000
Jones, C*	.167	6	1	0	0	1	0	.286	.167
Jordan, Brian	.167	6	1	1	2	0	2	.167	.667
Klesko, Ryan*	.000	2	0	0	0	3	2	.600	.000
Lankford, Ray*	.000	2	0	0	0	4	2	.667	.000
Lemke, Mark#	.250	8	2	0	0	1	1	.250	.250
Liriano, N#	.000	5	0	0	0	1	0	.000	.000
Lopez, Javy	.000	6	0	0	1	0	3	.000	.000
McGriff, Fred*	.500	4	2	0	2	2	0	.667	.750
McRae, Brian#	.125	8	1	0	0	1	1	.222	.125
Reed, Jody	.200	5	1	1	1	0	1	.200	.800
Sanchez, Rey	.000	5	0	0	0	0	1	.000	.000
Sandberg, R	.400	5	2	0	0	0	0	.400	.400
Servais, S	.125	8	1	0	1	1	4	.222	.125
Sosa, Sammy	.143	7	1	1	3	1	3	.250	.571
Whiten, Mark#	.200	5	1	0	0	0	3	.200	.200
Williams, Ma	.200	5	1	0	0	0	3	.200	.200
Zeile, Todd	.500	4	2	0	0	1	0	.600	.500

Jose Parra, Twins — RHP

Batter	Avg	AB	H	HR	BI	BB	SO	OBP	Slg
Anderson, G*	.500	6	3	0	2	0	0	.500	.667
Berroa, G	.167	6	1	0	0	1	1	.286	.167
Bordick, Mike	.333	6	2	0	1	0	0	.333	.333
Bragg, Darren*	.667	6	4	0	0	0	0	.667	.667
Buhner, Jay	.250	8	2	0	1	0	3	.250	.375
Clark, Will*	.333	12	4	2	3	0	1	.333	.917
Cora, Joey#	.000	6	0	0	0	0	1	.000	.000
Damon, Johnny*	.600	5	3	0	2	0	0	.600	1.000
Davis, Chili#	.000	5	0	0	1	0	2	.000	.000
Easley, D	.200	5	1	0	0	0	1	.200	.400

Jose Parra, Twins — RHP

Batter	Avg	AB	H	HR	BI	BB	SO	OBP	Slg
Edmonds, Jim*	.000	6	0	0	0	1	2	.143	.000
Elster, Kevin	.400	5	2	0	2	2	1	.571	.600
Frye, Jeff	.125	8	1	0	0	1	0	.222	.125
Gates, Brent#	.600	5	3	0	0	1	0	.667	.600
Giambi, Jason*	.500	4	2	0	1	2	1	.667	.500
Gonzalez, J	.444	9	4	2	4	1	2	.500	1.222
Greer, Rusty*	.500	8	4	0	1	1	0	.556	.625
Griffey Jr, K*	.143	7	1	0	1	2	2	.400	.143
Hamilton, D*	.182	11	2	0	1	0	1	.182	.273
Haselman, B	.000	5	0	0	0	0	2	.000	.000
Jaha, John	.167	6	1	0	0	2	0	.375	.167
Johnson, L*	.714	7	5	0	1	0	0	.714	1.286
Lockhart, K*	.400	5	2	0	0	0	0	.400	.400
Martinez, Da*	.167	6	1	1	3	1	0	.250	.667
Martinez, E	.143	7	1	0	0	0	2	.250	.286
McLemore, M	.167	12	2	0	1	1	0	.231	.167
Mouton, Lyle	.250	4	1	0	1	2	0	.500	.500
Myers, Greg*	.600	5	3	0	1	0	1	.600	.600
Nilsson, Dave*	.375	8	3	2	4	0	0	.375	1.125
Nixon, Otis#	.500	6	3	0	1	1	0	.571	.500
Palmer, Dean	.333	6	2	1	2	0	2	.333	.833
Phillips, T#	.143	7	1	1	1	1	1	.250	.571
Raines, Tim*	.250	4	1	0	1	2	1	.429	.750
Rodriguez, Al	.333	6	2	0	0	1	1	.333	.333
Rodriguez, I	.222	9	2	1	2	1	2	.300	.556
Salmon, Tim	.571	7	4	1	1	0	1	.571	1.000
Seltzer, K	.250	8	2	0	0	1	0	.333	.250
Snow, J.T.#	.000	7	0	0	0	0	1	.000	.000
Sorrento, P*	.000	5	0	0	0	1	3	.167	.000
Steinbach, T	.600	5	3	0	3	0	1	.667	.800
Tettleton, M#	.250	8	2	1	2	0	1	.333	.750
Thomas, Frank	.333	6	2	0	2	2	1	.500	.333
Tinsley, Lee#	.400	5	2	0	0	0	2	.400	.400
Valentin, Jse#	.250	4	1	0	1	1	0	.400	.250
Ventura, R*	.286	7	2	0	0	0	0	.286	.429
Wilson, Dan	.286	7	2	0	0	0	1	.286	.286
Young, Ernie	.400	5	2	2	5	0	2	.400	1.600

Jeff Parrett, Phillies — RHP

Batter	Avg	AB	H	HR	BI	BB	SO	OBP	Slg
Aldrete, Mike*	.000	2	0	0	0	3	0	.600	.000
Alicea, Luis*	.250	5	2	0	0	0	3	.250	.375
Alomar, R#	.400	5	2	0	2	7	0	.750	.400
Alou, Moises	.222	9	2	1	2	2	1	.364	.556
Andrews, S	.000	5	0	0	0	0	2	.000	.000
Baerga, C#	.200	5	1	0	1	0	0	.200	.200
Bagwell, Jeff	.250	8	2	0	0	0	3	.250	.375
Bell, Derek	.444	9	4	1	2	2	1	.500	.889
Bell, Jay	.250	16	4	0	2	0	6	.235	.313
Berry, Sean	.500	4	2	0	2	1	1	.600	.500
Bichette, D	.167	6	1	0	0	1	2	.286	.167
Biggio, Craig	.294	17	5	1	2	0	3	.294	.471
Blauser, Jeff	.250	8	2	1	3	4	5	.462	.625
Bonds, Barry*	.250	16	4	0	0	6	4	.455	.375
Bonilla, B#	.375	16	6	0	1	4	3	.500	.375
Borders, Pat	.000	6	0	0	0	0	2	.000	.000
Brogna, Rico*	.600	5	3	0	1	0	1	.600	1.000
Burks, Ellis	.667	6	4	1	3	1	0	.714	1.333
Butler, Brett*	.000	4	0	0	0	2	1	.333	.000
Caminiti, Ken#	.333	12	4	0	3	1	3	.385	.417
Candaele, C#	.500	6	3	0	3	0	0	.500	1.333
Cangelosi, J#	.143	14	2	0	0	1	1	.200	.214
Carreon, Mark	.429	14	6	1	4	0	1	.429	.714
Carter, Joe	.222	9	2	1	3	0	2	.222	.778
Castilla, G	.250	4	1	0	0	1	2	.400	.250
Clark, Dave*	.286	7	2	0	0	0	1	.286	.286
Clark, Will*	.286	7	2	1	2	1	0	.444	.857
Clayton, R	.167	6	1	0	0	1	3	.286	.167
Colbrunn, G	.000	4	0	0	1	0	2	.000	.000
Coleman, V#	.235	17	4	0	0	2	7	.316	.294
Conine, Jeff	.000	4	0	0	0	1	3	.200	.000
Daulton, D*	.143	7	1	0	0	1	1	.143	.143
Davis, Chili#	.250	4	1	0	2	1	0	.400	.250
Davis, Eric	.250	12	3	1	5	3	2	.400	.583
Dawson, Andre	.333	12	4	1	3	2	2	.467	.667
DeShields, D*	.600	5	3	0	3	1	1	.667	1.200
Devereaux, M	.000	6	0	0	0	0	2	.000	.000
Duncan, M	.167	12	2	0	1	0	3	.167	.167
Dunston, S	.231	13	3	0	0	0	4	.231	.308
Dykstra, L*	.364	11	4	0	3	1	0	.417	.455
Eisenreich, J*	.200	5	1	0	0	1	2	.333	.200
Elster, Kevin	.125	8	1	0	0	3	3	.364	.125
Eusebio, Tony	.500	6	3	1	4	0	1	.500	1.000
Gagne, Greg	.286	7	2	0	0	0	2	.286	.429
Galarraga, A	.467	15	7	1	4	0	4	.467	.800
Gant, Ron	.250	16	4	0	2	4	4	.333	.375
Garcia, C	.000	5	0	0	0	1	0	.167	.000
Gilkey, B	.286	7	2	0	1	4	1	.545	.286
Girardi, Joe	.429	7	3	0	2	1	2	.500	.429
Gomez, Leo	.250	4	1	0	0	1	0	.400	.250
Gonzalez, J	.000	3	0	0	1	1	1	.200	.000
Grace, Mark*	.429	14	6	0	6	2	0	.500	.429
Grissom, M	.364	11	4	0	2	1	4	.417	.364
Gwynn, Tony*	.579	19	11	0	3	5	1	.667	.684
Hamilton, D*	.000	4	0	0	1	0	0	.000	.000
Harris, Lenny*	.222	9	2	0	1	4	2	.462	.222
Hayes, C	.000	6	0	0	0	0	2	.000	.000
Hernandez, Jo	.500	4	2	0	0	1	0	.600	.500
Hill, G	.333	6	2	0	2	2	1	.500	.333
Howard, T*	.200	5	1	0	0	0	2	.200	.200
Hundley, Todd*	.250	4	1	0	0	1	0	.400	.250
Hunter, Bri L	.333	6	2	0	2	0	1	.333	.333
James, Dion*	.000	4	0	0	0	2	0	.333	.000
Javier, Stan#	.333	3	1	0	0	2	0	.600	.333
Jefferies, G#	.143	21	3	0	1	5	2	.308	.143
Joyner, Wally*	.250	4	1	0	1	1	1	.400	.250
Justice, Dave*	.200	5	1	0	0	1	1	.333	.200
Karros, Eric	.500	4	2	1	1	2	0	.667	1.250
Kelly, R	.500	8	4	0	1	0	0	.500	.750
Kent, Jeff	.333	6	2	0	0	1	3	.429	.333
King, Jeff	.385	13	5	1	4	1	2	.429	.692
Kingery, Mike*	.444	9	4	1	2	2	1	.545	1.111
Knoblauch, C	.400	5	2	0	2	2	0	.571	.600
Lankford, Ray*	.000	5	0	0	0	1	2	.167	.000
Lansing, Mike	.429	7	3	0	1	0	1	.429	.571
Larkin, Barry	.231	26	6	0	1	1	2	.259	.231
Lemke, Mark#	.400	10	4	0	0	1	2	.455	.600
Lewis, Mark	.000	4	0	0	0	1	2	.200	.000
Listach, Pat#	.000	4	0	0	0	1	3	.200	.000
Lopez, Javy	.167	6	1	0	0	0	4	.167	.167
Magadan, Dave*	.222	18	4	1	4	2	7	.300	.444
Manwaring, K	.400	5	2	0	4	0	2	.429	.400
Martin, Al*	.500	4	2	0	0	1	0	.600	.500
Martinez, Da*	.333	6	2	0	0	0	3	.333	.333
May, Derrick*	.250	8	2	0	1	0	1	.250	.375
McGee, Willie#	.267	15	4	0	0	3	3	.267	.333
McGriff, Fred*	.500	4	2	0	3	2	1	.667	.500
McRae, Brian#	.444	9	4	0	1	0	2	.444	.556
Merced, O*	.286	7	2	0	1	0	0	.286	.429
Miller, Orl	.375	8	3	0	0	0	0	.375	.625
Mitchell, K	.286	14	4	1	3	2	2	.375	.643
Morandini, M*	.600	5	3	0	2	1	0	.667	.600
Morris, Hal*	.556	9	5	1	3	1	0	.545	.889
Mouton, James	.000	5	0	0	0	0	0	.000	.000
Murray, Eddie#	.111	9	1	0	0	1	4	.200	.111
Nixon, Otis#	.500	6	3	0	5	2	1	.625	.667
O'Neill, Paul*	.000	15	0	0	0	1	6	.063	.000
Pagnozzi, Tom	.429	7	3	0	2	2	1	.500	.571
Palmeiro, R*	.250	4	1	0	0	1	0	.400	.250
Pena, Tony	.250	12	3	0	2	2	3	.357	.250
Pendleton, T#	.207	29	6	0	4	2	10	.258	.241
Phillips, T#	.000	4	0	0	0	1	2	.200	.000
Raines, Tim#	.538	13	7	0	6	0	2	.538	.769
Reed, Jeff*	.600	5	3	0	1	0	0	.667	1.000
Reed, Jody	.286	7	2	0	3	1	2	.333	.429
Roberts, Bip#	.222	9	2	0	3	1	0	.417	.222
Sabo, Chris	.154	13	2	0	1	0	4	.154	.231
Samuel, Juan	.250	12	3	0	1	2	4	.357	.417
Sandberg, R	.182	22	4	0	0	1	3	.217	.182
Sanders, R	.200	5	1	0	0	0	2	.200	.200
Santiago, B	.333	24	8	1	4	0	4	.360	.500
Schu, Rick	.200	5	1	0	0	1	1	.333	.400
Segui, David#	.000	6	0	0	0	1	1	.143	.000
Servais, S	.250	4	1	1	1	1	1	.400	1.000
Shipley, C	.600	5	3	0	2	0	0	.600	.600
Smith, Dwight*	.000	9	0	0	0	1	2	.100	.000
Smith, Ozzie#	.318	22	7	0	4	2	0	.360	.318
Sosa, Sammy	.222	9	2	0	1	0	2	.200	.222
Strawberry, D*	.385	13	5	1	1	2	2	.467	.692
Thompson, Mil*	.385	13	5	0	5	3	5	.500	.615
Thompson, Rob	.167	12	2	1	1	2	4	.286	.417
Vizcaino, J#	.222	9	2	0	1	0	2	.222	.333
Walker, Larry*	.000	6	0	0	0	2	2	.250	.000
Wallach, Tim	.308	13	4	0	2	1	2	.400	.538
Walton, J	.200	10	2	0	0	0	3	.200	.200
Weiss, Walt#	.125	8	1	0	0	1	1	.125	.125
White, Devon#	.200	5	1	0	1	1	2	.333	.400
White, R	.200	5	1	0	0	0	2	.200	.200
Whiten, Mark#	.000	10	0	0	0	2	5	.167	.000
Wilkins, Rick*	.167	6	1	1	3	2	3	.375	.667
Williams, Ma	.214	14	3	0	1	1	5	.267	.286
Young, Eric	.200	5	1	0	0	2	1	.429	.200
Zeile, Todd	.368	19	7	2	7	1	4	.381	.684

Steve Parris, Pirates — RHP

Batter	Avg	AB	H	HR	BI	BB	SO	OBP	Slg
Alfonzo, E	.000	6	0	0	0	0	2	.000	.000
Bell, Derek	.500	6	3	1	4	0	0	.500	1.167
Biggio, Craig	.250	4	1	0	0	2	0	.500	.250
Boone, Bret	.250	8	2	0	2	0	2	.400	.800
Caminiti, Ken#	.200	5	1	0	0	0	2	.200	.200
Eisenreich, J*	.429	7	3	0	2	1	2	.500	.571

Steve Parris, Pirates — RHP

Batter	Avg	AB	H	HR	BI	BB	SO	OBP	Slg
Finley, Steve*	.500	6	3	0	0	1	0	.571	.500
Gwynn, Tony*	.286	7	2	0	1	0	0	.286	.429
Hayes, C	.333	3	1	0	3	1	1	.400	.333
Howard, T*	.600	5	3	0	0	1	0	.667	.800
Hunter, Bri L	.500	6	3	0	0	0	0	.500	.667
Jefferies, R	.333	6	2	0	0	1	0	.429	.500
Larkin, Barry	.600	5	3	0	1	0	0	.600	.800
Lewis, Darren	.400	5	2	0	0	0	0	.400	.400
Livingstone*	.286	7	2	0	1	0	0	.286	.286
Magadan, Dave*	.000	4	0	0	0	2	1	.333	.000
Morandini, M*	.375	8	3	0	1	1	0	.444	.500
Morris, Hal*	.200	5	1	0	2	0	0	.200	.200
Sanders, R	.600	5	3	3	5	1	0	.667	2.400
Shipley, C	.000	6	0	0	0	0	2	.000	.000
Taubensee, E*	.200	5	1	0	1	0	3	.333	.400
Veras, Q#	.250	4	1	0	2	1	1	.500	.250
Wilkins, Rick*	.200	5	1	0	1	0	2	.200	.200
Zeile, Todd	.600	5	3	0	1	1	2	.667	.600

Bob Patterson, Cubs — LHP

Batter	Avg	AB	H	HR	BI	BB	SO	OBP	Slg
Alomar, R#	.154	13	2	0	0	0	5	.154	.154
Amaro, Ruben#	.400	5	2	0	1	1	1	.500	.400
Anderson, Brd*	.000	9	0	0	0	0	6	.000	.000
Anthony, Eric*	.000	8	0	0	0	0	3	.000	.000
Baerga, C#	.250	4	1	0	0	2	0	.500	.250
Bagwell, Jeff	.250	4	1	1	1	1	2	.400	1.000
Baines, H*	.167	6	1	0	0	0	1	.167	.167
Belliard, R	.000	6	0	0	0	0	1	.000	.000
Benard, M*	.250	4	1	0	0	1	1	.400	.500
Blowers, Mike	.200	5	1	0	0	0	0	.200	.400
Boggs, Wade*	.222	9	2	0	0	0	0	.222	.222
Bonds, Barry*	.000	2	0	0	1	2	0	.400	.000
Butler, Brett*	.308	13	4	0	0	1	1	.357	.308
Caminiti, Ken#	.455	11	5	1	5	1	0	.500	1.000
Candaele, C#	.583	12	7	0	1	0	0	.583	.750
Carreon, Mark	.250	4	1	0	0	1	0	.400	.250
Carter, Joe	.333	6	2	0	1	1	1	.429	.333
Clark, Will*	.250	16	4	0	3	1	6	.294	.375
Coleman, V#	.300	20	6	0	0	1	3	.333	.450
Cora, Joey#	.222	9	2	0	1	0	2	.222	.222
Dascenzo, D*	.500	10	5	0	1	0	0	.500	.500
Daulton, D*	.077	13	1	0	0	1	2	.143	.077
Davis, Eric	.167	6	1	0	0	1	5	.286	.167
Dawson, Andre	.294	17	5	2	5	0	3	.294	.647
DeShields, D*	.300	10	3	1	5	1	4	.364	.700
Devereaux, M	.200	5	1	0	0	0	0	.200	.400
Duncan, M	.500	8	4	0	1	0	0	.500	.875
Dunston, S	.308	13	4	1	5	0	1	.286	.538
Dykstra, L*	.154	13	2	0	0	5	3	.389	.154
Elster, Kevin	.200	5	1	0	0	1	1	.333	.200
Finley, Steve*	.250	8	2	0	0	0	2	.250	.250
Fletcher, D*	.400	5	2	0	0	0	2	.400	.400
Galarraga, A	.286	7	2	0	0	0	2	.286	.286
Gant, Ron	.000	7	0	0	0	0	4	.000	.000
Gates, Brent#	.200	5	1	0	0	0	0	.200	.200
Gilkey, B	.200	5	1	0	0	0	0	.200	.200
Girardi, Joe	.333	9	3	0	1	0	1	.300	.444
Grace, Mark*	.267	15	4	0	3	0	2	.267	.333
Greenwell, M*	.000	8	0	0	0	0	1	.000	.000
Griffey Jr, K*	.400	5	2	1	2	1	2	.500	1.000
Guillen, O*	.000	7	0	0	0	1	2	.125	.000
Gwynn, Tony*	.375	16	6	0	1	4	1	.500	.375
Harris, Lenny*	.250	4	1	0	0	1	1	.400	.250
Hayes, C	.000	6	0	0	0	0	1	.000	.000
Hollins, Dave#	.125	8	1	0	0	0	0	.125	.125
Hundley, Todd#	.429	6	2	0	1	1	2	.429	.333
Javier, Stan#	.143	7	1	0	0	0	1	.143	.286
Jefferies, G#	.333	15	5	0	1	0	1	.333	.400
Johnson, L*	.214	14	3	0	1	0	1	.214	.214
Joyner, Wally*	.143	7	1	0	0	1	1	.250	.143
Justice, Dave*	.286	7	2	0	0	1	2	.375	.571
Klesko, Ryan*	.250	4	1	0	0	1	1	.400	.250
Lankford, Ray*	.077	13	1	0	1	0	3	.077	.231
Larkin, Barry	.500	4	2	1	1	1	0	.600	1.250
Lemke, Mark#	.286	7	2	0	1	0	0	.286	.429
Magadan, Dave*	.111	9	1	0	3	2	4	.273	.222
Martinez, Da*	.000	5	0	0	0	1	1	.167	.000
Martinez, T*	.333	9	3	0	5	0	2	.333	.556
McGee, Willie#	.125	8	1	0	1	0	3	.125	.125
McGriff, Fred*	.333	6	2	0	1	1	1	.333	.375
McRae, Brian#	.000	4	0	0	0	0	2	.000	.200
Merced, O*	.200	5	1	0	0	0	2	.200	.200
Mitchell, K	.429	7	3	1	4	2	0	.500	.857
Morandini, M*	.143	14	2	0	0	0	5	.143	.143
Morris, Hal*	.400	5	2	0	1	1	2	.500	.400
Murray, Eddie#	.143	14	2	0	1	0	3	.133	.143
Naehring, Tim	.000	1	0	0	1	0	0	.333	.200
Nixon, Otis*	.333	6	2	0	1	0	2	.333	.333
O'Neill, Paul*	.150	20	3	0	2	1	5	.190	.200
Olerud, John*	.182	11	2	0	3	0	2	.182	.182

Bob Patterson, Cubs — LHP (continued)

Batter	Avg	AB	H	HR	BI	BB	SO	OBP	Slg
Oliver, Joe	.125	8	1	0	0	1	2	.222	.125
Palmeiro, R*	.444	9	4	2	3	1	1	.500	1.333
Pendleton, T#	.308	13	4	0	1	1	0	.357	.308
Polonia, Luis*	.000	5	0	0	0	0	3	.000	.000
Raines, Tim#	.250	12	3	0	2	0	3	.308	.333
Ripken, Cal	.000	1	0	0	1	3	0	.600	.000
Roberts, Bip#	.111	9	1	0	2	0	1	.111	.111
Sabo, Chris	.300	10	3	0	0	1	1	.364	.400
Samuel, Juan	.267	15	4	1	3	1	4	.313	.533
Sandberg, R	.417	12	5	0	0	0	0	.417	.500
Santiago, B	.667	3	2	0	2	1	0	.600	1.000
Sierra, Ruben#	.429	7	3	0	0	0	0	.429	.429
Smith, Ozzie#	.400	15	6	1	2	2	3	.471	.800
Sprague, Ed	.000	6	0	0	0	0	2	.000	.000
Steinbach, T	.000	4	0	0	1	0	1	.000	.000
Strawberry, D*	.208	24	5	1	7	3	7	.321	.375
Surhoff, B.J.*	.200	5	1	0	0	1	1	.333	.200
Taubensee, E*	.143	7	1	0	0	1	1	.143	.143
Tettleton, M#	.500	4	2	2	3	1	1	.600	2.000
Thompson, Mil*	.182	11	2	0	1	0	2	.182	.273
Thompson, Rob	.500	6	3	0	0	1	1	.500	.500
Valentin, Jhn	.167	6	1	0	0	0	0	.167	.333
Vaughn, Mo*	.125	8	1	0	0	0	3	.125	.250
Ventura, R*	.200	5	1	0	1	0	0	.286	.200
Walker, Larry*	.000	4	0	0	1	1	1	.167	.000
Wallach, Tim	.250	4	1	0	1	1	1	.400	.250
Walton, J	.143	7	1	0	0	1	0	.250	.143
White, Devon#	.167	6	1	0	0	1	5	.286	.167
Williams, Ber#	.400	5	2	1	3	1	1	.500	1.000
Williams, Ma	.364	11	4	0	0	1	2	.417	.364
Zeile, Todd	.333	12	4	1	4	0	2	.333	.750

Roger Pavlik, Rangers — RHP

Batter	Avg	AB	H	HR	BI	BB	SO	OBP	Slg
Aldrete, Mike*	.000	5	0	0	0	1	0	.167	.000
Alomar, R#	.240	25	6	0	4	2	2	.296	.280
Alomar Jr, S	.273	11	3	1	1	0	1	.333	.545
Amaral, Rich	.222	9	2	0	0	1	1	.300	.222
Anderson, Brd*	.222	18	4	1	3	1	0	.250	.556
Anderson, G*	.154	13	2	0	0	2	5	.267	.231
Ausmus, Brad	.000	6	0	0	0	0	2	.000	.000
Baerga, C#	.316	19	6	1	3	0	2	.350	.632
Baines, H*	.412	17	7	1	5	1	2	.421	.706
Bartee, K	.000	7	0	0	0	1	2	.125	.000
Becker, Rich*	.333	21	7	2	6	3	4	.417	.714
Belle, Albert	.250	20	5	2	5	5	2	.400	.650
Berroa, G	.211	19	4	0	1	1	6	.250	.263
Blowers, Mike	.091	11	1	0	0	2	2	.231	.091
Bonilla, B*	.167	6	1	0	0	0	1	.167	.167
Boone, Bret	.333	9	3	2	3	0	3	.333	1.000
Borders, Pat	.333	9	3	0	2	0	2	.333	.444
Bordick, Mike	.308	13	4	1	1	3	0	.438	.538
Bournigal, R	.333	9	3	0	1	0	1	.333	.444
Brosius, S	.412	17	7	2	5	4	5	.545	.765
Buhner, Jay	.304	23	7	2	9	2	8	.370	.696
Burks, Ellis	.400	5	2	0	0	1	2	.500	.600
Burnitz, J*	.167	6	1	0	0	0	0	.167	.167
Canseco, Jose	.125	8	1	0	0	1	2	.222	.125
Carreon, Mark	.000	5	0	0	0	1	0	.167	.000
Carter, Joe	.048	21	1	0	0	6	7	.259	.048
Cedeno, D#	.571	7	4	0	2	1	2	.625	.714
Cirillo, Jeff	.556	9	5	1	4	1	0	.600	1.333
Clark, Tony#	.333	9	3	0	0	0	5	.333	.333
Cole, Alex*	.000	8	0	0	1	1	3	.111	.000
Coleman, V#	.000	11	0	0	2	2	1	.143	.000
Cora, Joey#	.200	20	4	0	2	3	1	.304	.350
Cordova, M	.429	14	6	1	4	0	1	.429	.714
Curtis, Chad	.176	17	3	0	1	3	0	.286	.176
Damon, Johnny*	.400	10	4	0	0	1	0	.455	.500
Davis, Chili#	.313	16	5	0	2	1	3	.353	.313
Dawson, Andre	.300	10	3	0	2	0	0	.300	.300
Deer, Rob	.200	10	2	0	0	3	6	.385	.200
Delgado, C*	.667	9	6	2	6	1	2	.700	1.556
Devereaux, M	.429	7	3	1	4	0	1	.429	1.000
Diaz, Alex#	.286	7	2	0	0	0	1	.286	.429
DiSarcina, G	.538	13	7	0	1	0	0	.538	.538
Durham, Ray#	.182	11	2	0	0	1	2	.250	.273
Easley, D	.400	10	4	0	2	5	3	.600	.400
Edmonds, Jim*	.000	4	0	0	0	2	2	.500	.000
Erstad, Darin*	.000	5	0	0	0	1	2	.167	.000
Fabregas, Jor*	.200	5	1	0	1	0	0	.200	.200
Fermin, Felix	.286	14	4	0	0	1	1	.375	.357
Fielder, C	.091	22	2	2	4	1	4	.130	.364
Flaherty, John*	.444	9	4	0	0	0	3	.444	.556
Fox, Andy*	.000	7	0	0	0	1	3	.125	.000
Franco, Julio	.182	11	2	0	0	0	1	.182	.182
Fryman, T	.308	26	8	1	4	2	6	.379	.462
Gaetti, Gary	.235	17	4	0	3	0	7	.235	.353
Gagne, Greg	.273	22	6	0	1	1	5	.304	.318
Gallego, Mike	.143	7	1	0	1	1	2	.222	.143

Roger Pavlik, Rangers — RHP

Batter	Avg	AB	H	HR	BI	BB	SO	OBP	Slg
Gates, Brent#	.000	8	0	0	0	1	2	.111	.000
Giambi, Jason*	.077	13	1	0	0	1	4	.143	.077
Giles, B*	.429	7	3	1	2	0	0	.429	1.143
Girardi, Joe	.300	10	3	0	0	0	2	.300	.400
Gonzalez, A	.200	5	1	1	1	0	1	.200	.800
Goodwin, C*	.000	5	0	0	0	0	2	.200	.600
Goodwin, Tom*	.273	11	3	0	0	0	1	.273	.273
Grebeck, C	.000	4	0	0	0	1	3	.200	.000
Green, Shawn*	.273	11	3	0	0	2	3	.385	.455
Greenwell, M*	.444	9	4	1	1	2	2	.545	.778
Griffey Jr, K*	.318	22	7	2	8	5	5	.444	.591
Guillen, O*	.217	23	5	0	2	0	3	.217	.217
Gwynn, Chris*	.375	8	3	0	0	0	2	.375	.500
Hale, Chip*	.200	5	1	0	0	0	1	.200	.200
Hamelin, Bob*	.222	9	2	0	0	2	3	.364	.333
Hamilton, D*	.100	10	1	0	0	0	0	.100	.100
Henderson, R	.500	8	4	1	2	1	0	.600	1.000
Herrera, Jose*	.111	9	1	0	1	1	0	.200	.111
Higginson, B*	.118	17	2	1	1	1	6	.190	.294
Hoiles, Chris	.000	5	0	0	0	2	1	.286	.000
Hollins, Dave#	.286	7	2	0	2	3	3	.500	.429
Hulse, David*	.143	7	1	0	0	0	1	.143	.143
Jaha, John	.167	12	2	1	3	3	3	.333	.417
James, Dion*	.273	11	3	0	0	1	2	.333	.273
Javier, Stan#	.333	6	2	1	1	3	1	.556	.833
Jefferies, G#	.333	6	2	0	0	1	1	.429	.333
Jefferson, R	.250	12	3	2	4	3	3	.400	.750
Jeter, Derek	.000	6	0	0	1	1	0	.000	.000
Johnson, L*	.120	25	3	0	1	1	3	.154	.120
Joyner, Wally*	.238	21	5	0	4	5	3	.346	.286
Karkovice, R	.294	17	5	1	2	1	5	.368	.588
Kelly, Pat	.286	7	2	0	0	2	2	.375	.429
Kelly, R	.200	10	2	0	1	0	1	.200	.300
Kirby, Wayne*	.111	9	1	0	0	1	2	.200	.111
Knoblauch, C	.500	28	14	2	4	6	0	.600	.857
Koslofski, K*	.286	7	2	0	2	0	4	.286	.286
Kreuter, Chad#	.200	5	1	0	0	0	2	.200	.200
Levis, Jesse*	.000	4	0	0	0	1	0	.200	.000
Lewis, Darren	.000	4	0	0	0	0	0	.200	.000
Lewis, Mark	.417	12	5	1	3	2	2	.467	.917
Leyritz, Jim	.333	6	2	1	1	0	3	.333	.833
Livingstone*	.286	7	2	0	1	0	1	.286	.286
Lockhart, K*	.333	12	4	1	2	0	1	.333	.583
Lofton, Kenny*	.167	18	3	0	1	3	4	.286	.167
Macfarlane, M	.333	12	4	0	1	0	2	.429	.333
Magadan, Dave*	.000	5	0	0	0	1	0	.167	.000
Martinez, Da*	.357	14	5	0	0	2	2	.471	.571
Martinez, E	.313	16	5	0	3	4	3	.450	.500
Martinez, S*	.286	7	2	0	0	1	2	.375	.714
Martinez, T*	.296	27	8	2	6	1	5	.310	.556
May, Derrick*	.500	4	2	0	1	1	1	.600	.750
Mayne, Brent*	.077	13	1	0	2	3	3	.250	.077
McCarty, Dave	.300	10	3	1	2	2	4	.417	.700
McGwire, Mark	.308	13	4	1	3	0	0	.438	.692
McRae, Brian#	.250	20	5	0	1	0	3	.250	.250
Meares, Pat	.222	18	4	0	1	0	1	.211	.333
Molitor, Paul	.423	26	11	1	4	5	2	.516	.654
Mouton, Lyle	.000	5	0	0	1	0	1	.000	.000
Murray, Eddie#	.667	6	4	0	0	0	0	.667	.667
Myers, Greg*	.143	14	2	0	1	0	3	.133	.143
Naehring, Tim	.000	7	0	0	0	3	1	.300	.000
Nieves, M#	.200	5	1	0	1	1	1	.333	.200
Nilsson, Dave*	.333	6	2	1	3	2	0	.500	.833
Nunnally, Jon*	.167	6	1	0	0	2	3	.375	.333
O'Leary, Troy*	.429	7	3	1	1	2	2	.556	.857
O'Neill, Paul*	.474	19	9	1	2	2	2	.524	.737
Olerud, John*	.261	23	6	0	3	3	3	.346	.348
Oliver, Joe	.600	5	3	0	0	1	1	.667	.600
Palmeiro, R*	.545	11	6	1	3	1	2	.571	.818
Pena, Tony	.000	5	0	0	0	0	0	.000	.000
Perez, Tomas#	.400	5	2	0	0	0	0	.400	.400
Phillips, T#	.286	21	6	1	2	7	4	.464	.429
Polonia, Luis*	.231	13	3	1	1	1	3	.286	.462
Pride, Curtis*	.600	5	3	0	1	1	1	.667	1.200
Raines, Tim#	.368	19	7	0	2	3	4	.455	.526
Ramirez, M	.000	12	0	0	1	0	3	.000	.000
Reboulet, J	.417	12	5	0	2	2	0	.533	.417
Ripken, Cal	.154	13	2	0	0	3	1	.313	.154
Salmon, Tim	.214	14	3	0	0	3	3	.389	.214
Samuel, Juan	.500	6	3	0	0	0	1	.500	1.333
Seltzer, K	.143	7	1	0	0	2	2	.333	.286
Shumpert, T	.200	5	1	0	0	0	0	.200	.200
Sierra, Ruben#	.227	22	5	0	1	5	6	.370	.318
Snow, J.T.#	.167	18	3	0	0	0	2	.167	.167
Sojo, Luis	.500	4	2	0	1	1	0	.600	.500
Sorrento, P*	.286	14	4	1	4	1	5	.333	.571
Sprague, Ed	.182	22	4	1	1	1	6	.250	.318
Stahoviak, S*	.158	19	3	0	3	2	5	.238	.158
Stairs, Matt*	.200	5	1	0	0	2	0	.429	.200
Stanley, Mike	.357	14	5	1	4	2	3	.412	.571
Steinbach, T	.231	13	3	0	1	0	4	.231	.308

Roger Pavlik, Rangers — RHP (continued)

Batter	Avg	AB	H	HR	BI	BB	SO	OBP	Slg
Surhoff, B.J.*	.143	7	1	0	1	2	0	.333	.429
Tartabull, D	.118	17	2	0	2	5	5	.318	.176
Tettleton, M#	.400	10	4	1	3	2	5	.455	.800
Thomas, Frank	.250	24	6	3	8	9	2	.455	.667
Thome, Jim*	.143	14	2	1	2	4	6	.333	.357
Tinsley, Lee#	.000	4	0	0	0	1	2	.200	.000
Trammell, A	.182	11	2	0	1	1	0	.250	.182
Tucker, M*	.111	9	1	0	0	1	6	.200	.111
Valentin, Jhn	.333	15	5	0	1	3	2	.444	.400
Valentin, Jse#	.000	9	0	0	0	1	2	.100	.000
Valle, Dave	.286	7	2	0	0	2	1	.444	.286
Vaughn, Greg	.400	10	4	1	4	0	0	.400	.800
Vaughn, Mo*	.500	18	9	1	3	1	4	.526	.667
Velarde, R	.167	12	2	0	0	1	3	.231	.167
Ventura, R*	.357	28	10	1	3	6	6	.471	.536
Vina, F*	.231	13	3	0	1	0	2	.286	.231
Vizcaino, J#	.500	6	3	0	0	1	0	.500	.500
Vizquel, Omar#	.174	23	4	0	0	2	4	.240	.174
Ward, Turner#	.125	8	1	0	0	1	4	.222	.125
White, Devon#	.222	18	4	0	1	0	3	.222	.389
Williams, Ber#	.333	18	6	2	3	4	2	.455	.667
Williams, Geo#	.250	4	1	0	0	1	1	.400	.250
Williams, Ger	.000	6	0	0	0	0	2	.000	.000
Wilson, Dan	.375	8	3	0	1	0	1	.333	.625
Young, Ernie	.286	7	2	0	0	1	2	.375	.286
Zaun, Greg#	.143	7	1	0	0	1	0	.250	.143

Alejandro Pena, Marlins — RHP

Batter	Avg	AB	H	HR	BI	BB	SO	OBP	Slg
Aldrete, Mike*	.200	5	1	0	0	1	0	.200	.200
Alicea, Luis#	.500	4	2	1	1	1	1	.600	1.250
Alomar, R#	.250	8	2	0	0	0	0	.250	.250
Bagwell, Jeff	.250	4	1	0	0	1	1	.400	.250
Bell, Jay	.357	14	5	1	1	0	4	.357	.714
Belliard, R	.167	6	1	0	0	2	1	.375	.167
Biggio, Craig	.462	13	6	0	2	2	4	.533	.538
Bonds, Barry*	.111	9	1	0	0	8	3	.529	.111
Bonilla, B#	.250	12	3	0	1	3	4	.400	.250
Butler, Brett*	.300	10	3	0	0	1	1	.300	.300
Caminiti, Ken#	.429	14	6	1	1	1	2	.467	.857
Candaele, C#	.333	12	4	0	0	0	2	.333	.500
Cangelosi, J#	.000	4	0	0	0	2	2	.333	.000
Cedeno, A	.200	5	1	0	0	0	2	.200	.400
Clark, Will*	.333	15	5	2	3	3	7	.444	.800
Coleman, V#	.313	16	5	0	0	2	3	.389	.438
Conine, Jeff	.167	6	1	0	0	0	3	.167	.167
Dascenzo, D	.143	7	1	0	0	0	0	.143	.143
Daulton, D*	.500	8	4	1	7	2	2	.545	1.000
Davis, Chili#	.250	8	2	0	1	0	2	.250	.375
Davis, Eric	.211	19	4	1	1	1	4	.250	.368
Dawson, Andre	.214	28	6	0	1	1	2	.241	.250
DeShields, D*	.000	9	0	0	0	1	5	.100	.000
Duncan, M	.000	5	0	0	0	0	1	.000	.000
Dunston, S	.143	21	3	1	2	0	5	.143	.286
Dykstra, L*	.200	5	1	0	1	2	0	.375	.400
Elster, Kevin	.200	5	1	1	1	0	0	.200	.800
Finley, Steve*	.333	6	2	0	0	0	0	.333	.333
Galarraga, A	.316	19	6	1	5	0	6	.316	.579
Gant, Ron	.077	13	1	0	0	4	0	.077	.077
Gilkey, B	.167	6	1	0	0	0	0	.167	.167
Girardi, Joe	.000	11	0	0	0	0	3	.000	.000
Gonzalez, L*	.125	8	1	0	0	0	2	.125	.125
Grace, Mark	.316	19	6	0	1	4	1	.435	.316
Grissom, M	.222	9	2	0	0	0	2	.222	.222
Gwynn, Tony*	.348	23	8	0	1	1	0	.400	.435
Harris, Lenny*	.100	10	1	0	0	0	1	.100	.100
Hayes, Charlie	.091	11	1	0	0	1	5	.167	.091
James, Dion*	.400	5	2	0	1	2	0	.571	.400
Jefferies, G#	.000	5	0	0	0	0	0	.000	.000
Jordan, Ricky	.455	11	5	1	5	0	1	.500	.909
Kent, Jeff	.200	5	1	0	2	0	0	.200	.200
King, Jeff	.429	7	3	0	1	1	1	.500	.714
Lankford, Ray*	.333	9	3	0	0	0	3	.333	.444
Larkin, Barry	.286	21	6	1	3	0	3	.286	.429
Lewis, Darren	.250	8	2	0	2	0	3	.250	.250
Magadan, Dave*	.111	9	1	0	1	1	0	.111	.444
Martinez, Da*	.143	14	2	0	1	1	3	.200	.143
McGee, Willie#	.313	16	5	0	0	1	0	.353	.375
Merced, O*	.286	7	2	1	2	1	2	.375	.857
Mitchell, K	.167	18	3	1	1	2	6	.250	.333
Morandini, M*	.167	6	1	0	0	0	2	.167	.167
Murray, Eddie#	.143	7	1	0	0	0	2	.143	.143
O'Neill, Paul*	.154	13	2	0	0	0	3	.154	.154
Oliver, Joe	.200	5	1	0	0	0	1	.200	.200
Orsulak, Joe*	.250	8	2	0	0	2	1	.455	.500
Pagnozzi, Tom	.375	8	3	0	4	0	0	.375	.625
Palmeiro, R*	.500	6	3	0	0	0	0	.500	.500
Pena, G#	.200	5	1	0	0	0	2	.200	.400
Pena, Tony	.190	19	7	0	1	5	1	.500	.474
Pendleton, T#	.286	14	4	0	2	3	2	.368	.286
Raines, Tim#	.235	17	4	1	1	2	1	.316	.529
Reed, Jeff*	.143	7	1	0	0	1	0	.143	.143

Alejandro Pena, Marlins — RHP

Batter	Avg	AB	H	HR	BI	BB	SO	OBP	Slg
Roberts, Bip#	.000	6	0	0	0	2	0	.250	.000
Sabo, Chris	.385	13	5	0	3	2	1	.438	.462
Samuel, Juan	.320	25	8	1	5	1	6	.346	.440
Sandberg, R	.361	36	13	3	8	2	2	.395	.722
Sanders, R	.167	6	1	0	0	0	2	.167	.167
Santiago, B	.211	19	4	0	1	0	7	.211	.263
Smith, Dwight*	.400	5	2	0	1	1	0	.500	.400
Smith, Ozzie#	.292	24	7	0	3	1	1	.308	.292
Sosa, Sammy	.333	6	2	2	4	0	2	.333	1.333
Stillwell, K#	.286	7	2	0	1	1	0	.375	.286
Strawberry, D*	.091	11	1	1	2	2	5	.231	.364
Thompson, Mil*	.200	20	4	0	0	4	5	.333	.250
Thompson, Rob	.500	12	6	0	2	1	0	.538	.667
Thompson, Ry	.250	4	1	0	0	1	2	.400	.500
Vizcaino, J#	.200	5	1	0	0	0	0	.200	.200
Walker, Larry*	.182	11	2	1	2	0	4	.182	.455
Wallach, Tim	.259	27	7	1	4	0	3	.286	.407
Walton, J	.455	11	5	0	0	1	1	.538	.455
Williams, Ma	.235	17	4	1	2	2	5	.316	.588
Zeile, Todd	.125	8	1	0	1	1	0	.200	.250

Brad Pennington, Angels — LHP

Batter	Avg	AB	H	HR	BI	BB	SO	OBP	Slg
Jaha, John	.000	4	0	0	0	1	2	.000	.000
Myers, Greg*	.400	5	2	0	0	0	0	.400	.400

Troy Percival, Angels — RHP

Batter	Avg	AB	H	HR	BI	BB	SO	OBP	Slg
Alomar Jr, S	.143	7	1	1	1	0	2	.143	.571
Belle, Albert	.200	5	1	1	0	0	0	.200	.800
Berroa, G	.333	6	2	1	4	4	2	.600	.833
Brosius, S	.111	9	1	0	0	0	3	.111	.111
Cirillo, Jeff	.500	4	2	0	0	1	1	.600	.500
Cordova, M	.000	5	0	0	0	0	5	.000	.000
Curtis, Chad	.400	5	2	0	0	0	2	.400	.400
Gates, Brent#	.000	7	0	0	0	0	4	.000	.000
Guillen, O*	.429	7	3	0	3	0	0	.429	.429
Hale, Chip*	.167	6	1	0	0	0	1	.167	.167
Hoiles, Chris	.143	7	1	0	0	0	4	.143	.143
Lockhart, K*	.400	5	2	0	2	0	0	.400	.600
Macfarlane, M	.333	6	2	2	3	0	2	.333	1.333
Martinez, Da*	.000	5	0	0	0	0	2	.000	.000
McGwire, Mark	.000	9	0	0	0	3	4	.250	.000
Naehring, Tim	.200	5	1	0	2	1	0	.200	.400
O'Neill, Paul*	.200	5	1	0	0	0	3	.200	.200
Raines, Tim#	.200	5	1	1	1	0	0	.200	.800
Ripken, Cal	.200	5	1	0	1	0	0	.200	.200
Seitzer, K	.167	6	1	0	0	0	3	.286	.167
Steinbach, T	.333	9	3	1	2	1	3	.400	.667
Thomas, Frank	.250	4	1	1	2	2	2	.500	1.000
Thome, Jim*	.400	5	2	1	2	0	2	.400	1.000
Vaughn, Greg	.000	6	0	0	0	0	3	.000	.000
Ventura, R*	.750	4	3	0	0	1	1	.800	.750
Wilson, Dan	.167	6	1	0	1	0	3	.167	.167

Mike Perez, Cubs — RHP

Batter	Avg	AB	H	HR	BI	BB	SO	OBP	Slg
Abbott, Kurt	.167	6	1	0	0	0	2	.167	.167
Alou, Moises	.000	6	0	0	0	1	2	.143	.000
Arias, Alex	.375	8	3	0	1	0	1	.375	.375
Bagwell, Jeff	.667	6	4	1	6	2	0	.750	1.333
Barberie, B#	.714	7	5	1	3	0	1	.750	1.286
Bell, Jay	.286	14	4	0	2	0	2	.333	.429
Belliard, R	.125	8	1	0	0	0	2	.125	.125
Berry, Sean	.200	5	1	0	0	1	0	.200	.200
Bichette, D	.600	5	3	0	1	0	0	.600	.800
Biggio, Craig	.333	12	4	0	0	1	0	.385	.500
Blauser, Jeff	.125	8	1	1	1	0	2	.125	.500
Bonds, Barry*	.429	7	3	0	0	1	1	.500	.429
Bonilla, B#	.286	7	2	0	1	1	2	.375	.429
Boone, Bret	.000	5	0	0	0	0	3	.000	.000
Branson, Jeff	.333	6	2	0	0	0	0	.333	.333
Brumfield, J	.400	5	2	0	0	0	0	.400	.600
Butler, Brett*	.500	8	4	0	1	0	1	.500	.500
Caminiti, Ken#	.333	6	2	0	1	1	0	.429	.500
Cangelosi, J#	.500	4	2	0	1	0	0	.600	.500
Cedeno, A	.625	8	5	1	5	0	3	.625	1.125
Cianfrocco, A	.429	7	3	0	2	1	1	.500	.429
Clayton, R	.300	10	3	0	1	1	3	.364	.300
Colbrunn, G	.500	4	2	0	1	1	0	.600	1.000
Coleman, V#	.333	6	2	1	4	0	0	.333	.833
Conine, Jeff	.143	7	1	0	0	2	4	.333	.143
Cordero, Wil	.200	10	2	0	0	2	1	.333	.500
Daulton, D*	.000	4	0	0	0	2	1	.333	.000
Dawson, Andre	.375	8	3	0	0	2	0	.500	.500
DeShields, D*	.444	9	4	0	1	1	0	.500	.556
Duncan, M	.200	5	1	0	0	0	1	.200	.200
Dunston, S	.167	6	1	0	0	0	0	.167	.167
Dykstra, L*	.000	5	0	0	0	0	0	.000	.000
Finley, Steve*	.200	5	1	0	2	0	2	.429	.200
Fletcher, D*	.167	6	1	0	0	0	0	.167	.167
Frazier, Lou#	.600	5	3	0	0	0	0	.600	1.000
Galarraga, A	.364	11	4	1	4	1	2	.417	.727
Gant, Ron	.500	10	5	0	0	2	4	.583	.500
Garcia, C	.250	4	1	0	1	1	0	.333	.250
Girardi, Joe	.222	9	2	0	1	0	1	.200	.222
Grace, Mark*	.250	8	2	0	1	1	0	.333	.375
Grissom, M	.353	17	6	1	4	1	3	.389	.588
Gutierrez, R	.400	5	2	0	0	0	0	.400	.600
Harris, Lenny*	.167	6	1	0	0	0	2	.167	.167
Hayes, C	.444	9	4	0	4	0	2	.400	.556
Hernandez, Ca	.000	5	0	0	0	0	3	.000	.000
Hill, G	.000	6	0	0	0	0	1	.000	.000
Hollins, Dave#	.250	4	1	0	0	1	1	.500	.250
Howard, T*	.000	5	0	0	0	1	0	.167	.000
Hundley, Todd#	.000	4	0	0	0	2	1	.333	.000
Hunter, Bri L	.200	5	1	0	0	0	3	.200	.200
Incaviglia, P	.375	8	3	2	6	0	1	.375	1.125
Jordan, Ricky	.600	5	3	0	1	0	0	.600	1.000
Justice, Dave*	.200	5	1	0	0	2	2	.429	.200
Karros, Eric	.125	8	1	0	0	3	3	.364	.125
King, Jeff	.357	14	5	1	4	0	1	.333	.571
Lansing, Mike	.333	6	2	0	1	0	1	.375	.333
Larkin, Barry	.364	11	4	1	1	1	4	.417	.636
Lemke, Mark#	.455	11	5	0	2	0	0	.455	.455
Lewis, Darren	.250	8	2	0	1	1	2	.333	.250
Magadan, Dave*	.429	7	3	0	0	1	0	.500	.429
Manwaring, K	.125	8	1	0	0	1	1	.222	.125
Martinez, Da*	.000	7	0	0	0	1	0	.125	.000
May, Derrick*	.000	5	0	0	0	1	0	.167	.000
McGee, Willie#	.000	6	0	0	0	2	2	.250	.000
Merced, O*	.600	10	6	0	1	1	0	.636	.600
Mondesi, Raul	.333	9	3	0	1	0	4	.300	.444
Morandini, M*	.400	5	2	0	0	1	1	.500	.400
Morris, Hal*	.429	7	3	1	1	1	0	.500	.857
Murray, Eddie*	.333	6	2	0	0	1	2	.429	.333
Nixon, Otis#	.286	7	2	0	3	3	0	.500	.429
Offerman, J*	.000	7	0	0	0	1	2	.125	.000
Oliver, Joe	.143	7	1	0	0	1	0	.250	.143
Pendleton, T#	.273	11	3	0	0	0	0	.273	.455
Phillips, J*	.400	5	2	0	0	0	0	.400	.400
Piazza, Mike	.125	8	1	0	1	0	4	.125	.125
Reed, Jody	.000	3	0	0	0	2	0	.400	.000
Rodriguez, H*	.200	5	1	0	0	0	0	.200	.400
Sabo, Chris	.500	6	3	1	1	0	0	.500	1.333
Sandberg, R	.250	12	3	0	3	0	0	.231	.333
Sanders, R	.167	6	1	0	2	1	1	.286	.333
Schofield, D	.200	5	1	0	0	1	0	.333	.200
Slaught, Don	.000	5	0	0	0	1	0	.167	.000
Smith, Dwight*	.167	6	1	0	0	0	0	.286	.167
Sosa, Sammy	.000	7	0	0	0	0	0	.000	.000
Thompson, Mil*	.250	4	1	0	0	1	1	.500	.500
Thompson, Rob	.286	7	2	0	1	1	2	.375	.286
Vizcaino, J#	.333	6	2	1	3	0	0	.429	.833
Walker, Larry*	.250	4	1	0	0	0	0	.250	.750
Wallach, Tim	.105	19	2	0	2	2	4	.182	.105
Walton, J	.286	7	2	0	0	0	0	.286	.429
Weiss, Walt#	.500	4	2	0	1	0	1	.600	1.000
Williams, E	.400	5	2	0	0	0	1	.400	.400
Williams, Ma	.111	9	1	0	0	2	1	.273	.111

Yorkis Perez, Marlins — LHP

Batter	Avg	AB	H	HR	BI	BB	SO	OBP	Slg
Alicea, Luis#	.333	6	2	0	0	0	0	.333	.500
Bell, Jay	.500	4	2	0	0	1	0	.600	1.000
Bonds, Barry*	.400	5	2	0	2	2	1	.571	.400
Boone, Bret	.333	6	2	0	1	0	2	.333	.333
Brogna, Rico*	.200	5	1	0	1	0	3	.200	.200
Butler, Brett*	.250	4	1	0	0	0	1	.250	.250
Caminiti, Ken#	.250	4	1	0	0	2	1	.500	.333
Daulton, D*	.250	4	1	1	2	1	1	.400	1.000
DeShields, D*	.000	4	0	0	1	1	2	.167	.000
Dykstra, L*	.000	3	0	0	0	2	2	.400	.000
Eisenreich, J	.214	14	3	0	2	0	3	.214	.214
Finley, Steve*	.250	4	1	0	0	1	1	.400	.750
Galarraga, A	.000	3	0	0	0	2	2	.400	.000
Gonzalez, L*	.000	4	0	0	0	0	4	.000	.000
Grace, Mark*	.250	8	2	0	2	0	2	.250	.250
Hundley, Todd#	.000	4	0	0	0	2	2	.333	.000
Jefferies, G#	.500	6	3	0	0	0	0	.500	.667
Jones, C#	.000	4	0	0	0	3	2	.429	.000
Justice, Dave*	.400	5	2	1	2	4	0	.667	1.400
King, Jeff	.667	3	2	0	1	3	0	.833	1.000
Kingery, Mike*	.333	6	2	0	0	0	1	.333	.333
Klesko, Ryan*	.125	8	1	0	0	1	2	.300	.125
Lankford, Ray*	.000	4	0	0	0	1	4	.125	.250
Lemke, Mark#	.000	4	0	0	0	1	1	.200	.000
Mabry, John*	.200	5	1	0	0	0	1	.200	.200
Martin, Al*	.333	6	2	0	2	1	0	.429	.333
McGriff, Fred*	.313	16	5	1	5	2	1	.389	.563
Merced, O*	.111	9	1	0	0	1	1	.200	.111
Morandini, M*	.200	10	2	0	0	0	1	.273	.200

Yorkis Perez, Marlins — LHP

Batter	Avg	AB	H	HR	BI	BB	SO	OBP	Slg
Morris, Hal*	.167	6	1	0	1	1	2	.286	.333
Mouton, James	.200	5	1	0	0	1	1	.333	.400
Taubensee, E*	.333	6	2	1	2	0	2	.333	.833
Walker, Larry*	.200	5	1	1	1	0	2	.200	.800
Weiss, Walt#	.200	5	1	0	1	0	0	.200	.200
Whiten, Mark*	.167	6	1	0	0	0	0	.167	.500
Wilkins, Rick*	.000	6	0	0	0	0	3	.000	.000
Zeile, Todd	.333	6	2	0	0	4	0	.600	.500

Robert Person, Mets — RHP

Batter	Avg	AB	H	HR	BI	BB	SO	OBP	Slg
Amaro, Ruben#	.000	4	0	0	0	1	0	.333	.000
Aurilia, Rich	.000	3	0	0	1	1	0	.200	.000
Bell, Jay	.400	5	2	0	0	1	2	.500	.400
Benard, M*	.667	3	2	0	2	2	1	.800	1.000
Bonds, Barry*	.333	3	1	0	0	2	1	.600	.667
Boone, Bret	.286	7	2	0	0	0	2	.286	.571
Branson, Jeff*	.400	5	2	0	0	1	1	.500	.400
Clark, Dave*	.500	4	2	1	3	1	2	.600	1.250
Clayton, R	.400	5	2	0	1	0	0	.400	.600
Davis, Eric	.167	6	1	0	0	0	1	.167	.500
Dye, Jermaine	.200	5	1	0	0	0	1	.200	.200
Greene, W*	.250	4	1	0	0	1	0	.400	.250
Grissom, M	.400	5	2	0	1	0	0	.333	.600
Harris, Lenny*	.200	5	1	0	1	0	2	.200	.400
Hill, G	.200	5	1	0	0	0	2	.200	.400
Johnson, Mark*	.200	5	1	0	0	1	2	.333	.400
Jones, C#	.200	5	1	0	0	2	1	.429	.200
Lemke, Mark#	.400	5	2	0	0	0	0	.400	.400
Liriano, N#	.200	5	1	0	1	0	1	.167	.200
Lopez, Javy	.200	5	1	1	1	0	1	.200	.800
Magee, W	.167	6	1	0	0	0	0	.167	.333
Martin, Al*	.167	6	1	0	0	0	3	.167	.167
McGriff, Fred*	.167	6	1	0	1	0	0	.167	.167
Morris, Hal*	.143	7	1	1	1	0	2	.143	.571
Mueller, Bill#	.200	5	1	0	0	0	2	.200	.200
Otero, Ricky#	.000	5	0	0	0	0	0	.000	.000
Pendleton, T#	.286	7	2	2	3	0	3	.286	1.143
Relaford, D#	.167	6	1	0	0	1	2	.286	.167
Sanders, R	.125	8	1	1	1	1	1	.222	.500
Sefcik, Kevin	.400	5	2	0	0	0	0	.400	.400
Stocker, K*	.000	5	0	0	0	0	3	.000	.000
Wilkins, Rick*	.000	6	0	0	0	0	3	.000	.000
Zuber, Jon*	.200	5	1	1	2	0	1	.333	.800

Chris Peters, Pirates — LHP

Batter	Avg	AB	H	HR	BI	BB	SO	OBP	Slg
Bagwell, Jeff	.500	4	2	0	0	3	1	.714	.750
Batiste, Kim	.333	6	2	0	0	0	0	.333	.667
Bell, Derek	.400	5	2	0	0	2	1	.571	.400
Berry, Sean	.333	6	2	0	4	1	0	.429	.333
Biggio, Craig	.400	5	2	0	0	2	2	.571	.400
Caminiti, Ken#	.400	5	2	1	1	0	0	.400	1.000
Eusebio, Tony	.000	5	0	0	0	0	1	.000	.000
Gwynn, Tony*	.200	5	1	0	0	0	0	.200	.200
Hill, G	.333	6	2	1	1	0	0	.333	1.000
Hunter, Bri L	.286	7	2	0	0	0	0	.286	.286
Jones, Dax	.286	7	2	0	1	0	1	.286	.571
McCarty, Dave	.167	6	1	0	0	0	1	.167	.167
Mouton, James	.500	4	2	0	0	1	0	.600	.500

Mark Petkovsek, Cardinals — RHP

Batter	Avg	AB	H	HR	BI	BB	SO	OBP	Slg
Abbott, Kurt	.000	8	0	0	0	0	1	.000	.000
Alfonzo, E	.143	7	1	0	1	0	0	.143	.143
Ashley, Billy	.000	6	0	0	0	0	3	.000	.000
Aurilia, Rich	.167	6	1	0	0	0	1	.167	.167
Bagwell, Jeff	.750	4	3	0	3	2	0	.833	1.000
Bates, Jason#	.286	7	2	0	1	0	0	.286	.286
Bell, Derek	.250	4	1	0	2	1	0	.400	.250
Bell, Jay	.286	7	2	1	2	0	0	.286	1.000
Benard, M*	.286	7	2	0	0	0	1	.286	.286
Bichette, D	.200	20	4	2	4	1	6	.238	.500
Biggio, Craig	.400	5	2	0	0	0	2	.500	.400
Bonds, Barry*	.111	9	1	1	1	3	1	.333	.444
Boone, Bret	.250	4	1	0	0	1	0	.333	.250
Branson, Jeff*	.250	8	2	0	1	0	0	.250	.250
Brito, Jorge	.250	4	1	0	1	0	0	.400	.500
Brogna, Rico*	.222	9	2	0	1	0	0	.222	.222
Burks, Ellis	.250	8	2	0	0	5	1	.538	.250
Butler, Brett*	.444	9	4	0	0	1	1	.500	.889
Carr, Chuck	.000	5	0	0	0	1	1	.167	.000
Carreon, Mark	.250	8	2	1	2	0	1	.250	.625
Castilla, V	.150	20	3	0	1	0	3	.150	.150
Clayton, R	.000	6	0	0	0	0	2	.000	.000
Colbrunn, G	.444	9	4	0	2	0	1	.444	.556
Conine, Jeff	.000	6	0	0	0	0	0	.000	.000
Davis, Eric	.286	7	2	0	0	0	0	.286	.286
DeShields, D*	.273	11	3	0	0	1	0	.333	.273
Fonville, C#	.167	6	1	0	0	0	1	.167	.167
Gagne, Greg	.400	5	2	0	1	0	1	.500	.400

Mark Petkovsek, Cardinals — RHP

Batter	Avg	AB	H	HR	BI	BB	SO	OBP	Slg
Galarraga, A	.409	22	9	1	4	2	5	.480	.727
Gant, Ron	.400	5	2	0	0	1	1	.500	.600
Gilkey, B	.400	5	2	1	3	1	0	.500	1.000
Girardi, Joe	.286	7	2	0	1	0	2	.286	.286
Gonzalez, L*	.222	9	2	0	2	0	0	.222	.222
Grace, Mark*	.333	9	3	1	2	1	0	.364	.667
Grissom, M	.200	5	1	0	0	3	0	.500	.400
Gutierrez, R	.000	3	0	0	1	1	0	.200	.000
Gwynn, Tony*	.250	4	1	0	0	1	0	.400	.250
Hansen, Dave*	.200	5	1	0	2	1	0	.333	.400
Hayes, C	.400	5	2	0	0	0	0	.400	.400
Hernandez, Jo	.000	5	0	0	1	0	2	.000	.000
Hill, G	.143	7	1	0	0	0	1	.250	.286
Hollandsworth*	.333	6	2	0	1	0	2	.333	.500
Hundley, Todd#	.600	5	3	0	3	2	1	.625	.800
Huskey, Butch	.250	4	1	0	0	1	1	.400	.250
Johnson, Char	.400	5	2	0	1	0	1	.400	.400
Jones, C#	.167	6	1	0	1	1	0	.286	.167
Jones, Chris	.143	7	1	0	1	0	0	.143	.143
Karros, Eric	.267	15	4	1	3	3	2	.389	.533
Kelly, R	.455	11	5	0	2	2	2	.538	.455
Kent, Jeff	.200	5	1	0	0	0	0	.200	.400
Kingery, Mike*	.333	12	4	0	2	0	0	.333	.333
Klesko, Ryan*	.200	5	1	0	2	0	0	.200	.400
Larkin, Barry	.286	7	2	0	0	0	0	.286	.286
Lemke, Mark#	.167	6	1	0	0	0	0	.167	.167
Manwaring, K	.000	6	0	0	0	0	1	.000	.000
McGriff, Fred*	.200	5	1	0	2	0	0	.200	.200
McRae, Brian#	.375	8	3	0	0	4	0	.583	.500
Mondesi, Raul	.273	11	3	0	1	2	0	.429	.273
Morris, Hal*	.600	5	3	1	1	2	0	.714	1.200
Offerman, J#	.333	12	6	0	2	0	0	.500	.667
Orsulak, Joe*	.333	3	1	0	0	2	0	.600	.333
Pendleton, T#	.333	6	2	1	2	0	1	.333	.833
Piazza, Mike	.333	18	6	1	6	0	2	.333	.500
Reed, Jeff*	.400	5	2	0	1	0	0	.400	.600
Reed, Jody	.000	8	0	0	0	0	1	.000	.000
Sanders, Deion*	.500	4	2	1	2	1	1	.600	1.250
Sanders, R	.333	6	2	1	2	1	1	.429	.833
Santiago, B	.286	7	2	0	0	1	1	.375	.429
Servais, S	.125	8	1	0	0	1	2	.222	.125
Sosa, Sammy	.400	10	4	2	5	1	0	.455	1.100
Thompson, Rob	.429	7	3	1	2	0	2	.429	1.143
Veras, Q#	.000	5	0	0	0	0	1	.167	.000
Vizcaino, J#	.429	7	3	0	0	0	0	.429	.571
Walker, Larry*	.333	15	5	1	7	1	1	.353	.667
Wallach, Tim	.500	8	4	0	3	1	1	.556	.750
Weiss, Walt#	.188	16	3	0	0	1	2	.235	.188
Wilkins, Rick*	.200	5	1	0	2	1	0	.333	.400
Williams, Ma	.833	6	5	2	2	1	0	.857	2.167
Young, Eric	.429	14	6	0	0	1	0	.500	.429
Zeile, Todd	.286	7	2	0	1	2	0	.444	.429

Andy Pettitte, Yankees — LHP

Batter	Avg	AB	H	HR	BI	BB	SO	OBP	Slg
Alicea, Luis#	.000	6	0	0	0	0	1	.000	.000
Alomar, R#	.250	8	2	0	0	1	2	.333	.250
Alomar Jr, S	.500	6	3	0	1	0	1	.500	.500
Amaral, Rich	.000	7	0	0	0	0	0	.000	.000
Anderson, Brd*	.333	15	5	0	0	1	1	.412	.533
Anderson, G*	.286	14	4	0	0	0	5	.286	.286
Baerga, C#	.333	15	5	0	1	2	3	.412	.467
Batista, Tony	.250	8	2	0	1	0	2	.250	.500
Battle, Allen	.400	4	0	0	0	2	1	.333	.000
Bautista, D	.182	11	2	0	0	0	3	.182	.182
Belle, Albert	.400	15	6	1	2	2	1	.471	.800
Berroa, G	.600	15	9	2	4	3	2	.632	1.133
Blowers, Mike	.167	6	1	0	0	0	3	.167	.167
Bonilla, B#	.438	16	7	1	4	0	2	.438	.625
Borders, Pat	.375	8	3	0	0	1	1	.444	.500
Bordick, Mike	.200	15	3	0	0	2	1	.294	.200
Bragg, Darren*	.200	5	1	0	0	2	0	.200	.200
Brosius, S	.400	10	4	0	1	0	2	.400	.500
Brumfield, J	.125	16	2	0	1	0	7	.125	.125
Buford, Damon	.333	6	2	0	0	0	1	.333	.333
Buhner, Jay	.167	6	1	1	3	2	1	.375	.667
Canseco, Jose	.333	12	4	1	2	0	2	.333	.583
Carter, Joe	.250	20	5	1	1	1	1	.286	.400
Cedeno, D#	.000	6	0	0	0	1	3	.143	.000
Cirillo, Jeff	.500	12	6	1	2	2	2	.571	1.000
Clark, Tony*	.000	5	0	0	0	1	1	.167	.000
Clark, Will*	.286	7	2	0	2	0	1	.250	.429
Coleman, V#	.000	10	0	0	0	0	2	.000	.000
Coomer, Ron	.000	5	0	0	0	1	0	.000	.000
Cordova, M	.750	4	3	0	1	2	0	.833	.750
Curtis, Chad	.308	13	4	0	0	4	0	.308	.308
Damon, Johnny*	.250	4	1	0	0	2	1	.500	.250
Davis, Chili#	.125	16	2	1	2	8	6	.222	.313
Devereaux, M	.100	10	1	0	1	1	2	.182	.100
DiSarcina, M	.333	12	4	0	2	0	0	.308	.417
Durham, Ray#	.273	11	3	0	2	1	2	.333	.455

164

Batter	Avg	AB	H	HR	BI	BB	SO	OBP	Slg
Easley, D	.300	10	3	0	2	0	1	.300	.400
Edmonds, Jim*	.067	15	1	0	0	1	3	.125	.200
Elster, Kevin	.286	7	2	0	0	1	1	.375	.429
Espinoza, A	.286	7	2	0	0	1	1	.375	.286
Fabregas, Jor*	.286	7	2	0	0	0	2	.286	.286
Fielder, C	.545	11	6	0	1	1	1	.583	.727
Flaherty, J	.273	11	3	0	2	0	0	.273	.364
Franco, Julio	.556	9	5	0	0	1	1	.600	.667
Frye, Jeff	.429	7	3	0	1	0	0	.429	.571
Fryman, T	.286	14	4	0	1	1	4	.333	.357
Gaetti, Gary	.143	7	1	0	1	1	3	.250	.143
Garciaparra	.200	5	1	0	0	0	2	.200	.200
Gates, Brent#	.444	9	4	0	0	1	1	.444	.556
Giambi, Jason*	.429	7	3	0	1	0	2	.429	.571
Gomez, Chris	.333	9	3	0	1	4	3	.538	.333
Gonzalez, A	.095	21	2	1	2	0	8	.095	.286
Gonzalez, J	.545	11	6	1	3	0	2	.545	1.000
Goodwin, C*	.000	5	0	0	0	0	0	.000	.000
Goodwin, Tom*	.143	7	1	0	0	0	2	.143	.143
Greenwell, M*	.417	12	5	0	2	1	1	.462	.667
Greer, Rusty*	.250	8	2	1	2	0	3	.250	.625
Griffey Jr, K*	.286	7	2	0	0	2	1	.444	.286
Guillen, O*	.600	5	3	0	0	0	1	.600	.600
Hamelin, Bob*	.375	8	3	0	0	0	3	.375	.375
Hamilton, D*	.500	10	5	0	3	0	2	.500	.500
Hammonds, J	.500	4	2	0	1	0	0	.500	.500
Haselman, B	.111	9	1	0	0	0	0	.111	.222
Henderson, R	.286	7	2	0	2	1	1	.375	.286
Hiatt, Phil	.375	8	3	0	1	0	1	.375	.500
Higginson, B*	.200	5	1	0	0	0	0	.200	.200
Hoiles, Chris	.200	10	2	1	1	2	2	.333	.500
Hollins, Dave#	.400	5	2	0	1	1	1	.500	.600
Howard, Dave#	.167	6	1	0	1	1	2	.286	.167
Hudler, Rex	.286	7	2	0	0	0	3	.286	.429
Huff, Michael	.400	5	2	0	0	1	0	.500	.600
Jaha, John	.167	6	1	0	0	1	0	.167	.333
Javier, Stan#	.286	7	2	0	1	0	0	.286	.429
Joyner, Wally*	.375	8	3	0	0	1	1	.444	.500
Karkovice, R	.400	5	2	0	0	2	1	.571	.400
Kelly, R	.000	5	0	0	0	0	3	.000	.000
Knoblauch, C	.200	5	1	0	0	1	0	.333	.200
Lesher, Brian	.167	6	1	0	1	0	3	.167	.167
Lewis, Darren	.143	7	1	0	0	0	2	.143	.286
Listach, Pat#	.200	10	2	0	2	1	1	.273	.300
Lofton, Kenny*	.176	17	3	0	0	1	2	.222	.176
Lovullo, T#	.200	5	1	0	1	0	1	.200	.200
Manto, N	.000	9	0	0	0	0	3	.000	.000
Martin, N	.333	6	2	0	0	0	1	.333	.333
Martinez, E	.333	6	2	2	5	3	1	.556	1.333
Matheny, Mike	.167	6	1	0	0	0	1	.167	.167
McGee, Willie*	.429	7	3	0	0	0	2	.429	.714
McGwire, Mark	.294	17	5	2	5	1	3	.333	.824
McLemore, M#	.167	12	2	0	2	1	1	.214	.167
Meares, Pat	.667	6	4	0	1	0	0	.667	1.000
Mieske, Matt	.333	12	4	0	0	2	2	.429	.417
Molitor, Paul	.071	14	1	0	0	0	3	.071	.071
Mouton, Lyle	.286	7	2	0	1	0	3	.286	.286
Murray, Eddie*	.438	16	7	0	5	0	2	.438	.438
Naehring, Tim	.500	6	3	0	0	2	0	.625	.500
Nevin, Phil	.250	4	1	0	1	1	1	.400	.250
Nilsson, Dave*	.333	6	2	0	0	1	0	.429	.333
Nixon, Otis*	.412	17	7	0	0	1	0	.412	.529
O'Brien, C	.400	10	4	0	0	2	3	.500	.500
Offerman, J#	.000	5	0	0	0	0	3	.000	.000
Olerud, John*	.125	8	1	0	0	1	1	.222	.250
Palmeiro, R*	.250	20	5	1	4	0	1	.238	.400
Palmer, Dean	.500	4	2	0	0	1	1	.600	.750
Paquette, J	.333	6	2	0	1	0	2	.333	.500
Pena, Tony	.000	4	0	0	0	1	0	.200	.000
Perez, Robert	.389	18	7	0	2	0	2	.389	.389
Perez, Tomas#	.250	12	3	0	2	0	3	.250	.250
Perry, H	.500	6	3	2	2	0	1	.500	1.500
Phillips, T#	.167	12	2	0	1	4	2	.353	.250
Ramirez, M	.467	15	7	2	5	0	3	.467	.933
Randa, Joe	.400	5	2	0	0	0	0	.400	.400
Ripken, Billy	.000	5	0	0	0	0	0	.000	.000
Ripken, Cal	.267	15	4	0	0	2	2	.353	.467
Rodriguez, A	.167	6	1	1	1	0	2	.167	.667
Rodriguez, I	.357	14	5	2	3	0	1	.357	.786
Salmon, Tim	.188	16	3	0	1	3	2	.333	.421
Samuel, Juan	.263	19	5	1	3	2	7	.333	.421
Seitzer, K	.200	10	2	0	1	3	2	.385	.200
Sierra, Ruben#	.444	9	4	2	6	0	0	.444	1.222
Slaught, Don	.600	5	3	0	0	1	0	.667	.800
Smith, Mark	.250	8	2	0	0	0	3	.250	.250
Snopek, Chris	.286	7	2	0	0	2	1	.444	.429
Snow, J.T.#	.188	16	3	0	0	2	5	.235	.188
Sprague, Ed	.313	16	5	3	7	4	2	.450	1.000
Steinbach, T	.200	15	3	0	0	0	5	.200	.200
Stevens, Lee*	.400	5	2	0	2	0	2	.400	.400
Surhoff, B.J.*	.533	15	8	0	3	0	1	.533	.600

Batter	Avg	AB	H	HR	BI	BB	SO	OBP	Slg
Tartabull, D	.000	7	0	0	1	1	3	.125	.000
Tettleton, M#	.500	4	2	0	0	4	1	.750	.750
Thomas, Frank	.556	9	5	1	2	4	0	.692	1.000
Tinsley, Lee#	.000	5	0	0	0	0	2	.000	.000
Trammell, A	.333	9	3	0	0	0	1	.333	.556
Valentin, Jhn	.125	8	1	0	1	1	1	.222	.250
Valentin, Jse#	.429	7	3	0	2	3	1	.545	.429
Vaughn, Greg	.500	10	5	1	5	3	0	.615	.900
Vaughn, Mo*	.250	12	3	0	0	2	5	.357	.250
Velarde, R	.571	7	4	2	3	1	1	.700	1.571
Vizquel, Omar#	.167	12	2	0	0	2	1	.286	.167
Voigt, Jack	.400	5	2	1	3	0	2	.400	1.200
Wallach, Tim	.167	6	1	1	1	0	1	.167	.667
Wilson, Dan	.500	4	2	0	2	1	0	.600	.500
Young, Ernie	.154	13	2	1	1	0	2	.154	.385

Batter	Avg	AB	H	HR	BI	BB	SO	OBP	Slg
Aldrete, Mike*	.000	5	0	0	0	0	0	.000	.000
Alomar, R#	.500	14	7	0	1	0	0	.533	.643
Alomar Jr, S	.167	6	1	0	1	0	0	.167	.167
Amaral, Rich	.111	9	1	0	0	1	1	.200	.111
Anderson, Brd*	.417	12	5	1	1	2	0	.500	.833
Anderson, G*	.400	5	2	0	0	0	0	.400	.400
Baerga, C	.077	13	1	0	4	1	1	.125	.154
Baines, H*	.333	12	4	0	1	0	1	.333	.333
Belle, Albert	.235	17	4	0	0	6	4	.458	.353
Berroa, G	.125	8	1	0	0	0	1	.125	.125
Boggs, Wade*	.154	13	2	0	0	2	2	.267	.154
Borders, Pat	.556	9	5	0	0	0	0	.556	.778
Bordick, Mike	.462	13	6	0	6	0	0	.500	.538
Buhner, Jay	.357	14	5	1	3	2	4	.471	.643
Burks, Ellis	.375	8	3	0	0	1	1	.500	.375
Canseco, Jose	.300	10	3	0	2	1	1	.364	.400
Carter, Joe	.133	15	2	0	1	0	2	.188	.133
Cedeno, D#	.500	6	3	0	0	0	0	.500	.833
Cora, Joey#	.333	12	4	0	1	1	0	.357	.333
Cordova, M	.400	5	2	0	2	0	1	.400	.600
Curtis, Chad	.333	18	6	0	0	4	4	.455	.389
Cuyler, Milt*	.000	5	0	0	0	0	2	.000	.000
Davis, Chili*	.222	18	4	1	5	0	2	.222	.444
Devereaux, M	.250	16	4	0	2	1	0	.278	.250
Diaz, Alex#	.000	5	0	0	1	0	0	.000	.000
DiSarcina, G	.231	13	3	0	3	2	0	.333	.385
Durham, Ray#	.333	6	2	0	0	0	0	.333	.500
Easley, D	.250	4	1	0	0	1	0	.400	.250
Edmonds, Jim*	.167	12	2	1	1	1	4	.231	.500
Fabregas, Jor*	.000	5	0	0	0	0	0	.000	.000
Fermin, Felix	.077	13	1	0	0	0	0	.143	.077
Fielder, C	.273	11	3	0	4	2	1	.429	.364
Franco, Julio	.273	11	3	0	2	2	3	.385	.273
Fryman, T	.375	16	6	0	4	3	6	.474	.500
Gaetti, Gary	.500	6	3	0	1	0	1	.500	.833
Gates, Brent#	.667	12	8	0	2	0	0	.667	.750
Gomez, Chris	.000	5	0	0	0	0	0	.000	.000
Gomez, Leo	.455	11	5	1	2	2	2	.538	.818
Gonzales, R	.333	3	1	0	0	2	0	.600	.333
Gonzalez, J	.333	18	6	2	4	0	3	.333	.833
Grebeck, C	.333	3	1	0	0	2	0	.600	.667
Green, Shawn*	.000	4	0	0	0	1	1	.200	.000
Griffey Jr, K*	.273	22	6	0	1	2	0	.333	.273
Guillen, O*	.182	11	2	0	1	0	1	.182	.273
Hall, Mel*	.143	7	1	0	0	0	1	.143	.143
Hamilton, D*	.267	15	4	0	0	1	0	.267	.333
Hammonds, J	.500	5	1	0	0	1	0	.200	.200
Henderson, R	.000	2	0	0	0	2	1	.600	.000
Hill, G	.500	6	3	0	0	0	0	.500	.500
Hoiles, Chris	.500	6	3	2	4	1	0	.571	1.500
Hulse, David*	.333	6	2	0	0	0	2	.333	.333
Huson, Jeff*	.333	6	2	0	0	0	1	.333	.333
Jaha, John	.385	13	5	0	2	1	1	.429	.538
James, Dion*	.125	8	1	0	2	1	0	.200	.250
Jefferson, R*	.200	5	1	0	0	2	2	.429	.400
Johnson, L*	.333	12	4	0	1	1	0	.385	.333
Karkovice, R	.067	15	1	0	0	0	4	.067	.067
Kelly, Pat	.200	10	2	0	1	0	3	.200	.200
Kelly, R	.250	4	1	0	1	0	2	.400	.750
Kirby, Wayne*	.300	10	3	0	1	0	0	.300	.300
Knoblauch, C	.385	13	5	0	1	4	2	.529	.692
Knorr, Randy	.000	5	0	0	0	0	2	.000	.000
Kreuter, Chad#	.000	8	0	0	0	1	0	.000	.000
Leius, Scott	.200	5	1	0	2	1	0	.333	.200
Lewis, Mark	.143	7	1	0	0	1	3	.250	.143
Listach, Pat#	.250	4	1	0	1	1	2	.400	.250
Livingstone*	.286	7	2	0	0	0	0	.286	.286
Lofton, Kenny*	.211	19	4	0	0	2	0	.286	.211
Lovullo, T#	.143	7	1	0	0	1	0	.250	.143
Martinez, Da*	.000	6	0	0	0	1	0	.143	.000
Martinez, E	.500	12	6	2	5	4	0	.625	1.083
Martinez, T*	.250	12	3	0	2	1	1	.357	.250
McGwire, Mark	.250	4	1	1	3	1	2	.400	1.000

Hipolito Pichardo, Royals — RHP

Batter	Avg	AB	H	HR	BI	BB	SO	OBP	Slg
McLemore, M#	.455	11	5	0	2	0	2	.455	.636
Molitor, Paul	.261	23	6	0	2	2	2	.320	.391
Munoz, Pedro	.167	6	1	0	0	0	3	.167	.167
Myers, Greg*	.714	7	5	2	4	2	0	.778	1.571
Naehring, Tim	.333	9	3	0	1	2	1	.455	.333
Nilsson, Dave*	.600	5	3	0	1	0	1	.600	1.000
Nixon, Otis#	.000	4	0	0	1	0	2	.000	.000
O'Leary, Troy*	.571	7	4	0	1	1	1	.625	.571
O'Neill, Paul*	.125	8	1	0	0	3	0	.364	.125
Olerud, John*	.500	12	6	0	2	3	2	.600	.667
Palmeiro, R*	.500	14	7	2	3	1	1	.563	1.071
Palmer, Dean	.133	15	2	0	1	3	2	.316	.200
Pena, Tony	.286	7	2	0	0	0	1	.286	.286
Perez, E	.286	7	2	0	0	0	1	.286	.286
Phillips, T#	.462	13	6	0	0	4	0	.588	.538
Plantier, P*	.111	9	1	1	2	0	1	.111	.444
Polonia, Luis*	.222	18	4	0	1	5	2	.375	.278
Raines, Tim*	.429	14	6	0	1	3	1	.529	.714
Reboulet, J	.000	7	0	0	0	1	1	.125	.000
Reed, Jody	.182	11	2	1	1	0	1	.182	.455
Ripken, Billy	.143	7	1	0	0	1	1	.250	.143
Ripken, Cal	.235	17	4	0	2	2	1	.300	.353
Rodriguez, Al	.400	5	2	1	2	0	1	.400	1.000
Rodriguez, I	.300	20	6	0	1	1	0	.333	.400
Salmon, Tim	.368	19	7	0	3	2	2	.429	.421
Samuel, Juan	.400	5	2	0	1	0	2	.400	1.000
Schofield, D	.400	5	2	1	2	1	1	.500	1.000
Seitzer, K	.313	16	5	0	2	3	2	.421	.375
Sierra, Ruben#	.176	17	3	0	0	1	3	.222	.235
Snow, J.T.#	.154	13	2	0	0	1	3	.214	.154
Sojo, Luis	.533	15	8	0	4	0	1	.533	.600
Sorrento, P*	.250	16	4	1	3	1	1	.294	.500
Spiers, Bill*	.100	10	1	0	0	2	1	.250	.100
Sprague, Ed	.333	18	6	0	3	0	2	.333	.389
Stankiewicz	.286	7	2	0	0	0	0	.286	.429
Stanley, Mike	.571	7	4	0	1	2	2	.700	.714
Steinbach, T	.167	12	2	0	1	0	2	.167	.167
Strange, Doug#	.125	8	1	0	0	0	0	.125	.125
Surhoff, B.J.*	.545	11	6	0	2	1	0	.583	.818
Sveum, Dale*	.667	3	2	0	1	2	1	.800	1.333
Tartabull, D	.167	12	2	0	1	2	3	.286	.167
Tettleton, M	.143	14	2	0	1	2	5	.250	.214
Thomas, Frank	.227	22	5	1	4	3	6	.320	.409
Thome, Jim*	.333	12	4	0	2	1	2	.357	.333
Trammell, A	.500	4	2	0	0	1	0	.667	.500
Turner, Chris	.200	5	1	0	0	0	0	.333	.400
Valentin, Jse#	.714	7	5	0	4	1	0	.750	1.000
Valle, Dave	.250	8	2	0	0	1	0	.333	.250
Vaughn, Greg	.154	13	2	0	2	3	1	.313	.154
Vaughn, Mo*	.000	10	0	0	0	1	2	.091	.000
Velarde, R	.444	9	4	0	1	1	1	.455	.556
Ventura, R*	.143	21	3	0	0	2	2	.217	.143
Vizquel, Omar#	.385	13	5	0	0	2	1	.467	.385
Ward, Turner#	.182	11	2	0	3	0	1	.154	.182
White, Devon*	.231	13	3	0	0	0	1	.231	.231
Whiten, Mark#	.286	7	2	0	1	1	2	.375	.286
Williams, Ber#	.462	13	6	0	3	2	2	.533	.615
Williams, Ger	.000	5	0	0	0	0	1	.000	.000
Wilson, Dan	.000	3	0	0	1	0		.250	.000

Dan Plesac, Pirates — LHP

Batter	Avg	AB	H	HR	BI	BB	SO	OBP	Slg
Abbott, Kurt	.200	5	1	0	1	0	2	.200	.400
Alomar, R#	.077	13	1	0	1	1	2	.143	.077
Anthony, Eric*	.333	6	2	0	0	0	2	.333	.333
Arias, Alex	.400	5	2	0	0	0	1	.400	.400
Baerga, C#	.250	8	2	0	3	0	0	.250	.375
Baines, H*	.143	7	1	0	0	0	3	.143	.286
Belle, Albert	.200	5	1	0	0	0	0	.200	.200
Bichette, D	.400	10	4	1	3	0	2	.400	.800
Boggs, Wade*	.375	16	6	0	5	1	5	.412	.625
Bonds, Barry*	.333	15	5	1	4	2	2	.412	.667
Boone, Bret	.222	9	2	0	1	0	1	.222	.333
Borders, Pat	.077	13	1	0	0	2	1	.200	.077
Branson, Jeff*	.250	8	2	0	0	2	2	.400	.375
Buhner, Jay	.200	5	1	0	0	0	1	.200	.200
Burks, Ellis	.125	8	1	1	1	2	2	.222	.444
Butler, Brett*	.400	15	6	0	1	2	7	.471	.533
Caminiti, Ken#	.250	8	2	1	3	1	1	.333	.625
Cangelosi, J#	.143	7	1	0	0	0	4	.143	.143
Canseco, Jose	.182	11	2	0	1	0	6	.182	.182
Carreon, Mark	.167	6	1	0	0	0	3	.286	.167
Carter, Joe	.286	21	6	0	0	2	4	.348	.333
Castilla, V	.571	7	4	1	1	1	2	.625	1.143
Cedeno, A	.000	5	0	0	0	0	1	.000	.000
Clark, Phil	.333	3	1	0	2	1	1	.400	.333
Clayton, R	.250	8	2	0	1	1	1	.333	.250
Cuyler, Milt#	.571	7	4	0	0	1	0	.625	.714
Daulton, D*	.222	9	2	0	1	3	3	.417	.222
Davis, Chili#	.000	5	0	0	0	1	0	.167	.000
Deer, Rob	.000	11	0	0	0	0	5	.000	.000
DeShields, D*	.167	6	1	0	1	1	3	.286	.167
Duncan, M	.400	5	2	0	2	1	1	.500	.600
Dykstra, L*	.143	7	1	0	1	1	3	.250	.143
Eisenreich, J*	.316	19	6	0	2	2	6	.381	.316
Espinoza, A	.600	5	3	0	3	2	0	.714	.800
Fermin, Felix	.167	6	1	0	0	0	0	.167	.167
Fielder, C	.167	12	2	1	2	4	3	.353	.417
Finley, Steve*	.462	13	6	0	3	0	0	.462	.692
Fletcher, D*	.143	7	1	0	0	0	1	.143	.143
Franco, Julio	.455	11	5	1	1	2	1	.538	.727
Fryman, T	.111	9	1	0	0	0	0	.200	.111
Gaetti, Gary	.286	14	4	0	2	2	0	.412	.429
Gagne, Greg	.364	11	4	0	2	0	3	.333	.364
Galarraga, A	.400	5	2	1	3	0	0	.400	1.000
Gallego, Mike	.333	3	1	0	0	2	1	.600	.333
Gilkey, B	.286	7	2	1	2	1	2	.375	.714
Gomez, Leo	.167	6	1	0	0	1	2	.286	.333
Gonzalez, J	.500	4	2	1	1	1	0	.600	1.250
Gonzalez, L*	.167	6	1	0	3	0	1	.143	.333
Grace, Mark*	.333	9	3	0	2	0	3	.333	.333
Greenwell, M*	.375	8	3	0	2	0	0	.444	.375
Griffey Jr, K*	.167	12	2	0	1	0	2	.167	.250
Guillen, O*	.273	11	3	0	4	0	4	.333	.273
Gutierrez, R	.250	4	1	0	2	1	1	.400	.250
Gwynn, Tony*	.778	9	7	0	3	0	0	.700	1.111
Hall, Mel*	.250	8	2	0	2	1	1	.333	.375
Hayes, C	.000	5	0	0	0	0	3	.000	.000
Henderson, R	.273	11	3	0	0	2	3	.385	.273
Hernandez, Jo	.400	5	2	0	0	1	1	.400	.800
Hollins, Dave#	.200	5	1	0	0	0	0	.200	.200
Howard, T*	.200	10	2	0	2	0	2	.200	.200
Howell, Jack*	.000	5	0	0	0	2	1	.286	.000
Hundley, Todd#	.000	10	0	0	0	1	6	.091	.000
Incaviglia, P	.048	21	1	0	2	1	5	.091	.048
Javier, Stan#	.400	5	2	0	2	0	1	.400	.400
Jefferies, G#	.222	18	4	0	0	0	0	.222	.333
Johnson, L*	.167	12	2	0	1	1	3	.231	.167
Joyner, Wally	.385	26	10	0	5	1	5	.414	.538
Justice, Dave*	.143	7	1	0	1	2	2	.250	.143
Kelly, R	.222	9	2	0	1	2	3	.364	.222
Kent, Jeff	.222	9	2	1	2	0	2	.222	.556
King, Jeff	.200	5	1	1	1	0	0	.200	.800
Kingery, Mike*	.000	7	0	0	0	1	4	.125	.000
Klesko, Ryan*	.429	7	3	1	2	0	3	.375	.857
Lankford, Ray*	.333	12	4	1	6	0	7	.333	.917
Larkin, Barry	.000	6	0	0	0	2	0	.250	.000
Lewis, Darren	.500	6	3	0	1	0	1	.500	.500
Lewis, Mark	.222	9	2	0	0	0	2	.222	.222
Leyritz, Jim	.400	5	2	0	2	2	2	.571	.400
Liriano, N#	.143	7	1	0	0	1	4	.250	.143
Mabry, John*	.200	5	1	0	0	0	3	.200	.200
Macfarlane, M	.000	6	0	0	0	1	2	.143	.000
Magadan, Dave*	.000	6	0	0	0	1	2	.143	.000
Manwaring, K	.500	4	2	0	0	1	1	.600	.500
Marzano, John	.167	6	1	0	0	0	1	.167	.167
McGriff, Fred*	.192	26	5	1	3	3	7	.300	.385
McGwire, Mark	.333	9	3	1	2	0	4	.333	.667
McLemore, M#	.143	6	2	0	0	1	0	.429	.333
McRae, Brian*	.300	10	3	0	3	1	0	.364	.400
Merced, O*	.250	8	2	1	3	0	2	.250	.625
Miller, Orl	.500	4	2	0	0	1	0	.600	.750
Morandini, M*	.000	5	0	0	1	0	2	.000	.000
Morman, Russ	.600	5	3	0	1	1	0	.667	.600
Morris, Hal*	.154	13	2	1	2	0	6	.154	.385
Mouton, James	.600	5	3	1	3	0	0	.600	1.200
Murray, Eddie*	.250	12	3	0	1	1	2	.308	.250
Offerman, J#	.500	6	3	0	1	0	1	.571	.667
Olerud, John*	.400	5	2	0	1	1	2	.429	.400
Oliver, Joe	.375	8	3	1	4	0	1	.375	.750
Orsulak, Joe*	.167	12	2	0	1	0	1	.231	.250
Palmeiro, R	.273	11	3	2	6	1	2	.333	.818
Pena, Tony	.333	6	2	0	0	0	2	.333	.333
Pendleton, T#	.231	13	3	0	0	0	2	.231	.231
Phillips, T#	.182	11	2	0	1	7	2	.500	.182
Plantier, P*	.167	6	1	1	1	2	5	.375	.667
Polonia, Luis*	.000	5	0	0	0	1	1	.286	.000
Raines, Tim*	.333	3	1	0	0	2	0	.600	.333
Reed, Jody	.231	13	3	0	2	2	1	.333	.231
Ripken, Billy	.167	6	1	0	0	0	2	.167	.167
Ripken, Cal	.118	17	2	0	0	0	5	.118	.176
Roberts, Bip#	.200	5	1	0	1	0	0	.333	.200
Rodriguez, H*	.000	5	0	0	0	0	4	.000	.000
Sabo, Chris	.400	5	2	0	0	0	1	.400	.600
Sanders, R	.375	8	3	0	0	0	2	.375	.375
Scarsone, S	.000	5	0	0	0	0	4	.000	.000
Schofield, D	.182	11	2	0	3	1		.357	.364
Schu, Rick	.000	4	0	0	0	3	1	.200	.000
Segui, David#	.200	5	1	1	2	1	0	.333	.800
Seitzer, K	.200	5	1	0	0	2	2	.429	.200
Servais, S	.444	9	4	0	2	0	1	.444	.556
Shipley, C	.800	5	4	0	1	0	0	.800	.800

Dan Piesac, Pirates — LHP

Batter	Avg	AB	H	HR	BI	BB	SO	OBP	Slg
Sierra, Ruben#	.130	23	3	0	2	1	1	.167	.130
Slaught, Don	.182	11	2	0	2	0	4	.182	.273
Smith, Ozzie#	.200	10	2	0	1	0	1	.200	.300
Sosa, Sammy	.143	7	1	0	0	1	3	.250	.143
Stanley, Mike	.333	6	2	0	3	2	3	.500	.500
Steinbach, T	.300	10	3	0	1	0	4	.300	.400
Stevens, Lee*	.167	6	1	0	0	0	3	.167	.167
Stillwell, K#	.182	11	2	0	1	0	4	.182	.182
Stocker, K#	.400	5	2	0	0	0	0	.400	.400
Tartabull, D	.333	12	4	0	2	2	5	.429	.417
Taubensee, E*	.000	5	0	0	0	0	3	.000	.000
Tettleton, M#	.250	8	2	2	2	2	1	.400	1.000
Trammell, A	.091	11	1	1	2	0	1	.083	.364
Valle, Dave	.375	8	3	0	0	0	0	.375	.375
Velarde, R	.167	6	1	0	0	1	3	.286	.167
Ventura, R*	.429	7	3	1	4	0	0	.429	.857
Vizcaino, J#	.400	5	2	0	0	1	1	.500	.400
Walker, Larry*	.143	7	1	0	2	2	3	.333	.143
Weiss, Walt#	.182	11	2	0	0	0	2	.182	.182
White, Devon#	.167	24	4	0	1	0	5	.167	.292
Whiten, Mark&	.231	13	3	1	1	1	2	.286	.462
Williams, Ber#	.400	5	2	1	2	0	0	.400	1.000
Young, Eric	.375	8	3	1	1	3	0	.545	.875
Zeile, Todd	.400	5	2	0	3	1	0	.500	.600

Eric Plunk, Indians — RHP

Batter	Avg	AB	H	HR	BI	BB	SO	OBP	Slg
Aldrete, Mike*	.429	7	3	0	0	2	2	.556	.429
Alomar, R#	.412	17	7	1	1	1	3	.444	.765
Anderson, Brd*	.333	9	3	1	2	0	0	.333	.778
Baerga, C#	.000	5	0	0	0	1	1	.167	.000
Baines, H*	.583	12	7	0	2	4	2	.688	.583
Becker, Rich*	.364	11	4	0	3	0	2	.364	.455
Berroa, G	.400	5	2	0	0	1	1	.500	.600
Bichette, D	.300	10	3	1	1	0	2	.300	.600
Blowers, Mike	.000	5	0	0	0	1	2	.167	.000
Boggs, Wade*	.545	11	6	0	1	7	0	.722	.909
Bonilla, B#	.167	6	1	0	0	1	1	.286	.167
Borders, Pat	.400	10	4	0	2	1	1	.455	.400
Bordick, Mike	.000	9	0	0	0	1	2	.100	.000
Brosius, S	.250	8	2	0	0	0	2	.250	.250
Buhner, Jay	.316	19	6	1	4	5	4	.458	.474
Burks, Ellis	.250	8	2	0	0	1	3	.333	.375
Butler, Brett*	.167	6	1	0	0	1	1	.286	.167
Canseco, Jose	.300	20	6	1	7	3	6	.375	.500
Carter, Joe	.172	29	5	1	1	4	6	.294	.345
Cedeno, D#	.333	6	2	0	0	0	2	.333	.667
Clark, Will*	.400	5	2	0	1	1	0	.500	.600
Cole, Alex*	.000	12	0	0	0	2	4	.143	.000
Cora, Joey*	.333	9	3	0	1	0	0	.300	.333
Cordova, M	.167	6	1	1	1	2	3	.444	.667
Curtis, Chad	.000	6	0	0	0	0	0	.000	.000
Cuyler, Milt#	.333	9	3	0	0	1	2	.400	.556
Davis, Chili#	.313	16	5	1	1	2	3	.389	.563
Dawson, Andre	.167	6	1	0	0	0	2	.167	.333
Deer, Rob	.118	17	2	1	2	4	8	.286	.353
Devereaux, M	.143	14	2	2	4	2	6	.235	.571
Diaz, Alex#	.333	6	2	0	1	0	0	.333	.333
DiSarcina, G	.167	6	1	0	0	0	0	.167	.167
Durham, Ray#	.167	6	1	0	2	0	1	.167	.167
Easley, D	.500	4	2	0	1	1	1	.600	.500
Eisenreich, J*	.300	10	3	0	2	1	2	.364	.300
Fermin, Felix	.200	5	1	0	1	0	1	.200	.400
Fielder, C	.308	26	8	2	11	3	4	.400	.577
Finley, Steve*	.000	4	0	0	1	0	1	.000	.000
Franco, Julio	.222	18	4	0	4	1	4	.250	.222
Frye, Jeff	.125	8	1	0	0	0	2	.125	.125
Fryman, T	.250	16	4	2	7	5	8	.391	.625
Gaetti, Gary	.286	21	6	1	5	0	5	.286	.476
Gagne, Greg	.188	16	3	0	0	1	6	.235	.250
Gallego, Mike	.600	5	3	0	0	3	0	.750	.600
Gates, Brent#	.000	5	0	0	2	1	0	.286	.000
Girardi, Joe	.333	3	1	0	0	2	1	.600	.333
Gonzales, R	.167	6	1	0	0	0	0	.167	.167
Gonzalez, J	.286	18	3	0	1	3	6	.286	.222
Greenwell, M*	.200	15	3	0	3	4	4	.368	.467
Greer, Rusty*	.250	4	1	0	0	1	1	.400	.250
Griffey Jr, K*	.222	9	2	0	1	2	2	.364	.222
Guillen, O*	.158	19	3	0	1	1	2	.190	.211
Hall, Mel*	.444	9	4	0	3	0	2	.444	.444
Hamilton, D*	.455	11	5	0	1	1	2	.500	.545
Henderson, R	.238	21	5	1	2	14	3	.543	.381
Hill, G	.250	4	1	0	0	2	1	.500	.250
Hoiles, Chris	.000	5	0	0	1	3	1	.333	.000
Howard, Dave#	.125	8	1	0	0	0	4	.125	.125
Howell, Jack*	.000	11	0	0	0	2	9	.154	.000
Hulse, David*	.222	9	2	0	0	1	2	.300	.333
Incaviglia, P	.188	16	3	0	2	4	9	.381	.250
Jaha, John	.111	9	1	0	0	0	4	.111	.111
James, Dion*	.167	6	1	0	0	2	2	.375	.333
Jefferson, R*	.333	6	2	0	1	1	1	.429	.333

Eric Plunk, Indians — RHP

Batter	Avg	AB	H	HR	BI	BB	SO	OBP	Slg
Johnson, L*	.250	12	3	0	0	0	1	.250	.417
Joyner, Wally*	.625	16	10	3	8	3	1	.684	1.313
Karkovice, R	.429	7	3	1	2	0	4	.429	.857
Kelly, Pat	.333	3	1	0	1	1	1	.500	.667
Knoblauch, C	.250	16	4	0	2	1	4	.294	.250
Kreuter, Chad	.200	5	1	0	0	3	3	.500	.200
Leius, Scott	.250	8	2	0	0	0	2	.250	.250
Lewis, Mark	.286	7	2	0	1	0	2	.286	.286
Liriano, N#	.400	5	2	0	0	0	2	.400	.400
Listach, Pat#	.600	5	3	0	0	0	1	.600	.800
Livingstone*	.000	4	0	0	0	1	2	.200	.000
Macfarlane, M	.111	9	1	0	1	4	3	.385	.222
Martinez, E	.333	6	2	1	3	4	3	.600	.833
Martinez, T*	.333	6	2	0	0	1	3	.429	.500
Mayne, Brent*	.222	9	2	0	2	0	2	.222	.333
McCarty, Dave	.400	5	2	0	1	0	2	.400	.600
McGriff, Fred*	.000	6	0	0	0	0	4	.000	.000
McGwire, Mark	.200	10	2	0	3	2	7	.333	.200
McLemore, M#	.188	16	3	0	2	0	2	.188	.375
McRae, Brian#	.083	12	1	0	0	1	2	.214	.250
Meares, Pat	.333	9	3	0	1	0	3	.333	.444
Mieske, Matt	.000	5	0	0	0	0	3	.000	.000
Molitor, Paul	.458	24	11	2	7	6	4	.567	.833
Munoz, Pedro	.200	10	2	1	1	1	5	.273	.500
Murray, Eddie#	.357	14	5	0	1	0	4	.333	.357
Myers, Greg*	.250	8	2	0	0	1	3	.333	.375
Naehring, Tim	.333	9	3	0	0	1	4	.400	.333
Nilsson, Dave*	.400	5	2	1	1	0	1	.400	1.000
Nixon, Otis#	.375	8	3	0	1	1	2	.444	.500
O'Leary, Troy*	.167	6	1	0	2	1	1	.286	.333
O'Neill, Paul*	.200	5	1	1	3	1	1	.500	.800
Olerud, John*	.286	14	4	1	2	2	2	.375	.571
Oliver, Joe	.200	5	1	0	0	1	4	.333	.200
Orsulak, Joe*	.182	11	2	0	0	0	0	.182	.455
Palmeiro, R*	.250	12	3	1	2	1	3	.308	.667
Palmer, Dean	.143	7	1	0	2	5	1	.500	.143
Pena, Tony	.125	8	1	0	0	1	2	.222	.125
Phillips, T#	.313	16	5	0	1	3	2	.400	.375
Plantier, P*	.571	7	4	0	0	0	0	.571	.571
Polonia, Luis*	.333	9	3	0	1	1	1	.400	.333
Raines, Tim#	.375	8	3	0	3	0	1	.375	.375
Reboulet, J	.167	6	1	0	1	0	2	.167	.167
Reed, Jody	.308	13	4	1	3	1	2	.357	.538
Ripken, Billy	.200	10	2	0	1	0	2	.200	.200
Ripken, Cal	.143	35	5	1	5	3	5	.211	.229
Rodriguez, I	.250	12	3	1	2	0	2	.250	.500
Salmon, Tim	.333	9	3	1	1	3	3	.500	.667
Schofield, D	.154	13	2	0	2	2	2	.267	.231
Schu, Rick	.000	6	0	0	0	0	1	.000	.000
Segui, David#	.250	4	1	0	1	1	1	.400	.250
Seitzer, K	.174	23	4	0	1	6	6	.367	.261
Sheffield, G	.000	7	0	0	0	0	1	.000	.000
Shumpert, T	.111	9	1	0	0	0	3	.111	.111
Sierra, Ruben#	.194	31	6	1	5	1	11	.219	.419
Slaught, Don	.200	5	1	0	0	3	0	.500	.200
Sojo, Luis	.444	9	4	0	4	0	1	.444	.556
Spiers, Bill*	.182	11	2	0	0	0	2	.182	.273
Sprague, Ed	.125	8	1	0	1	3	4	.333	.125
Stahoviak, S*	.000	6	0	0	0	0	2	.000	.000
Stanley, Mike	.071	14	1	0	0	1	2	.133	.071
Steinbach, T	.167	18	3	0	0	1	2	.211	.167
Stillwell, K#	.833	6	5	0	0	1	1	.833	.833
Strange, Doug#	.250	8	2	0	1	3	4	.455	.500
Surhoff, B.J.*	.316	19	6	1	5	0	4	.316	.579
Sveum, Dale#	.200	10	2	1	1	3	2	.385	.500
Tartabull, D	.063	32	2	0	2	5	10	.189	.125
Taubensee, E*	.400	5	2	0	0	0	2	.400	.400
Tettleton, M#	.222	18	4	0	0	7	6	.462	.278
Thomas, Frank	.000	13	0	0	1	2	3	.133	.000
Thome, Jim*	.500	4	2	0	1	1	0	.600	.750
Tinsley, Lee#	.833	6	5	0	0	2	1	.875	1.000
Trammell, A	.077	26	2	0	1	3	5	.172	.077
Valentin, Jhn	.300	10	3	1	1	0	2	.300	.600
Valentin, Jse#	.125	8	1	0	0	3	6	.364	.125
Valle, Dave	.250	8	2	0	0	3	4	.455	.500
Vaughn, Greg	.053	19	1	0	0	2	6	.143	.105
Vaughn, Mo*	.100	10	1	0	1	2	4	.250	.200
Velarde, R	.000	8	0	0	0	0	3	.000	.000
Ventura, R*	.182	11	2	0	0	4	2	.400	.273
Vizquel, Omar#	.200	10	2	0	0	1	1	.273	.200
Walbeck, Matt#	.125	8	1	1	2	1	2	.222	.500
Weiss, Walt#	.444	9	4	0	1	1	1	.500	.444
White, Devon#	.188	16	3	0	1	1	8	.222	.250
Whiten, Mark#	.125	8	1	0	0	0	2	.125	.125
Williams, Ber#	.222	9	2	0	0	2	1	.364	.222
Wilson, Dan	.200	5	1	0	0	0	3	.200	.200
Worthington	.375	8	3	1	2	0	2	.375	.875

Jim Poole, Giants — LHP

Batter	Avg	AB	H	HR	BI	BB	SO	OBP	Slg
Aldrete, Mike*	.500	4	2	0	0	1	1	.600	.500

Jim Poole, Giants — LHP

Batter	Avg	AB	H	HR	BI	BB	SO	OBP	Slg
Baerga, C#	.200	5	1	0	2	2	2	.429	.400
Baines, H*	.400	5	2	1	2	0	0	.400	1.200
Boggs, Wade*	.077	13	1	0	0	4	5	.294	.154
Buhner, Jay	.250	4	1	1	3	1	1	.333	1.000
Clark, Will*	.167	6	1	0	0	0	2	.167	.333
Cora, Joey#	.143	7	1	0	0	2	0	.333	.143
Durham, Ray#	.400	5	2	0	0	0	0	.400	.600
Gates, Brent#	.500	4	2	0	5	1	2	.600	.750
Gomez, Chris	.000	6	0	0	0	0	2	.000	.000
Greenwell, M*	.063	16	1	0	0	0	0	.063	.063
Griffey Jr, K*	.250	8	2	0	2	0	1	.250	.375
Guillen, O*	.300	10	3	0	0	2	0	.417	.400
Hamilton, D*	.300	10	3	0	1	0	1	.300	.300
Hulse, David*	.333	6	2	0	0	0	0	.333	.500
Johnson, L*	.400	10	4	0	3	0	0	.400	.800
Joyner, Wally*	.182	11	2	0	1	0	2	.167	.182
Karkovice, R	.333	9	3	0	2	0	1	.333	.333
Knoblauch, C	.200	5	1	0	0	1	0	.200	.200
Listach, Pat#	.750	4	3	0	1	0	0	.750	.750
Macfarlane, M	.200	5	1	1	2	0	0	.200	.800
Martinez, T*	.250	8	2	1	4	1	1	.333	.625
McRae, Brian#	.333	3	1	0	0	2	0	.600	.333
O'Neill, Paul*	.182	11	2	0	1	2	4	.308	.182
Olerud, John*	.429	7	3	0	2	1	2	.500	.714
Palmeiro, R*	.000	11	0	0	1	1	1	.083	.000
Phillips, T#	.000	5	0	0	0	4	3	.444	.000
Raines, Tim#	.300	10	3	0	1	1	1	.364	.300
Reed, Jody	.200	5	1	0	0	1	0	.333	.200
Seitzer, K	.250	4	1	0	0	2	1	.500	.500
Sierra, Ruben#	.333	6	2	0	0	0	1	.333	.333
Surhoff, B.J.*	.154	13	2	0	3	1	4	.214	.154
Tettleton, M#	.333	6	2	2	3	1	3	.500	1.333
Thomas, Frank	.286	7	2	0	1	2	1	.444	.286
Valentin, Jse#	.000	5	0	0	0	0	2	.000	.000
Vaughn, Greg	.500	4	2	1	2	2	0	.667	1.250
Vaughn, Mo*	.200	10	2	0	0	0	5	.200	.200
Ventura, R*	.545	11	6	1	5	0	0	.500	1.091
Williams, Ber#	.286	7	2	0	1	0	0	.286	.286

Mark Portugal, Reds — RHP

Batter	Avg	AB	H	HR	BI	BB	SO	OBP	Slg
Dawson, Andre	.391	23	9	0	3	2	1	.423	.478
Decker, Steve	.500	6	3	0	0	0	1	.500	.667
DeShields, D*	.276	29	8	0	1	7	8	.417	.276
Doster, David	.143	7	1	0	0	0	1	.143	.143
Duncan, M	.333	18	6	1	1	1	2	.368	.611
Dunston, S	.192	26	5	0	1	0	5	.192	.231
Dykstra, L*	.313	16	5	0	0	2	1	.389	.313
Eisenreich, J*	.250	24	6	0	1	4	2	.357	.292
Elster, Kevin	.083	12	1	0	1	0	1	.077	.083
Eusebio, Tony	.250	8	2	1	2	1	0	.333	.625
Finley, Steve*	.333	18	6	0	1	1	2	.368	.389
Fletcher, D*	.261	23	6	2	3	1	2	.320	.522
Floyd, Cliff*	.100	10	1	0	0	0	3	.100	.200
Franco, Julio	.273	11	3	0	1	3	1	.429	.455
Frazier, Lou#	.167	6	1	0	0	1	2	.286	.167
Gaetti, Gary	.250	4	1	1	2	1	0	.400	1.000
Galarraga, A	.393	28	11	0	3	1	1	.419	.571
Gallego, Mike	.000	4	0	0	0	0	0	.000	.000
Gant, Ron	.452	31	14	1	7	5	6	.514	.613
Garcia, C	.375	16	6	0	0	3	0	.412	.500
Gilkey, B	.333	15	5	0	1	2	1	.412	.467
Girardi, Joe	.452	31	14	0	6	0	1	.469	.581
Gomez, Leo	.333	6	2	0	2	2	1	.500	.500
Gonzalez, L*	.273	11	3	0	2	3	0	.400	.273
Grace, Mark*	.205	44	9	1	4	5	1	.280	.295
Greenwell, M*	.333	6	2	0	0	2	0	.500	.333
Grissom, M	.167	42	7	2	6	4	2	.239	.310
Grudzielanek	.154	13	2	0	0	0	1	.154	.231
Gutierrez, R	.462	13	6	0	2	0	2	.462	.538
Gwynn, Chris*	.125	8	1	0	0	0	0	.125	.125
Gwynn, Tony*	.375	48	18	0	5	4	3	.423	.417
Hall, Mel*	.091	11	1	0	1	1	4	.167	.091
Hansen, Dave*	.154	13	2	1	2	0	3	.154	.385
Harris, Lenny*	.406	32	13	1	5	4	4	.472	.500
Hayes, C	.258	31	8	0	1	3	4	.324	.290
Henderson, R	.333	12	4	1	3	2	0	.400	.667
Hernandez, Jo	.000	5	0	0	0	0	0	.000	.000
Hollandsworth	.429	7	3	1	2	0	0	.429	1.000
Hollins, Dave#	.000	6	0	0	0	5	2	.455	.000
Howard, T*	.313	16	5	0	1	0	3	.313	.438
Howell, Jack*	.300	10	3	1	3	2	3	.385	.600
Hundley, Todd#	.227	22	5	0	1	1	9	.261	.318
Hunter, Bri L	.417	12	5	0	0	0	0	.417	.417
Hyers, Tim*	.000	6	0	0	1	1	3	.143	.000
Incaviglia, P	.200	25	5	1	3	0	8	.200	.360
Javier, Stan#	.143	7	1	0	0	1	0	.250	.143
Jefferies, G#	.298	47	14	2	3	4	2	.353	.468
Johnson, Bri	.500	10	5	1	4	0	0	.455	1.000
Johnson, Char	.000	5	0	0	0	3	0	.000	.000
Jones, C#	.154	13	2	1	2	1	1	.214	.385
Jones, Chris	.250	4	1	1	1	1	0	.400	1.000
Jordan, Brian	.348	23	8	0	3	0	4	.360	.435
Jordan, Ricky	.000	6	0	0	0	0	0	.000	.000
Joyner, Wally*	.333	15	5	0	2	2	0	.412	.400
Justice, Dave*	.320	25	8	2	8	2	7	.370	.600
Karros, Eric	.176	34	6	2	4	1	6	.200	.382
Kent, Jeff	.381	21	8	0	2	4	4	.458	.524
King, Jeff	.391	23	9	1	5	2	2	.440	.609
Kingery, Mike*	.250	28	7	1	1	2	2	.300	.393
Klesko, Ryan*	.231	13	3	1	1	1	5	.286	.615
Lampkin, Tom*	.000	6	0	0	0	0	2	.000	.000
Lankford, Ray*	.087	23	2	1	1	4	6	.222	.217
Lansing, Mike	.364	22	8	0	1	3	2	.462	.500
Larkin, Barry	.238	21	5	0	0	0	2	.238	.333
Lemke, Mark#	.200	20	4	1	3	5	2	.360	.350
Lewis, Darren	.143	7	1	0	0	0	0	.143	.429
Lieberthal, M	.167	6	1	0	0	0	0	.167	.167
Liriano, N#	.273	11	3	0	1	1	2	.333	.364
Livingstone*	.250	8	2	0	0	1	5	.250	.250
Lopez, Javy	.286	7	2	1	1	1	0	.375	.714
Mabry, John*	.400	10	4	1	4	1	2	.455	.800
Magadan, Dave*	.231	39	9	0	6	4	5	.295	.308
Manwaring, K	.333	18	6	1	2	0	1	.333	.500
Martin, Al*	.238	21	5	0	0	2	7	.304	.286
Martinez, Da*	.217	23	5	0	2	0	3	.217	.217
May, Derrick*	.286	14	4	0	2	4	1	.444	.357
McGee, Willie#	.419	31	13	0	3	0	3	.419	.452
McGriff, Fred*	.250	28	7	4	9	7	9	.389	.679
McRae, Brian#	.125	16	2	0	0	0	3	.125	.250
Merced, O*	.387	31	12	1	9	1	4	.394	.613
Miller, Orl	.222	9	2	1	3	0	2	.222	.556
Mitchell, K	.350	40	14	2	7	1	7	.366	.525
Molitor, Paul	.400	5	2	0	1	0	0	.400	.400
Mondesi, Raul	.278	18	5	0	2	2	1	.350	.333
Morandini, M*	.306	36	11	2	6	3	8	.359	.500
Morris, Hal*	.318	22	7	1	2	1	1	.348	.500
Mouton, James	.000	9	0	0	1	3	0	.100	.000
Murray, Eddie#	.190	42	8	2	6	3	5	.244	.357
Nixon, Otis#	.333	9	3	0	0	2	2	.455	.333
O'Brien, C	.375	8	3	0	0	0	0	.444	.500
O'Neill, Paul*	.267	15	4	2	5	6	2	.476	.733

Mark Portugal, Reds — RHP

Batter	Avg	AB	H	HR	BI	BB	SO	OBP	Slg
Abbott, Kurt	.333	6	2	1	2	0	1	.429	.833
Aldrete, Mike*	.250	4	1	0	0	2	0	.500	.250
Alfonzo, E	.250	8	2	1	3	0	0	.250	.625
Alicea, Luis#	.105	19	2	0	1	1	4	.150	.105
Alomar, R#	.313	16	5	1	1	2	3	.389	.500
Alou, Moises	.353	17	6	2	6	1	2	.350	.882
Andrews, J	.429	7	3	1	4	0	0	.429	1.000
Arias, Alex	.333	6	2	0	0	1	1	.429	.333
Ashley, Billy	.000	9	0	0	0	1	3	.100	.000
Bagwell, Jeff	.647	17	11	0	3	4	1	.727	.941
Barberie, B#	.250	16	4	0	2	1	2	.294	.313
Bell, Derek	.250	28	7	1	3	1	2	.276	.357
Bell, Jay	.278	36	10	0	2	1	3	.297	.306
Belliard, R	.214	14	3	0	1	1	1	.250	.286
Benjamin, M	.000	3	0	0	1	0	0	.200	.000
Berry, Sean	.474	19	9	0	3	1	1	.500	.632
Bichette, D	.474	19	9	4	7	0	1	.474	1.211
Biggio, Craig	.292	24	7	1	1	5	0	.346	.458
Blauser, Jeff	.300	30	9	3	6	4	5	.382	.633
Boggs, Wade*	.278	18	5	0	0	1	2	.316	.389
Bonds, Barry*	.190	21	4	0	0	4	1	.320	.286
Bonilla, B#	.214	42	9	2	6	3	10	.267	.405
Boone, Bret	.200	5	1	0	2	0	1	.167	.400
Bournigal, R	.400	5	2	0	2	0	0	.400	.400
Branson, Jeff*	.143	7	1	0	0	0	2	.143	.286
Brogna, Rico*	.167	6	1	0	1	1	2	.250	.167
Brumfield, J	.333	9	3	0	0	2	0	.333	.333
Burks, Ellis	1.000	4	4	0	2	2	0	1.000	2.250
Burnitz, J*	.143	7	1	1	1	3	3	.400	.571
Butler, Brett*	.295	78	23	1	5	10	13	.382	.449
Caminiti, Ken#	.438	16	7	2	5	1	5	.471	1.000
Cangelosi, J#	.214	14	3	0	0	3	2	.353	.214
Canseco, Jose	.667	6	4	0	1	0	1	.714	.833
Carr, Chuck	.267	15	4	0	2	2	3	.353	.333
Carreon, Mark	.222	9	2	1	1	0	0	.222	.556
Carter, Joe	.286	21	6	1	5	0	2	.273	.524
Castilla, V	.091	11	1	0	0	0	3	.091	.091
Cedeno, A	.357	14	5	0	2	1	1	.400	.429
Cianfrocco, A	.143	7	1	0	0	0	2	.143	.143
Clark, Dave*	.000	7	0	0	0	1	3	.125	.000
Clark, Will*	.306	36	11	2	4	7	6	.400	.583
Clayton, J	.154	13	2	0	0	0	2	.154	.154
Colbrunn, G	.571	7	4	1	3	0	0	.571	1.143
Cole, Alex*	.000	4	0	0	0	4	0	.500	.000
Coleman, V#	.545	11	6	0	0	1	2	.583	.818
Conine, Jeff	.222	18	4	0	0	3	2	.333	.389
Cordero, Wil	.286	14	4	0	2	2	1	.375	.357
Dascenzo, D#	.429	7	3	0	1	1	1	.500	.714
Daulton, D*	.154	26	4	0	1	2	5	.214	.192
Davis, Eric	.333	18	6	1	6	4	4	.435	.556

168

Mark Portugal, Reds — RHP

Batter	Avg	AB	H	HR	BI	BB	SO	OBP	Slg
Offerman, J*	.259	27	7	1	3	4	5	.344	.444
Oliver, Joe	.231	13	3	0	0	0	2	.231	.231
Orsulak, Joe*	.214	14	3	0	1	0	1	.267	.286
Otero, Ricky#	.143	7	1	0	1	1	1	.250	.429
Pagnozzi, Tom	.059	17	1	0	1	2	1	.150	.059
Parent, Mark	.000	6	0	0	0	0	1	.000	.000
Pendleton, T#	.360	25	9	0	3	3	5	.429	.440
Phillips, T#	.200	5	1	0	0	1	1	.333	.400
Piazza, Mike	.250	32	8	3	9	4	2	.333	.531
Plantier, P*	.235	17	4	0	1	2	3	.316	.235
Reed, Jeff*	.111	9	1	0	1	2	0	.273	.111
Reed, Jody	.211	19	4	0	3	3	1	.318	.263
Roberson, K#	.167	6	1	0	0	1	1	.286	.167
Roberts, Bip#	.324	34	11	0	0	4	5	.410	.353
Rodriguez, I*	.250	12	3	0	0	2	5	.357	.250
Sabo, Chris	.250	20	5	0	1	2	4	.318	.300
Samuel, Juan	.143	14	2	0	0	2	4	.250	.143
Sanchez, Rey	.429	14	6	0	0	0	1	.429	.571
Sandberg, R	.324	37	12	2	8	6	7	.419	.541
Sanders, R	.462	13	6	1	1	2	2	.533	.769
Santangelo, F#	.333	6	2	0	0	0	1	.333	.333
Santiago, B	.314	35	11	2	4	1	4	.333	.514
Schofield, D	.333	12	4	0	1	3	2	.438	.500
Segui, David#	.294	17	5	1	3	1	2	.333	.647
Servais, J	.111	9	1	0	0	1	1	.273	.111
Sheaffer, D	.000	4	0	0	0	2	0	.333	.000
Sheffield, G	.143	14	2	1	2	2	2	.250	.357
Sierra, Ruben#	.250	8	2	0	3	0	2	.250	.250
Slaught, Don	.333	15	5	0	2	1	2	.375	.333
Smith, Dwight*	.333	18	6	0	0	1	4	.368	.389
Smith, Ozzie#	.115	26	3	0	2	2	1	.179	.115
Sosa, Sammy	.211	19	4	0	2	2	4	.286	.263
Steinbach, T	.250	4	1	1	2	1	0	.400	1.000
Stillwell, K#	.200	5	1	1	3	0	2	.200	.800
Stocker, K#	.227	22	5	0	0	1	4	.261	.227
Strawberry, D*	.421	19	8	3	6	3	7	.500	.947
Tarasco, Tony*	.167	6	1	0	0	0	0	.167	.167
Tartabull, J	.000	6	0	0	0	1	2	.143	.000
Tettleton, M#	.200	5	1	0	0	1	3	.333	.200
Thompson, Mil*	.211	19	4	2	6	1	4	.250	.526
Thompson, Rob	.211	38	8	0	1	7	11	.333	.263
Thompson, Ry	.455	11	5	1	1	1	2	.500	.818
VanderWal, J*	.083	12	1	0	0	0	2	.083	.083
Veras, Q#	.143	7	1	0	0	1	1	.250	.143
Vizcaino, J#	.348	23	8	1	6	1	4	.375	.565
Walker, Larry*	.194	31	6	1	6	2	7	.235	.355
Wallach, Tim	.200	35	7	1	3	4	8	.282	.343
Walton, J	.278	18	5	0	1	1	3	.350	.278
Weiss, Walt*	.250	24	6	1	4	0	1	.250	.458
White, Devon#	.333	6	2	1	1	1	2	.429	.833
White, R	.182	11	2	0	0	0	2	.182	.182
Whiten, Mark#	.143	14	2	0	0	2	5	.250	.143
Wilkins, Rick*	.182	22	4	0	0	2	3	.250	.227
Williams, E	.000	5	0	0	1	0	1	.167	.000
Williams, Ma	.067	45	3	0	0	2	13	.106	.067
Young, Eric	.136	22	3	0	1	1	2	.174	.136
Young, Kevin	.083	12	1	0	1	2	2	.214	.083
Zeile, Todd	.364	33	12	0	4	3	6	.417	.455

Mike Potts, Brewers — LHP

Batter	Avg	AB	H	HR	BI	BB	SO	OBP	Slg
Baines, H*	.600	5	3	1	2	0	0	.600	1.200
Ventura, R*	.400	5	2	2	2	0	1	.400	1.600

Jay Powell, Marlins — RHP

Batter	Avg	AB	H	HR	BI	BB	SO	OBP	Slg
Alicea, Luis#	.200	5	1	0	0	0	3	.200	.600
Gaetti, Gary	.333	3	1	0	0	2	1	.600	.667
Hollandsworth*	.400	5	2	0	0	0	0	.400	.400
Jordan, Brian	.500	6	3	0	0	0	1	.500	.500
Stocker, K#	.400	5	2	0	0	1	0	.200	.100

Ariel Prieto, Athletics — RHP

Batter	Avg	AB	H	HR	BI	BB	SO	OBP	Slg
Alomar, R#	.300	10	3	0	0	1	1	.364	.300
Anderson, Brd*	.300	10	3	0	0	1	2	.364	.300
Anderson, G*	.400	5	2	1	1	1	0	.500	1.000
Arias, George	.000	5	0	0	0	0	1	.000	.000
Baerga, C#	.200	5	1	0	1	0	0	.200	.200
Baines, H*	.571	7	4	0	1	2	1	.667	.571
Becker, Rich*	.200	10	2	0	0	4	4	.429	.200
Belle, Albert	.600	5	3	0	0	0	1	.600	.600
Bonilla, B#	.222	9	2	0	2	0	0	.300	.444
Carter, Joe	.500	14	7	2	7	0	0	.500	1.000
Clark, Will*	.667	3	2	0	0	2	0	.800	1.000
Cordova, M	.455	11	5	0	2	2	0	.538	.636
Curtis, Chad	.400	5	2	0	0	1	0	.500	.400
Damon, Johnny*	.333	3	1	0	0	2	0	.600	.333
Davis, Chili#	.600	5	3	1	3	1	0	.667	1.200
Delgado, C*	.375	8	3	2	5	1	3	.444	1.125
Devereaux, M	.167	6	1	0	0	0	0	.167	.167

Ariel Prieto, Athletics — RHP

Batter	Avg	AB	H	HR	BI	BB	SO	OBP	Slg
DiSarcina, G	.333	6	2	0	0	0	1	.333	.500
Edmonds, Jim*	.375	8	3	1	2	0	1	.375	.875
Fabregas, Jor*	.600	5	3	0	0	0	0	.600	.600
Fielder, C	.250	4	1	0	1	0	0	.400	.250
Frye, Jeff	.143	7	1	0	0	1	3	.250	.143
Fryman, T	.000	5	0	0	0	1	1	.167	.000
Gonzalez, A	.111	9	1	1	3	0	4	.100	.444
Goodwin, Tom*	.300	10	3	0	0	1	1	.364	.300
Green, Shawn*	.250	8	2	0	0	2	0	.400	.250
Guillen, O*	.167	6	1	0	1	1	1	.250	.167
Higginson, B*	.000	5	0	0	0	0	2	.000	.000
Hoiles, Chris	.000	4	0	0	0	2	2	.333	.000
Hollins, Dave#	.333	6	2	0	1	2	1	.500	.500
Howard, Dave#	.333	6	2	0	1	0	0	.333	.667
Karkovice, R	.250	8	2	0	0	1	3	.333	.250
Kelly, R	.500	4	2	0	0	1	1	.667	.500
Kirby, Wayne*	.167	6	1	0	0	0	2	.167	.167
Knoblauch, C	.375	8	3	0	1	1	1	.500	.500
Lewis, Darren	.200	5	1	0	0	1	0	.333	.400
Lockhart, K*	.250	8	2	0	2	2	0	.400	.375
Macfarlane, M	.286	7	2	0	0	0	0	.286	.286
Martinez, Da*	.167	6	1	0	0	0	0	.167	.167
Martinez, S*	.429	7	3	0	1	0	3	.429	.429
Meares, Pat	.286	7	2	0	1	0	3	.250	.429
Molitor, Paul	.214	14	3	0	2	1	2	.267	.214
Murray, Eddie*	.167	6	1	0	1	0	1	.143	.167
Myers, Greg*	.125	8	1	0	1	1	1	.222	.125
Nixon, Otis#	.167	6	1	0	0	3	1	.444	.167
Offerman, J#	.300	10	3	0	0	1	1	.364	.600
Olerud, John*	.500	12	6	0	0	2	1	.571	.500
Palmeiro, R*	.333	6	2	2	4	4	1	.600	1.333
Paquette, C	.333	6	2	1	4	0	0	.429	1.167
Phillips, T#	.111	9	1	0	0	0	4	.111	.111
Ramirez, M	.250	4	1	0	0	1	0	.400	.250
Reboulet, J	.200	5	1	0	1	0	1	.200	.200
Ripken, Cal	.100	10	1	0	0	0	1	.100	.200
Roberts, Bip#	.429	7	3	0	1	1	1	.500	.429
Salmon, Tim	.429	7	3	0	1	1	0	.500	.571
Snow, J.T.#	.000	5	0	0	0	0	2	.000	.000
Sorrento, P*	.286	7	2	0	3	1	4	.375	.286
Sprague, Ed	.400	10	4	0	2	3	0	.571	.500
Stahoviak, S*	.200	10	2	0	1	1	1	.273	.300
Surhoff, B.J.*	.400	10	4	0	2	0	0	.571	.400
Sweeney, Mike	.000	6	0	0	1	0	0	.000	.000
Thomas, Frank	.500	8	4	0	3	0	1	.444	.625
Thome, Jim*	.000	4	0	0	0	1	1	.200	.000
Tucker, M*	.200	5	1	0	0	2	2	.429	.400
Valentin, Jhn	.167	6	1	0	0	0	0	.167	.167
Vaughn, Mo*	.167	6	1	0	0	0	2	.167	.167
Velarde, R	.143	7	1	0	0	0	2	.143	.143
Ventura, R*	.167	6	1	0	0	3	0	.444	.167
Vizquel, Omar#	.000	7	0	0	0	0	0	.000	.000
White, Devon#	.500	4	2	0	3	1	0	.600	.750

Tim Pugh, Reds — RHP

Batter	Avg	AB	H	HR	BI	BB	SO	OBP	Slg
Alou, Moises	.273	11	3	1	2	1	2	.333	.545
Andrews, S	.200	5	1	1	4	0	1	.200	.800
Anthony, Eric*	.400	5	2	0	1	0	1	.400	.400
Arias, Alex	.200	10	2	0	0	1	1	.333	.200
Bagwell, Jeff	.563	16	9	0	2	2	0	.611	.750
Bell, Derek	.417	12	5	0	3	1	0	.462	.667
Bell, Jay	.273	11	3	0	0	0	1	.333	.364
Berry, Sean	.444	9	4	0	3	0	2	.444	.444
Bichette, D	.400	10	4	0	1	0	0	.400	.500
Biggio, Craig	.158	19	3	0	3	2	3	.238	.158
Blauser, Jeff	.222	9	2	1	1	0	0	.222	.556
Bonds, Barry*	.500	6	3	0	0	0	0	.500	.667
Bonilla, B#	.250	20	5	1	5	1	3	.261	.400
Burnitz, J*	.571	7	4	1	3	1	0	.625	1.000
Butler, Brett*	.522	23	12	1	5	1	2	.542	.826
Caminiti, Ken#	.143	14	2	0	2	1	0	.200	.214
Cangelosi, J#	.250	4	1	0	0	1	0	.400	.250
Carr, Chuck	.273	11	3	0	0	0	2	.429	.273
Carreon, Mark	.200	5	1	0	1	0	0	.200	.200
Castilla, V	.583	12	7	2	5	0	0	.583	1.167
Cedeno, A	.083	12	1	0	0	1	3	.154	.083
Clark, Dave*	.500	6	3	0	0	0	0	.500	.667
Clark, Will*	.000	5	0	0	0	0	2	.000	.000
Clayton, O	.400	5	2	0	0	1	0	.500	.600
Colbrunn, G	.200	5	1	0	2	1	0	.333	.400
Cole, Alex*	.300	10	3	0	0	1	1	.364	.300
Coleman, V#	.143	7	1	0	0	1	1	.143	.286
Conine, Jeff	.462	13	6	1	3	2	3	.533	.692
Cordero, Wil	.300	10	3	0	2	0	0	.417	.300
DeShields, D*	.333	6	2	0	1	0	0	.333	.333
Dunston, S	.333	6	2	0	1	0	0	.333	.500
Dykstra, L*	.400	5	2	0	0	1	0	.500	.400
Eusebio, Tony	.600	5	3	0	0	1	0	.667	.600
Finley, Steve*	.400	10	4	0	0	1	1	.455	.500
Fletcher, D*	.000	10	0	0	0	1	0	.167	.000

Tim Pugh, Reds — RHP

Batter	Avg	AB	H	HR	BI	BB	SO	OBP	Slg
Galarraga, A	.600	5	3	1	2	0	0	.600	1.200
Gant, Ron	.400	5	2	0	0	0	1	.400	.600
Garcia, C	.167	6	1	0	1	0	1	.167	.167
Gilkey, B	.400	15	6	1	1	0	1	.400	.600
Girardi, Joe	.400	5	2	0	1	1	0	.500	.400
Gonzalez, L*	.333	12	4	0	3	2	0	.333	.333
Goodwin, Tom*	.000	4	0	0	0	2	0	.333	.000
Grace, Mark*	.100	10	1	0	1	0	0	.100	.200
Grissom, M	.500	12	6	1	1	0	2	.500	.750
Grudzielanek	.375	8	3	0	1	0	0	.375	.500
Gutierrez, R	.000	5	0	0	0	0	1	.000	.000
Gwynn, Tony*	.571	7	4	0	0	1	0	.625	.857
Hansen, Dave*	.400	10	4	0	1	0	2	.400	.500
Harris, Lenny*	.333	6	2	0	0	0	0	.333	.333
Hayes, C	.286	7	2	0	1	2	2	.455	.429
Hollins, Dave#	.500	6	3	0	1	2	0	.625	.500
Hundley, Todd#	.231	13	3	1	2	3	2	.375	.615
Hunter, Bri L	.600	5	3	0	0	0	0	.600	.800
Jefferies, G#	.429	7	3	0	0	0	2	.429	.857
Jones, C#	.000	6	0	0	0	0	2	.000	.000
Jordan, Brian	.250	8	2	0	1	0	3	.250	.375
Justice, Dave*	.333	9	3	1	2	2	1	.455	.667
Karros, Eric	.316	19	6	0	2	1	2	.333	.368
Kent, Jeff	.133	15	2	0	1	2	4	.222	.200
King, Jeff	.364	11	4	1	6	0	0	.364	.636
Klesko, Ryan*	.333	3	1	0	3	1	1	.400	.667
Lankford, Ray*	.250	8	2	0	0	2	3	.400	.250
Lansing, Mike	.231	13	3	0	0	2	1	.333	.385
Lemke, Mark#	.167	6	1	0	0	3	0	.444	.167
Lewis, Darren	.333	6	2	0	0	1	1	.429	.333
Lopez, Javy	.400	5	2	0	0	1	0	.500	.400
Magadan, Dave*	.556	9	5	0	0	1	0	.600	.667
Manwaring, K	.600	5	3	1	1	1	0	.667	1.200
Martin, Al*	.000	8	0	0	0	1	1	.111	.000
May, Derrick*	.375	8	3	0	0	2	0	.500	.500
McGee, Willie#	.250	4	1	0	0	2	1	.500	.250
McGriff, Fred*	.538	13	7	2	5	4	1	.647	1.154
Merced, O*	.500	8	4	1	2	2	1	.600	1.000
Miller, Orl	.500	6	3	0	1	2	0	.625	.500
Mondesi, Raul	.400	5	2	1	2	0	1	.400	1.200
Morandini, M*	.750	4	3	0	3	2	0	.833	1.250
Mouton, James	.750	4	3	0	3	2	0	.750	1.000
Murray, Eddie#	.333	12	4	0	1	2	1	.429	.417
O'Brien, C	.400	5	2	0	0	1	0	.571	.400
Offerman, J#	.200	15	3	0	1	4	1	.368	.267
Orsulak, Joe*	.429	14	6	0	2	0	0	.429	.643
Pendleton, T#	.250	8	2	0	0	0	1	.250	.375
Piazza, Mike	.545	11	6	1	3	0	0	.643	.818
Plantier, P*	.333	9	3	0	3	0	2	.333	.444
Reed, Jody	.250	8	2	0	1	3	1	.417	.375
Rodriguez, H*	.222	9	2	0	2	1	0	.273	.222
Sanchez, Rey	.222	9	2	0	2	0	0	.200	.222
Sandberg, R	.286	7	2	1	2	2	0	.444	.714
Santiago, B	.188	16	3	0	2	1	3	.235	.188
Segui, David#	.100	10	1	0	0	1	0	.182	.100
Sheaffer, D	.200	10	2	1	3	0	2	.200	.500
Sheffield, G	.250	16	4	2	5	0	1	.250	.688
Slaught, Don	.333	6	2	0	0	0	1	.429	.333
Smith, Ozzie#	.143	7	1	0	0	0	0	.143	.143
Sosa, Sammy	.462	13	6	2	6	0	1	.462	.923
Stillwell, K#	.167	6	1	0	0	0	1	.167	.167
Tarasco, Tony*	.000	5	0	0	0	0	1	.000	.000
Taubensee, E*	1.000	4	4	0	2	1	0	1.000	1.000
Thompson, Rob	.000	4	0	0	0	1	2	.200	.000
Thompson, Ry	.133	15	2	0	2	1	6	.188	.267
Vizcaino, J#	.125	8	1	0	0	4	1	.417	.125
Walker, Larry*	.286	7	2	1	1	1	2	.375	.714
Wallach, Tim	.200	10	2	0	0	0	2	.200	.200
Weiss, Walt#	.444	9	4	0	2	2	1	.545	.444
White, R	.222	9	2	0	0	1	3	.300	.222
Whiten, Mark#	.000	6	0	0	0	2	1	.250	.000
Wilkins, Rick*	.200	10	2	0	0	1	0	.273	.200
Williams, Ma	.000	6	0	0	0	0	3	.000	.000
Young, Eric	.357	14	5	0	0	0	0	.357	.357
Zeile, Todd	.385	13	5	0	2	2	0	.467	.538

Paul Quantrill, Blue Jays — RHP

Batter	Avg	AB	H	HR	BI	BB	SO	OBP	Slg
Abbott, Kurt	.400	5	2	0	0	0	1	.400	.400
Aldrete, Mike*	.429	7	3	1	3	0	1	.429	1.000
Alfonzo, E	.571	7	4	0	2	0	0	.571	1.143
Alomar, R#	.500	8	4	0	2	3	2	.667	.750
Alomar Jr, S	.222	9	2	0	0	1	0	.300	.222
Alou, Moises	.300	10	3	1	2	0	1	.364	.600
Amaral, Rich	.143	7	1	0	0	1	2	.250	.143
Anderson, Brd*	.286	14	4	1	1	0	3	.286	.643
Anderson, G*	.333	6	2	0	0	0	1	.333	.333
Baerga, C#	.571	14	8	1	1	3	0	.647	.786
Bagwell, Jeff	.300	10	3	0	1	1	1	.364	.400
Baines, H*	.111	9	1	1	1	0	2	.111	.444
Becker, Rich*	.750	4	3	0	1	0	0	.750	.750
Bell, Derek	.143	7	1	0	1	0	1	.143	.143
Bell, Jay	.182	11	2	0	0	1	2	.250	.182
Belle, Albert	.429	14	6	2	2	1	1	.500	.857
Berroa, G	.667	6	4	0	0	0	0	.667	.833
Bichette, D	.286	7	2	1	2	0	2	.286	.714
Biggio, Craig	.444	9	4	0	1	1	2	.500	.556
Blauser, Jeff	.333	6	2	0	0	1	1	.429	.500
Boggs, Wade*	.267	15	4	0	1	3	1	.389	.333
Bonds, Barry*	.250	8	2	1	1	4	1	.500	.625
Bonilla, B#	.333	12	4	1	1	1	5	.385	.750
Boone, Bret	.429	14	6	0	0	0	1	.429	.857
Borders, Pat	.500	8	4	0	1	2	1	.600	.625
Bordick, Mike	.500	10	5	0	0	0	1	.500	.600
Bournigal, R	.286	7	2	0	1	0	0	.375	.286
Brogna, Rico*	.333	9	3	1	3	1	3	.400	.667
Buhner, Jay	.313	16	5	1	4	5	5	.476	.500
Butler, Brett*	.143	14	2	0	0	3	3	.294	.214
Caminiti, Ken#	.250	4	1	0	1	2	1	.500	.250
Canseco, Jose	.400	5	2	0	0	0	0	.400	.600
Carreon, Mark	.417	12	5	1	2	1	0	.462	.667
Carter, Joe	.167	6	1	0	1	1	1	.286	.500
Clark, Dave*	.250	4	1	0	2	0	0	.167	.250
Clayton, R	.417	12	5	0	2	0	2	.385	.500
Colbrunn, G	.000	5	0	0	0	0	1	.000	.000
Conine, Jeff	.200	5	1	0	1	2	0	.429	.200
Cora, Joey*	.222	9	2	0	0	0	1	.300	.333
Cordero, Wil	.750	12	9	0	4	0	1	.750	.833
Cordova, M	.286	7	2	0	1	0	0	.286	.571
Cummings, M*	.143	7	1	0	0	0	1	.143	.286
Curtis, Chad	.200	5	1	0	1	0	0	.200	.200
Damon, Johnny*	.400	5	2	1	2	0	1	.400	1.200
Davis, Chili#	.571	7	4	0	2	1	0	.625	.571
DeShields, D*	.300	10	3	1	2	2	3	.417	.600
Devereaux, M	.222	9	2	0	0	1	0	.222	.333
Diaz, Alex#	.250	4	1	1	1	0	0	.250	1.000
DiSarcina, G	.375	8	3	0	2	0	1	.375	.375
Duncan, M	.556	9	5	1	1	1	1	.600	.889
Durham, Ray#	.000	5	0	0	1	0	0	.000	.000
Edmonds, Jim*	.333	3	1	0	1	2	0	.600	.333
Eusebio, Tony	.143	7	1	0	0	0	0	.143	.143
Fabregas, Jor*	.250	4	1	0	0	1	0	.400	.250
Fermin, Felix	.000	6	0	0	0	0	0	.000	.000
Fielder, C	.364	11	4	1	3	1	1	.417	.636
Finley, Steve*	.667	6	4	0	1	0	0	.667	.833
Fletcher, D*	.500	10	5	0	1	0	0	.500	.500
Franco, Julio	.300	10	3	1	5	0	2	.300	.600
Fryman, T	.250	4	1	0	2	0	0	.250	.250
Gaetti, Gary	.250	4	1	0	1	0	0	.200	.250
Gagne, Greg	.333	6	2	0	0	0	2	.333	.333
Gallego, Mike	.286	7	2	0	0	0	0	.286	.286
Garcia, C	.167	6	1	0	1	0	0	.167	.333
Gates, Brent#	.167	6	1	0	0	0	1	.167	.167
Gilkey, B	.333	6	2	0	1	0	0	.333	.667
Girardi, Joe	.000	4	0	0	0	0	2	.000	.000
Gomez, Leo	.200	5	1	0	0	0	2	.333	.400
Gonzalez, J	.571	7	4	1	3	0	0	.571	1.000
Gonzalez, L*	.500	10	5	0	2	1	1	.545	.900
Goodwin, Tom*	.000	5	0	0	0	1	1	.143	.000
Grace, Mark*	.333	6	2	0	3	0	0	.333	.500
Griffey Jr, K*	.333	15	5	1	1	2	4	.412	.800
Grissom, M	.000	7	0	0	0	1	0	.000	.000
Guillen, O*	.400	5	2	0	0	0	0	.400	.600
Gwynn, Chris*	.333	9	3	0	0	1	0	.455	.444
Gwynn, Tony*	.750	4	3	0	2	1	0	.800	.750
Hale, Chip*	.400	5	2	0	0	0	0	.400	.400
Hamilton, D*	.333	9	3	1	1	1	2	.400	.667
Hayes, C	.200	5	1	0	0	0	0	.200	.200
Henderson, R	.000	6	0	0	0	0	4	.000	.000
Hill, G	.308	13	4	0	1	0	1	.308	.308
Hocking, D#	.286	7	2	1	2	0	2	.286	.857
Howard, Dave#	.286	7	2	0	0	0	4	.286	.286
Hulse, David*	.333	6	2	0	2	0	0	.333	.333
Hundley, Todd#	.167	6	1	0	0	0	1	.167	.167
Jaha, John	.167	6	1	0	2	1	0	.286	.333
James, Dion*	.250	4	1	0	1	1	0	.400	.250
Jefferson, R*	.700	10	7	0	3	1	1	.727	1.000
Jeter, Derek	.556	9	5	0	1	0	2	.556	.667
Johnson, Mark*	.250	8	2	0	0	1	1	.333	.375
Jones, C	.250	4	1	1	1	0	1	.400	1.000
Justice, Dave*	.500	4	2	1	2	1	1	.600	1.250
Karros, Eric	.417	12	5	1	3	0	1	.417	.917
Kelly, Pat	.000	4	0	0	0	0	0	.000	.000
Kelly, R	.143	14	2	0	1	0	0	.133	.143
Kent, Jeff	.333	9	3	0	2	1	0	.400	.333
Knoblauch, C	.467	15	7	0	2	3	0	.526	.533
Lankford, Ray*	.200	5	1	1	3	0	0	.200	.800
Lansing, Mike	.222	9	2	0	0	0	0	.222	.222
Lemke, Mark#	.000	6	0	0	0	0	0	.000	.000
Lewis, Darren	.429	7	3	0	0	0	2	.429	.571
Leyritz, Jim	.182	11	2	0	0	1	3	.308	.273

Paul Quantrill, Blue Jays — RHP

Batter	Avg	AB	H	HR	BI	BB	SO	OBP	Slg
Liriano, N#	.444	9	4	1	1	0	0	.444	.778
Listach, Pat#	.286	7	2	0	2	0	1	.286	.429
Livingstone*	.375	8	3	0	0	0	0	.375	.500
Lockhart, K*	.429	7	3	0	0	1	0	.429	.429
Lofton, Kenny*	.250	8	2	0	1	0	1	.222	.250
Macfarlane, M	.333	9	3	0	0	0	1	.333	.444
Magadan, Dave*	.500	10	5	0	1	1	1	.545	.700
Manwaring, K	.273	11	3	0	0	1	1	.385	.455
Martin, Al*	.400	15	6	1	1	0	0	.400	.733
Martinez, E	.300	10	3	1	4	0	0	.300	.700
Martinez, T*	.150	20	3	1	2	0	1	.150	.300
McCarty, Dave	.200	5	1	0	0	0	0	.200	.200
McGriff, Fred*	.400	5	2	0	0	0	1	.400	.400
McGwire, Mark	.167	6	1	1	1	1	2	.286	.667
McLemore, M#	.222	9	2	0	0	0	1	.222	.333
McRae, Brian*	.273	11	3	0	1	1	1	.333	.364
Meares, Pat	.400	10	4	0	1	0	0	.400	.400
Merced, O*	.615	13	8	1	3	1	1	.643	1.154
Molitor, Paul	.188	16	3	0	0	3	1	.316	.188
Mondesi, Raul	.231	13	3	0	0	0	2	.231	.308
Mouton, James	.286	7	2	0	0	0	0	.286	.286
Munoz, Pedro	.333	9	3	0	1	0	0	.333	.333
Murray, Eddie*	.143	7	1	0	1	1	1	.250	.286
Myers, Greg*	.667	6	4	0	1	0	2	.667	1.333
Nilsson, Dave*	.143	7	1	1	1	0	1	.143	.571
O'Leary, Troy*	.250	4	1	0	0	1	0	.400	.250
O'Neill, Paul*	.231	13	3	1	1	0	4	.231	.538
Offerman, J#	.143	14	2	0	0	2	5	.250	.143
Olerud, John*	.250	4	1	0	0	1	0	.400	.500
Orsulak, Joe*	.333	3	1	0	0	1	0	.600	.333
Palmeiro, R*	.500	6	3	1	6	3	0	.545	1.167
Palmer, Dean	.000	7	0	0	0	1	1	.125	.000
Paquette, C	.143	7	1	0	0	0	2	.143	.143
Phillips, T#	.429	7	3	0	0	1	1	.500	.429
Piazza, Mike	.250	8	2	0	1	0	0	.250	.375
Plantier, P*	.200	5	1	1	2	1	2	.333	.800
Raines, Tim#	.375	8	3	3	7	0	0	.375	1.500
Ramirez, M	.667	6	4	1	1	1	1	.714	1.667
Reboulet, J	.182	11	2	0	0	2	1	.308	.182
Ripken, Cal	.300	10	3	0	1	1	1	.375	.300
Roberts, Bip#	.286	7	2	0	1	1	1	.375	.286
Rodriguez, Al	.400	5	2	0	0	0	2	.400	.800
Rodriguez, I	.222	9	2	1	3	0	2	.222	.556
Salmon, Tim	.400	10	4	2	4	1	2	.455	1.000
Segui, David#	.364	11	4	0	0	1	1	.417	.545
Seitzer, K	.125	8	1	0	0	1	0	.222	.125
Sierra, Ruben#	.000	15	0	0	0	1	4	.063	.000
Slaught, Don	.400	5	2	0	0	1	1	.500	.400
Snow, J.T.#	.167	6	1	1	1	0	3	.167	.667
Sorrento, P*	.600	10	6	2	3	1	0	.583	1.400
Sosa, Sammy	.000	3	0	0	0	2	1	.400	.000
Spiers, Bill*	.333	9	3	0	1	0	1	.333	.333
Sprague, Ed	.286	7	2	0	1	0	0	.286	.429
Stahoviak, S*	.222	9	2	0	0	0	2	.222	.333
Stankiewicz	.000	7	0	0	0	0	1	.000	.000
Stanley, Mike	.091	11	1	1	1	2	4	.231	.364
Steinbach, T	.444	9	4	1	2	0	1	.444	.889
Strange, Doug#	.500	6	3	0	0	1	0	.571	.667
Strawberry, D*	.250	4	1	0	1	0	0	.333	.250
Surhoff, B.J.*	.308	13	4	0	2	1	2	.357	.385
Tarasco, Tony*	.500	8	4	1	2	0	0	.500	1.000
Tartabull, D	.273	11	3	1	5	1	4	.333	.545
Tavarez, Je#	.286	7	2	0	0	0	3	.286	.286
Tettleton, M	.125	8	1	0	0	1	5	.125	.125
Thomas, Frank	.000	5	0	0	0	1	2	.167	.000
Thome, Jim*	.143	7	1	0	0	1	3	.250	.143
Thompson, Rob	.125	8	1	0	1	2	1	.300	.125
Tucker, M*	.000	4	0	0	0	1	1	.200	.000
Valle, Dave	.375	8	3	0	0	0	0	.375	.375
Vaughn, Greg	.417	12	5	2	3	1	0	.462	1.000
Velarde, R	.636	11	7	0	2	0	1	.636	.727
Ventura, R*	.500	4	2	1	1	1	1	.600	1.250
Vizcaino, J	.364	11	4	0	1	0	2	.364	.545
Vizquel, Omar#	.286	14	4	0	1	1	4	.333	.286
Walker, Larry*	.600	5	3	0	0	0	0	.600	.800
Wallach, Tim	.600	10	6	0	3	1	1	.636	.700
Weiss, Walt#	.000	4	0	0	0	1	0	.200	.000
White, Devon#	.375	8	3	0	0	0	3	.375	.375
White, R	.333	6	2	0	1	1	0	.429	.667
Williams, Ber#	.316	19	6	0	2	0	2	.316	.474
Williams, Ger	.250	8	2	0	0	0	0	.250	.375
Williams, Ma	.111	9	1	0	0	0	2	.111	.111
Wilson, Dan	.333	3	1	0	0	0	0	.333	.333
Zeile, Todd	.200	10	2	0	2	0	0	.200	.300

Scott Radinsky, Dodgers — LHP

Batter	Avg	AB	H	HR	BI	BB	SO	OBP	Slg
Alomar, R#	.571	7	4	1	2	0	1	.571	1.000
Anderson, Brd*	.143	7	1	0	0	1	2	.250	.143
Baerga, C*	.286	7	2	0	1	1	1	.375	.286
Baines, H*	.000	4	0	0	0	1	1	.200	.000

Scott Radinsky, Dodgers — LHP

Batter	Avg	AB	H	HR	BI	BB	SO	OBP	Slg
Bichette, D	.667	6	4	0	4	0	0	.667	.667
Boggs, Wade*	.250	8	2	0	2	3	1	.455	.250
Borders, Pat	.500	6	3	0	0	1	0	.571	.500
Buhner, Jay	.111	9	1	1	2	3	0	.333	.444
Burks, Ellis	.444	9	4	0	3	0	1	.444	.444
Carter, Joe	.167	6	1	0	1	0	0	.167	.167
Curtis, Chad	.250	4	1	0	1	3	0	.571	.250
Davis, Chili#	.556	9	5	1	8	3	3	.615	1.111
Deer, Rob	.250	4	1	0	1	2	1	.500	.500
Devereaux, M	.200	5	1	0	0	0	2	.200	.200
Edmonds, Jim*	.200	5	1	0	0	1	1	.333	.200
Eisenreich, J*	.222	9	2	0	1	1	2	.300	.222
Espinoza, A	.000	4	0	0	0	1	0	.200	.000
Fielder, C	.000	6	0	0	0	3	1	.333	.000
Finley, Steve*	.600	5	3	0	0	0	1	.600	.800
Flaherty, J	.333	6	2	0	0	0	0	.333	.333
Franco, Julio	.200	5	1	0	1	2	1	.429	.200
Fryman, T	.250	4	1	0	1	1	2	.333	.500
Gaetti, Gary	.167	6	1	0	0	0	0	.167	.167
Greenwell, M*	.375	8	3	1	4	0	0	.333	.875
Griffey Jr, K*	.067	15	1	0	0	0	6	.125	.133
Hall, Mel*	.154	13	2	0	1	0	2	.143	.231
Hamilton, D*	.125	8	1	0	0	0	3	.125	.125
Hill, G	.400	5	2	1	1	0	2	.400	1.000
Jefferies, G#	.400	5	2	0	1	0	0	.333	.400
Joyner, Wally*	.200	15	3	0	1	0	4	.200	.200
Kelly, Pat	.600	5	3	0	1	0	1	.600	.600
Kelly, R	.200	5	1	0	0	1	0	.333	.200
Knoblauch, C	.200	5	1	0	1	1	0	.429	.600
Leius, Scott	.333	3	1	0	0	2	0	.600	.333
Leyritz, Jim	.167	6	1	0	3	1	1	.286	.167
Lofton, Kenny*	.250	8	2	0	1	2	2	.333	.250
Macfarlane, M	.000	5	0	0	0	1	0	.167	.000
Martin, Al*	.000	5	0	0	0	0	2	.000	.000
Martinez, E	.500	2	1	0	0	2	0	.750	.500
Martinez, T*	.375	8	3	1	3	0	1	.333	.875
McCarty, Dave	.286	7	2	1	3	0	3	.286	.714
McGriff, Fred*	.000	4	0	0	0	1	1	.200	.000
McLemore, M#	.000	6	0	0	1	2	3	.250	.000
McRae, Brian*	.200	10	2	0	0	1	1	.273	.200
Molitor, Paul	.200	5	1	0	0	0	1	.200	.200
Morandini, M*	.250	4	1	0	0	1	1	.400	.250
Munoz, Pedro	.200	5	1	0	0	1	1	.333	.200
O'Neill, Paul*	.200	5	1	0	0	0	2	.200	.200
Olerud, John*	.167	12	2	0	2	2	3	.286	.250
Orsulak, Joe*	.333	3	1	0	1	2	1	.600	.333
Palmeiro, R*	.250	12	3	0	4	0	1	.231	.417
Phillips, T#	.417	12	5	1	3	1	0	.462	.667
Polonia, Luis*	.400	10	4	0	0	0	0	.400	.400
Reed, Jody	.200	5	1	0	0	0	0	.200	.200
Schofield, D	.250	4	1	0	0	1	0	.400	.250
Segui, David#	.167	6	1	0	1	0	1	.167	.333
Seitzer, K	.400	5	2	0	2	1	0	.500	.400
Sierra, Ruben#	.375	8	3	0	1	5	0	.615	.375
Snow, J.T.#	.600	5	3	0	2	1	0	.667	.600
Spiers, Bill*	.333	6	2	0	0	0	1	.333	.333
Stanley, Mike	.429	7	3	0	2	1	2	.444	.429
Surhoff, B.J.*	.400	10	4	2	4	0	2	.400	1.100
Tartabull, D	.375	8	3	1	1	1	2	.444	.750
Tettleton, M	.222	9	2	0	1	4	3	.462	.333
Trammell, A	.200	5	1	0	0	1	0	.333	.400
Valle, Dave	.250	4	1	0	0	2	0	.500	.250
Vaughn, Greg	.200	10	2	0	0	1	3	.273	.200
Vaughn, Mo*	.000	7	0	0	0	1	4	.125	.000
Velarde, R	.429	7	3	0	0	0	0	.429	.429
Vizquel, Omar#	.000	3	0	0	0	3	0	.500	.000
Weiss, Walt#	.167	6	1	0	0	1	0	.286	.167
Whiten, Devon	.000	4	0	0	0	1	2	.200	.000
Whiten, Mark#	.167	6	1	0	0	1	0	.286	.167
Williams, Ber#	.333	6	2	0	1	0	0	.333	.333

Brad Radke, Twins — RHP

Batter	Avg	AB	H	HR	BI	BB	SO	OBP	Slg
Alexander, M	.000	5	0	0	0	0	0	.000	.000
Alicea, Luis#	.000	4	0	0	1	0	0	.000	.000
Alomar, R#	.400	5	2	1	1	1	0	.500	1.200
Alomar Jr, S	.273	11	3	1	2	0	0	.273	.545
Anderson, Brd*	.250	12	3	0	0	0	2	.308	.417
Anderson, G*	.286	7	2	0	0	1	0	.286	.286
Arias, George	.000	4	0	0	0	1	2	.200	.000
Baerga, C#	.364	22	8	1	3	0	2	.364	.545
Baines, H*	.154	13	2	1	3	4	3	.353	.385
Belle, Albert	.421	19	8	1	5	2	3	.476	.789
Berroa, G	.250	16	4	2	5	0	3	.278	.688
Blowers, Mike	.125	8	1	0	0	0	1	.125	.125
Boggs, Wade*	.235	17	4	0	1	0	2	.235	.471
Bonilla, B#	.333	6	2	0	2	0	1	.333	.500
Bordick, Mike	.267	15	4	0	2	1	0	.294	.267
Bragg, Darren*	.444	9	4	1	2	3	0	.583	.778
Brosius, S	.000	9	0	0	0	3	0	.000	.000
Buhner, Jay	.417	12	5	3	5	1	4	.462	1.167

171

Brad Radke, Twins — RHP

Batter	Avg	AB	H	HR	BI	BB	SO	OBP	Slg
Burnitz, J*	1.000	4	4	2	3	2	0	1.000	2.750
Canseco, Jose	.222	9	2	0	1	0	2	.222	.222
Carter, Joe	.400	10	4	1	3	0	1	.364	1.000
Cedeno, D#	.333	6	2	0	0	0	1	.333	.333
Cirillo, Jeff	.182	11	2	0	1	1	3	.231	.364
Clark, Will*	.267	15	4	0	0	2	0	.353	.267
Cora, Joey#	.176	17	3	0	0	3	1	.333	.235
Curtis, Chad	.267	15	4	0	1	1	4	.313	.400
Damon, Johnny*	.200	10	2	0	0	0	1	.200	.200
Davis, Chili#	.091	11	1	0	0	0	1	.091	.091
Delgado, C*	.455	11	5	1	1	0	0	.455	.727
Devereaux, M	.333	6	2	0	0	0	0	.333	.667
Diaz, Alex*	.167	6	1	0	0	0	0	.167	.167
DiSarcina, G	.714	7	5	0	0	0	0	.714	1.000
Duncan, M	.250	4	1	0	0	0	1	.250	.250
Durham, Ray*	.267	15	4	1	2	0	3	.267	.600
Edmonds, Jim*	.091	11	1	0	0	0	4	.091	.182
Elster, Kevin	.200	5	1	0	1	0	2	.200	.200
Fabregas, Jor*	.167	6	1	0	0	0	0	.167	.167
Fielder, C	.167	12	2	0	3	0	2	.154	.333
Flaherty, J	.333	6	2	1	3	2	0	.444	.833
Fox, Andy*	.000	6	0	0	0	1	0	.167	.000
Frye, Jeff	.333	15	5	0	2	0	1	.333	.333
Fryman, T	.467	15	7	0	3	0	2	.467	.467
Gates, Brent#	.059	17	1	0	1	2	2	.158	.176
Giambi, Jason*	.294	17	5	0	1	0	1	.294	.412
Gil, Benji	.571	7	4	0	0	0	2	.571	.857
Gomez, Chris	.143	7	1	0	0	0	2	.143	.143
Gonzalez, A	.273	11	3	1	1	0	1	.273	.727
Gonzalez, J	.100	10	1	0	2	0	1	.100	.300
Goodwin, Tim*	.545	11	6	1	2	0	1	.545	.909
Green, Shawn*	.273	11	3	0	1	0	3	.273	.455
Greenwell, M	.333	9	3	1	2	0	1	.333	.667
Greer, Rusty*	.400	10	4	2	4	0	1	.400	1.100
Griffey Jr, K*	.200	15	3	2	4	2	5	.294	.667
Guillen, O*	.429	14	6	0	2	0	1	.429	.571
Hamelin, Bob*	.143	7	1	1	2	0	0	.143	.571
Hamilton, D*	.267	15	4	1	2	0	1	.267	.467
Henderson, R	.111	9	1	0	0	1	1	.200	.111
Herrera, Jose*	.000	4	0	0	0	0	0	.200	.000
Higginson, B*	.400	15	6	1	4	0	2	.400	.667
Howard, Dave#	.200	5	1	0	0	0	0	.200	.200
Jaha, John	.286	14	4	1	5	2	3	.375	.500
Javier, Stan*	.167	6	1	0	0	1	0	.375	.167
Jeter, Derek	.000	4	0	0	0	0	0	.000	.000
Karkovice, R	.167	6	1	0	0	0	2	.167	.167
Kelly, Pat	.250	4	1	0	0	0	0	.250	.250
Levis, Jesse*	.250	4	1	0	1	0	0	.400	.250
Lewis, Darren	.000	4	0	0	1	1	0	.200	.000
Lewis, Mark	.000	5	0	0	0	2	0	.000	.000
Leyritz, Jim	.429	7	3	1	1	0	1	.429	.857
Listach, Pat#	.125	8	1	0	0	0	1	.125	.125
Lockhart, K*	.357	14	5	1	6	0	1	.357	.786
Lofton, Kenny*	.278	18	5	1	2	1	3	.316	.500
Macfarlane, M	.200	5	1	0	1	1	1	.333	.200
Martinez, Da*	.231	13	3	1	1	0	2	.231	.462
Martinez, E	.286	14	4	1	1	2	2	.375	.500
Martinez, S*	.000	8	0	0	0	0	5	.000	.000
Martinez, T*	.313	16	5	1	4	2	3	.389	.563
McGwire, Mark	.357	14	5	2	5	5	2	.526	.929
McLemore, M#	.333	12	4	0	0	2	1	.429	.333
Mieske, Matt	.200	5	1	0	0	0	0	.200	.200
Murray, Eddie#	.333	15	5	2	3	1	1	.353	.733
Naehring, Tim	.200	10	2	0	1	2	0	.273	.200
Newfield, M	.333	9	3	0	0	0	1	.333	.333
Nilsson, Dave*	.091	11	1	0	1	2	0	.231	.182
Nixon, Otis#	.130	23	3	0	1	2	2	.200	.130
Nunnally, Jon*	.143	7	1	0	1	0	3	.143	.429
O'Leary, Troy*	.333	12	4	1	3	0	1	.333	.917
O'Neill, Paul*	.385	13	5	1	5	2	1	.438	.692
Offerman, J*	.250	8	2	0	1	1	0	.333	.375
Olerud, John*	.333	6	2	0	1	2	0	.500	.500
Oliver, Joe	.200	5	1	0	0	1	2	.333	.400
Palmeiro, R*	.455	11	5	1	2	0	2	.455	.818
Palmer, Dean	.500	12	6	2	2	0	3	.500	1.083
Paquette, C	.400	15	6	3	4	1	2	.438	1.000
Phillips, T#	.118	17	2	0	0	2	2	.211	.176
Plantier, P*	.600	5	3	1	3	1	0	.667	1.200
Polonia, Luis*	.500	6	3	0	1	0	0	.429	.667
Raines, Tim*	.600	5	3	0	1	0	0	.667	.800
Ramirez, M	.611	18	11	2	9	0	2	.579	1.111
Ripken, Cal	.333	9	3	0	1	1	1	.455	.556
Roberts, Bip#	.143	7	1	0	0	0	1	.143	.143
Rodriguez, Al	.111	9	1	1	1	1	5	.200	.444
Rodriguez, I	.364	11	4	1	1	0	1	.364	.727
Salmon, Tim	.100	10	1	1	1	2	1	.182	.400
Seitzer, K	.273	11	3	1	2	3	1	.429	.545
Sheets, Andy	.000	6	0	0	0	0	1	.000	.000
Sierra, Ruben#	.278	18	5	1	3	1	3	.316	.500
Snow, J.T.#	.000	5	0	0	0	2	1	.286	.000
Sojo, Luis	.286	7	2	0	1	0	0	.286	.286

Brad Radke, Twins — RHP

Batter	Avg	AB	H	HR	BI	BB	SO	OBP	Slg
Sorrento, P*	.429	21	9	1	3	0	2	.429	.714
Sprague, Ed	.182	11	2	0	1	0	1	.182	.364
Stairs, Matt*	.500	6	3	1	1	0	0	.500	1.000
Stanley, Mike	.375	8	3	0	3	0	0	.375	.625
Steinbach, T	.188	16	3	1	4	1	3	.235	.500
Surhoff, B.J.*	.417	12	5	2	4	0	2	.417	1.083
Tartabull, D	.400	15	6	3	6	0	2	.400	1.000
Tettleton, M	.091	11	1	0	0	1	2	.167	.091
Thomas, Frank	.333	9	3	2	3	1	2	.400	1.000
Thome, Jim*	.316	19	6	0	2	0	4	.316	.474
Tinsley, Lee#	.000	5	0	0	0	1	2	.167	.000
Tucker, M*	.250	8	2	0	1	2	0	.400	.250
Valentin, Jhn	.167	12	2	1	1	1	2	.231	.417
Valentin, Jose#	.300	10	3	1	1	2	0	.364	.800
Vaughn, Mo*	.417	12	5	1	1	0	3	.417	1.000
Velarde, R	.143	7	1	0	0	1	4	.250	.143
Ventura, R*	.143	14	2	0	0	1	1	.200	.143
Vina, F*	.200	10	2	0	0	0	0	.200	.200
Vizquel, Omar#	.278	18	5	0	1	1	3	.300	.444
Williams, Ber#	.267	15	4	1	4	1	0	.313	.533
Williams, Ger	.125	8	1	0	0	0	2	.222	.125
Wilson, Dan	.308	13	4	1	3	2	1	.400	.615
Young, Ernie	.333	9	3	0	1	1	0	.400	.333
Zaun, Greg#	.167	6	1	0	0	0	1	.167	.167

Pat Rapp, Marlins — RHP

Batter	Avg	AB	H	HR	BI	BB	SO	OBP	Slg
Alfonzo, E	.364	11	4	0	1	1	1	.417	.364
Alicea, Luis#	.429	7	3	0	2	1	0	.444	.571
Alou, Moises	.200	15	3	0	2	6	1	.429	.200
Andrews, S	.143	7	1	0	0	2	3	.333	.286
Anthony, Eric*	.333	6	2	0	3	1	0	.375	.667
Ausmus, Brad	.143	7	1	0	2	1	1	.250	.143
Bagwell, Jeff	.500	8	4	1	4	2	2	.600	.875
Bates, Jason#	.143	7	1	0	2	3	1	.400	.286
Batiste, Kim	.125	8	1	0	0	0	0	.125	.125
Bell, Derek	.267	15	4	0	1	6	0	.313	.333
Bell, Jay	.667	6	4	0	2	0	0	.667	1.000
Belliard, R	.200	5	1	0	0	1	0	.333	.200
Berry, Sean	.313	16	5	1	3	1	3	.389	.625
Bichette, D	.375	32	12	0	6	1	6	.382	.594
Biggio, Craig	.364	11	4	0	2	3	1	.500	.455
Blauser, Jeff	.267	15	4	0	1	2	0	.389	.333
Bonds, Barry*	.417	12	5	1	4	5	0	.556	.833
Bonilla, B#	.333	15	5	1	3	1	4	.375	.533
Boone, Bret	.385	13	5	1	2	2	1	.438	.615
Branson, Jeff*	.143	14	2	0	0	0	1	.143	.143
Brogna, Rico*	.308	13	4	1	1	0	2	.308	.615
Brumfield, J	.200	5	1	0	1	1	0	.200	.200
Bullett, S*	.500	6	3	1	3	1	0	.571	1.000
Burks, Ellis	.400	15	6	2	6	2	2	.471	.867
Burnitz, J*	.125	8	1	0	0	2	1	.300	.125
Butler, Brett*	.000	10	0	0	0	3	2	.231	.000
Caminiti, Ken#	.222	9	2	0	0	1	3	.300	.222
Cangelosi, J#	.000	4	0	0	0	1	0	.400	.000
Castilla, V	.389	18	7	1	4	1	1	.421	.611
Cedeno, A	.000	4	0	0	0	0	0	.200	.000
Cianfrocco, A	.333	6	2	0	3	2	2	.556	.667
Clayton, R	.556	18	10	0	3	2	2	.600	.611
Cordero, Wil	.375	16	6	0	1	6	0	.412	.375
Daulton, D*	.143	7	1	0	3	3	0	.364	.286
DeShields, D*	.083	12	1	0	0	5	2	.353	.083
Duncan, M	.500	8	4	0	3	2	0	.545	.750
Dunston, S	.500	8	4	0	1	0	0	.500	.500
Dykstra, L*	.188	16	3	0	0	2	1	.278	.250
Eisenreich, J*	.421	19	8	1	7	3	1	.500	.737
Eusebio, Tony	.000	4	0	0	0	1	0	.200	.000
Everett, Carl#	.000	4	0	0	0	3	2	.429	.000
Finley, Steve*	.111	9	1	0	0	0	0	.200	.111
Fletcher, D*	.250	28	7	0	1	0	0	.267	.357
Floyd, Cliff*	.286	14	4	0	0	2	2	.375	.286
Gaetti, Gary	.375	8	3	0	4	0	1	.333	.625
Gagne, Greg	.000	3	0	0	0	2	2	.400	.000
Galarraga, A	.130	23	3	1	4	1	8	.259	.261
Gant, Ron	.000	5	0	0	0	3	3	.375	.000
Garcia, C	.286	7	2	0	0	0	2	.286	.429
Gilkey, B	.273	11	3	0	1	1	0	.333	.273
Girardi, Joe	.000	6	0	0	1	2	0	.143	.000
Gonzalez, L*	.231	13	3	0	0	1	1	.231	.308
Grace, Mark*	.462	13	6	0	6	1	0	.533	.769
Greene, W*	.500	6	3	0	1	0	2	.500	.500
Grissom, M	.071	28	2	0	0	2	5	.133	.071
Grudzielanek	.091	11	1	0	2	4	4	.231	.091
Gutierrez, R	.214	14	3	0	1	0	0	.267	.214
Gwynn, Tony*	.231	13	3	0	1	0	0	.231	.231
Haney, Todd	.400	5	2	0	0	0	0	.400	.400
Hansen, Dave*	.250	4	1	0	2	2	0	.500	.250
Harris, Lenny*	.143	7	1	0	0	1	0	.250	.143
Hayes, C	.222	18	4	0	3	2	1	.286	.222
Henderson, R*	.500	4	2	0	0	2	1	.714	.500
Hill, G	.000	8	0	0	0	1	0	.111	.000

Pat Rapp, Marlins — RHP

Batter	Avg	AB	H	HR	BI	BB	SO	OBP	Slg
Hollandsworth*	.200	10	2	0	0	0	3	.200	.200
Hollins, Dave*	.250	8	2	0	2	2	1	.400	.250
Howard, T*	.000	7	0	0	0	0	0	.000	.000
Hundley, Todd#	.200	15	3	1	4	1	2	.294	.400
Hunter, Bri L	.333	6	2	0	1	0	2	.333	.500
Incaviglia, P	.000	5	0	0	0	2	1	.286	.000
Jefferies, G#	.167	12	2	0	2	4	0	.375	.250
Johnson, L*	.667	6	4	0	1	0	1	.667	.667
Johnson, Mark*	.250	4	1	0	0	1	1	.400	.250
Jones, C#	.071	14	1	0	1	1	1	.133	.071
Jordan, Brian	.143	7	1	0	0	1	2	.333	.286
Joyner, Wally*	.600	5	3	0	1	0	0	.667	.600
Justice, Dave*	.429	14	6	0	0	2	0	.500	.500
Karros, Eric	.235	17	4	0	2	0	4	.235	.294
Kelly, R	.364	11	4	0	3	0	5	.364	.455
Kent, Jeff	.348	23	8	4	10	2	4	.400	.913
King, Jeff	.375	8	3	0	3	1	0	.500	.500
Kingery, Mike*	.353	17	6	1	3	2	0	.421	.706
Klesko, Ryan*	.385	13	5	1	2	5	0	.556	.692
Lankford, Ray*	.222	9	2	1	2	7	3	.563	.556
Lansing, Mike	.355	31	11	0	2	1	1	.375	.452
Larkin, Barry	.294	17	5	1	3	2	2	.368	.529
Lemke, Mark#	.267	15	4	1	0	3	2	.389	.267
Lewis, Darren	.538	13	7	0	1	3	2	.625	.692
Lieberthal, M	.400	5	2	0	0	0	1	.400	.400
Liriano, N#	.000	10	0	0	0	1	2	.091	.000
Lopez, Javy	.300	10	3	0	0	0	2	.300	.300
Mabry, John*	.250	8	2	0	0	0	0	.250	.250
Magadan, Dave*	.364	11	4	0	0	2	1	.462	.364
Manwaring, K	.077	13	1	0	1	0	4	.077	.077
Martin, Al*	.375	8	3	0	2	3	2	.545	.375
Martinez, Da*	.500	6	3	1	1	1	1	.571	1.167
May, Derrick*	.250	8	2	0	1	3	0	.417	.250
McGee, Willie*	.438	16	7	0	1	2	1	.500	.563
McGriff, Fred*	.250	16	4	1	1	3	2	.368	.500
McRae, Brian#	.111	9	1	1	1	4	2	.385	.444
Merced, O*	.333	9	3	0	2	0	0	.333	.444
Mondesi, Raul	.364	11	4	0	1	2	0	.500	.455
Morandini, M*	.462	26	12	0	0	1	1	.481	.538
Morris, Hal*	.476	21	10	0	4	1	0	.500	.619
Mouton, James	.000	4	0	0	1	1	0	.200	.000
Murray, Eddie*	.500	6	3	0	1	1	0	.571	.667
O'Brien, Pete	.545	11	6	1	1	2	1	.643	.818
Ochoa, Alex	.400	5	2	0	0	0	0	.400	.800
Offerman, J#	.250	8	2	0	0	1	1	.333	.250
Oliver, Joe	.167	6	1	0	0	0	2	.167	.333
Orsulak, Joe*	.200	20	4	1	3	0	1	.200	.350
Otero, Ricky*	.300	10	3	0	1	1	0	.364	.300
Owens, J	.143	7	1	0	0	0	4	.250	.143
Pagnozzi, Tom	.167	12	2	1	2	1	1	.231	.500
Pena, G#	.200	5	1	0	0	3	1	.500	.200
Piazza, Mike	.214	14	3	0	1	4	2	.389	.214
Plantier, P*	.417	12	5	0	1	3	2	.533	.583
Polonia, Luis*	.500	8	4	0	0	0	1	.500	.500
Reed, Jeff*	.444	9	4	0	1	2	1	.545	.444
Reed, Jody	.143	7	1	0	0	1	1	.250	.143
Roberts, Bip#	.286	7	2	0	0	0	1	.286	.429
Rodriguez, H*	.222	9	2	0	0	2	2	.364	.222
Sanchez, Rey	.375	8	3	0	2	1	2	.444	.500
Sandberg, R	.250	4	1	0	0	1	0	.400	.250
Sanders, R	.182	11	2	1	2	2	4	.357	.545
Santangelo, F#	.286	7	2	0	0	0	0	.286	.286
Santiago, B	.222	9	2	0	0	1	1	.364	.222
Selcik, Kevin	.500	6	3	0	1	0	0	.500	.667
Segui, David#	.353	17	6	1	6	5	2	.500	.588
Servais, S	.500	6	3	1	3	1	1	.571	1.333
Sheaffer, D	.200	5	1	0	0	0	3	.200	.200
Shipley, J	.100	10	1	0	0	1	0	.182	.100
Smith, Dwight*	.200	5	1	0	1	3	1	.500	.400
Smith, Ozzie*	.400	5	2	0	0	2	0	.571	.400
Sosa, Sammy	.154	13	2	0	1	2	2	.313	.154
Stinnett, K	.333	3	1	0	0	1	2	.600	.333
Stocker, K#	.235	17	4	0	0	1	3	.278	.235
Sweeney, Mark*	.600	5	3	1	3	4	0	.778	1.200
Tarasco, Tony*	.333	6	2	0	1	4	0	.600	.667
Taubensee, E*	.444	9	4	0	0	0	2	.444	.444
Thompson, Mil*	.333	12	4	0	1	1	1	.385	.333
Thompson, Rob	.182	11	2	0	0	4	2	.400	.182
Thompson, Ry	.263	19	5	0	2	1	5	.300	.316
VanderWal, J*	.273	11	3	0	2	3	2	.429	.455
Vizcaino, J#	.313	16	5	0	1	2	0	.389	.563
Walker, Larry*	.263	19	5	0	5	1	5	.300	.421
Wallach, Tim	.143	7	1	1	3	0	1	.143	.571
Weiss, Walt*	.250	20	5	0	0	5	1	.400	.300
White, R	.308	13	4	0	1	1	3	.357	.385
Whiten, Mark#	.385	13	5	1	3	0	4	.385	.769
Wilkins, Rick*	.429	7	3	0	2	2	3	.556	.571
Williams, Ma	.125	16	2	0	2	1	5	.167	.188
Young, Eric	.267	15	4	1	1	4	0	.421	.533
Zeile, Todd	.154	13	2	0	1	4	3	.353	.154

Steve Reed, Rockies — RHP

Batter	Avg	AB	H	HR	BI	BB	SO	OBP	Slg
Abbott, Kurt	.125	8	1	0	0	0	5	.125	.125
Alfonzo, E	.400	5	2	0	2	0	0	.400	.400
Alou, Moises	.286	7	2	0	1	0	1	.375	.429
Anthony, Eric*	.167	6	1	0	0	0	0	.167	.167
Ausmus, Brad	.125	8	1	0	0	0	2	.125	.125
Bagwell, Jeff	.333	18	6	2	6	2	2	.429	.778
Bell, Derek	.333	15	5	1	3	0	3	.353	.600
Bell, Jay	.111	9	1	0	2	0	1	.091	.111
Benard, M*	.200	5	1	0	0	1	1	.333	.400
Benjamin, M	.167	6	1	0	0	0	2	.167	.167
Berry, Sean	.286	7	2	1	2	0	2	.286	.857
Biggio, Craig	.071	14	1	0	1	1	2	.188	.071
Blauser, Jeff	.231	13	3	0	1	0	4	.231	.231
Bonilla, B#	.500	2	1	0	1	2	1	.600	.500
Boone, Bret	.273	11	3	0	0	0	0	.273	.273
Branson, Jeff*	.500	8	4	1	3	0	0	.500	.875
Brumfield, J	.000	6	0	0	0	0	0	.000	.000
Bullett, S*	.000	4	0	0	0	1	1	.200	.000
Butler, Brett*	.333	9	3	0	0	0	0	.333	.556
Caminiti, Ken#	.400	5	2	1	1	1	0	.500	1.000
Carr, Chuck	.571	7	4	0	1	0	0	.571	.571
Cedeno, A	.167	6	1	0	0	1	0	.167	.333
Cianfrocco, A	.200	5	1	1	1	0	1	.200	.800
Clayton, R	.111	9	1	0	0	1	3	.200	.111
Colbrunn, G	.000	6	0	0	0	1	0	.000	.000
Conine, Jeff	.417	12	5	0	0	1	2	.462	.583
Cordero, Wil	.125	8	1	0	0	1	0	.222	.125
Davis, Eric	.200	5	1	1	2	1	1	.333	.800
Finley, Steve*	.333	6	2	0	1	0	0	.333	.500
Gant, Ron	.300	10	3	1	1	3	1	.462	.600
Garcia, C	.333	6	2	1	1	0	2	.333	.833
Gilkey, B	.250	8	2	0	4	0	3	.300	.250
Grace, Mark*	.444	9	4	0	3	1	1	.500	.556
Grissom, M	.500	10	5	0	0	2	1	.583	.800
Gutierrez, R	.143	7	1	0	0	0	1	.143	.143
Gwynn, Tony*	.800	5	4	1	2	0	0	.800	1.400
Hernandez, Jo	.200	5	1	0	0	0	3	.200	.200
Hill, G	.400	5	2	0	1	3	1	.625	.600
Hundley, Todd#	.167	6	1	0	1	0	0	.167	.167
Incaviglia, P	.200	5	1	0	0	1	1	.333	.400
Jefferies, G#	.333	6	2	0	2	0	1	.333	.333
Johnson, Char	.200	5	1	1	2	0	2	.200	.800
Jordan, Brian	.111	9	1	0	0	1	1	.111	.111
Justice, Dave*	.250	4	1	1	3	1	0	.400	1.000
Karros, Eric	.308	13	4	1	2	3	4	.438	.615
Kelly, R	.125	8	1	1	1	0	0	.125	.500
Kent, Jeff	.111	9	1	0	1	0	1	.100	.111
King, Jeff	.500	5	3	0	0	1	0	.571	.833
Klesko, Ryan*	.167	6	1	1	1	0	1	.167	.667
Lankford, Ray*	.250	4	1	0	0	2	2	.400	.250
Lansing, Mike	.455	11	5	1	4	0	0	.455	.818
Larkin, Barry	.000	9	0	0	0	2	1	.182	.000
Lemke, Mark*	.143	7	1	0	0	1	0	.250	.143
Lewis, Darren	.286	7	2	0	1	1	2	.375	.571
Lopez, Javy	.667	6	4	1	3	1	0	.714	1.333
Magadan, Dave*	.250	4	1	0	0	1	0	.400	.250
Manwaring, K	.231	13	3	0	0	0	2	.231	.231
May, Derrick*	.250	4	1	0	0	1	1	.400	.250
McGriff, Fred*	.600	5	3	2	2	1	0	.667	1.800
McRae, Brian#	.000	7	0	0	0	0	2	.000	.000
Merced, O*	.200	5	1	0	0	1	3	.333	.200
Mitchell, K	.200	5	1	0	0	0	0	.200	.200
Mondesi, Raul	.444	9	4	0	5	0	2	.444	.778
Morris, Hal*	.300	10	3	2	3	1	1	.385	.900
Offerman, J#	.000	4	0	0	0	1	1	.200	.000
Oliver, Joe	.000	5	0	0	0	0	2	.000	.000
Pagnozzi, Tom	.364	11	4	1	2	0	4	.364	.636
Pendleton, T#	.500	4	2	0	1	0	1	.600	.750
Piazza, Mike	.545	11	6	4	9	0	1	.615	1.727
Roberts, Bip#	.286	7	2	0	1	0	1	.286	.286
Rodriguez, H*	.750	4	3	0	1	0	0	.800	.750
Sanchez, Rey	.143	14	2	0	0	0	2	.143	.143
Sandberg, R	.250	8	2	0	0	0	1	.250	.375
Sanders, R	.077	13	1	1	2	2	2	.200	.308
Santiago, B	.000	16	0	0	1	1	4	.056	.000
Scarsone, S	.200	5	1	0	0	1	1	.200	.200
Servais, S	.200	5	1	0	0	0	3	.200	.200
Sheffield, G	.000	10	0	0	2	1	5	.083	.000
Shipley, C	.400	5	2	0	1	0	2	.400	.600
Sosa, Sammy	.182	11	2	0	1	0	3	.182	.182
Stocker, K#	.500	4	2	1	1	2	0	.600	1.250
Taubensee, E*	.500	6	3	1	2	0	1	.500	1.000
Tavarez, Je#	.000	5	0	0	0	0	2	.000	.000
Thompson, Ry	.125	8	1	0	3	0	2	.125	.375
Veras, Q#	.000	1	0	0	0	4	0	.800	.000
Vizcaino, J#	.143	7	1	0	0	0	1	.143	.143
Wallach, Tim	.143	7	1	0	1	1	1	.250	.143
Weiss, Walt*	.000	6	0	0	0	1	0	.000	.000
Wilkins, Rick*	.400	5	2	0	3	0	2	.400	.600
Williams, Ma	.375	8	3	0	3	0	0	.375	.375

Steve Reed, Rockies — RHP

Batter	Avg	AB	H	HR	BI	BB	SO	OBP	Slg
Young, Kevin	.000	6	0	0	0	0	2	.000	.000
Zeile, Todd	.400	15	6	2	6	1	0	.438	.867

Bryan Rekar, Rockies — RHP

Batter	Avg	AB	H	HR	BI	BB	SO	OBP	Slg
Abbott, Kurt	.250	4	1	0	0	1	1	.400	.250
Alou, Moises	.667	3	2	0	1	1	0	.800	1.000
Ausmus, Brad	.600	5	3	0	3	0	0	.600	.600
Benjamin, M	.000	6	0	0	0	0	0	.000	.000
Berry, Sean	.167	6	1	1	2	0	1	.167	.667
Bonds, Barry*	.429	7	3	1	4	1	1	.500	.857
Caminiti, Ken#	.000	4	0	0	1	0	1	.000	.000
Conine, Jeff	.333	6	2	0	2	0	1	.333	.667
Daulton, D*	.222	9	2	0	2	1	3	.300	.222
Dawson, Andre	.333	3	1	0	1	0	0	.400	.333
Dunston, S	.000	6	0	0	0	0	0	.000	.000
Dykstra, L*	.333	9	3	0	1	2	1	.500	.667
Eisenreich, J*	.000	5	0	0	0	0	1	.000	.000
Finley, Steve*	.600	5	3	0	0	0	1	.600	1.400
Gilkey, B	.286	7	2	1	1	0	1	.286	.857
Gonzalez, L*	.375	8	3	1	3	2	1	.500	.875
Grace, Mark*	.200	10	2	0	1	1	1	.273	.200
Grudzielanek	.833	6	5	0	3	0	0	.833	.833
Hayes, C	.000	7	0	0	0	0	2	.000	.000
Hill, G	.400	5	2	0	2	1	0	.429	.400
Jefferies, G#	.400	10	4	0	1	1	1	.455	.700
Jordan, Brian	.600	5	3	0	0	0	0	.600	.600
Lansing, Mike	.222	9	2	1	3	0	1	.222	.556
Manwaring, K	.000	4	0	0	1	0	1	.167	.000
McCarty, Dave	.200	5	1	0	0	0	0	.200	.400
McRae, Brian#	.300	10	3	1	1	2	2	.417	.600
Morandini, M*	.286	14	4	0	0	0	1	.286	.357
Pendleton, T#	.200	5	1	0	1	0	2	.200	.400
Reed, Jody	.750	4	3	0	0	1	0	.800	1.000
Rodriguez, H*	.000	5	2	0	1	0	1	.400	.600
Sanchez, Rey	.000	5	0	0	0	1	1	.167	.000
Sandberg, R	.000	4	0	0	1	0	0	.200	.000
Santiago, B	.000	5	0	0	0	0	1	.000	.000
Segui, David#	.286	7	2	0	1	1	1	.375	.429
Servais, S	.200	10	2	1	2	0	2	.200	.500
Sosa, Sammy	.455	11	5	2	4	0	0	.455	1.182
Stocker, K#	.250	8	2	0	1	0	1	.222	.375
Tavarez, Je#	.333	6	2	0	0	0	0	.333	.333
Veras, Q	.333	6	2	0	1	0	1	.333	.500
Whiten, Mark#	.200	5	1	0	1	0	2	.200	.200
Williams, Ma	.333	6	2	0	0	0	0	.333	.333
Zeile, Todd	.000	11	0	0	0	0	2	.000	.000

Mike Remlinger, Reds — LHP

Batter	Avg	AB	H	HR	BI	BB	SO	OBP	Slg
Arias, Alex	.333	3	1	0	0	2	0	.600	.333
Blauser, Jeff	.250	4	1	0	1	4	1	.625	.500
Bonds, Barry*	.286	7	2	1	1	1	1	.375	.714
Bournigal, R	.200	5	1	0	1	0	0	.200	.200
Butler, Brett*	.429	7	3	0	0	3	0	.600	.571
Castillo, L#	.200	5	1	1	1	1	1	.333	.800
Clayton, D	.000	4	0	0	0	0	2	.200	.000
Colbrunn, G	.200	5	1	1	1	1	1	.333	.800
Conine, Jeff	.429	7	3	1	2	2	1	.556	1.143
DeShields, D*	.333	6	2	0	1	0	1	.333	.333
Gilkey, B	.200	5	1	0	0	1	1	.333	.400
Grissom, M	.250	4	1	0	1	1	0	.400	.250
Gwynn, Tony*	.143	7	1	0	2	0	0	.143	.143
Jones, C#	.000	5	0	0	0	1	1	.167	.000
Jordan, Ricky	.600	5	3	0	3	0	1	.600	.800
Justice, Dave*	.000	4	0	0	0	3	1	.429	.000
Karros, Eric	.333	3	1	0	2	0	0	.600	.333
Lankford, Ray*	.000	6	0	0	1	0	2	.143	.000
Lemke, Mark#	.143	7	1	0	3	0	0	.400	.143
Lewis, Darren	.143	7	1	0	0	0	0	.143	.286
Lopez, Javy	.400	10	4	0	0	1	1	.455	.600
Manwaring, K	.250	4	1	0	0	1	0	.400	.250
McGriff, Fred*	.267	15	4	1	3	1	0	.313	.533
Mondesi, Raul	.286	7	2	1	2	0	3	.286	.857
Natal, Bob	.000	2	0	0	0	3	2	.600	.000
Pendleton, T	.273	11	3	0	0	0	2	.273	.364
Piazza, Mike	.500	4	2	1	1	3	1	.714	1.500
Renteria, O	.000	4	0	0	0	2	3	.333	.000
Santiago, B	.250	8	2	2	3	0	1	.250	1.000
Sheffield, G	.200	5	1	0	0	1	0	.333	.200
Smith, Ozzie#	.429	7	3	0	3	0	0	.429	.714
Wallach, Tim	.400	5	2	1	3	2	1	.571	1.000
White, Devon#	.500	4	2	0	2	0	1	.600	.750
Williams, Ma	.167	6	1	1	2	0	1	.167	.667

Carlos Reyes, Athletics — RHP

Batter	Avg	AB	H	HR	BI	BB	SO	OBP	Slg
Alicea, Luis#	.000	5	0	0	0	0	2	.000	.000
Alomar, R#	.429	7	3	0	1	4	0	.636	.857
Alomar Jr, S	.000	8	0	0	0	1	3	.111	.000
Anderson, Brd*	.167	12	2	0	0	0	3	.167	.250

Carlos Reyes, Athletics — RHP

Batter	Avg	AB	H	HR	BI	BB	SO	OBP	Slg
Baerga, C#	.250	8	2	0	1	0	0	.250	.375
Baines, H*	.200	10	2	0	1	1	0	.333	.200
Becker, Rich*	.000	5	0	0	0	0	2	.000	.000
Belle, Albert	.250	12	3	2	6	0	2	.250	.750
Boggs, Wade*	.300	10	3	0	1	2	1	.417	.400
Bonilla, B#	.167	6	1	0	0	2	3	.375	.167
Buhner, Jay	.143	7	1	1	3	0	0	.143	.571
Canseco, Jose	.400	5	2	2	4	2	0	.571	1.600
Carter, Joe	.000	4	0	0	0	2	0	.333	.000
Clark, Will*	.286	7	2	0	2	1	0	.333	.286
Cora, Joey#	.364	11	4	0	1	1	1	.385	.455
Cordova, M	.444	9	4	2	4	0	1	.444	1.111
Curtis, Chad	.167	12	2	1	2	1	0	.231	.417
Davis, Chili#	.800	5	4	0	3	0	0	.800	1.000
Delgado, C*	.250	4	1	0	1	1	1	.400	.250
DiSarcina, G	.143	7	1	1	1	0	1	.143	.571
Edmonds, Jim*	.167	6	1	0	1	0	0	.167	.167
Elster, Kevin	.286	7	2	0	2	1	0	.333	.429
Fielder, C	.333	12	4	1	1	1	2	.385	.667
Franco, Julio	.444	9	4	0	2	3	0	.538	.556
Fryman, T	.250	12	3	0	0	1	4	.308	.250
Gomez, Chris	.333	6	2	0	0	0	2	.333	.333
Gonzalez, A	.600	5	3	1	2	2	0	.714	1.200
Gonzalez, J	.250	8	2	0	3	1	1	.300	.250
Green, Shawn*	.200	5	1	0	0	0	1	.200	.200
Greenwell, M*	.600	5	3	0	0	1	0	.667	.600
Greer, Rusty*	.600	10	6	1	4	0	0	.600	1.200
Guillen, O*	.111	9	1	0	0	0	0	.111	.111
Hamelin, Bob*	.000	5	0	0	0	1	1	.167	.000
Hamilton, D*	.200	5	1	0	0	1	0	.333	.200
Hammonds, J	.200	5	1	0	1	0	1	.200	.400
Haselman, B	.000	4	0	0	0	1	0	.200	.000
Higginson, B*	.143	7	1	1	1	2	0	.333	.571
Hoiles, Chris	.333	9	3	3	8	3	2	.538	1.333
Hollins, Dave#	.000	5	0	0	0	1	3	.167	.000
Hudler, Rex	.600	5	3	0	0	0	0	.600	.800
Hulse, David*	.000	5	0	0	0	0	0	.000	.000
Jaha, John	.500	6	3	2	3	0	1	.429	1.500
Jeter, Derek	.167	6	1	0	0	0	2	.286	.167
Johnson, L*	.286	7	2	0	0	1	0	.375	.429
Karkovice, R	.000	3	0	0	0	3	1	.500	.000
Kelly, Pat	.000	4	0	0	0	0	2	.000	.000
Knoblauch, C	.400	5	2	0	1	3	0	.625	.600
Lewis, Mark	.200	5	1	0	0	0	1	.200	.200
Leyritz, Jim	.429	7	3	2	4	0	1	.429	1.429
Listach, Pat#	.500	4	2	0	1	1	1	.600	.500
Lockhart, K*	.400	5	2	1	2	0	0	.400	1.000
Lofton, Kenny*	.500	4	2	0	0	2	0	.667	.750
Macfarlane, M	.333	6	2	1	3	0	2	.333	.833
Martinez, Da*	.167	6	1	0	0	0	1	.167	.167
Martinez, E	.286	7	2	0	1	2	2	.444	.429
Martinez, T*	.333	9	3	0	1	0	1	.333	.444
Matheny, Mike	.200	5	1	0	2	0	2	.200	.200
McLemore, M#	.250	12	3	0	1	1	2	.308	.333
Meares, Pat	.143	7	1	0	1	0	0	.143	.143
Molitor, Paul	.375	8	3	0	1	2	3	.545	.375
Murray, Eddie*	.375	8	3	0	1	1	1	.444	.500
Myers, Greg*	.333	6	2	0	0	1	1	.429	.333
Naehring, Tim	.556	9	5	1	4	1	0	.600	1.111
Nixon, Otis#	.200	10	2	0	0	0	1	.200	.300
O'Leary, Troy*	.429	7	3	1	3	0	1	.429	1.000
O'Neill, Paul*	.556	9	5	0	2	3	1	.667	.556
Olerud, John*	.333	6	2	1	3	2	1	.500	1.000
Palmeiro, R*	.300	10	3	0	1	0	1	.364	.400
Palmer, Dean	.286	7	2	0	0	2	2	.444	.429
Phillips, T#	.333	9	3	0	0	1	2	.400	.333
Polonia, Luis*	.100	10	1	0	1	0	0	.100	.200
Raines, Tim*	.462	13	6	2	3	2	0	.533	1.000
Ramirez, M	.200	10	2	1	2	1	2	.250	.500
Ripken, Cal	.083	12	1	0	1	2	5	.214	.083
Rodriguez, Al	.400	5	2	0	0	0	0	.400	.400
Rodriguez, I	.556	9	5	0	3	0	0	.556	.889
Salmon, Tim	.200	5	1	0	0	2	1	.429	.200
Seitzer, K	.143	7	1	1	2	0	0	.143	.571
Sierra, Ruben#	.200	5	1	0	1	0	2	.200	.200
Snow, J.T.#	.143	7	1	1	2	0	2	.143	.571
Sojo, Luis	.000	5	0	0	0	0	1	.000	.000
Sorrento, P*	.000	5	0	0	0	0	4	.111	.000
Sprague, Ed	.200	5	1	0	1	2	2	.429	.200
Stahoviak, S*	.250	4	1	0	1	1	1	.333	.250
Surhoff, B.J.*	.250	8	2	0	0	0	2	.250	.375
Tartabull, D	.250	8	2	0	0	0	2	.250	.250
Tettleton, M#	.000	6	0	0	0	5	2	.455	.000
Thomas, Frank	.200	10	2	0	2	4	2	.429	.300
Thome, Jim*	.125	8	1	0	0	1	4	.222	.250
Valentin, Jhn	.286	7	2	0	1	0	1	.286	.286
Valentin, Jose	.200	5	1	0	0	0	1	.200	.200
Vaughn, Greg	.400	5	2	0	0	0	2	.400	.400
Vaughn, Mo*	.800	5	4	1	1	2	1	.875	1.400
Velarde, R	.400	5	2	0	1	1	2	.500	.400
Ventura, R*	.273	11	3	0	3	1	1	.308	.273

Carlos Reyes, Athletics — RHP

Batter	Avg	AB	H	HR	BI	BB	SO	OBP	Slg
Vizquel, Omar*	.286	7	2	0	0	1	2	.375	.286
Walbeck, Matt#	.333	6	2	0	1	0	1	.333	.500
White, Devon#	.500	4	2	0	0	1	0	.600	.750
Williams, Ber#	.250	8	2	0	2	2	0	.400	.250
Williams, E	.400	5	2	0	0	0	1	.400	.400
Williams, Ger	.400	5	2	0	0	0	0	.400	.400
Wilson, Dan	.429	7	3	0	1	0	1	.429	.571

Shane Reynolds, Astros — RHP

Batter	Avg	AB	H	HR	BI	BB	SO	OBP	Slg
Abbott, Kurt	.417	12	5	1	4	0	2	.417	.833
Alfonzo, E	.636	11	7	0	0	0	0	.636	.727
Alicea, Luis*	.375	16	6	0	1	1	4	.412	.438
Alou, Moises	.316	19	6	2	7	2	2	.381	.789
Andrews, S	.286	7	2	0	1	1	2	.375	.286
Anthony, Eric*	.000	6	0	0	0	1	1	.143	.000
Arias, Alex	.286	7	2	0	0	0	1	.286	.286
Ashley, Billy	.200	5	1	0	0	0	3	.200	.400
Ausmus, Brad	.154	13	2	0	0	1	0	.214	.154
Barberie, B#	.286	7	2	0	0	0	4	.375	.429
Bell, Derek	.100	10	1	0	1	0	1	.100	.100
Bell, Jay	.333	24	8	0	0	0	2	.333	.500
Benard, S	.333	6	2	0	0	1	1	.429	.333
Benjamin, M	.333	6	2	1	2	0	0	.333	1.167
Berry, Sean	.200	5	1	0	1	0	2	.200	.200
Bichette, D	.214	14	3	1	3	0	0	.214	.500
Blauser, Jeff	.500	8	4	0	0	1	1	.556	.875
Blowers, Mike	.000	5	0	0	0	1	2	.167	.000
Bonds, Barry*	.263	19	5	1	1	2	4	.333	.474
Boone, Bret	.357	14	5	0	2	2	0	.412	.429
Branson, Jeff*	.333	12	4	0	2	3	4	.438	.333
Brogna, Rico*	.333	12	4	1	4	0	4	.333	.667
Brumfield, J	.300	10	3	0	0	0	1	.300	.300
Buford, Damon	.000	6	0	0	0	1	2	.143	.000
Bullett, S*	.375	8	3	0	0	0	5	.375	.375
Burks, Ellis	.538	13	7	1	2	1	1	.571	.846
Butler, Brett*	.300	20	6	1	2	0	2	.300	.450
Caminiti, Ken#	.286	14	4	1	2	1	1	.333	.571
Carr, Chuck	.167	6	1	0	0	0	1	.167	.167
Carreon, Mark	.222	9	2	0	3	0	1	.222	.333
Castilla, V	.455	11	5	1	3	0	2	.417	.727
Castillo, L#	.200	5	1	0	0	1	2	.333	.200
Cedeno, A	.273	11	3	0	0	0	6	.273	.273
Cianfrocco, A	.167	6	1	0	0	0	4	.167	.167
Clark, Dave*	.091	11	1	0	0	0	5	.091	.091
Clayton, R	.273	22	6	0	2	0	4	.261	.318
Colbrunn, G	.500	10	5	0	3	0	0	.583	.600
Conine, Jeff	.467	15	7	1	7	1	3	.500	.800
Cordero, Wil	.182	11	2	0	1	1	4	.250	.182
Cummings, M*	.300	10	3	0	1	0	4	.300	.300
Davis, Eric	.667	3	2	0	0	4	0	.857	.667
Dawson, Andre	.400	5	2	1	4	0	0	.400	1.000
Decker, Steve	.333	6	2	0	1	0	0	.333	.333
DeShields, D*	.100	20	2	0	0	0	6	.100	.100
Duncan, M	.250	8	2	0	0	0	1	.250	.250
Dunston, S	.267	15	4	0	2	0	3	.267	.333
Dykstra, L*	.429	7	3	0	1	0	0	.429	.571
Eisenreich, J*	.250	16	4	0	1	1	1	.294	.250
Everett, Carl#	.200	10	2	0	0	1	5	.273	.200
Faneyte, R	.000	6	0	0	0	0	1	.000	.000
Finley, Steve*	.200	20	4	0	1	1	3	.238	.250
Fletcher, D*	.333	18	6	0	4	0	3	.316	.500
Floyd, Cliff*	.000	4	0	0	0	0	2	.000	.000
Gaetti, Gary	.154	13	2	1	2	0	6	.154	.385
Gagne, Greg	.600	5	3	1	1	3	1	.750	1.200
Galarraga, A	.125	8	1	0	1	0	3	.222	.375
Gant, Ron	.381	21	8	3	5	0	7	.381	1.000
Garcia, C	.250	16	4	0	0	0	3	.250	.313
Gilkey, B	.250	20	5	0	3	2	6	.348	.350
Gomez, Leo	.167	6	1	0	0	0	3	.167	.333
Gonzalez, L*	.214	14	3	1	1	2	1	.313	.571
Grace, Mark*	.409	22	9	1	6	2	0	.458	.682
Grissom, M	.250	16	4	0	0	0	2	.250	.313
Grudzielanek	.167	6	1	0	0	0	1	.167	.167
Gwynn, Tony*	.364	22	8	0	3	0	0	.364	.455
Hansen, Dave*	.222	9	2	0	1	1	2	.300	.333
Harris, Lenny*	.143	7	1	0	0	0	0	.143	.286
Hayes, C	.385	13	5	0	2	2	1	.467	.462
Henderson, R	.200	10	2	0	1	2	2	.333	.500
Hernandez, Jo	.333	12	4	0	2	1	3	.385	.333
Hill, G	.444	9	4	1	3	0	4	.400	1.222
Hollandsworth*	.500	6	2	0	5	0	3	.500	1.167
Howard, T*	.231	13	3	0	1	0	4	.231	.231
Hundley, Todd#	.333	18	6	1	3	1	4	.368	.500
Huskey, Butch	.250	12	3	1	1	0	3	.250	.667
Hyers, Tim*	.333	6	2	0	1	0	1	.333	.333
Incaviglia, P	.300	10	3	0	0	0	3	.300	.300
Jefferies, G#	.333	15	5	0	2	1	1	.412	.333
Johnson, Bri	.300	10	3	1	2	1	1	.364	.600
Johnson, L*	.231	13	3	1	1	0	2	.231	.538
Johnson, Mark*	.000	7	0	0	0	0	4	.000	.000
Jones, C#	.000	10	0	0	0	1	2	.091	.000
Jordan, Brian	.150	20	3	1	2	0	4	.150	.350
Joyner, Wally*	.000	9	0	0	0	1	1	.100	.000
Justice, Dave*	.000	5	0	0	0	1	1	.167	.000
Karros, Eric	.217	23	5	0	3	1	4	.250	.217
Kelly, R	.000	7	0	0	0	0	1	.000	.000
Kendall, J	.000	4	0	0	0	0	0	.333	.000
Kent, Jeff	.188	16	3	1	1	0	6	.188	.375
King, Jeff	.286	21	6	2	3	1	2	.318	.619
Kingery, Mike*	.400	5	2	0	1	0	1	.400	.400
Klesko, Ryan*	.444	9	4	0	0	1	3	.500	.556
Lankford, Ray*	.417	24	10	0	1	1	5	.462	.542
Lansing, Mike	.368	19	7	0	2	0	5	.368	.526
Larkin, Barry	.333	21	7	0	2	2	2	.391	.429
Lemke, Mark*	.154	13	2	0	0	1	0	.154	.154
Lewis, Darren	.200	10	2	1	1	0	0	.200	.500
Lieberthal, M	.167	6	1	0	2	0	0	.167	.167
Liriano, N#	.286	7	2	0	0	1	0	.375	.429
Livingstone*	.400	10	4	1	1	0	1	.400	.700
Lopez, Javy	.571	7	4	0	0	0	0	.571	.571
Lopez, Luis#	.000	8	0	0	0	0	3	.000	.000
Mabry, John*	.316	19	6	0	0	0	2	.316	.421
Magadan, Dave*	.400	5	2	0	0	1	0	.400	.400
Manwaring, K	.545	11	6	0	0	1	1	.545	.727
Martin, Al*	.214	14	3	0	3	0	5	.214	.357
Martinez, Da*	.333	9	3	0	1	0	2	.333	.444
McGriff, Fred*	.250	12	3	0	0	0	4	.250	.250
McRae, Brian#	.063	16	1	0	0	2	7	.167	.125
Merced, O*	.400	20	8	0	1	1	3	.429	.400
Mitchell, K	.000	5	0	0	0	0	2	.000	.000
Mondesi, Raul	.267	15	4	1	2	1	4	.313	.467
Morandini, M*	.190	21	4	0	0	0	3	.190	.238
Morris, Hal*	.458	24	11	0	1	2	5	.519	.500
Nieves, M#	.200	5	1	0	0	0	4	.200	.200
Ochoa, Alex	.286	7	2	0	1	0	0	.286	.429
Offerman, J#	.500	14	7	0	1	0	2	.500	.571
Ordonez, Rey	.273	11	3	0	0	0	1	.273	.273
Orsulak, Joe*	.111	9	1	0	0	0	1	.111	.111
Otero, Ricky#	.125	8	1	0	1	0	0	.125	.125
Pagnozzi, Tom	.267	15	4	0	0	0	2	.267	.333
Pendleton, T#	.714	7	5	0	2	0	0	.625	1.000
Piazza, Mike	.455	22	10	1	2	0	3	.455	.591
Plantier, P*	.143	7	1	0	1	2	3	.333	.143
Reed, Jeff*	.167	6	1	0	0	0	3	.167	.167
Reed, Jody	.118	17	2	0	1	1	1	.167	.118
Renteria, E	.800	5	4	0	1	0	0	.800	1.200
Roberts, Bip#	.571	14	8	0	4	2	2	.647	.857
Rodriguez, H*	.143	21	3	0	0	0	4	.182	.190
Sabo, Chris	.333	6	2	0	0	0	0	.333	.500
Sanchez, Rey	.133	15	2	0	2	0	5	.133	.133
Sandberg, R	.375	8	3	0	0	0	3	.375	.375
Sanders, R	.238	21	5	0	4	3	5	.333	.333
Santangelo, F#	.333	6	2	0	0	0	1	.333	.333
Santiago, B	.083	12	1	1	1	1	3	.154	.333
Scarsone, S	.125	8	1	0	1	0	3	.125	.125
Segui, David#	.200	10	2	0	0	0	1	.200	.400
Servais, S	.125	8	1	0	1	1	1	.222	.125
Sheaffer, D	.500	6	3	0	1	0	1	.500	.500
Sheffield, G	.143	7	1	0	0	2	3	.333	.143
Shipley, C	.000	8	0	0	0	0	1	.000	.000
Slaught, Don	.100	10	1	0	0	0	0	.100	.100
Smith, Ozzie#	.400	10	4	0	1	0	1	.400	.400
Snow, Sammy	.278	18	5	1	3	1	4	.316	.611
Stocker, K#	.222	9	2	0	1	0	2	.222	.222
Sweeney, Mark*	.167	6	1	0	1	0	3	.167	.167
Tarasco, Tony*	.125	8	1	0	0	1	4	.222	.125
Taubensee, E*	.533	15	8	0	1	1	4	.563	.867
Tavarez, Je#	.000	5	0	0	0	1	0	.000	.000
Thompson, Rob	.222	9	2	0	0	1	0	.222	.333
TuckerWal, J*	.571	7	4	0	2	0	1	.571	.714
Vizcaino, J	.063	16	1	0	1	2	1	.167	.125
Wallach, Tim	.000	9	0	0	0	0	1	.100	.000
Weiss, Walt*	.000	4	0	0	0	2	1	.333	.000
White, Devon#	.000	4	0	0	0	0	5	.000	.000
White, R	.375	8	3	0	0	1	3	.500	.375
Whiten, Mark#	.222	9	2	0	0	5	4	.500	.222
Wilkins, Rick*	.000	5	0	0	0	3	3	.375	.000
Williams, E	.500	6	3	0	1	0	1	.500	1.000
Williams, Ma	.500	6	3	2	3	2	0	.667	1.667
Young, Eric	.154	13	2	0	1	1	0	.267	.154
Zeile, Todd	.421	19	8	0	3	0	1	.421	.579

Armando Reynoso, Rockies — RHP

Batter	Avg	AB	H	HR	BI	BB	SO	OBP	Slg
Abbott, Kurt	.400	5	2	0	0	0	0	.400	.400
Alicea, Luis#	.083	12	1	0	0	0	0	.083	.167
Alou, Moises	.375	8	3	0	1	6	0	.643	.375
Andrews, S	.167	6	1	1	2	0	1	.143	.667
Anthony, Eric*	.375	16	6	0	2	2	1	.444	.500
Arias, Alex	.500	4	2	0	1	0	0	.600	.750
Ausmus, Brad	.375	8	3	0	0	0	1	.375	.375

Armando Reynoso, Rockies — RHP

Batter	Avg	AB	H	HR	BI	BB	SO	OBP	Slg
Bagwell, Jeff	.318	22	7	1	3	4	4	.423	.636
Bell, David	.750	4	3	0	3	2	0	.833	1.500
Bell, Derek	.368	19	7	2	4	0	3	.368	.789
Bell, Jay	.333	18	6	1	0	0	1	.333	.556
Benard, M*	.167	6	1	0	0	1	0	.286	.167
Benjamin, M	.091	11	1	0	0	0	1	.091	.091
Berry, Sean	.429	14	6	2	3	2	0	.500	.929
Biggio, Craig	.348	23	8	1	6	1	4	.385	.609
Blauser, Jeff	.462	13	6	1	3	2	1	.533	.692
Bonds, Barry*	.667	15	10	2	9	8	1	.783	1.400
Bonilla, B#	.333	6	2	0	0	1	1	.429	.500
Boone, Bret	.100	10	1	0	1	0	2	.100	.100
Branson, Jeff*	.143	7	1	0	2	1	3	.250	.143
Brogna, Rico*	.000	10	0	0	0	1	0	.000	.000
Brumfield, J	.400	5	2	0	1	4	1	.667	.400
Butler, Brett*	.250	12	3	0	0	3	3	.400	.417
Caminiti, Ken#	.250	24	6	2	4	5	2	.379	.583
Cangelosi, J#	.444	9	4	0	0	0	1	.444	.778
Carreon, Mark	.300	10	3	0	3	0	0	.300	.300
Cedeno, A	.176	17	3	0	1	2	5	.250	.176
Cianfrocco, A	.333	6	2	0	0	0	2	.333	.333
Clark, Will*	.429	14	6	0	1	0	2	.467	.571
Clayton, R	.625	16	10	1	5	5	0	.652	1.000
Conine, Jeff	.200	10	2	1	1	2	1	.333	.500
Cordero, Wil	.250	12	3	0	1	0	3	.250	.583
Daulton, D*	.167	10	2	0	0	3	0	.385	.500
Davis, Eric	.400	15	6	1	5	0	1	.400	.667
DeShields, D*	.200	5	1	0	0	0	0	.200	.200
Duncan, M	.538	13	7	2	5	1	0	.571	1.154
Dunston, S	.600	5	3	1	2	0	0	.600	1.200
Dykstra, L*	.300	10	3	1	3	1	1	.308	.600
Eisenreich, J*	.364	11	4	0	0	1	1	.417	.455
Eusebio, Tony	.333	9	3	0	1	2	1	.455	.333
Everett, Carl#	.400	5	2	0	1	0	0	.400	.400
Finley, Steve*	.355	31	11	1	4	1	2	.394	.677
Flaherty, J	.200	5	1	1	1	0	2	.200	.800
Fletcher, D*	.188	16	3	0	1	0	1	.188	.250
Floyd, Cliff*	.250	4	1	0	0	1	0	.400	.250
Gallego, Mike	.800	5	4	0	1	0	0	.833	1.000
Gant, Ron	.429	14	6	0	1	0	4	.429	.429
Garcia, C	.313	16	5	0	2	2	1	.421	.313
Gilkey, B	.120	25	3	1	1	4	1	.241	.240
Gomez, Chris	.400	5	2	0	0	0	0	.400	.400
Gonzalez, L*	.250	16	4	0	2	1	0	.368	.313
Grace, Mark*	.455	11	5	0	0	1	0	.500	.455
Grissom, M	.389	18	7	0	1	2	2	.450	.556
Grudzielanek	.000	7	0	0	0	0	1	.222	.000
Gutierrez, R	.000	5	0	0	0	0	0	.000	.000
Gwynn, Tony*	.385	13	5	0	1	1	1	.429	.462
Harris, Lenny*	.143	7	1	0	1	0	2	.143	.429
Hayes, C	.500	6	3	1	2	0	0	.500	1.167
Henderson, R	.000	6	0	0	0	0	0	.000	.000
Hill, G	.000	7	0	0	0	0	0	.125	.000
Hollins, Dave#	.125	8	1	1	1	2	3	.417	.500
Howard, T*	.583	12	7	0	0	0	1	.583	.917
Hundley, Todd#	.385	13	5	2	6	1	3	.429	.846
Hunter, Bri L	.182	11	2	0	1	0	2	.182	.273
Huskey, Butch	.143	7	1	0	0	1	1	.250	.143
Incaviglia, P	.438	16	7	1	4	3	3	.526	.750
Jefferies, G#	.211	19	4	0	0	0	0	.211	.211
Johnson, L*	.222	9	2	1	2	0	1	.222	.778
Jones, C#	.500	8	4	2	4	2	0	.600	1.375
Jordan, Brian	.375	16	6	0	1	1	2	.474	.500
Joyner, Wally*	.200	5	1	0	1	0	0	.200	.200
Justice, Dave*	.333	15	5	0	3	1	2	.375	.333
Karros, Eric	.364	11	4	1	1	0	0	.364	.727
Kelly, R	.250	8	2	0	1	0	0	.250	.375
Kendall, J	.400	5	2	0	1	0	0	.400	.400
Kent, Jeff	.286	14	4	1	3	0	1	.286	.500
King, Jeff	.125	16	2	0	1	0	3	.125	.188
Klesko, Ryan*	.111	9	1	0	0	1	0	.200	.222
Lankford, Ray*	.227	22	5	2	3	5	6	.370	.545
Lansing, Mike	.278	18	5	2	3	2	2	.350	.778
Larkin, Barry	.238	21	5	0	1	5	1	.385	.381
Lemke, Mark#	.188	16	3	0	4	0	3	.188	.188
Lewis, Darren	.364	11	4	0	0	3	1	.533	.455
Livingstone*	.444	9	4	0	2	0	0	.444	.667
Lopez, Javy	.167	6	1	1	1	2	0	.375	.667
Mabry, John*	.438	16	7	1	3	0	0	.438	.813
Magadan, Dave*	.444	9	4	0	0	1	0	.545	.556
Manwaring, K	.267	15	4	0	0	2	4	.389	.533
Martin, Al*	.375	16	6	0	3	1	4	.412	.500
Martinez, Da*	.333	9	3	0	2	1	2	.400	.556
May, Derrick*	.000	6	0	0	0	2	0	.333	.000
McGee, Willie#	.273	11	3	0	3	0	2	.250	.273
McGriff, Fred*	.125	16	2	1	2	4	0	.333	.313
McRae, Brian#	.000	5	0	0	0	1	0	.500	.800
Merced, O*	.563	16	9	2	8	1	2	.588	1.063
Miller, Orl	.000	5	0	0	0	2	1	.375	.000
Mitchell, K	.333	9	3	0	2	1	1	.400	.444
Morandini, M*	.400	5	2	0	1	1	1	.500	.800

Armando Reynoso, Rockies — RHP

Batter	Avg	AB	H	HR	BI	BB	SO	OBP	Slg
Morris, Hal*	.273	22	6	1	4	1	3	.304	.455
Mouton, James	.375	8	3	1	1	1	2	.444	.750
Newfield, M	.375	8	3	1	2	0	0	.375	.875
Ochoa, Alex	.333	6	2	0	1	0	0	.333	.500
Offerman, J#	.111	9	1	0	1	0	0	.111	.111
Oliver, Joe	.083	12	1	0	0	1	4	.154	.083
Ordonez, Rey	.200	10	2	0	0	0	3	.200	.300
Orsulak, Joe*	.571	7	4	1	3	0	0	.571	1.143
Otero, Ricky#	.333	6	2	1	2	0	1	.429	.833
Pagnozzi, Tom	.455	11	5	0	2	1	1	.500	.727
Pendleton, T#	.417	12	5	0	3	0	2	.417	.417
Piazza, Mike	.250	8	2	0	1	1	1	.333	.250
Plantier, P*	.273	11	3	0	5	0	3	.273	.455
Pride, Curtis*	.000	4	0	0	0	2	1	.333	.000
Reed, Jody	.353	17	6	0	1	4	0	.476	.412
Roberts, Bip#	.400	10	4	0	0	0	0	.500	.600
Rodriguez, H*	.273	11	3	1	2	0	0	.273	.636
Sabo, Chris	.273	11	3	0	1	1	0	.357	.273
Sandberg, R	.000	6	0	0	2	1	2	.111	.000
Sanders, R	.500	16	8	4	7	1	1	.529	1.375
Santiago, B	.188	16	3	0	2	4	2	.350	.188
Scarsone, S	.200	5	1	0	0	1	1	.333	.200
Segui, David#	.500	12	6	1	2	0	0	.500	.750
Servais, S	.400	5	2	0	1	1	1	.500	.400
Sheaffer, D	.200	5	1	0	0	0	0	.200	.200
Sheffield, G	.200	10	2	0	1	0	2	.273	.200
Smith, Dwight*	.200	5	1	0	0	0	1	.200	.400
Smith, Ozzie#	.250	12	3	0	2	1	1	.286	.250
Sosa, Sammy	.364	11	4	0	1	0	3	.364	.545
Stocker, K#	.000	5	0	0	0	1	3	.375	.000
Sweeney, Mark*	.333	6	2	0	0	1	2	.429	.333
Tarasco, Tony*	.000	6	0	0	0	0	1	.000	.000
Taubensee, E*	.111	9	1	0	1	1	2	.200	.111
Thompson, Rob	.231	13	3	0	0	2	3	.333	.231
Vizcaino, J#	.304	23	7	0	2	0	1	.304	.391
Walker, Larry*	.167	6	1	1	2	0	0	.375	.667
Wallach, Tim	.154	13	2	1	3	0	0	.154	.385
Weiss, Walt#	.333	6	2	0	2	0	1	.333	.333
White, R	.200	10	2	1	2	2	2	.333	.500
Whiten, Mark#	.429	7	3	1	3	1	2	.500	1.000
Wilkins, Rick*	.231	13	3	1	2	2	3	.333	.462
Williams, Ma	.176	17	3	1	1	2	6	.263	.353
Young, Kevin	.250	8	2	0	0	1	1	.250	.375
Zeile, Todd	.238	21	5	1	2	0	3	.238	.381

Arthur Rhodes, Orioles — LHP

Batter	Avg	AB	H	HR	BI	BB	SO	OBP	Slg
Alomar, R#	.235	17	4	0	2	3	3	.350	.353
Alomar Jr, S	.250	4	1	0	0	1	2	.400	.500
Amaral, Rich	.200	10	2	0	1	0	2	.200	.200
Baerga, C#	.467	15	7	1	2	1	3	.500	.667
Belle, Albert	.357	14	5	2	7	5	2	.526	.929
Berroa, G	.000	6	0	0	0	1	3	.143	.000
Blowers, Mike	.286	7	2	1	3	1	2	.375	.714
Boone, Bret	.167	6	1	0	1	2	1	.375	.167
Borders, Pat	.143	7	1	0	1	0	0	.143	.143
Brosius, S	.250	4	1	0	1	1	1	.400	.500
Buhner, Jay	.214	14	3	1	2	1	6	.267	.429
Canseco, Jose	.625	8	5	3	4	4	1	.750	1.750
Carter, Joe	.364	22	8	1	2	0	5	.364	.636
Cirillo, Jeff	.200	5	1	0	0	1	1	.333	.400
Clark, Will*	.250	4	1	0	1	0	0	.200	.250
Cole, Alex*	.286	7	2	0	0	3	1	.500	.286
Curtis, Chad	.286	14	4	0	2	0	3	.286	.429
Damon, Johnny*	.167	6	1	0	1	0	1	.143	.167
Davis, Chili*	.308	13	4	0	0	2	3	.400	.308
Davis, Russ	.333	6	2	0	0	0	4	.333	.333
Deer, Rob	.250	4	1	0	0	1	4	.400	.250
DiSarcina, G	.286	7	2	0	0	0	1	.286	.429
Easley, D	.200	10	2	1	1	1	2	.273	.600
Espinoza, A	.250	8	2	0	0	0	0	.250	.250
Fermin, Felix	.625	8	5	0	0	0	1	.625	.625
Fielder, C	.333	12	4	1	3	1	2	.385	.583
Franco, Julio	.300	10	3	0	2	1	3	.364	.500
Frye, Jeff	.250	8	2	1	1	1	0	.333	.750
Fryman, T	.250	12	3	0	3	1	4	.308	.250
Gaetti, Joe	.000	5	0	0	1	1	2	.143	.000
Gagne, Greg	.375	8	3	1	4	0	0	.375	.875
Gallego, Mike	.000	4	0	0	0	2	1	.333	.000
Girardi, Joe	.400	5	2	0	1	0	1	.400	.400
Gonzales, R	.200	5	1	0	0	0	2	.200	.400
Gonzalez, A	.333	3	1	0	1	1	1	.500	.333
Gonzalez, J	.059	17	1	0	2	0	8	.053	.059
Goodwin, Tom*	.000	7	0	0	0	2	0	.000	.000
Greenwell, M*	.250	8	2	0	0	0	0	.250	.375
Griffey Jr, K*	.125	16	2	2	3	2	5	.222	.500
Hamilton, D*	.333	3	1	0	1	3	0	.667	.333
Haselman, B	.200	5	1	0	0	1	0	.200	.400
Henderson, R	.000	5	0	0	0	3	3	.375	.000
Howard, Dave*	.111	9	1	0	0	1	1	.200	.333
Howard, T*	.286	7	2	0	0	0	3	.286	.429

176

Arthur Rhodes, Orioles — LHP

Batter	Avg	AB	H	HR	BI	BB	SO	OBP	Slg
Hudler, Rex	.200	5	1	0	1	0	3	.167	.200
Hulse, David*	.000	2	0	0	0	3	0	.600	.000
Jaha, John	.364	11	4	1	4	1	1	.417	.636
Javier, Stan#	.273	11	3	0	1	1	2	.333	.273
Jefferson, R*	.500	4	2	1	1	1	1	.600	1.250
Joyner, Wally*	.000	6	0	0	0	0	3	.000	.000
Kelly, Pat	.500	6	3	0	0	4	1	.700	1.000
Kelly, R	.200	10	2	1	1	1	3	.273	.500
Kirby, Wayne*	.000	5	0	0	1	1	0	.167	.000
Knoblauch, C	.250	20	5	0	4	2	5	.348	.400
Knorr, Randy	.571	7	4	0	5	2	1	.667	.714
Kreuter, Chad#	.167	6	1	0	0	1	1	.286	.167
Leius, Scott	.333	12	4	0	1	1	3	.385	.333
Lewis, Mark	.500	8	4	1	1	0	1	.500	1.125
Leyritz, Jim	.333	15	5	0	0	4	3	.474	.333
Lockhart, K*	.143	7	1	0	0	0	1	.143	.143
Lofton, Kenny*	.400	10	4	1	2	0	4	.400	.700
Martinez, E	.400	5	2	0	0	0	0	.400	.600
Martinez, T*	.333	12	4	0	0	2	4	.429	.417
McGwire, Mark	.167	6	1	1	2	1	2	.286	.667
Meares, Pat	.125	8	1	0	0	0	3	.125	.250
Mieske, Matt	.167	6	1	0	2	0	0	.167	.500
Molitor, Paul	.364	11	4	0	4	2	2	.462	.455
Munoz, Pedro	.278	18	5	2	2	0	6	.278	.611
Murray, Eddie#	.143	7	1	0	0	0	3	.143	.143
Naehring, Tim	.250	8	2	0	2	1	1	.333	.375
Nilsson, Dave*	.200	5	1	1	4	1	0	.333	.800
Nunnally, Jon*	.200	5	1	0	0	2	0	.429	.200
O'Leary, Troy*	.000	5	0	0	0	2	0	.000	.000
O'Neill, Paul*	.286	7	2	1	2	1	0	.375	.714
Offerman, J#	.000	4	0	0	0	1	2	.200	.000
Olerud, John*	.143	14	2	0	0	5	0	.368	.214
Palmeiro, R*	.462	13	6	1	1	0	1	.462	.692
Palmer, Dean	.333	15	5	1	4	3	6	.444	.600
Paquette, C	.500	4	2	1	2	1	1	.600	1.250
Phillips, T#	.417	12	5	0	0	1	5	.462	.583
Ramirez, M	.400	5	2	1	5	1	1	.500	1.200
Reboulet, J	.308	13	4	0	1	2	1	.400	.308
Reed, Jody	.333	6	2	0	0	1	1	.429	.333
Rodriguez, I	.214	14	3	1	4	3	1	.333	.500
Salmon, Tim	.500	10	5	1	6	4	2	.667	.800
Seitzer, K	.250	8	2	0	2	4	0	.500	.375
Sierra, Ruben*	.200	20	4	0	1	0	5	.200	.350
Snow, J.T.#	.429	7	3	1	3	0	2	.429	.857
Sojo, Luis	.143	7	1	0	1	0	0	.143	.143
Sprague, Ed	.222	9	2	1	2	2	0	.364	.556
Stankiewicz	.000	5	0	0	0	0	1	.000	.000
Stanley, Mike	.125	8	1	0	0	2	5	.300	.125
Strange, Doug*	.000	6	0	0	0	1	2	.143	.000
Surhoff, B.J.*	.200	5	1	0	1	2	0	.429	.400
Tartabull, D	.444	9	4	1	3	3	1	.583	.889
Tettleton, M#	.125	8	1	0	1	0	2	.125	.250
Thome, Jim*	.125	8	1	0	0	0	4	.125	.125
Tinsley, Lee*	.400	5	2	0	0	1	3	.500	.400
Trammell, A	.143	7	1	1	2	1	2	.250	.571
Valentin, Jhn	.222	9	2	1	4	2	3	.364	.556
Valentin, Jse#	.375	8	3	0	0	0	3	.375	.625
Valle, Dave	.100	10	1	1	1	3	2	.308	.400
Vaughn, Greg	.111	9	1	0	0	4	1	.385	.111
Vaughn, Mo*	.200	10	2	0	2	0	4	.200	.200
Velarde, R	.308	13	4	0	2	2	4	.400	.385
Vitiello, Joe	.400	5	2	0	0	0	3	.400	.400
Vizquel, Omar#	.063	16	1	0	0	1	1	.118	.063
Walbeck, Matt#	.000	9	0	0	0	1	0	.000	.000
White, Devon#	.429	21	9	1	6	0	6	.409	.667
Whiten, Mark#	.500	4	2	0	0	1	0	.600	.500
Williams, Ber#	.250	16	4	0	2	5	2	.429	.250
Williams, Ger	.500	10	5	1	5	0	1	.500	1.000

Bill Risley, Blue Jays — RHP

Batter	Avg	AB	H	HR	BI	BB	SO	OBP	Slg
Baines, H*	.200	5	1	0	0	0	0	.200	.200
Brosius, S	1.000	4	4	1	2	1	0	1.000	2.250
Coleman, V#	.000	4	0	0	0	1	1	.000	.000
Cora, Joey#	.400	5	2	0	0	0	0	.400	1.000
Curtis, Chad	.000	6	0	0	0	0	3	.000	.000
Durham, Ray#	.000	5	0	0	0	1	0	.167	.000
Edmonds, Jim*	.200	5	1	1	3	0	3	.200	.800
Fielder, C	.250	8	2	2	2	1	3	.333	1.000
Fryman, T	.667	6	4	1	2	1	0	.714	1.333
Gomez, Chris	.167	6	1	1	1	1	1	.375	.667
Gonzalez, J	.200	5	1	1	2	0	1	.200	.800
Greer, Rusty*	.143	7	1	0	0	2	1	.143	.286
Karkovice	.000	5	0	0	0	0	3	.000	.000
Leius, Scott	.200	5	1	0	0	1	2	.333	.200
Martin, N	1.000	4	4	0	1	1	0	1.000	1.000
McLemore, M#	.143	7	1	0	0	0	1	.143	.143
Naehring, Tim	.143	7	1	0	0	0	3	.143	.286
Nixon, Otis#	.200	5	1	0	0	1	0	.333	.200
Phillips, T#	.250	8	2	1	1	2	2	.400	.750
Raines, Tim#	.375	8	3	0	0	2	1	.500	.375
Ripken, Cal	.250	4	1	0	0	1	1	.400	.250
Salmon, Tim	.000	6	0	0	0	1	1	.143	.000
Sorrento, P*	.167	6	1	1	1	1	1	.286	.667
Strange, Doug#	.400	5	2	1	5	0	2	.400	1.200
Tettleton, M#	.200	5	1	0	0	1	1	.333	.200
Thomas, Frank	.333	6	2	1	2	2	1	.500	.833
Thome, Jim*	.000	4	0	0	1	2	0	.200	.000
Valentin, Jhn	.500	6	3	0	1	0	1	.500	.667
Ventura, R*	.429	7	3	0	1	0	2	.429	.429
Williams, Ber#	.000	5	0	0	0	0	0	.000	.000

Kevin Ritz, Rockies — RHP

Batter	Avg	AB	H	HR	BI	BB	SO	OBP	Slg
Abbott, Kurt	.538	13	7	1	4	2	2	.600	.923
Alfonzo, E	.000	14	0	0	1	1	0	.067	.000
Allensworth	.375	8	3	0	2	0	2	.375	.750
Anthony, Eric*	.500	6	3	0	2	2	1	.625	.500
Arias, Alex	.333	9	3	0	1	1	0	.455	.667
Ausmus, Brad	.222	9	2	0	1	2	0	.364	.333
Bagwell, Jeff	.200	15	3	0	0	4	5	.368	.267
Baines, H*	.182	11	2	0	0	4	1	.400	.182
Bell, Derek	.333	21	7	0	0	4	0	.440	.381
Bell, Jay	.200	20	4	1	3	3	4	.304	.400
Benard, M*	.125	8	1	0	0	0	0	.300	.125
Benjamin, M	.286	7	2	0	0	1	2	.444	.429
Berry, Sean	.267	15	4	1	2	0	1	.267	.467
Biggio, Craig	.294	17	5	0	5	3	2	.455	.412
Blauser, Jeff	.125	8	1	0	0	0	4	.125	.125
Blowers, Mike	.111	9	1	0	0	1	2	.200	.222
Boggs, Wade*	.286	7	2	0	1	4	1	.545	.286
Bonds, Barry*	.083	12	1	0	1	5	2	.353	.083
Bonilla, B#	.000	9	0	0	0	1	3	.100	.000
Boone, Bret	.250	16	4	0	3	1	5	.368	.250
Branson, Jeff*	.250	12	3	0	0	1	1	.308	.250
Brogna, Rico*	.444	9	4	0	3	3	2	.538	.556
Buhner, Jay	.250	4	1	0	2	0	3	.400	.250
Burks, Ellis	.375	8	3	0	1	0	1	.375	.375
Butler, Brett*	.333	18	6	0	1	1	2	.368	.444
Caminiti, Ken#	.250	16	4	2	6	4	3	.381	.625
Cangelosi, J#	.571	7	4	0	1	1	0	.625	.857
Canseco, Jose	.000	6	0	0	1	1	0	.125	.000
Carr, Chuck	.000	4	0	0	0	1	1	.200	.000
Carter, Joe	.000	5	0	0	0	1	2	.167	.000
Cedeno, A	.000	5	0	0	0	0	0	.000	.000
Clark, Dave*	.429	7	3	0	1	2	0	.556	.429
Clayton, R	.300	10	3	1	3	1	0	.364	.700
Colbrunn, G	.133	15	2	1	1	2	3	.235	.333
Conine, Jeff	.400	20	8	2	10	1	1	.429	.850
Curtis, Chad	.400	5	2	0	0	0	2	.400	.400
Daulton, D*	.667	3	2	0	1	3	0	.833	.667
Davis, Chili#	.333	3	1	0	2	1	0	.500	.333
Dawson, Andre	.250	5	1	0	0	0	3	.250	.250
DeShields, D*	.231	13	3	0	3	1	2	.250	.462
Devereaux, M	.400	5	2	0	0	1	0	.400	.400
Dorsett, B	.333	6	2	0	2	1	0	.333	.500
Doster, David	.500	6	3	0	1	0	0	.500	.667
Dunston, S	.125	8	1	0	0	1	4	.222	.125
Dykstra, L*	.250	8	2	0	0	3	3	.250	.250
Eisenreich, J*	.417	12	5	0	2	0	1	.417	.500
Eusebio, Tony	.125	8	1	0	0	1	1	.125	.125
Finley, Steve*	.563	16	9	2	6	4	0	.650	1.125
Fonville, C#	.154	13	2	0	1	4	1	.353	.154
Franco, Julio	.286	7	2	0	0	0	0	.286	.429
Gaetti, Gary	.250	8	2	0	2	5	2	.538	.375
Gagne, Greg	.200	5	1	0	0	2	1	.429	.200
Gant, Ron	.100	10	1	1	3	0	3	.100	.400
Garcia, C	.100	10	1	0	0	1	2	.182	.100
Gilkey, B	.167	18	3	0	1	1	3	.211	.222
Gomez, Chris	.444	9	4	1	1	1	1	.500	.778
Gonzalez, L*	.538	13	7	0	3	3	2	.667	.769
Grace, Mark*	.500	20	10	2	11	4	1	.560	1.050
Grebeck, C	.000	9	0	0	0	1	1	.100	.000
Greenwell, M*	.429	7	3	0	1	0	0	.429	.429
Griffey Jr, K*	.286	7	2	0	2	0	1	.286	.286
Gutierrez, R	.200	5	1	0	0	0	3	.200	.200
Gwynn, Tony*	.267	15	4	0	1	1	0	.294	.333
Hall, Mel*	.167	6	1	0	0	0	2	.167	.167
Hansen, Dave*	.500	4	2	0	0	1	0	.600	.500
Harris, Lenny*	.167	12	2	0	0	0	2	.167	.250
Hayes, C	.077	13	1	0	0	0	2	.077	.077
Henderson, R	.100	10	1	0	0	4	3	.357	.100
Hernandez, Jo	.333	15	5	0	1	0	4	.333	.467
Hill, G	.333	15	5	4	8	2	4	.588	1.133
Hollandsworth	.231	13	3	0	2	1	4	.286	.308
Howard, T*	.182	16	2	1	1	1	4	.250	.545
Hundley, Todd#	.400	10	4	0	2	2	2	.500	.600
Hunter, Bri L	.429	14	6	0	1	0	2	.429	.643
Huskey, Butch	.600	10	6	1	3	0	0	.600	1.000
Incaviglia, P	.273	11	3	1	5	4	4	.467	.545
Jefferies, G#	.333	9	3	0	2	2	1	.417	.556
Johnson, Bri	.250	8	2	0	0	0	1	.250	.250

Kevin Ritz, Rockies — RHP

Batter	Avg	AB	H	HR	BI	BB	SO	OBP	Slg
Johnson, Char	.400	10	4	1	2	0	2	.400	.700
Johnson, L*	.231	13	3	0	0	1	0	.286	.231
Johnson, Mark*	.444	9	4	0	1	3	1	.583	.556
Jordan, Brian	.400	5	2	1	3	0	0	.400	1.000
Joyner, Wally*	.636	11	7	0	1	4	0	.750	.636
Justice, Dave*	.200	5	1	0	0	2	0	.429	.200
Karros, Eric	.286	21	6	1	3	3	4	.375	.524
Kelly, R	.294	17	5	0	0	1	5	.333	.412
Kendall, J	.000	5	0	0	0	0	0	.000	.000
Kent, Jeff	.400	10	4	2	6	0	0	.364	1.000
King, Jeff	.450	20	9	1	6	1	0	.478	.650
Kingery, Mike*	.600	5	3	0	1	1	1	.667	.800
Klesko, Ryan*	.400	5	2	1	1	1	1	.500	1.000
Lankford, Ray*	.200	10	2	0	0	3	2	.429	.200
Larkin, Barry	.214	14	3	0	0	4	1	.389	.214
Lewis, Darren	.111	9	1	0	0	1	3	.200	.111
Liriano, N#	.571	7	4	0	3	3	0	.700	.571
Livingstone*	.111	9	1	0	0	0	1	.111	.222
Lopez, Javy	.167	6	1	0	0	0	1	.167	.167
Lopez, Luis#	.333	6	2	0	0	0	0	.333	.333
Mabry, John*	.111	9	1	0	0	1	1	.200	.111
Magadan, Dave*	.167	6	1	0	0	1	1	.286	.167
Manwaring, K	.333	6	2	0	0	1	0	.500	.333
Martin, Al*	.261	23	6	0	1	4	2	.370	.304
May, Derrick*	.231	13	3	0	3	2	1	.333	.308
McCarty, Dave	.333	6	2	0	1	1	1	.429	.333
McGriff, Fred*	.167	6	1	0	0	1	1	.286	.333
McGwire, Mark	.375	8	3	1	3	1	1	.400	.750
McRae, Brian#	.353	17	6	0	1	0	4	.389	.471
Merced, O*	.294	17	5	0	0	2	3	.368	.353
Miller, Orl	.118	17	2	0	1	0	3	.118	.118
Mitchell, K	.600	5	3	1	4	3	1	.667	1.200
Molitor, Paul	.000	6	0	0	0	2	1	.250	.000
Mondesi, Raul	.100	20	2	0	3	2	3	.182	.100
Morandini, M*	.200	5	1	1	1	2	0	.429	.800
Morris, Hal*	.389	18	7	0	5	1	0	.421	.556
Mueller, Bill#	.500	6	3	0	2	0	0	.500	.667
Nieves, M#	.000	3	0	0	0	2	3	.400	.000
O'Brien, C	.200	5	1	0	1	0	0	.200	.200
Offerman, J#	.429	7	3	0	1	4	0	.636	.429
Ordonez, Rey	.429	7	3	0	1	1	0	.500	.714
Orsulak, Joe*	.231	13	3	0	1	4	1	.412	.308
Osik, Keith	.333	6	2	0	0	0	1	.333	.333
Otero, Ricky*	.125	8	1	0	0	0	0	.125	.125
Pagnozzi, Tom	.625	8	5	0	2	1	0	.667	.750
Palmeiro, R*	.625	8	5	0	4	1	0	.667	1.250
Pena, G#	.167	6	1	0	1	0	2	.167	.167
Pena, Tony	.600	5	3	0	3	0	0	.600	.600
Pendleton, T#	.176	17	3	0	0	2	3	.263	.294
Petagine, Rob*	.600	5	3	0	2	1	0	.667	.600
Phillips, J*	.200	5	1	1	3	2	2	.429	.800
Piazza, Mike	.333	21	7	0	2	2	1	.391	.333
Plantier, P*	.067	15	1	0	0	8	8	.067	.067
Polonia, Luis*	.667	6	4	0	2	1	1	.750	.833
Reed, Jody	.318	22	7	0	4	0	0	.348	.364
Renteria, E	.571	7	4	0	1	0	1	.571	.571
Ripken, Cal	.167	6	1	0	3	1	0	.286	.333
Roberts, Bip#	.000	8	0	0	0	0	2	.000	.000
Sanchez, Rey	.222	18	4	0	0	0	1	.222	.278
Sandberg, R	.100	10	1	0	0	2	1	.250	.100
Sanders, R	.429	14	6	1	4	3	3	.529	.857
Santiago, B	.200	10	2	0	0	4	1	.429	.200
Scarsone, S	.000	5	0	0	0	0	1	.000	.000
Segui, David*	.333	6	2	1	2	0	1	.333	.833
Seitzer, K	.500	10	5	0	2	2	1	.538	.700
Servais, S	.333	9	3	1	7	0	1	.333	.778
Sheffield, G	.385	13	5	1	4	3	0	.500	.615
Sierra, Ruben#	.286	7	2	0	3	0	4	.222	.286
Sojo, Luis	.167	6	1	0	2	0	0	.167	.167
Sosa, Sammy	.391	23	9	4	10	1	6	.417	.957
Spiers, Bill*	.500	6	3	1	2	0	0	.500	1.000
Steinbach, T	.143	7	1	0	0	0	2	.143	.143
Stillwell, K#	.400	5	2	0	0	1	1	.500	.400
Stocker, K#	.250	4	1	1	1	1	1	.400	1.000
Sweeney, Mark*	.000	7	0	0	0	1	3	.125	.000
Tartabull, D	.111	9	1	0	0	0	4	.111	.111
Taubensee, E*	.375	8	3	1	2	1	3	.444	.750
Veras, Q#	.250	8	2	0	0	1	2	.333	.250
Vizcaino, J#	.333	12	4	0	1	0	1	.333	.333
Wallach, Tim	.571	7	4	0	1	0	0	.500	.571
Weiss, Walt#	.200	5	1	0	0	1	2	.333	.200
White, Devon#	.176	17	3	0	0	1	7	.222	.176
Whiten, Mark#	.333	6	2	0	2	3	2	.556	.833
Wilkins, Rick*	.182	11	2	1	1	3	6	.357	.545
Williams, E	.250	4	1	0	1	0	0	.250	.500
Williams, Ma	.364	11	4	1	3	3	3	.500	.818
Young, Kevin	.167	6	1	0	1	0	1	.167	.167
Zeile, Todd	.133	15	2	0	3	3	2	.316	.267

Mariano Rivera, Yankees — RHP

Batter	Avg	AB	H	HR	BI	BB	SO	OBP	Slg
Anderson, Brd*	.200	5	1	0	0	0	1	.200	.400
Baerga, C#	.400	5	2	0	0	0	0	.400	.400
Baines, H*	.000	7	0	0	0	0	2	.000	.000
Berroa, G	.273	11	3	1	4	1	3	.333	.545
Bonilla, B#	.250	8	2	1	5	0	1	.250	.625
Bordick, Mike	.500	6	3	0	0	1	0	.500	.500
Brosius, S	.125	8	1	0	1	0	2	.125	.250
Buhner, Jay	.000	7	0	0	0	4	4	.000	.000
Cirillo, Jeff	.250	4	1	0	0	1	1	.400	.250
Coleman, V#	.200	5	1	0	0	1	1	.333	.200
Cora, Joey#	.286	7	2	0	0	1	1	.286	.286
Cordova, M	.000	7	0	0	0	0	4	.125	.000
Damon, Johnny*	.200	5	1	0	0	0	0	.200	.200
Durham, Ray#	.000	9	0	0	0	1	1	.000	.000
Frye, Jeff	.125	8	1	0	0	0	3	.125	.250
Gates, Brent#	.200	10	2	0	2	0	0	.200	.200
Giambi, Jason*	.200	5	1	0	0	0	2	.200	.200
Gonzalez, J	.571	7	4	1	6	0	0	.571	1.571
Goodwin, Tom*	.286	7	2	0	0	0	0	.286	.286
Greer, Rusty*	.143	7	1	0	1	0	2	.143	.143
Griffey Jr, K*	.500	4	2	1	3	0	0	.714	1.250
Guillen, O*	.286	7	2	0	1	0	0	.375	.286
Jaha, John	.200	5	1	0	0	1	0	.200	.200
Javier, Stan#	.333	6	2	0	0	0	1	.333	.333
Karkovice, R	.000	6	0	0	0	0	5	.000	.000
Knoblauch, C	.333	6	2	0	0	3	1	.556	.500
Lockhart, K*	.200	5	1	0	2	2	0	.429	.400
Lofton, Kenny*	.250	4	1	0	0	1	0	.200	.250
Martinez, Da*	.000	6	0	0	0	1	5	.143	.000
Martinez, E	.875	8	7	2	5	1	1	.889	2.000
Martinez, T*	.167	6	1	0	0	0	2	.167	.167
McGwire, Mark	.250	8	2	0	1	5	3	.533	.250
McLemore, M#	.167	6	1	0	0	1	0	.286	.167
Meares, Pat	.333	6	2	0	0	0	2	.333	.333
Molitor, Paul	.200	5	1	0	2	0	1	.200	.400
Murray, Eddie#	.000	6	0	0	0	1	1	.143	.000
Myers, Greg*	.400	5	2	0	2	0	0	.400	.400
Nixon, Otis#	.500	4	2	0	1	0	0	.500	.500
Palmeiro, R*	.400	5	2	1	2	2	0	.571	1.000
Phillips, T#	.125	8	1	0	0	1	5	.222	.125
Ramirez, M	.000	5	0	0	1	0	5	.000	.000
Ripken, Cal	.333	6	2	0	2	1	0	.429	.500
Seitzer, K	.600	5	3	0	0	0	1	.600	.600
Sierra, Ruben*	.400	5	2	1	2	2	1	.571	1.000
Sojo, Luis	.200	5	1	1	0	0	0	.200	.400
Sorrento, P*	.750	4	3	0	1	2	1	.833	1.000
Stahoviak, S*	.200	5	1	0	0	1	2	.333	.200
Steinbach, T	.083	12	1	0	0	4	0	.083	.083
Strange, Doug*	.400	5	2	0	0	1	1	.500	.400
Tettleton, M#	.250	4	1	0	1	1	0	.400	.500
Thomas, Frank	.286	7	2	0	0	0	1	.286	.286
Thome, Jim*	.000	4	0	0	0	2	2	.333	.000
Vaughn, Mo*	.400	5	2	0	0	1	0	.400	.400
Ventura, R*	.250	8	2	0	1	1	1	.333	.250
Vizquel, Omar#	.500	6	3	0	2	0	0	.500	.500
Wilson, Dan	.000	6	0	0	1	0	4	.000	.000

Rich Robertson, Twins — LHP

Batter	Avg	AB	H	HR	BI	BB	SO	OBP	Slg
Alomar, R#	.200	10	2	0	0	1	0	.273	.300
Alomar Jr, S	.000	5	0	0	0	0	1	.167	.000
Amaral, Rich	.333	6	2	0	1	0	0	.333	.500
Anderson, Brd*	.286	7	2	0	2	3	0	.583	.286
Anderson, G*	.167	12	2	0	1	0	2	.167	.250
Arias, George	.143	7	1	0	0	0	1	.143	.143
Baerga, C#	.167	6	1	0	0	0	1	.286	.167
Bagwell, Jeff	.750	4	3	0	1	2	0	.833	1.250
Batista, Tony	.667	3	2	0	1	2	0	.800	.667
Belle, Albert	.833	6	5	1	3	2	0	.889	1.500
Berroa, G	.667	6	4	2	5	1	1	.625	1.667
Boggs, Wade*	.250	4	1	0	0	1	1	.400	.250
Bonilla, B#	.250	12	3	0	1	1	1	.308	.333
Bordick, Mike	.571	7	4	0	2	0	0	.571	1.000
Brosius, S	.250	4	1	0	0	2	2	.500	.250
Brumfield, J	.500	6	3	0	0	0	1	.571	.833
Buhner, Jay	.500	4	2	0	0	1	0	.600	.500
Caminiti, Ken*	.167	6	1	0	3	1	0	.286	.333
Carter, Joe	.083	12	1	0	0	1	2	.154	.167
Cedeno, A	1.000	5	5	0	0	0	0	1.000	1.000
Cedeno, D#	.000	7	0	0	0	0	0	.000	.000
Cirillo, Jeff	.222	9	2	0	1	0	1	.222	.333
Clark, Will*	.000	3	0	0	0	2	0	.400	.000
Curtis, Chad	.571	7	4	2	5	1	1	.625	1.429
Davis, Chili*	.250	8	2	0	1	2	3	.400	.500
Delgado, C*	.250	4	1	0	0	1	1	.400	.250
Devereaux, M	.333	12	4	0	1	1	0	.385	.417
DiSarcina, G	.167	12	2	0	0	0	1	.167	.167
Duncan, M	.125	8	1	0	0	0	1	.125	.250
Durham, Ray*	.091	11	1	0	0	1	3	.286	.091
Easley, D	.500	4	2	1	1	1	1	.600	1.250
Edmonds, Jim*	.375	8	3	1	2	2	2	.500	.750

178

Batter	Avg	AB	H	HR	BI	BB	SO	OBP	Slg
Eusebio, Tony	.000	4	0	0	1	0	0	.000	.000
Fielder, C	.250	4	1	1	1	0	1	.400	1.000
Finley, Steve*	.200	5	1	0	0	1	0	.333	.200
Flaherty, J	.500	6	3	0	0	0	0	.500	.500
Franco, Julio	.000	3	0	0	0	2	1	.400	.000
Fryman, T	.500	6	3	0	0	2	3	.625	.500
Giambi, Jason*	.167	6	1	0	0	0	1	.167	.167
Gonzalez, A	.200	5	1	0	0	1	3	.333	.200
Gonzalez, L*	.000	5	0	0	1	2	1	.286	.000
Goodwin, Tom*	.400	5	2	0	1	0	0	.400	.600
Greer, Rusty*	.333	3	1	0	2	2	2	.600	1.000
Guillen, O*	.000	5	0	0	0	0	0	.000	.000
Hamilton, D*	.000	5	0	0	0	2	1	.286	.000
Hammonds, J	.286	7	2	0	1	2	3	.444	.429
Higginson, B*	.500	4	2	0	1	2	0	.667	.500
Hoiles, Chris	.300	10	3	1	1	2	2	.417	.700
Howard, Dave#	.000	4	0	0	0	1	1	.200	.000
Hudler, Rex	.125	8	1	0	0	2	2	.125	.125
Hunter, Brian	.000	4	0	0	1	1	0	.200	.000
Jaha, John	.333	6	2	0	0	2	2	.500	.500
Jeter, Derek	.167	6	1	0	0	2	0	.375	.167
Johnson, L*	.400	10	4	0	0	2	0	.400	.400
Lewis, Darren	.500	2	1	0	1	2	0	.750	.500
Lewis, Mark	.600	5	3	0	0	0	1	.600	.600
Leyritz, Jim	.286	7	2	0	0	1	2	.375	.286
Listach, Pat#	.400	5	2	0	1	1	0	.500	.400
Martinez, E	.250	4	1	0	0	3	2	.571	.250
Martinez, T*	.250	8	2	0	1	1	0	.333	.375
Mashore, D	.500	4	2	0	1	0	1	.600	1.250
Matheny, Mike	.333	6	2	0	2	0	3	.333	.333
McGwire, Mark	.500	6	3	1	3	2	1	.625	1.000
Mieske, Matt	.667	6	4	1	4	1	1	.556	1.333
Mouton, Lyle	.000	12	0	0	2	1	2	.071	.000
Murray, Eddie#	.250	8	2	1	2	1	1	.333	.625
Nixon, Otis#	.444	9	4	0	1	1	0	.444	.556
O'Brien, C	.250	4	1	0	1	1	1	.400	.250
O'Leary, Troy*	.000	4	0	0	1	1	1	.200	.000
O'Neill, Paul*	.444	9	4	0	0	0	1	.444	.556
Offerman, J#	1.000	3	3	0	0	2	0	1.000	1.333
Olerud, John*	.000	6	0	0	0	0	2	.000	.000
Palmeiro, R*	.167	12	2	1	4	3	1	.333	.417
Perez, Robert	.333	6	2	0	0	1	0	.429	.333
Phillips, T#	.500	6	3	0	0	2	1	.625	.500
Raines, Tim#	.500	4	2	1	1	1	1	.600	1.250
Ramirez, M	.400	10	4	1	4	0	1	.400	.900
Randa, Joe	.667	6	4	0	3	1	0	.714	.833
Ripken, Cal	.364	11	4	0	3	1	1	.500	.364
Rodriguez, Al	.250	4	1	0	1	1	0	.400	.500
Rodriguez, I	.167	6	1	0	1	0	0	.167	.167
Salmon, Tim	.333	9	3	1	2	3	2	.500	.778
Samuel, Juan	.222	9	2	0	1	4	4	.462	.444
Sierra, Ruben#	.286	7	2	0	0	0	1	.286	.286
Slaught, Don	.375	8	3	0	1	2	0	.500	.500
Snopek, Chris	.125	8	1	0	0	0	2	.125	.125
Snow, J.T.#	.083	12	1	0	0	0	2	.083	.083
Sprague, Ed	.091	11	1	0	0	1	3	.167	.091
Stanley, Mike	.000	4	0	0	0	2	2	.333	.000
Steinbach, T	.143	7	1	0	0	1	1	.250	.143
Surhoff, B.J.*	.083	12	1	0	0	1	2	.154	.083
Tartabull, D	.333	3	1	0	1	3	0	.667	.333
Thomas, Frank	.400	10	4	2	5	1	0	.455	1.000
Thome, Jim*	.333	6	2	0	0	1	0	.429	.333
Valentin, Jhn	.250	4	1	0	0	2	1	.500	.250
Valentin, Jse#	.111	9	1	0	0	1	4	.200	.111
Vaughn, Greg	.286	7	2	1	1	1	2	.375	.714
Vaughn, Mo*	.167	6	1	0	0	1	1	.286	.167
Velarde, R	.143	7	1	0	0	0	1	.143	.143
Ventura, R*	.273	11	3	0	0	1	2	.333	.364
Vina, F*	.250	4	1	0	1	1	0	.400	.750
Vitiello, Joe	.167	6	1	0	1	1	2	.250	.167
Vizquel, Omar#	.286	7	2	0	0	1	1	.375	.286
Whiten, Mark#	.500	6	3	1	2	0	1	.500	1.000
Williams, Ber#	.250	4	1	0	0	3	0	.571	.250
Williams, Ger	.222	9	2	1	2	0	1	.222	.556
Wilson, Dan	.500	4	2	1	2	0	0	.400	1.250
Young, Ernie	.143	7	1	0	1	0	3	.143	.143

Batter	Avg	AB	H	HR	BI	BB	SO	OBP	Slg
Brosius, S	.500	4	2	0	0	0	1	.600	.500
Buhner, Jay	.091	11	1	1	3	0	5	.091	.364
Canseco, Jose	.250	4	1	0	1	0	2	.200	.250
Carreon, Mark	.714	7	5	1	2	0	0	.714	1.429
Carter, Joe	.182	11	2	0	1	0	1	.182	.364
Cedeno, D#	.250	12	3	0	1	0	0	.250	.333
Cirillo, Jeff	.214	14	3	0	1	1	1	.313	.357
Clark, Tony#	.222	9	2	0	0	0	3	.222	.222
Clark, Will*	.222	9	2	0	1	2	1	.364	.222
Coleman, V#	.400	10	4	0	0	0	2	.400	.500
Cora, Joey*	.200	10	2	1	2	2	1	.333	.600
Curtis, Chad	.133	15	2	0	2	2	1	.235	.133
Delgado, C*	.333	6	2	0	1	0	1	.286	.500
DiSarcina, M	.143	7	1	0	1	1	0	.250	.143
Duncan, M	.667	6	4	0	1	0	0	.667	1.000
Durham, Ray#	.250	8	2	0	4	2	1	.400	.250
Edmonds, Jim*	.000	6	0	0	0	1	3	.143	.000
Elster, Kevin	.000	4	0	0	0	0	2	.000	.000
Espinoza, A	.200	5	1	1	1	0	1	.333	.800
Fabregas, Jor*	.000	8	0	0	0	0	2	.000	.000
Fasano, Sal	.000	5	0	0	0	0	1	.000	.000
Fielder, C	.500	16	8	4	7	1	3	.529	1.313
Fryman, T	.412	17	7	1	5	0	1	.444	.706
Gates, Brent#	.333	9	3	0	1	2	1	.417	.556
Giambi, Jason*	.182	11	2	0	1	1	1	.250	.273
Giles, B*	.400	5	2	1	1	1	0	.500	1.000
Girardi, Joe	.222	9	2	0	1	0	3	.222	.333
Gomez, Chris	.286	7	2	0	0	1	1	.375	.571
Gonzalez, J	.111	9	1	1	1	0	1	.111	.444
Goodwin, Tom*	.167	6	1	0	0	3	1	.444	.167
Green, Shawn*	.000	9	0	0	1	0	4	.000	.000
Greer, Rusty*	.333	9	3	0	3	1	1	.400	.444
Griffey Jr, K*	.250	8	2	0	0	2	0	.400	.250
Hamilton, D*	.455	11	5	0	1	3	0	.571	.545
Hammonds, J	.000	4	0	0	0	1	0	.200	.000
Henderson, R	.333	6	2	0	0	1	0	.429	.333
Herrera, Jose*	.000	7	0	0	0	1	2	.125	.000
Higginson, B*	.400	15	6	2	7	1	1	.438	.933
Hoiles, Chris	.167	6	1	0	0	0	2	.167	.167
Howard, Dave#	.400	5	2	0	0	1	1	.500	.400
Hudler, Rex	.143	7	1	0	1	0	2	.143	.143
Jaha, John	.375	8	3	0	1	3	3	.583	.500
Javier, Stan#	.000	5	0	0	0	1	2	.167	.000
Jefferson, R*	.200	5	1	0	1	0	1	.200	.200
Jeter, Derek	.111	9	1	0	0	0	4	.111	.222
Johnson, L*	.200	5	1	0	1	0	0	.200	.200
Levis, Jesse*	.286	7	2	0	0	0	0	.286	.286
Lewis, Mark	.143	7	1	0	0	0	1	.250	.143
Lockhart, K*	.200	10	2	0	0	0	0	.200	.200
Lofton, Kenny*	.455	11	5	1	1	0	0	.455	.818
Martinez, Da*	.333	6	2	0	0	3	1	.556	.333
Martinez, E	.143	7	1	0	1	2	1	.333	.286
Martinez, T*	.364	11	4	0	2	0	2	.364	.545
Matheny, Mike	.000	3	0	0	0	1	0	.250	.000
McGwire, Mark	.300	10	3	2	3	1	2	.364	.900
McLemore, M#	.400	10	4	0	2	0	0	.400	.500
Mieske, Matt	.000	7	0	0	0	1	1	.000	.000
Molitor, Paul	.000	5	0	0	0	0	1	.000	.000
Mouton, Lyle	.333	6	2	1	2	0	1	.333	.833
Murray, Eddie#	.333	6	2	1	1	0	1	.333	.833
Naehring, Tim	.333	3	1	0	1	0	0	.400	.333
Newfield, M	.167	6	1	1	3	1	0	.286	.667
Newson, W*	.400	5	2	0	0	0	1	.400	.400
Nieves, M#	.400	5	2	0	0	0	1	.400	.600
Nilsson, Dave*	.308	13	4	0	1	3	2	.438	.308
Nixon, Otis#	.286	7	2	0	0	0	1	.375	.286
O'Brien, C	.333	6	2	0	0	0	0	.333	.667
O'Leary, Troy*	.000	7	0	0	1	0	1	.000	.000
O'Neill, Paul*	.385	13	5	1	3	3	0	.500	.692
Offerman, J#	.429	7	3	0	0	1	1	.429	.714
Olerud, John*	.000	8	0	0	1	3	0	.273	.000
Palmeiro, R*	.273	11	3	0	3	1	1	.333	.455
Palmer, Dean	.750	4	3	1	3	0	0	.857	1.500
Paquette, C	.250	8	2	0	1	0	3	.222	.250
Pena, Tony	.333	6	2	0	0	0	1	.333	.333
Plantier, P*	.500	6	3	1	1	0	0	.500	1.000
Polonia, Luis*	.333	9	3	0	0	0	1	.333	.333
Raines, Tim#	.091	11	1	0	0	2	1	.231	.091
Ramirez, M	.556	9	5	0	2	0	2	.556	.556
Ripken, Cal	.222	9	2	0	1	2	4	.364	.333
Rodriguez, Al	.000	5	0	0	0	0	1	.000	.000
Rodriguez, I	.273	11	3	0	0	0	2	.273	.364
Salmon, Tim	.222	9	2	1	2	2	2	.364	.556
Seitzer, K	.294	17	5	0	1	0	2	.294	.353
Sierra, Ruben#	.091	11	1	0	0	3	2	.286	.091
Slaught, Don	.000	5	0	0	0	1	0	.000	.000
Snow, J.T.#	.500	10	5	1	1	1	0	.545	1.000
Sojo, Luis	.200	5	1	0	0	0	0	.200	.200
Sorrento, P*	.400	5	2	0	1	0	0	.400	.400
Sprague, Ed	.222	9	2	0	2	2	3	.417	.222
Stanley, Mike	.333	6	2	0	4	2	1	.500	.833

Batter	Avg	AB	H	HR	BI	BB	SO	OBP	Slg
Aldrete, Mike*	.000	6	0	0	0	2	1	.250	.000
Alomar, R#	.125	8	1	0	1	2	0	.273	.125
Anderson, Brd*	.333	12	4	1	3	0	0	.333	.667
Anderson, G*	.200	10	2	1	2	1	0	.273	.500
Baerga, C#	.222	9	2	0	1	1	1	.300	.222
Baines, H*	.143	7	1	0	1	1	0	.250	.143
Belle, Albert	.200	10	2	1	4	1	0	.333	.500
Berroa, G	.182	11	2	1	2	0	3	.250	.455
Blowers, Mike	.400	5	2	1	1	0	0	.400	1.000
Boggs, Wade*	.462	13	6	0	1	3	0	.563	.462
Bonilla, B#	.000	6	0	0	0	1	0	.143	.000
Bordick, A	.444	9	4	0	1	2	0	.545	.556

Frank Rodriguez, Twins — RHP

Batter	Avg	AB	H	HR	BI	BB	SO	OBP	Slg
Steinbach, T	.300	10	3	0	0	1	0	.364	.500
Strange, Doug#	.500	4	2	0	1	0	0	.400	.500
Surhoff, B.J.*	.417	12	5	1	5	1	0	.462	.667
Tartabull, D	.167	6	1	0	1	0	4	.167	.167
Tettleton, M#	.667	6	4	1	5	1	1	.714	1.500
Thomas, Frank	.714	7	5	2	5	1	1	.750	1.714
Thome, Jim*	.300	10	3	1	2	2	3	.417	.700
Tucker, M*	.200	5	1	0	0	1	0	.333	.400
Valentin, Jse#	.273	11	3	0	1	2	2	.385	.273
Vaughn, Mo*	.400	5	2	0	1	3	2	.625	.600
Ventura, R*	.500	6	3	0	2	0	2	.625	.500
Vina, F*	.231	13	3	0	1	0	1	.214	.231
Vizquel, Omar*	.167	6	1	0	0	0	0	.167	.333
Wallach, Tim	.500	6	3	0	2	0	2	.500	.500
Williams, Ber#	.273	11	3	0	1	3	2	.429	.273
Williams, Geo#	.200	5	1	0	0	0	1	.200	.200
Wilson, Dan	.167	6	1	0	0	1	0	.286	.167
Young, Ernie	.375	8	3	1	2	1	2	.444	.750

Kenny Rogers, Yankees — LHP

Batter	Avg	AB	H	HR	BI	BB	SO	OBP	Slg
Alomar, R#	.222	45	10	1	3	3	11	.271	.422
Alomar Jr, S	.353	17	6	2	6	0	1	.353	.882
Amaral, R	.333	12	4	1	1	1	2	.385	.583
Anderson, Brd*	.161	31	5	2	5	4	11	.250	.355
Anderson, G*	.333	15	5	0	2	2	4	.412	.467
Arias, George	.167	6	1	0	0	0	1	.167	.167
Baerga, C#	.300	30	9	0	4	1	2	.323	.400
Baines, H*	.077	13	1	0	0	1	3	.143	.077
Bartee, K	.400	5	2	0	1	1	0	.500	.400
Battle, Allen	.000	6	0	0	0	1	0	.143	.000
Bautista, D	.333	6	2	1	1	0	2	.333	.833
Becker, Rich*	.200	10	2	0	0	0	4	.200	.200
Belle, Albert	.320	25	8	0	1	3	10	.393	.440
Berroa, G	.300	20	6	0	4	4	2	.440	.350
Bichette, D	.333	9	3	0	2	0	3	.333	.444
Blowers, Mike	.357	14	5	1	3	1	2	.400	.643
Boggs, Wade*	.448	29	13	0	3	1	2	.467	.621
Bonilla, B#	.273	11	3	0	1	1	1	.333	.273
Borders, Pat	.200	30	6	0	1	4	6	.294	.233
Bordick, Mike	.207	29	6	0	2	3	1	.281	.207
Bournigal, R	.200	5	1	0	0	1	0	.200	.400
Brosius, S	.409	22	9	2	4	4	4	.435	.727
Buhner, Jay	.333	24	8	3	10	5	5	.448	.708
Burks, Ellis	.278	18	5	1	4	2	2	.350	.556
Cameron, Mike	.200	5	1	0	0	0	1	.200	.200
Canseco, Jose	.222	9	2	1	1	5	2	.533	.556
Carter, Joe	.273	33	9	0	4	6	8	.385	.394
Cirillo, Jeff	.313	16	5	0	0	2	2	.389	.375
Clark, Tony#	.111	9	1	0	1	0	3	.111	.111
Cole, Alex*	.333	6	2	0	1	0	0	.333	.333
Coleman, V#	.214	14	3	1	1	1	2	.267	.429
Coomer, Ron	.091	11	1	0	0	0	2	.091	.091
Cora, Joey#	.294	17	5	0	0	2	1	.368	.412
Cordova, M	.200	15	3	0	2	2	4	.278	.200
Curtis, Chad	.367	30	11	0	1	1	2	.387	.433
Cuyler, Milt#	.125	8	1	0	0	0	2	.125	.125
Davis, Chili#	.318	44	14	1	5	3	11	.362	.455
Davis, Russ	.400	5	2	0	0	0	1	.400	.600
Deer, Rob	.100	20	2	0	1	1	10	.143	.150
Devereaux, M	.351	37	13	1	3	2	8	.385	.486
DiSarcina, G	.091	33	3	0	2	0	1	.091	.121
Durant, Mike	.500	4	2	0	0	1	0	.600	.500
Durham, Ray#	.063	16	1	0	0	0	8	.063	.063
Easley, D	.294	17	5	0	1	3	2	.381	.294
Edmonds, Jim*	.148	27	4	2	2	4	10	.258	.481
Eisenreich, J*	.364	11	4	0	2	0	1	.364	.636
Elster, Kevin	.200	5	1	0	0	1	0	.200	.200
Espinoza, A	.467	15	7	0	0	0	2	.467	.467
Fabregas, Jor*	.000	4	0	0	0	2	0	.333	.000
Fermin, Felix	.269	26	7	0	3	1	3	.321	.346
Fielder, C	.333	33	11	3	9	5	10	.421	.727
Flaherty, J	.154	13	2	0	1	0	3	.214	.231
Franco, Julio	.556	9	5	0	0	2	1	.636	.667
Frye, Jeff	.000	6	0	0	0	1	0	.000	.000
Fryman, T	.313	32	10	2	6	4	8	.405	.625
Gaetti, Gary	.200	25	5	0	1	2	3	.286	.240
Gagne, Greg	.350	20	7	0	2	4	3	.458	.350
Gallego, Mike	.400	15	6	1	2	1	3	.412	.667
Gates, Brent#	.250	28	7	0	3	1	4	.276	.357
Gomez, Chris	.167	18	3	0	2	4	3	.333	.176
Gomez, Leo	.417	12	5	1	4	1	3	.429	.833
Gonzales, R	.250	12	3	0	1	2	3	.357	.333
Gonzalez, A	.167	6	1	0	0	1	2	.286	.167
Gonzalez, J*	.600	5	3	2	4	0	0	.600	1.800
Grebeck, C	.286	21	6	2	7	3	3	.375	.667
Greene, Todd	.167	6	1	0	0	0	0	.167	.167
Greenwell, M*	.182	22	4	0	1	1	4	.217	.273
Greer, Rusty*	.429	7	3	0	1	0	2	.429	.429
Griffey Jr, K*	.314	35	11	1	3	3	9	.385	.457
Guillen, O*	.067	15	1	0	2	0	0	.067	.067
Hall, Mel*	.222	9	2	0	0	0	1	.222	.333
Hamilton, D*	.174	23	4	0	2	1	5	.208	.174
Haselman, D	.125	8	1	0	3	1	2	.222	.250
Henderson, R	.273	11	3	1	1	4	2	.467	.545
Hiatt, Phil	.000	7	0	0	0	0	4	.000	.000
Hill, G	.167	12	2	1	3	1	4	.231	.583
Hoiles, Chris	.167	18	3	2	4	4	6	.304	.500
Hollins, Dave#	.400	5	2	1	1	3	0	.625	1.000
Howard, Dave#	.429	7	3	0	1	1	0	.500	.429
Howard, T*	.250	4	1	0	0	1	1	.400	.250
Hudler, Rex	.222	18	4	0	2	1	1	.250	.278
Huff, Michael	.000	5	0	0	0	3	0	.375	.000
Hulse, David*	.000	5	0	0	0	0	1	.000	.000
Jaha, John	.353	17	6	0	4	3	1	.429	.412
Javier, Stan*	.250	24	6	0	2	2	4	.308	.333
Jefferson, R*	.143	7	1	0	2	1	2	.333	.143
Johnson, L*	.344	32	11	0	1	0	3	.344	.406
Joyner, Wally*	.250	24	6	0	2	1	6	.280	.333
Karkovice, R	.263	19	5	0	1	3	7	.364	.368
Kelly, Pat	.429	14	6	1	2	1	2	.467	.714
Kelly, R	.300	20	6	0	2	2	5	.364	.400
Knoblauch, C	.314	35	11	0	1	3	4	.368	.400
Knorr, Randy	.143	7	1	0	0	0	1	.143	.143
Kreuter, Chad#	.167	6	1	1	2	0	4	.167	.667
Leius, Scott	.167	18	3	0	0	1	5	.211	.278
Lewis, Mark	.571	7	4	0	1	0	1	.500	.571
Leyritz, Jim	.188	16	3	0	2	3	2	.316	.188
Liriano, N#	.000	5	0	0	0	1	2	.167	.000
Listach, Pat#	.261	23	6	0	4	1	4	.292	.391
Lofton, Kenny*	.294	17	5	0	1	5	4	.455	.412
Lovullo, T#	.000	8	0	0	1	0	0	.100	.000
Macfarlane, M	.231	26	6	0	2	2	7	.310	.308
Manto, Jeff	.000	7	0	0	1	0	1	.000	.000
Martin, N	.235	17	4	0	0	0	2	.235	.294
Martinez, E	.462	26	12	0	6	6	1	.563	.538
Martinez, T*	.133	15	2	0	2	0	3	.133	.267
Mayne, Brent*	.000	3	0	0	1	1	0	.200	.000
McCarty, Dave	.333	18	6	0	1	0	2	.333	.500
McGee, Willie#	.222	9	2	1	1	0	5	.222	.667
McGriff, Fred*	.250	8	2	0	1	0	4	.333	.500
McGwire, Mark	.273	22	6	4	10	8	4	.500	.864
McLemore, M#	.000	13	0	0	0	1	2	.071	.000
McRae, Brian*	.381	21	8	0	3	3	5	.458	.524
Meares, Pat	.125	16	2	1	3	1	2	.167	.375
Mercedes, H	.400	5	2	0	0	0	1	.400	.400
Mieske, Matt	.211	19	4	0	1	0	2	.211	.368
Molitor, Paul	.417	36	15	3	6	7	1	.512	.667
Mouton, Lyle	.412	17	7	0	2	0	0	.412	.529
Munoz, Pedro	.333	27	9	1	4	3	6	.400	.481
Murray, Eddie#	.200	10	2	2	3	1	1	.273	.800
Myers, Greg*	.000	7	0	0	0	1	5	.125	.000
Naehring, Tim	.208	24	5	1	4	3	5	.296	.417
Nevin, Phil	.143	7	1	0	0	0	3	.143	.143
Nilsson, Dave*	.400	10	4	1	3	0	1	.400	.700
Nixon, Otis#	.200	10	2	0	0	0	1	.200	.200
O'Neill, Paul*	.333	6	2	0	0	2	1	.500	.333
Obando, S	.200	5	1	0	0	1	1	.333	.200
Olerud, John*	.095	21	2	0	2	3	6	.240	.190
Oliver, Joe	.200	10	2	0	0	0	3	.200	.200
Orsulak, Joe*	.333	6	2	0	1	0	2	.333	.333
Ortiz, Luis	.429	7	3	0	3	0	2	.429	.571
Palmeiro, R*	.278	18	5	1	3	3	5	.381	.444
Palmer, Dean	.200	5	1	1	2	0	3	.200	.800
Paquette, C	.176	17	3	1	3	1	7	.222	.353
Parent, Mark	.143	7	1	0	0	0	1	.143	.143
Pena, Tony	.500	12	6	0	1	0	0	.538	.667
Perez, E	.333	6	2	1	2	1	1	.429	.833
Perez, Robert	.000	5	0	0	0	0	0	.000	.000
Phillips, T#	.289	45	13	0	3	10	3	.418	.400
Polonia, Luis*	.000	14	0	0	1	1	3	.067	.000
Raines, Tim#	.091	11	1	0	1	3	1	.286	.091
Ramirez, M	.200	15	3	0	2	1	2	.250	.333
Randa, Joe	.333	6	2	0	0	0	2	.333	.333
Reboulet, J	.286	21	6	0	0	1	3	.318	.333
Reed, Jody	.294	17	5	0	0	2	0	.368	.294
Ripken, Billy	.364	11	4	0	0	1	0	.364	.364
Ripken, Cal	.270	37	10	1	5	2	4	.308	.405
Rodriguez, Al	.600	5	3	1	2	0	1	.600	1.400
Rodriguez, I	.286	7	2	0	0	0	0	.286	.429
Salmon, Tim	.324	34	11	4	9	5	5	.410	.765
Samuel, Juan	.077	13	1	1	1	0	3	.143	.308
Schofield, D	.056	18	1	0	0	1	5	.105	.056
Schu, Rick	.000	6	0	0	0	0	1	.000	.000
Segui, David*	.444	9	4	0	1	0	1	.444	.667
Seitzer, K	.346	26	9	0	1	4	4	.433	.500
Sierra, Ruben#	.259	27	7	1	3	3	1	.323	.370
Snopek, Chris	.333	9	3	0	0	1	1	.400	.333
Snow, J.T.#	.235	34	8	0	2	2	4	.278	.235
Sojo, Luis	.250	12	3	0	3	1	1	.571	.250
Sorrento, P*	.250	4	1	0	2	1	0	.400	.500
Sosa, Sammy	.500	4	2	0	0	1	0	.600	.500

Kenny Rogers, Yankees — LHP

Batter	Avg	AB	H	HR	BI	BB	SO	OBP	Slg
Spiers, Bill*	.000	6	0	0	0	0	1	.000	.000
Sprague, Ed	.400	25	10	1	2	3	2	.464	.640
Stanley, Mike	.278	18	5	1	4	5	2	.435	.500
Steinbach, T	.250	28	7	1	3	4	5	.333	.393
Stevens, Lee*	.000	4	0	0	0	1	0	.200	.000
Stillwell, K#	.000	7	0	0	0	1	2	.111	.000
Surhoff, B.J.*	.182	22	4	0	0	4	4	.333	.182
Sveum, Dale#	.125	8	1	0	0	1	1	.222	.125
Tartabull, D	.333	18	6	2	6	7	5	.520	.722
Tettleton, M#	.471	17	8	0	2	5	4	.591	.647
Thomas, Frank	.393	28	11	3	9	4	2	.455	.786
Thome, Jim*	.300	10	3	0	2	2	3	.417	.500
Tinsley, Lee#	.143	14	2	1	1	0	5	.143	.357
Trammell, A	.192	26	5	0	4	4	2	.281	.231
Turner, Chris	.222	9	2	0	1	1	1	.300	.222
Valentin, Jhn	.176	17	3	0	0	1	0	.222	.176
Valentin, Jse#	.125	8	1	0	1	0	3	.125	.250
Valle, Dave	.200	10	2	1	1	2	0	.333	.600
Vaughn, Greg	.250	24	6	2	5	3	4	.333	.500
Vaughn, Mo*	.286	21	6	2	4	3	7	.400	.619
Velarde, R	.308	26	8	0	1	2	3	.357	.423
Ventura, R*	.242	33	8	2	6	6	6	.350	.424
Vizquel, Omar#	.182	22	4	0	5	1	4	.200	.273
Voigt, Jack	.333	9	3	2	3	0	0	.400	1.000
Walbeck, Matt#	.154	13	2	0	2	0	2	.154	.231
Wallach, Tim	.167	6	1	0	0	0	3	.167	.167
Ward, Turner#	.143	7	1	0	1	1	1	.250	.286
Webster, L	.444	9	4	0	1	1	2	.500	.444
Weiss, Walt#	.250	8	2	0	1	1	1	.250	.375
White, Devon#	.207	29	6	0	1	4	4	.303	.276
Whiten, Mark#	.333	9	3	1	3	2	0	.455	.778
Williams, Ber#	.462	13	6	1	6	3	1	.563	.846
Williams, E	.250	8	2	0	2	2	1	.364	.375
Williams, Geo#	.500	6	3	0	1	0	0	.500	.500
Williams, Ger	.125	8	1	0	0	0	1	.125	.125
Wilson, Dan	.200	5	1	0	2	1	2	.333	.200
Worthington	.286	7	2	0	1	1	0	.375	.286
Young, Ernie	.167	12	2	0	1	0	2	.231	.250

Mel Rojas, Expos — RHP

Batter	Avg	AB	H	HR	BI	BB	SO	OBP	Slg
Hansen, Dave*	.000	9	0	0	1	1	5	.100	.000
Harris, Lenny*	.125	8	1	0	1	1	1	.200	.125
Hayes, C	.286	14	4	0	1	1	3	.333	.286
Hill, G	.500	4	2	0	3	1	2	.600	1.000
Hollins, Dave#	.091	11	1	0	0	1	3	.167	.091
Howard, T*	.333	6	2	0	0	0	1	.333	.500
Hudler, Rex	.571	7	4	0	0	0	1	.571	.571
Hundley, Todd#	.250	8	2	1	1	1	2	.333	.625
Hunter, Brian	.000	5	0	0	0	1	1	.167	.000
Incaviglia, P	.100	10	1	0	0	0	2	.182	.200
Jefferies, G#	.308	13	4	0	3	1	1	.357	.385
Johnson, Char	.333	3	1	0	0	2	1	.600	.333
Johnson, L*	.400	5	2	0	4	0	1	.400	1.200
Jordan, Brian	.000	8	0	0	0	1	3	.111	.000
Jordan, Ricky	.000	7	0	0	0	0	0	.000	.000
Justice, Dave*	.286	7	2	2	3	0	1	.286	1.143
Karros, Eric	.231	13	3	0	3	1	2	.286	.308
Kelly, R	.125	8	1	0	1	0	1	.125	.125
Kent, Jeff	.222	9	2	0	1	1	3	.300	.333
King, Jeff	.133	15	2	0	2	2	1	.278	.267
Kingery, Mike*	.333	6	2	1	1	0	1	.333	.833
Klesko, Ryan*	.500	6	3	1	2	1	1	.625	1.167
Lankford, Ray*	.125	16	2	0	1	2	7	.222	.313
Larkin, Barry	.333	15	5	0	2	0	1	.333	.400
Lemke, Mark#	.100	10	1	0	0	1	6	.182	.100
Lewis, Darren	.333	9	3	0	1	0	0	.400	.444
Lieberthal, M	.333	6	2	0	0	0	0	.333	.333
Livingstone*	.750	4	3	0	1	1	0	.800	.750
Magadan, Dave*	.222	9	2	0	0	0	4	.222	.333
Manwaring, K	.167	6	1	0	1	0	2	.167	.167
Martin, Al*	.286	7	2	0	0	2	2	.444	.286
Martinez, Da*	.143	7	1	0	0	1	0	.250	.143
May, Derrick*	.333	6	2	0	3	1	1	.429	.500
McGee, Willie#	.400	5	2	0	0	1	0	.500	.400
McGriff, Fred*	.111	9	1	0	0	1	3	.200	.111
McRae, Brian*	.286	7	2	0	2	0	1	.286	.286
Merced, O*	.231	13	3	0	3	3	3	.375	.308
Mitchell, K	.200	10	2	0	1	0	3	.200	.300
Mondesi, Raul	.125	8	1	0	0	0	2	.222	.125
Morandini, M*	.250	16	4	0	1	3	2	.368	.313
Morris, Hal*	.588	17	10	1	3	0	1	.556	.882
Mouton, James	.400	5	2	0	0	0	0	.400	.800
Murray, Eddie#	.300	10	3	0	1	1	2	.364	.300
Nixon, Otis#	.000	5	0	0	0	0	0	.000	.000
O'Neill, Paul*	.200	5	1	0	0	1	1	.333	.200
Offerman, J#	.375	8	3	0	0	1	1	.444	.375
Oliver, Joe	.143	7	1	0	0	0	2	.143	.286
Orsulak, Joe*	.000	9	0	0	0	0	2	.100	.000
Pagnozzi, Tom	.071	14	1	0	0	0	3	.071	.071
Pena, G#	.091	11	1	0	0	1	2	.167	.182
Pendleton, T#	.000	9	0	0	0	3	0	.000	.000
Phillips, J*	.200	5	1	0	1	0	2	.200	.200
Piazza, Mike	.091	11	1	0	1	0	6	.091	.091
Plantier, P*	.000	6	0	0	0	0	1	.000	.000
Reed, Jeff*	.222	9	2	0	0	2	4	.364	.333
Roberts, Bip#	.111	9	1	0	1	3	3	.333	.111
Sabo, Chris	.143	14	2	1	1	2	4	.250	.357
Samuel, Juan	.333	6	2	0	0	0	0	.333	.333
Sanchez, Rey	.200	5	1	0	0	1	1	.200	.200
Sandberg, R	.250	12	3	1	1	1	2	.308	.500
Sanders, R	.077	13	1	0	0	1	4	.143	.077
Santiago, B	.100	10	1	0	0	0	5	.100	.100
Scarsone, S	.500	2	1	0	0	2	0	.750	.500
Sheffield, G	.385	13	5	0	2	4	1	.529	.692
Slaught, Don	.333	9	3	0	2	0	1	.333	.556
Smith, Dwight*	.167	6	1	0	0	1	3	.286	.333
Smith, Ozzie#	.250	12	3	0	1	2	0	.357	.333
Sosa, Sammy	.375	8	3	0	0	0	0	.444	.625
Stocker, K#	.286	7	2	0	0	2	2	.444	.286
Strawberry, D*	.143	7	1	0	1	0	1	.143	.143
Taubensee, E*	.143	7	1	0	0	0	4	.143	.286
Thompson, Mil*	.286	14	4	1	5	3	0	.412	.643
Thompson, Rob	.200	10	2	0	1	3	0	.200	.200
Veras, Q#	.200	5	1	0	1	1	0	.200	.200
Vizcaino, J#	.400	10	4	0	2	1	3	.455	.400
Wallach, Tim	.143	7	1	0	0	1	3	.333	.143
Weiss, Walt#	.222	9	2	0	1	0	2	.222	.444
Whiten, Mark#	.444	9	4	1	4	1	0	.500	.778
Wilkins, Rick*	.154	13	2	0	1	3	1	.313	.154
Williams, Ma	.375	8	3	0	2	1	0	.444	.500
Young, Eric	.400	5	2	0	1	0	0	.333	.400
Zeile, Todd	.313	16	5	2	9	1	2	.350	.688

Mel Rojas, Expos — RHP

Batter	Avg	AB	H	HR	BI	BB	SO	OBP	Slg
Abbott, Kurt	.286	7	2	0	0	0	2	.286	.286
Alicea, Luis#	.125	8	1	0	2	2	3	.300	.375
Anthony, Eric*	.000	8	0	0	0	1	1	.111	.000
Ausmus, Brad	.400	5	2	0	1	0	2	.400	.400
Bagwell, Jeff	.333	12	4	0	2	4	4	.500	.417
Batiste, Kim	.000	5	0	0	0	0	3	.000	.000
Bell, Derek	.000	12	0	0	0	0	4	.000	.000
Bell, Jay	.250	16	4	0	1	2	6	.333	.313
Bichette, D	.143	7	1	0	1	1	0	.333	.143
Biggio, Craig	.286	14	4	0	1	1	4	.333	.357
Blauser, Jeff	.000	10	0	0	0	0	2	.091	.000
Bonds, Barry*	.421	19	8	1	3	3	4	.522	.684
Bonilla, B#	.294	17	5	2	2	3	5	.400	.706
Boone, Bret	.167	6	1	0	1	0	0	.167	.167
Branson, Jeff*	.111	9	1	0	0	1	2	.200	.111
Bullett, S*	.167	6	1	0	0	0	2	.167	.500
Butler, Brett*	.200	10	2	0	1	0	3	.200	.200
Caminiti, Ken#	.000	9	0	0	0	3	2	.250	.000
Candaele, C	.429	7	3	0	0	0	0	.429	.714
Cangelosi, J#	.167	6	1	0	1	1	2	.286	.167
Carr, Chuck	.200	5	1	0	0	1	3	.333	.400
Carreon, Mark	.167	6	1	1	0	0	0	.167	.167
Castilla, V	.286	7	2	0	0	0	2	.286	.286
Cedeno, A	.375	8	3	0	0	1	2	.444	.375
Clark, Dave*	.250	8	2	0	2	1	2	.333	.500
Clark, Will*	.333	6	2	0	0	2	0	.500	.667
Clayton, R	.333	9	3	0	0	3	0	.333	.333
Colbrunn, G	.111	9	1	0	0	0	1	.111	.111
Coleman, V#	.333	6	2	0	2	0	2	.333	.833
Conine, Jeff	.154	13	2	0	2	2	1	.313	.231
Daulton, D*	.200	15	3	0	0	3	3	.333	.200
Davis, Eric	.000	4	0	0	0	1	0	.200	.000
Dawson, Andre	.231	13	3	0	2	0	1	.286	.308
DeShields, D*	.286	7	2	0	0	1	1	.375	.286
Duncan, M	.133	15	2	1	4	1	3	.188	.400
Dunston, S	.333	6	2	2	2	0	3	.429	1.333
Dykstra, L*	.133	15	2	1	3	3	2	.250	.333
Eisenreich, J	.143	14	2	1	4	0	1	.143	.357
Everett, Carl#	.143	7	1	1	1	0	6	.143	.571
Finley, Steve*	.385	13	5	1	6	2	0	.438	.769
Galarraga, A	.778	9	7	1	5	0	2	.778	1.333
Gant, Ron	.111	9	1	1	1	0	2	.111	.444
Garcia, C	.000	7	0	0	0	0	1	.000	.000
Gilkey, B	.154	13	2	0	0	1	5	.214	.154
Girardi, Joe	.333	6	2	0	1	0	0	.333	.500
Gonzalez, L*	.000	8	0	0	0	0	2	.000	.000
Grace, Mark*	.167	12	2	0	2	2	0	.286	.167
Gutierrez, R	.333	6	2	0	0	1	1	.429	.333
Gwynn, Chris*	.200	5	1	0	0	2	1	.429	.400
Gwynn, Tony*	.118	17	2	0	2	0	0	.105	.176

Jose Rosado, Royals — LHP

Batter	Avg	AB	H	HR	BI	BB	SO	OBP	Slg
Amaral, Rich	.000	8	0	0	0	0	1	.000	.000
Anderson, G*	.800	5	4	0	0	0	0	.800	1.000
Ausmus, Brad	.167	6	1	0	0	1	1	.286	.167
Bartee, K	.571	7	4	1	1	1	2	.625	1.000
Belle, Albert	.333	6	2	0	0	0	0	.333	.500
Boggs, Wade*	.167	6	1	0	0	1	0	.286	.167

Jose Rosado, Royals — LHP

Batter	Avg	AB	H	HR	BI	BB	SO	OBP	Slg
Brumfield, J	.250	8	2	0	0	0	1	.250	.375
Buhner, Jay	.167	6	1	0	0	0	2	.167	.167
Carter, Joe	.143	7	1	0	0	0	0	.143	.429
Clark, Tony#	.143	7	1	1	2	0	2	.143	.571
Davis, Chili#	.200	5	1	0	0	0	3	.200	.400
Duncan, M	.200	5	1	0	2	0	0	.200	.400
Durham, Ray#	.125	8	1	0	0	0	0	.125	.250
Easley, D	.167	6	1	0	0	0	0	.167	.167
Fryman, T	.200	5	1	0	0	2	4	.400	.200
Gonzalez, A	.000	7	0	0	0	0	1	.000	.000
Griffey Jr, K*	.500	6	3	0	0	0	1	.500	.667
Hunter, Brian	.333	6	2	0	0	0	0	.333	.500
Jeter, Derek	.800	5	4	0	1	0	0	.833	.800
Lewis, Darren	.000	5	0	0	0	1	0	.167	.000
Lewis, Mark	.143	7	1	0	1	0	1	.143	.286
Martinez, Da*	.400	5	2	0	1	0	0	.500	.400
Martinez, E	.500	6	3	1	2	0	1	.500	1.000
Martinez, T*	.600	5	3	0	0	0	1	.600	.600
Nevin, Phil	.333	6	2	0	0	0	1	.429	.333
Nieves, M#	.143	7	1	0	0	0	0	.143	.143
O'Neill, Paul*	.167	6	1	1	1	0	1	.167	.667
Perez, Robert	.333	6	2	0	1	1	0	.429	.333
Phillips, T#	.429	7	3	0	0	1	2	.500	.571
Rodriguez, Al	.200	5	1	0	0	1	0	.333	.400
Salmon, Tim	.500	2	1	0	2	3	0	.800	1.000
Seitzer, K	.333	6	2	0	0	0	1	.333	.500
Sierra, Ruben#	.222	9	2	0	1	0	1	.200	.222
Snopek, Chris	.600	5	3	0	3	0	1	.667	1.200
Snow, J.T.#	.000	5	0	0	0	0	1	.000	.000
Sprague, Ed	.200	5	1	0	1	1	0	.286	.200
Tartabull, D	.400	5	2	0	2	1	1	.500	.600
Thome, Jim*	.400	5	2	1	3	1	1	.500	1.000
Williams, Ber#	.200	5	1	0	0	0	0	.200	.200
Williams, Ger	.000	4	0	0	1	0	1	.000	.000
Wilson, Dan	.167	6	1	0	1	0	3	.167	.167

Matt Ruebel, Pirates — LHP

Batter	Avg	AB	H	HR	BI	BB	SO	OBP	Slg
Bell, Derek	.250	4	1	0	0	1	0	.400	.250
Bichette, D	.167	6	1	0	0	1	0	.286	.333
Burks, Ellis	.500	6	3	0	1	1	1	.571	.667
Caminiti, Ken#	.333	6	2	1	1	0	0	.429	1.000
Castilla, V	.167	6	1	0	0	0	0	.286	.167
Cianfrocco, A	.200	5	1	0	2	0	1	.200	.400
Finley, Steve*	.143	7	1	0	0	0	0	.143	.143
Galarraga, A	.333	6	2	1	3	1	1	.375	.833
Gwynn, Tony*	.200	5	1	0	1	0	0	.333	.200
Henderson, R	.667	3	2	0	3	2	0	.667	1.000
Hunter, Bri L	.400	5	2	0	0	0	0	.400	.800
Owens, J	.167	6	1	0	0	0	0	.167	.167
Walker, Larry*	.333	6	2	1	2	0	0	.500	1.000
Weiss, Walt#	.600	5	3	0	0	1	1	.714	.800
Young, Eric	.286	7	2	0	1	0	0	.375	.429

Kirk Rueter, Giants — LHP

Batter	Avg	AB	H	HR	BI	BB	SO	OBP	Slg
Alicea, Luis#	.250	8	2	0	0	0	1	.250	.250
Arias, Alex	.375	8	3	0	0	0	0	.375	.375
Ausmus, Brad	.200	5	1	0	0	0	0	.200	.200
Bagwell, Jeff	.385	13	5	0	2	2	1	.467	.462
Barberie, B#	.250	4	1	0	0	1	1	.400	.250
Bates, Jason#	.200	5	1	0	0	0	0	.200	.200
Bell, Derek	.357	14	5	0	2	0	2	.357	.357
Bell, Jay	.083	12	1	0	1	4	2	.313	.083
Bichette, D	.154	13	2	0	1	0	1	.143	.231
Biggio, Craig	.182	11	2	0	1	1	0	.286	.182
Blauser, Jeff	.125	8	1	0	0	1	1	.222	.125
Bonds, Barry*	.200	10	2	0	0	1	1	.273	.200
Boone, Bret	.250	8	2	1	2	0	0	.250	.625
Burks, Ellis	.300	10	3	0	0	1	4	.364	.300
Butler, Brett*	.400	10	4	0	0	2	1	.500	.400
Caminiti, Ken#	.000	7	0	0	0	0	1	.000	.000
Carr, Chuck	.300	10	3	0	3	1	1	.364	.400
Carreon, Mark	.286	7	2	0	0	0	1	.286	.286
Castilla, V	.182	11	2	1	4	1	1	.250	.455
Clark, Will*	.000	4	0	0	0	1	1	.200	.000
Clayton, R	.133	15	2	0	0	1	0	.188	.133
Colbrunn, G	.429	7	3	0	0	1	0	.500	.429
Conine, Jeff	.364	11	4	0	1	1	1	.417	.545
Daulton, D*	.600	5	3	0	1	0	0	.600	.800
Davis, Eric	.000	6	0	0	0	0	1	.000	.000
DeShields, D*	.182	11	2	0	0	0	1	.182	.182
Duncan, M	.500	10	5	0	0	1	1	.545	.800
Dykstra, L*	.400	10	4	0	0	1	2	.455	.400
Finley, Steve*	.250	4	1	0	0	1	0	.400	.250
Gaetti, Gary	.286	7	2	0	1	1	1	.375	.571
Galarraga, A	.455	11	5	1	2	1	2	.500	.909
Gant, Ron	.133	15	2	0	0	2	2	.235	.133
Garcia, C	.250	16	4	0	3	0	1	.250	.313
Gilkey, B	.300	10	3	0	1	0	0	.300	.300
Grace, Mark*	.273	11	3	0	0	0	0	.273	.273

Kirk Rueter, Giants — LHP

Batter	Avg	AB	H	HR	BI	BB	SO	OBP	Slg
Grissom, M	.200	5	1	0	1	0	0	.200	.400
Gutierrez, R	.000	8	0	0	0	0	1	.000	.000
Gwynn, Tony*	.125	8	1	1	1	1	1	.222	.500
Hayes, C	.333	12	4	0	1	0	2	.333	.333
Hill, G	.000	6	0	0	0	0	0	.000	.000
Hollins, Dave#	.333	3	1	1	2	2	0	.600	1.333
Hunter, Bri L	.400	5	2	0	0	0	0	.400	.600
Huskey, Butch	.500	4	2	0	1	1	0	.600	.500
Incaviglia, P	.625	8	5	0	1	0	0	.625	.625
Jefferies, G#	.400	10	4	2	2	0	0	.400	1.100
Jones, C#	.250	4	1	0	1	1	0	.400	.250
Jones, Chris	.400	5	2	0	0	0	0	.400	.400
Jordan, Brian	.300	10	3	0	0	0	1	.300	.400
Justice, Dave*	.200	5	1	0	2	0	0	.200	.400
Karros, Eric	.455	11	5	1	2	2	0	.538	.909
Kelly, R	.400	5	2	0	0	1	0	.500	.400
Kendall, J	.200	5	1	0	0	2	0	.429	.200
Kent, Jeff	.667	6	4	0	2	1	0	.714	.833
King, Jeff	.143	14	2	1	1	0	2	.143	.357
Klesko, Ryan*	.800	5	4	0	0	0	0	.800	.800
Lankford, Ray*	.364	11	4	0	2	1	2	.417	.455
Larkin, Barry	.200	5	1	0	1	1	1	.286	.200
Lemke, Mark#	.125	8	1	0	0	1	0	.222	.250
Lewis, Darren	.091	11	1	0	1	1	1	.167	.091
Mabry, John*	.429	7	3	0	2	0	0	.429	.429
Manwaring, N	.200	10	2	0	1	0	4	.200	.200
Martin, Al*	.273	11	3	1	2	0	1	.273	.545
McGriff, Fred*	.444	9	4	0	2	2	0	.545	.667
McRae, Brian*	.000	5	0	0	0	0	0	.000	.000
Merced, O*	.333	15	5	0	2	0	1	.333	.333
Mondesi, Raul	.333	9	3	1	3	0	2	.300	.667
Morandini, M*	.200	5	1	0	0	0	0	.200	.200
Morris, Hal*	.200	5	1	0	1	0	1	.333	.200
Mouton, James	.429	7	3	0	0	0	0	.429	.429
Offerman, J#	.000	6	0	0	1	1	0	.143	.000
Owens, J	.200	5	1	1	1	0	1	.200	.800
Pagnozzi, Tom	.200	5	1	0	0	0	0	.200	.200
Pendleton, T#	.300	10	3	0	2	0	1	.300	.400
Piazza, Mike	.455	11	5	0	1	0	0	.500	.455
Plantier, P*	.000	6	0	0	0	2	1	.250	.000
Roberson, K#	.000	6	0	0	0	0	2	.000	.000
Roberts, Bip#	.556	9	5	0	1	0	1	.556	.556
Sanchez, Rey	.300	10	3	0	0	0	0	.300	.300
Sandberg, R	.571	7	4	0	0	1	0	.625	.571
Sanders, R	.333	9	3	0	2	0	4	.333	.444
Santiago, B	.375	8	3	1	1	0	0	.375	1.000
Scarsone, S	.429	7	3	0	2	1	2	.444	.714
Servais, S	.000	8	0	0	1	0	0	.000	.000
Sheaffer, D	.375	8	3	1	1	0	0	.375	.750
Sheffield, G	.444	9	4	1	3	1	1	.500	.778
Shipley, C	.500	6	3	0	0	0	0	.500	.667
Slaught, Don	.667	6	4	0	1	1	0	.714	.667
Sosa, Sammy	.455	11	5	1	2	0	3	.455	1.091
Stinnett, K	.000	4	0	0	0	1	0	.200	.000
Stocker, K#	.167	6	1	0	0	1	1	.286	.333
Thompson, Rob	.500	5	2	1	1	1	0	.500	1.000
Vizcaino, J#	.444	9	4	0	0	1	1	.500	.444
Walker, Larry*	.000	5	0	0	0	0	0	.000	.000
Wallach, Tim	.111	9	1	0	1	0	0	.111	.111
Walton, J	.400	5	2	0	0	0	0	.400	.400
Wehner, John	.286	7	2	0	2	0	1	.286	.429
Weiss, Walt#	.556	9	5	0	0	2	0	.636	.667
Whiten, Mark#	.357	14	5	2	3	0	1	.357	.857
Williams, E	.200	5	1	0	0	1	0	.200	.200
Williams, Ma	.000	5	0	0	0	0	0	.000	.000
Young, Eric	.333	6	2	0	0	2	1	.500	.667
Zeile, Todd	.250	12	3	0	0	0	0	.250	.250

Scott Ruffcorn, White Sox — RHP

Batter	Avg	AB	H	HR	BI	BB	SO	OBP	Slg
Vizquel, Omar*	.400	5	2	0	0	0	0	.400	.400

Bruce Ruffin, Rockies — LHP

Batter	Avg	AB	H	HR	BI	BB	SO	OBP	Slg
Aldrete, Mike*	.625	8	5	0	1	1	0	.667	.750
Alicea, Luis#	.111	9	1	0	0	0	1	.200	.222
Alomar, R#	.200	10	2	0	0	1	2	.273	.200
Alou, Moises	.222	9	2	0	0	0	2	.222	.222
Anthony, Eric*	.111	9	1	0	0	0	2	.111	.111
Ausmus, Brad	.000	5	0	0	0	0	1	.167	.000
Bagwell, Jeff	.083	12	1	0	2	3	5	.267	.167
Bell, Derek	.111	9	1	0	2	1	2	.200	.111
Bell, Jay	.270	37	10	0	2	2	6	.308	.270
Belliard, R	.800	5	4	0	0	2	1	.857	.800
Benjamin, M	.200	5	1	0	1	0	2	.200	.200
Biggio, Craig	.357	28	10	0	4	4	4	.438	.429
Blauser, Jeff	.273	22	6	1	4	4	8	.370	.455
Bonds, Barry*	.212	33	7	0	4	7	4	.333	.303
Bonilla, B#	.404	52	21	2	9	5	4	.441	.615
Boone, Bret	.400	5	2	1	1	0	1	.400	1.000
Branson, Jeff*	.000	5	0	0	0	0	2	.000	.000

Batter	Avg	AB	H	HR	BI	BB	SO	OBP	Slg
Butler, Brett*	.350	20	7	0	4	13	3	.606	.350
Caminiti, Ken#	.235	34	8	1	4	0	6	.229	.412
Candaele, C#	.348	23	8	0	1	4	3	.444	.391
Cangelosi, J#	.259	27	7	0	3	9	0	.444	.296
Carr, Chuck	.286	7	2	0	0	0	3	.286	.429
Carreon, Mark	.267	15	4	1	4	0	1	.267	.467
Cedeno, A	.500	12	6	0	1	0	2	.500	.583
Clark, Phil	.364	11	4	0	1	0	0	.364	.545
Clark, Will*	.280	25	7	1	5	3	5	.345	.480
Clayton, R	.182	11	2	0	1	0	4	.182	.182
Coleman, V#	.264	53	14	0	2	2	8	.291	.358
Conine, Jeff	.286	7	2	0	1	1	0	.333	.286
Cordero, Wil	.000	7	0	0	0	0	2	.000	.000
Dascenzo, D*	.000	3	0	0	1	2	0	.500	.000
Daulton, D*	.250	8	2	0	1	1	2	.333	.250
Davis, Chili#	.375	8	3	0	1	1	1	.444	.500
Davis, Eric	.417	24	10	1	5	5	6	.500	.750
Dawson, Andre	.282	39	11	1	7	2	3	.310	.436
DeShields, D*	.421	19	8	0	3	1	2	.450	.474
Duncan, M	.364	22	8	1	8	1	6	.391	.636
Dunston, S	.185	54	10	0	1	0	4	.185	.278
Dykstra, L*	.143	14	2	0	0	7	1	.455	.214
Eisenreich, J*	.000	9	0	0	0	0	1	.000	.000
Elster, Kevin	.167	12	2	0	1	2	2	.286	.167
Fermin, Felix	.400	5	2	0	0	0	0	.400	.400
Finley, Steve*	.143	14	2	0	0	0	5	.143	.214
Fletcher, D*	.000	5	0	0	0	2	1	.286	.000
Galarraga, A	.423	26	11	1	5	2	2	.448	.654
Gallego, Mike	.400	5	2	0	1	0	1	.400	.600
Gant, Ron	.476	21	10	1	8	3	2	.542	.905
Garcia, C	.100	10	1	0	0	1	3	.182	.200
Gilkey, B	.400	10	4	0	1	1	4	.455	.500
Girardi, Joe	.500	12	6	1	4	1	2	.538	.917
Gonzales, R	.200	5	1	1	3	0	1	.200	.800
Gonzalez, L*	.182	11	2	0	0	0	1	.182	.273
Grace, Mark*	.297	37	11	0	6	7	3	.409	.405
Grissom, M	.294	17	5	0	1	3	6	.400	.412
Gutierrez, R	.571	7	4	0	1	2	1	.667	.571
Gwynn, Tony*	.306	36	11	0	3	6	1	.405	.306
Hall, Mel*	.000	5	1	0	0	1	0	.333	.000
Hayes, C	.286	7	2	1	1	0	2	.286	.714
Hernandez, Jo	.200	5	1	0	0	0	0	.200	.200
Hill, G	.167	6	1	0	1	0	3	.167	.167
Hollins, Dave#	.167	6	1	0	2	1	1	.250	.167
Howard, T*	.400	5	2	0	3	1	1	.500	.400
Hudler, Rex	.375	16	6	0	0	0	5	.375	.625
Hundley, Todd#	.333	12	4	0	1	1	3	.385	.583
Hunter, Brian	.286	7	2	0	0	0	2	.286	.286
Incaviglia, P	.000	5	0	0	0	0	1	.000	.000
James, Dion*	.000	3	0	0	1	3	1	.500	.000
Jefferies, G#	.200	25	5	2	4	4	2	.310	.440
Johnson, L*	.000	5	0	0	1	0	1	.000	.000
Jones, C#	.167	6	1	0	0	1	1	.286	.167
Jordan, Brian	.200	5	1	1	2	0	3	.200	.800
Joyner, Wally*	.000	5	0	0	0	1	0	.167	.000
Justice, Dave*	.238	21	5	2	6	3	2	.333	.571
Karros, Eric	.250	4	1	0	1	1	1	.400	.250
Kelly, R	.500	8	4	0	4	3	3	.636	.625
Kent, Jeff	.222	9	2	0	1	0	2	.222	.222
King, Jeff	.281	32	9	1	8	2	3	.314	.531
Lankford, Ray*	.105	19	2	0	0	3	5	.227	.105
Lansing, Mike	.333	6	2	0	0	1	2	.429	.333
Larkin, Barry	.194	31	6	0	3	3	6	.265	.226
Lemke, Mark#	.250	16	4	0	1	3	3	.368	.313
Lewis, Darren	.500	8	4	0	2	0	0	.500	.500
Lopez, Javy	.250	4	1	0	2	1	0	.400	.250
Mabry, John*	.250	4	1	0	1	1	0	.400	.250
Magadan, Dave*	.357	14	5	0	1	4	2	.500	.500
Manwaring, K	.333	15	5	0	0	2	3	.412	.400
Martin, Al*	.250	4	1	0	0	2	3	.500	.250
McGee, Willie*	.395	38	15	1	8	4	7	.452	.658
McGriff, Fred*	.316	19	6	0	0	1	6	.350	.368
McRae, Brian#	.167	6	1	0	0	0	3	.167	.167
Merced, O*	.200	5	1	0	2	1	0	.333	.200
Mitchell, K	.400	30	12	0	4	1	1	.406	.667
Mondesi, Raul	.400	5	2	1	3	0	1	.400	1.200
Morris, Hal*	.125	8	1	0	1	0	1	.125	.125
Murray, Eddie*	.385	13	5	0	2	1	0	.467	.462
Nixon, Otis#	.200	10	2	0	0	3	0	.200	.200
O'Brien, C	.333	6	2	1	2	0	2	.333	.833
O'Neill, Paul*	.273	11	3	0	4	1	2	.333	.364
Oliver, Joe	.182	11	2	1	1	3	2	.357	.455
Pagnozzi, Tom	.263	19	5	0	3	2	3	.318	.263
Palmeiro, R*	.462	13	6	0	2	3	2	.563	.462
Parker, Rick	.400	5	2	0	1	1	2	.500	.600
Pena, G#	.000	5	0	0	0	4	4	.000	.000
Pena, Tony	.313	16	5	0	0	2	1	.389	.313
Pendleton, T#	.296	54	16	1	11	1	3	.309	.426
Plantier, P*	.200	5	1	1	1	2	2	.333	.800
Polonia, Luis*	.000	4	0	0	0	1	1	.200	.000
Raines, Tim#	.238	21	5	0	0	0	3	.238	.333
Reed, Jody	.000	7	0	0	0	4	1	.364	.000
Roberts, Bip#	.261	23	6	0	3	3	3	.346	.304
Sabo, Chris	.409	22	9	0	3	1	2	.435	.455
Samuel, Juan	.278	18	5	1	1	0	4	.278	.500
Sandberg, R	.288	52	15	0	3	6	7	.362	.365
Sanders, R	.125	8	1	0	0	1	2	.222	.125
Santiago, B	.292	24	7	0	2	2	2	.333	.375
Scarsone, S	.429	7	3	0	0	0	3	.429	.429
Servais, S	.167	6	1	0	2	1	2	.286	.167
Sheffield, G	.600	5	3	1	3	0	0	.600	1.200
Shipley, C	.333	9	3	0	0	0	1	.333	.333
Slaught, Don	.353	17	6	0	1	2	3	.400	.412
Smith, Ozzie#	.196	51	10	0	4	13	9	.359	.235
Sosa, Sammy	.625	8	5	0	1	0	2	.625	.750
Spehr, Tim	.000	3	0	0	0	1	0	.250	.000
Stillwell, K#	.500	8	4	0	0	1	2	.556	.625
Stocker, K#	.400	5	2	0	1	0	0	.400	.400
Strawberry, D*	.325	40	13	0	7	5	12	.400	.425
Tartabull, D	.333	3	1	1	4	3	1	.667	1.333
Thompson, Mil*	.214	14	3	0	1	1	3	.267	.429
Thompson, Rob	.328	28	10	0	4	5	5	.455	.357
Vizcaino, J#	.500	6	3	0	1	3	2	.667	.500
Walker, Larry*	.278	18	5	2	7	1	5	.316	.667
Wallach, Tim	.429	28	12	2	8	1	2	.448	.821
Walton, J	.219	32	7	0	2	2	5	.257	.281
Weiss, Walt*	.333	6	2	0	0	1	1	.429	.333
Whiten, Mark#	.250	8	2	1	3	1	3	.333	.625
Wilkins, Rick*	.000	8	0	0	0	1	4	.111	.000
Williams, Ma	.318	22	7	3	5	3	2	.400	.727
Young, Kevin	.000	8	0	0	0	0	5	.000	.000
Zeile, Todd	.308	26	8	1	4	3	3	.379	.462

Johnny Ruffin, Reds RHP

Batter	Avg	AB	H	HR	BI	BB	SO	OBP	Slg
Alou, Moises	.556	9	5	1	2	0	0	.556	.889
Bagwell, Jeff	.333	3	1	1	3	2	1	.600	1.333
Bell, Derek	.250	8	2	0	1	0	1	.250	.250
Bell, Jay	.000	5	0	0	0	1	3	.167	.000
Berry, Sean	.333	6	2	0	1	0	2	.333	.333
Bichette, D	.143	7	1	1	1	1	2	.250	.571
Biggio, Craig	.400	5	2	0	0	1	1	.500	.600
Bonds, Barry*	.500	4	2	1	1	2	1	.667	1.500
Carr, Chuck	.000	4	0	0	0	1	0	.200	.000
Castilla, V	.500	6	3	0	0	0	3	.500	.667
Clayton, R	.000	4	0	0	1	1	1	.200	.000
Conine, Jeff	.000	7	0	0	0	3	0	.000	.000
Cordero, Wil	.000	5	0	0	0	0	1	.000	.000
Daulton, D*	.000	5	0	0	0	1	3	.167	.000
Dykstra, L*	.600	5	3	0	1	0	0	.600	1.200
Eisenreich, J*	.333	6	2	0	0	0	1	.333	.333
Finley, Steve*	.000	4	0	0	0	1	2	.200	.000
Fletcher, D*	.000	5	0	0	0	0	0	.000	.000
Galarraga, A	.250	8	2	0	1	0	5	.333	.250
Gant, Ron	.600	5	3	1	2	0	0	.600	1.200
Garcia, C	.143	7	1	0	0	0	1	.143	.143
Gilkey, B	.444	9	4	1	2	1	0	.500	1.000
Gonzalez, L*	.600	5	3	0	2	1	0	.667	.800
Grace, Mark*	.500	4	2	0	0	3	1	.714	.500
Grissom, M	.667	6	4	1	1	0	0	.667	1.167
Gutierrez, R	.286	7	2	0	1	0	2	.286	.286
Hayes, C	.375	8	3	1	2	0	1	.375	.750
Hollins, Dave#	.200	5	1	0	0	1	1	.333	.400
Hundley, Todd#	.000	4	0	0	0	2	1	.333	.000
Jefferies, G#	.600	5	3	0	1	1	0	.667	.600
Karros, Eric	.000	7	0	0	0	0	1	.000	.000
Kent, Jeff	.125	8	1	1	1	0	3	.125	.500
King, Jeff	.167	6	1	0	1	2	2	.375	.167
Lansing, Mike	.000	4	0	0	1	0	1	.167	.000
Magadan, Dave*	.333	3	1	0	0	3	0	.667	.333
Manwaring, K	.400	5	2	0	1	0	1	.400	.600
Martin, Al*	.200	5	1	0	0	0	0	.200	.200
McGriff, Fred*	.500	4	2	1	2	1	2	.600	1.250
Merced, O*	.200	5	1	0	2	0	1	.200	.400
Orsulak, Joe*	.333	6	2	0	1	0	0	.333	.333
Pendleton, T#	.250	4	1	1	1	0	0	.400	1.000
Piazza, Mike	.000	5	0	0	0	3	0	.000	.000
Rodriguez, H*	.200	5	1	0	0	0	0	.200	.200
Sanchez, Rey	.143	7	1	0	0	0	2	.143	.143
Santangelo, F#	.000	5	0	0	0	1	0	.167	.000
Sheffield, G	.000	4	0	0	0	3	2	.375	.000
Smith, Ozzie#	.600	5	3	0	0	0	0	.600	1.000
Sosa, Sammy	.222	9	2	1	3	0	4	.222	.556
Stocker, K*	.400	5	2	0	1	1	3	.500	.400
Walker, Larry*	.600	5	3	0	1	2	1	.714	.600
Whiten, Mark#	.333	6	2	0	0	0	0	.333	.333
Wilkins, Rick*	.250	4	1	0	0	2	0	.500	.250
Williams, Ma	.571	7	4	2	5	0	1	.571	1.429
Young, Eric	.500	4	2	1	1	1	0	.600	1.250
Zeile, Todd	.000	7	0	0	0	1	2	.125	.000

Jeff Russell, Rangers — RHP

Batter	Avg	AB	H	HR	BI	BB	SO	OBP	Slg
Aldrete, Mike*	.143	7	1	0	1	1	0	.250	.143
Alomar, R#	.364	11	4	0	2	0	0	.364	.455
Alomar Jr, S	.300	10	3	0	1	0	1	.300	.400
Anderson, Brd*	.222	9	2	0	1	0	2	.222	.222
Baerga, C#	.375	8	3	0	1	2	0	.583	.625
Baines, H*	.188	16	3	1	4	2	4	.278	.375
Becker, Rich*	.250	4	1	0	0	1	1	.400	.250
Belle, Albert	.250	12	3	1	4	0	4	.250	.500
Berroa, G	.429	7	3	1	2	2	1	.556	.857
Bichette, D	.167	6	1	0	0	0	1	.167	.167
Boggs, Wade*	.429	14	6	1	1	4	1	.556	.786
Borders, Pat	.200	5	1	0	0	0	0	.200	.200
Bordick, Mike	.500	4	2	0	0	1	1	.600	.500
Buhner, Jay	.273	11	3	1	4	4	4	.438	.545
Burks, Ellis	.450	20	9	2	6	2	3	.500	.850
Canseco, Jose	.240	25	6	3	7	4	5	.345	.600
Carter, Joe	.105	19	2	0	3	0	4	.095	.105
Cora, Joey#	.444	9	4	0	2	0	1	.444	.556
Curtis, Chad	.250	4	1	0	1	0	0	.250	.500
Cuyler, Milt*	.333	3	1	0	1	2	0	.600	.333
Davis, Chili#	.333	27	9	1	4	4	7	.419	.556
Dawson, Andre	.143	7	1	1	1	0	2	.143	.571
Deer, Rob	.154	13	2	1	2	0	2	.154	.385
Devereaux, M	.250	8	2	1	1	1	4	.333	.625
Fermin, Felix	.400	5	2	0	1	0	0	.400	.400
Fielder, C	.364	11	4	0	3	0	4	.364	.364
Franco, Julio	.333	12	4	0	1	0	3	.333	.417
Frye, Jeff	.400	5	2	0	0	0	0	.400	.400
Fryman, T	.167	18	3	0	0	0	4	.167	.167
Gaetti, Gary	.043	23	1	0	1	1	7	.080	.043
Gagne, Greg	.294	17	5	1	3	0	4	.333	.471
Gallego, Mike	.100	10	1	0	0	3	5	.308	.100
Gates, Brent#	.000	6	0	0	0	0	1	.000	.000
Gomez, Leo	.100	10	1	0	0	0	4	.100	.100
Gonzalez, A	.000	4	0	0	0	1	1	.200	.000
Greenwell, M*	.615	13	8	2	11	2	2	.667	1.154
Griffey Jr, K*	.500	8	4	1	2	1	1	.556	1.000
Guillen, O*	.292	24	7	0	4	1	1	.308	.458
Gwynn, Tony*	.500	8	4	0	2	0	0	.500	.625
Hale, Chip*	.000	6	0	0	0	2	0	.000	.000
Hall, Mel*	.250	12	3	1	3	0	1	.250	.583
Hamilton, D*	.000	7	0	0	0	1	2	.125	.000
Henderson, R	.316	19	6	2	3	6	6	.480	.684
Hoiles, Chris	.000	7	0	0	0	0	4	.000	.000
Hollins, Dave#	.500	4	2	1	2	1	1	.600	1.250
Howell, Jack*	.250	20	5	1	4	0	7	.250	.450
Jaha, John	.500	4	2	0	0	2	0	.667	.500
Javier, Stan#	.200	10	2	0	1	2	2	.333	.400
Johnson, L*	.250	8	2	0	1	1	0	.300	.250
Joyner, Wally*	.208	24	5	1	1	1	4	.240	.375
Karkovice, R	.222	9	2	0	1	0	2	.222	.222
Kelly, R	.143	7	1	0	0	0	1	.143	.143
Kingery, Mike*	.111	9	1	0	2	0	1	.111	.111
Knoblauch, C	.133	15	2	0	2	4	1	.350	.133
Listach, Pat#	.400	5	2	0	0	1	0	.500	.400
Lofton, Kenny*	.333	3	1	0	0	2	0	.600	.333
Macfarlane, M	.125	8	1	1	3	1	1	.222	.500
Martinez, E	.500	6	3	1	3	2	0	.667	1.333
Martinez, T*	.250	8	2	0	0	0	1	.250	.250
Marzano, John	.200	5	1	0	1	0	0	.200	.400
Mayne, Brent*	.200	5	1	0	0	0	0	.200	.200
McGriff, Fred*	.500	8	4	1	1	2	1	.600	1.000
McGwire, Mark	.095	21	2	0	1	3	5	.208	.095
McLemore, M#	.154	13	2	0	2	3	1	.353	.154
McRae, Brian#	.286	7	2	0	1	0	0	.286	.429
Mieske, Matt	.000	5	0	0	0	0	1	.000	.000
Molitor, Paul	.278	36	10	1	5	2	4	.316	.361
Murray, Eddie#	.500	12	6	0	3	1	1	.538	.500
Myers, Greg*	.455	11	5	0	4	0	1	.455	.636
Naehring, Tim	.200	5	1	0	0	0	0	.200	.200
Newson, W*	.333	6	2	0	2	0	3	.333	.333
O'Brien, Pete	.571	7	4	0	0	0	0	.571	.571
Olerud, John*	.250	8	2	0	1	0	1	.333	.375
Orsulak, Joe*	.417	12	5	0	0	3	1	.533	.500
Pena, Tony	.154	13	2	0	2	0	1	.154	.385
Phillips, T#	.154	26	4	0	2	4	6	.267	.192
Polonia, Luis*	.222	9	2	0	0	1	1	.300	.222
Raines, Tim#	.231	13	3	0	0	1	1	.286	.231
Ramirez, M	.200	5	1	1	4	1	0	.333	.800
Reed, Jody	.357	14	5	0	1	2	1	.438	.429
Ripken, Billy	.333	6	2	0	0	1	0	.429	.333
Ripken, Cal	.250	20	5	0	2	1	3	.286	.350
Salmon, Tim	.333	6	2	0	1	1	3	.429	.333
Samuel, Juan	.333	9	3	0	0	0	2	.333	.444
Sandberg, R	.200	5	1	0	0	2	3	.429	.400
Schofield, D	.280	25	7	0	4	1	1	.296	.320
Seitzer, K	.231	26	6	0	5	2	4	.286	.231
Sierra, Ruben#	.200	5	1	0	1	2	1	.375	.200
Slaught, Don	.571	7	4	0	3	1	0	.667	.571
Sorrento, P*	.500	6	3	0	2	0	2	.429	.500
Spiers, Bill*	.167	6	1	0	0	0	0	.167	.167

Jeff Russell, Rangers — RHP

Batter	Avg	AB	H	HR	BI	BB	SO	OBP	Slg
Steinbach, T	.400	10	4	0	2	2	2	.500	.400
Stillwell, K#	.333	12	4	0	1	0	2	.333	.333
Surhoff, B.J.*	.176	17	3	0	1	0	0	.176	.235
Sveum, Dale#	.125	8	1	0	0	1	3	.222	.125
Tartabull, D	.286	21	6	1	6	2	4	.348	.619
Tettleton, M#	.154	13	2	0	0	3	4	.353	.154
Thomas, Frank	.333	9	3	0	3	1	2	.400	.444
Tinsley, Lee*	.200	5	1	0	0	0	2	.200	.200
Trammell, A	.211	19	4	0	0	1	2	.250	.316
Valentin, Jhn	.333	6	2	0	2	0	0	.333	.500
Valle, Dave	.154	13	2	0	4	0	0	.143	.154
Vaughn, Greg	.125	8	1	0	0	1	2	.222	.125
Velarde, R	.000	6	0	0	1	2	1	.222	.000
Ventura, R*	.167	12	2	0	3	2	3	.267	.167
Vizquel, Omar#	.500	8	4	0	1	1	1	.556	.500
Wallach, Tim	.333	9	3	0	1	1	3	.400	.444
White, Devon#	.250	36	9	1	3	2	13	.289	.444
Wilson, Dan	.000	5	0	0	0	0	0	.000	.000
Worthington	.000	8	0	0	0	1	3	.111	.000

Ken Ryan, Phillies — RHP

Batter	Avg	AB	H	HR	BI	BB	SO	OBP	Slg
Alomar, R#	.200	5	1	0	2	0	2	.200	.400
Alomar Jr, S	.167	6	1	0	0	0	0	.167	.167
Baerga, C#	.333	6	2	0	1	0	1	.333	.333
Belle, Albert	.250	4	1	1	3	1	1	.500	1.000
Bichette, D	.200	5	1	0	0	1	2	.333	.400
Carter, Joe	.400	5	2	0	0	0	1	.400	.600
Cole, Alex*	.250	4	1	0	0	1	1	.400	.250
Curtis, Chad	.000	5	0	0	0	3	0	.375	.000
Davis, Chili#	.400	5	2	0	0	2	2	.571	.400
DiSarcina, G	.200	5	1	0	1	0	1	.200	.200
Fermin, Felix	.143	7	1	0	2	0	0	.143	.143
Gaetti, Gary	.400	5	2	1	2	0	2	.333	1.000
Hale, Chip*	.600	5	3	0	2	0	0	.600	.800
Henderson, R	.000	8	0	0	0	1	1	.111	.000
Hill, G	.333	6	2	0	2	2	2	.444	.333
Huskey, Butch	.600	5	3	0	0	0	0	.600	1.200
Javier, Stan#	.429	7	3	0	0	0	1	.429	.571
Jefferson, R*	.200	5	1	0	1	0	0	.333	.200
Kirby, Wayne*	.167	6	1	0	2	4	4	.500	.167
Knoblauch, C	.000	4	0	0	1	0	0	.200	.000
Leyritz, Jim	.167	6	1	0	0	0	3	.167	.167
Lofton, Kenny*	.250	8	2	0	0	1	2	.333	.375
Martinez, T*	.200	5	1	0	1	0	1	.200	.200
McRae, Brian#	.250	4	1	0	2	3	0	.571	.250
Molitor, Paul	.400	5	2	0	0	1	0	.500	.400
Newfield, M	.400	5	2	0	0	0	0	.400	.600
Ochoa, Alex	.400	5	2	1	1	0	0	.400	1.000
Olerud, John*	.400	5	2	0	1	1	1	.500	.400
Palmer, Dean	.200	5	1	1	1	0	2	.200	.800
Polonia, Luis*	.333	6	2	0	1	0	1	.333	.333
Ramirez, M	.500	4	2	2	2	1	2	.600	2.000
Reboulet, J	.000	5	0	0	0	0	2	.400	.000
Rodriguez, I	.200	5	1	0	0	0	3	.200	.200
Salmon, Tim	.375	8	3	0	1	0	1	.375	.500
Smith, Dwight*	.000	5	0	0	0	1	0	.000	.000
Snow, J.T.#	.500	4	2	0	1	1	1	.600	.500
Sorrento, P*	.500	4	2	1	3	1	2	.600	1.500
Stanley, Mike	.400	5	2	0	1	0	2	.400	.400
Tartabull, D	.333	6	2	0	0	1	1	.429	.333
Thome, Jim*	.143	7	1	0	0	0	5	.143	.143
Valle, Dave	.400	5	2	0	0	0	0	.400	.400
Vizquel, Omar#	.200	10	2	0	1	0	0	.200	.200
White, Devon#	.200	5	1	0	1	0	2	.200	.200
Williams, Ber#	.333	6	2	0	1	1	1	.429	.333

A.J. Sager, Tigers — RHP

Batter	Avg	AB	H	HR	BI	BB	SO	OBP	Slg
Abbott, Kurt	.600	5	3	0	2	0	0	.600	.800
Belle, Albert	.400	5	2	1	4	0	1	.400	1.000
Blauser, Jeff	.667	6	4	0	1	0	0	.667	.667
Brumfield, J	.000	5	0	0	0	0	1	.000	.000
Canseco, Jose	.000	4	0	0	0	1	1	.200	.000
Carter, Joe	.167	6	1	0	0	1	1	.286	.167
Cirillo, Jeff	.625	8	5	0	2	0	1	.625	1.000
Cora, Joey#	.500	6	3	0	2	0	1	.500	.500
Delgado, C*	.200	5	1	0	0	3	2	.500	.200
Duncan, M	.200	5	1	0	0	0	2	.200	.400
Fielder, C	.200	5	1	1	3	0	1	.200	.800
Girardi, Joe	.200	5	1	0	0	0	1	.333	.200
Gonzalez, A	.143	7	1	0	0	0	1	.143	.286
Green, Shawn*	.333	6	2	0	0	1	0	.429	.500
Jaha, John	.333	6	2	0	0	0	1	.333	.500
Jeter, Derek	.200	5	1	0	0	0	1	.200	.200
Kelly, R	.333	6	2	0	0	0	1	.333	.333
Kent, Jeff	.400	5	2	0	0	1	2	.500	.400
Lemke, Mark#	.600	5	3	0	0	0	0	.600	.600
Lofton, Kenny*	.200	5	1	0	0	0	0	.200	.200
Nilsson, Dave*	.250	4	1	0	1	2	0	.500	.250
Olerud, John*	.000	3	0	0	0	3	1	.500	.000
Pendleton, T#	.250	4	1	0	1	1	1	.400	.500
Perez, Tomas#	.143	7	1	0	0	0	1	.143	.143
Rodriguez, Al	.600	5	3	0	0	0	0	.600	.600
Sprague, Ed	.250	8	2	0	2	0	2	.250	.375
Thome, Jim*	.500	4	2	1	1	1	1	.600	1.250
Valentin, Jse*	.200	5	1	0	0	0	0	.200	.200
Vina, F*	.333	6	2	0	0	1	0	.429	.333
Vizcaino, J#	.167	6	1	0	0	0	2	.167	.167
Vizquel, Omar*	.600	5	3	0	0	0	1	.600	.600
Williams, Ber#	.600	5	3	0	0	0	0	.600	.600

Roger Salkeld, Reds — RHP

Batter	Avg	AB	H	HR	BI	BB	SO	OBP	Slg
Alou, Moises	.000	7	0	0	0	0	1	.000	.000
Anderson, Brd*	.200	10	2	1	3	0	2	.200	.700
Aurilia, Rich	.500	6	3	0	1	2	1	.625	.500
Baines, H*	.400	5	2	0	0	1	0	.500	.400
Benard, M*	.222	9	2	0	0	1	2	.300	.222
Bonds, Barry*	.222	9	2	1	1	0	1	.222	.556
Canseco, Jose	.000	4	0	0	0	1	2	.200	.000
Coleman, V#	.250	8	2	0	0	0	0	.250	.250
Cora, Joey#	.500	4	2	0	2	2	1	.571	.750
Franco, Julio	.500	4	2	0	2	2	1	.667	.750
Gaetti, Gary	.300	10	3	0	1	0	3	.364	.300
Gagne, Greg	.375	8	3	0	1	1	2	.444	.500
Gallego, Mike	.250	4	1	0	0	2	0	.500	.250
Gant, Ron	.000	4	0	0	0	2	2	.333	.000
Gilkey, B	.250	4	1	1	3	1	1	.400	1.000
Gomez, Leo	.000	7	0	0	0	1	3	.125	.000
Gonzalez, J	.500	5	3	0	1	0	0	.600	.800
Grebeck, C	.000	7	0	0	0	0	0	.000	.000
Greer, Rusty*	.750	4	3	0	2	1	0	.800	1.000
Grudzielanek	.500	6	3	0	0	0	0	.500	.833
Guillen, O*	.500	4	2	0	0	1	0	.500	.500
Hamelin, Bob*	.400	5	2	1	2	1	1	.500	1.200
Hill, G	.000	4	0	0	0	2	2	.333	.000
Hoiles, Chris	.250	4	1	0	1	3	1	.571	.250
Hollandsworth*	.200	5	1	1	1	0	0	.200	.400
Hulse, David*	.500	6	3	0	0	0	0	.500	.500
Hundley, Todd*	.500	5	1	1	2	0	2	.200	.800
Huskey, Butch	.000	4	0	0	0	1	2	.200	.000
Javier, Stan#	.000	5	0	0	0	0	3	.000	.000
Johnson, L*	.333	9	3	0	1	1	0	.455	.333
Jordan, Brian	.400	5	2	0	2	0	1	.400	.400
Joyner, Wally*	.750	4	3	0	1	3	1	.857	1.500
Lampkin, Tom*	.200	5	1	0	0	0	1	.200	.400
Lankford, Ray*	.400	5	2	0	0	0	0	.400	.600
Lansing, Mike	.500	6	3	1	4	1	0	.571	1.167
Lieberthal, M	.250	4	1	0	1	1	1	.400	.250
Mabry, John*	.000	3	0	0	0	2	0	.400	.000
Mayne, Brent*	.500	2	1	0	0	3	0	.800	1.000
McLemore, M#	.286	7	2	0	0	1	0	.375	.286
McRae, Brian#	.000	6	0	0	0	4	2	.400	.000
Palmeiro, R*	1.000	4	4	2	2	1	0	1.000	2.750
Pendleton, T#	.000	5	0	0	0	1	0	.000	.000
Piazza, Mike	.667	3	2	0	1	2	1	.800	.667
Polonia, Luis*	.167	6	1	0	0	0	0	.167	.167
Raines, Tim#	.250	8	2	0	0	2	1	.400	.500
Ripken, Cal	.400	5	2	0	1	1	1	.429	.400
Rodriguez, H*	.200	5	1	0	0	1	0	.333	.400
Rodriguez, I	.500	4	2	0	1	1	0	.600	.500
Thomas, Frank	.400	5	2	1	1	1	2	.500	1.000
Ventura, R*	.625	8	5	2	5	0	0	.625	1.500
Vizcaino, J#	.800	5	4	0	2	1	0	.833	.800
White, Devon#	.400	5	2	0	1	0	0	.400	.600
Wilkins, Rick*	.333	6	2	1	3	1	1	.429	1.000
Young, Eric	.250	4	1	0	0	1	0	.400	.250
Zeile, Todd	.333	3	1	0	1	3	1	.667	.333

Scott Sanders, Padres — RHP

Batter	Avg	AB	H	HR	BI	BB	SO	OBP	Slg
Abbott, Kurt	.250	4	1	0	0	0	2	.400	.250
Alfonzo, E	.000	7	0	0	0	0	2	.000	.000
Alicea, Luis#	.250	4	1	0	0	1	0	.400	.750
Alou, Moises	.235	17	4	0	2	0	1	.235	.235
Andrews, S	.143	7	1	1	2	1	4	.250	.571
Bagwell, Jeff	.385	13	5	0	2	2	2	.438	.538
Barberie, B#	.571	7	4	0	4	1	0	.667	.857
Bell, Derek	.143	7	1	0	1	1	4	.333	.143
Bell, Jay	.400	15	6	1	2	1	3	.438	.600
Benard, M*	.143	7	1	0	0	0	1	.143	.143
Benjamin, M	.250	4	1	0	1	0	2	.400	.500
Berry, Sean	.273	11	3	0	1	0	1	.273	.364
Bichette, D	.200	15	3	0	1	2	4	.294	.267
Biggio, Craig	.125	16	2	0	1	3	4	.250	.188
Blauser, Jeff	.250	4	1	0	0	1	0	.500	.250
Bonds, Barry*	.400	15	6	3	5	1	4	.438	1.067
Bonilla, B#	.100	10	1	0	1	2	1	.250	.100
Boone, Bret	.100	10	1	0	0	0	5	.100	.100
Branson, Jeff*	.273	11	3	0	0	1	2	.333	.364
Brogna, Rico*	.300	10	3	1	2	3	3	.417	.800
Burks, Ellis	.167	6	1	1	2	1	0	.286	.667
Butler, Brett*	.143	7	1	0	2	0	0	.143	.143
Caminiti, Ken#	.333	6	2	1	2	2	2	.500	.833
Carr, Chuck	.444	9	4	0	0	0	1	.444	.444
Carreon, Mark	.500	6	3	1	4	1	2	.571	1.333
Castilla, V	.200	15	3	0	1	0	3	.200	.200
Cedeno, A	.273	11	3	0	0	1	3	.333	.364
Clark, Dave*	.222	9	2	1	1	1	2	.300	.556
Clayton, R	.125	8	1	0	0	1	2	.222	.125
Conine, Jeff	.188	16	3	0	0	0	7	.188	.188
Cordero, Wil	.167	12	2	0	0	0	3	.167	.167
DeShields, D*	.400	5	2	0	2	2	0	.500	.400
Dunston, S	.143	7	1	1	0	2	0	.143	.571
Eisenreich, J*	.200	5	1	0	1	1	1	.286	.400
Finley, Steve*	.286	7	2	0	0	2	1	.444	.286
Fletcher, D*	.300	10	3	0	0	2	1	.417	.300
Floyd, Cliff*	.222	9	2	0	1	1	1	.300	.222
Frazier, Lou#	.571	7	4	0	0	0	0	.571	.857
Gagne, Greg	.400	5	2	0	0	1	3	.500	.400
Galarraga, A	.364	11	4	1	4	2	3	.500	.818
Gant, Ron	.250	4	1	0	2	0	1	.200	.250
Garcia, C	.273	11	3	0	0	0	4	.333	.273
Gilkey, B	.333	9	3	2	5	1	2	.364	1.000
Gonzalez, L*	.000	11	0	0	0	1	3	.083	.000
Grace, Mark*	.250	8	2	0	2	1	1	.333	.500
Grissom, M	.083	12	1	0	1	0	4	.083	.083
Grudzielanek	.000	10	0	0	0	0	5	.000	.000
Harris, Lenny*	.000	5	0	0	0	0	0	.000	.000
Hayes, C	.300	10	3	0	1	2	3	.417	.300
Hernandez, Jo	.167	6	1	0	0	0	3	.167	.167
Hill, G	.154	13	2	0	0	0	8	.154	.154
Hollandsworth*	.143	7	1	0	0	0	4	.143	.143
Howard, T*	.364	11	4	0	0	0	0	.364	.455
Hundley, Todd#	.111	9	1	0	2	2	5	.273	.111
Hunter, Brian	.400	5	2	1	3	0	0	.333	1.200
Jefferies, G#	.500	14	7	1	3	0	2	.500	.857
Johnson, Mark*	.167	6	1	0	0	2	1	.375	.333
Jordan, Brian	.182	11	2	0	0	0	5	.182	.182
Jordan, Kevin	.400	5	2	0	0	0	0	.400	.600
Justice, Dave*	.500	6	3	0	1	1	0	.571	.500
Karros, Eric	.500	8	4	1	1	1	1	.556	.875
Kendall, J	.500	6	3	0	0	0	0	.500	.500
Kent, Jeff	.083	12	1	0	0	0	4	.083	.083
King, Jeff	.250	12	3	1	3	1	2	.308	.583
Kingery, Mike*	.364	11	4	1	3	3	2	.467	.727
Kirby, Wayne	.500	4	2	0	0	2	1	.667	.750
Lankford, Ray*	.300	10	3	1	1	1	2	.364	.700
Lansing, Mike	.071	14	1	0	0	1	3	.133	.071
Larkin, Barry	.273	11	3	1	3	3	3	.400	.545
Lewis, Darren	.000	9	0	0	0	0	2	.000	.000
Liriano, N#	.286	7	2	0	0	1	1	.375	.286
Manwaring, K	.333	9	3	0	0	0	1	.333	.333
Martin, Al*	.333	15	5	2	2	2	6	.412	.400
May, Derrick*	.333	12	4	0	2	0	1	.333	.333
McGriff, Fred*	.200	5	1	1	3	2	2	.429	.800
McMillon, B*	1.000	1	1	0	0	4	0	1.000	1.000
McRae, Brian#	1.000	5	5	0	0	0	0	1.000	1.000
Merced, O*	.300	10	3	0	5	4	0	.467	.500
Miller, Orl	.000	6	0	0	0	0	0	.000	.000
Mitchell, K	.200	5	1	0	0	1	0	.333	.200
Mondesi, Raul	.250	8	2	0	0	3	0	.250	.375
Morandini, M*	.182	11	2	0	0	1	1	.250	.182
Morris, Hal*	.333	15	5	1	3	0	3	.333	.333
Mouton, James	.125	8	1	0	0	0	3	.125	.125
Orsulak, Joe*	.182	11	2	0	0	1	0	.182	.273
Otero, Ricky#	.286	7	2	0	0	1	0	.375	.571
Owens, J	.200	5	1	0	0	0	2	.200	.200
Pagnozzi, Tom	.250	8	2	1	2	0	4	.250	.625
Pendleton, T#	.182	11	2	1	2	0	2	.167	.455
Piazza, Mike	.250	8	2	0	2	1	5	.333	.250

Scott Sanders, Padres — RHP

Batter	Avg	AB	H	HR	BI	BB	SO	OBP	Slg
Renteria, E	.000	4	0	0	0	2	0	.333	.000
Rodriguez, H*	.200	10	2	1	1	0	5	.200	.500
Rolen, Scott	.333	6	2	0	0	0	2	.333	.500
Sanchez, Rey	.364	11	4	0	0	0	4	.364	.364
Sanders, R	.250	12	3	0	2	1	5	.308	.333
Santiago, B	.154	13	2	0	2	0	2	.154	.154
Segui, David#	.100	10	1	0	0	1	2	.182	.000
Servais, A	.333	6	2	1	1	0	2	.333	.833
Sheffield, G	.200	10	2	0	0	1	1	.273	.400
Smith, Ozzie*	.333	6	2	0	3	3	0	.556	.500
Sosa, Sammy	.375	8	3	1	2	1	1	.444	.750
Stocker, K#	.200	10	2	0	0	1	4	.273	.200
Tarasco, Tony*	.000	5	0	0	0	1	3	.167	.000
Taubensee, E*	.125	16	2	0	1	2	3	.222	.125
Thompson, Mil*	.400	10	4	0	2	1	2	.455	.500
Thompson, Rob	.111	9	1	0	0	0	3	.111	.111
Thompson, Ry	.167	6	1	1	1	0	3	.167	.667
Veras, Q#	.286	7	2	0	0	1	3	.375	.286
Vizcaino, J#	.400	10	4	0	0	0	2	.400	.400
Walker, Larry*	.400	10	4	2	4	1	2	.455	1.100
Wallach, Tim	.200	5	1	0	1	0	1	.200	.200
Weiss, Walt#	.300	10	3	0	0	3	1	.462	.500
White, Devon#	.286	7	2	0	2	0	1	.286	.429
White, R	.167	6	1	0	0	1	2	.286	.167
Whiten, Mark#	.200	5	1	0	0	1	2	.333	.200
Wilkins, Rick*	.133	15	2	0	0	1	2	.188	.200
Williams, Ma	.091	11	1	0	1	0	4	.091	.091
Young, Eric	.125	16	2	0	1	1	2	.176	.125
Zeile, Todd	.143	14	2	1	2	4	5	.333	.357

Scott Sanderson, Angels — RHP

Batter	Avg	AB	H	HR	BI	BB	SO	OBP	Slg
Gates, Brent#	.400	5	2	0	1	0	0	.333	.600
Gil, Benji	.200	5	1	0	0	0	1	.200	.200
Gomez, Leo	.200	10	2	0	0	1	1	.273	.300
Gonzales, R	.333	12	4	0	0	0	3	.333	.333
Gonzalez, J	.429	14	6	0	5	1	2	.467	.643
Grace, Mark*	1.000	4	4	0	1	1	0	1.000	1.000
Greenwell, M*	.200	40	8	3	4	2	1	.238	.500
Griffey Jr, K*	.342	38	13	2	6	2	4	.366	.579
Guillen, O*	.429	14	6	0	0	0	0	.429	.500
Gwynn, Tony*	.379	29	11	0	4	2	1	.419	.414
Hale, Chip*	.400	5	2	0	0	0	1	.500	.600
Hall, Mel*	.222	9	2	0	0	0	1	.222	.444
Hamelin, Bob*	.200	5	1	0	0	0	0	.200	.400
Hamilton, D*	.333	12	4	0	3	3	3	.467	.583
Hayes, C	.167	6	1	0	2	0	1	.167	.333
Henderson, R	.400	10	4	1	2	3	2	.538	.700
Hoiles, Chris	.143	7	1	0	0	1	1	.250	.143
Howard, T*	.167	6	1	1	1	0	2	.167	.667
Howell, Jack*	.167	6	1	0	0	0	2	.167	.167
Hudler, Rex	.000	5	0	0	0	0	2	.000	.000
Huson, Jeff*	.625	8	5	0	0	0	1	.625	.625
Incaviglia, P	.286	7	2	1	2	0	0	.286	.714
James, Dion*	.333	24	8	1	3	2	1	.407	.542
Javier, Stan*	.250	4	1	0	0	2	1	.500	.250
Jefferies, G#	.333	12	4	0	0	0	0	.333	.417
Jefferson, R*	.222	18	4	0	0	5	5	.222	.222
Johnson, L*	.192	26	5	0	1	0	1	.192	.269
Jordan, Ricky	.429	7	3	3	5	0	1	.429	1.714
Joyner, Wally*	.333	21	7	1	6	2	2	.391	.476
Karkovice, R	.143	7	1	0	0	0	0	.143	.143
Kelly, Pat	.500	8	4	0	1	0	0	.500	.875
Kelly, R	.250	8	2	0	1	0	2	.222	.375
King, Jeff	.286	7	2	1	1	0	0	.286	.857
Kirby, Wayne*	.571	7	4	1	3	1	0	.625	1.000
Knoblauch, C	.478	23	11	0	4	0	1	.500	.565
Larkin, Barry	.400	10	4	0	0	0	1	.400	.400
Leius, Scott	.200	5	1	1	2	0	0	.200	.800
Lewis, Mark	.000	11	0	0	0	0	6	.000	.000
Listach, Pat#	.375	8	3	0	0	3	0	.545	.375
Livingstone*	.231	13	3	0	0	0	5	.231	.308
Lofton, Kenny*	.350	20	7	1	2	0	0	.350	.600
Macfarlane, M	.300	10	3	0	0	0	2	.300	.400
Magadan, Dave*	.571	7	4	0	0	1	0	.625	.714
Martinez, Da*	.200	10	2	0	0	0	3	.200	.200
Martinez, E	.241	29	7	1	3	3	5	.313	.448
Martinez, T*	.143	14	2	0	1	0	1	.133	.143
May, Derrick*	.200	5	1	0	0	0	1	.200	.200
Mayne, Brent*	.385	13	5	0	1	1	3	.429	.538
McGee, Willie*	.364	33	12	1	5	1	1	.371	.576
McGriff, Fred*	.167	6	1	1	1	0	2	.167	.667
McGwire, Mark	.417	12	5	0	2	1	1	.533	.750
McLemore, M#	.143	7	1	0	0	0	1	.143	.286
McRae, Brian*	.235	17	4	0	1	0	2	.316	.235
Meares, Pat	.556	9	5	0	0	1	0	.556	.667
Mieske, Matt	.400	5	2	0	0	0	3	.400	.600
Mitchell, K	.316	19	6	1	4	2	7	.381	.526
Molitor, Paul	.240	25	6	0	0	2	4	.296	.360
Munoz, Pedro	.125	8	1	0	0	0	0	.125	.125
Murray, Eddie*	.308	13	4	1	3	1	3	.357	.692
Myers, Greg*	.222	9	2	1	3	0	1	.222	.556
Naehring, Tim	.182	11	2	0	1	2	4	.308	.273
Nilsson, Dave*	.000	5	0	0	0	1	0	.167	.000
Nixon, Otis#	.200	10	2	0	0	1	2	.273	.200
O'Neill, Paul*	.308	13	4	1	1	0	2	.308	.538
Olerud, John*	.207	29	6	1	4	2	7	.250	.310
Orsulak, Joe*	.276	29	8	3	6	2	2	.323	.655
Palmeiro, R*	.269	26	7	2	8	2	2	.310	.654
Palmer, Dean	.182	11	2	1	2	0	3	.182	.545
Parent, Mark	.250	4	1	1	1	1	2	.400	1.000
Pena, Tony	.254	59	15	0	0	1	11	.267	.356
Pendleton, T#	.200	30	6	2	5	2	4	.242	.400
Phillips, T#	.314	35	11	2	3	8	8	.442	.543
Plantier, P*	.294	17	5	3	4	2	3	.368	.941
Polonia, Luis*	.400	30	12	0	3	0	4	.387	.633
Raines, Tim#	.409	22	9	0	2	4	3	.481	.455
Ramirez, M	.000	4	0	0	0	1	2	.200	.000
Reed, Jody	.455	33	15	2	3	2	1	.486	.727
Ripken, Billy	.444	9	4	0	0	0	0	.444	.444
Ripken, Cal	.208	24	5	1	2	2	2	.269	.375
Roberts, Bip#	.200	5	1	0	0	1	4	.333	.200
Rodriguez, I	.333	12	4	0	1	0	4	.333	.583
Salmon, Tim	.273	11	3	2	3	0	4	.273	.818
Samuel, Juan	.250	28	7	1	4	0	4	.250	.464
Sandberg, R	.200	5	1	0	0	0	0	.200	.200
Santiago, B	.333	9	3	0	1	0	3	.300	.333
Schofield, D	.222	9	2	0	1	0	2	.222	.333
Segui, David#	.000	5	0	0	0	0	1	.000	.000
Seitzer, K	.185	27	5	0	5	0	4	.185	.333
Sheffield, G	.000	7	0	0	1	1	0	.000	.000
Shumpert, T	.357	14	5	0	0	0	4	.357	.429
Sierra, Ruben#	.391	23	9	0	5	1	4	.417	.478

Scott Sanderson, Angels — RHP

Batter	Avg	AB	H	HR	BI	BB	SO	OBP	Slg
Aldrete, Mike*	.333	18	6	1	1	1	2	.368	.611
Alomar, R	.522	23	12	1	5	3	3	.556	.826
Alomar Jr, S	.350	20	7	1	2	0	3	.350	.600
Amaral, Rich	.000	6	0	0	0	0	1	.000	.000
Anderson, Brd*	.400	20	8	0	4	4	0	.500	.650
Anthony, Eric*	.400	5	2	1	1	1	2	.500	1.200
Baerga, C#	.318	22	7	1	2	2	5	.375	.545
Baines, H*	.333	18	6	1	4	3	3	.429	.500
Barberie, B#	.250	8	2	0	1	0	0	.250	.250
Bell, Jay	.000	8	0	0	0	0	4	.000	.000
Belle, Albert	.350	20	7	3	9	2	1	.391	.900
Belliard, R	.250	12	3	0	3	1	3	.308	.417
Bichette, D	.389	18	7	0	2	0	1	.389	.389
Biggio, Craig	.125	8	1	0	2	0	2	.125	.125
Blowers, Mike	.143	7	1	0	0	0	2	.143	.286
Boggs, Wade*	.188	32	6	0	1	1	2	.206	.281
Bonds, Barry*	.348	23	8	2	4	3	3	.423	.739
Bonilla, B#	.444	18	8	1	4	4	1	.545	.611
Borders, Pat	.438	16	7	1	1	0	2	.438	.750
Bordick, Mike	.111	9	1	0	0	1	1	.200	.111
Buhner, Jay	.176	17	3	3	3	0	4	.176	.706
Burks, Ellis	.200	20	4	1	1	1	3	.238	.450
Butler, Brett*	.400	5	2	0	0	0	0	.400	.400
Caminiti, Ken#	.250	8	2	1	2	0	2	.250	.750
Candaele, C#	.200	5	1	0	1	1	0	.333	.200
Cangelosi, J#	.500	6	3	0	2	2	0	.625	.833
Canseco, Jose	.313	16	5	1	2	0	3	.353	.625
Carr, Chuck	.333	6	2	1	1	0	0	.333	.833
Carreon, Mark	.083	12	1	1	2	0	4	.083	.083
Carter, Joe	.423	26	11	2	10	1	1	.414	.769
Clark, Will*	.294	17	5	0	1	1	1	.333	.471
Cole, Alex*	.364	11	4	0	1	1	1	.417	.364
Coleman, V#	.308	39	12	0	1	3	6	.357	.436
Conine, Jeff	.333	6	2	0	0	0	2	.333	.333
Cora, Joey*	.333	6	2	0	0	1	1	.429	.500
Curtis, Chad	.250	12	3	1	2	0	1	.250	.500
Cuyler, Milt*	.250	16	4	0	0	1	4	.294	.313
Daulton, D*	.286	7	2	0	2	0	3	.286	.429
Davis, Chili#	.282	39	11	4	5	4	9	.349	.692
Davis, Eric	.176	17	3	1	4	3	5	.300	.412
Dawson, Andre	.261	23	6	1	1	1	3	.292	.522
Deer, Rob	.056	18	1	0	0	2	8	.150	.056
Devereaux, M	.250	12	3	0	2	0	6	.231	.417
DiSarcina, G	.273	11	3	0	1	1	0	.333	.364
Duncan, M	.200	15	3	0	0	0	7	.200	.267
Dykstra, L*	.300	30	9	3	4	1	2	.323	.733
Easley, D	.111	9	1	0	1	0	0	.111	.111
Eisenreich, J*	.286	14	4	1	3	3	1	.412	.643
Espinoza, A	.467	15	7	0	2	0	0	.467	.533
Fermin, Felix	.240	25	6	0	1	0	1	.240	.320
Fielder, C	.220	41	9	4	12	1	7	.238	.585
Finley, Steve*	.200	5	1	0	0	2	0	.429	.200
Flaherty, J	.000	5	0	0	0	0	3	.000	.000
Franco, Julio	.476	21	10	2	5	3	0	.542	.810
Fryman, T	.216	37	8	1	2	0	8	.216	.351
Gaetti, Gary	.250	24	6	0	1	0	3	.250	.292
Gagne, Greg	.278	18	5	0	0	0	4	.278	.333
Galarraga, A	.188	16	3	0	1	2	5	.278	.188
Gallego, Mike	.375	8	3	1	1	0	0	.375	.750

Scott Sanderson, Angels — RHP

Batter	Avg	AB	H	HR	BI	BB	SO	OBP	Slg
Smith, Dwight*	.143	7	1	1	1	2	2	.333	.571
Smith, Ozzie#	.297	37	11	0	1	1	3	.316	.405
Sojo, Luis	.316	19	6	0	1	0	1	.316	.474
Sorrento, P*	.263	19	5	0	1	0	1	.263	.263
Sosa, Sammy	.412	17	7	0	2	0	5	.421	.529
Spiers, Bill*	.200	10	2	0	0	1	0	.273	.200
Sprague, Ed	.231	13	3	1	1	0	1	.231	.462
Stanley, Mike	.200	5	1	0	1	0	0	.200	.400
Steinbach, T	.333	9	3	1	4	0	0	.300	.889
Stevens, Lee*	.462	13	6	0	1	1	4	.500	.538
Stillwell, K#	.214	14	3	0	0	2	2	.313	.286
Strange, Doug#	.500	4	2	0	1	0	0	.600	.500
Strawberry, D*	.143	21	3	0	1	4	4	.280	.190
Surhoff, B.J.*	.400	15	6	1	3	0	2	.375	.733
Tartabull, D	.250	24	6	2	6	0	5	.250	.542
Tettleton, M#	.192	26	5	1	2	7	5	.364	.308
Thomas, Frank	.313	16	5	3	4	0	2	.389	.875
Thome, Jim*	.556	9	5	3	5	0	0	.556	1.667
Thompson, Mil*	.200	10	2	0	1	1	2	.273	.200
Thompson, Rob	.143	14	2	0	1	1	4	.250	.214
Trammell, A	.111	18	2	0	0	1	0	.158	.167
Valentin, Jhn	.333	18	6	0	2	1	2	.350	.500
Valentin, Jse#	.250	4	1	0	0	1	0	.400	.500
Valle, Dave	.250	20	5	0	2	1	4	.286	.300
Vaughn, Greg	.385	13	5	0	3	0	4	.385	.769
Vaughn, Mo*	.192	26	5	1	3	2	3	.250	.346
Velarde, R	.250	4	1	0	0	1	2	.400	.250
Ventura, R*	.400	20	8	2	8	3	3	.478	.750
Vizquel, Omar#	.241	29	7	0	2	2	2	.290	.241
Walbeck, Matt#	.800	5	4	1	2	0	0	.800	1.800
Wallach, Tim	.313	16	5	0	2	3	1	.421	.500
Weiss, Walt#	.357	14	5	0	1	0	1	.357	.429
White, Devon#	.353	34	12	0	3	1	3	.371	.441
Whiten, Mark#	.222	9	2	2	4	0	0	.222	.889
Wilkins, Rick*	.200	5	1	1	1	0	2	.200	.800
Williams, Ber#	.000	7	0	0	0	0	2	.000	.000
Wilson, Dan	.125	8	1	0	0	0	1	.125	.125

Bob Scanlan, Royals — RHP

Batter	Avg	AB	H	HR	BI	BB	SO	OBP	Slg
Alicea, Luis#	.333	3	1	0	1	0	1	.500	.333
Alomar, R#	.222	9	2	0	0	1	0	.300	.333
Alomar Jr, S	.600	5	3	1	1	0	0	.600	1.200
Alou, Moises	.500	6	3	0	2	2	2	.625	.667
Anderson, Brd*	.182	11	2	0	2	2	3	.357	.273
Baerga, C#	.286	7	2	0	1	0	0	.286	.286
Bagwell, Jeff	.333	9	3	0	1	1	1	.400	.444
Baines, H*	.400	10	4	1	4	2	0	.500	.700
Barberie, B#	.182	11	2	0	2	4	2	.400	.273
Becker, Rich*	.455	11	5	0	3	1	1	.462	.636
Bell, Jay	.000	7	0	0	0	1	1	.125	.000
Belle, Albert	.600	10	6	1	4	0	0	.600	1.000
Belliard, R	.000	5	0	0	0	0	1	.000	.000
Biggio, Craig	.400	5	2	0	0	2	0	.571	.600
Blauser, Jeff	.286	7	2	0	0	1	1	.375	.286
Boggs, Wade*	.600	5	3	0	2	0	0	.600	.800
Bonilla, B#	.333	6	2	0	1	0	0	.333	.500
Butler, Brett*	.600	5	3	0	1	5	0	.800	1.000
Caminiti, Ken#	.200	5	1	0	1	0	1	.200	.200
Carter, Joe	.333	6	2	0	1	0	0	.333	.500
Cianfrocco, A	.333	6	2	0	0	1	2	.429	.333
Clark, Will*	.143	14	2	0	1	1	1	.200	.143
Clayton, R	.111	9	1	0	1	0	1	.111	.111
Cole, Alex*	.375	8	3	0	1	1	3	.444	.500
Coleman, V#	.273	11	3	0	2	0	1	.250	.455
Conine, Jeff	.250	4	1	0	1	1	0	.400	.250
Cordova, M	.333	6	2	0	1	2	0	.444	.333
Curtis, Chad	.200	5	1	0	0	0	1	.200	.400
Daulton, D*	.500	6	3	0	0	0	0	.500	.667
Davis, Eric	.250	4	1	0	0	3	1	.571	.250
Dawson, Andre	.400	5	2	0	0	0	1	.400	.600
Decker, Steve	.200	5	1	0	1	0	0	.333	.200
DeShields, D*	.222	9	2	0	2	4	1	.429	.222
Devereaux, M	.250	4	1	0	0	1	0	.400	.250
Duncan, M	.600	5	3	0	0	0	0	.600	1.000
Durham, Ray#	.333	3	1	0	0	2	0	.600	.333
Eisenreich, J*	.000	4	0	0	0	1	1	.200	.000
Elster, Kevin	.167	6	1	0	1	1	1	.286	.167
Espinoza, A	.250	4	1	0	0	0	1	.400	.250
Fielder, C	.333	6	2	0	0	1	0	.429	.333
Finley, Steve*	.000	4	0	0	0	2	1	.333	.000
Fletcher, D*	.286	7	2	0	0	0	0	.286	.286
Franco, Julio	.200	5	1	0	3	0	1	.200	.200
Frye, Jeff	.000	5	0	0	0	1	0	.167	.000
Fryman, T	.429	7	3	0	2	0	1	.429	.571
Gaetti, Gary	.429	7	3	1	3	0	2	.429	.857
Gagne, Greg	.200	10	2	0	0	0	2	.200	.300
Galarraga, A	.429	14	6	0	3	0	0	.429	.500
Gallego, Mike	.000	5	0	0	1	0	0	.000	.000
Gant, Ron	.267	15	4	1	4	0	3	.250	.467
Gil, Benji	.600	5	3	0	2	0	1	.600	.600

Bob Scanlan, Royals — RHP

Batter	Avg	AB	H	HR	BI	BB	SO	OBP	Slg
Gilkey, B	.500	6	3	1	1	0	0	.500	1.000
Gomez, Leo	.333	9	3	1	2	0	1	.400	.667
Gonzalez, L*	.400	5	2	0	2	0	0	.500	.800
Goodwin, Tom*	.333	6	2	0	0	1	0	.429	.333
Greenwell, M*	.222	9	2	0	2	1	1	.300	.222
Grissom, M	.348	23	8	0	7	0	2	.333	.609
Guillen, O*	.625	8	5	0	5	0	1	.625	1.125
Gwynn, Tony*	.200	5	1	0	1	0	0	.200	.200
Hale, Chip*	.000	6	0	0	1	0	2	.000	.000
Hamelin, Bob*	.167	6	1	1	2	0	0	.167	.667
Hammonds, J	.286	7	2	0	1	0	0	.286	.429
Harris, Lenny	.250	8	2	0	3	0	2	.250	.250
Hayes, C	.167	6	1	0	0	1	2	.286	.333
Hoiles, Chris	.375	8	3	0	0	4	1	.583	.500
Hollins, Dave#	.375	8	3	3	6	0	2	.444	1.500
Howard, Dave#	.400	5	2	0	0	1	0	.500	.400
Hundley, Todd#	.000	4	0	0	0	0	3	.000	.000
Javier, Stan#	.222	9	2	0	0	0	1	.222	.333
Jefferies, G#	.250	8	2	0	1	0	1	.250	.250
Jefferson, R*	.600	5	3	1	3	1	2	.667	1.200
Johnson, L*	.375	8	3	0	2	0	1	.375	.375
Joyner, Wally*	.500	6	3	0	0	1	1	.571	.667
Justice, Dave*	.571	7	4	0	2	2	2	.667	.571
Karros, Eric	.400	10	4	1	1	0	1	.400	.800
King, Jeff	.333	6	2	1	2	0	0	.333	.833
Knoblauch, C	.167	12	2	0	0	4	2	.412	.250
Lankford, Ray*	.167	6	1	0	2	0	0	.143	.500
Leius, Scott	.214	14	3	1	2	1	0	.267	.429
Lemke, Mark#	.600	5	3	0	1	0	0	.600	.600
Lewis, Darren	.000	7	0	0	0	1	0	.125	.000
Lofton, Kenny*	.571	7	4	0	1	2	1	.667	.857
Macfarlane, M	.143	7	1	0	0	2	0	.400	.143
Magadan, Dave*	.500	4	2	0	2	1	0	.600	.500
Manwaring, K	.143	7	1	0	0	2	1	.333	.143
Martinez, Da*	.429	14	6	0	4	1	1	.467	.786
Mayne, Brent*	.333	6	2	0	1	0	0	.333	.667
McGee, Willie#	.364	11	4	0	4	0	0	.364	.545
McLemore, M#	.273	11	3	0	2	2	1	.357	.364
McRae, Brian#	.286	7	2	0	0	0	1	.286	.286
Meares, Pat	.333	15	5	1	1	0	0	.333	.600
Merced, O*	.400	5	2	0	2	0	0	.400	.800
Molitor, Paul	.571	7	4	0	2	0	2	.571	.571
Morandini, M*	.250	8	2	0	0	0	2	.250	.250
Munoz, Pedro	.300	10	3	0	1	0	1	.300	.300
Murray, Eddie*	.353	17	6	0	0	0	1	.353	.412
Nixon, Otis#	.188	16	3	0	1	1	5	.235	.250
Nunnally, Jon*	.000	4	0	0	0	1	1	.200	.000
O'Neill, Paul*	.400	10	4	1	3	1	2	.455	.800
Offerman, J#	.000	3	0	0	1	1	1	.200	.000
Olerud, John*	.200	5	1	0	1	1	0	.333	.200
Oliver, Joe	.250	8	2	0	2	0	1	.250	.375
Pagnozzi, Tom	.100	10	1	0	0	0	1	.182	.100
Palmeiro, R*	.300	10	3	0	0	1	1	.364	.400
Pena, G#	.167	6	1	0	0	0	1	.167	.167
Pendleton, T#	.273	11	3	0	0	0	2	.385	.364
Piazza, Mike	.333	6	2	0	1	1	0	.429	.333
Polonia, Luis*	.571	7	4	0	0	0	0	.571	.571
Raines, Tim#	.429	7	3	0	0	1	2	.500	.571
Ramirez, M	.400	5	2	1	2	0	0	.400	1.200
Rebouiet, J	.625	8	5	0	1	0	0	.625	.625
Ripken, Cal	.200	10	2	1	2	1	0	.333	.500
Rodriguez, I	.556	9	5	0	1	0	0	.556	.667
Sabo, Chris	.250	12	3	0	1	1	2	.286	.333
Samuel, Juan	.333	9	3	0	0	2	0	.333	.333
Sanders, R	.000	3	0	0	0	2	2	.400	.000
Santiago, B	.222	9	2	0	1	0	1	.222	.333
Slaught, Don	.200	5	1	0	0	0	0	.200	.200
Smith, Ozzie#	.571	7	4	0	0	0	0	.571	.714
Sorrento, P*	.200	5	1	0	0	0	3	.200	.200
Sprague, Ed	.333	6	2	0	0	0	0	.333	.333
Stahoviak, S*	.250	8	2	0	0	1	1	.333	.250
Tartabull, D	.286	7	2	0	2	0	1	.286	.286
Tettleton, M#	.167	6	1	0	0	1	0	.286	.167
Thomas, Frank	.143	7	1	0	1	2	0	.300	.143
Thome, Jim*	.143	7	1	1	3	1	2	.250	.571
Thompson, Mil*	.125	8	1	0	1	2	1	.300	.125
Thompson, Rob	.333	12	4	0	0	0	1	.333	.333
Tucker, M*	.333	3	1	0	0	2	1	.600	.333
Valentin, Jhn	.250	8	2	1	1	1	0	.400	.750
VanderWal, J*	.125	8	1	0	1	0	0	.125	.125
Vaughn, Mo*	.500	8	4	2	4	1	2	.500	1.250
Ventura, R*	.222	9	2	0	0	1	2	.300	.222
Vizquel, Omar#	.250	4	1	0	0	1	1	.400	.250
Walbeck, Matt#	.100	10	1	0	1	2	2	.250	.100
Walker, Larry*	.250	12	3	0	1	4	1	.438	.417
Wallach, Tim	.125	15	3	0	1	0	3	.188	.267
Williams, Ma	.125	16	2	0	2	0	2	.125	.188
Zeile, Todd	.600	10	6	0	3	1	0	.636	.800

Curt Schilling, Phillies — RHP

Batter	Avg	AB	H	HR	BI	BB	SO	OBP	Slg
Abbott, Kurt	.462	13	6	2	3	1	1	.500	1.000
Alfonzo, E	.000	4	0	0	0	1	2	.200	.000
Alicea, Luis#	.357	14	5	0	5	0	3	.357	.643
Allensworth	.333	6	2	0	0	2	2	.500	.333
Alou, Moises	.308	26	8	0	3	2	3	.367	.423
Andrews, S	.000	4	0	0	0	1	4	.111	.000
Anthony, Eric*	.200	20	4	0	0	1	5	.238	.300
Arias, Alex	.300	10	3	0	0	0	2	.300	.300
Ausmus, Brad	.000	8	0	0	0	0	1	.000	.000
Baerga, C#	.200	5	1	0	1	0	0	.200	.200
Bagwell, Jeff	.205	39	8	0	3	3	9	.262	.231
Barberie, B#	.167	18	3	0	1	2	5	.250	.167
Bell, Derek	.048	21	1	0	1	2	4	.125	.048
Bell, Jay	.294	17	5	0	1	4	2	.429	.471
Belliard, R	.286	7	2	0	0	0	0	.286	.286
Berry, Sean	.357	14	5	1	2	0	2	.333	.643
Bichette, D	.214	14	3	1	2	1	4	.313	.500
Biggio, Craig	.237	38	9	0	2	3	7	.286	.289
Blauser, Jeff	.172	29	5	0	2	3	4	.250	.172
Blowers, Mike	.833	6	5	0	0	0	0	.833	1.167
Boggs, Wade*	.286	7	2	0	1	3	0	.500	.286
Bonds, Barry*	.214	28	6	1	4	8	4	.389	.464
Bonilla, B#	.150	20	3	1	3	1	4	.190	.300
Boone, Bret	.429	7	3	1	2	0	2	.375	.857
Branson, Jeff*	.333	18	6	0	1	0	4	.333	.389
Burks, Ellis	.313	16	5	2	5	2	3	.368	.688
Burnitz, J*	.333	9	3	1	1	0	3	.333	.778
Butler, Brett*	.286	14	4	0	0	6	3	.500	.286
Caminiti, Ken#	.304	23	7	2	3	0	6	.304	.652
Candaele, C#	.200	5	1	0	0	0	0	.200	.200
Cangelosi, J#	.000	7	0	0	0	1	1	.125	.000
Carr, Chuck	.333	15	5	0	0	2	1	.412	.400
Carreon, Mark	.125	8	1	0	1	0	3	.125	.125
Castilla, V	.077	13	1	0	0	0	3	.077	.077
Cedeno, A	.063	16	1	0	0	1	2	.118	.063
Cedeno, Roger#	.333	6	2	0	0	0	1	.333	.667
Cianfrocco, A	.300	10	3	1	1	0	3	.300	.600
Clark, Dave*	.500	8	4	0	2	1	0	.556	.625
Clark, Will*	.158	19	3	0	0	2	6	.238	.158
Clayton, R	.440	25	11	1	6	0	6	.440	.680
Colbrunn, G	.222	9	2	1	1	0	3	.222	.556
Cole, Alex*	.429	7	3	0	0	1	1	.500	.429
Coleman, V#	.273	11	3	0	0	1	2	.333	.273
Conine, Jeff	.250	20	5	1	3	2	2	.333	.350
Cordero, Wil	.333	15	5	0	2	0	5	.333	.467
Dascenzo, D#	.250	8	2	1	1	1	1	.333	.500
Davis, Eric	.308	13	4	1	4	1	5	.333	.538
Dawson, Andre	.111	9	1	0	0	0	2	.111	.111
Decker, Steve	.400	5	2	1	2	0	2	.333	1.000
DeShields, D*	.303	33	10	2	6	5	6	.395	.515
Dorsett, B	.333	6	2	0	1	0	1	.333	.333
Dunston, S	.143	14	2	0	0	1	1	.200	.214
Eusebio, Tony	.300	10	3	0	1	1	0	.364	.300
Finley, Steve*	.280	25	7	1	3	4	3	.367	.520
Fletcher, D*	.036	28	1	0	4	1	5	.067	.036
Floyd, Cliff*	.167	6	1	0	1	0	2	.167	.500
Gaetti, Gary	.000	5	0	0	0	0	2	.000	.000
Gagne, Greg	.143	7	1	0	2	0	4	.143	.286
Galarraga, A	.167	24	4	1	4	0	6	.259	.333
Gant, Ron	.200	25	5	0	1	2	4	.259	.320
Garcia, C	.333	9	3	1	2	0	1	.333	.667
Gilkey, B	.367	30	11	2	5	2	5	.406	.700
Girardi, Joe	.200	10	2	0	0	2	0	.333	.200
Gonzalez, L*	.167	36	6	1	5	3	9	.225	.250
Grace, Mark*	.214	28	6	0	2	6	1	.353	.250
Greene, W*	.375	8	3	1	1	1	3	.375	.875
Greenwell, M	.167	6	1	0	1	0	0	.286	.333
Grissom, M	.450	40	18	2	7	1	5	.463	.675
Grudzielanek	.273	11	3	0	0	1	3	.333	.273
Gwynn, Tony*	.400	25	10	1	3	0	1	.423	.640
Hansen, Dave*	.167	6	1	0	0	0	3	.167	.167
Harris, Lenny*	.176	17	3	0	3	1	2	.222	.176
Hayes, Charlie	.412	17	7	0	3	0	1	.412	.529
Henderson, R	.500	4	2	0	2	1	0	.600	.750
Hill, G	.133	15	2	0	1	2	6	.235	.133
Hollandsworth	.273	11	3	0	2	2	5	.385	.364
Houston, T*	.000	7	0	0	0	0	1	.000	.000
Howard, T*	.444	18	8	0	2	1	1	.474	.556
Hubbard, T	.000	5	0	0	0	1	3	.167	.000
Hundley, Todd*	.161	31	5	0	1	1	7	.188	.161
Hunter, Brian	.000	5	0	0	0	0	0	.000	.000
Hunter, Bri L	.300	10	3	0	1	1	2	.364	.400
Incaviglia, P	.444	9	4	0	2	1	1	.500	.556
Javier, Stan#	.500	6	3	0	0	1	0	.571	.833
Jefferies, G#	.667	9	6	1	5	0	0	.667	1.000
Johnson, Char	.444	9	4	1	1	2	5	.545	.778
Johnson, L*	.333	9	3	0	1	0	1	.300	.333
Johnson, Mark*	.000	7	0	0	0	0	1	.000	.000
Jones, C#	.250	8	2	0	1	2	4	.400	.250
Jordan, Brian	.455	11	5	0	3	1	2	.462	.455
Justice, Dave*	.360	25	9	3	11	6	5	.484	.800
Karros, Eric	.286	28	8	1	7	0	2	.286	.429
Kelly, R	.125	8	1	0	0	2	1	.300	.125
Kendall, J	.400	5	2	0	0	1	1	.500	.400
Kent, Jeff	.250	12	3	0	0	0	4	.250	.333
King, Jeff	.235	17	4	1	2	4	1	.364	.412
Kingery, Mike*	.500	6	3	0	0	1	1	.571	.833
Kirby, Wayne*	.600	5	3	0	1	0	1	.600	1.000
Klesko, Ryan*	.000	10	0	0	0	2	4	.167	.000
Lampkin, Tom*	.286	7	2	1	1	0	3	.286	.714
Lankford, Ray*	.300	30	9	3	6	5	7	.400	.700
Lansing, Mike	.320	25	8	0	3	1	5	.370	.440
Larkin, Barry	.208	24	5	0	0	4	3	.321	.208
Lemke, Mark#	.464	28	13	2	4	3	4	.516	.714
Lewis, Darren	.346	26	9	0	0	1	3	.370	.346
Liriano, N#	.200	5	1	0	1	0	1	.200	.600
Lopez, Javy	.167	6	1	0	0	0	1	.167	.167
Mabry, John*	.333	6	2	0	1	1	0	.429	.500
Magadan, Dave*	.333	21	7	0	0	4	4	.440	.476
Manwaring, K	.278	18	5	0	5	2	0	.350	.389
Martin, Al*	.000	12	0	0	0	0	3	.000	.000
Martinez, Da*	.294	17	5	0	2	0	2	.294	.412
May, Derrick*	.417	24	10	0	3	0	3	.417	.583
McGee, Willie#	.182	11	2	0	1	1	3	.250	.182
McGriff, Fred*	.233	30	7	2	6	5	6	.333	.500
McRae, Brian#	.200	15	3	1	1	0	4	.200	.467
Merced, O*	.235	17	4	1	2	1	0	.316	.529
Miller, Orl	.313	16	5	0	2	0	3	.313	.375
Mitchell, K	.111	9	1	0	1	2	1	.273	.222
Mondesi, Raul	.333	15	5	1	2	0	2	.333	.533
Morris, Hal*	.353	17	6	0	1	0	1	.353	.529
Murray, Eddie*	.077	26	2	0	0	2	6	.143	.077
Nieves, M#	.250	4	1	1	1	1	3	.400	1.000
Nixon, Otis*	.267	15	4	0	0	2	5	.353	.267
O'Brien, C	.429	7	3	0	4	2	1	.556	.714
O'Neill, Paul*	.111	9	1	0	0	1	1	.200	.111
Offerman, J#	.083	12	1	0	0	1	5	.154	.083
Oliver, Joe	.000	7	0	0	0	1	3	.125	.000
Ordonez, Rey	.000	5	0	0	0	0	1	.000	.000
Orsulak, Joe*	.435	23	10	1	2	1	4	.458	.609
Pagnozzi, Tom	.188	16	3	0	1	2	1	.278	.188
Pena, G#	.200	10	2	0	0	1	1	.273	.200
Pendleton, T#	.268	41	11	0	4	1	14	.286	.341
Piazza, Mike	.294	17	5	0	0	1	4	.333	.294
Plantier, P*	.571	7	4	2	5	0	1	.571	1.714
Prince, Tom	.000	3	0	0	1	0	0	.000	.000
Reed, Jeff*	.222	9	2	1	2	0	1	.222	.500
Reed, Jody	.214	14	3	0	0	1	1	.313	.286
Roberts, Bip#	.167	12	2	0	0	3	5	.333	.167
Rodriguez, H*	.154	13	2	1	4	1	4	.214	.385
Sabo, Chris	.222	9	2	1	3	0	3	.222	.556
Samuel, Juan	.167	6	1	0	0	3	0	.444	.167
Sanchez, Rey	.200	20	4	0	0	1	0	.200	.250
Sandberg, R	.250	24	6	0	5	1	7	.280	.292
Sanders, R	.300	20	6	1	2	1	7	.364	.500
Santangelo, F#	.125	8	1	0	0	1	2	.222	.125
Santiago, B	.231	13	3	0	0	0	3	.231	.231
Scarsone, S	.429	7	3	0	0	0	3	.429	.429
Schofield, D	.000	5	0	0	0	1	1	.167	.000
Segui, David#	.091	11	1	0	0	1	3	.167	.091
Servais, S	.222	9	2	1	3	1	1	.300	.667
Sheffield, G	.368	19	7	1	3	6	2	.520	.579
Shipley, C	.143	7	1	0	2	0	1	.143	.143
Slaught, Don	.333	6	2	0	3	0	0	.333	.667
Smith, Dwight*	.385	13	5	1	2	0	2	.385	.769
Smith, Ozzie#	.185	27	5	0	0	3	2	.267	.185
Sosa, Sammy	.333	21	7	1	2	2	8	.391	.571
Spiers, Bill*	.500	6	3	0	0	0	2	.500	.667
Stillwell, K#	.167	6	1	0	0	1	1	.143	.167
Strawberry, D*	.222	9	2	0	1	3	3	.417	.222
Taubensee, E*	.188	16	3	0	2	1	2	.222	.188
Thompson, Mil*	.200	10	2	0	0	1	4	.273	.200
Thompson, Rob	.154	26	4	1	2	2	11	.214	.385
Thompson, Ry	.182	11	2	0	1	1	4	.250	.364
Timmons, O	.143	7	1	0	0	0	3	.143	.143
VanderWal, J*	.273	11	3	1	3	1	1	.333	.636
Velarde, R	.000	3	0	0	0	1	1	.250	.000
Veras, Q#	.077	13	1	0	0	2	8	.200	.077
Vizcaino, J#	.320	25	8	0	4	0	4	.320	.360
Walker, Larry*	.292	24	7	2	3	7	4	.452	.625
Wallach, Tim	.286	28	8	0	2	5	5	.333	.321
Webster, L	.200	5	1	0	0	1	0	.333	.400
Weiss, Walt#	.278	18	5	0	0	1	4	.316	.278
Whiten, Mark#	.000	5	0	0	0	0	1	.000	.000
Wilkins, Rick*	.059	17	1	0	0	2	4	.158	.059
Williams, E	.400	5	2	0	0	0	1	.400	.800
Williams, Ma	.257	35	9	3	6	0	7	.278	.571
Young, Eric	.267	15	4	0	0	1	1	.313	.267
Zeile, Todd	.261	23	6	0	3	1	4	.292	.391

Jason Schmidt, Pirates — RHP

Batter	Avg	AB	H	HR	BI	BB	SO	OBP	Slg
Alfonzo, E	.500	6	3	0	3	0	2	.429	.500
Alicea, Luis#	.250	4	1	0	1	1	0	.400	.500
Aurilia, Rich	.200	5	1	0	0	0	1	.200	.200
Bagwell, Jeff	.400	5	2	1	2	1	0	.500	1.200
Bell, Derek	.200	5	1	0	0	1	1	.333	.200
Benard, M*	.400	5	2	0	1	1	1	.500	.600
Berry, Sean	.200	5	1	0	1	0	1	.200	.200
Biggio, Craig	.167	6	1	0	0	0	1	.167	.167
Bonds, Barry*	.000	1	0	0	1	3	0	.600	.000
Brogna, Rico*	.600	5	3	0	1	1	1	.667	.800
Clayton, R	.000	4	0	0	1	1	1	.167	.000
Colbrunn, G	.375	8	3	0	2	0	0	.375	.500
Conine, Jeff	.667	6	4	2	6	1	1	.714	1.667
DeShields, D*	.200	5	1	0	0	1	2	.333	.400
Dunston, S	.800	5	4	0	0	0	1	.800	.800
Finley, Steve*	.333	6	2	0	2	0	0	.333	.333
Gant, Ron	.000	4	0	0	0	2	3	.333	.000
Gilkey, B	.250	4	1	0	2	2	0	.429	.250
Gonzalez, L*	.222	9	2	1	3	2	1	.364	.556
Grace, Mark*	.200	5	1	1	1	3	0	.500	.800
Hill, G	.200	5	1	0	1	1	1	.333	.200
Hollandsworth*	.000	5	0	0	0	1	3	.167	.000
Hundley, Todd#	.571	7	4	1	6	0	0	.500	1.286
Jennings, R*	.286	7	2	0	0	1	1	.375	.286
Johnson, Char	.200	5	1	0	0	1	0	.200	.200
Johnson, L*	.571	7	4	0	1	0	0	.571	.857
Joyner, Wally*	1.000	4	4	0	3	2	0	1.000	1.500
Karros, Eric	.000	5	0	0	2	0	3	.000	.000
Kent, Jeff	.500	6	3	0	2	0	1	.500	.667
Mabry, John*	.200	5	1	0	0	0	3	.200	.200
McRae, Brian#	.333	12	4	0	0	1	1	.385	.500
Mondesi, Raul	.286	7	2	0	1	0	1	.286	.286
Ordonez, Rey	.000	5	0	0	0	0	0	.000	.000
Pendleton, T#	.000	5	0	0	0	0	2	.000	.000
Piazza, Mike	.600	5	3	2	2	1	1	.667	1.800
Reed, Jody	.000	6	0	0	0	0	0	.000	.000
Sanchez, Rey	.200	10	2	0	1	0	2	.182	.200
Sandberg, R	.500	8	4	0	1	0	1	.500	.500
Servais, S	.429	7	3	0	1	0	1	.429	.429
Sheaffer, D	.400	5	2	0	1	0	2	.400	.600
Sheffield, G	.200	5	1	0	1	2	1	.375	.200
Veras, Q#	.200	5	1	0	0	3	0	.500	.200
White, Devon#	.333	6	2	0	0	0	0	.333	.333
Wilkins, Rick*	.333	3	1	0	1	2	0	.600	.333

Pete Schourek, Reds — LHP

Batter	Avg	AB	H	HR	BI	BB	SO	OBP	Slg
Encarnacion	.000	6	0	0	0	0	0	.000	.000
Eusebio, Tony	.111	9	1	0	2	0	3	.111	.333
Everett, Carl#	.000	5	0	0	0	1	3	.167	.000
Finley, Steve*	.286	14	4	0	0	3	0	.412	.286
Fletcher, D*	.333	6	2	0	0	1	0	.429	.333
Fonville, C#	.125	8	1	0	0	0	1	.125	.250
Galarraga, A	.211	19	4	0	1	3	7	.348	.211
Gant, Ron	.250	8	2	0	2	1	1	.333	.375
Garcia, C	.300	20	6	0	4	1	5	.333	.400
Gilkey, B	.364	22	8	0	1	2	1	.417	.500
Girardi, Joe	.000	8	0	0	0	1	3	.111	.000
Gonzalez, L*	.292	24	7	0	4	1	3	.320	.375
Grace, Mark*	.333	24	8	0	2	1	5	.360	.417
Grissom, M	.190	21	4	1	2	0	4	.190	.333
Grudzielanek	.308	13	4	0	2	0	2	.286	.385
Gutierrez, R	.000	12	0	0	0	2	3	.143	.000
Gwynn, Tony*	.385	26	10	0	3	1	1	.407	.462
Hayes, C	.273	11	3	0	0	1	2	.333	.545
Hernandez, Ca	.000	4	0	0	0	2	0	.333	.000
Hill, G	.250	8	2	0	1	2	4	.400	.375
Hollins, Dave#	.167	12	2	0	1	0	1	.231	.250
Hubbard, Mike	.000	5	0	0	0	0	0	.000	.000
Hudler, Rex	.250	4	1	1	1	1	0	.400	1.000
Hundley, Todd#	.125	8	1	1	2	1	2	.222	.500
Hunter, Brian	.364	11	4	3	7	1	2	.417	1.273
Hunter, Bri L	.286	7	2	0	0	0	2	.286	.286
Huskey, Butch	.200	5	1	0	1	0	0	.200	.200
Incaviglia, P	.250	8	2	0	2	0	1	.222	.375
Javier, Stan#	.250	4	1	0	0	1	1	.400	.250
Jefferies, G#	.167	12	2	0	0	0	1	.167	.167
Johnson, Char	.167	6	1	0	0	1	1	.286	.167
Johnson, L*	.286	7	2	0	0	0	0	.286	.286
Jones, C#	.333	9	3	0	1	0	1	.333	.444
Jordan, Brian	.364	11	4	0	2	2	1	.500	.455
Justice, Dave*	.333	9	3	0	1	0	1	.333	.333
Karros, Eric	.250	16	4	0	3	2	3	.333	.500
Kelly, Mike	.500	6	3	1	2	0	2	.500	1.000
Kelly, R	.176	17	3	0	0	0	1	.176	.235
Kent, Jeff	.200	10	2	0	1	3	1	.385	.200
King, Jeff	.243	37	9	2	8	3	2	.300	.486
Klesko, Ryan*	.200	5	1	0	0	1	0	.333	.200
Lankford, Ray*	.270	37	10	0	2	2	3	.308	.405
Lansing, Mike	.273	11	3	0	0	2	1	.385	.364
Larkin, Barry	.286	14	4	1	3	3	1	.444	.500
Lemke, Mark#	.222	9	2	0	2	2	1	.364	.444
Lewis, Darren	.182	11	2	0	1	0	2	.182	.182
Lopez, Javy	.143	7	1	0	0	1	2	.250	.143
Mabry, John*	.250	4	1	0	1	1	1	.400	.250
Magadan, Dave*	.429	7	3	0	1	1	0	.500	.571
Manwaring, K	.333	9	3	0	0	3	1	.500	.333
Martin, Al*	.300	10	3	1	2	0	2	.300	.700
McGriff, Fred*	.387	31	12	2	6	1	5	.406	.645
McRae, Brian#	.429	7	3	0	0	0	1	.429	.571
Merced, O*	.083	12	1	0	1	0	1	.083	.167
Miller, Orl	.250	8	2	0	1	0	2	.250	.500
Mitchell, K	.250	4	1	0	0	1	0	.400	.250
Mondesi, Raul	.188	16	3	0	2	0	4	.176	.250
Morandini, M*	.250	16	4	1	3	1	1	.294	.438
Morris, Hal*	.286	7	2	0	3	1	3	.455	.429
Mouton, James	.308	13	4	0	0	0	4	.308	.385
Natal, Bob	.500	6	3	1	1	0	1	.500	1.167
Nixon, Otis#	.400	5	2	0	1	1	0	.500	.400
O'Neill, Paul*	.500	4	2	0	2	1	2	.600	.750
Offerman, J#	.467	15	7	0	3	0	1	.467	.467
Oliver, Joe	.545	11	6	1	4	0	2	.545	1.091
Owens, J	.200	5	1	0	2	0	1	.200	.400
Pagnozzi, Tom	.438	16	7	2	6	0	1	.471	1.000
Parent, Mark	.200	5	1	0	0	1	1	.333	.200
Pena, G#	.333	18	6	0	2	1	3	.368	.389
Pendleton, T#	.429	21	9	0	3	0	1	.429	.476
Piazza, Mike	.200	10	2	2	4	0	3	.200	.800
Plantier, P*	.125	8	1	0	0	0	1	.125	.125
Roberts, Bip#	.200	25	5	0	2	0	1	.231	.200
Sabo, Chris	.385	13	5	0	0	3	0	.500	.538
Samuel, Juan	.000	4	0	0	0	1	3	.200	.000
Sanchez, Rey	.091	11	1	0	1	1	1	.167	.091
Sandberg, R	.182	11	2	0	0	2	2	.308	.182
Sanders, R	.400	10	4	0	1	1	3	.417	.600
Santiago, B	.364	11	4	1	1	4	1	.533	.636
Scarsone, S	.091	11	1	0	1	1	4	.167	.091
Segui, David#	.091	11	1	0	2	2	1	.231	.182
Servais, S	.333	9	3	0	2	2	0	.417	.667
Sheaffer, D	.000	6	0	0	0	0	4	.000	.000
Sheffield, G	.238	21	5	2	2	3	5	.333	.571
Shipley, C	.364	11	4	0	0	0	1	.364	.364
Slaught, Don	.304	23	7	0	2	0	2	.304	.348
Smith, Ozzie!	.381	21	8	0	3	1	0	.409	.524
Sosa, Sammy	.200	10	2	0	0	2	3	.333	.300
Stillwell, K#	.200	5	1	0	0	1	0	.200	.200
Stocker, K#	.250	8	2	0	1	0	3	.250	.375
Strawberry, D*	.167	6	1	0	0	2	1	.375	.167

Pete Schourek, Reds — LHP

Batter	Avg	AB	H	HR	BI	BB	SO	OBP	Slg
Abbott, Kurt	.188	16	3	2	4	1	5	.235	.625
Alfonzo, E	.500	6	3	0	3	1	0	.571	.667
Alou, Moises	.333	6	2	0	1	0	0	.286	.500
Andrews, S	.000	5	0	0	0	0	4	.000	.000
Anthony, Eric*	.000	4	0	0	0	1	1	.200	.000
Arias, Alex	.000	11	0	0	1	0	3	.154	.000
Ausmus, Brad	.571	7	4	0	2	1	2	.625	.714
Bagwell, Jeff	.160	25	4	0	5	3	4	.267	.240
Barberie, B#	.222	9	2	0	0	1	0	.300	.333
Bell, Derek	.462	26	12	0	4	1	4	.481	.500
Bell, Jay	.447	38	17	0	7	8	2	.542	.632
Benitez, Y	.333	6	2	1	1	0	2	.333	1.000
Berry, Sean	.250	12	3	0	5	2	3	.333	.417
Bichette, D	.308	13	4	2	7	0	3	.286	.769
Biggio, Craig	.385	26	10	1	2	3	3	.448	.577
Blauser, Jeff	.188	16	3	1	3	2	2	.316	.375
Bogar, Tim	.250	8	2	0	0	0	1	.250	.250
Bonds, Barry*	.290	31	9	5	11	7	6	.400	.774
Bonilla, B#	.400	10	4	1	3	1	0	.455	.700
Brumfield, J	.364	11	4	0	0	1	1	.417	.455
Burks, Ellis	.250	12	3	0	0	0	0	.250	.250
Butler, Brett*	.313	16	5	0	1	2	3	.389	.438
Caminiti, Ken#	.467	15	7	2	6	2	1	.529	.867
Candaele, C#	.143	7	1	0	0	0	0	.143	.143
Carr, Chuck	.227	22	5	0	0	4	5	.393	.227
Carreon, Mark	.455	11	5	1	4	0	1	.417	.818
Castilla, V	.455	11	5	1	2	0	0	.455	.818
Cedeno, A	.500	8	4	2	5	0	1	.500	1.500
Cedeno, Roger#	.333	6	2	0	0	0	2	.333	.333
Clark, Will*	.300	10	3	1	3	2	0	.417	.600
Clayton, R	.429	14	6	0	2	1	1	.467	.429
Colbrunn, G	.214	14	3	0	0	0	2	.214	.286
Conine, Jeff	.154	26	4	3	6	2	5	.214	.500
Cordero, Wil	.250	8	2	0		1	3	.400	.250
Daulton, D*	.200	15	3	0	1	2	1	.294	.267
Davis, Eric	.500	2	1	0	0	3	1	.800	.500
Dawson, Andre	.286	21	6	1	3	0	4	.273	.524
DeShields, D*	.429	14	6	0	2	2	2	.500	.500
Duncan, M	.250	16	4	0	1	0	2	.250	.313
Dunston, S	.091	11	1	0	1	0	1	.154	.091
Dye, Jermaine	.500	6	3	1	1	0	0	.500	1.000
Dykstra, L*	.429	14	6	0	2	0	1	.429	.429
Eisenreich, J*	.375	8	3	0	2	0	1	.300	.375
Elster, Kevin	.167	6	1	0	0	0	2	.167	.333

Pete Schourek, Reds — LHP

Batter	Avg	AB	H	HR	BI	BB	SO	OBP	Slg
Thompson, Mil*	.750	4	3	0	0	2	0	.833	.750
Thompson, Rob	.200	10	2	0	1	1	2	.273	.200
Veras, Q#	.000	6	0	0	0	0	1	.000	.000
Vizcaino, J#	.077	13	1	0	0	0	0	.077	.077
Walker, Larry*	.364	22	8	2	2	3	4	.440	.682
Wallach, Tim	.133	15	2	1	3	1	2	.188	.400
Webster, L	.000	9	0	0	0	3	2	.250	.000
Wehner, John	.200	10	2	0	1	0	2	.200	.200
Weiss, Walt*	.375	16	6	0	1	3	3	.474	.375
White, R	.714	14	10	1	4	1	1	.733	1.214
Whiten, Mark#	.077	13	1	0	1	2	5	.200	.077
Wilkins, Rick*	.375	8	3	0	1	1	0	.444	.375
Williams, Ma	.364	11	4	0	2	1	2	.462	.455
Young, Eric	.333	9	3	1	1	2	0	.455	.889
Young, Kevin	.462	13	6	0	0	0	1	.462	.538
Zeile, Todd	.267	30	8	0	4	5	7	.361	.367

Tim Scott, Giants — RHP

Batter	Avg	AB	H	HR	BI	BB	SO	OBP	Slg
Abbott, Kurt	.400	5	2	0	0	0	1	.400	.400
Alicea, Luis*	.167	6	1	0	1	2	1	.375	.333
Anthony, Eric*	.400	5	2	2	3	0	1	.400	1.600
Bagwell, Jeff	.833	6	5	0	2	1	0	.778	1.167
Barberie, B#	.000	4	0	0	0	1	3	.333	.000
Bell, Derek	.250	4	1	0	0	1	1	.400	.250
Bell, Jay	.364	11	4	1	3	2	4	.462	.636
Bichette, D	.500	8	4	2	3	0	0	.500	1.250
Biggio, Craig	.500	12	6	1	2	0	3	.538	.750
Blauser, Jeff	.250	4	1	0	1	0	1	.400	.250
Bonds, Barry*	.000	5	0	0	0	1	0	.167	.000
Bonilla, B#	.286	7	2	1	1	0	1	.286	.714
Boone, Bret	.375	8	3	0	5	0	0	.375	.750
Branson, Jeff*	.200	5	1	0	1	1	1	.333	.200
Brogna, Rico*	.400	5	2	1	2	0	2	.400	1.000
Burks, Ellis	.000	5	0	0	0	0	0	.000	.000
Butler, Brett*	.250	4	1	0	1	3	0	.571	.500
Caminiti, Ken#	.200	10	2	0	1	1	1	.273	.300
Carr, Chuck	.000	7	0	0	0	0	1	.125	.000
Castilla, A	.167	6	1	0	1	1	0	.286	.333
Cedeno, A	.000	9	0	0	0	0	4	.100	.000
Clayton, D	.300	10	3	0	1	2	1	.417	.400
Colbrunn, G	.600	5	3	0	1	0	0	.600	.600
Conine, Jeff	.167	6	1	0	0	1	2	.286	.333
Daulton, D*	.167	6	1	0	0	1	4	.286	.167
Davis, Eric	.167	6	1	0	1	0	1	.167	.167
Dawson, Andre	.400	5	2	0	0	0	1	.400	.400
DeShields, D*	.250	8	2	0	1	2	0	.400	.250
Dykstra, L*	.167	6	1	0	0	0	1	.167	.333
Eisenreich, J*	.000	8	0	0	0	0	1	.000	.000
Everett, Carl*	.500	4	2	0	1	1	2	.600	.500
Finley, Steve*	.222	9	2	0	1	0	3	.222	.333
Galarraga, A	.111	9	1	0	0	0	3	.111	.111
Gant, Ron	.400	5	2	1	2	2	1	.625	1.400
Garcia, C	.222	9	2	0	0	0	0	.222	.222
Gilkey, B	.333	9	3	0	2	1	0	.400	.444
Girardi, Joe	.000	5	0	0	0	0	2	.000	.000
Gonzalez, L*	.167	6	1	0	1	0	2	.143	.167
Grace, Mark*	.500	6	3	0	0	1	0	.571	.500
Gwynn, Tony*	.000	5	0	0	1	0	1	.000	.000
Harris, Lenny*	.750	4	3	0	0	2	0	.833	1.000
Hayes, C	.214	14	3	0	0	0	1	.214	.357
Hill, G	.167	6	1	0	0	0	2	.167	.167
Hollins, Dave#	.375	8	3	1	2	2	2	.500	.750
Hundley, Todd#	.400	10	4	1	2	0	1	.400	.700
Hunter, Bri L	.333	6	2	0	0	0	0	.333	.333
Jefferies, G#	.308	13	4	1	6	0	1	.308	.538
Johnson, Mark*	.000	4	0	0	0	0	2	.000	.000
Jordan, Brian	.286	7	2	0	0	1	0	.286	.571
Justice, Dave*	.000	4	0	0	0	1	0	.200	.000
Karros, Eric	.500	12	6	0	2	1	0	.538	.583
Kelly, R	.400	5	2	0	0	0	0	.400	.600
Kent, Jeff	.167	6	1	1	3	0	1	.167	.667
King, Jeff	.400	10	4	1	4	2	0	.500	.800
Lankford, Ray*	.375	8	3	0	1	2	1	.500	.375
Larkin, Barry	.375	8	3	0	0	1	0	.444	.375
Lemke, Mark#	.222	9	2	0	0	1	1	.300	.222
Lewis, Darren	.667	6	4	0	1	0	1	.667	1.167
Magadan, Dave*	.143	7	1	0	0	0	1	.143	.143
May, Derrick*	.200	5	1	0	0	3	1	.500	.200
McGee, Willie*	.500	4	2	0	3	1	0	.600	1.000
Merced, C*	1.000	10	1	0	0	2	5	.250	.100
Mitchell, K	.400	4	4	1	5	1	0	.833	2.250
Mondesi, Raul	.500	12	6	0	3	0	2	.500	.667
Morandini, M*	.286	7	2	0	1	0	3	.286	.286
Morris, Hal*	.333	6	2	0	2	1	1	.429	.500
Murray, Eddie*	.000	4	0	0	0	1	0	.200	.000
Offerman, J#	.400	5	2	0	0	1	1	.500	.400
Oliver, Joe	.111	9	1	0	0	0	3	.111	.111
Pagnozzi, Tom	.500	12	6	0	1	0	2	.500	.750
Pena, Geronimo	.200	5	1	1	1	1	1	.429	.800
Pendleton, T#	.000	4	0	0	1	1	3	.167	.000

Tim Scott, Giants — RHP

Batter	Avg	AB	H	HR	BI	BB	SO	OBP	Slg
Piazza, Mike	.091	11	1	0	1	0	4	.091	.182
Reed, Jeff*	.000	7	0	0	0	0	1	.000	.000
Reed, Jody	.333	6	2	0	2	1	0	.429	.333
Sabo, Chris	.200	5	1	0	1	0	3	.200	.400
Sandberg, R	.000	8	0	0	1	0	1	.111	.000
Sanders, R	.364	11	4	1	3	1	4	.417	.909
Santiago, B	.286	7	2	0	0	1	1	.375	.286
Servais, S	.000	5	0	0	0	1	0	.167	.000
Slaught, Don	.500	6	3	0	0	1	1	.571	.500
Smith, Ozzie#	.600	5	3	0	0	2	0	.714	.600
Sosa, Sammy	.167	6	1	0	0	0	2	.167	.167
Stocker, K#	.250	8	2	0	1	1	2	.333	.250
Thompson, Rob	.167	6	1	0	1	2	1	.333	.167
Vizcaino, J#	.400	5	2	0	1	1	1	.500	.800
Wallach, Tim	.286	7	2	0	1	2	0	.444	.286
Weiss, Walt*	.429	7	3	0	0	2	1	.556	.429
Whiten, Mark#	.250	8	2	0	1	0	2	.250	.250
Williams, Ma	.625	8	5	1	1	1	1	.667	1.125
Young, Eric	.286	7	2	0	1	1	0	.375	.286
Young, Kevin	.200	5	1	0	0	0	2	.200	.200
Zeile, Todd	.273	11	3	0	3	1	2	.333	.455

Aaron Sele, Red Sox — RHP

Batter	Avg	AB	H	HR	BI	BB	SO	OBP	Slg
Aldrete, Mike*	.125	8	1	0	1	0	1	.125	.125
Alomar, R#	.333	12	4	0	0	5	0	.529	.417
Alomar Jr, S	.455	11	5	0	0	3	1	.600	.455
Anderson, Brd*	.385	13	5	0	2	4	2	.529	.462
Anderson, G*	.667	6	4	0	5	0	0	.667	1.167
Ausmus, Brad	.200	5	1	0	0	1	1	.333	.200
Baerga, C#	.389	18	7	1	1	3	2	.450	.611
Baines, H*	.214	14	3	1	3	3	2	.353	.500
Becker, Rich*	.200	5	1	0	0	0	0	.200	.200
Belle, Albert	.250	16	4	0	3	1	6	.294	.313
Berroa, G	.250	12	3	0	1	0	0	.250	.250
Boggs, Wade*	.208	24	5	0	3	4	2	.321	.292
Bonilla, B#	.286	7	2	0	3	1	3	.333	.429
Borders, Pat	.000	8	0	0	0	0	0	.000	.000
Bordick, Mike	.211	19	4	0	0	2	0	.286	.211
Brosius, S	.273	11	3	1	4	0	3	.273	.545
Buhner, Jay	.500	6	3	1	4	0	1	.500	1.167
Burks, Ellis	.200	5	1	0	0	1	0	.333	.200
Carter, Joe	.357	14	5	1	2	1	2	.400	.714
Cedeno, D#	.200	5	1	0	0	1	2	.333	.200
Clark, Tony#	.429	7	3	1	3	1	3	.500	1.000
Clark, Will*	.667	6	4	0	4	1	0	.714	1.000
Coleman, V#	.167	6	1	0	0	0	1	.167	.167
Cora, Joey#	.111	9	1	0	0	2	0	.273	.111
Cordova, M	.182	11	2	0	1	1	6	.250	.273
Curtis, Chad	.154	13	2	0	0	1	3	.214	.154
Damon, Johnny*	.556	9	5	1	4	0	2	.556	1.222
Davis, Chili#	.133	15	2	1	2	3	2	.278	.400
Delgado, C*	.333	3	1	0	0	2	1	.600	.333
Devereaux, M	.200	10	2	0	1	1	3	.273	.200
DiSarcina, G	.267	15	4	0	0	1	0	.313	.267
Durham, Ray#	.250	8	2	0	0	1	0	.250	.500
Easley, D	.200	10	2	0	1	2	0	.333	.300
Edmonds, Jim*	.333	9	3	0	1	2	4	.400	.333
Espinoza, A	.000	5	0	0	0	0	3	.000	.000
Fermin, Felix	.300	10	3	0	1	0	0	.300	.300
Fielder, C	.188	16	3	1	3	2	2	.278	.375
Franco, Julio	.455	11	5	0	3	0	3	.455	.636
Fryman, T	.250	12	3	1	3	2	5	.357	.500
Gaetti, Gary	.222	9	2	0	0	0	3	.222	.222
Gallego, Mike	.455	11	5	0	3	1	1	.462	.455
Gates, Brent#	.154	13	2	0	0	2	1	.267	.154
Giambi, Jason*	.375	8	3	0	0	1	2	.444	.500
Girardi, Joe	.167	6	1	0	1	0	0	.286	.167
Gomez, Chris	.167	6	1	0	2	0	3	.167	.167
Gomez, Leo	.167	6	1	0	0	1	1	.286	.167
Gonzalez, A	.500	4	2	0	3	1	1	.600	.500
Gonzalez, J	.333	9	3	0	2	0	1	.300	.333
Goodwin, Tom*	.444	9	4	0	1	0	0	.444	.444
Green, Shawn*	.600	5	3	0	2	2	0	.625	.800
Greer, Rusty*	.167	6	1	0	0	1	1	.286	.167
Griffey Jr, K*	.286	7	2	1	1	2	2	.444	.714
Guillen, O*	.417	12	5	0	0	0	0	.417	.583
Hale, Chip*	.000	5	0	0	0	0	0	.000	.000
Hamelin, Bob*	.375	8	3	0	1	5	0	.615	.375
Hamilton, D*	.500	8	4	0	1	1	0	.600	.625
Henderson, R	.143	14	2	2	2	1	1	.250	.571
Herrera, Jose*	.286	7	2	0	0	0	2	.286	.429
Higginson, B*	.300	10	3	0	1	1	1	.364	.400
Hoiles, Chris	.231	13	3	1	3	0	2	.231	.462
Howard, Dave#	.200	5	1	0	0	0	0	.333	.200
Jaha, John	.429	14	6	0	3	0	3	.429	.500
James, Dion*	.300	10	3	0	0	0	0	.300	.400
Javier, Stan#	.222	9	2	0	3	3	2	.462	.333
Jefferson, R*	.000	6	0	0	0	1	0	.000	.000
Jeter, Derek	.333	6	2	0	0	1	3	.429	.333
Johnson, L*	.286	7	2	0	0	0	0	.286	.286

Aaron Sele, Red Sox — RHP

Batter	Avg	AB	H	HR	BI	BB	SO	OBP	Slg
Joyner, Wally*	.429	7	3	1	4	2	0	.556	.857
Karkovice, R	.143	7	1	0	0	1	3	.250	.143
Kelly, Pat	.250	12	3	0	0	0	4	.250	.250
Kirby, Wayne*	.182	11	2	0	0	1	1	.250	.182
Knoblauch, C	.235	17	4	0	0	3	2	.350	.294
Kreuter, Chad#	.500	4	2	0	0	1	1	.667	.500
Lawton, Matt*	.400	5	2	1	2	1	0	.500	1.000
Lewis, Darren	.375	8	3	0	1	0	1	.375	.375
Lewis, Mark	.167	6	1	0	1	0	2	.286	.167
Leyritz, Jim	.000	7	0	0	0	1	3	.125	.000
Listach, Pat#	.333	6	2	0	1	0	0	.333	.333
Lockhart, K*	.286	7	2	1	3	1	1	.333	.714
Lofton, Kenny*	.438	16	7	0	4	0	1	.368	.563
Lovullo, T#	.333	6	2	0	1	0	2	.333	.333
Macfarlane, M	.444	9	4	0	1	2	2	.545	.556
Martinez, Da*	.167	6	1	0	0	0	2	.167	.167
Martinez, E	.500	6	3	0	2	2	1	.556	.667
Martinez, T*	.200	15	3	0	0	0	1	.200	.200
McGwire, Mark	.375	8	3	0	1	3	2	.583	.625
McLemore, M#	.000	9	0	0	0	1	2	.100	.000
McRae, Brian#	.200	5	1	0	0	3	1	.500	.600
Meares, Pat	.200	15	3	0	0	0	2	.200	.200
Mieske, Matt	.750	4	3	0	1	0	0	.600	1.000
Molitor, Paul	.176	17	3	0	0	3	3	.300	.176
Murray, Eddie#	.357	14	5	0	3	0	3	.357	.429
Myers, Greg*	.250	12	3	1	1	0	3	.250	.583
Nilsson, Dave*	.000	4	0	0	0	3	2	.429	.000
Nixon, Otis*	.167	6	1	0	0	0	1	.167	.167
O'Neill, Paul*	.429	21	9	1	5	3	6	.480	.714
Offerman, J*	.500	4	2	0	0	2	2	.667	.500
Olerud, John*	.273	11	3	0	3	3	0	.429	.455
Palmeiro, R*	.158	19	3	0	1	0	5	.200	.211
Palmer, Dean	.333	6	2	0	0	0	1	.333	.333
Paquette, C	.333	6	2	1	2	0	1	.333	1.000
Perez, E	.200	5	1	0	0	1	0	.333	.200
Phillips, T#	.357	14	5	0	2	1	4	.400	.357
Plantier, P*	.000	5	0	0	1	0	2	.167	.000
Polonia, Luis*	.323	31	10	0	2	0	2	.323	.452
Pride, Curtis*	.667	3	2	1	2	2	0	.800	1.667
Raines, Tim#	.545	11	6	1	1	2	1	.615	.818
Ramirez, M	.231	13	3	0	0	0	6	.231	.231
Randa, Joe	.250	4	1	0	2	1	2	.333	.250
Rebouleit, J	.333	6	2	0	2	0	2	.333	.333
Ripken, Cal	.250	16	4	0	1	1	2	.294	.313
Roberts, Bip#	.400	5	2	0	0	1	0	.500	.400
Rodriguez, I	.286	7	2	0	0	0	1	.286	.286
Salmon, Tim	.222	18	4	0	1	1	7	.263	.278
Schofield, D	.200	5	1	0	0	0	2	.333	.200
Seitzer, K	.167	6	1	0	0	0	2	.167	.333
Sierra, Ruben#	.286	14	4	2	5	2	5	.375	.786
Slaught, Don	.400	5	2	0	0	1	1	.500	.400
Smith, Dwight*	.200	5	1	0	2	1	2	.333	.200
Snow, J.T.#	.000	10	0	0	0	2	4	.167	.000
Sojo, Luis	.200	5	1	0	1	0	1	.200	.200
Sorrento, P	.200	10	2	1	2	4	3	.429	.500
Spiers, Bill*	.000	4	0	0	1	4	0	.500	.000
Sprague, Ed	.400	10	4	0	2	0	1	.500	.500
Stahoviak, S*	.500	8	4	0	1	1	3	.600	.625
Stanley, Mike	.300	10	3	2	3	2	3	.417	.900
Steinbach, T	.231	13	3	1	2	0	3	.231	.462
Surhoff, B.J.*	.286	14	4	1	4	2	2	.375	.500
Tartabull, D	.182	22	4	0	1	2	9	.250	.182
Thomas, Frank	.267	15	4	2	5	4	1	.421	.667
Thome, Jim*	.235	17	4	0	0	3	6	.350	.353
Trammell, A	.750	4	3	0	1	1	0	.800	.750
Tucker, M*	.250	8	2	0	1	0	4	.250	.250
Valentin, Jose*	.286	7	2	0	0	0	0	.286	.286
Vaughn, Greg	.083	12	1	0	1	1	2	.214	.167
Velarde, R	.200	15	3	0	0	0	5	.200	.200
Ventura, R*	.357	14	5	2	3	3	3	.471	.857
Vizquel, Omar#	.700	10	7	1	6	0	1	.700	1.100
Ward, Turner#	.167	6	1	0	0	0	1	.167	.167
White, Devon#	.000	8	0	0	0	0	5	.111	.000
Williams, Ber#	.316	19	6	0	3	2	3	.409	.579
Wilson, Dan	.143	7	1	0	0	0	1	.250	.143
Young, Ernie	.167	6	1	0	1	0	3	.167	.167

Scott Service, Reds — RHP

Batter	Avg	AB	H	HR	BI	BB	SO	OBP	Slg
Bagwell, Jeff	.167	6	1	0	1	0	3	.167	.167
Bichette, D	.250	4	1	1	1	2	1	.500	1.000
Biggio, Craig	.167	6	1	0	0	1	4	.286	.167
Burks, Ellis	.200	5	1	0	2	0	1	.200	.200
Caminiti, Ken#	.400	5	2	0	0	0	1	.400	.400
Finley, Steve*	.667	3	2	0	1	2	0	.800	2.000
Grace, Mark*	.400	5	2	1	1	2	1	.571	1.200
Hayes, C	.000	5	0	0	0	1	1	.167	.000
Hill, G	.250	4	1	0	0	0	0	.400	.250
Incaviglia, P	.333	6	2	0	1	0	2	.333	.333
Karros, Eric	.000	7	0	0	0	0	3	.000	.000
Lemke, Mark#	.250	4	1	0	0	1	0	.400	.250

Jeff Shaw, Reds — RHP

Batter	Avg	AB	H	HR	BI	BB	SO	OBP	Slg
Abbott, Kurt	.143	7	1	0	1	1	1	.250	.143
Alicea, Luis#	.375	8	3	0	0	0	0	.444	.500
Arias, Alex	.143	7	1	0	1	0	1	.143	.286
Aurilia, Rich	.167	6	1	0	0	0	0	.167	.167
Ausmus, Brad	.500	6	3	0	1	0	0	.571	.500
Bagwell, Jeff	.429	7	3	0	3	2	1	.556	.571
Baines, H*	.400	10	4	0	1	0	1	.400	.500
Bell, Derek	.308	13	4	0	2	0	2	.308	.308
Bell, Jay	.167	6	1	0	0	0	1	.167	.333
Benjamin, M	.000	5	0	0	0	0	1	.167	.000
Berry, Sean	.600	5	3	0	2	1	0	.667	.800
Bichette, D	.286	14	4	1	6	0	2	.286	.571
Biggio, Craig	.500	8	4	1	1	1	1	.556	.875
Blauser, Jeff	.250	8	2	0	1	0	2	.333	.375
Bonds, Barry*	.417	12	5	1	3	3	1	.533	.750
Bonilla, B#	.500	8	4	1	2	0	2	.500	.875
Boone, Bret	.167	6	1	0	1	0	1	.167	.333
Borders, Pat	.375	8	3	0	1	0	0	.333	.375
Burks, Ellis	.250	8	2	0	0	0	2	.250	.375
Butler, Brett*	.500	4	2	0	0	0	1	.500	.750
Caminiti, Ken#	.571	7	4	0	1	2	0	.667	.714
Carr, Chuck	.444	9	4	0	2	1	0	.500	.556
Carreon, Mark	.250	8	2	0	1	0	2	.250	.250
Castilla, V	.400	5	2	1	1	0	1	.400	1.000
Cianfrocco, A	.375	8	3	0	0	1	4	.444	.375
Clark, Dave*	.167	6	1	0	0	1	1	.286	.167
Clayton, R	.063	16	1	0	0	1	0	.118	.063
Colbrunn, G	.400	5	2	0	1	0	1	.400	.800
Conine, Jeff	.250	8	2	0	1	1	3	.300	.375
Curtis, Chad	.167	6	1	0	0	0	1	.167	.167
Daulton, D*	.333	6	2	0	0	1	1	.429	.333
Davis, Eric	.250	4	1	0	0	1	1	.400	.500
DeShields, D*	.286	7	2	0	0	3	0	.286	.286
Duncan, M	.286	7	2	0	1	0	0	.286	.429
Dye, Jermaine	.200	5	1	0	0	0	2	.200	.200
Dykstra, L*	.286	7	2	0	1	0	1	.375	.571
Eisenreich, J*	.300	10	3	0	0	1	1	.364	.400
Everett, Carl#	.286	7	2	0	1	0	1	.286	.429
Fielder, C	.600	5	3	1	2	0	0	.600	1.400
Finley, Steve*	.600	5	3	0	1	0	0	.600	.600
Franco, Julio	.250	8	2	0	1	2	1	.400	.375
Fryman, T	.500	4	2	0	0	1	0	.600	.750
Gaetti, Gary	.500	8	4	0	2	1	2	.556	.500
Gagne, Greg	.400	5	2	1	1	0	2	.400	.400
Galarraga, A	.250	12	3	1	2	0	2	.250	.583
Gallego, Mike	.500	6	3	1	1	0	1	.500	1.167
Gant, Ron	.571	7	4	2	3	2	1	.667	1.429
Garcia, C	.400	5	2	0	1	0	1	.400	.600
Gilkey, B	.167	12	2	0	1	0	3	.167	.167
Girardi, Joe	.750	4	3	0	3	0	0	.600	.750
Gomez, Leo	.200	5	1	0	2	0	1	.200	.200
Gonzalez, L*	.600	5	3	2	3	1	0	.667	1.800
Grace, Mark*	.273	11	3	0	0	1	0	.333	.273
Grissom, M	.200	5	1	0	2	1	0	.333	.400
Gwynn, Tony*	.429	7	3	0	0	0	0	.429	.429
Hamilton, D*	.400	5	2	0	0	0	0	.400	.400
Hayes, C	.000	6	0	0	0	1	3	.143	.000
Henderson, R	.143	7	1	0	0	1	1	.333	.143
Hernandez, Jo	.333	6	2	0	1	0	2	.333	.333
Hill, G	.333	12	4	1	2	1	2	.385	.667
Hollins, Dave#	.333	3	1	0	1	2	0	.600	.667
Hundley, Todd#	.286	7	2	0	0	0	2	.286	.286
Huson, Jeff*	.400	5	2	0	0	3	0	.625	.400
Incaviglia, P	.273	11	3	0	3	1	5	.385	.273
Jefferies, G#	.500	6	3	1	2	0	0	.500	1.000
Johnson, L*	.500	4	2	0	1	0	0	.500	.500
Jones, C#	.500	4	2	0	0	1	1	.600	.750
Jordan, Brian	.375	8	3	0	0	1	2	.444	.625
Joyner, Wally*	.200	5	1	0	0	1	1	.333	.400
Justice, Dave*	.500	4	2	0	3	1	1	.600	.750
Karros, Eric	.222	9	2	0	0	1	0	.222	.556
Kelly, R	.125	8	1	0	1	1	2	.300	.125
Kent, Jeff	.364	11	4	0	2	0	3	.364	.545

Jeff Shaw, Reds — RHP

Batter	Avg	AB	H	HR	BI	BB	SO	OBP	Slg
King, Jeff	.000	8	0	0	0	1	2	.111	.000
Knoblauch, C	.000	4	0	0	0	1	0	.200	.000
Lankford, Ray*	.250	8	2	1	2	3	1	.455	.625
Larkin, Barry	.222	9	2	0	0	0	0	.222	.222
Lemke, Mark#	.000	8	0	0	0	0	3	.000	.000
Lewis, Darren	.200	10	2	0	0	0	1	.200	.200
Lopez, Javy	.167	6	1	0	0	0	1	.167	.167
Magadan, Dave*	.000	4	0	0	1	2	1	.333	.000
Manwaring, K	.167	6	1	0	1	0	0	.286	.167
Martin, Al*	.400	5	2	2	2	0	0	.400	1.600
Martinez, Da*	.000	4	0	0	1	1	0	.200	.000
Martinez, E	.600	5	3	0	2	0	0	.600	.800
May, Derrick*	.222	9	2	0	1	1	0	.273	.222
Mayne, Brent*	.250	4	1	0	0	1	1	.400	.500
McGee, Willie#	.200	5	1	0	0	0	1	.333	.200
McGriff, Fred*	.333	9	3	0	0	0	0	.333	.333
McRae, Brian#	.286	7	2	0	1	1	0	.333	.429
Merced, O*	.333	9	3	0	1	0	0	.400	.333
Molitor, Paul	.167	6	1	0	1	0	2	.167	.167
Mondesi, Raul	.167	6	1	0	0	0	1	.167	.500
Morandini, M*	.286	7	2	0	1	2	0	.444	.571
Morris, Hal*	.333	6	2	0	0	1	1	.429	.333
Offerman, J#	.250	4	1	0	2	0	0	.200	.250
Oliver, Joe	.200	5	1	1	1	0	2	.200	.800
Orsulak, Joe*	.333	9	3	0	0	0	0	.333	.333
Pagnozzi, Tom	.231	13	3	0	3	0	3	.231	.231
Palmeiro, R*	.250	12	3	0	1	1	3	.308	.250
Pendleton, T#	.333	3	1	0	1	1	0	.364	.444
Phillips, T*	.500	4	2	0	2	1	1	.600	.750
Piazza, Mike	.100	10	1	0	1	0	1	.182	.100
Plantier, P*	.444	9	4	1	3	0	1	.444	.778
Polonia, Luis*	.250	8	2	0	0	0	0	.250	.250
Reed, Jeff*	.500	6	3	0	0	1	1	.500	.667
Reed, Jody	.250	4	1	0	1	0	0	.400	.250
Roberts, Bip#	.333	3	1	0	0	2	0	.600	.333
Sanchez, Rey	.143	7	1	0	0	0	1	.143	.143
Sandberg, R	.222	9	2	0	2	1	2	.300	.444
Sanders, R	.111	9	1	1	1	0	3	.111	.444
Santiago, B	.167	6	1	0	2	0	1	.167	.500
Scarsone, S	.250	8	2	0	0	2	5	.400	.375
Segui, David#	.250	4	1	0	0	2	2	.500	.500
Seitzer, K	.000	4	0	0	0	1	2	.200	.000
Sheffield, G	.375	8	3	2	3	0	0	.375	1.125
Shipley, C	.200	5	1	0	0	1	1	.429	.200
Sierra, Ruben#	.000	10	0	0	0	1	1	.091	.000
Smith, Dwight*	.429	7	3	0	0	0	1	.429	.571
Smith, Ozzie*	.250	8	2	0	0	1	1	.333	.250
Sojo, Luis	.167	6	1	0	0	0	0	.167	.333
Sosa, Sammy	.158	19	3	1	2	0	5	.158	.368
Spiers, Bill*	.000	3	0	0	0	2	1	.400	.000
Steinbach, T	.400	5	2	0	1	0	0	.400	.400
Stocker, K#	.333	6	2	0	1	1	1	.375	.333
Thompson, Mil*	.200	5	1	0	0	0	0	.200	.200
Vaughn, Greg	.000	6	0	0	0	1	3	.143	.000
Vizcaino, J#	.222	9	2	0	2	2	0	.364	.333
Walker, Larry*	.167	6	1	0	0	1	1	.286	.167
Wallach, Tim	.200	5	1	1	2	1	0	.333	.800
Weiss, Walt*	.154	13	2	0	0	2	2	.154	.154
White, Devon*	.222	9	2	0	0	1	1	.300	.333
Whiten, Mark#	.400	5	2	1	2	0	1	.571	.600
Wilkins, Rick*	.333	12	4	0	2	5	2	.529	.417
Williams, Ma	.250	8	2	0	2	1	2	.333	.250
Young, Eric	.000	7	0	0	1	0	0	.000	.000
Zeile, Todd	.222	9	2	1	3	0	0	.222	.556

Paul Shuey, Indians — RHP

Batter	Avg	AB	H	HR	BI	BB	SO	OBP	Slg
Berroa, G	.000	5	0	0	0	0	0	.000	.000
Molitor, Paul	.000	5	0	0	0	0	0	.000	.000
Vaughn, Mo*	.400	5	2	0	2	0	1	.400	.400

Bill Simas, White Sox — RHP

Batter	Avg	AB	H	HR	BI	BB	SO	OBP	Slg
Alomar, R#	.000	5	0	0	0	1	0	.167	.000
Belle, Albert	.333	3	1	0	2	2	1	.600	.667
Berroa, G	.400	5	2	0	1	0	1	.400	.800
Bordick, Mike	.200	5	1	0	2	0	2	.200	.200
Carter, C	.333	6	2	0	1	0	2	.333	.400
Fielder, C	.400	5	2	0	1	1	2	.500	.400
Fryman, T	.400	5	2	0	0	2	0	.571	.800
Gonzalez, A	.250	4	1	0	0	1	0	.400	.250
Gonzalez, J	.667	6	4	1	3	0	0	.667	1.167
Martinez, E	.000	5	0	0	0	0	1	.000	.000
Molitor, Paul	.400	5	2	0	0	0	2	.400	.400
Murray, Eddie#	.500	4	2	0	1	1	0	.600	.500
Rodriguez, I	.000	5	0	0	0	1	0	.000	.000

Mike Sirotka, White Sox — LHP

Batter	Avg	AB	H	HR	BI	BB	SO	OBP	Slg
Anderson, G*	.167	6	1	0	1	0	2	.167	.167
Becker, Rich*	.143	7	1	0	0	0	2	.143	.143
Coomer, Ron	.400	5	2	2	3	0	0	.400	1.600
Cordova, M	.167	6	1	0	1	1	1	.250	.333
Davis, Chili*	.400	5	2	0	2	1	0	.429	.400
Easley, D	.200	5	1	0	0	0	3	.200	.200
Kelly, R	.200	5	1	0	1	0	1	.200	.200
Knoblauch, C	.667	9	6	0	2	1	0	.700	1.000
Molitor, Paul	.500	6	3	0	4	1	0	.571	.667
Salmon, Tim	.667	3	2	1	3	4	0	.857	1.667
Snow, J.T.#	.429	7	3	1	8	0	1	.429	1.286
Walbeck, Matt#	.143	7	1	0	0	0	0	.143	.143

Heathcliff Slocumb, Red Sox — RHP

Batter	Avg	AB	H	HR	BI	BB	SO	OBP	Slg
Abbott, Kurt	.333	6	2	0	0	0	2	.500	.333
Alou, Moises	.200	10	2	0	1	0	2	.200	.300
Anderson, Brd*	.500	4	2	0	0	1	0	.600	.500
Arias, Alex	.167	6	1	0	0	2	2	.375	.167
Ausmus, Brad	.000	5	0	0	0	0	3	.000	.000
Bagwell, Jeff	.125	8	1	0	1	2	1	.300	.125
Barberie, B#	.667	9	6	0	4	1	1	.727	.667
Bell, Derek	.333	6	2	0	1	0	3	.333	.333
Bell, Jay	.188	16	3	0	2	1	7	.235	.375
Berry, Sean	.400	5	2	0	1	0	1	.400	.400
Biggio, Craig	.167	6	1	0	1	4	0	.500	.167
Blauser, Jeff	.167	6	1	0	0	0	2	.167	.167
Bonds, Barry*	.143	7	1	0	3	3	1	.200	.143
Bonilla, B#	.214	14	3	0	0	1	4	.267	.214
Burks, Ellis	.400	5	2	0	1	0	0	.400	.400
Burnitz, J*	.667	3	2	0	2	2	0	.800	.667
Caminiti, Ken#	.400	5	2	0	0	1	0	.500	.400
Carr, Chuck	.400	5	2	0	0	1	2	.500	.400
Carter, Joe	.000	3	0	0	0	2	0	.400	.000
Clayton, R	.400	5	2	0	2	1	1	.500	.400
Conine, Jeff	.375	8	3	0	2	2	1	.500	.500
Cordero, Wil	.333	6	2	0	1	1	1	.429	.333
Dawson, Andre	.000	2	0	0	0	3	0	.600	.000
DeShields, D*	.250	8	2	0	2	0	3	.250	.250
Devereaux, M	.400	5	2	0	0	0	0	.400	.400
Duncan, M	.571	7	4	0	1	0	0	.571	.714
Dunston, S	.500	4	2	1	3	1	0	.600	1.250
Fielder, C	.250	4	1	0	0	1	2	.400	.250
Finley, Steve*	.375	8	3	0	0	0	2	.375	.375
Fletcher, D*	.667	6	4	0	3	1	0	.714	.667
Fryman, T	.250	4	1	0	1	1	0	.400	.250
Galarraga, A	.333	6	2	0	0	0	3	.333	.333
Gant, Ron	.400	5	2	0	0	1	1	.500	.400
Garcia, C	.000	7	0	0	0	0	1	.125	.000
Gilkey, B	.250	8	2	0	3	0	4	.222	.375
Girardi, Joe	.286	7	2	0	1	0	1	.286	.286
Gonzalez, L*	.167	6	1	0	0	2	2	.375	.167
Grissom, M	.429	7	3	0	1	0	2	.429	.571
Hayes, C	.167	6	1	0	3	2	0	.375	.333
Hoiles, Chris	.500	4	2	0	0	1	2	.600	.750
Hollins, Dave*	.714	7	5	0	0	0	0	.714	.857
Hundley, Todd#	.000	5	0	0	0	0	4	.000	.000
Hunter, Brian	.250	4	1	0	2	1	1	.400	.500
Jeter, Derek	.000	6	0	0	0	0	1	.000	.000
Jordan, Brian	.143	7	1	0	1	1	2	.250	.143
Jordan, Ricky	.000	4	0	0	0	1	0	.200	.000
Justice, Dave*	.500	2	1	0	0	3	0	.800	1.000
Karros, Eric	.167	6	1	0	0	0	0	.167	.167
Kelly, R	.600	5	3	0	1	0	0	.600	1.000
Kent, Jeff	.333	6	2	0	1	0	1	.333	.500
King, Jeff	.444	9	4	0	4	0	2	.444	.556
Kingery, Mike*	.250	4	1	0	0	1	0	.250	.250
Knoblauch, C	.167	6	1	0	0	0	1	.167	.167
Lankford, Ray*	.250	8	2	0	1	1	2	.333	.250
Lansing, Mike	.200	5	1	0	0	0	0	.200	.200
Larkin, Barry	.167	6	1	0	0	0	1	.167	.167
Lemke, Mark#	.500	6	3	0	2	1	0	.571	.500
Lewis, Darren	.125	8	1	0	0	0	4	.125	.125
Lopez, Javy	.400	5	2	0	1	0	3	.400	.400
Magadan, Dave*	.200	5	1	0	0	0	0	.333	.200
Manwaring, K	.200	5	1	0	0	0	2	.200	.200
Martin, Al*	.167	6	1	0	0	1	1	.286	.167
Martinez, Da*	.000	5	0	0	0	2	2	.286	.000
McGriff, Fred*	.000	3	0	0	0	2	2	.400	.000
Meares, Pat	.333	6	2	0	0	0	1	.333	.333
Merced, O*	.083	12	1	0	0	0	7	.083	.083
Morris, Hal*	.250	4	1	0	0	0	1	.250	.250
Murray, Eddie#	.167	6	1	0	1	2	1	.375	.167
Nieves, M#	.000	4	0	0	0	1	2	.200	.000
Nilsson, Dave*	.000	4	0	0	0	1	1	.200	.000
Nixon, Otis#	.500	4	2	0	1	0	0	.600	.500
Offerman, J#	.143	7	1	0	0	0	2	.143	.143
Oliver, Joe	.250	4	1	0	0	1	1	.400	.250
Orsulak, Joe*	.600	5	3	0	0	1	0	.600	.600
Pagnozzi, Tom	.200	10	2	0	0	0	3	.200	.200
Parker, Rick	.000	4	0	0	0	0	0	.000	.000
Pena, G#	.286	7	2	0	0	1	3	.375	.286
Pendleton, T#	.500	6	3	0	1	1	2	.571	.500

Heathcliff Slocumb, Red Sox — RHP

Batter	Avg	AB	H	HR	BI	BB	SO	OBP	Slg
Piazza, Mike	.000	4	0	0	0	1	1	.200	.000
Plantier, P*	.167	6	1	0	0	0	2	.167	.333
Raines, Tim#	.200	5	1	0	0	0	0	.200	.200
Ripken, Cal	.200	5	1	0	0	2	0	.429	.200
Roberts, Bip#	.000	5	0	0	0	2	1	.250	.000
Rodriguez, Al	.000	4	0	0	0	2	2	.333	.000
Rodriguez, I	.000	4	0	0	2	0	0	.000	.000
Samuel, Juan	.200	5	1	0	0	1	3	.333	.200
Sanders, R	.400	5	2	0	1	0	2	.400	.600
Santiago, B	.167	6	1	0	2	0	0	.125	.167
Segui, David#	.429	7	3	0	0	0	0	.429	.429
Sheffield, G	.222	9	2	1	6	2	3	.364	.556
Shipley, C	.600	5	3	0	0	0	1	.600	.600
Slaught, Don	.286	7	2	0	1	2	0	.444	.429
Strange, Doug#	.200	5	1	0	0	2	2	.429	.200
Strawberry, D*	.667	6	4	0	1	1	1	.714	.667
Thomas, Frank	.167	6	1	0	2	0	5	.143	.167
Thompson, Rob	.400	5	2	0	1	0	0	.500	.600
Thompson, Ry	.400	5	2	0	1	0	0	.400	.800
Vaughn, Greg	.000	5	0	0	0	0	3	.000	.000
Walker, Larry*	.200	5	1	1	1	0	1	.200	.800
Wallach, Tim	.111	9	1	0	1	1	5	.182	.111
Weiss, Walt#	.000	5	0	0	0	0	1	.000	.000
Zeile, Todd	.444	9	4	0	2	1	1	.500	.667

Aaron Small, Athletics — RHP

Batter	Avg	AB	H	HR	BI	BB	SO	OBP	Slg
Clark, Will*	.000	3	0	0	0	2	0	.400	.000
Rodriguez, I	.400	5	2	0	0	0	1	.400	.600

John Smiley, Reds — LHP

Batter	Avg	AB	H	HR	BI	BB	SO	OBP	Slg
Abbott, Kurt	.444	9	4	0	0	0	1	.444	.444
Aldrete, Mike*	.250	4	1	0	0	1	1	.400	.250
Alfonzo, E	.375	8	3	0	1	1	0	.444	.625
Alicea, Luis#	.286	7	2	0	2	0	0	.286	.286
Alomar, R#	.313	16	5	1	1	2	3	.421	.500
Alou, Moises	.400	15	6	3	6	1	4	.438	1.067
Anderson, Brd*	.200	5	1	0	0	2	0	.429	.600
Andrews, S	.333	3	1	0	1	1	1	.400	.333
Arias, Alex	.143	14	2	0	0	0	2	.143	.143
Ashley, Billy	.200	10	2	0	0	0	6	.200	.200
Aude, Rich	.143	7	1	0	0	0	2	.143	.143
Aurilia, Rich	.222	9	2	0	0	0	3	.222	.222
Baerga, C#	.273	11	3	0	0	0	1	.333	.273
Bagwell, Jeff	.231	26	6	3	9	5	2	.375	.577
Barberie, B#	.000	11	0	0	0	1	4	.083	.000
Bates, Jason#	.333	6	2	0	1	0	1	.333	.333
Batiste, Kim	.455	11	5	1	2	0	2	.455	.818
Bell, David	.333	6	2	0	2	0	0	.333	.333
Bell, Derek	.440	25	11	1	4	0	3	.440	.680
Bell, Jay	.276	29	8	1	4	5	4	.371	.414
Belle, Albert	.286	7	2	0	0	0	1	.286	.571
Belliard, R	.364	11	4	0	1	0	2	.364	.364
Berroa, G	.800	5	4	0	1	0	0	.800	.800
Berry, Sean	.375	16	6	0	1	1	4	.412	.500
Bichette, D	.333	18	6	4	9	1	4	.350	1.056
Biggio, Craig	.378	37	14	0	5	9	3	.490	.514
Blauser, Jeff	.167	30	5	1	1	8	12	.359	.267
Bogar, Tim	.500	6	3	0	0	0	1	.500	.500
Boggs, Wade*	.200	5	1	0	0	1	0	.333	.200
Bonds, Barry*	.286	14	4	3	6	7	2	.524	.929
Bonilla, B#	.313	16	5	1	2	0	3	.313	.563
Borders, Pat	.250	8	2	0	2	0	2	.250	.250
Bordick, Mike	.200	10	2	0	0	2	2	.333	.200
Brogna, Rico*	.333	6	2	0	3	0	3	.333	.500
Brumfield, J	.500	6	3	0	1	0	1	.500	.667
Burks, Ellis	.231	13	3	1	2	1	2	.286	.462
Butler, Brett*	.231	39	9	1	3	4	2	.302	.385
Caminiti, Ken#	.143	35	5	1	3	1	5	.167	.229
Candaele, C#	.222	9	2	0	1	1	0	.300	.333
Cangelosi, J	.200	5	1	0	0	1	1	.333	.400
Canizaro, Jay	.500	6	3	0	0	0	2	.500	.500
Canseco, Jose	.167	6	1	1	1	1	3	.286	.667
Carr, Chuck	.286	7	2	0	0	1	2	.444	.429
Carreon, Mark	.222	36	8	2	3	0	4	.222	.389
Carter, Joe	.231	13	3	1	3	0	2	.231	.538
Castilla, V	.182	11	2	0	0	2	2	.308	.182
Cedeno, Andu	.333	18	6	0	0	0	8	.333	.389
Cianfrocco, A	.222	9	2	0	0	0	2	.222	.333
Clark, Phil	.222	9	2	0	0	0	0	.300	.222
Clark, Will*	.204	54	11	0	5	1	6	.232	.259
Clayton, R	.200	20	4	0	1	0	4	.200	.200
Colbrunn, G	.250	16	4	0	0	0	5	.250	.375
Coleman, V#	.343	35	12	0	5	1	5	.378	.514
Conine, Jeff	.333	21	7	1	4	1	3	.364	.476
Cora, Joey*	.000	8	0	0	0	2	1	.273	.000
Cordero, Wil	.222	9	2	0	0	2	1	.364	.222
Curtis, Chad	.167	12	2	0	1	1	2	.231	.250
Dascenzo, D#	.125	8	1	0	0	0	1	.125	.125
Daulton, D*	.118	17	2	0	1	4	3	.318	.176
Davis, Chili#	.000	2	0	0	0	3	2	.600	.000
Davis, Eric	.429	14	6	1	8	1	3	.412	.643
Dawson, Andre	.447	38	17	4	9	0	4	.447	.842
Decker, Steve	.000	10	0	0	1	1	3	.083	.000
Deer, Rob	.444	9	4	3	4	0	2	.444	1.556
DeShields, D*	.333	18	6	0	1	3	3	.429	.500
Devereaux, M	.600	10	6	0	0	0	1	.600	.800
DiSarcina, G	.333	6	2	0	0	0	1	.333	.333
Duncan, M	.323	31	10	1	3	0	6	.323	.452
Dunston, S	.304	46	14	3	6	1	4	.333	.587
Dye, Jermaine	.200	5	1	1	1	0	0	.200	.800
Dykstra, L*	.229	35	8	0	2	3	4	.289	.429
Eisenreich, J*	.500	6	3	0	0	0	0	.500	.500
Elster, Kevin	.160	25	4	2	2	2	2	.222	.400
Eusebio, Tony	.389	18	7	1	2	0	1	.389	.667
Fielder, C	.200	10	2	1	3	0	5	.200	.500
Finley, Steve*	.143	14	2	0	1	0	0	.143	.143
Fonville, C#	.333	6	2	0	1	0	1	.333	.333
Frazier, Lou#	.200	5	1	0	1	0	0	.200	.200
Frye, Jeff	.000	7	0	0	0	0	1	.000	.000
Fryman, T	.111	9	1	0	0	1	3	.200	.111
Gaetti, Gary	.133	15	2	0	0	0	4	.133	.267
Gagne, Greg	.000	5	0	0	0	0	2	.000	.000
Galarraga, A	.333	57	19	2	6	4	13	.377	.544
Gallego, Mike	.125	8	1	0	0	1	1	.222	.125
Gant, Ron	.219	32	7	2	5	4	5	.306	.438
Garcia, C	.389	36	14	0	3	0	4	.389	.444
Gilkey, B	.143	28	4	0	2	2	5	.200	.250
Girardi, Joe	.316	19	6	0	0	0	2	.316	.474
Gomez, Leo	.400	5	2	0	2	3	2	.625	.400
Gonzalez, J	.000	7	0	0	0	0	3	.000	.000
Gonzalez, L*	.300	10	3	0	3	1	1	.417	.600
Grace, Mark*	.362	47	17	1	5	4	4	.404	.447
Grebeck, C	.250	8	2	0	1	1	3	.333	.250
Grissom, M	.286	49	14	2	8	4	8	.340	.531
Grudzielanek	.600	10	6	0	1	1	1	.636	.600
Gutierrez, R	.286	21	6	0	1	0	3	.318	.381
Gwynn, Tony*	.167	36	6	1	2	2	6	.211	.250
Hall, Mel*	.333	6	2	1	2	1	2	.429	.833
Hamilton, D	.200	5	1	0	1	0	0	.200	.200
Hayes, C	.318	44	14	2	7	2	6	.348	.545
Henderson, R	.063	16	1	0	0	2	2	.167	.063
Hernandez, Jo	.200	5	1	0	0	1	2	.333	.400
Hill, G	.222	18	4	1	1	1	6	.263	.500
Hollins, Dave#	.235	17	4	0	0	1	3	.278	.412
Howard, Dave#	.167	6	1	0	0	0	2	.167	.167
Howard, T*	.417	12	5	1	3	0	4	.417	.750
Hudler, Rex	.333	18	6	0	1	0	4	.333	.500
Huff, Michael	.333	6	2	0	1	1	1	.429	.500
Hundley, Todd#	.154	13	2	2	3	3	5	.313	.615
Hunter, Brian	.278	18	5	1	4	1	3	.316	.500
Hunter, Bri L	.105	19	2	0	0	0	4	.105	.105
Huskey, Butch	.125	8	1	0	0	1	1	.222	.125
Incaviglia, P	.200	10	2	0	0	1	2	.273	.200
Javier, Stan#	.364	11	4	0	2	1	2	.417	.545
Jefferies, G#	.295	44	13	3	4	1	1	.311	.523
Johnson, Bri	.143	7	1	0	0	1	1	.125	.143
Johnson, Char	.462	13	6	0	1	0	0	.462	.538
Johnson, L*	.294	17	5	0	3	1	0	.333	.529
Jones, C#	.063	16	1	0	0	2	4	.167	.063
Jones, Chris	.125	8	1	1	2	0	4	.125	.500
Jones, Dax	.143	7	1	0	0	0	1	.143	.143
Jordan, Brian	.176	17	3	0	1	0	4	.176	.294
Jordan, Ricky	.217	23	5	0	3	1	3	.240	.261
Joyner, Wally*	.231	13	3	0	0	1	3	.286	.385
Justice, Dave*	.118	17	2	0	2	4	0	.286	.235
Karkovice, R	.000	6	0	0	0	1	1	.000	.000
Karros, Eric	.211	19	4	0	2	0	4	.200	.263
Kelly, Mike	.300	10	3	0	3	1	1	.364	.500
Kelly, Pat	.167	6	1	0	0	0	3	.167	.167
Kelly, R	.421	19	8	1	3	0	1	.421	.579
Kendall, J	.222	9	2	0	0	0	0	.300	.333
Kent, Jeff	.250	24	6	0	1	2	8	.308	.333
King, Jeff	.364	33	12	1	3	2	4	.400	.667
Klesko, Ryan*	.000	5	0	0	0	1	4	.167	.000
Lankford, Ray*	.280	25	7	0	4	0	11	.333	.400
Lansing, Mike	.176	17	3	0	1	0	4	.176	.235
Larkin, Barry	.238	21	5	0	0	2	0	.304	.286
Lemke, Mark#	.240	25	6	1	2	2	5	.296	.360
Lewis, Darren	.267	15	4	0	0	1	0	.313	.267
Lewis, Mark	.143	7	1	0	2	2	0	.300	.286
Leyritz, Jim	.333	6	2	1	1	0	0	.333	.833
Listach, Pat#	.000	5	0	0	0	2	0	.400	.000
Lofton, Kenny*	.375	8	3	0	0	0	0	.375	.500
Lopez, Javy	.000	18	0	0	0	0	2	.000	.000
Mabry, John*	.375	8	3	0	0	1	0	.375	.500
Macfarlane, M	.333	9	3	0	0	0	2	.333	.444
Magadan, Dave*	.214	28	6	1	4	6	2	.353	.357
Manwaring, K	.280	25	7	0	3	0	1	.280	.320
Martin, Al*	.308	13	4	1	3	1	5	.357	.615
Martinez, Da*	.250	4	1	0	0	0	2	.400	.250

John Smiley, Reds — LHP

Batter	Avg	AB	H	HR	BI	BB	SO	OBP	Slg
McGee, Willie#	.278	36	10	0	4	2	9	.316	.333
McGriff, Fred*	.351	37	13	3	5	3	4	.400	.622
McGwire, Mark	.500	10	5	2	2	3	2	.615	1.300
McRae, Brian#	.240	25	6	0	0	0	6	.240	.320
Merced, O*	.300	30	9	0	2	2	4	.344	.467
Miller, Orl	.125	8	1	0	0	0	1	.125	.125
Mitchell, K	.171	35	6	3	5	6	5	.310	.429
Molitor, Paul	.286	7	2	0	3	1	0	.333	.714
Mondesi, Raul	.059	17	1	0	0	1	2	.111	.118
Mordecai, M	.600	5	3	1	2	0	0	.600	1.400
Mouton, James	.318	22	7	0	1	1	4	.348	.364
Murray, Eddie#	.240	25	6	0	3	0	2	.240	.240
Nixon, Otis#	.300	30	9	0	2	6	3	.417	.367
O'Brien, C	.238	21	5	0	2	1	2	.273	.238
O'Neill, Paul*	.273	11	3	0	1	0	4	.273	.273
Ochoa, Alex	.500	10	5	0	0	0	1	.500	.600
Offerman, J#	.333	9	3	0	2	1	2	.400	.333
Oliver, Joe	.250	12	3	1	2	1	2	.308	.500
Ordonez, Rey	.222	9	2	0	0	0	0	.222	.222
Owens, J	.375	8	3	0	0	1	2	.444	.375
Pagnozzi, Tom	.333	27	9	1	4	2	7	.379	.556
Palmeiro, R*	.050	20	1	0	0	4	2	.208	.050
Palmer, Dean	.091	11	1	0	0	0	3	.091	.091
Parent, Mark	.222	18	4	1	3	4	4	.364	.500
Parker, Rick	.000	7	0	0	0	2	1	.182	.000
Pena, G#	.333	6	2	0	0	0	0	.333	.333
Pena, Tony	.348	23	8	1	3	0	1	.348	.522
Pendleton, T#	.267	45	12	1	11	1	2	.277	.422
Phillips, T#	.273	11	3	0	1	0	2	.273	.273
Piazza, Mike	.222	18	4	1	2	2	6	.300	.500
Plantier, P*	.333	9	3	0	0	1	2	.400	.333
Polonia, Luis*	.625	8	5	0	1	0	1	.625	.625
Raines, Tim#	.182	33	6	0	0	5	4	.289	.242
Reed, Jody	.353	17	6	0	0	1	0	.389	.471
Renteria, E	.222	9	2	0	0	1	2	.300	.222
Ripken, Cal	.200	5	1	0	0	0	1	.333	.200
Roberts, Bip#	.429	7	3	0	1	1	0	.500	.714
Rodriguez, I	.571	7	4	0	1	0	1	.571	.571
Sabo, Chris	.217	23	5	1	2	0	2	.217	.348
Samuel, Juan	.241	29	7	0	1	3	5	.313	.241
Sanchez, Rey	.429	14	6	0	2	0	1	.429	.571
Sandberg, R	.227	44	10	1	4	1	7	.244	.341
Santiago, B	.214	14	3	1	2	0	2	.267	.429
Segui, David#	.353	17	6	1	4	1	4	.389	.588
Seitzer, K	.400	5	2	1	1	2	2	.571	1.000
Servais, S	.250	8	2	1	1	0	3	.250	.750
Sheaffer, D	.462	13	6	0	2	0	0	.462	.538
Sheffield, G	.357	14	5	2	4	5	0	.526	.857
Shipley, C	.286	14	4	0	2	0	2	.286	.357
Sierra, Ruben#	.273	11	3	0	2	0	0	.273	.273
Simms, Mike	.200	5	1	1	3	0	0	.200	.800
Slaught, Don	.571	14	8	1	5	1	2	.563	1.000
Smith, Ozzie#	.300	60	18	0	5	2	5	.317	.350
Sojo, Luis	.286	7	2	0	2	0	0	.286	.286
Sosa, Sammy	.364	22	8	0	2	1	4	.391	.455
Stankiewicz	.000	4	0	0	0	2	0	.333	.000
Steinbach, T	.556	9	5	1	5	0	0	.556	1.111
Stillwell, K#	.200	5	1	0	0	1	0	.333	.200
Stinnett, K	.222	9	2	0	0	0	3	.222	.222
Stocker, K#	.182	11	2	0	1	2	5	.308	.182
Strawberry, D*	.179	28	5	1	4	4	6	.281	.500
Surhoff, B.J.*	.000	6	0	0	1	0	1	.000	.000
Tartabull, D	.000	6	0	0	0	0	3	.000	.000
Tettleton, M#	.111	9	1	0	0	0	3	.111	.111
Thomas, Frank	.300	10	3	0	1	0	1	.300	.500
Thompson, Mil*	.389	18	7	0	2	1	1	.421	.444
Thompson, Rob	.288	52	15	3	5	3	10	.339	.538
Thompson, Ry	.231	13	3	1	4	0	2	.231	.462
Timmons, O	.222	9	2	0	1	0	2	.222	.333
Vaughn, Greg	.200	5	1	0	1	2	0	.429	.200
Ventura, R*	.333	9	3	0	1	2	0	.455	.444
Veras, Q#	.667	6	4	0	2	0	0	.667	1.167
Vizcaino, J#	.421	19	8	0	2	0	5	.421	.421
Walker, Larry*	.263	19	5	0	1	3	5	.364	.421
Wallach, Tim	.276	58	16	1	6	2	5	.300	.379
Walton, J	.400	20	8	2	4	1	5	.429	.700
Wehner, John	.385	13	5	0	1	0	3	.385	.462
Weiss, Walt#	.200	20	4	0	2	1	3	.238	.200
White, Devon#	.222	18	4	1	4	0	4	.200	.389
White, R	.636	11	7	0	1	0	2	.636	.909
Whiten, Mark#	.235	17	4	0	0	2	6	.350	.353
Wilkins, Rick*	.250	12	3	2	3	1	3	.286	.750
Williams, E	.375	8	3	0	1	1	1	.444	.750
Williams, Ma	.429	35	15	7	15	3	7	.474	1.114
Worthington	.143	7	1	0	0	0	0	.143	.143
Young, Eric	.364	11	4	0	0	2	2	.462	.455
Young, Kevin	.250	12	3	0	1	0	4	.250	.250
Zeile, Todd	.200	30	6	3	6	3	1	.265	.567

Lee Smith, Reds — RHP

Batter	Avg	AB	H	HR	BI	BB	SO	OBP	Slg
Aldrete, Mike*	.200	5	1	0	0	1	2	.333	.200
Alomar, R#	.714	7	5	0	0	2	1	.778	.857
Alou, Moises	.111	9	1	0	0	0	2	.111	.111
Anderson, Brd*	.000	6	0	0	0	1	4	.143	.000
Anthony, Eric*	.143	7	1	0	1	1	2	.250	.143
Bagwell, Jeff	.200	5	1	0	0	0	2	.200	.200
Baines, H*	.400	5	2	0	0	2	0	.571	.400
Barberie, J	.556	9	5	0	0	1	0	.600	.556
Bell, Jay	.000	11	0	0	0	1	5	.083	.000
Biggio, Craig	.111	9	1	0	0	1	3	.200	.111
Blauser, Jeff	.143	7	1	0	0	0	3	.143	.143
Blowers, Mike	.400	5	2	0	1	0	2	.400	.400
Boggs, Wade*	.200	5	1	0	1	0	1	.200	.200
Bonds, Barry*	.400	10	4	2	4	1	3	.455	1.100
Bonilla, B#	.308	13	4	2	3	0	2	.308	.769
Borders, Pat	.167	6	1	0	0	0	1	.167	.167
Buhner, Jay	.286	7	2	0	0	1	2	.375	.429
Butler, Brett*	.375	8	3	0	0	1	1	.375	.375
Caminiti, Ken#	.222	9	2	0	0	0	3	.222	.222
Candaele, C#	.250	8	2	0	1	0	2	.250	.250
Canseco, Jose	.000	5	0	0	0	0	3	.000	.000
Carter, Joe	.125	8	1	0	1	1	1	.200	.375
Clark, Dave*	.375	8	3	0	0	2	1	.500	.375
Clark, Will*	.286	7	2	0	2	2	0	.444	.429
Coleman, V#	.385	13	5	0	0	3	4	.500	.462
Cora, Joey#	.200	5	1	0	0	1	0	.200	.200
Cordero, Wil	.000	5	0	0	0	0	2	.000	.000
Daulton, D*	.083	12	1	1	1	1	8	.154	.333
Davis, Chili#	.231	13	3	1	1	2	6	.333	.538
Davis, Eric	.231	13	3	1	4	0	4	.231	.538
Dawson, Andre	.250	16	4	0	0	1	1	.294	.313
Deer, Rob	.000	4	0	0	0	2	3	.333	.000
DeShields, D*	.111	9	1	0	1	1	3	.200	.111
Devereaux, M	.200	5	1	0	0	1	3	.333	.200
Duncan, M	.500	16	8	1	7	0	1	.500	.938
Dunston, S	.125	8	1	0	0	0	1	.125	.250
Dykstra, L*	.278	18	5	0	2	2	6	.350	.278
Fermin, Felix	.000	5	0	0	0	0	0	.000	.000
Finley, Steve*	.000	6	0	0	0	1	1	.000	.000
Fletcher, D*	.167	6	1	0	0	0	1	.286	.167
Franco, Julio	.429	7	3	0	2	1	0	.500	.571
Gaetti, Gary	.250	12	3	2	6	1	4	.308	.750
Gagne, Greg	.143	7	1	0	0	2	4	.333	.143
Galarraga, A	.091	11	1	0	0	2	5	.231	.091
Gant, Ron	.250	8	2	2	2	0	0	.250	1.000
Girardi, Joe	.000	4	0	0	1	1	1	.200	.000
Gonzalez, L*	.167	6	1	0	0	1	1	.286	.167
Grace, Mark*	.500	8	4	0	3	2	0	.600	.625
Grissom, M	.100	10	1	0	0	0	0	.100	.100
Guillen, O*	.333	9	3	0	1	0	2	.333	.333
Gwynn, Tony*	.200	20	4	0	3	2	3	.273	.300
Hale, Chip*	.500	4	2	0	1	0	1	.400	.500
Hall, Mel*	.400	5	2	0	1	0	0	.400	.400
Hansen, Dave*	.400	5	2	0	1	0	0	.400	.400
Harris, Lenny*	.250	8	2	0	1	3	0	.455	.250
Hayes, C	.444	9	4	0	1	0	2	.444	.778
Henderson, R	.091	11	1	0	0	3	5	.286	.091
Hollins, Dave#	.000	5	0	0	0	1	2	.167	.000
Howell, Jack*	.000	4	0	0	1	1	4	.167	.000
Hundley, Todd#	.250	8	2	0	0	0	1	.250	.250
Javier, Stan#	.200	15	3	0	0	3	7	.333	.333
Jefferies, G#	.250	8	2	0	2	0	1	.250	.250
Johnson, L*	.250	4	1	0	0	1	0	.400	.250
Jordan, Ricky	.273	11	3	0	1	0	3	.273	.455
Joyner, Wally*	.375	8	3	0	1	1	0	.444	.500
Karros, Eric	.111	9	1	0	1	2	1	.273	.222
King, Jeff	.429	7	3	0	2	0	1	.429	.571
Larkin, Barry	.385	13	5	0	2	0	3	.385	.462
Lemke, Mark#	.000	7	0	0	0	0	1	.000	.000
Lewis, Darren	.000	6	0	0	0	0	4	.000	.000
Magadan, Dave*	.286	14	4	0	1	2	1	.375	.357
Martinez, Da*	.125	8	1	0	0	0	4	.125	.125
McGee, Willie#	.300	20	6	0	5	3	6	.391	.550
McGriff, Fred*	.143	7	1	0	1	2	2	.333	.286
McGwire, Mark	.222	9	2	2	6	1	2	.300	.889
McLemore, M#	.333	3	1	0	0	2	2	.600	.333
Merced, O*	.286	7	2	1	3	1	1	.375	.714
Mitchell, K	.222	9	2	0	0	0	5	.222	.222
Molitor, Paul	.000	3	0	0	0	2	0	.400	.000
Mondesi, Raul	.000	5	0	0	0	0	0	.000	.000
Morandini, M*	.200	5	1	0	1	1	1	.333	.400
Morris, Hal*	.364	11	4	0	1	0	2	.364	.545
Murray, Eddie#	.250	12	3	0	2	5	2	.471	.333
Nixon, Otis#	.000	7	0	0	0	2	3	.222	.000
O'Leary, Troy*	.200	5	1	0	0	0	0	.200	.400
O'Neill, Paul*	.286	7	2	1	2	5	1	.583	.714
Oliver, Joe	.200	10	2	0	0	1	1	.273	.200
Orsulak, J*	.316	19	6	0	4	1	2	.318	.368
Pena, Tony	.231	13	3	0	0	1	3	.286	.308
Pendleton, T#	.118	17	2	1	2	2	6	.211	.353
Phillips, T#	.400	5	2	1	3	2	1	.571	1.000

Lee Smith, Reds — RHP

Batter	Avg	AB	H	HR	BI	BB	SO	OBP	Slg
Polonia, Luis*	.364	11	4	0	1	0	3	.364	.364
Raines, Tim#	.357	14	5	0	1	0	0	.333	.429
Reed, Jeff*	.333	6	2	0	1	0	1	.333	.333
Reed, Jody	.200	5	1	0	1	0	1	.200	.200
Ripken, Cal	.222	9	2	0	2	0	2	.182	.222
Roberts, Bip#	.500	6	3	0	1	1	1	.571	.667
Rodriguez, H*	.400	5	2	0	1	0	0	.400	.400
Rodriguez, I	.250	4	1	0	2	0	1	.333	.250
Sabo, Chris	.800	5	4	0	1	0	0	.800	.800
Samuel, Juan	.238	21	5	1	2	1	8	.273	.381
Sandberg, R	.385	13	5	1	3	0	3	.385	.615
Santiago, B	.167	6	1	0	0	0	3	.286	.167
Schofield, D	.400	5	2	0	0	0	1	.400	.600
Schu, Rick	.000	4	0	0	0	1	2	.200	.000
Seitzer, K	.429	7	3	0	2	1	0	.500	.714
Sheffield, G	.600	5	3	1	0	0	0	.600	.600
Sierra, Ruben‡	.143	7	1	0	0	0	3	.143	.143
Slaught, Don	.143	7	1	0	1	0	1	.143	.143
Smith, Dwight	.364	11	4	1	3	2	3	.429	.636
Smith, Ozzie‡	.267	15	4	0	2	5	1	.450	.267
Sosa, Sammy	.273	11	3	0	1	0	3	.273	.273
Steinbach, T	.286	7	2	0	2	0	1	.286	.286
Stillwell, K#	.222	9	2	1	2	1	4	.300	.556
Strawberry, D*	.182	22	4	1	3	1	6	.217	.318
Surhoff, B.J.*	.000	4	0	0	1	1	1	.167	.000
Tartabull, D	.143	7	1	0	0	2	3	.333	.286
Tettleton, M#	.000	4	0	0	0	3	2	.429	.000
Thomas, Frank	.500	4	2	0	0	1	1	.600	.500
Thome, Jim*	.500	4	2	0	0	1	2	.600	.750
Thompson, Mil*	.429	7	3	0	0	1	4	.500	.571
Thompson, Rob	.167	6	1	0	0	0	1	.167	.167
Trammell, A	.200	5	1	1	2	0	2	.200	.800
VanderWal, J*	.000	6	0	0	0	0	5	.000	.000
Vaughn, Greg	.250	4	1	0	0	1	2	.400	.500
Ventura, R*	.286	7	2	0	2	0	1	.286	.286
Vizcaino, J#	.250	8	2	0	2	0	1	.250	.250
Walker, Larry*	.182	11	2	0	1	2	5	.308	.273
Wallach, Tim	.286	28	8	2	3	3	5	.355	.571
Weiss, Walt‡	.143	7	1	0	0	2	1	.333	.286
White, Devon#	.333	6	2	0	0	1	1	.429	.333
Wilkins, Rick*	.500	4	2	1	1	1	0	.600	1.250
Williams, E	.250	4	1	0	0	1	0	.400	.250
Williams, Ma	.222	9	2	0	0	0	3	.222	.333

Zane Smith, Pirates — LHP

Batter	Avg	AB	H	HR	BI	BB	SO	OBP	Slg
Abbott, Kurt	.200	5	1	0	0	0	0	.200	.200
Aldrete, Mike*	.500	6	3	0	0	0	0	.500	.500
Alicea, Luis#	.250	16	4	0	0	0	1	.250	.375
Alomar, R#	.455	11	5	0	2	1	2	.538	.636
Alou, Moises	.150	20	3	0	1	1	2	.190	.200
Amaral, Rich	.143	7	1	0	0	0	1	.143	.286
Amaro, Ruben‡	.200	15	3	1	2	4	2	.368	.533
Anderson, Brd*	.400	5	2	0	0	0	2	.400	.600
Andrews, S	.200	5	1	0	1	3	3	.500	.400
Bagwell, Jeff	.364	33	12	0	3	5	5	.447	.545
Barberie, B#	.409	22	9	0	2	2	2	.458	.545
Batiste, Kim	.000	8	0	0	0	0	1	.000	.000
Bautista, D	.000	6	0	0	1	0	0	.000	.000
Bell, David	.500	6	3	0	0	0	0	.500	.667
Bell, Derek	.222	9	2	1	1	0	1	.222	.667
Bell, Jay	.294	17	5	0	2	0	5	.294	.412
Belliard, R	.273	11	3	0	0	1	1	.333	.273
Berroa, G	.300	10	3	0	0	0	1	.300	.400
Berry, Sean	.250	16	4	0	0	0	1	.250	.250
Bichette, D	.250	12	3	0	1	0	1	.250	.333
Biggio, Craig	.280	50	14	1	4	3	2	.321	.540
Blauser, Jeff	.200	20	4	0	1	1	4	.238	.200
Blowers, Mike	.400	5	2	0	0	0	0	.400	.400
Bogar, Tim	.167	6	1	0	0	0	2	.167	.167
Bonds, Barry*	.314	35	11	2	7	5	4	.400	.629
Bonilla, B#	.200	50	10	1	4	1	10	.216	.280
Boone, Bret	.167	6	1	0	1	1	1	.286	.167
Bordick, Mike	.200	5	1	0	0	0	0	.200	.200
Brosius, S	.333	6	2	0	0	1	0	.429	.333
Brumfield, J	.167	6	1	0	0	0	0	.167	.167
Buhner, Jay	.200	5	1	0	2	0	0	.167	.200
Burks, Ellis	.429	7	3	0	0	1	1	.500	.429
Burnitz, J*	.000	5	0	0	0	1	2	.167	.000
Butler, Brett*	.148	27	4	0	3	4	6	.258	.148
Caminiti, Ken#	.367	49	18	0	6	4	6	.415	.429
Candaele, C#	.174	23	4	0	0	1	1	.208	.174
Cangelosi, J#	.111	9	1	0	1	4	1	.385	.222
Carr, Chuck	.375	8	3	0	0	0	1	.375	.375
Carreon, M	.429	14	6	0	4	1	0	.429	.571
Carter, Joe	.500	6	3	0	1	1	0	.571	.667
Castilla, V	.167	6	1	0	1	1	1	.286	.333
Cedeno, A	.267	15	4	3	7	0	1	.267	.933
Cianfrocco, A	.222	9	2	0	0	1	2	.300	.222
Clark, Will*	.324	37	12	1	8	0	1	.342	.432
Clayton, R	.375	16	6	1	2	0	1	.375	.688

Zane Smith, Pirates — LHP

Batter	Avg	AB	H	HR	BI	BB	SO	OBP	Slg
Coleman, V#	.424	59	25	0	8	5	5	.477	.508
Conine, Jeff	.400	10	4	0	1	0	1	.400	.700
Cordero, Wil	.375	8	3	0	2	1	0	.444	.500
Cordova, M	.400	5	2	0	0	0	1	.400	.600
Curtis, Chad	.250	8	2	0	0	0	2	.250	.375
Dascenzo, D#	.353	17	6	0	2	1	0	.389	.412
Daulton, D*	.167	18	3	0	2	0	3	.167	.389
Davis, Chili*	.207	29	6	1	5	2	4	.250	.345
Davis, Eric	.188	48	9	1	7	8	6	.304	.313
Dawson, Andre	.273	44	12	1	4	2	3	.304	.432
Decker, Steve	.167	6	1	0	1	0	1	.143	.167
Deer, Rob	.500	4	2	0	0	1	1	.600	.500
DeShields, D*	.240	25	6	1	3	2	7	.296	.480
Devereaux, M	.167	6	1	0	1	0	0	.167	.333
Dorsett, B	.167	6	1	0	0	0	0	.167	.167
Duncan, M	.250	56	14	0	4	4	10	.295	.321
Dunston, S	.216	37	8	1	5	2	6	.244	.351
Dykstra, L*	.257	35	9	0	3	2	4	.289	.343
Elster, Kevin	.405	37	15	0	0	0	5	.405	.405
Fielder, C	.000	5	0	0	0	1	0	.167	.000
Finley, Steve*	.179	28	5	0	0	0	7	.179	.179
Flaherty, J	.167	6	1	0	0	0	0	.167	.333
Fletcher, D*	.556	9	5	0	3	0	0	.556	.667
Fryman, T	.000	6	0	0	0	0	1	.000	.000
Gaetti, Gary	.286	7	2	0	3	1	1	.333	.286
Galarraga, A	.413	46	19	4	14	5	7	.471	.783
Gant, Ron	.292	24	7	1	6	5	4	.414	.542
Gates, Brent#	.167	6	1	0	0	1	1	.286	.167
Gilkey, B	.286	35	10	0	2	1	1	.306	.371
Gonzalez, L*	.429	7	3	1	5	0	1	.333	1.000
Grace, Mark*	.316	38	12	0	3	2	3	.350	.368
Grissom, M	.344	32	11	0	3	6	2	.447	.469
Grudzielanek	.167	6	1	0	0	0	1	.167	.333
Gutierrez, R	.250	4	1	0	0	2	0	.500	.750
Gwynn, Tony*	.351	57	20	1	9	5	3	.403	.491
Harris, Lenny*	.250	8	2	0	0	0	0	.250	.250
Hayes, C	.261	23	6	2	2	2	4	.320	.565
Henderson, R	.182	11	2	0	0	1	0	.250	.182
Hill, G	.556	9	5	1	1	0	1	.556	.889
Hollins, Dave#	.318	22	7	2	5	2	3	.400	.591
Hudler, Rex	.188	16	3	0	1	2	2	.278	.250
Hundley, Todd#	.300	10	3	0	0	0	3	.300	.400
Hunter, Brian	.333	9	3	0	1	0	0	.333	.444
Hunter, Bri L	.333	6	2	0	0	0	1	.333	.333
Huskey, Butch	.250	4	1	0	2	0	0	.200	.250
Incaviglia, P	.300	10	3	1	1	1	1	.364	.700
Javier, Stan#	.385	13	5	0	3	0	0	.385	.462
Jefferies, G#	.229	35	8	0	3	0	3	.222	.257
Johnson, L*	.000	10	0	0	0	1	0	.000	.000
Jones, Chris	.444	9	4	0	0	0	2	.444	.444
Jordan, Brian	.538	13	7	0	4	1	0	.571	.769
Jordan, Ricky	.316	19	6	0	2	0	0	.316	.316
Justice, Dave*	.200	15	3	0	0	2	1	.294	.267
Karros, Eric	.429	7	3	0	1	1	0	.500	.571
Kelly, R	.375	8	3	0	0	0	1	.375	.500
Kent, Jeff	.529	17	9	0	1	0	0	.529	.647
King, Jeff	.400	10	4	0	2	2	0	.500	.500
Knoblauch, C	.500	4	2	0	1	0	0	.400	.500
Lankford, Ray*	.226	31	7	1	2	1	9	.250	.323
Lansing, Mike	.500	12	6	0	1	1	0	.538	.500
Larkin, Barry	.408	49	20	4	12	2	4	.423	.694
Lemke, Mark#	.278	18	5	0	0	4	0	.409	.333
Lewis, Darren	.222	9	2	0	1	1	1	.300	.222
Magadan, Dave*	.320	25	8	0	3	2	2	.370	.360
Manwaring, K	.000	16	0	0	0	1	0	.059	.000
Martinez, Da*	.200	5	1	0	1	1	1	.333	.200
Martinez, E	.800	5	4	0	0	1	0	.833	1.000
McGee, Willie*	.333	60	20	2	15	1	8	.349	.533
McGriff, Fred*	.227	22	5	0	2	2	5	.292	.227
McGwire, Mark	1.000	4	4	3	3	1	0	1.000	3.250
Miller, Orl	.200	5	1	0	1	0	2	.200	.200
Mitchell, K	.222	27	6	2	5	1	3	.250	.481
Mondesi, Raul	.167	6	1	0	1	0	0	.167	.167
Morandini, M*	.250	8	2	0	0	0	2	.250	.250
Morris, Hal*	.167	18	3	0	0	2	0	.167	.167
Mouton, James	.250	8	2	0	1	0	1	.250	.500
Munoz, Pedro	.500	5	3	1	3	0	0	.600	1.200
Murray, Eddie‡	.200	20	4	1	3	3	4	.304	.450
Nixon, Otis#	.333	24	8	0	0	2	3	.385	.375
O'Brien, C	.154	13	2	0	0	0	1	.154	.231
O'Neill, Paul*	.125	16	2	0	1	4	1	.176	.188
Obando, S	.167	6	1	0	0	0	0	.167	.333
Offerman, J#	.250	8	2	0	0	0	1	.250	.250
Oliver, Joe	.406	32	13	3	3	0	4	.406	.750
Pagnozzi, Tom	.214	28	6	0	3	2	4	.267	.250
Palmeiro, R*	.333	9	3	0	1	1	0	.400	.444
Parent, Mark	.333	6	2	0	0	0	1	.333	.333
Pena, G#	.167	6	1	0	1	0	0	.167	.167
Pena, Tony	.176	17	3	1	2	1	1	.263	.412
Pendleton, T#	.492	65	32	2	15	1	3	.500	.662
Phillips, T#	.600	5	3	0	0	0	0	.600	.600

195

Zane Smith, Pirates — LHP

Batter	Avg	AB	H	HR	BI	BB	SO	OBP	Slg
Piazza, Mike	.500	6	3	0	1	0	0	.500	.500
Raines, Tim*	.364	22	8	0	0	5	4	.481	.500
Reed, Jeff*	.200	5	1	1	2	0	2	.200	.800
Reed, Jody	.000	3	0	0	0	0	0	.400	.000
Ripken, Cal	.500	4	2	0	1	0	0	.400	.500
Roberts, Bip#	.368	19	7	0	1	0	0	.368	.474
Rodriguez, H*	.200	5	1	0	1	0	1	.200	.400
Sabo, Chris	.302	43	13	2	11	1	2	.318	.535
Salmon, Tim	.750	4	3	0	1	1	0	.800	1.000
Samuel, Juan	.289	38	11	2	7	4	12	.349	.632
Sanchez, Rey	.200	10	2	0	2	0	0	.200	.200
Sandberg, R	.279	43	12	0	2	5	6	.354	.326
Sanders, R	.350	20	7	0	0	1	0	.350	.500
Santiago, B	.419	31	13	5	10	2	3	.455	1.032
Schu, Rick	.167	6	1	0	0	1	2	.286	.167
Segui, David#	.545	11	6	0	1	0	0	.545	.636
Servais, S	.294	17	5	0	1	0	2	.294	.294
Sheaffer, D	.200	5	1	0	0	1	0	.333	.200
Sheffield, G	.300	10	3	2	3	0	0	.300	.900
Shipley, C	.500	6	3	0	1	0	1	.500	.500
Sierra, Ruben*	.375	8	3	0	2	0	1	.375	.500
Slaught, Don	.300	10	3	0	1	0	1	.300	.300
Smith, Ozzie#	.338	77	26	0	3	5	3	.378	.390
Snow, J.T.#	.000	5	0	0	0	0	2	.000	.000
Sojo, Luis	.600	5	3	0	0	0	0	.667	.800
Sosa, Sammy	.333	12	4	1	4	0	2	.333	.750
Steinbach, T	.400	5	2	0	3	1	2	.500	.600
Stillwell, K#	.238	21	5	0	1	3	5	.333	.286
Stinnett, K	.250	8	2	0	0	0	0	.250	.250
Strawberry, D*	.159	44	7	1	5	2	14	.196	.227
Thompson, Mil*	.000	7	0	0	0	1	4	.125	.000
Thompson, Rob	.214	42	9	0	3	2	9	.283	.286
Thompson, Ry	.143	14	2	0	0	0	2	.143	.143
Trammell, A	.000	5	0	0	0	1	0	.167	.000
Vizcaino, J#	.100	20	2	0	0	1	1	.143	.100
Walker, Larry*	.238	21	5	0	4	0	2	.238	.476
Wallach, Tim	.268	56	15	1	15	5	6	.323	.393
Walton, J	.200	15	3	0	0	0	4	.200	.267
Webster, L	.375	8	3	0	1	2	0	.545	.750
Weiss, Walt#	.231	13	3	0	1	2	0	.333	.231
White, R	.200	10	2	0	0	0	0	.200	.400
Whiten, Mark#	.200	10	2	0	0	1	0	.273	.200
Wilkins, Rick*	.000	6	0	0	1	0	2	.000	.000
Williams, Ber#	.000	4	0	0	0	1	0	.200	.000
Williams, Ma	.333	30	10	2	6	3	6	.382	.667
Young, Eric	.000	9	0	0	0	0	0	.100	.000
Zeile, Todd	.107	28	3	0	3	4	6	.219	.179

John Smoltz, Braves — RHP

Batter	Avg	AB	H	HR	BI	BB	SO	OBP	Slg
Abbott, Kurt	.333	12	4	1	1	0	5	.333	.667
Aldrete, Mike*	.500	8	4	0	1	3	0	.636	.875
Alfonzo, E	.111	9	1	0	0	0	3	.111	.111
Alicea, Luis#	.100	10	1	0	1	1	2	.231	.100
Allensworth	.000	7	0	0	1	0	0	.000	.000
Alomar, R#	.231	26	6	1	3	0	4	.222	.423
Alou, Moises	.120	25	3	0	0	6	7	.290	.120
Anthony, Eric*	.320	25	8	0	2	5	7	.433	.320
Arias, Alex	.188	16	3	0	0	1	1	.188	.188
Ashley, Billy	.429	7	3	1	1	3	3	.600	1.000
Aurilia, Rich	.167	6	1	0	0	1	1	.167	.333
Ausmus, Brad	.125	8	1	0	1	0	3	.125	.125
Bagwell, Jeff	.293	58	17	0	4	6	9	.359	.362
Barberie, B#	.250	12	3	0	0	2	3	.357	.250
Bates, Jason#	.000	7	0	0	0	0	3	.000	.000
Batiste, Kim	.364	11	4	0	1	0	3	.364	.364
Bell, David	.000	5	0	0	0	0	2	.000	.000
Bell, Derek	.207	29	6	3	6	0	9	.200	.517
Bell, Jay	.120	50	6	0	4	4	15	.185	.160
Benard, M*	.000	7	0	0	0	1	2	.125	.000
Benjamin, M	.250	8	2	0	0	1	0	.250	.250
Berry, Sean	.200	25	5	1	3	2	10	.259	.440
Bichette, D	.118	17	2	0	1	2	6	.211	.118
Biggio, Craig	.234	77	18	2	7	6	18	.294	.351
Blowers, Mike	.167	6	1	0	0	0	5	.167	.167
Bogar, Tim	.143	7	1	0	0	1	3	.250	.143
Bonds, Barry*	.295	44	13	4	8	14	9	.466	.636
Bonilla, B#	.279	43	12	1	3	4	6	.340	.442
Boone, Bret	.071	14	1	0	0	0	8	.071	.071
Branson, Jeff	.304	23	7	3	5	1	1	.333	.696
Brogna, Rico*	.556	9	5	0	2	2	2	.636	.778
Brumfield, J	.200	10	2	1	2	0	3	.182	.500
Bullett, S*	.182	11	2	0	1	1	2	.250	.364
Burks, Ellis	.429	14	6	2	7	1	4	.467	1.000
Butler, Brett*	.348	66	23	0	1	15	9	.476	.455
Caminiti, Ken#	.220	59	13	0	2	5	11	.273	.237
Candaele, C#	.056	18	1	0	1	3	1	.190	.056
Cangelosi, J#	.556	18	10	0	1	5	2	.679	.556
Carr, Chuck	.375	8	3	0	0	2	1	.500	.375
Carreon, Mark	.154	13	2	0	0	1	1	.214	.231
Carter, Joe	.571	7	4	1	3	1	2	.625	1.000

John Smoltz, Braves — RHP (continued)

Batter	Avg	AB	H	HR	BI	BB	SO	OBP	Slg
Castilla, V	.200	20	4	0	0	0	7	.200	.200
Cedeno, A	.270	37	10	0	4	1	12	.289	.351
Cianfrocco, A	.000	9	0	0	0	0	4	.000	.000
Clark, Dave*	.231	26	6	0	4	2	8	.300	.231
Clark, Will*	.273	55	15	1	7	3	5	.300	.345
Clayton, R	.200	15	3	0	0	1	4	.250	.200
Colbrunn, G	.200	10	2	0	2	1	0	.273	.200
Coleman, V#	.333	27	9	1	3	1	5	.357	.556
Conine, Jeff	.238	21	5	1	4	3	11	.333	.381
Cordero, Wil	.316	19	6	2	5	0	5	.316	.789
Dascenzo, D#	.250	24	6	1	2	0	6	.250	.375
Daulton, D*	.167	36	6	2	6	6	8	.286	.361
Davis, Eric	.438	32	14	5	8	5	5	.514	.969
Dawson, Andre	.074	27	2	1	1	0	9	.107	.185
Decker, Steve	.143	14	2	0	1	2	2	.200	.214
DeShields, D*	.256	39	10	0	3	7	9	.370	.282
Duncan, M	.211	19	4	0	1	1	6	.250	.263
Dunston, S	.271	48	13	2	9	0	11	.265	.438
Dykstra, L*	.333	43	12	0	2	5	5	.367	.349
Eisenreich, J*	.080	25	2	0	1	3	4	.172	.080
Elster, Kevin	.182	11	2	0	2	2	2	.308	.364
Eusebio, Tony	.333	6	2	0	0	0	3	.333	.333
Everett, Carl#	.333	12	4	0	2	1	3	.385	.333
Finley, Steve*	.207	58	12	1	3	1	16	.220	.293
Fletcher, D*	.240	25	6	1	3	2	3	.321	.440
Floyd, Cliff*	.143	7	1	0	0	2	3	.333	.286
Frazier, Lou#	.200	5	1	0	0	1	0	.333	.200
Gaetti, Gary	.600	5	3	0	0	2	1	.714	.800
Gagne, Greg	.200	5	1	0	1	1	3	.333	.200
Galarraga, A	.135	37	5	1	6	2	16	.195	.297
Gant, Ron	.200	15	3	2	5	2	5	.278	.667
Garcia, C	.313	16	5	0	1	1	4	.333	.313
Gilkey, B	.304	23	7	0	3	2	4	.360	.435
Girardi, Joe	.227	22	5	0	1	3	4	.320	.227
Goff, Jerry*	.167	6	1	0	0	0	1	.167	.167
Gonzalez, L*	.231	52	12	1	4	8	11	.333	.365
Grace, Mark*	.317	60	19	5	8	11	6	.423	.683
Greene, W*	.400	5	2	0	0	0	1	.400	.400
Grissom, M	.258	31	8	0	0	0	4	.258	.290
Grudzielanek	.333	12	4	0	2	0	3	.333	.500
Gutierrez, R	.400	5	2	0	0	1	1	.500	.400
Gwynn, Chris*	.278	18	5	0	0	1	5	.316	.333
Gwynn, Tony*	.453	53	24	2	10	1	1	.463	.717
Hansen, Dave*	.200	15	3	0	1	1	5	.250	.200
Harris, Lenny*	.321	56	18	0	6	6	6	.387	.375
Hayes, C	.200	40	8	2	6	7	7	.319	.400
Hill, G	.000	6	0	0	0	0	6	.000	.000
Hollandsworth*	.500	6	3	0	0	1	2	.625	.500
Hollins, Dave#	.400	10	4	0	4	7	1	.611	.600
Howard, T*	.211	19	4	0	1	0	4	.211	.316
Howell, Jack*	.000	5	0	0	0	1	2	.167	.000
Hudler, Rex	.400	5	2	0	1	0	1	.400	.400
Hundley, Todd#	.250	32	8	1	5	0	6	.242	.406
Hunter, Brian	.000	6	0	0	1	0	0	.000	.000
Hunter, Bri L	.286	7	2	0	2	1	3	.375	.429
Incaviglia, P	.154	13	2	1	2	0	6	.154	.385
Javier, Stan#	.167	18	3	0	1	0	2	.167	.167
Jefferies, G#	.194	36	7	1	4	1	1	.216	.333
Johnson, Char	.000	7	0	0	0	0	3	.000	.000
Johnson, L*	.286	7	2	0	0	0	2	.286	.429
Johnson, Mark*	.250	16	4	0	1	2	2	.368	.375
Jones, Chris	.167	6	1	1	2	2	3	.667	.667
Jordan, Brian	.250	16	4	1	10	0	2	.235	.625
Jordan, Ricky	.217	23	5	0	2	0	6	.217	.304
Joyner, Wally*	.000	6	0	0	0	1	2	.143	.000
Karros, Eric	.216	37	8	2	4	2	15	.256	.405
Kelly, R	.000	13	0	0	1	0	1	.071	.000
Kendall, J	.333	12	4	0	0	0	0	.333	.417
Kent, Jeff	.286	21	6	1	2	1	4	.318	.476
King, Jeff	.158	38	6	1	2	4	7	.238	.289
Kingery, Mike*	.150	20	3	0	0	2	3	.190	.150
Lampkin, Tom*	.000	5	0	0	1	0	2	.000	.000
Lankford, Ray*	.289	45	13	1	5	2	7	.306	.467
Lansing, Mike	.182	22	4	0	0	2	5	.250	.182
Larkin, Barry	.286	63	18	3	6	5	3	.338	.460
Lewis, Darren	.263	19	5	0	0	2	2	.263	.263
Lieberthal, M	.167	6	1	0	0	0	2	.167	.167
Liriano, N#	.000	10	0	0	0	0	2	.000	.000
Mabry, John*	.300	10	3	1	2	2	3	.417	.600
Magadan, Dave*	.333	39	13	1	5	7	4	.435	.513
Manwaring, K	.125	24	3	1	3	0	6	.125	.250
Martin, Al*	.586	29	17	1	7	5	5	.647	.931
Martinez, Da*	.302	43	13	1	6	5	9	.375	.488
May, Derrick*	.235	34	8	0	0	1	3	.257	.265
McCracken, Q#	.000	5	0	0	0	0	2	.000	.000
McGee, Willie*	.250	52	13	0	7	3	8	.281	.346
McGriff, Fred*	.320	25	8	4	3	7	3	.393	.520
McRae, Brian*	.143	14	2	0	2	0	3	.143	.143
Merced, Q*	.344	32	11	1	3	9	7	.488	.531
Miller, Orl	.313	16	5	1	1	4	2	.353	.563
Mitchell, K	.317	41	13	4	11	5	8	.391	.732

John Smoltz, Braves — RHP

Batter	Avg	AB	H	HR	BI	BB	SO	OBP	Slg
Mondesi, Raul	.222	18	4	2	2	1	6	.263	.611
Morandini, M*	.311	45	14	0	8	3	12	.354	.378
Morris, Hal*	.313	48	15	1	6	7	6	.393	.417
Mouton, James	.182	11	2	0	0	0	4	.182	.182
Murray, Eddie#	.295	44	13	1	4	3	3	.333	.386
Newfield, M	.143	7	1	0	0	1	2	.250	.286
O'Neill, Paul*	.205	39	8	1	4	9	5	.354	.282
Offerman, J#	.143	28	4	0	0	1	7	.172	.143
Oliver, Joe	.292	24	7	1	1	2	6	.346	.417
Ordonez, Rey	.167	6	1	0	0	0	2	.167	.167
Orsulak, Joe*	.400	20	8	0	1	1	2	.429	.400
Pagnozzi, Tom	.229	35	8	0	2	2	8	.263	.314
Pena, G#	.333	9	3	0	0	0	0	.333	.667
Pena, Tony	.143	7	1	0	0	0	3	.143	.143
Pendleton, T#	.194	31	6	0	5	3	8	.265	.194
Petagine, Rob*	.143	7	1	0	1	0	2	.143	.286
Phillips, J*	.143	7	1	1	3	1	4	.250	.571
Piazza, Mike	.148	27	4	1	3	2	11	.207	.296
Plantier, P*	.000	14	0	0	0	5	.000	.000
Prince, Tom	.111	9	1	0	1	2	.200	.222
Raines, Tim#	.125	8	1	0	3	1	0	.222	.375
Reed, Jeff*	.208	24	5	0	1	5	3	.345	.250
Reed, Jody	.154	26	4	0	0	1	6	.185	.154
Roberson, K#	.333	6	2	1	2	1	0	.429	.833
Roberts, Bip#	.382	34	13	0	1	11	4	.533	.500
Rodriguez, H*	.105	19	2	0	0	2	7	.190	.158
Sabo, Chris	.158	38	6	0	1	3	12	.220	.237
Samuel, Juan	.255	47	12	1	4	1	17	.271	.319
Sanchez, Rey	.208	24	5	0	0	4	.208	.333
Sandberg, R	.279	43	12	6	11	7	7	.392	.698
Sanders, R.	.147	34	5	1	2	0	15	.147	.235
Santangelo, F#	.200	5	1	0	0	0	2	.200	.200
Santiago, B	.245	49	12	5	10	2	19	.275	.551
Schofield, D	.250	4	1	0	0	3	0	.571	.250
Segui, David#	.308	13	4	1	3	1	.438	.538
Servais, S	.158	19	3	1	1	0	6	.200	.316
Sheaffer, D	.286	14	4	0	2	0	3	.286	.429
Sheffield, G	.188	32	6	1	5	7	5	.333	.375
Shipley, C	.000	6	0	0	0	0	5	.000	.000
Simms, Mike	.125	8	1	0	2	0	3	.125	.250
Slaught, Don	.000	9	0	0	0	0	2	.100	.000
Smith, Dwight*	.000	19	0	0	0	0	2	.000	.000
Smith, Ozzie#	.322	59	19	0	4	3	4	.365	.390
Sosa, Sammy	.040	25	1	0	0	2	14	.111	.120
Stillwell, K#	.000	13	0	0	1	0	3	.000	.000
Stocker, K#	.211	19	4	0	1	1	2	.250	.263
Strange, Doug*	.333	6	2	0	0	1	1	.429	.333
Strawberry, D*	.182	33	6	0	4	3	5	.250	.303
Taubensee, E*	.300	30	9	1	3	3	9	.364	.433
Thompson, Mil*	.276	29	8	0	2	5	4	.382	.310
Thompson, Rob	.237	59	14	2	5	3	16	.286	.424
Thompson, Ry	.182	11	2	2	8	1	4	.250	.727
VanderWal, J*	.333	12	4	0	1	3	.500	.333
Veras, Q#	.500	10	5	0	1	2	3	.583	1.200
Vizcaino, J#	.171	35	6	0	1	3	5	.237	.171
Walker, Larry*	.326	46	15	0	7	4	13	.380	.500
Wallach, Tim	.205	44	9	0	2	5	14	.286	.318
Walton, J	.333	18	6	0	0	0	3	.333	.444
Webster, L	.222	9	2	0	0	0	2	.222	.333
Weiss, Walt#	.083	24	2	0	0	2	5	.154	.083
White, Devon#	.000	5	0	0	0	1	1	.167	.000
Whiten, Mark#	.267	15	4	2	6	3	5	.389	.667
Wilkins, Rick*	.323	31	10	4	7	1	8	.333	.742
Williams, Ma	.290	62	18	1	13	1	14	.292	.419
Young, Eric	.300	20	6	0	3	1	3	.318	.350
Zeile, Todd	.250	44	11	0	7	6	11	.340	.318

Steve Soderstrom, Giants — RHP

Batter	Avg	AB	H	HR	BI	BB	SO	OBP	Slg
Castilla, V	.167	6	1	0	0	0	2	.167	.167
Galarraga, A	.500	4	2	0	1	2	1	.571	.500
McCracken, Q#	.600	5	3	0	1	1	0	.667	.600
Perez, Neifi#	.000	6	0	0	0	0	0	.000	.000
Reed, Jeff*	.400	5	2	0	2	0	0	.400	.400

Clint Sodowsky, Tigers — RHP

Batter	Avg	AB	H	HR	BI	BB	SO	OBP	Slg
Berroa, G	.200	5	1	0	0	0	0	.200	.200
Giambi, Jason*	.400	5	2	0	0	0	0	.400	.400
Jefferson, R*	.667	6	4	2	5	0	0	.667	1.667
Knoblauch, C	.500	2	1	0	0	1	0	.800	.500
Molitor, Paul	.143	7	1	0	2	0	2	.143	.143
O'Leary, Troy*	.600	5	3	0	0	0	0	.600	.600
Valentin, Jhn	.500	4	2	0	1	2	0	.667	.500
Vaughn, Mo*	.167	6	1	0	1	0	1	.167	.167
Young, Ernie	.600	5	3	0	2	0	0	.600	.600

Steve Sparks, Brewers — RHP

Batter	Avg	AB	H	HR	BI	BB	SO	OBP	Slg
Aldrete, Mike*	.400	5	2	0	1	2	.500	.400
Alomar, R#	.286	7	2	0	0	1	0	.375	.286

Steve Sparks, Brewers — RHP

Batter	Avg	AB	H	HR	BI	BB	SO	OBP	Slg
Anderson, Brd*	.375	8	3	1	2	4	1	.583	.750
Anderson, G*	.222	9	2	0	2	0	1	.222	.222
Baerga, C#	.400	15	6	0	1	0	1	.400	.600
Baines, H*	.077	13	1	0	1	2	1	.200	.077
Becker, Rich*	.100	10	1	0	0	1	1	.182	.100
Belle, Albert	.462	13	6	1	3	0	0	.429	.769
Berroa, G	.250	8	2	0	3	0	1	.250	.375
Boggs, Wade*	.364	11	4	1	1	0	2	.364	.636
Bonilla, B#	.167	6	1	0	0	1	2	.286	.333
Bordick, Mike	.429	7	3	0	0	0	1	.429	.571
Brosius, S	.750	4	3	2	4	1	0	.800	2.250
Buhner, Jay	.333	6	2	2	5	1	1	.500	1.333
Canseco, Jose	.375	8	3	0	3	0	2	.375	.500
Carter, Joe	.571	7	4	1	2	0	0	.625	1.000
Cedeno, D*	.400	5	2	0	0	0	0	.400	.600
Clark, Tony#	.333	6	2	0	0	2	2	.500	.333
Clark, Will*	.333	9	3	0	0	2	1	.455	.556
Cora, Joey*	.125	8	1	0	1	0	1	.125	.125
Cordova, M	.300	10	3	1	3	2	0	.417	.700
Curtis, Chad	.300	10	3	0	1	0	1	.273	.500
Damon, Johnny*	.300	10	3	0	0	0	1	.300	.500
Davis, Chili#	.000	3	0	0	0	2	1	.400	.000
Davis, Russ	.200	5	1	1	1	0	0	.200	.800
Devereaux, M	.400	5	2	0	0	1	0	.500	.400
DiSarcina, G	.111	9	1	0	0	0	0	.111	.111
Durham, Ray#	.231	13	3	0	3	0	0	.231	.385
Easley, D	.143	7	1	0	1	0	0	.125	.143
Edmonds, Jim*	.286	7	2	0	1	2	1	.444	.429
Fabregas, Jor*	.167	6	1	0	0	1	0	.286	.167
Fasano, Sal	.000	6	0	0	0	0	1	.000	.000
Fielder, C	.222	9	2	0	3	3	3	.417	.222
Frye, Jeff	.200	5	1	0	0	2	2	.429	.200
Fryman, T	.125	8	1	0	3	1	.364	.250
Gaetti, Gary	.286	7	2	0	1	0	2	.286	.286
Gagne, Greg	.250	8	2	0	0	0	0	.250	.250
Gates, Brent#	.000	6	0	0	0	0	1	.000	.000
Giambi, Jason*	.500	6	3	1	3	1	0	.571	1.500
Gil, Benji	.300	10	3	0	0	0	1	.300	.400
Gonzalez, A	.000	5	0	0	0	0	0	.000	.000
Gonzalez, J	.800	8	4	2	5	0	1	.500	1.250
Goodwin, C*	.000	7	0	0	0	2	3	.222	.000
Goodwin, Tom*	.214	14	3	0	0	2	3	.313	.214
Green, Shawn*	.250	5	1	0	1	0	3	.333	.200
Greenwell, M*	.000	7	0	0	0	0	2	.000	.000
Greer, Rusty*	.455	11	5	1	3	1	1	.462	.909
Griffey Jr, K*	.000	4	0	0	0	4	1	.500	.000
Guillen, O*	.500	12	6	0	0	0	0	.500	.500
Hamelin, Bob*	.400	5	2	0	0	2	1	.571	.400
Hammonds, J	.750	4	3	1	2	1	0	.800	1.500
Henderson, R	.000	4	0	0	0	1	2	.200	.000
Higginson, B*	.143	7	1	0	0	3	4	.400	.143
Hocking, D#	.000	3	0	0	0	1	0	.250	.000
Hoiles, Chris	.667	3	2	0	0	2	0	.800	.667
Hollins, Dave#	.250	4	1	0	0	1	0	.400	.250
Hosey, Dwayne*	.286	7	2	0	0	1	2	.375	.571
Howard, Dave#	.167	6	1	0	0	0	0	.167	.500
Huff, Michael	.231	13	3	0	1	2	1	.667	.750
Javier, Stan#	.500	4	2	0	0	1	0	.600	.500
Jefferson, R*	.000	7	0	0	0	1	1	.125	.000
Johnson, L*	.286	7	2	1	1	0	0	.286	.714
Joyner, Wally*	.286	7	2	1	2	0	0	.250	.714
Karkovice, B	.300	10	3	2	4	0	1	.300	.900
Kelly, Pat	.500	4	2	0	1	1	1	.500	.500
Knoblauch, C	.111	9	1	0	1	1	1	.182	.333
Lockhart, K*	.111	9	1	0	1	1	0	.182	.111
Lofton, Kenny*	.231	13	3	0	1	2	1	.333	.231
Martinez, E	.200	5	1	0	0	1	2	.333	.200
Mayne, Brent*	.000	6	0	0	0	0	0	.000	.000
McGwire, Mark	.333	3	1	0	0	4	0	.750	.667
McLemore, M#	.400	10	4	0	3	2	1	.462	.600
Meares, Pat	.375	8	3	0	1	0	0	.375	.500
Molitor, Paul	.636	11	7	0	3	0	0	.636	.818
Munoz, Pedro	.400	5	2	0	0	0	0	.400	.400
Murray, Eddie#	.357	14	5	0	4	1	0	.357	.429
Myers, Greg*	.444	9	4	1	2	1	0	.500	1.111
Naehring, Tim	.333	6	2	0	0	0	0	.333	.333
Nixon, Otis#	.200	10	2	0	0	1	1	.273	.200
Nunnally, Jon*	.000	4	0	0	1	2	1	.333	.000
O'Neill, Paul*	.444	9	4	0	1	2	0	.545	.444
Olerud, John*	.400	5	2	0	0	1	1	.500	.400
Palmeiro, R*	.375	8	3	0	2	1	0	.400	.625
Palmer, Dean	.500	6	3	1	2	0	0	.500	1.000
Pena, Tony	.300	10	3	0	1	1	0	.364	.400
Phillips, T#	.333	15	5	1	3	4	.444	.533
Polonia, Luis*	.000	8	0	0	1	0	.000	.000
Raines, Tim#	.167	6	1	0	0	0	0	.286	.333
Ramirez, M	.250	12	3	1	2	1	1	.308	.500
Ripken, Cal	.222	9	2	0	0	1	0	.300	.222
Rodriguez, I	.333	9	3	0	0	0	1	.333	.444
Salmon, Tim	.000	7	0	0	1	1	1	.111	.000
Sierra, Ruben#	.500	6	3	1	1	1	0	.571	1.000

Steve Sparks, Brewers — RHP

Batter	Avg	AB	H	HR	BI	BB	SO	OBP	Slg
Snow, J.T.#	.400	5	2	0	1	2	0	.571	.400
Sorrento, P*	.467	15	7	2	8	2	0	.529	1.067
Sprague, Ed	.429	7	3	0	3	0	2	.500	.429
Stahoviak, S*	.444	9	4	0	3	0	1	.444	.667
Stairs, Matt*	.333	6	2	0	1	0	1	.286	.333
Stanley, Mike	.375	8	3	1	1	0	3	.375	.875
Steinbach, T	.000	5	0	0	0	0	0	.000	.000
Tartabull, D	.000	10	0	0	0	2	5	.167	.000
Tettleton, M#	.100	10	1	0	0	3	0	.308	.100
Thomas, Frank	.333	12	4	1	2	3	1	.467	.667
Thome, Jim*	.364	11	4	1	1	2	1	.462	.727
Trammell, A	.250	4	1	0	0	1	0	.400	.250
Tucker, M*	.333	9	3	1	3	0	0	.333	.778
Valentin, Jhn	.286	7	2	0	1	1	0	.375	.571
Valle, Dave	.400	5	2	0	1	1	0	.500	.400
Vaughn, Mo*	.375	8	3	1	2	0	0	.375	.750
Ventura, R*	.333	12	4	0	1	2	0	.429	.500
Vitiello, Joe	.000	4	0	0	0	0	0	.000	.000
Vizquel, Omar#	.200	15	3	1	2	1	0	.333	.000
Williams, Ber#	.200	10	2	0	1	1	1	.273	.300
Wilson, Dan	.400	5	2	2	3	3	0	.625	1.600

Paul Spoljaric, Blue Jays — LHP

Batter	Avg	AB	H	HR	BI	BB	SO	OBP	Slg
Anderson, Brd*	.400	5	2	0	0	0	3	.400	.600
Palmeiro, R*	.000	4	0	0	0	1	3	.200	.000

Jerry Spradlin, Reds — RHP

Batter	Avg	AB	H	HR	BI	BB	SO	OBP	Slg
Young, Eric	.333	3	1	1	3	1	1	.400	1.333

Dennis Springer, Angels — RHP

Batter	Avg	AB	H	HR	BI	BB	SO	OBP	Slg
Abbott, Kurt	.400	5	2	1	3	0	0	.400	1.000
Alomar, R#	.333	6	2	0	0	0	0	.333	.333
Anderson, Brd*	.500	6	3	1	1	1	0	.571	1.000
Boggs, Wade*	.250	4	1	0	0	1	1	.400	.250
Bonilla, B#	.333	6	2	0	0	0	2	.333	.333
Bragg, Darren*	.000	5	0	0	0	1	0	.167	.000
Buhner, Jay	.000	5	0	0	0	1	1	.286	.000
Colbrunn, G	.200	5	1	0	0	0	0	.200	.400
Conine, Jeff	.000	5	0	0	0	0	1	.000	.000
Cora, Joey*	.375	8	3	0	2	0	0	.375	.625
Duncan, M	.500	8	4	2	5	0	0	.500	1.375
Fielder, C	.250	8	2	0	2	0	2	.333	.250
Griffey Jr, K*	.333	6	2	1	4	1	1	.429	.833
Hollins, Dave#	.200	5	1	0	1	1	0	.333	.200
Jeter, Derek	.200	5	1	0	0	0	0	.200	.200
Leyritz, Jim	.400	5	2	2	3	0	0	.400	1.600
Lofton, Kenny*	.400	5	2	1	1	1	0	.500	1.200
Martinez, E	.400	5	2	0	1	1	0	.400	.400
Martinez, T*	.250	4	1	0	1	2	1	.400	1.000
Murray, Eddie*	.400	5	2	0	0	1	0	.500	.600
O'Neill, Paul*	.400	5	2	1	1	0	0	.400	1.200
Palmeiro, R*	.000	6	0	0	0	2	0	.000	.000
Pendleton, T#	.250	4	1	0	0	1	1	.400	.250
Rodriguez, Al	.500	6	3	0	0	1	2	.571	.500
Seltzer, K	.200	5	1	0	0	2	0	.429	.200
Sorrento, P*	.167	6	1	0	0	0	3	.167	.167
Strawberry, D*	.400	5	2	1	2	1	1	.500	1.000
Surhoff, B.J.*	.000	6	0	0	0	0	2	.000	.000
Tavarez, Je#	.400	5	2	0	0	0	0	.400	.800
Williams, Ber#	.000	5	0	0	0	0	1	.000	.000
Wilson, Dan	.200	5	1	0	0	0	1	.200	.200

Russ Springer, Phillies — RHP

Batter	Avg	AB	H	HR	BI	BB	SO	OBP	Slg
Abbott, Kurt	.250	4	1	0	0	0	2	.200	.250
Aldrete, Mike*	.200	5	1	0	0	0	1	.333	.200
Alfonzo, E	.200	5	1	0	1	0	1	.333	.200
Alicea, Luis#	.250	4	1	0	0	1	0	.400	.250
Alomar, R#	.200	5	1	1	1	0	0	.200	.800
Anderson, Brd*	.000	5	0	0	0	1	2	.167	.000
Baerga, C#	.143	7	1	0	1	1	1	.250	.143
Bagwell, Jeff	.500	4	2	2	3	1	0	.600	2.000
Baines, H*	1.000	4	4	0	0	1	0	1.000	1.250
Bell, Jay	.000	4	0	0	0	1	3	.200	.000
Belle, Albert	.167	6	1	1	1	1	0	.286	.667
Bichette, D	.400	5	2	0	2	0	0	.400	.400
Biggio, Craig	.333	6	2	1	3	0	1	.333	.833
Boggs, Wade*	.333	6	2	0	0	1	0	.429	.500
Bordick, Mike	.500	4	2	0	0	0	1	.600	.500
Brosius, S	.000	5	0	0	0	0	2	.000	.000
Burks, Ellis	.200	5	1	1	2	1	2	.333	.800
Canseco, Jose	.167	6	1	0	0	0	2	.167	.167
Carter, Joe	.000	4	0	0	0	1	1	.200	.000
Colbrunn, G	.000	6	0	0	0	1	1	.200	.000
Conine, Jeff	.286	7	2	1	1	0	0	.375	.429
Cora, Joey#	.429	7	3	0	2	0	1	.375	.429
Curtis, Chad	.200	5	1	0	1	0	0	.200	.400
Dawson, Andre	.125	8	1	0	1	0	0	.125	.125
DeShields, D*	.200	5	1	1	2	0	3	.200	.800
Fermin, Felix	.125	8	1	0	0	0	0	.125	.125
Fielder, C	.125	8	1	1	2	0	3	.125	.500
Fryman, T	.571	7	4	0	2	1	1	.625	1.000
Gaetti, Gary	.200	5	1	0	0	0	1	.200	.200
Gagne, Greg	.250	4	1	0	1	0	1	.200	.200
Gallego, Mike	.000	3	0	0	1	1	1	.200	.000
Gates, Brent*	.375	8	3	1	4	1	0	.444	.875
Gilkey, B	.500	4	2	0	0	1	0	.600	.500
Gonzalez, J	.000	7	0	0	0	0	0	.000	.000
Greenwell, M*	.250	8	2	0	0	1	0	.333	.375
Grissom, M	.600	5	3	0	1	0	0	.600	.800
Guillen, O*	.400	5	2	0	0	0	2	.400	.600
Hale, Chip*	.429	7	3	0	1	1	2	.500	.571
Hayes, C	.000	5	0	0	0	0	0	.000	.000
Henderson, R	.200	5	1	0	0	5	1	.600	.200
Hoiles, Chris	.200	5	1	1	2	0	1	.200	.800
Hulse, David*	.000	4	0	0	0	1	1	.200	.000
Hunter, Bri L	.333	6	2	0	0	1	0	.333	.500
Huskey, Butch	.400	5	2	0	1	0	2	.400	.400
James, Dion*	.200	5	1	0	0	0	1	.200	.200
Jefferson, R*	.400	5	2	2	2	1	1	.500	1.600
Johnson, L*	.417	12	5	1	1	0	0	.417	.750
Jones, C#	.600	5	3	0	1	0	0	.600	1.000
Kelly, Pat	.000	5	0	0	0	0	0	.000	.000
King, Jeff	.600	5	3	0	3	0	0	.600	1.600
Kirby, Wayne*	.200	5	1	1	2	0	0	.333	.800
Klesko, Ryan*	.167	6	1	0	1	0	1	.167	.167
Knoblauch, C	.417	12	5	0	2	2	3	.500	.500
Kreuter, Chad#	.000	4	0	0	0	1	0	.200	.000
Lankford, Ray*	.400	5	2	0	1	0	1	.400	.800
Lemke, Mark*	.600	5	3	0	2	0	0	.600	1.000
Livingstone*	.400	5	2	0	0	0	2	.400	.400
Lofton, Kenny*	.600	5	3	0	0	1	0	.667	.600
Martinez, T*	.600	5	3	0	0	1	0	.667	.800
Mayne, Brent*	.200	5	1	0	0	3	0	.200	.200
McCarty, Dave	.200	5	1	0	0	0	1	.200	.200
McGriff, Fred*	.200	5	1	0	0	0	1	.200	.200
McLemore, M#	.000	5	0	0	0	1	0	.000	.000
Meares, Pat	.200	5	1	0	0	1	2	.333	.200
Molitor, Paul	.429	7	3	0	1	0	0	.429	.429
Mouton, James	.200	5	1	0	0	0	0	.200	.200
Naehring, Tim	.600	5	3	0	2	2	0	.714	.800
Nixon, Otis*	.200	5	1	0	0	1	0	.200	.200
O'Neill, Paul*	.333	6	2	1	1	0	0	.333	.833
Ochoa, Alex	.600	5	3	0	2	0	0	.600	.600
Olerud, John*	.333	3	1	0	0	2	1	.600	.333
Oliver, Joe	.000	5	0	0	0	0	0	.000	.000
Ordonez, Rey	.200	5	1	0	0	0	1	.200	.200
Palmeiro, R*	.500	8	4	2	5	0	0	.500	1.250
Paquette, C	.000	5	0	0	0	0	0	.000	.000
Pendleton, T#	.200	5	1	0	0	2	1	.429	.200
Raines, Tim*	.500	6	3	0	1	0	0	.500	.667
Reed, Jody	.000	4	0	0	1	1	0	.167	.000
Ripken, Cal	.286	7	2	1	2	1	0	.375	.714
Sabo, Chris	.600	5	3	0	0	0	2	.600	.800
Sheffield, G	.600	5	3	1	4	2	1	.714	1.400
Sierra, Ruben#	.444	9	4	1	3	1	2	.500	.778
Sojo, Luis	.333	6	2	1	3	1	0	.429	.833
Sorrento, P*	.167	6	1	0	0	1	3	.286	.167
Sprague, Ed	1.000	3	3	0	1	1	0	1.000	1.333
Stahoviak, S*	.750	4	3	0	1	0	0	.800	1.000
Steinbach, T	.286	7	2	0	0	0	0	.286	.429
Sweeney, Mark*	.000	5	0	0	0	0	0	.000	.000
Tartabull, D	.667	6	4	1	4	1	2	.714	1.500
Tettleton, M#	.500	4	2	1	1	2	0	.667	1.250
Thomas, Frank	.600	5	3	0	3	0	0	.600	.600
Valentin, Jhn	.333	9	3	0	1	1	0	.400	.556
Vaughn, Mo*	.143	7	1	0	0	1	3	.250	.143
Ventura, R*	.000	5	0	0	0	0	1	.167	.000
Veras, Q#	.250	4	1	0	0	3	0	.571	.250
Vizcaino, J#	.000	8	0	0	1	1	0	.000	.000
Wallach, Tim	.400	5	2	0	0	1	0	.400	.800
White, Devon#	.200	10	2	0	1	1	2	.273	.400
Whiten, Mark*	.750	4	3	0	2	2	0	.833	1.000
Williams, Ber#	.125	8	1	0	0	0	1	.125	.125

Mike Stanton, Rangers — LHP

Batter	Avg	AB	H	HR	BI	BB	SO	OBP	Slg
Alicea, Luis#	.250	4	1	0	0	1	0	.500	.250
Anderson, Brd*	.000	5	0	0	0	1	2	.167	.000
Anderson, G*	.500	4	2	0	2	0	1	.500	.750
Anthony, Eric*	.000	3	0	0	1	1	2	.200	.000
Bagwell, Jeff	.400	5	2	0	2	1	1	.571	.600
Bell, Derek	.600	5	3	0	1	0	1	.600	.600
Bell, Jay	.400	5	2	0	1	1	0	.500	.600
Biggio, Craig	.143	14	2	0	1	1	3	.200	.143
Bonds, Barry*	.300	10	3	0	1	5	1	.533	.500
Bonilla, B#	.273	11	3	0	2	1	1	.308	.273
Butler, Brett*	.091	11	1	0	1	3	0	.286	.091
Caminiti, Ken*	.222	18	4	0	3	0	4	.222	.333

Mike Stanton, Rangers — LHP

Batter	Avg	AB	H	HR	BI	BB	SO	OBP	Slg
Carr, Chuck	.400	5	2	0	0	0	1	.400	.400
Cedeno, A	.375	8	3	0	2	1	0	.500	.375
Clark, Will*	.364	11	4	0	3	2	3	.462	.545
Damon, Johnny*	.250	4	1	0	1	1	0	.400	.250
Daulton, D*	.385	13	5	1	1	3	3	.500	.769
Davis, Eric	.000	6	0	0	0	1	4	.143	.000
DeShields, D*	.000	10	0	0	0	2	3	.167	.000
Duncan, A	.222	9	2	0	1	1	2	.300	.222
Dykstra, L*	.100	10	1	0	0	1	3	.250	.100
Eisenreich, J*	.000	6	0	0	0	1	2	.143	.000
Finley, Steve*	.357	14	5	0	0	2	3	.438	.429
Garcia, C	.500	6	3	0	1	0	0	.500	.667
Gilkey, B	.333	6	2	0	2	1	2	.429	.500
Gonzalez, L*	.100	10	1	0	1	3	3	.286	.100
Grace, Mark*	.333	15	5	0	2	4	2	.474	.400
Grissom, M	.375	8	3	0	5	1	1	.444	.625
Guillen, O*	.600	5	3	1	0	0	0	.600	.600
Gwynn, Tony*	.231	13	3	0	0	1	0	.286	.231
Hollins, Dave#	.333	12	4	1	1	2	2	.429	.750
Javier, Stan#	.000	5	0	0	0	1	0	.167	.000
Jefferies, G#	.500	8	4	1	2	0	0	.600	.625
Jordan, Ricky	.375	8	3	0	0	0	0	.375	.500
King, Jeff	.400	5	2	0	1	0	1	.400	.400
Lankford, Ray*	.455	11	5	1	3	1	4	.500	.727
Larkin, Barry	.200	10	2	0	1	0	1	.200	.200
Lewis, Darren	.167	6	1	0	1	1	2	.286	.167
Lofton, Kenny*	.364	11	4	0	3	0	2	.364	.545
Magadan, Dave*	.200	5	1	0	0	0	1	.200	.200
Martinez, Da*	.500	8	4	1	3	0	2	.500	.875
Martinez, T*	.250	4	1	0	0	1	0	.400	.250
May, Derrick*	.400	5	2	1	7	0	1	.333	1.200
McGee, Willie*	.167	6	1	0	1	0	2	.167	.167
McGriff, Fred*	.143	14	2	1	1	0	4	.143	.357
Merced, O*	.222	9	2	0	3	0	1	.222	.333
Morandini, M*	.429	7	3	1	3	0	0	.444	.857
Morris, Hal*	.333	12	4	0	0	4	4	.556	.333
Murray, Eddie*	.071	14	1	0	0	0	1	.071	.071
O'Neill, Paul*	.214	14	3	0	4	0	6	.214	.214
Offerman, J#	.167	12	2	0	0	1	2	.231	.167
Olerud, John*	.200	5	1	0	0	0	0	.200	.200
Oliver, Joe	.600	5	3	0	1	0	0	.571	.600
Palmeiro, R*	.000	5	0	0	1	1	1	.167	.000
Pena, G#	.200	5	1	0	0	0	2	.200	.200
Plantier, P*	.286	7	2	0	0	0	1	.286	.286
Roberts, Bip#	.250	12	3	0	1	0	3	.250	.250
Samuel, Juan	.333	6	2	0	2	0	1	.333	.667
Sandberg, R	.333	9	3	0	1	0	1	.333	.444
Sanders, R	.600	5	3	0	3	1	1	.667	.600
Santiago, B	.444	9	4	0	1	0	0	.444	.444
Sheffield, G	.400	5	2	1	2	1	0	.571	1.000
Smith, Ozzie*	.222	9	2	0	0	0	2	.222	.222
Snow, J.T.#	.200	5	1	0	0	0	2	.200	.400
Sosa, Sammy	.000	4	0	0	0	2	0	.333	.000
Strawberry, D*	.000	11	0	0	0	2	4	.154	.000
Surhoff, B.J.*	.286	7	2	0	0	0	0	.286	.286
Thome, Jim*	.200	5	1	0	2	0	3	.200	.200
Thompson, Mil*	.125	8	1	0	2	0	2	.125	.125
Ventura, R*	.333	6	2	0	1	0	1	.333	.333
Vizcaino, Jo	.286	7	2	0	2	0	2	.286	.429
Vizquel, Omar#	.500	4	2	0	0	2	0	.667	.500
Walker, Larry*	.250	12	3	1	2	0	2	.250	.500
Wallach, Tim	.125	8	1	1	1	0	1	.125	.500
Wilkins, Rick*	.167	6	1	0	0	0	3	.167	.167
Williams, Ma	.500	8	4	0	2	0	0	.500	.750
Wilson, Dan	.400	5	2	0	3	0	1	.400	.600
Young, Eric	.000	5	0	0	0	1	2	.167	.000
Zeile, Todd	.333	3	1	0	1	2	0	.600	.333

Garrett Stephenson, Phillies — RHP

Batter	Avg	AB	H	HR	BI	BB	SO	OBP	Slg
Belle, Albert	.000	4	0	0	0	0	1	.200	.000
Carreon, Mark	.750	4	3	0	0	1	0	.800	.750

Dave Stevens, Twins — RHP

Batter	Avg	AB	H	HR	BI	BB	SO	OBP	Slg
Alomar, R#	.000	4	0	0	0	1	0	.200	.000
Baerga, C#	.200	5	1	0	0	0	1	.200	.200
Belle, Albert	.375	8	3	0	1	0	0	.375	.500
Berroa, G	.571	7	4	2	4	1	0	.625	1.571
Boggs, Wade*	.400	5	2	0	1	0	1	.400	.600
Brosius, S	.250	4	1	0	0	4	0	.625	.500
Buhner, Jay	.400	5	2	2	4	4	1	.667	1.600
Carter, Joe	.167	6	1	1	1	0	3	.167	.667
Cirillo, Jeff	.333	6	2	1	1	0	0	.333	.833
Clark, Will*	.444	9	4	0	2	0	0	.444	.667
Curtis, Chad	.333	6	2	0	0	1	1	.429	.333
Davis, Chili#	.333	6	2	0	2	2	0	.500	.333
DiSarcina, G	.286	7	2	0	2	0	3	.286	.571
Durham, Ray#	.200	5	1	1	2	1	1	.333	.800
Edmonds, Jim*	.143	7	1	0	0	0	2	.143	.143
Espinoza, A	.600	5	3	1	2	0	0	.600	1.200

Dave Stevens, Twins — RHP

Batter	Avg	AB	H	HR	BI	BB	SO	OBP	Slg
Frye, Jeff	.000	5	0	0	0	2	1	.286	.000
Gates, Brent#	.600	5	3	0	3	0	2	.600	1.200
Giambi, Jason*	.200	5	1	0	0	2	3	.429	.200
Gomez, Leo	.000	5	0	0	0	0	2	.000	.000
Gonzalez, J	.125	8	1	0	0	0	0	.125	.250
Greenwell, M*	.250	4	1	0	0	1	0	.400	.250
Greer, Rusty*	.000	5	0	0	0	1	0	.167	.000
Hoiles, Chris	.000	4	0	0	1	0	0	.000	.000
Howard, Dave#	.400	5	2	0	1	1	0	.429	.400
Hudler, Rex	.250	4	1	0	0	0	1	.250	.250
Jaha, John	.600	5	3	2	4	0	0	.600	1.800
Javier, Stan#	.400	5	2	0	3	0	0	.400	.600
Kelly, Pat	.167	6	1	0	0	0	1	.167	.167
Martinez, E	.000	5	0	0	0	0	0	.000	.000
McLemore, M#	.000	3	0	0	1	1	0	.200	.000
Mieske, Matt	.125	8	1	0	2	0	2	.111	.125
Murray, Eddie#	.400	5	2	2	2	1	0	.500	1.600
Nilsson, Dave*	.571	7	4	0	1	0	0	.571	.857
Nixon, Otis#	.667	6	4	0	0	1	0	.714	.833
Palmer, Dean	.000	6	0	0	1	0	2	.143	.000
Paquette, C	.250	4	1	0	1	0	1	.200	.250
Phillips, T#	.571	7	4	0	3	2	0	.667	.571
Ramirez, M	.200	5	1	1	1	3	4	.500	.800
Salmon, Tim	.333	6	2	1	2	2	2	.500	1.000
Seitzer, K	.286	7	2	0	0	1	0	.375	.286
Snow, J.T.#	.143	7	1	0	1	1	2	.250	.286
Sorrento, P*	.286	7	2	0	0	0	0	.286	.286
Steinbach, T	.000	7	0	0	0	1	0	.000	.000
Tettleton, M#	.167	6	1	0	0	0	1	.286	.167
Thomas, Frank	.571	7	4	0	4	1	0	.625	.571
Thome, Jim*	.333	6	2	0	0	0	2	.333	.333
Valentin, Jhn	.000	6	0	0	0	0	0	.000	.000
Valentin, Jse#	.000	5	0	3	3	1	0	.571	1.333
Vaughn, Greg	.143	7	1	0	0	1	3	.250	.143
Ventura, R*	.286	7	2	0	1	0	0	.286	.286
Vizquel, Omar#	.375	8	3	0	3	1	0	.444	.375
Williams, Ber#	.250	4	1	0	0	1	0	.400	.500
Wilson, Dan	.167	6	1	0	1	1	0	.167	.167

Todd Stottlemyre, Cardinals — RHP

Batter	Avg	AB	H	HR	BI	BB	SO	OBP	Slg
Alfonzo, E	.000	5	0	0	0	0	1	.000	.000
Alicea, Luis#	.250	8	2	0	0	3	1	.455	.250
Alomar Jr, S	.308	26	8	1	6	1	2	.321	.462
Alou, Moises	.125	8	1	1	3	1	1	.222	.500
Amaral, Rich	.143	7	1	0	1	0	0	.143	.143
Anderson, Brd*	.316	38	12	2	4	3	7	.366	.500
Anderson, G*	.250	8	2	1	2	0	2	.222	.625
Andrews, S	.167	6	1	0	0	0	2	.286	.333
Arias, Alex	.125	8	1	1	3	0	2	.125	.500
Baerga, C#	.378	37	14	1	5	5	4	.452	.541
Bagwell, Jeff	.444	9	4	1	1	5	0	.667	.778
Baines, H*	.395	38	15	5	13	5	6	.465	.868
Becker, Rich*	.100	11	1	0	0	1	6	.182	.100
Bell, Derek	.267	15	4	0	0	0	2	.267	.333
Bell, Jay	.250	8	2	0	2	0	2	.222	.250
Belle, Albert	.457	35	16	3	8	5	7	.525	.800
Belliard, R	.143	7	1	0	0	0	0	.143	.143
Bichette, D	.071	14	1	0	0	0	4	.071	.071
Biggio, Craig	.125	16	2	0	1	1	4	.176	.125
Blowers, Mike	.000	12	0	0	0	4	3	.250	.000
Boggs, Wade*	.304	46	14	1	2	15	5	.484	.413
Boone, Bret	.125	8	1	1	1	0	4	.125	.500
Bordick, Mike	.167	12	2	0	2	0	0	.167	.167
Brogna, Rico*	.333	6	2	0	0	1	1	.429	.333
Buhner, Jay	.115	26	3	1	2	9	9	.148	.231
Burks, Ellis	.250	36	9	2	4	5	4	.357	.472
Caminiti, Ken#	.000	7	0	0	0	3	2	.300	.000
Cangelosi, J#	.286	7	2	0	0	3	1	.500	.286
Canseco, Jose	.306	36	11	8	15	4	12	.390	.972
Carreon, Mark	.000	2	0	0	0	3	0	.600	.000
Carter, Joe	.000	14	0	0	0	0	4	.000	.000
Castillo, L#	.250	4	1	0	0	2	0	.500	.250
Clark, Dave*	.385	13	5	0	5	0	2	.385	.538
Clark, Will*	.357	14	5	2	2	1	4	.400	.929
Colbrunn, G	.333	6	2	1	2	0	1	.333	.833
Cole, Alex*	.500	20	10	0	0	1	1	.524	.550
Coleman, V#	.133	15	2	0	0	3	0	.133	.133
Conine, Jeff	.125	8	1	0	0	0	5	.125	.125
Cora, Joey#	.292	24	7	0	2	0	5	.292	.292
Cordova, M	.200	10	2	0	0	1	3	.273	.200
Curtis, Chad	.391	23	9	1	3	2	3	.440	.652
Cuyler, Milt*	.222	9	2	0	0	1	1	.300	.444
Davis, Chili#	.314	35	11	1	7	4	3	.385	.486
Davis, Eric	.250	8	2	0	0	2	2	.400	.250
Dawson, Andre	.000	4	0	0	1	0	2	.375	.000
Deer, Rob	.154	13	2	1	1	3	8	.313	.385
DeShields, D*	.400	5	2	0	1	1	1	.500	.400
Devereaux, M	.214	28	6	1	3	3	2	.290	.321
DiSarcina, G	.083	24	2	0	1	0	0	.083	.083
Durham, Ray#	.250	4	1	0	0	1	0	.400	.250

199

Batter	Avg	AB	H	HR	BI	BB	SO	OBP	Slg
Easley, D	.556	9	5	0	1	1	2	.600	.667
Edmonds, Jim*	.364	11	4	0	1	2	6	.462	.636
Eisenreich, J*	.370	27	10	0	4	0	1	.370	.444
Espinoza, A	.167	36	6	0	3	0	7	.162	.167
Eusebio, Tony	.286	7	2	0	1	0	0	.286	.286
Fabregas, Jor*	.222	9	2	0	1	0	3	.222	.222
Fermin, Felix	.310	29	9	0	3	2	1	.344	.414
Fielder, C	.364	22	8	2	7	3	6	.423	.636
Finley, Steve*	.154	13	2	0	0	1	2	.214	.231
Flaherty, J	.273	11	3	0	1	0	1	.250	.273
Fletcher, D*	.333	9	3	1	1	1	1	.400	.667
Franco, Julio	.225	40	9	0	1	2	3	.262	.250
Frye, Jeff	.333	6	2	0	1	0	1	.333	.500
Fryman, T	.267	15	4	0	4	0	5	.294	.267
Gaetti, Gary	.270	37	10	6	8	0	7	.293	.324
Gagne, Greg	.302	53	16	2	6	1	7	.315	.491
Gallego, Mike	.238	21	5	0	2	4	1	.346	.333
Gil, Benji	.125	8	1	0	0	0	2	.125	.125
Gilkey, B	.333	9	3	2	5	3	2	.500	1.111
Gomez, Chris	.250	12	3	1	6	1	2	.286	.583
Gomez, Leo	.125	24	3	1	1	1	2	.160	.292
Gonzales, R	.200	5	1	0	0	1	2	.333	.400
Gonzalez, J	.269	26	7	2	3	4	5	.367	.538
Gonzalez, L*	.333	9	3	1	2	1	1	.400	.778
Goodwin, C*	.000	4	0	0	0	1	1	.200	.000
Goodwin, Tom*	.375	8	3	2	2	0	1	.375	1.125
Grace, Mark*	.000	8	0	0	0	2	2	.200	.000
Grebeck, C	.625	8	5	0	1	0	0	.625	.625
Greenwell, M*	.275	51	14	3	8	3	2	.309	.471
Greer, Rusty*	.200	10	2	0	1	3	2	.385	.200
Griffey Jr, K*	.294	34	10	0	3	5	3	.400	.382
Grissom, M	.444	9	4	3	3	1	1	.500	1.444
Grudzielanek	.333	12	4	0	1	0	1	.333	.583
Guillen, O*	.333	24	8	0	4	0	2	.333	.333
Gwynn, Chris*	.600	10	6	0	2	1	1	.636	.700
Gwynn, Tony*	.333	6	2	0	1	0	1	.286	.500
Hall, Mel*	.500	42	21	1	5	2	2	.523	.690
Hamelin, Bob*	.300	10	3	0	0	0	3	.300	.500
Hamilton, D*	.222	27	6	0	1	1	3	.250	.296
Hammonds, J	.300	10	3	0	0	0	1	.300	.300
Haselman, B	.111	9	1	0	0	0	2	.111	.111
Hayes, C	.000	7	0	0	0	1	2	.125	.000
Henderson, R	.263	19	5	2	3	9	6	.500	.579
Hernandez, Jo	.200	5	1	0	1	0	2	.200	.400
Hiatt, Phil	.250	8	2	0	0	0	2	.333	.250
Hill, G	.300	10	3	1	4	0	4	.300	.700
Hoiles, Chris	.176	17	3	1	4	2	2	.263	.353
Hollandsworth*	.286	7	2	0	0	1	2	.375	.286
Houston, T*	.571	7	4	0	0	0	2	.571	.571
Howard, Dave*	.333	9	3	0	2	0	3	.333	.556
Howard, T*	.273	11	3	0	0	1	1	.273	.455
Howell, Jack*	.300	10	3	1	2	2	0	.417	.600
Hudler, Rex	.200	5	1	0	0	0	2	.200	.200
Hulse, David*	.143	21	3	0	0	1	3	.182	.190
Hundley, Todd#	.300	10	3	1	3	0	1	.300	.700
Hunter, Bri L	.444	9	4	0	0	0	2	.444	.444
Huskey, Butch	.000	9	0	0	0	0	3	.000	.000
Huson, Jeff*	.167	12	2	0	0	1	3	.333	.167
Incaviglia, P	.143	21	3	0	0	1	10	.182	.238
Jaha, John	.200	5	1	0	1	2	2	.500	.200
James, Dion*	.462	26	12	0	1	7	2	.576	.500
Javier, Stan#	.385	13	5	0	3	1	0	.429	.462
Jefferson, R*	.400	10	4	1	3	0	1	.400	.700
Johnson, L*	.229	48	11	0	0	3	0	.275	.292
Johnson, Mark*	.667	6	4	1	1	2	1	.750	1.333
Jones, C#	.300	10	3	2	2	1	1	.364	.900
Joyner, Wally*	.295	44	13	1	8	5	7	.367	.432
Karkovice, A	.313	16	5	1	5	2	3	.389	.563
Karros, Eric	.167	6	1	0	1	1	2	.250	.167
Kelly, Pat	.091	33	3	0	2	1	7	.118	.152
Kelly, R	.394	33	13	1	6	2	6	.405	.636
Kendall, J	.125	8	1	0	0	0	2	.125	.250
Kent, Jeff	.167	6	1	0	0	0	0	.286	.333
King, Jeff	.250	4	1	0	0	1	0	.400	.250
Kirby, Wayne*	.238	21	5	1	3	0	2	.238	.381
Klesko, Ryan*	.222	9	2	0	1	1	2	.300	.333
Knoblauch, C	.250	40	10	0	6	5	3	.348	.275
Lampkin, Tom*	.200	5	1	0	0	2	1	.429	.200
Lansing, Mike	.444	9	4	0	2	2	2	.545	.444
Leius, Scott	.375	32	12	0	1	1	9	.394	.469
Lemke, Mark#	.125	8	1	0	1	2	0	.273	.125
Lewis, Mark	.300	10	3	0	2	1	5	.364	.300
Leyritz, Jim	.318	22	7	1	8	0	3	.318	.455
Liriano, N	.333	12	4	0	0	1	0	.385	.417
Listach, Pat#	.600	10	6	1	4	1	1	.636	1.000
Lofton, Kenny*	.350	20	7	0	1	0	3	.381	.500
Lopez, Javy	.125	8	1	0	1	0	2	.200	.125
Macfarlane, M	.300	20	6	1	4	3	2	.462	.600
Magadan, Dave*	.250	12	3	0	0	0	4	.250	.333
Martin, Al*	.444	9	4	1	2	0	1	.444	.778
Martinez, Da*	.400	5	2	0	1	1	1	.571	.600

Batter	Avg	AB	H	HR	BI	BB	SO	OBP	Slg
Martinez, E	.370	27	10	2	5	3	3	.452	.593
Martinez, T*	.313	16	5	0	1	1	4	.450	.313
May, Derrick*	.182	11	2	0	0	3	2	.357	.182
Mayne, Brent*	.238	21	5	0	3	5	5	.385	.286
McGriff, Fred*	.375	8	3	0	2	3	1	.545	.500
McGwire, Mark	.118	17	2	0	0	3	6	.250	.176
McLemore, M#	.333	30	10	1	5	2	7	.375	.567
McRae, Brian#	.182	33	6	0	4	5	6	.289	.242
Meares, Pat	.333	12	4	1	3	0	3	.333	.667
Merced, O*	.444	9	4	2	4	0	3	.444	1.111
Miller, Orl	.267	15	4	1	2	0	2	.267	.467
Molitor, Paul	.391	23	9	2	5	2	4	.462	.696
Mondesi, Raul	.250	8	2	0	1	0	2	.250	.500
Morris, Hal*	.200	5	1	0	0	0	0	.200	.400
Munoz, Pedro	.188	16	3	1	5	1	4	.235	.438
Murray, Eddie*	.000	7	0	0	0	3	2	.300	.000
Myers, Greg*	.250	8	2	0	1	1	1	.300	.250
Naehring, Tim	.286	21	6	0	2	2	6	.348	.381
Nilsson, Dave*	.500	4	2	0	0	2	1	.667	.750
Nixon, Otis#	.313	16	5	0	1	3	5	.421	.500
Nunnally, Jon*	.125	8	1	0	0	0	5	.125	.125
O'Brien, C	.333	3	1	0	0	1	1	.600	.333
O'Leary, Troy*	.231	13	3	0	0	1	4	.286	.231
O'Neill, Paul*	.333	21	7	0	3	2	1	.417	.429
Oliver, Joe	.500	6	3	1	5	0	2	.500	1.167
Ordonez, Rey	.222	9	2	0	0	0	1	.222	.222
Orsulak, Joe*	.250	28	7	0	3	1	1	.276	.357
Palmeiro, R*	.375	40	15	3	9	9	6	.490	.775
Palmer, Dean	.409	22	9	1	1	0	4	.409	.636
Pena, Tony	.182	33	6	1	7	1	9	.200	.303
Perez, E	.300	10	3	0	4	0	1	.273	.600
Perry, H	.667	6	4	0	1	0	0	.667	.667
Phillips, T#	.297	37	11	0	3	3	9	.350	.378
Piazza, Mike	.000	5	0	0	0	3	3	.375	.000
Plantier, P*	.300	10	3	1	1	0	2	.300	.600
Polonia, Luis*	.295	44	13	1	5	7	2	.404	.409
Raines, Tim#	.200	20	4	1	1	3	4	.333	.350
Ramirez, M	.286	7	2	1	3	2	0	.444	.714
Reboulet, J	.286	7	2	0	0	1	0	.375	.571
Reed, Jody	.294	34	10	0	2	4	4	.368	.353
Renteria, E	.000	6	0	0	0	0	2	.000	.000
Ripken, Billy	.176	17	3	0	0	0	2	.176	.294
Ripken, Cal	.349	43	15	0	7	4	4	.388	.488
Rodriguez, Al	.200	5	1	0	1	0	1	.200	.200
Rodriguez, H*	.333	9	3	3	6	2	2	.455	1.333
Rodriguez, I	.185	27	5	0	2	1	5	.207	.333
Salmon, Tim	.364	22	8	1	4	2	6	.417	.682
Sandberg, R	.300	5	1	0	0	1	1	.333	.400
Santangelo, F#	.000	3	0	0	0	1	0	.400	.000
Schofield, D	.313	16	5	0	1	1	4	.353	.438
Segui, David#	.286	14	4	0	1	2	2	.353	.357
Seitzer, K	.172	29	5	0	4	4	10	.265	.207
Sheffield, G	.273	11	3	2	4	4	4	.467	.818
Shumpert, T	.000	9	0	0	0	1	0	.100	.000
Sierra, Ruben#	.355	31	11	2	5	1	5	.375	.613
Slaught, Don	.143	7	1	0	0	0	0	.143	.286
Smith, Dwight*	.273	11	3	1	1	1	2	.333	.545
Snow, J.T.#	.294	17	5	1	2	2	4	.368	.529
Sojo, Luis	.286	7	2	1	1	0	0	.286	.714
Sorrento, P*	.324	37	12	4	8	4	12	.390	.676
Sosa, Sammy	.167	12	2	0	0	0	4	.167	.333
Spiers, Bill*	.273	33	9	0	1	3	3	.333	.303
Stahoviak, S*	.143	7	1	0	0	0	2	.143	.143
Stankiewicz	.200	5	1	0	0	1	0	.333	.200
Stanley, Mike	.182	11	2	0	1	0	2	.182	.273
Steinbach, T	.222	9	2	0	0	1	2	.300	.333
Stevens, Lee*	.200	5	1	0	0	0	1	.200	.400
Stillwell, K#	.300	20	6	0	4	1	4	.318	.450
Strange, Doug*	.333	12	4	0	1	3	1	.467	.333
Surhoff, B.J.*	.286	28	8	2	8	0	1	.276	.571
Tartabull, D	.294	34	10	1	8	8	10	.429	.500
Tettleton, M#	.241	29	7	0	3	7	8	.405	.310
Thomas, Frank	.333	27	9	1	9	9	9	.514	.519
Thome, Jim*	.333	21	7	0	1	3	3	.391	.333
Tinsley, Lee#	.143	7	1	0	0	0	0	.143	.286
Trammell, A	.258	31	8	0	7	2	5	.314	.323
Valentin, Jhn	.423	26	11	3	6	2	2	.464	.885
Valentin, Jse#	.000	7	0	0	0	1	3	.125	.000
Valle, Dave	.111	9	1	0	0	1	0	.200	.333
Vaughn, Greg	.269	26	7	1	5	6	3	.406	.462
Vaughn, Mo*	.250	32	8	2	2	4	11	.368	.438
Velarde, R	.083	12	1	0	0	2	4	.214	.167
Ventura, R*	.276	29	8	0	2	4	8	.343	.310
Vina, F*	.000	7	0	0	0	0	0	.000	.000
Vizcaino, J#	.000	5	0	0	0	0	0	.000	.000
Vizquel, Omar#	.179	28	5	0	0	1	5	.207	.250
Voigt, Jack	.400	5	2	0	0	1	1	.500	.400
Walbeck, Matt#	.125	16	2	1	2	0	1	.125	.313
Ward, Turner#	.600	5	3	0	0	2	2	.714	.800
Webster, L*	.143	7	1	0	0	0	0	.143	.143
Weiss, Walt*	.400	15	6	0	1	1	4	.471	.400

Todd Stottlemyre, Cardinals — RHP

Batter	Avg	AB	H	HR	BI	BB	SO	OBP	Slg
White, Devon#	.200	20	4	1	2	1	8	.238	.350
White, R	.250	8	2	1	3	0	2	.250	.625
Whiten, Mark#	.263	19	5	0	1	2	3	.333	.368
Wilkins, Rick*	.167	6	1	0	0	2	3	.375	.167
Williams, Ber#	.214	28	6	0	2	1	10	.241	.286
Wilson, Dan	.625	8	5	0	1	0	1	.625	.750
Worthington	.000	6	0	0	0	1	2	.143	.000

Jeff Suppan, Red Sox — RHP

Batter	Avg	AB	H	HR	BI	BB	SO	OBP	Slg
Becker, Rich*	.200	5	1	0	4	0	0	.167	.400
Cirillo, Jeff	.250	4	1	0	1	0	1	.200	.250
Knoblauch, C	.600	5	3	0	2	2	1	.714	1.000
Seitzer, K	.500	4	2	0	1	1	0	.600	1.000
Stahoviak, S*	.400	5	2	0	0	1	1	.400	.800
Walbeck, Matt#	.600	5	3	0	1	0	0	.600	1.000

Bill Swift, Rockies — RHP

Batter	Avg	AB	H	HR	BI	BB	SO	OBP	Slg
Abbott, Kurt	.143	7	1	0	0	1	2	.250	.143
Alicea, Luis#	.000	12	0	0	0	0	4	.000	.000
Alomar Jr, S	.125	8	1	0	0	0	1	.125	.125
Alou, Moises	.222	9	2	0	0	0	1	.222	.333
Anderson, Brd*	.143	7	1	0	0	1	0	.250	.143
Anthony, Eric*	.000	5	0	0	0	1	1	.167	.000
Arias, Alex	.000	5	0	0	0	0	1	.000	.000
Ausmus, Brad	.308	13	4	0	1	0	0	.308	.308
Baerga, C#	.000	5	0	0	0	0	1	.000	.000
Bagwell, Jeff	.333	6	2	0	2	3	1	.600	.500
Baines, H*	.452	31	14	2	7	3	0	.486	.742
Barberie, B#	.286	14	4	0	1	1	1	.333	.429
Bell, Derek	.143	7	1	0	1	0	1	.143	.143
Bell, Jay	.200	20	4	0	3	1	3	.238	.200
Belle, Albert	.250	4	1	0	0	1	2	.400	.250
Belliard, R	.286	7	2	0	0	0	2	.286	.286
Benard, M*	.600	5	3	0	0	0	0	.600	.800
Berry, Sean	.667	6	4	1	2	0	0	.667	1.167
Bichette, D	.417	12	5	2	3	1	2	.462	1.083
Biggio, Craig	.313	16	5	0	0	0	0	.313	.313
Blauser, Jeff	.313	16	5	1	4	2	1	.389	.625
Bogar, Tim	.000	5	0	0	0	0	1	.000	.000
Boggs, Wade*	.429	28	12	0	3	1	2	.433	.536
Bonds, Barry*	.000	3	0	0	0	3	0	.500	.000
Bonilla, B	.391	23	9	1	2	3	1	.462	.609
Boone, Bret	.111	9	1	1	1	0	2	.111	.444
Borders, Pat	.000	5	0	0	0	0	2	.000	.000
Branson, Jeff	.273	11	3	0	0	0	3	.250	.273
Brogna, Rico*	.444	9	4	1	2	0	1	.444	1.000
Brumfield, J	.167	6	1	0	0	0	1	.167	.167
Burks, Ellis	.250	28	7	0	2	0	4	.250	.286
Burnitz, J*	.556	9	5	1	3	0	2	.556	.889
Butler, Brett*	.250	36	9	0	4	5	1	.341	.361
Caminiti, Ken#	.357	14	5	1	6	1	0	.400	.643
Cangelosi, J	.400	5	2	0	0	0	0	.500	.400
Canseco, Jose	.300	20	6	0	4	1	4	.318	.400
Carr, Chuck	.063	16	1	0	0	0	3	.063	.063
Carter, Joe	.375	16	6	0	4	4	2	.500	.500
Castilla, V	.222	9	2	0	0	0	0	.222	.222
Cedeno, A	.091	11	1	0	0	0	1	.091	.091
Clark, Dave*	.200	15	3	0	1	3	2	.333	.200
Colbrunn, G	.176	17	3	0	0	0	7	.176	.176
Cole, Alex*	.125	8	1	0	0	1	0	.222	.125
Coleman, V#	.444	9	4	0	0	1	2	.500	.444
Conine, Jeff	.381	21	8	1	2	1	3	.409	.524
Cordero, Wil	.182	11	2	0	1	1	4	.250	.182
Daulton, D*	.391	23	9	2	8	4	2	.481	.870
Davis, Chili#	.182	11	2	0	1	1	0	.250	.182
Davis, Eric	.111	9	1	0	0	1	1	.200	.111
Deer, Rob	.167	18	3	0	0	3	5	.286	.167
DeShields, D*	.214	28	6	0	1	3	3	.290	.286
Devereaux, M	.000	5	0	0	0	0	4	.000	.000
Duncan, M	.091	22	2	0	1	0	7	.091	.091
Dunston, S	.429	7	3	0	1	0	2	.429	.429
Dykstra, L*	.440	25	11	0	2	3	4	.517	.720
Eisenreich, J	.207	29	6	0	0	1	1	.233	.207
Fermin, Felix	.125	8	1	0	1	0	0	.125	.125
Fielder, C	.250	8	2	0	1	3	0	.455	.250
Finley, Steve*	.259	27	7	0	1	1	4	.286	.333
Fletcher, D*	.118	17	2	0	0	1	1	.167	.118
Fonville, C#	.000	7	0	0	0	0	3	.000	.000
Franco, Julio	.276	29	8	1	3	0	6	.276	.483
Fryman, T	.167	6	1	0	0	0	1	.167	.167
Gaetti, Gary	.200	35	7	2	6	1	3	.222	.400
Gagne, Greg	.375	24	9	0	5	3	1	.464	.458
Galarraga, A	.000	9	0	0	0	0	6	.000	.000
Gallego, Mike	.200	10	2	0	1	1	1	.273	.200
Gant, Ron	.308	13	4	0	2	1	3	.357	.308
Garcia, C	.364	11	4	0	2	0	0	.364	.455
Gilkey, B	.273	11	3	1	1	1	2	.333	.636
Girardi, Joe	.333	6	2	0	0	0	1	.333	.333
Gonzalez, J	.167	6	1	0	2	0	0	.167	.167

Bill Swift, Rockies — RHP

Batter	Avg	AB	H	HR	BI	BB	SO	OBP	Slg
Gonzalez, L*	.286	14	4	0	2	0	2	.286	.429
Grace, Mark*	.471	17	8	1	5	2	1	.526	.706
Greene, W*	.400	5	2	0	1	1	0	.500	.600
Greenwell M*	.261	23	6	1	2	2	2	.320	.391
Grissom, M	.143	21	3	0	0	1	1	.182	.190
Guillen, O*	.296	27	8	0	4	1	1	.310	.370
Gutierrez, R	.182	11	2	0	0	1	1	.250	.182
Gwynn, Chris*	.200	5	1	0	2	0	2	.200	.600
Gwynn, Tony*	.360	25	9	1	4	2	0	.407	.520
Hall, Mel*	.214	14	3	0	1	0	0	.214	.286
Hansen, Dave*	.333	18	6	0	2	1	1	.368	.333
Harris, Lenny*	.389	18	7	1	2	0	1	.389	.556
Hayes, C	.176	17	3	0	1	2	5	.263	.294
Henderson, R	.167	24	4	0	3	3	2	.259	.208
Hollins, Dave*	.286	21	6	0	1	2	5	.400	.381
Howard, T*	.286	8	2	0	1	1	0	.300	.375
Howell, Jack*	.455	11	5	0	2	2	0	.500	.636
Hundley, Todd#	.300	20	6	1	6	2	0	.364	.500
Hunter, Brian	.333	6	2	1	1	0	0	.333	.833
Huson, Jeff*	.500	6	3	0	0	0	1	.500	.500
Incaviglia, P	.217	23	5	0	2	0	2	.250	.304
Javier, Stan#	.000	5	0	0	0	2	0	.286	.000
Jefferies, G#	.400	10	4	1	5	2	0	.500	.700
Jones, C#	.167	6	1	0	1	0	1	.167	.167
Joyner, Wally*	.250	16	4	0	0	1	3	.294	.250
Justice, Dave*	.286	14	4	2	4	2	5	.375	.714
Karkovice, R	.143	7	1	0	0	0	1	.143	.286
Karros, Eric	.286	28	8	2	5	2	8	.333	.500
Kelly, R	.190	21	4	0	0	2	7	.261	.286
Kent, Jeff	.143	14	2	1	4	0	2	.143	.357
King, Jeff	.385	13	5	0	1	0	1	.385	.462
Kreuter, Chad#	.333	3	1	0	0	2	0	.600	.333
Lankford, Ray*	.556	9	5	0	1	1	1	.600	.778
Larkin, Barry	.217	23	5	0	1	1	0	.250	.261
Lemke, Mark#	.250	8	2	0	2	1	2	.333	.500
Liriano, N#	.357	14	5	0	0	1	2	.400	.500
Livingstone, S	.286	7	2	0	0	1	0	.375	.286
Macfarlane, M	.273	11	3	0	1	0	0	.273	.455
Magadan, Dave*	.500	14	7	0	3	3	0	.588	.571
Martin, Al*	.250	16	4	1	2	1	4	.294	.438
Martinez, Da*	.200	5	1	0	1	0	0	.167	.400
May, Derrick*	.214	14	3	0	1	2	2	.313	.286
McGriff, Fred*	.379	29	11	3	7	3	1	.438	.759
McGwire, Mark	.357	14	5	0	0	1	1	.400	.357
McLemore, M#	.000	6	0	0	0	0	2	.000	.000
McRae, Brian*	.000	7	0	0	0	1	0	.000	.000
Merced, O*	.125	16	2	0	1	0	1	.125	.188
Mitchell, K	.333	15	5	1	3	2	2	.412	.600
Molitor, Paul	.348	23	8	0	3	2	3	.400	.391
Mondesi, Raul	.389	18	7	0	1	0	5	.389	.444
Morandini, M*	.368	19	7	0	1	3	1	.455	.474
Morris, Hal*	.333	18	6	1	3	0	1	.333	.556
Murray, Eddie*	.304	23	7	0	4	3	0	.385	.304
Nixon, Otis#	.333	9	3	0	0	2	3	.455	.333
O'Brien, C	.429	7	3	0	0	0	1	.429	.571
O'Neill, Paul*	.200	5	1	0	0	0	0	.200	.200
Offerman, J#	.182	22	4	0	1	7	1	.379	.182
Olerud, John*	.200	5	1	0	0	0	2	.200	.200
Oliver, Joe	.063	16	1	0	0	0	1	.063	.063
Orsulak, Joe*	.333	15	5	0	2	2	1	.412	.467
Pagnozzi, Tom	.250	8	2	0	0	0	1	.250	.375
Palmeiro, R*	.200	10	2	0	2	1	0	.250	.200
Pena, Tony	.000	7	0	0	0	1	3	.125	.000
Pendleton, T#	.286	14	4	0	1	5	3	.450	.357
Phillips, J*	.200	5	1	0	0	0	1	.200	.200
Phillips, T#	.308	13	4	0	1	1	3	.357	.308
Piazza, Mike	.300	20	6	1	7	1	3	.333	.500
Plantier, P*	.389	18	7	1	3	3	1	.476	.667
Reed, Jeff*	.222	9	2	0	0	0	1	.222	.222
Reed, Jody	.150	20	3	0	0	2	1	.227	.150
Ripken, Billy	.000	6	0	0	0	2	0	.333	.000
Ripken, Cal	.111	18	2	0	1	4	1	.273	.111
Roberts, Bip#	.250	12	3	0	1	2	2	.333	.250
Rodriguez, H*	.105	19	2	0	0	1	2	.150	.158
Sabo, Chris	.200	10	2	0	0	0	1	.273	.300
Samuel, Juan	.167	6	1	0	0	0	2	.167	.182
Sanchez, Rey	.182	11	2	0	0	1	0	.250	.182
Sandberg, R	.308	13	4	0	4	0	3	.308	.308
Sanders, R	.238	21	5	0	1	1	7	.273	.286
Santiago, R	.389	18	7	0	0	0	6	.389	.444
Scarsone, S	.200	5	1	0	0	0	1	.200	.200
Schofield, D	.421	19	8	1	7	0	2	.450	.632
Segui, David#	.333	6	2	0	0	1	1	.429	.333
Seitzer, K	.417	24	10	0	1	4	0	.500	.417
Servais, S	.167	6	1	0	0	0	4	.167	.167
Sheffield, G	.179	28	5	2	5	3	5	.258	.393
Shipley, C	.000	5	0	0	0	0	0	.000	.000
Sierra, Ruben*	.455	22	10	0	2	7	0	.455	.773
Slaught, Don	.375	8	3	0	2	1	1	.444	.375
Smith, Dwight*	.385	13	5	0	0	0	0	.385	.385
Smith, Ozzie#	.417	12	5	0	0	2	0	.500	.417

Bill Swift, Rockies — RHP

Batter	Avg	AB	H	HR	BI	BB	SO	OBP	Slg
Sosa, Sammy	.100	10	1	1	2	2	5	.250	.400
Spiers, Bill*	.111	9	1	0	0	2	1	.273	.111
Steinbach, T	.417	12	5	0	5	0	0	.462	.500
Stillwell, K#	.241	29	7	0	2	1	1	.267	.276
Stocker, K#	.250	8	2	0	0	1	1	.333	.250
Strawberry, D*	.286	7	2	1	3	0	0	.286	.714
Surhoff, B.J.*	.364	11	4	0	2	1	0	.385	.545
Sveum, Dale#	.143	7	1	0	0	0	0	.143	.143
Tartabull, D	.235	17	4	1	2	1	1	.278	.412
Taubensee, E*	.385	13	5	1	1	1	4	.429	.692
Tettleton, M#	.278	18	5	0	0	4	1	.409	.333
Thompson, Mil*	.167	12	2	0	1	0	3	.231	.167
Thompson, Ry	.143	7	1	0	0	1	3	.250	.143
Trammell, A	.286	21	6	1	2	3	0	.375	.476
VanderWal, J*	.333	12	4	1	1	2	0	.429	.583
Vaughn, Greg	.286	7	2	1	3	1	0	.375	.714
Veras, Q#	.800	5	4	0	2	1	0	.833	.800
Vizcaino, J#	.467	15	7	0	0	1	0	.500	.533
Walker, Larry*	.333	15	5	1	2	2	2	.412	.692
Wallach, Tim	.250	20	5	0	0	0	3	.250	.300
Weiss, Walt	.273	22	6	0	0	1	0	.304	.318
White, Devon#	.357	14	5	1	3	0	2	.357	.571
Whiten, Mark#	.417	12	5	0	2	1	0	.462	.417
Wilkins, Rick*	.353	17	6	1	1	3	1	.450	.529
Worthington	.300	10	3	0	3	2	2	.417	.300
Young, Eric	.000	8	0	0	0	1	0	.000	.000
Young, Kevin	.333	6	2	0	2	0	0	.333	.500
Zeile, Todd	.182	11	2	0	2	1	0	.250	.273

Greg Swindell, Indians — LHP

Batter	Avg	AB	H	HR	BI	BB	SO	OBP	Slg
Finley, Steve*	.107	28	3	0	0	1	6	.138	.179
Fonville, C#	.333	6	2	0	1	0	2	.333	.333
Franco, Julio	.286	21	6	1	6	0	2	.286	.476
Fryman, T	.500	6	3	0	1	0	0	.500	.667
Gaetti, Gary	.310	42	13	3	13	3	10	.348	.571
Gagne, Greg	.278	36	10	1	3	1	8	.297	.556
Galarraga, A	.474	19	9	2	6	1	5	.500	.947
Gallego, Mike	.129	31	4	0	0	2	9	.182	.129
Gant, Ron	.273	22	6	0	5	4	2	.357	.364
Garcia, C	.429	14	6	0	2	0	1	.429	.500
Gilkey, B	.435	23	10	0	2	4	2	.519	.435
Girardi, Joe	.417	12	5	0	0	0	1	.417	.500
Gomez, Leo	.600	5	3	0	0	0	1	.600	.800
Gonzalez, L*	.250	8	2	0	0	2	2	.400	.375
Grace, Mark*	.273	22	6	0	2	0	1	.273	.409
Grebeck, C	.000	6	0	0	0	0	3	.000	.000
Greenwell, M*	.400	15	6	1	4	2	0	.471	.733
Griffey Jr, K*	.333	9	3	2	2	0	2	.333	1.000
Grissom, M	.476	21	10	5	9	0	3	.476	1.381
Grudzielanek	.333	9	3	0	0	0	1	.333	.444
Guillen, O*	.300	30	9	0	0	1	5	.323	.400
Gutierrez, R	.308	13	4	0	0	1	2	.357	.385
Gwynn, Tony*	.344	32	11	1	2	0	0	.344	.500
Hamilton, D*	.333	3	1	0	1	1	1	.400	.333
Hansen, Dave*	.000	5	0	0	0	0	1	.000	.000
Hayes, C	.571	14	8	1	2	0	1	.571	1.071
Henderson, R	.316	38	12	3	4	11	3	.469	.579
Hernandez, Ca	.167	6	1	0	0	0	2	.167	.167
Hernandez, Jo	.143	7	1	0	1	1	2	.250	.143
Hill, G	.280	25	7	1	4	4	5	.379	.520
Hoiles, Chris	.143	7	1	1	3	0	4	.143	.571
Hollandsworth*	.143	7	1	0	0	0	2	.143	.143
Hollins, Dave#	.300	20	6	0	4	0	4	.273	.450
Howard, Dave#	.400	5	2	0	1	0	1	.333	.400
Howell, Jack*	.000	5	0	0	0	0	2	.000	.000
Hunter, Brian	.200	20	4	2	2	0	4	.200	.500
Incaviglia, P	.167	42	7	1	5	3	18	.222	.286
Javier, Stan#	.227	22	5	0	1	0	5	.227	.273
Jefferies, G#	.313	16	5	1	3	0	1	.294	.625
Johnson, Bri	.125	8	1	0	2	0	1	.125	.250
Johnson, Char	.500	6	3	0	1	1	0	.571	.667
Johnson, L*	.000	7	0	0	0	0	0	.000	.000
Jones, Chris	.222	9	2	0	0	0	2	.222	.222
Jordan, Brian	.333	21	7	2	5	2	4	.391	.714
Jordan, Ricky	.143	7	1	0	0	0	1	.143	.143
Joyner, Wally*	.345	29	10	0	4	2	5	.387	.379
Justice, Dave*	.412	17	7	3	3	2	2	.474	.941
Karkovice, R	.071	14	1	0	0	1	7	.133	.071
Karros, Eric	.433	30	13	1	4	2	3	.455	.600
Kelly, Pat	.200	5	1	0	0	0	0	.200	.200
Kelly, R	.216	51	11	2	4	0	12	.212	.353
Kent, Jeff	.100	10	1	0	0	1	0	.100	.100
King, Jeff	.316	19	6	2	5	0	2	.316	.684
Lankford, Ray*	.321	28	9	0	1	4	6	.406	.464
Lansing, Mike	.381	21	8	0	2	0	0	.381	.476
Larkin, Barry	.350	20	7	1	3	1	2	.364	.550
Leius, Scott	.400	5	2	0	0	0	0	.400	.400
Lemke, Mark#	.182	22	4	1	2	2	2	.250	.364
Lewis, Darren	.370	27	10	1	8	1	0	.393	.667
Lewis, Mark	1.000	5	5	0	2	0	0	1.000	1.600
Leyritz, Jim	.214	14	3	0	1	0	5	.214	.286
Liriano, N#	.615	13	8	1	3	0	3	.615	.923
Lopez, Javy	.286	7	2	0	0	0	2	.286	.286
Mabry, John*	.400	5	2	0	0	0	0	.400	.800
Macfarlane, M	.143	21	3	0	1	0	5	.143	.143
Magadan, Dave*	.214	14	3	0	2	1	3	.267	.286
Manwaring, K	.294	17	5	2	2	2	3	.368	.647
Martinez, E	.500	14	7	1	1	1	1	.533	.857
Martinez, T*	.400	5	2	0	0	1	1	.400	.400
May, Derrick*	.333	6	2	0	1	0	0	.333	.333
McGee, Willie*	.273	11	3	0	0	0	0	.273	.455
McGriff, Fred*	.419	31	13	2	9	9	7	.537	.710
McGwire, Mark	.325	40	13	3	10	5	6	.391	.625
McLemore, M#	.200	5	1	0	0	1	2	.333	.400
McRae, Brian#	.316	19	6	0	2	0	4	.316	.368
Merced, O*	.571	7	4	0	1	1	2	.556	.714
Mitchell, K	.500	12	6	2	3	0	0	.500	1.083
Molitor, Paul	.308	26	8	0	3	2	3	.357	.538
Mondesi, Raul	.313	16	5	1	2	2	3	.389	.750
Morman, Russ	.250	16	4	1	2	0	2	.250	.438
Morris, Hal*	.350	20	7	0	2	1	4	.381	.400
Murray, Eddie#	.261	23	6	1	2	1	3	.292	.391
Nixon, Otis#	.250	20	5	0	2	0	5	.250	.250
O'Brien, C	.143	14	2	0	1	2	1	.250	.286
O'Neill, Paul*	.250	4	1	0	0	1	1	.400	.500
Offerman, J#	.231	26	6	0	1	2	4	.286	.231
Oliver, Joe	.231	13	3	0	1	0	1	.231	.231
Orsulak, Joe*	.091	11	1	0	0	1	0	.091	.091
Pagnozzi, Tom	.313	16	5	0	1	0	3	.313	.375
Palmeiro, R*	.346	26	9	1	3	1	2	.370	.500
Parent, Mark	.364	11	4	2	4	2	1	.462	1.091

Greg Swindell, Indians — LHP

Batter	Avg	AB	H	HR	BI	BB	SO	OBP	Slg
Abbott, Kurt	.286	14	4	0	1	0	5	.286	.286
Alomar, R#	.250	12	3	0	4	1	1	.308	.500
Alou, Moises	.273	22	6	1	4	1	2	.333	.500
Anderson, Brd*	.091	11	1	1	1	0	4	.091	.364
Andrews, S	.167	6	1	0	0	1	1	.286	.167
Anthony, Eric*	.250	8	2	0	0	3	2	.250	.250
Arias, Alex	.300	10	3	0	1	1	3	.364	.500
Ashley, Billy	.125	8	1	0	1	1	3	.222	.250
Ausmus, Brad	.250	8	2	0	0	1	1	.333	.375
Bagwell, Jeff	.417	12	5	0	1	2	2	.462	.500
Baines, Harold*	.211	19	4	0	4	2	3	.286	.316
Barberie, B#	.444	18	8	1	1	0	4	.444	.667
Batiste, Kim	.167	6	1	0	0	0	0	.167	.167
Bell, Derek	.467	15	7	2	4	0	1	.467	.867
Bell, Jay	.269	26	7	1	1	0	3	.269	.462
Benjamin, M	.125	8	1	0	0	0	6	.125	.250
Berry, Sean	.077	13	1	0	2	1	4	.143	.154
Bichette, D	.464	28	13	1	2	0	8	.464	.714
Biggio, Craig	.308	13	4	0	0	2	2	.400	.385
Blauser, Jeff	.321	28	9	0	0	4	6	.406	.393
Boggs, Wade*	.214	28	6	0	2	1	1	.241	.357
Bonds, Barry*	.300	20	6	1	4	3	2	.375	.550
Bonilla, B	.316	19	6	1	4	2	4	.316	.474
Boone, Bret	.583	12	7	2	7	1	0	.571	1.250
Borders, Pat	.321	28	9	0	2	1	4	.345	.429
Branson, Jeff*	.100	10	1	0	0	0	4	.100	.100
Brogna, Rico*	.200	5	1	0	0	1	2	.333	.200
Brumfield, J	.267	15	4	0	1	1	1	.294	.333
Buhner, Jay	.250	8	2	1	2	0	3	.250	.625
Burks, Ellis	.167	24	4	0	3	3	7	.259	.167
Butler, Brett*	.324	34	11	0	0	3	1	.395	.412
Caminiti, Ken#	.409	22	9	1	4	1	2	.435	.682
Candaele, C#	.333	9	3	0	0	1	0	.400	.333
Canseco, Jose	.378	37	14	6	12	3	5	.415	.892
Carr, Chuck	.143	28	4	1	4	0	1	.143	.286
Carreon, Mark	.125	8	1	0	1	1	4	.200	.125
Carter, Joe	.182	11	2	1	3	0	1	.167	.545
Castilla, V	.222	9	2	0	1	0	1	.222	.333
Cedeno, A	.000	6	0	0	0	0	5	.000	.000
Cianfrocco, A	.455	11	5	0	2	0	1	.455	.545
Clark, Phil	.200	10	2	0	0	0	1	.200	.200
Clark, Will*	.313	16	5	0	2	0	1	.294	.375
Clayton, R	.320	25	8	1	4	0	4	.320	.440
Colbrunn, G	.412	17	7	0	0	0	2	.412	.529
Conine, Jeff	.160	25	4	1	1	3	10	.250	.320
Cordero, Wil	.278	18	5	0	2	0	4	.263	.333
Daulton, D*	.417	12	5	0	0	1	3	.462	.667
Davis, Chili#	.190	21	4	0	1	0	4	.182	.190
Davis, Eric	.500	8	4	0	0	2	1	.600	.625
Dawson, Andre	.364	11	4	0	1	0	1	.364	.364
Deer, Rob	.200	21	4	1	3	3	8	.308	.333
DeShields, D*	.211	19	4	0	1	3	1	.318	.211
Devereaux, M	.355	31	11	0	3	3	1	.400	.452
Dorsett, B	.182	11	2	0	0	0	2	.182	.182
Duncan, M	.269	26	7	0	2	0	9	.269	.385
Dunston, S	.333	9	3	1	2	0	1	.333	.778
Dykstra, L*	.529	17	9	0	0	1	2	.556	.824
Eisenreich, J*	.462	13	6	0	0	0	3	.462	.538
Espinoza, A	.333	24	8	0	5	0	2	.320	.375
Fielder, C	.316	19	6	4	9	0	7	.316	.947

Greg Swindell, Indians — LHP

Batter	Avg	AB	H	HR	BI	BB	SO	OBP	Slg
Pena, G#	.385	13	5	1	3	0	2	.357	.692
Pena, Tony	.200	15	3	1	4	0	1	.188	.400
Pendleton, T#	.147	34	5	0	2	0	2	.147	.176
Phillips, T#	.273	22	6	0	1	3	3	.346	.455
Piazza, Mike	.500	22	11	3	8	2	1	.542	.955
Plantier, P*	.308	13	4	2	2	0	3	.308	.769
Polonia, Luis*	.286	21	6	0	0	0	5	.286	.286
Prince, Tom	.500	4	2	0	1	1	0	.600	.500
Raines, Tim#	.714	7	5	0	0	0	0	.714	.714
Reed, Jody	.375	32	12	0	1	2	2	.412	.406
Ripken, Billy	.359	39	14	0	3	1	6	.375	.462
Ripken, Cal	.367	49	18	6	11	3	5	.404	.755
Roberts, B#	.222	9	2	0	0	1	2	.300	.222
Sabo, Chris	.091	11	1	0	3	3	1	.286	.091
Samuel, Juan	.364	11	4	0	1	1	2	.417	.364
Sanchez, Rey	.083	12	1	0	0	0	0	.083	.083
Sandberg, R	.364	11	4	1	4	1	0	.417	.727
Sanders, R	.391	23	9	1	4	4	4	.464	.652
Santangelo, F#	.167	6	1	0	0	0	0	.167	.167
Santiago, B	.250	28	7	0	2	1	3	.276	.286
Scarsone, S	.000	7	0	0	0	0	0	.000	.000
Schofield, D	.115	26	3	1	3	2	5	.172	.269
Schu, Rick	.143	14	2	1	2	0	5	.143	.357
Segui, David#	.267	15	4	0	1	0	1	.267	.267
Seitzer, K	.233	30	7	0	2	5	6	.343	.267
Servais, K	.000	6	0	0	0	0	0	.000	.000
Sheffield, G	.281	32	9	2	8	4	4	.361	.531
Shipley, C	.545	11	6	0	1	1	1	.538	.818
Shumpert, T	.250	8	2	0	1	0	2	.250	.375
Sierra, Ruben#	.250	36	9	1	5	1	10	.270	.444
Slaught, Don	.200	25	5	0	2	1	3	.222	.280
Smith, Ozzie#	.200	20	4	0	0	2	0	.273	.250
Sojo, Luis	.400	15	6	0	2	0	2	.400	.533
Sosa, Sammy	.270	37	10	1	2	3	9	.325	.405
Spehr, Tim	.250	8	2	0	0	1	4	.333	.375
Spiers, Bill*	.167	6	1	0	1	0	1	.167	.333
Sprague, Ed	.375	8	3	1	3	0	3	.375	.750
Stanley, Mike	.150	20	3	0	0	2	10	.227	.200
Steinbach, T	.318	22	7	1	3	1	4	.348	.545
Stillwell, K#	.286	28	8	0	1	1	6	.310	.357
Stinnett, K	.143	7	1	1	1	1	1	.250	.571
Stocker, K#	.333	6	2	0	1	0	1	.333	.333
Strawberry, D*	.500	6	3	0	1	0	1	.500	.500
Surhoff, B.J.*	.125	16	2	0	1	0	1	.125	.188
Sveum, Dale#	.263	19	5	2	4	0	8	.263	.789
Tartabull, D	.391	23	9	1	3	5	2	.500	.652
Tavarez, Je#	.333	6	2	0	0	1	1	.333	.333
Tettleton, M#	.316	19	6	1	3	6	3	.480	.526
Thomas, Frank	.545	11	6	1	5	1	2	.583	.909
Thompson, Rob	.154	13	2	0	0	2	2	.267	.308
Thompson, Ry	.667	6	4	1	3	0	1	.667	1.500
Trammell, A	.333	24	8	1	2	1	3	.360	.458
Valle, Dave	.350	20	7	1	5	2	1	.409	.700
Vaughn, Greg	.133	15	2	0	0	12	13	.333	.200
Ventura, R*	.250	8	2	0	0	3	2	.455	.250
Veras, Q#	.125	8	1	0	0	1	1	.222	.125
Vizcaino, J#	.455	11	5	0	1	2	1	.538	.545
Vizquel, Omar#	.250	4	1	0	0	0	0	.250	.250
Walker, Larry*	.250	12	3	0	1	0	1	.308	.250
Wallach, Tim	.273	22	6	1	5	0	8	.261	.636
Walton, J	.300	10	3	1	1	0	3	.364	.600
Wehner, John	.333	6	2	0	2	1	1	.429	.500
Weiss, Walt#	.185	27	5	0	3	2	6	.233	.333
White, Devon#	.357	28	10	1	2	1	3	.400	.500
White, R	.429	14	6	1	2	1	1	.467	.714
Whiten, Mark#	.333	12	4	2	4	1	2	.385	.833
Williams, Ber#	.143	7	1	0	1	0	1	.125	.143
Williams, E	.385	13	5	1	0	1	0	.357	.615
Williams, Ma	.438	16	7	2	5	1	2	.471	.875
Worthington,	.000	8	0	0	0	1	1	.111	.000
Young, Eric	.200	20	4	0	1	2	2	.273	.200
Young, Kevin	.000	6	0	0	0	1	4	.143	.000
Zeile, Todd	.313	16	5	2	4	1	2	.333	.813

Jeff Tabaka, Astros — LHP

Batter	Avg	AB	H	HR	BI	BB	SO	OBP	Slg
Alou, Moises	.429	7	3	1	1	0	2	.429	.857
Bonds, Barry*	.333	3	1	0	2	2	1	.600	.333
Boone, Bret	.250	4	1	0	1	0	1	.400	.250
Branson, J	.167	6	1	0	1	3	0	.444	.167
Butler, Brett*	.000	5	0	0	0	0	2	.000	.000
Caminiti, Ken#	.200	5	1	0	1	0	0	.200	.200
Cordero, Wil	.000	5	0	0	0	0	1	.000	.000
DeShields, D*	.500	4	2	0	0	1	1	.600	.500
Fletcher, D*	.000	5	0	0	0	0	0	.000	.000
Grace, Mark*	.500	6	3	0	1	2	1	.625	.500
Justice, Dave*	.200	5	1	0	2	3	0	.500	.600
Lansing, Mike	.400	5	2	0	0	0	0	.400	.600
Larkin, Barry	.429	7	3	0	0	0	2	.429	.429
Lewis, Darren	.167	6	1	0	0	0	1	.167	.167
McGriff, Fred*	.667	6	4	0	2	1	0	.714	.833

Jeff Tabaka, Astros — LHP

Batter	Avg	AB	H	HR	BI	BB	SO	OBP	Slg
Morandini, M*	.333	3	1	0	0	2	1	.600	.667
Morris, Hal*	.364	11	4	0	4	0	2	.364	.455
Segui, David#	.167	6	1	0	0	0	3	.167	.333
Taubensee, E*	.750	4	3	0	2	1	0	.800	1.500

Kevin Tapani, White Sox — RHP

Batter	Avg	AB	H	HR	BI	BB	SO	OBP	Slg
Aldrete, Mike*	.222	9	2	0	0	1	2	.300	.222
Alicea, Luis#	.000	5	0	0	1	0	0	.167	.000
Alomar, R#	.341	41	14	0	6	8	7	.423	.439
Alomar Jr, S	.348	23	8	2	4	1	1	.375	.696
Amaral, Rich	.235	17	4	0	2	0	1	.235	.353
Anderson, Brd*	.258	31	8	2	5	4	9	.378	.452
Anderson, G*	.167	6	1	1	3	0	3	.167	.667
Baerga, C#	.262	42	11	3	13	0	2	.267	.524
Baines, H*	.314	35	11	1	3	3	4	.368	.543
Becker, Rich*	.375	8	3	1	2	0	2	.375	.750
Bell, Jay	.333	6	2	0	1	0	1	.333	.333
Belle, Albert	.194	36	7	2	5	3	9	.293	.389
Berroa, G	.389	18	7	1	3	2	2	.450	.611
Bichette, D	.200	15	3	2	7	1	3	.235	.667
Blowers, Mike	.167	12	2	0	0	0	3	.167	.167
Boggs, Wade*	.380	50	19	1	4	5	3	.436	.540
Bonilla, B#	.167	6	1	0	1	1	2	.286	.167
Boone, Bret	.000	11	0	0	1	0	2	.077	.000
Borders, Pat	.320	25	8	2	3	0	1	.320	.600
Bordick, Mike	.375	24	9	0	1	0	2	.375	.375
Bournigal, R	.167	6	1	0	0	1	0	.286	.167
Bragg, Darren*	.250	12	3	0	2	4	0	.438	.500
Brosius, S	.294	17	5	0	1	2	2	.368	.353
Brumfield, J	.375	8	3	0	0	1	2	.444	.375
Buhner, Jay	.315	54	17	2	7	3	18	.362	.500
Burks, Ellis	.350	20	7	1	3	0	2	.350	.550
Caminiti, Ken#	.500	4	2	0	0	1	0	.600	.750
Canseco, Jose	.306	36	11	5	11	1	11	.324	.750
Carreon, Mark	.250	8	2	0	1	1	1	.333	.250
Carter, Joe	.244	41	10	0	7	8	6	.367	.317
Casanova, R#	.200	5	1	0	0	1	1	.333	.200
Castilla, V	.167	6	1	1	0	0	0	.167	.667
Cirillo, Jeff	.455	11	5	0	0	1	0	.500	.545
Clark, Tony#	.000	3	0	0	0	2	3	.400	.000
Clark, Will*	.286	7	2	1	3	0	2	.286	.714
Cole, Alex*	.000	4	0	0	0	1	2	.200	.000
Coleman, V#	.286	7	2	0	1	0	0	.286	.714
Cora, Joey#	.486	35	17	1	5	0	2	.486	.771
Cordova, M	.286	7	2	0	0	0	2	.286	.429
Curtis, Chad	.229	35	8	0	4	0	3	.250	.314
Cuyler, Milt*	.125	8	1	0	2	0	4	.125	.250
Davis, Chili#	.333	30	10	1	9	2	8	.375	.500
Dawson, Andre	.000	7	0	0	0	1	0	.000	.000
Deer, Rob	.063	16	1	0	0	2	5	.167	.063
Delgado, C*	.385	13	5	0	4	0	5	.357	.538
Devereaux, M	.214	28	6	1	3	0	6	.214	.393
Diaz, Alex#	.286	7	2	0	0	0	0	.286	.286
DiSarcina, G	.207	29	6	0	0	0	3	.207	.310
Easley, D	.300	10	3	0	0	2	1	.462	.400
Edmonds, Jim*	.300	10	3	2	4	0	3	.300	.900
Eisenreich, J*	.455	22	10	1	4	0	3	.455	.636
Espinoza, A	.278	18	5	1	1	0	1	.278	.500
Fabregas, Jor*	.333	6	2	0	0	0	2	.333	.500
Fermin, Felix	.348	23	8	0	0	1	0	.375	.435
Fielder, C	.200	30	6	1	6	1	12	.219	.300
Finley, Steve*	.667	6	4	0	1	1	1	.714	1.000
Fox, Andy*	.000	5	0	0	0	1	0	.000	.000
Franco, Julio	.458	24	11	0	3	5	2	.552	.500
Frye, Jeff	.417	12	5	0	0	1	0	.462	.500
Fryman, T	.400	30	12	1	2	0	2	.419	.533
Gaetti, Gary	.225	40	9	4	5	0	10	.225	.425
Gagne, Greg	.435	23	10	0	2	1	2	.458	.522
Galarraga, A	.333	6	2	0	0	0	1	.333	.333
Gallego, Mike	.214	14	3	1	3	3	1	.353	.429
Gates, Brent#	.364	11	4	1	2	2	0	.462	.727
Giambi, Jason*	.214	14	3	0	1	0	1	.214	.286
Gil, Benji	.333	6	2	0	1	0	1	.333	.500
Girardi, Joe	.125	8	1	0	0	0	1	.125	.125
Gomez, Chris	.222	9	2	0	0	0	1	.222	.222
Gomez, Leo	.353	17	6	0	1	0	4	.353	.471
Gonzales, A	.188	16	3	1	1	0	2	.188	.375
Gonzalez, A	.182	11	2	0	0	1	2	.250	.273
Gonzalez, J	.259	27	7	0	1	1	5	.286	.296
Goodwin, Tom*	.000	10	0	0	1	0	2	.000	.000
Grebeck, C	.273	11	3	0	1	0	1	.273	.455
Green, Shawn*	.364	11	4	1	2	2	2	.462	.636
Greenwell, M*	.474	19	9	0	2	2	2	.500	.684
Greer, Rusty*	.143	7	1	0	0	0	2	.143	.143
Griffey Jr, K*	.207	58	12	3	10	1	11	.210	.431
Guillen, O*	.235	17	4	0	2	0	1	.222	.294
Gwynn, Chris*	.000	6	0	0	0	1	0	.000	.000
Hall, Mel*	.320	25	8	1	3	0	5	.320	.600
Hamelin, Bob*	.100	10	1	0	0	1	4	.182	.200
Hamilton, D*	.464	28	13	1	7	3	3	.516	.714

Batter	Avg	AB	H	HR	BI	BB	SO	OBP	Slg
Hammonds, J	.083	12	1	0	0	0	2	.083	.083
Haselman, B	.200	5	1	0	0	0	1	.200	.200
Hayes, C	.143	7	1	0	0	0	4	.143	.286
Henderson, R	.276	29	8	0	1	5	3	.382	.310
Hiatt, Phil	.500	12	6	3	6	0	3	.500	1.250
Higginson, B*	.200	10	2	1	3	0	1	.200	.500
Hill, G	.000	12	0	0	1	0	2	.000	.000
Hoiles, Chris	.350	20	7	0	1	7	1	.519	.350
Howard, Dave#	.143	7	1	0	0	0	1	.143	.143
Howell, Jack*	.333	6	2	0	0	0	1	.333	.667
Huff, Michael	.500	4	2	0	2	1	0	.600	1.000
Hulse, David*	.176	17	3	0	0	2	4	.263	.176
Huson, Jeff*	.042	24	1	0	1	0	3	.042	.083
Incaviglia, P	.333	6	2	0	2	0	1	.286	.333
Jaha, John	.167	18	3	1	1	1	5	.250	.333
James, Dion*	.519	27	14	2	6	0	2	.519	.963
Javier, Stan#	.273	11	3	0	1	0	0	.273	.455
Jefferies, G#	.100	10	1	0	0	0	1	.100	.100
Jefferson, R*	.400	10	4	1	1	1	3	.455	.800
Jeter, Derek	.375	8	3	0	0	0	1	.375	.500
Johnson, L*	.233	30	7	0	2	0	3	.233	.367
Joyner, Wally*	.159	44	7	0	1	6	8	.260	.205
Karkovice, R	.222	18	4	1	2	2	1	.300	.389
Kelly, Pat	.176	17	3	0	1	2	1	.263	.235
Kelly, R	.263	19	5	1	1	0	4	.263	.474
King, Jeff	.571	7	4	0	4	0	0	.571	.714
Kirby, Wayne*	.353	17	6	0	2	1	2	.389	.412
Knoblauch, C	.429	7	3	0	2	1	1	.500	.571
Kreuter, Chad#	.364	11	4	0	1	0	1	.364	.455
Levis, Jesse*	.000	5	0	0	0	0	1	.000	.000
Lewis, Mark	.214	14	3	0	1	0	1	.214	.286
Leyritz, Jim	.125	16	2	0	0	1	3	.222	.125
Liriano, N	.273	11	3	0	1	0	2	.273	.364
Listach, Pat#	.222	9	2	0	0	3	1	.417	.222
Livingstone*	.250	12	3	0	2	0	3	.250	.333
Lockhart, K*	.200	5	1	0	1	1	0	.286	.400
Lofton, Kenny*	.475	40	19	0	1	2	3	.500	.600
Lovullo, T#	.231	13	3	0	1	0	4	.231	.308
Macfarlane, M	.240	25	6	2	3	3	4	.321	.520
Magadan, Dave*	.500	8	4	0	1	0	2	.500	.625
Martin, Al*	.143	7	1	0	0	0	2	.143	.143
Martinez, E	.347	49	17	0	3	11	6	.467	.429
Martinez, S*	.333	6	2	0	1	0	3	.333	.333
Martinez, T*	.139	36	5	0	2	5	6	.244	.194
Matheny, Mike	.444	9	4	0	1	0	1	.444	.667
Mayne, Brent*	.182	22	4	0	2	1	5	.217	.227
McGriff, Fred*	.500	6	3	0	1	3	1	.667	.667
McGwire, Mark	.409	22	9	2	3	5	2	.519	.727
McLemore, M#	.184	38	7	0	3	5	7	.279	.237
McRae, Brian#	.405	42	17	1	9	0	8	.409	.571
Meares, Pat	.167	6	1	0	0	0	1	.167	.167
Merced, O*	.400	5	2	0	1	1	2	.429	.600
Mieske, Matt	.286	14	4	0	1	0	2	.286	.500
Molitor, Paul	.317	63	20	2	8	3	8	.348	.556
Munoz, Pedro	.167	6	1	0	0	0	2	.167	.167
Murray, Eddie#	.231	26	6	1	5	1	5	.259	.423
Myers, Greg*	.357	28	10	0	0	2	2	.400	.429
Naehring, Tim	.300	20	6	1	3	1	2	.333	.450
Nevin, Phil	.200	5	1	0	2	0	3	.200	.200
Newfield, M	.000	6	0	0	0	0	2	.000	.000
Newson, W*	.353	17	6	0	2	1	6	.389	.412
Nieves, M#	.222	9	2	1	4	0	1	.300	.556
Nilsson, Dave*	.292	24	7	0	2	0	5	.280	.292
Nixon, Otis#	.190	21	4	0	0	1	3	.227	.238
Nunnally, Jon*	.000	5	0	0	0	1	4	.167	.000
O'Brien, C	.250	8	2	0	1	0	1	.333	.250
O'Leary, Troy*	.167	12	2	0	0	1	2	.231	.333
O'Neill, Paul*	.423	26	11	2	7	3	6	.467	.769
Offerman, J#	.400	5	2	0	0	1	2	.500	.400
Olerud, John*	.367	49	18	1	8	1	6	.380	.551
Orsulak, Joe*	.278	18	5	1	2	0	0	.289	.500
Palmeiro, R*	.321	53	17	4	9	2	8	.339	.660
Palmer, Dean	.304	23	7	1	4	2	6	.360	.565
Paquette, C	.000	5	0	0	0	0	0	.000	.000
Pena, Tony	.111	18	2	0	0	1	2	.158	.167
Perez, E	.333	9	3	0	1	0	1	.333	.333
Perez, Tomas#	.500	4	2	0	1	0	0	.400	.500
Phillips, T#	.270	37	10	0	2	3	6	.325	.351
Plantier, P*	.188	16	3	0	1	0	5	.188	.250
Polonia, Luis*	.333	48	16	0	2	1	6	.347	.354
Pride, Curtis*	.500	6	3	1	1	0	2	.500	1.000
Raines, Tim*	.300	30	9	1	4	2	3	.344	.500
Ramirez, M	.235	17	4	1	2	1	1	.278	.529
Randa, Joe	.200	5	1	0	0	0	3	.200	.200
Reed, Jody	.233	30	7	0	1	1	5	.258	.300
Ripken, Billy	.000	3	0	0	0	1	0	.400	.000
Ripken, Cal	.273	44	12	1	5	2	2	.304	.409
Rodriguez, Al	.333	12	4	0	1	0	2	.333	.333
Rodriguez, I	.143	14	2	0	0	0	0	.143	.143
Salmon, Tim	.316	19	6	1	2	4	5	.435	.526
Schofield, D	.167	12	2	0	0	0	1	.167	.167

Batter	Avg	AB	H	HR	BI	BB	SO	OBP	Slg
Segui, David#	.091	11	1	0	1	0	1	.091	.182
Seitzer, K	.206	34	7	0	4	2	2	.250	.294
Sheffield, G	.286	7	2	0	0	0	0	.286	.286
Shumpert, T	.300	10	3	0	0	0	1	.300	.400
Sierra, Ruben#	.310	42	13	1	7	1	4	.326	.500
Smith, Dwight*	.143	7	1	1	2	0	3	.143	.571
Snow, J.T.#	.400	15	6	0	1	1	4	.438	.467
Sojo, Luis	.174	23	4	0	0	0	0	.174	.217
Sorrento, P*	.400	35	14	3	9	2	7	.421	.829
Spiers, Bill*	.136	22	3	0	4	0	8	.136	.182
Sprague, Ed	.385	26	10	1	3	1	3	.407	.577
Stankiewicz	.500	6	3	0	1	1	0	.571	.667
Stairs, Matt*	.167	6	1	0	0	0	2	.286	.167
Stanley, Mike	.154	13	2	0	2	0	2	.154	.231
Steinbach, T	.355	31	11	4	7	3	4	.412	.871
Stevens, Lee*	.071	14	1	0	0	2	3	.188	.071
Stillwell, K#	.091	11	1	0	1	1	0	.167	.091
Strange, Doug#	.167	12	2	0	1	0	5	.167	.167
Surhoff, B.J.*	.286	42	12	1	4	1	3	.302	.381
Sveum, Dale#	.222	9	2	0	0	1	3	.300	.444
Tartabull, D	.200	20	4	0	1	2	8	.273	.200
Tettleton, M#	.250	28	7	4	8	5	7	.364	.750
Thomas, Frank	.174	23	4	0	3	4	7	.296	.261
Thome, Jim*	.240	25	6	3	6	5	8	.355	.640
Tinsley, Lee#	.250	12	3	0	2	1	4	.308	.250
Trammell, A	.333	15	5	0	1	1	1	.375	.400
Valentin, Jhn	.158	19	3	1	1	4	2	.304	.368
Valentin, Jse#	.176	17	3	2	4	2	5	.263	.588
Valle, Dave	.281	32	9	1	2	1	4	.324	.469
Vaughn, Greg	.318	44	14	2	7	4	13	.380	.523
Vaughn, Mo*	.355	31	11	3	9	1	4	.353	.742
Velarde, R	.316	19	6	1	3	2	3	.381	.474
Ventura, R*	.387	31	12	4	9	1	5	.394	.806
Vina, F*	.200	10	2	0	0	0	2	.200	.200
Vizquel, Omar#	.231	52	12	0	3	4	7	.293	.308
Walker, Larry*	.333	6	2	0	0	0	1	.333	.333
Ward, Turner#	.667	9	6	1	3	1	2	.700	1.000
Weiss, Walt#	.286	14	4	0	1	1	2	.333	.357
White, Devon#	.283	46	13	1	5	3	9	.327	.457
Whiten, Mark#	.176	17	3	1	1	0	3	.176	.353
Williams, Ber#	.237	38	9	1	5	2	7	.275	.474
Wilson, Dan	.235	17	4	0	1	0	2	.235	.235
Young, Eric	.400	5	2	0	0	2	0	.571	1.000
Young, Ernie	.143	7	1	0	0	3	3	.400	.143

Julian Tavarez, Indians — RHP

Batter	Avg	AB	H	HR	BI	BB	SO	OBP	Slg
Aldrete, Mike*	.200	5	1	0	0	0	2	.200	.400
Alomar, R#	.333	6	2	0	0	0	0	.333	.333
Anderson, G*	.000	4	0	0	0	1	1	.200	.000
Baines, H*	.333	3	1	0	0	2	0	.600	.333
Becker, Rich*	.750	8	6	0	2	0	1	.750	1.125
Berroa, G	.000	7	0	0	0	2	0	.222	.000
Bordick, Mike	.200	5	1	0	0	1	0	.333	.200
Buhner, Jay	.000	5	0	0	2	0	0	.000	.000
Canseco, Jose	.000	5	0	0	0	0	3	.000	.000
Carter, Joe	.400	10	4	1	3	1	1	.455	.700
Cirillo, Jeff	.750	4	3	0	1	1	0	.800	1.250
Cora, Joey#	.200	5	1	0	0	1	0	.200	.200
Cordova, M	.286	7	2	0	0	0	1	.286	.429
Damon, Johnny*	.400	5	2	0	1	0	0	.400	.800
Devereaux, M	.200	5	1	0	0	0	2	.200	.400
Gaetti, Gary	.400	5	2	1	1	0	1	.400	1.000
Gates, Brent#	.250	4	1	0	0	0	0	.400	.750
Giambi, Jason*	.000	3	0	0	0	2	0	.400	.000
Gonzalez, J	.143	7	1	1	1	0	0	.143	.571
Goodwin, Tom*	.833	6	5	0	1	0	0	.833	1.333
Greenwell, M*	.231	13	3	0	0	0	1	.231	.385
Greer, Rusty*	.400	5	2	1	2	0	2	.400	1.000
Guillen, O*	.000	3	0	0	1	0	0	.200	.000
Hulse, David*	.500	6	3	0	0	0	0	.500	.500
Jaha, John	.286	7	2	0	0	3	3	.286	.286
Jeter, Derek	.333	6	2	0	0	0	1	.333	.333
Knoblauch, C	.250	12	3	1	2	2	3	.400	.500
Leyritz, Jim	.286	7	2	0	0	0	1	.250	.429
Lockhart, K*	.600	5	3	0	1	0	0	.600	.600
Macfarlane, M	.500	8	4	1	1	1	1	.556	.875
Martinez, T*	.200	5	1	0	0	0	0	.200	.200
McGwire, Mark	.333	3	1	1	1	2	1	.600	1.333
McLemore, M#	.600	5	3	0	2	1	0	.667	.800
Meares, Pat	.300	10	3	0	2	1	1	.417	.500
Molitor, Paul	.273	11	3	0	4	0	2	.273	.364
Naehring, Tim	.444	9	4	1	2	1	1	.500	.778
Nixon, Otis#	.333	6	2	0	0	1	0	.429	.333
O'Neill, Paul*	.600	5	3	1	3	1	0	.667	1.200
Offerman, J#	.200	5	1	0	0	0	0	.200	.200
Olerud, John*	.429	7	3	0	1	2	0	.555	.429
Palmeiro, R*	.000	5	0	0	0	0	0	.000	.000
Palmer, Dean	.250	4	1	0	0	1	1	.500	.250
Randa, Joe	.200	5	1	0	0	0	1	.200	.200

Julian Tavarez, Indians — RHP

Batter	Avg	AB	H	HR	BI	BB	SO	OBP	Slg
Ripken, Cal	.200	5	1	1	3	0	4	.200	.800
Rodriguez, I	.429	7	3	0	1	0	0	.429	.571
Salmon, Tim	.000	4	0	0	0	1	2	.000	.000
Seitzer, K	.250	8	2	0	0	0	0	.250	.250
Sierra, Ruben#	.200	5	1	0	0	0	1	.200	.200
Sprague, Ed	.125	8	1	0	0	0	3	.125	.125
Stahoviak, S*	.250	4	1	0	1	2	1	.500	.500
Steinbach, T	.500	6	3	0	3	0	2	.500	.667
Surhoff, B.J.*	.250	4	1	0	0	1	2	.400	.250
Tettleton, M#	.400	5	2	1	2	1	1	.500	1.000
Thomas, Frank	.167	6	1	0	3	1	0	.286	.333
Tucker, M*	.400	5	2	1	1	0	1	.500	1.000
Valentin, Jhn	.286	14	4	0	1	1	2	.333	.357
Valentin, Jse#	.400	5	2	0	2	1	1	.500	.400
Vaughn, Greg	.333	6	2	0	0	0	1	.333	.333
Vaughn, Mo*	.583	12	7	0	2	2	1	.643	.583
Velarde, R	.400	5	2	0	2	0	1	.400	.600
Vina, F*	.167	6	1	0	0	0	1	.167	.167
White, Devon#	.250	4	1	0	0	1	2	.400	.250
Williams, Ber#	.500	6	3	0	1	1	1	.571	.667
Williams, Ger	.400	5	2	0	0	0	3	.400	.400
Wilson, Dan	.143	7	1	1	1	0	2	.143	.571

Billy Taylor, Athletics — RHP

Batter	Avg	AB	H	HR	BI	BB	SO	OBP	Slg
Belle, Albert	.500	4	2	0	0	2	1	.667	.500
Buhner, Jay	.200	5	1	1	3	2	2	.429	.800
Canseco, Jose	.000	4	0	0	0	1	2	.000	.000
Devereaux, M	.333	6	2	0	1	0	2	.333	.333
DiSarcina, G	.000	6	0	0	0	0	3	.000	.000
Gonzalez, J	.000	8	0	0	0	0	4	.000	.000
Hammonds, J	.333	3	1	0	1	1	2	.500	.333
Hoiles, Chris	.400	5	2	1	3	0	1	.400	1.000
Martinez, E	.167	6	1	0	0	1	0	.286	.167
Molitor, Paul	.600	5	3	0	3	0	0	.600	1.000
Murray, Eddie*	.200	5	1	0	0	0	2	.200	.200
Palmer, Dean	.400	5	2	0	0	3	1	.625	.400
Polonia, Luis*	.250	4	1	0	0	1	0	.400	.250
Ramirez, M	.200	5	1	0	2	1	3	.286	.200
Ripken, Cal	.333	3	1	0	3	2	2	.600	.667
Rodriguez, I	.200	5	1	0	0	0	0	.200	.200
Sorrento, P*	.286	7	2	0	0	1	2	.375	.429
Sprague, Ed	.000	3	0	0	1	1	1	.400	.000
Stanley, Mike	.200	5	1	0	0	0	3	.200	.200
Strange, Doug#	.000	5	0	0	0	0	2	.000	.000
Velarde, R	.286	7	2	0	0	0	2	.286	.286

Amaury Telemaco, Cubs — RHP

Batter	Avg	AB	H	HR	BI	BB	SO	OBP	Slg
Alfonzo, E	.600	5	3	0	0	0	0	.600	.600
Bell, Jay	.400	5	2	0	2	0	0	.400	.600
Blauser, Jeff	.250	4	1	0	0	0	1	.400	.250
Castilla, V	.500	4	2	2	2	0	2	.600	2.000
Cianfrocco, A	.000	4	0	0	1	0	1	.000	.000
Espinoza, A	.000	6	0	0	0	1	0	.000	.000
Finley, Steve*	.333	6	2	1	1	0	0	.333	1.000
Galarraga, A	.333	6	2	2	4	0	1	.333	1.333
Gilkey, B	.167	6	1	0	0	0	3	.167	.167
Grissom, M	.667	6	4	1	2	1	0	.714	1.333
Gwynn, Tony*	.333	6	2	1	1	0	0	.333	.833
Henderson, R	.333	6	2	1	1	0	1	.333	.833
Johnson, L*	.333	6	2	2	2	0	0	.333	1.333
Jones, C#	.000	5	0	0	0	1	0	.167	.000
Klesko, Ryan*	.400	5	2	1	4	1	0	.500	1.000
Lopez, Javy	.000	5	0	0	0	0	1	.000	.000
McCracken, Q#	.333	3	1	1	2	0	1	.333	1.333
McGriff, Fred*	.500	6	3	0	1	0	1	.500	.667
Reed, Jody	.200	5	1	0	1	0	1	.200	.200
Smith, Dwight*	.167	6	1	0	2	0	0	.167	.167
Weiss, Walt*	.500	4	2	0	0	2	1	.667	.750

Dave Telgheder, Athletics — RHP

Batter	Avg	AB	H	HR	BI	BB	SO	OBP	Slg
Alomar Jr, S	.400	5	2	0	0	0	0	.400	.600
Becker, Rich*	.400	5	2	0	0	1	2	.500	.400
Belle, Albert	.333	6	2	0	0	0	1	.333	.333
Berry, Sean	.167	6	1	1	1	1	1	.286	.667
Biggio, Craig	.250	4	1	0	1	1	0	.400	.500
Blauser, Jeff	.200	5	1	0	0	1	1	.333	.200
Boggs, Wade*	.400	5	2	0	0	0	1	.400	.400
Bonds, Barry*	.333	6	2	0	2	2	1	.500	.667
Bragg, Darren*	.125	8	1	0	0	0	2	.125	.250
Buhner, Jay	.125	8	1	1	2	0	0	.125	.500
Butler, Brett*	.429	7	3	0	0	0	0	.429	.571
Carreon, Mark	.222	9	2	0	2	0	1	.222	.444
Clark, Will*	.333	6	2	0	0	0	0	.333	.500
Clayton, R	.500	10	5	2	6	0	0	.500	1.100
Cora, Joey#	.429	7	3	0	1	0	0	.500	.714
Cordero, Wil	.200	5	1	0	0	0	0	.333	.200
Cordova, M	.000	4	0	0	1	0	0	.000	.000
DeShields, D*	.333	9	3	0	0	2	0	.455	.444

Dave Telgheder, Athletics — RHP

Batter	Avg	AB	H	HR	BI	BB	SO	OBP	Slg
Fielder, C	.000	4	0	0	0	1	1	.200	.000
Finley, Steve*	.200	5	1	0	2	0	1	.200	.200
Fletcher, D*	.167	6	1	0	0	1	1	.286	.500
Frye, Jeff	.250	4	1	0	0	1	1	.400	.750
Griffey Jr, K*	.125	8	1	1	1	0	4	.125	.500
Grissom, M	.333	9	3	0	1	2	1	.455	.444
Hill, G	.400	5	2	0	0	0	2	.400	.400
Hollins, Dave#	.200	5	1	0	1	0	1	.200	.400
Justice, Dave*	.333	6	2	0	0	0	0	.333	.333
Karros, Eric	.833	6	5	2	5	1	0	.857	1.833
Knoblauch, C	.500	4	2	1	1	2	1	.667	1.250
Lemke, Mark#	.167	6	1	0	1	0	0	.167	.167
Lewis, Darren	.143	7	1	0	0	1	0	.333	.143
Lofton, Kenny*	.333	6	2	0	2	1	0	.429	.333
Manwaring, K	.400	5	2	0	0	0	0	.500	.400
Martinez, E	.429	7	3	1	1	1	0	.500	1.000
McGee, Willie#	.333	6	2	0	0	0	0	.333	.333
Molitor, Paul	.000	4	0	0	0	1	1	.200	.000
Mondesi, Raul	.200	5	1	0	0	0	0	.200	.200
Morandini, M*	.400	5	2	0	0	0	1	.400	.400
O'Brien, C	.400	5	2	0	0	0	0	.400	.400
Offerman, J#	.667	6	4	0	0	0	1	.667	.833
Piazza, Mike	.429	7	3	0	2	0	1	.429	.571
Ramirez, M	.167	6	1	1	2	0	0	.167	.667
Rodriguez, Al	.375	8	3	1	1	0	0	.375	.750
Seitzer, K	.167	6	1	0	0	1	1	.286	.167
Sojo, Luis	.250	4	1	0	0	0	0	.250	.500
Sorrento, P*	.600	5	3	2	3	2	0	.625	1.667
Stahoviak, S*	.200	5	1	0	0	0	0	.200	.200
Thome, Jim*	.400	5	2	0	3	1	1	.500	.600
Thompson, Rob	.222	9	2	0	1	0	2	.222	.444
Vizcaino, J#	.200	5	1	0	0	0	0	.200	.200
Vizquel, Omar#	.600	5	3	0	0	1	0	.667	.800
Walker, Larry*	.000	4	0	0	0	3	0	.429	.000
Weiss, Walt#	.000	3	0	0	0	2	0	.400	.000
White, R	.250	4	1	0	0	1	0	.400	.250
Whiten, Mark#	.333	9	3	0	1	0	3	.333	.333
Williams, Ma	.000	3	0	0	0	2	1	.400	.000

Bob Tewksbury, Padres — RHP

Batter	Avg	AB	H	HR	BI	BB	SO	OBP	Slg
Abbott, Kurt	.000	6	0	0	0	0	3	.000	.000
Aldrete, Mike*	.400	5	2	0	0	0	1	.400	.400
Alicea, Luis#	.000	5	0	0	0	0	0	.000	.000
Allensworth	.333	6	2	0	0	0	1	.429	.333
Alomar, R#	.267	15	4	0	1	0	1	.267	.467
Alou, Moises	.133	30	4	2	3	2	4	.212	.333
Andrews, S	.000	5	0	0	0	1	1	.167	.000
Anthony, Eric*	.222	18	4	0	0	0	1	.222	.278
Arias, Alex	.111	9	1	0	0	0	2	.111	.111
Aurilia, Rich	.400	5	2	0	0	0	1	.400	.400
Ausmus, Brad	.556	9	5	0	0	0	0	.556	.889
Bagwell, Jeff	.240	25	6	1	5	3	4	.300	.440
Baines, H*	.444	9	4	0	1	1	1	.500	.444
Barberie, B#	.364	22	8	0	0	3	1	.440	.455
Batiste, Kim	.556	9	5	0	3	0	0	.556	.667
Bell, Derek	.200	15	3	1	4	0	3	.250	.467
Bell, Jay	.357	56	20	0	4	1	5	.373	.429
Belliard, R	.273	11	3	0	1	0	0	.273	.364
Benard, M*	.231	13	3	0	1	1	1	.286	.231
Benjamin, M	.200	5	1	0	0	0	1	.200	.200
Berry, Sean	.250	16	4	0	2	0	5	.235	.375
Bichette, D	.259	27	7	1	3	1	7	.286	.370
Biggio, Craig	.320	25	8	0	5	1	3	.357	.400
Blauser, Jeff	.280	25	7	0	0	1	1	.308	.400
Blowers, Mike	.143	7	1	1	0	1	0	.143	.143
Boggs, Wade*	.412	17	7	1	1	0	0	.412	.706
Bonds, Barry*	.326	46	15	3	13	3	4	.346	.587
Bonilla, B#	.310	42	13	1	7	0	4	.289	.452
Boone, Bret	.455	11	5	0	1	0	1	.455	.545
Branson, Jeff*	.286	7	2	0	0	0	0	.286	.286
Brumfield, J	.500	10	5	0	1	0	1	.500	.800
Burks, Ellis	.190	21	4	1	2	1	4	.227	.476
Burnitz, J*	.143	7	1	0	0	0	0	.143	.143
Butler, Brett*	.400	20	8	1	2	1	1	.429	.650
Caminiti, Ken#	.263	19	5	0	3	1	2	.300	.316
Candaele, C#	.071	14	1	0	0	1	4	.133	.143
Cangelosi, J	.200	5	1	0	0	1	0	.200	.600
Carr, Chuck	.250	8	2	0	1	0	1	.333	.250
Carreon, Mark	.182	11	2	0	1	1	2	.250	.273
Carter, Joe	.333	18	6	2	3	1	2	.368	.667
Castilla, V	.333	15	5	1	1	0	3	.333	.600
Cedeno, A	.182	11	2	0	2	1	1	.308	.273
Cianfrocco, A	.100	10	1	1	3	0	2	.100	.400
Clark, Dave*	.269	26	7	1	3	2	3	.310	.500
Clark, Will*	.261	23	6	0	1	0	1	.261	.435
Clayton, R	.333	21	7	0	0	0	1	.333	.381
Colbrunn, A	.167	6	1	0	1	0	1	.167	.167
Cole, Alex*	.368	19	7	0	2	0	6	.368	.526
Coleman, V*	.292	24	7	0	0	0	3	.292	.375
Conine, Jeff	.250	16	4	0	2	0	2	.250	.375

Batter	Avg	AB	H	HR	BI	BB	SO	OBP	Slg
Cora, Joey#	.333	6	2	0	0	0	0	.333	.500
Cordero, Wil	.462	13	6	0	0	1	3	.500	.500
Damon, Johnny*	.571	7	4	1	1	0	0	.571	1.143
Dascenzo, D#	.167	6	1	0	1	0	0	.143	.167
Daulton, D*	.324	34	11	2	6	2	5	.378	.588
Davis, Eric	.381	21	8	1	3	0	1	.364	.619
Dawson, Andre	.324	34	11	1	3	1	5	.343	.471
Decker, Steve	.500	8	4	0	1	1	0	.556	.625
DeShields, D*	.211	38	8	0	6	1	5	.231	.316
DiSarcina, G	.400	5	2	0	0	0	0	.400	.400
Dorsett, B	.200	5	1	0	0	0	0	.200	.200
Duncan, A	.227	22	5	0	2	0	3	.261	.227
Dunston, S	.382	34	13	0	4	1	2	.400	.618
Dye, Jermaine	.333	6	2	0	1	0	0	.333	.500
Dykstra, L*	.324	34	11	0	1	2	1	.361	.412
Easley, D	.400	5	2	0	1	0	1	.400	.400
Edmonds, Jim*	.667	6	4	0	4	0	0	.667	.667
Eisenreich, J*	.333	12	4	0	1	0	0	.385	.500
Eusebio, Tony	.167	6	1	0	0	0	2	.167	.167
Finley, Steve*	.318	22	7	0	0	0	1	.318	.409
Fletcher, D*	.270	37	10	0	2	1	4	.282	.297
Floyd, Cliff*	.182	11	2	0	0	0	2	.182	.273
Franco, Julio	.375	8	3	0	1	1	1	.444	.625
Frazier, Lou#	.400	5	2	0	2	0	0	.400	.600
Gaetti, Gary	.294	17	5	1	5	1	2	.300	.588
Gagne, Greg	.278	18	5	0	2	1	1	.316	.389
Galarraga, A	.158	38	6	2	3	0	10	.179	.316
Gallego, Mike	.500	6	3	0	1	0	1	.500	.667
Gant, Ron	.357	28	10	0	1	1	3	.379	.393
Garcia, C	.450	20	9	1	6	1	1	.476	.700
Giovanola, Ed*	.200	5	1	0	0	0	1	.200	.200
Girardi, Joe	.056	18	1	0	0	0	1	.150	.056
Gomez, Leo	.000	5	0	0	0	1	2	.167	.000
Gonzalez, L*	.276	29	8	2	5	1	1	.300	.517
Goodwin, Tom*	.462	13	6	0	1	0	0	.462	.538
Grace, Mark*	.296	54	16	0	10	3	4	.328	.389
Green, Shawn*	.000	6	0	0	0	0	2	.000	.000
Grissom, M	.351	37	13	0	1	0	1	.342	.514
Grudzielanek	.200	10	2	0	1	0	1	.200	.300
Guillen, O*	.667	9	6	0	2	0	0	.600	.778
Gutierrez, R	.167	6	1	0	0	1	1	.286	.333
Gwynn, Tony*	.303	33	10	1	3	1	0	.324	.485
Hall, Mel*	.000	6	0	0	0	1	2	.143	.000
Hamelin, Bob*	.143	7	1	0	0	1	1	.250	.143
Hansen, Dave*	.333	6	2	0	0	0	0	.333	.333
Harris, Lenny*	.500	16	8	0	2	0	0	.500	.688
Hayes, C	.385	39	15	1	6	1	6	.400	.590
Hernandez, Ca	.333	6	2	0	0	0	0	.333	.333
Hernandez, Jo	.222	9	2	0	1	0	1	.222	.222
Hill, G	.333	9	3	2	3	0	2	.333	1.000
Hollandsworth*	.167	6	1	0	0	1	0	.286	.167
Hollins, Dave#	.250	20	5	0	4	0	3	.250	.250
Howard, T*	.370	27	10	0	3	3	1	.433	.556
Hundley, Todd#	.353	17	6	1	2	1	3	.389	.647
Hunter, Brian	.111	9	1	0	0	1	4	.200	.111
Hunter, Bri L	.333	6	2	0	0	0	0	.333	.333
Incaviglia, R	.273	11	3	0	0	0	3	.273	.364
James, Dion*	.429	7	3	0	0	1	1	.429	.429
Javier, Stan#	.250	8	2	0	0	2	0	.400	.375
Jefferies, G#	.267	15	4	1	5	2	0	.333	.600
Johnson, Char	.400	5	2	0	0	0	2	.400	.600
Johnson, L*	.286	7	2	1	3	0	0	.286	.714
Johnson, Mark*	.385	13	5	0	1	0	2	.385	.385
Jones, C#	.000	7	0	0	0	0	0	.000	.000
Jordan, Brian	.556	9	5	1	3	0	1	.556	.889
Jordan, Ricky	.600	10	6	2	3	0	2	.600	1.300
Joyner, Wally*	.273	11	3	0	4	4	1	.467	.364
Justice, Dave*	.323	31	10	0	1	1	3	.344	.387
Karros, Eric	.190	21	4	0	1	0	1	.182	.190
Kelly, R	.500	14	7	0	1	1	1	.533	.500
Kendall, J	.375	8	3	1	2	1	1	.444	.750
Kent, Jeff	.400	5	2	1	1	1	0	.500	1.200
King, Jeff	.217	23	5	0	3	2	0	.280	.261
Kingery, Mike*	.300	10	3	0	1	0	1	.364	.300
Kirby, Wayne*	.300	10	3	0	0	0	0	.300	.300
Klesko, Ryan*	.500	18	9	0	4	1	2	.526	.611
Lankford, Ray*	.333	6	2	0	1	1	3	.429	.333
Lansing, Mike	.393	28	11	1	3	2	2	.433	.536
Larkin, Barry	.250	36	9	0	2	3	2	.289	.278
Lemke, Mark#	.129	31	4	0	2	3	1	.182	.161
Lewis, Darren	.188	16	3	0	0	1	1	.188	.313
Liriano, N#	.000	6	0	0	0	1	3	.143	.000
Lockhart, K*	.000	6	0	0	1	0	0	.125	.000
Lopez, Javy	.125	16	2	0	1	0	2	.125	.125
Mabry, John*	.250	8	2	0	2	0	2	.222	.375
Magadan, Dave*	.375	24	9	0	4	2	2	.379	.417
Manwaring, K	.250	16	4	0	0	1	1	.333	.250
Martin, Al*	.240	25	6	0	2	0	4	.231	.320
Martinez, Da*	.364	33	12	1	2	0	3	.382	.485
Martinez, E	.400	5	2	0	0	0	0	.400	.600
Martinez, T*	.200	5	1	0	0	0	0	.200	.200

Batter	Avg	AB	H	HR	BI	BB	SO	OBP	Slg
May, Derrick*	.324	37	12	0	1	1	1	.342	.351
Mayne, Brent*	.250	12	3	0	1	0	0	.250	.333
McCracken, Q#	.400	5	2	0	0	0	2	.400	.400
McGee, Willie#	.400	25	10	0	2	0	2	.400	.440
McGriff, Fred*	.270	37	10	1	3	3	7	.325	.351
Merced, O*	.342	38	13	1	4	3	3	.390	.553
Miller, Orl	.333	9	3	1	2	0	1	.333	.667
Mitchell, K	.333	18	6	0	2	0	0	.316	.611
Molitor, Paul	.500	10	5	0	1	1	0	.545	.700
Mondesi, Raul	.556	9	5	0	0	0	1	.556	.556
Morandini, M*	.133	30	4	0	0	3	0	.133	.133
Morris, Hal*	.206	34	7	1	6	1	3	.222	.353
Mouton, James	.571	7	4	0	0	0	2	.571	.714
Murray, Eddie#	.207	29	6	1	3	1	5	.233	.379
Myers, Greg*	.000	4	0	0	0	1	2	.200	.000
Nixon, Otis*	.462	13	6	0	0	1	0	.500	.462
Nunnally, Jon*	.000	6	0	0	0	0	2	.000	.000
O'Brien, C	.444	9	4	2	5	0	0	.500	1.111
O'Neill, Paul*	.286	28	8	1	1	2	3	.333	.500
Offerman, J#	.313	16	5	0	0	1	1	.353	.375
Olerud, John*	.286	7	2	0	1	1	1	.375	.429
Oliver, Joe	.290	31	9	0	2	0	1	.290	.387
Orsulak, Joe*	.333	6	2	0	1	0	0	.286	.333
Pagnozzi, Tom	.000	6	0	0	1	0	1	.000	.000
Pendleton, T#	.281	32	9	2	5	0	2	.273	.531
Phillips, T#	.429	7	3	0	0	0	1	.429	.571
Piazza, Mike	.385	13	5	0	1	0	1	.385	.462
Plantier, P*	.667	9	6	1	2	1	2	.700	1.222
Polonia, Luis*	.143	7	1	0	0	0	1	.143	.143
Raines, Tim#	.188	16	3	0	0	1	3	.235	.250
Reed, Jeff*	.400	20	8	0	2	1	1	.429	.400
Reed, Jody	.375	8	3	0	1	0	0	.333	.375
Ripken, Cal	.091	11	1	0	1	3	0	.286	.091
Roberts, Bip#	.321	28	9	0	4	0	0	.310	.500
Rodriguez, H*	.167	18	3	1	4	0	2	.167	.389
Sabo, Chris	.296	27	8	2	3	0	1	.321	.519
Salmon, Tim	.800	5	4	1	2	0	0	.800	1.600
Samuel, Juan	.083	12	1	0	0	1	2	.154	.083
Sanchez, Rey	.400	10	4	0	2	0	0	.455	.400
Sandberg, R	.310	42	13	4	9	1	2	.333	.714
Sanders, R	.333	9	3	1	1	0	3	.400	.778
Santangelo, F#	.333	6	2	0	1	1	0	.429	.667
Santiago, B	.303	33	10	1	2	0	4	.303	.485
Scarsone, S	.500	6	3	0	1	0	0	.500	.667
Schofield, D	.182	11	2	0	0	0	0	.182	.182
Segui, David#	.357	14	5	0	0	1	1	.400	.500
Seitzer, K	.600	5	3	0	0	0	0	.600	.600
Sheaffer, D	.286	14	4	0	1	0	1	.286	.357
Sheffield, G	.071	14	1	0	1	2	2	.176	.071
Sierra, Ruben#	.222	9	2	0	0	0	2	.222	.556
Slaught, Don	.333	12	4	1	3	1	2	.385	.583
Smith, Dwight*	.250	28	7	1	3	2	3	.300	.429
Snow, J.T.#	.200	5	1	0	2	0	1	.200	.400
Sosa, Sammy	.360	25	9	2	4	0	6	.385	.600
Sprague, Ed	.667	6	4	0	0	0	1	.667	1.000
Stanley, Mike	.000	4	0	0	0	1	0	.200	.000
Stillwell, K#	.333	6	2	0	0	0	0	.333	.500
Strawberry, D*	.417	12	5	0	2	0	1	.417	.583
Taubensee, E*	.286	14	4	1	2	0	4	.267	.500
Thompson, Mil*	.385	13	5	0	3	1	0	.429	.385
Thompson, Rob	.219	32	7	0	4	0	8	.219	.313
Thompson, Ry	.200	5	1	0	0	0	2	.200	.200
Tinsley, Lee#	.000	5	0	0	0	0	2	.000	.000
Tucker, M*	.000	10	2	0	1	0	1	.200	.200
VanderWal, J*	.214	14	3	0	2	0	2	.200	.286
Veras, Q#	.333	6	2	0	0	0	1	.333	.333
Vizcaino, J#	.172	29	5	0	0	0	2	.172	.207
Walker, Larry*	.250	40	10	4	11	2	5	.279	.600
Wallach, Tim	.211	38	8	0	4	1	1	.231	.368
Walton, J	.353	17	6	1	2	0	4	.353	.588
Weiss, Walt#	.360	25	9	0	2	1	3	.370	.440
White, Devon#	.273	11	3	0	2	1	0	.333	.364
White, R	.167	6	1	0	0	0	1	.286	.167
Wilkins, Rick*	.324	34	11	2	9	0	5	.324	.676
Williams, Ber#	.000	5	0	0	0	1	2	.167	.000
Williams, Ma	.286	42	12	2	8	0	8	.289	.524
Wilson, Dan	.125	8	1	0	0	0	1	.125	.250
Young, Eric	.263	19	5	0	2	2	1	.333	.316
Young, Kevin	.667	6	4	0	0	0	3	.667	.833

Larry Thomas, White Sox — LHP

Batter	Avg	AB	H	HR	BI	BB	SO	OBP	Slg
Anderson, G*	.200	5	1	0	0	0	2	.200	.200
Giambi, Jason*	.750	4	3	0	1	0	0	.800	.750
Goodwin, Tom*	.250	4	1	0	1	0	0	.250	.500
Martinez, T*	.333	3	1	0	0	3	1	.667	.333
O'Neill, Paul*	.200	5	1	0	1	0	0	.200	.400
Olerud, John*	.500	4	2	0	0	1	2	.600	.500
Snow, J.T.#	.167	6	1	0	0	0	0	.167	.167

Justin Thompson, Tigers — LHP

Batter	Avg	AB	H	HR	BI	BB	SO	OBP	Slg
Belle, Albert	.667	3	2	0	1	2	0	.800	1.333
Goodwin, Tom*	.222	9	2	0	0	0	2	.222	.222
Howard, Dave#	.167	6	1	0	1	0	2	.167	.167
Kent, Jeff	.000	3	0	0	1	1	1	.200	.000
Lofton, Kenny*	.167	6	1	0	0	0	1	.167	.167
Macfarlane, M	.500	4	2	0	1	0	1	.600	1.000
Offerman, J#	.333	6	2	1	1	3	1	.556	.833
Paquette, C	.111	9	1	0	0	0	3	.111	.111
Ramirez, M	.000	2	0	0	1	2	1	.400	.000
Randa, Joe	.000	6	0	0	0	1	3	.143	.000
Thome, Jim*	.833	6	5	2	4	0	1	.833	2.000
Vitiello, Joe	.200	5	1	0	1	1	2	.333	.200
Vizcaino, J#	.167	6	1	0	0	0	3	.167	.167
Young, Kevin	.200	5	1	0	0	0	2	.200	.200

Mark Thompson, Rockies — RHP

Batter	Avg	AB	H	HR	BI	BB	SO	OBP	Slg
Abbott, Kurt	.500	4	2	1	1	2	0	.667	1.500
Alicea, Luis#	.167	6	1	0	0	0	1	.167	.167
Allensworth	.333	6	2	0	1	0	1	.286	.500
Alou, Moises	.167	6	1	0	0	0	0	.167	.333
Aurilia, Rich	.667	3	2	0	2	1	0	.600	.667
Bagwell, Jeff	.200	5	1	0	1	3	1	.500	.200
Bell, Derek	.273	11	3	0	2	0	2	.273	.273
Bell, Jay	.000	6	0	0	0	1	1	.143	.000
Berry, Sean	.000	2	0	0	1	1	1	.400	.000
Biggio, Craig	.333	6	2	0	1	1	0	.500	.500
Blauser, Jeff	.286	7	2	0	1	0	2	.286	.286
Blowers, Mike	.333	6	2	0	0	2	0	.500	.667
Bonds, Barry*	.333	6	2	1	1	3	2	.556	.833
Boone, Bret	.250	8	2	1	2	0	2	.250	.625
Brogna, Rico*	.600	5	3	0	3	1	0	.667	.800
Butler, Brett*	.143	7	1	0	1	0	1	.143	.143
Caminiti, Ken#	.286	7	2	0	0	0	2	.286	.429
Clark, Dave*	.400	5	2	1	2	0	0	.400	1.200
Clayton, R	.250	8	2	0	0	1	2	.333	.250
Conine, Jeff	.222	9	2	0	3	1	1	.300	.444
Davis, Eric	.625	8	5	2	7	0	0	.625	1.625
DeShields, D*	.444	9	4	0	0	2	0	.545	.667
Finley, Steve*	.250	8	2	0	0	0	2	.250	.375
Fletcher, D*	.600	5	3	0	1	0	0	.600	.800
Fonville, C#	.250	12	3	0	0	1	2	.308	.250
Gaetti, Gary	.286	7	2	0	2	0	1	.286	.429
Garcia, C	.400	5	2	0	1	0	1	.400	1.000
Gilkey, B	.333	9	3	1	3	1	1	.400	.667
Gomez, Chris	.000	4	0	0	0	1	0	.200	.000
Gonzalez, L*	.000	6	0	0	0	0	1	.143	.000
Grace, Mark*	.500	6	3	0	1	0	1	.500	.833
Grissom, M	.417	12	5	0	1	0	2	.417	.500
Grudzielanek	.143	7	1	0	1	0	0	.143	.286
Gutierrez, R	.000	4	0	0	0	0	1	.200	.000
Gwynn, Tony*	.750	4	3	0	0	0	0	.875	1.250
Hollandsworth*	.444	9	4	0	2	0	2	.500	.667
Hundley, Todd#	.556	9	5	1	4	2	0	.636	.889
Hunter, Bri L	.222	9	2	0	0	0	1	.222	.222
Huskey, Butch	.143	7	1	0	0	1	2	.250	.143
Incaviglia, P	.000	5	0	0	0	0	2	.000	.000
Johnson, Bri	.333	6	2	0	2	0	0	.333	.833
Johnson, L*	.125	8	1	0	0	0	0	.125	.125
Johnson, Mark*	.333	6	2	1	3	1	1	.429	.833
Jones, C#	.444	9	4	1	3	1	2	.500	1.000
Jordan, Brian	.286	7	2	0	2	1	0	.375	.286
Karros, Eric	.286	14	4	1	1	0	2	.286	.643
Kendall, J	.600	5	3	0	0	0	0	.600	.800
Kent, Jeff	.333	6	2	0	0	1	3	.429	.333
King, Jeff	.000	7	0	0	0	1	1	.125	.000
Klesko, Ryan*	.250	8	2	1	2	0	3	.250	.625
Lankford, Ray*	.375	8	3	1	4	1	1	.400	.875
Lansing, Mike	.333	6	2	0	0	0	2	.429	.500
Larkin, Barry	.444	9	4	1	3	0	1	.444	.778
Lemke, Mark#	.286	7	2	0	2	0	1	.286	.286
Livingstone*	.200	5	1	0	1	2	1	.429	.200
Lopez, Javy	.333	3	1	0	0	2	0	.667	.333
Mabry, John*	.167	6	1	0	0	1	0	.286	.167
Magadan, Dave*	.333	9	3	0	0	2	0	.455	.333
Manwaring, K	.667	3	2	0	1	1	1	.600	1.333
Martin, Al*	.375	8	3	0	0	0	0	.375	.375
May, Derrick*	.200	5	1	0	0	0	1	.200	.200
McGee, Willie*	.333	6	2	0	0	1	1	.429	.333
McGriff, Fred*	.375	8	3	0	0	1	1	.444	.375
McRae, Brian*	.222	9	2	1	1	2	3	.364	.556
Mitchell, K	.400	5	2	0	0	1	0	.500	.800
Mondesi, Raul	.357	14	5	3	6	0	2	.357	1.071
Morandini, M*	.429	7	3	0	0	0	0	.429	.571
Morris, Hal*	.286	7	2	0	1	2	1	.444	.286
Offerman, J#	.200	5	1	0	1	0	0	.200	.200
Ordonez, Rey	.000	7	0	0	0	0	1	.000	.000
Orsulak, Joe*	.333	9	3	0	1	1	1	.400	.667
Otero, Ricky*	.400	5	2	0	0	0	0	.400	.400
Pagnozzi, Tom	.400	5	2	0	0	0	0	.400	.600
Pendleton, T#	.375	8	3	1	5	2	1	.500	.750

Mark Thompson, Rockies — RHP

Batter	Avg	AB	H	HR	BI	BB	SO	OBP	Slg
Piazza, Mike	.462	13	6	1	2	1	2	.500	.692
Plantier, P*	.600	5	3	0	1	0	0	.600	.800
Reed, Jody	.400	5	2	0	0	0	0	.400	.600
Renteria, E	.286	7	2	0	0	1	1	.375	.286
Rodriguez, H*	.600	5	3	1	2	2	0	.714	1.400
Sanchez, Rey	.111	9	1	0	0	0	1	.111	.111
Sandberg, R	.143	7	1	0	0	0	2	.143	.143
Segui, David#	.167	6	1	0	0	0	1	.167	.167
Sheffield, G	.400	5	2	0	1	6	1	.727	.600
Sosa, Sammy	.200	10	2	1	1	0	2	.273	.600
Taubensee, E*	.200	5	1	0	0	0	0	.200	.400
Veras, Q#	.250	4	1	0	0	1	0	.400	.250
Vizcaino, J#	.333	9	3	0	3	1	0	.400	.556
White, Devon#	.000	7	0	0	0	1	2	.125	.000
Wilkins, Rick*	.286	7	2	1	2	1	1	.375	1.000
Williams, Ma	.333	6	2	1	4	0	0	.333	.833
Zeile, Todd	.400	5	2	0	0	2	0	.571	.400

Mike Timlin, Blue Jays — RHP

Batter	Avg	AB	H	HR	BI	BB	SO	OBP	Slg
Aldrete, Mike*	.667	3	2	0	0	2	0	.800	.667
Alomar Jr, S	.286	7	2	0	0	1	1	.375	.286
Anderson, Brd*	.125	8	1	0	0	1	2	.222	.125
Baerga, C#	.167	12	2	0	2	1	3	.214	.167
Baines, H*	.364	11	4	0	2	1	1	.417	.455
Belle, Albert	.500	10	5	2	3	2	1	.583	1.100
Boggs, Wade*	.125	8	1	0	2	2	1	.300	.375
Bordick, Mike	.300	10	3	0	0	0	2	.300	.300
Buhner, Jay	.143	7	1	0	1	0	3	.250	.143
Canseco, Jose	.250	12	3	1	2	1	4	.308	.583
Cole, Alex*	.222	9	2	0	1	1	2	.300	.222
Curtis, Chad	.000	3	0	0	0	2	1	.500	.000
Cuyler, Milt#	.286	7	2	0	0	2	2	.444	.286
Damon, Johnny*	.000	5	0	0	0	0	0	.000	.000
Davis, Chili*	.444	9	4	0	0	1	0	.500	.444
Deer, Rob	.111	9	1	1	2	2	6	.273	.444
Devereaux, M	.167	6	1	0	3	1	0	.286	.333
DiSarcina, A	.571	7	4	0	0	1	2	.625	.571
Durham, Ray*	.000	4	0	0	0	1	1	.200	.000
Espinoza, A	.000	4	0	0	0	0	1	.200	.000
Fermin, Felix	.286	7	2	0	0	0	2	.286	.286
Fielder, C	.286	14	4	1	3	1	4	.313	.500
Franco, Julio	.182	11	2	0	1	3	3	.357	.182
Fryman, T	.154	13	2	1	3	2	2	.267	.385
Gaetti, Gary	.000	9	0	0	1	0	3	.100	.000
Gagne, Greg	.143	7	1	0	1	0	0	.143	.143
Gallego, Mike	.444	9	4	0	3	2	1	.545	.444
Gomez, Leo	.429	7	3	1	4	0	2	.500	.857
Gonzalez, J	.385	13	5	1	2	1	5	.429	.615
Goodwin, Tom*	.333	3	1	0	0	1	2	.500	.333
Greenwell, M*	.286	7	2	0	0	1	1	.375	.429
Greer, Rusty*	.000	5	0	0	0	1	1	.167	.000
Griffey Jr, K*	.400	5	2	0	1	0	1	.500	.400
Guillen, O*	.500	4	2	0	1	0	0	.400	.500
Hall, Mel*	.000	4	0	0	0	1	1	.200	.000
Hamelin, Bob*	.400	5	2	0	0	0	0	.400	.600
Hamilton, D*	.222	9	2	0	5	1	0	.300	.222
Henderson, R	.333	6	2	0	0	1	2	.429	.333
Hoiles, Chris	.429	7	3	1	4	0	4	.429	.857
Howard, Dave#	.000	7	0	0	0	0	2	.000	.000
Hulse, David*	.200	10	2	0	0	0	2	.200	.200
Jaha, John	.500	6	3	0	0	0	1	.500	.500
Johnson, L*	.500	8	4	0	2	1	1	.556	.500
Joyner, Wally*	.333	6	2	0	1	0	1	.333	.333
Karkovice, R	.000	4	0	0	0	1	4	.200	.000
Kelly, Pat	.000	10	0	0	1	0	1	.000	.000
Kelly, R	.000	6	0	0	0	0	0	.143	.000
Kirby, Wayne*	.600	5	3	1	1	0	0	.600	1.400
Knoblauch, C	.167	6	1	0	2	0	1	.286	.167
Leius, Scott	.200	5	1	0	0	0	1	.200	.200
Lewis, Mark	.200	5	1	0	0	1	0	.333	.200
Leyritz, Jim	.000	5	0	0	0	1	2	.167	.000
Listach, Pat#	.167	6	1	0	1	0	3	.167	.167
Livingstone*	.400	5	2	0	0	0	0	.400	.600
Lofton, Kenny*	.125	8	1	0	0	1	0	.222	.125
Macfarlane, M	.000	5	0	0	0	1	1	.167	.000
Martinez, Da*	.400	5	2	0	1	0	0	.400	.600
Martinez, E	.333	6	2	0	0	0	0	.333	.333
Mayne, Brent*	.250	4	1	0	1	1	1	.400	.250
McGwire, Mark	.200	10	2	0	3	1	5	.273	.200
McLemore, M#	.429	7	3	0	1	0	1	.500	.429
McRae, Brian#	.167	6	1	0	0	1	1	.286	.167
Molitor, Paul	.143	7	1	0	0	0	0	.143	.143
Murray, Eddie#	.167	6	1	0	1	0	4	.167	.333
Naehring, Tim	.400	5	2	0	0	1	0	.500	.400
Nilsson, Dave*	.000	4	0	0	0	1	2	.200	.000
Nixon, Otis#	.250	4	1	0	0	1	2	.400	.250
O'Neill, Paul*	.000	4	0	0	0	1	0	.200	.000
Palmeiro, R*	.308	13	4	1	2	1	0	.357	.538
Palmer, Dean	.111	9	1	0	2	0	5	.111	.111
Pena, Tony	.000	6	0	0	0	1	0	.143	.000

207

Mike Timlin, Blue Jays — RHP

Batter	Avg	AB	H	HR	BI	BB	SO	OBP	Slg
Phillips, T#	.200	5	1	0	3	5	3	.600	.200
Polonia, Luis*	.500	10	5	0	0	4	1	.643	.500
Raines, Tim#	.000	6	0	0	0	1	1	.143	.000
Ramirez, M	.400	5	2	1	1	1	2	.500	1.000
Ripken, Cal	.167	12	2	0	0	1	1	.231	.167
Rodriguez, I	.182	11	2	0	1	0	5	.182	.182
Salmon, Tim	.400	5	2	0	2	2	1	.571	.400
Seitzer, K	.250	8	2	0	2	0	2	.250	.250
Sierra, Ruben&	.273	11	3	0	1	1	4	.333	.273
Sojo, Luis	.000	6	0	0	0	0	3	.000	.000
Sorrento, P*	.333	12	4	1	4	0	2	.333	.583
Stanley, Mike	.111	9	1	0	0	1	3	.200	.111
Steinbach, T	.000	7	0	0	0	0	1	.000	.000
Strange, Doug#	.250	4	1	0	0	1	1	.400	.250
Surhoff, B.J.*	.429	7	3	0	3	0	1	.429	.571
Tartabull, D	.333	9	3	0	2	1	2	.364	.556
Tettleton, M#	.000	4	0	0	0	3	1	.429	.000
Thomas, Frank	.000	10	0	0	0	4	5	.333	.000
Trammell, A	.400	5	2	0	0	1	0	.571	.400
Valentin, Jhn	.200	5	1	1	1	1	0	.333	.800
Valle, Dave	.200	5	1	0	0	1	1	.200	.200
Vaughn, Greg	.231	13	3	0	4	1	5	.286	.231
Vaughn, Mo*	.000	8	0	0	0	0	3	.000	.000
Velarde, R	.250	8	2	0	1	0	2	.250	.250
Ventura, R*	.333	12	4	0	0	1	6	.385	.333
Vizquel, Omar#	.333	6	2	0	1	1	0	.429	.333
Williams, Ber#	.111	9	1	0	3	4	2	.385	.333

Salomon Torres, Mariners — RHP

Batter	Avg	AB	H	HR	BI	BB	SO	OBP	Slg
Alicea, Luis#	.000	8	0	0	0	2	1	.200	.000
Anderson, G*	.000	6	0	0	0	0	2	.000	.000
Baerga, C#	.667	6	4	0	2	1	1	.714	.667
Barberie, B#	.250	8	2	0	0	1	1	.333	.250
Batista, Tony	.000	4	0	0	0	1	2	.200	.000
Becker, Rich*	.200	5	1	0	0	1	0	.200	.400
Belle, Albert	.167	6	1	0	1	1	0	.286	.333
Berroa, G	.200	5	1	0	1	1	0	.286	.200
Bichette, D	.200	5	1	0	0	0	0	.200	.200
Boggs, Wade*	.250	4	1	0	0	1	0	.400	.250
Butler, Brett*	.333	3	1	0	0	2	2	.600	.333
Caminiti, Ken#	.250	4	1	0	0	2	0	.500	.250
Carr, Chuck	.200	10	2	0	0	1	1	.273	.200
Conine, Jeff	.500	12	6	2	7	0	3	.500	1.167
Cordova, M	.333	6	2	0	1	0	2	.333	.500
Damon, Johnny*	.600	5	3	0	2	0	1	.600	.600
DiSarcina, G	.200	5	1	0	0	1	0	.333	.200
Dunston, S	.600	5	3	1	1	0	1	.667	1.200
Edmonds, Jim*	.167	6	1	0	0	0	0	.167	.167
Gaetti, Gary	.000	4	0	0	0	1	2	.200	.000
Galarraga, A	.167	6	1	1	2	0	2	.286	.667
Giambi, Jason*	.250	4	1	0	0	1	1	.400	.250
Gilkey, B	.500	8	4	1	2	2	1	.600	1.000
Girardi, Joe	.333	6	2	0	0	0	0	.333	.333
Gonzalez, L*	.500	4	2	0	2	0	0	.400	1.000
Goodwin, Tom*	.333	9	3	0	0	0	0	.333	.333
Grace, Mark*	.500	8	4	0	3	1	0	.556	.625
Grissom, M	.500	4	2	0	1	1	0	.600	.750
Hamelin, Bob*	.333	3	1	1	2	2	1	.600	1.333
Jefferies, G#	.100	10	1	0	1	0	0	.100	.200
Joyner, Wally*	.333	6	2	0	1	0	0	.333	.333
Karros, Eric	.333	3	1	0	1	1	1	.600	.667
Kelly, R	.250	4	1	0	0	1	1	.500	.500
Kirby, Wayne*	.400	5	2	0	0	0	1	.400	.400
Knoblauch, C	.333	6	2	0	0	1	2	.429	.333
Liriano, N#	.750	4	3	1	2	1	0	.800	2.000
Lockhart, K*	.222	9	2	0	1	1	1	.300	.333
Magadan, Dave*	.200	5	1	0	0	2	0	.429	.200
May, Derrick*	.600	5	3	0	1	1	0	.667	.600
Molitor, Paul	.000	7	0	0	0	0	0	.125	.000
Nunnally, Jon*	.250	4	1	0	0	4	1	.625	.500
Offerman, J#	.100	10	1	0	1	0	2	.100	.100
Pena, Tony	.000	4	0	0	0	1	0	.200	.000
Piazza, Mike	.500	4	2	0	0	1	1	.600	.500
Ramirez, M	.200	5	1	1	3	1	1	.333	.800
Roberts, Bip#	.500	4	2	0	1	1	0	.600	.750
Rodriguez, H*	.250	4	1	1	2	1	1	.400	1.000
Salmon, Tim	.000	4	0	0	0	2	1	.333	.000
Santiago, B	.000	6	0	0	0	0	0	.000	.000
Sheffield, G	.625	8	5	2	4	4	0	.750	1.625
Smith, Ozzie#	.000	5	0	0	0	2	0	.286	.000
Snow, J.T.#	.286	7	2	0	1	0	0	.286	.429
Sorrento, P*	.333	6	2	0	0	2	0	.333	.500
Sosa, Sammy	.222	9	2	0	0	0	3	.222	.333
Stahoviak, S*	.000	5	0	0	0	1	2	.167	.000
Thome, Jim*	.000	4	0	0	0	2	0	.333	.000
Valentin, Jhn	.500	6	3	0	0	2	0	.500	.667
Vaughn, Mo*	.250	4	1	0	0	3	1	.571	.250
Velarde, R	.400	5	2	1	1	0	2	.400	1.200
Vina, F*	.286	7	2	0	0	0	2	.286	.429
Vizcaino, J#	.167	6	1	0	0	0	0	.167	.167

Salomon Torres, Mariners — RHP

Batter	Avg	AB	H	HR	BI	BB	SO	OBP	Slg
Vizquel, Omar#	.400	5	2	0	0	1	0	.500	.600
Weiss, Walt#	.143	7	1	0	0	1	1	.143	.143
Whiten, Mark#	.222	9	2	0	0	1	1	.300	.222
Wilkins, Rick*	.500	8	4	2	4	0	1	.500	1.500
Young, Eric	.000	2	0	0	0	3	0	.600	.000
Zeile, Todd	.222	9	2	0	0	1	1	.300	.333

Steve Trachsel, Cubs — RHP

Batter	Avg	AB	H	HR	BI	BB	SO	OBP	Slg
Abbott, Kurt	.167	12	2	1	3	2	5	.286	.583
Alfonzo, E	.333	9	3	0	1	0	0	.333	.333
Alicea, Luis#	.100	10	1	1	2	1	7	.182	.400
Allensworth	.333	6	2	0	1	1	2	.429	.667
Alou, Moises	.400	15	6	0	0	1	2	.438	.600
Anthony, Eric*	.000	5	0	0	0	1	3	.167	.000
Arias, Alex	.600	5	3	0	1	0	1	.667	.800
Ashley, Billy	.000	8	0	0	0	1	1	.111	.000
Ausmus, Brad	.571	7	4	1	2	3	1	.700	1.000
Bagwell, Jeff	.292	24	7	3	5	4	1	.414	.708
Barberie, B#	.222	9	2	0	2	2	1	.364	.222
Batiste, Kim	.600	5	3	0	0	1	0	.667	.600
Bell, David	.000	6	0	0	0	0	0	.000	.000
Bell, Derek	.316	19	6	0	2	2	3	.364	.421
Bell, Jay	.231	13	3	0	0	2	5	.333	.308
Benard, M*	.000	6	0	0	0	0	1	.000	.000
Berry, Sean	.125	8	1	0	0	1	1	.300	.250
Bichette, D	.435	23	10	1	5	1	3	.458	.696
Biggio, Craig	.231	26	6	1	4	3	3	.310	.423
Blauser, Jeff	.400	5	2	0	0	1	0	.400	.600
Blowers, Mike	.222	9	2	0	1	0	0	.222	.333
Bonds, Barry*	.250	16	4	1	1	4	2	.400	.500
Bonilla, B#	.600	5	3	0	0	1	0	.667	1.000
Boone, Bret	.333	18	6	1	2	2	2	.400	.556
Branson, Jeff*	.500	8	4	2	2	0	2	.500	1.250
Brogna, Rico*	.143	7	1	0	1	0	2	.143	.143
Burks, Ellis	.308	13	4	1	1	0	5	.308	.615
Butler, Brett*	.353	17	6	0	1	0	1	.353	.353
Caminiti, Ken#	.176	17	3	1	1	3	4	.333	.412
Cangelosi, J#	.333	6	2	0	0	1	1	.429	.333
Carr, Chuck	.167	12	2	0	0	1	1	.231	.167
Carreon, Mark	.750	4	3	1	5	2	0	.833	2.000
Castilla, V	.400	10	4	2	6	2	1	.462	1.100
Cedeno, A	.400	15	6	1	3	0	2	.400	.600
Cedeno, Roger*	.143	7	1	0	1	0	0	.143	.143
Cianfrocco, A	.571	7	4	1	1	0	0	.571	1.143
Clark, Dave*	.200	5	1	0	0	1	2	.333	.200
Clayton, R	.300	20	6	1	1	0	1	.300	.450
Colbrunn, G	.400	15	6	0	2	1	1	.438	.400
Conine, Jeff	.333	18	6	1	1	2	6	.400	.500
Cordero, Will	.400	5	2	1	1	0	2	.500	1.200
Daulton, D*	.333	6	2	1	3	0	2	.333	.833
Decker, Steve	.333	3	1	0	0	2	0	.600	.333
DeShields, D*	.412	17	7	1	1	2	3	.474	.647
Duncan, M	.286	7	2	0	0	0	1	.286	.286
Dunston, S	.000	3	0	0	0	2	0	.400	.000
Dykstra, L*	.333	6	2	0	0	1	0	.429	.333
Eusebio, Tony	.182	11	2	0	0	1	1	.250	.182
Finley, Steve*	.231	13	3	1	1	2	2	.333	.462
Fletcher, D*	.250	8	2	1	2	0	2	.250	.625
Floyd, Cliff*	.000	7	0	0	1	0	1	.000	.000
Fonville, C#	.143	7	1	0	0	0	1	.143	.143
Gaetti, Gary	.167	6	1	1	1	2	2	.375	.667
Gagne, Greg	.000	5	0	0	0	0	2	.000	.000
Galarraga, A	.444	18	8	0	5	3	1	.500	.611
Gallego, Mike	.400	5	2	0	1	0	0	.400	.400
Gant, Ron	.167	12	2	1	1	2	5	.286	.417
Garcia, C	.563	16	9	1	4	0	0	.563	.875
Gilkey, B	.133	15	2	0	0	0	5	.133	.133
Girardi, Joe	.333	6	2	0	0	1	1	.429	.333
Gonzalez, L*	.300	10	3	1	1	0	2	.300	.700
Grissom, M	.188	16	3	0	3	1	4	.235	.250
Grudzielanek	.333	9	3	0	0	1	0	.400	.556
Gutierrez, R	.333	9	3	1	1	2	2	.455	.778
Gwynn, Chris*	.200	5	1	0	0	2	1	.333	.200
Gwynn, Tony*	.500	6	3	0	3	0	0	.500	.500
Harris, Lenny*	.200	5	1	0	0	0	1	.200	.400
Hayes, C	.200	20	4	1	3	1	3	.238	.350
Hill, G	.333	9	3	0	2	1	0	.400	.444
Hollandsworth*	.167	6	1	0	0	1	1	.286	.167
Howard, T*	.200	15	3	0	1	1	2	.250	.267
Hundley, Todd#	.375	8	3	3	3	0	1	.375	1.500
Hunter, Bri L	.222	18	4	0	0	0	3	.263	.278
Jefferies, G#	.467	15	7	2	3	2	0	.529	.933
Johnson, Bri	.000	6	0	0	0	0	1	.000	.000
Johnson, Char	.000	6	0	0	1	2	1	.250	.000
Johnson, Mark*	.125	8	1	0	0	0	1	.125	.125
Jones, C#	.375	8	3	2	2	2	1	.500	1.125
Jones, Chris	.000	5	0	0	0	1	0	.000	.000
Jordan, Brian	.333	21	7	0	0	2	0	.417	.381
Karros, Eric	.278	18	5	0	1	2	2	.350	.333
Kelly, R	.250	8	2	0	0	1	0	.250	.250

Batter	Avg	AB	H	HR	BI	BB	SO	OBP	Slg
Kendall, J	.667	3	2	1	2	1	0	.800	2.333
King, Jeff	.125	8	1	0	0	1	1	.222	.125
Kingery, Mike*	.100	10	1	0	1	0	0	.091	.100
Klesko, Ryan*	.400	10	4	1	4	0	3	.400	.700
Lankford, Ray*	.231	26	6	3	4	4	9	.333	.654
Lansing, Mike	.125	16	2	0	0	0	1	.125	.125
Larkin, Barry	.350	20	7	2	3	3	2	.435	.900
Lemke, Mark#	.600	5	3	0	2	2	1	.714	1.200
Lewis, Darren	.167	12	2	0	0	0	1	.167	.167
Liriano, Nel	.333	9	3	0	0	0	3	.333	.667
Livingstone*	.143	7	1	0	0	1	1	.250	.143
Lopez, Javy	.200	5	1	1	1	0	0	.200	.800
Mabry, John*	.231	13	3	1	3	1	1	.267	.462
Magadan, Dave*	.250	8	2	0	0	0	1	.250	.375
Magee, W	.000	6	0	0	0	0	0	.000	.000
Manwaring, K	.300	10	3	0	3	1	0	.364	.300
Martin, Al*	.400	10	4	0	1	1	0	.455	.500
May, Derrick*	.333	6	2	1	1	0	0	.333	1.167
McGee, Willie#	.286	7	2	0	0	0	0	.286	.429
McGriff, Fred*	.375	8	3	0	2	1	0	.400	.375
Merced, O*	.000	15	0	0	0	0	2	.000	.000
Miller, Orl	.333	12	4	0	1	0	3	.333	.500
Mondesi, Raul	.278	18	5	1	4	1	4	.316	.444
Morandini, M*	.429	14	6	1	2	3	1	.529	.714
Morris, Hal*	.267	15	4	1	2	4	2	.421	.467
Mouton, James	.100	10	1	1	2	1	4	.182	.400
Newfield, M	.500	4	2	0	0	1	1	.600	.500
Offerman, J#	.167	12	2	0	0	4	3	.375	.167
Orsulak, Joe*	.250	8	2	0	0	0	1	.250	.250
Otero, Ricky#	.700	10	7	1	2	0	0	.636	1.200
Owens, J	.000	6	0	0	0	0	2	.000	.000
Pagnozzi, Tom	.467	15	7	1	3	2	3	.529	1.067
Pendleton, T#	.364	11	4	0	0	2	3	.462	.364
Piazza, Mike	.286	21	6	0	2	3	4	.375	.333
Plantier, P*	.100	10	1	0	0	1	3	.182	.100
Reed, Jody	.417	12	5	1	1	1	1	.462	.667
Renteria, E	.429	7	3	0	0	0	0	.429	.571
Roberts, Bip*	.167	6	1	0	0	1	1	.286	.167
Rodriguez, H*	.143	14	2	0	1	1	5	.200	.214
Sanders, R	.182	11	2	0	0	3	5	.357	.273
Santangelo, F#	.250	8	2	0	0	1	0	.250	.750
Santiago, B	.350	20	7	2	3	3	7	.435	.800
Segui, David#	.500	8	4	1	3	0	0	.500	1.000
Sheaffer, D	.250	12	3	0	0	1	0	.308	.333
Sheffield, G	.538	13	7	2	4	3	1	.625	1.077
Silvestri, D	.000	5	0	0	0	1	1	.000	.000
Smith, Ozzie#	.154	13	2	0	0	0	0	.154	.154
Spiers, Bill*	.125	8	1	0	1	0	1	.125	.125
Stocker, K#	.273	11	3	0	0	0	2	.273	.273
Sweeney, Mark*	.000	7	0	0	0	0	2	.000	.000
Taubensee, E*	.100	10	1	0	0	0	1	.100	.100
Thompson, Rob	.500	6	3	0	0	0	1	.500	.500
Veras, Q#	.200	5	1	0	0	1	1	.333	.400
Vizcaino, J#	.143	7	1	0	0	1	1	.250	.143
Walker, Larry*	.111	9	1	1	1	3	3	.333	.444
Wallach, Tim	.167	12	2	1	3	0	0	.167	.500
Webster, L*	.125	8	1	0	1	1	2	.222	.125
Weiss, Walt#	.389	18	7	0	1	4	5	.478	.389
White, Devon#	.333	6	2	0	0	1	0	.429	.667
Whiten, Mark#	.000	10	0	0	0	0	5	.000	.000
Wilkins, Rick*	.167	6	1	0	1	2	1	.375	.167
Williams, Ma	.000	12	0	0	0	4	1	.235	.000
Young, Eric	.167	12	2	1	2	4	1	.375	.417
Zeile, Todd	.250	8	2	0	0	0	0	.250	.250

Batter	Avg	AB	H	HR	BI	BB	SO	OBP	Slg
Dykstra, L*	.333	6	2	0	2	1	0	.429	.500
Morandini, M*	.286	7	2	0	0	0	2	.286	.286
Pendleton, T#	.200	5	1	0	0	0	0	.200	.200
Thompson, Mil*	.000	6	0	0	0	1	3	.143	.000

Batter	Avg	AB	H	HR	BI	BB	SO	OBP	Slg
Alomar, R#	.364	11	4	0	1	2	0	.429	.364
Amaral, Rich	.222	9	2	0	0	1	0	.222	.222
Anderson, Brd*	.667	9	6	1	1	2	2	.727	1.444
Anderson, G*	.200	5	1	1	3	0	1	.200	.800
Baerga, C#	.308	13	4	0	1	0	0	.308	.462
Baines, H*	.429	7	3	0	1	0	1	.375	.571
Belle, Albert	.400	15	6	2	4	0	4	.400	1.067
Berroa, G	.500	10	5	2	6	0	1	.500	1.300
Blowers, Mike	.333	9	3	0	1	2	1	.455	.444
Boggs, Wade*	.286	7	2	0	3	3	0	.500	.286
Borders, Pat	.273	11	3	0	1	0	0	.273	.455
Bordick, Mike	.385	13	5	0	2	0	0	.467	.385
Brosius, S	.143	7	1	0	2	0	1	.125	.143
Buhner, Jay	.000	6	0	0	0	2	5	.200	.000
Canseco, Jose	.000	6	0	0	0	2	2	.250	.000
Carter, Joe	.214	14	3	0	1	0	3	.214	.357
Cirillo, Jeff	.111	9	1	1	1	2	0	.273	.444

Batter	Avg	AB	H	HR	BI	BB	SO	OBP	Slg
Clark, Will*	.000	5	0	0	0	1	1	.167	.000
Coleman, V#	.400	5	2	0	1	1	3	.500	.400
Cora, Joey#	.364	11	4	1	1	2	2	.462	.727
Curtis, Chad	.375	16	6	0	2	1	4	.412	.500
Cuyler, Milt*	.167	6	1	0	0	1	4	.286	.167
Damon, Johnny*	.600	5	3	0	0	0	0	.600	1.000
Davis, Chili#	.667	6	4	0	5	1	1	.714	.833
Dawson, Andre	.143	7	1	0	1	0	1	.143	.143
Deer, Rob	.125	8	1	0	1	0	2	.125	.250
Devereaux, M	.250	12	3	0	1	0	3	.250	.250
Diaz, Alex#	.286	7	2	0	1	1	0	.375	.286
DiSarcina, G	.000	6	0	0	0	0	0	.000	.000
Durham, Ray#	.167	6	1	0	0	0	1	.167	.167
Easley, D	.200	10	2	0	2	1	2	.273	.300
Fermin, Felix	.571	7	4	0	3	0	0	.571	.571
Fielder, C	.250	16	4	2	3	1	6	.294	.625
Fryman, T	.118	17	2	0	0	0	4	.167	.176
Gaetti, Gary	.375	8	3	0	0	1	2	.444	.375
Gagne, Greg	.444	9	4	0	4	0	1	.444	.667
Gallego, Mike	.167	6	1	0	0	0	1	.167	.167
Gates, Brent#	.333	9	3	1	2	2	3	.455	.667
Gomez, Chris	.167	6	1	1	2	0	0	.167	.667
Gomez, Leo	.000	4	0	0	0	1	2	.200	.000
Gonzalez, J	.214	14	3	0	1	0	5	.214	.214
Goodwin, Tom*	.000	7	0	0	1	2	1	.125	.000
Greenwell, M*	.333	6	2	0	0	1	1	.429	.500
Greer, Rusty*	.333	5	2	1	2	0	0	.400	1.000
Griffey Jr, K*	.200	5	1	0	0	2	1	.429	.400
Guillen, O*	.400	5	2	0	1	0	0	.400	.800
Hamelin, Bob*	.400	5	2	0	1	0	0	.400	.600
Hamilton, D*	.273	11	3	0	0	0	1	.273	.364
Hammonds, J	.143	7	1	0	0	1	1	.250	.286
Henderson, R	.571	7	4	0	2	3	0	.700	.571
Higginson, B*	.400	5	2	1	2	1	1	.571	1.000
Hoiles, Chris	.333	6	2	1	3	0	2	.333	.833
Howard, Dave#	.333	3	1	0	0	2	1	.600	.333
Hulse, David*	.333	9	3	0	1	0	1	.333	.667
Huson, Jeff*	.400	5	2	0	0	0	1	.400	.800
Jaha, John	.583	12	7	3	9	1	1	.615	1.500
James, Dion*	.500	6	3	0	0	1	0	.571	.500
Javier, Stan*	.500	6	3	1	3	2	2	.625	1.000
Johnson, L*	.500	6	3	0	0	0	0	.500	.667
Joyner, Wally*	.182	11	2	0	1	2	4	.308	.273
Kelly, Pat	.143	7	1	0	1	0	3	.143	.143
Kirby, Wayne*	.333	6	2	1	3	0	0	.286	1.000
Kreuter, Chad#	.286	7	2	0	1	1	1	.375	.429
Lewis, Mark	.200	5	1	0	0	1	1	.200	.200
Livingstone*	.500	4	2	0	1	2	0	.667	.750
Lockhart, K*	.500	8	4	0	2	0	0	.500	.875
Lofton, Kenny*	.455	11	5	0	3	2	1	.538	.545
Macfarlane, M	.167	12	2	0	0	0	2	.286	.250
Martinez, E	.667	6	4	1	4	2	1	.750	1.333
Martinez, T*	.000	5	0	0	0	0	0	.000	.000
Mayne, Brent*	.333	6	2	0	2	0	0	.500	.333
McGwire, Mark	.000	7	0	0	0	1	5	.125	.000
McLemore, M#	.500	10	5	0	2	2	2	.583	.700
McRae, Brian#	.600	5	3	0	1	1	0	.667	1.200
Molitor, Paul	.222	9	2	0	1	0	1	.222	.333
Murray, Eddie#	.111	9	1	0	0	1	0	.200	.111
Naehring, Tim	.167	6	1	0	0	2	1	.375	.167
Newson, W*	.375	8	3	1	1	0	2	.375	.750
Nilsson, Dave*	.308	13	4	1	3	2	1	.400	.692
Nixon, Otis#	.200	5	1	0	0	1	2	.333	.200
Nunnally, Jon*	.000	5	0	0	1	2	1	.286	.000
O'Neill, Paul*	.250	8	2	1	2	0	0	.250	.625
Offerman, J#	.250	4	1	0	2	0	0	.400	.750
Olerud, John*	.400	10	4	0	2	1	1	.417	.600
Oliver, Joe	.250	4	1	0	0	1	0	.400	.250
Palmeiro, R*	.250	12	3	1	3	5	2	.471	.667
Palmer, Dean	.400	10	4	1	3	1	4	.455	.700
Paquette, C	.333	9	3	0	2	0	1	.333	.667
Pena, Tony	.111	9	1	0	1	0	3	.111	.111
Phillips, T#	.308	13	4	1	1	3	5	.438	.538
Polonia, Luis*	.231	13	3	0	0	2	1	.333	.231
Raines, Tim#	.400	5	2	0	0	1	1	.500	.400
Ramirez, M	.200	10	2	0	3	2	2	.333	.500
Randa, Joe	.250	4	1	0	1	1	0	.400	.250
Reed, Jody	.000	4	0	0	0	1	1	.200	.000
Ripken, Cal	.111	9	1	0	0	2	0	.273	.111
Rodriguez, I	.143	14	2	0	1	0	6	.143	.214
Salmon, Tim	.286	7	2	0	0	1	1	.286	.286
Seitzer, K	.300	10	3	0	0	1	1	.364	.400
Sierra, Ruben#	.091	11	1	0	4	0	1	.091	.182
Snow, J.T.#	.000	5	0	0	0	2	2	.286	.000
Sojo, Luis	.111	9	1	1	1	0	1	.111	.444
Sorrento, P*	.100	10	1	0	2	1	3	.167	.200
Sprague, Ed	.300	10	3	1	3	0	2	.364	.700
Stanley, Mike	.400	10	4	1	3	2	4	.462	.700
Steinbach, T	.333	12	4	0	1	0	1	.385	.417
Stevens, Lee*	.333	3	1	0	1	3	0	.667	.333

Mike Trombley, Twins — RHP

Batter	Avg	AB	H	HR	BI	BB	SO	OBP	Slg
Strange, Doug#	.154	13	2	1	1	3	5	.313	.462
Tartabull, D	.100	10	1	0	0	1	2	.182	.200
Tettleton, M#	.300	10	3	2	7	0	5	.300	1.000
Thomas, Frank	.167	6	1	0	0	3	1	.444	.167
Thome, Jim*	.625	8	5	0	3	3	2	.727	.625
Tucker, M*	.000	4	0	0	0	2	1	.333	.000
Valentin, Jhn	.200	10	2	1	1	0	2	.200	.500
Valentin, Jse#	.250	8	2	0	2	1	6	.300	.250
Valle, Dave	.167	6	1	0	0	0	2	.286	.333
Vaughn, Greg	.000	7	0	0	0	0	2	.000	.000
Vaughn, Mo*	.500	8	4	1	1	3	0	.636	1.000
Ventura, R*	.111	9	1	1	3	0	0	.111	.444
Vina, F*	.500	6	3	0	0	0	0	.500	.667
Vitiello, Joe	.143	7	1	0	0	0	0	.143	.143
Vizquel, Omar#	.500	10	5	0	2	1	1	.583	.800
Ward, Turner#	.000	6	0	0	0	1	3	.143	.000
White, Devon#	.429	7	3	1	1	1	1	.500	1.000
Williams, Ber#	.625	8	5	0	0	1	1	.667	.625
Wilson, Dan	.000	5	0	0	0	0	1	.000	.000

Tom Urbani, Tigers — LHP

Batter	Avg	AB	H	HR	BI	BB	SO	OBP	Slg
Alou, Moises	.600	10	6	0	1	0	0	.600	.700
Ausmus, Brad	.400	5	2	0	2	1	0	.500	.400
Bell, Jay	.667	12	8	1	5	0	0	.667	1.083
Belliard, R	.600	5	3	0	2	0	0	.600	.800
Berry, Sean	.700	10	7	2	6	0	0	.700	1.500
Blauser, Jeff	.222	9	2	0	0	1	2	.300	.222
Bonds, Barry*	.111	9	1	0	0	4	1	.429	.111
Bonilla, B#	.111	9	1	0	2	0	2	.111	.444
Brogna, Rico*	.400	5	2	0	0	0	1	.400	.600
Brumfield, J	.333	6	2	0	0	0	0	.333	.333
Burnitz, J*	.167	6	1	1	2	0	3	.167	.667
Butler, Brett*	.000	8	0	0	0	1	1	.111	.000
Caminiti, Ken#	.125	8	1	0	0	2	1	.300	.125
Carreon, Mark	.500	6	3	1	2	0	0	.500	1.000
Cedeno, A	.500	6	3	0	0	0	1	.500	.500
Clark, Phil	.000	5	0	0	1	0	1	.000	.000
Clayton, R	.100	10	1	0	0	0	1	.100	.100
Cordero, Wil	.300	10	3	0	2	0	3	.300	.400
Daulton, D*	.600	5	3	0	3	0	1	.600	1.000
Duncan, M	.333	12	4	0	0	0	2	.333	.333
Dykstra, L*	.385	13	5	0	0	3	2	.500	.462
Finley, Steve*	.444	9	4	0	1	1	1	.500	.667
Garcia, C	.300	10	3	1	1	1	2	.364	.700
Grace, Mark*	.600	5	3	0	2	0	0	.667	1.000
Grissom, M	.273	11	3	1	1	0	1	.273	.545
Gwynn, Tony*	.333	9	3	0	0	1	0	.400	.333
Hayes, C	.400	5	2	1	3	2	0	.571	1.000
Hill, G	.444	9	4	0	1	1	1	.500	.444
Hundley, Todd#	.333	6	2	0	0	1	0	.333	.333
Incaviglia, P	.125	8	1	1	1	0	1	.125	.500
Johnson, Bri	.167	6	1	0	1	0	1	.167	.167
Jordan, Brian	.500	8	4	0	3	0	0	.500	.625
Justice, Dave*	.286	7	2	0	2	1	0	.375	.286
Karros, Eric	.429	7	3	1	3	0	1	.429	.857
Kelly, Mike	.333	6	2	0	0	0	1	.333	.333
Kelly, R	.000	6	0	0	0	0	2	.000	.000
Kent, Jeff	.143	7	1	0	0	1	0	.250	.143
King, Jeff	.556	9	5	0	4	0	1	.692	.778
Klesko, Ryan*	.286	7	2	0	0	0	1	.286	.286
Lansing, Mike	.222	9	2	0	0	1	0	.300	.333
Lemke, Mark#	.273	11	3	0	0	1	2	.333	.545
Lewis, Darren	.188	16	3	0	1	0	2	.188	.188
Lopez, Javy	.429	7	3	0	1	2	1	.500	.429
Manwaring, K	.455	11	5	1	2	0	4	.455	.818
Martin, Al*	.400	5	2	1	4	0	1	.400	1.000
McGee, Willie#	.143	7	1	0	0	0	1	.250	.143
McGriff, Fred*	.364	11	4	2	3	1	2	.417	.909
McRae, Brian#	.200	5	1	0	0	1	1	.333	.200
Merced, O*	.222	9	2	1	1	1	1	.300	.556
Morandini, M*	.400	5	2	0	1	0	0	.400	.400
Morris, Hal*	.667	3	2	0	0	2	0	.800	.667
O'Brien, C	.500	4	2	0	0	2	0	.667	.750
Offerman, J*	.143	7	1	0	1	1	1	.250	.143
Oliver, Joe	.500	4	2	0	1	0	0	.400	.500
Piazza, Mike	.167	6	1	0	1	0	0	.286	.167
Reed, Jody	.385	13	5	0	1	0	2	.385	.462
Roberts, Bip#	.100	10	1	0	0	2	1	.250	.100
Sanchez, Rey	.333	6	2	0	1	0	0	.333	.333
Santiago, B	.200	5	1	0	0	0	0	.200	.200
Scarsone, S	.625	8	5	1	1	0	2	.625	1.125
Schall, Gene	.200	5	1	0	0	0	0	.200	.200
Segui, David#	.000	8	0	0	0	1	0	.200	.000
Shipley, C	.400	5	2	0	1	0	0	.400	.600
Slaught, Don	.250	4	1	0	0	2	0	.500	.250
Sosa, Sammy	.143	7	1	0	1	2	2	.333	.143
Stocker, K#	.333	6	2	0	0	0	0	.333	.500
Tarasco, Tony*	.167	6	1	0	0	1	0	.167	.167
Thompson, Rob	.500	8	4	0	2	3	2	.636	.750
Thompson, Ry	.000	7	0	0	1	0	3	.000	.000

Tom Urbani, Tigers — LHP

Batter	Avg	AB	H	HR	BI	BB	SO	OBP	Slg
Tinsley, Lee#	.000	5	0	0	0	0	2	.000	.000
Vizcaino, J#	.571	7	4	0	1	0	0	.571	.571
Walker, Larry*	.000	4	0	0	0	1	0	.200	.000
Wallach, Tim	.200	5	1	1	1	1	2	.333	.800
Webster, L	.600	5	3	0	1	0	0	.600	.800
White, R	.333	6	2	0	0	0	0	.333	.333
Williams, E	.429	7	3	0	0	0	1	.429	.429
Williams, Ma	.500	12	6	1	5	0	1	.500	1.083
Young, Kevin	.400	5	2	0	0	0	0	.400	.800
Zeile, Todd	.000	5	0	0	0	0	1	.000	.000

Ugueth Urbina, Expos — RHP

Batter	Avg	AB	H	HR	BI	BB	SO	OBP	Slg
Bates, Jason#	.200	5	1	0	0	0	0	.200	.400
Bichette, D	.143	7	1	0	2	1	0	.250	.143
Burks, Ellis	.000	5	0	0	0	1	2	.167	.000
Caminiti, Ken#	.429	7	3	1	4	0	1	.429	1.000
Castilla, V	.200	5	1	0	0	0	2	.200	.200
Cedeno, A	.000	5	0	0	0	0	0	.000	.000
Colbrunn, G	.500	4	2	0	0	1	1	.600	.750
Eisenreich, J*	.800	5	4	0	0	1	1	.833	1.200
Finley, Steve*	.333	9	3	1	2	0	1	.333	.667
Gaetti, Gary	.000	5	0	0	0	1	0	.167	.000
Galarraga, A	.250	8	2	1	1	0	2	.250	.750
Gilkey, B	.750	4	3	0	1	2	0	.833	1.250
Gonzalez, L*	.400	5	2	0	0	2	0	.571	.400
Grace, Mark*	.800	5	4	0	0	1	0	.833	.800
Grissom, M	.000	4	0	0	0	1	1	.200	.000
Gwynn, Tony*	.500	8	4	0	2	0	0	.444	.625
Henderson, R	.167	6	1	0	1	1	1	.286	.167
Hollandsworth*	.500	6	3	0	1	0	1	.500	.500
Jefferies, G#	.250	4	1	0	0	1	1	.400	.250
Johnson, Bri	.167	6	1	0	0	0	2	.167	.167
Jones, C#	.600	5	3	1	1	0	1	.600	1.200
Jordan, Brian	.333	6	2	1	1	0	1	.333	1.000
Joyner, Wally*	.429	7	3	0	0	1	2	.500	.429
Karros, Eric	.500	2	1	3	1	0	0	.600	1.250
Lankford, Ray*	.333	6	2	1	1	3	0	.556	.833
Mabry, John*	.143	7	1	1	1	1	1	.250	.571
McRae, Brian#	.600	5	3	0	0	2	0	.714	.800
Mondesi, Raul	.200	5	1	0	1	0	3	.200	.200
Morandini, M*	.500	6	3	0	1	0	1	.500	.667
Otero, Ricky#	.167	6	1	0	0	0	1	.167	.167
Pagnozzi, Tom	.500	4	2	2	3	1	0	.600	2.000
Reed, Jeff*	.167	6	1	0	0	0	1	.167	.167
Renteria, E	.167	6	1	1	1	0	3	.167	.667
Sheffield, G	.333	6	2	1	1	1	0	.429	1.000
Smith, Ozzie#	.167	6	1	0	0	0	1	.167	.167
Sosa, Sammy	.000	6	0	0	0	0	3	.000	.000
Weiss, Walt#	.500	6	2	0	1	2	0	.500	.667
Young, Eric	.000	6	0	0	0	0	0	.000	.000
Zeile, Todd	.143	7	1	0	0	1	1	.250	.143

Ismael Valdes, Dodgers — RHP

Batter	Avg	AB	H	HR	BI	BB	SO	OBP	Slg
Abbott, Kurt	.429	7	3	0	0	1	3	.500	.429
Alfonzo, E	.000	6	0	0	0	1	2	.143	.000
Alicea, Luis#	.333	6	2	0	2	0	2	.286	.500
Alou, Moises	.000	7	0	0	0	0	3	.000	.000
Ausmus, Brad	.000	8	0	0	0	1	1	.000	.000
Bagwell, Jeff	.000	14	0	0	0	1	1	.067	.000
Bell, David	.000	6	0	0	0	0	2	.000	.000
Bell, Derek	.308	13	4	0	2	0	2	.333	.385
Bell, Jay	.077	13	1	0	0	0	6	.077	.077
Berry, Sean	.400	15	6	0	1	2	0	.471	.533
Bichette, D	.154	13	2	1	2	0	1	.143	.385
Biggio, Craig	.286	14	4	0	0	1	1	.286	.429
Blauser, Jeff	.267	15	4	0	1	0	3	.267	.267
Bonds, Barry*	.000	8	0	0	0	3	3	.273	.000
Boone, Bret	.167	12	2	0	2	1	1	.231	.333
Branson, Jeff*	.000	3	0	0	0	2	0	.400	.000
Brogna, Rico*	.000	5	0	0	0	0	2	.000	.000
Brumfield, J	.375	8	3	0	0	0	3	.375	.750
Bullett, S*	.333	6	2	0	0	1	1	.429	.333
Burks, Ellis	.308	13	4	1	3	0	3	.308	.615
Caminiti, Ken#	.400	20	8	4	8	2	5	.455	1.000
Carr, Chuck	.286	7	2	0	0	1	1	.375	.429
Carreon, Mark	.286	7	2	0	2	0	1	.286	.286
Castilla, V	.286	14	4	0	1	0	0	.286	.429
Cedeno, A	.286	7	2	0	0	2	2	.444	.286
Clark, Dave*	.500	4	2	1	2	2	0	.667	1.250
Clayton, R	.091	11	1	0	0	0	2	.091	.091
Colbrunn, G	.286	14	4	1	1	0	0	.286	.571
Conine, Jeff	.188	16	3	0	0	1	5	.235	.188
Cordero, Wil	.462	13	6	0	1	1	4	.500	.538
Davis, Eric	.750	4	3	1	2	2	1	.833	1.750
Dunston, S	.000	9	0	0	0	0	2	.000	.000
Eisenreich, J*	.474	19	9	1	5	2	0	.524	.632
Elster, Kevin	.250	4	1	0	1	0	1	.200	.500
Finley, Steve*	.136	22	3	0	0	2	2	.208	.136
Flaherty, J	.200	5	1	0	1	0	1	.167	.200

Ismael Valdes, Dodgers — RHP

Batter	Avg	AB	H	HR	BI	BB	SO	OBP	Slg
Fletcher, D*	.000	9	0	0	0	1	0	.100	.000
Frazier, Lou#	.333	6	2	0	0	2	1	.556	.333
Galarraga, A	.154	13	2	1	1	2	8	.267	.462
Gant, Ron	.200	5	1	1	3	1	2	.286	.800
Garcia, C	.167	6	1	0	0	0	0	.167	.167
Gilkey, B	.462	13	6	2	7	2	1	.500	1.077
Girardi, Joe	.400	5	2	0	0	0	0	.400	.400
Gomez, Chris	.125	8	1	0	0	1	3	.222	.125
Gomez, Leo	.333	6	2	1	2	0	2	.333	1.000
Gonzalez, L*	.357	14	5	1	3	3	2	.471	.571
Goodwin, J	.000	7	0	0	0	0	1	.000	.000
Grace, Mark*	.316	19	6	0	1	1	1	.350	.526
Grissom, M	.286	21	6	0	1	2	1	.348	.286
Grudzielanek	.000	9	0	0	0	1	0	.000	.000
Gwynn, Tony*	.450	20	8	1	3	1	1	.429	.700
Haney, Todd	.000	5	0	0	0	0	1	.000	.000
Hayes, C	.429	7	3	0	4	2	3	.556	.429
Henderson, R	.250	8	2	0	0	0	1	.250	.250
Hernandez, Jo	.182	11	2	0	0	1	4	.250	.182
Hill, G	.143	7	1	0	0	1	0	.250	.143
Howard, T*	.500	8	4	0	1	0	1	.500	.625
Hundley, Todd#	.143	7	1	0	0	2	2	.333	.286
Hunter, Bri L	.182	11	2	0	0	0	3	.182	.182
Incaviglia, P	.143	7	1	1	3	0	3	.143	.571
Jefferies, G#	.364	11	4	0	0	0	1	.364	.364
Johnson, Bri	.200	5	1	0	0	0	0	.200	.200
Johnson, Char	.333	12	4	1	1	1	3	.385	.583
Johnson, L*	.364	11	4	0	1	0	0	.364	.636
Johnson, Mark*	.444	9	4	0	6	1	0	.667	.444
Jones, C#	.200	20	4	0	1	0	4	.200	.200
Jones, Chris	.333	6	2	0	0	0	2	.333	.500
Jordan, Brian	.429	7	3	0	1	1	3	.500	.571
Jordan, Kevin	.000	5	0	0	0	1	0	.167	.000
Joyner, Wally*	.111	9	1	0	0	0	1	.111	.111
Justice, Dave*	.167	12	2	1	1	0	2	.167	.500
Kendall, J	.000	5	0	0	0	1	2	.167	.000
Kent, Jeff	.182	11	2	0	0	0	3	.182	.182
King, Jeff	.267	15	4	1	2	1	3	.353	.533
Kingery, Mike*	.154	13	2	1	2	1	0	.214	.538
Klesko, Ryan*	.333	15	5	1	3	3	2	.421	.600
Lankford, Ray*	.333	9	3	0	1	0	1	.333	.556
Lansing, Mike	.375	8	3	0	3	0	1	.333	.500
Larkin, Barry	.300	10	3	0	1	2	1	.385	.300
Lemke, Mark#	.308	13	4	1	2	1	1	.357	.538
Liriano, N#	.000	7	0	0	1	1	2	.111	.000
Livingstone*	.300	10	3	0	0	0	1	.300	.400
Lopez, Javy	.273	11	3	1	2	0	0	.273	.545
Mabry, John*	.000	10	0	0	0	0	0	.000	.000
Magee, Wendell	.429	7	3	0	1	0	0	.429	.429
Manwaring, K	.375	8	3	0	1	0	1	.375	.375
Martin, Al*	.222	18	4	1	2	0	3	.222	.500
May, Derrick*	.286	7	2	0	0	0	2	.286	.429
McCracken, Q#	.000	5	0	0	1	1	1	.167	.000
McGee, Willie#	.400	5	2	0	0	1	0	.400	.400
McGriff, Fred*	.158	19	3	1	3	0	5	.158	.421
McRae, Brian#	.192	26	5	0	3	2	2	.250	.231
Merced, O*	.429	7	3	0	1	0	2	.429	.571
Miller, Orl	.182	11	2	0	0	0	5	.167	.182
Morandini, M*	.273	22	6	0	1	1	3	.304	.318
Morris, Hal*	.333	9	3	0	4	1	1	.400	.556
Mouton, James	.400	5	2	0	0	1	0	.500	.400
Nieves, M#	.222	9	2	0	0	0	1	.222	.222
Oliver, Joe	.400	5	2	0	0	1	0	.500	.400
Ordonez, Rey	.200	5	1	0	0	1	1	.333	.200
Orsulak, Joe*	.167	6	1	1	2	0	0	.167	.667
Otero, Ricky#	.400	5	2	0	0	0	0	.400	.400
Parent, Mark	.167	6	1	0	0	0	2	.167	.167
Pendleton, T#	.143	14	2	0	0	2	1	.250	.143
Petagine, Rob*	.143	7	1	0	0	1	2	.250	.286
Reed, Jeff*	.167	12	2	0	0	1	2	.231	.250
Reed, Jody	.368	19	7	1	4	0	1	.368	.579
Rolen, Scott	.286	7	2	0	0	0	3	.286	.286
Sanchez, Rey	.300	20	6	0	2	0	2	.300	.400
Sandberg, R	.000	6	0	0	0	1	2	.143	.000
Sanders, R	.286	7	2	1	4	1	3	.375	.857
Santangelo, F#	.400	5	2	0	0	1	0	.400	.400
Santiago, B	.267	15	4	0	1	0	1	.267	.400
Segui, David#	.625	8	5	1	5	1	0	.667	1.250
Servais, J	.500	4	2	0	1	0	1	.500	.500
Sheffield, G	.444	9	4	2	2	1	0	.500	1.333
Smith, Ozzie#	.000	7	0	0	0	1	0	.125	.000
Sosa, Sammy	.136	22	3	0	1	1	11	.174	.136
Stocker, K#	.067	15	1	0	0	1	2	.125	.067
Tarasco, Tony*	.143	14	2	1	1	0	2	.143	.357
Taubensee, E*	.333	6	2	0	2	0	0	.333	.500
Thompson, Ron	.250	8	2	0	0	2	2	.400	.250
VanderWal, J*	.200	5	1	0	0	0	1	.333	.200
Veras, Q#	.182	11	2	0	0	0	2	.182	.182
Vizcaino, O	.250	8	2	0	0	0	4	.333	.250
Walker, Larry*	.200	5	1	0	1	0	3	.200	.400
Weiss, Walt#	.333	12	4	0	1	0	1	.333	.417

Ismael Valdes, Dodgers — RHP

Batter	Avg	AB	H	HR	BI	BB	SO	OBP	Slg
White, R	.111	9	1	0	0	0	1	.111	.222
Whiten, Mark#	.222	9	2	0	2	0	2	.222	.222
Wilkins, Rick*	.125	8	1	0	0	2	2	.300	.125
Williams, Ma	.200	5	1	0	0	0	2	.200	.200
Young, Eric	.538	13	7	0	1	2	1	.625	.615
Zeile, Todd	.316	19	6	0	1	0	7	.316	.316

Marc Valdes, Marlins — RHP

Batter	Avg	AB	H	HR	BI	BB	SO	OBP	Slg
Alicea, Luis*	.667	3	2	0	0	2	0	.800	1.000
Biggio, Craig	.400	5	2	0	0	1	0	.571	.600
Cangelosi, J#	.333	3	1	0	0	2	0	.600	.333
Gaetti, Gary	.000	5	0	0	0	0	0	.000	.000
Gant, Ron	.200	5	1	1	2	1	1	.333	.800
Hunter, Bri L	.400	5	2	0	0	0	0	.400	.600
Jordan, Brian	.333	6	2	0	0	0	0	.333	.500
Mabry, John*	.333	6	2	0	0	0	0	.333	.333
Magadan, Dave*	.429	7	3	0	2	0	0	.429	.429
May, Derrick*	.500	4	2	1	2	1	0	.600	1.250
Pagnozzi, Tom	.200	5	1	0	0	0	1	.200	.200
Shipley, C	.000	5	0	0	0	0	0	.000	.000
Smith, Ozzie#	.667	6	4	0	1	0	0	.667	.667

Fernando Valenzuela, Padres — LHP

Batter	Avg	AB	H	HR	BI	BB	SO	OBP	Slg
Abbott, Kurt	.333	9	3	0	0	0	1	.333	.444
Aldrete, Mike*	.000	8	0	0	1	3	2	.250	.000
Alfonzo, E	.000	8	0	0	0	2	3	.200	.000
Alicea, Luis*	.250	8	2	0	1	0	1	.400	.250
Alomar, R#	.147	34	5	0	3	2	6	.184	.206
Alou, Moises	.364	11	4	0	1	0	0	.364	.455
Aude, Rich	.375	8	3	1	4	0	3	.375	.875
Baerga, C#	.385	13	5	0	3	1	2	.429	.385
Bagwell, Jeff	.143	7	1	0	0	1	0	.250	.143
Bell, Derek	.273	11	3	0	0	0	4	.273	.364
Bell, Jay	.176	17	3	1	2	4	1	.333	.353
Belle, Albert	.286	7	2	0	1	1	1	.400	.286
Belliard, R	.100	20	2	0	2	0	1	.100	.100
Berroa, G	.333	9	3	1	0	0	4	.333	.667
Berry, Sean	.375	8	3	1	2	1	1	.444	.875
Bichette, Dante	.222	9	2	1	2	1	0	.273	.556
Biggio, Craig	.375	24	9	1	7	2	4	.393	.583
Blauser, Jeff	.364	22	8	1	5	2	4	.417	.545
Blowers, Mike	.333	9	3	1	2	0	2	.333	.778
Bogar, Tim	.000	8	0	0	0	0	0	.000	.000
Bonds, Barry*	.222	27	6	2	3	5	5	.344	.519
Bonilla, B#	.320	25	8	1	4	4	1	.414	.480
Boone, Bret	.167	12	2	0	0	1	2	.231	.250
Borders, Pat	.333	9	3	0	1	0	0	.333	.333
Bordick, Mike	.000	5	0	0	0	2	0	.375	.000
Bournigal, R	.000	4	0	0	1	0	0	.000	.000
Brogna, Rico*	.143	14	2	0	1	1	3	.200	.143
Brumfield, J	.375	8	3	0	0	1	0	.444	.625
Buhner, Jay	.250	4	1	1	2	3	0	.571	1.000
Burks, Ellis	.500	10	5	0	3	0	0	.615	.700
Butler, Brett*	.286	42	12	0	3	5	3	.362	.381
Caminiti, Ken#	.158	19	3	0	0	4	3	.304	.263
Candaele, C#	.476	21	10	2	4	2	1	.522	.857
Cangelosi, J#	.125	8	1	0	0	2	0	.222	.250
Carreon, Mark	.200	10	2	0	2	0	1	.182	.300
Carter, Joe	.217	23	5	1	4	0	5	.217	.348
Castilla, V	.300	10	3	1	1	0	0	.300	.600
Clark, Will*	.327	49	16	0	5	7	10	.404	.449
Clayton, R	.308	13	4	1	1	0	1	.357	.615
Colbrunn, G	.250	4	1	0	0	0	0	.400	.250
Coleman, V#	.133	60	8	0	2	6	11	.212	.183
Conine, Jeff	.167	6	1	0	3	1	0	.250	.167
Cora, Joey*	.286	14	4	0	1	0	1	.333	.286
Cordero, Wil	.750	4	3	0	0	1	1	.800	1.500
Curtis, Chad	.500	2	1	1	3	0	0	.800	2.000
Dascenzo, D#	.250	8	2	0	0	0	1	.250	.250
Daulton, D*	.125	8	1	0	0	5	3	.364	.250
Davis, Chili*	.300	50	15	3	6	4	14	.352	.500
Davis, Eric	.188	48	9	3	7	12	14	.350	.396
Dawson, Andre	.282	39	11	2	8	5	4	.378	.615
Decker, Steve	.333	6	2	0	2	2	2	.500	.333
Deer, Rob	.286	7	2	0	0	2	2	.444	.286
DeShields, D*	.105	19	2	0	0	2	7	.190	.105
Duncan, M	.320	25	8	1	3	2	7	.370	.480
Dunston, S	.143	28	4	1	1	3	3	.172	.250
Dykstra, L*	.400	15	6	0	1	0	1	.400	.467
Encarnacion	.200	5	1	1	3	0	3	.200	.800
Espinoza, A	.300	10	3	0	1	0	1	.300	.500
Eusebio, Tony	.333	6	2	1	1	0	5	.429	1.000
Fermin, Felix	.133	15	2	0	0	0	5	.133	.133
Fielder, C	.500	4	2	0	1	2	0	.600	.750
Fonville, C#	.200	5	1	0	0	0	0	.200	.400
Fryman, T	.800	5	4	0	2	0	0	.800	1.000
Gaetti, Gary	.200	5	1	0	1	3	1	.500	.200
Gagne, Greg	.250	8	2	0	2	1	0	.333	.500
Galarraga, A	.283	53	15	3	16	4	7	.333	.547

Fernando Valenzuela, Padres — LHP

Batter	Avg	AB	H	HR	BI	BB	SO	OBP	Slg
Gant, Ron	.292	24	7	0	0	3	4	.370	.417
Garcia, C	.200	5	1	0	0	0	0	.200	.400
Gates, Brent#	.444	9	4	0	0	1	2	.500	.556
Gilkey, B	.071	14	1	0	1	1	3	.133	.143
Girardi, Joe	.600	10	6	0	2	0	0	.600	.800
Glanville, D	.200	5	1	0	1	0	0	.167	.200
Gomez, Leo	.200	5	1	0	0	0	0	.200	.200
Grace, Mark*	.250	20	5	1	5	3	3	.348	.400
Grebeck, C	.200	5	1	0	0	0	0	.200	.200
Greenwell, M*	.364	11	4	0	0	1	2	.417	.364
Griffey Jr, K*	.167	6	1	0	1	1	2	.286	.333
Grissom, M	.111	27	3	0	2	1	3	.143	.148
Grudzielanek	.333	6	2	0	0	1	1	.429	.333
Gwynn, Tony*	.329	73	24	1	7	4	4	.359	.425
Hayes, C	.304	23	7	0	3	2	2	.360	.435
Henderson, R	.222	9	2	0	1	0	1	.222	.222
Hernandez, Jo	.200	5	1	1	2	1	0	.333	.800
Hiatt, Phil	.000	4	0	0	0	1	1	.200	.000
Hill, G	.154	13	2	1	1	1	3	.214	.462
Hundley, Todd#	.231	13	3	1	2	2	3	.333	.462
Huskey, Butch	.500	10	5	1	1	0	1	.500	.900
James, Dion*	.222	18	4	0	2	1	4	.263	.278
Javier, Stan#	.125	8	1	0	0	2	1	.300	.250
Jefferies, G#	.294	17	5	0	3	0	0	.400	.353
Johnson, L*	.267	15	4	0	0	0	0	.267	.267
Jones, C	.250	8	2	1	1	0	2	.250	.625
Jones, Chris	.333	6	2	0	0	4	0	.333	.500
Jordan, Brian	.375	8	3	0	0	0	1	.375	.500
Jordan, Ricky	.167	12	2	0	1	0	0	.167	.167
Joyner, Wally*	.000	4	0	0	0	2	1	.333	.000
Justice, Dave*	.333	9	3	1	3	0	2	.333	.667
Karkovice, R	.250	4	1	0	1	1	2	.400	.500
Karros, Eric	.571	14	8	2	5	0	1	.571	1.000
Kent, Jeff	.182	11	2	0	1	2	1	.308	.273
King, Jeff	.400	15	6	0	0	4	1	.526	.667
Kirby, Wayne*	.444	9	4	0	0	1	1	.500	.556
Klesko, Ryan*	.400	5	2	0	1	1	2	.500	.600
Knoblauch, C	.125	8	1	0	1	0	0	.125	.250
Knorr, Randy	.500	4	2	0	1	0	0	.600	.500
Lankford, Ray*	.400	5	2	0	0	1	0	.500	.400
Lansing, Mike	.250	12	3	1	1	0	3	.250	.500
Larkin, Barry	.229	48	11	1	6	2	9	.260	.333
Lemke, Mark#	.429	14	6	2	4	2	2	.500	.929
Lewis, Darren	.286	7	2	0	0	0	0	.286	.429
Lewis, Mark	.667	3	2	0	2	1	0	.600	1.000
Listach, Pat#	.600	5	3	0	0	1	0	.667	.600
Lofton, Kenny*	.500	8	4	0	1	3	1	.636	.875
Mabry, John*	.400	5	2	0	3	0	1	.400	.400
Macfarlane, M	.167	6	1	0	2	0	1	.167	.333
Magadan, Dave*	.125	8	1	0	0	0	1	.125	.125
Manwaring, K	.174	23	4	0	0	0	2	.208	.174
Martin, Al*	.000	4	0	0	0	2	0	.250	.000
McCarty, Dave	.188	16	3	0	1	0	1	.188	.250
McCracken, Q#	.444	9	4	0	4	0	2	.444	.778
McGee, Willie#	.278	54	15	2	4	5	14	.350	.500
McGriff, Fred*	.273	11	3	0	0	0	2	.273	.364
McRae, Brian#	.357	14	5	0	1	2	2	.438	.643
Meares, Pat	.500	6	3	0	0	0	1	.500	.500
Mitchell, K	.294	51	15	4	14	5	6	.345	.627
Molitor, Paul	.375	16	6	1	2	2	0	.444	.563
Mondesi, Raul	.182	11	2	0	1	2	2	.308	.273
Morris, Hal*	.231	13	3	0	0	0	3	.231	.231
Mottola, Chad	.400	5	2	2	4	0	0	.400	1.600
Mouton, James	.714	7	5	1	2	2	0	.778	1.143
O'Neill, Paul*	.176	17	3	1	2	1	6	.211	.353
Obando, S	.250	8	2	0	1	0	3	.250	.500
Ochoa, Alex	.400	5	2	0	0	1	0	.500	.400
Olerud, John*	.444	9	4	1	1	3	0	.583	.778
Oliver, Joe	.333	24	8	0	6	2	0	.385	.500
Ordonez, Rey	.400	10	4	0	1	0	0	.400	.400
Orsulak, Joe*	.000	4	0	0	0	0	0	.000	.000
Owens, Eric	.400	5	2	0	1	0	0	.333	.400
Owens, J	.250	4	1	0	0	2	1	.500	.500
Pagnozzi, Tom	.214	14	3	0	2	1	2	.267	.286
Palmeiro, R*	.417	12	5	0	2	1	2	.462	.417
Paquette, J	.286	7	2	0	1	0	2	.286	.571
Parent, Mark	.583	12	7	2	4	0	1	.583	1.167
Pena, Tony	.275	51	14	0	8	4	7	.321	.333
Pendleton, T#	.226	62	14	1	9	6	9	.290	.306
Phillips, T#	.800	5	4	1	1	0	0	.800	1.800
Piazza, Mike	.222	9	2	0	4	1	2	.273	.222
Raines, Tim#	.311	61	19	1	6	7	6	.382	.426
Reboulet, J	.000	4	0	0	0	0	0	.000	.000
Roberts, Bip#	.226	31	7	0	0	0	7	.226	.258
Rodriguez, H*	.143	7	1	0	0	1	2	.250	.143
Sabo, Chris	.357	28	10	2	7	3	1	.406	.643
Samuel, Juan	.143	35	5	1	5	2	12	.184	.286
Sandberg, R	.273	44	12	3	11	10	9	.407	.523
Santiago, B	.211	38	8	1	4	6	6	.318	.316
Scarsone, S	.455	11	5	0	1	0	2	.455	.636
Schall, Gene	.500	6	3	0	0	0	1	.500	.667
Schofield, D	.167	6	1	0	0	2	0	.375	.167
Schu, Rick	.200	15	3	1	1	0	7	.200	.400
Segui, David#	.125	8	1	0	0	1	2	.222	.125
Servais, S	.400	5	2	0	0	0	0	.400	.400
Sheffield, G	.375	8	3	0	0	0	0	.375	.500
Shipley, C	.000	5	0	0	0	0	1	.000	.000
Shumpert, T	.500	4	2	1	1	1	0	.600	1.250
Sierra, Ruben#	.429	7	3	1	3	1	0	.500	1.143
Silvestri, D	.333	6	2	1	3	1	0	.429	.833
Slaught, Don	.286	7	2	0	1	0	1	.286	.429
Smith, Ozzie#	.293	58	17	0	1	9	5	.397	.379
Sosa, Sammy	.000	8	0	0	0	0	4	.000	.000
Sprague, Ed	.083	12	1	0	0	0	1	.083	.083
Stankiewicz	.167	6	1	0	0	0	1	.167	.167
Steinbach, T	.250	4	1	0	0	1	1	.400	.250
Stillwell, K#	.200	5	1	0	3	0	2	.200	.400
Stinnett, K	.143	7	1	0	0	0	2	.143	.286
Stocker, K#	.375	8	3	0	0	2	1	.500	.375
Strawberry, D*	.298	47	14	3	7	9	10	.404	.511
Thomas, Frank	.200	5	1	1	3	0	0	.200	.800
Thompson, Mil*	.200	10	2	1	2	0	3	.200	.500
Thompson, Rob	.377	61	23	3	8	5	14	.424	.607
Thompson, Ry	.143	7	1	0	0	1	2	.250	.143
Valentin, Jhn	.200	5	1	0	1	1	1	.333	.200
Valle, Dave	.200	5	1	0	0	1	0	.333	.200
Vaughn, Greg	.500	4	2	0	1	0	4	.750	.500
Vaughn, Mo*	.333	9	3	1	2	1	3	.400	.778
Ventura, R*	.200	5	1	0	0	0	1	.200	.200
Vizcaino, J#	.429	7	3	0	0	1	0	.500	.429
Walker, Larry*	.625	8	5	1	2	0	0	.625	1.125
Wallach, Tim	.208	53	11	0	3	9	5	.323	.264
Walton, J	.417	12	5	0	0	1	2	.462	.500
Webster, L	.294	17	5	0	3	3	2	.400	.412
Wehner, John	.125	8	1	0	0	0	3	.125	.125
Weiss, Walt#	.125	8	1	0	0	0	2	.125	.125
White, Devon#	.211	19	4	0	1	1	2	.238	.263
White, R	.000	5	0	0	0	1	1	.167	.000
Whiten, Mark#	.286	7	2	1	1	1	1	.375	.714
Williams, Ma	.220	41	9	4	9	4	12	.289	.561
Young, Eric	.100	10	1	0	0	1	0	.182	.100
Zeile, Todd	.000	4	0	0	0	2	0	.333	.000

Julio Valera, Royals — RHP

Batter	Avg	AB	H	HR	BI	BB	SO	OBP	Slg
Alomar, R#	.375	16	6	2	6	1	1	.444	.750
Anderson, Brd*	.294	17	5	0	2	0	3	.294	.353
Baerga, C#	.571	7	4	0	1	0	0	.571	.571
Baines, H*	.154	13	2	0	0	2	2	.267	.231
Belle, Albert	.400	5	2	1	4	2	1	.571	1.000
Boggs, Wade*	.250	4	1	0	0	2	1	.500	.250
Bonilla, B#	.286	7	2	0	1	0	1	.286	.429
Borders, Pat	.250	8	2	1	2	1	0	.333	.625
Bordick, Mike	.182	11	2	0	0	0	1	.182	.273
Buhner, Jay	.500	4	2	0	1	1	1	.600	.750
Burks, Ellis	.167	6	1	0	0	2	3	.375	.167
Canseco, Jose	.444	9	4	0	0	1	1	.444	.556
Carreon, Mark	.000	7	0	0	1	0	0	.000	.000
Carter, Joe	.267	15	4	1	2	1	4	.333	.467
Cora, Joey#	.600	5	3	0	1	2	1	.714	.600
Davis, Chili*	.167	6	1	0	0	0	1	.167	.167
Devereaux, M	.188	16	3	1	1	0	1	.188	.563
Eisenreich, J*	.375	8	3	0	1	1	0	.444	.375
Fielder, C	.250	8	2	0	0	1	2	.333	.250
Fryman, T	.222	9	2	0	0	0	4	.222	.222
Gagne, Greg	.375	8	3	0	0	1	3	.444	.375
Gomez, Leo	.200	10	2	0	0	2	0	.200	.300
Gonzalez, J	.222	9	2	1	2	0	3	.222	.556
Greenwell, M*	.000	6	0	0	0	2	0	.000	.000
Griffey Jr, K*	.500	6	3	1	2	1	2	.571	1.000
Hall, Mel*	.455	11	5	0	0	0	0	.455	.455
Hamilton, D*	.200	5	1	0	0	0	0	.200	.200
Hayes, C	.222	9	2	0	4	0	3	.222	.333
Henderson, R	.091	11	1	0	0	1	3	.167	.091
Hoiles, Chris	.333	12	4	0	0	4	1	.500	.333
Hollins, Dave#	.000	4	0	0	0	1	0	.200	.000
Howard, T*	.500	5	3	0	1	0	0	.600	.600
Huson, Jeff*	.500	6	3	1	1	0	0	.500	.667
Jefferies, G#	.833	6	5	0	3	0	0	.833	.833
Johnson, L*	.286	7	2	0	0	0	0	.286	.286
Joyner, Wally*	.364	11	4	1	1	1	1	.417	.636
Karkovice, R	.167	6	1	0	0	0	0	.167	.167
Kelly, Pat	.000	5	0	0	0	2	3	.200	.000
Kelly, R	.250	8	2	0	0	3	2	.455	.250
Kent, Jeff	.167	6	1	1	3	0	2	.167	.667
Knoblauch, C	.500	8	4	0	0	0	0	.444	.625
Leius, Scott	.250	8	2	0	0	1	0	.250	.375
Leyritz, Jim	.333	3	1	0	0	1	0	.600	.333
Listach, Pat#	.375	8	3	0	0	0	1	.444	.375
Livingstone*	.429	7	3	0	1	0	0	.429	.571
Lofton, Kenny*	.333	6	2	0	0	1	0	.429	.500
Macfarlane, M	.600	5	3	0	1	1	0	.667	.600

Julio Valera, Royals — RHP

Batter	Avg	AB	H	HR	BI	BB	SO	OBP	Slg
Martinez, E	.200	5	1	0	0	1	0	.333	.200
Martinez, T*	.600	5	3	1	4	0	0	.600	1.200
Mayne, Brent*	.200	5	1	0	0	0	0	.200	.400
McGwire, Mark	.200	10	2	1	1	1	4	.273	.600
McLemore, M#	.429	7	3	1	3	1	1	.500	1.000
McRae, Brian#	.182	11	2	0	0	1	5	.250	.182
Mitchell, K	.500	4	2	0	2	1	1	.600	.750
Molitor, Paul	.250	12	3	0	1	0	1	.250	.417
Munoz, Pedro	.000	7	0	0	1	0	1	.000	.000
Myers, Greg*	.333	6	2	0	0	1	0	.429	.500
Newson, W*	.500	3	1	0	3	0	2	.500	.625
Olerud, John*	.400	10	4	0	0	1	0	.455	.500
Palmeiro, R*	.000	7	0	0	0	1	1	.125	.000
Palmer, Dean	.222	9	2	0	1	1	4	.300	.222
Pena, Tony	.143	7	1	0	0	0	3	.143	.286
Phillips, T#	.667	9	6	0	1	2	2	.727	.889
Plantier, P*	.000	5	0	0	0	2	0	.286	.000
Reboulet, J	.286	7	2	0	2	0	1	.286	.429
Reed, Jody	.286	7	2	0	1	0	2	.286	.429
Ripken, Billy	.200	5	1	0	0	0	1	.200	.400
Ripken, Cal	.235	17	4	0	2	2	2	.316	.294
Rodriguez, I	.400	10	4	0	0	0	1	.400	.400
Seitzer, K	.222	9	2	0	0	0	2	.222	.333
Sierra, Ruben#	.375	8	3	0	2	5	1	.615	.500
Sorrento, P*	.286	7	2	0	0	1	0	.375	.286
Sprague, Ed	.200	5	1	0	2	1	2	.429	.400
Steinbach, T	.000	8	0	0	0	0	1	.000	.000
Surhoff, B.J.*	.125	8	1	0	1	1	1	.222	.125
Sveum, Dale#	.400	5	2	0	0	0	1	.400	.400
Tartabull, D	.111	9	1	0	0	2	3	.273	.111
Tettleton, M#	.143	7	1	0	0	2	0	.333	.143
Thomas, Frank	.400	10	4	1	3	1	0	.455	1.000
Vaughn, Greg	.000	5	0	0	0	1	2	.167	.000
Velarde, R*	.286	7	2	0	0	0	2	.286	.429
Ventura, R*	.167	6	1	0	0	3	0	.444	.167
Vizquel, Omar#	.333	6	2	0	0	0	1	.333	.500
Weiss, Walt#	.286	7	2	0	0	2	1	.444	.286
White, Devon#	.308	13	4	1	1	2	2	.400	.538
Williams, Ber#	.750	1	3	1	2	1	0	.800	1.750

Todd Van Poppel, Tigers — RHP

Batter	Avg	AB	H	HR	BI	BB	SO	OBP	Slg
Alomar, R#	.143	7	1	0	1	3	1	.364	.286
Alomar Jr, S	.250	8	2	1	1	0	2	.250	.625
Amaral, Rich	.429	7	3	0	1	0	1	.375	.429
Anderson, Brd*	.263	19	5	2	5	2	4	.333	.632
Baerga, C#	.182	11	2	0	0	0	1	.182	.182
Baines, H*	.190	21	4	0	2	7	4	.393	.238
Becker, Rich*	.500	2	1	0	0	6	0	.875	1.000
Belle, Albert	.429	7	3	1	2	3	0	.600	1.000
Blowers, Mike	.222	9	2	0	1	1	2	.300	.333
Boggs, Wade*	.333	9	3	0	1	4	3	.538	.556
Buhner, Jay	.167	12	2	0	1	2	1	.286	.250
Canseco, Jose	.200	10	2	0	0	3	3	.385	.200
Carter, Joe	.000	14	0	0	0	1	2	.067	.000
Cedeno, D#	.429	7	3	0	0	1	2	.500	.857
Cirillo, Jeff	.000	3	0	0	0	2	1	.400	.000
Clark, Will*	.538	13	7	2	4	4	1	.611	1.154
Coleman, V#	.333	15	5	1	4	3	1	.444	.733
Cora, Joey#	.143	14	2	0	0	1	1	.200	.286
Cordova, M	.375	8	3	1	3	2	2	.500	.750
Curtis, Chad	.222	9	2	0	2	0	4	.364	.222
Damon, Johnny*	.200	10	2	0	0	0	3	.200	.200
Davis, Chili#	.250	4	1	0	2	2	1	.500	.500
Dawson, Andre	.100	10	1	0	0	0	1	.100	.200
Delgado, C*	.400	5	2	0	0	1	0	.500	.400
Devereaux, M	.200	10	2	0	0	0	1	.200	.200
DiSarcina, G	.125	8	1	0	0	0	0	.222	.250
Duncan, M	.200	5	1	0	0	0	1	.200	.200
Durham, Ray#	.400	15	6	1	2	0	4	.400	.800
Easley, D	.500	6	3	0	2	0	1	.500	.833
Edmonds, Jim*	.500	6	3	1	3	0	1	.500	1.333
Espinoza, A	.000	6	0	0	1	1	1	.143	.000
Fielder, C	.143	14	2	0	1	1	5	.200	.143
Franco, Julio	.100	10	1	0	0	2	1	.250	.100
Frye, Jeff	.250	4	1	1	4	0	2	.200	1.000
Fryman, T	.182	11	2	1	1	3	3	.357	.455
Gaetti, Gary	.286	14	4	0	2	0	3	.267	.357
Gagne, Greg	.059	17	1	0	1	1	11	.111	.118
Gil, Benji	.111	9	1	0	0	0	5	.111	.111
Gonzalez, A	.143	7	1	0	0	0	3	.143	.143
Gonzalez, J	.211	19	4	2	3	1	4	.286	.526
Goodwin, Tom*	.273	11	3	0	0	3	0	.429	.273
Green, Shawn*	.364	11	4	1	3	0	0	.364	.727
Greenwell, M*	.091	11	1	1	1	5	2	.375	.364
Greer, Rusty*	.200	15	3	1	4	4	3	.368	.400
Griffey Jr, K*	.273	11	3	1	2	3	2	.429	.636
Guillen, O*	.056	18	1	0	0	1	0	.105	.056
Hale, Chip*	.500	6	3	0	2	0	0	.625	.833
Hamelin, Bob*	.313	16	5	3	5	5	1	.476	.938
Hamilton, D*	.286	7	2	1	2	2	0	.500	.714

Todd Van Poppel, Tigers — RHP

Batter	Avg	AB	H	HR	BI	BB	SO	OBP	Slg
Hammonds, J	.286	7	2	0	1	0	1	.286	.429
Haselman, B	.667	6	4	1	1	0	1	.667	1.333
Higginson, B*	.600	5	3	1	5	0	0	.600	1.400
Hoiles, Chris	.083	12	1	0	1	3	3	.267	.167
Hulse, David*	.273	11	3	0	1	1	2	.333	.273
Jaha, John	.429	7	3	2	2	3	1	.636	1.286
Jeter, Derek	.500	6	3	0	1	1	1	.571	1.167
Johnson, L*	.231	13	3	0	0	1	1	.286	.231
Joyner, Wally*	.500	16	8	0	3	2	3	.556	.625
Karkovice, R	.200	5	1	0	0	0	1	.200	.200
Kirby, Wayne*	.250	4	1	0	0	2	2	.500	.250
Knoblauch, C	.500	12	6	0	4	2	2	.533	.667
Kreuter, Chad#	.400	5	2	0	2	1	0	.429	.600
Leius, Scott	.333	9	3	0	2	0	2	.333	.333
Lewis, Darren	.250	4	1	0	0	2	0	.500	.250
Livingstone*	.000	3	0	0	1	1	1	.200	.000
Lockhart, K*	.333	12	4	1	3	0	0	.333	.667
Lofton, Kenny*	.500	4	2	0	0	3	0	.714	.500
Lovullo, T#	.000	5	0	0	0	1	1	.167	.000
Macfarlane, M	.286	14	4	0	2	1	2	.333	.500
Martinez, Da*	.500	10	5	0	2	3	1	.615	.800
Martinez, E	.300	10	3	2	2	1	1	.364	.900
Martinez, S*	.000	10	0	0	1	0	0	.000	.000
Martinez, T*	.167	12	2	1	3	1	5	.214	.417
Mayne, Brent*	.200	5	1	0	0	0	3	.200	.200
McCarty, Dave	.000	4	0	0	0	1	1	.200	.000
McLemore, M#	.091	22	2	0	0	7	7	.310	.091
McRae, Brian#	.188	16	3	0	2	0	3	.188	.313
Meares, Pat	.273	11	3	0	1	1	2	.308	.364
Molitor, Paul	.400	10	4	0	2	1	2	.500	.500
Munoz, Pedro	.200	10	2	0	1	1	4	.273	.300
Murray, Eddie#	.333	6	2	0	0	1	1	.429	.333
Naehring, Tim	.273	11	3	0	1	1	3	.385	.364
Nilsson, Dave*	.333	6	2	0	4	2	2	.444	.333
Nixon, Otis#	.200	15	3	0	1	6	2	.409	.200
Nunnally, Jon*	.000	7	0	0	0	1	2	.125	.000
O'Leary, Troy*	.500	4	2	0	1	0	1	.400	.500
O'Neill, Paul*	.400	10	4	2	8	3	1	.538	1.100
Offerman, J#	.286	7	2	0	0	0	0	.286	.286
Olerud, John*	.364	11	4	0	1	2	1	.462	.455
Palmeiro, R*	.214	14	3	3	5	4	3	.368	.857
Palmer, Dean	.125	16	2	1	2	1	3	.176	.313
Paquette, C	.000	7	0	0	0	0	2	.000	.000
Phillips, T#	.300	20	6	2	6	3	4	.391	.650
Polonia, Luis*	.500	8	4	0	3	1	0	.556	.500
Raines, Tim#	.313	16	5	0	0	1	2	.353	.438
Ramirez, M	.167	6	1	0	0	2	2	.375	.167
Ripken, Cal	.150	20	3	1	3	0	2	.150	.300
Rodriguez, I	.348	23	8	1	5	0	3	.348	.609
Sabo, Chris	.333	6	2	0	0	2	0	.500	.333
Salmon, Tim	.286	7	2	0	1	3	1	.500	.429
Segui, David#	.750	4	3	0	3	1	0	.800	1.000
Seitzer, K	.600	5	3	1	3	0	0	.600	1.200
Sierra, Ruben#	.200	5	1	0	1	2	1	.429	.200
Smith, Dwight*	.200	5	1	0	0	0	2	.200	.200
Snow, J.T.#	.200	5	1	1	2	1	1	.333	.800
Sojo, Luis	.111	9	1	0	0	1	1	.200	.111
Sorrento, P*	.000	8	0	0	0	1	2	.111	.000
Sprague, Ed	.364	11	4	2	3	1	1	.417	1.000
Stahoviak, S*	.000	7	0	0	0	3	5	.300	.000
Stanley, Mike	.333	9	3	0	3	1	3	.400	.444
Strange, Doug#	.154	13	2	1	2	1	3	.214	.462
Strawberry, D*	.000	3	0	0	0	2	2	.400	.000
Surhoff, B.J.*	.000	7	0	0	0	1	1	.000	.000
Tartabull, D	.444	9	4	1	3	1	2	.500	.778
Tettleton, M#	.462	13	6	3	10	9	3	.682	1.308
Thomas, Frank	.261	23	6	1	3	5	6	.393	.391
Thome, Jim*	.143	7	1	1	1	4	0	.250	.571
Trammell, A	.375	8	3	0	0	0	0	.375	.375
Valentin, Jhn	.353	17	6	0	4	2	0	.450	.412
Valentin, Jse#	.500	6	3	1	6	3	1	.667	1.333
Vaughn, Greg	.000	7	0	0	0	4	4	.364	.000
Vaughn, Mo*	.500	14	7	2	6	4	2	.611	1.000
Velarde, R	.400	5	2	0	0	1	0	.500	.400
Ventura, R*	.333	18	6	3	7	8	5	.556	.833
Vina, F*	.571	7	4	0	3	0	0	.500	.857
Vitiello, Joe	.167	6	1	0	0	1	0	.286	.167
Vizquel, Omar#	.400	5	2	0	0	1	0	.500	.600
Walbeck, Matt#	.182	11	2	1	0	1	0	.182	.182
White, Devon#	.500	8	4	0	1	0	2	.500	.625
Williams, Ber#	.091	11	1	0	1	3	4	.286	.091
Wilson, Dan	.300	10	3	0	0	0	1	.300	.300

Tim VanEgmond, Brewers — RHP

Batter	Avg	AB	H	HR	BI	BB	SO	OBP	Slg
Baines, H*	.200	5	1	0	0	1	1	.333	.200
Becker, Rich*	.800	5	4	1	1	0	0	.800	1.400
Bragg, Darren*	.250	4	1	0	0	1	0	.400	.250
Brosius, S	.750	4	3	0	0	1	0	.800	1.000
Buhner, Jay	.167	6	1	1	1	1	0	.286	.667
Cora, Joey#	.000	4	0	0	1	0	0	.000	.000

213

Tim VanEgmond, Brewers — RHP

Batter	Avg	AB	H	HR	BI	BB	SO	OBP	Slg
Curtis, Chad	.250	4	1	1	2	0	0	.200	1.000
Davis, Chili#	.286	7	2	1	1	3	1	.500	.714
Diaz, Alex#	.000	5	0	0	1	1	0	.143	.000
DiSarcina, G	.571	7	4	0	1	1	0	.625	.714
Durham, Ray#	.333	6	2	0	0	0	0	.333	.333
Easley, D	.400	5	2	0	0	0	0	.400	.800
Edmonds, Jim*	.286	7	2	0	2	3	1	.500	.429
Griffey Jr, K*	.000	7	0	0	0	1	0	.000	.000
Guillen, O*	.000	4	0	0	0	0	0	.000	.000
Jaha, John	.286	7	2	1	1	0	2	.286	.714
Jefferson, R	.500	6	3	1	1	0	1	.500	1.333
Knoblauch, C	.200	5	1	1	1	0	2	.200	.800
Martinez, Da*	.167	6	1	0	0	0	1	.167	.500
Martinez, T*	.500	6	3	2	5	2	1	.625	1.500
Meares, Pat	.200	5	1	0	0	0	0	.200	.200
Mieske, Matt	.000	7	0	0	0	0	3	.000	.000
Molitor, Paul	.444	9	4	0	1	0	1	.444	.667
Myers, Greg*	.500	4	2	0	1	3	0	.714	.500
Nilsson, Dave*	.500	6	3	0	2	1	1	.571	.833
Phillips, T#	.000	8	0	0	1	0	4	.000	.000
Reed, Jody	.125	8	1	0	0	0	1	.125	.125
Rodriguez, Al	.333	6	2	0	0	0	0	.333	.333
Salmon, Tim	.286	7	2	0	1	1	1	.375	.286
Seitzer, K	.286	7	2	0	0	1	1	.375	.286
Snow, J.T.#	.500	8	4	2	6	1	0	.556	1.250
Sojo, Luis	.200	5	1	0	1	0	1	.200	.200
Tartabull, D	.000	4	0	0	0	2	2	.333	.000
Valentin, Jse#	.000	5	0	0	0	1	2	.167	.000
Vaughn, Greg	.286	7	2	1	2	0	1	.286	.857
Ventura, R*	.333	6	2	0	1	0	1	.333	.667

William VanLandingham, Giants — RHP

Batter	Avg	AB	H	HR	BI	BB	SO	OBP	Slg
Abbott, Kurt	.286	7	2	1	1	1	2	.375	.714
Alfonzo, E	.167	6	1	0	2	0	1	.167	.333
Alicea, Luis#	.000	5	0	0	0	0	1	.000	.000
Alou, Moises	.200	10	2	1	3	2	3	.333	.600
Anthony, Eric*	.222	9	2	1	1	0	2	.222	.556
Bagwell, Jeff	.316	19	6	1	5	4	4	.435	.737
Bell, Derek	.250	16	4	0	1	2	4	.316	.375
Bell, Jay	.400	10	4	0	3	2	1	.571	.500
Berry, Sean	.294	17	5	2	7	0	2	.294	.882
Bichette, D	.222	9	2	0	1	0	1	.222	.333
Biggio, Craig	.250	24	6	2	5	1	0	.280	.542
Blauser, Jeff	.000	2	0	0	0	4	0	.667	.000
Bonilla, B#	.000	6	0	0	0	0	1	.000	.000
Boone, Bret	.250	12	3	0	0	3	1	.400	.333
Brogna, Rico*	.273	11	3	2	4	1	1	.333	.818
Brumfield, J	.429	7	3	0	1	2	0	.556	.571
Butler, Brett*	.167	6	1	0	0	3	0	.444	.333
Caminiti, Ken#	.538	13	7	1	7	1	3	.600	.923
Cedeno, A	.400	5	2	0	0	1	0	.400	.800
Colbrunn, G	.385	13	5	1	3	0	1	.385	.692
Conine, Jeff	.222	9	2	0	0	1	5	.300	.222
Cordero, Wil	.200	10	2	0	0	0	2	.200	.300
Cummings, M*	.286	7	2	1	1	0	0	.286	.714
Davis, Eric	.250	8	2	0	1	1	4	.333	.375
DeShields, S	.313	16	5	0	1	3	1	.421	.438
Dunston, S	.000	6	0	0	0	1	0	.000	.000
Eisenreich, J	.357	14	5	1	3	0	1	.357	.714
Eusebio, Tony	.000	5	0	0	1	1	2	.143	.000
Finley, Steve*	.417	12	5	1	3	0	1	.462	.667
Flaherty, J	.667	6	4	0	2	0	1	.667	.833
Fletcher, D*	.313	16	5	1	4	0	1	.313	.563
Floyd, Cliff*	.000	6	0	0	0	0	0	.000	.000
Fonville, C#	.143	7	1	0	1	0	0	.143	.143
Gaetti, Gary	.000	4	0	0	0	1	0	.200	.000
Gagne, Greg	.000	6	0	0	0	1	2	.143	.000
Galarraga, A	.167	6	1	0	0	3	3	.167	.167
Gant, Ron	.000	4	0	0	0	2	1	.333	.000
Gilkey, B	.333	12	4	1	4	1	1	.429	.667
Girardi, J	.333	6	2	0	2	0	1	.333	.667
Gomez, Chris	.667	3	2	0	2	2	1	.800	.667
Gomez, Leo	.400	5	2	0	0	0	1	.500	.600
Gonzalez, L*	.467	15	7	0	3	4	1	.579	.600
Goodwin, C*	.600	5	3	0	0	2	0	.714	.800
Grace, Mark*	.333	21	7	0	2	0	2	.333	.333
Greene, W*	.222	9	2	0	3	0	2	.222	.444
Grudzielanek	.333	12	4	0	0	1	3	.385	.417
Gwynn, Tony*	.400	10	4	0	0	0	0	.400	.400
Harris, Lenny*	.143	7	1	0	1	0	0	.143	.143
Hayes, C	.000	15	0	0	0	2	4	.118	.000
Henderson, R	.250	4	1	0	0	1	3	.500	.250
Hill, G	.200	5	1	1	3	0	2	.429	.800
Hollandsworth*	.182	11	2	1	1	0	1	.182	.455
Howard, T.	.800	10	8	0	3	0	0	.727	.900
Hundley, Todd#	.214	14	3	0	2	0	4	.267	.214
Hunter, Bri L	.143	14	2	0	2	0	4	.133	.143
Jefferies, G#	.143	14	2	0	0	1	2	.200	.143
Johnson, Char	.286	7	2	0	2	0	0	.286	.286
Johnson, L*	.500	8	4	0	0	0	0	.500	.500

William VanLandingham, Giants — RHP

Batter	Avg	AB	H	HR	BI	BB	SO	OBP	Slg
Johnson, Mark*	.286	7	2	0	0	2	2	.444	.286
Jordan, Brian	.429	7	3	0	1	1	1	.500	.714
Justice, Dave*	.200	5	1	0	1	1	0	.333	.200
Karros, Eric	.222	18	4	0	2	1	3	.300	.278
Kelly, R	.111	9	1	0	1	0	3	.100	.222
Kendall, J	.500	4	2	0	0	1	0	.600	.500
Kent, Jeff	.364	11	4	1	2	1	3	.417	.636
King, Jeff	.000	8	0	0	0	2	1	.200	.000
Kingery, Mike*	.167	6	1	0	0	0	0	.167	.167
Kirby, Wayne*	.333	6	2	0	0	1	0	.429	.333
Klesko, Ryan*	.200	5	1	1	1	0	0	.200	.800
Lankford, Ray*	.500	8	4	2	4	0	0	.500	1.375
Lansing, Mike	.182	11	2	0	0	2	2	.308	.182
Larkin, Barry	.200	15	3	2	4	1	2	.250	.600
Lemke, Mark#	.250	4	1	0	0	1	0	.400	.250
Liriano, N#	.333	9	3	0	1	0	2	.333	.444
Livingstone*	.667	9	6	0	0	0	0	.667	.667
Lopez, Javy	.600	5	3	0	0	0	1	.600	.600
Lopez, Luis#	.200	5	1	0	2	0	0	.200	.200
Mabry, John*	.286	7	2	0	0	1	0	.375	.286
Magadan, Dave*	.167	6	1	0	0	1	1	.286	.167
Martin, Al*	.333	15	5	0	2	1	1	.375	.467
May, Derrick*	.429	14	6	0	3	1	0	.467	.571
McGriff, Fred*	.400	5	2	0	4	0	0	.333	.600
McRae, Brian#	.143	14	2	0	1	2	1	.235	.143
Merced, O*	.222	9	2	0	3	2	1	.364	.444
Miller, Orl	.364	11	4	0	2	1	2	.417	.364
Mondesi, Raul	.353	17	6	2	2	2	6	.421	.765
Morandini, M*	.308	13	4	0	0	4	1	.471	.462
Morris, Hal*	.333	12	4	0	1	0	3	.333	.333
Mouton, James	.300	10	3	0	2	1	0	.300	.400
Offerman, J#	.429	7	3	0	0	0	1	.429	.429
Oliver, Joe	.429	7	3	0	3	2	1	.556	1.000
Ordonez, Rey	.400	5	2	0	0	0	0	.400	.600
Owens, Eric	.000	6	0	0	0	1	1	.143	.000
Parent, Mark	.600	5	3	2	5	1	1	.667	1.800
Pendleton, T#	.200	15	3	0	3	0	2	.200	.267
Piazza, Mike	.375	16	6	0	1	5	1	.524	.375
Reed, Jody	.167	6	1	0	0	0	1	.167	.167
Rodriguez, H*	.143	7	1	0	0	0	1	.143	.286
Rolen, Scott	.000	5	0	0	0	0	1	.000	.000
Sanchez, Rey	.133	15	2	0	1	2	2	.222	.200
Sandberg, R	.143	14	2	0	0	2	3	.250	.143
Sanders, R	.200	5	1	0	1	2	2	.429	.200
Santangelo, F#	.111	9	1	0	0	0	1	.111	.111
Santiago, B	.000	8	0	0	0	0	3	.000	.000
Segui, David#	.333	12	4	0	1	2	0	.429	.500
Servais, S	.333	12	4	0	2	0	0	.333	.583
Sheaffer, D	.600	5	3	0	0	0	0	.600	.800
Sheffield, G	.333	9	3	1	2	0	2	.333	.667
Sosa, Sammy	.412	17	7	1	5	2	2	.474	.588
Stankiewicz	.000	4	0	0	0	2	1	.333	.000
Stocker, K#	.250	12	3	0	0	2	0	.308	.250
Tarasco, Tony*	.333	9	3	0	0	0	0	.333	.444
Thompson, Ry	.167	6	1	1	1	0	4	.167	.667
Veras, Q#	.111	9	1	0	0	1	2	.200	.222
Vizcaino, J#	.600	10	6	0	0	1	0	.636	.700
Wallach, Tim	.091	11	1	1	2	1	4	.167	.364
Webster, L	.286	7	2	0	1	2	0	.444	.571
Weiss, Walt#	.350	4	1	0	2	3	1	.571	.350
White, Devon#	.125	8	1	0	0	1	0	.222	.125
White, R	.286	14	4	1	3	3	2	.412	.571
Whiten, Mark#	.250	4	1	0	0	4	1	.625	.500
Wilkins, Rick*	.286	7	2	1	2	4	1	.545	.714
Young, Eric	.200	5	1	0	0	1	0	.333	.200
Zeile, Todd	.400	5	2	0	2	3	1	.625	.600

Dave Veres, Expos — RHP

Batter	Avg	AB	H	HR	BI	BB	SO	OBP	Slg
Abbott, Kurt	.167	6	1	0	2	0	1	.167	.500
Alfonzo, E	.200	5	1	0	0	0	2	.200	.200
Alou, Moises	.333	6	2	0	2	0	1	.333	.500
Arias, Alex	.600	5	3	0	0	0	0	.667	.600
Bagwell, Jeff	.250	4	1	0	0	1	0	.400	.250
Bell, Derek	.500	6	3	0	2	0	0	.500	.667
Bell, Jay	.250	8	2	1	2	0	3	.250	.625
Berry, Sean	.600	5	3	0	1	0	0	.600	.600
Bichette, D	.111	9	1	1	2	0	3	.111	.444
Blauser, Jeff	.000	5	0	0	0	2	4	.286	.000
Boone, Bret	.000	5	0	0	0	0	0	.000	.000
Brumfield, J	.000	5	0	0	0	1	1	.167	.000
Burks, Ellis	.143	7	1	1	1	0	3	.143	.571
Castilla, V	.429	7	3	0	2	0	2	.375	.429
Clayton, R	.222	9	2	0	0	0	3	.222	.333
Colbrunn, G	.444	9	4	0	1	0	0	.444	.556
Conine, Jeff	.500	4	2	0	0	2	1	.667	.500
Cordero, Wil	.167	6	1	0	1	1	0	.286	.333
Dunston, S	.429	7	3	0	0	0	1	.429	.571
Eisenreich, J*	.600	5	3	0	0	0	0	.600	.600
Fletcher, D*	.400	5	2	0	0	0	1	.400	.600

214

Dave Veres, Expos — RHP

Batter	Avg	AB	H	HR	BI	BB	SO	OBP	Slg
Galarraga, A	.667	6	4	2	2	0	0	.714	1.833
Gant, Ron	.429	7	3	1	2	1	2	.500	1.000
Garcia, C	.333	6	2	0	0	0	1	.333	.500
Gilkey, B	.000	7	0	0	0	0	3	.000	.000
Girardi, Joe	.400	5	2	0	1	0	0	.400	.400
Grace, Mark*	.333	9	3	0	0	0	0	.333	.444
Grissom, M	.222	9	2	0	3	0	0	.200	.222
Grudzielanek	.000	4	0	0	0	1	2	.200	.000
Gwynn, Tony*	.600	5	3	0	0	1	0	.667	.600
Hayes, C	.222	9	2	0	1	1	1	.300	.333
Hernandez, Jo	.333	6	2	0	1	0	1	.333	.333
Hill, G	.000	10	0	0	0	0	5	.000	.000
Hundley, Todd#	.200	5	1	0	0	1	1	.333	.200
Jefferies, Gr	.167	6	1	0	0	0	0	.167	.167
Johnson, Bri	.000	4	0	0	3	0	1	.000	.000
Johnson, Char	.500	4	2	0	0	2	1	.667	.500
Jones, C#	.400	5	2	1	1	2	0	.571	1.400
Jordan, Brian	.600	5	3	0	2	0	0	.667	.800
Karros, Eric	.500	4	2	0	1	1	1	.500	.750
Kent, Jeff	.200	5	1	0	0	0	2	.200	.200
King, Jeff	.400	10	4	0	2	0	1	.400	.400
Kingery, Mike*	.200	5	1	0	0	2	1	.429	.200
Lankford, Ray*	.333	9	3	0	1	0	2	.333	.444
Lansing, Mike	.429	7	3	0	1	0	0	.429	.429
Larkin, Barry	.625	8	5	1	2	0	2	.625	1.000
Lemke, Mark#	.000	5	0	0	0	0	2	.000	.000
Lewis, Darren	.000	5	0	0	0	1	0	.000	.000
Lewis, Mark	.200	5	1	0	0	0	3	.200	.200
Liriano, N#	.333	6	2	0	0	0	1	.429	.333
Lopez, Javy	.000	5	0	0	0	0	0	.167	.000
Mabry, John*	.000	5	0	0	0	0	2	.000	.000
Manwaring, K	.400	5	2	0	1	0	1	.400	.400
McRae, Brian#	.667	6	4	0	1	0	0	.667	.833
Merced, O*	.000	6	0	0	0	0	2	.000	.000
Mondesi, Raul	.167	6	1	1	1	0	1	.167	.667
Morris, Hal*	.400	5	2	0	0	3	2	.625	.800
Orsulak, Joe*	.000	5	0	0	0	0	0	.000	.000
Pagnozzi, Tom	.000	5	0	0	0	0	2	.000	.000
Parent, Mark	.167	6	1	0	1	0	2	.167	.333
Pendleton, T#	.286	7	2	1	1	1	2	.375	.714
Piazza, Mike	.600	5	3	1	2	1	1	.667	1.200
Reed, Jody	.000	4	0	0	0	1	1	.200	.000
Santiago, B	.000	8	0	0	0	4	0	.111	.000
Scarsone, S	.286	7	2	0	0	0	3	.286	.429
Sheffield, G	.000	5	0	0	0	1	3	.167	.000
Sosa, Sammy	.143	7	1	0	2	1	1	.222	.143
Spiers, Bill*	.333	3	1	0	1	1	0	.400	.333
Stocker, K#	.000	5	0	0	0	0	1	.000	.000
Tavarez, Je#	.400	5	2	0	0	1	0	.400	.400
VanderWal, J*	.400	5	2	0	0	1	2	.500	.400
Vizcaino, J#	.200	5	1	0	0	0	2	.200	.200
Weiss, Walt#	.286	7	2	0	0	0	1	.286	.286
White, R	.333	6	2	0	0	0	2	.333	.333
Young, Eric	.111	9	1	0	0	1	0	.111	.111
Zeile, Todd	.000	6	0	0	1	0	0	.000	.000

Randy Veres, Tigers — RHP

Batter	Avg	AB	H	HR	BI	BB	SO	OBP	Slg
Bichette, D	.200	5	1	0	0	0	1	.200	.200
Kelly, R	.600	5	3	0	3	0	1	.500	.800
Liriano, N#	.500	4	2	0	0	0	0	.714	.500
Munoz, Pedro	.400	5	2	0	2	0	1	.400	.400
Polonia, Luis*	.500	4	2	0	1	1	0	.600	.750
Weiss, Walt#	.200	5	1	0	0	2	1	.429	.200

Ron Villone, Brewers — LHP

Batter	Avg	AB	H	HR	BI	BB	SO	OBP	Slg
Alomar, R#	.250	4	1	1	2	1	1	.400	1.000
Anderson, Brd*	.333	3	1	0	1	2	0	.600	.333
Gonzalez, L*	.250	4	1	0	0	1	1	.400	.250
Palmeiro, R*	.000	5	0	0	0	0	1	.000	.000
Ventura, R*	.000	4	0	0	0	1	2	.333	.000

Frank Viola, Blue Jays — LHP

Batter	Avg	AB	H	HR	BI	BB	SO	OBP	Slg
Alomar, R#	.269	26	7	0	3	2	7	.321	.269
Alomar Jr, S	.333	12	4	1	4	1	2	.400	.583
Amaral, Rich	.300	10	3	0	2	1	2	.364	.300
Anderson, Brd*	.238	21	5	0	2	3	4	.360	.238
Anthony, Eric*	.200	10	2	0	0	0	1	.200	.200
Baerga, C#	.235	17	4	0	2	1	2	.300	.235
Bagwell, Jeff	.375	8	3	0	1	2	1	.500	.375
Baines, H*	.304	46	14	1	8	4	4	.360	.478
Bell, Jay	.289	38	11	0	1	4	5	.308	.368
Belle, Albert	.200	20	4	1	6	1	4	.208	.400
Belliard, R	.300	10	3	0	0	0	1	.300	.400
Bichette, D	.429	14	6	1	4	0	1	.400	.857
Biggio, Craig	.235	17	4	0	0	1	3	.278	.235
Blauser, Jeff	.143	7	1	0	0	2	4	.333	.143
Blowers, Mike	.200	10	2	0	0	1	4	.273	.300
Boggs, Wade*	.300	60	18	0	6	4	4	.344	.317

Frank Viola, Blue Jays — LHP

Batter	Avg	AB	H	HR	BI	BB	SO	OBP	Slg
Bonds, Barry*	.188	16	3	0	2	2	4	.316	.188
Bonilla, B#	.355	31	11	1	5	1	4	.364	.548
Borders, Pat	.192	26	5	0	5	1	3	.222	.269
Bordick, Mike	.211	19	4	0	1	1	1	.250	.263
Brosius, S	.125	8	1	0	0	1	1	.222	.125
Brumfield, J	.333	6	2	0	0	0	0	.333	.333
Buhner, Jay	.294	17	5	1	8	2	4	.364	.529
Burks, Ellis	.217	23	5	0	3	0	5	.208	.261
Butler, Brett*	.333	57	19	0	1	5	6	.387	.386
Caminiti, Ken#	.118	17	2	0	1	4	4	.167	.118
Candaele, C#	.357	14	5	0	0	0	2	.357	.357
Cangelosi, J#	.200	10	2	0	0	2	1	.333	.200
Canseco, Jose	.400	35	14	2	4	8	7	.512	.657
Carter, Joe	.300	70	21	6	13	0	12	.300	.600
Clark, Will*	.263	19	5	0	1	1	4	.300	.263
Cole, Alex*	.200	5	1	0	0	1	1	.333	.200
Coleman, V#	.200	25	5	0	2	0	4	.192	.320
Cora, Joey#	.143	7	1	0	0	3	1	.400	.143
Cordero, Wil	.333	3	1	0	3	2	1	.600	.333
Curtis, Chad	.389	18	7	1	1	2	4	.450	.611
Cuyler, Milt#	.167	12	2	0	0	0	2	.167	.167
Dascenzo, D#	.471	17	8	0	5	0	3	.444	.471
Daulton, D*	.267	15	4	0	1	3	6	.389	.333
Davis, Chili#	.267	30	8	0	8	2	9	.313	.267
Davis, Eric	.111	9	1	0	0	1	2	.200	.111
Dawson, Andre	.240	25	6	0	2	1	1	.269	.240
Decker, Steve	.600	5	3	0	3	0	0	.600	.800
Deer, Rob	.261	46	12	3	8	3	14	.306	.565
DeShields, D*	.296	27	8	0	1	0	6	.296	.333
Devereaux, M	.333	18	6	1	3	2	4	.400	.500
DiSarcina, M	.133	15	2	0	0	1	1	.188	.200
Duncan, M	.308	13	4	1	2	0	1	.308	.615
Dunston, S	.269	26	7	0	2	0	4	.259	.308
Dykstra, L*	.250	20	5	0	2	5	5	.400	.300
Easley, D	.500	10	5	0	1	0	0	.545	.500
Espinoza, A	.250	8	2	0	0	0	2	.250	.250
Fermin, Felix	.300	20	6	0	1	0	1	.300	.300
Fielder, C	.333	33	11	2	14	5	9	.421	.667
Finley, Steve*	.143	7	1	0	1	0	0	.125	.143
Franco, Julio	.420	50	21	2	4	4	5	.463	.620
Fryman, T	.286	14	4	0	2	1	1	.313	.357
Gaetti, Gary	.143	14	2	0	0	1	0	.200	.143
Gagne, Greg	.000	11	0	0	1	5		.083	.000
Galarraga, A	.217	23	5	1	1	1	6	.250	.391
Gallego, Mike	.238	21	5	2	4	0	2	.227	.571
Gant, Ron	.313	16	5	0	1	1	1	.353	.375
Garcia, C	.333	6	2	0	0	0	1	.333	.333
Gilkey, B	.167	6	1	0	0	1	0	.286	.167
Girardi, Joe	.188	16	3	0	2	0	2	.188	.188
Gomez, Leo	.111	9	1	0	0	0	0	.111	.222
Gonzales, R	.300	10	3	1	1	3	3	.500	.600
Gonzalez, J	.133	15	2	0	1	2	2	.188	.133
Grace, Mark*	.419	31	13	1	7	1	3	.438	.677
Grebeck, C	.333	12	4	0	0	1	0	.385	.333
Greenwell, M*	.304	23	7	0	1	1	1	.333	.348
Griffey Jr, K*	.400	15	6	1	3	2	1	.471	.667
Grissom, M	.179	28	5	0	1	2	5	.233	.214
Guillen, O*	.250	28	7	1	4	0	1	.250	.357
Gwynn, Tony*	.300	20	6	0	3	1	2	.333	.300
Hall, Mel*	.167	12	2	0	0	1	1	.231	.167
Hamilton, D*	.143	7	1	0	0	0	0	.143	.143
Hayes, C	.216	37	8	1	4	3	5	.275	.297
Henderson, R	.323	62	20	2	7	11	8	.425	.468
Hill, G	.400	10	4	0	1	0	0	.400	.500
Hoiles, Chris	.222	9	2	0	1	2	1	.364	.444
Hollins, Dave#	.333	6	2	0	0	2	0	.333	.667
Howard, Dave#	.200	5	1	0	2	2	1	.375	.200
Howard, T*	.286	7	2	0	0	0	1	.286	.429
Howell, Jack*	.250	12	3	0	1	0	3	.250	.583
Hudler, Rex	.364	11	4	0	1	1	0	.417	.455
Huff, Michael	.286	7	2	0	0	0	2	.286	.429
Hunter, Brian	.364	11	4	1	5	0	3	.364	.727
Huson, Jeff*	.400	5	2	0	1	0	0	.400	1.000
Incaviglia, P	.154	39	6	1	2	1	21	.175	.256
Javier, Stan*	.136	22	3	0	0	4	7	.269	.136
Jefferies, G#	.200	10	2	0	1	4	1	.273	.200
Johnson, L*	.333	12	4	0	2	0	0	.333	.333
Jordan, Ricky	.294	17	5	0	1	3	3	.400	.529
Joyner, Wally*	.229	48	11	1	4	3	3	.288	.313
Justice, Dave*	.125	8	1	1	1	0	2	.222	.500
Karkovice, R	.188	16	3	1	2	2	7	.278	.250
Kelly, Pat	.125	8	1	0	1	0	2	.111	.125
Kelly, R	.522	23	12	1	5	1	2	.542	.783
King, Jeff	.417	24	10	1	3	1	3	.440	.542
Knoblauch, C	.400	15	6	0	3	0	0	.500	.467
Kreuter, Chad*	.222	9	2	0	0	4	1	.462	.222
Lankford, Ray*	.250	12	3	0	2	0	2	.250	.333
Larkin, Barry	.308	13	4	0	1	1	2	.357	.385
Leius, Scott	.400	5	2	0	0	1	2	.500	.400
Lemke, Mark#	.000	7	0	0	0	0	1	.000	.000
Lewis, Darren	.286	7	2	0	0	1	0	.444	.429

Frank Viola, Blue Jays — LHP

Batter	Avg	AB	H	HR	BI	BB	SO	OBP	Slg
Leyritz, Jim	.111	9	1	0	0	2	1	.273	.111
Liriano, N#	.333	9	3	0	0	0	3	.333	.444
Listach, Pat#	.222	9	2	0	1	0	3	.222	.222
Lofton, Kenny*	.286	14	4	0	0	1	1	.333	.357
Lovullo, T#	.143	7	1	0	0	1	0	.250	.143
Macfarlane, M	.154	13	2	0	0	0	2	.214	.154
Manwaring, K	.167	6	1	0	0	0	0	.167	.333
Martinez, Da*	.286	7	2	0	1	0	1	.286	.429
Martinez, E	.571	7	4	0	2	1	1	.556	.857
Martinez, T*	.273	11	3	0	1	0	2	.273	.364
Marzano, John	.200	5	1	0	0	1	0	.200	.200
McGee, Willie*	.250	8	2	0	0	0	1	.250	.250
McGriff, Fred*	.261	23	6	2	5	1	4	.292	.565
McGwire, Mark	.111	27	3	1	1	4	12	.226	.222
McLemore, M#	.154	13	2	0	0	2	4	.267	.154
McRae, Brian#	.158	19	3	0	4	0	2	.200	.158
Meares, Pat	.400	5	2	0	0	2	0	.571	.400
Merced, O*	.286	7	2	0	1	0	0	.286	.286
Mitchell, K	.273	22	6	2	4	5	4	.407	.545
Molitor, Paul	.340	50	17	1	4	4	6	.382	.480
Morman, Russ	.333	9	3	0	0	0	2	.333	.333
Munoz, Pedro	.273	11	3	0	1	1	2	.385	.273
Murray, Eddie#	.220	59	13	2	4	4	10	.270	.322
Naehring, Tim	.333	3	1	0	0	2	0	.600	.333
Nixon, Otis#	.235	17	4	0	0	1	2	.278	.235
O'Brien, C	.250	12	3	0	0	0	0	.250	.250
O'Leary, Troy*	.000	5	0	0	0	0	1	.000	.000
O'Neill, Paul*	.333	18	6	1	2	1	3	.368	.611
Offerman, J#	.400	5	2	0	0	0	1	.400	.400
Olerud, John*	.250	8	2	0	0	3	1	.455	.375
Oliver, Joe	.300	10	3	0	2	2	2	.417	.300
Orsulak, Joe*	.000	5	0	0	1	0	0	.000	.000
Pagnozzi, Tom	.444	9	4	0	1	0	1	.444	.667
Palmeiro, R*	.227	22	5	0	0	1	0	.227	.273
Palmer, Dean	.273	11	3	0	1	3	2	.429	.273
Paquette, C	.400	5	2	1	1	0	1	.400	1.000
Parent, Mark	.000	5	0	0	0	2	0	.286	.000
Pena, G#	.600	5	3	0	0	0	0	.600	.800
Pena, Tony	.200	5	1	0	0	1	2	.333	.200
Pendleton, T#	.208	24	5	1	2	1	3	.240	.333
Phillips, T#	.295	44	13	1	4	11	6	.446	.432
Polonia, Luis*	.261	23	6	0	0	0	5	.261	.261
Raines, Tim#	.226	31	7	1	1	2	4	.273	.323
Ramirez, M	.250	4	1	0	1	1	1	.333	.250
Reed, Jody	.100	10	1	0	0	2	4	.250	.100
Ripken, Bill	.263	19	5	0	2	0	2	.333	.368
Ripken, Cal	.297	64	19	4	13	7	7	.356	.578
Roberts, Bip#	.227	22	5	0	0	0	4	.227	.273
Rodriguez, I	.267	15	4	1	1	0	1	.267	.533
Sabo, Chris	.545	11	6	1	2	4	2	.667	.909
Salmon, Tim	.250	12	3	0	2	1	3	.308	.250
Samuel, Juan	.250	16	4	0	0	1	2	.294	.250
Sandberg, R	.375	24	9	3	5	7	6	.500	.792
Santiago, B	.353	17	6	1	1	1	4	.389	.529
Schofield, D	.182	44	8	1	2	3	9	.229	.273
Schu, Rick	.167	6	1	0	0	2	1	.375	.167
Segui, David#	.286	7	2	0	0	0	0	.286	.286
Seitzer, K	.304	23	7	0	0	6	4	.448	.348
Sheffield, G	.182	11	2	0	1	1	1	.250	.273
Shipley, C	.000	5	0	0	0	0	0	.000	.000
Sierra, Ruben#	.288	59	17	1	2	5	5	.344	.407
Simms, Mike	.250	4	1	1	3	2	1	.500	1.000
Slaught, Don	.222	36	8	0	4	2	10	.256	.250
Smith, Ozzie#	.138	29	4	0	0	3	1	.219	.172
Snow, J.T.#	.500	6	3	0	0	0	0	.500	.500
Sprague, Ed	.143	7	1	0	0	2	1	.333	.286
Stankiewicz	.250	8	2	0	0	0	0	.250	.250
Stanley, Mike	.342	38	13	2	4	7	7	.444	.579
Steinbach, T	.146	41	6	0	2	3	4	.217	.146
Stillwell, K	.143	7	1	0	0	0	1	.143	.143
Strange, Doug#	.111	9	1	0	0	0	2	.111	.111
Strawberry, D*	.167	6	1	1	2	1	0	.286	.667
Surhoff, B.J.*	.364	11	4	1	2	0	0	.364	.727
Sveum, Dale#	.176	17	3	0	1	1	6	.211	.294
Tartabull, D	.333	33	11	2	10	5	8	.421	.636
Tettleton, M#	.083	24	2	0	3	3	7	.185	.167
Thomas, Frank	.304	23	7	1	2	1	2	.333	.565
Thome, Jim*	.000	4	0	0	0	1	1	.000	.000
Thompson, Mil*	.333	12	4	0	0	0	3	.333	.417
Thompson, Rob	.263	19	5	1	4	1	3	.300	.579
Trammell, A	.298	57	17	4	8	4	1	.344	.596
Valentin, Jhn	.500	6	3	0	2	0	1	.500	.667
Valle, Dave	.360	25	9	2	3	4	4	.467	.600
Vaughn, Greg	.429	7	3	0	1	0	2	.429	.571
Vaughn, Mo*	.400	5	2	0	1	1	3	.500	.400
Velarde, R	.143	14	2	0	0	0	2	.143	.214
Ventura, R*	.118	17	2	0	2	2	5	.190	.176
Vizquel, Omar*	.200	15	3	0	1	0	5	.250	.267
Walker, Larry*	.083	12	1	0	0	0	5	.083	.167
Wallach, Tim	.333	30	10	2	3	1	5	.355	.600
Walton, J	.238	21	5	0	2	0	6	.238	.286
Wehner, John	.167	6	1	0	0	0	1	.167	.167
Weiss, Walt#	.364	11	4	0	2	0	0	.364	.364
White, Devon#	.132	38	5	1	3	1	10	.154	.211
Williams, Ber#	.308	13	4	0	1	1	3	.400	.308
Williams, Ma	.273	22	6	3	7	0	5	.273	.727
Worthington	.000	5	0	0	0	0	3	.000	.000
Young, Kevin	.000	4	1	1	2	0	0	.200	1.000
Zeile, Todd	.286	21	6	0	4	1	3	.318	.333

Ed Vosberg, Rangers — LHP

Batter	Avg	AB	H	HR	BI	BB	SO	OBP	Slg
Anderson, Brd*	.500	6	3	1	3	1	0	.571	1.500
Baines, H*	.167	6	1	1	4	2	2	.375	.667
Boggs, Wade*	.400	5	2	0	1	1	2	.500	.400
Bonilla, B#	.167	6	1	0	0	0	2	.167	.167
Cirillo, Jeff	.750	4	3	0	1	1	0	.800	1.000
Coleman, V#	.600	5	3	1	1	0	0	.600	1.200
Davis, Chili#	.000	5	0	0	0	1	0	.000	.000
Griffey Jr, K*	.000	3	0	0	0	2	0	.400	.000
Guillen, O*	.167	6	1	0	0	0	0	.167	.167
Leyritz, Jim	.200	5	1	0	2	0	1	.200	.200
Lofton, Kenny*	.200	5	1	0	2	0	1	.200	.200
Martinez, T*	.333	6	2	0	0	0	2	.333	.500
O'Neill, Paul*	.250	8	2	0	0	0	2	.250	.250
Palmeiro, R*	.000	7	0	0	2	1	1	.222	.000
Phillips, T#	.000	5	0	0	0	0	0	.000	.000
Ripken, Cal	.167	6	1	0	0	0	2	.167	.167
Samuel, Juan	.400	5	2	1	3	1	1	.500	1.000
Snow, J.T.#	.333	3	1	0	1	1	0	.400	.333
Thome, Jim*	.500	4	2	0	1	1	1	.600	.500
Velarde, R	.000	4	0	0	1	0	1	.000	.000
Ventura, R*	.111	9	1	0	1	0	2	.100	.111
Vina, F*	.000	4	0	0	1	0	0	.200	.000
Vizquel, Omar#	.000	6	0	0	0	1	0	.000	.000
Williams, Ber#	.143	7	1	0	0	0	1	.143	.143

Terrell Wade, Braves — LHP

Batter	Avg	AB	H	HR	BI	BB	SO	OBP	Slg
Bell, Jay	.250	4	1	0	0	1	2	.400	.250
Bonds, Barry*	.667	3	2	0	3	2	0	.800	1.000
Clayton, R	.333	6	2	0	0	0	2	.333	.333
Finley, Steve*	.400	5	2	0	1	0	0	.400	.400
Larkin, Barry	.250	4	1	0	0	1	1	.400	.250
Mabry, John*	.500	4	2	1	1	0	2	.500	1.250
Mitchell, K	.500	2	1	1		3	0	.800	2.000
Otero, Ricky#	.500	4	2	0	0	1	0	.600	.750
Reed, Jody	.400	5	2	0	0	1	0	.400	.600
Rolen, Scott	.667	3	2	0	1	2	1	.800	.667
Santiago, B	.500	6	3	1	3	0	2	.500	1.000
Weiss, Walt#	.000	2	0	0	0	3	0	.000	.000
Zeile, Todd	.333	3	1	0	0	2	1	.600	.333

Matt Wagner, Mariners — RHP

Batter	Avg	AB	H	HR	BI	BB	SO	OBP	Slg
Baines, H*	.333	6	2	0	1	1	1	.429	.333
Berroa, G	.500	6	3	1	3	0	1	.500	1.167
Bournigal, R	.400	5	2	0	1	1	0	.500	.400
Brosius, S	.200	5	1	0	0	1	0	.333	.400
Durham, Ray#	.400	5	2	0	0	2	0	.571	.400
Fryman, T	.000	4	0	0	0	1	1	.200	.000
Giambi, Jason*	.400	5	2	0	2	0	1	.400	.800
Guillen, O*	.167	6	1	0	0	0	0	.167	.167
Herrera, Jose*	.000	5	0	0	0	1	2	.167	.000
Higginson, B*	.200	5	1	0	0	0	0	.200	.200
Karkovice, R	.000	6	0	0	0	0	0	.000	.000
Martinez, Da*	.286	7	2	1	1	1	1	.375	.714
Murray, Eddie#	.667	3	2	0	0	2	0	.800	.667
Steinbach, T	.333	3	1	1	3	2	0	.600	1.333
Tartabull, D	.400	5	2	0	0	2	0	.571	.600
Thomas, Frank	.500	8	4	1	3	0	1	.500	1.000
Ventura, R*	.167	6	1	0	0	1	1	.286	.167

Paul Wagner, Pirates — RHP

Batter	Avg	AB	H	HR	BI	BB	SO	OBP	Slg
Abbott, Kurt	.333	9	3	1	4	1	2	.455	.778
Alicea, Luis#	.400	5	2	0	4	1	2	.429	.600
Alou, Moises	.385	13	5	0	3	0	1	.385	.538
Anthony, Eric*	.286	7	2	0	2	0	0	.286	.286
Arias, Alex	.200	5	1	0	1	1	0	.286	.200
Ausmus, Brad	.231	13	3	0	2	2	1	.333	.462
Bagwell, Jeff	.545	11	6	1	2	3	3	.667	.909
Barberie, B#	.333	9	3	0	0	1	3	.333	.444
Bates, Jason#	.333	6	2	0	1	1	0	.429	.500
Bell, David	.500	6	3	0	1	0	1	.500	.500
Bell, Derek	.333	15	8	0	1	1	1	.563	.600
Benjamin, M	.000	5	0	0	0	0	3	.000	.000
Bichette, D	.281	21	8	2	9	0	7	.391	.762
Biggio, Craig	.417	12	5	0	0	4	2	.563	.500
Blauser, Jeff	.263	19	5	1	2	4	7	.391	.421
Bonds, Barry*	.500	8	4	1	3	0	1	.571	.667
Bonilla, B#	.364	11	4	0	2	0	2	.364	.545

Paul Wagner, Pirates — RHP

Batter	Avg	AB	H	HR	BI	BB	SO	OBP	Slg
Boone, Bret	.286	14	4	0	0	1	1	.375	.357
Branson, Jeff*	.400	10	4	0	1	0	1	.400	.400
Brogna, Rico*	.444	9	4	0	3	1	3	.500	.444
Burks, Ellis	.143	7	1	0	1	4	2	.455	.143
Burnitz, J*	.250	4	1	0	0	1	2	.400	.250
Butler, Brett*	.250	12	3	0	0	1	1	.308	.250
Caminiti, Ken#	.200	15	3	0	2	4	5	.368	.267
Cangelosi, J#	.200	5	1	0	0	2	0	.429	.200
Carr, Chuck	.182	11	2	0	0	3	3	.357	.182
Castilla, V	.308	13	4	2	3	2	3	.438	.769
Cedeno, A	.300	10	3	0	1	0	1	.300	.300
Cianfrocco, A	.400	5	2	0	0	0	2	.500	.600
Clayton, R	.429	7	3	0	2	1	1	.500	.429
Colbrunn, G	.333	9	3	0	1	0	1	.333	.444
Cole, Alex*	.600	5	3	0	1	1	0	.667	.600
Conine, Jeff	.211	19	4	2	7	0	5	.250	.579
Cordero, Wil	.455	11	5	0	2	2	2	.538	.636
Daulton, D*	.667	3	2	0	0	4	0	.857	1.000
Davis, Eric	.571	7	4	0	3	0	2	.571	.571
DeShields, D*	.263	19	5	0	1	3	3	.364	.263
Dunston, S	.200	10	2	0	2	1	2	.333	.400
Dykstra, L*	.500	8	4	0	3	0	3	.636	.875
Eisenreich, J*	.667	6	4	1	1	2	0	.750	1.167
Finley, Steve*	.381	21	8	2	7	0	4	.381	.667
Fletcher, D*	.294	17	5	0	5	0	1	.294	.412
Floyd, Cliff*	.143	7	1	0	1	0	1	.143	.143
Fonville, C#	.500	6	3	0	1	1	1	.571	.667
Galarraga, A	.261	23	6	1	2	1	7	.320	.478
Gant, Ron	.200	15	3	1	2	1	4	.250	.400
Gilkey, B	.375	16	6	1	1	2	3	.474	.688
Girardi, Joe	.000	11	0	0	0	0	4	.000	.000
Gonzalez, L*	.154	13	2	0	1	2	2	.267	.231
Grace, Mark*	.476	21	10	0	4	3	2	.542	.524
Greene, W*	.000	5	0	0	0	3	3	.375	.000
Grissom, M	.412	17	7	1	2	1	3	.444	.647
Gutierrez, R	.167	6	1	0	0	3	1	.444	.167
Gwynn, Tony*	.438	16	7	2	6	2	1	.500	.938
Hansen, Dave*	.250	4	1	0	0	1	1	.400	.250
Harris, Lenny*	.125	8	1	0	1	0	2	.125	.375
Hayes, C	.067	15	1	0	4	1	2	.176	.067
Hernandez, Jo	.500	6	3	0	2	2	0	.625	.833
Hill, G	.333	6	2	0	2	0	0	.333	.333
Howard, T*	.167	12	2	0	1	1	0	.231	.250
Hundley, Todd#	.125	16	2	0	1	0	3	.125	.125
Jefferies, G#	.455	11	5	0	0	1	1	.500	.455
Jones, C*	.286	7	2	0	1	0	1	.286	.286
Jordan, Brian	.125	8	1	1	1	1	3	.222	.500
Jordan, Ricky	.000	5	0	0	1	0	2	.000	.000
Justice, Dave*	.368	19	7	3	6	1	3	.400	.842
Karros, Eric	.125	16	2	0	2	3	4	.263	.125
Kelly, R	.133	15	2	1	2	2	3	.235	.333
Kent, Jeff	.188	16	3	1	2	0	3	.176	.438
Kingery, Mike*	.333	12	4	0	0	4	1	.500	.417
Klesko, Ryan*	.231	13	3	1	2	2	3	.313	.462
Lankford, Ray*	.250	16	4	0	1	2	6	.333	.250
Lansing, Mike	.188	16	3	0	2	1	3	.235	.250
Larkin, Barry	.524	21	11	1	4	4	0	.600	.905
Lemke, Mark#	.294	17	5	0	1	0	1	.294	.353
Lewis, Darren	.600	5	3	0	0	3	0	.778	1.000
Liriano, N#	.000	6	0	0	0	0	2	.000	.000
Livingstone*	.600	5	3	0	1	1	0	.667	.600
Lopez, Javy	.556	9	5	3	5	1	3	.600	1.667
Mabry, John*	.333	9	3	0	1	3	1	.500	.444
Magadan, Dave*	.143	7	1	0	0	2	0	.333	.286
Manwaring, K	.333	6	2	0	0	0	1	.333	.333
May, Derrick*	.571	14	8	0	4	2	0	.588	.571
McGee, Willie#	.250	4	1	0	0	2	3	.500	.250
McGriff, Fred*	.286	14	4	1	3	0	4	.412	.500
McRae, Brian#	.250	8	2	0	0	1	0	.333	.500
Miller, Orl	.429	7	3	0	0	1	3	.500	.429
Mitchell, K	.333	6	2	0	1	0	1	.429	.333
Mondesi, Raul	.300	10	3	2	4	0	4	.300	.900
Morandini, M*	.167	12	2	0	0	2	5	.286	.250
Morris, Hal*	.467	15	7	1	5	0	2	.471	.733
Offerman, J#	.714	7	5	0	0	3	2	.800	1.000
Oliver, Joe	.400	5	2	2	3	0	1	.400	1.600
Orsulak, Joe*	.313	16	5	0	1	0	1	.294	.313
Pagnozzi, Tom	.500	6	3	0	3	1	1	.571	.667
Pendleton, T#	.250	20	5	0	1	0	6	.250	.250
Phillips, J*	.333	6	2	1	3	0	2	.333	1.000
Piazza, Mike	.353	17	6	3	7	1	3	.389	.882
Plantier, P*	.300	10	3	1	4	1	2	.364	.600
Reed, Jeff*	.000	6	0	0	0	0	3	.000	.000
Reed, Jody	.286	14	4	0	1	2	3	.353	.286
Roberson, Kd	.714	7	5	1	6	0	0	.714	1.286
Roberts, Bip#	.333	12	4	0	0	2	1	.429	.333
Rodriguez, H*	.143	7	1	0	0	0	0	.143	.286
Sabo, Chris	.500	4	2	0	2	0	1	.400	1.000
Sanchez, Rey	.500	8	6	0	1	0	0	.750	1.000
Sandberg, R	.273	11	3	0	1	2	2	.385	.364
Sanders, R	.389	18	7	1	5	4	5	.500	.667

Paul Wagner, Pirates — RHP

Batter	Avg	AB	H	HR	BI	BB	SO	OBP	Slg
Santiago, B	.125	16	2	0	1	1	4	.176	.188
Servais, J	.182	11	2	0	1	0	2	.182	.273
Sheaffer, D	.385	13	5	0	2	1	1	.429	.538
Sheffield, G	.250	4	1	0	0	1	0	.400	.250
Smith, Dwight*	.300	10	3	0	0	0	5	.300	.300
Smith, Ozzie*	.143	7	1	0	0	3	0	.400	.143
Sosa, Sammy	.125	24	3	0	1	1	8	.160	.208
Stocker, K#	.300	10	3	0	5	1	1	.364	.300
Sweeney, Mark*	.000	5	0	0	0	0	1	.000	.000
Tarasco, Tony*	.250	4	1	0	0	0	1	.400	.250
Taubensee, E*	.267	15	4	1	3	0	4	.267	.467
Tavarez, Je#	.000	5	0	0	0	0	2	.000	.000
Thompson, Mil*	.250	4	1	0	2	1	1	.400	.500
Thompson, Rob	.143	7	1	0	0	0	1	.143	.143
Thompson, Ry	.364	11	4	0	0	0	4	.364	.455
Veras, Q#	.250	4	1	0	0	2	0	.500	.250
Vizcaino, J#	.208	24	5	0	2	0	4	.208	.250
Walker, Larry*	.167	18	3	1	1	1	3	.211	.444
Wallach, Tim	.333	6	2	0	0	3	2	.556	.500
Weiss, Walt#	.000	17	0	0	1	7	3	.292	.000
White, R	.000	9	0	0	1	1	1	.100	.000
Whiten, Mark#	.250	12	3	0	0	3	4	.400	.250
Wilkins, Rick*	.267	15	4	0	2	0	4	.267	.467
Williams, E	.400	5	2	0	2	1	0	.500	.400
Young, Eric	.100	10	1	0	0	4	2	.357	.100
Zeile, Todd	.133	15	2	0	0	0	2	.133	.200

Tim Wakefield, Red Sox — RHP

Batter	Avg	AB	H	HR	BI	BB	SO	OBP	Slg
Alexander, M	.167	6	1	0	0	1	1	.286	.167
Alomar, R#	.182	11	2	0	1	0	2	.167	.364
Alomar Jr, S	.333	6	2	0	0	0	0	.333	.333
Alou, Moises	.600	5	3	0	0	0	1	.600	.600
Amaro, Ruben#	.000	6	0	0	0	2	2	.250	.000
Anderson, Brd*	.105	19	2	1	3	2	1	.190	.368
Anderson, G*	.385	13	5	1	2	1	2	.429	.615
Arias, Alex	.500	4	2	0	1	1	0	.600	.750
Baerga, C#	.286	14	4	0	3	1	0	.333	.357
Baines, H*	.222	18	4	0	1	3	1	.333	.222
Barberie, B#	.500	4	2	0	1	1	0	.600	.500
Battle, Allen	.429	7	3	0	0	1	2	.500	.429
Bautista, D	.143	7	1	0	0	0	1	.143	.143
Becker, Rich*	.250	8	2	0	1	1	3	.333	.375
Belle, Albert	.200	10	2	1	3	1	3	.231	.500
Belliard, R	.250	4	1	0	0	1	0	.500	.500
Benjamin, M	.000	4	0	0	0	0	0	.000	.000
Berroa, G	.250	12	3	1	3	0	3	.250	.500
Bichette, D	.556	9	5	0	3	0	1	.556	1.000
Blauser, Jeff	.500	8	4	0	1	2	0	.636	.500
Blowers, Mike	.500	8	4	2	7	1	1	.556	1.250
Boggs, Wade*	.200	5	1	0	0	2	0	.429	.200
Bonds, Barry*	.000	7	0	0	0	0	2	.000	.000
Bonilla, B	.231	13	3	0	0	4	3	.444	.308
Borders, Pat	.143	7	1	0	0	0	2	.143	.143
Bordick, Mike	.200	15	3	0	0	3	2	.333	.267
Bragg, Darren*	.250	8	2	1	2	1	1	.400	.625
Branson, Jeff*	.000	2	0	0	1	2	0	.400	.000
Brosius, S	.091	11	1	1	2	1	2	.154	.364
Buhner, Jay	.143	14	2	0	2	1	7	.200	.143
Butler, Brett*	.286	7	2	0	3	1	0	.375	.571
Carr, Chuck	.500	4	2	0	2	1	0	.600	.500
Carter, Joe	.313	16	5	1	5	0	5	.313	.563
Cedeno, A	.250	4	1	0	1	0	0	.200	.500
Cedeno, D#	.333	12	4	0	2	1	1	.357	.333
Cirillo, Jeff	.182	11	2	0	0	1	1	.308	.273
Clark, Tony#	.500	6	3	0	0	1	2	.571	.667
Clark, Will*	.318	22	7	1	3	6	3	.464	.545
Clayton, R	.385	13	5	0	0	0	0	.385	.385
Colbrunn, G	.167	6	1	0	0	1	0	.286	.333
Coleman, V#	.286	7	2	0	0	1	0	.500	.286
Cora, Joey#	.385	13	5	0	1	1	0	.400	.538
Cordova, M	.400	5	2	0	0	1	2	.500	.600
Curtis, Chad	.188	16	3	0	1	1	1	.235	.250
Davis, Chili*	.333	15	5	2	4	4	5	.474	.800
Davis, Russ	.400	5	2	1	1	0	1	.500	1.000
Dawson, Andre	.200	5	1	0	0	0	0	.200	.200
Delgado, C*	.133	15	2	0	2	1	3	.188	.267
DeShields, D*	.143	7	1	0	0	1	2	.250	.143
Devereaux, M	.200	10	2	0	0	0	0	.200	.200
Diaz, Alex#	.000	5	0	0	0	0	0	.000	.000
DiSarcina, G	.000	9	0	0	0	0	0	.000	.000
Duncan, M	.500	8	4	0	2	1	0	.556	.500
Durham, Ray#	.231	13	3	0	3	1	4	.286	.308
Easley, D	.000	5	0	0	0	0	2	.000	.000
Edmonds, Jim*	.533	15	8	1	1	0	1	.533	.933
Elster, Kevin	.125	8	1	0	0	2	5	.300	.250
Fabregas, Jor*	.429	7	3	0	0	0	0	.556	.429
Fermin, Felix	.286	7	2	0	0	0	0	.286	.286
Fielder, C	.158	19	3	0	0	1	7	.200	.211

Tim Wakefield, Red Sox — RHP

Batter	Avg	AB	H	HR	BI	BB	SO	OBP	Slg
Flaherty, J	.143	7	1	0	0	0	2	.143	.143
Fletcher, D*	.000	5	0	0	0	0	0	.000	.000
Franco, Julio	.429	7	3	0	4	1	2	.500	.429
Frye, Jeff	.500	8	4	0	0	0	2	.500	.625
Fryman, T	.333	15	5	2	4	0	2	.313	.800
Galarraga, A	.417	12	5	0	1	1	1	.462	.417
Gant, Ron	.250	8	2	0	0	1	0	.333	.250
Gates, Brent#	.154	13	2	0	0	0	1	.154	.231
Giambi, Jason*	.308	13	4	1	1	1	0	.357	.692
Gil, Benji	.167	6	1	0	0	0	1	.167	.167
Gilkey, B	.333	9	3	0	1	2	0	.417	.444
Girardi, Joe	.000	8	0	0	0	1	1	.111	.000
Gomez, Chris	.200	10	2	1	1	0	1	.200	.700
Gonzalez, A	.556	9	5	0	1	1	1	.600	.556
Gonzalez, J	.308	13	4	1	2	1	5	.357	.538
Goodwin, C*	.111	9	1	0	0	0	1	.111	.111
Goodwin, Tom*	.100	10	1	0	0	1	1	.182	.100
Grace, Mark*	.300	10	3	0	1	0	0	.273	.400
Green, Shawn*	.353	17	6	0	2	0	2	.353	.529
Greer, Rusty*	.353	17	6	1	4	1	2	.389	.647
Griffey Jr, K*	.500	10	5	0	2	1	1	.545	.700
Grissom, M	.500	6	3	1	3	0	0	.429	1.000
Guillen, O*	.143	7	1	0	0	0	1	.143	.143
Hamilton, D*	.429	7	3	0	1	2	0	.500	.571
Hayes, C	.556	8	4	0	1	1	2	.556	.625
Herrera, Jose*	.200	10	2	0	0	1	0	.273	.200
Higginson, B*	.357	14	5	1	3	1	3	.400	.714
Hoiles, Chris	.200	10	2	0	0	2	1	.385	.300
Hollins, Dave#	.333	12	4	0	0	0	0	.333	.417
Howard, Dave#	.167	6	1	0	0	0	1	.167	.167
Hudler, Rex	.000	8	0	0	0	0	1	.200	.000
Hundley, Todd#	.222	9	2	0	0	3	0	.222	.222
Incaviglia, P	.200	5	1	0	0	0	0	.200	.200
Jaha, John	.357	14	5	1	3	2	2	.471	.714
Javier, Stan#	.364	11	4	0	2	1	0	.417	.545
Jefferies, G	.500	6	3	0	4	1	1	.571	.500
Jeter, Derek	.500	6	3	0	0	0	0	.500	.667
Justice, Dave*	.167	12	2	0	1	0	0	.231	.250
Karkovice, R	.286	7	2	1	1	0	0	.375	.714
Karros, Eric	.000	8	0	0	0	1	1	.000	.000
Knoblauch, C	.222	9	2	0	0	0	1	.364	.444
Lankford, Ray*	.444	9	4	0	3	1	2	.500	.778
Lansing, Mike	.400	5	2	0	0	0	0	.400	.600
Larkin, Barry	.250	8	2	0	0	1	0	.333	.250
Leius, Scott	.000	6	0	0	0	1	2	.143	.000
Lemke, Mark#	.333	6	2	0	2	2	0	.500	.500
Lewis, Darren	.429	7	3	0	0	0	0	.429	.571
Lewis, Mark	.800	5	4	1	1	0	0	.800	1.400
Liriano, N#	.600	5	3	0	0	1	0	.667	.800
Listach, Pat#	.000	10	0	0	0	0	0	.000	.000
Lofton, Kenny*	.267	15	4	0	1	0	0	.267	.267
Loretta, Mark	.333	6	2	0	0	0	0	.333	.500
Magadan, Dave*	.400	5	2	0	1	0	0	.400	.600
Manto, Jeff	.167	6	1	0	0	1	0	.286	.167
Martinez, Da*	.308	13	4	0	3	3	1	.438	.385
Martinez, E	.125	8	1	0	1	6	3	.533	.125
Martinez, S*	.143	7	1	0	0	2	3	.333	.143
Martinez, T*	.545	11	6	0	2	5	2	.688	.818
Matheny, Mike	.000	13	0	0	0	0	3	.000	.000
May, Derrick*	.200	5	1	0	0	0	2	.200	.200
McGee, Willie*	.133	15	2	0	1	0	4	.133	.133
McGwire, Mark	.250	16	4	3	5	4	4	.429	.813
McLemore, M#	.833	6	5	0	2	2	1	.778	.833
Mieske, Matt	.300	10	3	0	1	0	4	.273	.400
Mitchell, K	.200	5	1	1	1	0	1	.200	.800
Molitor, Paul	.000	5	0	0	0	0	1	.167	.000
Morandini, M*	.182	11	2	0	0	0	1	.182	.182
Munoz, Pedro	.400	10	4	1	1	0	1	.400	.700
Murray, Eddie#	.190	21	4	1	1	3	3	.292	.333
Newson, W*	.400	5	2	2	3	0	0	.400	1.600
Nilsson, Dave*	.688	16	11	1	4	1	0	.706	1.125
Nixon, Otis#	.241	29	7	0	2	4	8	.353	.310
O'Neill, Paul*	.200	5	1	0	3	3	0	.400	.400
Offerman, J	.250	8	2	0	0	3	2	.455	.250
Olerud, John*	.333	12	4	1	3	3	2	.467	.667
Pagnozzi, Tom	.000	6	0	0	0	0	1	.000	.000
Palmeiro, R*	.111	18	2	2	3	4	4	.273	.444
Palmer, Dean	.444	9	4	1	1	2	2	.545	.889
Pena, Tony	.000	3	0	0	0	2	0	.400	.000
Pendleton, T#	.231	13	3	0	0	0	1	.231	.231
Perez, Tomas#	.143	7	1	0	0	0	1	.143	.143
Phillips, T#	.222	18	4	0	0	4	3	.364	.222
Plantier, P*	.000	8	0	0	0	2	2	.200	.000
Ramirez, M	.091	11	1	0	0	1	4	.167	.091
Reboulet, J	.600	5	3	0	1	1	1	.667	.600
Reed, Jeff*	.333	3	1	0	0	2	0	.600	.333
Ripken, Cal	.150	20	3	1	3	1	3	.190	.350
Roberts, Bip#	.167	6	1	0	1	3	2	.444	.167
Rodriguez, I	.176	17	3	1	1	0	0	.222	.294
Sabo, Chris	.200	5	1	0	3	1	1	.286	.400
Salmon, Tim	.188	16	3	2	3	2	6	.316	.563

Tim Wakefield, Red Sox — RHP

Batter	Avg	AB	H	HR	BI	BB	SO	OBP	Slg
Sandberg, R	.429	7	3	2	3	0	0	.429	1.286
Sanders, R	.167	6	1	0	2	1	1	.286	.167
Schofield, D	.000	4	0	0	1	1	1	.200	.000
Seitzer, K	.667	9	6	0	1	2	0	.727	.667
Sierra, Ruben#	.000	7	0	0	0	0	2	.000	.000
Singleton, D*	.000	5	0	0	0	0	1	.000	.000
Smith, Dwight*	.667	6	4	1	1	1	0	.714	1.500
Smith, Mark	.500	4	2	0	0	1	0	.667	.500
Smith, Ozzie#	.250	8	2	0	2	2	3	.455	.500
Snow, J.T.#	.222	18	4	1	3	1	3	.263	.389
Sojo, Luis	.250	4	1	0	0	0	0	.400	.250
Sorrento, P*	.273	11	3	0	2	0	1	.273	.364
Sosa, Sammy	.167	6	1	0	0	0	2	.167	.333
Sprague, Ed	.250	16	4	0	6	2	3	.300	.375
Stahoviak, S*	.250	8	2	1	2	0	1	.250	.750
Steinbach, T	.105	19	2	0	1	1	2	.190	.158
Strawberry, D*	.385	13	5	2	6	0	1	.385	.846
Surhoff, B.J.*	.308	13	4	0	2	0	0	.308	.308
Tartabull, D	.333	9	3	1	3	2	1	.417	.667
Tettleton, M#	.143	14	2	2	4	4	5	.333	.571
Thomas, Frank	.357	14	5	3	3	1	0	.400	1.000
Thome, Jim*	.308	13	4	1	1	0	1	.308	.615
Thompson, Rob	.400	5	2	1	3	2	0	.571	1.200
Trammell, A	.250	4	1	0	0	2	0	.500	.250
Valentin, Jose#	.000	5	0	0	0	0	3	.000	.000
Velarde, R	.250	8	2	0	0	2	2	.400	.375
Ventura, R*	.429	14	6	1	3	1	1	.467	.714
Vina, F*	.353	17	6	0	0	1	2	.389	.353
Vizcaino, J#	.500	6	3	0	1	0	0	.500	.500
Vizquel, Omar#	.417	12	5	0	1	1	1	.462	.500
Walbeck, Matt#	.000	5	0	0	0	0	1	.000	.000
Walker, Larry*	.286	7	2	1	1	0	0	.286	.714
Wallach, Tim	.200	5	1	0	0	1	0	.333	.200
Whiten, Mark#	.000	5	0	0	0	1	1	.167	.000
Wilkins, Rick*	.400	10	4	0	3	0	0	.400	.700
Williams, Ber#	.500	8	4	0	2	1	1	.600	.625
Williams, Ger	.000	6	0	0	0	0	1	.000	.000
Williams, Ma	.250	12	3	2	5	0	1	.286	.750
Wilson, Dan	.091	11	1	1	2	0	1	.167	.364
Young, Eric	.167	6	1	0	0	1	1	.286	.167
Zaun, Greg#	.000	6	0	0	0	0	0	.000	.000
Zeile, Todd	.417	12	5	1	3	2	2	.500	.750

Mike Walker, Tigers — RHP

Batter	Avg	AB	H	HR	BI	BB	SO	OBP	Slg
Bagwell, Jeff	.000	3	0	0	0	2	0	.400	.000
Biggio, Craig	.750	4	3	0	2	0	0	.600	1.000
Boggs, Wade*	.750	4	3	0	0	1	0	.800	.750
Burks, Ellis	.500	4	2	1	3	1	1	.500	1.250
Devereaux, M	.200	5	1	1	1	1	1	.333	.400
Gaetti, Gary	.000	6	0	0	0	0	2	.000	.000
Gagne, Greg	.250	4	1	0	0	1	0	.400	.250
Greenwell, M*	.400	5	2	0	1	1	0	.500	.400
Johnson, Char	.000	3	0	0	0	2	0	.400	.000
Kelly, R	.214	14	3	0	1	0	1	.267	.357
Leyritz, Jim	.333	6	2	0	1	2	1	.500	.333
Liriano, N#	.714	7	5	0	1	1	0	.750	1.000
Palmeiro, R*	.500	4	2	0	0	1	0	.600	.750
Pena, Tony	.250	4	1	0	0	1	0	.400	.250
Phillips, T#	.000	4	0	0	1	1	0	.200	.000
Reed, Jody	.200	5	1	0	0	1	0	.333	.200
Ripken, Billy	.600	5	3	0	1	0	0	.600	.800
Ripken, Cal	.333	6	2	1	3	1	1	.429	1.000
Seitzer, K	.600	5	3	1	2	0	0	.600	1.800

Donne Wall, Astros — RHP

Batter	Avg	AB	H	HR	BI	BB	SO	OBP	Slg
Allensworth	.143	7	1	0	0	0	0	.250	.143
Bell, Jay	.300	10	3	0	0	0	1	.300	.400
Bichette, D	.615	13	8	0	4	0	0	.615	1.000
Boone, Bret	.400	5	2	0	1	0	0	.400	.400
Burks, Ellis	.250	8	2	0	2	1	2	.333	.250
Castilla, V	.000	7	0	0	1	1	1	.111	.000
Clark, Dave*	.200	5	1	0	0	0	0	.200	.400
Conine, Jeff	.167	6	1	0	0	0	1	.167	.333
Cummings, M*	.400	5	2	0	0	0	0	.400	.400
DeShields, D*	.000	6	0	0	0	0	0	.000	.000
Dunston, S	.286	7	2	1	2	0	0	.286	.714
Gaetti, Gary	.500	6	3	0	1	0	1	.500	.667
Gagne, Greg	.400	5	2	0	1	0	0	.500	.400
Galarraga, A	.364	11	4	1	4	1	2	.417	.818
Gant, Ron	.143	7	1	0	0	1	2	.250	.143
Garcia, C	.300	10	3	0	1	1	2	.364	.400
Gilkey, B	.200	5	1	0	0	1	3	.333	.200
Gomez, Leo	.400	5	2	0	0	0	0	.400	.400
Gonzalez, L*	.300	10	3	1	4	1	1	.364	.800
Grace, Mark*	.400	10	4	1	2	0	2	.364	.500
Grissom, M	.429	7	3	0	0	1	0	.500	.429
Haney, Todd	.333	6	2	0	0	0	0	.333	.500
Hayes, C	.000	8	0	0	1	0	1	.000	.000
Hollandsworth*	.167	6	1	0	0	0	0	.167	.167

Donne Wall, Astros — RHP

Batter	Avg	AB	H	HR	BI	BB	SO	OBP	Slg
Hundley, Todd#	.400	5	2	0	1	0	2	.400	.600
Johnson, Mark*	.250	8	2	0	0	1	1	.333	.375
Jones, C#	.000	4	0	0	1	2	1	.286	.000
Jordan, Brian	.000	6	0	0	2	1	0	.222	.000
Karros, Eric	.400	5	2	2	3	1	0	.500	1.600
Kendall, J	.400	5	2	0	1	0	0	.400	.600
King, Jeff	.333	9	3	0	1	1	1	.364	.333
Klesko, Ryan*	.250	4	1	1	1	1	2	.400	1.000
Lankford, Ray*	.167	6	1	0	0	2	0	.444	.167
Lemke, Mark#	.375	8	3	0	0	0	1	.375	.500
Liriano, N#	.000	1	0	0	0	0	0	.000	.000
Mabry, John*	.222	9	2	1	2	0	1	.222	.556
Martin, Al*	.200	15	3	1	1	0	1	.200	.400
McCracken, Q#	.286	7	2	0	2	0	2	.286	.857
McGriff, Fred*	.286	7	2	1	2	0	0	.286	.714
McRae, Brian*	.167	12	2	0	0	0	0	.167	.250
Merced, O*	.333	9	3	0	1	0	2	.333	.333
Mondesi, Raul	.167	6	1	0	0	0	3	.167	.167
Morris, Hal*	.250	4	1	0	0	0	1	.250	.500
Orsulak, Joe*	.333	6	2	0	2	0	0	.333	.333
Osik, Keith	.333	6	2	0	1	0	1	.333	.667
Pagnozzi, Tom	.333	6	2	2	2	0	0	.333	1.333
Pendleton, T#	.667	6	4	0	1	1	1	.714	.833
Perez, Eddie	.500	6	3	0	2	0	0	.500	.833
Piazza, Mike	.667	6	4	0	0	0	1	.667	.833
Reed, Jeff*	.125	8	1	0	0	0	3	.125	.250
Sanchez, Rey	.000	7	0	0	0	0	0	.000	.000
Sandberg, R	.333	6	2	0	0	0	0	.333	.333
Servais, S	.600	10	6	1	3	0	0	.600	.900
Sheffield, G	.667	6	4	1	2	0	1	.667	1.167
Sosa, Sammy	.222	9	2	2	4	1	4	.364	.889
VanderWal, J*	.200	5	1	0	0	0	1	.200	.200
Veras, Q#	.571	7	4	0	0	1	1	.625	.714
Weiss, Walt#	.000	9	0	0	0	1	2	.100	.000
White, Devon#	.200	5	1	0	2	0	1	.200	.400
Whiten, Mark#	.250	4	1	0	1	1	1	.400	.750
Young, Eric	.429	14	6	0	0	0	0	.429	.429

Jeff Ware, Blue Jays — RHP

Batter	Avg	AB	H	HR	BI	BB	SO	OBP	Slg
Clark, Tony*	.500	4	2	2	2	1	0	.600	2.000
Durham, Ray#	.000	4	0	0	0	1	0	.000	.000
Fielder, C	.400	5	2	1	4	0	1	.400	1.200
Fryman, T	.000	4	0	0	0	1	0	.200	.000
Gonzalez, J	.000	4	0	0	0	1	0	.200	.000
Greer, Rusty*	.600	5	3	0	2	0	1	.600	.600
Guillen, O*	.333	3	1	0	0	1	0	.500	.333
Higginson, B*	.000	2	0	0	0	3	0	.600	.000
Lewis, Darren	.333	3	1	0	0	2	0	.600	.667
McLemore, M#	.000	5	0	0	0	0	0	.000	.000
Tettleton, M#	.000	4	0	0	0	1	2	.200	.000
Thomas, Frank	.333	6	2	0	2	1	0	.429	.500
Velarde, R	.500	4	2	0	0	1	0	.667	.750
Ventura, R*	.333	6	2	1	2	0	1	.333	.833

John Wasdin, Athletics — RHP

Batter	Avg	AB	H	HR	BI	BB	SO	OBP	Slg
Alomar, R#	.000	5	0	0	0	1	1	.143	.000
Alomar Jr, S	.000	5	0	0	0	0	0	.000	.000
Anderson, Brd*	.000	4	0	0	0	1	0	.333	.000
Anderson, G*	.111	9	1	0	1	0	2	.111	.111
Ausmus, Brad	.200	5	1	0	0	0	3	.200	.200
Baines, H*	.333	6	2	0	2	0	0	.333	.500
Becker, Rich*	.400	4	1	0	0	2	1	.500	.250
Belle, Albert	.167	6	1	0	0	0	1	.167	.167
Bonilla, B#	.200	5	1	1	1	1	0	.333	.800
Borders, Pat	.000	5	0	0	0	0	1	.000	.000
Bragg, Darren*	.000	3	0	0	0	3	0	.500	.000
Buhner, Jay	.200	5	1	1	2	2	1	.429	.800
Cedeno, A	.000	6	0	0	0	0	1	.000	.000
Clark, Tony#	.167	6	1	1	4	0	2	.167	.667
Cora, Joey#	.500	6	3	0	0	0	0	.500	.833
Cordova, M	.600	5	3	0	2	0	0	.571	1.000
Curtis, Chad	.143	7	1	0	0	0	0	.143	.143
Damon, Johnny*	.500	4	2	0	1	0	0	.500	.750
Davis, Chili#	.333	9	3	2	5	0	1	.333	1.000
DiSarcina, G	.125	8	1	0	0	0	0	.125	.125
Durham, Ray#	.400	5	2	0	1	0	0	.400	.400
Erstad, Darin*	.286	7	2	0	1	1	0	.375	.286
Fielder, C	.167	6	1	0	0	0	2	.167	.167
Frye, Jeff	.000	6	0	0	0	0	0	.000	.000
Fryman, T	.143	7	1	0	0	0	1	.143	.143
Gonzalez, J	.500	6	3	0	2	0	0	.500	.667
Goodwin, Tom*	.286	7	2	0	0	0	1	.286	.286
Greenwell, M*	.250	4	1	0	2	0	0	.500	.500
Greer, Rusty*	.600	5	3	0	0	1	1	.667	.800
Griffey Jr, K*	.167	6	1	0	2	0	0	.143	.167
Guillen, O*	.250	4	1	0	1	0	0	.200	.250
Haselman, B	.300	10	3	0	0	0	3	.300	.300
Higginson, B*	.400	5	2	1	1	0	1	.500	1.000
Hoiles, Chris	.500	4	2	0	0	0	1	.600	.750
Hollins, Dave#	.167	6	1	0	0	0	0	.167	.167
Jefferson, R*	.167	6	1	0	0	0	3	.167	.333
Knoblauch, C	.167	6	1	0	0	0	1	.167	.167
Lewis, Mark	.167	6	1	0	0	0	1	.167	.167
Lockhart, K*	.286	7	2	0	2	0	0	.286	.429
Lofton, Kenny*	.400	5	2	1	1	0	1	.400	1.200
Martinez, Da*	.333	6	2	0	1	1	0	.429	.667
Martinez, E	.167	6	1	0	2	1	2	.286	.167
McLemore, M#	.400	5	2	0	0	0	1	.400	.400
Meares, Pat	.800	5	4	0	3	0	0	.800	.800
Murray, Eddie#	.250	4	1	0	1	1	0	.400	.250
Naehring, Tim	.333	12	4	0	0	0	1	.333	.417
O'Leary, Troy*	.083	12	1	1	1	0	3	.083	.333
Offerman, J#	.250	4	1	0	0	3	0	.571	.750
Palmeiro, R*	.333	6	2	1	3	0	0	.333	.833
Palmer, Dean	.200	5	1	0	0	0	1	.200	.200
Phillips, T#	.143	7	1	1	1	2	3	.333	.571
Ramirez, M	.250	4	1	0	0	1	3	.400	.250
Ripken, Cal	.400	5	2	0	0	0	0	.500	.400
Roberts, Bip#	.000	4	0	0	0	1	0	.200	.000
Rodriguez, Al	.200	5	1	0	0	0	1	.200	.200
Rodriguez, I	.000	6	0	0	0	1	1	.000	.000
Salmon, Tim	.429	7	3	1	1	1	2	.500	.857
Snow, J.T.#	.375	8	3	1	2	0	2	.375	.750
Sorrento, P*	.333	6	2	0	0	0	0	.333	.333
Surhoff, B.J.*	.750	4	3	0	0	1	0	.800	1.000
Tartabull, D	.333	3	1	1	3	2	0	.600	1.333
Tettleton, M#	.000	4	0	0	0	1	1	.200	.000
Thome, Jim*	.250	4	1	1	1	1	1	.400	1.000
Valentin, Jhn	.333	12	4	1	4	0	0	.333	.583
Vaughn, Mo*	.444	9	4	0	2	2	0	.583	.667
Velarde, R	.500	6	3	0	0	0	0	.571	.500
Ventura, R*	.333	3	1	0	0	2	0	.600	.333
Vizquel, Omar#	.250	4	1	0	0	1	1	.400	.250
Wilson, Dan	.000	5	0	0	0	0	0	.000	.000

Allen Watson, Giants — LHP

Batter	Avg	AB	H	HR	BI	BB	SO	OBP	Slg
Abbott, Kurt	.125	16	2	1	0	0	7	.125	.188
Alfonzo, E	.000	5	0	0	2	0	1	.000	.000
Alicea, Luis#	.500	4	2	0	0	1	0	.600	.750
Alou, Moises	.500	10	5	0	2	0	1	.500	1.000
Arias, Alex	.200	5	1	0	1	0	0	.200	.200
Aude, Rich	.500	8	4	0	2	0	2	.500	.625
Ausmus, Brad	.571	7	4	0	1	2	1	.667	.714
Bagwell, Jeff	.300	20	6	2	4	1	4	.333	.650
Barberie, B#	.200	10	2	0	0	2	1	.385	.300
Bates, Jason#	.333	6	2	0	1	3	2	.500	.500
Bell, David	.600	5	3	0	0	1	0	.667	.600
Bell, Derek	.133	15	2	0	0	1	5	.188	.267
Bell, Jay	.412	17	7	2	4	5	3	.583	.824
Belliard, R	.429	7	3	0	1	0	1	.429	.571
Berry, Sean	.222	9	2	0	0	2	0	.364	.222
Bichette, D	.385	13	5	0	2	1	3	.429	.615
Biggio, Craig	.286	21	6	2	5	6	2	.464	.619
Blauser, Jeff	.100	20	2	0	2	2	5	.182	.150
Bogar, Tim	.333	6	2	0	1	1	0	.429	.333
Bonds, Barry*	.222	9	2	0	1	3	0	.417	.222
Bonilla, B#	.364	11	4	1	3	1	0	.417	.818
Boone, Bret	.091	11	1	0	1	3	2	.286	.091
Borders, Pat	.200	5	1	0	0	0	0	.200	.200
Branson, Jeff*	.000	4	0	0	1	0	0	.000	.000
Brogna, Rico*	.000	6	0	0	1	0	2	.000	.000
Brumfield, J	.250	12	3	0	1	0	1	.250	.333
Burks, Ellis	.571	7	4	0	1	2	1	.667	.714
Butler, Brett*	.462	13	6	1	3	3	0	.563	.692
Caminiti, Ken#	.261	23	6	0	4	0	3	.261	.391
Cangelosi, J#	.000	8	0	0	0	1	1	.000	.000
Carr, Chuck	.200	15	3	0	0	2	1	.294	.200
Carreon, Mark	.667	6	4	1	1	0	0	.667	1.333
Castilla, V	.125	8	1	1	1	1	0	.222	.500
Cedeno, A	.235	17	4	0	3	1	2	.278	.353
Cianfrocco, A	.000	4	0	0	0	2	2	.333	.000
Clark, Phil	.222	9	2	0	2	0	1	.222	.333
Clayton, R	.250	20	5	1	0	5	3	.238	.350
Colbrunn, G	.294	17	5	1	1	0	3	.294	.471
Conine, Jeff	.444	18	8	1	4	2	4	.476	.611
Cordero, Wil	.333	6	2	0	0	0	0	.333	.500
Cummings, M*	.000	8	0	0	0	2	2	.000	.000
Davis, Eric	.400	5	2	0	0	0	2	.500	.600
Dorsett, B	.000	7	0	0	1	1	1	.125	.000
Dunston, S	.200	10	2	0	0	1	1	.273	.300
Dye, Jermaine	.167	6	1	0	0	0	1	.167	.167
Eusebio, Tony	.538	13	7	0	5	1	1	.571	.846
Everett, Carl#	.600	5	3	2	3	0	1	.600	1.800
Finley, Steve*	.222	18	4	1	3	3	4	.333	.389
Fletcher, D*	.000	3	0	0	0	2	1	.400	.000
Frazier, Lou#	.000	6	0	0	0	1	1	.143	.000
Gaetti, Gary	.167	6	1	0	0	0	1	.167	.167
Galarraga, A	.583	12	7	1	5	0	3	.615	1.000
Gant, Ron	.125	8	1	0	0	2	2	.300	.125

Batter	Avg	AB	H	HR	BI	BB	SO	OBP	Slg
Garcia, C	.211	19	4	0	0	0	3	.211	.263
Gilkey, B	.222	9	2	0	0	1	2	.300	.222
Girardi, Joe	.250	4	1	0	0	1	0	.400	.250
Gomez, Leo	.571	7	4	0	2	2	2	.667	.571
Gonzalez, L*	.250	12	3	1	1	1	2	.357	.583
Goodwin, C*	.000	3	0	0	0	2	1	.400	.000
Grace, Mark*	.250	20	5	0	1	0	1	.250	.250
Grissom, M	.250	24	6	2	7	1	3	.269	.583
Grudzielanek	.250	4	1	0	0	1	0	.400	.500
Gutierrez, R	.167	6	1	0	0	2	3	.375	.167
Gwynn, Tony*	.067	15	1	0	0	2	0	.176	.067
Henderson, R	.500	4	2	1	2	2	0	.667	1.250
Hernandez, Jo	.500	8	4	1	1	1	1	.556	1.125
Hill, G	.455	11	5	1	2	0	0	.455	.727
Hundley, Todd*	.200	10	2	0	0	0	2	.273	.300
Hunter, Brian	.000	5	0	0	0	0	0	.000	.000
Hunter, Bri L	.300	10	3	0	1	0	0	.273	.300
Huskey, Butch	.000	5	0	0	0	1	1	.167	.000
Johnson, Bri	.167	6	1	0	0	0	1	.167	.167
Johnson, Char	.375	8	3	1	1	2	1	.500	.750
Johnson, L*	.333	12	4	0	2	0	1	.333	.583
Jones, C#	.500	12	6	2	6	0	2	.500	1.083
Jones, Chris	.000	9	0	0	0	3	0	.000	.000
Jordan, Brian	.300	10	3	0	0	0	2	.300	.300
Justice, Dave*	.316	19	6	1	2	2	2	.381	.474
Karros, Eric	.545	11	6	1	2	1	4	.583	.909
Kelly, Mike	.400	5	2	0	0	0	2	.500	.600
Kelly, R	.143	7	1	0	1	0	3	.143	.143
Kendall, J	.500	4	2	0	1	1	0	.500	.500
Kent, Jeff	.267	15	4	0	1	1	2	.313	.400
King, Jeff	.294	17	5	1	3	2	1	.350	.471
Klesko, Ryan*	.111	9	1	0	0	0	0	.111	.111
Lankford, Ray*	.333	6	2	0	3	0	1	.286	.500
Lansing, Mike	.400	10	4	1	4	0	2	.400	.800
Larkin, Barry	.267	15	4	2	7	4	1	.421	.733
Lemke, Mark#	.111	18	2	0	0	6	0	.333	.167
Lewis, Darren	.333	9	3	0	0	0	0	.400	.333
Lewis, Mark	.333	6	2	0	2	0	1	.333	.500
Lopez, Javy	.375	16	6	0	1	0	3	.375	.438
Manwaring, K	.143	7	1	0	0	2	2	.333	.143
Martin, Al*	.000	4	0	0	0	2	0	.333	.000
May, Derrick*	.333	6	2	0	2	0	0	.333	.667
McCracken, Q#	.250	4	1	0	1	1	0	.400	.250
McGee, Willie#	.200	15	3	1	2	0	3	.200	.467
McGriff, Fred*	.125	24	3	3	7	1	6	.160	.500
McRae, Brian#	.455	11	5	1	8	1	1	.500	1.000
Merced, O*	.333	6	2	0	0	4	3	.600	.333
Miller, Orl	.333	6	2	0	0	1	2	.429	.667
Mitchell, K	.250	8	2	0	1	0	1	.250	.375
Mondesi, Raul	.222	9	2	0	0	0	3	.222	.444
Morris, Hal*	.200	10	2	0	0	0	4	.273	.300
Mouton, James	.300	20	6	0	2	6	3	.462	.300
Murray, Eddie#	.333	6	2	1	2	0	1	.333	.833
Newfield, M	.167	6	1	0	0	0	3	.167	.333
O'Brien, C	.375	8	3	0	1	0	0	.375	.625
Offerman, J#	.429	7	3	0	2	0	2	.429	.714
Oliver, Joe	.400	10	4	2	4	1	4	.455	1.000
Ordonez, Rey	.333	9	3	0	0	0	1	.333	.333
Owens, Eric	.400	10	4	0	0	0	1	.400	.500
Pagnozzi, Tom	.444	9	4	2	2	0	0	.444	1.222
Parent, Mark	.444	9	4	1	1	0	0	.444	.889
Pendleton, T#	.308	13	4	0	2	0	1	.308	.462
Perez, Eddie	.200	5	1	0	0	1	1	.333	.400
Perez, E	.333	6	2	0	0	0	2	.333	.333
Piazza, Mike	.429	7	3	2	3	1	3	.444	1.286
Plantier, P*	.167	6	1	1	1	0	1	.167	.667
Prince, Tom	.000	8	0	0	0	0	3	.111	.000
Reed, Jody	.286	14	4	0	0	0	1	.286	.357
Roberts, Bip#	.500	4	2	0	2	1	0	.600	1.000
Rodriguez, H*	.167	6	1	0	0	1	0	.167	.167
Sabo, Chris	.200	5	1	0	0	1	1	.333	.600
Sanchez, Rey	.167	12	2	0	1	1	1	.231	.167
Sandberg, R	.417	12	5	4	7	1	2	.462	1.500
Sanders, R	.400	10	4	0	1	3	4	.538	.700
Santiago, B	.381	21	8	1	5	3	3	.458	.571
Segui, David#	.400	5	2	1	3	2	0	.571	1.000
Servais, S	.250	8	2	0	1	0	0	.250	.250
Sheaffer, D	.222	9	2	0	1	0	0	.222	.444
Sheffield, G	.125	8	1	0	0	5	0	.462	.125
Shipley, C	.100	10	1	0	0	1	1	.250	.100
Simms, Mike	.000	6	0	0	0	0	0	.000	.000
Sosa, Sammy	.267	15	4	1	2	4	1	.421	.467
Stinnett, K	.333	6	2	1	1	0	0	.333	.833
Stocker, K#	.400	5	2	0	0	0	1	.400	.400
Thompson, Rob	.286	7	2	0	0	1	2	.375	.429
Thompson, Ry	.333	6	2	0	0	0	3	.333	.500
Timmons, O	.375	8	3	1	1	1	1	.444	.750
Veras, Q#	.167	6	1	1	1	1	1	.286	.667
Vizcaino, J#	.400	15	6	0	1	2	2	.471	.400
Walker, Larry*	.000	10	0	0	1	2	0	.167	.000
Wallach, Tim	.364	11	4	1	3	0	3	.364	.727

Batter	Avg	AB	H	HR	BI	BB	SO	OBP	Slg
Walton, J	.364	11	4	1	1	3	2	.500	.727
Wehner, John	.167	6	1	0	0	0	1	.167	.167
Weiss, Walt#	.375	8	3	0	0	0	1	.375	.625
Whiten, Mark#	.000	6	0	0	0	0	1	.000	.000
Wilkins, Rick*	.250	4	1	0	0	1	0	.400	.250
Williams, E	.400	5	2	0	1	1	0	.500	.600
Williams, Ma	.300	10	3	2	2	1	3	.417	.900
Young, Eric	.333	12	4	0	4	0	0	.385	.417
Young, Kevin	.167	6	1	0	0	1	0	.286	.333
Zeile, Todd	.600	5	3	1	1	1	1	.667	1.200

Batter	Avg	AB	H	HR	BI	BB	SO	OBP	Slg
Alicea, Luis#	.400	10	4	0	2	0	0	.400	.700
Alou, Moises	.000	5	0	0	1	1	1	.143	.000
Andrews, S	.000	6	0	0	0	0	5	.000	.000
Ausmus, Brad	.250	8	2	0	0	1	0	.333	.250
Bagwell, Jeff	.083	12	1	0	0	0	3	.083	.083
Baines, H*	.200	5	1	0	1	0	0	.200	.200
Bell, Derek	.200	10	2	1	1	1	2	.273	.500
Bell, Jay	.091	11	1	0	1	2	3	.231	.091
Belliard, R	.400	5	2	0	3	1	0	.500	.600
Benard, M*	.400	5	2	0	0	1	0	.500	.400
Berry, Sean	.000	6	0	0	0	0	1	.000	.000
Bichette, D	.333	9	3	0	0	1	1	.400	.444
Biggio, Craig	.400	10	4	0	2	1	1	.455	.400
Blauser, Jeff	.333	6	2	0	0	3	0	.556	.333
Bonds, Barry*	.545	11	6	1	1	3	1	.643	.909
Bonilla, B#	.400	10	4	1	5	3	1	.538	1.000
Boone, Bret	.250	8	2	0	2	2	0	.400	.250
Branson, Jeff*	.200	5	1	0	0	0	0	.200	.200
Brogna, Rico*	.250	4	1	0	1	1	0	.400	.250
Brumfield, J	.333	6	2	0	0	2	1	.500	.333
Burks, Ellis	.273	11	3	0	2	0	5	.273	.273
Burnitz, J*	.500	4	2	0	0	4	0	.750	.750
Butler, Brett*	.400	10	4	0	0	0	1	.400	.400
Caminiti, Ken#	.667	6	4	0	1	1	0	.714	.667
Carreon, Mark	.333	9	3	0	2	0	0	.333	.333
Castilla, V	.200	5	1	0	0	0	0	.200	.200
Cedeno, A	.000	9	0	0	0	0	3	.000	.000
Clark, Dave*	.667	15	10	1	4	0	0	.667	1.000
Clayton, R	.000	9	0	0	0	1	1	.100	.000
Cordero, Wil	.500	6	3	0	1	2	2	.625	.500
Cummings, M*	.167	6	1	1	1	0	3	.167	.667
Daulton, D*	.357	14	5	0	5	1	2	.400	.429
Duncan, M	.400	10	4	0	1	0	0	.400	.500
Dunston, S	.357	14	5	1	4	0	2	.357	.643
Dykstra, L*	.400	10	4	0	0	4	1	.571	.400
Eisenreich, J*	.143	14	2	0	3	3	1	.294	.214
Finley, Steve*	.333	6	2	0	0	0	0	.333	.833
Fletcher, D*	.750	4	3	0	3	0	0	.800	1.000
Gagne, Greg	.600	5	3	0	0	1	0	.600	.600
Galarraga, A	.333	9	3	1	4	0	2	.333	.667
Gant, Ron	.333	9	3	0	0	1	0	.333	.556
Garcia, C	.750	4	3	0	0	1	1	.750	1.000
Gilkey, B	.429	7	3	0	3	2	1	.556	.429
Girardi, Joe	.400	5	2	1	3	1	0	.500	1.000
Gonzalez, L*	.200	5	1	0	0	3	0	.500	.200
Grace, Mark*	.500	6	3	0	3	3	0	.600	.667
Grissom, M	.600	5	3	0	1	0	0	.667	.600
Gutierrez, R	.375	8	3	0	0	1	0	.375	.375
Harris, Lenny*	.000	6	0	0	0	0	1	.000	.000
Hayes, C	.083	12	1	0	0	3	2	.267	.167
Hill, G	.857	7	6	0	4	2	1	.800	1.143
Hollandsworth*	.667	3	2	0	3	3	1	.833	.667
Hollins, Dave#	.250	4	1	0	0	5	1	.667	.250
Howard, T*	.222	9	2	0	0	1	2	.222	.222
Hundley, Todd#	.273	11	3	0	0	2	3	.385	.273
Jefferies, G#	.455	11	5	0	2	4	0	.600	.636
Justice, Dave*	.375	8	3	0	3	1	2	.444	.750
Karros, Eric	.364	11	4	0	1	0	3	.364	.455
Kelly, R	.471	17	8	0	2	1	0	.500	.471
Kent, Jeff	.600	15	9	0	8	3	2	.684	.933
King, Jeff	.278	18	5	0	2	0	2	.278	.333
Kingery, Mike*	.000	4	0	0	0	1	0	.000	.000
Klesko, Ryan*	.000	5	0	0	0	2	0	.286	.000
Lankford, Ray*	.455	11	5	0	1	0	3	.500	.727
Lansing, Mike	.571	7	4	1	1	0	0	.571	1.000
Larkin, Barry	.250	16	4	0	2	1	3	.294	.313
Lemke, Mark#	.125	8	1	0	0	2	0	.300	.125
Lewis, Darren	.125	8	1	0	2	2	1	.300	.250
Liriano, N#	.667	9	6	0	2	1	0	.700	.889
Lopez, Javy	.429	7	3	2	3	1	2	.500	1.286
Manwaring, K	.000	7	0	0	0	1	1	.125	.000
Martin, Al*	.167	18	3	0	0	2	1	.250	.167
Martinez, Da*	.429	7	3	0	0	0	1	.429	.571
McGriff, Fred*	.222	9	2	1	4	0	3	.300	.556
McRae, Brian#	.250	8	2	0	0	0	4	.250	.250
Merced, O*	.375	16	6	0	0	0	1	.375	.438
Miller, Orl	.200	5	1	0	1	0	1	.200	.200
Mondesi, Raul	.455	11	5	0	2	0	2	.455	.545

Dave Weathers, Yankees — RHP

Batter	Avg	AB	H	HR	BI	BB	SO	OBP	Slg
Morandini, M*	.118	17	2	0	0	4	4	.318	.118
Morris, Hal*	.235	17	4	0	1	0	3	.235	.294
Mouton, James	.286	7	2	0	0	0	0	.286	.429
Murray, Eddie#	.400	5	2	0	2	0	0	.400	.600
O'Brien, C	.250	4	1	0	0	0	1	.400	.250
Offerman, J#	.545	11	6	0	2	1	0	.583	.636
Orsulak, Joe*	.364	11	4	0	0	0	0	.364	.545
Phillips, T#	.333	6	2	0	1	1	2	.429	.333
Piazza, Mike	.250	8	2	0	0	2	2	.400	.250
Plantier, P*	.429	7	3	1	3	1	0	.500	1.000
Reed, Jody	.364	11	4	0	1	0	0	.364	.364
Roberts, Bip#	.200	5	1	0	1	0	0	.167	.200
Rodriguez, H*	.143	7	1	0	0	0	0	.143	.143
Sabo, Chris	.250	4	1	0	0	1	0	.400	.500
Sanchez, Rey	.333	6	2	0	0	1	1	.429	.333
Sanders, R	.214	14	3	1	5	2	4	.313	.429
Santiago, B	.333	6	2	1	2	0	2	.333	.833
Scarsone, S	.375	8	3	0	1	0	1	.375	.625
Segui, David#	.167	6	1	0	0	2	0	.375	.167
Servais, S	.286	7	2	1	2	0	0	.250	.714
Sosa, Sammy	.625	8	5	2	6	1	0	.700	1.500
Stocker, K#	.071	14	1	0	1	1	2	.188	.071
Tarasco, Tony*	.600	10	6	0	1	1	1	.636	.800
Taubensee, E*	.400	10	4	0	1	1	1	.455	.400
Thomas, Frank	.000	3	0	0	0	3	0	.500	.000
Thompson, Mil*	.364	11	4	0	1	1	1	.417	.364
Thompson, Rob	.300	10	3	1	3	2	4	.417	.600
Thompson, Ry	.000	11	0	0	0	3	0	.000	.000
Ventura, R*	.500	6	3	1	4	0	1	.500	1.000
Vina, F*	.000	5	0	0	0	0	0	.000	.000
Vizcaino, J#	.200	15	3	0	1	1	1	.294	.267
Walker, Larry*	1.000	4	4	0	3	0	0	1.000	1.750
Wallach, Tim	.125	8	1	0	0	0	2	.125	.125
Weiss, Walt#	.143	7	1	0	0	1	0	.250	.143
Whiten, Mark#	.333	6	2	0	1	1	2	.429	.333
Wilkins, Rick*	.286	7	2	0	0	3	3	.500	.286
Young, Eric	.167	6	1	0	2	0	0	.167	.333
Young, Kevin	.400	5	2	0	0	0	1	.400	.400
Zeile, Todd	.200	10	2	1	4	3	3	.357	.500

Bob Wells, Mariners — RHP

Batter	Avg	AB	H	HR	BI	BB	SO	OBP	Slg
Kirby, Wayne*	.333	3	1	0	0	2	0	.600	.667
Knoblauch, C	.000	6	0	0	0	0	1	.143	.000
Listach, Pat#	.143	7	1	0	0	0	2	.143	.143
Martinez, Da*	.429	7	3	0	0	1	0	.500	.429
Matheny, Mike	.571	7	4	1	2	0	1	.571	1.429
McGwire, Mark	.333	6	2	2	4	0	0	.333	1.333
Meares, Pat	.167	6	1	0	0	0	0	.143	.167
Molitor, Paul	.583	12	7	0	1	1	1	.571	.667
Myers, Greg*	.500	8	4	2	4	1	1	.556	1.375
Naehring, Tim	.200	10	2	0	0	0	2	.200	.200
Nixon, Otis#	.400	5	2	0	0	1	0	.500	.400
O'Brien, C	.400	5	2	0	0	0	0	.400	.800
O'Leary, Troy*	.364	11	4	0	0	1	1	.417	.545
Palmeiro, R*	.625	8	5	0	3	1	1	.667	1.000
Palmer, Dean	.000	4	0	0	0	1	2	.200	.000
Phillips, T#	.143	7	1	0	1	2	2	.333	.143
Ramirez, M	.000	7	0	0	0	0	2	.000	.000
Reboulet, J	.000	5	0	0	0	0	2	.000	.000
Ripken, Cal	.857	7	6	0	2	0	0	.857	1.429
Rodriguez, I	.571	7	4	0	2	0	2	.571	.714
Salmon, Tim	.375	8	3	1	4	1	1	.500	.875
Seitzer, K	.444	9	4	1	0	0	3	.444	.889
Snow, J.T.#	.250	8	2	1	1	0	2	.250	.625
Sprague, Ed	.167	6	1	0	1	3	2	.444	.333
Stahoviak, S*	.333	6	2	0	1	2	1	.500	.333
Stanley, Mike	.000	7	0	0	0	0	2	.000	.000
Tartabull, D	.400	5	2	0	0	1	0	.400	.400
Thomas, Frank	.333	9	3	2	3	1	1	.400	1.000
Thome, Jim*	.375	8	3	0	1	2	2	.500	.500
Valentin, Jhn	.333	9	3	0	0	3	0	.500	.444
Valentin, Jse#	.167	6	1	1	1	2	1	.375	.667
Vaughn, Greg	.375	8	3	2	2	0	2	.375	1.125
Vaughn, Mo*	.125	8	1	0	0	2	2	.364	.125
Velarde, R	.200	10	2	0	1	0	1	.200	.200
Ventura, R*	.143	7	1	1	1	0	1	.143	.571
Vina, F*	.200	10	2	0	1	0	0	.200	.200
Vizquel, Omar#	.500	6	3	0	1	2	0	.556	.667

Bob Wells, Mariners — RHP

Batter	Avg	AB	H	HR	BI	BB	SO	OBP	Slg
Alicea, Luis#	.000	4	0	0	0	0	0	.000	.000
Alomar, R#	.600	5	3	0	2	1	1	.667	1.200
Alomar Jr, S	.286	7	2	0	1	0	0	.286	.286
Anderson, Brd*	.250	8	2	1	2	0	0	.250	.750
Anderson, G*	.000	5	0	0	0	0	0	.000	.000
Baerga, C#	.125	8	1	1	2	0	0	.125	.500
Baines, H*	.333	6	2	1	2	2	1	.444	.833
Becker, Rich*	.100	10	1	1	2	0	2	.100	.400
Belle, Albert	.333	9	3	0	1	1	1	.364	.444
Berroa, G	.111	9	1	0	1	1	3	.200	.111
Boggs, Wade*	.600	5	3	1	3	0	0	.600	1.200
Bordick, Mike	.000	5	0	0	0	0	1	.000	.000
Brosius, S	.400	5	2	0	0	1	2	.500	.400
Burnitz, J*	.000	2	0	0	0	3	0	.600	.000
Canseco, Jose	.143	7	1	0	0	2	2	.333	.286
Carter, Joe	.167	6	1	0	0	2	0	.375	.167
Cirillo, Jeff	.286	7	2	0	0	0	1	.286	.571
Cordova, M	.222	9	2	0	2	0	2	.222	.333
Curtis, Chad	.143	7	1	0	1	0	0	.143	.143
Davis, Chili#	.125	8	1	0	0	1	0	.222	.125
Delgado, C*	.500	4	2	0	0	1	1	.667	.750
DiSarcina, G	.429	7	3	0	0	0	0	.429	.857
Durham, Ray#	.800	5	4	0	0	1	1	.833	1.000
Edmonds, Jim*	.500	4	2	0	1	0	1	.400	.750
Erstad, Darin*	.200	5	1	0	0	0	0	.200	.200
Fabregas, Jor*	.000	5	0	0	0	0	0	.000	.000
Fielder, C	.571	7	4	2	8	3	1	.700	1.571
Flaherty, J	.286	7	2	1	1	0	0	.375	.714
Frye, Jeff	.200	5	1	1	2	1	0	.333	.800
Fryman, T	.111	9	1	0	0	4	1	.417	.111
Gates, Brent#	.333	6	2	0	0	2	0	.500	.333
Giambi, Jason*	.833	6	5	0	2	1	0	.857	1.000
Gomez, Chris	.500	4	2	0	3	0	2	.400	1.000
Gonzalez, A	.000	7	0	0	0	1	3	.125	.000
Gonzalez, J	.500	6	3	1	2	0	0	.500	1.000
Green, Shawn*	.167	6	1	0	0	0	1	.167	.167
Greenwell, M*	.571	7	4	1	4	0	0	.571	1.571
Greer, Rusty*	.286	7	2	0	1	0	0	.286	.286
Guillen, O*	.200	5	1	1	3	0	1	.200	.800
Hammonds, J	.200	5	1	0	0	1	0	.200	.200
Haselman, B	.250	4	1	1	2	1	0	.400	1.000
Henderson, R*	.000	5	0	0	0	1	0	.167	.000
Higginson, B*	.000	6	0	0	0	0	3	.000	.000
Hoiles, Chris	.250	8	2	0	0	2	2	.250	.250
Hollins, Dave#	.400	5	2	0	0	0	0	.400	.600
Jaha, John	.143	7	1	1	1	0	4	.143	.571
Jefferson, R*	.667	6	4	2	3	0	0	.667	1.667
Jeter, Derek	.500	4	2	0	1	1	0	.600	.750
Karkovice, R	.000	6	0	0	0	0	1	.000	.000

David Wells, Orioles — LHP

Batter	Avg	AB	H	HR	BI	BB	SO	OBP	Slg
Alexander, M	.200	5	1	0	0	1	1	.333	.200
Alomar, R#	.167	12	2	0	1	0	3	.167	.250
Alomar Jr, S	.313	16	5	0	0	1	5	.353	.375
Amaral, Rich	.190	21	4	0	1	3	2	.292	.286
Anderson, Brd*	.000	11	0	0	1	1	3	.200	.000
Anderson, G*	.333	15	5	1	2	1	2	.375	.533
Ausmus, Brad	.400	5	2	0	0	0	0	.400	.600
Baerga, C#	.242	33	8	0	4	1	3	.265	.333
Baines, H*	.316	19	6	0	3	1	.409	.316	
Bartee, K	.286	7	2	0	1	0	3	.286	.429
Batista, Tony	.400	5	2	0	0	1	1	.500	.600
Battle, Allen	.500	10	5	0	0	2	0	.500	.500
Becker, Rich*	.000	5	0	0	0	0	3	.000	.000
Bell, David	.286	7	2	0	0	1	1	.286	.429
Belle, Albert	.357	28	10	2	6	2	3	.387	.679
Beltre, E	.200	5	1	0	0	0	2	.200	.200
Benitez, Y	.500	6	3	1	2	0	0	.500	1.000
Berroa, G	.167	12	2	0	1	2	1	.267	.167
Berry, Sean	.250	4	1	0	1	1	0	.400	.500
Bichette, D	.235	17	4	0	1	1	3	.278	.294
Blowers, Mike	.150	20	3	0	1	0	3	.150	.350
Boggs, Wade*	.206	34	7	2	5	4	5	.289	.412
Borders, Pat	.125	8	1	0	0	2	0	.300	.125
Bordick, Mike	.250	24	6	0	1	0	1	.250	.333
Brosius, S	.333	15	5	2	6	0	4	.375	.800
Buford, Damon	.111	9	1	0	1	1	3	.182	.111
Buhner, Jay	.121	33	4	2	3	3	9	.194	.303
Burks, Ellis	.120	25	3	0	5	3	.267	.160	
Canseco, Jose	.261	23	6	0	2	1	8	.292	.391
Carreon, Mark	.375	8	3	0	2	1	0	.444	.375
Carter, Joe	.000	11	0	0	0	3	3	.214	.000
Cirillo, Jeff	.167	12	2	0	0	0	0	.167	.167
Clark, Tony#	.222	9	2	1	4	0	4	.222	.667
Clark, Will*	.250	16	4	1	3	1	2	.294	.500
Cole, Alex*	.125	8	1	0	1	0	1	.125	.125
Coleman, V#	.250	8	2	0	1	0	2	.250	.250
Coomer, Ron	.500	6	3	1	1	0	0	.500	1.000
Cora, Joey#	.400	10	4	0	0	0	2	.400	.400
Cordero, Wil	.250	8	2	0	1	1	3	.333	.250
Cordova, M	.000	9	0	0	0	0	2	.000	.000
Curtis, Chad	.286	21	6	1	4	2	6	.375	.619
Davis, Chili#	.314	51	16	4	12	3	13	.352	.627
Davis, Russ	.571	7	4	1	1	0	1	.571	1.286
Dawson, Andre	.471	17	8	0	2	0	2	.471	.765
Deer, Rob	.353	17	6	1	4	0	2	.353	.706
Devereaux, M	.143	21	3	1	2	0	2	.143	.333
DiSarcina, G	.259	27	7	2	3	0	1	.259	.556
Duncan, M	.455	11	5	0	1	0	0	.500	.545
Durham, Ray#	.467	15	7	1	2	0	0	.438	.867
Easley, D	.125	8	1	0	1	0	2	.125	.125
Edmonds, Jim*	.200	15	3	1	1	2	6	.294	.400

221

David Wells, Orioles — LHP

Batter	Avg	AB	H	HR	BI	BB	SO	OBP	Slg
Eisenreich, J*	.091	11	1	0	0	0	0	.091	.091
Elster, Kevin	.462	13	6	0	3	1	5	.467	.692
Espinoza, A	.290	31	9	1	2	0	3	.290	.387
Fasano, Sal	.000	6	0	0	0	0	3	.000	.000
Fermin, Felix	.233	30	7	0	5	0	2	.233	.300
Fielder, C	.381	21	8	4	10	5	4	.500	.952
Finley, Steve*	.091	11	1	0	0	0	3	.091	.273
Flaherty, J	.429	7	3	0	2	0	1	.375	.571
Fletcher, D*	.400	5	2	0	0	0	0	.400	.600
Franco, Julio	.316	38	12	0	5	4	3	.381	.447
Frye, Jeff	.000	12	0	0	2	0	1	.000	.000
Fryman, T	.333	21	7	1	4	2	7	.391	.524
Gaetti, Gary	.250	24	6	5	9	2	2	.296	.875
Gagne, Greg	.136	22	3	0	1	2	5	.208	.182
Gallego, Mike	.231	26	6	0	1	3	3	.310	.269
Gates, Brent#	.545	11	6	0	4	0	1	.545	.727
Giambi, Jason*	.333	3	1	0	0	0	0	.600	.667
Gilkey, R	.143	7	1	0	1	1	0	.250	.143
Girardi, Joe	.364	11	4	0	2	0	0	.364	.364
Gomez, Chris	.400	5	2	0	0	0	1	.500	.400
Gomez, Leo	.333	9	3	1	3	0	0	.333	.667
Gonzales, R	.077	13	1	0	0	0	1	.077	.154
Gonzalez, J	.296	27	8	2	7	3	3	.367	.556
Goodwin, Tom*	.400	5	2	0	0	0	1	.400	.400
Grebeck, D	.407	27	11	2	2	1	2	.429	.704
Greenwell, M*	.270	37	10	1	5	1	0	.317	.405
Greer, Rusty*	.071	14	1	0	0	1	0	.067	.071
Griffey Jr, K*	.308	39	12	3	6	2	10	.357	.641
Grudzielanek	.167	6	1	0	0	0	2	.167	.167
Guillen, O*	.370	27	10	0	2	1	1	.393	.481
Hall, Mel*	.333	12	4	2	3	0	0	.333	.917
Hamelin, Bob*	.333	6	2	0	1	0	1	.286	.333
Hamilton, D*	.343	35	12	0	3	1	2	.361	.429
Haselman, B	.167	6	1	1	1	0	2	.167	.667
Hayes, C	.167	6	1	0	1	0	3	.167	.167
Henderson, R	.222	27	6	0	1	5	7	.344	.296
Hiatt, Phil	.071	14	1	0	0	0	8	.071	.071
Higginson, B*	.250	4	1	0	1	1	0	.400	.250
Hill, G	.429	7	3	2	2	1	1	.500	1.429
Hoiles, Chris	.083	12	1	0	0	1	3	.154	.083
Hollins, Dave#	.333	6	2	0	0	0	1	.333	.500
Howard, Dave*	.167	12	2	0	0	0	0	.167	.250
Howard, Matt	.000	5	0	0	0	0	2	.000	.000
Howell, Jack*	.222	9	2	0	0	1	4	.364	.333
Hudler, Rex	.400	15	6	2	6	1	1	.438	.867
Huff, Michael	.235	17	4	0	2	2	1	.300	.235
Incaviglia, P	.188	16	3	0	4	0	5	.176	.188
Jaha, John	.350	20	7	1	2	1	2	.381	.600
Javier, Stan#	.167	12	2	0	0	1	2	.231	.167
Jefferies, G#	.000	4	0	0	0	1	2	.200	.000
Jefferson, R*	.500	8	4	0	1	1	2	.556	.625
Jeter, Derek	.333	15	5	0	0	0	2	.333	.400
Johnson, L*	.154	26	4	0	2	0	3	.154	.192
Joyner, Wally*	.258	31	8	0	3	2	2	.324	.323
Karkovice, R	.318	22	7	3	6	1	5	.333	.727
Kelly, Pat	.333	18	6	0	1	1	3	.368	.444
Kelly, R	.160	25	4	0	0	2	8	.222	.200
Kent, Jeff	.500	6	3	0	0	0	0	.500	.500
Knoblauch, C	.345	29	10	0	3	2	2	.387	.414
Knorr, Randy	.500	6	3	0	2	0	1	.500	.833
Lankford, Ray*	.000	8	0	0	0	0	4	.000	.000
Lansing, Mike	.200	5	1	0	1	0	0	.200	.200
Leius, Scott	.273	11	3	0	1	0	0	.273	.364
Lewis, Darren	.000	6	0	0	0	0	0	.000	.000
Lewis, Mark	.250	20	5	0	1	1	4	.286	.350
Leyritz, Jim	.143	28	4	1	1	4	10	.250	.250
Listach, Pat#	.316	19	6	0	3	2	4	.381	.421
Livingstone*	.400	5	2	0	2	0	0	.400	.400
Lofton, Kenny*	.350	20	7	0	1	0	3	.350	.400
Mabry, John*	.250	8	2	1	1	0	1	.250	.625
Macfarlane, M	.143	21	3	1	2	2	1	.250	.286
Malave, Jose	.167	6	1	1	3	0	1	.167	.667
Manto, Jeff	.353	17	6	2	5	0	5	.353	.706
Martin, N	.000	10	0	0	0	0	1	.000	.000
Martinez, Da*	.250	8	2	0	0	0	1	.250	.625
Martinez, E	.341	41	14	2	2	3	4	.386	.537
Martinez, T*	.200	20	4	0	1	0	5	.227	.250
McCarty, Dave	.286	7	2	0	0	1	1	.375	.286
McGwire, Mark	.346	26	9	3	11	2	5	.379	.731
McLemore, M#	.500	16	8	0	1	1	1	.529	.500
McRae, Brian#	.435	23	10	0	0	3	3	.435	.565
Meares, Pat	.313	16	5	0	1	0	3	.313	.375
Mieske, Jeff	.231	13	3	1	1	2	3	.333	.462
Mitchell, Kei	.200	5	1	0	0	1	0	.333	.200
Mitchell, K	.429	7	3	0	2	1	2	.500	.571
Molitor, Paul	.441	34	15	1	5	3	2	.486	.706
Munoz, Pedro	.333	12	4	1	3	0	2	.333	.667
Murray, Eddie#	.143	14	2	2	4	1	3	.200	.571
Naehring, Tim	.182	11	2	0	0	1	1	.250	.182
Nevin, Phil	.600	5	3	2	4	0	1	.600	1.800
Newfield, M	.429	7	3	0	1	0	1	.429	.571

David Wells, Orioles — LHP

Batter	Avg	AB	H	HR	BI	BB	SO	OBP	Slg
Nieves, M#	.000	5	0	0	0	0	1	.000	.000
Nilsson, Dave*	.143	7	1	0	0	0	0	.143	.143
Nixon, Otis#	.250	8	2	0	0	1	0	.333	.250
O'Leary, Troy*	.000	7	0	0	0	1	1	.125	.000
O'Neill, Paul*	.071	14	1	0	0	0	1	.071	.071
Obando, S	.333	6	2	0	1	1	0	.429	.500
Offerman, J#	.286	7	2	0	0	0	1	.286	.429
Olerud, John*	.400	10	4	0	4	0	2	.400	.500
Oliver, Joe	.250	8	2	0	0	0	1	.250	.500
Orsulak, Joe*	.000	6	0	0	0	0	2	.000	.000
Palmeiro, R*	.129	31	4	0	5	2	3	.206	.226
Palmer, Dean	.394	33	13	3	8	2	6	.459	.788
Paquette, C	.333	12	4	0	2	0	4	.333	.333
Pena, Tony	.250	28	7	0	2	1	6	.276	.321
Phillips, T#	.167	30	5	0	1	2	6	.219	.200
Plantier, P*	.333	9	3	0	0	0	2	.333	.333
Polonia, Luis*	.238	21	5	0	3	1	7	.261	.381
Raines, Tim#	.250	16	4	0	1	5	5	.429	.250
Ramirez, M	.333	15	5	1	3	2	2	.412	.533
Randa, Joe	.333	6	2	0	1	1	1	.429	.500
Reboulet, J	.154	13	2	0	0	1	4	.214	.154
Reed, Jody	.148	27	4	0	1	3	1	.233	.185
Ripken, Billy	.412	17	7	1	1	3	0	.500	.706
Ripken, Cal	.345	29	10	3	6	1	2	.387	.724
Rodriguez, Al	.500	6	3	1	3	1	1	.571	1.167
Rodriguez, I	.333	27	9	3	6	3	5	.387	.741
Salmon, Tim	.188	16	3	2	5	6	3	.417	.563
Schofield, D	.182	22	4	0	2	1	6	.217	.182
Schu, Rick	.400	10	4	0	0	0	2	.400	.400
Segui, David#	.273	11	3	0	1	1	0	.333	.364
Seitzer, K	.258	31	8	0	4	4	5	.333	.387
Sheffield, G	.250	8	2	0	1	0	0	.222	.250
Shumpert, T	.111	9	1	0	0	0	1	.111	.111
Sierra, Ruben#	.360	50	18	1	6	4	6	.407	.520
Slaught, Don	.333	12	4	0	2	0	3	.333	.417
Smith, Ozzie*	.286	7	2	0	0	0	0	.286	.286
Snow, J.T.#	.056	18	1	0	1	1	4	.105	.111
Sojo, Luis	.133	15	2	0	3	1	1	.188	.267
Sorrento, P*	.400	5	2	0	0	0	0	.400	.400
Sosa, Sammy	.286	7	2	0	1	0	1	.286	.286
Spiers, Bill*	.250	8	2	1	2	3	2	.455	.625
Sprague, Ed	.200	10	2	0	2	0	1	.200	.400
Stanley, Mike	.257	35	9	1	4	3	11	.316	.400
Steinbach, T	.313	32	10	2	4	2	7	.353	.594
Stilwell, K#	.182	11	2	0	0	0	2	.182	.273
Stinnett, K	.000	4	0	0	0	0	3	.200	.000
Stynes, Chris	.250	8	2	0	2	0	1	.250	.375
Surhoff, B.J.*	.375	24	9	0	4	0	3	.400	.458
Tartabull, D	.289	38	11	4	8	3	9	.341	.684
Tettleton, M#	.353	17	6	1	4	6	0	.500	.647
Thomas, Frank	.368	38	14	4	7	10	7	.500	.816
Thome, Jim*	.143	14	2	0	0	1	3	.200	.143
Tinsley, Lee#	.100	10	1	0	0	0	2	.100	.100
Trammell, A	.350	20	7	0	1	3	5	.435	.500
Turner, Chris	.400	4	2	0	1	1	2	.600	1.250
Valentin, Jhn	.409	22	9	0	0	4	3	.500	.455
Valentin, Jse#	.111	9	1	0	0	1	2	.200	.111
Valle, Dave	.286	28	8	2	5	2	4	.333	.571
Vaughn, Greg	.154	26	4	1	3	9	6	.361	.308
Vaughn, Mo*	.414	29	12	4	7	4	8	.500	.828
Velarde, R	.107	28	3	0	0	2	9	.167	.107
Ventura, R*	.208	24	5	0	3	4	3	.300	.292
Vitiello, Joe	.000	4	0	0	0	2	1	.429	.000
Vizcaino, J#	.571	7	4	0	0	0	0	.571	.714
Vizquel, Omar#	.043	23	1	0	0	1	4	.083	.043
Walbeck, Matt#	.333	6	2	0	0	0	1	.333	.333
Wallach, Tim	.400	5	2	0	0	0	1	.400	.600
Ward, Turner*	.000	8	0	0	0	0	3	.000	.000
Webster, J	.200	5	1	0	0	0	0	.200	.200
Weiss, Walt*	.077	13	1	0	2	1	1	.143	.077
White, Devon#	.250	20	5	0	1	0	5	.250	.350
White, R	.000	4	0	0	1	2	0	.333	.000
Whiten, Mark#	.273	11	3	1	0	1	1	.273	.545
Williams, Ber#	.227	44	10	2	4	3	6	.277	.386
Williams, E	.200	5	1	0	0	0	0	.200	.200
Williams, Ger	.333	18	6	2	4	4	3	.478	.833
Wilson, Dan	.182	11	2	0	0	0	2	.182	.182
Worthington	.167	6	1	0	0	1	1	.286	.167
Young, Ernie	.333	6	2	0	0	2	3	.500	.333
Young, Kevin	.167	6	1	0	1	0	1	.167	.167

Turk Wendell, Cubs — RHP

Batter	Avg	AB	H	HR	BI	BB	SO	OBP	Slg
Alicea, Luis#	.500	4	2	0	0	1	1	.600	.750
Ausmus, Brad	.200	5	1	1	3	0	1	.200	.800
Bagwell, Jeff	.200	5	1	0	0	2	3	.429	.400
Bell, Derek	.333	9	3	0	1	0	0	.400	.444
Bell, Jay	.429	7	3	0	1	3	2	.600	.429
Bichette, D	.333	6	2	1	2	1	2	.429	.333
Biggio, Craig	.333	6	2	1	2	1	2	.429	.833
Boone, Bret	.400	5	2	0	2	1	1	.500	.600

Turk Wendell, Cubs — RHP

Batter	Avg	AB	H	HR	BI	BB	SO	OBP	Slg
Branson, Jeff*	.167	6	1	0	0	0	0	.167	.167
Castilla, V	.667	6	4	2	5	0	1	.667	1.667
Cianfrocco, A	.000	11	0	0	0	0	4	.000	.000
Clayton, R	.000	5	0	0	0	0	2	.000	.000
Colbrunn, G	.333	6	2	0	1	0	1	.333	.333
Conine, Jeff	.600	5	3	0	2	1	0	.714	1.000
Finley, Steve*	.250	4	1	0	0	1	1	.400	.250
Fonville, C#	.400	5	2	0	1	0	1	.400	.400
Galarraga, A	.333	6	2	1	2	0	0	.333	1.000
Gant, Ron	.000	7	0	0	0	1	2	.143	.000
Garcia, C	.400	5	2	0	0	1	1	.571	.600
Gilkey, B	.000	6	0	0	0	2	2	.250	.000
Gutierrez, R	.333	6	2	0	0	1	2	.429	.500
Gwynn, Tony*	.600	5	3	0	0	1	0	.667	1.000
Hill, G	.200	5	1	1	2	0	1	.200	.800
Howard, T*	.429	7	3	1	3	0	1	.429	.857
Jefferies, G#	.333	9	3	0	1	2	0	.455	.333
Johnson, Char	.500	4	2	0	1	1	1	.600	.500
Jones, C#	.600	5	3	1	2	0	0	.600	1.200
Jones, Chris	.400	5	2	0	2	0	0	.400	.400
Jordan, Brian	.250	8	2	1	2	1	3	.333	.625
Karros, Eric	.111	9	1	1	1	0	3	.111	.444
Kelly, R	.333	3	1	0	1	1	0	.400	.333
Lankford, Ray*	.333	9	3	1	2	0	3	.333	.667
Larkin, Barry	.222	9	2	1	2	2	2	.364	.556
Lemke, Mark#	.167	6	1	0	0	0	1	.167	.167
Lopez, Javy	.200	5	1	0	2	0	1	.200	.200
Lopez, Luis#	.200	5	1	0	0	0	2	.200	.400
Mabry, John*	.200	5	1	0	0	0	0	.200	.400
Martin, Al*	.000	4	0	0	0	2	0	.333	.000
McGriff, Fred*	.167	6	1	0	0	1	4	.286	.167
Merced, O*	.714	7	5	0	3	0	0	.714	.857
Mondesi, Raul	.625	8	5	0	1	0	1	.625	.750
Morris, Hal*	.400	5	2	0	0	2	0	.571	.400
Nieves, M#	.400	5	2	1	2	0	1	.400	1.000
Pagnozzi, Tom	.500	8	4	1	3	1	0	.556	1.000
Pendleton, T#	.125	8	1	0	1	1	4	.222	.250
Piazza, Mike	.200	5	1	1	3	0	1	.200	.800
Plantier, P*	.000	6	0	0	0	1	2	.143	.000
Reed, Jody	.250	8	2	0	1	1	1	.333	.250
Sanders, R	.167	6	1	0	0	1	2	.286	.167
Santiago, B	.250	4	1	1	2	1	1	.333	1.000
Shipley, C	.200	5	1	0	0	0	0	.200	.200
Smith, Ozzie#	.625	8	5	0	4	1	0	.667	.750
Walker, Larry*	.400	5	2	0	0	1	0	.500	.400
Wallach, Tim	.000	5	0	0	0	2	2	.000	.000
Weiss, Walt#	.333	6	2	0	1	1	1	.429	.333
Zeile, Todd	.400	5	2	1	5	0	0	.400	1.000

Don Wengert, Athletics — RHP

Batter	Avg	AB	H	HR	BI	BB	SO	OBP	Slg
Alomar, R#	.455	11	5	1	1	0	0	.455	.727
Anderson, Brd*	.200	10	2	0	1	2	0	.333	.400
Anderson, G*	.200	5	1	0	1	0	0	.200	.400
Baerga, C#	.400	5	2	0	1	0	0	.400	.400
Becker, Rich*	.333	9	3	0	1	2	2	.455	.333
Belle, Albert	.286	7	2	1	1	0	0	.286	.714
Bonilla, B#	.400	10	4	0	0	2	0	.500	.500
Bowers, Brent*	.571	7	4	0	0	0	0	.571	.714
Buhner, Jay	.143	7	1	0	0	2	1	.333	.143
Canseco, Jose	.429	7	3	2	2	0	0	.429	1.286
Carter, Joe	.286	7	2	0	2	1	1	.375	.571
Cedeno, D#	.400	5	2	0	0	0	1	.400	.400
Cirillo, M	.600	5	3	0	0	0	0	.600	.600
Cora, Joey#	.625	8	5	1	1	0	0	.625	1.125
Cordova, M	.200	10	2	0	0	0	3	.200	.300
Curtis, Chad	.286	7	2	0	0	2	2	.444	.571
Damon, Johnny*	.000	5	0	0	0	1	0	.000	.000
Davis, Chili#	.200	5	1	0	0	0	0	.200	.200
Delgado, C*	.000	6	0	0	0	1	0	.000	.000
DiSarcina, G	.200	5	1	0	0	0	0	.200	.400
Elster, Kevin	.429	7	3	1	1	0	0	.429	1.000
Fielder, C	.286	7	2	0	0	1	1	.375	.429
Flaherty, J	.400	5	2	0	1	0	1	.400	.600
Franco, Julio	.200	5	1	0	1	0	2	.200	.400
Fryman, T	.333	6	2	1	2	1	0	.429	1.000
Gonzalez, A	.200	5	1	0	0	0	1	.200	.200
Gonzalez, J	.600	5	3	2	2	0	0	.714	1.800
Goodwin, Tom*	.375	8	3	0	2	0	0	.444	.375
Green, Shawn*	.200	5	1	0	0	0	0	.200	.400
Greer, Rusty*	.125	8	1	0	0	1	1	.222	.125
Griffey Jr, K*	.750	4	3	0	0	1	0	.800	.750
Hamelin, Bob*	.429	7	3	0	1	0	0	.429	.429
Hamilton, D*	.400	5	2	0	1	0	1	.500	.400
Higginson, B*	.800	5	4	2	6	0	0	.667	2.200
Hoiles, Chris	.333	9	3	1	2	2	2	.455	.667
Hollins, Dave#	.250	12	3	0	1	1	0	.308	.333
Jaha, John	.400	5	2	0	0	0	0	.500	.400
Jeter, Derek	.333	3	1	0	3	0	1	.400	.333
Knoblauch, C	.375	8	3	0	0	1	2	.444	.375
Lewis, Darren	.000	4	0	0	0	2	1	.333	.000

Don Wengert, Athletics — RHP

Batter	Avg	AB	H	HR	BI	BB	SO	OBP	Slg
Lewis, Mark	.500	6	3	0	3	0	0	.500	.667
Listach, Pat#	.600	5	3	0	1	0	1	.600	.600
Lockhart, K*	.250	8	2	0	0	0	0	.250	.375
Lofton, Kenny*	.600	5	3	0	0	1	0	.667	.800
Macfarlane, M	.500	8	4	0	1	0	1	.500	.750
Martinez, E	.250	4	1	0	1	4	0	.667	.250
Martinez, T*	.333	3	1	0	0	2	1	.600	.667
McLemore, M#	.250	8	2	1	2	2	0	.400	.625
Meares, Pat	.000	5	0	0	0	0	1	.000	.000
Mieske, Matt	.333	6	2	0	0	0	0	.333	.500
Molitor, Paul	.333	12	4	0	1	0	1	.333	.417
Murray, Eddie*	.125	8	1	0	0	2	1	.300	.125
Myers, Greg*	.222	9	2	1	1	0	2	.222	.667
Newson, W*	.333	6	2	0	0	0	3	.333	.667
O'Neill, Paul*	.500	4	2	1	2	1	0	.600	1.250
Offerman, J#	.286	7	2	0	1	2	2	.444	.571
Olerud, John*	.000	6	0	0	0	1	1	.143	.000
Palmeiro, R*	.222	9	2	0	1	2	0	.417	.333
Palmer, Dean	.500	6	3	0	1	0	2	.429	.500
Paquette, C	.375	8	3	0	0	0	1	.375	.500
Phillips, T#	.333	6	2	0	1	1	1	.429	.333
Ramirez, M	.400	5	2	1	1	1	1	.500	1.000
Randa, Joe	.333	6	2	0	0	0	2	.333	.333
Reboulet, J	.167	6	1	0	0	0	0	.167	.167
Ripken, Cal	.364	11	4	0	1	1	1	.417	.455
Rodriguez, Al	.222	9	2	0	0	0	1	.222	.444
Rodriguez, I	.222	9	2	0	0	0	1	.222	.333
Seitzer, K	.667	3	2	0	3	2	0	.800	1.000
Snow, J.T.#	.333	6	2	1	2	0	0	.333	.833
Sorrento, P*	.286	7	2	0	3	2	2	.444	.286
Sprague, Ed	.375	8	3	1	2	0	1	.375	1.000
Stahoviak, S*	.600	5	3	1	2	1	1	.667	1.200
Stanley, Mike	.200	5	1	0	1	1	1	.333	.200
Strawberry, D*	.000	3	0	0	0	2	0	.400	.000
Surhoff, B.J.*	.250	8	2	1	1	0	0	.333	.625
Thome, Jim*	.167	6	1	0	2	1	0	.286	.333
Trammell, A	.167	6	1	0	2	0	0	.167	.167
Valentin, Jhn	.000	5	0	0	0	1	1	.286	.000
Valentin, Jse#	.143	7	1	0	1	0	2	.143	.143
Vaughn, Greg	.200	5	1	0	1	0	0	.286	.400
Vaughn, Mo*	.571	7	4	2	4	0	2	.571	1.571
Vina, F*	.333	6	2	1	2	0	0	.333	.833
Vizquel, Omar*	.500	4	2	0	0	1	0	.600	.500
Whiten, Mark#	.800	5	4	1	3	0	0	.800	1.600
Williams, Ber#	.000	4	0	0	0	1	1	.200	.000
Wilson, Dan	.286	7	2	0	0	0	3	.286	.429

David West, Phillies — LHP

Batter	Avg	AB	H	HR	BI	BB	SO	OBP	Slg
Alfonzo, E	.400	5	2	0	1	0	1	.400	.400
Alicea, Luis*	.250	4	1	1	3	2	0	.500	1.000
Alomar, R#	.167	6	1	0	1	2	1	.375	.167
Alou, Moises	.273	11	3	0	2	0	3	.273	.364
Arias, Alex	.200	5	1	0	0	0	0	.333	.200
Baerga, C#	.286	7	2	1	3	0	0	.375	.714
Bagwell, Jeff	.444	9	4	1	3	1	0	.500	.778
Barberie, B#	.600	5	3	0	0	1	0	.600	.600
Bell, Derek	.250	12	3	0	1	2	3	.357	.250
Bell, Jay	.143	7	1	0	0	1	1	.250	.286
Belle, Albert	.375	8	3	1	5	0	0	.375	.875
Belliard, R	.200	5	1	0	0	0	0	.200	.200
Berry, Sean	.000	6	0	0	0	2	3	.250	.000
Bichette, D	.300	10	3	0	1	1	3	.364	.500
Biggio, Craig	.200	10	2	1	1	2	1	.333	.500
Blauser, Jeff	.143	7	1	0	1	0	0	.250	.286
Bogar, Tim	.333	6	2	0	1	0	0	.333	.333
Boggs, Wade*	.417	12	5	0	0	1	1	.417	.583
Bonds, Barry*	.143	7	1	0	0	4	2	.455	.143
Bonilla, B#	.077	13	1	0	1	0	2	.077	.077
Borders, Pat	.176	17	3	0	1	0	2	.176	.294
Bordick, Mike	.000	3	0	0	1	1	0	.250	.000
Bournigal, R	.333	6	2	0	2	0	0	.333	.500
Brumfield, J	.500	4	2	0	0	1	1	.600	.750
Buhner, Jay	.000	8	0	0	0	3	0	.000	.000
Burks, Ellis	.100	10	1	0	1	1	0	.182	.200
Butler, Brett*	.143	7	1	0	2	5	1	.600	.200
Caminiti, Ken#	.444	9	4	0	0	1	0	.444	.556
Canseco, Jose	.429	7	3	3	5	0	3	.429	1.714
Carr, Chuck	.375	8	3	0	1	0	2	.375	.500
Carter, Joe	.429	7	3	1	4	0	0	.375	1.000
Cedeno, A	.000	5	0	0	0	2	3	.286	.000
Cianfrocco, A	.000	5	0	0	0	0	3	.000	.000
Clark, Phil	.333	6	2	1	2	1	2	.429	1.000
Clark, Will*	.200	5	1	0	0	2	0	.429	.200
Clayton, G	.000	5	0	0	0	0	3	.000	.000
Colbrunn, G	.000	4	0	0	0	0	1	.200	.000
Cole, Alex*	.200	5	1	0	0	0	2	.333	.200
Coleman, V#	.200	5	1	0	0	0	3	.200	.200
Conine, Jeff	.111	9	1	1	2	2	4	.273	.444
Cordero, Wil	.333	6	2	0	1	2	1	.500	.500
Curtis, Chad	.000	4	0	0	0	1	0	.200	.000

David West, Phillies — LHP

Batter	Avg	AB	H	HR	BI	BB	SO	OBP	Slg
Cuyler, Milt#	.000	4	0	0	0	1	1	.200	.000
Davis, Chili#	.200	5	1	1	3	3	1	.500	.800
Davis, Eric	.000	3	0	0	0	2	2	.400	.000
Deer, Rob	.375	8	3	1	2	0	2	.375	1.000
DeShields, D*	.154	13	2	0	0	3	4	.313	.231
Espinoza, A	.400	5	2	0	0	0	1	.400	.400
Fermin, Felix	.000	6	0	0	0	3	0	.333	.000
Fielder, C	.111	9	1	0	0	1	3	.200	.222
Finley, Steve*	.375	8	3	0	3	1	3	.444	.875
Franco, Julio	.364	11	4	0	4	2	1	.400	.364
Frazier, Lou#	.400	4	0	0	0	2	0	.333	.000
Fryman, T	.400	5	2	0	1	2	1	.571	.800
Gaetti, Gary	.250	4	1	0	0	1	1	.400	.250
Galarraga, A	.500	4	2	0	0	1	1	.600	.500
Garcia, C	.333	6	2	0	0	1	1	.429	.333
Gilkey, R	.000	5	0	0	0	2	0	.375	.000
Gonzales, R	.000	4	0	0	2	0	0	.000	.000
Gonzalez, J	.200	5	1	0	0	3	2	.200	.200
Gonzalez, L*	.250	8	2	0	1	3	4	.455	.250
Grace, Mark*	.143	7	1	0	2	1	2	.250	.286
Grebeck, C	.000	4	0	0	0	0	1	.000	.000
Greenwell, M*	.250	4	1	0	0	1	3	.200	.250
Griffey Jr, K*	.400	15	6	2	3	1	3	.438	.867
Grissom, M	.154	13	2	0	1	1	2	.214	.154
Guillen, O*	.400	10	4	0	2	1	0	.455	.500
Gutierrez, R	.000	4	0	0	0	1	1	.200	.000
Gwynn, Tony*	.400	5	2	1	3	0	0	.400	1.000
Hall, Mel*	.333	6	2	0	0	0	1	.333	.333
Hayes, C	.375	8	3	0	0	0	1	.375	.500
Henderson, R	.222	9	2	1	3	2	2	.364	.556
Hill, G	.167	12	2	1	2	2	2	.286	.417
Howell, Jack*	.600	5	3	0	2	0	0	.667	.600
Hundley, Todd#	.143	7	1	0	0	0	1	.143	.143
Incaviglia, P	.143	7	1	0	1	0	1	.125	.143
Jefferies, G#	.000	5	0	0	0	0	0	.000	.000
Johnson, L*	.222	9	2	0	0	1	3	.300	.444
Jones, Chris	.000	4	0	0	0	1	1	.200	.000
Jordan, Brian	.400	5	2	0	1	2	0	.571	.400
Joyner, Wally*	.364	11	4	1	2	0	1	.364	.636
Justice, Dave*	.250	8	2	1	4	3	1	.455	.625
Karkovice, R	.364	11	4	1	5	1	2	.417	.727
Karros, Eric	.000	12	0	0	0	0	3	.000	.000
Kelly, R	.308	13	4	0	0	1	2	.357	.308
Kent, Jeff	.300	10	3	0	0	0	1	.300	.300
King, Jeff	.111	9	1	1	2	3	0	.308	.444
Lankford, Ray*	.000	7	0	0	0	3	4	.300	.000
Lansing, Mike	.375	8	3	0	1	1	2	.400	.375
Larkin, Barry	.333	6	2	0	2	1	0	.429	.333
Lemke, Mark#	.250	8	2	0	1	1	1	.333	.375
Lewis, Darren	.167	6	1	0	0	1	1	.286	.167
Liriano, N#	.200	5	1	0	3	1	1	.333	.400
Macfarlane, M	.200	5	1	0	2	0	2	.167	.200
Manwaring, K	.333	3	1	0	0	2	1	.600	.333
Martin, Al*	.143	7	1	0	0	2	2	.333	.143
Martinez, Da*	.000	5	0	0	0	1	2	.167	.000
Martinez, E	.375	8	3	0	0	0	0	.375	.500
McGriff, Fred*	.238	21	5	0	4	3	5	.320	.333
McGwire, Mark	.500	4	2	1	1	2	1	.667	1.500
Merced, O*	.000	4	0	0	0	1	0	.200	.000
Molitor, Paul	.200	5	1	0	2	0	0	.167	.400
Mondesi, Raul	.100	10	1	0	0	0	1	.100	.100
Morris, Hal*	.000	5	0	0	0	0	2	.000	.000
Mouton, James	.250	8	2	0	1	1	1	.333	.250
O'Brien, C	.400	5	2	0	2	1	1	.500	.800
Offerman, J#	.500	4	2	0	2	1	0	.600	.500
Orsulak, Joe*	.250	8	2	0	2	1	0	.333	.500
Pagnozzi, Tom	.600	5	3	0	0	1	0	.667	1.000
Palmeiro, R*	.250	4	1	0	0	1	0	.400	.250
Parent, Mark	.200	5	1	1	1	1	1	.333	.800
Pena, Tony	.571	7	4	1	2	1	1	.625	1.286
Pendleton, T#	.273	11	3	0	0	0	1	.273	.273
Phillips, T#	.364	11	4	1	3	0	1	.364	.727
Piazza, Mike	.364	11	4	1	3	0	3	.364	.636
Plantier, P*	.200	5	1	1	2	1	0	.500	.800
Polonia, Luis*	.200	5	1	0	1	0	2	.167	.200
Reed, Jeff*	.000	4	0	0	0	1	0	.200	.000
Reed, Jody	.500	10	5	0	1	1	1	.545	.600
Ripken, Billy	.500	4	2	0	0	1	0	.600	.500
Ripken, Cal	.143	7	1	0	1	1	1	.222	.143
Roberts, Bip#	.000	4	0	0	0	1	2	.200	.000
Sandberg, R	.400	5	2	0	0	0	0	.400	.400
Santiago, B	.250	4	1	0	0	2	3	.500	.250
Scarsone, S	.500	4	2	0	0	1	1	.600	.500
Segui, David#	.222	9	2	0	0	2	2	.333	.222
Seitzer, K	.250	4	1	0	0	0	1	.400	.375
Servais, S	.400	5	2	1	6	0	2	.400	1.000
Sheffield, G	.125	8	1	0	2	1	0	.300	.125
Shipley, C	.333	9	3	0	0	0	2	.333	.444
Sierra, Ruben#	.364	11	4	0	2	3	1	.500	.545
Slaught, Don	.400	5	2	0	0	0	0	.400	.600
Smith, Ozzie	.400	10	4	0	1	1	0	.455	.500

David West, Phillies — LHP (continued)

Batter	Avg	AB	H	HR	BI	BB	SO	OBP	Slg
Sosa, Sammy	.412	17	7	1	2	2	5	.474	.824
Stanley, Mike	.667	9	6	0	2	1	1	.700	.889
Steinbach, T	.200	5	1	0	0	2	2	.429	.200
Stillwell, K#	.000	4	0	0	0	1	1	.200	.000
Stinnett, K	.000	2	0	0	1	3	2	.500	.000
Tartabull, D	.200	5	1	0	1	2	3	.375	.200
Tettleton, M#	.200	10	2	0	1	3	4	.385	.300
Thomas, Frank	.333	6	2	0	0	1	2	.429	.500
Thompson, Ry	.375	8	3	0	0	1	3	.444	.500
Valle, Dave	.182	11	2	0	1	3	1	.357	.273
Vaughn, Greg	.400	5	2	0	0	1	1	.500	.400
Velarde, R	.400	5	2	0	2	0	1	.400	.400
Ventura, R*	.333	9	3	0	2	4	2	.538	.333
Vizcaino, J#	.333	12	4	0	1	0	2	.333	.333
Vizquel, Omar*	.500	4	2	1	5	1	0	.600	1.250
Walker, Larry*	.286	7	2	0	1	4	1	.583	.429
Wallach, Tim	.091	11	1	0	0	0	1	.091	.091
Webster, L	.000	5	1	0	0	1	0	.333	.400
Weiss, Walt*	.333	6	2	0	0	1	0	.429	.500
White, Devon#	.188	16	3	0	1	0	5	.235	.188
White, R	.125	8	1	0	0	1	1	.222	.250
Whiten, Mark#	.300	10	3	1	2	1	1	.364	.600
Williams, Ma	.167	6	1	1	1	1	1	.286	.667
Worthington	.000	4	0	0	0	1	0	.200	.000
Zeile, Todd	.333	6	2	0	1	0	2	.333	.500

John Wetteland, Yankees — RHP

Batter	Avg	AB	H	HR	BI	BB	SO	OBP	Slg
Alicea, Luis#	.250	4	1	0	0	4	1	.625	.250
Alomar, R#	.353	17	6	0	1	1	4	.368	.353
Alomar Jr, S	.250	4	1	0	1	0	1	.250	.500
Anthony, Eric*	.000	6	0	0	0	0	4	.000	.000
Baerga, C#	.500	8	4	0	2	0	0	.500	.500
Bagwell, Jeff	.000	6	0	0	0	0	2	.000	.000
Barberie, B#	.000	6	0	0	0	0	3	.000	.000
Bell, Jay	.267	15	4	0	3	3	4	.389	.333
Belle, Albert	.333	6	2	0	0	0	1	.333	.667
Belliard, R	.143	7	1	0	0	1	3	.250	.143
Benjamin, M	.000	5	0	0	0	0	2	.000	.000
Berroa, G	.400	5	2	0	0	1	1	.500	.600
Biggio, Craig	.417	12	5	2	6	3	4	.533	.917
Blauser, Jeff	.222	9	2	1	1	1	3	.300	.333
Bonds, Barry*	.250	12	3	1	1	1	3	.357	.583
Bonilla, B#	.176	17	3	1	4	1	4	.222	.353
Branson, Jeff*	.333	6	2	0	0	1	1	.429	.333
Burnitz, J*	.500	6	3	2	4	0	0	.500	1.667
Butler, Brett*	.250	16	4	0	3	4	3	.368	.250
Caminiti, Ken#	.500	10	5	1	2	0	3	.500	.900
Canseco, Jose	.000	7	0	0	0	0	1	.000	.000
Carr, Chuck	.200	5	1	0	1	0	2	.333	.400
Carter, Joe	.125	8	1	1	1	0	3	.125	.500
Cedeno, A	.333	6	2	0	1	0	3	.333	.500
Clark, Dave*	.000	8	0	0	0	2	4	.200	.000
Clark, Will*	.133	15	2	1	1	0	5	.188	.333
Coleman, V#	.143	7	1	0	0	2	4	.333	.143
Daulton, D*	.167	6	1	1	2	3	2	.375	.333
Davis, Eric	.125	8	1	0	1	1	1	.222	.125
Delgado, C*	.000	5	0	0	0	0	2	.000	.000
Devereaux, M	.000	4	0	0	0	1	3	.200	.000
Duncan, M	.625	8	5	0	4	0	1	.667	.875
Dykstra, L*	.000	5	0	0	1	4	2	.444	.000
Eisenreich, J*	.000	4	0	0	0	1	0	.000	.000
Elster, Kevin	.333	9	3	1	4	2	4	.417	.667
Finley, Steve*	.286	7	2	0	0	1	2	.375	.286
Frye, Jeff	.250	4	1	0	1	1	3	.400	.250
Galarraga, A	.333	6	2	1	4	1	1	.429	.833
Gant, Ron	.125	8	1	0	0	2	5	.300	.125
Gates, Brent#	.250	4	1	0	0	1	2	.400	.500
Gilkey, B	.222	9	2	1	2	0	1	.222	.556
Grace, Mark*	.300	10	3	1	2	2	0	.417	.600
Gwynn, Tony*	.267	15	4	1	3	0	2	.267	.467
Hale, Chip*	.500	6	3	0	1	0	0	.500	.500
Harris, Lenny*	.222	9	2	0	1	0	1	.222	.222
Higginson, B*	.167	6	1	1	1	0	3	.167	.667
Hoiles, Chris	.000	5	0	0	0	2	1	.400	.000
Hollins, Dave#	.000	5	0	0	0	2	1	.286	.000
Howard, T*	.250	4	1	0	0	0	1	.250	.250
Hunter, Brian	.200	5	1	0	0	0	4	.200	.200
Javier, Stan#	.200	5	1	0	1	0	2	.200	.200
Jefferies, G#	.154	13	2	0	1	3	3	.313	.231
Jefferson, R*	.000	4	0	0	0	1	2	.000	.000
Jordan, Ricky	.000	4	0	0	1	0	0	.000	.000
Justice, Dave*	.000	4	0	0	1	0	1	.000	.000
Karros, Eric	.286	7	2	0	0	0	0	.286	.286
Kent, Jeff	.200	5	1	0	0	1	0	.200	.200
King, Jeff	.059	17	1	0	1	1	7	.105	.059
Knoblauch, C	.000	4	0	0	0	1	0	.200	.000
Lankford, Ray*	.273	11	3	0	1	1	6	.333	.545
Larkin, Barry	.077	13	1	0	3	0	0	.071	.154
Lemke, Mark#	.200	5	1	0	0	0	1	.200	.400
Lockhart, K*	.333	6	2	0	0	0	0	.333	.333

224

John Wetteland, Yankees — RHP

Batter	Avg	AB	H	HR	BI	BB	SO	OBP	Slg
Lofton, Kenny*	.333	6	2	0	2	1	1	.429	.667
Macfarlane, M	.000	5	0	0	0	0	1	.000	.000
Magadan, Dave*	.400	5	2	0	2	0	1	.400	.600
Martin, Al*	.286	7	2	0	0	0	3	.286	.286
Martinez, Da*	.375	8	3	0	0	1	2	.444	.375
May, Derrick*	.000	10	0	0	0	0	4	.000	.000
McGee, Willie#	.600	5	3	0	2	1	0	.667	.600
McGriff, Fred*	.182	11	2	0	0	0	3	.182	.182
Merced, O*	.250	8	2	0	1	0	1	.250	.250
Mieske, Matt	.000	5	0	0	0	0	2	.000	.000
Mitchell, K	.444	9	4	0	1	3	2	.583	.444
Morandini, M*	.167	6	1	0	0	0	2	.167	.500
Morris, Hal*	.143	7	1	0	1	0	0	.125	.143
Murray, Eddie#	.167	12	2	0	0	1	5	.231	.250
Naehring, Tim	.000	3	0	0	0	2	1	.400	.000
O'Leary, Troy*	.167	6	1	0	2	0	1	.167	.333
O'Neill, Paul*	.143	7	1	0	0	3	0	.400	.286
Offerman, J#	.500	4	2	0	1	2	1	.667	.750
Oliver, Joe	.286	7	2	0	1	2	2	.375	.571
Orsulak, Joe*	.500	6	3	1	4	1	0	.571	1.000
Pagnozzi, Tom	.000	6	0	0	1	1	1	.143	.000
Pendleton, T#	.286	7	2	0	0	0	2	.375	.286
Piazza, Mike	.600	5	3	0	1	0	1	.600	.800
Plantier, P*	.000	4	0	0	0	1	2	.200	.000
Polonia, Luis*	.400	5	2	0	0	0	1	.400	.400
Ramirez, M	.111	9	1	0	0	0	4	.111	.111
Reed, Jeff*	.000	6	0	0	0	0	2	.000	.000
Roberts, Bip#	.217	23	5	0	4	1	4	.250	.217
Sabo, Chris	.091	11	1	0	1	0	1	.091	.182
Samuel, Juan	.200	5	1	0	0	0	2	.200	.200
Sanchez, Rey	.800	5	4	0	0	1	1	.833	.800
Sandberg, R	.100	10	1	0	1	3	1	.308	.100
Sanders, R	.167	6	1	0	1	1	5	.286	.167
Santiago, B	.438	16	7	0	1	1	4	.471	.500
Sheffield, G	.125	8	1	0	0	0	1	.222	.125
Slaught, Don	.143	7	1	0	1	0	2	.143	.286
Smith, Dwight*	.000	8	0	0	0	3	0	.000	.000
Smith, Ozzie#	.556	9	5	0	2	2	1	.636	.556
Sosa, Sammy	.000	6	0	0	1	1	3	.125	.000
Sprague, Ed	.222	9	2	1	1	0	4	.222	.667
Strawberry, D*	.429	7	3	0	1	1	3	.500	.714
Surhoff, B.J.*	.000	5	0	0	0	1	2	.167	.000
Taubensee, E*	.000	5	0	0	0	0	0	.000	.000
Thome, Jim*	.250	4	1	0	2	0	1	.200	.750
Thompson, Mil*	.333	9	3	0	1	3	0	.455	.333
Thompson, Rob	.231	13	3	0	0	1	6	.286	.231
Vina, F*	.167	6	1	0	0	0	1	.167	.167
Wallach, Tim	.333	6	2	0	1	0	0	.333	.500
Weiss, Walt	.200	5	1	0	0	0	2	.200	.200
Whiten, Mark#	.111	9	1	0	0	2	4	.273	.333
Wilkins, Rick*	.111	9	1	0	0	1	5	.200	.111
Williams, Ma	.333	18	6	1	4	1	6	.368	.556
Zeile, Todd	.231	13	3	1	2	0	2	.231	.462

Wally Whitehurst, Yankees — RHP

Batter	Avg	AB	H	HR	BI	BB	SO	OBP	Slg
Alicea, Luis#	.333	6	2	0	0	0	1	.333	.667
Alou, Moises	.500	10	5	0	2	0	0	.500	.700
Anthony, Eric*	.125	8	1	0	2	2	1	.300	.125
Bagwell, Jeff	.200	10	2	0	2	0	1	.200	.200
Barberie, B#	.250	8	2	0	0	3	1	.455	.625
Bell, Jay	.667	9	6	0	1	0	0	.667	1.000
Belliard, R	.273	11	3	0	1	0	3	.273	.273
Berry, Sean	.714	7	5	0	1	1	0	.667	.857
Bichette, D	.000	6	0	0	0	0	0	.000	.000
Biggio, Craig	.438	16	7	0	1	1	2	.471	.563
Blauser, Jeff	.200	10	2	0	0	2	1	.333	.200
Bogar, Tim	.200	5	1	0	0	0	1	.200	.200
Bonds, Barry*	.600	10	6	2	3	4	0	.714	1.200
Bonilla, B#	.250	12	3	1	1	1	1	.308	.500
Burnitz, J*	.143	7	1	0	0	1	3	.250	.143
Butler, Brett*	.316	19	6	0	0	1	3	.350	.316
Caminiti, Ken#	.214	14	3	0	2	0	2	.200	.286
Candaele, C#	.250	4	1	0	1	1	0	.400	.250
Carr, Chuck	.250	8	2	0	1	1	1	.333	.250
Cedeno, A	.143	7	1	0	1	1	2	.250	.429
Clark, Will*	.250	12	3	0	2	1	2	.308	.333
Clayton, R	.143	7	1	0	1	0	0	.250	.143
Coleman, V#	.000	5	0	0	1	0	1	.000	.000
Conine, Jeff	.400	5	2	0	3	2	2	.571	.400
Cordero, Wil	.125	8	1	0	2	0	4	.125	.125
Dascenzo, D#	.286	7	2	0	0	0	1	.286	.286
Daulton, D*	.333	9	3	2	3	0	3	.333	1.000
Davis, Eric	.333	9	3	0	3	0	1	.333	.444
Dawson, Andre	.400	15	6	2	6	1	1	.412	.867
DeShields, B*	.188	16	3	0	1	1	3	.235	.313
Duncan, M	.333	9	3	0	1	0	1	.333	.333
Dunston, S	.333	12	4	0	0	0	2	.333	.417
Dykstra, L*	.333	9	3	1	1	1	0	.400	.667
Finley, Steve*	.182	11	2	0	1	0	0	.182	.182
Fletcher, D*	.300	10	3	0	0	1	1	.364	.300

Wally Whitehurst, Yankees — RHP

Batter	Avg	AB	H	HR	BI	BB	SO	OBP	Slg
Floyd, Cliff*	.429	7	3	1	1	1	0	.500	1.000
Galarraga, A	.111	18	2	0	0	0	3	.158	.111
Gant, Ron	.263	19	5	2	7	0	3	.263	.632
Gilkey, B	.250	8	2	0	0	0	0	.333	.375
Gonzalez, L*	.200	10	2	0	0	1	1	.273	.400
Grace, Mark*	.310	29	9	0	3	2	0	.375	.379
Grissom, M	.286	21	6	1	4	0	1	.286	.476
Gwynn, Chris*	.167	6	1	0	0	0	2	.167	.167
Gwynn, Tony*	.500	8	4	0	1	0	0	.500	.625
Harris, Lenny*	.125	8	1	0	0	0	1	.125	.125
Hayes, C	.357	14	5	0	2	1	2	.400	.429
Hollins, Dave#	.300	10	3	0	2	1	3	.364	.400
Hundley, Todd#	.750	4	3	1	2	0	0	.833	1.500
Javier, Stan#	.000	7	0	0	0	0	1	.000	.000
Jefferies, G#	.571	7	4	0	0	0	1	.571	.571
Jordan, Brian	.000	5	0	0	1	0	1	.167	.000
Justice, Dave*	.267	15	4	1	2	2	4	.353	.467
Karros, Eric	.364	11	4	0	0	0	1	.364	.455
Kelly, R	.500	4	2	0	1	0	1	.400	.500
Kent, Jeff	.625	8	5	0	3	0	0	.625	1.000
King, Jeff	.100	10	1	0	1	0	2	.100	.300
Lankford, Ray*	.235	17	4	1	1	4	5	.381	.471
Lansing, Mike	.200	10	2	0	0	0	0	.200	.200
Larkin, Barry	.316	19	6	1	5	0	1	.316	.474
Lemke, Mark#	.500	10	5	0	0	3	0	.615	.900
Lewis, Darren	.200	15	3	0	1	1	1	.250	.200
Manwaring, K	.375	8	3	0	1	1	0	.444	.375
Martinez, Da*	.182	11	2	0	1	0	2	.182	.273
May, Derrick*	.400	20	8	0	3	0	2	.400	.450
McGee, Willie#	.143	7	1	0	2	1	2	.250	.143
McGriff, Fred*	.375	8	3	0	2	2	3	.500	.500
Mitchell, K	.500	12	6	0	3	0	1	.500	.500
Morandini, M*	.125	8	1	0	0	1	3	.222	.125
Morris, Hal*	.400	15	6	0	1	0	2	.400	.533
Murray, Eddie#	.200	10	2	1	2	0	1	.200	.500
Nixon, Otis#	.267	15	4	0	3	2	3	.333	.333
O'Neill, Paul*	.500	8	4	0	2	2	1	.600	.625
Offerman, J#	.273	11	3	0	2	3	3	.429	.273
Oliver, Joe	.400	5	2	0	2	0	1	.400	.600
Pagnozzi, Tom	.300	10	3	0	1	2	2	.462	.500
Pena, G#	.222	9	2	0	0	0	3	.222	.222
Pendleton, T#	.348	23	8	0	3	1	7	.375	.478
Piazza, Mike	.400	5	2	2	4	0	0	.429	1.600
Reed, Jeff*	.273	11	3	0	1	0	2	.273	.364
Reed, Jody	.400	5	2	0	0	0	0	.333	.400
Roberts, Bip#	.000	12	0	0	1	0	3	.000	.000
Sabo, Chris	.200	15	3	0	1	0	3	.200	.200
Sanchez, Rey	.235	17	4	0	1	0	2	.235	.294
Sandberg, R	.464	28	13	2	8	2	3	.500	.964
Sanders, R	.250	4	1	0	0	1	2	.400	.250
Santiago, B	.273	11	3	0	1	1	1	.333	.273
Servais, S	.167	6	1	0	0	0	1	.167	.167
Sheffield, G	.556	9	5	2	5	1	0	.600	1.444
Slaught, Don	.500	6	3	0	4	0	0	.500	.667
Smith, Dwight*	.333	12	4	0	1	1	3	.385	.500
Smith, Ozzie#	.368	19	7	0	2	1	0	.400	.368
Sosa, Sammy	.500	10	5	2	4	1	2	.545	1.200
Strawberry, D*	.000	8	0	0	0	1	0	.000	.000
Thompson, Mil*	.429	7	3	0	0	2	1	.556	.571
Thompson, Rob	.100	10	1	0	1	2	1	.182	.100
Vizcaino, J#	.250	12	3	0	1	2	2	.333	.333
Walker, Larry*	.000	18	0	0	0	0	7	.000	.000
Wallach, Tim	.227	22	5	2	4	1	4	.261	.500
Walton, J	.333	9	3	0	0	0	3	.333	.333
Weiss, Walt#	.800	5	4	0	0	1	0	.833	.800
Whiten, Mark#	.143	7	1	0	0	0	2	.143	.143
Wilkins, Rick*	.375	8	3	2	4	2	2	.438	.857
Williams, Ma	.333	15	5	1	2	0	3	.313	.600
Zeile, Todd	.143	21	3	0	1	0	3	.182	.143

Matt Whiteside, Rangers — RHP

Batter	Avg	AB	H	HR	BI	BB	SO	OBP	Slg
Alomar, R#	.429	7	3	0	1	0	0	.429	.429
Amaral, Rich	.200	5	1	0	2	0	1	.200	.200
Baerga, C#	.167	6	1	0	0	0	0	.167	.167
Belle, Albert	.400	5	2	0	0	0	0	.400	.400
Berroa, G	.444	9	4	0	2	2	2	.545	.444
Blowers, Mike	.125	8	1	0	1	2	3	.300	.125
Boggs, Wade*	.286	7	2	0	1	1	1	.375	.429
Borders, Pat	.286	7	2	0	1	1	1	.375	.429
Bordick, Mike	.421	19	8	0	1	2	1	.476	.421
Bournigal, R	.500	4	2	0	1	0	0	.500	1.000
Brosius, S	.250	8	2	1	1	2	1	.400	.750
Buhner, Jay	.214	14	3	0	1	2	3	.313	.214
Carter, Joe	.222	9	2	0	0	1	0	.222	.222
Coleman, V#	.600	5	3	0	0	1	0	.600	.600
Cora, Joey*	.143	7	1	0	0	0	0	.143	.143
Curtis, Chad	.000	5	0	0	0	0	0	.000	.000
Davis, Chili*	.429	7	3	0	2	1	0	.500	.571
Devereaux, M	.167	6	1	0	0	0	1	.167	.167
Diaz, Alex#	.000	3	0	0	0	1	1	.250	.000

Matt Whiteside, Rangers — RHP

Batter	Avg	AB	H	HR	BI	BB	SO	OBP	Slg
DiSarcina, G	.333	9	3	0	2	0	0	.333	.333
Fermin, Felix	.375	8	3	0	1	0	0	.375	.375
Fielder, C	.077	13	1	1	2	1	5	.143	.308
Fryman, T	.429	14	6	2	5	0	3	.429	.929
Gagne, Greg	.333	6	2	1	2	0	2	.333	.833
Gallego, Mike	.375	8	3	1	3	0	2	.375	.750
Gates, Brent#	.556	9	5	1	2	0	1	.556	.889
Giambi, Jason*	.167	6	1	0	3	2	0	.375	.167
Gomez, Chris	.000	4	0	0	1	0	0	.000	.000
Griffey Jr, K*	.571	7	4	2	4	1	0	.625	1.714
Henderson, R	.125	8	1	0	0	2	2	.300	.125
Herrera, Jose*	.400	5	2	0	0	0	0	.400	.400
Jaha, John	.000	4	0	0	0	2	0	.333	.000
Javier, Stan#	.000	0	0	0	0	3	0	.000	.000
Joyner, Wally*	.500	6	3	0	0	0	1	.500	.667
Kelly, Pat	.375	8	3	0	0	2	2	.500	.500
Knoblauch, L	.167	12	2	0	0	0	0	.167	.250
Kreuter, Chad#	.000	3	0	0	0	2	1	.400	.000
Leyritz, Jim	.333	9	3	0	0	0	3	.333	.333
Martinez, E	.400	10	4	1	1	3	0	.538	.700
Martinez, T*	.545	11	6	0	5	1	1	.583	.636
McCarty, Dave	.400	5	2	0	0	0	1	.400	.400
McGwire, Mark	.182	11	2	1	0	1	3	.250	.182
Meares, Pat	.400	5	2	0	1	1	1	.500	.600
Molitor, Paul	.200	5	1	1	2	1	1	.429	.800
Munoz, Pedro	.444	9	4	1	2	2	3	.545	.778
Paquette, C	.000	5	0	0	0	0	1	.000	.000
Pena, Tony	.200	5	1	0	1	0	0	.200	.200
Phillips, T#	.286	7	2	0	0	3	2	.500	.429
Polonia, Luis*	.200	5	1	0	0	0	0	.200	.200
Ramirez, M	.000	4	0	0	0	1	1	.000	.000
Ripken, Cal	.200	5	1	0	0	1	0	.333	.200
Salmon, Tim	.333	6	2	1	1	2	2	.500	.833
Schofield, D	.200	5	1	0	0	1	1	.200	.200
Seitzer, K	.200	5	1	0	0	1	0	.333	.200
Sierra, Ruben#	.286	7	2	0	0	0	1	.286	.286
Snow, J.T.#	.000	5	0	0	0	1	1	.167	.000
Sojo, Luis	.286	7	2	0	1	0	1	.286	.286
Sorrento, P*	.143	7	1	0	0	0	1	.143	.143
Sprague, Ed	.444	9	4	0	1	0	1	.444	.556
Stanley, Mike	.100	10	1	0	0	0	2	.100	.100
Steinbach, T	.250	12	3	0	3	0	3	.250	.250
Tartabull, D	.429	7	3	1	3	0	2	.429	1.143
Tettleton, M#	.500	4	2	0	1	0	0	.600	.500
Thomas, Frank	.500	6	3	1	3	1	1	.571	1.167
Trammell, A	.000	8	0	0	0	1	0	.000	.000
Vaughn, Greg	.250	4	1	0	0	1	0	.400	.250
Velarde, R	.000	6	0	0	0	1	3	.143	.000
Vizquel, Omar#	.222	9	2	0	0	0	1	.222	.222
Ward, Turner#	.500	4	2	0	0	1	0	.600	.500
White, Devon#	.000	5	0	0	0	0	2	.000	.000
Williams, Ber#	.429	7	3	0	1	0	2	.556	.429
Williams, Ger	.167	6	1	1	2	1	1	.286	.667
Wilson, Dan	.357	14	5	1	3	1	2	.400	.643
Young, Ernie	.333	6	2	0	0	1	0	.333	.333

Kevin Wickander, Brewers — LHP

Batter	Avg	AB	H	HR	BI	BB	SO	OBP	Slg
Baines, H*	.400	5	2	0	4	0	0	.333	.400
Boggs, Wade*	.333	6	2	0	3	2	2	.444	.333
Borders, Pat	.400	5	2	0	0	0	1	.400	.400
Eisenreich, J*	.500	4	2	0	1	0	1	.400	.750
Gonzalez, J	.200	5	1	0	2	0	1	.200	.200
Griffey Jr, K*	.143	7	1	1	1	2	2	.333	.571
Hollins, Dave*	.400	5	2	0	0	0	1	.400	.400
Johnson, L*	.500	4	2	0	0	2	0	.667	.500
Martinez, Da*	.250	4	1	0	2	1	0	.400	.250
Martinez, T*	.600	5	3	0	4	2	1	.714	.800
Olerud, John*	.500	6	3	0	0	2	0	.625	.500
Palmeiro, R*	.333	6	2	0	1	1	0	.429	.333
Palmer, Dean	.250	4	1	0	0	1	2	.400	.250
Rodriguez, I	.200	5	1	0	1	0	1	.200	.200
Sierra, Ruben#	.200	5	1	1	2	1	0	.286	.800
Tartabull, D	.333	6	2	0	1	1	1	.429	.500
Thomas, Frank	.500	4	2	0	1	2	1	.667	.500
Valle, Dave	.400	5	2	0	0	0	0	.400	.400
Vaughn, Mo*	.200	5	1	0	1	0	1	.333	.200
Ventura, R*	.250	4	1	0		4	1	.625	.250

Bob Wickman, Brewers — RHP

Batter	Avg	AB	H	HR	BI	BB	SO	OBP	Slg
Aldrete, Mike*	.375	8	3	1	1	1	3	.444	.750
Alicea, Luis#	.667	3	2	0	0	1	0	.750	.667
Alomar, R#	.400	10	4	0	2	1	1	.455	.500
Alomar Jr, S	.125	8	1	0	0	0	3	.125	.125
Amaral, Rich	.286	7	2	0	1	1	2	.375	.429
Anderson, Brd*	.091	11	1	0	0	2	2	.231	.091
Baerga, C#	.222	9	2	0	3	0	1	.200	.222
Baines, H*	.286	7	2	0	1	2	2	.444	.429
Becker, Rich*	.286	7	2	0	0	1	0	.286	.286
Belle, Albert	.429	14	6	1	6	3	4	.500	.714

Bob Wickman, Brewers — RHP

Batter	Avg	AB	H	HR	BI	BB	SO	OBP	Slg
Berroa, G	.222	9	2	1	2	0	4	.222	.556
Bonilla, B#	.000	5	0	0	0	0	1	.000	.000
Borders, Pat	.000	12	0	0	1	0	1	.000	.000
Bordick, Mike	.176	17	3	1	3	3	5	.364	.353
Brosius, S	.250	8	2	1	1	2	0	.400	.625
Buhner, Jay	.222	9	2	0	3	1	1	.273	.444
Burks, Ellis	.250	4	1	0	1	0	0	.400	.250
Canseco, Jose	.250	8	2	0	2	2	2	.400	.375
Carter, Joe	.300	10	3	0	1	1	2	.333	.300
Cirillo, Jeff	.111	9	1	0	0	0	3	.111	.111
Cora, Joey#	.400	5	2	0	0	2	0	.571	.400
Cordova,	.375	8	3	0	2	0	1	.375	.500
Curtis, Chad	.444	9	4	0	1	0	1	.455	.556
Cuyler, Milt#	.200	5	1	0	0	1	1	.333	.200
Davis, Chili*	.182	11	2	0	1	4	3	.400	.273
Devereaux, M	.300	10	3	0	1	0	1	.364	.400
DiSarcina, G	.333	9	3	0	2	0	2	.333	.333
Easley, D	.400	5	2	0	3	1	0	.429	.400
Edmonds, Jim*	.250	4	1	0	0	1	1	.400	.250
Fabregas, Jor*	.400	5	2	0	1	0	0	.400	.400
Fermin, Felix	.000	5	0	0	0	1	1	.167	.000
Fielder, C	.333	15	5	0	2	3	2	.444	.400
Franco, Julio	.333	6	2	0	3	2	1	.500	.667
Frye, Jeff	.000	4	0	0	1	1	1	.200	.000
Fryman, T	.353	17	6	0	5	1	2	.389	.647
Gaetti, Gary	.200	5	1	0	1	0	2	.200	.200
Gagne, Greg	.222	9	2	0	2	1	1	.300	.333
Gates, Brent#	.417	12	5	0	2	0	1	.417	.500
Gomez, Chris	.000	6	0	0	0	1	2	.143	.000
Gomez, Leo	.462	13	6	0	3	1	0	.500	.538
Gonzalez, J	.235	17	4	1	4	0	4	.278	.529
Goodwin, Tom*	.000	4	0	0	0	0	0	.000	.000
Greenwell, M*	.167	6	1	0	0	2	1	.375	.167
Greer, Rusty*	.333	6	2	0	1	2	1	.500	.667
Griffey Jr, K*	.500	6	3	1	2	2	1	.625	1.000
Guillen, O*	.250	12	3	0	3	1	1	.308	.250
Hale, Chip*	.364	11	4	0	1	1	1	.417	.364
Hamilton, D*	.167	12	2	0	2	2	0	.267	.167
Hammonds, J	.400	5	2	0	0	1	1	.400	.600
Henderson, R	.200	10	2	0	1	6	1	.500	.200
Higginson, B*	.333	6	2	1	2	2	1	.500	.833
Hoiles, Chris	.500	12	6	2	3	3	3	.588	1.000
Howard, Dave#	.429	7	3	0	0	0	2	.429	.571
Hudler, Rex	.286	7	2	1	2	0	4	.286	.714
Jaha, John	.308	13	4	0	0	0	4	.308	.308
Javier, Stan#	.143	7	1	0	1	0	0	.143	.143
Johnson, L*	.273	11	3	0	3	0	1	.273	.455
Joyner, Wally*	.333	9	3	0	1	0	1	.333	.333
Karkovice, R	.200	10	2	0	1	2	4	.333	.300
Kirby, Wayne*	.250	4	1	0	0	2	0	.500	.250
Knoblauch, C	.333	18	6	0	1	6	0	.500	.333
Leius, Scott	.167	6	1	0	1	4	0	.500	.167
Listach, Pat#	.250	8	2	0	0	0	3	.250	.250
Livingstone*	.400	5	2	0	0	1	1	.400	.600
Lofton, Kenny*	.200	5	1	0		3	0	.500	.200
Macfarlane, M	.200	5	1	0	3	0	3	.500	.200
Martinez, Da*	.400	5	2	0	0	0	1	.400	.400
Martinez, E	.556	9	5	0	6	1	0	.600	.889
Martinez, T*	.600	5	3	1	4	1	0	.667	1.600
Mayne, Brent*	.000	7	0	0	1	0	0	.000	.000
McCarty, Dave	.167	6	1	0	0	1	1	.167	.167
McGwire, Mark	.000	7	0	0	0	2	2	.300	.000
McLemore, M#	.250	20	5	0	3	2	1	.318	.250
McRae, Brian#	.429	7	3	0	1	2	0	.556	.571
Meares, Pat	.583	12	7	0	5	2	0	.643	.750
Molitor, Paul	.278	18	5	0	3	1	3	.316	.333
Munoz, Pedro	.400	10	4	0	0	0	2	.455	.400
Murray, Eddie#	.143	7	1	0	0	0	2	.143	.143
Myers, Greg*	.400	5	2	0	1	0	1	.400	.600
Naehring, Tim	.429	7	3	0	1	1	1	.500	.429
Nieves, M#	.200	5	1	0	1	0	3	.333	.200
Nilsson, Dave*	.500	8	4	1	3	0	0	.500	.875
Nixon, Otis#	.000	4	0	0	1	1	1	.200	.000
O'Leary, Troy*	.500	6	3	0	1	1	1	.571	.500
Olerud, John*	.556	9	5	0	2	2	0	.636	1.000
Oliver, Joe	.200	5	1	0	0	2	0	.200	.400
Palmeiro, R*	1.000	6	6	1	2	0	0	1.000	1.500
Palmer, Dean	.273	11	3	0	2	1	2	.357	.364
Paquette, C	.125	8	1	0	0	0	3	.222	.125
Pena, Tony	.250	4	1	0	0	1	0	.400	.250
Phillips, T#	.375	8	3	0	0	6	0	.643	.375
Raines, Tim#	.333	9	3	0	0	2	0	.455	.556
Ramirez, M	.364	11	4	0	1	1	2	.417	.364
Ripken, Cal	.095	21	2	0	2	1	4	.136	.095
Rodriguez, Al	.400	5	2	0	0	1	0	.400	.400
Rodriguez, I	.357	14	5	0	0	1	1	.400	.357
Salmon, Tim	.300	10	3	1	2	0	1	.300	.600
Segui, David#	.286	7	2	0	4	0	1	.286	.571
Seitzer, K	.100	20	2	1	1	1	4	.143	.095
Sierra, Ruben#	.235	17	4	0	1	2	1	.316	.353
Sorrento, P*	.500	4	2	0	2	0	0	.600	.500

Batter	Avg	AB	H	HR	BI	BB	SO	OBP	Slg
Spiers, Bill*	.000	4	0	0	0	0	1	.200	.000
Sprague, Ed	.077	13	1	1	4	1	2	.143	.308
Steinbach, T	.211	19	4	1	1	1	5	.250	.368
Strange, Doug#	.000	6	0	0	0	0	1	.000	.000
Surhoff, B.J.*	.333	12	4	0	0	0	0	.333	.333
Sveum, Dale#	.000	4	0	0	1	0	0	.000	.000
Tettleton, M#	.400	15	6	3	7	5	3	.550	1.000
Thomas, Frank	.333	15	5	1	5	2	0	.400	.600
Thome, Jim*	.167	6	1	0	0	1	1	.286	.333
Tinsley, Lee#	.250	8	2	0	1	1	0	.333	.375
Trammell, A	.222	9	2	0	0	0	0	.222	.222
Valentin, Jhn	.375	8	3	1	4	1	1	.400	1.000
Vaughn, Greg	.133	15	2	1	2	0	4	.133	.333
Vaughn, Mo*	.556	9	5	1	3	1	1	.636	1.222
Ventura, R*	.100	10	1	0	3	2	0	.250	.100
Vizquel, Omar#	.333	9	3	0	0	1	1	.333	.333
Walbeck, Matt#	.143	7	1	0	0	1	2	.250	.286
Webster, L	.400	5	2	1	1	0	0	.400	1.000
White, Devon#	.444	9	4	0	1	0	1	.444	.667
Williams, E	.200	5	1	0	1	0	1	.200	.200

Batter	Avg	AB	H	HR	BI	BB	SO	OBP	Slg
Bell, Derek	.200	5	1	0	0	1	0	.333	.200
Berry, Sean	.400	5	2	0	2	0	0	.400	.600
Bichette, D	.250	4	1	0	1	1	2	.400	.250
Colbrunn, G	.800	5	4	0	1	0	1	.800	1.000
Conine, Jeff	.500	4	2	0	1	1	0	.600	.500
Karros, Eric	.000	4	0	0	1	0	1	.000	.000

Batter	Avg	AB	H	HR	BI	BB	SO	OBP	Slg
Alicea, Luis#	.500	4	2	0	0	1	1	.667	.500
Alou, Moises	.500	6	3	0	0	1	0	.571	.500
Anderson, Brd*	.286	7	2	0	1	0	1	.286	.429
Anderson, G*	.200	5	1	0	0	0	0	.200	.200
Baerga, C#	.000	6	0	0	1	0	0	.000	.000
Batiste, Kim	.667	6	4	0	1	0	1	.667	.667
Bell, Derek	.286	7	2	0	1	1	1	.375	.286
Bell, Jay	.250	8	2	0	1	1	3	.455	.250
Belle, Albert	.286	7	2	2	6	0	2	.375	1.143
Belliard, R	.250	4	1	0	0	1	1	.400	.250
Berry, Sean	.167	6	1	0	1	1	2	.250	.167
Bichette, D	.714	7	5	0	2	0	0	.714	.714
Biggio, Craig	.167	6	1	0	1	0	5	.167	.167
Blauser, Jeff	.333	6	2	1	2	1	3	.429	.833
Boggs, Wade*	.400	5	2	0	0	0	0	.400	.400
Bonds, Barry*	.455	11	5	0	1	3	3	.571	.545
Bonilla, B#	.500	8	4	2	6	1	1	.556	1.250
Boone, Bret	.222	9	2	0	2	0	1	.222	.333
Bournigal, R	.400	5	2	0	2	0	0	.400	.600
Brumfield, J	.400	5	2	0	1	1	1	.500	.600
Butler, Brett*	.250	8	2	1	2	2	0	.455	.750
Canseco, Jose	.500	4	2	1	3	2	1	.667	1.250
Carter, Joe	.250	4	1	0	1	1	1	.400	.250
Castilla, V	.500	4	2	0	1	1	1	.600	1.000
Cirillo, Jeff	.400	5	2	0	3	0	0	.333	.400
Clark, Will*	.412	17	7	2	4	1	3	.444	.824
Clayton, R	.167	6	1	0	0	1	3	.286	.333
Cole, Alex*	.333	9	3	0	1	0	1	.333	.556
Cordero, Wil	.214	14	3	0	0	1	1	.267	.357
Cordova, M	.250	4	1	0	0	2	2	.500	.500
Daulton, D*	.100	10	1	0	1	4	3	.357	.100
Davis, Chili#	.500	4	2	0	0	1	0	.600	.500
DeShields, D*	.600	5	3	0	2	1	0	.750	.800
Devereaux, M	.000	4	0	0	1	1	0	.200	.000
Duncan, M	.250	20	5	0	3	0	4	.250	.350
Dunston, S	.250	4	1	0	0	1	0	.400	.250
Dykstra, L*	.300	10	3	0	0	1	0	.364	.400
Eisenreich, J	.286	7	2	0	0	1	1	.286	.286
Elster, Kevin	.286	7	2	0	0	0	0	.286	.429
Fletcher, D*	.600	5	3	0	1	0	0	.600	.600
Floyd, Cliff*	.333	6	2	0	1	0	1	.333	.500
Franco, Julio	.000	4	0	0	0	2	2	.333	.000
Frye, Jeff	.333	3	1	0	1	2	1	.667	.333
Galarraga, R	.143	7	1	0	1	2	0	.400	.143
Gant, Ron	.250	8	2	0	0	2	2	.400	.375
Garcia, C	.250	4	1	0	0	1	2	.400	.250
Giambi, Jason*	.500	4	2	0	1	1	0	.600	.750
Gilkey, B	.333	9	3	0	1	0	0	.400	.333
Girardi, Joe	.333	6	2	1	4	3	1	.556	.833
Gonzalez, J	.143	7	1	0	0	1	2	.250	.429
Grace, Mark*	.583	12	7	0	4	6	0	.722	.750
Greer, Rusty*	.400	5	2	1	2	2	1	.571	1.000
Grissom, M	.125	8	1	0	0	1	4	.385	.125
Gwynn, Tony*	.250	8	2	1	3	1	1	.333	.625
Hamilton, D*	.500	8	2	1	3	1	1	.333	.778
Hansen, Dave*	.857	7	6	1	4	2	0	.889	1.571
Harris, Lenny*	.000	5	0	0	1	0	0	.167	.000
Hayes, C	.250	8	2	0	1	1	1	.333	.375
Hernandez, Ca	.000	5	0	0	0	0	1	.000	.000

Batter	Avg	AB	H	HR	BI	BB	SO	OBP	Slg
Hernandez, Jo	.250	4	1	0	1	1	0	.400	.250
Hollins, Dave#	.273	11	3	0	1	1	2	.333	.364
Howell, Jack*	.125	8	1	0	2	0	0	.125	.125
Hundley, Todd#	.200	5	1	0	2	0	0	.200	.400
Incaviglia, P	.167	6	1	1	2	0	3	.167	.667
Jaha, John	.250	4	1	0	0	1	3	.500	.250
Javier, Stan#	.571	7	4	0	1	1	0	.625	.714
Jefferies, G#	.571	14	8	1	4	3	1	.647	1.000
Jefferson, R*	.500	4	2	1	1	1	1	.600	1.250
Jeter, Derek	.333	3	1	0	3	1	0	.400	.333
Jordan, Ricky	.125	8	1	0	2	0	0	.125	.250
Justice, Dave*	.154	13	2	1	3	0	3	.154	.385
Karros, Eric	.000	7	0	0	0	2	1	.222	.000
Kelly, R	.250	4	1	0	2	0	1	.200	.500
Kent, Jeff	.250	4	1	0	1	1	1	.500	.500
King, Jeff	.167	6	1	1	1	3	1	.444	.667
Knoblauch, C	.250	4	1	0	0	1	0	.400	.250
Lankford, Ray*	.200	15	3	1	2	3	5	.333	.400
Lansing, Mike	.200	10	2	0	0	2	1	.385	.200
Larkin, Barry	.471	17	8	0	5	3	3	.550	.471
Lawton, Matt*	.167	6	1	0	1	0	0	.167	.167
Lemke, Mark*	.250	4	1	0	0	2	0	.400	.250
Levis, Jesse*	.250	4	1	0	2	2	0	.500	.250
Lewis, Darren	.400	10	4	0	1	1	0	.455	.500
Lofton, Kenny*	.167	6	1	0	0	0	2	.375	.167
Magadan, Dave*	.500	4	2	0	0	3	1	.714	.500
Manwaring, K	.300	10	3	0	0	2	1	.417	.400
Martinez, Da*	.500	10	5	0	1	1	0	.545	.600
Martinez, T*	.250	4	1	0	0	1	1	.400	.250
May, Derrick*	.167	12	2	0	2	1	4	.231	.250
McGriff, Fred*	.250	8	2	2	3	0		.455	1.000
McLemore, M#	.500	4	2	0	0	2	0	.667	.750
Meares, Pat	.167	6	1	0	1	0	1	.143	.167
Merced, O*	.364	11	4	0	1	1	2	.417	.545
Miller, Orl	.000	5	0	0	0	0	2	.000	.000
Mitchell, K	.000	3	0	0	0	3	0	.571	.000
Molitor, Paul	.000	4	0	0	1	1	1	.200	.000
Mondesi, Raul	.286	7	2	0	0	1	1	.286	.286
Morandini, M*	.444	9	4	0	1	0	0	.500	.444
Morris, Hal*	.438	16	7	0	5	1	1	.471	.625
Murray, Eddie*	.375	8	3	1	2	1	1	.444	.875
Myers, Greg*	.250	4	1	0	2	1	2	.400	.250
Nilsson, Dave*	.167	6	1	0	0	0	2	.167	.167
Nixon, Otis#	.444	9	4	0	0	1	2	.500	.556
O'Leary, Troy*	.500	4	2	0	0	1	0	.600	1.000
O'Neill, Paul*	.300	10	3	0	3	1	0	.364	.400
Offerman, J#	.222	9	2	0	0	4	1	.462	.222
Oliver, Joe	.200	10	2	0	0	1	0	.200	.300
Pagnozzi, Tom	.100	10	1	0	0	0	0	.100	.200
Palmeiro, R*	.333	6	2	1	3	1	1	.429	.833
Palmer, Dean	.000	6	0	0	0	1	0	.143	.000
Parent, Mark	.750	4	3	0	0	1	1	.800	.750
Pena, G#	.100	10	1	0	0	0	2	.100	.200
Pendleton, T#	.571	14	8	1	7	0	3	.571	.857
Piazza, Mike	.222	9	2	1	2	0	2	.222	.556
Plantier, P*	.286	7	2	0	1	2	3	.444	.429
Ramirez, M	.333	6	2	0	1	1	0	.429	.667
Reb*oulet, J	1.000	2	2	0	1	3	0	1.000	1.500
Ripken, Cal	.333	6	2	0	0	1	2	.333	.833
Roberts, Bip#	.467	15	7	0	1	3	2	.556	.467
Rodriguez, H*	.400	5	2	0	0	1	0	.500	.600
Rodriguez, I	.000	10	0	0	2	1	0	.091	.000
Sabo, Chris	.000	4	0	0	1	1	2	.167	.000
Salmon, Tim	.000	4	0	0	0	1	1	.200	.000
Sanchez, Rey	.462	13	6	0	1	1	0	.500	.538
Sandberg, R	.333	9	3	0	2	2	0	.455	.556
Sanders, R	.667	12	8	2	5	2	2	.714	1.333
Santiago, B	.444	9	4	1	2	0	0	.444	.778
Scarsone, S	.000	6	0	0	1	0	3	.000	.000
Segui, David*	.333	3	1	0	0	1	0	.500	.333
Sheffield, G	.571	7	4	2	5	0	0	.571	1.571
Shipley, C	.333	6	2	0	0	0	1	.333	.333
Sierra, Ruben#	.400	5	2	1	1	0	0	.400	1.000
Slaught, Don	.500	4	2	0	0	0	1	.600	.500
Smith, Ozzie#	.167	6	1	0	0	2	0	.375	.167
Snow, J.T.#	.600	5	3	0	2	0	0	.600	.800
Sosa, Sammy	.182	11	2	0	3	2	3	.286	.182
Sprague, Ed	.400	5	2	1	2	1	0	.400	1.000
Stahoviak, S*	.167	6	1	0	0	2	0	.167	.333
Stanley, Mike	.333	3	1	0	1	0	0	.500	.333
Stillwell, K#	.000	6	0	0	1	0	0	.000	.000
Stocker, K#	.000	5	0	0	1	0	0	.167	.000
Tettleton, M#	.600	5	3	1	1	0	0	.667	1.200
Thome, Jim*	.800	5	4	1	2	2	0	.857	1.600
Thompson, Mil*	.250	4	1	0	1	1	0	.400	.250
Thompson, Rob	.333	9	3	1	2	0	1	.333	.778
Thompson, Ry	.000	5	0	0	0	1	0	.000	.000
Valentin, Jhn	.600	5	3	1	1	1	1	.571	1.200
Valentin, Jse#	1.000	5	5	0	2	1	0	1.000	1.000
Vaughn, Greg	.000	6	0	0	0	1	0	.000	.000
Vaughn, Mo*	.333	3	1	0	0	2	1	.667	.333

Brian Williams, Tigers — RHP

Batter	Avg	AB	H	HR	BI	BB	SO	OBP	Slg
Velarde, R	.200	5	1	0	0	0	1	.200	.200
Vina, F*	.444	9	4	0	1	2	2	.545	.444
Vizcaino, J#	.364	11	4	1	4	1	2	.417	.636
Vizquel, Omar#	.400	5	2	0	0	1	0	.500	.400
Walker, Larry*	.222	9	2	0	1	0	2	.222	.222
Wallach, Tim	.333	6	2	0	1	1	2	.429	.333
Weiss, Walt#	.250	4	1	0	1	2	0	.500	.250
Whiten, Mark#	.667	9	6	1	4	1	1	.700	1.111
Wilkins, Rick*	.250	8	2	0	1	1	4	.333	.250
Williams, Ber#	.667	6	4	0	1	1	1	.714	1.500
Williams, Ger	.250	4	1	0	1	6	1	.286	.250
Williams, Ma	.364	11	4	1	3	0	2	.417	.636
Young, Eric	.429	7	3	0	0	1	0	.500	.714
Young, Kevin	.600	5	3	0	5	1	1	.500	1.000
Zeile, Todd	.500	16	8	3	7	0	2	.500	1.250

Mike Williams, Phillies — RHP

Batter	Avg	AB	H	HR	BI	BB	SO	OBP	Slg
Abbott, Kurt	.182	11	2	0	1	0	2	.167	.273
Alicea, Luis*	.556	9	5	1	4	0	1	.556	1.222
Alou, Moises	.143	7	1	0	0	1	3	.250	.286
Andrews, S	.300	10	3	1	1	0	5	.300	.600
Anthony, Eric*	.000	4	0	0	0	2	1	.333	.000
Aurilia, Rich	.500	4	2	0	1	0	1	.400	.500
Ausmus, Brad	.333	3	1	0	0	1	0	.600	.667
Bagwell, Jeff	.455	11	5	1	3	1	2	.500	.727
Barberie, B#	.333	3	1	1	1	2	0	.600	1.333
Bell, Jay	.143	7	1	0	0	1	0	.250	.143
Benard, M*	.400	5	2	0	1	0	1	.400	.800
Berry, Sean	.167	6	1	0	1	0	2	.286	.167
Bichette, D	.400	5	2	0	0	0	0	.400	.400
Biggio, Craig	.182	11	2	0	1	2	2	.308	.364
Blauser, Jeff	.286	7	2	0	0	1	0	.286	.429
Blowers, Mike	.250	4	1	0	1	1	0	.400	.750
Bonds, Barry*	.333	6	2	1	2	3	0	.556	.833
Bonilla, B#	.400	5	2	0	1	1	3	.500	.400
Boone, Bret	.250	12	3	0	2	1	4	.286	.333
Branson, Jeff*	.143	7	1	0	0	1	0	.250	.143
Buford, Damon	.000	5	0	0	0	3	0	.000	.000
Bullett, S*	.400	5	2	0	1	0	0	.400	.800
Burks, Ellis	.333	6	2	1	2	0	0	.333	.833
Butler, Brett*	.375	16	6	0	3	2	0	.444	.563
Caminiti, Ken#	.100	10	1	0	0	3	1	.308	.200
Cangelosi, J	.111	9	1	0	0	2	0	.111	.222
Carr, Chuck	.000	5	0	0	0	1	0	.000	.000
Carreon, Mark	.200	5	1	0	0	1	1	.200	.200
Castilla, V	.600	5	3	1	1	0	2	.600	1.200
Cedeno, A	.600	10	6	0	1	2	0	.667	.700
Cedeno, Roger#	.200	5	1	0	0	1	0	.333	.200
Clark, Dave*	.167	6	1	0	0	1	1	.286	.333
Clayton, R	.333	6	2	0	0	2	1	.500	.500
Colbrunn, G	.273	11	3	0	2	1	1	.385	.273
Coleman, V#	.200	5	1	0	1	1	1	.333	.400
Conine, Jeff	.214	14	3	0	0	2	3	.375	.214
Davis, Eric	.286	14	4	0	1	0	1	.375	.429
DeShields, D*	.308	13	4	0	1	2	2	.400	.462
Dunston, S	.375	8	3	0	1	0	1	.375	.375
Finley, Steve*	.133	15	2	0	2	0	1	.133	.200
Fletcher, D*	.100	10	1	0	0	1	0	.182	.200
Floyd, Cliff*	.000	4	0	0	0	3	1	.429	.000
Fonville, C#	.000	5	0	0	0	1	1	.167	.000
Gagne, Greg	.167	6	1	0	0	1	0	.167	.167
Gant, Ron	.333	12	4	1	4	1	3	.385	.750
Garcia, C	.333	6	2	0	0	1	0	.333	.333
Gilkey, B	.222	9	2	0	1	0	1	.222	.333
Gonzalez, L*	.222	9	2	0	3	2	0	.333	.333
Grace, Mark*	.333	12	4	2	2	2	1	.429	.833
Greene, W*	.167	6	1	1	4	1	1	.286	.667
Grissom, M	.429	7	3	0	2	2	2	.556	.429
Grudzielanek	.556	9	5	0	0	3	1	.667	.556
Gutierrez, R	.400	5	2	0	0	0	0	.400	.400
Gwynn, Tony*	.417	12	5	0	0	1	0	.462	.500
Hansen, Dave*	.125	8	1	0	1	1	0	.125	.125
Harris, Lenny*	.214	14	3	0	1	0	0	.214	.357
Hayes, C	.600	5	3	0	2	0	0	.600	.600
Hernandez, Jo	.000	5	0	0	0	0	2	.000	.000
Hill, G	.462	13	6	0	0	0	2	.462	.538
Hollandsworth	.417	12	5	1	2	1	2	.462	.667
Howard, T*	.154	13	2	0	0	0	0	.154	.231
Hubbard, Tr	.000	3	0	0	0	2	0	.400	.000
Hundley, Todd#	.250	12	3	0	1	2	2	.357	.250
Hunter, Bri L	.333	9	3	1	1	0	4	.333	.667
Jefferies, G#	.200	5	1	0	0	2	0	.429	.400
Johnson, Char	.222	9	2	1	3	0	1	.222	.556
Jones, C#	.500	4	2	0	2	1	0	.600	.750
Jordan, Brian	.286	7	2	0	1	0	0	.286	.571
Justice, Dave*	.333	6	2	2	5	1	1	.429	1.333
Karros, Eric	.200	25	5	3	4	1	6	.231	.560
Kelly, R	.250	8	2	0	0	0	1	.250	.250
Kent, Jeff	.250	12	3	0	0	1	0	.308	.250
King, Jeff	.167	12	2	1	1	0	1	.167	.417

Mike Williams, Phillies — RHP

Batter	Avg	AB	H	HR	BI	BB	SO	OBP	Slg
Kirby, Wayne*	.167	6	1	0	0	1	1	.286	.167
Klesko, Ryan*	.400	5	2	2	3	0	0	.400	1.600
Lankford, Ray*	.462	13	6	2	3	1	4	.500	1.077
Lansing, Mike	.308	13	4	0	2	1	1	.357	.462
Larkin, Barry	.357	14	5	0	3	2	3	.471	.643
Lemke, Mark#	.273	11	3	0	2	1	2	.333	.364
Lopez, Javy	.400	5	2	0	0	0	1	.400	.400
Mabry, John*	.600	5	3	1	2	1	1	.667	1.400
Magadan, Dave*	.125	8	1	0	3	2	1	.300	.500
Manwaring, K	.167	6	1	0	1	0	1	.167	.333
Martin, Al*	.333	9	3	0	1	1	1	.400	.333
May, Derrick*	.200	5	1	0	0	1	0	.333	.200
McGriff, Fred*	.417	12	5	2	4	1	0	.462	1.000
McRae, Brian#	.273	11	3	0	0	2	0	.385	.545
Merced, O*	.400	5	2	0	1	0	1	.333	.400
Mondesi, Raul	.333	15	5	1	3	0	2	.333	.600
Morris, Hal*	.400	10	4	0	2	1	1	.455	.600
Mueller, Bill#	.000	3	0	0	2	0	0	.400	.000
Nieves, M#	.000	5	0	0	0	1	1	.167	.000
Offerman, J#	.308	13	4	0	1	1	0	.357	.462
Oliver, Joe	.286	7	2	0	3	0	2	.286	.429
Orsulak, Joe*	.167	6	1	0	1	1	1	.250	.167
Pagnozzi, Tom	.429	7	3	1	1	2	0	.556	1.000
Pendleton, T#	.500	12	6	0	3	1	0	.538	.833
Piazza, Mike	.417	12	5	1	4	3	1	.533	.917
Prince, Tom	.500	4	2	0	0	1	0	.600	.750
Roberts, Bip#	.200	5	1	0	0	1	1	.200	.400
Rodriguez, H*	.071	14	1	0	0	0	2	.071	.143
Sanchez, Rey	.200	7	3	0	1	1	0	.500	.429
Sandberg, R	.200	10	2	1	1	0	1	.200	.500
Sanders, R	.250	12	3	2	4	1	4	.308	.750
Santangelo, F#	.250	4	1	0	0	1	1	.400	.250
Santiago, B	.400	5	2	0	0	1	0	.400	.400
Scarsone, S	.667	6	4	1	3	0	0	.667	1.333
Segui, David#	.462	13	6	0	4	1	0	.500	.462
Servais, S	.286	7	2	0	1	0	1	.250	.429
Sheffield, G	.273	11	3	0	2	4	2	.467	.455
Sosa, Sammy	.400	10	4	2	6	1	0	.417	1.000
Spiers, Bill*	.000	5	0	0	0	1	0	.167	.000
Taubensee, E*	.167	6	1	0	0	0	2	.167	.167
Thompson, Ry	.333	6	2	0	1	2	0	.500	.500
Timmons, O	.000	5	0	0	0	1	0	.000	.000
VanderWal, J*	.500	6	3	2	4	2	0	.625	1.667
Veras, Q#	.000	6	0	0	0	3	1	.333	.000
Vizcaino, J#	.333	12	4	0	2	0	1	.308	.333
Wallach, Tim	.143	7	1	0	0	1	0	.250	.143
Weiss, Walt#	.000	5	0	0	0	2	0	.286	.000
White, Devon#	.625	8	5	1	4	2	1	.700	1.000
White, R	.300	10	3	0	3	0	2	.300	.500
Whiten, Mark#	.125	8	1	0	2	0	3	.125	.375
Wilkins, Rick*	.273	11	3	0	1	2	2	.385	.455
Wilson, Desi*	.000	5	0	0	0	1	0	.000	.000
Young, Eric	.286	7	2	0	2	0	0	.375	.286
Zeile, Todd	.333	6	2	0	2	2	0	.444	.500

Woody Williams, Blue Jays — RHP

Batter	Avg	AB	H	HR	BI	BB	SO	OBP	Slg
Alomar, R#	.286	5	0	0	0	2	0	.286	.000
Anderson, Brd*	.273	11	3	1	1	1	4	.385	.545
Baines, H*	.444	9	4	0	0	2	1	.545	.556
Boggs, Wade*	.500	8	4	0	0	1	0	.500	.750
Bonilla, B#	.000	5	0	0	0	2	0	.286	.000
Bordick, Mike	.000	3	0	0	1	3	0	.500	.000
Bragg, Darren*	.667	3	2	1	2	1	0	.600	2.000
Clark, Will*	.286	7	2	1	3	1	1	.375	.714
Coleman, V#	.200	5	1	0	0	1	0	.200	.200
Damon, Johnny*	.333	9	3	0	0	3	0	.333	.333
Davis, Chili#	.400	5	2	0	3	1	2	.500	.600
Devereaux, M	.600	5	3	0	1	0	1	.600	.800
Durham, Ray#	.167	6	1	0	0	0	1	.167	.167
Fielder, C	.000	11	0	0	0	5	0	.000	.000
Frye, Jeff	.000	7	0	0	0	1	0	.400	.000
Fryman, T	.000	7	0	0	0	2	1	.222	.000
Gallego, Mike	.250	8	2	0	0	0	3	.250	.250
Gonzalez, J	.333	6	2	0	1	0	0	.333	.500
Goodwin, Tom*	.200	5	1	0	0	1	0	.333	.200
Greenwell, M*	.000	6	0	0	0	2	1	.250	.000
Greer, Rusty*	.250	4	1	0	0	1	1	.400	.250
Guillen, O*	.200	5	1	0	0	0	0	.200	.200
Hamelin, Bob*	.100	10	1	0	0	1	4	.182	.100
Hamilton, D*	.333	6	2	0	0	0	0	.333	.333
Henderson, R	.000	6	0	0	0	1	1	.143	.000
Hoiles, Chris	.250	8	2	1	0	0	2	.250	.625
Howard, Dave#	.200	5	1	0	0	2	1	.429	.200
Jaha, John	.333	6	2	1	1	0	1	.333	.833
Javier, Stan#	.000	7	0	0	0	1	4	.125	.000
Jefferson, R*	.143	7	1	1	2	0	2	.143	.571
Kelly, Pat	.500	8	4	0	0	1	2	.556	.625
Listach, Pat#	.200	5	1	0	0	1	0	.200	.400
Lockhart, K*	.400	5	2	0	1	3	0	.625	.400
Macfarlane, M	.000	4	0	0	0	2	0	.333	.000

Woody Williams, Blue Jays — RHP

Batter	Avg	AB	H	HR	BI	BB	SO	OBP	Slg
Martinez, Da*	.500	4	2	0	1	1	1	.600	.500
McLemore, M#	.250	8	2	0	0	0	0	.250	.250
Murray, Eddie#	.000	6	0	0	0	1	2	.143	.000
Naehring, Tim	.125	8	1	0	0	0	2	.125	.125
Nixon, Otis#	.286	7	2	0	1	0	4	.286	.286
O'Leary, Troy*	.286	7	2	0	0	3	0	.500	.429
O'Neill, Paul*	.300	10	3	0	0	0	0	.300	.300
Offerman, J#	.143	7	1	0	1	2	2	.333	.143
Palmeiro, R*	.250	12	3	0	2	3	4	.400	.417
Palmer, Dean	.167	6	1	0	1	1	3	.250	.167
Paquette, C	.143	7	1	0	0	0	3	.143	.143
Phillips, T#	.571	7	4	0	0	2	1	.667	.714
Polonia, Luis*	.000	5	0	0	0	1	1	.167	.000
Raines, Tim#	.286	7	2	0	1	0	2	.286	.286
Ripken, Cal	.214	14	3	2	4	0	0	.214	.643
Rodriguez, I	.200	5	1	0	1	0	1	.200	.200
Seitzer, K	.125	8	1	0	0	1	0	.222	.125
Stanley, Mike	.625	8	5	1	3	2	0	.700	1.000
Steinbach, T	.167	6	1	0	0	0	2	.167	.167
Surhoff, B.J.*	.364	11	4	0	1	0	2	.364	.455
Sweeney, Mike	.333	6	2	0	0	0	0	.333	.333
Tartabull, D	.111	9	1	0	1	2	3	.273	.111
Tettleton, M#	.286	7	2	1	2	1	3	.375	.714
Thomas, Frank	.500	10	5	1	3	0	0	.500	.900
Tinsley, Lee#	.000	4	0	0	0	1	2	.200	.000
Valentin, Jhn	.143	7	1	0	1	1	0	.250	.143
Vaughn, Greg	.500	6	3	0	4	3	1	.667	.667
Vaughn, Mo*	.222	9	2	0	1	3	5	.417	.333
Ventura, R*	.571	7	4	0	2	1	0	.625	.571
Williams, Ber#	.222	9	2	1	2	2	2	.364	.667
Zeile, Todd	.000	7	0	0	0	0	3	.000	.000

Paul Wilson, Mets — RHP

Batter	Avg	AB	H	HR	BI	BB	SO	OBP	Slg
Sheffield, G	.500	6	3	1	3	2	1	.625	1.000
Sosa, Sammy	.429	7	3	2	4	0	2	.429	1.286
Taubensee, E*	.333	6	2	1	4	0	0	.333	1.000
Wallach, Tim	.333	6	2	1	2	0	2	.333	.833
White, Devon#	.429	7	3	0	1	1	1	.500	.571
Williams, Ma	.167	6	1	0	1	0	1	.167	.167

Bobby Witt, Rangers — RHP

Batter	Avg	AB	H	HR	BI	BB	SO	OBP	Slg
Alfonzo, E	.286	7	2	0	0	0	1	.286	.571
Alomar, R#	.333	33	11	0	2	1	6	.353	.545
Alomar Jr, S	.333	21	7	1	3	2	0	.417	.571
Amaral, Rich	.500	10	5	0	1	1	2	.545	.500
Anderson, Brd*	.313	32	10	3	5	9	6	.476	.750
Baerga, C#	.222	36	8	1	6	1	5	.243	.361
Bagwell, Jeff	.500	4	2	0	1	1	1	.600	.750
Baines, H*	.388	49	19	3	13	4	9	.434	.735
Battle, Allen	.500	6	3	1	2	1	0	.571	1.167
Becker, Rich*	.333	15	5	0	0	2	2	.412	.333
Bell, Derek	.600	5	3	0	2	0	0	.600	1.000
Bell, Jay	.333	6	2	0	0	4	2	.600	.500
Belle, Albert	.273	33	9	0	6	4	11	.351	.394
Berroa, G	.750	4	3	1	1	1	0	.800	1.500
Bichette, D	.333	18	6	0	2	0	5	.333	.389
Blauser, Jeff	.200	5	1	0	0	1	1	.333	.200
Blowers, Mike	.176	17	3	2	8	4	11	.333	.588
Boggs, Wade*	.368	57	21	0	3	22	7	.538	.509
Bonds, Barry*	.400	5	2	0	0	1	0	.500	.600
Bonilla, B#	.063	16	1	1	2	0	3	.059	.250
Boone, Bret	.167	6	1	0	1	0	1	.167	.333
Borders, Pat	.125	16	2	0	0	0	0	.125	.125
Bordick, Mike	.286	7	2	0	1	3	0	.500	.286
Brogna, Rico*	.400	10	4	0	1	3	3	.538	.600
Brosius, S	.500	8	4	0	0	0	1	.500	.625
Buhner, Jay	.267	30	8	4	11	4	7	.333	.700
Burks, Ellis	.235	34	8	2	3	6	8	.350	.441
Burnitz, J*	.300	10	3	0	1	1	5	.364	.300
Butler, Brett*	.417	12	5	0	1	3	0	.533	.667
Cangelosi, J#	.000	6	0	0	0	3	4	.333	.000
Canseco, Jose	.243	37	9	1	3	12	20	.429	.378
Carreon, Mark	.286	7	2	0	2	0	0	.444	.429
Carter, Joe	.188	48	9	0	9	5	14	.255	.250
Cedeno, D#	.231	13	3	0	0	0	2	.231	.231
Cirillo, Jeff	.200	10	2	0	0	0	2	.200	.200
Clark, Dave*	.077	13	1	0	0	3	1	.250	.077
Clark, Will*	.500	6	3	1	5	0	0	.500	1.000
Clayton, S	.333	6	2	0	1	0	1	.333	.333
Cole, Alex*	.182	11	2	0	1	7	5	.500	.364
Coleman, V#	.267	15	4	0	3	1	4	.313	.267
Coomer, Ron	.000	5	0	0	0	0	0	.000	.000
Cora, Joey#	.333	36	12	0	5	10	3	.478	.361
Cordero, Wil	.200	5	1	1	1	0	1	.200	.800
Cordova, M	.250	8	2	1	2	1	1	.333	.625
Curtis, Chad	.300	10	3	0	1	3	0	.462	.300
Cuyler, Milt#	.286	7	2	1	2	2	1	.444	1.000
Damon, Johnny*	.625	8	5	0	2	0	0	.625	1.000
Davis, Chili#	.143	35	5	0	2	6	8	.268	.229
Dawson, Andre	.417	12	5	0	0	0	2	.417	.500
Deer, Rob	.231	39	9	2	6	17	7	.388	.436
Delgado, C*	.357	14	5	1	3	1	6	.400	.643
Devereaux, M	.053	19	1	0	1	1	3	.095	.053
Diaz, Alex#	.500	4	2	0	3	1	1	.600	.750
DiSarcina, G	.267	15	4	0	2	0	0	.250	.400
Duncan, M	.200	5	1	0	1	1	1	.200	.200
Durham, Ray#	.267	15	4	0	2	1	2	.313	.467
Easley, D	.182	11	2	0	1	1	1	.250	.182
Edmonds, Jim*	.200	15	3	0	1	1	6	.250	.267
Eisenreich, J*	.286	14	4	0	3	1	1	.333	.357
Espinoza, A	.217	23	5	0	2	1	4	.250	.304
Fabregas, Jor*	.200	5	1	0	1	0	1	.200	.200
Fermin, Felix	.542	24	13	0	5	4	0	.607	.625
Fielder, C	.304	23	7	3	9	5	9	.414	.783
Finley, Steve*	.222	18	4	0	4	0	3	.211	.389
Franco, Julio	.278	36	10	1	6	2	8	.316	.389
Frye, Jeff	.333	6	2	0	0	1	0	.429	.333
Fryman, T	.185	27	5	0	1	3	7	.267	.222
Gaetti, Gary	.189	37	7	0	2	2	10	.231	.216
Gagne, Greg	.156	45	7	1	4	4	16	.224	.222
Gallego, Mike	.174	23	4	1	1	2	6	.240	.304
Giambi, Jason*	.667	6	4	0	1	1	0	.714	.833
Girardi, Joe	.200	5	1	0	0	0	2	.200	.400
Gomez, Chris	.000	4	0	0	0	0	1	.000	.000
Gomez, Leo	.286	14	4	1	2	1	4	.375	.500
Gonzales, R	.385	13	5	0	2	1	4	.400	.385
Gonzalez, A	.100	10	1	0	1	2	7	.250	.200
Gonzalez, J	.250	12	3	0	0	0	2	.250	.333
Gonzalez, L*	.000	4	0	0	0	2	1	.000	.000
Goodwin, Tom*	.286	7	2	0	0	2	1	.444	.286
Grebeck, C	.250	4	1	0	0	2	1	.500	.500
Green, Shawn*	.400	15	6	1	3	0	4	.400	.733
Greenwell, M*	.283	46	13	0	3	10	6	.421	.348

Paul Wilson, Mets — RHP

Batter	Avg	AB	H	HR	BI	BB	SO	OBP	Slg
Arias, Alex	.600	5	3	1	2	1	1	.667	1.200
Bagwell, Jeff	.667	3	2	1	3	2	1	.800	1.667
Bell, Derek	.400	5	2	0	0	0	1	.400	.400
Bell, Jay	.000	3	0	0	2	1	0	.200	.000
Biggio, Craig	.250	4	1	0	1	0	1	.400	.250
Bonds, Barry*	.500	6	3	0	1	0	0	.500	.667
Boone, Bret	.200	5	1	0	2	1	2	.333	.200
Caminiti, Ken*	.600	5	3	2	5	2	2	.714	1.800
Carreon, Mark	.000	4	0	0	0	0	0	.000	.000
Castillo, L#	.500	4	2	0	0	1	1	.600	.500
Conine, Jeff	.125	8	1	0	0	0	2	.125	.125
Davis, Eric	.250	4	1	1	1	1	0	.500	1.000
DeShields, D*	.000	4	0	0	0	2	0	.333	.000
Dunston, S	.200	5	1	0	0	0	1	.200	.200
Finley, Steve*	.364	11	4	0	5	2	0	.462	.818
Gagne, Greg	.200	5	1	0	0	0	1	.200	.200
Gomez, Chris	.333	6	2	0	0	0	1	.333	.333
Gomez, Leo	.000	5	0	0	0	1	1	.167	.000
Grace, Mark*	.400	5	2	1	2	2	1	.571	1.000
Greene, W*	.400	5	2	0	0	1	2	.500	.400
Grissom, M	.000	7	0	0	0	1	1	.125	.000
Gwynn, Tony*	.333	9	3	0	1	0	0	.333	.333
Hayes, C	.167	6	1	0	1	0	0	.167	.167
Henderson, R	.333	9	3	0	0	3	1	.538	.333
Hollandsworth*	.167	6	1	1	2	1	0	.286	.667
Howard, T*	.167	6	1	0	0	0	3	.167	.167
Hunter, Bri L	.333	3	1	0	2	0	0	.600	.333
Javier, Stan#	.333	6	2	0	0	1	1	.333	.333
Jefferies, G#	.500	6	3	0	2	0	0	.500	.833
Johnson, Bri	.333	12	4	0	1	0	1	.333	.583
Johnson, Char	.167	6	1	0	0	0	2	.167	.167
Johnson, Mark*	.250	4	1	0	0	2	2	.500	.250
Jones, C#	.375	8	3	0	2	0	1	.375	.375
Joyner, Wally*	.182	11	2	0	3	2	2	.308	.273
Karros, Eric	.400	5	2	0	1	1	1	.500	.400
Kendall, J	.000	5	0	0	1	0	0	.000	.000
Kirby, Wayne*	.400	5	2	0	1	2	0	.571	.400
Klesko, Ryan*	.500	6	3	1	2	1	2	.571	1.167
Larkin, Barry	.500	6	3	0	1	3	0	.667	.500
Livingstone*	.250	4	1	0	1	2	1	.500	.250
Lopez, Javy	.000	5	0	0	0	1	0	.000	.000
Martin, Al*	.333	6	2	0	0	0	1	.333	.333
McGriff, Fred*	.333	6	2	0	2	1	1	.429	.500
McRae, Brian#	.167	6	1	0	0	0	3	.167	.167
Merced, O*	.167	6	1	0	0	0	3	.167	.167
Mondesi, Raul	.333	6	2	0	0	0	1	.333	.500
Morandini, M*	.000	6	0	0	0	1	1	.143	.000
Morris, Hal*	.200	5	1	0	0	0	0	.200	.200
Otero, Ricky*	.600	5	3	0	2	0	0	.714	.800
Pendleton, T#	.143	7	1	0	1	1	3	.250	.286
Piazza, Mike	.500	5	2	0	1	1	1	.500	.500
Reed, Jody	.286	7	2	0	2	2	2	.444	.429
Renteria, E	.200	5	1	0	0	1	0	.200	.200
Sandberg, R	.500	6	3	0	1	1	2	.571	.833
Sanders, R	.600	5	3	0	1	1	0	.667	.600
Santiago, B	.400	5	2	0	0	0	1	.400	.400
Servais, S	.000	6	0	0	0	0	3	.000	.000

Bobby Witt, Rangers — RHP

Batter	Avg	AB	H	HR	BI	BB	SO	OBP	Slg
Greer, Rusty*	.333	6	2	0	0	0	1	.333	.333
Griffey Jr, K*	.406	32	13	2	8	9	5	.537	.656
Guillen, O*	.250	56	14	1	4	5	11	.306	.357
Gwynn, Chris*	.400	5	2	0	0	0	3	.400	.400
Hale, Chip*	.385	13	5	0	3	1	1	.400	.385
Hall, Mel*	.296	27	8	1	6	2	3	.345	.519
Hamelin, Bob*	.400	15	6	1	5	0	3	.375	.800
Hamilton, D*	.250	24	6	0	4	3	4	.310	.292
Hammonds, J	.400	5	2	0	0	0	0	.400	.400
Haselman, B	.200	5	1	0	0	0	3	.200	.200
Henderson, R	.382	34	13	1	4	13	4	.553	.588
Herrera, Jose*	.200	5	1	0	0	0	2	.200	.200
Higginson, B*	.250	4	1	0	0	2	0	.500	.250
Hill, G	.125	8	1	0	0	0	4	.125	.125
Hoiles, Chris	.389	18	7	1	6	4	4	.500	.611
Hollandsworth*	.167	6	1	0	0	0	3	.286	.167
Howard, Dave*	.111	9	1	0	1	0	1	.111	.111
Howell, Jack*	.286	21	6	0	3	2	2	.348	.333
Hulse, David*	.235	17	4	0	0	2	2	.316	.235
Hundley, Todd*	.167	6	1	0	0	1	1	.286	.167
Incaviglia, D	.000	5	0	0	0	2	2	.286	.000
Jaha, John	.273	22	6	1	3	3	3	.360	.455
James, Dion*	.308	26	8	0	0	2	3	.357	.346
Javier, Stan*	.333	12	4	0	2	2	1	.429	.417
Jefferson, R*	.333	6	2	0	2	0	1	.333	.500
Johnson, L*	.400	50	20	0	5	6	4	.456	.600
Johnson, Mark*	.400	5	2	0	1	0	3	.400	.400
Jones, C#	.250	4	1	0	0	2	1	.500	.250
Jordan, Brian	.429	7	3	0	0	0	0	.429	.429
Joyner, Wally*	.233	30	7	1	6	7	9	.368	.400
Justice, Dave*	.000	4	0	0	0	1	2	.200	.000
Karkovice, R	.161	31	5	2	4	5	8	.270	.355
Karros, Eric	.167	6	1	0	1	1	3	.286	.333
Kelly, Pat	.214	14	3	0	0	0	6	.214	.214
Kelly, R	.125	24	3	1	4	1	5	.160	.250
Kent, Jeff	.357	14	5	0	0	1	0	.400	.357
King, Jeff	.333	3	1	0	1	0	0	.600	.667
Kingery, Mike*	.444	9	4	0	0	0	0	.444	.556
Kirby, Wayne*	.400	5	2	0	2	0	2	.400	.400
Knoblauch, C	.257	35	9	0	3	7	5	.364	.286
Lankford, Ray*	.429	7	3	1	2	0	2	.429	.857
Lawton, Matt*	.000	5	0	0	0	1	1	.167	.000
Leius, Scott	.333	9	3	0	2	0	0	.333	.444
Lewis, Darren	.167	6	1	0	1	0	1	.167	.167
Lewis, Mark	.385	13	5	0	1	1	3	.429	.385
Leyritz, Jim	.222	9	2	0	0	2	0	.200	.333
Liriano, N#	.300	10	3	1	4	3	2	.462	.600
Listach, Pat#	.125	8	1	0	0	3	2	.364	.125
Livingstone*	.125	8	1	0	1	0	1	.125	.125
Lockhart, K*	.333	6	2	1	2	2	1	.500	.833
Lofton, Kenny*	.368	19	7	0	3	7	1	.538	.474
Lovullo, T#	.000	4	0	0	0	1	3	.200	.000
Mabry, John*	.500	6	3	0	1	0	0	.500	.500
Macfarlane, M	.250	16	4	2	5	0	4	.294	.625
Manto, Jeff	.375	8	3	0	3	2	1	.545	.625
Martin, Al*	.333	6	2	0	0	1	1	.429	.500
Martinez, Da*	.313	16	5	0	1	2	2	.389	.375
Martinez, E	.281	32	9	0	2	7	8	.410	.375
Martinez, S*	.444	9	4	0	1	0	1	.444	.667
Martinez, T*	.348	23	8	1	2	2	5	.400	.565
Marzano, John	.200	5	1	0	0	1	4	.333	.200
Matheny, Mike	.000	6	0	0	0	1	4	.000	.000
Mayne, Brent*	.222	9	2	0	1	2	1	.364	.333
McCarty, Dave	.111	9	1	0	0	0	1	.111	.111
McGriff, Fred*	.304	23	7	1	3	4	7	.393	.565
McGwire, Mark	.250	24	6	1	3	10	4	.471	.375
McLemore, M#	.438	16	7	0	4	3	1	.500	.625
McRae, Brian#	.273	22	6	0	2	2	8	.320	.364
Meares, Pat	.333	18	6	0	0	0	1	.333	.333
Merced, O*	.667	6	4	0	3	0	1	.667	1.167
Mieske, Matt	.167	6	1	0	0	0	1	.167	.167
Molitor, Paul	.292	72	21	2	6	12	10	.388	.403
Mondesi, Raul	.286	7	2	0	0	0	0	.286	.286
Munoz, Pedro	.095	21	2	0	1	0	10	.095	.095
Murray, Eddie#	.176	17	3	0	0	6	4	.391	.176
Myers, Greg*	.286	14	4	0	2	2	4	.375	.357
Newfield, M	.286	7	2	0	0	0	1	.286	.429
Newson, W*	.100	10	1	0	0	1	4	.182	.100
Nilsson, Dave*	.500	20	10	0	3	2	4	.545	.600
Nixon, Otis#	.308	13	4	0	0	1	1	.357	.385
O'Brien, C	.211	19	4	2	5	4	4	.273	.526
O'Neill, Paul*	.381	21	8	1	4	1	5	.409	.619
Offerman, J#	.429	7	3	1	4	3	0	.600	1.000
Olerud, John*	.345	29	10	2	5	10	3	.525	.690
Orsulak, Joe*	.348	23	8	1	3	3	1	.423	.522
Palmeiro, R*	.208	24	5	3	5	5	4	.345	.625
Palmer, Dean	.417	12	5	3	6	2	3	.500	1.250
Parent, Mark	.200	5	1	0	0	0	1	.200	.400
Peitier, Dan*	.500	6	3	0	2	1	0	.571	.667
Pena, Tony	.259	27	7	0	2	1	4	.286	.407
Phillips, T#	.277	47	13	3	10	7	7	.364	.532

Bobby Witt, Rangers — RHP

Batter	Avg	AB	H	HR	BI	BB	SO	OBP	Slg
Piazza, Mike	.333	6	2	0	1	1	3	.429	.500
Plantier, P*	.125	8	1	0	0	2	0	.300	.125
Polonia, Luis*	.225	40	9	0	1	14	7	.426	.325
Raines, Tim#	.297	37	11	0	7	5	0	.381	.405
Ramirez, M	.200	10	2	0	1	1	2	.273	.200
Reboulet, J	.167	6	1	1	1	1	1	.286	.667
Reed, Jeff*	.000	6	0	0	0	2	2	.000	.000
Reed, Jody	.323	31	10	0	3	9	5	.475	.419
Ripken, Billy	.148	27	4	0	1	4	5	.258	.185
Ripken, Cal	.320	50	16	1	5	14	10	.469	.420
Roberts, Bip#	.400	5	2	0	2	1	1	.500	.400
Rodriguez, Al	.364	11	4	0	1	1	3	.417	.455
Rodriguez, I	.250	8	2	1	1	0	0	.250	.625
Salmon, Tim	.583	12	7	1	5	2	4	.643	.833
Schofield, D	.211	19	4	1	2	1	3	.238	.368
Schu, Rick	.500	4	2	0	0	1	1	.600	.500
Segui, David#	.250	8	2	0	2	1	1	.333	.250
Seitzer, K	.222	36	8	0	4	10	8	.391	.278
Sheffield, G	.091	11	1	0	1	2	0	.231	.091
Shumpert, T	.200	10	2	1	3	3	2	.385	.500
Sierra, Ruben#	.000	7	0	0	0	3	3	.300	.000
Smith, Dwight*	.167	6	1	0	0	0	1	.167	.167
Smith, Mark	.400	5	2	0	0	0	0	.400	.400
Smith, J.T.#	.500	12	6	1	1	1	2	.538	.833
Snow, J.T.#	.316	19	6	0	0	4	0	.350	.316
Sojo, Luis	.316	19	6	0	0	0	0	.350	.316
Sorrento, P*	.609	23	14	1	3	8	5	.710	.783
Spiers, Bill*	.294	34	10	1	3	1	6	.314	.412
Sprague, Ed	.280	25	7	0	1	2	7	.333	.320
Stahoviak, S*	.471	17	8	1	4	1	1	.500	.706
Stairs, Matt*	.500	4	2	0	0	1	0	.600	.750
Stanley, Mike	.222	9	2	1	2	3	3	.417	.778
Steinbach, T	.217	23	5	0	1	0	6	.217	.261
Stevens, Lee*	.600	5	3	1	2	0	2	.500	1.200
Stillwell, K#	.176	17	3	0	0	1	5	.222	.176
Strange, Doug#	.143	7	1	0	0	3	1	.400	.286
Surhoff, B.J.*	.316	57	18	3	11	8	4	.394	.526
Sveum, Dale#	.167	24	4	0	1	3	9	.250	.208
Tarasco, Tony*	.250	8	2	1	1	0	1	.250	.625
Tartabull, D	.246	57	14	3	12	7	12	.318	.474
Tettleton, M#	.250	36	9	0	4	9	16	.391	.278
Thomas, Frank	.333	39	13	2	7	7	5	.426	.538
Thome, Jim*	.385	13	5	1	7	1	4	.429	.923
Thompson, Rob	.200	5	1	0	0	1	4	.333	.200
Thompson, Ry	.000	7	0	0	0	0	2	.000	.000
Trammell, A	.175	40	7	0	3	6	3	.271	.200
Tucker, M*	.250	4	1	0	2	1	1	.286	.250
Valentin, Jhn	.167	18	3	0	0	6	3	.375	.167
Valentin, Jse#	.071	14	1	1	1	1	5	.133	.286
Valle, Dave	.125	16	2	0	1	3	4	.263	.188
Vaughn, Greg	.214	28	6	4	6	7	7	.361	.643
Vaughn, Mo*	.368	19	7	1	2	4	5	.458	.526
Ventura, R*	.333	48	16	1	4	11	6	.458	.438
Vina, F*	.273	11	3	0	0	0	0	.273	.273
Vizcaino, J*	.125	8	1	0	1	0	0	.125	.125
Vizquel, Omar#	.174	23	4	0	1	7	4	.367	.174
Walbeck, Matt#	.125	8	1	0	0	0	2	.125	.125
Wallach, Tim	.000	6	0	0	0	2	4	.250	.000
Ward, Turner#	.154	13	2	0	0	2	4	.267	.231
Webster, L	.500	8	4	0	1	0	1	.500	.625
Weiss, Walt*	.071	14	1	0	1	4	2	.278	.214
White, Devon#	.268	41	11	1	4	6	13	.362	.366
Whiten, Mark#	.364	11	4	0	1	1	5	.417	.364
Williams, Ber#	.211	19	4	1	4	1	4	.238	.421
Williams, E	.200	5	1	0	0	0	1	.200	.200
Williams, Ger*	.000	6	0	0	0	1	1	.143	.000
Wilson, Dan	.438	16	7	0	2	0	3	.438	.563
Worthington	.235	17	4	0	1	0	5	.235	.294

Mark Wohlers, Braves — RHP

Batter	Avg	AB	H	HR	BI	BB	SO	OBP	Slg
Abbott, Kurt	.500	5	0	0	0	0	4	.000	.000
Anthony, Eric*	.250	4	1	1	3	1	1	.400	1.000
Bagwell, Jeff	.143	7	1	0	1	1	1	.364	.143
Bell, Derek	.333	6	2	0	2	0	1	.286	.667
Bell, Jay	.333	9	3	0	3	3	2	.500	.556
Benjamin, M	.000	5	0	0	0	0	2	.000	.000
Berry, Sean	.500	4	2	0	1	1	2	.600	.500
Bichette, D	.500	12	6	0	4	0	3	.500	.583
Biggio, Craig	.250	12	3	0	0	2	2	.250	.250
Bonds, Barry*	.000	4	0	0	0	4	1	.500	.000
Bonilla, B#	.000	5	0	0	0	0	1	.167	.000
Boone, Bret	.400	5	2	0	2	2	3	.571	.400
Branson, Jeff*	.250	8	2	0	0	0	4	.250	.250
Bullett, S*	.000	6	0	0	0	0	6	.000	.000
Burks, Ellis	.333	6	2	0	0	0	3	.333	.333
Butler, Brett*	.200	5	1	0	1	1	2	.333	.200
Caminiti, Ken#	.333	9	3	0	1	3	1	.400	.333
Candaele, C#	.250	4	1	0	2	0	0	.250	.250
Cangelosi, J#	.250	4	1	0	0	0	1	.400	.250
Carr, Chuck	.250	4	1	0	0	0	0	.250	.250
Carreon, Mark	.167	6	1	0	0	0	1	.167	.167

230

Mark Wohlers, Braves — RHP

Batter	Avg	AB	H	HR	BI	BB	SO	OBP	Slg
Castilla, V	.364	11	4	1	2	0	2	.364	.636
Cedeno, A	.250	4	1	1	2	1	2	.400	1.000
Clark, Dave*	.600	5	3	1	2	0	1	.500	1.400
Clayton, R	.000	4	0	0	0	0	2	.000	.000
Conine, Jeff	.111	9	1	0	0	1	3	.200	.111
Daulton, D*	.400	5	2	0	1	0	1	.400	.600
DeShields, D*	.000	1	0	0	0	3	1	.750	.000
Duncan, M	.222	9	2	0	1	0	0	.222	.222
Dykstra, L*	.333	6	2	0	0	1	1	.429	.667
Eisenreich, J*	.167	6	1	0	2	0	2	.167	.167
Eusebio, Tony	.600	5	3	0	1	1	2	.667	.600
Finley, Steve*	.167	6	1	0	0	0	0	.167	.167
Fletcher, D*	.300	10	3	0	1	0	1	.300	.300
Floyd, Cliff*	.600	5	3	0	0	0	1	.600	.800
Galarraga, A	.417	12	5	1	3	1	3	.462	.750
Garcia, C	.500	6	3	0	2	2	1	.667	.500
Gilkey, B	.400	5	2	0	1	1	1	.500	.400
Girardi, Joe	.000	5	0	0	0	0	1	.000	.000
Gonzalez, L*	.000	7	0	0	0	0	3	.000	.000
Grace, Mark*	.333	3	1	0	0	2	1	.600	.333
Grissom, M	.250	4	1	0	1	1	1	.400	.250
Grudzielanek	.167	6	1	0	0	0	3	.167	.167
Gutierrez, R	.000	5	0	0	0	1	2	.167	.000
Gwynn, Tony*	.000	5	0	0	0	1	0	.167	.000
Hansen, Dave*	.000	5	0	0	0	2	0	.286	.000
Harris, Lenny*	.167	6	1	0	1	0	1	.167	.333
Hayes, C	.200	10	2	0	4	1	2	.273	.300
Hollins, Dave#	.250	4	1	0	0	2	1	.500	.250
Hundley, Todd#	.000	7	0	0	0	3	1	.300	.000
Incaviglia, P	.500	4	2	0	1	1	2	.600	.500
Jefferies, G#	.167	6	1	0	1	0	1	.167	.333
Jordan, Brian	.200	5	1	0	0	1	3	.333	.400
Jordan, Ricky	.167	6	1	0	1	0	0	.143	.333
Karros, Eric	.200	5	1	0	1	0	1	.167	.200
Kent, Jeff	.000	4	0	0	0	0	2	.000	.000
King, Jeff	.125	8	1	0	2	0	2	.111	.125
Kingery, Mike*	.250	8	2	0	0	0	2	.250	.500
Lankford, Ray*	.000	4	0	0	0	1	1	.200	.000
Lansing, Mike	.250	8	2	0	1	0	2	.250	.250
Larkin, Barry	.167	6	1	0	0	2	2	.375	.167
Lewis, Darren	.400	5	2	0	2	1	0	.571	.400
Liriano, N#	.167	6	1	0	0	0	1	.167	.167
Mabry, John*	.167	6	1	0	0	0	2	.167	.167
Magadan, Dave*	.400	5	2	0	0	3	2	.625	.400
Martin, Al*	.500	6	3	0	0	1	2	.571	.500
May, Derrick*	.000	5	0	0	0	0	1	.000	.000
McGee, Willie#	.000	3	0	0	0	2	2	.400	.000
McRae, Brian#	.143	7	1	0	1	0	2	.143	.143
Miller, Orl	.400	5	2	0	1	0	1	.400	.400
Mitchell, K	.750	4	3	0	3	1	0	.800	.750
Mondesi, Raul	.400	5	2	1	1	0	0	.400	1.400
Morandini, M*	.500	8	4	0	1	1	3	.556	.500
Morris, Hal*	.200	10	2	0	0	0	4	.200	.200
Mouton, James	.000	5	0	0	0	0	4	.000	.000
Offerman, J#	.000	5	0	0	0	2	2	.286	.000
Oliver, Joe	.000	5	0	0	0	0	0	.000	.000
Orsulak, Joe*	.000	6	0	0	1	2	1	.250	.000
Pagnozzi, Tom	.000	5	0	0	0	0	2	.000	.000
Pendleton, T#	.000	5	0	0	0	0	1	.000	.000
Piazza, Mike	.333	6	2	0	2	2	1	.556	.500
Reed, Jeff*	.250	4	1	1	1	1	2	.400	1.000
Reed, Jody	.500	6	3	0	1	1	0	.571	.500
Rodriguez, H*	.250	8	2	0	0	1	4	.333	.375
Sabo, Chris	.333	3	1	0	1	2	1	.600	.333
Sanchez, Rey	.000	5	0	0	0	0	2	.000	.000
Sanders, R	.100	10	1	0	0	0	5	.100	.100
Santiago, B	.222	9	2	0	0	0	5	.222	.222
Sheffield, G	.071	14	1	0	0	1	4	.133	.143
Smith, Ozzie*	.250	4	1	0	0	1	1	.400	.250
Sosa, Sammy	.167	6	1	0	2	0	3	.167	.333
Stocker, K#	.000	4	0	0	1	0	1	.000	.000
Taubensee, E*	.200	5	1	0	0	2	3	.429	.200
Thompson, Rob	.000	4	0	0	0	1	3	.200	.000
Vizcaino, J#	.600	5	3	0	3	0	0	.600	.600
Wallach, Tim	.000	6	0	0	1	0	2	.000	.000
Weiss, Walt*	.429	7	3	0	1	3	2	.600	.571
White, R	.000	6	0	0	1	0	3	.000	.000
Wilkins, Rick*	.143	7	1	0	1	0	5	.143	.143
Williams, Ma	.222	9	2	0	1	1	2	.300	.222
Young, Eric	.333	6	2	0	0	1	1	.500	.333
Young, Kevin	.000	5	0	0	0	0	2	.000	.000
Zeile, Todd	.200	5	1	0	2	0	2	.167	.200

Steve Wojciechowski, Athletics — LHP

Batter	Avg	AB	H	HR	BI	BB	SO	OBP	Slg
Anderson, G*	.500	6	3	1	1	0	0	.500	1.000
Becker, Rich*	.200	5	1	0	0	0	1	.200	.400
Boggs, Wade*	.111	9	1	0	0	0	0	.111	.111
Cirillo, Jeff	.167	6	1	0	1	0	0	.286	.167
Coomer, Ron	.333	9	3	1	2	0	1	.333	.667
Cordova, M	.250	8	2	1	2	1	0	.333	.625
Curtis, Chad	.167	6	1	0	0	0	0	.167	.167
Cuyler, Milt#	.000	5	0	0	0	0	1	.000	.000
Davis, Chili#	.333	6	2	0	1	0	0	.333	.333
DiSarcina, G	.000	4	0	0	0	1	1	.200	.000
Durant, Mike	.500	2	1	0	0	2	1	.750	1.000
Fielder, C	.333	3	1	1	2	2	1	.667	1.333
Fryman, T	.500	6	3	0	1	0	0	.500	.500
Girardi, Joe	.000	5	0	0	0	1	1	.167	.000
Green, Shawn*	.750	4	3	0	2	0	0	.800	1.500
Hamilton, D*	.333	3	1	0	1	2	0	.600	1.000
Jaha, John	.200	5	1	0	0	1	1	.333	.200
Kelly, R	.600	5	3	0	0	0	1	.600	.800
Knoblauch, C	.400	5	2	0	1	1	0	.429	.400
Lewis, Mark	.400	5	2	0	2	1	1	.500	.400
Leyritz, Jim	.200	5	1	0	0	1	0	.333	.200
Listach, Pat#	.500	8	4	0	0	1	1	.556	.625
Martinez, T*	.222	9	2	0	1	0	1	.222	.222
Matheny, Mike	.500	4	2	0	2	1	0	.600	.750
Meares, Pat	.286	7	2	1	2	0	2	.286	.714
Mieske, Matt	.600	5	3	0	0	2	0	.714	1.000
Molitor, Paul	.286	7	2	0	0	0	1	.286	.286
O'Neill, Paul*	.143	7	1	0	1	2	0	.333	.143
Reboulet, J	.200	5	1	0	1	1	0	.333	.200
Salmon, Tim	.333	6	2	0	1	0	0	.333	.500
Seitzer, K	.222	9	2	0	1	0	1	.222	.333
Sierra, Ruben#	.125	8	1	0	0	0	0	.125	.125
Snow, J.T.#	.750	4	3	0	1	1	0	.800	1.000
Stanley, Mike	.167	6	1	0	0	2	0	.375	.167
Valentin, Jhn	.200	5	1	0	1	0	0	.200	.200
Valentin, Jse#	.000	7	0	0	0	0	2	.000	.000
Vaughn, Greg	.429	7	3	0	0	2	0	.556	.571
Vaughn, Mo*	.500	4	2	1	2	1	1	.600	1.250
Velarde, R	.250	8	2	0	1	1	0	.333	.375
Vitiello, Joe	.333	6	2	0	1	1	1	.429	.333
Wallach, Tim	.000	5	0	0	0	1	0	.000	.000
Williams, Ber#	.571	7	4	1	2	1	1	.667	1.000
Williams, Ger	.286	7	2	0	0	1	0	.375	.286

Bob Wolcott, Mariners — RHP

Batter	Avg	AB	H	HR	BI	BB	SO	OBP	Slg
Alicea, Luis#	.400	5	2	0	0	1	0	.500	.600
Alomar, R#	.333	3	1	0	0	2	0	.600	.333
Anderson, Brd*	.286	7	2	1	1	0	0	.286	.857
Baines, H*	.333	9	3	0	0	0	0	.333	.556
Becker, Rich*	.444	9	4	0	0	3	2	.583	.444
Berroa, G	.143	7	1	1	1	0	1	.143	.571
Bonilla, B#	.571	7	4	0	1	0	0	.571	1.143
Bournigal, R	.250	8	2	0	1	0	1	.250	.375
Brosius, S	.000	6	0	0	0	1	3	.143	.000
Canseco, Jose	.200	10	2	0	1	1	1	.273	.400
Carter, Joe	.222	9	2	2	4	0	0	.222	.889
Cedeno, D#	.500	6	3	0	0	0	2	.500	.833
Clark, Tony#	.500	6	3	1	1	0	0	.500	1.000
Clark, Will*	.250	4	1	0	1	2	0	.500	.250
Cordova, M	.556	9	5	0	2	0	1	.556	.667
Curtis, Chad	.000	4	0	0	0	1	1	.200	.000
Cuyler, Milt#	.000	3	0	0	0	2	0	.400	.000
Damon, Johnny*	.333	9	3	0	1	1	0	.400	.333
Delgado, C*	.167	6	1	1	3	2	1	.444	.667
DiSarcina, G	.000	6	0	0	0	0	0	.167	.000
Durham, Ray#	.000	5	0	0	0	1	0	.000	.000
Erstad, Darin*	.500	4	2	0	0	1	0	.600	.500
Fielder, C	.200	5	1	0	0	0	1	.200	.200
Frye, Jeff	.000	5	0	0	0	0	0	.000	.000
Fryman, T	.571	7	4	1	4	0	0	.500	1.000
Giambi, Jason*	.143	7	1	0	0	0	2	.143	.143
Gonzalez, A	.000	6	0	0	0	0	0	.000	.000
Gonzalez, J	.200	5	1	0	0	0	1	.200	.200
Goodwin, Tom*	.300	10	3	0	1	1	1	.364	.400
Green, Shawn*	.375	8	3	0	1	0	0	.375	.875
Greenwell, M*	.400	5	2	1	3	0	0	.400	1.000
Guillen, O*	.375	8	3	0	1	0	1	.375	.500
Hamelin, Bob*	.286	7	2	1	3	2	0	.444	.714
Herrera, Jose*	.375	8	3	1	2	0	0	.375	.750
Higginson, B*	.400	5	2	0	0	1	1	.500	.800
Hoiles, Chris	.400	5	2	0	0	1	1	.500	.600
Hollins, Dave#	.000	8	0	0	0	0	1	.000	.000
Howard, Dave*	.143	7	1	0	0	0	2	.143	.143
Jefferson, R*	.000	4	0	0	0	1	2	.000	.000
Knoblauch, C	.000	10	0	0	0	1	0	.000	.000
Lewis, Darren	.333	6	2	0	3	2	0	.500	.667
Lewis, Mark	.000	6	0	0	0	0	3	.000	.000
Lockhart, K*	.750	8	6	0	2	2	0	.800	1.000
Macfarlane, M	.111	9	1	0	1	0	1	.100	.222
Manto, Jeff	.200	5	1	0	0	0	2	.200	.200
Martinez, Da*	.500	4	2	0	2	0	1	.400	.750
McGwire, Mark	.167	6	1	1	1	1	1	.286	.444
Meares, Pat	.444	9	4	1	4	0	0	.400	.889
Molitor, Paul	.333	12	4	0	0	0	1	.333	.333
Myers, Greg*	.111	9	1	0	2	1	1	.200	.111
Naehring, Tim	.500	10	5	0	0	3	1	.643	.600

Bob Wolcott, Mariners — RHP

Batter	Avg	AB	H	HR	BI	BB	SO	OBP	Slg
Nieves, M#	.250	4	1	1	2	1	0	.400	1.000
Nixon, Otis#	.222	9	2	0	0	0	1	.222	1.222
O'Brien, C	.250	4	1	0	1	0	1	.500	.250
O'Leary, Troy*	.417	12	5	0	0	0	3	.417	.417
Offerman, J#	.250	4	1	0	0	1	1	.400	.250
Olerud, John*	.000	6	0	0	0	3	0	.333	.000
Palmeiro, R*	.714	7	5	2	5	0	0	.714	1.714
Phillips, T#	.625	8	5	1	2	1	1	.667	1.250
Polonia, Luis*	.400	5	2	1	2	0	0	.400	1.000
Ripken, Cal	.400	5	2	1	1	0	0	.500	1.000
Rodriguez, I	.400	5	2	1	1	0	0	.500	1.000
Salmon, Tim	.200	5	1	0	2	0	0	.200	.200
Sierra, Ruben#	.167	6	1	0	0	0	2	.167	.167
Snow, J.T.#	.500	4	2	0	1	1	0	.600	.500
Sprague, Ed	.000	8	0	0	0	0	3	.000	.000
Stahoviak, S	.300	10	3	0	1	0	2	.300	.500
Stairs, Matt*	.500	6	3	0	0	0	0	.500	.667
Stanley, Mike	.200	5	1	0	0	1	3	.333	.200
Steinbach, T	.143	7	1	0	0	0	3	.143	.143
Tartabull, D	.000	5	0	0	0	0	0	.000	.000
Tettleton, R	.800	5	4	1	1	0	0	.800	1.600
Thomas, Frank	.222	9	2	1	3	2	1	.364	.556
Valentin, Jhn	.273	11	3	1	2	2	2	.385	.636
Vaughn, Mo*	.273	11	3	0	1	3	3	.429	.455
Velarde, R	.000	6	0	0	0	0	1	.000	.000
Ventura, R*	.300	10	3	0	1	0	1	.300	.400
Williams, E	.750	4	3	0	0	1	0	.800	.750

Tim Worrell, Padres — RHP

Batter	Avg	AB	H	HR	BI	BB	SO	OBP	Slg
Alou, Moises	.600	5	3	2	4	2	1	.714	2.000
Anthony, Eric*	.200	5	1	1	2	0	1	.200	.800
Bagwell, Jeff	.375	8	3	0	0	1	1	.444	.375
Bell, Derek	.500	6	3	0	0	0	1	.500	.667
Bell, Jay	.250	12	3	0	1	1	4	.308	.333
Benard, M*	.333	6	2	0	1	0	1	.333	.667
Berry, Sean	.250	8	2	2	3	0	2	.250	1.000
Bichette, D	.400	5	2	0	1	0	2	.400	.400
Biggio, Craig	.250	4	1	0	0	2	1	.571	.250
Blauser, Jeff	.000	10	0	0	1	0	3	.000	.000
Bonds, Barry*	.667	3	2	1	4	1	1	.857	1.667
Branson, Jeff*	.500	4	2	0	1	1	0	.600	.500
Brown, Brant*	.429	7	3	0	1	0	1	.429	.429
Burks, Ellis	.400	5	2	0	1	1	2	.500	.400
Clark, Dave*	.571	7	4	0	1	0	0	.571	.714
Clayton, R	.286	7	2	0	1	1	1	.375	.571
Conine, Jeff	.200	5	1	0	0	0	0	.200	.200
Davis, Eric	.000	6	0	0	0	3	0	.000	.000
DeShields, D*	.357	14	5	0	0	1	2	.400	.429
Fletcher, D*	.200	5	1	0	3	1	0	.286	.200
Fonville, C*	.400	5	2	0	0	0	1	.400	.600
Gaetti, Gary	.200	5	1	1	1	0	1	.200	.600
Gagne, Greg	.000	5	0	0	0	1	3	.167	.000
Galarraga, A	.500	6	3	0	1	0	2	.571	.667
Gant, Ron	.222	9	2	0	0	1	0	.222	.222
Garcia, C	.600	5	3	0	1	0	1	.600	.600
Gilkey, B	.375	8	3	0	2	0	2	.375	.625
Gonzalez, L*	.000	7	0	0	0	1	1	.125	.000
Grace, Mark*	.429	7	3	1	2	1	0	.500	.857
Grissom, M	.300	10	3	0	1	2	1	.417	.400
Hansen, Dave*	.400	5	2	0	0	1	0	.500	.400
Hernandez, Jo	.200	5	1	0	1	1	2	.333	.400
Hollandsworth*	.600	5	3	0	0	0	1	.600	.600
Howard, T*	.167	6	1	0	0	1	0	.286	.167
Hundley, Todd#	.286	7	2	0	1	1	0	.375	.429
Jefferies, G#	.000	5	0	0	0	2	2	.286	.000
Jones, C#	.400	5	2	0	0	2	1	.500	.800
Jordan, Brian	.286	7	2	0	1	0	2	.286	.429
Justice, Dave*	.250	12	3	0	0	0	2	.250	.250
Karros, Jeff	.182	11	2	1	2	0	2	.182	.455
Kent, Jeff	.000	4	0	0	1	0	1	.000	.000
King, Jeff	.200	5	1	0	0	0	1	.200	.200
Kingery, Mike*	.750	4	3	0	4	1	0	.800	1.250
Klesko, Ryan*	.111	9	1	0	1	1	1	.200	.222
Lankford, Ray*	.000	9	0	0	0	4	3	.000	.000
Lansing, Mike	.167	6	1	0	0	0	1	.167	.167
Larkin, Barry	.143	7	1	0	0	0	0	.250	.286
Lemke, Mark#	.100	10	1	0	0	1	0	.182	.100
Liriano, N#	.286	7	2	0	0	1	0	.286	.286
Lopez, Javy	.222	9	2	1	2	0	0	.222	.556
Mabry, John*	.200	5	1	0	1	0	2	.333	.400
Manwaring, A	.200	5	1	0	1	0	1	.200	.200
Martin, Al*	.500	8	4	0	2	0	0	.500	.875
McGriff, Fred*	.333	12	4	1	3	4	0	.500	.667
McRae, Brian#	.125	8	1	0	0	0	0	.125	.250
Merced, O*	.250	4	1	0	0	2	0	.500	.250
Mondesi, Raul	.222	9	2	0	2	1	0	.222	.222
Morandini, M*	.250	8	2	0	0	2	3	.400	.250
Morris, Hal*	.556	9	5	1	5	2	1	.636	1.000
Nixon, Otis#	.286	7	2	0	0	1	0	.375	.286
Offerman, J#	.500	4	2	0	0	1	1	.600	.500

Tim Worrell, Padres — RHP

Batter	Avg	AB	H	HR	BI	BB	SO	OBP	Slg
Oliver, Joe	.286	7	2	0	0	1	2	.375	.286
Ordonez, Rey	.400	5	2	0	1	0	1	.400	.400
Orsulak, Joe*	.000	4	0	0	0	1	0	.200	.000
Pagnozzi, Tom	.333	9	3	0	0	0	0	.333	.667
Pendleton, T#	.364	11	4	0	0	0	3	.364	.455
Piazza, Mike	.625	8	5	2	5	2	0	.700	1.500
Sabo, Chris	.000	5	0	0	0	2	0	.286	.000
Sanchez, Rey	.500	6	3	0	0	0	0	.500	.667
Sandberg, R	.111	9	1	0	0	1	0	.111	.111
Sanders, R	.200	5	1	0	1	1	1	.333	.400
Sosa, Sammy	.385	13	5	1	3	1	4	.429	.615
Thompson, Rob	.167	6	1	0	0	1	3	.286	.167
Walker, Larry*	.000	5	0	0	0	3	2	.375	.000
Wallach, Tim	.000	6	0	0	0	0	2	.000	.000
Weiss, Walt*	.286	7	2	1	1	2	2	.444	.714
Williams, Ma	.400	5	2	0	1	0	1	.500	.600
Young, Eric	.500	4	2	0	3	1	0	.600	.500
Zeile, Todd	.143	7	1	1	1	2	1	.333	.571

Todd Worrell, Dodgers — RHP

Batter	Avg	AB	H	HR	BI	BB	SO	OBP	Slg
Aldrete, Mike*	.000	3	0	0	0	1	1	.250	.000
Alfonzo, E	.200	5	1	0	0	1	0	.200	.200
Alicea, Luis#	.200	5	1	0	0	1	0	.333	.200
Alomar, R#	.000	6	0	0	0	0	1	.000	.000
Alou, Moises	.333	6	2	0	3	1	2	.429	.333
Anthony, Eric*	.400	5	2	1	1	0	2	.400	1.000
Ausmus, Brad	.400	5	2	0	0	1	0	.400	.400
Bagwell, Jeff	.400	5	2	0	0	1	0	.500	.400
Barberie, B#	.125	8	1	0	1	0	2	.125	.125
Bell, Derek	.286	7	2	0	0	0	1	.286	.429
Bell, Jay	.222	9	2	1	1	0	2	.222	.556
Bichette, D	.400	5	2	0	0	1	0	.400	.400
Blauser, Jeff	.571	7	4	0	3	0	1	.571	.714
Bonds, Barry*	.333	12	4	0	1	3	3	.467	.333
Bonilla, B#	.176	17	3	0	0	1	9	.222	.235
Boone, Bret	.000	5	0	0	1	0	1	.000	.000
Branson, Jeff*	.000	4	0	0	0	1	0	.200	.000
Butler, Brett*	.000	8	0	0	0	1	1	.111	.000
Caminiti, Ken#	.143	7	1	0	0	3	0	.143	.286
Candaele, C#	.000	5	0	0	0	1	0	.000	.000
Cangelosi, Ja	.500	6	3	0	1	1	1	.571	.500
Carr, Chuck	.400	5	2	0	2	1	0	.429	.600
Castilla, V	.571	7	4	0	2	0	0	.500	.571
Cedeno, A	.000	4	0	0	0	1	2	.200	.000
Clark, Will*	.500	10	5	1	3	3	2	.615	1.000
Clayton, R	.000	4	0	0	0	1	0	.000	.000
Colbrunn, G	.250	4	1	0	1	1	1	.400	.250
Conine, Jeff	.429	7	3	0	1	0	2	.429	.429
Cordero, Wil	.200	5	1	0	0	1	0	.200	.200
Daulton, D*	.133	15	2	1	4	1	5	.188	.400
Davis, Chili*	.500	8	4	0	2	4	1	.615	.500
Davis, Eric	.067	15	1	1	1	4	2	.263	.267
Dawson, Andre	.174	23	4	1	5	1	5	.208	.304
Duncan, M	.182	11	2	0	0	0	3	.182	.273
Dunston, S	.211	19	4	0	2	0	5	.211	.211
Dykstra, L*	.231	13	3	0	0	2	1	.333	.231
Eisenreich, J*	.333	6	2	1	1	1	0	.429	.833
Elster, Kevin	.167	6	1	0	0	1	0	.286	.167
Everett, Carl#	.167	6	1	0	0	0	3	.167	.167
Finley, Steve*	.000	6	0	0	0	0	1	.000	.000
Fletcher, D*	.200	5	1	1	3	2	1	.375	.800
Galarraga, A	.360	25	9	1	5	1	5	.385	.680
Gant, Ron	.000	12	0	0	0	2	4	.143	.000
Garcia, C	.600	5	3	0	2	1	0	.714	.600
Girardi, Joe	.429	7	3	0	2	0	1	.429	.571
Gonzalez, L*	.250	4	1	0	1	2	1	.500	.250
Grace, Mark*	.167	6	1	0	0	1	0	.286	.167
Grissom, M	.444	9	4	1	2	2	2	.545	.778
Grudzielanek	.200	5	1	0	0	0	0	.200	.200
Gwynn, Tony*	.300	10	3	0	0	2	1	.417	.400
Harris, Lenny*	.200	5	1	0	0	1	0	.200	.200
Hollins, Dave#	.333	6	2	0	0	1	2	.429	.333
Hundley, Todd#	.000	7	0	0	0	0	4	.125	.000
James, Dion*	.333	6	2	0	0	0	2	.333	.500
Jefferies, G#	.000	6	0	0	0	1	2	.143	.000
Johnson, Char	.333	6	2	1	2	0	1	.333	.833
Jordan, Brian	.250	8	2	0	0	0	2	.333	.375
Jordan, Ricky	.125	8	1	0	0	3	1	.364	.250
Justice, Dave*	.250	4	1	0	1	3	1	.400	.250
Kent, Jeff	.286	7	2	1	3	0	2	.286	.714
King, Jeff	.143	7	1	0	1	1	1	.250	.143
Lankford, Ray*	.429	7	3	0	0	1	1	.429	.571
Lansing, Mike	.250	4	1	0	0	0	0	.400	.250
Larkin, Barry	.286	14	4	0	0	0	0	.333	.357
Lemke, Mark#	.250	8	2	0	0	0	2	.250	.250
Magadan, Dave*	.167	6	1	0	0	3	1	.444	.167
Martin, Al*	.500	4	2	0	0	2	1	.667	.500
Martinez, Da*	.273	11	3	0	1	1	4	.333	.455
McGriff, Fred*	.200	5	1	1	1	1	0	.800	.600
McRae, Brian#	.250	4	1	0	0	1	0	.400	.250

Todd Worrell, Dodgers — RHP

Batter	Avg	AB	H	HR	BI	BB	SO	OBP	Slg
Miller, Orl	.200	5	1	0	0	0	2	.200	.400
Mitchell, K	.357	14	5	1	4	2	3	.438	.571
Morandini, M*	.222	9	2	0	0	0	4	.222	.222
Morris, Hal*	.400	10	4	1	4	0	0	.400	.800
Murray, Eddie#	.500	4	2	2	4	1	1	.600	2.000
Nixon, Otis#	.333	6	2	0	0	1	1	.429	.667
O'Neill, Paul*	.222	9	2	0	0	0	2	.222	.333
Oliver, Joe	.400	5	2	0	1	0	1	.400	.400
Orsulak, Joe*	.667	6	4	0	2	1	0	.625	.667
Pena, Tony	.000	5	0	0	0	0	2	.000	.000
Pendleton, T#	.111	9	1	0	2	1	3	.200	.111
Plantier, P*	.143	7	1	1	1	0	4	.250	.571
Raines, Tim#	.071	14	1	0	0	3	4	.235	.214
Reed, Jeff*	.429	7	3	0	1	0	2	.429	.571
Roberts, Bip#	.286	7	2	0	0	0	1	.286	.286
Samuel, Juan	.368	19	7	1	7	0	3	.368	.789
Sanchez, Rey	.250	4	1	0	0	0	0	.250	.250
Sandberg, R	.364	22	8	0	4	1	3	.375	.455
Santiago, B	.174	23	4	1	2	2	9	.240	.348
Segui, David#	.375	8	3	0	2	0	2	.375	.500
Sosa, Sammy	.250	8	2	0	0	0	1	.250	.250
Stocker, K#	.000	8	0	0	0	1	4	.111	.000
Strawberry, D*	.333	9	3	0	1	2	4	.455	.556
Taubensee, E*	.286	7	2	0	1	0	2	.286	.429
Thompson, Mil*	.133	15	2	0	0	1	8	.188	.200
Thompson, Rob	.125	16	2	0	2	1	3	.176	.125
VanderWal, J*	.400	10	4	1	2	1	4	.455	.700
Vizcaino, J	.250	8	2	1	3	0	5	.250	.625
Walker, Larry*	.400	5	2	0	0	2	1	.571	.600
Wallach, Tim	.231	26	6	0	4	1	9	.250	.308
Weiss, Walt#	.556	9	5	0	5	0	2	.556	.667
Whiten, Mark#	.500	6	3	1	1	1	0	.571	1.000
Wilkins, Rick*	.000	5	0	0	0	0	1	.000	.000
Williams, Ma	.556	9	5	0	0	0	1	.556	.667
Young, Kevin	.200	5	1	0	2	0	0	.200	.200
Zeile, Todd	.400	5	2	2	2	0	0	.400	1.600

Jamey Wright, Rockies — RHP

Batter	Avg	AB	H	HR	BI	BB	SO	OBP	Slg
Alicea, Luis#	.167	6	1	0	0	0	1	.167	.500
Aurilia, Rich	.333	6	2	0	1	0	0	.333	.333
Benard, M*	.125	8	1	0	0	1	0	.300	.125
Bonds, Barry*	.000	5	0	0	0	3	1	.375	.000
Clayton, R	.167	6	1	0	0	1	0	.286	.333
Gaetti, Gary	.200	5	1	0	0	1	0	.333	.200
Gant, Ron	.200	5	1	0	1	2	0	.429	.200
Grissom, M	.167	6	1	0	0	1	0	.286	.167
Jones, C#	.500	6	3	1	3	1	0	.571	1.000
Jordan, Brian	.167	6	1	0	1	0	0	.167	.167
Klesko, Ryan*	.800	5	4	0	0	1	0	.833	1.200
Lankford, Ray*	.429	7	3	0	1	0	1	.429	.857
Lemke, Mark#	.200	5	1	0	0	0	1	.200	.200
Lopez, Javy	.200	5	1	0	1	0	0	.333	.200
Mabry, John*	.167	6	1	0	0	0	1	.167	.167
McGriff, Fred*	.429	7	3	0	2	0	0	.429	.714
Pagnozzi, Tom	.333	6	2	0	2	0	0	.333	.500
Williams, Ma	.200	5	1	1	1	1	1	.333	.800

Anthony Young, Astros — RHP

Batter	Avg	AB	H	HR	BI	BB	SO	OBP	Slg
Alicea, Luis#	.083	12	1	0	0	0	1	.083	.167
Alou, Moises	.231	13	3	1	2	1	3	.313	.462
Amaro, Ruben#	.000	5	0	0	0	0	0	.000	.000
Bagwell, Jeff	.273	11	3	0	5	1	2	.308	.364
Barberie, B#	.800	5	4	0	3	2	1	.857	1.000
Batiste, Kim	.455	11	5	1	7	0	1	.455	.727
Bell, Derek	.125	8	1	0	0	0	3	.125	.125
Bell, Jay	.077	13	1	0	0	4	4	.294	.077
Belliard, R	.250	12	3	0	1	0	2	.250	.250
Benjamin, M	.200	5	1	0	1	0	1	.333	.200
Bichette, D	.273	11	3	0	4	0	1	.273	.545
Biggio, Craig	.333	15	5	2	2	1	4	.375	.867
Blauser, Jeff	.333	6	2	0	4	0	0	.333	.833
Bonds, Barry*	.308	13	4	0	3	5	1	.500	.385
Boone, Bret	.400	5	2	0	0	2	0	.400	.800
Branson, Jeff*	.600	5	3	0	2	0	0	.600	.600
Butler, Brett*	.308	13	4	0	0	1	3	.357	.385
Caminiti, Ken#	.200	10	2	1	3	0	1	.200	.600
Carreon, Mark	.125	8	1	0	1	0	0	.125	.250
Castilla, V	.000	7	0	0	0	0	1	.000	.000
Cedeno, A	.143	7	1	0	0	1	1	.250	.143
Cianfrocco, A	.273	11	3	1	4	0	2	.273	.545
Clark, Dave*	.500	5	2	0	1	1	1	.500	.600
Clark, Will*	.273	11	3	0	2	2	2	.385	.273
Clayton, R	.267	15	4	0	2	3	2	.389	.267
Cordero, Wil	.375	8	3	0	1	1	0	.444	.500
Dascenzo, D#	.250	4	1	0	0	1	0	.400	.250
Daulton, D*	.455	11	5	0	2	2	1	.500	.909
Davis, Eric	.300	10	3	0	1	1	2	.364	.500
Dawson, Andre	.111	9	1	1	2	1	1	.200	.444
DeShields, D*	.500	18	9	0	4	1	1	.526	.778
Duncan, M	.357	14	5	0	0	1	3	.400	.357
Dunston, S	.167	6	1	0	0	0	1	.167	.167
Dykstra, L*	.250	12	3	0	0	4	2	.438	.333
Eisenreich, J*	.250	8	2	0	2	2	0	.400	.375
Finley, Steve*	.250	8	2	0	0	2	1	.400	.375
Fletcher, D*	.333	6	2	0	1	1	0	.429	.333
Galarraga, A	.250	12	3	0	2	0	2	.308	.333
Gant, Ron	.111	9	1	1	2	3	2	.385	.444
Garcia, C	.143	14	2	0	1	0	2	.143	.286
Gilkey, B	.429	7	3	1	3	2	0	.600	1.286
Girardi, Joe	.200	5	1	0	0	1	1	.333	.400
Gonzalez, L*	.400	10	4	0	1	1	0	.455	.800
Grace, Mark*	.211	19	4	0	4	4	3	.333	.316
Grissom, M	.261	23	6	0	0	1	2	.292	.348
Gutierrez, R	.250	8	2	0	0	1	2	.333	.250
Gwynn, Tony*	.083	12	1	0	1	0	0	.083	.083
Hansen, Dave*	.167	6	1	0	2	2	1	.375	.167
Harris, Lenny	.250	4	1	0	0	2	0	.500	.250
Hayes, C	.143	7	1	0	0	0	1	.143	.143
Hill, G	.500	4	2	2	2	1	0	.600	2.000
Hollins, Dave#	.429	14	6	0	3	0	3	.429	.500
Hunter, Brian	.167	6	1	0	0	0	0	.167	.167
Incaviglia, P	.200	10	2	0	1	1	2	.250	.300
Jefferies, G#	.250	8	2	0	1	2	1	.400	.375
Jordan, Brian	.200	10	2	0	3	0	0	.250	.300
Jordan, Ricky	.250	8	2	1	2	0	2	.250	.625
Justice, Dave*	.385	13	5	2	5	1	3	.429	.846
Karros, Eric	.286	7	2	1	2	1	0	.375	.714
Kelly, R	.000	6	0	0	0	1	3	.143	.000
King, Jeff	.214	14	3	0	2	2	0	.313	.286
Kingery, Mike*	.600	5	3	0	0	2	0	.714	.600
Klesko, Ryan*	.500	4	2	0	1	1	1	.600	1.000
Lankford, Ray*	.316	19	6	0	0	2	7	.381	.368
Lansing, Mike	.222	9	2	0	2	1	2	.300	.222
Larkin, Barry	.300	10	3	0	1	1	1	.364	.300
Lemke, Mark#	.273	11	3	0	0	1	1	.273	.364
Lewis, Darren	.412	17	7	0	1	3	2	.500	.471
Lopez, Javy	.000	5	0	0	0	0	1	.000	.000
Magadan, Dave*	.250	4	1	0	0	1	1	.400	.500
Manwaring, K	.294	17	5	0	2	1	0	.368	.412
Martin, Al*	.222	9	2	1	2	2	2	.364	.556
Martinez, Da*	.111	9	1	0	1	2	3	.273	.111
May, Derrick*	.273	11	3	0	1	1	1	.333	.273
McGee, Willie*	.500	8	4	0	1	1	0	.556	.500
McGriff, Fred*	.273	11	3	1	3	2	2	.385	.636
Merced, O*	.133	15	2	1	1	2	1	.235	.333
Mondesi, Raul	.500	6	3	1	1	0	0	.500	1.000
Morandini, M*	.278	18	5	0	0	0	5	.278	.444
Morris, Hal*	.250	8	2	0	0	1	1	.333	.250
Nixon, Otis#	.375	8	3	0	1	0	0	.333	.375
O'Neill, Paul*	.250	4	1	0	1	1	0	.400	.500
Offerman, J#	.385	13	5	0	3	1	2	.429	.538
Oliver, Joe	.667	6	4	1	2	0	1	.667	1.167
Pagnozzi, Tom	.273	11	3	0	1	1	1	.333	.364
Pena, G#	.375	8	3	0	1	0	1	.375	.375
Pendleton, T#	.211	19	4	2	2	0	2	.211	.526
Piazza, Mike	.250	8	2	0	1	1	0	.333	.250
Plantier, P*	.333	6	2	1	2	0	2	.333	.833
Roberson, K#	.000	5	0	0	0	1	2	.167	.000
Roberts, Bip#	.167	6	1	0	0	0	0	.167	.167
Rodriguez, H*	.750	8	6	1	2	0	0	.750	1.250
Sabo, Chris	.500	8	4	2	6	0	1	.500	1.250
Sanchez, Rey	.375	8	3	0	1	1	0	.444	.500
Sandberg, R	.286	21	6	0	1	1	1	.348	.286
Sanders, R	.182	11	2	0	0	2	1	.308	.273
Santiago, B	.500	4	2	0	2	1	1	.600	.500
Scarsone, S	.333	6	2	0	0	0	0	.333	.500
Servais, S	.333	6	2	0	1	1	1	.429	.333
Slaught, Don	.154	13	2	0	0	0	0	.154	.154
Smith, Dwight*	.176	17	3	0	0	4	2	.333	.176
Smith, Ozzie#	.167	12	2	0	0	0	0	.167	.167
Sosa, Sammy	.125	8	1	0	0	1	3	.222	.125
Stocker, K#	.000	5	0	0	0	2	2	.286	.000
Thompson, Mil*	.400	10	4	1	2	0	0	.400	.700
Thompson, Rob	.400	10	4	0	2	1	1	.455	.600
VanderWal, J*	.286	7	2	0	0	1	1	.375	.429
Vizcaino, J	.200	15	3	0	0	2	2	.188	.267
Walker, Larry*	.421	19	8	2	4	1	2	.450	.842
Wallach, Tim	.111	9	1	1	3	0	3	.333	.444
Webster, L	.400	5	2	0	0	0	0	.400	.400
Weiss, Walt#	.000	8	0	0	0	2	2	.200	.000
Whiten, Mark#	.417	12	5	0	2	1	0	.462	.583
Wilkins, Rick*	.375	16	6	2	6	1	3	.412	.813
Williams, Ma	.105	19	2	1	3	1	3	.150	.263
Young, Kevin	.000	5	0	0	0	0	0	.000	.000
Zeile, Todd	.313	16	5	0	1	2	1	.368	.313

Batters at Parks

Do the terms "home field advantage" and "the friendly confines" have any basis in reality? The answer could lie in the following pages. This section highlights batter performances at every stadium in the majors.

Our park data goes back as far as 1987. So for the newer parks—like The Ballpark In Arlington or Jacobs Field—the numbers cover the park's entire history. Each batter must have logged at least 35 plate appearances at an individual park in order to make the list.

Atlanta, Georgia — Grass

Batter	Avg	AB	H	HR	BI	BB	SO	OBP	Slg
Abbott, Kurt	.235	51	12	2	4	6	18	.316	.392
Aldrete, Mike*	.364	55	20	0	14	7	7	.415	.418
Alicea, Luis#	.212	85	18	0	5	8	15	.277	.259
Alomar, R#	.311	103	32	1	11	7	13	.355	.437
Alou, Moises	.227	97	22	2	11	13	9	.315	.330
Anthony, Eric*	.228	57	13	2	8	9	17	.333	.351
Arias, Alex	.350	40	14	0	6	4	2	.391	.450
Bagwell, Jeff	.316	114	36	8	20	19	22	.409	.561
Bell, Derek	.320	75	24	3	13	4	12	.354	.493
Bell, Jay	.239	163	39	4	17	8	35	.275	.380
Belliard, R	.218	551	120	0	26	24	69	.259	.254
Berroa, G	.238	80	19	1	4	3	19	.265	.300
Berry, Sean	.190	63	12	1	5	5	10	.250	.302
Bichette, D	.239	71	17	2	5	2	15	.267	.380
Biggio, Craig	.244	213	52	5	20	11	32	.283	.329
Blauser, Jeff	.260	1667	433	41	188	222	318	.353	.400
Bogar, Tim	.361	36	13	2	10	3	6	.390	.611
Bonds, Barry*	.268	194	52	11	32	22	30	.352	.490
Bonilla, B#	.252	147	37	6	20	15	23	.315	.429
Boone, Bret	.294	51	15	1	6	3	9	.339	.412
Branson, Jeff*	.228	57	13	3	7	4	13	.279	.421
Brogna, Rico*	.333	33	11	1	4	3	7	.389	.455
Brumfield, J	.342	38	13	2	5	4	9	.395	.579
Burks, Ellis	.286	42	12	4	8	5	10	.362	.667
Butler, Brett*	.314	210	66	2	16	40	28	.425	.400
Caminiti, Ken#	.284	218	62	3	18	20	32	.346	.376
Candaele, C#	.214	98	21	0	9	6	7	.264	.265
Cangelosi, J#	.255	55	14	0	4	13	13	.408	.345
Carr, Chuck#	.279	43	12	0	1	7	6	.380	.302
Carreon, Mark	.286	63	18	2	7	4	5	.328	.444
Carter, Joe	.258	31	8	2	9	9	3	.405	.484
Castilla, V	.207	92	19	3	12	2	19	.229	.326
Cedeno, A	.330	88	29	3	19	4	16	.351	.523
Clark, Dave*	.237	38	9	0	4	4	12	.318	.237
Clark, Will*	.374	198	74	10	41	27	29	.454	.596
Clayton, R	.260	96	25	2	9	9	21	.315	.396
Colbrunn, G	.277	65	18	0	9	4	15	.314	.354
Coleman, V#	.250	108	27	0	4	6	21	.289	.296
Conine, Jeff	.337	86	29	2	14	12	17	.414	.477
Cordero, Wil	.323	62	20	3	11	4	7	.364	.548
Dascenzo, D#	.273	44	12	1	5	3	4	.313	.341
Daulton, D*	.215	130	28	6	23	25	17	.338	.454
Davis, Chili#	.273	33	9	3	6	6	6	.385	.545
Davis, Eric	.290	183	53	11	33	23	43	.368	.557
Dawson, Andre	.224	134	30	11	27	7	23	.259	.545
Decker, Steve	.111	36	4	1	3	2	6	.154	.250
DeShields, D*	.221	131	29	1	15	13	33	.290	.298
Duncan, M	.281	146	41	3	17	4	28	.310	.377
Dunston, S	.306	170	52	4	21	3	31	.318	.429
Dye, Jermaine	.310	126	39	4	17	3	19	.326	.468
Dykstra, L*	.276	174	48	0	19	27	26	.376	.345
Eisenreich, J*	.217	46	10	0	6	6	5	.296	.304
Elster, Kevin	.315	73	23	2	15	5	8	.359	.479
Everett, Carl#	.219	32	7	0	6	4	14	.324	.281
Finley, Steve*	.240	150	36	1	12	6	26	.270	.333
Fletcher, D*	.137	51	7	0	1	3	8	.214	.137
Galarraga, A	.295	190	56	10	32	7	64	.330	.495
Gant, Ron	.272	1591	432	82	258	159	286	.340	.493
Garcia, C	.243	37	9	0	2	2	9	.275	.324
Gilkey, B	.358	95	34	3	16	15	12	.445	.495
Giovanola, Ed*	.140	43	6	0	4	5	9	.229	.186
Girardi, Joe	.219	64	14	2	6	7	11	.296	.313
Gonzalez, L*	.182	110	20	3	8	13	18	.283	.309
Grace, Mark*	.277	184	51	6	22	21	15	.350	.435
Grissom, M	.274	715	196	16	61	52	83	.326	.410
Grudzielanek	.149	47	7	0	2	0	10	.167	.191
Gutierrez, R	.256	39	10	0	0	1	11	.275	.282
Gwynn, Tony*	.379	261	99	4	41	24	5	.430	.529
Harris, Lenny*	.286	105	30	1	7	10	11	.348	.343
Hayes, C	.296	135	40	9	21	14	21	.360	.563
Hill, G	.304	46	14	2	8	1	14	.319	.500
Hollins, Dave#	.338	65	22	3	15	18	10	.477	.554
Howard, T*	.173	52	9	0	1	1	8	.189	.269
Hudler, Rex	.209	43	9	3	4	0	4	.209	.419
Hundley, Todd#	.342	79	27	3	11	4	19	.373	.481
Hunter, Brian	.243	317	77	16	63	29	56	.301	.451
Incaviglia, P	.283	60	17	4	16	6	17	.343	.567
James, Dion*	.306	506	155	6	56	82	58	.405	.437
Javier, Stan#	.173	81	14	1	4	6	12	.227	.222
Jefferies, G#	.268	138	37	6	17	10	7	.315	.449
Jones, Andruw	.269	52	14	3	6	2	13	.296	.577
Jones, C#	.308	562	173	33	115	76	88	.387	.555
Jones, Chris	.327	49	16	2	8	7	13	.411	.571
Jordan, Brian	.333	66	22	4	14	4	13	.366	.606
Jordan, Ricky	.288	73	21	2	13	4	8	.313	.466
Justice, Dave*	.287	1413	405	88	267	210	244	.378	.539
Karros, Eric	.260	104	27	2	21	5	23	.283	.404
Kelly, Mike	.147	75	11	0	3	6	19	.217	.187

Atlanta, Georgia — **Grass**

Batter	Avg	AB	H	HR	BI	BB	SO	OBP	Slg
Kelly, R	.299	157	47	3	15	15	18	.358	.427
Kent, Jeff	.258	66	17	0	9	1	9	.279	.333
King, Jeff	.202	124	25	2	15	12	16	.271	.315
Kingery, Mike*	.333	39	13	0	8	1	2	.350	.359
Klesko, Ryan*	.299	575	172	44	114	59	125	.366	.581
Lankford, Ray*	.233	146	34	2	16	14	40	.296	.349
Lansing, Mike	.220	91	20	1	3	5	10	.258	.264
Larkin, Barry	.350	237	83	8	31	27	17	.414	.557
Lemke, Mark#	.263	1416	373	18	130	145	134	.330	.348
Lewis, Darren	.297	101	30	1	8	8	13	.357	.406
Liriano, N#	.147	34	5	0	3	5	7	.250	.206
Lopez, Javy	.282	563	159	22	73	25	91	.316	.442
Mabry, John*	.275	40	11	1	2	2	10	.310	.375
Magadan, Dave*	.241	141	34	2	11	21	25	.337	.326
Manwaring, K	.218	124	27	1	9	8	27	.274	.258
Martin, Al*	.407	54	22	1	6	7	9	.475	.611
Martinez, Da*	.322	87	28	2	8	11	19	.398	.506
May, Derrick*	.255	51	13	2	11	0	6	.250	.392
McGee, Willie#	.227	181	41	0	18	4	36	.243	.276
McGriff, Fred*	.291	970	282	58	195	118	166	.367	.528
McRae, Brian*	.294	51	15	1	4	3	8	.333	.412
Merced, O*	.254	71	18	1	9	7	14	.321	.338
Mitchell, K	.333	162	54	11	35	19	23	.413	.593
Mondesi, Raul	.271	48	13	2	5	1	10	.294	.438
Morandini, M*	.299	97	29	0	14	7	18	.349	.361
Mordecai, M	.185	92	17	2	11	9	20	.257	.293
Morris, Hal*	.308	107	33	1	10	15	21	.398	.383
Murray, Eddie#	.254	142	36	3	13	8	11	.288	.359
Nixon, Otis#	.302	693	209	2	42	85	72	.376	.352
O'Brien, C	.269	193	52	11	32	19	34	.344	.508
O'Neill, Paul*	.207	111	23	1	14	15	24	.302	.279
Offerman, J#	.136	81	11	1	6	9	17	.222	.173
Oliver, Joe	.266	124	33	4	19	9	21	.313	.403
Orsulak, Joe*	.152	46	7	0	1	2	9	.188	.174
Pagnozzi, Tom	.220	100	22	1	11	4	16	.248	.320
Palmeiro, R*	.286	35	10	1	7	6	2	.390	.486
Parent, Mark	.143	49	7	0	5	2	11	.176	.184
Pena, G#	.298	47	14	1	2	4	13	.353	.447
Pena, Tony	.233	43	10	0	7	5	6	.313	.279
Pendleton, T#	.292	1252	365	42	190	81	172	.332	.458
Perez, Eddie	.308	78	24	2	15	4	9	.345	.487
Piazza, Mike	.333	60	20	5	15	10	13	.437	.633
Plantier, P*	.093	43	4	1	2	5	13	.188	.186
Polonia, Luis*	.175	40	7	0	2	3	6	.227	.275
Prince, Tom	.133	30	4	0	0	6	7	.297	.233
Raines, Tim#	.254	71	18	1	11	14	8	.368	.352
Reed, Jeff*	.227	66	15	2	7	9	9	.316	.364
Reed, Jody	.214	56	12	0	1	3	8	.254	.250
Roberts, Bip#	.351	148	52	2	13	15	10	.415	.466
Rodriguez, H*	.242	33	8	1	2	1	12	.286	.394
Sabo, Chris	.285	158	45	7	26	14	17	.352	.468
Samuel, Juan	.226	164	37	4	22	15	45	.297	.329
Sanchez, Rey	.178	73	13	0	0	3	7	.211	.205
Sandberg, R	.274	179	49	11	23	16	18	.333	.508
Sanders, R	.258	120	31	4	10	10	29	.321	.442
Santiago, B	.272	206	56	14	41	13	39	.315	.524
Segui, David#	.390	41	16	2	8	5	8	.457	.610
Servais, S	.304	56	17	1	7	8	4	.391	.482
Sheaffer, D	.222	36	8	0	3	1	6	.237	.250
Sheffield, G	.284	109	31	6	18	19	20	.395	.541
Shipley, C	.327	49	16	0	4	4	8	.370	.347
Simms, Mike	.200	45	9	3	8	3	10	.265	.444
Slaught, Don	.243	74	18	0	6	2	10	.278	.257
Smith, Dwight*	.193	181	35	4	21	20	40	.278	.298
Smith, Ozzie#	.281	203	57	0	15	13	15	.323	.355
Sosa, Sammy	.256	78	20	4	12	8	24	.326	.474
Stillwell, K#	.218	55	12	1	3	4	7	.271	.309
Stocker, K#	.255	51	13	0	5	3	9	.291	.294
Strawberry, D*	.243	136	33	10	18	14	24	.318	.522
Tarasco, Tony*	.299	97	29	2	10	5	13	.333	.392
Taubensee, E*	.306	62	19	2	9	4	20	.348	.468
Thompson, Mil*	.245	94	23	1	3	6	21	.290	.319
Thompson, Rob	.280	246	69	9	24	27	50	.361	.480
Thompson, Ry	.234	47	11	0	3	3	11	.280	.298
Veras, Q#	.267	45	12	0	2	2	9	.306	.356
Vizcaino, J#	.286	84	24	0	8	3	13	.303	.321
Walker, Larry*	.326	132	43	7	23	12	24	.382	.545
Wallach, Tim	.278	198	55	12	48	14	24	.326	.540
Walton, J	.299	97	29	1	2	7	22	.349	.402
Weiss, Walt#	.211	71	15	0	0	11	12	.317	.225
White, R	.260	50	13	1	4	5	13	.339	.440
Whiten, Mark#	.312	93	29	4	24	14	24	.402	.548
Wilkins, Rick*	.217	46	10	3	6	8	19	.327	.413
Williams, Ma	.258	213	55	3	28	7	38	.278	.347
Young, Eric	.227	88	20	0	5	6	9	.281	.284
Zeile, Todd	.217	152	33	2	17	10	32	.264	.309

Batter	Avg	AB	H	HR	BI	BB	SO	OBP	Slg
Aldrete, Mike*	.303	33	10	1	6	1	4	.324	.485
Alexander, M	.192	151	29	2	12	8	30	.238	.258
Alomar, R#	.340	376	128	14	62	60	45	.422	.529
Alomar Jr, S	.265	68	18	3	13	2	7	.286	.441
Amaral, Rich	.179	56	10	1	3	5	10	.246	.250
Anderson, Brd*	.261	1369	357	53	179	194	253	.362	.454
Baerga, C#	.219	96	21	2	8	5	12	.265	.323
Baines, H*	.320	562	180	31	103	90	70	.412	.541
Barberie, B#	.244	119	29	1	12	26	29	.395	.336
Bautista, D	.261	46	12	1	3	2	11	.292	.413
Belle, Albert	.313	115	36	11	25	14	15	.386	.670
Berroa, G	.238	63	15	0	7	7	16	.310	.317
Blowers, Mike	.250	64	16	2	11	3	18	.290	.422
Boggs, Wade*	.237	93	22	2	10	7	7	.287	.366
Bonilla, B#	.297	418	124	16	81	50	60	.366	.476
Borders, Pat	.230	61	14	1	6	4	11	.277	.311
Bordick, Mike	.262	107	28	5	14	12	5	.333	.449
Brosius, S	.250	56	14	3	9	3	14	.283	.482
Buford, Damon	.127	55	7	1	4	8	15	.246	.200
Buhner, Jay	.323	93	30	8	19	11	19	.396	.624
Canseco, Jose	.296	98	29	6	21	13	20	.381	.592
Carter, Joe	.256	117	30	6	17	6	18	.296	.479
Clark, Will*	.207	29	6	0	6	6	6	.324	.310
Cora, Joey#	.178	73	13	1	10	6	8	.247	.247
Curtis, Chad	.265	98	26	2	8	10	20	.333	.347
Davis, Chili#	.217	92	20	5	13	21	17	.363	.413
Devereaux, M	.244	862	210	34	143	78	145	.305	.429
DiSarcina, G	.266	94	25	0	7	1	5	.278	.298
Easley, D	.236	55	13	1	3	6	10	.311	.382
Edmonds, Jim*	.274	62	17	3	6	2	14	.297	.484
Espinoza, A	.217	60	13	1	5	1	7	.242	.367
Fermin, Felix	.217	46	10	0	2	2	5	.250	.217
Fielder, C	.281	96	27	6	22	10	19	.346	.500
Franco, Julio	.278	54	15	1	8	5	9	.339	.389
Frye, Jeff	.162	37	6	1	3	4	8	.244	.297
Fryman, T	.325	123	40	3	17	8	28	.366	.463
Gaetti, Gary	.250	48	12	3	7	4	8	.302	.458
Gagne, Greg	.115	52	6	0	2	2	10	.145	.192
Gallego, Mike	.311	45	14	1	4	5	8	.380	.467
Gates, Brent#	.258	66	17	0	7	6	11	.329	.348
Gomez, Chris	.314	51	16	0	4	5	9	.375	.373
Gomez, Leo	.246	532	131	27	75	74	97	.345	.442
Gonzalez, A	.297	37	11	3	5	6	14	.395	.568
Gonzalez, J	.252	103	26	8	23	6	22	.297	.515
Goodwin, C*	.294	143	42	0	13	6	29	.327	.357
Goodwin, Tom*	.324	37	12	0	1	5	11	.405	.324
Grebeck, C	.290	31	9	0	1	6	4	.405	.290
Greenwell, M*	.256	82	21	3	9	10	6	.333	.390
Greer, Rusty*	.158	38	6	0	3	5	3	.256	.211
Griffey Jr, K*	.279	104	29	5	17	7	27	.321	.500
Guillen, O*	.246	57	14	1	6	3	2	.283	.404
Hamelin, Bob*	.172	29	5	2	6	5	9	.286	.379
Hamilton, D*	.342	76	26	0	3	12	9	.432	.434
Hammonds, J	.277	383	106	13	49	25	65	.322	.441
Haselman, B	.147	34	5	1	2	1	8	.189	.265
Henderson, R	.267	60	16	1	5	16	5	.416	.367
Hiatt, Phil	.176	34	6	0	4	1	13	.200	.235
Higginson, B*	.294	34	10	3	6	2	5	.333	.588
Hill, G	.171	35	6	0	0	1	8	.194	.200
Hoiles, Chris	.269	916	246	57	159	163	196	.384	.489
Howard, Dave#	.256	39	10	0	2	2	3	.293	.359
Hudler, Rex	.265	34	9	5	9	0	6	.257	.735
Hulse, David*	.297	37	11	0	1	3	5	.350	.351
Huson, Jeff*	.289	97	28	1	9	10	13	.355	.351
Jaha, John	.308	78	24	5	16	12	17	.407	.590
Javier, Stan#	.310	42	13	1	5	5	6	.396	.452
Jefferson, R*	.375	40	15	2	5	3	8	.432	.600
Johnson, L*	.300	80	24	1	7	1	7	.309	.388
Joyner, Wally*	.262	61	16	1	9	11	10	.365	.361
Karkovice, R	.193	57	11	3	8	7	19	.273	.351
Kelly, Pat	.333	48	16	1	7	3	14	.396	.438
Kelly, R	.255	51	13	1	8	2	7	.273	.373
Kirby, Wayne*	.310	42	13	0	1	2	2	.341	.357
Knoblauch, C	.286	91	26	2	9	13	13	.387	.451
Leius, Scott	.341	41	14	0	7	4	6	.400	.439
Lewis, Mark	.235	51	12	2	3	2	13	.264	.412
Leyritz, Jim	.277	47	13	3	7	8	9	.393	.489
Listach, Pat#	.338	71	24	0	6	7	8	.397	.451
Lofton, Kenny*	.316	117	37	0	9	7	18	.360	.385
Macfarlane, M	.246	65	16	2	8	1	14	.258	.446
Manto, Jeff	.256	133	34	12	24	14	35	.327	.556
Martinez, E	.393	84	33	5	22	19	11	.495	.690
Martinez, T*	.250	104	26	4	11	9	24	.313	.442
Mayne, Brent*	.176	34	6	1	4	1	6	.194	.294
McGwire, Mark	.212	66	14	5	13	12	24	.329	.439
McLemore, M#	.276	597	165	4	64	61	85	.342	.350
McRae, Brian#	.306	49	15	0	4	4	9	.358	.388
Meares, Pat	.298	57	17	2	8	1	11	.310	.491

ORIOLE PARK AT CAMDEN YARDS
Home of the Baltimore Orioles
Baltimore, Maryland — Grass

Batter	Avg	AB	H	HR	BI	BB	SO	OBP	Slg
Mieske, Matt	.319	47	15	2	8	4	10	.365	.553
Molitor, Paul	.263	118	31	0	16	13	10	.328	.322
Munoz, Pedro	.286	49	14	6	15	1	10	.294	.673
Murray, Eddie#	.224	147	33	11	25	20	22	.310	.469
Myers, Greg*	.200	35	7	0	1	5	4	.293	.229
Naehring, Tim	.295	61	18	1	6	5	11	.343	.393
Nilsson, Dave*	.246	61	15	3	15	3	10	.292	.475
Nixon, Otis#	.348	46	16	0	4	2	9	.375	.370
O'Leary, Troy*	.217	46	10	0	3	3	9	.265	.217
O'Neill, Paul*	.257	70	18	3	8	12	12	.366	.429
Obando, S	.254	71	18	2	10	3	18	.289	.366
Olerud, John*	.293	99	29	2	12	12	11	.375	.394
Orsulak, Joe*	.278	180	50	2	18	18	13	.347	.361
Palmeiro, R*	.317	826	262	54	169	127	123	.404	.575
Palmer, Dean	.312	77	24	9	19	9	20	.393	.727
Paquette, C	.300	50	15	2	15	1	10	.314	.460
Parent, Mark	.308	52	16	1	9	3	17	.339	.423
Pena, Tony	.290	62	18	2	7	3	9	.323	.419
Phillips, T#	.275	109	30	4	8	21	23	.392	.477
Polonia, Luis*	.278	162	45	2	10	8	15	.312	.358
Raines, Tim#	.254	59	15	0	3	7	8	.333	.288
Ramirez, M	.320	50	16	2	15	7	12	.404	.520
Reed, Jody	.167	36	6	0	1	3	3	.231	.167
Ripken, Billy	.240	229	55	4	29	17	20	.300	.323
Ripken, Cal	.263	1408	370	44	207	144	154	.334	.409
Rodriguez, I	.322	90	29	4	12	7	12	.364	.567
Sabo, Chris	.227	132	30	3	20	7	22	.277	.379
Salmon, Tim	.260	100	26	7	20	14	22	.364	.510
Segui, David#	.264	311	82	7	47	39	41	.341	.399
Seitzer, K	.310	87	27	2	17	11	6	.376	.483
Sierra, Ruben#	.271	133	36	4	15	8	15	.312	.459
Smith, Dwight*	.395	38	15	0	5	2	4	.439	.474
Smith, Mark	.220	100	22	4	11	9	29	.291	.390
Snow, J.T.#	.292	72	21	2	5	7	9	.354	.472
Sojo, Luis	.286	42	12	0	2	1	1	.318	.381
Sorrento, P*	.250	84	21	2	15	8	16	.315	.357
Sprague, Ed	.260	96	25	1	8	8	14	.349	.375
Stankiewicz	.138	29	4	0	3	5	4	.257	.241
Stanley, Mike	.304	69	21	5	13	9	16	.385	.609
Steinbach, T	.253	87	22	3	13	6	21	.292	.414
Strange, Doug#	.341	41	14	3	8	5	5	.426	.634
Surhoff, B.J.*	.269	320	86	14	47	27	42	.333	.478
Tarasco, Tony*	.234	47	11	1	6	3	9	.280	.340
Tartabull, D	.281	96	27	8	27	14	33	.378	.604
Tettleton, M#	.270	89	24	7	19	20	26	.404	.584
Thomas, Frank	.293	82	24	8	20	22	7	.439	.598
Thorne, Jim*	.250	68	17	4	11	14	21	.378	.471
Tinsley, Lee#	.278	36	10	2	3	6	9	.409	.472
Trammell, A	.170	47	8	2	2	4	8	.235	.340
Valentin, Jhn	.318	88	28	0	7	6	16	.362	.352
Valentin, Jse#	.209	43	9	2	5	4	12	.271	.395
Valle, Dave	.342	38	13	1	5	5	3	.432	.500
Vaughn, Greg	.272	92	25	5	20	14	23	.370	.435
Vaughn, Mo*	.235	102	24	8	22	11	26	.319	.500
Velarde, R	.261	69	18	3	14	9	14	.354	.420
Ventura, R*	.289	97	28	3	13	10	9	.352	.454
Vina, F*	.250	36	9	0	0	2	1	.289	.306
Vizquel, Omar#	.224	85	19	0	2	2	9	.250	.235
Voigt, Jack	.258	159	41	6	25	24	35	.353	.421
White, Devon#	.180	100	18	2	11	11	23	.259	.260
Whiten, Mark#	.241	29	7	1	2	8	5	.405	.414
Williams, Ber#	.348	112	39	5	16	11	18	.407	.589
Williams, Ger	.333	45	15	2	8	3	7	.375	.578
Wilson, Dan	.250	52	13	3	7	3	14	.304	.481
Zaun, Greg#	.225	102	23	2	11	12	15	.314	.324
Zeile, Todd	.200	45	9	1	9	5	3	.280	.333

FENWAY PARK
Home of the Boston Red Sox
Boston, Massachusetts — Grass

Batter	Avg	AB	H	HR	BI	BB	SO	OBP	Slg
Aldrete, Mike*	.194	31	6	1	4	8	6	.359	.355
Alicea, Luis#	.255	208	53	0	17	23	29	.332	.327
Alomar, R#	.276	134	37	1	7	10	22	.326	.373
Alomar Jr, S	.299	107	32	2	7	8	13	.364	.393
Amaral, Rich	.324	37	12	0	5	3	8	.375	.432
Anderson, Brd*	.272	217	59	3	30	27	47	.367	.429
Baerga, C#	.277	177	49	7	26	12	20	.328	.463
Baines, H*	.328	201	66	7	27	30	28	.414	.463
Bautista, D	.349	43	15	1	10	1	8	.356	.442
Becker, Rich*	.211	38	8	0	7	3	10	.279	.289
Belle, Albert	.242	157	38	12	37	14	31	.314	.510
Beltre, E	.184	38	7	0	4	3	10	.238	.211
Berroa, G	.208	53	11	0	5	3	16	.250	.264
Bichette, D	.366	71	26	3	9	1	12	.375	.577
Blowers, Mike	.319	69	22	1	8	7	17	.382	.420
Boggs, Wade*	.361	1734	626	29	207	349	134	.466	.528

Batter	Avg	AB	H	HR	BI	BB	SO	OBP	Slg
Bonilla, B#	.222	36	8	0	4	6	7	.341	.278
Borders, Pat	.252	107	27	1	10	5	25	.283	.299
Bordick, Mike	.274	113	31	1	10	6	11	.308	.345
Bragg, Darren*	.260	127	33	4	19	15	24	.342	.441
Brosius, S	.207	58	12	2	4	4	11	.254	.328
Buhner, Jay	.266	173	46	7	36	21	48	.343	.434
Burks, Ellis	.294	1363	401	48	199	137	205	.360	.484
Butler, Brett*	.375	32	12	0	2	3	1	.429	.500
Canseco, Jose	.313	508	159	36	113	14	40	.341	.622
Carter, Joe	.304	230	70	17	45	14	40	.341	.622
Cedeno, D#	.158	38	6	0	1	3	12	.220	.158
Cirillo, Jeff	.317	41	13	2	5	4	7	.378	.561
Clark, Dave*	.263	38	10	2	6	5	8	.349	.500
Clark, Will*	.500	40	20	0	13	4	4	.545	.600
Cole, Alex*	.223	103	23	0	10	13	14	.305	.291
Cora, Joey#	.213	80	17	0	9	9	9	.286	.288
Cordero, Wil	.307	101	31	2	19	5	13	.343	.455
Cordova, M	.176	34	6	0	2	1	8	.200	.206
Curtis, Chad	.250	108	27	1	11	6	28	.287	.343
Cuyler, Milt#	.174	92	16	0	7	8	21	.248	.217
Davis, Chili#	.318	198	63	6	31	31	46	.405	.480
Dawson, Andre	.290	393	114	15	70	14	48	.322	.491
Deer, Rob	.210	181	38	10	24	30	61	.329	.420
Delgado, C*	.195	41	8	0	4	2	8	.227	.268
Devereaux, M	.228	162	37	4	20	15	34	.292	.327
Diaz, Alex#	.226	31	7	0	4	2	2	.257	.290
DiSarcina, G	.216	97	21	1	10	5	11	.300	.396
Durham, Ray#	.271	48	13	1	2	2	16	.300	.333
Easley, D	.310	58	18	0	4	4	8	.375	.362
Edmonds, Jim*	.308	65	20	1	4	8	18	.384	.446
Eisenreich, J*	.271	70	19	0	5	4	9	.307	.386
Espinoza, A	.164	73	12	1	5	4	16	.205	.233
Fabregas, Jor*	.405	37	15	0	7	2	6	.415	.405
Fermin, Felix	.203	172	35	0	10	9	9	.243	.215
Fielder, C	.239	176	42	9	30	24	47	.330	.432
Flaherty, J	.183	82	15	0	2	3	15	.218	.232
Franco, Julio	.322	152	49	5	21	22	19	.411	.461
Frye, Jeff	.287	251	72	3	18	29	37	.365	.382
Fryman, T	.292	161	47	9	34	11	45	.328	.503
Gaetti, Gary	.231	160	37	11	31	12	35	.277	.500
Gagne, Greg	.230	126	29	1	10	10	42	.290	.333
Gallego, Mike	.313	96	30	1	8	10	15	.391	.375
Garciaparra, N	.209	43	9	3	7	0	6	.205	.535
Gates, Brent#	.260	77	20	1	6	5	9	.305	.312
Gomez, Chris	.314	35	11	1	7	4	9	.385	.543
Gomez, Leo	.283	60	17	6	13	7	12	.352	.650
Gonzales, R	.178	45	8	0	2	5	4	.250	.200
Gonzalez, A	.472	36	17	1	8	3	1	.525	.694
Gonzalez, J	.282	124	35	12	31	6	30	.321	.629
Goodwin, Tom*	.353	34	12	0	2	1	3	.371	.353
Grebeck, C	.205	39	8	0	3	2	8	.244	.231
Green, Shawn*	.302	43	13	0	5	3	4	.333	.442
Greenwell, M*	.311	2257	703	63	383	239	163	.378	.489
Greer, Rusty*	.353	51	18	1	10	9	4	.459	.510
Griffey Jr, K*	.326	193	63	7	31	23	32	.397	.528
Guillen, O*	.257	175	45	0	8	1	15	.260	.309
Hale, Chip*	.353	34	12	0	6	2	1	.405	.412
Hall, Mel*	.281	135	38	4	20	4	17	.300	.422
Hamilton, D*	.258	93	24	0	9	7	13	.307	.290
Haselman, B	.278	187	52	8	28	22	35	.354	.455
Henderson, R	.305	164	50	5	21	27	29	.412	.482
Higginson, B*	.333	42	14	1	7	4	8	.375	.524
Hill, G	.378	37	14	3	10	5	8	.422	.649
Hoiles, Chris	.299	97	29	6	15	14	30	.386	.526
Hosey, Dwayne#	.238	63	15	1	3	8	17	.324	.365
Howell, Jack*	.215	79	17	2	9	6	25	.271	.380
Hudler, Rex	.441	34	15	2	10	1	6	.472	.765
Huff, Michael	.296	54	16	1	6	7	11	.381	.370
Huson, Jeff*	.258	66	17	0	5	4	9	.296	.348
Incaviglia, P	.209	86	18	3	13	10	28	.292	.337
Jaha, John	.333	93	31	3	19	8	18	.392	.527
James, Dion*	.262	61	16	0	4	7	0	.338	.295
Javier, Stan#	.261	69	18	1	5	8	16	.338	.420
Jefferson, R*	.386	316	122	16	68	20	65	.420	.677
Johnson, L*	.264	125	33	0	12	5	11	.298	.304
Joyner, Wally*	.301	146	44	3	15	16	15	.368	.473
Karkovice, R	.234	64	15	3	8	10	22	.355	.422
Kelly, Pat	.300	40	12	0	5	2	8	.349	.375
Kelly, R	.209	110	23	5	12	5	20	.250	.391
Kirby, Wayne*	.219	32	7	0	5	5	7	.342	.281
Knoblauch, C	.273	121	33	0	15	16	16	.369	.364
Kreuter, Chad#	.333	54	18	2	11	6	15	.429	.574
Leius, Scott	.300	50	15	1	3	5	11	.364	.460
Leyritz, Jim	.244	78	19	2	14	7	18	.310	.385
Liriano, N#	.352	54	19	0	8	2	7	.386	.389
Listach, Pat#	.232	69	16	1	4	3	20	.264	.319
Livingstone, S	.278	36	10	0	4	1	5	.289	.333
Lofton, Kenny*	.310	100	31	1	8	14	15	.388	.410

Boston, Massachusetts — **Grass**

Batter	Avg	AB	H	HR	BI	BB	SO	OBP	Slg
Macfarlane, M	.253	281	71	11	46	30	58	.344	.427
Malave, Jose	.200	40	8	1	2	2	9	.256	.300
Manto, Jeff	.259	54	14	3	7	9	11	.375	.500
Martinez, Da*	.310	29	9	0	1	6	8	.429	.379
Martinez, E	.313	144	45	4	20	19	23	.402	.465
Martinez, T*	.307	127	39	4	17	11	22	.364	.488
Marzano, John	.216	231	50	5	24	5	49	.241	.333
McGee, Willie#	.274	117	32	1	10	9	24	.323	.376
McGriff, Fred*	.404	99	40	3	12	16	26	.487	.626
McGwire, Mark	.271	181	49	18	42	38	45	.390	.602
McLemore, M#	.270	100	27	0	9	9	15	.333	.350
McRae, Brian#	.308	78	24	3	9	5	9	.349	.526
Meares, Pat	.250	40	10	1	1	2	7	.302	.375
Mieske, Matt	.300	60	18	2	7	2	15	.317	.433
Mitchell, K	.339	62	21	2	15	7	5	.414	.484
Molitor, Paul	.326	239	78	5	34	20	26	.373	.464
Munoz, Pedro	.196	46	9	0	3	0	13	.196	.217
Murray, Eddie*	.271	129	35	4	16	14	21	.338	.419
Myers, Greg*	.167	66	11	2	4	5	11	.225	.273
Naehring, Tim	.297	781	232	20	122	106	145	.384	.439
Newfield, M	.268	41	11	2	6	0	4	.286	.463
Newson, W*	.353	34	12	2	5	7	11	.463	.618
Nilsson, Dave*	.261	92	24	1	12	11	18	.346	.359
Nixon, Otis#	.292	267	78	0	24	33	43	.370	.330
O'Leary, Troy#	.321	480	154	15	81	41	59	.378	.535
O'Neill, Paul*	.242	62	15	2	9	14	13	.377	.435
Olerud, John*	.290	138	40	4	24	30	20	.420	.464
Orsulak, Joe*	.241	83	20	1	8	11	13	.337	.325
Palmeiro, R*	.307	176	54	5	21	16	22	.371	.460
Palmer, Dean	.304	79	24	3	12	11	21	.385	.506
Paquette, C	.235	34	8	1	2	2	10	.278	.353
Pena, Tony	.239	855	204	8	86	73	124	.300	.324
Phillips, T#	.273	205	56	2	16	19	43	.333	.371
Plantier, P*	.268	306	82	11	45	33	71	.338	.428
Polonia, Luis*	.274	190	52	2	16	9	32	.305	.379
Raines, Tim#	.277	94	26	3	12	9	11	.340	.415
Ramirez, M	.293	58	17	4	9	9	13	.388	.552
Reboulet, J	.289	38	11	0	4	3	5	.341	.368
Reed, Jody	.286	1393	399	12	134	172	132	.367	.393
Ripken, Billy	.214	98	21	0	6	7	15	.264	.265
Ripken, Cal	.318	236	75	6	25	23	23	.379	.475
Rodriguez, Al	.314	51	16	1	7	2	13	.333	.412
Rodriguez, I	.287	94	27	2	11	4	13	.327	.457
Rodriguez, T	.212	33	7	1	6	3	4	.278	.333
Salmon, Tim	.323	99	32	4	15	9	22	.373	.515
Schofield, D	.225	89	20	0	5	7	19	.281	.292
Schu, Rick	.289	38	11	1	3	2	6	.325	.368
Segui, David#	.342	38	13	0	10	6	5	.413	.395
Seitzer, K	.328	192	63	1	23	25	23	.405	.438
Selby, Bill*	.200	50	10	0	1	5	8	.273	.240
Sheffield, G	.333	54	18	1	8	2	5	.357	.500
Shumpert, T	.255	47	12	0	4	2	12	.286	.319
Sierra, Ruben#	.275	211	58	4	28	13	37	.316	.412
Snow, J.T.#	.177	79	14	0	7	8	24	.253	.203
Sojo, Luis	.322	59	19	0	2	2	1	.344	.390
Sorrento, P*	.314	86	27	3	14	11	19	.388	.547
Sosa, Sammy	.227	44	10	1	1	1	11	.244	.341
Spiers, Bill*	.288	80	23	1	9	5	11	.337	.413
Sprague, Ed	.253	91	23	1	15	9	20	.327	.352
Stahoviak, S*	.325	40	13	0	7	4	9	.378	.475
Stairs, Matt*	.280	50	14	0	12	3	7	.321	.460
Stanley, Mike	.259	278	72	10	46	59	56	.384	.417
Steinbach, T	.204	157	32	7	22	7	24	.242	.382
Stillwell, K#	.261	69	18	2	10	4	9	.301	.391
Strange, Doug#	.186	43	8	0	2	7	7	.300	.209
Surhoff, B.J.*	.335	188	63	2	33	10	10	.363	.468
Sveum, Dale#	.270	63	17	0	5	8	20	.361	.365
Tartabull, D	.222	180	40	6	28	26	58	.321	.372
Tettleton, M#	.241	166	40	9	28	36	48	.377	.458
Thomas, Frank	.326	138	45	13	33	27	24	.426	.681
Thome, Jim*	.260	77	20	3	11	14	16	.380	.455
Tinsley, Lee#	.270	345	93	6	44	34	79	.335	.380
Trammell, A	.329	143	47	4	17	14	15	.390	.503
Valentin, Jhn	.310	998	309	34	155	149	137	.403	.504
Valentin, Jse#	.237	59	14	1	3	12	15	.366	.373
Valle, Dave	.263	133	35	6	26	16	23	.344	.466
Vaughn, Greg	.218	142	31	5	34	10	43	.266	.387
Vaughn, Mo*	.321	1378	443	79	287	206	339	.415	.566
Velarde, R	.260	127	33	4	13	12	30	.329	.425
Ventura, R*	.235	149	35	6	21	22	26	.331	.423
Vina, F*	.258	31	8	0	2	3	1	.343	.258
Vizquel, Omar	.291	158	46	1	21	11	15	.337	.367
Walbeck, Matt#	.237	38	9	0	5	0	7	.237	.289
Ward, Turner#	.211	38	8	0	1	9	7	.375	.211
Weiss, Walt#	.333	42	14	0	0	9	9	.451	.405
White, Devon#	.235	179	42	4	13	13	39	.289	.341
Whiten, Mark#	.187	91	17	1	7	13	24	.288	.275
Williams, Ber#	.340	94	32	2	17	17	13	.451	.489

FENWAY PARK
Home of the Boston Red Sox
Boston, Massachusetts Grass

Batter	Avg	AB	H	HR	BI	BB	SO	OBP	Slg
Williams, E	.121	33	4	0	1	4	7	.211	.121
Wilson, Dan	.172	58	10	1	8	4	13	.234	.241
Worthington	.205	39	8	0	4	4	9	.295	.333

ANAHEIM STADIUM
Home of the Anaheim Angels
Anaheim, California Grass

Batter	Avg	AB	H	HR	BI	BB	SO	OBP	Slg
Aldrete, Mike*	.150	60	9	0	3	6	10	.224	.167
Alomar, R#	.289	121	35	5	21	10	9	.356	.455
Alomar Jr, S	.294	85	25	3	13	2	9	.318	.459
Amaral, Rich	.263	76	20	1	9	5	11	.305	.355
Anderson, Brd*	.277	155	43	4	18	24	26	.379	.432
Anderson, G*	.305	495	151	14	68	28	84	.342	.455
Arias, George	.304	125	38	5	22	9	21	.351	.432
Baerga, C#	.262	122	32	3	14	3	12	.287	.369
Baines, H*	.282	174	49	7	22	19	20	.357	.454
Becker, Rich*	.333	36	12	1	3	3	10	.400	.472
Belle, Albert	.260	131	34	10	29	15	19	.333	.504
Berroa, G	.274	73	20	6	17	8	22	.341	.562
Bichette, D	.238	281	67	11	42	7	60	.263	.395
Blowers, Mike	.307	75	23	3	18	3	22	.333	.467
Boggs, Wade*	.302	199	60	4	20	25	20	.382	.417
Bonilla, B#	.389	36	14	2	5	5	5	.465	.583
Borders, Pat	.264	144	38	5	14	8	20	.303	.389
Bordick, Mike	.262	122	32	0	8	9	18	.323	.295
Brosius, S	.250	72	18	3	14	8	15	.329	.403
Buhner, Jay	.244	160	39	11	31	28	34	.361	.494
Burks, Ellis	.248	133	33	1	16	12	25	.311	.353
Canseco, Jose	.274	168	46	16	39	18	45	.358	.601
Carter, Joe	.276	199	55	10	35	16	33	.329	.467
Cirillo, Jeff	.333	33	11	1	6	4	6	.421	.485
Clark, Will*	.188	48	9	2	7	5	8	.268	.375
Coleman, V#	.194	36	7	0	0	3	7	.256	.250
Cora, Joey#	.337	86	29	1	9	10	5	.406	.430
Cordova, M	.175	40	7	0	3	3	7	.250	.250
Curtis, Chad	.276	782	216	17	85	86	127	.352	.398
Cuyler, Milt#	.081	37	3	0	3	3	6	.167	.081
Damon, Johnny*	.270	37	10	1	10	1	5	.289	.432
Davis, Chili#	.282	1783	503	83	319	263	364	.372	.471
Dawson, Andre	.220	41	9	2	5	1	9	.238	.390
Deer, Rob	.241	137	33	6	17	13	47	.312	.409
Devereaux, M	.297	145	43	5	18	10	24	.354	.497
DiSarcina, G	.245	1195	293	9	113	47	97	.278	.321
Durham, Ray*	.200	40	8	1	1	4	9	.289	.300
Easley, D	.237	532	126	7	56	56	74	.314	.336
Edmonds, Jim*	.303	697	211	36	129	73	167	.369	.525
Eisenreich, J*	.225	71	16	0	1	2	9	.247	.225
Erstad, Darin*	.263	95	25	1	8	9	16	.327	.337
Espinoza, A	.224	58	13	0	3	2	6	.250	.224
Fabregas, Jor*	.256	313	80	2	27	24	36	.307	.300
Fermin, Felix	.278	115	32	0	7	6	4	.311	.322
Fielder, C	.193	145	28	3	16	23	49	.310	.297
Finley, Steve*	.324	34	11	1	7	1	3	.343	.441
Franco, Julio	.335	167	56	3	29	13	32	.384	.473
Frye, Jeff	.283	60	17	1	7	3	7	.333	.383
Fryman, T	.344	131	45	7	26	12	32	.405	.611
Gaetti, Gary	.254	676	172	26	86	41	131	.302	.402
Gagne, Greg	.255	161	41	2	12	10	27	.299	.360
Gallego, Mike	.176	119	21	4	13	11	22	.254	.294
Gates, Brent#	.155	58	9	0	4	4	8	.203	.190
Gomez, Chris	.163	49	8	1	4	4	8	.241	.224
Gomez, Leo	.219	64	14	1	3	7	19	.292	.297
Gonzales, R	.278	399	111	7	47	50	51	.360	.398
Gonzalez, A	.163	43	7	0	2	5	9	.260	.209
Gonzalez, J	.277	119	33	10	34	6	24	.312	.563
Goodwin, Tom*	.275	40	11	0	5	2	6	.310	.325
Grebeck, C	.175	57	10	1	5	8	8	.277	.281
Greene, Todd	.171	35	6	1	2	2	5	.237	.286
Greenwell, M*	.272	184	50	5	24	16	15	.338	.397
Greer, Rusty*	.311	45	14	2	9	2	9	.347	.489
Griffey Jr, K*	.280	164	46	13	42	13	28	.330	.561
Guillen, O*	.255	192	49	0	22	5	12	.271	.344
Hall, Mel*	.268	97	26	4	10	2	12	.280	.412
Hamelin, Bob*	.258	31	8	1	8	7	8	.375	.387
Hamilton, D*	.198	86	17	1	6	4	13	.242	.291
Hammonds, J	.283	53	15	2	8	2	6	.309	.453
Henderson, R	.206	170	35	4	9	32	32	.335	.329
Hill, G	.217	60	13	4	8	5	17	.277	.467
Hoiles, Chris	.320	100	32	8	23	11	20	.397	.630
Howard, Dave#	.217	46	10	1	9	2	11	.245	.304
Howell, Jack*	.241	963	232	40	131	104	240	.316	.416
Hudler, Rex	.283	300	85	14	37	15	59	.322	.510
Huff, Michael	.276	29	8	0	1	7	6	.417	.310
Hulse, David*	.257	35	9	0	3	3	7	.316	.314
Huson, Jeff*	.275	40	11	0	5	4	5	.333	.275
Incaviglia, P	.299	87	26	6	8	6	25	.358	.552

ANAHEIM STADIUM
Home of the Anaheim Angels
Anaheim, California   Grass

Batter	Avg	AB	H	HR	BI	BB	SO	OBP	Slg
Jaha, John	.211	57	12	3	9	15	7	.384	.386
Javier, Stan#	.262	195	51	3	24	21	41	.332	.364
Jefferson, R*	.250	40	10	3	8	4	8	.318	.525
Johnson, L*	.323	130	42	0	10	10	5	.371	.377
Joyner, Wally*	.274	1375	377	51	209	149	144	.344	.439
Karkovice, R	.255	102	26	3	10	8	28	.315	.392
Kelly, Pat	.263	76	20	2	9	2	17	.296	.368
Kelly, R	.299	77	23	3	11	5	19	.341	.455
Knoblauch, C	.336	128	43	2	16	15	14	.418	.414
Kreuter, Chad#	.175	57	10	1	4	7	15	.266	.281
Leius, Scott	.212	66	14	5	12	9	9	.307	.485
Lewis, Mark	.245	53	13	1	3	5	8	.310	.396
Leyritz, Jim	.175	103	18	4	14	10	35	.261	.320
Liriano, N#	.278	36	10	1	2	1	6	.297	.444
Listach, Pat#	.211	71	15	0	4	8	13	.300	.239
Lofton, Kenny*	.374	91	34	2	8	11	7	.441	.495
Lovullo, T#	.239	180	43	4	16	23	21	.322	.356
Macfarlane, M	.263	160	42	6	23	17	34	.351	.450
Manto, Jeff	.227	44	10	0	1	2	12	.292	.273
Martinez, E	.324	145	47	4	16	22	13	.417	.462
Martinez, T*	.354	96	34	9	20	5	16	.392	.688
Mayne, Brent*	.216	37	8	0	1	3	4	.275	.243
McGriff, Fred*	.253	79	20	6	13	11	24	.341	.532
McGwire, Mark	.271	166	45	11	35	40	36	.417	.524
McLemore, M#	.238	475	113	4	45	55	71	.316	.309
McRae, Brian#	.250	100	25	2	8	3	17	.272	.320
Meares, Pat	.230	61	14	3	6	3	14	.273	.393
Molitor, Paul	.267	187	50	4	25	26	17	.355	.364
Munoz, Pedro	.190	79	15	0	9	3	14	.235	.228
Murray, Eddie#	.262	84	22	3	7	7	8	.315	.393
Myers, Greg*	.263	377	99	12	54	25	75	.307	.414
Naehring, Tim	.312	93	29	2	12	6	12	.350	.409
Nilsson, Dave*	.250	32	8	1	3	4	5	.324	.344
Nixon, Otis#	.153	59	9	0	3	3	10	.190	.203
O'Leary, Troy*	.273	44	12	1	7	1	5	.289	.432
O'Neill, Paul*	.236	72	17	1	8	13	12	.349	.361
Olerud, John*	.287	101	29	5	18	12	16	.376	.515
Orsulak, Joe*	.234	64	15	2	4	6	4	.310	.375
Palmeiro, R*	.311	190	59	16	42	20	25	.377	.632
Palmer, Dean	.274	113	31	10	20	10	29	.333	.602
Paquette, C	.178	45	8	0	2	4	11	.255	.200
Pena, Tony	.197	71	14	1	8	6	13	.260	.310
Perez, E	.180	178	32	5	22	20	34	.264	.331
Phillips, T	.268	436	117	19	55	84	111	.389	.450
Polonia, Luis*	.272	1098	299	3	78	80	121	.323	.334
Raines, Tim#	.321	137	44	3	16	13	16	.386	.453
Ramirez, M	.333	42	14	3	9	5	10	.404	.690
Reboulet, J	.119	42	5	1	3	4	7	.213	.214
Reed, Jody	.194	124	24	0	4	8	16	.242	.258
Ripken, Billy	.225	111	25	1	9	3	18	.243	.324
Ripken, Cal	.270	244	66	8	32	23	18	.330	.406
Rodriguez, Al	.395	38	15	2	6	3	8	.452	.658
Rodriguez, I	.327	98	32	0	5	4	16	.352	.378
Salmon, Tim	.284	1037	294	69	192	162	250	.383	.540
Samuel, Juan	.224	49	11	2	12	1	15	.235	.388
Schofield, D	.235	1072	252	9	91	101	147	.305	.296
Schu, Rick	.316	79	25	4	9	6	11	.360	.544
Segui, David#	.237	38	9	1	4	5	3	.341	.368
Seitzer, K	.307	189	58	4	19	23	24	.380	.434
Sheffield, G	.345	58	20	2	10	1	3	.371	.483
Shumpert, T	.256	39	10	2	6	1	10	.275	.462
Sierra, Ruben#	.304	230	70	10	39	26	30	.368	.491
Slaught, Don	.288	125	36	3	19	11	17	.345	.400
Smith, Dwight*	.208	77	16	3	8	4	11	.247	.351
Snow, J.T.#	.279	899	251	39	151	94	168	.348	.443
Sojo, Luis	.262	423	111	4	38	21	23	.298	.322
Sorrento, P*	.220	59	13	4	9	11	12	.347	.441
Sosa, Sammy	.298	47	14	2	6	2	12	.327	.553
Spiers, Bill*	.226	53	12	1	3	7	9	.328	.321
Sprague, Ed	.167	72	12	3	13	8	19	.267	.319
Stanley, Mike	.281	139	39	4	20	13	31	.348	.432
Steinbach, T	.297	212	63	9	35	13	34	.339	.472
Stevens, Lee*	.226	336	76	6	49	24	85	.275	.339
Stillwell, K#	.260	104	27	1	9	9	15	.313	.385
Strange, Doug#	.279	43	12	0	7	1	9	.289	.326
Surhoff, B.J.*	.252	163	41	4	26	14	13	.306	.350
Sveum, Dale#	.172	58	10	0	4	3	15	.206	.172
Tartabull, D	.265	211	56	14	35	30	59	.354	.517
Tettleton, M#	.244	156	38	8	19	29	43	.367	.449
Thomas, Frank	.367	147	54	12	34	41	29	.503	.667
Thome, Jim*	.378	45	17	5	10	3	12	.417	.778
Trammell, A	.263	156	41	4	21	7	20	.293	.372
Turner, Chris	.222	108	24	1	8	7	25	.267	.315
Valentin, Jhn	.207	87	18	2	12	6	14	.250	.345
Valentin, Jse#	.214	42	9	2	5	5	17	.298	.357
Valle, Dave	.281	121	34	7	26	15	18	.362	.479
Vaughn, Greg	.147	136	20	6	13	16	33	.242	.324
Vaughn, Mo*	.300	100	30	6	19	11	26	.386	.530

ANAHEIM STADIUM
Home of the Anaheim Angels

Anaheim, California									Grass
Batter	Avg	AB	H	HR	BI	BB	SO	OBP	Slg
Velarde, R	.316	380	120	9	30	44	80	.391	.447
Ventura, R*	.263	167	44	7	31	19	27	.333	.425
Vizquel, Omar#	.197	117	23	0	10	13	15	.275	.214
Wallach, Tim	.258	89	23	5	14	7	23	.320	.461
Weiss, Walt#	.265	68	18	0	8	6	6	.324	.294
White, Devon#	.237	1166	276	30	116	80	257	.287	.376
Whiten, Mark#	.177	62	11	0	3	7	20	.261	.226
Williams, Ber#	.336	116	39	4	14	13	22	.403	.517
Williams, E	.219	32	7	0	1	4	7	.306	.250
Wilson, Dan	.271	59	16	1	6	2	13	.306	.373
Worthington	.213	47	10	1	3	10	7	.351	.340

WRIGLEY FIELD
Home of the Chicago Cubs

Chicago, Illinois									Grass
Batter	Avg	AB	H	HR	BI	BB	SO	OBP	Slg
Abbott, Kurt	.150	40	6	1	5	5	14	.261	.300
Aldrete, Mike*	.193	57	11	0	9	7	17	.281	.281
Alicea, Luis#	.282	71	20	1	8	11	18	.378	.408
Alomar, R#	.303	66	20	0	4	3	8	.333	.379
Alou, Moises	.191	110	21	2	6	9	18	.252	.309
Amaro, Ruben#	.143	28	4	0	0	5	6	.314	.179
Anthony, Eric*	.128	86	11	2	9	9	27	.211	.233
Arias, Alex	.222	99	22	2	9	4	11	.260	.333
Ausmus, Brad	.148	54	8	1	3	3	12	.193	.259
Bagwell, Jeff	.273	128	35	5	23	30	22	.413	.453
Barberie, B#	.252	103	26	1	8	9	24	.313	.340
Batiste, Kim	.257	35	9	1	2	1	4	.278	.343
Bell, Derek	.276	87	24	2	12	2	14	.292	.425
Bell, Jay	.295	193	57	2	18	17	39	.354	.425
Belliard, R	.288	118	34	0	12	8	20	.339	.347
Benjamin, M	.450	40	18	3	9	2	6	.476	.750
Berry, Sean	.367	49	18	4	13	4	8	.426	.755
Bichette, D	.300	100	30	1	13	4	9	.327	.440
Biggio, Craig	.342	193	66	7	22	22	25	.416	.534
Blauser, Jeff	.300	120	36	11	25	15	20	.390	.658
Bonds, Barry*	.271	277	75	17	41	48	36	.376	.549
Bonilla, B#	.345	252	87	18	60	28	56	.411	.683
Boone, Bret	.317	63	20	4	10	3	20	.348	.556
Branson, Jeff*	.258	66	17	1	7	9	12	.347	.485
Brumfield, J	.232	56	13	2	5	0	9	.246	.393
Bullett, S*	.236	148	35	4	20	13	45	.301	.372
Burks, Ellis	.273	33	9	3	5	2	11	.314	.636
Butler, Brett*	.238	202	48	0	12	22	22	.310	.302
Caminiti, Ken#	.231	186	43	4	17	14	35	.289	.376
Candaele, C#	.275	80	22	0	8	10	10	.352	.438
Cangelosi, J#	.302	43	13	0	6	6	6	.388	.372
Carr, Chuck*	.295	61	18	0	2	4	7	.338	.361
Carreon, Mark	.351	74	26	6	21	6	8	.400	.676
Castilla, V	.254	71	18	2	11	5	14	.308	.380
Cedeno, A	.220	59	13	3	7	1	17	.233	.390
Cianfrocco, A	.205	44	9	2	6	4	17	.271	.386
Clark, Dave*	.234	141	33	3	14	7	33	.268	.348
Clark, Will*	.190	121	23	1	6	18	32	.310	.248
Clayton, R	.257	105	27	0	10	9	18	.322	.257
Colbrunn, G	.242	66	16	4	14	2	6	.286	.485
Coleman, V#	.275	207	57	1	9	16	41	.326	.324
Conine, Jeff	.261	88	23	3	10	11	23	.340	.420
Cordero, Wil	.371	62	23	3	9	3	8	.418	.597
Dascenzo, D#	.248	561	139	1	41	48	50	.308	.316
Daulton, D*	.279	165	46	8	30	21	34	.354	.473
Davis, Eric	.241	145	35	7	21	16	45	.327	.441
Dawson, Andre	.302	1613	487	94	304	114	214	.350	.541
Decker, Steve	.364	33	12	2	8	3	5	.417	.576
DeShields, D*	.288	139	40	4	22	20	26	.372	.417
Dorsett, B	.143	35	5	0	2	1	9	.162	.171
Duncan, M	.315	111	35	0	20	10	21	.369	.459
Dunston, S	.273	1606	438	35	174	62	256	.301	.405
Dykstra, L*	.266	199	53	6	21	20	26	.333	.442
Eisenreich, J*	.250	32	8	0	7	6	1	.359	.313
Elster, Kevin	.231	78	18	1	14	5	6	.264	.385
Finley, Steve*	.257	144	37	4	12	9	18	.299	.396
Fletcher, D*	.235	68	16	2	7	6	5	.297	.368
Galarraga, A	.269	245	66	9	32	11	66	.305	.416
Gant, Ron	.199	151	30	5	16	10	44	.248	.318
Garcia, C	.333	93	31	5	13	5	12	.382	.570
Gilkey, B	.346	104	36	5	12	17	19	.439	.654
Girardi, Joe	.274	485	133	3	50	34	64	.323	.336
Glanville, D	.179	39	7	1	3	1	2	.195	.308
Gomez, Leo	.233	193	45	10	33	33	45	.358	.446
Gonzalez, L*	.318	462	147	19	90	65	53	.403	.543
Grace, Mark*	.320	2515	806	40	344	313	188	.393	.437
Grissom, M	.259	166	43	3	12	16	14	.319	.398
Gutierrez, R	.286	49	14	0	4	11	7	.417	.388
Gwynn, Tony*	.339	227	77	3	24	22	4	.398	.441
Haney, Todd	.261	92	24	1	4	8	15	.327	.348
Harris, Lenny*	.289	114	33	3	23	6	9	.320	.465

Batter	Avg	AB	H	HR	BI	BB	SO	OBP	Slg
Hayes, C	.232	151	35	5	15	6	28	.259	.344
Hernandez, Jo	.229	349	80	10	42	27	104	.282	.358
Hill, G	.263	209	55	10	32	24	50	.339	.464
Hollins, Dave#	.306	85	26	5	17	9	13	.372	.553
Houston, T*	.293	41	12	0	4	3	5	.341	.341
Howard, T*	.270	63	17	2	3	2	9	.292	.429
Hudler, Rex	.318	44	14	0	8	3	3	.340	.409
Hundley, Todd#	.245	94	23	6	15	7	19	.297	.489
Hunter, Brian	.162	37	6	3	6	3	9	.225	.405
Hunter, Bri L	.255	47	12	0	1	1	6	.271	.298
Incaviglia, P	.245	49	12	3	9	3	14	.288	.469
James, Dion*	.238	42	10	2	6	7	8	.353	.405
Jefferies, G#	.375	184	69	3	23	13	7	.415	.495
Johnson, Mark*	.200	35	7	1	3	5	4	.293	.286
Jones, C#	.256	43	11	1	9	9	8	.370	.349
Jordan, Brian	.343	70	24	5	15	2	7	.361	.600
Jordan, Ricky	.314	121	38	5	27	4	16	.326	.496
Justice, Dave*	.322	87	28	3	13	13	14	.412	.460
Karros, Eric	.248	113	28	6	13	7	22	.295	.478
Kelly, R	.234	47	11	2	5	4	5	.288	.383
Kent, Jeff	.269	52	14	2	8	3	7	.309	.481
King, Jeff	.222	135	30	3	14	10	21	.272	.333
Kingery, Mike*	.250	48	12	0	6	4	6	.308	.250
Klesko, Ryan*	.289	45	13	2	11	7	13	.377	.489
Lankford, Ray*	.297	155	46	7	29	26	39	.393	.548
Lansing, Mike	.261	69	18	1	3	3	8	.311	.377
Larkin, Barry	.280	182	51	6	14	21	23	.354	.473
Lemke, Mark#	.253	83	21	0	6	12	8	.347	.337
Lewis, Darren	.193	83	16	0	5	7	7	.256	.241
Liriano, N#	.406	32	13	0	10	5	8	.486	.531
Lopez, Javy	.280	50	14	1	6	2	9	.308	.400
Mabry, John*	.277	47	13	1	5	4	7	.327	.383
Magadan, Dave*	.266	244	65	3	30	37	37	.359	.369
Manwaring, K	.230	100	23	3	10	12	9	.322	.360
Martin, Al*	.184	76	14	1	9	9	13	.261	.250
Martinez, Da*	.271	479	130	11	40	48	82	.341	.407
May, Derrick*	.303	696	211	15	107	44	67	.344	.431
McGee, Willie*	.315	165	52	3	20	9	26	.349	.467
McGriff, Fred*	.323	124	40	6	26	13	32	.381	.556
McRae, Brian*	.288	587	169	15	63	65	85	.366	.441
Merced, O*	.298	151	45	7	32	10	21	.339	.497
Miller, Orl	.333	39	13	2	4	2	10	.381	.564
Mitchell, K	.291	103	30	8	23	15	24	.392	.583
Mondesi, Raul	.310	71	22	3	7	2	14	.329	.493
Morandini, M*	.299	117	35	0	4	13	12	.379	.410
Morris, Hal*	.271	107	29	1	13	18	18	.375	.346
Mouton, James	.258	31	8	1	5	5	7	.351	.452
Murray, Eddie#	.395	119	47	6	26	17	16	.464	.647
Nixon, Otis#	.349	83	29	0	4	5	12	.386	.398
O'Brien, C	.196	46	9	0	5	1	4	.208	.239
O'Neill, Paul*	.322	115	37	4	24	12	16	.383	.557
Offerman, J#	.258	62	16	0	4	8	11	.338	.290
Oliver, Joe	.278	79	22	2	16	2	11	.296	.418
Orsulak, Joe*	.224	49	11	0	8	4	5	.286	.306
Pagnozzi, Tom	.295	132	39	2	18	9	23	.336	.432
Palmeiro, R*	.310	378	117	13	47	28	31	.355	.489
Parent, Mark	.235	102	24	4	16	10	16	.301	.412
Pena, G#	.356	59	21	2	17	6	18	.397	.593
Pena, Tony	.274	95	26	1	13	7	10	.327	.389
Pendleton, T#	.307	241	74	7	34	19	39	.359	.461
Piazza, Mike	.287	87	25	1	11	12	14	.370	.345
Plantier, P*	.195	41	8	2	4	4	11	.267	.341
Raines, Tim#	.260	96	25	3	10	13	11	.348	.385
Reed, Jeff*	.255	98	25	1	7	15	8	.360	.316
Reed, Jody	.203	59	12	0	1	4	5	.254	.237
Roberson, K#	.150	140	21	8	17	10	45	.222	.343
Roberts, Bip#	.299	97	29	2	8	14	7	.384	.392
Rodriguez, H*	.265	49	13	0	2	3	11	.308	.327
Sabo, Chris	.297	138	41	7	22	10	20	.347	.536
Samuel, Juan	.304	158	48	3	15	5	42	.329	.405
Sanchez, Rey	.261	789	206	2	56	37	84	.299	.318
Sandberg, R	.296	2409	714	110	376	252	345	.362	.500
Sanders, R	.154	65	10	3	9	10	20	.282	.308
Santiago, B	.298	151	45	9	28	13	31	.351	.563
Segui, David#	.244	41	10	1	6	7	3	.347	.341
Servais, S	.278	360	100	14	54	27	65	.338	.436
Sheffield, G	.288	80	23	6	17	15	9	.406	.613
Slaught, Don	.303	76	23	4	12	6	7	.354	.513
Smith, Dwight*	.315	639	201	19	92	57	98	.373	.487
Smith, Ozzie#	.264	231	61	0	26	23	13	.328	.364
Sosa, Sammy	.276	1184	327	83	223	94	263	.332	.542
Stocker, K#	.378	37	14	0	4	4	3	.439	.514
Strange, Doug*	.180	61	11	0	5	6	7	.261	.213
Strawberry, D*	.219	155	34	7	21	23	34	.322	.400
Taubensee, E*	.310	58	18	3	10	3	10	.333	.500
Thompson, Mil*	.290	186	54	3	20	16	27	.353	.387
Thompson, Rob	.278	151	42	1	14	11	23	.341	.351
Thompson, Ry	.250	36	9	3	6	4	8	.325	.611

Batter	Avg	AB	H	HR	BI	BB	SO	OBP	Slg
Timmons, O	.226	164	37	11	21	15	39	.294	.451
VanderWal, J*	.224	49	11	1	5	2	12	.250	.408
Vizcaino, J#	.297	518	154	2	43	42	67	.345	.369
Walker, Larry*	.300	150	45	7	27	35	18	.431	.500
Wallach, Tim	.254	240	61	9	24	14	34	.300	.408
Walton, J	.278	587	163	8	43	51	89	.336	.375
Weiss, Walt#	.219	73	16	1	2	11	12	.321	.329
Whiten, Mark#	.250	52	13	1	6	5	12	.316	.365
Wilkins, Rick*	.232	715	166	23	70	83	181	.318	.375
Williams, E	.235	34	8	3	5	4	3	.316	.500
Williams, Ma	.293	167	49	13	37	11	34	.335	.569
Young, Eric	.219	64	14	2	2	5	5	.275	.359
Zeile, Todd	.241	257	62	9	28	37	35	.336	.397

Batter	Avg	AB	H	HR	BI	BB	SO	OBP	Slg
Aldrete, Mike*	.233	43	10	1	6	1	10	.244	.372
Alomar, R#	.339	127	43	3	17	15	17	.406	.472
Alomar Jr, S	.302	43	13	2	3	2	6	.333	.465
Amaral, Rich	.242	62	15	0	3	8	8	.333	.290
Anderson, Brd*	.243	74	18	2	4	9	14	.333	.351
Anderson, G*	.200	35	7	0	1	1	8	.216	.229
Baerga, C#	.342	120	41	6	20	13	10	.412	.550
Baines, H*	.269	309	83	13	52	59	46	.384	.430
Becker, Rich*	.375	32	12	1	5	3	10	.444	.563
Belle, Albert	.269	130	35	8	16	14	20	.340	.477
Beltre, E	.160	75	12	1	7	2	11	.179	.213
Berroa, G	.339	56	19	3	11	5	6	.391	.589
Blowers, Mike	.176	68	12	2	5	7	21	.250	.294
Boggs, Wade*	.258	97	25	1	9	18	10	.368	.309
Borders, Pat	.279	104	29	1	4	6	18	.318	.337
Bordick, Mike	.273	88	24	1	11	11	12	.360	.341
Brosius, S	.295	44	13	1	8	9	7	.436	.455
Buhner, Jay	.221	122	27	3	12	17	28	.317	.352
Burks, Ellis	.288	257	74	7	42	36	52	.379	.451
Canseco, Jose	.214	70	15	5	16	6	19	.276	.443
Carter, Joe	.186	118	22	3	14	10	21	.252	.288
Cirillo, Jeff	.324	37	12	0	5	6	5	.419	.486
Cole, Alex*	.147	34	5	0	3	3	9	.216	.176
Coleman, V#	.339	56	19	1	7	5	5	.381	.518
Cora, Joey#	.283	614	174	2	58	71	55	.365	.358
Cordova, M	.217	46	10	2	8	4	4	.288	.413
Curtis, Chad	.280	107	30	1	11	11	14	.345	.364
Cuyler, Milt#	.222	45	10	0	2	3	12	.271	.311
Davis, Chili#	.274	113	31	5	18	22	26	.388	.442
Deer, Rob	.217	60	13	8	16	8	19	.309	.667
Devereaux, M	.246	256	63	6	37	20	47	.300	.371
DiSarcina, G	.330	88	29	1	8	2	10	.352	.409
Durham, Ray#	.248	505	125	4	51	45	79	.314	.345
Easley, D	.263	57	15	1	6	4	10	.306	.386
Edmonds, Jim*	.216	37	8	3	7	7	12	.370	.459
Espinoza, A	.304	46	14	0	3	3	6	.360	.370
Fermin, Felix	.255	98	25	1	4	3	5	.277	.316
Fielder, C	.282	142	40	14	34	23	33	.382	.599
Franco, Julio	.352	256	90	12	59	32	35	.421	.551
Frye, Jeff	.245	53	13	0	6	3	5	.286	.321
Fryman, T	.222	162	36	2	19	11	30	.269	.321
Gaetti, Gary	.237	118	28	3	12	4	19	.268	.339
Gagne, Greg	.234	107	25	3	10	9	18	.297	.374
Gallego, Mike	.236	55	13	1	9	4	11	.288	.327
Gates, Brent#	.282	71	20	0	11	8	14	.341	.366
Giambi, Jason*	.243	37	9	1	4	2	9	.282	.324
Gomez, Chris	.265	34	9	1	5	2	3	.306	.382
Gomez, Leo	.278	54	15	2	14	5	13	.333	.463
Gonzales, R	.306	36	11	2	11	4	6	.375	.528
Gonzalez, J	.279	104	29	7	18	5	15	.306	.519
Goodwin, Tom*	.351	37	13	0	2	4	4	.429	.378
Grebeck, C	.291	467	136	5	52	67	57	.383	.398
Green, Shawn*	.359	39	14	0	2	4	7	.419	.513
Greenwell, M*	.290	62	18	0	8	9	3	.375	.339
Greer, Rusty*	.317	63	20	2	8	4	13	.368	.476
Griffey Jr, K*	.212	118	25	6	18	7	19	.256	.407
Guillen, O*	.274	1095	300	5	119	31	85	.289	.356
Hall, Mel*	.250	44	11	1	4	0	4	.250	.409
Hamilton, D*	.250	104	26	2	12	9	18	.304	.337
Hammonds, J	.170	53	9	2	7	5	6	.241	.358
Henderson, R	.396	53	21	3	9	18	7	.556	.717
Hoiles, Chris	.304	79	24	5	14	11	12	.385	.570
Howard, Dave#	.239	46	11	0	3	1	8	.255	.348
Huff, Michael	.217	143	31	1	18	16	29	.304	.294
Hulse, David*	.279	43	12	1	2	3	5	.326	.349
Huson, Jeff*	.302	43	13	1	3	5	6	.367	.419
Jaha, John	.197	76	15	0	5	4	15	.232	.250
Javier, Stan#	.319	47	15	0	4	5	6	.385	.362
Johnson, L*	.279	1331	372	5	116	83	76	.321	.357

COMISKEY PARK
Home of the Chicago White Sox
Chicago, Illinois   Grass

Batter	Avg	AB	H	HR	BI	BB	SO	OBP	Slg
Joyner, Wally*	.280	82	23	4	11	15	7	.388	.476
Karkovice, R	.222	873	194	27	107	75	226	.288	.370
Kelly, Pat	.204	49	10	0	5	2	14	.231	.224
Kelly, R	.267	45	12	0	4	7	4	.365	.333
Kirby, Wayne*	.156	32	5	0	3	5	6	.263	.188
Knoblauch, C	.339	118	40	1	13	17	10	.413	.475
Kreuter, Chad#	.267	75	20	2	12	6	18	.317	.480
Leius, Scott	.220	41	9	2	6	4	6	.283	.439
Lewis, Darren	.209	172	36	0	24	23	18	.296	.244
Lewis, Mark	.188	48	9	0	3	6	5	.273	.250
Listach, Pat#	.203	69	14	0	4	8	12	.286	.232
Lofton, Kenny*	.290	124	36	2	12	9	19	.336	.355
Macfarlane, M	.275	80	22	7	16	12	19	.381	.563
Martin, N	.325	209	68	1	25	6	28	.339	.416
Martinez, Da*	.281	342	96	5	38	45	44	.367	.415
Martinez, E	.286	119	34	3	15	24	15	.406	.445
Martinez, T*	.301	93	28	7	17	13	13	.383	.591
Mayne, Brent*	.195	41	8	1	5	4	8	.255	.293
McGwire, Mark	.315	54	17	7	15	7	10	.397	.722
McLemore, M#	.230	74	17	0	9	9	13	.310	.257
McRae, Brian*	.289	90	26	0	4	9	13	.366	.356
Meares, Pat	.244	41	10	0	3	0	2	.256	.268
Mieske, Matt	.306	49	15	3	11	3	9	.346	.592
Molitor, Paul	.308	133	41	1	16	17	22	.391	.429
Mouton, Lyle	.319	188	60	8	33	23	43	.388	.516
Munoz, Pedro	.325	80	26	4	15	3	21	.345	.525
Murray, Eddie#	.174	69	12	2	10	5	13	.224	.290
Myers, Greg*	.263	38	10	1	4	1	3	.282	.368
Naehring, Tim	.230	61	14	1	6	3	15	.266	.295
Newson, W*	.246	264	65	9	37	54	70	.376	.379
Nilsson, Dave*	.329	70	23	0	5	7	7	.385	.386
Nixon, Otis#	.231	52	12	0	3	9	8	.344	.288
O'Neill, Paul*	.362	58	21	4	14	10	3	.456	.655
Olerud, John*	.324	105	34	6	13	20	11	.425	.524
Orsulak, Joe*	.420	50	21	1	7	3	4	.455	.620
Palmeiro, R*	.259	116	30	5	18	17	15	.355	.448
Palmer, Dean	.241	87	21	5	10	7	14	.313	.437
Paquette, C	.232	56	13	4	13	2	20	.259	.500
Pena, Tony	.316	79	25	2	8	3	9	.349	.418
Phillips, T#	.300	400	120	10	40	94	72	.433	.430
Plantier, P*	.226	31	7	1	1	4	8	.314	.355
Polonia, Luis*	.299	77	23	0	7	8	13	.360	.364
Raines, Tim#	.285	1163	331	23	121	175	102	.379	.401
Ramirez, M	.259	58	15	2	7	8	12	.348	.397
Reboulet, J	.229	35	8	0	2	5	4	.317	.286
Reed, Jody	.261	69	18	0	7	11	5	.354	.319
Ripken, Billy	.294	34	10	1	4	2	3	.324	.441
Ripken, Cal	.210	119	25	3	15	12	6	.289	.328
Rodriguez, Al	.156	32	5	3	7	7	13	.308	.438
Rodriguez, I	.277	112	31	3	16	3	15	.296	.375
Sabo, Chris	.211	38	8	1	4	0	5	.225	.342
Salmon, Tim	.239	92	22	1	11	18	25	.366	.315
Samuel, Juan	.233	43	10	1	2	2	6	.267	.326
Schofield, D	.138	29	4	0	4	3	8	.212	.138
Seitzer, K	.306	134	41	4	28	10	15	.352	.418
Sierra, Ruben&	.231	134	31	4	26	11	26	.282	.366
Slaught, Don	.200	35	7	0	1	2	3	.243	.200
Snopek, Chris	.276	87	24	4	11	9	17	.344	.425
Snow, J.T.#	.194	72	14	3	8	6	15	.256	.319
Sojo, Luis	.187	75	14	0	3	3	2	.218	.227
Sorrento, P*	.220	82	18	5	17	5	27	.261	.451
Sosa, Sammy	.186	145	27	3	10	7	44	.222	.297
Spiers, Bill*	.265	49	13	1	3	2	5	.294	.388
Sprague, Ed	.291	86	25	3	12	11	17	.384	.442
Stanley, Mike	.180	50	9	2	12	5	15	.237	.340
Steinbach, T	.278	97	27	5	17	11	13	.364	.485
Stevens, Lee*	.205	39	8	0	4	3	4	.262	.308
Strange, Doug#	.211	38	8	0	3	5	5	.302	.289
Surhoff, B.J.*	.269	104	28	2	2	9	14	.327	.404
Sveum, Dale#	.200	65	13	1	9	10	16	.303	.308
Tartabull, D	.246	309	76	20	62	40	90	.330	.482
Tettleton, M#	.177	113	20	4	11	28	36	.345	.310
Thomas, Frank	.333	1515	505	113	332	363	212	.461	.626
Thome, Jim*	.259	54	14	1	6	10	15	.369	.407
Trammell, A	.274	62	17	2	10	4	4	.313	.403
Valentin, Jhn	.286	49	14	2	5	4	7	.340	.490
Valentin, Jse#	.100	40	4	1	3	10	15	.280	.200
Valle, Dave	.236	72	17	0	3	8	10	.313	.250
Vaughn, Greg	.223	121	27	6	16	7	24	.264	.430
Vaughn, Mo*	.217	83	18	2	11	9	23	.281	.289
Velarde, R	.253	75	19	3	9	5	12	.296	.427
Ventura, R*	.289	1532	443	64	276	240	212	.382	.463
Vina, F*	.257	35	9	0	3	3	4	.316	.286
Vizquel, Omar#	.200	110	22	0	6	14	13	.288	.236
Walbeck, Matt#	.268	41	11	0	2	8	9	.380	.268
Ward, Turner#	.182	44	8	0	6	6	9	.280	.250
White, Devon#	.256	86	22	2	10	4	19	.297	.372
Whiten, Mark#	.304	46	14	0	0	6	8	.385	.326

COMISKEY PARK
Home of the Chicago White Sox
Chicago, Illinois — Grass

Batter	Avg	AB	H	HR	BI	BB	SO	OBP	Slg
Williams, Ber#	.274	95	26	3	11	7	20	.320	.474
Wilson, Dan	.311	61	19	2	7	3	8	.338	.475

CINERGY FIELD
Home of the Cincinnati Reds
Cincinnati, Ohio — Artificial

Batter	Avg	AB	H	HR	BI	BB	SO	OBP	Slg
Abbott, Kurt	.182	33	6	0	2	2	11	.229	.333
Aldrete, Mike*	.283	60	17	0	7	5	10	.338	.383
Alicea, Luis#	.222	36	8	0	5	4	9	.293	.306
Alomar, R#	.305	82	25	3	5	13	13	.400	.537
Alou, Moises	.287	94	27	7	18	3	14	.310	.543
Anthony, Eric*	.239	176	42	6	20	22	40	.317	.381
Arias, Alex	.133	45	6	0	0	5	5	.220	.133
Bagwell, Jeff	.297	138	41	8	27	25	25	.407	.536
Bell, Derek	.418	98	41	2	16	1	22	.424	.582
Bell, Jay	.333	174	58	5	22	17	25	.403	.471
Belliard, R	.244	86	21	0	10	6	14	.301	.267
Berry, Sean	.254	63	16	2	16	3	10	.294	.444
Bichette, D	.351	77	27	8	22	5	16	.376	.740
Biggio, Craig	.307	218	67	5	22	26	25	.390	.436
Blauser, Jeff	.268	198	53	4	21	18	44	.332	.389
Bonds, Barry*	.321	184	59	19	50	55	24	.477	.728
Bonilla, B#	.301	163	49	12	30	23	30	.382	.601
Boone, Bret	.260	681	177	18	104	59	121	.322	.413
Branson, Jeff*	.263	563	148	17	63	39	102	.308	.423
Brumfield, J	.262	221	58	5	18	24	36	.331	.398
Burks, Ellis	.268	41	11	2	8	0	6	.268	.488
Butler, Brett*	.283	240	68	1	13	36	42	.377	.371
Caminiti, Ken#	.239	205	49	5	26	19	35	.306	.390
Candaele, C#	.259	81	21	1	3	6	10	.310	.321
Cangelosi, J#	.205	39	8	1	2	8	8	.354	.308
Carr, Chuck#	.161	31	5	0	0	3	7	.278	.226
Carreon, Mark	.273	55	15	1	7	2	6	.293	.382
Carter, Joe	.289	38	11	3	15	2	6	.325	.605
Castilla, V	.333	75	25	5	7	2	6	.351	.560
Cedeno, A	.165	79	13	0	6	1	20	.175	.215
Cianfrocco, A	.200	35	7	3	6	0	9	.200	.486
Clark, Dave*	.319	47	15	1	9	1	13	.333	.447
Clark, Will*	.303	198	60	11	36	33	30	.401	.535
Clayton, R	.329	79	26	0	5	7	19	.391	.392
Colbrunn, G	.246	61	15	1	8	3	7	.288	.328
Coleman, V#	.264	159	42	2	11	12	30	.316	.377
Conine, Jeff	.315	92	29	3	13	8	23	.366	.446
Cordero, Wil	.268	56	15	1	5	3	9	.305	.339
Dascenzo, D#	.256	43	11	0	6	4	2	.313	.326
Daulton, D*	.250	112	28	5	22	14	20	.336	.491
Davis, Eric	.267	1175	314	73	236	216	327	.381	.500
Dawson, Andre	.257	136	35	9	28	5	14	.287	.471
DeShields, D*	.255	106	27	0	9	18	22	.363	.330
Dorsett, B	.237	131	31	4	20	12	16	.303	.366
Duncan, M	.304	578	176	20	82	26	98	.335	.478
Dunston, S	.294	163	48	4	11	7	26	.331	.442
Dykstra, L*	.292	130	38	1	7	18	14	.378	.346
Eisenreich, J*	.462	52	24	0	4	3	6	.491	.558
Elster, Kevin	.178	73	13	1	7	10	13	.277	.260
Everett, Carl#	.158	38	6	0	3	5	11	.256	.184
Finley, Steve*	.258	151	39	0	9	12	22	.315	.351
Fletcher, D*	.306	72	22	2	11	6	8	.367	.472
Galarraga, A	.285	179	51	5	21	7	53	.312	.469
Gant, Ron	.245	376	92	23	65	55	85	.338	.497
Garcia, C	.261	88	23	1	9	1	13	.270	.295
Gilkey, B	.360	125	45	2	21	11	13	.409	.480
Girardi, Joe	.292	72	21	0	3	4	6	.329	.361
Gonzalez, L*	.226	137	31	9	23	10	21	.287	.504
Goodwin, C*	.225	80	18	0	4	13	24	.333	.263
Grace, Mark*	.347	193	67	8	40	19	13	.398	.554
Greene, W*	.234	261	61	15	45	29	83	.309	.448
Grissom, M	.309	165	51	6	18	8	21	.345	.491
Grudzielanek,	.370	54	20	1	7	0	5	.375	.481
Gutierrez, R	.280	50	14	0	5	2	7	.302	.360
Gwynn, Tony*	.354	263	93	3	36	14	13	.383	.483
Hansen, Dave*	.325	40	13	0	7	6	10	.404	.400
Harris, Lenny*	.273	472	129	4	40	37	42	.325	.345
Hayes, C	.200	115	23	2	13	10	22	.260	.348
Hill, G	.324	37	12	2	4	3	8	.390	.595
Hollins, Dave#	.288	73	21	3	15	17	20	.424	.479
Howard, T*	.286	486	139	8	51	34	72	.333	.430
Hudler, Rex	.286	42	12	0	1	1	7	.302	.373
Hundley, Todd#	.227	88	20	6	17	9	25	.296	.500
Hunter, Brian	.200	105	21	6	21	7	28	.246	.419
Hunter, Bri L	.306	36	11	0	0	2	6	.342	.361
Incaviglia, P	.175	63	11	3	8	4	20	.224	.349
James, Dion*	.357	42	15	1	6	6	8	.429	.571
Javier, Stan#	.318	66	21	1	3	4	13	.357	.515
Jefferies, G#	.285	123	35	2	11	9	5	.331	.374
Johnson, Char	.394	33	13	1	8	2	5	.417	.576

248

CINERGY FIELD
Home of the Cincinnati Reds
Cincinnati, Ohio   **Artificial**

Batter	Avg	AB	H	HR	BI	BB	SO	OBP	Slg
Johnson, L*	.344	32	11	0	4	4	2	.421	.469
Jones, C#	.180	50	9	3	7	6	12	.268	.380
Jones, Chris	.243	70	17	1	3	4	26	.293	.314
Jordan, Brian	.333	45	15	2	9	1	10	.347	.578
Jordan, Ricky	.238	84	20	2	14	4	13	.275	.357
Justice, Dave*	.247	150	37	8	31	23	25	.347	.453
Karros, Eric	.226	124	28	5	18	11	21	.285	.452
Kelly, Mike	.231	52	12	1	8	8	12	.344	.385
Kelly, R	.295	261	77	6	39	17	43	.340	.418
Kent, Jeff	.273	77	21	0	4	9	22	.356	.299
King, Jeff	.227	128	29	6	20	15	15	.306	.406
Kingery, Mike*	.271	59	16	2	5	1	6	.295	.475
Klesko, Ryan*	.195	41	8	1	5	6	13	.286	.390
Lankford, Ray*	.287	122	35	4	17	16	29	.374	.475
Lansing, Mike	.282	78	22	0	4	6	9	.341	.346
Larkin, Barry	.297	2418	717	73	339	313	239	.378	.454
Lemke, Mark#	.319	116	37	1	10	15	20	.394	.457
Lewis, Darren	.259	162	42	0	10	17	20	.333	.290
Lewis, Mark	.312	93	29	1	13	11	18	.385	.430
Lopez, Javy	.214	42	9	1	1	3	10	.283	.333
Mabry, John*	.281	32	9	4	7	3	4	.343	.656
Magadan, Dave*	.297	118	35	0	9	31	13	.444	.381
Manwaring, K	.198	111	22	1	6	12	17	.276	.279
Martin, Al*	.250	72	18	0	2	5	8	.299	.306
Martinez, Da*	.292	274	80	8	32	28	34	.353	.471
May, Derrick*	.194	62	12	0	5	8	6	.282	.242
McGee, Willie#	.234	137	32	1	8	14	25	.314	.292
McGriff, Fred*	.320	150	48	16	34	34	26	.443	.680
McRae, Brian#	.186	43	8	1	2	4	10	.255	.326
Merced, O*	.295	112	33	5	20	16	13	.383	.500
Miller, Orl	.242	33	8	2	3	4	9	.324	.455
Mitchell, K	.329	554	182	45	126	84	92	.412	.644
Mondesi, Raul	.206	68	14	0	5	2	16	.233	.294
Morandini, M*	.192	73	14	0	2	14	17	.326	.247
Morris, Hal*	.322	1411	454	35	216	118	181	.374	.490
Mottola, Chad	.219	32	7	1	2	4	7	.306	.344
Mouton, James	.302	43	13	0	3	4	12	.388	.419
Murray, Eddie#	.281	139	39	5	31	18	13	.358	.446
Nixon, Otis*	.172	93	16	0	9	7	16	.228	.183
O'Brien, C	.254	59	15	2	10	5	10	.313	.390
O'Neill, Paul*	.273	1305	356	63	220	151	211	.349	.479
Offerman, J#	.267	90	24	0	7	18	17	.389	.311
Oliver, Joe	.242	1036	251	32	159	81	187	.297	.394
Orsulak, Joe*	.304	46	14	0	8	1	3	.313	.457
Owens, Eric	.238	122	29	0	6	14	19	.314	.279
Pagnozzi, Tom	.204	98	20	1	9	7	15	.255	.316
Parent, Mark	.171	35	6	1	4	3	12	.237	.314
Pena, G#	.333	33	11	3	8	4	8	.395	.667
Pena, Tony	.212	52	11	2	6	1	3	.226	.385
Pendleton, T#	.251	251	63	6	33	18	36	.298	.394
Piazza, Mike	.297	74	22	6	17	13	10	.398	.581
Plantier, P*	.235	34	8	2	6	5	12	.333	.441
Raines, Tim*	.269	67	18	1	9	6	10	.324	.358
Reed, Jeff*	.231	442	102	5	40	48	74	.305	.326
Reed, Jody	.281	32	9	0	7	6	1	.390	.344
Roberts, Bip#	.310	477	148	3	41	60	62	.388	.407
Rodriguez, H*	.276	58	16	2	13	6	17	.338	.466
Sabo, Chris	.283	1481	419	61	201	138	196	.346	.488
Samuel, Juan	.269	223	60	5	23	16	42	.318	.390
Sanchez, Rey	.250	60	15	0	5	4	5	.292	.300
Sandberg, R	.302	192	58	3	15	25	37	.382	.411
Sanders, R	.271	1031	279	40	161	140	266	.362	.472
Santiago, B	.270	341	92	12	46	27	65	.326	.440
Scarsone, S	.222	36	8	1	4	3	14	.282	.333
Segui, David#	.265	49	13	1	8	3	6	.308	.408
Servais, S	.239	67	16	2	5	2	16	.257	.358
Sheffield, G	.185	108	20	6	18	15	17	.281	.361
Shipley, C	.294	34	10	1	3	2	4	.333	.412
Slaught, Don	.317	63	20	3	8	8	8	.405	.524
Smith, Dwight*	.211	57	12	1	5	4	18	.262	.333
Smith, Ozzie#	.289	180	52	0	18	28	11	.386	.350
Sosa, Sammy	.269	93	25	3	7	5	18	.313	.398
Stillwell, K#	.261	188	49	3	12	15	26	.315	.404
Stocker, K#	.209	43	9	0	8	3	13	.255	.209
Strawberry, D*	.240	100	24	6	18	17	26	.356	.480
Taubensee, E*	.275	357	98	13	60	35	74	.339	.454
Thompson, Mil*	.255	98	25	1	7	6	17	.295	.316
Thompson, Rob	.245	196	48	3	18	20	54	.326	.357
Thompson, Ry	.245	49	12	1	5	0	10	.255	.408
VanderWal, J*	.333	36	12	3	6	5	5	.415	.667
Vizcaino, J#	.321	84	27	1	14	9	11	.389	.464
Walker, Larry*	.278	126	35	10	26	16	28	.359	.587
Wallach, Tim	.283	198	56	11	35	16	21	.336	.515
Walton, J	.256	176	45	5	25	12	27	.307	.409
Weiss, Walt*	.183	71	13	1	7	12	8	.314	.282
White, R	.368	38	14	1	3	3	5	.415	.553
Whiten, Mark#	.275	51	14	4	13	6	12	.351	.529
Wilkins, Rick*	.295	78	23	2	9	15	13	.415	.436

CINERGY FIELD
Home of the Cincinnati Reds
Cincinnati, Ohio — Artificial

Batter	Avg	AB	H	HR	BI	BB	SO	OBP	Slg
Williams, Ma	.260	173	45	18	48	10	38	.308	.607
Wilson, Dan	.279	68	19	0	7	6	13	.338	.324
Young, Eric	.262	84	22	0	4	10	5	.340	.333
Young, Kevin	.175	40	7	0	1	0	10	.171	.175
Zeile, Todd	.212	137	29	4	16	21	22	.314	.336

JACOBS FIELD
Home of the Cleveland Indians
Cleveland, Ohio — Grass

Batter	Avg	AB	H	HR	BI	BB	SO	OBP	Slg
Aldrete, Mike*	.344	32	11	1	5	3	8	.389	.469
Alomar, R#	.296	71	21	0	6	2	1	.315	.380
Alomar Jr, S	.278	436	121	11	52	27	43	.328	.417
Amaro, Ruben#	.087	46	4	1	2	2	3	.125	.174
Anderson, Brd*	.269	67	18	1	5	4	10	.306	.388
Anderson, G*	.216	37	8	2	9	1	8	.237	.405
Baerga, C#	.304	662	201	20	118	31	44	.331	.459
Baines, H*	.333	60	20	4	10	6	7	.394	.617
Becker, Rich*	.292	48	14	0	5	6	10	.370	.354
Belle, Albert	.334	746	249	68	181	112	118	.423	.713
Berroa, G	.304	46	14	1	5	2	8	.333	.435
Boggs, Wade*	.250	56	14	0	8	7	5	.333	.321
Bonilla, B#	.375	32	12	4	9	5	7	.447	.813
Bordick, Mike	.262	42	11	0	3	2	3	.311	.357
Brosius, S	.206	34	7	1	2	2	8	.250	.324
Buhner, Jay	.340	47	16	4	15	4	9	.392	.702
Burnitz, J*	.298	57	17	4	12	11	11	.420	.614
Canseco, Jose	.279	68	19	1	12	9	23	.359	.382
Carreon, Mark	.278	54	15	1	7	3	2	.328	.389
Carter, Joe	.303	66	20	4	11	4	14	.343	.515
Clark, Will*	.370	46	17	0	5	6	5	.444	.391
Cole, Alex*	.256	39	10	0	1	2	4	.293	.308
Cora, Joey#	.276	58	16	0	3	4	4	.323	.328
Cordova, M	.340	53	18	3	9	5	7	.397	.604
Curtis, Chad	.116	43	5	1	2	3	10	.174	.186
Cuyler, Milt#	.209	43	9	0	5	4	6	.292	.302
Durham, Ray#	.220	41	9	0	3	2	6	.256	.268
Espinoza, A	.254	205	52	2	19	5	28	.272	.337
Fielder, C	.200	60	12	0	4	5	22	.273	.217
Franco, Julio	.346	246	85	8	47	42	44	.443	.488
Fryman, T	.250	76	19	2	4	7	20	.313	.382
Gates, Brent#	.293	41	12	0	6	4	7	.362	.366
Giambi, Jason*	.189	37	7	0	2	3	9	.250	.189
Giles, B*	.328	61	20	2	13	9	6	.408	.508
Gonzalez, A	.250	36	9	1	1	3	8	.308	.333
Gonzalez, J	.339	59	20	5	20	2	9	.361	.661
Goodwin, Tom*	.400	35	14	1	5	1	4	.417	.571
Green, Shawn*	.309	55	17	2	7	3	7	.350	.527
Greenwell, M*	.278	54	15	2	5	2	3	.304	.426
Greer, Rusty*	.405	42	17	1	7	6	4	.469	.619
Griffey Jr, K*	.303	33	10	1	5	4	11	.378	.515
Guillen, O*	.271	70	19	0	0	2	5	.292	.329
Hamilton, D*	.306	36	11	1	4	2	3	.333	.500
Hammonds, J	.300	50	15	2	5	4	15	.352	.480
Hoiles, Chris	.300	40	12	2	10	6	15	.375	.475
Hulse, David*	.224	49	11	0	6	0	3	.240	.265
Jaha, John	.289	45	13	3	6	7	8	.407	.533
Johnson, L*	.250	40	10	1	3	2	1	.286	.375
Karkovice, R	.286	42	12	0	5	2	10	.318	.333
Kent, Jeff	.283	60	17	2	11	6	10	.333	.467
Kirby, Wayne*	.276	156	43	3	18	15	24	.343	.404
Knoblauch, C	.292	72	21	1	6	5	13	.363	.361
Leius, Scott	.182	44	8	1	4	3	6	.234	.341
Lewis, Mark	.211	57	12	1	5	2	9	.237	.316
Leyritz, Jim	.250	28	7	2	7	8	3	.421	.571
Lofton, Kenny*	.340	794	270	22	95	79	84	.397	.513
Macfarlane, M	.267	45	12	3	9	6	10	.411	.533
Martinez, Da*	.216	37	8	1	1	3	6	.275	.351
Martinez, E	.324	34	11	3	7	11	9	.500	.647
Martinez, T*	.308	52	16	3	11	7	5	.390	.558
McGwire, Mark	.308	26	8	5	10	8	13	.486	.885
McLemore, M#	.250	48	12	0	6	5	9	.321	.354
Meares, Pat	.318	44	14	2	9	2	6	.367	.591
Molitor, Paul	.232	69	16	1	6	8	14	.321	.348
Murray, Eddie#	.291	584	170	25	99	54	74	.348	.473
Nilsson, Dave*	.250	48	12	2	5	6	7	.327	.458
Nixon, Otis#	.298	47	14	0	3	4	5	.353	.383
O'Leary, Troy*	.250	44	11	1	5	1	13	.283	.386
O'Neill, Paul*	.291	55	16	3	15	12	9	.406	.527
Olerud, John*	.297	64	19	2	6	7	4	.366	.453
Palmeiro, R*	.242	62	15	1	5	8	6	.329	.387
Palmer, Dean	.282	39	11	2	9	2	8	.302	.487
Pena, Tony	.220	245	54	2	22	20	42	.278	.310
Perry, H	.307	88	27	3	9	5	15	.354	.511
Phillips, T#	.214	56	12	1	4	8	14	.308	.304
Raines, Tim#	.304	56	17	2	9	2	3	.328	.482
Ramirez, M	.282	638	180	40	141	104	145	.382	.553

JACOBS FIELD
Home of the Cleveland Indians
Cleveland, Ohio   **Grass**

Batter	Avg	AB	H	HR	BI	BB	SO	OBP	Slg
Ripken, Cal	.308	65	20	1	8	3	12	.333	.431
Rodriguez, I	.290	62	18	2	10	3	2	.333	.484
Salmon, Tim	.297	37	11	1	1	6	11	.409	.405
Seitzer, K	.333	105	35	1	16	13	19	.412	.467
Sierra, Ruben#	.319	47	15	2	10	3	5	.353	.532
Snow, J.T.#	.400	35	14	3	8	2	2	.432	.771
Sorrento, P*	.264	333	88	20	71	42	68	.345	.486
Sprague, Ed	.172	58	10	1	3	7	14	.262	.293
Stahoviak, S*	.139	36	5	1	6	6	12	.262	.222
Stanley, Mike	.361	36	13	2	4	6	6	.467	.611
Steinbach, T	.256	39	10	3	6	0	6	.250	.538
Surhoff, B.J.	.316	57	18	1	3	1	7	.328	.404
Tartabull, D	.282	39	11	1	3	9	9	.408	.513
Tettleton, M#	.178	45	8	2	7	15	15	.391	.311
Thomas, Frank	.303	66	20	4	18	21	14	.466	.576
Thome, Jim*	.298	621	185	41	123	137	158	.429	.576
Valentin, Jhn	.250	64	16	1	1	2	3	.294	.359
Valentin, Jse#	.267	60	16	3	12	5	17	.318	.533
Vaughn, Greg	.191	47	9	1	1	6	9	.283	.298
Vaughn, Mo*	.313	64	20	3	14	6	17	.366	.453
Velarde, R	.333	42	14	2	6	5	7	.404	.548
Ventura, R*	.324	71	23	3	13	9	12	.402	.479
Vizcaino, J#	.299	97	29	0	10	4	12	.324	.320
Vizquel, Omar#	.287	673	193	5	87	68	53	.349	.373
Walbeck, Matt#	.180	50	9	1	10	2	6	.226	.300
White, Devon#	.250	40	10	1	6	2	6	.273	.375
Williams, Ber#	.298	57	17	3	11	10	9	.403	.544
Wilson, Dan	.243	37	9	0	5	2	6	.282	.324

COORS FIELD
Home of the Colorado Rockies
Denver, Colorado   **Grass**

Batter	Avg	AB	H	HR	BI	BB	SO	OBP	Slg
Abbott, Kurt	.216	37	8	0	2	3	10	.275	.324
Alou, Moises	.282	39	11	1	3	4	5	.378	.436
Anthony, Eric*	.296	54	16	1	10	8	9	.381	.426
Ausmus, Brad	.375	32	12	1	9	3	5	.429	.625
Bagwell, Jeff	.303	33	10	1	9	6	4	.400	.485
Bates, Jason#	.309	230	71	5	35	37	48	.409	.478
Bell, Derek	.250	36	9	2	7	2	7	.300	.472
Bell, Jay	.311	45	14	4	10	6	5	.385	.600
Benard, M*	.289	38	11	1	4	4	6	.372	.474
Bichette, D	.371	638	237	53	182	39	87	.406	.697
Biggio, Craig	.375	32	12	2	6	6	2	.500	.563
Blauser, Jeff	.353	34	12	2	9	2	6	.389	.618
Bonds, Barry*	.359	39	14	2	9	10	3	.490	.590
Boone, Bret	.289	45	13	1	6	2	5	.340	.378
Branson, Jeff*	.229	35	8	1	3	4	8	.308	.343
Brogna, Rico*	.242	33	8	1	3	4	7	.324	.424
Burks, Ellis	.360	472	170	31	111	50	99	.425	.680
Caminiti, Ken#	.333	54	18	5	16	8	9	.400	.685
Castilla, V	.362	602	218	50	132	37	75	.400	.691
Clayton, R	.286	35	10	0	0	3	4	.359	.371
Conine, Jeff	.413	46	19	6	14	7	7	.491	.935
DeShields, D*	.263	38	10	0	2	7	7	.378	.316
Finley, Steve*	.387	62	24	1	7	4	5	.441	.677
Fletcher, D*	.324	34	11	2	10	3	1	.378	.588
Galarraga, A	.331	593	196	50	158	42	140	.390	.661
Gant, Ron	.421	38	16	2	8	4	7	.476	.632
Gilkey, B	.391	46	18	7	12	5	6	.442	.870
Girardi, Joe	.291	247	72	6	41	15	32	.333	.417
Gonzalez, L*	.359	39	14	2	11	5	4	.468	.590
Grace, Mark*	.348	46	16	2	16	10	2	.441	.587
Grissom, M	.358	53	19	1	7	6	8	.424	.491
Grudzielanek	.455	33	15	0	6	1	3	.486	.576
Hayes, C	.200	40	8	2	4	0	10	.200	.375
Hollandsworth*	.341	44	15	3	12	2	7	.362	.659
Hubbard, Tr	.313	67	21	3	16	13	13	.432	.537
Hundley, Todd#	.455	33	15	3	14	6	7	.538	.879
Hunter, Bri L	.265	34	9	0	3	1	4	.306	.382
Jones, C#	.235	51	12	1	4	7	12	.328	.392
Jordan, Brian	.224	49	11	2	10	1	3	.255	.367
Karros, Eric	.393	56	22	6	13	7	10	.460	.786
Kent, Jeff	.273	33	9	2	7	3	6	.324	.485
King, Jeff	.440	50	22	4	17	2	6	.472	.840
Kingery, Mike*	.264	174	46	4	19	29	17	.368	.425
Klesko, Ryan*	.488	41	20	4	15	4	10	.532	.927
Lankford, Ray*	.170	47	8	3	7	10	9	.310	.404
Lansing, Mike	.326	43	14	4	13	1	7	.341	.674
Larkin, Barry	.297	37	11	0	5	8	5	.422	.324
Lemke, Mark#	.286	35	10	0	5	2	1	.324	.314
Lopez, Javy	.419	31	13	2	10	4	5	.500	.710
Mabry, John*	.524	42	22	2	11	2	1	.556	.857
Manwaring, K	.233	30	7	0	4	3	4	.306	.267
Martin, Al*	.333	48	16	1	3	7	8	.429	.500
McCracken, Q#	.329	140	46	2	28	20	27	.410	.486
McGriff, Fred*	.519	52	27	3	13	4	7	.561	.788

251

COORS FIELD
Home of the Colorado Rockies
Denver, Colorado — Grass

Batter	Avg	AB	H	HR	BI	BB	SO	OBP	Slg
McRae, Brian#	.310	58	18	3	6	3	10	.344	.586
Merced, O*	.256	39	10	1	6	5	4	.341	.385
Mondesi, Raul	.367	60	22	5	21	3	11	.397	.717
Morris, Hal*	.220	50	11	3	10	5	3	.298	.460
Owens, J	.299	127	38	6	16	12	32	.364	.488
Pagnozzi, Tom	.250	36	9	2	7	2	4	.308	.528
Pendleton, T#	.222	45	10	2	9	7	11	.327	.422
Piazza, Mike	.431	58	25	7	20	4	9	.476	.828
Reed, Jeff*	.304	184	56	7	25	24	32	.383	.484
Reed, Jody	.282	39	11	0	6	9	2	.429	.385
Rodriguez, H*	.395	43	17	1	9	3	11	.435	.605
Sanchez, Rey	.304	46	14	0	4	2	2	.333	.326
Sanders, R	.405	37	15	3	4	3	5	.450	.784
Santiago, B	.156	32	5	0	3	3	6	.229	.188
Segui, David#	.356	45	16	2	10	6	2	.431	.533
Sheffield, G	.441	34	15	5	13	3	3	.500	.971
Sosa, Sammy	.373	59	22	6	18	4	12	.422	.797
VanderWal, J*	.342	117	40	7	37	19	18	.428	.632
Veras, Q#	.308	39	12	0	1	5	3	.386	.359
Vizcaino, J#	.286	42	12	0	5	2	9	.318	.381
Walker, Larry*	.361	393	142	36	104	30	65	.419	.756
Weiss, Walt#	.312	478	149	5	52	101	64	.433	.389
Williams, Ma	.326	43	14	6	16	2	9	.356	.744
Young, Eric	.384	477	183	12	77	54	26	.457	.543
Zeile, Todd	.277	47	13	2	8	8	3	.393	.532

TIGER STADIUM
Home of the Detroit Tigers
Detroit, Michigan — Grass

Batter	Avg	AB	H	HR	BI	BB	SO	OBP	Slg
Aldrete, Mike*	.231	39	9	1	9	5	2	.311	.359
Alomar, R#	.285	137	39	3	13	21	14	.380	.431
Alomar Jr, S	.304	79	24	4	12	1	12	.309	.506
Amaral, Rich	.234	47	11	0	3	3	6	.294	.298
Anderson, Brd*	.306	160	49	6	22	24	23	.402	.500
Anderson, G*	.395	43	17	3	8	1	4	.409	.721
Ausmus, Brad	.240	121	29	2	13	16	30	.329	.331
Baerga, C#	.292	144	42	9	29	9	15	.338	.563
Baines, H*	.355	172	61	9	44	22	30	.421	.570
Bartee, K	.271	129	35	0	8	8	48	.314	.302
Bautista, D	.185	232	43	5	21	13	52	.229	.293
Belle, Albert	.236	148	35	10	33	19	30	.327	.520
Berroa, G	.305	59	18	3	9	5	9	.358	.492
Bichette, D	.209	43	9	0	3	2	11	.244	.302
Blowers, Mike	.203	64	13	3	7	2	14	.227	.406
Boggs, Wade*	.296	196	58	1	21	28	11	.380	.403
Bonilla, B#	.486	37	18	5	15	7	0	.565	.946
Borders, Pat	.266	109	29	3	16	6	12	.299	.431
Bordick, Mike	.198	101	20	0	5	7	12	.255	.218
Brosius, S	.288	66	19	3	9	5	12	.351	.515
Buhner, Jay	.288	139	40	10	35	20	43	.378	.547
Burks, Ellis	.289	149	43	2	15	7	26	.318	.389
Canseco, Jose	.258	182	47	9	28	26	52	.362	.456
Carreon, Mark	.212	151	32	5	19	14	30	.278	.364
Carter, Joe	.236	203	48	4	24	16	32	.300	.389
Casanova, R#	.205	44	9	1	4	2	13	.239	.295
Cedeno, A	.205	88	18	6	13	2	21	.222	.455
Cirillo, Jeff	.306	62	19	1	10	5	6	.358	.516
Clark, Phil	.424	33	14	0	3	5	6	.500	.485
Clark, Tony#	.246	244	60	17	53	21	78	.301	.508
Clark, Will*	.323	62	20	0	9	14	9	.442	.419
Cole, Alex*	.463	54	25	2	8	4	6	.508	.630
Coleman, V#	.244	45	11	0	3	3	6	.292	.267
Cora, Joey#	.227	75	17	2	6	7	7	.310	.347
Cordova, M	.319	47	15	1	7	11	11	.448	.447
Curtis, Chad	.262	504	132	14	58	68	83	.350	.405
Cuyler, Milt#	.234	629	147	3	49	65	121	.314	.300
Davis, Chili#	.261	153	40	6	28	20	27	.349	.431
Davis, Eric	.259	108	28	6	17	19	32	.370	.472
Deer, Rob	.228	587	134	38	97	105	217	.345	.475
Devereaux, M	.233	133	31	6	16	8	27	.277	.391
Diaz, Alex#	.293	41	12	0	4	0	7	.302	.341
DiSarcina, G	.225	71	16	2	5	6	7	.278	.394
Durham, Ray#	.500	44	22	2	9	4	8	.551	.795
Easley, D	.261	46	12	0	2	5	8	.346	.283
Edmonds, Jim*	.283	53	15	5	13	6	15	.377	.623
Eisenreich, J*	.286	63	18	0	4	3	8	.318	.333
Espinoza, A	.345	84	29	0	6	4	7	.389	.405
Fermin, Felix	.186	102	19	0	1	5	2	.222	.206
Fielder, C	.261	1800	470	127	402	277	437	.362	.514
Flaherty, J	.240	250	60	8	37	17	44	.294	.424
Franco, Julio	.250	184	46	5	22	26	31	.343	.364
Frye, Jeff	.317	41	13	0	8	6	8	.404	.439
Fryman, T	.269	1757	473	64	264	191	384	.342	.441
Gaetti, Gary	.241	170	41	9	27	14	34	.310	.441
Gagne, Greg	.228	162	37	3	14	4	34	.246	.327
Gallego, Mike	.200	95	19	0	10	6	14	.260	.242

Batter	Avg	AB	H	HR	BI	BB	SO	OBP	Slg
Gates, Brent#	.333	45	15	2	7	7	11	.423	.644
Gomez, Chris	.244	471	115	11	74	53	85	.325	.386
Gonzales, R	.167	66	11	1	5	5	11	.222	.227
Gonzalez, A	.306	36	11	0	5	2	8	.333	.444
Gonzalez, J	.333	150	50	7	35	12	22	.376	.533
Goodwin, Tom*	.343	35	12	0	2	1	3	.361	.343
Grebeck, C	.354	48	17	2	9	6	3	.426	.563
Green, Shawn*	.282	39	11	2	5	2	6	.349	.513
Greenwell, M*	.283	166	47	4	25	21	18	.368	.428
Greer, Rusty*	.271	59	16	2	6	8	5	.358	.390
Griffey Jr, K*	.308	159	49	8	23	26	27	.401	.522
Guillen, O*	.261	203	53	3	21	7	13	.284	.335
Hall, Mel*	.244	127	31	6	25	2	19	.252	.417
Hamelin, Bob*	.237	38	9	2	5	11	9	.408	.447
Hamilton, D*	.369	111	41	1	12	1	4	.375	.486
Hayes, C	.395	38	15	3	9	2	2	.425	.684
Henderson, R	.295	132	39	3	17	21	14	.390	.447
Higginson, B*	.279	438	122	25	63	60	98	.365	.523
Hill, G	.238	42	10	5	6	4	10	.319	.619
Hoiles, Chris	.222	72	16	4	8	13	12	.352	.403
Howard, Dave#	.176	51	9	0	3	1	7	.208	.196
Howell, Jack*	.208	53	11	3	9	11	8	.344	.434
Huff, Michael	.297	37	11	1	6	2	8	.333	.432
Hulse, David*	.255	55	14	1	6	7	6	.339	.309
Huson, Jeff*	.298	47	14	1	7	8	6	.411	.404
Incaviglia, P	.201	268	54	7	29	24	87	.268	.343
Jaha, John	.354	82	29	4	14	6	15	.389	.573
James, Dion*	.294	34	10	0	4	7	4	.415	.353
Javier, Stan#	.189	74	14	2	10	3	11	.218	.297
Jefferson, R*	.306	62	19	3	9	8	11	.394	.516
Johnson, L*	.302	126	38	1	11	11	5	.355	.357
Joyner, Wally*	.288	163	47	4	25	21	17	.367	.436
Karkovice, R	.300	120	36	10	26	11	31	.358	.583
Kelly, Pat	.292	65	19	1	9	6	7	.361	.385
Kelly, R	.330	100	33	4	19	8	19	.376	.530
Kirby, Wayne*	.239	46	11	0	6	3	8	.286	.283
Knoblauch, C	.323	130	42	3	17	15	18	.400	.454
Kreuter, Chad#	.258	388	100	12	47	52	98	.343	.397
Leius, Scott	.280	50	14	2	4	6	4	.357	.460
Lewis, Mark	.249	321	80	8	36	16	61	.292	.383
Leyritz, Jim	.175	57	10	2	4	8	10	.324	.298
Liriano, N#	.286	42	12	0	5	4	4	.375	.381
Listach, Pat#	.231	39	9	0	2	2	5	.268	.256
Livingstone*	.263	388	102	4	54	27	47	.307	.335
Lofton, Kenny*	.339	109	37	2	12	14	8	.411	.514
Lovullo, T#	.164	55	9	1	4	10	12	.299	.236
Macfarlane, M	.261	119	31	8	20	12	20	.338	.496
Martinez, Da*	.290	31	9	2	10	3	3	.343	.581
Martinez, E	.281	114	32	1	8	17	17	.379	.386
Martinez, T*	.209	115	24	6	17	10	17	.270	.409
McGriff, Fred*	.213	75	16	3	10	14	20	.330	.387
McGwire, Mark	.301	153	46	20	44	21	36	.384	.732
McLemore, M#	.283	113	32	0	5	12	17	.349	.319
McRae, Brian#	.274	95	26	3	13	5	15	.307	.421
Meares, Pat	.288	59	17	0	7	2	10	.328	.373
Mieske, Matt	.265	34	9	1	8	6	10	.375	.412
Molitor, Paul	.292	212	62	13	40	36	19	.394	.538
Munoz, Pedro	.266	79	21	5	15	6	18	.310	.544
Murray, Eddie#	.315	108	34	3	18	16	10	.400	.444
Myers, Greg*	.234	64	15	1	8	2	11	.254	.328
Naehring, Tim	.280	75	21	4	14	10	7	.379	.507
Nevin, Phil	.261	115	30	5	13	11	39	.336	.461
Newson, W*	.310	42	13	1	4	12	13	.463	.452
Nieves, M#	.231	199	46	10	22	18	76	.303	.432
Nilsson, Dave*	.241	79	19	1	12	11	10	.333	.380
Nixon, Otis#	.308	52	16	0	3	9	5	.410	.346
O'Brien, C	.250	36	9	0	2	2	7	.308	.306
O'Leary, Troy*	.349	43	15	3	7	5	9	.417	.628
O'Neill, Paul*	.289	83	24	4	10	7	14	.344	.482
Olerud, John*	.361	97	35	4	16	36	12	.529	.557
Orsulak, Joe*	.273	88	24	2	9	11	8	.354	.386
Palmeiro, R*	.330	200	66	11	40	20	22	.394	.555
Palmer, Dean	.232	95	22	5	13	4	28	.272	.453
Paquette, C	.263	38	10	1	5	1	9	.282	.421
Parent, Mark	.243	74	18	6	15	1	19	.250	.541
Pena, Tony	.170	94	16	1	9	3	13	.192	.234
Phillips, T#	.275	1413	388	33	165	294	264	.399	.393
Polonia, Luis*	.337	172	58	0	25	8	14	.365	.384
Pride, Curtis*	.303	142	43	5	20	16	30	.373	.528
Raines, Tim#	.400	115	46	5	25	28	14	.517	.609
Ramirez, M	.323	62	20	4	12	7	10	.389	.597
Reboulet, J	.275	40	11	0	6	12	9	.453	.300
Reed, Jody	.293	133	39	2	13	12	7	.354	.398
Ripken, Billy	.209	110	23	1	2	5	8	.250	.291
Ripken, Cal	.302	248	75	12	50	21	24	.357	.528
Rodriguez, Al	.371	35	13	1	8	2	9	.405	.600
Rodriguez, I	.252	115	29	5	17	9	13	.313	.443
Salmon, Tim	.254	63	16	3	15	17	15	.415	.444

253

TIGER STADIUM
Home of the Detroit Tigers
Detroit, Michigan — **Grass**

Batter	Avg	AB	H	HR	BI	BB	SO	OBP	Slg
Samuel, Juan	.370	154	57	10	32	16	31	.434	.708
Schofield, D	.224	107	24	1	8	12	17	.314	.280
Schu, Rick	.191	136	26	3	11	11	20	.252	.301
Segui, David#	.275	51	14	1	5	5	7	.339	.353
Seitzer, K	.314	194	61	2	21	16	15	.372	.423
Sheffield, G	.256	39	10	1	3	3	2	.318	.359
Shumpert, T	.263	38	10	0	3	3	5	.317	.342
Sierra, Ruben#	.239	297	71	12	48	27	43	.294	.431
Slaught, Don	.211	38	8	2	3	4	10	.302	.421
Snow, J.T.#	.208	53	11	2	9	4	8	.271	.377
Sojo, Luis	.302	63	19	1	6	2	2	.328	.508
Sorrento, P*	.282	85	24	3	17	12	19	.367	.459
Spiers, Bill*	.164	61	10	2	8	10	9	.282	.311
Sprague, Ed	.277	94	26	3	13	4	16	.313	.468
Stanley, Mike	.305	105	32	8	21	17	22	.408	.562
Steinbach, T	.279	147	41	7	24	16	22	.358	.490
Stillwell, K#	.295	78	23	0	4	11	9	.389	.359
Strange, Doug#	.219	137	30	1	11	14	23	.294	.277
Surhoff, B.J.*	.318	170	54	4	31	10	16	.350	.482
Sveum, Dale#	.276	58	16	2	6	6	9	.354	.379
Tartabull, D	.221	195	43	9	29	33	62	.336	.395
Tettleton, M#	.249	997	248	60	166	235	280	.391	.487
Thomas, Frank	.346	127	44	8	39	31	15	.458	.630
Thorne, Jim*	.333	66	22	8	12	24	17	.511	.727
Tinsley, Lee#	.319	47	15	1	5	8	12	.418	.404
Trammell, A	.298	1858	553	51	284	186	155	.362	.440
Valentin, Jhn	.347	98	34	6	22	6	14	.404	.602
Valentin, Jse#	.212	52	11	1	7	12	15	.359	.288
Valle, Dave	.233	90	21	6	14	15	11	.352	.478
Vaughn, Greg	.225	142	32	9	26	12	29	.290	.451
Vaughn, Mo*	.228	101	23	7	20	14	28	.345	.436
Velarde, R	.234	128	30	4	12	10	20	.288	.375
Ventura, R*	.302	149	45	11	35	20	23	.376	.577
Vina, F*	.297	37	11	2	4	3	4	.357	.541
Vizquel, Omar#	.305	141	43	1	11	13	11	.359	.376
Walbeck, Matt#	.297	37	11	0	3	1	5	.316	.351
Ward, Turner#	.154	39	6	1	3	1	7	.186	.282
Weiss, Walt#	.216	51	11	1	4	8	6	.322	.294
White, Devon#	.231	195	45	3	12	12	45	.286	.333
Whiten, Mark#	.267	45	12	1	7	3	6	.300	.333
Williams, Ber#	.326	132	43	7	32	7	16	.355	.545
Williams, E	.208	106	22	3	11	9	25	.282	.321
Wilson, Dan	.235	34	8	3	6	1	8	.257	.529
Worthington	.158	38	6	1	6	9	17	.333	.263

PRO PLAYER STADIUM
Home of the Florida Marlins
Miami, Florida — **Grass**

Batter	Avg	AB	H	HR	BI	BB	SO	OBP	Slg
Abbott, Kurt	.284	525	149	22	71	40	145	.340	.503
Alicea, Luis#	.224	49	11	0	3	5	7	.309	.306
Alou, Moises	.185	54	10	0	5	7	10	.290	.241
Arias, Alex	.304	352	107	4	46	34	44	.373	.386
Bagwell, Jeff	.210	62	13	0	7	11	14	.316	.242
Barberie, B#	.259	378	98	4	29	30	60	.328	.365
Bell, Derek	.290	69	20	2	12	4	14	.329	.449
Bell, Jay	.225	71	16	2	9	7	16	.288	.352
Belliard, R	.235	34	8	0	4	2	5	.270	.265
Berry, Sean	.356	59	21	5	15	6	10	.418	.712
Bichette, D	.260	96	25	2	12	4	19	.301	.385
Biggio, Craig	.300	70	21	2	6	16	7	.437	.429
Blauser, Jeff	.309	55	17	2	9	13	11	.466	.436
Bonds, Barry*	.304	56	17	2	11	19	12	.474	.518
Bonilla, B#	.286	35	10	3	7	8	8	.419	.629
Boone, Bret	.220	59	13	1	6	6	10	.294	.322
Branson, Jeff*	.171	41	7	0	0	2	11	.209	.171
Brumfield, J	.250	36	9	0	2	3	10	.300	.472
Burks, Ellis	.229	48	11	3	4	5	10	.315	.438
Butler, Brett*	.321	53	17	1	4	11	8	.438	.453
Caminiti, Ken#	.293	75	22	2	13	10	12	.384	.427
Carr, Chuck#	.272	643	175	5	46	58	92	.334	.341
Carreon, Mark	.350	40	14	2	14	3	3	.386	.600
Castilla, V	.333	57	19	3	10	7	7	.406	.561
Castillo, L#	.247	93	23	0	3	7	25	.300	.280
Cedeno, A	.356	59	21	1	2	4	8	.415	.508
Clark, Dave*	.375	40	15	0	6	3	6	.419	.375
Clayton, R	.326	46	15	0	4	4	8	.380	.391
Colbrunn, G	.291	588	171	22	93	29	94	.335	.451
Conine, Jeff	.310	1072	332	41	190	103	218	.367	.482
Cordero, Wil	.294	68	20	4	13	6	11	.364	.515
Daulton, D*	.283	46	13	4	16	9	9	.393	.587
Dawson, Andre	.265	136	36	3	22	4	29	.299	.390
Decker, Steve	.268	71	19	2	8	10	9	.354	.394
DeShields, D*	.170	53	9	0	2	8	11	.279	.283
Duncan, M	.340	50	17	1	8	2	8	.352	.520
Dunston, S	.367	49	18	2	6	1	6	.380	.571
Dykstra, L*	.203	69	14	0	3	19	11	.389	.232

254

PRO PLAYER STADIUM
Home of the Florida Marlins

Miami, Florida — Grass

Batter	Avg	AB	H	HR	BI	BB	SO	OBP	Slg
Eisenreich, J*	.293	75	22	2	15	11	9	.379	.467
Everett, Carl#	.163	43	7	2	5	7	14	.280	.326
Finley, Steve*	.303	89	27	1	8	7	8	.354	.494
Fletcher, D*	.234	64	15	1	16	8	6	.320	.391
Floyd, Cliff*	.250	44	11	1	2	6	10	.340	.318
Galarraga, A	.287	87	25	4	17	11	27	.366	.460
Gant, Ron	.268	41	11	1	5	9	8	.400	.463
Garcia, C	.259	58	15	2	5	4	9	.302	.466
Gilkey, B	.298	84	25	4	20	12	13	.392	.524
Girardi, Joe	.200	50	10	1	7	6	6	.286	.300
Gonzalez, L*	.266	79	21	3	14	7	15	.322	.481
Grace, Mark*	.181	83	15	1	8	11	2	.289	.301
Grebeck, C	.200	55	11	0	4	1	7	.224	.218
Grissom, M	.278	97	27	3	8	10	11	.346	.454
Grudzielanek	.244	41	10	0	4	3	6	.295	.268
Gutierrez, R	.242	33	8	0	4	5	6	.342	.364
Gwynn, Tony*	.302	53	16	0	14	1	2	.304	.415
Harris, Lenny*	.237	38	9	0	4	1	6	.256	.316
Hayes, C	.185	92	17	0	4	7	23	.257	.239
Hollandsworth*	.290	31	9	1	6	5	7	.405	.419
Hollins, Dave#	.234	47	11	0	6	18	10	.446	.298
Howard, T*	.244	41	10	0	4	1	7	.279	.341
Hundley, Todd#	.290	69	20	5	16	9	18	.370	.565
Incaviglia, P	.344	32	11	4	9	7	8	.450	.844
Jefferies, G#	.338	77	26	2	17	10	6	.414	.506
Johnson, Char	.231	376	87	13	38	39	80	.307	.372
Jones, C#	.205	44	9	0	8	5	11	.280	.250
Jordan, Brian	.229	35	8	0	2	5	6	.317	.229
Justice, Dave*	.294	68	20	4	13	14	10	.422	.588
Karros, Eric	.309	81	25	3	21	9	15	.370	.506
Kelly, R	.375	56	21	2	9	4	11	.410	.607
Kent, Jeff	.297	74	22	4	11	6	13	.354	.486
King, Jeff	.207	82	17	1	10	10	14	.298	.293
Kingery, Mike*	.240	50	12	1	2	6	5	.321	.340
Klesko, Ryan*	.267	45	12	3	7	8	7	.370	.578
Lankford, Ray*	.312	77	24	2	10	16	24	.432	.494
Lansing, Mike	.375	80	30	0	10	4	9	.412	.500
Larkin, Barry	.310	71	22	3	10	10	9	.395	.479
Lemke, Mark#	.338	74	25	1	9	13	9	.427	.432
Lopez, Javy	.333	51	17	3	9	5	10	.393	.588
Magadan, Dave*	.304	260	79	5	32	54	29	.420	.415
Manwaring, K	.167	48	8	0	4	3	14	.212	.208
Martin, Al*	.274	73	20	2	9	13	11	.384	.425
May, Derrick*	.152	66	10	0	3	4	9	.197	.182
McGee, Willie#	.295	44	13	2	8	4	3	.354	.477
McGriff, Fred*	.342	79	27	5	17	5	11	.384	.595
McRae, Brian#	.268	41	11	1	6	6	3	.354	.390
Merced, O*	.197	76	15	0	7	9	12	.282	.224
Mondesi, Raul	.313	64	20	3	7	7	7	.389	.531
Morandini, M*	.235	81	19	1	8	4	10	.287	.383
Morman, Russ	.204	54	11	1	4	4	12	.283	.315
Morris, Hal*	.295	88	26	2	11	8	13	.347	.398
Mouton, James	.125	40	5	0	4	4	8	.205	.150
Natal, Bob	.182	148	27	2	10	15	36	.274	.270
Offerman, J#	.352	54	19	0	3	9	12	.444	.444
Orsulak, Joe*	.274	175	48	3	25	8	23	.303	.366
Pagnozzi, Tom	.409	44	18	4	10	5	8	.469	.705
Pendleton, T#	.284	518	147	12	79	28	93	.319	.415
Piazza, Mike	.358	67	24	4	14	10	13	.436	.582
Plantier, P*	.317	41	13	1	9	3	3	.356	.463
Reed, Jody	.238	63	15	0	5	6	10	.310	.286
Renteria, E	.309	188	58	2	17	22	24	.385	.415
Rodriguez, H*	.225	40	9	1	1	4	2	.295	.325
Sanchez, Rey	.262	61	16	1	2	6	10	.338	.344
Sandberg, R	.263	38	10	2	6	3	5	.326	.474
Sanders, R	.230	87	20	4	14	9	26	.299	.448
Santiago, B	.247	434	107	12	54	35	88	.306	.406
Segui, David#	.321	53	17	1	9	6	8	.390	.434
Servais, S	.240	50	12	2	8	8	11	.356	.440
Sheffield, G	.304	639	194	43	139	147	96	.443	.565
Shipley, C	.235	34	8	0	2	2	3	.278	.324
Smith, Dwight*	.219	32	7	2	2	5	7	.324	.500
Smith, Ozzie#	.311	45	14	0	5	3	1	.354	.400
Sosa, Sammy	.307	75	23	5	12	4	14	.358	.573
Stocker, K#	.149	47	7	1	8	8	5	.322	.319
Taubensee, E*	.306	49	15	3	8	4	9	.358	.510
Tavarez, Je#	.314	153	48	1	17	10	21	.358	.399
Thompson, Mil*	.410	39	16	0	4	10	2	.540	.410
Thompson, Rob	.345	55	19	2	4	8	17	.429	.564
Thompson, Ry	.268	41	11	1	4	2	7	.318	.415
VanderWal, J*	.219	32	7	0	2	5	9	.324	.406
Veras, Q#	.249	321	80	3	23	63	52	.383	.333
Vizcaino, J#	.273	77	21	0	3	4	10	.317	.390
Walker, Larry*	.320	75	24	2	14	7	11	.381	.493
Wallach, Tim	.283	46	13	3	7	6	14	.365	.478
Weiss, Walt*	.234	299	70	0	23	58	44	.362	.278
White, Devon#	.255	282	72	5	34	17	55	.297	.394
White, R	.267	60	16	1	5	5	11	.328	.400

PRO PLAYER STADIUM
Home of the Florida Marlins
Miami, Florida   Grass

Batter	Avg	AB	H	HR	BI	BB	SO	OBP	Slg
Whiten, Mark#	.286	77	22	1	10	6	22	.337	.468
Wilkins, Rick*	.359	39	14	2	8	8	9	.468	.615
Williams, Ma	.254	59	15	2	9	3	9	.281	.390
Young, Eric	.234	64	15	0	0	12	5	.372	.328
Zeile, Todd	.219	73	16	5	19	19	17	.385	.466

THE ASTRODOME
Home of the Houston Astros
Houston, Texas   Artificial

Batter	Avg	AB	H	HR	BI	BB	SO	OBP	Slg
Abbott, Kurt	.208	53	11	0	6	2	16	.246	.264
Aldrete, Mike*	.294	68	20	1	11	5	9	.342	.441
Alicea, Luis#	.324	74	24	0	7	6	16	.370	.446
Alomar, R#	.330	112	37	3	13	7	21	.367	.509
Alou, Moises	.267	75	20	4	14	4	14	.317	.507
Andrews, S	.206	34	7	0	4	6	11	.325	.235
Anthony, Eric*	.236	666	157	21	89	66	159	.306	.381
Arias, Alex	.275	40	11	0	3	5	5	.356	.400
Bagwell, Jeff	.309	1535	475	72	287	257	281	.414	.533
Barberie, B#	.250	36	9	1	2	4	11	.333	.389
Batiste, Kim	.219	32	7	0	2	2	9	.257	.219
Bell, Derek	.275	582	160	12	105	45	107	.334	.399
Bell, Jay	.316	190	60	6	23	21	35	.382	.500
Belliard, R	.256	90	23	0	5	4	19	.292	.278
Berry, Sean	.254	213	54	5	36	18	33	.316	.399
Bichette, D	.274	95	26	2	17	2	19	.286	.421
Biggio, Craig	.285	2200	626	37	229	291	326	.378	.410
Blauser, Jeff	.257	183	47	5	19	18	45	.325	.399
Bonds, Barry*	.324	207	67	14	44	48	27	.451	.638
Bonilla, B#	.251	167	42	5	27	24	30	.342	.407
Boone, Bret	.373	59	22	1	9	6	12	.418	.508
Branson, Jeff*	.291	55	16	0	7	4	16	.328	.345
Brumfield, J	.195	41	8	0	3	3	8	.261	.220
Burks, Ellis	.326	46	15	2	7	5	10	.392	.500
Butler, Brett*	.268	213	57	3	11	35	26	.381	.380
Caminiti, Ken#	.275	1779	489	35	250	153	299	.332	.405
Candaele, C#	.255	611	156	3	58	64	71	.326	.350
Cangelosi, J#	.299	291	87	3	23	55	53	.418	.399
Carr, Chuck*	.078	51	4	0	1	3	11	.130	.118
Carreon, Mark	.155	71	11	3	11	4	12	.208	.324
Carter, Joe	.297	37	11	1	8	3	6	.366	.486
Castilla, V	.213	61	13	1	6	1	12	.222	.295
Cedeno, A	.255	713	182	17	84	62	191	.322	.405
Cianfrocco, A	.368	38	14	1	8	0	11	.385	.500
Clark, Dave*	.263	57	15	2	4	3	9	.300	.456
Clark, Will*	.308	211	65	10	38	32	37	.399	.526
Clayton, R	.145	110	16	1	9	3	24	.168	.182
Colbrunn, G	.266	64	17	3	11	4	3	.315	.438
Cole, Alex*	.206	34	7	0	0	7	6	.341	.206
Coleman, V#	.206	126	26	0	4	7	28	.248	.238
Conine, Jeff	.288	80	23	1	11	6	15	.352	.413
Cordero, Wil	.258	62	16	0	3	4	13	.324	.371
Dascenzo, D#	.167	30	5	0	1	3	6	.235	.167
Daulton, D*	.214	103	22	4	19	24	12	.359	.369
Davis, Eric	.252	155	39	8	21	20	48	.335	.471
Dawson, Andre	.281	128	36	5	23	5	16	.309	.500
DeShields, D*	.265	113	30	2	15	14	23	.346	.372
Duncan, M	.211	123	26	2	9	5	28	.240	.293
Dunston, S	.221	172	38	3	13	6	37	.244	.343
Dykstra, L*	.322	149	48	0	12	10	20	.377	.450
Eisenreich, J*	.256	43	11	2	7	5	3	.333	.419
Elster, Kevin	.177	62	11	1	4	5	11	.235	.274
Eusebio, Tony	.267	348	93	7	51	24	67	.313	.379
Finley, Steve*	.275	1080	297	10	88	81	133	.326	.384
Fletcher, D*	.219	73	16	3	9	3	9	.275	.370
Galarraga, A	.288	170	49	7	27	7	42	.315	.471
Gant, Ron	.265	226	60	12	36	20	52	.325	.504
Garcia, C	.305	82	25	0	4	5	14	.360	.402
Gilkey, B	.190	105	20	1	10	10	29	.267	.257
Girardi, Joe	.270	100	27	0	7	2	23	.284	.310
Gonzalez, L*	.265	1033	274	22	153	88	166	.326	.413
Grace, Mark*	.314	207	65	5	23	29	18	.398	.459
Grissom, M	.214	145	31	6	13	16	22	.288	.386
Grudzielanek	.135	37	5	0	0	2	11	.220	.135
Gutierrez, R	.297	209	62	1	16	15	47	.352	.349
Gwynn, Chris*	.171	35	6	1	5	1	6	.194	.343
Gwynn, Tony*	.378	246	93	1	34	28	10	.440	.459
Hansen, Dave*	.217	46	10	2	6	4	9	.275	.370
Harris, Lenny*	.257	105	27	0	12	8	9	.316	.371
Hayes, C	.218	142	31	2	16	8	21	.260	.296
Hernandez, Jo	.250	36	9	0	3	2	11	.308	.278
Hill, G	.273	44	12	4	9	2	10	.304	.682
Hollins, Dave#	.286	70	20	3	9	10	14	.390	.500
Howard, T*	.156	43	11	0	5	3	13	.304	.372
Hundley, Todd#	.159	82	13	1	7	1	23	.169	.268
Hunter, Bri L	.289	429	124	1	20	18	73	.318	.357
Incaviglia, P	.300	213	64	7	30	10	69	.341	.474

Batter	Avg	AB	H	HR	BI	BB	SO	OBP	Slg
James, Dion*	.200	40	8	0	3	5	6	.283	.250
Jefferies, G#	.259	162	42	4	19	11	15	.305	.364
Johnson, Bri	.175	40	7	1	10	2	11	.209	.300
Johnson, Char	.233	30	7	0	3	7	10	.378	.367
Jones, C#	.256	43	11	2	7	12	9	.418	.419
Jones, Chris	.197	61	12	1	7	7	20	.271	.295
Jordan, Brian	.260	73	19	2	11	7	20	.337	.452
Jordan, Ricky	.248	109	27	1	11	3	15	.281	.330
Justice, Dave*	.237	139	33	7	19	37	24	.400	.410
Karros, Eric	.274	95	26	2	9	2	17	.289	.379
Kelly, R	.295	44	13	1	3	3	9	.347	.500
Kent, Jeff	.211	57	12	2	8	3	12	.308	.351
King, Jeff	.287	129	37	10	29	10	18	.329	.543
Kingery, Mike*	.253	79	20	0	7	6	13	.302	.342
Klesko, Ryan*	.333	45	15	3	12	5	14	.400	.667
Knorr, Randy	.262	42	11	1	5	2	10	.304	.405
Lankford, Ray*	.238	143	34	5	13	13	44	.313	.392
Lansing, Mike	.276	76	21	0	9	9	12	.356	.382
Larkin, Barry	.344	224	77	4	22	15	27	.393	.464
Lemke, Mark#	.169	142	24	0	9	12	18	.231	.183
Lewis, Darren	.284	102	29	0	9	10	9	.348	.314
Liriano, N#	.294	51	15	2	3	6	7	.368	.431
Lofton, Kenny*	.176	34	6	0	0	2	13	.222	.176
Lopez, Javy	.262	42	11	0	2	4	11	.326	.262
Mabry, John*	.365	52	19	2	7	3	5	.400	.577
Magadan, Dave*	.321	268	86	0	33	47	34	.420	.392
Manwaring, K	.284	155	44	0	10	9	33	.333	.329
Martin, Al*	.213	61	13	1	6	8	15	.310	.344
Martinez, Da*	.320	128	41	2	18	8	18	.370	.430
May, Derrick*	.244	238	58	5	40	31	31	.332	.370
McGee, Willie*	.320	194	62	4	17	14	30	.365	.454
McGriff, Fred*	.345	139	48	10	36	21	30	.432	.669
McLemore, M#	.088	34	3	0	1	3	8	.158	.088
McRae, Brian#	.204	49	10	1	2	5	12	.278	.306
Merced, O*	.323	130	42	2	20	16	25	.395	.438
Miller, Orl	.236	402	95	8	49	13	97	.268	.351
Mitchell, K	.244	156	38	8	26	20	34	.328	.455
Mondesi, Raul	.204	54	11	1	1	0	13	.204	.296
Morandini, M*	.281	89	25	1	7	8	17	.347	.348
Morris, Hal*	.228	158	36	2	10	11	23	.281	.285
Mouton, James	.266	443	118	5	35	39	86	.329	.359
Murray, Eddie#	.261	153	40	6	27	18	23	.337	.431
Nixon, Otis#	.289	97	28	0	1	6	8	.330	.289
O'Neill, Paul*	.178	146	26	1	12	23	28	.292	.226
Offerman, J#	.230	74	17	0	4	9	14	.306	.324
Oliver, Joe	.190	100	19	2	8	9	22	.255	.260
Orsulak, Joe*	.235	51	12	1	4	8	8	.350	.353
Pagnozzi, Tom	.188	128	24	0	7	7	24	.230	.242
Palmeiro, R*	.243	37	9	0	0	0	4	.243	.378
Parent, Mark	.216	51	11	4	8	8	8	.322	.471
Pena, G#	.175	40	7	1	2	1	10	.209	.300
Pena, Tony	.255	51	13	0	0	4	5	.321	.275
Pendleton, T#	.263	209	55	2	27	12	34	.304	.330
Piazza, Mike	.417	72	30	3	8	4	7	.447	.556
Plantier, P*	.327	55	18	4	10	9	15	.448	.600
Raines, Tim#	.294	51	15	1	8	6	6	.373	.392
Reed, Jeff*	.181	105	19	1	12	11	14	.258	.286
Reed, Jody	.257	70	18	0	7	8	5	.338	.286
Roberts, Bip#	.310	142	44	1	9	23	22	.417	.415
Rodriguez, H*	.250	48	12	2	6	1	18	.275	.458
Sabo, Chris	.277	173	48	4	16	17	29	.345	.416
Samuel, Juan	.201	154	31	4	17	17	53	.279	.338
Sanchez, Rey	.188	96	18	0	5	3	13	.228	.219
Sandberg, R	.249	169	42	8	26	16	39	.317	.432
Sanders, R	.278	97	27	6	16	9	30	.336	.505
Santiago, B	.255	200	51	4	25	12	39	.296	.375
Scarsone, S	.178	45	8	0	3	2	16	.213	.267
Segui, David#	.244	41	10	0	2	3	5	.295	.293
Servais, S	.207	445	92	10	55	30	75	.264	.333
Sheffield, G	.284	95	27	5	13	8	17	.337	.474
Shipley, C	.286	168	48	3	9	6	24	.318	.387
Simms, Mike	.215	181	39	7	30	15	61	.281	.376
Slaught, Don	.271	70	19	2	14	9	7	.350	.429
Smith, Dwight*	.305	59	18	0	8	3	11	.349	.407
Smith, Ozzie#	.242	186	45	2	19	21	9	.317	.312
Sosa, Sammy	.179	95	17	4	14	5	31	.225	.316
Spiers, Bill*	.271	129	35	3	17	11	27	.336	.411
Stankiewicz	.125	48	6	1	4	9	11	.276	.229
Stillwell, K#	.271	59	16	0	6	2	13	.306	.339
Stocker, K#	.328	58	19	0	4	2	8	.381	.448
Strawberry, D*	.235	136	32	8	20	19	44	.325	.456
Taubensee, E*	.264	330	87	8	33	33	66	.332	.412
Thompson, Mil*	.267	202	54	3	20	22	49	.341	.386
Thompson, Rob	.201	194	39	5	14	18	44	.276	.345
VanderWal, J*	.185	54	10	1	5	6	16	.267	.296
Veras, Q#	.333	33	11	0	1	9	3	.476	.485
Vizcaino, J#	.297	64	19	1	8	7	8	.361	.406
Walker, Larry*	.212	99	21	1	7	9	26	.291	.323

THE ASTRODOME
Home of the Houston Astros
Houston, Texas — **Artificial**

Batter	Avg	AB	H	HR	BI	BB	SO	OBP	Slg
Wallach, Tim	.250	160	40	3	19	9	35	.298	.356
Walton, J	.208	77	16	1	4	5	18	.262	.273
Weiss, Walt#	.241	58	14	0	4	12	13	.370	.259
White, R	.293	41	12	1	6	2	12	.341	.463
Whiten, Mark#	.333	48	16	3	10	7	10	.418	.625
Wilkins, Rick*	.212	198	42	6	18	32	63	.316	.348
Williams, Ma	.179	207	37	7	30	11	59	.228	.319
Young, Eric	.317	82	26	0	8	6	6	.378	.366
Young, Kevin	.263	38	10	0	4	2	8	.293	.316
Zeile, Todd	.295	139	41	1	15	12	19	.342	.410

EWING M. KAUFFMAN STADIUM
Home of the Kansas City Royals
Kansas City, Missouri — **Grass**

Batter	Avg	AB	H	HR	BI	BB	SO	OBP	Slg
Aldrete, Mike*	.400	50	20	1	7	4	5	.444	.600
Alomar, R#	.279	122	34	3	14	22	18	.395	.426
Alomar Jr, S	.288	66	19	1	6	4	6	.329	.424
Amaral, Rich	.191	47	9	0	2	5	5	.269	.255
Anderson, Brd*	.304	184	56	9	27	26	33	.396	.565
Baerga, C#	.306	121	37	1	19	4	16	.326	.421
Baines, H*	.268	205	55	6	22	21	37	.336	.400
Becker, Rich*	.220	50	11	0	5	4	10	.278	.240
Belle, Albert	.258	128	33	6	22	10	22	.319	.445
Berroa, G	.167	60	10	1	5	3	10	.219	.250
Bichette, D	.217	46	10	0	1	3	11	.265	.261
Blowers, Mike	.250	32	8	1	7	3	10	.306	.469
Boggs, Wade*	.338	216	73	2	18	29	10	.415	.403
Borders, Pat	.232	142	33	2	16	5	27	.262	.359
Bordick, Mike	.269	119	32	1	17	13	12	.351	.311
Brosius, S	.239	71	17	0	9	3	12	.266	.366
Buhner, Jay	.192	120	23	1	14	8	42	.252	.258
Burks, Ellis	.248	149	37	4	17	11	28	.304	.430
Canseco, Jose	.295	173	51	12	32	15	36	.358	.590
Carter, Joe	.249	225	56	3	30	10	33	.282	.378
Cedeno, D#	.257	35	9	1	4	3	5	.293	.343
Cirillo, Jeff	.245	49	12	0	7	3	2	.296	.265
Clark, Will*	.283	53	15	1	9	9	11	.375	.415
Cole, Alex*	.232	56	13	0	2	5	9	.295	.304
Coleman, V#	.296	375	111	3	32	27	57	.343	.424
Conine, Jeff	.250	32	8	0	6	5	5	.351	.344
Cora, Joey#	.218	110	24	0	6	2	8	.237	.282
Cordova, M	.308	52	16	0	8	2	10	.333	.385
Curtis, Chad	.274	73	20	2	6	5	13	.316	.438
Cuyler, Milt#	.292	48	14	1	3	1	12	.306	.396
Damon, Johnny*	.267	352	94	4	32	19	42	.307	.381
Davis, Chili#	.272	195	53	11	35	22	43	.344	.503
Dawson, Andre	.211	38	8	0	3	3	5	.279	.237
Deer, Rob	.157	127	20	5	17	15	42	.255	.307
Delgado, C*	.212	33	7	2	3	3	8	.297	.424
Devereaux, M	.310	158	49	1	18	3	23	.319	.418
DiSarcina, G	.318	85	27	1	8	3	10	.341	.424
Easley, D	.222	45	10	1	7	3	7	.286	.311
Edmonds, Jim*	.314	51	16	2	7	3	12	.345	.569
Eisenreich, J*	.277	969	268	12	122	75	87	.325	.404
Espinoza, A	.310	84	26	0	11	1	5	.326	.393
Fasano, Sal	.208	77	16	1	4	8	6	.291	.260
Fermin, Felix	.281	89	25	0	5	7	7	.347	.337
Fielder, C	.283	159	45	9	27	16	44	.356	.516
Franco, Julio	.265	166	44	4	16	19	28	.348	.367
Frye, Jeff	.209	43	9	0	1	4	4	.271	.279
Fryman, T	.291	127	37	8	31	18	27	.377	.583
Gaetti, Gary	.268	653	175	28	102	42	119	.319	.472
Gagne, Greg	.294	749	220	7	88	56	108	.344	.398
Gallego, Mike	.231	108	25	2	11	11	16	.303	.333
Gates, Brent#	.304	56	17	1	8	8	4	.379	.393
Giambi, Jason*	.364	33	12	4	8	1	1	.400	.758
Gomez, Leo	.268	71	19	3	8	20	13	.438	.437
Gonzales, R	.169	71	12	0	4	6	10	.241	.183
Gonzalez, J	.328	119	39	12	28	6	20	.365	.731
Goodwin, Tom*	.264	500	132	2	25	32	73	.315	.326
Green, Shawn*	.289	38	11	3	5	3	5	.341	.553
Greenwell, M*	.327	156	51	3	20	12	13	.372	.500
Greer, Rusty*	.357	42	15	0	2	4	7	.426	.500
Griffey Jr, K*	.229	170	39	6	19	26	21	.332	.394
Guillen, O*	.354	178	63	0	19	9	9	.383	.433
Gwynn, Chris*	.317	164	52	0	18	11	18	.356	.433
Hall, Mel*	.321	112	36	3	24	2	15	.330	.518
Hamelin, Bob*	.241	394	95	19	65	67	80	.354	.467
Hamilton, D*	.257	136	35	0	7	5	11	.282	.287
Henderson, R	.298	141	42	4	15	31	19	.436	.447
Hiatt, Phil	.265	189	50	5	27	8	62	.302	.413
Hoiles, Chris	.319	69	22	6	16	6	16	.390	.667
Howard, Dave#	.248	649	161	4	69	64	117	.314	.331
Howell, Jack*	.238	80	19	0	5	5	20	.282	.388
Hulse, David*	.170	47	8	0	0	0	11	.170	.213
Huson, Jeff*	.222	36	8	0	3	5	5	.310	.222

EWING M. KAUFFMAN STADIUM
Home of the Kansas City Royals
Kansas City, Missouri   **Grass**

Batter	Avg	AB	H	HR	BI	BB	SO	OBP	Slg
Incaviglia, P	.154	104	16	2	10	7	40	.207	.250
Jaha, John	.288	73	21	5	11	6	12	.350	.562
James, Dion*	.329	73	24	1	7	5	4	.372	.452
Javier, Stan#	.255	98	25	2	10	12	14	.342	.367
Jefferies, G#	.289	280	81	3	37	26	12	.346	.396
Johnson, L*	.240	146	35	1	15	11	9	.293	.356
Joyner, Wally*	.323	1040	336	14	157	109	105	.386	.454
Karkovice, R	.250	96	24	3	12	11	25	.327	.417
Kelly, Pat	.286	42	12	1	6	1	7	.295	.429
Kelly, R	.250	92	23	1	16	6	20	.307	.359
Kirby, Wayne*	.261	46	12	0	5	4	5	.320	.326
Knoblauch, C	.317	145	46	1	17	20	17	.405	.503
Koslofski, K*	.206	107	22	1	9	12	20	.295	.252
Kreuter, Chad#	.211	38	8	1	5	4	12	.295	.421
Leius, Scott	.246	61	15	0	5	7	9	.319	.311
Lewis, Mark	.217	46	10	0	0	1	9	.250	.239
Leyritz, Jim	.266	64	17	6	9	6	17	.319	.578
Liriano, N#	.239	67	16	0	5	2	9	.261	.254
Listach, Pat#	.340	53	18	1	8	10	7	.444	.604
Livingstone*	.327	49	16	0	1	1	4	.340	.388
Lockhart, K*	.302	321	97	7	43	26	22	.354	.439
Lofton, Kenny*	.256	90	23	0	3	9	11	.323	.256
Lovullo, T#	.158	38	6	0	2	4	6	.238	.211
Macfarlane, M	.271	1228	333	41	183	97	202	.340	.466
Martinez, Da*	.250	32	8	1	2	2	2	.294	.375
Martinez, E	.275	167	46	5	24	18	24	.349	.425
Martinez, T*	.205	122	25	2	14	11	20	.271	.336
Mayne, Brent*	.278	561	156	4	63	50	80	.338	.360
McGriff, Fred*	.300	70	21	5	6	5	20	.347	.614
McGwire, Mark	.282	163	46	6	25	25	27	.381	.479
McLemore, M#	.294	109	32	1	9	7	14	.336	.367
McRae, Brian*	.274	1198	328	13	144	87	188	.326	.389
Meares, Pat	.295	61	18	1	8	4	16	.358	.426
Mercedes, H	.276	29	8	0	6	6	8	.378	.310
Molitor, Paul	.296	233	69	5	22	24	23	.362	.442
Morman, Russ	.194	36	7	0	1	3	6	.256	.250
Munoz, Pedro	.250	80	20	2	8	2	22	.268	.363
Murray, Eddie#	.333	87	29	3	19	6	10	.376	.598
Myers, Greg*	.313	83	26	1	10	5	6	.356	.422
Myers, Rod*	.333	39	13	1	8	2	12	.366	.538
Naehring, Tim	.183	82	15	0	6	7	8	.253	.244
Newson, W*	.324	34	11	0	3	10	10	.477	.382
Nilsson, Dave*	.159	63	10	3	7	2	9	.182	.333
Nixon, Otis#	.333	60	20	0	1	5	6	.379	.400
Norman, Les	.163	49	8	0	3	5	9	.241	.204
Nunnally, Jon*	.210	186	39	8	23	33	53	.330	.414
O'Brien, C	.122	41	5	0	1	1	6	.140	.195
O'Neill, Paul*	.313	83	26	7	16	10	10	.379	.639
Offerman, J#	.305	275	84	1	28	30	45	.371	.411
Olerud, John*	.247	150	37	3	17	12	19	.305	.360
Orsulak, Joe*	.242	99	24	1	11	5	9	.279	.313
Palmeiro, R*	.283	173	49	4	23	20	21	.360	.480
Palmer, Dean	.165	97	16	5	11	7	30	.226	.361
Paquette, C	.265	211	56	12	45	11	48	.304	.488
Pena, Tony	.217	92	20	1	4	2	15	.232	.272
Phillips, T#	.263	186	49	6	27	36	31	.384	.441
Polonia, Luis*	.361	194	70	0	24	21	20	.417	.454
Pulliam, H	.269	52	14	2	5	5	10	.333	.462
Raines, Tim#	.298	114	34	1	18	21	11	.407	.430
Ramirez, M	.298	47	14	3	10	2	7	.327	.596
Randa, Joe	.310	203	63	3	35	20	24	.372	.443
Reboulet, J	.190	42	8	0	4	5	9	.277	.214
Reed, Jody	.259	108	28	0	7	9	9	.325	.370
Ripken, Billy	.260	96	25	1	13	8	9	.317	.354
Ripken, Cal	.279	222	62	6	26	33	19	.371	.473
Roberts, Bip#	.284	155	44	0	26	11	16	.331	.368
Rodriguez, Al	.290	31	9	0	1	3	4	.353	.387
Rodriguez, I	.351	114	40	3	11	4	11	.370	.500
Salmon, Tim	.299	67	20	4	17	10	11	.392	.582
Samuel, Juan	.248	101	25	1	13	6	28	.303	.347
Schofield, D	.262	107	28	3	11	13	21	.352	.393
Segui, David*	.250	32	8	0	3	4	2	.333	.313
Seitzer, K	.314	1435	450	19	162	184	147	.393	.436
Sheffield, G	.189	53	10	1	11	4	3	.237	.302
Shumpert, T	.210	367	77	3	32	23	70	.262	.308
Sierra, Ruben#	.294	238	70	4	36	15	25	.332	.445
Slaught, Don	.240	50	12	0	4	6	12	.333	.340
Snow, J.T.#	.230	74	17	4	8	7	13	.305	.419
Sojo, Luis	.333	72	24	0	8	2	5	.360	.417
Sorrento, P*	.237	76	18	1	6	9	10	.314	.329
Sosa, Sammy	.195	41	8	0	7	1	18	.227	.244
Spehr, Tim	.200	25	5	1	10	8	6	.394	.400
Spiers, Bill*	.220	59	13	0	5	2	8	.246	.288
Sprague, Ed	.221	86	19	4	12	6	18	.268	.407
Stanley, Mike	.238	105	25	2	13	11	20	.322	.352
Steinbach, T	.275	167	46	0	18	11	21	.326	.359
Stillwell, K#	.252	903	228	10	113	81	124	.314	.369
Strange, Doug#	.206	63	13	0	5	1	8	.219	.302

EWING M. KAUFFMAN STADIUM
Home of the Kansas City Royals
Kansas City, Missouri — Grass

Batter	Avg	AB	H	HR	BI	BB	SO	OBP	Slg
Stynes, Chris	.339	59	20	0	5	2	3	.361	.424
Surhoff, B.J.*	.235	170	40	0	15	4	13	.253	.282
Sveum, Dale#	.147	68	10	0	10	7	23	.227	.265
Sweeney, Mike	.257	70	18	1	9	5	7	.329	.343
Tartabull, D	.283	1182	335	60	196	178	278	.376	.502
Tettleton, M#	.181	182	33	5	17	27	53	.286	.297
Thomas, Frank	.299	134	40	5	24	24	24	.390	.463
Thome, Jim*	.270	63	17	3	7	6	16	.329	.429
Trammell, A	.306	111	34	1	15	9	6	.366	.432
Tucker, M*	.252	254	64	3	27	30	56	.338	.378
Valentin, Jhn	.224	49	11	1	10	6	6	.293	.388
Valentin, Jse#	.333	51	17	0	6	7	9	.414	.549
Valle, Dave	.216	97	21	1	6	8	10	.303	.289
Vaughn, Greg	.237	139	33	8	21	14	36	.312	.439
Vaughn, Mo*	.274	84	23	4	20	17	17	.394	.500
Velarde, R	.318	85	27	2	9	8	20	.379	.471
Ventura, R*	.221	163	36	2	18	23	18	.312	.288
Vitiello, Joe	.259	212	55	6	31	27	50	.350	.401
Vizquel, Omar#	.233	116	27	1	8	14	9	.313	.293
Walbeck, Matt#	.233	43	10	0	6	4	2	.292	.256
Ward, Turner#	.190	63	12	1	12	7	5	.274	.317
Weiss, Walt#	.279	68	19	0	6	6	6	.329	.294
White, Devon#	.256	172	44	0	11	13	32	.317	.337
Whiten, Mark#	.185	54	10	1	6	7	11	.279	.278
Williams, Ber#	.248	113	28	2	10	9	22	.303	.354
Wilson, Dan	.222	45	10	1	3	1	9	.234	.289
Worthington	.213	47	10	1	7	6	9	.302	.319
Young, Kevin	.236	72	17	4	10	7	19	.304	.458

DODGER STADIUM
Home of the Los Angeles Dodgers
Los Angeles, California — Grass

Batter	Avg	AB	H	HR	BI	BB	SO	OBP	Slg
Abbott, Kurt	.216	37	8	1	2	0	14	.216	.378
Aldrete, Mike*	.311	61	19	1	11	6	10	.362	.377
Alicea, Luis#	.265	49	13	0	4	13	8	.406	.306
Alomar, R#	.253	95	24	0	6	6	16	.294	.295
Alou, Moises	.316	79	25	1	7	5	12	.349	.405
Anthony, Eric*	.163	49	8	2	7	3	15	.208	.306
Ashley, Billy	.279	247	69	13	37	30	85	.357	.470
Ausmus, Brad	.227	44	10	0	2	1	8	.244	.250
Bagwell, Jeff	.277	141	39	8	29	18	20	.345	.461
Barberie, B#	.208	48	10	1	4	4	9	.269	.292
Bell, Derek	.295	88	26	2	20	1	18	.309	.420
Bell, Jay	.253	146	37	1	17	9	30	.295	.363
Belliard, R	.237	76	18	0	2	5	15	.284	.276
Benjamin, M	.100	40	4	0	0	4	9	.182	.100
Berry, Sean	.254	71	18	1	6	5	12	.312	.366
Bichette, D	.193	88	17	2	14	7	16	.250	.295
Biggio, Craig	.276	210	58	2	17	21	37	.346	.381
Blauser, Jeff	.207	169	35	3	13	13	45	.276	.290
Blowers, Mike	.262	168	44	4	20	15	35	.324	.405
Bonds, Barry*	.262	202	53	9	34	35	39	.364	.446
Bonilla, B#	.284	169	48	10	27	22	33	.361	.515
Boone, Bret	.213	47	10	2	5	1	7	.229	.404
Bournigal, R	.299	67	20	0	6	6	5	.365	.358
Branson, Jeff*	.265	49	13	2	5	3	9	.308	.408
Brogna, Rico*	.260	50	13	4	12	4	8	.315	.540
Brumfield, J	.313	32	10	0	1	4	8	.389	.406
Burks, Ellis	.206	34	7	0	6	4	4	.282	.235
Butler, Brett*	.307	1294	397	6	90	221	145	.407	.376
Caminiti, Ken#	.318	239	76	11	40	27	43	.383	.510
Candaele, C#	.341	91	31	2	9	6	9	.378	.440
Cangelosi, J#	.313	32	10	1	4	4	3	.389	.438
Carr, Chuck*	.250	48	12	0	4	4	10	.302	.292
Carter, Joe	.278	36	10	1	6	4	4	.350	.389
Castilla, V	.208	72	15	1	6	3	17	.237	.264
Castro, Juan	.208	48	10	0	1	5	7	.283	.250
Cedeno, A	.237	97	23	3	16	7	20	.292	.381
Cedeno, Roger#	.233	120	28	0	6	10	25	.295	.283
Clark, Dave*	.214	56	12	1	7	6	9	.290	.286
Clark, Will*	.322	199	64	7	35	25	44	.392	.467
Clayton, R	.213	94	20	0	6	5	21	.253	.287
Colbrunn, G	.286	35	10	2	4	2	7	.342	.486
Cole, Alex*	.351	37	13	0	0	4	5	.415	.405
Coleman, V#	.237	156	37	0	11	15	20	.304	.256
Conine, Jeff	.236	72	17	2	8	1	19	.243	.347
Cora, Joey#	.182	33	6	0	0	3	5	.250	.182
Cordero, Wil	.263	57	15	0	3	5	9	.333	.316
Curtis, Chad	.157	51	8	1	5	7	6	.259	.235
Daulton, D*	.215	107	23	3	16	24	25	.353	.327
Davis, Chili*	.257	35	9	2	8	1	8	.278	.486
Davis, Eric	.240	480	115	17	70	68	108	.333	.379
Dawson, Andre	.291	134	39	9	28	5	18	.312	.545
Decker, Steve	.211	38	8	1	3	2	8	.250	.289
DeShields, D*	.244	717	175	9	61	98	131	.333	.324
Devereaux, M	.224	49	11	0	4	2	9	.255	.224

DODGER STADIUM
Home of the Los Angeles Dodgers
Los Angeles, California — **Grass**

Batter	Avg	AB	H	HR	BI	BB	SO	OBP	Slg
Duncan, M	.221	290	64	3	27	13	69	.257	.303
Dunston, S	.264	140	37	5	20	7	27	.302	.421
Dykstra, L*	.347	118	41	1	9	16	20	.430	.458
Eisenreich, J*	.395	81	32	2	14	5	6	.430	.543
Elster, Kevin	.213	47	10	1	3	4	8	.269	.319
Finley, Steve*	.308	182	56	5	23	14	22	.354	.451
Fletcher, D*	.274	95	26	3	12	9	5	.336	.411
Fonville, C#	.240	263	63	0	13	23	41	.301	.259
Frazier, Lou#	.161	31	5	0	1	6	7	.316	.194
Gagne, Greg	.212	198	42	3	24	23	49	.293	.288
Galarraga, A	.195	185	36	5	24	11	55	.240	.308
Gant, Ron	.244	201	49	5	23	18	38	.311	.373
Garcia, C	.217	60	13	2	5	2	10	.250	.317
Gilkey, B	.325	80	26	3	22	16	16	.434	.513
Girardi, Joe	.292	89	26	0	7	4	12	.330	.348
Gonzalez, L*	.232	142	33	3	11	12	19	.301	.331
Goodwin, Tom*	.255	47	12	0	1	1	5	.271	.255
Grace, Mark*	.295	166	49	3	23	20	16	.367	.428
Grissom, M	.224	161	36	1	8	10	26	.280	.292
Grudzielanek	.200	45	9	0	2	2	5	.245	.200
Gutierrez, R	.212	33	7	0	1	4	5	.297	.273
Gwynn, Chris*	.267	243	65	4	24	16	39	.314	.346
Gwynn, Tony*	.346	246	85	2	23	36	13	.425	.427
Hansen, Dave*	.263	422	111	3	34	48	63	.338	.303
Harris, Lenny*	.264	784	207	3	56	53	68	.312	.315
Hayes, C	.235	98	23	2	11	7	17	.286	.316
Hernandez, Ca	.231	242	56	3	16	15	39	.282	.302
Hill, G	.217	46	10	2	6	3	13	.265	.435
Hollandsworth*	.284	261	74	5	25	20	54	.337	.379
Hollins, Dave#	.217	69	15	1	10	9	13	.313	.319
Howard, T*	.279	43	12	1	5	1	11	.295	.419
Hundley, Todd#	.165	91	15	2	4	10	20	.262	.253
Incaviglia, P	.179	56	10	0	2	1	20	.207	.196
James, Dion*	.218	78	17	2	10	7	13	.279	.321
Javier, Stan#	.260	281	73	2	29	37	48	.343	.310
Jefferies, G#	.255	153	39	1	9	10	11	.301	.327
Johnson, Bri	.184	38	7	0	2	2	7	.220	.184
Johnson, Mark*	.161	31	5	0	1	4	9	.257	.161
Jones, C#	.195	41	8	0	3	7	7	.313	.220
Jordan, Brian	.180	61	11	2	7	4	19	.242	.311
Jordan, Ricky	.225	71	16	0	4	2	9	.263	.282
Justice, Dave*	.211	123	26	8	24	18	27	.308	.431
Karros, Eric	.264	1301	343	59	209	112	208	.320	.447
Kelly, R	.262	206	54	2	15	8	29	.290	.350
Kent, Jeff	.256	78	20	2	10	4	14	.302	.372
King, Jeff	.271	85	23	2	13	12	12	.354	.388
Kingery, Mike*	.310	71	22	0	5	9	6	.388	.380
Kirby, Wayne*	.218	87	19	0	5	10	6	.299	.241
Klesko, Ryan*	.213	47	10	2	6	10	11	.351	.404
Lankford, Ray*	.283	120	34	2	9	17	26	.372	.400
Lansing, Mike	.230	74	17	0	6	6	10	.296	.270
Larkin, Barry	.309	204	63	2	17	12	26	.346	.402
Lemke, Mark#	.144	125	18	0	4	23	14	.275	.152
Lewis, Darren	.273	88	24	0	2	6	8	.319	.318
Liriano, N#	.213	47	10	1	6	5	4	.288	.340
Livingstone*	.256	39	10	1	6	1	4	.268	.410
Lopez, Javy	.256	43	11	4	8	1	12	.283	.581
Mabry, John*	.250	32	8	0	1	3	7	.314	.281
Magadan, Dave*	.316	98	31	0	7	9	9	.380	.347
Manwaring, K	.238	101	24	0	8	3	17	.267	.257
Martin, Al*	.294	85	25	2	6	5	18	.341	.471
Martinez, Da*	.270	122	33	1	12	10	23	.323	.344
May, Derrick*	.311	45	14	2	7	4	8	.367	.489
McGee, Willie#	.299	137	41	3	17	15	32	.368	.423
McGriff, Fred*	.266	143	38	3	17	22	37	.355	.371
McRae, Brian#	.231	52	12	0	2	4	6	.298	.288
Merced, O*	.278	97	27	0	14	10	21	.343	.351
Miller, Orl	.212	33	7	1	5	1	7	.257	.333
Mitchell, K	.244	172	42	7	22	17	38	.306	.413
Mondesi, Raul	.295	808	238	36	114	40	144	.328	.496
Morandini, M*	.248	125	31	0	11	9	24	.304	.312
Morris, Hal*	.355	110	39	2	14	10	14	.405	.482
Mouton, James	.250	32	8	0	2	5	9	.351	.313
Murray, Eddie#	.287	890	255	31	144	130	119	.375	.438
Nixon, Otis#	.123	65	8	0	1	7	14	.208	.138
O'Neill, Paul*	.248	153	38	6	26	20	25	.335	.418
Offerman, J#	.272	988	269	5	74	142	146	.365	.344
Oliver, Joe	.189	95	18	2	12	4	16	.220	.305
Orsulak, Joe*	.313	67	21	3	9	6	9	.365	.448
Pagnozzi, Tom	.265	117	31	1	18	4	22	.295	.333
Parent, Mark	.245	53	13	1	5	3	13	.281	.321
Pena, Tony	.327	52	17	0	7	4	5	.368	.385
Pendleton, T#	.263	224	59	3	22	17	32	.314	.362
Piazza, Mike	.305	975	297	58	188	89	178	.363	.515
Plantier, P*	.212	52	11	2	7	6	13	.311	.404
Prince, Tom	.209	43	9	0	5	3	11	.271	.256
Raines, Tim#	.376	93	35	2	10	13	11	.453	.495
Reed, Jeff*	.262	107	28	0	7	6	17	.301	.308

DODGER STADIUM
Home of the Los Angeles Dodgers
Los Angeles, California — **Grass**

Batter	Avg	AB	H	HR	BI	BB	SO	OBP	Slg
Reed, Jody	.302	285	86	0	24	26	27	.361	.354
Roberts, Bip#	.273	143	39	1	8	16	27	.346	.364
Rodriguez, H*	.256	367	94	12	54	22	79	.298	.401
Sabo, Chris	.239	159	38	3	13	8	13	.280	.333
Samuel, Juan	.257	651	167	12	70	59	157	.323	.366
Sanchez, Rey	.300	50	15	0	5	4	6	.345	.380
Sandberg, R	.224	174	39	2	15	13	33	.275	.316
Sanders, R	.286	63	18	3	6	6	11	.357	.508
Santiago, B	.245	204	50	9	35	12	38	.295	.412
Segui, David#	.300	50	15	1	11	5	5	.364	.480
Servais, S	.161	62	10	1	7	0	9	.161	.242
Sheffield, G	.293	82	24	3	12	12	14	.379	.439
Shipley, C	.234	64	15	1	8	0	12	.246	.281
Slaught, Don	.267	45	12	0	8	4	9	.314	.356
Smith, Dwight*	.159	69	11	0	3	3	16	.194	.188
Smith, Ozzie#	.249	177	44	0	11	28	13	.354	.282
Sosa, Sammy	.340	94	32	6	17	10	26	.406	.574
Stillwell, K#	.216	51	11	0	4	4	7	.273	.333
Stocker, K#	.273	66	18	0	4	5	12	.324	.288
Strawberry, D*	.252	460	116	23	83	65	102	.346	.454
Tarasco, Tony*	.258	31	8	2	5	4	5	.333	.516
Taubensee, E*	.133	45	6	0	4	1	11	.170	.133
Thompson, Mil*	.204	196	40	2	15	15	38	.264	.255
Thompson, Rob	.196	189	37	1	11	10	53	.235	.254
VanderWal, J*	.214	56	12	3	7	6	18	.290	.375
Veras, Q#	.273	33	9	1	1	8	6	.429	.455
Vizcaino, J#	.229	144	33	1	9	12	28	.293	.278
Walker, Larry*	.308	133	41	5	16	10	32	.359	.481
Wallach, Tim	.239	786	188	20	93	62	151	.299	.358
Weiss, Walt#	.270	74	20	0	8	8	10	.337	.284
Whiten, Mark#	.283	60	17	1	6	5	16	.333	.383
Wilkins, Rick*	.250	96	24	5	16	9	26	.321	.448
Williams, Ma	.276	221	61	12	31	16	51	.329	.525
Young, Eric	.293	123	36	1	14	11	10	.370	.366
Zeile, Todd	.253	154	39	1	14	15	36	.314	.325

COUNTY STADIUM
Home of the Milwaukee Brewers
Milwaukee, Wisconsin — **Grass**

Batter	Avg	AB	H	HR	BI	BB	SO	OBP	Slg
Alomar, R#	.313	134	42	3	15	18	13	.395	.463
Alomar Jr, S	.317	63	20	2	13	5	4	.366	.492
Amaral, Rich	.294	51	15	1	6	4	9	.357	.451
Anderson, Brd*	.297	155	46	3	18	23	23	.395	.419
Anderson, G*	.429	42	18	1	13	0	2	.400	.571
Baerga, C#	.243	144	35	6	25	9	10	.295	.382
Baines, H*	.265	196	52	5	27	13	26	.311	.398
Becker, Rich*	.234	47	11	1	3	5	8	.321	.319
Belle, Albert	.326	138	45	12	36	20	20	.420	.688
Berroa, G	.234	47	11	2	8	5	13	.308	.447
Bichette, D	.243	424	103	9	58	26	87	.284	.375
Boggs, Wade*	.285	221	63	2	29	28	19	.358	.348
Borders, Pat	.247	93	23	5	14	4	17	.276	.484
Bordick, Mike	.282	78	22	1	10	9	7	.341	.372
Brosius, S	.184	38	7	0	0	5	6	.279	.211
Buhner, Jay	.277	119	33	8	17	14	35	.353	.529
Burks, Ellis	.232	112	26	3	12	9	18	.295	.330
Burnitz, J*	.256	39	10	1	6	4	7	.341	.385
Canseco, Jose	.262	149	39	7	31	18	38	.339	.450
Carr, Chuck#	.324	37	12	0	1	1	10	.342	.405
Carter, Joe	.298	208	62	13	35	11	23	.332	.553
Cirillo, Jeff	.293	499	146	13	64	63	60	.375	.453
Clark, Will*	.259	54	14	0	6	7	6	.355	.333
Cole, Alex*	.195	41	8	0	6	6	3	.313	.220
Cora, Joey#	.244	82	20	0	8	9	5	.330	.317
Cordova, M	.245	49	12	1	5	4	4	.296	.347
Curtis, Chad	.294	102	30	3	9	8	11	.342	.441
Cuyler, Milt#	.293	75	22	0	11	7	10	.345	.427
Davis, Chili#	.263	167	44	5	29	32	31	.376	.395
Deer, Rob	.216	984	213	52	149	140	336	.323	.416
Devereaux, M	.227	154	35	3	14	14	19	.290	.305
Diaz, Alex#	.254	142	36	0	8	9	12	.294	.338
DiSarcina, G	.289	76	22	0	8	0	5	.299	.395
Durham, Ray#	.319	47	15	1	8	5	5	.377	.468
Easley, D	.205	44	9	1	5	2	2	.255	.295
Eisenreich, J*	.289	97	28	0	10	8	14	.340	.309
Espinoza, A	.321	106	34	2	13	2	13	.333	.443
Fermin, Felix	.270	111	30	0	7	1	3	.283	.279
Fielder, C	.256	156	40	11	22	14	34	.316	.513
Franco, Julio	.316	196	62	5	44	25	21	.390	.459
Frye, Jeff	.450	40	18	1	8	4	4	.489	.650
Fryman, T	.355	152	54	3	38	10	17	.395	.507
Gaetti, Gary	.276	145	40	8	29	10	33	.327	.510
Gagne, Greg	.337	181	61	4	19	9	30	.370	.503
Gallego, Mike	.234	128	30	2	14	8	19	.285	.313
Gates, Brent#	.229	48	11	0	5	3	2	.269	.333
Gomez, Chris	.282	39	11	0	5	5	7	.364	.385

Batter	Avg	AB	H	HR	BI	BB	SO	OBP	Slg
Gomez, Leo	.218	78	17	3	13	10	12	.307	.372
Gonzales, R	.293	58	17	1	9	7	7	.369	.414
Gonzalez, A	.167	30	5	0	2	6	6	.297	.200
Gonzalez, J	.290	107	31	9	26	11	15	.358	.589
Goodwin, Tom*	.293	41	12	0	1	5	4	.370	.341
Grebeck, C	.271	59	16	0	13	4	7	.343	.322
Green, Shawn*	.261	46	12	2	7	4	9	.320	.413
Greenwell, M*	.243	181	44	2	19	13	14	.298	.304
Greer, Rusty*	.325	40	13	1	6	5	6	.391	.500
Griffey Jr, K*	.306	144	44	7	30	21	24	.391	.500
Guillen, O*	.308	182	56	1	16	4	20	.319	.379
Hall, Mel*	.234	107	25	2	18	4	10	.254	.336
Hamelin, Bob*	.222	36	8	2	5	7	12	.341	.444
Hamilton, D*	.295	1100	324	12	131	128	97	.368	.394
Hammonds, J	.283	46	13	3	11	3	5	.358	.543
Henderson, R	.238	126	30	2	5	20	25	.342	.341
Higginson, B*	.255	47	12	2	8	12	7	.410	.426
Hill, G	.179	39	7	0	5	2	13	.209	.231
Hoiles, Chris	.276	98	27	4	12	20	16	.398	.449
Howard, Dave#	.174	46	8	0	1	4	12	.240	.217
Howell, Jack*	.237	76	18	4	8	11	18	.333	.474
Hulse, David*	.293	266	78	1	34	19	46	.334	.372
Huson, Jeff*	.329	73	24	2	13	5	4	.367	.562
Incaviglia, P	.269	93	25	7	20	5	21	.310	.538
Jaha, John	.273	864	236	36	138	103	207	.357	.446
James, Dion*	.259	54	14	1	7	3	5	.310	.389
Javier, Stan#	.253	83	21	0	5	3	14	.284	.289
Jefferson, R*	.268	56	15	4	13	3	12	.317	.536
Johnson, L*	.336	146	49	0	16	8	12	.368	.438
Joyner, Wally*	.292	219	64	8	25	15	24	.342	.461
Karkovice, R	.283	106	30	4	19	9	30	.347	.491
Kelly, Pat	.237	59	14	1	5	6	9	.328	.407
Kelly, R	.283	99	28	4	15	11	22	.372	.455
Kirby, Wayne*	.257	35	9	1	4	1	4	.270	.457
Knoblauch, C	.268	123	33	1	11	20	14	.379	.374
Kreuter, Chad#	.209	43	9	0	3	6	7	.320	.279
Lampkin, Tom*	.178	73	13	1	7	8	13	.256	.260
Leius, Scott	.262	65	17	1	5	10	8	.360	.369
Levis, Jesse*	.242	128	31	0	13	18	9	.340	.281
Lewis, Mark	.255	47	12	0	3	1	5	.271	.277
Leyritz, Jim	.283	60	17	2	8	9	11	.386	.433
Liriano, N#	.233	73	17	0	1	6	6	.291	.288
Listach, Pat#	.251	805	202	1	78	80	149	.319	.298
Livingstone*	.308	39	12	0	1	0	2	.308	.333
Lofton, Kenny*	.260	127	33	1	11	17	15	.347	.386
Loretta, Mark	.318	110	35	0	8	9	9	.370	.355
Lovullo, T#	.295	44	13	0	5	3	7	.333	.386
Macfarlane, M	.232	112	26	5	13	9	21	.313	.402
Martinez, Da*	.471	34	16	1	6	0	4	.486	.676
Martinez, E	.271	107	29	1	11	17	18	.373	.374
Martinez, T*	.284	74	21	0	8	3	11	.313	.338
Marzano, John	.229	35	8	0	1	1	6	.250	.286
Matheny, Mike	.258	279	72	6	40	18	54	.308	.391
May, Derrick*	.272	81	22	1	8	5	10	.322	.370
Mayne, Brent*	.262	42	11	1	8	4	7	.319	.405
McGriff, Fred*	.122	82	10	2	4	19	18	.287	.220
McGwire, Mark	.307	150	46	11	37	25	36	.397	.633
McIntosh, Tim	.194	36	7	2	5	3	11	.275	.389
McLemore, M#	.298	121	36	2	16	16	16	.376	.430
McRae, Brian#	.291	103	30	0	4	6	13	.327	.320
Meares, Pat	.214	70	15	1	8	2	10	.243	.329
Mieske, Matt	.246	479	118	20	69	42	88	.310	.418
Molitor, Paul	.320	1721	550	41	209	212	184	.393	.476
Munoz, Pedro	.311	106	33	3	9	3	25	.336	.443
Murray, Eddie#	.323	124	40	3	25	7	17	.351	.484
Myers, Greg*	.207	58	12	2	3	3	5	.246	.345
Naehring, Tim	.233	43	10	1	2	8	7	.365	.349
Newfield, M	.263	95	25	4	14	3	16	.284	.442
Newson, W*	.216	37	8	1	5	11	13	.396	.324
Nilsson, Dave*	.298	781	233	20	136	86	116	.363	.452
Nixon, Otis*	.254	59	15	0	2	5	5	.313	.305
O'Brien, C	.226	226	51	9	32	18	26	.286	.412
O'Leary, Troy*	.259	81	21	1	11	7	16	.318	.333
O'Neill, Paul*	.247	93	23	4	13	8	16	.301	.419
Olerud, John*	.375	120	45	7	28	20	12	.465	.675
Oliver, Joe	.286	140	40	4	21	8	19	.338	.436
Orsulak, Joe*	.274	106	29	3	9	3	6	.294	.415
Palmeiro, R*	.327	211	69	9	36	20	20	.383	.545
Palmer, Dean	.181	94	17	2	11	8	25	.260	.298
Paquette, C	.200	40	8	0	3	3	8	.256	.300
Pena, Tony	.278	90	25	0	11	9	14	.343	.311
Phillips, T#	.263	186	49	1	16	23	31	.344	.333
Plantier, P*	.281	32	9	2	6	7	5	.410	.531
Polonia, Luis*	.301	166	50	0	12	9	13	.335	.361
Raines, Tim#	.291	110	32	2	14	20	6	.405	.427
Ramirez, M	.373	51	19	4	11	13	9	.500	.745
Reboulet, J	.340	53	18	2	9	5	4	.397	.566
Reed, Jody	.267	307	82	1	33	42	23	.354	.322

COUNTY STADIUM
Home of the Milwaukee Brewers
Milwaukee, Wisconsin — Grass

Batter	Avg	AB	H	HR	BI	BB	SO	OBP	Slg
Ripken, Billy	.259	112	29	0	5	6	13	.306	.286
Ripken, Cal	.277	256	71	14	49	26	23	.340	.512
Rodriguez, I	.302	86	26	1	11	7	8	.358	.360
Salmon, Tim	.289	83	24	3	16	15	21	.394	.494
Schofield, D	.258	97	25	0	7	15	14	.357	.351
Seitzer, K	.275	1080	297	18	130	142	114	.362	.380
Sheffield, G	.260	543	141	8	50	54	56	.328	.374
Sierra, Ruben#	.226	234	53	5	32	10	29	.252	.350
Slaught, Don	.279	61	17	3	11	5	8	.333	.426
Snow, J.T.#	.196	51	10	1	5	7	6	.305	.294
Sojo, Luis	.347	72	25	2	8	2	7	.373	.444
Sorrento, P*	.167	102	17	1	7	10	19	.248	.225
Sosa, Sammy	.167	42	7	1	4	1	11	.186	.286
Spiers, Bill*	.284	793	225	6	98	61	122	.334	.364
Sprague, Ed	.208	77	16	1	10	9	13	.303	.286
Stanley, Mike	.216	102	22	2	9	14	15	.316	.333
Steinbach, T	.331	142	47	4	19	12	26	.385	.507
Stillwell, K#	.329	82	27	0	4	1	17	.341	.427
Strange, Doug#	.238	42	10	0	3	0	6	.238	.262
Surhoff, B.J.*	.281	1939	545	35	290	173	160	.337	.400
Sveum, Dale#	.253	719	182	16	93	59	184	.309	.388
Tartabull, D	.294	153	45	5	20	27	37	.404	.464
Tettleton, M#	.196	163	32	8	28	26	37	.305	.374
Thomas, Frank	.322	146	47	9	37	35	17	.451	.623
Thome, Jim*	.306	49	15	4	14	13	13	.460	.612
Trammell, A	.333	153	51	3	13	14	12	.391	.444
Valentin, Jhn	.250	68	17	1	7	10	8	.363	.441
Valentin, Jse#	.248	621	154	22	109	73	139	.328	.446
Valle, Dave	.230	126	29	1	16	11	20	.292	.349
Vaughn, Greg	.258	1554	401	82	288	226	359	.350	.478
Vaughn, Mo*	.212	113	24	8	26	19	13	.336	.451
Velarde, R	.371	97	36	4	17	12	17	.441	.557
Ventura, R*	.278	176	49	7	36	19	17	.348	.483
Vina, F*	.278	418	116	4	48	34	32	.345	.380
Vizquel, Omar#	.291	134	39	1	8	9	13	.340	.328
Walbeck, Matt#	.167	48	8	1	8	1	11	.180	.250
Ward, Turner#	.263	274	72	9	47	44	51	.362	.427
Weiss, Walt#	.313	64	20	0	6	3	7	.353	.344
White, Devon#	.224	165	37	2	14	11	29	.275	.333
Whiten, Mark#	.244	41	10	1	6	4	5	.298	.341
Williams, Ber#	.197	117	23	4	20	18	20	.300	.325
Williams, Ger	.204	54	11	0	2	1	12	.218	.278
Wilson, Dan	.294	34	10	2	5	4	3	.368	.529
Worthington	.305	59	18	2	5	5	7	.359	.441

HUBERT H. HUMPHREY METRODOME
Home of the Minnesota Twins
Minneapolis, Minnesota — Artificial

Batter	Avg	AB	H	HR	BI	BB	SO	OBP	Slg
Aldrete, Mike*	.300	30	9	0	3	5	2	.400	.333
Alomar, R#	.271	107	29	3	14	21	9	.386	.411
Alomar Jr, S	.218	78	17	4	11	2	7	.238	.372
Amaral, Rich	.425	40	17	0	4	1	4	.439	.575
Anderson, Brd*	.273	150	41	4	12	20	24	.377	.460
Anderson, G*	.294	34	10	1	6	1	2	.314	.412
Baerga, C#	.270	159	43	6	23	7	16	.330	.453
Baines, H*	.302	182	55	7	28	20	31	.368	.484
Becker, Rich*	.283	498	141	10	62	54	115	.352	.400
Belle, Albert	.312	141	44	9	38	15	26	.390	.610
Berroa, G	.407	59	24	6	18	6	12	.456	.797
Bichette, D	.328	61	20	1	7	1	13	.328	.459
Blowers, Mike	.250	48	12	1	7	4	11	.308	.354
Boggs, Wade*	.294	218	64	4	29	23	16	.358	.436
Borders, Pat	.256	117	30	2	11	1	23	.263	.436
Bordick, Mike	.276	105	29	0	16	8	10	.328	.343
Brosius, S	.302	63	19	1	12	9	9	.382	.397
Buhner, Jay	.248	161	40	9	34	20	55	.330	.503
Burks, Ellis	.254	122	31	2	12	7	25	.295	.377
Canseco, Jose	.256	176	45	12	32	18	59	.328	.500
Carreon, Mark	.375	32	12	1	3	5	3	.474	.563
Carter, Joe	.258	190	49	11	36	10	27	.304	.521
Cirillo, Jeff	.327	49	16	2	8	6	5	.411	.571
Clark, Will*	.295	61	18	4	8	8	8	.377	.525
Cole, Alex*	.352	250	88	2	22	34	44	.430	.480
Coleman, V#	.281	32	9	1	2	5	5	.378	.438
Coomer, Ron	.276	170	47	7	29	11	21	.319	.471
Cora, Joey#	.323	93	30	2	9	7	7	.376	.484
Cordova, M	.305	522	159	26	110	57	111	.381	.533
Curtis, Chad	.278	115	32	2	11	11	15	.344	.383
Cuyler, Milt#	.276	58	16	0	7	2	10	.300	.345
Davis, Chili#	.285	648	185	29	115	106	116	.382	.492
Dawson, Andre	.211	38	8	2	4	0	9	.211	.421
Deer, Rob	.243	136	33	8	25	16	41	.322	.478
Devereaux, M	.306	134	41	2	15	6	17	.338	.433
DiSarcina, G	.263	76	20	0	6	6	4	.325	.355
Durant, Mike	.206	34	7	0	3	6	8	.317	.265
Durham, Ray#	.237	38	9	2	9	4	7	.318	.500

Batter	Avg	AB	H	HR	BI	BB	SO	OBP	Slg
Easley, D	.349	43	15	3	6	5	8	.417	.605
Edmonds, Jim*	.200	50	10	3	7	3	13	.245	.440
Eisenreich, J*	.307	75	23	1	9	3	8	.333	.453
Espinoza, A	.253	91	23	3	6	3	17	.277	.352
Fermin, Felix	.333	96	32	1	9	7	4	.379	.427
Fielder, C	.237	152	36	9	32	17	44	.310	.480
Franco, Julio	.301	156	47	2	21	21	23	.387	.423
Frye, Jeff	.250	52	13	0	4	5	6	.305	.288
Fryman, T	.288	139	40	5	29	8	25	.320	.496
Gaetti, Gary	.274	1145	314	51	198	73	187	.320	.472
Gagne, Greg	.248	1305	324	25	139	84	253	.298	.386
Gallego, Mike	.224	125	28	4	14	11	22	.285	.352
Gates, Brent*	.263	76	20	2	9	9	8	.345	.421
Giambi, Jason*	.268	41	11	0	3	5	8	.348	.293
Gomez, Chris	.163	49	8	1	5	3	7	.212	.265
Gomez, Leo	.221	77	17	1	6	7	16	.286	.312
Gonzales, R	.213	61	13	0	1	1	12	.238	.246
Gonzalez, J	.250	116	29	8	22	3	23	.269	.509
Goodwin, Tom*	.244	41	10	1	6	7	11	.354	.463
Grebeck, C	.125	48	6	0	2	4	11	.192	.146
Greenwell, M*	.289	149	43	5	23	10	11	.335	.477
Greer, Rusty	.314	51	16	6	12	5	8	.375	.745
Griffey Jr, K*	.307	163	50	10	30	15	31	.365	.571
Guillen, O*	.278	169	47	0	20	4	17	.291	.343
Hale, Chip*	.285	281	80	1	34	33	35	.361	.352
Hall, Mel*	.281	89	25	2	12	3	15	.312	.449
Hamilton, D*	.238	122	29	1	14	7	11	.279	.320
Hammonds, J	.357	42	15	2	9	3	9	.400	.595
Henderson, R	.312	189	59	5	25	36	25	.419	.471
Higginson, B*	.189	37	7	0	4	6	7	.295	.270
Hill, G	.306	36	11	1	3	2	5	.342	.556
Hocking, D#	.263	114	30	0	12	8	20	.311	.360
Hoiles, Chris	.243	74	18	3	10	11	13	.348	.446
Hollins, Dave#	.250	216	54	6	28	44	51	.385	.403
Howard, Dave#	.237	38	9	0	3	10	8	.396	.289
Howell, Jack*	.351	74	26	2	10	9	15	.437	.595
Huff, Michael	.293	41	12	1	6	6	5	.383	.463
Hulse, David*	.242	33	8	0	1	2	4	.286	.364
Huson, Jeff*	.174	69	12	0	4	10	6	.278	.217
Incaviglia, P	.220	100	22	3	10	2	33	.238	.370
Jaha, Chris	.313	80	25	7	23	11	13	.402	.650
James, Dion*	.317	41	13	1	7	4	3	.391	.488
Javier, Stan#	.316	95	30	3	12	9	12	.387	.432
Johnson, L*	.357	143	51	0	25	6	8	.383	.524
Joyner, Wally*	.320	194	62	8	37	21	22	.382	.495
Karkovice, M	.181	83	15	3	8	12	25	.292	.325
Kelly, Pat	.297	74	22	2	8	6	11	.346	.473
Kelly, R	.306	255	78	7	31	17	47	.360	.459
Kirby, Wayne*	.333	57	19	1	10	3	6	.361	.474
Knoblauch, C	.321	1697	545	15	173	225	176	.404	.426
Kreuter, Chad#	.250	36	9	2	3	2	5	.289	.417
Lawton, Matt*	.256	133	34	2	25	17	18	.355	.383
Leius, Scott	.256	703	180	13	88	78	101	.330	.366
Lewis, Mark	.300	50	15	0	2	3	8	.352	.400
Leyritz, Jim	.286	56	16	3	7	4	10	.355	.464
Liriano, N#	.258	124	32	2	13	11	22	.316	.419
Listach, Pat#	.222	63	14	0	3	7	15	.300	.270
Lockhart, K*	.357	42	15	1	5	0	3	.357	.643
Lofton, Kenny*	.375	112	42	2	14	11	10	.431	.491
Lovullo, T#	.246	57	14	3	8	4	12	.295	.474
Macfarlane, M	.198	116	23	2	7	3	32	.225	.310
Martinez, Da*	.313	32	10	2	6	3	5	.378	.531
Martinez, E	.352	122	43	4	17	17	18	.437	.541
Martinez, T*	.256	86	22	1	14	6	15	.295	.384
Mayne, Brent*	.286	56	16	0	7	7	10	.365	.339
McCarty, Dave	.218	271	59	3	20	19	68	.278	.325
McGriff, Fred*	.319	72	23	6	12	17	21	.456	.611
McGwire, Mark	.272	162	44	13	30	37	32	.412	.549
McLemore, M#	.259	147	38	0	13	22	25	.355	.306
McRae, Brian*	.305	105	32	3	12	2	19	.324	.514
Meares, Pat	.265	731	194	6	81	21	122	.292	.361
Mieske, Matt	.326	46	15	3	13	4	9	.365	.630
Molitor, Paul	.342	546	187	10	86	36	57	.383	.502
Munoz, Pedro	.275	767	211	29	112	52	193	.324	.456
Murray, Eddie#	.325	114	37	12	27	13	13	.394	.684
Myers, Greg*	.298	248	74	5	28	11	36	.326	.435
Naehring, Tim	.189	53	10	1	4	2	5	.232	.264
Newson, W*	.256	43	11	2	4	8	10	.373	.419
Nilsson, Dave*	.267	75	20	7	18	7	9	.325	.600
Nixon, Otis#	.273	77	21	0	2	4	13	.309	.312
O'Brien, C	.225	40	9	0	2	2	6	.262	.300
O'Leary, Troy*	.273	33	9	4	7	3	8	.324	.697
O'Neill, Paul*	.314	86	27	5	18	10	10	.388	.581
Olerud, John*	.281	96	27	3	20	10	9	.333	.458
Orsulak, Joe*	.315	89	28	0	8	4	12	.344	.438
Palmeiro, R*	.284	194	55	5	28	13	29	.333	.448
Palmer, Dean	.368	87	32	13	28	11	21	.436	.874
Paquette, C	.242	66	16	4	15	5	16	.288	.485

HUBERT H. HUMPHREY METRODOME
Home of the Minnesota Twins
Minneapolis, Minnesota — Artificial

Batter	Avg	AB	H	HR	BI	BB	SO	OBP	Slg
Pena, Tony	.226	93	21	1	10	4	8	.255	.312
Phillips, T#	.277	195	54	6	25	33	29	.383	.441
Polonia, Luis*	.288	146	42	0	14	5	20	.307	.349
Raines, Tim#	.252	115	29	4	20	9	15	.307	.417
Ramirez, M	.373	67	25	5	18	7	15	.432	.687
Reboulet, J	.258	484	125	4	47	59	74	.342	.329
Reed, Jody	.273	99	27	0	6	19	11	.395	.343
Ripken, Billy	.207	58	12	0	6	4	6	.270	.207
Ripken, Cal	.296	226	67	6	36	31	20	.384	.456
Rodriguez, I	.273	88	24	2	11	6	13	.326	.398
Salmon, Tim	.313	64	20	5	10	19	14	.476	.672
Schofield, D	.352	108	38	0	10	16	12	.435	.398
Segui, David#	.289	38	11	1	3	4	3	.357	.421
Seitzer, K	.284	204	58	4	19	23	24	.355	.402
Sheffield, G	.262	42	11	1	8	5	1	.360	.381
Sierra, Ruben#	.268	257	69	9	37	23	37	.326	.455
Slaught, Don	.207	58	12	0	4	4	10	.258	.207
Snow, J.T.#	.290	62	18	1	7	7	13	.371	.452
Sojo, Luis	.264	87	23	2	7	3	7	.286	.391
Sorrento, P*	.264	193	51	5	28	19	45	.333	.404
Sosa, Sammy	.262	42	11	2	5	4	11	.326	.452
Spiers, Bill*	.120	50	6	0	2	3	12	.167	.120
Sprague, Ed	.259	81	21	3	14	5	20	.318	.469
Stahoviak, S*	.285	375	107	9	42	45	95	.362	.432
Stanley, Mike	.240	104	25	4	17	15	30	.342	.481
Steinbach, T	.253	186	47	7	31	14	33	.316	.425
Stillwell, K#	.355	76	27	6	24	10	14	.437	.645
Strange, Doug#	.233	60	14	1	5	4	9	.281	.350
Surhoff, B.J.*	.289	149	43	2	25	11	15	.333	.383
Sveum, Dale#	.257	70	18	1	6	4	25	.299	.400
Tartabull, D	.282	188	53	14	43	28	46	.375	.553
Tettleton, M#	.248	153	38	6	16	26	39	.359	.431
Thomas, Frank	.273	132	36	8	27	17	25	.349	.538
Thome, Jim*	.395	86	34	6	16	10	25	.454	.674
Tinsley, Lee*	.235	34	8	0	3	4	9	.316	.265
Trammell, A	.322	143	46	4	16	7	14	.353	.434
Tucker, M*	.219	32	7	3	6	2	8	.286	.500
Valentin, Jhn	.260	73	19	2	7	7	9	.321	.425
Valentin, Jse#	.291	55	16	2	10	3	15	.322	.509
Valle, Dave	.185	108	20	4	9	7	12	.267	.333
Vaughn, Greg	.302	116	35	5	18	16	26	.393	.534
Vaughn, Mo*	.290	93	27	5	18	7	26	.337	.548
Velarde, R	.192	78	15	0	4	10	24	.292	.256
Ventura, R*	.277	141	39	6	15	20	15	.366	.482
Vina, F*	.278	36	10	1	3	3	2	.325	.444
Vizquel, Omar#	.309	165	51	2	15	20	17	.385	.436
Walbeck, Matt#	.234	462	108	2	44	27	70	.278	.301
Ward, Turner#	.244	41	10	2	7	7	8	.354	.439
Webster, L	.239	163	39	3	17	11	21	.286	.356
Weiss, Walt#	.302	53	16	1	7	5	6	.362	.434
White, Devon#	.247	194	48	7	23	11	50	.295	.423
Whiten, Mark#	.367	30	11	3	7	4	7	.444	.733
Williams, Ber#	.274	106	29	4	13	12	18	.347	.481
Wilson, Dan	.316	57	18	2	13	0	6	.310	.456
Worthington	.238	63	15	2	9	5	14	.294	.397

OLYMPIC STADIUM
Home of the Montreal Expos
Montreal, Quebec — Artificial

Batter	Avg	AB	H	HR	BI	BB	SO	OBP	Slg
Abbott, Kurt	.189	37	7	0	1	2	13	.231	.243
Aldrete, Mike*	.272	173	47	1	19	44	30	.420	.358
Alicea, Luis#	.182	88	16	0	7	6	18	.247	.216
Alomar, R#	.176	74	13	1	2	6	11	.238	.270
Alou, Moises	.304	987	300	43	207	96	137	.365	.521
Andrews, S	.214	271	58	10	47	26	86	.285	.384
Anthony, Eric*	.221	77	17	2	4	7	25	.286	.312
Arias, Alex	.158	38	6	0	1	3	8	.220	.158
Ausmus, Brad	.308	39	12	0	4	4	9	.372	.333
Bagwell, Jeff	.281	135	38	3	20	21	25	.385	.415
Barberie, B#	.275	193	53	2	20	32	34	.385	.326
Bell, Derek	.243	70	17	0	10	2	21	.274	.257
Bell, Jay	.202	188	38	2	12	18	32	.275	.271
Belliard, R	.221	77	17	0	4	9	13	.333	.273
Berry, Sean	.283	474	134	16	74	50	93	.350	.443
Bichette, D	.195	77	15	3	7	2	11	.210	.325
Biggio, Craig	.291	172	50	4	16	23	30	.376	.448
Blauser, Jeff	.222	90	20	1	12	13	20	.360	.300
Bonds, Barry*	.348	279	97	24	58	38	35	.430	.692
Bonilla, B#	.291	244	71	9	41	36	52	.381	.504
Boone, Bret	.170	47	8	1	7	0	9	.170	.298
Branson, Jeff*	.226	53	12	0	5	5	8	.288	.245
Butler, Brett*	.238	172	41	0	6	18	24	.314	.285
Caminiti, Ken#	.294	153	45	5	20	16	19	.359	.471
Candaele, C#	.247	340	84	1	15	26	27	.304	.321
Cangelosi, J#	.255	47	12	0	3	8	6	.375	.255
Carr, Chuck#	.284	67	19	1	11	8	11	.360	.448

266

Batter	Avg	AB	H	HR	BI	BB	SO	OBP	Slg
Carreon, Mark	.267	60	16	1	5	4	7	.323	.367
Castilla, V	.282	39	11	3	8	0	8	.300	.513
Cedeno, A	.185	81	15	1	8	6	25	.241	.259
Cianfrocco, A	.190	142	27	3	17	10	41	.248	.296
Clark, Dave*	.174	46	8	1	5	10	10	.321	.261
Clark, Will*	.266	154	41	4	17	15	28	.333	.435
Clayton, R	.227	97	22	1	8	7	14	.279	.299
Colbrunn, G	.285	221	63	4	34	14	34	.329	.416
Coleman, V#	.264	163	43	0	9	14	30	.326	.344
Conine, Jeff	.338	71	24	2	9	8	13	.413	.535
Cordero, Wil	.269	702	189	16	85	62	117	.334	.426
Dascenzo, D#	.222	54	12	0	3	3	5	.263	.259
Daulton, D*	.286	140	40	6	21	23	31	.395	.471
Davis, Eric	.243	144	35	7	27	15	38	.315	.417
Dawson, Andre	.324	179	58	7	32	11	23	.378	.564
DeShields, D*	.293	1046	306	10	77	144	208	.381	.385
Duncan, M	.230	135	31	0	11	9	24	.283	.341
Dunston, S	.274	146	40	2	16	7	15	.308	.425
Dykstra, L*	.285	228	65	7	25	25	30	.352	.482
Eisenreich, J*	.196	46	9	1	5	2	10	.229	.326
Elster, Kevin	.200	100	20	4	11	6	18	.245	.380
Eusebio, Tony	.250	36	9	0	7	3	7	.308	.278
Everett, Carl#	.333	36	12	2	7	2	10	.385	.611
Finley, Steve*	.307	127	39	4	14	9	13	.358	.496
Fletcher, D*	.268	766	205	19	118	61	72	.322	.419
Floyd, Cliff*	.244	311	76	6	41	34	65	.328	.379
Frazier, Lou#	.299	194	58	1	21	20	24	.361	.361
Galarraga, A	.277	1370	379	49	219	107	348	.338	.472
Gant, Ron	.252	151	38	5	21	16	34	.329	.424
Garcia, C	.255	47	12	0	2	0	4	.271	.319
Gilkey, B	.235	119	28	2	6	16	22	.326	.361
Girardi, Joe	.221	95	21	0	7	4	13	.250	.232
Goff, Jerry*	.222	63	14	1	5	15	18	.372	.270
Gonzalez, L*	.187	75	14	0	4	10	16	.279	.267
Grace, Mark*	.297	195	58	3	22	17	21	.352	.410
Grissom, M	.294	1294	380	28	146	97	182	.343	.426
Grudzielanek	.327	416	136	6	37	21	45	.370	.457
Gutierrez, R	.179	39	7	0	3	2	9	.238	.308
Gwynn, Tony*	.344	215	74	3	27	15	8	.386	.465
Harris, Lenny*	.281	96	27	1	4	4	6	.307	.365
Hayes, C	.240	154	37	2	16	6	33	.268	.318
Hill, G	.160	50	8	1	4	4	14	.222	.240
Hollins, Dave#	.197	71	14	2	6	11	12	.310	.380
Howard, T*	.184	38	7	0	3	5	6	.273	.237
Hudler, Rex	.268	205	55	5	17	11	33	.311	.415
Hundley, Todd#	.271	70	19	7	16	9	19	.350	.586
Hunter, Brian	.214	42	9	0	4	2	15	.267	.286
Hunter, Bri L	.283	46	13	1	9	1	8	.288	.435
Huson, Jeff*	.239	67	16	0	2	9	6	.329	.299
Incaviglia, P	.245	53	13	3	13	7	13	.349	.415
James, Dion*	.262	42	11	0	3	8	3	.380	.310
Javier, Stan#	.304	46	14	0	2	7	10	.407	.370
Jefferies, G#	.315	165	52	5	25	12	11	.360	.473
Johnson, Char	.220	41	9	2	6	6	13	.319	.439
Johnson, L*	.314	35	11	0	5	1	3	.333	.400
Jones, C#	.279	43	12	2	6	7	6	.380	.512
Jordan, Brian	.265	68	18	1	6	1	13	.275	.412
Jordan, Ricky	.185	92	17	0	9	5	12	.232	.239
Justice, Dave*	.245	94	23	2	16	20	16	.374	.372
Karros, Eric	.264	110	29	4	15	13	25	.341	.436
Kelly, R	.356	101	36	0	14	5	13	.398	.416
Kent, Jeff	.341	91	31	4	16	5	18	.381	.538
King, Jeff	.289	121	35	2	15	7	13	.331	.405
Kingery, Mike*	.208	48	10	2	7	4	11	.259	.396
Klesko, Ryan*	.303	33	10	2	5	5	6	.395	.636
Lankford, Ray*	.237	135	32	6	16	21	29	.352	.415
Lansing, Mike	.269	993	267	11	94	79	123	.329	.372
Larkin, Barry	.293	188	55	2	25	16	12	.349	.410
Lemke, Mark#	.208	106	22	0	4	16	16	.311	.226
Lewis, Darren	.156	77	12	0	4	10	6	.261	.221
Lopez, Javy	.297	37	11	3	7	1	5	.333	.595
Magadan, Dave*	.270	141	38	0	16	22	22	.372	.369
Manwaring, K	.196	92	18	1	6	10	19	.308	.261
Marrero, O*	.250	40	10	1	2	7	3	.362	.400
Martin, Al*	.273	66	18	2	10	5	20	.324	.500
Martinez, Da*	.260	726	189	11	64	50	103	.308	.368
May, Derrick*	.250	72	18	2	10	4	13	.291	.403
McGee, Willie#	.295	149	44	1	24	8	23	.335	.389
McGriff, Fred*	.266	124	33	5	20	17	21	.357	.468
McRae, Brian#	.314	35	11	0	4	7	2	.429	.400
Merced, O*	.267	86	23	1	11	13	16	.366	.395
Mitchell, K	.233	116	27	7	12	17	23	.333	.474
Mondesi, Raul	.286	70	20	2	12	4	18	.342	.486
Morandini, M*	.269	108	29	1	10	12	17	.347	.426
Morris, Hal*	.269	119	32	2	10	8	14	.318	.353
Mouton, James	.293	41	12	0	1	5	5	.370	.317
Murray, Eddie#	.242	120	29	1	13	14	16	.316	.358
Nixon, Otis#	.230	430	99	0	30	53	58	.314	.291

267

268

OLYMPIC STADIUM
Home of the Montreal Expos

Montreal, Quebec								Artificial
Batter	Avg	AB	H	HR	BI	BB	SO	OBP	Slg
O'Brien, C	.167	54	9	1	4	4	11	.220	.296
O'Neill, Paul*	.236	106	25	3	18	9	27	.293	.415
Obando, S	.283	92	26	6	16	11	19	.362	.533
Offerman, J#	.215	79	17	0	8	3	18	.247	.304
Oliver, Joe	.241	79	19	2	7	9	19	.319	.316
Orsulak, Joe*	.327	49	16	1	5	3	7	.370	.469
Pagnozzi, Tom	.215	135	29	2	10	5	17	.239	.296
Palmeiro, R*	.317	41	13	2	6	2	3	.364	.585
Pena, G#	.321	53	17	2	6	4	12	.390	.528
Pena, Tony	.294	85	25	4	10	6	7	.341	.459
Pendleton, T#	.212	203	43	2	27	17	40	.271	.291
Piazza, Mike	.373	67	25	7	13	8	12	.440	.746
Plantier, P*	.103	39	4	1	2	0	10	.103	.179
Pride, Curtis*	.243	37	9	0	3	2	11	.282	.351
Raines, Tim#	.301	938	282	26	115	142	92	.392	.459
Reed, Jeff*	.229	192	44	3	19	15	30	.281	.333
Reed, Jody	.167	36	6	0	3	1	2	.211	.222
Roberts, Bip#	.368	125	46	1	9	15	14	.430	.512
Rodriguez, H*	.258	333	86	21	64	25	97	.310	.523
Sabo, Chris	.250	108	27	4	17	9	16	.311	.454
Samuel, Juan	.253	150	38	3	13	13	33	.319	.427
Sanchez, Rey	.224	67	15	0	5	5	8	.274	.299
Sandberg, R	.262	244	64	9	22	31	45	.348	.434
Sanders, R	.247	77	19	4	14	12	19	.356	.442
Santangelo, F#	.325	249	81	6	43	39	33	.428	.514
Santiago, B	.206	175	36	5	22	8	31	.253	.349
Scarsone, S	.269	52	14	2	4	6	15	.345	.442
Schofield, D	.222	27	6	0	1	8	6	.432	.370
Segui, David#	.295	421	124	11	60	45	45	.363	.458
Servais, S	.355	31	11	0	8	4	2	.450	.484
Sheffield, G	.329	82	27	4	10	21	6	.462	.561
Shipley, C	.270	37	10	0	5	1	4	.300	.351
Silvestri, D	.250	120	30	0	13	33	30	.406	.308
Slaught, Don	.254	67	17	1	7	11	9	.367	.313
Smith, Dwight*	.271	85	23	2	10	3	20	.295	.376
Smith, Ozzie#	.329	213	70	2	16	28	5	.406	.418
Sosa, Sammy	.256	86	22	2	9	5	22	.309	.384
Spehr, Tim	.202	94	19	1	10	9	25	.279	.319
Stankiewicz	.321	53	17	0	7	7	9	.429	.415
Stillwell, K#	.280	50	14	1	9	3	7	.309	.520
Stocker, K#	.310	58	18	0	2	13	9	.453	.379
Strawberry, D*	.290	162	47	12	36	21	39	.376	.556
Tarasco, Tony*	.252	238	60	7	20	24	46	.321	.403
Taubensee, E*	.231	52	12	3	11	2	12	.255	.423
Thompson, Mil*	.235	149	35	3	20	11	31	.292	.336
Thompson, Rob	.171	146	25	5	10	7	34	.219	.342
Thompson, Ry	.175	40	7	1	3	5	9	.261	.275
VanderWal, J*	.241	191	46	3	23	25	28	.332	.346
Vizcaino, J#	.226	93	21	0	6	7	20	.280	.269
Walker, Larry*	.284	1111	316	48	191	124	226	.363	.496
Wallach, Tim	.270	1737	469	43	252	152	263	.332	.423
Walton, J	.246	65	16	2	8	5	14	.315	.385
Webster, L	.259	170	44	3	19	14	17	.337	.382
Weiss, Walt#	.164	67	11	0	0	10	10	.273	.179
White, R	.301	452	136	10	61	48	81	.375	.442
Whiten, Mark#	.308	78	24	4	11	5	21	.349	.551
Wilkins, Rick*	.306	72	22	2	10	12	20	.395	.486
Williams, Ma	.239	163	39	9	22	9	38	.276	.442
Young, Eric	.213	47	10	0	1	4	3	.302	.298
Young, Kevin	.167	36	6	0	0	1	15	.211	.194
Zeile, Todd	.247	162	40	7	27	16	20	.309	.426

SHEA STADIUM
Home of the New York Mets

Flushing, New York								Grass
Batter	Avg	AB	H	HR	BI	BB	SO	OBP	Slg
Abbott, Kurt	.262	42	11	0	6	2	10	.319	.310
Aldrete, Mike*	.229	35	8	0	4	4	11	.308	.314
Alfonzo, E	.269	349	94	2	34	25	43	.315	.347
Alicea, Luis#	.179	56	10	0	3	6	8	.270	.196
Alomar, R#	.271	70	19	0	5	7	8	.338	.329
Alou, Moises	.288	66	19	5	17	7	6	.355	.561
Amaro, Ruben#	.256	43	11	0	4	6	2	.353	.372
Andrews, S	.231	39	9	1	5	2	8	.262	.385
Anthony, Eric*	.221	77	17	4	13	9	18	.299	.416
Arias, Alex	.237	59	14	0	3	7	4	.328	.271
Ausmus, Brad	.389	36	14	0	2	5	5	.442	.417
Bagwell, Jeff	.331	130	43	7	33	13	23	.384	.569
Barberie, B#	.286	56	16	1	7	9	13	.385	.393
Batiste, Kim	.412	34	14	1	6	1	5	.429	.588
Bell, Derek	.329	76	25	4	15	2	11	.338	.579
Bell, Jay	.274	190	52	3	18	19	32	.344	.411
Belliard, R	.308	91	28	0	2	4	16	.337	.352
Berry, Sean	.259	58	15	4	5	5	9	.323	.552
Bichette, D	.318	66	21	3	8	4	14	.361	.515
Biggio, Craig	.243	177	43	5	17	12	37	.298	.367
Blauser, Jeff	.298	114	34	2	6	15	21	.400	.421

Batter	Avg	AB	H	HR	BI	BB	SO	OBP	Slg
Bogar, Tim	.216	231	50	1	16	17	49	.278	.273
Bonds, Barry*	.264	292	77	9	43	41	39	.355	.428
Bonilla, B#	.279	936	261	43	149	102	154	.348	.481
Boone, Bret	.308	52	16	2	5	2	10	.327	.519
Branson, Jeff*	.250	48	12	0	3	7	14	.339	.313
Brogna, Rico*	.308	383	118	20	64	32	92	.360	.540
Brumfield, J	.278	36	10	0	1	2	5	.316	.417
Buford, Damon	.208	72	15	2	5	7	17	.288	.333
Burnitz, J*	.250	204	51	8	25	29	55	.345	.441
Butler, Brett*	.304	368	112	2	30	36	47	.365	.391
Caminiti, Ken#	.241	145	35	4	22	11	26	.291	.379
Candaele, C#	.234	77	18	1	3	2	11	.250	.273
Cangelosi, J#	.198	96	19	0	1	22	20	.364	.229
Carr, Chuck#	.259	85	22	0	8	5	14	.300	.329
Carreon, Mark	.261	341	89	10	32	24	41	.319	.396
Castilla, V	.279	43	12	3	8	2	8	.304	.558
Cedeno, A	.203	74	15	0	3	2	14	.234	.297
Cianfrocco, A	.333	42	14	2	12	2	8	.378	.500
Clark, Dave*	.348	46	16	3	10	9	7	.446	.543
Clark, Will*	.274	157	43	4	20	16	25	.339	.414
Clayton, R	.309	97	30	2	11	3	16	.337	.464
Colbrunn, G	.309	81	25	2	8	2	17	.333	.457
Coleman, V#	.264	537	142	5	40	62	104	.340	.341
Conine, Jeff	.269	104	28	4	19	8	22	.316	.433
Cordero, Wil	.159	69	11	1	4	2	12	.194	.217
Dascenzo, D#	.239	67	16	0	4	5	7	.301	.299
Daulton, D*	.241	145	35	4	24	22	33	.353	.372
Davis, Eric	.241	108	26	4	11	13	35	.322	.398
Dawson, Andre	.211	209	44	6	27	11	39	.252	.340
DeShields, D*	.238	172	41	2	14	18	47	.311	.366
Duncan, M	.301	146	44	2	15	1	26	.320	.425
Dunston, S	.259	162	42	4	16	6	39	.279	.426
Dykstra, L*	.269	590	159	12	54	63	68	.345	.407
Eisenreich, J*	.333	57	19	0	6	9	8	.412	.351
Elster, Kevin	.223	789	176	16	88	65	123	.284	.338
Espinoza, A	.324	68	22	2	10	3	8	.352	.485
Everett, Carl#	.304	230	70	10	30	32	48	.395	.478
Finley, Steve*	.268	142	38	5	17	11	11	.318	.444
Fletcher, D*	.256	86	22	2	8	6	8	.309	.360
Floyd, Cliff*	.259	58	15	3	7	1	8	.283	.414
Galarraga, A	.260	246	64	9	30	19	75	.311	.427
Gant, Ron	.261	153	40	9	32	15	32	.326	.516
Garcia, C	.354	48	17	0	5	0	3	.367	.500
Gilkey, B	.327	361	118	16	54	40	75	.394	.540
Girardi, Joe	.169	77	13	0	3	2	8	.200	.182
Gonzalez, L*	.257	113	29	2	8	9	19	.317	.398
Grace, Mark*	.303	231	70	5	35	27	29	.374	.476
Grissom, M	.267	191	51	3	17	11	29	.307	.372
Grudzielanek	.257	35	9	0	3	0	5	.257	.371
Gutierrez, R	.278	54	15	0	5	4	11	.333	.333
Gwynn, Chris*	.205	39	8	2	8	5	8	.289	.385
Gwynn, Tony*	.301	236	71	2	14	14	13	.345	.390
Harris, Lenny*	.344	96	33	2	15	5	12	.376	.448
Hayes, C	.255	149	38	2	12	9	20	.296	.336
Hill, G	.354	48	17	2	6	5	11	.415	.521
Hollins, Dave#	.237	59	14	2	8	4	17	.286	.356
Howard, T*	.268	71	19	1	3	4	11	.303	.338
Hudler, Rex	.173	52	9	0	3	2	14	.204	.212
Hundley, Todd#	.237	961	228	42	138	105	199	.317	.415
Hunter, Bri L	.323	31	10	1	4	6	7	.421	.452
Huskey, Butch	.275	295	81	11	39	15	57	.305	.424
Incaviglia, P	.206	34	7	2	6	0	13	.194	.412
James, Dion*	.348	46	16	1	4	6	10	.423	.522
Javier, Stan#	.245	53	13	0	4	4	7	.293	.321
Jefferies, G#	.308	916	282	24	110	87	64	.370	.468
Johnson, Bri	.281	32	9	1	5	2	6	.343	.438
Johnson, Char	.242	33	8	0	1	4	10	.333	.303
Johnson, L*	.294	337	99	1	30	11	25	.314	.409
Johnson, Mark*	.297	37	11	1	6	2	7	.341	.405
Jones, C#	.327	49	16	2	5	7	7	.404	.551
Jones, Chris	.213	164	35	6	18	11	49	.271	.366
Jordan, Brian	.333	51	17	2	8	3	9	.370	.510
Jordan, Ricky	.311	103	32	4	12	1	14	.321	.524
Justice, Dave*	.225	111	25	7	19	10	23	.289	.459
Karros, Eric	.188	112	21	6	14	6	20	.235	.393
Kelly, R	.262	61	16	0	0	3	9	.308	.311
Kent, Jeff	.284	894	254	34	141	51	169	.330	.472
King, Jeff	.243	152	37	4	17	13	22	.304	.401
Kingery, Mike*	.286	49	14	1	8	3	5	.315	.429
Klesko, Ryan*	.209	43	9	2	4	8	11	.333	.395
Lankford, Ray*	.283	145	41	4	17	15	31	.350	.476
Lansing, Mike	.297	64	19	4	16	4	3	.343	.516
Larkin, Barry	.269	197	53	3	22	7	14	.311	.376
Lemke, Mark#	.231	117	27	0	5	12	7	.300	.291
Lewis, Darren	.302	86	26	0	7	5	9	.348	.395
Liriano, N#	.409	44	18	1	8	2	2	.417	.591
Livingstone*	.343	35	12	0	4	4	2	.410	.371
Lopez, Javy	.208	53	11	2	4	3	12	.263	.377

269

Batter	Avg	AB	H	HR	BI	BB	SO	OBP	Slg
Magadan, Dave*	.292	1054	308	13	135	182	126	.393	.387
Manwaring, K	.200	80	16	0	8	3	17	.247	.200
Martin, Al*	.313	64	20	3	6	7	14	.375	.469
Martinez, Da*	.267	150	40	2	18	11	23	.317	.380
May, Derrick*	.346	81	28	3	15	8	5	.404	.556
Mayne, Brent*	.236	55	13	0	3	6	14	.311	.255
McGee, Willie#	.313	176	55	3	15	12	29	.360	.420
McGriff, Fred*	.282	142	40	9	22	13	32	.338	.493
McRae, Brian#	.366	41	15	3	5	4	9	.435	.707
Merced, O*	.245	110	27	2	15	9	23	.300	.364
Miller, Orl	.314	35	11	4	6	3	6	.368	.657
Mitchell, K	.274	117	32	9	19	17	29	.363	.530
Mondesi, Raul	.313	67	21	3	10	2	13	.338	.567
Morandini, M*	.254	118	30	0	7	4	21	.288	.339
Morris, Hal*	.272	92	25	3	13	7	16	.314	.478
Murray, Eddie#	.259	649	168	26	107	51	82	.311	.431
Nixon, Otis#	.248	105	26	0	7	10	19	.308	.267
O'Brien, C	.196	276	54	4	22	34	25	.294	.272
O'Neill, Paul*	.356	87	31	4	9	12	25	.434	.586
Ochoa, Alex	.272	169	46	1	14	11	19	.317	.343
Offerman, J#	.235	81	19	0	5	6	17	.303	.259
Oliver, Joe	.311	61	19	3	13	3	14	.344	.557
Ordonez, Rey	.228	246	56	0	11	15	21	.275	.252
Orsulak, Joe*	.296	446	132	10	59	36	20	.344	.408
Otero, Ricky#	.218	55	12	0	6	5	8	.283	.236
Pagnozzi, Tom	.254	118	30	0	18	4	20	.278	.364
Palmeiro, R*	.182	55	10	0	1	3	7	.237	.218
Pena, G#	.324	71	23	1	8	2	21	.338	.479
Pena, Tony	.136	66	9	0	5	6	15	.208	.197
Pendleton, T#	.294	252	74	7	31	15	36	.331	.429
Petagine, Rob*	.268	56	15	2	11	8	14	.364	.393
Piazza, Mike	.373	67	25	5	11	13	9	.481	.642
Plantier, P*	.310	42	13	5	10	4	9	.370	.714
Prince, Tom	.311	45	14	2	7	5	8	.373	.578
Raines, Tim#	.307	114	35	5	16	18	15	.406	.526
Reed, Jeff*	.193	88	17	0	3	9	16	.273	.216
Reed, Jody	.243	37	9	0	2	7	5	.364	.297
Roberts, Bip#	.242	149	36	0	5	7	20	.274	.275
Rodriguez, H*	.333	51	17	2	11	1	11	.340	.510
Sabo, Chris	.225	111	25	1	8	5	26	.252	.288
Samuel, Juan	.213	301	64	3	26	21	71	.272	.272
Sanchez, Rey	.176	51	9	1	4	3	2	.236	.294
Sandberg, R	.263	255	67	11	38	25	46	.325	.427
Sanders, R	.325	80	26	4	13	9	20	.389	.550
Santiago, B	.260	173	45	4	19	9	40	.301	.353
Schofield, D	.214	201	43	3	18	32	37	.323	.303
Segui, David#	.257	222	57	8	30	27	25	.337	.419
Servais, S	.189	53	10	1	6	10	8	.333	.264
Sheffield, G	.333	72	24	2	12	13	8	.427	.486
Slaught, Don	.436	55	24	0	9	3	4	.475	.491
Smith, Dwight*	.280	75	21	1	4	9	10	.357	.413
Smith, Ozzie#	.238	189	45	0	12	18	13	.304	.275
Sosa, Sammy	.205	78	16	3	13	8	26	.295	.321
Spiers, Bill*	.308	39	12	0	8	8	5	.417	.359
Stillwell, K#	.242	33	8	0	1	2	4	.306	.273
Stinnett, K	.212	156	33	1	8	20	43	.315	.269
Stocker, K#	.340	53	18	1	6	10	9	.453	.453
Strawberry, D*	.277	1047	290	83	228	156	234	.372	.575
Taubensee, E*	.208	48	10	3	5	4	8	.264	.438
Thompson, Mil*	.300	150	45	0	5	12	36	.364	.380
Thompson, Rob	.291	179	52	5	19	11	40	.332	.430
Thompson, Ry	.214	487	104	16	63	38	151	.277	.359
Tomberlin, A*	.290	31	9	2	6	4	12	.371	.548
VanderWal, J*	.220	41	9	1	6	1	9	.233	.341
Vina, F*	.264	72	19	0	5	4	7	.354	.333
Vizcaino, J#	.266	681	181	5	63	51	95	.319	.327
Walker, Larry*	.209	148	31	4	20	11	38	.268	.372
Wallach, Tim	.288	271	78	8	39	21	51	.339	.446
Walton, J	.269	67	18	0	3	9	14	.388	.328
Wehner, John	.188	32	6	0	1	2	4	.235	.344
Weiss, Walt*	.385	65	25	0	5	8	7	.452	.446
White, R	.364	44	16	0	4	5	6	.420	.500
Whiten, Mark#	.160	50	8	1	6	5	9	.236	.240
Wilkins, Rick*	.261	92	24	6	20	13	25	.343	.500
Williams, E	.250	32	8	3	7	2	6	.294	.563
Williams, Ma	.266	169	45	7	23	10	35	.313	.450
Young, Eric	.245	49	12	0	1	2	3	.275	.265
Zeile, Todd	.285	151	43	4	16	12	28	.333	.457

Batter	Avg	AB	H	HR	BI	BB	SO	OBP	Slg
Aldrete, Mike*	.317	60	19	4	8	3	19	.349	.617
Alomar, R#	.325	123	40	3	11	8	19	.364	.504
Alomar Jr, S	.248	105	26	1	14	6	12	.292	.352
Amaral, Rich	.317	63	20	1	7	6	7	.371	.413

Grass

Batter	Avg	AB	H	HR	BI	BB	SO	OBP	Slg
Anderson, Brd*	.231	156	36	4	20	25	18	.346	.365
Anderson, G*	.231	39	9	0	6	0	3	.231	.256
Baerga, C#	.329	161	53	6	28	8	16	.358	.540
Baines, H*	.253	174	44	6	27	30	28	.361	.425
Belle, Albert	.331	136	45	12	27	16	29	.396	.676
Berroa, G	.373	67	25	9	23	13	14	.469	.866
Bichette, D	.318	66	21	2	4	4	13	.357	.455
Blowers, Mike	.229	140	32	2	10	13	42	.292	.293
Boggs, Wade*	.337	1098	370	14	116	153	89	.415	.434
Bonilla, B#	.308	39	12	1	5	5	3	.386	.436
Borders, Pat	.248	113	28	1	10	6	16	.283	.327
Bordick, Mike	.263	114	30	1	8	8	20	.317	.342
Bragg, Darren*	.367	30	11	1	3	6	5	.486	.500
Brosius, S	.175	57	10	2	7	5	13	.250	.281
Buhner, Jay	.280	164	46	15	48	16	46	.340	.616
Burks, Ellis	.199	146	29	3	14	11	24	.255	.322
Canseco, Jose	.253	198	50	13	44	24	47	.332	.515
Carter, Joe	.259	212	55	14	36	8	29	.290	.514
Cirillo, Jeff	.343	35	12	1	1	4	4	.410	.457
Clark, Will*	.343	35	12	0	12	5	6	.405	.486
Cole, Alex*	.273	55	15	0	2	9	7	.369	.291
Cora, Joey#	.246	61	15	1	5	7	4	.319	.295
Cordova, M	.351	37	13	0	6	2	9	.400	.432
Curtis, Chad	.232	99	23	0	7	12	21	.313	.273
Cuyler, Milt*	.190	42	8	0	2	6	9	.306	.286
Davis, Chili#	.283	184	52	11	30	24	45	.365	.527
Davis, Russ	.264	53	14	2	7	4	13	.316	.415
Deer, Rob	.229	153	35	8	20	14	54	.292	.464
Devereaux, M	.273	139	38	4	9	11	23	.329	.453
DiSarcina, G	.317	82	26	1	13	7	6	.380	.463
Duncan, M	.406	160	65	5	31	5	21	.423	.613
Durham, Ray#	.290	31	9	0	2	3	3	.371	.387
Easley, D	.338	74	25	2	11	4	6	.370	.459
Edmonds, Jim*	.222	54	12	0	5	9	9	.333	.315
Eisenreich, J*	.321	84	27	0	9	5	10	.363	.452
Elster, Kevin	.125	40	5	0	3	3	10	.186	.175
Espinoza, A	.253	768	194	2	47	26	82	.279	.314
Fermin, Felix	.305	95	29	0	9	8	4	.365	.326
Fielder, C	.256	281	72	17	51	27	73	.324	.484
Fox, Andy*	.178	90	16	1	6	9	13	.253	.222
Franco, Julio	.257	167	43	2	13	21	27	.344	.341
Frye, Jeff	.132	38	5	0	3	4	8	.214	.211
Fryman, T	.247	170	42	6	20	14	34	.305	.447
Gaetti, Gary	.209	172	36	6	28	9	32	.246	.349
Gagne, Greg	.281	146	41	6	14	4	21	.300	.527
Gallego, Mike	.259	463	120	8	46	58	74	.350	.387
Gates, Brent#	.274	62	17	0	7	1	4	.297	.306
Girardi, Joe	.304	214	65	1	20	14	22	.353	.374
Gomez, Chris	.282	39	11	0	4	6	11	.378	.282
Gomez, Leo	.253	91	23	2	10	14	17	.349	.396
Gonzales, R	.191	68	13	0	4	6	15	.257	.191
Gonzalez, A	.167	42	7	2	3	4	14	.239	.310
Gonzalez, J	.221	113	25	6	22	6	19	.270	.416
Grebeck, C	.250	44	11	0	1	2	6	.283	.341
Greenwell, M*	.282	216	61	6	24	18	21	.346	.435
Greer, Rusty*	.220	41	9	1	4	1	8	.238	.415
Griffey Jr, K*	.311	161	50	9	31	13	25	.369	.528
Guillen, O*	.239	159	38	0	12	3	13	.258	.277
Hall, Mel*	.268	952	255	37	141	51	77	.304	.432
Hamilton, D*	.296	81	24	2	7	7	10	.348	.407
Haselman, B	.290	31	9	1	3	2	6	.353	.548
Hayes, C	.220	259	57	7	32	14	48	.264	.347
Henderson, R	.294	686	202	21	69	137	77	.413	.448
Hill, G	.216	37	8	1	4	2	10	.256	.297
Hoiles, Chris	.237	97	23	4	14	12	24	.324	.412
Howard, Dave#	.255	51	13	0	5	5	6	.316	.294
Howell, Jack*	.257	74	19	4	13	13	12	.368	.527
Hudler, Rex	.244	45	11	1	5	0	11	.255	.400
Huff, Michael	.205	39	8	1	3	7	7	.326	.359
Hulse, David*	.326	43	14	1	4	3	9	.383	.465
Incaviglia, P	.241	79	19	3	10	4	26	.282	.443
Jaha, John	.303	66	20	3	8	7	14	.370	.500
James, Dion*	.324	361	117	9	46	34	29	.379	.468
Javier, Stan#	.238	63	15	0	6	4	12	.284	.238
Jefferson, R*	.188	69	13	1	8	2	13	.222	.246
Jeter, Derek	.293	321	94	3	45	31	51	.358	.389
Johnson, L*	.333	102	34	1	13	5	10	.361	.441
Joyner, Wally*	.280	157	44	9	36	22	15	.368	.516
Karkovice, M	.301	103	31	7	21	9	40	.357	.583
Kelly, Pat	.247	807	199	12	78	65	154	.311	.359
Kelly, R	.292	1141	333	25	124	87	197	.345	.422
Kirby, Wayne*	.171	41	7	0	3	5	6	.255	.195
Knoblauch, C	.302	116	35	1	7	13	8	.382	.405
Kreuter, Chad#	.192	52	10	1	5	7	10	.288	.288
Leius, Scott	.167	60	10	0	2	6	11	.242	.217
Lewis, Mark	.254	59	15	0	4	5	12	.308	.288
Leyritz, Jim	.279	755	211	20	110	94	161	.372	.411
Liriano, N#	.240	50	12	1	6	4	4	.296	.300

YANKEE STADIUM
Home of the New York Yankees
Bronx, New York   Grass

Batter	Avg	AB	H	HR	BI	BB	SO	OBP	Slg
Listach, Pat#	.232	69	16	1	5	10	10	.329	.304
Lofton, Kenny*	.344	128	44	1	16	10	16	.393	.500
Lovullo, T#	.271	59	16	2	5	4	2	.313	.424
Macfarlane, M	.228	123	28	5	18	8	32	.280	.431
Manto, Jeff	.216	37	8	1	6	8	8	.356	.378
Martinez, E	.364	118	43	7	29	21	12	.468	.627
Martinez, T*	.305	361	110	17	82	36	53	.366	.488
Marzano, John	.311	45	14	0	3	3	4	.360	.422
Mayne, Brent*	.094	32	3	0	2	2	6	.147	.125
McGriff, Fred*	.342	76	26	9	14	17	27	.462	.711
McGwire, Mark	.238	193	46	14	34	35	48	.362	.503
McLemore, M#	.205	122	25	1	10	9	17	.260	.303
McRae, Brian#	.141	71	10	1	6	3	9	.197	.211
Meares, Pat	.250	48	12	1	7	3	9	.294	.396
Mieske, Matt	.310	58	18	2	6	3	11	.344	.500
Molitor, Paul	.288	222	64	4	19	23	21	.356	.369
Munoz, Pedro	.366	71	26	6	20	3	11	.387	.648
Murray, Eddie#	.302	129	39	5	18	12	20	.359	.496
Myers, Greg*	.294	68	20	3	8	1	12	.304	.515
Naehring, Tim	.244	78	19	3	7	6	16	.298	.410
Nilsson, Dave*	.311	61	19	3	12	10	5	.408	.508
Nixon, Otis#	.410	61	25	0	5	5	7	.455	.475
O'Brien, C	.263	38	10	0	5	4	7	.349	.342
O'Neill, Paul*	.340	903	307	37	179	145	131	.427	.539
Olerud, John*	.270	111	30	2	13	22	20	.390	.414
Orsulak, Joe*	.321	84	27	2	5	6	7	.363	.440
Palmeiro, R*	.321	187	60	10	41	21	18	.394	.583
Palmer, Dean	.312	77	24	5	16	9	21	.386	.584
Paquette, C	.289	45	13	0	3	1	15	.313	.356
Pena, Tony	.277	83	23	0	3	9	12	.362	.349
Phillips, T#	.259	193	50	2	17	46	29	.399	.332
Plantier, P*	.263	38	10	2	7	7	9	.378	.474
Polonia, Luis*	.312	516	161	3	47	58	57	.382	.399
Raines, Tim#	.281	203	57	10	24	35	22	.384	.473
Ramirez, M	.295	78	23	7	14	7	19	.345	.615
Reboulet, J	.281	32	9	0	4	3	2	.361	.281
Reed, Jody	.374	123	46	1	14	21	2	.459	.496
Ripken, Billy	.179	106	19	1	6	3	17	.216	.236
Ripken, Cal	.298	265	79	7	29	19	26	.346	.445
Rodriguez, Al	.293	41	12	2	5	3	12	.333	.463
Rodriguez, I	.286	91	26	2	12	4	6	.309	.396
Salmon, Tim	.300	100	30	5	15	10	26	.360	.500
Schofield, D	.256	82	21	1	6	9	11	.344	.354
Segui, David#	.347	49	17	0	5	8	2	.439	.408
Seitzer, K	.255	184	47	3	27	31	29	.364	.370
Sheffield, G	.255	55	14	1	6	9	4	.348	.382
Shumpert, T	.273	33	9	2	5	1	6	.286	.455
Sierra, Ruben#	.282	490	138	18	96	50	75	.344	.449
Silvestri, D	.158	38	6	1	2	8	12	.304	.316
Slaught, Don	.281	356	100	11	51	25	55	.329	.469
Snow, J.T.#	.205	83	17	2	9	15	14	.337	.301
Sojo, Luis	.375	72	27	2	14	5	5	.410	.569
Sorrento, P*	.267	75	20	4	13	9	16	.353	.453
Sosa, Sammy	.229	48	11	2	5	4	9	.302	.396
Spiers, Bill*	.203	59	12	0	2	0	11	.217	.271
Sprague, Ed	.227	97	22	4	19	8	14	.287	.423
Stankiewicz	.284	215	61	2	15	20	19	.345	.381
Stanley, Mike	.298	667	199	46	156	105	148	.396	.559
Steinbach, T	.234	175	41	4	19	9	32	.274	.349
Stillwell, K#	.152	46	7	0	1	7	5	.264	.196
Strange, Doug#	.120	50	6	0	5	2	12	.151	.180
Strawberry, D*	.317	142	45	11	31	18	35	.393	.613
Surhoff, B.J.*	.292	168	49	1	13	13	17	.343	.339
Sveum, Dale#	.173	75	13	4	8	4	15	.213	.373
Tartabull, D	.251	813	204	39	160	139	221	.359	.456
Tettleton, M#	.298	141	42	12	36	25	44	.404	.589
Thomas, Frank	.352	105	37	4	22	32	12	.504	.543
Thome, Jim*	.250	60	15	4	13	11	10	.370	.517
Tinsley, Lee#	.213	47	10	1	4	3	16	.260	.340
Trammell, A	.235	119	28	2	15	8	14	.285	.370
Valentin, Jhn	.308	78	24	3	18	15	9	.421	.474
Valentin, Jse#	.167	42	7	2	4	3	15	.217	.405
Valle, Dave	.169	77	13	0	4	8	16	.253	.195
Vaughn, Greg	.216	134	29	6	21	11	29	.275	.403
Vaughn, Mo*	.260	123	32	9	25	19	27	.381	.537
Velarde, R	.272	922	251	17	106	100	165	.349	.386
Ventura, R*	.211	114	24	6	21	25	23	.353	.404
Vizquel, Omar#	.225	142	32	1	8	9	14	.268	.254
Weiss, Walt#	.343	67	23	1	9	8	5	.413	.478
White, Devon#	.294	180	53	7	26	8	28	.325	.478
Whiten, Mark#	.237	76	18	4	12	5	12	.280	.408
Williams, B#	.294	1272	374	32	170	178	169	.381	.445
Williams, E	.161	31	5	0	3	4	6	.278	.194
Williams, Ger	.251	311	78	11	49	24	50	.301	.457
Wilson, Dan	.278	36	10	1	3	1	5	.297	.389
Worthington	.229	35	8	1	3	0	8	.229	.400

Batter	Avg	AB	H	HR	BI	BB	SO	OBP	Slg
Aldrete, Mike*	.223	282	63	9	33	42	61	.321	.340
Alomar, R#	.363	124	45	2	17	24	6	.467	.548
Alomar Jr, S	.143	84	12	1	5	6	9	.226	.214
Amaral, Rich	.325	40	13	0	6	4	9	.386	.375
Anderson, Brd*	.235	170	40	6	21	23	34	.333	.441
Anderson, G*	.327	49	16	2	8	2	6	.353	.469
Baerga, C#	.265	132	35	1	13	7	12	.310	.326
Baines, H*	.278	665	185	28	136	97	104	.364	.444
Batista, Tony	.255	110	28	1	14	13	20	.336	.355
Battle, Allen	.196	46	9	0	0	6	10	.302	.217
Becker, Rich*	.152	46	7	0	1	7	15	.264	.174
Belle, Albert	.300	110	33	10	29	13	19	.365	.627
Berroa, G	.296	695	206	33	117	82	127	.368	.488
Bichette, D	.219	32	7	3	8	5	7	.333	.531
Blowers, Mike	.254	67	17	3	16	8	19	.338	.403
Boggs, Wade*	.225	200	45	1	14	32	21	.336	.275
Bonilla, B#	.293	41	12	1	11	5	5	.383	.488
Borders, Pat	.250	108	27	4	20	3	25	.268	.426
Bordick, Mike	.260	1270	330	10	109	111	129	.327	.334
Bournigal, R	.206	126	26	0	8	10	6	.265	.270
Brosius, S	.263	720	189	38	100	66	116	.330	.471
Buhner, Jay	.236	127	30	11	24	15	30	.315	.512
Burks, Ellis	.281	139	39	3	16	11	21	.336	.417
Canseco, Jose	.280	1409	394	90	276	205	376	.373	.521
Carter, Joe	.169	183	31	7	27	18	30	.262	.295
Clark, Will*	.339	56	19	2	14	11	6	.456	.536
Coleman, V#	.172	29	5	0	2	4	7	.294	.276
Cora, Joey#	.271	107	29	0	8	13	16	.350	.346
Cordova, M	.326	43	14	2	9	4	8	.388	.535
Curtis, Chad	.135	52	7	1	3	13	4	.308	.231
Cuyler, Milt#	.288	52	15	1	8	4	13	.339	.462
Davis, Chili#	.340	147	50	11	37	19	27	.413	.626
Dawson, Andre	.205	39	8	0	1	0	5	.225	.231
Deer, Rob	.195	113	22	10	17	17	45	.311	.496
Devereaux, M	.279	140	39	5	20	12	22	.333	.443
DiSarcina, G	.179	84	15	0	0	6	11	.233	.214
Durham, Ray#	.295	44	13	2	6	2	11	.354	.523
Easley, D	.139	36	5	0	3	1	6	.200	.194
Edmonds, Jim*	.161	56	9	3	6	4	15	.217	.357
Eisenreich, J*	.283	92	26	4	14	7	8	.333	.489
Espinoza, A	.198	81	16	1	5	3	13	.226	.272
Fermin, Felix	.375	72	27	1	8	4	4	.416	.472
Fielder, C	.230	135	31	6	22	16	38	.314	.378
Finley, Steve*	.184	38	7	0	2	4	2	.262	.184
Franco, Julio	.263	171	45	2	19	16	28	.330	.327
Frye, Jeff	.284	67	19	1	9	5	12	.338	.388
Fryman, T	.206	107	22	2	9	7	26	.252	.308
Gaetti, Gary	.232	181	42	8	24	9	27	.273	.392
Gagne, Greg	.238	147	35	6	15	8	33	.282	.408
Gallego, Mike	.246	890	219	11	82	114	121	.335	.328
Gates, Brent#	.276	704	194	8	72	66	110	.335	.365
Giambi, Jason*	.283	307	87	9	42	43	51	.377	.466
Gomez, Leo	.220	50	11	0	2	6	10	.298	.260
Gonzales, R	.208	53	11	1	4	8	9	.302	.302
Gonzalez, J	.232	125	29	9	23	13	26	.300	.504
Goodwin, Tom*	.200	50	10	1	4	1	4	.216	.260
Greenwell, M*	.301	173	52	3	22	19	14	.366	.393
Greer, Rusty*	.315	73	23	1	10	14	12	.420	.479
Griffey Jr, K*	.261	153	40	6	24	24	26	.356	.412
Guillen, O*	.231	221	51	0	23	3	17	.241	.253
Hall, Mel*	.244	123	30	2	18	1	15	.248	.366
Hamelin, Bob*	.256	39	10	3	7	7	9	.383	.538
Hamilton, D*	.321	106	34	1	10	6	11	.357	.425
Haselman, B	.263	38	10	1	1	3	10	.317	.395
Henderson, R	.294	1379	405	50	161	320	193	.429	.456
Herrera, Jose*	.295	176	52	3	16	13	32	.344	.386
Hill, G	.190	42	8	1	4	2	11	.222	.286
Hoiles, Chris	.267	105	28	8	18	18	23	.384	.552
Hollins, Dave#	.176	34	6	0	3	3	6	.243	.235
Howard, Dave#	.302	43	13	0	4	1	9	.318	.302
Howell, Jack*	.230	87	20	5	9	15	21	.343	.437
Hulse, David*	.294	68	20	0	5	5	12	.342	.353
Huson, Jeff*	.275	40	11	0	2	6	5	.370	.325
Incaviglia, P	.143	63	9	2	4	7	20	.229	.270
Jaha, John	.200	50	10	2	6	5	14	.322	.340
James, Dion*	.340	53	18	0	3	4	9	.386	.377
Javier, Stan#	.260	836	217	6	77	104	127	.343	.344
Jefferson, R*	.270	37	10	2	6	1	11	.308	.486
Johnson, L*	.273	165	45	1	15	8	12	.310	.388
Joyner, Wally*	.247	158	39	2	19	18	23	.330	.329
Karkovice, R	.185	81	15	5	10	7	24	.258	.420
Kelly, Pat	.222	81	18	1	8	5	20	.308	.333
Kelly, R	.357	84	30	1	5	3	18	.379	.464
Kingery, Mike*	.208	48	10	0	3	8	6	.321	.229
Knoblauch, C	.256	117	30	1	11	15	11	.355	.359
Kreuter, Chad#	.286	42	12	1	8	4	11	.340	.429
Leius, Scott	.200	50	10	0	3	3	17	.245	.220
Lesher, Brian	.200	40	8	2	8	2	9	.233	.375

OAKLAND-ALAMEDA COUNTY COLISEUM
Home of the Oakland Athletics
Oakland, California — Grass

Batter	Avg	AB	H	HR	BI	BB	SO	OBP	Slg
Lewis, Darren	.103	29	3	0	0	6	1	.257	.103
Lewis, Mark	.306	49	15	1	8	4	12	.358	.429
Leyritz, Jim	.351	37	13	2	11	5	8	.444	.541
Liriano, N#	.146	41	6	0	1	1	3	.167	.195
Listach, Pat#	.298	47	14	0	2	4	11	.353	.319
Livingstone*	.179	28	5	0	2	4	5	.265	.179
Lockhart, K*	.258	31	8	0	2	4	4	.333	.355
Lofton, Kenny*	.352	91	32	1	10	10	10	.416	.571
Lovullo, T#	.194	67	13	0	3	7	14	.280	.224
Macfarlane, M	.221	113	25	4	15	8	19	.286	.354
Martinez, Da*	.432	37	16	0	5	6	4	.512	.649
Martinez, E	.216	148	32	4	13	25	21	.346	.338
Martinez, T*	.280	107	30	6	16	9	17	.342	.495
Mashore, D	.271	48	13	1	8	10	15	.390	.417
Mayne, Brent*	.185	54	10	0	1	3	10	.228	.204
McGee, Willie#	.264	72	19	0	6	5	12	.312	.292
McGriff, Fred*	.253	79	20	5	16	8	19	.322	.481
McGwire, Mark	.247	1947	481	148	400	395	462	.378	.520
McLemore, M#	.212	137	29	2	12	24	33	.327	.285
McRae, Brian#	.220	91	20	0	9	6	20	.263	.264
Meares, Pat	.193	57	11	1	6	4	8	.246	.316
Molitor, Paul	.327	168	55	5	25	23	22	.407	.500
Munoz, Pedro	.244	82	20	3	11	6	22	.295	.378
Murray, Eddie#	.268	82	22	3	15	12	12	.358	.439
Myers, Greg*	.226	62	14	1	8	6	13	.294	.323
Naehring, Tim	.323	65	21	0	4	10	11	.423	.400
Newson, W*	.263	38	10	0	2	5	12	.349	.368
Nilsson, Dave*	.313	64	20	1	10	7	7	.375	.391
Nixon, Otis#	.366	41	15	0	4	9	5	.471	.366
O'Leary, Troy*	.208	48	10	1	5	3	10	.255	.313
O'Neill, Paul*	.282	78	22	4	13	20	14	.430	.487
Olerud, John*	.279	111	31	3	12	17	20	.372	.405
Orsulak, Joe*	.215	65	14	0	3	6	7	.282	.308
Palmeiro, R*	.293	198	58	11	40	21	16	.363	.520
Palmer, Dean	.241	108	26	4	17	18	23	.359	.389
Paquette, C	.227	361	82	16	37	13	102	.252	.418
Pena, Tony	.203	74	15	1	5	7	11	.272	.257
Phillips, T#	.257	638	164	11	66	96	128	.353	.356
Plantier, P*	.270	126	34	2	21	10	33	.326	.373
Polonia, Luis*	.287	609	175	2	51	55	66	.346	.374
Raines, Tim#	.285	123	35	0	13	25	13	.400	.390
Ramirez, M	.302	43	13	1	6	7	11	.392	.419
Reboulet, J	.250	36	9	2	7	4	5	.325	.444
Reed, Jody	.388	80	31	1	13	12	3	.457	.500
Ripken, Billy	.176	85	15	0	5	6	8	.228	.212
Ripken, Cal	.215	256	55	9	26	16	31	.261	.355
Rodriguez, Al	.200	50	10	2	5	2	10	.231	.380
Rodriguez, I	.282	117	33	3	12	3	14	.301	.427
Salmon, Tim	.400	65	26	3	10	6	9	.444	.646
Schofield, D	.211	76	16	1	4	6	11	.286	.276
Segui, David*	.313	32	10	1	2	4	2	.378	.469
Seitzer, K	.233	287	67	2	22	36	34	.319	.310
Sheffield, G	.180	61	11	1	3	3	5	.219	.262
Sierra, Ruben#	.240	847	203	30	137	72	125	.295	.393
Slaught, Don	.184	38	7	0	3	3	6	.262	.263
Snow, J.T.#	.296	81	24	8	16	10	21	.370	.642
Sojo, Luis	.211	57	12	1	3	3	4	.274	.333
Sorrento, P*	.299	97	29	5	18	10	25	.364	.536
Sosa, Sammy	.157	51	8	1	7	1	20	.182	.275
Spiers, Bill*	.253	79	20	1	10	6	14	.314	.342
Sprague, Ed	.333	78	26	5	14	7	5	.398	.590
Stairs, Matt*	.268	71	19	4	11	9	11	.346	.479
Stanley, Mike	.255	98	25	2	7	13	22	.345	.388
Steinbach, T	.274	1962	538	57	281	146	314	.326	.414
Stevens, Lee*	.237	38	9	2	4	7	12	.356	.474
Stillwell, K#	.259	81	21	0	8	4	6	.291	.321
Strange, Doug#	.130	46	6	1	4	3	9	.184	.217
Surhoff, B.J.*	.262	187	49	5	27	15	23	.314	.385
Sveum, Dale#	.119	84	10	3	13	8	30	.194	.238
Tartabull, D	.319	232	74	15	41	28	63	.393	.573
Tettleton, M#	.224	272	61	13	40	51	80	.349	.401
Thomas, Frank	.308	133	41	9	34	32	27	.444	.564
Thome, Jim*	.361	36	13	2	11	9	9	.478	.694
Tomberlin, A*	.204	54	11	3	8	3	15	.246	.370
Trammell, A	.239	134	32	3	11	14	18	.311	.351
Valentin, Jhn	.288	104	30	2	19	7	7	.336	.404
Valentin, Jse#	.250	48	12	4	12	1	13	.260	.521
Valle, Dave	.202	89	18	4	12	9	16	.290	.348
Vaughn, Greg	.259	108	28	10	25	25	19	.403	.611
Vaughn, Mo*	.324	108	35	4	19	14	26	.413	.481
Velarde, R	.247	93	23	1	8	6	21	.290	.323
Ventura, R*	.218	165	36	5	18	28	24	.333	.352
Vina, F*	.179	39	7	0	2	1	3	.200	.205
Vizquel, Omar#	.188	133	25	0	1	9	9	.239	.211
Walbeck, Matt#	.270	37	10	0	8	0	2	.263	.324
Ward, Turner#	.206	34	7	0	1	7	6	.341	.206
Weiss, Walt#	.221	802	177	3	52	76	118	.293	.268
White, Devon#	.291	199	58	5	22	9	47	.322	.427

OAKLAND-ALAMEDA COUNTY COLISEUM
Home of the Oakland Athletics
Oakland, California — Grass

Batter	Avg	AB	H	HR	BI	BB	SO	OBP	Slg
Whiten, Mark#	.246	61	15	2	6	8	11	.343	.426
Williams, Ber#	.267	101	27	3	17	17	22	.383	.446
Williams, Geo#	.196	107	21	1	8	16	23	.302	.271
Wilson, Dan	.347	49	17	0	9	3	3	.385	.388
Worthington	.229	35	8	0	0	7	7	.357	.257
Young, Ernie	.239	276	66	12	33	26	71	.308	.424

VETERANS STADIUM
Home of the Philadelphia Phillies
Philadelphia, Pennsylvania — Artificial

Batter	Avg	AB	H	HR	BI	BB	SO	OBP	Slg
Abbott, Kurt	.236	55	13	2	6	2	17	.263	.400
Aldrete, Mike*	.362	47	17	0	5	7	4	.446	.426
Alfonzo, E	.216	37	8	2	4	0	6	.216	.486
Alicea, Luis#	.286	63	18	1	9	9	10	.392	.397
Alomar, R#	.329	70	23	1	7	10	6	.413	.386
Alou, Moises	.305	131	40	3	21	10	20	.352	.481
Amaro, Ruben#	.254	248	63	6	26	20	42	.321	.407
Anthony, Eric*	.314	86	27	4	15	11	17	.388	.523
Arias, Alex	.313	48	15	0	3	4	6	.358	.375
Ausmus, Brad	.257	35	9	1	1	6	6	.381	.429
Bagwell, Jeff	.323	130	42	5	27	17	24	.401	.523
Barberie, B#	.220	59	13	0	3	7	14	.319	.237
Batiste, Kim	.226	266	60	2	24	3	47	.234	.293
Bell, Derek	.225	80	18	1	8	6	22	.270	.300
Bell, Jay	.240	229	55	2	19	11	52	.280	.341
Belliard, R	.218	78	17	0	4	9	15	.307	.269
Benjamin, M	.227	75	17	0	9	6	18	.293	.333
Berry, Sean	.261	69	18	3	8	3	15	.301	.464
Bichette, D	.254	63	16	5	16	5	19	.304	.635
Biggio, Craig	.311	167	52	2	14	29	23	.417	.449
Blauser, Jeff	.254	126	32	4	21	8	24	.299	.444
Bonds, Barry*	.312	260	81	23	61	71	33	.458	.650
Bonilla, B#	.358	265	95	11	52	33	35	.423	.596
Boone, Bret	.366	41	15	1	7	1	7	.386	.512
Branson, Jeff*	.178	45	8	0	3	6	12	.269	.244
Brogna, Rico*	.243	37	9	2	5	1	9	.263	.432
Burks, Ellis	.389	36	14	5	10	4	5	.463	.861
Butler, Brett*	.309	175	54	0	10	39	22	.438	.354
Caminiti, Ken#	.263	152	40	3	30	21	25	.351	.382
Candaele, C#	.200	80	16	0	2	14	10	.319	.263
Cangelosi, J#	.258	66	17	0	4	21	8	.432	.333
Carr, Chuck#	.151	73	11	0	2	9	10	.244	.192
Carreon, Mark	.242	66	16	1	1	5	14	.296	.333
Castilla, V	.196	46	9	2	3	4	11	.275	.348
Cedeno, A	.308	65	20	0	3	7	15	.375	.385
Cianfrocco, A	.271	59	16	0	5	3	16	.302	.390
Clark, Dave*	.271	48	13	0	5	7	10	.357	.333
Clark, Will*	.297	145	43	6	36	15	30	.364	.517
Clayton, R	.310	84	26	0	20	15	21	.412	.393
Colbrunn, G	.129	62	8	2	8	2	9	.156	.258
Coleman, V#	.266	173	46	0	10	28	30	.369	.387
Conine, Jeff	.241	79	19	2	10	14	10	.365	.405
Cordero, Wil	.292	65	19	0	3	6	7	.361	.385
Dascenzo, D#	.190	58	11	1	4	8	6	.284	.276
Daulton, D*	.252	1478	372	57	251	251	279	.361	.442
Davis, Eric	.259	147	38	10	29	13	36	.319	.524
Dawson, Andre	.289	201	58	5	28	17	38	.344	.433
Decker, Steve	.250	36	9	0	3	5	9	.341	.250
DeShields, D*	.294	194	57	4	19	31	37	.402	.407
Doster, David	.298	57	17	1	4	5	10	.355	.456
Duncan, M	.259	810	210	17	95	26	168	.288	.389
Dunston, S	.211	194	41	1	12	5	31	.233	.253
Dykstra, L*	.296	1468	435	36	136	259	134	.402	.453
Eisenreich, J*	.346	650	225	12	90	61	63	.403	.489
Elster, Kevin	.258	89	23	1	9	17	21	.385	.337
Eusebio, Tony	.355	31	11	0	4	6	4	.447	.419
Finley, Steve*	.279	122	34	5	19	16	13	.362	.475
Fletcher, D*	.188	138	26	2	16	11	17	.245	.275
Galarraga, A	.251	235	59	7	30	12	57	.305	.421
Gant, Ron	.280	157	44	8	26	18	36	.356	.516
Garcia, C	.222	63	14	0	2	1	14	.234	.270
Gilkey, B	.321	112	36	5	16	14	11	.402	.571
Girardi, Joe	.268	82	22	1	5	6	12	.318	.378
Gonzalez, L*	.253	95	24	1	13	14	15	.351	.347
Grace, Mark*	.247	227	56	7	29	38	13	.353	.366
Grissom, M	.246	207	51	5	18	19	33	.307	.372
Grudzielanek	.182	33	6	0	1	1	7	.229	.182
Gutierrez, R	.184	49	9	0	4	10	12	.317	.224
Gwynn, Chris*	.211	38	8	2	8	3	9	.268	.474
Gwynn, Tony*	.323	229	74	3	35	19	9	.370	.445
Hansen, Dave*	.258	31	8	0	0	6	9	.378	.323
Harris, Lenny*	.258	89	23	1	7	10	10	.333	.326
Hayes, C	.264	994	262	19	138	56	163	.303	.381
Hill, G	.227	66	15	2	7	5	16	.292	.379
Hollins, Dave#	.246	861	212	34	124	133	171	.358	.427
Howard, T*	.239	46	11	1	5	3	7	.286	.391

	VETERANS STADIUM								
	Home of the Philadelphia Phillies								
Philadelphia, Pennsylvania									Artificial

Batter	Avg	AB	H	HR	BI	BB	SO	OBP	Slg
Hudler, Rex	.316	57	18	2	3	0	5	.316	.474
Hundley, Todd#	.209	91	19	1	8	9	22	.280	.308
Hunter, Brian	.271	48	13	0	4	2	9	.294	.396
Hunter, Bri L	.225	40	9	1	6	2	9	.262	.425
Incaviglia, P	.255	444	113	28	82	37	107	.316	.500
James, Dion*	.357	28	10	1	3	8	3	.500	.464
Javier, Stan#	.325	151	49	0	13	14	21	.383	.444
Jefferies, G#	.294	548	161	15	87	53	37	.352	.445
Jones, C#	.378	45	17	2	8	9	7	.481	.578
Jones, Chris	.429	42	18	2	8	0	7	.419	.619
Jordan, Brian	.231	39	9	1	5	4	7	.318	.308
Jordan, Kevin	.230	87	20	3	10	3	14	.261	.391
Jordan, Ricky	.290	1023	297	30	163	29	149	.310	.434
Justice, Dave*	.272	103	28	6	25	28	19	.436	.515
Karros, Eric	.228	123	28	4	18	7	25	.265	.350
Kelly, R	.233	60	14	0	0	4	12	.292	.267
Kent, Jeff	.295	78	23	0	7	5	11	.337	.410
King, Jeff	.240	171	41	3	20	19	18	.325	.380
Klesko, Ryan*	.250	40	10	3	9	5	9	.326	.550
Lankford, Ray*	.248	133	33	2	19	12	37	.310	.376
Lansing, Mike	.260	100	26	2	7	6	16	.308	.380
Larkin, Barry	.255	184	47	8	19	29	17	.360	.435
Lemke, Mark#	.304	92	28	2	15	8	5	.360	.467
Lewis, Darren	.307	88	27	0	5	10	17	.374	.364
Liebertha, M	.242	157	38	5	21	5	22	.268	.382
Liriano, N#	.257	35	9	1	5	2	8	.297	.429
Lopez, Javy	.242	33	8	0	3	2	8	.278	.273
Mabry, John*	.342	38	13	1	4	2	4	.375	.500
Magadan, Dave*	.292	154	45	4	22	26	18	.394	.468
Magee, W	.276	76	21	2	9	6	15	.329	.434
Manwaring, K	.307	75	23	0	13	14	4	.426	.440
Martin, Al*	.258	62	16	2	4	5	12	.309	.371
Martinez, Da*	.255	145	37	2	9	14	24	.321	.338
May, Derrick*	.268	71	19	5	17	2	6	.293	.521
McGee, Willie#	.277	166	46	2	19	13	35	.330	.386
McGriff, Fred*	.329	143	47	5	21	17	30	.398	.517
McRae, Brian*	.300	50	15	1	4	3	5	.340	.460
Merced, O*	.223	112	25	2	8	13	22	.302	.330
Mitchell, K	.214	98	21	3	12	12	18	.319	.347
Mondesi, Raul	.263	80	21	3	10	4	14	.298	.438
Morandini, M*	.264	1286	340	12	103	110	200	.327	.365
Morris, Hal*	.420	100	42	4	23	9	10	.464	.650
Mouton, James	.233	43	10	1	7	2	9	.283	.349
Murray, Eddie#	.256	129	33	3	15	10	14	.309	.403
Murray, Glenn	.182	55	10	2	5	3	22	.224	.309
Nixon, Otis#	.198	96	19	0	5	13	16	.300	.260
O'Brien, C	.246	61	15	0	13	7	10	.333	.328
O'Neill, Paul*	.187	107	20	3	18	8	19	.239	.290
Offerman, J#	.321	81	26	0	3	16	14	.433	.395
Oliver, Joe	.319	72	23	1	12	13	12	.424	.417
Orsulak, Joe*	.232	56	13	0	3	1	7	.246	.250
Otero, Ricky#	.270	230	62	0	13	20	18	.329	.361
Pagnozzi, Tom	.293	123	36	1	15	8	22	.328	.366
Palmeiro, R*	.349	43	15	0	4	6	3	.429	.488
Pena, G*	.197	61	12	0	2	12	17	.342	.230
Pena, Tony	.365	74	27	2	12	8	7	.422	.541
Pendleton, T#	.235	217	51	2	30	21	36	.303	.313
Phillips, J*	.188	48	9	4	8	6	22	.278	.521
Piazza, Mike	.416	77	32	7	23	5	13	.446	.792
Prince, Tom	.184	49	9	0	4	4	11	.259	.245
Raines, Tim#	.282	103	29	1	8	20	9	.398	.417
Reed, Jeff*	.227	44	10	0	3	4	7	.286	.318
Reed, Jody	.154	39	6	0	1	4	4	.233	.179
Roberts, Bip#	.250	100	25	1	11	21	13	.380	.350
Rodriguez, H*	.162	37	6	1	7	2	6	.205	.297
Rolen, Scott	.253	87	22	2	12	11	17	.340	.379
Sabo, Chris	.231	121	28	3	10	10	21	.290	.380
Samuel, Juan	.271	838	227	28	118	79	184	.340	.477
Sanchez, Rey	.345	58	20	1	8	5	6	.397	.500
Sandberg, R	.271	240	65	9	23	29	47	.352	.454
Sanders, R	.259	81	21	6	13	9	28	.333	.556
Santiago, B	.260	389	101	12	46	38	70	.323	.401
Scarsone, S	.326	43	14	1	8	6	11	.408	.488
Schall, Gene	.296	71	21	1	9	8	19	.367	.437
Schu, Rick	.223	112	25	5	14	10	23	.293	.420
Selcik, Kevin	.333	66	22	0	5	4	10	.380	.470
Segui, David#	.234	64	15	1	4	6	10	.300	.328
Servais, S	.169	59	10	3	10	4	12	.239	.373
Sheffield, G	.304	79	24	4	16	10	11	.385	.494
Shipley, C	.346	52	18	1	5	0	6	.370	.462
Slaught, Don	.284	67	19	0	8	5	6	.338	.328
Smith, Dwight*	.208	72	15	2	10	6	15	.278	.389
Smith, Ozzie#	.226	217	49	1	17	35	22	.331	.286
Sosa, Sammy	.278	79	22	1	8	11	19	.367	.380
Stillwell, K#	.256	43	11	0	0	2	6	.289	.302
Stocker, K#	.256	672	172	4	68	83	119	.347	.345
Strawberry, D*	.250	164	41	9	37	25	31	.345	.476
Sveum, Dale#	.108	65	7	0	6	10	17	.224	.138

276

VETERANS STADIUM
Home of the Philadelphia Phillies
Philadelphia, Pennsylvania   **Artificial**

Batter	Avg	AB	H	HR	BI	BB	SO	OBP	Slg
Taubensee, E*	.262	42	11	1	7	5	6	.340	.405
Thompson, Mil*	.297	792	235	9	92	88	127	.365	.407
Thompson, Rob	.228	136	31	3	10	16	27	.327	.331
Thompson, Ry	.196	46	9	0	2	5	10	.283	.304
VanderWal, J*	.200	30	6	2	9	6	8	.333	.433
Veras, Q#	.222	45	10	1	2	6	10	.314	.289
Vizcaino, J#	.292	113	33	1	14	5	15	.319	.354
Walker, Larry*	.275	153	42	5	18	18	31	.351	.438
Wallach, Tim	.254	279	71	5	31	20	38	.309	.380
Walton, J	.216	74	16	1	10	7	15	.286	.324
Webster, L	.284	95	27	1	12	10	13	.352	.389
Wehner, John	.306	36	11	0	1	6	8	.405	.361
Weiss, Walt#	.219	64	14	0	2	10	12	.324	.234
White, R	.317	41	13	1	8	4	8	.378	.585
Whiten, Mark*	.274	212	58	12	41	38	65	.389	.491
Wilkins, Rick*	.183	71	13	1	4	10	19	.289	.282
Williams, Ma	.237	156	37	16	30	18	32	.328	.615
Young, Eric	.162	37	6	0	1	4	5	.244	.162
Zeile, Todd	.279	383	107	14	62	43	63	.351	.433
Zuber, Jon*	.246	57	14	1	6	3	7	.283	.298

THREE RIVERS STADIUM
Home of the Pittsburgh Pirates
Pittsburgh, Pennsylvania   **Artificial**

Batter	Avg	AB	H	HR	BI	BB	SO	OBP	Slg
Abbott, Kurt	.279	61	17	2	6	3	15	.313	.492
Aldrete, Mike*	.196	56	11	1	6	5	9	.258	.268
Alicea, Luis#	.325	80	26	0	21	6	8	.356	.488
Allensworth	.248	105	26	4	19	13	24	.331	.429
Alomar, R#	.261	69	18	0	2	5	8	.311	.319
Alou, Moises	.336	125	42	3	23	3	16	.359	.504
Amaro, Ruben#	.208	48	10	1	6	7	9	.321	.333
Anthony, Eric*	.231	39	9	2	8	6	11	.326	.462
Arias, Alex	.413	46	19	0	2	4	1	.462	.522
Aude, Rich	.173	81	14	1	8	2	21	.193	.247
Ausmus, Brad	.297	37	11	0	2	4	3	.357	.378
Bagwell, Jeff	.367	128	47	8	26	11	24	.417	.688
Barberie, B#	.415	65	27	0	4	6	5	.472	.569
Batiste, Kim	.147	34	5	1	3	1	4	.167	.265
Bell, Derek	.316	79	25	2	12	8	14	.379	.443
Bell, Jay	.271	2059	559	35	194	232	375	.347	.403
Belliard, R	.189	370	70	0	20	31	65	.259	.227
Benjamin, M	.171	35	6	0	0	1	7	.216	.200
Berry, Sean	.233	60	14	0	9	7	10	.313	.233
Bichette, D	.373	83	31	2	17	3	18	.400	.542
Biggio, Craig	.284	190	54	1	19	19	24	.354	.389
Blauser, Jeff	.297	138	41	4	16	15	27	.376	.442
Bonds, Barry*	.268	1588	425	78	243	283	267	.379	.490
Bonilla, B#	.278	1465	408	56	237	177	193	.355	.477
Boone, Bret	.273	66	18	0	9	4	10	.333	.348
Branson, Jeff*	.305	59	18	2	13	8	6	.400	.508
Brumfield, J	.272	283	77	4	18	23	49	.333	.399
Bullett, S*	.188	48	9	1	3	2	10	.220	.292
Burks, Ellis	.293	41	12	2	7	5	7	.370	.512
Butler, Brett*	.241	166	40	1	10	17	19	.314	.295
Caminiti, Ken#	.255	161	41	6	21	21	20	.341	.422
Candaele, C#	.195	77	15	0	2	7	3	.262	.260
Cangelosi, J#	.266	301	80	2	21	60	45	.395	.352
Carr, Chuck#	.279	61	17	1	5	4	7	.323	.377
Carreon, Mark	.402	87	35	8	21	7	8	.448	.759
Castilla, V	.148	54	8	2	6	4	7	.220	.333
Cedeno, A	.200	60	12	1	7	4	10	.246	.283
Cianfrocco, A	.326	43	14	0	7	1	8	.356	.465
Clark, Dave*	.288	465	134	25	93	64	105	.373	.514
Clark, Will*	.267	146	39	6	17	9	18	.321	.438
Clayton, R	.263	76	20	0	7	1	12	.275	.329
Colbrunn, G	.296	81	24	4	13	1	12	.298	.494
Cole, Alex*	.307	101	31	0	10	11	23	.375	.426
Coleman, V#	.288	156	45	1	5	11	25	.339	.391
Conine, Jeff	.295	78	23	3	14	12	9	.372	.474
Cordero, Wil	.231	65	15	0	3	6	4	.320	.323
Cummings, M*	.253	190	48	4	23	14	38	.303	.368
Dascenzo, D#	.197	66	13	0	2	6	2	.264	.227
Daulton, D*	.194	134	26	2	14	23	31	.310	.284
Davis, Eric	.326	135	44	8	32	13	32	.384	.615
Dawson, Andre	.215	209	45	10	27	6	35	.239	.397
Decker, Steve	.333	30	10	0	2	6	5	.444	.333
DeShields, D*	.272	169	46	2	15	21	36	.349	.373
Duncan, M	.304	125	38	6	17	5	21	.336	.512
Dunston, S	.283	173	49	4	28	10	27	.319	.434
Dykstra, L*	.287	188	54	2	15	23	19	.368	.410
Eisenreich, J*	.292	48	14	2	8	6	3	.370	.438
Elster, Kevin	.213	89	19	3	14	8	10	.276	.371
Encarnacion	.200	85	17	2	7	9	22	.277	.318
Eusebio, Tony	.258	31	8	0	7	3	4	.306	.323
Fermin, Felix	.282	85	24	0	2	8	6	.361	.306
Finley, Steve*	.331	142	47	5	20	10	15	.377	.521

Batter	Avg	AB	H	HR	BI	BB	SO	OBP	Slg
Fletcher, D*	.272	81	22	3	11	6	8	.337	.420
Galarraga, A	.300	303	91	17	48	15	66	.339	.521
Gant, Ron	.221	149	33	4	20	19	30	.310	.349
Garcia, C	.286	935	267	18	100	57	147	.329	.407
Gilkey, B	.290	138	40	5	16	18	12	.381	.486
Girardi, Joe	.179	84	15	0	4	1	16	.198	.226
Goff, Jerry*	.220	50	11	2	6	7	15	.316	.400
Gonzalez, L*	.330	112	37	4	25	10	9	.391	.563
Grace, Mark*	.294	231	68	3	25	24	17	.360	.420
Grissom, M	.324	173	56	5	23	16	22	.379	.480
Gutierrez, R	.214	42	9	0	3	2	3	.244	.262
Gwynn, Tony*	.356	225	80	4	33	13	12	.388	.520
Harris, Lenny*	.172	87	15	0	7	8	6	.273	.207
Hayes, C	.269	334	90	10	51	31	54	.333	.437
Hernandez, Jo	.231	39	9	2	7	4	13	.302	.487
Hill, G	.365	74	27	5	14	4	15	.397	.635
Hollins, Dave#	.263	76	20	2	5	8	6	.349	.382
Howard, T*	.347	72	25	0	9	6	9	.400	.458
Hudler, Rex	.214	70	15	2	5	1	15	.225	.414
Hundley, Todd#	.216	102	22	3	12	7	29	.264	.373
Hunter, Brian	.270	137	37	6	32	10	29	.311	.482
Hunter, Bri L	.289	45	13	0	0	0	7	.289	.356
Incaviglia, P	.234	47	11	1	6	8	11	.333	.383
James, Dion*	.288	52	15	0	6	6	6	.362	.423
Javier, Stan#	.300	40	12	0	5	6	7	.391	.425
Jefferies, G#	.270	174	47	5	21	17	14	.335	.397
Johnson, Mark*	.261	257	67	17	38	44	62	.379	.525
Jones, C#	.410	39	16	1	6	3	6	.452	.538
Jones, Chris	.324	37	12	1	7	0	10	.324	.405
Jordan, Brian	.267	60	16	5	16	3	8	.328	.533
Jordan, Ricky	.186	59	11	1	3	5	12	.250	.254
Justice, Dave*	.323	96	31	7	18	17	9	.421	.583
Karros, Eric	.314	105	33	1	12	7	19	.357	.429
Kelly, R	.299	67	20	2	10	3	11	.333	.433
Kendall, J	.306	216	66	2	26	9	15	.350	.417
Kent, Jeff	.260	77	20	3	8	0	9	.263	.455
King, Jeff	.261	1609	420	48	265	148	212	.320	.421
Kingery, Mike*	.272	151	41	3	16	18	19	.347	.404
Klesko, Ryan*	.342	38	13	4	9	9	11	.468	.711
Lankford, Ray*	.248	165	41	4	20	15	49	.317	.370
Lansing, Mike	.283	92	26	0	6	8	4	.347	.413
Larkin, Barry	.329	210	69	5	23	19	16	.384	.533
Lemke, Mark#	.248	105	26	2	12	8	6	.296	.371
Lewis, Darren	.357	70	25	0	5	9	5	.438	.386
Liriano, N#	.251	219	55	5	24	19	27	.315	.338
Lopez, Javy	.214	42	9	3	3	2	15	.250	.476
Mabry, John*	.364	44	16	0	6	1	5	.362	.386
Magadan, Dave*	.278	169	47	1	14	30	14	.385	.337
Manwaring, K	.184	76	14	0	5	4	11	.253	.197
Martin, Al*	.296	932	276	37	127	86	210	.355	.494
Martinez, Da*	.261	165	43	2	14	15	31	.320	.376
May, Derrick*	.263	57	15	2	9	3	2	.295	.439
McGee, Willie#	.318	173	55	2	22	7	29	.346	.474
McGriff, Fred*	.205	122	25	5	13	17	36	.300	.361
McRae, Brian*	.280	50	14	1	4	3	4	.333	.420
Merced, O*	.281	1256	353	33	172	178	200	.370	.435
Miller, Orl	.375	48	18	3	14	3	14	.444	.646
Mitchell, K	.277	130	36	11	28	14	15	.347	.562
Mondesi, Raul	.286	56	16	5	15	2	5	.305	.625
Morandini, M*	.302	116	35	0	2	12	17	.377	.414
Morris, Hal*	.354	113	40	2	19	18	17	.447	.478
Mouton, James	.237	38	9	0	3	4	8	.310	.474
Murray, Eddie#	.269	108	29	1	15	12	12	.333	.352
Nixon, Otis#	.330	112	37	0	5	13	12	.400	.366
O'Brien, C	.234	47	11	1	4	2	4	.280	.404
O'Neill, Paul*	.186	86	16	1	13	11	14	.270	.279
Offerman, J#	.233	60	14	0	8	2	7	.270	.350
Oliver, Joe	.299	97	29	4	16	3	15	.320	.474
Orsulak, Joe*	.250	44	11	0	1	2	4	.283	.295
Osik, Keith	.288	59	17	0	6	7	9	.364	.390
Pagnozzi, Tom	.224	161	36	4	17	9	28	.265	.342
Palmeiro, R*	.304	56	17	4	6	3	3	.339	.607
Parent, Mark	.224	156	35	5	20	14	41	.287	.359
Pena, G#	.217	46	10	1	5	7	15	.368	.326
Pena, Tony	.304	69	21	2	10	3	3	.338	.435
Pendleton, T#	.289	232	67	4	30	13	20	.324	.418
Piazza, Mike	.367	90	33	8	22	4	15	.394	.667
Plantier, P*	.324	34	11	6	16	8	13	.442	.853
Prince, Tom	.172	163	28	2	21	19	34	.258	.264
Raines, Tim#	.258	120	31	4	15	20	9	.369	.408
Reed, Jeff*	.167	78	13	0	5	7	9	.235	.192
Reed, Jody	.206	63	13	0	6	7	6	.292	.286
Roberts, Bip#	.241	79	19	0	5	17	12	.375	.266
Sabo, Chris	.228	127	29	4	22	10	10	.279	.378
Samuel, Juan	.256	160	41	4	18	12	37	.316	.394
Sanchez, Rey	.286	56	16	0	6	3	6	.355	.339
Sandberg, R	.296	240	71	7	27	14	23	.335	.458
Sanders, R	.346	107	37	5	20	7	22	.379	.570

THREE RIVERS STADIUM
Home of the Pittsburgh Pirates
Pittsburgh, Pennsylvania   **Artificial**

Batter	Avg	AB	H	HR	BI	BB	SO	OBP	Slg
Santiago, B	.302	162	49	5	21	11	30	.345	.481
Segui, David#	.235	34	8	1	2	3	6	.297	.353
Servais, S	.258	62	16	1	10	0	11	.281	.371
Sheffield, G	.316	76	24	8	20	7	4	.376	.658
Shipley, C	.273	44	12	0	2	1	6	.289	.318
Slaught, Don	.302	733	221	5	89	75	94	.368	.412
Smith, Dwight*	.237	97	23	1	9	8	20	.299	.330
Smith, Ozzie#	.280	243	68	1	15	17	13	.326	.346
Sosa, Sammy	.245	98	24	3	12	2	19	.260	.398
Stocker, K#	.200	50	10	0	4	6	6	.298	.280
Strawberry, D*	.223	121	27	9	25	26	30	.362	.504
Taubensee, E*	.267	60	16	0	10	6	10	.328	.400
Tavarez, Je#	.222	36	8	0	0	2	5	.263	.250
Thompson, Mil*	.305	154	47	1	16	14	20	.363	.377
Thompson, Rob	.321	156	50	3	19	6	24	.358	.436
Thompson, Ry	.286	49	14	3	8	2	11	.308	.571
Veras, Q#	.281	32	9	2	6	10	5	.452	.531
Vizcaino, J#	.241	108	26	0	8	9	16	.297	.306
Walker, Larry*	.218	170	37	3	16	12	32	.278	.329
Wallach, Tim	.228	250	57	3	29	29	39	.307	.336
Walton, J	.304	115	35	1	8	11	22	.370	.383
Webster, L	.241	29	7	0	0	6	7	.371	.345
Wehner, John	.290	252	73	1	20	14	49	.325	.369
Weiss, Walt#	.239	67	16	1	5	10	8	.346	.343
White, R	.218	55	12	1	10	2	8	.246	.345
Whiten, Mark#	.258	62	16	3	9	9	9	.342	.435
Wilkins, Rick*	.353	68	24	6	18	7	11	.421	.691
Williams, Ma	.267	131	35	5	24	10	22	.317	.473
Womack, Tony*	.214	28	6	0	2	5	5	.333	.286
Young, Eric	.213	75	16	0	7	8	9	.298	.293
Young, Kevin	.237	384	91	12	56	34	79	.304	.401
Zeile, Todd	.223	188	42	4	22	25	30	.316	.356

SAN DIEGO/JACK MURPHY STADIUM
Home of the San Diego Padres
San Diego, California   **Grass**

Batter	Avg	AB	H	HR	BI	BB	SO	OBP	Slg
Aldrete, Mike*	.167	30	5	0	1	10	6	.375	.200
Alicea, Luis#	.264	53	14	1	5	8	7	.355	.415
Alomar, R#	.290	863	250	12	91	75	112	.347	.379
Alou, Moises	.330	103	34	4	14	5	13	.361	.563
Anthony, Eric*	.210	81	17	7	19	6	20	.261	.494
Ausmus, Brad	.267	484	129	12	47	41	87	.327	.399
Bagwell, Jeff	.309	136	42	8	25	23	27	.409	.544
Barberie, B#	.245	49	12	1	9	9	12	.362	.408
Bell, Derek	.283	526	149	22	69	39	110	.340	.451
Bell, Jay	.297	165	49	4	21	12	31	.341	.461
Belliard, R	.181	83	15	1	8	1	17	.200	.253
Benjamin, M	.148	54	8	1	2	4	12	.220	.259
Berry, Sean	.362	69	25	4	16	2	13	.380	.638
Bichette, D	.255	102	26	4	9	4	23	.290	.422
Biggio, Craig	.222	212	47	6	17	24	33	.311	.344
Blauser, Jeff	.217	207	45	4	16	20	46	.281	.333
Bonds, Barry*	.380	205	78	20	48	51	28	.496	.751
Bonilla, B#	.235	179	42	9	31	23	35	.316	.436
Boone, Bret	.289	76	22	3	15	4	12	.325	.474
Branson, Jeff*	.317	63	20	2	7	11	7	.419	.460
Brogna, Rico*	.184	49	9	3	6	3	16	.226	.388
Burks, Ellis	.246	57	14	2	4	6	11	.317	.439
Butler, Brett*	.319	238	76	2	22	32	29	.399	.408
Caminiti, Ken#	.290	689	200	39	128	79	122	.361	.508
Candaele, C#	.243	74	18	0	5	5	13	.288	.311
Cangelosi, J#	.143	35	5	0	1	5	6	.250	.171
Carr, Chuck#	.278	36	10	0	6	4	4	.341	.361
Carreon, Mark	.140	57	8	1	5	4	9	.197	.263
Carter, Joe	.220	322	71	12	53	18	49	.263	.366
Castilla, V	.247	73	18	1	6	0	11	.247	.356
Cedeno, A	.213	320	68	7	27	27	73	.282	.306
Cianfrocco, A	.251	402	101	10	53	20	93	.291	.398
Clark, Dave*	.278	36	10	1	5	5	13	.366	.389
Clark, Phil	.291	244	71	11	43	15	32	.339	.475
Clark, Will*	.321	224	72	11	48	20	37	.378	.571
Clayton, R	.255	102	26	1	12	4	17	.290	.353
Coleman, V#	.277	119	33	0	5	11	29	.338	.286
Conine, Jeff	.224	58	13	3	9	7	23	.308	.431
Cora, Joey#	.235	170	40	0	7	21	19	.321	.265
Cordero, Wil	.221	68	15	3	12	8	15	.312	.368
Daulton, D*	.232	112	26	3	13	16	25	.326	.375
Davis, Eric	.291	172	50	12	33	30	47	.402	.535
Dawson, Andre	.338	133	45	8	31	11	14	.381	.602
Decker, Steve	.286	28	8	1	2	6	5	.412	.429
DeShields, D*	.242	153	37	1	13	22	28	.337	.346
Duncan, M	.319	116	37	3	12	5	31	.360	.491
Dunston, S	.188	138	26	4	7	3	29	.211	.290
Dykstra, L*	.218	142	31	2	5	9	14	.270	.303
Eisenreich, J*	.271	59	16	0	5	4	6	.313	.322
Elster, Kevin	.224	49	11	2	8	7	8	.316	.367

SAN DIEGO/JACK MURPHY STADIUM
Home of the San Diego Padres
San Diego, California   Grass

Batter	Avg	AB	H	HR	BI	BB	SO	OBP	Slg
Finley, Steve*	.304	635	193	19	62	64	80	.369	.479
Flaherty, J	.325	120	39	5	19	2	14	.336	.500
Fletcher, D*	.319	91	29	4	13	11	8	.402	.505
Frazier, Lou#	.400	35	14	0	5	4	6	.462	.514
Galarraga, A	.294	201	59	16	45	10	47	.329	.587
Gant, Ron	.261	180	47	9	33	21	35	.333	.456
Garcia, C	.299	77	23	1	14	3	9	.345	.429
Gilkey, B	.271	96	26	3	15	5	15	.308	.438
Girardi, Joe	.230	74	17	1	5	7	10	.301	.297
Gomez, Chris	.237	135	32	1	13	21	28	.342	.289
Gonzalez, L*	.189	106	20	1	13	9	19	.246	.255
Grace, Mark*	.339	177	60	5	28	20	15	.400	.508
Greene, W*	.229	35	8	1	3	7	8	.357	.400
Grissom, M	.296	159	47	2	20	16	17	.360	.377
Grudzielanek	.146	48	7	0	1	3	13	.196	.167
Gutierrez, R	.254	370	94	6	28	46	87	.343	.324
Gwynn, Chris*	.116	69	8	1	3	4	17	.164	.188
Gwynn, Tony*	.345	2526	872	33	283	255	125	.403	.463
Hansen, Dave*	.316	38	12	0	4	4	7	.381	.421
Harris, Lenny*	.311	103	32	1	9	9	6	.366	.388
Hayes, C	.256	121	31	0	13	10	19	.311	.306
Henderson, R	.268	228	61	6	15	62	38	.431	.386
Hernandez, Jo	.238	42	10	2	6	4	8	.304	.500
Hill, G	.289	45	13	5	7	6	11	.373	.711
Hollandsworth*	.294	34	10	1	3	1	7	.314	.500
Hollins, Dave#	.284	81	23	5	23	6	18	.344	.531
Howard, T*	.252	214	54	4	19	13	41	.298	.336
Howell, Jack*	.197	76	15	3	9	11	13	.299	.342
Hudler, Rex	.366	41	15	1	3	2	2	.395	.512
Hundley, Todd#	.179	84	15	2	6	8	23	.258	.310
Hunter, Brian	.235	51	12	3	12	2	8	.246	.529
Hunter, Bri L	.368	38	14	0	4	1	9	.385	.421
Hyers, Tim*	.163	49	8	0	0	3	9	.212	.163
Incaviglia, P	.209	43	9	1	2	1	11	.227	.326
James, Dion*	.281	64	18	0	3	5	7	.333	.391
Javier, Stan#	.255	55	14	0	1	9	9	.359	.309
Jefferies, G#	.284	141	40	1	12	6	12	.309	.348
Johnson, Bri	.272	243	66	6	32	6	42	.293	.391
Jones, C#	.275	40	11	2	4	5	4	.356	.500
Jordan, Brian	.246	65	16	3	7	4	13	.290	.400
Jordan, Ricky	.258	89	23	4	12	2	14	.283	.438
Joyner, Wally*	.243	185	45	5	27	32	34	.355	.368
Justice, Dave*	.279	140	39	3	18	15	25	.350	.407
Karros, Eric	.288	118	34	6	12	9	27	.344	.492
Kelly, R	.316	38	12	2	4	1	6	.333	.526
Kent, Jeff	.239	71	17	3	12	2	23	.267	.394
King, Jeff	.253	99	25	3	17	17	12	.356	.384
Kingery, Mike*	.309	55	17	1	10	6	6	.365	.400
Klesko, Ryan*	.385	52	20	4	11	5	10	.439	.712
Lampkin, Tom*	.265	83	22	1	6	4	12	.307	.373
Lankford, Ray*	.155	84	13	0	3	8	27	.228	.214
Lansing, Mike	.300	70	21	1	7	2	8	.329	.414
Larkin, Barry	.296	233	69	6	28	17	30	.349	.464
Lemke, Mark#	.281	89	25	3	9	12	10	.363	.393
Lewis, Darren	.275	69	19	0	7	7	8	.351	.377
Livingstone*	.293	249	73	2	20	15	31	.333	.398
Lockhart, K*	.258	31	8	2	6	2	4	.294	.452
Lopez, Javy	.286	49	14	3	12	0	8	.294	.510
Lopez, Luis#	.223	197	44	3	20	14	40	.272	.330
Magadan, Dave*	.315	92	29	2	10	19	22	.434	.380
Manwaring, K	.254	114	29	0	11	10	13	.328	.325
Martin, Al*	.320	75	24	3	12	6	16	.361	.493
Martinez, Da*	.260	127	33	1	14	14	28	.331	.346
May, Derrick*	.236	55	13	2	7	4	8	.288	.364
McGee, Willie#	.310	203	63	1	20	14	39	.358	.389
McGriff, Fred*	.274	723	198	49	139	141	159	.392	.523
McRae, Brian#	.333	51	17	0	2	4	7	.414	.412
Merced, O*	.252	115	29	3	24	21	17	.360	.374
Miller, Orl	.188	32	6	1	1	3	10	.257	.313
Mitchell, K	.291	230	67	15	49	22	41	.353	.561
Mondesi, Raul	.281	64	18	3	14	3	11	.313	.469
Morandini, M*	.198	106	21	2	7	5	19	.241	.283
Morris, Hal*	.247	174	43	3	19	13	33	.298	.333
Murray, Eddie#	.321	137	44	11	26	20	18	.398	.606
Newfield, M	.245	102	25	2	16	8	15	.298	.353
Nieves, M#	.170	165	28	7	21	9	68	.219	.309
Nixon, Otis#	.328	67	22	1	5	8	9	.400	.373
O'Neill, Paul*	.297	138	41	2	16	15	28	.361	.420
Offerman, J#	.220	82	18	0	7	9	16	.290	.232
Oliver, Joe	.255	98	25	1	13	5	22	.288	.347
Orsulak, Joe*	.183	60	11	0	1	2	8	.210	.217
Pagnozzi, Tom	.248	101	25	2	12	3	10	.269	.396
Palmeiro, R*	.400	35	14	1	3	2	1	.421	.571
Parent, Mark	.230	226	52	16	36	13	49	.269	.482
Pena, Tony	.182	44	8	0	5	9	9	.321	.205
Pendleton, T#	.283	230	65	6	29	13	24	.322	.404
Petagine, Rob*	.244	45	11	2	8	18	11	.460	.467
Piazza, Mike	.338	77	26	7	21	7	13	.388	.675

SAN DIEGO/JACK MURPHY STADIUM
Home of the San Diego Padres
San Diego, California — Grass

Batter	Avg	AB	H	HR	BI	BB	SO	OBP	Slg
Plantier, P*	.213	478	102	25	72	56	121	.302	.416
Raines, Tim#	.226	84	19	1	7	21	6	.398	.310
Reed, Jeff*	.245	106	26	2	8	18	25	.355	.349
Reed, Jody	.260	457	119	5	44	66	40	.353	.335
Roberts, Bip#	.296	1091	323	12	87	78	149	.349	.390
Rodriguez, H*	.120	50	6	1	5	0	8	.118	.240
Sabo, Chris	.278	169	47	3	13	9	19	.318	.391
Samuel, Juan	.247	162	40	8	19	12	33	.301	.444
Sanchez, Rey	.373	59	22	0	2	1	3	.377	.441
Sandberg, R	.254	169	43	7	24	13	24	.312	.444
Sanders, R	.329	82	27	3	13	11	23	.421	.561
Santiago, B	.265	1482	392	43	196	66	259	.295	.404
Segui, David#	.195	41	8	0	0	2	10	.233	.293
Servais, S	.224	58	13	1	2	5	8	.297	.293
Sheaffer, D	.268	41	11	2	4	5	6	.340	.415
Sheffield, G	.356	450	160	31	87	47	34	.417	.651
Shipley, C	.261	364	95	4	40	13	51	.287	.360
Slaught, Don	.386	44	17	2	8	4	8	.438	.636
Smith, Dwight*	.293	58	17	3	6	2	16	.317	.517
Smith, Ozzie#	.257	191	49	0	18	15	13	.309	.319
Sosa, Sammy	.330	88	29	9	22	4	26	.368	.648
Stillwell, K#	.227	278	63	2	25	28	47	.297	.291
Stocker, K#	.265	68	18	0	5	10	26	.358	.309
Strawberry, D*	.237	139	33	6	13	19	28	.325	.460
Taubensee, E*	.288	59	17	1	5	4	10	.333	.373
Thompson, Mil*	.281	146	41	2	16	15	23	.352	.404
Thompson, Rob	.220	227	50	10	30	29	47	.305	.401
Thompson, Ry	.256	39	10	1	2	4	11	.370	.333
Vaughn, Greg	.233	60	14	5	9	7	16	.324	.533
Vizcaino, J#	.225	89	20	0	4	1	20	.242	.247
Walker, Larry*	.258	132	34	10	29	17	23	.344	.530
Wallach, Tim	.267	206	55	8	28	14	32	.315	.422
Walton, J	.302	43	13	1	4	5	6	.388	.395
Weiss, Walt#	.261	92	24	2	2	11	14	.340	.380
Whiten, Mark#	.264	53	14	3	6	7	12	.350	.491
Wilkins, Rick*	.288	59	17	1	5	9	12	.382	.441
Williams, E	.298	225	67	10	37	21	42	.367	.498
Williams, Ma	.269	219	59	7	29	9	44	.306	.402
Young, Eric	.177	79	14	0	4	9	8	.267	.228
Young, Kevin	.225	40	9	0	1	4	9	.295	.300
Zeile, Todd	.228	127	29	3	17	18	23	.331	.362

3COM PARK
Home of the San Francisco Giants
San Francisco, California — Grass

Batter	Avg	AB	H	HR	BI	BB	SO	OBP	Slg
Abbott, Kurt	.206	34	7	1	6	1	8	.250	.294
Aldrete, Mike*	.266	372	99	10	43	54	62	.359	.382
Alfonzo, E	.294	34	10	2	9	1	5	.306	.500
Alicea, Luis#	.241	58	14	1	5	10	7	.357	.362
Alomar, R#	.160	81	13	1	6	7	7	.233	.222
Alou, Moises	.318	66	21	5	10	6	14	.370	.636
Anthony, Eric*	.236	110	26	9	21	12	25	.309	.491
Aurilia, Rich	.260	181	47	1	13	12	31	.309	.298
Ausmus, Brad	.375	40	15	2	5	1	8	.405	.575
Bagwell, Jeff	.408	142	58	9	35	29	30	.517	.725
Barberie, B#	.321	53	17	1	6	6	6	.379	.453
Batiste, Kim	.171	82	14	1	3	2	22	.200	.256
Bell, Derek	.282	71	20	0	9	4	12	.321	.324
Bell, Jay	.237	139	33	5	16	21	34	.346	.388
Belliard, R	.149	94	14	0	2	4	18	.184	.191
Benard, M*	.251	267	67	2	9	35	44	.341	.315
Benjamin, M	.184	304	56	8	25	18	77	.231	.306
Berry, Sean	.286	63	18	3	17	5	10	.342	.476
Bichette, D	.247	85	21	3	8	2	14	.273	.388
Biggio, Craig	.282	220	62	7	25	23	18	.358	.409
Blauser, Jeff	.323	161	52	4	15	17	25	.392	.472
Bogar, Tim	.194	36	7	0	1	3	7	.256	.222
Bonds, Barry*	.300	1056	317	79	219	254	151	.436	.594
Bonilla, B#	.263	194	51	7	21	21	33	.335	.433
Boone, Bret	.286	56	16	4	8	3	10	.339	.554
Branson, Jeff*	.217	46	10	2	8	1	12	.229	.370
Brogna, Rico*	.243	37	9	2	4	2	8	.282	.459
Brumfield, J	.238	42	10	1	1	4	7	.319	.333
Burks, Ellis	.159	44	7	2	4	8	15	.288	.318
Butler, Brett*	.310	1022	317	8	73	149	100	.399	.387
Caminiti, Ken#	.261	249	65	12	43	25	41	.332	.458
Candaele, C#	.254	71	18	2	7	6	7	.312	.352
Canizaro, Jay	.200	55	11	1	5	4	19	.250	.309
Carr, Chuck#	.255	51	13	0	2	4	8	.309	.255
Carreon, Mark	.279	488	136	16	82	39	58	.336	.445
Carter, Joe	.176	34	6	0	2	4	4	.300	.235
Castilla, V	.254	71	18	0	5	3	12	.286	.338
Cedeno, A	.231	65	15	4	11	4	20	.286	.477
Clark, Will*	.303	1940	588	86	341	248	329	.379	.515
Clayton, R	.253	926	234	11	91	70	171	.305	.349
Colbrunn, G	.259	81	21	3	12	3	15	.295	.420

3COM PARK
Home of the San Francisco Giants
San Francisco, California — Grass

Batter	Avg	AB	H	HR	BI	BB	SO	OBP	Slg
Coleman, V#	.304	125	38	0	4	13	20	.367	.344
Conine, Jeff	.253	75	19	5	16	12	14	.356	.493
Cordero, Wil	.338	68	23	3	10	2	7	.357	.544
Cruz, Jacob*	.213	47	10	3	6	8	17	.339	.426
Daulton, D*	.187	107	20	2	8	16	18	.310	.280
Davis, Chili#	.242	223	54	9	28	38	50	.352	.404
Davis, Eric	.288	198	57	12	43	28	48	.381	.510
Dawson, Andre	.266	143	38	8	29	5	18	.291	.469
Decker, Steve	.196	224	44	5	27	17	40	.255	.299
DeShields, D*	.228	162	37	1	8	19	31	.308	.278
Duncan, M	.185	151	28	3	11	3	26	.205	.318
Dunston, S	.299	261	78	10	38	12	36	.336	.475
Dykstra, L*	.278	144	40	2	12	15	14	.346	.396
Eisenreich, J*	.236	72	17	2	9	4	9	.286	.389
Elster, Kevin	.200	50	10	1	3	3	9	.245	.320
Faneyte, R	.190	63	12	0	4	12	22	.320	.238
Finley, Steve*	.326	144	47	7	19	13	9	.390	.507
Fletcher, D*	.289	90	26	2	11	3	11	.312	.389
Galarraga, A	.255	192	49	7	26	14	31	.324	.411
Gant, Ron	.246	199	49	13	32	21	36	.320	.472
Garcia, C	.281	64	18	0	3	8	11	.365	.281
Gilkey, B	.340	100	34	6	17	8	13	.393	.600
Girardi, Joe	.286	91	26	1	8	6	16	.333	.385
Gonzalez, L*	.352	125	44	2	24	12	20	.397	.512
Grace, Mark*	.275	193	53	2	20	10	16	.309	.363
Greene, W*	.275	40	11	1	9	4	13	.341	.500
Grissom, M	.250	136	34	3	11	8	21	.295	.375
Grudzielanek,	.231	52	12	0	2	4	9	.298	.250
Gutierrez, R	.244	41	10	0	3	6	7	.340	.244
Gwynn, Chris*	.389	54	21	1	12	4	10	.431	.500
Gwynn, Tony*	.302	242	73	1	25	16	11	.342	.393
Hansen, Dave*	.212	52	11	1	5	1	8	.222	.308
Harris, Lenny*	.314	121	38	0	7	6	5	.344	.372
Hayes, C	.274	135	37	6	19	8	22	.313	.467
Hill, G	.272	437	119	23	91	34	89	.327	.501
Hollandsworth*	.344	32	11	1	5	3	5	.400	.563
Hollins, Dave#	.260	77	20	3	8	8	16	.352	.429
Hudler, Rex	.133	30	4	0	0	3	6	.235	.133
Hundley, Todd#	.235	68	16	6	19	6	16	.316	.529
Hunter, Brian	.206	63	13	3	9	5	11	.261	.397
Incaviglia, P	.243	37	9	2	4	1	10	.282	.459
James, Dion*	.215	65	14	1	1	9	13	.311	.277
Javier, Stan#	.244	156	38	1	12	17	29	.326	.340
Jefferies, G#	.238	122	29	2	8	12	5	.301	.328
Johnson, Char	.194	36	7	0	3	5	11	.293	.250
Jones, Chris	.308	39	12	1	5	3	10	.349	.538
Jones, Dax	.097	31	3	0	3	4	8	.194	.097
Jordan, Brian	.180	61	11	2	6	3	14	.239	.311
Jordan, Ricky	.250	84	21	2	6	3	17	.276	.369
Justice, Dave*	.243	136	33	5	14	20	23	.338	.390
Karros, Eric	.250	136	34	10	26	10	24	.320	.544
Kelly, R	.250	56	14	3	6	5	11	.323	.500
Kent, Jeff	.259	81	21	4	9	8	15	.330	.432
King, Jeff	.259	112	29	6	23	11	13	.325	.464
Kingery, Mike*	.246	207	51	0	16	21	21	.322	.300
Lampkin, Tom*	.221	140	31	6	26	20	17	.323	.379
Lankford, Ray*	.213	108	23	5	13	12	24	.301	.435
Lansing, Mike	.277	65	18	3	8	6	9	.342	.477
Larkin, Barry	.249	193	48	8	28	24	13	.332	.420
Lemke, Mark#	.151	126	19	0	7	9	11	.204	.190
Lewis, Darren	.232	896	208	8	63	80	95	.303	.300
Liriano, N#	.261	46	12	2	7	5	4	.327	.457
Lopez, Javy	.412	34	14	3	6	1	0	.429	.735
Magadan, Dave*	.269	108	29	0	18	16	11	.357	.324
Manwaring, K	.257	1019	262	9	107	64	157	.309	.340
Martin, Al*	.221	77	17	0	5	6	22	.277	.312
Martinez, Da*	.232	353	82	3	27	31	56	.297	.314
May, Derrick*	.333	63	21	1	9	6	5	.400	.476
McCarty, Dave	.250	96	24	5	18	7	19	.308	.438
McGee, Willie*	.296	850	252	5	72	60	114	.341	.368
McGriff, Fred*	.226	115	26	7	13	14	23	.313	.452
McRae, Brian#	.304	46	14	0	6	3	5	.365	.457
Merced, O*	.372	86	32	2	15	11	11	.449	.488
Miller, Orl	.219	32	7	0	5	3	9	.278	.313
Mitchell, K	.282	1164	328	69	214	135	191	.357	.530
Mondesi, Raul	.241	83	20	1	4	9	20	.315	.337
Morandini, M*	.295	95	28	1	8	9	13	.362	.379
Morris, Hal*	.293	116	34	6	16	7	13	.331	.517
Mouton, James	.195	41	8	0	3	2	4	.250	.195
Mueller, Bill#	.308	107	33	0	8	12	16	.377	.374
Murray, Eddie#	.254	138	35	10	34	14	15	.316	.464
Nixon, Otis#	.284	88	25	1	8	9	16	.347	.352
O'Neill, Paul*	.239	155	37	6	21	16	22	.308	.374
Offerman, J#	.216	111	24	2	18	18	18	.318	.315
Oliver, Joe	.159	82	13	1	9	5	21	.207	.268
Pagnozzi, Tom	.313	96	30	0	9	5	13	.347	.354
Parent, Mark	.250	40	10	1	4	4	7	.318	.325
Parker, Rick	.189	53	10	0	2	4	9	.246	.189

3COM PARK
Home of the San Francisco Giants
San Francisco, California — Grass

Batter	Avg	AB	H	HR	BI	BB	SO	OBP	Slg
Pena, Tony	.103	39	4	0	0	1	6	.125	.128
Pendleton, T#	.273	227	62	8	28	15	32	.316	.436
Phillips, J*	.185	162	30	5	17	7	51	.219	.296
Piazza, Mike	.284	109	31	3	19	8	16	.336	.431
Plantier, P*	.209	43	9	2	9	9	10	.327	.395
Raines, Tim#	.300	90	27	2	12	14	7	.390	.489
Reed, Jeff*	.256	281	72	5	24	31	42	.331	.335
Reed, Jody	.307	75	23	2	10	4	8	.342	.440
Roberts, Bip#	.313	112	35	0	10	15	14	.388	.366
Rodriguez, H*	.253	83	21	7	13	7	18	.311	.542
Sabo, Chris	.238	122	29	4	9	11	16	.311	.418
Samuel, Juan	.237	135	32	2	9	9	34	.281	.356
Sanchez, Rey	.313	67	21	0	3	7	3	.373	.388
Sandberg, R	.351	171	60	5	13	15	19	.399	.468
Sanders, R	.208	77	16	1	7	9	23	.284	.299
Santangelo, F#	.226	31	7	1	5	3	5	.286	.323
Santiago, B	.308	221	68	13	38	13	38	.345	.534
Scarsone, S	.243	367	89	12	47	29	114	.305	.409
Segui, David#	.293	58	17	3	11	11	4	.406	.517
Servais, S	.345	58	20	2	11	4	9	.415	.552
Sheaffer, D	.147	34	5	0	3	1	2	.171	.147
Sheffield, G	.289	83	24	10	25	13	13	.390	.699
Shipley, C	.178	45	8	2	5	0	7	.178	.333
Slaught, Don	.319	47	15	2	5	3	5	.360	.511
Smith, Dwight*	.373	75	28	1	5	4	8	.413	.453
Smith, Ozzie!	.257	148	38	0	8	11	10	.306	.318
Sosa, Sammy	.226	84	19	3	13	8	27	.293	.417
Stillwell, K#	.122	49	6	0	3	1	5	.137	.163
Stocker, K#	.170	53	9	0	1	5	14	.267	.170
Strawberry, D*	.208	173	36	7	23	32	41	.333	.364
Taubensee, E*	.182	55	10	1	3	6	13	.262	.273
Thompson, Mil*	.231	130	30	2	6	9	12	.296	.338
Thompson, Rob	.263	2003	526	64	222	219	422	.344	.433
Thompson, Ry	.275	51	14	4	6	1	17	.302	.529
VanderWal, J*	.377	53	20	3	7	8	3	.468	.585
Veras, Q#	.156	32	5	0	0	7	4	.308	.219
Vizcaino, J#	.326	92	30	1	8	4	7	.351	.467
Walker, Larry*	.262	126	33	8	22	15	24	.352	.484
Wallach, Tim	.220	173	38	5	25	12	34	.269	.341
Walton, J	.238	42	10	0	2	4	5	.304	.310
Weiss, Walt#	.250	76	19	0	6	16	10	.380	.303
White, R	.412	51	21	3	9	2	7	.444	.765
Whiten, Mark#	.214	56	12	1	3	9	11	.323	.304
Wilkins, Rick*	.241	141	34	8	22	23	37	.343	.461
Williams, Ma	.267	2041	544	129	371	141	432	.317	.514
Wilson, Desi*	.310	58	18	0	5	4	14	.355	.328
Young, Eric	.338	71	24	1	6	7	7	.413	.423
Zeile, Todd	.267	135	36	5	23	13	29	.333	.407

THE KINGDOME
Home of the Seattle Mariners
Seattle, Washington — Artificial

Batter	Avg	AB	H	HR	BI	BB	SO	OBP	Slg
Aldrete, Mike*	.286	28	8	2	7	6	5	.400	.571
Alomar, R#	.357	126	45	2	23	14	16	.423	.516
Alomar Jr, S	.185	81	15	1	11	3	12	.218	.272
Amaral, Rich	.271	584	158	4	54	67	82	.351	.351
Anderson, Brd*	.264	159	42	8	26	23	25	.364	.528
Anderson, G*	.263	38	10	2	4	5	6	.349	.526
Anthony, Eric*	.281	114	32	3	15	14	31	.359	.456
Baerga, C#	.258	128	33	0	10	6	18	.314	.336
Baines, H*	.246	175	43	2	22	26	26	.335	.354
Becker, Rich*	.273	55	15	0	5	9	18	.375	.382
Belle, Albert	.317	120	38	9	21	13	23	.390	.600
Berroa, G	.220	50	11	0	6	4	9	.278	.260
Bichette, D	.211	57	12	1	8	4	14	.258	.351
Blowers, Mike	.273	564	154	28	103	82	165	.367	.489
Boggs, Wade*	.317	202	64	3	26	29	13	.397	.455
Bonilla, B#	.273	33	9	4	10	5	6	.350	.758
Boone, Bret	.257	191	49	9	27	9	47	.294	.471
Borders, Pat	.266	94	25	3	7	4	17	.296	.436
Bordick, Mike	.230	100	23	0	9	16	16	.339	.260
Bragg, Darren*	.248	202	50	5	22	23	42	.328	.386
Brosius, S	.233	60	14	1	4	9	16	.361	.333
Buhner, Jay	.259	1681	436	102	322	269	458	.365	.508
Burks, Ellis	.294	143	42	7	23	13	26	.357	.517
Canseco, Jose	.214	173	37	8	28	23	54	.302	.434
Carter, Joe	.255	200	51	8	38	13	40	.302	.440
Cirillo, Jeff	.121	33	4	0	1	3	6	.216	.212
Clark, Will*	.204	49	10	0	7	13	8	.385	.265
Coleman, V#	.273	110	30	1	6	7	27	.322	.382
Cora, Joey#	.295	522	154	3	44	44	39	.358	.395
Cordova, M	.306	49	15	0	8	4	10	.382	.469
Curtis, Chad	.322	115	37	6	19	15	16	.410	.583
Cuyler, Milt#	.281	57	16	3	7	5	8	.359	.509
Davis, Chili#	.292	161	47	4	24	21	40	.372	.441
Davis, Russ	.231	104	24	3	12	10	37	.304	.385

283

THE KINGDOME
Home of the Seattle Mariners
Seattle, Washington   **Artificial**

Batter	Avg	AB	H	HR	BI	BB	SO	OBP	Slg
Deer, Rob	.250	108	27	6	15	19	46	.357	.472
Devereaux, M	.248	149	37	3	22	13	29	.307	.356
Diaz, Alex#	.264	197	52	4	18	7	22	.298	.355
DiSarcina, G	.355	107	38	1	14	4	5	.384	.449
Durham, Ray#	.349	43	15	1	5	7	11	.440	.465
Easley, D	.170	47	8	0	2	2	11	.200	.170
Edmonds, Jim*	.289	38	11	2	5	1	8	.317	.474
Eisenreich, J*	.236	89	21	3	13	6	5	.278	.393
Espinoza, A	.264	87	23	0	7	2	13	.286	.356
Fermin, Felix	.285	309	88	0	24	6	17	.309	.346
Fielder, C	.273	165	45	10	32	30	44	.387	.521
Finley, Steve*	.265	34	9	0	1	4	4	.342	.265
Franco, Julio	.282	177	50	8	27	13	35	.325	.475
Frye, Jeff	.306	36	11	0	3	7	6	.444	.417
Fryman, T	.277	141	39	3	27	11	38	.327	.411
Gaetti, Gary	.213	202	43	7	20	14	37	.261	.356
Gagne, Greg	.228	145	33	2	8	9	45	.282	.324
Gallego, Mike	.250	96	24	2	12	11	24	.345	.365
Gates, Brent#	.411	56	23	0	11	7	12	.462	.554
Gomez, Chris	.341	41	14	3	6	2	9	.378	.634
Gomez, Leo	.245	49	12	1	7	7	15	.344	.347
Gonzales, R	.276	76	21	1	5	8	11	.368	.368
Gonzalez, A	.154	39	6	0	3	1	14	.175	.231
Gonzalez, J	.266	143	38	10	27	10	32	.323	.552
Goodwin, Tom*	.415	41	17	0	5	10	6	.519	.463
Grebeck, C	.226	53	12	1	2	8	9	.328	.377
Greenwell, M*	.302	172	52	6	40	24	20	.398	.459
Greer, Rusty*	.410	39	16	2	7	3	7	.452	.692
Griffey Jr, K*	.314	1925	604	128	376	263	290	.398	.589
Guillen, O*	.247	162	40	2	21	7	15	.275	.358
Hall, Mel*	.308	91	28	2	9	9	14	.363	.440
Hamilton, D*	.339	118	40	2	14	13	8	.409	.492
Haselman, B	.225	142	32	4	17	10	28	.282	.380
Henderson, R	.304	148	45	4	18	30	21	.420	.466
Higginson, B*	.281	32	9	1	5	2	8	.343	.469
Hill, G	.154	39	6	0	2	5	9	.244	.179
Hoiles, Chris	.236	106	25	3	14	17	30	.352	.377
Hollins, Dave*	.349	63	22	2	13	10	11	.455	.524
Howard, Dave#	.130	54	7	0	6	3	12	.172	.185
Howell, Jack*	.265	83	22	5	12	6	21	.319	.518
Hudler, Rex	.425	40	17	2	7	1	10	.452	.650
Huff, Michael	.212	33	7	1	3	3	9	.289	.333
Hulse, David*	.122	41	5	0	2	1	4	.143	.171
Hunter, Brian	.281	96	27	2	15	7	21	.330	.417
Huson, Jeff*	.160	50	8	1	1	5	7	.236	.280
Incaviglia, P	.329	79	26	5	19	3	16	.391	.608
Jaha, John	.235	51	12	5	12	6	15	.339	.549
James, Dion*	.361	61	22	2	8	3	5	.391	.492
Javier, Stan#	.290	93	27	2	16	6	14	.330	.462
Jefferson, R*	.261	119	31	6	24	12	36	.326	.445
Jeter, Derek	.281	32	9	1	4	3	5	.333	.406
Johnson, L*	.333	144	48	1	18	14	13	.388	.451
Joyner, Wally*	.262	168	44	6	27	24	28	.359	.429
Karkovice, J	.216	88	19	3	9	9	32	.290	.364
Kelly, Pat	.129	62	8	0	10	2	16	.162	.210
Kelly, R	.278	97	27	2	10	10	21	.346	.412
Kingery, Mike*	.265	283	75	8	35	23	41	.322	.452
Knoblauch, C	.208	120	25	1	10	11	22	.289	.308
Kreuter, Chad#	.253	99	25	2	10	13	24	.339	.404
Leius, Scott	.246	57	14	2	6	11	10	.368	.386
Lewis, Mark	.200	60	12	1	4	5	15	.269	.267
Leyritz, Jim	.319	72	23	4	16	8	11	.402	.583
Liriano, N#	.186	59	11	0	2	8	9	.284	.254
Listach, Pat#	.220	82	18	0	9	5	17	.264	.256
Lofton, Kenny*	.244	90	22	0	3	5	12	.284	.267
Lovullo, T#	.269	52	14	2	6	6	10	.345	.500
Macfarlane, M	.222	108	24	4	11	14	32	.325	.398
Magadan, Dave*	.255	102	26	0	14	24	12	.391	.333
Manto, Jeff	.214	42	9	2	6	6	12	.327	.429
Martinez, E	.321	1528	490	57	239	277	225	.428	.529
Martinez, T*	.258	897	231	45	162	112	136	.341	.465
Marzano, John	.232	56	13	0	2	2	5	.267	.286
Matheny, Mike	.265	34	9	1	2	2	9	.306	.441
Mayne, Brent*	.231	39	9	0	2	3	9	.302	.256
McGriff, Fred*	.333	72	24	12	32	8	24	.412	.875
McGwire, Mark	.237	156	37	13	34	32	33	.368	.519
McLemore, M#	.264	121	32	1	12	20	15	.373	.339
McRae, Brian#	.143	91	13	0	5	13	18	.250	.231
Meares, Pat	.328	67	22	4	18	3	14	.366	.567
Mitchell, Kei	.184	38	7	2	4	10	5	.347	.342
Mitchell, K	.319	207	66	5	41	17	25	.368	.473
Molitor, Paul	.339	189	64	4	26	21	26	.400	.513
Munoz, Pedro	.367	60	22	2	9	1	19	.387	.550
Murray, Eddie*	.276	87	24	3	11	4	6	.308	.425
Myers, Greg*	.253	91	23	1	21	5	10	.293	.374
Naehring, Tim	.269	52	14	2	4	12	11	.415	.442
Newfield, M	.184	103	19	1	11	6	18	.227	.252
Newson, W*	.302	53	16	1	6	13	12	.439	.415

THE KINGDOME
Home of the Seattle Mariners
Seattle, Washington — Artificial

Batter	Avg	AB	H	HR	BI	BB	SO	OBP	Slg
Nilsson, Dave*	.385	52	20	5	19	3	3	.439	.788
Nixon, Otis*	.356	45	16	0	2	7	10	.442	.444
O'Brien, C	.270	37	10	1	5	3	4	.400	.405
O'Neill, Paul*	.304	69	21	0	12	14	14	.422	.406
Olerud, John*	.224	107	24	6	19	20	26	.341	.411
Orsulak, Joe*	.364	55	20	2	11	6	6	.435	.600
Palmeiro, R*	.331	172	57	9	20	14	23	.389	.552
Palmer, Dean	.224	98	22	5	14	10	33	.296	.459
Paquette, C	.189	74	14	4	12	5	27	.238	.405
Pena, Tony	.269	78	21	2	6	5	10	.321	.385
Phillips, T#	.263	205	54	10	28	38	32	.380	.459
Pirkl, Greg	.177	62	11	3	9	2	15	.212	.387
Polonia, Luis*	.283	145	41	1	6	12	24	.335	.393
Raines, Tim#	.221	86	19	2	9	9	14	.295	.360
Ramirez, M	.262	42	11	3	9	6	9	.354	.500
Reboulet, J	.306	49	15	0	4	6	13	.368	.388
Reed, Jody	.210	81	17	0	0	10	10	.312	.272
Ripken, Billy	.300	100	30	3	18	7	16	.349	.450
Ripken, Cal	.323	232	75	8	36	27	22	.392	.487
Rodriguez, Al	.348	368	128	19	65	37	74	.407	.595
Rodriguez, I	.261	111	29	1	6	9	12	.320	.342
Salmon, Tim	.207	92	19	4	17	15	30	.321	.370
Samuel, Juan	.125	32	4	1	2	7	12	.282	.219
Schofield, D	.225	80	18	1	7	14	13	.340	.300
Seitzer, K	.333	177	59	4	23	27	28	.411	.446
Sheets, Andy	.167	42	7	0	1	5	17	.255	.190
Sheffield, G	.255	47	12	0	6	3	5	.288	.298
Shumpert, T	.294	51	15	1	8	4	10	.357	.471
Sierra, Ruben#	.327	251	82	12	45	31	42	.392	.550
Snow, J.T.#	.228	57	13	0	4	10	11	.362	.263
Sojo, Luis	.222	454	101	10	52	24	42	.264	.333
Sorrento, P*	.277	274	76	15	55	35	66	.363	.522
Sosa, Sammy	.229	35	8	1	7	1	7	.263	.371
Spiers, Bill*	.243	70	17	0	5	6	8	.295	.271
Sprague, Ed	.183	71	13	2	6	8	26	.266	.324
Stanley, Mike	.237	131	31	5	20	18	26	.329	.374
Steinbach, T	.263	175	46	4	23	12	33	.323	.406
Stillwell, K#	.271	85	23	1	8	6	12	.315	.424
Strange, Doug#	.239	142	34	3	17	12	27	.304	.331
Surhoff, B.J.*	.182	137	25	0	7	6	14	.214	.263
Sveum, Dale#	.286	49	14	1	5	4	12	.340	.367
Tartabull, D	.265	185	49	7	35	40	56	.398	.454
Tettleton, M#	.177	186	33	6	24	24	62	.274	.323
Thomas, Frank	.336	137	46	11	27	38	24	.477	.635
Thome, Jim*	.282	39	11	0	3	7	11	.391	.385
Trammell, A	.246	134	33	1	12	21	16	.346	.306
Valentin, Jhn	.225	89	20	3	11	12	15	.314	.393
Valentin, Jse#	.114	35	4	1	2	4	14	.205	.229
Valle, Dave	.233	1215	283	26	144	102	169	.307	.355
Vaughn, Greg	.173	104	18	3	16	18	35	.295	.317
Vaughn, Mo*	.258	97	25	7	23	14	25	.371	.536
Velarde, R	.295	129	38	4	24	12	29	.368	.512
Ventura, R*	.315	146	46	6	22	24	27	.409	.500
Vina, F*	.238	63	15	0	2	3	6	.284	.333
Vizquel, Omar#	.257	1064	273	4	70	86	117	.312	.321
Walbeck, Matt#	.200	35	7	1	5	2	11	.243	.371
Weiss, Walt#	.161	62	10	0	4	6	11	.232	.194
White, Devon#	.303	208	63	6	24	15	44	.347	.471
Whiten, Mark#	.283	113	32	5	20	8	29	.339	.469
Williams, Ber#	.237	97	23	2	9	16	18	.357	.381
Wilson, Dan	.256	558	143	13	76	44	103	.311	.401
Worthington	.246	57	14	2	11	4	15	.295	.404

BUSCH STADIUM
Home of the St. Louis Cardinals
St. Louis, Missouri — Grass

Batter	Avg	AB	H	HR	BI	BB	SO	OBP	Slg
Abbott, Kurt	.225	40	9	2	6	3	9	.279	.425
Aldrete, Mike*	.341	44	15	0	2	4	5	.396	.364
Alicea, Luis#	.252	778	196	12	88	93	122	.336	.387
Alomar, R#	.333	69	23	0	5	2	8	.347	.420
Alou, Moises	.247	93	23	3	10	10	12	.333	.398
Amaro, Ruben#	.265	34	9	1	3	3	5	.316	.500
Anthony, Eric*	.250	60	15	3	9	9	13	.348	.500
Arias, Alex	.227	44	10	1	6	6	2	.327	.295
Bagwell, Jeff	.205	117	24	1	18	16	24	.307	.325
Barberie, B#	.363	80	29	1	5	12	7	.463	.463
Battle, Allen	.294	51	15	0	1	6	11	.368	.373
Bell, David	.231	147	34	2	17	6	25	.272	.313
Bell, Derek	.250	84	21	1	6	3	13	.308	.310
Bell, Jay	.230	191	44	3	24	23	34	.320	.377
Belliard, R	.183	93	17	0	6	1	15	.191	.194
Berry, Sean	.365	63	23	3	10	1	6	.369	.651
Bichette, D	.196	92	18	3	17	7	25	.260	.326
Biggio, Craig	.329	170	56	6	29	19	20	.406	.506
Blauser, Jeff	.173	127	22	1	7	15	30	.257	.228
Bonds, Barry*	.289	246	71	7	40	34	36	.372	.496

285

BUSCH STADIUM
Home of the St. Louis Cardinals
St. Louis, Missouri   **Grass**

Batter	Avg	AB	H	HR	BI	BB	SO	OBP	Slg
Bonilla, B#	.237	262	62	12	43	33	37	.317	.443
Boone, Bret	.167	54	9	0	5	2	12	.193	.204
Branson, Jeff*	.250	52	13	0	4	1	8	.264	.288
Brogna, Rico*	.345	55	19	2	10	1	9	.357	.564
Burks, Ellis	.350	40	14	2	7	6	10	.435	.600
Butler, Brett*	.305	197	60	2	18	10	17	.344	.452
Caminiti, Ken#	.207	164	34	4	14	13	30	.264	.311
Candaele, C#	.180	61	11	0	4	2	5	.206	.246
Cangelosi, J#	.250	48	12	0	5	9	5	.383	.313
Carr, Chuck#	.278	72	20	0	3	8	8	.366	.319
Carreon, Mark	.360	75	27	3	13	4	3	.392	.533
Castilla, V	.217	60	13	2	5	3	12	.254	.367
Cedeno, A	.204	54	11	0	7	5	9	.283	.259
Cianfrocco, A	.146	41	6	2	8	1	12	.182	.293
Clark, Dave*	.341	44	15	1	10	6	9	.412	.523
Clark, Will*	.287	129	37	8	26	10	24	.338	.558
Clayton, R	.252	305	77	6	23	20	63	.300	.370
Colbrunn, G	.328	64	21	3	13	1	12	.333	.531
Coleman, V#	.279	1199	335	11	99	104	206	.339	.389
Conine, Jeff	.253	75	19	1	9	8	18	.333	.333
Cordero, Wil	.377	69	26	1	6	7	13	.442	.507
Dascenzo, D#	.192	73	14	0	7	6	4	.250	.247
Daulton, D*	.230	161	37	3	21	18	29	.304	.348
Davis, Eric	.245	110	27	3	8	12	29	.320	.355
Dawson, Andre	.274	175	48	7	26	8	26	.312	.440
DeShields, D*	.237	177	42	2	17	19	37	.315	.328
Duncan, M	.281	146	41	1	7	3	18	.298	.363
Dunston, S	.307	192	59	4	22	5	22	.327	.500
Dykstra, L*	.269	234	63	0	14	31	17	.358	.346
Eisenreich, J*	.357	56	20	0	9	2	8	.373	.429
Elster, Kevin	.265	98	26	2	7	9	12	.327	.398
Eusebio, Tony	.500	40	20	0	11	2	1	.524	.700
Finley, Steve*	.256	129	33	3	9	13	14	.326	.349
Fletcher, D*	.265	83	22	1	8	2	10	.282	.361
Gaetti, Gary	.303	244	74	13	45	17	52	.357	.566
Galarraga, A	.248	412	102	11	48	19	93	.300	.374
Gallego, Mike	.205	78	16	0	3	6	18	.271	.231
Gant, Ron	.267	378	101	25	66	58	77	.364	.534
Garcia, C	.225	71	16	1	8	1	7	.230	.366
Gilkey, B	.262	1084	284	18	119	104	147	.330	.389
Girardi, Joe	.319	91	29	0	3	5	12	.364	.440
Gonzalez, L*	.279	104	29	2	8	11	14	.353	.433
Grace, Mark*	.286	217	62	1	24	24	18	.361	.392
Grissom, M	.299	194	58	4	20	8	12	.325	.448
Gutierrez, R	.278	36	10	0	2	1	9	.297	.417
Gwynn, Tony*	.292	216	63	3	23	8	7	.314	.403
Harris, Lenny*	.281	96	27	0	8	10	10	.349	.375
Hayes, C	.314	156	49	4	24	9	24	.359	.436
Hernandez, Jo	.256	43	11	2	5	3	9	.298	.488
Hill, G	.328	67	22	4	12	7	7	.392	.537
Hollins, Dave#	.272	81	22	3	13	8	17	.326	.420
Howard, T*	.340	50	17	2	5	3	3	.377	.520
Hudler, Rex	.252	266	67	6	20	14	45	.291	.391
Hundley, Todd#	.270	74	20	4	11	7	12	.337	.473
Hunter, Brian	.200	35	7	1	4	3	5	.263	.371
Hunter, Bri L	.343	35	12	2	5	3	3	.395	.514
Incaviglia, P	.216	51	11	4	7	1	12	.231	.471
James, Dion*	.178	45	8	0	1	4	10	.245	.222
Javier, Stan#	.250	48	12	0	6	7	9	.345	.354
Jefferies, G#	.314	560	176	17	85	61	43	.384	.475
Johnson, L*	.288	66	19	2	10	5	6	.338	.470
Jones, C#	.239	46	11	1	6	5	7	.314	.326
Jordan, Brian	.307	847	260	28	149	47	144	.350	.498
Jordan, Ricky	.365	137	50	2	20	12	15	.416	.562
Justice, Dave*	.268	127	34	5	21	14	25	.338	.417
Karros, Eric	.266	109	29	5	20	10	21	.322	.431
Kelly, R	.220	59	13	0	6	1	10	.226	.237
Kent, Jeff	.314	70	22	5	12	5	11	.368	.600
King, Jeff	.295	139	41	4	16	7	8	.324	.439
Kingery, Mike*	.340	53	18	1	6	4	4	.386	.509
Klesko, Ryan*	.173	52	9	1	3	6	8	.259	.288
Lankford, Ray*	.286	1526	437	57	245	202	340	.367	.493
Lansing, Mike	.274	62	17	0	3	5	9	.338	.290
Larkin, Barry	.315	184	58	4	21	15	11	.367	.413
Lemke, Mark#	.184	125	23	1	7	14	13	.262	.240
Lewis, Darren	.205	83	17	0	3	4	16	.250	.325
Liriano, N#	.273	44	12	0	3	3	8	.319	.318
Lopez, Javy	.405	42	17	3	13	4	8	.447	.667
Mabry, John*	.286	476	136	5	55	34	68	.334	.393
Magadan, Dave*	.285	151	43	1	24	25	16	.385	.384
Manwaring, K	.222	63	14	0	5	4	9	.268	.302
Martin, Al*	.344	64	22	3	6	2	10	.364	.516
Martinez, Da*	.301	146	44	1	13	12	20	.358	.404
May, Derrick*	.311	90	28	1	9	4	10	.340	.400
McGee, Willie#	.312	1180	368	12	157	62	179	.345	.421
McGriff, Fred*	.265	117	31	7	30	18	21	.365	.521
McRae, Brian#	.200	50	10	2	4	6	10	.298	.340
Merced, O*	.343	140	48	5	28	15	20	.408	.550

BUSCH STADIUM
Home of the St. Louis Cardinals
St. Louis, Missouri   **Grass**

Batter	Avg	AB	H	HR	BI	BB	SO	OBP	Slg
Miller, Orl	.206	34	7	0	2	2	6	.250	.294
Mitchell, K	.347	95	33	8	23	16	14	.434	.726
Mondesi, Raul	.371	62	23	2	9	4	10	.426	.645
Morandini, M*	.212	104	22	0	8	9	13	.281	.279
Morris, Hal*	.347	101	35	4	14	10	13	.411	.495
Mouton, James	.283	60	17	1	9	9	13	.386	.383
Murray, Eddie#	.265	113	30	3	11	13	15	.341	.407
Nixon, Otis#	.272	114	31	0	7	13	10	.346	.316
O'Brien, C	.196	51	10	1	4	4	6	.268	.353
O'Neill, Paul*	.263	95	25	2	19	13	14	.360	.421
Offerman, J#	.279	61	17	0	9	5	10	.328	.426
Oliver, Joe	.231	78	18	1	3	6	7	.286	.308
Orsulak, Joe*	.238	42	10	1	3	3	5	.304	.333
Pagnozzi, Tom	.256	1269	325	22	140	98	182	.311	.366
Palmeiro, R*	.410	39	16	0	6	5	1	.467	.590
Parent, Mark	.184	38	7	1	3	3	5	.238	.342
Pena, G#	.270	489	132	15	58	57	112	.359	.444
Pena, Tony	.240	643	154	8	57	50	71	.294	.327
Pendleton, T#	.266	1128	300	25	158	93	135	.322	.406
Piazza, Mike	.274	73	20	4	12	10	9	.361	.493
Plantier, P*	.425	40	17	6	12	7	10	.511	1.000
Prince, Tom	.147	34	5	0	2	2	9	.231	.206
Raines, Tim#	.340	106	36	1	17	19	3	.430	.509
Reed, Jeff*	.345	84	29	0	12	12	9	.427	.393
Reed, Jody	.197	61	12	0	1	3	7	.231	.230
Roberts, Bip#	.308	117	36	1	12	10	14	.359	.436
Rodriguez, H*	.222	45	10	2	6	5	10	.300	.467
Sabo, Chris	.282	103	29	1	7	6	13	.327	.437
Samuel, Juan	.232	155	36	2	12	11	30	.298	.342
Sanchez, Rey	.297	74	22	0	5	1	4	.316	.338
Sandberg, R	.273	253	69	12	38	34	32	.356	.482
Sanders, R	.302	53	16	2	7	6	15	.383	.509
Santiago, B	.233	159	37	4	10	8	24	.274	.371
Segui, David#	.270	37	10	1	8	2	5	.300	.405
Servais, S	.186	59	11	2	6	3	10	.238	.322
Sheaffer, D	.234	205	48	4	25	20	31	.310	.376
Sheffield, G	.247	73	18	2	12	6	6	.313	.384
Shipley, C	.244	41	10	0	3	1	5	.279	.317
Slaught, Don	.354	48	17	1	3	3	3	.426	.479
Smith, Dwight*	.271	85	23	1	15	10	13	.344	.388
Smith, Ozzie#	.289	2378	687	9	234	298	142	.367	.365
Sosa, Sammy	.192	104	20	6	13	3	26	.213	.375
Stillwell, K#	.282	39	11	0	3	1	6	.300	.333
Stocker, K#	.211	38	8	0	3	3	5	.279	.263
Strawberry, D*	.336	137	46	6	21	18	26	.410	.547
Sweeney, Mark*	.273	99	27	0	15	17	16	.376	.303
Taubensee, E*	.283	46	13	1	6	4	13	.333	.370
Thompson, Mil*	.268	821	220	12	97	65	117	.324	.391
Thompson, Rob	.221	131	29	1	11	9	30	.282	.328
Thompson, Ry	.344	32	11	3	5	3	9	.417	.719
VanderWal, J*	.164	55	9	0	6	4	16	.213	.200
Vizcaino, J#	.250	100	25	0	4	6	5	.292	.320
Walker, Larry*	.248	157	39	6	23	15	22	.322	.439
Wallach, Tim	.264	265	70	9	52	18	40	.305	.438
Walton, J	.261	92	24	2	11	12	24	.349	.457
Weiss, Walt#	.382	76	29	0	8	11	7	.461	.500
White, R	.211	38	8	1	6	1	4	.231	.316
Whiten, Mark#	.241	431	104	19	72	50	97	.322	.397
Wilkins, Rick*	.318	85	27	3	12	12	24	.408	.529
Williams, Ma	.326	132	43	9	25	12	23	.385	.614
Young, Eric	.229	70	16	0	5	4	5	.280	.243
Young, Kevin	.286	35	10	0	2	2	9	.316	.400
Zeile, Todd	.277	1341	372	39	207	173	189	.358	.430

THE BALLPARK IN ARLINGTON
Home of the Texas Rangers
Arlington, Texas   **Grass**

Batter	Avg	AB	H	HR	BI	BB	SO	OBP	Slg
Alomar, R#	.270	74	20	0	6	7	11	.333	.432
Alomar Jr, S	.349	43	15	4	9	2	6	.378	.698
Amaral, Rich	.341	44	15	0	6	6	9	.420	.364
Anderson, Brd*	.318	44	14	5	10	6	11	.423	.795
Anderson, G*	.313	48	15	1	10	2	9	.340	.396
Baerga, C#	.343	67	23	2	10	2	4	.366	.463
Baines, H*	.528	36	19	5	19	3	2	.564	1.083
Becker, Rich*	.294	51	15	1	5	5	10	.357	.431
Belle, Albert	.303	76	23	5	15	5	11	.346	.553
Beltre, E	.304	125	38	0	15	13	23	.370	.376
Berroa, G	.354	65	23	2	10	6	8	.405	.523
Blowers, Mike	.263	38	10	2	6	0	8	.263	.474
Boggs, Wade*	.205	39	8	1	4	7	5	.326	.282
Bordick, Mike	.237	59	14	1	7	6	9	.308	.339
Brosius, S	.422	45	19	2	6	7	8	.500	.667
Buford, Damon	.309	81	25	3	11	10	16	.380	.481
Buhner, Jay	.265	83	22	5	18	6	23	.319	.518
Canseco, Jose	.275	258	71	21	60	42	62	.377	.566
Carter, Joe	.235	68	16	0	4	7	8	.303	.294

Batter	Avg	AB	H	HR	BI	BB	SO	OBP	Slg
Cedeno, D#	.358	53	19	2	7	0	13	.358	.509
Cirillo, Jeff	.346	52	18	1	10	4	4	.393	.577
Clark, Will*	.312	648	202	28	133	107	88	.407	.509
Coleman, V#	.280	50	14	1	6	4	6	.327	.380
Cora, Joey#	.305	59	18	0	8	6	5	.364	.390
Cordova, M	.304	46	14	2	9	1	8	.313	.522
Curtis, Chad	.309	68	21	1	7	4	5	.351	.426
Davis, Chili#	.219	64	14	4	13	4	10	.261	.453
Delgado, C*	.235	34	8	1	4	1	15	.278	.412
Devereaux, M	.270	37	10	1	6	3	6	.325	.405
DiSarcina, G	.313	67	21	2	7	2	2	.329	.507
Durham, Ray#	.317	41	13	1	9	5	9	.396	.561
Easley, D	.224	49	11	1	7	4	12	.304	.286
Edmonds, Jim*	.323	62	20	3	9	8	14	.400	.532
Elster, Kevin	.238	244	58	9	48	27	70	.313	.410
Fabregas, Jor*	.314	35	11	0	5	3	5	.368	.371
Fermin, Felix	.243	37	9	0	6	3	2	.293	.270
Fielder, C	.172	64	11	4	7	8	16	.264	.359
Franco, Julio	.261	46	12	3	8	4	10	.333	.478
Frazier, Lou#	.264	53	14	0	9	8	9	.381	.302
Frye, Jeff	.335	251	84	2	23	37	26	.425	.458
Fryman, T	.219	73	16	1	10	5	14	.268	.342
Gaetti, Gary	.257	35	9	1	8	0	5	.250	.400
Gagne, Greg	.244	41	10	1	8	0	7	.238	.390
Gates, Brent#	.113	53	6	1	7	1	8	.140	.208
Gil, Benji	.257	206	53	5	23	14	71	.303	.408
Gomez, Chris	.061	33	2	0	2	3	10	.158	.091
Gonzales, R	.236	55	13	1	3	6	7	.306	.345
Gonzalez, J	.307	626	192	44	150	56	93	.371	.602
Goodwin, Tom*	.286	42	12	0	2	2	9	.333	.310
Greenwell, M*	.265	34	9	0	2	1	2	.286	.382
Greer, Rusty*	.301	604	182	19	113	93	104	.388	.460
Griffey Jr, K*	.403	62	25	6	15	13	7	.507	.742
Guillen, O*	.350	60	21	0	6	0	0	.344	.517
Hamelin, Bob*	.294	34	10	0	3	5	5	.390	.382
Hamilton, D*	.313	332	104	2	30	34	36	.376	.392
Henderson, R	.286	28	8	1	3	7	3	.429	.429
Higginson, B*	.200	35	7	0	1	5	6	.300	.229
Hulse, David*	.288	184	53	1	16	11	33	.330	.364
Jaha, John	.382	55	21	4	19	8	11	.453	.655
Javier, Stan#	.342	38	13	3	6	1	6	.350	.658
Johnson, L*	.300	50	15	3	8	1	6	.314	.520
Joyner, Wally*	.250	32	8	1	3	6	5	.368	.438
Karkovice, R	.175	40	7	0	1	4	13	.250	.225
Knoblauch, C	.397	68	27	2	5	13	7	.494	.574
Leius, Scott	.273	33	9	0	5	2	5	.333	.364
Lewis, Mark	.444	27	12	0	6	6	3	.529	.667
Listach, Pat#	.317	41	13	0	1	2	4	.364	.366
Lockhart, K*	.286	35	10	0	2	2	2	.333	.400
Lofton, Kenny*	.288	66	19	0	4	5	12	.333	.364
Martinez, Da*	.302	43	13	1	3	4	4	.362	.395
Martinez, E	.343	70	24	4	13	17	7	.461	.600
Martinez, T*	.279	68	19	2	12	7	12	.338	.426
McGwire, Mark	.333	36	12	6	10	16	5	.547	.861
McLemore, M#	.290	500	145	6	50	85	75	.391	.392
Meares, Pat	.302	53	16	0	3	3	7	.333	.377
Molitor, Paul	.304	69	21	2	10	3	6	.333	.449
Mouton, Lyle	.447	38	17	0	7	4	7	.523	.579
Murray, Eddie#	.304	56	17	2	6	2	5	.328	.446
Myers, Greg*	.114	35	4	0	3	1	11	.139	.114
Naehring, Tim	.163	43	7	2	5	7	5	.294	.326
Newson, W*	.250	120	30	5	20	16	38	.336	.425
Nilsson, Dave*	.262	42	11	2	9	5	9	.340	.452
Nixon, Otis#	.272	320	87	0	29	35	48	.342	.309
O'Neill, Paul*	.413	46	19	3	10	6	6	.481	.696
Olerud, John*	.227	44	10	1	8	6	7	.327	.386
Ortiz, Luis	.303	66	20	2	15	2	9	.319	.530
Palmeiro, R*	.341	44	15	5	10	6	7	.412	.727
Palmer, Dean	.266	533	142	35	109	56	137	.338	.510
Paquette, C	.262	42	11	0	1	0	8	.262	.286
Phillips, T#	.311	61	19	1	6	9	9	.400	.459
Raines, Tim#	.206	34	7	0	2	3	5	.270	.265
Ramirez, M	.340	53	18	1	11	9	10	.435	.434
Ripken, Billy	.390	59	23	0	5	2	8	.410	.458
Ripken, Cal	.262	42	11	1	6	5	4	.354	.357
Rodriguez, I	.312	734	229	22	108	48	71	.359	.475
Salmon, Tim	.565	62	35	5	19	11	9	.640	.935
Seitzer, K	.442	52	23	0	7	7	6	.508	.577
Sierra, Ruben#	.186	59	11	1	7	8	10	.284	.271
Snow, J.T.#	.193	57	11	0	11	2	8	.222	.263
Sojo, Luis	.321	53	17	1	4	3	2	.357	.491
Sorrento, P*	.303	66	20	6	25	5	16	.338	.606
Sprague, Ed	.309	68	21	3	10	5	12	.351	.471
Stahoviak, S*	.333	33	11	3	8	3	7	.405	.667
Stanley, Mike	.188	32	6	3	8	4	8	.282	.531
Steinbach, T	.339	62	21	4	13	7	10	.400	.597
Stevens, Lee*	.308	39	12	2	8	4	13	.386	.590
Stillwell, K#	.261	46	12	1	2	4	8	.320	.391

THE BALLPARK IN ARLINGTON
Home of the Texas Rangers
Arlington, Texas — Grass

Batter	Avg	AB	H	HR	BI	BB	SO	OBP	Slg
Strange, Doug#	.223	139	31	3	20	13	23	.301	.360
Tartabull, D	.231	52	12	1	9	9	15	.339	.365
Tettleton, M#	.270	492	133	37	106	117	126	.409	.553
Thomas, Frank	.344	61	21	4	13	17	7	.475	.590
Thome, Jim*	.277	65	18	3	11	7	23	.351	.492
Trammell, A	.152	33	5	0	2	5	5	.263	.212
Valentin, Jhn	.267	30	8	0	3	6	2	.389	.333
Valle, Dave	.273	88	24	0	8	9	18	.340	.352
Vaughn, Mo*	.286	49	14	2	6	3	10	.340	.408
Velarde, R	.057	35	2	0	1	4	11	.150	.057
Ventura, R*	.301	73	22	6	19	11	14	.393	.589
Vina, F*	.286	42	12	2	4	1	2	.362	.476
Vizquel, Omar#	.246	65	16	0	4	7	6	.319	.277
Voigt, Jack	.188	48	9	2	5	5	9	.278	.354
Walbeck, Matt#	.233	43	10	2	6	2	7	.267	.372
White, Devon#	.190	42	8	2	8	2	8	.227	.405
Williams, Ber#	.255	51	13	5	14	8	13	.350	.608
Williams, Ger	.194	36	7	0	1	3	4	.275	.278
Wilson, Dan	.328	58	19	0	7	3	9	.371	.414
Worthington	.250	40	10	2	7	8	5	.360	.425

SKYDOME
Home of the Toronto Blue Jays
Toronto, Ontario — Artificial

Batter	Avg	AB	H	HR	BI	BB	SO	OBP	Slg
Aldrete, Mike*	.279	43	12	2	9	14	11	.466	.488
Alomar, R#	.312	1325	414	31	187	167	129	.389	.471
Alomar Jr, S	.275	102	28	3	17	4	17	.312	.392
Amaral, Rich	.319	47	15	0	5	7	8	.404	.426
Anderson, Brd*	.243	140	34	8	18	27	34	.369	.457
Anderson, G*	.325	40	13	1	3	1	6	.341	.525
Baerga, C#	.273	172	47	5	25	9	25	.310	.424
Baines, H*	.319	119	38	6	11	13	10	.386	.513
Becker, Rich*	.256	43	11	0	5	4	10	.319	.326
Bell, Derek	.152	99	15	2	5	10	21	.270	.263
Belle, Albert	.338	136	46	9	33	19	24	.414	.640
Berroa, G	.259	54	14	3	10	2	7	.298	.500
Bichette, D	.262	42	11	2	6	2	9	.295	.429
Blowers, Mike	.191	47	9	1	10	6	10	.283	.319
Boggs, Wade*	.273	172	47	2	16	33	14	.391	.372
Bonilla, B#	.265	34	9	2	4	4	4	.342	.529
Borders, Pat	.252	1002	253	29	130	54	127	.292	.399
Bordick, Mike	.308	91	28	0	13	13	18	.398	.396
Brito, Tilson	.250	36	9	1	4	3	7	.341	.444
Brosius, S	.250	72	18	2	11	3	16	.286	.389
Brumfield, J	.284	148	42	8	28	8	36	.323	.527
Buhner, Jay	.254	122	31	4	20	18	27	.350	.393
Burks, Ellis	.360	75	27	2	7	11	10	.455	.560
Canseco, Jose	.256	125	32	12	36	16	38	.345	.592
Carter, Joe	.264	1746	461	111	352	115	328	.313	.525
Cedeno, D#	.243	267	65	1	19	19	61	.297	.330
Cirillo, Jeff	.271	48	13	1	3	4	11	.327	.375
Clark, Will*	.319	69	22	3	10	5	8	.364	.478
Cole, Alex*	.214	56	12	1	1	10	12	.333	.286
Cora, Joey#	.238	84	20	1	3	5	10	.281	.321
Cordova, M	.275	40	11	2	4	5	6	.348	.475
Curtis, Chad	.247	97	24	5	20	16	18	.362	.454
Cuyler, Milt#	.294	68	20	0	1	8	8	.368	.382
Damon, Johnny*	.265	34	9	1	3	4	5	.375	.471
Davis, Chili*	.349	129	45	7	24	22	18	.441	.566
Deer, Rob	.171	117	20	7	12	13	49	.258	.359
Delgado, C*	.262	366	96	19	59	54	116	.361	.475
Devereaux, M	.256	117	30	2	10	13	19	.331	.385
DiSarcina, G	.235	85	20	1	9	6	8	.286	.341
Durham, Ray#	.209	43	9	1	5	5	5	.292	.302
Easley, D	.222	36	8	0	3	3	7	.300	.278
Edmonds, Jim*	.291	55	16	1	5	2	10	.316	.436
Eisenreich, J*	.250	56	14	1	9	3	5	.283	.375
Espinoza, A	.219	73	16	3	7	0	11	.219	.370
Fermin, Felix	.265	98	26	0	13	6	6	.302	.286
Fielder, C	.266	188	50	15	41	24	51	.346	.553
Flaherty, J	.286	35	10	3	7	1	5	.306	.543
Franco, Julio	.274	117	32	4	15	15	16	.356	.402
Frye, Jeff	.212	33	7	0	0	2	5	.278	.212
Fryman, T	.216	162	35	4	23	14	49	.289	.358
Gaetti, Gary	.287	101	29	4	18	7	21	.354	.495
Gagne, Greg	.236	127	30	6	22	5	26	.263	.441
Gallego, Mike	.183	71	13	1	11	11	11	.294	.282
Gates, Brent#	.302	63	19	0	15	5	12	.343	.397
Giambi, Jason*	.364	33	12	1	3	4	5	.432	.606
Gomez, Chris	.254	59	15	1	10	9	15	.348	.339
Gomez, Leo	.227	75	17	3	7	7	16	.298	.360
Gonzales, R	.173	75	13	1	4	15	12	.326	.240
Gonzalez, A	.224	513	115	11	65	48	150	.295	.382
Gonzalez, J	.233	133	31	4	17	9	26	.289	.353
Goodwin, Tom*	.318	44	14	0	2	5	8	.388	.364
Grebeck, C	.216	37	8	1	2	3	3	.275	.351

SKYDOME
Home of the Toronto Blue Jays
Toronto, Ontario   **Artificial**

Batter	Avg	AB	H	HR	BI	BB	SO	OBP	Slg
Green, Shawn*	.254	397	101	12	47	28	79	.309	.431
Greenwell, M*	.296	169	50	7	25	8	16	.330	.462
Greer, Rusty*	.313	48	15	3	10	4	8	.377	.583
Griffey Jr, K*	.298	121	36	8	16	11	16	.353	.545
Guillen, O*	.243	103	25	1	8	3	10	.264	.320
Hall, Mel*	.288	73	21	3	9	4	9	.325	.493
Hamelin, Bob*	.184	38	7	4	7	7	15	.340	.500
Hamilton, D*	.278	133	37	2	16	13	12	.340	.368
Hayes, C	.257	35	9	0	1	0	3	.257	.257
Henderson, R	.247	174	43	6	19	35	26	.379	.391
Higginson, B*	.250	44	11	0	3	13	10	.421	.341
Hill, G	.257	241	62	14	34	17	57	.306	.494
Hoiles, Chris	.141	85	12	2	5	8	18	.215	.247
Howard, Dave#	.172	58	10	2	6	4	15	.226	.293
Howell, Jack*	.282	39	11	1	3	7	5	.404	.410
Huff, Michael	.224	196	44	1	12	26	22	.324	.316
Hulse, David*	.197	71	14	0	1	5	13	.250	.239
Huson, Jeff*	.171	35	6	0	2	7	2	.302	.229
Incaviglia, P	.220	50	11	1	8	3	10	.273	.340
Jaha, John	.272	81	22	4	10	14	20	.379	.469
James, Dion*	.333	57	19	0	7	14	5	.465	.351
Javier, Stan*	.250	44	11	0	5	5	9	.314	.273
Jefferson, R*	.333	45	15	1	6	0	11	.333	.444
Johnson, L*	.258	124	32	1	8	4	12	.287	.347
Joyner, Wally*	.362	130	47	7	27	16	14	.432	.608
Karkovice, R	.157	83	13	5	12	5	28	.205	.386
Kelly, Pat	.289	83	24	2	13	4	19	.319	.458
Kelly, R	.336	113	38	2	18	6	16	.358	.469
Kent, Jeff	.232	99	23	2	10	14	21	.328	.394
Kirby, Wayne*	.256	39	10	3	4	1	13	.275	.513
Knoblauch, C	.283	113	32	2	12	18	21	.391	.451
Knorr, Randy	.226	177	40	8	28	17	44	.292	.401
Kreuter, Chad#	.150	40	6	0	4	6	6	.261	.150
Leius, Scott	.229	48	11	0	4	6	13	.321	.313
Lewis, Mark	.260	50	13	0	4	3	13	.296	.280
Leyritz, Jim	.297	74	22	3	14	12	20	.409	.446
Liriano, N#	.238	231	55	3	31	32	27	.332	.346
Listach, Pat#	.289	90	26	1	8	6	25	.333	.400
Livingstone*	.341	44	15	0	7	2	6	.370	.432
Lockhart, K*	.222	36	8	0	4	4	5	.286	.222
Lofton, Kenny*	.277	119	33	0	11	12	13	.341	.345
Macfarlane, M	.214	103	22	5	12	9	19	.291	.388
Martinez, E	.318	107	34	6	20	20	11	.430	.589
Martinez, S*	.228	197	45	3	19	11	49	.278	.350
Martinez, T*	.253	75	19	4	11	15	14	.378	.440
Mayne, Brent*	.175	57	10	1	9	7	12	.266	.246
McGriff, Fred*	.276	446	123	28	69	96	74	.404	.509
McGwire, Mark	.202	89	18	6	12	11	19	.287	.438
McLemore, M#	.322	87	28	1	10	8	7	.379	.448
McRae, Brian#	.270	89	24	4	14	11	17	.356	.461
Meares, Pat	.158	57	9	0	1	3	21	.213	.158
Mieske, Matt	.234	47	11	2	7	1	11	.250	.426
Molitor, Paul	.342	937	320	32	155	105	100	.408	.527
Munoz, Pedro	.160	50	8	0	1	6	14	.263	.200
Murray, Eddie#	.183	60	11	0	6	5	12	.246	.200
Myers, Greg*	.261	356	93	8	44	34	53	.320	.399
Naehring, Tim	.333	60	20	1	6	15	9	.467	.433
Nilsson, Dave*	.242	33	8	3	8	4	7	.324	.545
Nixon, Otis#	.272	294	80	1	14	52	43	.383	.303
O'Brien, C	.234	184	43	8	26	15	37	.325	.424
O'Leary, Troy*	.231	52	12	1	4	9	8	.339	.327
O'Neill, Paul*	.264	72	19	2	12	5	7	.321	.431
Olerud, John*	.292	1548	452	47	220	260	209	.398	.461
Orsulak, Joe*	.273	66	18	1	12	3	6	.304	.424
Palmeiro, R*	.304	168	51	3	22	13	25	.354	.405
Palmer, Dean	.245	94	23	5	20	3	32	.265	.489
Paquette, C	.122	41	5	1	4	1	14	.140	.220
Pena, Tony	.236	106	25	2	16	4	15	.259	.349
Perez, Robert	.310	129	40	1	12	6	10	.338	.388
Perez, Tomas#	.205	210	43	2	18	17	29	.263	.305
Phillips, T#	.274	164	45	6	16	32	46	.395	.445
Polonia, Luis*	.299	134	40	0	10	10	17	.352	.358
Raines, Tim#	.200	105	21	2	12	14	16	.300	.295
Ramirez, M	.283	53	15	4	10	11	8	.400	.547
Reboulet, J	.146	41	6	0	2	6	4	.255	.220
Reed, Jody	.278	115	32	0	9	9	10	.331	.330
Ripken, Billy	.261	69	18	1	2	2	7	.282	.406
Ripken, Cal	.270	196	53	9	34	8	17	.300	.464
Rodriguez, Al	.294	34	10	2	9	2	5	.324	.647
Rodriguez, I	.297	118	35	4	20	5	15	.325	.475
Salmon, Tim	.273	77	21	3	7	14	20	.385	.455
Samuel, Juan	.295	88	26	4	9	8	29	.361	.545
Schofield, D	.236	237	56	2	18	28	54	.322	.321
Segui, David#	.261	46	12	1	6	3	6	.306	.413
Seitzer, K	.333	135	45	1	16	22	22	.431	.430
Sheffield, G	.175	40	7	0	5	1	2	.190	.200
Sierra, Ruben#	.279	129	36	3	24	11	20	.333	.419
Snow, J.T.#	.250	64	16	0	7	4	9	.290	.297

Batter	Avg	AB	H	HR	BI	BB	SO	OBP	Slg
Sojo, Luis	.179	56	10	0	6	5	3	.246	.196
Sorrento, P*	.241	112	27	10	22	17	24	.338	.545
Sosa, Sammy	.353	34	12	1	5	0	9	.353	.500
Spiers, Bill*	.191	89	17	2	8	8	12	.263	.337
Sprague, Ed	.253	1126	285	47	162	92	244	.323	.433
Stahoviak, S*	.188	32	6	0	1	4	10	.278	.219
Stanley, Mike	.262	84	22	3	9	18	20	.385	.440
Steinbach, T	.326	132	43	3	14	6	27	.355	.477
Stillwell, K#	.243	37	9	0	3	2	6	.300	.324
Strange, Doug#	.290	69	20	1	11	5	9	.338	.377
Surhoff, B.J.*	.306	147	45	3	29	11	18	.354	.435
Tartabull, D	.300	120	36	6	23	23	30	.410	.550
Tettleton, M#	.252	139	35	4	20	42	36	.427	.403
Thomas, Frank	.275	120	33	6	21	23	22	.405	.475
Thome, Jim*	.239	67	16	2	5	18	21	.407	.373
Tinsley, Lee#	.189	37	7	0	3	5	11	.286	.270
Trammell, A	.275	80	22	3	8	11	10	.363	.450
Valentin, Jhn	.313	83	26	6	21	15	7	.418	.614
Valentin, Jse*	.311	45	14	5	13	6	15	.392	.667
Valle, Dave	.271	48	13	1	7	9	4	.417	.417
Vaughn, Greg	.270	137	37	8	23	20	35	.373	.482
Vaughn, Mo*	.326	95	31	6	20	11	29	.404	.632
Velarde, R	.211	90	19	1	1	9	27	.290	.344
Ventura, R*	.290	131	38	6	21	20	16	.382	.489
Vina, F*	.310	42	13	1	1	6	3	.408	.524
Vizquel, Omar#	.285	130	37	5	17	13	10	.352	.469
Walbeck, Matt#	.294	34	10	1	4	1	4	.314	.412
Ward, Turner#	.196	143	28	2	14	13	25	.266	.294
Weiss, Walt#	.306	36	11	0	7	9	1	.426	.417
White, Devon#	.283	1371	388	36	146	108	289	.342	.462
Whiten, Mark#	.224	143	32	3	16	12	36	.288	.357
Williams, Ber#	.269	119	32	1	9	14	29	.351	.378
Wilson, Dan	.294	34	10	1	6	4	8	.368	.412
Worthington	.227	44	10	2	6	6	12	.320	.386

Pitchers at Parks

This section highlights pitcher performances at every stadium in the majors.

Just like with the hitters, our pitcher park data goes back as far as 1987. A minimum of 12 innings pitched was required to make the list at a particular park.

ATLANTA-FULTON COUNTY STADIUM
Home of the Atlanta Braves

Atlanta, Georgia — Grass

Pitcher	W	L	ERA	G	GS	Sv	IP	H	BB	SO	HR	Avg
Assenmacher*	8	8	4.18	97	0	7	114.0	121	36	104	8	.268
Astacio, P	0	5	6.26	6	4	0	23.0	29	8	15	3	.319
Avery, Steve*	39	25	3.51	101	101	0	620.1	596	180	412	50	.255
Beck, Rod	0	2	2.87	11	0	4	15.2	11	7	15	2	.204
Belcher, Tim	2	3	4.04	12	11	1	64.2	54	27	48	7	.228
Benes, Andy	3	2	3.12	10	10	0	66.1	57	26	42	9	.227
Bielecki, M	8	5	3.32	46	13	1	114.0	109	47	90	5	.254
Blair, Willie	0	2	2.35	11	2	0	23.0	23	4	8	2	.261
Boever, Joe	5	8	4.02	81	0	12	109.2	101	50	87	10	.250
Borbon, Pedro*	3	1	3.46	52	0	3	41.2	35	12	41	2	.227
Borowski, Joe	1	1	2.19	6	0	0	12.1	10	2	8	3	.227
Boskie, Shawn	1	3	4.40	6	4	0	28.2	28	8	16	2	.262
Brantley, J	2	3	4.54	29	2	4	41.2	42	16	29	6	.268
Brocail, Doug	1	1	4.02	3	3	0	15.2	15	3	9	3	.250
Brown, Kevin	0	2	5.27	2	2	0	13.2	16	5	6	2	.286
Bullinger, J	2	1	6.75	6	3	0	20.0	19	7	13	6	.257
Burba, Dave	2	3	7.45	10	3	0	19.1	30	8	14	6	.357
Burkett, John	3	6	4.46	15	14	0	82.2	95	32	52	7	.289
Candiotti, T	1	3	4.39	6	5	0	26.2	24	6	17	2	.238
Carpenter, C	0	0	1.15	8	0	0	15.2	10	4	12	1	.179
Castillo, F	0	3	7.13	4	4	0	17.2	24	7	11	2	.316
Castillo, T*	1	1	6.21	32	1	0	37.2	52	13	34	5	.329
Charlton, N*	4	1	2.45	16	1	1	25.2	16	9	25	1	.184
Clark, Mark	1	1	3.21	2	2	0	14.0	9	4	8	2	.184
Clontz, Brad	8	3	3.16	71	0	2	82.2	74	28	60	6	.243
Cone, David	4	1	2.55	7	6	0	42.1	31	26	44	4	.201
Cook, Dennis*	2	1	2.53	8	3	0	21.1	15	6	9	3	.195
Cooke, Steve*	0	2	2.50	3	3	0	18.0	18	8	10	3	.265
Cormier, R*	0	2	2.12	6	2	0	17.0	17	3	5	1	.262
Darwin, Danny	4	2	3.26	12	4	1	38.2	38	8	27	1	.260
Drabek, Doug	5	4	3.64	10	10	0	64.1	56	18	29	10	.234
Eichhorn, M	1	3	5.40	23	0	0	31.2	35	11	22	4	.292
Fassero, Jeff	0	3	3.52	9	4	0	30.2	34	7	30	6	.270
Fernandez, S*	2	2	3.77	7	7	0	43.0	26	21	48	5	.173
Foster, Kevin	1	1	2.57	2	2	0	14.0	10	2	9	1	.208
Franco, John*	0	2	1.61	22	0	13	22.1	19	11	14	1	.229
Freeman, M	6	4	3.47	70	3	2	103.2	94	34	78	9	.242
Gardner, Mark	2	2	4.28	5	4	0	27.1	26	7	20	4	.257
Glavine, Tom*	70	44	3.47	147	147	0	970.1	943	315	575	79	.256
Gooden, D	3	1	3.16	5	5	0	37.0	40	13	18	3	.278
Gross, Kevin	2	3	6.56	13	7	2	48.0	66	32	27	3	.335
Hamilton, J	0	3	6.63	3	3	0	19.0	24	5	13	4	.316
Hammond, C*	2	0	4.57	4	4	0	21.2	27	6	5	1	.318
Hampton, Mike*	0	2	5.52	4	3	0	14.2	20	3	6	4	.328
Harnisch, P	4	4	3.86	9	9	0	51.1	51	26	40	5	.251
Heredia, Gil	2	0	2.25	8	2	0	20.0	15	3	20	4	.200
Hernandez, X	1	1	1.71	18	0	2	21.0	16	9	21	0	.213
Hershiser, O	8	2	2.89	12	12	0	87.1	69	28	50	7	.217
Hill, Ken	2	4	3.48	9	9	0	54.1	44	23	30	6	.223
Isringhausen	1	0	6.28	3	3	0	14.1	13	6	8	2	.232
Jackson, Dan*	4	5	3.53	10	10	0	66.1	63	19	36	7	.263
Jackson, Mike	1	1	1.84	13	0	1	14.2	14	2	14	2	.237
Jones, Bobby	0	3	6.75	5	5	0	24.0	30	7	7	6	.306
Jones, Doug	2	1	5.50	12	0	4	18.0	26	2	17	2	.329
Juden, Jeff	0	2	9.75	7	2	0	12.0	16	8	7	4	.320
Kile, Darryl	3	2	2.88	9	8	0	56.1	47	25	46	7	.227
Leiper, Dave*	1	2	10.54	13	0	0	13.2	25	7	8	2	.397
Lilliquist, D*	7	11	4.07	29	25	0	148.1	180	31	75	15	.298
Maddux, Greg	38	15	2.33	70	68	0	514.1	408	80	378	26	.215
Maddux, Mike	0	4	3.82	14	3	1	33.0	36	17	17	3	.290
Magrane, Joe*	2	1	4.74	4	4	0	24.2	26	4	14	5	.271
Martinez, De	6	2	2.53	9	9	0	53.1	59	14	34	5	.285
Martinez, PJ	2	1	3.62	8	5	0	37.1	28	16	35	5	.212
Martinez, R	4	3	2.51	7	7	0	46.2	36	19	36	4	.214
McDowell, R	0	2	2.61	18	0	6	31.0	30	19	12	1	.256
McElroy, C*	1	1	5.94	16	0	0	16.2	21	14	9	1	.309
McMichael, G	9	7	3.40	134	0	18	159.0	156	44	140	11	.254
Mercker, Kent*	18	9	3.82	121	25	14	261.1	229	121	219	26	.237
Mimbs, M*	1	0	3.14	4	2	0	14.1	11	10	11	0	.216
Micki, Dave	1	2	4.60	4	2	0	15.2	22	5	16	3	.338
Morgan, Mike	2	5	4.68	10	9	0	57.2	56	21	27	5	.263
Moyer, Jamie*	0	2	10.22	2	2	0	12.1	19	8	7	4	.352
Mulholland, T*	3	4	4.92	10	10	0	53.0	69	12	19	7	.317
Myers, Randy*	2	1	3.00	18	1	8	27.0	22	15	25	3	.218
Navarro, J	1	0	2.66	3	3	0	20.1	20	5	10	3	.260
Neagle, Denny*	3	1	3.38	10	6	0	42.2	38	16	30	5	.236
Nied, Dave	1	1	4.50	5	3	0	20.0	17	7	20	1	.227
Nomo, Hideo	1	0	1.35	2	2	0	13.1	7	6	16	0	.146
Olivares, O	1	2	4.25	8	5	0	29.2	38	11	11	4	.319
Osborne, D*	1	1	3.10	3	3	0	20.1	21	1	10	4	.266
Parrett, Jeff	5	5	4.19	40	0	2	53.2	62	32	44	3	.292
Pena, Alej	3	3	3.48	40	0	11	44.0	38	12	34	6	.229
Portugal, M	2	3	5.20	9	9	0	45.0	46	20	32	8	.264
Rapp, Pat	1	0	4.96	3	3	0	16.1	19	10	4	2	.306
Reed, Steve	1	0	2.84	10	0	0	12.2	11	3	8	3	.239
Reynolds, S	3	0	1.65	5	3	0	27.1	27	6	21	0	.262
Reynoso, A	1	4	4.97	10	7	1	38.0	43	14	18	7	.287
Rojas, Mel	0	1	2.55	14	0	3	17.2	8	4	16	2	.136

294

ATLANTA-FULTON COUNTY STADIUM
Home of the Atlanta Braves

Atlanta, Georgia — Grass

Pitcher	W	L	ERA	G	GS	Sv	IP	H	BB	SO	HR	Avg
Ruffin, Bruce*	2	5	5.79	16	6	3	46.2	59	14	36	7	.307
Sanderson, S	1	1	1.54	5	3	0	23.1	12	4	16	1	.146
Schilling, C	3	1	3.44	12	7	2	52.1	46	14	37	5	.231
Schmidt, J	3	4	6.31	13	9	0	51.1	59	32	44	6	.295
Shaw, Jeff	0	1	2.03	8	1	0	13.1	11	5	9	1	.224
Slocumb, H	1	1	5.84	13	0	4	12.1	15	5	12	1	.278
Smiley, John*	2	5	4.60	13	9	0	58.2	56	22	31	8	.253
Smith, Zane	11	17	4.24	43	42	0	271.2	297	92	129	22	.281
Smoltz, John	55	44	3.53	133	133	0	912.1	783	304	767	92	.232
Stanton, Mike*	11	8	3.24	153	0	26	161.1	149	58	121	10	.246
Swift, Bill	1	1	4.22	4	3	0	21.1	21	10	16	1	.250
Swindell, G*	2	1	3.67	5	4	0	27.0	27	5	17	4	.257
Tewksbury, B	3	2	2.23	6	6	0	44.1	42	11	16	2	.253
Urbani, Tom*	0	1	3.31	5	2	0	16.1	18	5	4	3	.295
Valdes, I	2	1	3.63	3	3	0	22.1	22	3	9	4	.272
Valenzuela, F*	5	2	4.07	10	8	0	55.1	51	22	35	6	.244
Viola, Frank*	1	2	3.48	3	3	0	20.2	20	7	10	1	.270
Wade, Terrell*	1	0	2.65	22	3	0	34.0	25	19	36	4	.210
Wagner, Paul	1	2	4.85	6	4	1	26.0	28	11	18	4	.280
Watson, Allen*	3	0	4.50	4	4	0	26.0	22	6	13	5	.227
Wetteland, J	0	0	2.04	9	1	7	17.2	9	5	22	1	.150
Whitehurst, W	1	3	4.15	8	4	0	26.0	29	6	19	2	.279
Williams, Mk	0	1	6.75	5	1	0	13.1	18	7	11	4	.340
Wohlers, Mark	17	11	3.64	150	0	38	163.1	137	65	164	9	.231
Worrell, Todd	0	1	2.16	17	0	9	16.2	15	5	10	0	.234
Young, A	1	1	2.70	5	3	1	20.0	19	6	11	1	.260

ORIOLE PARK AT CAMDEN YARDS
Home of the Baltimore Orioles

Baltimore, Maryland — Grass

Pitcher	W	L	ERA	G	GS	Sv	IP	H	BB	SO	HR	Avg
Abbott, Jim*	2	1	5.01	5	5	0	32.1	39	7	7	5	.302
Aguilera, R	1	1	5.28	10	1	4	15.1	15	7	12	1	.259
Alvarez, W*	1	2	5.30	6	6	0	37.1	39	22	19	5	.281
Appier, Kevin	2	4	3.92	7	7	0	39.0	40	13	39	2	.268
Belcher, Tim	2	0	1.99	3	3	0	22.2	15	9	12	1	.197
Benitez, A	1	1	4.38	32	0	2	39.0	28	22	47	4	.201
Bere, Jason	2	1	8.79	3	3	0	14.1	18	14	9	2	.305
Bones, Ricky	1	4	9.57	6	5	0	26.1	35	17	7	10	.327
Bosio, Chris	2	3	3.79	6	6	0	35.2	42	14	13	4	.298
Boskie, Shawn	2	1	2.20	3	3	0	16.1	13	6	16	3	.203
Brown, Kevin	7	6	3.93	16	16	0	107.2	102	23	80	9	.251
Castillo, T*	0	0	2.30	12	0	1	15.2	13	6	12	3	.213
Clark, Mark	0	0	9.00	4	2	0	12.0	14	6	2	3	.298
Clark, Terry	1	3	3.33	27	0	0	24.1	26	10	11	2	.277
Clemens, R	2	4	3.00	7	7	0	48.0	44	23	43	4	.240
Cone, David	0	3	5.40	4	4	0	25.0	28	13	23	4	.295
Cook, Dennis*	1	2	5.63	10	2	0	16.0	13	7	6	0	.224
Coppinger, R	3	2	6.75	10	9	0	49.1	56	26	46	11	.287
Darwin, Danny	4	0	1.61	5	4	0	28.0	19	6	14	1	.192
Doherty, John	1	0	1.05	4	3	0	25.2	22	5	9	0	.237
Eckersley, D	0	0	3.00	12	0	10	12.0	8	1	7	0	.190
Eichhorn, M	2	2	1.87	26	0	1	43.1	35	8	24	0	.222
Eldred, Cal	3	1	4.36	6	6	0	43.1	35	21	35	6	.224
Erickson, S	12	9	4.40	28	28	0	188.0	193	68	84	21	.270
Fernandez, A	2	1	3.73	4	4	0	31.1	33	7	22	5	.273
Fernandez, S*	3	5	4.62	12	11	0	74.0	65	27	58	15	.234
Finley, Chuck*	0	2	4.26	3	3	0	19.0	17	10	16	3	.239
Flener, Huck*	0	1	3.95	4	1	0	13.2	10	4	10	2	.189
Frohwirth, T	8	2	2.87	70	0	3	116.0	103	39	56	7	.242
Gordon, Tom	1	0	4.63	7	2	0	23.1	24	13	18	2	.264
Groom, Buddy*	0	2	5.29	7	2	1	17.0	17	6	9	2	.262
Guardado, E*	0	1	5.84	5	1	0	12.1	11	4	11	1	.239
Gubicza, Mark	0	1	8.10	4	3	0	16.2	28	5	8	4	.384
Guthrie, Mark*	0	0	5.25	8	0	0	12.0	12	1	10	2	.261
Guzman, Juan	2	1	4.19	3	3	0	19.1	19	6	14	0	.250
Haney, Chris*	0	2	5.32	4	4	0	22.0	29	8	16	4	.319
Hanson, Erik	0	2	8.15	3	3	0	17.2	23	11	12	6	.343
Haynes, Jimmy	3	4	5.97	17	7	0	60.1	75	36	42	9	.310
Hentgen, Pat	3	1	3.07	5	4	0	29.1	34	12	17	3	.288
Hernandez, R	0	2	1.32	10	0	5	13.2	10	10	14	0	.213
Hershiser, O	2	2	8.10	4	4	0	20.0	28	9	7	4	.350
Hill, Ken	0	0	4.97	2	2	0	12.2	16	8	9	4	.333
Hitchcock, S*	1	3	9.12	7	5	0	24.2	31	20	25	8	.298
Johns, Doug*	2	0	3.46	3	2	0	13.0	13	6	8	4	.255
Johnson, R*	1	1	5.01	4	3	0	23.1	11	16	24	2	.136
Jones, Doug	1	4	7.83	26	0	10	23.0	30	10	27	4	.306
Kamieniecki	1	1	2.42	4	3	0	26.0	22	11	17	2	.237
Karl, Scott*	1	0	4.30	3	2	0	14.2	11	7	9	1	.200
Key, Jimmy*	5	5	1.78	5	5	0	35.1	26	15	25	1	.206
Klingenbeck	3	1	4.45	5	5	0	30.1	30	15	15	5	.263
Krivda, Rick*	1	5	4.95	15	10	0	72.2	70	28	40	13	.258
Langston, M*	4	0	1.96	5	5	0	36.2	25	11	30	2	.188
Leiter, Al*	2	2	3.42	5	4	1	26.1	26	12	19	2	.255
Leiter, Mark	1	1	5.54	4	2	0	13.0	15	7	10	1	.294
Lira, Felipe	0	3	11.30	4	3	0	14.1	21	6	6	4	.350
Magnante, M*	0	0	6.59	7	1	0	13.2	22	4	7	2	.373

ORIOLE PARK AT CAMDEN YARDS
Home of the Baltimore Orioles
Baltimore, Maryland — Grass

Pitcher	W	L	ERA	G	GS	Sv	IP	H	BB	SO	HR	Avg
Martinez, De	3	0	1.82	3	3	0	24.2	12	7	19	2	.141
McCaskill, K	0	0	6.32	7	2	0	15.2	18	7	6	0	.290
McDonald, Ben	23	18	3.88	54	54	0	354.2	320	123	241	43	.240
McDowell, J	5	0	3.43	6	6	0	42.0	39	16	30	3	.245
McDowell, R	1	2	3.58	23	0	2	32.2	36	14	11	3	.288
Mercker, Kent*	1	4	7.75	9	7	0	33.2	45	20	14	8	.317
Mesa, Jose	4	2	4.50	18	7	4	52.0	42	27	24	5	.225
Milacki, Bob	5	4	5.92	13	11	0	65.1	81	21	35	10	.296
Mills, Alan	14	6	3.44	98	0	5	162.0	130	82	116	22	.226
Moyer, Jamie*	10	13	5.09	38	35	0	212.0	222	58	122	35	.271
Mussina, Mike	40	20	4.01	77	77	0	531.2	532	119	368	72	.261
Myers, Randy*	1	1	1.61	28	0	16	28.0	24	15	35	1	.233
Nagy, Charles	2	2	4.70	4	4	0	23.0	22	7	12	1	.265
Navarro, J	2	0	1.45	3	2	0	18.2	12	3	10	2	.179
Ogea, Chad	0	0	4.74	4	1	0	19.0	15	6	7	5	.221
Olson, Gregg	2	3	1.78	59	0	33	60.2	41	25	60	3	.192
Oquist, Mike	3	4	6.19	23	6	0	64.0	77	40	39	9	.304
Orosco, Jesse*	2	3	2.69	81	0	3	67.0	42	30	70	7	.179
Pavlik, Roger	0	0	4.60	3	3	0	15.2	13	8	5	1	.224
Pennington, B*	1	2	8.90	32	0	3	29.1	34	34	31	7	.291
Pettitte, A*	4	0	4.97	5	4	0	25.1	29	7	12	3	.302
Plunk, Eric	0	1	3.86	11	0	2	14.0	8	3	19	1	.160
Poole, Jim*	3	0	3.30	59	0	0	46.1	38	22	28	2	.230
Reyes, Carlos	2	1	4.85	7	0	0	13.0	12	4	9	3	.235
Rhodes, A*	12	14	6.01	46	27	1	184.1	184	98	168	28	.263
Robertson, R*	1	1	6.00	2	2	0	12.0	16	5	5	3	.320
Rodriguez, Fr	2	0	3.71	4	2	0	17.0	13	3	9	2	.210
Rogers, Kenny*	1	0	3.81	8	4	0	28.1	28	11	25	5	.248
Salkeld, R	0	1	6.14	3	3	0	14.2	17	10	14	3	.288
Sanderson, S	2	0	3.75	2	2	0	12.0	10	6	8	1	.222
Scanlan, Bob	0	1	3.86	4	2	0	14.0	9	11	5	1	.191
Sele, Aaron	2	0	3.57	3	3	0	22.2	16	9	19	0	.203
Smith, Lee	0	2	2.74	24	0	17	23.0	21	10	21	2	.247
Stottlemyre, T	2	2	6.03	6	6	0	34.1	49	17	14	4	.336
Tapani, Kevin	2	4	5.30	6	6	0	35.2	42	19	21	5	.296
Trombley, M	1	0	1.23	5	1	1	14.2	14	7	8	0	.246
Valenzuela, F*	5	3	4.40	15	15	0	88.0	89	33	37	6	.268
Valera, Julio	0	2	5.14	4	2	0	14.0	16	6	8	2	.286
Van Poppel, T	1	0	7.24	5	2	0	13.2	17	7	9	0	.321
Viola, Frank*	1	1	5.68	2	2	0	12.2	13	7	3	2	.271
Wakefield, T	1	1	2.08	3	3	0	21.2	14	11	12	2	.182
Wells, David*	7	7	3.37	20	19	0	139.0	130	25	93	13	.253
Wengert, Don	1	0	1.17	3	2	0	15.1	15	5	6	0	.254
Wickman, Bob	1	3	7.11	12	2	2	19.0	27	10	12	2	.338
Williams, W	0	1	5.54	6	1	0	13.0	8	9	6	1	.170
Witt, Bobby	3	2	4.33	6	6	0	35.1	35	18	23	7	.255

FENWAY PARK
Home of the Boston Red Sox
Boston, Massachusetts — Grass

Pitcher	W	L	ERA	G	GS	Sv	IP	H	BB	SO	HR	Avg
Abbott, Jim*	2	2	3.07	6	6	0	44.0	43	20	27	2	.259
Aguilera, R	3	2	3.62	25	1	16	32.1	41	2	25	4	.304
Aldred, Scott*	1	1	2.57	2	2	0	14.0	14	3	9	1	.264
Alvarez, W*	2	2	2.73	5	4	0	26.1	25	10	17	2	.248
Appier, Kevin	5	2	3.22	10	10	0	64.1	62	24	61	5	.254
Bailey, Cory	0	2	5.09	13	0	0	17.2	21	12	14	2	.318
Bautista, J	1	1	3.63	4	3	0	22.1	20	8	8	3	.247
Belcher, Tim	2	1	2.51	4	4	0	28.2	27	5	13	3	.250
Belinda, Stan	6	0	3.38	56	0	3	64.0	49	33	44	4	.214
Bere, Jason	1	2	2.20	3	3	0	16.1	10	13	16	2	.161
Bielecki, M	0	2	8.53	4	2	0	12.2	17	7	7	2	.321
Boever, Joe	2	1	1.35	8	0	1	13.1	7	7	12	0	.156
Bones, Ricky	2	2	4.71	9	9	0	49.2	53	19	20	9	.285
Bosio, Chris	4	5	3.59	14	11	0	67.2	76	21	43	5	.285
Boskie, Shawn	0	2	9.82	6	3	0	18.1	33	9	8	2	.398
Brandenburg	2	2	4.96	17	0	0	16.1	15	4	15	2	.234
Brown, Kevin	1	4	5.98	8	8	0	49.2	61	23	24	4	.292
Candiotti, T	3	3	4.39	7	7	0	41.0	44	15	19	6	.272
Castillo, T*	1	1	2.45	13	0	1	22.0	23	0	20	3	.258
Clemens, R	75	48	3.16	155	155	0	1132.1	991	341	1090	71	.234
Cone, David	3	0	3.26	4	4	0	30.1	22	10	31	3	.202
Cormier, R*	4	4	4.60	24	6	0	58.2	64	15	36	6	.283
Darwin, Danny	20	15	4.54	57	40	1	279.1	305	72	197	37	.280
DeLucia, Rich	0	1	8.31	3	3	0	13.0	17	11	5	2	.327
Doherty, John	0	2	6.30	8	3	2	30.0	45	9	12	1	.344
Eckersley, D	0	4	4.39	17	1	8	26.2	30	2	18	2	.286
Eichhorn, M	1	0	0.78	18	0	2	23.0	16	6	19	1	.193
Eldred, Cal	2	2	3.63	5	5	0	34.2	31	13	21	2	.244
Erickson, S	4	5	4.07	10	10	0	59.2	66	22	27	5	.286
Eshelman, V*	6	1	5.73	31	11	0	77.0	89	44	46	8	.288
Farrell, John	1	4	6.68	5	5	0	31.0	35	14	15	7	.285
Fernandez, A	1	5	4.95	7	7	0	43.2	53	17	30	5	.291
Fetters, Mike	1	0	1.38	12	0	6	13.0	11	4	7	0	.250
Finley, Chuck*	3	7	4.23	16	13	0	87.1	84	47	50	5	.260
Fossas, Tony*	4	3	2.68	124	0	2	84.0	69	40	66	4	.224
Frohwirth, T	1	2	4.55	22	0	1	27.2	30	9	14	2	.275

Pitcher	W	L	ERA	G	GS	Sv	IP	H	BB	SO	HR	Avg
Garces, Rich	3	1	3.12	27	0	0	34.2	30	24	47	1	.234
Garcia, Ramon	2	1	8.76	3	2	0	12.1	20	3	8	5	.370
Gibson, Paul*	0	1	6.62	13	0	0	17.2	27	4	2	1	.351
Gordon, Tom	9	7	5.16	30	26	0	169.1	200	84	128	19	.292
Groom, Buddy*	1	0	5.11	6	1	0	12.1	11	4	8	3	.234
Gross, Kevin	2	1	4.50	3	3	0	22.0	22	12	12	3	.250
Gubicza, Mark	2	2	4.75	8	7	0	41.2	51	20	25	1	.311
Guetterman, L*	0	1	3.22	13	1	1	22.1	25	9	12	3	.291
Gunderson, E*	1	1	5.94	27	0	0	16.2	17	6	11	2	.274
Guthrie, Mark*	1	0	0.56	10	1	2	16.0	12	1	11	0	.211
Guzman, Juan	1	2	3.16	5	5	0	31.1	25	18	33	1	.212
Habyan, John	0	1	7.62	9	1	0	13.0	24	6	7	1	.414
Hanson, Erik	8	7	4.11	24	24	0	146.2	157	49	95	12	.276
Harnisch, P	0	3	4.87	3	3	0	20.1	17	18	11	2	.239
Henneman, M	2	3	5.17	26	0	3	31.1	46	16	22	4	.329
Hentgen, Pat	4	2	3.72	8	6	0	48.1	46	14	23	5	.256
Hernandez, R	0	1	1.35	13	0	5	13.1	7	4	20	1	.146
Hershiser, O	1	0	3.46	2	2	0	13.0	13	2	5	0	.260
Hill, Ken	0	0	7.43	2	2	0	13.1	15	7	8	1	.273
Hitchcock, S*	2	0	2.51	4	2	0	14.1	9	5	11	1	.173
Honeycutt, R*	1	0	3.57	14	0	2	17.2	14	5	14	2	.219
Hudson, Joe	1	2	2.50	37	0	2	54.0	51	25	30	2	.263
Jackson, Mike	1	1	5.95	15	0	3	19.2	14	12	15	2	.200
Johnson, R*	3	1	4.97	7	6	0	38.0	30	22	49	2	.213
Jones, Doug	0	0	0.98	15	0	9	18.1	20	2	18	1	.270
Kamieniecki	0	4	5.88	6	5	0	33.2	37	20	13	5	.280
Karl, Scott*	1	1	1.71	3	3	0	21.0	19	8	9	0	.241
Key, Jimmy*	7	3	3.97	11	11	0	77.0	79	14	40	7	.265
Krivda, Rick*	1	1	3.46	2	2	0	13.0	10	4	12	3	.217
Langston, M*	6	3	3.08	10	10	0	64.1	67	32	45	3	.268
Leftwich, P	0	2	5.79	2	2	0	14.0	15	5	9	2	.273
Leiter, Al*	0	4	9.00	8	6	0	27.0	35	15	21	4	.318
Lilliquist, D*	1	0	5.09	22	1	1	23.0	36	6	17	7	.356
Maddux, Mike	4	1	3.15	30	5	0	74.1	77	19	41	7	.264
Mahomes, Pat	1	1	5.60	10	2	1	17.2	18	12	10	2	.265
Martinez, De	2	0	1.19	3	3	0	22.2	16	6	13	2	.198
McCaskill, K	3	7	4.26	14	10	0	63.1	78	29	25	5	.308
McDonald, Ben	2	1	3.96	6	6	0	36.1	25	24	27	3	.200
McDowell, J	5	2	2.77	9	9	0	65.0	71	20	42	3	.274
Meacham, R	1	1	1.32	7	1	2	13.2	15	6	7	1	.288
Mesa, Jose	0	2	4.93	14	5	4	45.2	51	13	23	4	.291
Milacki, Bob	0	3	4.07	5	5	0	24.1	28	12	16	3	.280
Mills, Alan	0	0	2.25	5	1	1	12.0	10	6	9	1	.222
Minchey, Nate	1	4	7.12	7	6	0	30.1	52	17	17	3	.388
Miranda, A*	1	2	6.65	7	4	0	23.0	27	15	14	3	.297
Montgomery, J	0	1	2.05	19	0	11	26.1	20	17	15	1	.213
Moyer, Jamie*	5	2	5.00	18	8	0	68.1	86	21	32	7	.308
Mussina, Mike	3	2	4.63	7	7	0	46.2	55	15	26	0	.306
Nagy, Charles	3	0	1.11	5	5	0	40.2	25	5	21	2	.179
Navarro, J	5	2	4.50	10	8	0	56.0	66	22	30	6	.299
Nelson, Jeff	0	2	4.50	16	0	0	16.0	18	5	15	1	.286
Olson, Gregg	0	1	3.45	12	0	6	15.2	14	6	11	2	.241
Orosco, Jesse*	0	1	4.70	20	0	0	23.0	23	12	19	3	.261
Pall, Donn	2	1	4.64	12	0	1	21.1	26	10	10	3	.302
Pavlik, Roger	0	2	9.60	4	4	0	15.0	24	16	7	3	.358
Plesac, Dan*	0	0	4.96	11	1	3	16.1	23	6	13	1	.338
Plunk, Eric	2	4	2.95	23	0	0	36.2	32	11	44	1	.239
Quantrill, P	5	8	3.33	51	9	2	129.2	143	40	62	8	.285
Radke, Brad	1	1	3.00	2	2	0	12.0	11	4	10	1	.234
Rodriguez, Fr	0	3	9.15	7	3	0	19.2	26	12	10	1	.333
Rogers, Kenny*	4	1	3.77	16	5	2	45.1	44	13	27	5	.254
Russell, Jeff	1	5	4.66	57	1	28	58.0	70	25	42	6	.299
Ryan, Ken	4	6	5.45	64	0	11	71.0	79	37	61	4	.286
Sanderson, S	3	5	4.58	10	9	0	57.0	70	8	33	9	.295
Sele, Aaron	13	13	4.33	36	36	0	222.1	228	96	187	17	.267
Slocumb, H	2	3	4.78	37	0	15	37.2	29	24	38	1	.213
Smith, Lee	10	2	3.04	79	0	36	97.2	75	40	128	8	.206
Smith, Zane*	5	3	4.39	12	12	0	67.2	81	14	28	6	.302
Sparks, Steve	1	1	3.60	2	2	0	15.0	13	5	9	1	.220
Stanton, Mike*	3	2	3.48	35	0	1	31.0	33	13	18	5	.275
Stottlemyre	4	3	3.94	11	10	0	64.0	61	26	37	7	.256
Suppan, Jeff	0	3	7.86	8	5	0	26.1	37	8	19	5	.339
Swift, Bill	0	1	5.24	10	2	1	22.1	28	12	13	2	.318
Swindell, G*	1	3	4.99	5	5	0	30.2	40	8	23	2	.313
Tapani, Kevin	3	0	4.60	5	5	0	29.1	34	11	12	7	.286
Tavarez, Ju	3	1	3.44	7	2	0	18.1	21	4	11	2	.288
Tewksbury, B	0	0	7.30	2	2	0	12.1	12	3	4	3	.245
Timlin, Mike	0	0	1.50	9	0	2	12.0	6	7	9	0	.154
Trombley, M	1	1	4.41	5	2	0	16.1	18	8	10	3	.277
Valenzuela, F*	1	1	3.86	2	2	0	16.1	12	7	9	1	.211
Van Poppel, T	0	2	9.95	5	2	0	12.2	14	12	7	2	.286
Vanegmond, T	2	1	4.73	7	5	0	32.1	31	16	16	6	.248
Viola, Frank*	17	13	3.49	42	42	0	268.0	280	94	149	12	.271
Wakefield, T	15	10	4.25	29	29	0	201.0	215	66	131	31	.271
Wells, Bob	1	1	7.04	4	1	0	15.1	19	4	10	5	.306
Wells, David*	3	8	6.28	18	10	0	71.2	80	25	38	18	.284
Wickman, Bob	1	3	4.50	10	2	1	18.0	23	7	12	2	.307
Williams, W	1	1	3.86	7	1	0	16.1	12	8	15	3	.194

FENWAY PARK
Home of the Boston Red Sox
Boston, Massachusetts — Grass

Pitcher	W	L	ERA	G	GS	Sv	IP	H	BB	SO	HR	Avg
Witt, Bobby	4	4	4.22	13	12	0	81.0	83	58	74	7	.269

ANAHEIM STADIUM
Home of the Anaheim Angels
Anaheim, California — Grass

Pitcher	W	L	ERA	G	GS	Sv	IP	H	BB	SO	HR	Avg
Abbott, Jim*	20	39	4.40	85	83	0	552.0	607	186	300	53	.285
Aguilera, R	2	2	3.52	19	1	11	23.0	18	2	17	5	.209
Alvarez, W*	2	4	4.06	8	6	1	44.1	40	20	30	8	.245
Anderson, Brn*	6	6	4.67	21	18	0	113.2	114	31	52	16	.264
Appier, Kevin	5	3	3.22	10	10	0	72.2	70	23	71	4	.257
Belcher, Tim	2	2	6.46	4	4	0	23.2	39	11	7	6	.375
Bere, Jason	2	1	7.80	6	6	0	30.0	39	18	42	7	.310
Bielecki, M	1	3	6.16	11	4	0	30.2	30	15	16	6	.259
Boever, Joe	1	0	5.63	7	0	0	16.0	18	5	6	3	.286
Bones, Ricky	1	1	4.09	7	5	0	33.0	33	11	12	7	.258
Bosio, Chris	4	3	4.12	10	8	1	59.0	50	13	38	7	.228
Boskie, Shawn	8	9	5.89	27	24	0	142.0	170	44	96	31	.293
Brown, Kevin	4	3	3.79	9	9	0	61.2	55	25	28	6	.238
Candiotti, T	2	2	6.41	6	6	0	26.2	33	13	17	2	.300
Castillo, T*	0	0	5.54	8	0	0	13.0	14	4	7	3	.275
Clark, Terry	4	3	4.62	9	8	0	50.2	66	13	21	5	.327
Clemens, R	8	3	3.04	15	15	0	106.2	85	32	107	12	.219
Cone, David	3	2	2.70	5	5	0	40.0	29	16	27	2	.209
Darwin, Danny	1	2	3.16	6	4	1	31.1	26	8	16	4	.215
DeLucia, Rich	0	1	3.45	4	2	0	15.2	17	6	10	2	.279
Dickson, J	0	3	7.16	3	3	0	16.1	22	7	12	4	.319
Eckersley, D	0	1	1.82	23	0	19	24.2	16	3	23	0	.184
Eichhorn, M	7	7	2.21	103	0	6	138.1	126	24	102	2	.247
Eldred, Cal	2	0	1.00	2	2	0	18.0	9	5	16	0	.145
Erickson, S	6	0	2.60	6	6	0	45.0	38	7	20	2	.232
Farrell, John	4	8	6.23	13	12	0	69.1	81	33	39	10	.298
Fernandez, A	1	2	3.81	8	8	0	52.0	63	11	36	8	.303
Fernandez, S*	2	0	2.35	2	2	0	15.1	7	4	13	3	.135
Fetters, Mike	2	2	3.51	26	0	4	51.1	57	18	25	7	.286
Finley, Chuck*	71	53	3.27	163	148	0	1086.2	992	401	918	104	.245
Frey, Steve*	4	3	2.77	56	0	9	52.0	47	20	25	4	.239
Frohwirth, T	0	1	6.59	10	0	2	13.2	14	10	6	1	.259
Gibson, Paul*	0	1	2.18	9	1	0	20.2	18	9	12	2	.228
Gohr, Greg	1	0	4.26	10	2	0	25.1	28	10	17	2	.275
Gordon, Tom	5	4	3.15	15	10	0	74.1	64	36	60	5	.239
Grimsley, J	5	1	5.08	18	10	0	79.2	73	38	52	7	.236
Guardado, E*	1	1	7.11	5	2	1	12.2	15	8	11	1	.300
Gubicza, Mark	5	4	3.78	10	10	0	66.2	67	20	46	7	.263
Guetterman, L*	0	0	1.56	10	0	1	17.1	15	4	7	0	.250
Guzman, Juan	1	3	6.75	4	4	0	25.1	28	9	19	6	.277
Habyan, John	1	2	3.91	17	0	1	23.0	23	11	14	3	.256
Hancock, Ryan	2	0	2.81	4	1	0	16.0	13	4	12	1	.224
Hanson, Erik	2	5	5.04	10	10	0	60.2	62	31	40	5	.267
Harnisch, P	1	0	1.13	2	2	0	16.0	12	9	12	1	.214
Harris, Pep	1	0	2.57	7	2	0	21.0	15	8	12	3	.200
Henneman, M	1	3	3.12	22	0	9	26.0	26	14	15	0	.265
Hentgen, Pat	3	2	5.50	6	5	0	37.2	39	17	28	5	.277
Hernandez, R	2	1	3.94	11	1	1	16.0	15	5	14	2	.238
Hershiser, O	1	1	4.41	3	3	0	16.1	15	10	9	2	.250
Hill, Ken	1	0	2.40	2	2	0	15.0	17	5	11	1	.298
Hitchcock, S*	2	2	5.40	5	4	1	18.1	28	7	18	4	.341
Holtz, Mike*	2	1	2.70	13	0	0	13.1	10	13	15	1	.217
Holzemer, M*	0	2	7.09	22	2	0	33.0	41	15	18	5	.299
Honeycutt, R*	0	1	2.25	14	0	0	16.0	9	6	6	0	.167
Jackson, Mike	3	0	3.44	14	0	3	18.1	19	10	11	0	.275
James, Mike	5	1	1.83	63	0	1	68.2	49	28	47	6	.198
Johns, Doug*	1	1	2.35	2	2	0	15.1	13	4	8	1	.236
Johnson, R*	5	2	3.23	9	9	0	64.0	60	19	65	8	.241
Jones, Doug	1	1	4.15	9	0	5	13.0	13	2	8	3	.260
Kamieniecki	2	1	3.08	4	4	0	26.1	27	12	12	2	.273
Key, Jimmy*	6	1	2.85	11	11	0	79.0	66	18	44	7	.226
Langston, M*	48	36	3.83	108	108	0	768.2	679	264	624	89	.240
Leftwich, P	5	10	5.06	19	19	0	112.0	125	34	58	11	.284
Leiter, Al*	2	1	4.57	4	4	0	21.2	12	19	24	2	.167
Leiter, Mark	5	7	4.30	28	6	0	75.1	78	23	49	10	.264
Lilliquist, D*	1	1	1.98	10	0	0	13.2	7	4	13	2	.163
Linton, Doug	2	0	4.94	10	1	0	23.2	26	8	16	4	.277
Magrane, Joe*	3	4	6.25	18	10	0	72.0	78	38	33	13	.278
McCaskill, K	28	25	3.67	71	63	1	410.0	403	136	224	35	.258
McDonald, Ben	6	1	1.65	8	8	0	60.0	42	14	46	2	.197
McDowell, J	5	5	4.18	11	11	0	75.1	78	22	50	6	.273
McElroy, C*	2	0	3.68	22	0	0	22.0	17	7	20	1	.215
Meacham, R	1	0	2.77	7	1	0	13.0	16	5	11	2	.291
Mesa, Jose	2	1	4.05	10	3	5	26.2	34	5	14	2	.312
Milacki, Bob	0	1	4.30	3	2	0	14.2	19	2	8	3	.306
Monteleone, R	1	2	3.21	20	0	0	33.2	35	9	10	4	.265
Montgomery, J	0	1	2.59	20	0	12	24.1	17	9	14	1	.195
Moyer, Jamie*	1	1	9.00	6	4	0	19.0	32	10	8	6	.368
Mussina, Mike	5	1	2.98	7	7	0	51.1	39	11	46	3	.207
Nagy, Charles	2	1	4.50	5	5	0	34.0	33	8	16	4	.258
Navarro, J	0	3	3.86	4	3	0	21.0	21	9	11	0	.269

Anaheim, California — Grass

Pitcher	W	L	ERA	G	GS	Sv	IP	H	BB	SO	HR	Avg
Orosco, Jesse*	2	0	3.52	17	0	1	15.1	7	8	15	2	.140
Pall, Donn	1	3	2.41	13	0	2	18.2	21	3	8	1	.273
Patterson, B*	4	3	2.93	57	0	0	55.1	46	17	39	7	.230
Pavlik, Roger	2	0	1.08	2	2	0	16.2	19	5	11	0	.292
Percival, T	1	2	2.04	65	0	18	75.0	37	31	110	9	.145
Pettitte, A*	2	0	3.60	2	2	0	15.0	16	4	13	3	.271
Pichardo, H	3	1	3.24	11	3	1	33.1	29	14	18	2	.234
Plesac, Dan*	1	1	0.95	14	1	5	28.1	13	10	22	0	.135
Plunk, Eric	0	1	2.96	16	0	4	27.1	24	13	31	3	.235
Quantrill, P	1	1	5.68	3	2	0	12.2	16	6	8	2	.302
Ritz, Kevin	0	1	4.15	3	2	0	13.0	11	10	7	0	.234
Robertson, R*	1	1	1.89	3	2	0	19.0	12	6	12	1	.174
Rogers, Kenny*	4	3	2.45	14	7	0	62.1	41	30	44	5	.191
Russell, Jeff	4	1	2.90	19	2	2	40.1	36	11	31	2	.237
Sanderson, S	7	7	5.00	23	22	0	126.0	153	23	64	20	.300
Sele, Aaron	1	1	2.25	3	3	0	20.0	15	7	17	1	.203
Smith, Lee	0	3	2.89	36	0	21	37.1	32	10	35	2	.237
Springer, D	3	4	6.49	10	9	0	52.2	48	23	31	12	.244
Springer, R	3	5	6.49	29	11	2	86.0	110	42	54	19	.313
Stottlemyre	2	7	4.84	12	10	0	61.1	71	19	34	4	.291
Swindell, G*	3	0	0.63	6	5	0	42.2	25	4	40	1	.166
Tapani, Kevin	4	4	3.39	9	9	0	61.0	53	14	45	5	.235
Trombley, M	1	1	4.60	4	3	0	15.2	16	7	9	1	.271
Valera, Julio	9	6	3.20	26	16	2	129.1	137	31	76	10	.274
Viola, Frank*	1	3	3.19	6	6	0	42.1	45	10	23	5	.278
Wakefield, T	2	0	2.74	3	3	0	23.0	19	9	13	4	.229
Wells, David*	4	3	5.44	14	7	1	48.0	54	14	31	6	.287
Witt, Bobby	2	1	3.52	3	3	0	15.1	14	6	11	1	.237

Chicago, Illinois — Grass

Pitcher	W	L	ERA	G	GS	Sv	IP	H	BB	SO	HR	Avg
Abbott, Kyle*	0	2	8.76	3	2	0	12.1	14	4	7	4	.286
Adams, Terry	3	5	3.90	49	0	2	64.2	54	35	46	6	.230
Ashby, Andy	1	1	5.58	6	5	0	30.2	33	11	24	5	.280
Assenmacher*	15	6	3.04	161	0	16	192.2	171	59	189	16	.236
Astacio, P	0	3	5.96	7	4	0	22.2	29	9	15	3	.315
Avery, Steve*	2	2	3.48	6	6	0	41.1	42	9	33	3	.268
Bautista, J	8	2	2.99	66	2	1	99.1	94	23	63	12	.252
Beck, Rod	0	1	2.70	15	0	9	16.2	19	7	12	3	.288
Belcher, Tim	4	2	2.13	11	9	0	67.2	58	16	34	3	.227
Belinda, Stan	1	3	4.67	13	0	4	17.1	10	9	17	4	.169
Benes, Andy	6	5	2.95	12	12	0	76.1	71	18	50	5	.244
Bielecki, M	20	18	3.97	65	52	0	328.2	316	114	210	33	.255
Blair, Willie	2	2	3.49	11	2	1	28.1	28	13	22	3	.264
Boever, Joe	0	1	3.80	12	0	2	21.1	22	7	18	2	.265
Boskie, Shawn	13	14	4.34	62	29	0	213.2	228	82	98	30	.280
Bottenfield	2	1	1.90	26	1	0	42.2	36	9	20	5	.234
Brantley, J	0	2	3.34	21	1	9	29.2	37	13	26	5	.303
Bullinger, J	12	16	4.64	72	33	6	246.1	250	116	158	22	.266
Burba, Dave	3	3	2.38	13	4	0	34.0	27	7	35	1	.218
Burkett, John	3	1	2.33	8	7	0	46.1	43	9	18	3	.251
Candiotti, T	1	2	0.62	4	4	0	29.0	17	8	19	1	.167
Carpenter, C	4	0	1.04	13	1	0	26.0	20	6	14	1	.220
Casian, Larry*	0	0	2.01	40	0	0	22.1	21	9	10	1	.259
Castillo, F	22	28	3.90	73	73	0	441.1	429	124	324	50	.252
Charlton, N*	2	0	1.47	9	1	1	18.1	11	6	15	0	.183
Clark, Mark	0	2	4.50	4	4	0	22.0	21	7	16	3	.256
Cone, David	2	5	5.40	10	9	0	58.1	68	15	55	5	.289
Cooke, Steve*	0	1	4.50	4	2	0	16.0	17	3	16	1	.279
Darwin, Danny	0	2	4.71	5	3	0	21.0	28	5	14	4	.322
Drabek, Doug	5	6	4.28	16	15	0	96.2	109	26	46	8	.288
Fassero, Jeff*	2	1	1.58	13	4	2	40.0	28	10	33	3	.194
Fernandez, S*	0	3	7.30	5	5	0	24.2	30	7	14	5	.291
Foster, Kevin	13	7	3.76	29	26	0	170.0	149	54	131	26	.237
Franco, John*	1	3	1.93	20	0	7	23.1	19	6	15	2	.226
Freeman, M	4	0	3.02	12	5	0	41.2	31	13	25	3	.207
Gardner, Mark	5	3	5.90	12	10	0	58.0	59	10	40	15	.266
Glavine, Tom*	5	2	2.41	9	9	0	59.2	46	16	45	2	.207
Gooden, D	8	1	4.63	14	13	1	89.1	107	25	72	7	.296
Gross, Kevin	3	6	5.52	12	11	0	62.0	76	23	41	7	.305
Hamilton, J	2	1	4.80	5	5	0	30.0	30	11	22	4	.250
Hammond, C*	2	1	3.21	6	4	0	28.0	32	9	15	0	.299
Hampton, Mike*	1	0	1.33	5	2	0	20.1	17	8	9	0	.230
Hanson, Erik	1	0	0.75	2	2	0	12.0	10	5	11	0	.217
Harnisch, P	2	1	3.96	6	6	0	38.2	33	14	34	3	.231
Heredia, Gil	2	0	1.29	4	2	0	14.0	11	3	8	0	.229
Hernandez, X	0	0	4.12	11	0	2	19.2	21	4	10	4	.273
Hershiser, O	2	3	4.30	10	8	1	52.1	55	13	36	6	.266
Hill, Ken	3	3	2.90	10	10	0	62.0	57	17	39	8	.242
Hoffman, T	0	1	1.32	12	0	6	13.2	11	3	19	1	.220
Jackson, Dan*	5	6	4.10	23	21	0	131.2	137	54	60	10	.269
Jackson, Mike	2	3	7.36	15	1	0	18.1	20	8	15	7	.274
Jones, Bobby	4	0	4.01	5	5	0	33.2	30	6	19	5	.240
Jones, Doug	2	0	3.12	23	0	4	26.0	30	3	12	2	.283
Jones, Todd	0	1	3.65	10	0	4	12.1	10	6	14	0	.233

WRIGLEY FIELD
Home of the Chicago Cubs

Chicago, Illinois — Grass

Pitcher	W	L	ERA	G	GS	Sv	IP	H	BB	SO	HR	Avg
Kile, Darryl	3	3	5.75	10	6	0	36.0	39	24	29	4	.285
Langston, M*	1	1	2.57	2	2	0	14.0	11	8	12	0	.250
Leskanic, C	1	1	4.74	11	2	3	19.0	15	10	17	3	.211
Loaiza, E	1	0	2.84	2	2	0	12.2	14	5	7	1	.269
Maddux, Greg	48	32	3.22	103	102	0	728.2	672	229	488	43	.246
Maddux, Mike	2	1	5.64	12	2	2	30.1	36	11	21	3	.300
Magrane, Joe*	3	0	1.85	5	5	0	34.0	25	8	31	2	.198
Martinez, De	4	4	4.88	10	10	0	66.1	65	16	41	7	.255
Martinez, PJ	2	2	5.24	6	3	0	22.1	20	7	25	2	.235
Martinez, R	5	1	3.19	10	10	0	62.0	60	14	34	8	.252
McDowell, R	2	3	2.01	25	0	5	31.1	31	15	13	0	.267
McElroy, C*	7	6	2.94	104	0	4	134.2	115	69	110	8	.239
Mercker, Kent*	2	2	3.38	6	2	0	16.0	23	6	12	2	.338
Morgan, Mike	20	14	2.51	47	47	0	326.2	284	102	172	18	.241
Moyer, Jamie*	8	15	4.26	34	31	0	209.1	214	75	146	29	.267
Mulholland, T*	4	5	7.55	13	10	0	62.0	82	17	37	10	.309
Myers, Randy*	1	8	4.11	102	0	57	105.0	103	51	109	14	.261
Myers, Rodney	0	0	5.34	20	0	0	28.2	34	12	20	3	.288
Navarro, J	10	11	3.78	31	31	0	212.0	213	65	153	19	.260
Neagle, Denny*	3	1	4.43	10	6	1	40.2	37	9	30	5	.240
Olivares, O	1	0	8.10	8	5	0	30.0	40	16	23	8	.333
Osborne, D*	1	2	5.50	3	3	0	18.0	19	5	14	2	.260
Parrett, Jeff	3	4	7.82	22	1	0	25.1	35	8	21	4	.347
Patterson, B*	4	1	2.91	51	0	4	43.1	44	11	37	5	.267
Pavlas, Dave	2	0	3.00	7	0	0	12.0	15	0	4	3	.313
Pena, Alej	2	2	3.51	20	0	7	33.1	37	7	21	3	.276
Perez, Mike	3	5	3.26	64	0	0	66.1	64	29	38	5	.256
Plesac, Dan*	3	2	4.59	62	0	1	66.2	64	20	66	10	.250
Portugal, M	4	5	4.92	10	10	0	56.2	63	27	26	3	.288
Pugh, Tim	1	2	5.50	4	3	0	18.0	23	6	9	4	.315
Rapp, Pat	2	2	7.58	4	4	0	19.0	26	14	9	3	.329
Reed, Steve	0	0	0.00	15	0	1	17.0	8	3	18	0	.133
Rekar, Bryan	1	1	0.75	2	2	0	12.0	8	5	9	1	.186
Reynolds, S	0	1	7.62	6	2	0	13.0	15	5	10	2	.273
Reynoso, A	2	2	4.07	4	4	0	24.1	25	8	12	2	.281
Ritz, Kevin	3	0	3.92	3	3	0	20.2	18	6	21	3	.234
Rojas, Mel	1	0	3.15	18	0	5	20.0	17	6	13	1	.233
Rueter, Kirk*	1	2	5.19	3	3	0	17.1	19	1	10	3	.284
Ruffin, Bruce*	1	3	5.27	22	7	1	54.2	61	18	34	4	.289
Sanders, S	1	1	7.50	4	2	0	12.0	9	6	15	1	.200
Sanderson, S	9	9	4.52	39	19	1	139.1	161	38	95	19	.291
Scanlan, Bob	8	11	4.72	89	8	4	135.1	151	49	65	11	.289
Schilling, C	1	2	4.34	9	5	1	37.1	38	9	27	3	.259
Schourek, P*	1	2	2.76	5	2	0	16.1	14	6	16	1	.250
Shaw, Jeff	1	1	1.35	11	1	0	20.0	15	5	12	0	.224
Slocumb, H	2	3	3.79	48	0	2	59.1	58	26	41	3	.262
Smiley, John*	6	3	5.03	12	11	0	62.2	75	10	33	10	.288
Smith, Lee	4	5	4.35	41	0	25	51.2	64	15	54	5	.308
Smith, Zane	3	1	3.66	9	7	0	46.2	43	9	20	2	.246
Smoltz, John	6	3	2.73	12	12	0	85.2	54	30	76	10	.182
Stanton, Mike*	1	1	8.03	16	0	1	12.1	13	6	8	2	.265
Swartzbaugh	0	0	0.92	8	2	0	19.2	14	7	10	1	.209
Swift, Bill	0	1	5.68	2	2	0	12.2	16	4	10	3	.320
Swindell, G*	2	0	2.77	4	2	0	13.0	14	5	7	1	.275
Telemaco, A	2	4	5.98	12	10	0	46.2	56	16	36	8	.296
Tewksbury, B	3	5	4.95	11	11	0	63.2	84	11	29	8	.311
Thompson, Mar	1	1	2.13	2	2	0	12.2	11	3	10	1	.229
Trachsel, S	12	21	3.83	46	45	0	279.2	280	102	190	49	.260
Valdes, I	1	2	4.68	4	4	0	25.0	28	9	26	3	.269
Valenzuela, F*	2	2	5.14	7	6	0	35.0	42	13	21	4	.300
VanLandingham	2	2	3.91	5	4	0	25.1	28	10	13	2	.267
Viola, Frank*	2	2	3.82	5	5	0	30.2	37	10	20	3	.303
Wagner, Paul	1	0	4.43	6	2	0	20.1	22	4	9	2	.272
Walker, Mike	0	0	3.76	24	0	0	26.1	29	17	13	2	.276
Watson, Allen*	1	3	4.01	4	4	0	24.2	27	8	10	7	.278
Wendell, Turk	5	4	3.87	68	1	8	93.0	79	47	87	9	.230
Wetteland, J	0	1	1.84	8	0	4	14.2	10	7	14	1	.196
Whitehurst, W	0	3	6.00	11	7	1	39.0	53	9	25	6	.331
Williams, Bri	1	3	5.40	6	4	0	21.2	26	13	14	0	.295
Williams, Mk	1	0	6.08	4	2	0	13.1	16	4	6	3	.314
Wilson, Paul	0	2	5.40	2	2	0	13.1	12	4	16	3	.235
Worrell, Todd	0	0	0.99	20	0	11	27.1	23	9	23	0	.237
Young, A	5	8	3.52	40	15	3	120.1	107	50	59	14	.242

COMISKEY PARK
Home of the Chicago White Sox

Chicago, Illinois — Grass

Pitcher	W	L	ERA	G	GS	Sv	IP	H	BB	SO	HR	Avg
Abbott, Jim*	3	6	3.00	12	12	0	84.0	74	29	37	8	.233
Aguilera, R	1	1	4.15	10	1	5	17.1	19	7	11	3	.275
Alvarez, W*	30	19	3.89	75	64	0	432.1	396	217	305	42	.247
Anderson, Brn*	2	1	6.50	3	3	0	18.0	25	2	9	3	.338
Andujar, Luis	0	2	4.91	4	4	0	22.0	26	12	8	2	.302
Appier, Kevin	5	1	2.05	6	6	0	44.0	33	18	32	1	.217
Assenmacher	2	3	4.34	24	0	0	18.2	16	6	17	1	.229
Baldwin, J	6	4	4.30	18	17	0	106.2	103	41	76	18	.252
Belcher, Tim	3	5	5.24	11	11	0	67.0	78	24	31	7	.290

Chicago, Illinois   **Grass**

Pitcher	W	L	ERA	G	GS	Sv	IP	H	BB	SO	HR	Avg
Bere, Jason	14	10	4.73	39	39	0	217.0	192	140	183	25	.239
Bertotti, M*	2	1	9.16	8	3	0	18.2	24	13	13	4	.312
Boever, Joe	0	1	6.00	9	0	0	15.0	14	11	7	3	.255
Bohanon, B*	0	0	2.57	4	1	0	14.0	12	4	4	0	.231
Bones, Ricky	1	3	5.12	6	5	0	31.2	37	10	10	4	.291
Bosio, Chris	1	3	5.40	7	7	0	36.2	36	29	17	3	.263
Brown, Kevin	0	3	5.44	7	7	0	44.2	52	19	21	4	.295
Candiotti, T	0	2	3.21	2	2	0	14.0	16	4	11	1	.267
Castillo, T*	2	0	1.44	18	0	1	25.0	20	7	9	1	.233
Clark, Mark	1	0	4.38	2	2	0	12.1	13	2	5	0	.260
Clemens, R	1	2	4.11	5	5	0	35.0	31	12	20	2	.238
Cone, David	3	1	3.64	4	4	0	29.2	25	16	16	3	.223
Cook, Dennis*	1	0	2.16	22	1	0	33.1	23	12	25	1	.192
Darwin, Danny	1	1	3.92	5	2	0	20.2	13	6	15	2	.171
Darwin, Jeff	0	0	3.18	11	0	0	17.0	13	5	8	5	.213
DeLucia, Rich	0	4	7.47	5	4	0	15.2	15	12	9	3	.254
Doherty, John	0	1	3.50	4	2	0	18.0	18	6	7	2	.261
Eckersley, D	0	0	2.25	11	0	10	12.0	8	4	10	3	.182
Eichhorn, M	0	1	2.57	11	0	0	14.0	13	2	9	1	.250
Eldred, Cal	4	3	3.65	7	7	0	44.1	50	19	26	4	.281
Erickson, S	1	3	6.00	6	6	0	33.0	44	22	7	0	.341
Fernandez, A	41	29	3.52	95	93	0	659.0	579	193	463	71	.236
Finley, Chuck*	3	4	6.44	8	8	0	43.1	61	17	26	3	.335
Garcia, Ramon	2	2	6.50	11	9	0	45.2	49	19	21	10	.277
Gordon, Tom	3	0	4.67	5	3	0	17.1	17	10	10	1	.266
Grimsley, J	0	1	3.21	3	2	0	14.0	12	7	7	0	.240
Groom, Buddy*	1	1	4.05	9	1	0	13.1	17	10	6	2	.327
Gross, Kevin	2	0	4.66	3	3	0	19.1	18	10	11	1	.240
Gubicza, Mark	1	5	6.27	8	6	0	33.0	51	14	11	4	.345
Guzman, Juan	1	3	3.51	5	5	0	33.1	30	13	23	4	.240
Haney, Chris*	1	1	3.38	3	2	0	13.1	16	5	6	3	.302
Hanson, Erik	2	3	5.40	5	4	0	30.0	35	12	19	2	.294
Henneman, M	1	2	4.26	11	0	6	12.2	15	8	3	1	.319
Hentgen, Pat	3	1	2.76	5	4	0	29.1	27	6	19	2	.233
Hernandez, R	14	9	2.25	154	1	72	183.2	154	51	181	10	.226
Hill, Ken	1	0	1.59	2	2	0	17.0	11	5	11	1	.180
Johnson, R*	4	0	3.10	4	4	0	29.0	19	16	35	3	.184
Kamieniecki	0	1	8.62	4	3	0	15.2	15	16	7	3	.246
Karchner, M	3	5	6.60	38	0	0	43.2	54	26	32	8	.310
Key, Jimmy*	3	1	2.20	5	5	0	32.2	29	10	20	2	.230
Keyser, Brian	2	5	5.16	26	6	0	82.0	102	28	38	8	.308
Langston, M*	4	1	2.43	8	8	0	63.0	50	21	37	3	.216
Leiter, Al*	2	1	2.66	4	3	0	20.1	16	12	14	0	.216
Leiter, Mark	2	1	4.70	4	2	0	15.1	14	6	8	4	.241
Linton, Doug	1	1	6.75	3	3	0	14.2	17	6	13	3	.288
Magnante, M*	1	0	1.59	9	1	0	17.0	16	7	8	2	.258
Magrane, Joe*	0	2	5.40	8	4	0	26.2	28	9	7	5	.272
Mahomes, Pat	0	2	4.87	4	3	0	20.1	19	5	10	4	.253
Martinez, De	1	0	0.95	3	3	0	19.0	7	6	10	1	.113
McCaskill, K	19	14	3.69	94	26	3	275.1	272	111	154	21	.260
McDonald, Ben	1	6	6.05	7	7	0	38.2	41	19	23	4	.272
McDowell, J	35	22	3.55	68	68	0	504.0	505	138	329	39	.263
Milacki, Bob	2	0	5.19	3	3	0	17.1	20	4	8	3	.278
Mills, Alan	0	1	7.64	9	0	0	17.2	17	15	10	4	.274
Miranda, A*	1	0	4.34	5	2	0	18.2	16	11	8	3	.235
Montgomery, J	1	1	2.65	16	0	11	17.0	12	12	9	1	.207
Moyer, Jamie*	2	0	0.59	2	2	0	15.1	9	3	6	0	.173
Mussina, Mike	4	3	3.86	8	8	0	51.1	49	14	29	6	.250
Nagy, Charles	4	5	4.56	9	9	0	53.1	72	15	27	4	.324
Navarro, J	0	2	4.07	4	3	0	24.1	18	8	13	1	.212
Nelson, Jeff	0	0	0.61	15	0	0	14.2	10	8	13	0	.200
Olson, Gregg	0	1	4.05	14	0	6	13.1	22	4	4	0	.373
Pall, Donn	10	2	4.18	70	0	2	103.1	111	32	51	11	.278
Pavlik, Roger	2	2	3.15	7	7	0	45.2	37	22	37	6	.227
Pichardo, H	1	2	1.93	14	4	2	37.1	29	15	20	2	.213
Plunk, Eric	2	1	4.50	11	0	1	18.0	21	6	13	2	.288
Radinsky, S*	8	7	3.36	131	0	18	123.1	122	40	92	11	.257
Radke, Brad	2	0	4.73	2	2	0	13.1	14	3	7	3	.269
Reyes, Carlos	1	1	3.75	4	2	0	12.0	11	13	4	1	.262
Rivera, M	1	0	0.00	4	1	1	14.1	5	5	18	0	.106
Robertson, R*	0	1	4.41	4	2	0	16.1	13	6	9	3	.224
Rogers, Kenny*	1	1	4.78	9	4	0	32.0	32	14	18	4	.267
Ruffcorn, S	0	2	6.59	4	2	0	13.2	17	10	4	3	.327
Russell, Jeff	1	1	5.68	11	0	4	12.2	17	9	7	2	.327
Sanderson, S	5	1	4.91	10	10	0	55.0	73	9	22	9	.323
Scanlan, Bob	0	2	11.93	5	2	0	14.1	26	7	8	0	.377
Sele, Aaron	0	1	3.00	4	4	0	21.0	21	13	18	2	.276
Shaw, Jeff	0	0	6.75	7	0	0	12.0	16	4	7	3	.333
Simas, Bill	2	3	4.60	38	0	0	47.0	46	27	43	4	.253
Sirotka, Mike*	1	3	4.55	10	6	0	29.2	35	10	8	3	.313
Smiley, John*	0	3	6.00	2	2	0	12.0	14	4	5	0	.286
Sparks, Steve	0	3	7.08	3	3	0	20.1	25	10	4	3	.305
Stottlemyre	1	3	6.91	5	5	0	27.1	32	14	13	2	.291
Tapani, Kevin	9	5	4.33	21	21	0	141.1	149	47	89	18	.273
Thomas, Larry*	2	2	2.10	40	0	0	25.2	24	10	19	2	.250
Van Poppel, T	2	0	4.43	4	4	0	22.1	21	13	14	2	.256
Viola, Frank*	0	1	3.77	2	2	0	14.1	16	4	7	1	.281
Wakefield, T	2	1	4.03	3	3	0	22.1	29	9	9	1	.309

Pitcher	W	L	ERA	G	GS	Sv	IP	H	BB	SO	HR	Avg
Wells, David*	2	4	4.38	9	8	0	51.1	58	20	26	7	.286
Wickman, Bob	2	0	5.93	8	1	1	13.2	14	8	7	1	.259
Witt, Bobby	2	5	5.30	9	9	0	54.1	66	30	28	6	.301
Wolcott, Bob	0	2	5.63	3	3	0	16.0	19	5	5	2	.306

Pitcher	W	L	ERA	G	GS	Sv	IP	H	BB	SO	HR	Avg
Ashby, Andy	0	4	11.72	5	4	0	17.2	24	15	12	4	.343
Assenmacher*	0	1	5.87	14	0	1	15.1	16	8	13	1	.291
Astacio, P	3	0	1.57	8	6	0	46.0	33	12	17	1	.201
Avery, Steve*	4	5	4.71	11	11	0	63.0	60	23	54	7	.253
Ayala, Bobby	6	7	4.74	26	8	1	76.0	81	27	55	8	.278
Beck, Rod	0	0	2.40	13	0	5	15.0	14	3	11	1	.246
Belcher, Tim	18	14	4.61	43	38	2	234.1	224	91	175	25	.251
Belinda, Stan	1	0	4.50	9	0	4	12.0	10	6	10	3	.233
Benes, Andy	6	3	3.81	9	9	0	54.1	57	20	47	5	.271
Bielecki, M	3	2	2.97	7	5	0	33.1	26	12	27	1	.210
Blair, Willie	0	3	7.66	12	3	0	24.2	32	8	15	3	.305
Boever, Joe	1	4	6.23	16	0	1	17.1	23	8	14	3	.315
Boskie, Shawn	1	1	6.46	3	2	0	15.1	17	5	4	3	.283
Brantley, J	5	8	3.59	101	1	40	133.0	107	54	109	21	.226
Bullinger, J	1	1	4.24	8	1	0	17.0	14	11	12	2	.237
Burba, Dave	10	10	3.32	33	25	0	165.1	133	86	131	10	.220
Burkett, John	5	3	3.42	8	8	0	50.0	51	12	31	4	.258
Candiotti, T	0	3	5.61	5	5	0	25.2	26	10	17	2	.268
Carrasco, H	4	6	3.23	84	0	6	108.2	89	51	70	8	.223
Castillo, F	1	2	6.39	6	5	0	25.1	32	7	12	5	.314
Castillo, T*	1	0	6.57	10	0	0	12.1	18	6	8	2	.346
Charlton, N*	13	12	3.19	117	19	15	239.2	211	94	182	20	.236
Cone, David	4	0	1.50	6	4	0	36.0	20	13	41	2	.159
Cook, Dennis*	1	0	4.24	6	2	0	17.0	21	5	15	3	.323
Cormier, R*	0	2	10.06	4	4	0	17.0	31	5	10	6	.391
Darwin, Danny	1	5	4.31	12	7	0	56.1	51	19	33	11	.244
DeLucia, Rich	0	1	3.68	9	1	0	14.2	16	7	16	2	.262
Dewey, Mark	0	0	2.77	10	0	0	13.0	13	6	7	1	.271
Drabek, Doug	5	3	2.25	11	11	0	76.0	67	21	42	11	.233
Fassero, Jeff*	1	2	3.68	10	2	0	22.0	21	10	14	1	.269
Fernandez, S*	4	2	1.75	8	8	0	51.1	34	25	46	3	.190
Foster, Kevin	0	2	6.75	3	3	0	14.2	18	5	22	5	.300
Franco, John*	13	8	2.97	110	0	60	136.1	123	41	86	0	.245
Freeman, M	0	1	2.45	8	1	0	14.2	12	4	10	2	.226
Gardner, Mark	1	3	7.50	5	5	0	24.0	39	11	19	2	.386
Glavine, Tom*	14	2	2.41	17	17	0	123.0	92	40	73	7	.208
Gooden, D	2	5	5.02	8	8	0	43.0	48	14	44	4	.281
Gross, Kevin	6	2	2.90	12	9	0	68.1	60	25	51	7	.235
Hamilton, J	1	2	3.00	3	3	0	21.0	17	7	9	1	.230
Hammond, C*	8	12	4.98	33	28	0	161.0	177	75	85	19	.281
Hampton, Mike*	1	2	5.30	6	3	0	18.2	18	11	13	3	.269
Hanson, Erik	1	1	3.58	9	8	0	50.1	52	5	43	7	.264
Harnisch, P	2	4	5.65	8	8	0	43.0	51	27	34	9	.293
Heredia, Gil	0	1	4.42	6	3	0	18.1	23	6	13	1	.311
Hernandez, X	6	2	4.28	48	1	2	67.1	75	26	58	5	.281
Hershiser, O	6	2	3.18	9	9	0	65.0	71	16	36	9	.275
Hill, Ken	1	4	5.31	7	7	0	39.0	35	20	32	8	.238
Jackson, Dan*	17	13	3.81	43	42	0	269.1	237	105	159	18	.235
Jackson, Mike	6	1	1.34	31	0	2	40.1	29	15	44	3	.201
Jarvis, Kevin	7	5	5.75	23	17	0	108.0	126	31	54	15	.287
Jones, Bobby	2	2	3.90	5	5	0	32.1	27	11	15	2	.233
Jones, Todd	2	0	5.52	11	0	0	14.2	12	12	15	3	.222
Juden, Jeff	0	3	6.48	5	2	0	16.2	18	10	10	2	.295
Kile, Darryl	1	2	5.68	6	3	0	19.0	21	13	15	1	.292
Leiper, Dave*	1	0	1.42	11	0	1	12.2	11	6	7	0	.234
Lieber, Jon	1	2	7.63	4	3	0	15.1	21	2	10	3	.344
Lilliquist, D*	2	0	1.84	7	2	0	14.2	16	3	8	1	.291
Loaiza, E	0	1	1.29	2	2	0	14.0	7	6	9	1	.146
Maddux, Greg	7	4	2.62	16	16	0	113.1	103	18	85	3	.243
Maddux, Mike	0	0	3.68	12	0	3	14.2	14	5	8	0	.241
Magrane, Joe*	3	1	1.96	6	6	0	46.0	35	12	28	2	.212
Martinez, De	5	3	4.12	10	10	0	63.1	64	20	34	8	.269
Martinez, PJ	1	1	2.13	6	3	1	25.1	15	3	30	1	.163
Martinez, R	8	3	3.18	11	11	0	73.2	66	24	55	6	.235
McDowell, R	3	1	2.59	19	0	7	24.1	23	9	8	1	.253
McElroy, C*	4	4	4.10	64	0	4	68.0	60	19	50	4	.240
Mercker, Kent*	0	1	2.13	6	1	0	12.2	11	1	10	3	.239
Minor, Blas	0	1	4.15	9	0	0	13.0	14	7	9	3	.280
Moore, Marcus	1	1	6.75	16	0	0	18.2	23	14	16	1	.303
Morgan, Mike	7	4	3.86	14	12	0	72.1	81	25	40	7	.286
Moyer, Jamie*	1	2	3.77	3	3	0	14.1	13	8	9	2	.250
Mulholland, T*	1	3	3.19	6	6	0	36.2	44	15	20	3	.297
Myers, Randy*	6	10	2.91	84	5	28	136.0	117	69	118	8	.238
Neagle, Denny*	2	3	5.64	10	7	0	44.2	53	15	35	5	.296
Nitkowski, C*	0	2	9.00	6	4	0	15.0	23	9	6	2	.354
Olivares, O	2	0	4.01	5	4	0	24.2	34	10	7	3	.354
Osborne, D*	1	1	5.73	4	4	0	22.0	28	9	13	5	.326
Osuna, Al*	0	1	4.05	12	0	0	13.1	12	8	10	0	.261

CINERGY FIELD
Home of the Cincinnati Reds

Cincinnati, Ohio — Artificial

Pitcher	W	L	ERA	G	GS	Sv	IP	H	BB	SO	HR	Avg
Parrett, Jeff	1	1	1.45	11	1	0	18.2	12	7	19	0	.185
Pena, Alej	0	0	0.43	12	0	4	21.0	11	1	23	0	.157
Perez, Mike	0	0	3.12	12	0	2	17.1	11	2	11	2	.180
Plesac, Dan*	1	0	1.80	13	0	3	15.0	11	3	13	1	.193
Portugal, M	9	10	3.68	26	26	0	161.1	144	40	80	23	.237
Pugh, Tim	12	9	4.41	42	27	0	196.0	218	76	93	21	.286
Rapp, Pat	2	1	4.08	3	3	0	17.2	19	10	7	1	.275
Reed, Steve	3	1	2.51	11	0	0	14.1	9	8	6	3	.184
Remlinger, M*	0	1	5.93	8	2	0	13.2	13	10	12	2	.250
Reynolds, S	1	3	4.06	8	5	0	31.0	40	14	29	0	.323
Reynoso, A	2	1	6.26	5	5	0	27.1	36	10	10	3	.340
Ritz, Kevin	0	4	8.20	4	4	0	18.2	26	12	15	2	.347
Rojas, Mel	1	1	3.96	14	0	4	25.0	23	3	22	4	.240
Ruffin, Bruce*	2	2	5.12	16	6	2	45.2	52	24	34	3	.291
Ruffin, J	4	1	3.21	68	0	5	95.1	94	37	72	10	.260
Salkeld, R	5	3	3.99	14	9	0	65.1	58	23	46	8	.240
Sanders, S	0	0	1.15	3	2	0	15.2	9	6	15	0	.173
Sanderson, S	1	1	3.94	3	3	0	16.0	17	6	12	4	.270
Schilling, C	2	2	3.31	8	5	2	35.1	34	9	26	4	.250
Schourek, P*	22	5	3.06	32	27	0	185.0	155	44	158	15	.229
Scott, Tim	1	1	6.35	16	0	0	17.0	20	7	20	2	.286
Service, S	1	1	3.80	30	0	1	45.0	51	15	40	8	.290
Shaw, Jeff	6	3	2.47	41	0	3	54.2	44	16	34	7	.220
Slocumb, H	1	2	2.92	8	0	1	12.1	16	4	6	1	.320
Smiley, John*	22	20	3.88	57	56	1	355.1	350	101	247	34	.265
Smith, Lee	2	2	3.69	34	0	9	39.0	38	13	27	5	.252
Smith, Zane*	4	3	4.05	15	11	0	80.0	78	29	32	9	.263
Smoltz, John	4	5	2.88	10	10	0	68.2	59	22	62	4	.232
Spradlin, J	1	0	3.67	21	0	2	27.0	23	7	12	2	.240
Stanton, Mike*	2	0	2.41	20	0	2	18.2	18	5	13	0	.271
Swift, Bill	2	1	1.21	5	4	0	29.2	21	5	17	1	.200
Swindell, G*	8	4	3.15	21	21	0	143.0	151	31	85	12	.276
Tewksbury, B	4	3	4.02	8	8	0	47.0	54	10	14	3	.287
Trachsel, S	2	0	2.78	4	4	0	22.2	21	9	17	5	.241
Valenzuela, F*	4	3	5.94	8	8	0	50.0	60	21	25	8	.302
VanLandingham	1	0	3.38	3	3	0	18.2	22	10	9	1	.301
Viola, Frank*	0	2	5.79	3	3	0	18.2	26	7	10	3	.329
Wagner, Paul	1	3	6.31	5	4	0	25.2	27	11	17	5	.267
Watson, Allen*	0	3	5.84	4	4	0	24.2	31	11	16	4	.316
Weathers, D	2	0	4.02	6	3	0	15.2	12	7	8	1	.222
Wells, David*	4	2	3.05	6	6	0	41.1	42	9	29	3	.266
West, David*	0	1	2.13	6	1	0	12.2	7	7	14	1	.163
Wetteland, J	0	0	0.63	9	0	3	14.1	6	4	19	0	.128
Whitehurst, W	1	1	2.55	7	3	0	17.2	18	1	11	1	.257
Wickander, K*	0	0	10.05	18	0	0	14.1	21	13	11	3	.333
Williams, Bri	3	2	5.87	9	4	0	23.0	31	14	14	1	.337
Worrell, Todd	1	2	3.98	18	0	9	20.1	15	7	13	2	.208
Young, A	0	5	8.15	7	2	0	17.2	23	7	11	4	.329

JACOBS FIELD
Home of the Cleveland Indians

Cleveland, Ohio — Grass

Pitcher	W	L	ERA	G	GS	Sv	IP	H	BB	SO	HR	Avg
Abbott, Jim*	1	1	3.46	2	2	0	13.0	14	5	3	2	.269
Aguilera, R	0	1	3.46	7	1	3	13.0	12	0	10	3	.231
Alvarez, W*	3	0	2.79	4	4	0	29.0	26	7	12	3	.236
Anderson, Brn*	3	1	5.22	7	7	0	39.2	44	14	15	8	.291
Appier, Kevin	1	3	6.97	5	5	0	31.0	34	14	28	4	.286
Assenmacher*	6	2	2.61	67	0	2	51.2	49	13	53	2	.253
Belcher, Tim	0	4	4.94	4	4	0	31.0	31	11	11	5	.261
Bones, Ricky	1	2	6.05	3	3	0	19.1	22	7	6	3	.286
Bosio, Chris	0	3	6.61	3	3	0	16.1	22	7	7	2	.333
Boskie, Shawn	0	2	4.85	2	2	0	13.0	12	4	5	3	.226
Brown, Kevin	0	2	4.61	2	2	0	13.2	14	8	7	0	.264
Clark, Mark	11	3	4.12	21	20	0	133.1	146	36	58	15	.281
Clemens, R	0	2	7.01	4	4	0	25.2	33	12	22	6	.320
Cone, David	2	1	3.90	4	4	0	27.2	29	12	13	3	.276
Cook, Dennis*	0	0	3.68	12	0	0	14.2	14	10	18	0	.255
Embree, Alan*	4	1	4.15	24	0	0	26.0	21	18	20	5	.241
Erickson, S	0	4	7.31	5	5	0	28.1	46	13	12	4	.371
Fernandez, A	1	3	4.94	4	4	0	27.1	34	8	12	5	.306
Finley, Chuck*	0	2	2.77	2	2	0	13.0	14	3	5	1	.264
Gordon, Tom	0	3	19.50	3	3	0	12.0	30	11	9	3	.462
Graves, Danny	2	0	4.15	9	0	0	17.1	16	8	15	1	.239
Grimsley, J	2	0	6.11	15	9	1	66.1	81	41	41	7	.313
Gross, Kevin	0	1	3.77	3	2	0	14.1	16	5	9	1	.291
Guzman, Juan	1	2	3.70	4	4	0	24.1	24	10	16	3	.258
Haney, Chris*	1	0	5.25	4	4	0	24.0	28	7	8	3	.301
Hanson, Erik	3	1	2.57	4	4	0	28.0	26	8	14	1	.245
Hershiser, O	15	4	3.37	25	25	0	165.2	160	46	108	13	.254
Hill, Ken	1	1	3.75	6	6	0	36.0	39	12	16	2	.279
Hitchcock, S*	0	0	4.12	4	3	0	19.2	21	6	19	3	.269
Johnson, R*	1	0	2.12	2	2	0	17.0	10	5	15	0	.175
Karl, Scott*	1	0	4.63	5	3	0	23.1	24	7	14	1	.273
Krivda, Rick*	0	1	3.75	2	2	0	12.0	12	4	2	0	.279
Lilliquist, D*	0	0	4.15	17	0	0	17.1	16	5	7	3	.254
Lira, Felipe	0	1	2.51	3	2	0	14.1	10	6	11	1	.204

JACOBS FIELD
Home of the Cleveland Indians

Cleveland, Ohio											Grass
Pitcher	W	L	ERA	G	GS	Sv	IP	H	BB	SO	HR	Avg
Lopez, Albie	2	1	3.86	6	6	0	37.1	38	9	29	3	.262
Martinez, De	11	10	3.74	35	35	0	235.2	244	49	100	24	.267
McDonald, Ben	0	0	6.06	3	3	0	16.1	21	7	3	2	.339
McDowell, J	9	5	5.76	17	17	0	106.1	121	44	80	13	.287
Mesa, Jose	6	9	2.27	91	0	41	115.0	85	40	101	3	.207
Mulholland, T*	1	1	4.15	2	2	0	13.0	16	5	9	1	.327
Mussina, Mike	0	2	10.95	2	2	0	12.1	17	3	7	4	.340
Nagy, Charles	23	8	3.37	43	43	0	307.0	290	88	244	27	.249
Ogea, Chad	12	2	3.47	29	19	0	145.1	135	37	92	12	.246
Oliver, D*	2	0	1.93	4	1	0	14.0	9	5	10	1	.180
Pettitte, A*	1	1	5.25	2	2	0	12.0	16	5	4	3	.327
Plunk, Eric	12	2	3.13	71	0	3	92.0	70	41	88	6	.211
Poole, Jim*	2	1	2.14	39	0	0	42.0	31	17	38	3	.203
Radke, Brad	1	2	6.87	3	3	0	18.1	27	2	11	3	.351
Shuey, Paul	4	2	3.16	32	0	5	37.0	36	18	39	4	.254
Sparks, Steve	0	2	7.90	2	2	0	13.2	20	3	4	4	.339
Stottlemyre	0	0	2.57	2	2	0	14.0	15	5	10	1	.268
Swindell, G*	1	0	4.74	7	0	0	19.0	17	5	15	4	.243
Tapani, Kevin	0	1	8.31	4	4	0	17.1	30	7	11	5	.380
Tavarez, Ju	8	4	3.40	54	3	0	87.1	92	17	67	9	.271
Van Poppel, T	0	0	1.35	4	1	0	13.1	7	6	9	2	.156
Wakefield, T	0	1	3.75	2	2	0	12.0	13	5	8	2	.265
Wells, David*	1	0	3.00	2	2	0	15.0	19	2	8	1	.311
Witt, Bobby	0	3	7.53	3	3	0	14.1	21	11	6	3	.339

COORS FIELD
Home of the Colorado Rockies

Denver, Colorado											Grass
Pitcher	W	L	ERA	G	GS	Sv	IP	H	BB	SO	HR	Avg
Ashby, Andy	1	1	8.64	3	3	0	16.2	23	4	13	5	.329
Astacio, P	0	2	10.50	4	2	0	12.0	17	6	14	5	.321
Bailey, Roger	7	2	6.86	32	8	1	82.2	102	41	36	10	.307
Benes, Andy	0	2	10.05	3	3	0	14.1	26	5	12	1	.419
Burba, Dave	1	0	6.89	5	3	0	15.2	20	6	12	3	.313
Burkett, John	0	3	9.35	3	3	0	17.1	29	2	14	1	.377
Castillo, F	2	0	2.87	2	2	0	15.2	14	1	10	4	.233
Drabek, Doug	0	1	13.15	3	3	0	13.0	30	4	10	5	.455
Foster, Kevin	1	0	7.82	3	3	0	12.2	12	8	13	6	.250
Freeman, M	7	7	6.92	28	24	0	128.2	180	59	62	28	.338
Glavine, Tom*	1	0	3.95	4	4	0	27.1	34	10	10	2	.318
Habyan, John	1	0	6.00	12	0	0	18.0	24	9	15	3	.338
Harnisch, P	2	0	4.76	3	3	0	17.0	20	0	13	5	.299
Hawblitzel, R	0	0	4.50	6	0	0	12.0	14	3	4	1	.286
Holmes, D	8	1	3.62	68	0	9	79.2	83	23	75	7	.265
Jones, Bobby	0	1	11.68	3	3	0	12.1	25	4	8	6	.439
Leiter, Mark	0	2	8.24	4	3	0	19.2	31	8	11	5	.365
Leskanic, C	8	1	4.42	73	0	0	89.2	92	27	83	9	.265
Lieber, Jon	1	1	5.27	4	2	0	13.2	17	0	12	3	.315
Loaiza, E	1	0	3.29	2	2	0	13.2	17	3	4	0	.321
Martinez, PJ	0	1	6.00	2	2	0	12.0	12	6	12	5	.261
Martinez, R	1	2	7.41	3	3	0	17.0	22	11	17	5	.319
Morgan, Mike	1	1	7.24	3	3	0	13.2	18	7	7	5	.321
Mulholland, T*	0	3	8.62	3	3	0	15.2	23	8	12	3	.348
Munoz, Mike*	4	0	8.04	61	0	0	47.0	66	22	45	10	.333
Navarro, J	1	1	9.56	3	3	0	16.0	29	4	12	5	.392
Neagle, Denny*	0	3	9.60	3	3	0	15.0	29	3	11	3	.403
Nomo, Hideo	1	0	5.79	3	3	0	18.2	18	10	24	5	.243
Olivares, O	0	2	8.40	8	2	0	15.0	23	4	8	3	.365
Painter, L*	6	0	5.71	39	1	0	58.1	72	21	44	10	.304
Petkovsek, M	1	0	4.30	5	2	0	23.0	23	6	14	1	.258
Rapp, Pat	1	1	6.26	4	4	0	23.0	23	15	14	3	.280
Reed, Steve	6	2	3.05	70	0	2	82.2	66	25	73	10	.224
Rekar, Bryan	2	5	10.35	16	14	0	68.2	114	23	33	15	.371
Reynolds, S	0	1	6.00	2	2	0	12.0	15	5	8	4	.300
Reynoso, A	8	7	5.36	24	22	0	126.0	166	39	55	24	.319
Ritz, Kevin	13	8	5.72	32	29	2	181.0	208	78	113	27	.288
Ruffin, Bruce*	6	3	3.83	55	0	14	54.0	51	27	51	3	.246
Schilling, C	1	1	5.54	2	2	0	13.0	14	4	11	3	.269
Schourek, P*	0	1	8.78	3	3	0	13.1	17	6	9	4	.315
Smoltz, John	1	1	6.91	2	2	0	14.1	19	4	15	2	.328
Swift, Bill	5	2	5.24	14	12	1	68.2	82	27	42	10	.304
Thompson, Mar	6	6	6.79	31	16	0	112.2	154	52	65	20	.334
Valdes, I	3	0	4.91	5	3	0	22.0	26	4	13	4	.302
Wright, Jamey	2	1	6.38	7	7	0	42.1	49	20	22	5	.302

TIGER STADIUM
Home of the Detroit Tigers

Detroit, Michigan											Grass
Pitcher	W	L	ERA	G	GS	Sv	IP	H	BB	SO	HR	Avg
Abbott, Jim*	1	1	5.14	8	7	0	42.0	46	18	23	7	.274
Aguilera, R	0	1	1.09	16	1	12	24.2	18	8	17	1	.202
Aldred, Scott*	2	10	7.40	20	18	0	90.0	111	53	57	16	.307
Alvarez, W*	3	0	3.66	5	5	0	32.0	28	9	36	5	.231
Appier, Kevin	4	3	3.76	10	7	0	55.0	50	23	66	5	.238
Belcher, Tim	4	6	5.70	12	12	0	79.0	90	39	48	11	.283
Bere, Jason	3	1	2.39	4	4	0	26.1	17	17	27	1	.179

TIGER STADIUM
Home of the Detroit Tigers

Detroit, Michigan   **Grass**

Pitcher	W	L	ERA	G	GS	Sv	IP	H	BB	SO	HR	Avg
Bergman, Sean	5	7	4.94	19	19	0	98.1	108	49	61	10	.283
Boever, Joe	11	4	4.37	62	0	4	111.1	125	46	76	15	.289
Bohanon, B*	1	0	6.22	26	5	0	46.1	56	23	31	7	.296
Bones, Ricky	0	4	6.68	6	5	0	32.1	38	20	10	6	.302
Bosio, Chris	4	4	4.15	16	11	2	82.1	76	21	49	12	.247
Brown, Kevin	5	3	3.48	10	10	0	67.1	59	24	53	6	.229
Candiotti, T	2	4	3.02	8	8	0	50.2	43	22	39	3	.225
Christopher	3	0	5.62	27	0	0	41.2	44	14	26	12	.270
Clark, Mark	2	1	3.38	3	3	0	21.1	16	5	16	0	.205
Clemens, R	6	6	3.81	12	12	0	82.2	63	28	100	12	.209
Cone, David	4	1	3.32	5	5	0	38.0	26	15	38	2	.202
Cook, Dennis*	0	0	3.79	9	2	0	19.0	17	10	15	6	.243
Cummings, J*	1	3	7.94	12	0	0	17.0	25	11	18	3	.342
Darwin, Danny	1	1	2.59	5	3	0	24.1	15	6	13	2	.174
DeLucia, Rich	0	3	9.00	4	3	0	12.0	10	10	7	2	.222
Doherty, John	19	14	4.95	79	34	4	278.1	331	78	100	29	.298
Eckersley, D	0	1	2.14	19	0	13	21.0	18	4	22	1	.222
Eichhorn, M	0	1	4.15	19	0	0	21.2	28	8	15	5	.326
Eischen, Joey*	1	0	3.45	13	0	0	15.2	14	8	10	2	.246
Eldred, Cal	2	3	7.85	5	5	0	28.2	35	19	27	9	.292
Erickson, S	7	1	3.53	10	10	0	63.2	59	27	32	5	.242
Farrell, John	1	5	9.58	8	8	0	31.0	43	18	8	9	.331
Fernandez, A	5	1	3.91	8	8	0	50.2	51	21	40	7	.260
Fetters, Mike	0	2	5.14	11	1	4	14.0	20	5	6	3	.357
Finley, Chuck*	5	3	4.79	13	10	0	67.2	69	37	44	9	.264
Frohwirth, T	0	2	6.75	10	0	1	13.1	19	12	10	1	.328
Gibson, Paul*	12	8	3.17	105	7	6	227.0	206	98	146	13	.243
Gohr, Greg	1	6	5.04	25	9	0	69.2	88	25	56	12	.303
Gordon, Tom	5	6	6.35	12	9	0	56.2	62	36	61	9	.278
Grimsley, J	1	1	6.75	5	3	0	17.1	19	13	14	1	.279
Groom, Buddy*	0	5	7.16	47	8	0	71.2	107	41	46	7	.355
Gross, Kevin	2	1	3.12	4	4	0	26.0	17	5	14	5	.187
Gubicza, Mark	2	5	5.37	10	9	0	53.2	52	23	32	9	.260
Guthrie, Mark*	2	1	2.16	9	3	0	33.1	30	9	33	3	.242
Guzman, Juan	2	2	4.13	5	5	0	32.2	24	22	36	4	.209
Habyan, John	1	1	2.97	14	1	1	30.1	23	10	21	3	.202
Haney, Chris*	0	1	3.55	2	2	0	12.2	10	5	9	2	.233
Hanson, Erik	5	2	3.25	8	8	0	61.0	50	21	54	9	.228
Henneman, M	39	12	2.97	253	0	79	348.1	295	106	267	27	.229
Hentgen, Pat	3	2	5.40	9	6	0	46.2	44	20	31	10	.246
Hernandez, R	1	2	3.45	13	0	6	15.2	11	6	20	2	.190
Hershiser, O	1	2	3.86	3	3	0	21.0	21	5	15	3	.259
Hill, Ken	2	0	0.53	2	2	0	17.0	8	2	14	1	.140
Honeycutt, R*	0	0	4.26	13	0	0	12.2	14	7	5	1	.280
Howe, Steve*	0	0	0.00	9	0	0	12.1	3	3	7	0	.077
Hurtado, E	1	1	6.00	2	2	0	12.0	16	11	7	3	.314
Jackson, Mike	0	1	2.70	13	0	2	16.2	9	8	22	3	.158
Johnson, R*	1	5	5.98	7	7	0	40.2	42	31	52	5	.273
Jones, Doug	1	1	4.76	9	1	1	17.0	27	5	13	2	.365
Kamieniecki	1	2	4.50	5	2	0	16.0	17	17	13	2	.288
Keagle, Greg	2	2	7.89	14	3	0	43.1	57	28	36	8	.315
Key, Jimmy*	4	5	3.36	10	10	0	67.0	65	15	52	9	.257
Langston, M*	3	5	3.66	12	12	0	86.0	69	36	72	12	.218
Leiter, Al*	1	1	3.26	5	4	0	19.1	13	16	14	0	.203
Leiter, Mark	9	10	4.52	55	19	1	187.0	186	74	145	25	.259
Lewis, Richie	3	3	5.40	38	0	1	48.1	42	39	40	5	.235
Lima, Jose	3	8	6.23	28	9	1	78.0	91	14	60	16	.288
Linton, Doug	2	1	2.76	5	2	0	16.1	14	6	16	3	.226
Lira, Felipe	9	14	3.77	35	29	0	191.0	173	59	110	27	.242
Lopez, Albie	1	0	2.63	2	1	0	13.2	7	2	11	2	.152
MacDonald, B*	4	2	6.91	41	0	2	41.2	43	26	23	8	.274
Magrane, Joe*	2	0	3.65	2	2	0	12.1	12	10	8	1	.267
Mahomes, Pat	2	0	3.00	5	1	1	12.0	12	7	8	1	.250
Martinez, De	3	0	3.13	4	4	0	23.0	27	10	18	1	.300
Maxcy, Brian	3	1	7.92	22	0	0	30.2	42	15	11	4	.328
McCaskill, K	2	3	2.79	12	5	1	48.1	46	18	27	6	.256
McDonald, Ben	2	3	6.04	9	8	0	44.2	40	25	38	9	.237
McDowell, J	5	2	4.18	8	8	0	51.2	45	23	45	5	.231
Meacham, R	1	2	7.91	9	2	0	19.1	30	10	9	5	.361
Mesa, Jose	3	3	6.92	10	6	2	39.0	54	21	24	7	.333
Milacki, Bob	3	4	4.30	9	8	0	52.1	35	32	25	6	.193
Mills, Alan	1	1	3.86	14	0	1	23.1	14	14	19	2	.167
Montgomery, J	1	1	2.96	19	0	8	24.1	20	11	22	3	.233
Moyer, Jamie*	2	1	2.63	6	3	0	24.0	22	9	14	4	.242
Mulholland, T*	0	0	2.84	2	2	0	12.2	13	5	9	0	.265
Munoz, Mike*	0	2	4.97	36	0	0	29.0	36	16	15	2	.308
Mussina, Mike	4	1	2.32	6	6	0	42.2	28	13	40	5	.188
Myers, Mike*	1	2	5.94	45	0	0	36.1	42	20	40	3	.286
Nagy, Charles	4	2	5.12	6	6	0	38.2	39	11	33	6	.253
Navarro, J	0	2	9.58	5	4	0	20.2	37	8	14	6	.398
Nelson, Jeff	0	1	4.40	10	0	0	14.1	18	2	20	1	.305
Nitkowski, C*	2	5	7.01	11	9	0	43.2	62	28	26	7	.344
Olivares, O	4	4	4.35	11	11	0	70.1	72	37	39	6	.271
Olson, Gregg	2	2	4.41	32	0	9	32.2	27	22	22	4	.225
Orosco, Jesse*	1	0	2.08	16	0	2	17.1	10	5	16	1	.169
Pall, Donn	1	2	2.45	12	0	0	18.1	16	3	9	1	.232
Pavlik, Roger	3	2	2.86	5	5	0	34.2	26	9	36	3	.208
Pichardo, H	1	1	5.87	6	2	0	15.1	20	6	10	1	.317

TIGER STADIUM
Home of the Detroit Tigers

Detroit, Michigan — Grass

Pitcher	W	L	ERA	G	GS	Sv	IP	H	BB	SO	HR	Avg
Plesac, Dan*	2	0	3.09	14	2	7	23.1	16	10	20	4	.203
Plunk, Eric	2	1	3.69	26	1	0	39.0	41	32	42	6	.275
Radke, Brad	1	2	10.80	3	3	0	15.0	19	4	7	1	.306
Reyes, Carlos	1	1	3.95	3	2	0	13.2	12	6	10	1	.235
Rhodes, A*	2	0	3.07	3	2	0	14.2	11	7	13	0	.200
Ritz, Kevin	5	5	4.46	26	15	0	103.0	106	61	74	5	.266
Rodriguez, Fr	1	0	9.69	4	3	0	13.0	18	4	9	6	.321
Rogers, Kenny*	2	2	5.27	15	6	2	42.2	41	19	40	7	.247
Russell, Jeff	0	0	2.00	18	1	8	27.0	19	10	25	2	.194
Sager, A.J.	1	4	5.29	12	3	0	32.1	37	15	24	4	.301
Sanderson, S	5	2	3.98	7	7	0	43.0	38	13	34	10	.228
Sele, Aaron	2	0	3.63	3	3	0	17.1	18	12	17	3	.261
Smiley, John*	0	1	5.79	2	2	0	14.0	14	3	18	4	.264
Sodowsky, C	2	1	7.23	5	5	0	18.2	19	12	9	3	.253
Sparks, Steve	2	0	1.76	3	2	0	15.1	12	4	12	1	.214
Stottlemyre	4	1	4.58	9	6	0	35.1	37	25	35	4	.276
Swift, Bill	1	0	1.47	9	1	1	18.1	8	10	3	1	.136
Swindell, G*	0	2	9.00	3	3	0	15.0	29	9	12	3	.414
Tapani, Kevin	3	1	6.92	5	5	0	26.0	32	6	21	7	.294
Thompson, Ju*	0	3	5.40	6	6	0	30.0	34	17	25	4	.288
Trombley, M	1	0	7.07	6	2	0	14.0	16	3	18	3	.276
Urbani, Tom*	1	1	9.53	9	2	0	17.0	23	9	13	7	.319
Van Poppel, T	2	4	9.95	9	8	0	31.2	41	30	19	8	.313
Veres, Randy	0	2	5.19	12	0	0	17.1	16	9	15	4	.239
Viola, Frank*	3	2	3.43	6	6	0	42.0	36	15	24	3	.232
Walker, Mike	0	0	9.18	11	0	0	16.2	24	10	9	8	.338
Wells, David*	21	9	3.61	47	38	0	284.0	262	66	197	31	.244
West, David*	1	1	3.07	2	2	0	14.2	9	6	13	1	.170
Whiteside, M	0	0	4.85	9	0	2	13.0	12	9	9	3	.250
Wickander, K*	0	0	2.81	18	0	1	16.0	18	10	8	1	.300
Wickman, Bob	3	0	2.08	9	1	0	26.0	25	13	14	1	.258
Williams, Bri	3	3	5.42	22	10	2	79.2	82	52	49	11	.272
Witt, Bobby	3	4	4.91	10	10	0	62.1	50	46	60	6	.215

PRO PLAYER STADIUM
Home of the Florida Marlins

Miami, Florida — Grass

Pitcher	W	L	ERA	G	GS	Sv	IP	H	BB	SO	HR	Avg
Ashby, Andy	1	1	3.62	5	5	0	27.1	26	4	17	4	.263
Astacio, P	2	1	3.28	6	3	0	24.2	21	9	10	2	.231
Avery, Steve*	0	3	6.84	5	5	0	26.1	33	5	19	3	.308
Benes, Andy	3	1	2.93	4	4	0	27.2	22	5	23	1	.216
Blair, Willie	2	1	3.86	8	1	0	14.0	16	8	14	0	.286
Borland, Toby	0	0	4.26	7	0	0	12.2	12	4	16	2	.231
Bottenfield	1	1	3.46	3	2	0	13.0	13	4	8	1	.283
Brown, Kevin	12	4	1.69	19	19	0	138.1	101	20	89	5	.204
Burba, Dave	0	2	5.93	7	2	0	13.2	16	7	10	2	.296
Burkett, John	11	13	4.57	29	29	0	183.1	200	58	127	19	.281
Candiotti, T	2	0	3.66	3	3	0	19.2	20	8	16	1	.274
Carpenter, C	0	0	2.95	13	0	0	18.1	15	6	13	0	.224
Carrasco, H	0	1	0.69	7	0	1	13.0	7	8	15	0	.156
Castillo, F	1	3	4.24	5	5	0	34.0	33	8	22	3	.260
Clark, Mark	1	1	4.61	2	2	0	13.2	14	4	12	1	.269
Cooke, Steve*	1	0	2.89	4	3	0	18.2	17	11	15	0	.246
Cormier, R*	2	1	4.03	4	4	0	22.1	22	10	14	2	.256
Drabek, Doug	0	1	3.38	3	3	0	18.2	14	6	13	2	.209
Fassero, Jeff*	1	3	3.58	6	5	0	32.2	41	9	29	1	.313
Foster, Kevin	1	1	7.62	3	3	0	13.0	16	9	10	1	.302
Freeman, M	0	3	5.63	3	3	0	16.0	19	8	5	3	.302
Gardner, Mark	3	6	5.38	31	15	0	108.2	127	50	72	18	.293
Glavine, Tom*	2	4	3.89	6	6	0	37.0	40	18	28	2	.272
Gooden, D	1	1	4.50	2	2	0	16.0	14	1	15	1	.230
Gross, Kevin	1	0	2.77	2	2	0	13.0	16	3	14	0	.314
Hamilton, J	0	1	6.38	3	3	0	18.1	27	8	17	2	.351
Hammond, C*	14	12	3.82	49	35	0	230.2	234	64	157	17	.264
Harnisch, P	2	1	3.92	4	4	0	20.2	17	10	14	1	.230
Helling, Rick	2	0	1.13	3	2	0	16.0	7	2	16	0	.127
Heredia, Gil	0	0	3.86	4	2	1	14.0	17	3	7	0	.309
Hernandez, X	0	0	4.12	10	0	2	19.2	16	6	19	3	.222
Hershiser, O	1	1	4.85	2	2	0	13.0	18	2	7	1	.316
Hill, Ken	1	1	2.92	2	2	0	12.1	10	6	6	0	.217
Hoffman, T	2	1	2.61	19	0	2	20.2	17	8	15	2	.218
Hutton, Mark	1	0	2.50	4	3	0	18.0	19	3	5	1	.275
Jarvis, Kevin	1	1	4.40	2	2	0	14.1	12	5	6	1	.214
Johnstone, J	1	3	6.17	18	0	0	23.1	33	19	14	2	.320
Jones, Bobby	0	2	7.62	2	2	0	13.0	19	3	4	3	.352
Kile, Darryl	2	1	3.00	3	3	0	18.0	12	10	21	1	.182
Klink, Joe*	0	0	4.05	32	0	0	20.0	14	13	13	0	.194
Leiter, Al*	11	3	2.08	17	17	0	116.2	67	62	115	7	.168
Leiter, Mark	1	1	0.83	3	3	0	21.2	10	9	16	1	.143
Leskanic, C	0	3	7.82	9	1	0	12.2	14	9	11	2	.269
Lewis, Richie	5	4	4.13	67	1	0	98.0	88	56	81	14	.242
Maddux, Greg	4	0	2.48	5	5	0	29.0	22	11	25	3	.210
Mantei, Matt	0	0	5.52	10	0	0	14.2	15	11	18	1	.263
Martinez, PJ	1	1	2.25	4	2	0	16.0	12	8	17	1	.211
Martinez, R	3	0	3.00	4	4	0	24.0	21	13	21	1	.239
Mathews, T	3	5	3.51	71	1	3	97.1	85	31	85	7	.237

PRO PLAYER STADIUM
Home of the Florida Marlins

Miami, Florida — Grass

Pitcher	W	L	ERA	G	GS	Sv	IP	H	BB	SO	HR	Avg
McMichael, G	1	0	2.63	12	0	2	13.2	8	7	12	0	.170
Mercker, Kent*	1	0	5.87	4	3	0	15.1	23	7	12	3	.338
Miller, Kurt	2	1	4.25	11	5	0	36.0	37	13	22	2	.272
Morgan, Mike	2	0	2.10	4	4	0	25.2	19	12	12	1	.200
Navarro, J	3	0	2.21	3	3	0	20.1	18	6	14	2	.243
Neagle, Denny*	1	3	3.46	7	6	0	39.0	38	10	25	3	.264
Nen, Robb	7	7	3.39	109	1	36	138.0	126	44	145	10	.240
Nied, Dave	0	0	4.50	2	2	0	14.0	13	9	9	1	.265
Nomo, Hideo	0	2	4.19	3	3	0	19.1	14	5	20	4	.200
Olivares, O	2	0	3.29	3	2	0	13.2	18	7	9	1	.310
Pena, Alej	2	1	2.25	13	0	0	16.0	11	2	20	2	.186
Perez, Mike	0	0	5.25	11	0	3	12.0	18	5	13	1	.346
Perez, Yorkis*	6	3	2.67	92	0	1	81.0	56	34	87	5	.194
Portugal, M	2	1	6.91	3	3	0	14.1	14	8	11	3	.255
Powell, Jay	3	0	2.82	38	0	2	38.1	34	21	22	1	.234
Pugh, Tim	1	2	9.22	4	3	0	13.2	26	11	10	3	.406
Rapp, Pat	20	17	4.07	49	48	0	285.1	298	126	170	22	.278
Reed, Steve	0	2	1.76	11	0	0	15.1	16	5	12	0	.286
Reynolds, S	0	4	10.18	5	4	0	20.1	33	15	23	4	.359
Ritz, Kevin	1	3	5.09	4	4	0	23.0	26	8	13	2	.295
Rojas, Mel	0	0	1.76	11	0	4	15.1	14	7	16	1	.241
Rueter, Kirk*	1	1	3.52	3	3	0	15.1	13	4	7	1	.241
Schilling, C	2	1	4.56	4	4	0	23.2	26	9	29	4	.271
Schourek, P*	2	1	2.81	6	4	0	32.0	29	10	29	4	.238
Shaw, Jeff	2	0	5.02	12	0	0	14.1	15	0	10	1	.273
Slocumb, H	1	0	2.45	9	0	2	14.2	16	8	8	1	.296
Smoltz, John	2	1	4.97	4	4	0	25.1	31	9	22	2	.307
Swift, Bill	2	1	3.05	3	3	0	20.2	20	7	13	1	.256
Swindell, G*	2	1	2.53	5	5	0	32.0	27	6	28	1	.218
Torres, S	1	0	4.38	2	2	0	12.1	11	4	10	2	.229
Trachsel, S	2	1	2.41	3	3	0	18.2	19	11	11	1	.264
Valdes, I	2	0	0.41	4	3	0	22.0	18	7	17	1	.217
Valdes, Marc	1	3	4.78	6	6	0	26.1	33	16	6	2	.303
Veres, Randy	3	0	3.38	23	0	0	21.1	20	7	17	5	.244
Wagner, Paul	2	1	2.49	4	4	0	21.2	18	8	16	1	.231
Watson, Allen*	0	3	4.62	5	4	0	25.1	33	13	14	5	.314
Weathers, D	9	11	5.75	45	25	0	164.1	206	86	85	11	.315
Williams, Mk	1	2	5.49	5	3	0	19.2	21	14	10	2	.273
Witt, Bobby	2	3	3.98	9	9	0	54.1	44	26	46	3	.224
Wohlers, Mark	1	0	1.46	12	0	3	12.1	9	3	12	1	.209

THE ASTRODOME
Home of the Houston Astros

Houston, Texas — Artificial

Pitcher	W	L	ERA	G	GS	Sv	IP	H	BB	SO	HR	Avg
Ashby, Andy	3	2	2.92	7	6	1	37.0	33	9	25	1	.241
Assenmacher*	1	0	1.06	13	0	1	17.0	11	9	15	0	.200
Astacio, P	2	1	2.22	5	4	0	28.1	24	8	26	2	.238
Avery, Steve*	3	2	3.08	8	8	0	49.2	45	13	26	4	.245
Bautista, J	0	1	6.39	9	0	0	12.2	13	5	6	0	.283
Beck, Rod	1	0	3.38	11	0	6	16.0	16	5	10	1	.267
Belcher, Tim	4	1	2.55	9	9	0	67.0	50	24	57	5	.208
Belinda, Stan	1	0	3.95	13	0	2	13.2	9	9	12	0	.200
Benes, Alan	1	1	3.07	2	2	0	14.2	10	2	8	1	.192
Benes, Andy	4	6	2.69	12	12	0	83.2	69	29	80	4	.223
Bielecki, M	0	1	4.84	5	4	0	22.1	27	11	10	2	.318
Blair, Willie	3	2	2.47	19	3	0	47.1	37	15	34	0	.214
Boever, Joe	1	3	2.41	53	0	3	74.2	74	35	47	3	.262
Boskie, Shawn	2	1	2.59	5	3	0	24.1	17	5	15	1	.195
Bottenfield	0	1	4.38	5	1	0	12.1	12	1	6	1	.261
Brantley, J	4	3	2.78	16	3	2	32.1	19	7	29	3	.167
Brocail, Doug	5	3	4.06	35	7	0	82.0	81	24	57	9	.255
Bullinger, J	1	1	5.14	5	2	0	14.0	16	11	8	1	.302
Burba, Dave	0	1	6.30	6	2	0	20.0	25	12	19	3	.316
Burkett, John	4	2	3.50	8	8	0	46.1	44	5	29	2	.259
Candiotti, T	2	1	2.65	5	5	0	34.0	35	9	24	1	.267
Carpenter, C	3	2	7.50	13	1	0	18.0	22	11	10	3	.310
Carrasco, H	0	0	0.00	7	0	1	12.2	5	2	12	0	.122
Castillo, F	2	3	4.57	7	7	0	41.1	47	11	22	0	.290
Charlton, N*	0	1	2.34	16	3	2	34.2	26	13	37	2	.218
Cone, David	3	2	3.26	6	6	0	38.2	34	16	31	2	.234
Cormier, R*	0	3	6.46	5	5	0	23.2	31	7	14	5	.326
Corsi, Jim	0	3	4.66	24	0	0	38.2	34	6	28	4	.234
Darwin, Danny	23	11	2.86	112	37	6	380.2	330	107	282	21	.234
Dougherty, J	3	1	4.63	30	0	0	35.0	34	12	21	2	.260
Drabek, Doug	22	25	3.42	71	71	0	481.1	482	132	366	34	.265
Fassero, Jeff*	2	1	3.09	11	4	1	32.0	31	9	34	2	.248
Fernandez, S*	1	5	3.91	9	9	0	46.0	37	17	35	3	.214
Foster, Kevin	1	1	3.75	2	2	0	12.0	10	8	14	1	.227
Franco, John*	2	3	2.89	17	0	8	18.2	13	4	13	0	.191
Freeman, M	1	1	6.23	6	2	0	13.0	13	10	11	1	.241
Gardner, Mark	3	2	3.35	9	6	1	40.1	34	13	20	1	.233
Glavine, Tom*	4	8	2.96	16	16	0	103.1	96	36	69	2	.249
Gooden, D	2	2	3.40	7	7	0	50.1	50	15	45	2	.259
Gross, Kevin	4	5	3.84	11	10	0	61.0	53	30	40	5	.227
Hamilton, J	1	1	2.30	3	2	0	15.2	9	9	14	0	.170
Hammond, C*	3	4	3.10	9	8	0	49.1	40	13	32	4	.226

Houston, Texas   **Artificial**

Pitcher	W	L	ERA	G	GS	Sv	IP	H	BB	SO	HR	Avg
Hampton, Mike*	12	9	3.09	46	25	0	186.1	180	50	147	12	.256
Harnisch, P	28	16	2.96	66	66	0	444.2	339	132	362	37	.209
Hartgraves, D*	2	0	0.55	33	0	0	33.0	16	15	26	0	.147
Heredia, Gil	1	1	3.70	7	4	0	24.1	25	3	17	1	.278
Hernandez, X	14	8	2.59	132	3	16	204.2	150	65	183	9	.202
Hershiser, O	3	8	4.08	13	12	0	90.1	85	23	76	7	.248
Hill, Ken	4	2	2.89	9	8	0	56.0	52	22	34	1	.249
Hoffman, T	1	0	3.68	10	0	4	14.2	8	5	17	1	.154
Holmes, D	0	1	1.26	10	0	2	14.1	11	7	14	1	.208
Hudek, John	4	1	3.07	39	0	10	41.0	24	16	48	4	.167
Jackson, Dan*	0	4	7.03	5	5	0	24.1	33	8	19	3	.330
Jackson, Mike	1	3	4.73	10	1	0	13.1	10	6	7	1	.217
Jones, Bobby	2	0	1.73	4	4	0	26.0	20	11	12	0	.217
Jones, Doug	9	9	3.41	76	0	25	100.1	100	21	86	8	.262
Jones, Todd	11	8	2.57	92	0	17	133.0	106	52	122	6	.219
Juden, Jeff	2	1	3.22	6	3	0	22.1	21	8	17	2	.256
Kile, Darryl	25	31	3.76	87	76	0	485.1	452	236	401	30	.249
Leiter, Mark	2	0	3.86	2	2	0	14.0	15	3	7	2	.300
Lilliquist, D*	1	1	5.87	3	3	0	15.1	18	4	6	1	.295
Maddux, Greg	8	2	1.68	13	13	0	107.0	80	27	64	2	.209
Maddux, Mike	0	3	6.23	9	2	0	13.0	18	5	4	2	.340
Magrane, Joe*	3	4	2.63	7	7	0	51.1	38	17	21	1	.208
Martinez, De	4	2	3.44	8	8	0	52.1	43	17	41	3	.219
Martinez, PJ	1	3	5.40	6	3	0	23.1	26	11	15	3	.292
Martinez, PA*	1	0	6.11	16	0	0	17.2	17	12	13	3	.258
Martinez, R	2	1	4.57	7	7	0	43.1	41	15	30	6	.253
McDowell, R	1	2	2.77	21	0	3	26.0	22	15	12	0	.239
Mercker, Kent*	2	2	3.52	11	5	0	30.2	21	16	28	0	.188
Miicki, Dave	1	1	2.00	4	2	0	18.0	16	2	9	1	.235
Morgan, Mike	4	6	3.61	15	12	0	77.1	74	21	50	3	.254
Morman, Alvin*	3	0	5.94	23	0	0	16.2	15	11	11	4	.238
Moyer, Jamie*	2	1	1.66	4	3	0	21.2	18	6	14	0	.231
Mulholland, T*	2	4	3.40	9	7	0	50.1	49	13	20	2	.257
Myers, Randy*	2	6	6.39	23	0	9	31.0	38	13	34	6	.297
Navarro, J	2	1	3.86	4	4	0	25.2	30	10	15	3	.294
Neagle, Denny*	2	3	3.72	9	5	0	36.1	36	11	27	1	.259
Nen, Robb	0	1	4.97	9	0	3	12.2	14	7	11	1	.280
Nied, Dave	2	1	3.15	4	3	0	20.0	25	2	5	1	.321
Olivares, O	1	0	2.18	5	3	0	20.2	16	11	13	2	.225
Osborne, D*	3	1	2.65	5	5	0	34.0	27	12	22	1	.218
Osuna, Al*	11	4	3.63	97	0	6	86.2	66	42	60	8	.214
Painter, L*	1	0	8.31	5	2	0	13.0	16	5	3	4	.308
Parrett, Jeff	3	3	5.10	19	1	3	30.0	36	14	27	3	.300
Pena, Alej	2	3	3.44	24	0	8	34.0	39	13	35	2	.291
Perez, Mike	0	1	6.08	13	0	0	13.1	19	7	2	2	.345
Portugal, M	32	11	2.55	71	61	1	405.2	357	133	302	22	.238
Pugh, Tim	1	2	8.84	5	3	0	18.1	33	6	7	0	.398
Rapp, Pat	0	1	4.20	3	3	0	15.0	21	6	9	1	.339
Reed, Steve	1	0	3.86	16	0	0	16.1	19	5	12	4	.288
Reynolds, S	17	11	3.27	47	40	0	278.1	264	49	265	19	.247
Reynoso, A	1	2	2.55	4	4	0	24.2	25	10	20	1	.272
Ritz, Kevin	2	1	4.50	4	4	0	20.0	22	10	13	1	.278
Rojas, Mel	2	1	1.84	15	0	2	14.2	15	7	13	0	.259
Rueter, Kirk*	2	0	1.27	4	3	0	21.1	13	3	6	0	.181
Ruffin, Bruce*	2	4	2.75	18	4	5	39.1	37	13	24	2	.243
Sanders, S	1	1	4.76	7	4	0	28.1	28	13	30	1	.255
Sanderson, S	2	0	5.11	4	3	0	12.1	13	3	8	1	.265
Schilling, C	5	4	3.56	38	6	3	91.0	90	39	78	0	.263
Schourek, P*	0	2	8.14	6	4	0	24.1	38	10	12	3	.349
Smiley, John*	5	3	5.32	13	11	0	67.2	79	19	36	6	.298
Smith, Lee	0	0	1.17	14	0	11	15.1	8	4	22	1	.151
Smith, Zane*	2	5	4.70	12	11	1	61.1	71	21	33	4	.297
Smoltz, John	8	3	2.56	14	14	0	98.1	83	30	98	4	.224
Stanton, Mike*	1	1	1.72	16	0	5	15.2	8	3	17	2	.154
Stottlemyre	1	1	2.87	2	2	0	15.2	18	10	13	2	.310
Swift, Bill	3	1	3.54	6	4	0	28.0	28	7	25	0	.262
Swindell, G*	13	19	3.99	49	43	0	275.1	313	52	174	37	.287
Tabaka, Jeff*	0	1	2.03	20	0	0	26.2	21	14	20	1	.216
Tewksbury, B	2	2	3.96	6	6	0	36.1	43	8	22	3	.301
Trachsel, S	1	0	4.43	3	3	0	20.1	20	6	13	3	.260
Valdes, I	0	0	2.70	2	2	0	13.1	18	1	5	0	.327
Valenzuela, F*	0	3	4.62	7	6	0	37.0	48	14	22	3	.314
VanLandingham	0	2	5.12	3	3	0	19.1	17	12	12	1	.239
Veres, Dave	6	0	2.49	57	0	1	76.0	66	21	61	6	.241
Viola, Frank*	1	1	1.69	3	3	0	16.0	9	5	10	1	.170
Wagner, Billy*	2	1	2.40	21	0	4	30.0	13	24	39	2	.137
Wagner, Paul	1	0	4.50	7	2	0	16.0	18	11	17	2	.295
Wall, Donne	15	14	3.83	15	14	0	91.2	86	20	75	9	.247
Watson, Allen*	1	1	4.32	4	4	0	25.0	26	7	14	2	.274
Weathers, D	1	0	3.45	4	2	0	15.2	15	4	11	0	.263
Wetteland, J	1	1	5.03	12	1	2	19.2	16	9	23	4	.216
Whitehurst, W	1	1	1.93	5	3	0	18.2	17	6	9	0	.233
Williams, Bri	6	8	4.67	37	16	2	123.1	136	55	85	13	.285
Williams, Mk	0	3	3.38	4	3	0	18.2	15	6	18	0	.221
Worrell, Todd	0	0	2.51	14	0	9	14.1	13	3	11	0	.245
Young, A	2	1	2.88	19	0	2	25.0	20	12	13	2	.220

Pitcher	W	L	ERA	G	GS	Sv	IP	H	BB	SO	HR	Avg
Abbott, Jim*	1	6	5.97	11	11	0	63.1	79	31	25	5	.307
Aguilera, R	0	1	2.82	14	1	8	22.1	21	4	17	0	.250
Aldred, Scott*	1	1	3.75	3	2	0	12.0	15	5	9	1	.319
Alvarez, W*	1	5	3.38	6	5	0	40.0	44	16	22	2	.291
Appier, Kevin	46	33	3.25	104	99	0	689.2	574	227	543	44	.225
Bautista, J	0	2	5.50	5	2	0	18.0	23	8	12	3	.311
Belcher, Tim	7	8	4.75	22	22	0	140.1	169	48	60	18	.303
Belinda, Stan	1	1	4.28	30	0	2	40.0	36	15	34	4	.237
Bere, Jason	1	1	5.04	4	4	0	25.0	19	15	25	1	.209
Boever, Joe	1	0	3.38	6	0	0	16.0	16	6	10	1	.254
Bohanon, B*	1	1	3.38	8	2	0	24.0	22	5	9	0	.239
Bones, Ricky	4	2	3.65	7	7	0	49.1	46	12	10	5	.251
Bosio, Chris	4	2	2.81	9	8	0	57.2	54	11	38	3	.248
Boskie, Shawn	0	0	2.81	2	2	0	16.0	15	3	8	1	.259
Brewer, Billy*	5	4	3.44	77	0	2	68.0	56	28	31	7	.229
Brown, Kevin	4	4	4.14	10	10	0	63.0	67	14	30	2	.271
Candiotti, T	4	2	1.85	6	6	0	43.2	37	10	18	0	.239
Castillo, T*	1	1	4.30	11	0	0	14.2	14	4	6	0	.269
Clark, Mark	1	1	3.29	2	2	0	13.2	14	4	4	1	.269
Clark, Terry	1	0	4.95	8	1	0	20.0	23	3	7	1	.280
Clemens, R	6	3	1.94	12	12	0	93.0	76	23	73	1	.224
Cone, David	14	9	3.46	31	31	0	234.1	199	101	170	18	.231
Darwin, Danny	1	1	7.03	5	4	0	24.1	37	8	17	3	.346
Eckersley, D	1	0	3.81	22	0	13	26.0	29	5	28	1	.271
Eichhorn, M	0	1	3.00	16	0	2	18.0	18	14	9	0	.257
Eldred, Cal	0	2	7.71	2	2	0	14.0	17	7	5	2	.298
Erickson, S	2	1	3.38	5	5	0	32.0	36	6	17	3	.281
Farrell, John	0	3	5.47	4	4	0	26.1	29	11	12	2	.282
Fernandez, A	6	0	1.80	8	8	0	65.0	57	13	43	0	.238
Fetters, Mike	1	2	2.76	13	1	3	16.1	13	10	10	1	.217
Finley, Chuck*	6	3	3.27	13	13	0	82.2	73	33	50	3	.239
Gardner, Mark	3	2	6.30	7	7	0	40.0	47	13	18	7	.301
Gibson, Paul*	0	0	3.00	13	1	2	27.0	22	15	18	1	.224
Gordon, Tom	39	35	3.50	140	71	2	591.1	498	283	498	33	.228
Granger, Jeff*	0	1	7.71	10	1	0	14.0	18	9	8	1	.310
Gross, Kevin	0	3	9.75	3	2	0	12.0	19	2	9	2	.358
Guardado, E*	0	1	7.36	8	1	0	14.2	16	5	14	2	.271
Gubicza, Mark	52	54	3.84	157	130	2	910.0	932	290	537	54	.267
Guetterman, L*	1	2	6.55	10	2	0	22.0	34	7	6	3	.354
Guthrie, Mark*	2	3	6.04	13	2	0	22.1	26	14	14	3	.295
Guzman, Juan	2	1	2.00	5	5	0	36.0	29	15	24	0	.218
Habyan, John	0	0	2.20	12	0	0	16.1	19	2	9	0	.297
Haney, Chris*	12	19	5.39	44	43	0	260.1	303	62	127	30	.291
Hanson, Erik	3	2	4.91	5	5	0	33.0	43	12	22	2	.319
Harnisch, P	0	1	5.68	2	2	0	12.2	13	11	7	1	.265
Henneman, M	0	2	4.78	24	0	8	26.1	27	11	15	0	.265
Hentgen, Pat	3	1	3.41	4	4	0	29.0	27	9	20	4	.257
Hernandez, R	1	2	3.46	10	0	5	13.0	11	1	11	2	.224
Hershiser, O	1	2	4.50	3	3	0	20.0	20	9	9	2	.263
Hill, Ken	1	2	3.52	2	2	0	15.1	18	1	12	1	.295
Honeycutt, R*	0	2	3.48	18	0	2	20.2	19	7	8	0	.257
Huisman, Rick	1	1	2.37	12	0	0	19.0	12	6	17	4	.176
Jackson, Dan*	6	9	4.30	19	18	0	121.1	117	57	86	6	.254
Jackson, Mike	1	1	1.80	11	0	2	15.0	9	4	11	0	.173
Jacome, Jason*	4	4	4.98	30	9	0	65.0	79	25	25	7	.303
Johnson, R*	1	4	2.33	7	7	0	46.1	32	20	55	4	.200
Jones, Doug	0	0	0.00	9	0	7	13.1	5	1	9	0	.114
Kamieniecki, J	1	2	4.19	3	3	0	19.1	21	7	11	0	.292
Karl, Scott*	0	1	3.55	2	2	0	12.2	10	6	4	0	.222
Key, Jimmy*	6	3	2.93	10	10	0	67.2	66	7	39	4	.250
Langston, M*	3	4	4.13	9	9	0	65.1	72	18	54	5	.275
Leiter, Al*	1	1	4.19	3	3	0	19.1	17	17	9	1	.243
Leiter, Mark	1	1	3.63	6	4	0	22.1	25	5	8	3	.281
Linton, Doug	3	4	4.88	16	9	0	66.1	68	16	45	8	.266
Lloyd, Graeme*	0	2	4.38	10	0	0	12.1	11	3	6	2	.234
Magnante, M*	7	6	2.99	95	8	0	171.2	161	54	100	7	.249
Martinez, De	1	1	3.86	2	2	0	14.0	13	3	10	0	.250
McCaskill, K	2	3	5.95	11	6	0	42.1	49	15	21	3	.288
McDonald, Ben	3	2	4.11	6	6	0	35.0	40	16	24	1	.286
McDowell, J	5	0	2.45	8	8	0	58.2	58	14	27	0	.260
Meacham, R	11	5	4.38	88	1	3	137.2	149	25	88	13	.274
Mesa, Jose	1	2	2.82	11	5	4	38.1	40	11	25	2	.263
Milacki, Bob	1	5	4.91	11	11	0	66.0	64	21	28	3	.255
Monteleone, R	0	1	3.55	8	0	0	12.2	13	3	8	3	.255
Montgomery, J	31	18	2.48	271	0	109	362.2	306	89	316	28	.228
Moyer, Jamie*	2	3	3.43	8	6	0	42.0	40	8	15	2	.250
Mulholland, T*	1	1	7.50	2	2	0	12.0	16	5	6	2	.320
Mussina, Mike	6	0	2.20	8	8	0	61.1	50	10	28	4	.223
Nagy, Charles	2	1	2.15	4	4	0	29.1	24	8	23	1	.231
Navarro, J	4	3	5.40	9	8	0	50.0	66	15	26	4	.316
Ogea, Chad	1	1	0.71	3	2	0	12.2	13	1	11	1	.260
Oliver, D*	0	1	4.15	3	2	0	13.0	15	5	2	2	.300
Olson, Gregg	3	3	2.82	29	0	9	38.1	30	16	25	2	.216
Orosco, Jesse*	0	0	1.32	17	0	1	13.2	12	11	15	0	.240
Pall, Donn	0	2	2.63	7	0	0	13.2	14	2	5	0	.269
Pavlik, Roger	1	2	4.38	4	4	0	24.2	33	10	20	1	.347
Pettitte, A*	2	0	1.69	4	2	0	16.0	12	6	17	0	.211
Pichardo, H	19	12	4.39	102	26	3	262.2	291	80	119	16	.283

Kansas City, Missouri   **Grass**

Pitcher	W	L	ERA	G	GS	Sv	IP	H	BB	SO	HR	Avg
Plesac, Dan*	1	3	3.28	15	1	6	24.2	17	13	18	0	.202
Plunk, Eric	0	1	3.03	19	1	3	29.2	28	18	28	2	.248
Prieto, Ariel	0	2	3.21	2	2	0	14.0	14	6	4	1	.269
Pugh, Tim	0	1	6.88	10	1	0	17.0	20	6	13	6	.286
Quantrill, P	2	0	0.00	5	0	0	12.0	7	3	7	0	.175
Radinsky, S*	0	1	2.03	14	0	1	13.1	8	1	5	1	.170
Radke, Brad	1	1	5.57	3	3	0	21.0	26	3	7	1	.302
Reyes, Carlos	0	2	3.14	3	2	0	14.1	16	4	6	1	.281
Rogers, Kenny	3	4	3.44	13	4	0	34.0	40	11	18	2	.310
Rosado, Jose*	5	3	3.03	9	9	0	62.1	56	16	36	5	.242
Russell, Jeff	2	3	7.31	15	0	2	16.0	22	5	12	2	.328
Sanderson, S	3	1	4.24	5	4	0	23.1	28	10	8	0	.298
Scanlan, Bob	1	1	1.89	8	1	0	19.0	16	4	8	2	.239
Sele, Aaron	0	0	1.86	3	3	0	19.1	16	9	14	1	.235
Sparks, Steve	1	0	2.35	4	3	0	23.0	23	4	7	1	.261
Stottlemyre	5	5	4.03	14	11	0	73.2	83	18	44	4	.287
Swift, Bill	1	2	2.73	9	3	2	29.2	26	6	6	2	.236
Swindell, G*	2	3	3.55	5	5	0	33.0	36	10	21	1	.293
Tapani, Kevin	3	5	4.68	10	10	0	65.1	73	11	41	8	.285
Tewksbury, B	2	0	4.67	3	2	0	17.1	20	5	3	0	.303
Timlin, Mike	2	1	2.87	13	0	4	15.2	19	7	10	0	.317
Trombley, M	3	0	4.07	7	3	0	24.1	31	10	13	0	.307
Valera, Julio	1	3	6.05	18	2	0	38.2	45	19	15	1	.298
Van Poppel, T	3	1	5.73	5	4	0	22.0	24	11	12	2	.286
Viola, Frank*	3	4	4.19	9	9	0	58.0	58	17	36	4	.259
Wakefield, T	2	0	3.31	2	2	0	16.1	15	6	10	4	.242
Wells, David*	3	2	4.91	10	6	1	40.1	48	7	16	2	.304
Wickman, Bob	2	1	6.91	8	1	1	14.1	24	8	6	0	.369
Witt, Bobby	2	4	4.98	8	7	0	47.0	44	31	40	4	.247
Wojciechowski*	2	0	5.11	2	2	0	12.1	15	6	4	1	.294

Los Angeles, California   **Grass**

Pitcher	W	L	ERA	G	GS	Sv	IP	H	BB	SO	HR	Avg
Ashby, Andy	3	1	1.81	8	7	0	49.2	45	9	28	3	.245
Assenmacher*	0	3	3.98	18	0	0	20.1	21	7	20	2	.288
Astacio, P	22	16	2.94	72	54	0	386.1	339	116	258	27	.238
Avery, Steve*	4	4	2.39	8	8	0	52.2	42	14	34	4	.214
Bautista, J	1	1	4.43	6	3	0	22.1	30	2	8	5	.330
Beck, Rod	0	0	1.84	13	0	9	14.2	9	2	15	2	.173
Belcher, Tim	33	16	2.49	68	59	2	434.0	358	115	345	28	.225
Benes, Andy	1	6	3.45	9	9	0	57.1	59	16	36	6	.266
Bielecki, M	2	1	1.45	7	4	0	37.1	22	6	33	1	.164
Blair, Willie	1	3	4.26	7	4	1	31.2	30	9	18	2	.250
Boever, Joe	1	4	6.14	15	0	1	14.2	23	11	12	2	.343
Boskie, Shawn	0	2	7.27	5	2	0	17.1	23	5	7	3	.324
Bottenfield	1	0	1.93	3	2	0	14.0	9	7	3	2	.191
Brantley, J	2	0	2.95	22	1	5	36.2	31	15	27	2	.237
Bullinger, J	1	1	3.16	8	3	0	25.2	21	9	13	5	.219
Burba, Dave	0	1	7.50	8	1	0	18.0	18	8	15	7	.257
Burkett, John	6	3	2.76	10	10	0	65.1	56	22	47	2	.229
Candiotti, T	22	27	3.44	68	65	0	442.0	432	123	308	35	.257
Castillo, F	3	1	3.35	7	6	0	37.2	34	15	26	4	.241
Charlton, N*	1	3	3.13	15	2	3	31.2	29	17	19	2	.250
Clark, Mark	2	1	1.83	3	3	0	19.2	19	8	13	0	.244
Cone, David	4	3	2.50	8	8	0	57.2	43	15	46	4	.210
Cook, Dennis*	1	3	7.46	13	5	0	25.1	33	13	11	5	.320
Cormier, R*	1	0	2.19	4	4	0	24.2	29	2	26	1	.282
Cummings, J*	2	0	2.14	17	0	0	21.0	17	4	8	1	.213
Daal, Omar*	1	3	4.93	48	0	0	34.2	36	22	22	5	.281
Darwin, Danny	4	0	1.38	12	4	1	52.0	38	4	41	1	.201
Drabek, Doug	5	6	3.70	12	12	0	82.2	77	25	39	8	.249
Dreifort, D	0	3	4.84	19	0	2	22.1	24	11	24	2	.273
Eischen, Joey*	0	0	3.27	19	0	0	33.0	31	16	25	1	.242
Fassero, Jeff*	0	4	5.45	10	6	0	39.2	45	13	46	2	.278
Fernandez, S*	3	3	3.61	8	8	0	47.1	46	20	37	3	.257
Franco, John*	2	4	2.91	18	0	8	21.2	23	17	18	2	.250
Freeman, M	1	2	8.27	12	3	0	20.2	31	9	10	2	.365
Gardner, Mark	2	3	3.69	7	6	0	39.0	36	16	30	2	.250
Glavine, Tom*	5	7	3.91	17	17	0	103.2	126	35	80	7	.303
Gooden, D	4	2	2.94	7	7	0	49.0	46	14	38	1	.253
Gross, Kevin	27	22	2.99	73	55	2	407.0	362	119	311	24	.237
Guthrie, Mark*	1	3	2.06	41	0	1	43.2	38	11	41	0	.232
Hamilton, J	1	0	3.15	3	3	0	20.0	18	6	16	2	.231
Hammond, C*	3	1	2.43	6	5	0	37.0	23	9	26	3	.173
Harnisch, P	2	1	3.82	5	5	0	33.0	26	9	23	6	.213
Hernandez, X	1	2	4.37	16	1	0	22.2	20	13	18	2	.230
Hershiser, O	47	39	2.84	110	110	0	764.2	697	216	498	45	.242
Hill, Ken	2	2	2.70	6	6	0	40.0	32	9	30	0	.218
Holmes, D	0	1	5.02	13	0	1	14.1	12	8	12	1	.240
Honeycutt, R*	2	7	3.86	14	11	1	65.1	75	18	50	8	.278
Jackson, Dan*	4	5	4.26	13	12	0	76.0	89	30	44	3	.300
Jones, Bobby	1	0	1.13	2	2	0	16.0	13	3	14	0	.220
Jones, Doug	0	2	6.08	14	0	7	13.1	17	3	9	0	.321
Kile, Darryl	1	2	3.69	9	8	0	53.2	50	28	35	4	.249
Leiter, Mark	2	2	5.91	4	4	0	21.1	29	9	17	1	.326

Los Angeles, California   Grass

Pitcher	W	L	ERA	G	GS	Sv	IP	H	BB	SO	HR	Avg
Lilliquist, D*	1	0	2.77	2	2	0	13.0	11	2	7	1	.229
Loaiza, E	0	0	5.63	3	3	0	16.0	17	5	6	3	.279
Maddux, Greg	4	2	2.84	9	9	0	63.1	59	20	27	3	.252
Maddux, Mike	0	2	4.74	16	3	2	38.0	44	15	26	1	.299
Magrane, Joe*	1	1	2.79	3	3	0	19.1	23	5	10	0	.299
Martinez, De	2	6	2.70	9	9	0	60.0	60	13	35	5	.261
Martinez, PJ	7	4	2.59	35	3	2	66.0	52	27	79	6	.216
Martinez, R	54	38	3.43	120	117	0	801.1	687	314	612	63	.231
McDowell, R	10	8	3.04	100	0	15	133.1	158	53	73	7	.298
McElroy, C*	0	0	0.68	11	0	2	13.1	9	9	15	1	.196
Mercker, Kent*	1	1	0.61	10	3	0	29.2	17	16	28	2	.160
Micki, Dave	2	0	3.14	4	2	0	14.1	20	7	18	0	.317
Morgan, Mike	16	19	3.17	55	46	1	331.2	298	77	175	29	.242
Moyer, Jamie*	1	1	5.17	3	3	0	15.2	22	7	11	1	.328
Mulholland, T*	3	2	1.56	6	5	0	40.1	35	8	15	2	.232
Myers, Randy*	3	1	1.32	23	1	12	34.0	19	11	40	1	.167
Navarro, J	2	0	3.52	2	2	0	15.1	13	4	8	1	.224
Neagle, Denny*	3	2	2.63	6	3	0	27.1	28	5	27	2	.262
Nomo, Hideo	17	8	2.32	32	32	0	233.0	157	82	255	16	.191
Orosco, Jesse*	1	1	3.57	24	0	2	22.2	17	10	17	1	.200
Osborne, D*	2	2	4.42	7	7	0	38.2	43	14	22	4	.287
Osuna, Al*	3	0	1.29	17	0	2	14.0	5	8	17	0	.116
Osuna, A	3	5	2.90	55	0	3	62.0	37	21	65	2	.177
Park, Chan Ho	2	3	2.38	20	5	0	56.2	33	30	68	1	.167
Parrett, Jeff	1	1	2.35	13	0	1	15.1	9	6	16	2	.170
Pena, Alej	3	9	2.40	83	5	15	146.1	129	40	137	10	.236
Perez, Mike	0	0	0.61	12	0	1	14.2	13	2	17	0	.250
Portugal, M	4	5	6.14	11	10	0	51.1	61	25	37	7	.299
Pugh, Tim	1	2	4.22	4	4	0	21.1	25	7	9	2	.309
Quantrill, P	1	1	1.50	2	2	0	12.0	10	3	8	0	.222
Radinsky, S*	4	1	1.35	28	0	0	26.2	25	8	26	0	.253
Rapp, Pat	1	2	2.00	3	3	0	18.0	15	9	17	0	.227
Reed, Steve	1	0	3.00	9	0	1	12.0	10	3	9	4	.227
Reynolds, S	2	3	3.76	7	6	0	38.1	37	4	30	5	.252
Ritz, Kevin	2	3	4.22	5	5	0	32.0	29	19	15	0	.244
Rojas, Mel	0	1	1.02	13	0	8	17.2	12	6	22	0	.190
Rueter, Kirk*	1	0	4.20	3	3	0	15.0	18	3	6	2	.305
Ruffin, Bruce*	0	5	6.15	11	4	1	26.1	38	11	12	3	.330
Sanderson, S	2	0	2.91	6	3	0	21.2	26	2	17	2	.310
Scanlan, Bob	0	1	2.93	9	1	2	15.1	12	7	5	0	.231
Schilling, C	1	1	2.13	5	3	0	25.1	17	6	23	1	.187
Schourek, P*	0	1	3.63	4	3	0	17.1	15	7	16	2	.234
Shaw, Jeff	1	1	4.38	9	0	0	12.1	8	4	8	3	.190
Smiley, John*	3	5	2.21	9	8	1	57.0	45	9	44	2	.213
Smith, Lee	0	1	1.25	18	0	14	21.2	18	5	10	0	.225
Smith, Zane*	2	5	3.73	9	8	0	50.2	54	20	20	1	.284
Smoltz, John	4	7	3.50	14	14	0	87.1	83	43	76	8	.255
Stanton, Mike*	0	3	3.52	16	0	2	15.1	13	8	13	1	.241
Swift, Bill	4	1	1.63	6	5	0	38.2	30	11	25	1	.217
Swindell, G*	2	2	5.30	6	6	0	35.2	43	13	24	5	.314
Tapani, Kevin	1	1	9.47	6	4	0	19.0	36	7	13	3	.409
Tewksbury, B	2	3	3.48	8	7	0	41.1	52	8	17	2	.319
Thompson, Mar	1	0	1.23	2	2	0	14.2	11	2	8	0	.208
Trachsel, S	1	2	4.02	5	5	0	31.1	25	8	19	2	.217
Trlicek, R	1	1	2.03	18	0	0	26.2	21	7	17	1	.219
Valdes, I	15	8	2.58	43	29	0	230.0	179	57	186	17	.211
Valenzuela, F*	19	24	3.85	63	61	1	411.2	402	194	234	25	.257
VanLandingham	1	2	3.47	4	4	0	23.1	19	8	14	2	.224
Viola, Frank*	2	1	1.08	3	3	0	25.0	16	3	15	1	.182
Wagner, Paul	0	1	4.20	5	3	0	15.0	18	9	14	1	.290
Wakefield, T	1	1	4.20	2	2	0	15.0	19	4	4	1	.317
West, David*	1	1	1.80	4	2	0	15.0	8	5	9	0	.167
Wetteland, J	6	7	3.52	34	7	4	71.2	64	23	66	7	.239
Whitehurst, W	1	2	5.82	7	3	1	21.2	26	6	16	5	.317
Williams, Bri	1	1	3.14	7	1	1	14.1	8	8	6	0	.163
Williams, Mk	1	1	4.08	6	4	0	28.2	22	9	11	4	.206
Worrell, Tim	2	0	0.69	6	0	1	13.0	7	4	10	0	.156
Worrell, Todd	11	6	3.43	108	0	44	115.1	100	29	112	9	.234
Young, A	0	2	3.95	7	1	1	13.2	12	5	11	0	.250

Milwaukee, Wisconsin   Grass

Pitcher	W	L	ERA	G	GS	Sv	IP	H	BB	SO	HR	Avg
Abbott, Jim*	5	5	4.70	12	12	0	61.1	62	44	41	1	.265
Aguilera, R	3	4	5.82	15	0	6	17.0	25	9	10	3	.347
Aldred, Scott*	3	1	2.10	4	4	0	25.2	24	8	18	2	.250
Alvarez, W*	1	0	6.35	4	3	0	17.0	19	14	13	1	.284
Anderson, Brn*	2	0	2.35	2	2	0	15.1	12	3	6	1	.226
Appier, Kevin	5	2	4.01	11	10	0	60.2	65	28	49	3	.278
Bere, Jason	2	1	5.56	4	4	0	22.2	21	15	20	3	.250
Bohanon, B*	1	0	1.88	5	2	0	14.1	11	8	12	0	.208
Bones, Ricky	23	27	4.44	70	63	0	425.1	451	135	161	49	.271
Bosio, Chris	34	29	3.58	102	84	3	611.1	616	144	381	49	.261
Boze, M	0	0	4.41	12	0	1	16.1	15	14	9	0	.273
Brown, Kevin	3	2	3.92	6	6	0	43.2	49	8	27	2	.288
Candiotti, T	5	1	2.65	7	7	0	54.1	56	12	36	6	.264

COUNTY STADIUM
Home of the Milwaukee Brewers

Milwaukee, Wisconsin Grass

Pitcher	W	L	ERA	G	GS	Sv	IP	H	BB	SO	HR	Avg
Clemens, R	7	3	1.89	12	12	0	90.1	64	22	85	2	.195
Cone, David	2	1	2.86	3	3	0	22.0	18	7	10	0	.225
Cook, Dennis*	1	1	2.00	5	1	0	18.0	12	4	10	3	.200
D'Amico, Jeff	3	4	5.65	9	9	0	43.0	45	13	30	15	.263
Darwin, Danny	2	2	3.06	5	4	1	32.1	25	7	21	1	.216
Doherty, John	2	2	5.48	6	3	1	21.1	27	8	8	2	.310
Eckersley, D	0	0	5.79	13	0	4	14.0	22	4	13	1	.344
Eichhorn, M	2	0	6.26	19	0	0	27.1	42	9	15	3	.353
Eldred, Cal	25	13	3.20	49	49	0	348.1	286	118	220	31	.223
Erickson, S	2	3	6.27	8	8	0	47.1	57	16	19	6	.310
Farrell, John	2	1	4.31	5	5	0	31.1	30	11	17	1	.254
Fernandez, A	3	3	5.74	10	10	0	58.0	73	21	42	9	.307
Fetters, Mike	9	7	3.18	127	0	23	147.1	132	74	100	6	.250
Finley, Chuck*	4	3	5.43	10	9	0	63.0	77	26	52	6	.302
Florie, Bryce	0	1	7.30	8	0	0	12.1	15	6	10	3	.294
Fossas, Tony*	2	0	3.17	53	0	1	59.2	60	17	47	4	.255
Garcia, Ramon	2	2	4.75	19	0	2	36.0	33	8	12	5	.244
Gibson, Paul*	3	2	2.48	12	2	0	36.1	30	10	15	1	.226
Givens, Brian*	4	5	5.77	10	10	0	53.0	69	23	33	6	.312
Gordon, Tom	4	6	4.70	13	7	0	61.1	66	22	52	7	.277
Gross, Kevin	1	2	7.64	3	3	0	17.2	23	10	6	2	.311
Guardado, E*	0	1	8.47	9	3	0	17.0	25	6	8	5	.347
Gubicza, Mark	2	5	3.26	11	10	0	66.1	63	24	33	3	.257
Guetterman, L*	2	0	1.96	11	0	1	18.1	14	2	7	0	.206
Guthrie, Mark*	3	0	1.32	12	2	0	27.1	16	6	21	0	.172
Guzman, Juan	2	2	4.99	6	6	0	30.2	25	20	24	4	.229
Habyan, John	0	0	3.38	13	0	0	21.1	15	6	10	2	.188
Haney, Chris*	2	2	3.80	4	4	0	23.2	21	16	11	0	.253
Hanson, Erik	6	3	3.84	10	10	0	65.2	57	18	45	2	.234
Harnisch, P	1	1	7.82	3	3	0	12.2	13	8	10	3	.260
Haynes, Jimmy	1	1	3.45	2	2	0	15.2	5	11	12	0	.100
Henneman, M	3	2	4.13	20	0	5	28.1	30	12	18	1	.275
Henry, Doug	5	4	4.04	97	0	33	100.1	94	48	80	13	.247
Hentgen, Pat	5	0	2.48	6	5	0	36.1	37	12	26	2	.261
Hernandez, R	1	1	1.84	12	0	4	14.2	11	5	18	0	.208
Hershiser, O	0	2	8.04	3	3	0	15.2	26	8	8	4	.371
Hill, Ken	2	1	3.66	3	3	0	19.2	19	12	12	2	.264
Hitchcock, S*	3	0	3.38	5	5	0	32.0	31	10	14	1	.261
Holmes, D	3	3	4.37	41	0	4	59.2	68	17	46	4	.293
Honeycutt, R*	0	1	4.91	17	0	1	14.2	13	5	8	2	.250
Howe, Steve*	1	0	0.64	9	0	1	14.0	13	3	10	1	.241
Jackson, Mike	1	0	3.45	8	0	1	15.2	12	6	13	1	.211
Johns, Doug*	1	0	6.00	2	2	0	12.0	12	5	8	1	.279
Johnson, R*	4	3	3.74	10	10	0	65.0	47	44	65	4	.205
Jones, Doug	4	3	3.23	24	1	5	39.0	38	11	30	2	.257
Kamieniecki	2	3	2.58	5	5	0	38.1	29	16	13	0	.210
Karl, Scott*	10	9	4.81	29	26	0	168.1	197	57	89	20	.295
Key, Jimmy*	5	4	4.08	10	10	0	64.0	64	11	34	8	.261
Kiefer, Mark	3	0	5.32	26	0	0	45.2	45	29	31	8	.260
Langston, M*	5	4	4.14	12	12	0	82.2	79	36	62	6	.260
Leiter, Mark	1	2	3.67	4	4	0	27.0	29	10	17	1	.284
Lloyd, Graeme*	4	7	4.38	94	0	3	96.2	116	24	48	7	.304
Mahomes, Pat	0	1	5.27	4	2	0	13.2	15	6	4	1	.278
Martinez, De	3	0	5.04	4	4	0	25.0	30	5	15	2	.288
McCaskill, K	1	4	5.08	10	6	1	39.0	45	16	29	4	.288
McDonald, Ben	8	11	3.79	26	25	0	161.2	151	58	109	16	.244
McDowell, J	5	1	2.56	7	7	0	56.1	42	11	30	4	.205
Mercedes, J	2	1	4.39	22	0	0	41.0	40	17	16	7	.265
Mesa, Jose	2	3	4.30	12	5	3	37.2	37	15	21	0	.259
Milacki, Bob	1	1	3.43	4	3	0	21.0	20	13	2	0	.267
Mills, Alan	2	0	2.12	11	0	2	17.0	12	8	12	0	.197
Miranda, A*	8	11	4.19	54	26	2	186.2	169	106	120	17	.248
Monteleone, R	1	0	4.86	9	0	0	16.2	15	6	17	2	.234
Montgomery, J	2	1	1.71	21	0	14	31.2	20	8	22	1	.180
Moyer, Jamie*	4	2	3.12	7	6	0	40.1	34	17	16	3	.225
Mussina, Mike	4	1	3.40	5	5	0	39.2	32	10	20	1	.227
Nagy, Charles	1	1	5.51	4	4	0	16.1	26	5	14	1	.351
Navarro, J	34	25	4.14	88	71	1	502.2	528	156	259	28	.272
Ogea, Chad	2	0	1.69	2	2	0	16.0	10	1	7	1	.169
Olivares, O	0	0	0.69	2	2	0	13.0	8	7	3	0	.190
Orosco, Jesse*	5	6	3.99	97	0	6	85.2	77	39	90	7	.237
Pavlik, Roger	2	0	3.38	2	2	0	13.1	14	4	11	1	.264
Pettitte, A*	0	2	7.62	2	2	0	13.0	19	9	6	0	.358
Pichardo, H	1	2	4.60	8	1	0	15.2	15	8	8	0	.242
Plesac, Dan*	8	12	3.71	150	6	56	203.2	182	68	188	18	.239
Plunk, Eric	1	2	2.45	20	1	2	36.2	23	18	34	2	.176
Potts, Mike*	1	2	8.87	12	0	1	22.1	34	15	10	1	.374
Radinsky, S*	4	0	3.21	12	0	2	14.0	10	3	11	1	.208
Radke, Brad	0	1	3.21	2	2	0	14.0	11	8	2	2	.216
Reyes, Al	1	1	1.93	18	0	1	23.1	12	13	18	1	.154
Rhodes, A*	3	0	2.00	3	2	0	18.0	11	11	8	0	.180
Rodriguez, Fr	1	1	4.50	2	2	0	12.0	17	5	5	1	.321
Rogers, Kenny*	3	3	3.60	11	4	1	35.0	27	11	18	3	.218
Ruffin, Bruce*	1	3	7.88	11	2	0	16.0	20	11	14	1	.328
Russell, Jeff	2	3	1.19	20	1	6	30.1	21	6	16	1	.189
Sanderson, S	3	2	4.65	7	7	0	40.2	44	18	17	2	.284
Scanlan, Bob	3	7	6.00	26	14	1	99.0	128	33	43	16	.318
Sele, Aaron	2	1	6.57	3	3	0	12.1	19	3	4	0	.358

COUNTY STADIUM
Home of the Milwaukee Brewers

Pitcher	W	L	ERA	G	GS	Sv	IP	H	BB	SO	HR	Avg
Sparks, Steve	4	8	6.54	25	17	0	129.1	151	74	53	15	.303
Stottlemyre	1	2	6.38	5	5	0	24.0	27	9	17	4	.278
Swift, Bill	0	1	4.32	5	2	0	16.2	23	2	10	2	.333
Swindell, G*	1	0	5.54	4	4	0	26.0	27	4	20	2	.262
Tapani, Kevin	1	6	5.74	11	10	0	58.0	75	11	41	6	.314
Trombley, M	0	1	5.27	5	1	0	13.2	13	10	6	1	.260
Vanegmond, T	2	4	5.59	8	6	0	38.2	37	15	23	6	.252
Veres, Randy	0	3	3.75	15	0	1	24.0	23	10	12	4	.264
Villone, Ron*	0	0	3.46	13	0	2	13.0	8	6	11	3	.182
Viola, Frank*	2	2	3.08	6	6	0	38.0	41	7	31	8	.272
Wakefield, T	1	1	1.80	2	2	0	15.0	13	1	13	2	.224
Wells, David*	2	4	6.34	12	6	1	44.0	52	17	27	3	.287
Wickander, K*	0	0	3.94	16	0	0	16.0	18	9	12	0	.290
Wickman, Bob	3	0	1.29	16	2	0	28.0	22	8	23	3	.222
Witt, Bobby	6	4	4.52	16	16	0	95.2	84	50	78	9	.239

HUBERT H. HUMPHREY METRODOME
Home of the Minnesota Twins

Pitcher	W	L	ERA	G	GS	Sv	IP	H	BB	SO	HR	Avg
Abbott, Jim*	8	2	4.04	11	11	0	71.1	87	27	40	2	.307
Aguilera, R	12	14	3.73	175	15	91	262.2	239	64	244	33	.239
Aldred, Scott*	3	2	7.15	14	8	0	56.2	65	20	36	15	.289
Alvarez, W*	2	1	3.79	8	5	0	38.0	38	14	33	2	.255
Appier, Kevin	3	0	1.86	4	4	0	29.0	23	8	25	1	.211
Belcher, Tim	3	1	4.98	5	5	0	34.1	34	19	14	2	.266
Bennett, Erik	0	0	8.27	14	0	1	16.1	21	8	5	4	.313
Bere, Jason	1	1	5.14	2	2	0	14.0	12	8	16	1	.235
Bohanon, B*	0	1	6.88	5	3	0	17.0	21	9	5	4	.300
Bones, Ricky	3	2	5.74	9	9	0	47.0	62	19	13	9	.326
Bosio, Chris	2	2	2.36	8	7	0	53.1	51	14	25	3	.249
Brown, Kevin	5	1	3.74	8	8	0	55.1	55	14	29	1	.261
Candiotti, T	1	3	3.52	5	5	0	30.2	30	6	20	5	.246
Casian, Larry*	4	3	5.56	58	2	1	77.2	98	20	31	14	.314
Clark, Mark	2	0	3.60	5	3	0	15.0	17	7	15	1	.233
Clemens, R	4	3	2.48	9	9	0	69.0	57	23	50	3	.227
Cone, David	3	1	2.12	4	4	0	29.2	17	14	33	1	.165
DeLucia, Rich	0	1	2.77	3	2	0	13.0	11	7	9	2	.229
Doherty, John	3	0	1.75	6	3	0	25.2	24	2	6	1	.258
Dyer, Mike	2	3	7.09	6	6	0	26.2	38	12	22	0	.339
Eckersley, D	0	0	4.10	20	0	13	26.1	26	1	20	3	.255
Eichhorn, M	0	1	3.09	19	0	1	23.1	21	9	13	1	.259
Eldred, Cal	0	0	6.32	3	3	0	15.2	21	11	8	3	.323
Erickson, S	36	30	4.26	82	81	0	532.0	573	169	317	43	.277
Farrell, John	3	1	2.48	5	4	0	32.2	27	7	12	1	.220
Fernandez, A	4	1	4.31	7	7	0	48.0	53	19	36	4	.286
Fetters, Mike	0	1	3.60	14	0	8	15.0	19	3	13	0	.311
Finley, Chuck*	6	7	4.72	14	13	0	89.2	107	32	50	5	.301
Frohwirth, T	0	1	6.43	12	0	0	21.0	16	14	14	2	.208
Gibson, Paul*	0	0	5.82	13	0	1	17.0	23	10	6	2	.348
Gordon, Tom	3	2	5.67	11	5	0	39.2	46	20	36	2	.291
Grimsley, J	0	3	6.27	5	3	0	18.2	20	12	8	4	.278
Guardado, E*	7	11	5.47	78	9	4	126.2	139	54	87	20	.284
Gubicza, Mark	6	3	3.26	11	10	0	66.1	59	11	32	2	.252
Guthrie, Mark*	13	11	4.09	119	21	5	235.2	245	89	210	23	.273
Guzman, Juan	5	2	3.60	8	8	0	50.0	42	24	41	5	.225
Haney, Chris*	2	1	5.87	5	4	0	23.0	27	12	12	4	.300
Hansell, Greg	2	0	5.36	31	0	2	48.2	54	19	31	6	.286
Hanson, Erik	3	3	2.82	8	8	0	54.1	55	16	35	1	.261
Harnisch, P	0	2	9.82	3	3	0	14.2	25	6	5	1	.368
Hawkins, L	1	2	8.00	6	6	0	27.0	36	5	14	8	.327
Henneman, M	0	5	4.00	21	0	9	27.0	33	10	19	1	.311
Hentgen, Pat	3	1	1.74	5	4	0	31.0	19	7	19	1	.179
Hernandez, R	0	1	5.68	11	0	6	12.2	12	8	8	1	.255
Hershiser, O	1	0	1.32	2	2	0	13.2	13	1	11	0	.236
Hill, Ken	2	0	3.32	3	3	0	21.2	20	10	22	1	.244
Jackson, Mike	0	1	3.10	16	0	1	20.1	22	8	6	1	.293
Johnson, R*	4	4	3.64	10	10	0	64.1	59	27	64	5	.241
Jones, Doug	1	2	4.76	14	0	5	17.0	20	10	12	1	.294
Karl, Scott*	1	1	5.14	2	2	0	14.0	16	4	3	3	.286
Key, Jimmy*	5	1	1.80	9	9	0	60.0	50	8	39	2	.227
Klingenbeck	1	0	6.93	12	3	0	37.2	49	12	23	12	.316
Klink, Joe*	1	1	2.45	12	0	0	22.0	26	5	15	1	.299
Langston, M*	4	4	3.59	8	8	0	57.2	54	22	40	4	.248
Leiter, Al*	2	0	4.80	3	3	0	15.0	21	13	11	1	.344
Lira, Felipe	1	2	5.82	3	3	0	17.0	22	7	9	1	.328
Magnante, M*	1	2	11.15	6	2	0	15.1	26	10	5	3	.361
Mahomes, Pat	8	15	6.81	63	28	0	190.1	220	108	120	35	.295
Martinez, De	3	0	3.72	4	4	0	29.0	25	8	19	1	.238
McCaskill, K	5	3	5.11	11	7	0	49.1	54	18	34	5	.284
McDonald, Ben	0	3	6.00	4	4	0	21.0	24	3	17	2	.279
McDowell, J	5	4	3.47	12	12	0	80.1	82	29	54	8	.261
Meacham, R	2	2	4.11	12	0	0	15.1	17	4	7	1	.283
Mesa, Jose	3	1	2.39	11	3	2	26.1	24	9	17	1	.238
Milacki, Bob	3	2	4.14	7	7	0	45.2	55	12	13	4	.302
Milchin, Mike*	1	0	9.49	14	0	0	12.1	19	7	11	3	.358
Mills, Alan	0	0	6.75	9	0	0	14.2	15	10	10	1	.278

HUBERT H. HUMPHREY METRODOME
Home of the Minnesota Twins

Pitcher	W	L	ERA	G	GS	Sv	IP	H	BB	SO	HR	Avg
Monteleone, R	1	1	2.16	9	0	0	16.2	10	7	10	0	.175
Montgomery, J	0	3	2.89	25	0	14	28.0	27	10	29	2	.243
Morgan, Mike	1	3	7.00	5	3	0	18.0	21	5	7	6	.292
Moyer, Jamie*	1	1	5.53	7	4	0	27.2	35	5	15	5	.315
Mussina, Mike	6	1	2.28	7	7	0	55.1	52	9	34	4	.244
Nagy, Charles	0	4	6.75	7	7	0	41.1	66	19	29	3	.379
Naulty, Dan	2	1	1.47	24	0	1	30.2	17	17	32	1	.160
Navarro, J	3	5	5.27	10	9	0	54.2	65	12	21	5	.294
Neagle, Denny*	0	1	4.50	6	3	0	18.0	27	7	13	3	.346
Nelson, Jeff	0	0	4.80	13	0	1	15.0	14	9	13	0	.255
Olson, Gregg	0	3	4.32	15	0	3	16.2	21	8	18	0	.313
Pall, Donn	0	0	3.95	12	0	0	13.2	16	5	7	2	.281
Parra, Jose	4	3	6.99	20	8	0	65.2	86	26	38	13	.315
Pavlik, Roger	2	2	7.23	4	4	0	23.2	35	8	16	7	.347
Pichardo, H	1	0	6.11	6	2	0	17.2	19	8	9	0	.284
Plesac, Dan*	0	1	1.26	13	0	8	14.1	10	4	9	1	.189
Plunk, Eric	1	2	2.64	22	1	1	30.2	28	13	36	3	.237
Portugal, M	2	4	7.63	20	4	1	48.1	77	19	33	13	.363
Prieto, Ariel	0	1	4.40	2	2	0	14.1	17	7	5	1	.321
Quantrill, P	0	2	3.52	6	2	0	15.1	21	2	7	0	.318
Radke, Brad	12	15	4.09	34	33	0	228.2	221	54	134	40	.251
Reyes, Carlos	1	1	3.29	5	0	0	13.2	12	3	7	1	.235
Rhodes, A*	2	2	5.56	5	4	0	22.2	25	9	16	0	.275
Robertson, R*	4	11	5.04	33	21	0	130.1	136	88	91	11	.271
Rodriguez, Fr	9	8	4.25	26	26	0	161.0	152	71	90	15	.250
Rogers, Kenny*	2	3	3.74	15	6	1	43.1	48	16	27	2	.281
Russell, Jeff	4	2	2.80	25	2	11	45.0	40	15	21	2	.238
Sanderson, S	1	3	5.09	6	6	0	35.1	49	9	20	4	.336
Scanlan, Bob	2	0	3.92	4	3	0	20.2	20	11	12	0	.256
Sele, Aaron	2	1	1.93	3	3	0	18.2	23	7	13	0	.295
Smiley, John*	10	4	2.83	19	19	0	136.2	117	40	94	8	.234
Springer, R	0	1	5.84	3	1	0	12.1	13	6	13	1	.271
Stevens, Dave	8	5	7.30	69	0	10	90.0	111	46	55	22	.301
Stottlemyre	3	5	5.88	12	10	0	64.1	81	26	40	6	.320
Swift, Bill	2	1	5.28	13	3	0	29.0	38	8	8	1	.311
Swindell, G*	1	3	6.00	4	4	0	27.0	30	8	15	3	.297
Tapani, Kevin	45	30	3.65	91	91	0	628.0	637	134	398	48	.262
Tavarez, Ju	0	0	4.11	7	1	0	15.1	18	5	12	0	.286
Trombley, M	9	8	4.87	71	14	5	186.2	186	55	148	30	.256
Valera, Julio	0	1	7.82	4	2	0	12.2	19	7	7	1	.358
Van Poppel, T	1	0	8.10	6	3	0	20.0	26	15	18	2	.321
Viola, Frank*	30	12	2.62	51	51	0	385.0	334	99	294	36	.231
Wakefield, T	1	1	5.11	2	2	0	12.1	11	4	6	2	.244
Wells, David*	3	2	3.46	10	5	0	39.0	39	10	26	6	.262
West, David*	6	10	6.33	30	23	0	128.0	131	66	108	19	.264
Wickman, Bob	2	2	4.99	12	3	0	30.2	30	18	17	1	.265
Witt, Bobby	7	4	3.38	12	12	0	82.2	79	38	62	6	.253
Wojciechowski*	0	1	4.73	2	2	0	13.1	15	4	4	1	.313

OLYMPIC STADIUM
Home of the Montreal Expos

Pitcher	W	L	ERA	G	GS	Sv	IP	H	BB	SO	HR	Avg
Alvarez, Tavo	1	4	6.67	9	6	0	28.1	38	13	16	2	.311
Ashby, Andy	0	3	4.29	4	4	0	21.0	20	9	13	3	.253
Assenmacher*	3	0	0.36	17	0	2	25.1	13	8	27	0	.155
Astacio, P	0	2	9.00	5	4	0	19.0	28	7	12	0	.337
Avery, Steve*	1	4	5.48	8	7	0	42.2	45	13	34	2	.265
Beck, Rod	0	1	3.26	16	0	6	19.1	18	4	15	2	.250
Belcher, Tim	2	4	4.17	8	8	0	49.2	44	18	34	3	.238
Benes, Andy	1	7	4.18	8	8	0	51.2	49	14	38	5	.255
Bielecki, M	4	1	4.42	12	6	0	36.2	45	11	23	3	.308
Blair, Willie	1	0	2.70	6	1	0	13.1	12	4	12	0	.255
Boever, Joe	1	0	3.06	13	0	4	17.2	11	12	19	2	.177
Boskie, Shawn	1	0	3.72	7	5	0	29.0	29	7	20	1	.257
Bottenfield	1	3	3.67	20	9	1	68.2	69	26	32	7	.261
Brantley, J	2	0	1.97	20	0	6	32.0	24	12	27	4	.214
Brocail, Doug	1	0	1.53	4	3	0	17.2	12	6	8	3	.200
Brown, Kevin	0	1	1.98	2	2	0	13.2	16	1	10	0	.302
Bullinger, J	1	2	7.15	7	3	0	22.2	29	9	15	2	.312
Burba, Dave	1	2	6.11	9	2	0	17.2	22	9	19	1	.306
Burkett, John	5	0	4.38	6	6	0	37.0	47	12	22	3	.305
Candiotti, T	1	2	3.06	5	5	0	32.1	24	10	24	3	.205
Castillo, F	0	2	4.76	4	4	0	22.2	28	7	18	2	.322
Charlton, N*	1	0	2.12	10	1	1	17.0	15	2	13	0	.259
Cone, David	5	3	1.92	12	11	0	79.2	66	31	67	3	.228
Cooke, Steve*	0	1	7.27	3	2	0	17.1	21	7	13	1	.300
Cormier, R*	8	9	4.07	24	20	0	119.1	112	31	84	13	.246
Daal, Omar*	2	2	3.02	40	2	0	50.2	39	24	46	4	.215
Darwin, Danny	3	2	3.79	9	5	1	35.2	37	8	18	6	.261
Drabek, Doug	9	4	2.71	17	17	0	123.0	92	26	86	9	.204
Dyer, Mike	3	3	3.13	35	0	1	37.1	35	18	28	2	.255
Fassero, Jeff*	33	24	3.40	133	51	4	434.0	379	167	371	29	.236
Fernandez, S*	0	5	6.95	10	9	0	44.0	47	21	48	8	.276
Franco, John*	2	1	2.96	21	0	12	27.1	28	9	19	3	.275
Freeman, M	1	0	6.16	9	3	0	19.0	19	13	16	1	.260
Frey, Steve*	5	1	2.83	56	0	7	57.1	52	29	34	3	.251

Pitcher	W	L	ERA	G	GS	Sv	IP	H	BB	SO	HR	Avg
Gardner, Mark	16	15	3.41	52	46	0	285.0	252	102	242	20	.237
Glavine, Tom*	5	5	3.57	14	14	0	95.2	77	30	68	6	.223
Gooden, D	3	5	4.24	10	10	0	63.2	62	19	53	3	.255
Grimsley, J	2	1	1.88	4	4	0	24.0	16	18	17	0	.198
Gross, Kevin	12	13	4.20	38	34	0	222.2	224	89	161	14	.265
Hamilton, J	2	0	2.70	3	3	0	23.1	21	4	16	0	.239
Hammond, C*	1	0	3.51	6	4	0	25.2	23	15	9	1	.253
Haney, Chris*	3	5	4.12	12	11	0	63.1	67	21	37	5	.272
Harnisch, P	0	2	3.86	5	5	0	28.0	26	13	21	2	.243
Heredia, Gil	8	4	4.23	50	9	0	110.2	125	20	78	10	.284
Hernandez, X	0	0	7.23	14	0	0	18.2	23	11	16	2	.307
Hershiser, O	4	4	2.65	9	9	0	68.0	59	20	51	2	.236
Hill, Ken	18	15	3.12	44	43	0	286.0	263	109	150	16	.245
Hoffman, T	1	0	3.75	10	0	3	12.0	8	3	16	2	.182
Isringhausen, J	1	1	6.11	3	3	0	17.2	23	10	11	2	.319
Jackson, Dan*	2	3	3.88	8	8	0	48.2	46	20	24	2	.251
Jackson, Mike	0	2	3.44	13	1	0	18.1	18	6	15	2	.257
Johnson, R*	2	1	2.53	5	5	0	32.0	24	17	30	3	.209
Jones, Bobby	2	0	2.11	3	3	0	21.1	19	6	14	1	.241
Jones, Doug	0	0	3.46	10	0	4	13.0	11	2	11	1	.234
Jones, Todd	0	0	4.40	9	0	2	14.1	17	7	5	2	.298
Juden, Jeff	0	0	3.38	12	0	0	16.0	10	8	10	1	.185
Kile, Darryl	3	2	3.92	7	7	0	41.1	42	17	32	4	.280
Langston, M*	6	3	2.62	10	10	0	79.0	66	39	76	7	.227
Leiper, Dave*	0	1	4.02	19	0	0	15.2	13	2	10	1	.220
Leiter, Mark	2	2	3.50	10	10	0	64.1	55	11	52	11	.226
Maddux, Greg	7	6	2.39	18	18	0	128.0	115	29	78	3	.243
Maddux, Mike	1	0	0.75	13	0	0	24.0	14	6	17	0	.171
Magrane, Joe*	3	7	6.06	10	9	0	52.0	63	24	32	7	.301
Manuel, Barry	2	0	2.87	26	0	0	37.2	27	8	27	4	.193
Martinez, De	49	29	2.74	106	104	1	751.2	638	176	449	58	.229
Martinez, PJ	18	13	3.41	43	39	0	264.0	212	90	259	17	.221
Martinez, R	5	4	3.36	10	10	0	64.1	60	37	44	0	.255
McDowell, R	0	0	2.33	22	0	9	38.2	32	11	21	0	.235
Mercker, Kent*	1	1	4.80	9	2	0	15.0	19	8	9	0	.317
Morgan, Mike	1	6	4.19	10	9	0	58.0	55	22	25	3	.253
Moyer, Jamie*	3	1	2.51	6	5	0	32.1	37	10	19	2	.287
Mulholland, T*	6	2	3.29	11	11	0	82.0	81	11	33	6	.257
Myers, Randy*	0	1	3.52	19	0	5	23.0	19	12	28	2	.229
Navarro, J	0	2	5.25	2	2	0	12.0	15	4	3	2	.319
Neagle, Denny*	1	2	5.05	10	5	0	35.2	34	14	26	6	.250
Nomo, Hideo	1	1	2.70	2	2	0	13.1	10	11	15	0	.217
Olivares, O	2	1	2.57	9	3	0	28.0	25	8	14	1	.238
Osborne, D*	2	2	3.60	6	6	0	35.0	34	5	22	4	.258
Painter, L*	0	2	5.54	4	2	0	13.0	14	5	15	1	.269
Paniagua, J	1	1	4.64	5	5	0	21.1	27	11	15	5	.314
Parrett, Jeff	9	9	3.40	70	0	8	103.1	76	46	85	8	.208
Pena, Alej	4	2	1.08	15	0	2	25.0	13	3	21	1	.153
Perez, Mike	0	0	5.82	17	0	1	17.0	18	6	10	1	.281
Portugal, M	4	3	4.60	8	8	0	45.0	51	15	20	6	.287
Pugh, Tim	2	1	3.91	6	3	0	23.0	18	10	14	2	.220
Rapp, Pat	1	2	1.55	5	5	0	29.0	23	17	15	2	.225
Reynolds, S	2	0	3.32	3	3	0	19.0	22	4	11	1	.301
Reynoso, A	1	2	3.52	4	4	0	23.0	20	10	13	3	.238
Rojas, Mel	17	9	3.44	183	0	48	238.1	196	77	192	20	.223
Rueter, Kirk*	11	7	4.81	30	30	0	147.2	173	41	65	17	.299
Ruffin, Bruce*	2	3	3.49	11	4	0	28.1	36	11	16	1	.313
Sanders, S	2	0	1.96	4	3	0	18.1	8	4	19	2	.127
Sanderson, S	1	2	4.26	4	2	0	12.2	11	6	10	2	.234
Scanlan, Bob	0	2	5.17	8	1	1	15.2	21	9	6	0	.333
Schilling, C	4	1	2.35	7	5	0	38.1	28	11	35	1	.206
Schourek, P*	1	1	7.15	8	3	1	22.2	34	6	15	2	.366
Scott, Tim	7	5	2.91	90	0	5	105.0	85	41	83	4	.224
Service, S	1	1	6.92	10	0	0	13.0	16	7	16	2	.296
Shaw, Jeff	4	7	4.02	75	6	2	121.0	119	41	68	9	.258
Smiley, John*	4	5	4.17	12	8	0	58.1	60	17	44	3	.260
Smith, Lee	0	0	0.00	17	0	14	21.0	9	5	24	0	.125
Smith, Zane*	6	9	3.51	35	20	1	146.0	169	46	89	4	.294
Smoltz, John	7	3	2.72	11	11	0	76.0	58	32	72	2	.214
Swift, Bill	2	1	1.80	3	3	0	20.0	15	5	7	2	.200
Swindell, G*	1	3	3.51	5	5	0	25.2	35	4	14	3	.324
Tewksbury, B	5	3	2.95	9	9	0	64.0	53	12	24	2	.232
Trachsel, S	1	0	1.77	3	3	0	20.1	14	6	15	1	.189
Urbina, U	6	2	3.40	21	13	0	84.2	69	41	72	11	.216
Valdes, I	1	1	1.20	3	2	0	15.0	10	3	12	1	.200
Valenzuela, F*	1	4	4.62	8	6	0	37.0	42	23	26	1	.278
VanLandingham	1	1	5.21	3	3	0	19.0	15	7	10	2	.214
Veres, Dave	4	1	3.89	36	0	2	41.2	43	12	31	2	.272
Viola, Frank*	3	0	1.13	3	3	0	24.0	23	2	19	1	.258
Wagner, Paul	0	3	7.71	4	3	0	16.1	20	5	6	2	.303
Watson, Allen*	1	1	5.79	3	3	0	14.0	17	6	7	2	.309
Weathers, D	1	1	5.40	3	2	0	13.1	20	4	12	1	.345
Wetteland, J	12	7	2.91	101	0	53	123.2	95	38	137	8	.212
Whitehurst, W	1	0	1.10	11	3	0	32.2	22	5	18	0	.198
Williams, Bri	2	0	1.72	4	1	0	15.2	14	4	11	0	.241
Williams, Mk	1	1	4.50	5	3	0	18.0	19	8	11	3	.279
Worrell, Todd	1	2	2.31	23	0	7	23.1	22	11	26	1	.253
Young, A	1	3	4.70	10	2	1	23.0	26	9	12	2	.280

Pitcher	W	L	ERA	G	GS	Sv	IP	H	BB	SO	HR	Avg
Abbott, Kyle*	0	2	3.77	3	2	0	14.1	15	6	8	1	.283
Aguilera, R	11	6	3.27	35	12	3	118.1	109	31	100	10	.248
Ashby, Andy	1	2	4.10	5	5	0	26.1	36	10	17	3	.330
Assenmacher*	2	1	1.91	18	0	4	28.1	18	10	40	2	.176
Astacio, P	2	1	5.40	5	4	0	21.2	21	15	12	5	.269
Avery, Steve*	4	2	2.19	11	11	0	74.0	53	25	42	2	.199
Beck, Rod	0	2	2.65	15	0	9	17.0	18	1	19	1	.257
Belcher, Tim	1	2	3.72	6	6	0	29.0	26	11	24	2	.236
Belinda, Stan	0	0	2.25	13	0	3	12.0	7	7	9	0	.167
Benes, Andy	3	0	1.97	7	7	0	50.1	27	14	48	4	.155
Bielecki, M	1	1	3.30	11	5	0	30.0	27	17	19	2	.245
Blair, Willie	2	2	3.26	7	2	1	19.1	21	4	13	2	.273
Boskie, Shawn	0	1	6.00	4	2	0	12.0	17	4	8	0	.370
Brantley, J	0	1	4.19	14	1	4	19.1	19	12	18	3	.257
Brocail, Doug	0	1	6.00	6	1	1	12.0	15	5	5	2	.333
Bullinger, J	1	1	6.60	5	2	0	15.0	14	5	6	1	.241
Burba, Dave	2	2	8.69	8	2	0	19.2	25	10	11	2	.321
Burkett, John	2	5	5.65	10	9	0	43.0	52	15	25	8	.301
Byrd, Paul	1	1	3.49	27	0	0	28.1	33	8	22	3	.295
Candiotti, T	1	3	2.35	10	9	0	65.0	48	20	39	1	.207
Carpenter, C	2	2	4.02	11	1	0	15.2	14	5	6	4	.250
Castillo, F	1	3	4.71	5	5	0	28.2	34	6	18	3	.301
Castillo, T*	0	0	2.40	5	2	0	15.0	21	4	10	1	.323
Charlton, N*	1	2	2.70	11	0	2	13.1	10	5	11	0	.222
Clark, Mark	6	6	3.17	17	17	0	110.2	105	20	69	14	.254
Cone, David	40	22	3.05	84	79	0	585.0	487	191	588	43	.225
Cooke, Steve*	2	0	1.40	4	2	1	19.1	15	4	10	2	.211
Cormier, R*	0	3	3.35	7	7	0	43.0	40	9	27	4	.241
Darwin, Danny	1	2	4.44	7	4	1	24.1	27	4	16	2	.293
Dewey, Mark	1	0	3.09	15	0	1	23.1	23	8	12	2	.264
Dipoto, Jerry	5	2	3.94	60	0	4	82.1	82	39	58	2	.273
Drabek, Doug	8	8	4.04	20	20	0	120.1	124	41	53	12	.264
Fassero, Jeff*	2	2	3.08	9	3	1	26.1	33	4	23	2	.303
Fernandez, S*	42	21	2.49	91	90	0	603.0	388	197	596	48	.181
Franco, John*	19	12	2.51	182	0	102	201.0	198	66	158	11	.256
Freeman, M	0	1	3.57	5	3	0	17.2	19	7	7	2	.275
Gardner, Mark	2	3	4.91	8	6	0	36.2	32	25	25	5	.237
Gibson, Paul*	0	1	3.90	23	0	0	32.1	33	4	30	2	.262
Glavine, Tom*	3	2	3.54	8	8	0	53.1	53	16	44	3	.256
Gooden, D	56	34	3.30	109	109	0	769.0	683	232	614	50	.239
Gross, Kevin	3	4	5.21	14	9	0	67.1	76	25	37	9	.289
Guetterman, L*	2	3	5.13	20	0	1	26.1	33	9	11	2	.303
Gunderson, E*	0	1	3.38	22	0	0	13.1	13	9	9	1	.271
Hamilton, J	2	0	1.50	4	4	0	30.0	19	5	20	2	.179
Hammond, C*	3	1	2.45	7	5	0	33.0	33	10	21	1	.258
Hampton, Mike*	0	3	8.31	4	3	0	13.0	22	5	7	2	.361
Harnisch, P	7	10	3.22	31	31	0	198.2	182	66	134	24	.243
Henry, Doug	4	4	3.77	54	0	4	71.2	66	24	57	10	.241
Heredia, Gil	1	0	1.46	4	1	1	12.1	9	0	12	0	.220
Hernandez, X	1	1	6.92	10	0	0	13.0	16	6	12	6	.291
Hershiser, O	3	2	3.02	7	7	0	47.2	38	13	33	2	.221
Hill, Ken	5	3	2.83	9	9	0	60.1	45	18	41	3	.199
Hoffman, T	0	2	4.26	10	0	4	12.2	9	9	12	1	.200
Isringhausen	10	8	3.05	22	22	0	153.2	145	53	102	8	.253
Jackson, Dan*	2	3	1.71	8	8	0	47.1	31	17	25	0	.183
Jackson, Mike	2	0	4.91	15	0	0	14.2	14	6	9	3	.255
Jacome, Jason*	2	3	4.99	5	5	0	30.2	34	11	13	3	.288
Jones, Bobby	14	16	3.78	46	46	0	307.1	332	94	188	28	.278
Jones, Doug	1	2	1.50	9	0	5	12.0	7	1	12	1	.171
Jones, Todd	0	1	1.42	9	0	3	12.2	11	6	7	1	.250
Kile, Darryl	1	1	3.60	5	4	0	30.0	34	7	29	5	.286
Leiter, Al*	1	0	2.25	2	2	0	12.0	12	3	15	1	.261
Leiter, Mark	1	1	2.25	2	2	0	16.0	11	6	12	2	.200
Linton, Doug	3	1	3.97	14	2	0	22.2	35	9	14	2	.354
Maddux, Greg	9	6	3.17	17	17	0	119.1	106	32	72	7	.237
Maddux, Mike	4	4	4.22	48	0	2	70.1	73	15	44	9	.266
Magrane, Joe*	3	1	5.25	7	7	0	36.0	40	13	25	1	.290
Martinez, De	5	3	2.77	10	10	0	65.0	61	26	36	3	.242
Martinez, PJ	5	0	0.95	6	4	0	38.0	18	8	27	1	.143
Martinez, R	2	3	4.82	9	9	0	52.1	51	22	33	7	.256
McDowell, R	9	11	3.88	81	0	22	120.2	125	37	58	10	.265
McElroy, C*	0	1	1.65	12	0	0	16.1	12	7	10	1	.218
Mercker, Kent*	1	0	1.11	11	3	0	24.1	20	8	21	0	.220
Mimbs, M*	1	1	3.72	3	3	0	19.1	22	5	9	2	.297
Minor, Blas	4	2	4.33	33	0	1	43.2	49	9	37	8	.283
Milicki, Dave	7	7	3.54	36	13	1	127.0	116	40	103	18	.245
Morgan, Mike	3	2	5.19	9	8	0	50.1	47	15	33	7	.246
Moyer, Jamie*	1	1	1.80	2	2	0	15.0	11	2	5	1	.208
Mulholland, T*	1	5	4.22	8	8	0	49.0	46	14	26	3	.249
Myers, Randy*	11	3	2.46	107	1	44	139.0	88	54	146	6	.183
Navarro, J	2	0	1.80	2	2	0	15.0	11	2	8	2	.204
Neagle, Denny*	4	1	1.94	11	4	0	41.2	35	10	34	1	.227
Nied, Dave	1	1	2.25	2	2	0	12.0	10	10	6	1	.227
Nomo, Hideo	0	1	5.54	2	2	0	13.0	14	4	20	4	.269
Olivares, O	2	0	2.57	4	3	0	21.0	18	8	7	2	.228
Orosco, Jesse*	2	4	2.98	28	0	8	45.1	41	16	54	3	.240
Osborne, D*	0	0	3.78	3	3	0	16.2	19	3	11	4	.297
Painter, L*	1	0	1.88	4	1	0	14.1	12	0	11	1	.222

SHEA STADIUM
Home of the New York Mets
Flushing, New York   Grass

Pitcher	W	L	ERA	G	GS	Sv	IP	H	BB	SO	HR	Avg
Parrett, Jeff	0	0	3.05	15	0	0	20.2	21	4	20	1	.266
Patterson, B*	1	2	2.64	19	2	3	30.2	32	10	25	2	.271
Pena, Alej	7	3	3.11	60	0	6	81.0	69	28	72	9	.229
Perez, Mike	1	1	4.73	13	0	1	13.1	8	5	8	3	.174
Person, R	3	2	3.26	12	6	0	47.0	42	15	47	7	.233
Portugal, M	3	3	4.42	13	12	0	75.1	79	24	46	10	.280
Pugh, Tim	2	3	4.50	5	4	0	24.0	25	7	16	4	.269
Rapp, Pat	1	3	3.94	5	5	0	29.2	28	14	17	5	.248
Remlinger, M*	1	2	3.68	8	4	0	29.1	25	19	17	3	.231
Reynolds, S	2	1	3.26	3	3	0	19.1	21	5	15	3	.273
Reynoso, A	1	1	7.11	4	4	0	19.0	20	4	12	3	.267
Ritz, Kevin	2	1	3.38	3	3	0	16.0	18	6	8	1	.286
Rojas, Mel	2	1	4.57	15	0	6	21.2	18	5	25	2	.222
Ruffin, Bruce*	1	3	5.27	15	5	2	42.2	46	19	35	5	.274
Sanders, S	0	2	3.24	4	2	1	16.2	13	7	14	0	.197
Sanderson, S	1	1	3.94	3	3	0	16.0	19	6	6	2	.297
Schilling, C	3	1	3.16	7	3	0	31.1	24	10	25	3	.216
Schourek, P*	10	13	4.09	53	26	0	211.0	222	78	111	15	.270
Scott, Tim	2	1	5.40	9	0	0	13.1	9	6	8	3	.191
Smiley, John*	7	5	2.78	19	14	0	103.2	88	16	73	9	.231
Smith, Lee	0	3	3.60	16	0	10	15.0	14	7	15	2	.241
Smith, Zane*	5	4	2.31	12	9	0	66.1	53	12	43	3	.218
Smoltz, John	3	4	4.17	9	9	0	58.1	54	19	38	7	.244
Stottlemyre	2	0	2.93	2	2	0	15.1	11	5	9	2	.200
Swift, Bill	3	3	3.86	5	5	0	32.2	32	9	18	3	.258
Swindell, G*	1	0	3.29	2	2	0	13.2	9	3	8	1	.184
Telgheder, D	4	2	5.79	15	6	0	51.1	57	17	25	8	.279
Tewksbury, B	3	3	4.58	9	8	0	53.0	62	6	24	5	.295
Thompson, Mar	0	2	3.38	4	2	0	16.0	14	6	8	1	.237
Urbani, Tom*	1	0	2.25	2	2	0	12.0	10	5	6	1	.244
Valenzuela, F*	3	0	3.00	7	6	0	42.0	31	24	39	5	.209
Valera, Julio	1	0	4.15	4	2	0	13.0	13	9	6	1	.260
Viola, Frank*	22	16	3.50	41	41	0	280.1	294	60	199	23	.269
Wagner, Paul	1	1	3.00	4	2	0	18.0	17	3	13	0	.258
Wakefield, T	1	0	0.69	2	2	0	13.0	4	6	8	0	.103
Wallace, D	2	1	1.20	12	0	3	15.0	14	6	9	0	.241
Watson, Allen*	0	2	3.96	4	4	0	25.0	26	3	15	3	.274
Weathers, D	0	2	4.79	5	4	0	20.2	28	11	13	0	.318
West, David*	2	3	7.22	11	4	0	28.2	28	15	20	4	.250
Wetteland, J	0	2	3.60	9	2	6	15.0	17	8	17	0	.298
Whitehurst, W	8	11	3.53	65	16	1	163.0	157	41	116	9	.233
Wilson, Paul	3	4	2.93	12	12	0	73.2	62	33	58	1	.223
Witt, Bobby	0	0	3.77	2	2	0	14.1	16	7	11	1	.286
Wohlers, Mark	1	1	2.57	14	0	1	14.0	5	7	16	0	.114
Worrell, Todd	2	1	4.15	18	0	5	17.1	18	9	18	3	.269
Young, A	2	20	4.27	52	18	9	141.1	168	48	83	12	.297

YANKEE STADIUM
Home of the New York Yankees
Bronx, New York   Grass

Pitcher	W	L	ERA	G	GS	Sv	IP	H	BB	SO	HR	Avg
Abbott, Jim*	17	14	3.43	37	37	0	270.1	250	68	145	27	.250
Aguilera, R	0	1	3.94	13	1	9	16.0	17	3	9	1	.258
Aldred, Scott*	2	1	5.48	6	4	0	21.1	25	16	9	3	.309
Alvarez, W*	2	1	4.47	8	8	0	46.1	42	32	36	9	.239
Anderson, Bm*	1	1	6.23	3	3	0	17.1	21	4	8	4	.296
Appier, Kevin	2	0	1.51	5	5	0	35.2	21	16	28	1	.172
Assenmacher*	1	1	3.45	23	0	0	15.2	12	8	10	1	.218
Belcher, Tim	1	4	4.82	5	5	0	28.0	31	19	12	1	.279
Boehringer, B	1	3	8.14	9	2	0	24.1	27	16	16	5	.287
Bohanon, B*	0	2	8.20	9	3	0	18.2	30	11	13	1	.361
Bones, Ricky	2	1	4.22	7	4	0	32.0	32	6	14	2	.260
Bosio, Chris	1	2	5.59	10	7	0	48.1	57	16	23	6	.302
Brown, Kevin	4	3	3.98	7	7	0	43.0	44	13	17	3	.267
Campbell, Mi	1	1	1.93	2	2	0	14.0	10	5	6	2	.189
Candiotti, T	2	2	2.95	6	6	0	36.2	25	8	19	5	.197
Clemens, R	8	3	2.97	14	14	0	100.0	93	30	87	3	.245
Cone, David	11	3	3.11	16	16	0	115.2	87	54	108	11	.207
Cook, Dennis*	1	1	6.89	8	2	0	15.2	20	7	10	3	.328
Cummings, J*	1	2	5.87	4	2	0	15.1	11	10	6	2	.208
Darwin, Danny	1	1	2.14	4	3	0	21.0	12	6	12	5	.162
Eckersley, D	1	1	4.55	20	1	11	27.2	30	1	31	4	.275
Eichhorn, M	0	3	2.95	18	0	0	21.1	14	8	12	2	.184
Eldred, Cal	1	2	5.12	3	3	0	19.1	18	10	5	3	.247
Erickson, S	2	1	2.21	5	5	0	36.2	31	9	20	0	.231
Fernandez, A	1	3	6.67	5	5	0	28.1	34	5	12	8	.288
Fetters, Mike	0	1	5.60	8	1	2	17.2	20	7	12	3	.286
Finley, Chuck*	5	5	3.75	12	10	0	74.1	73	27	50	9	.259
Fossas, Tony*	0	0	3.75	18	0	0	12.0	7	7	6	2	.175
Gibson, Paul*	2	2	4.78	30	0	0	43.1	46	16	35	12	.274
Gooden, D	8	1	3.56	16	16	0	101.0	90	37	74	8	.241
Gordon, Tom	2	2	2.92	6	3	0	24.2	20	12	28	3	.230
Guardado, E*	1	1	5.02	7	1	0	14.1	11	7	8	2	.212
Gubicza, Mark	3	6	2.94	12	11	0	79.2	79	17	49	5	.259
Guetterman, L*	17	4	3.96	131	1	13	206.2	207	60	96	15	.267
Guthrie, Mark*	1	0	3.05	8	1	1	20.2	19	7	12	2	.250
Guzman, Juan	1	3	5.17	7	7	0	38.1	35	25	30	4	.238

YANKEE STADIUM
Home of the New York Yankees

Bronx, New York   Grass

Pitcher	W	L	ERA	G	GS	Sv	IP	H	BB	SO	HR	Avg
Habyan, John	10	4	3.33	81	1	6	113.2	117	30	75	6	.272
Haney, Chris*	1	3	5.33	5	5	0	25.1	31	14	14	2	.310
Hanson, Erik	4	4	4.33	9	8	0	54.0	55	15	31	7	.262
Harnisch, P	0	2	4.15	2	2	0	13.0	13	7	9	0	.250
Henneman, M	0	3	2.90	18	0	4	31.0	27	7	16	4	.248
Hentgen, Pat	2	3	5.71	7	6	0	41.0	54	17	31	5	.321
Hernandez, X	1	3	7.79	15	0	5	17.1	22	9	16	3	.314
Hershiser, O	1	0	3.77	2	2	0	14.1	13	3	9	1	.245
Hill, Ken	1	1	2.93	2	2	0	15.1	11	6	8	1	.204
Hitchcock, S*	8	10	4.81	30	23	1	144.0	152	59	102	10	.274
Howe, Steve*	10	4	3.82	106	0	16	110.2	113	19	51	10	.262
Hutton, Mark	1	1	5.79	9	3	0	23.1	23	14	14	2	.277
Johnson, R*	4	4	2.72	12	11	0	76.0	70	43	79	6	.247
Jones, Doug	0	0	1.69	15	0	10	21.1	19	4	21	1	.235
Kamieniecki	21	15	4.33	58	48	0	322.0	336	127	171	35	.273
Karl, Scott*	0	2	6.39	2	2	0	12.2	14	4	7	3	.264
Key, Jimmy*	25	14	3.74	53	53	0	337.0	342	84	219	27	.264
Langston, M*	4	3	4.79	9	9	0	56.1	58	30	42	5	.266
Leiter, Al*	3	7	5.23	14	12	1	63.2	54	43	71	5	.227
Leiter, Mark	2	1	5.91	11	6	1	42.2	46	16	35	7	.272
Lira, Felipe	0	3	8.06	4	4	0	22.1	32	14	12	1	.344
MacDonald, B*	1	1	3.52	22	0	0	30.2	27	11	25	5	.237
Magnante, M*	0	3	4.97	12	2	0	25.1	29	10	9	2	.309
Martinez, De	0	5	6.84	5	5	0	26.1	37	14	10	4	.339
McCaskill, K	2	3	4.91	7	6	0	29.1	30	11	16	7	.265
McDonald, Ben	4	2	3.15	8	8	0	54.1	53	17	31	5	.259
McDowell, J	8	10	4.60	22	22	0	154.2	154	60	114	25	.262
Mecir, Jim	1	1	4.30	16	0	0	23.0	23	12	21	3	.267
Mendoza, R	0	2	9.69	3	3	0	13.0	25	3	6	1	.410
Mesa, Jose	0	1	3.90	13	3	4	27.2	32	12	17	2	.286
Milacki, Bob	2	2	4.38	6	6	0	39.0	41	11	18	5	.270
Mills, Alan	1	5	3.22	28	1	0	44.2	48	22	23	4	.289
Monteleone, R	7	5	4.47	66	0	0	114.2	115	36	79	17	.260
Montgomery, J	1	0	2.25	14	0	8	20.0	14	7	20	3	.197
Moyer, Jamie*	3	3	4.28	8	7	0	48.1	58	10	30	7	.297
Mulholland, T*	4	2	6.87	11	9	0	55.0	62	14	29	16	.287
Munoz, Bobby	3	1	3.70	18	0	0	24.1	20	11	18	0	.225
Mussina, Mike	1	3	3.68	5	5	0	29.1	28	15	21	2	.246
Nagy, Charles	3	3	4.08	7	7	0	46.1	46	12	20	6	.261
Navarro, J	2	2	3.99	8	7	0	47.1	54	14	16	5	.287
Nelson, Jeff	2	3	4.97	42	0	1	41.2	36	27	47	4	.232
Olson, Gregg	0	0	0.98	17	0	10	18.1	13	8	13	0	.200
Oquist, Mike	0	0	1.46	3	0	0	12.1	7	2	11	0	.159
Orosco, Jesse*	1	2	5.14	17	0	1	14.0	16	7	13	3	.286
Pall, Donn	2	0	2.62	19	0	0	34.1	35	10	20	4	.263
Pavlas, Dave	0	0	2.75	12	0	1	19.2	20	6	15	0	.270
Pavlik, Roger	3	1	4.50	5	5	0	28.0	35	18	17	3	.315
Pettitte, A*	18	6	2.94	31	30	0	220.1	197	68	147	19	.243
Plesac, Dan*	1	2	5.84	13	0	2	12.1	13	8	16	3	.260
Plunk, Eric	10	5	3.37	70	9	0	149.2	148	87	123	18	.259
Polley, Dale*	0	2	8.25	19	0	0	12.0	12	6	7	2	.255
Quantrill, P	1	2	2.41	6	2	0	18.2	18	1	12	2	.257
Radke, Brad	1	2	5.40	3	3	0	18.1	18	3	4	3	.257
Reyes, Carlos	0	2	8.78	6	2	0	13.1	25	6	6	2	.424
Rhodes, A*	2	1	4.23	6	5	0	27.2	25	13	20	4	.243
Rivera, M	9	4	3.86	38	5	0	81.2	69	33	84	7	.228
Rogers, Kenny*	11	8	4.76	31	22	3	141.2	158	64	80	12	.282
Russell, Jeff	1	2	3.21	15	0	1	14.0	15	8	8	1	.294
Sanderson, S	16	13	4.65	37	37	0	224.1	247	53	126	35	.280
Sele, Aaron	0	2	4.20	5	5	0	30.0	38	11	16	3	.311
Smith, Lee	0	1	0.86	21	0	11	21.0	14	11	21	1	.189
Sparks, Steve	1	1	2.81	4	2	0	16.0	16	9	8	2	.281
Springer, R	0	1	9.00	9	1	0	15.0	16	8	9	2	.262
Stottlemyre	5	2	4.37	10	8	0	55.2	60	18	24	7	.275
Swift, Bill	1	1	1.61	6	2	2	22.1	16	3	14	1	.198
Swindell, G*	2	4	4.43	9	7	0	42.2	52	12	33	8	.301
Tapani, Kevin	4	6	5.05	11	11	0	73.0	81	9	41	10	.279
Tewksbury, B	1	3	6.75	6	5	0	26.2	37	7	17	3	.339
Timlin, Mike	0	0	0.55	12	0	2	16.1	4	8	8	0	.080
Viola, Frank*	4	3	3.58	8	8	0	50.1	42	18	35	5	.235
Wakefield, T	1	1	3.86	2	2	0	14.0	7	12	8	2	.159
Walker, Mike	1	0	2.19	2	1	0	12.1	9	6	3	0	.209
Wells, David*	9	1	2.84	18	9	0	79.1	64	16	69	9	.218
Wetteland, J	2	4	3.00	59	0	33	60.0	40	19	56	8	.187
Whiteside, M	0	1	7.20	8	0	0	15.0	20	7	10	2	.333
Wickman, Bob	18	3	3.84	112	12	3	210.2	204	82	129	14	.258
Witt, Bobby	1	5	7.56	6	6	0	33.1	37	23	22	2	.276

OAKLAND-ALAMEDA COUNTY COLISEUM
Home of the Oakland Athletics

Oakland, California   Grass

Pitcher	W	L	ERA	G	GS	Sv	IP	H	BB	SO	HR	Avg
Abbott, Jim*	2	4	5.30	9	8	0	52.2	61	34	33	7	.298
Acre, Mark	3	2	5.36	45	0	1	50.1	51	22	34	7	.262
Adams, Willie	3	2	2.90	6	6	0	40.1	35	12	38	6	.226
Aguilera, R	2	0	2.55	13	2	9	24.2	23	10	25	5	.237
Alvarez, W*	2	1	3.48	10	8	0	54.1	40	29	54	6	.214

OAKLAND-ALAMEDA COUNTY COLISEUM
Home of the Oakland Athletics

Oakland, California   Grass

Pitcher	W	L	ERA	G	GS	Sv	IP	H	BB	SO	HR	Avg
Appier, Kevin	4	3	1.80	11	11	0	70.0	54	28	59	1	.210
Bautista, J	1	0	1.29	2	2	0	14.0	7	5	3	0	.156
Belcher, Tim	0	1	3.93	3	3	0	18.1	20	5	10	0	.286
Bere, Jason	2	2	4.57	5	5	0	21.2	24	9	13	1	.279
Bielecki, M	2	0	2.70	3	2	0	13.1	9	6	14	0	.184
Boever, Joe	4	3	4.05	23	0	0	40.0	47	14	23	3	.292
Bones, Ricky	2	3	4.46	7	6	0	34.1	35	18	21	4	.259
Bosio, Chris	3	3	3.99	13	10	1	65.1	59	23	41	6	.242
Boskie, Shawn	2	1	4.37	4	3	0	22.2	21	6	13	3	.241
Briscoe, John	1	2	5.73	42	1	1	55.0	50	46	47	10	.246
Brown, Kevin	4	3	3.22	9	9	0	64.1	56	31	39	1	.237
Candiotti, T	1	4	7.28	5	5	0	29.2	45	16	19	3	.354
Chouinard, B	3	1	5.11	5	4	0	24.2	27	12	15	3	.284
Clark, Mark	3	0	1.50	3	3	0	18.0	17	7	14	2	.243
Clemens, R	5	5	2.70	10	10	0	73.1	51	29	75	7	.195
Cone, David	2	2	3.07	4	4	0	29.1	21	4	33	2	.196
Corsi, Jim	9	5	3.24	69	1	1	94.1	85	38	50	5	.253
Darwin, Danny	3	2	4.55	6	4	0	27.2	31	6	18	6	.277
DeLucia, Rich	0	3	3.94	3	2	0	16.0	14	5	14	3	.233
Doherty, John	1	2	3.46	4	2	0	13.0	14	4	2	3	.292
Eckersley, D	34	16	2.39	272	0	155	335.0	245	59	381	28	.201
Eichhorn, M	0	1	7.45	17	0	0	19.1	36	11	15	2	.424
Eldred, Cal	2	1	5.03	3	3	0	19.2	15	5	8	2	.203
Erickson, S	4	3	2.97	9	9	0	60.2	62	21	29	4	.270
Farrell, John	1	2	4.08	4	4	0	28.2	33	7	33	4	.284
Fernandez, A	4	3	3.93	8	8	0	52.2	43	30	49	6	.226
Fetters, Mike	0	1	7.36	10	1	3	14.2	24	8	10	3	.375
Finley, Chuck*	2	8	3.52	14	12	0	84.1	80	43	59	10	.261
Gordon, Tom	2	4	3.07	13	9	0	70.1	57	43	59	6	.225
Groom, Buddy*	0	0	5.55	37	0	1	35.2	46	16	26	6	.319
Gross, Kevin	0	3	10.80	3	3	0	13.1	15	14	6	4	.283
Gubicza, Mark	5	5	2.55	13	10	0	81.1	71	19	62	2	.234
Guzman, Juan	4	1	4.64	7	7	0	42.2	36	23	33	2	.231
Habyan, John	0	3	5.93	10	0	0	13.2	15	2	16	2	.288
Haney, Chris*	1	1	4.38	4	4	0	24.2	24	11	7	3	.255
Hanson, Erik	3	2	3.19	8	8	0	53.2	51	21	48	3	.252
Harris, R	0	0	1.71	8	0	0	21.0	11	8	15	1	.159
Henneman, M	1	1	4.11	13	0	4	15.1	16	12	12	0	.267
Hentgen, Pat	4	0	2.27	6	5	0	35.2	28	13	27	3	.211
Hernandez, R	2	0	6.75	15	0	7	14.2	16	10	15	2	.281
Hitchcock, S*	0	2	5.40	4	4	0	23.1	19	14	14	4	.232
Honeycutt, R*	10	11	2.69	192	0	19	197.1	154	60	125	13	.219
Jackson, Dan*	0	1	4.26	2	2	0	12.2	15	6	8	0	.306
Jackson, Mike	0	2	3.66	16	0	1	19.2	14	11	21	2	.206
Johns, Doug*	6	7	4.50	27	16	1	116.0	112	48	45	11	.256
Johnson, R*	5	2	3.19	8	8	0	59.1	31	35	72	5	.154
Jones, Doug	0	2	3.00	11	0	4	12.0	12	6	14	0	.255
Kamieniecki	1	1	3.55	6	3	1	25.1	26	12	9	4	.271
Karl, Scott*	1	0	2.92	2	2	0	12.1	11	9	8	2	.234
Key, Jimmy*	3	4	3.78	10	10	0	66.2	66	15	48	8	.267
Klink, Joe*	4	1	3.16	51	0	1	51.1	43	12	27	2	.230
Krivda, Rick*	2	0	3.45	3	3	0	15.2	15	5	10	2	.259
Langston, M*	2	4	3.97	8	8	0	56.2	57	23	38	6	.269
Leiper, Dave*	2	1	1.32	52	0	0	54.2	37	20	35	2	.190
Leiter, Al*	0	1	5.93	4	3	0	13.2	19	9	13	1	.345
Leiter, Mark	2	0	2.89	4	2	0	18.2	16	5	18	0	.232
Mahomes, Pat	0	3	5.19	5	2	0	17.1	16	13	7	6	.267
McCaskill, K	1	4	4.31	12	8	1	48.0	53	30	31	3	.283
McDonald, Ben	3	2	2.95	7	7	0	39.2	25	21	31	1	.177
McDowell, J	6	4	2.91	14	14	0	96.0	82	33	75	8	.233
Mesa, Jose	2	2	3.77	8	4	2	28.2	23	15	15	2	.228
Milacki, Bob	2	2	2.29	6	5	0	35.1	26	17	11	3	.213
Mills, Alan	2	0	3.45	10	0	0	15.2	9	17	14	1	.167
Mohler, Mike*	1	5	4.48	65	5	3	74.1	67	38	58	9	.246
Montgomery, J	1	3	4.79	20	0	8	20.2	23	9	23	3	.291
Moyer, Jamie*	2	2	4.50	7	6	0	32.0	36	6	17	4	.275
Mussina, Mike	6	1	2.62	7	7	0	55.0	45	19	35	4	.223
Nagy, Charles	3	2	4.35	7	7	0	51.2	61	13	26	6	.292
Navarro, J	2	2	2.30	8	6	0	47.0	31	24	25	1	.189
Nelson, Jeff	0	3	6.59	12	0	0	13.2	11	17	7	2	.244
Olson, Gregg	0	2	2.12	14	0	10	17.0	9	6	17	0	.164
Pall, Donn	1	0	4.02	8	0	0	15.2	20	9	7	1	.308
Parrett, Jeff	4	0	3.29	37	0	0	52.0	47	23	41	3	.241
Pavlik, Roger	1	0	2.01	6	6	0	40.1	26	24	26	2	.194
Pettitte, A*	2	2	6.38	4	4	0	18.1	30	6	17	2	.366
Piesac, Dan*	0	3	4.50	11	0	4	14.0	13	9	15	3	.255
Plunk, Eric	7	6	4.28	61	8	5	117.2	97	79	106	10	.226
Prieto, Ariel	6	5	4.30	14	13	0	83.2	80	32	60	7	.256
Quantrill, P	1	2	3.93	5	2	0	18.1	21	3	17	5	.284
Radke, Brad	0	2	8.00	3	3	0	18.0	20	7	8	4	.286
Reyes, Carlos	3	3	3.71	52	8	0	126.0	102	59	89	12	.220
Rodriguez, Fr	1	2	5.87	3	2	0	15.1	16	6	7	3	.276
Rogers, Kenny*	2	1	5.06	16	6	2	42.2	57	18	21	9	.326
Russell, Jeff	5	0	1.29	26	0	13	35.0	23	17	26	3	.184
Sanderson, S	6	8	3.44	18	17	0	110.0	93	32	67	14	.225
Sele, Aaron	2	1	4.95	4	4	0	20.0	17	7	16	3	.224
Small, Aaron	1	1	7.50	4	2	0	12.0	15	8	8	2	.306
Smiley, John*	1	1	3.07	2	2	0	14.2	11	5	8	2	.208

OAKLAND-ALAMEDA COUNTY COLISEUM
Home of the Oakland Athletics

Oakland, California — Grass

Pitcher	W	L	ERA	G	GS	Sv	IP	H	BB	SO	HR	Avg
Stottlemyre	7	6	4.22	22	20	0	143.0	143	61	143	16	.261
Swift, Bill	2	0	1.50	7	2	1	24.0	25	4	10	0	.269
Swindell, G*	3	4	4.41	8	7	0	51.0	55	10	40	9	.268
Tapani, Kevin	3	0	3.83	7	7	0	42.1	49	14	17	5	.292
Taylor, Billy	5	4	5.04	47	0	7	55.1	51	27	55	5	.241
Telgheder, D	3	5	4.43	9	8	0	44.2	50	15	22	5	.286
Timlin, Mike	0	0	0.54	11	0	4	16.2	11	7	14	0	.186
Trombley, M	2	0	4.19	6	2	0	19.1	21	7	16	2	.284
Van Poppel, T	8	15	5.01	49	28	0	206.2	189	112	166	31	.246
Viola, Frank*	3	3	3.02	9	9	0	56.2	48	33	32	2	.239
Wakefield, T	2	1	4.43	3	3	0	22.1	17	7	13	5	.210
Wasdin, John	7	3	4.66	15	13	0	87.0	83	31	37	13	.250
Wells, David*	2	2	4.24	11	5	2	34.0	34	9	24	4	.268
Wengert, Don	4	4	5.00	23	13	0	95.1	111	30	47	19	.292
Whiteside, M	1	2	4.09	14	0	2	22.0	24	9	17	1	.270
Wickman, Bob	0	1	3.92	8	2	0	20.2	15	12	14	3	.197
Witt, Bobby	17	13	3.93	41	41	0	268.0	242	136	212	21	.244
Wojciechowski*	3	4	5.37	13	9	0	52.0	59	23	18	7	.284

VETERANS STADIUM
Home of the Philadelphia Phillies

Philadelphia, Pennsylvania — Artificial

Pitcher	W	L	ERA	G	GS	Sv	IP	H	BB	SO	HR	Avg
Abbott, Kyle*	2	7	5.21	27	11	0	95.0	105	36	72	14	.286
Aguilera, R	1	1	4.41	4	2	0	16.1	20	6	11	1	.308
Ashby, Andy	2	8	5.94	16	15	0	83.1	84	41	63	6	.263
Assenmacher*	0	3	5.63	23	0	2	24.0	31	12	23	4	.313
Astacio, P	1	2	7.71	7	5	0	28.0	36	18	16	6	.319
Avery, Steve*	4	2	4.43	7	7	0	42.2	41	15	33	7	.252
Beck, Rod	0	2	2.75	17	0	6	19.2	11	4	21	3	.159
Beech, Matt*	0	3	7.57	5	5	0	27.1	32	8	24	7	.299
Belcher, Tim	1	4	4.15	5	5	0	30.1	27	19	19	3	.235
Belinda, Stan	3	1	1.80	14	0	2	15.0	9	3	15	2	.170
Benes, Andy	4	3	2.77	9	9	0	65.0	46	24	43	6	.197
Bielecki, M	3	2	3.71	12	6	0	43.2	47	21	27	3	.283
Blair, Willie	2	1	4.50	7	2	0	20.0	26	9	12	3	.310
Blazier, Ron	2	1	6.43	14	0	0	21.0	26	7	14	3	.299
Boever, Joe	3	3	2.72	62	0	6	92.2	73	40	78	2	.215
Borland, Toby	3	8	3.63	77	0	4	106.2	105	49	83	6	.259
Boskie, Shawn	3	4	4.43	14	10	0	63.0	64	24	42	7	.262
Bottalico, R	6	5	2.76	65	0	15	84.2	51	33	100	8	.172
Brantley, J	1	1	4.99	21	1	8	30.2	28	17	32	3	.237
Bullinger, J	2	2	4.95	7	3	1	20.0	17	15	14	1	.221
Burba, Dave	3	0	0.57	9	1	0	15.2	7	7	17	1	.132
Burkett, John	3	2	4.62	10	10	0	60.1	71	20	34	6	.300
Candiotti, T	2	3	4.11	7	7	0	35.0	34	24	27	1	.252
Carpenter, C	2	0	2.15	14	2	0	29.1	24	5	13	2	.222
Castillo, F	0	2	6.27	7	6	0	33.0	37	10	21	8	.278
Charlton, N*	2	2	6.00	22	1	0	30.0	34	15	32	4	.288
Clark, Mark	1	0	5.16	4	4	0	22.2	36	5	16	1	.356
Cone, David	4	2	3.94	12	9	0	61.2	50	27	66	7	.220
Cook, Dennis*	8	5	3.19	37	16	1	149.2	119	52	77	19	.219
Cooke, Steve*	0	3	4.05	4	3	0	20.0	22	5	13	5	.278
Cormier, R*	1	0	2.42	5	2	0	22.1	16	2	18	0	.195
Daal, Omar*	1	0	2.45	11	1	0	14.2	13	2	15	0	.241
Darwin, Danny	2	1	2.05	8	3	1	26.1	17	6	14	1	.183
Drabek, Doug	6	4	3.92	13	13	0	82.2	73	22	64	9	.230
Fassero, Jeff*	4	2	1.01	13	3	0	35.2	28	10	33	0	.215
Fernandez, S*	9	8	3.52	23	22	0	135.1	106	48	146	16	.212
Foster, Kevin	0	1	4.61	3	2	0	13.2	11	9	9	0	.220
Franco, John*	2	3	1.14	23	0	15	23.2	16	9	23	0	.195
Freeman, M	1	3	6.54	18	9	1	53.2	56	36	39	4	.267
Frey, Steve*	1	0	2.15	24	0	1	29.1	24	9	11	3	.222
Frohwirth, T	2	0	3.21	38	0	0	47.2	42	14	34	4	.237
Gardner, Mark	2	2	3.57	7	6	0	35.1	39	17	33	2	.269
Glavine, Tom*	7	3	3.41	11	11	0	71.1	60	31	39	4	.229
Gooden, D	4	3	3.35	11	10	0	75.1	67	24	65	3	.238
Grace, Mike	4	0	2.98	6	6	0	42.1	38	7	28	2	.239
Grimsley, J	1	5	4.14	11	11	0	58.2	47	40	38	4	.223
Gross, Kevin	13	20	3.84	43	40	0	269.2	232	119	182	30	.233
Hamilton, J	0	2	7.56	3	3	0	16.2	26	5	13	2	.371
Hammond, C*	1	1	5.51	4	3	0	16.1	16	9	13	2	.254
Hampton, Mike*	2	0	2.84	6	4	0	25.1	26	10	16	1	.260
Harnisch, P	1	4	7.09	6	6	0	33.0	43	12	21	6	.309
Heredia, Gil	0	2	7.24	6	3	0	13.2	23	6	6	1	.377
Hernandez, X	0	1	5.02	10	0	1	14.1	13	8	15	0	.241
Hershiser, O	2	2	2.35	6	6	0	38.1	36	21	22	0	.254
Hill, Ken	7	4	4.52	12	11	0	65.2	57	36	33	6	.236
Honeycutt, R*	1	0	1.42	4	2	0	12.2	17	6	9	0	.321
Hunter, Rich	1	6	6.75	8	8	0	40.0	44	20	20	7	.280
Jackson, Dan*	21	12	3.69	41	41	0	280.1	285	82	187	18	.261
Jackson, Mike	2	4	2.44	33	2	2	62.2	36	28	58	2	.167
Jones, Bobby	2	2	4.81	4	4	0	24.1	35	3	12	0	.333
Jones, Doug	2	2	1.36	33	0	21	39.2	39	6	25	0	.245
Jordan, R*	0	1	1.29	12	0	0	14.0	9	7	10	0	.184
Juden, Jeff	3	2	3.93	10	8	0	50.1	42	25	43	4	.226
Kile, Darryl	4	1	4.02	5	5	0	31.1	31	15	20	2	.261

Philadelphia, Pennsylvania — Artificial

Pitcher	W	L	ERA	G	GS	Sv	IP	H	BB	SO	HR	Avg
Langston, M*	0	1	1.20	2	2	0	15.0	9	5	17	2	.170
Lieber, Jon	1	1	2.14	4	3	0	21.0	15	3	18	0	.200
Lilliquist, D*	1	0	1.46	2	2	0	12.1	11	3	7	0	.244
Maddux, Greg	9	5	2.89	16	16	0	112.0	100	16	99	3	.234
Maddux, Mike	5	3	4.11	33	9	0	92.0	95	24	72	4	.268
Magrane, Joe*	2	5	5.06	9	9	0	48.0	59	21	25	4	.303
Martinez, De	6	3	2.47	13	13	0	91.0	74	22	52	13	.214
Martinez, PJ	2	0	1.85	8	5	0	34.0	28	13	29	1	.222
Martinez, R	4	4	4.77	11	11	0	66.0	66	38	42	8	.259
McDowell, R	7	11	3.50	87	0	21	108.0	113	46	59	2	.272
McElroy, C*	1	1	3.94	31	0	1	29.2	37	20	30	0	.301
Mercker, Kent*	0	1	2.93	9	1	1	15.1	12	7	15	2	.211
Mimbs, M*	7	12	4.97	33	21	1	139.1	138	69	90	16	.264
Morgan, Mike	3	2	3.35	7	6	0	43.0	38	18	30	4	.241
Moyer, Jamie*	2	4	5.74	6	6	0	31.1	30	17	28	4	.256
Mulholland, T*	33	24	3.85	84	80	0	549.2	544	119	314	44	.259
Munoz, Bobby	4	3	4.64	14	10	0	66.0	80	23	27	3	.308
Myers, Randy*	3	2	2.25	21	1	14	32.0	20	13	34	3	.175
Navarro, J	3	0	0.77	3	3	0	23.1	12	8	12	1	.148
Neagle, Denny*	0	2	4.30	5	2	1	14.2	17	8	8	1	.304
Nomo, Hideo	0	1	4.50	3	3	0	16.0	15	6	19	2	.254
Olivares, O	2	1	4.62	10	3	0	37.0	34	13	29	4	.246
Osborne, D*	0	3	5.53	5	5	0	27.2	36	13	15	5	.308
Pall, Donn	1	0	2.13	6	0	0	12.2	9	2	9	0	.200
Parrett, Jeff	11	5	2.98	71	3	4	121.0	108	57	93	10	.243
Patterson, B*	3	3	5.12	18	1	1	19.1	22	7	10	3	.289
Pena, Alej	1	1	6.12	16	1	1	25.0	29	8	27	5	.305
Portugal, M	5	1	2.53	8	8	0	57.0	52	18	42	2	.235
Quantrill, P	6	7	5.12	26	16	1	109.0	133	35	63	15	.306
Rapp, Pat	2	3	4.88	6	6	0	31.1	32	24	18	0	.267
Rekar, Bryan	1	1	5.14	2	2	0	14.0	15	4	12	2	.283
Reynolds, S	2	0	1.46	5	5	0	37.0	33	5	26	1	.236
Reynoso, A	0	2	5.59	4	4	0	19.1	20	12	14	2	.270
Rojas, Mel	1	0	1.11	23	0	7	32.1	18	12	21	0	.159
Ruffin, Bruce*	23	26	4.46	102	61	3	407.1	448	179	237	32	.284
Ryan, Ken	2	3	2.68	33	0	6	50.1	34	23	39	3	.192
Sanders, S	1	0	0.66	3	2	0	13.2	11	2	9	0	.220
Scanlan, Bob	0	2	2.60	9	1	0	17.1	15	6	12	2	.234
Schilling, C	23	23	3.18	62	55	0	413.0	345	109	355	31	.224
Schourek, P*	3	1	2.97	8	4	0	30.1	30	10	21	1	.263
Scott, Tim	1	1	2.19	10	0	0	12.1	8	0	14	2	.178
Shepherd, K	1	0	2.19	6	0	1	12.1	12	3	5	0	.286
Slocumb, H	3	1	3.30	59	0	13	73.2	68	39	68	0	.243
Smiley, John*	3	1	4.70	16	10	0	67.0	73	16	54	7	.284
Smith, Lee	1	3	4.66	17	0	11	19.1	20	8	21	2	.253
Smith, Zane*	1	4	4.47	9	8	0	48.1	46	13	26	8	.251
Smoltz, John	5	3	2.43	9	9	0	63.0	43	21	59	1	.189
Springer, D	0	1	3.46	2	2	0	13.0	8	8	7	1	.178
Springer, R	3	2	2.85	33	3	0	66.1	51	23	67	6	.213
Swift, Bill	1	1	8.35	4	4	0	18.1	35	5	8	2	.412
Swindell, G*	2	2	2.05	5	4	0	30.2	31	4	18	0	.272
Tewksbury, B	2	4	5.32	11	8	1	47.1	66	12	18	3	.338
Trachsel, S	0	1	3.38	2	2	0	11.1	11	6	9	1	.220
Valdes, I	1	2	7.71	5	3	0	12.2	30	4	11	2	.341
Valenzuela, F*	5	0	2.98	10	9	0	57.1	56	16	24	6	.262
VanLandingham	1	0	4.15	2	2	0	13.0	11	7	5	0	.239
Viola, Frank*	2	1	1.90	6	6	0	42.2	31	16	30	1	.205
Wagner, Paul	1	2	4.22	6	3	0	21.1	23	13	16	1	.277
Weathers, D	0	1	4.22	5	4	0	21.1	24	9	12	1	.282
West, David*	8	7	3.18	60	12	2	130.1	96	74	120	8	.202
Wetteland, J	1	2	3.21	9	1	4	14.0	9	11	17	2	.184
Williams, Bri	2	0	6.53	6	3	0	20.2	30	7	10	1	.337
Williams, Mk	8	9	4.89	51	27	0	202.1	211	74	115	25	.271
Wohlers, Mark	0	1	2.57	15	0	2	14.0	13	5	18	1	.241
Worrell, Todd	6	3	3.06	27	0	10	32.1	31	21	32	4	.250
Young, A	1	3	4.70	9	3	2	23.0	26	9	15	3	.280

Pittsburgh, Pennsylvania — Artificial

Pitcher	W	L	ERA	G	GS	Sv	IP	H	BB	SO	HR	Avg
Ashby, Andy	2	2	3.38	5	5	0	32.0	30	10	27	1	.248
Assenmacher, P	2	1	8.02	21	1	1	21.1	27	10	22	5	.307
Astacio, P	3	1	1.63	4	4	0	27.2	26	6	22	1	.252
Avery, Steve*	3	3	5.11	8	8	0	44.0	51	24	31	4	.290
Bautista, J	2	0	4.15	5	1	0	13.0	11	1	8	4	.220
Beck, Rod	1	1	7.80	13	0	7	15.0	19	2	13	5	.302
Belcher, Tim	4	2	2.76	9	9	0	62.0	41	19	58	2	.191
Belinda, Stan	8	6	3.49	105	0	31	129.0	111	44	107	9	.232
Benes, Alan	1	1	9.00	3	3	0	14.0	18	7	13	2	.310
Benes, Andy	6	3	4.20	10	10	0	64.1	53	26	39	8	.229
Bielecki, M	3	4	3.97	16	10	1	70.1	69	20	35	8	.258
Blair, Willie	0	1	3.45	6	1	0	15.2	12	3	8	1	.214
Boever, Joe	0	3	5.89	19	0	3	18.1	24	8	10	2	.316
Boskie, Shawn	0	5	8.31	5	5	0	21.2	33	8	12	5	.359
Brantley, J	1	2	1.50	18	1	6	24.0	15	12	19	1	.176
Brocail, Doug	2	0	1.80	4	2	0	15.0	15	4	12	0	.254

Pitcher	W	L	ERA	G	GS	Sv	IP	H	BB	SO	HR	Avg
Burba, Dave	3	0	2.66	7	2	0	20.1	20	7	13	0	.267
Burkett, John	3	4	6.64	8	8	0	40.2	52	14	20	6	.310
Candiotti, T	2	3	5.14	6	6	0	35.0	45	13	18	2	.328
Carpenter, C	1	0	1.15	10	0	0	15.2	9	4	12	0	.173
Castillo, F	0	3	5.23	8	8	0	43.0	46	14	28	8	.277
Charlton, N*	2	3	5.04	12	3	2	30.1	29	10	28	4	.248
Christiansen*	2	2	4.93	46	0	0	49.1	56	27	53	3	.290
Clark, Mark	0	1	4.05	3	2	0	13.1	13	7	5	0	.255
Cone, David	5	1	3.02	10	9	0	65.2	52	28	51	4	.217
Cooke, Steve*	9	10	4.45	33	29	0	196.1	210	53	103	23	.279
Cordova, F	2	5	4.56	31	3	5	51.1	57	12	48	5	.281
Cormier, R*	1	0	5.90	7	5	0	29.0	34	5	14	2	.293
Darwin, Danny	4	7	3.68	17	13	0	93.0	91	19	67	11	.253
Dewey, Mark	3	1	3.20	37	0	1	50.2	51	17	36	4	.267
Drabek, Doug	60	28	2.70	99	97	0	703.0	611	163	464	55	.236
Dyer, Mike	3	3	4.53	44	0	2	57.2	65	26	35	6	.293
Ericks, John	6	5	3.97	24	11	4	88.1	83	37	79	6	.243
Fassero, Jeff*	2	2	3.00	13	4	1	36.0	31	10	27	2	.235
Fernandez, S*	5	2	2.18	12	11	0	74.1	55	27	42	8	.202
Foster, Kevin	2	2	5.86	5	5	0	27.2	34	18	21	4	.312
Franco, John*	3	2	3.14	25	0	14	28.2	35	16	22	1	.294
Freeman, M	3	0	2.78	8	3	0	22.2	20	10	21	1	.230
Gardner, Mark	2	2	5.59	7	6	0	38.2	36	18	23	5	.245
Glavine, Tom*	4	7	4.04	13	13	0	82.1	86	38	43	3	.276
Gooden, D	1	5	6.23	7	7	0	39.0	52	15	30	3	.327
Gross, Kevin	2	6	5.54	12	12	0	66.2	84	25	55	9	.307
Hammond, C*	2	4	5.03	9	9	0	53.2	48	19	32	5	.242
Hampton, Mike*	0	1	4.96	6	3	0	16.1	20	7	9	2	.299
Hancock, Lee*	0	0	5.12	14	0	0	19.1	17	8	11	3	.230
Hanson, Erik	2	0	2.84	2	2	0	12.2	13	3	13	1	.265
Harnisch, P	2	1	2.00	4	4	0	27.0	15	10	17	1	.156
Heredia, Gil	1	0	2.16	7	2	1	16.2	11	8	14	0	.186
Hernandez, X	3	0	2.12	9	0	0	17.0	12	7	16	3	.197
Hershiser, O	2	4	4.78	8	7	0	43.1	42	23	27	4	.261
Hill, Ken	4	4	4.53	10	9	0	51.2	58	20	34	3	.302
Hope, John	0	4	6.09	13	7	0	44.1	52	18	19	5	.304
Jackson, Dan*	5	3	3.36	15	14	0	85.2	83	35	42	0	.257
Jackson, Mike	0	1	2.08	11	0	0	13.0	7	4	12	0	.159
Jones, Bobby	3	0	2.77	4	4	0	26.0	26	10	10	3	.260
Kile, Darryl	3	4	4.41	8	7	0	49.0	48	22	39	3	.265
Leiter, Mark	0	1	5.40	2	2	0	13.1	14	3	9	2	.259
Lieber, Jon	11	10	4.70	43	26	0	184.0	215	43	120	21	.292
Loaiza, E	3	9	5.89	21	20	0	107.0	136	36	63	19	.317
Maddux, Greg	5	8	3.60	16	16	0	100.0	100	34	59	9	.265
Maddux, Mike	2	0	2.67	19	1	1	33.2	27	8	24	0	.221
Magrane, Joe*	5	3	2.44	9	9	0	62.2	54	20	29	2	.232
Martinez, De	6	2	3.11	15	15	0	98.1	85	24	54	3	.230
Martinez, PJ	3	2	3.27	7	5	0	33.0	27	14	25	3	.227
Martinez, R	3	3	3.48	7	7	0	44.0	38	17	34	5	.230
McCurry, Jeff	1	1	7.08	29	0	0	34.1	53	20	14	6	.371
McDowell, R	2	1	3.13	22	0	3	23.0	18	25	11	0	.225
McElroy, C*	0	0	2.70	17	0	0	16.2	14	15	18	2	.233
Mercker, Kent*	1	1	3.60	12	1	1	25.0	12	11	22	2	.146
Miceli, Danny	6	7	4.86	76	4	13	92.2	85	47	88	14	.241
Minor, Blas	5	3	5.06	45	0	1	58.2	64	19	55	3	.283
Morel, Ramon	0	0	6.75	17	0	0	24.0	35	9	11	2	.350
Morgan, Mike	2	10	5.77	13	13	0	73.1	96	30	42	1	.322
Moyer, Jamie*	1	3	7.86	7	5	0	26.1	35	12	19	7	.310
Mulholland, T*	3	2	3.66	10	9	0	66.1	57	14	24	4	.225
Myers, Randy*	1	5	4.06	25	0	6	31.0	25	25	35	2	.248
Navarro, J	2	1	4.87	3	3	0	20.1	25	4	13	0	.298
Neagle, Denny*	21	12	4.03	89	43	0	319.1	333	97	263	39	.269
Nomo, Hideo	2	0	3.60	2	2	0	15.0	14	4	21	1	.237
Olivares, O	0	2	3.71	7	5	0	34.0	31	14	17	3	.250
Osborne, D*	1	3	3.04	5	4	0	26.2	21	11	18	3	.214
Parrett, Jeff	2	2	2.67	21	0	3	27.0	21	13	22	3	.221
Parris, Steve	4	6	4.66	12	11	0	65.2	71	23	52	7	.284
Patterson, B*	13	9	3.97	99	10	10	167.2	154	57	127	19	.245
Pena, Alej	1	3	5.12	27	0	6	31.2	27	25	33	3	.225
Peters, Chris*	2	2	5.65	8	4	0	28.2	37	8	13	2	.322
Petkovsek, M	1	0	3.62	17	0	0	27.1	23	8	8	4	.228
Plesac, Dan*	4	4	3.44	69	0	6	73.1	71	30	78	5	.253
Portugal, M	2	2	4.35	7	7	0	39.1	34	16	19	1	.234
Quantrill, P	1	1	5.65	4	2	0	14.1	21	3	5	1	.350
Reynolds, S	2	1	2.25	4	1	0	16.0	14	2	11	0	.233
Ritz, Kevin	2	1	2.84	3	3	0	19.0	17	7	5	0	.246
Robertson, R*	0	1	6.28	10	0	0	14.1	19	8	7	1	.328
Rojas, Mel	2	1	1.76	21	0	3	30.2	24	21	25	1	.212
Ruebel, Matt*	1	0	3.12	14	4	0	34.2	33	16	15	2	.246
Rueter, Kirk*	2	1	2.42	4	4	0	22.1	20	4	10	1	.235
Ruffin, Bruce*	2	5	2.80	16	9	3	64.1	60	21	30	2	.249
Sanders, S	2	1	2.87	3	2	0	15.2	12	5	13	2	.218
Sanderson, S	0	2	4.23	7	3	0	27.2	30	10	16	2	.283
Schilling, C	0	1	3.33	5	3	1	24.1	23	9	9	2	.261
Schmidt, J	1	1	4.35	3	3	0	20.2	17	12	17	1	.215
Schourek, P*	2	3	4.69	11	7	0	48.0	50	15	29	3	.273
Scott, Tim	1	0	4.26	14	0	0	12.2	14	7	8	0	.280
Shaw, Jeff	0	1	2.84	13	0	0	12.2	9	3	8	2	.209

THREE RIVERS STADIUM
Home of the Pittsburgh Pirates
Pittsburgh, Pennsylvania   **Artificial**

Pitcher	W	L	ERA	G	GS	Sv	IP	H	BB	SO	HR	Avg
Slocumb, H	0	1	6.08	11	0	0	13.1	9	8	1	.240
Smiley, John*	33	26	3.24	96	60	2	450.1	402	131	284	39	.239
Smith, Lee	1	2	8.36	14	0	5	14.0	18	8	11	5	.305
Smith, Zane*	28	18	2.96	73	69	0	459.2	453	75	240	31	.260
Smoltz, John	3	5	4.07	11	11	0	66.1	62	35	46	3	.245
Stanton, Mike*	0	0	6.59	16	0	4	13.2	12	8	11	1	.240
Swift, Bill	1	1	6.38	4	4	0	18.1	22	4	6	1	.282
Swindell, G*	3	1	4.03	6	4	0	29.0	26	7	15	2	.232
Tewksbury, B	3	3	3.97	12	9	0	56.2	77	7	21	4	.324
Trachsel, S	1	1	3.29	2	2	0	13.2	10	6	9	1	.200
Urbani, Tom*	1	0	6.14	4	3	0	14.2	19	8	4	4	.317
Valdes, I	1	1	3.86	2	2	0	14.0	12	3	14	2	.235
Valenzuela, F*	3	3	4.50	9	9	0	52.0	54	29	31	6	.273
VanLandingham	1	0	4.26	3	3	0	12.2	14	9	7	2	.286
Viola, Frank*	2	2	5.26	6	6	0	37.2	47	10	27	6	.305
Wagner, Paul	16	22	4.53	64	37	0	266.1	281	92	219	23	.274
Wakefield, T	9	3	2.76	18	16	0	117.1	105	67	62	5	.243
Wall, Donne	1	0	2.08	2	2	0	13.0	16	1	5	0	.296
Watson, Allen*	2	1	4.91	4	4	0	22.0	22	6	13	3	.268
Weathers, D	0	1	3.10	4	3	0	20.1	20	4	12	2	.263
West, David*	1	0	4.40	6	2	0	14.1	12	5	10	3	.226
Wetteland, J	1	0	1.78	16	1	10	25.1	16	11	30	1	.176
Wilkins, Marc	0	0	5.23	24	0	1	32.2	35	13	25	4	.273
Worrell, Tim	0	1	2.81	4	2	0	16.0	19	6	12	0	.288
Worrell, Todd	0	1	4.11	16	0	7	15.1	16	5	19	2	.267
Young, A	1	2	2.55	6	3	0	24.2	23	5	8	2	.245

SAN DIEGO/JACK MURPHY STADIUM
Home of the San Diego Padres
San Diego, California   **Grass**

Pitcher	W	L	ERA	G	GS	Sv	IP	H	BB	SO	HR	Avg
Ashby, Andy	15	11	2.80	42	40	0	270.1	239	71	199	32	.238
Assenmacher*	1	0	3.68	15	0	1	14.2	10	9	11	3	.192
Astacio, P	1	0	2.08	3	2	0	13.0	13	2	10	0	.260
Avery, Steve*	2	2	4.04	9	9	0	49.0	45	20	27	4	.251
Beck, Rod	0	0	1.29	14	0	7	14.0	5	2	10	1	.111
Belcher, Tim	3	3	2.89	9	8	0	56.0	43	16	37	2	.211
Belinda, Stan	0	1	4.15	11	0	2	13.0	15	4	15	1	.283
Benes, Andy	34	36	3.87	94	93	0	618.1	600	195	557	64	.254
Bergman, Sean	1	5	4.75	19	7	0	55.0	61	19	44	8	.290
Berumen, A	2	1	3.74	20	0	1	21.2	11	18	22	1	.147
Bielecki, M	2	4	4.24	9	5	0	34.0	45	16	18	4	.326
Blair, Willie	3	6	3.95	57	9	1	123.0	124	47	88	12	.262
Bochtler, D	4	4	4.14	50	0	1	58.2	49	29	57	8	.236
Boever, Joe	1	3	3.79	14	0	3	19.0	24	3	11	2	.320
Bones, Ricky	3	3	5.40	7	7	0	33.1	38	9	20	1	.281
Brantley, J	3	2	2.66	27	1	7	44.0	46	17	40	3	.280
Brocail, Doug	2	6	4.50	19	12	0	80.0	90	22	45	7	.283
Bullinger, J	0	1	4.38	6	1	0	12.1	13	7	6	0	.277
Burba, Dave	1	0	3.68	8	1	0	14.2	11	6	8	2	.216
Burkett, John	2	2	4.55	6	5	1	31.2	35	6	11	2	.289
Candiotti, T	2	4	3.97	8	8	0	47.2	52	15	33	8	.281
Carrasco, H	1	2	0.73	9	0	1	12.1	6	13	6	0	.150
Castillo, F	4	0	2.34	6	5	0	34.2	33	9	18	3	.248
Charlton, N*	3	2	1.30	10	2	1	27.2	22	15	19	0	.237
Cone, David	4	3	2.31	7	7	0	50.2	35	15	47	3	.197
Cook, Dennis*	1	1	3.00	4	2	0	12.0	12	7	5	1	.261
Cooke, Steve*	1	1	9.69	4	3	0	13.0	21	5	8	3	.350
Cormier, R*	0	2	2.77	4	4	0	26.0	25	4	16	3	.253
Darwin, Danny	1	3	5.55	9	3	0	24.1	28	5	14	6	.295
Dishman, G*	2	3	4.47	9	7	0	44.1	41	16	17	4	.258
Drabek, Doug	4	6	5.71	11	11	0	63.0	79	26	34	8	.315
Fassero, Jeff*	5	0	1.30	10	5	1	41.2	28	7	42	1	.189
Fernandez, S*	2	2	3.12	8	8	0	52.0	44	13	49	9	.232
Florie, Bryce	0	2	3.23	48	0	1	61.1	54	38	68	4	.233
Foster, Kevin	0	3	5.73	4	4	0	22.0	25	10	17	4	.291
Franco, John*	1	1	1.80	21	0	13	25.0	20	10	23	1	.220
Freeman, M	1	2	1.55	10	3	0	29.0	18	12	20	0	.175
Gardner, Mark	1	2	5.16	5	4	0	22.2	23	7	15	4	.261
Glavine, Tom*	10	4	3.42	15	15	0	102.2	89	25	55	6	.237
Gooden, D	6	2	2.15	8	8	0	62.2	58	18	48	2	.250
Gross, Kevin	2	5	4.72	14	11	0	68.2	82	31	56	7	.296
Hamilton, J	18	12	3.08	41	40	0	266.0	237	84	191	21	.239
Hammond, C*	2	4	3.63	7	5	0	34.2	33	16	21	2	.258
Hampton, Mike*	0	1	2.03	3	2	0	13.1	15	6	6	0	.283
Harnisch, P	2	3	3.64	7	7	0	42.0	52	12	28	4	.308
Hermanson, D	3	0	6.85	19	0	0	23.2	27	12	15	5	.287
Hernandez, X	1	1	4.70	18	1	1	30.2	27	15	33	3	.231
Hershiser, O	3	4	2.41	10	10	0	71.0	66	23	45	5	.250
Hill, Ken	6	0	2.83	9	9	0	60.1	52	17	39	7	.231
Hoffman, T	15	7	2.76	106	0	46	127.1	95	38	138	11	.202
Holmes, D	0	1	7.50	14	0	2	12.0	11	5	13	2	.234
Isringhausen	1	1	1.20	2	2	0	15.0	11	5	5	0	.229
Jackson, Dan*	5	6	5.03	11	11	0	59.0	61	33	43	6	.277
Jackson, Mike	2	1	4.58	11	1	0	19.2	16	13	15	2	.222
Jarvis, Kevin	1	1	4.50	3	3	0	14.0	18	6	8	1	.310
Jones, Bobby	1	1	4.50	3	3	0	20.0	15	7	15	2	.205

323

SAN DIEGO/JACK MURPHY STADIUM
Home of the San Diego Padres
San Diego, California   Grass

Pitcher	W	L	ERA	G	GS	Sv	IP	H	BB	SO	HR	Avg
Jones, Doug	1	2	2.19	10	0	4	12.1	12	1	13	2	.235
Kile, Darryl	2	1	3.19	6	4	0	31.0	24	15	26	1	.214
Leiper, Dave*	2	0	3.19	36	0	1	53.2	47	16	29	5	.237
Leiter, Al*	1	0	0.60	2	2	0	15.0	9	6	8	1	.184
Leiter, Mark	1	1	4.40	3	2	0	14.1	13	9	13	2	.228
Lieber, Jon	1	1	5.63	3	3	0	16.0	25	4	10	1	.357
Lilliquist, D*	1	3	7.83	12	4	0	33.1	40	17	20	7	.303
Maddux, Greg	6	7	2.90	14	14	0	93.0	83	28	73	3	.239
Maddux, Mike	7	2	2.14	67	1	3	96.2	68	33	62	3	.203
Magrane, Joe*	2	2	1.96	6	6	0	46.0	34	16	22	3	.213
Martinez, De	3	1	2.13	7	7	0	55.0	45	11	33	2	.228
Martinez, PJ	1	1	5.27	7	4	0	27.1	24	8	26	4	.238
Martinez, PA*	4	2	1.81	41	0	1	54.2	28	31	49	4	.143
Martinez, R	5	2	1.99	12	11	0	77.0	59	25	62	3	.208
McDowell, R	1	2	1.07	24	0	9	33.2	28	8	13	0	.243
McElroy, C*	2	0	4.26	11	0	1	12.2	14	6	9	2	.269
McMichael, G	2	0	2.19	9	0	1	12.1	9	2	10	0	.205
Mercker, Kent*	0	2	3.38	9	2	0	18.2	13	8	13	5	.194
Mimbs, M*	0	0	3.00	4	2	0	15.0	23	5	6	0	.343
Morgan, Mike	5	1	2.67	11	9	0	57.1	57	22	28	7	.265
Moyer, Jamie*	1	2	4.76	3	3	0	17.0	23	9	12	1	.324
Mulholland, T*	4	3	5.30	9	8	0	52.2	71	12	31	6	.329
Myers, Randy*	3	5	3.68	53	0	29	58.2	63	19	54	5	.273
Neagle, Denny*	1	0	0.59	7	1	0	15.1	11	2	5	1	.208
Nomo, Hideo	1	1	2.77	2	2	0	13.0	13	5	14	1	.265
Olivares, O	1	0	1.54	5	2	0	23.1	15	7	5	1	.188
Osborne, D*	3	1	4.22	6	6	0	32.0	34	8	16	5	.274
Parrett, Jeff	1	3	4.50	20	0	0	22.0	26	13	23	2	.306
Patterson, B*	1	1	5.11	9	1	0	12.1	10	5	12	2	.222
Pena, Alej	1	1	1.10	13	0	3	16.1	8	7	14	1	.145
Portugal, M	1	4	5.06	9	8	0	53.1	52	21	35	7	.257
Pugh, Tim	2	0	2.74	5	3	0	23.0	16	9	11	0	.195
Rapp, Pat	1	1	3.63	3	3	0	17.1	17	8	7	0	.279
Reynolds, S	2	2	0.99	5	4	0	27.1	23	5	18	2	.228
Reynoso, A	2	3	4.60	6	6	0	31.1	36	7	21	5	.288
Ritz, Kevin	2	2	2.90	5	5	0	31.0	28	8	14	4	.233
Rojas, Mel	1	1	0.41	19	0	10	22.0	15	9	17	1	.195
Ruffin, Bruce*	2	2	2.27	18	2	5	31.2	21	25	20	3	.184
Sager, A.J.	0	1	4.03	11	1	0	22.1	23	7	12	3	.271
Sanders, S	13	10	4.28	51	32	0	208.1	192	80	201	24	.242
Schilling, C	4	2	3.18	10	4	0	34.0	29	5	22	5	.232
Schourek, P*	2	2	4.61	6	4	1	27.1	31	10	19	3	.279
Scott, Tim	5	1	3.23	37	0	0	47.1	44	14	37	4	.244
Slocumb, H	0	1	2.13	10	0	0	12.2	9	5	12	0	.220
Smiley, John*	4	0	3.08	11	7	0	49.2	49	7	38	5	.262
Smith, Lee	2	1	0.71	13	0	6	12.2	5	6	10	0	.114
Smith, Zane*	3	4	4.00	9	8	0	54.0	54	16	23	7	.266
Smoltz, John	4	3	3.00	10	10	0	66.0	46	21	68	4	.192
Stanton, Mike*	2	1	1.23	13	0	1	14.2	13	2	9	1	.232
Swift, Bill	3	0	3.71	5	4	1	26.2	28	7	7	3	.267
Swindell, G*	4	2	4.74	6	6	0	38.0	50	10	23	5	.314
Tabaka, Jeff*	1	0	3.09	23	0	1	23.1	17	10	15	1	.213
Tewksbury, B	8	7	3.66	22	19	0	135.1	137	23	95	12	.262
Thompson, Mar	2	0	3.95	4	2	0	13.2	17	8	5	1	.327
Trachsel, S	1	2	5.56	4	4	0	22.2	24	11	18	4	.282
Urbani, Tom*	0	1	3.14	3	3	0	14.1	20	4	8	0	.328
Valdes, I	1	0	3.24	4	2	0	16.2	12	5	14	3	.190
Valenzuela, F*	13	9	3.96	38	33	0	182.0	196	71	112	24	.277
Veras, Dario	1	0	2.84	11	0	0	12.2	13	3	7	2	.283
Villone, Ron*	1	1	1.11	21	0	0	24.1	21	5	28	1	.231
Viola, Frank*	1	2	2.74	3	3	0	23.0	17	2	19	2	.200
Wagner, Paul	0	0	4.57	6	3	1	21.2	21	10	17	2	.263
Watson, Allen*	1	2	5.48	5	3	0	23.0	23	11	12	2	.280
Weathers, D	1	1	2.35	4	2	0	15.1	11	5	9	3	.204
Wendell, Turk	1	1	4.79	9	2	1	20.2	20	5	14	3	.253
West, David*	0	3	6.75	7	2	0	12.0	13	11	13	3	.271
Wetteland, J	3	2	2.89	14	2	2	28.0	24	7	29	2	.231
Whitehurst, W	4	8	3.80	18	17	0	90.0	98	26	58	13	.281
Williams, Bri	1	7	5.44	25	4	0	46.1	43	24	48	7	.244
Williams, Mk	0	1	3.65	3	2	0	12.1	16	3	5	0	.308
Wohlers, Mark	1	0	0.55	15	0	6	16.1	12	7	15	0	.211
Worrell, Tim	7	9	4.19	44	19	0	148.1	139	48	108	17	.245
Worrell, Todd	1	2	4.91	19	0	9	22.0	22	4	27	5	.268

3COM PARK
Home of the San Francisco Giants
San Francisco, California   Grass

Pitcher	W	L	ERA	G	GS	Sv	IP	H	BB	SO	HR	Avg
Abbott, Kyle*	0	2	2.70	3	2	0	13.1	13	3	6	0	.250
Ashby, Andy	3	1	2.55	6	5	0	35.1	36	6	14	4	.269
Assenmacher*	0	2	4.85	22	0	3	26.0	31	10	25	3	.313
Astacio, P	1	1	3.58	6	4	0	27.2	28	5	18	2	.257
Avery, Steve*	2	4	4.14	8	7	0	45.2	41	12	25	5	.240
Barton, Shawn*	3	0	2.73	27	0	0	29.2	25	10	15	2	.234
Bautista, J	5	7	4.13	50	5	0	106.2	103	25	51	19	.252
Beck, Rod	11	14	3.00	182	0	80	207.0	180	40	181	24	.236
Belcher, Tim	2	4	4.14	10	9	0	54.1	58	20	40	4	.274

3COM PARK
Home of the San Francisco Giants
San Francisco, California   **Grass**

Pitcher	W	L	ERA	G	GS	Sv	IP	H	BB	SO	HR	Avg
Benes, Andy	7	3	2.70	11	11	0	76.2	61	29	67	8	.216
Bielecki, M	2	1	7.52	7	3	0	20.1	26	9	9	4	.321
Blair, Willie	2	1	6.14	10	1	0	22.0	15	9	16	3	.190
Boever, Joe	1	1	2.96	20	0	2	24.1	14	13	16	1	.173
Boskie, Shawn	1	2	5.74	3	3	0	15.2	18	10	11	3	.281
Bottenfield	0	1	2.63	4	2	0	13.2	10	6	6	1	.213
Bourgeois, S	0	0	4.20	7	1	0	15.0	18	6	4	1	.286
Brantley, J	18	8	2.72	146	9	24	251.1	210	100	202	22	.227
Brocail, Doug	0	3	4.82	5	3	0	18.2	24	9	11	3	.312
Bullinger, J	1	1	4.91	3	3	0	14.2	18	4	15	0	.295
Burba, Dave	10	7	3.46	88	9	0	153.1	134	77	142	11	.236
Burkett, John	35	20	3.53	85	83	0	560.2	539	115	361	51	.254
Candiotti, T	1	5	5.31	9	9	0	57.2	67	26	42	8	.291
Castillo, F	1	1	3.27	3	3	0	22.0	17	6	17	2	.210
Charlton, N*	3	1	2.42	12	1	0	26.0	22	6	30	3	.220
Cone, David	2	3	3.16	6	6	0	37.0	32	15	49	5	.225
Cook, Dennis*	3	1	2.30	5	4	0	27.1	22	5	16	3	.222
Cooke, Steve*	1	1	2.38	4	3	0	22.2	17	9	12	3	.213
Cormier, R*	2	3	4.08	5	5	0	28.2	28	4	16	5	.262
Creek, Doug*	0	2	6.41	26	0	0	19.2	18	16	14	3	.228
Darwin, Danny	4	3	3.23	13	4	1	47.1	36	18	34	6	.207
DeLucia, Rich	3	4	5.26	34	0	0	39.1	37	17	31	4	.252
Dewey, Mark	6	2	3.22	65	0	1	78.1	69	27	60	5	.241
Drabek, Doug	4	2	4.31	10	10	0	64.2	67	14	48	9	.272
Estes, Shawn*	1	4	4.57	7	7	0	43.1	45	20	41	5	.260
Fassero, Jeff	2	1	3.38	7	3	0	26.2	30	6	19	2	.275
Fernandez, O	2	6	3.94	15	14	0	93.2	99	29	62	7	.274
Fernandez, S*	2	3	4.32	6	5	0	25.0	27	5	23	3	.273
Foster, Kevin	2	2	4.88	4	4	0	24.0	21	9	19	5	.228
Franco, John*	2	2	1.95	27	0	13	32.1	26	7	23	5	.220
Freeman, M	2	1	2.91	8	2	1	21.2	15	6	15	1	.197
Frey, Steve*	0	3	4.33	34	0	0	27.0	27	14	16	5	.278
Gardner, Mark	7	3	3.84	23	19	0	133.2	132	43	107	19	.261
Glavine, Tom*	4	2	3.46	8	8	0	52.0	52	23	35	2	.254
Gooden, D	5	2	2.95	8	8	0	58.0	49	21	44	4	.230
Grimsley, J	1	1	3.00	2	2	0	12.0	12	4	6	2	.261
Gross, Kevin	4	5	2.72	10	8	0	59.2	58	27	46	1	.253
Gunderson, E*	0	1	4.05	5	2	0	13.1	17	7	11	1	.315
Hamilton, J	1	0	5.68	3	3	0	19.0	23	9	10	2	.307
Hammond, C*	0	3	10.27	5	5	0	23.2	33	10	16	8	.330
Harnisch, P	0	2	3.48	4	4	0	20.2	16	8	14	2	.211
Heredia, Gil	1	5	5.68	16	6	0	50.2	50	14	19	7	.262
Hernandez, X	2	0	4.05	16	0	2	20.0	25	6	16	4	.309
Hershiser, O	7	4	3.46	15	15	0	101.1	97	26	73	6	.257
Hill, Ken	2	1	5.14	5	4	0	28.0	30	10	19	4	.261
Hoffman, T	1	1	1.08	14	0	9	16.2	8	6	20	1	.140
Hook, Chris	5	1	4.85	29	0	0	39.0	39	21	23	5	.269
Jackson, Dan*	3	5	4.43	11	11	0	69.0	75	27	50	6	.284
Jackson, Mike	8	5	3.25	94	1	4	108.0	86	41	110	11	.222
Jones, Bobby	4	0	2.52	5	5	0	35.2	29	7	31	4	.223
Juden, Jeff	3	2	4.46	20	2	0	34.1	31	12	32	6	.246
Kile, Darryl	3	4	7.36	10	9	0	47.2	58	30	41	5	.294
Leiter, Mark	8	9	4.63	28	28	0	175.0	179	60	137	20	.269
Leskanic, C	1	1	4.20	8	1	1	15.0	12	7	4	2	.250
Lieber, Jon	1	0	1.32	3	2	0	13.2	14	0	7	0	.269
Lilliquist, D*	0	2	6.60	4	3	0	15.0	18	5	7	2	.300
Loaiza, E	1	0	4.60	3	3	0	15.2	21	7	9	1	.328
Maddux, Greg	6	7	3.00	14	14	0	93.0	83	27	77	5	.239
Maddux, Mike	0	0	3.00	13	0	3	21.0	22	4	20	3	.272
Magrane, Joe*	1	3	4.15	5	5	0	30.1	30	11	21	0	.256
Martinez, De	3	5	3.84	9	9	0	58.2	66	13	47	5	.280
Martinez, PJ	3	0	4.00	8	6	0	36.0	37	16	47	3	.280
Martinez, R	4	4	4.50	10	10	0	66.0	65	20	46	8	.258
McDowell, R	2	2	4.67	25	0	6	34.2	34	13	20	2	.250
McElroy, C*	1	1	4.50	13	0	1	12.0	12	10	13	2	.250
McMichael, G	1	0	1.46	8	0	3	12.1	6	2	10	1	.146
Monteleone, R	2	1	3.38	19	0	0	24.0	27	3	10	4	.281
Morgan, Mike	4	4	2.83	10	8	0	60.1	58	11	33	4	.257
Moyer, Jamie*	1	1	1.32	2	2	0	13.2	8	4	5	0	.182
Mulholland, T*	7	10	3.38	29	20	0	149.1	165	28	72	19	.279
Myers, Randy*	1	2	1.93	19	1	5	28.0	21	5	29	1	.204
Navarro, J	2	1	1.08	3	3	0	25.0	17	5	20	1	.189
Neagle, Denny*	4	1	3.82	7	5	0	33.0	25	11	25	5	.212
Nied, Dave	0	3	9.69	5	3	0	13.0	15	7	7	3	.294
Nomo, Hideo	2	0	1.23	3	3	0	22.0	6	11	26	1	.085
Olivares, O	0	1	4.19	3	3	0	19.1	16	8	14	1	.239
Osborne, D*	1	2	1.96	3	3	0	23.0	16	7	19	1	.193
Parrett, Jeff	0	0	6.62	17	0	0	17.2	20	8	15	3	.282
Patterson, B*	2	0	2.45	12	1	0	18.1	18	3	16	1	.257
Pena, Alej	0	1	2.00	14	0	5	18.0	16	4	17	1	.235
Perez, Mike	2	0	0.69	12	0	2	13.0	12	6	12	0	.250
Petkovsek, M	1	1	2.08	3	2	0	13.0	8	3	15	1	.174
Plesac, Dan*	1	1	4.50	8	0	0	12.0	14	4	11	1	.286
Poole, Jim*	1	1	3.00	19	0	0	15.0	9	3	13	1	.173
Portugal, M	9	9	3.30	28	28	0	185.1	170	54	130	24	.244
Quantrill, P	0	0	3.95	3	2	0	13.2	15	5	9	1	.273
Rapp, Pat	0	2	2.66	5	3	0	20.1	18	9	9	5	.247
Reed, Steve	1	0	2.33	16	0	0	19.1	11	5	17	0	.167

3COM PARK
Home of the San Francisco Giants

Pitcher	W	L	ERA	G	GS	Sv	IP	H	BB	SO	HR	Avg
Remlinger, M*	1	1	2.12	4	4	0	29.2	21	12	16	5	.194
Reynolds, S	1	1	5.21	3	3	0	19.0	21	1	18	3	.280
Reynoso, A	3	1	4.76	6	6	0	34.0	35	15	19	6	.280
Ritz, Kevin	1	3	7.29	4	4	0	21.0	21	13	11	1	.266
Rojas, Mel	2	3	5.25	18	0	5	24.0	26	11	16	1	.283
Rueter, Kirk*	1	3	2.97	5	5	0	30.1	28	5	19	1	.246
Ruffin, Bruce*	1	3	3.20	17	4	2	39.1	45	22	24	2	.304
Sanders, S	0	1	2.91	4	3	0	21.2	17	5	22	3	.213
Sanderson, S	4	3	4.02	10	7	1	47.0	44	8	34	12	.244
Scanlan, Bob	1	0	1.13	7	1	2	16.0	9	6	5	0	.173
Schilling, C	1	2	2.50	10	6	1	54.0	42	13	48	6	.212
Schourek, P*	1	1	7.56	5	3	0	16.2	20	10	14	5	.299
Scott, Tim	2	1	6.61	17	0	0	16.1	21	10	10	3	.323
Service, S	1	0	4.58	16	0	0	17.2	11	10	22	3	.180
Shaw, Jeff	0	0	2.18	10	0	1	20.2	20	9	13	1	.247
Smiley, John*	5	3	3.51	14	12	0	84.2	72	21	52	12	.230
Smith, Zane*	2	6	3.19	10	8	0	53.2	49	11	23	4	.249
Smoltz, John	7	3	3.35	14	14	0	102.0	87	27	72	8	.230
Swift, Bill	21	9	2.26	42	38	1	266.1	217	72	155	17	.226
Swindell, G*	2	1	6.75	5	5	0	28.0	36	4	14	7	.316
Tewksbury, B	5	1	2.17	9	8	0	58.0	60	7	25	3	.264
Torres, S	3	10	5.67	14	14	0	74.2	77	47	40	12	.278
Urbani, Tom*	1	1	3.95	4	2	0	13.2	14	8	7	2	.264
Valenzuela, F*	6	6	3.20	13	12	0	81.2	81	31	60	10	.256
VanLandingham,	13	9	4.26	34	34	0	215.1	213	80	148	20	.258
Veres, Dave	0	0	0.00	7	0	1	12.1	8	1	20	0	.178
Viola, Frank*	0	3	5.04	4	4	0	25.0	26	8	16	4	.271
Wagner, Paul	0	1	3.75	2	2	0	12.0	12	3	12	1	.245
Wakefield, T	0	2	6.75	2	2	0	12.0	12	5	6	3	.273
Watson, Allen*	3	4	4.37	13	13	0	82.1	73	39	65	11	.246
Weathers, D	0	1	5.75	6	3	0	20.1	23	9	17	3	.295
Wetteland, J	1	0	2.25	9	1	1	20.0	13	6	19	1	.181
Williams, Bri	3	0	4.64	6	3	0	21.1	22	7	22	2	.265
Williams, Mk	1	1	3.46	2	2	0	13.0	15	3	9	1	.300
Worrell, Todd	0	2	3.52	18	0	8	23.0	22	9	25	3	.242
Wright, Jamey	0	1	1.50	2	2	0	12.0	12	5	5	0	.273
Young, A	0	0	3.38	9	2	1	18.2	14	11	11	1	.209

THE KINGDOME
Home of the Seattle Mariners

Pitcher	W	L	ERA	G	GS	Sv	IP	H	BB	SO	HR	Avg
Abbott, Jim*	4	4	5.11	9	9	0	56.1	66	20	29	4	.296
Aguilera, R	1	1	1.26	11	0	9	14.1	9	6	12	1	.173
Aldred, Scott*	0	2	5.52	3	3	0	14.2	14	10	4	3	.250
Alvarez, W*	3	4	3.61	9	7	0	42.1	39	32	33	3	.247
Appier, Kevin	4	1	3.06	8	8	0	53.0	44	20	34	4	.222
Ayala, Bobby	11	3	4.47	81	0	20	98.2	78	37	119	10	.212
Belcher, Tim	6	8	4.45	17	17	0	111.1	116	51	62	16	.262
Benes, Andy	3	1	5.19	6	6	0	34.2	35	23	21	4	.259
Bohanon, B*	0	0	6.86	7	2	1	21.0	24	7	17	5	.293
Bones, Ricky	2	1	4.21	4	4	0	25.2	30	9	9	6	.291
Bosio, Chris	18	18	4.30	56	44	1	301.2	309	92	209	28	.265
Boskie, Shawn	2	1	6.75	4	4	0	22.2	31	7	9	4	.326
Brown, Kevin	2	2	3.43	9	9	0	60.1	62	26	37	3	.272
Burba, Dave	1	1	3.92	15	0	1	20.2	19	8	13	2	.247
Campbell, Mi	3	9	6.09	20	20	0	109.1	118	45	68	22	.271
Candiotti, T	1	0	2.16	4	4	0	25.0	23	12	20	0	.242
Carmona, R	5	3	3.22	34	2	2	72.2	77	47	51	8	.280
Charlton, N*	6	3	2.55	68	0	24	88.1	49	40	101	7	.163
Clark, Mark	1	0	5.84	3	2	0	12.1	16	5	7	1	.314
Clemens, R	8	2	1.84	11	11	0	88.0	62	26	62	6	.200
Cone, David	3	0	1.91	4	4	0	33.0	19	12	30	3	.164
Cook, Dennis*	0	2	5.14	12	1	0	14.0	17	6	10	2	.293
Cummings, J*	0	5	9.87	10	6	0	34.2	48	19	15	7	.329
Darwin, Danny	1	1	6.75	4	2	0	14.2	17	4	4	4	.298
Davis, Tim*	4	2	5.12	44	2	1	51.0	50	27	33	6	.265
DeLucia, Rich	13	8	4.72	50	21	1	171.2	180	62	117	28	.271
Doherty, John	0	2	8.53	6	2	0	19.0	25	5	5	2	.333
Eckersley, D	2	3	4.10	23	0	16	26.1	25	4	28	5	.248
Eichhorn, M	1	2	3.00	12	0	1	18.0	18	9	8	0	.269
Eldred, Cal	2	2	3.78	5	5	0	33.1	30	10	24	3	.246
Erickson, S	1	6	7.61	10	9	0	49.2	67	28	28	7	.335
Farrell, John	1	0	2.59	6	6	0	41.2	41	18	18	3	.255
Fernandez, A	3	1	3.88	8	8	0	51.0	50	22	29	6	.259
Fetters, Mike	1	1	3.71	11	0	2	17.0	17	12	11	0	.262
Finley, Chuck*	8	3	2.50	15	12	0	93.2	74	42	53	5	.223
Gibson, Paul*	0	3	7.07	13	0	1	14.0	19	5	5	3	.317
Gordon, Tom	8	2	3.88	12	9	0	67.1	49	38	58	10	.198
Gross, Kevin	1	0	2.12	2	2	0	17.0	13	7	7	3	.210
Gubicza, Mark	4	2	3.97	7	7	0	45.1	54	18	33	6	.293
Guetterman, L*	7	1	3.62	37	8	2	79.2	78	32	36	8	.257
Guthrie, Mark*	1	3	5.13	12	3	0	26.1	36	10	21	2	.319
Guzman, Juan	6	0	3.34	8	8	0	56.2	40	31	54	4	.196
Habyan, John	0	0	3.92	14	1	0	20.2	20	10	16	1	.263
Haney, Chris*	1	1	8.76	3	3	0	12.1	17	12	8	1	.340
Hanson, Erik	30	27	3.89	77	77	0	507.1	524	137	407	47	.268

THE KINGDOME
Home of the Seattle Mariners

Pitcher	W	L	ERA	G	GS	Sv	IP	H	BB	SO	HR	Avg
Henneman, M	2	1	2.55	16	0	5	17.2	18	10	13	1	.265
Hentgen, Pat	2	1	2.87	3	2	0	15.2	14	15	14	0	.237
Hershiser, O	2	0	3.54	3	3	0	20.1	17	4	12	5	.224
Hill, Ken	0	1	2.77	2	2	0	13.0	11	8	7	0	.229
Hitchcock, S*	6	6	5.67	19	19	0	112.2	131	42	73	17	.295
Honeycutt, R*	0	0	2.60	16	0	1	17.1	13	4	6	2	.224
Howe, Steve*	2	0	2.76	18	0	2	16.1	18	2	8	2	.281
Hurtado, E	2	3	7.32	11	3	1	35.2	46	18	24	7	.324
Jackson, Mike	14	11	3.33	167	0	14	224.0	173	90	202	25	.211
Johnson, R*	55	27	3.17	113	109	2	763.1	551	370	899	56	.203
Jones, Doug	1	2	2.84	13	0	7	19.0	15	6	17	3	.211
Kamieniecki	4	1	4.29	6	6	0	35.2	35	18	21	5	.255
Karl, Scott*	2	1	6.05	3	3	0	19.1	24	9	14	4	.304
Key, Jimmy*	4	2	3.65	8	8	0	44.1	45	10	26	7	.265
Knackert, B	1	1	7.23	14	1	0	18.2	31	9	16	2	.353
Langston, M*	20	20	4.05	49	49	0	364.0	326	149	332	42	.242
Lira, Felipe	0	0	4.02	3	2	0	15.2	14	4	15	3	.230
Lopez, Albie	1	1	6.57	3	2	0	12.1	13	5	11	6	.265
Magnante, M*	0	1	6.00	11	1	0	15.0	18	6	8	1	.305
Mahomes, Pat	4	1	4.30	8	2	0	23.0	17	10	15	5	.213
Martinez, De	1	0	3.38	2	2	0	13.1	11	2	4	2	.220
McCaskill, K	4	7	5.00	21	11	0	72.0	81	27	38	7	.284
McDonald, Ben	1	4	5.73	7	7	0	37.2	40	22	30	7	.270
McDowell, J	3	1	2.96	6	6	0	48.2	41	9	40	2	.227
Meacham, R	1	1	6.91	15	3	1	28.2	41	9	17	7	.345
Menhart, Paul	2	1	5.28	6	5	0	29.0	36	14	14	6	.324
Mesa, Jose	1	2	6.43	12	2	8	21.0	31	7	12	5	.365
Milacki, Bob	1	2	6.33	7	5	0	27.0	37	14	15	3	.325
Mills, Alan	1	1	3.45	11	0	1	15.2	12	8	14	1	.211
Minor, Blas	0	0	5.19	7	0	0	17.1	18	8	8	4	.273
Monteleone, R	1	2	9.39	9	0	0	15.1	27	9	6	5	.403
Montgomery, J	0	0	3.65	22	0	14	24.2	25	7	21	3	.263
Morgan, Mike	7	10	4.87	19	19	0	131.1	152	26	58	16	.291
Moyer, Jamie*	4	1	3.48	10	8	0	54.1	55	16	35	6	.261
Mulholland, T*	4	3	4.36	8	7	0	43.1	43	15	18	3	.261
Mussina, Mike	2	0	3.43	3	3	0	21.0	24	4	13	2	.289
Nagy, Charles	1	5	6.05	7	7	0	41.2	55	21	19	3	.322
Navarro, J	2	5	6.15	7	7	0	41.0	55	10	22	7	.324
Nelson, Jeff	9	4	2.87	111	0	7	141.0	114	46	145	9	.229
Olson, Gregg	1	2	3.54	20	0	8	20.1	25	12	18	1	.298
Orosco, Jesse*	2	1	9.60	20	0	0	15.0	25	8	14	1	.368
Pall, Donn	1	1	2.14	12	0	1	21.0	17	3	9	2	.230
Parra, Jose	2	0	1.80	3	2	0	15.0	13	2	12	1	.236
Pavlik, Roger	0	4	8.17	6	6	0	25.1	33	21	13	5	.330
Pichardo, H	1	1	3.54	9	2	0	20.1	22	13	11	2	.301
Plesac, Dan*	0	1	1.65	13	0	5	16.1	19	2	9	1	.311
Plunk, Eric	5	1	1.69	20	2	0	32.0	22	23	30	1	.195
Quantrill, P	1	0	3.32	5	2	0	19.0	16	6	11	3	.219
Radke, Brad	2	1	5.13	4	4	0	26.1	23	10	20	8	.235
Rhodes, A*	2	1	3.79	4	3	0	19.0	19	8	20	3	.260
Risley, Bill	7	3	2.93	44	0	1	55.1	45	18	72	6	.221
Rogers, Kenny*	1	1	4.81	14	2	1	24.1	26	8	18	3	.280
Russell, Jeff	2	1	4.01	17	1	6	24.2	22	14	18	4	.242
Salkeld, R	2	3	4.34	6	6	0	29.0	26	23	24	2	.234
Sanderson, S	5	1	2.09	6	6	0	43.0	31	5	28	3	.200
Stottlemyre	2	2	4.05	7	7	0	40.0	33	16	26	4	.228
Swift, Bill	12	9	3.16	97	23	9	262.0	264	73	82	13	.267
Swindell, G*	1	1	4.32	5	5	0	33.1	32	5	26	4	.256
Tapani, Kevin	1	2	3.53	11	11	0	71.1	58	14	44	7	.223
Torres, S	2	5	5.63	11	9	0	56.0	63	28	43	8	.278
Van Poppel, T	2	0	4.15	4	3	0	21.2	17	10	15	3	.224
Viola, Frank*	2	2	7.06	4	4	0	21.2	27	6	16	7	.303
Wagner, Matt	1	1	6.67	6	5	0	29.2	30	21	18	6	.261
Wells, Bob	5	5	5.64	31	9	0	95.2	105	38	61	15	.279
Wells, David*	1	3	3.79	15	8	0	59.1	53	17	37	8	.233
West, David*	2	1	2.25	4	2	0	20.0	10	9	8	3	.147
Whiteside, M	0	2	5.17	11	0	0	15.2	23	6	7	2	.338
Witt, Bobby	3	5	6.14	9	9	0	51.1	60	30	51	6	.290
Wolcott, Bob	3	8	5.81	19	18	0	91.1	112	37	50	13	.306

BUSCH STADIUM
Home of the St. Louis Cardinals

Pitcher	W	L	ERA	G	GS	Sv	IP	H	BB	SO	HR	Avg
Ashby, Andy	0	3	5.91	4	4	0	21.1	23	10	9	2	.284
Assenmacher*	0	1	2.01	23	0	2	22.1	23	12	12	1	.274
Astacio, P	2	3	6.14	6	4	0	22.0	21	7	14	2	.263
Avery, Steve*	2	3	5.72	8	8	0	45.2	50	13	30	6	.281
Bailey, Cory	2	1	2.33	28	0	0	27.0	23	11	20	0	.237
Bailey, Roger	1	2	2.16	3	2	0	16.2	11	8	8	2	.193
Barber, Brian	1	1	8.31	6	3	0	17.1	18	13	16	2	.281
Batchelor, R	1	0	2.84	9	0	0	12.2	9	3	8	0	.196
Bautista, J	2	1	1.88	13	1	0	24.0	13	4	6	3	.157
Belcher, Tim	0	2	8.82	4	3	0	16.1	24	9	8	1	.358
Belinda, Stan	2	1	1.32	11	0	3	13.2	8	10	15	0	.170
Benes, Alan	8	4	3.52	15	14	0	94.2	79	40	72	15	.232
Benes, Andy	9	7	4.06	23	21	1	146.1	137	51	105	16	.247

327

BUSCH STADIUM
Home of the St. Louis Cardinals

St. Louis, Missouri   Grass

Pitcher	W	L	ERA	G	GS	Sv	IP	H	BB	SO	HR	Avg
Bielecki, M	3	0	3.12	13	6	1	52.0	43	17	25	2	.222
Blair, Willie	0	0	7.04	8	1	0	15.1	19	6	19	3	.306
Boever, Joe	0	1	4.97	11	0	3	12.2	10	10	7	2	.222
Boskie, Shawn	1	0	0.60	4	2	0	15.0	8	4	7	0	.154
Brantley, J	1	0	2.05	16	0	5	22.0	17	9	13	0	.213
Bullinger, J	3	1	2.95	10	6	2	42.2	35	22	25	1	.224
Burkett, John	2	2	2.87	8	8	0	53.1	51	16	26	6	.259
Candiotti, T	5	0	2.11	8	8	0	59.2	40	14	43	4	.197
Carpenter, C	7	6	4.09	85	7	1	134.1	127	41	75	9	.249
Castillo, F	4	2	3.99	8	8	0	47.1	45	13	31	2	.257
Charlton, N*	1	2	3.58	12	3	1	27.2	27	11	22	0	.257
Clark, Mark	3	7	4.58	14	11	0	72.2	67	25	26	10	.241
Cone, David	3	3	4.00	14	11	1	78.2	73	26	74	5	.244
Cook, Dennis*	2	2	6.04	5	5	0	28.1	30	10	9	2	.278
Cooke, Steve*	0	1	5.06	3	2	0	16.0	18	4	12	1	.290
Cormier, R*	15	8	3.70	39	31	0	209.1	225	33	106	14	.278
Darwin, Danny	2	3	4.22	8	4	0	32.0	33	3	11	2	.270
DeLucia, Rich	4	3	4.54	30	0	0	41.2	34	19	42	7	.221
Drabek, Doug	6	5	2.86	18	18	0	119.2	103	28	73	3	.238
Eckersley, D	0	1	2.70	35	0	14	33.1	32	3	27	5	.256
Fassero, Jeff	3	1	2.05	12	2	0	26.1	20	6	24	1	.202
Fernandez, S*	3	7	4.46	14	14	0	76.2	69	27	67	5	.240
Fossas, Tony*	2	2	1.40	59	0	1	45.0	30	18	42	2	.186
Franco, John*	1	5	3.54	24	0	10	28.0	33	16	28	1	.297
Freeman, M	2	4	4.50	9	2	1	20.0	24	8	22	2	.296
Frey, Steve*	1	0	4.80	10	0	0	15.0	18	5	7	2	.305
Gardner, Mark	3	3	2.70	8	6	0	40.0	33	15	31	5	.228
Glavine, Tom*	5	1	4.45	11	11	0	64.2	64	27	41	2	.256
Gooden, D	4	2	3.56	9	9	0	65.2	62	14	43	3	.247
Gross, Kevin	1	6	4.67	11	8	0	52.0	63	20	34	2	.306
Guetterman, L*	3	1	2.38	20	0	0	22.2	17	6	12	1	.213
Habyan, John	3	0	2.15	44	0	1	50.1	45	15	41	1	.242
Hamilton, J	1	1	0.82	3	3	0	22.0	12	8	9	1	.171
Hammond, C*	1	4	7.71	8	5	0	23.1	43	10	9	2	.417
Hampton, Mike*	2	0	1.76	4	2	0	15.1	9	2	10	1	.164
Haney, Chris*	1	2	3.50	3	3	0	18.0	18	5	15	0	.250
Harnisch, P	1	4	6.49	8	8	0	43.0	57	11	24	3	.320
Hernandez, X	0	2	5.82	15	1	0	21.2	25	6	16	5	.298
Hershiser, O	0	2	3.66	7	5	1	32.0	34	15	19	1	.274
Hill, Ken	15	16	4.16	53	52	0	315.2	303	135	181	17	.255
Honeycutt, R*	1	2	2.51	33	1	2	32.1	22	5	29	2	.195
Jackson, Dan*	4	7	5.13	24	17	0	107.0	126	40	54	8	.301
Jackson, Mike	0	3	3.38	12	0	0	16.0	12	5	12	3	.203
Jones, Bobby	1	1	2.25	2	2	0	16.0	16	4	7	0	.267
Jones, Todd	2	0	4.26	11	0	1	12.2	13	9	11	1	.271
Kile, Darryl	1	2	6.43	7	5	0	28.0	41	17	17	3	.345
Leiter, Al*	1	1	7.11	2	2	0	12.2	16	6	11	1	.333
Leskanic, C	0	2	9.49	9	1	0	12.1	18	7	17	3	.327
Lieber, Jon	1	0	2.30	7	1	1	15.2	13	3	10	1	.236
Lilliquist, D*	0	1	5.40	3	3	0	16.2	22	4	5	3	.314
Maddux, Greg	9	6	2.78	15	15	0	107.0	100	22	83	4	.251
Magrane, Joe*	22	26	3.23	71	68	0	462.2	442	142	225	19	.255
Martinez, De	2	5	2.78	11	11	0	74.1	63	25	40	3	.227
Martinez, PJ	2	1	3.82	6	4	0	33.0	27	9	35	4	.221
Martinez, R	4	1	1.13	5	5	0	39.2	25	14	30	1	.182
Mathews, T.J.	3	2	1.85	44	0	3	58.1	35	17	53	4	.172
McDowell, R	4	6	5.26	28	0	5	37.2	48	20	18	2	.308
McElroy, C*	0	0	2.89	18	0	1	18.2	16	11	17	0	.239
McMichael, G	1	0	1.06	10	0	1	17.0	10	3	14	2	.175
Mercker, Kent*	1	2	2.88	12	2	2	25.0	18	18	21	2	.196
Mlicki, Dave	0	1	10.13	5	2	0	13.1	19	10	10	4	.339
Morgan, Mike	4	10	4.03	21	21	0	129.2	139	34	66	12	.278
Moyer, Jamie*	0	2	4.97	5	5	0	25.1	30	10	13	2	.319
Mulholland, T*	1	2	4.25	11	9	0	48.2	51	6	25	3	.279
Myers, Randy*	1	2	2.20	25	0	17	41.0	32	15	35	2	.209
Navarro, J	0	0	5.50	3	3	0	18.0	24	7	7	1	.348
Neagle, Denny*	0	3	6.48	8	4	1	25.0	22	11	21	5	.242
Nied, Dave	1	0	4.85	2	2	0	13.0	16	3	10	2	.291
Nomo, Hideo	2	1	2.95	3	3	0	21.1	16	5	24	1	.200
Olivares, O	15	16	4.16	73	45	3	333.1	326	120	180	25	.259
Osborne, D*	23	11	3.19	55	51	0	335.2	324	81	210	29	.254
Parrett, Jeff	8	4	3.45	66	1	1	94.0	81	43	78	8	.237
Pena, Alej	3	1	2.81	15	1	2	25.2	24	7	19	2	.255
Perez, Mike	14	5	3.27	97	0	8	115.2	112	33	61	4	.257
Petkovsek, M	13	3	3.06	41	15	0	126.1	120	35	60	10	.255
Portugal, M	4	0	1.65	7	7	0	49.0	34	14	23	0	.194
Pugh, Tim	2	0	1.93	2	2	0	14.0	11	2	4	2	.212
Rapp, Pat	0	1	3.43	3	3	0	21.0	17	11	10	1	.236
Reed, Steve	1	0	1.42	11	0	1	12.2	6	0	13	0	.143
Reynolds, S	1	1	4.99	8	4	0	30.2	39	4	24	3	.305
Reynoso, A	1	1	2.96	4	4	0	24.1	25	8	10	1	.266
Ritz, Kevin	1	0	4.00	3	3	0	18.0	15	6	9	1	.231
Rojas, Mel	3	2	2.11	13	0	2	21.1	22	8	16	1	.275
Rueter, Kirk*	2	0	1.50	2	2	0	12.0	9	0	6	3	.196
Ruffin, Bruce*	1	2	4.22	21	5	5	49.0	54	21	38	2	.284
Sanderson, S	1	2	3.98	4	4	0	20.1	23	6	10	3	.284
Schilling, C	1	1	6.30	8	7	0	40.0	45	11	27	4	.283
Schourek, P*	1	2	5.40	8	5	0	33.1	35	11	27	3	.267

328

BUSCH STADIUM
Home of the St. Louis Cardinals
St. Louis, Missouri — Grass

Pitcher	W	L	ERA	G	GS	Sv	IP	H	BB	SO	HR	Avg
Smiley, John*	2	2	3.82	12	9	0	61.1	60	11	35	2	.262
Smith, Lee	12	16	2.86	139	0	76	157.1	149	43	154	10	.248
Smith, Zane	6	4	3.44	15	14	0	89.0	97	18	41	4	.278
Smoltz, John	3	5	5.10	11	11	0	67.0	77	22	48	2	.285
Stottlemyre	6	7	4.01	20	19	0	128.0	108	55	112	16	.229
Swift, Bill	1	0	3.14	2	2	0	14.1	14	3	6	0	.264
Swindell, G*	0	4	6.94	5	4	0	23.1	28	9	12	4	.318
Tewksbury, B	35	23	3.39	80	73	0	509.2	519	60	217	38	.267
Trachsel, S	4	1	2.27	5	5	0	31.2	21	10	36	2	.186
Urbani, Tom*	3	10	4.90	32	16	0	119.1	143	33	67	13	.300
Valdes, I	2	1	2.38	3	3	0	22.2	17	5	22	1	.205
Valenzuela, F*	2	4	4.20	7	7	0	45.0	43	17	22	2	.264
Veres, Dave	0	0	2.25	10	0	0	12.0	12	3	15	0	.255
Viola, Frank*	2	1	3.65	5	5	0	37.0	35	14	16	2	.252
Wagner, Paul	2	2	5.12	5	3	0	19.1	23	13	18	3	.307
Watson, Allen*	13	10	4.53	32	32	0	180.2	183	76	95	20	.268
Wendell, Turk	0	1	6.39	9	1	2	12.2	13	8	8	3	.265
West, David*	2	0	3.06	6	3	0	17.2	15	10	9	1	.234
Wetteland, J	0	3	6.23	11	1	5	13.0	16	9	15	1	.308
Whitehurst, W	2	2	3.67	12	3	0	34.1	40	8	23	2	.286
Williams, Bri	1	2	4.80	5	2	0	15.0	14	7	7	4	.246
Williams, Mk	0	3	5.27	5	2	0	13.2	19	6	13	3	.339
Worrell, Todd	14	13	2.43	141	0	45	163.0	117	59	143	11	.200
Young, A	1	1	1.66	8	2	0	21.2	19	2	7	0	.260

THE BALLPARK IN ARLINGTON
Home of the Texas Rangers
Arlington, Texas — Grass

Pitcher	W	L	ERA	G	GS	Sv	IP	H	BB	SO	HR	Avg
Abbott, Jim*	1	2	2.90	4	4	0	31.0	23	10	16	1	.204
Alberro, Jose	0	0	8.44	8	0	0	16.0	24	9	7	1	.338
Alvarez, W*	2	2	4.32	4	4	0	25.0	30	14	13	2	.303
Anderson, Brn*	1	0	2.25	2	2	0	12.0	13	2	5	0	.277
Appier, Kevin	1	2	5.29	4	4	0	17.0	18	14	12	2	.277
Ayala, Bobby	1	0	2.70	8	0	3	13.1	11	4	14	1	.224
Belcher, Tim	1	2	3.48	3	3	0	20.2	18	6	11	2	.222
Bere, Jason	2	0	2.84	2	2	0	12.2	8	7	11	4	.178
Bohanon, B*	2	2	7.58	11	4	0	29.2	41	8	25	4	.325
Bosio, Chris	2	0	1.10	3	3	0	16.1	17	7	5	2	.266
Brandenburg	0	4	4.28	20	0	0	40.0	49	15	36	6	.299
Brown, Kevin	5	5	4.03	15	14	0	102.2	124	28	72	8	.305
Burkett, John	2	1	6.30	3	3	0	20.0	22	5	12	3	.286
Burrows, T*	2	0	3.64	16	2	1	29.2	31	7	14	4	.270
Carpenter, C	0	2	3.41	24	0	5	34.1	40	7	23	3	.299
Cone, David	1	0	0.61	2	2	0	14.2	7	4	10	1	.135
Cook, Dennis*	4	2	4.62	49	0	1	60.1	58	23	49	8	.261
Darwin, Danny	2	3	11.33	6	5	0	27.0	46	5	16	11	.374
Doherty, John	0	1	5.40	4	1	0	13.1	15	7	6	1	.283
Erickson, S	1	1	4.43	3	3	0	22.1	24	7	14	1	.282
Fernandez, A	2	1	3.12	5	5	0	34.2	35	10	32	3	.263
Finley, Chuck*	2	3	6.30	5	5	0	30.0	38	22	24	7	.311
Gordon, Tom	2	2	7.17	4	4	0	21.1	26	11	18	2	.306
Gross, Kevin	10	9	5.71	28	22	0	138.2	167	63	85	20	.304
Gubicza, Mark	0	3	9.56	3	3	0	16.0	27	5	8	4	.365
Guzman, Juan	1	3	6.52	4	4	0	19.1	20	17	21	2	.260
Haney, Chris*	1	1	2.45	3	3	0	22.0	21	4	11	1	.253
Hanson, Erik	0	3	6.41	3	3	0	19.2	26	9	18	1	.310
Helling, Rick	3	3	7.52	10	7	0	40.2	59	16	20	13	.343
Henneman, M	0	3	3.75	26	0	15	24.0	19	7	23	3	.218
Heredia, Gil	0	2	3.89	26	0	1	44.0	42	9	26	3	.253
Hershiser, O	1	1	9.24	3	3	0	12.2	20	5	8	3	.351
Hill, Ken	9	7	4.45	18	18	0	121.1	136	49	79	8	.287
Hitchcock, S*	1	1	4.58	3	2	0	17.2	19	9	16	5	.275
Honeycutt, R*	0	1	8.03	22	0	0	12.1	21	6	5	2	.382
Johnson, R*	2	0	3.33	4	4	0	24.1	25	9	30	2	.266
Key, Jimmy*	1	2	7.16	3	3	0	16.1	23	10	12	3	.343
Langston, M*	1	2	6.29	4	4	0	24.1	27	13	24	3	.281
Leiter, Al*	0	3	4.71	3	3	0	21.0	21	14	18	1	.266
Lira, Felipe	1	1	4.38	3	2	0	12.1	11	4	5	1	.244
Mahomes, Pat	2	0	3.63	5	3	0	22.1	18	11	12	4	.217
McDonald, Ben	3	0	3.80	3	3	0	21.1	26	2	12	3	.295
McDowell, J	1	4	5.60	5	5	0	35.1	41	10	19	7	.287
McDowell, R	4	1	4.15	34	0	1	47.2	40	23	25	2	.233
Miranda, A*	0	1	3.68	5	2	0	14.2	20	6	13	3	.323
Mussina, Mike	2	0	3.14	2	2	0	14.1	10	6	10	0	.196
Nagy, Charles	3	1	4.83	5	5	0	31.2	38	14	23	6	.292
Oliver, D*	14	3	4.10	49	22	2	155.2	155	67	123	16	.259
Pavlik, Roger	16	12	5.61	39	39	0	228.0	234	91	151	28	.265
Rodriguez, Fr	1	2	12.41	3	3	0	12.1	21	8	7	1	.382
Rogers, Kenny*	16	6	3.32	31	31	0	216.2	197	74	153	23	.239
Russell, Jeff	1	2	3.63	45	0	11	44.2	51	14	20	1	.282
Sparks, Steve	1	0	0.63	2	2	0	14.1	13	6	7	0	.250
Stanton, Mike*	1	0	7.30	14	0	0	12.1	18	6	8	3	.340
Stottlemyre	1	1	5.21	3	3	0	19.0	21	6	23	5	.273
Tewksbury, B	3	3	3.72	9	9	0	65.1	77	7	26	4	.296
Van Poppel, T	1	4	7.71	6	3	1	21.0	23	12	12	5	.280
Vosberg, Ed*	3	4	1.48	47	0	7	48.2	43	12	36	4	.239

THE BALLPARK IN ARLINGTON
Home of the Texas Rangers

Arlington, Texas — Grass

Pitcher	W	L	ERA	G	GS	Sv	IP	H	BB	SO	HR	Avg
Wakefield, T	1	2	5.21	3	3	0	19.0	21	12	15	1	.284
Wells, David*	0	3	6.23	3	3	0	17.1	25	8	4	4	.347
Whiteside, M	5	2	4.10	54	0	2	83.1	81	23	54	10	.256
Wickman, Bob	0	0	4.38	8	0	0	12.1	12	7	7	2	.255
Witt, Bobby	12	5	5.48	23	22	0	141.1	179	60	104	18	.315

SKYDOME
Home of the Toronto Blue Jays

Toronto, Ontario — Artificial

Pitcher	W	L	ERA	G	GS	Sv	IP	H	BB	SO	HR	Avg
Abbott, Jim*	3	7	4.11	11	11	0	76.2	86	26	43	9	.293
Aguilera, R	1	2	2.38	12	2	2	22.2	22	10	17	1	.253
Alvarez, W*	3	0	1.61	3	3	0	22.1	17	7	10	1	.210
Appier, Kevin	3	2	2.31	7	7	0	50.2	42	12	47	1	.222
Belcher, Tim	4	0	3.52	4	4	0	30.2	22	9	20	2	.195
Bergman, Sean	1	0	3.18	3	3	0	17.0	19	8	10	2	.279
Blair, Willie	3	2	3.90	18	2	0	32.1	25	15	21	1	.210
Bohanon, B*	0	1	7.31	18	2	1	28.1	32	19	15	5	.286
Bones, Ricky	3	2	4.02	6	6	0	40.1	37	15	14	9	.243
Bosio, Chris	2	3	4.74	7	7	0	43.2	42	15	23	6	.251
Boskie, Shawn	1	0	0.57	2	2	0	15.2	9	3	11	0	.161
Brow, Scott	0	2	6.08	25	3	2	50.1	62	30	28	8	.308
Brown, Kevin	2	3	7.32	6	6	0	35.2	51	9	23	6	.323
Burkett, John	1	0	0.60	2	2	0	15.0	14	3	14	0	.241
Candiotti, T	4	4	3.14	12	12	0	77.1	79	30	64	5	.266
Carrara, G	2	3	11.37	15	3	0	31.2	52	25	19	10	.377
Castillo, T*	8	9	3.93	92	0	5	132.2	126	57	78	15	.254
Clark, Mark	1	0	8.27	3	3	0	16.1	27	6	8	5	.403
Clemens, R	3	3	4.03	11	11	0	73.2	72	29	54	7	.259
Cone, David	5	6	3.43	14	13	0	94.1	82	38	78	10	.232
Coppinger, R	2	0	1.88	2	2	0	14.1	9	2	11	2	.180
Crabtree, Tim	4	4	1.98	40	0	1	50.0	45	20	33	3	.237
Cummings, J*	0	1	2.84	2	1	0	12.2	14	6	7	2	.286
Darwin, Danny	0	6	7.17	11	7	0	47.2	59	16	30	11	.309
DeLucia, Rich	1	1	2.77	3	2	0	13.0	9	5	12	1	.191
Eckersley, D	0	0	1.04	15	0	10	17.1	10	1	17	1	.167
Eichhorn, M	6	2	3.10	49	0	2	72.2	75	24	58	4	.266
Eldred, Cal	2	0	1.69	2	2	0	16.0	10	1	8	0	.175
Erickson, S	2	6	4.84	9	9	0	57.2	57	17	36	5	.265
Farrell, John	0	0	6.48	5	3	0	16.2	20	7	10	4	.294
Fernandez, A	1	4	2.52	9	9	0	64.1	55	24	53	6	.230
Fetters, Mike	1	1	3.74	13	2	5	21.2	25	7	12	2	.281
Finley, Chuck*	1	3	3.48	5	5	0	31.0	28	11	25	8	.239
Flener, Huck*	2	1	3.69	11	6	0	46.1	42	23	30	4	.241
Frohwirth, T	1	1	2.60	8	0	1	17.1	10	9	20	1	.169
Gibson, Paul*	1	1	4.67	12	0	0	17.1	16	10	14	2	.254
Gordon, Tom	6	3	3.54	19	19	0	68.2	56	31	69	6	.220
Gubicza, Mark	3	5	5.40	9	7	0	38.1	46	19	29	3	.309
Guetterman, L*	0	2	7.07	7	0	0	14.0	17	5	8	4	.315
Guthrie, Mark*	0	1	6.46	6	2	0	15.1	17	6	10	4	.293
Guzman, Juan	32	18	4.03	79	79	0	504.1	489	193	439	42	.255
Hall, Darren	1	2	4.43	22	0	8	22.1	29	12	18	3	.319
Haney, Chris*	1	0	3.20	3	3	0	19.2	16	4	12	0	.219
Hanson, Erik	7	8	5.04	19	19	0	125.0	125	53	89	11	.263
Harnisch, P	1	0	3.86	2	2	0	14.0	13	1	7	1	.245
Henneman, M	0	1	1.42	18	0	10	25.1	19	9	18	0	.211
Hentgen, Pat	30	26	4.00	84	67	0	500.0	492	190	347	58	.256
Hernandez, R	1	2	2.93	11	0	6	15.1	11	5	16	2	.193
Hernandez, X	0	0	7.62	5	0	0	13.0	15	4	5	2	.278
Hershiser, O	4	0	3.21	4	4	0	28.0	27	5	28	4	.250
Hitchcock, S*	2	0	5.40	3	3	0	15.0	16	10	13	2	.276
Honeycutt, R*	1	0	1.32	17	0	0	13.2	11	6	13	1	.234
Hurtado, E	2	2	4.26	6	3	0	38.0	37	20	17	4	.261
Janzen, Marty	4	4	6.32	10	6	0	47.0	57	25	32	9	.305
Johnson, R*	3	1	4.72	5	5	0	34.1	27	14	35	5	.209
Kamieniecki	2	2	3.86	4	4	0	25.2	25	9	15	2	.263
Karl, Scott*	1	1	4.58	3	3	0	19.2	18	7	10	2	.243
Key, Jimmy*	28	24	3.88	69	69	0	412.2	429	101	247	40	.268
Langston, M*	3	5	4.89	9	9	0	57.0	60	25	43	3	.270
Leiter, Al*	16	8	3.69	48	29	0	219.1	205	109	183	16	.246
Leiter, Mark	0	1	9.22	6	2	0	13.2	21	7	9	2	.362
Linton, Doug	1	1	6.75	8	2	0	22.2	24	15	10	1	.276
MacDonald, B*	1	2	3.99	42	0	0	58.2	68	23	26	6	.297
Magnante, M*	0	0	1.46	6	1	0	12.1	15	3	5	0	.313
Mahomes, Pat	1	0	3.00	4	2	0	18.0	19	6	17	3	.268
Martinez, De	2	0	0.90	3	3	0	20.0	16	9	7	0	.219
McCaskill, K	1	2	5.40	9	4	0	30.0	37	14	14	4	.296
McDonald, Ben	3	1	7.33	5	4	0	23.1	30	3	17	11	.300
McDowell, J	1	5	6.75	6	6	0	36.0	49	15	22	6	.327
Menhart, Paul	1	2	5.52	14	6	0	44.0	37	26	36	3	.230
Mesa, Jose	2	3	6.13	13	6	5	39.2	49	17	24	3	.314
Milacki, Bob	1	2	5.79	5	4	0	23.1	28	4	18	5	.289
Mills, Alan	2	0	2.92	6	1	0	12.1	16	6	11	1	.308
Miranda, A*	1	1	4.84	5	3	0	22.1	23	6	20	2	.258
Montgomery, J	0	2	5.14	17	0	9	21.0	24	9	16	3	.293
Moyer, Jamie*	1	1	4.84	4	4	0	22.1	27	7	11	4	.300
Mussina, Mike	2	1	2.37	5	5	0	38.0	30	7	22	3	.221

Pitcher	W	L	ERA	G	GS	Sv	IP	H	BB	SO	HR	Avg
Nagy, Charles	4	4	4.19	10	10	0	62.1	69	19	49	5	.276
Navarro, J	3	1	4.09	7	6	0	44.0	50	7	24	4	.294
Nelson, Jeff	0	1	2.19	13	0	0	12.1	11	4	14	0	.234
Oliver, D*	2	0	1.98	3	2	0	13.2	13	8	9	0	.255
Olson, Gregg	1	4	4.66	16	0	6	19.1	29	11	19	1	.341
Orosco, Jesse*	1	0	1.56	18	0	0	17.1	7	7	21	0	.125
Pall, Donn	0	2	5.68	9	0	0	12.2	15	3	5	2	.300
Pavlik, Roger	1	2	4.45	5	5	0	30.1	27	16	29	3	.231
Pettitte, A*	3	0	3.09	4	3	0	23.1	19	5	17	1	.213
Pichardo, H	1	3	6.65	10	2	0	21.2	31	4	14	3	.330
Plunk, Eric	0	3	3.91	14	0	1	23.0	17	9	23	3	.205
Prieto, Ariel	1	2	10.38	3	3	0	13.0	19	5	8	3	.345
Quantrill, P	1	9	6.04	24	10	0	70.0	102	37	42	16	.349
Rhodes, A*	0	1	5.68	4	3	0	19.0	18	5	14	3	.247
Risley, Bill	0	0	5.63	13	0	0	16.0	18	13	8	3	.300
Robertson, R*	1	0	0.00	2	1	0	13.2	9	4	11	0	.184
Robinson, Ken	0	1	4.18	13	0	0	23.2	16	13	20	3	.186
Rodriguez, Fr	1	0	3.46	2	2	0	13.0	11	5	4	0	.234
Rogers, Kenny*	2	2	2.76	17	5	0	45.2	36	17	36	7	.220
Russell, Jeff	0	3	2.81	15	0	4	16.0	16	4	7	1	.267
Sanderson, S	0	2	3.62	5	5	0	32.1	36	3	15	2	.290
Scanlan, Bob	0	0	3.29	3	2	0	13.2	15	2	6	0	.294
Sele, Aaron	1	0	2.93	3	3	0	15.1	14	6	9	1	.246
Spoljaric, P*	1	2	5.31	14	0	0	20.1	18	11	17	6	.228
Stottlemyre	37	26	4.06	83	78	1	527.1	513	167	306	53	.255
Swindell, G*	0	3	7.71	4	3	0	18.2	26	6	9	6	.317
Tapani, Kevin	3	5	5.47	9	9	0	52.2	66	17	31	4	.307
Timlin, Mike	13	8	3.20	139	2	16	188.1	179	80	163	10	.251
Trombley, M	1	2	5.51	6	2	0	16.1	17	5	5	4	.283
Valenzuela, F*	0	0	3.45	2	2	0	15.2	13	5	6	2	.228
Valera, Julio	0	2	9.22	4	2	0	13.2	16	6	9	5	.286
Van Poppel, T	0	1	3.74	4	3	0	21.2	21	9	11	3	.253
Viola, Frank*	2	2	4.50	7	7	0	44.0	42	27	26	6	.255
Wakefield, T	0	1	4.73	2	2	0	13.1	14	8	13	0	.259
Ware, Jeff	2	1	6.00	7	3	0	24.0	20	21	14	3	.227
Wells, Bob	2	0	0.64	3	1	0	14.0	12	4	10	0	.226
Wells, David*	16	14	3.68	81	30	4	271.2	262	68	161	36	.254
West, David*	2	0	3.60	3	2	0	20.0	14	7	12	1	.189
Williams, W	6	5	4.31	52	7	0	112.2	106	58	87	14	.251
Witt, Bobby	3	2	4.70	5	5	0	30.2	27	15	35	3	.237

Leader Boards

It's hard to work your way through this section of the book without thinking about pitcher Larry Jaster and his 1966 season. Jaster was a 22-year-old southpaw who, after performing well in limited action the previous year, started the season with the St. Louis Cardinals. Despite a six-week stint in the minors, he managed to go 11-5 for the Redbirds with an impressive five shutouts—*all five* coming against the National League champion Los Angeles Dodgers. Jaster, who beat Don Drysdale (twice), Claude Osteen (twice), and Don Sutton, threw just two shutouts the remainder of his major league career and was out of baseball five years later. But for one amazing summer, Jaster could look at the Dodgers and say, "I've got your number."

That's what this section is about—who's got somebody's number. Mark McGwire has Kevin Gross' number. Wally Whitehurst has Larry Walker's number. And Tim Salmon has *everybody's* number—as long as he's hitting in Arlington.

The Leader Boards are made up of five distinctive sections. The first part consists of straight batter/pitcher match-ups. The next two show how batters fare in their home parks and on the road, while the final two examine pitchers in the same manner. "Home Park" is defined as a player's home park only while he is a member of that team.

Batter vs. Pitcher

Highest Batting Average
(Minimum 15 PA)

Match-Up	AB	H	BA
Edgar Martinez vs. Brian Anderson	17	13	.765
David Segui vs. Marvin Freeman	14	10	.714
Rondell White vs. Pete Schourek	14	10	.714
Dave Nilsson vs. Tim Wakefield	16	11	.688
Barry Bonds vs. Armando Reynoso	15	10	.667
Jeff Conine vs. Marvin Freeman	15	10	.667
Chili Davis vs. Mike Jackson	9	6	.667
Dave Clark vs. Dave Weathers	15	10	.667
Frank Thomas vs. Buddy Groom	6	4	.667
Jeff Bagwell vs. Mark Portugal	17	11	.647

Highest On-Base Average
(Minimum 15 PA)

Match-Up	PA*	OB	OBA
Frank Thomas vs. Buddy Groom	15	13	.867
Mark McGwire vs. Kevin Gross	15	12	.800
Edgar Martinez vs. Brian Anderson	19	15	.789
Barry Bonds vs. Armando Reynoso	23	18	.783
Chili Davis vs. Mike Jackson	17	13	.765
David Segui vs. Marvin Freeman	17	13	.765
Orlando Merced vs. Jeff Brantley	16	12	.750
Wally Joyner vs. Kevin Ritz	16	12	.750
Chipper Jones vs. Michael Mimbs	16	12	.750
Edgar Martinez vs. Kevin Gross	19	14	.737

Highest Slugging Average
(Minimum 15 PA)

Match-Up	AB	TB	SLG
Mark McGwire vs. Kevin Gross	8	17	2.125
Edgar Martinez vs. Erik Hanson	11	17	1.545
Edgar Martinez vs. Joe Magrane	8	12	1.500
Edgar Martinez vs. Brian Anderson	17	25	1.471
Barry Bonds vs. Armando Reynoso	15	21	1.400
Jeff Conine vs. Marvin Freeman	15	21	1.400
Pete Incaviglia vs. Bob Milacki	13	18	1.385
Brent Gates vs. Pat Mahomes	13	18	1.385
Marquis Grissom vs. Greg Swindell	21	29	1.381
Reggie Sanders vs. Armando Reynoso	16	22	1.375

Hits

Match-Up	H
Ryne Sandberg vs. Dwight Gooden	35
Rickey Henderson vs. Jimmy Key	35
Mark Grace vs. Doug Drabek	33
Cal Ripken vs. Mark Langston	32
Terry Pendleton vs. Zane Smith	32
Paul Molitor vs. Roger Clemens	31
Andres Galarraga vs. Doug Drabek	31
Wade Boggs vs. Mark Gubicza	29
Brett Butler vs. Doug Drabek	29
Tony Gwynn vs. Greg Maddux	28

Doubles

Match-Up	2B
Tony Gwynn vs. Doug Drabek	9
Barry Larkin vs. Greg Maddux	9
9 Match-ups tied with	8

Triples

Match-Up	3B
Lance Johnson vs. Bobby Witt	4
Mickey Morandini vs. Greg Maddux	4
15 Match-ups tied with	3

Home Runs

Match-Up	HR
Rickey Henderson vs. Jimmy Key	9
Jose Canseco vs. Todd Stottlemyre	8
Cecil Fielder vs. Jimmy Key	7
Barry Bonds vs. Greg Maddux	7
Ryne Sandberg vs. Terry Mulholland	7
Matt Williams vs. John Smiley	7
Matt Williams vs. Ramon Martinez	7
Cecil Fielder vs. Pat Hentgen	7
11 Match-ups tied with	6

Total Bases

Match-Up	TB
Rickey Henderson vs. Jimmy Key	68
Andres Galarraga vs. Doug Drabek	54
Barry Bonds vs. Greg Maddux	51
Matt Williams vs. Ramon Martinez	50
Mark Grace vs. Doug Drabek	49
Ryne Sandberg vs. Dwight Gooden	46
Paul Molitor vs. Mark Langston	45
Ryne Sandberg vs. Dennis Martinez	44
Tim Wallach vs. Tom Glavine	44
Robby Thompson vs. Tom Glavine	44

Runs Batted In

Match-Up	RBI
Gary Gaetti vs. Roger Clemens	18
Joe Carter vs. Mark Langston	18
Terry Steinbach vs. Chuck Finley	18
Frank Thomas vs. Ricky Bones	17
Andres Galarraga vs. Fernando Valenzuela	16
Benito Santiago vs. Greg Maddux	16
Barry Bonds vs. Andy Benes	16
11 Match-ups tied with	15

Sacrifice Hits

Match-Up	SH
Ron Karkovice vs. Mark Gubicza	4
Jay Bell vs. Bob Tewksbury	4
Jay Bell vs. David Cone	4
Jay Bell vs. Greg Maddux	4
Rafael Belliard vs. Andy Benes	4
Jay Bell vs. Andy Benes	4
Jay Bell vs. Shawn Boskie	4
Kimera Bartee vs. David Wells	4
35 Match-ups tied with	3

Sacrifice Flies

Match-Up	SF
Barry Bonds vs. Mike Morgan	3
18 Match-ups tied with	3

Walks

Match-Up	BB
Wade Boggs vs. Bobby Witt	22
Danny Tartabull vs. Randy Johnson	19
Wade Boggs vs. Mark Gubicza	17
Tony Phillips vs. Mark Langston	17
Frank Thomas vs. Mark Langston	17
Rickey Henderson vs. Randy Johnson	17
Barry Bonds vs. Kevin Gross	16
Mark McGwire vs. Chuck Finley	16
5 Match-ups tied with	15

Hit By Pitch

Match-Up	HBP
Robby Thompson vs. Dennis Martinez	4
Jeff Kent vs. Tom Candiotti	4
John Cangelosi vs. John Smoltz	4
Craig Biggio vs. Mark Gardner	4
Brady Anderson vs. Felipe Lira	4
27 Match-ups tied with	3

Strikeouts

Match-Up	K
Chili Davis vs. Roger Clemens	28
Tim Wallach vs. Dwight Gooden	27
Juan Samuel vs. Dwight Gooden	24
Ryne Sandberg vs. Dwight Gooden	23
Devon White vs. Roger Clemens	23
Danny Tartabull vs. Chuck Finley	23
Mickey Tettleton vs. Mark Langston	22
Rob Deer vs. Jimmy Key	22
Greg Vaughn vs. Jack McDowell	22
Tony Phillips vs. Kevin Appier	22

At-Bats per Home Run
(Minimum 15 PA)

Match-Up	AB	HR	RAT
Mark McGwire vs. Kevin Gross	8	4	2.0
Edgar Martinez vs. Erik Hanson	11	4	2.8
Andre Dawson vs. Stan Belinda	13	4	3.3
Mickey Tettleton vs. Mark Eichhorn	15	4	3.8
Jeff Kent vs. Mike Morgan	15	4	3.8
Reggie Sanders vs. Armando Reynoso	16	4	4.0
Cecil Fielder vs. Frank Rodriguez	16	4	4.0
Dean Palmer vs. Bobby Witt	12	3	4.0
Edgar Martinez vs. Joe Magrane	8	2	4.0
Marquis Grissom vs. Greg Swindell	21	5	4.2

Strikeouts Per At-Bat
(Minimum 15 PA)

Match-Up	K	AB	RAT
Greg Vaughn vs. Greg Swindell	12	15	.800
Michael Huff vs. Randy Johnson	9	12	.750
Mark McGwire vs. Jose Mesa	7	10	.700
Dean Palmer vs. David Cone	11	16	.688
Pete Incaviglia vs. Roger Clemens	15	22	.682
Cecil Fielder vs. Dennis Eckersley	10	15	.667
Randy Velarde vs. Pat Hentgen	11	17	.647
Mike Blowers vs. Bobby Witt	11	17	.647
Greg Gagne vs. Todd Van Poppel	11	17	.647
Mickey Tettleton vs. Jason Bere	9	14	.643

Lowest Batting Average
(Minimum 15 PA)

Match-Up	AB	H	BA
Dick Schofield vs. Mark Gubicza	28	0	.000
Greg Gagne vs. Al Leiter	20	0	.000
Stan Javier vs. Mark Gubicza	19	0	.000
Stan Javier vs. Tom Glavine	19	0	.000
Dwight Smith vs. John Smoltz	19	0	.000
Kevin Stocker vs. Andy Benes	19	0	.000
5 Match-ups tied with	18	0	.000

Lowest On-Base Average
(Minimum 15 PA)

Match-Up	PA*	OB	OBA
Stan Javier vs. Mark Gubicza	19	0	.000
Dwight Smith vs. John Smoltz	19	0	.000
Kevin Stocker vs. Andy Benes	19	0	.000
Javy Lopez vs. John Smiley	18	0	.000
Larry Walker vs. Wally Whitehurst	18	0	.000
Ed Sprague vs. Chris Bosio	15	0	.000
Orlando Merced vs. Steve Trachsel	15	0	.000
Pat Meares vs. Pat Hentgen	14	0	.000
Ozzie Guillen vs. Dennis Martinez	24	1	.042
Jeff Huson vs. Kevin Tapani	24	1	.042

Batter @ Home Park

Batting Average
(Minimum 300 PA)

Match-Up	AB	H	BA
Eric Young @ Coors Field	477	183	.384
Dante Bichette @ Coors Field	638	237	.371
Vinny Castilla @ Coors Field	602	218	.362
Wade Boggs @ Fenway Park	1679	608	.362
Larry Walker @ Coors Field	393	142	.361
Gary Sheffield @ Jack Murphy	405	146	.360
Ellis Burks @ Coors Field	472	170	.360
Paul Molitor @ Metrodome	334	120	.359
Roberto Alomar @ Camden Yards	283	101	.357
Kevin Mitchell @ Cinergy Field	418	147	.352

On-Base Average
(Minimum 300 PA)

Match-Up	PA*	OB	OBA
Wade Boggs @ Fenway Park	2041	951	.466
Frank Thomas @ Comiskey Park	1900	876	.461
Eric Young @ Coors Field	549	251	.457
Barry Bonds @ 3Com Park	1193	533	.447
Gary Sheffield @ Pro Player	795	354	.445
Kevin Mitchell @ Cinergy Field	494	216	.437
Roberto Alomar @ Camden Yards	336	146	.435
Walt Weiss @ Coors Field	589	255	.433
Rickey Henderson @ Oakland-Alameda	1651	710	.430
Jim Thome @ Jacobs Field	767	329	.429

Slugging Average
(Minimum 300 PA)

Match-Up	AB	TB	SLG
Larry Walker @ Coors Field	393	297	.756
Albert Belle @ Jacobs Field	746	532	.713
Dante Bichette @ Coors Field	638	445	.697
Vinny Castilla @ Coors Field	602	416	.691
Ellis Burks @ Coors Field	472	321	.680
Kevin Mitchell @ Cinergy Field	418	281	.672
Andres Galarraga @ Coors Field	593	392	.661
Gary Sheffield @ Jack Murphy	405	266	.657
Frank Thomas @ Comiskey Park	1515	948	.626
Barry Bonds @ 3Com Park	941	578	.614

Hits

Match-Up	H
Tony Gwynn @ Jack Murphy	872
Mark Grace @ Wrigley Field	806
Barry Larkin @ Cinergy Field	717
Ryne Sandberg @ Wrigley Field	714
Mike Greenwell @ Fenway Park	703
Ozzie Smith @ Busch Stadium	687
Craig Biggio @ Astrodome	626
Wade Boggs @ Fenway Park	608
Ken Griffey Jr @ Kingdome	604
Will Clark @ 3Com Park	588

Doubles

Match-Up	2B
Wade Boggs @ Fenway Park	165
Mike Greenwell @ Fenway Park	163
Mark Grace @ Wrigley Field	153
Edgar Martinez @ Kingdome	139
Tony Gwynn @ Jack Murphy	139
Craig Biggio @ Astrodome	136
Jay Bell @ Three Rivers	129
Ken Griffey Jr @ Kingdome	128
Barry Larkin @ Cinergy Field	125
Will Clark @ 3Com Park	122

Triples

Match-Up	3B
Tony Gwynn @ Jack Murphy	30
Lance Johnson @ Comiskey Park	29
Vince Coleman @ Busch Stadium	25
Mike Greenwell @ Fenway Park	24
Ryne Sandberg @ Wrigley Field	24
Devon White @ SkyDome	23
Steve Finley @ Astrodome	23
Ray Lankford @ Busch Stadium	23
Robby Thompson @ 3Com Park	22
2 Match-ups tied with	21

Home Runs

Match-Up	HR
Mark McGwire @ Oakland-Alameda	148
Matt Williams @ 3Com Park	129
Ken Griffey Jr @ Kingdome	128
Cecil Fielder @ Tiger Stadium	127
Frank Thomas @ Comiskey Park	113
Joe Carter @ SkyDome	110
Ryne Sandberg @ Wrigley Field	110
Jay Buhner @ Kingdome	102
Andre Dawson @ Wrigley Field	94
Dave Justice @ Atlanta-Fulton	88

Total Bases

Match-Up	TB
Ryne Sandberg @ Wrigley Field	1205
Tony Gwynn @ Jack Murphy	1170
Ken Griffey Jr @ Kingdome	1134
Mike Greenwell @ Fenway Park	1103
Mark Grace @ Wrigley Field	1099
Barry Larkin @ Cinergy Field	1097
Matt Williams @ 3Com Park	1050
Mark McGwire @ Oakland-Alameda	1012
Will Clark @ 3Com Park	1000
Frank Thomas @ Comiskey Park	948

Runs Batted In

Match-Up	RBI
Mark McGwire @ Oakland-Alameda	400
Cecil Fielder @ Tiger Stadium	398
Mike Greenwell @ Fenway Park	383
Ken Griffey Jr @ Kingdome	376
Ryne Sandberg @ Wrigley Field	376
Matt Williams @ 3Com Park	371
Joe Carter @ SkyDome	351
Mark Grace @ Wrigley Field	344
Will Clark @ 3Com Park	341
Barry Larkin @ Cinergy Field	339

Sacrifice Hits

Match-Up	SH
Jay Bell @ Three Rivers	59
Ozzie Smith @ Busch Stadium	43
Robby Thompson @ 3Com Park	41
Dick Schofield @ Anaheim	32
Greg Gagne @ Metrodome	30
B.J. Surhoff @ County Stadium	28
Mike Bordick @ Oakland-Alameda	28
Craig Biggio @ Astrodome	28
Omar Vizquel @ Kingdome	27
Brett Butler @ Dodger Stadium	27

Sacrifice Flies

Match-Up	SF
Will Clark @ 3Com Park	34
Joe Carter @ SkyDome	30
B.J. Surhoff @ County Stadium	29
Barry Larkin @ Cinergy Field	29
Mark McGwire @ Oakland-Alameda	26
Mark Grace @ Wrigley Field	26
Jeff King @ Three Rivers	25
Mike Greenwell @ Fenway Park	24
Robin Ventura @ Comiskey Park	24
Ryne Sandberg @ Wrigley Field	24

Walks

Match-Up	BB
Mark McGwire @ Oakland-Alameda	395
Frank Thomas @ Comiskey Park	363
Wade Boggs @ Fenway Park	333
Mark Grace @ Wrigley Field	313
Barry Larkin @ Cinergy Field	313
Rickey Henderson @ Oakland-Alameda	306
Ozzie Smith @ Busch Stadium	298
Craig Biggio @ Astrodome	291
Tony Phillips @ Tiger Stadium	285
Edgar Martinez @ Kingdome	277

Hit By Pitch

Match-Up	HBP
Craig Biggio @ Astrodome	52
Mike Macfarlane @ Kauffman Stadium	38
Robby Thompson @ 3Com Park	35
Dave Valle @ Kingdome	32
Brady Anderson @ Camden Yards	31
Ed Sprague @ SkyDome	30
Mark McGwire @ Oakland-Alameda	29
Chuck Knoblauch @ Metrodome	27
Jeff Bagwell @ Astrodome	26
2 Match-ups tied with	24

Strikeouts

Match-Up	K
Mark McGwire @ Oakland-Alameda	462
Jay Buhner @ Kingdome	458
Matt Williams @ 3Com Park	432
Cecil Fielder @ Tiger Stadium	427
Robby Thompson @ 3Com Park	422
Travis Fryman @ Tiger Stadium	384
Jay Bell @ Three Rivers	375
Jose Canseco @ Oakland-Alameda	360
Chili Davis @ Anaheim	359
Greg Vaughn @ County Stadium	359

At-Bats per Home Run
(Minimum 300 PA)

Match-Up	AB	HR	RAT
Larry Walker @ Coors Field	393	36	10.9
Albert Belle @ Jacobs Field	746	68	11.0
Andres Galarraga @ Coors Field	593	50	11.9
Dante Bichette @ Coors Field	638	53	12.0
Vinny Castilla @ Coors Field	602	50	12.0
Barry Bonds @ 3Com Park	941	75	12.5
Darryl Strawberry @ Shea Stadium	1009	80	12.6
Kevin Mitchell @ Cinergy Field	418	33	12.7
Ryan Klesko @ Atlanta-Fulton	575	44	13.1
Mickey Tettleton @ Arlington	471	36	13.1

Batter @ Road Park

Batting Average
(Minimum 35 PA)

Match-Up	AB	H	BA
Tim Salmon @ Arlington	62	35	.565
Harold Baines @ Arlington	36	19	.528
John Mabry @ Coors Field	42	22	.524
Fred McGriff @ Coors Field	52	27	.519
Marquis Grissom @ Olympic Stadium	45	23	.511
Ray Durham @ Tiger Stadium	44	22	.500
Will Clark @ Fenway Park	40	20	.500
Tony Eusebio @ Busch Stadium	40	20	.500
Ryan Klesko @ Coors Field	41	20	.488
Bobby Bonilla @ Tiger Stadium	37	18	.486

On-Base Average
(Minimum 35 PA)

Match-Up	PA*	OB	OBA
Tim Salmon @ Arlington	75	48	.640
Bobby Bonilla @ Tiger Stadium	46	26	.565
Harold Baines @ Arlington	39	22	.564
Fred McGriff @ Coors Field	57	32	.561
Rickey Henderson @ Comiskey Park	72	40	.556
John Mabry @ Coors Field	45	25	.556
Ray Durham @ Tiger Stadium	49	27	.551
Marquis Grissom @ Olympic Stadium	51	28	.549
Mark McGwire @ Arlington	53	29	.547
Will Clark @ Fenway Park	44	24	.545

Slugging Average
(Minimum 35 PA)

Match-Up	AB	TB	SLG
Harold Baines @ Arlington	36	39	1.083
Phil Plantier @ Busch Stadium	40	40	1.000
Gary Sheffield @ Coors Field	34	33	.971
Bobby Bonilla @ Tiger Stadium	37	35	.946
Tim Salmon @ Arlington	62	58	.935
Jeff Conine @ Coors Field	46	43	.935
Ryan Klesko @ Coors Field	41	38	.927
Mark McGwire @ Jacobs Field	26	23	.885
Todd Hundley @ Coors Field	33	29	.879
Fred McGriff @ Kingdome	72	63	.875

Hits

Match-Up	H
Tony Gwynn @ Atlanta-Fulton	99
Barry Bonds @ Olympic Stadium	97
Bobby Bonilla @ Veterans Stadium	95
Tony Gwynn @ Cinergy Field	93
Tony Gwynn @ Astrodome	93
Andres Galarraga @ Three Rivers	91
Bobby Bonilla @ Wrigley Field	87
Tony Gwynn @ Dodger Stadium	85
Barry Larkin @ Atlanta-Fulton	83
Ruben Sierra @ Kingdome	82

Doubles

Match-Up	2B
Bobby Bonilla @ Veterans Stadium	24
Barry Bonds @ Busch Stadium	24
Barry Larkin @ Atlanta-Fulton	21
Bobby Bonilla @ Wrigley Field	21
Barry Bonds @ Shea Stadium	21
6 Match-ups tied with	20

Triples

Match-Up	3B
Brett Butler @ Busch Stadium	10
Lance Johnson @ Metrodome	7
Brady Anderson @ Kauffman Stadium	6
Chuck Knoblauch @ Kauffman Stadium	6
Tony Gwynn @ Olympic Stadium	6
Juan Samuel @ Olympic Stadium	6
14 Match-ups tied with	5

Home Runs

Match-Up	HR
Barry Bonds @ Olympic Stadium	24
Barry Bonds @ Veterans Stadium	23
Mark McGwire @ Tiger Stadium	20
Barry Bonds @ Jack Murphy	20
Barry Bonds @ Cinergy Field	19
Mark McGwire @ Fenway Park	18
Bobby Bonilla @ Wrigley Field	18
Matt Williams @ Cinergy Field	18
3 Match-ups tied with	17

Total Bases

Match-Up	TB
Barry Bonds @ Olympic Stadium	193
Bobby Bonilla @ Wrigley Field	172
Barry Bonds @ Veterans Stadium	169
Bobby Bonilla @ Veterans Stadium	158
Andres Galarraga @ Three Rivers	158
Barry Bonds @ Jack Murphy	154
Barry Bonds @ Wrigley Field	152
Joe Carter @ Fenway Park	143
Ruben Sierra @ Kingdome	138
Tony Gwynn @ Atlanta-Fulton	138

Runs Batted In

Match-Up	RBI
Barry Bonds @ Veterans Stadium	61
Bobby Bonilla @ Wrigley Field	60
Barry Bonds @ Olympic Stadium	58
Bobby Bonilla @ Veterans Stadium	52
Tim Wallach @ Busch Stadium	52
Cal Ripken @ Tiger Stadium	50
Barry Bonds @ Cinergy Field	50
Cal Ripken @ County Stadium	49
5 Match-ups tied with	48

Sacrifice Hits

Match-Up	SH
Jay Bell @ Wrigley Field	11
Jay Bell @ Busch Stadium	9
Jay Bell @ Shea Stadium	8
Brett Butler @ Veterans Stadium	8
Ozzie Guillen @ Kauffman Stadium	7
Steve Finley @ 3Com Park	7
11 Match-ups tied with	6

Sacrifice Flies

Match-Up	SF
Ruben Sierra @ Tiger Stadium	8
Frank Thomas @ Tiger Stadium	8
Tim Wallach @ Busch Stadium	8
Mark Grace @ Cinergy Field	7
Frank Thomas @ Kauffman Stadium	6
Ruben Sierra @ County Stadium	6
Ruben Sierra @ Kingdome	6
Will Clark @ Dodger Stadium	6
Jeff Bagwell @ Dodger Stadium	6
Bobby Bonilla @ Veterans Stadium	6

Walks

Match-Up	BB
Barry Bonds @ Veterans Stadium	71
Barry Bonds @ Cinergy Field	55
Barry Bonds @ Jack Murphy	51
Barry Bonds @ Wrigley Field	48
Barry Bonds @ Astrodome	48
Tony Phillips @ Yankee Stadium	46
Mickey Tettleton @ SkyDome	42
Frank Thomas @ Anaheim	41
Barry Bonds @ Shea Stadium	41
3 Match-ups tied with	40

Hit By Pitch

Match-Up	HBP
Carlos Baerga @ Metrodome	8
Jeff Blauser @ Olympic Stadium	7
Andres Galarraga @ Veterans Stadium	7
Andres Galarraga @ Busch Stadium	7
Mike Macfarlane @ Anaheim	6
Joe Carter @ Oakland-Alameda	6
Brett Butler @ Astrodome	6
Barry Larkin @ Shea Stadium	6
Andres Galarraga @ 3Com Park	6
21 Match-ups tied with	5

Strikeouts

Match-Up	K
Andres Galarraga @ Shea Stadium	75
Andres Galarraga @ Wrigley Field	66
Andres Galarraga @ Three Rivers	66
Andres Galarraga @ Atlanta-Fulton	64
Danny Tartabull @ Tiger Stadium	62
Mickey Tettleton @ Kingdome	62
Danny Tartabull @ Anaheim	59
Jose Canseco @ Metrodome	59
Matt Williams @ Astrodome	59
Danny Tartabull @ Fenway Park	58

At-Bats per Home Run
(Minimum 35 PA)

Match-Up	AB	HR	RAT
Mark McGwire @ Jacobs Field	26	5	5.2
Phil Plantier @ Three Rivers	34	6	5.7
Fred McGriff @ Kingdome	72	12	6.0
Mark McGwire @ Arlington	36	6	6.0
Bernard Gilkey @ Coors Field	46	7	6.6
Phil Plantier @ Busch Stadium	40	6	6.7
Dean Palmer @ Metrodome	87	13	6.7
Gary Sheffield @ Coors Field	34	5	6.8
Rex Hudler @ Camden Yards	34	5	6.8
Matt Williams @ Coors Field	43	6	7.2

Pitcher @ Home Park

Wins

Match-Up	W
Roger Clemens @ Fenway Park	75
Chuck Finley @ Anaheim	71
Tom Glavine @ Atlanta-Fulton	70
Dwight Gooden @ Shea Stadium	56
Randy Johnson @ Kingdome	55
John Smoltz @ Atlanta-Fulton	55
Ramon Martinez @ Dodger Stadium	54
Mark Gubicza @ Kauffman Stadium	52
Dennis Martinez @ Olympic Stadium	49
Doug Drabek @ Three Rivers	49

Losses

Match-Up	L
Mark Gubicza @ Kauffman Stadium	54
Chuck Finley @ Anaheim	53
Roger Clemens @ Fenway Park	48
Tom Glavine @ Atlanta-Fulton	44
John Smoltz @ Atlanta-Fulton	44
Orel Hershiser @ Dodger Stadium	39
Jim Abbott @ Anaheim	38
Ramon Martinez @ Dodger Stadium	38
Andy Benes @ Jack Murphy	36
2 Match-ups tied with	35

Earned Run Average
(Minimum 100 IP)

Match-Up	ER	IP	ERA
Kevin Brown @ Pro Player	26	138.1	1.69
Al Leiter @ Pro Player	27	116.2	2.08
Greg Maddux @ Atlanta-Fulton	111	457.1	2.18
Roberto Hernandez @ Comiskey Park	46	183.2	2.25
Jose Mesa @ Jacobs Field	29	115.0	2.27
Alejandro Pena @ Dodger Stadium	34	133.0	2.30
Greg Swindell @ Cinergy Field	28	109.0	2.31
Hideo Nomo @ Dodger Stadium	60	233.0	2.32
Bill Swift @ 3Com Park	67	259.1	2.33
Mark Eichhorn @ Anaheim	33	127.1	2.33

Games

Match-Up	G
Dennis Eckersley @ Oakland-Alameda	272
Jeff Montgomery @ Kauffman Stadium	271
Mike Henneman @ Tiger Stadium	251
Rick Honeycutt @ Oakland-Alameda	189
Mel Rojas @ Olympic Stadium	183
Rod Beck @ 3Com Park	182
John Franco @ Shea Stadium	175
Rick Aguilera @ Metrodome	174
Mike Jackson @ Kingdome	167
Chuck Finley @ Anaheim	163

Games Started

Match-Up	GS
Roger Clemens @ Fenway Park	155
Chuck Finley @ Anaheim	148
Tom Glavine @ Atlanta-Fulton	147
John Smoltz @ Atlanta-Fulton	133
Mark Gubicza @ Kauffman Stadium	130
Ramon Martinez @ Dodger Stadium	117
Orel Hershiser @ Dodger Stadium	110
Randy Johnson @ Kingdome	109
Dwight Gooden @ Shea Stadium	109
Dennis Martinez @ Olympic Stadium	104

Saves

Match-Up	Sv
Dennis Eckersley @ Oakland-Alameda	155
Jeff Montgomery @ Kauffman Stadium	109
John Franco @ Shea Stadium	98
Rick Aguilera @ Metrodome	90
Rod Beck @ 3Com Park	80
Mike Henneman @ Tiger Stadium	77
Lee Smith @ Busch Stadium	74
Roberto Hernandez @ Comiskey Park	72
Dan Plesac @ County Stadium	56
3 Match-ups tied with	53

Innings Pitched

Match-Up	IP
Roger Clemens @ Fenway Park	1132.1
Chuck Finley @ Anaheim	1086.2
Tom Glavine @ Atlanta-Fulton	970.1
John Smoltz @ Atlanta-Fulton	912.1
Mark Gubicza @ Kauffman Stadium	910.0
Ramon Martinez @ Dodger Stadium	801.1
Dwight Gooden @ Shea Stadium	769.0
Orel Hershiser @ Dodger Stadium	764.2
Randy Johnson @ Kingdome	763.1
Dennis Martinez @ Olympic Stadium	751.2

Hits

Match-Up	H
Chuck Finley @ Anaheim	992
Roger Clemens @ Fenway Park	991
Tom Glavine @ Atlanta-Fulton	943
Mark Gubicza @ Kauffman Stadium	932
John Smoltz @ Atlanta-Fulton	783
Orel Hershiser @ Dodger Stadium	697
Ramon Martinez @ Dodger Stadium	687
Dwight Gooden @ Shea Stadium	683
Greg Maddux @ Wrigley Field	653
Mark Langston @ Anaheim	650

Walks

Match-Up	BB
Chuck Finley @ Anaheim	401
Randy Johnson @ Kingdome	370
Roger Clemens @ Fenway Park	341
Tom Glavine @ Atlanta-Fulton	315
Ramon Martinez @ Dodger Stadium	314
John Smoltz @ Atlanta-Fulton	304
Mark Gubicza @ Kauffman Stadium	290
Tom Gordon @ Kauffman Stadium	283
Mark Langston @ Anaheim	251
Darryl Kile @ Astrodome	236

Strikeouts

Match-Up	K
Roger Clemens @ Fenway Park	1090
Chuck Finley @ Anaheim	918
Randy Johnson @ Kingdome	899
John Smoltz @ Atlanta-Fulton	767
Dwight Gooden @ Shea Stadium	614
Ramon Martinez @ Dodger Stadium	612
Sid Fernandez @ Shea Stadium	596
Mark Langston @ Anaheim	593
David Cone @ Shea Stadium	588
Tom Glavine @ Atlanta-Fulton	575

Wild Pitches

Match-Up	WP
John Smoltz @ Atlanta-Fulton	49
Juan Guzman @ SkyDome	40
Chuck Finley @ Anaheim	36
Mark Gubicza @ Kauffman Stadium	36
Tom Gordon @ Kauffman Stadium	31
Randy Johnson @ Kingdome	28
David Cone @ Shea Stadium	28
Roger Clemens @ Fenway Park	26
3 Match-ups tied with	24

At-Bats per Home Run
(Minimum 100 IP)

Match-Up	AB	HR	RAT
Mark Eichhorn @ Anaheim	475	2	237.5
Jose Mesa @ Jacobs Field	411	3	137.0
Mike Perez @ Busch Stadium	429	4	107.3
John Habyan @ Yankee Stadium	401	4	100.3
Kevin Brown @ Pro Player	494	5	98.8
Mike Magnante @ Kauffman Stadium	646	7	92.3
Joe Magrane @ Busch Stadium	1736	19	91.4
Tim Scott @ Olympic Stadium	365	4	91.3
John Franco @ Cinergy Field	451	5	90.2
Tim Wakefield @ Three Rivers	432	5	86.4

Pitcher @ Road Park

Wins

Match-Up	W
Tom Glavine @ Cinergy Field	14
Tom Glavine @ Jack Murphy	10
David Wells @ Yankee Stadium	9
Doug Drabek @ Olympic Stadium	9
Greg Maddux @ Shea Stadium	9
Greg Maddux @ Veterans Stadium	9
Greg Maddux @ Busch Stadium	9
12 Match-ups tied with	8

Losses

Match-Up	L
Mike Morgan @ Three Rivers	10
David Wells @ Fenway Park	8
Chuck Finley @ Oakland-Alameda	8
Orel Hershiser @ Astrodome	8
Tom Glavine @ Astrodome	8
Doug Drabek @ Shea Stadium	8
Greg Maddux @ Three Rivers	8
14 Match-ups tied with	7

Earned Run Average
(Minimum 9 IP)

Match-Up	ER	IP	ERA
Lee Smith @ Olympic Stadium	0	21.0	0.00
Steve Reed @ Wrigley Field	0	17.0	0.00
Mariano Rivera @ Comiskey Park	0	14.1	0.00
Rich Robertson @ SkyDome	0	13.2	0.00
Doug Jones @ Kauffman Stadium	0	13.1	0.00
Hector Carrasco @ Astrodome	0	12.2	0.00
Steve Howe @ Tiger Stadium	0	12.1	0.00
Dave Veres @ 3Com Park	0	12.1	0.00
Paul Quantrill @ Kauffman Stadium	0	12.0	0.00
Rod Beck @ Busch Stadium	0	11.1	0.00

Games

Match-Up	G
Jeff Brantley @ Atlanta-Fulton	29
Roger McDowell @ Busch Stadium	28
Todd Worrell @ Veterans Stadium	27
Jeff Brantley @ Jack Murphy	27
John Franco @ 3Com Park	27
Mike Henneman @ Fenway Park	26
Eric Plunk @ Tiger Stadium	26
Randy Myers @ Busch Stadium	26
6 Match-ups tied with	25

Games Started

Match-Up	GS
Doug Drabek @ Shea Stadium	20
Greg Maddux @ Olympic Stadium	18
Doug Drabek @ Busch Stadium	18
Tom Glavine @ Cinergy Field	17
Tom Glavine @ Dodger Stadium	17
Doug Drabek @ Olympic Stadium	17
Greg Maddux @ Shea Stadium	17
5 Match-ups tied with	16

Saves

Match-Up	Sv
Dennis Eckersley @ Anaheim	19
Randy Myers @ Busch Stadium	17
Dennis Eckersley @ Kingdome	16
John Franco @ Veterans Stadium	15
7 Match-ups tied with	14

Innings Pitched

Match-Up	IP
Greg Maddux @ Olympic Stadium	128.0
Tom Glavine @ Cinergy Field	123.0
Doug Drabek @ Olympic Stadium	123.0
Doug Drabek @ Shea Stadium	120.1
Doug Drabek @ Busch Stadium	119.2
Greg Maddux @ Shea Stadium	119.1
Greg Maddux @ Cinergy Field	113.1
Greg Maddux @ Veterans Stadium	112.0
Greg Maddux @ Astrodome	107.0
Greg Maddux @ Busch Stadium	107.0

Hits

Match-Up	H
Tom Glavine @ Dodger Stadium	126
Doug Drabek @ Shea Stadium	124
Greg Maddux @ Olympic Stadium	115
Doug Drabek @ Wrigley Field	109
Chuck Finley @ Metrodome	107
Dwight Gooden @ Wrigley Field	107
Greg Maddux @ Shea Stadium	106
Greg Maddux @ Cinergy Field	103
Doug Drabek @ Busch Stadium	103
3 Match-ups tied with	100

Walks

Match-Up	BB
Bobby Witt @ Fenway Park	58
Bobby Witt @ County Stadium	50
Chuck Finley @ Fenway Park	47
Bobby Witt @ Tiger Stadium	46
Randy Johnson @ County Stadium	44
Jim Abbott @ County Stadium	44
Randy Johnson @ Yankee Stadium	43
Chuck Finley @ Oakland-Alameda	43
Tom Gordon @ Oakland-Alameda	43
John Smoltz @ Dodger Stadium	43

Strikeouts

Match-Up	K
Roger Clemens @ Anaheim	107
Roger Clemens @ Tiger Stadium	100
Greg Maddux @ Veterans Stadium	99
John Smoltz @ Astrodome	98
Roger Clemens @ Yankee Stadium	87
Doug Drabek @ Olympic Stadium	86
Roger Clemens @ County Stadium	85
Greg Maddux @ Cinergy Field	85
Greg Maddux @ Busch Stadium	83
2 Match-ups tied with	80

Wild Pitches

Match-Up	WP
John Smoltz @ Cinergy Field	10
Mark Langston @ Yankee Stadium	8
David Wells @ Yankee Stadium	8
Doug Drabek @ Shea Stadium	8
John Smoltz @ 3Com Park	8
Roger Pavlik @ Comiskey Park	7
Mark Portugal @ Dodger Stadium	7
John Smoltz @ Three Rivers	7
15 Match-ups tied with	6

At-Bats per Home Run
(Minimum 9 IP)

Match-Up	AB	HR	RAT
Alex Fernandez @ Kauffman Stadium	239	0	-
Ramon Martinez @ Olympic Stadium	235	0	-
Jack McDowell @ Kauffman Stadium	223	0	-
Zane Smith @ Olympic Stadium	210	0	-
Mark Portugal @ Busch Stadium	175	0	-
Danny Jackson @ Shea Stadium	169	0	-
Mike Mussina @ Fenway Park	180	0	-
Curt Schilling @ Astrodome	161	0	-
Tom Candiotti @ Kauffman Stadium	155	0	-
Frank Castillo @ Astrodome	162	0	-

About STATS, Inc.

STATS, Inc. is the nation's leading independent sports information and statistical analysis company, providing detailed sports services for a wide array of clients.

As one of the fastest-growing sports companies—in 1994, we ranked 144th on the "Inc. 500" list of fastest-growing privately held firms—STATS provides the most up-to-the-minute sports information to professional teams, print and broadcast media, software developers and interactive service providers around the country. Some of our major clients are ESPN, the Associated Press, *The Sporting News*, Electronic Arts, Motorola, SONY and Topps. Much of the information we provide is available to the public via STATS On-Line. With a computer and a modem, you can follow action in the four major professional sports, as well as NCAA football and basketball. . . as it happens!

STATS Publishing, a division of STATS, Inc., produces 11 annual books, including the *Major League Handbook*, *The Scouting Notebook*, the *Pro Football Handbook*, the *Pro Basketball Handbook* and the *Hockey Handbook*. These publications deliver STATS' expertise to fans, scouts, general managers and media around the country.

In addition, STATS offers the most innovative—and fun—fantasy sports games around, from *Bill James Fantasy Baseball* and *Bill James Classic Baseball* to *STATS Fantasy Football* and *STATS Fantasy Hoops*.

Information technology has grown by leaps and bounds in the last decade, and STATS will continue to be at the forefront as both a vendor and supplier of the most up-to-date, in-depth sports information available. For those of you on the information superhighway, you can always catch STATS at our site on America Online (Keyword: STATS).

For more information on our products, or on joining our reporter network, write us at:

STATS, Inc.
8131 Monticello Ave.
Skokie, IL 60076-3300

. . . or call us at 1-800-63-STATS (1-800-637-8287). Outside the U.S., dial 1-847-676-3383.

Glossary

Most of the information in this book is pretty straightforward. But for the sake of completeness, here is a rundown of all the abbreviations and formulas:

For Hitters:
*=Bats left-handed, #=switch hitter, Avg=batting average, AB=at-bats, H=hits, HR=home runs, BI=runs batted in, BB=walks, SO=strikeouts, OBP=on-base percentage, SLG=slugging percentage, PA=plate appearances, SH=sacrifice hits, SF=sacrifice flies, RAT=ratio of AB/HR.

For Pitchers:
*=throws left-handed, W=wins, L=losses, ERA=earned run average, G=games pitched, GS=games started, Sv=saves, IP=innings pitched, H=hits allowed, BB=walks issued, SO=strikeouts, HR=home runs allowed, Avg=batting average allowed by the pitcher, ER=earned runs allowed, WP=wild pitches, RAT=ratio of SO/AB.

Formulas and Definitions:
PA = (AB + BB + HBP + SF + SH + defensive interference), or the total number of times a batter came up to the plate.
PA* = (AB + BB + HBP + SF), or the divisor for OBP
TOTAL BASES = [H + 2B + (2 x 3B) + (3 x HR)]
AVG = H / AB
OBP = (H + BB + HBP) / (AB + BB + HBP + SF)
SLG = TB / AB

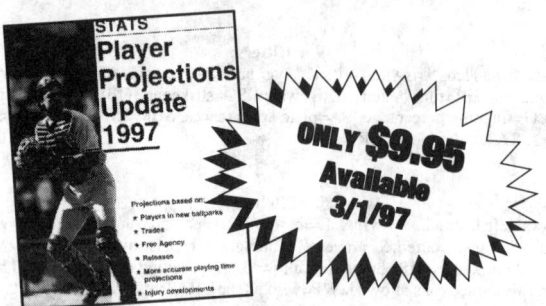

STATS Fantasy Hoops

Soar into the 1995-96 season with STATS Fantasy Hoops! SFH puts YOU in charge. Don't just sit back and watch Grant Hill, Shawn Kemp, and Jason Kidd - get in the game and coach your team to the top!

How to Play SFH:
1. Sign up to coach a team.
2. STATS sends you a set of rules and a draft form.
3. Complete the draft form and return it to STATS.
4. You will take part in the draft with 9 other owners.
5. You make unlimited weekly transactions including trades, free agent signings, and benchings.
6. Six teams in your league make the postseason.

SFH mirrors the real thing. Weekly reports tell you everything you need to know to lead your team to the SFH Championship!

STATS Fantasy Football

STATS Fantasy Football puts YOU in charge! You draft, trade, bench, activate players and sign free agents each week. SFF pits you head-to-head against 11 other owners.

STATS' scoring system applies realistic values, tested against actual NFL results. Each week, you'll receive a superb in-depth report telling you all about both team and league performances.

How to Play SFF:
1. Sign up today!
2. STATS sends you a draft list of NFL players.
3. Fill out the draft form and take part in the draft along with 11 other team owners.
4. Go head-to-head against the other owners. You'll make weekly roster moves and transactions!

Order from STATS INC. **Today!**

Use Order Form in This Book, or Call 1-800-63-STATS or

708-676-3383!

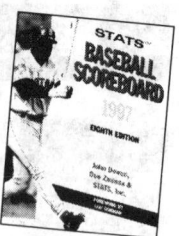

STATS INC. Order Form

Name_____ Phone_____

Address_____ Fax_____

City_____ State_____ Zip_____

Method of Payment (U.S. Funds Only):

❑ Check/Money Order   ❑ Visa   ❑ MasterCard

Cardholder Name_____

Credit Card Number_____ Exp. _____

Signature_____

BOOKS

Qty	Product Name	Item #	Price	Total
	STATS Major League Handbook 1997	HB97	$19.95	
	Major League Hndbk. 1997 (Comb-bnd)	HC97	$21.95	
	STATS Projections Update 1997	PJUP	$9.95	
	The Scouting Notebook: 1997	SN97	$18.95	
	STATS Player Profiles 1997	PP97	$19.95	
	Player Profiles 1997 (Comb-bound)	PC97	$21.95	
	STATS Minor Lg. Scouting Ntbk. 1997	MN97	$18.95	
	STATS Minor League Handbook 1997	MH97	$19.95	
	Minor League Hndbk. 1997 (Comb-bnd)	MC97	$21.95	
	STATS 1997 BVSP Match-Ups!	BP97	$14.95	
	STATS Baseball Scoreboard 1997	SB97	$18.95	
	STATS Pro Basketball Hndbk. 1996-97	BH97	$17.95	
	Pro Football Revealed (1997 Edition)	PF97	$18.95	
	STATS Pro Football Handbook 1997	FH97	$19.95	
	STATS Hockey Handbook 1996-97	HH97	$17.95	
	For previous editions, circle appropriate years:			
	Major League Handbook 91 92 93 94 95 96		$9.95	
	Scouting Report/Notebook 92 94 95 96		$9.95	
	Player Profiles 93 94 95 96		$9.95	
	Minor League Handbook 92 93 94 95 96		$9.95	
	Baseball Scoreboard 92 93 94 95 96		$9.95	
	Basketball Scoreboard 94 95 96		$9.95	
	Pro Football Handbook 95 96		$9.95	
	Pro Football Revealed 94 95 96		$9.95	

STATS ON-LINE

Qty	Product Name	Item #	Price	Total
	STATS On-Line	ONLE	$30.00	

FANTASY GAMES & STATSfax (STATSfax prices reflect the monthly charge for service)

Qty.	Product Name	Item Number	Price	Total
	Bill James Classic Baseball	BJCB	$129.00	
	How to Win the Classic Game	CGBK	$16.95	
	Classic Game STATSfax	CFX5	$20.00	
	STATS Fantasy Hoops	SFH	$85.00	
	STATS Fantasy Hoops STATSfax—5-Day	SFH5	$20.00	
	STATS Fantasy Hoops STATSfax—7-Day	SFH7	$25.00	
	STATS Fantasy Football	SFF	$69.00	
	STATS Fantasy Football STATSfax—3-Day	SFF3	$15.00	
	Bill James Fantasy Baseball	BJFB	$89.00	
	Fantasy Baseball STATSfax—5-Day	SFX5	$20.00	
	Fantasy Baseball STATSfax—7-Day	SFX7	$25.00	

For faster service, call 1-800-63-STATS, or fax this form to STATS at 847-676-0821, or e-mail to info@stats.com

FREE Information Kits:

❑ STATS Reporter Networks   ❑ Bill James Classic Baseball
❑ Bill James Fantasy Baseball ❑ STATS On-Line
❑ STATS Fantasy Hoops   ❑ STATS Fantasy Football
❑ STATS Year-end Reports   ❑ STATSfax

BP97

TOTALS

	Price	Total
Product Total (excl. Fantasy Games and On-Line)		
For first class mailing in U.S. add:	+$2.50/book	
Canada—all orders—add:	+$3.50/book	
Order 2 or more books—subtract:	-$1.00/book	
IL residents add 8.5% sales tax		
Subtotal		
Fantasy Games & On-Line Total		
GRAND TOTAL		

Mail to: STATS, Inc., 8131 Monticello Ave., Skokie, IL 60076-3300